Abbreviations for Units

A	ampere	h	hour	N	newton
Å	angstrom (10^{-10} m)	Hz	hertz	nm	nanometer (10^{-9} m)
atm	atmosphere	in.	inch	Pa	pascal
BTU	British thermal unit	J	joule	rad	radians
Bq	becquerel	K	kelvin	rev	revolution
C	coulomb	kg	kilogram	R	roentgen
°C	degree Celsius	km	kilometer	Sv	sievert
cal	calorie	keV	kilo-electron volt	s	second
Ci	curie	lb	pound	T	tesla
cm	centimeter	L	liter	u	unified mass unit
eV	electron volt	m	meter	V	volt
°F	degree Fahrenheit	MeV	mega-electron volt	W	watt
fm	femtometer, fermi (10^{-15} m)	mi	mile	Wb	weber
ft	foot	min	minute	y	year
G	gauss	mm	millimeter	μm	micrometer (10^{-6} m)
Gy	gray	mmHg	millimeters of mercury	μs	microsecond
g	gram	mol	mole	μC	microcoulomb
H	henry	ms	millisecond	Ω	ohm

Some Conversion Factors

Length
1 m = 39.37 in. = 3.281 ft = 1.094 yard
1 m = 10^{15} fm = 10^{10} Å = 10^9 nm
1 km = 0.6214 mi
1 mi = 5280 ft = 1.609 km
1 light-year = 1 $c \cdot$ y = 9.461×10^{15} m
1 in. = 2.540 cm

Volume
1 L = 10^3 cm^3 = 10^{-3} m^3 = 1.057 qt

Time
1 h = 3600 s = 3.6 ks
1 y = 365.24 day = 3.156×10^7 s

Speed
1 km/h = 0.278 m/s = 0.6214 mi/h
1 ft/s = 0.3048 m/s = 0.6818 mi/h

Angle–angular speed
1 rev = 2π rad = 360°
1 rad = 57.30°
1 rev/min (rpm) = 0.1047 rad/s

Force–pressure
1 N = 10^5 dyn = 0.2248 lb
1 lb = 4.448 N
1 atm = 101.3 kPa = 1.013 bar = 760 mmHg = 14.70 lb/in.^{2}

Mass
1 u = [(10^{-3} mol^{-1})/N_A] kg = 1.661×10^{-27} kg
1 tonne = 10^3 kg = 1 Mg
1 kg = 2.205 lb

Energy–power
1 J = 10^7 erg = 0.7376 ft $\cdot$ lb = 9.869×10^{-3} L $\cdot$ atm
1 kW $\cdot$ h = 3.6 MJ
1 cal = 4.186 J
1 L $\cdot$ atm = 101.325 J = 24.22 cal
1 eV = 1.602×10^{-19} J
1 BTU = 778 ft $\cdot$ lb = 252 cal = 1054 J
1 horsepower = 550 ft $\cdot$ lb/s = 746 W

Thermal conductivity
1 W/(m $\cdot$ K) = 6.938 BTU $\cdot$ in./(h $\cdot$ ft$^2 \cdot$ °F)

Magnetic field
1 T = 10^4 G

Viscosity
1 Pa $\cdot$ s = 10 poise

COLLEGE PHYSICS

Roger A. Freedman
Todd G. Ruskell
Philip R. Kesten
David L. Tauck

W. H. FREEMAN AND COMPANY
New York

Publisher: *Jessica Fiorillo*
Development Editor: *Blythe Robbins*
Acquisitions Editor: *Alicia Brady*
Associate Director of Marketing: *Debbie Clare*
Senior Market Development Manager: *Kirsten Watrud*
Media Acquisitions Editor: *Dave Quinn*
Media Producer: *Jenny Chiu*
Associate Editor: *Heidi Bamatter*
Assistant Editor: *Courtney Lyons*
Editorial Assistant: *Tue Tran*
Marketing Assistant: *Samantha Zimbler*
Senior Project Editor: *Georgia Lee Hadler*
Copy Editor: *Betty Pessagno*
Photo Editor: *Ted Szczepanski*
Photo Researcher: *Christina Micek*
Text and Cover Designer: *Blake Logan*
Illustration Coordinator: *Janice Donnola*
Illustrations: *Precision Graphics*
Production Coordinator: *Julia DeRosa*
Composition: *cMPreparé*
Printing and Binding: *Quad Graphics*

Cover photo by Kim Taylor/Hotspot Media
Barn Owl (Tyto alba) landing. Three images at 20 millisecond intervals.

Library of Congress Control Number: 2013939077

First Edition:
ISBN-10: 1-4641-3562-2
ISBN-13: 978-1-4641-3562-0

Printed in the United States of America
First printing

MCAT® is a registered trademark of the Association of American Medical Colleges. MCAT material included is printed with permission of the AAMC. Additional duplication is prohibited without written permission of the AAMC. The appearance of MCAT material in this book does not constitute sponsorship or endorsement by the AAMC.

W. H. Freeman and Company
41 Madison Avenue
New York, NY 10010
Houndmills, Basingstoke RG21 6XS, England
www.whfreeman.com

Roger:

To the memory of S/Sgt Ann Kazmierczak Freedman,
WAC and Pvt. Richard Freedman, AUS

Todd:

I dedicate this book to Susan and Allison, whose never-ending patience,
love, and support made it possible. And to my parents, from whom I learned
so much—especially my father, who so effectively demonstrates what it means
to be an effective teacher both in and out of the classroom.

Phil:

To my parents, for instilling in me a love of learning, to my wife for her
unconditional support, and to my children for letting their kooky dad
infuse so much of their lives with science.

Dave:

To my parents, Bill and Jean, for showing me how to lead a wonderful life,
and to my sister and friends, teachers and students for helping me do it.

Contents in Brief

Contents

Biological Applications

Unique and fully integrated physiological and biological applications are found throughout the text and are indicated by an owl icon. Below is a list of select biological applications organized by chapter section for easy reference.

Biological Applications

A UNIQUE AUTHOR TEAM

This ground-breaking text boasts an exceptionally strong writing team that is uniquely qualified to write a college physics textbook. The *College Physics* author team is led by **Roger Freedman**, accomplished textbook author of such bestselling titles as *Universe* (W. H. Freeman), *Investigating Astronomy* (W. H. Freeman), and *University Physics* (Pearson). Dr. Freedman is a Lecturer in Physics at the University of California, Santa Barbara. He was an undergraduate at the University of California campuses in San Diego and Los Angeles, and did his doctoral research in theoretical nuclear physics at Stanford University. He came to UCSB in 1981 after three years of teaching and doing research at the University of Washington. At UCSB, Dr. Freedman has taught in both the Department of Physics and the College of Creative Studies, a branch of the university intended for highly gifted and motivated undergraduates. In recent years, he has helped to develop computer-based tools for learning introductory physics and astronomy and has been a pioneer in the use of classroom response systems and the "flipped" classroom model at UCSB. Roger holds a commercial pilot's license and was an early organizer of the San Diego Comic-Con, now the world's largest popular culture convention.

As a Teaching Professor of Physics at the Colorado School of Mines, **Todd Ruskell** focuses on teaching at the introductory level, and continually develops more effective ways to help students learn. One method used in large enrollment introductory courses is Studio Physics. This collaborative, hands-on environment helps students develop better intuition about, and conceptual models of, physical phenomena through an active learning approach. Dr. Ruskell brings his experience in improving students' conceptual understanding to the text, as well as a strong liberal arts perspective. Dr. Ruskell's love of physics began with a B.A. in physics from Lawrence University in Appleton, Wisconsin. He went on to receive an M.S. and Ph.D. in optical sciences from the University of Arizona. He has received awards for teaching excellence, including Colorado School of Mines' Alumni Teaching Award. Dr. Ruskell currently serves on the physics panel and advisory board for the NANSLO (North American Network of Science Labs Online) project.

Philip Kesten, Associate Professor of Physics and Associate Provost for Residential Learning Communities at Santa Clara University, holds a B.S. in physics from the Massachusetts Institute of Technology and received his Ph.D. in high-energy particle physics from the University of Michigan. Since joining the Santa Clara faculty in 1990, Dr. Kesten has also served as Chair of Physics, Faculty Director of the ATOM and da Vinci Residential Learning Communities, and Director of the Ricard Memorial Observatory. He has received awards for teaching excellence and curriculum innovation, was Santa Clara's Faculty Development Professor for 2004–2005, and was named the California Professor of the Year in 2005 by the Carnegie Foundation for the Advancement of Education. Dr. Kesten is co-founder of Docutek (A SirsiDynix Company), an Internet software company, and has served as the Senior Editor for *Modern Dad*, a newsstand magazine.

Unlike any other physics text on the market, this project includes a physiologist as primary author. **David Tauck**, Associate Professor of Biology, holds both a B.A. in biology and an M.A. in Spanish from Middlebury College. He earned his Ph.D. in physiology at Duke University and completed postdoctoral fellowships at Stanford University and Harvard University in anesthesia and neuroscience, respectively. Since joining the Santa Clara University faculty in 1987, he has served as Chair of the Biology Department, the College Committee on Rank and Tenure, and the Institutional Animal Care and Use Committee; he has also served as president of the local chapter of Phi Beta Kappa. Dr. Tauck currently serves as the Faculty Director in Residence of the da Vinci Residential Learning Community.

Dear Students and Instructors,

Welcome to *College Physics*! We are excited to bring you this innovative text. No other college physics text presents material in quite this way. Our unique author team includes an experienced and highly successful textbook author, physicists who have spent years focusing on how students learn physics best, and even a biology professor who brings his perspective on what makes physics interesting to the students who take this course.

Our innovations help students master concepts and succeed in developing and practicing the problem-solving skills they need to do well in this course. The visual impact of this text is something totally new: Word balloons throughout the text highlight key physics concepts in figures and equations so that students can learn the concepts in easy-to-manage pieces.

In addition, numerous features in the text are also designed to help students succeed in this course. Look for the **Chapter Goals** outlined at the beginning of each chapter, **Watch Out!** boxes that address misconceptions; **Got the Concept?** questions that test students' understanding of the material; **Take-Home Messages** that directly link to the chapter goals and help students focus on the important concepts presented in each chapter section; **Examples** that are broken down into key steps with an easy-to-follow *Set-Up, Solve, Reflect* structure; **Questions and Problems** at the end of each chapter; and we even have a special **MCAT Appendix** to help pre-med students prepare for this important test.

Our aim is to instill in students a deeper appreciation of physics—by showing them how it connects to their lives and their future careers, but also by helping them succeed in the course. We hope you enjoy exploring and using this text!

Best Regards,

Todd Ruskell

Roger, Todd, Phil, Dave

Preface

TEXT FEATURES

College Physics provides instructors and students with a fresh approach to the algebra-based physics course. With art designed to teach and a focus on real-life biological and medical applications, *College Physics* provides students with a deeper understanding of physics principles and a greater appreciation for why physics is important to their future work in the life sciences.

A Focus on Developing Problem-Solving Skills

Many textbooks encourage memorization of equations over comprehension of concepts, allowing students to look for shortcuts in doing—and therefore learning—physics. To better align physics concepts with problem solving, *College Physics* incorporates student-friendly pedagogy by presenting worked examples in a model that emphasizes reasoning and analysis. Presented in a flexible format that easily demonstrates text, equations, and figures, the worked examples use a common procedure throughout to help build students' confidence when approaching problem solving. This procedure, summarized by the key phrases "Set Up," "Solve," and "Reflect," mirrors the approach scientists take in solving problems:

Set Up. The first step in each problem is to determine an overall approach and to gather the necessary pieces of information needed to solve it. These might include sketches, equations related to the physics, and concepts. The authors rely heavily on diagrams since they can be extraordinarily beneficial in helping students understand how to approach a problem.

Solve. Rather than simply summarizing the mathematical manipulations required to move from first principles to the final answer, the authors show many intermediate steps in working out solutions to the sample problems, highlighting a crucial part of the problem-solving process that is otherwise often overlooked. While many other texts only include figures in the Set Up portion of the worked example, the authors use sketches throughout each section whenever they are helpful in clarifying the physics for students.

Reflect. An important part of the process of solving a problem is to reflect on the meaning, implications, and validity of the answer. Is it physically reasonable? Do the units make sense? Is there a deeper or wider understanding that can be drawn from the result? The authors address these and related questions when appropriate.

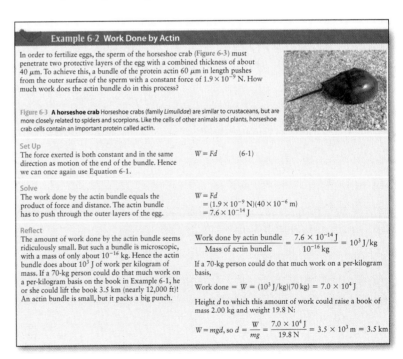

Example 6-2 Work Done by Actin

In order to fertilize eggs, the sperm of the horseshoe crab (Figure 6-3) must penetrate two protective layers of the egg with a combined thickness of about 40 μm. To achieve this, a bundle of the protein actin 60 μm in length pushes from the outer surface of the sperm with a constant force of 1.9×10^{-9} N. How much work does the actin bundle do in this process?

Figure 6-3 **A horseshoe crab** Horseshoe crabs (family *Limulidae*) are similar to crustaceans, but are more closely related to spiders and scorpions. Like the cells of other animals and plants, horseshoe crab cells contain an important protein called actin.

Set Up
The force exerted is both constant and in the same direction as motion of the end of the bundle. Hence we can once again use Equation 6-1.

$$W = Fd \qquad (6\text{-}1)$$

Solve
The work done by the actin bundle equals the product of force and distance. The actin bundle has to push through the outer layers of the egg.

$$W = Fd$$
$$= (1.9 \times 10^{-9}\text{ N})(40 \times 10^{-6}\text{ m})$$
$$= 7.6 \times 10^{-14}\text{ J}$$

Reflect
The amount of work done by the actin bundle seems ridiculously small. But such a bundle is microscopic, with a mass of only about 10^{-16} kg. Hence the actin bundle does about 10^3 J of work per kilogram of mass. If a 70-kg person could do that much work on a per-kilogram basis on the book in Example 6-1, he or she could lift the book 3.5 km (nearly 12,000 ft)! An actin bundle is small, but it packs a big punch.

$$\frac{\text{Work done by actin bundle}}{\text{Mass of actin bundle}} = \frac{7.6 \times 10^{-14}\text{ J}}{10^{-16}\text{ kg}} = 10^3\text{ J/kg}$$

If a 70-kg person could do that much work on a per-kilogram basis,

Work done $= W = (10^3\text{ J/kg})(70\text{ kg}) = 7.0 \times 10^4\text{ J}$

Height d to which this amount of work could raise a book of mass 2.00 kg and weight 19.8 N:

$$W = mgd, \text{ so } d = \frac{W}{mg} = \frac{7.0 \times 10^4\text{ J}}{19.8\text{ N}} = 3.5 \times 10^3\text{ m} = 3.5\text{ km}$$

Relaxed spring

d

If you stretch the spring a distance d, it exerts a force $\vec{F}$ on you.

$\vec{F}$

$2d$

$2\vec{F}$

If you double the distance that you stretch the spring, the force doubles.

Figure 6-17 **Hooke's law** If you stretch an ideal spring, the force that it exerts on you is directly proportional to its extension.

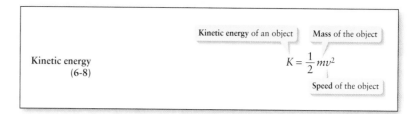

Kinetic energy
(6-8)

Kinetic energy of an object

Mass of the object

$$K = \frac{1}{2}mv^2$$

Speed of the object

Innovative Visual Features

This text incorporates groundbreaking visual features that bridge physics concepts to equations and figures throughout the book. In the form of "balloon art," the authors break down important equations and figures into smaller amounts of information.

The visual word balloons reinforce key ideas from the text and guide students to understanding the physics principles that are important to grasp in each chapter. The figures are simple, colorful, and approachable, inviting students to explore them rather than intimidating students into ignoring them.

A Seamless Blend of Physics and Biology

This book guides students through the fundamentals of introductory physics, weaving physiology and biomedical topics throughout the text and helping life science students discover the reasons why learning physics is important to their own fields of study. The authors' aim is to instill in students a deeper appreciation of physics by showing how it determines many characteristics of living systems. A complete list of biological applications can be found at the beginning of this Preface, and these applications are marked throughout the chapters with a brown owl icon like the one below. We offer an electronic biology appendix that professors can reference to learn more about the biology included in the text.

Muscles and Doing Work

Pick up a book or other heavy object and hold it in your hand at arm's length (Figure 6-4). After awhile you'll notice your arm getting tired: It feels like you're doing work to hold the object in midair. But Equation 6-1 says that you're doing *no* work on the book, because the book isn't moving (its displacement d is zero). So if you're not doing any work, why does your arm feel tired?

To see the explanation for this seeming paradox, notice that the muscles in your arm (and elsewhere in your body) exert forces on their ends by contracting. Skeletal muscles (those that control the motions of your arms, legs, fingers, toes, and other structures) are made up of bundles of muscle cells (Figure 6-5a). Muscle cells consist of bundles of myofibrils that are segmented into thousands of tiny structures called sarcomeres. Connected to each other, end to end, sarcomeres contain interdigitated filaments of the contractile proteins actin and myosin (Figure 6-5b). As the filaments slide past each other the sarcomeres can shorten, resulting in the muscle contracting; when the muscle relaxes, sarcomeres lengthen.

Figure 6-4 **Getting tired while doing zero work** Weights that you hold stationary in your outstretched arms undergo no displacement, so you do zero work on them. Why, then, do your arms get tired?

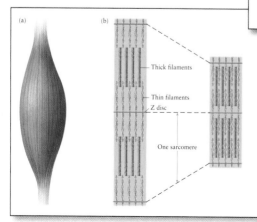

Thick filaments

Thin filaments

Z disc

One sarcomere

Figure 6-5 **Muscles and muscle function** (a) The muscles of your body are composed of many individual muscle fibers. (b) The internal structure of a muscle fiber when relaxed (left) and contracted (right).

LEARNING TOOLS

Carefully crafted to support students new to college-level physics, learning tools placed throughout the text guide students in developing the crucial conceptual foundation that they need to be successful in the course.

Outcome-Based Learning Objectives

To help outline assessment criteria and key goals throughout the chapter, the beginning of each chapter highlights outcome-based learning objectives that allow students to judge if they've reached the objective set forth for each chapter section. The listed learning objectives include both short-term (chapter sections) goals and long-term comprehensive (chapter) goals that highlight the important pedagogy that students should focus on throughout the text. The learning objectives of each chapter section are reinforced by Take-Home Messages at the end of each chapter section.

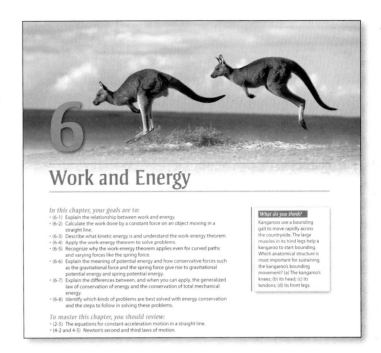

6

Work and Energy

In this chapter, your goals are to:
- (6-1) Explain the relationship between work and energy.
- (6-2) Calculate the work done by a constant force on an object moving in a straight line.
- (6-3) Describe what kinetic energy is and understand the work-energy theorem.
- (6-4) Apply the work-energy theorem to solve problems.
- (6-5) Recognize why the work-energy theorem applies even for curved paths and varying forces like the spring force.
- (6-6) Explain the meaning of potential energy and how conservative forces such as the gravitational force and the spring force give rise to gravitational potential energy and spring potential energy.
- (6-7) Explain the differences between, and when you can apply, the generalized law of conservation of energy and the conservation of total mechanical energy.
- (6-8) Identify which kinds of problems are best solved with energy conservation and the steps to follow in solving these problems.

To master this chapter, you should review:
- (2-5) The equations for constant-acceleration motion in a straight line.
- (4-2 and 4-5) Newton's second and third laws of motion.

What do you think?
Kangaroos use a bounding gait to move rapidly across the countryside. The large muscles in its hind legs help a kangaroo to start bounding. Which anatomical structure is most important for sustaining the kangaroo's bounding movement? (a) The kangaroo's knees; (b) its head; (c) its tendons; (d) its front legs.

Take-Home Messages

This boxed feature appears at the end of each chapter section and summarizes the main physics principles introduced in that section. These **Take-Home Messages** are directly tied to the outcome-based learning objectives listed at the beginning of each chapter, so that students can check for understanding before moving on to the next chapter section.

Special Attention to Common Misconceptions

Having taught physics for many years, the authors know which topics are prone to cause misunderstandings for students. So they created the "**Watch Out!**" boxed feature, which draws attention to these misconceptions and corrects them immediately as students read the text. By addressing these head on, students will have a deeper grasp of the physics presented throughout the text.

Conceptual Problems Built into the Flow of the Text

Health sciences and biological sciences students are used to a conceptual approach to both problem solving and learning in general. For that reason, the authors created a similar approach with the "**Got the Concept?**" questions that appear throughout the text. These questions almost never require numeric calculations but instead invite students to think through the implications or connections of a physics concept.

Take-Home Message for Section 6-2

✔ If a force acts on an object that undergoes a displacement, the force can do work on that object.

✔ For a constant force and straight-line displacement, the amount of work done is given by the displacement multiplied by the component of the the force parallel to that displacement.

✔ Whether the work done is positive, negative, or zero depends on the angle between the direction of the force and the direction of the displacement.

✔ If one object does negative work on a second object, the second object must do an equal amount of positive work on the first object.

! Watch Out!   Displacement and distance are not the same thing.

The fundamental difference is that distance tells you "how far," while displacement tells you "how far and in what direction." Displacement is a vector. That's why displacements can be positive or negative, but distances are *always* positive. (If you were asked, "How far is it from New York to Boston?" you wouldn't answer "Negative 300 km.") In Figure 2-2 each swimmer travels the same distance, 50.0 m, but their displacements are different (+50.0 m for swimmer A, −50.0 m for swimmer B) because the *directions* of their motion are different.

? Got the Concept? 2-2   Average Velocity

It takes you 15 min to drive 6.0 mi in a straight line to the local hospital. It takes 10 min to go the last 3.0 mi, 2.0 min to go the last mile, and only 30 s (= 0.50 min) to go the last 0.50 mile. What is your average velocity for the trip? Take the positive x direction to be from your starting point toward the hospital.

End-of-Chapter Summary

The end-of-chapter summary incorporates the key concepts from each chapter into an easy-to-follow table. Each table identifies the important topics covered in the chapter and provides students with a quick summary of each concept, as well as the important equation(s) or figure(s) associated with the topic.

Chapter Summary

Topic	Equation or Figure
Work done by a force in the direction of displacement: If an object moves in a straight line while a constant force is applied in the same direction as the displacement, the work is just equal to the force times the displacement.	Work done on an object by a constant force $\vec{F}$ that points in the same direction as the object's displacement $\vec{d}$ — Magnitude of the constant force $\vec{F}$ $$W = Fd \qquad (6\text{-}1)$$ Magnitude of the displacement $\vec{d}$
Work done by a constant force at an angle θ to the straight-line displacement: If an object moves in a straight line while a constant force is applied at some angle θ to the displacement, the work is equal to the force times the displacement multiplied by the cosine of the angle between the force and displacement.	Work done on an object by a constant force $\vec{F}$ that points at an angle θ to the object's displacement $\vec{d}$ — Magnitude of the constant force $\vec{F}$ $$W = (F \cos \theta)d \qquad (6\text{-}2)$$ Angle between the directions of $\vec{F}$ and $\vec{d}$ — Magnitude of the displacement $\vec{d}$

End-of-Chapter Problems

To reinforce the problem-solving skills taught in the chapters, the end-of-chapter problems incorporate conceptual questions and problems in the following format:

Conceptual Problems
Multiple-Choice Problems
Estimation/Numerical Analysis
Problems by Chapter Section
General Problems

Problems include three levels of difficulty: basic or single-concept problems (•), intermediate problems that may require synthesis of concepts and multiple steps (••), and challenging problems (•••). Problems are also designated when they pertain to certain topics, such as Biology, Medical, Sports, and Astronomy.

See the Math Tutorial for more information on trigonometry

Math Tutorial

Students may find that it's been a while since they studied a particular math concept and they need a reminder. Margin notes link concepts in the text to the **Math Appendix** found in the back of the book. The Math Tutorial serves as a refresher and includes worked examples as well as practice problems.

Special MCAT Appendix

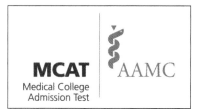

Since many students taking this course are preparing for a medical career, there is a special MCAT appendix in the back of the book to help students prepare for the MCAT test. This appendix includes actual MCAT problems provided by the Association of American Medical Colleges (AAMC) for students to practice with before taking the actual test.

MCAT® Appendix

The section that follows includes material from previously administered MCAT® items and is reprinted with permission of the Association of American Medical Colleges (AAMC).

Passage 13 (81–85)

Tennis balls must pass a rebound test before they can be certified for tournament play. To qualify, balls dropped from a given height must rebound within a specified range of heights. Measuring rebound height can be difficult because the ball is at its maximum height for only a brief time. It is possible to perform a simpler indirect measurement to calculate the height of rebound by measuring how long it takes the ball to rebound and hit the floor again. The diagram below illustrates the experimental setup used to make the measurement.

The ball is dropped from a height of 2.0 m, and it hits the floor and then rebounds to a height h. A microphone detects the sound of the ball each time it hits the floor, and a timer connected to the microphone measures the time (t) between the two impacts. The height of the rebound is $h = gt^2/8$ where $g = 9.8 \text{ m/s}^2$ is the acceleration due to gravity. Care must be taken so that the measured times do not contain systematic error. Both the speed of sound and the time of impact of the ball with the floor must be considered. Four balls were tested using the method. The results are listed in the table below.

Ball	Time (s)
A	1.01
B	1.05
C	0.97
D	1.09

81. If NO air resistance is present, which of the following quantities remains constant while the ball is in the air between the first and second impacts?

A. Kinetic energy of the ball
B. Potential energy of the ball
C. Momentum of the ball
D. Horizontal speed of the ball

STUDENT ANCILLARY SUPPORT

Supplemental learning materials allow students to interact with concepts in a variety of scenarios. By analyzing figures, reinforcing problem-solving methods, reviewing chapter objectives, and reading through worked-out solutions, students obtain a practical understanding of the core concepts. With that in mind, W. H. Freeman has developed the most comprehensive student learning package—both printed and online—available today.

Printed Student Resources

- **Problem-Solving Guide with Solutions** by Timothy A. French, DePaul University
  Volume I (Chapters 1–15) ISBN: 1-4641-0137-X
  Volume II (Chapters 16–28) ISBN: 1-4641-0138-8

The *Problem-Solving Guide with Solutions* takes a unique approach to promoting students' problem-solving skills by providing detailed and annotated solutions to selected problems. Unlike other solutions manuals, this guide follows the "Set Up," "Solve," and "Reflect" format outlined in the Worked Examples in the text for worked-out solutions to selected odd-numbered end-of-chapter problems in the textbook. It also includes integrated media icons which point to selected problem-solving tools that can be accessed.

- **Student Workbook** by Jason Bryslawskyj, CUNY Graduate Center, CUNY Baruch College and Mark Kanner, CUNY Graduate Center, CUNY City College
  Volume I (Chapters 1–15) ISBN: 1-4641-4957-7
  Volume II (Chapters 16–28) ISBN: 1-4641-4958-5

This workbook helps students put concepts from the text into practice before applying them to homework problems. Short exercises highlight the main goals in each chapter section, allowing students to develop the skills they need to apply these concepts when problem solving. By reiterating the key concepts, problem-solving strategies, and learning objectives from the main text, the workbook allows students to build the confidence they need to successfully tackle homework problems.

Premium Media Resources

The *College Physics* Companion Website, www.whfreeman.com/collegephysics1e, provides a range of tools for problem solving and conceptual support. These Premium Media Resources can be purchased for a small fee. Select resources are also embedded in the Multimedia-Enhanced e-Book and WebAssign Premium.

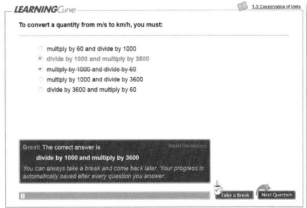

- **LearningCurve** incorporates adaptive question selection, personalized study plans, and state-of-the-art question analysis reports in activities with a game-like feel that keeps students engaged with the material. Integrated e-Book sections give students additional exposure to the course text. An innovative scoring system ensures that students who need more help with the material spend more time quizzing themselves than students who are already proficient. There is a LearningCurve activity available for each chapter in the book.

- **P'Casts** are videos that emulate the face-to-face experience of watching an instructor work a problem. Using a virtual whiteboard, the P'Casts' tutors demonstrate the steps involved in solving key worked examples, while explaining concepts along the way. The worked examples were chosen with the input of physics students and instructors across the country. There are 250 P'Casts total, all of which can be viewed online or downloaded to portable media devices.

- **Interactive Exercises** are active learning, problem-solving activities. Each Interactive Exercise consists of a parent problem accompanied by a Socratic-dialog "help" sequence designed to encourage critical thinking as users do a guided conceptual analysis before attempting the mathematics. Immediate feedback for both correct and incorrect responses is provided through each problem-solving step. Over 75 Interactive Exercises are available.

- **Balloon Art Concept Checks** guide students through the process of identifying important physics concepts in key figures and equations. Based on the colorful unique "balloon art" featured in *College Physics,* these interactive questions reinforce key ideas from the text, highlight important physics principles they must grasp in each chapter, and invite students to explore physics in an exciting and colorful way.

- **PhET Simulations** take the University of Colorado at Boulder's renowned research-based physics simulations and add a layer of inquiry-based questions unique to the *College Physics* book. To help students visually comprehend concepts and illustrate cause-and-effect relationships, PhET simulations animate what is invisible to the eye through the use of graphics and intuitive controls such as click-and-drag manipulation, sliders, and radio buttons. The tutorial questions further encourage this quantitative exploration, while addressing specific problem-solving needs.

- **Math Tutorial** offers improved mathematic support for students who may need a little math refresher. The comprehensive Math Tutorial reviews basic results of algebra, geometry, trigonometry, and calculus; links mathematical concepts to physics concepts in the text; and provides Examples and Practice Problems so students may check their understanding of mathematical concepts.

- **Picture Its** help bring static figures from the text to life. By manipulating variables within each animated figure, students visualize a variety of physics concepts. Approximately 50 activities are available.

- **Pocket Worked Examples** put the problem-solving worked examples in the palm of your hand. All Worked Examples from the *College Physics* text are available as downloadable PDF files, which can be printed or sent to your mobile device.

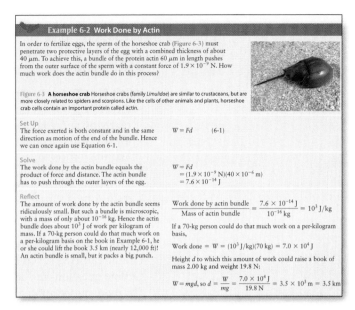

Example 6-2 Work Done by Actin

In order to fertilize eggs, the sperm of the horseshoe crab (Figure 6-3) must penetrate two protective layers of the egg with a combined thickness of about 40 μm. To achieve this, a bundle of the protein actin 60 μm in length pushes from the outer surface of the sperm with a constant force of 1.9×10^{-9} N. How much work does the actin bundle do in this process?

Figure 6-3 **A horseshoe crab** Horseshoe crabs (family *Limulidae*) are similar to crustaceans, but are more closely related to spiders and scorpions. Like the cells of other animals and plants, horseshoe crab cells contain an important protein called actin.

Set Up

The force exerted is both constant and in the same direction as motion of the end of the bundle. Hence we can once again use Equation 6-1.

$$W = Fd \qquad (6\text{-}1)$$

Solve

The work done by the actin bundle equals the product of force and distance. The actin bundle has to push through the outer layers of the egg.

$$W = Fd$$
$$= (1.9 \times 10^{-9}\ \text{N})(40 \times 10^{-6}\ \text{m})$$
$$= 7.6 \times 10^{-14}\ \text{J}$$

Reflect

The amount of work done by the actin bundle seems ridiculously small. But such a bundle is microscopic, with a mass of only about 10^{-16} kg. Hence the actin bundle does about 10^3 J of work per kilogram of mass. If a 70-kg person could do that much work on a per-kilogram basis on the book in Example 6-1, he or she could lift the book 3.5 km (nearly 12,000 ft)! An actin bundle is small, but it packs a big punch.

$$\frac{\text{Work done by actin bundle}}{\text{Mass of actin bundle}} = \frac{7.6 \times 10^{-14}\ \text{J}}{10^{-16}\ \text{kg}} = 10^3\ \text{J/kg}$$

If a 70-kg person could do that much work on a per-kilogram basis,

$$\text{Work done} = W = (10^3\ \text{J/kg})(70\ \text{kg}) = 7.0 \times 10^4\ \text{J}$$

Height d to which this amount of work could raise a book of mass 2.00 kg and weight 19.8 N:

$$W = mgd,\ \text{so}\ d = \frac{W}{mg} = \frac{7.0 \times 10^4\ \text{J}}{19.8\ \text{N}} = 3.5 \times 10^3\ \text{m} = 3.5\ \text{km}$$

- **PhysicsNews** from *Scientific American* provides an up-to-the-minute streaming feed of new physics-related stories direct from *Scientific American* magazine. Stay on top of the latest happenings in physics all in one easy place.

SCIENTIFIC AMERICAN™

ELECTRONIC TEXTBOOKS

For students interested in digital textbooks, W. H. Freeman offers the complete *College Physics* book in two easy-to-use formats.

The Multimedia-Enhanced e-Book

The Multimedia-Enhanced e-Book contains the complete text with a wealth of helpful interactive functions. All student Premium Resources are linked directly from the e-Book pages. Students are thus able to access supporting resources when they need them, taking advantage of the "teachable moment" as they read. Customization functions include instructor and student notes, highlighting, document linking, and editing capabilities. Access to the Multimedia-Enhanced e-Book can be purchased from the Book Companion Website.

The CourseSmart eTextbook

Though it does not include any Premium Resources, the CourseSmart eTextbook does provide the full digital text, along with tools to take notes, search, and highlight passages. A free app allows access to CourseSmart eTextbooks on Android and Apple devices, such as the iPad. They can also be downloaded to your computer and accessed without an Internet connection, removing any limitations for students when it comes to reading digital text. The CourseSmart eTextbook can be purchased at www.coursesmart.com.

ONLINE TUTORING

W. H. Freeman knows that learning physics can be hard and that sometimes students need some extra support. That's why we've partnered with NetTutor to bring students tutoring they can access anytime, anywhere.

NetTutor®

www.nettutor.com

NetTutor® is an online tutoring service that specializes in a customized tutoring experience. Using the Socratic Method, tutors guide students through problems or concepts, but never present answers. This approach develops critical thinking skills and encourages students to persevere. Powered by an easy-to-use interactive interface, NetTutor® provides the most student-friendly online tutoring environment available, conducted by local tutors who really understand how to help today's students learn.

With NetTutor®, students get:

- Expert, U.S.-based tutors, ready to help your students with problems from your textbook and your assignments.
- Tutors who use questions and familiar concepts to guide students through the learning process.
- A virtual whiteboard, which enables students to interact with tutors as they work with you to solve problems, share information, and ask questions.
- The ability to print or save copies of each tutoring session for reference.
- The option for students to extend access via direct online purchase.

Assistance is always available!

Online tutoring seven days a week.
Offline question-and-answer 24 hours a day.
For more information about packaging tutoring access with your *College Physics* text, please contact your Publisher's Representative.

INSTRUCTOR RESOURCES

For instructors using *College Physics*, W. H. Freeman provides a complete suite of assessment tools and course materials for the taking.

Computerized Test Bank

ISBN: 1-4641-0133-7
The Test Bank offers over 2,000 multiple-choice questions, tackling both core physics concepts and various life-science applications. While the Test Bank is also available in downloadable Word files on the book companion website, the easy-to-use CD includes Windows and Macintosh versions of the widely used Diploma test generation software, allowing instructors to add, edit, and sequence questions to suit their testing needs.

Electronic Instructor Resources

Instructors can access valuable teaching tools through www.whfreeman.com/collegephysics1e. These password-protected resources are designed to enhance lecture presentations, and include Textbook Images (available in .JPEG and PowerPoint format), Clicker Questions, Lecture PowerPoint slides, Art PowerPoint slides, Instructor Solutions, Biology Appendix, and more.

Course Management System Cartridges

W. H. Freeman provides seamless integration of resources in your Course Management Systems. Four cartridges are available (Blackboard, Canvas, Desire2Learn, and Angel), and other select cartridges (Moodle, Sakai, etc.) can be produced upon request.

ONLINE HOMEWORK SYSTEMS

W. H. Freeman offers the widest variety of online homework options on the market.

www.saplinglearning.com

Sapling Learning provides highly effective interactive homework and instruction that improve student learning outcomes for the problem-solving disciplines. They offer an enjoyable teaching and effective learning experience that is distinctive in three important ways:

- **Targeted Instructional Content:** Sapling Learning increases student engagement and comprehension by delivering immediate feedback and targeted instructional content.
- **Performance Tracking:** Sapling Learning grades assignments, tracks student participation and progress, and compiles performance analytics—helping instructors save time and tailor assignments to address student needs.

- **Proven Results:** Independent university studies have shown Sapling Learning improves student performance by three-fourths to a full letter grade.
- **Unsurpassed Service and Support:** Sapling Learning makes teaching more enjoyable by providing a dedicated Master's- and Ph.D.-level colleague who provides software, course development, and consulting support throughout the semester. Our Tech TAs help instructors to:

  - Customize assignments by editing our existing questions or creating new questions that support the course, not just the text.
  - Choose point values and grading policies to help achieve educational goals, analyze class statistics, and apply the results to help students learn more efficiently.
  - Provide instructors with one-on-one training on use of Sapling Learning's online homework system and customization tools.
  - Resolve any issues that may arise with the software or online assignments so that instructors spend less time managing technology and more time with their students.

Sapling Learning is not tied to a specific textbook or edition, giving instructors freedom to customize Sapling to their syllabus and students the flexibility to choose more affordable used or rental textbooks.

www.webassign.com

For instructors interested in online homework management, WebAssign Premium features a time-tested secure online environment already used by millions of students worldwide. Featuring algorithmic problem generation and supported by a wealth of physics-specific learning tools, WebAssign Premium for *College Physics* presents instructors with a powerful assignment manager and student environment. WebAssign Premium provides the following resources:

- **Algorithmically generated problems:** Students receive homework problems containing unique values for computation, encouraging them to work out the problems on their own.
- **Complete access to the Multimedia-Enhanced e-Book** is available from a live table of contents, as well as from relevant problem statements.
- **Links to select Premium Multimedia Resources** (P'Casts, Interactive Exercises, and Picture Its) are provided as hints and feedback to ensure a clearer understanding of the problems and the concepts they reinforce.
- **Personal Study Plan** allowing students to review key prerequisite algebra concepts at their own pace.
- **Additional Resource Question Collections** from expert physics education researchers that have been thoroughly class-tested and researched are also available to add to your WebAssign course at no extra charge.

For budget-conscious students, a lower-priced, homework-only option is also available. This version does not include the e-Book or any of the Premium Multimedia Resources.

ACKNOWLEDGMENTS

Creating a first edition textbook requires the coordinated effort of an enormous number of talented professionals. We are grateful for the dedicated support of our in-house team at W. H. Freeman; thank you for transforming our concept into a beautiful book.

We especially want to thank our development editor, Blythe Robbins, for guiding us through the process of creating a textbook. We would also like to thank Associate Publisher Jessica Fiorillo for encouraging us and leading our editorial team, Media Acquisitions Editor Dave Quinn for producing gorgeous ancillaries and contributing significantly to the design of the book and cover, and of course, we thank Associate Editor Heidi Bamatter for coordinating reviews, in addition to Assistant Editor Courtney Lyons and Editorial Assistant Tue Tran for their hard work on the project. Randi Rossignol and Susan Brennan made important contributions to the early stages of this project, and they deserve special thanks for motivating many of the unique features of this book. Special thanks also go to our skilled in-house production team, Julia DeRosa, Ted Szczepanski, Bill Page, Janice Donnola, Blake Logan, and Georgia Hadler, for their patience, dedication, and attention to detail. And of course, Senior Market Development Manager Kirsten

Watrud and Senior Marketing Manager Alicia Brady deserve a special thank you for providing us with key market data.

We are particularly grateful for the substantial contributions of Accuracy Checker Valerie Walters, Problems Editor Mark Hollabaugh, Solutions Manual Author Tim French, Workbook Authors Jason Bryslawskyj and Mark Kanner. Francesca Monaco of cMPreparé also deserves a special thank you for coordinating the compositor process.

Friends and Family
One of us (RAF) thanks his wife Caroline Robillard for her patience with the seemingly endless hours that went into preparing this textbook. I also thank my students at the University of California, Santa Barbara, for giving me the opportunity to test and refine new ideas for making physics more accessible.

One of us (TGR) thanks his wife Susan and daughter Allison for their limitless patience and understanding with the countless hours spent working on this book. I also thank my parents who showed me how to live a balanced life.

One of us (PRK) would like to acknowledge valuable and insightful conversations on physics and physics teaching with Richard Barber, John Birmingham, and J. Patrick Dishaw of Santa Clara University, and to offer these colleagues my gratitude. Finally, I offer my gratitude to my wife Kathy and my children Sam and Chloe for their unflagging support during the arduous process that led to the book you hold in your hands.

One of us (DLT) thanks his family and friends for accommodating my tight schedule during the years that writing this book consumed. I especially want to thank my parents, Bill and Jean, for their boundless encouragement and support, and for teaching me everything I've ever really needed to know; they've shown me how to live a good life, be happy, and age gently. I greatly appreciate my sister for encouraging me not to abandon a healthy lifestyle just to write a book. I also want to thank my nonbiological family, Holly and Geoff, for leading me to Sonoma County and for making Sebastopol feel like home.

Accuracy Review
We know that instructors have particular concerns about using first edition texts because they are prone to errors. We have done everything in our power to alleviate this concern in using our text by submitting chapters and end-of-chapter problem sets to several rounds of accuracy reviews and detailed error-checking, by the following:

Wayne R. Anderson
Sacramento City College

Marisa Bauza Roman
Drexel University

Kevin W. Cooper
Ohio University

Mark Hollabaugh
Normandale Community College

Dr. Guy Letteer
Sacred Heart Preparatory and Santa Clara University

Linghong Li
The University of Tennessee at Martin

Alan Meert
University of Pennsylvania

Dr. Valerie A. Walters
V Walters Consulting

Class Testers
We thank the faculty below and their students for class testing the text.

Miah Muhammad Adel, *University of Arkansas, Pine Bluff*
Jeremy Armstrong, *Winona State University*
Harold Bank, *Clayton State University*
Jeff J. Bechtold, *Austin Community College*
Michael Bates, *Moraine Valley Community College*
Bill Brandon, *University of North Carolina, Pembroke*
Allison Bruce, *El Paso Community College*
Andrew Cahoon, *Colby Sawyer College*
Zengjun Chen, *Tuskegee University*
Kathryn Devine, *The College of Idaho*
Carl Drake, *Jackson State University*
Diana Driscoll, *Case Western Reserve University*
Greg Falabella, *Wagner College*
Brian Geislinger, *Gadsden State Community College*
Zvonko Hlousek, *California State University, Long Beach*
Olenka Hubrickyj Cabot, *San Jose State University*
Charles Johnson, *South Georgia College*
Anthony Karmis, *University of California, Santa Barbara*
Elena Kuchina, *Thomas Nelson Community College*
Cecille Labuda, *University of Mississippi*
Shelly R. Lesher, *University of Wisconsin, La Crosse*
Susannah Lomant, *Georgia Perimeter College*
Ron MacTaylor, *Salem State University*
Firas Mansour, *University of Waterloo*
Maxim Marienko, *Hofstra University/Queens College CUNY*
Eric Martell, *Millikin University*
Karie A. Meyers, *Pima Community College*
Tamar More, *University of Portland*
Sandra J. Rhoades, *Kennesaw State University*
Bill Robinson, *North Carolina State University*
Michael Sampogna, *Pima Community College*
Tumer Sayman, *Eastern Michigan University*
Pete Schwart, *California Polytechnic State University*
Malav Shah, *Macon State College*
Peter Sheldon, *Randolph College*
Jason Shulman, *Richard Stockton College of New Jersey*
Glenn Spiczak, *University of Wisconsin, River Falls*
Melody Thomas, *Northwest Arkansas Community College*
Greg Thompson, *Adrian University*
Vijayalakshmi Varadarajan, *Des Moines Area Community College*
Brian Zulkoskey, *University of Saskatchewan, Saskatoon*

Reviewers

We would also like to thank the many colleagues who carefully reviewed chapters for us. Their insightful comments significantly improved our book.

Don Abernathy, *North Central Texas College*
Elise Adamson, *Wayland Baptist University*
Miah Muhammad Adel, *University of Arkansas, Pine Bluff*
Ricardo Alarcon, *Arizona State University*
Z. Altounian, *McGill University*
Abu Amin, *Riverland Community College*
Sanjeev Arora, *Fort Valley State University*
Llani Attygalle, *Bowling Green State University*
Yiyan Bai, *Houston Community College*
Michael Bates, *Moraine Valley Community College*
Luc Beaulieu, *Memorial University*
Jeff J. Bechtold, *Austin Community College*
David Bennum, *University of Nevada*
Satinder Bhagat, *University of Maryland*
Dan Boye, *Davidson University*
Jeff Bronson, *Blinn College*
Douglas Brumm, *Florida State College at Jacksonville*
Mark S. Bruno, *Gateway Community College*
Brian K. Bucklein, *Missouri Western State University*
Michaela Burkardt, *New Mexico State University*
Kris Byboth, *Blinn College*
Joel W. Cannon, *Washington & Jefferson College*
Kapila Clara Castoldi, *Oakland University*
Paola M. Cereghetti, *Lehigh University*
Hong Chen, *University of North Florida*
Zengjun Chen, *Tuskegee University*
Uma Choppali, *Dallas County Community College*
Todd Coleman, *Century College*
José D'Arruda, *University of North Carolina, Pembroke*
Tinanjan Datta, *Georgia Regents University*
Chad L. Davies, *Gordon College*
Brett DePaola, *Kansas State University*
Sandra Doty, *Ohio University*
James Dove, *Metro Community College*
Carl T. Drake, *Jackson State University*
Rodney Dunning, *Longwood University*
Vernessa M. Edwards, *Alabama A & M University*
Davene Eyres, *North Seattle Community College*
Hasan Fakhruddin, *Ball State University*
Paul Fields, *Pima Community College*
Lewis Ford, *Texas A & M University*
J.A. Forrest, *University of Waterloo*
Scott Freedman, *Philadelphia Academy Charter High School*
Tim French, *Harvard University*
James Friedrichsen III, *Austin Community College*
Sambandamurthy Ganapathy, *SUNY, Buffalo*
J. William Gary, *University of California, Riverside*
L. Gasparov, *University of North Florida*
Gasparyan, *California State University, Bakersfield*
Brian Geislinger, *Gadsden State Community College*
Oommen George, *San Jacinto College*
Anindita Ghosh, *Suffolk County Community College*
Alan I. Goldman, *Iowa State University*
Richard Goulding, *Memorial University of Newfoundland*

Morris C. Greenwood, *San Jacinto College Central*
Thomas P. Guella, *Worcester State University*
Alec Habig, *University of Minnesota, Duluth*
Edward Hamilton, *Gonzaga University*
C. A. Haselwandter, *University of Southern California*
Zvonko Hlousek, *California State University, Long Beach*
Micky Holcomb, *West Virginia University*
Kevin M. Hope, *University of Montevallo*
J. Johanna Hopp, *University of Wisconsin, Stout*
Leon Hsu, *University of Minnesota*
Olenka Hubickyj Cabot, *San Jose State University*
Richard Ignace, *East Tennessee State University*
Elizabeth Jeffery, *James Madison University*
Yong Joe, *Ball State University*
Darrin Eric Johnson, *University of Minnesota, Duluth*
David Kardelis, *Utah State University, College of Eastern Utah*
Agnes Kim, *Georgia State College*
Ju H. Kim, *University of North Dakota*
Seth T. King, *University of Wisconsin, La Crosse*
Kathleen Koenig, *University of Cincinnati*
Olga Korotkova, *University of Miami*
Minjoon Kouh, *Drew University*
Tatiana Krivosheev, *Clayton State University*
Michael Kruger, *University of Missouri, Kansas City*
Jessica C. Lair, *Eastern Kentucky University*
Josephine M. Lamela, *Middlesex County College*
Patrick M. Len, *Cuesta College*
Shelly R. Lesher, *University of Wisconsin, La Crosse*
Zhujun Li, *Richland College*
Bruce W. Liby, *Manhattan College*
David M. Lind, *Florida State University*
Jeff Loats, *Metropolitan State College of Denver*
Susannah E. Lomant, *Georgia Perimeter College*
Jia Grace Lu, *University of Southern California*
Mark Lucas, *Ohio University*
Lianxi Ma, *Blinn College*
Aklilu Maasho, *Dyersburg State Community College*
Ron MacTaylor, *Salem State University*
Eric Mandell, *Bowling Green State University*
Maxim Marienko, *Hofstra University*
Mark Matlin, *Bryn Mawr College*
Dan Mattern, *Butler Community College*
Mark E. Mattson, *James Madison University*
Jo Ann Merrell, *Saddleback College*
Michael R. Meyer, *Michigan Technological University*
Karie A. Meyers, *Pima Community College*
Andrew Meyertholen, *University of the Redlands*
John H. Miller, Jr., *University of Houston*
Ronald C. Miller, *University of Central Oklahoma*
Ronald Miller, *Texas State Technical College System*
Hector Mireles, *California State University, Pomona*
Ted Monchesky, *Dalhousie University*
Steven W. Moore, *California State University, Monterey Bay*
Mark Morgan-Tracy, *University of New Mexico*
Dennis Nemeschansky, *University of Southern California*
Terry F. O'Dwyer, *Nassau Community College*
John S. Ochab, *J. Sargeant Reynolds Community College*

COLLEGE PHYSICS

1

Introduction to Physics

In this chapter, your goals are to:
- (1-1) Explain the roles that concepts and equations play in physics.
- (1-2) Describe three key steps in solving any physics problem.
- (1-3) Identify the fundamental units used for measuring physical quantities and convert from one set of units to another.
- (1-4) Use significant figures in calculations.
- (1-5) Use dimensional analysis to check algebraic results.

To master this chapter, you should review:
- The principles of algebra and how to solve an equation for a particular variable.

What do you think?

The size of a hummingbird's head is closest to which of these lengths? (a) one micrometer (1 μm); (b) one millimeter (1 mm); (c) one centimeter (1 cm); (d) one meter (1 m).

The answer to the *What do you think?* question can be found at the end of the chapter.

1-1 Physicists use a special language—part words, part equations—to describe the natural world

A hummingbird is a beautiful sight to anyone. As seen through the eyes of a physicist, however, a hummingbird is a remarkable illustration of several physical principles at work. The beating of the hummingbird's wings pushes downward on the air, which causes the air to push upward in response and keep the bird aloft. The flow of blood through the hummingbird's body is governed by the properties of moving fluids, including the interplay of pressure and friction in the narrowest blood vessels. The bending of light rays as they enter the bird's eye forms an image on the retina, providing the hummingbird with vision. And the subtle interference of light waves reflecting off the feathers at the bird's throat gives them their characteristic iridescence. To truly understand and appreciate hummingbirds or any other living organism, we need to understand the principles of physics. The purpose of this book is to help you gain that understanding.

Learning physics is somewhat like learning a foreign language. If you're paying a brief visit to a foreign country, you may just memorize a few key phrases such as "Where is the hotel?" in the local language. But if you want to be fluent in the language, you don't memorize millions of phrases for the countless situations you might encounter. Instead, you learn the language by internalizing a vocabulary of useful words and the grammar that allows you to combine those words into meaningful sentences. Using those basic tools, you can express an enormous variety of ideas, even those no one else has expressed before. In the same way, it may seem at the outset that physics is a long compilation of rules, equations, definitions, and concepts. By taking a closer look, we will discover that this long list of physics "phrases" are created from a much smaller set of physics "grammar" and the key vocabulary of physics. Your goal is to become fluent

1

Figure 1-1 $E = mc^2$ When you burn natural gas in a kitchen range, you are converting some of the rest energy of methane and oxygen into light and heat.

in physics by understanding how to use the rules of physics grammar to connect the vocabulary of physics.

The vocabulary of physics is often expressed in terms of mathematical quantities, and the grammar that relates these quantities are the equations of physics. Like most physics books, this one contains many equations. Not all of these equations are equally important, however. A much smaller set of *fundamental* equations express the key ideas of physics. By starting with these fundamental equations and combining them using the rules of algebra, you'll be able to solve all of the physics problems that you encounter in this book.

It's tempting to view the equations in this book, even the fundamental ones, as being all there is to learning physics. If you adopt this view, you'll get the idea that solving a physics problem is simply a hunt to find the correct equation. Not so! Each of the equations of physics is shorthand for a *concept* that can be much more profound than the equation might suggest. One example is Albert Einstein's famous equation

$$E = mc^2$$

In this equation E represents energy, m represents mass, and c represents the speed at which light travels in a vacuum. But what the equation *means* is something deeper. In this book we'll often write fundamental equations with explanations attached, such as this one:

Einstein's equation for rest energy
(1-1)

The rest energy of an object is the amount of energy it possesses simply as a consequence of having mass. (Einstein was the first physicist to deduce that energy of this kind existed.) Equation 1-1 shows that rest energy is *directly proportional* to mass: The greater the mass of an object, the greater its rest energy and vice versa. If the rest energy of an object decreases, its mass must decrease as well. You can find an example of this in many kitchens (Figure 1-1). In a gas range, natural gas (mostly methane, CH_4) combines with oxygen to produce carbon dioxide (CO_2) and water (H_2O). The chemical reaction that takes place is

See the Math Tutorial for more information on equations

$$CH_4 + 2O_2 \longrightarrow CO_2 + 2H_2O$$

This process releases energy in the form of heat and light. This energy comes from rest energy, so the combined rest energy of the products (a CO_2 molecule and two H_2O molecules) is less than the rest energy of the reactants (a CH_4 molecule and two O_2 molecules). Equation 1-1 then tells us that the combined mass of the molecules present after the reaction is slightly *less* than the combined mass of the molecules present before the reaction. This is a remarkable statement, but sensitive measurements reveal it to be true. When you look at a flame, Equation 1-1 itself isn't the important part of this story: It's the *concept* behind this equation that's truly important. This is an important idea that can be easy to forget. When we come across an important idea like this one, or a situation that requires special care, we'll put it in a **Watch Out!** box like the one on the left side of this page.

 Watch Out!

You need to be careful.

When we come across a situation that requires special care, we'll put it in a **Watch Out!** box like this one.

Take-Home Message for Section 1-1

✔ Like all other sciences, physics is a collection of interlinked concepts.

✔ The equations of physics help us summarize complex ideas in mathematical shorthand.

✔ It's essential to understand the concepts behind each fundamental equation.

1-2 Success in physics requires well-developed problem-solving skills

More than just broadening our understanding of the world, the process of learning physics involves learning to solve problems. Physics problems can appear challenging because they usually can't be done simply by selecting an equation and plugging in values. Solving physics problems is easier, however, if you build up a set of tools and techniques, and then apply a consistent strategy. Our strategy for solving problems involves three steps that we refer to as *Set Up, Solve,* and *Reflect.* We'll use these steps in all of the worked examples in this book.

Example 1-1 Strategy for Solving Problems

Set Up

At the beginning of any problem, ask yourself these questions: What is the problem asking for? Which quantities are known, and which are unknowns whose values you need to determine to solve the problem? What concepts will help solve the problem, and which equations should you use to apply these principles? Once you've answered these questions, you'll have a good idea of how to get started with solving the problem. Here are some helpful hints for setting up any problem:

Draw a picture. Physicists rely heavily on diagrams. You'll find one or more in many of the worked examples in this book. A good problem-solving picture should capture the motion, the process, the geometry, or whatever else defines the problem. You don't need an artistic masterpiece; it's perfectly okay to represent most complex objects as squares or circles or even dots.

Label all quantities. It makes sense to label all quantities such as length, speed, and temperature right on the picture you've drawn. But be careful! First, more than one of a given kind of variable is often in a problem. For example, if two objects are moving at different speeds, but you use the same symbol v for the speeds of both objects, confusion is bound to result. Subscripts are useful in such a case, for example, v_A and v_B for the speeds of the two objects. Also, don't hesitate to label lengths, velocities, and other quantities even if you haven't been given a value for them. You might be able to figure out the value of one of these quantities and use it later in the problem, or you might gain an insight that will guide you to a solution.

Look for connections. Often the best strategy for solving a physics problem is to look for connections between quantities. These connections could be relationships between two or more variables or a statement that a certain parameter has the same value for two objects. Furthermore, these connections will often enable you either to eliminate variables or to find a value for an unknown variable. As a result, you sometimes will have an equation that defines the variable of interest only in terms of variables that are known. So we'll always be on the lookout for connections such as these when starting a problem.

Solve

Once you've sized up the situation and selected the concepts and equations to use, finding the answer is often just an exercise in mathematics. During this step in the worked examples, we'll break down and show many intermediate steps as we describe our reasoning and thought processes. In this way, we'll model good problem solving, which will lead you to develop your own problem-solving skills and habits.

Reflect

An important but often overlooked part of problem solving is to review the answer to see what it tells you. If the problem calls for a numerical answer, it's important to ask, "Do the number and the units make sense?" This is often a good way for you to check the accuracy of your calculations. For example, if you've been asked to calculate the diameter of Earth and you come up with 40 centimeters, or if you come up with an answer in kilograms (the unit of mass), it's time to go back and check your calculations. If your answer is a formula rather than a single number, check that what the formula says is reasonable. As an example, if you've found a formula that relates the weight of a cat to its volume, your answer should show that a heavier cat has a larger volume than a lightweight one. If it doesn't, there's an error in your calculations that you need to find and fix.

Learning physics will be easier if you study the many worked examples in this book and get in the habit of following the same steps of *Set Up, Solve,* and *Reflect* in your own problem solving.

1-3 Measurements in physics are based on standard units of time, length, and mass

To the average person, physics calls to mind speculative theories about the nature of matter and the origins of space and time. But at its heart physics is an *experimental* science based on measurements of the natural world. Over a century ago the renowned Scottish physicist Lord Kelvin (1824–1907) expressed this viewpoint: "If you can measure that of which you speak, and can express it by a number, you know something of your subject; but if you cannot measure it, your knowledge is unsatisfactory."

Any measurement requires a standard of comparison. If you want to compare the heights of two children, for example, you might stand them side by side and use one child's height as a reference for the other. A better and more reliable standard would be to use a vertical rod with equally spaced markings (in other words, a ruler) that acts as a standard of length.

In physics, three fundamental quantities for which it is essential to have standards are *time*, *length*, and *mass*. The standards or **units** for these three quantities are the *second*, the *meter*, and the *kilogram*, respectively, and the system of units based on these quantities is called the **Système International**, or **SI** for short. By understanding how these standards are defined, we'll get a sense of the precision toward which physicists strive in their measurements. Table 1-1 lists all of the fundamental SI quantities, including others that we'll encounter in later chapters.

The definition of the **second** (abbreviated s) is based on the properties of the cesium atom. When such atoms are excited, they emit radio waves of a very definite frequency. The second is defined to be the amount of time required for cesium to emit 9,192,631,770 complete cycles of these waves. This may seem like a bizarre way to measure time, but modern radio technology is highly refined and it's relatively easy to prepare a gas of cesium atoms with the right properties. Hence a physicist anywhere in the world could readily repeat these measurements.

In the past, objects such as metal bars were used as standards of length. These were not very good standards, however, because their length changes slightly but measurably when the temperature changes. Today, radio technology is used to define the **meter** (abbreviated m), the SI standard of length. The speed of light in a vacuum is defined to be precisely 299,792,458 meters per second, so that the meter is the distance that light (or radio waves, which are a form of light) travels in 1/299,792,458 of a second. This is a robust and repeatable standard because light in a vacuum travels at the same speed anywhere on Earth and, as best we can tell, everywhere in the universe. (We specify a vacuum because light travels more slowly in a material such as glass, water, or even air.)

Mass is a measure of the amount of material in an object. A feather has less mass than a baseball, which in turn has less mass than a cinder block. The ideal standard for mass would be one that is, like the standards for time and length, based on something that is the same throughout the universe—for example, the mass of a hydrogen atom. Unfortunately, physicists' present-day ability to measure masses on the atomic scale is not yet precise enough to give a really satisfactory standard of mass. For the time being, the **kilogram** (abbreviated kg) is defined to be the mass of a special cylinder of platinum-iridium alloy kept in a repository near Paris, France (Figure 1-2). This standard kilogram isn't very portable, and physicists look forward to the day when a mass standard can be based on the properties of atoms. (The *gram*, equal to 1/1000 of a kilogram, is not a fundamental SI unit.)

Table 1-1 Fundamental Quantities and Their SI Units

Quantity	Unit	Abbreviation
time	second	s
length	meter	m
mass	kilogram	kg
temperature	kelvin	K
electric current	ampere	A
amount of substance	mole	mol
luminous intensity	candela	cd

Figure 1-2 **The international mass standard** This cylinder is defined to have a mass of precisely one kilogram. To ensure that repeated measurements of its mass give the same value, the cylinder has to be treated very carefully to prevent even a small number of atoms from being scraped off.

> ❗ **Watch Out! Mass and weight are different quantities.**
>
> It's important not to confuse *mass* and *weight*. While an object's mass tells you how much material that object contains, its weight tells you how strongly gravity pulls on that object's material. Consider a person who weighs 110 pounds on Earth, corresponding to a mass of 50 kilograms. Gravity is only about one-sixth as strong on the Moon as it is on Earth, so on the Moon this person would weigh only one-sixth of 110 pounds, or about 18 pounds. But that person's mass of 50 kilograms is the same on the Moon; wherever you go in the universe, you take all of your material along with you. We'll explore the relationship between mass and weight in Chapter 4.

Units for many other physical quantities can be derived from the fundamental units of time, length, and mass. For example, speed is measured in meters per second (m/s) and weight is measured in kilograms times meters per second per second, or kilogram-meters per second squared ($kg \cdot m/s^2$). Some derived quantities are used so frequently that physicists have named a new unit to represent them. For example, the SI unit of weight is the newton (N), equal to $1 \ kg \cdot m/s^2$ or about 0.225 pounds.

When we begin our study of heat and temperature in Chapter 14, we will need to introduce another unit called the *kelvin*, which is the fundamental unit of temperature. We'll also need another unit called the *ampere*, a unit of electric current, when we begin our study of electricity in Chapter 16. Until then, all of the units we'll work with will be based on seconds, meters, and kilograms.

Unit Conversions

In science and in ordinary life, a variety of other units are used for time, length, and mass. As we'll see, it's straightforward to convert between different units for the same quantity.

In addition to the second, some other common units of time include the following:

$$1 \text{ minute (min)} = 60 \text{ s}$$
$$1 \text{ hour (h)} = 3600 \text{ s}$$
$$1 \text{ day (d)} = 86,400 \text{ s}$$

Some other units of length that are handy when discussing sizes and distances include millimeters (mm), centimeters (cm), and kilometers (km). These units of length are related to the meter as follows:

$$1 \text{ mm} = 0.001 \text{ m}$$
$$1 \text{ cm} = 0.01 \text{ m}$$
$$1 \text{ km} = 1000 \text{ m}$$

Although the English system of inches (in), feet (ft), and miles (mi) is much older than the SI, today the English system is actually based on the SI system: The inch is *defined* to be exactly 2.54 cm. A useful set of conversions is as follows:

$$1 \text{ in} = 2.54 \text{ cm}$$
$$1 \text{ ft} = 0.3048 \text{ m}$$
$$1 \text{ mi} = 1.609 \text{ km}$$

You'll find more conversion factors in Appendix A.

We can use conversions such as these to convert any quantity from one set of units to another. For example, the *Saturn V* rocket used to send astronauts to the Moon stood about 363 feet tall (Figure 1-3). How can we convert this height to meters? Figure 1-4 shows the technique. When doing unit conversions or other multiplication and division calculations involving units, you can treat the unit associated with the number as a variable. Units can get multiplied together, and they can also cancel if the same unit appears in the numerator and denominator.

Figure 1-3 **From feet to meters**
The *Saturn V* rocket that sent the first humans to the Moon stood 363 feet tall. How tall is this in meters?

Figure 1-4 Converting units
To convert units, remember that a quantity does not change if you multiply by 1. The only thing to remember is to write 1 in an appropriate way.

(1) To convert units—for example, to convert a distance in feet (ft) to a distance in meters (m)—multiply by 1 in the appropriate form. Multiplying a number by 1 does not change the number.

$$363 \text{ ft} = 363 \text{ ft} \times 1$$

(2) To find the appropriate form of 1, begin with the conversion between the two units...

(3) ...and divide one side by the other. (If you divide a number by an equal number, the result is always equal to 1.) This gives two ways to express the conversion between feet and meters.

$$1 \text{ ft} = 0.3048 \text{ m, so} \quad \frac{1 \text{ ft}}{0.3048 \text{ m}} = 1 \text{ and } \frac{0.3048 \text{ m}}{1 \text{ ft}} = 1$$

INCORRECT APPROACH:

(4) If you try multiplying 363 ft by the first form of 1...

(5) ...the result is not in the desired units.

$$363 \text{ ft} = 363 \text{ ft} \times 1 = 363 \text{ ft} \times \frac{1 \text{ ft}}{0.3048 \text{ m}} = 1190 \, \frac{\text{ft}^2}{\text{m}} \quad \times$$

CORRECT APPROACH:

To convert a quantity from one set of units to another, multiply the quantity by 1 (equal to the ratio of the two units). Choose the ratio so that the unwanted units cancel out.

(6) If instead you multiply 363 ft by the second form of 1...

(7) ...the units of ft cancel and the result is in meters, as desired.

$$363 \text{ ft} = 363 \text{ ft} \times 1 = 363 \, \cancel{\text{ft}} \times \frac{0.3048 \text{ m}}{1 \, \cancel{\text{ft}}} = 111 \text{ m} \quad \text{OK}$$

! Watch Out! Take care with conversions that have multiple steps.

Some conversions cannot be easily carried out in a single step. As an illustration, let's verify the number of seconds in a day. Since 1 day (d) equals 24 hours (h), 1 h equals 60 minutes (min), and 1 min equals 60 seconds (s), we convert units three times:

Notice that we were careful to check the cancellation of each pair of like units (d and d, h and h, min and min). We strongly recommend that you carry out conversions such as this one in an equally methodical way.

$$1 \text{ d} = 1 \, \cancel{\text{d}} \left(\frac{24 \, \cancel{\text{h}}}{1 \, \cancel{\text{d}}} \right) \left(\frac{60 \, \cancel{\text{min}}}{1 \, \cancel{\text{h}}} \right) \left(\frac{60 \text{ s}}{1 \, \cancel{\text{min}}} \right) = 86{,}400 \text{ s}$$

Example 1-2 The World's Fastest Bird

The white-throated needletail (*Hirundapus caudacutus*) can move at speeds up to 47.0 m/s in level flight. (Falcons can go even faster, but they must dive to do so.) What is this speed in km/h? in mi/h?

Set Up

This is a problem in converting units. To find the speed in km/h, we will have to convert meters (m) to kilometers (km) and seconds (s) to hours (h). To then find the speed in mi/h, we will have to convert km to miles (mi). In each stage of the conversion, we'll follow the procedure shown in Figure 1-4.

Conversions:
  1 h = 3600 s
  1 km = 1000 m
  1 mi = 1.609 km

Solve

We write the first two conversions above as a ratio equal to 1, such as (1 km)/(1000 m) = 1. We then multiply each of these by 47.0 m/s to find the speed in km/h. Note that we must set up the ratios so that the units of meters (m) and seconds (s) cancel as shown.

$$47.0 \text{ m/s} = \left(47.0 \, \frac{\cancel{\text{m}}}{\cancel{\text{s}}} \right) \left(\frac{3600 \, \cancel{\text{s}}}{1 \text{ h}} \right) \left(\frac{1 \text{ km}}{1000 \, \cancel{\text{m}}} \right)$$

$$= 169 \text{ km/h}$$

To convert this speed to mi/h, we use the ratio $(1 \text{ mi})/(1.609 \text{ km}) = 1$. $169 \text{ km/h} = \left(169 \dfrac{\cancel{\text{km}}}{\text{h}}\right)\left(\dfrac{1 \text{ mi}}{1.609 \cancel{\text{km}}}\right)$

$$= 105 \text{ mi/h}$$

Reflect

Since there are 3600 s in an hour, an object that moves at 1 m/s will travel 3600 m, or 3.6 km, in 1 h. So 1 m/s = 3.6 km/h. This says that *any* speed in km/h will be 3.6 times greater than the speed in m/s. You can check our first result by verifying that 169 is just 3.6 times 47.0.

To check our second result, note that a mile is a greater distance than a kilometer. Hence our fast-flying bird will travel fewer miles than kilometers in a one-hour time interval, and the speed in mi/h will be less than in km/h. This is just what we found.

❗ Watch Out! Use the correct conversion factor.

You can get into trouble if you are careless in applying the method of taking the number whose units are to be converted and multiplying it by a conversion factor equal to 1. For example, suppose we tried to find the speed in mi/h by multiplying 169 km/h by the conversion factor $1 = (1.609 \text{ km})/(1 \text{ mi})$.

We would then get a result with strange units (kilometers squared per hour per mile) because the unwanted units of kilometers didn't cancel. What's more, the speed in mi/h should be less than in km/h, not more. If you *always* keep track of units when doing conversions, you'll avoid mistakes of this kind.

$$169 \text{ km/h} = \left(169 \dfrac{\text{km}}{\text{h}}\right)\left(\dfrac{1.609 \text{ km}}{1 \text{ mi}}\right) = 272 \text{ km}^2/(\text{h} \cdot \text{mi})$$

Quantities versus Units

In this book we'll often use symbols to denote the values of physical quantities. We'll always write these symbols using *italics*. Some examples include the symbols v for speed, B for magnetic field, and E for energy. (As these examples show, the symbol is not always the first letter of the name of the quantity.) By contrast, the letters that we use to denote units, such as m (meters), s (seconds), and kg (kilograms) are not italicized. If the unit is named for a person, the letter is capitalized. An example is the unit of power, the watt (abbreviated W), named for the Scottish inventor James Watt.

In some cases the same symbol is used for more than one quantity. One example is the symbol T, which can denote a temperature, a period of time, or the tension in a stretched rope. The letter T (not italicized) is also used as an abbreviation for the unit of magnetic field, the tesla (named for the Serbian-American physicist Nikola Tesla). You'll often need to pay careful attention to the context in which a symbol is used to discern the quantity or unit it represents.

Scientific Notation

Physicists investigate objects that vary in size from the largest structures in the universe, including galaxies and clusters of galaxies, down to atomic nuclei and the particles found within nuclei. The time intervals that they analyze range from the age of the universe to a tiny fraction of a second. To describe such a wide range of phenomena, we need an equally wide range of both large and small numbers.

To avoid such confusing terms as "a million billion billion," physicists use a standard shorthand system called **scientific notation**. All the cumbersome zeros that accompany a large number are consolidated into one term consisting of 10 followed by an **exponent**, which is written as a superscript. The exponent indicates how many zeros you would need to write out the long form of the number. The exponent also tells you how many tens must be multiplied together to give the desired number, which is why the exponent is also called the **power of ten**. For example, ten thousand can be written as 10^4 ("ten to the fourth" or "ten to the fourth power") because $10^4 = 10 \times 10 \times 10 \times 10 = 10{,}000$. Some powers of ten are so common that we have created abbreviations for them that appear as a prefix to the actual unit. For example, rather than writing 10^9 watts (10^9 W), we can write 1 gigawatt, or 1 GW. **Table 1-2** lists the prefix and its abbreviation for several common powers of ten.

Table 1-2 Prefixes

Factor	Prefix	Symbol
10^{-24}	yocto	y
10^{-21}	zepto	z
10^{-18}	atto	a
10^{-15}	femto	f
10^{-12}	pico	p
10^{-9}	nano	n
10^{-6}	micro	μ
10^{-3}	milli	m
10^{-2}	centi	c
10^{-1}	deci	d
10^{1}	deka	da
10^{2}	hecto	h
10^{3}	kilo	k
10^{6}	mega	M
10^{9}	giga	G
10^{12}	tera	T
10^{15}	peta	P
10^{18}	exa	E
10^{21}	zetta	Z
10^{24}	yotta	Y

? Got the Concept? 1-1
Smallest to Biggest

Each of these numbers represents the size of something. Arrange them from smallest to largest. (a) 0.1 mm; (b) 7 μm; (c) 6380 km; (d) 165 cm; (e) 200 nm.

Answers to *Got the Concept?* questions can be found at the end of the chapter.

In scientific notation, numbers are usually written as a figure between 1 and 10 multiplied by the appropriate power of ten. The approximate distance between Earth and the Sun, for example, can be written as 1.5×10^8 km. This is far more convenient than writing "150,000,000 km" or "one hundred and fifty million kilometers." A power output of 2500 watts (2500 W) can be written in scientific notation as 2.5×10^3 W. (Alternatively, we can write this as 2.5 kW, where 1 kW = 1 kilowatt = 10^3 W.)

Note that most electronic calculators use a shorthand for scientific notation. To enter the number 1.5×10^8, you first enter 1.5, then press a key labeled "EXP," "EE," or "10^x," then enter the exponent 8. (The EXP, EE, or 10^x key takes care of the "$\times$ 10" part of the expression.)

The number will then appear on your calculator's display as "1.5 E 8," "1.5 8," or some variation of these; typically the "$\times$ 10" is not displayed as such. There are some variations from one calculator to another, so you should spend a few minutes to make sure you know the correct procedure for working with numbers in scientific notation. You will be using this notation continually in your study of physics, so this is time well spent.

! Watch Out! Know how your calculator expresses scientific notation.

Confusion can result from the way calculators display scientific notation. Since 1.5×10^8 is displayed as "1.5 8" or "1.5 E 8," it is not uncommon to think that 1.5×10^8 is the same as 1.5^8. That is not correct, however; 1.5^8 is equal to 1.5 multiplied by itself eight times, or 25.63, which is not even close to $150,000,000 = 1.5 \times 10^8$. Another common mistake is to write 1.5×10^8 as 15^8. If you are inclined to do this, perhaps you are thinking that you can multiply 1.5 by 10, then tack on the exponent later. This also does not work; 15^8 is equal to 15 multiplied by itself eight times, or 2,562,890,625, which again is nowhere near 1.5×10^8. Reading over the manual for your calculator will help you to avoid these common errors.

? Got the Concept? 1-2
Comparing Sizes

For each pair, determine which quantity is bigger and find the ratio of the larger quantity to the smaller quantity.
(a) 1 mg, 1 kg
(b) 1 mm, 1 cm
(c) 1 MW, 1 kW
(d) 10^{-10} m, 10^{-14} m
(e) 10^{10} m, 10^{14} m

You can use scientific notation for numbers that are less than one by using a minus sign in front of the exponent. A negative exponent tells you to *divide* by the appropriate number of tens. For example, 10^{-2} ("ten to the minus two") means to divide by 10 twice, so $10^{-2} = (1/10) \times (1/10) = 1/100 = 0.01$. Table 1-2 also includes negative powers of ten.

You can also use scientific notation to express a number such as 0.00245: $0.00245 = 2.45 \times 0.001 = 2.45 \times 10^{-3}$. (Again, the standard for scientific notation is that the first figure is a number between 1 and 10.) This notation is particularly useful when dealing with very small numbers. A good example is the diameter of a hydrogen atom, which is much more convenient to state in scientific notation (1.1×10^{-10} m) than as a decimal (0.00000000011 m) or a fraction (110 trillionths of a meter).

Example 1-3 Hair Growth

The hair on a typical person's head grows at an average rate of 1.5 cm per month (Figure 1-5). Approximately how far (in meters) will the ends of your hair move during a 50-min physics class? Express the answer using scientific notation.

Figure 1-5 **Hair growth** How much does a person's hair grow during a 50-minute class period?

Set Up

Like Example 1-2, this is a problem in converting units. We'll again follow the procedure shown in Figure 1-4. Not all months have the same number of days, so we'll assume an average 30-day month. We'll use the idea that since speed equals distance

Conversions:

$$1 \text{ min} = 60 \text{ s}$$
$$1 \text{ d} = 86,400 \text{ s}$$
$$1 \text{ month (average)} = 30 \text{ d}$$

per time, the distance the hair moves equals the growth speed multiplied by the time in one class period.

$$1 \text{ cm} = 0.01 \text{ m}$$

$$speed = \frac{distance}{time}$$

$$so \ distance = speed \times time$$

Solve

Let's first express the speed at which hair grows in SI units (m/s). We use the conversion factors relating meters to centimeters, months to days, and days to seconds, and cancel units. We must move the decimal point to the right by nine steps to put the result in scientific notation, so the exponent is -9.

To find the distance that hair grows in 50 min, we multiply this speed by 50 min and include the conversion factor relating seconds and minutes. We then put the result into scientific notation. Note that the first number in the result is between 1 and 10. Note also that when multiplying together powers of ten, we simply add the exponents.

1.5 cm/month

$$= \left(1.5 \, \frac{\cancel{cm}}{\cancel{month}}\right)\left(\frac{0.01 \text{ m}}{1 \, \cancel{cm}}\right)\left(\frac{1 \, \cancel{month}}{30 \, \cancel{d}}\right)\left(\frac{1 \, \cancel{d}}{86,400 \text{ s}}\right)$$

$$= 0.0000000058 \text{ m/s} = 5.8 \times 10^{-9} \text{m/s}$$

$$distance = \left(5.8 \times 10^{-9} \, \frac{m}{\cancel{s}}\right)(50 \, \cancel{min})\left(\frac{60 \, \cancel{s}}{1 \, \cancel{min}}\right)$$

$$= (5.8 \times 10^{-9})(3 \times 10^3) \text{ m}$$

$$= 5.8 \times 3 \times 10^{-9} \times 10^3 \text{ m}$$

$$= 17 \times 10^{-9} \times 10^3 \text{ m}$$

$$= 1.7 \times 10^1 \times 10^{-9} \times 10^3 \text{ m}$$

$$= 1.7 \times 10^{1-9+3} \text{ m}$$

$$= 1.7 \times 10^{-5} \text{ m}$$

Reflect

You can also express this result in micrometers (μm). Note that when dividing powers of ten, we subtract the exponents. A distance of 17 μm is about 1/40 mm. Do you think you could notice this change in length with the unaided eye?

$$1.7 \times 10^{-5} \text{ m} = (1.7 \times 10^{-5} \text{ m})\left(\frac{1 \, \mu m}{10^{-6} \text{ m}}\right)$$

$$= 1.7 \times \frac{10^{-5}}{10^{-6}} \, \mu m$$

$$= 1.7 \times 10^{-5-(-6)} \, \mu m$$

$$= 1.7 \times 10^1 \, \mu m = 17 \, \mu m$$

Take-Home Message for Section 1-3

✔ Many physical quantities can be measured in units that are combinations of the SI units seconds, meters, and kilograms.

✔ To convert a physical quantity from one set of units to another, multiply it by an appropriate conversion factor equal to 1.

✔ In scientific notation, quantities are expressed as a number between 1 and 10 multiplied by 10 raised to a power.

✔ Prefixes can be used instead of scientific notation to indicate 10 raised to a power.

1-4 Correct use of significant figures helps keep track of uncertainties in numerical values

Although physicists strive to make their measurements as precise as possible, the unavoidable fact is that there is always some uncertainty in every measurement. This is not a result of sloppiness or of a lack of care on the part of the person doing the measurement; rather, it is due to fundamental limitations in how well measurements can be carried out.

If you try to measure the size of your thumbnail using a ruler with markings in millimeters, you might find that it's between 15 and 16 mm in length. With keen eyes and a little judgment, you might be able to tell that the length is very nearly halfway between those two markings on the ruler, so you might say that the length is approximately 15.5 mm. However, armed only with your ruler it would be impossible to say whether the length was 15.47 mm, 15.51 mm, or 15.54 mm. We would say that the fourth digit is *not significant*, that is, it does not contain meaningful information. Hence this measurement has only three **significant figures**. We specify this implicitly by giving the measured value as 15.5 mm, by which we mean that it's between 15.4 and 15.6 mm. More precise measurements have more significant figures; less precise measurements have fewer significant figures.

An alternative way to present the number would be to give the length of your thumbnail as 15.5 $\pm$ 0.1 mm, with the number after the $\pm$ sign representing the uncertainty. This

$\sqrt{x}$ *See the Math Tutorial for more information on significant figures* kind of presentation is very common in experimental work. In this book, however, we'll use significant figures to represent uncertainty.

Note that some numbers are *exact*, with no uncertainty whatsoever. Three examples are the number of meters in a kilometer (exactly 1000), the speed of light (defined to be exactly 299,792,458 m/s, as we learned in Section 1-3), and the value of π. The value of any measured quantity, however, will have some uncertainty.

Scientific notation is helpful in representing the number of significant figures in a measurement. When we say that the radius of the Moon at its equator is 3476 km, we imply that there are four significant figures in the value and that the uncertainty in the diameter is only about 1 km. Since there are 1000 m in 1 km, we could also express the diameter as 3,476,000 m. This is misleading, however, since it gives the impression that there are *seven* significant figures in the value. That isn't correct; we do *not* know the value of the Moon's equatorial radius to within 1 meter. A better way to express the diameter in meters is as 3.476×10^6 m, which makes it explicit that there are only four significant figures in the value. The radius of the minor planet Eris is less well known and is about 1300 km; only the first two digits are significant, so it's more accurate to express this dimension as 1.3×10^3 km.

There are special rules to help determine whether or not zeroes in a number are significant. *Leading zeroes* are not significant, so the number 0.0035 has only two significant figures. *Trailing zeroes* to the right of the decimal point are significant, so the number 0.3500 has four significant figures. When we have trailing zeroes to the left of the decimal point, as in 350, things get ambiguous. To make it clear that the trailing zero is significant, it is best to write 3.50×10^2. We will attempt to do just that throughout this text. However, there may be times when it is more expedient to write exact numbers without scientific notation. For example, there are exactly 60 s in 1 min, so the 60 has as many significant figures as we need, and we won't bother writing 6.0000×10^1 s or 60.000 to indicate that the value should have five significant figures.

In most problems in this book we'll use numbers with two, three, or four significant figures. For example, you might be asked about the motion of an ostrich that runs 43.9 m (three significant figures) in 2.3 s (two significant figures). If you use your calculator to find the speed of this ostrich (the distance traveled divided by the elapsed time), the result will be

$$\frac{43.9 \text{ m}}{2.3 \text{ s}} = 19.08695652 \text{ m/s (incorrect)}$$

This answer is incorrect because there are *not* 10 significant figures in the answer. In no way do you know the result that precisely! The general rule for *multiplying or dividing* numbers is that the result has the same number of significant figures as the input number with the *fewest* significant figures. In our example the elapsed time of 2.3 s has fewer significant figures (two) than the distance of 43.9 m, so the result has only two significant figures. Rounding our result, we get

| 3 significant figures | Result has only 2 significant figures |

$$\frac{43.9 \text{ m}}{2.3 \text{ s}} = 19 \text{ m/s} \quad \text{(correct)}$$

| 2 significant figures |

Following the same rule, if a strip of cloth is 35.65 cm long and 2.49 cm wide, the area (length times width) has only three significant figures: (35.65 cm)(2.49 cm) = 88.7685 cm^2, which rounds to 88.8 cm^2.

There's a slightly different rule for *adding or subtracting* numbers. Suppose that you drive 44.3 km (according to the odometer of your car) from Central City to the parking lot at the Metropolis shopping mall, then walk an additional 108 m or 0.108 km (according to your pedometer) to your favorite clothing store. The total distance you have traveled is (44.3 km) + (0.108 km), which according to your calculator is 44.408 km.

? Got the Concept? 1-3
Significant Figures

All of these numbers have the same value but are written with a different number of significant figures: (a) 123, (b) 1.230×10^2, (c) 123.000, (d) 1.23×10^2, (e) 0.12300×10^3. Rank them in order of least to most significant figures.

This isn't quite right, however, because you only know your driving distance to the nearest tenth of a kilometer. As a result, you need to round off the answer to the nearest tenth of a kilometer, or 44.4 km. So

1 digit to the right of the decimal point   3 digits to the right of the decimal point

$$44.3 \text{ km} + 0.108 \text{ km} = 44.4 \text{ km}$$

Result has only 1 digit to the right of the decimal point

Thus the general rule for adding or subtracting numbers is that the result can have no less uncertainty than the most uncertain input number. In our example that's the 44.3-km distance, which has an uncertainty of about 0.1 km. Stated another way, the answer may have no more digits to the right of the decimal point than the input number with the fewest digits to the right of the decimal point when all numbers are expressed in scientific notation with the same exponent.

Let's summarize our general rules for working with significant figures:

Rule 1 When multiplying or dividing numbers, the result should have the same number of significant figures as the input number with the fewest significant figures. The same rule applies to squaring, taking the square root, calculating sines and cosines, and so on.

Rule 2 When adding or subtracting numbers, the result should have the same number of digits to the right of the decimal point as the input number with the fewest digits to the right of the decimal point when all numbers are expressed in scientific notation with the same exponent.

We'll use these rules for working with significant figures in all of the worked examples in the book. (If you look back, you'll see that we actually used them in Examples 1-2 and 1-3 in Section 1-3.) Make sure that you follow these same rules in your own problem solving.

❗ Watch Out! **Be mindful of significant figures when rounding numbers.**

If you're doing a calculation with several steps, it's best to retain *all* of the digits in your calculation until the very end. Then you can round off the result as necessary to give the answer to the correct number of significant figures. For example, suppose you want to calculate $32.1 \times 4.998 \times 4.87$. Our general rules tell us that the final answer has only three significant figures. The product of the first two numbers is $32.1 \times 4.998 = 160.4358$, which if you round off at this point becomes 160. If you multiply this rounded number by 4.87, you get 779.2, which rounds to 779. If, however, you calculate $32.1 \times 4.998 \times 4.87$ directly using your calculator *without* rounding the intermediate answer, you get 781.322346. Rounding this to three significant figures gives the correct answer, which is 781. Moral: Don't round until the end of your calculation!

Example 1-4 Combining Volumes

What is the volume (in cubic kilometers) of Earth? What is the volume of the Moon? What is the combined volume of the two worlds together? The radius of Earth is 6378 km, and the radius of the Moon is 1738 km.

Set Up

From the Math Tutorial, the volume of a sphere of radius R is $4\pi R^3/3$. Since we multiply the radius by itself, the answer can have no more significant figures than the value of the radius.

Radius of Earth $R_E = 6378$ km
Radius of Moon $R_M = 1738$ km

Solve

For Earth, R_E has four significant figures, so the volume has only four significant figures.

Volume of Earth:

$$V_E = \frac{4\pi \left(6378 \text{ km}\right)^3}{3}$$

$$= 1.086781293 \times 10^{12} \text{ km}^3$$

Round to four significant figures:

$$V_E = 1.087 \times 10^{12} \text{ km}^3$$

The radius of the Moon also has four significant figures, and so its volume does as well.

Volume of Moon:

$$V_M = \frac{4\pi \left(1738 \text{ km}\right)^3}{3}$$

$$= 2.199064287 \times 10^{10} \text{ km}^3$$

Round to four significant figures:

$$V_M = 2.199 \times 10^{10} \text{ km}^3$$

To find the combined volume, we add V_E and V_M. To make sure we retain the correct number of significant figures in our answer, we express both numbers in scientific notation with the same exponent. According to Rule 2 for addition, our answer must have only three significant figures to the right of the decimal point.

$$V_E = 1.087 \times 10^{12} \text{ km}^3$$
$$V_M = 2.199 \times 10^{10} \text{ km}^3$$
$$= 0.02199 \times 10^{12} \text{ km}^3$$

To avoid intermediate rounding errors we will use the unrounded values and then round the result to three digits to the right of the decimal point at the end of the calculation.

$$V_E + V_M = (1.086781293 \times 10^{12} \text{ km}^3)$$
$$+ (0.02199064287 \times 10^{12} \text{ km}^3)$$
$$= (1.086781293 + 0.02199064287) \times 10^{12} \text{ km}^3$$
$$= 1.10877193587 \times 10^{12} \text{ km}^3$$

This has too many significant figures, so we round to the final answer of

$$V_E + V_M = 1.109 \times 10^{12} \text{ km}^3$$

Reflect

In this problem we had to use both the significant figure rule for multiplication and the significant figure rule for addition. You should be prepared to use both of these rules in solving problems on your own. In this example, if we had used the rounded values of the volumes, we would have gotten $V_E + V_M = 1.087 \times 10^{12} \text{ km}^3 + 0.02199 \times 10^{12} \text{ km}^3 = 1.10899 \times 10^{12} \text{ km}^3$, which still rounds to $1.109 \times 10^{12} \text{ km}^3$. But this is not always the case, so don't round until you have finished all your calculations.

Take-Home Message for Section 1-4

✔ Significant figures characterize the precision of a measurement or the uncertainty of a numerical value.

✔ When multiplying or dividing numbers, the result has the same number of significant figures as the input number with the fewest significant figures.

✔ When adding or subtracting numbers, the result has the same number of digits to the right of the decimal point as the input number with the fewest number of digits to the right of the decimal point *when all numbers are expressed in scientific notation with the same exponent.*

✔ When writing a number, all trailing zeroes to the right of the decimal point are significant figures.

1-5 Dimensional analysis is a powerful way to check the results of a physics calculation

Once you've done a problem, it's useful to be able to quickly determine how likely it is that you've done the problem correctly. One valuable approach is to do a **dimensional analysis**. This approach is particularly useful when you calculate an algebraic result and want to check it before substituting numerical values.

To see what we mean, first note that any physical quantity has a *dimension*: Three quantities that we introduced in Section 1-3 are mass, length, and time. (Table 1-1 in Section 1-3 lists additional physical quantities.) We say that the mass of a hydrogen atom has dimensions of mass, the diameter of the atom has dimensions of length, and the amount of time it takes light to travel that diameter has dimensions of time. Mass, length, and time are *fundamental* dimensions because they cannot be expressed in terms of other, more fundamental quantities. (We'll encounter a few other fundamental dimensions in later chapters.)

Dimensions *have* units but are not units themselves. Units are used to help express the numerical value of a dimension. A dimension of length may be expressed in units of meters; for example, the length of a typical house cat is 0.65 m. The dimension of time might be expressed in units of nanoseconds, and the dimension of mass might be expressed in units of kilograms.

The dimensions of many quantities are made up of a combination of fundamental dimensions. One example is speed, which has dimensions of distance per time, or (distance)/(time) for short. Another is volume, which has dimensions of distance cubed or (distance)^3.

Here's the key to using dimensional analysis: *In any equation, the dimensions must be the same on both sides of the equation.* As an example, suppose you hold a ball at height h above the ground and then let it fall. The ball takes a time t to reach the ground. You calculate that the relationship between the height h and the time t is

$$h = vt^2 \qquad\qquad (1\text{-}2)$$

where v is the speed of the ball just before it hits the ground. Is Equation 1-2 dimensionally correct? To find out, replace each symbol by the dimensions of the quantity that it represents. The height h has dimensions of length or distance, speed v has dimensions of (distance)/(time), and time t has dimensions of time. Dimensions cancel just like algebraic quantities, so if we simplify this, we get

$$\text{distance} = \frac{\text{distance}}{\text{time}} \times (\text{time})^2$$
$$= \frac{\text{distance}}{\text{time}} \times \text{time} \times \text{time}$$
$$= \text{distance} \times \text{time}$$

This is *inconsistent:* The left-hand side of Equation 1-2 (h) has dimensions of distance, while the right-hand side (vt^2) has dimensions of distance multiplied by time. So Equation 1-2 *cannot* be correct.

It turns out that the correct relationship between the height h from which the ball is dropped and the time t it takes to reach the ground is

$$h = \frac{1}{2}gt^2 \qquad\qquad (1\text{-}3)$$

where g is a constant. Let's use dimensional analysis to figure out the dimensions of g. Again h has units of distance and t has units of time. The number $1/2$ has no dimensions at all, so it can be ignored (it is a pure number with no units, so it is *dimensionless*). We rewrite Equation 1-3 in terms of dimensions and solve for the dimensions of g:

$$\text{distance} = (\text{dimensions of } g) \times (\text{time})^2$$
$$(\text{dimensions of } g) = \frac{\text{distance}}{(\text{time})^2}$$

The SI units of g must then be m/s^2 (meters per second squared, or meters per second per second). We'll learn the significance of the quantity g (called the *acceleration due to gravity*) in Chapter 2.

Watch Out!

Dimensions are not the same as units.

Be careful to make the distinction between *dimensions* and *units*. For example, volume may be expressed in any number of different units such as m^3, cm^3, mm^3, or km^3. But no matter what units are used, volume *always* has dimensions of (distance)^3.

! Watch Out! Dimensional analysis can't tell you everything.

Suppose that as a result of an algebraic error we failed to include the factor of $1/2$ in Equation 1-3 and instead found $h = gt^2$. Because the pure number $1/2$ has no dimensions, it wouldn't change the dimensional analysis we did above. So a dimensional analysis would not catch this mistake. Performing dimensional analysis can tell you whether an answer is wrong, but even if the dimensions of your answer are correct, the numerical value might still be wrong.

? Got the Concept? 1-4 Dimensional Analysis

A block of mass m oscillates back and forth on the end of a spring. (Flip forward in the book and look at Figure 12-2.) You'll find that the time T that the block takes for one full back-and-forth cycle depends on a constant k that has dimensions of mass divided by time squared according to

$$T = 2\pi\sqrt{\frac{m}{k}}$$

Use dimensional analysis to determine whether this result could be correct.

Take-Home Message for Section 1-5

✔ Dimensional analysis is the technique of checking the dimensions of your algebraic answer before you substitute values to compute a numeric result.

✔ The dimensions of any quantity can be put together from a few fundamental dimensions, including mass, distance, and time.

✔ The key to using dimensional analysis: *In any equation, the dimensions must be the same on both sides of the equation.*

Key Terms

units
Système International
second
meter

mass
kilogram
scientific notation
exponent

power of ten
significant figures
dimensional analysis

Chapter Summary

Topic	Equation or Figure
Problem-Solving Strategy: We'll solve all problems using a strategy that incorporates three steps.	*Set Up* the problem *Solve* for the desired quantities *Reflect* on the answer
Unit Conversion: Units can be converted by multiplying any value by an appropriate representation of 1.	$47.0 \text{ m/s} = \left(47.0\dfrac{\text{m}}{\text{s}}\right)\left(\dfrac{3600 \text{ s}}{1 \text{ h}}\right)\left(\dfrac{1 \text{ km}}{1000 \text{ m}}\right)$ $= 169 \text{ km/h}$
Scientific Notation: Any number can be written in scientific notation, which usually consists of a number between 1 and 10 multiplied by 10 raised to some power. Prefixes can be used as abbreviations for many powers of ten.	$150{,}000{,}000 \text{ km} = 1.5 \times 10^8 \text{ km}$ $2500 \text{ watts} = 2.5 \times 10^3 \text{ W}$ $= 2.5 \text{ kilowatts} = 2.5 \text{ kW}$

Significant Figures: Any measured quantity has a finite number of significant digits. You need to keep track of the number of significant digits in all your calculations. There are different rules for addition/subtraction and multiplication/division.

Rule 1 When multiplying or dividing numbers, the result should have the same number of significant figures as the input number with the fewest significant figures. The same rule applies to squaring, taking the square root, calculating sines and cosines, and so on.

Rule 2 When adding or subtracting numbers, the result should have the same number of digits to the right of the decimal point as the input number with the fewest digits to the right of the decimal point when all numbers are expressed in scientific notation with the same exponent.

3 significant figures | Result has only 2 significant figures

$$\frac{43.9 \text{ m}}{2.3 \text{ s}} = 19 \text{ m/s} \quad (\text{correct})$$

2 significant figures

1 digit to the right of the decimal point | 3 digits to the right of the decimal point

$$44.3 \text{ km} + 0.108 \text{ km} = 44.4 \text{ km}$$

Result has only 1 digit to the right of the decimal point

Dimensional Analysis: Analyzing the dimensions of an equation can provide a clue as to the correctness of that equation. Dimensions and units are not the same thing.

$$h = \frac{1}{2}gt^2 \tag{1-3}$$

$$\text{distance} = (\text{dimensions of } g) \times (\text{time})^2$$

$$(\text{dimensions of } g) = \frac{\text{distance}}{(\text{time})^2}$$

Answer to What do you think? Question

(c) 1 cm. The length of a typical hummingbird is 7.5 to 13 cm, and the head is 1 or 2 cm in length.

Answers to Got the Concept? Questions

1-1 From smallest to largest, the order is (e), (b), (a), (d), and (c). Some examples of objects of about the size of the five distances include: 200 nanometers (e) is the diameter of a typical virus; 7 μm (b) is the diameter of a human red blood cell; 0.1 mm (a) is the diameter of a typical human hair; 165 cm (d) is the average height of a woman in the United States; and (c) 6380 km is the mean radius of Earth.

1-2 (a) One kilogram is bigger than one milligram by a factor of 1 million; 1 mg equals 0.001 g equals 0.000001 kg. (b) One centimeter is 10 times bigger than 1 mm; 1 mm equals 0.001 m and 1 cm equals 0.01 m. (c) One megawatt is 1 thousand times bigger than 1 kW; 1 MW equals 1,000,000 W and 1 kW equals 1,000 W. (d) A distance of 10^{-10} m is 10^4 (10,000) times bigger than 10^{-14} m: $(10^{-10}$ m$)/(10^{-14}$ m$) = 10^{-10-(-14)} = 10^{-10+14} = 10^4$. (e) A distance 10^{14} m is 10^4 (10,000) times bigger than 10^{10} m; $(10^{14}$ m$)/(10^{10}$ m$) = 10^{14-10} = 10^4$.

1-3 123 has three significant digits, as does 1.23×10^2. 1.230×10^2 is written with four significant digits, 0.12300×10^3 has five significant digits, and 123.000 has six.

1-4 Since m has dimensions of mass, k has dimensions of mass per time squared, and 2π is dimensionless, the dimensions of the right-hand side of the equation $T = 2\pi\sqrt{m/k}$ are

$$\sqrt{\frac{\text{mass}}{\text{mass}/(\text{time})^2}} = \sqrt{\text{mass} \times \frac{(\text{time})^2}{\text{mass}}}$$

$$= \sqrt{(\text{time})^2} = \text{time}$$

The left-hand side of the equation, T, also has dimensions of time. Hence you can have some confidence that this relationship is correct. You cannot say, however, that this equation is *exactly* correct because the pure number 2π has no dimensions and therefore does not play a role in the dimensional analysis. Had the equation been, say, $T = 5\sqrt{m/k}$ the dimensional analysis would be exactly the same.

Questions and Problems

In a few problems, you are given more data than you actually need; in a few other problems, you are required to supply data from your general knowledge, outside sources, or informed estimate.

For all problems, use $g = 9.80 \text{ m/s}^2$ for the free-fall acceleration due to gravity. Neglect friction and air resistance unless instructed to do otherwise.

* Basic, single-concept problem
** Intermediate-level problem, may require synthesis of concepts and multiple steps
*** Challenging problem
SSM *Solution is in Student Solutions Manual*

Conceptual Questions

1. •Define the following basic quantities in physics (length, mass, and time) and list the appropriate SI unit that is used for each quantity.

2. •Is it possible to define a system of units in which length is not one of the fundamental properties?

3. •Why do physicists and other scientists prefer to use metric units and prefixes (for example, micro, milli, and centi) to American Standard Units, for example, inches and pounds? SSM

4. •If you use a calculator to divide 3411 by 62.0, you will get something like 55.016129. (Exactly what you get will depend on your calculator.) Of course, you know that all those decimal places aren't significant. How should you write the answer?

5. •All valid equations in physics have consistent units. Are all equations that have consistent units valid? Support your answer with examples. SSM

6. •What properties should an object, system, or process have for it to be a useful standard of measurement of a physical quantity such as length or time?

7. •Acceleration has dimensions L/T^2, where L is length and T is time. What are the SI units of acceleration? SSM

8. •Consider the number 61,000. (a) What is the least number of significant figures this might have? (b) The greatest number? (c) If the same number is expressed as 6.10×10^4, how many significant figures does it have?

Multiple-Choice Questions

9. •Which of the following are fundamental quantities?
   A. mass density
   B. length
   C. area
   D. resistance
   E. all of the above

10. •Which length is the largest?
   A. 10 nm
   B. 10 cm
   C. 10^2 mm
   D. 10^{-2} m
   E. 1

11. •One nanosecond is
   A. 10^{-15} s
   B. 10^{-6} s
   C. 10^{-9} s
   D. 10^{-3} s
   E. 10^9 s

12. •How many cubic meters are there in a cubic centimeter?
   A. 10^2
   B. 10^6
   C. 10^{-2}
   D. 10^{-3}
   E. 10^{-6}

13. •How many square centimeters are there in a square meter?
   A. 10
   B. 10^2
   C. 10^4
   D. 10^{-2}
   E. 10^{-4} SSM

14. •Calculate $1.4 + 15 + 7.15 + 8.003$ using the proper number of significant figures.
   A. 31.553
   B. 31.550
   C. 31.55
   D. 31.6
   E. 32

15. •Calculate $0.688/0.28$ using the proper number of significant figures.
   A. 2.4571
   B. 2.457
   C. 2.46
   D. 2.5
   E. 2

16. •Which of the following relationships is dimensionally consistent with a value for acceleration that has dimensions of distance per time per time? In these equations, x is distance, t is time, and v is speed.
   A. v^2/t
   B. v/t
   C. v/t^2
   D. v/x^2
   E. v^2/x^2

17. •Calculate 25.8×70.0 using the proper number of significant figures.
   A. 1806.0
   B. 1806
   C. 1810
   D. 1800
   E. 2000 SSM

Estimation/Numerical Analysis

18. •Estimate the distance from your dorm or apartment to your physics lecture room. Give your answer in meters.

19. •Estimate the time required for a baseball to travel from home plate to the center field fence in a major league baseball game.

20. •Estimate the number of laptop computers on your campus.

21. •Estimate the volume (in liters) of water used daily by each student at your school. SSM

22. •Estimate the amount (in kg) of nonrecyclable and non-compostable garbage that each student at your school produces each day.

23. •Estimate the height (in m) of the tallest building on your campus.

24. •Enrico Fermi once estimated the length of all the sidewalks in Chicago in the 1940s. Estimate the length (in km) of sidewalks in present-day Chicago.

25. •**Biology** Although human cells vary in size, the volume of a typical cell is equivalent to the volume of a sphere that has an approximately 10^{-5} m radius. Estimate the number of cells in your body. (*Hint*: Consider your body as a collection of cylinders.) SSM

26. •**Biology** Estimate the volume flow rate (in units of m^3/s) of the air that fills your lungs as you take a deep breath.

Problems

1-3 Measurements in physics are based on standard units of time, length, and mass

27. •Write the following numbers in scientific notation:
    A. 237
    B. 0.00223
    C. 45.1
    D. 1115
    E. 14,870
    F. 214.78
    G. 0.00000442
    H. 12,345,678

28. •Write the following numbers using decimals:
    A. 4.42×10^{-3}
    B. 7.09×10^{-6}
    C. 8.28×10^2
    D. 6.02×10^6
    E. 456×10^3
    F. 22.4×10^{-3}
    G. 0.375×10^{-4}
    H. 138×10^{-6}

29. •Write the metric prefixes for the following powers of ten:
    A. $10^3 =$ _____
    B. $10^9 =$ _____
    C. $10^6 =$ _____
    D. $10^{12} =$ _____
    E. $10^{-3} =$ _____
    F. $10^{-12} =$ _____
    G. $10^{-6} =$ _____
    H. $10^{-9} =$ _____ SSM

30. •What are the numerical values for the following prefixes:
    A. p = _____
    B. m = _____
    C. M = _____
    D. μ = _____
    E. f = _____
    F. G = _____
    G. T = _____
    H. c = _____

31. •Complete the following conversions:
    A. 125 cm = _____ m
    B. 233 g = _____ kg
    C. 786 ms = _____ s
    D. 454 kg = _____ mg
    E. 208 cm^2 = _____ m^2
    F. 444 m^2 = _____ cm^2
    G. 12.5 cm^3 = _____ m^3
    H. 144 m^3 = _____ cm^3

32. •Complete the following conversions:
    A. 238 ft = _____ m
    B. 772 in = _____ cm
    C. 1220 in^2 = _____ cm^2
    D. 559 oz = _____ L
    E. 973 lb = _____ g
    F. 122 ft^3 = _____ m^3
    G. 1.28 mi^2 = _____ km^2
    H. 442 in^3 = _____ cm^3

33. •Complete the following conversions:
    A. 125 cm = _____ in
    B. 233 in = _____ cm
    C. 553 ms = _____ h
    D. 454 in = _____ m
    E. 355 cm^2 = _____ in^2
    F. 333 m^2 = _____ ft^2
    G. 424 in^3 = _____ cm^3
    H. 172 m^3 = _____ in^3

34. •Complete the following conversions:
    A. 118 gal = _____ ft^3
    B. 1.3 ft^3 = _____ gal
    C. 14,400 fl oz = _____ L
    D. 128 fl oz = _____ m^3
    E. 487 in^3 = _____ cm^3
    F. 0.0032 gal = _____ L
    G. 129 in^3 = _____ m^3
    H. 324 pints = _____ L

35. •Complete the following conversions:
    A. 328 cm^3 = _____ L
    B. 112 L = _____ m^3
    C. 220 hectares = _____ m^2
    D. 44,300 m^2 = _____ hectares
    E. 225 L = _____ m^3
    F. 17.2 hectares · m = _____ L
    G. 225,300 L = _____ hectares · m
    H. 2000 m^3 = _____ mL SSM

36. •Complete the following conversions:
    A. 33.5 gal = _____ L
    B. 62.8 L = _____ gal
    C. 216 acre · ft = _____ L
    D. 1770 gal = _____ m^3
    E. 22.8 fl oz = _____ cm^3
    F. 54.2 cm^3 = _____ cups
    G. 1.25 hectares = _____ acre
    H. 664 mm^3 = _____ qt

37. •Write the following quantities in scientific notation without prefixes: (a) 300 km, (b) 33.7 μm, and (c) 77.5 GW.

38. •Write the following with prefixes and not using scientific notation: (a) 3.45×10^{-4} s, (b) 2.00×10^{-11} W, (c) 2.337×10^8 m, and (d) 6.54×10^4 g.

39. •The United States is about the only country in the world that still uses the units feet, miles, and gallons. You might see some car specifications in a magazine that give fuel efficiency as 7.6 km per kilogram of fuel. Given that a mile is 1.609 km, a gallon is 3.785 liters, and a liter of gasoline has a mass of 0.729 kg, what is the car's fuel efficiency in miles per gallon? SSM

40. •You hire a printer to print concert tickets. He delivers them in circular rolls labeled as 1000 tickets each. You want to check the number of tickets in each roll without counting thousands of tickets. You decide to do it by measuring the diameter of the rolls. If the tickets are 2 in long and 0.22 mm thick and are rolled on a core 3 cm in diameter, what should be the diameter of a roll of 1000 tickets?

1-4 Correct use of significant figures helps keep track of uncertainties in numerical values

41. •Give the number of significant figures in each of the following numbers:

    A. 112.4
    B. 10
    C. 3.14159
    D. 700
    E. 1204.0
    F. 0.0030
    G. 9.33×10^3
    H. 0.02240

42. •Complete the following operations using the correct number of significant figures:

    A. $5.36 \times 2.0 = $ _____
    B. $\dfrac{14.2}{2} = $ _____
    C. $2 \times 3.14159 = $ _____
    D. $4.040 \times 5.55 = $ _____
    E. $4.444 \times 3.33 = $ _____
    F. $\dfrac{1000}{333.3} = $ _____
    G. $2.244 \times 88.66 = $ _____
    H. $133 \times 2.000 = $ _____

43. •Complete the following operations using the correct number of significant figures:

A.	B.	C.	D.
4.55	80.00	71.1	200
+ 21.6	− 112.3	+ 3.70	+ 33.7 SSM

1-5 Dimensional analysis is a powerful way to check the results of a physics calculation

44. •The equation that describes motion of an object is $x = \frac{1}{2}at^2 + v_0 t + x_0$, where x is the position of the object, a is the acceleration, t is time, v_0 is the initial speed, and x_0 is the initial position. Show that the dimensions in the equation are consistent.

45. •The equation that describes motion of an object is $x = vt + x_0$, where x is the position of the object, v is its speed, t is time, and x_0 is the initial position. Show that the dimensions in the equation are consistent. SSM

46. •The motion of a vibrating system is described by $y(x, t) = A_0 e^{-\alpha t} \sin(kx - \omega t)$. Find the SI units for k, ω, and α.

47. •The equation that describes the kinetic energy of a moving particle is $K = \frac{1}{2}mv^2$, where m is the mass of the particle and v is its speed. Show that 1 joule (J), the SI unit of energy, is equivalent to 1 $kg \cdot m^2/s^2$.

48. •The period T of a simple pendulum, the time for one complete oscillation, is given by $T = 2\pi\sqrt{(L/g)}$, where L is the length of the pendulum and g is the acceleration due to gravity. Show that the dimensions in the equation are consistent.

49. •Which of the following could be correct based on a dimensional analysis?
    A. The volume flow rate is 64 m^3/s.
    B. The height of the Transamerica building is 332 m^2.
    C. The time required for a fortnight is 66 m/s.
    D. The speed of the train is 9.8 m/s^2.
    E. The weight of a standard kilogram mass is 2.2 lb.
    F. The density of gold is 19.3 kg/m^2. SSM

General Problems

50. •**Biology** A typical human cell is approximately 10 μm in diameter and enclosed by a membrane that is 5.0 nm thick. (a) What is the volume of the cell? (b) What is the volume of the cell membrane? (c) What percent of the cell volume does its membrane occupy? To simplify the calculations, model the cell as a sphere.

51. •**Medical** Express each quantity in the standard SI units requested. (a) An adult should have no more than 2500 mg of sodium per day. What is the limit in kg? (b) A 240-mL cup of whole milk contains 35 mg of cholesterol. Express the cholesterol concentration in the milk in kg/m^3 and in mg/mL. (c) A typical human cell is about 10 μm in diameter, modeled as a sphere. Express its volume in cubic meters. (d) A low-strength aspirin tablet (sometimes called a "baby aspirin") contains 81 mg of the active ingredient. How many kg of the active ingredient does a 100-tablet bottle of baby aspirin contain? (e) The average flow rate of urine out of the kidneys is typically 1.2 L/min. Express the rate in m^3/s. (f) The density of blood proteins is about 1.4 g/cm^3. Express the density in kg/m^3.

52. •**Medical** The concentration of PSA (prostate-specific antigen) in the blood is sometimes used as a screening test for possible prostate cancer in men. The value is normally reported as the number of nanograms of PSA per milliliter of blood. A PSA of 1.7 (ng/mL) is considered low. Express that value in (a) g/L, (b) standard SI units of kg/m^3, and (c) μg/L.

53. •When a woman who is 2 m tall stands near a flagpole, the shadow of her head and the shadow of the top of the flagpole are

superimposed (**Figure 1-6**). The woman's shadow is 10 m long, as shown in the figure. Determine the height of the flagpole.

—— 10 m ——

—— 22 m ——

Figure 1-6 Problem 53

54. • The acceleration g of a falling object near a planet is given by the following equation $g = GM/R^2$. If the planet's mass M is expressed in kg and the distance of the object from the planet's center R is expressed in meters, determine the units of the gravitational constant G. The acceleration g must have units of m/s^2.

55. • **Medical** At a resting pulse rate of 75 beats per minute, the human heart typically pumps about 70 mL of blood per beat. Blood has a density of 1060 kg/m^3. Circulating all of the blood in the body through the heart takes about 1 min in a person at rest. (a) How much blood (in L and m^3) is in the body? (b) On average, what mass of blood (in g and kg) does the heart pump each beat? SSM

56. • During a certain experiment, light is found to take 37.1 μs to traverse a measured distance of 11.12 km. Determine the speed of light from the data. Express your answer in SI units and in scientific notation, using the appropriate number of significant figures.

57. •• **Medical** The body mass index (BMI) estimates the amount of fat in a person's body. It is defined as the person's mass m in kg divided by the square of the person's height h in m. (a) Write the formula for BMI in terms of m and h. (b) In the United States, most people measure weight in pounds and height in feet and inches. Show that with weight W in pounds and height h in inches, the BMI formula is BMI = $703\,W/h^2$. (c) A person with a BMI between 25.0 and 30.0 is considered overweight. If a person is 5′11″ tall, for what range of mass will he be considered overweight?

58. •• **Medical** A typical prostate gland has a mass of about 20 g and is about the size of a walnut. The gland can be modeled as a sphere 4.50 cm in diameter and of uniform density. (a) What is the density of the prostate? Express your answer in g/cm^3 and in standard SI units. (b) How does the density compare to that of water? (c) During a biopsy of the prostate, a thin needle is used to remove a series of cylindrical tissue samples. If the cylinders have a total length of 28.0 mm and a diameter of 0.100 mm, what is the total mass (in g) of tissue taken? (d) What percentage of the mass of the prostate is removed during the biopsy?

2 Linear Motion

In this chapter, your goals are to:
- (2-1) State and explain the definition of linear motion.
- (2-2) Explain the meanings of and relationships among displacement, average velocity, and constant velocity.
- (2-3) Solve problems involving linear motion with constant velocity.
- (2-4) Explain the distinction between velocity and acceleration, and interpret graphs of velocity versus time.
- (2-5) Use and interpret the equations and graphs for linear motion with constant acceleration.
- (2-6) Apply Know/Don't Know tables to help solve constant-acceleration linear motion problems.
- (2-7) Describe the special case of free-fall motion.
- (2-8) Solve problems involving objects in free fall.

To master this chapter, you should review:
- (1-2) The three key steps in solving any physics problem.
- (1-4) How to use significant figures in calculations.

2-1 Studying motion in a straight line is the first step in understanding physics

We live in a universe of motion. We are surrounded by speeding cars, scampering animals, and moving currents of air. Our planet is in motion as it spins on its axis and orbits the Sun. There is motion, too, within our bodies, including the pulsations of the heart and the flow of blood through the circulatory system. One of the principal tasks of physics is to describe motion in all of its forms and all of its variety, and it is with the description of motion—a subject called *kinematics*—that we begin our study of physics.

In general, objects can move in all three dimensions: forward and back, left and right, and up and down. In this chapter, however, we'll just consider the comparatively simple case of **linear motion** (also called *one-dimensional motion*), or motion in a straight line. There are many situations in nature and technology in which objects move very nearly along a straight line: an airliner accelerating down the runway before it takes off, a blood cell moving along a capillary, or a rocket climbing upward from the launch pad. All of the concepts that we'll study in this chapter apply directly to motion in two or three dimensions, which we'll study in Chapter 3. You'll use the ideas of this chapter and the next throughout your study of physics, so the time you spend understanding them now will be an excellent investment for the future.

2-2 Constant velocity means moving at a steady speed in the same direction

Figure 2-1 shows objects in linear motion: Three swimmers traveling down the lanes of a swimming pool. Their motion is particularly simple because each swimmer has a **constant velocity**: The swimmer's speed stays the same, and the swimmer always moves in the same direction. Let's look at this kind of motion more closely.

Each swimmer moves with a steady speed and always moves in the same direction. Hence each swimmer has a constant velocity.

Figure 2-1 **Constant velocity** An object has a constant velocity when its speed remains the same (it neither speeds up nor slows down) and its direction of motion remains the same. These three swimmers all move in the same direction, yet have different constant velocities because their speeds are different: The middle swimmer (who reaches the end of the pool first) is the fastest.

Coordinates, Displacement, and Average Velocity

To measure how fast and in what direction an object (such as a swimmer) moves, we first need a way to measure the object's position at different times. We do this using a **coordinate system** as shown in Figure 2-2a to identify and label positions. We use the symbol x to denote the position of the object at a given time t. The value of x can be positive or negative, depending on where the object is relative to an **origin** or a **reference position** that we take to be at $x = 0$. We can choose the reference position to be anywhere that's convenient. For example, we might choose $x = 0$ to be the point where we're sitting alongside a swimming pool. If our seat is 10.0 meters (10.0 m for short) from one end of a swimming pool with a length of 50.0 m, then one end of the pool is at $x = -10.0$ m and the other end is at $x = +40.0$ m.

The **coordinates**, or **position**, of an object relative to an origin are what we call **vector** quantities. Vectors are special quantities that contain two kinds of information: size, or **magnitude**, and direction. For instance, if you asked a person located at the origin in Figure 2-2a where the near end of the swimming pool is, an answer of "10 m" is not very helpful. If you wanted to walk to that end of the pool, you would also need to know in which direction to walk! The magnitude of the position of the end of the pool relative to the origin is 10 m. The direction of the end of the pool is specified by the minus sign of the coordinate, which is why we need to use $x = -10$ m to fully describe the position of the end of the pool. The position of the far end of the pool relative to the

Figure 2-2 Coordinate systems and displacement (a) The displacement of two swimmers. (b) Displacement is independent of the coordinate system.

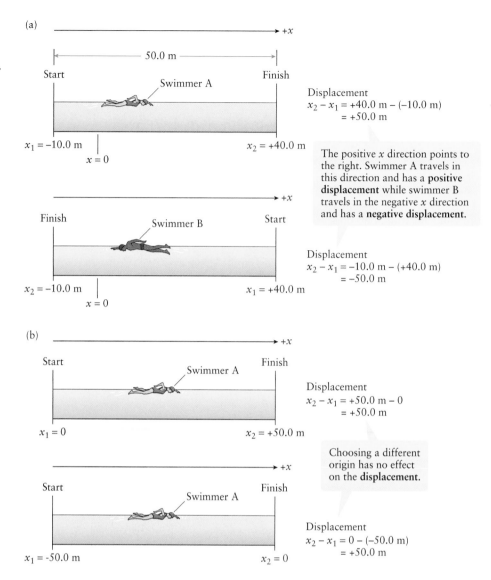

(a)

50.0 m

Start   Finish

Swimmer A

$x_1 = -10.0$ m $x_2 = +40.0$ m

$x = 0$

Displacement
$x_2 - x_1 = +40.0$ m $-$ (-10.0 m)
$= +50.0$ m

The positive x direction points to the right. Swimmer A travels in this direction and has a **positive displacement** while swimmer B travels in the negative x direction and has a **negative displacement**.

Finish   Start

Swimmer B

$x_2 = -10.0$ m $x_1 = +40.0$ m

$x = 0$

Displacement
$x_2 - x_1 = -10.0$ m $-$ ($+40.0$ m)
$= -50.0$ m

(b)

Start   Finish

Swimmer A

$x_1 = 0$ $x_2 = +50.0$ m

Displacement
$x_2 - x_1 = +50.0$ m $- 0$
$= +50.0$ m

Choosing a different origin has no effect on the **displacement**.

Start   Finish

Swimmer A

$x_1 = -50.0$ m $x_2 = 0$

Displacement
$x_2 - x_1 = 0 - (-50.0$ m)
$= +50.0$ m

origin is 40 m in the positive direction, or $x = +40.0$ m. For motion along a straight line, the direction is always given by the sign of the quantity.

❚ Watch Out! How can you tell if a quantity is a vector?

When we write positive numbers we often don't explicitly write the "+" sign, although we'll do our best in this book. For instance, referring to Figure 2-2a, we could say the position of the far end of the pool is $x = 40.0$ m. Position requires you to know a direction, so this would be a vector. We could also say the far end of the pool is a distance $d = 40.0$ m away. This number is written the same way as the position. However, a distance does not contain direction information, so it is not a vector.

In addition, negative numbers do not always indicate a direction. For instance, on a cold winter day the temperature might be $-10°$C. Temperature is just a number, which might be positive or negative. There is no direction such as "up" or "right" associated with temperature. Temperature is not a vector. You need to rely on the context to decide whether the sign of a quantity refers to a direction or simply a negative number.

The **displacement** of an object is the difference between its positions at two different times. It tells us how far and in what direction the object moves, so displacement, like position, is a vector. For example, if swimmer A travels the length of the swimming pool from left to right (Figure 2-2a), she starts at $x_1 = -10.0$ m and ends at $x_2 = +40.0$ m. (The subscripts "1" and "2" help us keep track of which position is which.) Her displacement is the *later* position minus the *earlier* position: $x_2 - x_1 = +40.0$ m $- (-10.0$ m) $=$

+50.0 m. The positive value of displacement means that her value of x increased; we say that she moved 50.0 m in the positive x direction. By comparison, swimmer B (Figure 2-2a) travels the length of the pool in the opposite direction. For him $x_1 = +40.0$ m and $x_2 = -10.0$ m, and his displacement is $x_2 - x_1 = (-10.0 \text{ m}) - 40.0 \text{ m} = -50.0 \text{m}$. Swimmer B moves 50.0 m in the negative x direction, and his displacement is negative. You can see that the *sign* (plus or minus) of the displacement tells you the *direction* in which each swimmer moves.

❗ Watch Out! Displacement and distance are not the same thing.

The fundamental difference is that distance tells you "how far," while displacement tells you "how far and in what direction." Displacement is a vector. That's why displacements can be positive or negative, but distances are *always* positive. (If you were asked, "How far is it from New York to Boston?" you wouldn't answer "Negative 300 km.") In Figure 2-2 each swimmer travels the same distance, 50.0 m, but their displacements are different (+50.0 m for swimmer A, −50.0 m for swimmer B) because the *directions* of their motion are different.

Note that the displacement of either swimmer does *not* depend on our choice of reference position (**Figure 2-2b**). As an example, if we choose $x = 0$ to be at the left-hand end of the pool, the right-hand end is at $x = 50.0$ m and the displacement of swimmer A is $x_2 - x_1 = 50.0 \text{ m} - 0 = 50.0$ m. If instead we choose $x = 0$ to be at the right-hand end of the pool, the left-hand end is at $x = -50.0$ m and swimmer A has displacement $x_2 - x_1 = 0 - (-50.0 \text{ m}) = 50.0$ m.

To determine how *fast* an object moves, we need to define a new quantity, **average speed**, which is the total distance the object travels divided by the amount of time it takes the object to travel that distance—that is, the **elapsed time** or *duration* of that **time interval**. We use the symbol t to denote a value of the time, and the symbol $v_{average}$ ("v-average") for average speed. For example, suppose you start timing swimmer A just as she starts off at $x_1 = -10.0$ m, so the time at this instant is $t_1 = 0$ (Figure 2-2a). Your watch says she reaches the other end of the pool at time $t_2 = 25.0$ s. The elapsed time is $t_2 - t_1 = 25.0 \text{ s} - 0 = 25.0$ s. And she traveled a total distance of 50.0 m in that time, so her average speed is

$$v_{average} = \frac{\text{distance}}{\text{time interval}} = \frac{50.0 \text{ m}}{25.0 \text{ s}} = 2.00 \text{ m/s for swimmer A}$$

Slow-moving swimmer B also travels from one end of the pool to the other, a distance of 50.0 m. If it takes him 100.0 s to do so, as measured by your stopwatch, his average speed is

$$v_{average} = \frac{\text{distance}}{\text{time interval}} = \frac{50.0 \text{ m}}{100.0 \text{ s}} = 0.500 \text{ m/s for swimmer B}$$

Note that the average speed does not contain any direction information. The average speed of both swimmers is a positive number, independent of the direction they swim.

To get direction information, we need to calculate the **average velocity** of an object, which is a vector quantity. We use the symbol $v_{average,x}$ ("v-average-x") for average velocity. This symbol is very close to the symbol used to denote the average speed. But it includes the subscript x to remind us that the object is moving in either the positive or negative x direction. The average velocity is given by the displacement divided by the time interval required for that displacement to occur. Consider swimmer A again, who starts at position $x = -10.0$ m and ends at position $x = +40.0$ m in 25.0 s. Her average velocity is then

$$v_{average,x} = \frac{x_2 - x_1}{t_2 - t_1} = \frac{40.0 \text{ m} - (-10.0 \text{ m})}{25.0 \text{ s} - 0}$$
$$= \frac{50.0 \text{ m}}{25.0 \text{ s}} = +2.00 \text{ m/s for swimmer A}$$

So that swimmer A moves in the positive x direction (as shown by the positive sign of $v_{average,x}$), or from left to right in Figure 2-2a, at an average *speed* of 2.00 meters per second. The standard SI units for average velocity and average speed are meters per second (m/s). **Table 2-1** lists some other common units for these quantities.

Watch Out!

Speed and velocity are not the same thing.

Note that average speed and average velocity are related but are *not* the same quantity. Average speed is equal to the *distance* traveled divided by the elapsed time. Distances are always positive, so average speed is always positive. Average velocity can be positive or negative, depending on the direction in which the object moves. Average velocity is a vector.

Table 2-1 Units of velocity and speed

The SI unit of velocity and speed is the meter per second (m/s). Here are some other common units:

1 kilometer per hour (km/h) = 0.2778 m/s
1 mile per hour (mi/h) = 0.4470 m/s = 1.609 km/h
1 foot per second (ft/s) = 0.3048 m/s = 1.097 km/h = 0.6818 mi/h
1 knot = 1 nautical mile per hour = 0.5148 m/s = 1.853 km/h = 1.152 mi/h = 1.689 ft/s

By comparison, swimmer B starts at the right-hand side of the pool at $x_1 = +40.0$ m, at $t_1 = 0$, and at $t_2 = 100$ s he reaches the left-hand side of the pool at $x_2 = -10.0$ m (Figure 2-2a). Hence for swimmer B the average velocity for the trip along the length of the pool is

$$v_{\text{average},x} = \frac{x_2 - x_1}{t_2 - t_1} = \frac{-10.0 \text{ m} - 40.0 \text{ m}}{100 \text{ s} - 0}$$

$$= \frac{-50.0 \text{ m}}{100 \text{ s}} = -0.500 \text{ m/s for swimmer B}$$

Swimmer B moves at only 0.500 m/s. The minus sign of $v_{\text{average},x}$ says that he travels in the negative x direction, or from right to left in Figure 2-2a. Equation 2-1 summarizes these ideas about average velocity:

Average velocity for linear motion
(2-1)

Average velocity of an object in linear motion

Displacement (change in position) of the object over a certain time interval: The object moves from x_1 to x_2, so $\Delta x = x_2 - x_1$.

$$v_{\text{average},x} = \frac{x_2 - x_1}{t_2 - t_1} = \frac{\Delta x}{\Delta t}$$

For both the displacement and the elapsed time, subtract the earlier value (x_1 or t_1) from the later value (x_2 or t_2).

Elapsed time for the time interval: The object is at x_1 at time t_1, and x_2 at time t_2, so the elapsed time is $\Delta t = t_2 - t_1$.

Watch Out!

Be sure you understand the meaning of Δ.

The symbol Δx does *not* mean a quantity Δ multiplied by a quantity x! Instead, it means the *change* in the value of x.

In Equation 2-1 Δx ("delta-x") is an abbreviation for the change $x_2 - x_1$ in the position x, and Δt ("delta-t") is an abbreviation for the change $t_2 - t_1$ in the time t; that is, the elapsed time. Throughout our study of physics we'll use the symbol Δ ("delta") to represent the change in a quantity.

Watch Out! Average speed is not the magnitude of the average velocity.

The example of the swimmers may make you think that the average speed is simply the magnitude of the average velocity. As long as the object travels in a straight line and does not turn around, this is true. But consider the average speed and average velocity of a swimmer who does a complete lap in the pool. This swimmer starts and ends at the same location. Her total displacement is then zero. This means her average velocity is also zero. But does it mean her average speed was also zero? No! She traveled two lengths of the pool—this distance is definitely *not* zero. So her average speed is not zero either.

Constant Velocity, Motion Diagrams, and Graphs of *x* versus *t*

We've calculated the average velocity for each swimmer's entire trip from one end of the pool to the other. But we can also calculate the average velocity for any *segment* of a swimmer's trip between the two ends. A swimmer has *constant velocity* if the average velocity calculated for *any* segment of the trip has the same value as for any other segment. As an example, in Figure 2-3a swimmer A is at $x_1 = 0.0$ m at $t_1 = 5.0$ s and at $x_2 = 30.0$ m at $t_2 = 20.0$ s. Her average velocity for this part of her motion is

$$v_{average,x} = \frac{x_2 - x_1}{t_2 - t_1} = \frac{30.0 \text{ m} - 0.0 \text{ m}}{20.0 \text{ s} - 5.0 \text{ s}}$$

$$= \frac{30.0 \text{ m}}{15.0 \text{ s}} = +2.00 \text{ m/s for swimmer A}$$

That's the same as we calculated above for the entire trip from one end of the pool to the other. If the average velocity has the same value for all segments, we call it simply the *velocity* and give it the symbol v_x ("*v-x*").

Figure 2-3a shows how to depict swimmer A's entire motion in a way that makes it clear that her velocity is constant. We draw a dot to represent her position at equal time intervals (say, $t = 0$, $t = 5.0$ s, $t = 10.0$ s, $t = 15.0$ s, and so on). Taken together, these dots make up a **motion diagram**. The spacing between adjacent dots shows you the distance that the object traveled during the corresponding time interval. The spacing is the same between any two adjacent dots in Figure 2-3a, which tells you that swimmer A travels equal distances in the $+x$ direction—that is, has equal displacement—in equal time intervals. That's just what we mean by saying that swimmer A has constant velocity.

Figure 2-3b shows a motion diagram for swimmer B. Since he moves more slowly than swimmer A (speed 0.500 m/s compared to 2.00 m/s), he travels a smaller distance in the same time interval. Hence the dots in swimmer B's motion diagram are more closely spaced than those for swimmer A.

Yet another useful way to depict motion is in terms of a graph of position versus time, also known as an *x–t* **graph**. In Figure 2-4a, we've turned swimmer A's motion diagram on its side so that the x axis now runs upward. Then to emphasize that each dot in the diagram corresponds to a specific time t, we've moved each dot to the right by an amount that corresponds to the value of t. We add a horizontal axis for time to make it easy to read the value of t that corresponds to each dot. The result is a graph of the swimmer's coordinate x versus the time t, which as mentioned earlier is also called an *x–t* graph. To finish the graph, we draw a smooth curve connecting the dots. For this constant-velocity motion, the graph is a straight line.

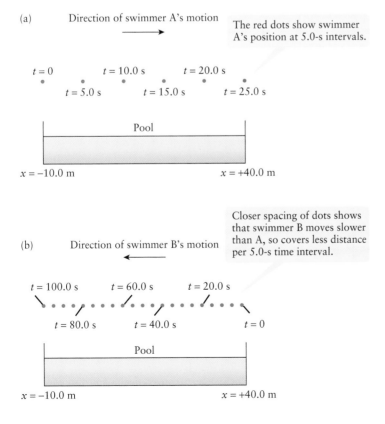

Figure 2-3 **Motion diagrams for constant velocity** A series of dots shows the positions of (a) swimmer A and (b) swimmer B at equal time intervals.

> ### ⚠ Watch Out! Horizontal motion can be graphed on the vertical axis.
>
> ● Although the swimmer's motion in the *x* direction in Figure 2-3a is *horizontal*, we've drawn the *x*–*t* graph of Figure 2-4a with the *x* axis *vertical*. We do this because in graphs that show how a quantity varies with time, we always put time on the horizontal axis. For example, a graph of how a stock mutual fund performs shows time (that is, different dates) on the horizontal axis and the value of the fund on the vertical axis. Hence we're forced to put the coordinate *x* on the vertical axis, no matter how the object's motion is actually oriented in space.

Figure 2-4b shows the *x*–*t* graph for swimmer B. This swimmer also has a constant velocity, and the *x*–*t* graph is again a straight line. However, this graph differs from the *x*–*t* graph for swimmer A (Figure 2-4a) in two ways: where the line touches the vertical axis, and the *slope* of the line (how steep it is and whether it slopes up or down).

The point on the graph where the line touches the vertical (*x*) axis shows you the position *x* of the object at *t* = 0. We give this the symbol x_0 ("*x*-zero"). If the motion starts at *t* = 0, then x_0 represents the *initial position* of the object. The slope of the line tells you something equally important: the value of the object's velocity. If you consider two points on the line, corresponding to times t_1 and t_2 and positions x_1 and x_2, the slope is the vertical difference $x_2 - x_1$ between those two points (the "rise" of the graph) divided by the horizontal difference $t_2 - t_1$ (the "run" of the graph). But that's just our definition of the average velocity, Equation 2-1. The *x*–*t* graph in Figure 2-4a has a steep

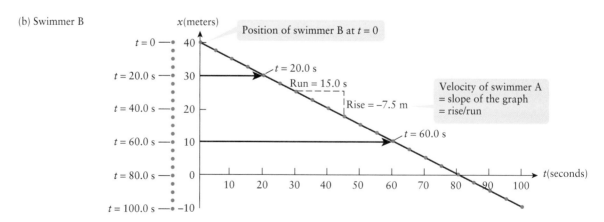

Figure 2-4 From motion diagrams to *x*–*t* graphs: Constant velocity How to convert the motion diagrams from Figure 2-3 for (a) swimmer A and (b) swimmer B into graphs of position *x* versus time *t*. If the velocity is constant, the *x*–*t* graph is a straight line.

slope (which means swimmer A is moving rapidly) and slopes upward (which means she is moving in the positive x direction). By contrast, the x–t graph in Figure 2-4b has a shallow slope (so swimmer B is moving slowly) and slopes downward (so he is moving in the negative x direction).

The Equation for Constant-Velocity Linear Motion

We can write a simple and useful equation for constant-velocity motion by starting with Equation 2-1, $v_{average,x} = (x_2 - x_1)/(t_2 - t_1)$. Since the velocity is constant, we replace $v_{average,x}$ by v_x. We choose the earlier time t_1 in this equation to be $t = 0$, and use x_0 instead of x_1 as the symbol for the object's position at this time. We also use the symbols t and x instead of t_2 and x_2 to represent the later time and the object's position at that time. Then Equation 2-1 becomes

$$v_x = \frac{x - x_0}{t - 0} = \frac{x - x_0}{t}$$

We multiply both sides of this equation by t, then add x_0 to both sides. The result is

Position at time t of an object in linear motion with constant velocity

Position at time $t = 0$ of the object

$$x = x_0 + v_x t$$

Constant velocity of the object   Time at which the object is at position x

Position versus time for linear motion with constant velocity (2-2)

This equation gives the position x of the object as a function of the time t. In the following section we'll see how to use Equation 2-2 to solve problems about linear motion with constant velocity. But even with this equation, an essential part of solving any such problem is drawing x–t graphs like those shown in Figure 2-4.

? Got the Concept? 2-1 Interpreting x–t Graphs

Figure 2-5 shows x–t graphs for four objects, all drawn on the same axes. Each object moves at a constant velocity from $t = 0$ to $t = 5.0$ s. (a) Which object moves at the greatest speed? (b) Which one travels the greatest distance from $t = 0$ to $t = 5.0$ s? (c) Which one has the most positive displacement from $t = 0$ to $t = 5.0$ s? (d) Which one has the most negative displacement from $t = 0$ to $t = 5.0$ s? (e) Which one ends up at the most positive value of x? (f) Which one ends up at the most negative value of x?

(Answers to *Got the Concept?* questions can be found at the end of the chapter.)

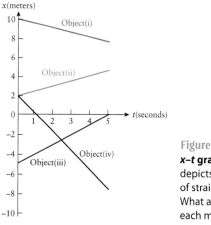

Figure 2-5 **Four different x–t graphs** Each graph depicts a different example of straight-line motion. What are the properties of each motion?

Take-Home Message for Section 2-2

✔ The displacement Δx of an object in linear motion is the difference between the object's position x at two different times (displacement Δx is the *later* position minus the *earlier* position).

✔ The average velocity of the object between those two different times, $v_{average,x}$, is the displacement Δx (the difference between the two positions) divided by the elapsed time Δt (the difference between the two times).

✔ An object has constant velocity if $v_{average,x}$ has the same value for any time interval. If the velocity is constant, the object always moves in the same direction and maintains a steady speed.

✔ Motion diagrams and x–t graphs are important tools for interpreting what happens during linear motion.

2-3 Solving straight-line motion problems: Constant velocity

▶ Go to Interactive Exercise 2-1 for more practice dealing with velocity

Let's see how to apply the ideas of Section 2-2 to some problems involving linear motion.

Example 2-1 Average Velocity

You drive from Bismarck, North Dakota, to Fargo, North Dakota, on Interstate Highway 94, an approximately straight road 315 km in length. You leave Bismarck and travel 210 km at constant velocity in 2.50 h, then stop for 0.50 h at a rest area. You then drive the remaining 105 km to Fargo at constant velocity in 1.00 h. You then turn around immediately and drive back to Bismarck nonstop at constant velocity in 2.75 h. (a) Draw an x–t graph for the entire round trip. Then calculate the average velocity for (b) the trip from Bismarck to the rest area, (c) the trip from the rest area to Fargo, (d) the entire outbound trip from Bismarck to Fargo, (e) the return trip from Fargo to Bismarck, and (f) the round trip from Bismarck to Fargo and back to Bismarck.

Set Up

This is an example of linear motion along the straight highway between Bismarck and Fargo. We set up our coordinates as shown, with $x = 0$ at the starting position (Bismarck) and the positive x direction from Bismarck toward Fargo. We also choose $t = 0$ to be when the car leaves Bismarck. Equation 2-1 will tell us the average velocity for each portion of the trip.

Average velocity for linear motion:

$$v_{average,x} = \frac{x_2 - x_1}{t_2 - t_1} = \frac{\Delta x}{\Delta t} \quad (2\text{-}1)$$

Solve

(a) To draw the x–t graph for the car's motion, we first put a dot on the graph for the car's positions and the corresponding times at the beginning and end of each leg of the trip. The velocity is constant on each leg, so we draw straight lines connecting successive points. The slope of the graph is positive (upward) for the legs in which the car moves in the positive x direction toward Fargo, and negative (downward) in which the car moves in the negative x direction back toward Bismarck. The slope is *zero* (the line is flat) during the time when the car is at the rest area and not moving.

(b) Calculate the average velocity for the trip from Bismarck (position $x_1 = 0$ at time $t_1 = 0$) to the rest area (position $x_2 = 210$ km at time $t_2 = 2.50$ h).

Bismarck to rest area:

$$v_{average,x} = \frac{\Delta x}{\Delta t} = \frac{x_2 - x_1}{t_2 - t_1}$$

$$= \frac{210 \text{ km} - 0}{2.50 \text{ h} - 0} = +84.0 \text{ km/h}$$

(c) Calculate the average velocity for the trip from the rest area (position $x_3 = 210$ km at time $t_3 = 2.50$ h + 0.50 h = 3.00 h) to Fargo (position $x_4 = 315$ km at time $t_4 = 3.00$ h + 1.00 h = 4.00 h).

Rest area to Fargo:

$$v_{average,x} = \frac{\Delta x}{\Delta t} = \frac{x_4 - x_3}{t_4 - t_3}$$

$$= \frac{315 \text{ km} - 210 \text{ km}}{4.00 \text{ h} - 3.00 \text{ h}} = +105 \text{ km/h}$$

(d) Calculate the average velocity for the entire outbound trip from Bismarck (position $x_1 = 0$ at time $t_1 = 0$) to Fargo (position $x_4 = 315$ km at time $t_4 = 4.00$ h).

Bismarck to Fargo:

$$v_{average,x} = \frac{\Delta x}{\Delta t} = \frac{x_4 - x_1}{t_4 - t_1}$$

$$= \frac{315 \text{ km} - 0}{4.00 \text{ h} - 0} = +78.8 \text{ km/h}$$

(e) Calculate the average velocity for the return trip from Fargo (position $x_4 = 315$ km at time $t_4 = 4.00$ h) to Bismarck (position $x_5 = 0$ at time $t_5 = 4.00$ h + 2.75 h = 6.75 h).

Fargo back to Bismarck:

$$v_{average,x} = \frac{\Delta x}{\Delta t} = \frac{x_5 - x_4}{t_5 - t_4}$$

$$= \frac{0 - 315 \text{ km}}{6.75 \text{ h} - 4.00 \text{ h}} = -115 \text{ km/h}$$

(f) For the round trip from Bismarck (position $x_1 = 0$ at time $t_1 = 0$) to Fargo and back to Bismarck (position $x_5 = 0$ at time $t_5 = 6.75$ h), the net displacement $\Delta x = x_5 - x_1$ is *zero*: The car ends up back where it started. Hence the average velocity for the round trip is also zero.

Bismarck to Fargo and back to Fargo:

$$v_{average,x} = \frac{\Delta x}{\Delta t} = \frac{x_5 - x_1}{t_5 - t_1}$$

$$= \frac{0 - 0}{6.75 \text{ h} - 0} = 0$$

Reflect

The average velocity is positive for the trips from Bismarck toward Fargo (since the car moves in the positive x direction) and negative for the trip from Fargo back to Bismarck (since the car moves in the negative x direction). The result $v_{average, x} = 0$ for the round trip means that the net displacement for the round trip was zero. The average *speed* for the trip was definitely not zero, however: The car traveled a total distance of 2(315 km) = 630 km in a total elapsed time of 6.75 h, so the average speed was (630 km)/(6.75 h) = 93.3 km/h. Displacement and distance are not the same thing; likewise, average velocity and average speed are not the same thing.

Example 2-2 When Swimmers Pass

Consider again swimmers A and B, whose motion is depicted in Figure 2-3. Both of them begin swimming at $t = 0$. (a) Write the position-versus-time equation, Equation 2-2, for each swimmer. Use the coordinate system shown in Figure 2-3. (b) Calculate the position of each swimmer at $t = 10.0$ s. (c) Calculate the time when each swimmer is at $x = 15.0$ m. (d) At what time and position do the two swimmers pass each other?

Set Up

We can use Equation 2-2 because each swimmer is in linear motion with constant velocity. Figure 2-3 shows where each swimmer starts and each swimmer's constant velocity, which are just the quantities we need to substitute into Equation 2-2. (We use subscripts A and B to denote the quantities that pertain to each swimmer.)

$$x = x_0 + v_x t \qquad (2-2)$$

Swimmer A starts at $x = -10.0$ m at $t = 0$ and has velocity +2.00 m/s, so

$$x_{A0} = -10.0 \text{ m}$$
$$v_{Ax} = +2.00 \text{ m/s}$$

Swimmer B starts at $x = +40.0$ m at $t = 0$ and has velocity −0.500 m/s, so

$$x_{B0} = +40.0 \text{ m}$$
$$v_{Bx} = -0.500 \text{ m/s}$$

Solve

(a) Use the given information to write down Equation 2-2 for each swimmer. It's useful to draw the x–t graphs for both swimmers on the same graph (see Figure 2-4).

Swimmer A:
$$x_A = x_{A0} + v_{Ax}t \quad \text{so}$$
$$x_A = -10.0 \text{ m} + (2.00 \text{ m/s})t$$

Swimmer B:
$$x_B = x_{B0} + v_{Bx}t \quad \text{so}$$
$$x_B = +40.0 \text{ m} + (-0.500 \text{ m/s})t$$

(b) To find the position of each swimmer at $t = 10.0$ s, just substitute this value of t into the equations for x_A and x_B from (a).

Swimmer A:
$$x_A = -10.0 \text{ m} + (2.00 \text{ m/s})(10.0 \text{ s})$$
$$= -10.0 \text{ m} + 20.0 \text{ m}$$
$$= +10.0 \text{ m}$$

Swimmer B:
$$x_B = +40.0 \text{ m} + (-0.500 \text{ m/s})(10.0 \text{ s})$$
$$= +40.0 \text{ m} + (-5.00 \text{ m})$$
$$= +35.0 \text{ m}$$

$t = 10.0$ s
swimmer A at $x = 10.0$ m
swimmer B at $x = 35.0$ m

(c) In order to solve for the times when the two swimmers are at $x = 15.0$ m, we must first rearrange the equations from (a) so that t (the quantity we are trying to find) is by itself on one side of each equation. We then substitute 15.0 m for both x_A and x_B.

Swimmer A:
$$x_A = -10.0 \text{ m} + (2.00 \text{ m/s})t \quad \text{so}$$
$$x_A + 10.0 \text{ m} = (2.00 \text{ m/s})t$$
$$t = \frac{x_A + 10.0 \text{ m}}{2.00 \text{ m/s}}$$

Substitute $x_A = 15.0$ m:
$$t = \frac{15.0 \text{ m} + 10.0 \text{ m}}{2.00 \text{ m/s}} = 12.5 \text{ s for A}$$

$x = 20.0$ m
swimmer A at $t = 15.0$ s
swimmer B at $t = 40.0$ s

Swimmer B:
$$x_B = +40.0 \text{ m} + (-0.500 \text{ m/s})t \quad \text{so}$$
$$x_B - 40.0 \text{ m} = (-0.500 \text{ m/s})t$$
$$t = \frac{x_B - 40.0 \text{ m}}{(-0.500 \text{ m/s})}$$

Substitute $x_B = 15.0$ m:
$$t = \frac{15.0 \text{ m} - 40.0 \text{ m}}{(-0.500 \text{ m/s})} = 50.0 \text{ s for B}$$

(d) The two swimmers pass when they are at the *same* value of x (so $x_A = x_B$) at the *same* time t. First find the time *when* this happens by setting the expressions for x_A and x_B from (a) equal to each other, then solving for the corresponding value of t.

Swimmer A:
$$x_A = -10.0 \text{ m} + (2.00 \text{ m/s})t$$

Swimmer B:
$$x_B = +40.0 \text{ m} + (-0.500 \text{ m/s})t$$

When the two swimmers pass, $x_A = x_B$:
$$-10.0 \text{ m} + (2.00 \text{ m/s})t$$
$$= 40.0 \text{ m} + (-0.500 \text{ m/s})t$$
$$(2.00 \text{ m/s})t - (-0.500 \text{ m/s})t$$
$$= 40.0 \text{ m} - (-10.0 \text{ m})$$
$$(2.50 \text{ m/s})t = 50.0 \text{ m}$$
$$t = \frac{50.0 \text{ m}}{2.50 \text{ m/s}} = 20.0 \text{ s}$$

point where swimmers A and B pass each other:
$x = 30.0$ m at $t = 20.0$ s

To find *where* the two swimmers pass, substitute the value of t for when they pass into either the equation for x_A or the equation for x_B.

At $t = 20.0$ s, swimmer A's position is
$$x_A = -10.0 \text{ m} + (2.00 \text{ m/s})t$$
$$= -10.0 \text{ m} + (2.00 \text{ m/s})(20.0 \text{ s})$$
$$= 30.0 \text{ m}$$

(Both should give the same answer, since at this time $x_A = x_B$.)

$t = 20.0$ s is the time when the two swimmers pass, so the position where they pass is $x = 30.0$ m.

Reflect

We can check our results by noting that swimmer B moves 1/4 as fast as swimmer A. This checks out for part (b): In 10.0 s, swimmer A moves 20.0 m in the positive x direction from her starting point at $x_{A0} = -10.0$ m and swimmer B moves 5.00 m (that is, 1/4 as far) in the negative x direction from his starting point at $x_{B0} = +40.0$ m. It also checks out for part (c): $x = 15.0$ m is at the midpoint of the pool, so each swimmer has to travel 25.0 m (half the length of the pool) which takes swimmer B four times longer than swimmer A (50.0 s versus 12.5 s). And in part (d), the position where the two swimmers meet is 10.0 m from where swimmer B started but 40.0 m (four times farther) from where swimmer A started.

You can also check the answer to part (d) by substituting $t = 20.0$ s into the equation for x_B. You should find $x_B = 30.0$ m, the same as x_A (since $t = 20.0$ s is when the two swimmers pass). Do you?

? Got the Concept? 2-2   Average Velocity

It takes you 15 min to drive 6.0 mi in a straight line to the local hospital. It takes 10 min to go the last 3.0 mi, 2.0 min to go the last mile, and only 30 s (= 0.50 min) to go the last 0.50 mile. What is your average velocity for the trip? Take the positive x direction to be from your starting point toward the hospital.

Take-Home Message for Section 2-3

✔ You can solve many problems that involve straight-line motion by using Equation 2-1, which relates average velocity, displacement, and elapsed time.

✔ If the velocity is constant, you can also use Equation 2-2 to relate velocity, position, and time.

2-4 Velocity is the rate of change of position, and acceleration is the rate of change of velocity

In Sections 2-2 and 2-3 we considered linear motion with constant velocity: an object that moves in a straight line with unvarying speed and always in the same direction. But in many important situations the speed, the direction of motion, or both, can change as an object moves. Some examples include a car speeding up to get through an intersection before the light turns red; the same car slowing down as a police officer signals the driver to pull over; or a dog that runs away from you to pick up a thrown stick, then changes direction and returns the stick to you.

Whenever an object changes its speed or direction of motion—that is, whenever its velocity changes—we say that the object *accelerates* and undergoes an *acceleration*. Before we study acceleration, however, we first need to take a closer look at the idea of velocity.

Instantaneous Velocity

Figure 2-6 is a motion diagram of an object that moves with a changing velocity: a jogger who starts at rest, speeds up, then slows down toward the end of a 100-m run. The dots of this motion diagram are *not* equally spaced, which means that at different points during his jog he covers different distances in a given amount of elapsed time. Hence her average velocity over a 2.0-s interval is *not* constant.

The red dots show the jogger's position at 2.0-second intervals

These dots are close together—the jogger was moving slowly, and hence covered only a short distance during the time interval between dots.

These dots are farther apart—the jogger was moving faster, and hence covered a greater distance during the time interval between dots.

Figure 2-6 **Motion with varying velocity** A jogger's velocity changes as he speeds up and slows down. This motion diagram shows these velocity changes.

Figure 2-7 **From motion diagram to *x*–*t* graph: Varying velocity**
Converting the jogger's motion diagram from Figure 2-6 to an *x*–*t* graph. Compare to Figure 2-4.

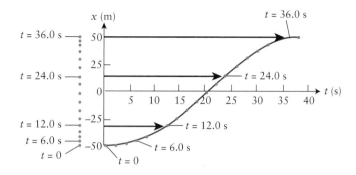

Figure 2-7 **From motion diagram to *x*–*t* graph: Varying velocity**
Converting the jogger's motion diagram from Figure 2-6 to an *x*–*t* graph. Compare to Figure 2-4.

Figure 2-7 shows the *x*–*t* graph for the jogger. The graph is not a straight line because the velocity is not constant. In Section 2-2 we saw that if the velocity *is* constant, as for the two swimmers whose motion is graphed in Figure 2-4, the slope of the straight-line *x*–*t* graph tells us the value of the velocity. We'll now show that the same is true when the velocity is not constant.

In Figure 2-8a, we've picked out two points during the jogger's motion. If we draw a straight line connecting the two corresponding points on the *x*–*t* graph, the vertical traverse or "rise" of this straight line is equal to the displacement Δx, and the horizontal traverse or "run" is equal to the duration Δt of the time interval. Now, Equation 2-1 tells us that the average velocity $v_{\text{average},x}$ for the time interval between these two points equals Δx divided by Δt. Hence, the average velocity is equal to the "rise" divided by the "run," which is just the *slope* of this straight line. For the case shown in Figure 2-8a, the rise is $\Delta x = 59.5$ m and the run is $\Delta t = 18.0$ s, so $v_{\text{average},x} = (59.5 \text{ m})/(18.0 \text{ s}) = +3.31 \text{ m/s}$. The plus sign means that the straight line slopes upward, which tells us that *x* increased during the time interval and the jogger moved in the positive *x* direction.

The straight line in Figure 2-8a doesn't exactly match the shape of the *x*–*t* curve between the two points. However, if we decrease the time interval between the two points, as in Figure 2-8b, the straight line is a better match to the *x*–*t* curve. If we imagine making the time interval *very* short—say, between $t = 6.000000000$ s and $t = 6.000000001$ s—the straight line would become an *exact* match to the actual *x*–*t* curve. Such a straight line has the same slope as a line tangent to the *x*–*t* curve, as in Figure 2-8c. The slope of such a tangent line equals the object's average velocity over an extremely short time interval. If we make this time interval infinitesimally small, the slope gives us the **instantaneous velocity** v_x at the instant in question. This tells us how fast and in what direction the object is moving at that instant. (We used the same symbol v_x in Section 2-2 when we discussed objects that move with constant velocity. If the velocity is constant, v_x has the same value at all times.)

Note that the symbol v_x does not contain the subscript "average" because it doesn't denote an average. Rather, it tells you the speed and direction of motion of the object at that particular instant. The subscript *x* reminds us that v_x is the *velocity* of the object in the positive or negative *x* direction; this can be positive or negative. The absolute value or magnitude of v_x is the **instantaneous speed** of the object, which we denote by the symbol *v* without a subscript. Instantaneous speed is always positive or zero, never negative. A car's speedometer is a familiar device for measuring instantaneous speed.

As an example, consider the jogger whose motion is graphed in Figure 2-8c. Careful measurement shows that the slope of the tangent line to the *x*–*t* curve at $t = 6.0$ s is $+1.50 \text{ m/s}$. (You can verify this by measuring the "rise" and "run" of the tangent line as in Figures 2-8a and 2-8b, then taking their quotient.) So, the jogger's instantaneous velocity is $v_x = +1.50 \text{ m/s}$ at $t = 6.0$ s; she was moving in the positive *x* direction at speed $v = 1.50 \text{ m/s}$. As a shorthand, we'll simply use the term **velocity** to stand for instantaneous velocity, which we'll use much more often than average velocity. Likewise, we'll use **speed** to refer to instantaneous speed.

Mathematically, an object's velocity v_x is the *rate of change* of the object's position as given by the coordinate *x*. The faster the position changes, the greater the magnitude of the velocity v_x and the greater the speed of the object. A positive value of v_x means that *x* is increasing—that is, the object is moving in the positive *x* direction; a negative value of v_x means that *x* is decreasing—that is, the object is moving in the negative *x* direction.

! Watch Out!

Instantaneous speed is the magnitude of instantaneous velocity.

Unlike average speed, which is generally not the absolute value of the average velocity, the *instantaneous* speed is always equal to the absolute value of the *instantaneous* velocity.

(a) Average *x* velocity on an *x–t* graph

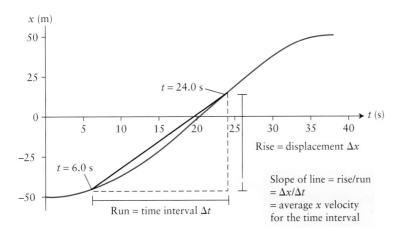

(b) Average *x* velocity for a shorter time interval

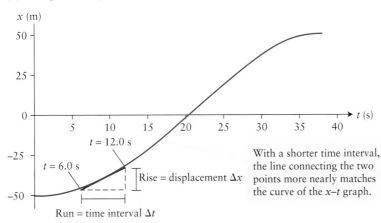

With a shorter time interval, the line connecting the two points more nearly matches the curve of the *x–t* graph.

(c) Instantaneous *x* velocity on an *x–t* graph

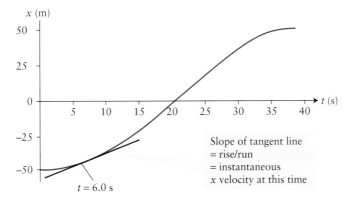

Example 2-3 Decoding an *x–t* Graph

Figure 2-9 shows an *x–t* graph for the motion of an object. (a) Determine the direction in which the object is moving at $t = 0$, 10 s, 20 s, 30 s, and 40 s. (b) Describe the object's motion in words, and draw a motion diagram for the object for the period from $t = 0$ to $t = 40$ s.

Figure 2-9 **An *x–t* graph to interpret** How must an object move to produce this *x–t* graph?

Set Up

We'll use the idea that the slope of the x–t graph for an object tells us the object's velocity v_x. The algebraic sign of the velocity (plus or minus) tells us whether the object is moving in the positive or negative x direction.

$v_x =$ slope of x–t graph

Solve

(a) On a copy of Figure 2-9, we've drawn green lines tangent to the blue x–t curve at the five times of interest. The slope is negative at $t = 0$ (point 1 in the figure), so $v_x < 0$ and the object is moving in the negative x direction. The object is momentarily at rest ($v_x = 0$) at $t = 10$ s (point 2 in the figure), so it is not moving in either direction. At $t = 20$ s and 30 s (points 3 and 4 in the figure) the object is moving in the positive x direction ($v_x > 0$); at $t = 40.0$ s (point 5 in the figure) the object is again at rest ($v_x = 0$).

(b) The motion diagram depicts how the object moves. At time $t = 0$, the object is at $x = 0$ and moving in the negative x direction. The curve has a negative slope until $t = 10$ s, so the object continues to move in the negative x direction; because the slope of the x–t curve becomes shallower, the speed is decreasing and the object is slowing down so that the dots are closer together. At $t = 10$ s, the object comes to rest momentarily at $x = -50$ m. After $t = 10$ s, the x–t graph has a positive slope, so the object moves in the positive x direction. From $t = 10$ s to 20 s, the object is speeding up because the slope of the x–t curve is increasing. The object has the fastest speed (because the curve has the greatest slope) at $t = 20$ s when the object again passes through $x = 0$. After $t = 20$ s the slope of the x–t curve is still positive but getting shallower; so, the object is still moving in the positive x direction but its speed is decreasing so that the dots again get closer together. The object finally comes to rest at $x = +50$ m at $t = 40$ s.

Reflect

It's a common mistake to look at a graph like Figure 2-9 and say that the velocity at $t = 10$ s is negative. For this value of time, the curve in Figure 2-9 is below the horizontal axis and so the *coordinate* x is negative. However, the x–t curve has zero *slope* at $t = 10$ s, so at this instant the coordinate x is neither increasing nor decreasing and the velocity is *zero*. Remember that the *value* of an x–t graph shows you the object's *position* (in other words, where the object is), while the *slope* of the x–t graph tells you its *velocity* (that is, how fast and in which direction the object is moving).

Average Acceleration and Instantaneous Acceleration

Just as velocity is the rate of change of position, acceleration is the rate of change of velocity. Suppose an object like the jogger in Figure 2-6 has velocity v_{1x} at time t_1 and velocity v_{2x} at time t_2. We define the object's **average acceleration** $a_{\text{average},x}$ over this time interval to be the change in velocity $\Delta v_x = v_{2x} - v_{1x}$ divided by the elapsed time $\Delta t = t_2 - t_1$:

Average acceleration of an object in linear motion

Change in **velocity** of the object over a certain time interval: The velocity changes from v_{1x} to v_{2x}.

Average acceleration for linear motion
(2-3)

$$a_{\text{average},x} = \frac{\Delta v_x}{\Delta t} = \frac{v_{2x} - v_{1x}}{t_2 - t_1}$$

Elapsed time for the time interval: The object has velocity v_{1x} at time t_1, and has velocity v_{2x} at time t_2.

This definition agrees with our intuitive understanding of acceleration. If a race car initially at rest blasts away from the starting line and rapidly comes to its top speed, its velocity changes substantially (Δv_x is large) in a short time (Δt is small) and its average acceleration $a_{average,x}$ has a large magnitude. If, instead, an elderly horse starts from rest and gradually speeds up to a slow amble, the horse's velocity changes only a little (Δv_x is small) and takes a long time to change (Δt is large). In this case, the horse's average acceleration $a_{average,x}$ has only a small magnitude.

Velocity has units of meters per second (m/s) and time has units of seconds (s), so the SI units of acceleration are meters per second per second, or meters per second squared (m/s^2). Saying that an object has an acceleration of 2.0 m/s^2 means that the object's velocity becomes more positive by 2.0 m/s every second; an acceleration of -4.5 m/s^2 means that the velocity becomes more negative by 4.5 m/s every second. Because average velocity is a vector, average acceleration is also a vector, containing direction information.

Interpreting Positive and Negative Acceleration

We saw in Section 2-2 that a positive velocity means that the object is moving in the positive x direction; a negative velocity means the object is moving in the negative x direction. In a similar way, the sign of the average acceleration $a_{average,x}$ tells us the direction in which the object is *accelerating*: in the positive x direction if $a_{average,x}$ is positive and in the negative direction if $a_{average,x}$ is negative. To see what this means, let's look again at the jogger's motion (Figure 2-10a). He moves in the positive x direction at all

(a)

(b)

Figure 2-10 **Interpreting positive and negative acceleration** You must consider the algebraic signs (plus or minus) of acceleration *and* velocity to determine whether an object is slowing down or speeding up.

- If velocity v_x and acceleration a_x have the same sign (both + as in **1** or both − as in **3**), the jogger speeds up.
- If velocity v_x and acceleration a_x have the opposite signs (one + and one − as in **2** or **4**), the jogger slows down.

times. His instantaneous velocity increases from $+3.00$ m/s to $+4.00$ m/s during the interval from $t_1 = 12.0$ s to $t_2 = 24.0$ s, so the change in his velocity during this interval is positive: $\Delta v_x = v_{2x} - v_{1x} = (+4.00 \text{ m/s}) - (+3.00 \text{ m/s}) = +1.00$ m/s. The jogger's average acceleration for this time interval is also positive: $a_{\text{average},x} = \Delta v_x / \Delta t = (+1.00 \text{ m/s})/(24.0 \text{ s} - 12.0 \text{ s}) = +0.0833$ m/s^2. We say that he accelerates in the positive x direction. In this case, the acceleration is in the *same direction* as the jogger's motion and the jogger *speeds up*.

By contrast, the jogger's instantaneous velocity decreases from $+4.00$ m/s to $+0.80$ m/s during the time interval from $t_2 = 24.0$ s to $t_3 = 36.0$ s, so the jogger's velocity change during this interval is *negative:* $\Delta v_x = v_{3x} - v_{2x} = (+0.80 \text{ m/s}) - (+4.00 \text{ m/s}) = -3.20$ m/s. This means that the average acceleration for this time interval is also negative: $a_{\text{average},x} = \Delta v_x / \Delta t = (-3.20 \text{ m/s})/(36.0 \text{ s} - 24.0 \text{ s}) = -0.267$ m/s^2. We say that the jogger accelerates in the negative x direction. In this case, the acceleration is *opposite* to the direction of the jogger's motion and the jogger *slows down*.

It's common to think that positive acceleration always corresponds to speeding up and that negative acceleration always corresponds to slowing down. That's *not* always true, however! Figure 2-10b shows an example: The jogger from Figure 2-10a repeats the same motion but in the negative x direction, so her velocity is negative at all times. The figure shows that the jogger has *negative* average acceleration when she is speeding up and *positive* acceleration when she is slowing down. Here's a simple rule to help you understand when an object is speeding up and when it is slowing down:

When an object moving in a straight line speeds up, its velocity and acceleration have the same sign (both plus or both minus). When an object moving in a straight line slows down, its velocity and acceleration have opposite signs (one plus and the other minus).

! Watch Out! Acceleration doesn't have to mean increasing speed.

In everyday language, *acceleration* is used to mean "speeding up" and *deceleration* is used to mean "slowing down." In physics, however, acceleration refers to *any* change in velocity and so includes *both* speeding up and slowing down. Speeding up is "accelerating forward" (that is, in the direction of motion) and slowing down is "accelerating backward" (that is, opposite to the direction of motion).

Example 2-4 Calculating Average Acceleration

The object described in Example 2-3 has velocity $v_x = -10$ m/s at $t = 0$, $v_x = 0$ at $t = 10$ s, $v_x = +10$ m/s at $t = 20$ s, $v_x = +1.4$ m/s at $t = 30$ s, and $v_x = 0$ at $t = 40$ s. Find the object's average acceleration for the time intervals (a) $t = 0$ to 10 s, (b) $t = 10$ s to 20 s, (c) $t = 20$ s to 30 s, and (d) $t = 30$ s to 40 s.

Set Up

The figures in Example 2-3 show the x–t graph and motion diagram for this object. For each time interval we'll use the definition of average acceleration, Equation 2-3.

Average acceleration for linear motion:

$$a_{\text{average},x} = \frac{\Delta v_x}{\Delta t} = \frac{v_{2x} - v_{1x}}{t_2 - t_1}$$

(2-3)

Solve

(a) For the time interval $t_1 = 0$ to $t_2 = 10$ s (from point 1 to point 2 in the x–t graph), we have $v_{x1} = -10$ m/s and $v_{x2} = 0$. Because the velocity becomes more positive (it goes from negative to zero), the average x acceleration is positive.

$$a_{\text{average},x} = \frac{v_{2x} - v_{1x}}{t_2 - t_1}$$
$$= \frac{0 - (-10 \text{ m/s})}{10 \text{ s} - 0} = \frac{+10 \text{ m/s}}{10 \text{ s}}$$
$$= +1.0 \text{ m/s}^2$$

(b) For the time interval $t_2 = 10$ s to $t_3 = 20$ s (from point 2 to point 3 in the x–t graph), we have $v_{x2} = 0$ and $v_{x3} = +10$ m/s. The velocity again becomes more positive (it goes from zero to a positive value), so the average x acceleration is again positive.

$$a_{\text{average},x} = \frac{v_{3x} - v_{2x}}{t_3 - t_2}$$
$$= \frac{(+10 \text{ m/s}) - 0}{20 \text{ s} - 10 \text{ s}} = \frac{+10 \text{ m/s}}{10 \text{ s}}$$
$$= +1.0 \text{ m/s}^2$$

(c) For the time interval $t_3 = 20$ s to $t_4 = 30$ s (from point 3 to point 4 in the x–t graph), we have $v_{x3} = +10$ m/s and $v_{x4} = +1.4$ m/s. The velocity becomes more negative (less positive), so the average x acceleration is negative.

$$a_{\text{average},x} = \frac{v_{4x} - v_{3x}}{t_4 - t_3}$$
$$= \frac{(+1.4 \text{ m/s}) - (+10 \text{ m/s})}{30 \text{ s} - 20 \text{ s}} = \frac{-8.6 \text{ m/s}}{10 \text{ s}}$$
$$= -0.86 \text{ m/s}^2$$

(d) For the time interval $t_4 = 30$ s to $t_5 = 40$ s (from point 4 to point 5 in the x–t graph), we have $v_{x4} = +1.4$ m/s and $v_{x5} = 0$. Again the velocity becomes more negative and the average acceleration is negative.

$$a_{\text{average},x} = \frac{v_{5x} - v_{4x}}{t_5 - t_4}$$
$$= \frac{0 - (+1.4 \text{ m/s})}{40 \text{ s} - 30 \text{ s}} = \frac{-1.4 \text{ m/s}}{10 \text{ s}}$$
$$= -0.14 \text{ m/s}^2$$

Reflect

Let's check these results to see how they agree with the general rule about the algebraic signs of velocity v_x and average acceleration $a_{\text{average},x}$. From $t_1 = 0$ to $t_2 = 10$ s, v_x is negative (the x–t graph slopes downward) but $a_{\text{average},x} = +1.0$ m/s^2 is positive. Because the signs are different, the speed must decrease during this interval, and indeed it does (from 10 m/s to zero). From $t_2 = 10$ s to $t_3 = 20$ s, v_x is positive (the x–t graph slopes upward) and $a_{\text{average},x} = +1.0$ m/s^2 is also positive. During this interval the signs of v_x and $a_{\text{average},x}$ are the same and the speed increases (from 0 to 10 m/s), in accordance with the rule. During the intervals from $t_3 = 20$ s to $t_4 = 30$ s (for which $a_{\text{average},x} = -0.86$ m/s^2) and from $t_4 = 30$ s to $t_5 = 40$ s (for which $a_{\text{average},x} = -0.14$ m/s^2), v_x and $a_{\text{average},x}$ have opposite signs (v_x is positive and $a_{\text{average},x}$ is negative) and the speed decreases (from 10 m/s to 1.4 m/s to zero) as it should. When looking at changes in speed, the sign of the acceleration alone isn't what's important—what matters is how the signs of velocity and acceleration compare.

Instantaneous Acceleration and the v_x–t Graph

An object's acceleration can change from one moment to the next. For example, a car can accelerate forward and gain speed, cruise at a steady velocity with zero acceleration, then accelerate backward when the driver steps on the brakes. The **instantaneous acceleration**, or simply **acceleration**, describes how the velocity is changing at a given instant. We use the symbol a_x (without the word "average") to denote acceleration.

Just as an object's velocity v_x is the rate of change of its position as expressed by its coordinate x, the object's acceleration a_x is the rate of change of its velocity. In other words, *acceleration is to velocity as velocity is to position*. The slope of a graph of an object's position versus time (an x–t graph) indicates its velocity v_x. In the same way, the slope of a graph of the object's velocity versus time—that is, a v_x–t **graph**—tells us its acceleration a_x. If the v_x–t graph has an upward (positive) slope, the velocity is becoming more positive and the acceleration is positive; if the v_x–t graph has a downward

(a) Jogger's x-t graph

At each point on an x-t curve, the slope equals the instantaneous velocity v_x.

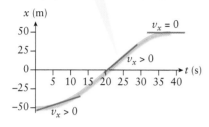

(b) Jogger's v_x-t graph

At each point on an v_x-t curve, the slope equals the instantaneous acceleration a_x.

Figure 2-11 From x–t graph to v_x–t graph Graphs of a jogger's (a) position versus time and (b) velocity versus time.

(negative) slope, the velocity is becoming more negative and the acceleration is negative. If the velocity is not changing so that the acceleration is zero, the v_x–t graph is horizontal and has zero slope.

You can see these properties of the v_x–t graph by inspecting Figure 2-11, which shows both the x–t graph and the v_x–t graph for the jogger whose motion we depicted in Figures 2-6, 2-7 and 2-10a. From $t = 0$ to $t = 16$ s his velocity becomes more positive, which we can see in two ways: The x–t graph has an *increasing* slope (which means v_x is becoming more positive), and the v_x–t graph has a *positive* slope (which means a_x is positive). From $t = 16$ s to $t = 28$ s, the jogger has a constant velocity, which is why the x–t graph has a *constant* slope (which means v_x is not changing) and the v_x–t graph is a horizontal line with *zero* slope (which means a_x is zero) during these times. Finally, from $t = 28$ s to $t = 38$ s, the jogger's velocity is becoming more negative, so the x–t graph has a *decreasing* slope (which means v_x is becoming more negative) and the v_x–t graph has a *negative* slope (which means a_x is negative). Table 2-2 summarizes these key features of x–t and v_x–t graphs.

Table 2-2 Interpreting x–t graphs and v_x–t graphs

A graph of coordinate x versus time t (x–t graph) and a graph of x velocity v_x versus time t (v_x–t graph) are different ways to depict the motion of an object along a straight line.

Type of graph	x–t graph	v_x–t graph
The *value* of the graph tells you. . .	the coordinate x of the object at a given time t	the velocity v_x of the object at a given time t
The *slope* of the graph tells you. . .	the velocity v_x of the object at a given time t	the acceleration a_x of the object at a given time t
Changes in the slope of the graph tell you. . .	the acceleration a_x of the object at a given time t	whether the acceleration is changing

Example 2-5 Decoding a v_x–t Graph

Figure 2-12 shows both the x–t graph and the v_x–t graph for the motion of the same object that we examined in Examples 2-3 and 2-4. Using these graphs alone, determine whether the object's acceleration a_x is positive, negative, or zero at (a) $t = 0$, (b) $t = 10$ s, (c) $t = 20$ s, (d) $t = 30$ s, and (e) $t = 40$ s.

Figure 2-12 Two graphs to interpret The x–t graph and v_x–t graph for the object from Examples 2-3 and 2-4.

Set Up
We use two ideas: (i) acceleration is the rate of change of velocity, and (ii) the value of the acceleration equals the slope of the v_x–t graph (Table 2-2).

Solve
(a) At $t = 0$, the v_x–t graph has a positive (upward) slope, which means that v_x is increasing and hence that a_x is positive. The x–t graph shows the same thing. This graph has a steep negative slope at $t = 0$, which means v_x is negative, but as time increases the slope becomes shallower as the slope and v_x become closer to zero. Because v_x is changing from a negative value toward zero, the velocity is increasing and a_x is positive.

(b) At $t = 10$ s, the v_x–t graph has the same upward slope as at $t = 0$, which means that the acceleration a_x is again positive. The velocity is zero at this instant, so the object is momentarily at rest. It's still accelerating, however; the object has a negative velocity just before $t = 10$ s, and the velocity is positive just after $t = 10$ s. This is the time at which the object turns around. You can also see this from the x–t graph, the slope of which is changing from negative to zero to positive around $t = 10$ s.

(c) At $t = 20$ s, the v_x–t graph has zero slope, so the acceleration is zero. At this instant, the velocity is neither increasing nor decreasing. That's why the x–t graph at this time is nearly a straight line of constant slope, indicating that the velocity isn't changing at this instant.

(d) At $t = 30$ s, the v_x–t graph has a negative (downward) slope, so a_x is negative. The x–t graph has a positive slope at this instant (v_x is positive) but is flattening out, so the slope and v_x are both becoming more negative, which is another way of saying that the acceleration is negative.

(e) At $t = 40$ s, the v_x–t graph is horizontal, so its slope is zero and the acceleration is likewise zero. At this time, the velocity is not changing. The x–t graph also reveals that the velocity is not changing, because the slope of this curve is constant at $t = 40$ s. (The slope of the x–t curve is also zero, which means that the constant value of v_x is zero. In other words, the object is at rest and is remaining at rest.)

Reflect

We can check our answers by seeing what they tell us about how the *speed* of the object is changing. At $t = 0$, the object has negative velocity and positive acceleration. Because v_x and a_x have opposite signs, the object is slowing down. At $t = 20$ s, the velocity is positive but the acceleration is zero; the velocity is not changing at this instant, so the object is neither speeding up nor slowing down. At $t = 30$ s, the velocity is positive and the acceleration is negative, so the object is once again slowing down. Finally, at $t = 40$ s, the object is at rest ($v_x = 0$) and is remaining at rest, so it is neither speeding up nor slowing down. You can confirm these conclusions by comparing with the motion diagram in Example 2-3. Are they consistent?

❓ Got the Concept? 2-3   Interpreting the Sign of Acceleration

Which statement about the motion depicted in Figure 2-12 is correct? (a) At $t = 5$ s, a_x is positive and the object is speeding up; (b) at $t = 5$ s, a_x is positive and the object is slowing down; (c) at $t = 5$ s, a_x is negative and the object is speeding up; (d) at $t = 5$ s, a_x is negative and the object is slowing down.

Take-Home Message for Section 2-4

✔ Instantaneous velocity v_x (or *velocity* for short) tells you an object's speed and direction of motion at a given instant. It is equal to the rate of change of the object's position and equals the slope of the object's x–t graph.

✔ The average acceleration of an object, $a_{\text{average},x}$, is the change in its velocity v_x over a given time interval divided by the duration Δt of the interval.

✔ Instantaneous acceleration a_x (or *acceleration* for short) equals the rate of change of an object's velocity at a given instant. It also equals the slope of the object's v_x–t graph.

✔ An object speeds up when its velocity and acceleration have the same sign, and slows down when they have opposite signs.

2-5 Constant acceleration means velocity changes at a steady rate

When a basketball falls from a player's hand or a car comes to a halt with the brakes applied, the acceleration of the object turns out to be nearly *constant*—that is, the velocity of the object changes at a steady rate (Figure 2-13). This situation is so common that it's worth deriving a set of kinematic equations that describe motion in a straight line with **constant acceleration**. These equations turn out to be useful even in situations where the acceleration isn't strictly constant.

If the acceleration is constant, the *instantaneous* acceleration a_x at any instant of time is the same as the *average* acceleration $a_{\text{average},x}$ for any time interval. Thus, we can use a_x in place of $a_{\text{average},x}$ in any equation. In particular, let's consider a time interval from $t = 0$ to some other time t. We use the symbol v_{0x} for the velocity at $t = 0$, which we call the initial velocity, and the symbol v_x (with no zero) for the velocity at time t. From the definition of average acceleration given in Equation 2-3,

$$a_x = \frac{v_x - v_{0x}}{t - 0} \tag{2-4}$$

Figure 2-13 **An object with constant acceleration** The velocity of this vehicle is not constant. But its acceleration—the rate of change of velocity—*is* constant.

We can rewrite Equation 2-4 to get an expression for the velocity v_x at any time t. Multiply both sides of the equation by t, and add v_{0x} to both sides of the equation:

$$a_x t = v_x - v_{0x}$$
$$v_{0x} + a_x t = v_x$$

Velocity, acceleration, and time for constant acceleration only (2-5)

Velocity at time t of an object in linear motion with constant acceleration

Velocity at time $t = 0$ of the object

$$v_x = v_{0x} + a_x t$$

Constant acceleration of the object

Time at which the object has velocity v_x

Equation 2-5 tells us how the object's velocity v_x varies with time. If $a_x = 0$ so that the object is not accelerating, v_x at any time t is the same as the velocity v_{0x} at $t = 0$: in other words, the velocity is constant. If a_x is not zero and the object is accelerating, the term $a_x t$ in this equation says that the velocity changes with time.

We'd also like to have an expression that shows how the object's x coordinate varies with time. (Equation 2-2 is an equation of this sort for the case of constant *velocity*—that is, zero acceleration.) To obtain such an expression, first note that if the object is at coordinate x_0 at $t = 0$ and at coordinate x at time t, its x displacement during the time interval from 0 to t is $\Delta x = x - x_0$. From Equation 2-1, Δx divided by the duration $\Delta t = t - 0$ of the time interval equals the average velocity for this time interval:

$$v_{\text{average},x} = \frac{\Delta x}{\Delta t} = \frac{x - x_0}{t - 0}$$

We can rewrite this expression using the same steps we used in writing Equation 2-5. The result is

(2-6)

$$x = x_0 + v_{\text{average},x} t$$

Equation 2-6 tells us that to determine where the object is at time t—that is, what its x coordinate is—we need to know the average velocity $v_{\text{average},x}$ for the time interval from 0 to t.

The average velocity is easy to find if the acceleration is constant. For example, suppose that the initial velocity is $v_{0x} = 3.0$ m/s and the acceleration is $a_x = 2.0$ m/s^2. From Equation 2-5, the velocity is

$$v_x = (3.0 \text{ m/s}) + (2.0 \text{ m/s}^2)(0 \text{ s}) = 3.0 \text{ m/s at } t = 0$$
$$v_x = (3.0 \text{ m/s}) + (2.0 \text{ m/s}^2)(1.0 \text{ s}) = 5.0 \text{ m/s at } t = 1.0 \text{ s}$$
$$v_x = (3.0 \text{ m/s}) + (2.0 \text{ m/s}^2)(2.0 \text{ s}) = 7.0 \text{ m/s at } t = 2.0 \text{ s}$$

To find the average of these three velocities—that is, the average velocity $v_{\text{average},x}$ for the time interval from $t = 0$ to $t = 2.0$ s—we add them together and divide by 3:

$$v_{\text{average},x} = \frac{3.0 \text{ m/s} + 5.0 \text{ m/s} + 7.0 \text{ m/s}}{3} = \frac{15.0 \text{ m/s}}{3} = 5.0 \text{ m/s}$$

Notice that $v_{\text{average},x} = 5.0$ m/s is also the value of the instantaneous velocity v_x at the midpoint of the interval ($t = 1.0$ s). Furthermore, $v_{\text{average},x}$ is equal to the average of the instantaneous velocities at the *beginning and end* of the time interval ($v_x = 3.0$ m/s at $t = 0$ and $v_x = 7.0$ m/s at $t = 2.0$ m/s; the average of these is $(3.0 \text{ m/s} + 7.0 \text{ m/s})/2 = (10.0 \text{ m/s})/2 = 5.0$ m/s). You will *always* get this result if the acceleration is constant. So for constant a_x, the average velocity for the time interval from time 0 to time t is the average of v_{0x} and v_x:

(2-7)

$$v_{\text{average},x} = \frac{v_{0x} + v_x}{2}$$

If we substitute the expression for v_x from Equation 2-5 into Equation 2-7, we get

(2-8)

$$v_{\text{average},x} = \frac{v_{0x} + v_{0x} + a_x t}{2} = \frac{2v_{0x} + a_x t}{2} = v_{0x} + \frac{1}{2} a_x t$$

Equation 2-8 gives the average velocity of an object moving with constant acceleration for the interval from 0 to t.

> **Watch Out!** Instantaneous velocity and average velocity are different quantities.
>
> Equations 2-5 and 2-8 look quite similar, but they describe two very different things. The first of these, $v_x = v_{0x} + a_x t$, tells us the *instantaneous velocity* at the *end* of the time interval from 0 to t. The second of these, $v_{average,x} = v_{0x} + (1/2)a_x t$, is a formula for the *average velocity during* this time interval.

If we substitute the expression for $v_{average,x}$ from Equation 2-8 into Equation 2-6, we get an equation for the coordinate of the object x at time t:

$$x = x_0 + v_{average,x}t = x_0 + \left(v_{0x} + \frac{1}{2}a_x t\right)t$$

or, simplifying,

Position at time t of an object in linear motion with constant acceleration

Velocity at time $t = 0$ of the object

Constant acceleration of the object

$$x = x_0 + v_{0x}t + \frac{1}{2}a_x t^2$$

Position at time $t = 0$ of the object

Time at which the object has position x

Position, acceleration, and time for constant acceleration only (2-9)

If we know the object's initial position x_0, its initial velocity v_{0x}, and its constant acceleration a_x, Equation 2-9 tells us its position x at any time t.

A good way to check Equation 2-9 is to consider a couple of special cases. If $v_{0x} = 0$ (the object is initially at rest) and $a_x = 0$ (the object's velocity doesn't change), Equation 2-9 says that $x = x_0$ at any time t. In other words, the object doesn't move! If v_{0x} is not zero (the object is moving initially) but $a_x = 0$ (the acceleration is zero), the object has a constant velocity $v_x = v_{0x}$ and its position at time t is $x = x_0 + v_{0x}t = x_0 + v_x t$. This relationship is the same as Equation 2-2 for linear motion with constant velocity, which we found in Section 2-2. Note that if there is a nonzero acceleration a_x, Equation 2-9 shows that there is an additional displacement of $(1/2)a_x t^2$ during the time interval from 0 to t compared to the case of constant velocity.

Graphing Motion with Constant Acceleration

A good way to interpret what Equations 2-5 and 2-9 tell us is to draw the associated motion diagram, x–t graph, and v_x–t graph. **Figure 2-14** shows three examples of these motion diagrams and graphs. In each case, the spacing between the dots of the motion

Figure 2-14 Motion with constant acceleration: Three examples Each of these three sets of an x–t graph and an v_x–t graph depicts a different example of linear motion with constant acceleration.

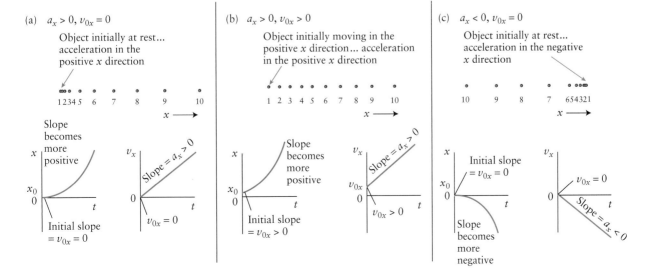

(a) $a_x > 0$, $v_{0x} = 0$

Object initially at rest... acceleration in the positive x direction

(b) $a_x > 0$, $v_{0x} > 0$

Object initially moving in the positive x direction... acceleration in the positive x direction

(c) $a_x < 0$, $v_{0x} = 0$

Object initially at rest... acceleration in the negative x direction diagram changes as the object's velocity changes. In cases (a) and (b) the acceleration is positive, so the velocity is becoming more positive. In each of these cases, the x–t graph is a special curve called a **parabola** that curves upward (the slope, which denotes v_x, is increasing) and the v_x–t graph is a straight line that slants upward (the slope, which denotes a_x, is positive). In case (c) the acceleration is negative. The x–t graph in this case is a parabola that curves downward (because v_x is getting more negative, and thus the slope of this curve is also becoming more negative), and the v_x–t graph is a straight line that slants downward (because a_x, and thus the slope of this curve, is negative).

! Watch Out!   Know your graphs.

Be careful not to confuse the x–t graph and the v_x–t graph for constant acceleration. When the acceleration is not zero, the x–t graph is *curved* because its slope at each point represents the velocity at the corresponding time t. The velocity is continually changing, so the slope is different at each point and the graph is curved. (Remember that acceleration means a change in velocity, so constant acceleration means the velocity changes at all times at the same rate.) By contrast, the v_x–t graph is a *straight line* because its slope at each point represents the *acceleration* at the corresponding time. The acceleration is constant, so the v_x–t graph has a constant slope (which makes the graph a straight line).

? Got the Concept? 2-4   Drawing x–t and v_x–t Graphs

Draw the x–t graph and v_x–t for motion with constant acceleration for each of the following cases: (a) $a_x > 0$, $v_{0x} < 0$; (b) $a_x < 0$, $v_{0x} > 0$; and (c) $a_x < 0$, $v_{0x} < 0$. (Assume that x_0 is positive in each case.)

In each of the cases shown in Figure 2-14, we have assumed that x_0 is positive. You should redraw each of the x–t graphs assuming instead that x_0 is negative. (This change has no effect on the v_x–t graphs. Can you see why not?)

The Kinematic Equations for Motion with Constant Acceleration

Equations 2-5 and 2-9 give the object's x coordinate and velocity at a given time t. There is also a third equation which is often useful in analyzing linear motion with constant acceleration. This equation expresses the object's velocity when the object is at a given x coordinate, without reference to time. To create this equation, first solve Equation 2-5 for the time at which the object has velocity v_x:

$$t = \frac{v_x - v_{0x}}{a_x}$$

Then substitute this expression into Equation 2-9, $x = x_0 + v_{0x}t + \frac{1}{2}a_xt^2$, every place you see the quantity t:

(2-10)
$$x = x_0 + v_{0x}\left(\frac{v_x - v_{0x}}{a_x}\right) + \frac{1}{2}a_x\left(\frac{v_x - v_{0x}}{a_x}\right)^2$$

With a little algebra, you can rewrite this equation as

Velocity at position x of an object in linear motion with constant acceleration

Velocity at position x_0 of the object

Velocity, acceleration, and position for constant acceleration only
(2-11)

$$v_x^2 = v_{0x}^2 + 2a_x(x - x_0)$$

Constant acceleration of the object

Two positions of the object

(You should fill in the algebraic steps required to transform Equation 2-10 into Equation 2-11.)

Equations 2-5, 2-9, and 2-11 are tremendously important, because they allow you to solve *any* problem in kinematics that involves straight-line motion with constant acceleration. Situations with constant or nearly constant acceleration are actually quite common in nature and technology, so these equations will be useful to us throughout our study of physics. In the following section we'll see how to tackle problems of this kind.

? Got the Concept? 2-5 Interpreting Motion with Constant Acceleration

At $t = 0$ an object has velocity $+2.00$ m/s. Its acceleration is constant and equal to -1.00 m/s^2. State whether the object is (i) speeding up, (ii) slowing down, or (iii) neither at each of the following times: (a) $t = 1.00$ s, (b) $t = 2.00$ s, (c) $t = 3.00$ s. (*Hint*: Use Equation 2-5.)

Take-Home Message for Section 2-5

✔ If an object in linear motion has a constant acceleration a_x, its velocity v_x changes at a steady rate.

✔ The v_x–t graph for an object in linear motion with constant acceleration a_x is a straight line. The slope of the line tells you the acceleration.

✔ The x–t graph for an object in linear motion with constant acceleration a_x is a parabola. The parabola curves upward if a_x is positive and curves downward if a_x is negative. The slope of the parabola where it meets the vertical axis tells you the velocity at $t = 0$.

2-6 Solving straight-line motion problems: Constant acceleration

Table 2-3 summarizes the properties of Equations 2-5, 2-9, and 2-11 for linear motion with constant acceleration. The three equations in Table 2-3 involve six physical quantities: the time t, the object's initial position coordinate x_0 at time 0, the object's position x at time t, its velocity v_{0x} at time 0, its velocity v_x at time t, and its constant acceleration a_x. However, not all of these quantities appear in any one of the three constant-acceleration equations. How, then, do you decide which equation or equations to use to solve a particular problem involving linear motion with constant acceleration?

One answer to this conundrum is to create a **Know/Don't Know table**. As the name suggests, this table lists which of the quantities in the problem you know and which quantities you don't know. As an example, consider this typical problem:

A car accelerates from $v_{0x} = 20.0$ m/s to $v_x = 24.0$ m/s at a constant acceleration of $a_x = 2.00$ m/s^2 (Figure 2-15a). How far does it travel during that process?

The problem asks us to find "how far," which in the language of physics corresponds to the distance, or the absolute value of the displacement $|x - x_0|$. While we don't

(a)

As a car speeds up from 20.0 m/s to 24.0 m/s with an acceleration of 2.00 m/s^2, what distance does it travel?

$v_{0x} = 20.0$ m/s $v_x = 24.0$ m/s

$a_x = 2.00$ m/s^2

x_0 |——Distance = ?——| x →+x

(b)

Quantity	Know/Don't Know
t	X
x_0	0
x	?
v_{0x}	20.0 m/s
v_x	24.0 m/s
a_x	2.00 m/s^2

Figure 2-15 **A constant-acceleration problem** To help solve the problem depicted in (a), it helps to write (b) a Know/Don't Know table.

Table 2-3 Equations for linear motion with constant acceleration

By using one or more of these equations, you can solve any problem involving motion in a straight line for which the acceleration is constant. The check marks indicate which of the quantities t (time), x_0 (the x coordinate at time 0), x (the x coordinate at time t), v_{0x} (the velocity at time 0), v_x (the velocity at time t), and a_x (the constant acceleration) appear in each equation.

Equation		Which quantities the equation includes					
		t	x	x_0	v_{0x}	v_x	a_x
$v_x = v_{0x} + a_x t$	(2-5)	✔			✔	✔	✔
$x = x_0 + v_{0x}t + \frac{1}{2}a_x t^2$	(2-9)	✔	✔	✔	✔		✔
$v_x^2 = v_{0x}^2 + 2a_x(x - x_0)$	(2-11)		✔	✔	✔	✔	✔

know the value of x_0, we are free to choose a coordinate system in which the car starts at $x_0 = 0$. Now, if we can determine x, we know that its absolute value will be the same as the distance the car travels. We are given the values of v_{0x}, v_x, and a_x, but we don't know the value of t, which is how long it takes the car to accelerate from 20.0 m/s to 24.0 m/s. So x_0, v_{0x}, v_x, and a_x are in the "Know" category, while x and t are in the "Don't Know" category. To make a Know/Don't Know table, start by making two columns. List the six quantities in one column, and enter values of the known quantities in the other column (Figure 2-15b). Note that we've put a question mark next to the final position x, which is the quantity that we'd like to determine. We've also put an "X" next to the time t: We don't know how much time it takes for the car to accelerate, but we don't *need* to know it (it's not asked for in the problem). The "X" tells us that we should eliminate this quantity from the problem.

The Know/Don't Know table tells us that we need an equation that may involve x_0, x, v_{0x}, v_x, and a_x, but does *not* involve t. You can see from Table 2-3 that the equation we want is Equation 2-11, $v_x^2 = v_{0x}^2 + 2a_x(x - x_0)$. We rearrange this equation so that the quantity we're trying to determine is on one side of the equation, and then we substitute the known values from our Know/Don't Know table:

$$x = \frac{v_x^2 - v_{0x}^2}{2a_x} + x_0 = \frac{(24.0 \text{ m/s})^2 - (20.0 \text{ m/s})^2}{2(2.00 \text{ m/s}^2)} + 0$$

$$= 44.0 \frac{\text{m}^2/\text{s}^2}{\text{m/s}^2} = 44.0 \text{ m}$$

It's useful to make a Know/Don't Know table as part of *every* problem solution, not just those involving linear motion with constant acceleration.

Solving Problems with Constant-Acceleration Linear Motion

Here's a procedure you can use to solve any problem that involves linear motion with constant acceleration.

(1) In a constant-acceleration linear motion problem, you will be asked to find the values of one or more quantities that describe motion. These could be the acceleration a_x, the the position x at a certain point in the motion, the initial position x_0, the velocity v_x at a certain point in the motion, the initial velocity v_{0x}, or the time t at which the moving object is at a certain position or has a certain velocity.

   a. Draw a picture that shows the object's motion. This should include the x axis (which lies along the direction of motion), a choice of origin, and a motion diagram. It's usually easiest to choose the direction in which the object moves to be the positive x direction and its initial position to be at the origin, so $x_0 = 0$.

   b. Sketch x–t and v_x–t graphs for the object's motion. These can be a great help in solving the problem.

(2) Make a Know/Don't Know table like that in Figure 2-15b.

   a. Enter all known values. Make sure that all quantities are expressed in con-sistent units. It's best to use SI units and express x in meters, v_x in meters per second, and a_x in meters per second squared. If you need to convert units, use the techniques you learned in Section 1-3.

   b. Mark the unknown quantities of interest with a "?". (There may be more than one.)

   c. Mark any remaining unknown quantities with an "X".

(3) Use Table 2-3 to select equations that involve the unknown quantities of interest as well as the quantities whose values are known.

(4) Once you have the equations you need, solve them for the unknowns using your knowledge of algebra. Then substitute the known values and compute an answer.

(5) If there's more than one quantity of interest, you'll need to use your skills at solving simultaneous equations (see Math Tutorial). If you're solving Equation 2-9 for the value of the time t, note that this is a quadratic equation and has to be solved using the techniques given in Math Tutorial. Quadratic equations can have two, one, or no solutions—you'll have to inspect your solutions to decide which is correct.

 See the Math Tutorial for more information on solving simultaneous equations

(6) Check your answers to see whether they're reasonable.

(7) A good way to check your work is to follow a different sequence of steps to get the answer; if you get the same answer both ways, you're on the right track.

(8) Make sure your answers have the correct units. For example, velocities should be in m/s, not m or m/s^2.

Example 2-6 Motion with Constant Acceleration I: Cleared for Takeoff!

After winning the lottery, you are shopping for a corporate jet. During a demonstration flight with a salesperson, you notice that a particular type of jet takes off after traveling 1.20 km down the runway and after reaching a speed of 226 km/h (140 mi/h). (a) Sketch a motion diagram, an x–t graph, and a v_x–t graph for the jet's motion as it rolls down the runway. (b) What is the magnitude of the airplane's acceleration (assumed constant) during the takeoff roll? (c) How long does it take the airplane to reach takeoff speed?

Set Up

We take the positive x axis to point along the runway in the direction that the jet travels, choose the origin at the point where the jet starts to move, and choose $t = 0$ to be when it starts to move. We are told the jet's initial velocity ($v_{0x} = 0$, because the jet starts at rest) as well as its velocity $v_x = 226$ km/h at position $x = 1.20$ km. Our goals in parts (b) and (c) are to find the jet's acceleration a_x and the time t when the jet attains $v_x = 226$ km/h, so we make a Know/Don't Know table for these two parts of the problem.

We want to determine the values of *two* unknown quantities, a_x and t, so we need two equations. Table 2-3 tells us that to find a_x from x_0, x, v_x, and v_{0x}, we should use Equation 2-11. Once we know the value of a_x we can use Equation 2-5 to find the time t at which $v_x = 226$ km/h.

To find a_x from x_0, x, v_{0x}, and v_x:

$$v_x^2 = v_{0x}^2 + 2a_x(x - x_0) \quad (2\text{-}11)$$

To find t from v_{0x}, v_x, and a_x:

$$v_x = v_{0x} + a_x t \quad (2\text{-}5)$$

start of takeoff roll $v_{0x} = 0$ takeoff $v_x = 226$ km/h

Quantity	Know/Don't Know
t	?
x_0	0
x	1.20 km
v_{0x}	0
v_x	226 km/h
a_x	?

Solve

(a) Because the jet speeds up as it rolls down the runway, successive dots in its motion diagram are spaced increasingly far apart. The x–t graph is a parabola (because a_x is constant) that starts at $x_0 = 0$ at $t = 0$ (the jet is initially at the origin), has zero slope at $t = 0$ (the initial velocity is zero), and curves upward (the slope increases as v_x increases). The v_x–t graph starts at $v_{0x} = 0$ at $t = 0$ (the initial velocity is zero) and is a straight line that slopes upward (the acceleration is constant and positive). (Compare Figure 2-14a.) We only draw the graphs to the point of takeoff, because after that point the jet is flying and no longer simply moving along the x axis.

(b) We first convert $v_x = 226$ km/h to m/s and convert $x = 1.20$ km to m. We then solve Equation 2-11 for a_x and substitute in the known values.

$$v_x = (226 \text{ km/h})\left(\frac{1000 \text{ m}}{1 \text{ km}}\right)\left(\frac{1 \text{ h}}{60 \text{ min}}\right)\left(\frac{1 \text{ min}}{60 \text{ s}}\right) = 62.8 \text{ m/s}$$

$$x = (1.20 \text{ km})\left(\frac{1000 \text{ m}}{1 \text{ km}}\right) = 1.20 \times 10^3 \text{ m}$$

Substitute into Equation 2-11:

$$a_x = \frac{v_x^2 - v_{0x}^2}{2(x - x_0)} = \frac{(62.8 \text{ m/s})^2 - (0 \text{ m/s})^2}{2(1.20 \times 10^3 \text{ m} - 0 \text{ m})} = 1.64 \text{ m/s}^2$$

(c) We now know the value of a_x from part (b), so we can solve Equation 2-5 for the time t at which $v_x = 226$ km/h $= 62.8$ m/s. When you enter the values for v_x and a_x into your calculator, retain the extra digits from your calculations above, and round the value for the time t only at the end.

Substitute a_x from part (b) into Equation 2-5:

$$t = \frac{v_x - v_{0x}}{a_x} = \frac{(62.8 \text{ m/s}) - (0 \text{ m/s})}{1.64 \text{ m/s}^2} = 38.2 \text{ s}$$

Reflect

Both of our numerical answers have the correct units: a_x is in m/s^2 and t is in s. We can check our answers to part (b) and part (c) by substituting $x = 0$, $v_{0x} = 0$, $a_x = 1.64$ m/s^2, and $t = 38.2$ s into Equation 2-9, the one constant-acceleration equation that we haven't used yet. We get $x = 1.20$ km, which means that when the jet reaches takeoff speed, it is 1.20 km down the runway—just as we were told in the statement of the problem. That's good news because it tells us our results are consistent.

Substitute a_x from part (b) and t from part (c) into Equation 2-9:

$$x = x_0 + v_{0x}t + \frac{1}{2}a_x t^2$$

$$= 0 + (0)(38.2 \text{ s}) + \frac{1}{2}(1.64 \text{ m/s}^2)(38.2 \text{ s})^2$$

$$= 1.20 \times 10^3 \text{ m} = 1.20 \text{ km}$$

Example 2-7 Motion with Constant Acceleration II: Which Solution Is Correct?

Consider again the jet takeoff described in Example 2-6. There is a marker alongside the runway 328 m from the point where the jet starts to move. How long after beginning its takeoff roll does the jet pass the marker?

Set Up

We use the same x axis and choice of origin as in Example 2-6. Again we have $x_0 = 0$ and $v_{0x} = 0$, and we know the value of a_x from our work in Example 2-6. Our goal is to calculate the time t at which $x = 328$ m. We don't know the jet's velocity at this point, nor are we asked for its value, so we put a red "X" next to v_x in the table.

Table 2-3 tells us that the equation we need to find t from the given information is Equation 2-9.

Position, acceleration, and time for constant acceleration only:

$$x = x_0 + v_{0x}t + \frac{1}{2}a_x t^2 \qquad (2\text{-}9)$$

Quantity	Know/Don't Know
t	?
x_0	0
x	328 m
v_{0x}	0
v_x	X
a_x	1.64 m/s^2

Solve

First, let's substitute the known values $x = 328$ m, $x_0 = 0$, $v_{0x} = 0$, and $a_x = 1.64$ m/s^2 into Equation 2-9.

Substitute $x_0 = 0$ and $v_{0x} = 0$, then simplify:

$$x = 0 + (0)t + \frac{1}{2}a_x t^2 = \frac{1}{2}a_x t^2$$

Then substitute $x = 328$ m, $a_x = 1.64$ m/s^2:

$$328\text{ m} = \frac{1}{2}(1.64\text{ m/s}^2)t^2$$

Rearrange the equation to solve for t.

$$t^2 = \frac{2(328\text{ m})}{1.64\text{ m/s}^2} = 4.00 \times 10^2\text{ s}^2$$

$$t = \pm\sqrt{4.00 \times 10^2\text{ s}^2} = \pm 20.0\text{ s}$$

The $\pm$ symbol in front of 20.0 s means that the square of either $t = +20.0$ s or $t = -20.0$ s is equal to $t^2 = 4.00 \times 10^2$ s^2. In this case, we clearly want a positive value of time: The jet must reach the marker at $x = 328$ m some time *after* beginning its takeoff roll at $t = 0$. So the correct answer is $t = 20.0$ s.

Choose the value that corresponds to a time after the jet started moving:

$t = 20.0$ s

Reflect

In Example 2-6, we found that the jet takes 38.2 s to travel 1.20 km. Our answer says that it takes less time (20.0 s) to travel a shorter distance (328 m), which is reasonable.

What may not seem reasonable is that we got *two* answers to the problem, only one of which made sense. To see the meaning of the other answer, $t = -20.0$ s, remember that we assumed that the jet has *constant* acceleration $a_x = 1.64$ m/s^2. As far as the equations are concerned, the jet has *always* had this acceleration, even before $t = 0$! According to these equations, before $t = 0$, the jet had the same positive value of a_x but had a *negative* velocity v_x and was moving *backward* along the runway in the negative x direction. The answer $t = -20.0$ s refers to the time during this fictitious motion when the backward-moving jet passed through the point $x = 328$ m.

Example 2-8 Motion with Constant Acceleration III: Demolition Derby

As a stunt for a movie, two cars are to collide with each other head-on (Figure 2-16). The two cars initially are 125 m apart, car A is heading straight for car B at 30.0 m/s, and car B is at rest. Car A maintains the same velocity, while car B accelerates toward car A at a constant 4.00 m/s^2. (a) When do the cars collide? (b) Where do the cars collide? (c) How fast is car B moving at the moment of collision?

Figure 2-16 **A head-on collision** When and where will these two cars collide?

Set Up

This situation is similar to the two swimmers in Example 2-2 in Section 2-3. The two cars collide when they are at the same place—in other words, at the time t when they have the same x coordinate, as the motion diagram shows. We choose the x axis so that car B is initially at the origin and car A is initially at $x = x_{A0} = 125$ m. Then car A has initial velocity $v_{A0x} = -30.0$ m/s (it is moving in the negative x direction, toward the origin) and zero acceleration, while car B has zero initial velocity (it starts at rest) and constant acceleration $a_{Bx} = +4.00$ m/s^2 (it accelerates in the positive x direction).

   The two cars collide at the time t when their x–t graphs cross. Note from the v_x–t graph that the two cars never have the same *velocity*, because they move in opposite directions.

Our goals are to find the value of t when the two cars collide, the common value of x for the two cars at this time, and the velocity of car B at this time. (The Know/Don't Know tables for the two cars seem to show *five* unknowns. But remember that the two cars have the same values of t and the same values of x when they collide.) Because time is an essential quantity in this problem, we use the two equations from Table 2-3 that involve t.

Position, acceleration, and time for constant acceleration only:

$$x = x_0 + v_{0x}t + \frac{1}{2}a_xt^2 \qquad (2\text{-}9)$$

Velocity, acceleration, and time for constant acceleration only:

$$v_x = v_{0x} + a_xt \qquad (2\text{-}5)$$

For Car A:

Quantity	Know/Don't Know
t	?
x_0	125 m
x	?
v_{0x}	−30.0 m/s
v_x	−30.0 m/s
a_x	0

For Car B:

Quantity	Know/Don't Know
t	?
x_0	0
x	?
v_{0x}	0
v_x	?
a_x	4.00 m/s^2

Solve

(a) Write Equation 2-9 twice, once with the values for car A and once with the values for car B.

Car A ($x_{A0} = 125$ m, $v_{A0x} = -30.0$ m/s, $a_{Ax} = 0$):

$$x_A = 125 \text{ m} + (-30.0 \text{ m/s})t + \frac{1}{2}(0)t^2$$

$$= 125 \text{ m} - (30.0 \text{ m/s})t$$

Car B ($x_{B0} = 0$, $v_{B0x} = 0$, $a_{Bx} = +4.00$ m/s^2):

$$x_B = 0 + (0)t + \frac{1}{2}(4.00 \text{ m/s}^2)t^2 = (2.00 \text{ m/s}^2)t^2$$

The collision occurs when $x_A = x_B$. We rewrite the resulting equation in the standard form for a quadratic equation, $ax^2 + bx + c = 0$, but using t in place of x.

When the cars collide, $x_A = x_B$, so

$$125 \text{ m} - (30.0 \text{ m/s})t = (2.00 \text{ m/s}^2)t^2 \text{ or}$$

$$(2.00 \text{ m/s}^2)t^2 + (30.0 \text{ m/s})t - 125 \text{ m} = 0$$

In the quadratic equation for t, we have $a = 2.00$ m/s^2, $b = 30.0$ m/s, and $c = -125$ m. We substitute these values into the formula for the general solution to a quadratic equation, and get two solutions for t. The collision took place after the time we called $t = 0$, so we choose the positive solution for t.

Solve for time t:

$$t = \frac{-b \pm \sqrt{b^2 - 4ac}}{2a}$$

$$= \frac{-(30.0 \text{ m/s}) \pm \sqrt{(30.0 \text{ m/s})^2 - 4(2.00 \text{ m/s}^2)(-125 \text{ m})}}{2(2.00 \text{ m/s}^2)}$$

$$= \frac{-(30.0 \text{ m/s}) \pm \sqrt{1900 \text{ m}^2/\text{s}^2}}{2(2.00 \text{ m/s}^2)}$$

$$= \frac{-(30.0 \text{ m/s}) \pm (43.6 \text{ m/s})}{4.00 \text{ m/s}^2}$$

$$= 3.40 \text{ s or } -18.4 \text{ s}$$

The answer must be positive, so desired answer is $t = 3.40$ s

(b) To find where the collision took place, we can plug $t = 3.40$ s into either the equation for x_A or the equation for x_B, because at this time x_A and x_B are equal. Let's choose the first of these.

Solve for the position of car A at $t = 3.40$ s:

$$x_A = 125 \text{ m} - (30.0 \text{ m/s})t$$
$$= 125 \text{ m} - (30.0 \text{ m/s})(3.40 \text{ s})$$
$$= 23.1 \text{ m}$$

So the collision takes place 23.1 m from the origin (the place where car B started).

(c) To calculate how fast car B was moving when the collision occurred, we will use Equation 2-5, now that we know from part (a) the time at which the collision occurred.

Solve for the velocity of car B at $t = 3.40$ s. Its initial velocity is 0, and its acceleration is 4.00 m/s^2.

$$v_x = v_{0x} + a_x t = 0 + (4.00 \text{ m/s}^2)(3.40 \text{ s})$$
$$= 13.6 \text{ m/s}$$

Reflect

You can check the answer for part (b) by verifying that you get the same result if you substitute $t = 3.40$ s into the equation for x_B. Be sure to try this!

Here's another way to look at the answer to part (b). When the two cars collide, car B has moved 23.1 m (from the origin to $x = 23.1$ m) while car A has moved more than four times as far (from $x = 125$ m to $x = 23.1$ m). These results make sense: Car B started at rest and reached a speed of only 13.6 m/s, while car A moved at a faster steady speed of 30.0 m/s and so covered more distance in the same amount of time.

? Got the Concept? 2-6   Don't Trust Your Calculator Too Much

A calculator tells you that $(1/2)(1.64 \text{ m/s}^2)(38.2 \text{ s})^2 = 1196.5768$ m, or 1.1965768 km. Explain why we said in Example 2-6 that this product equals 1.20 km.

? Got the Concept? 2-7   Distance Traveled While Slowing

A racing cyclist on a straight track slows down at a steady rate from 15.0 m/s to 10.0 m/s in 4.00 s. How far do the cyclist and her bicycle travel while she is slowing down?

(a) 40.0 m; (b) 50.0 m; (c) 60.0 m; (d) not enough information given to decide

---

Take-Home Message for Section 2-6

✔ To solve problems that involve linear motion with constant acceleration, you need just three equations (see Table 2-3) that involve six quantities: time t, initial position x_0, position x at time t, velocity v_{0x} at time $t = 0$, velocity v_x at time t, and (constant) acceleration a_x.

✔ Using a Know/Don't Know table as part of solving any problem helps you to select which equations will help you find the desired quantity of interest.

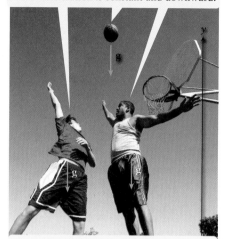

If we can ignore the effects of the air, the players and the ball are all in **free fall:** Their acceleration is constant and downward.

- An object in free fall has a constant downward acceleration.
- The magnitude g of the acceleration is the same no matter what the size of the object.
- The acceleration is the same whether the object is moving upward, moving downward, or momentarily at rest.

Figure 2-17 Free fall If an airborne object is large and heavy enough and moving relatively slowly, the effects of the air on the object can be ignored. Then the object moves with a constant acceleration due to gravity.

2-7 Objects falling freely near Earth's surface have constant acceleration

Perhaps the most important case of constant acceleration is the motion of falling objects near the surface of Earth (Figure 2-17). Experiment shows that if air resistance isn't important, an object falling near the surface has a constant, downward acceleration. We will learn later that this acceleration is due to a gravitational force exerted by Earth on the object.

To understand the importance of air resistance and the limitations it requires, take a sheet of notebook paper and let it fall. It speeds up for a second or so, then wafts downward at a slow, roughly constant speed. The speed doesn't keep increasing, so that's definitely *not* a case of constant acceleration. But now take a second, identical piece of notebook paper and wad it into a ball. If you drop the first sheet and the second, wadded sheet side by side, you'll find that the wadded one falls more rapidly and *does* keep on gaining speed as it falls. The difference is that by wadding up the second sheet, you've given it a smaller cross-sectional area and thus made it less susceptible to air resistance. Competition bicyclists use this same trick when they bend low over the handlebars. This reduces their cross section and the retarding effects of air resistance, enabling them to go faster for the same effort.

But even the wadded-up paper experiences some air resistance. Imagine, though, that you had superhuman strength and could crush the paper down to an infinitesimally small sphere. There would be essentially no air resistance on this tiny sphere, and only the pull of gravity would affect its fall. In this idealized situation, called **free fall**, the sphere would have a constant downward acceleration.

Free fall is an idealization, but many real-life situations come very close to this ideal. Some examples of nearly free fall include the basketball and players shown in Figure 2-17, a high diver descending toward the water, and a leaping frog in midair. In each of these cases, the falling object experiences minimal air resistance because it has a relatively slow speed, a small cross section, or both, and so falls with constant downward acceleration.

Watch Out! Be careful when falling isn't free.

If an object is falling at high speed, or has a relatively large cross section, we *cannot* ignore air resistance and so the motion is *not* free fall. Some examples include a sky diver descending under a parachute, a falling leaf, and a hawk with folded wings plummeting at high speed downward onto its prey. In each of these cases, the falling object reaches a maximum speed, or *terminal speed*, at which the retarding effects of air resistance balance the downward pull of gravity. We'll return to situations of this kind in Chapter 5.

Measuring Free-Fall Acceleration

You might be wondering how we can make the claim that the acceleration of a freely falling object near the surface of Earth is constant. The answer is simple—by experiment! Figure 2-18 shows a strobe photograph of a small sphere dropped from rest. The image of the sphere is recorded at intervals of 0.10 s. It's conventional to call the vertical axis the y axis (the horizontal axis is often called the x axis). It's also conventional to choose the positive y direction to point upward, so that increasing values of y correspond to increasing height. After the sphere is dropped from rest, it accelerates downward (in the negative y direction) and acquires a negative velocity v_y (the subscript y reminds us that we are now discussing motion along the y axis). We choose the initial position of the sphere to be $y_0 = 0$, so as the sphere descends its y coordinate becomes a larger and larger negative number.

Careful measurements of the y coordinate and velocity of the ball yield the values shown in Table 2-4. We plot the values of v_y and y versus time in Figure 2-19. We learned in Section 2-4 that the slope of an object's velocity–time graph tells us that object's

Table 2-4 Motion of a falling sphere

This table lists the y coordinate and y velocity at 0.10-s intervals for the falling sphere shown in Figure 2-17. Initially the sphere is at rest at $y = 0$. The positive y direction is upward, so as the sphere descends it has a negative y velocity and it moves to increasingly negative values of y.

Time t (s)	y coordinate (m)	y velocity (m/s)
0	0.00	0.00
0.10	−0.05	−0.98
0.20	−0.20	−1.96
0.30	−0.44	−2.94
0.40	−0.78	−3.92
0.50	−1.23	−4.91
0.60	−1.76	−5.89

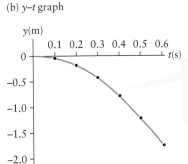

For free-fall problems, we choose the positive y direction to be upward. It's convenient to choose the starting position to be $y_0 = 0$.

When an object is dropped from rest and falls freely, it travels a greater distance in successive time intervals: That is, it accelerates downward.

Figure 2-18 **Analyzing a freely falling object** Measurements of this falling ball confirm that it has a constant acceleration.

acceleration. Because a straight line has a constant slope, we can conclude from Figure 2-19a that the acceleration of the falling sphere is constant. We can determine the value of this acceleration by measuring the slope of the v_x–t graph. Table 2-4 says that the velocity is $v_{1y} = -1.96$ m/s at $t_1 = 0.20$ s and the velocity is $v_{2y} = -3.92$ m/s at $t_2 = 0.40$ s, so the acceleration a_y of the falling sphere is

$$a_y = \text{slope of } v_y\text{–}t \text{ graph} = \frac{v_{2y} - v_{1y}}{t_2 - t_1} = \frac{-3.92 \text{ m/s} - (-1.96 \text{ m/s})}{0.40 \text{ s} - 0.20 \text{ s}} = -9.8 \text{ m/s}^2$$

We can confirm this value of acceleration in free fall by comparing the graph of position versus time in Figure 2-19b with the positions we can calculate by using the value $a_y = -9.8$ m/s^2. To make these calculations, we use Equation 2-9 for motion with constant acceleration, $x = x_0 + v_{0x}t + \frac{1}{2}a_x t^2$, but change every "$x$" in this equation to a "y." Using the initial velocity $v_{0y} = 0$ and initial y coordinate $y_0 = 0$, this equation becomes $y = \frac{1}{2}a_y t^2$. If we substitute $t = 0.30$ s and $a_y = -9.8$ m/s^2, our predicted position for the falling sphere is

$$y = \frac{1}{2}(-9.8 \text{ m/s}^2)(0.30 \text{ s})^2 = -0.44 \text{ m}$$

which agrees with the value in Table 2-4.

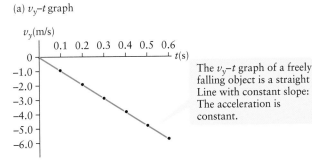

(a) v_y–t graph

The v_y–t graph of a freely falling object is a straight Line with constant slope: The acceleration is constant.

(b) y–t graph

The y–t graph of a freely falling object is a parabola, as it should be for an object that moves with constant acceleration.

Figure 2-19 **Graphing free fall** Graphs of velocity versus time and position versus time for the freely falling object shown in Figure 2-18.

Acceleration Due to Gravity

Experiments such as that depicted in Figure 2-18 show that an object in free fall near Earth's surface has a downward acceleration of approximate magnitude 9.80 m/s^2. (There are slight variations in this value from one place to another, related to differences in elevation and in the density of material beneath the surface. Keep in mind that 9.80 m/s^2 is an *average* value, which we state to three significant figures for convenience in calculation.) Physicists refer to this magnitude as the **acceleration due to gravity** and denote it by the symbol g:

$$(2\text{-}12) \qquad\qquad g = 9.80 \text{ m/s}^2$$

The value of g decreases very slightly with altitude: It is about 0.3% less at 10,000 m (32,800 ft) above sea level than at sea level. As we will learn in Chapter 10, a spacecraft journeying far beyond Earth encounters very different values of g. The value of g is also totally different on the surfaces of the Moon and other planets.

The downward acceleration due to gravity also acts on objects that are moving upward, or are even momentarily stationary. If a ball is tossed straight up, as it ascends its upward velocity is positive and its downward acceleration is negative. Because the velocity and acceleration have opposite signs, the ball slows down (see our discussion in Section 2-4). After the ball reaches the high point of its motion and starts to descend, its downward velocity and its downward acceleration are both negative. The signs of velocity and acceleration are the same, so the ball speeds up as it falls. The ball is in free fall throughout its motion, with the *same* magnitude and direction of acceleration at all times (Figure 2-20).

Watch Out!
! **g is always positive, never negative.**

Note that g is a *positive* number because it is the *magnitude* (absolute value) of the acceleration due to gravity. If we take the positive y direction to point upward, as we did in Figures 2-16 and 2-17, the acceleration due to gravity is negative: $a_y = -g = -9.80 \text{ m/s}^2$. But no matter whether you take the positive direction to be upward or downward, the quantity g is always positive.

Watch Out!   What happens when an object in free fall reaches its highest point?

!   It's a common error to think that if a ball is tossed upward, its acceleration at the high point of its motion is zero. It's true that the *velocity* is zero at this point, because the ball is momentarily at rest. The velocity is changing, however; the ball's velocity was upward a moment before reaching the high point, and the ball's velocity is downward a moment after. Whenever an object's velocity is changing, that object has an acceleration. Thus, the ball is still accelerating at the high point of the motion, with the same value of acceleration as on the way up and as on the way down (see Figure 2-19). If the acceleration at the high point of the motion actually *were* zero, the tossed ball would reach the high point of its motion and simply stop in midair: With no acceleration and therefore no change in velocity, the ball's zero velocity would remain zero forever! That doesn't happen in the real world, which tells us that the acceleration can't be zero at the high point.

? Got the Concept? 2-8
Interpreting Graphs for Free Fall

Figure 2-14 shows three possible combinations of x–t graphs and v_x–t graphs. If we interpret these as y–t graphs and v_y–t graphs, with the positive y direction chosen to be upward, which of these graph combinations are *not* possible for an object in free fall?

The Equations of Free Fall

Let's see how to describe free fall that involves motion that is straight up and down—that is, *one-dimensional* free fall or *linear* free fall. As we did in Figures 2-16, 2-17, and 2-19, it's conventional to call the vertical axis the y axis and to choose the positive y

$+y$

A freely falling object moving upward slows down: Its velocity and acceleration are in opposite directions.

A freely falling object instantaneously at rest will soon be moving downward: Its acceleration is downward.

A freely falling object moving downward speeds up: Its velocity and acceleration are in the same direction.

Object is moving upward: $v_y > 0$

Acceleration is downward: $a_y = -g$

Object is instantaneously at rest: $v_y = 0$

Acceleration is downward: $a_y = -g$

Object is moving downward: $v_y < 0$

Acceleration is downward: $a_y = -g$

Figure 2-20 Free fall acceleration
The acceleration due to gravity does not depend on how the object is moving.

 No matter how it is moving, an object in free fall has a constant downward acceleration of magnitude g.

direction to point upward. Then, the acceleration in free fall points in the negative y direction, so the acceleration is $a_y = -g$. (Remember from Equation 2-12 that g is a *positive* number.) We can write the equations for free fall by replacing all the x's in Equations 2-5, 2-9, and 2-11 with y's, and by using $-g$ for the acceleration a_y:

Velocity at time t of an object in free fall | Velocity at time $t = 0$ of the object

$$v_y = v_{0y} - gt$$

Acceleration due to gravity (g is positive) | Time at which the object has position v_y

Velocity, acceleration, and time for free fall
(2-13)

Position at time t of an object in free fall | Velocity at time $t = 0$ of the object | Acceleration due to gravity (g is positive)

$$y = y_0 + v_{0y}t - \frac{1}{2}gt^2$$

Position at time $t = 0$ of the object | Time at which the object is at position y

Position, acceleration, and time for free fall
(2-14)

Velocity at position y of an object in free fall | Velocity at position y_0 of the object | Position of object when it has velocity v_{0y}

$$v_y^2 = v_{0y}^2 - 2g\,(y - y_0)$$

Acceleration due to gravity (g is positive) | Position of object when it has velocity v_y

Velocity, acceleration, and position for free fall
(2-15)

Note the minus sign in front of each term containing g, which is a reminder that the acceleration is always *downward*, in the negative y direction. If a freely falling object is rising, it slows down; if the object is descending, it speeds up (Figure 2-19). When solving problems that involve free fall, make sure that you always check your answers to see that they agree with these common sense principles! If they don't—if, say, your answers tell you that a ball thrown straight up goes faster and faster as it climbs—you need to go back and check your work. In the following section we'll see how to solve a variety of free-fall problems.

Take-Home Message for Section 2-7

✔ An object is in free fall if its motion is influenced by gravity alone (that is, if air resistance is so small that it can be ignored).

✔ Free-fall motion near the surface of Earth is constant-acceleration motion, with a downward acceleration of magnitude $g = 9.80 \text{ m/s}^2$. The magnitude g is always a positive number.

✔ Our convention for discussing free fall is to always choose the positive y direction to be upward. Then the acceleration of an object in free fall is $a_y = -g$. The y–t graph for an object in free fall is a parabola with a downward curvature, and the v_y–t graph for an object in free fall is a straight line with downward (negative) slope.

2-8 Solving straight-line motion problems: Free fall

Table 2-5 summarizes the three equations we can use to answer questions about the motion of an object experiencing free fall. We use the same steps to solve problems that we used in Section 2-6. After all, the equations in Table 2-5 are the same equations as in Table 2-3, but for the special case of motion along the y axis, and with $a_y = -g$. As

Go to Interactive Exercise 2-2 for more practice dealing with free fall

you read through the following examples, keep in mind that that the process we use to solve each problem is no less important than the final answer.

Table 2-5 Equations for linear free fall

By using one or more of these equations, you can solve any problem involving free-fall motion that is straight up and down. The check marks indicate which of the quantities t (time), y_0 (the y coordinate at time 0), y (the y coordinate at time t), v_{0y} (the y velocity at time 0), v_y (the y velocity at time t), and $a_y = -g$ (the constant, downward y acceleration) appear in each equation. Note that g, the magnitude of the acceleration due to gravity, is a *positive* quantity.

Equation		t	y	y_0	v_{0y}	v_y	$a_y = -g$
				Which quantities the equation includes			
$v_y = v_{0y} - gt$	(2-13)	✔			✔	✔	✔
$y = y_0 + v_{0y}t - \frac{1}{2}gt^2$	(2-14)	✔	✔	✔	✔		✔
$v_y^2 = v_{0y}^2 - 2g(y - y_0)$	(2-15)		✔	✔	✔	✔	✔

Example 2-9 Free Fall I: A Falling Monkey

A monkey drops from a tree limb to grab a piece of fruit on the ground 1.80 m below (Figure 2-21). (a) How long does it take the monkey to reach the ground? (b) How fast is the monkey moving just before it reaches the ground? Neglect the effects of air resistance.

Monkey falls downward with increasing speed

Figure 2-21 **A monkey in free fall** What are the monkey's position and velocity as functions of time?

Set Up

We assume that the monkey falls freely with a constant downward acceleration of magnitude $g = 9.80 \text{ m/s}^2$. Then, we can use the equations in Table 2-5 as needed. Our goals are to find the time when he reaches the ground and the magnitude of his velocity just *before* reaching the ground. (Once the monkey is on the ground, his speed is zero.)

We choose the y direction to be upward as shown and choose the origin to be on the ground. Then, the monkey's initial y coordinate is $y_0 = 1.80$ m, his y coordinate when he reaches the ground is zero, and his initial velocity is $v_{0y} = 0$ (because he starts at rest). We've drawn the motion diagram, the y–t graph, and the v_y–t graph for the monkey's motion.

Note that because the acceleration is negative, the y–t graph curves downward (the slope, which represents the velocity v_y, becomes increasingly negative as time goes by), and the v_y–t graph has a downward (negative) slope.

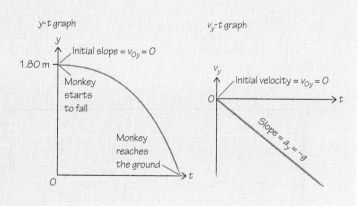

The Know/Don't Know table shows that we know the values of y_0, y, v_{0y}, and a_y, and want to find the values of (a) t and (b) v_y. To solve for t from the known information, we use Equation 2-14. Once we know the value of t, we can substitute it into Equation 2-13 to solve for the monkey's velocity v_y.

Position, acceleration, and time for free fall:

$$y = y_0 + v_{0y}t - \frac{1}{2}gt^2 \qquad (2\text{-}14)$$

Velocity, acceleration, and time for free fall:

$$v_y = v_{0y} - gt \qquad (2\text{-}13)$$

Quantity	Know/Don't Know
t	?
y_0	1.80 m
y	0
v_{0y}	0
v_y	?
$a_y = -g$	-9.80 m/s^2

Solve

(a) Substitute the known values from the Know/Don't Know table into Equation 2-14. Then, solve for t by rearranging the equation so that t^2 is by itself on the left-hand side of the equation, and by taking the square root.

To find the time t when the monkey reaches the ground, substitute values into Equation 2-14:

$$0 = 1.80\ \text{m} + (0)t - \frac{1}{2}(9.80\ \text{m/s}^2)t^2$$

Solve for t:

$$\frac{1}{2}(9.80\ \text{m/s}^2)t^2 = 1.80\ \text{m}$$

$$t^2 = \frac{1.80\ \text{m}}{(1/2)(9.80\ \text{m/s}^2)} = 0.367\ \text{s}^2$$

$$t = \pm\sqrt{0.367\ \text{s}^2} = \pm\,0.606\ \text{s}$$

The equation for t has both a positive solution and a negative solution. The monkey started to fall at $t = 0$ and we are looking for a time after this, so we must choose the positive value of t.

Choose the positive value of t:
$t = 0.606$ s

(b) To find the monkey's velocity v_y just before it reaches the ground, substitute the known values and $t = 0.606$ s from part (a) into Equation 2-13. We want the monkey's *speed*, which is a positive number and is just the absolute value of v_y.

To find the velocity just before reaching the ground, substitute into Equation 2-13:

$$v_y = 0 - (9.80\ \text{m/s}^2)(0.606\ \text{s})$$
$$= -5.94\ \text{m/s so}$$
Speed $= 5.94$ m/s

Reflect

The 1.80–m distance that the monkey falls is about the height of a human adult. Try dropping a pencil or a wadded-up piece of paper from this height and estimate the time of its fall. Our result in part (a) says that the fall takes less than a second. Can you verify that this is about right?

As a check on our result in part (b), we can also calculate the speed using Equation 2-15. If you substitute $v_{0y} = 0$, $g = 9.80$ m/s^2, y_0 = 1.80 m, and $y = 0$ into this equation, you should again find that the monkey's speed is 5.94 m/s. Do you? Check and find out!

Velocity, acceleration, and time for free fall:

$$v_y^2 = v_{0y}^2 - 2g(y - y_0) \qquad (2\text{-}15)$$

Example 2-10 Free Fall II: A Pronking Springbok

When startled, a springbok (*Antidorcas marsupialis*) like the one shown in Figure 2-22 leaps upward several times in succession, reaching a height of several meters. (This behavior, called *pronking*, may inform predators that the springbok knows of their presence.) During one such jump, a springbok leaves the ground at a speed of 6.00 m/s. (a) What maximum height above the ground does the springbok attain? (b) How long does it take the springbok to attain this height? (c) What is the springbok's velocity when it is 1.25 m above the ground? (d) At what times is the springbok 1.25 m above the ground?

Springbok moves upward with decreasing speed... ...comes momentarily to rest... ...then falls downward with increasing speed

Figure 2-22 Pronking When a springbok jumps into the air, it is in free fall.

Set Up

Like the monkey in Example 2-9, the springbok is in free fall once it leaves the ground. Unlike the monkey, however, the springbok is moving initially and so v_{0y} is *not* zero.

At the moment when the springbok attains its maximum height, its velocity is zero. So, parts (a) and (b) are really asking for the springbok's vertical coordinate and the time t when $v_y = 0$. In part (c) our goal is to find the springbok's velocity v_y at a certain vertical coordinate, and in part (d) we wish to find the times t at which the springbok is located at this coordinate.

We again choose the y axis to point upward, and again place the origin at ground level. Then the springbok has initial y coordinate $y_0 = 0$ and initial velocity $v_{0y} = +6.00$ m/s (positive because it's moving upward). The drawings show the springbok's motion diagram, y–t graph, and v_y–t graph. Because of the initial upward velocity, the y–t graph has an upward slope at $t = 0$ and the v_y–t graph starts with a positive value at $t = 0$.

The Know/Don't Know tables tell us that in parts (a) and (b) we want to calculate the value of y and the time t when the springbok reaches its highest point. We can use Equation 2-15 to find the position when the velocity is zero, and Equation 2-13 to determine how much time is required for the velocity to equal zero. In part (c) we want the value of v_y at a height corresponding to $y = 1.25$ m. We can again use Equation 2-15. In part (d) we'll use Equation 2-13 to find the time t when the springbok has this value of y. We expect the springbok to pass through this height twice, once moving upward and once moving back downward:

For parts (a) and (c):

$$v_y^2 = v_{0y}^2 - 2g(y - y_0) \quad (2\text{-}15)$$

For parts (b) and (d):

$$v_y = v_{0y} - gt \quad (2\text{-}13)$$

For parts (a) and (b)

Quantity	Know/Don't Know
t	?
y_0	0
y	?
v_{0y}	+6.00 m/s
v_y	0
$a_y = -g$	-9.80 m/s^2

For parts (c) and (d)

Quantity	Know/Don't Know
t	?
y_0	0
y	1.25 m
v_{0y}	+6.00 m/s
v_y	?
$a_y = -g$	-9.80 m/s^2

Solve

(a) To determine the value of y corresponding to the high point of the motion, we substitute the values from our Know/Don't Know table into Equation 2-15. Then we solve this equation for y, the height of the springbok above its launch point ($y_0 = 0$).

Substitute into Equation 2-15:

$$0^2 = (6.00 \text{ m/s})^2 - 2(9.80 \text{ m/s}^2)(y - 0)$$

Solve for y at the high point of the motion:

$$2(9.80 \text{ m/s}^2)y = (6.00 \text{ m/s})^2$$

$$y = \frac{(6.00 \text{ m/s})^2}{2(9.80 \text{ m/s}^2)} = 1.84 \text{ m}$$

(b) To find the time when the springbok is at the high point of its motion, use Equation 2-13 and substitute the values from the Know/Don't Know table.

Substitute into Equation 2-13:

$$0 = 6.00 \text{ m/s} - (9.80 \text{ m/s}^2)t$$

Solve for t at the high point of the motion:

$$(9.80 \text{ m/s}^2)t = 6.00 \text{ m/s}$$

$$t = \frac{6.00 \text{ m/s}}{9.80 \text{ m/s}^2} = \frac{6.00 \text{ m/s}}{9.80 \text{ m/s}^2} = 0.612 \text{ s}$$

(c) Now we want to determine the value of v_y when $y = 1.25$ m. Again, substitute the values from the Know/Don't Know table into Equation 2-15 to solve for v_y. When we take the square root of v_y^2, we get two solutions for v_y: A positive one corresponding to the springbok moving upward and a negative one corresponding to the springbok moving downward.

Substitute into Equation 2-15:

$$\begin{aligned} v_y^2 &= (6.00 \text{ m/s})^2 - 2(9.80 \text{ m/s}^2)(1.25 \text{ m} - 0) \\ &= 36.0 \text{ m}^2/\text{s}^2 - 24.5 \text{ m}^2/\text{s}^2 \\ &= 11.5 \text{ m}^2/\text{s}^2 \end{aligned}$$

Solve for v_y when $y = 1.25$ m:

$$v_y = \pm \sqrt{11.5 \text{ m}^2/\text{s}^2}$$

Solutions:
$v_y = +3.39 \text{ m/s}$ (springbok moving up)
$v_y = -3.39 \text{ m/s}$ (springbok moving down)

(d) From part (c), we know the two values of v_y for when the springbok passes through $y = 1.25$ m. To find the times t when it passes through this height, we substitute each value of v_y into Equation 2-13, along with $v_{0y} = 6.00$ m/s and $g = 9.80 \text{ m/s}^2$.

Substitute into Equation 2-13:
Springbok moving up ($v_y = +3.39 \text{ m/s}$):

$$+3.39 \text{ m/s} = +6.00 \text{ m/s} - (9.80 \text{ m/s}^2)t$$

Solve for t:

$$(9.80 \text{ m/s}^2)t = 6.00 \text{ m/s} - 3.39 \text{ m/s}$$

$$t = \frac{6.00 \text{ m/s} - 3.39 \text{ m/s}}{9.80 \text{ m/s}^2} = \frac{2.61 \text{ m/s}}{9.80 \text{ m/s}^2}$$

$$= 0.266 \text{ s}$$

Springbok moving down ($v_y = -3.39 \text{ m/s}$):

$$-3.39 \text{ m/s} = +6.00 \text{ m/s} - (9.80 \text{ m/s}^2)t$$

Solve for t:

$$(9.80 \text{ m/s}^2)t = 6.00 \text{ m/s} - (-3.39 \text{ m/s})$$

$$t = \frac{6.00 \text{ m/s} - (-3.39 \text{ m/s})}{9.80 \text{ m/s}^2} = \frac{9.39 \text{ m/s}}{9.80 \text{ m/s}^2}$$

$$= 0.958 \text{ s}$$

Reflect

A professional basketball player can jump to a height of about 1 m; our result in part (a) says a springbok can jump even higher. This makes sense, because a springbok has four powerful legs to propel it upward rather than just two!

We can check our result in part (c) by noticing that 3.39 m/s is less than 6.00 m/s. In other words, when the springbok is rising through $y = 1.25$ m it is going more slowly than when it left the ground—as it should be, because gravity slows the springbok as it ascends.

You can also check the times that we calculated in part (d) by solving for them directly without first calculating the values of v_y. You can do this with Equation 2-14: Substitute $y = 1.25$ m, $y_0 = 0$, $v_{0y} = 6.00$ m/s, and $g = 9.80 \text{ m/s}^2$ and solve for t in the same way that we did in Example 2-8 in Section 2-6. Try this! You should get the same two answers for t, 0.266 s and 0.958 s.

? Got the Concept? 2-9 How Many Times Does It Pass?

You throw a ball straight upward at an initial speed of 5.00 m/s. How many times does the ball pass through a point 2.00 m above the point where it left your hand? Ignore the effects of air resistance. (a) Two; (b) one; (c) zero; (d) not enough information given to decide.

Take-Home Message for Section 2-9

✔ You can use the three equations in Table 2-5 to solve any problems involving linear motion in free fall.

✔ The same techniques that we used in Section 2-6 for general constant-acceleration problems (including using a Know/Don't Know table) can also be used for free-fall problems.

Key Terms

acceleration
acceleration due to gravity
average acceleration
average speed
average velocity
constant acceleration
constant velocity
coordinates
coordinate system
displacement

elapsed time
free fall
instantaneous acceleration
instantaneous speed
instantaneous velocity
Know/Don't Know table
linear motion
magnitude
motion diagram
origin

parabola
position
reference position
speed
time interval
v_x–t graph
x–t graph
vector

Chapter Summary

Topic	Equation or Figure
Linear motion: We describe the motion of an object along a straight line by stating how its position x changes with the passage of time t. The change in the object's position over a time interval is called the displacement.	(a) Direction of swimmer A's motion The red dots show swimmer A's position at 5.0-s intervals. $t = 0$ $t = 10.0$ s $t = 20.0$ s $t = 5.0$ s $t = 15.0$ s $t = 25.0$ s Pool $x = -10.0$ m $x = +40.0$ m (Figure 2-3a)
Average velocity and instantaneous velocity: The average velocity of an object during a time interval describes how fast the object moved and in what direction. If the time interval is very short, the average velocity becomes the instantaneous velocity v_x (velocity for short).	**Average velocity** of an object in linear motion **Displacement** (change in position) of the object over a certain time interval: The object moves from x_1 to x_2, so $\Delta x = x_2 - x_1$. $$v_{\text{average},x} = \frac{x_2 - x_1}{t_2 - t_1} = \frac{\Delta x}{\Delta t}$$ (2-1) For both the displacement and the elapsed time, subtract the earlier value (x_1 or t_1) from the later value (x_2 or t_2). **Elapsed time** for the time interval: The object is at x_1 at time t_1, and x_2 at time t_2, so the elapsed time is $\Delta t = t_2 - t_1$.

Constant-velocity linear motion: If an object has the same velocity v_x at all times, it maintains a steady speed and always moves in the same direction. A graph of position x versus time t for constant-velocity motion is a straight line with slope v_x.

Position at time t of an object in linear motion with constant velocity

Position at time $t = 0$ of the object

$$x = x_0 + v_x t \qquad (2\text{-}2)$$

Constant velocity of the object

Time at which the object is at position x

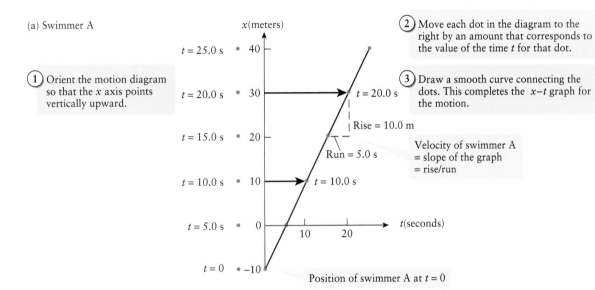

(a) Swimmer A

1 Orient the motion diagram so that the x axis points vertically upward.

2 Move each dot in the diagram to the right by an amount that corresponds to the value of the time t for that dot.

3 Draw a smooth curve connecting the dots. This completes the x–t graph for the motion.

Rise = 10.0 m

Run = 5.0 s

Velocity of swimmer A = slope of the graph = rise/run

Position of swimmer A at $t = 0$

(Figure 2-4a)

Average acceleration and instantaneous acceleration: An object's average acceleration over a time interval equals the average rate of change of the object's velocity during that interval. If the time interval is very short, average velocity becomes instantaneous velocity a_x (acceleration for short).

Average acceleration of an object in linear motion

Change in **velocity** of the object over a certain time interval: The velocity changes from v_{1x} to v_{2x}.

$$a_{\text{average},x} = \frac{\Delta v_x}{\Delta t} = \frac{v_{2x} - v_{1x}}{t_2 - t_1} \qquad (2\text{-}3)$$

Elapsed time for the time interval: The object has velocity v_{1x} at time t_1, and has velocity v_{2x} at time t_2.

Interpreting velocity and acceleration: The slope of an object's x–t graph (graph of position versus time) is its velocity v_x. The slope of its v_x–t graph (graph of velocity versus time) is its acceleration a_x. An object speeds up if v_x and a_x have the same sign, and slows down if v_x and a_x have opposite signs.

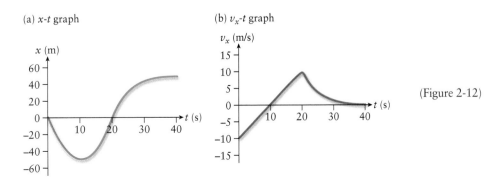

(a) x-t graph

(b) v_x-t graph

(Figure 2-12)

Motion with constant acceleration: The velocity of an object changes at the same rate at all times. The x–t graph for such an object is a parabola, and the v_x–t graph is a straight line.

Velocity at time t of an object in linear motion with constant acceleration | Velocity at time $t = 0$ of the object

$$v_x = v_{0x} + a_x t \tag{2-5}$$

Constant acceleration of the object | Time at which the object has velocity v_x

Position at time t of an object in linear motion with constant acceleration | Velocity at time $t = 0$ of the object | Constant acceleration of the object

$$x = x_0 + v_{0x} t + \frac{1}{2} a_x t^2 \tag{2-9}$$

Position at time $t = 0$ of the object | Time at which the object has position x

Velocity at position x of an object in linear motion with constant acceleration | Velocity at position x_0 of the object

$$v_x^2 = v_{0x}^2 + 2a_x (x - x_0) \tag{2-11}$$

Constant acceleration of the object | Two positions of the object

Free fall: An object that moves upward or downward under the influence of gravity alone is in free fall. It has a constant downward acceleration of magnitude g. Near the surface of Earth, $g = 9.80 \text{ m/s}^2$.

Velocity at time t of an object in free fall | Velocity at time $t = 0$ of the object

$$v_y = v_{0y} - gt \tag{2-13}$$

Acceleration due to gravity (g is positive) | Time at which the object has position v_y

Position at time t of an object in free fall | Velocity at time $t = 0$ of the object | Acceleration due to gravity (g is positive)

$$y = y_0 + v_{0y} t - \frac{1}{2} gt^2 \tag{2-14}$$

Position at time $t = 0$ of the object | Time at which the object is at position y

Velocity at position y of an object in free fall | Velocity at position y_0 of the object | Position of object when it has velocity v_{0y}

$$v_y^2 = v_{0y}^2 - 2g (y - y_0) \tag{2-15}$$

Acceleration due to gravity (g is positive) | Position of object when it has velocity v_y

Answer to What do you think? Question

The athlete is accelerating downward at this point, and in fact at *all* times from when her feet leave the ground to when they again touch the ground. This is a characteristic of free fall, discussed in Section 2-7.

Answers to Got the Concept? Questions

2-1 (a) (iv), (b) (iv), (c) (iii), (d) (iv), (e) (i), (f) (iv). Object (iv) has the steepest slope, so this object moves fastest *and* travels the greatest distance. The slope is negative, so the object moves in the negative x direction, but speed and distance are both positive quantities. Object (iii) has the most positive (upward) slope, so this object has the most positive velocity and hence the most positive displacement (from $x_1 = -5.0$ m to $x_2 = 0$ m, so $x_2 - x_1 = +5.0$ m). Object (iv) has the most negative (downward) slope, so this object has the most negative velocity and hence the most negative displacement (from $x_1 = +2.0$ m to $x_2 = -8.0$ m, so $x_2 - x_1 = -10.0$ m). The graphs show that at $t = 5.0$ s, object (i) ends up at the most positive value of x (7.5 m) and object (iv) ends up at the most negative value of x (-8.0 m).

2-2 24 mi/h. Average velocity equals the net displacement (6.0 mi) divided by the elapsed time (15 min = 0.25 h), or $v_x = (6.0 \text{ mi})/(0.25 \text{ h}) = 24.0$ mi/h. The other information tells you how the velocity varied during the trip but isn't relevant to the average velocity of the trip as a whole.

2-3 (b) We can determine the sign of the acceleration a_x from the slope of the v_x–t graph in Figure 2-12b. At $t = 5$ s, this graph has a positive slope, so a_x is positive and the velocity is becoming more positive. The v_x–t graph also shows that the value of the velocity v_x at $t = 5$ s is negative. Because v_x and a_x have opposite signs at $t = 5$ s, it follows that the object is slowing down at this time. You can confirm this result from Figure 2-12b: The object has $v_x = -10$ m/s at $t = 0$ and so is moving at 10 m/s in the negative x direction, while the object has $v_x = 0$ at $t = 10$ s and so is at rest. So, the speed decreases from $t = 0$ to $t = 10$ s and the object slows down.

2-4 (a) Because the acceleration is positive, the x–t graph is a parabola that curves upward, and the v_x–t graph slopes upward. The slope of the x–t graph is negative at $t = 0$ because $v_{0x} < 0$. (b) Because the acceleration is negative, the x–t graph is a parabola that curves downward, and the v_x–t graph slopes downward. The slope of the x–t graph is positive at $t = 0$ because $v_{0x} > 0$. (c) Because the acceleration is negative, the x–t graph is a parabola that curves downward, and the v_x–t graph slopes downward. The slope of the x–t graph is negative at $t = 0$ because $v_{0x} < 0$.

2-5 (a) (ii), (b) (iii), (c) (i) To decide how the speed of an accelerating object is changing, we need to compare the signs of its velocity and its acceleration. (a) At $t = 1.00$ s, $v_x = v_{0x} + a_x t = +2.00$ m/s + $(-1.00 \text{ m/s}^2)(1.00 \text{ s}) = +1.00$ m/s. The velocity is positive but the acceleration $a_x = -1.00$ m/s^2 is negative, so the object is slowing down. (b) At $t = 2.00$ s, $v_x = +2.00$ m/s + $(-1.00 \text{ m/s}^2)(2.00 \text{ s}) = 0$. The object is instantaneously at rest. It has just come to a stop (slowing down), but it is also speeding up because of the positive acceleration (c) At $t = 3.00$ s, $v_x = +2.00$ m/s + $(-1.00 \text{ m/s}^2)(3.00 \text{ s}) = -1.00$ m/s. The velocity and acceleration are both negative, so the object is speeding up.

2-6 We learned in Section 1-4 that when two numbers are multiplied together, the number with the smaller number of significant figures determines the number of significant figures in the product. Because 1.64 m/s^2 and 38.2 s each have only three significant figures, their product can only have three significant figures. (The factor of $1/2$ is an exact number, so it doesn't affect how many significant figures are in the result.)

2-7 (b) "Slowing down at a steady rate" means that the cyclist has a constant acceleration. In this situation, the average velocity over a certain time interval is just the average of the instantaneous velocities at the beginning and end of the interval (see Equation 2-7). Because $v_{0x} = 15.0$ m/s and $v_x = 10.0$ m/s, the average velocity over the 4.00-s time interval is

$$v_{\text{average},x} = \frac{v_{0x} + v_x}{2} = \frac{15.0 \text{ m/s} + 10.0 \text{ m/s}}{2} = 12.5 \text{ m/s}$$

The cyclist's displacement during the time interval equals the average velocity multiplied by the elapsed time, or (12.5 m/s)(4.00 s) = 50.0 m. You can find this same result using the equations in Table 2-3, but it's much easier to use this basic fact about the average velocity when acceleration is constant.

2-8 (a), (b) The acceleration in free fall is $a_y = -g$, which is negative. Hence the impossible graphs are (a) and (b), which assume positive acceleration. The possible case is (c): The y–t graph is a downward-curved parabola, and the v_y–t graph is a straight line with a negative slope.

2-9 (c) The ball *never* reaches a height 2.00 m above the release point. You can see this in more than one way. One is to calculate the maximum vertical height of the ball (where the ball comes momentarily to rest) by using Equation 2-15 and setting $v_y = 0$. Let the point where you release the ball be at $y = 0$.

$$v_y^2 = v_{0y}^2 - 2g(y - y_0)$$

$$0 = (5.00 \text{ m/s})^2 - 2(9.80 \text{ m/s}^2)(y - 0)$$

$$y = \frac{(5.00 \text{ m/s})^2}{2(9.80 \text{ m/s}^2)} = 1.28 \text{ m}$$

The maximum height attained is 1.28 m, so the ball never reaches a height of 2.00 m above the release point. Another way to reach the same conclusion is to use Equation 2-14 to calculate the time t when the ball is at $y = 2.00$ m:

$$y = y_0 + v_{0y}t - \frac{1}{2}gt^2$$

$$2.00 \text{ m} = 0 + (5.00 \text{ m/s})t - \frac{1}{2}(9.80 \text{ m/s}^2)t^2$$

$$(4.90 \text{ m/s}^2)t^2 + (-5.00 \text{ m/s})t + 2.00 \text{ m} = 0$$

$$t =$$

$$\frac{-(-5.00\ \text{m/s})\ \pm\ \sqrt{(-5.00\ \text{m/s})^2 - 4(4.90\ \text{m/s}^2)(2.00\ \text{m})}}{2(4.90\ \text{m/s}^2)}$$

The quantity inside the square root is

$$(-5.00\ \text{m/s})^2 - 4(4.90\ \text{m/s}^2)(2.00\ \text{m})$$
$$= 25.0\ \text{m}^2/\text{s}^2 - 39.2\ \text{m}^2/\text{s}^2 = -14.2\ \text{m}^2/\text{s}^2$$

The square root of a negative number is *imaginary:* There is no real number that is equal to $\sqrt{-14.2}$. So this problem has no solution, and we conclude that the ball never reaches a height of 2.00 m.

Questions and Problems

In a few problems, you are given more data than you actually need; in a few other problems, you are required to supply data from your general knowledge, outside sources, or informed estimate.

Interpret as significant all digits in numerical values that have trailing zeros and no decimal points. For all problems, use $g = 9.80\ \text{m/s}^2$ for the free-fall acceleration due to gravity. Neglect friction and air resistance unless instructed to do otherwise.

• Basic, single-concept problem

•• Intermediate-level problem, may require synthesis of concepts and multiple steps

••• Challenging problem

SSM *Solution is in Student Solutions Manual*

Conceptual Questions

1. •What happens to an object's velocity when the object's acceleration is in the opposite direction to the velocity? SSM

2. •Discuss the direction and magnitude of the velocity and acceleration of a ball that is thrown straight up, from the time it leaves your hand until it returns and you catch it.

3. •Explain the difference between average *speed* and average *velocity*.

4. •Under what circumstances will the displacement and the distance traveled be the same? When will they be different?

5. •Compare the concepts of *speed* and *velocity*. Do these two quantities have the same units? When can you interchange these two with no confusion? When would it be problematic? SSM

6. •Which speed gives the largest straight-line displacement in a fixed time: 1 m/s, 1 km/h, or 1 mi/h?

7. •The manufacturer of a high-end sports car plans to present its latest model's acceleration in units of m/s^2 rather than the customary units of miles/hour/second. Discuss the advantages and disadvantages of such an ad campaign in the global marketplace. Would you suggest making any modifications to this plan?

8. •The upper limit of the braking acceleration for most cars is about the same magnitude as the acceleration due to gravity on Earth. Compare the braking motion of a car with a ball thrown straight upward. Both have the same initial speed. Ignore air resistance.

9. •Under what circumstance(s) will the average velocity of a moving object be the same as the instantaneous velocity? SSM

10. •A video is made of a ball being thrown up into the air and then falling. Is there any way to tell whether the video is being played backward? Explain your answer.

11. •The velocity of a ball thrown straight up decreases as it rises. Does its acceleration increase, decrease, or remain the same as the ball rises? Explain your answer.

12. •Under what circumstances is it acceptable to omit the units during a physics calculation? What is the advantage of using SI units in *all* calculations, no matter how trivial?

13. •A device launches a ball straight up from the edge of a cliff so that the ball falls and hits the ground at the base of the cliff. The device is then turned so that a second, identical ball is launched straight down from the same height. Does the second ball hit the ground with a velocity that is higher than, lower than, or the same as the first ball? Explain your answer. SSM

14. •What are the units of the slopes of the following graphs: (a) displacement versus time? (b) velocity versus time? (c) distance fallen by a dropped rock versus time?

15. •Is there any consistent reason why "up" can't be labeled as "negative" or "left" as "positive"? Explain why many physics professors and textbooks recommend choosing *up* and *right* as the positive directions in a description of motion.

Multiple-Choice Questions

16. •Figure 2-23 shows a position versus time graph for a moving object. At which lettered point is the object moving the slowest?

A. A
B. B
C. C
D. D
E. E SSM

Figure 2-23 Problem 16

17. •Figure 2-24 shows a position versus time graph for a moving object. At which lettered point is the object moving the fastest?

A. A
B. B
C. C
D. D
E. E

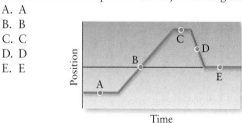

Figure 2-24 Problem 17

18. •A person is driving a car down a straight road. The instantaneous acceleration is constant and in the direction of the car's motion. The speed of the car is
    A. increasing.
    B. decreasing.
    C. constant.
    D. increasing but will eventually decrease.
    E. decreasing but will eventually increase.

19. •A person is driving a car down a straight road. The instantaneous acceleration is constant and directed opposite the direction of the car's motion. The speed of the car is
    A. increasing.
    B. decreasing.
    C. constant.
    D. increasing but will eventually decrease.
    E. decreasing but will eventually increase.

20. •A 1-kg ball and a 10-kg ball are dropped from a height of 10 m at the same time. In the absence of air resistance,
    A. the 1-kg ball hits the ground first.
    B. the 10-kg ball hits the ground first.
    C. the two balls hit the ground at the same time.
    D. the 10-kg ball will take 10 times the amount of time to reach the ground.
    E. there is not enough information to determine which ball hits the ground first.

21. •When throwing a ball straight up, which of the following are correct about the magnitudes of its velocity (v) and its acceleration (a) at the highest point in its path?
    A. both $v = 0$ and $a = 0$
    B. $v \neq 0$, but $a = 0$
    C. $v = 0$, but $a = 9.80 \text{ m/s}^2$
    D. $v \neq 0$, but $a = 9.80 \text{ m/s}^2$
    E. There is not enough information to determine the velocity (v) and acceleration (a).

Estimation/Numerical Analysis

22. •**Medical** Estimate the acceleration, upon hitting the ground, of a painter who loses his balance and falls from a step stool. Compare this to the acceleration he would experience if he bends his knees as he hits the ground.

23. •Estimate the time required for an average car to reach freeway speeds. Estimate the time required for an average car to slow down to zero from freeway speeds.

24. •**Sports** A marathon race is just over 26 mi in length. Estimate the average speed of a runner who completes the marathon in 5 h.

25. ••**Medical** The severity of many sports injuries is related to the magnitude of the acceleration that an athlete's body undergoes as it comes to rest, especially when joints (such as ankles and knees) are not properly aligned during falls. (a) Estimate the acceleration of a woman who falls while running at full speed and comes to rest on a muddy field. Compare the acceleration to that of the same woman who falls while running at full speed and comes to rest on a running track made from a synthetic material. (b) Repeat these estimates for a male athlete. Assume they both are world-class athletes. SSM

26. • Suppose a 1000-km airline trip takes 3 h with about 30 min of that spent taxiing, taking off, and landing. Estimate your average speed while airborne.

27. •**Biology** Estimate the acceleration that a cat undergoes as it jumps from the floor to a countertop.

28. •**Astronomy** Estimate the speed of Earth as it orbits the Sun. Explain any assumptions that you make in your estimation.

29. • Estimate the acceleration of a large cruise ship that is leaving port to head out to sea. SSM

30. • (a) Estimate the displacement of a swimmer during a typical workout. (b) Estimate the distance swam during the same workout.

31. •**Sports** (a) Estimate the acceleration of a thrown baseball. (b) Estimate the acceleration of a kicked soccer ball.

32. • A trainer times his racehorse as it completes a workout on a long, straight track. The position versus time data are given below. Plot an x–t graph and calculate the average speed of the horse between (a) 0 and 10 s, (b) 10 and 30 s, and (c) 0 and 50 s.

x(m)	t(s)	x(m)	t(s)
0	0	500	30
90	5	550	35
180	10	600	40
270	15	650	45
360	20	700	50
450	25		

33. • Write the equations for $x(t)$ for each interval of constant acceleration motion for the object whose position as a function of time is shown in the following table. (*Hint:* Graph the data on a graphing calculator or in a spreadsheet.) SSM

x(m)	t(s)	x(m)	t(s)	x(m)	t(s)
−12	0	18	9	85	18
−6	1	24	10	90	19
0	2	33	11	95	20
6	3	45	12	100	21
12	4	60	13	90	22
15	5	65	14	80	23
15	6	70	15	70	24
15	7	75	16	70	25
15	8	80	17		

34. • A coconut is dropped from a tall tree. Complete the following table. You may wish to program a spreadsheet to calculate these values more quickly.

t(s)	y(m)	v(m/s)	a(m/s^2)
0	0	0	0
1			
2			
3			
4			
5			
10			

Problems

2-3 Solving straight-line motion problems: Constant velocity

35. •Convert the following speeds:
    A. 30.0 m/s = _____ km/h
    B. 14.0 mi/h = _____ km/h
    C. 90.0 km/s = _____ mi/h
    D. 88.0 ft/s = _____ mi/h
    E. 100 mi/h = _____ m/s

36. •A bowling ball moves from $x_1 = 3.50$ cm to $x_2 = -4.70$ cm during the time interval from $t_1 = 3.00$ s to $t_2 = 5.50$ s. What is the ball's average velocity?

37. •What must a jogger's average speed be in order to travel 13.0 km in 3.25 h?

38. •**Sports** The Olympic record for the marathon set in 2008 is 2 h, 6 min, 32 s. The marathon distance is 26.2 mi. What was the average speed of the record-setting runner in km/h?

39. ••**Sports** Kevin completes his morning workout at the pool. He swims 4000 m (80 laps in the 50-m-long pool) in 1.00 h. (a) What is the average velocity of Kevin during his workout? (b) What is his average speed? (c) With a burst of speed, Kevin swims one 25.0-m stretch in 9.27 s. What is Kevin's average speed over those 25 m? SSM

40. ••A student rides her bicycle home from physics class to get her physics book and then heads back to class. It takes her 21.0 min to make the 12.2 km trip home and 13.0 min to get back to class. (a) Calculate the average velocity of the student for the round-trip (from the lecture hall to home and back to the lecture hall). (b) Calculate her average speed for the trip from the lecture hall to her home. (c) Calculate the average speed of the girl for the trip from her home back to the lecture hall. (d) Calculate her average speed for the round-trip.

41. •A school bus takes 0.700 h to reach the school from your house. If the average speed of the bus is 56.0 km/h, how far does the bus have to travel?

42. ••A car traveling 80.0 km/h is 1500 m behind a truck traveling at 70.0 km/h. How long will it take the car to catch up with the truck?

43. •**Medical** Alcohol consumption slows people's reaction times. In a controlled government test, it takes a certain driver 0.320 s to hit the brakes in a crisis when unimpaired and 1.00 s when drunk. When the car is initially traveling at 90.0 km/h, how much farther does the car travel before coming to a stop when the person is drunk compared to sober? SSM

44. ••A jet takes off from SFO (San Francisco, CA) and flies to ORD (Chicago, IL). The distance between the airports is 3000 km. After a 1-h layover, the jet returns to San Francisco. The total time for the round-trip (including the layover) is 9 h, 52 min. If the westbound trip (from ORD to SFO) takes 24 more minutes than the eastbound portion, calculate the time required for each leg of the trip. What is the average speed for the overall trip? What is the average speed *without* the layover?

45. •**Biology** The position versus time graph for a red blood cell leaving the heart is shown in **Figure 2-25**. Determine the instantaneous speed of the red blood cell when $t = 10$ ms. Recall, 1 ms = 0.001 s, 1 mm = 0.001 m.

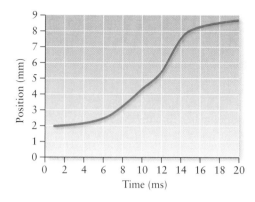

Figure 2-25
Problem 45

2-6 Solving straight-line motion problems: Constant acceleration

46. •Paola can flex her legs from a bent position through a distance of 20.0 cm. Paola leaves the ground when her legs are straight, at a speed of 4.43 m/s. Calculate the magnitude of her acceleration, assuming that it is constant.

47. •A runner starts from rest and achieves a maximum speed of 8.97 m/s. If her acceleration is 9.77 m/s², how long does it take her to reach that speed? SSM

48. •A car traveling at 35.0 km/h speeds up to 45.0 km/h in a time of 5.00 s. The same car later speeds up from 65.0 km/h to 75.0 km/h in a time of 5.00 s. (a) Calculate the magnitude of the constant acceleration for each of these intervals. (b) Determine the distance traveled by the car during each of these time intervals.

49. •A car starts from rest and reaches a maximum speed of 34.0 m/s in a time of 12.0 s. Calculate the magnitude of its average acceleration.

50. •The world's fastest cars are rated by the time required for them to accelerate from 0 to 60.0 mi/h. Convert 60.0 mi/h to kilometers per hour and then calculate the acceleration in m/s² for each of the cars on the following list:

1. Bugatti Veyron 16.4	2.4 s
2. Caparo T1	2.5 s
3. Ultima GTR	2.6 s
4. SSC Ultimate Aero TT	2.7 s
5. Saleen S7 Twin Turbo	2.8 s

51. ••Using the information for the Bugatti Veyron in the previous problem, calculate the distance that the car would travel in the time it takes to reach 90.0 km/h, which is the speed limit on many Canadian roads. Compare your answer to the distance that the Saleen S7 Twin Turbo would travel while accelerating to the same final speed. SSM

52. •A driver is traveling at 30.0 m/s when he sees a moose crossing the road 80.0 m ahead. The moose becomes distracted and stops in the middle of the road. If the driver of the car slams on the brakes, what is the minimum constant acceleration he must undergo to stop short of the moose and avert an accident? (In British Columbia, Canada, alone, there are over 4000 moose–car accidents each year.)

53. •**Biology** A sperm whale can accelerate at about 0.100 m/s² when swimming on the surface. How far will a whale travel if it starts at a speed of 1.00 m/s and accelerates to a speed of 2.25 m/s? Assume the whale travels in a straight line. SSM

54. •At the start of a race, a horse accelerates out of the gate at a rate of 3.00 m/s^2. How long does it take the horse to cover the first 25.0 m of the race?

55. ••Derive the equation that relates position to speed and acceleration but in which the time variable does not appear. Start with the basic equation for the definition of acceleration, $a = (v - v_0)/t$, solve for t, and substitute the resulting expression into the position versus time equation, $x = x_0 + v_0 t + \frac{1}{2}at^2$.

2-8 Solving straight-line motion problems: Free fall

56. •A ball is dropped from rest at a height of 25.0 m above the ground. (a) How fast is the ball moving when it is 10.0 m above the ground? (b) How much time is required for it to reach ground level? Ignore the effects of air resistance.

57. •Alex climbs to the top of a tall tree while his friend Gary waits on the ground below. Alex throws down a ball with an initial speed of 4.00 m/s from 50.0 m above the ground. At what speed must Gary throw a ball up in order for the two balls to cross paths 25.0 m above the ground? The starting height of the ball thrown upward is 1.50 m above the ground. Ignore the effects of air resistance. SSM

58. ••**Biology** A fox locates its prey, usually a mouse, under the snow by slight sounds the rodents make. The fox then leaps straight into the air and burrows its nose into the snow to catch its next meal. If a fox jumps to a height of 85.0 cm, calculate (a) the speed at which the fox leaves the snow and (b) how long the fox is in the air. Ignore the effects of air resistance.

59. •**Medical** More people end up in U.S. emergency rooms because of fall-related injuries than from any other cause. At what speed would someone hit the ground who accidentally steps off the top rung of a 6-ft-tall stepladder? (That step is usually embossed with the phrase "Warning! Do not stand on this step.") Ignore the effects of air resistance. SSM

60. ••Wes stands on the roof of a building, leans over the edge, and drops a rock. Lindsay waits 1.25 s after Wes releases his rock and throws her own rock straight down at 28.0 m/s. Both rocks hit the ground simultaneously. Calculate the common height from which the rocks were released. Ignore the effects of air resistance.

61. ••A ball is thrown straight up at 18.0 m/s. How fast is the ball moving after 1.00 s? After 2.00 s? After 5.00 s? When does the ball reach its maximum height? Ignore the effects of air resistance.

62. ••A tennis ball is hit straight up at 20.0 m/s from the edge of a sheer cliff. Sometime later, the ball passes the original height from which it was hit. (a) How fast is the ball moving at that time? (b) If the cliff is 30.0 m high, how long will it take the ball to reach the ground level? (c) What total distance did the ball travel? Ignore the effects of air resistance.

63. •••Mary spots Bill approaching the dorm at a constant rate of 2.00 m/s on the walkway that passes directly beneath Mary's window, 17.0 m above the ground. When Bill is 120 m away from the point below Mary's window she decides to drop an apple down to him. (See **Figure 2-26**.) (a) How long should Mary wait to drop the apple if Bill is to catch it 1.75 m above the ground, without either speeding up or slowing down? (b) How far from directly below the window should Bill be when Mary releases the apple? (c) What is the angle θ between the vertical and the line of sight between Mary and Bill at the instant Mary should release the apple? Ignore the effects of air resistance. SSM

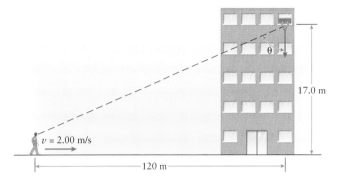

Figure 2-26 Problem 63

General Problems

64. •A car is driving at a speed of 40.0 km/h toward an intersection just as the light changes from green to yellow. If the driver has a reaction time of 0.750 s and the magnitude of the braking acceleration of the car is 5.50 m/s^2, find the minimum distance x_{min} the car travels before coming to a stop after the light changes.

65. ••Two trains, traveling toward one another on a straight track, are 300 m apart when the engineers on both trains become aware of the impending collision and hit their brakes. The eastbound train, initially moving at 98.0 km/h, slows down at 3.50 m/s^2. The westbound train, initially moving at 120 km/h, slows down at 4.20 m/s^2. Will the trains stop before colliding? If so, what is the distance between them once they stop? If not, what initial separation would have been needed to avert a disaster? SSM

66. ••**Biology** The cheetah is considered the fastest running animal in the world. Cheetahs can accelerate to a speed of 20.0 m/s in 2.50 s and can continue to accelerate to reach a top speed of 29.0 m/s. Assume the acceleration is constant until the top speed is reached and is zero thereafter. (a) Express the cheetah's top speed in mi/h. (b) Starting from a crouched position, how long does it take a cheetah to reach its top speed and how far does it travel in that time? (c) If a cheetah sees a rabbit 120 m away, how long will it take to reach the rabbit, assuming the rabbit does not move?

67. •**Medical** Very large accelerations can injure the body, especially if they last for a considerable length of time. One model used to gauge the likelihood of injury is the severity index (SI), defined as $SI = a^{5/2}t$, where a is the acceleration in multiples of g and t is the time the acceleration lasts (in seconds). In one set of studies of rear-end collisions, a person's velocity increases by 15.0 km/h with an acceleration of 35.0 m/s^2. (a) What is the severity index for the collision? (b) How far does the person travel during the collision if the car was initially moving forward at 5.00 km/h?

68. •••A man on a railroad platform attempts to measure the length of a train car by walking the length of the train and keeping the length of his stride a constant 82.0 cm per step. After he has paced off 12 steps from the front of the train car it begins to move, in the direction opposite to his, with an acceleration of 0.400 m/s^2. The end of the train passes him 10.0 s later, after he has walked another 20 steps. Determine the length of the train car.

69. ••Blythe and Geoff compete in a 1.00-km race. Blythe's strategy is to run the first 600 m of the race at a constant speed of 4.00 m/s, and then accelerate to her maximum speed of 7.50 m/s, which takes her 1.00 min, and then finish the race at that speed. Geoff decides to accelerate to his maximum speed of 8.00 m/s at the start of the race and to maintain that speed throughout the rest of the race. It takes Geoff 3.00 min to reach his maximum speed. Assuming all accelerations are constant, who wins the race?

70. ••Figure 2-27 is a graph of the velocity of a moving car. What is its instantaneous acceleration at times $t = 2$ s, $t = 4.5$ s, $t = 6$ s, and $t = 8$ s?

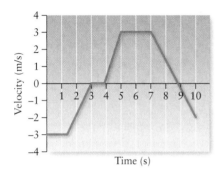

Figure 2-27
Problem 70

71. ••A ball is dropped from an upper floor, some unknown distance above your apartment. As you look out of your window, which is 1.50 m tall, you observe that it takes the ball 0.180 s to traverse the length of the window. Determine how high above the top of your window the ball was dropped. Ignore the effects of air resistance. SSM

72. •••A ball is thrown straight up at 15.0 m/s. (a) How much time does it take for the ball to be 5.00 m above its release point? (b) How fast is the ball moving when it is 7.00 m above its release point? (c) How much time is required for the ball to reach a point that is 7.00 m above its release point? Why are there two answers to part (c)?

73. ••In the book and film *Coraline*, the title character and her new friend Wybie discover a deep well. Coraline drops a rock into the well and hears the sounds of it hitting the bottom 5.50 s later. If the speed of sound is 340 m/s, determine the depth of the well.

74. •••Ten washers are tied to a long string at various locations, as in Figure 2-28. When the string is released some known height above the floor, the washers hit the floor with equal time intervals. Determine the distance between each washer ($y_n = ?$, $n = 1, 2, 3, …, 9, 10$) if the height between the lowest washer (#1) and the floor (before the string is dropped) is 10 cm.

Figure 2-28 Problem 74

75. •••A rocket is fired straight up. It contains two stages (Stage 1 and Stage 2) of solid rocket fuel that are designed to burn for 10.0 and 5.00 s, respectively, with no time interval between them. In Stage 1, the rocket fuel provides an upward acceleration of 15.0 m/s^2. In Stage 2, the acceleration is 12.0 m/s^2. Neglecting air resistance, calculate the maximum altitude above the surface of Earth of the payload and the time required for it to return to the surface. Assume the acceleration due to gravity is constant. SSM

76. •••A lacrosse ball is hurled straight up, leaving the head of the stick at a height of 2.00 m above the ground level. The ball passes by a 1.25-m-high window in a time of 0.400 s as it heads upward. Calculate the initial speed of the ball if it is 13.0 m from the ground to the bottom of the window. Ignore the effects of air resistance.

77. ••**Biology** A black mamba snake has a length of 4.30 m and a top speed of 8.90 m/s! Suppose a mongoose and a black mamba find themselves nose to nose. In an effort to escape, the snake accelerates at 18.0 m/s^2 from rest. (a) How much time does it take for the snake to reach its top speed? (b) How far does the snake travel in that time? (c) How much reaction time does the mongoose have before the tail of the mamba snake passes by?

78. ••**Sports** Kharissia wants to complete a 1000-m race with an average speed of 8.00 m/s. After 750 m, she has averaged 7.20 m/s. What average speed must she maintain for the remainder of the race in order to attain her goal?

79. ••**Sports** In April 1974, Steve Prefontaine completed a 10.0-km race in a time of 27 min, 43.6 s. Suppose "Pre" was at the 9.00-km mark at a time of 25.0 min even. If he accelerates for 60.0 s and maintains the increased speed for the duration of the race, calculate the acceleration that he had. Assume his instantaneous speed at the 9.00-km mark was the same as his overall average speed at that time.

80. ••A ball is thrown straight down at 1.50 m/s from a tall tower. Two seconds (2.00 s) later, a second ball is thrown straight up at 4.00 m/s. How far apart are the two balls 4.00 s after the second ball is thrown? What is the minimum separation between the balls and when does it occur? Ignore the effects of air resistance.

81. ••A two-stage rocket blasts off vertically from rest on a launch pad. During the first stage, which lasts for 15.0 s, the acceleration is a constant 2.00 m/s^2 upward. At the end of the first stage the second stage engine fires, producing an upward acceleration of 3.00 m/s^2 that lasts for 12.0 s. At the end of the second stage, the engines no longer fire and therefore cause no acceleration, so the rocket coasts to its maximum altitude. (a) What is the maximum altitude of the rocket? (b) Over the time interval from blastoff at the launch pad to the instant that the rocket falls back to the launch pad, what are its (i) average speed and (ii) average velocity? Ignore the effects of air resistance.

3

Motion in Two or Three Dimensions

In this chapter, your goals are to:

- (3-1) Recognize the differences among one-, two-, and three-dimensional motion.
- (3-2) Describe the properties of a vector and how to find the sum or difference of two vectors.
- (3-3) Relate the components of a vector to its magnitude and direction.
- (3-4) Use components in calculations involving vectors.
- (3-5) Explain how displacement, velocity, and acceleration are described in terms of vectors.
- (3-6) Identify the key features of projectile motion and how to interpret this kind of motion.
- (3-7) Solve problems involving projectile motion.
- (3-8) Describe why an object moving in a circle is always accelerating.
- (3-9) Solve problems that involve motion in a circle.
- (3-10) Explain how the structure of the ear helps us sense acceleration.

To master this chapter, you should review:

- (2-2, 2-3, and 2-4) The ideas of displacement, velocity, and acceleration for motion in a straight line.
- (2-5, 2-6) The concepts and equations of straight-line motion with constant acceleration.
- (2-7, 2-8) The concepts and equations of free fall.

What do you think?

If air resistance isn't a factor, does a clump of lava emerging from a volcano take more time to (a) climb to its maximum height or (b) descend from its maximum height back to the elevation from which it was launched? Or (c) do the climb and descent take the same amount of time?

3-1 The ideas of linear motion help us understand motion in two or three dimensions

The clumps of lava shown in the above photo follow *curved* paths. That means that we can't describe them simply by using the ideas of Chapter 2 for motion in a straight line (one-dimensional motion). But as we will see, we can extend the same concepts of displacement, velocity, and acceleration to motion along curved paths in two or three dimensions—that is, to motion in a plane or to generalized motion in space (Figure 3-1a).

One of the most common kinds of motion is that in which the acceleration is constant in both its magnitude and its direction. In this case, we'll find that the motion always lies in the same plane and hence is two-dimensional. A common example of two-dimensional motion is *projectile motion*, which occurs when the only source of an object's acceleration is the downward pull of gravity (Figure 3-1b). Projectile

This aircraft follows a complicated, three-dimensional path.

This motorcycle's path through the air is two-dimensional (in a plane): It moves left to right as well as up and down.

Each car on this Ferris wheel moves in the plane of the wheel, so its path is two-dimensional.

The most general kind of motion is three-dimensional. In many cases, however, the motion is in a plane and so is two-dimensional.

(a)   (b)   (c)

Figure 3-1 **Motion in three and two dimensions** Three examples of motion.

motion is not a perfect description of the flight of batted baseballs or thrown footballs, for which air resistance can be important, but it can still give useful approximate results.

We'll also examine the important case of motion in a circle (Figure 3-1c). We'll discover that even if an object travels around a circle at a constant speed, it is nonetheless accelerating. That's because the object is *turning*—the direction of its motion is continuously changing. In later chapters we'll use this observation to help explain why birds bank their wings when they turn, why cars sometimes skid when turning on a rain-slicked road, and other aspects of the natural and technological world.

You might worry that motion in two or three dimensions is two or three times harder to analyze than one-dimensional motion along a straight line. Not so! It turns out that we can use all of the same techniques to study two- and three-dimensional motions as we used for straight-line motion in Chapter 2. The difference is that the position, displacement, velocity, and acceleration of an object moving in two or three dimensions are best described using *vectors*—quantities that have both a magnitude and a direction that does not always point along a straight line. In the following section, we'll expand on the idea of vectors introduced in Chapter 2 and see how to use them to help analyze motion in two and three dimensions.

Take-Home Message for Section 3-1

✔ Motion in two or three dimensions uses the same ideas of velocity and acceleration as linear motion.

✔ In two- and three-dimensional motion, velocity and acceleration have to be treated as vector quantities.

3-2 A vector quantity has both a magnitude and a direction

One afternoon, you decide to take your textbook to study at your favorite coffee house. You could take a number of paths to the coffee house—the shortcut straight across the park, east along 1st Avenue and then north on Park Street, or a more scenic route through the park by way of the duck pond (Figure 3-2a). No matter which path you choose, however, the net result is that you end up 520 m from your apartment in a direction 60° north of east. This change in your position is your *displacement*, and it has both a *magnitude* (520 m) and a *direction* (60° north of east). This is an extension of the idea of displacement that we introduced in Chapter 2 for motion along a straight line. In that case, the sign of the displacement (positive or negative) told us whether the displacement was in the positive or negative *x* direction. Because your motion from apartment to coffee house is in a *plane*, however, we need to expand our definition of displacement.

(a)

No matter what path you take from your apartment to the coffee house...

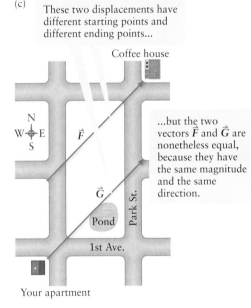

Figure 3-2 **Vectors** (a) Three paths from your apartment to your favorite coffee house. (b) Each path has the same displacement: from apartment to coffee house. (c) Two equal vectors. (d) Three unequal vectors.

(b)

...the displacement is the same. The displacement is represented by the vector $\vec{E}$.

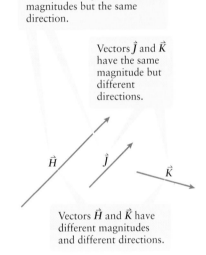

The **magnitude** of the displacement is the straight line distance from the starting point to the ending point.

The **direction** of this displacement is 60° north of east.

(c)

These two displacements have different starting points and different ending points...

...but the two vectors $\vec{F}$ and $\vec{G}$ are nonetheless equal, because they have the same magnitude and the same direction.

(d)

Vectors $\vec{H}$ and $\vec{J}$ have different magnitudes but the same direction.

Vectors $\vec{J}$ and $\vec{K}$ have the same magnitude but different directions.

Vectors $\vec{H}$ and $\vec{K}$ have different magnitudes and different directions.

A vector has only two attributes: magnitude and direction.

Vectors and Scalars

Any quantity that, like displacement, has both a magnitude and a direction is called a **vector**. An example is the **displacement vector** in **Figure 3-2b** that points from your starting point (your apartment) to your destination (the coffee house). As Figure 3-2b shows, we depict this vector by an arrow. The length of the arrow denotes the **magnitude** of the vector, which in this case is 520 m, the straight-line distance from starting point to destination. The **direction** of the displacement vector in this case is 60° north of east. We say that two vectors are equal *only* if they have the same magnitude and the same direction (**Figure 3-2c**). If two vectors differ in their magnitude, direction, or both, they are not equal to each other (**Figure 3-2d**).

Many important physical quantities have both a magnitude and a direction, and hence are vectors. When we say that a pigeon is flying at 10 m/s due west, we are

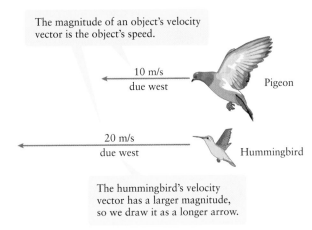

The magnitude of an object's velocity vector is the object's speed.

10 m/s
due west

Pigeon

20 m/s
due west

Hummingbird

The hummingbird's velocity vector has a larger magnitude, so we draw it as a longer arrow.

Figure 3-3 **Velocity vectors** The velocity of a flying bird is a vector: it has both a magnitude and a direction (the direction of the bird's travel).

stating its *velocity* vector (Figure 3-3). The pigeon's *speed* is the magnitude of this vector. Just as for the displacement vector, we use an arrow to denote the vector, and we use the length of the vector to denote the magnitude. That's why we draw the velocity vector for a hummingbird flying at 20 m/s as having twice the length of the velocity vector for the 10-m/s pigeon in Figure 3-3: The hummingbird's speed (the magnitude of its velocity) is twice as great. Other vectors that we will encounter in our study of physics include force (a push or pull), acceleration (which describes changes in velocity), and electric and magnetic fields.

Many important physical quantities have *no* direction associated with them, and so they are *not* vectors. These quantities are called **scalars** and can be described simply by stating a number and a unit. For example, the average temperature inside a home is 20°C, and the duration of a typical university lecture is 50 min. Other examples of scalar quantities are area, volume, mass, and density. Note that some scalar quantities can be negative: For example, the temperature inside a freezer can be less than -5°C.

To help us distinguish which quantities are scalars and which are vectors, we use different symbols for the two types of quantities. We will always use an *italic* letter to denote a scalar quantity, such as T for temperature or t for time. In handwriting you use ordinary letters for these quantities. By contrast, we always denote vectors using **boldface italic** letters with an arrow on top. Thus, we write displacement vectors like those shown in Figure 3-2 as $\vec{E}, \vec{F}, \vec{G}$, and so on. In handwriting, you should *always* draw an arrow over the symbol for a vector quantity.

Scalar: C — The symbol for a scalar is shown in *italic*.

Vector: $\vec{A}$ — The symbol for a vector is shown in **boldface italic** with an arrow.

The symbol for the magnitude of a vector is the same symbol as for the vector itself, but *without* the arrow over the symbol and in italic rather than boldface italic. For example, the magnitude of the displacement $\vec{E}$ shown in Figure 3-2b is $E = 520$ m. We also sometimes use absolute value signs to denote the magnitude of a vector: $|\vec{E}| = E = 520$ m.

Watch Out! Use vector notation correctly.

Note that it is *never* correct to write an equation such as $\vec{E} = 520$ m. A vector is not simply equal to its magnitude; its direction is just as important. You must instead say "$\vec{E}$ has magnitude 520 m and points 60° north of east." (Later in this chapter, we'll see a different, shorthand way to represent a vector mathematically.)

Like a scalar, the magnitude of a vector is given by a number and a unit. The unit is meters (m) for the displacement shown in Figure 3-2b. The magnitude of a vector can *never* be negative. If asked the distance from your apartment to the coffee house in Figure 3-2b, you would never say "it's negative 520 m from here"! In the same way, speed (the magnitude of velocity) is never negative, which is why there are no negative numbers on a speedometer.

Adding Vectors

Scalars add together according to the rules of ordinary arithmetic: If you have a house that has a floor area of 200 m^2 and you build an extra room that has a floor area of 15 m^2, the net result is a house that has a floor area of 200 m^2 + 15 m^2 = 215 m^2.

Vectors behave differently, however. As an example, suppose you walk due east from your apartment to the corner of 1st Avenue and Park Street, a displacement $\vec{A}$, then walk due north to the coffee house, a displacement $\vec{B}$ (Figure 3-4a). Your net displacement is from your apartment to the coffee house; the combined effect of these two displacements is the same as the single displacement $\vec{E}$. Combining $\vec{A}$ and $\vec{B}$ to get $\vec{E}$ is an example of **vector addition**, and we say that $\vec{E}$ is the **vector sum** of $\vec{A}$ and $\vec{B}$. That is, $\vec{E} = \vec{A} + \vec{B}$. You can see from Figure 3-4a that another way to get to the coffee house is to travel first from your apartment to the duck pond (displacement $\vec{C}$) and then from the duck pond to the coffee house (displacement $\vec{D}$). So it's also true that $\vec{E} = \vec{C} + \vec{D}$.

Figure 3-4a illustrates that to perform vector addition we draw the two vectors in sequence, with the tail of the second vector up against the tip of the first vector. The sum of these two vectors then points from the tail of the first vector to the tip of the second vector. Even if the two vectors are not originally tip to tip, you can make them that way by moving or *translating* one vector's tail to the other vector's tip while keeping the directions of the vectors the same, as Figure 3-4b shows. This figure also shows that the order in which you add vectors doesn't matter, so $\vec{A} + \vec{B} = \vec{B} + \vec{A}$. Ordinary scalar addition behaves the same way: for example, $3 + 4 = 4 + 3$.

(a)

Coffee house

$\vec{E}$

Park St.

$\vec{D}$

$\vec{B}$

Pond

$\vec{C}$

1st Ave.

$\vec{A}$

Your apartment

Traveling from your apartment to the corner of 1st Avenue to Park Street, then to the coffee house, gives you the same net displacement as traveling in a straight line from your apartment to the coffee house. So $\vec{E} = \vec{A} + \vec{B}$

A trip via the duck pond also gives you the same net displacement as a straight-line trip. So $\vec{E} = \vec{C} + \vec{D}$

Figure 3-4 Vector addition
(a) All three paths from your apartment to the coffee house give the same total displacement vector: $\vec{E} = \vec{A} + \vec{B} = \vec{C} + \vec{D}$. (b) How to place the vectors $\vec{A}$ and $\vec{B}$ so they can be added.

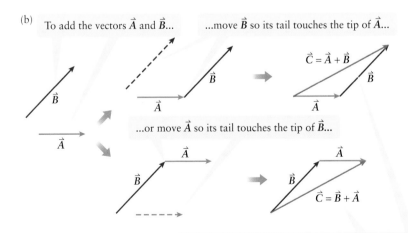

(b)   To add the vectors $\vec{A}$ and $\vec{B}$...   ...move $\vec{B}$ so its tail touches the tip of $\vec{A}$...

$\vec{B}$

$\vec{A}$

$\vec{B}$

$\vec{A}$

$\vec{C} = \vec{A} + \vec{B}$

$\vec{B}$

$\vec{A}$

...or move $\vec{A}$ so its tail touches the tip of $\vec{B}$...

$\vec{A}$

$\vec{B}$

$\vec{A}$

$\vec{B}$

$\vec{C} = \vec{B} + \vec{A}$

...and the sum $\vec{C}$ of the two vectors runs from the tail of the first vector to the tip of the second vector. You get the same result no matter which order you add the vectors: $\vec{C} = \vec{A} + \vec{B} = \vec{B} + \vec{A}$

When adding two vectors, place the tip of the first vector so it touches the tail of the second vector. The vector sum then extends from the tail of the first vector to the tip of the second vector.

Watch Out! Vector addition is not the same as ordinary addition.

It's a common error to conclude that the magnitude of $\vec{A} + \vec{B}$, the sum of two vectors, is equal to the sum of the magnitude of $\vec{A}$ and the magnitude of $\vec{B}$. This is usually *not* the case when adding vectors. As an example, in Figure 3-5a the vectors $\vec{A}$ and $\vec{B}$ are perpendicular, so these two vectors and their sum $\vec{C} = \vec{A} + \vec{B}$ make up three sides of a right triangle. In this case the Pythagorean theorem tells us that the magnitude of $\vec{C}$ is given by $C^2 = A^2 + B^2$,

so $C = \sqrt{A^2 + B^2}$. This is less than $A + B$. The one situation in which the magnitude $|\vec{A} + \vec{B}|$ *is* equal to the sum of magnitudes $A + B$ is when $\vec{A}$ and $\vec{B}$ point in the same direction (Figure 3-5b). Figure 3-5c shows that if $\vec{A}$ and $\vec{B}$ point in *opposite* directions, the magnitude $|\vec{A} + \vec{B}|$ is equal to the *difference* of A and B. In Section 3-3 we'll learn a technique for easily calculating the magnitude and direction of a vector sum.

(a)

$\vec{A}$ $\vec{C} = \vec{A} + \vec{B}$

Magnitude $A = 4$ m

$\vec{B}$
Magnitude $B = 3$ m

Magnitude of this vector sum:

$C = \sqrt{A^2 + B^2}$
$= \sqrt{(4\text{ m})^2 + (3\text{ m})^2}$
$= \sqrt{16\text{ m}^2 + 9\text{ m}^2}$
$= \sqrt{25\text{ m}^2} = 5$ m

(b) $\vec{A}$ Magnitude $A = 4$ m $\vec{B}$ Magnitude $B = 3$ m

$\vec{C} = \vec{A} + \vec{B}$

Magnitude of this vector sum:

$C = A + B$
$= 4$ m $+ 3$ m
$= 7$ m

(c) $\vec{A}$ Magnitude $A = 4$ m

$\vec{C} = \vec{A} + \vec{B}$ $\vec{B}$ Magnitude $B = 3$ m

Magnitude of this vector sum:

$C = A - B$
$= 4$ m $- 3$ m
$= 1$ m

The magnitude of the vector sum $\vec{A} + \vec{B}$ is equal to the sum of the magnitudes of $\vec{A}$ and $\vec{B}$ only if $\vec{A}$ and $\vec{B}$ point in the same direction, as in (b).

Figure 3-5 Special cases of vector addition The sum $\vec{A} + \vec{B}$ of two vectors that point (a) perpendicular to each other, (b) in the same direction, and (c) in opposite directions.

Subtracting Vectors

Go to Picture It 3-1 for more practice dealing with adding and subtracting vectors

A simple problem in arithmetic is "What is 7 minus 4?" What this problem is really asking is "What do I have to add to the second number (in our example, 4) to get the first number (in our example, 7)?" The answer is $7 - 4 = 3$, because 3 added to 4 gives 7. **Vector subtraction** works in much the same way. When we say that $\vec{D} - \vec{E} = \vec{F}$, we mean that the vector $\vec{F}$ is what we would have to add to the vector $\vec{E}$ to get the vector $\vec{D}$. Hence, the vectors $\vec{D}, \vec{E}$, and $\vec{F}$ are related as shown in Figure 3-6a.

(a) Subtracting vectors:

The difference $7 - 4 = 3$ is what you must add to 4 to get to 7.

$\vec{D}$ $\vec{F} = \vec{D} - \vec{E}$

$\vec{E}$

Similarly, the vector difference
$\vec{F} = \vec{D} - \vec{E}$
is what you must add to $\vec{E}$ to get $\vec{D}$.

(b) How to calculate $\vec{F} = \vec{D} - \vec{E}$:

① Form the vector $-\vec{E}$ (with the same magnitude as $\vec{E}$ but the opposite direction).

② Add $\vec{D}$ and $-\vec{E}$ by placing them tip to tail. Their sum is $\vec{D} + (-\vec{E}) = \vec{D} - \vec{E}$.

Figure 3-6 Vector subtraction Subtracting $\vec{E}$ from $\vec{D}$ is the same as adding $-\vec{E}$ to $\vec{D}$. (a) Subtracting one vector from another. (b) How to place the vectors $\vec{D}$ and $\vec{E}$ so they can be subtracted.

$\vec{E}$
$-\vec{E}$

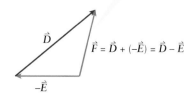
$\vec{D}$ $\vec{F} = \vec{D} + (-\vec{E}) = \vec{D} - \vec{E}$
$-\vec{E}$

To see how to carry out vector subtraction, let's first notice something about ordinary subtraction: When we *subtract* 4 from 7, we're really *adding* −4 to 7, so that $7 - 4 = 7 + (-4) = 3$. In the same way, when we *subtract* the vector $\vec{E}$ from the vector $\vec{D}$ to calculate the **vector difference** $\vec{D} - \vec{E}$, we're really *adding* the vector $-\vec{E}$ to the vector $\vec{D}$: that is, $\vec{D} - \vec{E} = \vec{D} + (-\vec{E})$. To take the *negative of a vector* we keep its magnitude the same and reverse its direction (Figure 3-6b). Thus, if $\vec{E}$ is a displacement vector of magnitude 600 m that points due *east*, the vector $-\vec{E}$ also has magnitude 600 m but points due *west*. Figure 3-6b then shows how to carry out the subtraction $\vec{D} - \vec{E}$ by adding $\vec{D}$ and $-\vec{E}$. If you know how to add two vectors, you also know how to subtract them!

A number of different animal species make use of vector addition and subtraction to navigate. As an example, honeybees like the one shown in Figure 3-7a fly along a jagged path from flower to flower in search of nectar, but they fly straight back—on a beeline—to their hive. A bee manages this feat by keeping track of the distances and directions it travels in moving from place to place. It then flies along the vector it has computed to go home. That is, if a honeybee's individual displacements from the hive are $\vec{A}$, $\vec{B}$, and $\vec{C}$, it knows that its net displacement from the hive is $\vec{A} + \vec{B} + \vec{C}$ and that it must travel through an additional displacement $-(\vec{A} + \vec{B} + \vec{C})$ to return to the hive (Figure 3-7b). Fiddler crabs, desert ants, and hamsters also use vector subtraction of this kind. We'll use vector subtraction in Section 3-5 to help us extend the ideas of velocity and acceleration to motion in two or three dimensions.

Multiplying a Vector by a Scalar

A third useful bit of mathematics involving vectors is **multiplying a vector by a scalar.** Figure 3-8 shows the simple rules for this. If c is a *positive* scalar, then the product of c and a vector $\vec{A}$ is a new vector $c\vec{A}$ that points in the same direction as $\vec{A}$ but has a different magnitude, equal to cA (the product of c and the magnitude of $\vec{A}$). If c is a *negative* scalar, then $c\vec{A}$ points in the direction opposite to $\vec{A}$ and has magnitude $|c|A$ (the absolute value of c multiplied by the magnitude of $\vec{A}$). We actually used this idea already when we defined the negative of a vector (Figure 3-6b): The vector $-\vec{E}$ equals the product of the negative scalar -1 and the vector $\vec{E}$, so $-\vec{E}$ points in the direction opposite to $\vec{E}$ and has magnitude $|-1|E = (1)E = E$ (that is, the same magnitude as $\vec{E}$).

We can also *divide* a vector by a scalar. This is really the same thing as multiplying by a scalar. As an example, dividing the vector $\vec{A}$ by 2 is the same as multiplying $\vec{A}$ by 1/2: $\vec{A}/2 = (1/2)\vec{A}$. So $\vec{A}/2$ is a vector that points in the same direction as $\vec{A}$ and has one-half the magnitude (Figure 3-8).

We'll use the multiplication of a vector by a scalar many times in our study of physics. In Section 3-5 we'll use it to define what we mean by the velocity and acceleration vectors.

(a)

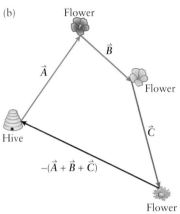

(b)

Figure 3-7 Honeybee vectors (a) A honeybee (genus *Apis*) visiting a flower. (b) Honeybees keep track of their vector displacements $\vec{A}, \vec{B}, \vec{C}, \ldots$ and use vector subtraction to calculate the direct route back to the hive.

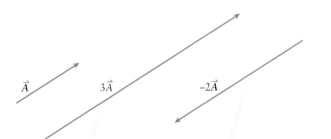

Figure 3-8 Multiplying a vector by a scalar How to multiply a vector $\vec{A}$ by a positive scalar or a negative scalar, and how to divide a vector by a scalar.

The number 3 is positive, so the vector $3\vec{A}$ points in the same direction as $\vec{A}$ but has 3 times the magnitude.

The number −2 is negative, so the vector $-2\vec{A}$ points in the direction opposite to $\vec{A}$ and has 2 times the magnitude.

Dividing a vector by 2 is the same as multiplying it by 1/2, so the vector $\vec{A}/2$ points in the same direction as $\vec{A}$ (since 1/2 is positive) and has 1/2 the magnitude.

? Got the Concept? 3-1   Adding and Subtracting Vectors

Vector $\vec{A}$ points due north, and vector $\vec{B}$ points due west. Both vectors have the same magnitude. Which of the following vectors points southwest? (a) $\vec{A} + \vec{B}$; (b) $\vec{A} - \vec{B}$; (c) $\vec{B} - \vec{A}$; (d) $-\vec{A} - \vec{B}$; (e) none of these.

Take-Home Message for Section 3-2

✔   Vectors are quantities that have both a magnitude and a direction. Scalars are ordinary numbers.

✔   To find the vector sum $\vec{A} + \vec{B}$ of two vectors, place the tail of the second vector ($\vec{B}$) against the tip of the first vector ($\vec{A}$). The vector sum points from the tail of the first vector to the tip of the second vector.

✔   The vector difference of two vectors, $\vec{A} - \vec{B}$, is the sum of $\vec{A}$ and $-\vec{B}$ (the negative of vector $\vec{B}$, which has the same magnitude as $\vec{B}$ but points in the opposite direction).

✔   The product of a scalar c and a vector $\vec{A}$ is a new vector that has magnitude $|c|A$ (the absolute value of c multiplied by the magnitude of $\vec{A}$). This vector points in the same direction as $\vec{A}$ if c is positive but in the opposite direction if c is negative.

3-3 Vectors can be described in terms of components

In Figure 3-5a the vectors $\vec{A}$ and $\vec{B}$ are perpendicular, so these two vectors and their sum $\vec{C} = \vec{A} + \vec{B}$ form three sides of a right triangle. Hence we could use the Pythagorean theorem to find the magnitude of $\vec{C}$. Unfortunately, in most situations vectors are not oriented in such a convenient manner. A powerful alternative technique for vector mathematics—that is just as easy to use no matter how vectors are arranged—is to use **vector components**. As an application, consider the arc of a thrown football. Gravity only pulls in the vertical direction, so it does not affect the football's horizontal motion. Likewise, wind blowing horizontally does not affect the vertical motion of the ball. As a result, we can analyze the two-dimensional motion of the football as two separate, one-dimensional motions—vertical motion and horizontal motion. (This isn't quite accurate if we include air resistance. Just as we did in our study of free fall in Section 2-7, however, we'll usually ignore the effects of air resistance.) We can describe the football's velocity as a vector, so it makes sense to break that vector into horizontal and vertical components.

Figure 3-9a shows a pair of mutually perpendicular coordinate axes labeled x and y. These two axes define a plane, and any point in the plane can be identified by its x and y coordinates. For instance, a point located at $x = 3$ and $y = 5$ has coordinates $(3, 5)$. The figure also shows a vector $\vec{A}$ whose direction lies in the x–y plane. If we place the tail of this vector at the **origin**—that is, at the point $x = 0$, $y = 0$—the coordinates of the tip of the vector $\vec{A}$ are (A_x, A_y) as shown in Figure 3-9a. The quantities A_x (we say "A-sub-x") and A_y (we say "A-sub-y") are called the **components** of the vector $\vec{A}$: A_x is

Figure 3-9 Components of a vector
(a) Determining the x component A_x and y component A_y of a vector $\vec{A}$.
(b), (c), (d) Whether the x and y components are positive or negative depends on the direction of the vector.

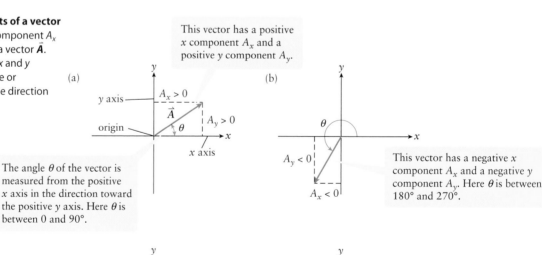

(a)

This vector has a positive x component A_x and a positive y component A_y.

$A_x > 0$
$\vec{A}$
$A_y > 0$
θ
y axis
origin
x axis

The angle θ of the vector is measured from the positive x axis in the direction toward the positive y axis. Here θ is between 0 and 90°.

(b)

θ
$A_y < 0$
$A_x < 0$

This vector has a negative x component A_x and a negative y component A_y. Here θ is between 180° and 270°.

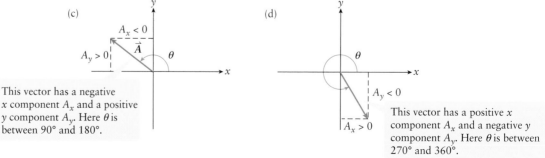

(c)

$A_x < 0$
$\vec{A}$
$A_y > 0$
θ

This vector has a negative x component A_x and a positive y component A_y. Here θ is between 90° and 180°.

(d)

θ
$A_y < 0$
$A_x > 0$

This vector has a positive x component A_x and a negative y component A_y. Here θ is between 270° and 360°.

called the **x component**, and A_y is called the **y component**. You can think of the components as the projections of the vector onto the x axis and y axis. Depending on the direction of the vector, the components can both be positive (Figure 3-9a), both negative (Figure 3-9b), or of different signs (Figures 3-9c and 3-9d).

Once you have stated the x component and y component of a vector, you have defined the vector completely. So you can describe a vector such as $\vec{A}$ in terms of either (1) its magnitude A and the angle θ or (2) its components A_x and A_y. You can use whichever description is more convenient. Figure 3-10 shows how to convert between these two descriptions. Note that the vector $\vec{A}$ of magnitude A, its x component A_x, and its y component A_y form three sides of a right triangle. From trigonometry, the cosine of the angle θ equals the adjacent side A_x divided by the hypotenuse A, the sine of θ equals the opposite side A_y divided by the hypotenuse A, and the tangent of θ equals the opposite side A_y divided by the adjacent side A_x. Furthermore, the Pythagorean theorem tells us that $A^2 = A_x^2 + A_y^2$. We can rewrite these relationships as

$$\cos \theta = \frac{A_x}{A}$$

$$\sin \theta = \frac{A_y}{A}$$

$$\tan \theta = \frac{A_y}{A_x}$$

$$A = \sqrt{A_x^2 + A_y^2}$$

With a slight rearrangement, the first two of these tell us how to find the components from the magnitude and direction, while the other two tell us how to find the magnitude and direction from the components:

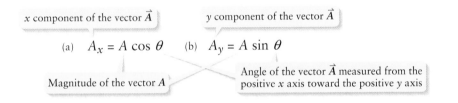

x component of the vector $\vec{A}$ y component of the vector $\vec{A}$

(a) $A_x = A \cos \theta$ (b) $A_y = A \sin \theta$

Magnitude of the vector A

Angle of the vector $\vec{A}$ measured from the positive x axis toward the positive y axis

Finding vector components from vector magnitude and direction (3-1)

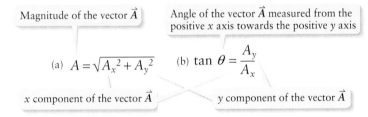

Magnitude of the vector $\vec{A}$

Angle of the vector $\vec{A}$ measured from the positive x axis towards the positive y axis

(a) $A = \sqrt{A_x{}^2 + A_y{}^2}$ (b) $\tan \theta = \frac{A_y}{A_x}$

x component of the vector $\vec{A}$ y component of the vector $\vec{A}$

Finding vector magnitude and direction from vector components (3-2)

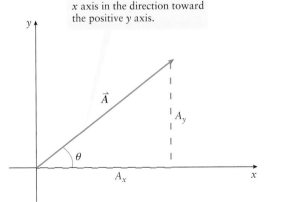

The angle θ of the vector is measured from the positive x axis in the direction toward the positive y axis.

To find the components A_x and A_y from the magnitude A and angle θ:

$A_x = A \cos \theta$

$A_y = A \sin \theta$

To find the magnitude A and angle θ from the components A_x and A_y:

$A = \sqrt{A_x{}^2 + A_y{}^2}$

$\tan \theta = \frac{A_y}{A_x}$

Figure 3-10 **Two ways to describe a vector** You can describe a vector $\vec{A}$ in terms of its magnitude A and direction θ or in terms of its components A_x and A_y.

! Watch Out! Use the angle properly when calculating vector components.

Equations 3-1 and 3-2 are valid *only* if the angle θ is measured from the positive x axis in the direction toward the positive y axis, as in Figures 3-9 and 3-10. We recom- mend that you always measure θ in that way. If you choose to measure the angle θ in some other way, you're on your own!

Vector Arithmetic with Components

Describing vectors in terms of their components greatly simplifies the vector arithmetic that we described in Section 3-2. Here are the rules:

(1) Figure 3-11 shows that if you add the vectors $\vec{A}$ and $\vec{B}$ to form the vector sum $\vec{C} = \vec{A} + \vec{B}$, each component of $\vec{C}$ is just the sum of the corresponding components of $\vec{A}$ and $\vec{B}$:

| x component of the vector $\vec{C} = \vec{A} + \vec{B}$ | x component of the vector $\vec{A}$ | x component of the vector $\vec{B}$ |

Rules for vector addition using components
(3-3)

(a) $C_x = A_x + B_x$

(b) $C_y = A_y + B_y$

| y component of the vector $\vec{C} = \vec{A} + \vec{B}$ | y component of the vector $\vec{A}$ | y component of the vector $\vec{B}$ |

(2) If we subtract $\vec{B}$ from $\vec{A}$ to form the vector difference $\vec{D} = \vec{A} - \vec{B} = \vec{A} + (-\vec{B})$, each component of $\vec{D}$ is equal to the sum of the corresponding components of $\vec{A}$ and $-\vec{B}$. The components of $-\vec{B}$ are $-B_x$ and $-B_y$, so the components of $\vec{D}$ are $D_x = A_x + (-B_x) = A_x - B_x$ and $D_y = A_y + (-B_y) = A_y - B_y$, or

| x component of the vector $\vec{D} = \vec{A} - \vec{B}$ | x component of the vector $\vec{A}$ | x component of the vector $\vec{B}$ |

Rules for vector subtraction using components
(3-4)

(a) $D_x = A_x - B_x$

(b) $D_y = A_y - B_y$

| y component of the vector $\vec{D} = \vec{A} - \vec{B}$ | y component of the vector $\vec{A}$ | y component of the vector $\vec{B}$ |

Figure 3-11 **Vector addition using components** The simplest way to add two vectors is in terms of their components.

The y component of the vector $\vec{C} = \vec{A} + \vec{B}$ equals the sum of the y components of $\vec{A}$ and $\vec{B}$:
$$C_y = A_y + B_y$$

The x component of the vector $\vec{C} = \vec{A} + \vec{B}$ equals the sum of the x components of $\vec{A}$ and $\vec{B}$:
$$C_x = A_x + B_x$$

 Each component of a vector sum $\vec{C} = \vec{A} + \vec{B}$ equals the sum of the corresponding components of the vectors $\vec{A}$ and $\vec{B}$.

That is, each component of $\vec{D} = \vec{A} - \vec{B}$ equals the difference between the corresponding components of $\vec{A}$ and $\vec{B}$.

(3) Finally, multiplying a vector $\vec{A}$ by a scalar c gives a new vector $\vec{E} = c\vec{A}$ whose components are just the components of $\vec{A}$ multiplied by c:

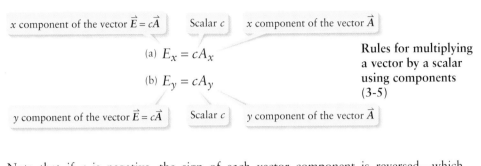

x component of the vector $\vec{E} = c\vec{A}$ Scalar c   x component of the vector $\vec{A}$

(a) $E_x = cA_x$

(b) $E_y = cA_y$

y component of the vector $\vec{E} = c\vec{A}$ Scalar c   y component of the vector $\vec{A}$

Rules for multiplying a vector by a scalar using components (3-5)

Note that if c is negative, the sign of each vector component is reversed—which means that the direction of the vector as a whole is reversed. That's just what we saw in Figure 3-8.

To use these rules you need to know the vectors $\vec{A}$ and $\vec{B}$ in terms of their components. If instead you're given $\vec{A}$ and $\vec{B}$ in terms of their magnitudes and directions, you can find their components using Equations 3-1. Once you've found the components of the desired result (such as a vector sum or a vector difference), you can determine its magnitude and direction using Equations 3-2. In the following section we'll look at several examples of this kind.

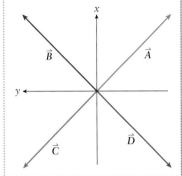

? Got the Concept? 3-2
Vector Components

Which of the vectors in the accompanying figure has a positive x component and a negative y component? (a) $\vec{A}$; (b) $\vec{B}$; (c) $\vec{C}$; (d) $\vec{D}$; (e) none of these.

? Got the Concept? 3-3 Zero Vectors and Zero Components

(a) Is it possible for a vector that has zero magnitude to have a nonzero component in some direction? (b) Is it possible for a vector that has nonzero magnitude to have a com-ponent in some direction that is equal to zero? In each case, draw an example if possible.

Take-Home Message for Section 3-3

✔ The components of a vector $\vec{A}$ are its projections onto two perpendicular axes: A_x is the projection onto the x axis, and A_y is the projection onto the y axis.

✔ Equations 3-1 let you find the components of a vector from its magnitude and direction, and Equations 3-2 let

you find the magnitude and direction of a vector from its components.

✔ Equations 3-3, 3-4, and 3-5 show how to add vectors, subtract vectors, and multiply a vector by a scalar using components.

3-4 Using components greatly simplifies vector calculations

The following examples show how to work with vectors in terms of components.

Example 3-1 Different Descriptions of a Vector

(a) Find the x and y components of a velocity vector $\vec{v}$ that has magnitude 35.0 m/s and points in a direction 36.9° west of north. (b) Find the magnitude and direction of a displacement vector $\vec{r}$ that has x component −24.0 m and y component −11.0 m. Choose the positive x direction to point east and choose the positive y direction to point north.

Set Up

Our drawing shows the two vectors and the x–y axes. We'll use Equations 3-1 to find the x and y components of the vector $\vec{v}$ in part (a) and Equations 3-2 to find the magnitude and direction of the vector $\vec{r}$ in part (b).

Finding vector components from vector magnitude and direction:

$$A_x = A \cos \theta \qquad (3\text{-}1a)$$
$$A_y = A \sin \theta \qquad (3\text{-}1b)$$

Finding vector magnitude and direction from vector components:

$$A = \sqrt{A_x^2 + A_y^2} \qquad (3\text{-}2a)$$

$$\tan \theta = \frac{A_y}{A_x} \qquad (3\text{-}2b)$$

Solve

(a) The angle 36.9° is measured from the positive y axis. To use Equations 3-1, the angle of the vector $\vec{v}$ must be measured from the positive x axis. The figure shows that the angle we need is $90° + 36.9° = 126.9°$. Use this angle in Equations 3-1 along with the magnitude $v = 35.0$ m/s of the vector $\vec{v}$.

$$v_x = (35.0 \text{ m/s}) \cos 126.9°$$
$$= (35.0 \text{ m/s})(-0.600)$$
$$= -21.0 \text{ m/s}$$

$$v_y = (35.0 \text{ m/s}) \sin 126.9°$$
$$= (35.0 \text{ m/s})(0.800)$$
$$= +28.0 \text{ m/s}$$

(b) The magnitude r of the vector $\vec{r}$ is the hypotenuse of a triangle whose other two sides are 11.0 m and 24.0 m in length. Hence we can use the Pythagorean theorem (which is Equation 3-2a) to calculate r.

$$r = \sqrt{r_x^2 + r_y^2}$$
$$= \sqrt{(-24.0 \text{ m})^2 + (-11.0 \text{ m})^2}$$
so $r = 26.4$ m

From Equation 3-2b, the tangent of the angle θ shown in the figure equals r_y divided by r_x, or 0.458. Use your calculator to find the inverse tangent of 0.458; the result is 24.6°. However, the tangent function has the property that $\tan \phi = \tan (180° + \phi)$. Hence 0.458 is equal to *both* $\tan 24.6°$ and $\tan (180° + 24.6°) = \tan 204.6°$. The figure shows that the angle of the vector $\vec{r}$ measured from the positive x axis is greater than 180°, so the answer we want is $\theta = 204.6°$, which we round to three significant digits.

$$\tan \theta = \frac{r_y}{r_x} = \frac{-11.0 \text{ m}}{-24.0 \text{ m}} = 0.458$$

$$\theta = \tan^{-1} 0.458 = 24.6° \text{ or}$$
$$= 204.6°$$

Reflect

The drawing of $\vec{v}$ in part (a) shows that this vector points in the negative x direction and the positive y direction. This agrees with our results, which show that v_x is negative and v_y is positive. The drawing of $\vec{r}$ in part (b) helped us decide which value of θ was the correct one. This shows the importance of always drawing a picture for any problem that involves vectors.

! Watch Out! **Make sure your calculator is calculating angles in degrees.**

Many students get frustrated trying to find a mistake in their physics, when the only problem is that their calculator was set to "radian" mode for angles. You should always check to make sure your calculator is in "degree" mode.

Example 3-2 At What Angle Is Your Heart?

In your heart, pacemaker cells generate electrical signals that trigger a contraction of the heart as the signals spread from the top of the heart to the bottom. The direction in which these signals travel is called the *electrical axis* of the heart, which reflects the angle at which the heart is positioned in the chest cavity.

The direction of a person's electrical axis is found using a technique called *electrocardiography*. In a simplified version of electrocardiography, electrodes are placed on the person's left wrist, right wrist, and right ankle. The electrical signal between the two wrist electrodes tells us the horizontal, right-to-left component of the heart's electrical activity. The signal between the right wrist and right ankle (which is recorded simultaneously with the signal between the wrists) gives us the vertical, top-to-bottom component. The vector found by combining these horizontal and vertical components points in the direction of the heart's electrical axis (Figure 3-12a).

The graphs in Figure 3-12b show sample recordings of the electrical signal versus time for these two pairs of electrodes. These graphs are called *electrocardiograms*, abbreviated ECG or EKG (after their German name *Elektrokardiogramm*). In this particular example, the maximum ECG signal between the wrists is 1.00 millivolt (mV) and the maximum ECG signal between the right wrist and right ankle is 1.40 mV. At what angle θ does the electrical signal propagate across the heart?

(a)

Electrode on right wrist

Electrode on left wrist

Electrode on right ankle

Horizontal

Vertical

(b)

1.00 mV — Horizontal component

1.40 mV — Vertical component

0 s   1.25 s

Figure 3-12 Electrocardiography and the electrical axis of the heart (a) Locating the electrical axis. (b) Horizontal and vertical electrocardiograms.

Set Up

Our goal is to find the angle θ shown in the figure, which is the direction of the heart's electrical axis measured relative to the horizontal. We choose the x axis to be horizontal and choose the y axis to be vertically downward. (We can choose the axes to be whatever we want, provided they're mutually perpendicular.) The sketch shows the electrical axis as a green vector; it has an x component of 1.00 mV (shown in red) and a y component of 1.40 mV (shown in purple). As in Example 3-1, we'll use Equation 3-2b to find this angle.

Finding vector direction from vector components:

$$\tan \theta = \frac{A_y}{A_x} \qquad (3\text{-}2b)$$

1.00 mV

θ

1.40 mV

electrical axis

Solve

The angle θ is measured from the positive x axis toward the positive y axis, so we can safely use Equation 3-2b. Using your calculator, you'll find that $\tan^{-1} 1.40 = 54.5°$. We saw in Example 3-1 that a second solution

$$\tan \theta = \frac{y \text{ component}}{x \text{ component}}$$

$$= \frac{1.40 \text{ mV}}{1.00 \text{ mV}} = 1.40$$

is 180° plus the result from your calculator, or 180° + 54.5°, or 234.5°. However, the figure above shows that θ is between 0 and 90°, so the correct answer is 54.5°.

$\theta = \tan^{-1} 1.40 = 54.5°$ or 234.5°

Correct answer: $\theta = 54.5°$

Reflect

If the horizontal and vertical signals were equally strong, the electrical axis would be tilted at an angle of 45° from the horizontal. In this example the vertical component is somewhat larger than the horizontal component, so the angle is a bit more than 45°. Normal clinical values are between −30° (that is, pointing 30° above the horizontal) and +90° (pointing straight down), so our result is reasonable.

Example 3-3 Adding Vectors Using Components

You travel 62.0 km in a direction 30.0° north of east, then turn to a direction 50.0° south of east and travel an additional 23.0 km (Figure 3-13). How far and in what direction are you from your starting point?

Figure 3-13 **A problem in vector addition** What is your net displacement?

Set Up

Each leg of the trip constitutes a displacement vector, which we show as $\vec{A}$ and $\vec{B}$ in the sketch. To find the magnitude and direction of the total displacement, which is just the vector sum $\vec{C} = \vec{A} + \vec{B}$, we will first find the x and y components of $\vec{A}$ and $\vec{B}$ using Equations 3-1. We'll then find the components of the vector sum $\vec{C}$ using Equations 3-3. Finally, we'll find the magnitude and direction of $\vec{C}$ using Equations 3-2.

$A_x = A \cos \theta$ (3-1a)
$A_y = A \sin \theta$ (3-1b)
$C_x = A_x + B_x$ (3-3a)
$C_y = A_y + B_y$ (3-3b)
$A = \sqrt{A_x^2 + A_y^2}$ (3-2a)
$\tan \theta = \dfrac{A_y}{A_x}$ (3-2b)

Solve

We choose the positive x axis to point east and the positive y axis to point north, and draw both $\vec{A}$ and $\vec{B}$ with their tails at the origin. The vector $\vec{A}$ points north of east at an angle of 30.0°, and the vector $\vec{B}$ points south of east at an angle −50.0° (negative since this angle is measured from the positive x axis in the direction *away from* the positive y axis). We use Equations 3-1 to find their components.

$A_x = (62.0 \text{ km}) \cos 30.0°$
   $= 53.7 \text{ km}$
$A_y = (62.0 \text{ km}) \sin 30.0°$
   $= 31.0 \text{ km}$

$B_x = (23.0 \text{ km}) \cos (-50.0°)$
   $= 14.8 \text{ km}$

$B_y = (23.0 \text{ km}) \sin (-50.0°)$
   $= -17.6 \text{ km}$

Given the components of $\vec{A}$ and $\vec{B}$, we can now find the components of $\vec{C} = \vec{A} + \vec{B}$ using Equations 3-3.

$C_x = A_x + B_x = 53.7 \text{ km} + 14.8 \text{ km} = 68.5 \text{ km}$
$C_y = A_y + B_y = 31.0 \text{ km} + (-17.6 \text{ km}) = 13.4 \text{ km}$

Now calculate the magnitude and direction of $\vec{C}$ using Equations 3-2. Both components of $\vec{C}$ are positive, so the vector points north of east and the angle θ_C is between 0 and 90°. Hence the desired angle is 11.1°, not 180° + 11.1° = 191.1°.

$C = \sqrt{C_x^2 + C_y^2}$
   $= \sqrt{(68.5 \text{ km})^2 + (13.4 \text{ km})^2}$
$C = 69.8 \text{ km}$

$\tan \theta_C = \dfrac{C_y}{C_x} = \dfrac{13.4 \text{ km}}{68.5 \text{ km}} = 0.195$

$\theta_C = \tan^{-1} 0.195 = 11.1°$

Reflect

The net displacement takes you 69.8 km from the starting point at an angle of 11.1° north of east. These numbers would be very difficult to get simply from the drawing of the two vectors shown above.

We now have all the mathematical tools that we need to study motion in two or three dimensions. In the next section, we'll begin this study by seeing how to relate the position, velocity, and acceleration of an object using vectors.

Take-Home Message for Section 3-4

✔ The easiest way to do arithmetic with vectors (adding, subtracting, and multiplying by a scalar) is to use components.

✔ For any problem involving vectors, it's essential to draw a sketch of the situation and to measure angles from the positive x direction toward the positive y direction.

✔ Be cautious using Equation 3-2b, $\tan \theta = A_y/A_x$. This equation actually gives two answers for the direction θ of a vector $\vec{A}$; your sketch will help you decide which answer is correct.

? Got the Concept? 3-4

Adding One Vector to Another Vector to Get a Third Vector

Vector $\vec{A}$ has components $A_x = 5$, $A_y = 3$ and vector $\vec{B}$ has components $B_x = 7$, $B_y = -2$. What are the components of the vector $\vec{D}$ that you must add to $\vec{A}$ to get $\vec{B}$?

3-5 For motion in a plane, velocity and acceleration are vector quantities

A hawk glides over a meadow at a shallow angle, then steepens its flight path to dive onto a mouse before sailing upward again (Figure 3-14a). How can an ornithologist describe the hawk's motion using the language of physics?

Just as for the straight-line motion that we discussed in Chapter 2, to have a complete description of the hawk's motion means that we must know its position at every instant of time. This knowledge requires that we have a reference point, or origin, from which to measure positions. Let's choose the origin to be at the point where the ornithologist stands and observes the motion. Then, at each instant we can visualize a **position vector** $\vec{r}$ that extends from the origin to the hawk's position at that instant. Figure 3-14b shows one such position vector. If we know what $\vec{r}$ is at each instant of time t, we know the path or **trajectory** that the hawk follows through space as well as what time the hawk passes through each point along that trajectory. In Figure 3-14b we have drawn dots to show the hawk's position at 1-s intervals, so this figure also shows the hawk's motion diagram.

For simplicity let's assume that our hawk moves in only two of the three dimensions of space, so it is in **two-dimensional motion**. This means that the hawk may move up and down as well as forward and back, but doesn't turn left or right. One key reason for making this simplifying assumption is that two-dimensional motion is a *lot* easier to

(a)

Figure 3-14 A hawk moving in a plane (a) Like all living creatures, hawks are able to move in more than one dimension. (b) The trajectory of a hawk's swooping flight. At any instant the hawk's position relative to the ornithologist is measured by a position vector $\vec{r}$.

(b)

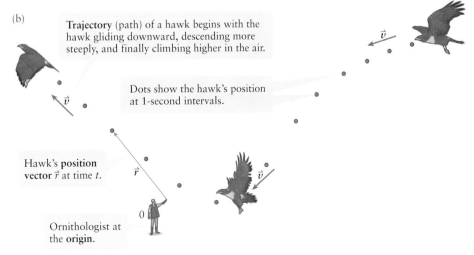

Trajectory (path) of a hawk begins with the hawk gliding downward, descending more steeply, and finally climbing higher in the air.

Dots show the hawk's position at 1-second intervals.

Hawk's **position vector** $\vec{r}$ at time t.

$\vec{r}$

Ornithologist at the **origin**.

$\vec{v}$

$\vec{v}$

$\vec{v}$

$\vec{v}$

draw than three-dimensional motion! More importantly, many real-life motions are two-dimensional. Some examples include the flight of a thrown baseball, the motion of a race car around a curved but level track, and Earth's orbit around the Sun. In these situations, all we need are two coordinate axes which we typically call x and y. In mathematics two such axes define a plane, so another name for two-dimensional motion is **motion in a plane**. If we use x and y to define the two perpendicular directions within the plane, we'll refer to this plane as the **x–y plane**.

The Velocity Vector

Just as for the one-dimensional motion that we studied in Chapter 2, understanding two- or three-dimensional motion means knowing how rapidly and in what direction the object moves along its trajectory. To see how to describe this type of trajectory, consider how the hawk shown in Figure 3-14b moves during a time interval between two instants of time that we call t_1 and t_2 (see Figure 3-15). The change of the hawk's position during that interval is its displacement vector $\Delta\vec{r}$ for that time interval. This vector points from the object's position at t_1 to its position at t_2, and is the difference between the object's position vector $\vec{r}_2$ at t_2 and its position vector $\vec{r}_1$ at t_1:

**Displacement vector equals the change in position vector over a time interval
(3-6)**

Displacement vector (change in position) of the object over the time interval from time t_1 to a later time t_2

Position vector of the object at later time t_2

$$\Delta\vec{r} = \vec{r}_2 - \vec{r}_1$$

Position vector of the object at earlier time t_1

To calculate the displacement vector, subtract the earlier value from the later value (just as for motion in a straight line).

If the time interval $t_2 - t_1$ between these two points is very small, $\Delta\vec{r}$ in Figure 3-15 is a very small vector and points very nearly along the hawk's trajectory, even if the trajectory is curved. By analogy to what we did for one-dimensional motion in Chapter 2, we define the hawk's **instantaneous velocity vector** $\vec{v}$ (or just **velocity vector** for short) at a given point along the trajectory as follows: Take the displacement $\Delta\vec{r} = \vec{r}_2 - \vec{r}_1$ for a very short time interval around that point and divide it by the duration $\Delta t = t_2 - t_1$ of the interval.

**Velocity vector equals displacement vector divided by time interval
(3-7)**

Velocity vector for the object over a very short time interval from time t_1 to a later time t_2

Displacement vector (change in position) of the object over the short time interval

$$\vec{v} = \frac{\Delta\vec{r}}{\Delta t} = \frac{\vec{r}_2 - \vec{r}_1}{t_2 - t_1}$$

For both the displacement and the elapsed time, subtract the earlier value from the later value.

Elapsed time for the time interval

Figure 3-15 The displacement vector and velocity vector The displacement and velocity vectors both point along the trajectory.

- An object's displacement during a short time interval is a vector that points from the object's position at the beginning of the interval to its position at the end of the interval.
- The object's velocity vector and displacement vector for that short time interval both point along the object's trajectory.

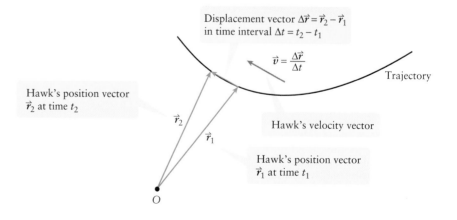

Displacement vector $\Delta\vec{r} = \vec{r}_2 - \vec{r}_1$ in time interval $\Delta t = t_2 - t_1$

$$\vec{v} = \frac{\Delta\vec{r}}{\Delta t}$$

Trajectory

Hawk's position vector $\vec{r}_2$ at time t_2

$\vec{r}_2$

$\vec{r}_1$

Hawk's velocity vector

Hawk's position vector $\vec{r}_1$ at time t_1

O

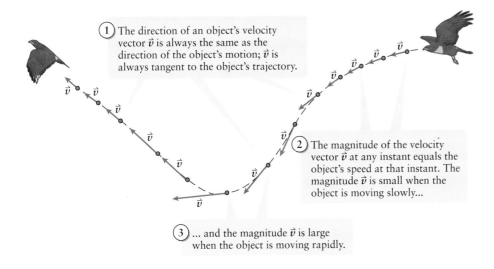

① The direction of an object's velocity vector $\vec{v}$ is always the same as the direction of the object's motion; $\vec{v}$ is always tangent to the object's trajectory.

② The magnitude of the velocity vector $\vec{v}$ at any instant equals the object's speed at that instant. The magnitude $\vec{v}$ is small when the object is moving slowly...

③ ... and the magnitude $\vec{v}$ is large when the object is moving rapidly.

Figure 3-16 **Velocity vectors on a curved trajectory** The varying velocity of the swooping hawk depicted in Figure 3-14.

The direction and magnitude at any instant of an object's velocity vector $\vec{v}$ tells you the direction of the object's motion and the object's speed at that instant.

This is the same as multiplying the displacement vector $\Delta\vec{r}$ by $1/\Delta t$ (see Figure 3-8). Since $1/\Delta t$ is positive, the velocity vector $\vec{v}$ defined by Equation 3-7 points in the same direction as $\Delta\vec{r}$. So the velocity vector at each point also points along the trajectory (Figure 3-16).

The *magnitude* v of the velocity vector is the magnitude of $\Delta\vec{r}$ divided by Δt: $v = |\vec{v}| = |\Delta\vec{r}|/\Delta t$. Note that $|\Delta\vec{r}|$ is just the distance that the hawk travels during the very short time interval of duration Δt. So the magnitude of the velocity vector, $v = |\Delta\vec{r}|/\Delta t$, is the instantaneous speed (distance per time) of the hawk at the instant in question. That's why the velocity vectors drawn in Figure 3-16 have different lengths at different points along the trajectory: $\vec{v}$ has a large magnitude where the hawk is moving rapidly and a small magnitude where the hawk is moving slowly (compare Figure 3-3). Like velocity and speed for motion in a straight line, the magnitude of the velocity vector $\vec{v}$ has units of meters per second (m/s).

Velocity Components

Just like any other vector, we can describe the velocity vector $\vec{v}$ of an object in terms of its components. The x component of $\vec{v}$, which we call v_x, equals the x component of displacement (the change in the x coordinate during the time interval, $\Delta x = x_2 - x_1$) divided by the time interval $\Delta t = t_2 - t_1$; we define v_y, the y component of $\vec{v}$, in a similar way. Thus

x component of the velocity vector $\vec{v}$

x component of the displacement during a short time interval

y component of the displacement during a short time interval

$$\text{(a) } v_x = \frac{\Delta x}{\Delta t} = \frac{x_2 - x_1}{t_2 - t_1}$$

$$\text{(b) } v_y = \frac{\Delta y}{\Delta t} = \frac{y_2 - y_1}{t_2 - t_1}$$

y component of the velocity vector $\vec{v}$

Elapsed time for the time interval

Components of the velocity vector (3-8)

You should recognize Equation 3-8a from Section 2-2: It's the same expression that we wrote for the average velocity along the x axis in straight-line motion. When the time interval is short, this expression also gives the instantaneous velocity. Equation 3-8b is the corresponding equation for straight-line motion along the y axis. Thus, we see that our two-dimensional vector definition of velocity is a natural extension of our definition of velocity for the case of straight-line motion.

Figure 3-17 An accelerating car Even if this car has a constant speed, it has an acceleration because its direction of motion—and hence the direction of its velocity $\vec{v}$—changes as it follows the curve of the road.

The Acceleration Vector and Its Direction

You are driving a car along a country road. You speed up along a straight part of the road, then slow down when you see a curve up ahead, and finally go around the curve at a constant speed (Figure 3-17). In which of these three cases are you accelerating?

The answer is that you are accelerating in *all* three of these cases: speeding up, slowing down, and turning. Remember from Section 2-4 that an object undergoes an acceleration whenever its velocity changes. Because velocity is a vector, this means that an object accelerates if there is a change in *any* aspect of the velocity vector $\vec{v}$. When your car speeds up (Figure 3-18a) or slows down (Figure 3-18b) while moving in a straight line, the *magnitude* of $\vec{v}$ changes and there is an acceleration. When your car is turning (Figures 3-18c and 3-18d), the *direction* of $\vec{v}$ changes and so there is also an acceleration, even if the car's speed doesn't change.

A car's throttle control or gas pedal is commonly called the accelerator, because depressing this pedal makes the car go faster. From the perspective of physics, however, a car has *three* "accelerator" controls: the gas pedal, which makes the car speed up; the brake pedal, which makes the car slow down; and the steering wheel, which changes the car's direction of motion.

What is the direction of a car's acceleration if it is turning? To see the answer, recall from Section 2-4 that for linear motion along the x axis, the acceleration a_x at a given time equals the change in velocity v_x during a very short time interval around that time divided by the duration of the time interval. For an object that moves in a plane, we have to consider the change in its velocity *vector* during a time interval. We again consider an infinitesimally short time interval from time t_1, when the object's velocity is $\vec{v}_1$, to a later time t_2, when the object has velocity $\vec{v}_2$. The object's **acceleration vector** $\vec{a}$ (short for **instantaneous acceleration vector**) at the time of this infinitesimal time interval is equal to the change in velocity $\Delta\vec{v} = \vec{v}_2 - \vec{v}_1$ divided by the duration $\Delta t = t_2 - t_1$ of the interval:

Acceleration vector equals change in velocity vector divided by time interval
(3-9)

Acceleration vector for the object over a very short time interval from time t_1 to a later time t_2

Change in velocity of the object over the short time interval

$$\vec{a} = \frac{\Delta\vec{v}}{\Delta t} = \frac{\vec{v}_2 - \vec{v}_1}{t_2 - t_1}$$

For both the velocity change and the elapsed time, subtract the earlier value from the later value.

Elapsed time for the time interval

(a) Speeding up in a straight line

The magnitude of the velocity vector is changing, so the object is accelerating.

(b) Slowing down in a straight line

The magnitude of the velocity vector is changing, so the object is accelerating.

(c) Turning right at a steady speed

(d) Turning left at a steady speed

An object accelerates if it speeds up, slows down, or changes direction. That's because in each case the velocity vector changes in either its magnitude or its direction.

The direction of the velocity vector is changing, so the object is accelerating.

Figure 3-18 Four different examples of acceleration An object is accelerating if *any* aspect of its velocity vector $\vec{v}$ is changing.

(a) Speeding up in a straight line

1. Add $\vec{v}_2$ and $-\vec{v}_1$ to form $\Delta\vec{v} = \vec{v}_2 - \vec{v}_1$:

2. Average acceleration $\vec{a}_{\text{average}}$ is in the same direction as $\Delta\vec{v}$ – in this case, in the direction of motion.

(c) Turning right at a steady speed

1. Add $\vec{v}_2$ and $-\vec{v}_1$ to form $\Delta\vec{v} = \vec{v}_2 - \vec{v}_1$:

2. Average acceleration $\vec{a}_{\text{average}}$ is in the same direction as $\Delta\vec{v}$ – in this case, toward the inside of the turn.

(b) Slowing down in a straight line

1. Add $\vec{v}_2$ and $-\vec{v}_1$ to form $\Delta\vec{v} = \vec{v}_2 - \vec{v}_1$:

2. Average acceleration $\vec{a}_{\text{average}}$ is in the same direction as $\Delta\vec{v}$ – in this case, opposite to the direction of motion.

(d) Turning left at a steady speed

1. Add $\vec{v}_2$ and $-\vec{v}_1$ to form $\Delta\vec{v} = \vec{v}_2 - \vec{v}_1$:

2. Average acceleration $\vec{a}_{\text{average}}$ is in the same direction as $\Delta\vec{v}$ – in this case, toward the inside of the turn.

The acceleration vector $\vec{a}$ points in the same direction as $\Delta\vec{v}$, and its magnitude equals the magnitude of $\Delta\vec{v}$ divided by Δt: $|\vec{a}| = |\Delta\vec{v}|/\Delta t$. Just like acceleration for motion in a straight line, the magnitude of the acceleration vector has units of meters per second squared (m/s^2).

While an object's velocity vector $\vec{v}$ always points along its trajectory, its acceleration vector may not. **Figure 3-19** shows how to find the direction of the acceleration vector $\vec{v} = \Delta\vec{v}/\Delta t$ for each situation shown in Figure 3-18. In **Figure 3-19a** a car is speeding up as it moves in a straight line. The velocity change $\Delta\vec{v}$ points in the same direction as the car's motion, and so its acceleration vector $\vec{a}$ is likewise in the direction of motion (the car "accelerates forward"). If instead the car slows down as it moves in a straight line as shown in **Figure 3-19b**, $\Delta\vec{v}$ and the acceleration both point opposite to the car's motion (it "accelerates backward"). In **Figures 3-19c** and **3-19d** the car is going around a curve at a constant speed. In this case the acceleration vector $\vec{a}$ is *perpendicular* to the car's trajectory and points toward the *inside* of the curve. If the car is turning to the right, as in Figure 3-19c, the acceleration $\vec{a}$ is to the right; if it is turning to the left, as in Figure 3-19d, the acceleration $\vec{a}$ is to the left. We can say that a car going around a curve "accelerates sideways." The same is true for a dog running in a circle or for a hawk circling in the sky above its prey.

You can convince yourself that the direction of acceleration is shown correctly in Figures 3-19c and 3-19d. To do this, note that *when you are riding in a vehicle that accelerates, you feel a push in the direction opposite the vehicle's acceleration.* (We'll see why this is so in Chapter 4.) If you're riding in a car that speeds up, you feel pushed *backward* into your seat. This push is opposite to the car's *forward* acceleration vector $\vec{a}$ (see Figure 3-19a). If the car brakes suddenly, you feel thrown *forward* in a direction opposite to the *backward* acceleration vector of the car (see Figure 3-19b). And if the car makes a turn at constant speed, you feel pushed to the *outside* of the turn. The acceleration vector $\vec{a}$ is opposite to this direction and hence must point to the *inside* of the turn as Figures 3-19c and 3-19d show.

Figure 3-19 Finding the direction of the acceleration vector An object's acceleration vector $\vec{a}$ for a given brief time interval points in the same direction as the difference $\Delta\vec{v} = \vec{v}_2 - \vec{v}_1$ between the object's velocities at the end and beginning of the interval. The four examples shown here correspond to the four situations in Figure 3-18.

Figure 3-20 shows another way to think about the direction of the acceleration vector $\vec{a}$. We can think of $\vec{a}$ at a given point along an object's trajectory as having two components: one that is perpendicular to the trajectory and one that points along the trajectory in the direction that the object is moving. The component of the object's acceleration perpendicular to the trajectory tells us about the change in the object's *direction*, and the component along the trajectory tells us about the change in the object's *speed*.

It's often useful to express the acceleration vector $\vec{a}$ of an object in terms of its x and y components. Use the symbols v_{1x} and v_{1y} for the velocity components of the object at time t_1, and the symbols v_{2x} and v_{2y} for the velocity components at time t_2. Then a_x, the x component of $\vec{a}$, equals the x component of velocity change ($\Delta v_x = v_{x2} - v_{x1}$) divided by the time interval $\Delta t = t_2 - t_1$, and the y component of $\vec{a}$ equals the y component of velocity change ($\Delta v_y = v_{y2} - v_{y1}$) divided by Δt:

Components of the acceleration
vector
(3-10)

x component of the
acceleration vector $\vec{a}$

Change in the x component of the
velocity during a short time interval

(a) $a_x = \dfrac{\Delta v_x}{\Delta t} = \dfrac{v_{x2} - v_{x1}}{t_2 - t_1}$

Change in the y component of the
velocity during a short time interval

(b) $a_y = \dfrac{\Delta v_y}{\Delta t} = \dfrac{v_{y2} - v_{y1}}{t_2 - t_1}$

Elapsed time for the time interval

y component of the
acceleration vector $\vec{a}$

In the next section, we'll use the component description of velocity and acceleration to help us analyze the motion of a *projectile*—an object moving through the air that is acted on by gravity alone.

Figure 3-20 Finding the acceleration of a swooping hawk How to find the acceleration vector of an object from its velocity vectors.

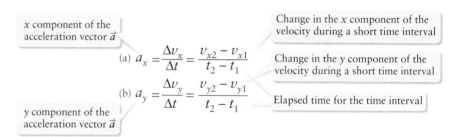

① Find the direction of $\vec{a}$ for (a) the interval from point 1 to point 2 and for (b) the interval from point 2 to point 3.

② For both intervals, there is a component of acceleration that points perpendicular to the trajectory (toward the inside of the turn). This describes changes in the hawk's direction of motion.

A hawk speeds up as it moves from point 1 to point 2, and slows down as it moves from point 2 to point 3.

For each interval we can break the acceleration a into a component along the trajectory and a component perpendicular to the trajectory.

④ For the interval from point 2 to point 3, there is a component of acceleration opposite to the direction of the hawk's motion. This describes the decrease in the hawk's speed.

③ For the interval from point 1 to point 2, there is a component of acceleration in the same direction as the hawk's motion. This describes the increase in the hawk's speed.

If an object's speed is increasing, $\vec{a}$ has a component in the direction of motion.
If an object's speed is decreasing, $\vec{a}$ has a component opposite to the direction of motion.
If an object's direction of motion is changing (the trajectory is curved), $\vec{a}$ has a component perpendicular to its trajectory that points towards the inside of the turn.

❓ Got the Concept? 3-5 Acceleration and Changing Speed

Figure 3-21 shows the acceleration vector $\vec{a}$ at several points along an object's curved trajectory. At each of points 1, 2, 3, and 4, is the object (a) speeding up, (b) slowing down, or (c) maintaining a constant speed?

At each point, the dashed line is perpendicular to the trajectory.

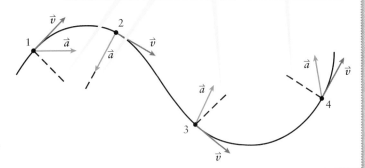

Figure 3-21 **Acceleration on a curved trajectory** At each of the points shown, is the object's speed increasing, decreasing, or staying the same?

Take-Home Message for Section 3-5

✔ If an object moves during a time interval, its displacement $\Delta\vec{r}$ is a vector that points from its position at the beginning of the interval to its position at the end of the interval.

✔ The velocity $\vec{v}$ of an object is a vector. It equals the displacement $\Delta\vec{r}$ for a very short interval multiplied by $1/\Delta t$ (1 divided by the duration of the interval). The velocity vector always points along the object's trajectory.

✔ The acceleration $\vec{a}$ of an object is also a vector. It equals the change in velocity $\Delta\vec{v}$ for a very short interval multiplied by $1/\Delta t$ (1 divided by the duration of the interval). The direction of the acceleration vector depends on how the object's speed is changing and on whether the object is changing direction.

3-6 A projectile moves in a plane and has a constant acceleration

We now have all the tools we need to analyze the kind of motion shown in the photograph that opens this chapter, in which clumps of molten lava fly through the air from a volcanic eruption. The curved paths followed by the lava are the same as those followed by streams of water from a fountain and by a leaping ballet dancer (Figure 3-22). If a path is curved, the direction of motion of an object which follows that path is constantly changing. Hence the object is *accelerating* at all points during the motion. What is the magnitude and direction of this acceleration?

If the object is moving through the air at a relatively slow speed so that air resistance can be neglected, the object's acceleration is due to gravity alone. Then the object is in *free fall* and has a constant downward acceleration, just as we discussed in Section 2-7. In that section, we looked only at motion that was straight up-and-down; now we want to consider **projectile motion**, which is free-fall motion that involves both vertical motion *and* horizontal motion. (We often refer to an object undergoing this kind of motion as a **projectile**.) Just as was the case for vertical free fall, the acceleration of a projectile is downward and has a magnitude g, called the *acceleration due to gravity*, for which we'll use the value $g = 9.80 \text{ m/s}^2$.

Projectile motion is always *two*-dimensional, so that the motion lies in a plane. To see why this is so, think about tossing a basketball upward and toward the east (Figure 3-23). When the ball leaves your hand, its velocity vector has a horizontal component toward the east, a vertical component that points upward, and zero component along the north–south direction. Because the acceleration vector points straight downward, there is *no* component of acceleration in a north–south direction. Therefore the north–south velocity doesn't change—this component of velocity starts at zero and remains zero. So the basketball always remains in a vertical plane that's oriented east–west, as Figure 3-23 shows.

(a)

(b)

Figure 3-22 **Two examples of projectile motion** (a) Water in a fountain. (b) A leaping ballet dancer.

Figure 3-23 Why projectile motion is two-dimensional motion The trajectory of a projectile is in a vertical plane because the acceleration due to gravity points downward.

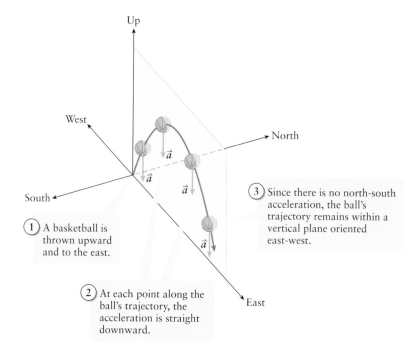

In Figure 3-24 we have drawn the acceleration vector at several points along a projectile's trajectory as well as the components of acceleration along and perpendicular to the trajectory. At *all* points, a perpendicular component of acceleration exists, so the projectile's direction of motion is changing at all points and the trajectory is curved all along its length. When the projectile is ascending, there is also a component of acceleration opposite to its motion, and so the projectile is slowing down. When the projectile is descending, there is an acceleration component in the direction of motion, which tells us that the projectile is speeding up. The only point at which the speed is instantaneously *not* changing is at the highest point of the trajectory, where the acceleration vector is entirely perpendicular to the trajectory. At this point the projectile has its *minimum* speed—just before reaching this point the speed is decreasing, and just after passing through this point the speed is increasing.

Figure 3-24 Projectile motion Acceleration components along and perpendicular to the trajectory.

• The acceleration $\vec{a}$ of a projectile is constant.
• Because the projectile's path is curved, $\vec{a}$ has varying components along and perpendicular to the direction of motion.

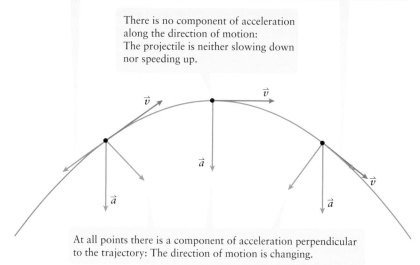

> # ! Watch Out! A projectile is a special case.
>
> Not every object in flight can be regarded as a projectile. As an example, a gliding bird is definitely *not* a projectile: The air exerts lift and drag forces on the bird that can't be ignored because these forces are comparable to the force of gravity. A batted baseball also feels a substantial drag force exerted by the air because of its high speed (much greater than the speed of the basketball in Figure 3-23), so this object isn't really a projectile either. Nonetheless, studying projectile motion is an important first step toward understanding these more complex kinds of motion.

The Equations of Projectile Motion

Let's be more quantitative about how a projectile's velocity changes during its flight. We use the x and y axes to define the plane in which the projectile moves, with the positive x axis pointing in a horizontal direction and the positive y axis pointing vertically upward (Figure 3-25). Because the constant acceleration vector $\vec{a}$ points vertically downward and has magnitude g, the components of $\vec{a}$ are

x component of the acceleration vector $\vec{a}$ for projectile motion

(a) $a_x = 0$

Zero value means that the x component of the velocity is constant.

(b) $a_y = -g$

y component of the acceleration vector $\vec{a}$ for projectile motion

Constant negative value means that the y component of the velocity is always decreasing, and decreases at a steady rate.

Components of the acceleration vector in projectile motion
(3-11)

> # ! Watch Out! Projectile motion means constant vertical acceleration.
>
> Just as for vertical free fall, it's important to remember that the vertical, y component of acceleration is the same ($a_y = -g$) at all times during projectile motion. This is true whether the projectile is moving upward, at the high point of its motion, or moving downward.

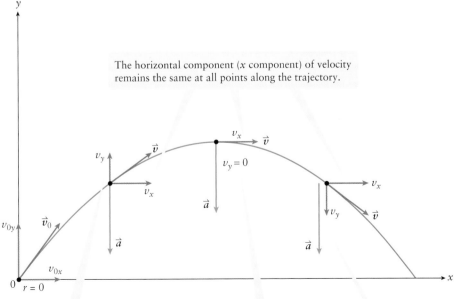

The horizontal component (x component) of velocity remains the same at all points along the trajectory.

The vertical component (y component) of velocity changes from positive (upward)... ... to zero (neither upward nor downward)... ... to negative (downward).

Figure 3-25 **Projectile motion: Horizontal and vertical components of velocity and acceleration** The acceleration due to gravity has a constant vertical component and no horizontal component. This determines how the velocity components vary with time.

Because both the x and y components of acceleration are constant, we can use our results from Chapter 2 to easily write down the equations that show how the x and y components of the projectile's velocity $\vec{v}$ vary with time. We'll let $t = 0$ represent the instant when the projectile begins its flight. At this moment, the projectile has x component of velocity v_{0x} and y component of velocity v_{0y}. (The "0" in the subscripts reminds us that these are the components at $t = 0$.) Equation 2-5 from Section 2-5 tells us that if the x component of acceleration is constant, the x component of velocity v_x as a function of time is $v_x = v_{0x} + a_x t$. The same equation rewritten for the y direction is $v_y = v_{0y} + a_y t$. If we substitute the values $a_x = 0$ and $a_y = -g$ from Equations 3-11, we get

Velocity, acceleration, and time for projectile motion
(3-12)

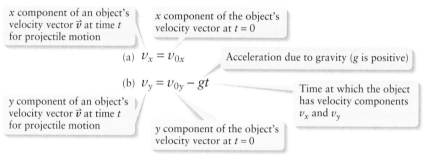

x component of an object's velocity vector $\vec{v}$ at time t for projectile motion

x component of the object's velocity vector at $t = 0$

(a) $v_x = v_{0x}$

Acceleration due to gravity (g is positive)

(b) $v_y = v_{0y} - gt$

Time at which the object has velocity components v_x and v_y

y component of an object's velocity vector $\vec{v}$ at time t for projectile motion

y component of the object's velocity vector at $t = 0$

Equation 3-12a tells us that *in projectile motion, the horizontal component of velocity doesn't change.* The acceleration due to gravity affects only the vertical component of velocity, so nothing acts to change the horizontal velocity. The vertical component of velocity *does* change with time, however; as Equation 3-12b shows, the y component of velocity decreases at a steady rate. If v_{0y} is positive as shown in Figure 3-25, v_y decreases to zero (at the high point of the trajectory) and then continues to decrease or becomes increasingly negative (that is, the projectile moves downward at an ever-faster rate).

We can use another equation from Chapter 2 to write down the equations for the projectile's x and y coordinates x and y at any time t. We let x_0 and y_0 be the projectile's coordinates at time $t = 0$. Because the x component of acceleration a_x is constant, we know that $x = x_0 + v_{0x}t + (1/2)a_x t^2$ from Equation 2-10 in Section 2-5. The same equation rewritten for the y direction is $y = y_0 + v_{0y}t + (1/2)a_y t^2$. For projectile motion $a_x = 0$ and $a_y = -g$, so these equations become

Position, acceleration, and time for projectile motion
(3-13)

x and y coordinates at time t of an object in projectile motion

x and y component at $t = 0$ of the object's velocity vector

(a) $x = x_0 + v_{0x}t$

Time at which the object has coordinates x and y

(b) $y = y_0 + v_{0y}t - \dfrac{1}{2}gt^2$

x and y coordinates at $t = 0$ of the object

Acceleration due to gravity (g is positive)

The shape of the curved path that the projectile follows in accordance with Equations 3-13 is called a **parabola**. You can see this shape in the photograph that opens this chapter and in Figure 3-22.

Interpreting Projectile Motion

You probably recognize Equations 3-12b and 3-13b from our discussion of free fall in Section 2-7; they're exactly the same as Equations 2-13 and 2-14, respectively. This result gives us the following interpretation of projectile motion:

Interpretation 1 Projectile motion can be regarded as a combination of two motions: (1) horizontal motion at a constant velocity and (2) vertical free fall.

The vertical and horizontal motions are *independent* of each other. To see this, notice that the expressions for v_x and x in Equations 3-12 and 3-13 involve only x quantities, while the expressions for y and v_y involve only y quantities. The multiflash photograph in Figure 3-26 helps to show how the horizontal and vertical parts of projectile motion are independent.

Another way to think about projectile motion is to first imagine what would happen if we could turn gravity off, so that $g = 0$. Then, a thrown projectile would have zero acceleration, its velocity would remain constant, and its trajectory would be a straight line. However, a projectile's trajectory curves downward because gravity *does* exist. Equation 3-13b tells us that after a time t, the projectile has been dragged downward by a distance $(1/2)gt^2$ from the straight-line path it would follow in the absence of gravity (**Figure 3-27**). We can summarize this view of projectile motion as follows:

Interpretation 2 Projectile motion can be regarded as a combination of two motions: (1) straight-line motion in the direction of the initial velocity and (2) a vertical motion that pulls the projectile downward a distance $(1/2)gt^2$ in time t.

Figure 3-28 illustrates this alternative interpretation. In this demonstration, a projectile is aimed directly at a hanging target. Just as the projectile starts its flight toward the target, the target is released and begins to fall. If gravity did not exist, the target wouldn't fall, the projectile would follow a straight-line path, and the projectile would score a direct hit on the target. Because gravity does exist, however, the target does fall and the projectile follows a curved path. But Figure 3-28 shows that the projectile still scores a direct hit. The reason is that gravity pulls *both* the projectile and the target downward by the *same* distance $(1/2)gt^2$ in a time t.

Equations 3-12 and 3-13 are the principal equations you will use in solving problems that involve projectile motion. We've compiled these equations into **Table 3-1**. However, you'll find that solving such problems is much easier if you keep in mind the ideas that went into Interpretations 1 and 2.

The yellow ball is projected horizontally.

At the same time, the red ball is dropped from rest.

The two balls have the same initial vertical velocity (zero) and the same vertical acceleration, so the vertical components of their motion are identical and they fall side by side.

Figure 3-26 Projectile motion: The vertical and horizontal components of motion are independent Although these two balls have different initial horizontal velocities, their initial vertical velocities—and hence their subsequent vertical motions—are identical.

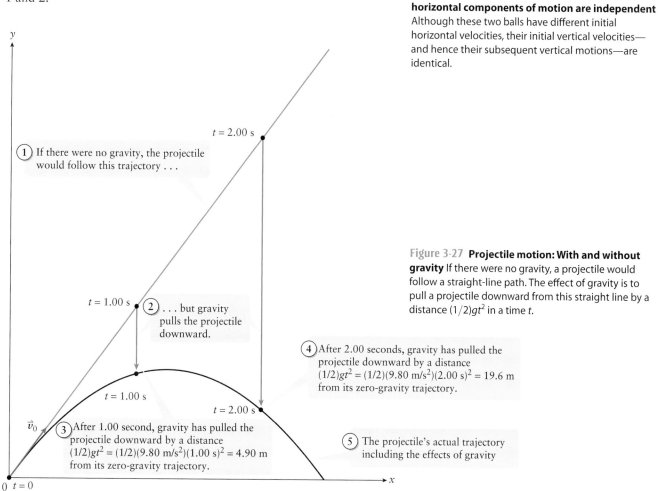

① If there were no gravity, the projectile would follow this trajectory . . .

$t = 2.00$ s

② . . . but gravity pulls the projectile downward.

$t = 1.00$ s

$t = 1.00$ s

$t = 2.00$ s

③ After 1.00 second, gravity has pulled the projectile downward by a distance $(1/2)gt^2 = (1/2)(9.80 \text{ m/s}^2)(1.00 \text{ s})^2 = 4.90$ m from its zero-gravity trajectory.

④ After 2.00 seconds, gravity has pulled the projectile downward by a distance $(1/2)gt^2 = (1/2)(9.80 \text{ m/s}^2)(2.00 \text{ s})^2 = 19.6$ m from its zero-gravity trajectory.

⑤ The projectile's actual trajectory including the effects of gravity

$\vec{v}_0$

$0 \quad t = 0$

Figure 3-27 Projectile motion: With and without gravity If there were no gravity, a projectile would follow a straight-line path. The effect of gravity is to pull a projectile downward from this straight line by a distance $(1/2)gt^2$ in a time t.

Figure 3-28 **Hitting a dropped target** This experiment demonstrates that all objects in free fall have the same downward acceleration.

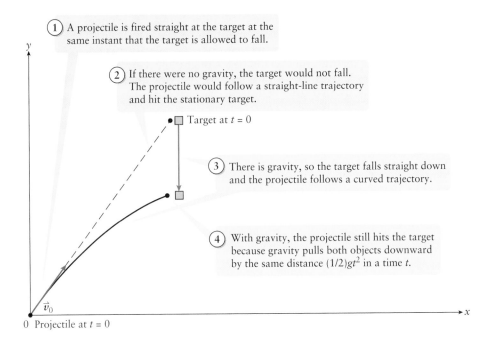

① A projectile is fired straight at the target at the same instant that the target is allowed to fall.

② If there were no gravity, the target would not fall. The projectile would follow a straight-line trajectory and hit the stationary target.

Target at $t = 0$

③ There is gravity, so the target falls straight down and the projectile follows a curved trajectory.

④ With gravity, the projectile still hits the target because gravity pulls both objects downward by the same distance $(1/2)gt^2$ in a time t.

$\vec{v}_0$

0 Projectile at $t = 0$

? Got the Concept? 3-6
The Changing Velocity of a Projectile

An object launched at some initial speed and angle follows a parabolic arc. At what point during the trajectory is the magnitude of its velocity the smallest? At what point, if any, will the velocity of the object be zero?

Table 3-1 Equations for projectile motion

By using one or more of these equations, you can solve any problem involving projectile motion. The check marks indicate which of the quantities t (time), x_0 (the x position at time 0), x (the x position at time t), v_{0x} (the x velocity at time 0), v_x (the x velocity at time t), y_0 (the y position at time 0), y (the y position at time t), v_{0y} (the y velocity at time 0), and v_y (the y velocity at time t) are present in each equation. Note that g, the magnitude of the acceleration due to gravity, is a *positive* quantity.

Equation		Which quantities the equation includes								
		t	x_0	x	v_{0x}	v_x	y_0	y	v_{0y}	v_y
$v_x = v_{0x}$	(3-12a)				✔	✔				
$v_y = v_{0y} - gt$	(3-12b)	✔							✔	✔
$x = x_0 + v_{0x}t$	(3-13a)	✔	✔	✔	✔					
$y = y_0 + v_{0y}t - \frac{1}{2}gt^2$	(3-13b)	✔					✔	✔	✔	

Take-Home Message for Section 3-6

✔   A projectile is an object that is launched and then falls freely (that is, moves without air resistance).

✔   Only gravity acts on a projectile, so the acceleration is downward and has the same magnitude throughout the motion.

✔   Projectile motion can be thought of as a combination of horizontal motion with constant velocity and vertical free fall.

✔   Projectile motion can also be thought of as straight-line motion in the direction of the initial velocity with an additional downward motion due to gravity.

Go to Interactive Exercise 3-1 for more practice dealing with projectile motion

3-7 You can solve projectile motion problems using techniques learned for straight-line motion

In this section we provide examples of solving problems involving projectile motion. You should strive to follow the general steps demonstrated here when you solve your own problems.

Example 3-4 Cliff Diving I

A diver leaps from a cliff in La Quebrada (Acapulco), Mexico. The cliff is 30.0 m above the surface of the water. He leaves the cliff moving at 2.00 m/s at a 40.0° angle above the horizontal. If air resistance can be neglected, (a) how long does it take him to hit the water and (b) how far does he travel in the horizontal direction before reaching the ocean?

Set Up

We can treat the diver as a projectile because air resistance is negligible. We choose the origin ($x_0 = 0$, $y_0 = 0$) to be where the diver leaves the cliff and starts to move as a projectile. The diver's initial velocity (of magnitude $v_0 = 2.00$ m/s and angle $\theta_0 = 40.0°$) has a positive x component and a positive y component that we can find using trigonometry. In part (a) we want to find the time t when he reaches the water at $y = -30.0$ m. Once we know the value of t, we'll use it in part (b) to find his x position at this time. This tells us how far he traveled horizontally during the dive. Table 3-1 tells us which equations to use for each part.

$$v_{0x} = v_0 \cos \theta_0$$
$$v_{0y} = v_0 \sin \theta_0$$

For part (a):
$$y = y_0 + v_{0y}t - \frac{1}{2}gt^2 \quad (3\text{-}13b)$$

For part (b):
$$x = x_0 + v_{0x}t \quad (3\text{-}13a)$$

Solve

(a) First find the x and y components of the diver's initial velocity.

$$v_{0x} = v_0 \cos \theta_0$$
$$= (2.00 \text{ m/s}) \cos 40.0°$$
$$= 1.53 \text{ m/s}$$

$$v_{0y} = v_0 \sin \theta_0$$
$$= (2.00 \text{ m/s}) \sin 40.0°$$
$$= 1.29 \text{ m/s}$$

Then, solve Equation 3-13b for time t and insert the known values $y_0 = 0$, $y = -30.0$ m, $v_{0y} = 1.29$ m/s, and $g = 9.80$ m/s^2.

$$y = y_0 + v_{0y}t - \frac{1}{2}gt^2 \quad \text{or} \quad \frac{1}{2}gt^2 - v_{0y}t + (y - y_0) = 0$$

This is a quadratic equation of the form $at^2 + bt + c = 0$, with $a = g/2$, $b = -v_{0y}$, and $c = y - y_0$.

$$t = \frac{-b \pm \sqrt{b^2 - 4ac}}{2a} = \frac{-(-v_{0y}) \pm \sqrt{(-v_{0y})^2 - 4\left(\frac{g}{2}\right)(y - y_0)}}{2\left(\frac{g}{2}\right)}$$

$$= \frac{v_{0y} \pm \sqrt{v_{0y}^2 - 2g(y - y_0)}}{g}$$

$$= \frac{(1.29 \text{ m/s}) \pm \sqrt{(1.29 \text{ m/s})^2 - 2(9.80 \text{ m/s}^2)(-30.0 \text{ m})}}{9.80 \text{ m/s}^2}$$

$$= \frac{(1.29 \text{ m/s}) \pm \sqrt{590 \text{ m}^2/\text{s}^2}}{9.80 \text{ m/s}^2} = \frac{(1.29 \text{ m/s}) \pm (24.3 \text{ m/s})}{9.80 \text{ m/s}^2}$$

$$= 2.61 \text{ s} \quad \text{or} \quad -2.35 \text{ s}$$

The diver reaches the water after leaving the cliff at $t = 0$, so the solution for t that we want is the positive one.

$$t = 2.61 \text{ s}$$

(b) The x and y components of projectile motion are independent of each other, so we didn't use the diver's constant x component of velocity v_{0x} at all in part (a) when we calculated the time t for him to fall to the water's surface. We do need the value $v_{0x} = 1.53$ m/s to find the diver's x coordinate during the fall, however. We substitute this value along with $t = 2.61$ s from part (a) into Equation 3-13a to determine the diver's final horizontal position.

$$x - x_0 = v_{0x}t$$
$$= (1.53 \text{ m/s})(2.61 \text{ s})$$
$$= 3.99 \text{ m}$$

Reflect

This example illustrates that projectile motion problems can have more than one solution, just like problems in linear motion with constant acceleration (see Example 2-8 in Section 2-6) or free-fall problems (see Example 2-10 in Section 2-8). Be on your guard for this!

If gravity did not exist, in time $t = 2.61$ s the diver would travel horizontally: $x - x_0 = v_{0x}t$
$$= (1.53 \text{ m/s})(2.61 \text{ s})$$
$$= 3.99 \text{ m}$$

vertically: $y - y_0 = v_{0y}t$
$$= (1.29 \text{ m/s})(2.61 \text{ s})$$
$$= 3.37 \text{ m}$$

We can check our results by using Interpretation 2 of projectile motion. If there were no gravity, the diver wouldn't fall but would continue along a straight line at an angle of 40.0° above the horizontal. Then, in 2.61 s the diver would rise 3.37 m above the cliff in 2.61 s. In fact the diver falls a distance $\frac{1}{2}gt^2 = 33.4$ m below his zero-gravity trajectory in 2.61 s. The net result is that the diver goes through a vertical displacement of -30.0 m—exactly the displacement from the height of the cliff to sea level.

When gravity is considered, the diver falls a distance

$$\frac{1}{2}gt^2 = \frac{1}{2}(9.80 \text{ m/s}^2)(2.61 \text{ s})^2 = 33.4 \text{ m}$$

so the diver's net vertical displacement in 2.61 s is

$$3.37 \text{ m} - 33.4 \text{ m} = -30.0 \text{ m}$$

Example 3-5 Cliff Diving II

What is the velocity (magnitude and direction) of the diver in Example 3-4 when he enters the water?

Set Up

From Example 3-4, we know the diver's initial ($t = 0$) velocity components, $v_{0x} = 1.53$ m/s and $v_{0y} = 1.29$ m/s, as well as the time $t = 2.61$ s that it takes for him to fall to the surface of the water. We'll use this information and Equations 3-12 to calculate his velocity components v_x and v_y when he reaches the water. We'll then use trigonometry to find the magnitude and direction of his velocity at that point.

Velocity, acceleration, and time for projectile motion:

$$v_x = v_{0x} \tag{3-12a}$$

$$v_y = v_{0y} - gt \tag{3-12b}$$

Solve

Equation 3-12a tells us that v_x doesn't change as the diver plummets toward the water, so it has the same value as when he left the cliff at $t = 0$. By contrast, Equation 3-12b tells us that v_y decreases by an amount gt.

$$v_x = v_{0x} = 1.53 \text{ m/s}$$
$$v_y = v_{0y} - gt$$
$$= 1.29 \text{ m/s} - (9.80 \text{ m/s}^2)(2.61 \text{ s})$$
$$= -24.3 \text{ m/s}$$

The diver's x and y components of velocity and his speed v make up the three sides of a right triangle, so we can find v from v_x and v_y using the Pythagorean theorem. Note from the sketch that because v_x is positive and v_y is negative, the angle θ must be between 0 and $-90°$.

Magnitude of $\vec{v}$:
$$v = \sqrt{v_x^2 + v_y^2}$$
$$= \sqrt{(1.53 \text{ m/s})^2 + (-24.3 \text{ m/s})^2}$$
$$= 24.3 \text{ m/s}$$

Direction of $\vec{v}$:
$$\tan \theta = \frac{v_y}{v_x}$$
$$= \frac{-24.3 \text{ m/s}}{1.53 \text{ m/s}} = -15.9$$
$$\theta = \tan^{-1}(-15.9)$$
$$= -86.4°$$

Reflect

To three significant figures, the diver's speed v is equal to the absolute value of his y component of velocity v_y. That's because the diver is descending at a very steep angle of almost $-90°$, so the x component of his velocity is very small compared to the y component.

The diver is moving at a substantial speed when he enters the water. You can show that $v = 87.5$ km/h or 54.4 mi/h, comparable to the highway driving speed of an automobile. (In fact the diver's speed will be somewhat less due to the effects of air resistance.) That's why it's essential that the diver enter the water with his body oriented at just the right angle to avoid a painful "belly flop."

Example 3-6 How High Does It Go?

A frog hops so that it leaves the ground at speed v_0 and at an angle θ_0 above the horizontal. What is the maximum height that the frog reaches during its leap? Ignore air resistance.

Set Up

We considered a similar problem in Example 2-10 (Section 2-8), in which a springbok jumped straight up. For both the springbok and the frog, the y component of velocity is zero at the peak of the motion (when the animal is moving neither up nor down). Unlike the springbok, the frog also has an x component of velocity, but this has no effect on the up-and-down motion. (Remember, the horizontal and vertical motions of a projectile are independent.)

We use a coordinate system as shown in the sketch, with the origin at the frog's starting point so that its initial coordinates are $x_0 = 0$, $y_0 = 0$. We'll use Equation 3-12b to find the time t_1 when the frog's y component of velocity is zero, so that it is at the highest point of its leap. We'll then use Equation 3-13b to find the frog's y coordinate y_1 at this time.

Velocity, acceleration, and time for projectile motion:
$$v_y = v_{0y} - gt \qquad (3\text{-}12b)$$

Position, acceleration, and time for projectile motion:
$$y = y_0 + v_{0y}t - \frac{1}{2}gt^2 \qquad (3\text{-}13b)$$

Solve

First express the frog's initial y component of velocity v_{0y} in terms of its initial speed v_0 and launch angle θ_0. Then, substitute this expression into Equation 3-12b and solve for the time t_1 when $v_y = 0$.

Set $v_y = 0$ (corresponding to the high point of the motion) at time $t = t_1$, then solve for t_1.

$$v_{0y} = v_0 \sin \theta_0 \text{ so}$$

$$v_y = v_0 \sin \theta_0 - gt$$

$$0 = v_0 \sin \theta_0 - gt_1$$

$$gt_1 = v_0 \sin \theta_0$$

$$t_1 = \frac{v_0 \sin \theta_0}{g}$$

Now use Equation 3-13b to solve for the frog's y coordinate at time t_1. Substitute $y_0 = 0$, $v_{0y} = v_0 \sin \theta_0$, and $t_1 = (v_0 \sin \theta_0)/g$ from above.

$$y_1 = 0 + (v_0 \sin \theta_0)\left(\frac{v_0 \sin \theta_0}{g}\right)$$

$$- \frac{1}{2}g\left(\frac{v_0 \sin \theta_0}{g}\right)^2$$

$$= \frac{v_0^2 \sin^2 \theta_0}{g} - \frac{v_0^2 \sin^2 \theta_0}{2g} \text{ so}$$

$$y_1 = \frac{v_0^2 \sin^2 \theta_0}{2g}$$

maximum height $= y_1 = \dfrac{v_0^2 \sin^2 \theta_0}{2g}$

Reflect

In this example, our result is a formula rather than a number. Can you verify that our answer for y_1 has the correct units?

To interpret what this formula tells us, let's look at how the maximum height y_1 depends on the values of the frog's initial speed v_0 and launch angle θ_0 as well as on the value of g. Because y_1 is proportional to the square of v_0, doubling the frog's launch speed makes it go *four* times as high. Note also that y_1 is proportional to $\sin^2 \theta_0$. The sine function has its maximum value for $\theta_0 = 90°$, which corresponds to the frog jumping straight up. Both the dependence on v_0 and the dependence on θ_0 make sense; the frog leaps higher if its launch speed is greater or if it jumps at a more vertical angle.

Finally, note that y_1 is *inversely* proportional to g (the factor of g is in the denominator). Hence, if the value of g were smaller, you would divide by a smaller number to calculate y_1 and you would get a larger answer. This result also makes sense: If gravity were weaker, the frog would reach a greater height.

 Go to Interactive Exercise 3-2 for more practice dealing with projectile motion

Notice that we didn't construct Know/Don't Know tables for Examples 3-5 and 3-6. That's because the tables are more complicated than the tables we've used in previous examples and we must now resolve all of the motion variables (excluding time) into x and y components. However, we still used the Know/Don't Know *approach* to determine which expressions would be useful in solving these problems. Going forward, then, we will continue to use the Know/Don't Know approach to solving problems, even if we don't explicitly create the table.

Example 3-7 How Long Is It in Flight?

How much time does the frog in Example 3-6 spend in the air before it returns to the ground?

Set Up

The key phrase in the problem statement is "returns to the ground," which means that the frog (which started its flight at $y_0 = 0$) returns to $y = 0$. We'll calculate the time t_2 when this happens using Equation 3-13b:

Position, acceleration, and time for projectile motion:

$$y = y_0 + v_{0y}t - \frac{1}{2}gt^2 \quad (3\text{-}13b)$$

Solve

From Example 3-6, we know that the frog's initial y component of velocity is $v_{0y} = v_0 \sin \theta_0$. We substitute this into Equation 3-8b along with $y = 0$ and $y_0 = 0$, the mathematical statement that the frog has returned to ground level, and set $t = t_2$ (the time when the frog returns to ground level).

$$v_{0y} = v_0 \sin \theta_0$$

Equation 3-13b becomes

$$0 = 0 + (v_0 \sin \theta_0)t_2 - \frac{1}{2}gt_2^2$$

Clearly one solution to the above equation is $t_2 = 0$. But we know the frog lands after it takes off. So we divide this expression by t_2, eliminating the quadratic, and making it much simpler to find the second solution for t_2, which will be the time the frog *returns* to the ground.

$$0 = (v_0 \sin \theta_0) - \frac{1}{2}gt_2 \text{ or}$$

$$t_2 = \frac{2v_0 \sin \theta_0}{g}$$

Reflect

The interesting thing we learn from our calculations is that the time $t_2 = (2v_0 \sin \theta_0)/g$ for the frog to return to its starting height is exactly *twice* the time $t_1 = (v_0 \sin \theta_0)/g$ that we calculated in Example 3-6 for the frog to reach its maximum height. In other words, a projectile takes just as long to ascend from its starting height to its maximum height as it does to descend from its maximum height back to its starting height.

Example 3-8 How Far Does It Go?

When the frog in Examples 3-6 and 3-7 returns to the ground, how far from its launch point does it land?

Set Up

In Example 3-7 we calculated the time t_2 when the frog returns to the ground. Now we want to know the frog's distance from the launch point at $x_0 = 0$, $y_0 = 0$ at time t_2. This is just the x component of its displacement $x_2 - x_0$ at this time. We'll use Equation 3-13a to find that displacement.

Position, velocity, acceleration, and time for projectile motion:

$$x = x_0 + v_{0x}t \qquad (3\text{-}13a)$$

Solve

To find the frog's x component of displacement when it returns to the ground, substitute $t = t_2$ into Equation 3-13a. We also need the frog's initial x component of velocity, which from Example 3-6 is $v_{0x} = v_0 \cos \theta_0$. We'll call the x coordinate x_2 at time t_2. The distance $x_2 - x_0$ that the frog travels horizontally during its projectile motion is called the *horizontal range*.

$$x_2 - x_0 = v_{0x}t_2$$

At time $t_2 = (2v_0 \sin \theta_0)/g$, find the displacement $x_2 - x_0$:

Horizontal range:

$$x_2 - x_0 = (v_0 \cos \theta_0)\left(\frac{2v_0 \sin \theta_0}{g}\right) = \frac{2v_0^2 \sin \theta_0 \cos \theta_0}{g}$$

Reflect

The horizontal range is proportional to v_0^2 (which says that increasing the launch speed makes the frog go farther) and inversely proportional to g (which says that the frog would also go farther if gravity were weaker).

To understand how the horizontal range depends on the launch angle θ_0, it's helpful to rewrite our result (using a formula from trigonometry) as $v_0^2 \sin 2\theta_0/g$. This expression shows that horizontal range is greatest for $\theta_0 = 45°$, so that $2\theta_0 = 90°$ and the function $\sin 2\theta_0$ has its greatest value ($\sin 90° = 1$). For launch angles less than 45°, the horizontal range is shorter because the projectile is in

Horizontal range

$$= \frac{2v_0^2 \sin \theta_0 \cos \theta_0}{g}$$

From trigonometry,

$$2 \sin \theta_0 \cos \theta_0 = \sin 2\theta_0$$

so

$$\text{horizontal range} = \frac{v_0^2 \sin 2\theta_0}{g}$$

the air for a relatively short time and so cannot travel as far horizontally. For launch angles greater than 45° the projectile spends more time in the air yet has a shorter horizontal range because its initial velocity is directly mostly upward (see the sketch).

Notice that for $\theta_0 = 90°$ the horizontal range is *zero*: the projectile lands right back where it started. However, with this launch angle the projectile reaches the greatest possible height, as we discussed in Example 3-6.

! Watch Out! Air resistance affects range.

The rule that a launch angle of 45° gives the greatest horizontal range doesn't work for objects such as thrown footballs or batted baseballs. The reason is that air resistance plays a significant role in the flight of these objects, so their acceleration is not constant, their trajectories are not parabolic, and the formulas we've developed in this section don't apply. Detailed calculations that account for air resistance show that a batted baseball has the greatest horizontal range for a launch angle of about 35° above the horizontal.

? Got the Concept? 3-7 How Fast Is a Flying Frog?

Suppose the frog in Examples 3-6, 3-7, and 3-8 leaves the ground at a launch angle $\theta_0 = 45°$. If the frog's speed is v_0 when it leaves the ground, what is its speed when it is at its maximum height? (a) v_0; (b) between v_0 and $v_0/2$; (c) $v_0/2$; (d) between $v_0/2$ and zero; (e) zero; (f) not enough information given to decide.

Take-Home Message for Section 3-7

✔ In solving problems that involve projectile motion, you can use many of the same techniques that we used in Section 2-8 to solve one-dimensional free-fall problems.

✔ Equations 3-12 and 3-13 are essential tools for solving any projectile motion problem.

3-8 An object moving in a circle is accelerating even if its speed is constant

Any driver knows that it takes a harder tug on the steering wheel to make a car round a tight corner at high speed than it does to take a gentle curve at low speed. We saw in Section 3-5 that a car following a curved path experiences an acceleration directed toward the inside of the curve, and that the driver causes this acceleration by turning the steering wheel. So the car's acceleration must be greater for a high-speed, tight turn than for a low-speed, gentle turn. What we'd like to know is *how much* greater the acceleration must be. Or what is the relationship between the car's acceleration, its speed, and the radius of its circular path?

To see the answer, let's look at the relatively simple case of an object going around a circular path at a constant speed, also called **uniform circular motion**. Because the object's speed is constant, its acceleration vector $\vec{a}$ is perpendicular to its trajectory and directed toward the inside of the circle. In other words, $\vec{a}$ points toward the *center* of the circle (Figure 3-29). An acceleration that points in this direction is called a **centripetal acceleration**, which comes from a Latin term meaning "seeking the center." Let's see how to calculate the magnitude of the centripetal acceleration vector.

Analyzing Motion in a Circle

Figure 3-30a shows two points along the trajectory of an object in uniform circular motion around a circular path of radius r. From point 1 to point 2, the object travels a distance Δs around the circle, and an imaginary line drawn from the center of the circle to the object rotates through an angle $\Delta\theta$. We can write a simple relationship between Δs and $\Delta\theta$ provided that we express $\Delta\theta$ in *radians*:

$$\Delta\theta = \frac{\Delta s}{r} \ (\Delta\theta \text{ in radians}) \tag{3-14}$$

You can check this formula by thinking about the case in which the object goes all the way around the circle so that the distance Δs equals $2\pi r$, the circumference of the circle. Then Equation 3-14 says that $\Delta\theta = (2\pi r)/r = 2\pi$, which is just the number of radians that make up a complete circle.

If the time interval between points 1 and 2 is very short, the angle $\Delta\theta$ is small and the curved arc of length Δs is nearly a straight line. Then the lines from the center of the circle to points 1 and 2 and the curved arc form a triangle with two sides of length r separated by an angle $\Delta\theta$ and a third side of length Δs given by Equation 3-14 (see Figure 3-30b). Thus, Equation 3-14 is a relationship between the length Δs of the short side of the triangle, the length r of the two long sides, and the angle $\Delta\theta$.

Figure 3-30c shows why Equation 3-14 is useful: The velocity vector rotates through the same angle $\Delta\theta$ as the object moves from point 1 (velocity $\vec{v}_1$) to point 2 (velocity $\vec{v}_2$). Because the motion is uniform (that is, the speed is constant), $\vec{v}_1$ and $\vec{v}_2$ have the same magnitude v. In Figure 3-30d, we've converted $\vec{v}_1$ into $-\vec{v}_1$ by reversing its direction and placed the head of $-\vec{v}_1$ against the tail of $\vec{v}_2$ to form the vector difference $\Delta\vec{v} = \vec{v}_2 - \vec{v}_1$. This vector diagram is equivalent to a triangle with two sides of length v separated by an angle $\Delta\theta$ and a third side of length Δv, which is the magnitude of the velocity change between points 1 and 2 (Figure 3-30e).

- In uniform circular motion, the speed is constant but the object accelerates because the velocity $\vec{v}$ is always changing direction.
- Because the speed is constant, the acceleration $\vec{a}$ is always perpendicular to the velocity $\vec{v}$.
- $\vec{a}$ always points toward the center of the circle.

Figure 3-29 **Uniform circular motion** An object moving around a circle at a constant speed.

(a)
An object in uniform circular motion moves a distance Δs from point 1 to point 2.

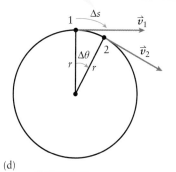

(b)
The three lengths r, r, and Δs approximate the three sides of a triangle.

(c)
The velocity vector of the object rotates throught the same angle $\Delta\theta$.

(d)
The vectors $-\vec{v}_1$, $\vec{v}_2$, and $\Delta\vec{v}$ form the three sides of a triangle... $\Delta\vec{v}$ is in the direction of the object's acceleration.

(e)
Both $-v_1$ and v_2 have the same magnitude v. This triangle is similar to that in part (b).

Figure 3-30 **Analyzing uniform circular motion**
(a) An object's circular path between points 1 and 2.
(b) A triangle relating the radius r of the circle, the distance traveled Δs, and the angle $\Delta\theta$. (c) Relating the velocity vectors at points 1 and 2. (d) Calculating the velocity change between points 1 and 2.
(e) A triangle relating the speed v, the magnitude Δv of the velocity change, and the angle $\Delta\theta$.

You can see that the triangle in Figure 3-30e is *similar* to the triangle in Figure 3-30b. Both triangles have two equal sides separated by the same angle, and so the relationship between the lengths of their sides is the same. Comparing the two figures shows that Δv and v in Figure 3-30e correspond to Δs and r, respectively, in Figure 3-30b. So, we can write an equation involving Δv and v that's the equivalent of Equation 3-14:

(3-15)
$$\Delta\theta = \frac{\Delta v}{v}$$

We'd like to calculate the magnitude of the object's acceleration, which is equal to $a_{\text{cent}} = \Delta v / \Delta t$. (We use the subscript "cent" to remind us that the acceleration is *centripetal*.) To do this calculation, substitute the expression for $\Delta\theta$ in Equation 3-15 into Equation 3-14:

$$\frac{\Delta v}{v} = \frac{\Delta s}{r}$$

To get an expression for $a_{\text{cent}} = \Delta v / \Delta t$, multiply both sides of this equation by v and divide both sides by Δt. Then we get

(3-16)
$$a_{\text{cent}} = \frac{\Delta v}{\Delta t} = \left(\frac{\Delta s}{r}\right)\left(\frac{v}{\Delta t}\right) = \left(\frac{\Delta s}{\Delta t}\right)\left(\frac{v}{r}\right)$$

Now, the object's speed v is equal to the distance Δs that it travels divided by the time interval Δt required to travel this distance: $v = \Delta s / \Delta t$. Therefore we can replace $\Delta s / \Delta t$ in Equation 3-16 by v, and our expression for the object's centripetal acceleration becomes $a_{\text{cent}} = v(v/r)$, or

Centripetal acceleration: Magnitude of the acceleration of an object in uniform circular motion

Speed of an object as it moves around the circle

Centripetal acceleration
(3-17)
$$a_{\text{cent}} = \frac{v^2}{r}$$

Radius of the circle

You should check for yourself that the expression v^2/r in this equation has the correct units for acceleration.

Equation 3-17 tells us that the magnitude of the centripetal acceleration is proportional to the square of the speed and inversely proportional to the radius of the circle. So, there is greater centripetal acceleration the greater the object's speed and the smaller the radius (and hence the tighter the turn). That's entirely consistent with our discussion at the beginning of this section.

Although we derived Equation 3-17 for the case of an object moving around a circle at constant speed, it's actually much more general than that. The same equation applies to an object that travels at constant speed around any *portion* of a circle. As an example, think of a bird initially flying north that makes a 90° right turn along a semicircular arc at constant speed until it is heading east, then levels out and flies straight. The part of the bird's flight during which it is turning constitutes uniform circular motion, with an acceleration directed toward the center of the circle of which the arc is part (Figure 3-31).

Equation 3-17 is also valid when the object's speed changes (a case called *nonuniform* circular motion). In this case, as we saw in Section 3-6, the acceleration vector has both a component along the direction of motion (which describes changes in the speed) and a component perpendicular to the motion (which describes changes in the direction of motion). It turns out that the magnitude of this perpendicular component at each point around the circular path is given correctly by Equation 3-17, $a_{\text{cent}} = v^2/r$, provided that we set v equal to the instantaneous value of the speed at that point (Figure 3-32).

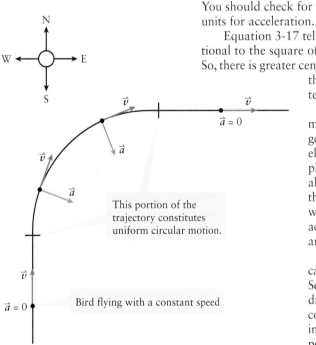

This portion of the trajectory constitutes uniform circular motion.

Bird flying with a constant speed

Figure 3-31 Uniform circular motion along an arc An object doesn't have to travel all the way around a complete circle to be in uniform circular motion.

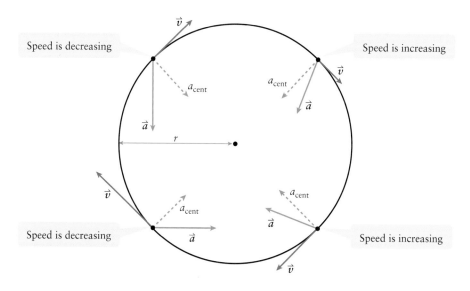

Speed is decreasing

Speed is increasing

Speed is decreasing

Speed is increasing

- If an object moves around a circle with varying speed, the acceleration $\vec{a}$ has a component along or opposite the direction of motion.
- Whether the speed is increasing, decreasing, or remaining constant, the acceleration has a component $a_{cent} = v^2/r$ directed toward the center of the circle.

Figure 3-32 Nonuniform circular motion If the speed varies in circular motion, the acceleration vector is not directed toward the center of the circle.

? Got the Concept? 3-8

Acceleration in Uniform Circular Motion

If an object is in uniform circular motion, its speed is constant. Is its *acceleration* constant?

Take-Home Message for Section 3-8

✔ If an object follows a curved trajectory, it has an acceleration even if its speed remains constant. Motion in a circle is an important example of motion of this kind.

✔ Uniform circular motion is motion around a circle at a constant speed. The acceleration of an object in uniform circular motion is centripetal: It points toward the center of the circle.

3-9 Any problem that involves uniform circular motion uses the idea of centripetal acceleration

Here are two examples of problems that involve motion around a circular path at constant speed.

Example 3-9 Around the Bend

A certain curve in a level road is signposted for a maximum recommended speed of 65 km/h. The curve is a circular arc with a radius of 95 m. What is the centripetal acceleration of a car that takes this curve at the maximum recommended speed?

Set Up
We are given the car's speed $v = 65$ km/h and the radius $r = 95$ m of its trajectory, so we can calculate its centripetal acceleration a_{cent} using Equation 3-17.

Centripetal acceleration:

$$a_{cent} = \frac{v^2}{r} \qquad (3\text{-}17)$$

Solve
We are given r in m and v in km/h. To calculate the car's acceleration in m/s², we must first convert v to m/s.

$$v = 65 \text{ km/h} \times \left(\frac{1000 \text{ m}}{1 \text{ km}}\right) \times \left(\frac{1 \text{ h}}{3600 \text{ s}}\right)$$
$$= 18 \text{ m/s}$$

Given the value of v, we calculate a_{cent} using Equation 3-17.

$$a_{cent} = \frac{v^2}{r} = \frac{(18 \text{ m/s})^2}{95 \text{ m}} = 3.4 \text{ m/s}^2$$

Reflect

The magnitude of the centripetal acceleration is just over one-third of the magnitude of the acceleration due to gravity during free fall. This certainly seems like a reasonable acceleration.

Example 3-10 Orbital Speed

The International Space Station (ISS) orbits Earth at an altitude of 360 km above Earth's surface. The acceleration required to keep the ISS in orbit along a circular path is provided by Earth's gravity, which is directed toward the center of Earth and hence toward the center of the orbit as shown in Figure 3-33. (Earth's gravitational pull decreases gradually with altitude, so the acceleration due to gravity that acts on the ISS is only 8.78 m/s^2.) (a) What is the orbital speed of the ISS in meters per second, kilometers per hour, and miles per hour? (b) How long (in minutes) does it take the ISS to complete an orbit? Note that the radius of Earth is 6378 km.

Figure 3-33 **An orbiting space station** The centripetal acceleration of an orbiting space station or other satellite is provided by Earth's gravity.

Set Up

We are given the ISS's centripetal acceleration a_{cent} and orbital radius r (the sum of Earth's radius and the altitude of the ISS, as the sketch shows). Using this information, we can calculate the speed v using Equation 3-17. Once we know v we can calculate the time T for the ISS to complete one orbit (that is, to travel a distance equal to the circumference of the orbit) using the relationship (speed) = (distance)/(time).

Centripetal acceleration:

$$a_{cent} = \frac{v^2}{r} \quad (3-17)$$

Solve

(a) We want an expression for the speed v of the space station, so we rearrange Equation 3-17 to put v by itself on the left-hand side.

$$a_{cent} = \frac{v^2}{r}$$
$$v^2 = ra_{cent}$$
$$v = \sqrt{ra_{cent}}$$

We calculate the orbital radius r by adding Earth's radius and the altitude of the ISS, then convert the result to meters.

$$r = 6378 \text{ km} + 360 \text{ km}$$
$$= 6738 \text{ km} \times \left(\frac{10^3 \text{ m}}{1 \text{ km}}\right) = 6.738 \times 10^6 \text{ m}$$

Substitute our calculated value of r into the expression for v.

$$v = \sqrt{(6.738 \times 10^6 \text{ m})(8.78 \text{ m/s}^2)}$$
$$= \sqrt{5.92 \times 10^7 \text{ m}^2/\text{s}^2} = 7.69 \times 10^3 \text{ m/s}$$

Convert the speed to km/h and mi/h:

$$v = 7.69 \times 10^3 \text{ m/s} \times \left(\frac{1 \text{ km}}{10^3 \text{ m}}\right) \times \left(\frac{3600 \text{ s}}{1 \text{ h}}\right)$$

$$= 2.77 \times 10^4 \text{ km/h}$$

$$v = 2.77 \times 10^4 \text{ km/h} \times \left(\frac{1 \text{ mi}}{1.609 \text{ km}}\right)$$

$$= 1.72 \times 10^4 \text{ mi/h}$$

(b) The distance that the ISS travels in one orbit is equal to the orbit circumference $2\pi r$. Because (speed) = (distance)/(time), the time T for one orbit equals the orbit circumference divided by the speed. We convert this answer to minutes.

$$\text{distance} = 2\pi(6.738 \times 10^6 \text{ m})$$

$$= 4.234 \times 10^7 \text{ m}$$

$$\text{time } T = \frac{\text{distance}}{\text{speed}} = \frac{4.234 \times 10^7 \text{ m}}{7.69 \times 10^3 \text{ m/s}}$$

$$= 5.51 \times 10^3 \text{ s} = (5.51 \times 10^3 \text{ s}) \times \left(\frac{1 \text{ min}}{60 \text{ s}}\right)$$

$$= 91.8 \text{ min}$$

Reflect

The sketch shows why there is one particular speed for a circular orbit of a given altitude. If you drop a ball, it falls straight downward. If you throw it horizontally, it follows a curved path before hitting the ground. The faster you throw the ball, the farther it travels prior to impact and the more gradually curved its trajectory. If you throw the ball with a sufficiently great speed, the curvature of its trajectory precisely matches the curvature of Earth. Then, the ball remains at the same height above Earth's surface and never falls to the ground. Putting a satellite such as the International Space Station into orbit works the same way, except that a rocket rather than a strong pitching arm is used to provide the necessary speed. Gravity is making the ISS "fall," but because of its high speed it falls *around* Earth rather than *toward* Earth. As we calculated in part (b), the ISS makes a complete orbit about every hour and a half.

Watch Out! What causes weightlessness—and what doesn't.

It's a common misconception that an object in orbit is "beyond the pull of Earth's gravity." It's true that an astronaut on board the International Space Station floats around the cabin *as though* she were weightless and unaffected by gravity. But if gravity didn't act on an orbiting satellite or its occupants, the satellite would have *zero* acceleration and hence couldn't stay in orbit: It would maintain a constant velocity and simply fly off into space in a straight line. In fact, a satellite such as the ISS remains in orbit precisely because it *does* feel the pull of gravity, which provides the acceleration necessary to make the satellite follow a circular trajectory around Earth. An astronaut on board the ISS *seems to* be weightless because she is really an independent satellite of Earth following the same orbit as the ISS does. Because the astronaut and the ISS are both following the same trajectory, there is nothing pushing the astronaut toward any of the station's walls. As a result, even though gravity is acting on the astronaut, she *feels* weightless.

Got the Concept? 3-9 Finding the Road Radius

If the car in Example 3-9 went around a curve at twice the speed assumed in that example, how much larger would the radius of the curve have to be in order that the centripetal acceleration be the same? (a) $\sqrt{2}$ times as large; (b) twice as large; (c) $2\sqrt{2}$ times as large; (d) 4 times as large; (e) 16 times as large.

3-10 The vestibular system of the ear allows us to sense acceleration

You can feel the effects of acceleration when you are pushed against the seat of an airplane during takeoff, thrown forward when the car you are riding in stops suddenly, or pushed into your seat when riding in a roller coaster car that makes a sharp turn. But you can also detect much more subtle accelerations, such as the gentle swaying of a hammock or a boat on a nearly still lake, even with your eyes closed. How do our bodies perceive such small accelerations?

The answer lies in the *vestibular system* of the ear (Figure 3-34). Part of the labyrinth of the ear, the vestibular system consists of a series of tiny, interconnected canals and chambers in the skull. Two structures sense the orientation of the head with respect to gravity, and three structures detect head rotation. Specialized cells in the vestibular system convert mechanical energy caused by movements of the head into electrical signals that are transmitted to the brain.

Any change in the motion of the head means that the head has experienced an acceleration, and two chambers at the center of the vestibular system detect the horizontal and vertical components of the acceleration vector. A layer of sensory cells is oriented vertically in one chamber and horizontally in the other. A bundle of microscopic, hair-like extensions called *cilia* stick up from each sensory cell into a gelatinous substance coated with a layer of calcium carbonate crystals. The rock-like appearance of these crystals gives them their name, *otoliths* ("ear stones" in Greek).

When the head accelerates, the relatively massive otoliths lag behind due to their inertia, which causes the cilia to bend. This bending causes the sensory cells to transmit an electrical signal to the brain. The sensory cells produce a maximum signal when the tip of a hair-cell bundle moves by less than 0.5 μm, so these cells are exquisitely sensitive to even gentle accelerations. In addition, each individual hair cell responds best to being bent in one particular direction. Any acceleration of the head therefore results in a unique pattern of nerve signals being sent to the brain, which enables you to tell both the magnitude and direction of the head's acceleration.

The other organs of the vestibular system detect *angular* acceleration (that is, the rate of change of your head's rotational motion). This is accomplished by three *semicircular canals* that are oriented perpendicular to one another (see Figure 3-34).

In a semicircular canal

Semicircular canals

Flow of fluid through semicircular canal

Cupula

Stereocilia

Hair cell

Support cell

Axon

Direction of body movement

Figure 3-34 **The inner ear** The organs that detect acceleration are located inside the fluid-filled chambers of the inner ear.

The interior of each canal is filled with fluid. Whenever the head rotates around the axis of one of the canals, the fluid inside it moves, bending a structure inside the canal called a *cupula* whose hair cells function like the cilia. The response of the brain to the resulting electrical signals it receives gives you the feeling of angular acceleration. Rotations of the head as small as 0.005° can be sensed in this way.

When the vestibular system functions normally, you are oblivious to its existence. If it malfunctions, however, you feel dizzy and may not be able to walk or even stand upright. In addition, if information from the vestibular system doesn't match the information from the eyes, the result is a sense of disorientation, like the feeling of seasickness some people experience in a small boat on choppy water.

> **Take-Home Message for Section 3-10**
>
> ✔ The vestibular system of the ear detects the acceleration vector of your head. It separately measures the horizontal and vertical components of acceleration.

Key Terms

acceleration vector (or instantaneous acceleration vector)
centripetal acceleration
component
direction
displacement vector
magnitude
motion in a plane
origin
parabola

position vector
projectile
projectile motion
scalar
trajectory
two-dimensional motion
uniform circular motion
vector
vector addition
vector components

vector difference
vector multiplication by a scalar
vector subtraction
vector sum
velocity vector (or instantaneous velocity vector)
x component
y component
x-*y* plane

Chapter Summary

Topic	Equation or Figure

Vectors and scalars: A vector quantity such as displacement or velocity has both a magnitude and a direction. By contrast, a scalar quantity such as temperature or time has no direction. We write a vector in boldface italic with an arrow above it. The magnitude of a vector $\vec{A}$ is written as A.

(d)

Vectors $\vec{H}$ and $\vec{J}$ have different magnitudes but the same direction.

Vectors $\vec{J}$ and $\vec{K}$ have the same magnitude but different directions.

Vectors $\vec{H}$ and $\vec{K}$ have different magnitudes and different directions.

 A vector has only two attributes: magnitude and direction.

(Figure 3-2d)

Vector arithmetic: To find the sum of two vectors $\vec{A}$ and $\vec{B}$, place them tip to tail. Then $\vec{A} + \vec{B}$ points from the tail of the first vector to the tip of the second vector. To find the difference $\vec{A} - \vec{B}$ of two vectors, add $\vec{A}$ and $-\vec{B}$ (a vector with the same magnitude as $\vec{B}$ that points opposite to $\vec{B}$). Multiplying a vector by a scalar can change the vector's magnitude, direction, or both.

(a)

$\vec{A}$

$\vec{C} = \vec{A} + \vec{B}$

Magnitude $A = 4$ m

$\vec{B}$

Magnitude $B = 3$ m

Magnitude of this vector sum:

$C = \sqrt{A^2 + B^2}$
$= \sqrt{(4\text{ m})^2 + (3\text{ m})^2}$
$= \sqrt{16\text{ m}^2 + 9\text{ m}^2}$
$= \sqrt{25\text{ m}^2} = 5$ m

(Figure 3-5a)

(Figure 3-8)

The number 3 is positive, so the vector $3\vec{A}$ points in the same direction as $\vec{A}$ but has 3 times the magnitude.

The number -2 is negative, so the vector $-2\vec{A}$ points in the direction opposite to $\vec{A}$ and has 2 times the magnitude.

Dividing a vector by 2 is the same as multiplying it by 1/2, so the vector $\vec{A}/2$ points in the same direction as $\vec{A}$ (since 1/2 is positive) and has 1/2 the magnitude.

Vector components: A vector can be expressed in terms of either its magnitude and direction or its components (the projections of the vector onto the x and y axes). The components can be calculated from the magnitude and direction, and the magnitude and direction can be calculated from the components.

(a)

This vector has a positive x component A_x and a positive y component A_y.

(Figure 3-9a)

The angle θ of the vector is measured from the positive x axis in the direction toward the positive y axis. Here θ is between 0 and 90°.

x component of the vector $\vec{A}$

y component of the vector $\vec{A}$

$$(a)\quad A_x = A \cos \theta \qquad (b)\quad A_y = A \sin \theta \tag{3-1}$$

Magnitude of the vector A

Angle of the vector $\vec{A}$ measured from the positive x axis toward the positive y axis

Magnitude of the vector $\vec{A}$

Angle of the vector $\vec{A}$ measured from the positive x axis towards the positive y axis

$$(a)\quad A = \sqrt{A_x^2 + A_y^2} \qquad (b)\quad \tan \theta = \frac{A_y}{A_x} \tag{3-2}$$

x component of the vector $\vec{A}$

y component of the vector $\vec{A}$

Vector arithmetic with components: To find the components of a vector sum $\vec{A} + \vec{B}$, add the respective components. To find the components of a vector difference $\vec{A} - \vec{B}$, subtract the respective components. To find the components of a vector $\vec{A}$ multiplied by a scalar c, multiply each component of $\vec{A}$ by c.

x component of the vector $\vec{C} = \vec{A} + \vec{B}$

x component of the vector $\vec{A}$

x component of the vector $\vec{B}$

$$(a)\quad C_x = A_x + B_x$$

$$(b)\quad C_y = A_y + B_y \tag{3-3}$$

y component of the vector $\vec{C} = \vec{A} + \vec{B}$

y component of the vector $\vec{A}$

y component of the vector $\vec{B}$

| x component of the vector $\vec{D} = \vec{A} - \vec{B}$ | x component of the vector $\vec{A}$ | x component of the vector $\vec{B}$ |

(a) $D_x = A_x - B_x$

(b) $D_y = A_y - B_y$

(3-4)

| y component of the vector $\vec{D} = \vec{A} - \vec{B}$ | y component of the vector $\vec{A}$ | y component of the vector $\vec{B}$ |

| x component of the vector $\vec{E} = c\vec{A}$ | Scalar c | x component of the vector $\vec{A}$ |

(a) $E_x = cA_x$

(b) $E_y = cA_y$

(3-5)

| y component of the vector $\vec{E} = c\vec{A}$ | Scalar c | y component of the vector $\vec{A}$ |

The displacement and velocity vectors: The displacement $\Delta\vec{r}$ of an object during a time interval is a vector that points from the object's position at the earlier time t_1 to its position at the later time t_2. The velocity vector $\vec{v}$ at a given time points along the object's trajectory; its magnitude is the object's speed. The components of $\vec{v}$ are given by the same expressions we used in Chapter 2 for velocity in linear motion.

Displacement vector (change in position) of the object over the time interval from time t_1 to a later time t_2

Position vector of the object at later time t_2

$$\Delta\vec{r} = \vec{r}_2 - \vec{r}_1$$

Position vector of the object at earlier time t_1

(3-6)

To calculate the displacement vector, subtract the earlier value from the later value (just as for motion in a straight line).

Velocity vector for the object over a very short time interval from time t_1 to a later time t_2

Displacement vector (change in position) of the object over the short time interval

$$\vec{v} = \frac{\Delta\vec{r}}{\Delta t} = \frac{\vec{r}_2 - \vec{r}_1}{t_2 - t_1}$$

Elapsed time for the time interval

For both the displacement and the elapsed time, subtract the earlier value from the later value.

(3-7)

x component of the velocity vector $\vec{v}$

x component of the displacement during a short time interval

(a) $v_x = \dfrac{\Delta x}{\Delta t} = \dfrac{x_2 - x_1}{t_2 - t_1}$

y component of the displacement during a short time interval

(b) $v_y = \dfrac{\Delta y}{\Delta t} = \dfrac{y_2 - y_1}{t_2 - t_1}$

y component of the velocity vector $\vec{v}$

Elapsed time for the time interval

(3-8)

The acceleration vector:
An object has a nonzero acceleration vector $\vec{a}$ whenever it is speeding up, slowing down, *or* changing direction. The x and y components of $\vec{a}$ are given by the same expressions we used in Chapter 2 for acceleration in linear motion. Alternatively, we can express $\vec{a}$ in terms of its component along the direction of motion (which describes changes in speed) and its component perpendicular to the direction of motion (which describes changes in direction).

Acceleration vector for the object over a very short time interval from time t_1 to a later time t_2

Change in velocity of the object over the short time interval   (3-9)

$$\vec{a} = \frac{\Delta\vec{v}}{\Delta t} = \frac{\vec{v}_2 - \vec{v}_1}{t_2 - t_1}$$

For both the velocity change and the elapsed time, subtract the earlier value from the later value.

Elapsed time for the time interval

x component of the acceleration vector $\vec{a}$

Change in the x component of the velocity during a short time interval

$$(a)\quad a_x = \frac{\Delta v_x}{\Delta t} = \frac{v_{x2} - v_{x1}}{t_2 - t_1}$$

Change in the y component of the velocity during a short time interval

$$(b)\quad a_y = \frac{\Delta v_y}{\Delta t} = \frac{v_{y2} - v_{y1}}{t_2 - t_1}$$

Elapsed time for the time interval

y component of the acceleration vector $\vec{a}$

(3-10)

Projectile motion: A projectile is a moving object acted on by gravity alone. It has a constant downward acceleration of magnitude g. In the equations for the motion of a projectile, we always choose the x axis to be horizontal and the y axis to point vertically upward.

- The acceleration $\vec{a}$ of a projectile is constant.
- Because the projectile's path is curved, $\vec{a}$ has varying components along and perpendicular to the direction of motion.

There is a component of acceleration opposite to the direction of motion: The projectile is slowing down.

There is a component of acceleration in the direction of motion: The projectile is speeding up.

There is no component of acceleration along the direction of motion: The projectile is neither slowing down nor speeding up.

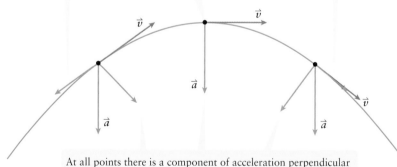

At all points there is a component of acceleration perpendicular to the trajectory: The direction of motion is changing.

(Figure 3-24)

x component of an object's velocity vector $\vec{v}$ at time t for projectile motion

x component of the object's velocity vector at $t = 0$

Acceleration due to gravity (g is positive)

(a) $v_x = v_{0x}$

(b) $v_y = v_{0y} - gt$

Time at which the object has velocity components v_x and v_y

(3-12)

y component of an object's velocity vector $\vec{v}$ at time t for projectile motion

y component of the object's velocity vector at $t = 0$

---

x and y coordinates at time t of an object in projectile motion

x and y component at $t = 0$ of the object's velocity vector

Time at which the object has coordinates x and y

(a) $x = x_0 + v_{0x}t$

(b) $y = y_0 + v_{0y}t - \dfrac{1}{2}gt^2$

(3-13)

x and y coordinates at $t = 0$ of the object

Acceleration due to gravity (g is positive)

Motion in a circle: For an object moving at constant speed around a circular path, the acceleration is centripetal (directed toward the center of the circle).

(Figure 3-29)

- In uniform circular motion, the speed is constant but the object accelerates because the velocity $\vec{v}$ is always changing direction.
- Because the speed is constant, the acceleration $\vec{a}$ is always perpendicular to the velocity $\vec{v}$.
- $\vec{a}$ always points toward the center of the circle.

Centripetal acceleration: Magnitude of the acceleration of an object in uniform circular motion

Speed of an object as it moves around the circle

(3-17)

$$a_{\text{cent}} = \frac{v^2}{r}$$

Radius of the circle

Answer to What do you think? Question

(c) The lava clump takes the *same* amount of time to climb to its maximum height as it does to descend from its maximum height back to its starting height. See Example 3-7 in Section 3-7.

Answers to Got the Concept? Questions

3-1 (c) The illustration shows the vectors $\vec{A}$ and $\vec{B}$ and the four combinations. One way to end up with a vector pointing southwest is to add a vector pointing west to a vector pointing south. Vector $\vec{B}$ points west. If we multiply vector $\vec{A}$ (which points north) by -1, the vector $-\vec{A}$ will point south. So $\vec{B} + (-\vec{A}) = \vec{B} - \vec{A}$ points southwest.

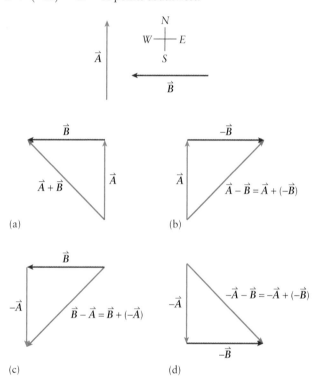

3-2 (a) You may have answered (d) if you assumed that the positive x direction points to the right and the positive y direction points upward. But the figure shows that in this case we've chosen the positive x direction to point upward and the positive y direction to point to the left. Hence the vector we want is $\vec{A}$, which points upward (in the positive x direction) and to the right (in the negative y direction). When thinking about vector components, always be mindful of the directions of the axes!

3-3 (a) no; (b) yes. A vector that has zero magnitude has zero length, and therefore cannot have components other than zero no matter what direction is chosen. However, any vector that has a nonzero magnitude will always have a component of zero length in the direction perpendicular to the vector. For example, a vector that points in the positive y direction has zero x component.

3-4 $D_x = 2$, $D_y = -5$ Our goal is to find a vector $\vec{D}$ with the property that $\vec{A} + \vec{D} = \vec{B}$, so $\vec{D} = \vec{B} - \vec{A}$. From Equations 3-4, the components of $\vec{D}$ are

$$D_x = B_x - A_x = 7 - 5 = 2$$
$$D_y = B_y - A_y = (-2) - 3 = -5$$

In other words, the x component of $\vec{D} = \vec{B} - \vec{A}$ is the x component of $\vec{B}$ minus the x component of $\vec{A}$, and similarly for the y component of $\vec{D} = \vec{B} - \vec{A}$. Our result tells us that the vector $\vec{D}$ has components $D_x = 2$, $D_y = -5$. If you wanted to, you could express $\vec{D}$ in terms of its magnitude and direction. But it's perfectly fine to write $\vec{D}$ in terms of its components as we have done here.

3-5 Point 1, (a); point 2, (c); point 3, (b); point 4, (a). At points 1 and 4 the object is speeding up, because its acceleration vector $\vec{a}$ points partially in the direction of motion (that is, partially in the direction of the velocity vector $\vec{v}$). At point 3 the acceleration vector points partially opposite to the direction of $\vec{v}$, so at this point the object is slowing down. At point 2, the object is neither speeding up nor slowing down, but is maintaining a constant speed. The acceleration vector is perpendicular to the velocity vector. Note that at all four points on this trajectory, the acceleration vector $\vec{a}$ points in whole or in part toward the inside of the trajectory's curve.

3-6 The magnitude of velocity is smallest at the peak of motion. At the peak the y component of velocity is zero, so regardless of the x component of velocity, the magnitude of $\vec{v}$ must be smallest. If the x component of velocity is zero, then the total velocity, both magnitude and direction, is zero at the peak. Because the x component of velocity v_x does not change, v_x can only be zero if the object initially has no x component of velocity ($v_{0x} = 0$; that is, if it is launched straight up).

3-7 (b) At its maximum height the y component of the frog's velocity is zero, and the x component of its velocity equals the x component of its initial velocity: $v_x = v_{0x} = v_0 \cos \theta_0$. Since $\cos 45° = 1/\sqrt{2} = 0.707$, at the frog's maximum height $v_x = 0.707 v_0$ and its speed is $0.707 v_0$—that is, between v_0 and $v_0/2$.

3-8 No. The *magnitude* of the acceleration $a_{cent} = v^2/r$ is constant, since the speed v is constant, but the *direction* of the acceleration vector is continually changing so that $\vec{a}$ points toward the center of the circle at all times (see Figure 3-29). Therefore the acceleration is *not* constant.

3-9 (d) The centripetal acceleration is given by Equation 3-17, $a_{cent} = v^2/r$. If the speed v is doubled, the numerator v^2 in the expression for a_{cent} increases by a factor of $2^2 = 4$. The radius r must also increase by a factor of 4 in order to maintain the same value of a_{cent}.

Questions and Problems

In a few problems, you are given more data than you actually need; in a few other problems, you are required to supply data from your general knowledge, outside sources, or informed estimate.

Interpret as significant all digits in numerical values that have trailing zeros and no decimal points. For all problems, use $g = 9.80 \text{ m/s}^2$ for the free-fall acceleration due to gravity.

• Basic, single-concept problem
•• Intermediate-level problem, may require synthesis of concepts and multiple steps
••• Challenging problem
SSM *Solution is in Student Solutions Manual*

Conceptual Questions

1. •(a) Can the sum of two vectors that have different magnitudes ever be equal to zero? If so, give an example. If not, explain why the sum of two vectors cannot be equal to zero. (b) Can the sum of three vectors that have different magnitudes ever be equal to zero? SSM

2. •What is the difference between a scalar and a vector? Give an example of a scalar and an example of a vector.

3. •Describe a situation in which the average velocity and the instantaneous velocity vectors are identical. Describe a situation in which these two velocity vectors are different.

4. •(a) Explain the difference between an object undergoing uniform circular motion and an object experiencing projectile motion. (b) In what ways are these kinds of motion similar?

5. •Consider the effects of air resistance on a projectile. Describe qualitatively how the projectile's velocities and accelerations in the vertical and horizontal directions differ when the effects of air resistance are ignored and when the effects are considered. SSM

6. •**Astronomy** If you were playing tennis on the Moon, what adjustments would you need to make in order for your shots to stay within the boundaries of the court? Would the trajectories of the balls look different on the Moon compared to on Earth?

7. •Explain what is meant by the magnitude of a vector.

8. •During the motion of a projectile, which of the following quantities are constant during the flight: x, y, vx, vy, ax, ay? (Neglect any effects due to air resistance.)

9. •For a given, fixed launch speed, at what angle should you launch a projectile to achieve (a) the longest range, (b) the longest time of flight, and (c) the greatest height? (Neglect any effects due to air resistance.) SSM

10. •A rock is thrown from a bridge at an angle 20° below horizontal. At the instant of impact, is the rock's speed greater than, less than, or equal to the speed with which it was thrown? Explain your answer. (Neglect any effects due to air resistance.)

11. •**Sports** A soccer player kicks a ball at an angle 60° from the ground. The soccer ball hits the ground some distance away. Is there any point at which the velocity and acceleration vectors are perpendicular to each other? Explain your answer. (Neglect any effects due to air resistance.)

12. •**Sports** Suppose you are the coach of a champion long jumper. Would you suggest that she take off at an angle less than 45°? Why or why not?

13. •An ape swings through the jungle by hanging from a vine. At the lowest point of its motion, is the ape accelerating? If so, what is the direction of its acceleration? SSM

14. •A cyclist rides around a flat, circular track at constant speed. Is his acceleration vector zero? Explain your answer.

15. •You are driving your car in a circular path on flat ground with a constant speed. At the instant you are driving north and turning right, are you accelerating? If so, what is the direction of your acceleration at that moment? If not, why not?

Multiple-Choice Questions

16. •Which of the following is not a vector?
    A. average velocity
    B. instantaneous velocity
    C. distance
    D. displacement
    E. acceleration

17. •Vector $\vec{A}$ has an x component and a y component that are equal in magnitude. Which of the following is the angle that vector $\vec{A}$ makes with respect to the x axis in the same x–y coordinate system?
    A. 0°
    B. 45°
    C. 60°
    D. 90°
    E. 120° SSM

18. •The vector in Figure 3-35 has a length of 4.00 units and makes a 30.0° angle with respect to the y axis as shown. What are the x and y components of the vector?
    A. 3.46, 2.00
    B. −2.00, 3.46
    C. −3.46, 2.00
    D. 2.00, −3.46
    E. −3.46, −2.00

Figure 3-35 Problem 18

19. •The acceleration of a particle in projectile motion
    A. points along the parabolic path of the particle.
    B. is directed horizontally.
    C. vanishes at the particle's highest point.
    D. is vertically downward.
    E. is zero.

20. •Adam drops a ball from rest from the top floor of a building at the same time that Bob throws a ball horizontally from the same location. Which ball hits the ground first? (Neglect any effects due to air resistance.)
    A. Adam's ball
    B. Bob's ball
    C. They both hit the ground at the same time.
    D. It depends on how fast Bob throws the ball.
    E. It depends on how fast the ball falls when Adam drops it.

21. •**Sports** Two golf balls are hit from the same point on a flat field. Both are hit at an angle of 30° above the horizontal. Ball 2 has twice the initial speed of ball 1. If ball 1 lands a distance d_1 from the initial point, at what distance d_2 does ball 2 land from the initial point? (Neglect any effects due to air resistance.)
A. $d_2 = 0.5d_1$
B. $d_2 = d_1$
C. $d_2 = 2d_1$
D. $d_2 = 4d_1$
E. $d_2 = 8d_1$ SSM

22. •A zookeeper is trying to shoot a monkey sitting at the top of a tree with a tranquilizer gun. If the monkey drops from the tree at the same instant that the zookeeper fires, where should the zookeeper aim if he wants to hit the monkey? (Neglect any effects due to air resistance.)
A. Aim straight at the monkey.
B. Aim lower than the monkey.
C. Aim higher than the monkey.
D. Aim to the right of the monkey.
E. It's impossible to determine.

23. •The acceleration vector of a particle in uniform circular motion
A. points along the circular path of the particle and in the direction of motion.
B. points along the circular path of the particle and opposite the direction of motion.
C. is zero.
D. points toward the center of the circle.
E. points outward from the center of the circle.

24. •If the speed of an object in uniform circular motion is constant and the radial distance is doubled, the magnitude of the radial acceleration decreases by what factor?
A. 2
B. 3
C. 4
D. 6
E. 1

25. •You toss a ball into the air at an initial angle 40° from the horizontal. At what point in the ball's trajectory does the ball have the smallest speed? (Neglect any effects due to air resistance.)
A. just after it is tossed
B. at the highest point in its flight
C. just before it hits the ground
D. halfway between the ground and the highest point on the rise portion of the trajectory
E. halfway between the ground and the highest point on the fall portion of the trajectory

Estimation/Numerical Analysis

26. •If $\vec{r}$ has a magnitude of 24 and points in a direction 36° south of west, find the vector components of $\vec{r}$. Use a protractor and some graph paper to verify your answer by drawing $\vec{r}$ and measuring the length of the lines representing its components.

27. •A vector $\vec{r}$ has a magnitude of 18 units and makes a 30° angle with respect to the x axis. Find the vector components of $\vec{r}$ using a protractor and some graph paper to verify your answer by drawing $\vec{r}$ and measuring the length of the lines representing its components.

28. •**Sports** In the 1970 National Basketball Association championship, Jerry West made a 60-ft shot from beyond half court to lead the Los Angeles Lakers to an improbable tie at the

buzzer with the New York Knicks. West threw the ball at an angle of 50.0° above the horizontal. The basket is 10 ft from the court floor. Neglecting air resistance, estimate the initial speed of the ball. (The Knicks won the game in overtime.)

29. •**Sports** In Detroit in 1971, Reggie Jackson hit one of the most memorable home runs in the history of the Major League Baseball All-Star Game. The approximate trajectory is plotted in **Figure 3-36**. (The asymmetry is due to air resistance.) Using the information in the graph, estimate the initial speed of the ball as it left Reggie's bat. SSM

Figure 3-36 Problem 29

30. •Use a spreadsheet program or a graphing calculator to make (a) a graph of v_x versus time, (b) a graph of v_y versus time, (c) a graph of a_x versus time, and (d) a graph of a_y versus time for an object that undergoes parabolic motion. Identify the points where the object reaches its highest point and where it hits the ground at the end of its flight.

Problems

3-2 A vector quantity has both a magnitude and a direction

3-3 Vectors can be described in terms of components

3-4 Using components greatly simplifies vector calculations

31. •Vector $\vec{A}$ has components $A_x = 6$ and $A_y = 9$. Vector $\vec{B}$ has components $B_x = 7$, $B_y = -3$, and vector $\vec{C}$ has components $C_x = 0$, $C_y = -6$. Determine the components of the following vectors: (a) $\vec{A} + \vec{B}$, (b) $\vec{A} - 2\vec{C}$, (c) $\vec{A} + \vec{B} - \vec{C}$, and (d) $\vec{A} + \frac{1}{2}\vec{B} - 3\vec{C}$.

32. •Calculate the magnitude and direction of the vector $\vec{r}$ using **Figure 3-37**.

Figure 3-37 Problem 32

33. •What are the components A_x and A_y of vector $\vec{A}$ in the three coordinate systems shown in **Figure 3-38**? SSM

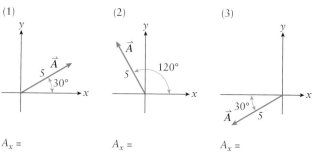

Figure 3-38 Problem 33

34. •Each of the following vectors is given in terms of its x and y components. Find the magnitude of each vector and the angle it makes with respect to the $+x$ axis.
    A. $A_x = 3, A_y = -2$
    B. $A_x = -2, A_y = 2$
    C. $A_x = 0, A_y = -2$

35. •$\vec{A}$ is 66.0 m long at a 28° angle with respect to the $+x$ axis. $\vec{B}$ is 40.0 m long at a 56° angle above the $-x$ axis. What is the sum of vectors $\vec{A}$ and $\vec{B}$ (magnitude and angle with the $+x$ axis)?

36. •Given the vector $\vec{A}$ with components $A_x = 2.00$ and $A_y = 6.00$, and the vector $\vec{B}$ with components $B_x = 3.00$ and $B_y = -2.00$, calculate the magnitude and angle with respect to the $+x$ axis of the vector sum $\vec{C} = \vec{A} + \vec{B}$.

37. •Given the vector $\vec{A}$ with components $A_x = 2.00$, $A_y = 6.00$, the vector $\vec{B}$ with components $B_x = 2.00$, $B_y = -2.00$, and the vector $\vec{D} = \vec{A} - \vec{B}$, calculate the magnitude and angle with the $+x$ axis of the vector $\vec{D}$. SSM

38. •Two velocity vectors are given as follows: $\vec{A} = 30$ m/s, 45° north of east and $\vec{B} = 40$ m/s, due north. Calculate each of the resultant velocity vectors: (a) $\vec{A} + \vec{B}$, (b) $\vec{A} - \vec{B}$, (c) $2\vec{A} + \vec{B}$.

39. •What are the magnitude and direction of the change in velocity if the initial velocity is 30 m/s south and the final velocity is 40 m/s west?

40. •Consider the set of vectors in Figure 3-39. Nathan says the magnitude of the resultant vector is 7, and the resultant vector points in a direction 37° in the northeasterly direction. What, if anything, is wrong with his statement? If something is wrong, explain the error(s) and how to correct it (them).

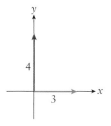

Figure 3-39 Problem 40

3-5 For motion in a plane, velocity and acceleration are vector quantities

41. ••The two vectors shown in Figure 3-40 represent the initial and final velocities of an object during a trip that took 5 s. Calculate the average acceleration during this trip. Is it possible to determine whether the acceleration was uniform from the information given in the problem? SSM

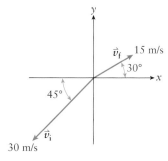

Figure 3-40 Problem 41

42. ••An object travels with a constant acceleration for 10 s. The vectors in Figure 3-41 represent the final and initial velocities. Carefully graph the x component of the velocity versus time, the y component of the velocity versus time, and the y component of the acceleration versus time.

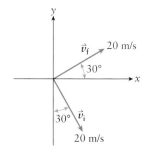

Figure 3-41 Problem 42

43. ••An object experiences a constant acceleration of 2.00 m/s² along the $-x$ axis for 2.70 s, attaining a velocity of 16.0 m/s in a direction 45° from the $+x$ axis. Calculate the initial velocity vector of the object.

44. ••Cody starts at a point 6.00 km to the east and 4.00 km to the south of a location that represents the origin of a coordinate system for a map. He ends up at a point 10.0 km to the west and 6.00 km to the north of the map origin. (a) What was his average velocity if the trip took him 4.00 h to complete? (b) Cody walks to his destination at a constant rate. His friend Marcus covers the distance with a combination of jogging, walking, running, and resting so that the total trip time is also 4.00 h. How do their average velocities compare?

3-6 A projectile moves in a plane and has a constant acceleration

3-7 You can solve projectile motion problems using techniques learned for straight-line motion

45. •An object is undergoing parabolic motion as shown from the side in Figure 3-42. Assume the object starts its motion at ground level. For the five positions shown, draw to scale vectors representing the magnitudes of (a) the x components of the velocity, (b) the y components of the velocity, and (c) the accelerations. (Neglect any effects due to air resistance.)

Figure 3-42 Problem 45

46. •An object undergoing parabolic motion travels 100 m in the horizontal direction before returning to its initial height. If the object is thrown initially at a 30° angle from the horizontal, determine the x component and the y component of the initial velocity. (Neglect any effects due to air resistance.)

47. •Five balls are thrown off a cliff at the angles shown in Figure 3-43. Each has the same initial velocity. Rank (a) the horizontal distance traveled, (b) the time required for each to hit the ground, and (c) the magnitude of the velocity when each hits the ground. (Neglect any effects due to air resistance.) SSM

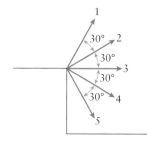

Figure 3-43 Problem 47

48. •Biology A Chinook salmon can jump out of water with a speed of 6.30 m/s. How far horizontally can a Chinook salmon travel through the air if it leaves the water with an initial angle of 40°? (Neglect any effects due to air resistance.)

49. •Biology A tiger leaps horizontally out of a tree that is 4.00 m high. If he lands 5.00 m from the base of the tree, calculate his initial speed. (Neglect any effects due to air resistance.) SSM

50. •A football is punted at 25.0 m/s at an angle of 30.0° above the horizon. What is the velocity vector of the ball when it is 5.00 m above ground level? Assume it starts 1.00 m above ground level. (Neglect any effects due to air resistance.)

51. •• A dart is thrown at a dartboard 2.37 m away. When the dart is released at the same height as the center of the

dartboard, it hits the center in 0.447 s. At what angle relative to the floor was the dart thrown? (Neglect any effects due to air resistance.)

3-8 An object moving in a circle is accelerating even if its speed is constant

3-9 Any problem that involves uniform circular motion uses the idea of centripetal acceleration

52. •A ball attached to a string is twirled in a circle of radius 1.25 m. If the constant speed of the ball is 2.25 m/s, what is the period of the circular motion?

53. •A ball spins on a 0.870-m-long string with a constant speed of 3.36 m/s. Calculate the acceleration of the ball. Be sure to specify the direction of the acceleration. SSM

54. •A washing machine drum 80.0 cm in diameter starts from rest and achieves 1200 rev/min in 22.0 s. Assuming the acceleration of the drum is constant, calculate the net acceleration (magnitude and direction) of a point on the drum after 1.00 s has elapsed.

55. •A 14.0-cm-diameter drill bit accelerates from rest up to 800 rev/min in 4.33 s. Calculate the acceleration of a point on the edge of the bit once it has achieved its operating speed.

56. •Riders on a Ferris wheel of diameter 16.0 m move in a circle with a radial acceleration of 2.00 m/s². What is the speed of the Ferris wheel?

57. •In 1892 George W. G. Ferris designed a carnival ride in the shape of a large wheel. This Ferris wheel had a diameter of 76 m and rotated one revolution every 20 min. What was the magnitude of the acceleration that riders experienced? SSM

58. •A car races at a constant speed of 330 km/h around a flat, circular track 1.00 km in diameter. What is the car's radial acceleration in m/s²?

59. ••Mary and Kelly decide they want to run side by side around a circular track. Mary runs in the inside lane of the track while Kelly runs in one of the outer lanes. What is the ratio of their accelerations?

60. •**Astronomy** We know that the Moon revolves around Earth during a period of 27.3 days. The average distance from the center of Earth to the center of the Moon is 3.84×10^8 m. What is the acceleration of the Moon due to its motion around Earth?

61. •**Astronomy** The space shuttle is in orbit about 300 km above the surface of Earth. The period of the orbit is about 5.43×10^3 s. What is the acceleration of the shuttle? (The radius of Earth is 6.38×10^6 m.) SSM

62. ••Calculate the accelerations of (a) Earth as it orbits the Sun, and (b) a car traveling along a circular path that has a radius of 50 m at a speed of 20 m/s.

63. •**Biology** In a vertical dive, a peregrine falcon can accelerate at 0.6 times the free-fall acceleration (that is, at $0.6g$) in reaching a speed of about 100 m/s. If a falcon pulls out of a dive into a circular arc at this speed and can sustain a radial acceleration of $0.6g$, what is the radius of the turn? SSM

64. •Commercial ultracentrifuges can rotate at rates of 100,000 rpm (revolutions per minute). As a consequence, they can create accelerations on the order of 800,000g. (A "g" represents an acceleration of 9.80 m/s².) Calculate the distance from the rotation axis of the sample chamber in such a device. What is the speed of an object traveling under the given conditions?

General Problems

65. ••You observe two cars traveling in the same direction on a long, straight section of Highway 5. The red car is moving at a constant v_R equal to 34 m/s and the blue car is moving at constant v_B equal to 28 m/s. At the moment you first see them, the blue car is 24 m ahead of the red car. (a) How long after you first see the cars does the red car catch up to the blue car? (b) How far did the red car travel between when you first saw it and when it caught up to the blue car? (c) Suppose the red car started to accelerate at a rate of a equal to 43 m/s² just at the moment you saw the cars. How long after that would the red car catch up to the blue car?

66. ••An experiment to measure the value of g is constructed using a tall tower outfitted with two sensing devices, one a distance H above the other. A small ball is fired straight up in the tower so that it rises to near the top and then falls back down; each sensing device reads out the time that elapses between the ball going up past the sensor and back down past the sensor. (a) It takes a time $2t_1$ for the ball to rise past and then come back down past the lower sensor, and a time $2t_2$ for the ball to rise past and then come back down past the upper sensor. Find an expression for g using these times and the height H. (b) Determine the value of g if H equals 25.0 m, t_1 equals 3.00 s, and t_2 equals 2.00 s.

67. ••**Sports** Steve Young stands on the 20-yard line, poised to throw long. He throws the ball at initial velocity v_0 equal to 15.0 m/s and releases it at an angle θ equal to 45.0°. (a) Having faked an end around, Jerry Rice comes racing past Steve at a constant velocity V_J equal to 8.00 m/s, heading straight down the field. Assuming that Jerry catches the ball at the same height above the ground that Steve throws it, how long must Steve wait to throw, after Jerry goes past, so that the ball falls directly into Jerry's hands? (b) As in part (a), Jerry is coming straight past Steve at V_J equal to 8.00 m/s. But just as Jerry goes past, Steve starts to run in the same direction as Jerry with V_S equal to 1.50 m/s. How long must Steve wait to release the ball so that it falls directly into Jerry's hands? SSM

68. ••You drop a rock from rest from the top of a tall building. (a) How far has the rock fallen in 2.50 s? (b) What is the velocity of the rock after it has fallen 11.0 m? (c) It takes 0.117 s for the rock to pass by a 2.00-m high window. How far from the top of the building is the top of the window?

69. ••You throw a ball from the balcony onto the court in the basketball arena. You release the ball at a height of 7.00 m above the court, with an initial velocity equal to 9.00 m/s at 33° above the horizontal. A friend of yours, standing on the court 11.0 m from the point directly beneath you, waits for a period of time after you release the ball and then begins to move directly away from you at an acceleration of 1.80 m/s². (She can only do this for a short period of time!) If you throw the ball in a line with her, how long after you release the ball should she wait to start running directly away from you so that she'll catch the ball exactly 1.00 m above the floor of the court?

70. ••Marcus and Cody want to hike to a destination 12.0 km north of their starting point. Before heading directly to the

destination, Marcus walks 10.0 km in a direction that is 30.0° north of east and Cody walks 15.0 km in a direction that is 45.0° north of west. How much farther must each hike on the second part of the trip?

71. •Nathan walks due east a certain distance and then walks due south twice that distance. He finds himself 15.0 km from his starting position. How far east and how far south does Nathan walk?

72. •••A group of campers must decide the quickest way to reach their next campsite. Figure 3-44 is a map of the area. One option is to walk directly to the site along a straight path 10.6 mi in length. Another option is to take a canoe down a river and then walk uphill 6.60 mi from the beach to the campsite. The campers estimate a hiking pace of 2.00 mi/h on the straight path and 0.500 mi/h walking up the hill. How fast would the canoe need to travel (assume a constant speed) in order for the second route to take less time than the first?

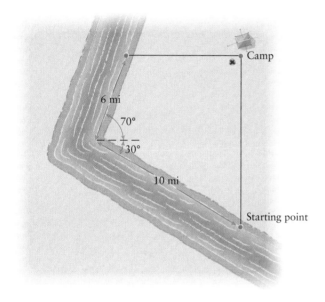

Figure 3-44 Problem 72

73. ••A water balloon is thrown horizontally at a speed of 2.00 m/s from the roof of a building that is 6.00 m above the ground. At the same instant the balloon is released, a second balloon is thrown straight down at 2.00 m/s from the same height. Determine which balloon hits the ground first and how much sooner it hits the ground than the other balloon. Which balloon is moving with the greatest speed at impact? (Neglect any effects due to air resistance.) SSM

74. •You throw a rock from the upper edge of a 75.0-m vertical dam with a speed of 25.0 m/s at 65.0° above the horizon. How long after throwing the rock will you (a) see it and (b) hear it hit the water flowing out at the base of the dam? The speed of sound in the air is 344 m/s. (Neglect any effects due to air resistance.)

75. •An airplane releases a ball as it flies parallel to the ground at a height of 255 m (Figure 3-45). If the ball lands on the ground at a horizontal displacement of exactly 255 m from the release point, calculate the airspeed of the plane. (Neglect any effects due to air resistance.)

255 m

255 m

Figure 3-45 Problem 75

76. ••An airplane flying upward at 35.3 m/s and an angle of 30.0° relative to the horizontal releases a ball when it is 255 m above the ground. Calculate (a) the time it takes the ball to hit the ground, (b) the maximum height of the ball, and (c) the horizontal distance the ball travels from the release point to the ground. (Neglect any effects due to air resistance.)

77. ••Sports In 1993, Javier Sotomayor set a world record of 2.45 m in the men's outdoor high jump. He is 193 cm (6 ft 4 in) tall. By treating his body as a point located at half his height, and given that he left the ground a horizontal distance from the bar of 1.5 m at a takeoff angle of 65°, determine Javier Sotomayor's takeoff speed. (Neglect any effects due to air resistance.)

78. ••Sports A boy runs straight off the end of a diving platform at a speed of 5.00 m/s. The platform is 10.0 m above the surface of the water. (a) Calculate the boy's speed when he hits the water. (b) How much time is required for the boy to reach the water? (c) How far horizontally will the boy travel before he hits the water? (Neglect any effects due to air resistance.)

79. •Sports Gabriele Reinsch threw a discus 76.80 m on July 9, 1988, to set the women's world record. Assume that she launched the discus with an elevation angle of 45° and that her hand was 2.0 m above the ground at the instant of launch. What was the initial speed of the discus required to achieve that range? (Neglect any effects due to air resistance.) SSM

80. •Astronomy The froghopper, a tiny insect, is a remarkable jumper. Suppose you raised a colony of the little critters on the Moon, where the acceleration due to gravity is only 1.62 m/s². If on Earth a froghopper's maximum jump height is h and maximum horizontal range is R, what would its maximum height and range be on the Moon in terms of h and R? Assume a froghopper's takeoff speed is the same on the Moon and on Earth.

81. ••Sports In 1998, Jason Elam kicked a record field goal. The football started on the ground 63.0 yards from the base of the goal posts and just barely cleared the 10-ft-high bar. If the initial trajectory of the football was 40.0° above the horizontal, (a) what was its initial speed and (b) how long after the ball was struck did it pass through the goal posts? (Neglect any effects due to air resistance.)

82. •••Sports In the hope that the Moon and Mars will one day become tourist attractions, a golf course is built on each. An average golfer on Earth can drive a ball from the tee about 63% of the distance to the hole. If this is to be true on the Moon and on Mars, by what factor should the dimensions of the golf courses on the Moon and Mars be changed relative to a course on Earth? (Neglect any effects due to air resistance.)

83. ••**Biology** Anne is working on a research project that involves the use of a centrifuge. Her samples must first experience an acceleration of $100g$, but then the acceleration must increase by a factor of 8. By how much will the rotation speed have to increase? Express your answer as a fraction of the initial rotation rate. SSM

84. •**Medical** In a laboratory test of tolerance for high angular acceleration, pilots were swung in a circle 13.4 m in diameter. It was found that they blacked out when they were spun at 30.6 rpm (rev/min). (a) At what acceleration (in SI units and in multiples of g) did the pilots black out? (b) If you want to decrease the acceleration by 25.0% without changing the diameter of the circle, by what percent must you change the time for the pilot to make one spin?

85. •**Medical** Modern pilots can survive radial accelerations up to $9g$ (88 m/s^2). Can a fighter pilot flying at a constant speed of 500 m/s and in a circle that has a diameter of 8800 m survive to tell about his experience?

86. •**Sports** A girl's fast-pitch softball player does a windmill pitch, moving her hand through a circular arc with her arm straight. She releases the ball at a speed of 24.6 m/s. Just before the ball leaves her hand, the ball's radial acceleration is 1960 m/s^2. What is the length of her arm from the pivot point at her shoulder?

4

Forces and Motion I: Newton's Laws

In this chapter, your goals are to:

- (4-1) Describe the importance of forces in determining how an object moves.
- (4-2) Use Newton's second law to relate the net force on an object to the object's acceleration.
- (4-3) Recognize the distinctions among mass, weight, and inertia.
- (4-4) Draw and use free-body diagrams in problems that involve forces.
- (4-5) Describe how Newton's third law relates forces that act on different objects.
- (4-6) Apply the sequence of steps used in solving all problems involving forces, including those that also involve kinematics.
- (4-7) Identify the forces that a fish uses for propulsion.

To master this chapter, you should review:

- (2-2, 2-3, and 2-4) The ideas of displacement, velocity, and acceleration for motion in a straight line.
- (2-5, 2-6) The concepts and equations of straight-line motion with constant acceleration.
- (3-2, 3-3, and 3-4) How to add vectors and how to do vector calculations using components.
- (3-5) The ideas of displacement, velocity, and acceleration in two dimensions.

> **What do you think?**
>
> If the sled dogs pull with double the force needed to maintain a constant velocity, what will happen to the sled? (a) It will move with a faster constant speed; (b) it will move for a while with a constant speed, and then its speed will increase; (c) its speed will increase continuously.

4-1 How objects move is determined by the forces that act on them

In the language of physics, the sled dogs in the above photo exert a *force* on the sled. Force is a vector: It has both magnitude and direction. For example, the force the dogs exert on the sled points in the direction of the sled's motion, while the ground exerts a friction force on the sled that points backwards (opposite to the sled's motion). The magnitude of each force is a measure of how strong it pushes or pulls on the sled.

What determines how the sled moves is not any one single force, but rather the combined effect of *all* the forces that act on it. If the forward force from the dogs has the same magnitude as the backwards friction force, these two oppositely directed force vectors cancel and add to zero. In this case, the sled moves with a constant velocity. But if the dogs pull harder than the force of friction, the forces do not cancel and there is a *net* force in the forward direction. Then the sled accelerates.

Experiment shows that no matter how hard the dogs pull on the sled, the sled pulls back on the dogs with an equally strong force. (The dogs feel this pull in their harnesses.) This turns out to be true for forces of all kinds: If one object exerts a force on a second object, the second object necessarily exerts a force on the first one.

These observations are at the heart of *Newton's laws of motion*, a time-tested set of physical principles that have a tremendous range of applicability. We'll use Newton's laws throughout the remainder of this book. We'll devote this chapter and the next to understanding these laws and some of their most important applications.

4-2 If a net external force acts on an object, the object accelerates

If you want to start a soccer ball rolling along the ground, you have to give it a push or kick. If you're a hockey goalie and want to deflect a puck away from the goal that you're defending, you have to hit the puck with your hockey stick. And if your dog runs off in pursuit of the neighbor's cat, you have to pull on the dog's leash to slow it down and bring it to a halt. In each of these cases you're changing the velocity of an object, either making it speed up (for the soccer ball), changing the direction of its motion (for the hockey puck), or making it slow down (for your dog). And in each case, to cause the object's velocity to change you have to exert a **force**—that is, a push or a pull—on that object.

Forces are *vectors* because they have both magnitude and direction. (You might pull a glass of your favorite beverage toward you or push a plate of cafeteria food away from you.) When more than one force acts on an object, the *directions* of the forces are just as important as their *magnitudes*; a force in one direction can cancel an equally strong force in the opposite direction. What determines how an object moves is the vector *sum* of all of the forces acting on that object, also called the **net external force** on the object (or, for short, the **net force**). If the individual forces acting on an object are $\vec{F}_1, \vec{F}_2, \vec{F}_3$, and so on, we can write the net force on that object as

The **net external force** acting on an object...   ...equals the **vector sum** of all of the individual forces that act on the object.

Net external force on an object (4-1)

$$\sum \vec{F}_{\text{ext}} = \vec{F}_1 + \vec{F}_2 + \vec{F}_3 + \ldots$$

The sum includes only external forces (forces exerted on the object by other objects).

For example, three forces act on a baseball player as he slides to get safely to base (Figure 4-1). One of these forces is the downward pull of Earth's gravity, called the **gravitational force** (denoted by a lowercase $\vec{w}$). The other two forces are exerted by the surface on which the player slides. The **friction force** on the player (which we denote by a lowercase $\vec{f}$) acts parallel to the surface and opposite to the player's motion. The friction force arises from chemical bonds that form between atoms on the ground and atoms on the player's uniform. These bonds resist being broken, so the player feels a

Figure 4-1 **Forces on a baseball player** (a) A baseball player sliding to get safely on base. (b) The vectors indicate the directions of each external force that acts on the player.

(a)

(b)
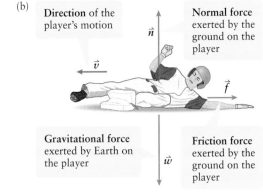

Direction of the player's motion

Normal force exerted by the ground on the player $\vec{n}$

$\vec{v}$

$\vec{f}$

Gravitational force exerted by Earth on the player $\vec{w}$

Friction force exerted by the ground on the player

 The **free-body diagram** of the player includes only forces exerted by other objects on the player (external forces). These include Earth's gravitational force (the player's weight) and forces from objects that the player is touching (in this case, the normal force and friction force exerted by the ground).

force slowing him down as he slides. The **normal force** on the player, by contrast, is directed perpendicular to the surface. (In physics and mathematics, "normal" is not the opposite of "abnormal"; rather, it's another word for "perpendicular.") Like the friction force, the normal force arises from interactions between atoms: The atoms in the player's uniform resist being squeezed into the atoms on the ground. This force, which we denote by a lowercase $\vec{n}$, prevents the player from falling through the ground below him. If you're sitting in a chair right now, you're feeling an upward normal force exerted by the chair on your rear end; if you're standing, you're feeling an upward normal force exerted on your feet by the ground.

The three forces that act on the baseball player in Figure 4-1 are called **external forces** because they are exerted by other objects outside of the player's body. The gravitational force is exerted by Earth as a whole, while the friction force and normal force are exerted by the ground that's in contact with the player.

Internal forces are also exerted by one part of the player's body on another. One example is the force that the player's shoulder exerts on his left arm to keep it from falling off. While internal forces are important for understanding the interactions of one part of the player's body with another, these forces are *not* included in the sum in Equation 4-1. That's why the left-hand side of that equation has the subscript "ext" for "external." In a moment, we'll see why it's appropriate to include only external forces in Equation 4-1.

Newton's Second Law

In the late seventeenth century, the English physicist and mathematician Sir Isaac Newton (1642–1727) published a treatise in which he described three fundamental relationships between force and motion. These relationships, called **Newton's laws of motion**, explain nearly all physical phenomena in our everyday experience. One of these relationships, commonly known as **Newton's second law**, is the most important for our discussion of forces. It states that

If a net external force acts on an object, the object accelerates. The net external force is equal to the product of the object's mass and the object's acceleration:

If a **net external force** acts on an object...   ... the object accelerates. The acceleration is in the same direction as the net force.

$$\sum \vec{F}_{ext} = m\vec{a}$$

Newton's second law of motion (4-2)

The magnitude of acceleration that the net external force causes depends on the mass m of the object (the quantity of material in the object). The greater the mass, the smaller the acceleration.

Newton's second law is simple to state but can be challenging to fully understand. Here are its three essential features:

(1) *A net force in a certain direction causes acceleration in that direction.* The baseball player shown in Figure 4-1 has a backward acceleration (he slows down) because the net force acting on him points opposite to the direction of his motion (Figure 4-2a). If we ignore air resistance, a falling basketball is acted on by only a single force, the downward gravitational force. So the net force on the ball is downward, and it accelerates downward (Figure 4-2b). This relationship between net force and acceleration is the reason why we devoted so much effort in Chapters 2 and 3 to understanding the nature of acceleration.

(2) *The magnitude of acceleration caused by the net force depends on the object's mass.* **Mass** is a measure of how much matter an object has. The SI unit of mass is the **kilogram**, abbreviated kg. A liter of water has a mass of one kilogram. Newton's second law says that the product of an object's mass and the object's acceleration equals the net external force on the object. So if you deliver identically strong kicks to a tennis ball (mass $m = 0.058$ kg) and to a soccer ball (mass $m = 0.43$ kg), the more massive soccer ball will experience less acceleration and will fly off with a slower speed.

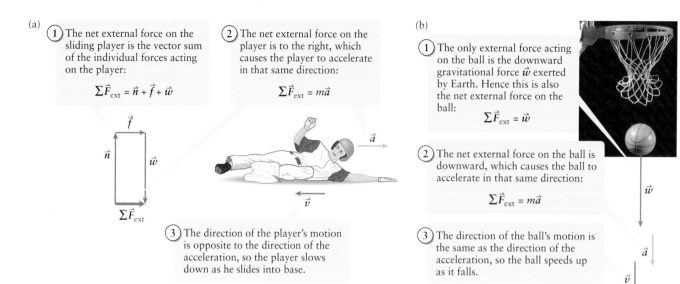

(a)

1 The net external force on the sliding player is the vector sum of the individual forces acting on the player:

$$\sum \vec{F}_{ext} = \vec{n} + \vec{f} + \vec{w}$$

2 The net external force on the player is to the right, which causes the player to accelerate in that same direction:

$$\sum \vec{F}_{ext} = m\vec{a}$$

3 The direction of the player's motion is opposite to the direction of the acceleration, so the player slows down as he slides into base.

(b)

1 The only external force acting on the ball is the downward gravitational force $\vec{w}$ exerted by Earth. Hence this is also the net external force on the ball:

$$\sum \vec{F}_{ext} = \vec{w}$$

2 The net external force on the ball is downward, which causes the ball to accelerate in that same direction:

$$\sum \vec{F}_{ext} = m\vec{a}$$

3 The direction of the ball's motion is the same as the direction of the acceleration, so the ball speeds up as it falls.

Figure 4-2 **The net external force determines acceleration** The net external force on an object is the vector sum $\sum \vec{F}_{ext}$ of the individual forces that act on that object. The acceleration $\vec{a}$ produced by the net external force is in the same direction as $\sum \vec{F}_{ext}$.

(3) *Only external forces acting on an object affect that object's acceleration.* As an example, sit in your chair with your feet off the ground and pull upward on your belt with both hands. No matter how hard you try, you can't lift yourself out of the chair! Your body has to accelerate to rise out of the chair (it has to go from being stationary to being in motion), but the force of your hands on your belt is an *internal* force (one part of your body pulls on another part). Thus, this force can't produce an acceleration. A helpful friend could lift you out of your chair, but that would happen by exerting an external force (one that originates outside your body).

To see the significance of mass more clearly, divide both sides of Equation 4-2 by the object's mass *m*:

Newton's second law, alternative form
(4-3)

The **acceleration** of an object...   ...is proportional to and in the same direction as the net external force on the object...

$$\vec{a} = \frac{1}{m} \sum \vec{F}_{ext}$$

... and inversely proportional to the mass of the object.

Figure 4-3 illustrates the ideas of Equation 4-3.

> **! Watch Out!** **Mass and weight are not the same thing.**
>
> An object's mass is the same no matter where the object is; for example, an astronaut walking on the Moon has the same mass as she has on Earth (the amount of matter in her body is exactly the same on either world). However, the astronaut has less *weight* on the Moon because gravity is weaker on the Moon than on Earth. We'll discuss the distinction between mass and weight in more detail in Section 4-3.)

The SI unit of force is the **newton**, abbreviated N. (An uppercase abbreviation is used for units that bear a person's name.) A net force of one newton applied to an object with a mass of one kilogram gives the object an acceleration of 1 m/s^2. Because $\sum \vec{F}_{ext} = m\vec{a}$ from Equation 4-2, it follows that

$$1 \text{ N} = 1 \text{ kg} \times 1 \text{ m/s}^2 = 1 \text{ kg} \cdot \text{m/s}^2$$

The English unit of force is the **pound** (abbreviated lb). To three significant figures, one pound equals 4.45 newtons and $1 \text{ N} = 0.225$ lb. One newton is a bit less than a quarter of a pound.

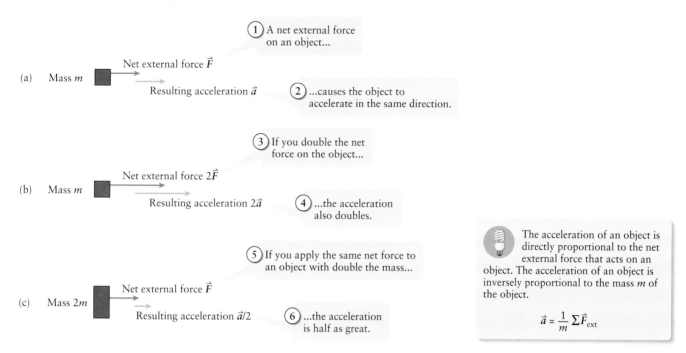

Figure 4-3 **Net force, mass, and acceleration** Newton's second law, $\sum \vec{F}_{ext} = m\vec{a}$ or $\vec{a} = (1/m)\sum \vec{F}_{ext}$, tells us how much acceleration results when a net external force $\sum \vec{F}_{ext}$ is applied to an object of mass m.

! **Watch Out!** It's the net force that matters.

Newton's second law tells us that a net force is required to make an object accelerate, that is, to *change* its velocity. However, your experience may suggest that a force has to act on an object to make it move even at a *constant* velocity. After all, you might reason, you have to exert a force to make a book slide across a table (Figure 4-4a). In fact, there's no contradiction between these two statements! The explanation is that the *net* force on the sliding book is zero. The forward force that you exert on the book just balances the backward force of friction that the table exerts on the book,

just as the upward normal force exerted on the book by the table just balances the downward gravitational force. Thus, the vector sum of *all* forces on the book is zero or $\sum \vec{F}_{ext} = 0$. From Newton's second law, this means that $\vec{a} = 0$, so the book moves over the table with a constant velocity (Figure 4-4a). If you push harder on the book, the force that you exert is greater in magnitude than the friction force and so the net force $\sum \vec{F}_{ext}$ points forward; then the book has a forward acceleration and speeds up (Figure 4-4b). If you let go of the sliding book, the net force $\sum \vec{F}_{ext}$ points backward, so the book has a backward acceleration and slows to a stop (Figure 4-4c). Just remember that it's the *net* force on an object that determines its acceleration, not any one particular force.

Figure 4-4 **It's the net external force that matters** (a) If you consider only the force that *you* apply to this book, you might think that a force is required to maintain constant velocity. If instead you consider *all* of the forces that act on the book, you'll see that a zero *net* external force keeps the book's velocity constant. If the net external force on the book is not zero, the book accelerates in the direction of the net force.

The sum $\sum \vec{F}_{\text{ext}}$ in Newton's second law involves vector addition. We saw in Chapter 3 that it's usually easiest to add vectors if we use components, so we'll often use Equation 4-2 in component form:

Sum of the x components of all external forces acting on the object

x component of the object's acceleration

Newton's second law in component form
(4-4)

(a) $\sum F_{\text{ext},x} = ma_x$

(b) $\sum F_{\text{ext},y} = ma_y$

Mass of the object

Sum of the y components of all external forces acting on the object

y component of the object's acceleration

The two examples below illustrate how to use Newton's second law to relate net force, mass, and acceleration.

Example 4-1 Small but Forceful

Microtubules are assembled from protein molecules (Figure 4-5). Microtubules help cells maintain their shape and are responsible for various kinds of movements within cells, such as pulling apart chromosomes during cell division. Measurements show that microtubules can exert forces from a few pN (1 pN = 1 piconewton = 10^{-12} N) up to hundreds of nN (1 nN = 1 nanonewton = 10^{-9} N). A particular bacterial chromosome has a mass of 2.00×10^{-17} kg. If a microtubule applies a force of 1.00 pN to the chromosome, what is the magnitude of the chromosome's acceleration? (Ignore any other forces that might act on the chromosome.)

Figure 4-5 **Microtubule** Microtubules (shown here in green within a fertilized sea urchin egg undergoing division) are protein molecules found within cells. They help cells hold their shape and are responsible for various kinds of movements within cells.

Set Up

Newton's second law tells us that the acceleration $\vec{a}_{\text{chromosome}}$ of the chromosome is determined by the net force acting on the chromosome and the chromosome's mass. We use this law to determine the magnitude of $\vec{a}_{\text{chromosome}}$.

Newton's second law of motion:

$$\sum \vec{F}_{\text{ext on chromosome}} = m_{\text{chromosome}} \vec{a}_{\text{chromosome}} \quad (4\text{-}2)$$

bacterial chromosome

net external force: $\vec{F}_{\text{ext on chromosome}}$

acceleration: $\vec{a}_{\text{chromosome}}$

mass: $m_{\text{chromosome}}$

Solve

Take the magnitude of both sides of Equation 4-2. (Note that mass is always positive.) Then solve for the magnitude $a_{\text{chromosome}}$ of the acceleration of the chromosome.

Magnitude of both sides of Equation 4-2:

$$\left| \sum \vec{F}_{\text{ext on chromosome}} \right| = m_{\text{chromosome}} \left| \vec{a}_{\text{chromosome}} \right| \text{ so}$$

$$\left| \sum \vec{F}_{\text{ext on chromosome}} \right| = m_{\text{chromosome}} a_{\text{chromosome}}$$

$$a_{\text{chromosome}} = \frac{\left| \sum \vec{F}_{\text{ext on chromosome}} \right|}{m_{\text{chromosome}}}$$

The net force on the chromosome is just the force exerted on it by the microtubule, of magnitude 1.00 pN. Use this value and $m_{\text{chromosome}} = 2.00 \times 10^{-17}$ kg to solve for the magnitude $a_{\text{chromosome}}$.

$$a_{\text{chromosome}} = \frac{1.00 \text{ pN}}{2.00 \times 10^{-17} \text{ kg}} = \frac{1.00 \times 10^{-12} \text{ N}}{2.00 \times 10^{-17} \text{ kg}}$$

$$= 5.00 \times 10^4 \text{ N/kg}$$

Use the definition $1\text{ N} = 1\text{ kg}\cdot\text{m/s}^2$:

$$a_{\text{chromosome}} = (5.00 \times 10^4\text{ N/kg})\left(\frac{1\text{ kg}\cdot\text{m/s}^2}{1\text{ N}}\right)$$

$$= 5.00 \times 10^4\text{ m/s}^2$$

Reflect

This acceleration is about 5000 times g, the acceleration due to gravity at the surface of Earth. These microtubules are quite strong! It is important to note, however, that the force exerted by the microtubule is opposed by resistive forces that we chose to neglect. The acceleration would not be quite this big in reality. Note also that the forces exerted by microtubules only act for very short periods of time.

Example 4-2   A Three-Person Tug-of-War

Jesse, Karim, and Luis, three hungry fraternity brothers, are each pulling on a cafeteria tray laden with desserts. The mass of the tray and its contents is 2.50 kg. The tray sits on a horizontal dining table, and each of the fraternity brothers pulls horizontally on the tray. Jesse pulls due south with a force of magnitude 85.0 N, and Karim pulls with a force of magnitude 90.0 N in a direction 35.0° north of east. If the tray accelerates due north at 20.0 m/s², how hard and in what direction does Luis pull on the tray? Ignore the effects of friction.

Set Up

The tray accelerates due to the net force that acts on it, which is the vector sum of the individual forces exerted on the tray by Jesse, Karim, and Luis. (We're told to ignore friction, so no other horizontal forces act on the tray. The tray doesn't accelerate vertically, so there's no net force in the vertical direction—the upward normal force exerted by the table top balances the downward gravitational force.) Because we know the mass and acceleration of the tray, we can use Newton's second law to calculate the net force on the tray. We'll then use the rules of vector addition and subtraction to determine the unknown force exerted by Luis.

$$\sum \vec{F}_{\text{ext on tray}} = m_{\text{tray}}\vec{a}_{\text{tray}} \quad (4\text{-}2)$$

In component form:

$$\sum F_{\text{ext on tray},x} = m_{\text{tray}}a_{\text{tray},x} \quad (4\text{-}4a)$$
$$\sum F_{\text{ext on tray},y} = ma_{\text{tray},y} \quad (4\text{-}4b)$$

Net force on tray = sum of forces exerted by Jesse, Karim, and Luis:

$$\sum \vec{F}_{\text{ext on tray}}$$
$$= \vec{F}_{\text{Jesse on tray}} + \vec{F}_{\text{Karim on tray}} + \vec{F}_{\text{Luis on tray}}$$

Solve

Vector arithmetic is easiest if we work in terms of vector components. The forces the three brothers exert are all in the horizontal plane, so we choose x and y axes that lie in this plane. The tray's acceleration vector $\vec{a}_{\text{tray}}$ points in the positive y direction.

$$a_{\text{tray},x} = 0$$
$$a_{\text{tray},y} = 20.0\text{ m/s}^2$$

Use Newton's second law in component form, Equations 4-4, to calculate the x and y components of the net force on the tray. Recall that $1\text{ kg}\cdot\text{m/s}^2 = 1\text{ N}$.

$$\sum F_{\text{ext on tray},x} = m_{\text{tray}}a_{\text{tray},x} = m_{\text{tray}}(0) = 0$$
$$\sum F_{\text{ext on tray},y} = m_{\text{tray}}a_{\text{tray},y} = (2.50\text{ kg})(20.0\text{ m/s}^2)$$
$$= 50.0\text{ kg}\cdot\text{m/s}^2 = 50.0\text{ N}$$

The x component of the net force on the tray is the sum of the x components of the individual forces on the tray, and similarly for the y component.

$$\sum F_{\text{ext on tray},x} = 0$$
$$= F_{\text{Jesse on tray},x} + F_{\text{Karim on tray},x} + F_{\text{Luis on tray},x}$$
$$\sum F_{\text{ext on tray},y} = 50.0\text{ N}$$
$$= F_{\text{Jesse on tray},y} + F_{\text{Karim on tray},y} + F_{\text{Luis on tray},y}$$

Solve for the components of the force that Luis exerts on the tray:

$$F_{\text{Luis on tray},x} = -F_{\text{Jesse on tray},x} - F_{\text{Karim on tray},x}$$
$$F_{\text{Luis on tray},y} = 50.0\text{ N} - F_{\text{Jesse on tray},y} - F_{\text{Karim on tray},y}$$

To proceed, we need to know the x and y components of the forces that Jesse and Karim exert on the tray.

$\vec{F}_{\text{Jesse on tray}}$:

magnitude 85.0 N, points due south (in the negative y direction) so

$$F_{\text{Jesse on tray},x} = 0$$

$$F_{\text{Jesse on tray},y} = -85.0 \text{ N}$$

$\vec{F}_{\text{Karim on tray}}$:

magnitude 90.0 N, points 35.0° north of east, so $F_{\text{Karim on tray},x}$ and $F_{\text{Karim on tray},y}$ are both positive

$$F_{\text{Karim on tray},x} = (90.0 \text{ N}) \cos 35.0°$$
$$= 73.7 \text{ N}$$
$$F_{\text{Karim on tray},y} = (90.0 \text{ N}) \sin 35.0°$$
$$= 51.6 \text{ N}$$

Substitute these values into the expressions for the components $F_{\text{Luis on tray},x}$ and $F_{\text{Luis on tray},y}$ and solve.

$$F_{\text{Luis on tray},x} = -(0) - (73.7 \text{ N})$$
$$= -73.7 \text{ N}$$
$$F_{\text{Luis on tray},y} = 50.0 \text{ N} - (-85.0 \text{ N}) - (51.6 \text{ N})$$
$$= 83.4 \text{ N}$$

The force that Luis exerts, $\vec{F}_{\text{Luis on tray}}$, has a negative x component and positive y component, so it points west of north. Calculate the magnitude of $\vec{F}_{\text{Luis on tray}}$ using the Pythagorean theorem and the direction of $\vec{F}_{\text{Luis on tray}}$ using trigonometry.

Magnitude of $\vec{F}_{\text{Luis on tray}}$:

$$F_{\text{Luis on tray}} = \sqrt{\left(F_{\text{Luis on tray},x}\right)^2 + \left(F_{\text{Luis on tray},y}\right)^2}$$
$$= \sqrt{(-73.7 \text{ N})^2 + (83.4 \text{ N})^2}$$
$$= 111 \text{ N}$$

Angle θ of $\vec{F}_{\text{Luis on tray}}$ measured west of north:

$$\tan \theta = \frac{73.7 \text{ N}}{83.4 \text{ N}} = 0.884$$

$$\theta = \tan^{-1} 0.884 = 41.5°$$

Reflect

Luis pulls on the tray with a force of 111 N at an angle of 41.5° west of north. In terms of components, Luis pulls west (in the negative x direction) with a force of 73.7 N, thus canceling Karim's 73.7-N pull to the east. Luis also pulls north (in the positive y direction) with a force of 83.4 N; combined with Karim's 51.6-N northward pull, Luis's pull overwhelms Jesse's 85.0-N pull toward the south. Hence, the net force on the tray and its delicious contents is northward, and its acceleration is northward as well.

Example 4-2 illustrates an important point: *It's always wise to choose coordinate axes that align with one or more of the vectors.* In this example we chose the axes to be east–west and north–south so that the tray's acceleration $\vec{a}_{\text{tray}}$ and the force $\vec{F}_{\text{Jesse on tray}}$ exerted by Jesse were both along one of the coordinate axes. This choice made it easy to express these vectors in terms of components and so simplified the calculation. Using a different choice of coordinate axes (say, one in which the positive x axis pointed 30° north of west and the positive y axis pointed 30° east of north), you would have ended up with the same result, but with a good deal more effort.

? Got the Concept? 4-1   Newton's Second Law

Rank the following objects in order of the magnitude of the net force that acts on the object, from greatest magnitude to smallest magnitude. (a) A 1250-kg automobile gaining speed at 2.00 m/s². (b) A 200,000-kg airliner flying in a straight line at a constant 280 m/s. (c) A 4500-kg truck slowing down at 0.600 m/s². (d) An 80.0-kg hiker climbing up a 4.00° slope at a constant 1.20 m/s.

? Got the Concept? 4-2   Measuring Mass in Zero Gravity

Imagine you are aboard a spacecraft far from any planet or star, so there is no gravitational force on you or anything else in the spacecraft. Floating in front of you are two spheres that are identical in size and appearance. One is made of lead and the other is made of plastic; the lead sphere is considerably more massive than the plastic one. Can you devise a simple experiment to determine which sphere is lead and which is plastic?

Take-Home Message for Section 4-2

✔ The net external force on an object is the vector sum of all of the individual forces that act on it from other objects.

✔ Newton's second law states that an object accelerates if the net external force on the object is not zero.

✔ The acceleration is in the same direction as the net force, is directly proportional to the magnitude of the net force, and is inversely proportional to the mass of the object (the quantity of material in the object).

4-3 Mass, weight, and inertia are distinct but related concepts

How much do you weigh? If you grew up in the United States, chances are your answer will be in pounds. If not, you'll probably use kilograms. We've already declared that the SI units of mass are kilograms. Does that mean that pounds and kilograms are both units of the same quantity? Are weight and mass the same?

The answer to both questions is "no!" Although people often use the terms *mass* and *weight* interchangeably in everyday conversation, they have different meanings in science. We'll use the ideas of mass and weight frequently, so it's important to distinguish between them.

As we discussed in Section 4-1, the mass of an object describes how much matter is contained in the object. By contrast, the **weight** of that object is the magnitude of the gravitational force that acts on the object. Because it's a force, weight is measured in newtons in the SI system and pounds in the English system. We'll use the symbols w for weight and $\vec{w}$ for gravitational force.

Consider an object that has mass m and is acted on by only the gravitational force. The object could be a ball falling in a vacuum, so there is no air resistance (Figure 4-6). Newton's second law, Equation 4-2, tells us that the gravitational force $\vec{w}$ equals the object's mass multiplied by its acceleration $\vec{a}$:

$$\vec{w} = m\vec{a}$$

The magnitude of the gravitational force is the weight w, so

$$w = ma$$

where a is the magnitude of the object's acceleration. We know from Section 2-7 that if only gravity acts on an object, the object's acceleration has magnitude g. So, we get the following expression for the weight of an object of mass m.

① If an object falls without air resistance, the net external force on the object equals the downward gravitational force on that object, which has magnitude w.

② An object falling without air resistance accelerates downward. The magnitude of the acceleration is g.

Mass m

$\Sigma\vec{F}_{ext} = \vec{w}$

$\vec{a} = \vec{g}$

③ Newton's second law, $\Sigma\vec{F}_{ext} = m\vec{a}$, tells us that $\vec{w} = m\vec{g}$ and so that $w = mg$.

Figure 4-6 Gravitational force Applying Newton's second law to a freely falling object shows that the magnitude of the gravitational force is $w = mg$.

Weight of an object of mass m

(4-5)

Weight of an object (equal to the magnitude of the gravitational force on that object)

$$w = mg$$

Mass of the object   Magnitude of the acceleration due to gravity

That is, *the weight of an object is equal to the object's mass multiplied by g, the acceleration due to gravity.* This statement makes it clear that the units of weight cannot be the same as the units of mass. In Chapters 2 and 3 we used an average value of $g = 9.80 \text{ m/s}^2$ but recognized that the exact value of g varies slightly from place to place on Earth. Therefore, the weight of an object must change as it is moved from place to place. *Hence weight is not an intrinsic property of an object.* Not only does the value of acceleration due to gravity change depending on where you are on Earth, but as we will see in Chapter 10, it can be significantly different on other worlds such as the Moon and Mars.

Watch Out! **Objects have weight even if they are not accelerating.**

We arrived at Equation 4-5 for the weight of an object by assuming that the object was falling freely. However, Equation 4-5 is true even if the object is not accelerating. A 10.0-kg object near Earth's surface has a weight of 98.0 N whether it's sitting on a table, falling off the table, or being pulled across the floor.

Got the Concept? 4-3 **Most Massive to Least Massive**

Rank the following objects according to their mass, from largest to smallest. The acceleration due to gravity at the equator of Mars is 3.69 m/s^2. (a) A rock on the Martian equator that weighs 10.0 N. (b) A rock at Earth's equator that weighs 10.0 N. (c) A rock on the Martian equator that has a mass of 10.0 kg. (d) A rock at Earth's equator that has a mass of 10.0 kg.

Mass m Mass $2m$

$w = mg$

$a = g$

$w = 2mg$

$a = g$

The gravitational force on an object is proportional to its mass. The more massive object experiences a greater gravitational force than the less massive object but has the same acceleration.

Figure 4-7 Greater mass means greater gravitational force Both of these objects are falling in a vacuum, so only the gravitational force acts on each object.

Consider dropping two different objects side by side in a vacuum, so that the only force acting on each object is the gravitational force (Figure 4-7). The heavier object weighs twice as much as the other, so it is subjected to twice as much gravitational force and hence twice as much net force as the lighter object.

So you might expect that the heavier object would have a greater downward acceleration $\vec{a}$. But Equation 4-5 tells us that the heavier object also has a greater mass, and that weight and mass are directly proportional. If the heavier object has twice the weight of the lighter one, it also has twice the mass. An object's acceleration is equal to the net force that acts on it divided by its mass (recall the alternative form of Newton's second law, $\vec{a} = \frac{1}{m}\sum \vec{F}_{\text{ext}}$, from Equation 4-3). Hence the quotient $\frac{1}{m}\sum \vec{F}_{\text{ext}}$ has the *same* value for both objects, and they both fall with the same acceleration in a vacuum.

Can you lift an object that weighs 10 N? How about a 1000-N object? In Section 4-2, we mentioned the following conversions, which are valid to three significant figures:

$$1\,\text{N} = 0.225\,\text{lb}$$
$$1\,\text{lb} = 4.45\,\text{N}$$

(You can find more precise conversion factors in Appendix A.) According to Equation 4-5, the mass of an object that weighs 10.0 N is $m = w/g = (10.0\,\text{N})/(9.80\,\text{m/s}^2) = 1.02\,\text{kg}$. A 1-L bottle of water has a mass of 1 kg; that is, it weighs about 10 N. In pounds, that's 10 multiplied by 0.225 lb or about 2.2 lb. You'd have no problem lifting that amount. This equivalence (1 liter of water = 1 kg = 10 N = about 2.2 lb) can help you get an intuitive feel for the answer when you encounter a new problem that involves forces.

Many people can lift an object that weighs 1000 N; that's a weight of 225 lb and a mass of about 100 kg.

Mass, Inertia, and Newton's First Law

The concept of mass is intertwined with the observation that all objects *resist changes* in their state of motion. We use the term **inertia** for the tendency of an object to resist a change in motion. For example, a *stationary* object (such as a rock lying on the ground or a roommate sleeping on the couch) tends to remain stationary. An object *in motion*, like a fast-moving hockey puck sliding on the ice, tends to keep moving in the same direction with the same speed.

Watch Out! Don't confuse mass, weight, and inertia.

Note the differences among mass, weight, and inertia. Mass is the *quantity of material* in an object; no matter where in the universe you take the object, its mass remains the same. Weight is the *magnitude of the gravitational force* on an object; it's proportional to the mass but depends on the value of *g* at the object's location. Inertia is the *tendency* of *all* objects to maintain the same motion. Unlike mass or weight, we do not give numerical values to the inertia of an object.

Newton described inertia as an intrinsic, unchanging: property of mass and of objects. This property is defined in **Newton's first law**:

An object at rest tends to stay at rest, and an object in uniform motion tends to stay in motion with the same speed and in the same direction unless acted upon by a net force.

Newton's first law contradicts the older theories of motion developed by the ancient Greeks, principally by the philosopher Aristotle (384 B.C.–322 B.C.). Aristotle believed that every object had a natural place in the world. For example, heavy objects, such as rocks, are naturally at rest on Earth, and light objects, such as clouds, are naturally at rest in the sky. In Aristotle's view, a moving object tended to stop when it found its natural rest position. To keep an object moving, reasoned Aristotle, a force had to be applied to it; to make it move faster, a greater force was required. Newton saw more deeply. He identified the concept of the *net* force on an object and realized that the net force on an object determines its acceleration rather than its speed. (This realization is Newton's second law.) If the net force on an object is zero, the object has zero acceleration and moves with a constant velocity—that is, with the same speed and in the same direction. (You should review the discussion of Figure 4-4 in Section 4-2.)

At this point, you can think of Newton's first law as a special case of the *second* law that applies when the net force on an object is zero. We'll nonetheless call these laws "first" and "second" in the same manner in which Newton numbered them. In equation form, we can write the first law as follows:

If the net external force on an object is zero...   ... the object does not accelerate...

$$\text{If } \sum \vec{F}_{\text{ext}} = 0, \text{ then } \vec{a} = 0 \text{ and } \vec{v} = \text{constant}$$

... and the velocity of the object remains constant. If the object is at rest, it remains at rest; if it is in motion, it continues in motion in a straight line at a constant speed.

Newton's first law of motion
(4-6)

We say that an object is in **equilibrium** if the net external force on it is zero. For example, a chandelier hanging from the ceiling is in equilibrium: The chain from which the chandelier is suspended exerts an upward force that exactly balances the downward gravitational force on the chandelier. The chandelier's velocity is zero and remains zero. But an airliner flying in a straight line at a constant speed is also in equilibrium, even though it is in motion. The forward thrust of the airliner's engines balances the backward drag force that the air exerts on the airliner, and the upward lift provided by air flowing around the wings balances the downward gravitational force. The airliner has a nonzero velocity, but its *acceleration* is zero and so the airliner is in equilibrium.

The following example illustrates how to use Newton's first law to analyze an object at rest.

 See the Math Tutorial for more information on trigonometry

Example 4-3 Let Sleeping Cats Lie

A cat that weighs 40.0 N has fallen asleep on a sloping ramp that is tilted by an angle of 15.0° from the horizontal. Three forces act on the cat: the downward gravitational force, a normal force perpendicular to the ramp, and a friction force directed uphill parallel to the ramp. The uphill friction force prevents the cat from sliding downhill, so the cat remains at rest while sleeping. Determine the magnitude of each force that acts on the cat.

Set Up

We are told that the cat's weight is $w = 40.0$ N, which is just the magnitude of the gravitational force on the cat ($\vec{w}_{cat}$). We also know the directions of the normal force $\vec{n}$ (perpendicular to the ramp) and the friction force $\vec{f}$ (uphill parallel to the ramp). Our task is to find the magnitudes of $\vec{n}$ and $\vec{f}$. We'll do this using the idea that the sum of $\vec{w}_{cat}$, $\vec{n}$, and $\vec{f}$ must be zero because the cat remains at rest (Newton's first law). So we can solve this problem by using vector addition.

Newton's first law of motion:

$$\sum \vec{F}_{ext\ on\ cat} = \vec{w}_{cat} + \vec{n} + \vec{f} = 0$$

$$(4\text{-}6)$$

Solve

Like most vector addition problems, this one is most easily solved using components. If $\sum \vec{F}_{ext\ on\ cat} = 0$, then each of the components of $\sum \vec{F}_{ext\ on\ cat}$ must also be equal to zero. It's convenient to choose the x axis to be along the tilted ramp and the y axis to be perpendicular to the ramp. (The x and y axes must be perpendicular to each other but don't have to be horizontal or vertical.) Using this choice, two of the vectors, $\vec{n}$ and $\vec{f}$, lie either directly along or directly opposite to one of the coordinate axes.

Newton's first law in component form:

$$\sum F_{ext\ on\ cat,x} = w_{cat,x} + n_x + f_x$$
$$\sum F_{ext\ on\ cat,y} = w_{cat,y} + n_y + f_y$$

Write down the x and y components of each of the external force vectors in terms of their magnitudes w, n, and f and the angle $\theta = 15.0°$ of the ramp. Note that $\vec{w}_{cat}$ has a positive x component (down the ramp) and a negative y component (into the ramp), $\vec{n}$ has only a positive y component (perpendicular to the ramp), and $\vec{f}$ has only a negative x component (up the ramp).

Components of gravitational force $\vec{w}_{cat}$:

$$w_{cat,x} = +w_{cat} \sin \theta$$
$$w_{cat,y} = -w_{cat} \cos \theta$$

Components of normal force $\vec{n}$:

$$n_x = 0$$
$$n_y = +n$$

Components of $\vec{f}$:

$$f_x = -f$$
$$f_y = 0$$

Substitute the expressions for $w_{cat,x}$, $w_{cat,y}$, n_x, n_y, f_x, and f_y into Newton's first law and solve for the magnitudes n and f.

Substitute into Newton's first law in component form:

$$\sum F_{ext\ on\ cat,x} = w_{cat} \sin \theta + 0 + (-f) = 0$$
$$\sum F_{ext\ on\ cat,y} = -w_{cat} \cos \theta + n + 0 = 0$$

From the y equation:

$$n = w_{cat} \cos \theta = (40.0\ N) \cos 15.0° = 38.6\ N$$

From the x equation:

$$f = w_{cat} \sin \theta = (40.0\ N) \sin 15.0° = 10.4\ N$$

Reflect

The downward gravitational force has magnitude 40.0 N, the normal force acting perpendicular to the ramp has magnitude 38.6 N, and the friction force acting uphill has magnitude 10.4 N. Note that no single force "balances" any of the other forces: All three forces are needed to mutually balance each other and keep the cat at rest.

$n = 38.6$ N
$f = 10.4$ N
$w_{cat} = 40.0$ N

! Watch Out! The normal force isn't always equal to the weight.

It's a common mistake to assume that the normal force on an object (in this case, the sleeping cat) has the same magnitude as the object's weight. That's clearly *not* true in this case: The normal-force magnitude $n = 38.6$ N is *less* than the cat's 40.0-N weight. As a general rule, it's *always* safest to treat the magnitude of the normal force as an unknown, as we have done in this example.

? Got the Concept? 4-4 Tilt the Cat, but Don't Wake It Up

You increase the angle θ of the ramp in Example 4-3 to a new value greater than 15.0°. The cat remains blissfully asleep and at rest at the new angle. What effect does this have on the magnitude n of the normal force and the magnitude f of the friction force? (a) n and f both increase; (b) n and f both decrease; (c) n increases and f decreases; (d) n decreases and f increases; (e) none of these; (f) The answer depends on the new value of θ.

Take-Home Message for Section 4-3

✔ The weight of an object is the magnitude of the gravitational force that acts on it.

✔ Newton's first law states that if the external forces on an object sum to zero, the object does not accelerate. If the object is stationary it remains at rest, and if it is in motion it continues to move in a straight line with constant velocity.

4-4 Making a free-body diagram is essential in solving any problem involving forces

A locked door is most easily opened when you have the right key. And you wouldn't think of walking around a foreign city without a map. The key that unlocks physics problems involving forces and the map that allows you to navigate these problems is the *free-body diagram*.

A **free-body diagram** is a graphical representation of all of the external forces acting on an object. It's useful because Newton's second law and Newton's first law both involve the sum of all external forces on an object, $\sum \vec{F}_{ext}$. The term *free body* means that we draw only the object on which the forces act, *not* the other objects that exert those forces. We drew a free-body diagram of the cat in the Set Up step in Example 4-3. As another example, Figure 4-8a shows a block on a horizontal table. A wind is blowing from left to right, and the wind pushes on the block and makes it slide. Figure 4-8b lists the steps involved in constructing this block's free-body diagram.

Often we'll label a force to indicate what object is exerting the force and what object the force acts on. For example, if a girl pushes on a book, we will label that force $\vec{F}_{girl\ on\ book}$. (We used a label of this kind in Figure 4-8b for the force of the wind blowing on the block.) However, we'll label some special forces in a different way to be in accordance with the convention that most physicists use. We'll use $\vec{w}$ for the gravitational force that Earth exerts on an object. If the object is in contact with a surface, we'll use $\vec{f}$ for the friction force on the object that acts parallel to the surface, and $\vec{n}$ for the normal force on the object that acts perpendicular to the surface (see Figure 4-8b). We'll refer to the friction force and normal force as **contact forces**: They arise only when two

(a) A block on a horizontal table

Wind → Motion of the block →

(b) Drawing the free-body diagram for the block

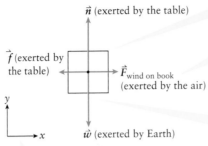

$\vec{n}$ (exerted by the table)

$\vec{f}$ (exerted by the table) ← → $\vec{F}_{\text{wind on book}}$ (exerted by the air)

y

→ x

$\vec{w}$ (exerted by Earth)

① Sketch the object on which the forces act.

② Identify what other objects exert forces on this object. This includes Earth (which exerts a gravitational force) and anything that touches the object.

③ For each force that acts on the object, draw the force vector with its tail at the center of the object. Make sure each vector points in the correct direction. Do not include forces that the object exerts on the other objects.

⑤ Choose, draw, and label the directions of the positive x and y axes. Choose the axes so that as many force vectors as possible lie along one of the axes.

④ Label each force with its symbol. Be certain that you can identify what other object exerts each force. If you're not sure what exerts a force, it's probably not a real force!

Figure 4-8 **Constructing a free-body diagram** (a) The wind pushes to the right on this block, which slides on a horizontal table. (b) How to create a free-body diagram that depicts all of the external forces that act on the block.

(a)

(b)

$\vec{n}$ Normal force exerted by the table on the box

y

→ x

$\vec{w}$ Gravitational force exerted by Earth on the box

The box exerts a downward force on the surface of the table, but we don't include this force in the free-body diagram of the box.

Figure 4-9 **A free-body diagram: A stationary box atop a table** (a) A box rests on a horizontal table top. (b) The free-body diagram for the box.

objects are in contact with each other. By contrast, the gravitational force is *not* a contact force: A basketball in midair is pulled downward by the gravitational force even though it's not in contact with the ground.

Examining Free-Body Diagrams

Let's look at some examples of free-body diagrams and what we can learn from them. In Figure 4-9a, a stationary box rests on a table with a horizontal top. The free-body diagram in Figure 4-9b shows the two forces that act on the box: the downward gravitational force $\vec{w}$ and the upward normal force $\vec{n}$ exerted by the table.

We choose the y axis to be vertical; then both forces lie along this axis. The sum of $\vec{w}$ and $\vec{n}$ must be zero in order for the box to remain at rest, so the free-body diagram tells us that $\vec{w}$ and $\vec{n}$ must be opposite in direction and have the same magnitude. Note that the *box* exerts a downward force on the surface of the *table*, but we don't include that force in the free-body diagram for the box. A diagram for the box includes only those forces that act *on* the box.

In Figure 4-10a a box is placed on an inclined ramp with a rough surface. There is friction between the box and the ramp, so the free-body diagram in Figure 4-10b includes a friction force $\vec{f}$ as well as the gravitational force $\vec{w}$ and the normal force $\vec{n}$. Because the ramp is tilted by an angle θ from the horizontal, the normal force (which is perpendicular to the ramp) is tilted from the vertical by the same angle θ. We've chosen the x axis to be parallel to the ramp and the y axis to be perpendicular to the ramp; then $\vec{f}$ has only an x component and $\vec{n}$ has only a y component. By assumption the block

(b)

① The box is at rest and doesn't accelerate, so the **net external force** must be zero:
$$\Sigma\vec{F}_{\text{ext}} = \vec{n} + \vec{f} + \vec{w} = 0$$

② With this choice of axes, the normal force has only a y component and the friction force has only an x component. (The gravitational force has both an x component and a y component.)

(a)

(exerted by the ramp) $\vec{n}$

(exerted by $\vec{f}$ the ramp)

y

→ x

θ

$\vec{w}$ (exerted by Earth)

③ The box also pushes on the ramp, but we don't include that force in the free-body diagram because it doesn't act on the box.

Figure 4-10 **A free-body diagram: A stationary box on a ramp** (a) Friction keeps the box from sliding down the ramp. (b) The free-body diagram for the box.

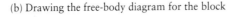

① With the friction force absent, the remaining normal force and gravitational force do not cancel. So the **net external force** $\Sigma \vec{F}_{ext} = \vec{n} + \vec{w}$ is not zero.

② The box neither leaps off the ramp nor sinks down into it, so it doesn't accelerate in the y direction. So the normal force must cancel the (negative) y component of the gravitational force.

③ Nothing cancels the positive x component of the gravitational force, so the net force is in the positive x direction...

④ ... and the acceleration of the block is in the positive x direction, the same as the direction of the net force.

Figure 4-11 A free-body diagram: A box sliding on a ramp The free-body diagram for a box sliding on a frictionless ramp.

y

(exerted by $\vec{n}$ the ramp)

x

$\Sigma \vec{F}_{ext} = \vec{n} + \vec{w}$

θ

$\vec{a}$ θ $\vec{w}$

(exerted by Earth)

remains at rest, so the net external force $\sum \vec{F}_{ext}$ on it—that is, the vector sum of $\vec{w}$, $\vec{n}$, and $\vec{f}$—must be zero. So the friction force $\vec{f}$ must point in the negative x direction in order to cancel the (positive) x component of the gravitational force $\vec{w}$; the normal force $\vec{n}$ points in the positive y direction and must cancel the (negative) y component of $\vec{w}$. (This is the same situation as in Example 4-3 in Section 4-3.) Note that the x and y components of the gravitational force $\vec{w}$ are less than the magnitude of the force, which is the box's weight w. The free-body diagram therefore tells us something useful: The magnitudes of the friction force and normal force are both *less* than the weight of the box. Compare this situation to the box on a horizontal surface shown in Figure 4-9, for which the magnitude of the normal force is just equal to the weight.

What happens if we grease the surface of the ramp so that there is no more friction? In this case the friction force $\vec{f}$ goes to zero, and the free-body diagram is as shown in Figure 4-11. Now the vector sum $\sum \vec{F}_{ext}$ of the external forces on the box cannot be zero: For the normal force and gravitational forces to cancel each other, they would have to point in opposite directions, which the free-body diagram in Figure 4-11 shows they do not. Instead the net external force points down the ramp in the positive x direction. According to Newton's second law, $\sum \vec{F}_{ext} = m\vec{a}$ (Equation 4-2), the box must therefore have a nonzero acceleration $\vec{a}$ down the ramp. We learn this not by having to do any calculations, but simply by examining the free-body diagram for the box.

Note that neither the normal force nor the gravitational force in Figure 4-11 depends on how fast or in what direction the box is moving. Whether the box is sliding up the ramp, momentarily at rest, or sliding down the ramp, these forces are the same. This means the acceleration is also the same in each of these cases. If the box is moving up the ramp, it slows down; if it is momentarily at rest, the box starts moving down the ramp; and if it is moving down the ramp, it speeds up. So, the free-body diagram also tells us that the box shown in Figure 4-11 moves in a straight line with a constant acceleration—which means we can analyze its motion using the techniques that we learned in Chapter 2.

Watch Out! Don't add nonexistent forces to a free-body diagram.

Students are sometimes tempted to add a force in a free-body diagram that is somehow associated with the motion. Common names for this force are "the force of velocity" or "the force of acceleration." If you feel this temptation, resist it! Remember that neither velocity nor acceleration is a force. Keep in mind also that acceleration is the *result* of force: For example, the acceleration of the box in Figure 4-11 is a result of the nonzero force in the x direction. (It's true that Newton's second law says that $\sum \vec{F}_{ext} = m\vec{a}$, which may mislead you into thinking that the quantity $m\vec{a}$ is itself a force. But remember the real meaning of Newton's second law: A net external force $\sum \vec{F}_{ext}$ on an object makes the object accelerate. So,

$m\vec{a}$ is *not* a force, and equation $\sum \vec{F}_{ext} = m\vec{a}$ just tells you the magnitude and direction of that resulting acceleration $\vec{a}$.) If you're still not convinced, ask yourself what external object could exert a "force of velocity" or a "force of acceleration" on the object you're analyzing. (Remember, only *external* forces can affect an object's motion. You may want to review the discussion in Section 4-2.) In Figure 4-11 we've already accounted for Earth's gravity, and we've already accounted for the one and only thing that touches the box (the surface of the ramp). So there can be no external forces on the box other than the two we've already drawn in Figure 4-11.

We'll use free-body diagrams throughout our study of forces and motion, and you should as well. Before we delve more deeply into how to solve problems using Newton's first and second laws, we'll introduce Newton's *third* law. This will give us deeper insight into the way in which objects exert forces on each other.

? Got the Concept? 4-5 **Choose the Correct Free-Body Diagram**

When a box is placed on an inclined ramp and released, it moves down the ramp with increasing speed. There is friction between the ramp and the box. Which of the free-body diagrams shown in **Figure 4-12** correctly depicts the forces on the box as it slides down the ramp?

(a)   (b)   (c)   (d)   (e)

Figure 4-12 **A box sliding down a ramp with friction** Which of these free-body diagrams is correct?

Take-Home Message for Section 4-5

✔ In order to solve a problem about how an object moves and the forces that act on it, you must draw a free-body diagram for the object. This diagram depicts all of the external forces that act on the object.

✔ Choose the *x* and *y* axes in a free-body diagram so that most of the forces point along one or the other of the axes.

(a)

Spring scales

(b)   Wall

No matter how hard you pull, the readings on the two scales are identical.

(c)   No matter how hard you pull, these forces have the same magnitude.

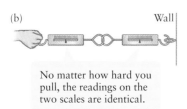

Force the wall exerts on you measured by the left-hand scale.

Force you exert on the wall measured by the right-hand scale.

Figure 4-13 **Comparing the forces that objects exert on each other** (a) Two spring scales connected together. Each scale measures the force exerted on it. (b) One scale is connected to a wall and you pull on the other end. (c) The force you exert on the wall with the scales is equal in magnitude to the force that the wall exerts back on you.

4-5 Newton's third law relates the forces that two objects exert on each other

If you hold a book, pick up a backpack, or dribble a basketball, in each case you're exerting a force on an object that affects that object's motion. However, you know from experience that the *object* exerts a force on *you* as well. You can feel the book pushing back against your palm; you can feel the straps of the backpack pulling on your fingers as you lift it; and you can feel the slap of the basketball against your hand as you push down on it. What is the connection between the force that you exert on an object and the force that the object exerts back on you?

Here's an experiment that offers an answer to this question. Take two spring scales (such as you might use for weighing a fish) and connect their upper ends together (**Figure 4-13a**). You hold the free end of one scale, and you attach the free end of the other scale to a hook mounted to the wall (**Figure 4-13b**). When you pull on the free end of the first scale, the wall pulls on the free end of the other scale. Remarkably, no matter how hard you pull, the reading on the scale that you hold (which measures the amount of force you exert) is *identical* to the reading on the scale attached to the wall (which measures the amount of force that the wall exerts). In other words, the force that you exert on the wall has the *same* magnitude as the force that the wall exerts back on you (**Figure 4-13c**).

In Figure 4-13 both you and the wall are stationary. We can try the same experiment with two objects in motion—say, a car and a trailer connected together by the same arrangement of two spring scales (**Figure 4-14**). The readings on each scale depend on whether the car and trailer are moving at a constant speed, speeding up, or slowing down. In all of these cases, however, experiment shows that the spring scale attached to the car reads *exactly* the same as the spring scale attached to the trailer. So, the force that the car exerts on the trailer always has the same magnitude as the force that the trailer exerts on the car. The only difference between the two forces is that they are in *opposite* directions: The car pulls forward on the trailer, while the trailer pulls backward on the car.

We can summarize these observations in the last of the basic laws of dynamics, known as **Newton's third law**:

If object A exerts a force on object B, object B exerts a force on object A that has the same magnitude but is in the opposite direction. These two forces act on different objects.

In declaring this law, Newton added: "If you press a stone with your finger, the finger is also pressed by the stone." This quote reminds us that Newton's third law refers to two forces that act on *different* objects. In Newton's example, these two forces are your finger pressing on the stone and the stone pressing on your finger. Physicists speak of the *interaction* between two objects, with the forces of the two objects on each other making up the interaction. The two forces involved in an interaction are referred to as a **force pair**. (These two forces are sometimes called the *action* and the *reaction*.)

We can express Newton's third law as an equation relating the force that an object A exerts on another object B (written as $\vec{F}_{A \text{ on } B}$) to the **reaction force** that object B exerts on object A (written as $\vec{F}_{B \text{ on } A}$):

Force that object A exerts on object B   Force that object B exerts on object A

$$\vec{F}_{A \text{ on } B} = -\vec{F}_{B \text{ on } A}$$

Newton's third law of motion (4-7)

 If object A exerts a force on object B, object B must exert a force on object A with the same magnitude but opposite direction.

The minus sign means that $\vec{F}_{B \text{ on } A}$ has the same magnitude as $\vec{F}_{A \text{ on } B}$ but is in the opposite direction (**Figure 4-15**). The two forces in a force pair are sometimes called "equal and opposite," which means that they are equal *in magnitude* and opposite *in direction*.

Comparing Newton's Three Laws

We've emphasized that Newton's third law is fundamentally different from the first and second laws because it tells us about forces that act on *two different* objects. By contrast, Newton's first and second laws tell us about the effect of the net external force acting on a *single* object. Here's an example that illustrates this important distinction. **Figure 4-16a** shows a ball held at rest in a person's hand. The drawing shows three forces: the gravitational force of Earth pulling down on the ball (the ball's weight), the force of the person's hand on the ball, and the force of the ball on the person's hand. All three forces have equal magnitudes but for different reasons!

(a) Holding a ball at rest

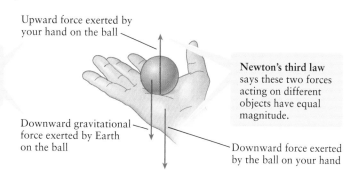

Newton's first law says these two forces acting on the same object (the ball) have equal magnitude.

Upward force exerted by your hand on the ball

Newton's third law says these two forces acting on different objects have equal magnitude.

Downward gravitational force exerted by Earth on the ball

Downward force exerted by the ball on your hand

(b) Accelerating a ball upward

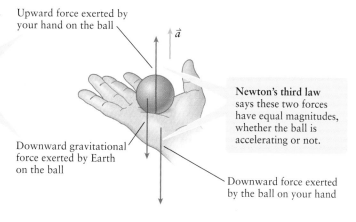

Newton's second law says these two forces acting on the ball do not have equal magnitudes. Their sum must be upward (in the direction of the acceleration).

Upward force exerted by your hand on the ball

$\vec{a}$

Newton's third law says these two forces have equal magnitudes, whether the ball is accelerating or not.

Downward gravitational force exerted by Earth on the ball

Downward force exerted by the ball on your hand

 The car and trailer are linked together by two spring scales (like those shown in Figure 4-13) connected end to end.

Each spring scale has the same reading: The force that the car exerts on the trailer always has the same magnitude as the force that the trailer exerts on the car. This is true no matter how the car and trailer move (and is also true if they aren't moving at all).

Figure 4-14 Comparing the forces that moving objects exert on each other A pair of spring scales like those shown in Figure 4-13a are used to connect a car and trailer.

These two forces are equal in magnitude but opposite in direction.

Figure 4-15 Newton's third law If object A exerts a force $\vec{F}_{A \text{ on } B}$ on object B, then object B necessarily exerts a force $\vec{F}_{B \text{ on } A}$ on object A with the same magnitude but the opposite direction.

Figure 4-16 Comparing Newton's three laws (a) Newton's first law and third law applied to a ball at rest in your palm. (b) Newton's second law and third law applied to a ball that you accelerate upward.

- The force of Earth on the ball and the force of the person's hand on the ball have equal magnitudes and opposite directions according to Newton's *first* law. These two forces are the only external forces acting *on* the ball, so their vector sum $\sum \vec{F}_{\text{ext}}$ must be zero (that is, the two forces must balance each other) in order that the ball remain at rest and not accelerate.
- The force of the person's hand on the ball and the force of the ball on the person's hand have equal magnitudes and opposite directions according to Newton's *third* law. These two forces are a force pair: If *A* represents the hand and *B* represents the ball, these are the forces of *A* on *B* and of *B* on *A*.

Figure 4-16b shows the situation when the person's hand is accelerating the ball upward. Now the vector sum $\sum \vec{F}_{\text{ext}}$ of external forces on the ball is not zero, so the force of Earth on the ball does *not* have the same magnitude as the force of the person's hand on the ball. However, the force of the person's hand on the ball still *does* have the same magnitude of the force of the ball on the hand because Newton's third law works at all times, even when the objects are accelerating.

Here's a general rule to keep in mind:

Use Newton's first law or second law when dealing with the forces that act on a given object. Use Newton's third law when relating the forces that act between two objects.

? Got the Concept? 4-6 Is Motion Impossible?

You ask a friend to push a large crate across a floor (Figure 4-17). Your friend declares that this feat isn't possible because whatever force he applies to the box will be met with an equal but opposite force. The vector sum of these forces, he argues, will be zero, so the crate will have zero acceleration and won't move. What's wrong with this argument?

Figure 4-17 Pushing a crate Do Newton's laws make it impossible to push this crate across the floor?

? Got the Concept? 4-7 Which Forces Act?

Two crates are at rest, one touching the other, on a horizontal surface. You push horizontally on crate 1 as shown by the red arrow in Figure 4-18. Which of the following is a force that acts on crate 2? (a) A force exerted by crate 1; (b) a force exerted by you; (c) a reaction force exerted by crate 2; (d) a force due to the acceleration of crate 2; (e) more than one of these.

Figure 4-18 Pushing two crates If you push on crate 1 as shown by the red arrow, what forces act on crate 2?

Newton's Third Law and Tension

We can use Newton's third law to help us understand another important type of contact force. **Tension** is the force exerted by a rope (or thread, string, cable, or wire) on an object to which the rope is connected. As an example, the rope shown in Figure 4-19a exerts a tension force on the sailor who holds on to the left-hand end of the rope and exerts a tension force on the boat tied to its right-hand end. We'll use the symbol $\vec{T}$ for a tension force.

Here's an important fact about tension: If a rope has sufficiently small mass, the tension forces that the rope exerts at its two ends have the *same* magnitude. To see why

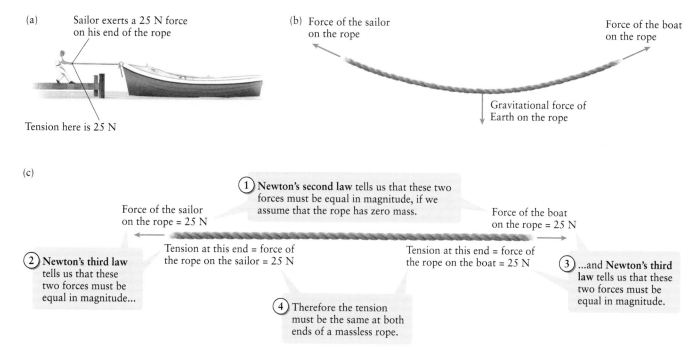

(a) Sailor exerts a 25 N force on his end of the rope

Tension here is 25 N

(b) Force of the sailor on the rope

Force of the boat on the rope

Gravitational force of Earth on the rope

(c)

1. **Newton's second law** tells us that these two forces must be equal in magnitude, if we assume that the rope has zero mass.

Force of the sailor on the rope = 25 N

Force of the boat on the rope = 25 N

2. **Newton's third law** tells us that these two forces must be equal in magnitude...

Tension at this end = force of the rope on the sailor = 25 N

Tension at this end = force of the rope on the boat = 25 N

3. ...and **Newton's third law** tells us that these two forces must be equal in magnitude.

4. Therefore the tension must be the same at both ends of a massless rope.

Figure 4-19 **Comparing the tensions at the two ends of a rope** (a) A sailor docking a boat pulls on one end of a rope. (b) The forces that act on the rope. (c) The forces that act on a massless rope. In this case the tension force must have the same magnitude at either end of the rope.

these forces have the same magnitude, consider a sailor who docks a boat by pulling on one end of a rope whose other end is tied to the boat (Figure 4-19a). If he pulls with a given force—say, 25 N—on his end of the rope, Newton's third law tells us that the rope pulls back on him with a force of 25 N. How much force does the *other* end of the rope exert on the boat?

To see the answer, consider Figure 4-19b, which shows the forces that act *on the* rope. The weight of the rope is a major complication. For one thing, it causes the rope to sag so that the angle of the rope is different at the two ends. However, in many situations the weight of the rope is very small compared to the pulling forces exerted on the rope by the objects attached to its ends. That's the case in Figure 4-19c. So, we can safely approximate the rope as having *zero* mass and hence *zero* weight. Using this approximation, the rope won't sag at all under its own weight (because it has none) and will be perfectly straight. Then the only forces acting on the rope are those at either end. Because the rope is straight, these two forces point in opposite directions (Figure 4-19c).

Newton's second law says that the sum of external forces on the rope, $\sum \vec{F}_{\text{ext}}$, is equal to $m\vec{a}$, the product of the rope's mass m and its acceleration $\vec{a}$. However, if the rope has zero mass ($m = 0$), the product $m\vec{a}$ is always equal to zero, even if the rope is accelerating. Therefore, the sum of external forces on the rope must be zero ($\sum \vec{F}_{\text{ext}} = 0$) under all circumstances. For this to be the case, the oppositely directed forces acting on either end of the rope (Figure 4-19c) must have the same magnitude whether the rope is accelerating or not.

Here's where Newton's third law applies: The law tells us that the force exerted *on* each end of the rope has the same magnitude as the tension forces exerted *by* each end of the rope. Because equal-magnitude forces act on each end of a massless rope, it follows that the tension is also the same at *both* ends: If the tension is 25 N at the left-hand end, it is 25 N at the right-hand end (Figure 4-19c). So we are left with the following general rule:

The tension is the same at both ends of a rope or string, provided the weight of the rope or string is much less than the forces exerted on the ends of the rope or string.

We now have all of the tools we need to solve problems that involve forces and acceleration. In the remainder of this chapter we'll look at techniques for solving problems of this kind.

Take-Home Message for Section 4-5

✔ Newton's third law tells us that if object A exerts a force on object B, object B has to exert a force on object A of the same magnitude but in the opposite direction.

✔ A rope exerts the same tension at both ends, provided the mass of the rope can be ignored.

4-6 All problems involving forces can be solved using the same series of steps

In this section, we'll use Newton's laws to solve a variety of problems that involve forces. In some problems the goal is to find an object's acceleration; in other cases, we want to find the magnitude of one or more of the forces acting on an object. Remarkably, we can set up *any* force problem using just two steps.

Method of Solving Force Problems

(1) Make a free-body diagram for the object or objects of interest using the rules that we outlined in Section 4-4. Choose the coordinate axes and label the positive directions. (As we've mentioned before, it's best to choose these axes so that one or more of the vectors in the problem—the acceleration and the individual forces—lie along one of the axes.)

(2) Write Newton's second law for each object and in each direction separately. Use the free-body diagram to make sure that for each object, all of the forces that act on that object are included in the sum of external forces. Then solve for the unknowns.

Problems Involving a Single Object

 See the Math Tutorial for more information on trigonometry

Our first few examples just involve a single object. In some problems, the goal is to find the object's acceleration; in other cases, you need to determine one or more of the forces acting on the object. Sometimes determining the acceleration or unknown force is not the goal itself, but just a necessary step to arrive at the final answer to a question. One thing to think about in these problems is the choice of x and y axes for your force diagram. If the object is on an incline, choose one of the axes to point along the incline. If the object is moving in a known direction, it's best to choose one of the axes to point in that direction. If you're not sure which way the object will accelerate (say, whether to the left or to the right), don't worry about it—choose an axis to point in one direction or the other. If it turns out that the acceleration is in the direction opposite to the one you chose, you'll know because the acceleration will turn out to be negative.

Example 4-4 What's the Angle?

A pair of fuzzy dice hangs on a lightweight thread from the rearview mirror of your high-performance sports car. At what angle from the vertical do the dice hang when the car is accelerating forward at a constant 6.50 m/s^2?

Set Up
The dice move along with the car and so have the same forward acceleration of 6.50 m/s^2. So, there must be a net forward force on the dice. The individual forces on the dice are the gravitational force $\vec{w}_{\text{dice}}$ exerted by Earth and the tension force $\vec{T}$ exerted by the thread. Because the thread is lightweight, the gravitational force on it is negligible and the thread will be straight when taut. So the angle of the thread from the vertical—which is the quantity we're trying to find—is the same as the angle θ of the tension force $\vec{T}$. We'll find this angle by applying Newton's second law to the dice.

Newton's second law in component form:

$$\sum F_{\text{ext on dice},x} = m_{\text{dice}} a_{\text{dice},x}$$
$$(4\text{-}4a)$$

$$\sum F_{\text{ext on dice},y} = m_{\text{dice}} a_{\text{dice},y}$$
$$(4\text{-}4b)$$

Net force on dice = sum of tension force and gravitational force:

$$\sum \vec{F}_{\text{ext on dice}} = \vec{T} + \vec{w}_{\text{dice}}$$

acceleration = 6.50 m/s^2

angle $\theta = ?$

$\vec{a}_{\text{dice}}$

acceleration is in the positive x direction

gravitational force is in the negative y direction

Solve

Write the x and y components of the external forces that act on the dice and the acceleration of the dice.

Components of tension force $\vec{T}$:

$$T_x = T \sin \theta$$
$$T_y = T \cos \theta$$

Components of gravitational force $\vec{w}_{dice}$: magnitude $w_{dice} = m_{dice}g$

$$w_{dice,x} = 0$$
$$w_{dice,y} = -w_{dice} = -m_{dice}g$$

Components of acceleration $\vec{a}_{dice}$:

$$a_{dice,x} = a_{dice} = 6.50 \text{ m/s}^2$$
$$a_{dice,y} = 0$$

Substitute the expressions for the components of $\vec{w}$, $\vec{T}$, and $\vec{a}_{dice}$ into Newton's second law. This gives two equations, one from the x components and one from the y components.

Newton's second law in component form:

$$x: \sum F_{\text{ext on dice},x} = T_x + w_{dice,x} = m_{dice}a_{dice,x}, \text{ so}$$

$$T \sin \theta + 0 = m_{dice}a_{dice}$$

$$y: \sum F_{\text{ext on dice},y} = T_y + w_{dice,y} = m_{dice}a_{dice,y}, \text{ so}$$

$$T \cos \theta + (-m_{dice}g) = 0$$

We don't know either the magnitude T or the angle θ of the tension force. All we are asked to solve for is the value of θ, so we eliminate T from the two equations above. We also use the definition of the tangent function, $\tan \theta = (\sin \theta)/(\cos \theta)$.

From the y equation:

$$T \cos \theta = m_{dice}g, \text{ so}$$

$$T = \frac{m_{dice}g}{\cos \theta}$$

Substitute this into the x equation:

$$T \sin \theta = m_{dice}a_{dice}, \text{ so}$$

$$\frac{m_{dice}g}{\cos \theta} \sin \theta = m_{dice}a_{dice}$$

Divide through by m_{dice} and g. Then apply the definition of tangent.

$$\frac{\sin \theta}{\cos \theta} = \frac{a_{dice}}{g}$$

$$\frac{\sin \theta}{\cos \theta} = \tan \theta = \frac{a_{dice}}{g}$$

Solve for θ:

$$\theta = \tan^{-1}\left(\frac{a_{dice}}{g}\right) = \tan^{-1}\left(\frac{6.50 \text{ m/s}^2}{9.80 \text{ m/s}^2}\right)$$

$$= \tan^{-1}(0.663)$$

$$= 33.6°$$

Reflect

Note that our answer doesn't depend on the mass m_{dice}. The angle θ would be the same whether the dice were made of lightweight plastic or solid gold.

We can check our result by using a range of values of acceleration. When the car is not accelerating (as would be the case if its velocity is constant), $a_{dice} = 0$ and $\theta = \tan^{-1} 0 = 0$. The dice hang straight down, which is expected. The greater the acceleration a_{dice}, the greater the value of θ—which is also what we would expect.

Watch Out!   Newton's laws apply only in inertial frames of reference.

You might argue that the dice in the preceding example accelerate *backward* rather than forward. After all, from your perspective as the driver, the dice swing backward when you step on the accelerator pedal. The driver's seat isn't a good place from which to apply Newton's laws, however, because you are yourself accelerating! It turns out that Newton's laws work *only* if you observe from a vantage point, or *frame of reference*, that is *not* accelerating. Such a vantage point is called an **inertial frame of reference**. (A more detailed study of Newton's first law than we can present in this book usually considers Newton's first law as a *definition* of inertial frames of reference. That's really why Newton's first law gets its own number.) One such frame of reference would be a person standing by the road as you accelerate away. The dice initially will lag behind the car due to their inertia, which is why the dice swing backward relative to the driver. Once the dice have stabilized, however, they move with the same acceleration as the car. The same inertial effect explains why you feel pushed back in your seat when the car accelerates forward and you feel thrown forward against your safety belt if the car brakes rapidly. No real force acts on you in either case: It's just your inertia. (If you think inertia *is* a real force, ask yourself what could be exerting it. If you think it's your own body, remember that only external forces affect motion; if you think it's "the force of acceleration" or "the force of velocity," remember from Section 4-4 that these forces don't exist.)

Example 4-5 Slipping and Sliding I

One wintry day, you accidentally drop your physics book (mass 2.50 kg) on a sidewalk that tilts at an angle of 10.0° below the horizontal. If the sidewalk is so icy as to be essentially frictionless, what is the book's acceleration as it slides downhill?

Set Up

We'll find the book's acceleration using Newton's second law. Because there is no friction in this situation, the only forces acting on the book are the gravitational force $\vec{w}_{\text{book}}$ (which points straight down) and the normal force $\vec{n}$ (which points perpendicular to the surface of the inclined sidewalk). This situation is similar to the block shown in Figure 4-11 (Section 4-4). Because the motion is down the ramp, we choose the x axis to be in that direction.

Newton's second law in component form applied to the book:

$$\sum F_{\text{ext on book},x} = m_{\text{book}}a_{\text{book},x} \quad (4\text{-}4a)$$
$$\sum F_{\text{ext on book},y} = m_{\text{book}}a_{\text{book},y} \quad (4\text{-}4b)$$

Net force on book = sum of normal force and gravitational force:

$$\sum \vec{F}_{\text{ext on book}} = \vec{n} + \vec{w}_{\text{book}}$$

Solve

Write the forces and the acceleration in component form. The book doesn't move perpendicular to the ramp, so the y component of its acceleration is zero.

Components of normal force $\vec{n}$:

$$n_x = 0$$
$$n_y = n$$

Components of gravitational force $\vec{w}_{\text{book}}$:

magnitude $w_{\text{book}} = m_{\text{book}}g$

$$w_{\text{book},x} = w_{\text{book}} \sin \theta$$
$$= m_{\text{book}}g \sin \theta$$

$$w_{\text{book},y} = -w_{\text{book}} \cos \theta$$
$$= -m_{\text{book}}g \cos \theta$$

Components of acceleration $\vec{a}_{\text{book}}$:

$a_{\text{book},x}$: to be determined
$a_{\text{book},y} = 0$

| Use the components to write Newton's second law for the book in component form. | Newton's second law in component form: |

$$x: \sum F_{\text{ext on book},x} = n_x + w_x = 0 + m_{\text{book}}g \sin \theta$$

$$= m_{\text{book}}a_{\text{book},x}, \text{ so}$$

$$m_{\text{book}}g \sin \theta = m_{\text{book}}a_{\text{book},x}$$

$$y: \sum F_{\text{ext on book},y} = n_y + w_y = n - m_{\text{book}}g \cos \theta = m_{\text{book}}a_{\text{book},y}, \text{ so}$$

$$n - m_{\text{book}}g \cos \theta = 0$$

| All we are asked to find is the acceleration of the book, so we only need the x equation. | Dividing the x equation by m_{book}: |

$$a_{\text{book},x} = g \sin \theta = (9.80 \text{ m/s}^2) \sin 10.0°$$
$$= 1.70 \text{ m/s}^2$$

Reflect

Our result tells us that the book accelerates in the positive x direction (downhill). This result makes sense: When no friction opposes its motion, the book should gain speed as it slides downhill. If the slope were steeper, θ and $\sin \theta$ would be greater and the acceleration $a_{\text{book},x} = g \sin \theta$ would be greater as well. Just as for an object in free fall, the acceleration doesn't depend on the book's mass.

Note also that our analysis would be exactly the same if you put the book near the bottom of the incline and gave it an upward push to start it moving. The gravitational force and normal force would be unchanged, so the magnitude and direction of the acceleration would likewise be unchanged. Because the acceleration is downhill and the velocity uphill, the book would slow down as it moved up the incline—again, just as we would expect.

book sliding downhill

acceleration of the book is the same

book sliding uphill

Example 4-6 Slipping and Sliding II

If there is friction between the book and the incline in the previous example, the book's downhill acceleration will be less than we calculated above. If the book gains speed at only 0.200 m/s^2 as it slides downhill, what is the magnitude of the friction force on the 2.50-kg book?

Set Up

The situation is much the same as in Example 4-5 but with an additional friction force $\vec{f}$ which points up the incline, opposing the book's motion. We are given the book's acceleration, so we'll use Newton's second law to determine the magnitude of the friction force.

Newton's second law in component form applied to the book:

$$\sum F_{\text{ext on book},x} = m_{\text{book}}a_{\text{book},x} \text{ (4-4a)}$$
$$\sum F_{\text{ext on book},y} = m_{\text{book}}a_{\text{book},y} \text{ (4-4b)}$$

Net force on book = sum of normal force, gravitational force, and friction force:

$$\sum \vec{F}_{\text{ext on book}} = \vec{n} + \vec{w}_{\text{book}} + \vec{f}$$

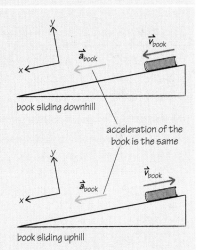

$a_{\text{book}} = 0.200 \text{ m/s}^2$

motion of book

$\theta = 10.0°$

Solve

The vectors $\vec{n}$, $\vec{w}_{\text{book}}$, and $\vec{a}_{\text{book}}$ break into components the same way that they did in Example 4-5. We complete the list with the vector components of $\vec{f}$.

Components of friction force $\vec{f}$:

$$f_x = -f$$
$$f_y = 0$$

Use the components to write Newton's second law for the book in component form.	Newton's second law in component form: x: $\sum F_{\text{ext on book},x} = n_x + w_x + f_x = 0 + m_{\text{book}}g \sin\theta - f = m_{\text{book}}a_{\text{book},x}$ so $$m_{\text{book}}g \sin\theta - f = m_{\text{book}}a_{\text{book},x}$$ y: $\sum F_{\text{ext on book},y} = n_y + w_y + f_y = n - m_{\text{book}}g \cos\theta + 0 = m_{\text{book}}a_{\text{book},y}$ so $$n - m_{\text{book}}g \cos\theta = 0$$
Solve the x equation for the magnitude f of the friction force.	$m_{\text{book}}g \sin\theta - f = m_{\text{book}}a_{\text{book},x}$ so $$\begin{aligned} f &= m_{\text{book}}g \sin\theta - m_{\text{book}}a_{\text{book},x} \\ &= m_{\text{book}}(g \sin\theta - a_{\text{book},x}) \\ &= (2.50 \text{ kg})\left[(9.80 \text{ m/s}^2)\sin 10.0° - 0.200 \text{ m/s}^2\right] \\ &= 3.75 \text{ kg} \cdot \text{m/s}^2 = 3.75 \text{ N} \end{aligned}$$

Reflect

This example is very much like Example 4-3 in Section 4-3. The only difference is that the net force on the cat in Example 4-3 is zero (the cat is at rest and remains at rest), while the net force on the book sliding down the incline in this example is *not* zero.

Example 4-7 How to "Lose Weight" the Easy Way

A 70.0-kg student stands on a bathroom scale in an elevator. What is the reading on the scale (a) when the elevator is moving upward at a constant 0.500 m/s? (b) When the elevator is accelerating downward at 1.00 m/s²?

Set Up

The reading on a bathroom scale tells you how hard you are pushing on it, which may not be the same as your weight. (Try pushing on a bathroom scale with your hand. The reading measures how strong you are, not how much you weigh.) Newton's third law tells us that the downward normal force of the student on the scale is equal in magnitude to the upward normal force exerted by the scale on the student, $\vec{n}_{\text{scale on student}}$. So, what we want to know is the magnitude of $\vec{n}_{\text{scale on student}}$ in each situation, which we'll find by applying Newton's second law to the student. The only other force acting on the student is the gravitational force $\vec{w}_{\text{student}}$. Both forces and the acceleration in part (b) are in the vertical direction, so we only need the y component.

y component of Newton's second law applied to the student:

$$\sum F_{\text{ext on student},y} = m_{\text{student}}a_{\text{student},y} \quad (4\text{-}4b)$$

Net force on student = sum of normal force and gravitational force:

$$\sum \vec{F}_{\text{ext on student}} = \vec{n}_{\text{scale on student}} + \vec{w}_{\text{student}}$$

Solve

(a) If the elevator is moving at a constant velocity, the student's acceleration is zero. So, the sum of the external forces on the student must be zero. We then solve for the magnitude of the normal force that the scale exerts on the student.

Student's y velocity is constant, so
$$a_{\text{student},y} = 0$$

Newton's second law in component form:

y: $\sum F_{\text{ext on student},y}$
$$= n_{\text{scale on student}} + (-w_{\text{student}})$$
$$= m_{\text{student}}a_{\text{student},y} = 0 \text{ so}$$

$n_{\text{scale on student}}$
$$\begin{aligned} &= w_{\text{student}} = m_{\text{student}}g \\ &= (70.0 \text{ kg})(9.80 \text{ m/s}^2) \\ &= 686 \text{ N} \end{aligned}$$

constant velocity: $a_{\text{student},\, y} = 0$

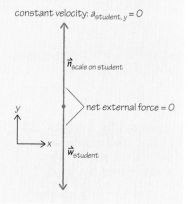

net external force = 0

(b) If the elevator, and so also the student, are accelerating downward (in the negative y direction) at 1.00 m/s^2, the net force on the student must be downward. The net force can only be downward if the upward normal force exerted by the scale is smaller than the downward gravitational force. Again we solve for the magnitude $n_{\text{scale on student}}$ using Newton's second law.

The student's acceleration has a downward (negative) y component:

$$a_{\text{student},y} = -1.00 \text{ m/s}^2$$

Newton's second law in component form:

$$y: \sum F_{\text{ext on student},y}$$
$$= n_{\text{scale on student}} + (-w_{\text{student}})$$
$$= m_{\text{student}}a_{\text{student},y} \text{ so}$$

$$n_{\text{scale on student}}$$
$$= w_{\text{student}} + m_{\text{student}}a_{\text{student},y}$$
$$= 686 \text{ N} + (70.0 \text{ kg})(-1.00 \text{ m/s}^2) = 616 \text{ N}$$

downward acceleration

$\vec{n}_{\text{scale on student}}$

net external force is downward

$\vec{w}_{\text{student}}$

$a_{\text{student},y} < 0$

Reflect

According to the scale, the student "weighs" 70 N less when the elevator accelerates downward. You've probably experienced this phenomenon in an elevator when it starts moving downward from rest, or when it comes to a halt when moving upward. A similar phenomenon occurs in an elevator that accelerates *upward*. Then $a_{\text{student},y}$ is positive, $n_{\text{scale on student}}$ is greater than the student's weight w_{student}, and the student feels heavier than normal.

What if the elevator is in free fall? Then $a_{\text{student},y} = -g = -9.80 \text{ m/s}^2$ (negative because the acceleration is downward). Substituting this value into our result gives $n_{\text{scale on student}} = 0$. The scale reads zero, and the student will feel weightless! This situation is called *apparent weightlessness*. (The student isn't truly weightless because the gravitational force still acts on her.) We'll see in Chapter 10 that astronauts in Earth orbit are also in free fall, so they *feel* weightless just like the student in the free-falling elevator.

If the elevator is in free fall,

$$a_{\text{student},y} = -g$$

$$n_{\text{scale on student}}$$
$$= w_{\text{student}} + m_{\text{student}}a_{\text{student},y}$$
$$= m_{\text{student}}g + m_{\text{student}}(-g)$$
$$= 0$$

free fall

normal force = 0

$\vec{w}_{\text{student}}$

$a_{\text{student},y} = -g$

Problems Involving Ropes and Tension

What object is pulling the water skier shown in Figure 4-20? You might be tempted to say that it's the boat—but that can't be correct because the boat doesn't touch her. Instead, the boat exerts a force on the tow rope, and it's the tow rope that pulls on the skier. The force that pulls the skier is therefore a *tension* force.

As we learned in Section 4-5, if the weight of the tow rope is small compared to the forces exerted by the objects to which it's attached (in this case, the boat and the water skier), we can ignore its mass altogether. In this case, the magnitude of the tension force is the *same* at both ends of the rope no matter how the boat, skier, and rope are moving. We'll use this principle in the next two examples, both of which involve moving objects that are connected by a lightweight string.

Figure 4-20 Towing a water skier
The boat exerts a force on the tow rope, and the tow rope pulls on the skier.

Go to Picture It 4-1 for more practice dealing with weight

Go to Interactive Exercises 4-1 and 4-2 for more practice dealing with tension

Example 4-8 Tension in a String

You pull two blocks connected by a lightweight string across a horizontal table. Block 1 has a mass of 1.00 kg and block 2 has a mass of 2.00 kg. There is negligible friction between the blocks and the table. The string is rather flimsy and will break if the tension is greater than 6.00 N. What is the maximum pull that you can apply to block 1 without breaking the string?

Set Up

As in the previous examples, we start by drawing a free-body diagram. Note that here there are *two* bodies (block 1 and block 2), so we have to be careful and draw *two* free-body diagrams to include the forces that act on each block. We choose the positive x axis to be in the direction of the blocks' horizontal motion and choose the positive y axis to be vertically upward.

$$\sum \vec{F}_{\text{ext on 1}} = m_1 \vec{a}_1$$
$$\sum \vec{F}_{\text{ext on 2}} = m_2 \vec{a}_2 \qquad (4\text{-}2)$$

Net force on block 1 = sum of force you exert, normal force, gravitational force, and tension:

$$\sum \vec{F}_{\text{ext on 1}} = \vec{F}_{\text{you on 1}} + \vec{n}_1 + \vec{w}_1 + \vec{T}_{\text{string on 1}}$$

We are told that the string connecting the blocks is lightweight, so the tension at either end of the string has the same magnitude: $T_{\text{string on 1}} = T_{\text{string on 2}}$. We'll call this magnitude T for short. Our goal is to find the maximum value of $F_{\text{you on 1}}$ (the magnitude of the force that you exert on block 1) so that T is no greater than 6.00 N.

Net force on block 2 = sum of normal force, gravitational force, and tension:

$$\sum \vec{F}_{\text{ext on 2}} = \vec{n}_2 + \vec{w}_2 + \vec{T}_{\text{string on 2}}$$

Tension is the same at both ends of the string:

$$T_{\text{string on 1}} = T_{\text{string on 2}} = T$$

Solve

We then write Newton's second law for each block in component form. If we assume that the string doesn't stretch, the two blocks move together and have the same x component of acceleration, which we call a_x.

Both blocks have the same x acceleration:

$$a_{1x} = a_{2x} = a_x$$

Both blocks have zero y acceleration.

Newton's second law in component form for block 1:

$$x: \sum F_{\text{ext on 1},x} = F_{\text{you on 1}} + (-T)$$
$$= m_1 a_x$$
$$y: \sum F_{\text{ext on 1},y} = n_1 + (-w_1) = 0$$

Newton's second law in component form for block 2:

$$x: \sum F_{\text{ext on 2},x} = T = m_2 a_x$$
$$y: \sum F_{\text{ext on 2},y} = n_2 + (-w_2) = 0$$

We want to find the value of $F_{\text{you on 1}}$ when $T = 6.00$ N (the maximum tension that will prevent the string from breaking). We use the x equation for block 2 to find the x acceleration a_x in this situation, and then we use this value of a_x in the x equation for block 1 to solve for $F_{\text{you on 1}}$.

First solve for the value of a_x when $T = 6.00$ N. Use the x equation for block 2:

$$T = m_2 a_x$$
$$a_x = \frac{T}{m_2} = \frac{6.00 \text{ N}}{2.00 \text{ kg}} = 3.00 \text{ N/kg} = 3.00 \text{ m/s}^2$$

Now substitute $a_x = 3.00 \text{ m/s}^2$ into the x equation for block 1 and solve for $F_{\text{you on 1}}$:

$$F_{\text{you on 1}} - T = m_1 a_x$$
$$F_{\text{you on 1}} = T + m_1 a_x = 6.00 \text{ N} + (1.00 \text{ kg})(3.00 \text{ m/s}^2)$$
$$= 6.00 \text{ N} + 3.00 \text{ kg} \cdot \text{m/s}^2 = 6.00 \text{ N} + 3.00 \text{ N} = 9.00 \text{ N}$$

Reflect

We can check our answers by referring back to Newton's second law in the x direction for each block. You exert a forward force $F_{\text{you on 1}} = 9.00$ N on block 1, and the string exerts a backward force of 6.00 N. So, the net forward force on block 1 is 9.00 N − 6.00 N = 3.00 N. This block has a mass of 1.00 kg, so the 3.00-N net force gives block 1 an acceleration of 3.00 m/s². The only horizontal force on block 2 is the forward tension force of 6.00 N; because block 2 has a mass of 2.00 kg, the forward acceleration produced is (6.00 N)/(2.00 kg) = 3.00 m/s². This acceleration is the same as for block 1, as it must be because the two blocks move together.

Because the two blocks move together, we could have treated the two blocks together as a single unit system with a mass equal to $m_1 + m_2 = 3.00$ kg. That wouldn't have helped us solve this problem, however. The reason is that the tension forces are *internal* forces (they involve one part of the combined unit pulling on another part) in this approach. As a result, there would be no way to apply the condition that the tension cannot exceed 6.00 N.

Here's the lesson: When solving problems that involve forces and accelerations for more than one object, it's safest to *always* apply Newton's laws to each object separately.

However, the combined system of two blocks can be used as another method to check your answer. Because both blocks have the same acceleration, the acceleration of the system of two blocks should also be the same.

Newton's second law in component form for the two blocks as a unit:

x: $\sum F_{\text{ext on unit},x}$
$= F_{\text{you on 1}} = (m_1 + m_2)a_{\text{on unit},x}$

y: $\sum F_{\text{ext on 1},y} = n + (-w) = 0$

We can't solve for $F_{\text{you on 1}}$ because the tension T does not appear in these equations.

But we can use the x equation of Newton's second law to check our answer for $F_{\text{you on 1}}$ solving for $a_{\text{on unit},x}$ of the two-block system.

$F_{\text{you on 1}} = (m_1 + m_2)a_{\text{on unit},x}$

$a_{\text{on unit},x} = \dfrac{F_{\text{you on 1}}}{m_1 + m_2} = \dfrac{9.00\text{ N}}{1.00\text{ kg} + 2.00\text{ kg}}$

$= 3.00\text{ N/kg} = 3.00\text{ m/s}^2$

which is the same acceleration we calculated for each block separately.

total mass = 3.00 kg

Example 4-9 Atwood's Machine

Two blocks are connected by a lightweight string that passes over a pulley as shown in Figure 4-21. (This arrangement is known as *Atwood's machine* after Rev. George Atwood, who devised it in 1784 as a way to demonstrate motion with constant acceleration.) Block 1 is more massive than block 2, so when released block 1 accelerates downward and block 2 accelerates upward. Assume that the mass of the pulley is so small that we can neglect it. Derive expressions for (a) the acceleration of each block and (b) the tension in the string.

Both the string and the pulley have negligible masses.

Figure 4-21 **Atwood's machine** When the blocks are released from rest, block 1 falls and block 2 rises. What are their accelerations, and what is the tension in the string?

Set Up

Each block has only two forces acting on it: a downward gravitational force and an upward tension force. We choose the positive y direction for block 1 to be downward and the positive y direction for block 2 to be upward. Using this choice, both blocks accelerate in the positive y direction, and both blocks have the same y component of acceleration (because we assume that the string doesn't stretch). One of our goals is to calculate this acceleration, which we call a_y.

Because we can neglect the mass of the pulley, the magnitude of the tension force has the same value T at both ends of the lightweight string. Our other goal is to calculate the value of T.

Newton's second law in the y direction applied to each block:

$\sum F_{\text{ext on 1},y} = m_1 a_{1y}$

$\sum F_{\text{ext on 2},y} = m_2 a_{2y}$

Net force on block 1 = sum of gravitational force and tension:

$\sum \vec{F}_{\text{ext on 1}} = \vec{w}_1 + \vec{T}_{\text{string on 1}}$

Net force on block 2 = sum of gravitational force and tension:

$\sum \vec{F}_{\text{ext on 2}} = \vec{w}_2 + \vec{T}_{\text{string on 2}}$

Both blocks have the same y acceleration:

$a_{1y} = a_{2y} = a_y$

Magnitude of tension is the same at both ends of the string:

$T_{\text{string on 1}} = T_{\text{string on 2}} = T$

Solve

Write the y component of Newton's second law for each block.

Newton's second law in component form for block 1:

$$y: \sum F_{\text{ext on }1,y} = w_1 + (-T) = m_1 a_y \text{ or}$$
$$m_1 g - T = m_1 a_y$$

Newton's second law in component form for block 2:

$$y: \sum F_{\text{ext on }2,y} = T + (-w_2) = m_2 a_y \text{ or}$$
$$T - m_2 g = m_2 a_y$$

We have two equations (one for block 1 and one for block 2) and two quantities that we want to find (a_y and T). One way to proceed is to first solve for one unknown in terms of the other. Let's solve the block 1 equation for T in terms of a_y. Then substitute this expression for T into the block 2 equation and solve for a_y.

Solve the block 1 equation for T:

$$m_1 g - T = m_1 a_y \text{ so}$$
$$T = m_1 g - m_1 a_y$$

Substitute this into the block 2 equation:

$$(m_1 g - m_1 a_y) - m_2 g = m_2 a_y$$

Solve for a_y:

$$m_1 g - m_2 g = m_1 a_y + m_2 a_y$$
$$(m_1 - m_2) g = (m_1 + m_2) a_y \text{ or}$$
$$a_y = \left(\frac{m_1 - m_2}{m_1 + m_2}\right)g$$

Now that we have an expression for a_y, substitute it back into the equation for T that we found from the block 1 equation. This resulting expression gives us our final answer for T.

From the block 1 equation for T:

$$T = m_1 g - m_1 a_y$$

Substitute our expression for a_y and simplify:

$$T = m_1 g - m_1 \left(\frac{m_1 - m_2}{m_1 + m_2}\right)g = m_1 g \left(1 - \frac{m_1 - m_2}{m_1 + m_2}\right)$$

$$= m_1 g \left(\frac{m_1 + m_2}{m_1 + m_2} - \frac{m_1 - m_2}{m_1 + m_2}\right) = m_1 g \left(\frac{m_1 + m_2 - m_1 + m_2}{m_1 + m_2}\right) \text{ or}$$

$$T = \frac{2 m_1 m_2 g}{m_1 + m_2}$$

Reflect

Do these results make sense? As a start, you should confirm that our expression for a_y (an acceleration) has units of m/s^2 and our expression for T (a force magnitude) has units of newtons. Do they?

To check our expression for acceleration a_y in more detail, notice that it depends on the difference $m_1 - m_2$ between the two masses. If $m_1 > m_2$ as we assumed here, a_y is positive; then both blocks accelerate in the positive y direction, so block 1 (the more massive and heavier one) accelerates downward and block 2 accelerates upward.

If instead $m_1 < m_2$ so that block 2 is more massive and heavier, the acceleration a_y is negative. Then, block 1 (which is now the lighter one) accelerates upward and block 2 downward. Finally, if the two blocks have equal mass so that $m_1 = m_2$, our expression says that $a_y = 0$ or the blocks don't accelerate at all. If the two equal-mass blocks begin at rest, they will remain at rest and in balance, just as we would expect.

What about our expression for the tension T? To check this out, let's choose some specific values of m_1 and m_2. With $m_1 = 4.00$ kg and $m_2 = 2.00$ kg, the tension is $T = 26.1$ N. That's less than the 39.2-N weight of block 1 but greater than the 19.6-N weight of block 2. This result makes sense because for block 1 the downward gravitational force overwhelms the upward tension force and the block accelerates downward, while for block 2 the upward tension force overwhelms gravity and the block accelerates upward. Note that because the tension force "holds back" the downward acceleration of block 1, the value of a_y is less than g.

Let $m_1 = 4.00$ kg and $m_2 = 2.00$ kg

Weight of block 1 $= m_1 g$
$= (4.00 \text{ kg})(9.80 \text{ m/s}^2)$
$= 39.2$ N

Weight of block 2 $= m_2 g$
$= (2.00 \text{ kg})(9.80 \text{ m/s}^2)$
$= 19.6$ N

Tension in string:

$$T = \frac{2 m_1 m_2 g}{m_1 + m_2}$$
$$= \frac{2(4.00 \text{ kg})(2.00 \text{ kg})(9.80 \text{ m/s}^2)}{4.00 \text{ kg} + 2.00 \text{ kg}}$$
$$= 26.1 \text{ N}$$

You should repeat these calculations for different values of the two masses. Try $m_1 = 1.00$ kg and $m_2 = 3.00$ kg: How does the tension compare to the weights of the two blocks in this case? Is the acceleration positive or negative in this case?

Acceleration of either block:

$$a_y = \left(\frac{m_1 - m_2}{m_1 + m_2}\right)g$$

$$= \left(\frac{4.00 \text{ kg} - 2.00 \text{ kg}}{4.00 \text{ kg} + 2.00 \text{ kg}}\right)(9.80 \text{ m/s}^2)$$

$$= 3.27 \text{ m/s}^2$$

Kinematics and Newton's Laws

All of the objects that we considered in Examples 4-4 through 4-9 move in straight lines. What's more, the forces acting on each object are constant. So the *accelerations* that these forces produce are constant as well. That means we can apply all of the kinematic formulas for straight-line motion with constant acceleration that we learned in Chapter 2. If you can solve problems that use these formulas, and can also solve problems that involve Newton's laws, it's straightforward to solve problems that involve both of these. Here's an example.

Example 4-10 Down the Slopes

A 60.0-kg skier starts from rest at the top of a hill with a 30.0° slope. She reaches the bottom of the slope 4.00 s later. If there is a constant 72.0-N friction force that resists her motion, how long is the hill?

Set Up

All three of the forces that act on the skier—the normal force $\vec{n}$, the gravitational force $\vec{w}_{\text{skier}}$, and the friction force $\vec{f}$—are constant. So, the net force on the skier is constant, as is her acceleration. We can therefore use a constant-acceleration formula to find the length of the hill. We'll find the skier's downhill acceleration using Newton's second law.

We choose the positive x axis to point down the slope and the positive y axis to point perpendicular to the slope as shown. (Compare Example 4-6.) Then, the skier's acceleration points along the x axis only.

$$x = x_0 + v_{0x}t + \frac{1}{2}a_xt^2 \qquad (2\text{-}9)$$

Newton's second law in component form for the skier:

x: $\sum F_{\text{ext on skier},x} = m_{\text{skier}}a_x$
y: $\sum F_{\text{ext on skier},y} = m_{\text{skier}}a_y$

Net force on skier = sum of normal force, gravitational force, and friction force:

$$\sum \vec{F}_{\text{ext on skier}} = \vec{n} + \vec{w}_{\text{skier}} + \vec{f}$$

Solve

The normal force $\vec{n}$ has only a positive y component. The gravitational force $\vec{w}_{\text{skier}}$ has a positive (downhill) x component and a negative y component, while the friction force has only a negative (uphill) x component. Use these components and Newton's second law to solve for the skier's x component of acceleration a_x.

Find the skier's x component of acceleration from the x component of Newton's second law:

$$\sum F_{\text{ext on skier},x} = w_{\text{skier}} \sin\theta + (-f)$$
$$= m_{\text{skier}}a_x$$

Weight of skier:

$w_{\text{skier}} = m_{\text{skier}}g$ so

$m_{\text{skier}}a_x = m_{\text{skier}}g \sin\theta - f$

$$a_x = g \sin\theta - \frac{f}{m_{\text{skier}}}$$

$$= (9.80 \text{ m/s}^2) \sin 30.0° - \frac{72.0 \text{ N}}{60.0 \text{ kg}}$$

$$= 4.90 \text{ m/s}^2 - 1.20 \text{ m/s}^2$$

$$= 3.70 \text{ m/s}^2$$

Now that we know the skier's acceleration in the x direction, we can use the kinematic equation to solve for her final position, which will be equal to the length of the hill as long as she starts at $x_0 = 0$. Because the skier starts at rest, her initial velocity is $v_{0x} = 0$.

Find the skier's final position after 4.00 s, assuming she starts at $x_0 = 0$.

$$x = x_0 + v_{0x}t + \frac{1}{2}a_xt^2$$

$$= 0 + 0 + \frac{1}{2}(3.70 \text{ m/s}^2)(4.00 \text{ s})^2$$

$$= 29.6 \text{ m}$$

Reflect

Is our answer consistent? With an acceleration of 3.70 m/s², our skier reaches a velocity of 14.8 m/s after 4.00 s. Because she started at rest, her average x component of velocity for the trip is half the final velocity, or 7.40 m/s. If you travel at 7.40 m/s for 4.00 s, you cover a distance of 29.6 m—which is just the answer that we obtained.

Skier's velocity at $t = 4.00$ s:

$$v_x = v_{0x} + a_xt \qquad (2-5)$$

The skier's initial velocity is $v_{0x} = 0$, so

$$v_x = 0 + (3.70 \text{ m/s}^2)(4.00 \text{ s}) = 14.8 \text{ m/s}$$

Average velocity for the skier's motion with constant acceleration:

$$v_{\text{average},x} = \frac{v_{0x} + v_x}{2} = \frac{0 + 14.8 \text{ m/s}}{2} = 7.40 \text{ m/s} \qquad (2-7)$$

Distance traveled in 4.00 s:

$$x = x_0 + v_{\text{average},x}t = 0 + (7.40 \text{ m/s})(4.00 \text{ s}) = 29.6 \text{ m}$$

By now you should have a pretty good sense of how to attack problems that involve force and acceleration. In the next chapter we'll use the same techniques to tackle problems involving a more detailed description of friction as well as motion in a circle.

Take-Home Message for Section 4-6

✔ To solve a problem that involves forces, begin by making a free-body diagram for the object (or objects) of interest and choosing coordinate axes.

✔ Once you have drawn the free-body diagram, write down Newton's second law for each coordinate axis and solve for the unknowns.

4-7 Fish use Newton's third law and a combination of forces to move through water

One biologically important application of Newton's laws is understanding how fish propel themselves. Some species of fish can swim long distances, often at high speeds. Many fish can speed up and slow down quickly and can maneuver with apparent ease in tight spaces. The mechanisms and physics that underlie fish propulsion are of interest not only to scientists, but also to engineers studying effective designs for underwater vehicles.

Fish typically have a number of fins of various shapes and sizes (Figure 4-22). In almost all species of fish, the side-to-side undulation or swishing of the *caudal fin* (and the rear part of the fish's body) is the primary means of propulsion. Figure 4-23 shows the fish from above and in the process of sweeping its caudal fin to the right. In doing so, the fish exerts a force on the surrounding water that acts perpendicular

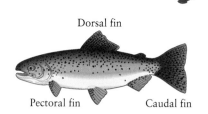

Figure 4-22 **Fish anatomy** Fish have a variety of fins for propulsion and directional control. The caudal fin is primarily responsible for pushing the fish forward through the water.

to the fish's body, in a manner similar to a normal force. Newton's third law requires that the water exert a force of equal magnitude on the fish in the opposite direction. This force on the fish, which we label $\vec{F}_{\text{water on fish}}$ in Figure 4-23, does not point in the direction that the fish is traveling. But $\vec{F}_{\text{water on fish}}$ *does* have a component in the direction of the fish's travel. This component, labeled F_{thrust} in Figure 4-23, propels the fish forward. In some fish the motion of the dorsal fin also contributes to forward locomotion.

The swishing of a fish's tail also results in a force perpendicular to the net motion of the fish (Figure 4-23). These lateral forces contribute to the stability of the fish, and help it turn and maneuver. Most fish can also make subtle adjustments to the orientation of the pectoral fins, one on each side of the fish, to enable it to stop, start, and change direction quickly. All of these aspects of fish propulsion are based on Newton's third law: Part of the fish's body exerts a force on the water, and the water responds by exerting a force on the fish.

Figure 4-23 **Propelling a fish** When a fish swishes its caudal fin back and forth, it exerts a force $\vec{F}_{\text{fish on water}}$ on the water. The reaction to this is the force $\vec{F}_{\text{water on fish}}$ that the water exerts on the fish. The forward component of this force (F_{thrust}) pushes the fish forward through the water.

Take-Home Message for Section 4-7

✔ Fish propel themselves by swishing their caudal fin and the rear end of their body back and forth, pushing on the surrounding water and so causing the water to exert a force on the fish. This force has a component that pushes the fish forward.

Key Terms

contact force
equilibrium
external force
force
force pair
free-body diagram
friction force
gravitational force

inertia
inertial frame of reference
internal force
kilogram
mass
net external force (net force)
newton
Newton's first law

Newton's laws of motion
Newton's second law
Newton's third law
normal force
pound
reaction force
tension
weight

Chapter Summary

Topic	Equation or Figure

Forces and Newton's second law of motion: The net external force on an object is the vector sum of all forces exerted on that object by other objects. Common forces include the gravitational force, the normal force, friction, and the tension force. Newton's second law states that if the net external force on an object is nonzero, the object accelerates.

The **net external force** acting on an object... ...equals the **vector sum** of all of the individual forces that act on the object.

$$\sum \vec{F}_{\text{ext}} = \vec{F}_1 + \vec{F}_2 + \vec{F}_3 + \ldots \tag{4-1}$$

The sum includes only external forces (forces exerted on the object by other objects).

If a **net external force** acts on an object... ... the object accelerates. The acceleration is in the same direction as the net force.

$$\sum \vec{F}_{\text{ext}} = m\vec{a} \tag{4-2}$$

The magnitude of acceleration that the net external force causes depends on the mass m of the object (the quantity of material in the object). The greater the mass, the smaller the acceleration.

The **acceleration** of an object... ...is proportional to and in the same direction as the net external force on the object...

$$\vec{a} = \frac{1}{m} \sum \vec{F}_{\text{ext}}$$

(4-3)

... and inversely proportional to the mass of the object.

Mass, weight, inertia, and Newton's first law of motion: The mass of an object is the quantity of material that it contains. Its weight is the magnitude of the gravitational force on the object. Inertia is the tendency of an object to maintain the same motion. Newton's first law states that if the net external force on an object is zero, it maintains a constant velocity.

Weight of an object (equal to the magnitude of the gravitational force on that object)

$$w = mg$$

(4-5)

Mass of the object   **Magnitude** of the acceleration due to gravity

If the net external force on an object is zero... ... the object does not accelerate...

If $\sum \vec{F}_{\text{ext}} = 0$, then $\vec{a} = 0$ and $\vec{v} = $ constant

(4-6)

... and the velocity of the object remains constant. If the object is at rest, it remains at rest; if it is in motion, it continues in motion in a straight line at a constant speed.

Free-body diagrams: A free-body diagram depicts all of the external forces that act on an object. The coordinate axes are chosen so that as many of the vectors as possible (force and acceleration) point along one of the axes.

① With the friction force absent, the remaining normal force and gravitational force do not cancel. So the **net external force** $\Sigma\vec{F}_{\text{ext}} = \vec{n} + \vec{w}$ is not zero.

② The box neither leaps off the ramp nor sinks down into it, so it doesn't accelerate in the y direction. So the normal force must cancel the (negative) y component of the gravitational force.

③ Nothing cancels the positive x component of the gravitational force, so the net force is in the positive x direction...

④ ... and the acceleration of the block is in the positive x direction, the same as the direction of the net force.

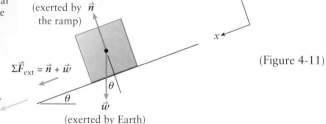

$\Sigma\vec{F}_{\text{ext}} = \vec{n} + \vec{w}$

(exerted by $\vec{n}$ the ramp)

$\vec{a}$ θ θ $\vec{w}$
(exerted by Earth)

(Figure 4-11)

Newton's third law of motion: The third law relates the forces that two objects exert on each other. This law is valid no matter how the objects move.

Force that object A exerts on object B   Force that object B exerts on object A

$$\vec{F}_{A \text{ on } B} = -\vec{F}_{B \text{ on } A}$$

(4-7)

 If object A exerts a force on object B, object B must exert a force on object A with the same magnitude but opposite direction.

Solving force problems: All problems that involve forces can be solved by: (1) first drawing a free-body diagram for the object in question, and (2) then writing out Newton's second law in component form and solving for the unknowns.

Sum of the x components of all external forces acting on the object

x component of the object's acceleration

(a) $\sum F_{\text{ext},x} = ma_x$

Mass of the object

(b) $\sum F_{\text{ext},y} = ma_y$

(4-4)

Sum of the y components of all external forces acting on the object

y component of the object's acceleration

Answer to What do you think? Question

(c) The forward force exerted on the sled by the dogs now exceeds the backward force of friction. Hence there is a net forward force on the sled, and it accelerates forward—that is, it speeds up.

Answers to Got the Concept? Questions

4-1   (c), (a), (b) and (d) [tie]. From Newton's second law, $\sum \vec{F}_{\text{ext}} = m\vec{a}$, the magnitude of the net force $\sum \vec{F}_{\text{ext}}$ equals the object's mass m multiplied by the magnitude of the object's acceleration $\vec{a}$. For case (a), this product is $(1250\,\text{kg})(2.00\,\text{m/s}^2) = 2500\,\text{kg} \cdot \text{m/s}^2 = 2500\,\text{N}$; for case (c), it is $(4500\,\text{kg})(0.600\,\text{m/s}^2) = 2700\,\text{N}$. (The truck is slowing down rather than speeding up, but all that counts is the *magnitude* of the acceleration.) So, there is a greater net force on the truck in (c) than on the automobile in (a). In cases (b) and (d) the objects are not accelerating (the velocities are constant), so $\vec{a} = 0$ and the net force on the object is zero.

4-2   Newton's second law holds everywhere in the universe, even in the absence of gravity. The second law says that if you apply the same force to each sphere, the massive lead sphere will have a smaller acceleration than the less massive plastic sphere. You can use this same principle here on Earth: Hold this textbook in one hand and a pencil in the other, then try to shake both hands side to side. The hand holding this textbook will move far less than the other hand because this book is quite a bit more massive than a pencil. So the acceleration of the book (and the hand holding it) will be much smaller than the acceleration of the pencil, assuming that each hand exerts roughly the same force.

4-3   (c) and (d) [tie], (a), (b). From Equation 4-5 an object's mass m is related to its weight w and the acceleration due to gravity g by $m = w/g$. So, the mass of rock (a) is $m_a = (10.0\,\text{N})/(3.69\,\text{m/s}^2) = 2.71\,\text{kg}$, and the mass of rock (b) is $m_b = (10.0\,\text{N})/(9.80\,\text{m/s}^2) = 1.02\,\text{kg}$. Both rock (c) and rock (d) have a mass of 10.0 kg.

4-4   (d) Example 4-3 shows that $n = w_{\text{cat}} \cos\theta$ and $f = w_{\text{cat}} \sin\theta$, where w_{cat} is the weight of the cat. As the value of θ increases, the value of $\cos\theta$ decreases and the value of $\sin\theta$ increases. This says that the steeper the angle, the greater the friction force that the ramp must exert to keep the cat from sliding. As we'll learn in Chapter 5, there is a limit to how much friction force a surface can exert. So if you increase the angle too much, the ramp will no longer be able to provide the needed amount of friction and the unhappy cat will start to slide.

4-5   (b) Three external forces act on the box: the gravitational force $\vec{w}$ (exerted by Earth), the normal force $\vec{n}$ (exerted by the surface of the ramp), and the friction force $\vec{f}$ (also exerted by the surface of the ramp). Acceleration is not a force, so the quantity $m\vec{a}$ doesn't belong in the free-body diagram. This rules out choices (d) and (e). The normal force $\vec{n}$ is not vertical in this situation but points perpendicular to the inclined surface of the ramp; this rules out choices (c) and (d). Finally, the friction force $\vec{f}$ opposes sliding, so if the box is sliding down the ramp it must be that $\vec{f}$ points up the ramp. This rules out choice (a). Hence only choice (b) is correct. Note that this is the same free-body diagram as shown in Figure 4-10b for a block at rest on the ramp. The difference here is that friction is weaker than in Figure 4-10b, so the block slides down the ramp rather than remaining stationary.

4-6   It is true that when your friend pushes on the crate, the crate pushes back on him according to Newton's third law. However, these two forces act on two *different* objects. The force exerted by the crate acts on your friend, *not* on the crate. So, we don't include it in the sum of external forces acting on the crate. (Remember that one of the keys to applying Newton's second law is considering *only* those external forces that act *on* the object you're considering—in this case, the crate.) The only horizontal forces that act on the crate are your friend's forward push and the backwards push of friction exerted by the floor. If your friend can overcome that friction force, the crate will accelerate and start moving!

4-7   (a) Crate 1 is in contact with crate 2 and so exerts a force on it. Answer (b) is incorrect: You do *not* exert a force on crate 2 because you are not in direct contact with it. (It's true that crate 1 only exerts a force on crate 2 because you push on crate 1, but crate 2 doesn't "know" that: All it "feels" is the push from crate 1.) Crate 2 does exert a reaction force to the push it receives from crate 1. But Newton's third law tells us that this reaction acts on crate 1, *not* on crate 2, so answer (c) is incorrect. As we discussed in Section 4-4, acceleration is caused by force, not the other way around, and there is no such thing as "the force of acceleration." So answer (d), too, is incorrect.

Questions and Problems

In a few problems, you are given more data than you actually need; in a few other problems, you are required to supply data from your general knowledge, outside sources, or informed estimate.

Interpret as significant all digits in numerical values that have trailing zeros and no decimal points.

For all problems, use $g = 9.80 \text{ m/s}^2$ for the free-fall acceleration due to gravity.

• Basic, single-concept problem

•• Intermediate-level problem, may require synthesis of concepts and multiple steps

••• Challenging problem

SSM *Solution is in Student Solutions Manual*

Conceptual Questions

1. •According to Newton's second law, does the direction of the net force always equal the direction of the acceleration? SSM

2. •If the sum of the forces acting on an object equals zero, does this imply that the object is at rest?

3. •What are the basic SI units (kg, m, s) for force according to Newton's second law $\sum \vec{F}_{\text{ext}} = m\vec{a}$?

4. •Medical, Sports Gymnastics routines are done over a padded floor to protect athletes who fall. Why is falling on padding safer than falling on concrete?

5. •A definition of the inertia of an object is that it is a measure of the quantity of matter. How does this definition compare with the definition discussed in the chapter?

6. •When constructing a free-body diagram, why is it a good idea to choose your coordinate system so that the motion of an object is along one of the axes?

7. •A certain rope will break under any tension greater than 800 N. How can it be used to lower an object weighing 850 N over the edge of a cliff without it breaking? SSM

8. •Sports A boxer claims that Newton's third law helps him while boxing. He says that during a boxing match, the force that his jaw feels is the same as the force that his opponent's fist feels (when the opponent is doing the punching). Therefore, his opponent will feel the same force as he feels and he will be able to fight on without any problems, no matter how many punches he receives or gives. It will always be an "even fight." Discuss any flaws in his reasoning.

9. •Astronomy We know that the Sun pulls on Earth. Does Earth also pull on the Sun? Why or why not? SSM

10. •Sports How can a fisherman land a 5-lb fish using fishing line that is rated at 4 lb?

11. •Tension is a very common force in day-to-day life. Identify five ordinary situations that involve the force of tension.

12. •Explain why the force that a horizontal surface exerts on an object at rest on it is called the normal force.

13. •A chair is mounted on a scale inside an elevator in the physics building. Describe the variation in the scale reading as the elevator begins to ascend, goes up at constant speed, stops, begins to descend, goes down at a constant speed, and stops again.

14. •List all the forces acting on a bottle of water if it were sitting on your desk.

15. •What is the net force on a bathroom scale when a 75-kg person stands on it? SSM

16. •An object of mass m is being weighed in an elevator that is moving upward with an acceleration a. What is the result if the weighing is done using (a) a spring balance and (b) a pan balance?

17. •Two forces of 30 N and 70 N act on an object. What are the minimum and maximum values for the sum of these two forces?

18. •You apply a 60-N force to push a box across the floor at constant speed. If you increase the applied force to 80 N, will the box speed up to some new constant speed, or will it continue to speed up until it hits the wall? Assume that the floor is horizontal and the surface is uniform. Explain your answer.

19. •Astronomy Why would it be easier to lift a truck on the Moon's surface than it is on Earth? SSM

20. •Medical Why should the driver and passengers in a car wear seatbelts? Explain your answer.

21. •Medical Why does the American Academy of Pediatrics recommend that all infants sit in rear-facing car seats starting with their first ride home from the hospital? Explain your answer.

22. •Medical Use Newton's third law to explain the forces involved in walking.

23. •Biology Use Newton's third law to explain how birds are able to fly forward. SSM

Multiple-Choice Questions

24. •Medical A car stops suddenly during a head-on collision, causing the driver's brain to slam into the skull. The resulting injury would most likely be to which part of the brain?

    A. frontal portion of the brain
    B. rear portion of the brain
    C. middle portion of the brain
    D. left side of the brain
    E. right side of the brain

25. •Medical During the sudden impact of a car accident, a person's neck can experience abnormal forces, resulting in an injury commonly known as *whiplash*. If a victim's head and neck move in the manner shown in Figure 4-24, his car was hit from the

    A. front.
    B. rear.
    C. right side.
    D. left side.
    E. top during a rollover. SSM

Time

Figure 4-24 Problem 25

26. •The net force on a moving object suddenly becomes zero and remains zero. The object will
   A. stop abruptly.
   B. reduce speed gradually.
   C. continue at constant velocity.
   D. increase speed gradually.
   E. reduce speed abruptly.

27. •Which has greater monetary value, a newton of gold on Earth or a newton of gold on the Moon?
   A. the newton of gold on Earth
   B. the newton of gold on the Moon
   C. the value is the same, regardless of location.
   D. One cannot say without checking the weight on the Moon.
   E. the newton of gold on the Moon but only when inside a spaceship

28. •According to Newton's second law of motion, when a net force acts on an object, the acceleration is
   A. zero.
   B. inversely proportional to the object's mass.
   C. independent of mass.
   D. inversely proportional to the net force.
   E. directly proportional to the object's mass.

29. •When a net force acts on an object, the object
   A. is at rest.
   B. is in motion with a constant velocity.
   C. has zero speed.
   D. is accelerating.
   E. at rest or in motion with a constant velocity.

30. •In the absence of a net force, an object cannot be
   A. at rest.
   B. in motion with a constant velocity.
   C. accelerating.
   D. moving with an acceleration of zero.
   E. experiencing opposite but equal forces.

31. •In the absence of a net force, an object can be
   A. at rest.
   B. in motion with a constant velocity.
   C. accelerating.
   D. at rest or in motion with a constant velocity.
   E. It's not possible to know without more information. SSM

32. •While an elevator traveling upward slows down to stop, the normal force on the feet of a passenger is _____ her weight. While an elevator traveling downward slows down to stop, the normal force on the feet of a passenger is _____ his weight.
   A. larger than; smaller than
   B. larger than; larger than
   C. smaller than; smaller than
   D. smaller than; larger than
   E. equal to; equal to

33. •How does the magnitude of the normal force exerted by the ramp in Figure 4-25 compare to the weight of the block? The normal force is
   A. equal to the weight of the block.
   B. greater than the weight of the block.
   C. less than the weight of the block.

D. possibly equal to or less than the weight of the block, depending on whether or not the ramp surface is smooth.
   E. possibly greater than or equal to the weight of the block, depending on whether or not the ramp surface is smooth.

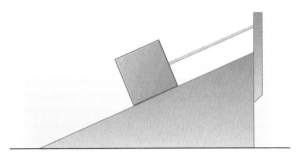

Figure 4-25 Problem 33

34. •Case (a) in Figure 4-26 shows block A accelerated across a frictionless table by a hanging 10-N block (1.02 kg). In case (b), the same block A is accelerated by a steady 10-N tension in the string. Treat the masses of the strings as negligible. The acceleration of block A in case (b) is
   A. greater than its acceleration in case (a).
   B. less than its acceleration in case (a).
   C. equal to its acceleration in case (a).
   D. twice its acceleration in case (a).
   E. half its acceleration in case (a).

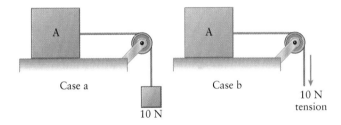

Case a

Case b

10 N

10 N tension

Figure 4-26 Problem 34

Estimation/Numerical Analysis

35. •Estimate the weight of five common objects using newtons (*not* pounds or ounces).

36. •Estimate the normal force acting on an apple that rests on a flat surface. What would this estimate be if the surface were tilted at an incline of 30° with the horizontal?

37. •**Sports** Give an estimate of the force that a major league baseball pitcher exerts on a baseball when he throws it. SSM

38. •Estimate the maximum tension in the cable that supports a typical elevator.

39. •**Sports** Estimate the force imparted on a tennis ball as it is fired from a tennis ball machine.

40. •**Sports** Estimate the tension in a rope that pulls you on water skis at a constant speed behind a speedboat.

41. •Estimate the force that is produced with the "jaws of life" (the pneumatic tool used to rip open the jammed doors of a vehicle that is involved in an accident).

42. •Estimate the force in newtons required to flip on a light switch.

43. •Estimate the force in newtons associated with snapping your fingers.

44. •**Medical** During an arthroscopic surgery repair of a patient's knee, a portion of healthy tendon is grafted in place of a damaged anterior cruciate ligament (ACL). To test the results, the surgeon applies a known force to the ligament and increases it at 1-s intervals for 10 s. Plot the data listed in the table as a function of time in a spreadsheet or on a graphing calculator and extrapolate the best-fit line to estimate the force that would correspond to a time of 15 s.

Time (s)	Force (mN)
0	0
1	2.28
2	5.73
3	11.28
4	12.27
5	12.54
6	12.38
7	14.11
8	16.79
9	21.08
10	28.51

45. ••Use a spreadsheet or graphing calculator to plot the velocity versus height of an express elevator. The elevator starts from rest on the ground floor, experiences a constant acceleration until reaching its maximum speed of 10 m/s at the 4th floor (the distance between each floor is 3.5 m), remains at this speed until the 20th floor, and then experiences a constant acceleration until it stops at the 30th floor. Identify the point(s) on the graph when the weight of a rider as measured by a spring scale will reach its maximum value. SSM

Problems

4-2 If a net external force acts on an object, the object accelerates

46. •What is the acceleration of a 2000-kg car if the net force on the car is 4000 N?

47. •What net force is needed to accelerate a 2000-kg car at 2.00 m/s^2?

48. ••Applying a constant net force to an object causes it to accelerate at 10 m/s^2. What will the acceleration of the object be if (a) the force is doubled, (b) the mass is halved, (c) the force is doubled and the mass is doubled, (d) the force is doubled and the mass is halved, (e) the force is halved, (f) the mass is doubled, (g) the force is halved and the mass is halved, and (h) the force is halved and the mass is doubled?

49. •Suppose that the engine of a car delivers a maximum force of 15,000 N. In the absence of any other forces, what is the maximum acceleration this engine can produce in a 1250-kg car? SSM

4-3 Mass, weight, and inertia are distinct but related concepts

50. •What is the weight on Earth of a wrestler who has a mass of 120 kg?

51. •A wrestler has a mass of 120 kg. What are (a) his mass and (b) weight on the Moon, where g is 1.62 m/s^2?

52. •(a) How does your mass differ as measured in Mexico City versus Los Angeles? (b) In which city is your weight greater?

53. •A bluefin tuna has a mass of 250 kg. What is its weight? SSM

54. ••**Astronomy** An astronaut has a mass of 80.0 kg. How much would the astronaut weigh on Mars where surface gravity is 38.0% of that on Earth?

55. •What is the net force on an apple that weighs 3.5 N when you hold it at rest in your hand?

4-4 Making a free-body diagram is essential in solving any problem involving forces

56. •Draw a free-body diagram for a heavy crate being lowered by a steel cable straight down at a constant speed.

57. •Draw a free-body diagram for a box being pushed horizontally by a person across a smooth floor at a steadily increasing speed. Ignore the friction between the box and the smooth floor. SSM

58. •Draw a free-body diagram for a bicycle rolling down a hill. Ignore the friction between the bicycle wheels and the hill, but consider any air resistance.

59. ••A tugboat uses its winch to pull up a sinking sailboat with an upward force of 4500 N. The mass of the boat is 200 kg and the water acts on the sailboat with a drag force of 2000 N. Draw a free-body diagram for the sailboat and describe the motion of the sailboat.

4-6 All problems involving forces can be solved using the same series of steps

60. ••Two forces are applied to a block of mass $M = 14.0$ kg that sits on a horizontal, frictionless table. One force $\vec{F}_1$ has a magnitude of 10.0 N and is directed at an angle θ_1 equal to 37.0° from the x direction as labeled in Figure 4-27. As a result of the forces, the block experiences an acceleration a equal to 0.500 m/s^2 in the x direction only. (a) What are the x and y components of the second force? (b) Draw the second force in its correct position and to scale on the picture.

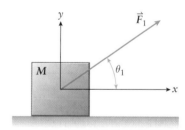

Figure 4-27 Problem 60

61. ••Three rugby players are pulling horizontally on ropes attached to a box, which remains stationary. Player 1 exerts a force F_1 equal to 100 N at an angle θ_1 equal to 60.0° with respect to the +x direction (Figure 4-28). Player 2 exerts a force F_2 equal to 200 N at an angle θ_2 equal to 37.0° with respect to the +x direction. The view in the figure is from above. Ignore friction and note that gravity plays no role in this problem! (a) Determine the force $\vec{F}_3$ exerted by Player 3. State your answer by giving the components of $\vec{F}_3$ in the directions perpendicular to and parallel to the positive x direction. (b) Redraw the

diagram and add the force $\vec{F}_3$ as carefully as you can. (c) Player 3's rope breaks, and Player 2 adjusts by pulling with a force of magnitude F_2' equal to 150 N at the same angle as before. In which direction is the acceleration of the box relative to the $+x$ direction shown? (d) In part (c), the acceleration is measured to be 10.0 m/s^2. What is the mass of the box? SSM

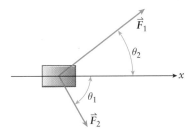

Figure 4-28   Problem 61

62. ••• Three forces act on a 2.00-kg object at angles $\theta_1 = 40.0°$, $\theta_2 = 60.0°$, and $\theta_3 = 20.0°$ as shown in Figure 4-29. Find the magnitude of $\vec{F}_2$ and $\vec{F}_3$ if the magnitude of F_1 is 1.00 N and the acceleration of the object is 1.50 m/s^2 toward the $+x$ direction.

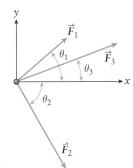

Figure 4-29   Problem 62

63. ••Box A weighs 80 N and rests on a table (Figure 4-30). A rope that connects boxes A and B drapes over a pulley so that box B hangs above the table, as shown in the figure. The pulley and rope are massless, and the pulley is frictionless. What force does the table exert on box A if box B weighs (a) 35 N; (b) 70 N; (c) 90 N?

Figure 4-30   Problem 63

64. ••Two forces act on an object of mass $M = 3.00$ kg as shown in Figure 4-31. Because of these forces, the object experiences an acceleration of $a = 7.00$ m/s^2 in the x direction. If $\theta_1 = 30.0°$, (a) calculate the magnitude of $\vec{F}_2$ and (b) make a careful drawing to show its direction, given that $F_1 = 20.0$ N.

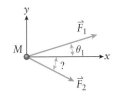

Figure 4-31   Problem 64

65. ••A 100-kg streetlight is supported equally by two ropes as shown in Figure 4-32. One rope pulls up and to the right, 40° above the horizontal; the other rope pulls up and to the left, 40° above the horizontal. What is the tension in each rope? SSM

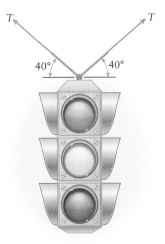

Figure 4-32   Problem 65

66. •••A 200-N sign is supported by two ropes as shown in Figure 4-33. If $\theta_L = 45.0°$ and $\theta_R = 30.0°$, what is the tension in each rope?

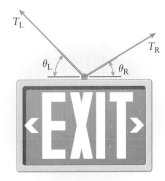

Figure 4-33   Problem 66

67. •• The distance between two telephone poles is 50 m. When a 0.500-kg bird lands on the telephone wire midway between the poles, the wire sags 0.15 m. How much tension does the bird produce in the wire? Ignore the weight of the wire.

68. •A locomotive pulls 10 identical freight cars with an acceleration of 2 m/s^2. How does the force between the third and fourth cars compare to the force between the seventh and eighth cars?

69. •A locomotive pulls 10 identical freight cars. The force between the locomotive and the first car is 100,000 N, and the acceleration of the train is 2 m/s^2. There is no friction to consider. Find the force between the ninth and tenth cars. SSM

70. •A block that has a mass of 0.0100 kg and a block that has a mass of 2.00 kg are attached to the ends of a rope. A student holds the 2.00-kg block and lets the 0.0100-kg block hang below it; then he lets go. What is the tension in the rope while the blocks are falling, before either hits the ground? Air resistance can be neglected.

71. •While parachuting, a 66.0-kg person experiences a downward acceleration of 2.50 m/s^2. What is the downward force on the parachute from the person?

72. •A bicycle and 50.0-kg rider accelerate at 1.00 m/s^2 up an incline of 10.0° above the horizontal. What is the magnitude of the force that the bicycle exerts on the rider?

73. •A car uniformly accelerates from 0 to 28.0 m/s. A 60.0-kg passenger experiences a horizontal force of 400 N. How much time does it take for the car to reach 28.0 m/s? SSM

74. •A car accelerates from 0 to 100 km/h in 4.50 s. What force does a 65.0-kg passenger experience during this acceleration?

75. •Adam and Ben pull hand over hand on opposite ends of a rope while standing on a frictionless frozen pond. Adam's mass is 75.0 kg and Ben's mass is 50.0 kg. If Adam's acceleration is 1.00 m/s^2 to the east, what are the magnitude and direction of Ben's acceleration?

76. ••Two blocks of masses M_1 and M_2 are connected by a massless string that passes over a massless pulley (Figure 4-34). M_2, which has a mass of 20.0 kg, rests on a long ramp of angle $\theta = 30.0°$. Friction can be ignored in this problem. (a) What is the value of M_1 for which the two blocks are in equilibrium (no acceleration)? (b) If the actual mass of M_1 is 5.00 kg and the system is allowed to move, what is the magnitude of the acceleration of the two blocks? (c) In part (b) does M_2 move up or down the ramp? (d) In part (b), how far does block M_2 move in 2.00 s?

Figure 4-34 Problem 76

77. ••In Figure 4-35, the block on the left incline is 6.00 kg. If $\theta_1 = 60.0°$ and $\theta_2 = 25°$, find the mass of the block on the right incline so that the system is in equilibrium (no acceleration). All surfaces are frictionless. SSM

Figure 4-35 Problem 77

General Problems

78. ••A child on a sled starts from rest at the top of a 20.0° slope. Assuming that there are no forces resisting the sled's motion, how long will the child take to reach the bottom of the slope, 210 m from the top?

79. ••A car is proceeding at a speed of 14.0 m/s when it collides with a stationary car in front. During the collision, the first car moves a distance of 0.300 m as it comes to a stop. The driver is wearing her seat belt, so she remains in her seat during the collision. If the driver's mass is 52.0 kg, how much force does the belt exert on her during the collision? Neglect any friction between the driver and the seat.

80. ••Your friend's car runs out of fuel, and you volunteer to push it to the nearest gas station. You carefully drive your car so that the bumpers of the two cars are in contact and then slowly accelerate to a speed of 2.00 m/s over the course of 1.00 min. If the mass of your friend's car is 1200 kg, what is the contact force between the two bumpers?

81. ••A 30.0-kg golden retriever stands on a scale in an elevator. Calculate the reading on the scale when the elevator (a) accelerates at 3.50 m/s^2 downward, (b) when the elevator cruises down at a steady speed, and (c) when the elevator accelerates at 4.00 m/s^2 upward. SSM

82. ••A person weighs 588 N. If she stands on a scale while riding on the Inclinator (the lift at the Luxor Hotel in Las Vegas), what will be the reading on the scale? Assume the Inclinator moves at a constant acceleration of 1.25 m/s^2, in a direction 39.0° above the horizontal, and that the rider stands vertically in the elevator car.

83. ••A rider in an elevator weighs 700 N. If this person stands on a scale in an elevator, describe the variation in the scale readings as the elevator initially starts from rest, accelerates upward at 3.00 m/s^2, cruises upward at 4.00 m/s, slows to a stop at 2.00 m/s^2, then free-falls all the way to the bottom of the elevator shaft before striking springs that bring the car to a safe stop.

84. ••A fuzzy die that has a weight of 1.80 N hangs from the ceiling of a car by a massless string. The car travels on a horizontal road and has an acceleration of 2.70 m/s^2 to the left. The string makes an angle θ with respect to the vertical, shown in Figure 4-36. What is the angle θ?

Figure 4-36 Problem 84

85. ••Biology On average, froghopper insects have a mass of 12.3 mg and jump to a height of 428 mm. The takeoff velocity is achieved as the little critter flexes its legs over a distance of approximately 2.00 mm. Assume a vertical jump with constant acceleration. (a) How long does the jump last (the jump itself, not the time in the air), and what is the froghopper's acceleration during that time? (b) Make a free-body diagram of the froghopper during its leap (but before it leaves the ground). (c) What force did the ground exert on the froghopper during the jump? Express your answer in millinewtons and as a multiple of the insect's weight. SSM

86. ••Medical A car traveling at 28.0 m/s hits a bridge abutment. A passenger in the car, who has a mass of 45.0 kg, moves forward a distance of 55.0 cm while being brought to rest by an inflated air bag. Assuming that the force that stops the

passenger is constant, what is the magnitude of force acting on the passenger?

87. ••Two mountain climbers are working their way up a glacier when one falls into a crevasse (Figure 4-37). The icy slope, which makes an angle of θ = 45.0° with the horizontal, can be considered frictionless. Sue's weight is pulling Paul up the 45.0° slope. If Sue's mass is 66.0 kg and she falls 2.00 m in 10.0 s starting from rest, calculate (a) the tension in the rope joining them and (b) Paul's mass. SSM

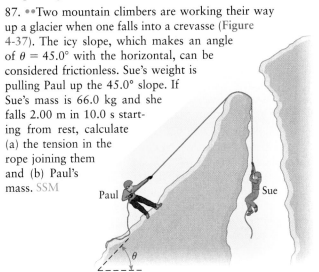

Figure 4-37 Problem 87

88. ••**Medical** During a front-end car collision, the acceleration limit for the chest is 60g as the car comes to rest. If a car was initially traveling at 48.0 km/h, (a) how much time does it take for the car to come to rest, assuming a constant acceleration equal to the threshold acceleration for damage to the chest? (b) Draw a free-body diagram of a person during the crash. (c) What force in newtons does the air bag exert on the chest of a 72.0-kg person? The trunk of the body comprises about 43.0% of body weight. (d) Why doesn't this force injure the person?

89. ••A window washer sits in a bosun's chair that dangles from a massless rope that runs over a massless, frictionless pulley and back down to the man's hand. The combined mass of man, chair, and bucket is 95.0 kg. With how much force must he pull downward to raise himself (a) slowly at constant speed and (b) with an upward acceleration 1.50 m/s²? SSM

90. ••A 200-kg block is hoisted up by two massless pulleys as shown in Figure 4-38. If a force of 1500 N is applied to the massless rope, what is the acceleration of the suspended mass?

1500 N

200 kg

Figure 4-38 Problem 90

91. •••Two blocks connected by a light string are being pulled across a frictionless horizontal tabletop by a hanging 10.0-N

weight (block C) (Figure 4-39). Block A has a mass of 2.00 kg. The mass of block B is only 1.00 kg. The blocks gain speed as they move toward the right, and the strings remain taut at all times. Assuming the pulley is massless and frictionless, what are the values of the tensions T_1 and T_2? SSM

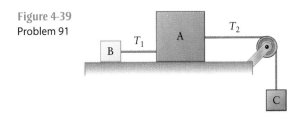

Figure 4-39
Problem 91

92. •••Three boxes are lined up so that they are touching each other as shown in Figure 4-40. Box A has a mass of 20.0 kg, box B has a mass of 30.0 kg, and box C has a mass of 50.0 kg. If an external force (F) pushes on box A toward the right, and the force that box B exerts on box C is 200 N, what is the acceleration of the boxes and the magnitude of the external force F?

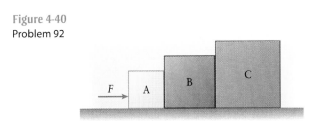

Figure 4-40
Problem 92

93. ••A 2.00-kg object A is connected with a massless string across a massless, frictionless pulley to a 3.00-kg object B (Figure 4-41). The smaller object rests on an inclined plane which is tilted at an angle of θ = 40.0° as shown. What are the acceleration of the system and the tension in the string?

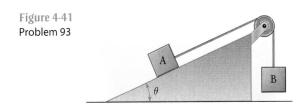

Figure 4-41
Problem 93

94. •••A 1.00-kg object A is connected with a string to a 2.00-kg object B, which is connected with a second string over a massless, frictionless pulley to a 4.00-kg object C (Figure 4-42). The 2.00-kg object is connected with a second string over a massless, frictionless pulley to a 4.00-kg object as shown. Calculate the acceleration of the system and the tension in both strings. Assume the strings have negligible mass and do not stretch, and assume the level tabletop is frictionless.

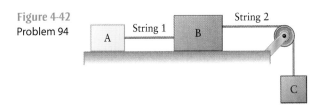

Figure 4-42
Problem 94

95. •••A 1.00-kg object A is connected with a string to a 2.00-kg object B, which is connected with a second string over a massless, frictionless pulley to a 4.00-kg object C (**Figure 4-43**). The first two objects are placed onto a frictionless inclined plane that makes an angle $\theta = 30.0°$ as shown. Calculate the acceleration of the masses and the tensions in both strings.

Figure 4-43
Problem 95

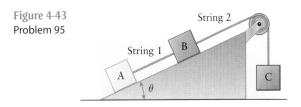

96. •••A compound Atwood's machine is constructed as shown in **Figure 4-44**. If block A has a mass of 2.00 kg, block B has a mass of 1.00 kg, and block C has a mass of 5.00 kg, calculate the acceleration of block A when the system is released from rest.

Figure 4-44 Problem 96

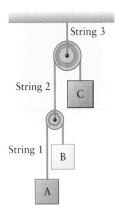

97. •**Medical, Astronomy** The space shuttle takes off vertically from rest with an acceleration of 29.0 m/s². What force is exerted on a 75.0-kg astronaut during takeoff? Express your answer in newtons and also as a multiple of the astronaut's weight on Earth.

98. •••**Sports** An athlete drops from rest from a platform 10.0 m above the surface of a 5.00-m-deep pool. Assuming that the athlete enters the water vertically and moves through the water with constant acceleration, what is the minimum average force the water must exert on a 62.0-kg diver to prevent her from hitting the bottom of the pool? Express your answer in newtons and also as a multiple of the diver's weight.

99. •••A person pulls three crates over a smooth horizontal floor as shown in **Figure 4-45**. The crates are connected to each other by identical horizontal strings A and B, each of which can support a maximum tension of 45.0 N before breaking. (a) What is the largest pulling force that can be exerted without breaking either of the strings? (b) What are the tensions in A and B just before one of the strings breaks?

Figure 4-45 Problem 99

100. •••A 275-g hard rubber ball falls from a height of 2.20 m. After each bounce, it rebounds to 75.0% of its previous height. High-speed photos reveal that the ball is in contact with the floor for 18.4 ms during each bounce. (a) Draw a free-body diagram of the ball before it hits the floor, (b) while it is in contact with the floor, and (c) after it has bounced and is rising. (d) What average force (magnitude and direction) does the floor exert on the ball during the first bounce?

Forces and Motion II: Applications

In this chapter, your goals are to:

- (5-1) Appreciate that Newton's laws apply to all forces and in all situations.
- (5-2) Recognize what determines the magnitude of the static friction force.
- (5-3) Be able to find the magnitude and direction of the force of kinetic friction.
- (5-4) Solve problems in which the forces on an object include static or kinetic friction.
- (5-5) Analyze situations in which fluid resistance is important.
- (5-6) Apply Newton's laws to objects in uniform circular motion.

To master this chapter, you should review:

- (3-5) The concepts and equations of motion in two or three dimensions.
- (3-8) The concepts and equations of uniform circular motion.
- (4-2 to 4-6) How to solve problems using Newton's laws of motion.

What do you think?

As a bicycle moves around a circular path at a constant speed, is there a nonzero *net* force on the bicycle? If so, does the net force point (a) inward toward the center of the circle, (b) outward away from the center of the circle, or (c) in some other direction?

5-1 We can use Newton's laws in situations beyond those we have already studied

In Chapter 4 we learned the basic laws that describe the motions of objects, and we saw how external forces acting on an object determine the magnitude and direction of the object's acceleration. In this chapter, we'll see how to apply these laws to a variety of very common situations. In particular, we'll take a much closer look at situations involving friction forces and drag forces—two forces that resist the motion of one object relative to another. We'll also analyze the direction of the forces acting on an object moving in a circular path and describe the resulting acceleration of that object.

The force of *friction* plays an important role in many physical situations. Friction acts in almost every case when two surfaces are in contact, and it can be present whether or not the two surfaces are sliding past each other. In Chapter 4 we used the friction force in some examples; in this chapter we'll learn more about the nature of friction and see how to solve more complex problems that involve friction. Another important situation arises when objects move through a fluid (a gas or liquid), such as a football flying through the air or a submarine cruising beneath the surface of the ocean. The fluid exerts a *drag force* on each of these objects. The drag force makes it more difficult for an object to move through a fluid and is greater the faster an object travels.

The forces of friction and drag are special *kinds* of forces. Another important situation is one that can involve forces of *any* kind: an object moving in a circular path at constant speed, like the bicycle shown in the photograph that opens this chapter. In this situation, no matter what forces act on the object, the net force must give the object an acceleration toward the center of the circle.

Take-Home Message for Section 5-1

✔ Newton's laws also apply in situations that involve frictional forces, drag forces, and motion in a circle.

(a)

The ground exerts a static friction force on the stationary children's feet. This force prevents their feet from sliding.

(b)

The water slide exerts a kinetic friction force on the moving child that slows him down. The water reduces the friction but doesn't eliminate it.

Figure 5-1 Static friction versus kinetic friction Both (a) static friction and (b) kinetic friction arise from the interaction between two surfaces in contact.

Magnitude of the static friction force

(5-1a)

(5-1b)

5-2 The static friction force changes magnitude to offset other applied forces

Friction is a force that resists the sliding of one object past another. If you push or pull on an object to make it slide but it doesn't move, we call the force that is preventing sliding a **static friction** force (Figure 5-1a). If the object is moving, we call the force that opposes this motion a **kinetic friction** force (Figure 5-1b). Both static and kinetic friction forces result from interactions between the microscopic irregularities (bumps) of the two surfaces in contact. Even surfaces that appear or feel smooth can be rough at the microscopic level. Irregularities on one surface can catch on or be impeded by irregularities on the other surface.

We'll concentrate on static friction in this section and analyze kinetic friction in Section 5-3.

Properties of Static Friction

To demonstrate some properties of static friction, gently rest your open palm and fingertips against a wall, and then try to drag your hand downward while maintaining contact with the wall. You'll find that it doesn't take much effort to make your hand slide. If you repeat the same experiment, but push a bit harder against the wall, you'll notice that it takes a bit more effort to get your hand to move. If you push as hard as you can on the wall, you'll find it very challenging to slide your hand down the wall. If the wall has a smooth surface, however, you'll find that your hands slip more easily than on a rough-surfaced wall.

Here's what we learn from this simple experiment:

(1) In each case the force that tries to keep your stationary hand from sliding is the force of static friction. We'll use the symbol $\vec{f}_s$ ("f-sub-s") for this force. (The subscript "s" reminds us that we're talking about *static* friction.) The static friction force $\vec{f}_s$ exerted on your hand by the wall acts parallel to your hand and parallel to the wall, that is, parallel to the surfaces in contact.

(2) You can overcome static friction by pushing against it with sufficient force. This says that in a given situation, the static friction force has a maximum magnitude $f_{s,max}$. You overcome the static friction force, and so start your hand sliding, if you apply a force in a direction parallel to the surfaces, whose magnitude is greater than $f_{s,max}$.

(3) The value of $f_{s,max}$ depends on how hard the two surfaces are pushed together—that is, on the *normal force* that acts perpendicular to the two surfaces. The greater the magnitude n of the normal force, the greater the maximum static friction force and the more difficult it is to make the surfaces slide past each other.

(4) The force of static friction depends on the properties of the surfaces in contact.

We can combine observations (ii), (iii), and (iv) into a simple mathematical relationship:

(1) The magnitude of the force of static friction on an object... (2) ... is less than or equal to a certain maximum value.

$$f_s \leq f_{s,max}$$

(3) The maximum force of static friction depends on... $$f_{s,max} = \mu_s n$$

(4) ... the coefficient of static friction (which depends on the properties of the two surfaces in contact)... (5) ... and the normal force pressing the object against a surface.

The quantity μ_s in Equation 5-1b is called the **coefficient of static friction**. Its value depends on the properties of both surfaces in contact; for example, μ_s has different values for steel on steel, for steel on glass, and for glass on glass. Because both f_s and n have units of force, Equation 5-1b tells us that μ_s must be dimensionless.

For common materials the coefficient of static friction ranges in value between about 0.1 and 0.8. For example, μ_s is approximately 0.1 for a ski on snow, approximately 0.5 for two pieces of wood in contact, and approximately 0.7 for two pieces of metal in contact. Lubrication reduces the frictional force between surfaces and hence the value of μ_s. In human joints, such as the elbow and knee, the presence of lubricating fluid results in a coefficient of static friction of about 0.01. This relatively low value of μ_s minimizes sticking and reduces wear and tear of the cartilage that supports these joints.

! Watch Out!   Static friction is described by an inequality, not an equality.

All of the mathematical relationships we've seen so far in our study of physics have been equalities, with an equals sign relating two quantities. But Equation 5-1a is an *inequality*. Figure 5-2 helps show why this is so. Imagine that you apply a horizontal force to a stationary block on a horizontal table. You find that if you apply a 20.0-N force, the block remains at rest. Therefore the static friction force must have the same 20.0-N magnitude to balance the force that you apply

(Figure 5-2a). What happens if you apply a lesser force, say only 10.0 N? The block would still remain at rest, so the force of static friction is now only 10.0 N in magnitude to exactly cancel the applied force (Figure 5-2b). The block also remains at rest if you don't push on it at all, so in this case the static friction force is zero (Figure 5-2c). If you push enough to overcome the maximum force of static friction given by Equation 5-1b, the object will slide. In Section 5-3 we'll discuss what happens then.

(a) You apply a force of 20.0 N to the right, but the block remains at rest...

20.0 N

20.0 N

...so the table must exert a static friction force of 20.0 N to the left on the block.

(b) You apply a force of 10.0 N to the right, but the block remains at rest...

10.0 N

10.0 N

...so the table must exert a static friction force of 10.0 N to the left on the block.

(c) You apply no force to the block and it remains at rest...

...so the table must exert no static friction force on the block.

 The static friction force adjusts its value to counteract whatever other forces are trying to make the object slide.

Figure 5-2 **The magnitude of the static friction force** For a given object at rest on a given surface, the magnitude of the static friction force is *not* always the same: It depends on the other forces acting on the object.

! Watch Out!   The direction of the static friction force is parallel to the contact surface.

Equations 5-1 relate only the *magnitudes* of the static friction force and the normal force. These forces are *not* in the same direction! The friction force always acts parallel to the

surface of contact, while the normal force always acts perpendicular to the surface. (Remember that "normal" is another word for "perpendicular.")

Static friction explains why a nail does not slide out of the wood into which it is hammered, even if the nail is upside down (Figure 5-3a). Because the nail is forced into the wood, strong normal forces are exerted on the side of the nail (Figure 5-3b). Equation 5-1b tells us that the maximum static friction force is quite large, more than enough to keep the nail in place. If you live in a wood-frame house, static friction deserves much of the credit for holding it together! The same effect explains why it is difficult to take off a tight-fitting pair of boots or to pull an overstuffed pillow out of its pillowcase.

Geckos (tropical lizards of the family *Gekkonidae*) use static friction to walk on vertical surfaces, even on a smooth plate of glass (Figure 5-4). At first glance this seems impossible: On a vertical surface there is nothing pushing the gecko into the surface, so the normal force would be zero and there would be zero static friction force (see Equation 5-1b).

(a)

(b)

The normal forces exerted on the sides of the nail by the surrounding wood...

...give rise to a static friction force...

f_s

n n

mg

...that prevents the nail from sliding out under the influence of the gravitational force.

Figure 5-3 **Static friction force on a nail** (a) Hammering a nail upward into a piece of wood. (b) Forces on the nail.

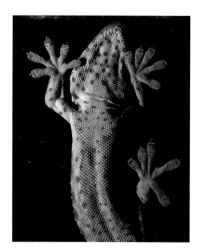

However, at the end of each of a gecko's toes are hundreds of thousands of tiny hairs or *setae*, each of which splits into hundreds of even smaller, flat pads. Each pad or *spatula* is only about 0.2 μm (2×10^{-7} m) across—so small that it can nestle in between the tiny crevices on the surface of a pane of glass. Like what happens to a nail in Figure 5-3, the normal force between a given spatula and the walls of its crevice give rise to a very weak static friction force. Multiply that tiny force by the millions of spatulae on a gecko's four feet, and the result is a maximum force of friction as great as 20 N—more than adequate to support the weight of an average gecko, which is less than 0.5 N.

Measuring the Coefficient of Static Friction

Here's a simple experiment for measuring the coefficient of static friction. Place a block of weight w on a ramp whose angle θ can be varied (**Figure 5-5a**). If the angle θ is small enough, the block will remain at rest. However, the block will start to slide if the angle is greater than a certain critical value. Let's see how to determine the value of μ_s from this critical angle, which we'll call θ_{slip}.

We'll follow the Method of Solving Force Problems that we used in Section 4-6. (You should review that strategy because we'll be using it a lot in this chapter.) Figure 5-5b shows the free-body diagram for the block when $\theta = \theta_{\text{slip}}$. Three forces act on the block: the normal force of magnitude n, which is perpendicular to the surface of the ramp; the gravitational force of magnitude w, which points downward; and the static friction force of magnitude f_s, which points opposite to the direction the block would move if it could. At this angle, the block is just about to slip, which means the friction force must be at its maximum value. So from Equations 5-1, $f_s = f_{s,\text{max}} = \mu_s n$.

We set the sum of the external forces on the block in each direction equal to mass multiplied by acceleration in that direction (Newton's second law). We take the positive x direction to point down the ramp and the positive y direction to point perpendicular to the ramp, as Figure 5-5b shows. The block remains at rest, so $a_x = a_y = 0$. Then the equations of Newton's second law are

(5-2)

$$\text{(a)} \quad x: \sum F_{\text{ext},x} = n_x + w_x + f_{s,\text{max},x} = ma_x = 0$$

$$\text{(b)} \quad y: \sum F_{\text{ext},y} = n_y + w_y + f_{s,\text{max},y} = ma_y = 0$$

Figure 5-5b shows that the gravitational force has a positive (downhill) x component $w_x = w \sin \theta_{\text{slip}}$ and a negative y component $w_y = -w \cos \theta_{\text{slip}}$. The normal force points in the positive y direction (so $n_x = 0$ and $n_y = n$), and the static friction force points in the negative x direction (so $f_{s,\text{max},x} = -f_{s,\text{max}}$ and $f_{s,\text{max},y} = 0$). So Equations 5-2 become

(5-3)

$$\text{(a)} \quad x: \sum F_{\text{ext},x} = 0 + w \sin \theta_{\text{slip}} + (-f_{s,\text{max}}) = 0$$

$$\text{(b)} \quad y: \sum F_{\text{ext},y} = n + (-w \cos \theta_{\text{slip}}) + 0 = 0$$

Our goal is to find the coefficient of static friction μ_s, and so we need to incorporate this quantity into our equations. We do this by substituting Equation 5-1b, $f_{s,\text{max}} = \mu_s n$, into Equation 5-3a. Then, by rearranging Equations 5-3, we get the following expressions

(5-4)

$$\text{(a)} \quad \mu_s n = w \sin \theta_{\text{slip}}$$

$$\text{(b)} \quad n = w \cos \theta_{\text{slip}}$$

Equation 5-4b tells us the value of n, the magnitude of the normal force, so we can substitute this quantity into Equation 5-4a and solve for μ_s:

$$\mu_s (w \cos \theta_{\text{slip}}) = w \sin \theta_{\text{slip}}$$
$$\mu_s \cos \theta_{\text{slip}} = \sin \theta_{\text{slip}}$$

(a) A block at rest on an inclined ramp

Block, weight w

Ramp whose angle θ
from the horizontal
can be varied

θ

(b) Free-body diagram for the block at
the angle where it is just about to slip

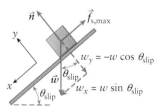

$\vec{n}$ $\vec{f}_{s,\text{max}}$

y

$w_y = -w \cos \theta_{\text{slip}}$

$\vec{w}$ θ_{slip}

x $w_x = w \sin \theta_{\text{slip}}$

θ_{slip}

Figure 5-5 **Measuring the coefficient of static friction** The angle at which a block on an incline just begins to slip tells you the coefficient of static friction μ_s.

Or, using $\tan \theta = (\sin \theta)/(\cos \theta)$,

Coefficient of static friction for an object at rest on a surface

Angle of the surface at which the object begins to slip

$$\mu_s = \tan \theta_{slip}$$

Angle at which an object slips on an incline

(5-5)

The greater the angle θ_{slip} beyond which the box begins to slide, the greater the value of $\tan \theta_{slip}$ and hence the greater the coefficient of static friction must be to provide the necessary friction force. Note that Equation 5-5 does *not* involve the weight of the block. A plastic block on a wooden ramp will begin to slide at the same angle θ regardless of its weight.

$\sqrt{x}$ *Go to the Math Tutorial for more information on trigonometry*

! **Watch Out!** **The coefficient of static friction can be greater than one.**

Because typical values of the coefficient of static friction are less than 1, it is tempting to assume that μ_s is *always* less than 1. Not so! **Figure 5-6** shows a wooden block that rests without slipping on a ramp covered with sandpaper. The ramp is set at a 50° angle; if this is the angle beyond which the block will slip, then from Equation 5-5 we find that $\mu_s = \tan 50° = 1.2$. Whenever θ_{slip} is greater than 45°, the coefficient of static friction is greater than $\tan 45° = 1$.

Figure 5-6 **A block on a sandpaper surface** This block can remain at rest at an angle of up to 50°, so the coefficient of static friction for this block on sandpaper is tan 50° = 1.2 (see Equation 5-5).

! **Watch Out!** **The normal force exerted on an object is not always equal to the object's weight.**

Since the maximum force of static friction is related to the normal force, it's important to remember that the normal force for an object on a surface is *not* always equal to the object's weight. (We cautioned you about this in Section 4-3). The situation shown in Figure 5-5 is an example of this caveat.

Equation 5-4b shows that the normal force on this object is the object's weight multiplied by the cosine of the angle of the incline. Resist the temptation to always set the normal force equal to the weight!

Example 5-1 Friction in Joints

The wrist is made up of eight small bones called *carpals* that glide back and forth as you wave your hand from side to side. A thin layer of cartilage covers the surfaces of the carpals, making them smooth and slippery. In addition, the spaces between the bones contain synovial fluid, which provides lubrication. During a laboratory experiment, a physiologist applies a compression force to squeeze the bones together along their nearly planar bone surfaces. She then measures the force that must be applied parallel to the surface of contact to make them move. (Figure 5-7 shows the contact region between these two carpal bone surfaces.) When the compression force is 11.2 N, the minimum force required to move the bones is 0.135 N. What is the coefficient of static friction in the joint?

Interface between two nearly planar carpal bone surfaces

Figure 5-7 **Static friction in the wrist** This X-ray image shows the carpal bones of the wrist.

Set Up

We begin by drawing the free-body diagram for one of the two carpals in question, which we call carpal A, when it is just about to slip relative to carpal B. The physiologist exerts two of the four forces acting on carpal A: the compression force $\vec{F}_{compression}$ (of magnitude 11.2 N) and the force $\vec{F}_{slide}$ applied parallel to the contact surface (of magnitude 0.135 N) to make bone A slide relative to bone B. The other two forces acting on carpal A are the normal force $\vec{n}$ and the static friction force $\vec{f}_{s,max}$, both exerted by Carpal B on Carpal A. (This friction force is the *maximum* force of static friction because the carpals are just about to slip.) Our goal is to find the value of μ_s, so we'll also use the relationship between $f_{s,max}$ and the normal force given by Equation 5-1b.

Newton's second law for carpal A:

$$\sum \vec{F}_{ext\ on\ A}$$
$$= \vec{F}_{compression} + \vec{F}_{slide} + \vec{n} + \vec{f}_{s,max}$$
$$= m_A \vec{a}_A$$

Magnitude of the static friction force:

$$f_{s,max} = \mu_s n \qquad (5\text{-}1b)$$

Solve

Let the positive x axis point up, and the positive y axis point to the left. Since we are considering the situation in which the carpals have not yet begun to slide, carpal A is at rest and $a_{A,x} = a_{A,y} = 0$. We use this information to write Newton's second law for carpal A in component form.

Newton's second law for carpal A in component form:

x: $\sum F_{ext\ on\ A,x}$
$$= 0 + F_{slide} + 0 + (-f_{s,max})$$
$$= m_A a_{A,x} = 0$$

y: $\sum F_{ext\ on\ A,y}$
$$= (-F_{compression}) + 0 + n + 0$$
$$= m_A a_{A,y} = 0$$

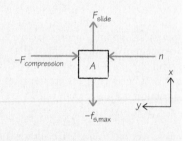

To find the value of μ_s using Equation 5-1b, we need to know the values of n and $f_{s,max}$. We find these quantities by using Newton's second law equations and the known values $F_{compression} = 11.2$ N and $F_{slide} = 0.135$ N.

Solve Equation 5-1b for μ_s:

$$\mu_s = \frac{f_{s,max}}{n}$$

Solve Newton's second law equations for $f_{s,max}$ and n. From the x component equation:

$$f_{s,max} = F_{slide} = 0.135\ N$$

From the y component equation:

$$n = F_{compression} = 11.2\ N\ \text{so}$$

$$\mu_s = \frac{0.135\ N}{11.2\ N} = 1.21 \times 10^{-2} = 0.0121$$

Reflect

This coefficient of static friction is very small, which means that very little effort is required to make your wrist move. The lubricating fluid between the bones is the key to keeping the friction so small. The fluid also helps reduce wear on the joints. If the bones or even the cartilage surfaces were in direct contact, our joints would wear down relatively quickly.

? Got the Concept? 5-1   Face to Face with Friction

A rectangular block made of steel has dimensions 1.00 cm × 2.00 cm × 3.00 cm. You place it on a wooden board, and then you tilt the board until the block begins to slide down the board. Which face of the block should be in contact with the board so that it begins to slide at the *shallowest* angle? (a) The 1.00 cm × 2.00 cm face, (b) the 1.00 cm × 3.00 cm face, (c) the 2.00 cm × 3.00 cm face. (d) The block will begin to slide at the same angle in each case. (e) The answer depends on the type of steel and the type of wood.

5-3 The kinetic friction force on a sliding object has a constant magnitude

In the previous section, we used a block on a tilted ramp (Figure 5-5) to help us explore the force of static friction. If the ramp is inclined by more than a certain critical angle, not even the maximum force of static friction will prevent the block from sliding. What happens if the ramp angle is increased even more? The block starts to move and still experiences a resistive force. However, this force is no longer static friction but kinetic friction, the frictional force between two surfaces that move relative to each other.

The Magnitude of the Kinetic Friction Force

Like static friction, the force of kinetic friction $\vec{f}_k$ ("f-sub-k") between two objects is proportional to the normal force that one object exerts on the other perpendicular to their surface of contact—in other words, it is proportional to how hard the two surfaces are pushed together. However, the kinetic friction force is typically less than the maximum force of static friction. We'll model the kinetic friction force as being independent of how fast the two objects slide past each other, as well as independent of the area of contact between the objects. (This model works well in many situations.) Then, we can write an expression for the magnitude f_k of the kinetic friction force:

The force of kinetic friction depends on...

$$f_k = \mu_k n$$

... the coefficient of kinetic friction (which depends on the properties of the two surfaces in contact)...

... and the normal force exerted on the object by the surface on which it slides.

Magnitude of the kinetic friction force
(5-6)

Like the coefficient of static friction μ_s, the value of the **coefficient of kinetic friction** μ_k depends on the kinds of surfaces that are in contact. For typical surfaces, μ_k is close to but less than μ_s. That's why it takes less force to keep a block sliding at constant speed over a horizontal surface than it does to start it moving in the first place (Figure 5-8). Values of the coefficient of kinetic friction for typical materials range between 0.1 and 0.8.

In Figure 5-9a, the block is moving at a constant velocity, so its acceleration is zero and the net force exerted on the block is zero as well. In this case the horizontal force that you apply just balances the force of kinetic friction of magnitude f_k opposing the motion. If the horizontal force that you apply is greater in magnitude than f_k, the net force points forward and the block speeds up (Figure 5-9b). If you apply a horizontal force with a magnitude less than f_k to the sliding block, the block slows down because the net force points backward (Figure 5-9c).

 Go to Interactive Exercises 5-1 and 5-2 for more practice dealing with kinetic friction

(a)

You push a stationary block with a horizontal force less than the maximum force of static friction.

$\vec{F}_{\text{applied}}$

$\vec{f}_s$

Static friction balances applied force: block remains at rest.

(b)

You push a stationary block with a horizontal force equal to the maximum force of static friction.

$\vec{F}_{\text{applied}}$

$\vec{f}_{s,\text{max}}$

Static friction just balances applied force: block is at rest but just about to slip.

(c)

Once the block is in motion, you can keep it moving by exerting a horizontal force equal to the force of kinetic friction.

$\vec{F}_{\text{applied}}$

$\vec{v}$ = constant

$\vec{f}_k$

Block moves at a constant velocity.

If you push hard enough on an object at rest, you can overcome the force of static friction.

Figure 5-8 From static friction to kinetic friction If you push hard enough on an object to overcome static friction and start the object sliding, the force of friction becomes the kinetic friction force.

(a)

You can keep a block sliding with constant velocity over a horizontal surface by exerting a horizontal force equal to the force of kinetic friction.

$\vec{F}_{\text{applied}}$

$\vec{v}$ = constant

$\vec{f}_k$

(b)

If you apply a horizontal force to the moving block greater than the force of kinetic friction, it speeds up.

$\vec{F}_{\text{applied}}$

$\vec{v}$

$\vec{a}$

$\vec{f}_k$

(c)

If you apply a horizontal force to the moving block less than the force of kinetic friction, it slows down.

$\vec{F}_{\text{applied}}$

$\vec{v}$

$\vec{a}$

$\vec{f}_k$

The kinetic friction force on a sliding object does not depend on how hard you push the object, nor does it depend on the speed of the object.

Figure 5-9 Kinetic friction: Three examples Depending on how hard you push on an object sliding with kinetic friction, it will either (a) maintain a constant velocity, (b) speed up, or (c) slow down.

Example 5-2 Sliding with Kinetic Friction

In Example 4-6 (see Section 4-6), we considered a book sliding down an incline with friction. In a variation of this problem, suppose the coefficient of kinetic friction between the incline and the sliding 2.50-kg book is 0.350. (a) What is the downhill acceleration of the book if the incline is at an angle from the horizontal of 30.0°? (b) What is the acceleration if the angle is 10.0°?

Set Up

The book is moving down the incline of angle θ, so the kinetic friction force (which always opposes sliding) must point up the incline. To find the net external force on the book and hence the book's acceleration, we need to determine the magnitude of the friction force by using Equation 5-6. Once we've found a general expression for the block's acceleration in terms of θ, we'll substitute the values $\theta = 30.0°$ and $\theta = 10.0°$.

Newton's second law applied to the book:

$$\sum \vec{F}_{\text{ext on block}} = \vec{n} + \vec{w}_{\text{book}} + \vec{f}_k$$
$$= m_{\text{block}}\vec{a}_{\text{block}}$$

Magnitude of the kinetic friction force:

$$f_k = \mu_k n \qquad (5\text{-}6)$$

Solve

Write Newton's second law for the block in component form. Because the block's acceleration is along the incline (that is, along the x direction), it follows that $a_{\text{block},y} = 0$.

Newton's second law for the book in component form:

$x:$ $\sum F_{\text{ext on book},x}$
$$= 0 + w_{\text{book}} \sin \theta + (-f_k)$$
$$= m_{\text{book}} a_{\text{book},x}$$

$y:$ $\sum F_{\text{ext on book},y}$
$$= n - w_{\text{book}} \cos \theta + 0$$
$$= m_{\text{book}} a_{\text{book},y} = 0$$

To find the magnitude of the kinetic friction force, we solve the y component equation for the magnitude of the normal force n and then substitute this expression into the equation for f_k. Next we substitute our result for f_k into the x component equation, giving an equation for the acceleration $a_{\text{book},x}$.

From the y component equation,
$$n = w_{\text{book}} \cos \theta$$
Substitute this into Equation 5-6:
$$f_k = \mu_k n = \mu_k(w_{\text{book}} \cos \theta)$$
Substitute this expression for f_k into the x equation:
$$w_{\text{book}} \sin \theta - \mu_k w_{\text{book}} \cos \theta = m_{\text{book}} a_{\text{book},x}$$

Now we can complete our solution for the book's acceleration $a_{\text{book},x}$. Use the relationship between gravitational force and mass.

Relationship between the mass m_{book} of the book and the gravitational force w_{book} on the book:

$$w_{\text{book}} = m_{\text{book}} g$$

Substitute into the x equation and solve for $a_{\text{book},x}$:
$$m_{\text{book}} g \sin \theta - \mu_k m_{\text{book}} g \cos \theta = m_{\text{book}} a_{\text{book},x}$$
The factor of m_{book} cancels, so
$$a_{\text{book},x} = g \sin \theta - \mu_k g \cos \theta \text{ or}$$
$$a_{\text{book},x} = g(\sin \theta - \mu_k \cos \theta)$$

Use this general formula for $a_{\text{book},x}$ for the given value of μ_k and the two given values of θ.

(a) Substitute $\theta = 30.0°$:
$$\begin{aligned} a_{\text{book},x} &= g(\sin \theta - \mu_k \cos \theta) \\ &= (9.80 \text{ m/s}^2)[\sin 30.0° - (0.350)(\cos 30.0°)] \\ &= (9.80 \text{ m/s}^2)[0.500 - (0.350)(0.866)] \\ &= 1.93 \text{ m/s}^2 \end{aligned}$$

(b) Substitute $\theta = 10.0°$:
$$\begin{aligned} a_{\text{book},x} &= g(\sin \theta - \mu_k \cos \theta) \\ &= (9.80 \text{ m/s}^2)[\sin 10.0° - (0.350)(\cos 10.0°)] \\ &= (9.80 \text{ m/s}^2)[0.174 - (0.350)(0.985)] \\ &= -1.68 \text{ m/s}^2 \end{aligned}$$

Reflect

The book has a positive (downhill) acceleration for $\theta = 30.0°$, which means the book speeds up as it slides downhill. However, when the incline is at a shallower angle of $\theta = 10.0°$, the book

Downhill component of gravitational force:
$$w_{\text{book},x} = w_{\text{book}} \sin \theta = m_{\text{book}} g \sin \theta$$

Uphill component of kinetic friction force:
$$f_k = \mu_k n = \mu_k m_{\text{book}} g \cos \theta$$

has a *negative* (uphill) acceleration: Its speed decreases as it moves down the incline.

To see why the speed decreases, let's calculate the downhill (x) component of the gravitational force and the uphill component of the kinetic friction force for each angle. The shallower the angle θ, the smaller the downhill gravitational force and the greater the uphill force of kinetic friction. If the angle is small enough, the friction force will dominate over the gravitational force—in which case the net force and acceleration point up the incline.

Can you show that the acceleration of the block will be zero (that is, it will slide down the incline with constant velocity) if $\theta = 19.3°$?

If $\theta = 30.0°$,

$$w_{\text{book},x} = (2.50 \text{ kg})(9.80 \text{ m/s}^2) \sin 30.0°$$
$$= 12.3 \text{ N}$$
$$f_k = (0.350)(2.50 \text{ kg})(9.80 \text{ m/s}^2) \cos 30.0°$$
$$= 7.43 \text{ N}$$

so gravity dominates over kinetic friction and the net force is downhill.

If $\theta = 10.0°$,

$$w_{\text{book},x} = (2.50 \text{ kg})(9.80 \text{ m/s}^2) \sin 10.0°$$
$$= 4.25 \text{ N}$$
$$f_k = (0.350)(2.50 \text{ kg})(9.80 \text{ m/s}^2) \cos 10.0°$$
$$= 8.44 \text{ N}$$

Kinetic friction dominates over gravity and so the net force is uphill.

Example 5-3 How Far Up the Incline?

You set the incline described in Example 5-2 at an angle of 30.0° from the horizontal, and then push the 2.50-kg book up the incline with an initial speed of 4.20 m/s. The coefficient of kinetic friction between block and ramp is again 0.350. How far up the incline does the book travel before coming to a stop?

Set Up

As in Example 5-2, the three forces acting on the sliding book are the normal force, gravitational force, and kinetic friction force. The difference here is that the friction force points downhill rather than uphill because the book is now sliding uphill. (Remember that the kinetic friction force always opposes the slipping.)

This problem asks for a distance, so it's really a kinematics problem. Because all three forces that act on the book are constant, the net external force is constant as well. Therefore the acceleration is constant and we can use one of the formulas from Section 2-5 for linear motion with constant acceleration. We choose an equation that relates the book's initial velocity v_{0x}, its final velocity v_x, and its acceleration $a_{\text{book},x}$ to its displacement $x - x_0$, which is what we are asked to find.

Newton's second law applied to the book:

$$\sum \vec{F}_{\text{ext on book}} = \vec{n} + \vec{w}_{\text{book}} + \vec{f}_k$$
$$= m_{\text{book}} \vec{a}_{\text{book}}$$

Magnitude of the kinetic friction force:

$$f_k = \mu_k n \qquad (5\text{-}6)$$

Velocity, acceleration, and position for constant acceleration only:

$$v_x^2 = v_{0x}^2 + 2a_{\text{book},x}(x - x_0) \quad (2\text{-}11)$$

Solve

Write Newton's second law for the book in component form. The equations are the same as in Example 5-2 except that the friction force now has a positive (downhill) x component.

Newton's second law for the book in component form:

x: $\sum F_{\text{ext on book},x}$
$$= 0 + w_{\text{book}} \sin \theta + f_k$$
$$= m_{\text{book}} a_{\text{book},x}$$

y: $\sum F_{\text{ext on book},y}$
$$= n - w_{\text{book}} \cos \theta + 0$$
$$= m_{\text{book}} a_{\text{book},y} = 0$$

(Book's acceleration is along the x axis only, so $a_{\text{book},y} = 0$.)

Use these equations and Equation 5-6 to solve for the acceleration of the book.

From the y component equation and $w_{book} = m_{book}g$,

$$n = w_{book} \cos \theta = m_{book} g \cos \theta$$

Substitute into Equation 5-6 and find the magnitude of the kinetic friction force:

$$f_k = \mu_k n = \mu_k m_{book} g \cos \theta$$

Substitute into x component equation and solve for $a_{book,x}$:

$$m_{book} g \sin \theta + \mu_k m_{book} g \cos \theta = m_{book} a_{book,x}$$

$$g \sin \theta + \mu_k g \cos \theta = a_{book,x}$$

$$a_{book,x} = g(\sin \theta + \mu_k \cos \theta)$$
$$= (9.80 \text{ m/s}^2)[\sin 30.0° + (0.350)(\cos 30.0°)]$$
$$= (9.80 \text{ m/s}^2)[0.500 + (0.350)(0.866)]$$
$$= 7.87 \text{ m/s}^2$$

(acceleration is positive because it points downhill)

Now we can solve for the displacement of the book from where it starts to where it stops. Its initial velocity v_{0x} is negative because the book starts off moving uphill. Its final velocity v_x is zero because it is at rest after traveling the maximum distance up the incline. Use Equation 2-11 to find $x - x_0$.

Equation 2-11:

$$v_x^2 = v_{0x}^2 + 2a_{book,x}(x - x_0)$$

with $v_{0x} = -4.20$ m/s, $v_x = 0$, and $a_{book,x} = 7.87$ m/s^2

Solve for $x - x_0$:

$$x - x_0 = \frac{v_x^2 - v_{0x}^2}{2a_{book,x}}$$
$$= \frac{0 - (-4.20 \text{ m/s})^2}{2(7.87 \text{ m/s}^2)}$$
$$= -1.12 \text{ m}$$

(Displacement is negative since the book moves uphill.)
So the book travels 1.12 m.

Reflect

The downhill acceleration of the book (7.87 m/s^2) is much greater than in Example 5-2 (1.93 m/s^2), because the force of kinetic friction now points downhill and so augments the downhill component of the gravitational force.

We can check our result by seeing how far the book would travel if the surface were horizontal, so $\theta = 0$. In this case, the book travels 2.57 m, which is more than twice the distance we found for the book on the 30.0° incline. It travels a greater distance if the surface is horizontal because the force of gravity is no longer helping to slow the book down. This result is physically reasonable and gives us confidence that our answer is correct.

If the surface is horizontal ($\theta = 0$):

$$a_{book,x} = g(\sin 0 + \mu_k \cos 0)$$
$$= g[0 + \mu_k(1)]$$
$$= \mu_k g$$
$$= (0.350)(9.80 \text{ m/s}^2)$$
$$= 3.43 \text{ m/s}^2$$

Then, the displacement of the book from where it starts to where it stops is

$$x - x_0 = \frac{v_x^2 - v_{0x}^2}{2a_{block,x}} = \frac{0 - (-4.20 \text{ m/s})^2}{2(3.43 \text{ m/s}^2)}$$
$$= -2.57 \text{ m}$$

So the book travels 2.57 m.

Rolling Friction

In addition to static friction and kinetic friction, a third important type of friction is **rolling friction**. If you start a billiard ball rolling across a horizontal surface, it will roll for quite a distance but will eventually come to a stop. A force must therefore act opposite to its motion, and it's this force that we call rolling friction (Figure 5-10). This force always acts opposite to the motion of a rolling object, whether it's rolling uphill, downhill, or on a horizontal surface.

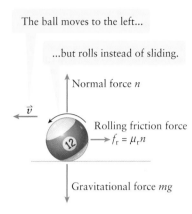

The ball moves to the left...

...but rolls instead of sliding.

Normal force n

$\vec{v}$

Rolling friction force
$f_r = \mu_r n$

Gravitational force mg

Figure 5-10 A rolling billiard ball
A ball can roll much farther on a horizontal surface than a block can slide on the same surface. The reason is that rolling friction is a much weaker force than kinetic friction.

Just as for static and kinetic friction, the force of rolling friction is proportional to the normal force that acts between the rolling object and the surface over which it rolls. So we can express the magnitude f_r of the rolling friction force as

(5-7) $$f_r = \mu_r n \quad (\text{force of rolling friction})$$

The **coefficient of rolling friction** μ_r can be a very small number—about 0.02 for rubber automobile tires on concrete and about 0.002 for the steel wheels of a railroad car on steel rails. As a result, rolling friction is generally much smaller than kinetic friction, so a round object will roll much farther than a brick-shaped object of the same size will slide. In general, the more rigid the rolling object and the more rigid the surface over which it rolls, the smaller the value of μ_r. The tires of your car are an example: If you don't keep them properly inflated, the coefficient of rolling friction for your tires will be greater than it should be and your fuel consumption will be greater as well.

Figure 5-11 summarizes the three varieties of friction force.

Figure 5-11 Three kinds of friction
Comparing (a) static friction, (b), kinetic friction, and (c) rolling friction.

(a) If an object is at rest on the ramp, the friction force that holds it in place is **static friction**.

$\vec{n}$

$\vec{f}_s$

$v = 0$

$\vec{w}$

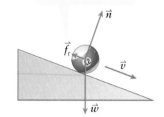

(b) If the object slides on the ramp, the friction force that acts on it is **kinetic friction**.

$\vec{n}$

$\vec{f}_k$

$\vec{v}$

$\vec{w}$

(c) If the object rolls on the ramp, the friction force that acts on it is **rolling friction**.

$\vec{n}$

$\vec{f}_r$

$\vec{v}$

$\vec{w}$

❓ Got the Concept? 5-2 A Question of Mass

Suppose the book in Examples 5-2 and 5-3 had a mass of 5.00 kg rather than 2.50 kg. How would this change the magnitude of the acceleration of the book as it moves along the ramp? (a) The magnitude would be greater going both downhill and uphill; (b) the magnitude would be less going both downhill and uphill; (c) the magnitude would be greater going downhill but less going uphill; (d) the magnitude would be less going downhill but greater going uphill; (e) none of these.

❓ Got the Concept? 5-3 Sliding Uphill to a Stop

Consider again the book sliding up the 30.0° incline in Example 5-3. For which of the following values of the coefficient of *static* friction will the book remain at rest after it stops? (a) 0.350 (the same as μ_k), (b) 0.600, (c) 0.750, (d) both (b) and (c), (e) all of (a), (b), and (c).

Take-Home Message for Section 5-3

✔ If an object is sliding over a surface, the kinetic friction force on the object acts in the direction that opposes the sliding.

✔ The magnitude of the kinetic friction force is proportional to the normal force exerted on the object by the surface on which it is sliding (Equation 5-6).

✔ Like kinetic friction, rolling friction opposes motion and is proportional to the normal force, but the coefficient of friction for rolling is much smaller than that for sliding.

5-4 Problems involving static and kinetic friction are like any other problem with forces

In this section we'll look at a number of problems that involve static friction, kinetic friction, or both. We'll solve these examples using the same two-step approach that we introduced in Section 4-6. First, draw a free-body diagram for each object of interest; second, use the diagram to write down a Newton's second law equation for each object and solve for the unknowns. The only new wrinkle for problems that involve friction are the expressions for the magnitudes of the static friction force ($f_s \leq f_{s,\max} = \mu_s n$) and the kinetic friction force ($f_k = \mu_k n$).

Example 5-4 Two Boxes, a String, and Friction

Two boxes are connected by a lightweight string that passes over a massless, frictionless pulley (Figure 5-12). Box 1 (mass $m_1 = 2.00$ kg) sits on a ramp inclined at 30.0° from the horizontal, while box 2 (mass $m_2 = 4.00$ kg) hangs from the other end of the string. When the boxes are released, the string remains taut, box 1 accelerates up the ramp, and box 2 accelerates downward. The coefficient of kinetic friction for box 1 sliding on the ramp is $\mu_k = 0.250$. What is the acceleration of each box?

Figure 5-12 **A pulley problem with friction** If there is friction between box 1 and the ramp, what is the acceleration of the boxes?

Set Up

Because box 2 has more mass than box 1, we expect that box 2 will fall, accelerating downward and pulling box 1 up the ramp. So we choose to have the positive x axis point up the ramp for box 1 and straight down for box 2. Box 1 has 4 forces acting on it: a normal force $\vec{n}_1$ from the surface of the ramp, its weight $\vec{w}_1$, the tension force from the string $\vec{T}_{\text{string on 1}}$, and the kinetic friction force from the ramp $\vec{f}_{k1}$. Two forces act on box 2: its weight $\vec{w}_2$ and the tension force from the string $\vec{T}_{\text{string on 2}}$. Because the string is lightweight and the pulley is massless and frictionless, the tensions $\vec{T}_{\text{string on 1}}$ and $\vec{T}_{\text{string on 2}}$ at either end have the same magnitude T. If the string doesn't stretch, the two boxes move together and their accelerations $\vec{a}_1$ and $\vec{a}_2$ have the same x component a_x. (Note that the positive x direction for each box is in the direction that the box moves.) Our goal is to calculate a_x.

Newton's second law applied to box 1:

$$\sum \vec{F}_{\text{ext on 1}} = \vec{n}_1 + \vec{w}_1 + \vec{T}_{\text{string on 1}} + \vec{f}_{k1} = m_1 \vec{a}_1$$

Magnitude of the kinetic friction force on box 1:

$$f_{k1} = \mu_k n_1$$

Newton's second law applied to box 2:

$$\sum \vec{F}_{\text{ext on 2}} = \vec{w}_2 + \vec{T}_{\text{string on 2}} = m_2 \vec{a}_2$$

Tensions have the same magnitude:

$$T_{\text{string on 1}} = T_{\text{string on 2}} = T$$

Accelerations have the same x component:

$$a_{1x} = a_{2x} = a_x$$

Solve

Write Newton's second law for each box in component form. Use T for the magnitude of each tension and a_x for the x component of each acceleration. Box 1 doesn't move in the y direction, so its y component of acceleration is zero and the net external force on box 1 has zero y component.

Newton's second law in component form for box 1:

$$x: 0 + (-w_1 \sin \theta) + T + (-f_k) = m_1 a_x$$
$$y: n_1 + (-w_1 \cos \theta) + 0 + 0 = 0$$

Newton's second law in component form for box 2:

$$x: w_2 + (-T) = m_2 g - T = m_2 a_x$$

Calculate the normal force n_1 that acts on box 1 from the y component equation for that box. Use this expression to find the magnitude of the kinetic friction force on box 1 and substitute the result into the x equation for that box.

From the y component equation for box 1,

$$n_1 = w_1 \cos \theta = m_1 g \cos \theta$$

So the kinetic friction force on box 1 has magnitude

$$f_{k1} = \mu_k n_1 = \mu_k m_1 g \cos \theta$$

Substitute this expression and $w_1 = m_1 g$ into the x component equation for box 1:

$$-m_1 g \sin \theta + T - \mu_k m_1 g \cos \theta = m_1 a_x$$

We now have two equations that involve the unknown quantities T and a_x. We're only asked to find the value of a_x, so we eliminate T between the two equations.

x component equation for box 1:

$$-m_1 g \sin \theta + T - \mu_k m_1 g \cos \theta = m_1 a_x$$

x component equation for box 2:

$$m_2 g - T = m_2 a_x$$

Solve for T using the x component equation for box 1:

$$T = m_1 g \sin \theta + \mu_k m_1 g \cos \theta + m_1 a_x$$

Substitute this into the x component equation for box 2:

$$m_2 g - m_1 g \sin \theta - \mu_k m_1 g \cos \theta - m_1 a_x = m_2 a_x$$

Rearrange and solve for a_x:

$$m_2 g - m_1 g \sin \theta - \mu_k m_1 g \cos \theta = m_1 a_x + m_2 a_x$$
$$(m_2 - m_1 \sin \theta - \mu_k m_1 \cos \theta)g = (m_1 + m_2)a_x$$

$$a_x = \frac{(m_2 - m_1 \sin \theta - \mu_k m_1 \cos \theta)}{(m_1 + m_2)}g$$

$$= \frac{(4.00 \text{ kg} - (2.00 \text{ kg}) \sin 30.0° - (0.250)(2.00 \text{ kg}) \cos 30.0°)}{(2.00 \text{ kg} + 4.00 \text{ kg})}$$

$$\times (9.80 \text{ m/s}^2)$$

$$= 4.19 \text{ m/s}^2$$

Reflect

If there were no friction to slow the boxes down, we would expect the acceleration to be greater. We can check this conclusion by looking at the case $\mu_k = 0$ (which implies zero kinetic friction). Sure enough, a_x is greater in this case.

Returning to the case where friction is present, you can imagine that if box 1 were sufficiently more massive than box 2, the kinetic friction force would be so great that the boxes would slow down rather than speed up as they move. In this case, a_x would be negative. Using $m_2 = 4.00$ kg and $\mu_k = 0.250$, can you show that a_x would be negative if m_1 were greater than 5.58 kg?

If there were no friction between box 1 and the ramp:
$\mu_k = 0$ so

$$a_x = \frac{(m_2 - m_1 \sin \theta)}{(m_1 + m_2)}g$$

$$= \frac{(4.00 \text{ kg} - (2.00 \text{ kg}) \sin 30.0°)}{(2.00 \text{ kg} + 4.00 \text{ kg})}(9.80 \text{ m/s}^2)$$

$$= 4.90 \text{ m/s}^2$$

Example 5-5 Pinned Against a Wall

You place a block of plastic that weighs 33.0 N against a vertical wall and push it toward the wall with a force of 55.0 N (Figure 5-13). The coefficients of static and kinetic friction between the plastic and the wall are $\mu_s = 0.420$ and $\mu_k = 0.400$, respectively. Does the block remain at rest? If not, with what acceleration does it slip down the wall?

Figure 5-13 **Pushing a block against a wall** If you push a block against a wall with a force of a given magnitude, will the block remain at rest or slide down the wall?

Set Up

Four forces act on the block: the gravitational force $\vec{w}_{block}$, the force $\vec{F}_{you\ on\ block}$ you exert to push it against the wall, the normal force $\vec{n}_{block}$ that the wall exerts, and the upward friction force $\vec{f}$ (which opposes the downward gravitational force). The block will only remain at rest if the force of static friction is large enough to balance the 33.0-N gravitational force.

We'll use Equation 5-1b to determine the maximum force of static friction, which will help us decide whether the block will slip. If the block slips, we'll use Equation 5-6 for the force of kinetic friction to determine its acceleration.

Newton's second law applied to the block:

$$\sum \vec{F}_{ext\ on\ block}$$
$$= \vec{w}_{block} + \vec{F}_{you\ on\ block} + \vec{n}_{block} + \vec{f}$$
$$= m_{block}\vec{a}_{block}$$

Magnitude of the static friction force:

$$f_{s,max} = \mu_s n \qquad (5\text{-}1b)$$

Magnitude of the kinetic friction force:

$$f_k = \mu_k n \qquad (5\text{-}6)$$

Solve

We use Newton's second law to determine the normal force that the wall exerts on the block and Equation 5-1b to find the maximum static friction force available. Only 23.1 N of static friction is available, which is less than the gravitational force on the block, so we conclude that the block will slip.

Newton's second law in component form for the block, assuming the block remains at rest (so the friction force is static friction):

x: $F_{you\ on\ block} + (-n_{block}) = 0$

y: $f_s + (-w_{block}) = 0$

From the x component equation,

$$n_{block} = F_{you\ on\ block} = 55.0\ \text{N}$$

From Equation 5-1b, the maximum static friction force available is

$$f_{s,max} = \mu_s n_{block} = (0.420)(55.0\ \text{N}) = 23.1\ \text{N}$$

From the y component equation, the required static friction force is

$$f_s = w_{block} = 33.0\ \text{N}$$

This force is more than the maximum static friction force available, so the block can't remain at rest.

We again apply Newton's second law to the block to find its acceleration as it slides down the wall. Again, we find the normal force that the wall exerts on the block, and we use this value to find the kinetic friction force. Note that we are given the block's weight, not its mass, so we have to calculate its mass m_{block}.

Newton's second law in component form for the block, assuming the block is sliding downward (so the friction force is kinetic friction):

$$x: F_{\text{you on block}} + (-n_{block}) = 0$$
$$y: f_k + (-w_{block}) = m_{block}a_{block,y}$$

From the x component equation,
$$n_{block} = F_{\text{you on block}} = 55.0 \text{ N}$$

From Equation 5-6,
$$f_k = \mu_k n_{block} = (0.400)(55.0 \text{ N}) = 22.0 \text{ N}$$

Find the mass of the block:
$$w_{block} = m_{block}g$$
$$m_{block} = \frac{w_{block}}{g} = \frac{33.0 \text{ N}}{9.80 \text{ m/s}^2} = 3.37 \text{ kg}$$

Substitute into the y equation and solve for $a_{block,y}$:
$$a_{block,y} = \frac{f_k - w_{block}}{m_{block}} = \frac{22.0 \text{ N} - 33.0 \text{ N}}{3.37 \text{ kg}} = -3.27 \text{ m/s}^2$$

Reflect

We chose the positive y direction to be upward, so the negative value of $a_{block,y}$ means that the block accelerates downward. The magnitude of the acceleration is somewhat less than $g = 9.80 \text{ m/s}^2$ because kinetic friction prevents the block from attaining free fall.

Can you show that the block would remain at rest if you pushed with a force of at least 78.6 N?

Example 5-6 A Sled Ride

Two children, Roberto (mass 35.0 kg) and Mary (mass 30.0 kg), go out sledding one winter day. Roberto sits on the sled of mass 5.00 kg, and Mary gives the sled a forward push (Figure 5-14). The coefficients of friction between Roberto and the upper surface of the sled are $\mu_s = 0.300$ and $\mu_k = 0.200$; the friction force between the sled and the icy ground is so small that we can ignore it. Mary finds that if she pushes too hard on the sled, Roberto slides toward the back of the sled. What is the maximum pushing force she can exert without this happening?

Figure 5-14 **Pushing a sled** How hard can Mary push without making Roberto slide toward the back of the sled?

Set Up

If Roberto doesn't slip, the friction force that acts between him and the sled is *static* friction. (The sled and Roberto are sliding over the ice, but they're not sliding relative to each other.) The maximum force of static friction sets a limit on how great the forward acceleration of Roberto and the sled together can be.

This suggests that we should consider two objects: (a) Roberto by himself and (b) Roberto and the sled considered as a unit. Roberto is pushed forward by the friction force exerted on him by the sled, while Roberto and the sled together are pushed forward by Mary's push $\vec{F}_{\text{Mary on unit}}$. (Note that Mary doesn't touch Roberto, so her push doesn't act on him directly.)

Newton's second law equation for Roberto:
$$\sum \vec{F}_{\text{ext on Roberto}}$$
$$= \vec{n}_{\text{sled on Roberto}} + \vec{w}_{\text{Roberto}}$$
$$+ \vec{f}_{\text{s,sled on Roberto}}$$
$$= m_{\text{Roberto}}\vec{a}_{\text{Roberto}}$$

Newton's second law equation for Roberto and the sled considered as a unit:
$$\sum \vec{F}_{\text{ext on unit}}$$
$$= \vec{n}_{\text{ground on unit}} + \vec{w}_{\text{unit}} + \vec{F}_{\text{Mary on unit}}$$
$$= m_{\text{unit}}\vec{a}_{\text{unit}}$$

We'll determine the maximum acceleration that will prevent Roberto from slipping, and then use the result to find the maximum forward force that Mary can exert.

Magnitude of the static friction force:

$$f_{s,\text{max}} = \mu_s n \qquad (5\text{-}1b)$$

Roberto and sled considered as a unit:

Solve

First let's consider just Roberto and the forces that act on him. He is pushed forward by the static friction force that the sled exerts on him. If Roberto is just about to slip, the static friction force has its maximum value. To determine this value, we first find the normal force that the sled exerts on Roberto.

Newton's second law in component form for Roberto, assuming that the static friction force has its maximum value:

$$x: f_{s,\text{max of sled on Roberto}} = m_{\text{Roberto}} a_{\text{Roberto},x}$$
$$y: n_{\text{sled on Roberto}} + (-w_{\text{Roberto}}) = 0$$

From the y component equation,

$$n_{\text{sled on Roberto}} = w_{\text{Roberto}} = m_{\text{Roberto}} g$$

So the maximum force of static friction that the sled exerts on Roberto is

$$f_{s,\text{max of sled on Roberto}} = \mu_s n_{\text{sled on Roberto}}$$
$$= \mu_s m_{\text{Roberto}} g$$

So from the x component equation, Roberto's maximum acceleration is

$$a_{\text{Roberto},x} = \frac{f_{s,\text{max of sled on Roberto}}}{m_{\text{Roberto}}}$$
$$= \frac{\mu_s m_{\text{Roberto}} g}{m_{\text{Roberto}}} = \mu_s g$$

Because Roberto does not slip, he and the sled have the same acceleration. So we can treat Roberto and the sled as a single unit that accelerates forward due to Mary's push. (For this combined unit, we don't have to consider the forces that Roberto and the sled exert on each other because these are *internal* forces.) Because we know Roberto's (and the sled's) maximum acceleration that will prevent slipping, we can calculate the maximum force that Mary can exert.

Newton's second law in component form applied to Roberto and the sled considered as a unit:

$$x: F_{\text{Mary on unit}} = m_{\text{unit}} a_{\text{unit},x}$$
$$y: n_{\text{ground on unit}} + (-w_{\text{unit}}) = 0$$

If Roberto has his maximum acceleration and does not slip on the sled,

$$a_{\text{unit},x} = a_{\text{Roberto},x} = \mu_s g$$

So the maximum force that Mary can exert without causing Roberto to slip is

$$F_{\text{Mary on unit}} = m_{\text{unit}} \mu_s g$$
$$= (m_{\text{Roberto}} + m_{\text{sled}}) \mu_s g$$
$$= [(35.0 \text{ kg}) + (5.00 \text{ kg})](0.300)(9.80 \text{ m/s}^2)$$
$$= 118 \text{ kg} \cdot \text{m/s}^2 = 118 \text{ N}$$

Reflect

What happens if Mary exerts a force greater than 118 N on the sled? There will not be enough static friction to prevent Roberto from sliding across the top of the sled. The net force on him will still be forward, but now it will be due to *kinetic* friction. This force has a smaller magnitude than the maximum force of static friction (we are told that μ_k has a smaller value than μ_s). So Roberto will not have as great an acceleration as the sled. From Mary's perspective, Roberto will slide backward relative to the sled.

? Got the Concept? 5-4 Speeding Up with Friction?

Can the force of friction cause an object to *speed up?* (a) Yes, but only the force of kinetic friction; (b) yes, but only the force of static friction; (c) yes, both kinetic and static friction can cause an object to speed up; (d) no.

5-5 An object moving through air or water experiences a drag force

When a solid object slides over another solid object, the force of kinetic friction provides resistance to its motion. Another important kind of resistance is the **fluid resistance** experienced by an object when it moves through a *fluid*—that is, a liquid or gas (Figure 5-15). The force that resists the motion of an object through a liquid like water or a gas like air is called a **drag force**.

This sea turtle feels a backward force of fluid resistance (drag) as it moves through the water.

(a)

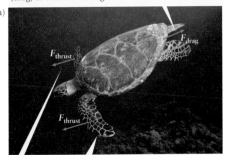

To maintain a constant forward velocity, the turtle pushes backward on the water. The water responds by exerting a forward force (thrust) on the flippers (Newton's third law).

These skydivers feel an upward force of fluid resistance (drag) as they move downward through the air.

(b)

Fluid resistance opposes gravity and slows their fall, giving them more time to enjoy the descent.

Figure 5-15 **Fluid resistance** When an object moves through either (a) a liquid such as water or (b) a gas such as air, it experiences fluid resistance (a drag force).

Drag Force on Microscopic Objects

Unlike the force of kinetic friction, the drag force depends crucially on the *speed* at which the object moves through the fluid. The faster the object's speed, the greater the magnitude of the drag force. For an object that is very small and is moving very slowly, such as a living cell or virus, the magnitude of the drag force is directly proportional to the speed v:

Drag force for small objects at low speeds (5-8)

Magnitude of the drag force on a small object moving at a low speed

$$F_{drag} = bv$$

Constant that depends on the properties of the object and of the fluid

Speed of the object relative to the fluid

The value of b in Equation 5-8 depends on the size, shape, and surface characteristics of the object and the properties of the liquid or gas through which the object is moving. As an example, for an algal spore (which has a spherical shape) of radius 0.020 mm moving in water, the coefficient b is 3.8×10^{-7} N·s/m. At a speed of 5.0×10^{-5} m/s, the drag force on this spore has magnitude

$$F_{\text{drag}} = bv = (3.8 \times 10^{-7}\,\text{N·s/m})(5.0 \times 10^{-5}\,\text{m/s}) = 1.9 \times 10^{-11}\,\text{N}$$

This force is so small that you might think it would have no effect on the spore at all. However, the mass of a spore with this size is only 3.6×10^{-11} kg. If the only force acting on the spore is the drag force (Figure 5-16), the resulting acceleration is

$$a_{\text{spore},x} = \frac{F_{\text{drag},x}}{m_{\text{spore}}} = \frac{-1.9 \times 10^{-11}\,\text{N}}{3.6 \times 10^{-11}\,\text{kg}} = -0.53\,\text{m/s}^2$$

The negative values of $F_{\text{drag},x}$ and $a_{\text{spore},x}$ mean that the drag force acts opposite to the spore's motion, as in Figure 5-16. This substantial acceleration brings the slow-moving spore nearly to a halt in a fraction of a second.

Drag Force on Larger Objects

For a larger object moving at a faster speed, such as the sea turtle or skydivers in Figure 5-15, the drag force has a different dependence on the speed v: Its magnitude is approximately proportional to the *square* of v. In this case, we can write

Magnitude of the drag force on a larger object moving at a faster speed

$$F_{\text{drag}} = cv^2$$

Constant that depends on the properties of the object and of the fluid

Speed of the object relative to the fluid

Drag force for larger objects at faster speeds
(5-9)

Like the coefficient b in Equation 5-8, the quantity c in Equation 5-9 depends on the fluid through which the object moves and the size, shape, and surface properties of the object. For a baseball flying through the air, $c = 1.3 \times 10^{-3}$ N·s²/m². If the baseball is traveling at 25 m/s (a relatively slow pitching speed for a professional player), the magnitude of the drag force on the ball is

$$F_{\text{drag}} = (1.3 \times 10^{-3}\,\text{N·s}^2/\text{m}^2)(25\,\text{m/s})^2 = 0.81\,\text{N}$$

This force is a bit more than half the weight of a regulation baseball (1.4 N or 5 ounces). So the drag force on this baseball is comparable in magnitude to the gravitational force! The drag force plays an important role in baseball and other ball sports.

The value of c is partially determined by how streamlined an object is. For example, the streamlined shape of a dolphin moving through the water gives it a value of c that is only about 1% as large as that of a sphere of the same cross-sectional area.

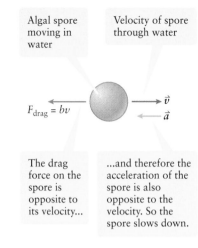

Algal spore moving in water

Velocity of spore through water

$F_{\text{drag}} = bv$ $\vec{v}$ $\vec{a}$

The drag force on the spore is opposite to its velocity...

...and therefore the acceleration of the spore is also opposite to the velocity. So the spore slows down.

Figure 5-16 Drag on a microscopic spore A spherical algal spore moves through water in the positive x direction.

Example 5-7 Terminal Speed

Consider a baseball dropped from rest so that it falls through the air. The downward gravitational force always acts on the ball, so at the instant it is released it has a downward acceleration of magnitude g. As a result of this acceleration, the ball's speed increases. According to Equation 5-9, the drag force (which points upward, opposite to the ball's motion) also increases. The drag force eventually becomes great enough that it has the same magnitude as the gravitational force. The net force on the ball is then zero, and the ball ceases to accelerate: It has reached its *terminal speed*, so it no longer speeds up nor does it slow down. Find the terminal speed of a baseball of mass $m = 0.14$ kg. Discuss how the terminal speed would change if the ball were made of iron or if the ball had a lightweight parachute. The coefficient c equals 1.3×10^{-3} N·s²/m².

Set Up

The free-body diagram shows the two forces acting on the baseball. We use Equation 5-9 to find the value of the speed v at which the sum of these forces is zero, so that the acceleration is zero and the downward velocity is constant.

$$\sum \vec{F}_{\text{ext on ball}}$$
$$= \vec{F}_{\text{drag on ball}} + \vec{w}_{\text{ball}}$$
$$= m\vec{a}_{\text{ball}} = 0$$

Drag force for larger objects at faster speeds:

$$F_{\text{drag}} = cv^2 \qquad (5\text{-}9)$$

Solve

Write Newton's second law in component form and solve for the terminal speed v_{term}.

Newton's second law in component form applied to the ball:

y: $F_{\text{drag on ball}} + (-w_{\text{ball}}) = 0$

At the terminal speed v_{term},

$F_{\text{drag on ball}} = cv_{\text{term}}^2$ so

$$cv_{\text{term}}^2 - w_{\text{ball}} = 0$$
$$cv_{\text{term}}^2 = w_{\text{ball}} = mg$$
$$v_{\text{term}}^2 = \frac{mg}{c}$$
$$v_{\text{term}} = \sqrt{\frac{mg}{c}}$$

Substitute the numerical values of m and c for the baseball.

Using $m = 0.14$ kg and $c = 1.3 \times 10^{-3}$ N·s²/m²,

$$v_{\text{term}} = \sqrt{\frac{(0.14\text{ kg})(9.80\text{ m/s}^2)}{1.3 \times 10^{-3}\text{ N·s}^2/\text{m}^2}}$$
$$= 32\text{ m/s}$$

Reflect

What would happen if we simultaneously dropped a baseball and an iron ball of the same shape and size? Both objects would have the same value of the coefficient c, but the iron ball would have a greater mass m and so a faster terminal speed. This difference in terminal speeds is the origin of the notion that "heavier objects fall faster"—which is a true statement if we take the drag force into account. If the baseball and iron ball were dropped side by side in a vacuum, however, they would accelerate together and always have the same speed.

If we added a parachute to the baseball, the drag force would be much greater for a given speed, and c would have a much larger value. The terminal speed of the baseball would then be greatly reduced. The same thing happens when a skydiver opens her parachute: Her terminal speed decreases dramatically, from about 60 m/s before opening the parachute to about 5 m/s afterward.

$$v_{\text{term}} = \sqrt{\frac{mg}{c}}$$

If two objects have the same shape and size (and hence the same value of c) but different masses, the more massive one will have a greater value of v_{term}.

! **Watch Out!** **The drag force is not a constant force.**

Unlike other forces we've considered, the magnitude of the drag force on an object changes as the object's speed changes. So if a drag force acts on an object, the net force on the object and hence the object's acceleration are *not* constant. As an example, a skydiver who falls without opening her parachute reaches half of her terminal speed ($v = v_{term}/2$) in 3 to 5 s. To achieve nearly terminal speed takes more than twice as long, about 15 to 20 s after beginning the fall. So her acceleration from rest to $v = v_{term}/2$ is much greater than that from $v = v_{term}/2$ to $v = v_{term}$. It would therefore be quite incorrect to try to apply the constant-acceleration formulas from Chapters 2 and 3.

? **Got the Concept? 5-5** **Comparing Drag Forces**

A baseball and a second object of the same mass are thrown into the air. When the second object is moving at one-half the speed of the baseball, the drag force on the second object is four times greater than the drag force on the baseball. Compared to the value of the quantity c for the baseball, the value of c for the second object is (a) 2 times greater, (b) 4 times greater, (c) 8 times greater, (d) 16 times greater, (e) none of these.

Take-Home Message for Section 5-5

✔ Microscopic objects moving through a fluid at low speeds experience a drag force that is proportional to the speed (Equation 5-8).

✔ Larger objects moving through a fluid at faster speeds experience a drag force that is proportional to the square of the speed (Equation 5-9).

✔ A falling object reaches its terminal speed when the upward drag force just balances the downward gravitational force.

5-6 In uniform circular motion, the net force points toward the center of the circle

Think of thrill seekers on a fast-moving amusement park ride or a motorcycle making a sharp turn (Figure 5-17). In both cases an object is following a curved path, so the direction of its velocity vector is changing. Because the direction of the velocity vector is changing, the object is *accelerating* (the object's speed can be constant or changing). In Section 3-5, we learned that when an object follows a curved path, the

(a)

Each person on this amusement park ride moves in a circle at constant speed...

...so the acceleration of each person and the net force on each person both point toward the center of the person's circular path.

(b)

This motorcycle rider also moves along a circular path at constant speed...

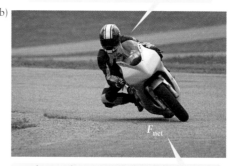

...so his acceleration and the net force on him both point toward the center of the circular path.

Figure 5-17 **Forces in uniform circular motion** An object moving on a circular path at a constant speed is in uniform circular motion. Since the object's direction of motion is continuously changing, the object is accelerating and a net external force must act on it.

acceleration vector $\vec{a}$ must have a component directed toward the inside of the curve. We went on to discover in Section 3-8 that the magnitude of this component, called the *centripetal acceleration*, depends on the radius of the curve and on the object's speed. From Section 4-2, we know that for an object to accelerate there must be a net external force that points in the direction of the acceleration vector $\vec{a}$. In this section, we'll put all of these ideas together and complete our analysis of objects that move along curved paths.

What kinds of force can provide the acceleration needed to make an object follow a curved path? The answer is simple: *any kind of force*, provided that it has a component perpendicular to the object's trajectory. In Figure 5-17a, for example, each person's acceleration arises from the normal force exerted on each person by the seat on which that person sits. For the motorcycle in Figure 5-17b, the acceleration is provided by the friction force that the ground exerts on the motorcycle's tires.

One of the simplest situations in which an object follows a curved trajectory is *uniform circular motion*, or motion around a circular path at a constant speed. We saw in Section 3-8 that in uniform circular motion, the acceleration at any point around the circle is directed toward the center of the circle (that is, it is *centripetal*) and has a magnitude a_{cent} that depends on the object's speed v and the radius r of the circle:

**Centripetal acceleration
(5-10)**

Centripetal acceleration: Magnitude of the acceleration of an object in uniform circular motion

Speed of the object as it moves around the circle

$$a_{\text{cent}} = \frac{v^2}{r}$$

Radius of the circle

Because the acceleration is always toward the center of the circle, it follows from Newton's second law that at any instant the net external force acting on the object of mass m must likewise be directed toward the center of the circle. Furthermore, the magnitude of the net external force must be equal to ma_{cent}. We can write this statement in equation form as

**Newton's second law equation
for uniform circular motion
(5-11)**

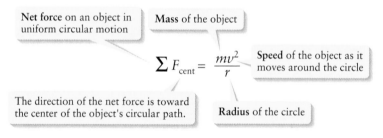

Net force on an object in uniform circular motion

Mass of the object

$$\sum F_{\text{cent}} = \frac{mv^2}{r}$$

Speed of the object as it moves around the circle

The direction of the net force is toward the center of the object's circular path.

Radius of the circle

Go to Interactive Exercise 5-3 for more practice dealing with centripetal acceleration

This equation says that in uniform circular motion, the net external force on the object is equal to the object's mass m multiplied by the centripetal acceleration $a_{\text{cent}} = v^2/r$.

Let's look at several examples of how to apply these ideas to problems in which an object moves around a circle at constant speed.

! Watch Out! **"Centripetal force" is not a special *kind* of force—it describes the *direction* of the net force.**

The force that points toward the inside of an object's curving trajectory and produces the centripetal acceleration is sometimes called the **centripetal force**. Keep in mind, however, that this is not a separate kind of force that you need to include in a free-body diagram. The word *centripetal* simply describes the direction of the force. Just as we might write

F_x to denote the x component of a force, we write F_{cent} to denote the component of force directed toward the center of an object's circular trajectory. As we'll see in the following examples, in different circumstances different forces play the role of the centripetal force.

Example 5-8 A Rock on a String

You tie one end of a lightweight string of length L around a rock of mass m. You hold the other end of the string in your hand and make the rock swing in a horizontal circle at constant speed. As you swing the rock, the string makes an angle θ with the vertical (Figure 5-18). Derive an expression for the speed at which the rock moves around the circle. Ignore the effect of drag forces.

Figure 5-18 **Moving in a circle** How fast must the rock move to make the string hang at an angle θ from the vertical?

Set Up

Because the rock moves at constant speed in a horizontal circle, its acceleration vector points horizontally toward the center of the circle. We choose the positive x axis to point in this direction, and the positive y axis to point upward.

    Only two forces act on the rock: the tension force $\vec{T}$ exerted by the string and the downward gravitational force $\vec{w}_{\text{rock}}$. The tension force is directed along the string and so points at an angle θ to the vertical. The vertical component of $\vec{T}$ balances the downward force of gravity, while the horizontal component of $\vec{T}$ provides the centripetal acceleration. Our goal is to solve for the rock's speed v.

Newton's second law equation for the rock:

$$\sum \vec{F}_{\text{ext on rock}} = \vec{T} + \vec{w}_{\text{rock}} = m_{\text{rock}}\vec{a}_{\text{rock}}$$

Centripetal acceleration:

$$a_{\text{rock,cent}} = \frac{v^2}{r} \qquad (5\text{-}10)$$

Solve

Write Newton's second law for the rock in component form. Note that the quantity v, which is what we're trying to find, doesn't appear in these equations. We'll introduce it in the next step through the expression for the rock's centripetal acceleration.

Newton's second law in component form applied to the rock:

x: $T \sin \theta = m_{\text{rock}}a_{\text{rock,cent}}$

y: $T \cos \theta + (-w)$
$\quad = T \cos \theta - m_{\text{rock}}g = 0$

Use Equation 5-10 to express the acceleration of the rock. Note that because the string is at an angle, the radius of the rock's circular path is *not* equal to the length of the string.

Radius of the rock's circular path:

$$r = L \sin \theta$$

so the rock's centripetal acceleration is

$$a_{\text{rock,cent}} = \frac{v^2}{r} = \frac{v^2}{L \sin \theta}$$

Substitute the expression for centripetal acceleration into the Newton's second law equation for the x direction and solve for v.

Newton's second law equations for the rock become

x: $T \sin \theta = m_{\text{rock}}a_{\text{rock,cent}} = \dfrac{m_{\text{rock}}v^2}{L \sin \theta}$

y: $T \cos \theta = m_{\text{rock}}g$

Solve the y component equation for T:

$$T = \frac{m_{\text{rock}}g}{\cos \theta}$$

Substitute this expression into the x component equation and solve for v:

$$\frac{m_{\mathrm{rock}}g}{\cos\theta}\sin\theta = \frac{m_{\mathrm{rock}}v^2}{L\sin\theta}$$

$$\frac{g\sin\theta}{\cos\theta} = \frac{v^2}{L\sin\theta}$$

$$v^2 = \frac{gL\sin^2\theta}{\cos\theta}$$

$$v = \sqrt{\frac{gL\sin^2\theta}{\cos\theta}}$$

Reflect

You can try this motion for yourself by tying a piece of string around an eraser or other small object and whirling it in a horizontal circle. You'll find that the faster the object moves, the greater the angle θ. Let's check that our answer agrees with this conclusion.

If θ is a small angle close to zero so that the string hangs down almost vertically, $\sin\theta$ is small and $\cos\theta$ is nearly equal to 1. (Remember that $\sin 0 = 0$ and $\cos 0 = 1$.) So the ratio $(\sin^2\theta)/(\cos\theta)$ is a small number, and the speed v will be small. If θ is a large angle close to $90°$ so that the string is nearly horizontal, $\sin\theta$ is a little less than 1 and $\cos\theta$ is small (recall $\sin 90° = 1$ and $\cos 90° = 0$). In this case, the ratio $(\sin^2\theta)/(\cos\theta)$ is a large number and the speed v will be large. So our formula agrees with the experiment!

! Watch Out! No "centrifugal force," please.

In Example 5-8, you may have been tempted to add a force that points toward the *outside* of the rock's curved trajectory (Figure 5-19a). Don't do it! If you felt this temptation, it's because you're thinking of the so-called centrifugal force you feel when riding in a car that makes a sharp turn. This "centrifugal force" seems to push you toward the outside of the turn ("centrifugal" means "fleeing the center"). This force is *fictitious*, however; nothing is exerting an outward force on you. Rather, you're just feeling your body's inertia, which is the tendency of all objects to want to continue in a straight line. Inertia explains what would happen if you

let go of the string attached to the rock: The rock would fly off in a straight line as seen from above (Figure 5-19b), and so it would move away from the center of its circular path. That's not because of a mysterious centrifugal force but rather because of the *absence* of the inward tension force. The lesson here is that you should never include a centrifugal force in any of your free-body diagrams. (If you still feel that you have to add an outward force to "keep the object in balance," remember that an object going around a curve is *not* in balance: The object is accelerating, so the net external force on it is *not* zero!)

(a) Incorrect free-body diagram of the rock

(b) A top view of the rock's trajectory

There is no object that exerts $F_{\mathrm{centrifugal}}$. So this force does not exist and should not be drawn.

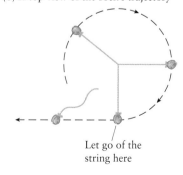

Let go of the string here

Figure 5-19 How *not* to draw a free-body diagram for uniform circular motion
(a) A free-body diagram should never include a "centrifugal force." (b) If the string is let go, the rock flies off in a straight line due to its inertia— *not* a "centrifugal force."

Example 5-9 Making an Airplane Turn

An airplane banks to one side in order to turn in that direction. By banking the plane, the *lift force*—a force that acts perpendicular to the direction of flight, caused by the motion of air over the airplane's wings—ends up with both a vertical component and a horizontal component (Figure 5-20). The horizontal component of this force provides the centripetal acceleration needed to make the airplane move around a circle. (a) If the airplane of mass $m_{airplane}$ is traveling at speed v and is banked by an angle θ, derive an expression for the radius of the turn. (b) The pilot of the airplane has mass m_{pilot} and weight $w_{pilot} = m_{pilot}g$. If the pilot is sitting on a scale as the airplane makes its banked turn, what does the scale read?

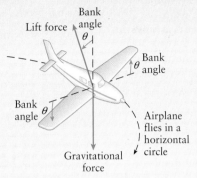

Figure 5-20 An airplane in a banked turn What mathematical expression describes the radius of the airplane's turn? The forward thrust force and the backward drag force cancel and are not shown.

Set Up

We draw two free-body diagrams, one for the airplane of mass $m_{airplane}$ and one for the pilot of mass m_{pilot}. (In both cases, the airplane and pilot are coming at us head on.) Both of these diagrams are almost identical to the free-body diagram for the rock in Example 5-8. Besides the gravitational force, a second force has a vertical component that balances the gravitational force (so that the airplane doesn't accelerate up or down) and a horizontal component that gives the object a centripetal acceleration. In part (a), we want to find the radius r of the turn; in part (b), our goal is to determine the value of the normal force n (the force that the scale exerts on the pilot, which is the same as the reading on the scale).

Newton's second law equation for the airplane:

$$\sum \vec{F}_{\text{ext on airplane}} = \vec{L} + \vec{w}_{airplane} = m_{airplane}\vec{a}_{airplane}$$

Newton's second law equation for the pilot:

$$\sum \vec{F}_{\text{ext on pilot}} = \vec{n} + \vec{w}_{pilot} = m_{pilot}\vec{a}_{pilot}$$

Centripetal acceleration:

$$a_{airplane} = a_{pilot} = a_{cent} = \frac{v^2}{r} \quad (5\text{-}10)$$

Solve

(a) Once again, we begin by writing Newton's second law in component form. The x component equation involves the radius r of the turn, but we don't know the value of the lift force L. We find this force from the y component equation, and we then substitute the value of L into the x equation and solve for r. The airplane's acceleration is directed toward the center of the turn, so it is a centripetal acceleration.

Newton's second law in component form applied to the airplane:

$$x\text{: } L \sin \theta = m_{airplane}a_{cent} = m_{airplane}\frac{v^2}{r}$$

$$y\text{: } L \cos \theta + (-w_{airplane}) = L \cos \theta - m_{airplane}g = 0$$

From the y equation,

$$L \cos \theta = m_{airplane}g$$

$$L = \frac{m_{airplane}g}{\cos \theta}$$

Substitute this expression for L into the x equation and solve for r:

$$m_{airplane}\frac{v^2}{r} = L \sin \theta = \frac{m_{airplane}g}{\cos \theta} \sin \theta = m_{airplane}g \tan \theta$$

$$\frac{v^2}{r} = g \tan \theta$$

$$r = \frac{v^2}{g \tan \theta}$$

(b) The component form of Newton's second law for the pilot is very similar to that for the airplane—the main difference is that the lift force L is replaced by the normal force n. Here, we only need the y component equation to solve for n. The pilot's acceleration is directed to the center of the turn, so it is a centripetal acceleration.

Newton's second law in component form applied to the pilot:

$$x: n \sin \theta = m_{\text{pilot}} a_{\text{cent}} = m_{\text{pilot}} \frac{v^2}{r}$$

$$y: n \cos \theta + (-w_{\text{pilot}}) = n \cos \theta - m_{\text{pilot}} g = 0$$

Solve the y component equation for n:

$$n \cos \theta = m_{\text{pilot}} g$$

$$n = \frac{m_{\text{pilot}} g}{\cos \theta}$$

Reflect

Our result in part (a) says that the faster the airplane's speed for a given bank angle θ, the larger the radius r of the turn. To make a tight turn at high speed (that is, to have r be small even though v is large), the quantity $\tan \theta$ has to be as large as possible. So the bank has to be steep to make a tight turn: the greater the bank angle θ, the greater the value of $\tan \theta$. (You should recall that $\tan 0 = 0$, $\tan 45° = 1$, and $\tan 90° = $ infinity.) Note that the airplane's mass doesn't appear in our result, so our conclusions are the same no matter whether the airplane is large or small.

Our result in part (b) shows the danger of too steep a bank angle. As θ increases, $\cos \theta$ decreases (recall that $\cos 0 = 1$, $\cos 60° = 1/2$, and $\cos 90° = 0$), so the scale reading becomes larger and larger. In other words, the pilot *feels* heavier than normal. The same is true for every part of the pilot's body, including her blood. If the bank angle is too steep, the pilot's heart can't pump this "heavy" blood up to her brain, and the pilot will lose consciousness.

To counter these effects, fighter pilots (who often make very sharp turns at steep bank angles) wear *g-suits*. These are garments that apply pressure to the legs and lower abdomen, thus preventing blood from pooling in the lower body even during extreme aerial maneuvers.

The greater the bank angle θ, the smaller the turning radius r of the airplane:

$$r = \frac{v^2}{g \tan \theta}$$

For $\theta = 45°$: $\tan 45° = 1$

$$r = \frac{v^2}{g}$$

For $\theta = 60°$: $\tan 60° = 1.73$

$$r = \frac{v^2}{1.73g} = 0.577 \frac{v^2}{g}$$

For $\theta = 80°$: $\tan 80° = 5.67$

$$r = \frac{v^2}{5.67g} = 0.176 \frac{v^2}{g}$$

The greater the bank angle θ, the greater the pilot's scale reading and the heavier she feels:

$$\text{"Normal" weight} = m_{\text{pilot}} g$$

$$\text{"Apparent" weight} = n = \frac{m_{\text{pilot}} g}{\cos \theta}$$

For $\theta = 45°$: $\cos 45° = 0.707$

$$n = \frac{m_{\text{pilot}} g}{0.707} = 1.41 m_{\text{pilot}} g$$

(The pilot feels "1.41 *g*".)

For $\theta = 60°$: $\cos 60° = 0.500$

$$n = \frac{m_{\text{pilot}} g}{0.500} = 2.00 m_{\text{pilot}} g$$

(The pilot feels "2.00 *g*".)

For $\theta = 80°$: $\cos 80° = 0.174$

$$n = \frac{m_{\text{pilot}} g}{0.174} = 5.76 m_{\text{pilot}} g$$

(The pilot feels "5.76 *g*" and might pass out.)

Example 5-10 A Turn on a Level Road

A car of mass m_{car} exits the freeway and travels around a circular off-ramp at a constant speed of 15.7 m/s (56.5 km/h, or 35.1 mi/h). The ramp is level (it is not banked), so the centripetal force has to be provided by the force of friction. If the coefficient of static friction between the car's tires and the road is 0.550 (a typical value when the road surface is wet), what radius of curvature is required for the off-ramp so that the car does not skid?

Set Up

This example is very similar to Example 5-6 in Section 5-4. In both examples, a static friction force produces an acceleration. The only difference is that in Example 5-6 the friction force gave Roberto a *forward* acceleration, while in this example the friction force causes a *centripetal* acceleration.

The free-body diagram shows the car head-on. Note that even though the car is rolling on its tires, the force that provides the centripetal acceleration is *static* friction rather than rolling friction. That's because the force of interest is the one that prevents the car from sliding sideways away from the center of its circular path. (By contrast, rolling friction acts opposite to the car's forward motion and so doesn't contribute to the centripetal acceleration.) The minimum value of the radius r corresponds to the maximum centripetal acceleration $a_{cent} = v^2/r$, which in turn corresponds to the maximum value $f_{s,max}$ of the static friction force.

Newton's second law equation for the car:

$$\sum \vec{F}_{ext\ on\ car}$$
$$= \vec{n} + \vec{w}_{car} + \vec{f}_s$$
$$= m_{car}\vec{a}_{car}$$

Centripetal acceleration:

$$a_{car} = a_{cent} = \frac{v^2}{r} \qquad (5\text{-}10)$$

Magnitude of the static friction force:

$$f_{s,max} = \mu_s n \qquad (5\text{-}1b)$$

Solve

We write Newton's second law for the car in component form, with the static friction force set equal to its maximum value $f_{s,max}$. The horizontal (x) acceleration equals the centripetal acceleration; there is zero vertical (y) acceleration. We then solve for the radius r of the car's circular path.

Newton's second law in component form for the car, assuming that the static friction force has its maximum value:

$$x: f_{s,max} = m_{car}a_{cent}$$
$$y: n + (-w_{car}) = 0$$

From the y component equation,

$$n = w_{car} = m_{car}g$$

So the maximum force of static friction of the tires is

$$f_{s,max} = \mu_s n = \mu_s m_{car}g$$

Substitute this expression and $a_{cent} = v^2/r$ into the x component equation, then solve for r:

$$\mu_s m_{car}g = m_{car}\frac{v^2}{r}$$

$$r = \frac{v^2}{\mu_s g}$$

Using $\mu_s = 0.550$ and $v = 15.7$ m/s,

$$r = \frac{(15.7 \text{ m/s})^2}{(0.550)(9.80 \text{ m/s}^2)} = 45.7 \text{ m}$$

Reflect

Our answer is the *minimum* radius of the off-ramp. If the radius is larger, the car will have a smaller centripetal acceleration $a_{cent} = v^2/r$ and the static friction force required will be less than the maximum force available.

Note that the minimum radius increases if the car is going faster (v is greater). Note also that for a given speed, the car can make a tighter turn (that is, r will be smaller) if the tires have a better "grip" on the road (so the coefficient of static friction μ_s is greater). The car would be able to make a tighter turn if the road were dry, in which case μ_s is about 1.0.

Example 5-11   A Turn on a Banked Road

Unlike the level off-ramp in Example 5-10, many freeway off-ramps, as well as corners at racetracks, are banked. As an example, the corners at the Indianapolis Motor Speedway are banked by 9.20°. The radius of each corner is 256 m. What is the fastest speed at which a race car could take one of these corners if the coefficient of static friction is $\mu_s = 0.550$, as in Example 5-10?

Set Up

In contrast to the situation in Example 5-10, the net centripetal force on the car comes from *two* forces exerted by the banked road: the horizontal component of the normal force and the horizontal component of the static friction force. Because we want the car to move as fast as possible and hence have the maximum possible centripetal acceleration, it has to have the maximum available centripetal force exerted on it. In this extreme case, the static friction force will be at its maximum value. Our goal is to find the value of v in this situation.

Newton's second law equation for the car:

$$\sum \vec{F}_{\text{ext on car}}$$
$$= \vec{n} + \vec{w}_{\text{car}} + \vec{f}_s$$
$$= m_{\text{car}} \vec{a}_{\text{car}}$$

Centripetal acceleration:

$$a_{\text{car}} = a_{\text{cent}} = \frac{v^2}{r} \qquad (5\text{-}10)$$

Magnitude of the static friction force:

$$f_{s,\text{max}} = \mu_s n \qquad (5\text{-}1b)$$

Solve

As in Example 5-10, we write Newton's second law for the car in component form, with the static friction force set equal to its maximum value $f_{s,\text{max}}$. Again, the horizontal (x) acceleration equals the centripetal acceleration; there is zero vertical (y) acceleration. The difference is that now the normal force and friction force have both x and y components.

Newton's second law in component form for the car, assuming that the static friction force has its maximum value:

$$x: n \sin \theta + f_{s,\text{max}} \cos \theta = m_{\text{car}} a_{\text{cent}}$$
$$y: n \cos \theta + (-w_{\text{car}})$$
$$+ (-f_{s,\text{max}} \sin \theta) = 0$$

Substitute the expressions for the maximum force of static friction, the centripetal acceleration, and the weight of the car:

$$f_{s,\text{max}} = \mu_s n$$
$$a_{\text{cent}} = \frac{v^2}{r}$$
$$w_{\text{car}} = m_{\text{car}} g$$

Then the Newton's law equations become

$$x: n \sin \theta + \mu_s n \cos \theta = m_{\text{car}} \frac{v^2}{r}$$
$$y: n \cos \theta - m_{\text{car}} g - \mu_s n \sin \theta = 0$$

Solve the y component equation for the normal force n.

Rearrange the y component equation to find n:

$$n \cos \theta - \mu_s n \sin \theta = m_{\text{car}} g$$
$$n(\cos \theta - \mu_s \sin \theta) = m_{\text{car}} g$$
$$n = \frac{m_{\text{car}} g}{\cos \theta - \mu_s \sin \theta}$$

Substitute this expression for n into the x component equation and solve for the speed v.

Rearrange the x component equation:

$$n \sin \theta + \mu_s n \cos \theta = m_{\text{car}} \frac{v^2}{r}$$
$$n(\sin \theta + \mu_s \cos \theta) = m_{\text{car}} \frac{v^2}{r}$$

Substitute the expression for n and solve for v:

$$\frac{m_{car}g}{\cos\theta - \mu_s \sin\theta}(\sin\theta + \mu_s \cos\theta)$$

$$= m_{car}\frac{v^2}{r} \qquad g\left(\frac{\sin\theta + \mu_s \cos\theta}{\cos\theta - \mu_s \sin\theta}\right) = \frac{v^2}{r}$$

$$v^2 = gr\left(\frac{\sin\theta + \mu_s \cos\theta}{\cos\theta - \mu_s \sin\theta}\right)$$

$$v = \sqrt{gr\left(\frac{\sin\theta + \mu_s \cos\theta}{\cos\theta - \mu_s \sin\theta}\right)}$$

Use the values of r, θ, and μ_s given for the Indianapolis Motor Speedway.

Using $r = 256$ m, $\theta = 9.20°$, and $\mu_s = 0.550$,
$\sin\theta = \sin 9.20° = 0.160$
$\cos\theta = \cos 9.20° = 0.987$

$$v = \sqrt{(9.80\ \text{m/s}^2)(256\ \text{m})\left(\frac{0.160 + (0.550)(0.987)}{0.987 - (0.550)(0.160)}\right)}$$

$$= 44.3\ \text{m/s}$$

$$= (44.3\ \text{m/s})\left(\frac{1\ \text{km}}{1000\ \text{m}}\right)\left(\frac{3600\ \text{s}}{1\ \text{h}}\right) = 159\ \text{km/h}$$

$$= (159\ \text{km/h})\left(\frac{1\ \text{mi}}{1.61\ \text{km}}\right) = 99.1\ \text{mi/h}$$

Reflect

This speed is quite a bit less than that reached by race cars on the straightaway (200 to 300 km/h), so it's necessary to slow down before turning this corner.

We can check our result by looking at two special cases: (a) If the curve is *not* banked, then $\theta = 0$, $\sin\theta = 0$, and $\cos\theta = 1$. In this case, our result reduces to what we found for the flat road in Example 5-10. (b) If the curve is banked but there is no friction, then $\mu_s = 0$ (because then the maximum force of friction is $f_{s,max} = \mu_s n = 0$). In this situation, our result simplifies to what we found for the airplane making a level turn in Example 5-9. (The airplane isn't on a road, but the lift force $\vec{L}$ on a turning airplane plays exactly the same role as the normal force $\vec{n}$ on a car on a frictionless banked curve.)

You can show that in case (a) the car's maximum speed would be only 37.1 m/s, while in case (b) it would be only 20.2 m/s. A banked curve with friction allows the highest speeds!

(a) If the curve is not banked (so $\theta = 0$):

$$v = \sqrt{gr\left(\frac{\sin 0 + \mu_s \cos 0}{\cos 0 - \mu_s \sin 0}\right)}$$

$$= \sqrt{gr\left(\frac{0 + \mu_s(1)}{1 - \mu_s(0)}\right)}$$

$$= \sqrt{\mu_s gr}$$

This equation is equivalent to what we found in Example 5-10 for a flat road:

$$r = \frac{v^2}{\mu_s g}, \text{so } v^2 = \mu_s gr \text{ and } v = \sqrt{\mu_s gr}$$

(b) If the curve is banked but there is no friction (so $\mu_s = 0$):

$$v = \sqrt{gr\left(\frac{\sin\theta + (0)\cos\theta}{\cos\theta - (0)\sin\theta}\right)}$$

$$= \sqrt{gr\left(\frac{\sin\theta}{\cos\theta}\right)}$$

$$= \sqrt{gr\tan\theta}$$

This equation is equivalent to what we found in Example 5-9 for an airplane making a banked turn:

$$r = \frac{v^2}{g\tan\theta}, \text{so } v^2 = gr\tan\theta \text{ and}$$

$$v = \sqrt{gr\tan\theta}$$

? Got the Concept? 5-6 Comparing Circular Motions

Five objects all move in uniform circular motion. The objects have different masses, move at different speeds, and travel in circular paths of different radii. Rank these objects in order of the magnitude of the centripetal force that acts on them, from greatest to least: (a) a 2.00-kg object moving at 10.0 m/s in a circle of radius 8.00 m, (b) a 2.00-kg object moving at 5.00 m/s in a circle of radius 4.00 m, (c) a 4.00-kg object moving at 5.00 m/s in a circle of radius 2.00 m, (d) a 4.00-kg object moving at 5.00 m/s in a circle of radius 8.00 m, and (e) an 8.00-kg object moving at 5.00 m/s in a circle of radius 1.00 m.

Take-Home Message for Section 5-6

✔ If an object is in uniform circular motion, its acceleration is directed toward the center of the circle and given by Equation 5-10.

✔ The net force on an object in uniform circular motion is also directed toward the center of the circle (Equation 5-11). The net force in this case is called the centripetal force.

✔ Any kind of force (or combination of forces) can provide the centripetal force on an object in uniform circular motion.

Key Terms

centripetal force
coefficient of kinetic friction
coefficient of rolling friction
coefficient of static friction

drag force
fluid resistance
friction
kinetic friction

rolling friction
static friction

Chapter Summary

Topic	Equation or Figure

Static friction: If an object is at rest on a surface, a static friction force $\vec{f}_s$ arises if other forces are trying to make the object move. The static friction force can have any magnitude up to a maximum value.

(a) You apply a force of 20.0 N to the right, but the block remains at rest...

20.0 N

20.0 N

...so the table must exert a static friction force of 20.0 N to the left on the block.

(b) You apply a force of 10.0 N to the right, but the block remains at rest...

10.0 N

10.0 N

...so the table must exert a static friction force of 10.0 N to the left on the block.

(c) You apply no force to the block and it remains at rest...

...so the table must exert no static friction force on the block.

The static friction force adjusts its value to counteract whatever other forces are trying to make the object slide.

(Figure 5-2)

(1) The magnitude of the force of static friction on an object... (2) ... is less than or equal to a certain maximum value.

$$f_s \leq f_{s,max}$$ (5-1a)

(3) The maximum force of static friction depends on...

$$f_{s,max} = \mu_s n$$ (5-1b)

(4) ... the coefficient of static friction (which depends on the properties of the two surfaces in contact)...

(5) ... and the normal force pressing the object against a surface.

An object at rest on an incline: Static friction will keep an object at rest on an inclined surface provided the angle θ of the incline is less than a critical value θ_{slip}.

(a) A block at rest on an inclined ramp

Block, weight w

Ramp whose angle θ from the horizontal can be varied

θ

(Figure 5-5a)

Coefficient of static friction for an object at rest on a surface

Angle of the surface at which the object begins to slip

$$\mu_{\text{s}} = \tan \theta_{\text{slip}}$$

(5-5)

Kinetic friction: If an object is sliding over a surface, that surface exerts a kinetic friction force $\vec{f}_{\text{k}}$ that opposes sliding. We model this force as being independent of the object's speed. There is a similar expression for the force of rolling friction; the difference is that the coefficient for rolling has a smaller value than that for sliding.

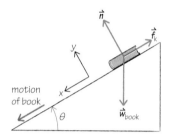

$\vec{n}$

$\vec{f}_{\text{k}}$

y

motion of book

x

θ

$\vec{w}_{book}$

(Example 5-2)

The force of kinetic friction depends on...

$$f_{\text{k}} = \mu_{\text{k}} n$$

(5-6)

... the coefficient of kinetic friction (which depends on the properties of the two surfaces in contact)...

... and the normal force exerted on the object by the surface on which it slides.

Drag force: An object moving through a fluid (gas or liquid) experiences a resistive force that opposes its motion. If the object is small and moving at a low speed v relative to the fluid, the magnitude of the drag force is proportional to v. For larger objects moving at faster speeds, the drag force is proportional to the square of v.

Magnitude of the drag force on a small object moving at a low speed

$$F_{\text{drag}} = bv$$

(5-8)

Constant that depends on the properties of the object and of the fluid

Speed of the object relative to the fluid

Magnitude of the drag force on a larger object moving at a faster speed

$$F_{\text{drag}} = cv^2$$

(5-9)

Constant that depends on the properties of the object and of the fluid

Speed of the object relative to the fluid

Uniform circular motion: If an object moves at constant speed around a circular path, the net force on the object points toward the center of the path. Any kind of force or combination of forces can contribute to this net force.

Centripetal acceleration: Magnitude of the acceleration of an object in uniform circular motion

Speed of the object as it moves around the circle

$$a_{cent} = \frac{v^2}{r}$$ (5-10)

Radius of the circle

Net force on an object in uniform circular motion

Mass of the object

$$\sum F_{cent} = \frac{mv^2}{r}$$

Speed of the object as it moves around the circle

(5-11)

The direction of the net force is toward the center of the object's circular path.

Radius of the circle

Answer to What do you think? Question

(a) There is a net force, and it points inward toward the center of the circle. Newton's second law tells us that the net force must be in the same direction as the bicycle's acceleration, and in uniform circular motion the acceleration is inward. If you're riding on the bicycle, it may *feel* as though a force is pushing you outward. This outward "force" isn't real, however; it's just a consequence of your body's inertia (see Section 5-6).

Answers to Got the Concept? Questions

5-1 (d) As shown in Equation 5-1b, the maximum static friction force between the block and board depends only on the normal force n and the coefficient of static friction μ_s. It does *not* depend on the area of contact between the block and board. Therefore the angle at which the block begins to slide will be the same no matter which face is in contact with the board.

5-2 (e) The acceleration of the book doesn't depend on its mass at all. The acceleration is caused by the kinetic friction force and the downhill component of the gravitational force. Both of these are proportional to the mass of the book. (The kinetic friction force has magnitude $f_k = \mu_k n$, and the normal force n is proportional to the block's weight and hence its mass.) The mass cancels out when we calculate the acceleration of the block, which is equal to the net external force on the block divided by its mass.

5-3 (d) We saw in Section 5-2 that an object at rest on a ramp with angle θ will just barely remain at rest (that is, the maximum force of static friction is just enough to balance the downhill component of the gravitational force), if $\mu_s = \tan \theta$. For an incline with $\theta = 30.0°$, $\mu_s = \tan 30.0° = 0.577$. If μ_s has a greater value than 0.577, the maximum static friction force available is greater than the force required and the object will still remain at rest. So both $\mu_s = 0.600$ and $\mu_s = 0.750$ will keep the object at rest. If $\mu_s = 0.350$, there isn't enough static friction and so the book will start sliding back downhill.

5-4 (c) Example 5-6 illustrates that both kinetic friction and static friction can cause an object to speed up. If Roberto doesn't slip on the upper surface of the sled, the force that accelerates him forward is the force of static friction. If he does slip, he nonetheless accelerates forward due to the force of kinetic friction. (In the latter case, it's true that he slips backward relative to the sled. However, both he and the sled are accelerating forward; it's just that Roberto's acceleration is less than the acceleration of the sled.)

5-5 (d) The drag force for both objects is given by $F_{drag} = cv^2$, so $c = F_{drag}/v^2$. Because the drag force on the second object is 4 times greater and $1/2$ the speed, the quantity c is $(4)/(1/2)^2 = 16$ times greater for the second object than for the baseball.

5-6 (e), (c), (a), (b) and (d) [tie] The centripetal force on an object of mass m moving at speed v in a circle of radius r is equal to mv^2/r—that is, to m multiplied by the object's centripetal acceleration $a_{cent} = v^2/r$. For the five cases this quantity is (a) $(2.00 \text{ kg})(10.0 \text{ m/s})^2/(8.00 \text{ m}) = 25.0$ N; (b) $(2.00 \text{ kg})(5.00 \text{ m/s})^2/(4.00 \text{ m}) = 12.5$ N; (c) $(4.00 \text{ kg})(5.00 \text{ m/s})^2/(2.00 \text{ m}) = 50.0$ N; (d) $(4.00 \text{ kg})(5.00 \text{ m/s})^2/(8.00 \text{ m}) = 12.5$ N; (e) $(8.00 \text{ kg})(5.00 \text{ m/s})^2/(1.00 \text{ m}) = 2.00 \times 10^2$ N.

Questions and Problems

In a few problems, you are given more data than you actually need; in a few other problems, you are required to supply data from your general knowledge, outside sources, or informed estimate.

Interpret as significant all digits in numerical values that have trailing zeros and no decimal points. For all problems, use $g = 9.80 \text{ m/s}^2$ for the free-fall acceleration due to gravity.

• Basic, single-concept problem

•• Intermediate-level problem, may require synthesis of concepts and multiple steps

••• Challenging problem

SSM *Solution is in Student Solutions Manual*

Conceptual Questions

1. •Complete the sentence: The static frictional force between two surfaces is (never/sometimes/always) less than the normal force. Explain your answer.

2. •You want to push a heavy box of books across a rough floor. You know that the maximum value of the coefficient of static friction (μ_s) is larger than the maximum value of the coefficient of kinetic friction (μ_k). Should you push the box for a short distance, rest, push the box another short distance, and then repeat the process until the box is where you want it, or will it be easier to keep pushing the box across the floor once you get it moving?

3. •If the force of friction always opposes the sliding of an object, how then can a frictional force cause an object to increase in speed? SSM

4. •A solid rectangular block has sides of three different areas. You can choose to rest any of the sides on the floor as you apply a horizontal force to the block. Does the choice of side on the floor affect how hard it is to push the block? Explain your answer.

5. • You're trying to press a book against a spot on the wall with your hand. As you get tired, you exert less force, but the book remains in the same spot on the wall. Do each of the following forces increase, decrease, or not change in magnitude when you reduce the force you are applying to the book: (a) weight, (b) normal force, (c) frictional force, and (d) maximum static frictional force?

6. •For an object moving in a circle, which of the following quantities are zero over one revolution: (a) displacement, (b) average velocity, (c) average acceleration, (d) instantaneous velocity, and (e) instantaneous centripetal acceleration?

7. •Why does water stay in a bucket that is whirled around in a vertical circle? Contrast the forces acting on the water when the bucket is at the lowest point on the circle to when the bucket is at the highest point on the circle. SSM

8. •An antilock braking system (ABS) prevents wheels from skidding while drivers stomp on the brakes in emergencies. How far will a car with an ABS move before finally stopping, as compared to a car without an ABS?

9. •Give two examples of two situations in which the normal force acting on an object is not equal to the object's weight.

10. •**Medical** A fluidlike substance called *synovial fluid* lubricates the surfaces where bones meet in joints, making the coefficient of friction between bones very small. Why is the minimum force required for moving bones in a typical knee joint different for different people, in spite of the fact that their joints have the same coefficient of friction? For simplicity, assume the surfaces in the knee are flat and horizontal.

11. •As a skydiver falls faster and faster through the air, does his acceleration increase, decrease, or remain the same? Explain your answer. SSM

12. •Why do raindrops fall from the sky at different speeds? Explain your answer.

13. •Why might your car start to skid if you drive too fast around a curve?

14. •What distinguishes the forces that act on a car driving over the top of a hill from those acting on a car driving through a dip in the road? Explain how the forces relate to the sensations passengers in the car experience during each situation.

15. •Explain how you might measure the centripetal acceleration of a car rounding a curve. SSM

16. •An object of mass M_1 rests on a horizontal table; friction exists between the object and the table (Figure 5-21). A ring of mass M_R is tied by massless strings both to the wall and to the object as shown. A second object of mass M_2 hangs from the ring. Draw free-body diagrams for the situation.

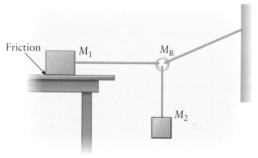

Figure 5-21
Problem 16

17. •Explain why curves in roads and cycling velodromes are banked. SSM

18. •At low speeds, the drag force on an object moving through a fluid is proportional to its velocity. According to Newton's second law, force is proportional to acceleration. As acceleration and velocity aren't the same quantity, is there a contradiction here?

19. •James Bond leaps without a parachute from a burning airplane flying at 15,000 ft. Ten seconds later his assistant, who was following behind in another plane dives after him, wearing her parachute and clinging to one for her hero. Is it possible for her to catch up with Bond and save him?

Multiple-Choice Questions

20. •If a sport utility vehicle (SUV) drives up a slope of 45°, what must be the minimum coefficient of static friction between the SUV's tires and the road?

   A. 1.0

   B. 0.5

   C. 0.7

   D. 0.9

   E. 0.05

21. •A block of mass m slides down a rough incline with constant speed. If a similar block that has a mass of $4m$ were placed on the same incline, it would
   A. slide down at constant speed.
   B. accelerate down the incline.
   C. slowly slide down the incline and then stop.
   D. accelerate down the incline with an acceleration four times greater than that of the smaller block.
   E. not move. SSM

22. •A 10-kg crate is placed on a horizontal conveyor belt moving with a constant speed. The crate does not slip. If the coefficients of friction between the crate and the belt are μ_s equal to 0.50 and μ_k equal to 0.30, what is the frictional force exerted on the crate?
   A. 98 N
   B. 49 N
   C. 29 N
   D. 9.8 N
   E. 0

23. •**Biology** The *Escherichia coli* (*E. coli*) bacterium propels itself through water by means of long, thin structures called flagella. If the force exerted by the flagella doubles, the velocity of the bacterium
   A. doubles.
   B. decreases by half.
   C. does not change.
   D. increases by a factor of four.
   E. cannot be determined without more information.

24. •A 1-kg wood ball and a 5-kg lead ball have identical sizes, shapes, and surface characteristics. They are dropped simultaneously from a tall tower. Air resistance is present. How do their accelerations compare?
   A. The 1-kg wood ball has the larger acceleration.
   B. The 5-kg lead ball has the larger acceleration.
   C. The accelerations are the same.
   D. The 5-kg ball accelerates at five times the acceleration of the 1-kg ball.
   E. The 1-kg ball accelerates at five times the acceleration of the 5-kg ball.

25. •A skydiver is falling at his terminal speed. Immediately after he opens his parachute
   A. his speed will be larger than his terminal speed.
   B. the drag force on the skydiver will decrease.
   C. the net force on the skydiver is in the downward direction.
   D. the drag force is larger than the skydiver's weight.
   E. the net force on the skydiver is zero. SSM

26. •Two rocks that are of equal mass are tied to massless strings and whirled in nearly horizontal circles at the same speed. One string is twice as long as the other. What is the tension T_1 in the shorter string compared to the tension T_2 in the longer one?
   A. $T_1 = 14T_2$
   B. $T_1 = 12T_2$
   C. $T_1 = T_2$
   D. $T_1 = 2T_2$
   E. $T_1 = 4T_2$

27. •You are on a Ferris wheel moving in a vertical circle. When you are at the bottom of the circle, how does the magnitude of the normal force N exerted by your seat compare to your weight mg?
   A. $N = mg$
   B. $N > mg$
   C. $N < mg$
   D. $N = 12mg$
   E. $N = 2mg$ SSM

28. •Two rocks are tied to massless strings and whirled in nearly horizontal circles so that the period of motion is the same for both. One string is twice as long as the other. The tension in the longer string is twice the tension in the shorter one. What is the mass m_1 of the rock at the end of the shorter string compared to the mass m_2 of the rock at the end of the longer one?
   A. $m_1 = 14m_2$
   B. $m_1 = 12m_2$
   C. $m_1 = m_2$
   D. $m_1 = 2m_2$
   E. $m_1 = 4m_2$

Estimation/Numerical Analysis

29. •Estimate the numerical value of the coefficient of static friction between a car's tires and dry pavement.

30. •Estimate the value of the coefficient of kinetic friction for a box of books on a carpeted floor.

31. •**Sports** Make a rough estimate of the value of the coefficient of kinetic friction between a baseball player's uniform and the infield surface as he slides into second base. SSM

32. •Give a numerical estimate of the minimum radius of curvature of an unbanked on-ramp for a typical freeway.

33. •**Sports** Estimate the size of the coefficient of kinetic friction between a hockey puck and the ice of a rink.

34. •(a) Estimate the magnitude of the coefficient of kinetic friction of a book as it slides across a tabletop. (b) Estimate the magnitude of the coefficient of static friction for the same book on the same tabletop.

35. •Estimate the magnitude of the coefficient of kinetic friction between you and the surface of a waterslide. SSM

36. •Estimate the magnitude of the coefficient of kinetic friction for a mug of root beer as it slides across a wooden bar.

37. •The following table lists the forces applied to a 1.00-kg crate at particular times. The crate begins at rest on a rough, horizontal surface but is then pushed with a constant force in the horizontal direction. Using the data, estimate the coefficient of static friction and the coefficient of kinetic friction between the crate and the surface.

t (s)	F (N)	t (s)	F (N)
0	0	0.25	8.26
0.01	1.33	0.30	7.84
0.05	3.28	0.35	5.17
0.10	8.11	0.40	5.21
0.15	8.20	0.45	5.22
0.20	8.24	0.50	5.37

Problems

5-2 The static friction force changes magnitude to offset other applied forces

38. •What is the minimum horizontal force that will cause a 5.00-kg box to begin to slide on a horizontal surface when the coefficient of static friction is 0.670?

39. •A 7.60-kg object rests on a level floor with a coefficient of static friction of 0.550. What minimum horizontal force will cause the object to start sliding? SSM

40. •Draw a free-body diagram for the situation shown in Figure 5-22. An object of mass M rests on a ramp; there is friction between the object and the ramp. The system is in equilibrium.

Figure 5-22 Problem 40

5-3 The kinetic friction force on a sliding object has a constant magnitude

41. •A book is pushed across a horizontal table at a constant speed. If the horizontal force applied to the book is equal to one-half of the book's weight, calculate the coefficient of kinetic friction between the book and the tabletop. SSM

42. •An object on a level surface experiences a horizontal force of 12.7 N due to kinetic friction. If the coefficient of kinetic friction is 0.37, what is the mass of the object?

43. •A 25.0-kg crate rests on a level floor. A horizontal force of 50.0 N accelerates the crate at 1.00 m/s². Calculate (a) the normal force on the crate, (b) the frictional force on the crate, and (c) the coefficient of kinetic friction between the crate and the floor.

44. •A block of mass M rests on a block of mass $M_1 = 5.00$ kg which is on a tabletop (Figure 5-23). A light string passes over a frictionless peg and connects the blocks. The coefficient of kinetic friction μ_k at both surfaces equals 0.330. A force of 60.0 N pulls the upper block to the left and the lower block to the right. The blocks are moving at a constant speed. Determine the mass of the upper block.

Figure 5-23
Problem 44

45. •A mop is pushed across the floor with a force F of 50.0 N at an angle of $\theta = 50.0°$ (Figure 5-24). The mass of the mop head is 3.75 kg. Calculate the acceleration of the mop head if the coefficient of kinetic friction between the head and the floor is 0.400.

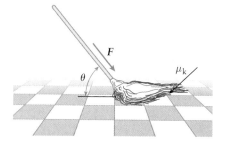

Figure 5-24
Problem 45

46. •If the coefficient of kinetic friction between an object with mass $M = 3.00$ kg and a flat surface is 0.400, what force will

cause the object to accelerate at 2.50 m/s²? The force is applied at an angle of $\theta = 30.0°$ (Figure 5-25).

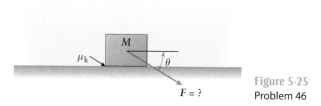

Figure 5-25
Problem 46

5-4 Problems involving static and kinetic friction are like any other problem with forces

47. ••A taut string connects a crate with mass $M_1 = 5.00$ kg to a crate with mass $M_2 = 12.0$ kg (Figure 5-26). The coefficient of static friction between the smaller crate and the floor is 0.573; the coefficient of static friction between the larger crate and the floor is 0.443. What is the minimum horizontal force F required to start the crates in motion? SSM

Figure 5-26 Problem 47

48. ••A box of mass $M_{box} = 2.00$ kg rests on top of a crate with mass $M_{crate} = 5.00$ kg (Figure 5-27). The coefficient of static friction between the box and the crate is 0.667. The coefficient of static friction between the crate and the floor is 0.400. Calculate the minimum force F that is required to move the crate to the right and the corresponding tension T in the rope that connects the box to the wall when the crate is moved.

Figure 5-27 Problem 48

49. •Two blocks are connected over a massless, frictionless pulley (Figure 5-28). The mass of block 2 is 8.00 kg, and the coefficient of kinetic friction between block 2 and the incline is 0.220. The angle θ of the incline is 28.0°. Block 2 slides down the incline at constant speed. What is the mass of block 1? SSM

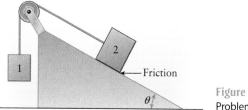

Figure 5-28
Problems 49 and 50

50. •Two blocks are connected over a massless, frictionless pulley (Figure 5-28). The mass of block 2 is 10.0 kg, and the

coefficient of kinetic friction between block 2 and the incline is 0.200. The angle θ of the incline is 30.0°. If block 2 moves up the incline at constant speed, what is the mass of block 1?

51. ••An object with mass M_1 of 2.85 kg is held in place on an inclined plane that makes an angle θ of 40.0° with the horizontal (Figure 5-29). The coefficient of static friction between the plane and the object is 0.552. A second object that has a mass M_2 of 4.75 kg is connected to the first object with a massless string over a massless, frictionless pulley. Calculate the initial acceleration of the system and the tension in the string once the objects are released.

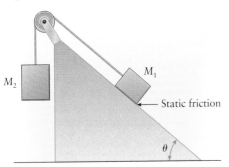

Static friction

Figure 5-29
Problem 51

52. •Draw free-body diagrams for the situation shown in Figure 5-30. An object of mass M_2 rests on a frictionless table, and an object of mass M_1 sits on it; there is friction between the objects. A horizontal force $\vec{F}$ is applied to the lower object as shown.

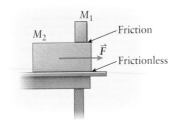

Figure 5-30 Problem 52

53. ••A horizontal force F of 10.0 N is applied to a stationary block with a mass M of 2.00 kg as shown in Figure 5-31. The coefficient of static friction between the block and the floor is 0.750; the coefficient of kinetic friction is 0.450. Find the acceleration of the box. SSM

Figure 5-31 Problem 53

5-5 An object moving through air or water experiences a drag force

54. •Biology A single-celled animal called a *paramecium* propels itself quite rapidly through water by using its hairlike *cilia*. A certain paramecium experiences a drag force of magnitude $F_{drag} = cv^2$ in water, where the drag coefficient c is approximately 0.310. What propulsion force does this paramecium generate when moving at a constant (terminal) speed v of 0.150×10^3 m/s?

55. •Biology The bacterium *Escherichia coli* propels itself with long, thin structures called flagella. When its flagella exert a force of 1.50×10^{-13} N, the bacterium swims through water at a speed of 20.0 μm/s. Find the speed of the bacterium in water when the force exerted by its flagella is 3.00×10^{-13} N.

56. ••We model the drag force of the atmosphere as proportional to the square of the speed of a falling object, $F_{drag} = cv^2$,

where the value of c for a 70.0-kg person with a parachute is 18.0 kg/m. (a) What is the person's terminal velocity? (b) Without a parachute, the same person's terminal velocity would be about 50.0 m/s. What would be the value of the proportionality constant c in that case?

57. ••A girl rides her scooter on a hill that is inclined at 10° with the horizontal. The combined mass of the girl and scooter is 50.0 kg. On the way down, she coasts at a constant speed of 12.0 m/s, while experiencing a drag force that is proportional to the square of her velocity. What force, parallel to the surface of the hill, is required to increase her speed to 20.0 m/s? Neglect any other resistive forces.

5-6 In uniform circular motion, the net force points toward the center of the circle

58. •A hockey puck that has a mass of 170 g is tied to a light string and spun in a circle of radius 1.25 m (on frictionless ice). If the string breaks under a tension that exceeds 5.00 N, what is the maximum speed of the puck without breaking the string?

59. •A 1500-kg truck rounds an unbanked curve on the highway at a speed of 20.0 m/s. If the maximum frictional force between the surface of the road and all four of the tires is 8000 N, calculate the minimum radius of curvature for the curve to prevent the truck from skidding off the road. SSM

60. •A 25.0-g metal washer is tied to a 60.0-cm-long string and whirled around in a vertical circle at a constant speed of 6.00 m/s. Calculate the tension in the string (a) when the washer is at the bottom of the circular path and (b) when it is at the top of the path.

61. •A centrifuge spins small tubes in a circle of radius 10.0 cm at a rate of 1200 rev/min. What is the centripetal force on a sample that has a mass of 1.00 g? SSM

62. •Astro What centripetal force is exerted on the Moon as it orbits about Earth at a center-to-center distance of 3.84×10^8 m with a period of 27.4 days? What is the source of the force? The mass of the Moon is equal to 7.35×10^{22} kg.

63. •Biology Very high-speed ultracentrifuges are useful devices to sediment materials quickly or to separate materials. An ultracentrifuge spins a small tube in a circle of radius 10.0 cm at 60,000 rev/min. What is the centripetal force experienced by a sample that has a mass of 0.00300 kg?

64. •At the Fermi National Accelerator Laboratory (Fermilab), a large particle accelerator, protons are made to travel in a circular orbit 6.3 km in circumference at a speed of nearly 3.0×10^8 m/s. What is the centripetal acceleration of one of the protons?

65. •In the game of tetherball, a 1.25-m rope connects a 0.750-kg ball to the top of a vertical pole so that the ball can spin around the pole as shown in Figure 5-32. What is the speed of the ball as it rotates around the pole when the angle θ of the rope is 35.0° with the vertical? SSM

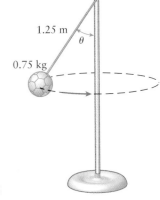

1.25 m

0.75 kg

Figure 5-32 Problem 65

66. •What is the force that a jet pilot feels against his seat as he completes a vertical loop that is 500 m in radius at a speed of 200 m/s? Assume his mass is 70.0 kg and that he is located at the bottom of the loop.

67. •The radius of Earth is 6.38×10^6 m, and it completes one revolution in 1 day. (a) What is the centripetal acceleration of an object located on the equator? (b) What is the centripetal acceleration of an object located at latitude 40.0° north?

68. ••A coin that has a mass of 25.0 g rests on a phonograph turntable that rotates at 78.0 rev/min. The center of the coin is 13.0 cm from the turntable axis. If the coin does not slip, what is the minimum value of the coefficient of static friction between the coin and the turntable surface?

69. •**Sports** In executing a windmill pitch, a fast-pitch softball player moves her hand through a circular arc of radius 0.310 m. The 0.190-kg ball leaves her hand at 24.0 m/s. What is the magnitude of the force exerted on the ball by her hand immediately before she releases it?

General Problems

70. ••A 150-kg crate rests in the bed of a truck that slows from 50.0 km/h to a stop in 12.0 s. The coefficient of static friction between the crate and the truck bed is 0.655. (a) Will the crate slide during the braking period? Explain your answer. (b) What is the minimum stopping time for the truck in order to prevent the crate from sliding?

71. ••The coefficient of static friction between a rubber tire and dry pavement is about 0.800. Assume that a car's engine only turns the two rear wheels and that the weight of the car is uniformly distributed over all four wheels. (a) What limit does the coefficient of static friction place on the time required for a car to accelerate from rest to 60 mph (26.8 m/s)? (b) How can friction accelerate a car *forward* when friction *opposes* motion? SSM

72. ••Two blocks are connected over a massless, frictionless pulley (Figure 5-33). Block m_1 has a mass of 1.00 kg and block m_2 has a mass of 0.400 kg. The angle θ of the incline is 30.0°. The coefficients of static friction and kinetic friction between block m_1 and the incline are μ_s equal to 0.500 and μ_k equal to 0.400, respectively. What is the value of the tension in the string?

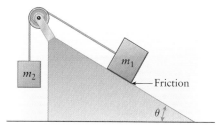

Figure 5-33
Problems 72 and 73

73. ••Two blocks are connected over a massless, frictionless pulley (Figure 5-33). Block m_1 has a mass of 1.00 kg and block m_2 has a mass of 2.00 kg. The angle θ of the incline is 30.0°. The coefficients of static friction and kinetic friction between block m_1 and the incline are μ_s equal to 0.500 and μ_k equal to 0.400. What is the acceleration of block m_1?

74. •A runaway ski slides down a 250-m-long slope inclined at 37.0° with the horizontal. If the initial speed is 10.0 m/s, how long does it take the ski to reach the bottom of the incline if

the coefficient of kinetic friction between the ski and snow is (a) 0.100 and (b) 0.150?

75. •In a mail-sorting facility, a 2.50-kg package slides down an inclined plane that makes an angle of 20.0° with the horizontal. The package has an initial speed of 2.00 m/s at the top of the incline, and it slides a distance of 12.0 m. What must the coefficient of kinetic friction between the package and the inclined plane be so that the package reaches the bottom with no speed? SSM

76. ••In Figure 5-34, two blocks are connected to each other by a massless string over a massless and frictionless pulley. The mass m_1 is 6.00 kg. Assuming the coefficient of static friction μ_s equals 0.542 for all surfaces, find the range of values of the mass m_2 of the second block so that the system is in equilibrium.

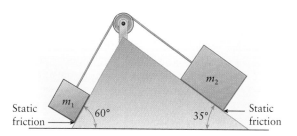

Figure 5-34 Problem 76

77. ••The terminal velocity of a raindrop that is 4.00 mm in diameter is approximately 8.50 m/s under controlled, windless conditions. The density of water is 1000 kg/m³. Recall that the density of an object is its mass divided by its volume. (a) If we model the air drag as being proportional to the square of the speed, $F_{\text{drag}} = cv^2$, what is the value of c? (b) Under the same conditions as above, what would be the terminal velocity of a raindrop that is 8.0 mm in diameter? Try to use your answer from part (a) to solve the problem by proportional reasoning instead of just doing the same calculation over again.

78. •Biomedical laboratories routinely use ultracentrifuges, some of which are able to spin at 100,000 rev/min about the central axis. The turning rotor in certain models is about 20.0 cm in diameter. At its top spin speed, what force does the bottom of the rotor exert on a 2.00-g sample that is in the rotor at the greatest distance from the axis of spin? Would the force be appreciably different if the sample were spun in a vertical or a horizontal circle? Why or why not?

79. ••An amusement park ride called the Rotor debuted in 1955 in Germany. Passengers stand in the cylindrical drum of the Rotor as it rotates around its axis. Once the Rotor reaches its operating speed, the floor drops but the riders remain pinned against the wall of the cylinder. Suppose the cylinder makes 25.0 rev/min and has a radius of 3.50 m. What is the coefficient of static friction between the wall of the cylinder and the backs of the riders?

80. •An object of mass m_1 undergoes constant circular motion and is connected by a massless string through a hole in a frictionless table to a larger object of mass m_2 (Figure 5-35). If the larger object is stationary, calculate the tension in the string and the speed of the circular motion of the smaller object. Assume that the objects have masses of 0.225 and 0.125 kg and the

radius R of the circular path of the smaller object is equal to 1.00 m.

Figure 5-35
Problem 80

81. •An object that has a mass M hangs from a support by a massless string of length L (Figure 5-36). The support is rotated so that the object follows a circular path at an angle θ from the vertical as shown. The object makes N revolutions per second. Derive an expression for the angle θ in terms of M, L, N, and any necessary physical constants. SSM

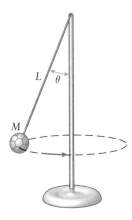

Figure 5-36 Problem 81

82. •Medical Occupants of cars hit from behind, even at low speed, often suffer serious neck injury from whiplash. During a low-speed rear-end collision, a person's head suddenly pivots about the base of the neck through a 60° angle, a motion that lasts 250 ms. The distance from the base of the neck to the center of the head is typically about 20 cm, and the head normally comprises about 6.0% of body weight. We can model the motion of the head as having uniform speed over the course of its pivot. Compute your answers to the following questions to two significant figures. (a) What is the acceleration of the head during the collision? (b) What force (in newtons and in pounds) does the neck exert on the head of a 75-kg person in the collision? (As a first approximation, neglect the force of gravity on the head.) (c) Would headrests mounted to the backs of the car seats help protect against whiplash? Why or why not?

83. •The wings of an airplane flying in a horizontal circle at a speed of 680 km/h are tilted 60.0° to the horizontal (Figure 5-37). What is the radius of the circle? Assume that the required force is provided entirely by the wings' lift, a force perpendicular to the surface of the wings.

Figure 5-37 Problem 83

84. •A curve that has a radius of 100 m is banked at an angle of 10.0° (Figure 5-38). If a 1000-kg car navigates the curve at 65 km/h without skidding, what is the minimum coefficient of static friction between the pavement and the tires?

Figure 5-38
Problem 84

6

Work and Energy

In this chapter, your goals are to:

- (6-1) Explain the relationship between work and energy.
- (6-2) Calculate the work done by a constant force on an object moving in a straight line.
- (6-3) Describe what kinetic energy is and understand the work-energy theorem.
- (6-4) Apply the work-energy theorem to solve problems.
- (6-5) Recognize why the work-energy theorem applies even for curved paths and varying forces like the spring force.
- (6-6) Explain the meaning of potential energy and how conservative forces such as the gravitational force and the spring force give rise to gravitational potential energy and spring potential energy.
- (6-7) Explain the differences between, and when you can apply, the generalized law of conservation of energy and the conservation of total mechanical energy.
- (6-8) Identify which kinds of problems are best solved with energy conservation and the steps to follow in solving these problems.

To master this chapter, you should review:

- (2-5) The equations for constant-acceleration motion in a straight line.
- (4-2 Newton's second and third laws of motion.
  and, 4-5)

> ### What do you think?
> Kangaroos use a bounding gait to move rapidly across the countryside. The large muscles in its hind legs help a kangaroo to start bounding. Which anatomical structure is most important for sustaining the kangaroo's bounding movement? (a) The kangaroo's knees; (b) its head; (c) its tendons; (d) its front legs.

6-1 The ideas of work and energy are intimately related

Life depends on energy. Energy is used in nearly every living process—moving, breathing, circulating blood, digesting food, and absorbing nutrients. There are different kinds of energy, including kinetic, potential, and internal. Energy can be transformed from one of these kinds into another. But what *is* energy?

In this chapter we'll see that if an object or system has **energy**, then that object or system may be able to do *work*. We need to have energy, for example, to push a stalled car or to lift a heavy box. Work has many different meanings in everyday life. In the language of physics, however, work has a very specific definition that describes what happens when a force is exerted on an object as it moves. One example of doing work is lifting a book from your desk to a high bookshelf; another is a football player pushing a blocking sled across the field (**Figure 6-1a**). By combining the definition of work with our knowledge of Newton's second law, we'll be led naturally to the idea of *kinetic*

The football player applies a force F to the sled while it moves a distance d. Hence he does an amount of work on the sled equal to Fd.

The girl does work on the basketball: She exerts a force on the ball as she pushes it away from her. As a result the ball acquires kinetic energy (energy of motion).

(a)

(b)

(c)

As the ball hits its target and slows down, work is done on the target. Some kinetic energy goes into deforming the ball and giving it elastic potential energy, which converts again to kinetic energy when the ball springs back.

Figure 6-1 **Work and energy** In this chapter we'll explore the ideas of (a) work, (b) kinetic energy, and (c) potential energy.

Take-Home Message for Section 6-1

✔ A force acting on an object in motion can do work on that object.

✔ An object or system's energy is related to its ability to do work.

✔ There are different kinds of energy, including kinetic, potential, and internal. Energy can be transformed from one of these kinds into another.

energy, which is the energy that an object has due to its motion (Figure 6-1b). An object with kinetic energy has the ability to do work: For example, a moving ball has the ability to displace objects in its path (Figure 6-1c).

Sometimes kinetic energy is lost—it gets converted to a form of energy that can't be recovered—such as when an egg thrown at high speed splatters against a wall. But if that egg is replaced with a rubber ball, the ball bounces off with nearly the same speed at which it was thrown and so we recover most of the ball's kinetic energy. We say that as the ball is compressed during its impact with the wall, the kinetic energy is converted into *potential energy*—energy associated not with the ball's motion but with its shape and postion—which in turn is again converted into kinetic energy as the ball bounces back (Figure 6-1c).

In this chapter we'll look at the ways in which kinetic energy, potential energy, and *internal energy*—energy stored within an object, sometimes in a way that can't easily be extracted—can transform into each other. (As an example, the energy you need to make it through today is extracted from energy stored in chemical bonds of the molecules of food that you consumed earlier.) In this way we'll discover the *law of conservation of energy*, which proves to be one of the great unifying principles of the natural sciences in general.

6-2 The work that a constant force does on a moving object depends on the magnitude and direction of the force

The man depicted in Figure 6-2 is doing *work* as he pushes a crate up a ramp. The amount of work that he does depends not only on how hard he pushes on the crate (that is, on the magnitude of the force that he exerts) but also the distance over which he moves the crate (that is, the displacement of the crate). In a similar way, cross-country skiing for 10 km requires more work and is more tiring than skiing for 1 km. The football players shown in Figure 6-1a will be more exhausted if the coach asks them to push the blocking sled all the way down the field rather than a short distance.

These examples suggest how we should define the **work** done by a force on an object. Suppose a constant force $\vec{F}$ acts on an object as it moves through a straight-line displacement $\vec{d}$, and the force $\vec{F}$ is in the same direction as $\vec{d}$. Then the work done by

The man exerts a constant force $\vec{F}$ on the crate. The direction of the force is parallel to the ramp.

As he exerts the force, the crate moves through a displacement $\vec{d}$ up the ramp.

 If the force $\vec{F}$ the man exerts on the crate is in the same direction as the displacement $\vec{d}$ of the crate, the work W that he does on the crate is the product of force and displacement: $W = Fd$.

Figure 6-2 **Work is force times distance** Calculating how much work the man does to push the crate up the ramp.

the force equals the product of the force magnitude F and the distance d over which the object moves:

Work done on an object by a constant force $\vec{F}$ that points in the same direction as the object's displacement $\vec{d}$

Magnitude of the constant force $\vec{F}$

$$W = Fd$$

Magnitude of the displacement $\vec{d}$

Work done by a constant force that points in the same direction as the straight-line displacement (6-1)

Note that Equation 6-1 refers only to situations in which the force acts in the *same* direction as the displacement. You've already seen two situations of this sort: The football players in Figure 6-1a push the sled backward as it moves backward, and the man in Figure 6-2 pushes the crate uphill as it moves uphill. Later we'll expand the definition of work to include the case in which force and displacement are *not* in the same direction.

We saw in Chapters 4 and 5 that it's important to keep track of what object *exerts* a given force and on what object that force is exerted. For the same reason, it's helpful to name both the object that exerts a force and the object on which the force does work. For example in Figure 6-2, the object exerting a force is the man and the object on which the force does work is the crate. The unit of work, the **joule** (J), is named after the nineteenth-century English physicist James Joule. His study of the relationship between motion and work was fundamental to the development of the scientific understanding of work and energy. From Equation 6-1,

$$1\,\text{J} = 1\,\text{N} \times 1\,\text{m or } 1\,\text{J} = 1\,\text{N}\cdot\text{m}$$

You do 1 J of work when you exert a 1-N push on an object as it moves through a distance of 1 m.

> ### ! Watch Out!
> **Work and weight have similar symbols.**
>
> Since *work* and *weight* begin with the same letter, it's important to use different symbols to represent them in equations. We'll use an uppercase W for work and a lowercase w for weight (the magnitude of the gravitational force), and we recommend that you do the same to prevent confusion.

Example 6-1 Lifting a Book

How much work must you do to lift a textbook with a mass of 2.00 kg—roughly the mass of this book—by 5.00 cm? (You lift the book at a constant speed.)

Set Up
Newton's first law tells us that the net force on the book must be zero if it is to move upward at a constant speed. Hence the upward force you apply must be constant and equal in magnitude to the gravitational force on the book. Since the applied force is constant and in the direction in which the book moves, we can use Equation 6-1 to calculate the work done.

Work done on an object, force in the same direction as displacement:

$$W = Fd \qquad (6\text{-}1)$$

Solve
Calculate the magnitude F of the force that you exert, then substitute this and the displacement $d = 5.00$ cm into Equation 6-1 to determine the work that you do.

$$F = mg = (2.00\,\text{kg})(9.80\,\text{m/s}^2)$$
$$= 19.6\,\text{N}$$

$$\begin{aligned} W = Fd &= (19.6\,\text{N})(5.00\,\text{cm}) \\ &= (19.6\,\text{N})(0.0500\,\text{m}) \\ &= 0.980\,\text{N}\cdot\text{m} \\ &= 0.980\,\text{J} \end{aligned}$$

Reflect
The work that you do is almost exactly one joule. The actual amount of energy that you would need to *expend* is several times more than 0.980 J, however. That's because your body isn't 100% efficient at converting energy into work. Some of the energy goes into heating your muscles. In fact, your muscles can consume energy even when they do *no* work, as we describe below. The value of 0.980 J that we calculated is just the amount of work that you do *on the book*.

Example 6-2 Work Done by Actin

In order to fertilize eggs, the sperm of the horseshoe crab (Figure 6-3) must penetrate two protective layers of the egg with a combined thickness of about 40 μm. To achieve this, a bundle of the protein actin 60 μm in length pushes from the outer surface of the sperm with a constant force of 1.9×10^{-9} N. How much work does the actin bundle do in this process?

Figure 6-3 **A horseshoe crab** Horseshoe crabs (family *Limulidae*) are similar to crustaceans, but are more closely related to spiders and scorpions. Like the cells of other animals and plants, horseshoe crab cells contain an important protein called actin.

Set Up

The force exerted is both constant and in the same direction as motion of the end of the bundle. Hence we can once again use Equation 6-1.

$$W = Fd \qquad (6\text{-}1)$$

Solve

The work done by the actin bundle equals the product of force and distance. The actin bundle has to push through the outer layers of the egg.

$$\begin{aligned} W &= Fd \\ &= (1.9 \times 10^{-9} \text{ N})(40 \times 10^{-6} \text{ m}) \\ &= 7.6 \times 10^{-14} \text{ J} \end{aligned}$$

Reflect

The amount of work done by the actin bundle seems ridiculously small. But such a bundle is microscopic, with a mass of only about 10^{-16} kg. Hence the actin bundle does about 10^3 J of work per kilogram of mass. If a 70-kg person could do that much work on a per-kilogram basis on the book in Example 6-1, he or she could lift the book 3.5 km (nearly 12,000 ft)! An actin bundle is small, but it packs a big punch.

$$\frac{\text{Work done by actin bundle}}{\text{Mass of actin bundle}} = \frac{7.6 \times 10^{-14} \text{ J}}{10^{-16} \text{ kg}} = 10^3 \text{ J/kg}$$

If a 70-kg person could do that much work on a per-kilogram basis,

$$\text{Work done} = W = (10^3 \text{ J/kg})(70 \text{ kg}) = 7.0 \times 10^4 \text{ J}$$

Height d to which this amount of work could raise a book of mass 2.00 kg and weight 19.8 N:

$$W = mgd, \text{ so } d = \frac{W}{mg} = \frac{7.0 \times 10^4 \text{ J}}{19.8 \text{ N}} = 3.5 \times 10^3 \text{ m} = 3.5 \text{ km}$$

Figure 6-4 **Getting tired while doing zero work** Weights that you hold stationary in your outstretched arms undergo no displacement, so you do zero work on them. Why, then, do your arms get tired?

Muscles and Doing Work

Pick up a book or other heavy object and hold it in your hand at arm's length (Figure 6-4). After awhile you'll notice your arm getting tired: It feels like you're doing work to hold the object in midair. But Equation 6-1 says that you're doing *no* work on the book, because the book isn't moving (its displacement d is zero). So if you're not doing any work, why does your arm feel tired?

To see the explanation for this seeming paradox, notice that the muscles in your arm (and elsewhere in your body) exert forces on their ends by contracting. Skeletal muscles (those that control the motions of your arms, legs, fingers, toes, and other structures) are made up of bundles of muscle cells (Figure 6-5a). Muscle cells consist of bundles of myofibrils that are segmented into thousands of tiny structures called sarcomeres. Connected to each other, end to end, sarcomeres contain interdigitated filaments of the contractile proteins actin and myosin (Figure 6-5b). As the filaments slide past each other the sarcomeres can shorten, resulting in the muscle contracting; when the muscle relaxes, sarcomeres lengthen.

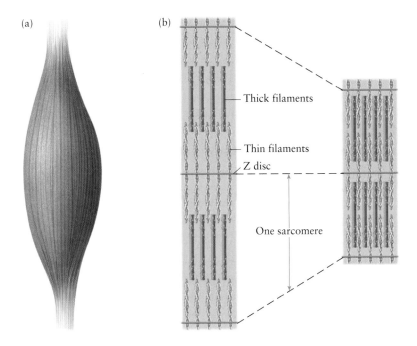

(a)   (b)

Thick filaments

Thin filaments

Z disc

One sarcomere

Figure 6-5 **Muscles and muscle function** (a) The muscles of your body are composed of many individual muscle fibers. (b) The internal structure of a muscle fiber when relaxed (left) and contracted (right).

The reason why your arm tires while holding the book is that the process of shortening the sarcomeres and maintaining the contraction against the load of the book requires energy. Metabolic pathways convert energy stored in the chemical bonds of fat and sugar to a form that your muscle cells can use, but these reactions generate waste products that change the conditions in the muscle. This leads to the feeling that you've been doing work—even though you're doing no work on the *book* itself.

If you again hold the book in one hand, but now rest your elbow on a table, you'll find that you can hold the book for a longer time without fatigue. That's because in this case you're using only the muscles of your hand and forearm, not those of your upper arm. Hence fewer muscle fibers have to stay contracted, fewer crossbridges between filaments have to be reattached to maintain the contraction, and you expend less energy.

Work by Forces Not Parallel to Displacement and Negative Work

How can we calculate the work done by a constant force that is *not* in the direction of the object's motion? As an example, in Figure 6-6a a groundskeeper is using a rope to pull a screen across a baseball diamond to smooth out the dirt. The net tension force $\vec{F}$ that the rope exerts on the screen is at an angle with respect to the direction in which the screen moves. In such a case, only the *component* of the force along the direction of motion contributes to the work done (Figure 6-6b).

If θ is the angle between the force $\vec{F}$ and the displacement $\vec{d}$, this component of the force is $F \cos \theta$. Hence the amount of work done by the force is

$\sqrt{x}$ *See the Math Tutorial for more information on trigonometry*

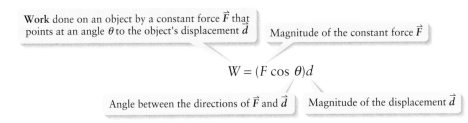

Work done on an object by a constant force $\vec{F}$ that points at an angle θ to the object's displacement $\vec{d}$ Magnitude of the constant force $\vec{F}$

$$W = (F \cos \theta)d$$

Angle between the directions of $\vec{F}$ and $\vec{d}$ Magnitude of the displacement $\vec{d}$

Work done by a constant force at an angle θ to the straight-line displacement
(6-2)

As a check on Equation 6-2, note that if $\vec{F}$ is in the same direction as the motion, $\theta = 0$ and $\cos \theta = \cos 0 = 1$. This is the same situation as shown in Figure 6-2, and in this case Equation 6-2 gives the same result as Equation 6-1: $W = Fd$. Note also that if

(a)

The man exerts a force $\vec{F}$ on the screen. The direction of the force is not parallel to the ground.

As he exerts the force, the screen undergoes a displacement $\vec{d}$ along the ground.

(b)

Screen

$\vec{F}$

θ

$F \cos \theta$

$\vec{d}$

Only the component of force parallel to the displacement contributes to the work that the man does on the screen.

If a constant force $\vec{F}$ acts on an object at an angle θ to the object's displacement $\vec{d}$, the work done by the force equals the force component $F \cos \theta$ parallel to the displacement multiplied by the displacement d: $W = (F \cos \theta) d$.

Figure 6-6 **When force is not aligned with displacement** (a) A man exerts a force on a screen to pull it across a baseball field. (b) Finding the work that the man does on the screen (seen from the side).

A lazy dog exerts a downward force on the screen.

$\vec{F}$ $\theta = 90°$ $\vec{d}$

The angle between the force and the displacement $\vec{d}$ of the screen is 90° (the force and displacement are perpendicular). Hence the force has zero component in the direction of $\vec{d}$ and does zero work.

Figure 6-7 **Doing zero work** A dog resting atop the screen exerts a force on the screen as it slides, but does zero work on the screen.

 See the Math Tutorial for more information about the dot product

$\vec{F}$ is perpendicular to the direction of motion, $\theta = 90°$ and $\cos \theta = \cos 90° = 0$. In this case Equation 6-2 tells us that force $\vec{F}$ does *zero* work. An example is the force exerted by a lazy dog lying on top of the screen from Figure 6-6a (Figure 6-7). The dog exerts a downward force on the screen as the screen moves horizontally, so $\theta = 90°$ and the lazy dog does no work at all.

Figure 6-8 shows a cart rolling along the floor as a person tries to slow it down. The force $\vec{F}$ that the person exerts on the cart is directed opposite to the cart's displacement $\vec{d}$, so the angle θ in Equation 6-2 is 180°. Since $\cos 180° = -1$, this means that the person does **negative work** on the cart: $W_{\text{person on cart}} = -Fd$, is negative. Negative work is done whenever the angle θ between the displacement of an object and the force acting on that object is greater than 90°, so $\cos \theta$ is less than zero.

What does it mean to do negative work on an object? From our discussions of kinematics and forces, we know that when the force on an object (and hence its acceleration) points in the opposite direction of the object's velocity and displacement, the object slows down (see Figure 2-10). So practically speaking, if you want to slow an object down, you must do negative work on it. Conversely, if you do positive work on an object, it speeds up. As we will see in Section 6-3, when you do negative work on an object, you remove some of its kinetic energy.

What else happens when you do negative work on an object? Newton's third law provides the answer: If the person in Figure 6-8 exerts a force $\vec{F}$ on the cart, the cart exerts a force $-\vec{F}$ on her (the same magnitude of force but in the opposite direction). The hands of the person have the same displacement $\vec{d}$ as the cart, and the force the cart exerts on her is in the *same* direction as her displacement ($\theta = 0$ and $\cos \theta = +1$ in Equation 6-2), so the work that the *cart* does on the *person* is $W_{\text{cart on person}} = +Fd$. *If object A does negative work on object B, then object B does an equal amount of positive work on object A.* So if you do negative work on an object, removing some of its energy, the object does positive work on you, adding to your energy.

A combination like that in Equation 6-2—the product of the magnitudes of two vectors and the cosine of the angle between them—shows up frequently in physics. Mathematically, this is one way to calculate the **dot product** of the vectors $\vec{F}$ and $\vec{d}$. To learn more about the dot product and its properties, you should explore Math Tutorial. However, in this chapter we will restrict ourselves to calculating the work done by a force using Equation 6-2.

Calculating Work Done by Multiple Forces

Any force acting on an object in a direction other than perpendicular to the direction of motion does work on the object. For example, four forces act on the screen in Fig-

1 As the person tries to make the cart slow down, the cart and the person's hands move together to the right (they have the same displacement).

$\vec{d}$

$\vec{F}_{\text{cart on person}} = -\vec{F}_{\text{person on cart}}$

$\vec{F}_{\text{person on cart}}$

If one object (like the person) does negative work on a second object (like the cart), the second object does an equal amount of positive work on the first object.

2 The force of the person on the cart is opposite to the cart's displacement. Hence $\theta = 180°$, $\cos \theta = -1$, and the person does negative work on the cart.

3 By Newton's third law, the cart exerts an equally strong force on the person, but in the opposite direction — that is, in the same direction of the displacement of the person's hands. So the cart does positive work on the person.

Figure 6-8 Doing negative work As the cart rolls to the right, the person pushes on the cart to the left in order to make it slow down. As a result, she does negative work on the cart.

ure 6-6a: The tension in the rope, the gravitational force, the normal force, and the force of friction. The free-body diagram in **Figure 6-9** shows all of these forces, as well as the displacement vector $\vec{d}$. Note that we draw $\vec{d}$ to one side in the diagram to avoid confusing it with the forces, and that the direction of motion is in the positive x direction as indicated by the dashed arrow.

The total work done on the object is the sum of the work done on the object by each force individually. We can determine the work that each force does on the screen by applying Equation 6-2:

Tension force: This force $\vec{T}$ (which we labeled $\vec{F}$ in Figure 6-6a) acts at an angle θ with respect to the direction of motion, so $W_{\text{tension}} = Td \cos \theta$.

Gravitational force: The acceleration due to gravity, and therefore the gravitational force $\vec{w}$, is perpendicular to the direction of motion, so the angle θ in Equation 6-2 is 90° for this force. Since $\cos 90° = 0$, the work done by the gravitational force is $W_{\text{gravity}} = 0$.

Normal force: The normal force $\vec{n}$ is also perpendicular to the direction of motion. So like the gravitational force, the normal force does no work at all: $W_{\text{normal}} = 0$.

Kinetic friction force: Because friction opposes sliding, the kinetic friction force vector $\vec{f}_k$ points in the direction opposite to the motion. The angle to use in Equation 6-2 is therefore 180°, and $W_{\text{friction}} = f_k d \cos 180° = -f_k d$. *When a force acts to oppose the motion of the object, the value of the work done by that force is negative.*

Note that if there were no friction present, the screen would *speed up* due to the tension force that does *positive* work on the screen. If there were friction but the tension force went to zero (for instance, if the groundskeeper shown in Figure 6-6a stopped pulling), the moving screen would *slow down* due to the friction force that does *negative* work on the screen.

$\vec{n}$ $\vec{T}$

θ

$\vec{f}_k$ ← - - - - →x

$\vec{d}$

$\vec{w}$

Always draw the displacement vector $\vec{d}$ to one side so you don't confuse it with the force vectors.

Figure 6-9 Calculating the work done by multiple forces The free-body diagram for the screen shown in Figure 6-6a. To find the work done by each force, draw the displacement vector $\vec{d}$ in the free-body diagram.

Example 6-3 Up the Hill

You need to push a box of supplies (weight 225 N) from your car to your campsite, a distance of 6.00 m up a 5.00° incline. You exert a force of 85.0 N parallel to the incline, and a 56.0-N kinetic friction force acts on the box. Calculate (a) how much work you do on the box, (b) how much work the force of gravity does on the box, (c) how much work the friction force does on the box, and (d) the net work done on the box by all forces.

Set Up

Since this problem involves forces, we draw a free-body diagram for the box. The forces do not all point along the direction of the box's displacement $\vec{d}$, so we'll have to use Equation 6-2 to calculate the work done by each force.

Work done by a constant force, straight-line displacement:

$$W = Fd \cos \theta \qquad (6\text{-}2)$$

Solve

(a) The force you exert on the box is in the same direction as the box's displacement, so $\theta = 0°$ in Equation 6-2.

$$\begin{aligned} W_{\text{you}} &= F_{\text{you}}d \cos 0° \\ &= (85.0 \text{ N})(6.00 \text{ m})(1) \\ &= 5.10 \times 10^2 \text{ N} \cdot \text{m} \\ &= 5.10 \times 10^2 \text{ J} \end{aligned}$$

(b) The angle between the gravitational force and the displacement is $\theta = 90.0° + 5.00° = 95.0°$. Since this is more than 90°, $\cos \theta$ is negative and the gravitational force does negative work on the box.

$$\begin{aligned} W_{\text{grav}} &= wd \cos 95.0° \\ &= (225 \text{ N})(6.00 \text{ m})(-0.0872) \\ &= -1.18 \times 10^2 \text{ J} \end{aligned}$$

(c) The friction force points opposite to the displacement, so for this force $\theta = 180°$ and $\cos \theta = -1$.

$$\begin{aligned} W_{\text{fric}} &= f_k d \cos 180° \\ &= (56.0 \text{ N})(6.00 \text{ m})(-1) \\ &= -3.36 \times 10^2 \text{ J} \end{aligned}$$

(d) The net work is the sum of the work done by all four forces that act on the box. The normal force points perpendicular to the displacement, so it does zero work (for this force, $\theta = 90°$ and $\cos \theta = 0°$).

$$\begin{aligned} W_{\text{total}} &= W_{\text{you}} + W_{\text{grav}} + W_{\text{fric}} + W_n \\ &= (5.10 \times 10^2 \text{ J}) + (-1.18 \times 10^2 \text{ J}) \\ &\quad + (-3.36 \times 10^2 \text{ J}) + 0 \\ &= 0.56 \times 10^2 \text{ J} = 56 \text{ J} \end{aligned}$$

Reflect

To check our result, let's calculate the *net* force that acts on the box and how much work is done by this net force. Our discussion of Equation 6-2 tells us that we only need the component of the net force in the direction of the displacement, which in our figure is the positive x component. So the work done by the net force is just $\sum F_x$ multiplied by d.

We learn two things from this. One, the work done by the net force has the *same* value as the sum of the work done by the individual forces. Two, in this case the net force is in the direction of the displacement, which means that the box picks up speed as it moves *and* the net work done on the box is positive. We'll use both of these observations in the next section to relate the net work done on an object to the change in its speed.

Net force up the incline:

$$\begin{aligned} \sum F_x &= F_{\text{you}} - f_k - w \sin 5.00° \\ &= 85.0 \text{ N} - 56.0 \text{ N} - (225 \text{ N})(0.0872) \\ &= 9.4 \text{ N} \end{aligned}$$

(positive, so the net force is uphill)

Work done by net force:

$$\begin{aligned} W_{\text{net}} &= \left(\sum F_x \right) d \\ &= (9.4 \text{ N})(6.00 \text{ m}) \\ &= 56 \text{ J} \end{aligned}$$

This equals the sum of the work done by the four forces individually.

❓ Got the Concept? 6-1   Work: Positive, Negative, or Zero?

For each of the following cases, state whether the work you do on the baseball is positive, negative, or zero. (a) You catch a baseball and your hand moves backward as you bring the ball to a halt; (b) you throw a baseball; (c) you carry a baseball in your hand as you ride your bicycle in a straight line at constant speed; (d) you carry a baseball in your hand as you ride your bicycle in a straight line at increasing speed.

6-3 Kinetic energy and the work-energy theorem give us an alternative way to express Newton's second law

In Example 6-3 we considered a box being pushed uphill that gained speed as it moved. We found that the total amount of work being done on this box was positive. Is there a general relationship between the total amount of work done on an object and the change in that object's speed? We'll find that the answer is yes, and that this answer leads us to a new and insightful way of thinking about the relationship between forces and motion. To do this we'll combine our definition of work from Section 6-1 with what we learned about one-dimensional motion in Chapter 2 and our knowledge of Newton's laws from Chapter 4.

Let's begin by considering an object that moves along a straight line that we'll call the x axis, traveling from initial coordinate x_i to final coordinate x_f with a constant acceleration a_x (Figure 6-10). Equation 2-11 gives us a relation between the object's velocity v_{ix} at x_i and its velocity v_{fx} at x_f:

$$v_{fx}^2 = v_{ix}^2 + 2a_x(x_f - x_i) \tag{6-3}$$

In Equation 6-3 v_{fx}^2 is the square of the velocity at x_f, but it also equals the square of the object's *speed* v_f at x_f. That's because v_{fx} is equal to $+v_f$ if the object is moving in the positive x direction and equal to $-v_f$ if moving in the negative x direction. In either case, $v_{fx}^2 = v_f^2$. For the same reason $v_{ix}^2 = v_i^2$, where v_i is the object's speed at x_i. So we can rewrite Equation 6-3 as

Speed at position x_f of an object in linear motion with constant acceleration   Speed at position x_i of the object

$$v_f^2 = v_i^2 + 2a_x\,(x_f - x_i)$$

Constant acceleration of the object   Two positions of the object

Speed, acceleration, and position for straight-line motion with constant acceleration
(6-4)

In Equation 6-4 $x_f - x_i$ is the displacement of the object, which moves along the x direction. Equation 6-2 tells us that if we multiply this by the x component of a force that acts on the object—that is, by the force component in the direction of the displacement—we get the work done by that force on the object. (This assumes that the net force on the object is constant, which is consistent with our assumption that the object's acceleration is constant.) Hence if we multiply $x_f - x_i$ by the x component of the *net* force on the object, $\sum F_x$, we get the work done on the object by the net force:

$$W_{net} = \left(\sum F_x \right)(x_f - x_i) \tag{6-5}$$

① A cart of mass m rolls along a straight line that we'll call the x axis.

② The cart slides from initial position x_i to final position x_f.

③ As the cart moves, a constant net force in the x direction acts on the cart.

Figure 6-10 Deriving the work-energy theorem A cart moves along a straight line, traveling from initial coordinate x_i to final coordinate x_f. The net force is constant, so the cart has a constant acceleration a_x.

Newton's second law tells us that $\sum F_x = ma_x$, where m is the mass of the object. So we can rewrite Equation 6-5 as

Work done by a constant net force, straight-line motion (6-6)

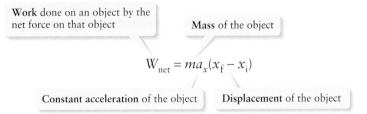

$$W_{\text{net}} = ma_x(x_f - x_i)$$

Work done on an object by the net force on that object

Mass of the object

Constant acceleration of the object

Displacement of the object

We can get another expression for the quantity $ma_x(x_f - x_i)$ by multiplying Equation 6-4 by $m/2$ and rearranging:

$$\frac{1}{2}mv_f^2 = \frac{1}{2}mv_i^2 + ma_x(x_f - x_i)$$

$$ma_x(x_f - x_i) = \frac{1}{2}mv_f^2 - \frac{1}{2}mv_i^2$$

We can now identify the left-hand side of this equation as the net work done on the object according to Equation 6-6. Making this substitution we get

(6-7)

$$W_{\text{net}} = \frac{1}{2}mv_f^2 - \frac{1}{2}mv_i^2$$

The right-hand side of Equation 6-7 is the *change* in the quantity $\frac{1}{2}mv^2$ over the course of the displacement (the value at the end of the displacement, where the speed is v_f, minus the value at the beginning where the speed is v_i). We call this quantity the **kinetic energy** K of the object:

Kinetic energy (6-8)

$$K = \frac{1}{2}mv^2$$

Kinetic energy of an object

Mass of the object

Speed of the object

The units of kinetic energy are $\text{kg} \cdot \text{m}^2/\text{s}^2$. Since $1\ \text{J} = 1\ \text{N} \cdot \text{m}$ and $1\ \text{N} = 1\ \text{kg} \cdot \text{m}/\text{s}^2$, you can see that kinetic energy is measured in joules, the same as work. Using the definition of kinetic energy given in Equation 6-8, we can rewrite Equation 6-7 as

The work-energy theorem (6-9)

$$W_{\text{net}} = K_f - K_i$$

Work done on an object by the net force on that object

Kinetic energy of the object after the work is done on it

Kinetic energy of the object before the work is done on it

When an object undergoes a displacement, the work done on it by the net force equals the object's kinetic energy at the end of the displacement minus its kinetic energy at the beginning of the displacement. This statement is called the **work-energy theorem**. It is valid as long as the object acted on is rigid—that is, it doesn't deform like a rubber ball might. Although we have derived this theorem for the special case of straight-line motion with constant forces, it turns out to be valid even if the object follows a curved path and is acted on by varying forces. (We'll justify this claim later in Section 6-5.)

The Meaning of the Work-Energy Theorem

What is kinetic energy, and how does the work-energy theorem help us solve physics problems? To answer these questions, let's first return to the cart from Figure 6-8 and imagine that it starts at rest on a horizontal frictionless surface. If you give the cart a push as in **Figure 6-11a**, the net force on the cart equals the force that you exert (the upward normal force on the cart cancels the downward gravitational force), so the work that you do is the work W_{net} done by the net force. The cart starts at rest, so $v_i = 0$ and the cart's initial kinetic energy $K_i = \frac{1}{2}mv_i^2$ is zero. After you've finished the push, the cart has final speed $v_f = v$ and kinetic energy $K_f = \frac{1}{2}mv^2$. So the work-energy theorem states that

$$W_{you\ on\ cart} = K_f - K_i = \frac{1}{2}mv^2 - 0 = \frac{1}{2}mv^2$$

In words, this gives us our first interpretation of kinetic energy: *An object's kinetic energy equals the work that was done to accelerate it from rest to its present speed.*

Now suppose your friend stands in front of the moving cart and brings it to a halt (**Figure 6-11b**). If we apply the work-energy theorem to the part of the motion where she exerts a force on the cart, the cart's initial kinetic energy is $K_i = \frac{1}{2}mv^2$ and its final kinetic energy is $K_f = 0$ (the cart ends up at rest). The net force on the cart is the force exerted by your friend, so the work she does equals the net work:

$$W_{friend\ on\ cart} = K_f - K_i = 0 - \frac{1}{2}mv^2 = -\frac{1}{2}mv^2$$

Our discussion in Section 6-2 tells us that the *cart* does an amount of work on your *friend* that's just the negative of the work that your friend does on the cart. So we can write

$$W_{cart\ on\ friend} = -W_{friend\ on\ cart} = \frac{1}{2}mv^2$$

This gives us a second interpretation of kinetic energy: *An object's kinetic energy equals the amount of work it can do in the process of coming to a halt from its present speed.*

This should remind you of the general definition of energy as the ability to do work, which we introduced in Section 6-1.

(a) Making the cart speed up

① The cart rolls without friction and the normal force balances the gravitational forces.

② The force you exert therefore equals the net force on the cart. You do positive work on the cart, and the cart gains speed and kinetic energy.

An object's kinetic energy equals the work that was done to accelerate it from rest to its present speed.

(b) Making the cart slow down

① The cart rolls without friction and the normal force balances the gravitational forces.

② The force your friend exerts therefore equals the net force on the cart. She does negative work on the cart, and the cart loses speed and kinetic energy.

③ As the cart loses kinetic energy, it pushes on your friend and does positive work on her.

An object's kinetic energy equals the work it can do in the process of coming to a halt from its present speed.

Figure 6-11 The meaning of kinetic energy We can interpret kinetic energy in terms of (a) what it takes to accelerate an object from rest or (b) what the object can do in slowing to a halt.

You already have a good understanding of this interpretation of kinetic energy. If you see a thrown basketball coming toward your head, you know intuitively that due to its mass and speed it has a pretty good amount of kinetic energy $K = \frac{1}{2}mv^2$, which means that it can do a pretty good amount of work on you (it can exert a force on your nose that pushes it inward a painful distance). You don't want this to happen, which is why you duck!

 ## Watch Out!   Kinetic energy is a scalar.

We've become comfortable breaking an object's motion into components, so you might be tempted to resolve kinetic energy into components as well. However, kinetic energy depends on *speed*, not velocity. Because speed is not a vector, kinetic energy is a *scalar* quantity and *not* a vector. It wouldn't be meaningful to set up components of kinetic energy in different directions. Note also that we've only discussed the kinetic energy associated with the motion of an object as a whole, which we call **translational kinetic energy**. Kinetic energy is also associated with the rotation of an object around its own axis. We'll return to this *rotational kinetic energy* in a later chapter.

Net Work and Net Force

In Equation 6-9 we interpret W_{net} as the work done by the net force. This might lead you to think that in any problem involving the work-energy theorem, you have to find the vector sum of the individual forces acting on the object. Not so! We saw in Example 6-3 in Section 6-2 that *the work done on an object by the net force equals the sum of the amount of work done by each individual force acting on the object*. Put another way, *the work done by the net force equals the net work done by all forces individually*. It turns out that this statement is true not just for the situation in Example 6-4; it applies to all situations.

This gives us a simplified statement of the work-energy theorem: *The net work done by all forces on an object, W_{net}, equals the difference between its final kinetic energy K_f and its initial kinetic energy K_i*. If the net work done is positive, then $K_f - K_i$ is positive, the final kinetic energy is greater than the initial kinetic energy, and the object gains speed. If the net work done is negative, then $K_f - K_i$ is negative, the final kinetic energy is less than the initial kinetic energy, and the object loses speed. If zero net work is done, the kinetic energy does not change and the object maintains the same speed (Table 6-1). This agrees with the observations we made in Section 6-1.

Example 6-4 shows how to use the work-energy theorem.

Table 6-1   The Work-Energy Theorem

If the net work done on an object is . . .	. . . then the change in the object's kinetic energy $K_f - K_i$ is. . .	. . . and the speed of the object. . .
$W_{net} > 0$ (positive net work)	$K_f - K_i > 0$ (kinetic energy increases)	increases (object speeds up)
$W_{net} < 0$ (negative net work)	$K_f - K_i < 0$ (kinetic energy decreases)	decreases (object slows down)
$W_{net} = 0$ (zero net work)	$K_f - K_i = 0$ (kinetic energy stays the same)	is unchanged (object maintains the same speed)

Example 6-4   Up the Hill Revisited

Consider again the box of supplies that you pushed up the incline in Example 6-3 (Section 6-2). Use the work-energy theorem to find how fast the box is moving when it reaches your campsite, assuming it is moving uphill at 0.75 m/s at the bottom of the incline.

Set Up

Our goal is to find the final speed v_f of the box. In Example 6-3 we were given the weight (and hence the mass m) of the box, and we found that the net work done on the box is $W_{net} = 56$ J. Since we're given $v_i = 0.75$ m/s, we can use Equations 6-8 and 6-9 to solve for v_f.

Work-energy theorem:
$$W_{net} = K_f - K_i \qquad (6-9)$$

Kinetic energy:
$$K = \frac{1}{2}mv^2 \qquad (6-8)$$

$v_f = ?$

$v_i = 0.75$ m/s

$W_{net} = 56$ J

$w = 225$ N

Solve
Use the work-energy theorem to solve for v_f in terms of the initial speed v_i, the net work done W_{net}, and the mass m.

Isolate the $\frac{1}{2}mv_f^2$ term on one side of the equation, then solve for v_f by multiplying through by $2/m$ and taking the square root.

Combine Equations 6-8 and 6-9:

$$W_{net} = \frac{1}{2}mv_f^2 - \frac{1}{2}mv_i^2$$

$$\frac{1}{2}mv_f^2 = \frac{1}{2}mv_i^2 + W_{net}$$

$$v_f^2 = v_i^2 + \frac{2W_{net}}{m}$$

$$v_f = \sqrt{v_i^2 + \frac{2W_{net}}{m}}$$

From Example 6-3 we know that $W_{net} = 56$ J. (This is the sum of the work done on the box by the individual forces, which is the same as the work done by the net force.) We find the mass m of the box from its known weight $w = 225$ N and the relationship $w = mg$. Use these to find the value of v_f.

$$m = \frac{w}{g} = \frac{225 \text{ N}}{9.80 \text{ m/s}^2} = 23.0 \text{ kg}$$

$$v_f = \sqrt{(0.75 \text{ m/s})^2 + \frac{2(56 \text{ J})}{23.0 \text{ kg}}}$$

$$= 2.3 \text{ m/s}$$

Reflect
We *could* have solved this problem by first finding the net force on the box, then calculating its acceleration from Newton's second law, and finally solving for v_f by using one of the kinematic equations from Chapter 2. But using the work-energy theorem is easier.

As a check on our result, note that we found in Example 6-3 that the net force on the box is 9.4 N uphill. Can you follow the procedure we just described to find the final velocity after moving 6.00 m up the incline?

Example 6-4 provides our first illustration of the usefulness of the work-energy theorem. In the following section we'll see more examples of how to apply this powerful theorem to various cases of straight-line motion. In Section 6-5 we'll see how the work-energy theorem can be applied to problems in which the motion is along a curved path and in which the forces are not constant.

? Got the Concept? 6-2 Slap Shot

A hockey player does work on a hockey puck in order to propel it from rest across the ice. When a constant force is applied over a certain distance, the puck leaves his stick at speed v. If instead he wants the puck to leave at speed $2v$, by what factor must he increase the distance over which he applies the same force? (a) $\sqrt{2}$; (b) 2; (c) $2\sqrt{2}$; (d) 4; (e) 8.

Take-Home Message for Section 6-3

✔ The net work done on an object (the sum of the work done on it by all forces) as it undergoes a displacement is equal to the change in the object's kinetic energy during that displacement.

✔ The formula for the kinetic energy of an object of mass m and speed v is $K = \frac{1}{2}mv^2$.

✔ The kinetic energy of an object is equal to the amount of work that was done to accelerate the object from rest to its present speed.

✔ The kinetic energy of an object is also equal to the amount of work the object can do in the process of coming to a halt from its present speed.

6-4 The work-energy theorem can simplify many physics problems

In this section we'll explore the relationships among work, force and speed by applying the definitions of work and kinetic energy (Equations 6-2 and 6-8) and the work-energy theorem (Equation 6-9) to a variety of physical situations. Even if the problem could be solved using Newton's second law, the work-energy theorem often makes the solution easier as well as giving additional insight.

When you work through problems using the work-energy theorem, you should keep the following ideas in mind: The work-energy theorem is a useful tool for problems that involve an object that moves a distance along a straight line while being acted on by constant forces. You can use this theorem to relate the forces, the distance traveled (the displacement), and the speed of the object at the beginning and end of the displacement.

Note that the work-energy theorem makes no reference to the *time* it takes the object to move through this displacement. If the problem requires you to use or find this time, you should use a different approach.

As you *Set Up* your solution, always begin by drawing a picture of the situation that shows the object's displacement. Include a free-body diagram that shows all of the forces that act on the object. Take care in drawing the direction of each force, since the direction plays a crucial role in determining how much work each force does on the object. Decide what quantity the problem is asking you to determine (for example, the object's final speed or the magnitude of one of the forces).

In the *Solve* step, use Equation 6-2 to find expressions for the work done by each force. The sum of the work done by each force is the total or net work done on the object, W_{net}. Then use Equations 6-8 and 6-9 to relate this to the object's initial and final kinetic energies. Solve the resulting equations for the desired unknown.

Finally, as you *Reflect* on your answer, remember to check whether the numbers have reasonable values and that each quantity has the correct units.

Example 6-5 How Far to Stop?

The U.S. National Highway Traffic Safety Administration lists the minimum braking distance for a car traveling at 40.0 mi/h to be 101 ft. If the braking force is the same at all speeds, what is the minimum braking distance for a car traveling at 65.0 mi/h?

Set Up

Three forces act on the car—the gravitational force, the normal force exerted by the road, and the braking force—but if the road is level, only the braking force does work on the car. (The other two forces are perpendicular to the displacement, so $Fd \cos 90° = 0$.) We'll use Equations 6-2, 6-8, and 6-9 to find the relationship among the initial speed v_i, the braking force, and the distance the car must travel to have the final speed be $v_f = 0$.

Work done by a constant force, straight-line displacement:

$$W = Fd \cos \theta \qquad (6\text{-}2)$$

Kinetic energy:

$$K = \frac{1}{2}mv^2 \qquad (6\text{-}8)$$

Work-energy theorem:

$$W_{net} = K_f - K_i \qquad (6\text{-}9)$$

Solve

The car ends up at rest, so its final kinetic energy is zero. So the work-energy theorem tells us that the net work done on the car (equal to the work done on it by the braking force) equals the negative of the initial kinetic energy.

Work-energy theorem with final kinetic energy equal to zero:

$$W_{net} = 0 - K_i = -\frac{1}{2}mv_i^2$$

The braking force of magnitude $F_{braking}$ is directed opposite to the displacement, so $\theta = 180°$ in the expression for the work $W_{braking}$ done by this force.

Net work = work done by the braking force:
$$W_{net} = W_{braking}$$
$$= F_{braking}d \cos 180° = -F_{braking}d$$

Substitute $W_{net} = -F_{braking}d$ into the work-energy theorem and solve for the braking distance d. The result tells us that d is proportional to the square of the initial speed v_i.

Work-energy theorem becomes

$$-F_{braking}d = -\frac{1}{2}mv_i^2$$

Solve for d:

$$d = \frac{mv_i^2}{2F_{braking}}$$

We aren't given the mass m of the car or the magnitude $F_{braking}$ of the braking force, but we can set up a ratio between the values of distance for $v_{i1} = 40.0$ mi/h and $v_{i2} = 65.0$ mi/h.

Use this expression to set up a ratio for the value of d at two different initial speeds. The mass of the car and the braking force are the same for both initial speeds:

$$\frac{d_2}{d_1} = \frac{v_{i2}^2}{v_{i1}^2}$$

Solve for the stopping distance d_2 corresponding to $v_{i2} = 65.0$ mi/h:

$$d_2 = d_1 \frac{v_{i2}^2}{v_{i1}^2} = (101 \text{ ft})\left(\frac{65.0 \text{ mi/h}}{40.0 \text{ mi/h}}\right)^2$$

$$= 267 \text{ ft}$$

Reflect

This example demonstrates what every driver training course stresses: The faster you travel, the more distance you should leave between you and the car ahead in case an emergency stop is needed. Increasing your speed by 62.5% (from 40.0 to 65.0 mi/h) increases your stopping distance by 164% (from 101 ft to 267 ft). The reason is that stopping distance is proportional to kinetic energy, which is proportional to the *square* of the speed.

Example 6-6 Work and Kinetic Energy: Force at an Angle

At the start of a race, a four-man bobsleigh crew pushes their sleigh as fast as they can down the 50.0-m straight, relatively flat starting stretch (**Figure 6-12**). The net force that the four men together apply to the 325-kg sleigh has magnitude 285 N and is directed at an angle of 20.0° below the horizontal. As they push, a 60.0-N kinetic friction force also acts on the sleigh. What is the speed of the sleigh right before the crew jumps in at the end of the starting stretch?

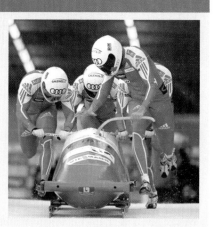

Figure 6-12 **Bobsleigh start** The success of a bobsleigh team depends on the team members giving the sleigh a competitive starting speed.

Set Up

Again we'll use the work-energy theorem, this time to determine the final speed v_f of the bobsleigh (which starts at rest, so its initial speed is $v_i = 0$). The normal force and gravitational forces do no work on the sleigh since they act perpendicular to the displacement. The four men of the crew do positive work, while the friction force does negative work. The new wrinkle is that the force exerted by the crew points at an angle to the displacement. We'll deal with this using Equation 6-2.

The sleigh gains speed and kinetic energy during the motion, so the net work done by these two forces must be positive.

Work done by a constant force, straight-line displacement:

$$W = Fd \cos \theta \qquad (6\text{-}2)$$

Kinetic energy:

$$K = \frac{1}{2}mv^2 \qquad (6\text{-}8)$$

Work-energy theorem:

$$W_{net} = K_f - K_i \qquad (6\text{-}9)$$

Solve

The sleigh starts at rest, so its initial kinetic energy is zero. From Equation 6-9 the net work done on the sleigh is therefore equal to its final kinetic energy, which is related to the final speed v_f.

Work-energy theorem with initial kinetic energy equal to zero:

$$W_{net} = K_f - 0 = \frac{1}{2}mv_f^2$$

The force of the crew is at $\theta = 20.0°$ to the displacement, and the friction force is at $\theta = 180°$. Use these in Equation 6-2 to find the net work done on the sleigh.

Net work = work done by the crew plus work done by friction

$$W_{net} = W_{crew} + W_{friction}$$
$$= F_{crew}d \cos 20.0° + f_k d \cos 180°$$
$$= (285\ \text{N})(50.0\ \text{m})(0.940)$$
$$\quad + (60.0\ \text{N})(50.0\ \text{m})(-1)$$
$$= 1.04 \times 10^4\ \text{J}$$

Substitute W_{net} into the work-energy theorem and solve for the final speed v_f.

Work-energy theorem says $W_{net} = \dfrac{1}{2}mv_f^2$

Solve for v_f: $v_f = \sqrt{\dfrac{2W_{net}}{m}} = \sqrt{\dfrac{2(1.04 \times 10^4\ \text{J})}{325\ \text{kg}}}$
$$= 8.00\ \text{m/s}$$

Reflect

This answer for v_f is relatively close to the speed of world-class sprinters, so it seems reasonable. In reality, the start of an Olympic four-man bobsleigh race is slightly downhill, so the sleigh's speed at the end of the starting stretch is typically even faster (11 or 12 m/s).

Example 6-7 Find the Work Done by an Unknown Force

An adventurous parachutist of mass 70.0 kg drops from the top of Angel Falls in Venezuela, the world's highest waterfall (Figure 6-13). The waterfall is 979 m (3212 ft) tall and the parachutist deploys his chute after falling 295 m, at which point his speed is 54.0 m/s. During the 295-m drop, (a) what was the net work done on him and (b) what was the work done on him by the force of air resistance?

Figure 6-13 **Falling with air resistance** As the parachutist falls, air resistance does negative work on him.

Set Up

We are given the parachutist's mass and the distance that he falls, so we can find the gravitational force that acts on him and the work done by that force using Equation 6-2. But the force of air resistance also acts on the parachutist. We don't know its magnitude, so we can't directly calculate the work done by air resistance. Instead, we'll use the work-energy theorem. We'll assume that the parachutist starts at rest, so his initial kinetic energy is zero.

Work done by a constant force, straight-line displacement:

$$W = Fd \cos \theta \qquad (6-2)$$

Work-energy theorem:

$$W_{net} = K_f - K_i \qquad (6-9)$$

Kinetic energy:

$$K = \frac{1}{2}mv^2 \qquad (6-8)$$

Solve

(a) Since $K_i = 0$, Equation 6-9 says that the net work done on the parachutist is just equal to his final kinetic energy.

$$W_{net} = K_f = \frac{1}{2}mv_f^2$$
$$= \frac{1}{2}(70.0\ \text{kg})(54.0\ \text{m/s})^2$$
$$= 1.02 \times 10^5\ \text{J}$$

(b) The net work is the sum of the work done by the gravitational force, W_{grav}, and the work done by air resistance, W_{air}. Hence W_{air} is the difference between W_{net} and W_{grav}.

Work done by the gravitational force: Displacement is in the same direction (downward) as the force, so

$$W_{grav} = mgd$$
$$= (70.0 \text{ kg})(9.80 \text{ m/s}^2)(295 \text{ m})$$
$$= 2.02 \times 10^5 \text{ J}$$

Hence the work done by air resistance is

$$W_{air} = W_{net} - W_{grav}$$
$$= 1.02 \times 10^5 \text{ J} - 2.02 \times 10^5 \text{ J}$$
$$= -1.00 \times 10^5 \text{ J}$$

Reflect

The work done by the force of air resistance is negative because the force is directed upward, opposite to the downward displacement. We can use the calculated value of W_{air} to find an average value of the air resistance force, considered as a constant. However, the force is *not* constant: The faster the parachutist falls, the greater the force of air resistance. In Section 6-5 we'll see how we can use the work-energy theorem with forces whose magnitude varies during the motion.

Average upward force of air resistance:

$$W_{air} = F_{air}d \cos 180° = -F_{air}d$$

Hence

$$F_{air} = -\frac{W_{air}}{d} = -\frac{(-1.00 \times 10^5 \text{ J})}{295 \text{ m}}$$
$$= 339 \text{ J/m} = 339 \text{ N}$$

? Got the Concept? 6-3 Pushing Boxes

You push two boxes from one side of a room to the other. Each box begins and ends at rest. The contact surfaces and areas between box and floor are the same for both, but one box is heavy while the other is light. There is friction between the box and the floor. (a) How does the work *you* do on each box compare? (i) You do more work on the heavy box; (ii) you do more work on the light box; (iii) you do the same amount of work on both boxes. (b) How does the *net* work done on each box compare? (i) There is more net work on the heavy box; (ii) there is more net work on the light box; (iii) there is the same net work on both boxes.

Take-Home Message for Section 6-4

✔ The work-energy theorem allows us to explore the relationship between force, distance, and speed in a variety of physical situations.

✔ To solve problems using the work-energy theorem, begin by drawing a free-body diagram that shows all the forces that act on the object in question. Then write expressions for the kinetic energies at the beginning and end of the displacement and for the total work done on the object (the sum of the work done by each force). Relate these using the work-energy theorem and solve for the unknown quantity.

6-5 The work-energy theorem is also valid for curved paths and varying forces

We've derived the work-energy theorem only for the special case of straight-line motion with constant forces. Since we already know how to solve problems for that kind of motion, you may wonder what good this theorem is. Here's the answer: The work-energy theorem also works for motion along a *curved* path and in cases where the forces are *not* constant (Figure 6-14a).

Figure 6-14 Motion along a curved path The weight travels in a curved path during the bicep curl.

(a)

A weightlifter doing bicep curls makes the weight move through a curved path. The force that he exerts on the weight varies during its travel.

(b)

An object's curved path from an initial point i to a final point f. We mark a larger number N of equally-spaced intermediate points 1, 2, 3, ..., N along the path and imagine breaking the path into short segments (from i to 1, from 1 to 2, from 2 to 3, ...).

To prove this, consider **Figure 6-14b**, which shows an object's curved path from an initial point i to a final point f. We mark a large number N of equally spaced intermediate points 1, 2, 3, . . . , N along the path and imagine breaking the path into short segments (for example, from i to 1, from 1 to 2, or from 2 to 3). If the length of each segment is sufficiently short, we can treat it as a straight line. Furthermore, the forces on the object don't change very much during the brief time the object is traversing one of these segments, so we can treat the forces as constant over that segment. (The forces may be different from one segment to the next.) Since each segment is a straight line with constant forces, we can safely apply the work-energy theorem in Equation 6-9 to every segment:

$$W_{\text{net, i to 1}} = K_1 - K_i$$
$$W_{\text{net, 1 to 2}} = K_2 - K_1$$
$$W_{\text{net, 2 to 3}} = K_3 - K_2$$
$$\cdots$$
$$W_{\text{net, N to f}} = K_f - K_N$$

Now add all of these equations together:

(6-10)
$$W_{\text{net, i to 1}} + W_{\text{net, 1 to 2}} + W_{\text{net, 2 to 3}} + \ldots + W_{\text{net, N to f}}$$
$$= (K_1 - K_i) + (K_2 - K_1) + (K_3 - K_2) + \ldots + (K_f - K_N)$$

The left-hand side of Equation 6-10 is the sum of the amounts of work done by the net force on each segment. This sum equals the *net* work done by the net force along the entire path from i to f, which we call simply W_{net}. On the right-hand side of the equation, $-K_1$ in the second term cancels K_1 in the first term, $-K_2$ in the third term cancels K_2 in the second term, and so on. The only quantities that survive on the right-hand side are $-K_i$ and K_f, so we are left with

$$W_{\text{net}} = K_f - K_i$$

This is *exactly* the same statement of the work-energy theorem as Equation 6-9. So we conclude that the work-energy theorem is valid for *any* path and for *any* forces, whether constant or not. This is why the work-energy theorem is so important: You can apply it to situations where using forces and Newton's laws would be difficult or impossible.

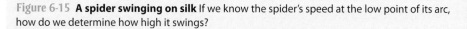

Example 6-8 A Swinging Spider

Figure 6-15 shows a South African kite spider (*Gasteracantha*) swinging on a strand of spider silk. Suppose a momentary gust of wind blows on a spider of mass 1.00×10^{-4} kg (0.100 gram) that's initially hanging straight down on such a strand. As a result, the spider acquires a horizontal velocity of 1.3 m/s. How high will the spider swing? Ignore air resistance.

Figure 6-15 **A spider swinging on silk** If we know the spider's speed at the low point of its arc, how do we determine how high it swings?

Set Up

Because the spider follows a curved path, this would be a very difficult problem to solve using Newton's laws directly. Instead, we can use the work-energy theorem. We are given the spider's initial speed $v_i = 1.3$ m/s (which means we know its initial kinetic energy), and we want to find its maximum height h. This is where the spider comes momentarily to rest (so its speed and kinetic energy are zero) before swinging back downward.

The free-body diagram shows that only two forces act on the swinging spider: The gravitational force and the tension force exerted by the strand of silk. All we have to do is figure out how to calculate the work done on the spider by these forces along this curved path. We'll do this by breaking the path into a large number of segments as in Figure 6-14.

Work-energy theorem:

$$W_{net} = K_f - K_i \qquad (6\text{-}9)$$

Kinetic energy:

$$K = \frac{1}{2}mv^2 \qquad (6\text{-}8)$$

Work done by a constant force, straight-line displacement:

$$W = Fd\cos\theta \qquad (6\text{-}2)$$

Solve

Rewrite the work-energy theorem in terms of the initial and final speeds of the spider and the work done by each force.

Combine Equations 6-9 and 6-8:

$$W_{net} = \frac{1}{2}mv_f^2 - \frac{1}{2}mv_i^2$$

Net work is the sum of the work done by the tension force T and the work done by the gravitational force:

$$W_{net} = W_{grav} + W_T$$

The final speed of the spider at the high point of its motion is $v_f = 0$, so the work-energy theorem becomes:

$$W_{grav} + W_T = -\frac{1}{2}mv_i^2$$

To calculate the work done by each force along the spider's curved path, break the path up into segments so short that each one can be considered as a straight line. On each segment the spider has a displacement $\Delta \vec{d}$ with horizontal component Δx and vertical component Δy. These are different for each individual segment.

On each segment of the path the tension force $\vec{T}$ points radially inward, perpendicular to the path and hence perpendicular to the displacement $\Delta\vec{d}$. Hence $\theta = 90°$ in Equation 6-2, which means that the tension force does *no* work during this displacement.

The gravitational force $\vec{w}$ always points straight downward (in the negative y direction) and has constant magnitude $w = mg$. We apply Equation 6-2 to the displacement and weight force drawn as shown, and use the identity $\cos(90° + \phi) = -\sin\phi$. Because the angle between the displacement and the weight force is greater than 90°, we expect the weight force to do negative work.

Work done by the tension force as the spider moves through a short segment of its path:

$$\Delta W_T = T\,\Delta d\,\cos 90° = 0$$

Work done by the gravitational force as the spider moves through a short segment of its path:

$$\Delta W_{\mathrm{grav}} = w\,\Delta d\,\cos\theta$$

The angle between the force and displacement is $\theta = 90° + \phi$ so

$$\Delta W_{\mathrm{grav}} = w\,\Delta d\,\cos(90° + \phi) = -w\,\Delta d\,\sin\phi$$

The figure shows

$\Delta d\,\sin\phi = \Delta y$, so

$$\Delta W_{\mathrm{grav}} = -w\,\Delta y = -mg\,\Delta y$$

Now we can calculate the *net* work done on the spider by each force as it moves along its curved path. This is just the sum of the individual bits of work done on it along the short segments.

The tension force does zero work on each short segment, so

$$W_T = 0$$

Work done by the gravitational force over the entire path:

$$W_{\mathrm{grav}} = (-mg\,\Delta y_1) + (-mg\,\Delta y_2) + (-mg\,\Delta y_3) + \dots$$
$$= -mg(\Delta y_1 + \Delta y_2 + \Delta y_3 + \dots)$$

The sum of all the Δy terms is the net vertical displacement $y_f - y_i = h - 0 = h$. So

$$W_{\mathrm{grav}} = -mgh$$

Substitute the expressions for W_T and W_{grav} into the work-energy theorem and solve for h.

Work-energy theorem:

$$W_{\mathrm{grav}} + W_T = -mgh + 0 = -\frac{1}{2}mv_i^2$$

$$v_i^2 = 2gh$$

$$h = \frac{v_i^2}{2g} = \frac{(1.3\ \mathrm{m/s})^2}{2(9.80\ \mathrm{m/s}^2)} = 0.086\ \mathrm{m} = 8.6\ \mathrm{cm}$$

Reflect

Our result says that the maximum height reached by the spider is the *same* as if the spider had initially been moving *straight up* at 1.3 m/s without being attached to the silk. In both cases the gravitational force does the same amount of (negative) work to reduce the spider's kinetic energy to zero.

   The tension force in this problem is complicated because its magnitude changes as the spider moves through its swing. The beauty of the work-energy approach is that we don't have to worry about the tension force at all, because it does no work on the spider.

If the spider is initially moving straight up:

$$W_{\mathrm{net}} = \frac{1}{2}mv_f^2 - \frac{1}{2}mv_i^2$$

$$W_{\mathrm{grav}} = -mgh = 0 - \frac{1}{2}mv_i^2$$

$$v_i^2 = 2gh$$

$$h = \frac{v_i^2}{2g} = 8.6\ \mathrm{cm}$$

Example 6-8 illustrates an important point: *If a force always acts perpendicular to an object's curved path, it does zero work on the object.* This enabled us to ignore the effects of the tension force. We'll use this same idea again in Section 6-6.

Work Done by a Varying Force

In Example 6-8 the tension force acting on the spider varied in magnitude but did no work (because it acts perpendicular to the spider's displacement). In many situations, however, a force of variable magnitude *does* do work on an object. As an example, you must do work to stretch a spring. The force you exert to do this is not constant: The farther you stretch the spring, the greater the magnitude of the force you must exert. How can we calculate the amount of work that you do while stretching the spring?

The key is to recognize that on a graph of force versus position, the work done by the force equals the *area* under the graph. To see why this is so, consider a *constant* force F that acts during a displacement d. The area under the graph of force versus position equals the area of the colored rectangle in **Figure 6-16**: That is, the height of the rectangle (the force F) multiplied by its width (the displacement d). This is indeed the same as the work done, $W = Fd$.

Let's apply this "area rule" to the work that you do in stretching a spring. Experiment shows that if you stretch a spring by a relatively small amount, the force that the *spring* exerts on you is directly proportional to the amount of stretch (**Figure 6-17**). We can write this relationship, known as **Hooke's law**, as

Work done by a constant force along direction of motion = Fd = area under graph of force versus position.

Figure 6-16 The "area rule" for work Finding the work done by a constant force using a graph of force versus position.

| Force exerted by an ideal spring | Spring constant of the spring (a measure of its stiffness) |

$$F_x = -kx$$

Extension of the spring ($x > 0$ if spring is stretched, $x < 0$ if spring is compressed)

Hooke's law
(6-11)

The minus sign in Equation 6-11 means that the force that the spring exerts on you is in the direction *opposite* to the stretch. If you pull one end of the spring in the positive x direction so $x > 0$, the spring pulls back on you in the negative x direction. (As we will see below, Hooke's law also describes situations in which the spring is compressed rather than stretched.) The quantity k in Equation 6-11, called the **spring constant**, depends on the stiffness of the spring: the greater the value of k, the stiffer the spring. As you can see from Equation 6-11, if the force is measured in newtons and the extension in meters, the spring constant has units of N/m.

To stretch the spring in Figure 6-17 at a steady speed, you must exert a force on the spring of the same magnitude as the force that the spring exerts on you, but in the opposite direction. Hence the force that you exert on the spring has the opposite sign from the force that the spring exerts on you:

$$F_{\text{you on spring},x} = +kx \text{ (force that you exert on the spring)} \qquad (6\text{-}12)$$

Stretching the spring means $x > 0$, and to do this you must exert a force in the same direction. So $F_{\text{you on spring},x} > 0$ if $x > 0$, which is just what Equation 6-12 tells us.

Figure 6-18 graphs the force that you exert as a function of the distance x that the spring has been stretched. If the spring is initially stretched a distance x_1 and you stretch

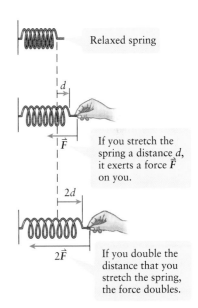

Relaxed spring

If you stretch the spring a distance d, it exerts a force $\vec{F}$ on you.

If you double the distance that you stretch the spring, the force doubles.

Figure 6-17 Hooke's law If you stretch an ideal spring, the force that it exerts on you is directly proportional to its extension.

Area under curve = work you do to stretch spring from x_1 to x_2.

Figure 6-18 Applying the "area rule" to an ideal spring We can use the same technique as in Figure 6-17 to find the work required to stretch a spring.

it further to x_2, the work W that you do is equal to the area of the colored trapezoid in Figure 6-18. From geometry, this area is equal to the *average* height of the graph multiplied by the width $x_2 - x_1$. Using Equation 6-12, we find

$$W = \left[\frac{(\text{force you exert at } x_1) + (\text{force you exert at } x_2)}{2} \right] (x_2 - x_1)$$

$$= \frac{(kx_1 + kx_2)}{2}(x_2 - x_1) = \frac{1}{2}k(x_1 + x_2)(x_2 - x_1)$$

▷ Go to Picture It 6-1 for more practice dealing with springs

We can simplify this to

Work that must be done on a spring to stretch it from $x = x_1$ to $x = x_2$.

Spring constant of the spring (a measure of its stiffness)

Work done to stretch a spring
(6-13)

$$W = \frac{1}{2}kx_2^2 - \frac{1}{2}kx_1^2$$

x_1 = initial stretch of the spring
x_2 = final stretch of the spring

❗ Watch Out! Who's doing the work?

Note that Equation 6-13 tells us the work that *you* do on the *spring*. The work that the *spring* does on *you* is equal to the negative of Equation 6-13.

Example 6-9 shows how to use Equation 6-13 to attack a problem that would have been impossible to solve with the force techniques from Chapters 4 and 5.

Example 6-9 Work Those Muscles!

An athlete stretches a set of exercise cords 47 cm from their unstretched length. The cords behave like a spring with spring constant 860 N/m. (a) How much force does the athlete exert to hold the cords in this stretched position? (b) How much work did he do to stretch them? (c) The athlete loses his grip on the cords. If the mass of the handle is 0.25 kg, how fast is it moving when it hits the wall to which the other end of the cords is attached? (You can ignore gravity and assume that the cords themselves have only a small mass.)

Set Up

In part (a) we'll use Equation 6-12 to find the force that the athlete exerts, and in part (b) Equation 6-13 will tell us the work that he does. In part (c) we'll see how much work the *cords* do as they go from being stretched to relaxed. This work goes into the kinetic energy of the handle. We're ignoring the mass of the cords and therefore assuming that they have no kinetic energy of their own.

$$F_{\text{athlete on cords},x} = +kx \quad (6\text{-}12)$$

$$W = \frac{1}{2}kx_2^2 - \frac{1}{2}kx_1^2 \quad (6\text{-}13)$$

$$W_{\text{net}} = K_f - K_i \quad (6\text{-}9)$$

$$K = \frac{1}{2}mv^2 \quad (6\text{-}8)$$

relaxed

←47 cm→

stretched

released

$v_f = ?$

Solve

(a) The force that the athlete exerts is proportional to the distance $x = 47$ cm that the cords are stretched.

Force exerted by the athlete to hold the cords stretched:

$$F_{\text{athlete on cords},x} = +kx$$

$$= (860 \text{ N/m})(47 \text{ cm})\left(\frac{1 \text{ m}}{100 \text{ cm}}\right)$$

$$= 4.0 \times 10^2 \text{ N}$$

$\vec{F}_{\text{cords on athlete}}$ $\vec{F}_{\text{athlete on cords}}$

(b) The cords are not stretched at all to start (so x_1 = 0) and end up stretched by 47 cm (so $x_2 = 47$ cm = 0.47 m).

Work done by the athlete to stretch the cords:

$$W_{\text{athlete on cords}} = \frac{1}{2}kx_2^2 - \frac{1}{2}kx_1^2$$

$$= \frac{1}{2}(860\,\text{N/m})(0.47\,\text{m})^2 - \frac{1}{2}(860\,\text{N/m})(0\,\text{m})^2$$

$$= 95\,\text{N}\cdot\text{m} = 95\,\text{J}$$

(c) When the athlete releases the handle, the cords relax from their new starting position ($x_1 = 0.47$ m) to their final, unstretched position ($x_2 = 0$). The work that the cords do on the handle is given by the negative of Equation 6-13.

Work done by the cords on the handle as they relax:

$W_{\text{cords on handle}}$

$$= -\left(\frac{1}{2}kx_2^2 - \frac{1}{2}kx_1^2\right)$$

$$= -\left(\frac{1}{2}(860\,\text{N/m})(0\,\text{m})^2 - \frac{1}{2}(860\,\text{N/m})(0.47\,\text{m})^2\right)$$

$$= -(-95\,\text{N}\cdot\text{m}) = 95\,\text{J}$$

We'll ignore the force of gravity (that is, we assume the handle flies back horizontally and doesn't fall). Then the net work done on the

Net work done on handle:

$$W_{\text{net}} = W_{\text{cords on handle}} = 95\,\text{J}$$

handle equals the work done by the cords. This is equal to the change in the handle's kinetic energy. Use this to find the handle's speed when the cords are fully relaxed.

Work-energy theorem applied to handle:

$$W_{\text{net}} = K_f - K_i = \frac{1}{2}mv_f^2 - \frac{1}{2}mv_i^2$$

Handle is initially at rest, so $v_i = 0$. Solve for final speed of the handle:

$$\frac{1}{2}mv_f^2 = W_{\text{net}} = 95\,\text{J}$$

$$v_f^2 = \frac{2W_{\text{net}}}{m}$$

$$v_f = \sqrt{\frac{2W_{\text{net}}}{m}} = \sqrt{\frac{2(95\,\text{J})}{0.25\,\text{kg}}} = 28\,\text{m/s}$$

Reflect

A common *incorrect* way to approach part (b) is to use the formula for the work done by a *constant* force: Multiply the force needed to hold the cords fully stretched by the cords' displacement. This gives the wrong answer because the force needed to pull the cords is *not* constant.

Notice that the amount of work that the athlete does to stretch the cords (95 J) is the *same* as the amount of work that the cords do on the handle when they relax. This suggests that the athlete stores energy in the cords by stretching them. We'll explore this idea in Section 6-6 as we introduce a new kind of energy, called *potential energy*.

Incorrect way to calculate work that the athlete does on the cords:

$$W_{\text{athlete on cords}} = F_x d = (4.0 \times 10^2\,\text{N})(0.47\,\text{m}) = 190\,\text{J}$$

(actual value: $W_{\text{athlete on cords}} = 95\,\text{J}$)

More on Hooke's Law and Its Limits

The spring in Figure 6-17 and the exercise cords in Example 6-9 exert a force when they are stretched. Springs also exert a force when they are *compressed* (Figure 6-19a). One example is a car's suspension, whose springs compress as you load passengers and luggage into the car. The force that an ideal spring exerts when compressed is

(a) A compressed spring ($x < 0$)
pushes in the +x direction.

(b) A stretched spring ($x > 0$)
pulls in the −x direction.

$x < 0$

$\vec{F}_{\text{by spring}}$

x

$x > 0$

$\vec{F}_{\text{by spring}}$

x

F_x

Force exerted
by a spring:
$F_x = -kx$

x

0

Figure 6-19 Compressing and stretching an ideal spring Hooke's law, $F_x = -kx$, applies equally well to an ideal spring whether it is (a) compressed or (b) stretched.

given by the Hooke's law relationship of Equation 6-11, $F_x = -kx$, the *same* equation that describes the force exerted by a *stretched* spring (**Figure 6-19b**). The only difference is that x is negative if the spring is compressed. Hence if you compress the spring (push its end in the negative x direction), the spring pushes back on you in the positive x direction.

Like Equation 6-11, Equation 6-13 is also valid when a spring is compressed. If a spring with spring constant $k = 1000 \text{ N/m}$ is initially relaxed (so $x_1 = 0$) and you stretch it by 20 cm (so $x_2 = +20 \text{ cm} = +0.20 \text{ m}$), the work that you do is

$$W = \frac{1}{2}kx_2^2 - \frac{1}{2}k(0)^2 = \frac{1}{2}(1000 \text{ N/m})(0.20 \text{ m})^2 = 20 \text{ J}$$

The work that you do to *compress* the same spring by 20 cm (so $x_2 = -20 \text{ cm} = -0.20 \text{ m}$) is

$$W = \frac{1}{2}kx_2^2 - \frac{1}{2}k(0)^2 = \frac{1}{2}(1000 \text{ N/m})(-0.20 \text{ m})^2 = 20 \text{ J}$$

So you have to do positive work to compress a spring as well as to stretch it.

It's important to recognize that Hooke's law and Equations 6-11, 6-12, and 6-13 are only *approximate* descriptions of how real springs, elastic cords, and tendons behave. As an example, **Figure 6-20** is a graph of the force needed to stretch a human patellar tendon (which connects the kneecap to the shin). The curve isn't a straight line, which means that the force isn't directly proportional to the amount of stretch. The force you have to apply to the tendon is also greater when you stretch than when

Figure 6-20 Tendons are not ideal springs This graph of force versus extension for a human patellar tendon is very different from that for an ideal spring (compare to Figure 6-19). The graph is not a straight line; there is a different graph for relaxing than for extending the tendon; and the graph for tendons that have undergone exercise (square data points) is different from that for tendons that have not (triangular data points).

you let it relax. What's more, the tendon can actually change its properties: The two sets of curves in Figure 6-20 are for males in their 70s before and after a 14-week course of physical training, which caused the patellar tendon to become much stronger and stiffer.

It's nonetheless true that Hooke's law is a useful approximation for the behavior of many materials when stretched or compressed, provided the amount of stretch or compression is small. We'll use this law in the next section and throughout our study of mechanics.

? Got the Concept? 6-4 Double the Work

In Example 6-9 the athlete did 95 J of work to stretch the exercise cords by 47 cm. How far would he have to stretch the cords to do double the amount of work (2×95 J $=$ 190 J)? (a) $\sqrt{2} \times 47$ cm $= 66$ cm; (b) 2×47 cm $= 94$ cm; (c) 4×47 cm $= 188$ cm.

Take-Home Message for Section 6-5

✔ The work-energy theorem applies even when the object follows a curved path or the forces that act on the object are not constant.

✔ A force that always acts perpendicular to an object's curved path does zero work on the object.

✔ An ideal spring exerts a force proportional to the distance that it is stretched or compressed (Hooke's law). The work required to stretch or compress a spring by a given distance is proportional to the square of that distance.

6-6 Potential energy is energy related to an object's position

We've seen that an object in motion has the ability to do work, as measured by its kinetic energy. But a *stationary* object can also have the ability to do work. An example is the barbell in Figure 6-21. When held at rest above the weight lifter's head, the barbell has no kinetic energy. If the weight lifter should drop the barbell, however, it will fall to the ground with a resounding crash and leave a dent in the floor. In other words, the barbell will exert a downward force on the floor over a distance, and so will do work. Thus, although the barbell is not moving and has no kinetic energy while the weight lifter holds it up, it has the *potential* to move and to do work simply because it's held so high. We use the term **potential energy** to refer to an ability to do work that's related to an object's *position*.

You'll find plenty of examples of potential energy in your environment. A heavy book on a high shelf has the potential to do painful work on your foot if it should fall. The spring in a mousetrap has the potential to do very destructive work on any mouse foolish enough to release the trap. And the positively charged protons in a uranium nucleus, which want to push away from each other but are prevented from doing so by the strong force between the constituents of the nucleus, have the potential to do work if the nucleus is broken apart—a process that provides the energy released in a nuclear reactor.

Gravitational Potential Energy

Let's see how to quantify the amount of potential energy associated with the barbell in Figure 6-21. If the barbell has mass m and is initially a height h above the floor, as it falls the gravitational force does an amount of work $W = Fh = mgh$ on it. From the work-energy theorem, this is equal to the kinetic energy that the dropped barbell has just before it hits the floor. (We're ignoring any effects of air resistance.) So we say that the potential energy of the Earth-barbell system before the barbell was dropped was mgh, and that this potential energy was converted to kinetic energy as the barbell fell. We use

Figure 6-21 **Potential energy** The barbell in this photo is at rest and so has zero kinetic energy. But it has the *potential* to acquire kinetic energy if the weight lifter should drop it, so there is potential energy in this situation.

Figure 6-22 Adding potential energy
The change in the kinetic energy of the barbell as it is raised by the weight lifter is zero. The work that he does to lift the barbell goes into increasing the potential energy.

the symbol U for potential energy, so we say that $U = mgh$. Note that potential energy has units of joules, the same as work and kinetic energy.

Where did the potential energy come from? To see the answer, consider what happens as the weight lifter *raises* the barbell from the floor to a height h (**Figure 6-22**). During the lifting, the barbell begins with zero kinetic energy (sitting on the floor) and ends up with zero kinetic energy (at rest above the weight lifter's head). The net *change* in its kinetic energy is zero, so the net work done on the barbell is also zero. Hence the positive work that the weight lifter did to raise the barbell must just balance the negative work done by the gravitational force of magnitude mg. The work done by gravity is $W_{\text{grav}} = -(mg)(h) = -mgh$ (negative since the displacement is upward but the gravitational force is downward). Hence the work done by the weight lifter to raise the barbell to height h is $W_{\text{weight lifter}} = +mgh$, which is exactly equal to the potential energy mgh associated with the barbell when it is at height h. So the weight lifter is the source of the potential energy. He provided this energy because he had to do work against the gravitational force, so we say that the Earth-barbell system has **gravitational potential energy**: an ability to do work that's related to the barbell's vertical position in the presence of gravity.

! Watch Out! To what object does gravitational potential energy "belong"?

We've been careful *not* to say "the barbell *has* gravitational potential energy." The reason is the gravitational potential energy is really a property of the *system* made up of the barbell and Earth (which exerts the gravitational force on the barbell). The weight lifter adds potential energy to this system by moving the barbell away from Earth. The gravitational potential energy mgh would be the same if the barbell remained at rest but Earth as a whole were pushed down a distance h. You should always be careful to define your system when using work and energy to solve problems.

There's nothing special about the particular height h of the barbell in Figure 6-22. In general, if the barbell of mass m is at a vertical coordinate y, the gravitational potential energy is

Gravitational potential energy (6-14)

Gravitational potential energy associated with an object   **Mass** of the object

$$U_{\text{grav}} = mgy$$

Acceleration due to gravity   **Height** of the object

When the weight lifter in Figure 6-22 raises the barbell (so y increases), the gravitational potential energy increases; when he lowers or drops the barbell, y decreases and the gravitational potential energy decreases.

Interpreting Potential Energy

Here's how the work-energy theorem describes what happens to a dropped barbell in the absence of air resistance: As the barbell falls, the gravitational force does work on it, and this work goes into changing the barbell's kinetic energy. In equation form,

(6-15) $$W_{\text{grav}} = \Delta K = K_{\text{f}} - K_{\text{i}} \quad \text{(only the gravitational force does work)}$$

Note that the work-energy theorem of Equation 6-15 restricts itself to the work done on the barbell and the change in kinetic energy of the barbell. It's true that Earth is exerting the force doing the work, but really, as far as the work-energy theorem is concerned, that force could come from any object.

Now let's *reinterpret* this statement in terms of gravitational potential energy, and generalize to the case in which the barbell follows a curved path (as would be the case if the barbell was thrown rather than dropped) rather than falling straight down. The barbell in **Figure 6-23** moves along a curve from an initial y coordinate y_i to a final coordinate y_f. As we did for the swinging spider in Example 6-8 (Section 6-5), we divide the path into a large number of short segments, each of which is small enough that we can treat it as a straight line. The displacement vector along this segment is $\Delta \vec{d}$, with horizontal component Δx and vertical component Δy. The work done along this segment by the force of gravity $\vec{w}$ is exactly the same as it was in Example 6-8:

$$\Delta W_{grav} = -mg\,\Delta y$$

The total work W_{grav} done by the force of gravity along the entire curved path is the sum of the ΔW_{grav} terms for each such element. The sum of all the Δy terms is the total change in the y coordinate, $y_f - y_i$, so

$$\begin{aligned} W_{grav} &= (-mg\,\Delta y_1) + (-mg\,\Delta y_2) + (-mg\,\Delta y_3) + \dots \\ &= -mg(\Delta y_1 + \Delta y_2 + \Delta y_3 + \dots) \\ &= -mg(y_f - y_i) = -mgy_f + mgy_i \end{aligned}$$

We can rewrite this in terms of the gravitational potential energy as given by Equation 6-14, $U_{grav} = mgy$:

$$\begin{aligned} W_{grav} &= -mgy_f + mgy_i = -(mgy_f - mgy_i) \\ &= -(U_{grav,f} - U_{grav,i}) = -\Delta U_{grav} \end{aligned} \qquad (6\text{-}16)$$

In other words, *the work done by gravity on an object equals the negative of the change in gravitational potential energy of the Earth-object system.* If an object descends, the gravitational force does positive work on it (the force is downward and the object moves downward) and the gravitational potential energy of the system decreases (its change is negative). If an object rises, the gravitational force does negative work on it (the force is downward but the object moves upward) and the gravitational potential energy of the system increases (its change is positive). If an object begins and ends its motion at the same height, the gravitational force does zero net work on it and there is zero net change in the system's gravitational potential energy.

We can now restate the work-energy theorem for the falling barbell. If we substitute W_{grav} from Equation 6-16 into Equation 6-15, we get

If the only force that does work on a moving object is the gravitational force...

$$\Delta K = -\Delta U_{grav}$$

... then the change in the object's kinetic energy K ...   ...is equal to the negative of the change in gravitational potential energy U_{grav}.

 If K increases, U_{grav} decreases and vice versa.

If the object rises, the gravitational potential energy of the Earth-object system increases and the kinetic energy decreases (the object slows down). If the object descends, the gravitational potential energy of the Earth-object system decreases and the kinetic energy increases (the object speeds up). From this perspective, we no longer need to talk about the *work* done by the gravitational force: that's accounted for completely by the change in the system's gravitational potential energy.

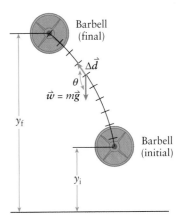

Figure 6-23 **Raising a barbell along a curved path** The work done on the barbell by the gravitational force $\vec{w}$ along a short segment $\Delta \vec{d}$ of this curved path is $\Delta W_{grav} = w\Delta d \cos\theta$. Adding up the work done along all such segments gives the net work done by the gravitational force between height y_i and height y_f.

 Go to Interactive Exercise 6-1 for more practice dealing with work, kinetic energy, and potential energy

Change in kinetic energy if only the gravitational force does work (6-17)

! Watch Out! **The choice of $y = 0$ for gravitational potential energy doesn't matter.**

The value of $U_{grav} = mgy$ depends on what height you choose to be $y = 0$. But Equation 6-17 shows that what matters is the *change* in gravitational potential energy, and that does *not* depend on your choice of $y = 0$. That's because the change in gravitational potential energy depends only on the *difference* between the initial and final heights, not the heights themselves: $\Delta U_{grav} = U_f - U_i = mgy_f - mgy_i = mg(y_f - y_i)$. Example 6-10 illustrates this important point.

Example 6-10 A Ski Jump

A skier of mass m starts at rest at the top of a ski jump ramp (Figure 6-24). The vertical distance from the top of the ramp to the lowest point is a distance H, and the vertical distance from the lowest point to where the skier leaves the ramp is D. The first part of the ramp is at an angle θ from the horizontal, and the second part is at an angle ϕ. Derive an expression for the speed of the skier when she leaves the ramp. Assume that her skis are well waxed, so that there is negligible friction between the skis and the ramp, and ignore air resistance.

Figure 6-24 Flying off the ramp What is the skier's speed when she leaves the frictionless ramp?

Set Up

The only forces that act on the skier are the gravitational force and the normal force exerted by the ramp. The normal force does no work on her because it always acts perpendicular to the ramp and hence perpendicular to her direction of motion. This means that only the gravitational force does work, so we can use Equation 6-17 for the Earth-skier system to calculate the change in the skier's kinetic energy and hence her final speed v_f.

Change in kinetic energy if only the gravitational force does work:

$$\Delta K = -\Delta U_{grav} \qquad (6\text{-}17)$$

Gravitational potential energy:

$$U_{grav} = mgy \qquad (6\text{-}14)$$

Kinetic energy:

$$K = \frac{1}{2}mv^2 \qquad (6\text{-}8)$$

Solve

Let's take $y = 0$ to be at the low point of the ramp. The skier then begins at rest ($v_i = 0$) at $y_i = H$ and is at $y_f = D$ when she leaves the ramp. Use Equations 6-8, 6-14 and 6-17 to solve for v_f.

At starting point:

$$K_i = \frac{1}{2}mv_i^2 = 0$$

$$U_{grav,\,i} = mgy_i = mgH$$

At the point where skier leaves the ramp:

$$K_f = \frac{1}{2}mv_f^2$$

$$U_{grav,\,f} = mgy_f = mgD$$

Use Equation 6-17:

$-\Delta U_{grav} = \Delta K$, Here

$$\Delta U_{grav} = U_{grav,\,f} - U_{grav,\,i} = mgD - mgH$$
$$= mg\,(D - H) = -mg\,(H - D)$$

(negative since $D < H$) and

$$\Delta K = K_f - K_i$$
$$= \frac{1}{2}mv_f^2 - 0 = \frac{1}{2}mv_f^2$$

(positive since skier is moving faster at the end of the ski jump than at the beginning). So

$$+\,mg\,(H - D) = \frac{1}{2}mv_f^2$$

$$v_f^2 = 2g(H - D)$$

$$v_f = \sqrt{2g(H - D)}$$

Reflect

The answer does *not* involve the angles θ or ϕ, or any other aspect of the ramp's shape. All that matters is the difference $H - D$ between the skier's initial and final heights. If the ramp had a different shape, the final speed v_f would be exactly the same.

As we mentioned in the **Watch Out!** feature just before this example, our answer also shouldn't depend on our having chosen $y = 0$ to be at the low point of the ramp. For example, if we instead chose $y = 0$ to be where the skier leaves the ramp, the result for v_f would be the same. Try this yourself: Take $y = 0$ to be at the skier's starting point, so the end of the ramp is at $y = -(H - D)$. Do you get the same ΔU_{grav} with this choice?

With $y = 0$ at the point where the skier leaves the ramp:
At starting point:

$$U_{grav, i} = mgy_i$$
$$= mg(H - D)$$

At the point where skier leaves the ramp:

$$U_{grav, f} = mgy_f = 0, \text{ So}$$

$$\Delta U_{grav} = U_{grav, f} - U_{grav, i}$$
$$= 0 - mg(H - D)$$
$$= -mg(H - D)$$

This is the same as with our previous choice of $y = 0$, so we'll find the same value of v_f.

? Got the Concept? 6-5   Choosing a Point of Reference

A ball is dropped from the top of an eleven-story building, 45 m above the ground, to a balcony on the back of the ninth floor, 36 m above the ground. In which case is the change in the ball's gravitational potential energy greatest?

(a) If we choose the ground to be at $y = 0$; (b) if we choose the balcony to be at $y = 0$; (c) if we choose the top of the building to be at $y = 0$; (d) the change is the same in all three cases.

Spring Potential Energy

In Example 6-10 the work done by the gravitational force on the skier is $W_{grav} = -\Delta U_{grav}$ (see Equation 6-16). We saw that this work depends only on the skier's final and initial positions, *not* on the path that she took between those two points. That's why we can express the work done by the gravitational force in terms of the difference ΔU_{grav} between the gravitational potential energy values at the two points.

The same is true for the work done by an ideal spring. We saw in Section 6-5 that the work you must do to stretch a spring from an extension x_i to an extension x_f is $\frac{1}{2}kx_f^2 - \frac{1}{2}kx_i^2$ (this is Equation 6-13, with 1 replaced by i and 2 replaced by f). The work that the *spring* does is the negative of this: $W_{spring} = -(\frac{1}{2}kx_f^2 - \frac{1}{2}kx_i^2)$. Note that this also depends on only the initial and final extensions of the spring, not on how you got from one to the other. (If the spring was initially relaxed—that is, $x_i = 0$—and you stretched the spring to $x_f = 1.00$ cm, the work done by the spring would be the same as if you first stretched the spring by 2.00 cm and then let it relax back to a 1.00-cm extension.) Hence just as we did for the work done by the gravitational force, we can write the work done by an ideal spring in terms of a change in potential energy:

$$W_{spring} = -\left(\frac{1}{2}kx_f^2 - \frac{1}{2}kx_i^2\right) \tag{6-18}$$
$$= -(U_{spring, f} - U_{spring, i}) = -\Delta U_{spring}$$

The quantity U_{spring} in Equation 6-18 is called the **spring potential energy:**

Spring potential energy of a stretched or compressed spring   Spring constant of the spring

Spring potential energy
(6-19)

$$U_{spring} = \frac{1}{2} kx^2$$

Extension of the spring ($x > 0$ if spring is stretched, $x < 0$ if spring is compressed)

The spring potential energy is zero if the spring is relaxed ($x = 0$) and positive if the spring is stretched ($x > 0$) or compressed ($x < 0$) (Figure 6-25). This says that we have to do work to either stretch the spring or compress it, and the work that we do goes into the spring potential energy.

Conservative and Nonconservative Forces

A force that can be associated with a potential energy, like the gravitational force or the force exerted by an ideal spring, is called a **conservative force**. (In Section 6-7 we'll see the reason for this term.) By contrast, the friction force is an example of a **nonconservative force** for which we *cannot* use the concept of potential energy. The reason is that unlike the gravitational force or the force exerted by an ideal spring, the work done by the friction force *does* depend on the path taken from the initial point to the final point. In Figure 6-26a we slide a book across a table top from an initial point to a final point along two different paths. Along either path the kinetic friction force has the same magnitude and points opposite to the direction of motion. Hence the friction force does more (negative) work along the curved path than along the straight path. Since the work done by friction depends on more than just the initial and final positions, we can't write it in terms of a change in potential energy. That's why there's no such thing as "friction potential energy."

Here's an equivalent way to decide whether a certain kind of force is conservative: If the work done by the force on a *round trip* (that is, one where the initial and final positions are the same) is *zero*, the force is conservative and we can use the idea of potential energy. This is the case for the gravitational force: if $y_f = y_i$, then $W_{grav} = -mgy_f + mgy_i = 0$. If you toss a ball straight up, the gravitational force does negative work on it as it rises and an equal amount of positive work as it falls back to your hand. The same is true for the spring force: If $x_f = x_i$, then $W_{spring} = \frac{1}{2}kx_f^2 - \frac{1}{2}kx_i^2 = 0$. But if you slide a book on a round trip on a table top, the total amount of work that the friction force does on the book is negative and *not* zero (Figure 6-26b). Hence the friction force is nonconservative. (To keep the book moving, you have to do an equal amount of positive work on the book as you push it.)

Figure 6-20 shows that the force exerted by a human tendon is also nonconservative. The tendon exerts more force on its end while it is being stretched than when it is relaxing to its original length, so it does more negative work on the muscle attached to its end as it stretches than it does positive work as it relaxes. So the tendon does a nonzero (and negative) amount of work on this "round trip." To make the tendon go through a complete cycle, the muscle has to do a nonzero amount of *positive* work on the tendon, just like the positive work you must do to push the book around the path in Figure 6-26b.

What happens to the work that you do in these cases? Before we can answer this question, we'll combine the ideas of kinetic energy and potential energy into yet another kind of energy, called *total mechanical energy*. This will lead us to one of the central ideas not just of physics but of science as a whole, the idea of *conservation of energy*.

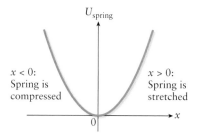

U_{spring}

$x < 0$:
Spring is
compressed

$x > 0$:
Spring is
stretched

0   x

Figure 6-25 Spring potential energy The potential energy in a spring is proportional to the square of its extension x. (See Equation 6-19.)

Figure 6-26 Kinetic friction is a nonconservative force Because the work done by kinetic friction depends on the path, and it does nonzero net work on a round trip, it is a nonconservative force.

(a) Friction does more negative work along path 2 than along path 1. Since the work done by friction depends on the path, we conclude that friction is not a conservative force.

(b) The book makes a round trip that begins and ends at this point. Friction does a nonzero, negative amount of work on the book for this round trip. So we again conclude that friction is not a conservative force.

6-7 If only conservative forces do work, total mechanical energy is conserved

Take a pencil in your hand and toss it upward. As the pencil ascends, it loses speed and its kinetic energy $K = \frac{1}{2}mv^2$ decreases. At the same time, the pencil gains height so that the gravitational potential energy $U_{grav} = mgy$ increases. After the pencil reaches its maximum height and falls downward, its kinetic energy increases as it gains speed and the gravitational potential energy decreases as it loses height. This way of thinking about the pencil's up-and-down motion suggests that energy is *transformed* from one form (kinetic) into a different form (gravitational potential) as the pencil rises, and is transformed back as the pencil descends.

Here's another example of energy transformation that's happening inside your body right now. When your heart contracts it pushes blood into the arteries, stretching their walls to accommodate the increased volume. The stretched arterial walls behave like a stretched spring and so possess spring potential energy. In between heart contractions the arterial walls relax back to their equilibrium size and lose their potential energy, just as a stretched spring does when it's allowed to relax to its unstretched length. As a result, blood gains kinetic energy as the arterial walls push on it between heartbeats. Thus spring potential energy of the arteries is transformed into kinetic energy of the blood. This energy transformation, which occurs about once per second in your body, is essential for life.

In both of these situations what's happening is that the *sum* of kinetic energy and potential energy—a sum that we call the *total mechanical energy*—keeps the same value and is *conserved*. When the system's kinetic energy increases, its potential energy decreases, and when its kinetic energy decreases, its potential energy increases. It's like having two bank accounts: You can transfer money from one account to the other, but the total amount of money in the bank (the sum of the amounts in the two accounts) remains the same. In this section we'll learn the special circumstances in which total mechanical energy is conserved, and we'll see how to express these ideas in equation form.

Suppose that as an object moves from an initial position to a final position, the only force that does work on the object is the gravitational force. [An example is the skier on a ski jump in Example 6-10 (Section 6-6). In addition to the gravitational force on the skier there is a normal force exerted by the ramp, but it does no work on the skier because this force is always perpendicular to the skier's path.] According to Equation 6-17, in this situation the work-energy theorem tells us that the change in the object's kinetic energy is equal to the negative of the change in its potential energy:

$$\Delta K = -\Delta U_{grav} \text{ (if only the gravitational force does work)} \tag{6-20}$$

The change in kinetic energy equals the final value minus the initial value, and likewise for the gravitational potential energy. So we can rewrite Equation 6-20 as

$$K_f - K_i = -(U_{grav,f} - U_{grav,i}) = -U_{grav,f} + U_{grav,i}$$
$$\text{(if only the gravitational force does work)}$$

Let's rearrange this equation so that all the terms involving the initial situation are on the left-hand side of the equals sign and all the terms involving the final situation are on the right-hand side. We get

$$K_i + U_{grav,i} = K_f + U_{grav,f} \text{ (if only the gravitational force does work)} \tag{6-21}$$

Equation 6-21 says something quite profound. If only the gravitational force does work on the object as it moves, its speed v and kinetic energy $K = \frac{1}{2}mv^2$ can change, and its height y and gravitational potential energy $U_{grav} = mgy$ can change. But the *sum* of kinetic energy and gravitational potential energy, $K + U$, has the same value at the end of the motion as at the beginning.

We can generalize these ideas and Equation 6-21 even more. Our results from Section 6-6 show that the work done by *any* conservative force can be written as the negative of the change in the associated potential energy. (Equations 6-18 and 6-19 show this for the case of the work done by an ideal spring: $W_{spring} = -\Delta U_{spring}$, where the spring potential energy is $U_{spring} = \frac{1}{2}kx^2$ and x is the extension of the spring.) If a number of conservative forces $\vec{F}_A, \vec{F}_B, \vec{F}_C, \ldots$ do work on an object as it moves, and the potential energies associated with each of these forces are $U_A, U_B, U_C, \ldots$, then the total work done by these forces is

$$
\begin{aligned}
W_{conservative} &= W_A + W_B + W_C + \ldots \\
&= (-\Delta U_A) + (-\Delta U_B) + (-\Delta U_C) + \ldots \\
&= (-U_{A,f} + U_{A,i}) + (-U_{B,f} + U_{B,i}) + (-U_{C,f} + U_{C,i}) + \ldots \\
&= -(U_{A,f} + U_{B,f} + U_{C,f} + \ldots) + (U_{A,i} + U_{B,i} + U_{C,i} + \ldots) \\
&= -U_f + U_i = -\Delta U
\end{aligned}
$$

(6-22)

In Equation 6-22 the quantity U is the *total* potential energy, which is just the sum of the individual potential energies $U_A, U_B, U_C, \ldots$ If these conservative forces are the only forces that do work on the object, then $W_{conservative}$ in Equation 6-22 equals the net work done on the object, which from the work-energy theorem equals $\Delta K = K_f - K_i$. So if only conservative forces do work, we have

$$K_f - K_i = -U_f + U_i$$

or, rearranging,

Values of the **kinetic energy** K of an object at two points (i and f) during its motion

$$K_i + U_i = K_f + U_f$$

Conservation of mechanical energy
(6-23)

Values of the **potential energy** U at the same two points

 If only conservative forces do work on an object, the sum $K + U$ maintains the same value throughout the motion. This sum is called the **total mechanical energy** E.

You can see that this is a more general form of Equation 6-21, which refers to the case in which only one conservative force—the gravitational force—does work. Note that we can take the initial point i and the final point f to be *any* two points during the motion, as long as only conservative forces do work.

So Equation 6-23 really says that **if only conservative forces do work on an object as it moves, the sum of the system's kinetic energy and potential energy has the same value at all times during the motion.** The sum of kinetic energy K and potential energy U is called the **total mechanical energy** E. So Equation 6-23 tells us that if only conservative forces do work on an object, the total mechanical energy is *conserved;* that is, it maintains the same value during the motion (see **Figure 6-27**). In order for this energy conservation to take place, your system must include the sources of the conservative forces—for example Earth and springs. You can now see the origin of the term *conservative* for

The kinetic energy K and the gravitational potential energy U_{grav} both change, but their sum E remains the same.

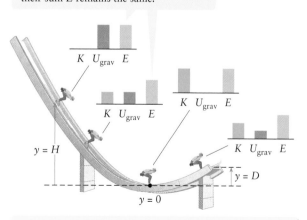

When only conservative forces like gravity act, the total mechanical energy E of the system is conserved.

Figure 6-27 Total mechanical energy is conserved As the skier moves on this frictionless ramp, the kinetic energy K and the gravitational potential energy U_{grav} both change, but their sum $E = K + U_{grav}$—the total mechanical energy—always has the same value.

forces like the gravitational force and the spring force: if only forces of this kind do work, the total mechanical energy of the system is conserved.

Another way to write Equation 6-23 is to move all of the terms in that equation to the same side of the equals sign:

$$K_f - K_i + U_f - U_i = 0$$

Since $K_f - K_i = \Delta K$ (the change in kinetic energy) and $U_f - U_i = \Delta U$ (the change in potential energy), we can rewrite this equation as

Change in the **kinetic energy** K of an object during its motion

Change in the **potential energy** U associated with an object during its motion

Conservation of mechanical energy—alternative version (6-24)

$$\Delta K + \Delta U = 0$$

 If only conservative forces do work on the object, the sum is zero: Total mechanical energy can transform between kinetic and potential forms, but there is no net change in the amount of total mechanical energy.

Equation 6-24 refers to the change in kinetic energy ΔK and the change in potential energy ΔU during the motion. If the only forces that do work on the object are conservative forces, the sum of these is zero: Any increase in kinetic energy comes with an equal decrease in potential energy, and vice versa. In other words, the total mechanical energy E remains constant as it transforms back and forth between the kinetic and potential forms.

 Go to Picture It 6-2 for more practice dealing with mechanical energy

---

! Watch Out! Total mechanical energy is a property of a system, not a single object.

We saw in Section 6-6 that gravitational potential energy for an object like a baseball is really a shared property of a *system* of two objects, the baseball and Earth. Thus the total mechanical energy for a baseball in flight, which incorporates gravitational potential energy, is likewise a property of that system. Likewise, if a weight is attached to a horizontal spring and allowed to oscillate back and forth, the total mechanical energy is a shared property of the weight (which has kinetic energy) and the spring (which has spring potential energy). Whenever you think about total mechanical energy, you should always be able to state to what system that mechanical energy belongs.

In Section 6-8 we'll use the idea of conservation of mechanical energy to solve a number of physics problems. First, however, let's see how this idea has to be modified if there are also *nonconservative* forces that do work.

Generalizing the Idea of Conservation of Energy: Nonconservative Forces

There are many situations in which total mechanical energy is not conserved. As an example, at the beginning of this section we asked you to toss a pencil into the air. During the toss you had to do *positive* work on the pencil: You exerted an upward force on the pencil as you pushed it upward. As a result, the total mechanical energy of the pencil increased (Figure 6-28). If you subsequently catch the pencil as it falls, you do *negative* work on the pencil because you exert an upward force on it as the pencil moves downward. As Figure 6-28 shows, the total mechanical energy decreases during the catch.

The total mechanical energy changes in these situations because the force exerted by your hand is not conservative. We can write a modified version of Equation 6-23 that can accommodate situations like these in which the total mechanical energy is *not* conserved. To do this, let's go back to the work-energy theorem, $W_{net} = K_f - K_i$. If both conservative and nonconservative forces do work on an object, the net work is the sum of the work done by the two kinds of forces:

$$W_{net} = W_{conservative} + W_{nonconservative} \tag{6-25}$$

Equation 6-22 says that the work done by conservative forces is $W_{conservative} = -U_f + U_i = -\Delta U$. Substituting this and Equation 6-25 into the work-energy theorem, we get

$$W_{net} = (-U_f + U_i) + W_{nonconservative} = K_f - K_i$$

We can rearrange this to

Change in mechanical energy
when nonconservative forces act
(6-26)

Values of the **kinetic energy** K of an object at two points (i and f) during its motion

$$K_i + U_i + W_{nonconservative} = K_f + U_f$$

Values of the **potential energy** U at the same two points

If nonconservative forces do work on an object, the total mechanical
energy $E = K + U$ changes its value.
If $W_{nonconservative} > 0$, $E_f > E_i$ and the total mechanical energy increases.
If $W_{nonconservative} < 0$, $E_f < E_i$ and the total mechanical energy decreases.

Equation 6-26 gives us more insight into the difference between conservative and nonconservative forces. While the pencil in Figure 6-28 is in flight—that is, during the time from when it leaves your hand to when it returns to your hand—the value of $E = K + U$ remains the same. Kinetic energy decreases and changes into potential energy as the pencil ascends, but the potential energy is turned back into kinetic energy as the pencil falls. Hence, because the gravitational force on the pencil is conservative, no energy is lost during the pencil's flight. If the force of your hand were also a conservative force, all of the energy you expended to toss the pencil would be returned to your body when you caught the pencil; you could toss the pencil up and down all day and you would never get tired. This is *not* the case, however, and you *do* get tired. (If you don't believe this, try it with a book rather than a pencil, and try tossing the book up and catching it a few dozen times.) Because the energy you expend in the toss is *not* returned to you in the catch, the force of your hand is nonconservative.

Here's an alternative way to think of the nonconservative forces depicted in Figure 6-28. To toss the pencil upward, you actually use potential energy stored in the chemical bonds of adenosine triphosphate (ATP), carbohydrates, and fat in the muscles of your arm. (Chemical bonds are fundamentally electric in nature, and we will learn in Chapter 17 that the electric force is conservative.) We don't include this kind of potential energy in the quantity U in Equation 6-26, which refers only to potential energy associated with the pencil. Instead, we'll use the symbol E_{other} for **internal energy**, a catch-all kind of energy that is not included in K or U in Equation 6-26. Not all of the released chemical energy goes into moving your muscles; some goes into warming your muscles (which is why you get warm when you exercise) and hence into **thermal energy**, which is energy associated with the random motion of atoms and molecules (in this case, inside your arm). Thermal energy is also considered part of E_{other}. So during the toss, some chemical energy is converted into thermal energy (and so remains within

Because you do work on
the pencil, the total
mechanical energy E—the
sum of kinetic energy K
and gravitational energy
U_{grav}—is not conserved
throughout this process.

While the pencil is in free fall, the value of the
total mechanical energy stays the same. The
energy shifts from kinetic energy to potential
energy, then back to kinetic energy.

When you toss the pencil
upward, you do positive
work on it and the total
mechanical energy of the
pencil increases.

Your hand does negative
work on the pencil,
decreasing the mechanical
energy of the system.

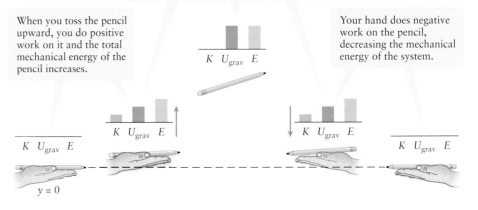

Figure 6-28 Tossing and catching a pencil The total mechanical energy associated with the pencil increases as you toss it upward, remains constant while the pencil is in flight, then decreases as you catch it.

E_{other}), and the rest is used to do work on the pencil (Figure 6-29). Hence during the toss, for which $W_{\text{nonconservative}} > 0$, E_{other} of your body decreases so $\Delta E_{\text{other}} < 0$.

When you catch the pencil, you again use your muscles and so you use more of the potential energy stored in chemical bonds. In the catch, however, there is a net *increase* in E_{other}: Both your arm and the pencil warm by a slight but measurable amount, corresponding to an increase in thermal energy, and this increase is greater than the loss of chemical energy (Figure 6-29). So during the catch, for which $W_{\text{nonconservative}} < 0$, E_{other} of you and the pencil increases so $\Delta E_{\text{other}} > 0$.

These observations suggest that the amount of nonconservative work done is related to the change in internal energy. Indeed, many careful measurements show that in *all* situations, $W_{\text{nonconservative}}$ is *exactly* equal to the negative of ΔE_{other}:

$$W_{\text{nonconservative}} = -\Delta E_{\text{other}} \qquad (6\text{-}27)$$

With Equation 6-27 in mind we can rewrite Equation 6-26 as

$$K_i + U_i - \Delta E_{\text{other}} = K_f + U_f$$

If we move all of the terms in this equation to the same side of the equals sign, we get

$$K_f - K_i + U_f - U_i + \Delta E_{\text{other}} = 0$$

Now, $K_f - K_i$ is the change in kinetic energy ΔK and $U_f - U_i$ is the change in potential energy ΔU. So we can rewrite this equation as

Change in the **kinetic energy** K of an object during its motion

Change in the **potential energy** U associated with an object during its motion

$$\Delta K + \Delta U + \Delta E_{\text{other}} = 0$$

The law of conservation of energy
(6-28)

Change in the **internal energy** E_{other} during the object's motion

Energy can transform between kinetic, potential, and internal forms, but there is no net change in the amount of energy.

Equation 6-28 suggests that we broaden our definition of energy to include both total mechanical energy ($E = K + U$) and internal energy E_{other}. In this case, we have to expand the system to include not only the object and the sources of the conservative forces that produce ΔU, but also the sources of the nonconservative forces that result in ΔE_{other} (like your hand in the case of the thrown pencil). As the object moves, K, U, and E_{other} can all change values, but the sum of these changes is zero: One kind of energy can transform into another, but the total amount of energy of all forms remains the same. This is the most general statement of the **law of conservation of energy.**

While the pencil is in free fall, the value of the total mechanical energy stays the same. The energy shifts from kinetic energy to potential energy, then back to kinetic energy.

When you catch the pencil, mechanical energy is converted to internal energy of your arm and the pencil (thermal energy), raising their temperatures.

When you toss the pencil upward, internal energy in your arm (chemical energy) is converted to mechanical energy.

Total energy—the sum of total mechanical energy (K plus U_{grav}) and internal energy E_{other}—is conserved in this process.

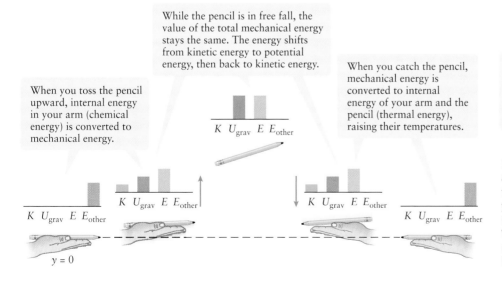

Figure 6-29 **Tossing and catching a pencil, revisited** When you toss the pencil some internal energy of your body in chemical form (E_{other}) is converted to mechanical energy. When you catch the pencil this added mechanical energy is converted back into internal energy.

Unlike the similar-appearing Equation 6-24, which applies only if nonconservative forces do no work, Equation 6-28 is *always* true as long as the system contains all objects that are exerting or feeling forces. Scientists have made an exhaustive search for situations in which the law of conservation of energy does not hold. No such situation has ever been found. So we conclude that conservation of energy is an absolute law of nature. In the following section we'll see how to apply this law to solve physics problems.

? Got the Concept? 6-6 How High?

A block is released from rest on the left-hand side of an asymmetric skateboard ramp at a height H (Figure 6-30). The angle from the horizontal of the left-hand side of the ramp is twice the angle of the right-hand side of the ramp. If the ramp is frictionless, to what height does the block rise on the right-hand side before stopping and sliding back down? (a) $2H$; (b) H; (c) $H/2$; (d) not enough information given to decide.

Figure 6-30 **An asymmetric skateboard ramp** If the block is released at height H on the left-hand side, to what height will it rise on the more gently sloped right-hand side?

Take-Home Message for Section 6-7

✔ If the only forces that do work on an object are conservative forces, then the total mechanical energy E (the sum of the kinetic energy K and the potential energy U) is conserved. The values of K and U may change as the object moves, but the value of E remains the same.

✔ If nonconservative forces also do work on the object, the total mechanical energy changes. The value of E increases if positive nonconservative work is done and decreases if negative nonconservative work is done.

✔ Work done by a nonconservative force is associated with a change in internal energy. The total energy—the sum of kinetic, potential, and internal energies—is always conserved.

6-8 Energy conservation is an important tool for solving a wide variety of problems

Go to Interactive Exercise 6-2 for more practice dealing with energy conservation

Let's now see how to use the energy conservation equations valid when only conservative forces do work (Equations 6-23 and 6-24) and those valid when nonconservative forces also do work (Equations 6-26 and 6-28). As a rule, if a problem involves a conserved quantity (that is, a quantity whose value remains unchanged), it simplifies the problem tremendously. Often the conservation equation, which relates the value of the conserved quantity at one point in an object's motion to the value at a different point, is all you need to solve for the desired unknown. We'll see several problems of that kind in this section.

Example 6-11 A Ski Jump, Revisited

As in Example 6-10 (Section 6-6), a skier of mass m starts at rest at the top of a ski jump ramp (Figure 6-31). (a) Use an energy conservation equation to find an expression for the skier's speed as she flies off the ramp. There is negligible friction between the skis and the ramp, and you can ignore air resistance. (b) After the skier reaches the ground at point P in Figure 6-32, she begins braking and comes to a halt at point Q. Find an expression for the magnitude of the constant friction force that acts on her between points P and Q.

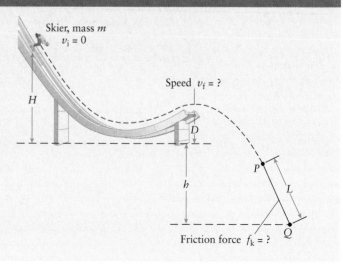

Figure 6-31 **Flying off the ramp and coming to a halt** What is the skier's speed as she leaves the ramp? How much friction is required to bring her to a halt?

Set Up

While the skier is on the ramp, both a normal force and the gravitational force act on her. The normal force is always perpendicular to her motion, so it does no work on her. So for part (a) of this problem, which takes us from the beginning to the end of the ramp, only the conservative force of gravity does work and so we can use Equation 6-23. (There are no springs, so there is no spring potential energy.) Our goal for this part is to find the skier's speed v_f as she leaves the ramp. In this part we take the initial point i to be at the top of the ramp and the final point f at the end of the ramp.

For part (b) we consider the skier's entire motion from the top of the ramp (which we again call point i) to where she finally comes to rest at point Q. A normal force also acts on her when she reaches the ground, but again this force does no work on her. Between points P and Q, a nonconservative *friction* force also acts and does negative work on her (the force is opposite to her motion). So for the motion as a whole we must use Equation 6-26. Our goal for part (b) is to find the magnitude f_k of the friction force.

Conservation of mechanical energy:

$$K_i + U_i = K_f + U_f \qquad (6\text{-}23)$$

Gravitational potential energy:

$$U_{grav} = mgy \qquad (6\text{-}14)$$

Change in mechanical energy when nonconservative forces act::

$$K_i + U_i + W_{nonconservative} = K_f + U_f \qquad (6\text{-}26)$$

Kinetic energy:

$$K = \frac{1}{2}mv^2 \qquad (6\text{-}8)$$

on ramp

in midair

between
P and Q

At the top of the ramp:
$$K_i = \frac{1}{2}mv_i^2 = 0$$
$$U_{grav,\,i} = mgy_i = mgH$$

At the end of the ramp:
$$K_f = \frac{1}{2}mv_f^2$$
$$U_{grav,\,f} = mgy_f = mgD$$

Now substitute the energies into Equation 6-23 and solve for v_f.

Equation 6-23:
$$K_i + U_i = K_f + U_f, \text{ so}$$

$$0 + mgH = \frac{1}{2}mv_f^2 + mgD$$

$$\frac{1}{2}mv_f^2 = mgH - mgD = mg\,(H - D)$$

$$v_f^2 = 2g(H - D)$$
$$v_f = \sqrt{2g(H - D)}$$

(b) Now the final position is at point Q, a distance h below the low point of the ramp so $y_Q = -h$. At this point the skier is again at rest, so $v_Q = 0$. The friction force f_k acts opposite to her motion as she moves a distance L, so this force does work $-f_kL$ on her.

At the top of the ramp:
$$K_i = \frac{1}{2}mv_i^2 = 0$$
$$U_{grav,\,i} = mgy_i = mgH$$

At point Q:
$$K_Q = \frac{1}{2}mv_Q^2 = 0$$
$$U_{grav,Q} = mgy_Q$$
$$= mg(-h) = -mgh$$

Work done by the friction force, which points opposite to the skier's displacement:

$$W_{nonconservative} = f_kL\cos 180° = f_kL(-1)$$
$$= -f_kL$$

Now use Equation 6-26 to solve for f_k.

Equation 6-26:

$$K_i + U_i + W_{nonconservative} = K_Q + U_Q \text{ so}$$

$$0 + mgH + (-f_k L) = 0 + (-mgh)$$

$$f_k L = mgH + mgh = mg(H + h)$$

$$f_k = mg\left(\frac{H + h}{L}\right)$$

Reflect

Our answer for part (a) is the same one that we found in Example 6-10, where we used the expression $W_{grav} = -\Delta U_{grav}$ for the work done by gravity. That's as it should be, since we used that expression in Section 6-7 to help derive Equation 6-23.

Our result for f_k in part (b) has the correct dimensions of force, the same as mg, since the dimensions of $H + h$ (the total vertical distance that the skier descends) cancel those of L (the skier's stopping distance). Note that the smaller the value of L compared to $H + h$, the greater the friction force required to bring the skier to a halt.

An alternative way to solve part (b) would be to treat the second part of the skier's motion separately, with the initial point at the end of the ramp [at height D, where the skier's speed is $\sqrt{2g(H - D)}$ as found in part (a)] and the final point is at point Q (at height $-h$, where the skier's speed is zero). You should try solving the problem this way using Equation 6-26 and $W_{nonconservative} = -f_k L$; you should get the same answer for f_k. Do you?

Example 6-12 Warming Skis and Snow

When the skier in Example 6-11 brakes to a halt, her skis and the snow over which she slides both warm up. What is the increase in the internal energy of the skis and snow in this process?

Set Up

This problem involves internal energy, so we'll use the most general statement of energy conservation. This says that during the skier's motion (from the top of the ramp to when she finally comes to rest at point Q), the sum of the changes in kinetic energy K, potential energy U, and internal energy E_{other} must be zero. We'll use this to find how much internal energy is added to the ski and snow during the braking.

The law of conservation of energy:

$$\Delta K + \Delta U + \Delta E_{other} = 0$$

(6-28)

Solve

Substitute the change in kinetic energy ΔK and the change in potential energy ΔU into Equation 6-28 and solve for the increase in internal energy. We'll refer to Example 6-11 for the initial and final values of y and v.

At the top of the ramp: $K_i = \frac{1}{2}mv_i^2 = 0$
$$U_{grav, i} = mgy_i = mgH$$

At point Q: $K_Q = \frac{1}{2}mv_Q^2 = 0$
$$U_{grav, Q} = mgy_Q = mg(-h) = -mgh$$

Change in kinetic energy: $\Delta K = K_Q - K_i = 0 - 0 = 0$

Change in potential energy: $\Delta U = U_{grav, Q} - U_{grav, i}$
$$= -mgh - mgH = -mg(H + h)$$

From Equation 6-28, $\Delta K + \Delta U + \Delta E_{other} = 0$
$$0 + [-mg(H + h)] + \Delta E_{other} = 0$$
$$\Delta E_{other} = mg(H + h)$$

Reflect

The overall motion of the skier begins and ends with zero kinetic energy. The net result is that the (gravitational) potential energy decreases by an amount $mg(H + h)$ and the internal energy increases by the same amount. This represents the amount of thermal energy that is added to

$$W_{nonconservative} = -\Delta E_{other}$$

(6-27)

From Example 6-11, $W_{nonconservative} = -f_k L$, and

$$f_k = mg\left(\frac{H + h}{L}\right), \text{ so}$$

the skier's skis and the snow over which she slides as she brakes to a halt.

We can check our result by using Equation 6-27, which relates the change in internal energy to the amount of nonconservative work done. We get the same answer with this approach, as we must.

$$W_{\text{nonconservative}} = -mg\left(\frac{H + h}{L}\right)L = -mg(H + h)$$

$$\Delta E_{\text{other}} = -W_{\text{nonconservative}} = mg(H + h)$$

Example 6-13 A Ramp and a Spring

A child's toy uses a spring with spring constant $k = 36$ N/m to shoot a block up a ramp inclined at $\theta = 30°$ from the horizontal (Figure 6-32). The mass of the block is $m = 8.0$ g. When the spring is compressed 4.2 cm and released, the block slides up the ramp, loses contact with the spring, and comes to rest a distance d along the ramp from where it started. Find the value of d. Neglect friction between the block and the surface of the ramp.

Figure 6-32 **Spring potential energy and gravitational potential energy** If the spring is compressed a certain distance, how far up the frictionless ramp will the block go?

Set Up

The forces on the block are a normal force, the gravitational force, and a spring force that acts during the part of the time that the block is in contact with the spring. The normal force does no work on the block (this force is always perpendicular to its motion). Therefore only conservative forces (gravity and the spring force) do work, and total mechanical energy is conserved. We'll use Equation 6-23 to solve for the distance d. The initial point i is where the block is released, and the final point f is a distance d up the ramp from the initial point.

$$K_i + U_i = K_f + U_f \qquad (6\text{-}23)$$

$$U_{\text{grav}} = mgy \qquad (6\text{-}14)$$

$$U_{\text{spring}} = \frac{1}{2}kx^2 \qquad (6\text{-}19)$$

$$K = \frac{1}{2}mv^2 \qquad (6\text{-}8)$$

in contact with spring

after losing contact with spring

Solve

The block is at rest with zero kinetic energy at both the initial point and the final point. If we take $y = 0$ to be the height of the block where it is released, then $y_i = 0$; the final height y_f is related to the distance d by trigonometry. We use Equation 6-14 to write the initial and final gravitational potential energies. The initial spring potential energy is given by Equation 6-19 with $k = 36$ N/m and $x_i = -4, 2$ cm; the final spring potential energy is zero because the spring is relaxed.

Before block is released:

$$K_i = \frac{1}{2}mv_i^2 = 0$$

$$U_{\text{grav, i}} = mgy_i = 0$$

$$U_{\text{spring, i}} = \frac{1}{2}kx_i^2$$

When block has traveled a distance d up the ramp: From Figure 6-33,

$$y_f = d \sin\theta, \text{ so}$$

$$K_f = \frac{1}{2}mv_f^2 = 0$$

$$U_{\text{grav, f}} = mgy_f = mgd \sin\theta$$

$$U_{\text{spring, f}} = \frac{1}{2}kx_f^2 = 0$$

Substitute the energies into Equation 6-23. (Remember that the *total* potential energy U is the sum of the gravitational and spring potential energies.) Then solve for the distance d.

Equation 6-23:

$$K_i + U_i = K_f + U_f, \text{ or}$$

$$K_i + U_{grav, i} + U_{spring, i} = K_f + U_{grav, f} + U_{spring, f}, \text{ so}$$

$$0 + 0 + \frac{1}{2}kx_i^2 = 0 + mgd \sin \theta + 0$$

$$d = \frac{kx_i^2}{2mg \sin \theta}$$

Insert numerical values (being careful to express distances in meters and masses in kilograms) and find the value of d. Recall that $1 \text{ N} = 1 \text{ kg} \cdot \text{m/s}^2$.

$$x_i = (4.2 \text{ cm})\left(\frac{1 \text{ m}}{100 \text{ m}}\right) = 0.042 \text{ m}$$

$$m = (8.0 \text{ g})\left(\frac{1 \text{ kg}}{1000 \text{ g}}\right) = 0.0080 \text{ kg}$$

$$d = \frac{(36 \text{ N/m})(0.042 \text{ m})^2}{2(0.0080 \text{ kg})(9.80 \text{ m/s}^2) \sin 30°}$$

$$= 0.81 \frac{\text{N} \cdot \text{s}^2}{\text{kg}} = 0.81 \frac{\text{kg} \cdot \text{m}}{\text{s}^2} \frac{\text{s}^2}{\text{kg}}$$

$$= 0.81 \text{ m} = 81 \text{ cm}$$

Reflect

In our solution we assumed that the final spring potential energy is zero, which means that the spring ends up neither compressed nor stretched. In other words, we assumed that the block moves so far up the ramp that it loses contact with the spring. That's consistent with our result: The block moves 81 cm up the ramp, much greater than the 4.2-cm distance by which the spring was originally compressed.

Our solution shows that the net effect of the block's motion is to convert spring potential energy at the initial position to gravitational potential energy at the final position. The block begins and ends with zero kinetic energy, just as the skier does in Examples 6-11 and 6-12. Note that the block *does* have kinetic energy at intermediate points during the motion, when it's moving up the ramp. However, we didn't need to worry about these intermediate stages of the motion.

This problem would have been impossible to solve using the techniques of Chapters 4 and 5 because the net force on the block isn't constant: The magnitude of the spring force starts off large, then decreases to zero as the block moves uphill and the spring relaxes. The energy approach is the *only* method that will lead us to the answer to this problem.

? Got the Concept? 6-7 Where Is It Zero?

In Example 6-13, which of the following are you free to choose as you see fit? (a) the point on the ramp where gravitational potential energy is zero; (b) the point on the ramp where spring potential energy is zero; (c) both of these; (d) neither of these.

Take-Home Message for Section 6-8

✔ The kinds of problems that are best solved using the law of conservation of energy are those in which an object moves from one place to another under the action of well-defined forces.

✔ Drawing a free-body diagram is essential for deciding which forces act and do work on the object.

✔ If only conservative forces do work, total mechanical energy is conserved. If nonconservative forces also do work, you must use the more general statement of energy conservation.

Key Terms

conservative force	kinetic energy	thermal energy
dot product	law of conservation of energy	total mechanical energy
energy	negative work	translational kinetic energy
gravitational potential energy	nonconservative force	work
Hooke's law	potential energy	work-energy theorem
internal energy	spring constant	
joule	spring potential energy	

Chapter Summary

Topic	Equation or Figure

Work done by a force in the direction of displacement: If an object moves in a straight line while a constant force is applied in the same direction as the displacement, the work is just equal to the force times the displacement.

Work done on an object by a constant force $\vec{F}$ that points in the same direction as the object's displacement $\vec{d}$

Magnitude of the constant force $\vec{F}$

$$W = Fd \tag{6-1}$$

Magnitude of the displacement $\vec{d}$

Work done by a constant force at an angle θ to the straight-line displacement: If an object moves in a straight line while a constant force is applied at some angle θ to the displacement, the work is equal to the force times the displacement multiplied by the cosine of the angle between the force and displacement.

Work done on an object by a constant force $\vec{F}$ that points at an angle θ to the object's displacement $\vec{d}$

Magnitude of the constant force $\vec{F}$

$$W = (F \cos \theta)d \tag{6-2}$$

Angle between the directions of $\vec{F}$ and $\vec{d}$ Magnitude of the displacement $\vec{d}$

Kinetic energy and the work-energy theorem: The work-energy theorem states that the net work done in a displacement—the sum of the work done on the object by individual forces—is equal to the change in the object's kinetic energy, or energy of motion, during that displacement. This theorem is valid whether the path is curved or straight and whether the forces are constant or varying.

Work done on an object by the net force on that object

$$W_{net} = K_f - K_i \tag{6-9}$$

Kinetic energy of the object after the work is done on it

Kinetic energy of the object before the work is done on it

Kinetic energy of an object   Mass of the object

$$K = \frac{1}{2}mv^2 \tag{6-8}$$

Speed of the object

The spring force and Hooke's law: An ideal spring exerts a force that is proportional to how far it is stretched or compressed, and it is always opposite to the stretch or compression. The spring force is not constant, so the work needed to stretch or compress a spring is not simply the force magnitude multiplied by the displacement.

Force exerted by an ideal spring   Spring constant of the spring (a measure of its stiffness)

$$F_x = -kx \tag{6-11}$$

Extension of the spring ($x > 0$ if spring is stretched, $x < 0$ if spring is compressed)

Work that must be done on a spring to stretch it from $x = x_1$ to $x = x_2$

Spring constant of the spring (a measure of its stiffness)

$$W = \frac{1}{2}kx_2^2 - \frac{1}{2}kx_1^2 \tag{6-13}$$

x_1 = initial stretch of the spring
x_2 = final stretch of the spring

Potential energy: Unlike kinetic energy, potential energy is associated with the position of an object. Gravitational potential energy increases with height. The potential energy of a spring increases with the stretch or compression of the spring. Only conservative forces, for which the work done does not depend on the path taken, are associated with a potential energy.

Gravitational potential energy associated with an object   Mass of the object

$$U_{\text{grav}} = mgy \qquad (6\text{-}14)$$

Acceleration due to gravity   Height of the object

Spring potential energy of a stretched or compressed spring   Spring constant of the spring

$$U_{\text{spring}} = \frac{1}{2}\,kx^2 \qquad (6\text{-}19)$$

Extension of the spring ($x > 0$ if spring is stretched, $x < 0$ if spring is compressed)

Total mechanical energy and its conservation: If only conservative forces do work on an object, the total mechanical energy is conserved. (Other forces can act on the object, but they cannot do any work.) The kinetic and potential energies can change, but their sum remains constant.

Values of the **kinetic energy** K of an object at two points (i and f) during its motion

$$K_{\text{i}} + U_{\text{i}} = K_{\text{f}} + U_{\text{f}} \qquad (6\text{-}23)$$

Values of the **potential energy** U at the same two points

 If only conservative forces do work on an object, the sum $K + U$ maintains the same value throughout the motion. This sum is called the **total mechanical energy** E.

Change in the **kinetic energy** K of an object during its motion   Change in the **potential energy** U associated with an object during its motion

$$\Delta K + \Delta U = 0 \qquad (6\text{-}24)$$

 If only conservative forces do work on the object, the sum is zero: Total mechanical energy can transform between kinetic and potential forms, but there is no net change in the amount of total mechanical energy.

Generalized law of conservation of energy: If nonconservative forces do work, total mechanical energy is not conserved. If we broaden our definition of energy to include the internal energy of the interacting objects, then total energy is conserved in *all* cases.

Values of the **kinetic energy** K of an object at two points (i and f) during its motion

$$K_{\text{i}} + U_{\text{i}} + W_{\text{nonconservative}} = K_{\text{f}} + U_{\text{f}} \qquad (6\text{-}26)$$

Values of the **potential energy** U at the same two points

 If nonconservative forces do work on an object, the total mechanical energy $E = K + U$ changes its value.
If $W_{\text{nonconservative}} > 0$, $E_{\text{f}} > E_{\text{i}}$ and the total mechanical energy increases.
If $W_{\text{nonconservative}} < 0$, $E_{\text{f}} < E_{\text{i}}$ and the total mechanical energy decreases.

Change in the **kinetic energy** K of an object during its motion

Change in the **potential energy** U associated with an object during its motion

$$\Delta K + \Delta U + \Delta E_{other} = 0 \qquad (6\text{-}28)$$

Change in the **internal energy** E_{other} during the object's motion

Energy can transform between kinetic, potential, and internal forms, but there is no net change in the amount of energy.

Answer to What do you think? Question

(c) The tendons in a kangaroo's legs and tail act like springs. When a bounding kangaroo lands on its feet, these tendons stretch and convert kinetic energy into elastic potential energy. When the kangaroo bounds back into the air, the tendons relax and the stored elastic energy is turned back into kinetic energy. Were it not for this form of energy storage, the kangaroo's leg muscles would have to push much harder on each bound to maintain the animal's motion.

Answers to Got the Concept? Questions

6-1   (a) negative, (b) positive, (c) zero, (d) positive. In (a) you exert a force opposite to the ball's displacement to slow it down, so the work you do on the ball is negative. In (b) the force you exert on the ball as you throw it is in the same direction as the ball's displacement, so you do positive work on the ball. In (c) you exert an upward force on the ball to keep it from falling, but there is no forward or backward force on the ball. Its displacement is forward, so the force you exert is perpendicular to the ball's displacement and no work is done. In (d) you must push the ball forward (in the direction of its displacement) to make the ball speed up, so you do positive work on the ball.

6-2   (d) The work-energy theorem equates the work done on an object to the change in its kinetic energy. The work done is proportional to the distance over which the force is applied, so this distance is directly proportional to the change in kinetic energy. When an object starts from rest, the change in kinetic energy (from Equation 6-9) equals the final kinetic energy, which is proportional to the square of the final speed. So the distance is proportional to the square of the final speed, and doubling the speed therefore requires that the force be applied over $2^2 = 4$ times the distance.

6-3   (a) (i), (b) (iii) The floor exerts a greater normal force n on the heavy box, so the kinetic friction force $f_k = \mu_k n$ is greater for the heavy box. Hence you must push harder on the heavy box to balance the greater kinetic friction force. You therefore do more work on the heavy box than on the light box, because you exert a greater force over the same distance. The work-energy theorem tells us that that *net* work done on *both* boxes is the same and equal to zero. That's because both boxes have initial kinetic energy $K_i = 0$ (they start at rest) and final kinetic energy $K_f = 0$ (they end at rest), so $W_{net} = K_f - K_i = 0 - 0 = 0$. You do positive work on each box, but the floor does an equal amount of negative work through the kinetic friction force.

6-4   (a) From Example 6-10, the work that the athlete must do to stretch the cords by a distance x_2 from their relaxed state ($x_1 = 0$) is $W_{athlete\ on\ cords} = \frac{1}{2}kx_2^2 - \frac{1}{2}kx_1^2 = \frac{1}{2}kx_2^2 - 0 = \frac{1}{2}kx_2^2$. This says that the work done is proportional to the square of the stretch. Equivalently, this says that the stretch is proportional to the square root of the work done. So to increase the work done by a factor of 2, the stretch must increase by a factor of $\sqrt{2}$.

6-5   (d) Equation 6-16 tells us that the change in gravitational potential energy as the ball moves from height y_i (the top of the building) to height y_f (the height of the balcony) is $\Delta U_{grav} = U_f - U_i = mgy_f - mgy_i = mg(y_f - y_i)$. The difference $y_f - y_i$ is 36 m − 45 m = −9 m; that is, the balcony is 9 m below the top of the building. This distance doesn't depend at all on where you choose $y = 0$! (If $y = 0$ is at the balcony, $y_i = 9$ m and $y_f = 0$, so $y_f - y_i = 0 - 9$ m = −9 m; if $y = 0$ is at the top of the building, $y_i = 0$ and $y_f = -9$ m, and $y_f - y_i = -9$ m − 0 = −9 m.) As far as *changes* in gravitational potential energy are concerned, you can choose the level $y = 0$ to be wherever you like.

6-6   (b) There is no friction, and the normal force does no work on the block (it always acts perpendicular to the path of the block). Hence only the conservative gravitational force does work, and so total mechanical energy is conserved. Let point i be where the block is released and point f be where it stops momentarily on the right-hand side of the ramp. The block is not moving at either point, so $K_i = K_f = 0$. Equation 6-23 then says that $U_i = U_f$, which means that the gravitational potential energy is the same at both points. Since $U_{grav} = mgy$, this means that the block is at the same height y at both points. Hence the block reaches the same height $y = H$ on the right-hand side of the ramp as on the left-hand side.

6-7   (a) We learned in Section 6-6 that we can choose $y = 0$ to be wherever we like when calculating gravitational potential energy $U_{grav} = mgy$. However, we do not have the same freedom when calculating spring potential energy $U_{spring} = \frac{1}{2}kx^2$; we *must* choose $x = 0$ to be where the spring is relaxed (neither stretched nor compressed).

Questions and Problems

In a few problems, you are given more data than you actually need; in a few other problems, you are required to supply data from your general knowledge, outside sources, or informed estimate.

Interpret as significant all digits in numerical values that have trailing zeros and no decimal points. For all problems, use $g = 9.80 \text{ m/s}^2$ for the free-fall acceleration due to gravity.

• Basic, single-concept problem

•• Intermediate-level problem, may require synthesis of concepts and multiple steps

••• Challenging problem

SSM *Solution is in Student Solutions Manual*

Conceptual Questions

1. •Using Equation 6-2, explain how the work done on an object by a force can be equal to zero.

2. •The energy that is provided by your electric company is *not* sold by the joule. Instead, you are charged by the kilowatt-hour (typically 1 kWh ≅ $0.25 including taxes). Explain why this makes sense for the average consumer. It might be helpful to read the electrical specifications of an appliance (such as a hair dryer or a blender).

3. •Why do seasoned hikers step *over* logs that have fallen in their path rather than stepping *onto* them? SSM

4. •A common classroom demonstration involves holding a bowling ball attached by a rope to the ceiling close to your face and releasing it from rest. In theory, you should not have to worry about being hit by the ball as it returns to its starting point. However, some of the most "exciting" demonstrations *have* involved the professor being hit by the ball! (a) Why should you expect not to be hit by the ball? (b) Why *might* you be hit if you actually perform the demonstration?

5. •One of your classmates in physics reasons, "If there is no displacement, then a force will perform no work." Suppose the student pushes with all of her might against a massive boulder, but the boulder doesn't move. (a) Does she expend energy pushing against the boulder? (b) Does she do work on the boulder? Explain your answer.

6. •Your roommate lifts a cement block, carries it across the room, and sets it back down on the floor. Is the net work she did on the block positive, negative, or zero? Explain your answer.

7. •Can the normal force ever do work on an object? Explain your answer. SSM

8. •Can kinetic energy ever have a negative value? Explain your answer.

9. •Can a change in kinetic energy ever have a negative value? Explain your answer.

10. •Define the concept of "nonconservative force" in your own words. Give three examples.

11. •Analyze the types of energy that are associated with the "circuit" that a snowboarder follows from the bottom of a mountain, to its peak, and back down again. Be sure to explain all changes in energy. SSM

12. •Why are the ramps for disabled people quite long instead of short and steep?

13. •A satellite orbits around Earth in a circular path at a high altitude. Explain why the gravitational force does zero work on the satellite.

14. •Model rockets are propelled by an engine containing a combustible solid material. Two rockets, one twice as heavy as the other, are launched using engines that contain the same amount of propellant. (a) Is the maximum kinetic energy of the heavier rocket less than, equal to, or more than the maximum kinetic energy of the lighter one? (b) Is the launch speed of the heavier rocket less than, equal to, or more than the launch speed of the lighter one?

15. •When does the kinetic energy of a rock that is dropped from the edge of a high cliff reach its maximum value? Answer the question (a) when the air resistance is negligible and (b) when there is significant air resistance. SSM

16. •Can gravitational potential energy have a negative value? Explain your answer.

17. •Bicycling to the top of a hill is much harder than coasting back down to the bottom. Do you have more gravitational potential energy at the top of the hill or at the bottom? Explain your answer.

18. •A rubber dart can be launched over and over again by the spring in a toy gun. Where is the energy generated to launch the dart?

Multiple-Choice Questions

19. •Box 2 is pulled up a rough incline by box 1 in an arrangement as shown in Figure 6-33. How many forces are doing work on box 2?

A. 1
B. 2
C. 3
D. 4
E. 5

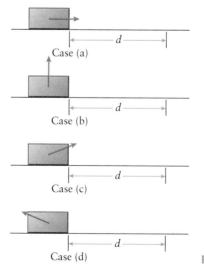

Figure 6-33
Problem 19

20. •Figure 6-34 shows four situations in which a box slides to the right a distance d across a frictionless floor as a result of applied forces, *one* of which is shown. The magnitudes of the forces shown are identical. Rank the four cases in order of increasing work done on the box by the force shown during the displacement.

Case (a)

Case (b)

Case (c)

Case (d)

Figure 6-34 Problem 20

21. •A box is dragged a distance d across a floor by a force $\vec{F}$ which makes an angle θ with the horizontal (Figure 6-35). If the magnitude of the force is held constant but the angle θ is increased up to 90°, the work done by the force in dragging the box
    A. remains the same.
    B. increases.
    C. decreases.
    D. first increases, then decreases.
    E. first decreases, then increases. SSM

Figure 6-35 Problem 21

22. •A car moves along a level road. If the car's velocity changes from 60 mph due east to 60 mph due west, the kinetic energy of the car
    A. remains the same.
    B. increases.
    C. decreases.
    D. first increases, then decreases.
    E. first decreases, then increases.

23. •A boy swings a ball on a string at constant speed in a horizontal circle that has a circumference equal to 6 m. What is the work done on the ball by the 10-N tension force in the string during one revolution of the ball?
    A. 190 J   D. 15 J
    B. 60 J   E. 0
    C. 30 J

24. •A spring that has a spring constant k is cut in half. What is the spring constant for each of the two resulting springs?
    A. 0.5k D. 2k
    B. k E. 2.5k
    C. 1.5k

25. •Adam and Bobby are twins who have the same weight. Adam drops to the ground from a tree at the same time that Bobby begins his descent down a frictionless slide. If they both start at the same height above the ground, how do their kinetic energies compare when they hit the ground?
    A. Adam has greater kinetic energy than Bobby.
    B. Bobby has greater kinetic energy than Adam.
    C. They have the same kinetic energy.
    D. Bobby has twice the kinetic energy as Adam.
    E. More information is required to compare their kinetic energies. SSM

26. •Three balls are thrown off a tall building with the same speed but in different directions. Ball A is thrown in the horizontal direction; ball B starts out at 45° above the horizontal; ball C begins its flight at 45° below the horizontal. Which ball has the greatest speed just before it hits the ground? Ignore any effects due to air resistance.
    A. Ball A
    B. Ball B
    C. Ball C
    D. All balls have the same speed.
    E. Balls B and C have the same speed, which is greater than the speed of ball A.

Estimation/Numerical Analysis

27. •About how many joules are required to lift a suitcase into the trunk of a car?

28. •If you always drive around with a 50-lb toolbox in your truck, about how much extra gas will you use over the life of your vehicle?

29. •How many joules of energy are required for an average adult to run a 5-K (5000 m) race? SSM

30. •(a) What is the kinetic energy of a commercial jet airplane when it "touches down" on a runway to land? (b) Where does the energy "go" when the plane stops?

31. •Estimate the kinetic energy of a cue ball during a typical billiards shot.

32. •Estimate the work done in carrying your backpack up one flight of stairs.

33. •Estimate the maximum kinetic energy of a puma, one of the best leapers of the animal kingdom. SSM

34. •Thor works as an express elevator attendant in the famed Empire State Building in New York City. If the potential energy that Thor gains during each ascent throughout his career were added and converted into kinetic energy, what would his speed be?

35. •The data below represent a changing force that acts on an object in the x direction (the force is parallel to the displacement). Graph F versus x using a graphing calculator or a spreadsheet. Calculate the work done by the force (a) in the first 0.100 m, (b) in the first 0.200 m, (c) from 0.100 m to 0.200 m, and (d) for the entire motion (for $0 < x < 0.250$ m).

x (m)	F (N)	x (m)	F (N)	x (m)	F (N)
0	0.00	0.0900	12.00	0.180	12.50
0.0100	2.00	0.100	12.48	0.190	12.50
0.0200	4.00	0.110	12.48	0.200	12.50
0.0300	6.00	0.120	12.48	0.210	12.48
0.0400	8.00	0.130	12.60	0.220	9.36
0.0500	10.00	0.140	12.60	0.230	6.24
0.0600	10.50	0.150	12.70	0.240	3.12
0.0700	11.00	0.160	12.70	0.250	0.00
0.0800	11.50	0.170	12.60		

Problems

6-2 The work that a constant force does on a moving object depends on the magnitude and direction of the force

36. •A crane slowly lifts a 200-kg crate a vertical distance of 15.0 m. How much work does the crane do on the crate? How much work does gravity do on the crate?

37. •**Sports** In the men's weight-lifting competition of the 2008 Beijing Olympics, Matthias Steiner made his record lift of 446 kg from the floor to over his head (2.0 m). How much work did Steiner do during the lift? SSM

38. • A 350-kg box is pulled 7.00 m up a 30.0° inclined plane by an external force of 5000 N that acts parallel to the frictionless plane. Calculate the work done by (a) the external force, (b) gravity, and (c) the normal force.

39. •Three clowns are trying to move a 300-kg crate 12.0 m across a smooth (frictionless) floor. Moe pushes to the right with a force of 500 N, Larry pushes to the left with 300 N, and Curly pushes straight down with 600 N. Calculate the work done by each of the clowns.

40. •An assistant for the football team carries a 30.0-kg cooler of water from the top row of the stadium, which is 20.0 m above the field level, down to the bench area on the field. (a) If the speed of the cooler is constant throughout the trip, calculate the work done by the assistant. (b) How much work is done by the force of gravity on the cooler of water?

41. ••The statue of Isaac Newton is crated and moved from the Oxford Museum of Natural History and Science for cleaning. The mass of the statue and the crate is 150 kg. As the statue slides down a ramp inclined at 40.0°, the curator pushes up, parallel to the ramp's surface, so that the crate does not acceler-ate (Figure 6-36). If the statue slides 3 m down
the ramp, and the coefficient of kinetic friction between the crate and the ramp is 0.54, calculate the work done on the crate by each of the following: (a) the gravitational force, (b) the curator, (c) the friction force, and (d) the normal force between the ramp and the crate. SSM

Figure 6-36 Problem 41

6-3 Kinetic energy and the work-energy theorem give us an alternative way to express Newton's second law

42. •A 1250-kg car moves at 20.0 m/s. How much work is required from the engine to increase the car's speed to 30.0 m/s?

43. •A bumblebee has a mass of about 0.25 g. If its speed is 10 m/s, calculate its kinetic energy. SSM

44. •A small truck has a mass of 2100 kg. How much work is required to decrease the speed of the vehicle from 22.0 m/s to 12.0 m/s on a level road?

45. ••Calculate the final speed of the 2.00-kg object that is pushed for 22.0 m by the 40.0-N force on a level, frictionless floor (Figure 6-37). Assume the object starts from rest. SSM

Figure 6-37 Problem 45

46. •A 10.0-kg block rests on a level floor; the coefficient of kinetic friction between the block and the floor is 0.440. A force of 200 N acts for 4 m. How fast is the block moving after being pushed 4 m? Assume it starts from rest.

6-4 The work-energy theorem can simplify many physics problems

47. •A force of 1200 N pushes a man on a bicycle forward. Air resistance pushes against him with a force of 800 N. If he starts from rest and is on a level road, how fast will he be moving after 20.0 m? The mass of the bicyclist and his bicycle is 90.0 kg.

48. •Sports A 0.145-kg baseball rebounds off of a wall. The re-bound speed is one-third of the original speed. By what percent does the kinetic energy of the baseball change in the collision with the wall? Where does the energy go?

49. •A book slides across a level, carpeted floor at an initial speed of 4.00 m/s and comes to rest after 3.25 m. Calculate the coefficient of kinetic friction between the book and the carpet. Assume the only forces acting on the book are friction, weight, and the normal force.

50. •A 325-g model boat floats on a pond. The wind on its sail provides a force of 1.85 N that points 25.0° north of east. The drag force of the water on the boat is 0.750 N, toward the west. If the boat starts from rest and heads east for a distance of 3.55 m, how fast is it moving?

51. •Sports A catcher in a baseball game stops a pitched ball that was originally moving at 44.0 m/s over a distance of 12.5 cm. The mass of the ball is 0.145 kg. What is the average force that the glove imparts to the ball during the catch? Com-ment on the force that the catcher's hand experiences during the catch. SSM

6-5 The work-energy theorem is also valid for curved paths and varying forces

52. •Calculate the work done from $x = 0$ to $x = 10$ m by the one-dimensional force depicted in the following graph (Figure 6-38).

Figure 6-38 Problem 52

53. •An object attached to the free end of a horizontal spring of constant 450 N/m is pulled from a position 12 cm beyond equilibrium to a position 18 cm beyond equilibrium. Calculate the work the spring does on the object. SSM

54. •A 5.00-kg object is attached to one end of a horizon-tal spring that has a negligible mass and a spring constant of 250 N/m. The other end of the spring is fixed to a wall. The spring is compressed by 10.0 cm from its equilibrium position and released from rest. (a) What is the speed of the object when it is 8.00 cm from equilibrium? (b) What is the speed when the object is 5.00 cm from equilibrium? (c) What is the speed when the object is at the equilibrium position?

6-6 Potential energy is energy related to an object's position

55. •What is the gravitational potential energy relative to the ground associated with a 1.00-N Gravenstein apple that is hanging from a limb 2.50 m above the ground?

56. •Pilings are driven into the ground at a building site by dropping a 2000-kg object onto them. What change in gravitational potential energy does the object undergo if it is released from rest 18.0 m above the ground and ends up 2.00 m above the ground?

57. •A 40.0-kg boy steps on a skateboard and pushes off from the top of a hill. What change in gravitational potential energy takes place as the boy glides down to the bottom of the hill, 4.35 m below the starting level? SSM

58. •How much additional potential energy is stored in a spring that has a spring constant of 15.5 N/m if the spring starts 10.0 cm from the equilibrium position and ends up 15.0 cm from the equilibrium position?

59. •A spring that has a spring constant of 200 N/m is oriented vertically with one end on the ground. (a) What distance does the spring compress when a 2.00-kg object is placed on its upper end? (b) By how much does the potential energy of the spring increase during the compression?

60. •An external force moves a 3.50-kg box at a constant speed up a frictionless ramp. The force acts in a direction parallel to the ramp. (a) Calculate the work done on the box by this force as it is pushed up the 5.00-m ramp to a height of 3.00 m. (b) Compare the value with the change in gravitational potential energy that the box undergoes as it rises to its final height.

61. •Over 630 m in height, the Burj Dubai is the world's tallest skyscraper. What is the change in gravitational potential energy of a $20 gold coin (33.5 g) when it is carried from ground level up to the top of the Burj Dubai? Neglect any slight variations in the acceleration due to gravity. SSM

62. •For a great view and a thrill, check out EdgeWalk at the CN Tower in Toronto, where you can walk on the roof of the tower's main pod, 356 m above the ground. What is the gravitational potential energy relative to the surface of Earth of a 65.0-kg sightseer on EdgeWalk? Neglect any slight variations in the acceleration due to gravity.

63. •A spring that is compressed 12.5 cm from its equilibrium position stores 3.33 J of potential energy. Determine the spring constant.

6-7 If only conservative forces do work, total mechanical energy is conserved

64. •A ball is thrown straight up at 15.0 m/s. At what height will the ball have one-half of its initial speed?

65. •A water balloon is thrown straight down at 12.0 m/s from a second floor window, 5.00 m above ground level. How fast is the balloon moving when it hits the ground? SSM

66. •A gold coin (33.5 g) is dropped from the top of the Burj Dubai building, 630 m above ground level. In the absence of air resistance, how fast would it be moving when it hit the ground?

67. •A 30.0-kg child rides a 9.00-kg sled down a frictionless ski slope. At the bottom of the hill, her speed is 7.00 m/s. If the slope makes an angle of 15.0° with the horizontal, how far did she slide on the sled?

68. •**Sports** During a long jump, four-time Olympic champion Carl Lewis's center of mass rose about 1.2 m from the launch point to the top of the arc. What minimum speed did he need at launch if he was traveling at 6.6 m/s at the top of the arc?

69. •A pendulum is constructed by attaching a small metal ball to one end of a 1.25-m-long string that hangs from the ceiling (Figure 6-39). The ball is released when it is raised high enough for the string to make an angle of 30.0° with the vertical. How fast is it moving at the bottom of its swing? Does the mass of the ball affect the answer? SSM

Figure 6-39 Problem 69

70. •An ice cube slides without friction down a track as shown in Figure 6-40. Calculate the speed of the cube at points B, C, D, and E. The ice cube starts at rest at point A.

Figure 6-40 Problem 70

71. •A driver loses control of her car when she slams on the brakes, leaving 88.0-m-long skid marks on the level road. The coefficient of kinetic friction is estimated to be 0.480. How fast was the car moving when the driver hit the brakes?

72. ••A 65.0-kg woman steps off a 10.0-m diving platform and drops straight down into the water. If she reaches a depth of 4.50 m, what is the average resistance force exerted on her by the water? Ignore any effects due to air resistance.

73. •A skier leaves the starting gate at the top of a ski jump with an initial speed of 4.00 m/s (Figure 6-41). The starting position is 120 m higher than the end of the ramp, which is 3.00 m above the snow. Find the final speed of the skier if he lands 145 m down the 20.0° slope. Assume there is no friction on the ramp, but air resistance causes a 50% loss in the final kinetic energy. The GPS reading of the elevation of the skier is 4212 m at the top of the jump and 4039 m at the landing point. SSM

Figure 6-41 Problem 73

6-8 Energy conservation is an important tool for solving a wide variety of problems

74. •An 18.0-kg suitcase falls from a hot-air balloon that is floating at a height of 385 m above the surface of Earth. The suitcase has an initial speed of 0 m/s, but it reaches a speed of

30.0 m/s just before it hits the ground. Calculate the percentage of the initial energy that is "lost" to air resistance.

75. •A bicyclist maintains a constant speed of 4.00 m/s up a hill that is inclined at 10.0° with the horizontal. Calculate the work done by the person and the work done by gravity if the bicycle moves a distance of 20.0 m up the hill. The combined mass of the rider and the bike is 90.0 kg.

76. •A child slides down a snow-covered slope on a sled. At the top of the hill, her mother gives her a push to start her off with a speed of 1.00 m/s. The frictional force acting on the sled is one-fifth of the combined weight of the child and the sled. If she travels for a distance of 25.0 m and her speed at the bottom is 4.00 m/s, calculate the angle that the hill makes with the horizontal.

77. ••The coefficient of restitution, e, of a ball hitting the floor is defined as the ratio of the speed of the ball right after it rebounds from the impact to the speed of the ball right before it hits the floor; that is, $e = v_{after}/v_{before}$. (a) Derive a formula for the coefficient of restitution when a ball is released from an initial height H and rebounds to a final height h. (b) Calculate the coefficient of restitution for a golf ball that bounces to a height of 60 cm after having been released from a height of 80 cm. SSM

General Problems

78. •You push a 20.0-kg crate at constant velocity up a ramp inclined at an angle of 33.0° to the horizontal. The coefficient of kinetic friction between the ramp and the crate, μ_k is equal to 0.200. How much work must you do to push the crate a distance of 2.00 m?

79. ••A 12.0-kg block (M) is released from rest on a frictionless incline that makes an angle of 28.0°, as shown in Figure 6-42. Below the block is a spring that has a spring constant of 13500 N/m. The block momentarily stops when it compresses the spring by 5.50 cm. How far does the block move down the incline from its rest position to the stopping point? SSM

Figure 6-42 Problem 79

80. •**Sports** A man on his luge (total mass of 88.0 kg) emerges onto the horizontal straight track at the bottom of the hill with a speed of 28.0 m/s. If the luge and rider slow at a constant rate of 2.80 m/s², what is the total work done on them by the force that slows them to a stop?

81. •**Biology** An adult dolphin is about 5.00 m long and weighs about 1600 N. How fast must he be moving as he leaves the water in order to jump to a height of 2.50 m? Ignore any effects due to air resistance.

82. •A 3.00-kg block is placed at the top of a track consisting of two frictionless quarter circles of radius R equal to 2.00 m connected by a 7.00-m-long, straight, horizontal surface (Figure 6-43). The coefficient of kinetic friction between the block and the horizontal surface is μ_k equal to 0.100. The block is released from rest. Find an expression that describes where the

block stops, as measured from the left end of the horizontal surface, marked $x = 0$ on the figure.

Figure 6-43 Problem 82

83. •An object is released from rest on a frictionless ramp of angle θ_1 equal to 60.0°, at a (vertical) height H_1 equal to 12.0 m above the base of the ramp (Figure 6-44). The bottom end of the ramp *merges smoothly* with a second frictionless ramp that rises at angle θ_2 equal to 37.0°. (a) How far up the second ramp, as measured along the ramp, does the object slide before coming to a momentary stop? (b) When the object is on its way back down the second ramp, what is its speed at the moment that it is a (vertical) height H_2 equal to 7.00 m above the base of the ramp? SSM

Figure 6-44 Problem 83

84. •**Biology** An average froghopper insect has a mass of 12.3 mg and reaches a maximum height of 290 mm when its takeoff angle is 58.0° above the horizontal. What is the takeoff speed of the froghopper?

85. •A 20.0-g object is placed against the free end of a spring (k equal to 25.0 N/m) that is compressed 10.0 cm (Figure 6-45). Once released, the object slides 1.25 m across the tabletop and eventually lands 1.60 m from the edge of the table on the floor, as shown. Is there friction between the object and the tabletop? If there is, what is the coefficient of kinetic friction? The sliding distance on the tabletop includes the 10.0-cm compression of the spring, and the tabletop is 1.00 m above the floor level.

Figure 6-45 Problem 85

86. ••A 1.00-kg object is attached by a thread of negligible mass, which passes over a pulley of negligible mass, to a 2.00-kg object. The objects are positioned so that they are the same height from the floor and then released from rest. What are the speeds of the objects when they are separated vertically by 1.00 m?

87. •You may have noticed runaway truck lanes while driving in the mountains. These gravel-filled lanes are designed to stop trucks that have lost their brakes on mountain grades. Typically such a lane is horizontal (if possible) and about 35.0 m long.

We can think of the ground as exerting a frictional drag force on the truck. If the truck enters the gravel lane with a speed of 55.0 mph (24.6 m/s), use the work-energy theorem to find the minimum coefficient of kinetic friction between the truck and the lane to be able to stop the truck.

88. •In 2006, the United States produced 282×10^9 kilowatt-hours (kWh) of electrical energy from 4138 hydroelectric plants (1.00 kWh $= 3.60 \times 10^6$ J). On average, each plant is 90% efficient at converting mechanical energy to electrical energy, and the average dam height is 50.0 m. (a) At 282×10^9 kWh of electrical energy produced in one year, what is the average power output per hydroelectric plant? (b) What total mass of water flowed over the dams during 2006? (c) What was the average mass of water per dam and the average volume of water per dam that provided the mechanical energy to generate the electricity? (The density of water is 1000 kg/m^3.) (d) A gallon of gasoline contains 45.0×10^6 J of energy. How many gallons of gasoline did the 4138 dams save?

89. •**Astronomy** In 2006, NASA's Mars Odyssey orbiter detected violent gas eruptions on Mars, where the acceleration due to gravity is 3.7 m/s^2. The jets throw sand and dust about 75.0 m above the surface. (a) What is the speed of the material just as it leaves the surface? (b) Scientists estimate that the jets originate as high-pressure gas speeds through vents just underground at about 160 km/h. How much energy per kilogram of material is lost due to nonconservative forces as the high-speed matter forces its way to the surface and into the air?

90. •A 3.00-kg block is sent up a ramp of angle θ equal to 37.0° with an initial velocity v_0 equal to 20.0 m/s. Between the block and the ramp, the coefficient of kinetic friction is μ_k equal to 0.50 and the coefficient of static friction is μ_s equal to 0.80. How far up the ramp (in the direction along the ramp) does the block go before it comes to a stop?

91. •A small block of mass M is placed halfway up on the inside of a frictionless, circular loop of radius R (Figure 6-46). The size of the block is very small compared to the radius of the loop. Determine an expression for the minimum downward speed with which the block must be released in order to guarantee that it will make a full circle.

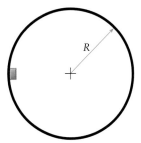

Figure 6-46 Problem 91

92. ••An object that weighs 25.0 N is placed on a horizontal, frictionless table in front of a spring that has a constant k (Figure 6-47). When the spring is compressed and released, the object shoots off the table and is caught on the end of a 3.00-m-long massless string. The object then moves in a circular path. The string doesn't break unless the spring is compressed more than 1.00 m. The maximum tension the string can sustain is 200 N. What is the value of the spring constant? (Ignore the fact that it would be odd for a string to be standing straight up as shown.)

Spring

Figure 6-47 Problem 92

7

Momentum, Collisions, and the Center of Mass

What do you think?

Cooper's hawk (*Accipiter cooperi*) is a species of raptor that hunts and captures other birds in flight. Suppose a fast-moving Cooper's hawk attacks a slow-moving pigeon from behind and captures the pigeon in its talons. Compared to the total kinetic energy of the two separate birds immediately before the capture, the kinetic energy of the system of two birds moving together immediately after the capture is (a) greater; (b) the same; (c) less.

In this chapter, your goals are to:
- (7-1) Comprehend the significance of momentum and the center of mass.
- (7-2) Define the linear momentum of an object and explain how it differs from kinetic energy.
- (7-3) Explain the conditions under which the total momentum of a system is conserved, and why total momentum is conserved in a collision.
- (7-4) Identify the differences and similarities between elastic, inelastic, and completely inelastic collisions.
- (7-5) Apply momentum conservation and energy conservation to problems about elastic collisions.
- (7-6) Relate the momentum change of an object, the force that causes the change, and the time over which the force acts.
- (7-7) Explain the physical significance of the center of mass, and describe how the net force on a system affects the motion of the system's center of mass.

To master this chapter, you should review:
- (3-2)   Multiplying a vector by a scalar.
- (3-5)   The definitions of the velocity and acceleration vectors.
- (4-2, 4-5) Newton's second and third laws of motion.
- (6-2, 6-3) The ideas of work, kinetic energy, and the work-energy theorem.

7-1 Newton's third law helps lead us to the idea of momentum

The ideas of kinetic energy and the work-energy theorem that we introduced in Chapter 6 gave us new ways to think about motion. These ideas derive fundamentally from Newton's second law, which states that the net external force on an object determines the object's acceleration. In this chapter we'll learn even more new physics by reconsidering Newton's *third* law. As we learned in Chapter 4, this law states that when two objects interact with each other, they exert forces of equal magnitude but opposite direction on each other. An important way to express this concept is in terms of the *momentum* of an object (written as $\vec{p}$), which is the product of an object's mass and its velocity. Since velocity is a vector, momentum is as well. We'll see that we can describe the behavior of two interacting objects, such as a baseball bat and a ball (Figure 7-1a) or a squid and the water it ejects to propel itself (Figure 7-1b), in terms of momentum: Each object in the pair undergoes a change in velocity and hence in momentum, and the

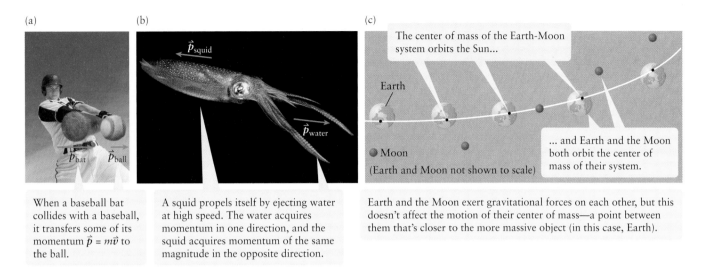

(a)

$\vec{p}_{bat}$ $\vec{p}_{ball}$

When a baseball bat collides with a baseball, it transfers some of its momentum $\vec{p} = m\vec{v}$ to the ball.

(b)

$\vec{p}_{squid}$

$\vec{p}_{water}$

A squid propels itself by ejecting water at high speed. The water acquires momentum in one direction, and the squid acquires momentum of the same magnitude in the opposite direction.

(c)

The center of mass of the Earth-Moon system orbits the Sun...

Earth

Moon

(Earth and Moon not shown to scale)

... and Earth and the Moon both orbit the center of mass of their system.

Earth and the Moon exert gravitational forces on each other, but this doesn't affect the motion of their center of mass—a point between them that's closer to the more massive object (in this case, Earth).

Figure 7-1 **Momentum and center of mass** In this chapter we'll begin by exploring (a) momentum, (b) conservation of momentum and (c) the center of mass of a system.

momentum changes are equal in magnitude but opposite in direction. This important observation will lead us to a physical principle called the *law of conservation of momentum*. This law will turn out to be an essential tool for analyzing what happens when two objects interact with each other.

Intimately related to the idea of momentum is the notion of *center of mass*. This is a point associated with an object or system of objects that behaves as though all of the mass of the system is concentrated at that point. For example, the center of mass of the Earth–Moon system is located along the line connecting the centers of these two objects; Earth and Moon orbit around this center of mass, which in turn orbits around the Sun as though the entire mass of the Earth–Moon system were concentrated there (Figure 7-1c). We'll develop these ideas about the center of mass by expanding on what we'll have learned about momentum.

We'll begin our exploration of the momentum concept by considering a simple system: a person standing on a skateboard who decides to jump off.

Take-Home Message for Section 7-1

✔ The idea of momentum is useful in situations where two or more objects interact with each other.

7-2 Momentum is a vector that depends on an object's mass, speed, and direction of motion

You're standing atop a stationary skateboard (Figure 7-2a). You then jump straight to the left off the back of the skateboard, and the skateboard rolls away to the right (Figure 7-2b). If you try this, you'll find that the skateboard rolls to the right much

(a)

(b)

When you jump off a skateboard, its speed is much greater than yours.

$\vec{v}_{you}$

$\vec{v}_{skateboard}$

The only horizontal forces on you and the skateboard are the forces you exert on each other.

(c)

The vertical forces on you cancel...

$\vec{w}_{Earth\ on\ you}$ $\vec{n}_{skateboard\ on\ you}$

$\vec{F}_{skateboard\ on\ you}$

...and the vertical forces on the skateboard cancel.

$\vec{n}_{ground\ on\ skateboard}$

$\vec{F}_{you\ on\ skateboard}$

$\vec{w}_{Earth\ on\ skateboard}$

$\vec{n}_{you\ on\ skateboard}$

Figure 7-2 **Jumping off a skateboard** You are (a) initially at rest atop a skateboard, then (b) jump off horizontally. (c) Free-body diagrams for you and the skateboard during the push-off.

faster than you fly through the air to the left. Why is this? What determines how much faster the skateboard moves than you do?

Like any question about motion, the best way to answer this question is by using Newton's laws. Figure 7-2c shows the free-body diagrams for you and your skateboard while you're pushing off the skateboard. The vertical forces on the skateboard cancel, as do the vertical forces on you, so the net force on the skateboard and the net force on you are both horizontal. (It's true that after your foot loses contact with the skateboard deck, only the gravitational force acts on you and so the net force is downward. But for now we're just interested in the forces that act while you're pushing off from the skateboard.) There is negligible friction between the ground and the wheels of the skateboard, so the only horizontal forces that act are the forces that you and the skateboard exert on each other. If we apply Newton's second law to the skateboard and to you, we get the equations

(7-1)
$$\sum \vec{F}_{\text{ext on skateboard}} = \vec{F}_{\text{you on skateboard}} = m_{\text{skateboard}}\vec{a}_{\text{skateboard}}$$
$$\sum \vec{F}_{\text{ext on you}} = \vec{F}_{\text{skateboard on you}} = m_{\text{you}}\vec{a}_{\text{you}}$$

The vectors $\vec{a}_{\text{skateboard}}$ and $\vec{a}_{\text{you}}$ are the accelerations of the skateboard and you, respectively, during the push-off.

Equations 7-1 involve the *accelerations* of the skateboard and you, but we're interested in the *velocities* of the skateboard and you after the push-off. To see how to get these, let's go back to the definition of the acceleration vector in Section 3-5. This definition tells us that

Acceleration vector equals change in velocity vector divided by time interval
(3-9)

Acceleration vector for the object over a very short time interval from time t_1 to a later time t_2

Change in velocity of the object over the short time interval

$$\vec{a} = \frac{\Delta\vec{v}}{\Delta t} = \frac{\vec{v}_2 - \vec{v}_1}{t_2 - t_1}$$

For both the velocity change and the elapsed time, subtract the earlier value from the later value.

Elapsed time for the time interval

In Equation 3-9 the elapsed time Δt is how long the push-off lasts. The initial velocity before the push-off is $\vec{v}_1 = 0$ for both the skateboard and you, since both begin at rest. We'll use the symbols $\vec{v}_{\text{skateboard}}$ and $\vec{v}_{\text{you}}$ for the velocities of the skateboard and you just after the push-off (corresponding to $\vec{v}_2$ in Equation 3-9). When we substitute these and Equation 3-9 into Equations 7-1, we get

$$\vec{F}_{\text{you on skateboard}} = m_{\text{skateboard}}\frac{\vec{v}_{\text{skateboard}}}{\Delta t}$$
$$\vec{F}_{\text{skateboard on you}} = m_{\text{you}}\frac{\vec{v}_{\text{you}}}{\Delta t}$$

Multiply both sides of these equations by Δt, the duration of the push-off:

(7-2)
$$\vec{F}_{\text{you on skateboard}}\Delta t = m_{\text{skateboard}}\vec{v}_{\text{skateboard}}$$
$$\vec{F}_{\text{skateboard on you}}\Delta t = m_{\text{you}}\vec{v}_{\text{you}}$$

Now remember that from Newton's third law, the force that the skateboard exerts on you has the same magnitude as the force that you exert on the skateboard, but points in the opposite direction (Figure 7-2c): $\vec{F}_{\text{skateboard on you}} = -\vec{F}_{\text{you on skateboard}}$. If we substitute this into Equations 7-2, you can see that the quantities $m_{\text{skateboard}}\vec{v}_{\text{skateboard}}$ and $m_{\text{you}}\vec{v}_{\text{you}}$ likewise have the same magnitude but point in opposite directions:

(7-3)
$$m_{\text{skateboard}}\vec{v}_{\text{skateboard}} = -m_{\text{you}}\vec{v}_{\text{you}}$$

This relationship is a direct consequence of Newton's second and third laws of motion. Here's how to interpret Equation 7-3:

- The minus sign in Equation 7-3 tells us that $\vec{v}_{\text{skateboard}}$ and $\vec{v}_{\text{you}}$ are in opposite directions. As Figure 7-2b shows, if you push the skateboard to the right, you must move to the left.

- If we take the magnitude of both sides of this equation, it gives us a relationship between the *speeds* of the skateboard and you just after the push-off:

$$m_{\text{skateboard}} v_{\text{skateboard}} = m_{\text{you}} v_{\text{you}} \quad \text{or} \quad v_{\text{skateboard}} = \left(\frac{m_{\text{you}}}{m_{\text{skateboard}}} \right) v_{\text{you}} \qquad (7\text{-}4)$$

The speed of the skateboard is equal to your speed multiplied by the ratio $m_{\text{you}}/m_{\text{skateboard}}$. You are much more massive than the skateboard, so this ratio is a large number and the skateboard moves much faster than you do.

- If you push off from the skateboard with greater force, both the skateboard and you will fly off at faster speeds. But this force doesn't appear in either Equation 7-3 or 7-4. That means the *ratio* of the skateboard's speed to yours will be the same no matter how hard you push.

Our analysis of the skateboard problem, and especially Equation 7-3, suggests that it's worthwhile to think about a quantity that's equal to the product of an object's mass m and its velocity vector $\vec{v}$. We'll call this quantity the object's **linear momentum**:

The **linear momentum** of an object is a vector.

The linear momentum points in the same direction as the **velocity vector** and is proportional to the velocity.

Linear momentum
(7-5)

$$\vec{p} = m\vec{v}$$

The linear momentum is also proportional to the object's **mass**.

We use the name *linear* momentum to distinguish this quantity from a related but fundamentally different quantity called *angular momentum* that we'll encounter when we study rotational motion in Chapter 8. For now, however, we'll call $\vec{p}$ simply the **momentum** of the object, which is how most physicists refer to it. Note that since the mass m is a positive scalar quantity, the momentum $\vec{p}$ points in the same direction as the velocity $\vec{v}$ (see Section 3-2). **Figure 7-3** compares the momentum vectors for three different objects.

Equation 7-5 shows that the units of momentum are the units of mass multiplied by the units of velocity, or $\text{kg} \cdot \text{m/s}$. This combination of units doesn't have a special name in the SI system, so we simply say that the momentum of a 1000-kg car driving at 20 m/s has magnitude $p = mv = (1000 \text{ kg})(20 \text{ m/s}) = 20{,}000 \text{ kg} \cdot \text{m/s}$, or "twenty thousand kilogram-meters per second."

We can use the definition of momentum, Equation 7-5, to rewrite Equation 7-3 for the skateboarder and you: $m_{\text{skateboard}} \vec{v}_{\text{skateboard}} = -m_{\text{you}} \vec{v}_{\text{you}}$ becomes

$$\vec{p}_{\text{skateboard}} = -\vec{p}_{\text{you}} \qquad (7\text{-}6)$$

Just after the push-off, you and the skateboard each have the same *magnitude* of momentum, but your momentum is directly opposite to the skateboard's momentum. We'll use this observation in Example 7-1.

(a)

These two objects have the same momentum $\vec{p} = m\vec{v}$: The magnitude of momentum is the same and they are both moving in the same direction.

$v = 6.0$ m/s

$p = mv = 6.0$ kg·m/s

$m = 1.0$ kg

(b)

These two objects have different momentum: The magnitude $p = mv$ is the same for both, but they move in different directions so the momentum vector $\vec{p} = m\vec{v}$ is different.

$v = 3.0$ m/s

$p = mv = 6.0$ kg·m/s

$m = 2.0$ kg

(c)

$v = 3.0$ m/s

$p = mv = 6.0$ kg·m/s

$m = 2.0$ kg

Figure 7-3 The momentum vector
Comparing the momentum vectors for three different objects.

> ## ! Watch Out! Don't confuse momentum and kinetic energy.
>
> Like momentum, the kinetic energy K of an object (introduced in Chapter 6) depends on its mass m and its speed v: $K = \frac{1}{2}mv^2$. But kinetic energy is a *scalar* quantity (it has no direction), while momentum $\vec{p} = m\vec{v}$ is a *vector* quantity. Furthermore, two objects with the same magnitude of momentum can have different kinetic energies. Example 7-1 explores this further.

Example 7-1 Momentum and Kinetic Energy

Suppose that you have a mass of 50.0 kg. Your skateboard has a mass of 2.50 kg. Just after you push off as in Figure 7-2, you are moving to the left at 0.600 m/s. (a) What is the magnitude of your momentum and the magnitude of the skateboard's momentum just after you push off? (b) What is the speed of the skateboard just after you push off? (c) What is your kinetic energy and the skateboard's kinetic energy just after you push off?

Set Up

We use the definitions of linear momentum and kinetic energy. Our discussion above and Equation 7-6 tell us how to find the speed of the skateboard from your speed.

$$\vec{p} = m\vec{v} \tag{7-5}$$

$$K = \frac{1}{2}mv^2 \tag{6-8}$$

$$\vec{p}_{\text{skateboard}} = -\vec{p}_{\text{you}} \tag{7-6}$$

Solve

(a) Equation 7-5 gives us the magnitude of your momentum. Equation 7-6 tells us that the skateboard has as much momentum to the right as you have to the left.

Your momentum vector:

$$\vec{p}_{\text{you}} = m_{\text{you}}\vec{v}_{\text{you}}$$

Magnitude of this vector:

$$\begin{aligned}
p_{\text{you}} &= m_{\text{you}}v_{\text{you}} \\
&= (50.0\text{ kg})(0.600\text{ m/s}) \\
&= 30.0\text{ kg} \cdot \text{m/s}
\end{aligned}$$

Since $\vec{p}_{\text{skateboard}} = -\vec{p}_{\text{you}}$, you and the skateboard have the same magnitude of momentum:

$$p_{\text{skateboard}} = m_{\text{skateboard}}v_{\text{skateboard}} = p_{\text{you}} = m_{\text{you}}v_{\text{you}} = 30.0\text{ kg} \cdot \text{m/s}$$

(b) We know the skateboard's mass and momentum, so we can solve for its speed.

$$p_{\text{skateboard}} = m_{\text{skateboard}}v_{\text{skateboard}}\text{ so}$$

$$\begin{aligned}
v_{\text{skateboard}} &= \frac{p_{\text{skateboard}}}{m_{\text{skateboard}}} \\
&= \frac{30.0\text{ kg} \cdot \text{m/s}}{2.50\text{ kg}} \\
&= 12.0\text{ m/s}
\end{aligned}$$

(c) Using Equation 6-8, we find the kinetic energies from the masses and speeds of the two objects.

Your kinetic energy:

$$\begin{aligned}
K_{\text{you}} &= \frac{1}{2}m_{\text{you}}v_{\text{you}}^2 \\
&= \frac{1}{2}(50.0\text{ kg})(0.600\text{ m/s})^2 \\
&= 9.00\text{ kg} \cdot \text{m}^2/\text{s}^2 = 9.00\text{ J}
\end{aligned}$$

$$K_{\text{skateboard}} = \frac{1}{2}m_{\text{skateboard}}v_{\text{skateboard}}^2 = \frac{1}{2}(2.50\text{ kg})(12.0\text{ m/s})^2 = 180\text{ J}$$

Reflect

The skateboard's speed is 12.0 m/s, about the same as the speed limit for cars in a residential neighborhood. It's not difficult to shove a skateboard hard enough to give it that speed.

As we discussed above, the skateboard moves much faster than you do after the push-off because it has much less mass. The ratio of your mass to that of the skateboard is 20.0 to 1: This same factor of 20.0 appears in the ratio of speeds (the skateboard is faster). It also appears in the ratio of kinetic energies: The skateboard has 20.0 times more kinetic energy than you do. If two objects have the same magnitude of momentum, the less massive one *always* has more kinetic energy.

$$\text{Skateboard speed: } v_{\text{skateboard}} = \left(12.0\frac{\text{m}}{\text{s}}\right)\left(\frac{1\text{ km}}{1000\text{ m}}\right)\left(\frac{3600\text{ s}}{1\text{ h}}\right)$$
$$= 43.2\text{ km/h} = 26.8\text{ mi/h}$$

$$\text{Ratio of masses: } \frac{m_{\text{you}}}{m_{\text{skateboard}}} = \frac{50.0\text{ kg}}{2.50\text{ kg}} = 20.0$$

$$\text{Ratio of speeds: } \frac{v_{\text{you}}}{v_{\text{skateboard}}} = \frac{0.600\text{ m/s}}{12.0\text{ m/s}} = 0.0500 = \frac{1}{20.0}$$

$$\text{Ratio of kinetic energies: } \frac{K_{\text{you}}}{K_{\text{skateboard}}} = \frac{9.00\text{ J}}{180\text{ J}} = 0.0500 = \frac{1}{20.0}$$

Example 7-1 further illustrates the idea that momentum and kinetic energy are not the same thing: Objects with the same momentum can have very different kinetic energies. To better understand the distinction, let's rewrite Equations 7-2 using the definition $\vec{p} = m\vec{v}$ for momentum:

$$\vec{F}_{\text{you on skateboard}}\Delta t = m_{\text{skateboard}}\vec{v}_{\text{skateboard}} = \vec{p}_{\text{skateboard}}$$
$$\vec{F}_{\text{skateboard on you}}\Delta t = m_{\text{you}}\vec{v}_{\text{you}} = \vec{p}_{\text{you}}$$

(7-7)

Both the skateboard and you begin at rest. Equations 7-7 say that the momentum that each object acquires during the push-off is equal to the net force that acts on it multiplied by the *time* over which the force acts. Newton's third law tells us that you and the skateboard exert forces of equal magnitude on each other, and that when one force is present the other one must be as well. Hence both forces act for the same time Δt, and the skateboard and you end up with equal magnitudes of momentum (although in opposite directions) (Figure 7-4).

We've seen how the idea of momentum is useful for the special case of a person pushing off a skateboard. In the next section we'll expand on this idea and see how to use the concept of momentum for the general case in which two objects interact and exert forces on each other.

$\vec{v}_{\text{you}}$
$\vec{F}_{\text{skateboard on you}}$
$\vec{v}_{\text{skateboard}}$
$\vec{F}_{\text{you on skateboard}}$

(1) $\vec{F}_{\text{skateboard on you}}$ and $\vec{F}_{\text{you on skateboard}}$ have the same magnitude.

(2) These forces act on you and the skateboard for the same amount of time, so you and the skateboard acquire the same magnitude of momentum.

(3) The skateboard moves faster and covers a greater distance while the forces act, so more work is done on the skateboard and it acquires more kinetic energy.

Figure 7-4 **Same momentum but different kinetic energy** During the push-off you and the skateboard acquire the same magnitude of momentum, but the skateboard acquires more kinetic energy.

? Got the Concept? 7-1 **Armed and Dangerous**

You are challenged to a skeet shooting competition while wearing rollerblades. You fire the rifle, and you recoil backwards. Compared to the kinetic energy of the bullet just after the shot, the kinetic energy of you and the rifle together is (a) greater; (b) the same; (c) less; (d) the answer depends on how powerful the rifle is.

Take-Home Message for Section 7-2

✔ The linear momentum of an object is a vector. It is equal to the product of the object's mass and its velocity.

✔ If two objects at rest push away from each other, each object acquires an equal amount of momentum in opposite directions (if no other net forces act on the objects).

✔ If two objects of different masses have the same magnitude of momentum, the object with the smaller mass has more kinetic energy than the other object.

7-3 The total momentum of a system of objects is conserved under certain conditions

In our analysis of you pushing off a skateboard in Section 7-2, our key discovery was that just after the push-off, your momentum and the momentum of the skateboard had the same magnitude but were in opposite directions. In terms of vectors (Equation 7-6), we wrote this as

$$\vec{p}_{skateboard} = -\vec{p}_{you}$$

Let's rearrange this equation so that both momentum vectors are on the same side of the equals sign:

(7-8)
$$\vec{p}_{you} + \vec{p}_{skateboard} = 0$$

The left-hand side of Equation 7-8 is the **total momentum** just after the push-off of you and the skateboard together. Since momentum is a vector, we have to use the rules of vector arithmetic to add them together, which is why these two vectors with equal magnitudes but opposite directions add to zero. That is, the system of you and the skateboard has zero total momentum just after the push-off.

Note also that the total momentum just *before* the push-off is also zero: Initially, neither you nor the skateboard is moving, so both objects have zero momentum and the sum of these is likewise zero. So for this special case, the total momentum of the system of you and the skateboard is *conserved*: It has the same value (in this case, zero) before and after the push-off (Figure 7-5).

We saw in Chapter 6 that problem-solving can be simplified tremendously if the *total mechanical energy E* of a system is conserved. We also saw that E is conserved only under special circumstances (if no work is done by nonconservative forces). Is something similar true for the total momentum of a system? And if so, what are the special circumstances under which total momentum is conserved? Let's find the answers to these questions, using our discussion from Section 7-2 as a guide.

 In this situation the total momentum of the system is conserved: The push-off does not affect its value.

① Before the push-off: No motion, so total momentum of the system of you and skateboard is zero:
$$\vec{p}_{you} + \vec{p}_{skateboard} = 0$$

$\vec{p}_{you} = 0$

$\vec{p}_{skateboard} = 0$

② After the push-off: Both objects have momentum, but the total momentum is still zero:
$$\vec{p}_{you} + \vec{p}_{skateboard} = 0$$

$\vec{p}_{you}$

$\vec{p}_{skateboard}$

Figure 7-5 **Total momentum** When you push off from the skateboard, your momentum and the momentum of the skateboard both change. But the *total* momentum of the system of you and the skateboard is unchanged.

A System of Several Objects: Internal and External Forces

Figure 7-6 shows a system of two objects. These objects could be billiard balls on a billiard table, oxygen molecules in the air around you, or a planet and its moon. Two kinds of forces can act on each object: forces exerted by other members of the system, which we call **internal forces**, and forces exerted by objects outside the system, which we call **external forces**. For the example of billiard balls on a billiard table, the internal forces are the forces that one ball exerts on another when they collide; the external forces are the normal and friction forces exerted by the table, the gravitational force exerted by Earth, and the force you exert on the cue ball with the cue. For the two objects A and B shown in Figure 7-6, we can write Newton's second law as

$$\sum \vec{F}_{\text{on A}} = \sum \vec{F}_{\text{external on A}} + \vec{F}_{\text{B on A}} = m_A \vec{a}_A \qquad (7\text{-}9)$$
$$\sum \vec{F}_{\text{on B}} = \sum \vec{F}_{\text{external on B}} + \vec{F}_{\text{A on B}} = m_B \vec{a}_B$$

We can reduce Equations 7-9 to a single equation by adding them together. This has several advantages. First, it leaves us with a single equation to analyze. Second, from Newton's third law, we know that $\vec{F}_{\text{B on A}} = -\vec{F}_{\text{A on B}}$. So when we add Equations 7-9, these two terms cancel each other out. Mathematically, we end up with

$$\sum \vec{F}_{\text{external on A}} + \sum \vec{F}_{\text{external on B}} = m_A \vec{a}_A + m_B \vec{a}_B \qquad (7\text{-}10)$$

You may think that it's simply convenient that the two internal forces cancel each other out. But it's actually very important. When two objects collide, we often know very little, if anything, about the details of the forces one object exerts on another. As a result, analyzing a collision would be nearly impossible if we needed to know these forces. So the fact that Newton's third law allows us to eliminate the internal forces from Equation 7-10 means we can actually calculate the effects of a collision.

Over a time interval Δt the velocity of A changes from $\vec{v}_{Ai}$ to $\vec{v}_{Af}$, and the velocity of B changes from $\vec{v}_{Bi}$ to $\vec{v}_{Bf}$. Using Equation 3-9, $\vec{a} = \Delta \vec{v}/\Delta t$, we can rewrite each of the accelerations in Equation 7-10 in terms of the changes in velocity:

$$\sum \vec{F}_{\text{external on A}} + \sum \vec{F}_{\text{external on B}} = \frac{m_A (\vec{v}_{Af} - \vec{v}_{Ai})}{\Delta t} + \frac{m_B (\vec{v}_{Bf} - \vec{v}_{Bi})}{\Delta t} \qquad (7\text{-}11)$$

We can further rewrite Equation 7-11 in terms of the momentum of each object before and after the time interval Δt. To do this, we begin by multiplying both sides of each equation by Δt and multiplying through by the the mass terms

$$\left(\sum \vec{F}_{\text{external on A}} + \sum \vec{F}_{\text{external on B}} \right) \Delta t = m_A \vec{v}_{Af} - m_A \vec{v}_{Ai} + m_B \vec{v}_{Bf} - m_B \vec{v}_{Bi}$$

and then use the definition of momentum, $\vec{p} = m\vec{v}$ to arrive at

$$\left(\sum \vec{F}_{\text{external on A}} + \sum \vec{F}_{\text{external on B}} \right) \Delta t = (\vec{p}_{Af} + \vec{p}_{Bf}) - (\vec{p}_{Ai} + \vec{p}_{Bi}) \qquad (7\text{-}12)$$

In Equation 7-12 $\vec{p}_{Ai}$ and $\vec{p}_{Bi}$ are the momenta of A and B, respectively, at the beginning of the time interval Δt, and $\vec{p}_{Af}$ and $\vec{p}_{Bf}$ are the momenta of A and B, respectively, at the end of the time interval.

The quantity in parentheses on the left-hand side of Equation 7-12 is the sum of all of the *external* forces that act on the *system* of objects A and B. We'll call this $\sum \vec{F}_{\text{external on system}}$ for short. The right-hand side of the equation is the difference between the *total* momentum of the system after the time interval Δt, $\vec{P}_f = \vec{p}_{Af} + \vec{p}_{Bf}$, and the *total* momentum of the system before the time interval, $\vec{P}_i = \vec{p}_{Ai} + \vec{p}_{Bi}$. So we can rewrite Equation 7-12 as

The sum of all external forces acting on a system of objects

Duration of a time interval over which the external forces act

$$\left(\sum \vec{F}_{\text{external on system}} \right) \Delta t = \vec{P}_f - \vec{P}_i = \Delta \vec{P}$$

Change during that time interval in the total momentum of the objects that make up the system

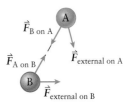

Figure 7-6 Internal forces and external forces If we treat the two objects A and B as a system, the forces that these objects exert on each other are *internal* forces. Forces exerted on A and B by other objects outside the system are *external* forces. The internal forces can either pull the objects together or push them apart.

External force and total momentum change for a system of objects
(7-13)

Equation 7-13 says something quite remarkable: *Only the external forces acting on a system can affect the system's total momentum.* The internal forces of one object on another allow momentum to be transferred between the objects (for example, when a moving cue ball hits an eight-ball at rest and sends the eight-ball flying), but they don't affect the value of the *total* momentum.

We now have the answer to the question "When is momentum conserved?" Equation 7-13 says that the total momentum does not change over the time interval Δt if the net external force on the system is zero. Then the left-hand side of Equation 7-13 is zero, and so there is zero difference between the final total momentum $\vec{P}_f = \vec{p}_{Af} + \vec{p}_{Bf}$ and the initial total momentum $\vec{P}_i = \vec{p}_{Ai} + \vec{p}_{Bi}$:

> If the net external force on a system of objects is zero...

> ... then the total momentum of the system at the end of a time interval...

Conservation of momentum
(7-14)

$$\vec{P}_f = \vec{P}_i$$

In this case, the total momentum of the system is conserved.

> ... is equal to the total momentum of the system at the beginning of that time interval.

Equation 7-14 is the **law of conservation of momentum**. It explains why the total momentum was conserved for the system of you and the skateboard in Section 7-2: There were external forces acting on you and on the skateboard, but the vector sum of these external forces was zero. Hence the total momentum of you and the skateboard had the same value (zero) both before and after the push-off.

Momentum Conservation and Collisions

The law of conservation of momentum turns out to be useful even when the net external force on a system is *not* zero. One example is a collision between two automobiles (Figure 7-7). During the collision the net vertical force on each car is zero: The upward normal force exerted by the ground balances the downward gravitational force. But the ground also exerts a horizontal friction force on each car, and there is nothing to balance the friction forces. So there is a net external force on the system of two cars. Does this mean we cannot use Equation 7-12? No. To see why this is so, let's rewrite Equation 7-12 the way it would appear if we didn't immediately cancel the internal forces when we added Equations 7-9 (the internal forces still appear on the left-hand side of the equation):

(7-15)

$$\left(\sum \vec{F}_{\text{external on A}} + \sum \vec{F}_{\text{external on B}} \right)\Delta t + \left(\vec{F}_{\text{B on A}} + \vec{F}_{\text{A on B}} \right)\Delta t$$
$$= \vec{p}_{Af} + \vec{p}_{Bf} - \vec{p}_{Ai} - \vec{p}_{Bi}$$

Figure 7-7 Forces in a collision
During a collision between two cars, the internal forces (the forces of one car on another) are so great that we can ignore the external forces on the system.

> ② The vertical forces on each car cancel.

> ① When the two cars collide, they exert strong forces on each other.

Car A

$\vec{n}_A$ $\vec{n}_B$

$\vec{F}_{\text{B on A}}$ $\vec{F}_{\text{A on B}}$ Car B

$\vec{f}_{kA}$ $\vec{f}_{kB}$

$\vec{w}_A$ $\vec{w}_B$

> ③ There is a kinetic friction force on each car, but these are very small compared to the forces that car A exerts on car B and car B exerts on car A.

So we can say that:
- The net force on car A is $\vec{F}_{\text{B on A}}$ and the net force on car B is $\vec{F}_{\text{A on B}}$.
- These forces are internal to the system of two cars.

Note that the forces $\vec{F}_{B \text{ on } A}$ and $\vec{F}_{A \text{ on } B}$ that the cars exert on each other are *very* large: They can deform metal and shatter both plastic and glass. By comparison, the external friction forces are much smaller in magnitude. So it's a very good approximation to ignore the relatively weak external friction forces during the brief duration Δt of the collision. That means that we can set the terms $\sum \vec{F}_{\text{external on } A}$ and $\sum \vec{F}_{\text{external on } B}$ in Equation 7-15 equal to zero:

$$(\vec{F}_{B \text{ on } A} + \vec{F}_{A \text{ on } B})\Delta t = \vec{p}_{Af} + \vec{p}_{Bf} - \vec{p}_{Ai} - \vec{p}_{Bi} \qquad (7\text{-}16)$$

But by Newton's third law, we still have $\vec{F}_{B \text{ on } A} = -\vec{F}_{A \text{ on } B}$, so the left-hand side of Equation 7-16 for the two colliding cars is zero. Thus the change in total momentum during the collision is still zero, or

$$\vec{p}_{Af} + \vec{p}_{Bf} = \vec{p}_{Ai} + \vec{p}_{Bi} \qquad (7\text{-}17)$$

This is the same as Equation 7-14, the law of conservation of momentum. So we conclude that

> If the internal forces during a collision are much greater in magnitude than the external forces, the total momentum of the colliding objects has the same value just before and just after the collision.

In *most* collisions the internal forces are much larger in magnitude than the external forces. For example, when two hockey players collide on the ice, the internal forces of one player on the other are strong enough to knock the wind out of the players or even cause injury. These forces are much greater than the friction forces that the ice exerts on the player. Similarly, the forces that act between a tennis ball and tennis racquet in a serve are so large that the ball distorts noticeably. The external forces that act on the ball and racquet during the time they are in contact—the gravitational forces and the force of the player's hand on the racquet—are very feeble by comparison. So it's almost always safe to say that the total momentum of a system of colliding objects just *after* the collision is the same as just *before* the collision.

Here's an experiment you can do to compare the magnitudes of internal and external forces during a collision. With your left hand, gently but firmly hold an empty aluminum soft drink can at its base so that the can is in the upright position. Use your right hand to give the side of the can a quick, karate-like chop. You'll notice that the can ends up with a permanent dent where you struck it with your right hand, but not where you held it with your left hand. The difference is that the chop you delivered to the can was a short-duration, large-force collision between your right hand and the empty can, which together make up a system of two colliding objects. The dent was caused by the strong force of your right hand on the can, which was an internal force between the two objects of the system. By contrast, the force of your left hand—an external force from outside the system—was far weaker and failed to produce a dent.

 Go to Interactive Exercise 7-1 for more practice dealing with conservation of momentum

---

! Watch Out! In a collision, momentum is conserved only *during* the collision.

The general rule that we have discovered says that the total momentum of colliding objects is conserved *only* during the very brief period during which the collision takes place. Once the collision is over, the strong internal forces no longer act, the external forces become dominant, and the total momentum is no longer conserved. For example, the two colliding cars shown in Figure 7-7 continued to move after the collision (with a total momentum just after the collision that equals their total momentum just before the collision). Once the collision has ended, however, friction with the track and grass soon caused the cars to come to a halt and lose all of their momentum.

! Watch Out! Remember, momentum is a vector.

It's important to note that Equation 7-14, the law of conservation of momentum, is a *vector* equation. If the vectors $\vec{P}_f$ and $\vec{P}_i$ are equal, it must be that the x components of the two vectors are equal *and* the y components of the two vectors are equal. Examples 7-2, 7-3, and 7-4 illustrate how to solve problems that involve the vector nature of momentum.

Example 7-2 Conservation of Momentum: A Collision on the Ice

Gordie, a 100-kg hockey player, is initially moving to the right at 5.00 m/s directly toward Mario, a stationary 80.0-kg player. After the two players collide head-on, Mario is moving to the right at 3.75 m/s. (a) In what direction and at what speed is Gordie moving after the collision? (b) What was the change in Gordie's momentum in the collision? What was the change in Mario's momentum?

Set Up

The system that we're considering is made up of the two players. The vertical forces on each player (the normal force exerted by the ice and the gravitational force) cancel each other, so there is no net external force in the vertical direction. The friction forces between the players and the ice are small compared to the forces that Gordie and Mario exert on each other. So we can treat the total momentum of the system as conserved during the collision. We'll use this to find Gordie's final velocity and the changes in momentum of each player. We choose the positive x direction to be to the right, as shown.

Momentum conservation:

$$\vec{P} = \vec{p}_G + \vec{p}_M \quad (7\text{-}14)$$

(G for Gordie, M for Mario) has the same value just before and just after the collision

$$\vec{p} = m\vec{v} \quad (7\text{-}5)$$

Gordie
$m_G = 100$ kg

Mario (at rest)
$m_M = 80.0$ kg

$v_{Gi} = 5.00$ m/s

$v_{Mi} = 0$
$\rightarrow +x$

before the collision

Solve

(a) Write the equation of momentum conservation, using the subscript i for values just before the collision and subscript f for values just after.

Just before the collision, the total momentum is

$$\vec{P}_i = \vec{p}_{Gi} + \vec{p}_{Mi} = m_G\vec{v}_{Gi} + m_M\vec{v}_{Mi}$$

Just after the collision, the total momentum is

$$\vec{P}_f = \vec{p}_{Gf} + \vec{p}_{Mf} = m_G\vec{v}_{Gf} + m_M\vec{v}_{Mf}$$

Momentum is conserved:

$$\vec{P}_f = \vec{P}_i$$

$$m_G\vec{v}_{Gf} + m_M\vec{v}_{Mf} = m_G\vec{v}_{Gi} + m_M\vec{v}_{Mi}$$

Note that $\vec{v}_{Mi} = 0$ since Mario is originally at rest. We need to find $\vec{v}_{Gf}$ (Gordie's velocity just after the collision).

Gordie
$v_{Gf} = ?$

Mario
$v_{Mf} = 3.75$ m/s

$\rightarrow +x$

after the collision

Since the motion is entirely along the x axis, we only need the x component of the momentum conservation equation. Solve for Gordie's final x velocity, v_{Gfx}; then substitute the values of the players' masses, Gordie's velocity before the collision, and Mario's velocity after the collision.

$$m_G v_{Gfx} + m_M v_{Mfx} = m_G v_{Gix} + m_M v_{Mix}$$

Mario is originally at rest, so $v_{Mix} = 0$ and

$$m_G v_{Gfx} + m_M v_{Mfx} = m_G v_{Gix}$$

$$m_G v_{Gfx} = m_G v_{Gix} - m_M v_{Mfx}$$

$$v_{Gfx} = v_{Gix} - \frac{m_M v_{Mfx}}{m_G}$$

Players' masses: $m_G = 100$ kg, $m_M = 80.0$ kg

Gordie's initial x velocity: $v_{Gix} = +5.00$ m/s

Mario's final x velocity: $v_{Mfx} = +3.75$ m/s

$$v_{Gfx} = (+5.00 \text{ m/s}) - \frac{(80.0 \text{ kg})(+3.75 \text{ m/s})}{100 \text{ kg}}$$

$$= +5.00 \text{ m/s} - 3.00 \text{ m/s}$$

$$= +2.00 \text{ m/s}$$

Gordie ends up moving at 2.00 m/s to the right (in the positive x direction).

(b) The change in each player's momentum equals his momentum after the collision minus his momentum before the collision.

Gordie: $\Delta p_{Gx} = m_G v_{Gfx} - m_G v_{Gix}$
$= (100 \text{ kg})(+ 2.00 \text{ m/s}) - (100 \text{ kg})(+ 5.00 \text{ m/s})$
$= 200 \text{ kg} \cdot \text{m/s} - 500 \text{ kg} \cdot \text{m/s}$
$= -300 \text{ kg} \cdot \text{m/s}$

Mario: $\Delta p_{Mx} = m_M v_{Mfx} - m_M v_{Mix}$
$= (80.0 \text{ kg})(+3.75 \text{ m/s}) - (80.0 \text{ kg})(0 \text{ m/s})$
$= +300 \text{ kg} \cdot \text{m/s}$

Reflect

Our answer to part (a) tells us that after the collision Gordie is still moving in the positive x direction, but with reduced speed: He has lost x momentum, while Mario (who was originally at rest) has gained x momentum. In fact, as part (b) shows, the amount of x momentum that Gordie loses (300 kg·m/s) is exactly the same as the amount of x momentum that Mario gains. Thus we can think of the collision between the two players as a *transfer* of momentum between Gordie and Mario. This is like a financial transaction in which one person gives money to another. No momentum is lost in the collision; it simply changes hands from one player to the other.

Notice that in this problem, we needed to know Mario's final x velocity v_{Mfx} in order to find Gordie's final x velocity v_{Gfx}. That's because the statement that momentum is conserved in the x direction gave us only one equation which relates v_{Mfx} and v_{Gfx}. Hence we were able to solve for only one unknown quantity. If we didn't know either of the players' final velocities, we would have needed additional information—in particular, the duration of the collision and the magnitude of the force that one player exerts on the other during the collision—which we unfortunately do not have. The law of conservation of momentum is a great tool, but by itself it can't tell you everything!

Although we used conservation of momentum in this example, note that neither player's *individual* momentum is conserved: Gordie's momentum after the collision is different than before the collision, and likewise for Mario's momentum. It's only the *total* momentum of Gordie and Mario's system that is conserved. *In general, the momentum of any particular object within a system will not be conserved.*

Example 7-3 A Collision at the Bowl-a-Rama

The sequence of images in Figure 7-8 shows a bowling ball striking a stationary pin. The second image shows that when the collision occurs, the ball strikes a bit to the left of the horizontal center of the pin. The third image shows what happens after the collision: The ball moves on a path to the left of its original direction and the pin shoots off to the right. Just after one such collision, the ball is moving off horizontally at a 10.0° angle and the pin is moving off horizontally at a 60.0° angle (measured relative to the original direction of motion of the ball). The mass of the ball is 3.50 times greater than the mass of the pin. Just after the collision, is the pin moving faster or slower than the ball, and by what factor?

Figure 7-8 Hitting a bowling pin off-center After the bowling ball strikes the left-hand side of the pin, the ball deflects to the left and the pin moves off to the right. How do their speeds compare?

Set Up

The forces that the ball and pin exert on each other are very strong (imagine what it would feel like if your finger were between the ball and pin when they hit!). Compared to these, we can ignore the external forces exerted on the system of ball and pin, so the total momentum of this system is conserved. The collision is two-dimensional, so we must account for the components of momentum in both the x and y directions.

Momentum conservation:

$$\vec{P} = \vec{p}_B + \vec{p}_P \qquad (7\text{-}14)$$

(B for ball, P for pin) has the same value just before and just after the collision

Linear momentum:

$$\vec{p} = m\vec{v} \qquad (7\text{-}5)$$

We are given the directions of motion of the ball and pin before and after the collision, and we want to find the *ratio* of the pin's final speed v_{Pf} to the ball's final speed v_{Bf}. We don't know the mass of either the ball or the pin, but we do know the ratio of their masses.

Ratio of the mass of the ball to the mass of the pin:

$$\frac{m_B}{m_P} = 3.50$$

Solve

The total momentum before the collision (subscript i) equals the total momentum after the collision (subscript f). Write this for both the *x* component and the *y* component of momentum.

Momentum conservation:

$$\vec{p}_{Bf} + \vec{p}_{Pf} = \vec{p}_{Bi} + \vec{p}_{Pi}, \text{ or}$$

$$m_B \vec{v}_{Bf} + m_P \vec{v}_{Pf} = m_B \vec{v}_{Bi} + m_P \vec{v}_{Pi}, \text{ or}$$

$$m_B v_{Bfx} + m_P v_{Pfx} = m_B v_{Bix} + m_P v_{Pix}$$
(total *x* momentum is conserved)

$$m_B v_{Bfy} + m_P v_{Pfy} = m_B v_{Biy} + m_P v_{Piy}$$
(total *y* momentum is conserved)

Just prior to the collision the ball has no component of velocity in the *y* direction (so $v_{Biy} = 0$) and the pin is at rest (so $v_{Pix} = v_{Piy} = 0$). Just after the collision the ball is moving at a 10.0° angle with positive *x* and *y* components of velocity, while the pin is moving at a 60.0° angle with a positive *x* velocity and a negative *y* velocity. Use these facts to rewrite the equations for the conservation of *x* and *y* momentum.

x equation:

$$m_B v_{Bf} \cos 10.0°$$
$$+ \, m_P v_{Pf} \cos 60.0° = m_B v_{Bi}$$

y equation:

$$m_B v_{Bf} \sin 10.0°$$
$$+ \, (-m_P v_{Pf} \sin 60.0°) = 0$$

Our goal is to find the ratio of the speed of the pin just after the collision (v_{Pf}) to the speed of the ball just after the collision (v_{Bf}). The equation for *x* momentum isn't useful for this because we aren't given the value of the ball's speed v_{Bi} before the collision. Instead, we use the equation for *y* momentum to solve for v_{Pf}/v_{Bf}, and then substitute the ratio of the masses of the two objects.

$$m_B v_{Bf} \sin 10.0° = m_P v_{Pf} \sin 60.0°$$

$$\frac{v_{Pf}}{v_{Bf}} = \frac{m_B}{m_P} \frac{\sin 10.0°}{\sin 60.0°} = (3.50)\frac{0.174}{0.866} = 0.702$$

After the collision, the speed of the pin is 0.702 times that of the ball.

Reflect

The pin moves relatively slowly because it suffered only a glancing blow from the ball. With a more head-on impact the pin can end up moving away from the collision at a much faster speed than the ball. We'll explore this in more detail in Section 7-5.

The most important direction in this problem is the positive *x* direction, since that is the direction of the total momentum vector. So although we used *x* and *y* to label the coordinate axes, it would have been more fitting to have called these the *parallel* and *perpendicular* axes based on their orientation relative to the total momentum vector. The equation for *y* momentum is just the statement that the total perpendicular momentum equals zero before and after the collision, and it was this statement that enabled us to find the pin's speed in terms of the speed of the ball.

Example 7-4 A Tricky Billiards Shot

On a billiards table, the 7-ball and the 8-ball are initially at rest and touching each other. You hit the cue ball in such a way that it acquires a speed of 1.7 m/s before hitting the 7-ball and 8-ball simultaneously. After the collision, the cue ball is at rest and the other two balls are each moving at 45° from the direction that the cue ball was moving. What are the speeds of the 7-ball and 8-ball immediately after the collision? Each billiard ball has a mass of 0.16 kg.

Set Up

This is a more complicated collision than in the previous two examples, but the fundamental principle is the same: Total momentum is conserved. Note that all three balls have the same mass $m = 0.16$ kg.

Initially all of the momentum is in the cue ball and points along the direction of its motion. After the collision, the 7-ball and 8-ball must travel on opposite sides of the cue ball's initial path as shown. (If they were on the same side, there would be a nonzero total momentum perpendicular to the cue ball's initial path, and momentum would not be conserved.)

As in Example 7-2, we know the directions of motion of the balls before and after the collision. We know the initial speed $v_{cue,i} = 1.7$ m/s and final speed $v_{cue,f} = 0$ of the cue ball, and we want to find the final speeds v_{7f} and v_{8f} of the 7-ball and 8-ball.

Momentum conservation:

$$\vec{P} = \vec{p}_{cue} + \vec{p}_7 + \vec{p}_8 \qquad (7\text{-}14)$$

(cue ball, 7-ball, and 8-ball) has the same value just before and just after the collision

Linear momentum:

$$\vec{p} = m\vec{v} \qquad (7\text{-}5)$$

Solve

Write in component form the momentum conservation equation, which says that the total momentum before the collision (subscript i) equals the total momentum after the collision (subscript f). Take the positive x axis to be in the direction that the cue ball was moving before the collision.

Momentum conservation:

$$\vec{p}_{cue,f} + \vec{p}_{7f} + \vec{p}_{8f} = \vec{p}_{cue,i} + \vec{p}_{7i} + \vec{p}_{8i}$$

The 7-ball and 8-ball are not moving before the collision, so $\vec{p}_{7i} = \vec{p}_{8i} = 0$, and the cue ball is not moving after the collision, so $\vec{p}_{cue,f} = 0$. So the momentum conservation equation becomes

$$\vec{p}_{7f} + \vec{p}_{8f} = \vec{p}_{cue,i}$$
$$m\vec{v}_{7f} + m\vec{v}_{8f} = m\vec{v}_{cue,i}$$

or in component form

$$mv_{7fx} + mv_{8fx} = mv_{cue,ix} \text{ (total } x \text{ momentum is conserved)}$$
$$mv_{7fy} + mv_{8fy} = mv_{cue,iy} \text{ (total } y \text{ momentum is conserved)}$$

The cue ball's initial velocity had zero y component (so $v_{cue,iy} = 0$). Of the 7-ball and 8-ball, one has positive y velocity and the other negative y velocity in order to satisfy the condition that total y momentum is conserved. Use these observations to simplify the momentum equations.

x equation:

$$mv_{7f} \cos 45° + mv_{8f} \cos 45° = mv_{cue,i}$$

y equation:

$$mv_{7f} \sin 45° + (-mv_{8f} \sin 45°) = 0$$

Solve the momentum conservation equations for the final speeds of the 7-ball and 8-ball.

From the y equation,

$$mv_{7f} \sin 45° = mv_{8f} \sin 45° \text{ so}$$

$$v_{7f} = v_{8f}$$

After the collision, the 7-ball and the 8-ball move with the same speed.

To find this common speed, replace v_{8f} in the x equation with v_{7f} and then solve for v_{7f}:

$$mv_{7f} \cos 45° + mv_{7f} \cos 45° = mv_{\text{cue,i}}$$

$$2mv_{7f} \cos 45° = mv_{\text{cue,i}}$$

$$v_{7f} = \frac{v_{\text{cue,i}}}{2 \cos 45°} = \frac{1.7 \text{ m/s}}{2 \cos 45°} = 1.2 \text{ m/s}$$

After the collision, both the 7-ball and the 8-ball are moving at 1.2 m/s.

Reflect

Note that we didn't need the value of the billiard ball mass. That's because all three balls have the same mass m, so m canceled out in the equations. That didn't happen in Example 7-3 because the bowling ball and pin had *different* masses.

There were three objects in this collision rather than two as in Examples 7-2 and 7-3. But the same ideas of momentum conservation apply no matter how many objects are involved in the collision.

? Got the Concept? 7-2 Which Way Did the Other One Go?

An object moving due west collides with a second object that is initially at rest. Just after the collision, the first object is moving toward the southeast. Just after the collision, the second object must be moving toward the (a) northeast; (b) southeast; (c) southwest; (d) northwest; (e) west.

Take-Home Message for Section 7-3

✔ In a system of objects, internal forces are those that one object in the system exerts on another object in the system. External forces are those exerted on objects in the system by other, outside objects.

✔ If the net external force on a system of objects is zero, the total momentum of the system is conserved. Objects within the system can exchange momentum with each other, but the vector sum of the momentum of all members of the system remains constant.

✔ During a collision, the internal forces are typically much larger in magnitude than any external forces. Hence the external forces can be ignored, and the total momentum just after the collision equals the total momentum just before the collision.

7-4 In an inelastic collision, some of the mechanical energy is lost

We've seen that momentum is conserved in collisions of all kinds, and that the law of conservation of momentum makes it straightforward to solve problems involving collisions. In a similar way we learned in Chapter 6 that *mechanical energy* is conserved in certain circumstances, and that the conservation of energy also simplifies the solution of a variety of problems. This leads us to ask the following: Are both mechanical energy and momentum conserved in collisions?

The answer to this question is "sometimes." In Section 6-7 we learned that mechanical energy is conserved if *only* conservative forces do work. An example of this is two objects that behave like ideal springs when they collide: They compress, converting some of the kinetic energy of the colliding objects into spring potential energy; then they relax and convert the potential energy back into kinetic energy (Figure 7-9a). (This idea is related to the one from Section 6-6 that a conservative force does zero net work on a *round* trip that takes an object back to where it started. If two ideal springs collide and bounce back, they return to the identical state they were in before the collision and so have undergone a "round trip.") A collision of this kind, in which the forces between

Because the ideal springs between these colliding objects exert conservative forces, mechanical energy is conserved in this **elastic collision**.

(a)

Before collision   During collision   After collision

(b)

The collision of the billiard balls is elastic: It does not cause any permanent deformation.

The forces between colliding ideal billiard balls are conservative. No mechanical energy is lost in this **elastic collision**.

(c)

The collision of the two cars is inelastic: It causes a permanent deformation.

The forces between colliding cars are not conservative. Mechanical energy is lost in this **inelastic collision**.

Figure 7-9 **Collision variations**
(a) The ideal springs between these colliding objects exert conservative forces. Mechanical energy is conserved in this elastic collision. (b) The forces between colliding billiard balls are very nearly conservative, and the collision is very nearly elastic. (c) The forces between colliding cars are not conservative. Mechanical energy is lost, and the collision is inelastic.

In elastic collisions, mechanical energy is conserved. In inelastic collisions, mechanical energy is lost.

the colliding objects are conservative, is called an **elastic collision**. In an elastic collision both total momentum *and* total mechanical energy are conserved.

Elastic collisions are happening all around you as you read these words: When oxygen and nitrogen molecules in the air collide with each other, the collisions are almost always elastic. That's because the forces between molecules (which are fundamentally electric in nature) are conservative forces. On a larger scale, a collision between billiard balls is very nearly elastic (Figure 7-9b). A billiard ball deforms slightly when hit, but immediately springs back to its original shape with very little of the energy being lost to thermal or acoustic energy.

Something very different usually happens when two automobiles collide: The bodies of the automobiles deform and do *not* spring back (Figure 7-9c). The forces involved in this deformation are *nonconservative*. That means the automobile bodies do *not* return to the same state they were in before the collision. Instead, mechanical energy is lost and is converted to internal energy. (This is by design. By absorbing mechanical energy as it deforms, the structure of an automobile prevents that energy from being used to do potentially harmful work on the automobile's occupants.) A collision in which mechanical energy is *not* conserved is called an **inelastic collision**.

If we know the masses of the colliding objects and their velocities before and after the collision, it's straightforward to determine whether the collision is elastic or inelastic. Here's the idea: By analogy to a collision between ideal springs (Figure 7-9a), there is zero potential energy just before and just after the collision (corresponding to the springs being relaxed). So just before and just after the collision, the total mechanical energy of the system is equal to the sum of the *kinetic energies* of the colliding objects. If the total kinetic energy has the same value before and after the collision, the collision is elastic; if there is less total kinetic energy after the collision, the collision is inelastic. Example 7-5 illustrates this technique for analyzing collisions.

Example 7-5 Elastic or Inelastic?

Determine whether the following collisions are elastic or inelastic: (a) The collision of two hockey players in Example 7-2 (Section 7-3); (b) the collision of three billiard balls in Example 7-4 (Section 7-3).

Set Up

For each collision we calculate the total kinetic energy (the sum of the individual kinetic energies of the colliding objects) just before and just after the collision. If these are equal, total mechanical energy is conserved and the collision is elastic; if they are not equal, the collision is inelastic.

Kinetic energy:

$$K = \frac{1}{2}mv^2 \qquad (6\text{-}8)$$

Solve

(a) The collision between the two hockey players in Example 7-2 is one-dimensional (that is, along a straight line). So the square of each player's speed v is the same as the square of each player's x velocity v_x.

Players' masses:

$m_G = 100$ kg, $m_M = 80.0$ kg

Before the collision, Gordie has x velocity $v_{Gix} = +5.00$ m/s and Mario is at rest. So the initial total kinetic energy is

$$K_{Gi} + K_{Mi} = \frac{1}{2}m_G v_{Gix}^2 + \frac{1}{2}m_M v_{Mix}^2$$

$$= \frac{1}{2}(100 \text{ kg})(5.00 \text{ m/s})^2$$

$$+ \frac{1}{2}(80.0 \text{ kg})(0 \text{ m/s})^2$$

$$= 1.25 \times 10^3 \text{ J}$$

After the collision, Gordie has x velocity $v_{Gfx} = +2.00$ m/s and Mario has x velocity $v_{Mfx} = +3.75$ m/s. So the final total kinetic energy is

$$K_{Gf} + K_{Mf} = \frac{1}{2}m_G v_{Gfx}^2 + \frac{1}{2}m_M v_{Mfx}^2$$

$$= \frac{1}{2}(100 \text{ kg})(2.00 \text{ m/s})^2 + \frac{1}{2}(80.0 \text{ kg})(3.75 \text{ m/s})^2$$

$$= 763 \text{ J}$$

The total kinetic energy is less after the collision than before, so this collision is inelastic.

(b) Repeat the calculation for the three billiard balls in Example 7-4, for which we know the masses, the speeds before the collision, and the speeds after the collision.

Each ball has mass $m = 0.16$ kg. Before the collision, the cue ball is moving at speed $v_{cue,i} = 1.7$ m/s and both the 7-ball and 8-ball are at rest. So the initial total kinetic energy is

$$K_{cue,i} + K_{7i} + K_{8i}$$

$$= \frac{1}{2}mv_{cue,i}^2 + \frac{1}{2}mv_{7i}^2 + \frac{1}{2}mv_{8i}^2$$

$$= \frac{1}{2}(0.16 \text{ kg})(1.7 \text{ m/s})^2$$

$$+ \frac{1}{2}(0.16 \text{ kg})(0 \text{ m/s})^2$$

$$+ \frac{1}{2}(0.16 \text{ kg})(0 \text{ m/s})^2 = 0.23 \text{ J}$$

After the collision the cue ball is at rest, the 7-ball is moving at 1.2 m/s, and the 8-ball is also moving at 1.2 m/s. So the final total kinetic energy is

$$K_{cue,f} + K_{7f} + K_{8f} = \frac{1}{2}mv_{cue,f}^2 + \frac{1}{2}mv_{7f}^2 + \frac{1}{2}mv_{8f}^2$$

$$= \frac{1}{2}(0.16 \text{ kg})(0)^2 + \frac{1}{2}(0.16 \text{ kg})(1.2 \text{ m/s})^2$$

$$+ \frac{1}{2}(0.16 \text{ kg})(1.2 \text{ m/s})^2$$

$$= 0.23 \text{ J}$$

The total kinetic energy is unchanged by the collision, so this collision is elastic.

Reflect

The human body is not as "springy" as a billiard ball, so the forces between Gordie and Mario when they collide are nonconservative. The lost mechanical energy went into increasing the two players' internal energies, which means that their temperatures increased slightly as a result of the collision.

Completely Inelastic Collisions

The type of collision in which the *most* mechanical energy is lost is a **completely inelastic collision**, in which two objects stick together after they collide. A collision between two cars is completely inelastic if the cars lock together and don't separate. (If the cars deform and then bounce apart, the collision is inelastic but not *completely* inelastic.) You are the result of a completely inelastic collision in which a sperm cell fused with an ovum, which nine months later led to your birth (Figure 7-10).

When an object of mass m_A and velocity $\vec{v}_{Ai}$ undergoes an inelastic collision with a second object of mass m_B and velocity $\vec{v}_{Bi}$, we can regard what remains after the collision as a single object of mass $m_A + m_B$. Momentum conservation then gives us an equation for the velocity $\vec{v}_f$ of this combined object just after the collision:

Figure 7-10 **A completely inelastic collision** A sperm cell and an ovum move together after they collide.

Velocities of objects A and B before they undergo a completely inelastic collision (in which they stick together)

$$m_A \vec{v}_{Ai} + m_B \vec{v}_{Bi} = (m_A + m_B)\vec{v}_f$$

Masses of objects A and B   Velocity of the two objects moving together after the collision

Momentum conservation in a completely inelastic collision (7-18)

 Go to Interactive Exercise 7-2 for more practice dealing with inelastic collisions

Examples 7-6 and 7-7 illustrate how to use this equation.

Example 7-6 A Head-On Collision

In a scene from an action movie, a 1.50×10^3-kg car moving north at 35.0 m/s collides head-on with a 7.50×10^3-kg truck moving south at 25.0 m/s. The car and truck stick together after the collision. (a) How fast and in what direction is the wreckage traveling just after the collision? (b) How much mechanical energy is lost in the collision?

Set Up

Since the two vehicles stick together, this is a completely inelastic collision. We'll use Equation 7-18 to find the final velocity $\vec{v}_f$ of the wreckage. We'll then compare the final kinetic energy of the wreckage to the combined kinetic energies of the car and truck before the collision; the difference is the amount of mechanical energy that's lost in the collision.

Momentum conservation in a completely inelastic collision:

$$m_{car} \vec{v}_{car,i} + m_{truck} \vec{v}_{truck,i}$$
$$= (m_{car} + m_{truck})\vec{v}_f \quad (7\text{-}18)$$

Kinetic energy:

$$K = \frac{1}{2}mv^2 \quad (6\text{-}8)$$

Solve

(a) The collision is along a straight line, which we call the x axis. We take the positive x axis to be to the north, in the direction of the car's motion before the collision. We use the x component of Equation 7-18 to solve for the final velocity.

Equation for conservation of x momentum in a completely inelastic collision:

$$m_{car}v_{car,ix} + m_{truck}v_{truck,ix} = (m_{car} + m_{truck})v_{fx}$$

Solve for final velocity of wreckage:

$$v_{fx} = \frac{m_{car}v_{car,ix} + m_{truck}v_{truck,ix}}{m_{car} + m_{truck}}$$

With our choice of x axis, we have

$$v_{car,ix} = +35.0 \text{ m/s}$$
$$v_{truck,ix} = -25.0 \text{ m/s}$$

Substitute values:

$$v_{fx} = \frac{\left[\begin{array}{l}(1.50 \times 10^3 \text{ kg})(+35.0 \text{ m/s}) \\ + (7.50 \times 10^3 \text{ kg})(-25.0 \text{ m/s})\end{array}\right]}{1.50 \times 10^3 \text{ kg} + 7.50 \times 10^3 \text{ kg}}$$
$$= -15.0 \text{ m/s}$$

The wreckage moves at 15.0 m/s to the south (in the negative x direction).

(b) Calculate the kinetic energies before and after the collision and compare.

Total kinetic energy before the collision:

$$K_{car,i} + K_{truck,i} = \frac{1}{2}m_{car}v_{car,i}^2 + \frac{1}{2}m_{truck}v_{truck,i}^2$$

$$= \frac{1}{2}(1.50 \times 10^3 \text{ kg})(35.0 \text{ m/s})^2$$

$$+ \frac{1}{2}(7.50 \times 10^3 \text{ kg})(25.0 \text{ m/s})^2$$

$$= 9.19 \times 10^5 \text{ J} + 2.34 \times 10^6 \text{ J}$$
$$= 3.26 \times 10^6 \text{ J}$$

Total kinetic energy after the collision:

$$K_{car,f} + K_{truck,f} = \frac{1}{2}(m_{car} + m_{truck})v_f^2$$

$$= \frac{1}{2}(1.50 \times 10^3 \text{ kg} + 7.50 \times 10^3 \text{ kg})(15.0 \text{ m/s})^2$$

$$= 1.01 \times 10^6 \text{ J}$$

The amount of mechanical energy lost in the collision is the difference between the initial and final energies:

$$(K_{car,i} + K_{truck,i}) - (K_{car,f} + K_{truck,f})$$
$$= 3.26 \times 10^6 \text{ J} - 1.01 \times 10^6 \text{ J}$$
$$= 2.25 \times 10^6 \text{ J}$$

Reflect

It makes sense that the wreckage moves in the direction of the truck's initial motion. Before the collision, the magnitude of the southbound truck's momentum was much greater than that of the northbound car, so the total momentum was to the south.

Our result in part (b) shows that more than two-thirds of the total mechanical energy is lost in the collision. This lost energy goes into doing work to deform the two vehicles,

Momentum of car before the collision:

$$p_{car,ix} = m_{car}v_{car,ix}$$
$$= (1.50 \times 10^3 \text{ kg})(+35.0 \text{ m/s})$$
$$= +5.25 \times 10^4 \text{ kg·m/s}$$

Momentum of truck before the collision:

$$p_{truck,ix} = m_{truck}v_{truck,ix}$$
$$= (7.50 \times 10^3 \text{ kg})(-25.0 \text{ m/s})$$
$$= -1.88 \times 10^5 \text{ kg·m/s}$$

which makes for a very impressive collision scene in the movie.

Total momentum before the collision:

$$P_{ix} = p_{car,ix} + p_{truck,ix}$$
$$= +5.25 \times 10^4 \text{ kg·m/s}$$
$$+(-1.88 \times 10^5 \text{ kg·m/s})$$
$$= -1.35 \times 10^5 \text{ kg·m/s}$$

Example 7-7 Drama in the Skies

The photograph that opens this chapter shows a Cooper's hawk attacking a pigeon from behind. Each bird has a mass of 0.600 kg. The pigeon is gliding due west at 8.00 m/s at a constant altitude, and the Cooper's hawk is diving on the pigeon at a speed of 12.0 m/s at an angle of 30.0° below the horizontal. Just after the Cooper's hawk grabs the pigeon in its talons, how fast and in what direction are the two birds moving?

Set Up

This is a completely inelastic collision because the two birds move together afterward. Unlike Example 7-6, this collision takes place in two dimensions, so we will need to consider more than one component of Equation 7-18 to find the final velocity $\vec{v}_f$ of the two birds after the collision.

Momentum conservation in a completely inelastic collision:

$$m_{pigeon}\vec{v}_{pigeon,i} + m_{hawk}\vec{v}_{hawk,i}$$
$$= (m_{pigeon} + m_{hawk})\vec{v}_f \quad (7\text{-}18)$$

Solve

We choose the positive x axis to be horizontal and to the west, and we choose the positive y axis to be upward. We write the components of the initial velocities of the hawk and pigeon.

Pigeon is initially moving in the positive x direction, so

$$v_{pigeon,ix} = v_{pigeon,i} = +8.00 \text{ m/s}$$
$$v_{pigeon,iy} = 0$$

Hawk is initially moving in the positive x direction and the negative y direction, so

$$v_{hawk,ix} = v_{hawk,i}\cos 30.0° = (12.0 \text{ m/s})\cos 30.0°$$
$$= +10.4 \text{ m/s}$$
$$v_{hawk,iy} = -v_{hawk,i}\sin 30.0° = -(12.0 \text{ m/s})\sin 30.0°$$
$$= -6.00 \text{ m/s}$$

Use conservation of momentum in component form to find the components of the final velocity of the two birds.

Equation for conservation of x momentum in the collision:

$$m_{pigeon}v_{pigeon,ix} + m_{hawk}v_{hawk,ix} = (m_{pigeon} + m_{hawk})v_{fx}$$

Solve for the final x velocity of the two birds:

$$v_{fx} = \frac{m_{pigeon}v_{pigeon,ix} + m_{hawk}v_{hawk,ix}}{m_{pigeon} + m_{hawk}}$$
$$= \frac{(0.600 \text{ kg})(+8.00 \text{ m/s}) + (0.600 \text{ kg})(+10.4 \text{ m/s})}{0.600 \text{ kg} + 0.600 \text{ kg}}$$
$$= +9.20 \text{ m/s}$$

Equation for conservation of y momentum in the collision:

$$m_{\text{pigeon}} v_{\text{pigeon,iy}} + m_{\text{hawk}} v_{\text{hawk,iy}} = (m_{\text{pigeon}} + m_{\text{hawk}}) v_{\text{fy}}$$

Solve for the final y velocity of the two birds:

$$v_{\text{fy}} = \frac{m_{\text{pigeon}} v_{\text{pigeon,iy}} + m_{\text{hawk}} v_{\text{hawk,iy}}}{m_{\text{pigeon}} + m_{\text{hawk}}}$$

$$= \frac{(0.600 \text{ kg})(0 \text{ m/s}) + (0.600 \text{ kg})(-6.00 \text{ m/s})}{0.600 \text{ kg} + 0.600 \text{ kg}}$$

$$= -3.00 \text{ m/s}$$

Given the components of the final velocity vector $\vec{v}_{\text{f}}$, use trigonometry to find the magnitude and direction of $\vec{v}_{\text{f}}$.

Speed after collision = magnitude of final velocity vector:

$$v_{\text{f}} = \sqrt{v_{\text{fx}}^2 + v_{\text{fy}}^2}$$

$$= \sqrt{(+9.20 \text{ m/s})^2 + (-3.00 \text{ m/s})^2}$$

$$= 9.67 \text{ m/s}$$

Direction of final velocity vector:

$$\tan \theta = \frac{v_{\text{fy}}}{v_{\text{fx}}} = \frac{-3.00 \text{ m/s}}{+9.20 \text{ m/s}} = -0.326$$

$$\theta = \arctan(-0.326) = -18.1°$$

After the collision, the two birds move at 9.67 m/s in a direction 18.1° below the horizontal.

$\theta = -18.1°$

$v_{\text{f}} = 9.67$ m/s

Reflect

The impact causes the hawk to slow down from 12.0 m/s to 9.67 m/s, and causes the pigeon to speed up from 8.00 m/s to 9.67 m/s. This is just what we would expect when a slow-moving pigeon is hit from behind by a fast-moving hawk.

! Watch Out! An inelastic collision doesn't have to be *completely* inelastic.

A common misconception is that a collision is inelastic if two objects come together and stick, and is elastic if they bounce off each other. Only the first part of this statement is true! Part (a) of Example 7-5 describes a collision between two hockey players that is inelastic even though the players bounce off each other. For a collision to be inelastic, some mechanical energy has to be lost in the collision, and this can happen even if the colliding objects don't stick together.

Three Special Cases of Completely Inelastic Collisions

Figure 7-11a shows an object of mass m_A moving with velocity $\vec{v}_{Ai}$ and about to collide with a second object of mass m_B that is initially at rest, so $\vec{v}_{Bi} = 0$. If the collision is

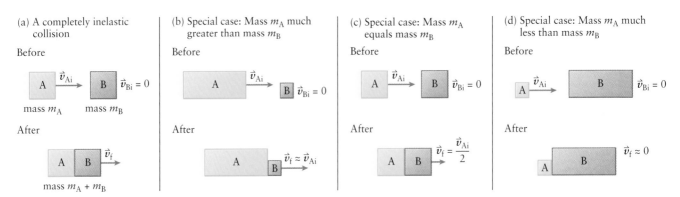

Figure 7-11 Analyzing a completely inelastic collision (a) Object A has a completely inelastic collision with object B (initially at rest). (b) If A is much more massive than B, the final velocity is almost the same as the initial velocity of A. (c) If A and B have the same mass, the final velocity is one-half the initial velocity of A. (d) If A is much less massive than B, the final velocity is nearly zero.

completely inelastic, we can use Equation 7-18 to find the velocity $\vec{v}_f$ after the collision. Since $\vec{v}_{Bi} = 0$,

$$m_A \vec{v}_{Ai} = (m_A + m_B)\vec{v}_f$$

and so

$$\vec{v}_f = \frac{m_A \vec{v}_{Ai}}{m_A + m_B} \qquad (7\text{-}19)$$

(completely inelastic collision, object B initially at rest)

Let's consider three important special cases of this equation.

(1) *The moving object has much greater mass than the object at rest* (Figure 7-11b). Whenever one quantity in an expression is significantly larger than another, it's a good approximation to ignore the smaller quantity if the two quantities are added or subtracted. So when the mass of object A is much larger than the mass of object B, we can safely replace $m_A + m_B$ in Equation 7-19 with m_A. In this approximation Equation 7-19 becomes

$$\vec{v}_f \approx \frac{m_A \vec{v}_{Ai}}{m_A} = \vec{v}_{Ai}$$

If a massive moving object collides with and sticks to a low-mass stationary object, the combined object moves away from the collision at the same velocity with which the first object approached. In this case the stationary object is so small that the moving object is essentially unaffected by the collision. If a fast-moving car runs into a hovering fly, the car slows down only imperceptibly.

(2) *The two objects have the same mass* (Figure 7-11c). If $m_A = m_B$, Equation 7-19 becomes

$$\vec{v}_f = \frac{\vec{v}_{Ai}}{2}$$

When a moving object collides with and sticks to a stationary one of the same mass, the combined system moves away from the collision at half the initial speed.

(3) *The moving object has much less mass than the object at rest* (Figure 7-11d). In this case the mass of object A is much less than the mass of object B, so the quantity m_A in the numerator of Equation 7-19 is very much less than the sum $m_A + m_B$ in the denominator. Therefore $m_A/(m_A + m_B)$ is close to zero, and in this approximation Equation 7-19 becomes

$$\vec{v}_f \approx 0$$

This says that because object A has so little mass, object B hardly moves at all when it is struck. As an example, suppose you drop a small blob of clay to the ground. The clay sticks to the surface, and so undergoes a completely inelastic collision with our planet. Because the mass of the clay is so small compared to Earth's mass, we don't observe any motion of the ground beneath our feet. (The same idea applies to the collision shown in Figure 7-10 between a sperm cell and a much more massive ovum.)

Our result also shows that if moving object A is much less massive than object B, almost all of the initial kinetic energy of object A is lost and converted to internal energy. An example is using an axe to split logs for the fireplace (Figure 7-12). Each impact is a completely inelastic collision between the axe (object A) and a large, stationary object B made up of the log. The lost kinetic energy of the axe goes into heating the axe and heating and ripping apart the log.

Figure 7-12 **Firewood physics** In splitting this log, why does the axe blade get hot as it is repeatedly strikes the log?

? Got the Concept? 7-3 How to Stop a Truck

In Example 7-6 a 1.50×10^3-kg car moving north at 35.0 m/s collides head-on with a 7.50×10^3-kg truck moving south. If the collision is completely inelastic, how fast must the truck be moving so that the wreckage is at rest immediately after the collision? (a) 20.0 m/s; (b) 14.0 m/s; (c) 10.0 m/s; (d) 7.0 m/s; (e) 5.0 m/s.

7-5 In an elastic collision, both momentum and mechanical energy are conserved

In Section 7-4 we introduced the idea of an *elastic* collision in which the forces between colliding objects are conservative and no mechanical energy is lost in the collision. Hence *both* total momentum (a vector) and total mechanical energy (a scalar) are conserved in an elastic collision. We call the two colliding objects A and B, with masses m_A and m_B. We then have two conservation equations that relate the velocities $\vec{v}_{Af}$ and $\vec{v}_{Bf}$ of the objects after the collision to the velocities $\vec{v}_{Ai}$ and $\vec{v}_{Bi}$ before the collision:

(a) $$m_A\vec{v}_{Af} + m_B\vec{v}_{Bf} = m_A\vec{v}_{Ai} + m_B\vec{v}_{Bi}$$
(momentum is conserved in an elastic collision)

(7-20)

(b) $$\frac{1}{2}m_A v_{Af}^2 + \frac{1}{2}m_B v_{Bf}^2 = \frac{1}{2}m_A v_{Ai}^2 + \frac{1}{2}m_B v_{Bi}^2$$
(mechanical energy is conserved in an elastic collision)

Equations 7-20 require some effort to solve. But even when you do solve them, they often don't tell the whole story of an inelastic collision. As an example, consider a collision on a pool table between a moving cue ball (A) with known initial velocity $\vec{v}_{Ai}$ and an 8-ball (B) that is initially at rest so $\vec{v}_{Bi} = 0$. Such a collision is almost perfectly elastic. If you're a pool player, you would like to know how fast and in what direction each ball will go after the collision, which means that you want to know the x and y components of their final velocities. So there are four unknowns in this problem: v_{Afx}, v_{Afy}, v_{Bfx}, and v_{Bfy}. But Equations 7-20 only give us *three* equations for these four unknowns: two from Equation 7-20a for the x and y components of momentum and one from Equation 7-20b. So these equations by themselves aren't enough to solve the problem. An experienced pool player knows that the final velocities also depend on whether the cue ball hits the 8-ball head-on or off-center, and this information isn't included in Equations 7-20.

One situation for which we can solve Equations 7-20 completely is that of a *one-dimensional* elastic collision, so all of the motions are along a straight line. To make the problem even simpler, we'll consider the case in which object B is initially at rest (Figure 7-13). An example is a moving cue ball that hits a stationary 8-ball head on. We call that axis along which the motion takes place the x axis. Then $v_{Bix} = 0$ (the initial velocity of object B is zero) and Equations 7-20 become

Figure 7-13 A head-on elastic collision If momentum and mechanical energy are both conserved in this head-on collision, what are the final velocities of the two objects?

(a) $$m_A v_{Afx} + m_B v_{Bfx} = m_A v_{Aix}$$
(momentum is conserved, head-on elastic collision, object B initially at rest)

(7-21)

(b) $$\frac{1}{2}m_A v_{Afx}^2 + \frac{1}{2}m_B v_{Bfx}^2 = \frac{1}{2}m_A v_{Aix}^2$$
(mechanical energy is conserved, head-on elastic collision, object B initially at rest)

Since each object moves along the x axis only, in Equation 7-21b we've replaced the square of each object's speed with the square of its x velocity.

The two unknowns in Equations 7-21 are the final velocities v_{Afx} and v_{Bfx} of the two objects. It turns out that solving these equations takes quite a few steps, so we'll just present the results:

$$v_{Afx} = v_{Aix}\left(\frac{m_A - m_B}{m_A + m_B}\right)$$

(7-22)

$$v_{Bfx} = v_{Aix}\left(\frac{2m_A}{m_A + m_B}\right)$$

(final velocities in a head-on elastic collision, object B initially at rest)

You can verify Equations 7-22 by substituting them into Equations 7-21 and simplifying.

Equations 7-22 show that the final velocity of each object is proportional to the initial velocity v_{Aix} of object A. The value of each final velocity also depends on a factor in parentheses that involves the masses of the two objects. In addition, the direction of each object's motion is given by the sign of its final velocity. If the sign of an object's final velocity is the same as the sign of v_{Aix}, the object leaves the collision in the same direction as object A was moving initially. If the final velocity has the opposite sign from v_{Aix}, the object is moving in the direction opposite to the initial motion. For example, if v_{Afx} is negative while v_{Aix} is positive, object A has bounced backward after colliding with initially stationary object B.

❗ Watch Out!   Some equations are less important than others.

Equations 7-22 are useful for solving a certain, very special kind of collision problem, but they are not *essential* equations that you should worry about trying to memorize or even remember in detail. What *is* worth remembering is the key physics of an elastic collision: Both momentum and kinetic energy are conserved.

Example 7-8 When Molecules Collide Elastically

In air, at room temperature, a typical molecule of oxygen (O_2) moves at about 500 m/s. (In Chapter 14 we'll explore the relationship between the temperature of a gas and the speeds of molecules in that gas.) The mass of an O_2 molecule is 32.0 u, where 1 u = 1 atomic mass unit = 1.66×10^{-27} kg. Suppose an O_2 molecule is initially moving at 5.00×10^2 m/s in the positive x direction and has a head-on elastic collision with a molecule of hydrogen (H_2, of mass 2.02 u) that is at rest. Determine the final velocity of each molecule, the initial and final momentum of each molecule, and the initial and final kinetic energy of each molecule.

Set Up

Since this is a one-dimensional elastic collision in which one object is initially at rest, we can find the final velocities using Equations 7-22. Here A represents the moving oxygen molecule and B represents the hydrogen molecule. We can then use the definitions of momentum and kinetic energy to find the initial and final values of these quantities.

Final velocities in a head-on elastic collision, object B initially at rest:

$$v_{Afx} = v_{Aix}\left(\frac{m_A - m_B}{m_A + m_B}\right)$$

$$v_{Bfx} = v_{Aix}\left(\frac{2m_A}{m_A + m_B}\right) \quad (7\text{-}22)$$

$$\vec{p} = m\vec{v} \quad (7\text{-}5)$$

$$K = \frac{1}{2}mv^2 \quad (6\text{-}8)$$

before

$v_{Aix} = +5.00 \times 10^2$ m/s $v_{Bix} = 0$

Ⓐ →   Ⓑ — →x

$m_A = m_{O_2} = 32.0$ u $m_B = m_{H_2} = 2.02$ u

after   Ⓐ   Ⓑ — — — →x

$v_{Afx} = ?$ $v_{Bfx} = ?$

Solve

Calculate the final velocities using Equations 7-22. Since these equations involve the ratios of the masses, we can use the mass values in atomic mass units without needing to convert to kilograms.

Oxygen molecule A is initially moving in the positive x direction, so

$$v_{Aix} = +5.00 \times 10^2 \text{ m/s}$$

Mass of molecule A (O_2) is $m_A = 32.0$ u
Mass of molecule B (H_2) is $m_B = 2.02$ u

Final velocity of O_2 molecule:

$$v_{Afx} = v_{Aix}\left(\frac{m_A - m_B}{m_A + m_B}\right)$$

$$= (+5.00 \times 10^2 \text{ m/s})\left(\frac{32.0 \text{ u} - 2.02 \text{ u}}{32.0 \text{ u} + 2.02 \text{ u}}\right)$$

$$= +4.41 \times 10^2 \text{ m/s}$$

$v_{Afx} = +4.41 \times 10^2$ m/s

Ⓐ → $v_{Bfx} = +9.41 \times 10^2$ m/s   Ⓑ →

$m_A = m_{O_2} = 32.0$ u $m_B = m_{H_2} = 2.02$ u

Final velocity of H_2 molecule:

$$v_{Bfx} = v_{Aix}\left(\frac{2m_A}{m_A + m_B}\right)$$

$$= (+5.00 \times 10^2 \text{ m/s})\left(\frac{2(32.0 \text{ u})}{32.0 \text{ u} + 2.02 \text{ u}}\right)$$

$$= +9.41 \times 10^2 \text{ m/s}$$

Both final velocities are positive, so after the collision both molecules are moving in the same direction as the initial motion of the O_2 molecule. The H_2 molecule is moving almost twice as fast as the initial velocity of the O_2 molecule.

We now know both the initial and final velocities, so we can calculate the initial and final values of momentum and kinetic energy for both molecules. For these calculations we need the masses in kilograms.

Masses of the molecules in kilograms:

m_A = mass of O_2 molecule
$$= (32.0 \text{ u})(1.66 \times 10^{-27} \text{ kg/u}) = 5.31 \times 10^{-26} \text{ kg}$$

m_B = mass of H_2 molecule
$$= (2.02 \text{ u})(1.66 \times 10^{-27} \text{ kg/u}) = 3.35 \times 10^{-27} \text{ kg}$$

Calculate the initial and final values of x momentum:

For molecule A (O_2):

$$p_{Aix} = m_A v_{Aix} = (5.31 \times 10^{-26} \text{ kg})(+5.00 \times 10^2 \text{ m/s})$$
$$= +2.66 \times 10^{-23} \text{ kg·m/s}$$

$$p_{Afx} = m_A v_{Afx} = (5.31 \times 10^{-26} \text{ kg})(+4.41 \times 10^2 \text{ m/s})$$
$$= +2.34 \times 10^{-23} \text{ kg·m/s} = 0.881 p_{Aix}$$

For molecule B (H_2):

$$p_{Bix} = m_B v_{Bix} = 0 \text{ (molecule B initially at rest)}$$
$$p_{Bfx} = m_B v_{Bfx} = (3.35 \times 10^{-27} \text{ kg})(+9.41 \times 10^2 \text{ m/s})$$
$$= +3.15 \times 10^{-24} \text{ kg·m/s} = 0.119 p_{Aix}$$

In the collision, the O_2 molecule transfers 0.119 of its initial momentum to the H_2 molecule, leaving 0.881 for itself.

Calculate the initial and final values of kinetic energy:

For molecule A (O_2):

$$K_{Ai} = \frac{1}{2}m_A v_{Aix}^2 = \frac{1}{2}(5.31 \times 10^{-26} \text{ kg})(+5.00 \times 10^2 \text{ m/s})^2$$

$$= 6.64 \times 10^{-21} \text{ J}$$

$$K_{Af} = \frac{1}{2}m_A v_{Afx}^2 = \frac{1}{2}(5.31 \times 10^{-26} \text{ kg})(+4.41 \times 10^2 \text{ m/s})^2$$

$$= 5.16 \times 10^{-21} \text{ J} = 0.777 K_{Ai}$$

For molecule B (H_2):

$$K_{Bi} = \frac{1}{2}m_B v_{Bix}^2 = 0 \text{ (molecule B initially at rest)}$$

$$K_{Bf} = \frac{1}{2}m_B v_{Bfx}^2 = \frac{1}{2}(3.35 \times 10^{-27} \text{ kg})(9.41 \times 10^2 \text{ m/s})^2$$

$$= 1.48 \times 10^{-21} \text{ J} = 0.223 K_{Ai}$$

In the collision, the O_2 molecule transfers 0.223 of its initial kinetic energy to the H_2 molecule, leaving 0.777 for itself.

Reflect

Our numerical answers show that both the *total* momentum and the *total* kinetic energy of the system of two molecules are conserved in this collision: Each of these quantities has the same value after the collision as before the collision.

In the case of an O_2 molecule (object A) hitting a stationary H_2 molecule (object B), moving object A is much more massive than stationary target object B. We found that object A slows down only slightly and loses only a little momentum and kinetic energy. Object B flies off moving faster than the original speed of object A.

We invite you to repeat these calculations for the case in which the moving O_2 molecule collides with a second O_2 molecule that is at rest. You'll find that the moving O_2 molecule ends up at rest and the stationary O_2 molecule ends up moving with the original velocity of the first molecule, 5.00×10^2 m/s. In this case the first O_2 molecule transfers all of its momentum and all of its kinetic energy to the second O_2 molecule.

We also invite you to repeat these calculations for the case in which the moving O_2 molecule collides with a protein molecule of mass 3.20×10^4 u that is at rest. In this case you'll find that the O_2 molecule has a final velocity of -4.99×10^2 m/s. The negative sign means that the O_2 molecule *bounces back*, and the magnitude means that the O_2 molecule ends up with nearly the same speed as it had originally (5.00×10^2 m/s). You'll also find that the massive protein molecule ends up with a final velocity of just $+0.999$ m/s, so it moves very slowly in the initial direction of motion of the O_2 molecule. Be sure to also calculate the final momentum and final kinetic energy of the protein molecule; you'll find that it ends up with about twice the initial momentum of the O_2 molecule, but has little kinetic energy.

Below we'll see that these results are just what we would expect for elastic collisions.

Example 7-8 suggests that just as we did in our exploration of completely inelastic collisions (Section 7-4), we can gain insight into the physics of elastic collisions by considering three special cases involving the relative masses of the two objects. Again, we consider a moving object A that has a head-on elastic collision with a stationary object B as is shown in Figure 7-14, so we can use Equations 7-22.

(1) *The moving object has much greater mass than the object at rest* (Figure 7-14a). If the mass of object A is much larger than the mass of object B, we can safely replace both $m_A - m_B$ and $m_A + m_B$ in Equations 7-22 with m_A. In this approximation Equations 7-22 become

$$v_{Afx} = v_{Aix}\left(\frac{m_A - m_B}{m_A + m_B}\right) \approx v_{Aix}\left(\frac{m_A}{m_A}\right) = v_{Aix}$$

$$v_{Bfx} = v_{Aix}\left(\frac{2m_A}{m_A + m_B}\right) \approx v_{Aix}\left(\frac{2m_A}{m_A}\right) = 2v_{Aix}$$

In this extreme case, the motion of the massive object A is unaffected by the collision, but the second, much smaller object B flies off at twice the initial speed of object A. That's what happens in the nearly elastic collision between a bowling ball and a stationary bowling pin, which only has about one-quarter the mass of the ball: The ball continues with nearly the same speed, while the pin flies off at a faster speed. That's also what happened in the collision between a moving oxygen molecule and a stationary, less-massive hydrogen molecule that we studied in Example 7-8.

Go to Picture It 7-1 for more practice dealing with elastic collisions

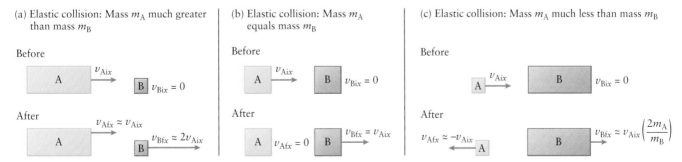

Figure 7-14 **Analyzing an elastic collision** Object A has a head-on elastic collision with object B (initially at rest). (a) If A is much more massive than B, A is almost unaffected and B flies off with twice the initial velocity of A. (b) If A and B have the same mass, A comes to rest and B flies off with the initial velocity of A. (c) If A is much less massive than B, A bounces back with nearly its initial speed and B moves forward very slowly.

(2) *The two objects have the same mass* (Figure 7-14b). If $m_A = m_B$, Equations 7-22 become

$$v_{Afx} = v_{Aix}\left(\frac{m_A - m_B}{m_A + m_B}\right) = 0$$

$$v_{Bfx} = v_{Aix}\left(\frac{2m_A}{m_A + m_B}\right) = v_{Aix}\left(\frac{2m_A}{2m_A}\right) = v_{Aix}$$

In this case, object A comes to a stop during the collision and object B leaves the collision with the initial velocity of A. This turns out to be the *only* possible result of the collision that conserves both momentum and kinetic energy. If a cue ball hits an 8-ball head-on, the result of this nearly elastic collision is that the cue ball stops and the 8-ball rolls away with the speed that the cue ball had before the collision.

(3) *The moving object has much less mass than the object at rest* (Figure 7-14c). In this case the mass of object A is small compared to the mass of object B, so $m_A - m_B$ is approximately equal to $-m_B$ and $m_A + m_B$ is approximately equal to m_B. Then Equations 7-22 become

$$v_{Afx} = v_{Aix}\left(\frac{m_A - m_B}{m_A + m_B}\right) \approx v_{Aix}\left(\frac{-m_B}{m_B}\right) = -v_{Aix}$$

$$v_{Bfx} = v_{Aix}\left(\frac{2m_A}{m_A + m_B}\right) \approx v_{Aix}\left(\frac{2m_A}{m_B}\right)$$

In this case object A is reflected back from the collision, moving with the same speed it had initially but in the opposite direction. Hence object A has lost almost no kinetic energy, but its momentum has changed from $p_{Aix} = +m_A v_{Aix}$ to $p_{Afx} = -m_A v_{Aix}$. Object B is moving very slowly since the ratio $2m_A/m_B$ is much less than 1 (remember that the mass of A is much less than that of B). Because object B has such a large mass, however, it has a substantial amount of momentum:

$$p_{Bfx} = m_B v_{Bfx} = m_B v_{Aix}\left(\frac{2m_A}{m_B}\right) = 2m_A v_{Aix}$$

Then the total momentum of the two objects after the collision is

$$p_{Afx} + p_{Bfx} = -m_A v_{Aix} + 2m_A v_{Aix} = m_A v_{Aix}$$

which is the same as the momentum of object A before the collision. So total momentum is conserved in this case, as it must be. An example is a pebble hitting a boulder: The pebble bounces back, while the recoil of the boulder is so little as to be imperceptible.

Figure 7-15 summarizes the differences between elastic collisions, inelastic collisions, and completely inelastic collisions.

? Got the Concept? 7-4 Classifying Collisions

For each of the following collisions, state whether it is elastic or inelastic. (a) A ball is dropped from rest and hits the ground. It rebounds to half of its original height. (b) After a ball with 200 J of kinetic energy hits a stationary ball on a horizontal surface, the first ball has 125 J of kinetic energy and the second has 75 J of kinetic energy. (c) A dog leaps in the air and catches a ball in its teeth.

(a) Elastic collision: Momentum conserved, mechanical energy conserved

Before

After

(b) Inelastic collision: Momentum conserved, mechanical energy not conserved

Before

After

(c) Completely inelastic collision: Momentum conserved, mechanical energy not conserved, colliding objects stick together

Before

After

Figure 7-15 **Three types of collision** Comparing (a) elastic, (b) inelastic, and (c) completely inelastic collisions.

7-6 What happens in a collision is related to the time the colliding objects are in contact

During a collision that brings a car to a sudden stop, the air bags installed in most cars inflate (Figure 7-16). Their purpose is to prevent serious injury by cushioning the impact between the car's occupants and hard surfaces in the vehicle.

The principle of the air bag is to minimize the *force* on the occupants by maximizing the *time* that it takes to bring the occupants to rest. To see how this works, let's look at the relationship between the net force on an object, the time that the net force acts, and the change in the object's momentum caused by the net force.

Collision Force, Contact Time, and Momentum Change

We learned in Section 7-3 that if external forces act on a *system* of objects for a time Δt, the result is a change in the momentum of the system from an initial value $\vec{P}_i$ to a final value $\vec{P}_f$. This change is given by Equation 7-13:

$$\left(\sum \vec{F}_{\text{external on system}} \right) \Delta t = \vec{P}_f - \vec{P}_i$$

Now suppose the system is made up of only a single object. Then we can replace the symbol $\vec{P}$ (for the momentum of a system) by $\vec{p}$ (for the momentum of a single object), and Equation 7-13 becomes

The sum of all external forces acting on an object

Duration of a time interval over which the external forces act

$$\left(\sum \vec{F}_{\text{external on object}} \right) \Delta t = \vec{p}_f - \vec{p}_i = \Delta \vec{p}$$

Change in the momentum $\vec{p}$ of the object during that time interval

External force and momentum change for an object
(7-23)

The left-hand side of Equation 7-23 is called the **impulse** that acts on the object. This equation tells us that to change the momentum of an *object* from $\vec{p}_i$ to $\vec{p}_f$, a certain amount of impulse is required. This impulse can be the result of a large external force $\sum \vec{F}_{\text{external on object}}$ that acts for a short time Δt or a smaller external force that acts for a longer time.

If the momentum change occurs as a result of a collision, the net external force on an object is predominantly due to the other object with which it is colliding; any other forces are very weak by comparison (see Section 7-3). So for the special case of a collision, Equation 7-23 becomes

Force exerted on an object during a collision

Duration of the collision = **contact time**

$$\vec{F}_{\text{collision}} \Delta t = \vec{p}_f - \vec{p}_i = \Delta \vec{p}$$

Change in the momentum $\vec{p}$ of the object during the collision

Collision force, contact time, and momentum change
(7-24)

The **contact time** in Equation 7-24 is the amount of time that the colliding objects are in contact, and hence the amount of time that the objects exert forces on each other.

Equation 7-24 is the tool we need to explain the principle of the air bag shown in Figure 7-16. If a car comes to a sudden stop, the momentum of one of its occupants

Figure 7-16 **A sudden stop with airbags** How does a deployed airbag help prevent serious injury?

(a)

$$\vec{F}_{collision} \Delta t = \vec{p}_f - \vec{p}_i = -\vec{p}_i$$

(b) $\vec{F}_{collision}$

(c)

$\vec{F}_{collision}$

As the crash test dummy comes to rest, its momentum changes from an initial value $\vec{p}_i$ to a final value $\vec{p}_f = 0$ (zero momentum). The product $\vec{F}_{collision} \Delta t$ equals the negative of $\vec{p}_i$.

If the crash test dummy strikes a hard surface, Δt is very short and $\vec{F}_{collision}$ is very large.

If the crash test dummy strikes an airbag, Δt is longer and $\vec{F}_{collision}$ is reduced.

Figure 7-17 Contact time (a) To bring a crash test dummy to rest requires that $\vec{F}_{collision} \Delta t$ have a certain large value. (b) A short contact time Δt means that the force $\vec{F}_{collision}$ will be large. (c) A longer contact time Δt reduces the magnitude of $\vec{F}_{collision}$.

changes from a large initial value $\vec{p}_i$ to a final value of zero ($\vec{p}_f = 0$). So the momentum change $\vec{p}_f - \vec{p}_i$ is large, which means the product $\vec{F}_{collision}\Delta t$ also has a large value (Figure 7-17a). If there are no air bags the occupant has a "hard" collision with the structure of the car and also comes to a sudden stop. In this case the contact time Δt is very short, and so $\vec{F}_{collision}$ must have a *very* large value: The car's structure exerts a tremendous force on the occupant that is likely to cause injury, as Figure 7-17b shows. (One of the authors of this book has a permanent scar from a collision in a car without air bags.) But if the car is equipped with air bags, the occupant covers a greater distance as it comes to rest and so is in contact with the air bag for a longer time Δt (Figure 7-17c). Hence $\vec{F}_{collision}$ (which represents the force exerted on the occupant by the air bag) is greatly reduced, and injury is avoided. For the same reason, if you jump down from a table it's less painful if you bend your knees when landing (so that your legs flex during the collision between your feet and the ground, thus maximizing the contact time Δt that it takes for you to come to a stop).

> **! Watch Out! Constant force or average force.**
>
> In deriving Equations 7-23 and 7-24, we have assumed that the forces acting on the object are *constant* forces that do not change during the time Δt. We can still use these equations even if the forces are not constant, however: Just treat $\sum \vec{F}_{external \ on \ object}$ in Equation 7-23 and $\vec{F}_{collision}$ in Equation 7-24 as the *average* values of these forces over the time interval Δt.

Example 7-9 shows how to apply the idea of contact time to a collision in which an object speeds up rather than slowing down.

Example 7-9 Follow-through

Tennis players are taught to *follow through* as they serve the ball—that is, to continue to swing the racket after first striking the ball. The rationale is that by increasing the time that the ball and racket are in contact, the ball might have a larger speed as it leaves the racket. Using her racket, a player can exert an average force of 560 N on a 57-g tennis ball during an overhand serve (Figure 7-18). At what speed does the ball leave her racket if the contact time between them is 0.0050 s? What would the speed of the ball be if she improved her follow-through and increased the contact time by a factor of 1.3 to 0.0065 s? During an overhand serve, the tennis ball is struck when it is essentially motionless.

Figure 7-18 Tennis physics How does an improved follow-through affect the speed of a tennis ball?

Set Up

We are given the force that the racket exerts on the ball and the contact time (the time that the ball is touching the racket). We also know that the ball starts at rest and so with zero momentum. We can use Equation 7-24 to calculate the final momentum of the ball, and then use Equation 7-5 to determine the final speed.

Collision force, contact time, and momentum change:

$$\vec{F}_{\text{collision}} \Delta t = \vec{p}_{\text{f}} - \vec{p}_{\text{i}} \qquad (7\text{-}24)$$

$$\vec{p} = m\vec{v} \qquad (7\text{-}5)$$

Solve

The racket follows a curved path during the serve. But since the collision between racket and ball lasts such a short time, the ball is in contact with the racket for just a short segment of that path, which we can treat as a straight line. We choose the positive x axis to be in the direction of the motion of the ball.

The collision is one-dimensional, so we just need the x component of Equation 7-24:

$$F_{\text{collision},x} \Delta t = p_{\text{f}x} - p_{\text{i}x}$$

The ball is initially at rest, so $v_{\text{i}x} = 0$ and

$$p_{\text{i}x} = 0$$

After the collision with the racket, the ball has (unknown) velocity $v_{\text{f}x}$, so

$$p_{\text{f}x} = mv_{\text{f}x}$$

Then the x component of Equation 7-24 becomes

$$F_{\text{collision},x} \Delta t = mv_{\text{f}x} - 0 = mv_{\text{f}x}$$

Solve for the final velocity of the ball in each case.

Rewrite the x component of Equation 7-24 to solve for $v_{\text{f}x}$:

$$v_{\text{f}x} = \frac{F_{\text{collision},x} \Delta t}{m}$$

In both cases, $F_{\text{collision},x} = 560$ N

$$m = 57 \text{ g} \left(\frac{1 \text{ kg}}{1000 \text{ g}} \right) = 0.057 \text{ kg}$$

Calculate $v_{\text{f}x}$ if the contact time is 0.0050 s. Recall that $1 \text{ N} = 1 \text{ kg} \cdot \text{m/s}^2$:

$$v_{\text{f}x} = \frac{F_{\text{collision},x} \Delta t}{m} = \frac{(560 \text{ N})(0.0050 \text{ s})}{0.057 \text{ kg}}$$

$$= 49 \frac{\text{N} \cdot \text{s}}{\text{kg}} \left(\frac{1 \text{ kg} \cdot \text{m/s}^2}{1 \text{ N}} \right) = 49 \text{ m/s}$$

With improved follow-through and a contact time of 0.0065 s,

$$v_{\text{f}x} = \frac{F_{\text{collision},x} \Delta t}{m} = \frac{(560 \text{ N})(0.0065 \text{ s})}{0.057 \text{ kg}} = 64 \text{ m/s}$$

Reflect

For a given force, the change in momentum and therefore the change in velocity during a collision are directly proportional to the contact time. Increasing the contact time Δt from 0.0050 s to $(1.3)(0.0050 \text{ s}) = 0.0065$ s results in an increase in the final speed of the tennis ball from 49 m/s to $(1.3)(49 \text{ m/s}) = 64 \text{ m/s}$.

Impulse and Momentum Versus Work and Kinetic Energy

Equation 7-23 says that the product of the net force on an object and the time that the force acts equals the change in momentum of the object. This should remind you of the work-energy theorem from Section 6-3, which we can write as

(7-25) $$W_{net} = Fd \cos \theta = K_f - K_i$$

This says that the net work on an object—which is the product of the net force on an object parallel to its displacement and the *displacement* of the object during the time that the force acts—equals the change in *kinetic energy* of the object. Equation 7-25 gives us an alternative way to think about the principle of the air bag shown in Figure 7-16. To bring a moving crash test dummy to rest, its kinetic energy $K = \frac{1}{2}mv^2$ must change from a large initial value K_i to a final value $K_f = 0$, so the required change in kinetic energy is $K_f - K_i = 0 - K_i = -K_i$. Hence a certain amount of (negative) work has to be done on the dummy to bring it to rest. Without an air bag, the dummy stops in a very short distance when it strikes the hard surfaces of the car, so the magnitude of the displacement d is small and the force F on the dummy must be large. With an air bag, however, the dummy travels a larger distance as it slows to a stop. In this case the magnitude of the displacement d is larger, and the force F is smaller and less injurious.

? Got the Concept? 7-5
Force of the Kick

A soccer player's foot is in contact with the 0.43-kg ball for 8.6×10^{-3} s. The ball is initially at rest. What is the speed of the ball immediately after being kicked if the player exerts a force of 1700 N on it? (a) 1.5 m/s; (b) 3.4 m/s; (c) 15 m/s; (d) 34 m/s.

Take-Home Message for Section 7-6

✔ The change in momentum of an object during a collision equals the force exerted on the object during the collision multiplied by the contact time—the length of time that the object touches another during the collision.

✔ The same change in momentum can be produced by a large force acting for a short time or by a small force acting for a longer time.

7-7 The center of mass of a system moves as though all of the system's mass were concentrated there

The concept of momentum can help us answer a question that may have been lurking in the back of your mind since Chapter 4. We learned in that chapter that the acceleration of an object is determined by the external forces on the object as described by Newton's second law: $\sum \vec{F}_{ext} = m\vec{a}$. But if the object is rotating, like a gymnast tumbling in midair or a barrel rolling downhill, different parts of the object have different accelerations. So the quantity $\vec{a}$ in $\sum \vec{F}_{ext} = m\vec{a}$ must refer to the acceleration of a specific point on the object. But what point is that?

The point we are looking for is called the **center of mass** of the object. As we will see, the center of mass moves as though all of the object's mass were squeezed into a tiny blob at that point and all of the external forces acted on that blob. We'll begin by showing how to calculate the position of the center of mass; then we'll use ideas about momentum to justify why the center of mass behaves as it does.

Averages and Weighted Averages

The position of an object's center of mass turns out to be a kind of *average* of the positions of all of the pieces that make up that object. If the object is a car, you can think of these pieces as the various components of a car, or the individual atoms that comprise the car. To see how this average is defined, let's first remind ourselves how to calculate an ordinary average.

To find the average of a set of N numbers, add them together and divide by N. For example, the average of the three numbers ($N = 3$) of 4, 8, and 18, for example, is $(4 + 8 + 18)/3 = 30/3 = 10$. The average of the set of six numbers $n_1 = 4$, $n_2 = 4$, $n_3 = 8$, $n_4 = 8$, $n_5 = 8$, $n_6 = 10$ is

$$\bar{n} = \frac{1}{6}\sum_{i=1}^{6} n_i = \frac{4 + 4 + 8 + 8 + 8 + 10}{6} = \frac{42}{6} = 7$$

Here n_i represents the *i*th value in the set, and the symbol $\bar{n}$ (*n* with a bar on top) denotes the average value of the numbers n_i. Notice that because some of the values in the set occur more than once, we could write this average as

$$\bar{n} = \frac{2(4) + 3(8) + 10}{6} = \frac{2}{6}(4) + \frac{3}{6}(8) + \frac{1}{6}(10) = 7 \qquad (7\text{-}26)$$

Each term in this sum includes the fraction of the entire set comprised of the value that follows it: 2/6 of the set has value 4, 3/6 of the set has value 8, and 1/6 of the set has value 10. In writing the sum this way, we have defined a **weighted average**, in which each value affects the result to a greater or lesser extent depending on how often it appears in the set. Here, *weight* does not refer to a force due to gravity, but rather to the amount that each value contributes to the result.

Let's see how to use a weighted average to define the center of mass of a complex object. Imagine a waiter who supports a tray on one hand. The tray has a bowl of soup on one side and a small mint on the other (Figure 7-19). To balance the combination of tray, soup bowl, and mint, the waiter supports the tray at a position much closer to the soup than the mint. This position is the center of mass of the three objects: If the tray, soup bowl, and mint were all squeezed into a single blob, the waiter would put his hand directly under the blob to support it. The position of the center of mass isn't the ordinary average of the positions of tray, soup bowl, and mint, which would be a point at the geometrical center of the tray. (If the waiter tried to balance the tray there, the result would be soup everywhere.) Instead, the center of mass is a *weighted* average that puts more emphasis on the position of the most massive member of the collection of objects (in this case, the soup bowl) and less emphasis on the least massive member (in this case, the mint).

Equation 7-26 provides some guidance as to how to write such a weighted average. Suppose we have a system of *N* objects with different masses $m_1, m_2, m_3, \ldots, m_N$. The total mass M_{tot} of the system is the sum of these *N* individual masses:

$$M_{\text{tot}} = m_1 + m_2 + m_3 + \ldots + m_N = \sum_{i=1}^{N} m_i \qquad (7\text{-}27)$$

The mass of each individual object represents a fraction m_i/M of the total mass. Now suppose the *N* objects are at different positions along the *x* axis: $x_1, x_2, x_3, \ldots, x_N$. (Figure 7-20). By analogy to Equation 7-26, we write the position of the center of mass as a weighted average of these positions:

Position of the center of mass of a system of N objects

m_i = masses of the individual objects

$$x_{\text{CM}} = \frac{m_1}{M_{\text{tot}}} x_1 + \frac{m_2}{M_{\text{tot}}} x_2 + \frac{m_3}{M_{\text{tot}}} x_3 + \ldots + \frac{m_N}{M_{\text{tot}}} x_N = \frac{1}{M_{\text{tot}}} \sum_{i=1}^{N} m_i x_i$$

Total mass of all N objects together

x_i = positions of the individual objects

Position of the center of mass of a system
(7-28)

The more massive a given object, the greater the ratio m_i/M_{tot}, and the greater the importance of that object's position x_i in the sum given by Equation 7-28. Example 7-10 illustrates this property of the position of the center of mass.

Lightweight mint   Heavier soup bowl

The system behaves as though all of its mass were concentrated at the center of mass. That's where the waiter supports the tray.

Figure 7-19 Center of mass at the restaurant The tray balances if it is supported at the center of mass of the system of tray, soup bowl, and mint.

Figure 7-20 A system of objects The position of the center of mass of this collection of objects depends on the masses and positions of the individual objects (Equation 7-28).

> Go to Picture It 7-2 for more practice dealing with center of mass

Example 7-10 Locating the Center of Mass

Two objects are located on the *x* axis at the positions $x_1 = 2.0$ m and $x_2 = 8.0$ m. For the system made up of these two objects, find the position of the center of mass (a) if m_1 and m_2 are both equal to 3.0 kg and (b) if $m_1 = 3.0$ kg and $m_2 = 33$ kg.

Set Up

Since there are just two objects, the total mass of the system is just the sum of their two masses. We use Equation 7-28 in each case to locate the center of mass.

Position of the center of mass of a system:

$$x_{CM} = \frac{m_1}{M_{tot}}x_1 + \frac{m_2}{M_{tot}}x_2 + \frac{m_3}{M_{tot}}x_3$$
$$+ \ldots + \frac{m_N}{M_{tot}}x_N$$

$$= \frac{1}{M_{tot}}\sum_{i=1}^{N} m_i x_i \qquad (7\text{-}28)$$

Total mass of the system of two objects:
$$M_{tot} = m_1 + m_2 \qquad (7\text{-}27)$$

(diagram: m_1 at $x_1 = 2.0$ m, m_2 at $x_2 = 8.0$ m, $x = 0$)

Solve

(a) Calculate the position of the center of mass for the case in which both objects have the same mass.

The two objects have equal masses:
$$m_1 = m_2 = 3.0 \text{ kg}$$
Total mass of the system:
$$M_{tot} = m_1 + m_2$$
$$= 3.0 \text{ kg} + 3.0 \text{ kg} = 6.0 \text{ kg}$$
Position of the center of mass:

$$x_{CM} = \frac{m_1}{M_{tot}}x_1 + \frac{m_2}{M_{tot}}x_2$$

$$= \frac{3.0 \text{ kg}}{6.0 \text{ kg}}(2.0 \text{ m}) + \frac{3.0 \text{ kg}}{6.0 \text{ kg}}(8.0 \text{ m}) = 5.0 \text{ m}$$

(diagram: $x = 5.0$ m, $m_1 = 3.0$ kg at $x_1 = 2.0$ m, $m_2 = 3.0$ kg at $x_2 = 8.0$ m, $x = 0$)

(b) Repeat part (a) for the case in which m_2 is much larger than m_1.

The two objects have different masses:
$$m_1 = 3.0 \text{ kg}, m_2 = 33 \text{ kg}$$
Total mass of the system:
$$M_{tot} = m_1 + m_2$$
$$= 3.0 \text{ kg} + 33 \text{ kg} = 36 \text{ kg}$$
Position of the center of mass:

$$x_{CM} = \frac{m_1}{M_{tot}}x_1 + \frac{m_2}{M_{tot}}x_2$$

$$= \frac{3.0 \text{ kg}}{36 \text{ kg}}(2.0 \text{ m}) + \frac{33 \text{ kg}}{36 \text{ kg}}(8.0 \text{ m}) = 7.5 \text{ m}$$

(diagram: $x_{cm} = 7.5$ m, $m_1 = 3.0$ kg at $x_1 = 2.0$ m, $m_2 = 33$ kg at $x_2 = 8.0$ m, $x = 0$)

Reflect

In part (a), the position $x_{CM} = 5.0$ m is 3.0 m from object 1 and 3.0 m from object 2—in other words, exactly halfway between the two identical objects. In part (b), by contrast, the center of mass is 5.5 m from the less massive object 1 ($m_1 = 3.0$ kg) and only 0.5 m from the more massive object 2 ($m_2 = 33$ kg). If one object in the system is much more massive than the others, the center of mass is closest to that most massive object. In both cases, if the two objects were connected by a rigid lightweight rod, you could balance the system in your hand if you supported it at the center of mass just like the tray shown in Figure 7-19.

It's important to note that the relative position of the center of mass does *not* depend on the choice of origin. As an example, suppose we choose $x = 0$ to be at the position of object 1, so that object 2 is at position $x_2 = 6.0$ m. In this case we find the center of mass in case (b) to be at $x_{CM} = 5.5$ m. That looks different from the value of 7.5 m that we found above, but is still 5.5 m from object 1 and 0.5 m from object 2—exactly as we found before.

Find the center of mass in case (b), with two objects of different mass, but now with the origin chosen to be at the position of object 1:

$$m_1 = 3.0 \text{ kg}, m_2 = 33 \text{ kg so } M_{tot} = 36 \text{ kg}$$
$$x_1 = 0, x_2 = 6.0 \text{ m}$$

Position of the center of mass:

$$x_{CM} = \frac{m_1}{M_{tot}}x_1 + \frac{m_2}{M_{tot}}x_2$$

$$= \frac{3.0 \text{ kg}}{36 \text{ kg}}(0) + \frac{33 \text{ kg}}{36 \text{ kg}}(6.0 \text{ m}) = 5.5 \text{ m}$$

(diagram: $x_{cm} = 5.5$ m, $m_1 = 3.0$ kg at $x_1 = 0$, $m_2 = 33$ kg at $x_2 = 6.0$ m)

More on the Position of the Center of Mass

In writing Equation 7-28, we assumed that all of the objects are arranged along a line that we call the x axis. If the objects are arranged in a plane defined by the x and y axes, we need to specify the x and y coordinates of the position of the center of mass. Equation 7-28 gives the x coordinate, and a very similar equation gives us the y coordinate:

$$y_{CM} = \frac{m_1}{M_{tot}}y_1 + \frac{m_2}{M_{tot}}y_2 + \frac{m_3}{M_{tot}}y_3 + \ldots + \frac{m_N}{M_{tot}}y_N = \frac{1}{M_{tot}}\sum_{i=1}^{N}m_i y_i \qquad (7\text{-}29)$$

$(y$ coordinate of the position of the center of mass)

If the objects are arranged in three dimensions, you would also need an equation similar to Equations 7-28 and 7-29 for the z coordinate z_{CM} of the center of mass.

The center of mass of the system in part (a) of Example 7-10 is midway between the two objects, at the *geometrical* center of the system. This is true whenever the system is *symmetrical* so that the mass is distributed in the same way on both sides of the center of mass. For example, the center of mass of a billiard ball is at its geometrical center, as is the center of mass of a uniform metal rod. In part (b) of Example 7-10 the center of mass is *not* at the geometrical center because the system is not symmetrical: Masses m_1 and m_2 have very different values.

> ! **Watch Out!** **There doesn't have to be any mass at the center of mass.**
>
> Note that in both parts (a) and (b) of Example 7-10, there's nothing physically located *at* the center of mass. The same is true for any symmetrical object with a hole at its center, like a Blu-ray disc, a doughnut, or a ping-pong ball: In each case the center of mass is located in the center of the empty hole.

Momentum, Force, and the Motion of the Center of Mass

It's now time to justify the statement that the center of mass as defined by Equation 7-28 moves as though all of the mass of the system were concentrated there. To begin, let's combine Equations 7-28 and 7-29 into a single *vector* equation for the position of the center of mass:

$$\vec{r}_{CM} = \frac{m_1}{M_{tot}}\vec{r}_1 + \frac{m_2}{M_{tot}}\vec{r}_2 + \frac{m_3}{M_{tot}}\vec{r}_3 + \ldots + \frac{m_N}{M_{tot}}\vec{r}_N = \frac{1}{M_{tot}}\sum_{i=1}^{N}m_i \vec{r}_i \qquad (7\text{-}30)$$

(vector position of the center of mass)

In Equation 7-30 $\vec{r}_{CM}$ is the position vector of the center of mass and the vectors $\vec{r}_1, \vec{r}_2, \vec{r}_3, \ldots, \vec{r}_N$ represent the positions of the N individual objects that make up the system. Each vector $\vec{r}_i$ has components x_i and y_i (and, if a third dimension is required, z_i), and $\vec{r}_{CM}$ has components x_{CM} and y_{CM} (and z_{CM} if required).

Let's now allow the objects that make up the system to move. (The objects need not be connected, so they may or may not move together.) During a time interval Δt each of the vectors $\vec{r}_i$ in Equation 7-30 changes by an amount $\Delta \vec{r}_i$, which can have a different value for each object. From Equation 7-30, the change $\Delta \vec{r}_{CM}$ in the position vector of the center of mass during Δt is

$$\Delta \vec{r}_{CM} = \frac{m_1}{M_{tot}}\Delta \vec{r}_1 + \frac{m_2}{M_{tot}}\Delta \vec{r}_2 + \frac{m_3}{M_{tot}}\Delta \vec{r}_3 + \ldots + \frac{m_N}{M_{tot}}\Delta \vec{r}_N = \frac{1}{M_{tot}}\sum_{i=1}^{N}m_i \Delta \vec{r}_i \qquad (7\text{-}31)$$

(change in vector position of the center of mass)

Equation 3-7 in Section 3-5 tells us that if an object changes its position by $\Delta \vec{r}$ during a time Δt, the velocity of the object is $\vec{v} = \Delta \vec{r}/\Delta t$. If we divide Equation 7-31 through by Δt, we get an expression for the velocity of the center of mass:

$$\vec{v}_{CM} = \frac{\Delta \vec{r}_{CM}}{\Delta t}$$

$$= \frac{1}{\Delta t}\left(\frac{m_1}{M_{tot}}\Delta \vec{r}_1 + \frac{m_2}{M_{tot}}\Delta \vec{r}_2 + \frac{m_3}{M_{tot}}\Delta \vec{r}_3 + \ldots + \frac{m_N}{M_{tot}}\Delta \vec{r}_N\right) \qquad (7\text{-}32)$$

$$= \frac{m_1}{M_{tot}}\vec{v}_1 + \frac{m_2}{M_{tot}}\vec{v}_2 + \frac{m_3}{M_{tot}}\vec{v}_3 + \ldots + \frac{m_N}{M_{tot}}\vec{v}_N = \frac{1}{M_{tot}}\sum_{i=1}^{N}m_i \vec{v}_i$$

(vector velocity of the center of mass)

Just as the position of the center of mass is a weighted average of the positions of the objects that make up the system, the *velocity* of the center of mass is a weighted average of the *velocities* of the objects.

The quantity $m_i\vec{v}_i$ on the right-hand side of Equation 7-32 should be familiar: This is just the *momentum* of the *i*th object in the system. So $\sum_{i=1}^{N} m_i\vec{v}_i$ is the vector sum of the momentum of all objects that make up the system. This is just the *total* momentum of the system, which we denote as $\vec{P}$. If we multiply Equation 7-32 by the total mass of the system M_{tot}, we get

Total momentum and the velocity of the center of mass (7-33)

The total momentum of a system...

... equals the vector sum of the momentum of all objects in the system...

$$\vec{P} = \sum_{i=1}^{N} m_i\vec{v}_i = M_{\text{tot}}\vec{v}_{\text{CM}}$$

... and also equals the total mass of the system multiplied by the velocity of the center of mass.

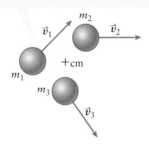

The total momentum of the system is $\vec{P} = m_1\vec{v}_1 + m_2\vec{v}_2 + m_3\vec{v}_3 \ldots$

$M_{\text{tot}} = m_1 + m_2 + m_3 + \ldots$

$\vec{v}_{\text{cm}}$

... which is the same as the momentum of all the mass moving together at the velocity of the center of mass: $\vec{P} = M_{\text{tot}}\vec{v}_{\text{cm}}$.

Figure 7-21 **Total momentum of a system** Two ways to represent the total momentum of a system of objects.

In other words, the total momentum of a system of objects of total mass M_{tot} is the *same* as if all of the objects were squeezed into a single blob moving at the velocity of the center of mass (Figure 7-21). This means that the total linear momentum of a football doesn't depend on how fast the football is spinning, but only on the velocity of the center of mass of the football (which is at the football's geometrical center because the football is symmetrical).

We can now use Equation 7-33 to see what affects the motion of the center of mass. This equation shows that in order for the velocity of the center of mass to change by an amount $\Delta\vec{v}_{\text{CM}}$, there must be a change in the total momentum of the system:

$$\Delta\vec{P} = M_{\text{tot}}\Delta\vec{v}_{\text{CM}}$$

(The mass M_{tot} doesn't change since the system always includes the same set of objects.) But Equation 7-13 in Section 7-3 tells us that the total momentum can change *only* if a net external force acts on the system during the time Δt over which the momentum changes:

$$\left(\sum \vec{F}_{\text{external on system}}\right)\Delta t = \Delta\vec{P}$$

Combining these two equations, we get

$$\left(\sum \vec{F}_{\text{external on system}}\right)\Delta t = M_{\text{tot}}\Delta\vec{v}_{\text{CM}}$$

Divide both sides of this equation by Δt, and recall that the acceleration $\vec{a}$ of an object equals the change in its velocity divided by the time over which the velocity changes: $\vec{a} = \Delta\vec{v}/\Delta t$ (Equation 3-9 in Section 3-5). The result is

How the net external force on a system affects the center of mass (7-34)

The net external force on a system...

... causes the center of mass of the system to accelerate.

$$\sum \vec{F}_{\text{external on system}} = M_{\text{tot}}\frac{\Delta\vec{v}_{\text{CM}}}{\Delta t} = M_{\text{tot}}\vec{a}_{\text{CM}}$$

Equation 7-34 looks almost exactly like Newton's second law for a single object of mass *m*:

$$\sum \vec{F}_{\text{ext}} = m\vec{a}$$

So what Equation 7-34 tells us is that *the center of mass of a system of objects moves exactly as if the entire mass M_{tot} of the system were concentrated at the center of mass, and all of the external forces on the system acted on that concentrated mass.*

This justifies the statements we made at the beginning of this section about the significance of the center of mass.

Equation 7-34 also says that only *external* forces affect the motion of the center of mass. If various parts of the system exert forces on each other, these forces can affect how those parts move relative to each other, but they have *no* effect on the motion of the center of mass. As an example, consider the ballet dancer shown in Figure 7-22. As he leaps from right to left, his arms, legs, head, and torso move in complicated ways relative to each other. But his center of mass, shown by the orange dots, moves in a simple parabolic trajectory. This is the same trajectory that would be followed by a blob with the same mass as the dancer that was acted on by only the external force of gravity. Figure 7-1c shows another example: The center of mass of the Earth–Moon system orbits the Sun as though both worlds were compressed into a blob at the center of mass and as though that blob were held in orbit by the Sun's gravitational attraction. The motion of the center of mass is unaffected by the gravitational forces between Earth and Moon, because these forces are internal to the Earth–Moon system.

If the net external force on a system is zero, Equation 7-34 says that the center of mass cannot accelerate even if the various parts of the system move relative to each other. Example 7-11 illustrates this principle.

The dancer's center of mass follows a parabolic trajectory, just as if all of the dancer's mass were concentrated there.

Figure 7-22 Center of mass of a ballet dancer The motion of the ballet dancer's body is very complex, but the motion of the dancer's center of mass is very simple.

Example 7-11 An Ant on a Twig

A narrow, uniform twig is 15 cm long and has a mass of 2.2 g. The twig floats in a swimming pool so that its left-hand end touches the edge of the pool (Figure 7-23a). A 0.35-g ant, initially resting at the right-hand end of the twig, crawls along the twig toward the left-hand end. Assuming that the twig experiences no resistive forces due to the water, how far is the left-hand end of the twig from the edge of the pool when the ant reaches that end (Figure 7-23b)?

(a) Initial

Twig $m_A = 0.35$ g
                            Ant
        $m_T = 2.2$ g
        |——— 15 cm ———|

(b) Final

$d = ?$

Figure 7-23 How far does the twig move? When the ant walks to the left along the length of the floating twig, how far to the right does the twig move?

Set Up

By assumption there are no horizontal resistive forces, and the water exerts an upward buoyant force that balances the downward gravitational force. So there is *zero* net external force on the system of ant and twig. (The ant and twig exert forces on each other as the ant walks. But these forces are *internal* to the system and so aren't included in the sum $\sum \vec{F}_{\text{external on system}}$.) So Equation 7-34 tells us that the center of mass of the system, which is initially at rest, does not accelerate and so remains at rest at the same position given by Equation 7-28. We'll use this to determine the final position of the ant.

How the net external force on a system affects the center of mass:

$$\sum \vec{F}_{\text{external on system}} = M_{\text{tot}}\frac{\Delta \vec{v}_{\text{CM}}}{\Delta t}$$

$$= M_{\text{tot}}\vec{a}_{\text{CM}} \quad (7\text{-}34)$$

In this situation $\sum \vec{F}_{\text{external on system}} = 0$, so the center of mass does not accelerate and so remains at rest at the same position.

Position of the center of mass of a system:

$$x_{\text{CM}} = \frac{m_1}{M_{\text{tot}}}x_1 + \frac{m_2}{M_{\text{tot}}}x_2 + \frac{m_3}{M_{\text{tot}}}x_3 + \ldots + \frac{m_N}{M_{\text{tot}}}x_N$$

$$= \frac{1}{M_{\text{tot}}}\sum_{i=1}^{N} m_i x_i \quad (7\text{-}28)$$

Total mass of the system of two objects:

$$M_{\text{tot}} = m_1 + m_2 \quad (7\text{-}27)$$

Length of twig is $L = 15$ cm $= 0.15$ m
Mass of ant: $m_A = 0.35$ g
Mass of twig: $m_T = 2.2$ g

B (buoyant force)

side view

$m_A g$

$m_T g$

Solve

First calculate the position of the center of mass when the ant and twig are in their initial positions. Since the center of mass doesn't move, this will also be its position when the ant begins walking.

Choose the x axis to lie along the length of the twig, with $x = 0$ at the edge of the pool.
The ant is small enough to treat as a point located at the end of the twig:

$$x_A = L$$

The twig is uniform, so its center of mass is at its geometrical center:

$$x_T = \frac{L}{2}$$

Total mass of the system:

$$M_{tot} = m_A + m_T$$

Position of the center of mass:

$$x_{CM} = \frac{m_A}{M_{tot}}x_A + \frac{m_T}{M_{tot}}x_T = \frac{m_A L + m_T L/2}{m_A + m_T}$$

$$= \frac{(0.35\text{ g})(15\text{ cm}) + (2.2\text{ g})(15\text{ cm})/2}{0.35\text{ g} + 2.2\text{ g}} = 8.5\text{ cm}$$

The center of mass is between the center of the twig and the position of the ant, and closer to the center of the more massive twig.

As the ant walks to the left, it pushes backward on the twig and so the twig moves to the right. However, the center of mass remains in the same position. Solve for the final distance d from the edge of the pool to the ant.

When the ant has completed its walk to the left-hand end of the twig, the new positions of the ant and the center of the twig are

$$x_A = d$$

$$x_T = d + \frac{L}{2}$$

The new position of the center of mass is

$$x_{CM} = \frac{m_A}{M_{tot}}x_A + \frac{m_T}{M_{tot}}x_T = \frac{m_A d + m_T(d + L/2)}{m_A + m_T}$$

This must be equal to the original position of the center of mass as found above, so

$$\frac{m_A d + m_T(d + L/2)}{m_A + m_T} = \frac{m_A L + m_T L/2}{m_A + m_T}$$

Multiply through by $m_A + m_T$:

$$m_A d + m_T(d + L/2) = m_A L + m_T L/2$$

The term $m_T L/2$ is on both sides of the equation, and so cancels:

$$m_A d + m_T d = m_A L$$

Solve for the distance d:

$$d = \frac{m_A L}{m_A + m_T} = \frac{(0.35\text{ g})(15\text{ cm})}{0.35\text{ g} + 2.2\text{ g}} = 2.1\text{ cm}$$

The ant and the left-hand end of the twig end up 2.1 cm from the edge of the pool.

Reflect

The ant was initially a distance $L = 15$ cm from the edge of the pool and ends up a distance $d = 2.1$ cm from the edge. Hence the ant moves a distance $L - d = 12.9$ cm. The twig, by contrast, moves away from the edge of the pool by only $d = 2.1$ cm. The twig moves a much shorter distance than the ant because the twig is far more massive.

The center of mass will play an important role when we discuss rotational motion in Chapter 8. We'll see that if an object is rotating as it moves through space, like a spinning football in flight or a spinning tire on a moving car, its motion can naturally be thought of as being in two pieces: the motion of the object's center of mass, plus rotation of the object around its center of mass.

? Got the Concept? 7-6 An Exploding Cannon Shell

An army artillery unit fires a cannon shell over level ground at a target 200 m away. The cannon is perfectly aimed to hit the target, and air resistance can be neglected. At the high point of the shell's trajectory, the shell explodes into two identical halves, both of which hit the ground at the same time. One half falls vertically downward from the point of the explosion. Where does the other half land? (a) On the target; (b) 50 m short of the target; (c) 50 m beyond the target; (d) 100 m beyond the target; (e) 150 m beyond the target.

Take-Home Message for Section 7-7

✔ The center of mass of a system of objects is a weighted average of the positions of the individual objects.

✔ The total momentum of the system equals the system's total mass multiplied by the velocity of the center of mass.

✔ If there is a net external force on the system, the center of mass accelerates as though all of the mass of the system was concentrated into a blob at the center of mass. If there is zero net external force on the system, the center of mass does not accelerate.

Key Terms

center of mass
completely inelastic collision
contact time
elastic collision
external forces

impulse
inelastic collision
internal forces
law of conservation of
    momentum

linear momentum (momentum)
momentum (linear momentum)
total momentum
weighted average

Chapter Summary

Topic	Equation or Figure

Linear momentum: The momentum of an object is a vector that points in the same direction as its velocity. It depends on both the mass and velocity of the object. Do not confuse momentum with kinetic energy, which is a scalar quantity.

The **linear momentum** of an object is a vector.

The linear momentum points in the same direction as the **velocity vector** and is proportional to the velocity.

$$\vec{p} = m\vec{v} \tag{7-5}$$

The linear momentum is also proportional to the object's **mass**.

External force and total momentum change for a system of objects: The total momentum of a system of objects is the vector sum of the individual momentum of each object in the system. Only external forces (which originate from objects outside the system) affect the total momentum; internal forces (exerted by one member of the system on another) do not.

The sum of all external forces acting on a system of objects

Duration of a time interval over which the external forces act

$$\left(\sum \vec{F}_{\text{external on system}} \right) \Delta t = \vec{P}_{\text{f}} - \vec{P}_{\text{i}} = \Delta \vec{P} \tag{7-13}$$

Change during that time interval in the total momentum of the objects that make up the system

Collisions and the law of conservation of momentum: The total momentum of a system is conserved (maintains the same value) if there is zero net external force on the system. If the internal forces during a collision are much greater in magnitude than the external forces, the total momentum of the colliding objects is conserved.

If the net external force on a system of objects is zero...	... then the total momentum of the system at the end of a time interval...

$$\vec{P}_{\mathrm{f}} = \vec{P}_{\mathrm{i}} \tag{7-14}$$

In this case, the total momentum of the system is conserved.	... is equal to the total momentum of the system at the beginning of that time interval.

Kinds of collisions: Momentum is conserved in collisions of all types. In an elastic collision, mechanical energy is also conserved. Mechanical energy is not conserved in an inelastic collision. In a completely inelastic collision, the colliding objects stick together after the collision.

(a) Elastic collision: Momentum conserved, mechanical energy conserved

(b) Inelastic collision: Momentum conserved, mechanical energy not conserved

(c) Completely inelastic collision: Momentum conserved, mechanical energy not conserved, colliding objects stick together

(Figure 7-15)

Completely inelastic collisions: The common final velocity in a completely inelastic collision depends on the masses and initial velocities of the colliding objects.

Velocities of objects A and B before they undergo a completely inelastic collision (in which they stick together)

$$m_{\mathrm{A}}\vec{v}_{\mathrm{Ai}} + m_{\mathrm{B}}\vec{v}_{\mathrm{Bi}} = (m_{\mathrm{A}} + m_{\mathrm{B}})\vec{v}_{\mathrm{f}} \tag{7-18}$$

Masses of objects A and B	Velocity of the two objects moving together after the collision

---

Impulse and external force: To cause a certain change in an object's momentum requires a certain impulse (the product of the net external force on an object and the time that those forces act).

The sum of all external forces acting on an object	Duration of a time interval over which the external forces act

$$\left(\sum \vec{F}_{\text{external on object}}\right) \Delta t = \vec{p}_{\mathrm{f}} - \vec{p}_{\mathrm{i}} = \Delta\vec{p} \tag{7-23}$$

Change in the momentum $\vec{p}$ of the object during that time interval

---

Contact time: The impulse in a collision is determined by the force in the collision and the contact time (the time that the colliding objects interact with each other). The same momentum change can be caused by a strong force with a short contact time or a weak force with a long contact time.

Force exerted on an object during a collision	Duration of the collision = **contact time**

$$\vec{F}_{\text{collision}} \Delta t = \vec{p}_{\mathrm{f}} - \vec{p}_{\mathrm{i}} = \Delta\vec{p} \tag{7-24}$$

Change in the momentum $\vec{p}$ of the object during the collision

Center of mass: The center of mass of a system of objects is a weighted average of the positions of the individual objects.

Position of the center of mass of a system of N objects

m_i = masses of the individual objects

$$x_{CM} = \frac{m_1}{M_{tot}}x_1 + \frac{m_2}{M_{tot}}x_2 + \frac{m_3}{M_{tot}}x_3 + \ldots + \frac{m_N}{M_{tot}}x_N = \frac{1}{M_{tot}}\sum_{i=1}^{N}m_i x_i$$

Total mass of all N objects together

x_i = positions of the individual objects

(7-28)

Total momentum and the motion of the center of mass: The total momentum of the system is the same as if all of the mass were concentrated at the center of mass and moving with the center-of-mass velocity.

The total momentum of a system...

... equals the vector sum of the momentum of all objects in the system...

$$\vec{P} = \sum_{i=1}^{N}m_i\vec{v}_i = M_{tot}\vec{v}_{CM}$$

(7-33)

... and also equals the total mass of the system multiplied by the velocity of the center of mass.

Motion of the center of mass: The center of mass of a system behaves as though all of the mass of the system were concentrated there and all of the external forces acted at that point. If there is no net external force on the system, the center of mass does not accelerate.

The net external force on a system...

... causes the center of mass of the system to accelerate.

$$\sum\vec{F}_{\text{external on system}} = M_{tot}\frac{\Delta\vec{v}_{CM}}{\Delta t} = M_{tot}\vec{a}_{CM}$$

(7-34)

Answer to What do you think? Question

(c) If two objects moving at different velocities collide and stick together, kinetic energy is always lost. That's because some portion of one or both of the objects is compressed in the collision. Hence negative work is done on the object or objects, and kinetic energy is lost. We discuss collisions of this kind (called *completely inelastic* collisions) in Section 7-4.

Answers to Got the Concept? Questions

7-1 (c) This situation is exactly like the case of you pushing off the skateboard. The rifle and the bullet exert forces of equal magnitude on each other, and these forces act for the same amount of time. So just after the shot, the rifle (with you and your rollerblades attached) has the same magnitude of *momentum* as does the bullet. Because the bullet has such a small mass, however, it ends up with much more kinetic energy than the combination of the rifle, you and your rollerblades. Since kinetic energy is a measure of how much work an object can do in coming to rest (see Section 6-3), it follows that the bullet will do much more damage to whatever it hits than will you recoiling on your rollerblades. (That's an important reason why a sharpshooter holds the rifle and lets the bullet fly rather than the other way around!)

7-2 (d) Momentum is conserved in this collision. The collision is two-dimensional, so we need both x and y axes; we'll take the positive x axis to point west (the direction in which the first object is moving initially) and the positive y axis to point north. Then before the collision the total momentum (which is equal to the momentum of the first object) has a positive x component and a zero y component. Because momentum is conserved, the total momentum after the collision must also point in the positive x direction. After the collision the first object has negative x momentum and negative y momentum, so the second object must have a large positive x momentum (so that the total x momentum can be positive) and a positive y momentum (so that the total y momentum can be zero). Therefore the second object is moving west and north.

7-3 (d) In order for the system of car and truck to be at rest after this completely inelastic collision, the total momentum of the system must be zero. The car has a northward momentum of magnitude $p_{car,i} = m_{car}v_{car,i} = (1.50 \times 10^3 \text{ kg})(35.0 \text{ m/s}) = 5.25 \times 10^4$ kg·m/s, so the truck must have a southward momentum of the same magnitude for the total momentum to be zero. Therefore $p_{truck,i} = m_{truck}v_{truck,i} = (7.50 \times 10^3 \text{ kg})v_{truck,i} = 5.25 \times 10^4 \text{ kg} \cdot \text{m/s}$, and $v_{truck,i} = (5.25 \times 10^4 \text{ kg} \cdot \text{m/s})/(7.50 \times 10^3 \text{ kg}) = 7.00 \text{ m/s}$.

7-4 (a) inelastic, (b) elastic, (c) inelastic. In (a) the ball collides with Earth, which is very much more massive than the ball. If the collision were elastic, the ball would rebound with nearly the same kinetic energy as it had just before hitting the ground, and so it would bounce back to its original height. Since this does not happen, mechanical energy must have been lost and the collision must have been inelastic. In (b) the total kinetic energy just after the collision is 125 J + 75 J = 200 J, the same as just before the collision. So mechanical energy is conserved and the collision is elastic. In (c) the colliding objects (the dog and the ball) move together after the collision, so this must be a *completely* inelastic collision as described in Section 7-4.

7-5 (d) This is the same situation as Example 7-9, so we can use the same equation for the final velocity of the ball: $v_{fx} = F_{collision,x}\Delta t/m = (1700 \text{ N})(8.6 \times 10^{-3} \text{ s})/(0.43 \text{ kg}) = 34 \text{ m/s}$ (about 120 km/h or 76 mi/h).

7-6 (d) If the shell did not explode, its center of mass would hit the target. The force that blows the cannon shell apart is *internal* to the shell, so it does not affect the motion of the center of mass. So the center of mass still hits the target. The explosion happens when the shell is halfway along its trajectory, so the half that falls vertically lands 100 m short of the target (half the horizontal distance from cannon to target). We saw in Example 7-10 that the center of mass of a system of two equal masses is halfway between the two masses. So the other mass must land 100 m on the other side of the target.

Questions and Problems

In a few problems, you are given more data than you actually need; in a few other problems, you are required to supply data from your general knowledge, outside sources, or informed estimate.

Interpret as significant all digits in numerical values that have trailing zeros and no decimal points.

For all problems, use $g = 9.80 \text{ m/s}^2$ for the free-fall acceleration due to gravity.

• Basic, single-concept problem

•• Intermediate-level problem, may require synthesis of concepts and multiple steps

••• Challenging problem

SSM *Solution is in Student Solutions Manual*

Conceptual Questions

1. •Using the common definition of the word *impulse*, comment on physicists' choice to define impulse as the change in momentum.

2. •Starting from Newton's second law, explain how a collision that is free from external forces conserves momentum. In other words, explain how the momentum of the system remains constant with time.

3. •If the mass of a basketball is 18 times that of a tennis ball, can they ever have the same momentum? Explain your answer. SSM

4. •Two objects have equal kinetic energies. Are the magnitudes of their momenta equal? Explain your answer.

5. •A glass will break if it falls onto a hardwood floor but not if it falls from the same height onto a padded, carpeted floor. Describe the different outcomes in the collision between a glass and the floor in terms of fundamental physical quantities.

6. •A child stands on one end of a long wooden plank that rests on a frictionless icy surface. (a) Describe the motion of the plank when she runs to the other end of the plank. (b) Describe the motion of the center of mass of the system. (c) How would your answers change if she had walked the plank rather than run down it?

7. •Based on what you know about center of mass, why is it potentially dangerous to step off of a small boat before it comes to a stop at the dock? SSM

8. •A man and his large dog sit at opposite ends of a rowboat, floating on a still pond. You notice from shore that the boat moves as the dog walks toward his owner. Describe the motion of the boat from your perspective.

9. •**Astronomy** An asteroid (2007 WD5) passed between Earth and Mars in 2007. Scientists initially estimated a 4% chance that the 50-m-wide asteroid would collide with Mars. If the asteroid had collided with Mars, could it have knocked the planet out of its orbit? Explain your answer. (For more information on Near Earth Objects, see neo.jpl.nasa.gov/index.html.)

10. •How would you determine if a collision is elastic or inelastic?

11. •A recent U.S. patent application describes a "damage avoidance system" for cell phones, which, upon detecting an impending, uncontrolled impact with a surface, deploys an air-filled bag around the phone. Explain how this could protect the cell phone from damage.

12. •Cite two examples of totally inelastic collisions that occur in your daily life.

13. •Why is conservation of energy alone not sufficient to explain the motion of a Newton's cradle toy, shown in **Figure 7-24**? Consider the case when two balls are raised and released together.

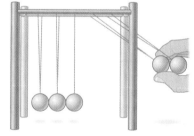

Figure 7-24 Problem 13

14. •After being thrown into the air, a lit firecracker explodes at the apex of its parabolic flight. (a) Is momentum conserved before or after the explosion? (b) Is the mechanical energy conserved? (c) What is the path of the center of mass? Neglect the effects of air resistance and explain your answers.

15. •An arrow shot into a straw target penetrates a distance that depends on the speed with which it strikes the target. How does the penetration distance change if the arrow's speed is doubled? Be sure to list all the assumptions you make while arriving at your answer.

Multiple-Choice Questions

16. •A large semitrailer truck and a small car have equal momentum. How do their speeds compare?
    A. The truck has a much higher speed than the car.
    B. The truck has only a slightly higher speed than the car.
    C. Both have the same speed.
    D. The truck has only a slightly lower speed than the car.
    E. The truck has a much lower speed than the car.

17. •A tennis player smashes a ball of mass m horizontally at a vertical wall. The ball rebounds at the same speed v with which it struck the wall. Has the momentum of the ball changed, and if so, what is the magnitude of the change?
    A. mv
    B. 0
    C. $12mv$
    D. $2mv$
    E. $4mv$ SSM

18. •You throw a bouncy rubber ball and a wet lump of clay, both of mass m, at a wall. Both strike the wall at speed v, but while the ball bounces off with no loss of speed, the clay sticks. What is the change in momentum of the clay and ball, respectively, assuming that toward the wall is the positive direction?
    A. 0; mv
    B. mv; 0
    C. 0; $-2mv$
    D. $-mv$; $-mv$
    E. $-mv$; $-2mv$

19. •Consider a completely inelastic, head-on collision between two particles that have equal masses and equal speeds. Describe the velocities of the particles after the collision.
    A. The velocities of both particles are zero.
    B. Both of their velocities are reversed.
    C. One of the particles continues with the same velocity and the other comes to rest.
    D. One of the particles continues with the same velocity and the other reverses direction at twice the speed.
    E. More information is required to determine the final velocities.

20. •An object is traveling in the positive x direction with speed v. A second object that has half the mass of the first is traveling in the opposite direction with the same speed. The two experience a completely inelastic collision. The final x component of the velocity is
    A. 0
    B. $v/2$
    C. $v/3$
    D. $2v/3$
    E. v

21. •Consider a completely elastic head-on collision between two particles that have the same mass and the same speed. What are the velocities after the collision?
    A. Both are zero.
    B. The magnitudes of the velocities are the same, but the directions are reversed.

C. One of the particles continues with the same velocity, and the other comes to rest.
D. One of the particles continues with the same velocity, and the other reverses direction at twice the speed.
E. More information is required to determine the final velocities. SSM

22. •Two small, identical steel balls collide completely elastically. Initially, ball 1 is moving with velocity v_1, and ball 2 is stationary. After the collision, the final velocities of ball 1 and ball 2 are
    A. $\frac{1}{2}v_1$; $\frac{1}{2}v_1$
    B. v_1; $2v_1$
    C. 0; v_1
    D. $-v_1$; 0
    E. $-v_1$; $2v_1$

23. •Two ice skaters, Lilly and John, face each other while stationary and push against each other's hands. John's mass is twice that of Lilly. How do their speeds compare after the push-off?
    A. Lilly's speed is one-fourth of John's speed.
    B. Lilly's speed is one-half of John's speed.
    C. Lilly's speed is the same as John's speed.
    D. Lilly's speed is twice John's speed.
    E. Lilly's speed is four times John's speed.

24. •A friend throws a heavy ball toward you while you are standing on smooth ice. You can either catch the ball or deflect it back toward your friend. Which of the following options will maximize your speed right after your interaction with the ball?
    A. You should catch the ball.
    B. You should deflect the ball back toward your friend at the same speed with which it hit your hand.
    C. You should let the ball go past you without touching it.
    D. It doesn't matter—your speed is the same regardless of what you do.
    E. You should deflect the ball back toward your friend at half the speed with which it hit your hand.

25. •Two blocks are released from rest on either side of a frictionless half-pipe (Figure 7-25). Block B is more massive than block A. The height H_B from which block B is released is less than H_A, the height from which block A is released. The blocks collide elastically on the flat section. After the collision, which is correct?
    A. Block A rises to a height greater than H_A and block B rises to a height less than H_B.
    B. Block A rises to a height less than H_A and block B rises to a height greater than H_B.
    C. Block A rises to height H_A and block B rises to height H_B.
    D. Block A rises to height H_B and block B rises to height H_A.
    E. The heights to which the blocks rise depends on where along the flat section they collide. SSM

Figure 7-25 Problem 25

Estimation/Numerical Analysis

26. •Estimate the momentum of a car driving the speed limit on a freeway.

27. •**Sports** Estimate the momentum of a fastball thrown by a major league pitcher.

28. •**Sports** Estimate the momentum of a tennis ball served by a professional tennis player.

29. •**Medical, Biology** Estimate the location of the center of mass of your body. SSM

30. •Estimate the momentum that a bumblebee has when it strikes a motorcycle rider.

31. •**Astronomy** Estimate the momentum of Earth as it orbits the Sun.

32. •**Sports** Compare the momentum of a fast-pitch softball to a major league fastball.

33. •Estimate the impulse delivered to a tennis ball that rebounds from a practice wall. SSM

34. •A car moving at 20 m/s slams into the back end of a car stopped at a red light. After the collision, the two cars stick together. If the cars have the same mass, estimate the distance the two cars travel before coming to rest. Assume that neither driver applies his brakes during the collision.

35. •The following gives the force (in newtons) acting on a 2-kg object as a function of time. (a) Make a graph of force versus time. (b) If the object starts from rest, what is its speed after 25 s?

t (s)	F (N)	t (s)	F (N)	t (s)	F (N)
0	−20	9	25	18	25
1	−20	10	25	19	25
2	−10	11	25	20	25
3	0	12	25	21	20
4	10	13	25	22	15
5	15	14	25	23	10
6	18	15	25	24	5
7	20	16	25	25	0
8	25	17	25		

Problems

7-2 Momentum is a vector that depends on an object's mass, speed, and direction of motion

36. •A 10,000-kg train car moves east at 15 m/s. Determine the momentum of the train car.

37. •**Sports** The magnitude of the instantaneous momentum of a 57-g tennis ball is 2.6 kg · m/s. What is its speed? SSM

38. •Determine the initial momentum, final momentum, and change in momentum of a 1250-kg car initially backing up at 5.00 m/s, then moving forward at 14.0 m/s.

39. •**Sports** What is the momentum of a 135-kg defensive lineman running at 7.00 m/s?

40. •One ball has four times the mass and twice the speed of another. (a) How does the momentum of the more massive ball compare to the momentum of the less massive one? (b) How does the kinetic energy of the more massive ball compare to the kinetic energy of the less massive one?

41. •A girl who has a mass of 55.0 kg rides her skateboard to class at a speed of 6.00 m/s. (a) What is her momentum? (b) If the momentum of the skateboard itself is 30.0 kg · m/s, what is its mass? SSM

7-3 The total momentum of a system of objects is conserved under certain conditions

42. •A 2.00-kg object is moving east at 4.00 m/s when it collides with a 6.00-kg object that is initially at rest. After the completely elastic collision, the larger object moves east at 1.00 m/s. What is the final velocity of the smaller object after the collision?

43. •A 3.00-kg object is moving toward the right at 6.00 m/s. A 5.00-kg object moves to the left at 4.00 m/s. After the two objects collide completely elastically, the 3.00-kg object moves toward the left at 2.00 m/s. What is the final velocity of the 5.00-kg object?

44. •Blythe and Geoff are ice skating together. Blythe has a mass of 50.0 kg and Geoff has a mass of 80.0 kg. Blythe pushes Geoff in the chest when both are at rest, causing him to move away at a speed of 4.00 m/s. (a) Determine Blythe's speed after she pushes Geoff. (b) In what direction does she move?

45. ••An object of mass $3M$, moving in the $+x$ direction at speed v_0, breaks into two pieces of mass M and $2M$ as shown in Figure 7-26. If $\theta_1 = 45°$ and $\theta_2 = 30°$, determine the final velocities of the resulting pieces in terms of v_0. SSM

Figure 7-26 Problem 45

46. •In a game of pool, the cue ball is rolling at 2.00 m/s in a direction 30.0° north of east when it collides with the eight ball (initially at rest). The mass of the cue ball is 170 g, but the mass of the eight ball is only 156 g. After the completely elastic collision, the cue ball heads off at 10.0° north of east and the eight ball moves off due north. What are the final speeds of each ball after the collision?

47. •**Biology** During mating season, male bighorn sheep establish dominance with head-butting contests which can be heard up to a mile away. When two males butt heads, the "winner" is the one that knocks the other backward. In one contest a sheep of a mass 95.0 kg and moving at 10.0 m/s runs directly into a sheep of mass 80.0 kg moving at 12.0 m/s. Which ram wins the head-butting contest? SSM

48. ••One way that scientists measure the mass of an unknown particle is to bounce a known particle, such as a proton or an electron, off the unknown particle in a bubble chamber. The initial and rebound velocities of the known particle are measured from photographs of the bubbles it creates as it moves; the information is used to determine the mass of the unknown particle. (a) If a known particle of mass m and initial speed v_0 collides elastically, head-on with a stationary unknown particle and then rebounds with speed v, find the mass of the unknown particle in terms of m, v, and v_0. (b) If the known particle is a proton and the unknown particle is a neutron, what will be the recoil speed of the proton and the final speed of the neutron?

7-4 In an inelastic collision, some of the mechanical energy is lost

49. •A 10,000-kg train car moving due east at 20.0 m/s collides with and couples to a 20,000-kg train car that is initially at rest. What is the common velocity of the two-car train after the collision?

50. •A large fish has a mass of 25.0 kg and swims at 1.00 m/s toward and then swallows a smaller fish that is not moving. If the smaller fish has a mass of 1.00 kg, what is the speed of the larger fish immediately after it finishes lunch?

51. •A 5.00-kg howler monkey is swinging due east on a vine. It overtakes and grabs onto a 6.00-kg monkey also moving east on a second vine. The first monkey is moving at 12.0 m/s at the instant it grabs the second, which is moving at 8.00 m/s. After they join on the same vine, what is their common speed? SSM

52. •A 1200-kg car is moving at 20.0 m/s due north. A 1500-kg car is moving at 18.0 m/s due east. The two cars simultaneously approach an icy intersection where, with no brakes or steering, they collide and stick together. Determine the speed and direction of the combined two-car wreck immediately after the collision.

53. •**Sports** An 85.0-kg linebacker is running at 8.00 m/s directly toward the sideline of a football field. He tackles a 75.0-kg running back moving at 9.00 m/s straight toward the goal line (perpendicular to the original direction of the linebacker). Determine their common speed and direction immediately after they collide.

7-5 In an elastic collision, both momentum and mechanical energy are conserved

54. •A 2.00-kg ball is moving at 3.00 m/s toward the right. It collides elastically with a 4.00-kg ball that is initially at rest. Determine the velocities of the balls after the collision.

55. •A 10.0-kg block of ice is sliding due east at 8.00 m/s when it collides elastically with a 6.00-kg block of ice that is sliding in the same direction at 4.00 m/s. Determine the velocities of the blocks of ice after the collision. SSM

56. •A 0.170-kg ball is moving at 4.00 m/s toward the right. It collides elastically with a 0.155-kg ball moving at 2.00 m/s toward the left. Determine the final velocities of the balls after the collision.

57. •A neutron traveling at 2.00×10^5 m/s collides elastically with a deuteron that is initially at rest. Determine the final speeds of the two particles after the collision. The mass of a neutron is 1.67×10^{-27} kg, and the mass of a deuteron is 3.34×10^{-27} kg.

7-6 What happens in a collision is related to the time the colliding objects are in contact

58. •A sudden gust of wind exerts a force of 20.0 N for 1.20 s on a bird that had been flying at 5.00 m/s. As a result, the bird ends up moving in the opposite direction at 7.00 m/s. What is the mass of the bird?

59. •Determine the average force exerted on your hand as you catch a 0.200-kg ball moving at 20.0 m/s. Assume the time of contact is 0.0250 s. SSM

60. •Determine the impulse delivered over the first 10 s to the object acted on by the force described by the graph (Figure 7-27).

Figure 7-27 Problem 60

61. •**Sports** A baseball of mass 0.145 kg is thrown at a speed of 40.0 m/s. The batter strikes the ball with a force of 25,000 N; the bat and ball are in contact for 0.500 ms. Assuming that the force is exactly opposite to the original direction of the ball, determine the final speed of the ball.

62. •A 5.00-kg object is constrained to move along a straight line. Its initial speed is 12.0 m/s in one direction, and its final speed is 8.00 m/s in the opposite direction. Complete the graph of force versus time with appropriate values for both variables (Figure 7-28). Several answers are correct; just be sure that your answer is internally consistent.

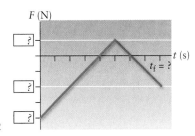

Figure 7-28 Problem 62

63. •**Sports** A baseball bat strikes a ball when both are moving at 31.3 m/s (relative to the ground) toward each other. The bat and ball are in contact for 1.20 ms, after which the ball is traveling at a speed of 42.5 m/s. The mass of the bat and the ball are 850 g and 145 g, respectively. Calculate the magnitude and direction of the impulse given to (a) the ball by the bat and (b) the bat by the ball. (c) What average force does the bat exert on the ball? (d) Why doesn't the force shatter the bat?

7-7 The center of mass of a system moves as though all of the system's mass were concentrated there

64. •Find the coordinates of the center of mass of the three objects shown in Figure 7-29 if $m_1 = 4.00$ kg, $m_2 = 2.00$ kg, and $m_3 = 3.00$ kg. Distances are in meters.

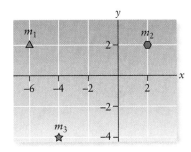

Figure 7-29 Problem 64

65. •What are the coordinates of the center of mass for the combination of the three objects shown in **Figure 7-30**? The uniform rod has a mass of 10.0 kg, has a length of 30.0 cm, and is located at $x = 50.0$ cm. The oval football has a mass of 2.00 kg, a semimajor axis of 15.0 cm, a semiminor axis of 8.00 cm, and is centered at $x = -50.0$ cm. The spherical volleyball has a mass of 1.00 kg, a radius of 10.0 cm, and is centered at $y = -30$ cm. SSM

Figure 7-30 Problem 65

66. •Four beads each of mass M are attached at various locations to a hoop of mass M and radius R (**Figure 7-31**). Find the center of mass of the hoop and beads.

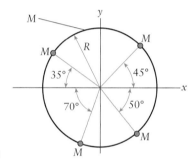

Figure 7-31 Problem 66

General Problems

67. •**Sports** A major league baseball has a mass of 0.145 kg. Neglecting the effects of air resistance, determine the momentum of the ball when it hits the ground if it falls from rest on the roof of the Metrodome in Minneapolis, Minnesota, a height of 60.0 m.

68. •Forensic scientists can determine the speed at which a rifle fires a bullet by shooting into a heavy block hanging by a wire. As the bullet embeds itself in the block, the block and embedded bullet swing up; the impact speed is determined from the maximum angle of the swing. (a) Which would make the block swing higher, a 0.204 Ruger bullet of mass 2.14 g and muzzle speed 1290 m/s or a 7-mm Remington Magnum bullet of mass 9.71 g and muzzle speed 948 m/s? Assume the bullets enter the block right after leaving the muzzle of the rifle. (b) Using your answer in part (a), determine the mass of the block so that when hit by the bullet it will swing through a 60.0° angle. The block hangs from wire of length 1.25 m and negligible mass. (c) What is the speed of an 8.41-g bullet that causes the block to swing upward through a 30.0° angle?

69. •A friend suggests that if all the people in the United States dropped down from a 1-m-high table at the same time, Earth would move in a noticeable way. To test the credibility of this proposal, (a) determine the momentum imparted to Earth by 300 million people, of an average mass of 65.0 kg, drop-

ping from 1.00 m above the surface. Assume no one bounces. (b) What change in Earth's speed would result? SSM

70. •Sally finds herself stranded on a frozen pond so slippery that she can't stand up or walk on it. To save herself, she throws one of her heavy boots horizontally, directly away from the closest shore. Sally's mass is 60 kg, the boot's mass is 5 kg, and Sally throws the boot with speed equal to 30.0 m/s. (a) What is Sally's speed immediately after throwing the boot? (b) Where is the center of mass of the Sally–boot system, relative to where she threw the boot, after 10.0 s? (c) How long does it take Sally to reach the shore, a distance of 30.0 m away from where she threw the boot? For all parts, assume the ice is frictionless.

71. •You have been called to testify as an expert witness in a trial involving a head-on collision. Car A weighs 680 kg and was traveling eastward. Car B weighs 500 kg and was traveling westward at 72.0 km/h. The cars locked bumpers and slid eastward with their wheels locked for 6.00 m before stopping. You have measured the coefficient of kinetic friction between the tires and the pavement to be 0.750. How fast (in miles per hour) was car A traveling just before the collision?

72. •A 5000-kg open train car is rolling at a speed of 20.0 m/s when it begins to rain heavily and 200 kg of water collects quickly in the car. If only the total mass has changed, what is the speed of the flooded train car? For simplicity, assume that all of the water collects at one instant and that the train tracks are frictionless.

73. •An 8000-kg open train car is rolling at a speed of 20.0 m/s when it begins to rain heavily. After water has collected in the car, it slows to 19.0 m/s. What mass of water has collected in the car? For simplicity, assume that all of the water collects at one instant and that the train tracks are frictionless. SSM

74. •An open rail car of initial mass 10,000 kg is moving at 5.00 m/s when rocks begin to fall into it from a conveyor belt. The rate at which the mass of rocks increases is 500 kg/s. Find the speed of the train car after rocks have fallen into the car for a total of 3.00 s.

75. •A skier and a snowboarder of equal mass collide in an area where the snow is level. Just before the collision, the skier was moving south at 8.00 m/s and the snowboarder was moving west at 12.0 m/s. After the unplanned meeting, the skier slid 45° south of west and the snowboarder slid 45° north of west. What was the speed of each athlete after the collision, assuming that the collision was completely elastic?

76. •**Sports** The sport of curling is quite popular in Canada. A curler slides a 19.1-kg stone so that it strikes a competitor's stationary stone at 6.40 m/s before moving at an angle of 120° from its initial direction. The competitor's stone moves off at 5.60 m/s. Determine the final speed of the first stone and the final direction of the second one.

77. ••**Biology** Lions can run at speeds up to approximately 80.0 km/h. A hungry 135-kg lion running northward at top speed attacks and holds onto a 29.0-kg Thomson's gazelle running eastward at 60.0 km/h. Find the speed and direction of travel of the lion–gazelle system just after the lion attacks. SSM

78. •**Biology** The mass of a pigeon hawk is twice that of the pigeons it hunts. Suppose a pigeon is gliding north at a speed of $v_P = 23.0$ m/s when a hawk swoops down, grabs the pigeon, and flies off (Figure 7-32). The hawk was flying north at speed of $v_H = 35.0$ m/s, at an angle $\theta = 45°$ below the horizontal, at the instant of the attack. Find the final velocity vector of the birds just after the attack.

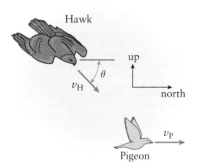

Figure 7-32 Problem 78

79. ••A 12.0-g bullet is fired into a block of wood with speed $v = 250$ m/s (Figure 7-33). The block is attached to a spring that has a spring constant of 200 N/m. The block with the embedded bullet compresses the spring a distance $d = 30.0$ cm to the right, before momentarily coming to a stop. Determine the mass of the wooden block. SSM

Figure 7-33 Problem 79

80. ••In a ballistic pendulum experiment, a small marble is fired into a cup attached to the end of a pendulum. If the mass of the marble is 0.00750 kg and the mass of the pendulum is 0.250 kg, how high will the pendulum swing if the marble has an initial speed of 6.00 m/s? Assume that the mass of the pendulum is concentrated at its end.

81. •••A 2.50-kg object (1) elastically collides with a 3.60-kg object (2) that is initially at rest. The less massive object has a speed of $v_1 = 4.00$ m/s and travels at an angle of θ_1 with its original direction after the collision; the more massive object has a speed of $v_2 = 2.50$ m/s and travels at an angle of θ_2 after the collision (Figure 7-34). What are the initial speed of the less massive object and the two scattering angles, θ_1 and θ_2?

Figure 7-34 Problem 81

82. ••A 0.0750-kg ball is thrown at 25.0 m/s toward a brick wall. (a) Determine the impulse that the wall imparts to the ball when it hits and rebounds at 25.0 m/s in the opposite direction. (b) Determine the impulse that the wall imparts to the ball when it hits and rebounds at an angle of 45.0°. (c) If the ball thrown in part (b) contacts the wall for 0.0100 s, determine the magnitude and direction of the force that the wall exerts on the ball.

83. ••The mass of an oxygen nucleus is about 16 times that of a proton. A proton traveling at 5.00×10^5 m/s collides completely elastically with an oxygen nucleus and leaves the interaction at 5.00×10^5 m/s. (a) What fraction of the initial kinetic energy is transferred to the oxygen nucleus? (b) Determine the final directions of the proton and the oxygen nucleus.

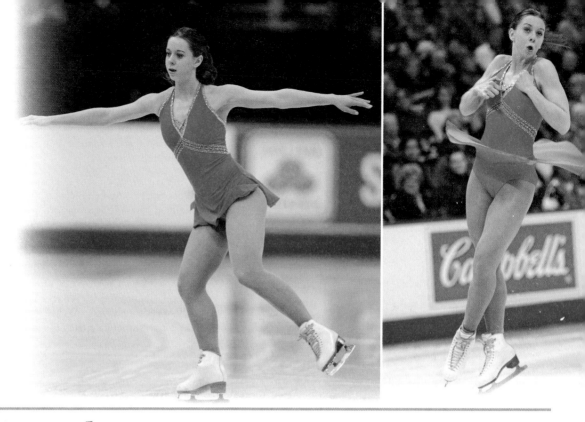

8

Rotational Motion

What do you think?

It's easier for a figure skater to rotate her body if she holds her arms by her side than if she holds her arms straight out. (You can try this yourself—spin around on your feet with your arms held in and with your arms held out.) Why does the orientation of her arms make a difference?

In this chapter, your goals are to:
- (8-1) Define translation and rotation.
- (8-2) Explain what is meant by the moment of inertia of an object and how to use it to calculate the rotational kinetic energy of a rotating object.
- (8-3) Describe the techniques for finding the moment of inertia of an object, including use of the parallel-axis theorem.
- (8-4) Apply the conservation of mechanical energy to rotating objects, including objects that roll without slipping.
- (8-5) Identify the equations of rotational kinematics and know how to use them to solve problems.
- (8-6) Define the concept of lever arm and know how to use it to calculate the torque generated by a force.
- (8-7) Explain the meaning of Newton's second law for rotational motion.
- (8-8) Define what is meant by the angular momentum of a rotating object and of a moving particle, and explain the circumstances under which angular momentum is conserved.
- (8-9) Explain how to find the direction of the angular momentum, angular velocity, and torque vectors.

To master this chapter, you should review:
- (2-2, 2-4) The definitions of average and instantaneous velocity and acceleration.
- (3-8)   The equation for the length of an arc in terms of its radius and angle.
- (4-2)   Newton's second law of motion.
- (6-3, 6-7) The definition of kinetic energy and the principle of conservation of energy.
- (7-2, 7-3) The concept of linear momentum and when linear momentum is conserved.
- (7-7)   The concept of the center of mass of an object.

8-1 Rotation is an important and ubiquitous kind of motion

Up to this point, we've considered the motions of objects such as a thrown baseball, a speeding car, or a soaring bird. We use the word **translation** to refer to these kinds of motion, in which an object as a whole moves through space. However, we haven't worried

A Ferris wheel rotates around a fixed (stationary) axis.

This mother-of-pearl moth caterpillar (*Pleurotya ruralis*) wraps itself into a circle for self-defense: It can roll away from predators 40 times faster than it can walk. As it rolls, the caterpillar moves as a whole (it translates) as well as rotates.

Our planet rotates to the east once per day around an axis that extends from the north pole to the south pole. Earth also translates: It takes one year to move in an orbit around the Sun.

(a)

(b)

(c)

Figure 8-1 **Rotational motion** Three examples of rotating objects.

much about the kind of motion called **rotation**, in which an object spins around an axis. (One example is the figure skater in the photograph above, who rotates around an axis that extends from her head to her toes. Figure 8-1 shows three more examples.) In this chapter we'll expand our horizons and investigate rotational motion.

In some situations, an object undergoes rotation but not translation. An example is the Ferris wheel shown in Figure 8-1a: The Ferris wheel as a whole remains at the same location in the amusement park, but the wheel rotates continuously to entertain its riders. Other objects that rotate without translation are a spinning ceiling fan or the rotating platter in a microwave oven. In other situations, like a rolling caterpillar (Figure 8-1b) or the wheels of a fast-moving bicycle, an object undergoes rotation and translation at the same time. And finally, you've spent your entire life on a planet that experiences both rotation and translation (Figure 8-1c). In this chapter we'll look at all three kinds of situations.

We saw in Chapter 6 that it can be easier to describe motion in terms of work and energy than in terms of forces. With this in mind, let's first ask the following question: How can we find the kinetic energy due to an object's rotation—that is, its *rotational kinetic energy*? Once we've answered this question, we'll be able to use conservation of energy to solve many problems involving rotational motion. Later in the chapter we'll look at an alternative approach involving *torque* and *angular acceleration*—quantities that bear the same relationship to rotational motion that force and acceleration do to translational motion.

> ## Take-Home Message for Section 8-1
>
> ✔ Translation refers to the motion of an object as a whole through space.
>
> ✔ Rotation refers to the spinning motion of an object.
>
> ✔ An object can rotate around a fixed axis (rotation without translation), or its axis can move as the object rotates (rotation with translation).

8-2 An object's rotational kinetic energy is related to its angular velocity and how its mass is distributed

To keep things simple, we'll begin our study of rotational motion by considering rotation without translation. To be specific, we'll examine a **rigid object**—that is, one whose shape doesn't change as it rotates. The spinning wind turbines shown in Figure 8-2 are examples of rotating rigid objects. (By contrast, the figure skater in the photograph that opens this chapter can change her shape as she spins.) We'll also assume that the rotation axis is *fixed*—that is, it keeps the same orientation in space. The wind turbines in Figure 8-2 rotate around fixed axes.

Each blade of this rotating wind turbine is rigid: It maintains the same shape at all times.

The wind turbine rotates around a fixed axis: The axis remains in the same place and keeps the same orientation.

While all parts of the blade rotate together, different parts move at different speeds: The blurring shows that the outer parts (at a greater distance *r* from the axis) move faster than the inner parts of the blade.

Figure 8-2 **A rotating rigid object** The blades of a wind turbine undergo rotation but do not undergo translation (the wind turbine as a whole doesn't go anywhere).

Figure 8-3 Angular velocity We define angular velocity by analogy to the way that we defined velocity for straight-line motion in Chapter 2.

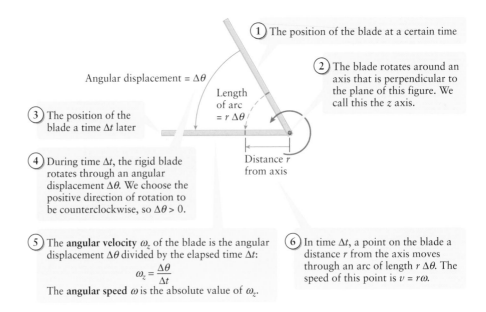

1. The position of the blade at a certain time

2. The blade rotates around an axis that is perpendicular to the plane of this figure. We call this the *z* axis.

Angular displacement = $\Delta\theta$

Length of arc = $r\,\Delta\theta$

3. The position of the blade a time Δt later

Distance *r* from axis

4. During time Δt, the rigid blade rotates through an angular displacement $\Delta\theta$. We choose the positive direction of rotation to be counterclockwise, so $\Delta\theta > 0$.

5. The **angular velocity** ω_z of the blade is the angular displacement $\Delta\theta$ divided by the elapsed time Δt:
$$\omega_z = \frac{\Delta\theta}{\Delta t}$$
The **angular speed** ω is the absolute value of ω_z.

6. In time Δt, a point on the blade a distance *r* from the axis moves through an arc of length $r\,\Delta\theta$. The speed of this point is $v = r\omega$.

$\sqrt{x}$ *See the Math Tutorial for more information on trigonometry*

Angular Velocity and Angular Speed

Let's see how to determine the rotational kinetic energy of the turbine shown in Figure 8-2. We'll begin by considering the motion of one of its blades, shown at two successive times in Figure 8-3.

Recall from Section 6-3 that an object's kinetic energy depends on its mass *m* and its speed *v*: $K = \frac{1}{2}mv^2$. However, we *cannot* use this formula directly to find the rotational kinetic energy of a turbine blade. Here's why: During a short time interval Δt, the entire blade rotates through a small angle $\Delta\theta$. However, different parts of the blade travel different distances during this time interval: A point near the rotation axis travels only a short distance, while a point farther from the axis travels a greater distance. Hence a point farther out along the blade moves faster and has a greater speed than a point closer to the axis. You can see this in the photograph in Figure 8-2: The blade is more blurred the farther it is from the axis. So the speed *v* is *different* for different parts of the blade. Hence we can't immediately use the formula $K = \frac{1}{2}mv^2$ from Section 6-3 to find the blade's kinetic energy because it's not clear which speed *v* we should use.

To see how to account for different speeds at different locations, let's see how the blade moves during a time interval Δt (Figure 8-3). During this time all parts of the rigid blade rotate through the same angle $\Delta\theta$ (pronounced "delta-theta"), which we call the **angular displacement** of the blade. Let's choose angles to increase in the counterclockwise direction; the blade in Figure 8-3 rotates counterclockwise, so with this choice the angular displacement $\Delta\theta$ in Figure 8-3 is positive. By analogy to how we defined average velocity for straight-line motion in Section 2-2, we define the **average angular velocity** of the blade to be

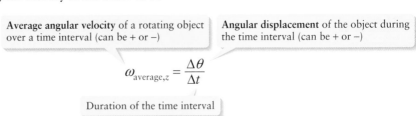

Average angular velocity of a rotating object over a time interval (can be + or −)

Angular displacement of the object during the time interval (can be + or −)

Average angular velocity
(8-1)

$$\omega_{\text{average},z} = \frac{\Delta\theta}{\Delta t}$$

Duration of the time interval

Here ω is the Greek letter omega, and the *z* in the subscript tells us that the blade is rotating around an axis that we call the *z* axis (Figure 8-3). For any rotating rigid object, the value of $\omega_{\text{average},z}$ is the same for all pieces of the object. The average angular velocity can be positive or negative, depending on the direction in which the object rotates. A common choice is to take counterclockwise rotation to be positive and clockwise rotation to be negative, but the choice is up to you.

Just as we did for ordinary velocity in Section 2-4, we'll define the *instantaneous* angular velocity ω_z, or just **angular velocity** for short, as the rate at which the object is rotating at a given instant. That is, the instantaneous angular velocity is the average angular velocity for a very short time interval.

The preferred units of angular velocity are radians per second, or rad/s. As we discussed in Section 3-8, radians are a measure of angle; there are 2π radians in a circle. We can also describe angle in terms of the number of revolutions (rev) that an object makes, so another common set of units for angular velocity is revolutions per second (rev/s). Since one revolution equals 2π radians, $1\,\text{rev/s} = 2\pi\,\text{rad/s}$.

We also use rad/s and rev/s as the units for **angular speed**, which is the magnitude or absolute value of angular velocity. An object that rotates 5.0 radians in one second has angular velocity $\omega_z = +5.0$ rad/s if it rotates in the positive direction and angular velocity $\omega_z = -5.0$ rad/s if it rotates in the negative direction, but in either case its angular speed is 5.0 rad/s. We'll use the symbol ω (with no subscript) for angular speed.

We now have the tools we need to find the *ordinary* speed in meters per second (m/s) of a point along the rotating blade. Figure 8-3 shows that a point (shown in red) a distance r from the rotation axis moves through a circular arc of radius r and angle $\Delta\theta$, which we've taken to be positive. We saw in Section 3-8 that if the angle $\Delta\theta$ is measured in radians and r is measured in meters, the length of such an arc in meters is $r\,\Delta\theta$ (see Figure 3-30). So, $r\,\Delta\theta$ is the distance that this point on the blade travels in a time Δt. The speed v of this point is the distance traveled divided by the time interval, or

$$v = \frac{r\,\Delta\theta}{\Delta t} \tag{8-2}$$

But $\Delta\theta/\Delta t$ is just the angular speed ω of the rotating blade. (Since the blade is rotating in the positive direction, its angular velocity $\omega_z = \Delta\theta/\Delta t$ is positive and so the angular speed ω—which is always positive—is the same as ω_z.) So we can rewrite Equation 8-2 for the speed of a point on the blade as

Speed (in m/s) of a point on a rotating rigid object

Distance (in m) from the axis of rotation to the point

$$v = r\omega$$

Angular speed (in rad/s) of the rotating rigid object

Speed of a point on a rotating rigid object
(8-3)

! **Watch Out!** Use correct units when relating speed and angular speed.

We derived Equation 8-3 from the statement that the length of the arc in Figure 8-3 is $r\,\Delta\theta$. This is true *only* if the angle $\Delta\theta$ is measured in radians (see Section 3-8). Hence you can safely use Equation 8-3 only if the angular speed ω is mea-sured in radians per second (rad/s). If you are given the angular speed in other units, such as revolutions per second (rev/s), revolutions per minute (rev/min), or degrees per second, you must convert it to rad/s before you can use Equation 8-3.

We derived Equation 8-3 assuming that the object is rotating in the positive direction. But it's equally valid if the object rotates in the negative direction, since the speed v and angular speed ω are always positive no matter what the direction of motion.

Equation 8-3 agrees with our observations about the wind turbine shown in Figure 8-2. All points on each turbine blade have the same angular speed ω, but points that are farther from the axis are at a greater distance r and so are moving at a greater speed $v = r\omega$.

Example 8-1 Speed versus Angular Speed

A turbine blade is rotating at 25.0 rev/min. How fast (in m/s) is a point on the blade moving that is (a) 0.500 m from the rotation axis and (b) 1.00 m from the rotation axis?

Set Up

For each point we are given the angular speed ω of the blade and the distance r from the rotation axis. We'll use Equation 8-3 to find the speed v of that piece.

Speed of a point on a rotating object:
$$v = r\omega \tag{8-3}$$

Solve

We are given the angular speed in revolutions per minute. We first need to convert this to radians per second so we can safely use Equation 8-3.

$\omega = 25.0$ rev/min
Convert revolutions to radians and minutes to seconds:

$$\omega = \left(25.0 \frac{\text{rev}}{\text{min}}\right)\left(\frac{2\pi \text{ rad}}{1 \text{ rev}}\right)\left(\frac{1 \text{ min}}{60 \text{ s}}\right)$$

$$= \frac{(25.0)(2\pi)}{60} \frac{\text{rad}}{\text{s}} = 2.62 \text{ rad/s}$$

For each case, substitute $\omega = 2.62$ rad/s and the value of the distance r of the point from the axis.

(a) $v_1 = r_1\omega = (0.500 \text{ m})(2.62 \text{ rad/s}) = 1.31 \text{ m/s}$
(b) $v_2 = r_2\omega = (1.00 \text{ m})(2.62 \text{ rad/s}) = 2.62 \text{ m/s}$

Reflect

Note that piece (b) is twice as far from the rotation axis as is piece (a) and has twice the speed. That's because in the same amount of time, piece (b) travels in a circle that has twice the radius and twice the circumference of the circle traveled by piece (a); so, piece (b) must cover twice as much distance as piece (a).

Note that the units of radians disappeared when we calculated the speed of each piece. We did this because a radian isn't truly a unit, but simply a way of counting the number of revolutions or fractions of a revolution through which an object has rotated.

radius r_1 = 0.500 m
circumference = $2\pi r_1$ = 3.14 m

radius r_2 = 1.00 m
circumference = $2\pi r_2$ = 6.28 m

Moment of Inertia and Rotational Kinetic Energy

Let's see how to use Equation 8-3 to find the kinetic energy of a rotating object such as a wind turbine blade. We'll assume the object is rigid, so all parts of the object rotate at the same angular speed ω. The speed v is different at different points along the blade, however. To account for this, let's imagine that the rigid blade is divided up into many small pieces (Figure 8-4). There are N such small pieces, where N is a large number. We label each piece using the subscript i, where i can equal any integer from 1 to N: $i = 1, 2, 3, \ldots, N$. The ith piece has mass m_i and is a distance r_i from the rotation axis. The reason that we have to use so many pieces is that we want each piece to be very small, so that there is only one value of the distance r_i for each piece. (If the pieces were too large, the distance from the axis would be different for different parts of the piece, and we wouldn't know what value of r to assign to the piece.)

- The total kinetic energy of the rotating blade is the sum of the kinetic energies of the N pieces:

$$K_{\text{rotational}} = K_1 + K_2 + K_3 + \ldots K_N$$

$$= \sum_{i=1}^{N} K_i = \sum_{i=1}^{N} \frac{1}{2}m_i r_i^2 \omega^2$$

- We can write this in terms of the moment of inertia of the blade:

$$K_{\text{rotational}} = \frac{1}{2}I\omega^2 \text{ where } I = \sum_{i=1}^{N} m_i r_i^2$$

① Divide the blade into N small pieces.

② The ith piece has mass m_i and is a distance r_i from the rotation axis.

Piece 1 Piece 3
Piece 2   ...and so on...

Piece N–1 Piece N

Distance r_i from axis

③ The blade is rotating with angular speed ω, so the speed of the ith piece is $v_i = r_i\omega$. The kinetic energy of this piece is

$$K_i = \frac{1}{2}m_i v_i^2 = \frac{1}{2}m_i(r_i\omega)^2 = \frac{1}{2}m_i r_i^2 \omega^2$$

Figure 8-4 **Calculating rotational kinetic energy and moment of inertia** The kinetic energy of a rotating object is the sum of the kinetic energies of all of its component pieces.

From Equation 8-3, the speed of the *i*th small piece of the blade is $v_i = r_i \omega$. If we measure ω in radians per second and r_i in meters, v_i will be in meters per second (m/s). The kinetic energy of the *i*th piece of the blade is therefore

$$K_i = \frac{1}{2} m_i v_i^2 = \frac{1}{2} m_i (r_i \omega)^2 = \frac{1}{2} m_i r_i^2 \omega^2$$

Kinetic energy is a scalar, not a vector, so we can find the total kinetic energy of the entire rotating turbine blade by simply adding together the kinetic energies of each piece of the blade:

$$K_{\text{rotational}} = K_1 + K_2 + K_3 + \dots + K_N = \sum_{i=1}^{N} K_i = \sum_{i=1}^{N} \frac{1}{2} m_i r_i^2 \omega^2 \qquad (8\text{-}4)$$

The subscript "rotational" in Equation 8-4 reminds us that this energy is the kinetic energy of the turbine blade due to its rotation. The quantities $\frac{1}{2}$ and ω^2 have the same values for each term in the sum, so we can factor them out of the sum. (If you're not sure whether it's correct to factor constant terms out of a sum, try it with a few numbers; for example, $2(3) + 2(4) + 2(5) = 2\,(3 + 4 + 5)$.) The result is

$$K_{\text{rotational}} = \frac{1}{2} \left(\sum_{i=1}^{N} m_i r_i^2 \right) \omega^2 \qquad (8\text{-}5)$$

What is the quantity in parentheses in Equation 8-5, $\sum_{i=1}^{N} m_i r_i^2$? Although it involves a sum over all the little pieces into which we've divided the turbine blade, it is *not* simply the total mass M of the blade. That sum would be $M = \sum_{i=1}^{N} m_i$, without the factor of r_i^2. Instead, the sum $\sum_{i=1}^{N} m_i r_i^2$ is a new quantity that tells us how the mass of the blade is *distributed*: It depends on both the mass of each small piece (m_i) and how far away from the rotation axis that piece is (r_i). This quantity is called the **moment of inertia** (sometimes called *rotational inertia*) of the turbine blade. We represent it by the symbol I:

To find the moment of inertia I of an object...   ...we imagine dividing the object into N small pieces, and calculate the sum...

$$I = \sum_{i=1}^{N} m_i r_i^2$$

Moment of inertia of an object (8-6)

...of the product of the mass m_i of the *i*th piece...   ...and the square of the distance r_i from the *i*th piece to the rotation axis.

The SI units of moment of inertia are kilograms multiplied by meters squared (kg · m^2).

 Watch Out! Take a moment to understand the meaning of "moment."

Despite its name, the term "*moment* of inertia" has nothing to do with a particular moment of time. Rather, "moment" is a mathematical term for a quantity that tells you how things are distributed. For example, when your class takes an exam, the average score on that exam (which tells you something about how the scores were distributed between zero and perfect) is an example of a moment.

We can use Equation 8-6 to write the expression for **rotational kinetic energy**, Equation 8-5, in terms of the moment of inertia:

Rotational kinetic energy of a rigid body spinning around an axis   **Moment of inertia** of the object for that rotation axis

$$K_{\text{rotational}} = \frac{1}{2} I \omega^2$$

Rotational kinetic energy of a rigid object (8-7)

Angular speed of the object

We've derived this formula for a rotating turbine blade, but it applies to *any* rotating rigid object. The rotational kinetic energy of a rigid object is equal to one-half the object's moment of inertia multiplied by the square of the object's angular speed. Note that in Equation 8-7 the value of the moment of inertia I is for a specific rotation axis. As we'll see in the next section, the value of I for a given object can be different depending on the axis around which that object rotates.

! Watch Out! Use correct units in calculating rotational kinetic energy.

In deriving Equation 8-7 we used Equation 8-3, $v = r\omega$, which is valid only if angles are measured in radians. To have the units of rotational kinetic energy work out properly with Equation 8-7, you *must* express angular speed ω in radians per second (rad/s). The following example illustrates the need to use correct units.

Example 8-2 Turbine Kinetic Energy

The blades of a wind turbine have a combined moment of inertia of 2.00×10^3 kg $\cdot$ m^2 for rotation around the turbine axis. If the blades make 4.00 complete revolutions every minute, what is the rotational kinetic energy of the blades?

Set Up

We use the definition of rotational kinetic energy from Equation 8-7. We are given the value of the moment of inertia I, but we are not told the value of the angular speed ω. Instead, we are told that the turbine makes 4.00 complete revolutions (4.00 rev for short) in 1 min. We can use this value to calculate the angular velocity from its definition (Equation 8-1). If we take the direction of rotation to be positive, the angular speed (which is the magnitude of angular velocity) is the same as $\omega_{average,z}$.

Rotational kinetic energy:

$$K_{rotational} = \frac{1}{2}I\omega^2 \qquad (8\text{-}7)$$

Angular velocity:

$$\omega_{average,z} = \frac{\Delta\theta}{\Delta t} \qquad (8\text{-}1)$$

Solve

First calculate the angular velocity and angular speed. Be careful to convert revolutions per minute to radians per second.

$$\omega_{average,z} = \frac{\Delta\theta}{\Delta t} = \left(\frac{4.00 \text{ rev}}{1 \text{ min}}\right)\left(\frac{2\pi \text{ rad}}{1 \text{ rev}}\right)\left(\frac{1 \text{ min}}{60 \text{ s}}\right)$$

$$= \frac{(4.00)(2\pi)}{60}\frac{\text{rad}}{\text{s}} = 0.419 \text{ rad/s}$$

The angular speed is the magnitude of this, which is equal to $\omega_{average,z}$ since its value is positive: $\omega = 0.419$ rad/s

Substitute this value of ω and the given value of I into the expression for rotational kinetic energy. We can drop the "rad" from the units of the final answer because radians aren't a true unit.

$$K_{rotational} = \frac{1}{2}I\omega^2 = \frac{1}{2}(2.00 \times 10^3 \text{ kg} \cdot \text{m}^2)(0.419 \text{ rad/s})^2$$

$$= 175 \text{ kg} \cdot \text{m}^2/\text{s}^2 = 175 \text{ J}$$

Reflect

This answer means that 175 J of work must be done on the turbine blades to bring them up to this angular speed. The blades are shaped so that the wind pushes on them and does the work for you. If you wanted to make the blades spin this fast on a day with no wind, you would have to push on the blades yourself to do 175 J of work. Remember that work equals force multiplied by distance, so if you pushed the tip of one blade a distance of 1.00 m to start it moving, you would have to exert a force of 175 N or 39.4 lb. (You'd actually have to exert even more force than that because there's bound to be some friction in the bearings of the turbine.)

Rotational Kinetic Energy versus Translational Kinetic Energy

It's useful to compare the formula for *rotational* kinetic energy from Equation 8-7 with the formula for *translational* kinetic energy that we learned in Section 6-3:

Translational kinetic energy

$$K_{translational} = \frac{1}{2}mv^2$$

Rotational kinetic energy

$$K_{rotational} = \frac{1}{2}I\omega^2$$

Notice that mass m in the translational kinetic energy equation corresponds to moment of inertia I in the rotational kinetic energy equation. Mass is a property of matter that represents the resistance of an object to a change in its velocity $\vec{v}$; by analogy, an object's moment of inertia represents the resistance of the object to a change in its *angular* velocity ω_z.

Both translational and rotational kinetic energy depend on the mass of the moving object. However, the moment of inertia (Equation 8-6) and therefore the rotational kinetic energy both depend on how the mass is *distributed* with respect to the axis of rotation. A bit of mass far from the rotation axis has a larger effect on the value of the moment of inertia than the same amount of mass close to the axis. The following example illustrates this effect.

Example 8-3 Whirling a Weight

The physicist in **Figure 8-5** whirls a small red object of mass 0.200 kg in a nearly horizontal circle at the end of a lightweight string. The object makes 5.00 revolutions per second. How much rotational kinetic energy must the physicist supply to cause this motion to occur if the string is (a) 0.300 m long or (b) 0.600 m long?

Figure 8-5 A weight moving in a circle What is the rotational kinetic energy of the small red weight moving in a horizontal circle?

Set Up

The statement that the string is "lightweight" means that we can ignore its mass and kinetic energy, so we need only calculate the kinetic energy of the red object. Figure 8-5 shows that the object is small compared to the length of the string, so it's reasonable to treat the object as though all its mass were concentrated at a single point. We'll use Equation 8-6 to find the moment of inertia I of the object in each case, then substitute its value into Equation 8-7 to calculate the rotational kinetic energy $K_{rotational}$. We're told that the angular speed is $\omega = 5.00$ rev/s.

Moment of inertia:

$$I = \sum_{i=1}^{N} m_i r_i^2 \quad (8\text{-}6)$$

Rotational kinetic energy:

$$K_{rotational} = \frac{1}{2}I\omega^2 \quad (8\text{-}7)$$

Solve

Because we can treat the red object as just a single point, the object consists of one piece. So there's only one term in the sum for moment of inertia (that is, $N = 1$). We then calculate the moment of inertia for each case.

$$I = \sum_{i=1}^{N} m_i r_i^2 = m_{object} r_{object}^2$$

(a) String 0.300 m long: $I = (0.200 \text{ kg})(0.300 \text{ m})^2 = 0.0180 \text{ kg} \cdot \text{m}^2$

(b) String 0.600 m long: $I = (0.200 \text{ kg})(0.600 \text{ m})^2 = 0.0720 \text{ kg} \cdot \text{m}^2$

We are given the angular speed in revolutions per second, so we must convert it to radians per second.

$$\omega = \left(5.00\,\frac{\text{rev}}{\text{s}}\right)\left(\frac{2\pi\ \text{rad}}{1\ \text{rev}}\right) = (5.00)(2\pi)\frac{\text{rad}}{\text{s}} = 31.4\ \text{rad/s}$$

Finally, insert the values of I and ω into the formula for rotational kinetic energy.

(a) String 0.300 m long:

$$K_{\text{rotational}} = \frac{1}{2}I\omega^2 = \frac{1}{2}(0.0180\ \text{kg}\cdot\text{m}^2)(31.4\ \text{rad/s})^2$$
$$= 8.88\ \text{kg}\cdot\text{m}^2/\text{s}^2 = 8.88\ \text{J}$$

(b) String 0.600 m long:

$$K_{\text{rotational}} = \frac{1}{2}I\omega^2 = \frac{1}{2}(0.0720\ \text{kg}\cdot\text{m}^2)(31.4\ \text{rad/s})^2$$
$$= 35.5\ \text{kg}\cdot\text{m}^2/\text{s}^2 = 35.5\ \text{J}$$

Reflect

The angular velocity ω is the same in both situations. However, the physicist must supply four times more kinetic energy to the rotating object—that is, he has to do four times as much work—when he uses the longer string: $4 \times 8.88\ \text{J} = 35.5\ \text{J}$. That's because doubling the length of the string makes the moment of inertia four times greater.

? Got the Concept? 8-1 Angular Speed of a DVD

On a digital video disc (DVD), video and audio data are stored in a series of tiny pits that are evenly spaced along a long spiral that spans most of the surface of the disc and extends from the inner edge of the DVD to the outer edge. The scanning laser in a DVD player reads this information at a constant rate. As the player reads information recorded closer and closer to the outer edge of the DVD, should the disc (a) rotate faster, (b) rotate slower, or (c) rotate at the same speed?

Take-Home Message for Section 8-2

✔ Angular velocity is a measure of how rapidly and in what direction an object rotates. Angular speed is the magnitude of angular velocity.

✔ The speed of a point on a rotating object depends on the point's distance from the rotation axis and the object's angular speed.

✔ The moment of inertia of an object depends on the object's mass and how that mass is distributed relative to the object's rotation axis.

✔ The rotational kinetic energy of an object spinning around an axis depends on its angular speed and its moment of inertia for that axis.

8-3 An object's moment of inertia depends on its mass distribution and the choice of rotation axis

Figure 8-6 **Moving a bank vault door** How easy or difficult it is to start this door moving depends on its moment of inertia for rotation around the hinges. The moment of inertia is determined by the mass of the door and how that mass is distributed.

We saw in Section 8-2 that the moment of inertia I of an object plays the same role for rotational motion that the object's mass m does for translational motion. The moment of inertia of an object is related to its mass, but also depends on how that mass is *distributed* throughout the object. An example is the door of a bank vault (Figure 8-6). The door takes effort to move in part because it's so massive. But an additional factor is that a substantial fraction of the door's mass is in its locking mechanism, and this mechanism is located a good distance away from the hinges around which the door rotates. The greater the fraction of the door's mass that's located far from the hinges, the more difficult it is to start the door rotating if it's at rest or to stop it moving if it's already in motion.

Because the moment of inertia of an object is such an important property, we should know how to calculate its value. In this section, we'll see some examples of how to determine moments of inertia. In particular, we'll see how the moment of inertia depends on the way in which the object's mass is distributed, and how the moment of inertia of a given object can change depending on the particular axis around which the object rotates.

Moment of Inertia of a Collection of Small Pieces

In Section 8-2 we introduced the formula for the moment of inertia of an object (Equation 8-6).

We imagine dividing the object into a large number of small objects of masses m_1, m_2, m_3, ... m_N, the moment of inertia I of the object is

$$I = \sum_{i=1}^{N} m_i r_i^2 \qquad (8\text{-}6)$$

In this expression r_i is the distance from the axis around which the object rotates to the position of the ith small piece.

From this definition, we can uncover three important properties of the moment of inertia:

(1) *The moment of inertia is additive.* If you know the moments of inertia of two objects around some rotation axis and you attach them to form a single object, the moment of inertia of the new object—around the same axis—is the sum of the moments of inertia of the two separate objects (Figure 8-7). Equation 8-6 above illustrates this principle: Each term $m_i r_i^2$ in the sum represents the moment of inertia of the ith piece of the object, and the total moment of inertia is the sum of the terms for all pieces.

(2) *The farther away from the rotation axis an object's mass lies, the greater the object's moment of inertia.* In Equation 8-6, the quantity r_i is the distance from the ith piece of the object to the rotation axis. The farther these pieces are from the rotation axis, the greater the values of r_i and the greater the moment of inertia. Example 8-4 demonstrates this idea.

(3) *The moment of inertia depends on the rotation axis.* If a different rotation axis is used, the quantities r_i in Equation 8-6 change and so the moment of inertia changes as well. In general, the moment of inertia for a given object is different for each different rotation axis. We'll see how this works in Example 8-5.

Let's illustrate these statements by looking at objects that we can describe as being composed of just a few pieces.

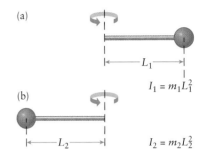

(a)

$$I_1 = m_1 L_1^2$$

(b)

$$I_2 = m_2 L_2^2$$

(c)

$$I = m_1 L_1^2 + m_2 L_2^2$$

Figure 8-7 Calculating moment of inertia The sum of the moments of inertia of the objects in (a) and (b) equals the moment of inertia of the composite object in (c).

Go to Picture It 8-1 for more practice dealing with moment of inertia

---

Example 8-4 Moment of Inertia for Dumbbells I

A dumbbell is made up of two small, massive spheres connected by a lightweight rod. Find the moment of inertia for each of the following two dumbbells. Each dumbbell is made with two identical 50.0-kg spheres, and each dumbbell rotates around its midpoint. (a) The two spheres are separated by 1.20 m. (b) The two spheres are separated by 2.40 m.

Set Up

The problem describes the rod connecting the spheres as "lightweight," so we can ignore the mass of the rod. In addition, the two spheres are described as "small," so we can treat each sphere as an infinitesimally small point object. Hence, we can use Equation 8-6 to find the moment of inertia I of each dumbbell. Because the dumbbell is made up of only two pieces, the sum in Equation 8-6 has only two terms, one for each sphere. That is, the moment of inertia of the dumbbell is the sum of the moments of inertia of the two spheres.

Moment of inertia:

$$I = \sum_{i=1}^{N} m_i r_i^2 = m_1 r_1^2 + m_2 r_2^2$$

$$(8\text{-}6)$$

Solve

Each sphere has mass 50.0 kg, so $m_1 = m_2 = 50.0$ kg in each case. For the first dumbbell, each sphere is one-half of 1.20 m from the rotation axis, so $r_1 = r_2 = 0.600$ m; similarly, in the second case each sphere is one-half of 2.40 m from the rotation axis, so $r_1 = r_2 = 1.20$ m. Substitute these values into the formula for moment of inertia I.

For both dumbbells,
$$I = m_1 r_1^2 + m_2 r_2^2 = (50.0 \text{ kg})r_1^2 + (50.0 \text{ kg})r_2^2$$

(a) For the first dumbbell:
$$I = (50.0 \text{ kg})(0.600 \text{ m})^2 + (50.0 \text{ kg})(0.600 \text{ m})^2 = 36.0 \text{ kg} \cdot \text{m}^2$$

(b) For the second dumbbell:
$$I = (50.0 \text{ kg})(1.20 \text{ m})^2 + (50.0 \text{ kg})(1.20 \text{ m})^2 = 144 \text{ kg} \cdot \text{m}^2$$

Reflect

Although both dumbbells have the same total mass $m_1 + m_2 = 50.0$ kg $+ 50.0$ kg $= 100.0$ kg, the mass is distributed in different ways. Hence, they have very different values of the moment of inertia. The farther the massive spheres are from the rotation axis, the greater the value of the moment of inertia.

Example 8-5 Moment of Inertia for Dumbbells II

Consider again the second dumbbell from Example 8-4, which has two small 50.0-kg spheres separated by 2.40 m. (a) Calculate the moment of inertia of this same dumbbell if it is rotated around the center of one of the spheres. (b) Determine the kinetic energy of this dumbbell if it rotates at 1.00 rad/s around its midpoint and if it rotates at 1.00 rad/s around the center of one of its spheres.

Set Up

As in Example 8-4, the moment of inertia I of the dumbbell is the sum of two terms, one for each sphere. We expect a different answer for I in part (a) because the values of r_1 and r_2 are different from those in Example 8-4. Once we know the value of I for each choice of axis, we can calculate the rotational kinetic energy using Equation 8-7.

Moment of inertia:
$$I = \sum_{i=1}^{N} m_i r_i^2 = m_1 r_1^2 + m_2 r_2^2 \quad (8\text{-}6)$$

Rotational kinetic energy:
$$K_{\text{rotational}} = \frac{1}{2} I \omega^2 \quad (8\text{-}7)$$

Solve

(a) Again, each sphere has mass 50.0 kg, so $m_1 = m_2 = 50.0$ kg in each case. Now one sphere is *on* the rotation axis, so $r_1 = 0$; the other sphere is 2.40 m from the rotation axis, so $r_2 = 2.40$ m. Substitute these values into the formula for I.

$$I = m_1 r_1^2 + m_2 r_2^2 = (50.0 \text{ kg})(0)^2 + (50.0 \text{ kg})(2.40 \text{ m})^2$$
$$= 288 \text{ kg} \cdot \text{m}^2$$

(b) In Example 8-4 we found that the moment of inertia of this dumbbell for rotation around its midpoint was $I = 144$ kg $\cdot$ m^2. Use this in

For rotation around the midpoint of the dumbbell,
$$I = 144 \text{ kg} \cdot \text{m}^2$$

Equation 8-7 to find the rotational kinetic energy when the dumbbell rotates around this axis at 1.00 rad/s.

Calculate the rotational kinetic energy for $\omega = 1.00$ rad/s:

$$K_{\text{rotational}} = \frac{1}{2}I\omega^2 = \frac{1}{2}(144 \text{ kg} \cdot \text{m}^2)(1.00 \text{ rad/s})^2 = 72.0 \text{ J}$$

Repeat the calculation for rotation around one of the spheres. We found above that for this axis, $I = 288$ kg $\cdot$ m^2.

For rotation around one of the spheres of the dumbbell,

$$I = 288 \text{ kg} \cdot \text{m}^2$$

Calculate the rotational kinetic energy for $\omega = 1.00$ rad/s:

$$K_{\text{rotational}} = \frac{1}{2}I\omega^2 = \frac{1}{2}(288 \text{ kg} \cdot \text{m}^2)(1.00 \text{ rad/s})^2 = 144 \text{ J}$$

Reflect

The dumbbell in this example is exactly the same object as the second dumbbell in Example 8-4, yet its moment of inertia is different. This shows that the moment of inertia of an object depends not only on its mass and how that mass is distributed, but also on the particular axis around which the object rotates.

We can check our results for rotational energy in the two cases by finding the *translational* kinetic energies of the individual spheres and adding them together. (Remember from Example 8-4 that we can treat each sphere as a point object, so we don't have to worry about the kinetic energy of a sphere spinning on its axis.) Our calculations show that changing the rotation axis while keeping the angular speed ω the same caused the speed v of the two spheres to change, and hence changed the total kinetic energy—with numerical values that exactly match the ones we calculated above.

For rotation around the midpoint of the dumbbell at angular speed $\omega = 1.00$ m/s: Each sphere is a distance $r = 1.20$ m from the rotation axis, so the speed of each sphere is

$$v = r\omega = (1.20 \text{ m})(1.00 \text{ rad/s}) = 1.20 \text{ m/s}$$

Each 50.0-kg sphere has translational kinetic energy

$$K_{\text{sphere}} = \frac{1}{2}mv^2 = \frac{1}{2}(50.0 \text{ kg})(1.20 \text{ m/s})^2 = 36.0 \text{ J}$$

So the total kinetic energy of the system of two spheres rotating around its midpoint is 36.0 J + 36.0 J = 72.0 J.

For rotation around one of the spheres at angular speed $\omega = 1.00$ rad/s: One sphere is at the rotation axis and is essentially at rest, so it has zero kinetic energy. The other sphere is a distance $r = 2.40$ m from the rotation axis, so the speed of this sphere is

$$v = r\omega = (2.40 \text{ m})(1.00 \text{ rad/s}) = 2.40 \text{ m/s}$$

The translational kinetic energy of this 50.0-kg sphere is

$$K_{\text{sphere}} = \frac{1}{2}mv^2 = \frac{1}{2}(50.0 \text{ kg})(2.40 \text{ m/s})^2 = 144 \text{ J}$$

So the total kinetic energy of the system of two spheres rotating around one of the spheres is 0 J + 144 J = 144 J.

! Watch Out!   An object has more than one moment of inertia.

If your friend points to an object and asks, "What is the moment of inertia of that object?" it could be a trick question! Example 8-5 shows that objects do *not* have a single moment of inertia; rather, the value of the moment of inertia depends on the specific rotation axis. Any object, even one like a DVD that commonly rotates around one particular axis (Figure 8-8a), can be made to rotate around any number of axes (Figure 8-8b). The axis does not even have to pass through the object that rotates around it—for example, imagine tying a string to the edge of a DVD and swinging it around in a circle above your head (Figure 8-8c). The DVD would be rotating around an axis that lies completely outside the DVD itself. The moment of inertia of the DVD will be different for each of the axes shown in Figure 8-8. *Always* make sure that you identify the axis of rotation before determining the moment of inertia of an object!

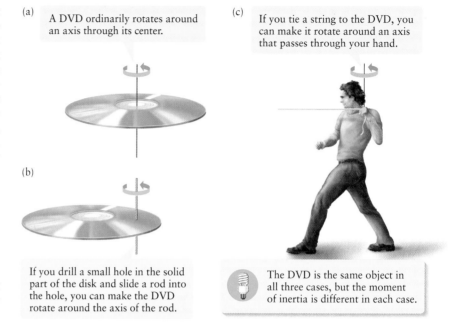

(a) A DVD ordinarily rotates around an axis through its center.

(b) If you drill a small hole in the solid part of the disk and slide a rod into the hole, you can make the DVD rotate around the axis of the rod.

(c) If you tie a string to the DVD, you can make it rotate around an axis that passes through your hand.

The DVD is the same object in all three cases, but the moment of inertia is different in each case.

Figure 8-8   **Three rotation axes for the same object** Changing the rotation axis of an object changes the value of its moment of inertia.

The Parallel-Axis Theorem

Finding the moment of inertia of an object can be challenging for certain choices of rotation axis. An example is a gymnast's hoop of mass M and radius R. The gymnast rotates the hoop around an axis that is perpendicular to the plane of the hoop and is near the hoop's rim (Figure 8-9a). If we imagine dividing the hoop into a large number of small pieces labeled $i = 1, 2, 3, \ldots, N$, every piece is a different distance r_i from the rotation axis, so it's very difficult to calculate the moment of inertia using Equation 8-6.

However, a remarkable and helpful relationship exists between the moment of inertia of any object for an axis through its *center of mass*, and the moment of inertia when the object rotates around any other parallel axis. (We introduced the idea of center of mass in Section 7-7. This would be a good time to go back and review that section.) This relationship, called the **parallel-axis theorem**, is useful because it's often relatively easy to determine an object's moment of inertia around its center of mass.

Here's the statement of the parallel-axis theorem: Suppose the moment of inertia of an object for a certain rotation axis is I. The moment of inertia of the same object for a second axis that's parallel to the first one but passes through the object's center of mass

Figure 8-9   **A gymnast's hoop**
(a) A hoop rotating around an axis that passes through its rim. (b) Calculating the hoop's moment of inertia for this axis.

(a)

(b)

Hoop

Rotation axis

Each piece of the loop is a different distance r_i from the rotation axis.

(a) Hoop rotating around an axis through its center

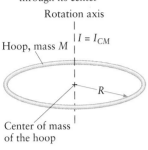

(b) Hoop rotating around an axis through its rim

(c) Top view of the hoop

Rotation axis perpendicular to plane of figure

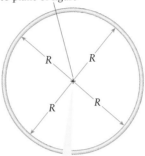

Rotation axis perpendicular to plane of figure

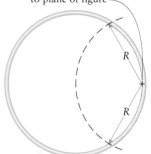

If the rotation axis passes through the center of the hoop, all parts of the hoop are a distance R from the axis.

With this choice of axis, most of the hoop is farther than R from the axis.

Figure 8-10 **Two moments of inertia for a hoop and the parallel-axis theorem** The parallel-axis theorem relates the hoop's moment of inertia for two different axes.

is I_{CM} (Figure 8-10). If the distance between the two axes is h and the mass of the object is M, the relationship between the two values of moment of inertia is

Moment of inertia of an object for a certain rotation axis

Moment of inertia of the same object for a second, parallel axis through its center of mass

$$I = I_{CM} + Mh^2$$

The parallel-axis theorem
(8-8)

Mass of the object

Distance between the two parallel axes

To see the parallel-axis theorem in action, let's return to the gymnast's hoop of mass M and radius R shown in Figure 8-9b. The theorem tells us that to determine the hoop's moment of inertia for an axis at its rim, we should first calculate its moment of inertia for a parallel axis that passes through its center of mass (Figure 8-10a). The center of mass of a symmetrical object such as a hoop is at the geometrical center of the object. (Recall from Section 7-7 that there doesn't actually have to be any mass *at* an object's center of mass.) If we divide the hoop into many small pieces, each of those pieces is the *same* distance R from this rotation axis. So in Equation 8-6 for the moment of inertia we can replace r_i for each value of i by R. This equation then becomes

$$I_{CM} = \sum_{i=1}^{N} m_i r_i^2 = \sum_{i=1}^{N} m_i R^2 = \left(\sum_{i=1}^{N} m_i \right) R^2 \tag{8-9}$$

The quantity $\sum_{i=1}^{N} m_i$ in Equation 8-9 is just the sum of the masses of all of the individual pieces that make up the hoop. This sum is just the mass M of the hoop as a whole, so we can rewrite Equation 8-9 as

$$I_{CM} = MR^2 \tag{8-10}$$

(moment of inertia of a hoop of mass M and radius R, axis through its center of mass and perpendicular to its plane)

Now we can use the parallel-axis theorem, Equation 8-8, to find the moment of inertia of this hoop for a parallel axis that passes through the rim of the hoop (Figure 8-10b). The distance between the two axes is just the radius R of the hoop, so we let $h = R$ in Equation 8-8. Using $I_{CM} = MR^2$ from Equation 8-10, we find

$$I = I_{CM} + MR^2 = MR^2 + MR^2$$

or

$$I = 2MR^2 \tag{8-11}$$

(moment of inertia of a hoop of mass M and radius R, axis through its rim and perpendicular to its plane)

This result would have been extremely difficult to obtain without using the parallel-axis theorem.

The results in Equations 8-10 and 8-11 are different for a simple reason: When the rotation axis is at the rim of a hoop of radius R, the average distance from the axis to the pieces that make up the hoop is greater than R (Figure 8-10c). (A portion of the hoop is closer than R, but a larger portion is farther away than R.) Hence the moment of inertia for this rotation axis is greater than for an axis that passes through the center of the hoop (Figure 8-10a), in which case all parts of the hoop are a distance R from the axis. As we have seen before, the farther an object's mass lies from the rotation axis, the greater its moment of inertia.

Example 8-6 Using the Parallel-Axis Theorem I

Use the parallel-axis theorem and the results of Example 8-4 to find the moment of inertia of the dumbbell in Example 8-5 rotated about one end of the dumbbell.

Set Up

The two spheres at the ends of the dumbbell have the same mass, so the center of mass of the dumbbell is at its midpoint. In Example 8-4, we found the moment of inertia of this dumbbell for an axis that passes through the midpoint, so this expression is I_{CM}. The dumbbell in Example 8-5 is identical but has a different, parallel rotation axis, so we can find its moment of inertia using the parallel-axis theorem, Equation 8-8.

Parallel-axis theorem:

$$I = I_{CM} + Mh^2 \qquad (8\text{-}8)$$

Solve

From Example 8-4, the moment of inertia of the dumbbell through its center of mass is $I_{CM} = 144 \text{ kg} \cdot \text{m}^2$. The axis of rotation for the dumbbell in Example 8-5 is a distance $h = 1.20 \text{ m}$ from the center of mass, and the total mass M of the dumbbell is the sum of the masses of the two 50.0-kg spheres. Substitute these values into the parallel-axis theorem.

$$I_{CM} = 144 \text{ kg} \cdot \text{m}^2$$
$$h = 1.20 \text{ m}$$
$$M = 50.0 \text{ kg} + 50.0 \text{ kg} = 100.0 \text{ kg}$$
$$I = I_{CM} + Mh^2 = 144 \text{ kg} \cdot \text{m}^2 + (100.0 \text{ kg})(1.20 \text{ m})^2$$
$$= 288 \text{ kg} \cdot \text{m}^2$$

Reflect

We get the same answer as in Example 8-5, which is a nice check that the parallel-axis theorem works.

Example 8-7 Using the Parallel-Axis Theorem II

A child's swing at a rustic amusement park is made up of an old tire hanging from a lightweight rope tied to a tree limb. The tire has a radius of 0.310 m and a mass of 11.0 kg, and hangs from a rope 2.50 m long. If the rope–tire combination is swinging around the tree limb at 1.20 rad/s at the low point of its motion, what is its kinetic energy?

Set Up

To find the kinetic energy due to the rotation of the rope–tire combination, we need to know its moment of inertia. The rope is lightweight, so we can ignore its mass. The tire is like a hoop that rotates around an axis at the position of the tree limb. We know the moment of inertia of a hoop for an axis through its center of mass (Equation 8-10), so we can find the tire's moment of inertia around the tree limb using the parallel-axis theorem, Equation 8-8. Then, we can find the rotational kinetic energy using Equation 8-7.

Moment of inertia of a hoop of mass M and radius R, axis through its center of mass and perpendicular to its plane:

$$I_{CM} = MR^2 \qquad (8\text{-}10)$$

Parallel-axis theorem:

$$I = I_{CM} + Mh^2 \qquad (8\text{-}8)$$

Rotational kinetic energy:

$$K_{\text{rotational}} = \frac{1}{2}I\omega^2 \qquad (8\text{-}7)$$

Solve

The tire has mass $M = 11.0$ kg and radius $R = 0.310$ m. The distance from the tree-limb axis to a parallel axis that passes through the center of the hoop (its center of mass) is $h = 0.310$ m $+ 2.50$ m $= 2.81$ m. Substitute these values into the formula for the tire's moment of inertia I for rotation around the tree limb.

$$
\begin{aligned}
I &= I_{CM} + Mh^2 \\
&= MR^2 + Mh^2 \\
&= (11.0 \text{ kg})(0.310 \text{ m})^2 + (11.0 \text{ kg})(2.81 \text{ m})^2 \\
&= 87.9 \text{ kg} \cdot \text{m}^2
\end{aligned}
$$

Then, substitute the moment of inertia and the angular speed $\omega = 1.20$ rad/s into the expression for rotational kinetic energy.

$$
\begin{aligned}
K_{\text{rotational}} &= \frac{1}{2} I \omega^2 \\
&= \frac{1}{2}(87.9 \text{ kg} \cdot \text{m}^2)(1.20 \text{ rad/s})^2 \\
&= 63.3 \text{ J}
\end{aligned}
$$

Reflect

Suppose we had been in a hurry and had neglected to apply the parallel-axis theorem. In this case, we might have used $I_{CM} = MR^2$ for the moment of inertia, and would have gotten an answer that was way off. The moment of inertia for the rope–tire combination rotating around the tree limb is *much* larger than that for the tire rotating around its center of mass. Hence, for a given angular speed, the kinetic energy for the rope–tire combination is much greater.

Incorrect calculation:

$$
\begin{aligned}
K_{\text{rotational}} &= \frac{1}{2} I_{CM}\, \omega^2 = \frac{1}{2} MR^2 \omega^2 \\
&= \frac{1}{2}(11.0 \text{ kg})(0.310 \text{ m})^2 (1.20 \text{ rad/s})^2 \\
&= 0.761 \text{ J (wrong!)}
\end{aligned}
$$

The Moment of Inertia for Common Shapes

It was straightforward to calculate the moment of inertia for the hoop shown in Figure 8-10 because all parts of the hoop are the same distance from its rotation axis. For solid objects with other shapes, calculating the moment of inertia is more difficult and requires the use of calculus, which is beyond our scope. Instead, we'll just present the results for some common shapes that show up in various situations involving rotation. Table 8-1 shows the moment of inertia for objects with some common shapes. We assume that these objects are *uniform*: That is, each object has the same composition throughout its volume.

You can see from Table 8-1 that the moment of inertia of a thin cylindrical shell of mass M and radius R around its central axis ($I = MR^2$) is twice that of a solid cylinder of the same mass and radius ($I = \frac{1}{2}MR^2$). You should expect the cylindrical shell to have a larger moment of inertia because the moment of inertia of an object is strongly influenced by how far the mass is from the rotation axis. In the case of the thin cylindrical shell, all of the mass is located a distance R from the axis, while for the solid cylinder only a fraction of the mass is that far from the axis. Hence the moment of inertia of the shell must be larger than the moment of inertia of the solid cylinder.

We can use the parallel-axis theorem to verify some of the results shown in Table 8-1. For example, consider a thin rod that has mass M and length L. The center of mass of this rod is at its geometric center. From Table 8-1, the moment of inertia of such a rod rotating around an axis perpendicular to the rod and through its center is

$$
I_{CM} = \frac{ML^2}{12}
$$

(moment of inertia of a thin uniform rod, rotation axis through its center)

What is the moment of inertia of this same rod for an axis through one end and perpendicular to the rod? This axis is parallel to an axis through the center of mass

Table 8-1 Moments of Inertia of Uniform Objects of Various Shapes

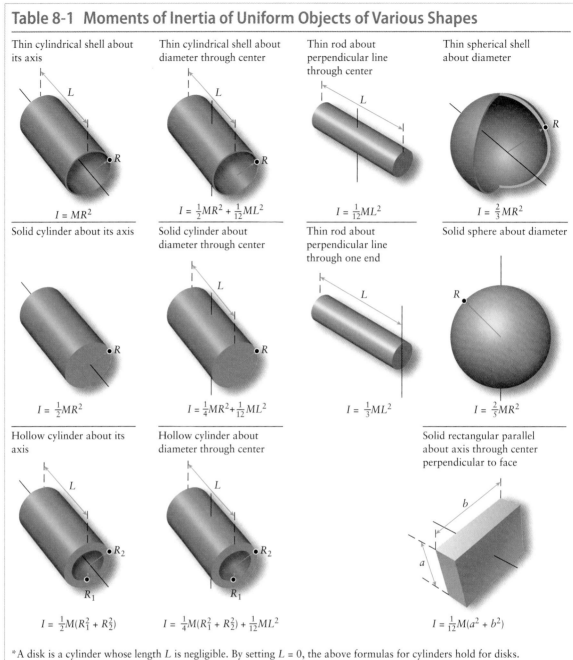

Thin cylindrical shell about its axis

$$I = MR^2$$

Thin cylindrical shell about diameter through center

$$I = \tfrac{1}{2}MR^2 + \tfrac{1}{12}ML^2$$

Thin rod about perpendicular line through center

$$I = \tfrac{1}{12}ML^2$$

Thin spherical shell about diameter

$$I = \tfrac{2}{3}MR^2$$

Solid cylinder about its axis

$$I = \tfrac{1}{2}MR^2$$

Solid cylinder about diameter through center

$$I = \tfrac{1}{4}MR^2 + \tfrac{1}{12}ML^2$$

Thin rod about perpendicular line through one end

$$I = \tfrac{1}{3}ML^2$$

Solid sphere about diameter

$$I = \tfrac{2}{5}MR^2$$

Hollow cylinder about its axis

$$I = \tfrac{1}{2}M(R_1^2 + R_2^2)$$

Hollow cylinder about diameter through center

$$I = \tfrac{1}{4}M(R_1^2 + R_2^2) + \tfrac{1}{12}ML^2$$

Solid rectangular parallel about axis through center perpendicular to face

$$I = \tfrac{1}{12}M(a^2 + b^2)$$

*A disk is a cylinder whose length L is negligible. By setting $L = 0$, the above formulas for cylinders hold for disks.

of the rod and a distance $h = L/2$ from that axis. From Equation 8-8, the moment of inertia for an axis through the end is

$$I = I_{CM} + Mh^2 = \frac{ML^2}{12} + M\left(\frac{L}{2}\right)^2$$

$$= \left(\frac{1}{12} + \frac{1}{4}\right)ML^2 = \left(\frac{1}{12} + \frac{3}{12}\right)ML^2 = \frac{4ML^2}{12}$$

or, simplifying,

$$I = \frac{ML^2}{3}$$

(moment of inertia of a thin uniform rod, axis through one end, perpendicular to rod)

This expression is just the result shown in Table 8-1 for the rod rotating around its end. Note that the moment of inertia for an axis passing through the end of the rod is four times the value of the moment of inertia when the rod rotates around a parallel axis through the center of the rod. For an axis through the center, no part of the rod is farther than $L/2$ from the axis; if the axis is through the end of the rod, one-half of the rod is farther than $L/2$ from the axis, so the moment of inertia is larger.

If one of the shapes shown in Table 8-1 rotates around an axis that is different than but parallel to the axis shown in the table, we can use the parallel-axis theorem to find the new moment of inertia. Because the moment of inertia is additive, you can also use the results shown in Table 8-1 to find the moment of inertia of a more complex object made up of two or more of the simple objects shown in the table.

Example 8-8 Earring Moment of Inertia

A woman's earring is a thin, uniform disk that has a mass M and a radius R. The earring hangs from the earring post by a small hole near the edge of the disk and is free to rotate. Find the moment of inertia of the disk around this rotation axis.

Set Up

A solid disk is an example of a solid cylinder like that shown in Table 8-1. This table shows that the moment of inertia of such a disk for an axis perpendicular to the plane of the disk and passing through its center is $I = MR^2/2$. (Unlike the cylinder shown in the table, the length L of the earring is much less than its radius R. But the length has no effect on the value of I.)

Because the disk is uniform, its geometrical center is its center of mass, so $MR^2/2$ equals I_{CM}. The axis we want is parallel to the axis through the disk's center, so we can use the parallel-axis theorem, Equation 8-8, to find the moment of inertia around the axis at the rim.

Parallel-axis theorem:

$$I = I_{CM} + Mh^2 \qquad (8\text{-}8)$$

rotation axis

disk, mass M

center of mass

Solve

The edge of the disk is a distance $h = R$ from the center of mass of the disk. Substitute this value and $I_{CM} = MR^2/2$ into the parallel-axis theorem.

$$I = \frac{MR^2}{2} + MR^2$$

or

$$I = \frac{3MR^2}{2}$$

Reflect

If the wearer of these earrings nods her head up and down while dancing at a club, she can make the disks rotate back and forth around the posts in an eye-catching way. The more massive the disks and the larger their radius, the greater their moment of inertia and the more effort will be required to get them moving (recall that rotational kinetic energy is given by $K_{rotational} = \frac{1}{2}I\omega^2$). Making the earrings small and lightweight will require less effort from the wearer!

❓ Got the Concept? 8-2 X Marks the Moment of Inertia, Part I

Two thin, uniform rods, each of which has mass M and length L, are attached at their centers to form an "X" or "+" shape. What is the moment of inertia when this configuration is rotated around an axis that passes through their centers, perpendicular to the plane of the two rods? (a) $ML^2/24$; (b) $ML^2/12$; (c) $ML^2/6$; (d) $ML^2/4$; (e) $ML^2/3$.

? Got the Concept? 8-3   X Marks the Moment of Inertia, Part II

Four thin, uniform rods, each of which has mass $M/2$ and length $L/2$, are attached at their ends to form an "X" or "+" shape. What is the moment of inertia when this configuration is rotated around the axis that passes through the center of the "X" perpendicular to the plane of the rods? (a) $ML^2/24$; (b) $ML^2/12$; (c) $ML^2/6$; (d) $ML^2/4$; (e) $ML^2/3$.

Take-Home Message for Section 8-3

✔ The moment of inertia of an object is additive and increases as the object's mass is moved farther from the rotation axis.

✔ An object's moment of inertia depends on the axis around which the object rotates.

✔ The parallel-axis theorem relates the moment of inertia for an axis through an object's center of mass to the moment of inertia for a second, parallel axis.

8-4 Conservation of mechanical energy also applies to rotating objects

Figure 8-11 **Soap box derby racers** These unpowered race cars roll downhill propelled only by gravity. How do the properties of a car's spinning wheels affect the car's speed?

Every year thousands of girls and boys race in the All-American Soap Box Derby in homemade cars powered only by the pull of gravity (Figure 8-11). In building their cars, competitors have the flexibility to be creative, but they can be disqualified for using wheels other than those officially approved. How would different kinds of wheels affect the outcome of the race? We can answer this and many related questions by using the conservation of energy.

We learned in Section 6-7 that the mechanical energy of a system—the sum of kinetic energy and potential energy—is conserved if no nonconservative forces do work on that system. This principle of *conservation of energy* makes it much easier to solve a wide variety of physics problems. In Sections 8-2 and 8-3 we introduced the *rotational* kinetic energy of a rigid body with moment of inertia I rotating with angular velocity ω: $K_{\text{rotational}} = \frac{1}{2}I\omega^2$. Does conservation of energy still hold true if we include rotational kinetic energy? And in particular, does it hold true for objects that are *both* translating (moving through space) *and* rotating, like a ball rolling downhill or the spinning wheels of a soap box derby car?

Happily, the answer to both questions is "yes," because rotational kinetic energy isn't really a new kind of energy. As we saw in Section 8-2, the rotational kinetic energy of a rigid body is just the combined kinetic energy of all of its component pieces due to the motion of those pieces around the rotation axis. So the principle of conservation of energy also holds if we include rotational kinetic energy.

We can also use the principle of conservation of energy for a rigid object that's both moving through space as a whole and rotating. In such a situation it turns out that we can write the object's *total* kinetic energy as the sum of two terms: the *translational* kinetic energy associated with the motion of the object's center of mass (see Section 7-7), and the *rotational* kinetic energy associated with the object's rotation around its center of mass (Figure 8-12). If the object has mass M and its center of mass is moving with speed v_{CM}, its translational kinetic energy is $K_{\text{translational}} = \frac{1}{2}Mv_{\text{CM}}^2$; if the object's moment of inertia for an axis through its center of mass is I_{CM} and it rotates with

1. The center of mass of this wrench (shown as a red cross) moves in a straight line...

2. ... and the wrench rotates around the center of mass.

Figure 8-12 **Combined translation and rotation** In this time-lapse image, you are looking down on a spinning wrench as it slides across a table. The wrench naturally rotates around its center of mass (shown by the red X), so we can think of its motion as the translation of the center of mass plus the rotation of the wrench around the center of mass.

angular speed ω, its rotational kinetic energy is $K_{\text{rotational}} = \frac{1}{2}I_{\text{CM}}\omega^2$. The total kinetic energy (translational plus rotational) of the object is then

(1) Total kinetic energy of a system that is both translating and rotating

(2) The translational kinetic energy is the same as if all of the mass of the system were moving at the speed of the center of mass.

$$K = K_{\text{translational}} + K_{\text{rotational}} = \frac{1}{2}Mv_{\text{CM}}^2 + \frac{1}{2}I_{\text{CM}}\omega^2$$

(3) The rotational kinetic energy is the same as if the system were not translating, and all of the mass were rotating around the center of mass.

Total kinetic energy for a rigid object undergoing both translation and rotation
(8-12)

Most of the objects we will encounter that undergo both translation and rotation will be symmetrical, like a rolling bowling ball or bicycle tire. In such a case the center of mass is at the object's geometrical center, and Table 8-1 in Section 8-3 will help you determine the value of I_{CM} for that object. (The wrench shown in Figure 8-12 is an exception: It has more mass at one end than the other, so its center of mass is *not* at its geometrical center.)

Whenever we have a situation involving a rigid object that undergoes both translation and rotation, we can make use of the energy relationships from Section 6-7 provided that we use Equation 8-12 as the expression for kinetic energy. If only conservative forces do work, mechanical energy (the sum of kinetic energy K and potential energy U) is conserved, so the value of $K + U$ is the same at any two times during the motion:

$$K_i + U_i = K_f + U_f \qquad (6\text{-}23)$$

(if only conservative forces do work)

If nonconservative forces also do work, the final mechanical energy $K_f + U_f$ is equal to the initial mechanical energy $K_i + U_i$ plus $W_{\text{nonconservative}}$, the amount of nonconservative work that is done during the motion:

$$K_i + U_i + W_{\text{nonconservative}} = K_f + U_f \qquad (6\text{-}26)$$

(if nonconservative forces do work)

In both Equations 6-23 and 6-26, the kinetic energy K is now given by Equation 8-12 and the potential energy U includes a term for each conservative force that acts (for example, the gravitational force or a spring force).

Example 8-9 illustrates how to use these ideas to solve a simple problem that involves both translational and rotational motion.

Example 8-9 Flying Disc Energy

A flying disc with a mass of 0.175 kg and a diameter 0.266 m is used in the team sport called Ultimate. A player takes a disc at rest and does 1.00 J of work on it, causing the disc to fly off in a horizontal direction. When the disc leaves the player's hand, nine-tenths of its kinetic energy is translational and one-tenth is rotational. Find (a) the speed of the flying disc's center of mass and (b) the angular speed of the rotating disc. Treat the disc as uniform.

Set Up

The work done by the player counts as nonconservative work, so we use Equation 6-26 to describe how the disc's energy changes. We use Equation 8-12 to describe the kinetic energy of the disc, which involves its moment of inertia I_{CM} for an axis through its center of mass (the same as its geometrical center). As in Example 8-8 in Section 8-3, this moment of inertia is $I_{\text{CM}} = MR^2/2$, where $M = 0.175$ kg and R is one-half of the disc's diameter (see the first entry in the second row of Table 8-1). Our goal is to find the values of v_{CM} and ω just after the disc leaves the player's hand.

If nonconservative forces do work:

$$K_i + U_i + W_{\text{nonconservative}} = K_f + U_f \qquad (6\text{-}26)$$

Total kinetic energy for a rigid object undergoing both translation and rotation:

$$K = K_{\text{translational}} + K_{\text{rotational}}$$

$$= \frac{1}{2}Mv_{\text{CM}}^2 + \frac{1}{2}I_{\text{CM}}\omega^2 \qquad (8\text{-}12)$$

mass M

radius R

before throw:
$v_{\text{CM}} = 0$, $\omega = 0$

ω

v_{CM}

after throw

Solve

During the throw, the disc moves horizontally, so its height stays the same and its gravitational potential energy is constant: that is, $U_f = U_i$. The disc starts at rest, so $K_i = 0$ (it has zero initial kinetic energy). So the work done on the disc by the player is transformed into the disc's final kinetic energy K_f.

$$K_i + U_i + W_{nonconservative} = K_f + U_f$$

Since $U_f = U_i$, $K_i = 0$, and $W_{nonconservative} = 1.00$ J, this becomes

$$1.00 \text{ J} = K_f$$

The disc's 1.00 J of kinetic energy is divided so that 9/10 is translational and 1/10 is rotational.

$$K_{translational} = \frac{1}{2}Mv_{CM}^2 = (9/10)(1.00 \text{ J}) = 0.900 \text{ J}$$

$$K_{rotational} = \frac{1}{2}I_{CM}\omega^2 = (1/10)(1.00 \text{ J}) = 0.100 \text{ J}$$

(a) Find the speed of the disc's center of mass.

From the expression for translational kinetic energy,

$$v_{CM}^2 = \frac{2K_{translational}}{M}$$

$$v_{CM} = \sqrt{\frac{2K_{translational}}{M}} = \sqrt{\frac{2(0.900 \text{ J})}{0.175 \text{ kg}}} = \sqrt{\frac{2(0.900 \text{ kg} \cdot \text{m}^2/\text{s}^2)}{0.175 \text{ kg}}}$$

$$= 3.21 \text{ m/s}$$

(b) Calculate the disc's moment of inertia for the axis of rotation through its center, then solve for its angular speed ω. Note that if $K_{rotational}$ is in joules and I_{CM} is in kg·m², ω is in radians per second.

Calculate the disc's moment of inertia through its center of mass:

$$I_{CM} = \frac{1}{2}MR^2 = \frac{1}{2}(0.175 \text{ kg})\left(\frac{0.266 \text{ m}}{2}\right)^2$$

$$= 1.55 \times 10^{-3} \text{ kg} \cdot \text{m}^2$$

From the expression for rotational kinetic energy,

$$\omega^2 = \frac{2K_{rotational}}{I_{CM}}$$

$$\omega = \sqrt{\frac{2K_{rotational}}{I_{CM}}} = \sqrt{\frac{2(0.100 \text{ J})}{1.55 \times 10^{-3} \text{ kg} \cdot \text{m}^2}}$$

$$= \sqrt{\frac{2(0.100 \text{ kg} \cdot \text{m}^2/\text{s}^2)}{1.55 \times 10^{-3} \text{ kg} \cdot \text{m}^2}} = 11.4 \text{ rad/s}$$

Reflect

This is a problem for which the conservation of energy equation is essential but not sufficient. In order to solve for the two unknowns, v_{CM} and ω, we needed a second relationship telling us how the kinetic energy was distributed—the statement that the disc's kinetic energy was 9/10 translational and 1/10 rotational.

We can check our results by first comparing v_{CM} to the average speed of a world-class sprinter who can typically run 100 m in 10 s or less, for an average speed of 10 m/s. Since 2π (just over 6) radians represents a full revolution, the value of ω tells us that the disc spins just under two times per second. Are these values what you might expect for a hand-thrown flying disc?

Rolling without Slipping

Let's return to one of the soap box derby cars that we thought about at the beginning of this section (Figure 8-11) and ask how we can use energy concepts to analyze its motion as it moves down the race course. For simplicity, let's think about a single wheel rolling downhill (Figure 8-13a) rather than the entire car. After the wheel has traveled a certain distance down the hill, how fast is it moving as a whole and how rapidly is it spinning?

Before the start of the race, the wheel has gravitational potential energy relative to the bottom of the hill but no kinetic energy. The wheel picks up speed as it rolls down the race course, a transformation of potential energy into kinetic. Unlike the flying disc

(a)

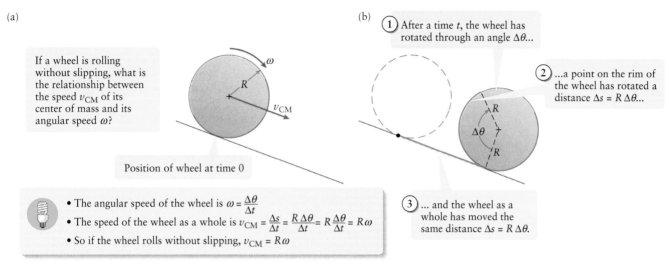

If a wheel is rolling without slipping, what is the relationship between the speed v_{CM} of its center of mass and its angular speed ω?

Position of wheel at time 0

(b)

① After a time t, the wheel has rotated through an angle $\Delta\theta$...

② ...a point on the rim of the wheel has rotated a distance $\Delta s = R\,\Delta\theta$...

③ ... and the wheel as a whole has moved the same distance $\Delta s = R\,\Delta\theta$.

- The angular speed of the wheel is $\omega = \dfrac{\Delta\theta}{\Delta t}$
- The speed of the wheel as a whole is $v_{CM} = \dfrac{\Delta s}{\Delta t} = \dfrac{R\,\Delta\theta}{\Delta t} = R\dfrac{\Delta\theta}{\Delta t} = R\omega$
- So if the wheel rolls without slipping, $v_{CM} = R\omega$

Figure 8-13 **A wheel rolling downhill** If a wheel rolls without slipping, there is a definite relationship between its angular speed and the speed of its center of mass.

in Example 8-9, however, we need to figure out how much of that kinetic energy is translational energy and how much is rotational. Furthermore, there must be friction between the wheel and the road in order for the wheel to roll. (If the road were frictionless, the wheel would simply slide downhill.) So we also need to know how much mechanical energy is lost due to friction as the wheel rolls.

To make further progress, we use the idea that the wheel is **rolling without slipping**—that is, the wheel does not skid or slide over the road. In this situation there is a specific relationship between the speed of the center of the wheel, v_{CM}, and the angular speed ω of the wheel's rotation. To see what this relationship is, consider what happens when the wheel rolls through a small angle $\Delta\theta$ over a time interval Δt (Figure 8-13b). Imagine that a thread has been wrapped around the circumference of the wheel and unwinds as the wheel rolls, marking the distance traveled. During the interval Δt a point on the rim of the wheel of radius R rotates a distance $\Delta s = R\,\Delta\theta$. Since the wheel doesn't slip on the road, $\Delta s = R\,\Delta\theta$ is also the length of thread that the wheel unwinds onto the road and hence the distance that the wheel as a whole moves down the road. Hence v_{CM}, the speed of the wheel as a whole, is equal to the distance Δs divided by the duration Δt of the time interval:

$$v_{CM} = \frac{\Delta s}{\Delta t} = \frac{R\,\Delta\theta}{\Delta t} = R\frac{\Delta\theta}{\Delta t}$$

But $\Delta\theta/\Delta t$ is just equal to ω, the angular speed of the wheel, so

Speed of the center of mass of a rolling object

$$v_{CM} = R\omega$$

Radius of the object   Angular speed of the object's rotation

Condition for rolling without slipping (8-13)

Equation 8-13 says that there is a direct proportionality between the linear speed v_{CM} and angular speed ω of a circular object that rolls without slipping. As the wheel in Figure 8-13 rolls downhill it gains speed so v_{CM} increases, and it rotates faster so ω increases, but these increases are always proportional to each other so that v_{CM} and ω are always related by Equation 8-13.

How much mechanical energy is lost due to friction if an object rolls without slipping, like the wheel in Figure 8-13? If the object and the surface are perfectly rigid, the answer is simple: The force of friction does *no* work at all, so *no* energy is lost. If an object *slides* over a surface, we saw in Section 6-7 that the kinetic friction force does work on the object and changes its mechanical energy. But there is no sliding if the object rolls without slipping, so friction does no work. The friction force still plays an important role: It's what makes the object roll. So as the wheel in Figure 8-13 rolls downhill and gravitational potential energy is converted to kinetic energy, the friction force ensures that a portion of the kinetic energy goes into the rotational form.

Nonrigid Objects and Rolling Friction

While friction does no work on an object that rolls without slipping, if the object or surface is not perfectly rigid—that is, if it can *deform*—there *is* a related force that does work on the object as it rolls. An example is a bicycle tire or automobile tire, which flexes and flattens on its bottom where it contacts the road. As the tire rolls, different parts of the tire successively get compressed as they touch the ground and relax as they lose contact with the ground. This flexing causes the tire to get warmer, which expends mechanical energy. The energy comes from the mechanical energy of the rolling tire, which means that left to itself on a horizontal surface the tire will lose kinetic energy and slow down. The net effect is the same as if a force were acting to oppose the rolling tire's motion. This is just the force that we called *rolling friction* in Section 5-3. Rolling friction is also present if the surface on which the object rolls is deformable, like a wrestling mat or the green baize that covers a billiards table.

You can minimize rolling friction on your bicycle or automobile by keeping tires properly inflated. Underinflated tires flex more, which means that they absorb more energy and reduce the car's mileage. That's also why transporting goods via railroad is more efficient than using trucks: Railroad cars have very rigid steel wheels, which flex much less than even properly inflated truck tires.

! Watch Out! **Rolling doesn't have to imply rolling friction.**

An object rolling on a surface experiences rolling friction *only* if the object, the surface, or both are deformable. In this chapter we'll assume that all rolling objects and the surface on which they roll are perfectly rigid. Then there's no rolling friction. A friction force may act on the rolling object, but it's the force of *static* friction (since the object rolls rather than slides over the surface). Static friction does no work on the object, so in this case mechanical energy is conserved.

We now see how to use the energy approach to solve problems involving objects that roll without slipping. Since no nonconservative work is done by the force of friction, we use Equation 6-23, $K_i + U_i = K_f + U_f$, which states that mechanical energy is conserved as the object rolls. The kinetic energy of the rolling object is given by Equation 8-12, $K = \frac{1}{2}Mv_{CM}^2 + \frac{1}{2}I_{CM}\omega^2$, and the speed v_{CM} and angular velocity ω are related by Equation 8-13, $v_{CM} = R\omega$. The following example makes use of these equations.

Example 8-10 Downhill Race: Disk versus Hoop

A uniform disk and a hoop are both allowed to roll without slipping down a ramp of height H (Figure 8-14). Both objects have the same radius R and the same mass M. If both objects start from rest at the same time, which one reaches the bottom of the ramp first?

Figure 8-14 **Who wins the race?** A competition between two objects rolling down a ramp.

Set Up

Both objects roll without slipping, so we can use Equations 6-23, 8-12, and 8-13 to describe their motion. The only real difference between the two objects is their moment of inertia: From Table 8-1, $I_{CM} = MR^2/2$ for the uniform disk, while $I_{CM} = MR^2$ for the hoop. To decide which one wins the race, we'll calculate v_{CM} at the bottom of the ramp for each object. The one with the faster speed will get to the bottom first and be declared the winner. We'll solve for $v_{CM,f}$ (the speed at the bottom of the ramp) for a general object that rolls down the ramp starting from rest: Only at the end will we plug in the value of I_{CM} for each object.

Conservation of mechanical energy:

$$K_i + U_i = K_f + U_f \qquad (6\text{-}23)$$

Kinetic energy for an object that undergoes both translation and rotation:

$$K = \frac{1}{2}Mv_{CM}^2 + \frac{1}{2}I_{CM}\omega^2 \qquad (8\text{-}12)$$

Condition for rolling without slipping:

$$v_{CM} = R\omega \qquad (8\text{-}13)$$

disk:
$I_{CM} = \frac{1}{2}MR^2$

mass M

hoop:
$I_{CM} = MR^2$

mass M

Solve

Initially the object is at rest with zero kinetic energy, so $K_i = 0$. The initial gravitational potential energy is $U_i = Mgy_i$, and the final gravitational potential energy is $U_f = Mgy_f$. The figure shows that $y_i - y_f = H$, so we can solve for the object's final kinetic energy K_f at the bottom of the ramp.

Conservation of energy equation:

$$0 + Mgy_i = K_f + Mgy_f, \text{ or}$$

$$K_f = Mgy_i - Mgy_f = Mg(y_i - y_f)$$

Since $y_i - y_f = H$,

$$K_f = MgH$$

The kinetic energy is part translational and part rotational. We can use Equation 8-13 to write ω_f (the angular velocity at the bottom of the ramp) in terms of $v_{CM,f}$ (the linear speed at the bottom of the ramp), and so can express the final kinetic energy in terms of the linear speed $v_{CM,f}$ only.

Kinetic energy at the bottom of the ramp:

$$K_f = \frac{1}{2}Mv_{CM,f}^2 + \frac{1}{2}I_{CM}\omega_f^2$$

Rolling without slipping:

$$v_{CM,f} = R\omega_f, \text{ so}$$

$$\omega_f = \frac{v_{CM,f}}{R}$$

Substitute into energy equation:

$$K_f = \frac{1}{2}Mv_{CM,f}^2 + \frac{1}{2}I_{CM}\left(\frac{v_{CM,f}}{R}\right)^2 = \frac{1}{2}Mv_{CM,f}^2 + \frac{1}{2}\left(\frac{I_{CM}}{R^2}\right)v_{CM,f}^2$$

$$= \frac{1}{2}\left(M + \frac{I_{CM}}{R^2}\right)v_{CM,f}^2$$

We now have two expressions for K_f. Set them equal to each other and solve for $v_{CM,f}$.

$$\frac{1}{2}\left(M + \frac{I_{CM}}{R^2}\right)v_{CM,f}^2 = MgH$$

$$v_{CM,f}^2 = \frac{2MgH}{M + \dfrac{I_{CM}}{R^2}}$$

$$v_{CM,f} = \sqrt{\frac{2MgH}{M + \dfrac{I_{CM}}{R^2}}}$$

Finally, substitute $I_{CM} = MR^2/2$ for the disk and $I_{CM} = MR^2$ for the hoop and find the final speed for each object.

The speed of the disk at the bottom of the ramp is faster than that of the hoop: $\sqrt{(4/3)gH}$ compared to $\sqrt{gH}$. Both objects will accelerate down the ramp, but at any given position down the ramp, the disk will be moving faster than the hoop. In a race, the disk would win.

For the uniform disk:

$$I_{CM} = \frac{MR^2}{2}$$

$$M + \frac{I_{CM}}{R^2} = M + \frac{M}{2} = \frac{3M}{2}$$

$$v_{CM,f} = \sqrt{\frac{2MgH}{3M/2}} = \sqrt{\left(\frac{2}{3M}\right)(2MgH)} = \sqrt{\frac{4gH}{3}}$$

For the hoop:

$$I_{CM} = MR^2$$

$$M + \frac{I_{CM}}{R^2} = M + M = 2M$$

$$v_{CM,f} = \sqrt{\frac{2MgH}{2M}} = \sqrt{gH}$$

Reflect

Why does the disk win? The only difference between the two objects is that the uniform disk has a smaller moment of inertia than the hoop ($MR^2/2$ compared to MR^2), so a smaller fraction of the gravitational potential energy is converted to rotational kinetic energy as it rolls down the ramp. That leaves more energy available for translational motion, which means that the disk travels faster down the ramp and wins the race.

We can verify this by calculating the ratio of rotational kinetic energy $K_{rotational}$ to translational kinetic energy $K_{translational}$ for a rolling object. This ratio is I_{CM}/MR^2, so the smaller the moment of inertia I_{CM} for a given mass M and radius R—like the uniform disk compared to the hoop—the smaller the rotational kinetic energy and the more energy is available for translation.

Note that our answers for the speeds of the disk and hoop don't depend on the mass or radius of either object. Even if the disk were larger and more massive than the hoop, it would still win the race!

Ratio of rotational kinetic energy to translational kinetic energy:

$$\frac{K_{rotational}}{K_{translational}} = \frac{\frac{1}{2}I_{CM}\omega^2}{\frac{1}{2}Mv_{CM}^2} = \frac{I_{CM}\omega^2}{Mv_{CM}^2}$$

If the object is rolling without slipping,

$$v_{CM} = R\omega$$

$$\omega = \frac{v_{CM}}{R}, \text{ so}$$

$$\frac{K_{rotational}}{K_{translational}} = \frac{I_{CM}\omega^2}{Mv_{CM}^2} = \frac{I_{CM}}{Mv_{CM}^2}\left(\frac{v_{CM}}{R}\right)^2 = \frac{I_{CM}}{MR^2}$$

Got the Concept? 8-4 Choose Your Wheels Wisely

Which wheels would allow a soap box derby car (Figure 8-11) to go faster: (a) uniform disks, or (b) ones that are like conventional bicycle tires with most of the mass along the rim of the wheels?

Got the Concept? 8-5 A Three-Way Downhill Race

A uniform disk, a uniform sphere, and a block are released from rest down adjacent ramps of identical angle. The disk and sphere roll without slipping, while the block slides without friction. All three objects start from the same height. Rank the three objects in the order in which they reach the bottom of the ramp, starting with the first to arrive.

Take-Home Message for Section 8-4

✔ The total kinetic energy K of an object of mass M is the sum of the translational kinetic energy of its center of mass, $K_{\text{translational}} = \frac{1}{2} M v_{\text{CM}}^2$, and the rotational kinetic energy of the object's rotation around its center of mass, $K_{\text{rotational}} = \frac{1}{2} I_{\text{CM}} \omega^2$.

✔ The same energy conservation equations we learned in Chapter 6 also apply when there is rotational motion. The

only difference is that the kinetic energy K now includes both translational and rotational kinetic energies.

✔ If an object rolls without slipping on a surface, the speed of its center of mass is directly proportional to its angular speed. If the rolling object is perfectly rigid, a friction force is present but does no work on the object as it rolls.

8-5 The equations for rotational kinematics are almost identical to those for linear motion

Up to this point we've discussed rotation by using the concepts of energy and energy conservation almost exclusively. However, in many situations we need to use **rotational kinematics**: a description not just of how rapidly an object rotates, but also how rapidly its angular velocity is changing, that is, its *angular acceleration.*

Angular acceleration is an important factor in the design of rotating machinery. When you turn on an electric fan on a sweltering hot day, you don't just want the fan to start spinning but to come up to speed right away. But if you're riding on a carnival merry-go-round, you want it to gain speed gradually and smoothly at the beginning of the ride (and lose speed in the same way at the end of the ride) rather than in a sudden jerk. In this section we'll see how angular acceleration is defined and how to do calculations using it. Just as motion in a straight line is easiest to analyze when the acceleration is constant, we'll see that the simplest kind of rotational motion is that with constant *angular* acceleration.

Defining Angular Acceleration

We'll define angular acceleration in much the same way that we defined the acceleration of an object moving in a straight line in Section 2-4. In that section, we described the average acceleration $a_{\text{average},x}$ of an object moving along the x axis as the change Δv_x in its x velocity during a time interval divided by the duration Δt of the time interval:

$$a_{\text{average},x} = \frac{\Delta v_x}{\Delta t} \ (\text{average } x \text{ acceleration})$$

If the duration Δt of the time interval becomes very short, the ratio $\Delta v_x / \Delta t$ becomes the *instantaneous* acceleration a_x or, for short, simply the acceleration.

Let's follow the same steps for rotational motion. Suppose a rigid object is rotating around the z axis with angular velocity ω_{1z} at time t_1 and with angular velocity ω_{2z} at a later time t_2 (Figure 8-15). The **average angular acceleration** $\alpha_{\text{average},z}$ (the Greek letter α, or alpha) for the time interval between t_1 and t_2 is the change in angular velocity, $\Delta \omega_z = \omega_{2z} - \omega_{1z}$, divided by the duration of the time interval, $\Delta t = t_2 - t_1$:

| Average angular acceleration of a rotating object | Change in angular velocity of the object over a certain time interval: The angular velocity changes from ω_{1z} to ω_{2z}. |

$$\alpha_{\text{average},z} = \frac{\omega_{2z} - \omega_{1z}}{t_2 - t_1} = \frac{\Delta \omega_z}{\Delta t}$$

Elapsed time for the time interval: The object has angular velocity ω_{1z} at time t_1, and has angular velocity ω_{2z} at time t_2.

At time t_1 an object rotates with angular velocity ω_{1z}.

At a later time t_2 the object rotates with a different angular velocity ω_{2z}.

ω_{1z}

ω_{2z}

The object's average angular acceleration equals the change in angular velocity divided by the elapsed time:

$$\alpha_{\text{average},z} = \frac{\omega_{2z} - \omega_{1z}}{t_2 - t_1} = \frac{\Delta \omega_z}{\Delta t}$$

Figure 8-15 Defining angular acceleration The greater the magnitude of the average angular acceleration $\alpha_{\text{average},z}$ of a rotating object, the more rapidly the angular velocity changes.

Average angular acceleration (8-14)

If the two times t_1 and t_2 are very close to each other, so that Δt is very short, this becomes the *instantaneous* angular acceleration α_z, or just **angular acceleration** for short. At any instant, angular acceleration is equal to the rate of change of angular velocity at that instant. Since angular velocity is measured in rad/s, angular acceleration is measured in rad/s^2.

Just as all pieces of a rigid object rotate with the same angular velocity ω_z at any time t, all pieces have the same angular acceleration. The value of α_z is positive if the angular velocity ω_z is becoming more positive and negative if ω_z is becoming more negative.

Watch Out! The sign of angular acceleration can be misleading.

Just as for the acceleration of an object moving along a straight line, a positive value of angular acceleration α_z does *not* necessarily correspond to speeding up and a negative value of α_z does not necessarily correspond to slowing down. An object's rotation speeds up if ω_z and α_z have the same algebraic sign—if both are positive, the object is rotating in the positive direction and speeding up, while if both are negative, the object is rotating in the negative direction and speeding up. If ω_z and α_z have opposite signs (one positive and one negative), the object's rotation is slowing down (Figure 8-16).

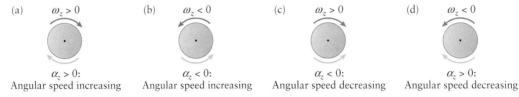

(a) $\omega_z > 0$

$\alpha_z > 0$:
Angular speed increasing

(b) $\omega_z < 0$

$\alpha_z < 0$:
Angular speed increasing

(c) $\omega_z > 0$

$\alpha_z < 0$:
Angular speed decreasing

(d) $\omega_z < 0$

$\alpha_z > 0$:
Angular speed decreasing

Figure 8-16 **The sign of angular acceleration** A rotating object is speeding up if its angular velocity ω_z and angular acceleration α_z are either (a) both positive or (b) both negative. It is slowing down if (c) ω_z is positive and α_z is negative or (d) ω_z is negative and α_z is positive.

Motion with Constant Angular Acceleration

We saw in Chapter 2 that an important case of motion in a straight line is when the acceleration a_x is constant, so that the velocity v_x changes at a steady rate. Let's look at the analogous situation of rotational motion with constant *angular* acceleration. This is important because a ball or wheel rolling downhill from rest moves with nearly constant angular acceleration, as do many types of rotating machinery as they start up or slow down.

It's straightforward to write down the equations for rotational motion with constant angular acceleration. To see how, take a look at the equations for linear velocity v_x and angular velocity ω_z, and the equations for linear acceleration a_x and angular acceleration α_z:

Go to Interactive Exercise 8-1 for more practice dealing with rotational kinematics

Linear motion	Rotational motion
$v_x = \dfrac{\Delta x}{\Delta t}$ (linear velocity)	$\omega_z = \dfrac{\Delta \theta}{\Delta t}$ (angular velocity)
$a_x = \dfrac{\Delta v_x}{\Delta t}$ (linear acceleration)	$\alpha_z = \dfrac{\Delta \omega_z}{\Delta t}$ (angular acceleration)

Comparing these equations shows that the rotational quantities θ, ω_z, and α_z are related to each other in exactly the same way that x, v_x, and a_x are related to each other. So we can take the equations for constant linear acceleration and convert them to the equations for constant angular acceleration by replacing x with θ, v_x with ω_z, and a_x with α_z. The equations for linear motion are

$$(2\text{-}5) \qquad v_x = v_{0x} + a_x t \text{ (constant } x \text{ acceleration only)}$$

$$(2\text{-}9) \qquad x = x_0 + v_{0x}t + \frac{1}{2}a_x t^2 \text{ (constant } x \text{ acceleration only)}$$

$$(2\text{-}11) \qquad v_x^2 = v_{0x}^2 + 2a_x(x - x_0) \text{ (constant } x \text{ acceleration only)}$$

Hence the equations for constant angular acceleration are

Angular velocity, angular acceleration, and time for constant angular acceleration only
(8-15)

Angular velocity at time t of a rotating object with constant angular acceleration

Angular velocity at time $t = 0$ of the object

$$\omega_z = \omega_{0z} + \alpha_z t$$

Constant angular acceleration of the object

Time at which the object has angular velocity ω_z

Angular position at time t of a rotating object with constant angular acceleration	Angular velocity at time $t = 0$ of the object	Constant angular acceleration of the object

$$\theta = \theta_0 + \omega_{0z}t + \frac{1}{2}\alpha_z t^2$$

Angular position at time $t = 0$ of the object	Time at which the object is at angular position θ

Angular position, angular acceleration, and time for constant angular acceleration only
(8-16)

Angular velocity at angular position θ of a rotating object with constant angular acceleration	Angular velocity at angular position θ_0 of the object

$$\omega_z^2 = \omega_{0z}^2 + 2\alpha_z(\theta - \theta_0)$$

Constant angular acceleration of the object	Two angular positions of the object

Angular velocity, angular acceleration, and angular position for constant angular acceleration only
(8-17)

To see what we mean by *angular position*, imagine a line drawn on the object outward from the rotation axis (Figure 8-17). The angle of this line from a reference direction changes as the object rotates, and it's this angle that we call the **angular position** θ. The angular displacement from time 0 to time t is $\theta - \theta_0$.

We can use Equations 8-17, 8-18, and 8-19 to solve a wide range of problems in rotational motion, just as we used Equations 2-5, 2-9, and 2-11 for linear motion problems in Chapter 2. Here's a representative example.

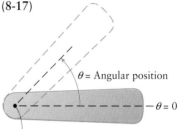

Figure 8-17 **Angular position** Imagine a line drawn on this rotating object from its rotation axis outward. The angle of this line at a given time is the object's angular position θ at that time.

> ! **Watch Out!** Equations 8-17, 8-18, and 8-19 are for rigid objects only.
>
> The three equations we've just presented can only be used if *all parts* of a rotating object have the same angular velocity and angular acceleration at any given time—in other words, only if the object is *rigid*. They *cannot* be used for a rotating object that isn't rigid, such as water in a bathtub as it swirls down the drain or a cake mix being stirred in a bowl. In Example 8-11, and in the problems at the end of the chapter, we'll always assume that the rotating objects are rigid.

Example 8-11 A Stopping Top

A top spinning at 4.00 rev/s comes to a complete stop in 64.0 s. Assuming the top slows down at a constant rate, how many revolutions does it make before coming to a stop?

Set Up

The statement that the top slows down at a constant rate means that its angular acceleration is constant, so we can use Equations 8-15 and 8-16. (We won't use Equation 8-17 because that equation doesn't involve time, which is one of the quantities we're given.)

To find constant angular acceleration α_z from $\omega_{0z}, \omega_z,$ and t:

$$\omega_z = \omega_{0z} + \alpha_z t \qquad (8\text{-}15)$$

Quantity	Know/Don't Know
t	64.0 s
θ_0	0
θ	?
ω_{0z}	4.00 rev/s
ω_z	0
α_z	X

These two equations involve six quantities ($t, \theta_0, \theta, \omega_{0z}, \omega_z,$ and α_z). Just as we did in Chapter 2 for linear motion with constant acceleration, we'll use a Know/Don't Know table to help keep track of which of these quantities are known and which we want to find.

To find the final angular postion θ from $\theta_0, \omega_{0z}, \alpha_z,$ and t:

$$\theta = \theta_0 + \omega_{0z}t + \frac{1}{2}\alpha_z t^2 \qquad (8\text{-}16)$$

In this case we are given the initial angular velocity $\omega_{0z} = 4.00$ rev/s, the final angular velocity $\omega_z = 0$, and the elapsed time $t = 64.0$ s. If we let the top start at an angular position of $\theta_0 = 0$, we want to find the top's final angular position θ during this time, but don't know the value of the angular acceleration α_z. We'll use Equation 8-15 to determine α_z from the known information, then substitute this value into Equation 8-16 to find the value of θ.

Solve

Rewrite Equation 8-15 to solve for α_z. Then substitute the values of ω_z, ω_{0z}, and t. (Note that we don't need to convert revolutions to radians: We just have to be consistent with units throughout our solution.)

Rewrite Equation 8-15: $\omega_z - \omega_{0z} = \alpha_z t$

$$\alpha_z = \frac{\omega_z - \omega_{0z}}{t}$$

The resulting value of α_z is negative while ω_{0z} is positive, which correctly says that the rotation is slowing down.

Substitute values: $\alpha_z = \dfrac{0 - 4.00 \text{ rev/s}}{64.0 \text{ s}} = -0.0625 \text{ rev/s}^2$

Solve for θ by plugging this value of α_z into Equation 8-16 along with the given values of ω_{0z} and t.

Equation 8-16: $\theta = \theta_0 + \omega_{0z} t + \dfrac{1}{2}\alpha_z t^2$

$= 0 \text{ rev} + (4.00 \text{ rev/s})(64.0 \text{ s}) + \dfrac{1}{2}(-0.0625 \text{ rev/s}^2)(64.0 \text{ s})^2$

$= 256 \text{ rev} - 128 \text{ rev}$

$= 128 \text{ rev}$

Reflect

We can check our answer by substituting the values for ω_z, ω_{0z}, and α_z into Equation 8-17 (which we did not use above) and solving for θ. This gives us the same answer for θ as above.

Note that by writing $\omega_{0z} = 4.00$ rev/s, we made the assumption that the top is initially rotating in the positive direction. Can you show that if you instead make $\omega_{0z} = -4.00$ rev/s, so that the top is initially rotating in the negative direction, you get $\theta - \theta_0 = -128$ rev? (This means that the top rotates 128 rev but in the negative direction.)

Equation 8-17: $\omega_z^2 = \omega_{0z}^2 + 2\alpha_z(\theta - \theta_0)$

Rewrite to solve for θ: $\omega_z^2 - \omega_{0z}^2 = 2\alpha_z(\theta - \theta_0)$

$\theta = \dfrac{\omega_z^2 - \omega_{0z}^2}{2\alpha_z} + \theta_0 = \dfrac{(0 \text{ rev/s})^2 - (4.00 \text{ rev/s})^2}{2(-0.0625 \text{ rev/s}^2)} + 0 \text{ rev}$

$= 128 \text{ rev}$

❓ Got the Concept? 8-6 Rate of Change of Angular Speed

Rank the following rotating objects in order of the rate at which the speed of their rotation is changing, from speeding up at the fastest rate to slowing down at the fastest rate. (a) A disk with $\omega_z = 2.00$ rad/s and $\alpha_z = -1.00$ rad/s^2; (b) a wheel with $\omega_z = 3.00$ rad/s and $\alpha_z = -2.00$ rad/s^2; (c) a ceiling fan with $\omega_z = -2.00$ rad/s and $\alpha_z = -1.00$ rad/s^2; (d) a flywheel with $\omega_z = 0$ and $\alpha_z = -0.750$ rad/s^2; (e) a circular saw with $\omega_z = 3.00$ rad/s and $\alpha_z = 0.750$ rad/s^2.

Take-Home Message for Section 8-5

✔ Just as acceleration in a straight line is the rate of change of velocity, angular acceleration is the rate of change of angular velocity.

✔ If the angular acceleration is constant for a rigid object, there are three simple equations that relate time, angular position, angular velocity, and angular acceleration.

8-6 Torque is to rotation as force is to translation

Where do you push or pull on a door to open it most easily? In what direction should you exert that push or pull? These may seem like odd questions to ask in a chapter about rotational motion. But keep in mind that when you open a door, you are giving it an *angular acceleration*: The door starts at rest and begins rotating around its hinges, so you're changing the door's angular velocity. So we can rephrase our questions like this: Where, and in what direction, should we push or pull on a door to give it an angular acceleration around its hinges?

Experience tells you that the best place to exert your push or pull on the door is at a spot far from the door hinges, and that the best direction to push or pull is perpendicular to the plane of the door (Figure 8-18a). You would never push near the hinges, like the student in Figure 8-18b, because experience has taught you that it's nearly impossible to open a door that way. (That's why a doorknob is located on the opposite end of a door from the hinges.) Experience also tells you that it would be hard to open the door by pushing or pulling in a direction parallel to the plane (Figure 8-18c).

This example shows that in order to give an object an angular acceleration, what matters is not just how hard you push or pull on the object, but also *where* and *in what direction* that push or pull is applied. A physical quantity that relates all of these aspects of an applied force is the *torque* associated with that force. In this section we'll find that just as the net force acting on an object determines its translational or linear acceleration (Newton's second law), the net *torque* acting on an object determines its *angular* acceleration.

(a) (b) (c)

Figure 8-18 **Opening a door**
(a) The easiest way to open a door is by exerting a force (push or pull) perpendicular to the door hinges at a point as far from the door hinges as possible. By contrast, it's very difficult to open the door if you exert a force (b) near the hinges or (c) in a direction parallel to the plane of the door.

Defining the Magnitude and Direction of Torque

Suppose that you exert a force $\vec{F}$ on an object as shown in Figure 8-19a. We use the symbol $\vec{r}$ to denote the vector from the rotation axis to the point where the force is applied, and we use the symbol ϕ (the Greek letter phi) for the angle between the directions of $\vec{r}$ and $\vec{F}$. The component of $\vec{F}$ that points straight out from the rotation axis, $F\cos\phi$, doesn't have any tendency to make the object rotate. But the perpendicular component of $\vec{F}$, $F\sin\phi$, *does* tend to make the object rotate—in this case in a clockwise direction. We describe the rotational effect of the force $\vec{F}$ by a quantity called the **torque** τ (the Greek letter tau) associated with the force. This is given by

Magnitude of the **torque** produced by a force acting on an object

Magnitude of the force

$$\tau = rF \sin \phi$$

Distance from the rotation axis of the object to where the force is applied

Angle between the vector $\vec{r}$ (from the rotation axis to where the force is applied) and the force vector $\vec{F}$

Magnitude of torque
(8-18)

Equation 8-18 tells us the *magnitude* of the torque, but torque also has *direction*. For the force shown in Figure 8-19a, we say that the associated torque is clockwise because it tends to make the object rotate clockwise. By contrast, the force depicted in Figure 8-19b tends to make the object rotate counterclockwise, so we say that the torque associated with this force is counterclockwise. (In Section 8-9 we'll see that torque itself can be regarded as a vector. But for rotation around an axis with fixed direction, like a door rotating around its hinges, all we need is the idea that torque can be clockwise or counterclockwise.)

Views of object from along its rotation axis

(a) A force that tends to cause
clockwise rotation

Point where
force is applied

The vector $\vec{r}$ points
from an object's
rotation axis to where
a force $\vec{F}$ is applied to
the object.

Rotation axis

(b) A force that tends to cause
counterclockwise rotation

(c) Determining the line of action of a
force and its lever arm

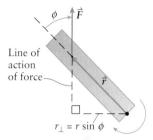

Line of
action
of force

$r_\perp = r \sin \phi$

The lever arm $r_\perp$ is perpendicular
to the line of action of the force,
and extends from the rotation axis
to the line of action of the force.

Figure 8-19 **Torque** (a) The vector $\vec{r}$ points from an object's rotation axis to where a force $\vec{F}$ is applied to the object. The torque produced by the force has magnitude $\tau = rF \sin \phi$. In this case the torque is clockwise because it tends to make the object rotate clockwise. (b) This torque is counterclockwise because it tends to make the object rotate counterclockwise. (c) Finding the torque in terms of the lever arm $r_\perp$.

Go to Interactive Exercise 8-2 for
more practice dealing with torque

In Section 8-2 we denoted the rotation axis as the z axis and used the symbol ω_z to denote angular velocity, a quantity that can be positive or negative depending on the direction of rotation. We did this to distinguish ω_z from the angular speed ω, which is the magnitude of angular velocity. In the same way we'll use τ_z as the symbol for torque and τ (with no subscript) to denote the magnitude of torque, as in Equation 8-18. If we choose the positive rotation direction to be counterclockwise, then in Figure 8-19a the torque is negative (it tends to cause clockwise rotation) and $\tau_z < 0$. In Figure 8-19b the torque has the same magnitude τ (the distance r, force magnitude F, and angle ϕ are the same as in Figure 8-19a), but the torque tends to cause counterclockwise rotation and so $\tau_z > 0$.

Figure 8-19c shows another way to calculate the magnitude of the torque for the situation in Figure 8-19a. As this figure shows, the **line of action** of the force is just an extension of the force vector $\vec{F}$ through the point where the force is applied. The **lever arm** of the force (also called the *moment arm*) is the perpendicular distance from the rotation axis to the line of action of the force, which is why we denote it by the symbol $r_\perp$ ($\perp$ is mathematical shorthand for "perpendicular"). Trigonometry shows that the lever arm $r_\perp$ equals $r \sin \phi$, the same quantity that appears in Equation 8-18. Hence we can rewrite that equation as

Magnitude of the **torque** produced
by a force acting on an object

Magnitude of the force

Magnitude of torque in
terms of lever arm
(8-19)

$$\tau = r_\perp F$$

Lever arm = perpendicular distance from the rotation
axis of the object to the line of action of the force

Equation 8-19 is mathematically equivalent to Equation 8-18, but defines torque in a slightly different way: It says that the magnitude of the torque produced by a force equals the lever arm of the force multiplied by the force magnitude. The longer the lever arm for a given force magnitude, the greater the torque.

Figure 8-20 illustrates these ideas about torque using the door that we discussed previously (see Figure 8-18). For a given force magnitude F, the lever arm $r_\perp$ and hence the torque magnitude τ will be as large as possible if r is as large as possible and if $\sin \phi$ has its maximum value of 1, which occurs if $\phi = 90°$. In other words, a force produces the maximum torque—and hence the maximum rotating effect—if it is applied as far from the rotation axis as possible and in a direction perpendicular to a line from the rotation axis to the point of application (see Figure 8-20a). That's just what we said in our discussion of the door. By contrast, if the force is applied close to the rotation axis so the distance r is small—like pushing on a door at a point close to the hinges—the lever arm $r_\perp = r \sin \phi$ is short, so the torque magnitude and rotating effect are small

(a) Pulling on a door far from the hinge (view as seen looking down on the door from above): Large lever arm $r_\perp$.

(b) Pulling on a door close to the hinge: Small lever arm $r_\perp$.

(c) Pushing on a door directly toward the hinge: Zero lever arm $r_\perp$.

Figure 8-20 Torques on a door
(a) For a force $\vec{F}$ of a given magnitude, the torque is greatest when r is large and $\phi = 90°$. The torque is small if (b) r is small or (c) sin ϕ is small.

(Figure 8-20b). The torque is also small if the force is applied in nearly the same direction as the vector $\vec{r}$ as in Figure 8-20c. In that case the angle ϕ is nearly zero, sin ϕ has a small value, and the lever arm $r_\perp = r \sin \phi$ is again short. This is like pulling on a door in a direction nearly parallel to the door's plane. (The same is true if the force is directed nearly opposite to $\vec{r}$, so ϕ is close to 180° and again sin ϕ is close to zero.)

From Equation 8-19, the SI units of torque are newtons multiplied by meters, or newton-meters (abbreviated N · m).

! Watch Out! Torque and work have the same units but are very different quantities.

Both torque and work have units of newton-meters. But you can't set one equal to the other. Work involves the product of the component of a force parallel to a displacement. Torque is the product of the component of a force perpendicular to a lever arm. Because physically they represent two very different things, it makes no sense to set one equal to the other.

? Got the Concept? 8-7 Using Torque to Loosen a Bolt

A socket wrench, like the one in Figure 8-21, can be used to loosen a bolt. If a bolt has become frozen in place and is especially difficult to loosen, a common trick is to slide a section of pipe over the handle of the wrench and turn the bolt while gripping the end of the pipe. Why does this work? Why do many experienced craftsmen tend to avoid using this trick?

Figure 8-21 Wrench torque
How does lengthening the handle of a wrench make it easier to loosen a bolt?

Lever Arms in Animal Anatomy

As Equation 8-19 shows, even a small force F can generate a large torque τ if the lever arm $r_\perp$ is long enough. Humans and other animals take advantage of this principle through the arrangement of their muscles and bones. As an example, Figure 8-22a shows that the point at which the masseter muscle is attached to the lower jawbone is far from the joint around which the jaw rotates. Hence the force exerted by the masseter muscle has a long lever arm, and so produces a large torque on the lower jawbone. This large torque enables you to crack a nut between your back teeth or use your front teeth to tear into the undercooked vegetables served at the campus cafeteria.

A very different arrangement is used in your forearm. One end of the biceps muscle attaches to the bone of the upper arm and the other to the lower arm just below the elbow (Figure 8-22b). Even though the biceps muscle can exert a large force, this muscle-joint

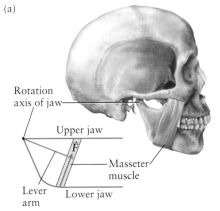

(a)

Rotation axis of jaw

Upper jaw

$\vec{F}$

Masseter muscle

Lever arm   Lower jaw

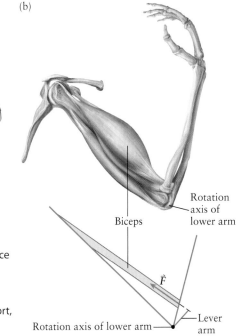

(b)

Rotation axis of lower arm

Biceps

$\vec{F}$

Lever arm

Figure 8-22 Lever arms in the human jaw and arm (a) The masseter muscle exerts a force on the lower jaw with a relatively long lever arm, so the torque on the lower jaw is quite large. (b) The lever arm for the force of the biceps muscle on the forearm is relatively short, so the torque is relatively small.

Rotation axis of lower arm

arrangement doesn't generate a large torque because the lever arm is relatively short. In chimpanzees the bicep is attached farther from the elbow joint, giving it the ability to generate more forearm torque than a human despite the chimpanzee's smaller size and smaller muscles.

Torque, Angular Acceleration, and Newton's Second Law for Rotation

We have suggested that a torque acting on an object (like the torque produced by pushing or pulling on a door) affects its rotation. What is the precise relationship between torque and the rotational effect that it causes? To find out, let's recall Newton's second law for *linear* motion along the *x* axis:

(4-4a)
$$\sum F_{\text{ext},x} = ma_x$$

This equation states that an object accelerates in response to the sum of all the external forces that act on the object: This sum $\sum F_{\text{ext},x}$ equals the object's mass *m* multiplied by its acceleration a_x. To find the rotational equivalent of this equation, remember from Section 8-2 that moment of inertia *I* plays the same role for rotational motion that mass *m* does for linear motion, and recall from Section 8-5 that angular acceleration α is the rotational equivalent of linear acceleration a_x. If torque plays the same role for rotational motion as force plays for translational motion, then we should be able to replace F_x with τ_z, *m* with *I*, and a_x with α_z in Equation 4-4a to get the rotational version of Newton's second law:

Newton's second law for rotational motion (8-20)

The net torque, or sum of all external torques acting on an object for the axis about which it can rotate

The angular acceleration produced by the net torque

$$\sum \tau_z = I\alpha_z$$

The object's moment of inertia for the axis about which it can rotate

Experiment shows that Equation 8-20 is, in fact, correct. An object acquires an *angular* acceleration α_z in response to the sum $\sum \tau_z$ of all of the external *torques* that act on the object, and this angular acceleration is directly proportional to the net torque. The magnitude of the angular acceleration also depends on the object's moment of inertia *I* around the rotation axis. The basic physics is the same as the original form of Newton's second law, Equation 4-4a.

❓ Got the Concept? 8-8   Rotating the Human Jaw

As Figure 8-23 shows, the human jaw can rotate around three axes as shown. Chewing is accomplished primarily by rotations around the axis labeled *y*, while moving your jaw from side to side involves rotating it around the axis labeled *z*. Measurements show that for a lower jaw with a mass of approximately 0.4 kg, typical values for the moments of inertia are $I_y = 3 \times 10^{-4}$ kg·m² and $I_z = 9 \times 10^{-4}$ kg·m². (a) Does the anatomy of the jaw favor (i) up-down motions or (ii) side-to-side motion? (b) Is more torque required (i) to open your jaw or (ii) to rotate it from side to side?

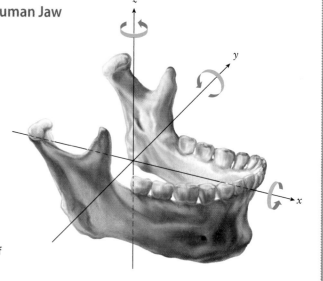

Figure 8-23 **The human jaw** The human jaw has a different moment of inertia for each of the three axes *x*, *y*, and *z*.

Got the Concept? 8-9 Insects versus Birds

The maneuverability of a flying insect or a bird depends in large part on the contributions their wings make to the moments of inertia around their roll, pitch, and yaw axes (Figure 8-24). As much as 15% of the total body mass of a bird can be in its wings, while the wings of a typical insect are a considerably smaller fraction of its total mass. Which would you expect to be able to maneuver more quickly in flight: (a) a flying insect or (b) a bird?

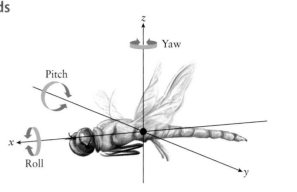

Figure 8-24 Rotation axes of an insect An insect can rotate in three ways: It can roll around its longitudinal *x* axis, pitch around its lateral *y* axis, or yaw around its *z* axis.

Take-Home Message for Section 8-6

✔ If a force acting on an object tends to change that object's rotation, the force generates a torque. The magnitude of the torque depends on where the force is applied relative to the rotation axis and on the orientation of the force.

✔ The magnitude of a torque is equal to the magnitude of the force that causes the torque multiplied by the lever arm of the force (the perpendicular distance from the rotation axis to the line of action of the force).

✔ Newton's second law for rotation says that if a net external torque $\sum \tau_z$ acts on an object, the object acquires an angular acceleration α_z. These are related via the moment of inertia I: $\sum \tau_z = I\alpha_z$.

8-7 The techniques used for solving problems with Newton's second law also apply to rotation problems

The examples in this section show how to use the rotational form of Newton's second law. Just as for the translational form of this law, in each example we'll begin our solution by drawing a free-body diagram.

In many problems it's necessary to use *both* the translational and rotational forms of Newton's second law. Examples 8-13 and 8-14 show how to tackle problems like these.

❗ Watch Out! In rotational problems, it matters *where* the force acts.

In problems that involve Newton's second law for translational motion, we draw all of the forces on an object as acting at a single point. But in problems that involve rotational motion, it's crucial to indicate in the free-body diagram *where* on the object each force acts. That's because the torque generated by a force depends on where the force is applied relative to the rotation axis. In the examples below, study closely how forces are depicted in free-body diagrams and how the corresponding torques are calculated.

Example 8-12 A Simple Pulley I

A pulley is a solid uniform cylinder of mass M_{pulley} and radius R that is free to rotate around an axis through its center. A lightweight rope is wound around the pulley. You exert a constant force of magnitude F on the rope, which makes the rope unwind and rotates the pulley (Figure 8-25). The rope does not stretch and does not slip on the pulley. What is the angular acceleration of the pulley about its axle?

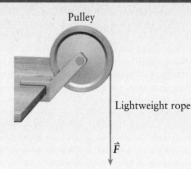

Figure 8-25 Exerting a torque on a pulley What is the angular acceleration of the pulley as the force *F* makes the rope unwind?

Set Up

We begin by drawing a free-body diagram for the pulley, taking care to draw each force at the point where it acts. We are told that the rope is lightweight (that is, it has much less mass than the pulley), so the force that you exert on the free end of the rope has the same magnitude F as the force that the rope exerts on the pulley. This force exerts a torque on the pulley and causes an angular acceleration. We'll use the rotational form of Newton's second law to determine this angular acceleration.

Newton's second law for rotational motion:

$$\sum \tau_z = I_{\text{pulley}} \alpha_{\text{pulley},z} \qquad (8\text{-}20)$$

Solve

The free-body diagram shows that only the tension force F exerts a torque on the pulley causing it to rotate around its axle. (The support force F_{support} and the weight of the pulley W_{pulley} both act at its rotation axis, so the lever arm is zero for both of these forces.) The lever arm for the tension force is R, so the tension torque is R multiplied by F.

Torque due to tension force:

$$\tau_z = r_\perp F = RF$$

(This torque makes the pulley rotate in the clockwise direction, so we take clockwise to be the positive rotation direction.)
This is the only torque acting on the pulley, so

$$\sum \tau_z = RF$$

$$\sum \tau_z = I_{\text{pulley}} \alpha_{\text{pulley},z}$$

From Table 8-1 in Section 8-3, the moment of inertia of a solid cylinder around its central axis is $I = MR^2/2$. Insert this into Newton's second law for rotational motion and solve for $\alpha_{\text{pulley},z}$.

Substitute values of $\sum \tau_z$ and $I_{\text{pulley}} = M_{\text{pulley}} R^2/2$:

$$RF = \frac{1}{2} M_{\text{pulley}} R^2 \alpha_{\text{pulley},z}$$

Solve for angular acceleration α_z: $\alpha_{\text{pulley},z} = \dfrac{2RF}{M_{\text{pulley}} R^2} = \dfrac{2F}{M_{\text{pulley}} R}$

Reflect

Our result for the angular acceleration $\alpha_{\text{pulley},z}$ depends on the pulling force F, the pulley mass M_{pulley}, and the pulley radius R. It makes sense that our result is proportional to the ratio F/M_{pulley}: A greater force F means a stronger pull and a greater angular acceleration, while a greater mass M_{pulley} means the pulley is more difficult to rotate and gives a smaller angular acceleration.

Our result also shows that the larger the pulley radius R, the smaller the angular acceleration $\alpha_{\text{pulley},z}$. This may seem backwards, since a larger radius means that the force F causes a larger torque $\tau = RF$. However, increasing the radius increases the moment of inertia $I = M_{\text{pulley}} R^2/2$ by a larger factor than it increases the torque. (Doubling the radius doubles the torque but quadruples the moment of inertia.) So the moment of inertia plays a more important role, which is why $\alpha_{\text{pulley},z}$ decreases with increasing pulley radius.

Example 8-13 A Simple Pulley II

You attach a block of mass M_{block} to the free end of the rope in Example 8-12 (Figure 8-26). When the block is released from rest and falls downward, the rope unwinds and the pulley rotates around its central axis. As in Example 8-12, the rope neither stretches nor slips on the pulley. Derive expressions for the acceleration of the block, the angular acceleration of the pulley, and the tension in the string.

Figure 8-26 **Block and pulley** What is the downward acceleration of the block as it falls, and what is the angular acceleration of the pulley as the rope unwinds?

Set Up

As in Example 8-12, the pulley has an angular acceleration because the tension of the rope exerts a torque on it. The difference here is that the tension is caused by the block attached to the rope's free end.

Another difference from Example 8-12 is that we have *two* moving objects: the pulley (which rotates) and the block (which moves in a straight line). Hence we have to write two Newton's second law equations: a rotational equation for the pulley, as in Example 8-12, and a translational equation for the block.

These two equations won't be enough to solve the problem, since we're trying to find *three* quantities: the block's acceleration $a_{block,x}$, the pulley's angular acceleration $\alpha_{pulley,z}$, and the string tension T. Happily, we can get a third equation because the string doesn't stretch. This tells us that the speed of the block equals the speed of a point on the pulley rim. We'll use this to find a relationship between $a_{block,x}$ and $\alpha_{pulley,z}$.

Newton's second law for rotational motion applies to the pulley:

$$\sum \tau_z = I_{pulley}\,\alpha_{pulley,z} \qquad (8\text{-}20)$$

Newton's second law for translational motion applies to the block:

$$\sum F_{ext,x} = M_{block}\,a_{block,x} \qquad (4\text{-}4a)$$

Statement that rope doesn't stretch:

$$v_{block} = v_{rim\ of\ pulley}$$

Solve

As in Example 8-12, the only force that exerts a torque on the pulley is the rope tension, which we call T. The lever arm of this force is R, so the net torque is $\sum \tau_z = RT$. Insert this and $I_{pulley} = M_{pulley}R^2/2$ into the rotational Newton's second law equation and solve for the tension.

For the pulley,

$$\sum \tau_z = I_{pulley}\,\alpha_{pulley,z}$$

Substitute values of $\sum \tau_z$ and I_{pulley}:

$$RT = \frac{1}{2}M_{pulley}R^2\alpha_{pulley,z}$$

(As in Example 8-12, this torque makes the pulley rotate in the clockwise direction. So we take clockwise to be the positive rotation direction.)

Divide through by R:

$$T = \frac{1}{2}M_{pulley}R\alpha_{pulley,z}$$

We want the block to accelerate in the positive direction when the pulley accelerates in the positive direction. So for the block, we take the positive x direction to point downward, which is the direction in which the block will move when the pulley rotates clockwise. Then the gravitational force $M_{block}g$ is in the positive x direction and the tension force T is in the negative x direction. (The rope has negligible mass, so the tension is the same throughout its length.) Use this to write Newton's second law equation for the block.

For the block,

$$\sum F_{ext,x} = M_{block}\,a_{block,x}$$

Substitute the individual forces:

$$M_{block}g - T = M_{block}\,a_{block,x}$$

Since the rope doesn't stretch, at any instant the speed of the block v_{block} equals the speed of a point on the pulley rim, which is equal to $R\omega$ (the product of the pulley radius and the pulley angular speed given by Equation 8-3). As the

At a certain time, $v_{block} = v_{rim\ of\ pulley}$ or

$$v_{block,x} = R\omega_{pulley} = R\omega_{pulley,z}$$

block falls, it gains speed and the pulley gains angular speed, but the speed of the block remains equal to the speed of the pulley's rim. Use this to relate the linear acceleration of the block to the angular acceleration of the pulley.

(The block is moving downward in the positive x direction, so its x velocity $v_{\text{block},x}$ is positive and equal to its speed v_{block}. The pulley is rotating in the positive direction, so its angular velocity $\omega_{\text{pulley},z}$ is positive and equal to the pulley's angular speed ω_{pulley}.)

A time Δt later,

$$v_{\text{block},x} + \Delta v_{\text{block},x} = R(\omega_{\text{pulley},z} + \Delta \omega_{\text{pulley},z})$$

so

$$v_{\text{block},x} + \Delta v_{\text{block},x} = R\omega_{\text{pulley},z} + R\, \Delta\omega_{\text{pulley},z}$$

Since $v_{\text{block},x} = R\omega_{\text{pulley},z}$ from above, it follows that

$$\Delta v_{\text{block},x} = R\, \Delta\omega_{\text{pulley},z}$$

Divide both sides by Δt:

$$\frac{\Delta v_{\text{block},x}}{\Delta t} = R\,\frac{\Delta \omega_{\text{pulley},z}}{\Delta t}$$

The ratios on the two sides are just the acceleration of the block and the angular acceleration of the pulley. So

$$a_{\text{block},x} = R\alpha_{\text{pulley},z} \text{ or } \alpha_{\text{pulley},z} = \frac{a_{\text{block},x}}{R}$$

Combine the three equations to solve for the three unknowns.

Substitute $\alpha_{\text{pulley},z} = a_{\text{block},x}/R$ into the pulley equation:

$$T = \frac{1}{2}M_{\text{pulley}}R\alpha_{\text{pulley},z} = \frac{1}{2}M_{\text{pulley}}R\left(\frac{a_{\text{block},x}}{R}\right) = \frac{1}{2}M_{\text{pulley}}a_{\text{block},x}$$

Substitute this expression for T into the block equation:

$$M_{\text{block}}g - T = M_{\text{block}}a_{\text{block},x} \text{ so}$$

$$M_{\text{block}}g - \frac{1}{2}M_{\text{pulley}}a_{\text{block},x} = M_{\text{block}}a_{\text{block},x}$$

Solve for $a_{\text{block},x}$:

$$M_{\text{block}}g = M_{\text{block}}a_{\text{block},x} + \frac{1}{2}M_{\text{pulley}}a_{\text{block},x}$$

$$M_{\text{block}}g = \left(M_{\text{block}} + \frac{1}{2}M_{\text{pulley}}\right)a_{\text{block},x}$$

$$a_{\text{block},x} = \left(\frac{M_{\text{block}}}{M_{\text{block}} + M_{\text{pulley}}/2}\right)g$$

Now find $\alpha_{\text{pulley},z}$ by substituting this into $\alpha_{\text{pulley},z} = a_{\text{block},x}/R$:

$$\alpha_{\text{pulley},z} = \frac{a_{\text{block},x}}{R}$$

$$\alpha_{\text{pulley},z} = \left(\frac{M_{\text{block}}}{M_{\text{block}} + M_{\text{pulley}}/2}\right)\frac{g}{R}$$

Finally, solve for T from the pulley equation:

$$T = \frac{1}{2}M_{\text{pulley}}R\alpha_{\text{pulley},z} = \frac{1}{2}M_{\text{pulley}}R\left(\frac{M_{\text{block}}}{M_{\text{block}} + M_{\text{pulley}}/2}\right)\frac{g}{R}$$

$$= M_{\text{block}}g\left(\frac{M_{\text{pulley}}}{2M_{\text{block}} + M_{\text{pulley}}}\right)$$

Reflect

The downward acceleration of the block is less than g, because the tension of the rope exerts an upward pull on the block that partially cancels the downward pull of gravity. The expression for tension T confirms this: T is less than $M_{block}g$, which says that the tension force doesn't completely balance out the gravitational force. If it did, the block would just hang there when released and wouldn't move at all!

Here's a way to check our results: If the pulley is very much lighter than the block, so M_{pulley} is nearly zero, it's as though the block is connected to nothing at all. In this case the block's downward acceleration would be g (it would be in free fall) and there would be no tension in the rope. Can you use our results for $a_{block,x}$ and T to show that this is the case?

$$a_{block,x} = \left(\frac{M_{block}}{M_{block} + M_{pulley}/2}\right)g:$$

Inside the parentheses the numerator M_{block} is less than the denominator $M_{block} + M_{pulley}/2$, so the ratio inside the parentheses is less than 1 and $a_{block,x} < g$

$$T = M_{block}g\left(\frac{M_{pulley}}{2M_{block} + M_{pulley}}\right):$$

Inside the parentheses the numerator M_{pulley} is less than the denominator $2M_{block} + M_{pulley}$, so the ratio inside the parentheses is less than 1 and $T < M_{block}g$.

Example 8-14 Rolling Without Slipping Revisited

In Example 8-10 in Section 8-4 we considered a uniform disk of mass M and radius R that rolls down a ramp without slipping. Use Newton's second law for rotational motion and for linear motion to determine the downhill acceleration of the disk's center of mass. The ramp is inclined at an angle θ to the horizontal.

Set Up

Unlike Example 8-13, in which we had one object (the pulley) undergoing purely rotational motion and another object (the block) undergoing purely translational motion, here we have *one* object that undergoes *both* rotational and translational motion. The principles are the same, however. We'll write down equations for both the rotational and translational forms of Newton's second law for the disk.

We also know from Section 8-4 that because the disk rolls without slipping, there's a relationship between the speed of the disk's center of mass v_{CM} and its angular speed ω. In a manner similar to what we did in Example 8-13, we'll use this to derive an equation that relates the disk's center of mass acceleration and its angular acceleration.

Newton's second law for rotational motion of the disk around its central axis (the z axis):

$$\sum \tau_z = I\alpha_z \qquad (8\text{-}20)$$

Newton's second law for linear motion of the disk—note that we include both x and y equations:

$$\sum F_{ext,x} = Ma_{CM,x}$$
$$\sum F_{ext,y} = Ma_{CM,y} \qquad (4\text{-}4)$$

Disk rolls without slipping:

$$v_{CM} = R\omega \qquad (8\text{-}13)$$

Solve

Three forces act on the disk as it rolls: the downward force of gravity Mg, the normal force n that acts perpendicular to the surface of the ramp, and the uphill force of friction f that keeps the disk from sliding downhill.

The force of gravity exerts no torque around the center of mass because it acts at the disk's center of mass, so its lever arm is $r_\perp = 0$. The normal force acts along a line that passes through the center of mass, so its lever arm is also zero and it exerts no torque. For the friction force, $r_\perp = R$ and $\tau_{friction,z} = Rf$. Substitute this and $I = MR^2/2$ into Newton's second law for rotation.

Newton's second law for rotation:

$$\sum \tau_z = I\alpha_z$$

Substitute $\sum \tau_z = \tau_{friction,z} = Rf$ and $I = MR^2/2$:

$$Rf = \frac{1}{2}MR^2\alpha_z$$

Divide both sides of this equation by R:

$$f = \frac{1}{2}MR\alpha_z$$

For translational motion, write the equations for the net force in the x and y directions. There is no acceleration in the y direction (perpendicular to the ramp) so $a_{CM,y} = 0$. The acceleration downhill in the x direction, $a_{CM,x}$, results from the forces of gravity and friction.

Net force in each direction:

$$\sum F_x = Mg \sin \theta - f$$
$$\sum F_y = n - Mg \cos \theta$$

Substitute into Newton's second law for translational motion:

$$Mg \sin \theta - f = Ma_{CM,x}$$
$$n - Mg \cos \theta = 0$$
(since $a_{CM,y} = 0$)

The y equation for linear motion isn't useful (it would only be of interest if we wanted to calculate the normal force n). The other two equations—one for rotational motion and one for linear motion along the x axis—involve three unknowns: f, α_z, and $a_{CM,x}$. So we need a third equation. This comes from the condition for rolling without slipping, $v_{CM} = R\omega$.

Rotation: $f = \dfrac{1}{2}MR\alpha_z$

Translational motion along x axis: $Mg \sin \theta - f = Ma_{CM,x}$

Rolling without slipping: $v_{CM} = R\omega$

In Example 8-13 the similar equation $v_{block} = R\omega$ led to $a_{block} = R\alpha$. The same mathematical steps (which we won't repeat here) lead us to the same relationship between $a_{CM,x}$ and α_z for the disk, which is our third equation.

Hence $a_{CM,x} = R\alpha_z$ or $\alpha_z = \dfrac{a_{CM,x}}{R}$

Combine the three equations to solve for $a_{CM,x}$.

Substitute $\alpha_z = a_{CM,x}/R$ into the rotational equation:

$$f = \frac{1}{2}MR\alpha_z = \frac{1}{2}MR\left(\frac{a_{CM,x}}{R}\right) \text{ so}$$

$$f = \frac{1}{2}Ma_{CM,x}$$

Substitute this expression for f into the linear motion equation and solve for $a_{CM,x}$:

$$Mg \sin \theta - f = Ma_{CM,x}$$

$$Mg \sin \theta - \frac{1}{2}Ma_{CM,x} = Ma_{CM,x}$$

$$Mg \sin \theta = Ma_{CM,x} + \frac{1}{2}Ma_{CM,x} = \frac{3}{2}Ma_{CM,x}$$

$$g \sin \theta = \frac{3}{2}a_{CM,x}$$

$$a_{CM,x} = \frac{2}{3}g \sin \theta$$

Reflect

If there were no friction, the disk would slide downhill rather than roll and its acceleration would be $g \sin \theta$ (the component along the ramp of the acceleration due to gravity) as in Example 4-5. Friction slows the disk's downhill motion, which is why its acceleration is only two-thirds of $g \sin \theta$. Can you show that the magnitude of the friction force is $(Mg/3) \sin \theta$?

    We can check our result for acceleration by asking how fast the disk will be moving at the bottom of the ramp if it starts from rest

Motion with constant x acceleration:

$$v_{CM,x}^2 = v_{CM,0x}^2 + 2a_{CM,x}(x - x_0)$$

Disk starts at rest: $v_{CM,0x} = 0$

Displacement down the ramp:

$$x - x_0 = \frac{H}{\sin \theta}$$

at a height H. The answer we get is $\sqrt{(4/3)gH}$. This is the same as we found in Example 8-10 in Section 8-4 using energy conservation—which is encouraging!

We calculated the acceleration above:

$$a_{CM,x} = \frac{2}{3}g\sin\theta, \text{ so}$$

$$v_{CM,x}^2 = 0 + 2\left(\frac{2}{3}g\sin\theta\right)\left(\frac{H}{\sin\theta}\right) = \frac{4gH}{3}$$

$$v_{CM,x} = \sqrt{\frac{4gH}{3}}$$

? Got the Concept? 8-10   Which Friction?

What kind of friction force acts on the disk in Example 8-14 as it rolls downhill: (a) static friction, (b) kinetic friction, or (c) a mixture of static and kinetic friction?

? Got the Concept? 8-11   A Uniform Sphere Rolling Downhill

Suppose we replace the disk in Example 8-14 with a uniform solid sphere like a billiard ball. Compared to the linear acceleration of the disk, what will be the linear acceleration of the sphere? (a) greater; (b) the same; (c) less.

Take-Home Message for Section 8-7

✔ Always draw a free-body diagram as part of the solution of any problem that involves forces and/or torques. In order to be able to calculate torques correctly, draw each force at the point where it is applied.

✔ In problems of this kind, apply Newton's second law for translation to any object that changes position and Newton's

second law for rotation to any object that rotates. Both laws must be applied to any object that undergoes both translation and rotation.

✔ In problems that involve both translation and rotation you will need to relate the translational acceleration to the rotational acceleration.

8-8 Angular momentum is conserved when there is zero net torque on a system

When a spinning figure skater pulls her arms and legs in close to her body, the rate at which she spins automatically increases (see the photographs that open this chapter). Even if you're not a figure skater, you can demonstrate this same effect by sitting in an office chair. Sit with your arms outstretched and hold a weight, like a brick or a full water bottle, in either hand. Now use your feet to start your body and the chair rotating, lift your feet off the ground, and then pull your arms inward. Your rotation will speed up quite noticeably!

   Why does this happen? For both cases, the figure skater and you in the office chair, there's no torque acting to make the object rotate faster. Instead, both of these situations are examples of the *conservation of angular momentum*. This principle is the rotational analog of the conservation of *linear* momentum that we introduced in Chapter 7.

Angular Momentum and Angular Momentum Conservation

To see what we mean by angular momentum, consider an object rotating around a fixed axis (that is, one that doesn't change its orientation). As in Section 8-2, we'll call this the z axis. The object's moment of inertia around this axis is I and its angular velocity is ω_z. We've seen that these quantities are analogous to the mass m and velocity v_x of an object in straight-line motion along the x axis. From Section 7-2, the linear momentum of such an object is

(8-21)
$$p_x = mv_x$$

By analogy to Equation 8-21, we'll define a new quantity called the **angular momentum** of an object rotating around the z axis. We'll give this the symbol L_z:

Angular momentum for rotation
around a fixed axis
(8-22)

The **angular momentum** of a rigid object rotating around a fixed axis...

...is proportional to the **angular velocity** at which the object rotates around that axis.

$$L_z = I\omega_z$$

The angular momentum is also proportional to the object's **moment of inertia** for that rotation axis.

The greater the moment of inertia and the faster the angular velocity, the greater the value of angular momentum. Note that like angular velocity, angular momentum can be positive or negative depending on which way the object is rotating and which direction of rotation you choose to be positive.

! Watch Out! Angular momentum and linear momentum are different quantities.

Although linear momentum p_x and angular momentum L_z are analogous to each other, they are *not* the same quantity and do not have the same units. Linear momentum has units of mass times velocity, or kg·m/s. The units of angular momentum are the units of moment of inertia (kg·m^2) multiplied by the units of angular velocity (rad/s), which we can write as kg·m^2/s. (We can eliminate the "rad" since radians are not a true unit.)

Why is angular momentum important? We saw in Section 7-3 that the total *linear* momentum of a system of two or more objects is *conserved* if there is no net external force on the system. The analogous statement about the angular momentum of a system is

If there is no net external torque on a system, the angular momentum of the system is conserved.

This is the principle of **conservation of angular momentum**. It explains what happens to a spinning figure skater when she pulls her limbs in. As she does so, her moment of inertia I decreases because more of her body's mass is closer to her rotation axis. There are no external torques on her—the force of gravity and the normal force don't have any effect on her rotation, and the friction force on her skates is very small. Hence her angular momentum L_z keeps the same value, and as I decreases her angular velocity ω_z has to increase so that the product $L_z = I\omega_z$ doesn't change. The same thing happens in the experiment we described at the beginning of this chapter with you sitting in an office chair.

 Got the Concept? 8-12 Tetherball Physics

In the child's game of tetherball, a rope attached to the top of a tall pole is tied to a ball. Players hit the ball in opposite directions in an attempt to wrap the rope around the pole. As the ball wraps around the pole, does the angular speed of the ball (a) decrease, (b) stay the same, or (c) increase? Explain in terms of angular momentum. Treat the rope as having negligible mass and neglect any resistive forces (such as air resistance and friction).

Example 8-15 Spinning Figure Skater

A figure skater executing a "scratch spin" (see the photographs that open this chapter) gradually pulls her arms in toward her body while spinning on one skate. During the spin her angular speed increases from 1.50 rad/s (approximately one revolution every four seconds) to 15.0 rad/s (approximately 2.5 rev/s). (a) By what factor does her moment of inertia around her central axis change as she pulls in her arms? (b) By what factor does her rotational kinetic energy change?

Set Up

There is very little friction between the skater and the ice, so the net torque on her is essentially zero and her angular momentum can be considered constant. We'll use this to determine her moment of inertia after she pulls her arms in, I_{after}, in terms of her moment of inertia before pulling them in, I_{before}. (Note that we are given the values $\omega_{before} = 1.50$ rad/s and $\omega_{after} = 15.0$ rad/s.) Then we'll compare her rotational kinetic energy before and after pulling her arms in by using Equation 8-7.

Angular momentum of the skater:

$$L_z = I\omega_z \qquad (8\text{-}22)$$

Rotational kinetic energy of the skater:

$$K_{rotational} = \frac{1}{2}I\omega^2 \qquad (8\text{-}7)$$

Solve

(a) Since angular momentum is conserved, we write an equation which says that the angular momentum after she pulls her arms in equals the angular momentum before she pulls them in. Then we solve for I_{after} in terms of I_{before}.

Conservation of angular momentum:

$$L_{after,z} = L_{before,z}$$

From Equation 8-22, this says

$$I_{after}\omega_{after,z} = I_{before}\omega_{before,z}$$

Let the direction of the skater's rotation be positive. Then her angular velocity ω_z at any instant is positive and equal to her angular speed ω at that instant. So the angular momentum conservation equation says

$$I_{after}\omega_{after} = I_{before}\omega_{before}$$

Rearrange to find the ratio of I_{after} to I_{before}:

$$\frac{I_{after}}{I_{before}} = \frac{\omega_{before}}{\omega_{after}}$$
$$= \frac{1.50 \text{ rad/s}}{15.0 \text{ rad/s}} = 0.100$$

The moment of inertia after she pulls her arms in is only 0.100 times (one-tenth) as large as the value before she pulls her arms in.

(b) Now we can use Equation 8-7 to compare the skater's rotational kinetic energy before and after she pulls her arms in.

$$K_{rotational,before} = \frac{1}{2}I_{before}\omega_{before}^2$$

$$K_{rotational,after} = \frac{1}{2}I_{after}\omega_{after}^2$$

Calculate the ratio of her rotational kinetic energy before and after:

$$\frac{K_{rotational,after}}{K_{rotational,before}} = \frac{(1/2)I_{after}\omega_{after}^2}{(1/2)I_{before}\omega_{before}^2} \text{ so}$$

$$\frac{K_{rotational,after}}{K_{rotational,before}} = \left(\frac{I_{after}}{I_{before}}\right)\left(\frac{\omega_{after}}{\omega_{before}}\right)^2 = (0.100)\left(\frac{15.0 \text{ rad/s}}{1.50 \text{ rad/s}}\right)^2$$

$$= (0.100)(10.0)^2 = 10.0$$

Her rotational kinetic energy after she pulls her arms in is 10.0 times as great as the value before she pulls her arms in.

Reflect

The skater's moment of inertia changes by a factor of $0.100 = 1/10.0$. This might seem large, because her arms (and one leg) are a relatively small fraction of her total mass. However,

Moment of inertia of the object:

$$I = \sum_{i=1}^{N} m_i r_i^2 \qquad (8\text{-}6)$$

the moment of inertia depends on the square of distance (see Equation 8-6), so holding her arms close to her body rather than extended has a significant effect on the skater's moment of inertia.

Although the skater's angular momentum maintains the same value as she pulls her arms in, her rotational kinetic energy does not. You can see why by rewriting the expression for rotational kinetic energy in terms of the angular momentum magnitude $L = I\omega$ and the angular speed ω. Since L is unchanged (it's conserved) and ω increases when the skater pulls her arms in, her rotational kinetic energy must increase.

The extra kinetic energy had to come from somewhere. In this case it comes from the skater herself as the chemical energy from the food she eats is used to flex muscles and bring her arms in.

Rotational kinetic energy:

$$K_{\text{rotational}} = \frac{1}{2}I\omega^2 = \frac{1}{2}(I\omega)\omega = \frac{1}{2}L\omega$$

The skater's angular speed ω increases while the magnitude L of her angular momentum stays the same, so $K_{\text{rotational}}$ increases.

Angular Momentum of a Particle

Example 8-15 demonstrates how the angular momentum concept helps us solve problems about rotating objects. It can also be useful to think about the angular momentum of a single *particle*. We've already seen the utility of this concept for the example of a tetherball moving around a pole (see Got the Concept? 8-12). Let's look at the general case of a particle of mass m moving with velocity $\vec{v}$, so that its linear momentum is $\vec{p} = m\vec{v}$. As an example, let's consider a girl (who we regard as a particle) running at constant speed toward a playground merry-go-round (Figure 8-27). We take the rotation axis to be the axis of the merry-go-round. At a given instant, the vector $\vec{r}$ points directly away from the rotation axis to the position of the girl, and there is an angle ϕ between the vectors $\vec{r}$ and $\vec{p}$. What is the girl's angular momentum around this rotation axis?

Figure 8-27 shows that only the component of the momentum $\vec{p}$ that's perpendicular to $\vec{r}$ contributes to the girl's rotation around the axis, so only this component $p_\perp = p \sin\phi$ contributes to the girl's angular momentum. We define the magnitude of her angular momentum as

| Magnitude of the angular momentum of a particle | Component of the particle's linear momentum perpendicular to the vector $\vec{r}$ from rotation axis to particle |

Magnitude of the angular momentum of a particle (8-23)

$$L = rp_\perp = rp \sin\phi$$

Distance from the rotation axis to the particle

Does this agree with our earlier definition $L_z = I\omega_z$ (Equation 8-22)? To find out, we can write $p_\perp = mv_\perp$, where $v_\perp$ is the component of the particle's velocity that's perpendicular to $\vec{r}$ in Figure 8-25. We can also write $v_\perp = r\omega$, where ω is the angular speed of the particle around the rotation axis. If we substitute these into Equation 8-23 for the magnitude of the particle's angular momentum, we get

(8-24)
$$L = rp_\perp = r(mv_\perp) = r(mr\omega) = mr^2\omega$$

Equation 8-6 tells us that if there's only a single particle of mass m a distance r from the rotation axis, its moment of inertia is $I = mr^2$. So Equation 8-24 for the magnitude of the particle's angular momentum becomes $L = I\omega$. But this is just the magnitude of the angular momentum $L_z = I\omega_z$ as given by Equation 8-22. So our definition of the angular momentum of a particle in Equation 8-23 is completely consistent with our earlier work.

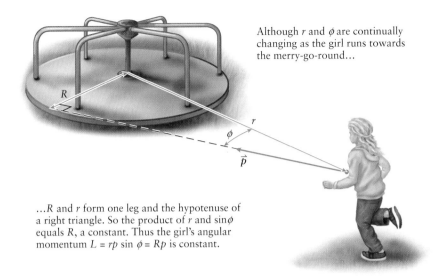

Although r and ϕ are continually changing as the girl runs towards the merry-go-round...

...R and r form one leg and the hypotenuse of a right triangle. So the product of r and $\sin\phi$ equals R, a constant. Thus the girl's angular momentum $L = rp \sin \phi = Rp$ is constant.

Figure 8-27 A girl running with constant linear momentum and angular momentum The distance from the rotation axis to the line along which the girl moves is $R = r \sin \phi$. (This is the opposite side of a right triangle with hypotenuse r and angle ϕ.) This distance has the same value no matter where the girl is along its straight-line path. If $p = mv$ is constant for the girl, her angular momentum $L = rp \sin \phi = (r \sin\ )p$ is also constant. If the girl then jumps onto the stationary merry-go-round, how fast does it rotate after she is on board?

! Watch Out! Angular momentum doesn't require the motion to be in a circle.

Note that a particle doesn't have to move in a circle, or even along a curved path, to have angular momentum. Consider the girl in Figure 8-27, who moves along a straight line at constant velocity. You can think of her as rotating around a fixed point (the axis of the merry-go-round) with an ever-changing radius from the axis. We can write the particle's angular momentum as $L = rp \sin \phi = (r \sin \phi)p = Rp$, where $R = r \sin \phi$ is the perpendicular distance from the fixed rotation axis to the path of the particle (see Figure 8-27). This distance is the same everywhere along the particle's path, so the angular momentum L in this case is constant.

There is zero net force and zero net torque acting on the girl in Figure 8-27, which is why she has a constant angular momentum. If there *is* a net force that acts on a particle, but if that force is always directed toward a fixed point that acts as a rotation axis, that force exerts zero torque (there is a 180° angle between the vector $\vec{r}$ from axis to particle and the force vector $\vec{F}$ that points from particle to axis, so the torque is $\tau = rF \sin \phi = rF \sin 180° = 0$). In that case the angular momentum is again conserved. One example of this is the motion of water as it circles the drain of a bathtub. The water is pulled directly toward the drain, so the force on each parcel of water exerts no torque and the angular momentum of the water is conserved. As the water approaches the drain, r decreases and so $p = mv$ increases to keep the angular momentum $L = rp_\perp$ constant. The same thing happens on a much more dramatic scale as air is drawn into the low pressure at the center of a hurricane. The circulating air gains tremendous speed, which gives the hurricane great destructive power.

Angular Momentum and a Rotational "Collision"

Here's another application of the angular momentum of a particle. The girl shown in Figure 8-27 runs across the playground and finally jumps onto the merry-go-round, so that both end up rotating together. This seems very much like the inelastic collisions we discussed in Section 7-4, in which a moving object collided with an initially stationary one and the two stuck together afterward. We approached those inelastic collisions by demanding that linear momentum is conserved. In Figure 8-27, however, the girl has linear momentum before the collision, and the system of girl and merry-go-round has *zero* total linear momentum after the collision (the system rotates but does not move bodily from one place to another). So *linear* momentum is not conserved in this collision.

However, the *angular* momentum of the system of girl and merry-go-round *is* conserved because there are no external torques acting on the system around the merry-go-round's rotation axis. (The vertical force of gravity and normal force don't affect the rotation, and there is very little friction in the bearings of the merry-go-round.) During the collision the girl and the merry-go-round exert torques on each other, but these torques are *internal* to the system of girl plus merry-go-round and so don't affect the

Go to Picture It 8-2 for more practice dealing with angular momentum

total angular momentum. All that happens in the collision is that angular momentum is transferred between the girl and the merry-go-round. Example 8-16 shows how to analyze what happens.

Example 8-16 A Girl on a Merry-Go-Round

The girl in Figure 8-27 has a mass of 30 kg. She runs toward the merry-go-round at 3.0 m/s, then jumps on. The merry-go-round is initially at rest, has a mass of 100 kg and a radius of 2.0 m, and can be treated as a uniform disk. Find the rotation speed of the merry-go-round after the girl jumps on.

Set Up

As we described above, angular momentum is conserved in this process. Before she jumps on, the girl has all of the angular momentum, with a magnitude given by Equation 8-23. After she jumps on, she and the merry-go-round rotate together with the same angular speed ω. Together they behave like a single object made up of a rotating disk with an extra mass (the girl) at its rim.

Angular momentum of the girl before jumping on:

$$L = rp_\perp = rp \sin \phi \qquad (8\text{-}23)$$

Angular momentum of the merry-go-round with the girl riding on it:

$$L_z = I\omega_z \qquad (8\text{-}22)$$

Moment of inertia of the merry-go-round plus girl:

$$I = I_{\text{merry-go-round}} + I_{\text{girl}} \qquad (8\text{-}6)$$

before girl jumps on
merry-go-round (top view)

after girl jumps on (top view)

Solve

Figure 8-27 shows that the distance $r \sin \phi$ is just equal to the radius of the merry-go-round, $R = 2.0$ m. Use this to find the magnitude of the angular momentum before she jumps on.

Before the girl jumps on, her linear momentum has magnitude

$$p = m_{\text{girl}}v_{\text{girl}} = (30 \text{ kg})(3.0 \text{ m/s}) = 90 \text{ kg} \cdot \text{m/s}$$

Her angular momentum is

$$L = rp \sin \phi = (r \sin \phi)p$$
$$= Rp = (2.0 \text{ m})(90 \text{ kg} \cdot \text{m/s}) = 180 \text{ kg} \cdot \text{m}^2/\text{s}$$

After she jumps on, the magnitude of the angular momentum is $L = I\omega$, where ω is what we are trying to find. Calculate the value of I for the system of merry-go-round plus girl.

Moment of inertia of the merry-go-round alone, considered as a uniform cylinder: From Table 8-1,

$$I_{\text{merry-go-round}} = \frac{1}{2}M_{\text{merry-go-round}}R^2 = \frac{1}{2}(100 \text{ kg})(2.0 \text{ m})^2 = 200 \text{ kg} \cdot \text{m}^2$$

Moment of inertia of the girl alone, considered as an object of mass m_{girl} rotating a distance R from the axis:

$$I_{\text{girl}} = m_{\text{girl}}R^2 = (30 \text{ kg})(2.0 \text{ m})^2 = 120 \text{ kg} \cdot \text{m}^2$$

Moment of inertia of the merry-go-round plus girl:

$$I = I_{\text{merry-go-round}} + I_{\text{girl}} = 200 \text{ kg} \cdot \text{m}^2 + 120 \text{ kg} \cdot \text{m}^2 = 320 \text{ kg} \cdot \text{m}^2$$

Angular momentum is conserved, so set the magnitude of angular momentum before the girl jumps on equal to the magnitude after she jumps on. Then solve for the final angular speed ω. Note that if L is in kg · m²/s and I is in kg·m², then ω is in rad/s.

Before the girl jumps on, $L = 180 \text{ kg} \cdot \text{m}^2/\text{s}$

After she jumps on, angular momentum is $L_z = I\omega_z$ with magnitude $L = I\omega = (320 \text{ kg} \cdot \text{m}^2)\omega$

Angular momentum is conserved, so the magnitude L is the same before and after:

$$180 \text{ kg} \cdot \text{m}^2/\text{s} = (320 \text{ kg} \cdot \text{m}^2)\omega$$
$$\omega = \frac{180 \text{ kg} \cdot \text{m}^2/\text{s}}{320 \text{ kg} \cdot \text{m}^2} = 0.56 \text{ rad/s}$$

Reflect

To get a better sense of our result, we convert it to rev/min. Our answer says that the merry-go-round spins 5.4 times per minute. In other words, it makes one revolution every (1/5.4) minute, or about once every 11 s—a reasonable pace for a merry-go-round.

Convert ω to revolutions per minute:

$$\omega = (0.56 \text{ rad/s}) \left(\frac{1 \text{ rev}}{2\pi \text{ rad}} \right) \left(\frac{60 \text{ s}}{1 \text{ min}} \right) = \frac{(0.56)(60)}{2\pi} \frac{\text{rev}}{\text{min}}$$

$$= 5.4 \text{ rev/min}$$

? Got the Concept? 8-13 Conserving angular momentum

For which of the following objects is angular momentum conserved as it rotates: (a) the pulley in Example 8-12 (Section 8-7), (b) the disk in Example 8-14 (Section 8-7), (c) both the pulley and the disk, or (d) neither the pulley nor the disk?

Take-Home Message for Section 8-8

✔ Just as an object's linear momentum is the product of its mass and velocity, a rotating object's angular velocity is the product of its moment of inertia around its rotation axis and its angular velocity.

✔ If there is no net external torque on a system, the angular momentum of the system is conserved. This holds true even if the system includes an object whose shape and moment of inertia change.

✔ A particle moving past a point has angular momentum relative to that point, even if the particle is not following a curved path.

8-9 Rotational quantities such as angular momentum and torque are actually vectors

Figure 8-28 shows an athlete doing the long jump. Although his body is essentially in an upright, running position at the beginning of the jump, while in midair his legs swing forward. By the time he lands, his legs are out in front of his torso. This significantly increases the distance of his jump. How does the athlete manage this in midair, with nothing to push against? What physics underlies his motion?

The answer is that there was no net torque acting on the athlete during his leap, so his angular momentum was conserved. (The force of gravity acted on him, but this acted at his center of mass and so exerted no torque around the center of mass.) As the athlete left the ground, the net angular momentum of his body around its center of mass was zero, or nearly so. Once in the air he rotated his legs up and forward (counterclockwise in Figure 8-28), giving them a nonzero angular momentum. In order for angular momentum to be conserved, some other part of his body had to rotate in such a way that the two contributions to his *net* angular momentum canceled. He rotated his arms rapidly clockwise while in the air, which helped rotate his upper torso clockwise in Figure 8-28. The angular momentum of the arms in one direction thus canceled the angular momentum of his legs in the opposite direction.

Figure 8-28 **Angular momentum during a long jump** This long jumper rotates his legs counterclockwise (upward) by swinging his arms clockwise. In this way he keeps the total angular momentum of his body equal to zero.

Angular Velocity and Angular Momentum as Vectors

We can understand this property of angular momentum most easily by considering angular momentum as a *vector* $\vec{L}$. In what direction does $\vec{L}$ point? We need to account for the direction of rotation, but there is no way to align a single vector in the plane of the rotation to indicate this direction (Figure 8-29a). Hence we take the angular momentum vector to point along the axis of rotation, which we call the z axis. By convention the specific direction of $\vec{L}$ is given by a **right-hand rule**. Curl the fingers of your right hand in the direction of motion and stick your thumb straight out. By the right-hand rule, your thumb points in the direction of the angular momentum vector (Figure 8-29b). We use this same rule to determine the direction of the angular *velocity* vector $\vec{\omega}$: This also points along the rotation axis. If the object rotates in the direction

Figure 8-29 The angular velocity and angular momentum vectors Rather than lying in (a) the plane of rotation, the angular velocity and angular momentum vectors of a rotating object are (b) oriented along the rotation axis. The directions of $\vec{L}$ and $\vec{\omega}$ are given by a right-hand rule.

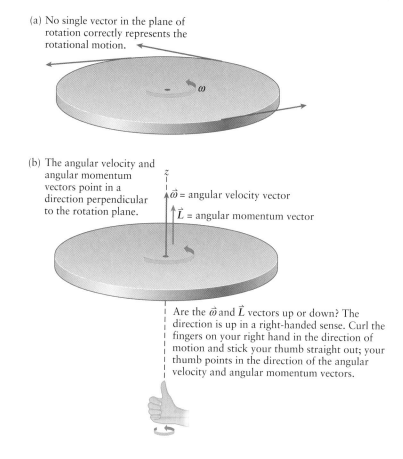

(a) No single vector in the plane of rotation correctly represents the rotational motion.

ω

(b) The angular velocity and angular momentum vectors point in a direction perpendicular to the rotation plane.

z

$\vec{\omega}$ = angular velocity vector

$\vec{L}$ = angular momentum vector

Are the $\vec{\omega}$ and $\vec{L}$ vectors up or down? The direction is up in a right-handed sense. Curl the fingers on your right hand in the direction of motion and stick your thumb straight out; your thumb points in the direction of the angular velocity and angular momentum vectors.

shown in Figure 8-29b, $\vec{\omega}$ and $\vec{L}$ point in the positive z direction and their components ω_z and L_z are positive; if the object rotates in the opposite direction, the vectors $\vec{\omega}$ and $\vec{L}$ point in the negative z direction and their components ω_z and L_z are negative. That's the origin of the positive and negative signs for ω_z and L_z that we introduced in Sections 8-2 and 8-8, respectively. (Strictly speaking, $\vec{L}$ points along the rotation axis only if the object's mass is arranged symmetrically around the rotation axis. We'll only consider situations of this kind, however, so you needn't worry about this point.)

How does this apply to the long jumper? If more than one element of a system is rotating, the net angular momentum $\vec{L}$ of the system is the vector sum of the angular momenta of each individual element. Therefore, the angular momentum of the jumper's arms and upper torso cancels out that of his legs. This stabilizes his motion so that both arms and legs are forward at the end of the jump, resulting in a longer flight and perhaps a gold medal.

Alligator Angular Momentum

Let's explore this physics more deeply by considering the feeding behavior of alligators, which involves rotations of their head, body, and tail. The structure of an alligator's jaws and teeth makes it impossible for these reptiles to cut the large prey on which they often feed into chunks small enough to swallow. To make matters worse, alligators have no leverage when they clamp onto their prey while swimming—their legs are too short to hold the food, and they can't push against the river bottom. However, by tightly biting the prey and then executing a special spinning maneuver, they can exert forces large enough to remove bite-sized pieces of food. This "death roll" arises from the conservation of angular momentum.

After the alligator has securely grabbed hold of its prey, it bends its tail and head to one side, forming a C-shape (Figure 8-30). This step is crucial to the execution of the "death roll" because it enables the animal to spin its head, body, and tail around different axes. The angular velocities of these three rotations are shown as large blue arrows in the figure. You can use the right-hand rule to verify that the angular momentum vectors associated with these three rotations, labeled $\vec{L}_{\text{Head}}$, $\vec{L}_{\text{Body}}$, and $\vec{L}_{\text{Tail}}$, point in the directions shown. The combined angular momentum of these three rotations is the vector sum $\vec{L}_{\text{Head}} + \vec{L}_{\text{Body}} + \vec{L}_{\text{Tail}}$, shown as a black arrow pointing directly upward in the figure.

The *total* angular momentum of the alligator remains constant because the alligator experiences no net torque. Therefore, as a result of rotating its head, body, and tail, the alligator as a whole must acquire a compensatory, net rotation *in the opposite direction* from the sum $\vec{L}_{\text{Head}} + \vec{L}_{\text{Body}} + \vec{L}_{\text{Tail}}$. This is the "death roll." As the alligator rotates around the "death roll" axis, its body acquires the angular momentum $\vec{L}_{\text{DeathRoll}}$ shown as a black arrow pointing downward in the figure. This angular momentum has the same magnitude as $\vec{L}_{\text{Head}} + \vec{L}_{\text{Body}} + \vec{L}_{\text{Tail}}$ but points in the opposite direction, so these two vectors cancel and the *total* angular momentum the alligator is $\vec{L}_{\text{Head}} + \vec{L}_{\text{Body}} + \vec{L}_{\text{Tail}} + \vec{L}_{\text{DeathRoll}} = 0$. During the death roll the alligator's tail, body, and head rotate into the page away from you in the orientation shown in Figure 8-30. This rotation results in a torque, and therefore a force, on the hapless prey in the alligator's mouth large enough to detach bite-sized pieces of meat. The force generated by this rolling maneuver on the alligator's prey is estimated to be well over 130 N.

Torque as a Vector

Like angular momentum $\vec{L}$, torque can be expressed as a vector $\vec{\tau}$ that has both a magnitude and a direction. So far, we have used Equation 8-18 in Section 8-6 to calculate the magnitude of the torque vector.

$$\tau = rF \sin \phi \qquad (8\text{-}18)$$

In Equation 8-18 r is the position from the rotation axis to the point where a force of magnitude F is applied. Both the position $\vec{r}$ and the force $\vec{F}$ are vectors, and ϕ is the angle between $\vec{r}$ and $\vec{F}$. The direction of $\vec{\tau}$ is given by a right-hand rule that's similar to the one we described to find the direction of the angular momentum or angular velocity vectors: Curl the fingers of your right hand in the direction that the torque would tend to make the object rotate, and your right thumb will point in the direction of $\vec{\tau}$ (**Figure 8-31**). Alternatively, point the fingers of your right hand along the direction of $\vec{r}$ so that your palm faces the vector $\vec{F}$, then curl your fingers from the direction of $\vec{r}$ to the direction of $\vec{F}$ along the shortest path. Your extended right thumb then points in the direction of $\vec{\tau}$. (Practice this with the two situations shown in Figure 8-31.)

Note that $\vec{\tau}$ is perpendicular to the plane defined by the vectors $\vec{r}$ and $\vec{F}$. Mathematically, a combination of two vectors $\vec{r}$ and $\vec{F}$ that has these properties is called the **cross product** or **vector product** of $\vec{r}$ and $\vec{F}$. You can learn more about the properties of the cross product in the Math Tutorial. In this text, though, we will rely on Equation 8-18 to calculate the magnitude of the torque and on the right-hand rule to determine its direction.

Figure 8-30 **The alligator 'death roll'** Alligators use the conservation of angular momentum to rotate in a 'death roll' that helps them consume their prey.

! Watch Out! There is no motion along the direction of torque.

It's important to recognize that no motion and no change in motion occur in the direction of the torque vector. For example, the torques shown in Figure 8-31 are directed either straight up or straight down, but they don't cause the bar on which the torque acts to *move* either up or down: Instead, the bar rotates around the rotation axis. The direction of the torque vector is simply a mathematical tool.

If the net torque on an object is zero—that is, if the *vector* sum $\sum \vec{\tau}$ of all external torques acting on the object is zero—the angular momentum of the object is conserved and its angular acceleration is zero. A special case of this is when the object is not rotating initially. In this case the object will remain at rest with zero angular momentum if the vector sum of all the torques on the object is zero. The following example illustrates how to use this principle.

To apply the right hand rule correctly, curl your fingers
from the direction of $\vec{r}$ to $\vec{F}$ along the shortest path.

Rotation axis

$\vec{\tau}$

$\vec{F}$

$\vec{r}$

ϕ

Rotational sense from $\vec{r}$ direction to
$\vec{F}$, and angle ϕ from $\vec{r}$ to $\vec{F}$.

Rotation axis

Angle φ from $\vec{r}$ to $\vec{F}$.

$\vec{r}$

ϕ

Rotational sense from $\vec{r}$ direction to $\vec{F}$.

$\vec{F}_2$

$\vec{\tau}$

Figure 8-31 The torque vector A force $\vec{F}$ acts on an object at a point that is separated from the rotation
axis by a vector $\vec{r}$. The torque $\vec{\tau}$ produced by this force is a vector that is perpendicular to both $\vec{r}$ and $\vec{F}$.
The magnitude of $\vec{\tau}$ is $\tau = rF \sin \phi$, and the direction of $\vec{\tau}$ is given by a right-hand rule.

Example 8-17 Balancing on a Seesaw

A seesaw is a uniform plank supported at its midpoint. Akeelah and her little sister Bree sit on opposite sides of the
seesaw. Akeelah weighs 1.50 times as much as Bree, and Akeelah sits 80.0 cm from the midpoint of the seesaw.
If the seesaw is tilted by an angle θ from the horizontal, where should Bree sit so that they just balance?

Set Up

When the system made up of Akeelah, Bree, and
the seesaw is balanced, the angular acceleration
of the system is zero: It has no tendency to start
rotating one way or the other. Hence the net
torque on the system must be zero.

We are told that Akeelah's distance from
the pivot is $r_A = 80.0$ cm $= 0.800$ m and that
Akeelah's weight is 1.50 times that of Bree: that
is, $w_A = 1.50 w_B$. Our goal is to find the distance r_B from the pivot to Bree that will satisfy
the condition of zero torque. We'll write this
condition in terms of the torque vector, using
Equation 8-18 to calculate the magnitudes of the
torques, and the right-hand rule to determine
their directions.

Condition that the net torque
is zero:

$$\sum \vec{\tau} = 0$$

Magnitude of the torque

$$\tau = rF \sin \phi \qquad (8\text{-}18)$$

Solve

Neither the weight of the seesaw nor the support
force exerts any torque on the system around
the pivot point, since both of these forces act at
the pivot and have $\vec{r} = 0$. The only torques are
due to the weight of Akeelah, $\vec{w}_A$, and the weight
of Bree, $\vec{w}_B$. The right-hand rule tells us that the
corresponding torques $\vec{\tau}_A$ and $\vec{\tau}_B$ are in opposite
directions, into and out of the page, respectively,
so their vector sum can be zero (as it must be to
keep the seesaw in balance).

Net torque on the system of
Akeelah, Bree, and the seesaw:

$$\sum \vec{\tau} = \vec{\tau}_A + \vec{\tau}_B = 0$$

For the net torque to be zero, the opposite torques $\vec{\tau}_A$ and $\vec{\tau}_B$ must have the same magnitude. The angle between $\vec{r}_A$ and $\vec{w}_A$ is $\phi_A = 90° - \theta$, and the angle between $\vec{r}_B$ and $\vec{w}_B$ is $\phi_B = 90° + \theta$. From trigonometry, $\sin(90° - \theta) = \sin(90° + \theta) = \cos\theta$.

Solve for Bree's distance from the pivot, r_B.

Opposite torques $\vec{\tau}_A$ and $\vec{\tau}_B$ have the same magnitude:

$\tau_A = \tau_B$

$r_A w_A \sin\phi_A = r_B w_B \sin\phi_B$

Substitute $\phi_A = 90° - \theta$, $\phi_B = 90° + \theta$:

$r_A w_A \sin(90° - \theta) = r_B w_B \sin(90° + \theta)$

$r_A w_A \cos\theta = r_B w_B \cos\theta$

$r_A w_A = r_B w_B$

From $r_A w_A = r_B w_B$, $r_B = r_A \dfrac{w_A}{w_B}$

Substitute $r_A = 0.800$ m, $w_A = 1.50 w_B$:

$$r_B = r_A \frac{w_A}{w_B} = (0.800 \text{ m})\left(\frac{1.50 w_B}{w_B}\right) = (0.800 \text{ m})(1.50)$$
$$= 1.20 \text{ m}$$

Bree must sit 1.20 m from the pivot in order to balance Akeelah.

Reflect

Notice the significance of the lever arm in this problem. Bree, who is lighter than Akeelah, can create a balance by sitting farther from the center. A small force can give rise to a large torque when the lever arm is large. Bree has $1/1.50$ the weight of Akeelah, so Bree's lever arm must be 1.50 times greater than Akeelah's and she must sit 1.50 times as far from the pivot as Akeelah.

Note also that the answer doesn't depend on the angle θ. The greater the value of θ, the shorter each girl's lever arm, but the *ratio* of the two lever arms is the same for any value of θ. So the seesaw will balance no matter what the angle θ.

Lever arm for Akeelah:

$r_{A\perp} = r_A \cos\theta$

Lever arm for Bree:

$r_{B\perp} = r_B \cos\theta$

Ratio of the two lever arms:

$\dfrac{r_{B\perp}}{r_{A\perp}} = \dfrac{r_B \cos\theta}{r_A \cos\theta} = \dfrac{r_B}{r_A} = 1.50$

This is the same for any value of θ.

? Got the Concept? 8-14
Danger! Falling Cat Zone

Everyone knows that a falling cat usually lands on its feet. This requires the cat to rotate itself into an upright position while falling (see Figure 8-32). The key to a cat's ability to start and stop rotating in midair is bending its body in the middle at the start of the fall. Explain how this helps the cat right itself while falling.

Figure 8-32 **A falling cat** How does this cat manage to right itself in midair so that it lands on its feet?

Take-Home Message for Section 8-8

✔ The angular velocity and angular momentum of a rotating object are vectors that lie along the object's rotation axis. The direction of these vectors is determined by a right-hand rule.

✔ Torque is also a vector whose direction is determined by a right-hand rule. If the object is free to rotate around an axis, the torque around that axis points along the axis.

Key Terms

angular acceleration
angular displacement
angular momentum
angular position
angular speed
angular velocity
average angular acceleration
average angular velocity

conservation of angular
  momentum
cross product (vector product)
lever arm
line of action
moment of inertia
parallel-axis theorem
right-hand rule

rigid object
rolling without slipping
rotation
rotational kinematics
rotational kinetic energy
torque
translation
vector product (cross product)

Chapter Summary

Topic	Equation or Figure

Angular velocity and angular speed: The angular velocity ω_z of a rigid object is the rate at which it rotates. (The z axis is the rotation axis of the object.) Angular velocity can be positive or negative, depending on which direction of rotation you choose to be positive. Angular speed ω is the magnitude of angular velocity. A point a distance r from the rotation axis has speed $v = r\omega$.

① The position of the blade at a certain time

② The blade rotates around an axis that is perpendicular to the plane of this figure. We call this the z axis.

Angular displacement $= \Delta\theta$

Length of arc $= r\,\Delta\theta$

③ The position of the blade a time Δt later

④ During time Δt, the rigid blade rotates through an angular displacement $\Delta\theta$. We choose the positive direction of rotation to be counterclockwise, so $\Delta\theta > 0$.

Distance r from axis

(Figure 8-3)

⑤ The **angular velocity** ω_z of the blade is the angular displacement $\Delta\theta$ divided by the elapsed time Δt:
$$\omega_z = \frac{\Delta\theta}{\Delta t}$$
The **angular speed** ω is the absolute value of ω_z.

⑥ In time Δt, a point on the blade a distance r from the axis moves through an arc of length $r\,\Delta\theta$. The speed of this point is $v = r\omega$.

Moment of inertia and rotational kinetic energy: The quantity that plays the role of mass for rotational motion is an object's moment of inertia. This depends on the mass of the object but also on how the components of the object are positioned relative to the rotation axis. (Table 8-1 lists the moments of inertia for various common shapes.) The rotational kinetic energy of an object is related to its moment of inertia and angular speed.

To find the moment of inertia I of an object...   ...we imagine dividing the object into N small pieces, and calculate the sum...

$$I = \sum_{i=1}^{N} m_i r_i^2 \tag{8-6}$$

...of the product of the mass m_i of the ith piece...   ...and the square of the distance r_i from the ith piece to the rotation axis.

Rotational kinetic energy of a rigid body spinning around an axis   **Moment of inertia** of the object for that rotation axis

$$K_{\text{rotational}} = \frac{1}{2} I \omega^2 \tag{8-7}$$

Angular speed of the object

Parallel-axis theorem: If an object's moment of inertia for an axis through its moment of inertia is I_{CM}, its moment of inertia for a second axis parallel to the center-of-mass axis and separated by a distance h is $I = I_{CM} + Mh^2$. Here M is the mass of the object.

(a) Hoop rotating around an axis through its center

Rotation axis

$I = I_{CM}$

Hoop, mass M

R

Center of mass of the hoop

(b) Hoop rotating around an axis through its rim

Rotation axis

$I = I_{CM} + Mh^2$

$\mid\!\leftarrow\!h = R\!\rightarrow\!\mid$

(Figure 8-10 a and b)

Total kinetic energy and conservation of energy: The total kinetic energy K of an object is the sum of its translational kinetic energy and rotational kinetic energy. With this expression for K, the same equations for conservation of energy that we learned in Chapter 6 apply for an object that is rotating, translating, or both.

① Total kinetic energy of a system that is both translating and rotating

② The translational kinetic energy is the same as if all of the mass of the system were moving at the speed of the center of mass.

$$K = K_{\text{translational}} + K_{\text{rotational}} = \frac{1}{2} M v_{CM}^2 + \frac{1}{2} I_{CM} \omega^2 \qquad (8\text{-}12)$$

③ The rotational kinetic energy is the same as if the system were not translating, and all of the mass were rotating around the center of mass.

Rolling without slipping: If an object rolls on a surface without slipping, the speed of the center of mass of the object must be related to the angular speed of the object's rotation. A friction force acts on this object to maintain this relationship. If the object is completely rigid, however, this friction force does no work on the object.

Speed of the center of mass of a rolling object

$$v_{CM} = R\omega \qquad (8\text{-}13)$$

Radius of the object   **Angular speed** of the object's rotation

Rotational kinematics: Angular acceleration is to angular velocity as ordinary acceleration is to velocity. If the angular acceleration of a rigid rotating object is constant, three basic equations relate the time, angular position, angular velocity, and angular acceleration of the object.

Angular velocity at time t of a rotating object with constant angular acceleration

Angular velocity at time $t = 0$ of the object

$$\omega_z = \omega_{0z} + \alpha_z t \qquad (8\text{-}15)$$

Constant angular acceleration of the object   **Time** at which the object has angular velocity ω_z

Angular position at time t of a rotatingobject with constant angular acceleration

Angular velocity at time $t = 0$ of the object

Constant angular acceleration of the object

$$\theta = \theta_0 + \omega_{0z} t + \frac{1}{2} \alpha_z t^2 \qquad (8\text{-}16)$$

Angular position at time $t = 0$ of the object   **Time** at which the object is at angular position θ

Angular velocity at angular position θ of a rotating object with constant angular acceleration

Angular velocity at angular position θ_0 of the object

$$\omega_z^2 = \omega_{0z}^2 + 2\alpha_z (\theta - \theta_0) \qquad (8\text{-}17)$$

Constant angular acceleration of the object   **Two angular positions** of the object

Views of object from along its rotation axis

(a) A force that tends to cause
    clockwise rotation

Point where
force is applied

The vector $\vec{r}$ points
from an object's
rotation axis to where
a force $\vec{F}$ is applied to
the object.

Rotation axis

(b) A force that tends to cause
    counterclockwise rotation

(c) Determining the line of action of a
    force and its lever arm

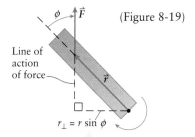

(Figure 8-19)

Line of
action
of force

$r_\perp = r \sin \phi$

The lever arm $r_\perp$ is perpendicular to the line of
action of the force, and extends from the
rotation axis to the line of action of the force.

Torque: If a force $\vec{F}$ acts at a position $\vec{r}$ from an object's rotation axis, it can change the rotation of the object. The torque associated with the force has magnitude $\tau = rF \sin \phi = r_\perp F$, where $r_\perp$ is the lever arm of the force. The torque τ_z can be positive or negative.

Rotational form of Newton's second law:
A net external torque on an object gives the object an angular acceleration. To analyze an object that is able to translate as well as rotate (such as one that rolls without slipping), both Newton's second law in its original form $\left(\sum \vec{F} = m\vec{a} \right)$ and this rotational form must be used.

The net torque, or sum of all external torques acting on an object for the axis about which it can rotate

The angular acceleration produced by the net torque

$$\sum \tau_z = I\alpha_z \qquad (8\text{-}20)$$

The object's moment of inertia for the axis about which it can rotate

---

Angular momentum and the conservation of angular momentum:
A rotating rigid object has an angular momentum L_z whose sign depends on the direction of rotation. A particle moving relative to an axis also has angular momentum around that axis. If there is no net external torque on an object or system of objects, its angular momentum remains constant.

The **angular momentum** of a rigid object rotating around a fixed axis...

...is proportional to the **angular velocity** at which the object rotates around that axis.

$$L_z = I\omega_z \qquad (8\text{-}22)$$

The angular momentum is also proportional to the object's **moment of inertia** for that rotation axis.

Magnitude of the angular momentum of a particle

Component of the particle's linear momentum perpendicular to the vector $\vec{r}$ from rotation axis to particle

$$L = rp_\perp = rp \sin \phi \qquad (8\text{-}23)$$

Distance from the rotation axis to the particle

Rotational quantities as vectors: The angular velocity $\vec{\omega}$, angular momentum $\vec{L}$, and torque $\vec{\tau}$ are actually all vector quantities that lie along the rotation axis. Their directions are given by a right-hand rule.

To apply the right hand rule correctly, curl your fingers from the direction of $\vec{r}$ to $\vec{F}$ along the shortest path.

Rotation axis

(Figure 8-31)

Rotational sense from $\vec{r}$ direction to $\vec{F}$, and angle ϕ from $\vec{r}$ to $\vec{F}$.

Answer to What do you think? Question

The resistance of an object to changes in its velocity—that is, its inertia—is determined by its mass: More mass means more inertia. By contrast, the resistance of an object to changes in its *rotation* is determined by its moment of inertia, which depends on both the object's mass and how that mass is distributed. The skater has a smaller moment of inertia with her arms pulled in, so it's easier to make her body spin rapidly than if her arms are extended. (See Section 8-2 and Section 8-6.)

Answers to Got the Concept? Questions

8-1 (b) In order to read information at a constant rate, the same linear distance along the spiral must pass the reader in a given amount of time regardless of radius. Distance in this case is the length of a circular arc, which is given by the product of angular displacement $\Delta\theta$ and radius r. In order for the product $r\,\Delta\theta$ to remain constant as r increases, the angular displacement $\Delta\theta$ in any fixed amount of time Δt must decrease. So as the scanning laser gets closer to the outer edge of the disc, the angular speed $\omega = \Delta\theta/\Delta t$ must decrease. Hence the motor that rotates the DVD inside the player must slow down as the scanning laser moves from the inner part of the disc to the outer part.

8-2 (c) Table 8-1 shows that the moment of inertia of a thin, uniform rod rotating around its center is $I_{\text{rod}} = ML^2/12$. Because the moment of inertia is additive, the moment of inertia of the two rods together is $I = 2I_{\text{rod}} = 2(ML^2/12) = ML^2/6$.

8-3 (c) The moment of inertia of a thin, uniform rod that has a mass m and a length l rotating around its end is $ml^2/3$. Each of the four rods in this problem (with $m = M/2$, $l = L/2$) rotates around its end, and so the system of four rods has a moment of inertia

$$I_{\text{rod}} = \frac{(M/2)(L/2)^2}{3} = \frac{ML^2}{24}$$

when rotating around its end. Because the moment of inertia is additive, the moment of inertia of the four rods together is

$$I = 4I_{\text{rod}} = 4\left(\frac{ML^2}{24}\right) = \frac{ML^2}{6}$$

Notice that the final configuration of the four rods in this *Got the Concept?* problem is identical to that of the two rods in the previous one. So it's not surprising that the result is the same.

8-4 (a) The car would go faster if its wheels were uniform disks. A wheel like a bicycle tire, with most of the mass far from the rotation axis, will have a larger moment of inertia than one with the mass uniformly distributed. (This is like the hoop and uniform disk in Example 8-10.) A larger moment of inertia means more energy is required to rotate the wheel, so less energy is available for translational kinetic energy and the speed of the car as a whole is less.

8-5 Block, uniform sphere, uniform disk. Because it does not rotate and has no work done on it by friction, *all* of the block's gravitational potential energy is transformed into translational kinetic energy. By contrast, as both the disk and the sphere roll downhill, part of the gravitational potential energy is transformed into rotational kinetic energy. That means that at any location, the hoop and sphere will be moving more slowly than the block. Hence the block reaches the bottom first. The sphere arrives second, since from Table 8-1 it has a smaller moment of inertia than the disk ($I_{\text{CM}} = 2MR^2/5$ for the sphere versus $I_{\text{CM}} = MR^2/2$ for the disk) and so less of the sphere's kinetic energy goes into rotation (see Example 8-10). The disk, with its large moment of inertia, comes in last.

8-6 (c), then (d) and (e) are tied for second place, then (a), then (b). The angular velocity ω_z and angular acceleration α_z have the same sign for objects (c) and (e), so the rotation is speeding up for both objects; (c) is speeding up at a greater rate because the absolute value of α_z is greater than for (e). Object (d) is at rest and has a nonzero α_z, so it must also be speeding up; its α_z has the same absolute value as object (e), so these two objects are speeding up at the same rate. Objects (a) and (b) are slowing down because ω_z and α_z have opposite signs; object (b) is slowing down at a faster rate because it has a larger absolute value of α_z.

8-7 Extending the handle of the wrench with the pipe lengthens the lever arm, because it increases the distance between the rotation axis and the point where the force is applied. Equation 8-21 shows that torque increases as the lever arm increases, even when the force remains the same, making it more likely that the bolt will rotate. The downside is that with this arrangement, applying even a small force may result in a torque large enough to break the bolt or the wrench!

8-8 (a) (i), (b) (ii) The torque required to create a certain angular acceleration is proportional to the moment of inertia (Equation 8-23). Because I_y is only about one-third as great as I_z, up-and-down motions (rotation around the y axis) are easier than side-to-side motions (rotation around the z axis). About three times as much torque is required to rotate the jaw from side to side (rotation around the z axis) as compared to the torque required to cause the jaw to open and close (rotation around the y axis).

8-9 (a) A typical bird has more of its mass farther from the roll axis compared to the insect, so its moment of inertia around that axis will be larger compared to its mass. Hence proportionally more effort is required to give the bird an angular acceleration around that axis. This makes the bird less responsive to the torques exerted by the aerodynamic forces on its wings. Thus a typical bird is less maneuverable than a flying insect, which can make rapid and abrupt turns.

8-10 (a) The disk moves down the ramp but doesn't *slide* down the ramp. Instead, as the disk rolls, each part of its rim sets down on the ramp and then lifts off again. Hence the friction force that acts on the disk is purely static friction, not kinetic (sliding) friction.

8-11 (a) The situation is the same as Example 8-14 but with a moment of inertia $I = (2/5)MR^2$ rather than $I = (1/2)MR^2$ (see Table 8-1). Since the sphere has a moment of inertia smaller than that of the disk, it requires a smaller torque to give it an angular acceleration. Hence the uphill friction force f acting on the sphere will be less than that on the disk. As a result, the net downhill force on the sphere, and thus its downhill acceleration, will be greater for the sphere than for the disk.

You can also get this result by redoing the calculation in Example 8-14 using $I = (2/5)MR^2$. The rotational form of Newton's second law becomes

$$Rf = \frac{2}{5}MR^2\alpha_z \text{ or } f = \frac{2}{5}MR\alpha_z$$

With $\alpha_z = a_{\text{CM},x}/R$, this becomes

$$f = \frac{2}{5}MR\left(\frac{a_{\text{CM},x}}{R}\right) = \frac{2}{5}Ma_{\text{CM},x}$$

Substitute this into the Newton's second law equation for the sphere's motion along the x axis:

$$Mg\sin\theta - f = Ma_{CM,\,x}$$

$$Mg\sin\theta - \frac{2}{5}Ma_{CM,\,x} = Ma_{CM,\,x}$$

$$Mg\sin\theta = Ma_{CM,\,x} + \frac{2}{5}Ma_{CM,\,x} = \frac{7}{5}Ma_{CM,\,x}$$

$$a_{CM,\,x} = \frac{5}{7}g\sin\theta$$

Since $5/7$ (about 0.714) is greater than $2/3$ (about 0.667), this is in fact greater than the disk's acceleration $a_{CM,\,x} = (2/3)g\sin\theta$.

8-12   (c) The angular speed of the ball increases. Once the ball has been hit and set in motion it has angular momentum around the pole, and because we neglect resistive forces there is no external torque on it. (Yes, there is a force on the ball due to tension in the rope. This force is straight inward toward the pole, however, so the angle ϕ between $\vec{r}$ and $\vec{F}$ in Equation 8-20, the definition of torque, is 180°. Hence the magnitude of the torque is zero: $\tau = rF\sin\phi = rF\sin 180° = 0$.) Angular momentum L_z is therefore conserved. As the rope loops around the pole, the ball gets closer to the rotational axis and its

moment of inertia I decreases. Hence the angular speed (which is the magnitude of the angular velocity ω_z) must increase in order for the magnitude of $L_z = I\omega_z$ to remain constant.

8-13   (d) The angular momentum L of a system is conserved only if no net torque acts on the system. This isn't the case for *either* the pulley or the disk: A net torque due to the tension force acts on the pulley as it rotates, and a net torque due to the force of friction acts on the disk as it rolls downhill. For both objects the moment of inertia I remains unchanged (the objects don't change shape) and the angular velocity ω_z increases, so $L_z = I\omega_z$ increases. Conservation laws are great when they apply, but remember that they do *not* apply in all situations!

8-14   By bending in the middle, the cat divides its body into two segments, each of which can rotate around a different axis. The cat uses its muscles to rotate its front section into an upright position while simultaneously rotating its hind quarters slightly in the same direction. This small twist cancels the angular momentum generated by the rotation of the front part of his body. Next, the opposite occurs: As the rear of the animal rotates into alignment with the front, it slightly twists its forequarters. Because the net angular momentum of the cat must remain zero, the cat's body must twist in order to cancel the angular momentum associated with the front and rear of its body separately.

Questions and Problems

In a few problems, you are given more data than you actually need; in a few other problems, you are required to supply data from your general knowledge, outside sources, or informed estimate. Interpret as significant all digits in numerical values that have trailing zeros and no decimal points.

For all problems, use $g = 9.80\ \mathrm{m/s^2}$ for the free-fall acceleration due to gravity.

• Basic, single-concept problem

•• Intermediate-level problem, may require synthesis of concepts and multiple steps

••• Challenging problem

SSM *Solution is in Student Solutions Manual*

Conceptual Questions

1. •Describe any inconsistencies in the following statement: *The units of torque are N · m, but that's not the same as the units of energy.*

2. •What are the units of angular velocity ($\vec{\omega}$)? Why are factors of 2π present in many equations describing rotational motion?

3. •Why is it critical to define the axis of rotation when you set out to find the moment of inertia of an object? SSM

4. •Explain how an object moving in a straight line can have a nonzero angular momentum.

5. •What are the units of the following quantities: (a) rotational kinetic energy, (b) moment of inertia, and (c) angular momentum?

6. •Explain which physical quantities change when an ice skater moves her arms in and out as she rotates in a pirouette. What causes her angular velocity to change, if it changes at all?

7. •While watching two people on a seesaw, you notice that the person at the top always leans backward, while the person at the bottom always leans forward. (a) Why do the riders do this? (b) Assuming they are sitting equidistant from the pivot point

of the seesaw, what, if anything, can you say about the relative masses of the two riders? SSM

8. •The four solids shown in **Figure 8-33** have equal heights, widths, and masses. The axes of rotation are located at the center of each object and are perpendicular to the plane of the paper. Rank the moments of inertia from greatest to least.

Hoop   Solid cylinder   Solid sphere   Hollow sphere

Figure 8-33   Problem 8

9. •Referring to the time-lapse photograph of a falling cat in Figure 8-32, do you think that a cat will fall on her feet if she does not have a tail? Explain your answer using the concepts of this chapter.

10. •What is the ratio of rotational kinetic energy for two balls, each tied to a light string and spinning in a circle with a radius equal to the length of the string? The first ball has a mass m and a string of length L, and rotates at a rate of ω. The second ball has a mass $2m$ and a string of length $2L$, and rotates at a rate of 2ω.

11. •A student cannot open a door at her school. She pushes with ever-greater force, and still the door will not budge! Knowing that the door does push open, is not locked, and a minimum torque is required to open the door, give a few reasons why this might be occurring.

12. •Analyze the following statement and determine if there are any physical inconsistencies: While rotating a ball on the end of a string of length L, the rotational kinetic energy remains constant as long as the length and angular speed are fixed. When the ball is pulled inward and the length of the string is

shortened, the rotational kinetic energy will remain constant due to conservation of energy, but the angular momentum will not because there is an external force acting on the ball to pull it inward. The moment of inertia and angular speed will, of course, remain the same throughout the process because the ball is rotating in the same plane throughout the motion.

13. •A freely rotating turntable moves at a steady angular velocity. A glob of cookie dough falls straight down and attaches to the very edge of the turntable. Describe which quantities (angular velocity, angular acceleration, torque, rotational kinetic energy, moment of inertia, or angular momentum) are conserved during the process and describe qualitatively what happens to the motion of the turntable. SSM

14. •Describe what a "torque wrench" is and discuss any difficulties that a Canadian auto or bicycle mechanic might have working with an American mechanic's tools (and vice versa).

15. •In describing rotational motion, it is often useful to develop an analogy with translational motion. First, write a set of equations describing translational motion. Then write the rotational analogs (for example, $\theta = \theta_0 \ldots$) of the translational equations (for example, $x = x_0 + v_0 t + \frac{1}{2}at^2$) using the following legend:

$$x \Leftrightarrow \theta \quad v \Leftrightarrow \omega \quad a \Leftrightarrow \alpha \quad F \Leftrightarrow \tau \quad m \Leftrightarrow I$$

$$p \Leftrightarrow L \quad K_{\text{translational}} \Leftrightarrow K_{\text{rotational}}$$

16. •In Chapter 4, you learned that the mass of an object determines how that object responds to an applied force. Write a rotational analog to that idea based on the concepts of this chapter.

17. •Using the rotational concepts of this chapter, explain why a uniform solid sphere beats a uniform solid cylinder which beats a ring when the three objects "race" down an inclined plane while rolling without slipping. SSM

18. •Which quantity is larger: the angular momentum of Earth rotating on its axis each day or the angular momentum of Earth revolving about the Sun each year? Try to determine the answer without using a calculator.

19. •Define the SI unit radian. The unit appears in some physical quantities (for example, the angular velocity of a turntable is 3.5 rad/s) and it is omitted in others (for example, the translational velocity at the rim of a turntable is 0.35 m/s). Because the formula relating rotational and translational quantities involves multiplying by a radian ($v = r\omega$), discuss when it is appropriate to include radians and when the unit should be dropped.

20. •A hollow cylinder rolls without slipping up an incline, stops, and then rolls back down. Which of the following graphs in Figure 8-34 shows the (a) angular acceleration and (b) angular velocity for the motion? Assume that up the ramp is the positive direction.

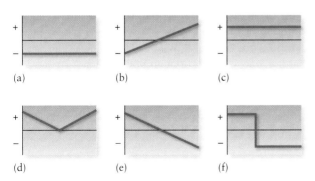

Figure 8-34 Problem 20

21. •Consider a situation in which a merry-go-round, starting from rest, speeds up in the counterclockwise direction. It eventually reaches and maintains a maximum angular velocity. After a short time the merry-go-round then starts to slow down and eventually stops. Assume the accelerations experienced by the merry-go-round have constant magnitudes. (a) Which graph in Figure 8-35 describes the angular velocity as the merry-go-round speeds up? (b) Which graph describes the angular position as the merry-go-round speeds up? (c) Which graph describes the angular velocity as the merry-go-round travels at its maximum velocity? (d) Which graph describes the angular position as the merry-go-round travels at its maximum velocity? (e) Which graph describes the angular velocity as the merry-go-round slows down? (f) Which graph describes the angular position as the merry-go-round slows down? (g) Draw a graph of the torque experienced by the merry-go-round as a function of time during the scenario described in the problem. SSM

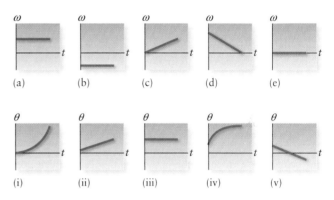

Figure 8-35 Problem 21

22. •Rank the torques exerted on the bolts in A–D (Figure 8-36) from least to greatest. Note that the forces in B and D make an angle of 45° with the wrench. Assume the wrenches and the magnitude of the force F are identical.

Figure 8-36 Problem 22

Multiple-Choice Questions

23. •A solid sphere of radius R, a solid cylinder of radius R, and a rod of length R all have the same mass, and all three are rotating with the same angular velocity. The sphere is rotating around an axis through its center. The cylinder is rotating around its long axis, and the rod is rotating around an axis through its center but perpendicular to the rod. Which one has the greatest rotational kinetic energy?

    A. the sphere
    B. the cylinder
    C. the rod
    D. the rod and cylinder have the same rotational kinetic energy
    E. they all have the same kinetic energy

24. •How would a flywheel's (spinning disk's) kinetic energy change if its moment of inertia were five times larger but its angular speed were five times smaller?
   A. 0.1 times as large as before
   B. 0.2 times as large as before
   C. same as before
   D. 5 times as large as before
   E. 10 times as large as before

25. •You have two steel spheres; sphere 2 has twice the radius of sphere 1. What is the ratio of the moment of inertia I_2:I_1?
   A. 2
   B. 4
   C. 8
   D. 16
   E. 32

26. •A solid ball, a solid disk, and a hoop, all with the same mass and the same radius, are set rolling without slipping up an incline, all with the same initial energy. Which goes farthest up the incline?
   A. the ball
   B. the disk
   C. the hoop
   D. the hoop and the disk roll to the same height, farther than the ball
   E. they all roll to the same height

27. •A solid ball, a solid disk, and a hoop, all with the same mass and the same radius, are set rolling without slipping up an incline, all with the same initial linear speed. Which goes farthest up the incline?
   A. the ball
   B. the disk
   C. the hoop
   D. the hoop and the disk roll to the same height, farther than the ball
   E. they all roll to the same height SSM

28. •Bob and Lily are riding on a merry-go-round. Bob rides on a horse toward the outside of the circular platform, and Lily rides on a horse toward the center of the circular platform. When the merry-go-round is rotating at a constant angular speed, Bob's angular speed is
   A. exactly half as much as Lily's.
   B. larger than Lily's.
   C. smaller than Lily's.
   D. the same as Lily's.
   E. exactly twice as much as Lily's.

29. •Bob and Lily are riding on a merry-go-round. Bob rides on a horse toward the outer edge of a circular platform. and Lily rides on a horse toward the center of the circular platform. When the merry-go-round is rotating at a constant angular speed ω, Bob's speed v is
   A. exactly half as much as Lily's.
   B. larger than Lily's.
   C. smaller than Lily's.
   D. the same as Lily's.
   E. exactly twice as much as Lily's.

30. •While a gymnast is in the air during a leap, which of the following quantities must remain constant for her?
   A. position
   B. velocity
   C. momentum
   D. angular velocity
   E. angular momentum about her center of mass

31. •The moment of inertia of a thin ring about its symmetry axis is $I_{CM} = MR^2$. What is the moment of inertia if you twirl a large ring around your finger, so that in essence it rotates about a point on the ring, about an axis parallel to the symmetry axis?
   A. $5MR^2$
   B. $2MR^2$
   C. MR^2
   D. $1.5MR^2$
   E. $0.5MR^2$ SSM

32. •You give a quick push to a ball at the end of a massless, rigid rod, causing the ball to rotate clockwise in a horizontal circle (Figure 8-37). The rod's pivot is frictionless. After the push has ended, the ball's angular velocity
   A. steadily increases.
   B. increases for a while, then remains constant.
   C. decreases for a while, then remains constant.
   D. remains constant.
   E. steadily decreases.

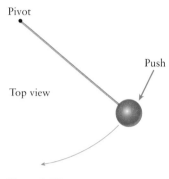

Figure 8-37 Problem 32

Estimation/Numerical Analysis

33. •Estimate the angular speed of a car moving around a cloverleaf on-ramp of a typical freeway. Cloverleaf ramps extend through approximately three-quarters of a circle to connect two orthogonal freeways. SSM

34. •A fan is designed to last for a certain time before it will have to be replaced (planned obsolescence). The fan only has one speed (at a maximum of 750 rpm), and it reaches the speed in 2 s (starting from rest). It takes the fan 10 s for the blade to stop once it is turned off. If the manufacturer specifies that the fan will operate up to 1 billion rotations, estimate how many days you will be able to use the fan.

35. •Estimate the torque you apply when you open a door in your house. Be sure to specify the axis to which your estimate refers.

36. •Make a rough estimate of the moment of inertia of a pencil that is spun about its center by a nervous student during an exam.

37. •Estimate the moment of inertia of a figure skater as she rotates about the longitudinal axis that passes straight down through the center of her body into the ice. Make this estimation for the extreme parts of a pirouette (arms fully extended and arms drawn in tightly).

38. •Estimate the angular displacement (in radians *and* degrees) of Earth in one day of its orbit around the Sun.

39. •Estimate the angular speed of the apparent passage of the Sun across the sky of Earth (from dawn until dusk).

40. •Estimate the angular acceleration of a lone sock that is inside a washing machine that starts from rest and reaches the maximum speed of its spin cycle in typical fashion.

41. •Estimate the angular momentum about the center of rotation for a "skip-it ball" that is spun around on the ankle of a small child (the child hops over the ball as it swings around and around her feet). SSM

42. •Estimate the moment of inertia of Earth about its central axis as it rotates once in a day. Try to recall (or guess) the mass and radius of Earth before you look up the data.

43. •Using a spreadsheet and the data below, calculate the average angular speed of the rotating object over the first 10 s. Calculate the average angular acceleration from 15 to 25 s. If the object has a moment of inertia of 0.25 kg · m² about the axis of rotation, calculate the average torque during the following time intervals: 0 < t < 10 s, 10 s < t < 15 s, and 15 s < t < 25 s.

t (s)	θ (rad)	t (s)	θ (rad)	t (s)	θ (rad)
0	0	9	3.14	18	6.48
1	0.349	10	3.50	19	8.53
2	0.700	11	3.50	20	11.0
3	1.05	12	3.49	21	14.1
4	1.40	13	3.50	22	17.6
5	1.75	14	3.51	23	21.6
6	2.10	15	3.51	24	26.2
7	2.44	16	3.98	25	31.0
8	2.80	17	5.01		

Problems

8-2 An object's rotational kinetic energy is related to its angular velocity and how its mass is distributed

44. •What is the angular speed of an object that completes 2.00 rev every 12.0 s? Give your answer in rad/s.

45. •A car rounds a curve with a translational speed of 12.0 m/s. If the radius of the curve is 7.00 m, calculate the angular speed in rad/s.

46. •Convert the following:

$$45.0 \text{ rev/min} = \underline{\hspace{1cm}} \text{rad/s}$$

$$33\tfrac{1}{3} \text{ rpm} = \underline{\hspace{1cm}} \text{rad/s}$$

$$2\pi \text{ rev/s} = \underline{\hspace{1cm}} \text{rad/s}$$

47. •Calculate the angular speed of the Moon as it orbits Earth (recall that the Moon completes one orbit about Earth in 27.4 days and the Earth–Moon distance is 3.84×10^8 m). SSM

48. •If a 0.250-kg point object rotates at 3.00 rev/s about an axis that is 0.500 m away, what is the kinetic energy of the object?

49. •What is the rotational kinetic energy of an object that has a moment of inertia of 0.280 kg · m² about the axis of rotation when its angular speed is 4.00 rad/s?

50. •What is the moment of inertia of an object that rotates at 13.0 rev/min about an axis and has a rotational kinetic energy of 18.0 J?

51. •What is the angular speed of a rotating wheel that has a moment of inertia of 0.330 kg · m² and a rotational kinetic energy of 2.75 J? Give your answer in both rad/s and rev/min. SSM

8-3 An object's moment of inertia depends on its mass distribution and the choice of rotation axis

52. •What is the combined moment of inertia for the three point objects about the axis O in Figure 8-38?

Figure 8-38
Problem 52

53. •What is the combined moment of inertia of three point objects ($m_1 = 1.00$ kg, $m_2 = 1.50$ kg, $m_3 = 2.00$ kg) tied together with massless strings and rotating about the axis O as shown in Figure 8-39?

Figure 8-39
Problem 53

54. ••A baton twirler in a marching band complains that her baton is defective (Figure 8-40). The manufacturer specifies that the baton should have an overall length of $L = 60.0$ cm and a total mass between 940 and 950 g (there is one 350-g objects on each end). Also according to the manufacturer, the moment of inertia about the central axis passing through the baton should fall between 0.0750 and 0.0800 kg · m². The twirler (who has completed a class in physics) claims this is impossible. Who's right? Explain your answer.

Figure 8-40
Problem 54

55. ••What is the moment of inertia of a steering wheel about the axis that passes through its center? Assume the rim of the wheel has a radius R and a mass M. Assume that there are five radial spokes that connect in the center as shown in Figure 8-41. The spokes are thin rods of length R and mass $\tfrac{1}{2}M$, and are evenly spaced around the wheel. SSM

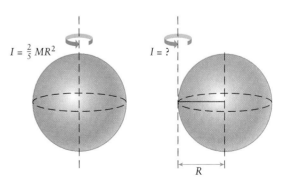

Figure 8-41
Problem 55

56. •Using the parallel-axis theorem, calculate the moment of inertia for a solid, uniform sphere about an axis that is tangent to its surface (Figure 8-42).

$I = \tfrac{2}{5} MR^2$ $I = ?$

Figure 8-42 Problem 56

57. •Calculate the moment of inertia for a uniform, solid cylinder (mass M, radius R) if the axis of rotation is tangent to the side of the cylinder as shown in Figure 8-43.

$I = \frac{1}{2} MR^2$ $I = ?$

Figure 8-43 Problem 57

58. •Calculate the moment of inertia for a thin rod that is 1.25 m long and has mass of 2.25 kg. The axis of rotation passes through the rod at a point one-third of the way from the left end (Figure 8-44).

$\frac{1}{3} L$ $\frac{2}{3} L$

Figure 8-44 Problem 58

59. •Calculate the moment of inertia of a thin plate that is 5.00 cm × 7.00 cm in area and has a mass density of 1.50 g/cm^2. The axis of rotation is located at the left side, as shown in Figure 8-45.

5.00 cm

7.00 cm

Figure 8-45 Problem 59

60. •Calculate the radius of a solid sphere of mass M that has the same moment of inertia about an axis through its center of mass as a second solid sphere of radius R and mass M which has the axis of rotation passing tangent to the surface and parallel to the center of mass axis (Figure 8-46).

M

$r = ?$

M

R

Figure 8-46
Problem 60

61. ••Two uniform, solid spheres (one has a mass M and a radius R and the other has a mass M and a radius $2R$) are connected by a thin, uniform rod of length $3R$ and mass M (Figure 8-47). Find the moment of inertia about the axis through the center of the rod. SSM

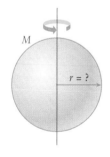

M M

$2R$ R

M

$3R$

Figure 8-47 Problem 61

62. ••What is the moment of inertia of the sphere–rod system shown in Figure 8-48 where the sphere has a radius R and a mass M and the rod is thin and massless, and has a length L? The sphere–rod system is spun about an axis A.

A

L

R

M

Figure 8-48 Problem 62

8-4 Conservation of mechanical energy also applies to rotating objects

63. •Calculate the final speed of a uniform, solid cylinder of radius 5.00 cm and mass 3.00 kg that starts from rest at the top of an inclined plane that is 2.00 m long and tilted at an angle of 25.0° with the horizontal. Assume the cylinder rolls without slipping down the ramp.

64. •Calculate the final speed of a uniform, solid sphere of radius 5.00 cm and mass 3.00 kg that starts with a translational speed of 2.00 m/s at the top of an inclined plane that is 2.00 m long and tilted at an angle of 25.0° with the horizontal. Assume the sphere rolls without slipping down the ramp.

65. •••A spherical marble that has a mass of 50.0 g and a radius of 0.500 cm rolls without slipping down a loop-the-loop track that has a radius of 20.0 cm. The marble starts from rest and *just barely* clears the loop to emerge on the other side of the track. What is the minimum height that the marble must start from to make it around the loop?

66. •••A billiard ball of mass 160 g and radius 2.50 cm starts with a translational speed of 2.00 m/s at point A on the track as shown in Figure 8-49. If point B is at the top of a hill that has a radius of curvature of 60 cm, what is the normal force acting on the ball at point B? Assume the billiard ball rolls without slipping on the track.

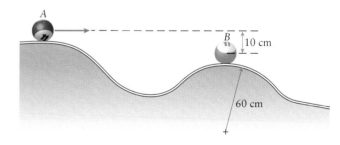

A

B 10 cm

60 cm

Figure 8-49 Problem 66

67. •**Sports** A bowling ball that has a radius of 11.0 cm and a mass of 5.00 kg rolls without slipping on a level lane at 2.00 rad/s. Calculate the ratio of the translational kinetic energy to the rotational kinetic energy of the bowling ball. SSM

68. •**Astronomy** Earth is approximately a solid sphere, has a mass of 5.98×10^{24} kg and a radius of 6.38×10^6 m, and completes one rotation about its central axis each day. Calculate the rotational kinetic energy of Earth as it spins on its axis.

69. •**Astronomy** Calculate the translational kinetic energy of Earth as it orbits the Sun once each year (the Earth–Sun distance

is 1.50×10^{11} m). Calculate the ratio of the translational kinetic energy to the rotational kinetic energy calculated in the previous problem.

70. •A potter's flywheel is made of a 5.00-cm-thick, round slab of concrete that has a mass of 60.0 kg and a diameter of 35.0 cm. This disk rotates about an axis that passes through its center, perpendicular to its round area. Calculate the angular speed of the slab about its center if the rotational kinetic energy is 15.0 J. Express your answer in both rad/s and rev/min.

71. ••**Sports** A flying disk (160 g, 25.0 cm in diameter) spins at a rate of 300 rpm with its center balanced on a fingertip. What is the rotational kinetic energy of the Frisbee if the disc has 70% of its mass on the outer edge (basically a thin ring 25.0-cm in diameter) and the remaining 30% is a nearly flat disk 25.0-cm in diameter? SSM

8-5 The equations for rotational kinematics are almost identical to those for linear motion

72. •Suppose a roulette wheel is spinning at 1 rev/s. (a) How long will it take for the wheel to come to rest if it experiences an angular acceleration of -0.02 rad/s^2? (b) How many rotations will it complete in that time?

73. •A spinning top completes 6000 rotations before it starts to topple over. The average speed of the rotations is 800 rpm. Calculate how long the top spins before it begins to topple.

74. •A child pushes a merry-go-round that has a diameter of 4.00 m and goes from rest to an angular speed of 18.0 rpm in a time of 43.0 s. (a) Calculate the angular displacement and the average angular acceleration of the merry-go-round. (b) What is the maximum tangential speed of the child if she rides on the edge of the platform?

75. •Jerry twirls an umbrella around its central axis so that it completes 24.0 rotations in 30.0 s. (a) If the umbrella starts from rest, calculate the angular acceleration of a point on the outer edge. (b) What is the maximum tangential speed of a point on the edge if the umbrella has a radius of 55.0 cm?

76. •Prior to the music CD, stereo systems had a phonographic turntable on which vinyl disk recordings were played. A particular phonographic turntable starts from rest and achieves a final constant angular speed of $33\frac{1}{3}$ rpm in a time of 4.5 s. How many rotations did the turntable undergo during that time? The classic Beatles album *Abbey Road* is 47 min and 7 s in duration. If the turntable requires 8 s to come to rest once the album is over, calculate the total number of rotations for the complete start-up, playing, and slowdown of the album.

77. •A CD player varies its speed as it moves to another circular track on the CD. A CD player is rotating at 300 rpm. To read another track, the angular speed is increased to 450 rpm in a time of 0.75 s. Calculate the average angular acceleration in rad/s^2 for the change to occur. SSM

78. •**Astronomy** A communication satellite circles Earth in a geosynchronous orbit such that the satellite remains directly above the same point on the surface of Earth. (a) What angular displacement (in radians) does the satellite undergo in 1 h of its orbit? (b) Calculate the angular speed of the satellite in rev/min and rad/s.

8-6 Torque is to rotation as force is to translation

79. •What is the torque about your shoulder axis if you hold a 10-kg barbell in one hand straight out and at shoulder height? Assume your hand is 75 cm from your shoulder. SSM

80. •A driver applies a horizontal force of 20.0 N (to the right) to the top of a steering wheel, as shown in Figure 8-50. The steering wheel has a radius of 18.0 cm and a moment of inertia of 0.0970 kg·m^2. Calculate the angular acceleration of the steering wheel about the central axis.

Figure 8-50
Problem 80

81. •**Medical** When the palmaris longus muscle in the forearm is flexed, the wrist moves back and forth (Figure 8-51). If the muscle generates a force of 45.0 N and it is acting with an effective lever arm of 22.0 cm, what is the torque that the muscle produces on the wrist? Curiously, over 15% of all Caucasians lack this muscle; a smaller percentage of Asians (around 5%) also lack it. Some studies correlate the absence of the muscle with carpal tunnel syndrome.

Palmaris longus muscle

Figure 8-51 Problem 81

82. •A torque wrench is used to tighten a nut on a bolt. The wrench is 25 cm long, and a force of 120 N is applied at the end of the wrench as shown in Figure 8-52. Calculate the torque about the axis that passes through the bolt.

$F = 120$ N   20°   25 cm

Figure 8-52 Problem 82

83. •An 85.0-cm-wide door is pushed open with a force of $F = 75.0$ N. Calculate the torque about an axis that passes through the hinges in each of the cases in Figure 8-53. SSM

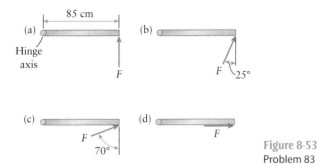

Figure 8-53
Problem 83

84. •••A 50.0-g meter stick is balanced at its midpoint (50 cm). Then a 200-g weight is hung with a light string from the 70.0-cm point, and a 100-g weight is hung from the 10.0-cm point (Figure 8-54). Calculate the clockwise and counterclockwise torques acting on the board due to the four forces shown about the following axes: (a) the 0-cm point, (b) the 50-cm point, and (c) the 100-cm point.

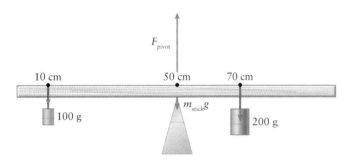

Figure 8-54 Problem 84

85. •A robotic arm lifts a barrel of radioactive waste (Figure 8-55). If the maximum torque delivered by the arm about the axis O is 3000 N · m and the distance r in the diagram is 3.00 m, what is the maximum mass of the barrel?

Figure 8-55 Problem 85

86. •A typical adult can deliver about 10 N · m of torque when attempting to open a twist-off cap on a bottle. What is the maximum force that the average person can exert with his fingers if most bottle caps are about 2 cm in diameter?

8-7 The techniques used for solving problems with Newton's second law also apply to rotation problems

87. •A potter's wheel is initially at rest. A constant external torque of 75.0 N · m is applied to the wheel for 15.0 s, giving the wheel an angular speed of 500 rev/min. (a) What is the

moment of inertia of the wheel? The external torque is then removed, and a brake is applied. If it takes the wheel 200 s to come to rest after the brake is applied, what is the magnitude of the torque exerted by the brake?

88. •A flywheel of mass 35.0 kg and diameter 60.0 cm spins at 400 rpm when it experiences a sudden power loss. The flywheel slows due to friction in its bearings during the 20.0 s the power is off. If the flywheel makes 200 complete revolutions during the power failure, (a) at what rate is the flywheel spinning when the power comes back on? (b) How long would it have taken for the flywheel to come to a complete stop?

89. ••A solid cylindrical pulley with a mass of 1.00 kg and a radius of 0.25 m is free to rotate about its axis. An object of mass 0.250 kg is attached to the pulley with a light string (Figure 8-56). Assuming the string does not stretch or slip, calculate the tension in the string and the angular acceleration of the pulley.

Figure 8-56 Problem 89

90. ••A block with mass $m_1 = 2.00$ kg rests on a frictionless table. It is connected with a light string over a pulley to a hanging block of mass $m_2 = 4.00$ kg. The pulley is a uniform disk with a radius of 4.00 cm and a mass of 0.500 kg (Figure 8-57). (a) Calculate the acceleration of each block and the tension in each segment of the string. (b) How long does it take the blocks to move a distance of 2.25 m? (c) What is the angular speed of the pulley at this time?

Figure 8-57 Problem 90

91. ••A yo-yo with a rolling radius of $r = 2.50$ cm rolls down a string with a linear acceleration of 6.50 m/s² (Figure 8-58). (a) Calculate the tension in the string and the angular acceleration of the yo-yo. (b) What is the moment of inertia of this yo-yo?

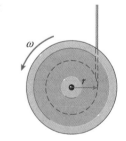

Figure 8-58 Problem 91

8-8 Angular momentum is conserved when there is zero net torque on a system

92. •What is the angular momentum about the central axis of a thin disk that is 18.0 cm in diameter, has a mass of 2.50 kg, and rotates at a constant 1.25 rad/s?

93. •What is the angular momentum of a 300-g tetherball when it whirls around the central pole at 60.0 rpm and at a radius of 125 cm?

94. •**Astronomy** Calculate the angular momentum of Earth as it orbits the Sun. Recall that the mass of Earth is 5.98×10^{24} kg, the distance between Earth and the Sun is 1.50×10^{11} m, and the time for one orbit is 365.3 days.

95. •**Astronomy** Calculate the angular momentum of Earth as it spins on its central axis once each day. Assume Earth is approximately a uniform, solid sphere that has a mass of 5.98×10^{24} kg and a radius of 6.38×10^{6} m.

96. •What is the speed of an electron in the lowest energy orbital of hydrogen, of radius equal to 5.29×10^{-11} m? The mass of an electron is 9.11×10^{-31} kg, and its angular momentum in this orbital is 1.055×10^{-34} J · s.

97. •What is the angular momentum of a 70.0-kg person riding on a Ferris wheel that has a diameter of 35.0 m and rotates once every 25.0 s? SSM

98. •A professor sits on a rotating stool that spins at 10.0 rpm while she holds a 1.00-kg weight in each of her hands. Her outstretched arms are 0.750 m from the axis of rotation, which passes through her head into the center of the stool. When she draws the weights in toward her body, her angular speed increases to 20.0 rpm. Neglecting the mass of her arms, how far are the weights from the rotational axis at the increased speed?

General Problems

99. •A baton is constructed by attaching two small objects that each have a mass M to the ends of a rod that has a length L and a uniform mass M. Find an expression for the moment of inertia of the baton when it is rotated around a point $(3/8)L$ from one end.

100. •The outside diameter of the playing area of an optical Blu-ray disc is 11.75 cm, and the inside diameter is 4.50 cm. When viewing movies, the disc rotates so that a laser maintains a constant linear speed relative to the disc of 7.50 m/s as it tracks over the playing area. (a) What are the maximum and minimum angular speeds (in rad/s and rpm) of the disc? (b) At which location of the laser on the playing area do these speeds occur? (c) What is the average angular acceleration of a Blu-ray disc as it plays an 8.0-h set of movies?

101. •A table saw has a 25.0-cm-diameter blade that rotates at a rate of 7000 rpm. It is equipped with a safety mechanism that can stop the blade within 5.00 ms if something like a finger is accidentally placed in contact with the blade. (a) What average angular acceleration occurs if the saw starts at 7000 rpm and comes to rest in this time? (b) How many rotations does the blade complete during the stopping period?

102. •In 1932 Albert Dremel of Racine, Wisconsin, created his rotary tool that has come to be known as a dremel. (a) Suppose a dremel starts from rest and achieves an operating speed of 35,000 rev/min. If it requires 1.20 s for the tool to reach operating speed and it is held at that speed for 45.0 s, how many rotations has the bit made? Suppose it requires another 8.50 s for the tool to return to rest. (b) What are the average angular accelerations for the start-up and the slow-down periods? (c) How many rotations does the tool complete from start to finish?

103. ••**Medical, Sports** On average, both arms and hands together account for 13% of a person's mass, while the head is 7.0% and the trunk and legs account for 80%. We can model a spinning skater with his arms outstretched as a vertical cylinder (head + trunk + legs) with two solid uniform rods (arms + hands) extended horizontally. Suppose a 62.0-kg skater is 1.80 m tall, has arms that are each 65.0 cm long (including the hands), and a trunk that can be modeled as being 35.0 cm in diameter. If the skater is initially spinning at 70.0 rpm with his arms outstretched, what will his angular velocity be (in rpm) when he pulls in his arms until they are at his sides parallel to his trunk?

104. •Derive an expression for the moment of inertia of a spherical shell (for example, the peel of an orange) that has a mass M and a radius R, and rotates about an axis that is tangent to the surface.

105. •Because of your success in physics class you are selected for an internship at a prestigious bicycle company in its research and development division. Your first task involves designing a wheel made of a hoop that has a mass of 1.00 kg and a radius of 50.0 cm, and spokes with a mass of 10.0 g each. The wheel should have a total moment of inertia 0.280 kg · m². (a) How many spokes are necessary to construct the wheel? (b) What is the mass of the wheel? SSM

106. ••Two beads that each have a mass M are attached to a thin rod that has a length $2L$ and a mass $M/8$. Each bead is initially a distance $L/4$ from the center of the rod. The whole system is set into uniform rotation about the center of the rod, with initial angular frequency $\omega = 20\pi$ rad/s. If the beads are then allowed to slide to the ends of the rod, what will the angular frequency become?

107. ••A uniform disk that has a mass M of 0.300 kg and a radius R of 0.270 m rolls up a ramp of angle θ equal to 55.0° with initial speed v of 4.8 m/s. If the disk rolls without slipping, how far up the ramp does it go?

108. •In a new model of a machine, a spinning solid spherical part of radius R must be replaced by a ring of the same mass which is to have the same kinetic energy. Both parts need to spin at the same rate, the sphere about an axis through its center and the ring about an axis perpendicular to its plane at its center. (a) What should the radius of the ring be in terms of R? (b) Will both parts have the same angular momentum? If not, which one will have more?

109. •Many 2.5-in-diameter (6.35-cm) computer hard disks spin at a constant 7200 rpm operating speed. The disks have a mass of about 7.50 g and are essentially uniform throughout with a very small hole at the center. If they reach their operating speed 2.50 s after being turned on, what average torque does the disk drive supply to the disk during the acceleration?

110. ••**Sports** At the 1984 Olympics, the great diver Greg Louganis won one of his 10 gold medals for the reverse $3\frac{1}{2}$ somersault tuck dive. In the dive, Louganis began his $3\frac{1}{2}$ turns with his body tucked in at a maximum height of approximately 2.0 m above the platform, which itself was 10.0 m above the water. He spun uniformly $3\frac{1}{2}$ times and straightened out his body just as he reached the water. A reasonable approximation is to model the diver as a thin uniform rod 2.0 m long when he is stretched out and as a uniform solid cylinder of diameter 0.75 m when he is tucked in. (a) What was Louganis's average angular speed as he fell toward the water with his body tucked in? *Hint:* How long did it take him to reach the water from his highest point? (b) What was his angular speed just as he stretched out? (c) How much did Louganis's rotational kinetic energy change while extending his body if his mass was 75 kg?

111. ••**Medical** The bones of the forearm (radius and ulna) are hinged to the humerus at the elbow (Figure 8-59). The biceps muscle connects to the bones of the forearm about 2 cm beyond the joint. Assume the forearm has a mass of 2 kg and a length of 0.4 m. When the humerus and the biceps are nearly vertical and the forearm is horizontal, if a person wishes to hold an object of mass M so that her forearm remains motionless, what is the relationship between the force exerted by the biceps muscle and the mass of the object?

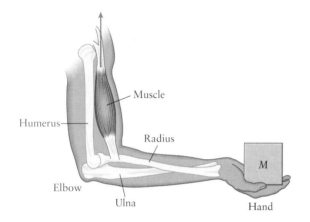

Muscle

Humerus

Radius

Elbow

Ulna

M

Hand

Figure 8-59 Problem 111

112. ••**Medical** The femur of a human leg (mass 10 kg, length 0.9 m) is in traction (Figure 8-60). The center of gravity of the leg is one-third of the distance from the pelvis to the bottom of the foot. Two objects, with masses m_1 and m_2, are hung at the ends of the leg using pulleys to provide upward support. A third object of 8 kg is hung to provide tension along the leg. The body provides tension as well. (a) What is the mathematical relationship between m_1 and m_2? Is this relationship unique in the sense that there is only one combination of m_1 and m_2 that maintains the leg in static equilibrium? (b) How does the relationship change if the tension force due to m_1 is applied at the leg's center of mass?

m_1 m_2

$\vec{F}_{body}$ 8 kg

Figure 8-60 Problem 112

113. •**Astronomy** It is estimated that 60,000 tons of meteors and other space debris accumulates on Earth each year. Assume the debris is accumulated uniformly across the surface of Earth. (a) How much does Earth's rotation rate change per year as a result of this accumulation? (That is, find the change

in angular velocity.) (b) How long would it take the accumulation of debris to change the rotation period by 1 s? SSM

114. •**Astronomy** Suppose we decided to use the rotation of Earth as a source of energy. (a) What is the maximum amount of energy we could obtain from this source? (b) By the year 2020 the projected rate at which the world uses energy is expected to be 6.4×10^{20} J/y. If energy use continues at that rate, for how many years would the spin of Earth supply our energy needs? Does this seem long enough to justify the effort and expense involved? (c) How long would it take before our day was extended to 48 h instead of 24 h? Assume that Earth is uniform throughout.

115. •**Astronomy** In a little over 5 billion years, our Sun will collapse to a white dwarf approximately 16,000 km in diameter. (Ignore the fact that the Sun will lose mass as it ages.) (a) What will our Sun's angular momentum and rotation rate be as a white dwarf? (Express your answers as multiples of its present-day values.) (b) Compared to its present value, will the Sun's rotational kinetic energy increase, decrease, or stay the same when it becomes a white dwarf? If it does change, by what factor will it change? The radius of the Sun is presently 6.96×10^8 m.

116. •**Astronomy** (a) If all the people in the world (~7 billion) lined up along the equator, would Earth's rotation rate increase or decrease? Justify your answer. (b) How would the rotation rate change if all people were no longer on Earth? Assume the average mass of a human is 70.0 kg.

117. •A 1000-kg merry-go-round (a flat, solid cylinder) supports 10 children, each with a mass of 50.0 kg, located at the axis of rotation (thus you may assume the children have no angular momentum at that location). Describe a plan to move the children such that the angular velocity of the merry-go-round decreases to one-half its initial value.

118. •One way for pilots to train for the physical demands of flying at high speeds is with a device called the "human centrifuge." It involves having the pilots travel in circles at high speeds so that they can experience forces greater than their own weight. The diameter of the NASA device is 17.8 m. (a) Suppose a pilot starts at rest and accelerates at a constant rate so that he undergoes 30 rev in 2 min. What is his angular acceleration (in rad/s^2)? (b) What is his angular velocity (in rad/s) at the end of that time? (c) After the 2-min period, the centrifuge moves at a constant speed. The g-force experienced is the centripetal force keeping the pilot moving along a circular path. What is the g-force experienced by the pilot? (1 g = mass × 9.80 m/s^2) (d) The pilot can tolerate 12 g's in the horizontal direction. How long would it take the centrifuge to reach that state if it starts at the angular speed found in part (c) and accelerates at the rate found in part (a)?

119. •••The moment of inertia of a rolling marble is $I = \frac{2}{5}MR^2$, where M is the mass of the marble and R is the radius. The marble is placed in front of a spring that has a constant k and has been compressed a distance x_c. The spring is released, and *as the marble comes off the spring* it begins to roll without slipping. *Note:* The static friction that causes rolling without slipping does not do work. (a) Derive an expression for the time it takes for the marble to travel a distance D along the surface after it has lost contact with the spring. (b) Show that your answer for part (a) has the correct units. SSM

9 Elastic Properties of Matter: Stress and Strain

In this chapter, your goals are to:

- (9-1) Explain the meaning of stress and strain in physics.
- (9-2) Define Hooke's law for an object under tension or compression.
- (9-3) Solve problems that involve the relationships between tensile stress and strain and between compressive stress and strain.
- (9-4) Explain the importance of the minus sign in the relationship between volume stress and volume strain.
- (9-5) Solve problems in which an object is under volume stress.
- (9-6) Define what is meant by shear, and explain what shear stress and shear strain are.
- (9-7) Solve problems that involve the relationship between shear stress and shear strain.
- (9-8) Explain what must happen to a material for it to go from elastic to plastic to failure, and why biological materials do not become plastic.
- (9-9) Solve problems concerning the stresses and strains on materials that may not obey Hooke's law.

To master this chapter, you should review:

- (1-4) The rules for working with significant figures.
- (6-5) Hooke's law for the force required to stretch or compress an ideal spring.

What do you think?

This mountain climber's arms actually shorten slightly as they support her weight. If the diameter of her arms was only half as much, would the amount that her arms shorten be (a) the same, (b) greater, or (c) less?

Figure 9-1 **Stress and strain** When an object such as an Achilles tendon is put under stress, it undergoes strain.

9-1 When an object is under stress, it deforms

So far in our study of physics we've treated objects as perfectly rigid. That is, an object's shape and size don't change no matter what forces we apply to it. But what about real objects that *do* change shape when forces are applied? As an example, look at the Achilles tendon that connects the heel bone to the muscles of the calf (Figure 9-1). When you bend your ankle to point your toes upward, the calf muscles pull upward on the top of the Achilles tendon just as hard as the heel bone pulls downward on the bottom of the tendon. Hence the net force on the tendon is zero, and the tendon as a whole doesn't accelerate. However, individual *parts* of the tendon move as the tendon stretches and deforms. In this

This Achilles tendon is relaxed.

This Achilles tendon is under **stress**: The muscles at its upper end exert an upward force *F*, and the heel bone at its lower end exerts an equally strong downward force. The tendon responds by undergoing **strain** (it stretches).

 Stress refers to forces that act to deform an object (change its size or shape). **Strain** refers to the deformation caused by these forces.

353

Figure 9-2 **Three kinds of stress**
You apply (a) tensile stress when you stretch an object along its length, (b) volume stress when you squeeze it on all sides, and (c) shear stress when you apply offset forces (as with a pair of shears).

(a)

This rope is under **tensile stress:** Forces are applied along its length to stretch it.

(b)

This orange is under **volume stress:** Forces are applied on all sides to squeeze it.

(c)

This branch is under **shear stress:** Offset forces are applied to deform it.

 Watch Out!

Stress and strain are different quantities.

In everyday language the words *stress* and *strain* can mean pretty much the same thing. You might say "I'm under a lot of stress" or "I'm under a lot of strain." In physics, however, **stress** refers to forces that make a body deform, and **strain** refers to how much deformation those forces cause.

chapter, we'll examine the physics of stretching, squeezing, compressing, and twisting materials.

We say that the applied forces in Figure 9-1 exert a *stress* on the tendon that makes it deform, and we call the resulting deformation the *strain*. We'll see that there are three distinct kinds of stress, which differ in the manner in which they are applied (Figure 9-2). One of our principal goals will be to see how much an object deforms when we apply a particular amount of stress—for example, how much a tendon stretches when you flex a muscle, or how much a skin diver's body compresses due to water pressure as she dives to the bottom of a lake.

Some materials, such as your Achilles tendon, your earlobes, or the tip of your nose, are *elastic*: If you apply a stress to stretch or squeeze them, they snap back to their original shape after the stress is removed. Other materials, like a well-chewed piece of bubble gum, are *plastic*: They exhibit a permanent change of shape when stretched. Even an elastic material like rubber can remain irreversibly deformed if large enough forces are applied. The material might even break apart and *fracture*, like a plastic fork that's bent too far. We'll look at the differences among these kinds of behavior later in this chapter.

Take-Home Message for Section 9-1

✔ An object is said to be under stress when forces act on the object to deform it (change its shape or size). The amount of deformation that results is called the strain.

✔ Elastic materials return to their original shape and size when the stress is removed, while plastic materials exhibit a permanent change in shape.

9-2 An object changes length when under tensile or compressive stress

(a)

This gymnast's upper leg is under **tension:** The ring pulls up on her leg and her hip pulls down on her leg.

(b)

This gymnast's arm is under **compression:** The shoulder pushes down on her arm and the ring in her hand pushes up on her arm.

Figure 9-3 **Tension and compression** (a) An object under tension tends to stretch along its length; (b) an object under compression tends to shorten along its length.

The Achilles tendon shown in Figure 9-1 and the rope shown in Figure 9-2a are under a kind of stress called **tension** or *tensile stress:* A force is applied at each end that makes the tendon or rope stretch. Figure 9-3a shows a gymnast whose upper legs are under tension. (Don't confuse this with the emotion of feeling "under tension," such as may happen before taking a physics exam!) A closely related kind of stress is **compression** or *compressive stress*, which occurs when a force is applied to each end of an object that tends to squeeze the object. The gymnast's arms in Figure 9-3b are under compression. If you grab each end of a pencil and try to pull the ends apart, you're putting the pencil under tension; if you push the ends toward each other, you're putting the pencil under compression.

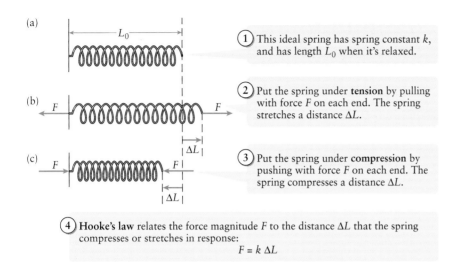

(a)

① This ideal spring has spring constant k, and has length L_0 when it's relaxed.

(b)

② Put the spring under **tension** by pulling with force F on each end. The spring stretches a distance ΔL.

(c)

③ Put the spring under **compression** by pushing with force F on each end. The spring compresses a distance ΔL.

④ **Hooke's law** relates the force magnitude F to the distance ΔL that the spring compresses or stretches in response:

$$F = k\,\Delta L$$

Figure 9-4 Hooke's law for an ideal spring When an ideal spring is under tension or compression, the change in the spring's length is directly proportional to the forces applied to its ends.

Most objects under compression or tension (not just ideal springs) obey Hooke's law, provided F and ΔL aren't too large.

Hooke's Law

How do objects behave when they are under tension or compression? We learned the answer to this question in Chapter 6 for one kind of object: an ideal spring (Figure 9-4a). When we stretch a spring along its length, we apply forces of the same magnitude F to both ends (Figure 9-4b). (This ensures that the net external force on the spring is zero, so the spring as a whole doesn't accelerate from rest.) According to **Hooke's law**, which we first encountered in Section 6-5, the force magnitude F is proportional to the distance ΔL that the spring stretches, provided that ΔL is small compared to the relaxed length of the spring, L_0:

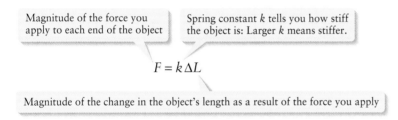

Magnitude of the force you apply to each end of the object

Spring constant k tells you how stiff the object is: Larger k means stiffer.

$$F = k\,\Delta L$$

Magnitude of the change in the object's length as a result of the force you apply

Hooke's law
(9-1)

(In Chapter 6 we used the symbol x for the amount that the spring stretches. We've changed this to ΔL to emphasize that this distance is the *change* in the overall length of the spring.)

The quantity k in Equation 9-1 is called the **spring constant**: It's a measure of the stiffness of the spring. To see this, note that we can rewrite Equation 9-1 as $k = F/\Delta L$. The stiffer the spring, the shorter the amount of stretch ΔL for a given force magnitude F, and so the greater the value of $k = F/\Delta L$. If the spring is loose and floppy, there is more stretch for a given force magnitude and $k = F/\Delta L$ has a smaller value. The SI units of k are newtons per meter (N/m).

Hooke's law also applies to an ideal spring under compression (Figure 9-4c): When compressed by forces of magnitude F, an ideal spring decreases in length by a distance ΔL given by Equation 9-1. The value of k for an ideal spring is the same for compression as for tension. Hence if stretching an ideal spring with forces of magnitude F makes its length increase by 1.00 mm, squeezing that spring with forces of the same magnitude F will make its length decrease by 1.00 mm.

Hooke's law is important because it doesn't just apply to ideal springs. Experiment shows that it holds true for most objects when they are stretched, provided that the amount of stretch is small. An example is a rubber strip made by cutting apart a rubber band (Figure 9-5a). When put under tension, the strip stretches by a distance ΔL that's directly proportional to the force magnitude F (Figure 9-5b). Likewise, when the strip is compressed, it shrinks by a distance ΔL that's directly proportional to F.

Experiment shows that the spring constant k for a given object depends on three things: its relaxed length L_0, its cross-sectional area A, and the material of which it

Figure 9-5 Hooke's law for tension and compression An object under tension obeys Hooke's law if the stress is not too great. The same is true for an object under compression.

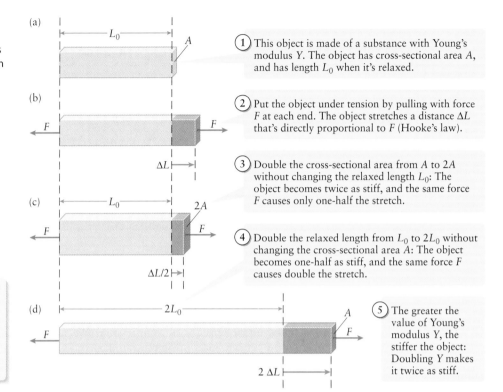

(a)

① This object is made of a substance with Young's modulus Y. The object has cross-sectional area A, and has length L_0 when it's relaxed.

(b)

② Put the object under tension by pulling with force F at each end. The object stretches a distance ΔL that's directly proportional to F (Hooke's law).

③ Double the cross-sectional area from A to $2A$ without changing the relaxed length L_0: The object becomes twice as stiff, and the same force F causes only one-half the stretch.

(c)

④ Double the relaxed length from L_0 to $2L_0$ without changing the cross-sectional area A: The object becomes one-half as stiff, and the same force F causes double the stretch.

(d)

⑤ The greater the value of Young's modulus Y, the stiffer the object: Doubling Y makes it twice as stiff.

The object's spring constant is proportional to its Young's modulus and its cross-sectional area, but inversely proportional to its length: $k = Y\dfrac{A}{L_0}$.

is made (for example, the particular kind of rubber). The last of these is given by a quantity called **Young's modulus** (or elastic modulus) for the material, denoted by the symbol Y. The greater the value of Y, the greater the intrinsic stiffness of the material. Experiment shows that k is directly proportional to Y and A but inversely proportional to L_0 (Figures 9-5c and 9-5d). The mathematical relationship that describes these observations is

Spring constant for an object under tension or compression (9-2)

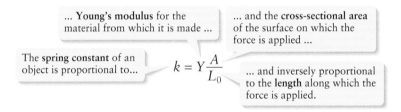

... **Young's modulus** for the material from which it is made ...

... and the **cross-sectional area** of the surface on which the force is applied ...

The **spring constant** of an object is proportional to...

$$k = Y\frac{A}{L_0}$$

... and inversely proportional to the **length** along which the force is applied.

This says that a short, thick object (small L_0, large A) is stiffer than a long, thin object (large L_0, small A) made of the same material and hence with the same value of Y. That's why a rubber eraser is harder to stretch than a rubber band. Equation 9-2 also says that the stiffer the material used to make an object—that is, the greater the value of Y—the stiffer the object will be.

! Watch Out! Young's modulus is not the same as the spring constant.

Don't confuse Young's modulus Y with the spring constant k. Young's modulus tells you how stiff a given *material* is; the spring constant refers to a particular *object* made of that material. If two objects have the same shape and size (and so the same values of A and L_0) but are made of different materials, Equation 9-2 says the object made of the material with greater Y will be harder to stretch or compress and will have a greater value of k. Equation 9-2 also says that if two objects are made of the same material (so Y is the same) but have different dimensions (so A, L_0, or both are different), their spring constants k can be different.

The first column of Table 9-1 gives specific values of Young's modulus Y for various materials. The SI units of Y are newtons per square meter, or N/m². This unit is

Table 9-1 Elastic Properties of Selected Materials

Material	Young's Modulus (10^9 N/m²)	Bulk Modulus (10^9 N/m²)	Shear Modulus (10^9 N/m²)
aluminum	70	76	26
brass	100	80	40
concrete	30	13	15
iron	211	170	82
nylon	3		4.1
rubber band	0.005		0.003
steel	200	140	78
air		1.41×10^5 N/m²	
ethyl alcohol		1.0	
water		2.2	
human ACL	0.1		
human lung		$1.5\text{–}9.8 \times 10^3$ N/m²	
pig endothelial cell			2×10^4 N/m²

also called the **pascal**, abbreviated Pa: 1 Pa $= 1$ N/m². As an example, $Y = 5 \times 10^6$ Pa for the rubber in a typical rubber band, while $Y = 2 \times 10^{11}$ Pa for steel. So compared to the force required to stretch a rubber band, the force required to stretch by the same amount a steel rod of the same cross-sectional area and length would be $(2 \times 10^{11})/(5 \times 10^6) = 4 \times 10^4$ times greater. Materials with different values of Y are found in the human body (Figure 9-6).

> **? Got the Concept? 9-1   Compare the Spring Constants**
>
> Rank the following four rods in order of how easy they are to stretch, from easiest to most difficult. All four rods are made of the same material. If any two rods are equally easy to stretch, say so. (a) A rod 5.00 cm long with cross-sectional area 2.00 mm²; (b) a rod 2.50 cm long with cross-sectional area 2.00 mm²; (c) a rod 5.00 cm long with cross-sectional area 1.00 mm²; (d) a rod 2.50 cm long with cross-sectional area 1.00 mm².

The anterior cruciate ligament (ACL) has a moderate value of Young's modulus: $Y =$ about 10^8 Pa for tension.

Quadriceps muscles

Femur

Anterior cruciate ligament

Meniscus

Fibula

Tibia

The meniscus, which is compressed between the femur and the tibia, has a small value of Young's modulus: $Y =$ about 10^6 Pa for compression, comparable to the silicone rubber nipple of a baby's pacifier.

An ACL is about 1/2000 as stiff as a steel rod ($Y = 2 \times 10^{11}$ Pa) of the same dimensions, but 20 times stiffer than a rubber band ($Y = 5 \times 10^6$ Pa). Hence your knee can bend freely (which an ACL of steel would not allow) without letting your tibia flop around loosely (as would happen with an ACL of rubber).

Figure 9-6 Young's modulus in the knee Comparing the values of Young's modulus for some common materials to the values for two components of the human knee.

Relating Stress and Strain

Here's a useful way to rewrite Hooke's law for an object under tension or compression. This will also help us define *stress* and *strain* more precisely. First we substitute k from Equation 9-2 into Equation 9-1.

$$F = \left(Y\frac{A}{L_0} \right)\Delta L$$

Then we divide both sides by the cross-sectional area A:

Tensile or compressive stress on the object: applied force F divided by the object's cross-sectional area A

Young's modulus Y tells you how stiff the material is of which the object is made: Larger Y means stiffer.

Hooke's law for an object under tension or compression (9-3)

$$\frac{F}{A} = Y\frac{\Delta L}{L_0}$$

Tensile or compressive strain of the object: resulting change in length ΔL divided by the object's relaxed length L_0

Figure 9-7 depicts the quantities included in Equation 9-3. The ratio F/A, equal to the force *per area* exerted on each end of the object, is called the **tensile stress** (if the object is being stretched) or **compressive stress** (if the object is being squeezed). Like Young's modulus, stress has units of newtons per square meter (N/m^2), or pascals (Pa).

The ratio $\Delta L/L_0$ that appears on the right-hand side of Equation 9-3 is called the **tensile strain** or **compressive strain**: It equals the distance that the object stretches or shrinks expressed as a fraction of its relaxed length. Tensile or compressive strain is a length divided by another length, so it's a dimensionless quantity.

Equation 9-3 tells us that we can express Hooke's law for tension or compression as follows:

$$(\text{Tensile or compressive stress}) =$$
(9-4) $$(\text{Young's modulus}) \times (\text{tensile or compressive strain})$$

That is, ***stress and strain are directly proportional,*** and the constant of proportionality is Young's modulus. This gives us an alternative way to interpret Figure 9-5. Compared to the object under tension in Figure 9-5b, the object in Figure 9-5c is under one-half the tensile stress (the force is the same but the cross-sectional area is twice as great). Hence the tensile strain is also reduced by one-half: Both objects have the same relaxed length L_0, so the object in Figure 9-5c stretches only half as far as the object in Figure 9-5b. The objects in Figures 9-5b and 9-5d have the same force at each end and the same cross-sectional area, so both objects are under the same tensile stress and the tensile strain is the same for both. Since the object in Figure 9-5d is twice as long, it stretches twice as far as the object in Figure 9-5b so that the ratio of the stretch distance to the relaxed length is the same.

Here's an analogy that illustrates the importance of the ratio of applied force (F) to the area over which it's applied (A). Consider how it feels to stand barefoot on a floor compared to how it might feel to stand barefoot on the head of a nail. In both cases the force of the supporting surface on you is equal to your weight, so the force F is the same. When that force is applied over the relatively large surface area of your feet, so F/A is small and there is little compressive stress on your foot, you will be comfortable. But if you stand on the small surface area of the nail head so F/A is large, it will definitely hurt!

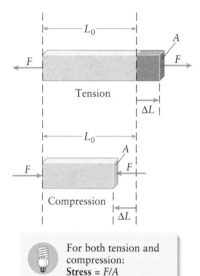

For both tension and compression:
Stress = F/A
Strain = ΔL/L₀
Hooke's law: Stress = Y × Strain

Figure 9-7 Stress and strain for tension or compression Hooke's law relates the stress on an object to the resulting strain of the object.

? Got the Concept? 9-2 Stress, Strain, and Young's Modulus

You apply the same force to each end of two rods of identical cross-sectional area. Both rods obey Hooke's law. Rod #1, made of material P, stretches 1.00 mm. Rod #2, made of material Q, stretches 2.00 mm. Which material has the greater value of Young's modulus? (a) Material P; (b) material Q; (c) they both have the same Young's modulus; (d) not enough information given to decide. *Hint:* Read the details of this question carefully.

Watch Out! Hooke's law has important limitations.

Hooke's law in Equation 9-3 applies *only* when the tensile strain is small, that is, when the change in length is small relative to the overall initial length. In Section 9-8 we'll investigate what can happen if the strain is *not* small. Hooke's law also applies only to materials that are of a uniform composition, like a solid bar of iron. Furthermore, for metals the value of Young's modulus is the same for compression as for tension; for other materials the values for compression and tension may be very different. In Section 9-8 we'll also look at biological materials like ligaments and tendons, which are not of uniform composition and so don't obey Hooke's law very faithfully. For many purposes, however, it's a reasonable approximation to apply Hooke's law even to biological materials like these.

Take-Home Message for Section 9-2

✔ Young's modulus Y is a measure of how easy it is to stretch or compress an object.

✔ Tensile stress equals the stretching force exerted on each end of an object divided by the object's cross-sectional area. The resulting change in length relative to the relaxed length, $\Delta L / L_0$, is called the tensile strain.

✔ We use the terms compressive stress and compressive strain for the case in which an object is squeezed along a single direction rather than stretched.

✔ If an object obeys Hooke's law, stress and strain are directly proportional.

9-3 Solving stress–strain problems: Tension and compression

Let's use the ideas of Section 9-2 to solve a problem that involves an object under tension.

Example 9-1 Tensile Stress and Strain

You are doing a laboratory experiment with a specimen cut from the sternoclavicular ligament in the shoulder of a cadaver (Figure 9-8). The segment is 2.00 mm by 2.00 mm in cross section and 30.0 mm long. When you apply a force of 1.00 N to each end of the specimen, the specimen stretches by 1.20 mm. Determine (a) the tensile stress on the specimen, (b) the tensile strain of the specimen, and (c) Young's modulus for the specimen. (d) If you repeated the experiment applying the same forces to a second specimen of ligament that has the same length but is 4.00 mm by 4.00 mm in cross section, how would the answers to (a), (b), and (c) change? How far would this specimen stretch?

Figure 9-8 **Sternoclavicular ligament** Ligaments connect one bone to another in the body; the sternoclavicular ligaments connect the sternum (breastbone) to the clavicles.

Set Up

We are given the dimensions of the specimen and the force $F = 1.00$ N applied to each end. We'll find the tensile stress and tensile strain using the definitions of these quantities, and we'll find Young's modulus Y using Hooke's law for tension.

$$\text{Tensile stress} = \frac{F}{A}$$

$$\text{Tensile strain} = \frac{\Delta L}{L_0}$$

$$(\text{Tensile stress}) = (\text{Young's modulus}) \times (\text{Tensile strain}) \quad (9\text{-}3)$$

Solve

(a) The tensile stress is the applied force $F = 1.00$ N divided by the cross-sectional area. We convert millimeters to meters.

Area $A = (2.00 \text{ mm}) \times (2.00 \text{ mm})$
$$= (2.00 \times 10^{-3} \text{ m}) \times (2.00 \times 10^{-3} \text{ m}) = 4.00 \times 10^{-6} \text{ m}^2$$

$$\text{Tensile stress} = \frac{F}{A} = \frac{1.00 \text{ N}}{4.00 \times 10^{-6} \text{ m}^2}$$
$$= 2.50 \times 10^5 \text{ N/m}^2 = 2.50 \times 10^5 \text{ Pa}$$

(b) The tensile strain is the change in length $\Delta L = 1.20$ mm divided by the relaxed length $L_0 = 30.0$ mm.

$$\text{Tensile strain} = \frac{\Delta L}{L_0} = \frac{1.20 \text{ mm}}{30.0 \text{ mm}}$$
$$= 0.0400 = 4.00 \times 10^{-2}$$

(c) Rearranging Hooke's law tells us that Young's modulus for this specimen equals the tensile stress divided by the tensile strain.

$$\text{Young's modulus } Y = \frac{\text{Tensile stress}}{\text{Tensile strain}} = \frac{2.50 \times 10^5 \text{ Pa}}{4.00 \times 10^{-2}}$$
$$= 6.25 \times 10^6 \text{ Pa}$$

(d) If each of the cross-sectional dimensions doubles from 2.00 mm to 4.00 mm, the cross-sectional area A increases by a factor of $2 \times 2 = 4$, so the tensile stress is $\frac{1}{4}$ as much as the previous value of 2.50×10^5 Pa. The value of Young's modulus is *unaffected*, since this depends on the type of material and not on its dimensions. From Hooke's law, the new tensile strain equals the new tensile stress divided by Y. Since Y is the same but the tensile stress is $\frac{1}{4}$ the previous value, the tensile strain is likewise $\frac{1}{4}$ of the previous value of 4.00×10^{-2}. The new specimen therefore stretches by $\frac{1}{4}$ as much as the first one.

New cross-sectional area A
$$= (4.00 \text{ mm}) \times (4.00 \text{ mm})$$
$$= (4.00 \times 10^{-3} \text{ m}) \times (4.00 \times 10^{-3} \text{ m})$$
$$= 1.60 \times 10^{-5} \text{ m}$$

New tensile stress
$$= \frac{F}{A} = \frac{1.00 \text{ N}}{1.60 \times 10^{-5} \text{ m}^2} = 6.25 \times 10^4 \text{ N/m}^2 = 6.25 \times 10^4 \text{ Pa}$$

Young's modulus $Y = 6.25 \times 10^6$ Pa

New tensile strain
$$= \frac{\text{New tensile stress}}{\text{Young's modulus}} = \frac{6.25 \times 10^4 \text{ Pa}}{6.25 \times 10^6 \text{ Pa}} = 1.00 \times 10^{-2}$$

$$\Delta L = (\text{new tensile strain}) \times L_0 = (1.00 \times 10^{-2})(30.0 \text{ mm})$$
$$= 0.300 \text{ mm}$$

Reflect

This example emphasizes the key message of Hooke's law: For relatively small stresses the stress is proportional to the strain. Note that the value of Young's modulus for the sternoclavicular ligament is quite a bit less than that for the ACL ($Y = 1 \times 10^8$ Pa). This is because different ligaments in different parts of the body are made of different materials.

For this 2.00 mm $\times$ 2.00 mm $\times$ 30.0 mm segment of sternoclavicular ligament, can you show that a stretching force of 0.025 N would be required to increase the 30.0-mm length of the segment by 0.10%?

? Got the Concept? 9-3 Compressive Stress and Strain

A brass rod ($Y = 1 \times 10^{11}$ Pa) and a steel rod ($Y = 2 \times 10^{11}$ Pa) of the same dimensions are subjected to identical squeezing forces on their ends. (a) Which experiences the greater compressive stress, the brass rod or the steel rod?

(b) Which undergoes the greater compressive strain, the brass rod or the steel rod? (c) Which undergoes the greatest change in length, the brass rod or the steel rod?

? Got the Concept? 9-4 Tensile Stress

Four rods that obey Hooke's law are each put under tension. Rank them according to the tensile stress on each rod, from smallest to largest value. (a) A rod 50.0 cm long with cross-sectional area 1.00 mm^2 and with a 200-N force applied on each end. (b) A rod 25.0 cm long with cross-sectional area 1.00 mm^2 and with a 200-N force applied on each end. (c) A rod with cross-sectional area 2.00 mm^2 with a 100-N force applied on each end. (d) A rod with Young's modulus 2.00×10^{10} Pa and relaxed length 50.0 cm that stretches 0.025 mm due to forces on its ends.

Take-Home Message for Section 9-3

✔ In problems involving tension or compression, use Hooke's law, Equation 9-3, to relate the stress (force divided by cross-sectional area) to the strain (change in length divided by relaxed length) and Young's modulus for the material. Then solve for the unknown quantity.

9-4 An object expands or shrinks when under volume stress

We saw in Sections 9-2 and 9-3 that applied forces can cause an object to stretch or compress along its length. Applied forces can also cause changes in an object's *volume*. You can see this effect when a fire extinguisher is discharged (Figure 9-9a). Inside the fire extinguisher, the gas (which is the object in question) is under high pressure, and this pressure keeps the gas confined within the small volume of the extinguisher cylinder. When you trigger the fire extinguisher, the released gas moves into the low-pressure outside air and expands to a much larger volume. The *volume stress* on the extinguisher gas is the *change* in the pressure that pushes on the gas, and the *volume strain* is a measure of how much the volume of this gas changes in response to that pressure change.

For the gas that escapes from the fire extinguisher in Figure 9-9a, the volume stress is negative (the pressure on the gas decreases) and the volume strain is positive (the volume of the gas increases). The reverse is true for a descending scuba diver (Figure 9-9b). The deeper in the ocean she dives, the greater the pressure on her body, so the volume stress is positive (the pressure on her body increases). This causes gases within her body to compress, so their volume strain is negative (the volume of the gas decreases). These compressed gases dissolve in her body fluids. If a diver ascends too quickly, the gases may pop out of solution and form bubbles that can cause excruciating pain (a condition called *decompression sickness*). To avoid this, scuba divers are trained to return to the surface at a gradual pace so that the pressure on their bodies decreases gradually. The dissolved gases then expand slowly and can safely be exhaled.

Relating Volume Stress and Volume Strain: Hooke's Law Revisited

Let's be more quantitative about volume stress and volume strain. First, notice that every object around you has forces exerted on it by the surrounding material (Figure 9-10a). Your body has forces exerted on it by the air around you; a submerged fish has forces exerted on it by the water in which it swims; and a rock buried below Earth's surface has forces exerted on it by the surrounding dirt. The magnitude of the force per unit area on the surface of the object is called the **pressure** p. (Unfortunately, we used this same symbol in Chapter 7 for momentum. We promise never to use these two quantities in the same equation!) The units of pressure are newtons per square meter (N/m^2) or pascals (Pa). This is the same unit we used for the tensile or compressive stress: F/A, which can also be thought of as a pressure.

As Figure 9-10 illustrates, an object's volume changes when the pressure p changes. We call the pressure change Δp the **volume stress**, and we call the resulting change in volume ΔV divided by the original volume V_0—that is, the quantity $\Delta V/V_0$—the **volume strain**. If the pressure increases so that the volume stress Δp is positive, then the object shrinks, and the volume strain is negative (Figure 9-10b). If the pressure decreases so that the volume stress is negative, then the object expands, and the volume strain is positive (Figure 9-10c). Note that volume stress, like pressure, has units of N/m^2 or Pa, while volume strain is dimensionless (it's a volume divided by another volume). These are the same units as the quantities tensile stress and tensile strain that we studied in Sections 9-2 and 9-3.

Experiment shows that if the volume stress on an object is not too large, the resulting volume strain is *directly proportional* to the volume stress. That is, Hooke's law relates volume stress and strain in the same manner as it does for tensile stress and strain:

$$(\text{Volume stress}) = -(\text{Bulk modulus}) \times (\text{volume strain})$$

(9-5)

That is, *volume stress and volume strain are directly proportional.* The proportionality constant in Equation 9-5 is called the **bulk modulus** of the material of which the object is made. Like Young's modulus, the bulk modulus B has units of N/m^2 or Pa. The

(a)

Triggering a fire extinguisher releases the high-pressure gases inside the tank. The pressure is much lower outside the tank, so the gases expand.

(b)

As this scuba diver descends, the pressure on her increases. This compresses gases inside her body and makes them dissolve in her body fluids.

 Volume stress refers to the change in pressure on an object.

Volume strain refers to the change in the object's volume caused by this pressure change.

Figure 9-9 **Volume stress and strain** Volume stress involves a change in pressure. (a) A pressure decrease makes the volume increase. (b) A pressure increase makes the volume decrease.

Figure 9-10 Hooke's law for volume stress An object under volume stress obeys Hooke's law if the stress is not too great.

① Initially this object has volume V_0. It is made of a material with bulk modulus B.

② The object's surroundings exert a force of magnitude F on each area A of the object's surface. The pressure is $p = F/A$.

(a)

A F

A

F

③ If the pressure on the object changes by Δp, the object's volume changes by ΔV.

(b)   (c)

④ If the pressure increases ($\Delta p > 0$), the volume decreases ($\Delta V < 0$).

⑤ If the pressure decreases ($\Delta p < 0$), the volume increases ($\Delta V > 0$).

Volume stress = Δp
Volume strain = $\Delta V/V_0$
Hooke's law:
Volume stress = $-B \times$ volume strain

second column of Table 9-1 lists the values of the bulk modulus of various substances. The minus sign in Equation 9-5 tells us that volume stress and volume strain have opposite signs; if one is positive, the other is negative (see parts b and c of Figure 9-10).

In terms of the quantities Δp, V_0, and ΔV depicted in Figure 9-10, we can rewrite Equation 9-5 as

Hooke's law for an object under volume stress (9-6)

Volume stress on the object: change in the pressure p on all sides of the object

Bulk modulus B: How difficult it is to compress the material of which the object is made; larger B means harder to compress.

$$\Delta p = -B \frac{\Delta V}{V_0}$$

Important minus sign!
If Δp is positive, then ΔV is negative; if Δp is negative, then ΔV is positive.

Volume strain of the object: resulting change in volume ΔV divided by the object's initial volume V_0

To get more insight into the meaning of Equation 9-6, multiply both sides by $-V_0/B$ to rewrite it so that ΔV is by itself on one side of the equation:

(9-7)

$$\Delta V = -\frac{\Delta p}{B} V_0$$

Equation 9-7 says that for a given pressure change Δp and initial volume V_0, making the bulk modulus B larger makes the change in volume ΔV smaller. A material that has a relatively large bulk modulus is relatively *incompressible*, which means that its volume doesn't change much even when it experiences a large volume stress. From the entries in Table 9-1 you can see that materials such as iron and concrete have very large bulk moduli; they are hard to compress, which makes them good materials for constructing buildings. By contrast, air has a bulk modulus more than a million times smaller than that of steel and is relatively easy to compress. The human lung is made of even more compressible material: Under physiologic conditions, the bulk modulus of the human lung varies between about 1500 and 10,000 Pa in young adults and increases with age. These low values of B minimize the effort needed to make the lungs expand and contract during respiration.

Another interpretation of the bulk modulus can be gained by examining Equation 9-7 in the case when Δp is equal to B. When this happens, we see that ΔV is equal to $-V_0$. That is, the object has shrunk to zero volume! So we can think of B as the change in pressure required to completely shrink an object made of that material. It's pretty challenging to shrink most objects to a point that has zero volume. That's one reason B is so large. If Δp is equal to $-B$, then ΔV is equal to V_0. That is, the volume of the object has doubled. So bulk modulus can also be interpreted as the change in pressure required for an object to double its volume.

? Got the Concept? 9-5   Volume Stress and Volume Strain

Two identical balloons are filled to the same size, one with water and one with air. When the two balloons are subjected to the same volume stress (the same force per unit surface area pushing in on the balloon), which of the two will exhibit the larger change in volume: (a) the water-filled balloon or (b) the air-filled balloon?

? Got the Concept? 9-6   Pressure and Force

You apply a pressure of $5.00 \times 10^6 \, \text{N/m}^2$ on all sides of a sphere of radius 2.00 m. What is the net force that is exerted on the sphere as a result? (a) 6.28×10^7 N; (b) 1.68×10^8 N; (c) 2.51×10^8 N; (d) zero.

Take-Home Message for Section 9-4

✔ Volume stress equals the *change* in pressure on an object.

✔ An object under volume stress either expands (if the stress is negative) or contracts (if the stress is positive); the volume strain is the change in the object's volume divided by its initial volume.

✔ If an object obeys Hooke's law, volume stress and volume strain are directly proportional; the constant of proportionality is the bulk modulus B for the material of which the object is made.

9-5 Solving stress–strain problems: Volume stress

In the following examples we'll look at two problems that involve volume stress and strain. Note that the ideas of volume stress and strain apply equally well to objects that are gases, liquids, and solids.

√x̄ *See the Math Tutorial for more information on geometry*

Example 9-2 A Submerged Cannonball

A solid iron cannonball falls into the Pacific near the Galapagos Islands, where the ocean is 2400 m deep and the pressure is 2.40×10^7 Pa at the bottom. (By contrast, air pressure at the surface is 1.01×10^5 Pa.) By what percentage does the cannonball shrink in volume as it sinks to the bottom?

Set Up

We use Hooke's law, Equation 9-6, to find the volume strain $\Delta V/V_0$ of the cannonball due to the additional pressure exerted on it (the volume stress Δp). Since $\Delta V/V_0$ expresses the change in volume as a fraction, we can convert it to a percentage by multiplying it by 100.

Hooke's law for an object under volume stress:

$$\Delta p = -B\frac{\Delta V}{V_0} \qquad (9\text{-}6)$$

cannonball at surface
$p = 1.01 \times 10^5$ Pa,
volume V_0

submerged cannonball
$p = 2.40 \times 10^7$ Pa,
volume $V = ?$

Solve

The volume stress is the difference between the pressure at the bottom of the ocean and the pressure at the surface.

Volume stress Δp
= (pressure at bottom) − (pressure at surface)
= 2.40×10^7 Pa − 1.01×10^5 Pa = 2.39×10^7 Pa

Use the value of B for iron from Table 9-1 and solve for $\Delta V/V_0$. Then convert this to a percentage.

$$\frac{\Delta V}{V_0} = -\frac{\Delta p}{B} = -\frac{2.39 \times 10^7 \, \text{Pa}}{1.7 \times 10^{11} \, \text{Pa}}$$
$$= -1.4 \times 10^{-4}$$

Percentage change in volume:

$$\frac{\Delta V}{V_0} \times 100\% = -1.4 \times 10^{-4} \times 100\%$$
$$= -0.014\%$$

Reflect

The minus sign tells us that $\Delta V < 0$ and so the volume of the cannonball decreases. Because iron has such a large bulk modulus B, even this immense pressure increase causes only a miniscule change in the cannonball's volume, just 14/1000 of 1%.

Note that while the volume stress Δp is given to three significant figures, the answer has only two significant figures. Can you see why? (See the discussion of significant figures in Section 1-4 if you're not sure.)

Example 9-3 Bubbles Rising

A scuba diver 10.0 m below the surface of a lake releases a spherical air bubble 2.00 cm in radius. As it rises to the surface, the pressure exerted by the surrounding water on the bubble decreases by 9.80×10^4 Pa due to the decreasing amount of water above the bubble. This pressure decrease causes the bubble to expand. Use Hooke's law to find the radius of the bubble as it breaks the surface.

Set Up

As in Example 9-2, we use the Hooke's law relationship between volume stress and volume strain, Equation 9-6. This gives us the change in volume ΔV versus the initial volume V_0. We assume that the amount of air in the bubble doesn't change as it rises. Thus, the change in volume of the bubble is due only to the volume stress, which equals the change in water pressure pushing on the outside of the bubble.

$$\Delta p = -B\frac{\Delta V}{V_0} \quad (9\text{-}6)$$

Volume stress $= \Delta p$
$\quad = -9.80 \times 10^4$ Pa
(negative because the pressure on the outside of the bubble decreases)

submerged air bubble

radius
$R_0 = 2.00$ cm

air bubble at surface

volume change $= \Delta V$

radius
$R = ?$

Solve

Use the bulk modulus of air from Table 9-1 and the value of Δp to solve for the volume strain $\Delta V/V_0$. The volume strain is positive because the bubble expands.

Bulk modulus of air from Table 9-1:
$B = 1.41 \times 10^5$ Pa, so

$$\frac{\Delta V}{V_0} = -\frac{\Delta p}{B} = -\frac{(-9.80 \times 10^4 \text{ Pa})}{1.41 \times 10^5 \text{ Pa}} = 0.695$$

Next we find the initial volume V_0 of the bubble using the formula for a sphere of radius $R_0 = 2.00$ cm (see Math Tutorial). The final volume of the bubble is the initial volume V_0 plus the volume change ΔV.

Initial volume of a spherical bubble:

$$V_0 = \frac{4\pi}{3}R_0^3 = \frac{4\pi}{3}(2.00 \text{ cm})^3$$
$$= 33.5 \text{ cm}^3$$

Final volume:

$$V = V_0 + \Delta V = V_0\left(1 + \frac{\Delta V}{V_0}\right)$$

$$= (33.5 \text{ cm}^3)(1 + 0.695) = (33.5 \text{ cm}^3)(1.695)$$
$$= 56.8 \text{ cm}^3$$

Solve for the final radius R of the bubble using the formula $V = (4\pi/3)R^3$ for the volume of a sphere of radius R.

$$V = \frac{4\pi}{3}R^3$$

$$R = \sqrt[3]{\frac{3V}{4\pi}} = \sqrt[3]{\frac{3(56.8 \text{ cm}^3)}{4\pi}} = 2.38 \text{ cm}$$

Reflect

Our calculation shows that as the bubble rises to the surface, its volume increases by a factor of 1.695 and its radius increases from 2.00 cm to 2.38 cm. Consider the implications of this result on decompression sickness (described in Section 9-4). When a diver ascends too quickly, not only do bubbles form, but also they get bigger as the diver rises to the surface.

It turns out that the answers we calculated here aren't exactly correct. The reason is that the air pressure *inside* the bubble also decreases as it expands, and as a result the bubble expands a bit less than we have calculated. A more detailed calculation shows that the volume actually increases by a factor of 1.623 and the final radius is 2.35 cm. Our calculations with Hooke's law are pretty close, however, which shows that this law can give quite useful results.

Take-Home Message for Section 9-5

✔ In problems involving volume stress and strain, use Hooke's law, Equation 9-6, to relate the stress (the change in pressure on an object) to the strain (change in the object's volume divided by its original volume) and the bulk modulus of the material. Then solve for the unknown quantity.

9-6 A solid object changes shape when under shear stress

When you run, play sports, or do any sort of physical activity, blood flow increases to your active tissues. The arteries need to expand or *dilate* to accommodate this increased blood flow. In addition to the dilation caused by increased blood pressure pushing outward against arterial walls, the deformation of endothelial cells that line the inside of the artery also leads to dilation of the vessel (Figure 9-11a, b). The force of blood pushing on the exposed surfaces of the cells deforms them in the direction of blood flow (Figure 9-11c). Because the cells are firmly attached to the arterial wall, the change in shape is neither a stretch nor a compression. Instead, the cells deform in a way similar to a cube of gelatin dessert being pushed parallel to the top face. In response to this deformation, the endothelial cells release nitric oxide gas. This gas diffuses to the muscle cells in the arterial wall and causes them to relax. As a result the artery dilates, thus relieving the stress on the endothelial cells (Figure 9-11d).

(a) Diagram of an artery

(b) Normal blood flow through the artery
— Endothelium
Blood →
— Endothelium

(c) Increased blood flow deforms the endothelial cells
F ←
→ F
Friction caused by blood rushing past
→ F
F ←
Endothelium held in place by force from arterial wall

(d) In response, surrounding muscle allows the artery to expand, relieving stress on the endothelium

Shear stress refers to forces that deform an object [like the endothelium in (c)] without making it expand or contract. **Shear strain** refers to the change in the object's shape caused by this stress.

Figure 9-11 Shear stress and strain When blood flow through an artery increases due to physical exertion, the endothelium deforms without becoming larger or smaller. This is an example of shear stress.

The kind of stress shown in Figure 9-11c is called **shear**. Unlike tensile stress and compressive stress (which are applied along a line within the object) or volume stress (which is applied over the entire surface of the object), shear stress is caused by forces applied *parallel* (tangential) to the faces of an object. As Figure 9-11c shows, these forces are *offset* from each other: They do not act along the same line. An object is said to experience shear when one face is made to move or slide relative to the opposite face.

Like the other types of stress we've encountered, **shear stress** is defined as a force per unit area. As an example, consider the object shown in Figure 9-12a. In Figure 9-12b opposite forces of the same magnitude $F_\parallel$ are applied to the upper and lower surfaces of this object. The subscript $\parallel$ means "parallel," and reminds us that these forces act parallel to the surfaces as in Figure 9-12b. (For the endothelial cells depicted in Figure 9-11c, one force is exerted by the blood that flows past the cells. The other force is exerted by the arterial wall to which the cells are attached.) The shear stress associated with these forces is the force magnitude $F_\parallel$ divided by the area A over which this force is applied, or $F_\parallel/A$. Just like tensile and volume stress, the units of shear stress are N/m^2 or Pa.

Figure 9-12 Shear stress and strain
Shear stress involves oppositely-directed forces that act on different surfaces of an object. These offset forces cause a twisting deformation (shear strain).

① This object has height h. Its upper and lower surfaces each have area A. It is made of a material with shear modulus S.

② Apply a force of magnitude $F_\parallel$ parallel to the upper surface...

③ ...and apply an opposite force of the same magnitude $F_\parallel$ parallel to the lower surface. Note that the two forces are offset (they do not act along the same line).

④ As a result of these forces, the upper and lower surfaces move a distance x relative to each other.

Shear stress = $F_\parallel/A$
Strain = x/h
Hooke's law:
Shear stress = S × shear strain

Figure 9-12 shows that this shear stress causes the object to deform. We measure the amount of deformation by the **shear strain**, which is the displacement of one surface relative to the other (shown as x in Figure 9-12b) divided by the distance between the surfaces (in Figure 9-12b, the distance h). Thus the shear strain equals x/h.

Experiment shows that for most materials the shear strain is proportional to the shear stress that produces it, provided that the stress is not too great. This is yet another version of Hooke's law, this time for shear:

(9-8)   Shear stress = Shear modulus × Shear strain

The **shear modulus** S is a measure of the rigidity and resistance to deformation of a material. The more rigid a material is, the larger its shear modulus. For example, the shear modulus for steel is about 7.8×10^{10} Pa, while that of rubber (which is much more deformable than steel) is only about 10^6 Pa.

We can use the above definitions of shear stress and shear strain (shown in Figure 9-12) to rewrite Equation 9-8 as

Hooke's law for an object under shear stress (9-9)

Shear stress on the object: force $F_\parallel$ applied to each of two opposite surfaces divided by the area A of each surface

Shear modulus S: How difficult it is to deform the material of which the object is made: larger S means more difficult.

$$\frac{F_\parallel}{A} = S\frac{x}{h}$$

Shear strain of the object: distance x that the two surfaces move relative to each other divided by the distance h between the surfaces

! Watch Out! There is no shear modulus for a liquid or gas.

While liquids and gases can sustain a *volume* stress that causes a change in volume, they cannot sustain a *shear* stress due to forces applied tangentially to their surfaces. Instead of deforming like the object shown in Figure 9-12, a force tangential to the surface of a liquid or gas causes it to flow rather than deform. This means that the shear modulus is defined *only* for solids.

? Got the Concept? 9-7   Shear Stress and Shear Strain

Figure 9-13 shows three objects that are all made of the same material. The forces applied to the three objects all have the same magnitude. (a) Rank the objects in order of the shear stress acting on them, from greatest to least. (b) Rank the objects in order of the shear strain that they will undergo, from greatest to least.

Figure 9-13 **Three objects under shear stress** The same forces act on all three objects, all of which are made of material with the same shear modulus. Which one experiences the greatest strain?

Take-Home Message for Section 9-6

✔ Shear stress occurs when a force is applied parallel to the face of an object and causes that face to move relative to the opposite face. Shear strain describes the extent to which an object is deformed by shear stress.

✔ The shear modulus measures the rigidity of a material and is only defined for solids.

9-7 Solving stress–strain problems: Shear stress

Here are two examples of how to solve problems involving shear stress and shear strain.

Example 9-4 Endothelial Cells and Shear

Endothelial cells in an artery experience shear stress as a result of blood flow. In an *in vitro* study of arterial endothelial cells from pigs, the shear strain was observed to be proportional to the shear stress when this stress was $8.6 \times 10^3 \, \text{N/m}^2$. The shear modulus of a typical endothelial cell is $2.0 \times 10^4 \, \text{N/m}^2$. Figure 9-14 shows a normal endothelial cell and a cell experiencing shear. At what angle ϕ does one surface of a cell move relative to the opposite surface? (The angle ϕ is labeled in Figure 9-14.)

Figure 9-14 **Shear stress on endothelial cells** A normal endothelial cell (left) and a cell experiencing shear stress (right).

Set Up

The observation that shear stress and shear strain are proportional means that Hooke's law applies in this situation, so we can use Equation 9-9. We are given the values of the shear stress and the shear modulus, so we can find the ratio x/h (the shear strain). Once we know this ratio, we'll use trigonometry to determine the angle ϕ shown in Figure 9-14.

Hooke's law for shear:

$$\frac{F_{\parallel}}{A} = S\frac{x}{h} \qquad (9\text{-}9)$$

Solve

Rearrange Equation 9-9 to calculate the shear strain. Then substitute $F_{\parallel}/A = 8.6 \times 10^3$ Pa for the shear stress and $S = 2.0 \times 10^4$ Pa for the shear modulus.

Divide both sides of Equation 9-9 by S:

$$\frac{x}{h} = \frac{(F_{\parallel}/A)}{S} = \frac{8.6 \times 10^3 \text{ Pa}}{2.0 \times 10^4 \text{ Pa}} = 0.43$$

The lengths x and h make up two sides of a right triangle with included angle ϕ. The tangent of ϕ equals the opposite side (x) divided by the adjacent side (h). Use this to solve for ϕ.

$$\tan \phi = \frac{x}{h} = 0.43$$

So ϕ is the angle whose tangent is 0.43, which means that ϕ is the inverse tangent of 0.43:

$$\phi = \tan^{-1} 0.43 = 23°$$

Reflect

The value of $\phi = 23°$ is quite large, which means that these endothelial cells undergo a dramatic change in shape (see Figure 9-14). This illustrates that endothelial cells in arteries, and the vascular system in general, are *very* sensitive to shear stress due to fluid flow. Note that, as we mention in Section 9-6, endothelial cells release nitric oxide gas when under shear stress; this gas release causes the underlying muscle to relax, thus expanding the artery. This increases blood flow while reducing the flow speed and relieving the shear stress on the endothelial cells—a classic example of negative feedback in physiology.

Example 9-5 Earthquake Damage

The dedication plate mounted to the base of a building was deformed during an earthquake. The plate, made from a metal alloy of shear modulus 4.00×10^{10} Pa, was originally 80.0 cm high, 50.0 cm long, and 5.00 mm thick. The earthquake shifted the top surface of the plate 0.100 mm relative to the bottom surface. What shear force did the plate experience during the earthquake?

Set Up

The displacement of the two surfaces of the plate ($x = 0.100$ mm) is small compared to the distance between them ($h = 80.0$ cm), so the shear strain x/h is very small. This suggests that we can use Hooke's law for shear, Equation 9-9. We are given the value of the shear modulus ($S = 4.00 \times 10^{10}$ Pa) and the dimensions of the plate, so we can solve for the shear force $F_{\parallel}$:

Hooke's law for shear:

$$\frac{F_{\parallel}}{A} = S\frac{x}{h} \qquad (9\text{-}9)$$

Solve

First calculate the shear stress $F_{\parallel}/A$ using Equation 9-9, making sure to convert to SI units.

$$\frac{F_{\parallel}}{A} = S\frac{x}{h} = (4.00 \times 10^{10} \text{ Pa})\left(\frac{0.100 \text{ mm}}{80.0 \text{ cm}}\right)$$

$$= (4.00 \times 10^{10} \text{ N/m}^2)\left(\frac{1.00 \times 10^{-4} \text{ m}}{0.800 \text{ m}}\right)$$

$$= (4.00 \times 10^{10} \text{ N/m}^2)(1.25 \times 10^{-4})$$

$$= 5.00 \times 10^{6} \text{ N/m}^2$$

The area A over which the force is applied is the area of the top or bottom surface of the plate. Multiply the shear stress by A to calculate the force magnitude $F_\parallel$:

$$A = (50.0 \text{ cm})(5.0 \text{ mm}) = (0.500 \text{ m})(5.00 \times 10^{-3} \text{ m})$$
$$= 2.50 \times 10^{-3} \text{ m}$$

$$F_\parallel = \frac{F_\parallel}{A}A = (5.00 \times 10^6 \text{ N/m}^2)(2.50 \times 10^{-3} \text{ m})$$
$$= 1.25 \times 10^4 \text{ N}$$

Reflect

The shear force was 12,500 N, or about 1.25 tons! This force is about the same as the weight of a small car. It takes a *lot* of force to deform metal.

Take-Home Message for Section 9-7

✔ In problems involving shear stress and strain, use Hooke's law, Equation 9-9, to relate the shear stress, the shear strain, and the shear modulus of the material. (It's very helpful to draw a picture of the situation.) Then solve for the unknown quantity.

9-8 Objects deform permanently or fail when placed under too much stress

Your arteries, ears, nose, and ligaments, as well as many other structures in your body, can be stretched, compressed, or bent without deforming them permanently. Somewhat like a rubber band, after you stretch your earlobe or squeeze the skin on your forearm by applying a modest force, it quickly returns to its original shape. Structures with this property are called **elastic**. (We used the term *elastic* in Chapter 7 to refer to collisions in which mechanical energy is conserved. Our new definition is really the same. If two elastic objects collide with each other, they may deform during the collision but will spring back to their original shapes afterward. Hence no energy is used up during the collision, and the total mechanical energy is conserved.) But if a structure is deformed too much, it will not spring back and may even tear or fracture. This is what can happen when too much force is applied to a human knee, making the anterior cruciate ligament (ACL) stretch too far and creating a tear in the ACL. How can we describe what happens when a structure or material is deformed so much that it is no longer elastic?

From Elastic to Plastic to Failure

If the tensile stress on an object is increased so that the change in the object's length ΔL becomes large relative to its initial length L_0, the deformation of the object becomes permanent. This is what happens if you a stretch a metal spring too far: The spring is permanently deformed and can no longer return to its original shape (Figure 9-15). The tensile stress at which this occurs is called the **yield strength**. If the tensile stress exceeds the yield strength and the object deforms permanently, we say that the object has become **plastic**.

Figure 9-15 A permanently deformed spring This spring has been stretched so far that it no longer returns to its original coiled shape. The metal of which the spring is made became plastic during the stretch.

⚠ Watch Out! When is a plastic object plastic?

The term *plastic* may seem like a strange one to use to describe objects that don't spring back to their original shape. After all, most objects that we think of as "plastic"—such as a plastic fork or a compact disc—are actually quite springy. But to make these objects the plastic material is heated so that it can flow into a mold, then cooled so that it solidifies into the desired shape. Strictly speaking, the material is only "plastic" when it is flowing into its new shape.

Figure 9-16 shows elastic and plastic behavior in an idealized graph of tensile stress versus tensile strain. In the elastic regime the tensile strain is *reversible*: If you increase the amount of stress by a small amount, then release that extra stress (say, by pulling a little harder on the ends of a spring, then easing off on the pull), the object will relax to the length it had before you increased the stress. By contrast, in the plastic region the

In the plastic region, the object is permanently deformed: It no longer springs back to its original length when the stress is released.

In this elastic region, the object springs back to its original length when the stress is released.

This idealized material obeys Hooke's law in the elastic region: Stress and strain are directly proportional, so the graph is a straight line.

Figure 9-16 Elastic behavior, plastic behavior, and failure This graph shows tensile stress versus tensile strain for an idealized material.

tensile strain is *irreversible*. If you pull a little harder on the ends of the object, it stretches a bit more and stays stretched even after you stop pulling.

When the strain on an object is large enough, it undergoes **failure**: The structure of the material starts to lose its integrity, which eventually leads to the object breaking apart. The maximum tensile stress that the material can withstand before failure is called the **ultimate strength**.

Biological Tissue: From Elastic to Failure

Most biological tissue, including your skin and ligaments—such as the anterior cruciate ligament, or ACL, in your knee (Figure 9-6) and the sternoclavicular ligament in your shoulder (Figure 9-8)—responds to increased tensile stress in a different way than the idealized material graphed in Figure 9-16. This tissue does *not* have a plastic regime: Once a stress is applied that exceeds the ability of biological tissue to spring back to its initial shape, it undergoes partial or complete failure. You can demonstrate this by holding each end of a string bean—a simple biological structure—with your fingertips and trying to pull the two ends apart. If you pull too hard, the string bean will break in two rather than acquire a permanent stretch.

The reason why biological tissue is different from metals has to do with its composition. As we discussed in Section 9-2, stretchable biological materials are *not* uniform but are composed of a combination of tiny fibrils of collagen and elastin (see Figure 9-17a). As a result, these materials do *not* obey Hooke's law if the tensile stress is small. If the tensile stress is too great, the fibrils do not acquire a permanent stretch but start breaking apart (Figure 9-17b).

Figure 9-18 shows an idealized curve of stress versus strain for biological tissue. The curve is not a straight line for small stresses (region I in Figure 9-18), which means that stress and strain are not directly proportional and Hooke's law is not strictly obeyed. Hooke's law *is* more valid for moderate stresses (region II in Figure 9-18). If the stress is too great and the elastin fibers begin to tear, the tissue fails (region III in Figure 9-18). This may be referred to as *fracture*, *rupture*, or *tearing*. That's what happens when an athlete suffers a knee injury and ends up with a partially or completely torn ACL.

(a)

Short section of a collagen fibril

Collagen molecule

50 nm

300 × 1.5 nm

1.5 nm

(b) Elastic fiber

Single elastin molecule

Cross-link

Stretch

Relax

Figure 9-17 Microscopic structure of biological tissue Connective tissues get their rigidity from the protein collagen and their elastic properties from the protein elastin.

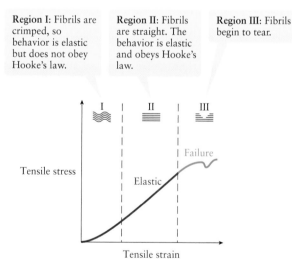

Region I: Fibrils are crimped, so behavior is elastic but does not obey Hooke's law.

Region II: Fibrils are straight. The behavior is elastic and obeys Hooke's law.

Region III: Fibrils begin to tear.

Tensile stress

I   II   III

Elastic

Failure

Tensile strain

Figure 9-18 Elastic behavior and failure for biological materials This graph shows tensile stress versus tensile strain for typical biological materials. Because such materials are made of elastin and collagen fibrils, this behavior is very different from that of the idealized material shown in Figure 9-16.

! Watch Out! Materials can be elastic yet not obey Hooke's law.

While biological tissue does not obey Hooke's law in the region of low tensile stress (region I in Figure 9-18), it is nonetheless elastic in this region. That's because it springs back to its original length when the tensile stress is removed.

The same is true for the larger stresses within region II in Figure 9-18, in which Hooke's law is more nearly valid. An object that obeys Hooke's law is necessarily elastic, but an elastic object does *not* necessarily obey Hooke's law!

In this section we've considered only the effects of *tensile* stress. Failure can also occur when an object is under compression (think of what would happen if you were to push the two ends of a peeled banana together). It can also happen under shear (which is what happens when you hold a piece of paper in your hands and tear it in two).

? Got the Concept? 9-8 Hooke's Law and Elastic Behavior

To stretch a certain object by 1.00 cm takes a force of 25.0 N applied at each end. To stretch the same object by 2.00 cm takes a force of 60.0 N applied at each end. In both cases the object returns to its initial length when the force is released. (a) Does the object obey Hooke's law? (b) Does the object display elastic behavior when the 60.0-N forces are applied?

Take-Home Message for Section 9-8

✔ When an object is subjected to a stress that results in a relatively small strain, it deforms but returns to its initial shape after the stress is removed (the elastic regime).

✔ If the stress on an object is increased so that the change in length becomes large relative to the object's initial length,

the deformation of the object becomes irreversible (the plastic regime) and represents the onset of failure, which eventually leads to the object breaking apart.

✔ Biological materials do not have a plastic regime: As the stress is increased, they go from the elastic regime directly to failure.

9-9 Solving stress–strain problems: From elastic behavior to failure

In the following three examples we'll examine the stress–strain behavior of a typical biological material, the anterior cruciate ligament (ACL) found in the human knee.

Example 9-6 Human ACL I: Maximum Force

A study of the properties of human ACLs revealed that the ultimate strength for an ACL in a younger person is, on average, 3.8×10^7 Pa. A typical cross-sectional area of the ACL is 4.4×10^{-5} m². What is the force exerted on the ACL when the tensile stress is at the maximum value that the ACL can withstand?

Set Up

The ultimate strength of an object is the maximum tensile stress, or maximum force per area, that the object can withstand. Use F_{max} to denote this maximum force, which is what we want to find. We use the definition of tensile stress from Equation 9-3 to relate the ultimate strength to the cross-sectional area A and the force F_{max}.

$$\text{Tensile stress} = \frac{F}{A}$$

so

$$\text{Ultimate strength} = \text{maximum tensile stress} = \frac{F_{max}}{A}$$

area $A = 4.4 \times 10^{-5}$ m²

F_{max} F_{max}

Solve

Rearrange the equation for ultimate strength to solve for F_{max}. Then substitute the known values and use 1 Pa = 1 N/m². Remember to convert to SI units.

$$\begin{aligned}
F_{max} &= (\text{ultimate strength}) \times A \\
&= (3.8 \times 10^7 \text{ Pa}) \times (4.4 \times 10^{-5} \text{ m}^2) \\
&= (3.8 \times 10^7 \text{ N/m}^2) \times (4.4 \times 10^{-5} \text{ m}^2) \\
&= 1.7 \times 10^3 \text{ N}
\end{aligned}$$

Reflect

Our result shows that a single knee ligament can withstand a sizeable force of 1.7×10^3 N. That's greater than the weight of the heaviest professional players in American football, those who play offensive tackle, who have an average mass of about 150 kg. Note that in normal use (walking, running, and so on) the forces that act on the ACL are only a fraction of F_{max}, the maximum force that the ACL can withstand.

Offensive tackle:

mass $m = 150$ kg

weight $mg = (150 \text{ kg})(9.80 \text{ m/s}^2)$

$= 1.5 \times 10^3$ N

Example 9-7 Human ACL II: Breaking Strain

A study of the properties of human anterior cruciate ligaments found that at the point of ACL failure in a younger person, the tensile strain of the ACL is approximately 0.60. The typical length of the ACLs studied was 2.7 cm. How far can the ACL stretch before it breaks?

Set Up

When an object is under tensile stress, its tensile strain equals how far it stretches ΔL divided by its total unstretched length L_0 (Equation 9-3). We know the tensile strain at the point at which the ACL fails (when the ACL is stretched as far as possible) as well as its unstretched length, so we can solve for its maximum stretch ΔL_{max}.

$$\text{Tensile strain} = \frac{\Delta L}{L_0}$$

so

Tensile strain at failure

$$= \text{maximum tensile strain} = \frac{\Delta L_{max}}{L_0}$$

Solve

Rearrange the equation for the tensile strain at failure and solve for ΔL_{max}.

$\Delta L_{max} = (\text{tensile strain at failure}) \times L_0$

$= (0.60)(2.7 \text{ cm}) = 1.6 \text{ cm}$

Reflect

If 1.6 cm (almost two-thirds of an inch) seems like a large stretch, it is! A maximum tensile stretch of 0.60 means that the ACL can stretch by 60% before failing.

Example 9-8 Human ACL III: The Point of No Return

A study of the properties of human anterior cruciate ligaments found that the **yield strength** of the ACL of a younger person is approximately 3.3×10^7 Pa. By what percentage of its initial length can the ACL stretch before it will no longer return to its original length intact? Use $Y_{ACL} = 1.1 \times 10^8$ Pa as the value for Young's modulus for an ACL.

Set Up

The yield strength of an object is the tensile stress beyond which the object is no longer elastic. In Figure 9-17, which shows a representative stress–strain curve for biological tissue, this corresponds to the boundary between region II and region III. While Hooke's law (Equation 9-4) is not strictly valid throughout the elastic regions I and II, we can use it to estimate the tensile strain at the point where the tensile stress equals the yield strength. This and the definition of tensile strain will tell us the percentage increase in the length of the ACL.

Hooke's law for tension expressed in terms of stress and strain:

Tensile stress

$= \text{Young's modulus} \times \text{tensile strain} \qquad (9-4)$

$$\text{Tensile strain} = \frac{\Delta L}{L_0}$$

Solve

We first solve Hooke's law, Equation 9-4, for the value of the tensile strain of the ACL when the tensile stress equals the yield strength.

$$\text{Tensile strain} = \frac{\text{tensile stress}}{\text{Young's modulus}}$$

Tensile stress = yield strength = 3.3×10^7 Pa

Young's modulus = $Y_{ACL} = 1.1 \times 10^8$ Pa

Hence when the tensile stress equals the yield strength,

$$\text{Tensile strain} = \frac{3.3 \times 10^7 \text{ Pa}}{1.1 \times 10^8 \text{ Pa}} = 0.30$$

Convert the tensile strain to a percentage increase in the length of the ACL.

$$\text{Tensile strain} = \frac{\Delta L}{L_0} = \text{fractional change in the length of the ACL}$$

To convert a fraction to a percentage, multiply by 100%:

$$\text{Tensile strain} = (0.30)(100\%) = 30\%$$

Reflect

We have found that the human ACL is elastic enough to withstand being stretched by a factor of 30% while still being able to return undamaged to its normal length. In Example 9-7 we discovered that a human ACL tears completely when stretched by about 60%. For strains between 30% and 60% some damage—for example, a partial tear—can occur.

Take-Home Message for Section 9-9

✔ The ideas of stress and strain are valid even for materials that do not obey Hooke's law. In this case we can still use Hooke's law to get rough estimates of the strain that corresponds to a given stress.

Key Terms

bulk modulus	pressure	tensile stress
compression	shear	tension
compressive strain	shear modulus	ultimate strength
compressive stress	shear strain	volume strain
elastic	shear stress	volume stress
failure	spring constant	yield strength
Hooke's law	strain	Young's modulus
pascal	stress	
plastic	tensile strain	

Chapter Summary

Topic	Equation or Figure
Stress and strain: An object is under stress when forces act to deform it (change its size or shape). Stress has units of force per area and is measured in pascals ($1 \text{ Pa} = 1 \text{ N/m}^2$). The amount of deformation that results is the strain, which is a dimensionless quantity.	This Achilles tendon is relaxed. This Achilles tendon is under **stress**: The muscles at its upper end exert an upward force F, and the heel bone at its lower end exerts an equally strong downward force. The tendon responds by undergoing **strain** (it stretches). (Figure 9-1) **Stress** refers to forces that act to deform an object (change its size or shape). **Strain** refers to the deformation caused by these forces.
Spring constant and material properties: The spring constant for an object, which we learned about in Chapter 6, is proportional to Young's modulus for the material and the cross-sectional area of the object, and inversely proportional to the length of the object.	... **Young's modulus** for the material from which it is made ... and the **cross-sectional area** of the surface on which the force is applied ... The **spring constant** of an object is proportional to... $k = Y\dfrac{A}{L_0}$ ... and inversely proportional to the **length** along which the force is applied. (9-2)

Tension, compression, and Hooke's law: An object is under tension if forces act to lengthen it along one dimension; it is under compression if forces act to shorten it along one dimension. If the object obeys Hooke's law, the strain is directly proportional to the stress; the constant of proportionality, called Young's modulus, depends on what the object is made of but not on its dimensions.

 For both tension and compression:
Stress = F/A
Strain = $\Delta L/L_0$
Hooke's law: Stress = $Y \times$ Strain

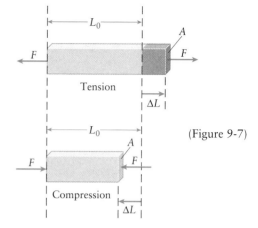

Tension

Compression

(Figure 9-7)

Volume stress and strain: An object is under volume stress if there is a *change* in the pressure p on the object. The stress is equal to the pressure change Δp. If Δp is small, Hooke's law applies and the strain (the fractional change in volume, $\Delta V/V_0$) is proportional to the stress. The proportionality constant is the bulk modulus of the material. The signs of stress and strain are opposite: Positive volume stress ($\Delta p > 0$) causes a negative volume strain ($\Delta V/V_0 < 0$) and vice versa.

(1) Initially this object has volume V_0. It is made of a material with bulk modulus B.

(2) The object's surroundings exert a force of magnitude F on each area A of the object's surface. The pressure is $p = F/A$.

(a)

(3) If the pressure on the object changes by Δp, the object's volume changes by ΔV.

(Figure 9-10)

(b)   (c)

 Volume stress = Δp
Volume strain = $\Delta V/V_0$
Hooke's law:
Volume stress = $-B \times$ volume strain

(4) If the pressure increases ($\Delta p > 0$), the volume decreases ($\Delta V < 0$).

(5) If the pressure decreases ($\Delta p < 0$), the volume increases ($\Delta V > 0$).

Shear stress and strain: An object is under shear stress if offset forces $F_\parallel$ act to twist the object's shape. If the shear stress is not too great, Hooke's law applies and the shear strain is proportional to the shear stress.

(1) This object has height h. Its upper and lower surfaces each have area A. It is made of a material with shear modulus S.

(a)

(2) Apply a force of magnitude $F_\parallel$ parallel to the upper surface...

(b)

(3) ...and apply an opposite force of the same magnitude $F_\parallel$ parallel to the lower surface. Note that the two forces are offset (they do not act along the same line).

(Figure 9-12)

 Shear stress = $F_\parallel/A$
Strain = x/h
Hooke's law:
Shear stress = $S \times$ shear strain

(4) As a result of these forces, the upper and lower surfaces move a distance x relative to each other.

Elasticity, plasticity, and failure:
Most materials return to their original size and shape when the stress is removed, provided the stress is not too great. This is called elastic behavior. If the stress is greater than a certain value, the material becomes plastic: It retains the deformation even after the stress is removed. Beyond a certain even greater value, the material undergoes failure (it ruptures or fractures). Biological materials do not become plastic but go from elastic behavior to failure if the stress is made too great.

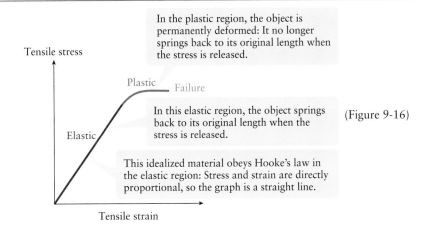

In the plastic region, the object is permanently deformed: It no longer springs back to its original length when the stress is released.

In this elastic region, the object springs back to its original length when the stress is released.

This idealized material obeys Hooke's law in the elastic region: Stress and strain are directly proportional, so the graph is a straight line.

(Figure 9-16)

Answer to What do you think? Question

(b) In Section 9-2 we learn that the amount that an object's length decreases due to compression is proportional to the compressive stress F/A, which is the force F applied (in this case, the climber's weight) divided by the object's cross-sectional area A. If the arms had one-half the diameter, they would have one-quarter the area A and the compressive stress F/A would be four times as much (assuming the climber's weight doesn't change, which means that F is unchanged). Hence her arms would shorten by four times the distance.

Answers to Got the Concept? Questions

9-1   (c), (a) and (d) [tie], (b) The easier a rod is to stretch, the smaller its spring constant k. Equation 9-2 tells us that $k = YA/L_0$. All four rods have the same Young's modulus Y (since they are all made of the same material). So the rod with the smallest value of k is the one with the smallest ratio A/L_0—that is, the one with the smallest cross-sectional area and the longest length. The values of this ratio for each of the four rods are (a) $(2.00 \text{ mm}^2)/(5.00 \text{ cm}) = 0.400 \text{ mm}^2/\text{cm}$, (b) $(2.00 \text{ mm}^2)/(2.50 \text{ cm}) = 0.800 \text{ mm}^2/\text{cm}$, (c) $(1.00 \text{ mm}^2)/(5.00 \text{ cm}) = 0.200 \text{ mm}^2/\text{cm}$, (d) $(1.00 \text{ mm}^2)/(2.50 \text{ cm}) = 0.400 \text{ mm}^2/\text{cm}$.

9-2   (d) Not enough information is given to decide. To see why not, rewrite Equation 9-3 as an equation for Young's modulus Y:

$$Y = \frac{F/A}{\Delta L/L_0} = \frac{\text{tensile stress}}{\text{tensile strain}}$$

To compare the value of Y for the two materials, we need to compare the ratio of tensile stress to tensile strain for the two rods. We are told that force F and cross-sectional area A are the same for both rods, so both are under the same tensile stress. We also know that ΔL is twice as great for rod #2 as for rod #1. But we don't know how the tensile *strain* compares for the two rods, because the statement of the question doesn't tell us anything about the relaxed lengths L_0 of the two rods. (That was the detail we asked you to look for.) So we don't have enough information to decide which material has the greater value of Y.

9-3   (a) Same for both, (b) brass rod, (c) brass rod. Each rod has the same cross-sectional area A and is subjected to forces of the same magnitude F, so the compressive *stress* F/A is the same for both. From Hooke's law, the compressive strain equals the compressive stress divided by Young's modulus Y: $\Delta L/L = (F/A)(1/Y)$. The brass rod has a smaller value of Y, so it will experience the greater compressive strain. The distance ΔL that each rod contracts equals the original length (which is the same for both rods) multiplied by the compressive strain, so the brass rod (which experiences greater strain) contracts more than the steel rod.

9-4   (c), then (d), then (a) and (b) (tie) For the first three cases, use the definition of tensile stress as force divided by cross-sectional area:

(a) Tensile stress $= \dfrac{F}{A} = \dfrac{200 \text{ N}}{(1.00 \text{ mm}^2)}\left(\dfrac{100 \text{ mm}}{1 \text{ m}}\right)^2$
$= 2.0 \times 10^6 \text{ N/m}^2$

(b) Same as (a); the length is different, but this has no effect on calculating the tensile stress

(c) Tensile stress $= \dfrac{F}{A} = \dfrac{100 \text{ N}}{(2.00 \text{ mm}^2)}\left(\dfrac{100 \text{ mm}}{1 \text{ m}}\right)^2$
$= 5.0 \times 10^5 \text{ N/m}^2$

(d) For the fourth case, we use Hooke's law, which states that

tensile stress $= $ (Young's modulus) $\times$ (tensile strain) $= Y\dfrac{\Delta L}{L_0} = $
$(2.00 \times 10^{10} \text{ Pa})\left(\dfrac{0.025 \text{ mm}}{50.0 \text{ cm}}\right)\left(\dfrac{1 \text{ cm}}{10 \text{ mm}}\right) = 1.0 \times 10^6 \text{ N/m}^2$

9-5 (b) The volume of the balloon filled with air will change the most. From Table 9-1 you can see that the bulk modulus of water is about 2×10^4 times larger than that of air. Water is therefore about 2×10^4 times *less* compressible than air.

9-6 (d) Because the pressure is the same on all sides, the forces pushing on opposite sides of the sphere are of equal magnitude but opposite direction. Hence the *net* force is zero!

9-7 (a) (iii), (i) and (ii) (tie); (b) (iii), (i) and (ii) (tie). In part (a), the shear stress equals $F_{\parallel}/A$. The force $F_{\parallel}$ is the same in each case. Hence object (iii) has the greatest shear stress since it has the smallest value of A. Objects (i) and (ii) have the same area and so have the same shear stress.

Part (b) uses Hooke's law: Shear stress and shear strain are proportional. All three objects are made of the same material with shear modulus S, so the constant or proportionality is the same in each case. Therefore, the ranking in order of shear strain is the same as the ranking in order of shear stress.

9-8 (a) No; (b) yes. If an object obeys Hooke's law, doubling the stretch (and hence doubling the tensile strain) would require double the force (and hence double the tensile stress). This object does *not* obey Hooke's law since doubling the stretch from 1.00 cm to 2.00 cm requires more than double the force (from 25.0 N to 60.0 N). The object *is* nonetheless elastic because it returns to its unstretched length when the tensile forces go away.

Questions and Problems

In a few problems, you are given more data than you actually need; in a few other problems, you are required to supply data from your general knowledge, outside sources, or informed estimate.

Interpret as significant all digits in numerical values that have trailing zeros and no decimal points. For all problems, use $g = 9.80 \text{ m/s}^2$ for the free-fall acceleration due to gravity. Neglect friction and air resistance unless instructed to do otherwise.
• Basic, single-concept problem
•• Intermediate-level problem, may require synthesis of concepts and multiple steps
••• Challenging problem
SSM *Solution is in Student Solutions Manual*

Conceptual Questions

1. •(a) What is the difference between Young's modulus and bulk modulus? (b) What are the units of these two physical quantities?

2. •Define the term *yield strength*.

3. •Is it possible for a long cable hung vertically to break under its own weight? Explain your answer. SSM

4. •Define the following terms: yield strength and ultimate strength.

5. •Devise a simple way of determining which modulus (Young's, bulk, or shear) is appropriate for any given stress–strain problem.

6. •Give a few reasons why Hooke's law is intuitively obvious and a few reasons why it is counterintuitive.

7. •In some recent studies, it has been shown that women are more susceptible to torn ACLs than men when competing in similar sports (most notably in soccer and basketball). What are some reasons why this disparity might exist?

8. •Describe the small stretch limit of Hooke's law for a spring.

9. •A $2'' \times 4''$ pine stud oriented horizontally is securely clamped at one end to an immovable object. A heavy weight hangs from the free end of the wood, causing it to bend. (a) Which part of the plank is under compression? (b) Which part of the plank is under tension? (c) Is there any part that is neither stretched nor compressed?

10. •(a) Describe some common features of strain that were defined in this chapter. (b) We encountered three types of strain (tensile, volume, and shear). What are some distinguishing features of these quantities?

11. •A steel wire and a brass wire, each of length L and diameter D, are joined together to form a wire of length $2L$. If this wire is then used to hang an object of mass m, describe the amount of stretch in the two segments of wire.

12. •Why are tall mountains typically shaped like cones rather than a straight vertical columnlike structure?

13. •Shear modulus (S) is sometimes known as *rigidity*. Can you explain why rigidity is an appropriate synonym for this physical quantity? SSM

14. •Is it possible, when tightening the lug nuts on the wheel of your car, to use too much torque and break off one of the bolts? Explain your answer.

15. •What can cause nylon tennis racket strings to break when they are hit by the ball?

16. •Human skin is under tension like a rubber glove that has had air blown into it. Why does skin acquire wrinkles as people get older?

17. •**Biology** The leg bone of a cow has an ultimate strength of about $150 \times 10^6 \text{ N/m}^2$ and a maximum strain of about 1.5%. The antler of a deer has an ultimate strength of about $160 \times 10^6 \text{ N/m}^2$ and a maximum strain of about 12%. Explain the relationship between structure and function in these data.

Multiple-Choice Questions

18. •The units for strain are
   A. N/m.
   B. N/m^2.
   C. N.
   D. $\text{N} \cdot \text{m}^2$.
   E. none of the above.

19. •The units for stress are
   A. N/m.
   B. N/m^2.
   C. N.
   D. $\text{N} \cdot \text{m}$.
   E. $\text{N} \cdot \text{m}^2$.

20. •When tension is applied to a metal wire of length L, it stretches by ΔL. If the same tension is applied to a wire of the same material with the same cross-sectional area, but of length $2L$, by how much will it stretch?
   A. ΔL
   B. $2 \, \Delta L$

C. $0.5 \, \Delta L$
D. $3 \, \Delta L$
E. $4 \, \Delta L$

21. •A steel cable lifting a heavy box stretches by ΔL. If you want the cable to stretch by only half of ΔL, by what factor must you increase its diameter?
   A. 2
   B. 4
   C. $\sqrt{2}$
   D. 1/2
   E. 1/4 SSM

22. •A wire is stretched just to its breaking point by a force F. A longer wire made of the same material has the same diameter. The force that will stretch it to its breaking point is
   A. larger than F.
   B. smaller than F.
   C. equal to F.
   D. much smaller than F.
   E. much larger than F.

23. •Two solid rods have the same length and are made of the same material with circular cross sections. Rod 1 has a radius r, and rod 2 has a radius $r/2$. If a compressive force F is applied to both rods, their lengths are reduced by ΔL_1 and ΔL_2, respectively. The ratio $\Delta L_1/\Delta L_2$ is
   A. 1/4.
   B. 1/2.
   C. 1.
   D. 2.
   E. 4.

24. •A wall mount for a television consists in part of a mounting plate screwed or bolted flush to the wall. Which kinds of stresses play a role in keeping the mount securely attached to the wall?
   A. compression stress
   B. tension stress
   C. shear stress
   D. bulk stress
   E. A, B, and C

25. •When choosing building construction materials, what kinds of materials would you choose, all other things being equal?
   A. materials with a relatively large bulk modulus
   B. materials with a relatively small bulk modulus
   C. either materials with a large or a small bulk modulus
   D. it doesn't matter as long as the building is not too tall
   E. materials with a relatively small shear modulus SSM

26. •A book is pushed sideways, deforming it as shown in Figure 9-19. To describe the relationship between stress and strain for the book in this situation, you would use
   A. Young's modulus.
   B. bulk modulus.
   C. shear modulus.
   D. both Young's modulus and bulk modulus.
   E. both shear modulus and bulk modulus.

Figure 9-19 Problem 26

27. •A steel cable supports an actor as he swings onto the stage. The weight of the actor stretches the steel cable. To describe the relationship between stress and strain for the steel cable, you would use
   A. Young's modulus.
   B. bulk modulus.
   C. shear modulus.
   D. both Young's modulus and bulk modulus.
   E. both shear modulus and bulk modulus.

Estimation/Numerical Analysis

28. •Estimate Young's modulus for (a) a rubber band and (b) a wooden pencil.

29. •Estimate Young's modulus for a strip of paper. SSM

30. •Estimate the shear modulus for a chilled stick of butter taken from a refrigerator. Describe how this value would change as the butter warms to room temperature.

31. •Estimate the force needed to break a bone in your arm.

32. •Estimate the force needed to bend a bar of 0.5-in. rebar. (Rebar is made from iron and is used to reinforce concrete.)

33. •Estimate the force needed to puncture a 0.5-cm-thick sheet of aluminum with a 1-cm diameter rivet.

34. •Estimate the shear strain experienced by a typical athletic shoe in a basketball game.

35. •The following data are associated with an alloy of steel. Plot a graph of stress versus strain for the alloy. What are (a) the yield strength, (b) the ultimate strength, and (c) Young's modulus, for the material? SSM

Strain (%)	Stress (10^9 N/m²)	Strain (%)	Stress (10^9 N/m²)
0	0	1.0	300
0.1	125	1.5	325
0.2	250	2.0	350
0.3	230	2.5	375
0.4	230	3.0	400
0.5	235	3.5	375
0.6	240	4.0	350
0.7	250	4.5	325
0.8	260	5.0	300
0.9	270		

36. •Biology A galloping horse experiences the following stresses and corresponding strains on its front leg bone. Plot a graph of the stress versus strain for the bone and identify (a) the elastic region, (b) the yield strength, and (c) Young's modulus for this type of bone.

Stress (10^6 N/m²)	Strain (%)
35	0.2
70	0.4
105	0.6
140	1.0
175	1.5

Problems

9-1 When an object is under stress, it deforms

9-2 An object changes length when under tensile or compressive stress

9-3 Solving stress–strain problems: Tension and compression

37. •A cylindrical steel rod is originally 250 cm long and has a diameter of 0.254 cm. A force is applied longitudinally and the rod stretches 0.85 cm. What is the magnitude of the force?

38. •A solid band of rubber, which has a circular cross section of radius 0.25 cm, is stretched a distance of 3 cm by a force of 87 N. Calculate the original length of the cylinder of rubber.

39. •A bar of aluminum has a cross section that is 1 cm × 1 cm and has a length of 88 cm. What force would be needed to stretch the bar to 100 cm? What is the tensile strain of the bar of aluminum at that point? SSM

40. •The tensile stress on a concrete block is $0.52 \times 10^9 \text{ N/m}^2$. What is its tensile strain under this force?

41. •A physicist examines a metal sample and measures the ratio of the tensile stress to the tensile strain to be $95 \times 10^9 \text{ N/m}^2$. From what material might the sample be made?

42. •A 10-m-long copper wire is pulled with a force of 1200 N and it stretches 10.0 cm. Calculate the radius of the copper if the value of Young's modulus is $110 \times 10^9 \text{ N/m}^2$. Assume the cross section of the wire is circular.

43. •(a) Calculate the ratio of the tensile strain on an aluminum bar to that on a steel bar if both bars have the same cross-sectional area and the same force is applied to each bar. (b) Does the original length of each bar affect your answer to part (a)? SSM

44. •The elastic limit of an alloy is $0.6 \times 10^9 \text{ N/m}^2$. What is the minimum radius of a 4-m-long wire made from the alloy if a single strand is designed to support a commercial sign that has a weight of 8000 N and hangs from a fixed point? To stay within safety codes, the wire cannot stretch more than 5 cm.

45. •A piece of steel piano wire is 1.60 m long and has a diameter of 0.20 cm. What is the magnitude of the tension required to break it? The strength of steel is $5.0 \times 10^8 \text{ N/m}^2$. SSM

46. •**Biology** What is the compressive stress on your feet if your weight is spread out evenly over both soles of your shoes? Assume your mass is 55 kg and each shoe has an area of 200 cm^2.

47. •**Biology** Compare the answer to Problem 9-46 to the case where each of your shoes only has an area of 10 cm^2 in contact with the floor (as might be the case for high-heeled shoes).

48. •**Medical** The anterior cruciate ligament in a woman's knee is 2.5 cm long and has a cross-sectional area of 0.54 cm^2. If a force of 3000 N is applied longitudinally, how much will the ligament stretch?

49. ••**Medical** One model for the length of a person's ACL (L_{ACL}, in millimeters) relates it to the person's height (h, in centimeters) with the linear function $L_{ACL} = 0.4606h - 41.29$. Age, gender, and weight do not significantly influence the relationship. If a basketball player has a height of 2.29 m, (a) approximately how long is his ACL? (b) If a pressure of $10 \times 10^6 \text{ N/m}^2$ is applied longitudinally to his ligament, how much will it stretch?

9-4 An object expands or shrinks when under volume stress

9-5 Solving stress–strain problems: Volume stress

50. •A cube of lead (each side is 5 cm) is pressed equally on all six sides with forces of 100,000 N. What will the new dimensions of the cube be after the forces are applied ($B = 46 \times 10^9 \text{ N/m}^2$ for lead)?

51. •A rigid cube (each side is 0.1 m) is filled with water and frozen solid. When water freezes it's volume expands about 9%. How much pressure is exerted on the sides of the

cube? *Hint:* Imagine trying to squeeze the block of ice back into the original cube. SSM

52. •A sphere of copper that has a radius of 5.00 cm is compressed uniformly by a force of $2.00 \times 10^8 \text{ N}$. Calculate the change in volume of the sphere and the sphere's final radius. The bulk modulus for copper is $140 \times 10^9 \text{ N/m}^2$.

53. •A spherical air bubble has a radius of 4.00 cm when it is 8.00 m below the surface of a freshwater lake. What is the radius of the bubble immediately before it reaches the surface?

9-6 A solid object changes shape when under shear stress

9-7 Solving stress–strain problems: Shear stress

54. •Shear forces act on a steel door during an earthquake (Figure 9-20). If the shear strain is 0.005, calculate the force acting on the door with dimensions 0.044 m × 0.81 m × 2.03 m.

Figure 9-20 Problem 54

55. •A brass nameplate is 2 cm × 10 cm × 20 cm in size. If a force of 200,000 N acts on the upper left side and the bottom right side (Figure 9-21), find the shear strain (x/h) and the angle ϕ. SSM

Figure 9-21 Problem 55

56. •**Medical** In asthmatic patients, an increased thickness of the airways causes a local reduction in stress through the airway walls. The effect can be as much as a 50% reduction in the local shear modulus of the airways of an asthmatic patient compared to those of a healthy person. Calculate the ratio of the shear strain in an asthmatic airway to that of a healthy airway.

57. ••A force of 5×10^6 N is applied tangentially at the center of one side of a brass cube. The angle of shear ϕ is measured to be 0.65°. Calculate the volume of the original cube.

58. •An enormous piece of granite that is 200 m thick and has a shear modulus of 50×10^9 N/m² is sheared from its geologic formation with an earthquake force of 275×10^9 N. The area on which the force acts is a square of side x as shown in Figure 9-22. Find the value of x if the shear force produces a shear strain of 0.125.

Figure 9-22
Problem 58

59. •**Medical** In regions of the cardiovascular system where there is steady laminar blood flow, the shear stress on cells lining the walls of the blood vessels is about 20 dyne/cm². If the shear strain is about 0.008, estimate the shear modulus for the affected cells. Note 1 dyne = $1\,\text{g} \cdot \text{cm/s}^2$ and 1 N = 105 dyne. SSM

9-8 Objects deform permanently or fail when placed under too much stress

9-9 Solving stress–strain problems: From elastic behavior to failure

60. •Steel will ultimately fail if the shear stress exceeds 400×10^6 N/m². Determine the force required to shear a steel bolt that is 0.50 cm in diameter.

61. •A theater rigging company uses a safety factor of 10 for all its ropes, which means that all ultimate breaking strengths will be overestimated by a factor of 10 just to be safe. Suppose a rope with an ultimate breaking strength of 10,000 N is tied with a knot that decreases rope strength by 50%. (a) If the rope is used to support a load of 1000 N, what is the safety factor? (b) Will the rigging company be able to use the rope with the knot? SSM

General Problems

62. •A 50-kg air-conditioning unit slips from its window mount, but the end of the electrical cord gets caught in the mounting bracket. In the process the cord (which is 0.5-cm in diameter) stretches from 3.0 m to 4.5 m. What is Young's modulus for the cord?

63. •**Medical** The largest tendon in the body, the Achilles tendon connects the calf muscle to the heel bone of the foot. This tendon is typically 25.0 cm long, is 5.0 mm in diameter, and has a Young's modulus of 1.47×10^9 N/m². If an athlete has stretched the tendon to a length of 26.1 cm, what is the tension (in newtons and pounds) in the tendon?

64. ••Two rods have the same diameter and are welded together as shown in Figure 9-23. The shorter rod has a Young's modulus of Y_1, and the longer one has a Young's modulus of Y_2. Calculate the combined Young's modulus for the system.

Figure 9-23 Problem 64

65. •**Biology** Many caterpillars construct cocoons from silk, one of the strongest naturally occurring materials known. Each thread is typically 2.0 μm in diameter and the silk has a Young's modulus of 4.0×10^9 N/m². (a) How many strands would be needed to make a rope 9.0 m long that would stretch only 1.00 cm when supporting a pair of 85-kg mountain climbers? (b) Assuming that there is no appreciable space between the parallel strands, what would be the diameter of the rope? Does the diameter seem reasonable for a rope that mountain climbers might carry? SSM

66. •• A brass sphere that has a radius of 6 cm sinks 2000 m to the bottom of the ocean. By how much does the volume shrink due to the enormous pressure at that depth, and what is the new radius? Neglect any temperature changes.

67. •A 2.8-carat diamond is grown under a high pressure of 58×10^9 N/m². (a) By how much does the volume of a spherical 2.8-carat diamond expand once it is removed from the chamber and exposed to atmospheric pressure? (b) What is the increase in the diamond's radius? One carat is 200 mg, and the density of diamond is 3.52 g/cm³. The bulk modulus for diamond is 200×10^9 N/m².

68. •A glass marble that has a diameter of 1 cm is dropped into a graduated cylinder that contains 20 cm of mercury. (a) By how much does the volume of the marble shrink while at the bottom of the mercury? (b) What is the corresponding change in radius associated with the compression? The bulk modulus of glass is 50×10^6 N/m².

69. •**Sports** During the 2004 Olympic clean-and-jerk weightlifting competition, Hossein Rezazadeh lifted 263.5 kg. Mr. Rezazadeh himself had a mass of 163 kg. Ultimately, the weight is all supported by the tibia (shin bone) of the lifter's legs. The average length of a tibia is 385 mm, and its diameter (modeling it as having a round cross section) is about 3.0 cm. Young's modulus for bone is typically about 2.0×10^{10} N/m². (a) By how much did the lift compress the athlete's tibia, assuming that the bone is solid? (b) Does this seem to be a significant compression? (c) Is it necessary to include the lifter's weight in your calculations? Why or why not? SSM

70. •When a house is moved, it is gradually raised and supported on wooden blocks. A typical house averages about 120,000 lb (54,000 kg). The house is supported uniformly on six stacks of blocks of Douglas fir wood (which has a Young's modulus of 13×10^9 N/m²). Each block is 25 cm by 75 cm. If the wood is stacked 1.5 m high, by how much will the house compress the supporting stack of blocks?

71. •• (a) What diameter is needed for a steel cable to support a large diesel engine with a mass of 4000 kg? (b) By how much will the 10-m-long cable stretch once the engine is raised up off the ground? Assume the ultimate breaking strength of steel is 400×10^6 N/m².

72. •**Sports** A runner's foot pushes backward on the ground as shown in Figure 9-24. This results in a 25-N shearing force exerted in the forward direction by the ground, and in the backward direction by the foot is distributed over an area of 15 cm^2 and a 1-cm-thick sole. If the shear angle θ is 5.0°, what is the shear modulus of the sole?

25 N

θ 25 N

Figure 9-24 Problem 72

73. The spherical bubbles near the surface of a glass of water are 2.5 mm at sea level where the atmosphere exerts a pressure of 1.01×10^5 N/m^2 over the surface of each bubble. If the glass of water is taken to the elevation of Golden, CO, where the atmosphere exerts a pressure of 8.22×10^4 N/m^2 over the bubble surface, what will be the diameter of the bubbles? SSM

74. •••**Biology** A particular human hair has a Young's modulus of 4.0×10^9 N/m^2 and a diameter of 150 μm. (a) If a 250-g object is suspended by the single strand of hair that is originally 20.0 cm long, by how much will the hair stretch? (b) If the same object were hung by an aluminum wire of the same dimensions as the hair, by how much would the aluminum stretch? (Try to do this part without repeating the previous calculation, but use proportional reasoning instead.) (c) If we think of the strand of hair as a spring, what is its spring constant? (d) How does the hair's spring constant compare with that of ordinary springs in your physics laboratory?

75. •**Medical** The femur bone in the human leg has a minimum effective cross section of 3.0 cm^2. How much compressive force can it withstand before breaking? Assume the ultimate strength of the bone to be 1.7×10^8 N/m^2.

76. •**Medical** At its narrowest point, the femur bone in the human leg resembles a hollow cylinder that has an outer radius of roughly 1.1 cm and an inner radius of just about 0.48 cm. Assuming that the ultimate strength of the bone is 1.7×10^8 N/m^2, how much force will be required to rupture it?

77. •••A beam is attached to a vertical wall with a hinge. The mass of the beam is 1000 kg and it is 4 m long. A steel support wire is tied from the end of the beam to the wall, making an angle of 30° with the beam (Figure 9-25). (a) By summing the torque about the axis passing through the hinge, calculate the tension in the support wire. Assume the beam is uniform so that the weight acts at its exact center. (b) What is the minimum cross-sectional area of the steel wire so that it is not permanently stretched? The yield strength (elastic limit) for steel is 290×10^6 N/m^2, and the ultimate breaking strength is 400×10^6 N/m^2.

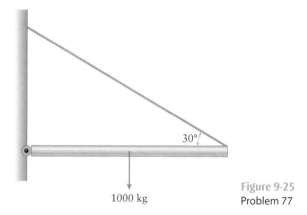

30°

1000 kg

Figure 9-25
Problem 77

78. ••Human bones have a typical compressive ultimate stress in the transverse direction of 133×10^6 N/m^2, and bovine bones have a typical compressive ultimate stress in the transverse direction of 178×10^6 N/m^2. (a) Is a human or a cow more likely to suffer a transverse break in a bone? Why? (b) The compressive longitudinal yield stress of human bones is approximately 182×10^6 N/m^2, and the compressive longitudinal ultimate stress is about 195×10^6 N/m^2. For cows, the compressive longitudinal yield stress of bone is about 196×10^6 N/m^2, and the compressive longitudinal ultimate stress is 237×10^6 N/m^2. Explain how a cow's bones are much more capable of supporting their extreme weight in comparison to a human's bones. (c) A bone in a woman's leg has an effective cross-sectional area of 3.00 cm^2. If the bone is 35 cm long, how much compressive force can it withstand before breaking? How much will her bone compress if it is subjected to a force one-tenth the magnitude of the force that breaks it? The longitudinal elastic modulus of human bone is about 9.6×10^9 N/m^2.

10 Gravitation

In this chapter, your goals are to:

- (10-1) Identify what it means to say that gravitation is universal.
- (10-2) Explain how Newton's law of universal gravitation describes the attractive gravitational force between any two objects.
- (10-3) Describe the general expression for gravitational potential energy and how to relate it to the expression used near Earth's surface.
- (10-4) Apply the law of universal gravitation and the expression for gravitational potential energy to analyze the orbits of satellites and planets.
- (10-5) Explain the origin of apparent weightlessness.

To master this chapter you should review:

- (3-2, 3-3) How to add vectors using components.
- (3-8) The properties of uniform circular motion.
- (3-10) How the inner ear senses acceleration.
- (4-3) The nature of the gravitational force near Earth's surface.
- (6-3, 6-6, The ideas of kinetic energy, potential energy, and the conservation of and 6-7) total mechanical energy.
- (8-2, 8-6, The concepts of angular speed, torque, and angular and 8-8) momentum.

What do you think?

The International Space Station (ISS) orbits Earth about 350 km (about 220 mi) above the surface of our planet, which has a radius of about 6370 km (3960 mi). Astronauts aboard the ISS feel as though they are weightless. Compared to the gravitational force that Earth exerts on an astronaut standing on our planet's surface, how great is the gravitational force that Earth exerts on the same astronaut when she is aboard the ISS? (a) The same; (b) about 10% less; (c) about 50% less; (d) about 75% less; (e) essentially zero.

10-1 Gravitation is a force of universal importance

Seventy years ago the idea of humans orbiting Earth or sending spacecraft to other worlds was regarded as science fiction. Today science fiction has become commonplace reality. Literally thousands of artificial satellites orbit our planet to track weather, relay signals for communications and entertainment, and collect scientific data about Earth and the universe. Humans live and work in Earth orbit aboard the International Space Station (see photograph above), have ventured as far as the Moon, and have sent robotic spacecraft to explore all the planets of the solar system.

While we think of spaceflight as an innovation of the twentieth century, we can trace its origins to Isaac Newton's revolutionary seventeenth-century notion of *universal gravitation*—the idea that all objects in the universe attract each other through the force of gravity. In Chapters 3 and 4 we learned that Earth's gravitational force acts on all objects near our planet's surface. In this chapter we'll extend our discussion to consider the gravitational forces exerted by any massive object on any other massive object. Gravitational forces between the components of our planet are partly responsible for holding Earth together (Figure 10-1a); gravitational forces exerted by Saturn

(a) Earth

(b) Saturn, its rings, and three of its moons

(c) Galaxy NGC 6744

Figure 10-1 Gravitation is universal The force of gravitation is responsible for (a) keeping our Earth from flying apart, (b) keeping the moons of the solar system in orbit around their planets, and (c) holding galaxies—among the largest structures in the universe—together.

Earth is held together by the mutual gravitational attraction of all its parts.

Saturn's rings are made of countless small objects that, like Saturn's moons, are held in orbit by the planet's gravitation.

This galaxy (a near-twin of our Milky Way) contains more than 10^{11} stars. The stars' gravitational attraction for each other holds the galaxy together.

keep its moons and other small bodies in orbit (Figure 10-1b); and gravitational forces between stars and the material between the stars hold entire galaxies of stars together (Figure 10-1c). All of these celestial bodies obey Newton's laws of motion, including the relationship between net force and acceleration, just as do objects here on Earth. The new wrinkle is the character of the dominant force that acts on them, the gravitational force.

In this chapter we will learn about the properties of the gravitational force, including how Newton deduced that this force must grow weaker as objects move farther apart. We will see how to treat the gravitational potential energy of a system of two objects interacting with each other, such as a satellite and Earth. We'll then use these ideas about gravitational force and gravitational potential energy to understand the nature of orbits. We'll find that the same ideas that apply to a satellite orbiting Earth also apply to planets orbiting the Sun. Indeed, we will see how Newton's idea of universal gravitation allowed him to explain three laws of planetary motion that had been discovered, but not understood, decades before. We'll also use the idea of universal gravitation to understand why astronauts in orbit feel weightless, and learn about some of the physiological challenges that astronauts face as a result.

10-2 Newton's law of universal gravitation explains the orbit of the Moon

Newton deduced much of what we now know about gravitation by considering the motion of Earth's Moon (Figure 10-2). It had been understood for centuries that the Moon orbits around Earth. Newton knew from his laws of motion that there must therefore be a force acting on the Moon to keep it from flying off into space, and that Earth must exert this force on the Moon. This is just the force of Earth's gravitation. But how strong is that force? Is it the same, weaker, or stronger than what Earth's gravitational force would be if the Moon were nearby? Let's see how Newton answered this question by using the ideas of circular motion.

It was well understood in the seventeenth century that the Moon orbits around Earth at a nearly constant speed in a nearly circular path. The evidence for this is that the Moon changes its position against the background stars. It moves against this background at a nearly constant rate (which tells us that its speed is nearly constant), and as it moves its apparent size changes very little (which tells us that the Moon maintains a roughly constant distance from Earth, and so its orbit is nearly circular).

The radius of the Moon's orbit—that is, the distance from Earth to the Moon—was also well known in Newton's time, even though travel to the Moon was centuries in the future. This was possible because as seen from different locations on Earth, the Moon appears to be in slightly different positions relative to the background of stars

Figure 10-2 The Moon Isaac Newton used the known distance to the Moon and the Moon's speed to deduce its acceleration, which he concluded was caused by Earth's gravitational attraction. This gave him an important clue about how the gravitational force depends on distance.

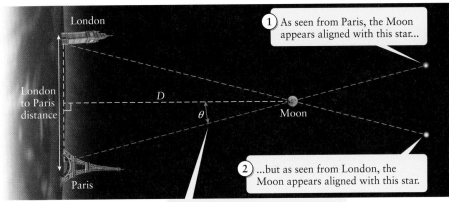

① As seen from Paris, the Moon appears aligned with this star...

② ...but as seen from London, the Moon appears aligned with this star.

③ Given the distance from London to Paris and the angle θ, the distance D to the Moon can be calculated.

Figure 10-3 Measuring the distance to the Moon The Moon is close enough that it appears to be in slightly different positions against the backdrop of distant stars when viewed from different locations on Earth. This made it possible to calculate the distance to the Moon many centuries before humans were able to send a spacecraft there.

(Figure 10-3). By measuring the differences in apparent position and using trigonometry, it's possible to measure the distance D in Figure 10-3. From these measurements, the distance from the center of Earth to the Moon (equal to Earth's radius $R = 6370$ km, which was also known in Newton's time, plus the distance D in Figure 10-3 from the surface of Earth to the Moon) turns out to be $384{,}000$ km $= 3.84 \times 10^8$ m. This is the radius r of the Moon's orbit.

As we learned in Section 3-8, an object that travels at constant speed v around a circular path of radius r—that is, an object in *uniform circular motion*—has an acceleration toward the center of the circle of magnitude

Centripetal acceleration: magnitude of the acceleration of an object in uniform circular motion

Speed of an object as it moves around the circle

$$a_{cent} = \frac{v^2}{r}$$

Radius of the circle

Centripetal acceleration
(3-17)

The Moon's acceleration is due to the gravitational pull of Earth on the Moon, so a_{cent} is equal to the value of g at the position of the Moon. Equation 3-17 shows that to determine the Moon's acceleration Newton had to know the values of the radius r of the Moon's orbit—that is, the distance from the center of Earth to the Moon—and the speed v of the Moon in its orbit.

From observations of the Moon's apparent motion relative to the stars, it was known in Newton's time that the Moon makes one complete orbit around Earth in a time $T = 27.3$ days, or 2.36×10^6 s. The speed v of the Moon in its orbit is therefore the circumference of its orbit, equal to 2π times the radius $r = 3.84 \times 10^8$ m of its orbit, divided by the time $T = 2.36 \times 10^6$ s to complete an orbit. The result turns out to be $v = 1.02 \times 10^3$ m/s (about 3670 km/h or 2280 mi/h). If you substitute these values for v and r into Equation 3-17, you'll find that the Moon's acceleration is, to two significant digits,

$$a_{cent} = \frac{v^2}{r} = \frac{(1.02 \times 10^3 \text{ m/s})^2}{3.84 \times 10^8 \text{ m}} = 2.7 \times 10^{-3} \text{ m/s}^2$$

This shows that a_{cent} is *very* much less than the value $g = 9.80$ m/s^2 at the surface of Earth. This implies that Earth's gravitational attraction—which is what exerts a force on the Moon to give it its centripetal acceleration—gets weaker with increasing distance. In fact, the Moon's acceleration is less than the value of g at Earth's surface by a factor of

$$\frac{a_{cent,Moon}}{g_{surface of Earth}} = \frac{2.7 \times 10^{-3} \text{ m/s}^2}{9.80 \text{ m/s}^2} = 2.8 \times 10^{-4} = \frac{1}{3600} = \frac{1}{60^2}$$

As it happens, the distance from the center of Earth to Earth's surface is smaller than the distance from the center of Earth to the Moon by a factor of

$$\frac{r_{Earth center to surface}}{r_{Earth center to Moon}} = \frac{6370 \text{ km}}{384{,}000 \text{ km}} = \frac{1}{60}$$

From this Newton deduced that

the acceleration due to Earth's gravity decreases in proportion to the square of the distance from Earth's center.

If you could stand atop a tower 6370 km tall—that is, a tower whose height equals the radius of Earth—you would be twice as far from Earth's center as a person at sea level and the acceleration due to gravity would be $1/(2)^2 = 1/4$ as great as at sea level. By contrast, if you were to stand atop Earth's tallest mountain, Mount Everest, you would be a little less than 9 km above sea level. The distance from Earth's center to the peak of Mount Everest is 6379 km as compared to 6370 km from Earth's center to sea level, which is greater by a factor of $(6379\,\text{km})/(6370\,\text{km}) = 1.0014$. So the value of g atop Mount Everest is about $1/(1.0014)^2 = 0.997$ of the value at sea level, or about 0.3% less than the sea-level value. This shows why there is only a small difference in the value of g with elevation on Earth.

The Law of Universal Gravitation

Here's how we can write in equation form Newton's observation that the acceleration g due to Earth's gravitation decreases in proportion to the square of the distance r from the center of Earth:

$$g = \frac{(\text{a constant})}{r^2}$$

The value of the constant in this equation is chosen so that at a point on Earth's surface, where r equals Earth's radius of 6370 km, the value of g equals $9.80\ \text{m/s}^2$. We learned in Section 4-3 that the magnitude of Earth's gravitational force on an object of mass m is mg. So if an object of mass m is located a distance r from Earth's center, the gravitational force of Earth on this object is

$$F_{\text{Earth on object}} = \frac{(\text{a constant})m}{r^2}$$

That is, Earth's gravitational force on an object of mass m is directly proportional to the mass m of the object that experiences the force.

Newton generalized this to say that *any* object of mass m_1 exerts a gravitational force on a second object of mass m_2, that this force is directly proportional to the mass m_2 of the object that experiences the force, and that this force is inversely proportional to the square of the distance r between the centers of the objects (Figure 10-4a):

(10-1)
$$F_{1\text{ on }2} = \frac{(\text{a constant})m_2}{r^2}$$

For the force of Earth on the Moon, m_2 is the Moon's mass and r is the Earth-Moon distance. If Equation 10-1 is true for *any* two objects, then it must also be true that the object of mass m_2 exerts a gravitational force on the object of mass m_1, and this force is directly proportional to the mass m_1. But Newton's third law (Section 4-5) tells us that the forces that the two objects exert on each other have opposite directions and the same magnitude: $F_{2\text{ on }1} = F_{1\text{ on }2}$. Hence the gravitational force that each object exerts on the other must be directly proportional to *both* m_1 and m_2. This chain of reasoning leads us to **Newton's law of universal gravitation:**

Newton's law of universal gravitation (10-2)

Gravitational constant (same for any two objects)   Masses of the two objects

Any two objects (1 and 2) exert equally strong gravitational forces on each other.

$$F_{1\text{ on }2} = F_{2\text{ on }1} = \frac{Gm_1m_2}{r^2}$$

Center-to-center distance between the two objects

The gravitational forces are attractive: $\vec{F}_{1\text{ on }2}$ pulls object 2 toward object 1 and $\vec{F}_{2\text{ on }1}$ pulls object 1 toward object 2.

As Figure 10-4a shows, the forces that the two objects exert on each other are attractive and are directed along the line that connects the centers of the two objects.

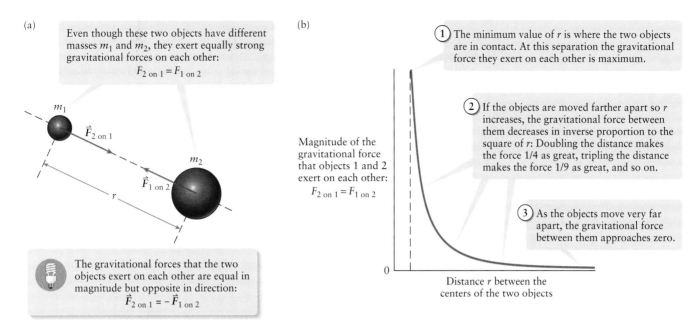

Figure 10-4 **The law of universal gravitation** (a) Any two objects exert gravitational forces on each other. These forces are equal in magnitude but opposite in direction: $\vec{F}_{2\text{ on }1} = -\vec{F}_{1\text{ on }2}$. (b) The magnitude of the gravitational force is inversely proportional to the square of the center-to-center distance r.

The proportionality constant G is called the **gravitational constant**. We'll see later in this section how the value of G (which Newton did not know) is determined. Its currently accepted value, to three significant figures, is

$$G = 6.67 \times 10^{-11}\ \text{N}\cdot\text{m}^2/\text{kg}^2$$

Figure 10-4b graphs the magnitude of the gravitational force between the two objects as a function of the distance r between their centers.

❗ Watch Out! Be sure to understand the limitations of Equation 10-2.

Strictly speaking, Equation 10-2 applies to two infinitesimally small objects with masses m_1 and m_2. It's much more challenging to calculate the gravitational force between two extended objects with complicated shapes, such as between Earth and the Moon (neither of which is a perfect sphere) or between Earth and the International Space Station (the shape of which you can see in the photograph that opens this chapter). However, in practice we can safely use Equation 10-2 if the *distance* between the two objects is large compared to the *size* of either object. That's the case for Earth and the Moon, which are separated by a distance of 384,000 km—much larger than the radius of either Earth (6370 km) or the Moon (1740 km).

It's also safe to use Equation 10-2 if one object is very much smaller than the other, as is the case for a satellite (like the International Space Station) orbiting Earth, as long as we can approximate the large object (in this case Earth) as being roughly uniform. In other situations, such as calculating the force between the two galaxies shown in Figure 10-1c (which are comparable in size and whose separation is comparable to the size of either galaxy), Equation 10-2 still gives useful estimates of the magnitude of the gravitational force. Note also that Equation 10-2 is not valid if one object is *inside* the other. For example, we can't use this equation to find the gravitational force on you when you're in a tunnel deep inside Earth's interior.

❗ Watch Out! The distance _r_ in Equation 10-2 is the center-to-center distance.

Always remember that r in Equation 10-2 is the distance between the *centers* of the two objects. If you're calculating the gravitational force that Earth exerts on a person standing on Earth's surface, the distance r equals the radius of Earth—that is, the distance from the center of Earth to that person.

For symmetrical objects like Earth or the Moon, the geometrical center is the same as the center of mass, so we'll often use the terms *center* and *center of mass* interchangeably when discussing gravitational forces.

As Equation 10-2 shows, the gravitational force that one object exerts on another is proportional to $1/r^2$, which is the reciprocal of the square of the distance r or "the inverse square" of r for short. That's why the law of universal gravitation is sometimes called *the inverse-square law for gravitation.* We'll learn in later chapters that the *electric* force that one charged particle exerts on another (for instance, the force between an electron and a proton) also obeys an inverse-square law.

Because the gravitational constant is such a small value, gravitational forces between two objects also tend to be pretty small unless at least one of the objects is relatively large (that is, planet-sized). The following examples illustrate this.

Example 10-1 You and Your Backpack

While you sit studying, what is the magnitude of the gravitational force that your 10-kg backpack sitting on your desk exerts on you? Assume that your mass is 70 kg and that your center of mass is 0.60 m from the center of your backpack.

Set Up
We'll use Newton's law of universal gravitation, Equation 10-2, to find the magnitude of the gravitational force.

Newton's law of universal gravitation:

$$F_{\text{bag on you}} = \frac{Gm_{\text{bag}}m_{\text{you}}}{r^2} \qquad (10\text{-}2)$$

Solve
Substitute the given values of G, $m_{\text{bag}} = 10$ kg, $m_{\text{you}} = 70$ kg, and $r = 0.60$ m into the expression for gravitational force. The masses and distance are given to only two significant figures, so our result has only two significant figures.

$$
\begin{aligned}
F_{\text{bag on you}} &= \frac{Gm_{\text{bag}}m_{\text{you}}}{r^2} \\
&= \frac{(6.67 \times 10^{-11}\,\text{N}\cdot\text{m}^2/\text{kg}^2)\,(10\,\text{kg})\,(70\,\text{kg})}{(0.60\,\text{m})^2} \\
&= 1.3 \times 10^{-7}\,\text{N}
\end{aligned}
$$

Reflect
The gravitational force your bag exerts on you is *very* small, about one ten-millionth of a newton. This is equivalent to the weight of a few specks of dust. This force is far smaller than the gravitational force Earth exerts on you (see the next example). It's also far smaller than the force of friction between you and your chair should you start to slide. That's why we generally neglect the gravitational force between everyday objects.

Example 10-2 Earth's Gravitational Force on You

Calculate the magnitude of the gravitational force that Earth exerts on you, again assuming you have a mass of 70 kg. Earth has mass 5.97×10^{24} kg and radius 6370 km.

Set Up
Again we'll find the magnitude of the gravitational force using Newton's law of universal gravitation, Equation 10-2. The distance r between the centers of the two objects (Earth and you) equals Earth's radius, 6370 km. The extra meter or so distance from Earth's surface to the center of your body is insignificant compared to the size of Earth's radius, so we ignore it.

Newton's law of universal gravitation:

$$F_{\text{Earth on you}} = \frac{Gm_{\text{Earth}}m_{\text{you}}}{r^2} \qquad (10\text{-}2)$$

r = distance from center of Earth to you
$= R_{\text{Earth}}$ = radius of Earth

Solve

To use the distance $r = R_{Earth} = 6370$ km in Equation 10-2, we first convert it to meters.

$$r = R_{Earth}$$
$$= (6370 \text{ km}) \times \frac{1000 \text{ m}}{1 \text{ km}} = 6.37 \times 10^6 \text{ m}$$

Substitute the values of G, m_{Earth}, m_{you}, and r into Equation 10-2. Again, our answer has only two significant figures.

$$F_{Earth \ on \ you} = \frac{Gm_{Earth}m_{you}}{r^2} = \frac{Gm_{Earth}m_{you}}{R_{Earth}^2}$$
$$= \frac{(6.67 \times 10^{-11} \text{ N} \cdot \text{m}^2/\text{kg}^2)(5.97 \times 10^{24} \text{ kg})(70 \text{ kg})}{(6.37 \times 10^6 \text{ m})^2}$$
$$= 6.9 \times 10^2 \text{ N}$$

Reflect

We can check our result by using the expression $w = mg$ for gravitational force that we introduced in Section 4-3. We get the same result as above, which shows that the values of G and m_{Earth} are compatible with the value of g at Earth's surface.

Using the expression $w = mg$ for gravitational force,

$$F_{Earth \ on \ you} = m_{you}g$$
$$= (70 \text{ kg})(9.80 \text{ m/s}^2)$$
$$= 6.9 \times 10^2 \text{ N}$$

Finding the Value of G and the Mass of Earth

Example 10-2 shows that there is a connection between the value of g at Earth's surface and the values of G and m_{Earth}, the gravitational constant and Earth's mass. To see this more clearly, take the two expressions for the gravitational force on you and set them equal to each other:

$$F_{Earth \ on \ you} = m_{you}g = \frac{Gm_{Earth}m_{you}}{R_{Earth}^2}$$

Then divide both sides of the equation by your mass, m_{you}, to get an expression for g:

Acceleration due to gravity at Earth's surface | Gravitational constant | Mass of Earth

$$g = \frac{Gm_{Earth}}{R_{Earth}^2}$$

Radius of Earth

Value of g at Earth's surface
(10-3)

This equation tells us that whenever we calculate a weight or an acceleration using g, we are simply using a shorthand form of the law of universal gravitation applied near Earth's surface. So the familiar expression $w = mg$ is just a special form of the general law of universal gravitation, Equation 10-2.

Equation 10-3 relates the value of g (which we can measure by observing a freely falling object) to the values of Earth's radius R_{Earth}, Earth's mass m_{Earth}, and the gravitational constant G. The value of R_{Earth} has been known since the third century B.C., when Eratosthenes, a scholar from Cyrene in modern-day Libya, first determined its value. (Figure 10-5 shows how Eratosthenes was able to do this.) But that leaves two unknown values in Equation 10-3, G and m_{Earth}. With only one equation to relate them, it seems impossible to determine the values of both of these unknowns.

The solution to this problem was provided by the British scientist Henry Cavendish in 1798, more than a century after Newton published the law of universal gravitation. Cavendish conducted the elegant experiment shown schematically in Figure 10-6, now known simply as the **Cavendish experiment**. The gravitational force of each large sphere on the nearby small sphere makes the wooden rod rotate, which twists the wire from which the rod is suspended. The wire resists being twisted and exerts a torque on the rod that tries to return the wire to its relaxed state, much as a stretched spring exerts a force that tries to return the spring to its unstretched length. In equilibrium the torque exerted by the wire just balances the gravitational torque. By measuring the wire beforehand, Cavendish knew how much torque the wire exerted for a given rotation angle, and thus he could determine the equal-magnitude gravitational torque. He could then determine the gravitational force on each small sphere required to cause this torque on

Figure 10-5 How Eratosthenes measured the radius of Earth Around 240 B.C. the scholar Eratosthenes measured Earth's radius by analyzing the shadows cast by the Sun at two different locations.

1 As the story is told, on the day of the summer solstice (when the sun is highest in the sky as seen from the Northern hemisphere) Eratosthenes observed the shadow cast by a column in the city of Alexandria.

2 Eratosthenes also knew that on the summer solstice the sun cast no shadow down a well in the Egyptian city of Syene (modern-day Aswan), so the sun was directly overhead there.

3 Given the known distance D_{AS} from Alexandria to Syene and his measurement of the angle θ, Eratosthenes was able to calculate the radius R_{Earth}.

Figure 10-6 The Cavendish experiment This experiment is used to determine the value of G. In the original (1798) version of the experiment, the wooden rod was 1.8 m in length, each small lead sphere had a mass of 0.73 kg, each large lead sphere had a mass of 158 kg, and the distance r was about 23 cm.

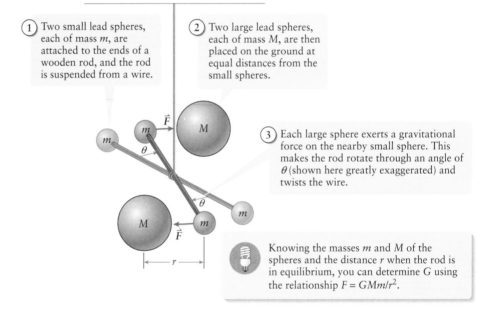

1 Two small lead spheres, each of mass m, are attached to the ends of a wooden rod, and the rod is suspended from a wire.

2 Two large lead spheres, each of mass M, are then placed on the ground at equal distances from the small spheres.

3 Each large sphere exerts a gravitational force on the nearby small sphere. This makes the rod rotate through an angle of θ (shown here greatly exaggerated) and twists the wire.

Knowing the masses m and M of the spheres and the distance r when the rod is in equilibrium, you can determine G using the relationship $F = GMm/r^2$.

the rod. With this technique Cavendish could measure extremely small forces on the order of 10^{-7} N, which made his experiment possible.

Given the magnitude of the force F, the masses m and M of the small and large spheres respectively, and the distance r between neighboring large and small spheres, we can use Newton's law of universal gravitation to solve for the value of G:

$$F = \frac{GMm}{r^2} \quad \text{so} \quad G = \frac{Fr^2}{Mm}$$

Modern experiments to measure G to great precision still use variations on Cavendish's original apparatus. Once the value of G is known, we can use Equation 10-3 to determine the value of Earth's mass, m_{Earth}. In this way Cavendish became the first person to determine the mass of our planet (now known to be 5.97×10^{24} kg).

Armed with knowledge of the value of G, we have all the tools we need to apply the law of universal gravitation to the orbits of satellites and planets. To analyze these orbits, it's important to first consider the potential energy associated with the gravitational force, which is the topic of the next section. First, however, here are two examples that make use of the law of universal gravitation.

Go to Picture It 10-1 for more practice dealing with gravitational force

Example 10-3 At What Altitude Is g Cut in Half?

At what height above Earth's surface is the value of g equal to one-half the value at the surface?

Set Up

Equation 10-3 tells us the value of g at Earth's surface, which we'll call $g_{surface}$. Our goal is to find the height h above the surface at which g has half this value. To find g at this altitude, we'll use the law of universal gravitation and the relationship between the gravitational force on an object and the value of g. Remember that the distance r in the law of universal gravitation is *not* the height above the surface, but rather the distance to Earth's center. This equals the radius of Earth plus the height of the object.

Value of g at Earth's surface:

$$g_{surface} = \frac{Gm_{Earth}}{R_{Earth}^2} \qquad (10\text{-}3)$$

Newton's law of universal gravitation:

$$F_{Earth\ on\ object} = \frac{Gm_{Earth}m_{object}}{r^2} \qquad (10\text{-}2)$$

Gravitational force on an object in terms of g:

$$F_{Earth\ on\ object} = m_{object}g$$

Distance from Earth's center to a height h above the surface:

$$r = R_{Earth} + h$$

Solve

Use the two expressions for the gravitational force on an object to solve for g at a height h above the surface.

Set the two expressions for $F_{Earth\ on\ object}$ equal to each other:

$$F_{Earth\ on\ object} = m_{object}g = \frac{Gm_{Earth}m_{object}}{r^2}$$

To solve for g, divide through by m_{object}:

$$g = \frac{Gm_{Earth}}{r^2}$$

Substitute $r = R_{Earth} + h$ in the expression for g:

$$g = \frac{Gm_{Earth}}{(R_{Earth} + h)^2}$$

We want to find the value of h at which g equals one-half of $g_{surface}$.

The value of g at height h equals $1/2$ the value of $g_{surface}$:

$$g = \frac{1}{2}g_{surface} \text{ so}$$

Substitute the expression for g we found above and the expression for $g_{surface}$ from Equation 10-3:

$$\frac{Gm_{Earth}}{(R_{Earth} + h)^2} = \frac{1}{2}\frac{Gm_{Earth}}{R_{Earth}^2}$$

Note that Gm_{Earth} cancels, leaving

$$\frac{1}{(R_{Earth} + h)^2} = \frac{1}{2R_{Earth}^2}$$

Take the reciprocal of both sides of this equation:

$$(R_{Earth} + h)^2 = 2R_{Earth}^2$$

To eliminate the squares, take the square root of both sides:

$$R_{Earth} + h = \sqrt{2}\,R_{Earth}$$

To get an expression for h, subtract R_{Earth} from both sides of this equation:

$$h = \sqrt{2}R_{Earth} - R_{Earth}$$
$$= (\sqrt{2} - 1)R_{Earth}$$

Substitute $R_{Earth} = 6370$ km:

$$h = (\sqrt{2} - 1)(6370 \text{ km}) = (1.414 - 1)(6370 \text{ km})$$
$$= 2640 \text{ km}$$

Reflect

Our calculation shows that g, like the gravitational force, is inversely proportional to the distance r from Earth's center. We can use this to check our result: At the height $h = (\sqrt{2} - 1)R_{Earth}$, the distance from Earth's center is $\sqrt{2}$ times Earth's radius R_{Earth} and so the value of g is $1/(\sqrt{2})^2 = 1/2$ the value at the surface—just as it must be according to the statement of the problem.

The altitude $h = 2640$ km is much higher than that of most Earth satellites (for the International Space Station shown in the photograph that opens this chapter, h is only about 350 km). That's why the value of g for these satellites is much closer to $g_{surface}$ than to $g_{surface}/2$.

How g depends on the distance r from Earth's center:

$$g = \frac{Gm_{Earth}}{r^2}$$

If the height above Earth's surface is $h = (\sqrt{2} - 1)R_{Earth}$, then the distance from Earth's center is

$$r = R_{Earth} + h$$
$$= R_{Earth} + (\sqrt{2} - 1)R_{Earth}$$
$$= \sqrt{2}R_{Earth}$$

and the value of g at this height is

$$g = \frac{Gm_{Earth}}{r^2} = \frac{Gm_{Earth}}{(\sqrt{2}R_{Earth})^2} = \frac{1}{(\sqrt{2})^2}\frac{Gm_{Earth}}{R_{Earth}^2}$$
$$= \frac{1}{2}\frac{Gm_{Earth}}{R_{Earth}^2} = \frac{1}{2}g_{surface}$$

Example 10-4 The Moons of Saturn

Figure 10-1b shows Saturn's moons Tethys, Dione, and Rhea. (Saturn's moons, of which 62 were known as of this writing, are named for mythological figures associated with the Roman god Saturn.) Their masses are 6.2×10^{20} kg for Tethys, 1.1×10^{21} kg for Dione, and 2.3×10^{21} kg for Rhea. All three of these moons are quite small compared to Earth's moon (mass 7.36×10^{22} kg). Tethys, Dione, and Rhea move in different orbits around Saturn and at different speeds, and on occasion form a right triangle (Figure 10-7). Calculate the *net* gravitational force on Tethys due to Dione and Rhea when the three moons are in this configuration. Compare this to the force that Saturn (mass 5.7×10^{26} kg) exerts on Tethys, which orbits 2.95×10^5 km from Saturn's center.

Figure 10-7 **Three moons of Saturn** What is the net gravitational force on Saturn's moon Tethys due to the other moons Dione and Rhea?

Set Up

Both Dione and Rhea exert gravitational forces on Tethys as given by Equation 10-2. As the figure shows, these forces act at right angles to each other. The *net* gravitational force on Tethys due to the two other moons is the vector sum of the two individual forces. We'll use the ideas of vector addition and vector components from Sections 3-2 and 3-3 to find this vector sum and determine the magnitude and direction of the net force.

Newton's law of universal gravitation:

$$F_{moon \text{ on } Tethys} = \frac{Gm_{moon}m_{Tethys}}{r^2_{moon \text{ to } Tethys}} \quad (10\text{-}2)$$

Solve

The easiest way to add vectors is by using components, so we choose x and y axes as shown. With this choice of axes, the force of Dione on Tethys has only a y component and the force of Rhea on Tethys has only an x component. Calculate these components using the values of r shown in Figure 10-7.

Convert the Dione-Tethys distance and Rhea-Tethys distance from kilometers to meters:

$$r_{\text{Dione to Tethys}} = r_{\text{Rhea to Tethys}} = 2.3 \times 10^5 \text{ km}$$

$$= (2.3 \times 10^5 \text{ km})\left(\frac{1000 \text{ m}}{1 \text{ km}}\right) = 2.3 \times 10^8 \text{ m}$$

The force of Dione on Tethys has zero x component and a positive y component:

$$F_{\text{Dione on Tethys},x} = 0$$

$$F_{\text{Dione on Tethys},y} = +\frac{Gm_{\text{Dione}}m_{\text{Tethys}}}{r^2_{\text{Dione to Tethys}}}$$

$$= +\frac{(6.67 \times 10^{-11} \text{ N} \cdot \text{m}^2/\text{kg}^2)(1.1 \times 10^{21} \text{ kg})(6.2 \times 10^{20} \text{ kg})}{(2.3 \times 10^8 \text{ m})^2}$$

$$= +8.6 \times 10^{14} \text{ N}$$

The force of Rhea on Tethys has a positive x component and zero y component:

$$F_{\text{Rhea on Tethys},x} = +\frac{Gm_{\text{Rhea}}m_{\text{Tethys}}}{r^2_{\text{Rhea to Tethys}}}$$

$$= +\frac{(6.67 \times 10^{-11} \text{ N} \cdot \text{m}^2/\text{kg}^2)(2.3 \times 10^{21} \text{ kg})(6.2 \times 10^{20} \text{ kg})}{(2.3 \times 10^8 \text{ m})^2}$$

$$= +1.8 \times 10^{15} \text{ N}$$

$$F_{\text{Rhea on Tethys},y} = 0$$

The net force on Tethys is the vector sum of the two individual forces. Find the components of the net force.

The x component of the net force on Tethys is the sum of the x components of the individual forces:

$$F_{\text{net on Tethys},x}$$
$$= F_{\text{Dione on Tethys},x} + F_{\text{Rhea on Tethys},x}$$
$$= 0 \text{ N} + 1.8 \times 10^{15} \text{ N}$$
$$= +1.8 \times 10^{15} \text{ N}$$

$F_{\text{net on Tethys, }y} = 8.6 \times 10^{14} \text{ N}$

$F_{\text{net on Tethys, }x} = 1.8 \times 10^{15} \text{ N}$

Similarly, the y component of the net force on Tethys is the sum of the y components of the individual forces:

$$F_{\text{net on Tethys},y} = F_{\text{Dione on Tethys},y} + F_{\text{Rhea on Tethys},y}$$
$$= +8.6 \times 10^{14} \text{ N} + 0 \text{ N}$$
$$= +8.6 \times 10^{14} \text{ N}$$

From the components of the net force, find its magnitude and direction using the techniques learned in Section 3-3.

Find the magnitude of the net force:

$$F_{\text{net on Tethys}} = \sqrt{(F_{\text{net on Tethys},x})^2 + (F_{\text{net on Tethys},y})^2}$$
$$= \sqrt{(+1.8 \times 10^{15} \text{ N})^2 + (+8.6 \times 10^{14} \text{ N})^2}$$
$$= 2.0 \times 10^{15} \text{ N}$$

Find the angle of the net force relative to the x axis:

$F_{\text{net on Tethys, }y}$
$= 8.6 \times 10^{14} \text{ N}$

$F_{\text{net on Tethys}}$
$= 2.0 \times 10^{15} \text{ N}$

$$\tan\theta = \frac{F_{\text{net on Tethys},y}}{F_{\text{net on Tethys},x}}$$

$$= \frac{+8.6 \times 10^{14} \text{ N}}{+1.8 \times 10^{15} \text{ N}} = 0.48$$

$\theta = 26°$

$F_{\text{net on Tethys, }x} = 1.8 \times 10^{15} \text{ N}$

so

$$\theta = \tan^{-1} 0.48 = 26°$$

Reflect

The net gravitational force on Tethys from Dione and Rhea is 2.0×10^{15} N, which seems tremendous. But the gravitational force that Saturn exerts on Tethys is about 1.4×10^5 (140,000) times greater than the force from the other moons. This means the orbit of Tethys around Saturn is affected hardly at all by the presence of the other moons.

Note that the net force on Tethys from the other two moons is not directed at either of those moons, but rather somewhere between the two. This isn't surprising: In general, the sum of two vectors doesn't point in the direction of either individual vector.

Convert the distance from the center of Saturn to Tethys from kilometers to meters:

$$r_{\text{Saturn to Tethys}} = (2.95 \times 10^5 \, \text{km})\left(\frac{1000 \, \text{m}}{1 \, \text{km}}\right) = 2.95 \times 10^8 \, \text{m}$$

Then the gravitational force that Saturn exerts on Tethys is

$$F_{\text{Saturn on Tethys}} = \frac{Gm_{\text{Saturn}}m_{\text{Tethys}}}{r_{\text{Saturn to Tethys}}^2}$$

$$= \frac{(6.67 \times 10^{-11} \, \text{N} \cdot \text{m}^2/\text{kg}^2)(5.7 \times 10^{26} \, \text{kg})(6.2 \times 10^{20} \, \text{kg})}{(2.95 \times 10^8 \, \text{m})^2}$$

$$= 2.7 \times 10^{20} \, \text{N}$$

This force is greater than the net force that Dione and Rhea together exert on Tethys by a factor of

$$\frac{F_{\text{Saturn on Tethys}}}{F_{\text{net on Tethys}}} = \frac{2.7 \times 10^{20} \, \text{N}}{2.0 \times 10^{15} \, \text{N}} = 1.4 \times 10^5$$

? Got the Concept? 10-1 Gravitational Force

Compared to the gravitational force that Earth exerts on a 50-kg object located three Earth radii above the North Pole, the gravitational force that Earth exerts on a 50-kg object located at the North Pole is (a) the same; (b) 3 times greater, (c) 4 times greater; (d) 9 times greater; (e) 16 times greater.

? Got the Concept? 10-2 Gravitational Acceleration

Compared to the acceleration due to Earth's gravity at a point three Earth radii above the North Pole, the acceleration due to Earth's gravity at the North Pole is (a) the same; (b) 3 times greater, (c) 4 times greater; (d) 9 times greater; (e) 16 times greater.

Take-Home Message for Section 10-2

✔ Newton's law of universal gravitation describes the gravitational force that any object exerts on another object. It states that the force is directly proportional to the product of the masses of two objects and inversely proportional to the square of the distance between their centers.

✔ The relationship we use for weight near Earth's surface, $w = mg$, is simply an application of the law of universal gravitation.

10-3 The gravitational potential energy of two objects is negative and increases toward zero as the objects are moved farther apart

In Chapter 6 we introduced the ideas of kinetic energy (Section 6-3) and potential energy (Section 6-6). We found that if a force is *conservative*—so that the work done by that force on an object as it moves depends only on the object's starting point and ending point, not on the path the object takes between them—then we can associate that force with potential energy. We also found that if only conservative forces do work on an object as it moves, the total mechanical energy—the sum of the kinetic energy and potential energy of the system—always keeps the same value and is *conserved* (Section 6-7).

One particularly important conservative force is the gravitational force on an object of mass m near Earth's surface, $w = mg$. We found that the potential energy associated with this force is $U_{grav} = mgy$, where y is the height of the object above some level that we choose to call $y = 0$. But because this simple expression for U_{grav} is based on the expression $w = mg$ for gravitational force, it *cannot* be correct for the more general form of the gravitational force between two objects, $F = Gm_1m_2/r^2$. What, then, is the correct expression for the gravitational potential energy of two objects of mass m_1 and m_2 separated by a distance r?

Deriving this expression from the law of universal gravitation is a task that requires calculus, which is beyond our scope. Instead we'll just present the answer, then examine it to see why it makes sense:

Gravitational constant (same for any two objects) | Masses of the two objects

Gravitational potential energy of a system of two objects (1 and 2)

$$U_{grav} = -\frac{Gm_1m_2}{r}$$

Center-to-center distance between the two objects

The gravitational potential energy is zero when the two objects are infinitely far apart. If the objects are brought closer together (so r is made smaller), U_{grav} decreases (it becomes more negative).

Gravitational potential energy (10-4)

The expression in Equation 10-4 looks nothing like the familiar formula $U_{grav} = mgy$. To understand the difference, let's consider two different cases in which gravitational potential energy changes (**Figure 10-8**).

In **Figure 10-8a** a woman on Earth's surface raises a book of mass m_{book} a vertical distance d. To do this she must work against a gravitational force on the book of magnitude $m_{book}g$, and so she must exert an upward force of the same magnitude. So she does an amount of work $m_{book}gd$ in the process. The book begins and ends at rest, so the work $m_{book}gd$ that she does goes into increasing the gravitational potential energy associated with the book: $\Delta U_{grav} = m_{book}gd$. If the woman stands on a ladder and once again lifts the book by a distance d, the gravitational force she works against is still $m_{book}g$ since the gravitational force exerted by Earth changes hardly at all near Earth's surface. So she again does work $m_{book}gd$, and the gravitational potential energy increases by the same amount $m_{book}gd$ as before. As **Figure 10-8b** shows, this means that the gravitational potential energy increases in direct proportion to the object's height y, and so the graph of U_{grav} versus height is a straight line: $U_{grav} = m_{book}gy$.

Now imagine the same person has donned a spacesuit and has brought the book with her to a point in space a distance r_A from the center of Earth (**Figure 10-8c**). At this point the gravitational force that Earth exerts on the book has magnitude $F_A = Gm_{Earth}m_{book}/r_A^2$. If she moves the book an additional distance d away from Earth, she has to exert a force of the same magnitude on the book and so does an amount of work $F_A d = (Gm_{Earth}m_{book}/r_A^2)d$. Just as on Earth, the work that she does goes into increasing the gravitational potential energy. If she now moves to a greater distance r_B from the center of Earth and repeats the process, Earth's gravitational force has a smaller magnitude $F_B = Gm_{Earth}m_{book}/r_B^2$. So at this greater distance she does a smaller amount of work $F_B d = (Gm_{Earth}m_{book}/r_B^2)d$, and so adds a smaller amount of gravitational potential energy. This means that at great distances, the gravitational potential energy does *not* increase in direct proportion to the distance r and the graph of U_{grav} versus distance is not a straight line. Instead, the graph becomes shallower with increasing values of r (**Figure 10-8d**). This is just what Equation 10-4 tells us, which helps to justify this expression for gravitational potential energy.

Figure 10-8 Gravitational potential energy near Earth's surface and far away (a) A woman lifts a book of mass m_{book} a distance d while standing on the ground. She then repeats the process while standing on a ladder. (b) The gravitational force and the change in gravitational potential energy is basically the same in both cases, so the graph of U_{grav} versus height is a straight line. (c) The woman again raises the book a distance d, first at distance r_A from Earth's center, then at distance r_B. (d) The gravitational force and the change in gravitational potential energy are less at distance r_B than at distance r_A, so the graph of U_{grav} versus distance is a curve that gets shallower as r increases.

(a)

Gravitational force on the book is essentially the same on the ground or on a ladder.

(b)

$$U_{grav} = m_{book}\,gy$$

$$\Delta U_{grav} = m_{book}\,gd$$

$$\Delta U_{grav} = m_{book}\,gd$$

ΔU_{grav} is essentially the same whether the woman stands on the ground or on a ladder.

(c)

Gravitational force on the book is less at distance r_B than at distance r_A.

(d)

$$U_{grav} = -\frac{Gm_{Earth}m_{book}}{r}$$

ΔU_{grav} at r_B

ΔU_{grav} at r_A

ΔU_{grav} is smaller at distance r_B than at distance r_A.

More on Gravitational Potential Energy

Here are three important attributes of Equation 10-4 for gravitational potential energy.

(1) *The gravitational potential energy of two objects interacting is a shared property of the two objects.* We learned in Section 6-6 that the gravitational potential energy $U_{grav} = mgy$ for an object of mass m near Earth's surface actually "belongs" to both Earth and the object, since it's associated with their mutual gravitational attraction. In the same way, $U_{grav} = -Gm_1m_2/r$ as given by Equation 10-4 "belongs" to the *system* made up of an object of mass m_1 and an object of mass m_2.

(2) *The gravitational potential energy as given by Equation 10-4 is never positive.* The minus sign in Equation 10-4 means that the value of U_{grav} given by this expression is always negative, except when the two objects are infinitely far apart so $r \rightarrow \infty$ and $U_{grav} = 0$ (see Figure 10-8d). Don't be concerned by this! We learned in Section 6-6 that what's really physically meaningful are not the values of potential energy, but rather the *differences* between the values of potential energy at two different points. That means we can choose the point where potential energy equals zero to be wherever it's convenient. Our choice is that $U_{grav} = 0$ when the two objects are infinitely far apart. With this choice, U_{grav} as given by Equation 10-4 decreases and becomes more and more negative as an object of mass m_1 and an object of mass m_2 move toward each other, just as gravitational potential energy decreases as a ball drops toward the ground (that is, toward Earth).

(3) *The gravitational potential energy as given by Equation 10-4 is consistent with the formula $U_{grav} = mgy$ from Section 6-6.* To see how this can be,

imagine an object of mass m a height y_i above Earth's surface—that is, at a distance $r = R_{Earth} + y_i$ from Earth's center. If you lift this object to a new height y_f above the surface, its new distance from Earth's center is $r = R_{Earth} + y_f$. The change in the gravitational potential energy in this process is

$$\Delta U_{grav} = U_{grav,f} - U_{grav,i} = \left(-\frac{Gm_{Earth}m}{R_{Earth} + y_f}\right) - \left(-\frac{Gm_{Earth}m}{R_{Earth} + y_i}\right)$$

$$= Gm_{Earth}m\left(\frac{1}{R_{Earth} + y_i} - \frac{1}{R_{Earth} + y_f}\right)$$

If we express this in terms of a common denominator, you should be able to show that we get

$$\Delta U_{grav} = m\left[\frac{Gm_{Earth}}{(R_{Earth} + y_i)(R_{Earth} + y_f)}\right](y_f - y_i) \qquad (10\text{-}5)$$

This looks like a horrible mess! But if the heights y_i and y_f are both small compared to Earth's radius R_{Earth}—that is, if the object of mass m remains close to Earth's surface—then the quantities $R_{Earth} + y_i$ and $R_{Earth} + y_f$ are both approximately equal to R_{Earth}. In that case the quantity in square brackets in Equation 10-5 becomes Gm_{Earth}/R_{Earth}^2, which we found in the previous section is equal to the value of g at Earth's surface (see Equation 10-3). Then Equation 10-5 becomes

$$\Delta U_{grav} = U_{grav,f} - U_{grav,i}$$
$$= mg(y_f - y_i) = mgy_f - mgy_i$$

That's precisely the result we would have obtained using $U_{grav} = mgy$. In other words, if we restrict ourselves to motion of the object near the surface of Earth, we can safely use the expression from Section 6-6 for gravitational potential energy.

Gravitational Potential Energy and Conservation of Total Mechanical Energy

Just like the gravitational force near the surface of Earth, the gravitational force given by the law of universal gravitation, Equation 10-2, is a conservative force. So it is still true that in situations in which only the gravitational force does work, the total mechanical energy E (the sum of the kinetic energy K and the gravitational potential energy U_{grav}) is *conserved*. An example is a rocket that's launched from Earth's surface with a certain initial speed. Earth is so massive compared to the rocket that we can assume that there is no effect on our planet. Then, if we ignore the effects of air resistance during the rocket's initial climb through the atmosphere, only gravity does work on the rocket and the total mechanical energy of the Earth-rocket system is conserved. The following example demonstrates how to use this idea.

Example 10-5 How High Does It Go?

You launch a rocket of mass 2.40×10^4 kg straight upward from Earth's surface. The rocket's engines burn for a short time, giving the rocket an initial speed of 9.00 km/s (32,400 km/h or 20,100 mi/h), then shut off (Figure 10-9). To what maximum height above Earth's surface will this rocket rise? Earth's mass is 5.97×10^{24} kg and its radius is 6370 km $= 6.37 \times 10^6$ m.

Figure 10-9 **A rocket launch** What is the relationship between the speed imparted to the rocket at launch and the maximum height that it reaches?

Set Up

We'll ignore the force of air resistance on the rocket as it ascends through the atmosphere (this force, like kinetic friction, is nonconservative). Then Earth's gravity is the only force that does work on the rocket, and total mechanical energy is conserved.

With such a tremendous launch speed, we expect the rocket to reach a very high altitude. So the rocket will not remain close to Earth's surface, and we must use the more general form for gravitational potential energy given by Equation 10-4.

Initially the rocket has speed $v_i = 9.00 \text{ km/s} = 9.00 \times 10^3 \text{ m/s}$ and is a distance r_i from Earth's center equal to the radius of Earth. At its maximum height the rocket is at rest ($v_f = 0$) and is a distance h above the surface. Our goal is to determine h.

Total mechanical energy is conserved:

$$K_i + U_{\text{grav,i}} = K_f + U_{\text{grav,f}} \qquad (6\text{-}23)$$

Gravitational potential energy:

$$U_{\text{grav}} = -\frac{Gm_{\text{Earth}}m_{\text{rocket}}}{r} \qquad (10\text{-}4)$$

Kinetic energy of rocket:

$$K = \frac{1}{2}m_{\text{rocket}}v^2 \qquad (6\text{-}8)$$

Solve

We first determine the total mechanical energy of the system using the given values for the rocket's initial speed and position.

When the rocket is initially launched at the surface, its kinetic energy is

$$K_i = \frac{1}{2}m_{\text{rocket}}v_i^2 = \frac{1}{2}(2.40 \times 10^4 \text{ kg})(9.00 \times 10^3 \text{ m/s})^2$$

$$= 9.72 \times 10^{11} \text{ kg} \cdot \text{m}^2/\text{s}^2 = 9.72 \times 10^{11} \text{ J}$$

(Recall that $1 \text{ J} = 1 \text{ kg} \cdot \text{m}^2/\text{s}^2$.)

The gravitational potential energy is

$$U_{\text{grav,i}} = -\frac{Gm_{\text{Earth}}m_{\text{rocket}}}{r_i} = -\frac{Gm_{\text{Earth}}m_{\text{rocket}}}{R_{\text{Earth}}}$$

$$= -\frac{(6.67 \times 10^{-11} \text{ N} \cdot \text{m}^2/\text{kg}^2)(5.97 \times 10^{24} \text{ kg})(2.40 \times 10^4 \text{ kg})}{6.37 \times 10^6 \text{ m}}$$

$$= -1.50 \times 10^{12} \text{ N} \cdot \text{m} = -1.50 \times 10^{12} \text{ J}$$

(Recall that $1 \text{ J} = 1 \text{ N} \cdot \text{m}$)

The total mechanical energy is

$$E_i = K_i + U_{\text{grav,i}} = (9.72 \times 10^{11} \text{ J}) + (-1.50 \times 10^{12} \text{ J}) = -5.28 \times 10^{11} \text{ J}$$

When the rocket is at the high point of its trajectory, it is momentarily at rest and its kinetic energy is zero. At this point the (conserved) total mechanical energy is equal to the gravitational potential energy. Use this to solve for the rocket's distance r_f from Earth's center at its high point.

At the high point of the trajectory, rocket speed is $v_f = 0$ and its kinetic energy is

$$K_f = \frac{1}{2}m_{\text{rocket}}v_f^2 = 0$$

The total mechanical energy has the same value as when the rocket was launched:

$$E_f = K_f + U_{\text{grav,f}} = E_i = -5.28 \times 10^{11} \text{ J}$$

Since $K_f = 0$, this means that

$$U_{\text{grav,f}} = -\frac{Gm_{\text{Earth}}m_{\text{rocket}}}{r_f} = E_i = -5.28 \times 10^{11} \text{ J}$$

$$\text{Solve for } r_f: r_f = -\frac{Gm_{Earth}m_{rocket}}{E_i}$$

$$= -\frac{(6.67 \times 10^{-11} \text{ N} \cdot \text{m}^2/\text{kg}^2)(5.97 \times 10^{24} \text{ kg})(2.40 \times 10^4 \text{ kg})}{(-5.28 \times 10^{11} \text{ J})}$$

$$= 1.81 \times 10^7 \text{ m} = 1.81 \times 10^4 \text{ km}$$

Subtract Earth's radius from r_f to find the rocket's final height above the surface.

The rocket's final distance from Earth's center, r_f, equals the radius of Earth (R_{Earth}) plus the rocket's final height h above Earth's surface:

$$r_f = R_{Earth} + h$$

Solve for h:

$$h = r_f - R_{Earth} = 1.81 \times 10^4 \text{ km} - 6.37 \times 10^3 \text{ km} = 1.17 \times 10^4 \text{ km}$$

Reflect

The final height is nearly twice the radius of Earth! This justifies our decision to use Equation 10-4 for gravitational potential energy. Had we used the expression from Chapter 6, $U_{grav} = m_{rocket}gy$, we would have gotten an incorrect answer because that expression assumes that g has the same value at all heights. In fact, g decreases substantially in value at greater distances from Earth, which means that the rocket climbs much higher than the expression $U_{grav} = m_{rocket}gy$ would predict.

From Example 10-3 (Section 10-2), the value of g at a distance r from Earth's center is

$$g = \frac{Gm_{Earth}}{r^2}$$

At the rocket's maximum distance,

$$g = \frac{Gm_{Earth}}{r_f^2}$$

$$= \frac{(6.67 \times 10^{-11} \text{ N} \cdot \text{m}^2/\text{kg}^2)(5.97 \times 10^{24} \text{ kg})}{(1.81 \times 10^7 \text{ m})^2}$$

$$= 1.22 \text{ m/s}^2$$

which is *much* less than $g = 9.80 \text{ m/s}^2$ at Earth's surface.

A common *incorrect* way to calculate h would be to use $U_{grav} = m_{rocket}gy$, which is based on the (false!) assumption that $g = 9.80 \text{ m/s}^2$ at all altitudes. Then conservation of total mechanical energy would have told us that

$$\frac{1}{2}m_{rocket}v_i^2 + m_{rocket}gy_i = \frac{1}{2}m_{rocket}v_f^2 + m_{rocket}gy_f$$

With $y_i = 0$ (rocket at surface), $y_f = h$ (rocket at maximum height), and $v_f = 0$ (rocket momentarily at rest at maximum height), this becomes

$$\frac{1}{2}m_{rocket}v_i^2 + 0 = 0 + m_{rocket}gh$$

$$h = \frac{v_i^2}{2g} = \frac{(9.00 \times 10^3 \text{ m/s})^2}{2(9.80 \text{ m/s}^2)} = 4.13 \times 10^6 \text{ m} = 4.13 \times 10^3 \text{ km}$$

(**Incorrect answer!**)

The actual height that the rocket reaches is almost three times higher, 1.17×10^4 km, because in fact the value of g decreases with altitude.

$g = 1.22 \text{ m/s}^2$

$h \approx 1.17 \times 10^4 \text{ km}$

$g = 9.80 \text{ m/s}^2$

Earth

Escape Speed

Like a ball thrown vertically upward, the rocket in Example 10-5 reaches a peak height and eventually returns to the surface. If the rocket is launched with a great enough speed, however, it will *never* return. That's a consequence of the law of universal gravitation, Equation 10-2. This says that the gravitational force that Earth exerts on the rocket decreases with increasing distance from Earth, and approaches zero as the rocket moves to infinitely great distances (see Figure 10-4b). As in Example 10-5 the rocket engines give it a certain initial speed, then shut off. The rocket then coasts upward and loses speed due to Earth's gravity. As the rocket climbs, the gravitational force on the rocket decreases, and so the rocket loses an ever-smaller amount of speed per second. If the initial speed of the rocket is great enough, there will still be some speed remaining when the rocket is very far from Earth and it will keep on going forever. We say that the rocket has *escaped* from Earth.

Watch Out!   You can never be "beyond the pull of Earth's gravity."

There's a common misconception that if a rocket travels far enough from Earth, it reaches a point where it's "beyond" the pull of our planet's gravity. But Equation 10-2 shows that in fact the gravitational force that Earth exerts on an object of mass m, $F = Gm_{Earth}m/r^2$, only becomes zero when the distance r from Earth to the object is *infinity*. The force gets progressively weaker as the object moves farther away from Earth, but it never entirely disappears. A rocket can escape from Earth if it has enough speed to overcome the attraction of Earth's gravity and travel to infinity. But the rocket still feels that attraction at all points along its infinite voyage.

We can find the minimum speed for a projectile to escape from Earth by using Equation 10-4 for gravitational potential energy. As in Example 10-5, we'll assume that the projectile (mass m) is launched from Earth's surface (that is, from a distance $r_i = R_{Earth}$ from Earth's center) with a speed v_i. The total mechanical energy just as the projectile is launched is then

$$(10\text{-}6) \qquad E_i = K_i + U_{grav,i} = \frac{1}{2}mv_i^2 + \left(-\frac{Gm_{Earth}m}{R_{Earth}}\right)$$

Just as in Example 10-5, we'll also ignore the effects of air resistance during the time that the projectile is passing through Earth's atmosphere. Then only the gravitational force does work on the projectile, and as in Example 10-5 we can use the principle that total mechanical energy is conserved. When the projectile is a distance r from Earth's center and moving at a speed v, the total mechanical energy is

$$(10\text{-}7) \qquad E = K + U_{grav} = \frac{1}{2}mv^2 + \left(-\frac{Gm_{Earth}m}{r}\right)$$

Since total mechanical energy is conserved, E_i as given by Equation 10-6 is equal to E as given by Equation 10-7:

$$(10\text{-}8) \qquad \frac{1}{2}mv_i^2 + \left(-\frac{Gm_{Earth}m}{R_{Earth}}\right) = \frac{1}{2}mv^2 + \left(-\frac{Gm_{Earth}m}{r}\right)$$

Now let's suppose that the projectile just barely escapes Earth, so its speed is zero when it is infinitely far away. That corresponds to replacing v with zero and r with infinity in Equation 10-8. The reciprocal of infinity is zero, so in this case both terms on the right-hand side of Equation 10-8 are zero: The projectile ends up with zero kinetic energy (it is at rest), and the gravitational potential energy ends up with a zero value (the projectile is infinitely far from Earth; see Figure 10-8d). Then Equation 10-8 becomes

$$(10\text{-}9) \qquad \frac{1}{2}mv_i^2 + \left(-\frac{Gm_{Earth}m}{R_{Earth}}\right) = 0$$

The initial speed v_i for which Equation 10-9 is true is called the **escape speed,** which we denote by the symbol v_{escape}. This is the minimum speed at which an object must be launched from Earth's surface to escape to infinity. To find its value, replace v_i in Equation 10-9 with v_{escape}, add $Gm_{Earth}m/R_{Earth}$ to both sides and multiply both sides by $2/m$.

$$\frac{1}{2}mv_{escape}^2 = \frac{Gm_{Earth}m}{R_{Earth}}$$

$$v_{escape}^2 = \frac{2Gm_{Earth}}{R_{Earth}}$$

Finally, take the square root of both sides:

Speed that a projectile must have at Earth's surface in order to escape Earth.

Gravitational constant   Mass of Earth

$$v_{escape} = \sqrt{\frac{2Gm_{Earth}}{R_{Earth}}}$$

Radius of Earth

Escape speed
(10-10)

If you substitute $G = 6.67 \times 10^{-11}\ \mathrm{N \cdot m^2/kg^2}$, $m_{Earth} = 5.97 \times 10^{24}$ kg, and $R_{Earth} = 6.37 \times 10^6$ m into Equation 10-10, you'll find that $v_{escape} = 1.12 \times 10^4$ m/s = 11.2 km/s (about 40,300 km/h or 25,000 mi/h). Rockets designed to send spacecraft to other planets must have powerful rocket engines (see Figure 10-9) in order to accelerate their payload to such high speeds.

Notice that the launch speed of the rocket in Example 10-5 was only 9.00 km/s, which is less than escape speed. That's why the rocket in that example did *not* escape, but reached a maximum distance from Earth before falling back. To have the rocket escape, it would have to be launched at 11.2 km/s or faster.

We can also use Equation 10-10 to find the escape speed from *any* planet or satellite: Just replace m_{Earth} and R_{Earth} with the mass and radius of the object from which the projectile is launched.

Example 10-6 Escaping from a Martian Moon

You have landed your spacecraft on Phobos, the larger of the two airless moons of Mars (Figure 10-10). Phobos is roughly spherical with an average radius of 11.1 km = 1.11×10^4 m. By dropping a baseball while standing on Phobos, you find that g has a very small value at the moon's surface, only 0.00580 m/s^2. At what speed would you have to throw the baseball to have it escape Phobos?

Figure 10-10 **Phobos** What is the escape speed from this miniature moon of Mars, just 11.1 km in radius?

Set Up

To find the escape speed v_{escape} using Equation 10-10, we need the radius of Phobos, which we are given, and the mass of Phobos, which we are *not* given. However, we recall from Equation 10-3 in Section 10-2 that the value of g on Earth's surface is related to Earth's mass and radius. We can write this same equation for Phobos, which will let us use the measured value of g on Phobos to determine its mass.

Escape speed from Phobos:

$$v_{escape} = \sqrt{\frac{2Gm_{Phobos}}{R_{Phobos}}} \quad (10\text{-}10)$$

Value of g at the surface of Phobos:

$$g = \frac{Gm_{Phobos}}{R_{Phobos}^2} \quad (10\text{-}3)$$

Solve

First use Equation 10-3 to determine the mass of Phobos.

From Equation 10-3, $g = \dfrac{Gm_{Phobos}}{R_{Phobos}^2}$

Solve this for the mass of Phobos:

$$m_{\text{Phobos}} = \frac{gR_{\text{Phobos}}^2}{G} = \frac{(0.00580 \text{ m/s}^2)(1.11 \times 10^4 \text{ m})^2}{6.67 \times 10^{-11} \text{ N} \cdot \text{m}^2/\text{kg}^2}$$

$$= 1.07 \times 10^{16} \frac{\text{kg}^2 \cdot \text{m/s}^2}{\text{N}} = 1.07 \times 10^{16} \text{ kg}$$

(Recall that $1 \text{ N} = 1 \text{ kg} \cdot \text{m/s}^2$.)

Then use Equation 10-10 to find the escape speed from Phobos.

Escape speed:

$$v_{\text{escape}} = \sqrt{\frac{2Gm_{\text{Phobos}}}{R_{\text{Phobos}}}}$$

$$= \sqrt{\frac{2(6.67 \times 10^{-11} \text{ N} \cdot \text{m}^2/\text{kg}^2)(1.07 \times 10^{16} \text{ kg})}{1.10 \times 10^4 \text{ m}}}$$

$$= \sqrt{127 \frac{\text{N} \cdot \text{m}}{\text{kg}}} = \sqrt{127 \frac{\text{kg} \cdot \text{m}}{\text{s}^2} \frac{\text{m}}{\text{kg}}} = \sqrt{127 \frac{\text{m}^2}{\text{s}^2}}$$

$$= 11.3 \text{ m/s} = 40.7 \text{ km/h} = 25.3 \text{ mi/h}$$

(We once again used $1 \text{ N} = 1 \text{ kg} \cdot \text{m/s}^2$.)

Reflect

The escape speed on Phobos is almost exactly 1/1000 the escape speed on Earth! In general, the smaller the planet or moon, the lower the escape speed.

A typical high school baseball pitcher can easily throw a baseball at more than 25 m/s (90 km/h or 56 mi/h), so a well-trained astronaut should have no problem throwing a baseball at the 11.3-m/s escape speed on Phobos.

❓ Got the Concept? 10-3   Which Direction for Escape?

In Example 10-6, suppose you throw the baseball with a speed faster than 11.3 m/s. **Figure 10-11** shows four possible directions in which you could throw the ball at that speed. In which of these directions would the ball escape from Phobos? (a) Direction A only; (b) direction A or B; (c) direction A, B, or C; (d) direction A, B, C, or D; (e) none of these.

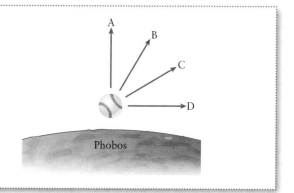

Figure 10-11 Four directions for escaping Phobos If a ball is thrown at escape speed, in what direction(s) can it be thrown so that it *will* escape?

Take-Home Message for Section 10-3

✔ When analyzing situations in which an object does not remain close to the surface of Earth, you must use the expression for gravitational potential energy that is derived from Newton's law of universal gravitation.

✔ Using Newton's law of universal gravitation, the gravitational potential energy of two objects is always negative or zero. It is zero when the two objects are infinitely far apart, and it becomes more and more negative as the objects move closer together.

✔ Escape speed is the speed at which a projectile must be launched from a planet or moon so that it never falls back to the world from which it was launched.

10-4 Newton's law of universal gravitation explains Kepler's laws for the orbits of planets and satellites

We saw in Section 10-2 that Newton deduced the law of universal gravitation from the properties of the Moon's orbit around Earth. Because gravitation is universal, the same principles apply to the orbit of *any* celestial object around another.

Circular Orbits: Orbital Speed and Orbital Period

The simplest type of orbit to analyze is a circular orbit. Many Earth satellites, including the International Space Station (see the photograph that opens this chapter) and the satellites that provide signals for Global Positioning System (GPS) navigation, are in circular or nearly circular orbits.

Although the first Earth satellite was put in orbit in 1957, Newton understood what was required to put a satellite in a circular orbit almost three centuries earlier (**Figure 10-12**). If a cannonball is dropped from a great height such as the top of a mountain, it will fall straight down. If it is thrown horizontally at a moderate speed, the cannonball will follow a curved arc before hitting the ground. But if it is thrown horizontally with just the right speed, the surface of Earth will fall away below the cannonball so that the cannonball always remains at the same height above the surface. Put another way, Earth's gravitational attraction will cause the cannonball to accelerate toward Earth's center. If the cannonball's speed is just right, the result will be uniform circular motion of the sort that we studied in Section 3-8, in which the acceleration is always directed toward the center of the cannonball's circular path (**Figure 10-13**).

We can find the speed v required for a circular orbit of radius r from Equation 3-17 for the acceleration in uniform circular motion: $a_{cent} = v^2/r$. For a satellite of mass m orbiting Earth, the acceleration is provided by Earth's gravitational force. From Newton's second law, this says

$$F_{\text{Earth on satellite}} = ma_{cent}$$

or, from Equation 3-17 for uniform circular motion and Equation 10-2 for the law of universal gravitation,

$$\frac{Gm_{\text{Earth}}m}{r^2} = m\frac{v^2}{r}$$

To solve for v, multiply both sides of this equation by r/m

$$\frac{Gm_{\text{Earth}}}{r} = v^2$$

and take the square root:

Gravitational constant   Mass of Earth

Speed of an Earth satellite in a circular orbit

$$v = \sqrt{\frac{Gm_{\text{Earth}}}{r}}$$

Radius of the satellite's orbit

Speed of an Earth satellite in a circular orbit
(10-11)

Many satellites, including the International Space Station, are in *low Earth orbit*: Their height above the surface is a few hundred kilometers, which is a short distance compared to Earth's radius of 6370 km. So we can find the approximate speed of a satellite in low Earth orbit by replacing r in Equation 10-11 with the radius of Earth and substituting the values $G = 6.67 \times 10^{-11} \text{ N} \cdot \text{m}^2/\text{kg}^2$, $m_{\text{Earth}} = 5.97 \times 10^{24}$ kg, and $R_{\text{Earth}} = 6.37 \times 10^6$ m:

$$v = \sqrt{\frac{Gm_{\text{Earth}}}{R_{\text{Earth}}}} = 7.91 \times 10^3 \text{ m/s} = 7.91 \text{ km/s}$$
(orbital speed for low Earth orbit)

This speed (about 28,500 km/h or 17,700 mi/h) is slower than the escape speed of 11.2 km/s (which we discussed in Section 10-3) by a factor of $1/\sqrt{2} = 0.707$.

Equation 10-11 shows that increasing the orbital radius r decreases the speed for a circular orbit. We saw an example of this in Section 10-2: The Moon orbits Earth at an average distance of 3.84×10^8 m, about 60 times Earth's radius, and its orbital speed is only 1.02×10^3 m/s $= 1.02$ km/s. You can understand why the speed decreases with increasing orbital radius by considering not a satellite orbiting Earth but a ball on the end of a string. Imagine whirling the ball on a string around your hand so that the ball makes a circular orbit around your hand. To make the ball move at high speed around a small circle, you have to exert a substantial pull on the string. But if you lengthen the string and make the same ball move at low speed

Page 6.

Figure 10-12 Newton's recipe for an Earth satellite Isaac Newton imagined that if a cannonball were fired horizontally from the top of a mountain with sufficient speed, the rate at which it fell could be made to match the rate at which Earth's surface fell away. The cannonball would therefore end up orbiting Earth. Newton created this illustration for the same 1687 book in which he presented the law of universal gravitation.

Figure 10-13 A circular orbit A satellite in a circular orbit is in uniform circular motion: The acceleration (due to Earth's gravitational force) has a constant magnitude and is always directed toward Earth's center, and the velocity has a constant magnitude.

around a large circle, much less pull is required. Similarly, a satellite that orbits close to Earth experiences a substantial gravitational pull and so moves at high speed, while a planet in a larger orbit experiences less gravitational force and moves at a lower speed.

Another useful way to describe how rapidly a satellite moves around its circular orbit is in terms of the **orbital period,** which is the time required to complete one orbit. In uniform circular motion the speed v is constant, so the orbital period T is just the circumference $2\pi r$ of the orbit (the distance around the circular orbit of radius r) divided by the speed: $T = 2\pi r/v$. Using Equation 10-11 for v, this becomes

$$T = \frac{2\pi r}{v} = 2\pi r \sqrt{\frac{r}{Gm_{\text{Earth}}}}$$

It's convenient to square both sides of this equation so as to eliminate the square root. Note that the square of r is r^2 and the square of $\sqrt{r}$ is r, so we end up with a factor of $r^2 \times r = r^3$ on the right-hand side of the equation:

Relationship between orbital period and radius for a circular orbit (10-12)

Period of an Earth satellite in a circular orbit   Radius of the satellite's orbit

$$T^2 = \frac{4\pi^2}{Gm_{\text{Earth}}} r^3$$

Gravitational constant   Mass of Earth

For an object in low Earth orbit, for which r equals R_{Earth}, this tells us that $T = 5.06 \times 10^3$ s $= 84.4$ min, or a little less than an hour and a half.

In words, Equation 10-12 says that the *square* of the orbital period T is directly proportional to the *cube* of the radius r of the orbit. By comparison, Equation 10-11 tells us that the orbital speed v is inversely proportional to the *square root* of the orbital radius r. As an example, consider a satellite that orbits at a distance $r = 4R_{\text{Earth}}$ from Earth's center (that is, at an altitude of $3R_{\text{Earth}}$ above Earth's surface). Since r is four times greater than for a satellite in low Earth orbit, the quantity r^3 is $4^3 = 4 \times 4 \times 4 = 64$ times greater. So the quantity T^2 is also 64 times greater than for an object in low Earth orbit, which means the period T is $\sqrt{64} = 8$ times longer. The orbital speed is proportional to $1/\sqrt{r}$, which is $1/\sqrt{4} = 1/2$ as great as for a satellite in low Earth orbit. These proportionality rules therefore tell us that for a satellite with $r = 4R_{\text{Earth}}$, the orbital period is 8×84.4 min $= 675$ min (11.2 hours) and the orbital speed is $(1/2) \times 7.91$ km/s $= 3.95$ km/s.

Watch Out! When a satellite orbits Earth, Earth moves too.

One aspect of orbital motion that we've ignored in this discussion is Newton's third law: If Earth exerts a gravitational force on a satellite, the satellite exerts an equally strong force on Earth. So Earth also moves in a small orbit. Strictly speaking, Earth and the satellite both orbit around the center of mass of the Earth–satellite system. However, even the larg-est satellite humans have ever placed in orbit has a tiny mass compared to the mass of Earth. So for all practical purposes the center of mass of the Earth–satellite system is at Earth's center. By contrast, the Moon's mass is a reasonable fraction of Earth's mass (about 1.2%), so for detailed calculations this effect must be taken into account (Figure 10-14).

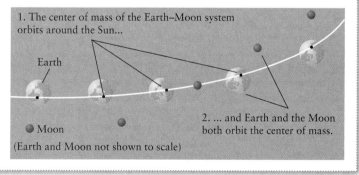

1. The center of mass of the Earth–Moon system orbits around the Sun...

Earth

Moon

(Earth and Moon not shown to scale)

2. ... and Earth and the Moon both orbit the center of mass.

Figure 10-14 **The motions of Earth and Moon** Because Earth and the Moon both exert gravitational forces on each other, it's not correct to say that the Moon orbits Earth. Rather, both objects move around their common center of mass.

Circular Orbits: Energy

Before placing a satellite into a circular orbit, an important question to ask is "How much energy will it take to put the satellite in the desired orbit?" The answer determines how powerful a rocket will be needed for the task. We have all the tools we need to answer this question: Equation 10-11 tells us the speed the satellite must have in its circular orbit, which allows us to determine the required kinetic energy, and Equation 10-4 tells us the gravitational potential energy. So the kinetic energy for a satellite of mass m in a circular orbit of radius r is

$$K = \frac{1}{2}mv^2 = \frac{1}{2}m\left(\sqrt{\frac{Gm_{\text{Earth}}}{r}}\right)^2 = \frac{Gm_{\text{Earth}}m}{2r}$$

Making the orbital radius r larger means the satellite moves more slowly and the kinetic energy decreases. The gravitational potential energy is

$$U_{\text{grav}} = -\frac{Gm_{\text{Earth}}m}{r}$$

As we discussed in Section 10-3, the gravitational potential energy is negative. Making the orbital radius r larger makes the gravitational potential energy less negative—that is, closer to zero—which means that the gravitational potential energy increases. The total mechanical energy is the sum of K and U_{grav}:

$$E = K + U_{\text{grav}} = \frac{1}{2}mv^2 + \left(-\frac{Gm_{\text{Earth}}m}{r}\right) = \frac{Gm_{\text{Earth}}m}{2r} + \left(-\frac{Gm_{\text{Earth}}m}{r}\right)$$

or

Gravitational constant   Mass of Earth

Total mechanical energy for a satellite in a circular orbit around Earth

Mass of satellite

$$E = -\frac{Gm_{\text{Earth}}m}{2r}$$

Radius of the satellite's orbit

The greater the radius r of the circular orbit, the greater (less negative) the total mechanical energy.

Total mechanical energy for a circular orbit
(10-13)

The total mechanical energy E is always negative because of the way we defined gravitational potential energy. A zero value of E corresponds to an infinite value of r, where the gravitational potential energy is zero and the satellite would have zero speed and zero kinetic energy.

As an example, for a satellite in low Earth orbit (with $r = R_{\text{Earth}}$) the total mechanical energy is $E = -Gm_{\text{Earth}}m/2R_{\text{Earth}}$. Before the spacecraft was launched and was sitting on Earth's surface, its kinetic energy was zero and E was equal to the gravitational potential energy: $E = U_{\text{grav}} = -Gm_{\text{Earth}}m/R$. So the amount of energy that had to be imparted to the satellite to put it into low Earth orbit was

$$\Delta E = E_{\text{in orbit}} - E_{\text{on surface}} = \left(-\frac{Gm_{\text{Earth}}m}{2R_{\text{Earth}}}\right) - \left(-\frac{Gm_{\text{Earth}}m}{R_{\text{Earth}}}\right) = +\frac{Gm_{\text{Earth}}m}{2R_{\text{Earth}}}$$

For a one-kilogram satellite ($m = 1.00$ kg), $\Delta E = 3.13 \times 10^7$ J. So 3.13×10^7 J of energy has to be imparted to each kilogram of a satellite placed into low Earth orbit. In practice, the energy requirements are much greater because the rocket and its fuel (which are much more massive than the satellite itself) also have to be given kinetic energy. One way to *reduce* the energy requirements is to take advantage of Earth's rotation. Every point on Earth's surface is rotating to the east (which is why we see the Sun rise in the east), and the speed in meters per second is greatest near the equator. That's why NASA and the European Space Agency launch satellites into orbit from locations relatively close to the equator (Florida and French Guiana, respectively) and launch them toward the east (Figure 10-15).

Figure 10-15 **Launching toward the east** This aerial photograph shows a space shuttle launch. Having climbed through the clouds, the spacecraft climbs upward and to the east (to the left in the photograph) from Florida. In this way the spacecraft takes advantage of Earth's eastward rotation, which gives the spacecraft 406 m/s of speed even before it lifts off.

> ## Watch Out! When a satellite falls to Earth, it's not just gravity's fault.
>
> Orbiting satellites do sometimes fall out of orbit and crash back to Earth. When this happens, however, the real culprit is not gravity but air resistance. A satellite in a relatively low orbit is actually flying through the tenuous outer wisps of Earth's atmosphere. Air resistance does negative work on the spacecraft, just like a kinetic friction force. This causes the total mechanical energy E to decrease and become more negative. From Equation 10-13, this means that the orbital radius r becomes smaller and the satellite sinks to a lower altitude, where it encounters more air resistance and sinks even lower. Eventually, the satellite either strikes Earth or burns up in flight due to air friction. By contrast, the Moon and planets orbit in the near-vacuum of interplanetary space. Hence, they are unaffected by this kind of air resistance, and they have remained in orbit around the Sun since the solar system formed 4.56 billion years ago.

Example 10-7 A Satellite for Satellite Television

The broadcasting satellites used in a satellite television system orbit Earth's equator with a period of exactly 24 hours, the same as Earth's rotation period. As a result, these satellites are *geostationary*: They always remain over the same spot on the equator, and so they always appear to be in the same position in the sky as seen from anywhere on Earth's surface. (A satellite TV receiver "dish" is aimed to receive the signal broadcast from one of these satellites.) (a) At what distance from Earth's center must a television satellite orbit? (b) What must be its orbital speed? (c) If a television satellite has a mass of 3.50×10^3 kg, how much energy must it be given to place it in orbit?

Set Up

A geostationary satellite has $T = 24$ h; we'll use this information and Equation 10-12 to find the radius r of the orbit. Once we find the value of r, we'll use Equation 10-11 to find the orbital speed of the satellite.

Equation 10-13 tells us the total mechanical energy of the spacecraft in orbit, and Equation 10-4 will tell us the total mechanical energy when the spacecraft is at rest on Earth's surface before being launched. The difference between these two values is the energy that must be given to the satellite.

Relationship between period and radius for a circular orbit:

$$T^2 = \frac{4\pi^2}{Gm_{\text{Earth}}} r^3 \quad (10\text{-}12)$$

Speed of an Earth satellite in a circular orbit:

$$v = \sqrt{\frac{Gm_{\text{Earth}}}{r}} \quad (10\text{-}11)$$

Total mechanical energy for a circular orbit:

$$E = -\frac{Gm_{\text{Earth}}m}{2r} \quad (10\text{-}13)$$

Gravitational potential energy:

$$U_{\text{grav}} = -\frac{Gm_1 m_2}{r} \quad (10\text{-}4)$$

Solve

(a) To use Equation 10-12 to find the orbital radius r, first convert the orbital period T to seconds.

Period of the satellite orbit:

$$T = 24 \text{ h}\left(\frac{60 \text{ min}}{1 \text{ h}}\right)\left(\frac{60 \text{ s}}{1 \text{ min}}\right) = 8.64 \times 10^4 \text{ s}$$

Solve Equation 10-12 for r^3:

$$r^3 = \frac{Gm_{\text{Earth}} T^2}{4\pi^2}$$

$$= \frac{(6.67 \times 10^{-11} \text{ N} \cdot \text{m}^2/\text{kg}^2)(5.97 \times 10^{24} \text{ kg})(8.64 \times 10^4 \text{ s})^2}{4\pi^2}$$

$$= 7.53 \times 10^{22} \frac{\text{N} \cdot \text{m}^2 \cdot \text{s}^2}{\text{kg}} = 7.53 \times 10^{22} \text{ m}^3$$

(We used $1 \text{ N} = 1 \text{ kg} \cdot \text{m/s}^2$.)

Take the cube root to find r:

$$r = \sqrt[3]{r^3} = \sqrt[3]{7.53 \times 10^{22}\,\text{m}^3}$$
$$= 4.22 \times 10^7\,\text{m} = 4.22 \times 10^4\,\text{km}$$

This is 6.63 times Earth's radius ($R_{\text{Earth}} = 6.37 \times 10^3\,\text{km}$).

(b) Then use Equation 10-11 to find the orbital speed of the satellite.

Orbital speed:

$$v = \sqrt{\frac{Gm_{\text{Earth}}}{r}}$$

$$= \sqrt{\frac{(6.67 \times 10^{-11}\,\text{N} \cdot \text{m}^2/\text{kg}^2)(5.97 \times 10^{24}\,\text{kg})}{4.22 \times 10^7\,\text{m}}}$$

$$= \sqrt{9.43 \times 10^6\,\frac{\text{N} \cdot \text{m}}{\text{kg}}} = \sqrt{9.43 \times 10^6\,\frac{\text{kg} \cdot \text{m}}{\text{s}^2}\frac{\text{m}}{\text{kg}}}$$

$$= \sqrt{9.43 \times 10^6\,\frac{\text{m}^2}{\text{s}^2}}$$

$$= 3.07 \times 10^3\,\text{m/s} = 1.11 \times 10^4\,\text{km/h} = 6.87 \times 10^3\,\text{mi/h}$$

(Again, we used $1\,\text{N} = 1\,\text{kg} \cdot \text{m/s}^2$.)

(c) Find the total mechanical energy in orbit, the total mechanical energy on Earth's surface, and the difference between these values for the satellite of mass $m = 3.50 \times 10^3$ kg.

When the satellite is in orbit, the total mechanical energy is

$$E_{\text{in orbit}} = -\frac{Gm_{\text{Earth}}m}{2r}$$

$$= -\frac{(6.67 \times 10^{-11}\,\text{N} \cdot \text{m}^2/\text{kg}^2)(5.97 \times 10^{24}\,\text{kg})(3.50 \times 10^3\,\text{kg})}{2(4.22 \times 10^7\,\text{m})}$$

$$= -1.65 \times 10^{10}\,\text{N} \cdot \text{m}$$

$$= -1.65 \times 10^{10}\,\text{J}$$

$E_{\text{in orbit}} = -1.65 \times 10^{10}$ J

$E_{\text{on surface}} = -2.19 \times 10^{11}$ J

Earth

With the spacecraft at rest on Earth's surface, the total mechanical energy is just the gravitational potential energy:

$$E_{\text{on surface}} = U_{\text{grav, on surface}} = -\frac{Gm_{\text{Earth}}m}{r}$$

$$= -\frac{(6.67 \times 10^{-11}\,\text{N} \cdot \text{m}^2/\text{kg}^2)(5.97 \times 10^{24}\,\text{kg})(3.50 \times 10^3\,\text{kg})}{6.37 \times 10^6\,\text{m}}$$

$$= -2.19 \times 10^{11}\,\text{N} \cdot \text{m} = -2.19 \times 10^{11}\,\text{J}$$

The amount of energy that must be given to the satellite to put it into orbit is

$$E_{\text{in orbit}} - E_{\text{on surface}} = (-1.65 \times 10^{10}\,\text{J}) - (-2.19 \times 10^{11}\,\text{J})$$

$$= 2.02 \times 10^{11}\,\text{J}$$

Reflect

Our answer to part (a) shows that geostationary broadcast satellites orbit at a tremendous distance from Earth. Part (c) shows that it takes a tremendous amount of energy to put them there.

You can check the result for part (b) by showing that the satellite's orbital speed v equals $2\pi r$ (the circumference of the circular orbit of radius r) divided by T (the time to complete one orbit). Does it?

Kepler's Laws of Planetary Motion

Decades before Newton published his law of universal gravitation, astronomers had carefully observed and recorded the positions of the planets as they traced out their orbits. While analyzing the observations made by the Danish astronomer Tycho Brahe, German mathematician and astronomer Johannes Kepler uncovered three laws that describe the orbit of one object around another, for example, the planets around the Sun.

Kepler's laws describe the shape of celestial orbits, the speed at which one object orbits another, and the time it takes an object to orbit another. However, these laws do not in themselves explain *why* the planetary orbits behave this way. While we write these laws in terms of a planet orbiting the Sun, they apply equally well to any object in orbit around another. One of Newton's great accomplishments was to show that his law of universal gravitation, in conjunction with his laws of motion, explained *why* the planets move according to Kepler's laws.

The first of Kepler's laws is the **law of orbits**:

> *The orbit of each planet is an ellipse with the Sun located at one focus of the ellipse.*

You can draw an ellipse by using a loop of string, two thumbtacks, and a pencil, as Figure 10-16a shows. Each thumbtack in the figure is at a *focus* (plural foci) of the ellipse; an ellipse has two foci. The longest diameter of an ellipse, called the *major axis*, passes through both foci. Half of that distance is called the **semimajor axis** and is usually designated by the symbol *a*. (Unfortunately, this is also the symbol for acceleration. We promise never to use semimajor axis and acceleration in the same equation!) A circle is a special case of an ellipse in which the two foci are at the same point; this corresponds to using only a single thumbtack in Figure 10-16a. The semimajor axis of a circle is equal to its radius.

Ellipses come in different shapes, depending on the elongation of the ellipse. The shape of an ellipse is described by its **eccentricity**, designated by the letter *e*. The value of *e* can range from 0 (a circle) to just under 1 (nearly a straight line). The greater the eccentricity, the more elongated the ellipse. Figure 10-16b shows a few examples of ellipses with different eccentricities. All of the objects that orbit the Sun have orbits that are at least slightly elliptical, with *e* greater than zero. The most circular of any planetary

Figure 10-16　Ellipses (a) To draw an ellipse, use two thumbtacks to secure the ends of a piece of string, then use a pencil to pull the string taut. If you move the pencil while keeping the string taut, the pencil traces out an ellipse. The thumbtacks are located at the two foci of the ellipse. The major axis is the greatest distance across the ellipse; the semimajor axis is half of this distance. (b) These ellipses have the same major axis but different eccentricities. An ellipse can have any eccentricity from *e* = 0 (a circle) to just under *e* = 1 (virtually a straight line).

(a) The geometry of an ellipse

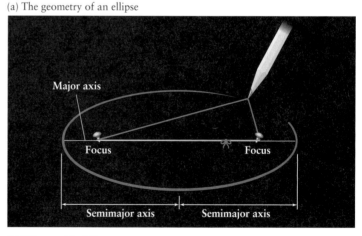

(b) Ellipses with different eccentricities

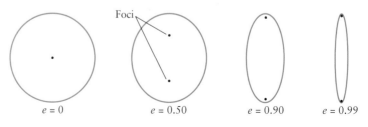

e = 0　　*e* = 0.50　　*e* = 0.90　　*e* = 0.99

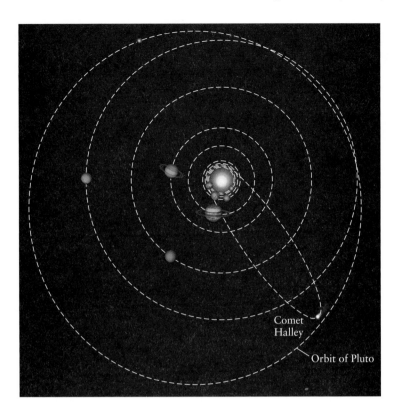

Figure 10-17 **Orbits in the solar system** The orbits of the planets and the minor planet Pluto are ellipses with relatively small eccentricities. Comet Halley, which moves around its elliptical orbit once every 76 years, has an eccentricity of 0.967.

orbit is that of Venus, with an eccentricity of just 0.007; Mercury's orbit has an eccentricity of 0.206. The minor planet Pluto has an eccentricity of 0.249, and a number of small bodies called comets move in very elongated orbits with eccentricities just less than 1 (Figure 10-17).

One of Newton's triumphs was to show that the planets can have elliptical orbits only if the force attracting them toward the Sun is in inverse proportion to the square of the distance r from Sun to planet. In other words, the elliptical shape of the planets is a verification of the law of universal gravitation, which states that this force has magnitude $F = Gm_{\text{sun}}m_{\text{planet}}/r^2$. (The proof is mathematically complex and beyond our scope.)

Kepler's second law states that unlike the case of a circular orbit, a planet does *not* move at a constant speed on an elliptical orbit. His **law of areas** describes how the speed changes around the orbit:

A line joining the Sun and a planet sweeps out equal areas in equal intervals of time, regardless of the position of the planet in the orbit.

Figure 10-18 illustrates this law. Suppose that it takes 30 days for a planet to go from point *A* to point *B*. During that time, an imaginary line joining the Sun and the planet sweeps out a nearly triangular area. Kepler discovered that a line joining the Sun and the planet also sweeps out exactly the same area during any other 30-day interval. In other words, if the planet also takes 30 days to go from point *C* to point *D*, then the two shaded segments in Figure 10-18 are equal in area.

The law of areas tells us that the planet moves fastest at *perihelion* (the point in its orbit closest to the Sun) and slowest at *aphelion* (the point when the planet is farthest from the Sun). This is what we would expect from the law of universal gravitation: A planet should speed up as it moves inward toward the Sun and approaches perihelion, and it should slow down as it moves outward away from the Sun and toward aphelion. But why does the speed vary in the particular manner described by the law of areas?

To answer this question, let's consider how a planet moves during a very short time interval Δt. Figure 10-19 shows that if Δt is short, an imaginary line from the Sun to

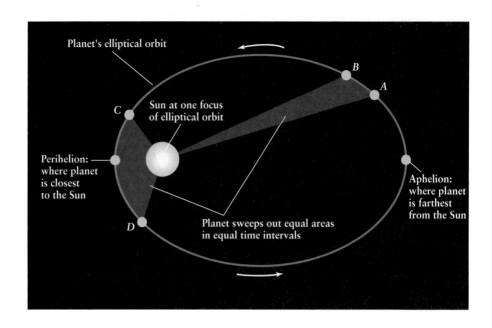

the planet moves through an angle $\Delta\theta$ and sweeps out an area $\Delta A = \frac{1}{2}r^2\Delta\theta$, where r is the distance from Sun to planet. Hence the *rate* at which this line sweeps out area is ΔA divided by Δt, or

$$\text{Rate at which area is swept out} = \frac{\Delta A}{\Delta t} = \frac{1}{2}r^2\frac{\Delta\theta}{\Delta t} = \frac{1}{2}r^2\omega$$

$\sqrt{x}$ *See the Math Tutorial for more information on geometry*

In this expression $\omega = \Delta\theta/\Delta t$ is the *angular speed* of the planet around the Sun (see Section 8-2). Kepler's law of areas says that $\Delta A/\Delta t$ has the same value at all points along the orbit, so

(10-14)

$$\frac{1}{2}r^2\omega = \text{constant (Kepler's law of areas)}$$

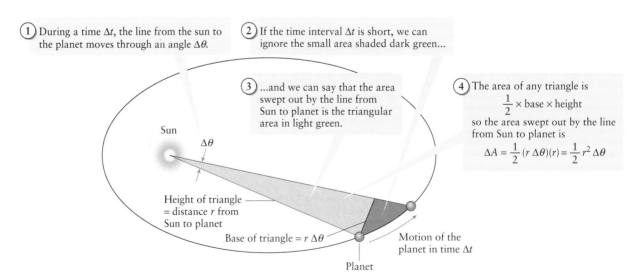

① During a time Δt, the line from the sun to the planet moves through an angle $\Delta\theta$.

② If the time interval Δt is short, we can ignore the small area shaded dark green...

③ ...and we can say that the area swept out by the line from Sun to planet is the triangular area in light green.

④ The area of any triangle is $\frac{1}{2} \times$ base $\times$ height so the area swept out by the line from Sun to planet is

$$\Delta A = \frac{1}{2}(r\,\Delta\theta)(r) = \frac{1}{2}r^2\,\Delta\theta$$

Sun

$\Delta\theta$

Height of triangle = distance r from Sun to planet

Base of triangle = $r\,\Delta\theta$

Motion of the planet in time Δt

Planet

Figure 10-19 Explaining Kepler's law of areas As a planet moves around its elliptical orbit, a line from the Sun to the planet sweeps out the same area $\Delta A = \frac{1}{2}r^2\Delta\theta$ in any time interval Δt. This turns out to be equivalent to the statement that the planet's angular momentum is conserved.

Now that we have the law of areas in equation form, we can understand how it arises. **Figure 10-20** shows that the gravitational force $\vec{F}$ exerted on a planet by the Sun is always directed opposite to the vector that points from the Sun to the planet. This means that the gravitational force exerts zero *torque* on the planet (see Section 8-6, where we learned that a force that acts either in the direction of $\vec{r}$ or opposite to $\vec{r}$ — as is the case in Figure 10-20 — produces zero torque).

We learned in Section 8-8 that the *angular momentum* of a system is conserved (that is, remains constant) if there is no net torque on it. Hence the angular momentum of a planet is conserved as it orbits the Sun. For a rotating object with moment of inertia I and angular speed ω, the magnitude of the angular momentum is $L = I\omega$. Furthermore, the moment of inertia of an object of mass m at a distance r from the rotation axis is $I = mr^2$ (see Section 8-2). So the statement that the angular momentum of an orbiting planet is conserved is

$$L = mr^2\omega = \text{constant}$$ (10-15)

(angular momentum of a planet is conserved)

If we divide Equation 10-15 by the planet's mass m (which does not change as it orbits) and also divide by 2, we get Equation 10-14. So the law of areas is a consequence of the gravitational force on a planet being directed toward the Sun, precisely as stated in the law of universal gravitation (see Figure 10-4a).

The first two of Kepler's laws describe how a given planet moves in its orbit. His third law, the **law of periods,** compares the orbital periods of orbits of different sizes:

The square of the period of a planet's orbit is proportional to the cube of the semimajor axis of the orbit.

This is precisely the relationship that we found for *circular* orbits in Equation 10-12. Newton was able to show that the law of periods follows from the law of universal gravitation even for elliptical orbits, if we replace the orbital radius r in Equation 10-12 with the semimajor axis a. For objects orbiting the Sun, we must also replace Earth's mass m_{Earth} with the mass of the Sun:

Period of an object in an elliptical orbit around the Sun

Semimajor axis of the object's orbit

$$T^2 = \frac{4\pi^2}{Gm_{\text{Sun}}} a^3$$

Gravitational constant

Mass of the Sun

Newton's form of Kepler's law of periods (10-16)

We've described Kepler's laws for the orbits of the planets. But the same laws apply to the orbits of satellites around Earth, to moons orbiting Saturn (see Figure 10-1b), and in general to any system where one object orbits another.

Newton's explanation of Kepler's three laws was perhaps his ultimate achievement. By extrapolating from the laws of nature that he saw here on Earth, he became the first human to understand the behavior of objects in the heavens.

Sun $\vec{r}$ $\vec{F}_{\text{Sun on planet}}$

Torque on planet = 0   Planet

Figure 10-20 The Sun's gravity produces zero torque The gravitational force of the Sun on a planet is directed toward the Sun. Hence this force produces no torque around the Sun, so the planet's angular momentum remains constant.

Watch Out! As the planets orbit, the Sun moves as well.

In this discussion we've ignored the forces that the planets exert on the Sun, and we have assumed that the Sun remains at rest. In fact, these forces cause the Sun to "wobble" around the center of mass of the solar system. Although this "wobble" is larger in amplitude than the radius of the Sun (6.96×10^5 km), we've neglected it because the amplitude is small compared to the semimajor axes of planetary orbits. However, astronomers have made use of this effect to search for planets orbiting other stars. By detecting the "wobble" of a star, astronomers have been able to detect the presence of that star's planets even though the planets themselves are too faint to be seen with even the most powerful telescopes. Hundreds of *extrasolar planets* have been discovered in this way.

The following example demonstrates one application of Equation 10-16.

Example 10-8 A Comet's Orbit

Distances in the solar system are typically measured not in meters or kilometers but in *astronomical units* (AU), where 1 AU is the semimajor axis of Earth's orbit around the Sun (1 AU = 1.50×10^8 km). Earth's orbital period around the Sun is one year. Find the orbital period of a comet that is 0.50 AU from the Sun at perihelion and 17.50 AU from the Sun at aphelion.

Set Up

We'll use the data about the comet to find its semimajor axis a. From this we'll use Newton's form of Kepler's law of periods to determine the period T.

Newton's form of Kepler's law of periods:

$$T^2 = \frac{4\pi^2}{Gm_{\text{Sun}}}a^3 \qquad (10\text{-}16)$$

Solve

The drawing shows that the length of the major axis of the comet's orbit is the sum of the perihelion and aphelion distances. The semimajor axis a is one-half the length of the major axis.

Length of the major axis:
(distance from Sun to comet at perihelion) + (distance from Sun to comet at aphelion)

$= 0.50 \text{ AU} + 17.50 \text{ AU} = 18.0 \text{ AU}$

Semimajor axis:

a_{comet}
$= \frac{1}{2} \times (\text{length of the major axis})$
$= 9.0 \text{ AU}$

We could calculate T directly from Equation 10-16 by substituting the values of G, m_{Sun}, and the semimajor axis of the comet's orbit (which we would have to convert to meters). But a much simpler approach is to compare the comet's orbit to that of Earth, for which the semimajor axis is one AU and the period is one year.

For Earth: $T_{\text{Earth}}^2 = \dfrac{4\pi^2}{Gm_{\text{Sun}}}a_{\text{Earth}}^3$

For the comet: $T_{\text{comet}}^2 = \dfrac{4\pi^2}{Gm_{\text{Sun}}}a_{\text{comet}}^3$

If we divide the second equation by the first one, the factor of $4\pi^2/Gm_{\text{Sun}}$ cancels out, leaving

$$\frac{T_{\text{comet}}^2}{T_{\text{Earth}}^2} = \frac{a_{\text{comet}}^3}{a_{\text{Earth}}^3}$$

Substitute values:

$$\frac{T_{\text{comet}}^2}{(1 \text{ y})^2} = \frac{(9.0 \text{ AU})^3}{(1 \text{ AU})^3} = 729$$

$$T_{\text{comet}} = \sqrt{729} \times 1 \text{ y} = 27 \text{ y}$$

Reflect

Our technique for solving this problem really used Kepler's original form of the law of periods: The square of the period is directly proportional to the cube of the semimajor axis. The semimajor axis for the comet's orbit is 9.0 times larger than that of Earth's orbit, so the square of the orbital period for the comet must be $(9.0)^3 = 729$ times larger than the square of the one-year orbital period of Earth. Therefore the comet's orbital period is $\sqrt{729}$ years, or 27 years.

? Got the Concept? 10-4 Comparing Orbits

Rank the following five objects in order of their orbital period around the Sun, from shortest period to longest period. (a) An asteroid in a circular orbit with radius 3.00×10^8 km; (b) an asteroid in a circular orbit with radius 4.00×10^8 km; (c) an asteroid in an elliptical orbit that is 3.00×10^8 km from the Sun at perihelion and 4.00×10^8 km from the Sun at aphelion; (d) an asteroid in an elliptical orbit that is 2.00×10^8 km from the Sun at perihelion and 5.00×10^8 km from the Sun at aphelion; and (e) an asteroid in an elliptical orbit that is 2.00×10^8 km from the Sun at perihelion and 4.00×10^8 km from the Sun at aphelion.

Take-Home Message for Section 10-4

✔ For an object in a circular orbit, the orbital speed is inversely proportional to the square root of the orbital radius. The square of the orbital period is directly proportional to the cube of the orbital radius.

✔ The total mechanical energy E for an object in a circular orbit is negative. The larger the orbital radius, the greater (less negative) the value of E.

✔ Kepler's three laws of planetary motion—the law of orbits, the law of areas, and the law of periods—were deduced from observations of how the planets move, but can all be explained by Newton's law of universal gravitation.

10-5 Apparent weightlessness can have major physiological effects on space travelers

Figure 10-21 shows astronauts floating inside an orbiting spacecraft. The astronauts *feel* as though they are weightless, but this is a misnomer: Earth's gravitation acts on them just as it acts on their spacecraft. As Figure 10-22 shows, because the astronauts are the same distance from Earth as their spacecraft, they have the same acceleration as the spacecraft and so "fall together" on their trajectory. Since the astronauts have no tendency to move toward the floor, ceiling, or any other part of the spacecraft, they are in a state of **apparent weightlessness.**

One of the ways in which we perceive our weight is through the force the floor exerts on our feet. As you gain mass, which increases your weight—the gravitational force Earth exerts on you—the force of the floor on your feet increases to keep you from sinking into the floor. We are aware not only of this increase in force, but also that our joints experience larger forces when we move, and our muscles must do more work to keep us standing upright and make us move. If you have ever been in an elevator that accelerated rapidly upward, you have experienced one or more of the above phenomena, giving you the sense of an apparent increase in weight as the elevator accelerated upward. If the elevator accelerates downward at a rapid rate, the force the floor exerts on your feet is reduced, your joints experience smaller forces when you move, and your muscles need to do less work to keep you standing upright or to make you move. In the extreme case when the elevator accelerates downward at 9.80 m/s^2, the force of the floor on your feet goes to zero, and you have a sense of apparent weightlessness, even though gravity still acts on you. As long as both you and your surroundings experience the same acceleration, you will feel "weightless."

So it's not necessary for a spacecraft to be in orbit around a planet for the occupants to experience apparent weightlessness. All that's needed is for the only external force on the spacecraft to be the gravitational force. Astronauts will feel weightless whether they are orbiting Earth aboard the International Space Station, on a mission from Earth to the Moon, or on an interplanetary voyage to Mars. (For a mission to Mars or any other planet, the spacecraft follows an elliptical orbit with the Sun at one focus, just as in Figure 10-18. This orbit is chosen so that it intersects the orbit of the destination planet.) The only times during the flight when the astronauts do not feel weightless is when the rockets are firing, either to put the spacecraft into the desired orbit or to take it out of orbit for landing.

At first glance, it might seem that being in a state of apparent weightlessness would be relaxing. In fact there are many very negative effects on an astronaut's body. One common problem is *space adaptation syndrome* (also called *space sickness*). About half

Figure 10-21 Astronauts in orbit In the apparent weightlessness aboard an orbiting spacecraft, there is no up or down.

Figure 10-22 The origin of apparent weightlessness If the only external force acting on a spacecraft is the gravitational force, then the spacecraft and its occupant have the same acceleration $a = F/m$. As a result, the spacecraft and the astronaut fall freely along the same trajectory and the astronaut feels "weightless."

$$F_{\text{Earth on astronaut}} = \frac{Gm_{\text{Earth}}m_{\text{astronaut}}}{r^2}$$

$$F_{\text{Earth on spacecraft}} = \frac{Gm_{\text{Earth}}m_{\text{spacecraft}}}{r^2}$$

Earth

Both the spacecraft and the astronaut have the same acceleration:

$$a_{\text{spacecraft}} = a_{\text{astronaut}} = \frac{Gm_{\text{Earth}}}{r^2}$$

of all astronauts suffer from this condition during their first few days of spaceflight. The symptoms include motion sickness and disorientation. Research suggests that space adaptation syndrome is related to the vestibular system of the inner ear, which senses gravity and acceleration (see Section 3-10). If an astronaut has a more sensitive vestibular system than normal and there is an asymmetry between the vestibular systems in the left and right ears, the astronaut is likely to be plagued by space adaptation syndrome.

Two problems that bedevil all astronauts are *loss of muscle mass* and *blood loss*. You exercise the muscles in your calves and spine simply by walking and standing. But in apparent weightlessness these muscles are not exercised and can lose as much as 5% of their mass per week. During a very long-duration spaceflight, such as a mission to Mars (which could take 10 months each way), astronauts might lose up to 40% of their capacity to do physical work, equivalent to a 40-year-old astronaut's muscles deteriorating to those of an 80-year-old. For this reason astronauts exercise as much as possible in space using special equipment designed to mimic gravity. (Building muscle mass before going into space does not appear to help: Astronauts who begin their missions with the greatest muscle mass also show the greatest decline while in space.)

The cause of blood loss is more subtle. When you stand upright on Earth, blood pools in your feet due to gravity, and so your blood pressure is higher in your feet than in your brain. (That's why blood pressure is always measured at the same vertical position in the body, typically at your upper arm at the same level as your heart.) In apparent weightlessness, however, blood distributes itself more evenly through the body: Blood moves out of the legs and into the large veins in the upper body where stretch receptors respond to the apparent increase in blood volume. (This gives astronauts in space a characteristic puffy-faced appearance.) Activation of these stretch receptors initiates a reflex to reduce blood volume. The reflex involves the release of a hormone from the heart, inhibition of the release of a hormone from the brain, partial inhibition of the neural signals that cause arteries to contract, and the production of copious amounts of a dilute urine. As a result astronauts can lose up to 22% of their blood volume within three days of apparent weightlessness. The weightless environment reduces demand on the heart because it does not have to overcome the effects of gravity to provide the brain with blood, so the heart muscle begins to atrophy as well. This is another reason for astronauts to do cardiovascular exercise while in space.

Astronauts recover muscle strength relatively quickly after returning from space (at a rate of about one day of recovery per day in space), and blood volume can be restored within a few days by drinking fluids. More problematic is recovery from the *bone loss* that occurs in space. Astronauts' bones atrophy at a rate of about 1% per month in apparent weightlessness, and recovery from a six-month mission may require two or three years back on Earth coupled with a program of strenuous exercise.

Another threat to astronauts' well-being is that while human muscle and bone tend to atrophy in apparent weightlessness, microbes such as *E. coli* and *Staphylococcus* actually reproduce more rapidly under these conditions. This leads to increased risk for contamination and serious infection during a long-duration spaceflight. Such are the biological challenges that confront the future of human exploration of space.

Take-Home Message for Section 10-5

✔ Astronauts in space feel apparent weightlessness because their acceleration is the same as that of the spacecraft.

✔ The physiological challenges of apparent weightlessness include space sickness; loss of muscle mass, blood, and bone; and increased risk of microbial infection.

Key Terms

apparent weightlessness	gravitational constant	Newton's law of universal
Cavendish experiment	law of areas	gravitation
eccentricity	law of orbits	orbital period
escape speed	law of periods	semimajor axis

Chapter Summary

Topic	Equation or Figure	

Newton's law of universal gravitation: Any two objects attract each other with a gravitational force. This force is proportional to the product of the masses of the objects, and inversely proportional to the square of the distance between the centers of the two objects.

Gravitational constant (same for any two objects) Masses of the two objects

Any two objects (1 and 2) exert equally strong gravitational forces on each other.

$$F_{1 \text{ on } 2} = F_{2 \text{ on } 1} = \frac{Gm_1 m_2}{r^2}$$

Center-to-center distance between the two objects   (10-2)

The gravitational forces are attractive: $\vec{F}_{1 \text{ on } 2}$ pulls object 2 toward object 1 and $\vec{F}_{2 \text{ on } 1}$ pulls object 1 toward object 2.

Value of g at Earth's surface: The acceleration due to gravity at our planet's surface is related to Earth's mass and radius. At greater distances r from Earth's center, the value of g decreases in inverse proportion to the square of r.

Gravitational constant   Mass of Earth

Acceleration due to gravity at Earth's surface

$$g = \frac{Gm_{\text{Earth}}}{R_{\text{Earth}}^2}$$

Radius of Earth   (10-3)

The Cavendish experiment: The value of the gravitational constant G in the law of universal gravitation can be determined by measuring the gravitational attraction between objects of known mass.

① Two small lead spheres, each of mass m, are attached to the ends of a wooden rod, and the rod is suspended from a wire.

② Two large lead spheres, each of mass M, are then placed on the ground at equal distances from the small spheres.

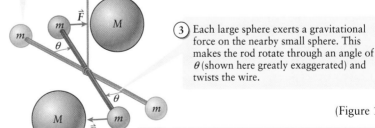

③ Each large sphere exerts a gravitational force on the nearby small sphere. This makes the rod rotate through an angle of θ (shown here greatly exaggerated) and twists the wire.

(Figure 10-6)

Knowing the masses m and M of the spheres and the distance r when the rod is in equilibrium, you can determine G using the relationship $F = GMm/r^2$.

Gravitational potential energy: The general expression for the gravitational potential energy of two objects follows from the law of universal gravitation. In this expression the potential energy is zero when the two objects are infinitely far apart; for any finite separation, U_{grav} is negative.

Gravitational constant (same for any two objects)   Masses of the two objects

Gravitational potential energy of a system of two objects (1 and 2)

$$U_{grav} = -\frac{Gm_1 m_2}{r}$$

Center-to-center distance between the two objects

(10-4)

The gravitational potential energy is zero when the two objects are infinitely far apart. If the objects are brought closer together (so r is made smaller), U_{grav} decreases (it becomes more negative).

Escape speed: If an object is launched from Earth's surface at the escape speed or faster, it will never fall back to Earth but will escape to infinity.

Gravitational constant   Mass of Earth

Speed that a projectile must have at Earth's surface in order to escape Earth.

$$v_{escape} = \sqrt{\frac{2Gm_{Earth}}{R_{Earth}}}$$

Radius of Earth

(10-10)

Circular orbits: A satellite in a circular orbit around Earth moves with a constant speed v. The orbital period T and the total mechanical energy E in a circular orbit both increase with increasing orbital radius r.

Gravitational constant   Mass of Earth

Speed of an Earth satellite in a circular orbit

$$v = \sqrt{\frac{Gm_{Earth}}{r}}$$

Radius of the satellite's orbit

(10-11)

Period of an Earth satellite in a circular orbit   Radius of the satellite's orbit

$$T^2 = \frac{4\pi^2}{Gm_{Earth}} r^3$$

Gravitational constant   Mass of Earth

(10-12)

Gravitational constant   Mass of Earth

Total mechanical energy for a satellite in a circular orbit around Earth

Mass of satellite

$$E = -\frac{Gm_{Earth}m}{2r}$$

Radius of the satellite's orbit

(10-13)

The greater the radius r of the circular orbit, the greater (less negative) the total mechanical energy.

Elliptical orbits: A circular orbit is actually a special case of an elliptical orbit. The planets move in elliptical orbits with the Sun at one focus. The speed varies in accordance with Kepler's law of areas, which is equivalent to the statement that the angular momentum of a planet is conserved. The orbital period is given by the same expression as for circular orbits around Earth, with Earth's mass replaced by the mass of

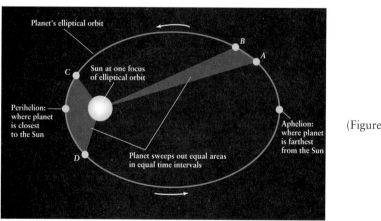

(Figure 10-18)

Planet's elliptical orbit

Sun at one focus of elliptical orbit

Perihelion: where planet is closest to the Sun

Aphelion: where planet is farthest from the Sun

Planet sweeps out equal areas in equal time intervals

the Sun and the orbital radius replaced by the semimajor axis (one-half the length of the long axis of the ellipse).

Period of an object in an elliptical orbit around the Sun

Semimajor axis of the object's orbit

Gravitational constant

$$T^2 = \frac{4\pi^2}{Gm_{Sun}} a^3$$

Mass of the Sun

(10-16)

Apparent weightlessness: Because gravitation is universal, astronauts riding in a spacecraft (with the rockets off) have the same acceleration as the spacecraft. As a result, they "fall" along with the spacecraft and feel as though they are weightless.

(Figure 10-22)

$F_{\text{Earth on astronaut}}$
$$= \frac{Gm_{\text{Earth}}m_{\text{astronaut}}}{r^2}$$

$F_{\text{Earth on spacecraft}}$
$$= \frac{Gm_{\text{Earth}}m_{\text{spacecraft}}}{r^2}$$

Earth

 Both the spacecraft and the astronaut have the same acceleration:

$$a_{\text{spacecraft}} = a_{\text{astronaut}} = \frac{Gm_{\text{Earth}}}{r^2}$$

Answer to What do you think? Question

(b) Newton's law of universal gravitation states that Earth's gravitational force is inversely proportional to the square of the distance from Earth's center. At the altitude of the ISS, the distance from Earth's center is 6370 km + 350 km = 6720 km, which is $(6720 \text{ km})/(6370 \text{ km}) = 1.055$ times Earth's radius. Hence the gravitational force at the altitude of the ISS is $1/(1.055)^2 = 0.90$ as great as at Earth's surface, or 10% less than at Earth's surface. It's true that an astronaut aboard the ISS *feels* weightless, but that's not because there is no gravitational force on her. Rather, there are gravitational forces on both the astronaut and the ISS, which give both objects the same acceleration. Hence both objects fall together around Earth in the same orbit. (See Sections 10-2 and 10-5.)

Answers to Got the Concept? Questions

10-1 (e) The gravitational force is inversely proportional to the square of the distance from Earth's center. A point at the North Pole is one Earth radius from the center, while the other point is four Earth radii from the center (three Earth radii from the surface). So the point at the North Pole is 1/4 the distance from Earth's center, and the gravitational force there is greater by a factor of $1/(1/4)^2 = 4^2 = 16$.

10-2 (e) The gravitational acceleration g is also inversely proportional to the square of the distance from Earth's center. By the same line of reasoning as in the previous question, the value of g is 16 times greater at the North Pole (one Earth radius from the planet's center) than at a point three Earth radii above the surface (four Earth radii from the center).

10-3 (d) If the ball has escape speed or greater, the total mechanical energy is enough for the ball to travel to infinity.

The total mechanical energy is a scalar, not a vector, so the direction in which the ball is thrown doesn't matter. Changing the direction in which the ball is thrown simply affects the path that the ball follows to infinity.

10-4 (a) and (e) [tie], (c) and (d) [tie], (b) The square of the orbital period T is proportional to the cube of the semimajor axis a. So a ranking in order of the orbital period is the same as a ranking in order of the semimajor axis. For a circular orbit, the semimajor axis is the orbital radius; for an elliptical orbit, the semimajor axis is half the major (long) axis, and the long axis is the sum of the distances at perihelion and aphelion. So the semimajor axes of the orbits are (a) 3.00×10^8 km, (b) 4.00×10^8 km, (c) $\frac{1}{2} \times (3.00 \times 10^8 \text{ km} + 4.00 \times 10^8 \text{ km}) = 3.50 \times 10^8$ km, (d) $\frac{1}{2} \times (2.00 \times 10^8 \text{ km} + 5.00 \times 10^8 \text{ km}) = 3.50 \times 10^8$ km, and (e) $\frac{1}{2} \times (2.00 \times 10^8 \text{ km} + 4.00 \times 10^8 \text{ km}) = 3.00 \times 10^8$ km.

Questions and Problems

In a few problems, you are given more data than you actually need; in a few other problems, you are required to supply data from your general knowledge, outside sources, or informed estimate.

Interpret as significant all digits in numerical values that have trailing zeros and no decimal points. For all problems, use $g = 9.80 \text{ m/s}^2$ for the free-fall acceleration due to gravity. Neglect friction and air resistance unless instructed to do otherwise. Refer to Appendix B for any required astronomical data like the masses or orbital radii of the planets.

• Basic, single-concept problem

•• Intermediate-level problem, may require synthesis of concepts and multiple steps

••• Challenging problem

SSM *Solution is in Student Solutions Manual*

Conceptual Questions

1. •Isaac Newton probably gained no insight by being hit on the head with a falling apple, but he did believe that "the Moon is falling." Explain this statement. SSM

2. •Would the magnitude of the acceleration due to gravity near Earth's surface increase more if Earth's mass were doubled or if Earth's radius were cut in half? Justify your answer.

3. •According to Equation 10-2, what happens to the force between two objects if (a) the mass of one object is doubled and (b) if both masses are halved? SSM

4. •Every object in the universe with mass experiences an attractive gravitational force due to every other object with mass. Why don't you feel a pull from objects close to you?

5. •The gravitational force acts on all objects in proportion to their mass. Why don't heavy objects fall faster than light ones, if you neglect air resistance?

6. •When powering a trip from Earth to the Moon, the thrusters of a ship don't have to get the ship all the way to the Moon. Why do the thrusters only have to get the ship partway there?

7. •The Sun gravitationally attracts the Moon. Does the Moon orbit the Sun?

8. •Imagine a world where the force of gravity were proportional to the inverse *cube* of the distance between two objects ($F_{\text{gravity}} \propto 1/r^3$). How would Kepler's law of periods be changed?

9. •Much attention has been devoted to the exact numerical power in Newton's law of universal gravitation ($F_{\text{gravity}} \propto 1/r^2$). Some theorists have investigated whether the dependence might be slightly larger or smaller than 2. What would be the significance (what impact would there be) if the power was not exactly 2?

10. •The fabrication of precision ball bearings may be better performed on the International Space Station than on the surface of Earth. Explain why.

11. •Why is the gravitational potential energy of two objects negative?

12. •When a frog is at the bottom of a well, the frog–Earth system has a negative amount of gravitational potential energy with respect to the ground level where we choose to set potential energy equal to zero. Can the frog escape from the well if it jumps upward with a positive amount of kinetic energy that is larger than the negative potential energy when the frog is at the bottom of the well? Explain.

13. •Earth moves faster in its orbit around the Sun during the winter in the Northern Hemisphere than it does during the summer in the Northern Hemisphere. Is Earth closer to the Sun during the Northern Hemisphere's winter or during the Northern Hemisphere's summer? Explain your answer. SSM

14. •A satellite is to be raised from one circular orbit to one further from Earth's surface. What will happen to its period?

15. •Describe some ways that Newton's law of gravity may have affected human evolution. SSM

16. •Geostationary satellites remain stationary over one point on Earth. How is this accomplished?

Multiple-Choice Questions

17. •Planet A orbits a star with a period T. Planet B circles the same star at four times the distance of Planet A. Planet B is four times as massive as Planet A. Planet B orbits the star with a period of

    A. $4T$.

    B. $8T$.

    C. $16T$.

    D. T.

    E. $T/4$.

18. •According to Newton's universal law of gravitation, $F = \dfrac{Gm_1 m_2}{r^2}$, if both masses are doubled, the force is

    A. four times as much as the original value.

    B. twice as much as the original value.

    C. the same as the original value.

    D. one-half of the original value.

    E. one-fourth of the original value.

19. •According to Newton's universal law of gravitation, $F = \dfrac{Gm_1 m_2}{r^2}$, if the distance r is doubled, the force is

    A. four times as much as the original value.

    B. twice as much as the original value.

    C. the same as the original value.

    D. one-half of the original value.

    E. one-fourth of the original value.

20. •Which is larger, the Sun's pull on Earth or Earth's pull on Sun?

    A. The Sun's pull on Earth is larger.

    B. Earth's pull on the Sun is larger.

    C. They pull on each other equally.

    D. The Sun's pull on Earth is twice as large as Earth's pull on the much larger Sun.

    E. There is no pull or force between Earth and the Sun.

21. •Compare the weight of a mountain climber when she is at the bottom of a mountain with her weight when she is at the top of the mountain. In which case is her weight larger?

    A. She weighs more at the bottom.

    B. She weighs more at the top.

    C. Both are the same.

D. She weighs twice as much at the top.

E. She weighs four times as much at the top. SSM

22. •A satellite and the International Space Station have the same mass and are going around Earth in concentric orbits. The distance of the satellite from Earth's center is twice that of the International Space Station's distance. What is the ratio of the centripetal force acting on the satellite compared to that acting on the International Space Station?

A. 1/4

B. 1/2

C. 1

D. 2

E. 4

23. •A satellite is in a circular orbit about Earth moving at a speed of v. In order to escape the planet, the satellite must attain a speed of

A. v.

B. $\sqrt{2}v$.

C. $2v$.

D. $v/2$.

E. $v/\sqrt{2}$. SSM

24. •The escape speed from planet X is v. Planet Y has the same radius as planet X but is twice as dense. The escape speed from planet Y is

A. v.

B. $\sqrt{2}v$.

C. $2v$.

D. $v/2$.

E. $v/\sqrt{2}$.

25. •Two satellites having equal masses are in circular orbits around Earth. Satellite A has a smaller orbital radius than satellite B. Which statement is true?

A. Satellite A has more kinetic energy, less potential energy, and less mechanical energy (kinetic energy plus potential energy) than satellite B.

B. Satellite A has less kinetic energy, less potential energy, and less mechanical energy than satellite B.

C. Satellite A has more kinetic energy, more potential energy, and less mechanical energy than satellite B.

D. Satellite A and satellite B have the same amount of mechanical energy.

E. Satellite A and satellite B have the same amount of kinetic energy and no potential energy because they are in motion. SSM

Estimation/Numerical Analysis

26. •Estimate the ratio between the maximum and minimum tidal forces on Earth due to the gravitational pull of the Moon.

27. •Estimate how close two 1-kg weights must be in an ordinary science lab in order to measure the gravitational force one exerts on the other. SSM

28. •Estimate the numerical range of the acceleration constant g between Earth's highest mountain peaks and its lowest valleys.

29. •Estimate the inaccuracy in using the acceleration constant g in kinematic formulas that describe terrestrial free-fall when you descend from the top of Mount Everest (8850 m elevation) to sea level.

30. •**Biology** Estimate the difference in height due to compression of the vertebrae when a 160-cm-tall sherpa at the peak of Mount Everest travels to sea level.

31. •Estimate the impact on the orbit of Earth about the Sun if Jupiter were not a part of our solar system. SSM

32. ••The eight planets, as well as Pluto and Halley's comet, orbit the Sun according to Newton's law of universal gravitation. The table has data for the periods (T) and semimajor axes (a) for each orbital ellipse. (a) Derive a best-fit constant, similar to that referred to in Kepler's law of periods. (b) Predict the value of a for the elliptical orbit of Halley's comet.

Planet	T (days)	a (AU)
Mercury	87.97	0.3871
Venus	224.7	0.7233
Earth	365.2	1.000
Mars	687.0	1.5234
Jupiter	4332	5.204
Saturn	10,832	9.582
Uranus	30,799	19.23
Neptune	60,190	30.10
Pluto	90,613.3	9.48
Halley	27,507	?

Problems

10-1 Gravitation is a force of universal importance

10-2 Newton's law of universal gravitation explains the orbit of the Moon

33. •A 500-kg tree stump is located 1000 m from a 12,000-kg boulder. Determine the magnitude and direction of the gravitational force exerted by the tree stump on the boulder.

34. •Kramer goes bowling and decides to employ the force of gravity to "pick up a spare." He rolls the 7.0-kg bowling ball very slowly so that it comes to rest a center-to-center distance of 0.2 m from the one remaining 1.5-kg bowling pin. Determine the force of gravity between the ball and the pin and comment on the efficacy of the technique. Treat the ball and pin as point objects for this problem.

35. •A 150-g baseball is 100 m from a 935-g bat. What is the force of gravitational attraction between the two objects? Ignore the size of the bat and ball (treat them as point objects) for this problem. SSM

36. •In 1994, the performer Rod Stewart drew over 3 million people to a concert in Rio de Janeiro, Brazil. (a) If the people in the group had an average mass of 80 kg, what collective gravitational force would the group have on a 4.5-kg eagle soaring 300 m above the throng? If you treat the group as a point object, you will get an upper limit for the gravitational force. (b) What is the ratio of that force of attraction to the force between Earth and the eagle?

37. •Compare the gravitational force on a 1-kg apple that is on the surface of Earth versus the gravitational force due to the Moon on the same apple in the same location on the surface of Earth. Assume that Earth and the Moon are spherical and that both have their masses concentrated at their respective centers.

38. •Determine the magnitude of the force of gravity between the Sun and Earth.

39. •Determine the net force of gravity acting on the Moon during an eclipse when it is directly between Earth and the Sun. SSM

40. •A star that has a mass equal to the mass of our Sun is located 50 AU from another star that has a mass that is one-half of the Sun's mass. At what point(s) will the gravitational force from the two stars on a 100,000-kg space probe be equal to zero?

41. •At what point between Earth and the Moon will a 50,000-kg space probe experience no net gravitational force? SSM

42. •Eight stars, all with the same mass as our Sun, are located on the vertices of an astronomically sized cube with sides of 100 AU. Determine the net gravitational force on one of the stars due to the other seven.

43. •Compare the weight of a 5.00-kg object on Earth's surface to the gravitational force between a 5.00-kg object that is one Earth radius from another object of mass equal to 5.98×10^{24} kg. Use Newton's universal law of gravitation for the second part of the question.

10-3 The gravitational potential energy of two objects is negative and increases toward zero as the objects are moved farther apart

44. •How much energy would be required to move the Moon from its present orbit around Earth to a location that is twice as far away? Assume the Moon's orbit around Earth is nearly circular and has a radius of 3.84×10^8 m, and that the Moon's orbital period is 27.3 days.

45. •How much work is done by the force of gravity as a 10-kg object moves from a point that is 6000 m above sea level to a point that is 1000 m above sea level? SSM

46. •(a) What is the escape velocity of a space probe that is launched from the surface of Earth? (b) Would the answer change if the launch occurs on top of a very tall mountain? Explain your answer.

47. •A small asteroid that has a mass of 100 kg is moving at 200 m/s when it is 1000 km above the Moon. (a) How fast will the meteorite be traveling when it impacts the lunar surface if it is heading straight toward the center of the Moon? (b) How much work does the Moon do in stopping the asteroid if neither the Moon nor the asteroid heats up in the process? The radius of the Moon is 1.737×10^6 m. SSM

48. ••The volume of water in the Pacific Ocean is about 7×10^8 km^3. The density of seawater is about 1030 kg/m^3. (a) Determine the gravitational potential energy of the Moon–Pacific Ocean system when the Pacific is facing away from the Moon. (b) Repeat the calculation when Earth has rotated so that the Pacific Ocean faces toward the Moon. (c) Estimate the maximum speed of the water in the Pacific Ocean due to the tidal influence of the Moon. For the sake of the calculations, treat the Pacific Ocean as a pointlike object (obviously a very rough approximation).

10-4 Newton's law of universal gravitation explains Kepler's laws for the orbits of planets and satellites

49. •The orbit of Mars around the Sun has a radius that is 1.524 times greater than the radius of Earth's orbit. Determine the time required for Mars to complete one revolution.

50. •The space shuttle usually orbited Earth at altitudes of around 300 km. (a) Determine the time for one orbit of the shuttle about Earth. (b) How many sunrises per day did the astronauts witness?

51. •What was the speed of a space shuttle that orbited Earth at an altitude of 300 km?

52. •A satellite orbits Earth at an altitude of 80,000 km. Determine the time for the satellite to orbit Earth once.

53. •A satellite requires 86.5 min to orbit Earth once. Assuming a circular orbit, what is the circumference of the satellite's orbit? SSM

54. •The orbital period of Saturn is 29.46 y. Determine the semimajor axis of its orbit.

55. •Determine the altitude of a geosynchronous satellite. Such a satellite will have precisely the same orbital period as Earth's rotational period.

56. •Given that Earth orbits the Sun with a semimajor axis of 1.000 AU and an approximate orbital period of 365.24 days, determine the mass of the Sun.

57. •The Moon orbits Earth in a nearly circular orbit that lasts 27.32 days. Determine the distance from the surface of the Moon to the surface of Earth. SSM

58. •A planet orbits a star with an orbital radius of 1 AU. If the star has a mass that is 1.75 times our own Sun's mass, determine the time for one revolution of the planet around the star.

General Problems

59. ••A satellite is launched into an elliptical orbit that has a period of 702 min. Aphelion of the orbit is 39,200 km and perihelion is 560 km. (a) Determine the gravitational potential energy at aphelion and perihelion of the satellite's orbit. (b) Estimate the energy required to place the satellite in orbit around the Earth.

60. ••**Astronomy** The four largest of Jupiter's moons are listed in the table below. Using these data, Kepler's three laws, and the law of universal gravitation, (a) complete the table and (b) determine the mass of Jupiter.

Moon	Semimajor Axis (km)	Orbital Period (days)
Io	421,700	1.769
Europa	671,034	?
Ganymede	?	7.155
Callisto	?	16.689

61. ••(a) What speed is needed to launch a rocket due east near the equator into a low Earth orbit? Assume the rocket skims along the surface of Earth, so $r \approx R_E$. (b) Repeat the calculation for a rocket fired due west. SSM

62. ••The former Soviet Union launched the first artificial Earth satellite, *Sputnik*, in 1957. Its mass was 84 kg, and it made one orbit every 96 min. (a) Determine the altitude of *Sputnik*'s orbit above Earth's surface, assuming circular orbits. (b) What was *Sputnik*'s weight in orbit and at Earth's surface?

63. •**Astronomy** The 2004 landings of the Mars rovers *Spirit* and *Opportunity* involved many stages, resulting in each probe having zero vertical velocity about 12 m above the surface of Mars. Determine (a) the time required for the final free-fall descent of the probes and (b) the vertical velocity at impact. The mass of Mars is 6.419×10^{23} kg and its radius is 3.397×10^6 m.

64. ••**Biology, Astronomy** On Earth, froghoppers can jump upward with a takeoff speed of 2.8 m/s. Suppose you took

some of the insects to an asteroid. If it is small enough, they can jump free of it and escape into space. (a) What is the diameter (in kilometers) of the largest spherical asteroid from which they could jump free? Assume a typical asteroid density of 2.0 g/cm³. (b) Suppose that one of the froghoppers jumped horizontally from a small hill on an asteroid. What would the diameter (in km) of the asteroid need to be so that the insect could go into a circular orbit just above the surface?

65. •**Astronomy** The International Space Station (ISS) orbits Earth in a nearly circular orbit that is 345 km above Earth's surface. (a) How many hours does it take for the ISS to make each orbit? (b) Some of the experiments performed by astronauts in the ISS involve the effects of "weightlessness" on objects. What gravitational force does Earth exert on a 10.0-kg object in the ISS? Express your answer in newtons and as a fraction of the force that Earth would exert on the object at Earth's surface. (c) Considering your answer in part (b), how can an object be considered *weightless* in the ISS?

66. ••**Astronomy** Measurements on the asteroid Apophis have shown that its aphelion (farthest distance from the Sun) is 1.099 AU, its perihelion (closest distance from the Sun) is 0.746 AU, and its mass is 2.7×10^{10} kg. (a) Determine the semimajor axis of Apophis in astronomical units and in meters. (b) How many days does it take Apophis to orbit the Sun? (c) At what point in its orbit is Apophis traveling fastest, and at what point is it traveling slowest? (d) Determine the ratio of its maximum speed to its minimum speed.

67. ••A rack of seven spherical bowling balls (each 8.00 kg, radius of 11.0 cm) is positioned along a line 100 cm from a point P, as shown in Figure 10-23. Determine the gravitational force the bowling balls exert on a ping-pong ball of mass 2.70 g centered at point P.

Figure 10-23 Problem 67

68. •**Astronomy** The Sun and solar system actually are not at rest in our Milky Way galaxy. We orbit around the center of the Milky Way galaxy once every 225,000,000 years, at a distance of 27,000 light-years. (One light-year is the distance that light travels in one year: 1 ly $= 9.46 \times 10^{12}$ km $= 9.46 \times 10^{15}$ m.) If the mass of the Milky Way were concentrated at the center of the galaxy, what would be the mass of the galaxy?

69. ••Locate the point(s) along the line $\overline{AB}$ where a small, 1.00-kg object could rest such that the net gravitational force on it due to the two objects shown is exactly zero (Figure 10-24). SSM

Figure 10-24 Problem 69

70. •••Find the net gravitational force exerted on a small, 1.00-kg object located at the point P by the three massive objects (Figure 10-25). Each of the massive objects lies on a coordinate axis as shown.

Figure 10-25 Problem 70

11 Fluids

What do you think?

The hot-air balloon in the photo is held up by a buoyant force exerted by the air surrounding the balloon. If the hot air inside the balloon were replaced by helium (which is less dense than hot air), would the magnitude of the buoyant force (a) increase, (b) decrease, or (c) remain the same?

In this chapter, your goals are to:
- (11-1) Describe the similarities and differences between liquids and gases.
- (11-2) Recognize how to apply the definition of density.
- (11-3) Explain the origin of fluid pressure in terms of molecular motion.
- (11-4) Calculate the pressure at a given depth in a fluid in hydrostatic equilibrium.
- (11-5) Explain the difference between absolute pressure and gauge pressure.
- (11-6) Calculate the force on an object due to a difference in pressure on its sides.
- (11-7) Explain how to apply Pascal's principle to a fluid at rest.
- (11-8) Apply Archimedes' principle to find the buoyant force on an object in a fluid.
- (11-9) Use the equation of continuity to analyze the flow of an incompressible fluid.
- (11-10) Apply Bernoulli's principle to relate fluid pressure and flow speed in an incompressible fluid.
- (11-11) Explain what happens in flows where viscosity is important.
- (11-12) Describe the role of surface tension in the behavior of liquids.

To master this chapter you should review:
- (6-7) What happens to the total mechanical energy of a system when nonconservative forces do work.
- (9-4) How pressure is defined.

11-1 Liquids and gases are both examples of fluids

Liquids and gases—collectively known as *fluids* for their ability to flow—are the most common states of matter in the universe. Indeed, much of our planet's interior, the entirety of our Sun, and most of your body are composed of fluids (Figure 11-1). Solid objects in our daily environment such as rocks and trees are exceptional cases in a universe dominated by fluids.

Solids are substances whose individual molecules cannot move freely, but remain in essentially fixed positions relative to one another. That's why a solid object maintains its shape, though it may bend or deform if you apply forces to it. In contrast, **fluids** are substances that can flow because their molecules can move freely with respect to each other and are not tied to fixed locations.

Fluids fall into two broad categories: liquids and gases. **Liquids** tend to maintain the same volume regardless of the shape and size of their container. For example, 1 cubic meter (1 m^3) of water taken from a storage tank will exactly fill a 1-m^3 container into which it is poured (Figure 11-2a). **Gases**, however, expand to fill whatever volume is available to them. If you place a cylinder containing 1 m^3 of compressed oxygen gas in

Much of Earth's interior is a thick liquid substance that sometimes comes to the surface as lava.

All of the material that makes up the Sun is in the form of a gas. The gas glows due to its high temperature.

The body of an adult human is mostly liquid (by mass, about 50 to 60 percent water). Hydration keeps the liquid level constant.

(a)

(b)

(c)

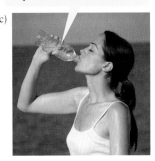

Figure 11-1 **Fluids** Materials that can flow make up (a) much of our Earth, (b) all of our Sun (as well as all of the stars visible in the night sky, which are objects like the Sun), and (c) most of our bodies. Note that the photo in (a) shows at least three different fluids: molten lava flowing down the rocks, liquid water in the ocean, and the air in our atmosphere.

a large room and open the valve, the oxygen gas spreads out over the entire room so that its volume is much greater than 1 m³ (Figure 11-2b). It can also be compressed further to fill an even smaller container.

What explains the difference between these two types of fluids? In a liquid, molecules are close to one another (almost touching). At close range the attractive forces between molecules are strong, keeping the molecules together so that the volume of the liquid stays the same. In a gas, however, the molecules are much farther apart; in the air you're breathing now, the average distance between molecules is about 10 times the size of a single molecule. At these greater separations the molecules exert little or no attractive forces on each other, so nothing prevents the molecules from spreading out to occupy all of the available volume.

In this chapter we will touch on many of the key aspects of fluids. The central concepts of *density* and *pressure*, coupled with the notion of what it means for a fluid to be in *equilibrium*, will help us understand why water pressure increases with increasing depth. They also explain the phenomenon of *buoyancy* that keeps the hot-air balloon in the opening photo aloft and that enables marine animals to float under water without

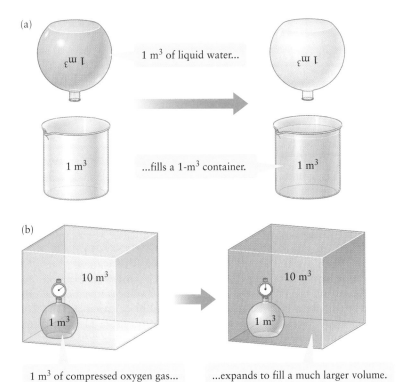

(a)

1 m³ of liquid water...

...fills a 1-m³ container.

(b)

1 m³ of compressed oxygen gas...

...expands to fill a much larger volume.

Figure 11-2 **Liquids versus gases** (a) A liquid maintains the same volume when you pour it from one container to another. (b) A gas expands to fill whatever volume is available.

sinking or rising. Fluids in *motion* are influenced not only by pressure and density but also by *viscous* forces, which are the frictional forces of one part of the fluid rubbing past another. By examining some of the myriad ways in which fluids flow, we will gain insight into the flight of airplanes and birds, the behavior of blood in the circulatory system, and the peculiar challenges that face very small swimming organisms. Finally, we will see how the mutual attraction of molecules in a liquid gives rise to surface tension, a phenomenon that impacts the function of your lungs.

Take-Home Message for Section 11-1

✔ Fluids (which include liquids and gases) do not have a definite shape. They can flow to take on the shape of their container because their molecules are in constant motion.

✔ Liquids maintain essentially the same volume as they flow, but gases will expand or contract as necessary to fill the available space.

✔ The attractive forces between molecules are strong in liquids, but are weak in gases because the molecules are farther apart.

11-2 Density measures the amount of mass per unit volume

One way to describe how tightly packed the molecules are in a gas, liquid, or solid is in terms of *density*. The **density** of a substance, denoted by the Greek letter ρ (rho), is the mass of the substance divided by the volume that it occupies. The greater the density of a substance, the more kilograms of that substance are packed into a given number of cubic meters of volume:

Definition of density
(11-1)

The **density** ρ ("rho") of a certain substance...

...equals the mass m of a given quantity of that substance...

$$\rho = \frac{m}{V}$$

...divided by the volume V of that quantity of the substance.

A given number of water molecules of combined mass m occupy a smaller volume V in liquid water than they do in water vapor (a gas). Hence the density $\rho = m/V$ of liquid water is greater than that of water vapor.

! Watch Out! Density doesn't tell you how closely packed the molecules are.

You need more information to figure out the space between molecules. A certain number of oxygen gas molecules have 14% greater density than the same number of nitrogen gas molecules with the same spacing between molecules. That's because density is *mass* per unit volume, and the mass of an oxygen molecule is 14% greater than that of a nitrogen molecule. To find the spacing between molecules in a given substance, you need to know both the density of the substance *and* the mass per molecule.

Density is usually stated in kilograms per cubic meter (kg/m^3). For this reason the density of a substance is often referred to as the *mass per unit volume* of the substance (that is, the number of kilograms of mass in $1\ m^3$, or one unit of volume). A common alternative choice of units is grams per cubic centimeter, or g/cm^3 ($1\ g/cm^3 = 1000\ kg/m^3$). As an example, one cubic meter of liquid water at a temperature of $4°C$ has a mass of 1000 kg and therefore a density $\rho = (1000\ kg)/(1\ m^3) = 1000\ kg/m^3$. Twice the mass of liquid water (2000 kg) occupies twice the volume ($2\ m^3$), and so its density is the same: $\rho = (2000\ kg)/(2\ m^3) = 1000\ kg/m^3$. This example shows that density depends only on the nature of the substance, *not* on how much of the substance is present. When we say that gold has a density of $19,300\ kg/m^3 = 1.93 \times 10^4\ kg/m^3$, we mean that *any* quantity of gold has this same density. Table 11-1 lists the densities of some common substances.

An alternative way to describe the density of a substance is to compare its density to that of another substance that serves as a standard. One common standard is liquid water at $4°C$ ($\rho = 1000\ kg/m^3$), and the **specific gravity** of a substance is equal to its density divided by that of 4°C liquid water. Human blood, for instance, has a specific gravity of 1.06, which means it is 1.06 times as dense as water: $\rho_{\text{blood}} = (1.06)(1000 \text{ kg/m}^3) = 1.06 \times 10^3 \text{ kg/m}^3$. The term *specific gravity* in this case means that a certain volume of blood weighs 1.06 times as much as the same volume of water—that is, it experiences 1.06 times as much gravitational force. On average, red blood cells make up about 38% of the volume of blood in women and 42% in men; these cells are only slightly denser than water, which is why the specific gravity of blood is just a little greater than 1.

In general, the density of a liquid depends on temperature. For example, if you take water from the refrigerator (temperature about 4°C) and let it warm to room temperature (about 20°C), the water expands slightly. Because the mass m of the water is the same but its volume V has increased, the density $\rho = m/V$ of 20°C water is slightly less (by about 0.2%) than that of 4°C water. Most liquids expand and become less dense when the temperature increases. Between 0°C and 4°C, water is a notable exception to this general rule: Within this temperature range, water *contracts* and becomes *more* dense as the temperature increases. That's why we give the densities of water and salt water in Table 11-1 at 4°C, the temperature at which these liquids are densest.

The density of gases is sensitive to both temperature and pressure. Heated air expands, which lowers its density; applying pressure to air to force it into an automobile tire makes the air occupy a smaller volume, which raises its density. Because gases can easily be compressed by squeezing, they are **compressible fluids**. By contrast, for most practical purposes liquids are **incompressible fluids**: The volume and the density of a liquid change very little when it is squeezed. (That's because the molecules of a liquid are almost touching and resist being squeezed much closer together.) You can easily compress air to a higher density using a hand pump of the sort used for inflating bicycle tires, but to compress water appreciably takes tremendous pressures like those found at the bottom of the ocean. (We introduced the idea of *pressure* in Section 9-4, and we'll describe it more carefully in Section 11-3.)

While the main focus of this chapter is on fluids, the idea of density applies to solids as well. The following examples show some applications of this idea.

Table 11-1 Densities of Various Substances

Substance	Density (kg/m³)
air at sea level at 15°C	1.23
dry timber (white pine)	370
fresh wood (red oak)	600
gasoline	680
ethanol (ethyl alcohol)	806
lipids (fats and oils)	915–945
ice at 0°C	917
fresh water at 4°C	1.000×10^3
fresh water at 20°C	998
seawater at 4°C	1.025×10^3
muscle	1.06×10^3
deer antler (low-density bone)	1.86×10^3
cow femur (typical bone)	2.06×10^3
tympanic bulla of a fin whale (densest bone)	2.47×10^3
aluminum (Al)	2.70×10^3
mollusk shell	2.7×10^3
calcite (mineral of shell)	2.8×10^3
tooth enamel, human	2.9×10^3
apatite (mineral of bone, tooth)	3.2×10^3
planet earth (average density)	5.52×10^3
iron (Fe)	7.8×10^3
mercury (Hg)	13.595×10^3
gold (Au)	19.3×10^3

Example 11-1 Density of Chicken

A typical whole chicken on sale at a supermarket has a mass of 2.3 kg and is approximately spherical in shape, with a radius of about 8.0 cm. What is the approximate density of such a chicken in kg/m³? Compare the result to the densities of the biological materials listed in Table 11-1.

Set Up

We are given the chicken's mass and its radius, and our goal is to calculate its density ρ. We use the definition of density in Equation 11-1, $\rho = m/V$.

The chicken is very nearly spherical, so to determine its volume we use the expression for the volume of a sphere of radius R (see the Math Tutorial).

Definition of density:

$$\rho = \frac{m}{V} \qquad (11\text{-}1)$$

Volume of a sphere of radius R:

$$V = \frac{4\pi R^3}{3}$$

Solve

To calculate the density in the desired units, we need to find the chicken's volume in cubic meters (m^3). To take this measure, we first express its radius in meters.

$$R = (8.0 \text{ cm})\left(\frac{1 \text{ m}}{100 \text{ cm}}\right) = 8.0 \times 10^{-2} \text{ m}$$

We then calculate the volume of the chicken in cubic meters (m^3).

$$V = \frac{4\pi R^3}{3} = \frac{4\pi (8.0 \times 10^{-2} \text{ m})^3}{3} = 2.1 \times 10^{-3} \text{ m}^3$$

The density is the mass of the chicken ($m = 2.3$ kg) divided by this volume.

$$\rho = \frac{m}{V} = \frac{2.3 \text{ kg}}{2.1 \times 10^{-3} \text{ m}^3} = 1.1 \times 10^3 \text{ kg/m}^3$$

Reflect

Our answer doesn't match up precisely with any of the values given in Table 11-1. That's because a chicken's body is not a pure substance, but a mixture of substances of different densities: fats, water, muscle, and bone. Our calculated density of 1.1×10^3 kg/m^3 is actually the *average* density of the chicken. (Most animals have approximately this average density.) We explore the idea of average density further in Example 11-2.

You may be wondering if it's reasonable to approximate a chicken as being spherical. If you look at the sketch, some parts of the chicken extend beyond the sphere, and some of the sphere is empty. But the volume of the chicken outside the sphere is nearly equal to the volume of the "empty" part of the sphere, so the volume of the chicken is actually pretty close to the volume of the sphere.

Example 11-2 Average Density

A submersible vessel used for deep-sea research has a metal hull with a large cavity in its interior for the crew and their equipment. Suppose that the hull is made of 1.130×10^3 m^3 of a particular steel alloy of density 7.910×10^3 kg/m^3, and that the cavity in the hull has volume 7.600×10^3 m^3 and is filled with air of density 1.200 kg/m^3. Find the *average* density of the submersible, that is, the density of the submersible as a whole.

Set Up

The submersible contains two materials—the steel of the hull and the air in the interior spaces—which have different densities and occupy different volumes. We want to find a third density, the *average* density of the entire submersible, equal to its total mass m_{sub} divided by its total volume V_{sub}. We again use the definition of density, Equation 11-1. We'll apply this definition three times, once for each density.

Definition of density:

$$\rho = \frac{m}{V} \qquad (11\text{-}1)$$

steel hull
density $\rho_{steel} = 7.910 \times 10^3$ kg/m^3
volume $V_{hull} = 1.130 \times 10^3$ m^3

interior spaces filled with air
density $\rho_{air} = 1.200$ kg/m^3
volume $V_{cavity} = 7.600 \times 10^3$ m^3

Solve

The submersible's average density $\rho_{average}$ is its total mass m_{sub} divided by its total volume V_{sub}, so we need to calculate both m_{sub} and V_{sub}. The volume of the submersible (V_{sub}) is the sum of the volume of the hull (V_{hull}) and the volume of the cavity (V_{cavity}).

Average density of the sub as a whole:

$$\rho_{average} = \frac{m_{sub}}{V_{sub}}$$

Total volume of the sub:

$$V_{sub} = V_{hull} + V_{cavity} = 1.130 \times 10^3 \text{ m}^3 + 7.600 \times 10^3 \text{ m}^3$$
$$= 8.730 \times 10^3 \text{ m}^3$$

From Equation 11-1, the mass of steel in the hull (m_{hull}) and the mass of air in the cavity (m_{cavity})

Rearrange Equation 11-1:
$$m = \rho V$$

are given by their respective densities multiplied by their respective volumes.

Solve for m_{hull} and m_{cavity}:

$$m_{hull} = \rho_{steel}V_{hull} = (7.910 \times 10^3 \text{ kg/m}^3)(1.130 \times 10^3 \text{ m}^3)$$
$$= 8.938 \times 10^6 \text{ kg}$$

$$m_{cavity} = \rho_{air}V_{cavity} = (1.200 \text{ kg/m}^3)(7.600 \times 10^3 \text{ m}^3)$$
$$= 9.120 \times 10^3 \text{ kg}$$

The total mass of the submersible (m_{sub}) is the sum of the mass of steel in the hull and the mass of air in the cavity.

$$m_{sub} = m_{hull} + m_{cavity} = 8.938 \times 10^6 \text{ kg} + 9.120 \times 10^3 \text{ kg}$$
$$= 8.947 \times 10^6 \text{ kg}$$

To get the average density, substitute the total volume V_{sub} and the total mass m_{sub} into the expression for $\rho_{average}$.

$$\rho_{average} = \frac{m_{sub}}{V_{sub}} = \frac{8.947 \times 10^6 \text{ kg}}{8.730 \times 10^3 \text{ m}^3}$$
$$= 1.025 \times 10^3 \text{ kg/m}^3$$

Reflect

No one component of the submersible has a density of 1.025×10^3 kg/m³; instead, this represents an average of the densities of the two components. Note that the average density is intermediate between the density of air (1.200 kg/m³) and the density of steel (7.910×10^3 kg/m³).

This particular value of average density is greater than the density of fresh water (1.000×10^3 kg/m³) but is the same as that of seawater (1.025×10^3 kg/m³). As we will see in Section 11-8, this means that the submersible will sink in fresh water but will float when submerged in seawater—which is a useful thing for a deep-sea research vessel to do.

Example 11-3 How Much Space for a Molecule?

A single molecule of water (H_2O) has a mass of 2.99×10^{-26} kg. Find the average volume per water molecule (a) in liquid water at 4°C and (b) in water vapor (that is, water in gas form) at 120°C, which has a density of 0.559 kg/m³. In each case, what is the length of each side of a cube with this volume? Compare to the size of a water molecule, which is about 2×10^{-10} m across.

Set Up

The density ρ of a substance tells us the mass per volume. We want to find the volume per *molecule* in the substance. We'll do this calculation by combining the value of ρ for each substance (liquid water at 4°C and water vapor at 120°C) with the mass per water molecule. We'll imagine that each molecule is at the center of a cube of side L, and we'll determine L from the formula for the volume of a cube.

Definition of density:

$$\rho = \frac{m}{V} \qquad (11\text{-}1)$$

Volume of a cube of side L:

$$V = L \times L \times L = L^3$$

Solve

Rewrite Equation 11-1 to solve for the volume occupied by a quantity m of the substance.

From Equation 11-1,

$$V = \frac{m}{\rho}, \text{ or}$$

$$\text{Volume occupied by a molecule} = \frac{(\text{mass of a molecule})}{(\text{density})}$$

(a) Table 11-1 tells us that water at 4°C has a density of 1.000×10^3 kg/m³. Use this to find the volume per molecule and the length L of a cube with this volume.

For water at 4°C,

Volume occupied by a molecule = V

$$= \frac{2.99 \times 10^{-26} \text{ kg}}{1.000 \times 10^3 \text{ kg/m}^3}$$
$$= 2.99 \times 10^{-29} \text{ m}^3$$

The volume V is equal to L^3; that is, V is the cube of L. So L is the cube *root* of V:

$$L = \sqrt[3]{V} = \sqrt[3]{2.99 \times 10^{-29}\,\text{m}^3}$$
$$= 3.10 \times 10^{-10}\,\text{m}$$

This is about 50% larger than the size of a water molecule (roughly 2×10^{-10} m).

(b) Repeat the calculation for water vapor at 120°C. The molecule is the same and so has the same mass, but the density is far less than that for the liquid at 4°C:

For water vapor at 120°C,

Volume occupied by a molecule = V

$$= \frac{2.99 \times 10^{-26}\,\text{kg}}{0.559\,\text{kg/m}^3}$$
$$= 5.35 \times 10^{-26}\,\text{m}^3$$

The length L of a cube with this volume is

$$L = \sqrt[3]{V} = \sqrt[3]{5.35 \times 10^{-26}\,\text{m}^3}$$
$$= 3.77 \times 10^{-9}\,\text{m}$$

This is larger than the size of a water molecule by a factor of $(3.77 \times 10^{-9}\,\text{m})/(2 \times 10^{-10}\,\text{m}) = 19$.

Reflect

In both liquids and gases, the molecules are in constant motion. That's why the volumes we calculated in this example are the *average* volume per molecule.

Our results show that in the liquid state a water molecule almost fills the volume that it occupies on average. So there is very little extra room to move the molecules closer together, which means that it is very difficult to compress a liquid. In the gaseous state, however, on average each molecule is surrounded by lots of empty space. In this state it's much easier to push the molecules closer together, and so a gas is relatively easy to compress.

? Got the Concept? 11-1 Weight and Density

Which is heavier, a block of iron or a block of ice? (a) the block of iron; (b) the block of ice; (c) they have the same weight; (d) not enough information given to decide.

Take-Home Message for Section 11-2

✔ The density of a substance describes how much mass of a particular substance occupies a given volume.

✔ The specific gravity of a substance equals the density of that substance relative to the density of fresh water at 4°C.

✔ An object's average density equals its total mass divided by its overall volume. It is intermediate in value between the densities of the least dense and most dense constituents of the object.

11-3 Pressure in a fluid is caused by the impact of molecules

Pressure is a commonplace idea. Everyone has had their blood pressure measured during a visit to the physician. An air-filled balloon bursts if the pressure within it is too great. And weather reports refer to low-pressure and high-pressure weather systems in the atmosphere. But what *is* pressure?

Figure 11-3 shows how pressure is defined. If you place a small, thin, flat plate in a fluid—a gas or a liquid—you'll find that the fluid exerts a force on either face of the plate. You can feel these forces if you stick your hand into a swimming pool or a sink full of water. (The same kind of forces act on your hand when it's surrounded by air, but are very feeble compared to the forces exerted by water.) The net force that the fluid exerts on either face of the plate acts perpendicular to the face. The **pressure** of the fluid acting on the face is the magnitude of this perpendicular force divided by the area of the face:

The **pressure** p exerted by a fluid on an object in the fluid...

...equals the force $F_\perp$ that the fluid exerts perpendicular to the face of the object...

$$p = \frac{F_\perp}{A}$$

...divided by the area A of that face.

Definition of pressure
(11-2)

! Watch Out! The symbols for pressure and density are not the same.

We use a lowercase p to represent pressure, and the lowercase Greek letter ρ (rho) to represent density. These variables look a lot alike, so you need to be careful, especially when you write them, that you properly distinguish between the two.

To understand why a fluid exerts forces like those shown in Figure 11-3, keep in mind that the molecules of a liquid or gas are in constant motion. Any object placed in a fluid is struck repeatedly by these moving molecules. The force of each individual impact is miniscule, but there are so many molecules and so many impacts that their combined effect is appreciable. It's that combined force that gives rise to the forces labeled $F_\perp$ in Figure 11-3. As an example, more than 10^{23} air molecules collide with a square centimeter of your skin every second, exerting a combined force of about 10 N on that square centimeter. In a fluid at rest (such as water in the kitchen sink that is not flowing or draining out, or the air in a room with no wind currents), the molecules of the fluid move in entirely random directions. At any point in the fluid there are as many molecules moving to the left as to the right, as many moving upward as downward, and so on. Hence a small, thin, flat plate placed in the fluid (Figure 11-3) experiences the same number of impacts, and hence the same magnitude of force, on each of its sides no matter which way the plate is oriented.

If we double the surface area A exposed to the fluid, the force magnitude $F_\perp$ also doubles because there is twice as much area to be hit by the molecules of the

A small, thin plate of area A is immersed in a fluid.

No matter how the plate is oriented, the fluid exerts the same magnitude of force $F_\perp$ and the same pressure $p = F_\perp/A$ on both sides of the plate.

Figure 11-3 **Pressure on a thin plate in a fluid** The fluid pressure on this plate does not depend on its orientation.

fluid. However, the pressure $p = F_\perp/A$ remains the same. Pressure is a property of the fluid, not of the object that's immersed in the fluid. Furthermore, because the pressure is the same no matter how the disk in Figure 11-3 is oriented, pressure has no direction: Unlike force, pressure is *not* a vector.

The SI units of pressure are newtons per square meter (N/m^2). As we discussed in Section 9-2, one newton per square meter is also called a **pascal** (abbreviated Pa): $1 \text{ Pa} = 1 \text{ N/m}^2$. We'll discuss other common units of pressure in Section 11-5.

Watch Out! Don't confuse force and pressure.

Although force and pressure are related, they are *not* the same quantity. Here's an example. If you take off your shoes and stand up, your mass is distributed evenly over the surface area of your two feet. The pressure on the soles of your feet is your mass divided by the surface area of the bottom of your two feet and is probably not uncomfortable. But if you stood on a bed of nails it would hurt! Your weight hasn't changed, so the force you exert on the surface supporting you hasn't changed. However, because the supporting surface—the tips of a few nails—has a much smaller surface area, the pressure on your feet is much greater (and much more painful) in this case. However, people can comfortably *lie* on a suitably prepared bed of nails. By lying flat, a person's weight is distributed over the area of the tips of many nails, resulting in a tolerable pressure (Figure 11-4).

Figure 11-4 **A bed of nails** It doesn't hurt to lie on this bed of nails. That's because the force that the nails exert is distributed over the area of many nails, resulting in a tolerable pressure on the person's back.

At sea level on Earth, the pressure of the atmosphere is about $1.01 \times 10^5 \text{ N/m}^2$, or 1.01×10^5 Pa. By contrast, the pressure at an altitude of 15,000 m (41,000 ft, about the highest altitude at which airliners fly) is only 1.78×10^4 Pa, or 17.6% of the pressure at sea level. One reason why the pressure is lower at high altitude is that the air is less dense there (0.289 kg/m^3 at 15,000 m versus 1.23 kg/m^3 at sea level). Hence there are fewer air molecules to produce pressure through collisions. A second reason is that the molecules at high altitude move more slowly than those near sea level, so when collisions do take place they are relatively gentle. We'll learn in Chapter 14 that gas molecules move more slowly in a cold gas than a warm gas. The air at 15,000 m is indeed quite cold: The average temperature there is $-56°C$ ($-69°F$) compared to $15°C$ ($59°F$) at sea level. The air pressure at 15,000 m is too low to sustain human life, which is why airliners have *pressurized* cabins: Air from the jet engine intakes is pumped into the cabin, increasing the pressure inside the cabin to what it would be at an altitude of $1800-2400$ m ($6000-8000$ ft) above sea level.

The variation of pressure with elevation isn't unique to our atmosphere. In the oceans, in lakes, and even in a glass of water there is greater pressure as you go deeper and lower pressure as you ascend. In the next section we'll learn more about how and why pressure increases with depth in a fluid.

? Got the Concept? 11-2 Something's Fishy

A tropical fish is at rest in the middle of an aquarium. Compared to the pressure on the left side of the fish, the pressure on the right side of the fish has (a) the same magnitude and the same direction; (b) the same magnitude and opposite direction; (c) a different magnitude and the same direction; (d) a different magnitude and opposite direction; (e) none of these.

Take-Home Message for Section 11-3

✔ A fluid exerts pressure on any object with which it is in contact.

✔ The pressure equals the force that the fluid exerts perpendicular to the object's face divided by the area of that face.

11-4 In a fluid at rest, pressure increases with increasing depth

Figure 11-5 shows the results of an experiment with air in our atmosphere. An empty plastic bottle is opened at an altitude of 9000 ft (2740 m) above sea level, so that the bottle fills with air at that altitude. The bottle is then tightly capped (Figure 11-5a). As the bottle is brought back to sea level, it compresses as though it had been squeezed by an invisible hand (see Figure 11-5b). (You can observe the reverse process if you buy a bag of potato chips at sea level and take it with you on a drive into the mountains. As you climb, you'll see the bag expand. If you go high enough, the bag may even pop open.)

Why do these things happen? The answer is that the pressure in a fluid *increases* as you go *deeper* into the fluid. For example, air pressure in the atmosphere is more than 25% greater at sea level than it is at an altitude of 2000 m. The air inside the bottle in Figure 11-5 was at the pressure found at 2740 m, so it compressed when it was brought to sea level and was surrounded by air at higher pressure. In this section we'll explore the relationship between pressure and depth in a fluid.

Hydrostatic Equilibrium

Let's consider a large tank filled with a fluid at rest (Figure 11-6). When a fluid is at rest (that is, not flowing), we say it is in **hydrostatic equilibrium.** The term *hydrostatic* specifically refers to water at rest, but it's common to use this term to refer to *any* kind of fluid in equilibrium.

Now imagine a box-shaped volume of fluid within the tank, as in Figure 11-6. The area of the top and bottom of the box is A and the height of the box is d. We won't put an actual box in the fluid; instead, we simply imagine a boundary that separates the box-shaped volume from the rest of the fluid.

The weight of the fluid above the box exerts a downward force of magnitude F_{down} on the box. Because fluids exert a force in all directions, the fluid below the box pushes upward on the box with a force of magnitude F_{up}. (We'll see in a moment that F_{up} is *not* equal to F_{down}.) The fluid also exerts forces on the sides of the box, but the *net* force on the sides is zero: There is as much force on the left side as on the right side, and these forces cancel. Finally, we must consider the force of gravity on the fluid inside the box. The fluid has weight. This weight appears as a downward force $\vec{w}$ on the fluid volume. Figure 11-6 shows the three remaining forces on the box—an upward force on the bottom, a downward force on the top, and the downward force of gravity.

(a)

(b)

Figure 11-5 Air pressure varies with elevation (a) This empty plastic bottle was opened to the air in a non-pressurized airplane at an altitude of 9000 ft (2740 m), then tightly capped. (b) Outside air pressure made the bottle collapse when it was returned to sea level.

Consider a box-shaped volume of fluid that is part of a larger quantity of fluid at rest.

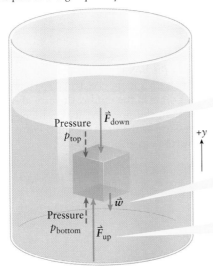

Pressure p_{top} $\vec{F}_{down}$

Downward force on the box due to the pressure at the top of the box

$+y$

$\vec{w}$

Downward gravitational force on the box

Pressure p_{bottom} $\vec{F}_{up}$

Upward force on the box due to the pressure at the bottom of the box

In order for the fluid to be in **hydrostatic equilibrium,** the net force on the box must be zero: $\Sigma \vec{F} = \vec{F}_{up} + \vec{F}_{down} + \vec{w} = 0$

Figure 11-6 Hydrostatic equilibrium We can derive the equation of hydrostatic equilibrium by considering a box-shaped portion of a fluid at rest. For the box to be in equilibrium, the pressure at its bottom must be greater than the pressure at its top.

We started with the assumption that the fluid in the tank is at rest. This requires that there be no *net* force on the fluid volume; that is, the vector sum of the three forces acting on the box must be zero:

$$\sum \vec{F} = \vec{F}_{\text{up}} + \vec{F}_{\text{down}} + \vec{w} = 0 \qquad (11\text{-}3)$$

All of these forces are vertically upward or downward, so we need only the y components of these forces. Taking the positive y direction to be upward, Equation 11-3 becomes

$$\sum F_y = F_{\text{up}} - F_{\text{down}} - w = 0 \qquad (11\text{-}4)$$

We can see that because the fluid in the box has a nonzero weight w, the forces F_{up} and F_{down} are *not* equal. From Equation 11-2, $p = F_{\perp}/A$, we can express the magnitude F_{up} of the upward force (which acts perpendicular to the underside of the box) as the pressure p_{bottom} at the bottom of the box multiplied by the area A of the bottom of the box. Similarly, the magnitude F_{down} of the downward force equals the pressure p_{top} at the top of the box multiplied by the area A of the top of the box. (The box is rectangular, so the top and bottom have the same area.) Furthermore, the weight w of the fluid in the box equals the product of the mass m of fluid in the box and the acceleration due to gravity g. So Equation 11-4 becomes

$$p_{\text{bottom}}A - p_{\text{top}}A - mg = 0 \quad \text{or} \quad p_{\text{bottom}}A = p_{\text{top}}A + mg \qquad (11\text{-}5)$$

Equation 11-5 tells us that because of the weight mg of the fluid in the box, the pressure p_{bottom} has to be greater than the pressure p_{top}. In other words, the pressure of the fluid is greater at a point that's deep in the fluid (the bottom of the box) than at a point that's less deep (the top of the box), and so pressure increases with increasing depth in the fluid.

A Uniform-Density Fluid: The Equation of Hydrostatic Equilibrium

We can simplify Equation 11-5 even further if we assume that the fluid has **uniform density**: That is, the density of the fluid has the same value throughout the fluid. The mass m of the volume of fluid in the box is the product of the density of the fluid, ρ, and the volume of the box. The height of the rectangular box is d, so its volume is $V = Ad$ and the mass of the fluid in the box is $m = \rho V = \rho Ad$. So Equation 11-5, the statement that the fluid in the box remains at rest, becomes

$$p_{\text{bottom}}A = p_{\text{top}}A + \rho Adg \qquad (11\text{-}6)$$

Now divide each term in Equation 11-6 by A:

$$p_{\text{bottom}} = p_{\text{top}} + \rho gd \qquad (11\text{-}7)$$

In other words, the pressure at the bottom of the box is greater than the pressure at the top of the box. Furthermore, the box is just an imaginary construct, so the real meaning of Equation 11-7 is as follows: At *any* two points in the fluid with vertical separation d, the pressure at the lower point is greater than the pressure at the upper point by an amount ρgd. In particular, let p_0 be the pressure at the upper point (Figure 11-6). Then the pressure p at a point a distance d below the upper point is

Variation of pressure with depth
in a fluid with uniform density
(equation of hydrostatic equilibrium)
(11-8)

Pressure at a certain point in a fluid at rest	Density of the fluid (same at all points in the fluid)

Pressure at a second, lower point in the fluid		Acceleration due to gravity

$$p = p_0 + \rho gd$$

Depth of the second point where the pressure is p below the point where the pressure is p_0

Equation 11-8 must be satisfied for a fluid to remain at rest, so this is also called the **equation of hydrostatic equilibrium**.

> ## ! Watch Out! Understand what Equation 11-8 tells you.
>
> Be careful with the sign of the $\rho g d$ term in Equation 11-8: Remember that the symbol d means *depth*. If the second point is *below* the point where the pressure is p_0, d is positive and p is greater than p_0. If the second point is *above* the point where the pressure is p_0, d is *negative* and p is less than p_0. In other words, pressure increases as you go deeper in a fluid like the ocean but decreases as you ascend. Note also that Equation 11-8 is based on the assumption that the fluid has the same density ρ at all points. If the density is noticeably different at different depths (as is the case for the air in our atmosphere), Equation 11-8 gives only approximate results.

Example 11-4 Air Pressure versus Water Pressure

You dig a swimming pool in your back yard that is 2.00 m deep. What is the pressure at the bottom of the pool (a) before you fill it with water; (b) after it is filled with water? At the time that you make the measurements, the air pressure at ground level is 1.0100×10^5 Pa.

Set Up

We are given the pressure $p_0 = 1.0100 \times 10^5$ Pa at the top of the pool and want to find the pressure p at a depth $d = 2.00$ m below the top of the pool. We'll use Equation 11-8 for this purpose. The only difference between parts (a) and (b) is the density ρ of the fluid: In part (a) we use the density of air, while in part (b) we use the density of water.

Variation of pressure with depth:

$$p = p_0 + \rho g d \qquad (11\text{-}8)$$

$d = 2.00$ m

Solve

(a) From Table 11-1 the density of air at sea level is $\rho = 1.23$ kg/m^3. Substitute this into Equation 11-8.

Pressure at the bottom of the pool filled with air:

$p = (1.0100 \times 10^5 \text{ Pa}) + (1.23 \text{ kg/m}^3)(9.80 \text{ m/s}^2)(2.00 \text{ m})$
$\quad = 1.0100 \times 10^5 \text{ Pa} + 24.1 \text{ kg/}(\text{m} \cdot \text{s}^2)$

Convert units: Recall that
$1 \text{ N} = 1 \text{ kg} \cdot \text{m/s}^2$ so
$1 \text{ Pa} = 1 \text{ N/m}^2 = 1 \text{ kg/}(\text{m} \cdot \text{s}^2)$

So the pressure at the bottom of the air-filled pool is
$p = 1.0100 \times 10^5 \text{ Pa} + 24.1 \text{ Pa}$
$\quad = 1.0100 \times 10^5 \text{ Pa} + 0.000241 \times 10^5 \text{ Pa}$
$\quad = 1.0102 \times 10^5 \text{ Pa}$

(b) When the pool is filled with water, the calculation is the same as in part (a) except that we use the density of water from Table 11-1, $\rho = 1.000 \times 10^3$ kg/m^3.

Pressure at the bottom of the pool filled with water:
$p = (1.0100 \times 10^5 \text{ Pa}) + (1.000 \times 10^3 \text{ kg/m}^3)(9.80 \text{ m/s}^2)(2.00 \text{ m})$
$\quad = 1.0100 \times 10^5 \text{ Pa} + 1.96 \times 10^4 \text{ kg/}(\text{m} \cdot \text{s}^2)$
$\quad = 1.0100 \times 10^5 \text{ Pa} + 0.196 \times 10^5 \text{ Pa}$
$\quad = 1.206 \times 10^5 \text{ Pa}$

Reflect

The pressure at the bottom of the air-filled pool is only 0.02% greater than at the top of the pool. That's such a tiny difference that we can ignore it. It takes a much greater variation in altitude than 2.00 m for the pressure difference in the air to be noticeable. (Your ears—which are sensitive pressure sensors—may "pop" when you drive up into the mountains, but they won't "pop" when you climb a ladder or a single flight of stairs.)

There *is* a noticeable pressure difference between the top and bottom of the water-filled pool: The pressure is about 20% greater at the bottom than at the surface. (You can definitely feel the increase in pressure when you dive to the bottom of a swimming pool.) The difference is that water is almost a thousand times denser than air. So a swimming pool full of water weighs almost a thousand times more than a swimming pool full of air, and so it produces an additional pressure almost a thousand times greater.

? Got the Concept? 11-3 Watching a U-tube

You pour water into a U-shaped tube as shown in Figure 11-7. The left-hand leg of the tube is 2.00 cm in radius, while the right-hand leg is 1.00 cm in radius. When the water is in equilibrium, how will the height of the water in the left-hand leg and the pressure at the bottom of the left-hand leg compare to the height of water in the right-hand leg and the pressure at the bottom of the right-hand leg? (a) greater height, greater pressure; (b) same height, same pressure; (c) lower height, lower pressure; (d) same height, greater pressure; (e) none of these.

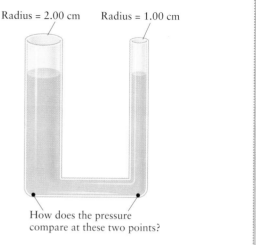

Radius = 2.00 cm   Radius = 1.00 cm

How does the pressure compare at these two points?

Figure 11-7 **A hollow U-tube** If water is poured into this hollow tube, how will the water level in each leg and the pressure at the bottom of each leg compare?

Take-Home Message for Section 11-4

✔ In a fluid in hydrostatic equilibrium (at rest), pressure increases as you go deeper into the fluid.

✔ The pressure difference between any two points within a uniform fluid in hydrostatic equilibrium depends only on the difference in the vertical height of the two points and the density of the fluid.

11-5 Scientists and medical professionals use various units for measuring fluid pressure

You might not be aware of it, but all of the air in the atmosphere directly above your head has weight, and that weight is pushing down on you right now. To be more precise, it's pushing in on you and exerting a pressure from every direction. Pressure on the surface of Earth due to the weight of air is considerable.

The air pressure at sea level varies somewhat due to the passage of weather systems, but on average is equal to 1.01325×10^5 Pa in SI units or about 14.7 pounds per square inch ($\mathrm{lb/in^2}$) in English units. This average value of atmospheric pressure at sea level is defined to be one **atmosphere**, abbreviated atm:

$$1 \text{ atm} = 1.01325 \times 10^5 \text{ Pa} = 14.7 \text{ lb/in}^2$$

To three significant figures, 1 atm = 1.01×10^5 Pa. Since 1 Pa = 1 $\mathrm{N/m^2}$, this means that if you paint a square one meter on a side onto the ground at sea level, the weight of the column of air that sits atop that square and extends to the upper limit of Earth's atmosphere is 1.01×10^5 N. A metric ton has a mass $m = 1000$ kg and a weight $mg = (1000 \text{ kg})(9.80 \text{ m/s}^2) = 9.80 \times 10^3$ N; the weight of air above that one-meter square is more than 10 times greater (to be precise, 10.3 metric tons). If you prefer to think in English units, paint a one-inch square onto the ground at sea level: The weight of air above that square is 14.7 pounds.

The atmosphere (atm) is a convenient unit for dealing with relatively large pressures. For example, the pressures found at the bottom of the ocean can exceed 10^3 atm, and high-pressure gas systems can operate at pressures of hundreds or even thousands of atmospheres. Very *low* pressures are often measured in pascals rather than atmospheres: For example, a high-quality vacuum pump can reduce the pressure inside a container to 10^{-5} Pa or lower. (A perfect vacuum would have a pressure of zero, since it would contain no molecules to cause collisions.)

Example 11-5 Diver's Rule of Thumb

To what depth in a freshwater lake would a diver have to descend for the pressure to be 1.00 atm greater than at the surface?

Set Up

Equation 11-8 from Section 11-4 tells us how the pressure p at a depth d below the lake's surface compares to the pressure p_0 at the surface. We can use this information to find the value of d such that p is greater than p_0 by 1.00 atm.

Variation of pressure with depth:

$$p = p_0 + \rho g d \qquad (11\text{-}8)$$

Solve

Rearrange Equation 11-8 to solve for the depth d at which the pressure has a certain value p.

From Equation 11-8,

$$p - p_0 = \rho g d$$
$$d = \frac{p - p_0}{\rho g}$$

We want the pressure p at depth d to be greater than the pressure p_0 at the surface by 1.00 atm, so $p - p_0 = 1.00$ atm. Substitute this value as well as the value of density ρ for fresh water from Table 11-1. Then use the conversion factors 1 atm $= 1.01 \times 10^5$ Pa $= 1.01 \times 10^5$ N/m^2 and 1 N $= 1$ kg $\cdot$ m/s^2:

Pressure difference:

$$p - p_0 = 1.00 \text{ atm}$$

Density of fresh water from Table 11-1:

$\rho = 1.000 \times 10^3$ kg/m^3 so

$$d = \frac{p - p_0}{\rho g}$$

$$= \frac{1.00 \text{ atm}}{(1.000 \times 10^3 \text{ kg/m}^3)(9.80 \text{ m/s}^2)} \times \left(\frac{1.01 \times 10^5 \text{ N/m}^2}{1 \text{ atm}} \right)$$

$$= 10.3 \frac{\text{m}^3}{\text{kg}} \frac{\text{s}^2}{\text{m}} \frac{\text{N}}{\text{m}^2} \times \left(\frac{1 \text{ kg} \cdot \text{m/s}^2}{1 \text{ N}} \right)$$

$$= 10.3 \text{ m}$$

Reflect

Our answer is a little bit more than 10 m, so it's a good approximation to say that our diver experiences a pressure change of 1 atmosphere going from the surface to a depth of 10 m. You can see that descending an additional 10 m would increase the pressure by another atmosphere, and so on. Divers use this as a "rule of thumb": Pressure increases by 1 atmosphere for every 10-m change in depth.

Measuring Pressure

You've almost certainly encountered pressure measurements when you've gone to the doctor or listened to a weather report. However, the value of pressure was probably not presented to you with units of atmospheres, Pa, or lb/in^2, but rather in either inches or millimeters of mercury. To understand these units of pressure, we'll examine how to construct a simple device called a *barometer* that's used to measure air pressure.

Fill a tube closed at one end with mercury, which has density ρ_{Hg} (Hg is the chemical symbol for mercury). While keeping the open end sealed, turn the tube upside down into a pan partially filled with mercury. (**Warning:** Mercury is poisonous, so do *not* try this experiment at home!) Now release the seal on the end of the tube, which is beneath the surface of the mercury in the pan. No air can get into the tube, so an equal volume of vacuum must remain in the place of whatever volume of fluid drains from the tube. Figure 11-8 shows this process.

Let's consider what happens once the system has come to hydrostatic equilibrium and a column of mercury of height H (measured from the surface of the mercury of the

Vacuum
$p_0 = 0$

Mercury of density ρ_{Hg}

H

p_{atm}

Fill a tube with mercury.

Plug the tube and invert it.

Put the inverted tube in a pan of mercury and remove the plug.

Not all the mercury drains into the pan because atmospheric pressure can support a column of mercury about three-quarters of a meter tall.

pan) remains in the tube. The pressure at the top of this column is $p_0 = 0$ because the pressure in a vacuum is zero. The pressure at the exposed surface of the mercury in the pan equals atmospheric pressure p_{atm}. Since the mercury is in hydrostatic equilibrium, the pressure at a point inside the mercury column at the same elevation as the exposed mercury surface is *also* equal to p_{atm}. From the equation of hydrostatic equilibrium, Equation 11-8, the pressure p_{atm} is greater than p_0 by $\rho_{Hg}gH$:

$$p_{atm} = p_0 + \rho_{Hg}gH$$

Since $p_0 = 0$ in the vacuum at the top of the mercury column, this equation becomes

(11-9)
$$p_{atm} = \rho_{Hg}gH$$
(atmospheric pressure measured with a mercury barometer)

As the atmospheric pressure p_{atm} rises and falls, the height H of the mercury column rises and falls along with it. Hence the height of the mercury column is a direct measure of atmospheric pressure.

A mercury barometer like that shown in Figure 11-8 is not a perfect instrument for measuring pressure: The density of mercury ρ_{Hg} changes with temperature, and the value of the acceleration due to gravity g depends on location. But at a temperature of 0°C so that the density of mercury is $\rho_{Hg} = 1.35951 \times 10^3 \text{ kg/m}^3$ and at a location where $g = 9.80665 \text{ m/s}^2$ (a "standard" value of g), the height of a column of mercury supported by exactly 1 atmosphere of pressure is found to be 760 mm. For that reason pressures are sometimes given in **millimeters of mercury,** or mmHg for short. Thus 1 atm = 760 mmHg. An equivalent (and preferred) unit is the **torr,** defined as 1/760 atm. This unit is named for the Italian scientist and mathematician Evangelista Torricelli, who invented the mercury barometer in the 1640s. The torr is a more appropriate unit than mmHg since most modern barometers work on different principles that don't involve columns of mercury.

If mercury is poisonous, why was it used in barometers? It's a case of convenience triumphing over safety. Equation 11-9 shows that the greater the density of the fluid, the lower the height H of the fluid column in the barometer. Because mercury is so dense—13.6 times denser than water—a mercury barometer is relatively compact and convenient to use. If you wanted to make a barometer like that shown in Figure 11-8 but using water rather than mercury, it would have to be 13.6 times taller than a mercury barometer. Can you show that if $p_{atm} = 1$ atm, the height of the liquid column in a water barometer would be 10.3 m—far too tall to be a convenient instrument?

Gauge Pressure

What is the air pressure inside a flat automobile tire? It's not zero: Rather, it's equal to atmospheric pressure (about 1 atm, 1.01×10^5 Pa, or 14.7 lb/in^2 at sea level). The same is true for a balloon that hasn't been inflated and for an empty, open bottle, because air at atmospheric pressure is inside these vessels. But if you use a tire pressure gauge to measure the air pressure in the deflated tire, it *will* read zero. This **gauge pressure** shows how much the pressure *exceeds* atmospheric pressure, which for many applications is a more intuitive way to think about pressure. The **absolute pressure**—that is to say, the true value of pressure—inside a deflated tire is equal to atmospheric pressure. If a tire pressure gauge shows that the air inside an inflated tire is at a pressure of 30.0 lb/in^2, that's the gauge pressure: The absolute pressure inside the tire equals the gauge pressure plus atmospheric pressure.

> **? Got the Concept? 11-4   Rank the Pressures**
>
> You have two balloons at sea level. One is deflated, and the other is inflated to 0.50 atm according to a pressure gauge connected to the mouth of the balloon. Rank the following from highest to lowest: (a) the gauge pressure inside the deflated balloon; (b) the absolute pressure inside the deflated balloon; (c) the gauge pressure inside the inflated balloon; (d) the absolute pressure inside the inflated balloon.

 ## Blood Pressure

Most of us encounter a pressure gauge when we visit the doctor and have our blood pressure measured (Figure 11-9). Blood pressure is usually given as two numbers, for example, "120 over 80." These values are measured in units of mmHg, and represent the high and low values of the *gauge* pressure in the arteries at the level of the heart. (Because the heart is a pump, the pressure in the system changes over the period of each heartbeat.)

Blood pressure is usually measured using a cuff around your upper arm, at the same elevation as your heart. We can understand why this is using the relationship between pressure and depth given by Equation 11-8. The blood within the body behaves rather like the fluid in the container shown in Figure 11-6: The farther down you go within the fluid, the greater the pressure. Since the heart is the principal organ of the circulatory system, let's have p_0 be the pressure at the position of the heart. Then Equation 11-8 tells us that the pressure of blood in the feet will be higher than the pressure in the heart and the pressure in the head will be lower. To measure the actual pressure produced by the heart's pumping action, it's important to measure that pressure at the same elevation as the heart itself—which explains the placement of a blood pressure cuff.

The average blood pressure (gauge pressure) in an upright person's feet is about 100 mmHg higher than when it leaves the heart, or about twice as great as the gauge pressure measured in a person's arm. In contrast, the pressure in the head is about 50 mmHg less than that at the heart. If you could somehow stretch your neck upward by a meter or so, the blood pressure in your head would drop to zero and no blood would reach your brain. So it's all for the best that you can't stretch your neck that far! (Some animals do have necks that are even longer: The head of an adult giraffe is about 2 m higher than his heart. To get blood to his brain, the giraffe heart has to generate much higher pressure than a human heart does—about 260 mmHg!)

These differences in pressure between different regions of the body affect the flow of blood in the veins returning to the heart from the head and neck. Blood pressure is always lower in veins than in arteries; if you can feel a pulse in your neck, you're feeling the carotid *artery* with its relatively high pressure. The gauge pressure of blood entering the heart is very close to zero. Since the pressure above the heart is even lower, the veins of the head and neck tend to collapse! How, then, does blood get back to the heart from the head and neck? As blood continues to enter the veins, pressure builds up and the vessels reopen. But as the blood flows through them, the pressure will again drop and the veins will collapse again. The result is intermittent venous blood flow in the head and neck.

You may be wondering why the gauge pressure of the blood entering the heart is so much lower than the gauge pressure of the blood leaving the heart, when the blood is

Figure 11-9 **Measuring blood pressure** A blood pressure cuff is applied around the upper arm, at the same elevation as the patient's heart. If the pressure were measured at a different elevation, the values would be either lower or higher than the actual pressures produced by the heart.

at essentially the same height. Equation 11-8 seems to indicate that these two pressures should be the same. However, you need to remember that Equation 11-8 is only valid under the conditions of *hydrostatic* equilibrium. Because blood is pumped by the heart and flows through the circulatory system, the blood is certainly *not* in hydrostatic equilibrium and we cannot use Equation 11-8. In Section 11-11 we'll discuss viscous flow, which helps to explain the difference in arterial and venous pressure.

Take-Home Message for Section 11-5

✔ The pressure exerted by air at sea level is approximately equal to 1 atm. This pressure is due to the weight of a column of air that extends to the top of our atmosphere.

✔ Gauge pressure is measured relative to some reference pressure. Usually this reference pressure is atmospheric pressure.

✔ Blood pressure is measured in mmHg, which is the height of a column of mercury the pressure could support. An equivalent unit to mmHg which physicists prefer is the torr.

11-6 A difference in pressure on opposite sides of an object produces a net force on the object

What makes a cork fly out of a champagne bottle? What makes the pistons move in the cylinders of an automobile engine? And what makes your beverage move up the straw into your mouth as you sip? In each case the cause is not strictly pressure, but rather pressure *difference*. The cork pops out because carbon dioxide gas inside the champagne bottle is at higher pressure than the air outside the bottle. Burning gasoline in the cylinder produces hot gas on one side of the piston that's at much higher pressure than the air on the other side, forcing the piston to move. And when you suck on a straw, you reduce the pressure in your mouth to a lower value than in the outside air, and the pressure difference drives liquid up the straw.

As a simple example of the force produced by a pressure difference, consider an object like a door with fluid on each side. The object has area A, there is pressure p_1 on one side of the object, and there is a greater pressure p_2 on the other side (Figure 11-10). By rearranging Equation 11-2, $p = F_\perp/A$, we can calculate the magnitude of the force that each fluid exerts perpendicular to the object's surface:

$$\text{Force on side 1: magnitude } F_{\perp 1} = p_1 A$$
$$\text{Force on side 2: magnitude } F_{\perp 2} = p_2 A$$

Since $p_2 > p_1$, the force $F_{\perp 2}$ on side 2 is greater than the force $F_{\perp 1}$ on side 1. These forces are in opposite directions, so the *net* force on the object has magnitude

$$F_{\text{net}} = F_{\perp 2} - F_{\perp 1} = p_2 A - p_1 A$$

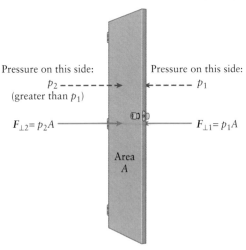

Pressure on this side:
p_2
(greater than p_1)

Pressure on this side:
p_1

$F_{\perp 2} = p_2 A$

$F_{\perp 1} = p_1 A$

Area A

Net force on the door due to the pressure difference:
$F_{\text{net}} = F_{\perp 2} - F_{\perp 1} = (p_2 - p_1)A$

Figure 11-10 Net force due to a pressure difference Because there are different pressures p_1 and p_2 on the two sides of this door, there is a net force on the door.

Net force on an object due to a pressure difference (11-10)

A pressure difference on two opposite sides of an object produces a net force.

Area of each side of the object

$$F_{\text{net}} = (p_2 - p_1)\, A$$

High pressure on one side of the object

Lower pressure on the other side of the object

That is, the net force on the object due to the pressures acting on it is proportional to the difference in pressure between the object's two sides. Note that Equation 11-10 refers *only* to the net force on an object due to a difference in pressure on its two sides. It doesn't include other forces that may act on the object, such as the force of gravity.

Example 11-6 Submarine Hatch

The air in the crew compartment of a research submarine is maintained at a pressure of 1.00 atm so that the crew can breathe normally. The sub operates at a depth of 85.0 m below the surface of the ocean. At this depth, what force would be required to push open a hatch of area 2.00 m²?

Set Up

There is 1.00 atm of air pressure on the inside of the hatch (call this p_{air}) pushing the hatch outward, but this is much less than the outside water pressure (call this p_{water}) pushing the hatch inward. The net inward force F_{net} due to this pressure difference is given by Equation 11-10; $A = 2.00$ m² is the surface area of the hatch. To open the hatch, the crew would have to exert an outward force of the same magnitude F_{net}.

To calculate F_{net}, we need to know the value of the water pressure p_{water}. We'll find this value using Equation 11-8 for the pressure at depth $d = 85.0$ m. In this equation, p_0 equals the pressure at the surface of the ocean (that is, at zero depth), which we also take to be 1.00 atm.

Net force on the hatch due to the pressure difference:

$$F_{net} = (p_{water} - p_{air})A \quad (11\text{-}10)$$

Variation of pressure with depth:

$$p_{water} = p_0 + \rho g d \quad (11\text{-}8)$$

$p_0 = 1.00$ atm

$d = 85.0$ m

p_{water}

$p_{air} = 1.00$ atm

hatch, area $A = 2.00$ m²

Solve

First find the pressure of the water at depth $d = 85$ m. Use the density of seawater from Table 11-1, $\rho = 1.025 \times 10^3$ kg/m³, convert atmospheres to newtons per square meter, and note that 1 kg/(m·s²) = 1 N/m².

Water pressure on the outside of the hatch:

$$p_{water} = p_0 + \rho g d$$

In this, $p_0 = 1.00$ atm $= 1.01 \times 10^5$ N/m², so

$$\begin{aligned}
p_{water} &= 1.01 \times 10^5 \text{ N/m}^2 \\
&\quad + (1.025 \times 10^3 \text{ kg/m}^3)(9.80 \text{ m/s}^2)(85.0 \text{ m}) \\
&= 1.01 \times 10^5 \text{ N/m}^2 + 8.54 \times 10^5 \text{ kg/(m·s}^2) \\
&= 1.01 \times 10^5 \text{ N/m}^2 + 8.54 \times 10^5 \text{ N/m}^2 \\
&= 9.55 \times 10^5 \text{ N/m}^2
\end{aligned}$$

Now we can calculate the magnitude of the net force on the hatch due to the pressure difference. This is the same as the force that the crew must exert to open the hatch.

Air pressure on the inside of the hatch:

$p_{air} = 1.00$ atm $= 1.01 \times 10^5$ N/m², so

$$\begin{aligned}
F_{net} &= (p_{water} - p_{air})A \\
&= (9.55 \times 10^5 \text{ N/m}^2 - 1.01 \times 10^5 \text{ N/m}^2)(2.00 \text{ m}^2) \\
&= (8.54 \times 10^5 \text{ N/m}^2)(2.00 \text{ m}^2) \\
&= 1.71 \times 10^6 \text{ N}
\end{aligned}$$

Reflect

This is an immense amount of force, equivalent to nearly 200 U.S. tons! Clearly the crew would not be able to open the hatch. In order for a crew member in diving gear to exit the submerged vessel, a portion of the crew compartment would have to be flooded with water from the outside. This action will equalize the inside and outside pressures and make it possible to open the hatch.

The Lungs

Pressure differences drive air into and out of the lungs. Frogs, for example, force air into their lungs by swallowing mouthfuls of air. In contrast, we humans suck air into our lungs by contracting the diaphragm and the muscles of the chest wall to increase the volume of our chest cavity. This pulls the lungs open, increasing their volume and therefore decreasing the pressure inside them. As this pressure becomes less than atmospheric pressure, the pressure difference pushes air through the airways and into the expanding lungs.

It takes energy for us to contract the muscles required for *inhalation*. However, normal *exhalation* does not require our muscles to do additional work on our chest wall. Relaxing the diaphragm and chest muscles allows the volume of the chest cavity to decrease. This process causes the pressure in the chest to rise above atmospheric pressure and forces air out of the lungs. Because atmospheric pressure is constant, changes in lung pressure determine the direction of airflow.

Breathing becomes more difficult if the chest is under pressure, such as if you're at the bottom of a football pile-on or if your body is submerged and you're trying to breathe through a tube that extends to the surface. The outside pressure on the chest makes it more difficult to expand the chest in order to inhale. Measurements show that if the pressure on a person's chest exceeds atmospheric pressure by 0.05 atm, the chest can't expand and inhalation is no longer possible. Example 11-7 shows that this places a limit on how deep underwater a person can be and still breathe through a hollow tube that opens above the surface.

Example 11-7 Breathing Underwater

Secret agent Steele Branson dives into a shallow freshwater pond to avoid capture by his nemesis. He intends to lie flat on his back on the bottom of the pond and breathe through a hollow reed. What is the length of the longest reed for which this could work?

Set Up

Branson needs to ensure that the difference between the water pressure p on his chest and the pressure p_0 of the atmosphere at the surface (where the open end of the reed is) does not exceed 0.05 atm. Equation 11-8 tells us how the water pressure varies with depth d, so our goal is to find the depth such that $p - p_0$ equals 0.05 atm.

Variation of pressure with depth:

$$p = p_0 + \rho g d \qquad (11\text{-}8)$$

Solve

Solve Equation 11-8 to find the depth d in terms of the water pressure on Branson's chest (p) and atmospheric pressure (p_0). Then find the depth d for which $p - p_0 = 0.05$ atm. Use the density of fresh water given in Table 11-1 as well as the definitions 1 atm = 1.01×10^5 N/m^2 and 1 N = 1 kg·m/s^2.

Rearrange Equation 11-8:

$$p - p_0 = \rho g d$$

Solve for d:

$$d = \frac{p - p_0}{\rho g}$$

$$= \frac{0.05\ \text{atm}}{(1.000 \times 10^3\ \text{kg/m}^3)(9.80\ \text{m/s}^2)} \times \frac{1.01 \times 10^5\ \text{N/m}^2}{1\ \text{atm}}$$

$$= 0.5\frac{\text{N·s}^2}{\text{kg}} \times \frac{1\ \text{kg·m/s}^2}{1\ \text{N}} = 0.5\ \text{m}$$

Reflect

The longest hollow reed through which Branson can breathe underwater is about half a meter—not that long, really. To check this result, let's calculate the weight of water half a meter deep on the area of a person's chest, about 30 cm × 60 cm. The answer is about 900 N or 200 lb. Certainly if a 200-lb person were sitting on your chest, you'd find it hard to breathe!

Scuba divers can descend to depths much greater than 0.5 m, but to do so they carry tanks of pressurized air. The regulator on a scuba tank delivers this air to the diver's mouth at the same pressure as the surrounding water, so $p - p_0 = 0$. Hence it's just as easy for a scuba diver to breathe underwater as on dry land.

Area of chest:

$$\begin{aligned} A &= 30\ \text{cm} \times 60\ \text{cm} \\ &= 0.30\ \text{m} \times 0.60\ \text{m} \\ &= 0.18\ \text{m}^2 \end{aligned}$$

Mass of water in a rectangular volume with base 0.18 m^2 and height 0.50 m:

$$\begin{aligned} m &= \rho V \\ &= (1.000 \times 10^3\ \text{kg/m}^3) \\ &\quad \times (0.18\ \text{m}^2)(0.50\ \text{m}) \\ &= 90\ \text{kg} \end{aligned}$$

Weight of that water:

$$\begin{aligned} mg &= (90\ \text{kg})(9.8\ \text{m/s}^2) \\ &= 900\ \text{N} = 200\ \text{lb} \end{aligned}$$

Take-Home Message for Section 11-6

✔ If the fluid pressure is different on two sides of an object, the result is a net force on the object. This net force is proportional to the pressure difference and to the area of the object.

11-7 A pressure increase at one point in a fluid causes a pressure increase throughout the fluid

When you squeeze one end of a tube of toothpaste, the pressure you apply is transmitted throughout the tube, and toothpaste comes out the other end. This is a simple example of a more general principle first proposed by the seventeenth-century French philosopher, mathematician, and scientist Blaise Pascal, who did pioneering investigations of the nature of pressure in fluids:

> *Pascal's principle:* Pressure applied to a confined, static fluid is transmitted undiminished to every part of the fluid as well as to the walls of the container.

We've already seen **Pascal's principle** in action in Section 11-4. There we learned that if a fluid is at rest—that is, in hydrostatic equilibrium—and the pressure at a certain point in the fluid is p_0, the pressure at a second point a distance d deeper in the fluid is $p = p_0 + \rho g d$ (Equation 11-8). If we were to increase the value of the pressure p_0 at the first point by, say, 50 Pa, the value of the pressure p at the second point would also have to increase by 50 Pa to maintain hydrostatic equilibrium.

A common practical application of Pascal's principle is a *hydraulic jack*. This device makes it possible to lift heavy objects using a force much less than the object's weight. You'll find these devices in operation wherever cars are being worked on: A hydraulic lift raises the car so that the mechanic can work on the car's underside. Smaller versions are used to raise and lower the chairs you sit in at the dentist and the barber. Figure 11-11 shows the construction of a simplified hydraulic lift. Start with a tube bent into a "U" shape. On the side labeled "1" the tube is much narrower than on the side labeled "2"; we'll call the cross-sectional areas of the two sides of the tube A_1 and A_2, respectively. We partially fill the tube with an incompressible liquid such as oil, so that its density does not change when pressure is applied. (This is a valid approximation for oil.) The liquid rises to the same height on both sides of the tube. (If you're not sure why, see the "Got the Concept" question at the end of Section 11-4.) We'll put a moveable cap at each end of the U-tube to keep the fluid from leaking out.

Now apply a downward force of magnitude F_1 to the cap on side 1. This causes the pressure in the fluid under the cap to increase by an amount $\Delta p = F_1/A_1$. According to Pascal's principle, this change in pressure is transmitted throughout the tube. We will therefore see this same pressure increase Δp below the cap on side 2, and that will cause an upward force $F_2 = \Delta p \times A_2$ on that cap. Substituting $\Delta p = F_1/A_1$ into this expression for F_2 gives

$$F_2 = \Delta p \times A_2 = \left(\frac{F_1}{A_1}\right)A_2$$

Area A_1 Area A_2

When a downward force is applied to the cap on side 1, the increase in pressure is transmitted undiminished throughout the fluid, forcing the cap on side 2 to rise.

Figure 11-11 A hydraulic jack Hydraulic jacks are used in workshops to elevate cars under repair and in dental offices to elevate the patient's chair. They operate using Pascal's principle.

or, rearranging,

$$(11\text{-}11) \qquad F_2 = F_1\left(\frac{A_2}{A_1}\right)$$

Since A_2 is greater than A_1, F_2 is greater than F_1, which means that a small force applied to side 1 results in a larger force applied to the cap on side 2. This is why a hydraulic jack is useful to auto mechanics: A relatively small force applied to side 1 can produce enough force on side 2 to raise a heavy car off the ground.

Equation 11-11 may make it seem like we get extra force "for free." However, there is a trade-off: The cap on side 1 must be pushed down a large distance to make the cap on side 2 move up a short distance. Here's why: When force F_1 is applied to the cap on side 1, that cap moves down a distance d_1 and displaces a volume of liquid $V_1 = d_1 A_1$. The increase in pressure throughout the tube causes liquid to rise on side 2, pushing up the cap on that side by a distance d_2. The increase in liquid volume under cap 2 is $V_2 = d_2 A_2$. Since the liquid used in the U-tube is assumed to be incompressible, these two volumes of liquid must be equal. Hence

$$d_2 A_2 = d_1 A_1$$

or

$$(11\text{-}12) \qquad d_2 = d_1\left(\frac{A_1}{A_2}\right)$$

$\sqrt{x}$ *See the Math Tutorial for more information on direct and inverse proportions*

The factor A_1/A_2 in Equation 11-12 is the reciprocal of the factor that relates F_2 to F_1 in Equation 11-11. Although the *force* that is applied on side 2 is larger than the force on side 1, the *distance* the cap on side 2 moves is smaller than the distance the cap on side 1 was moved.

? Got the Concept? 11-6   Work and a Hydraulic Lift

Consider a hydraulic lift like that shown in Figure 11-11. The cap on side 1 has a radius of 1.00 cm and the cap on side 2 has a radius of 5.00 cm. As you push down on the cap on side 1, you do a certain amount of work W_1. How much work is done on the cap on side 2 as it rises up? (a) $25\,W_1$; (b) $5\,W_1$; (c) W_1; (d) $W_1/5$; (e) $W_1/25$.

Take-Home Message for Section 11-7

✔ Pascal's principle states that pressure applied to a confined, static fluid is transmitted undiminished to every part of the fluid as well as to the walls of the container.

✔ Pascal's principle explains the hydraulic lift, which allows a small force exerted on a fluid at one location to translate into a larger force exerted by the fluid at another location.

11-8 Archimedes' principle helps us understand buoyancy

Drop a plastic toy into a pond, and you're not surprised when it pops back up to the surface. A boat anchor won't come back up—which is also not surprising. But why does the boat, which weighs much more than the anchor, float on the surface rather than sink?

To answer these questions, think of a fluid (gas or liquid) at rest. To maintain hydrostatic equilibrium of any portion of the fluid, like the shaded blob shown in Figure 11-12a, the net force on that portion of fluid must be zero. Hence the combined force due to the pressure of the surrounding fluid—greater pressure on the bottom, less pressure on top—must be an upward force that exactly balances the weight of the shaded blob of fluid. We call this combined upward force the **buoyant force**; it "buoys up" the blob of fluid just enough to keep it from sinking.

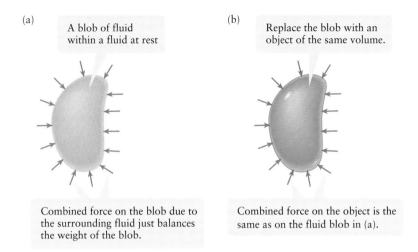

(a) A blob of fluid within a fluid at rest

(b) Replace the blob with an object of the same volume.

Combined force on the blob due to the surrounding fluid just balances the weight of the blob.

Combined force on the object is the same as on the fluid blob in (a).

Figure 11-12 **Archimedes' principle** (a) The blob is a portion of a fluid at rest. (b) If the blob is replaced by some other object of the same volume, that object feels the same upward (buoyant) force as did the blob.

Now we replace the blob of fluid in Figure 11-12a with an object of exactly the same dimensions (Figure 11-12b). We say that this object *displaces* a volume of fluid just equal to the volume of the object that's immersed in the fluid. For a boat floating in water, the displaced volume equals that portion of the boat's volume that's underwater. For a submarine under water, a balloon in air, or any other object that's totally immersed in a fluid, the displaced volume equals the total volume of the object.

Here's the critical observation: At each point on the object's surface, the *pressure* of the surrounding fluid is *exactly* the same as it was before we swapped the object for the blob of fluid. (Remember that the pressure on the object is caused by fluid molecules colliding with the object. The molecules move the same, and exert the same force in a collision, whether they're colliding with a solid object or with another part of the same fluid.) So the submerged object feels the *same* buoyant force as the blob of fluid did, with a magnitude just equal to the weight of that fluid blob. This statement about buoyant force is called **Archimedes' principle:**

The buoyant force on an object immersed in a fluid is equal to the weight of the fluid that the object displaces.

To be specific, suppose the object displaces a volume $V_{displaced}$ of fluid. If the fluid has density ρ_{fluid}, the fluid that the object displaces has mass $m_{fluid} = \rho_{fluid}V_{displaced}$ and weight $m_{fluid}g = \rho_{fluid}V_{displaced}g$. Hence the magnitude F_b of the buoyant force that acts on the object is

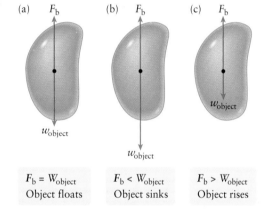

(a) F_b (b) F_b (c) F_b

w_{object} w_{object} w_{object}

| $F_b = W_{object}$ | $F_b < W_{object}$ | $F_b > W_{object}$ |
| Object floats | Object sinks | Object rises |

Figure 11-13 **Buoyancy: Floating, sinking, and rising** All three of these objects are immersed in the same fluid. All three have the same shape and size and so experience the same buoyant force F_b. Whether the object floats, sinks, or rises depends on its weight.

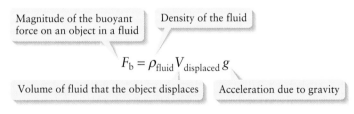

Magnitude of the buoyant force on an object in a fluid

Density of the fluid

$$F_b = \rho_{fluid}V_{displaced}\,g$$

Volume of fluid that the object displaces

Acceleration due to gravity

Buoyant force (11-13)

What effect does this buoyant force have? If the object's weight is exactly the same as the magnitude of the buoyant force F_b—that is, exactly the same as the weight of the displaced fluid—the net force on the object is zero and the object neither sinks nor rises; instead, it floats, remaining at the same height within the fluid. (Figure 11-13a). If the object weighs more than the displaced fluid, the object's weight overwhelms the buoyant force; hence the net force is downward and the object sinks (Figure 11-13b). If the object weighs less than the displaced fluid, the buoyant force overwhelms the object's weight so that the net force is upward and the object rises (Figure 11-13c).

Swimbladder

Figure 11-14 A fish with a swimbladder The gas-filled swimbladder gives this fish the same overall density as the surrounding water so that it floats while submerged.

Floating: Submarines, Fish, Ships, and Balloons

Many types of fish, as well as submarines, are able to float while submerged. In this case the volume $V_{\text{displaced}}$ of displaced fluid in Equation 11-13 is the same as the volume of the object. If the object has density ρ, its mass is $m = \rho V_{\text{displaced}}$ and its weight is $\rho V_{\text{displaced}} g$. Then the condition that the buoyant force on the object has the same magnitude as the object's weight is

$$\rho_{\text{fluid}} V_{\text{displaced}} g = \rho V_{\text{displaced}} g$$

or, dividing through by $V_{\text{displaced}} g$,

$$\rho_{\text{fluid}} = \rho$$
(condition that an object of density ρ floats while submerged in a fluid of density ρ_{fluid})

In words, *a submerged object can float only if its density is the same as the fluid in which it is immersed.*

Submarines and deep-sea research vessels are made of steel, which is far denser than water. They are nonetheless able to float underwater because they are hollow, with much of the internal volume filled with low-density air. The amount of air can be adjusted by filling ballast tanks with seawater or emptying the ballast tanks so that the submarine's *overall* density (the mass of the submarine divided by its volume) is equal to that of water (see Example 11-2 in Section 11-2). For the same reason, many species of fish (including salmon, herring, mackerel and cod) have a flexible gas-filled sac called a *swimbladder* (Figure 11-14). These fish are able to float while submerged because they can regulate the amount of gas in the swimbladder, to make their overall density equal to that of water. (In cod and other species, this regulation is done by exchanging gas between the swimbladder and the blood.)

Common aquarium fish have swimbladders and are able to float while submerged. But they move their fins constantly even if they are standing still. The reason is that the equilibrium provided by a swimbladder is *unstable*: If displaced even slightly upward or slightly downward, the fish tend to keep moving up or down. (A tightrope walker is in the same kind of unstable equilibrium. If he leans to the left, he will end up falling to the left.) If a water current displaces the fish slightly upward, the pressure at its new position is slightly less than before, and Pascal's principle (Section 11-7) tells us that this reduced pressure will be transmitted throughout the fish to the swimbladder. The reduced pressure makes the gas in the swimbladder expand, which decreases the average density of the fish as a whole. As a result, the fish is now less dense than the surrounding water and will continue to move upward. Similarly, if the fish should be displaced below its equilibrium position, the swimbladder will shrink in response to the increased pressure, thus increasing the density of the fish and making it sink even further. The continuous motions of the fish's fins are an effort to maintain a constant depth.

Fish that lack swimbladders are denser than water and hence cannot float; they must swim continuously to avoid sinking to the bottom. (The same is true for sharks.) This is not a hardship for fish such as flounder and dogfish, which lack a swimbladder but whose natural habitat is at the ocean bottom.

An object that is *less* dense than water floats on the surface with only part of its volume submerged; the lower the object's density relative to that of water, the higher it floats (see Example 11-8). Steel is denser than water, but ships made of steel are hollow inside; this makes their overall density less than that of water and so allows them to remain afloat while only partially submerged (Figure 11-15).

We've mostly been discussing objects in liquids such as water, but there is also a buoyant force on an object immersed in a gas such as the atmosphere. The buoyant force on a balloon filled with helium (which is less dense than air) is greater than the balloon's weight, which is why it rises if released. By contrast, a balloon filled with room-temperature air falls if released: The air inside the balloon is at higher pressure and has a higher density than the outside air, so the balloon's weight is more than the buoyant force acting on it. Hot air is less dense than cold air, so an air-filled balloon can be made to float if it's equipped with a burner to warm the balloon's contents. That's the principle of a hot-air balloon like that shown in the photograph that opens this chapter.

Ship (seen in cross section)

Hollow interior

Steel is denser than water, but ships made of steel are hollow inside; this makes their overall density less than that of water and so allows them to remain afloat while only partially submerged.

Figure 11-15 How steel ships float What determines whether an object floats is how its overall density compares to the density of water.

Example 11-8 What Lies Beneath the Surface?

A solid block of density ρ_{block} is placed in a liquid of density ρ_{liquid}. If the block is less dense than the liquid (that is, $\rho_{block} < \rho_{liquid}$), derive an expression for the fraction of the block's volume that is submerged.

Set Up

Archimedes' principle tells us that the buoyant force exerted on the block by the liquid equals the weight of the displaced liquid. In order for the block to float, the upward buoyant force must balance the weight of the block. We'll use this principle to compare the volume of displaced liquid $V_{displaced}$—equal to the volume of the block that's submerged in the liquid—to the total volume of the block.

Buoyant force:
$$F_b = \rho_{liquid} V_{displaced} g \qquad (11\text{-}13)$$

Solve

First write expressions for the block's mass m_{block} and weight w_{block}. When the block is in equilibrium, the upward buoyant force on the block equals the block's weight. Use this and the expression for w_{block} to solve for the ratio of $V_{displaced}$ to V_{block}.

Volume of block $= V_{block}$
Mass of block $=$ (density of block) $\times$ (volume of block):
$$m_{block} = \rho_{block} V_{block}$$

Weight of block $=$ (mass of block) $\times g$:
$$w_{block} = m_{block} g = \rho_{block} V_{block} g$$

Net force on the block in equilibrium is zero:
$$\sum F_y = F_b - w_{block} = 0 \text{ so}$$
$$F_b = w_{block}$$

From Equation 11-13,
$$F_b = \rho_{liquid} V_{displaced} g, \text{ so}$$
$$\rho_{liquid} V_{displaced} g = \rho_{block} V_{block} g$$

Divide through by g:
$$\rho_{liquid} V_{displaced} = \rho_{block} V_{block}$$

Solve for ratio of $V_{displaced}$ to V_{block}:

$$\text{fraction of block's volume that is submerged} = \frac{V_{displaced}}{V_{block}} = \frac{\rho_{block}}{\rho_{liquid}}$$

Reflect

The fraction of the block's volume that is submerged, $V_{displaced}/V_{block}$, is equal to the ratio of the block's density ρ_{block} to the density of the liquid, ρ_{liquid}. Let's try this for a couple of real-life examples: ice floating in fresh water and ice floating in salt water. We find that a cube of pure ice in a glass of water floats with 91.7% of its volume submerged, while an iceberg in salt water floats a bit higher with 89.5% of its volume below the surface.

Block of ice floating in fresh water:
$\rho_{block} =$ density of ice $= 917 \text{ kg/m}^3$
$\rho_{liquid} =$ density of fresh water $= 1.000 \times 10^3 \text{ kg/m}^3$

$$\text{fraction of ice that's submerged} = \frac{V_{displaced}}{V_{block}} = \frac{\rho_{block}}{\rho_{liquid}}$$

$$= \frac{917 \text{ kg/m}^3}{1.000 \times 10^3 \text{ kg/m}^3} = 0.917$$

So 91.7% of the ice is submerged.

Block of ice floating in salt water:
$\rho_{block} =$ density of ice $= 917 \text{ kg/m}^3$
$\rho_{liquid} =$ density of salt water $= 1.025 \times 10^3 \text{ kg/m}^3$

$$\text{fraction of ice that's submerged} = \frac{V_{displaced}}{V_{block}} = \frac{\rho_{block}}{\rho_{liquid}}$$

$$= \frac{917 \text{ kg/m}^3}{1.025 \times 10^3 \text{ kg/m}^3} = 0.895$$

so 89.5% of the ice is submerged.

Example 11-9 Underwater Float

A solid plastic ball of density $6.00 \times 10^2 \, \text{kg/m}^3$ and radius 2.00 cm is attached by a lightweight string to the bottom of an aquarium filled with fresh water. What is the tension in the string?

Set Up

Three forces act on the ball: the downward force of gravity, the upward buoyant force exerted by the water, and the downward tension force exerted by the string (which is what we want to find). We'll first use Equation 11-13 to determine the buoyant force on the ball, and then use Newton's first law to solve for the tension force.

Buoyant force:

$$F_b = \rho_{\text{water}} V_{\text{displaced}} g \qquad (11\text{-}13)$$

Solve

Newton's first law tells us that since the ball is at rest, the net force on the ball must be zero. Solve for the tension T in the string in terms of the buoyant force F_b and the weight of the ball $m_{\text{ball}}g$.

Newton's first law:

$$\sum F_y = F_b - T - m_{\text{ball}}g = 0 \text{ so}$$

$$T = F_b - m_{\text{ball}}g$$

The entire ball is submerged, so the volume of water that it displaces is equal to the volume of the ball of radius $R_{\text{ball}} = 2.00 \, \text{cm} = 2.00 \times 10^{-2}$ m. Use this to calculate the buoyant force.

Buoyant force:

$$F_b = \rho_{\text{water}} V_{\text{displaced}} g$$

$$V_{\text{displaced}} = V_{\text{ball}}$$

$$= \frac{4}{3}\pi R_{\text{ball}}^3 = \frac{4}{3}\pi (2.00 \times 10^{-2} \, \text{m})^3$$

$$= 3.35 \times 10^{-5} \, \text{m}^3 \text{ so}$$

$$F_b = (1.000 \times 10^3 \, \text{kg/m}^3)(3.35 \times 10^{-5} \, \text{m}^3)(9.80 \, \text{m/s}^2)$$

$$= 0.328 \, \text{kg} \cdot \text{m/s}^2 = 0.328 \, \text{N}$$

Use the density of the ball to calculate its weight.

$$\text{Weight of ball} = m_{\text{ball}}g = \rho_{\text{ball}} V_{\text{ball}} g$$

$$= (6.00 \times 10^2 \, \text{kg/m}^3)(3.35 \times 10^{-5} \, \text{m}^3)(9.80 \, \text{m/s}^2)$$

$$= 0.197 \, \text{kg} \cdot \text{m/s}^2 = 0.197 \, \text{N}$$

Finally, use the relationship that we derived from Newton's first law to solve for the tension T.

$$T = F_b - m_{\text{ball}}g = 0.328 \, \text{N} - 0.197 \, \text{N}$$

$$= 0.131 \, \text{N}$$

Reflect

The ball is less dense than water, so the buoyant force ($F_b = 0.328$ N) is greater than the weight of the ball ($m_{\text{ball}}g = 0.197$ N). Hence the string must exert a downward tension force to keep the ball from rising. If the string were to break, the ball would rise to the surface of the water. Can you see from Example 11-8 that the ball would end up floating with 60.0% of its volume submerged?

Apparent Weight

In Example 11-9 the submerged plastic ball is less dense than water and so has to be tethered to keep it from floating upward. Let's now think about a submerged object that's denser than water. The problem that now arises is how to keep the object from sinking, which we solve by suspending it from above. Figure 11-16a shows such a submerged object hanging from a spring balance, along with an identical object that isn't submerged. Although both objects have the same mass M and the same volume V, the weights registered on the spring balances are *not* the same. Why? The difference is that for the submerged object on the left, the buoyant force due to the displaced water opposes the force of gravity and makes the object seem to weigh less. Thus the scale reads the object's **apparent weight** rather than its true weight. (In Section 10-5 we saw that an object in orbit has an apparent weight of zero due to its acceleration. The kind of apparent weight we're discussing here is for an object that's *not* accelerating—instead, it's submerged in a fluid and acted on by a buoyant force.)

You can experience the difference between apparent weight and true weight in a swimming pool. If you swim below the surface of the water, you feel as though you weigh less than normal. Just as for the plastic ball in Figure 11-16, the upward buoyant force on you partially cancels the force of gravity. Astronauts use this effect to train for working in low gravity: They practice by working while submerged in an immense pool of water.

How is the apparent weight related to the true weight? **Figure 11-16b** shows the free-body diagram for the submerged object on the left in Figure 11-16a. The three forces acting on the object are the downward force of gravity (whose magnitude is the object's true weight w), the upward buoyant force F_b exerted by the water, and the upward force exerted by the spring balance. The scale on the spring balance measures how much force the balance exerts, so this force is just equal to the apparent weight w_{app}. The net force on the hanging object is zero (because the object is at rest), so

$$\sum F_y = w_{app} + F_b - w = 0$$

and

$$w_{app} = w - F_b$$
(apparent weight of a submerged object)

$(11\text{-}14)$

The apparent weight of a submerged object equals its true weight minus the buoyant force exerted on the object by the surrounding fluid.

If the object is completely submerged, the volume of fluid that it displaces equals the volume V of the object. Then we can replace $V_{displaced}$ in Equation 11-13 (the statement of Archimedes' principle) by V, and Equation 11-14 becomes

$$w_{app} = w - \rho_{fluid} V g$$
(apparent weight of an object of weight w
and volume V completely submerged in a fluid of density ρ_{fluid})

$(11\text{-}15)$

So by measuring the apparent weight of an object while submerged (w_{app}) and its true weight when not submerged (w), you can determine the object's volume. This knowledge can be quite handy when the object is irregularly shaped!

We can also write the apparent weight in terms of the density ρ of the object. Since the object has volume V, its mass is $m = \rho V$ and its true weight is $w = mg = \rho V g$. Then Equation 11-15 becomes

$$w_{app} = \rho V g - \rho_{fluid} V g = (\rho - \rho_{fluid}) V g$$
(apparent weight of an object of density ρ
and volume V completely submerged in a fluid of density ρ_{fluid})

$(11\text{-}16)$

Equation 11-16 says that if we know an object's volume V, we can determine its density ρ by measuring its apparent weight w_{app} when submerged in a fluid of density ρ_{fluid}. According to legend, Archimedes came to this realization while he was himself submerged in his bathtub—a discovery that led him to his understanding of buoyancy.

A useful application of Equation 11-16 is to find the *average* density ρ of an object composed of two materials of known density. This makes it possible to determine what fraction of the object is composed of each material. Example 11-10 shows how to use this technique to find the ratio of lean tissue to fat tissue in a person's body.

An object submerged in a fluid that is denser than air has an apparent weight less than its weight when submerged in air.

(a)

(b)

Upward force exerted by spring
= apparent weight w_{app}

Buoyant force F_b

Gravitational force w

Figure 11-16 Apparent weight
(a) An object hung from a spring balance has an apparent weight that depends on the fluid in which it is submerged. The reading on the scale indicates the force exerted by the spring, which is equal in magnitude to the object's apparent weight. (b) A free-body diagram showing the three forces acting on the submerged object in (a).

 Go to Picture It 11-1 for more practice dealing with the buoyant force

 Go to Interactive Exercise 11-1 and 11-2 for more practice dealing with the buoyant force

Example 11-10 Measuring Body Fat

In the human body the density of lean muscle is about 1.06×10^3 kg/m³, and the density of fat tissue is about 9.30×10^2 kg/m³. If a person who weighs 833 N in air has an apparent weight of 27.4 N when submerged in water, what percent of his body mass is fat? (Assume that the person is made of muscle and fat only.)

Set Up

To determine what fraction of this person's body mass is fat, we'll first determine the average density ρ of his body. To do this, we'll first find his volume V using Equation 11-15 and the measured values $w = 833$ N and $w_{app} = 27.4$ N. Then we can use Equation 11-16 to calculate his density ρ. We'll next compare ρ to the given densities of muscle and fat to determine the fat fraction.

Two equations for the apparent weight w_{app} of an object of weight w, volume V, and density ρ submerged in fluid of density ρ_{fluid}:

$$w_{app} = w - \rho_{fluid}Vg \qquad (11\text{-}15)$$
$$w_{app} = (\rho - \rho_{fluid})Vg \qquad (11\text{-}16)$$

fat mass: m_{fat}
muscle mass: m_{muscle}
total mass: $m = m_{fat} + m_{muscle}$

Solve

Solve Equation 11-15 for the person's volume V, then substitute the given values of w_{app}, w, g, and $\rho_{fluid} = 1.000 \times 10^3$ kg/m³ (the density of water).

Rearrange Equation 11-15 to solve for V:

$$\rho_{fluid}Vg = w - w_{app}$$

$$V = \frac{w - w_{app}}{\rho_{fluid}g} = \frac{833 \text{ N} - 27.4 \text{ N}}{(1.000 \times 10^3 \text{ kg/m}^3)(9.80 \text{ m/s}^2)}$$

$$= 0.0822 \text{ m}^3$$

Now use this value of V in Equation 11-16 and solve for the person's density ρ. We'll keep an extra significant figure for this intermediate calculation and adjust them at the end.

Rearrange Equation 11-16 to solve for ρ:

$$(\rho - \rho_{fluid})Vg = w_{app}$$

$$\rho - \rho_{fluid} = \frac{w_{app}}{Vg}$$

$$\rho = \rho_{fluid} + \frac{w_{app}}{Vg}$$

$$= 1.000 \times 10^3 \text{ kg/m}^3 + \frac{27.4 \text{ N}}{(0.0822 \text{ m}^3)(9.80 \text{ m/s}^2)}$$

$$= 1.034 \times 10^3 \text{ kg/m}^3$$

The overall density ρ is less than the density of lean muscle but greater than the density of fat, so the body is a mixture of these two quantities. Use the definition of density, $\rho = m/V$, to calculate the fraction x of the person's mass that is fat.

Let x = fraction of body mass m that is fat.

Then the mass of fat in the body is

$$m_{fat} = xm$$

The remaining mass in the body is muscle:

$$m_{muscle} = m - m_{fat} = m - xm = (1 - x)m$$

Volume of body fat = (mass of fat)/(density of fat), so

$$V_{fat} = \frac{m_{fat}}{\rho_{fat}} = \frac{xm}{\rho_{fat}}$$

Volume of body muscle = (mass of muscle)/(density of muscle), so

$$V_{muscle} = \frac{m_{muscle}}{\rho_{muscle}} = \frac{(1 - x)m}{\rho_{muscle}}$$

Overall volume of body = (mass of body)/(overall density of body), so

$$V = \frac{m}{\rho}$$

The total volume of the body equals the sum of the volume of fat and the volume of muscle:

$V = V_{fat} + V_{muscle}$, so

$$\frac{m}{\rho} = \frac{xm}{\rho_{fat}} + \frac{(1-x)m}{\rho_{muscle}}$$

Rearrange this equation and solve for x:

$$\frac{1}{\rho} = \frac{x}{\rho_{fat}} + \frac{(1-x)}{\rho_{muscle}}$$

$$\frac{1}{\rho} - \frac{1}{\rho_{muscle}} = \frac{x}{\rho_{fat}} - \frac{x}{\rho_{muscle}} = x\left(\frac{1}{\rho_{fat}} - \frac{1}{\rho_{muscle}}\right)$$

$$x = \frac{\left(\dfrac{1}{\rho} - \dfrac{1}{\rho_{muscle}}\right)}{\left(\dfrac{1}{\rho_{fat}} - \dfrac{1}{\rho_{muscle}}\right)}$$

$$= \frac{\left(\dfrac{1}{1.034 \times 10^3 \text{ kg/m}^3} - \dfrac{1}{1.06 \times 10^3 \text{ kg/m}^3}\right)}{\left(\dfrac{1}{9.30 \times 10^2 \text{ kg/m}^3} - \dfrac{1}{1.06 \times 10^3 \text{ kg/m}^3}\right)}$$

$$= 0.180$$

Reflect

Our result tells us that 0.180 (or 18.0%) of this person's mass is fat. Two-thirds of Americans have a percent body fat of 25% or more and are therefore overweight or obese. Adult men with between 18 and 24% body fat are considered healthy.

We can check our result for the person's density by calculating it in a different way: Take the person's weight of 833 N and divide by g to get the mass, then divide that by the volume that we calculated above from Equation 11-15. Happily, we get the same result as we did using Equation 11-16.

Note that the method outlined here is only an approximation of an actual body fat calculation; we ignored the volumes of the lungs and bones.

Second calculation of density:

$$\rho = \frac{m}{V}$$

Determine mass from weight:

$$w = mg, \text{ so } m = \frac{w}{g} = \frac{833 \text{ N}}{9.80 \text{ m/s}^2} = 85.0 \text{ kg}$$

From above, $V = 0.0822 \text{ m}^3$. So the person's density is

$$\rho = \frac{85.0 \text{ kg}}{0.0822 \text{ m}^3} = 1.03 \times 10^3 \text{ kg/m}^3$$

? Got the Concept? 11-7   Buoyancy I

A plastic cube with a coin taped to its top surface is floating partially submerged in water. Mark the level of the water on the cube, then remove the coin and tape it to the *bottom* of the cube. Will the cube sit (a) higher in the water, (b) lower in the water, or (c) the same as it was when the coin was on the top of the cube? *Hint:* The buoyant force on an object is the weight of the fluid that it displaces, and in this problem water is displaced by whatever is below the surface.

? Got the Concept? 11-8   Buoyancy II

An open, glass soda bottle will float in a tub of water as long as it is empty. Place an empty, open glass bottle into a tub of water so that it floats, and mark the level of the water on the wall of the tub. Now submerge the bottle so that it fills with water and sinks to the bottom. Is the level of the water in the tub (a) higher, (b) lower, or (c) the same as it was when the bottle was floating?

11-9 Fluids in motion behave differently depending on the flow speed and the fluid viscosity

In the preceding two sections we have considered fluids at rest. All around us, however, we find fluids in *motion*. Masses of air shift through the atmosphere to bring today's weather, river water courses downhill, and the oceans move in and out with the tides. Within our bodies, moving fluids—blood, lymph, and the air used in respiration—play essential roles in sustaining life.

In a wind tunnel, smoke trails display the smooth, steady pattern of laminar flow around this automobile.

The smoke rising from these incense sticks changes from laminar flow to chaotic, turbulent flow.

Although air rotates around the center of a hurricane, the flow is largely irrotational (a physicist's way of saying that the flow velocity changes in a special and gradual way from one point to another).

(a)   (b)   (c)

Figure 11-17 **Some examples of fluid flow** Three very different situations in which air (a fluid) is in motion.

Fluid flows in both nature and technology are breathtaking in their diversity (Figure 11-17). We'll begin our study of fluids in motion by examining how physicists classify different types of fluid flow.

Steady Flow and Unsteady Flow

The simplest type of fluid flow is one in which the flow pattern doesn't change with time, like a stream in which water moves very smoothly with no variations. Such fluid motion is called **steady flow**. The direction and speed of the flow can be different from one point in the fluid to another (Figure 11-18). At any one point, however, the flow velocity remains constant from one moment to the next.

In **unsteady flow** the velocity at a given point can change with time. You experience the unsteady flow of air when you stand outside on a gusty day: The direction and speed of the wind at your position changes erratically. A less erratic example of unsteady flow is the pulsing motion of blood as it exits your heart through the aorta. Ocean waves, too, involve an unsteady pulsing motion that carries water (and anyone bobbing in the water) alternately up and down.

As a particle of fluid moves through this pipe from (a) to (b) to (c), its velocity changes in direction and magnitude...

...but at any individual point in the fluid, the velocity of the fluid at that point is always the same. We call this steady flow.

Figure 11-18 **Steady flow of fluid in a pipe** In steady fluid flow the velocity can be different at different points in the flow, but the velocity at any one point maintains the same value at all times.

! **Watch Out!** Steady flow doesn't mean that the fluid velocity is the same everywhere.

Note that even though the fluid velocity at any one position in steady flow remains constant, the velocity of any given quantity of fluid *can* change as it moves. For example, water flowing through a curved pipe such as the one shown in Figure 11-18 changes its direction of motion as it follows the bends of the pipe. When we say that the flow is steady, we mean that when the next quantity of fluid passes through the same point in the pipe, its velocity at that given point will be the same as the previous quantity of fluid that passed through that same point.

Laminar Flow and Turbulent Flow

Imagine a multi-lane highway filled with moving cars. If none of the cars ever changed lanes, you'd have an efficient, smooth-running transportation system in which each car would follow exactly the same trajectory as the one in front of it and the one behind it (Figure 11-19a). If you now replace the cars with bits of fluid, you would have a type of fluid motion called **laminar flow**. Each bit of fluid follows a path called a **streamline** that is the direct equivalent of one of the lanes of our idealized highway (Figure 11-19b). The smoke trails in Figure 11-17a show the streamlines of laminar flow in a wind tunnel.

Real highways are not as well organized as those in our imaginary example. Some cars change lanes while others do not, some cars move faster than others in the same lane, and occasionally there are collisions (Figure 11-20a). A fluid that behaves in this way is undergoing **turbulent flow** (Figure 11-20b). There are no streamlines in this case, since adjacent bits of fluid can follow very different paths. Figure 11-17b shows the turbulent flow of smoke.

Generally speaking, a given type of flow changes from laminar to turbulent if the flow speed exceeds some critical value (which depends on the particular type of fluid). That's why airliners approaching Denver, which is downwind of the Rocky Mountains, can have a smooth ride when the wind is light and the airflow is laminar but a much bumpier ride when the wind is howling and the airflow turbulent.

Turbulence is much noisier than laminar flow. As an example, when you make a hissing or "S" sound you blow air past your teeth in a way that produces turbulence. By contrast, if you form your lips into an "o" and blow with equal force, your teeth are out the way, the airflow is more laminar, and the sound is much softer. Your diastolic blood pressure—the second of the two numbers in a blood pressure report such as 120/80 (see Section 11-5)—is measured by putting a cuff around your upper arm, gradually lowering the pressure of the cuff, and listening for a change in sound. At pressures just above the diastolic value, the artery is partially compressed, making the flow turbulent and noisy; at the diastolic pressure and below, the noise disappears because the artery is fully expanded and the flow is once again in its normal laminar state.

Viscous Flow and Inviscid Flow

When adjacent parts of a fluid move at different velocities, the parts rub and exert frictional forces on each other. Just as kinetic friction opposes the sliding motion of a block on a ramp, this rubbing opposes the sliding of one bit of fluid past another. This intrinsic resistance to flow is called **viscosity**. Motor oil is more *viscous*—that is, it has a greater viscosity—than water, which in turn is more viscous than air. Many liquids are less viscous at high temperatures; for example, warm maple syrup flows more easily than cold. Most automobiles with gasoline engines use a *multi-viscosity* oil designed to flow (and hence lubricate the engine's moving parts) equally well over a broad range of temperatures.

Fluids also experience friction when they flow past a solid surface. This friction is so great that it leads to what is called the **no-slip condition**: Right next to the solid surface, the velocity of the fluid is *zero* so the fluid does not "slip" over the surface. Instead, if fluid is flowing past the surface with a speed v, there is a **boundary layer** next to the surface within which the fluid speed increases from zero at the solid surface to the full speed v at the edge of the layer (Figure 11-21). A boundary layer of this kind develops around an automobile in motion, which is why driving even at freeway speeds doesn't blow dirt off the car. Any dirt particles lie well within the boundary layer, where the air is hardly moving at all. Even running water over the car won't dislodge all of the dirt particles, since there is also a boundary layer for water flow; only scrubbing with a sponge will complete the job.

Figure 11-21 shows that at different depths within the boundary layer, the fluid flows at different speeds. Hence frictional (viscous) forces act in the boundary layer, and these forces oppose the flow past the solid surface. This effect is called *viscous drag*, and

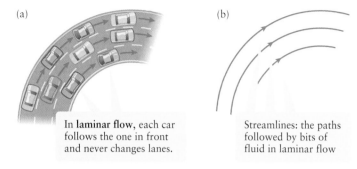

(a)   (b)

In **laminar flow**, each car follows the one in front and never changes lanes.

Streamlines: the paths followed by bits of fluid in laminar flow

Figure 11-19 **Laminar flow of cars and a fluid** (a) An idealized highway in which cars move in laminar flow. (b) Streamlines in a fluid with laminar flow.

(a)

In **turbulent flow**, each car follows its own path with frequent lane changes.

(b)

There are no streamlines for a fluid in turbulent flow.

Figure 11-20 **Turbulent flow of cars and a fluid** (a) A less-than-ideal highway in which cars move in turbulent flow. (b) In a fluid with turbulent flow, bits of fluid move in a haphazard and seemingly unpredictable way.

Figure 11-21 **A boundary layer in a viscous fluid** A boundary layer in a fluid moving past a flat surface.

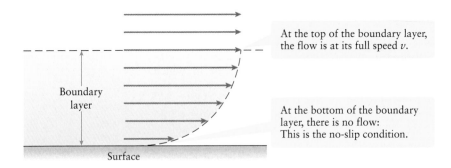

At the top of the boundary layer, the flow is at its full speed v.

At the bottom of the boundary layer, there is no flow: This is the no-slip condition.

Boundary layer

Surface

it makes an important contribution to the force of air resistance felt by a moving car. If the flow in the boundary layer is turbulent, there is a greater difference in flow speeds between bits of fluid close to the car's skin, so the viscous forces are greater and the vehicle experiences more drag. Giving a car a "streamlined" shape is a way to make the flow of air around the car less turbulent and more laminar so that the air follows streamlines, as in Figure 11-17a. This reduces the drag so that less power has to be provided by the engine, and the car gets better mileage.

While every fluid has some viscosity, in many physical situations the viscosity is relatively unimportant. (An example is the airflow around a bird in flight. The viscous forces are much less important than the forces due to the pressure of air on the bird.) In these situations it's reasonable to simplify the problem by imagining that the moving fluid has *zero* viscosity. Such **inviscid flow** is an idealization, just like the frictionless ramps and massless strings that we considered in Chapter 4. We'll make use of this idealization in Section 11-10.

Finally, as we did in our earlier consideration of static fluids, we'll examine only the special case of incompressible fluids—that is, fluids in which changes in pressure do not affect the density of the fluid. Flowing water, blood, and air usually behave as incompressible fluids. All of these fluids *can* be compressed by exerting pressure on them, but in many practical situations the pressures are low enough that the compression can be ignored.

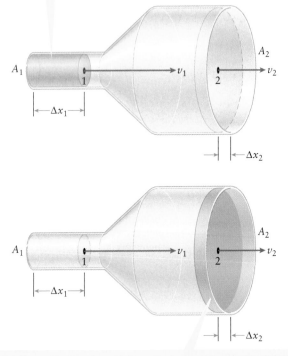

During the time it takes this quantity of fluid to move a distance Δx_1...

...this identical quantity of fluid moves a distance Δx_2. The amount of fluid between points 1 and 2 remains constant.

Figure 11-22 **The equation of continuity** This illustration shows the flow of an incompressible fluid through a pipe of varying diameter. A slug of fluid of volume $A_1 \Delta x_1$ moving at speed v_1 enters the region between points 1 and 2, which causes a slug of fluid of volume $A_2 \Delta x_2$ moving at speed v_2 to exit the region. The equation of continuity says that fluid enters the region at the same volume flow rate that it leaves the region.

The Equation of Continuity

No matter what other properties a moving fluid may have, it must obey the following restriction: Mass can neither be created nor destroyed as the fluid flows. Therefore, in a *steady* flow, if a certain mass of fluid flows *into* a given region of space (say, the interior of a certain segment of a pipe) in a given time interval, the same amount of mass must flow *out of* that region during that same time interval. This is called the *principle of continuity*. For example, if one kilogram of fluid flows into one end of a pipe each second, then one kilogram per second must flow out the other end. (If the principle of continuity were violated, the amount of fluid within the pipe would either increase or decrease. But in this case the flow wouldn't be steady as we originally assumed it to be.)

We can make a simple mathematical statement of the principle of continuity for the case of an *incompressible* fluid. The principle of continuity tells us that in a given time interval the same *volume* of incompressible fluid must flow into a certain region of space as flows out of that region. Figure 11-22 illustrates this principle for a pipe whose cross-sectional area varies along its length. Let 1 and 2 be two different points along the pipe, and consider the segment of the pipe between these two points. While a slug of fluid of volume $A_1 \Delta x_1$ enters the pipe segment at point 1, a slug of volume $A_2 \Delta x_2$ exits the segment at point 2. The principle of continuity then tells us that

$$A_1 \Delta x_1 = A_2 \Delta x_2 \qquad (11\text{-}17)$$

It takes some time interval Δt for the slug of fluid to enter the region at point 1. And since the volume of fluid between the points must remain constant, the slug of fluid at point 2 must exit the region in the same time interval. If we divide Equation 11-17 by the time interval Δt it takes for the slugs of fluid to enter or exit the region, we arrive at

$$A_1 \frac{\Delta x_1}{\Delta t} = A_2 \frac{\Delta x_2}{\Delta t} \qquad (11\text{-}18)$$

To see why we divided through by Δt, note that the fluid at point 1 moves a distance Δx_1 during the time interval Δt and so has speed $v_1 = \Delta x_1 / \Delta t$. Similarly, the fluid at point 2 (which moves a distance Δx_2 during the same time interval) has speed $v_2 = \Delta x_2 / \Delta t$. So we can rewrite Equation 11-18 as the following relationship, called the **equation of continuity**:

Cross-sectional area of the flow at point 1 | Flow speed at point 1

$$A_1 v_1 = A_2 v_2$$

Cross-sectional area of the flow at point 2 | Flow speed at point 2

In other words, the product of the pipe's cross-sectional area A and the flow speed v has the same value at point 1 as at point 2. The choice of these points is quite arbitrary; they could be any two points along the pipe's length. So Equation 11-19 tells us that the product Av has the same value *everywhere* along the pipe. *Where a pipe is narrow, an incompressible fluid moves rapidly; where the pipe is broad, the fluid moves more slowly.* If the flow is laminar, the "pipe" doesn't have to be a solid object with walls; it can be a volume enclosed by a set of streamlines (Figure 11-23). It follows that *where streamlines are close together, an incompressible fluid moves rapidly; where streamlines are far apart, the fluid moves more slowly.* The airflow around the car shown in Figure 11-17a is mostly incompressible, so the flow is rapid over the roof of the car where streamlines are close together.

The equation of continuity explains what happens when you put your thumb over the end of a garden hose. This action reduces the area through which water can flow out of the hose, and so the water emerges at a faster speed. The same principle explains why there are often strong winds through mountain passes, where the air is forced into a "pipe" of narrow cross section.

Note that the product Av in Equation 11-19 has units of $(m^2)(m/s) = m^3/s$, or volume per unit time. This quantity, called the **volume flow rate,** tells you the number of cubic meters of fluid that pass a given point each second. For example, the average volume flow rate of blood through the aorta of a resting human is about $10^{-4} \, m^3/s$, or 6 liters per minute. (This is an *average* volume flow rate since the flow is in pulses rather than steady.) So another way to restate the equation of continuity is that *the volume flow rate of an incompressible fluid moving through a pipe is the same at all points.*

This principle needs a little restatement if the pipe branches into a number of small pipes. An example is the human circulatory system, where the flow of oxygenated blood from the aorta is spread out into an enormous number of narrow capillaries (Figure 11-24). In this case the volume flow rate in the aorta is the same as the *combined* volume flow rate through all of the tiny capillaries. If the combined cross-sectional area of the capillaries, A_c, were the same as the cross-sectional area A_a of the aorta, blood would flow at the same speed throughout the system. In fact, in the human circulatory system A_c for the capillaries is greater than A_a for the aorta,

Figure 11-23 Streamline spacing and flow speed In laminar flow of an incompressible fluid, the spacing between streamlines tells you about the flow speed.

In laminar flow, fluid enclosed by these streamlines remains in the enclosed volume.

Fluid moves fastest where streamlines are closest together.

Fluid moves slowest where streamlines are far apart.

Equation of continuity for steady flow of an incompressible fluid (11-19)

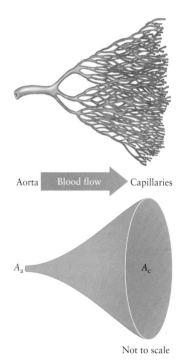

Aorta | Blood flow | Capillaries

A_a | | A_c

Not to scale

Figure 11-24 The human circulatory system Blood leaving the heart flows first through a single vessel, the aorta. Branches off the aorta eventually lead to billions of capillaries. Although each capillary is very small, the total cross-sectional area of all capillaries taken together is much larger than that of the aorta.

so the flow speed in the capillaries is *slower* than in the aorta. This slower speed gives the blood in the capillaries more time for exchange of nutrients, gases, and waste products between the blood and the surrounding tissues.

! Watch Out! **The continuity equation is for incompressible flow only.**

Note that Equation 11-19 applies only if the flow is *incompressible*, so its density is the same in all circumstances. In certain cases of fluid motion, however, the fluid does change density and we say that the flow is *compressible*. Air flowing faster than sound behaves like a compressible fluid: When such fast-moving air enters a constriction such as a narrow pipe, it slows down and the molecules of the fluid get squeezed together so that the density of the fluid increases. In such a case, Equation 11-19 doesn't apply. An analogy for a compressible fluid is how automobiles behave on a highway. You can think of the cars as "molecules" that make up a "fluid" that "flows" along the highway. In light traffic the cars in this "fluid" are far apart, but when this "fluid" passes through a narrower "pipe"—for example, a section of a two-lane highway where one lane is closed due to construction—the flow slows down, the cars get squeezed together, and a traffic jam results.

Example 11-11 Flow in a Constriction

An incompressible fluid in a pipe of cross-sectional area 4.0×10^{-4} m^2 flows at a speed of 3.0 m/s. What is the flow speed in a part of the pipe that is constricted and has a cross-sectional area of 2.0×10^{-4} m^2?

Set Up

We are given the cross-sectional area and flow speed at one point in the pipe, and we wish to determine the flow speed at another point in the same pipe that has a different cross-sectional area. Since the fluid is incompressible, we can use the equation of continuity, Equation 11-19.

Equation of continuity for steady flow of an incompressible fluid:

$$A_1 v_1 = A_2 v_2 \qquad (11\text{-}19)$$

point 1
area = 4.0×10^{-4} m^2
speed = 3.0 m/s

point 2
area = 2.0×10^{-4} m^2
speed = ?

Solve

Let point 1 be a location where the pipe has its full cross-sectional area. Then $A_1 = 4.0 \times 10^{-4}$ m^2 and $v_1 = 3.0$ m/s. Choose point 2 to be in the constriction, where $A_2 = 2.0 \times 10^{-4}$ m^2. Use the equation of continuity to solve for v_2.

Rearrange Equation 11-19 to solve for v_2:

$$v_2 = \frac{A_1}{A_2} v_1$$

Substitute values:

$$v_2 = \frac{(4.0 \times 10^{-4} \text{ m}^2)}{(2.0 \times 10^{-4} \text{ m}^2)} (3.0 \text{ m/s})$$

$$= 6.0 \text{ m/s}$$

Reflect

Our result shows that the speed in the narrow constriction is faster than in the broad part of the pipe, just as the equation continuity tells us it must be.

Example 11-12 How Many Capillaries?

The inner diameter of the human aorta is about 2.50 cm, while that of a typical capillary is about 6.00 μm = 6.00×10^{-6} m (see Figure 11-24). In a person at rest, the average flow speed of blood is about 20.0 cm/s in the aorta and about 1.00 mm/s in a capillary. Calculate (a) the volume flow rate of blood in the aorta, (b) the volume flow rate in a single capillary, and (c) the total number of open capillaries into which blood from the aorta is distributed at any one time.

Set Up

Figure 11-24 shows the situation. We are given the dimensions of the aorta and each capillary as well as the flow speed in each of these pipes. Our goal is to determine the volume flow rate (in volume per unit time, or m^3/s) in the aorta and in a capillary as well as the number of capillaries into which the aorta empties. The volume flow rate in a pipe is related to its cross-sectional area and the speed of the fluid moving in the pipe. Like water, blood acts like an incompressible fluid. (It will only compress appreciably under pressures much higher than those found in the body.) So we can use the ideas of the equation of continuity, including the idea that the volume flow rate through the aorta must be equal to the flow rate through all of the open capillaries combined.

Equation of continuity for steady flow of an incompressible fluid:

$$A_1 v_1 = A_2 v_2 \qquad (11\text{-}19)$$

1 = aorta
2 = all open capillaries combined

volume flow rate = Av

Solve

(a) The volume flow rate in the aorta is equal to the product of its cross-sectional area and the flow speed of aortal blood ($v_{\text{aorta}} = 20.0$ cm/s $= 0.200$ m/s).

Radius of aorta:
$$r_{\text{aorta}} = 1/2 \times (\text{diameter of aorta}) = 1/2 \times 2.50 \text{ cm}$$
$$= 1.25 \text{ cm} = 1.25 \times 10^{-2} \text{ m}$$

Cross-sectional area of aorta:
$$A_{\text{aorta}} = \pi r_{\text{aorta}}^2 = \pi (1.25 \times 10^{-2} \text{ m})^2$$
$$= 4.91 \times 10^{-4} \text{ m}^2$$

Volume flow rate in aorta:
$$A_{\text{aorta}} v_{\text{aorta}} = (4.91 \times 10^{-4} \text{ m}^2)(0.200 \text{ m/s})$$
$$= 9.82 \times 10^{-5} \text{ m}^3/s$$

(b) Do the same calculations for a capillary, in which the flow speed is $v_{\text{capillary}} = 1.00$ mm/s $= 1.00 \times 10^{-3}$ m/s.

Radius of a capillary:
$$r_{\text{capillary}} = 1/2 \times (\text{diameter of capillary}) = 1/2 \times 6.00 \times 10^{-6} \text{ m}$$
$$= 3.00 \times 10^{-6} \text{ m}$$

Cross-sectional area of a capillary:
$$A_{\text{capillary}} = \pi r_{\text{capillary}}^2 = \pi (3.00 \times 10^{-6} \text{ m})^2$$
$$= 2.83 \times 10^{-11} \text{ m}^2$$

Volume flow rate in a capillary:
$$A_{\text{capillary}} v_{\text{capillary}} = (2.83 \times 10^{-11} \text{ m}^2)(1.00 \times 10^{-3} \text{ m/s})$$
$$= 2.83 \times 10^{-14} \text{ m}^3/s$$

(c) Our results from (a) and (b) show that compared to the volume flow rate through a *single* capillary, the volume flow rate through the aorta is 3.47×10^9 times greater. The idea of continuity tells us that the combined volume flow rate through *all* the open capillaries must be equal to the volume flow rate through the aorta. We therefore learn the total number of open capillaries.

$$\frac{\text{Volume flow rate in aorta}}{\text{Volume flow rate in a capillary}} = \frac{9.82 \times 10^{-5} \text{ m}^3/s}{2.83 \times 10^{-14} \text{ m}^3/s}$$
$$= 3.47 \times 10^9$$

(Volume flow rate in aorta) = (total volume flow rate in all open capillaries combined)
... so there must be 3.47×10^9 open capillaries.

Reflect

Our results show that the human circulatory system is truly extensive!

As a check on our results, note that the *combined* cross-sectional areas of all capillaries is 9.82×10^{-2} m^2, which is 200 times greater

Total cross-sectional area of all open capillaries combined:
$$A_{\text{all open capillaries}} = (3.47 \times 10^9) A_{\text{capillary}}$$
$$= (3.47 \times 10^9)(2.83 \times 10^{-11} \text{ m}^2)$$
$$= 9.82 \times 10^{-2} \text{ m}^2$$

than the cross-sectional area of the aorta. By the equation of continuity, the flow speed in the capillaries should therefore be *slower* than in the aorta by a factor of $1/(2.00 \times 10^2)$: That is, $v_{capillary} = v_{aorta}/(2.00 \times 10^2) = (0.200 \text{ m/s})/(2.00 \times 10^2) = 1.00 \times 10^{-3}$ m/s. This gives us back one of the numbers we started with, so our calculation is consistent.

$$\frac{\text{Area of all open capillaries combined}}{\text{Area of aorta}} = \frac{9.82 \times 10^{-2} \text{ m}^2}{4.91 \times 10^{-4} \text{ m}^2}$$
$$= 2.00 \times 10^2$$

Example 11-13 From Capillaries to the Vena Cavae

Blood returns to the heart from the capillaries through two veins known as the *vena cavae*. The combined cross-sectional area of the vena cavae is 10.0 cm². At what average speed does blood move through these veins?

Set Up
We know the net volume flow rate of blood in the aorta from Example 11-12, and we're given the cross-sectional area $A_{vc} = 10.0$ cm² for the vena cavae. We'll use the equation of continuity to find the flow speed of blood in the vena cavae, v_{vc}.

Equation of continuity for steady flow of an incompressible fluid:

$$A_1 v_1 = A_2 v_2 \qquad (11\text{-}19)$$
1 = aorta
2 = vena cavae

superior vena cava
aorta
inferior vena cava

Solve
If we assume no blood volume is lost as it circulates through the body, the volume flow rate in the aorta is the same as in the vena cavae.

From Example 11-12,

volume flow rate in aorta $= A_{aorta} v_{aorta}$
$$= (4.91 \times 10^{-4} \text{ m}^2)(0.200 \text{ m/s})$$
$$= 9.82 \times 10^{-5} \text{ m}^3/\text{s}$$

Volume flow rate in venae cavae $= A_{vc} v_{vc}$, where

$$A_{vc} = (10.0 \text{ cm}^2)\left(\frac{1 \text{ m}}{100 \text{ cm}}\right)^2$$
$$= 1.00 \times 10^{-3} \text{ m}^2$$

The two volume flow rates are the same, so

$$A_{aorta} v_{aorta} = A_{vc} v_{vc}$$
$$v_{vc} = \frac{A_{aorta} v_{aorta}}{A_{vc}}$$
$$= \frac{9.82 \times 10^{-5} \text{ m}^3/\text{s}}{1.00 \times 10^{-3} \text{ m}^2}$$
$$= 9.82 \times 10^{-2} \text{ m/s} = 9.82 \text{ cm/s}$$

Reflect
Our results tell us that blood flows more slowly in the vena cavae (9.82×10^{-2} m/s) than in the aorta (0.200 m/s). That makes sense, for the venae cavae have a larger cross-sectional area than the aorta.

Speed of blood in vena cavae compared to speed of blood in capillaries is

$$\frac{v_{vc}}{v_{all open capillaries}} = \frac{9.82 \times 10^{-2} \text{ m/s}}{1.00 \times 10^{-3} \text{ m/s}} = 98.2$$

It's a common misconception that the slow-moving blood in the capillaries continues to move slowly as it returns to the heart. This example shows that this isn't the case! Compared to an average speed of 1.00 mm/s in the capillaries, blood moves 98.2 times faster in the vena cavae. The reason is that the cross-sectional area of the vena cavae is 1/98.2 as great as the combined cross-sectional area of the open capillaries, and the blood has to speed up as it returns to the heart to compensate for the decreased cross-sectional area.

Explanation: Cross-sectional area of vena cavae compared to cross-sectional area of all open capillaries combined is

$$\frac{A_{vc}}{A_{\text{all open capillaries}}} = \frac{1.00 \times 10^{-3} \text{ m}^2}{9.82 \times 10^{-2} \text{ m}^2}$$

$$= \frac{1}{98.2}$$

? Got the Concept? 11-9 How Diameter Goes with the Flow

While walking past a construction site, you notice a pipe sticking out of a second floor window, with water rushing out. As the water flows to the ground, it must speed up due to the effect of gravity. How does the diameter of the flowing stream of water change as it descends? If we assume that the flow remains laminar, (a) the diameter increases; (b) the diameter stays the same; (c) the diameter decreases.

Take-Home Message for Section 11-9

✔ In steady flow, the flow velocity at any one point remains constant from one moment to the next.

✔ In laminar flow, each bit of fluid follows a streamline. In turbulent flow, adjacent bits of fluid can follow very different paths.

✔ The viscosity of a fluid is a measure of its resistance to flow. It results in the formation of a boundary layer next to a solid surface. Fluid speed increases from zero at the solid surface to the full speed v of the flow at the edge of the boundary layer.

✔ In steady, incompressible flow, the product of the cross-sectional area of the flow and the speed of the flow is constant: If the cross-sectional area increases, the speed of the flow decreases, and vice versa.

11-10 Bernoulli's equation helps us relate pressure and speed in fluid motion

Hold a piece of notebook paper by two corners so that the paper droops downward. Then blow on the top of the paper as shown in Figure 11-25. You might expect that the force of the air expelled from your mouth would push the paper downward. But remarkably, the paper actually lifts *up* where it is struck by the moving air.

What's happened is that by making air move over the top of the paper, you've lowered the pressure of that air. Hence there is greater air pressure on the underside of the paper than on the top, and the paper lifts up. This simple experiment illustrates that certain kinds of fluid flow have a property described by **Bernoulli's principle: In a moving fluid, the pressure is low where the fluid is moving rapidly.** This principle was first identified by the eighteenth-century mathematician Daniel Bernoulli.

Bernoulli's principle explains why an open door may swing closed on a windy day. The pressure in the moving air outside the house is lower than the pressure of the still air inside the house. The difference in air pressure on the two sides of the door pulls the door toward the outside, slamming it shut. An umbrella bulges upward in the wind for the same reason; there is low-pressure, fast-moving air on top of the umbrella, but high-pressure still air in the space underneath.

Figure 11-26 illustrates the origins of Bernoulli's principle. A pipe of varying diameter carries an incompressible fluid from left to right. According to the equation of continuity that we discussed in Section 11-9, the fluid moves fastest in the narrow part of the pipe (point 2). Hence a parcel of fluid must speed up as it enters the narrow part.

Blowing on the top of a sheet of paper lowers the pressure there.

Higher pressure below pushes the paper up.

Figure 11-25 **Bernoulli's principle** A piece of paper lifts up if you blow over the top of the paper.

A net force must act on the fluid to change its velocity (that is, cause it to accelerate). This net force must be to the right as a parcel of fluid enters the narrow part. If we assume that there is negligible viscosity (see Section 11-9), the only forces that could be acting are those due to differences in pressure on the left and right sides of the parcel. As Figure 11-26 shows, to produce the required acceleration, the pressure must be lower in the narrow part of the pipe (where the fluid moves rapidly) than in the wide part (where the fluid moves slowly). This is just what Bernoulli's principle says: The pressure is lowest where the fluid moves the fastest.

> ## ⚠ Watch Out! Pressure differences cause velocity changes, not the other way around.
>
> It's *not* correct to say that the pressure differences in Figure 11-26 are *caused* by the changing velocity of the fluid. In fact, just the reverse is true: The changes in fluid velocity are caused by the pressure differences! Recall the meaning of Newton's second law: An object accelerates (that is, changes its velocity) in response to a net force acting on it. In other words, a change in velocity is a result of a net force, not the other way around. In the same way, the meaning of Bernoulli's principle is that a fluid undergoes a change in velocity as a result of pressure differences, not the reverse.

Fluid must move faster at point 2 than at point 1 to satisfy the equation of continuity.

To make the fluid speed up between point 1 and point 2, there must be a higher pressure at 1 than at 2.

Figure 11-26 Interpreting Bernoulli's principle Pressure differences drive a fluid through a constriction. The larger pressure on the left means that a parcel of fluid entering the constriction has a stronger force pushing it to the right than to the left, so the parcel speeds up as it approaches the constriction.

Bernoulli's Equation

Let's expand on these ideas and see how to express Bernoulli's principle as a rather simple and useful equation. By seeing where this equation comes from, we'll be able to understand why Bernoulli's principle only holds under certain special conditions. Many kinds of flow satisfy these conditions, but many others—including, for example, the flow of blood in the circulatory system—do not.

The shaded volume in Figure 11-27a shows a quantity of a fluid in motion. (This could be water flowing in a lazy river or air moving in a gentle breeze.) If we assume that the flow is *laminar* (see Section 11-9), we can think of this quantity of fluid as being enclosed within streamlines just as though it was flowing inside a pipe. As time goes by, this quantity of fluid moves along its "pipe," displacing other fluid at its front end and being displaced by fluid at its back end. Figure 11-27b shows our quantity of fluid a brief time interval Δt after the instant shown in Figure 11-27a. The fluid has vacated a volume $A_1 \Delta x_1$ at its back end and has moved into a volume $A_2 \Delta x_2$ at its front end.

Let's further assume that the flow is *steady*, so that the fluid velocity at any fixed position in the fluid remains the same. In this case, the motion of the shaded volume of fluid from the situation in Figure 11-27a to that in Figure 11-27b is the same as if the fluid had "lost" the volume $A_1 \Delta x_1$ at its back end and "gained" the volume $A_2 \Delta x_2$ at its

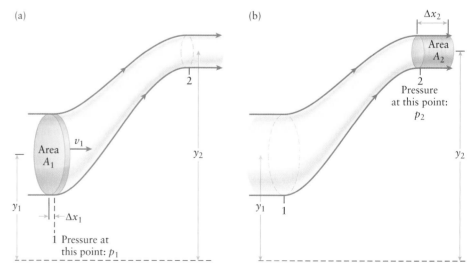

Figure 11-27 Deriving Bernoulli's equation (a) A slug of incompressible fluid of volume $A_1 \Delta x_1$ moving at speed v_1 enters the region between points 1 and 2. (b) A short time later, a slug of fluid of volume $A_2 \Delta x_2$ moving at speed v_2 exits the region. The equation of continuity says that fluid enters the region at the same rate that it exits. (Compare Figure 11-26.)

front end, with no other changes. If we make an additional assumption that the fluid is *incompressible*—so that its density ρ is the same at all points in the fluid—then the volume "lost" at the back end must be the same as the volume "gained" at the front end:

$$\text{volume "lost"} = A_1 \Delta x_1 = A_2 \Delta x_2 = \text{volume "gained"} \tag{11-20}$$

While the volume of the moving incompressible fluid remains the same, its *energy* can change. Over the time interval Δt, the shaded volume of fluid has lost the kinetic energy and gravitational potential energy associated with the "lost" volume at point 1, but has gained the kinetic and potential energies associated with the "gained" volume at point 2. In general, the back and front ends of the fluid may move at different speeds (think of the fluid moving through a pipe of varying diameter, as in Figure 11-27) and may be at different heights. Hence the amount of energy lost may be different from the amount gained, and the total mechanical energy of the shaded volume of fluid can change as it moves. The total energy change associated with the shaded volume of fluid is

$$\Delta E = \Delta K + \Delta U \tag{11-21}$$

We can write the mass of this volume of fluid as $\rho A_1 \Delta x_1$ (when it is at point 1) or $\rho A_2 \Delta x_2$ (when it is at point 2). We'll use the symbols v_1 and v_2 to denote the fluid speed at points 1 and 2, respectively, and use the symbols y_1 and y_2 for the heights at points 1 and 2. Then, using the familiar formulas $K = \frac{1}{2}mv^2$ for kinetic energy and $U = mgy$ for gravitational potential energy of the fluid-Earth system, we can write ΔK and ΔU in Equation 11-21 as

$$\Delta K = \text{change in kinetic energy} = +\frac{1}{2}(\rho A_2 \Delta x_2)v_2^2 - \frac{1}{2}(\rho A_1 \Delta x_1)v_1^2 \tag{11-22}$$

$$\Delta U = \text{change in gravitational potential energy} = +(\rho A_2 \Delta x_2)gy_2 - (\rho A_1 \Delta x_1)gy_1 \tag{11-23}$$

We learned in Section 6-7 that the total mechanical energy of a system (in this case, Earth and the shaded volume of fluid) changes only when work is done on it by nonconservative forces. What forces of this kind could be acting here? One possibility is friction within the shaded volume of fluid itself, or friction between this fluid and the fluid that surrounds it. If the fluid is flowing in a pipe, there could also be friction with the pipe walls. For simplicity we'll assume that there's no friction at all, so that the fluid is *inviscid* (that is, it has zero viscosity). Then the only nonconservative forces that could act on the shaded volume of fluid are forces from the surrounding fluid. There is pressure on all sides of the shaded volume of fluid, but work is done only by those forces that act on the *moving* parts of the fluid. From Figure 11-27, we can determine that the forces on the back and front ends of the shaded volume of fluid are $p_1 A_1$ and $p_2 A_2$, respectively. (In each case, force equals pressure times area.) The force on the back end pushes in the same direction as the displacement Δx_1 and so does positive work; the force on the front end does negative work because it pushes opposite to the displacement Δx_2. Hence the total nonconservative work done on the shaded volume of fluid in Figure 11-27 is

$$W_{\text{nonconservative}} = +(p_1 A_1)\Delta x_1 - (p_2 A_2)\Delta x_2 \tag{11-24}$$

Now we can put all the pieces together. From Section 6-7, the total change in mechanical energy given by Equations 11-21, 11-22, and 11-23 is equal to the nonconservative work done on the fluid given by Equation 11-24. That is

$$\Delta K + \Delta U = W_{\text{nonconservative}}$$

or

$$+\frac{1}{2}(\rho A_2 \Delta x_2)v_2^2 - \frac{1}{2}(\rho A_1 \Delta x_1)v_1^2 + (\rho A_2 \Delta x_2)gy_2 - (\rho A_1 \Delta x_1)gy_1$$
$$= +(p_1 A_1)\Delta x_1 - (p_2 A_2)\Delta x_2 \tag{11-25}$$

Equation 11-25 looks like a horrible mess. But because we assumed the fluid is incompressible, the volume "lost" is the same as the volume "gained" and $A_1 \Delta x_1$ is equal to $A_2 \Delta x_2$ (see Equation 11-20). Hence we can divide out all the factors of $A_1 \Delta x_1$ and $A_2 \Delta x_2$, leaving the simpler expression

$$+\frac{1}{2}\rho v_2^2 - \frac{1}{2}\rho v_1^2 + \rho g y_2 - \rho g y_1 = p_1 - p_2$$

We can rearrange this expression to read

(11-26)

$$p_1 + \frac{1}{2}\rho v_1^2 + \rho g y_1 = p_2 + \frac{1}{2}\rho v_2^2 + \rho g y_2$$

Equation 11-26 says that the quantity $p + \frac{1}{2}\rho v^2 + \rho g y$ has the same value at point 1 (the back end of the shaded volume of fluid) as at point 2 (the front end). But we could have chosen the back and front ends to be *anywhere* along the length of the shaded volume of fluid in Figure 11-27. So the quantity $p + \frac{1}{2}\rho v^2 + \rho g y$ must have the same value at *any* point within the streamlines that enclose this shaded volume.

What about a volume of fluid immediately adjacent to the shaded one we've been discussing (Figure 11-28)? In principle, this fluid could be moving at a very different speed than the fluid in the shaded volume. But in real fluids in which the flow is laminar, there is enough viscosity—that is, enough frictional force within the fluid—that adjoining bits of fluid move at nearly the same speed. That doesn't mean all of the fluid has to move at the same speed, but just that the speed varies gradually from one part of the fluid to another, with no abrupt jumps. Physicists say that such a flow is **irrotational**. This does *not* mean that the fluid can't rotate—it certainly can, like the hurricane in Figure 11-17c or like water swirling as it goes down the drain. Rather, the curious term *irrotational* refers to what would happen to a little paddlewheel that was put in the fluid and allowed to move with it. If the fluid speed on one side of the paddlewheel were sharply different from that on the other side, the paddlewheel would start turning. In the idealized case we're discussing, there are no such differences and the paddlewheel wouldn't rotate—which is why we call the flow irrotational.

Let's now make a final assumption that the fluid flow shown in Figure 11-28 is irrotational. (This assumption is actually in contradiction to our earlier approximation that the flow is inviscid; to make a fluid flow be irrotational, *some* viscosity must be present. So our approximation is really that the fluid has a little viscosity, but not too much!) With this additional assumption, the quantity $p + \frac{1}{2}\rho v^2 + \rho g y$ has the same value in the shaded volume in Figure 11-27 as it does in any adjacent volume. It also has the same value in the next volume over, and so on. So our idealized fluid has the same value of $p + \frac{1}{2}\rho v^2 + \rho g y$ at *all* points in the fluid. Put another way, points 1 and 2 in Equation 11-26 could be any two points in the fluid.

Our final result is **Bernoulli's equation:**

For this "tube" of fluid, $p + \frac{1}{2}\rho v^2 + \rho g y$ = a constant.

For this "tube" of fluid, $p + \frac{1}{2}\rho v^2 + \rho g y$ = another constant.

If the flow is irrotational, the constant is the same for all tubes of fluid.

Figure 11-28 Irrotational flow and Bernoulli's equation Two adjacent tubes of fluid. If the flow is irrotational, the quantity $p + \frac{1}{2}\rho v^2 + \rho g y$ has the same value for both tubes and for *all* parts of the fluid.

Bernoulli's equation
(11-27)

Fluid pressure at a given point in the fluid

Speed of the fluid at that point

Vertical coordinate of that point

$$p + \frac{1}{2}\rho v^2 + \rho g y = \text{a constant with the same}$$
$$\text{value throughout the fluid}$$

Density of the fluid (uniform throughout the fluid)

Acceleration due to gravity

Note that if the fluid is at rest, so that $v = 0$ at all points, Equation 11-27 becomes $p + \rho g y = $ constant: That is, as y decreases and you go deeper in a static fluid, the quantity $\rho g y$ decreases and the pressure p increases. This is just the relationship for pressure at various depths in a static fluid that we found in Section 11-4. Note also that if we compare two points at the same height y, Equation 11-27 tells us that the pressure p is high where the fluid speed v is low—which is just the statement of Bernoulli's principle that we made at the beginning of this section.

In order to derive Bernoulli's equation, we had to make a long laundry list of approximations: The fluid flow had to be *laminar, steady, incompressible, inviscid,* and *irrotational.* In many real-life situations these assumptions aren't valid. For example, the flow of water down a waterfall is turbulent, not laminar; viscosity is important for blood flow in capillaries; and the air flowing around a supersonic airplane undergoes substantial compression. But remarkably, there are a number of situations where Bernoulli's equation gives reasonably good results. In the examples that follow we'll look at some of these situations and examine how to use Bernoulli's equation in practical problems.

Example 11-14 Lift on a Wing

Figure 11-29 shows a computer simulation of air flowing around an airplane wing (seen end-on). As the figure shows, air flows faster over the top of the wing so that there is lower pressure on the top of the wing than on the bottom. Suppose the air (density 1.20 kg/m³) moves at 75 m/s past the lower surface of a small airplane's wing and at 85 m/s past the upper surface. If the area of the wing as seen from above is 10.0 m² and the top-to-bottom thickness of the wing is 7.0 cm, what is the overall upward force (the *lift*) that the air exerts on the wing?

Figure 11-29 **A computer simulation of airflow around a wing** A vertical column of parcels of air (shown by colored dots) starts at the left and moves to the right, flowing around a wing. The parcels passing over the top of the wing go faster than those passing below the bottom of the wing (they're spaced further apart horizontally), so there must be lower pressure on the top. (The dots are colored red in regions of low pressure.)

Set Up

The pressure on the bottom of the wing exerts an upward force, and the pressure on the top exerts a downward force. Our goal is to calculate the *combined* vertical force that these pressures exert on the wing. We use Bernoulli's equation to relate the pressure on the two surfaces of the wing. We also use the idea that pressure is force per area, so that the force on either surface of the wing is the pressure multiplied by the wing area.

Bernoulli's equation:

$$p + \frac{1}{2}\rho v^2 + \rho g y = \text{a constant} \tag{11-27}$$

Definition of pressure:

$$p = \frac{F_\perp}{A} \tag{11-2}$$

Solve

We want to calculate the net upward force on the wing, or the lift L. Let p_{bottom} and p_{top} be the pressures on the bottom and top of the wing respectively. Express L in terms of these pressures and the wing area A.

From Equation 11-2, the upward force on the bottom of the wing is

$$F_{\text{bottom}} = p_{\text{bottom}} A$$

and the downward force on the top of the wing is

$$F_{\text{top}} = p_{\text{top}} A$$

Combined upward force on the wing:

$$L = F_{\text{bottom}} - F_{\text{top}}$$
$$= p_{\text{bottom}} A - p_{\text{top}} A$$
$$= (p_{\text{bottom}} - p_{\text{top}})A$$

Use Bernoulli's equation to write an expression for the pressure difference $p_{\text{bottom}} - p_{\text{top}}$.

$p + \frac{1}{2}\rho v^2 + \rho g y$ has the same value on the top and bottom of the wing, so

$$p_{\text{bottom}} + \frac{1}{2}\rho v_{\text{bottom}}^2 + \rho g y_{\text{bottom}} = p_{\text{top}} + \frac{1}{2}\rho v_{\text{top}}^2 + \rho g y_{\text{top}}$$

Solve for $p_{\text{bottom}} - p_{\text{top}}$:

$$p_{\text{bottom}} - p_{\text{top}} = \frac{1}{2}\rho v_{\text{top}}^2 - \frac{1}{2}\rho v_{\text{bottom}}^2 + \rho g y_{\text{top}} - \rho g y_{\text{bottom}}$$

Calculate the pressure difference using $\rho = 1.20$ kg/m³, $v_{\text{top}} = 85$ m/s, $v_{\text{bottom}} = 75$ m/s, and $y_{\text{top}} - y_{\text{bottom}} = 7.0$ cm $= 7.0 \times 10^{-2}$ m (the top-to-bottom thickness of the wing).

$$\frac{1}{2}\rho v_{\text{top}}^2 - \frac{1}{2}\rho v_{\text{bottom}}^2 = \frac{1}{2}\rho(v_{\text{top}}^2 - v_{\text{bottom}}^2)$$
$$= \frac{1}{2}(1.20 \text{ kg/m}^3)\left[(85 \text{ m/s})^2 - (75 \text{ m/s})^2\right]$$
$$= 9.6 \times 10^2 \text{ kg/(m} \cdot \text{s}^2) = 9.6 \times 10^2 \text{ N/m}^2$$

$$\rho g y_{top} - \rho g y_{bottom} = \rho g (y_{top} - y_{bottom})$$
$$= (1.20 \text{ kg/m}^3)(9.80 \text{ m/s}^2)(7.0 \times 10^{-2} \text{ m})$$
$$= 0.82 \text{ kg/(m·s}^2) = 0.82 \text{ N/m}^2 \text{ so}$$

$$p_{bottom} - p_{top} = 9.6 \times 10^2 \text{ N/m}^2 + 0.82 \text{ N/m}^2$$
$$= 9.6 \times 10^2 \text{ N/m}^2 \text{ to two significant figures}$$

Calculate the lift L by multiplying the pressure difference by the wing area.

$$L = (p_{bottom} - p_{top})A = (9.6 \times 10^2 \text{ N/m}^2)(10.0 \text{ m}^2)$$
$$= 9.6 \times 10^3 \text{ N}$$

Reflect

In straight-and-level flight, the airplane is not accelerating either up or down, so the upward force of lift must exactly balance the weight of the airplane. So our wing can keep an airplane of weight 9.6×10^3 N (about 2200 lb) in the air.

Our result shows that for given speeds of airflow along the top and bottom of the wing, the lift L is proportional to the wing area A. The heavier the airplane, the larger the wing required to maintain flight. The same principle applies to gliding birds: An eagle or vulture weighs more than a hawk and so has a larger wing.

Even if the airplane were not moving, there would still be a small pressure difference of $\rho g y_{top} - \rho g y_{bottom} = 0.82$ N/m^2 between the upper and lower surfaces of the wing. This pressure difference means that the air exerts a small buoyant force on the wing. Our calculations show that this small pressure difference is totally negligible compared to the pressure difference $\frac{1}{2}\rho v_{top}^2 - \frac{1}{2}\rho v_{bottom}^2 = 9.6 \times 10^2$ N/m^2 due to air traveling faster past the top of the wing than past the bottom of the wing.

▌ Watch Out! Air molecules don't meet at the trailing edge of a wing.

Why does air travel at different speeds over the two surfaces of the wing? A common misconception is that air traveling along the top of the wing takes just as much time to go from the wing's leading edge to its trailing edge as does the air that travels along the bottom. According to this misconception, air has to move faster along the top of the wing because the upper surface is curved more than the lower, and molecules that parted company at the leading edge must somehow meet up at the trailing edge. But the computer simulation in Figure 11-29 shows that this isn't the case at all. Air travels over the upper surface of the wing *much* faster than the common misconception would have us believe, and the molecules *don't* meet up at the trailing edge. A better explanation is that air follows the curvature of the wing due to its (slight) viscosity. This curvature is such that the wing pushes air downward. By Newton's third law, the air must push the wing *upward* equally hard. To produce this upward force, or lift, there has to be a pressure difference between the two surfaces of the wing, and this pressure difference is what causes the air to flow at different speeds over the top and bottom of the wing.

Example 11-15 A Venturi Meter

Figure 11-30 shows a simple device called a *Venturi meter* for measuring fluid velocity in a gas such as air. When gas passes from left to right through the horizontal pipe, it speeds up as it passes through the constriction at point 2. Bernoulli's principle tells us that the gas pressure must be lower at point 2 than at point 1, and the pressure difference causes the liquid in the U-tube to drop on the left-hand side and rise on the right-hand side. Suppose the gas is air (density 1.20 kg/m^3) that enters the left-hand side of the Venturi meter at 25.0 m/s. The horizontal tube has cross-sectional area 2.00 cm^2 at point 1 and cross-sectional area 1.00 cm^2 at point 2. If the liquid in the U-tube is water, what is the difference in height between the water columns on the left-hand and right-hand sides of the tube?

Figure 11-30 **A Venturi meter** A Venturi meter, or flow meter, can be used to measure the flow speed of a gas.

Set Up

In this problem there are *two* fluids, the air that flows through the horizontal pipe and the water in the U-tube. Hence we'll use Bernoulli's equation twice: once to relate the moving air at point 1 to the moving air at point 2, and once to relate the heights of the water on the two sides of the U-tube (which is what we're trying to find). We'll also use the equation of continuity to relate the speeds of the air at points 1 and 2.

Bernoulli's equation:

$$p + \frac{1}{2}\rho v^2 + \rho g y = \text{a constant} \tag{11-27}$$

Equation of continuity for steady flow of an incompressible fluid:

$$A_1 v_1 = A_2 v_2 \tag{11-19}$$

relate properties of air here and here

relate properties of water here and here

Solve

We need to find the difference in air pressure at points 1 and 2, since this is what causes the difference in height of the water on the two sides of the U-tube. Find this difference using Bernoulli's equation and the equation of continuity applied to the air in the horizontal pipe, keeping in mind that we know the values of v_1, A_1, and A_2.

Bernoulli's equation for the air at points 1 and 2:

$$p_1 + \frac{1}{2}\rho_{\text{air}} v_1^2 + \rho_{\text{air}} g y_1 = p_2 + \frac{1}{2}\rho_{\text{air}} v_2^2 + \rho_{\text{air}} g y_2$$

At the center of the horizontal pipe, $y_1 = y_2$, so

$$p_1 + \frac{1}{2}\rho_{\text{air}} v_1^2 = p_2 + \frac{1}{2}\rho_{\text{air}} v_2^2$$

$$p_1 - p_2 = \frac{1}{2}\rho_{\text{air}} v_2^2 - \frac{1}{2}\rho_{\text{air}} v_1^2$$

From the equation of continuity,

$$v_2 = \frac{A_1}{A_2}v_1 \text{ so}$$

$$p_1 - p_2 = \frac{1}{2}\rho_{\text{air}}(v_2^2 - v_1^2) = \frac{1}{2}\rho_{\text{air}}\left[\left(\frac{A_1}{A_2}\right)^2 v_1^2 - v_1^2\right]$$

$$= \frac{1}{2}\rho_{\text{air}} v_1^2\left[\left(\frac{A_1}{A_2}\right)^2 - 1\right]$$

$$= \frac{1}{2}(1.20 \text{ kg/m}^3)(25.0 \text{ m/s})^2\left[\left(\frac{2.00 \text{ cm}^2}{1.00 \text{ cm}^2}\right)^2 - 1\right]$$

$$= 1.13 \times 10^3 \text{ kg/(m·s}^2) = 1.13 \times 10^3 \text{ N/m}^2$$

The pressure difference between points 1 and 2 is also the pressure difference between the water at two points: the top of the water column on the left-hand side of the U-tube and the water column on the right-hand side. The water is at rest ($v = 0$) at both points. Use this technique to find the height difference between the two water columns.

Bernoulli's principle for the water at the tops of the two columns:

$$p_1 + \frac{1}{2}\rho_{\text{water}} v_{\text{water},1}^2 + \rho_{\text{water}} g y_{\text{water},1}$$

$$= p_2 + \frac{1}{2}\rho_{\text{water}} v_{\text{water},2}^2 + \rho_{\text{water}} g y_{\text{water},2}$$

Water is at rest: $v_{\text{water},1} = v_{\text{water},2} = 0$

Solve for the height difference of the two water columns:

$$p_1 + \rho_{\text{water}} g y_{\text{water},1} = p_2 + \rho_{\text{water}} g y_{\text{water},2}$$

$$\rho_{\text{water}} g y_{\text{water},2} - \rho_{\text{water}} g y_{\text{water},1} = p_1 - p_2$$

$$y_{\text{water},2} - y_{\text{water},1} = \frac{p_1 - p_2}{\rho_{\text{water}} g} = \frac{1.13 \times 10^3 \text{ kg/(m·s}^2)}{(1.000 \times 10^3 \text{ kg/m}^3)(9.80 \text{ m/s}^2)}$$

$$= 0.115 \text{ m} = 11.5 \text{ cm}$$

Reflect
This height difference is large enough to easily measure, so the Venturi meter is a practical device.

We made an approximation in our solution that the pressure difference between points 1 and 2 within the horizontal pipe is the same as the pressure difference between the two water columns. This isn't exactly correct, because there is a greater weight of air above the column on the left-hand side. However, the resulting additional pressure difference is so small that we can ignore it.

Additional pressure difference between the tops of the two water columns due to the extra weight of air on the left-hand side:

$$\rho_{air}g(y_{water,2} - y_{water,1}) = (1.20\,\text{kg/m}^3)(9.80\,\text{m/s}^2)(0.115\,\text{m})$$
$$= 1.35\,\text{kg/}(\text{m}\cdot\text{s}^2) = 1.35\,\text{N/m}^2$$

This is 0.12% of the pressure difference calculated above $(p_1 - p_2 = 1.13 \times 10^3\,\text{N/m}^2)$, so we can neglect it.

Applications of Bernoulli's Principle

Can a thrown baseball be a "curveball"—that is, can it be made to follow a path that curves left or right? In the early days of baseball, most people thought a curveball was just an optical illusion. It wasn't until 1941, when *Life* magazine published photographs of a curveball taken with a strobe light, that baseball fans (and everyone else) had proof that a properly thrown baseball can be made to curve. Bernoulli's principle helps to explain why.

Imagine a baseball thrown without any spin, what ball players call a "knuckleball." As the ball flies, the air rushes past the left and right sides of the ball at the same speed. Since the speed of the air is same on both sides, according to Bernoulli's equation the air pressure in the air is also the same on both sides. Hence there is no tendency for the ball's trajectory to curve either right or left.

Now imagine the ball spinning as it moves (Figure 11-31). In this figure we're looking at the ball from above, and it is rotating counterclockwise as seen from this vantage point. The ball is moving in the direction shown by the arrow, and air rushes past it in the opposite direction. Because the surface of the ball is rough, and because the baseball has raised seams that hold the leather cover of the ball together, viscosity drags a layer of air around in the same direction as the spin of the ball (compare Figure 11-21). As a result, the net speed of air relative to the ball is slower on the right-hand side of the ball than on the left-hand side. Bernoulli's principle tells us that a speed difference corresponds to a pressure difference, and the slower speed to the right of the ball means that there is higher pressure there. This pressure difference means that as viewed from above, this baseball feels a force to the left and will curve to the left! (You can convince yourself that the ball would curve to the right if it rotated in the opposite direction.)

Bernoulli's principle can help baseball pitchers win games; it also helps fish such as mackerel stay alive. A mackerel swims with its mouth open, allowing water to enter through the mouth, pass through the gills where oxygen is extracted, and exit through an aperture called the *operculum*. The streamlines of water flow around the mackerel to follow the contours of its body. Figure 11-32 shows that these streamlines are close together near the operculum. As we learned in Section 11-9, flow in an incompressible fluid such as water is rapid where streamlines are close together but slow where the streamlines are far apart. Hence the water flow is *faster* at the operculum than at the mouth, and so according to Bernoulli's principle the pressure at the operculum is *lower* than at the mouth. This pressure difference helps to force water from mouth to operculum by way of the mackerel's gills. This effect, called *ram ventilation*, is essential to the mackerel's existence. If a mackerel stops swimming, the gills are unable to extract sufficient oxygen and the fish suffocates. Other species of fish use ram ventilation only at high swimming speeds; at lower speeds, where ram ventilation is less effective, they use muscular action to pump water through their gills.

As the ball rotates counterclockwise (in this picture) a layer of air close to the ball is also dragged around counterclockwise. This boundary layer moves in the same direction as the air rushing past the ball on the left, but opposes the air flow on the right.

Motion of ball from the pitcher toward the batter

Motion of air relative to the ball

According to Bernoulli's equation, higher net air speed on the left results in lower pressure. The pressure difference between the right and left sides of the ball results in a net force, so this ball will curve to the left!

Figure 11-31 What makes a curveball curve If a baseball rotates, viscosity drags a layer of air around the ball in the same direction as the ball's rotation.

❓ Got the Concept? 11-10   Bernoulli in Action

Imagine holding two pieces of paper vertically, with a small gap between them, and then blowing gently into the gap. Would you expect the pieces of paper to (a) be drawn together, (b) be pushed apart, or (c) be unaffected? (Try it!)

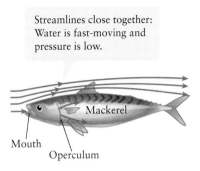

Streamlines close together: Water is fast-moving and pressure is low.

Mackerel

Mouth

Operculum

Figure 11-32 **Bernoulli's principle and fish respiration** Mackerel breathe by letting water flow from the mouth through the gills (where oxygen is extracted from the water) and out the operculum. Bernoulli's principle tells us that the water pressure at the operculum is lower when the fish is in motion, thus facilitating flow through the gills.

11-11 Viscosity is important in many types of fluid flow

We saw in Section 11-10 that Bernoulli's equation only holds true under certain very special assumptions. In particular, we saw that the fluid had to have a little bit of viscosity to make the laminar flow be irrotational. But we couldn't allow the fluid to have too much viscosity, since that would mean that *viscous forces*—that is, forces on fluid due to friction—would play an important role in determining the acceleration of a bit of moving fluid.

Water exiting hose

Open end of hose: Pressure is actually lower here than at the faucet.

Faucet end of hose

Figure 11-33 **When Bernoulli's equation doesn't work** A horizontal garden hose attached to a faucet. If Bernoulli's equation held true, the water pressure would be the same everywhere along the length of the hose. Bernoulli's equation does not apply here because viscous forces are important in this situation.

For many situations involving fluid flow there is "too much" viscosity, and Bernoulli's equation is *not* valid. One example is water flowing in a garden hose (Figure 11-33). The hose has the same cross-sectional area A throughout its length, so in order to satisfy the equation of continuity (which says that the product Av is a constant) the flow speed v must be the same at all points along the hose's length. Furthermore, if the hose is horizontal, then all points along the hose are at the same height y. If Bernoulli's equation, Equation 11-27 (which says that $p + \frac{1}{2}\rho v^2 + \rho g y$ is a constant), applied to this situation, then the water pressure p would also have to have the same value everywhere inside the hose. But in fact the pressure at the open end of the hose is substantially *lower* than at the end attached to the faucet. The reason is that frictional forces oppose the flow of water through the hose, so there has to be additional pressure at the faucet to sustain the flow.

The human circulatory system is another situation where Bernoulli's equation doesn't hold. The speed of blood flow in capillaries (about 10^{-3} m/s) is hundreds of times slower than in the aorta (about 0.2 m/s), so the term $\frac{1}{2}\rho v^2$ in Equation 11-27 has a much smaller value in the capillaries. Bernoulli's equation would therefore predict that blood pressure is much higher in the capillaries than in the aorta. In fact, the pressure is higher in the *aorta*; this is necessary to push against the frictional forces that the blood encounters on its way to the capillaries.

Let's be more quantitative about viscosity and its consequences. Figure 11-34 shows one way that physicists measure the viscosity of a fluid. Two glass plates, each of area A, are separated by a distance d and have a quantity of fluid filling the space between them. The lower plate is held stationary while the upper plate is pulled sideways at a constant

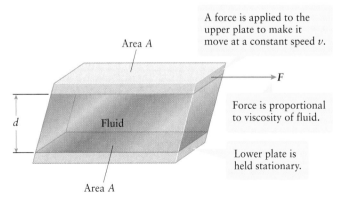

A force is applied to the upper plate to make it move at a constant speed v.

Area A

F

Fluid

d

Area A

Force is proportional to viscosity of fluid.

Lower plate is held stationary.

Figure 11-34 **Measuring viscosity** An experiment to measure the viscosity of a fluid.

speed v. Experiment shows that if the speed v is not too great, the fluid at the top remains attached to the upper plate and the fluid at the bottom remains attached to the lower plate, while the fluid in between slides sideways in sheets like a deck of cards. The force (magnitude F) that must be applied to the upper plate to make the fluid move in this way is relatively large for a viscous fluid like oil, but relatively low for a fluid like water. The force magnitude F is also proportional to the speed v and the area A but inversely proportional to the plate spacing d. We can summarize these observations in the following expression for F, which defines what we mean by the viscosity η (the Greek letter eta):

Definition of viscosity (11-28)

$$F = \frac{\eta A v}{d}$$

Force required to pull the upper plate in Figure 11-34

Viscosity of the fluid

Area of either plate in Figure 11-34

Spacing between the plates

Speed of one plate relative to the other

Table 11-2 Viscosities of Various Substances

Substance	Viscosity (Pa · s)
air at 0°C	1.709×10^{-5}
air at 20°C	1.808×10^{-5}
air at 40°C	1.904×10^{-5}
fresh water at 0°C	1.787×10^{-3}
fresh water at 20°C	1.002×10^{-3}
fresh water at 40°C	6.53×10^{-4}
seawater at 20°C	1.072×10^{-3}
mercury (Hg) at 20°C	1.554×10^{-3}
blood at 37°C	0.003–0.004
typical motor oil at 20°C	0.1
glycerin at 20°C	1.490
chocolate syrup at 20°C	1.5
ketchup at 20°C	5.1
honey at 20°C	10
peanut butter at 20°C	25.5

Equation 11-28 says that the greater the viscosity η, the greater the force that must be applied to move one plate relative to the other. The units of viscosity are pascals times seconds, or Pa · s for short. Viscosities are also sometimes given in *poise*, named for the nineteenth-century French scientist Jean Poiseuille; 1 poise equals 0.1 Pa · s.

Table 11-2 lists values of viscosity for several common fluids. Note that the viscosity of a fluid generally depends on temperature; liquids such as maple syrup and motor oil become less viscous and so flow more easily at higher temperatures.

Reynolds Number: Comparing Viscous Forces and Forces due to Pressure Differences

The experiment shown in Figure 11-34 is useful for measuring viscosity because the only forces making the fluid move are the frictional (viscous) forces that act between parts of the fluid and between the fluid and plates. In most real-life situations, however, there are also forces due to pressure differences acting on the fluid (for example, the pressure difference between the two ends of a garden hose as you water the lawn). To describe the relative importance of forces due to pressure difference and viscous forces in fluid flow, physicists use a dimensionless quantity—that is, a pure number with no units—called the **Reynolds number**:

Reynolds number (11-29)

$$Re = \frac{\rho l v}{\eta}$$

Reynolds number of a certain fluid flow

Density of the fluid

A length characteristic of the situation

Viscosity of the fluid

Speed of the flow

Roughly speaking, the Reynolds number Re (*not* R_e) is the ratio of the forces due to pressure differences acting on a small piece of the fluid to the viscous forces acting on the same piece of fluid. Because the viscosity η is in the denominator in this expression, the Reynolds number increases as the viscosity *decreases*, and vice versa. Thus Re has a large value if viscosity is relatively unimportant, but it has a small value if viscosity plays a dominant role.

Definition of the length l in Equation 11-29 depends on the situation. For a fluid flowing in a tube, such as water in a pipe or air through your nostrils, l could be the diameter of the tube; the narrower the pipe, the smaller the Reynolds number, the more important the role of viscosity, and the less likely it is that Bernoulli's equation will be valid.

For a fluid flowing *around* an object, such as air around a bird's wing or water around a fish, the length l could be the front-to-back dimension of the wing or fish.

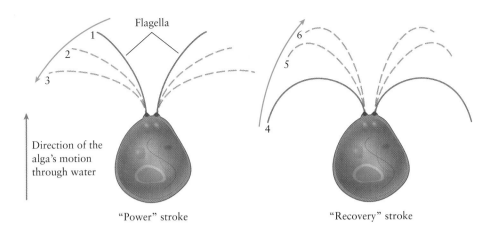

Flagella

1
2
3

Direction of the
alga's motion
through water

"Power" stroke

6
5
4

"Recovery" stroke

Figure 11-35 **Viscous forces on swimming algae** (a) The tiny flagellate *Chlamydomonas*, which is just a few micrometers in diameter, moves forward through water during a power stroke. (b) Due to the viscosity of water, *Chlamydomonas* actually moves backward during the recovery stroke.

Hence the Reynolds number *Re* is smaller, and viscosity more important, for a small organism moving through water than for a larger organism moving through water at the same speed. If the small organism moves at a slow speed v, the Reynolds number is even smaller and viscosity can become extremely important. As an example, the viscosity of water is relatively unimportant for a human doing the breaststroke underwater. The swimmer accelerates forward when she pulls her arms back in a "power stroke," pushing against the water, and continues forward even when she pulls her arms forward in the "recovery stroke." By contrast, viscosity is a huge effect for the single-celled alga *Chlamydomonas*, which propels itself slowly through water in a breaststroke-like way using two flagella (Figure 11-35). When the cell pulls its flagella back in the "recovery stroke," the cell actually *backs up* by about a third of the distance that it moves forward during a "power stroke." You can better empathize with the plight of *Chlamydomonas* by imagining yourself swimming in a tub of molasses!

Low Reynolds Number: Laminar Flow

If the viscosity of a flowing fluid is sufficiently high, and hence *Re* is sufficiently low, the flow will be laminar but will not obey Bernoulli's equation. An important example of this is the flow of fluids within pipes, such as the flow of vaccine in a hypodermic needle or of blood in the veins and arteries in your circulatory system. (Blood vessels can curve and can vary in diameter along their length, but for simplicity we'll consider straight pipes with circular cross sections.) To sustain a steady flow, there must be a pressure difference between the ends of the pipe; the fluid flows from the high-pressure end to the low-pressure end. That's why a hypodermic syringe is equipped with a plunger; the force of a thumb on the plunger provides the necessary high pressure on one end of the needle.

Figure 11-36 shows the laminar flow of fluid within a circular pipe seen in cross section. Due to friction, the fluid that's right up against the inside walls of the pipe doesn't move at all. This is the *no-slip condition* that we described in Section 11-9. (The fluid in contact with the lower plate in Figure 11-34 behaved the same way.) The fluid a small distance from the walls moves a little, the fluid a bit farther away moves a bit faster, and so on. The fastest flow is at the very center of the pipe. This flow pattern is called *parabolic* (since the dashed curve in Figure 11-36 is a parabola lying on its side). A derivation using calculus gives the following expression, called the **Hagen-Poiseuille equation,** relating the pressure difference between the two ends of the pipe to the resulting flow rate. (Non-French speakers can pronounce Poiseuille as "pwa-zoo-yah.")

Cross section
of a pipe

Figure 11-36 **Laminar flow of a viscous liquid in a circular pipe** The viscous fluid moves fastest at the center of the pipe, and does not move at all at the pipe walls.

Volume flow rate of
fluid through a pipe

Radius of the pipe

Pressure difference between
the two ends of the pipe

$$Q = \frac{\pi R^4}{8\eta L} \Delta p$$

Viscosity of the fluid

Length of the pipe

Hagen-Poiseuille equation for
laminar flow of a viscous fluid
(11-30)

Turbulent flow over the top of the bird's wing makes these feathers deflect upward.

Figure 11-37 Turbulent air flow over a buzzard's wings The airflow over the top of this buzzard's wings is largely turbulent, causing some of the small feathers near mid-span to be pushed up.

The longer the pipe (greater L) and the smaller its radius (smaller R), the less the volume flow rate Q caused by a given pressure difference Δp. You can appreciate why this is the case by comparing a volume of fluid that fills the inside of a short, wide pipe to the same volume of fluid that fills a long, narrow pipe. More of the fluid in the long, narrow pipe is in contact with the pipe walls and hence is not in motion, so the flow rate is less.

Equation 11-30 states that for the same pressure difference Δp, using a slightly wider pipe gives a much larger flow rate. Doubling the radius increases the flow rate by a factor of $2^4 = 16$! This equation also tells us that if we want to get the same volume flow rate Q through a narrower pipe (smaller R), we have to apply a greater pressure difference Δp between the two ends of the pipe. This helps explain how a diet high in cholesterol can lead to *hypertension*, or high blood pressure; cholesteric plaque building up within arteries decreases their inner radius R. Also, because the plaque build-up makes the arteries less elastic, hardened arteries expand less than healthy ones to accommodate blood pumped into them by the heart. Therefore, the heart must supply higher pressure to sustain the same blood flow.

High Reynolds Number: Turbulent Flow

Suppose fluid is moving through a circular pipe with the flow pattern shown in Figure 11-36. If there's a small imperfection in the pipe walls (biological pipes are never perfectly circular) or if something should disturb the flow, what happens? If the Reynolds number is low enough (that is, if the flow is sufficiently slow or the viscosity sufficiently high), the answer is "not much": The flow pattern is deformed a little, but thanks to viscous forces the pattern recovers its parabolic shape a short distance downstream of the disturbance. If the Reynolds number is greater than a certain value, however, the flow loses its regularity and becomes *turbulent* like the smoke trails in Figure 11-17b. For fluid flow in circular pipes, the critical value of the Reynolds number is about $Re = 2000$, where l in Equation 11-29 is the diameter (not the radius) of the pipe.

Unlike laminar flow, turbulent flow is messy as well as difficult to describe mathematically. It is also very common in nature. The flow of air around the wing of a gliding bird is laminar near the wing's leading edge, but becomes turbulent as the air moves along the wing's upper surface. The effect is more pronounced if the bird glides at a slower speed, in which case its wings are inclined at a greater angle to the direction of flight to provide enough lift. The turbulent air moving over the wing's upper surface can cause individual wing feathers to deflect upward (Figure 11-37). If the bird flies too slowly and tilts the wing up too sharply, the air on the upper surface becomes so turbulent that it no longer follows the contours of the wing. Since the wing produces lift by forcing air downward, this onset of turbulence means that the lifting force of the wing decreases dramatically (a phenomenon called an *aerodynamic stall*) and the bird drops suddenly. (You can sometimes see this happen to hawks or other predatory birds as they orbit slowly over a field, looking for a meal.) Birds recover from this drop by dipping their wings slightly to restore a more laminar flow. Airplane wings are subject to the same effect, which pilots deal with in the same way.

Blood flow in the human circulatory system is often approximately laminar. But the Reynolds number in the larger blood vessels is close to the critical value that separates laminar and turbulent flows. Hence a relatively small obstruction in the aorta—the large artery that carries blood from the heart to the rest of the body—can trigger turbulence. Turbulent flow in the aorta generates noise, which is one thing that a physician listens for (and hopes not to hear) when using a stethoscope to check your heart. A totally benign noise caused by turbulence is the sound you hear on a windy day as turbulent air blows past your ears.

Example 11-16 Laminar or Turbulent?

Is the flow of water at 20°C laminar or turbulent if (a) the pipe has radius 0.500 mm $= 5.00 \times 10^{-4}$ m and the average flow speed is 0.800 m/s; (b) the radius is 0.125 mm $= 1.25 \times 10^{-4}$ m and the average flow speed is 12.8 m/s? At this temperature the density of water is 998 kg/m³.

Set Up

The key to solving this problem is the Reynolds number, which for flow in a pipe of circular cross section is given by Equation 11-29. In this equation l is the diameter of the pipe. The flow is laminar if Re is less than 2000; otherwise it is turbulent.

Reynolds number:

$$Re = \frac{\rho l v}{\eta} \qquad (11\text{-}29)$$

Solve

(a) Use the diameter of the pipe (twice the radius) and the flow speed to calculate the Reynolds number. We use Table 11-2 to find the viscosity of water.

$l = 2(5.00 \times 10^{-4}\,\text{m}) = 1.00 \times 10^{-3}\,\text{m}$

Reynolds number of the flow:

$$Re = \frac{(9.98 \times 10^2\,\text{kg/m}^3)(1.00 \times 10^{-3}\,\text{m})(0.800\,\text{m/s})}{1.002 \times 10^{-3}\,\text{Pa·s}}$$

$= 797$

Since the Reynolds number is less than 2000, the flow is laminar.

(b) Repeat the calculation for the new pipe diameter and flow speed.

$l = 2(1.25 \times 10^{-4}\,\text{m}) = 2.50 \times 10^{-4}\,\text{m}$

Reynolds number of the flow:

$$Re = \frac{(9.98 \times 10^2\,\text{kg/m}^3)(2.50 \times 10^{-4}\,\text{m})(12.8\,\text{m/s})}{1.002 \times 10^{-3}\,\text{Pa·s}}$$

$= 3.19 \times 10^3$

In this case the Reynolds number is greater than 2000, so the flow is turbulent.

Reflect

Notice that compared to the pipe in (a), the pipe in (b) has 1/4 the radius and hence 1/16 the cross-sectional area (which is proportional to the square of the radius). Notice also that the average flow speed in (b) is 16 times that in (a). So the volume flow rate (the product of cross-sectional area A and flow speed v) is the *same* in both (a) and (b), but the flow is turbulent in the narrower pipe of (b). In a similar way, an obstruction in a blood vessel (which reduces the vessel's radius) doesn't change the flow rate, but does increase the Reynolds number and so can induce turbulence.

Volume flow rate in first pipe:

$$A_1 v_1 = \pi R_1^2 v_1$$
$$= \pi (5.00 \times 10^{-4}\,\text{m})^2$$
$$\times (0.800\,\text{m/s})$$
$$= 6.28 \times 10^{-7}\,\text{m}^3/\text{s}$$

Volume flow rate in second pipe:

$$A_2 v_2 = \pi R_2^2 v_2$$
$$= \pi (1.25 \times 10^{-4}\,\text{m})^2 (12.8\,\text{m/s})$$
$$= 6.28 \times 10^{-7}\,\text{m}^3/\text{s}$$

same volume flow rate, different Reynolds numbers

Example 11-17 Viscous Laminar Flow in a Long, Narrow Pipe

Water at 20°C moves in laminar flow at an average flow speed of 0.800 m/s through a pipe of radius 0.500 mm = 5.00×10^{-4} m. The pipe is 2.00 m long. Determine what the pressure difference must be between the two ends of the pipe.

Set Up

We saw in part (a) of Example 11-16 that the flow is laminar for water at this temperature moving through such a pipe at this speed. Because the pipe is long and narrow, viscosity is important and laminar flow is an example of Hagen-Poiseuille flow. (The density and viscosity are given in Example 11-16.) Our goal is to find the pressure difference Δp between the ends of the pipe, and we use the Hagen-Poiseuille equation, Equation 11-30.

Hagen-Poiseuille equation for laminar flow of a viscous fluid:

$$Q = \frac{\pi R^4}{8\eta L}\Delta p \qquad (11\text{-}30)$$

Solve
In Example 11-16 we calculated the volume flow rate.

Volume flow rate:

$$Q = 6.28 \times 10^{-7}\,\text{m}^3/\text{s}$$

Solve the Hagen-Poiseuille equation for the pressure difference Δp and substitute values.

$$\Delta p = \frac{8\eta L Q}{\pi R^4}$$

$$= \frac{8\,(1.002 \times 10^{-3}\,\text{Pa·s})\,(2.00\,\text{m})\,(6.28 \times 10^{-7}\,\text{m}^3/\text{s})}{\pi\,(5.00 \times 10^{-4}\,\text{m})^4}$$

$$= 5.13 \times 10^4\,\text{Pa}$$

Reflect
Even though the viscosity of water is low, the pressure required to sustain the flow is substantial (about half an atmosphere) because the pipe is so narrow and long.

$$\Delta p = (5.13 \times 10^4\,\text{Pa})\left(\frac{1\,\text{atm}}{1.01325 \times 10^5\,\text{Pa}}\right)$$

$$= 0.506\,\text{atm}$$

❓ Got the Concept? 11-11   When Is Viscosity More Important?

Two identical tubes have fluid flowing through them at the same speed. In one tube the fluid is air, and in the other tube the fluid is fresh water. In which tube is viscosity more important? (a) the tube with water; (b) the tube with air; (c) viscosity is equally important in each tube; (d) not enough information given to decide.

Take-Home Message for Section 11-11

✔ The Reynolds number for a fluid flow is large if viscous forces are relatively unimportant in the flow, and small if viscous forces play a dominant role.

✔ If a fluid flow has a sufficiently low Reynolds number, the flow is laminar. A sufficiently high Reynolds number means that the flow is turbulent.

✔ The Hagen-Poiseuille equation describes the laminar flow of a viscous fluid. This equation relates the pressure difference between the two ends of a pipe to the resulting flow rate.

11-12 Surface tension explains the shape of raindrops and how respiration is possible

Why does rain fall in droplets? Why does water roll off a duck's back? And why is it useful to use detergent when washing clothes? We can answer all of these questions by examining an important property of liquids called *surface tension*.

Unlike a gas, whose molecules easily spread out to fill the volume available, a liquid maintains an essentially constant volume because its molecules exert strong attractive forces on each other. As a result, the molecules try to huddle close to each other. The potential energy associated with these forces is lowest if as many of the molecules as possible are completely surrounded by other molecules, and if as few as possible are on the surface (where they are surrounded by other molecules on one side only). Therefore, to minimize this potential energy, the molecules arrange themselves so as to minimize the surface area of the liquid (Figure 11-38). A sphere has the smallest surface area for a given volume, which is why raindrops are spherical. The drop behaves as though its surface were a membrane that resists being stretched, which is why this behavior is called **surface tension**.

An irregular blob of liquid tends to become spherical due to surface tension.

Figure 11-38 **Surface tension** The effect of surface tension on a liquid blob or drop.

A spherical drop of radius R has volume $(4\pi/3)R^3$ and surface area $4\pi R^2$. The importance of surface tension is proportional to the ratio of the drop's surface area (which is the size of the "membrane" enclosing the drop) to its volume (which tells you the total amount of fluid in the drop). This ratio is $4\pi R^2/[(4\pi/3)R^3] = 3/R$, which *increases* as the radius R *decreases*. Hence surface tension is more important for small drops than for large ones. If you pour enough liquid into a container, surface tension is overwhelmed by gravitational forces and the liquid assumes a shape that fills the container and has a horizontal upper surface. In zero gravity even large quantities of liquid form spherical drops (Figure 11-39).

The surface tension of water enables ducks to remain warm and dry even after submerging themselves in search of a meal. A duck's feather has a crisscross grid of tiny barbules that form a fine mesh (Figure 11-40a). To push through this mesh, the water surface must stretch as shown in Figure 11-40b. Surface tension resists such stretching of the surface "membrane," so water does not penetrate the mesh and the duck's skin remains dry. (This is the origin of phrases like "Criticism rolls off him like water off a duck's back.") The same effect makes it difficult for water to penetrate between the closely spaced fibers of clothing. That's why clothing is best washed using a detergent, which is a substance that reduces the surface tension of water. One of the jobs of detergents is to make it easier for water to do its job.

Surface tension also plays an important role in human respiration. In the lungs, oxygen exchange takes place across the walls of tiny, balloon-like structures called *alveoli* (Figure 11-41). The inside surface of the alveoli is wet and the surface tension of this fluid generates a pressure that tends to pull the walls of the alveoli inward. The magnitude of this pressure is proportional to the surface tension and inversely proportional to the radius of the alveolus:

$$\text{Pressure} = (2 \times \text{Surface tension})/(\text{Alveolar radius})$$

Figure 11-39 **Surface tension on a weightless water drop** In the apparent weightlessness of an orbiting spacecraft, surface tension allows rather large quantities of water to form spherical drops.

Figure 11-40 **Surface tension and bird feathers** (a) This drawing of a bird feather shows the tiny interlocking barbules. (b) Due to surface tension, water cannot easily pass through the tiny spaces between barbules.

(a)

A duck's feather has a crisscross grid of tiny barbules that form a fine mesh...

Shaft

Barb

Barbules

Barb

...to push through this mesh, the water surface must stretch.

(b)

Water

Barbules (seen end-on)

Figure 11-41 **Alveoli** This illustration shows a cluster of the tiny balloon-like sacs called alveoli. A human lung contains about 3×10^8 alveoli.

Take-Home Message for Section 11-12

✔ The molecules of a liquid minimize their energy by surrounding themselves with their fellow molecules. As a result, liquids tend to form spherical drops.

✔ The surface of a liquid drop resists being stretched. This behavior is called surface tension.

The problem is that the alveoli do not all have the same radius, so smaller alveoli experience a greater pressure than larger ones. As a result, small alveoli would tend to collapse into larger ones if not for a substance called a *surfactant* that coats the inside surface of each alveolus. This remarkable substance decreases surface tension as a function of its concentration in the fluid lining the inside of the alveoli. As the radius of the alveolus decreases during exhalation, the concentration of surfactant increases on the surface of the fluid lining the alveolus and therefore decreases surface tension and the resulting pressure in the alveolus. This prevents smaller alveoli from collapsing into larger ones. Also, during inhalation the reduced surface tension makes it easier to inflate the lungs with the relatively small pressure difference between inhaled air and the low-pressure air in the thoracic cavity—about 130 Pa, or 0.13% of atmospheric pressure. A condition called respiratory distress syndrome occurs in premature infants whose lungs are deficient in surfactant; the increased surface tension pressure can make their alveoli collapse. Administering a replacement surfactant helps these newborn babies survive.

Key Terms

absolute pressure	gas	pressure
apparent weight	gauge pressure	Reynolds number
Archimedes' principle	Hagen-Poiseuille equation	solid
atmosphere (unit of pressure)	hydrostatic equilibrium	specific gravity
Bernoulli's equation	incompressible fluid	steady flow
Bernoulli's principle	inviscid flow	streamline
boundary layer	irrotational flow	surface tension
buoyant force	laminar flow	torr
compressible fluid	liquid	uniform density
density	millimeters of mercury	unsteady flow
equation of continuity	no-slip condition	turbulent flow
equation of hydrostatic equilibrium	pascal	viscosity
fluid	Pascal's principle	volume flow rate

Chapter Summary

Topic	Equation or Figure

Fluids: The molecules in a fluid are not arranged in any organized structure. A fluid does not have any shape of its own, and flows to conform to the shape of the container in which it is placed. A quantity of liquid maintains nearly the same volume, while a quantity of gas expands to fill the volume available.

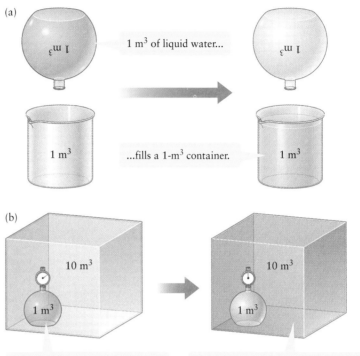

(Figure 11-2)

Density: The density ρ of a substance is its mass per volume. Density depends on how closely packed the molecules of the substance are, as well as on the mass of the individual molecules. An object's density does not directly indicate its mass—a small, dense object can have more mass than a large, less dense one.

The **density** ρ ("rho") of a certain substance... ...equals the mass m of a given quantity of that substance...

$$\rho = \frac{m}{V}$$ ...divided by the volume V of that quantity of the substance.

(11-1)

Pressure: The pressure p exerted by a fluid is the perpendicular force it exerts on a given area in the fluid divided by the area. Unlike force, pressure is not a vector. Pressure measured relative to atmospheric pressure is called gauge pressure.

The **pressure** p exerted by a fluid on an object in the fluid... ...equals the force $F_\perp$ that the fluid exerts perpendicular to the face of the object...

$$p = \frac{F_\perp}{A}$$ ...divided by the area A of that face.

(11-2)

Fluids at rest: A stationary fluid must be in hydrostatic equilibrium, so that the sum of the forces on any parcel of fluid is zero. In a fluid of uniform density, the pressure at a given point increases with depth to support the weight of the fluid above that point.

Pressure at a certain point in a fluid at rest   Density of the fluid (same at all points in the fluid)

Pressure at a second, lower point in the fluid   Acceleration due to gravity

$$p = p_0 + \rho g d$$

(11-8)

Depth of the second point where the pressure is p below the point where the pressure is p_0

Pressure difference: If there are different pressures on the two sides of an object, the different pressures produce a net force.

A pressure difference on two opposite sides of an object produces a net force.

Area of each side of the object

$$F_{net} = (p_2 - p_1) A \qquad (11\text{-}10)$$

High pressure on one side of the object

Lower pressure on the other side of the object

Pascal's principle: Pressure applied to a confined, static fluid is transmitted undiminished to every part of the fluid as well as to the walls of the container. A hydraulic jack, which converts a small force acting over a large distance into a large force acting over a small distance, relies on Pascal's principle.

When a downward force is applied to the cap on side 1, the increase in pressure is transmitted undiminished throughout the fluid, forcing the cap on side 2 to rise.

(Figure 11-11)

Buoyancy: An object immersed in a fluid feels an upward buoyant force F_b equal to the weight of fluid that the object displaces. A submerged object will remain submerged and neither sink nor rise if its average density is the same as that of the fluid.

Magnitude of the buoyant force on an object in a fluid

Density of the fluid

$$F_b = \rho_{fluid} V_{displaced} g \qquad (11\text{-}13)$$

Volume of fluid that the object displaces

Acceleration due to gravity

Fluid flow: The motion of a fluid is classified as being steady or unsteady; and as laminar or turbulent; viscous (with internal friction) or inviscid (without internal friction).

(b)

(b)

Streamlines: the paths followed by bits of fluid in laminar flow

There are no streamlines for a fluid in turbulent flow.

(Figure 11-19b)

(Figure 11-20b)

Equation of continuity: Fluid can neither be created nor destroyed as it flows. If an incompressible (constant-density) fluid flows through a pipe, the size of the pipe and the flow speed may change, but the volume flow rate (the cross-sectional area of the flow multiplied by the flow speed) remains the same.

Cross-sectional area of the flow at point 1

Flow speed at point 1

$$A_1 v_1 = A_2 v_2 \qquad (11\text{-}19)$$

Cross-sectional area of the flow at point 2

Flow speed at point 2

Bernoulli's principle and Bernoulli's equation: The pressure in a moving fluid is reduced at locations where the fluid moves rapidly. The mathematical statement of this principle, called Bernoulli's equation, is only accurate for idealized laminar, inviscid flows.

Fluid pressure at a given point in the fluid

Speed of the fluid at that point

Vertical coordinate of that point

$$p + \frac{1}{2} \rho v^2 + \rho g y = \text{a constant with the same value throughout the fluid} \qquad (11\text{-}27)$$

Density of the fluid (uniform throughout the fluid)

Acceleration due to gravity

Viscosity: The viscosity η of a fluid is a measure of how much friction is present when different parts of the fluid slide past one another. One way to measure viscosity is to see how much force is required to slide one plate relative to another, parallel plate if there is fluid between the plates.

Force required to pull the upper plate in Figure 11-34

Viscosity of the fluid

Area of either plate in Figure 11-34

$$F = \frac{\eta A v}{d}$$

(11-28)

Spacing between the plates

Speed of one plate relative to the other

Turbulent viscous flow: The flow of a viscous liquid becomes turbulent if the Reynolds number Re of the flow is too large. This happens if the flow speed is too great, the characteristic dimension of the flow (for example, the diameter of the pipe through which the fluid moves) is too large, or both.

Reynolds number of a certain fluid flow

Density of the fluid

A length characteristic of the situation

$$Re = \frac{\rho l v}{\eta}$$

(11-29)

Viscosity of the fluid

Speed of the flow

Laminar viscous flow: To make a viscous fluid flow through a pipe, there must be a pressure difference between the two ends of the pipe. A greater pressure difference is required for long, thin pipes than for short, broad ones.

Volume flow rate of fluid through a pipe

Radius of the pipe

Pressure difference between the two ends of the pipe

$$Q = \frac{\pi R^4}{8\eta L} \Delta p$$

(11-30)

Viscosity of the fluid

Length of the pipe

Surface tension: Attractive forces between the molecules of a liquid make it favorable for the liquid to minimize its surface area. This effect causes water to form droplets and makes it difficult to force water through small apertures.

(Figure 11-38)

An irregular blob of liquid tends to become spherical due to surface tension.

Answer to What do you think? Question

(c) A hot-air balloon is an object immersed in air (a fluid), and the upward buoyant force on an immersed object is equal in magnitude to the weight of the fluid that the object displaces. The balloon floats because the combined weight of the balloon, the air inside the balloon, the basket, and the passengers is balanced by the buoyant force. The balloon is the same size whether it is filled with hot air or helium, so it displaces the same *volume* of air and hence the same *weight* of air in either case. So the buoyant force is unaffected by replacing the hot air with helium. What changes as a result of filling the balloon with low-density helium is the total *weight* of the balloon. So the upward buoyant force on a helium-filled balloon opposes a weaker downward gravitational force than does the (identical) upward buoyant force on a balloon filled with hot air, and the helium-filled balloon will accelerate upward rather than float. (See Section 11-8.)

Answers to Got the Concept? Questions

11-1 (d) If you chose the block of iron, be careful! Table 11-1 tells us that iron has a much greater density ρ (7.8×10^3 kg/m^3) than does ice (0.917×10^3 kg/m^3), but the mass m (and hence the weight) of each block depends on its volume V. From Equation 11-1, $m = \rho V$. If the two blocks have the same volume, the block of iron will weigh more than the block of ice. But if the block of ice is the size of a house while the block of iron is the size of your fingernail, the ice will definitely outweigh the iron.

11-2 (e) Remember that, unlike force, pressure is *not* a vector and so has no direction. Therefore any statement that refers to the direction of pressure is an incorrect and misleading one! The pressure on each side of the fish is the same.

11-3 (b) In hydrostatic equilibrium, the pressure in the water depends only on the vertical position. To convince yourself of this assertion, let p_0 be the pressure at the bottom of the left-hand leg, and p be the pressure at the bottom of the right-hand leg. These two pressures are related by Equation 11-8, $p = p_0 + \rho g d$. Since both points are at the same height, $d = 0$, and $p = p_0$. That is, the pressure p at the bottom of the left-hand tube must be the *same* as the pressure at the bottom of the right-hand tube, since these points are at the same level. (If the pressure was higher on one side or the other, water would flow from the region of high pressure to the region of low pressure until the pressures equalized.) To see that the height of each column is the same, now let the pressure at the top of each column of water, which is equal to air pressure, be written as p_0. Since the pressure p_0 at the top of the water column is the same on both sides and the pressure p at the bottom of the water column is the same on both sides, it follows from $p = p_0 + \rho g d$ that the depth of water d must be the same on both sides as well.

11-4 (d), (b), (c), (a). The deflated balloon has air at atmospheric pressure inside, so its gauge pressure is zero and its absolute pressure is about 1.0 atm. The inflated balloon has a gauge pressure of 0.50 atm, and its absolute pressure is about $(0.50 \text{ atm}) + (1.0 \text{ atm}) = 1.5$ atm.

11-5 (a) We know from Section 11-4 that pressure increases with increasing depth in a fluid, including the atmosphere. So the air pressure on the bottom of the paper is slightly greater than the pressure on the top, and the net force due to these pressures is upward (although very small). It's true that the sum of *all* forces acting on the paper—including the force of gravity and the force exerted by your hands—is zero, because the paper is at rest. But that's not what the question is asking.

11-6 (c) The cap on side 2 has 5 times the radius and so 25 times the area of the cap on side 1 (that is, $A_2/A_1 = 25$). So from Equation 11-11 the force on side 2 (F_2) is 25 times greater than the force on side 1 (F_1). But from Equation 11-12, the displacement of the cap on side 2 (d_2) is only $1/25$ as much as the displacement of the cap on side 1 (d_1). Since work equals the product of force and displacement, the work done on side 2 is the *same* as the work done on side 1, because $25 \times (1/25) = 1$. The hydraulic jack doesn't increase the amount of work that you can do: It just makes it possible for you to do that work by applying a relatively small force F_1.

11-7 (a) Regardless of whether the coin is on the top or bottom of the cube, since the cube and coin are floating, the buoyant force of the water displaced must equal the weight of the cube plus the weight of the coin. (If that weren't true, the cube and coin would sink.) So the amount of water displaced is the same in both cases. However, when the coin is on the top, only the cube is displacing water, but when the coin is on the bottom, both the cube and the coin displace water. In this second case, then, the volume of the coin is contributing to the buoyant force, which means that the cube itself won't displace as much water as when the buoyant force was due totally to the amount of the cube that was submerged. For that reason, more of the cube will be above the surface of the water when the coin is taped to the bottom, and the cube will sit higher in the water.

11-8 (b) When the bottle was floating, it displaced a volume of water equal to its weight. That's because in order to float, the buoyant force must equal the bottle's weight, and according to Archimedes' principle, the buoyant force is also equal to the weight of the displaced water. However, when the bottle has sunk to the bottom of the tub, the volume of water it displaces is equal only to the volume of the glass that forms the bottle. Since the bottle sank, we know that the glass must be denser than water, which means the glass itself takes up less volume than the equivalent weight of water. The net result is that when the bottle sinks, the water level goes down.

11-9 (c) According to the equation of continuity, the product of the cross-sectional area of a flow of fluid and the speed of flow is constant. For that reason, as the speed of the flow increases, the cross-sectional area must decrease. This "neck-down" effect is visible even for height differences of about a meter and is quite noticeable in waterfalls before the flow turns turbulent.

11-10 (a) According to Bernoulli's principle, when two regions in a flowing fluid have different flow speed, the pressure must be lower in the region in which the flow is faster. In the experiment in which you blow between two papers, because air flows faster between the papers than in the region surrounding the papers, the pressure between them is lower than in the surrounding region, causing the papers to be drawn together—not pushed apart.

11-11 (b) The Reynolds number $Re = \rho l v / \eta$ is a measure of the relative importance of pressure forces and viscous forces in a flowing fluid. The smaller the value of Re, the more important viscosity is. The two tubes have the same dimensions (so the length l is the same), and the fluid flows at the same speed (so v is the same). Hence what's different between the two flows is the value of ρ/η, the ratio of density to viscosity. From Tables 11-1 and 11-2, the values of this ratio for the two fluids are as follows.

Water at 20°C:

$$\rho/\eta = (998 \text{ kg/m}^3)/(1.002 \times 10^{-3} \text{ Pa} \cdot \text{s})$$
$$= 9.96 \times 10^5 \text{ kg}/(\text{m}^3 \cdot \text{Pa} \cdot \text{s})$$

Air at around 15 to 20°C:

$$\rho/\eta = (1.23 \text{ kg/m}^3)/(1.808 \times 10^{-5} \text{ kg/m}^3)$$
$$= 6.80 \times 10^4 \text{ kg}/(\text{m}^3 \cdot \text{Pa} \cdot \text{s})$$

The value of ρ/η for air is less than one-tenth of the value for water, so viscous effects are actually more important for air than for water.

Questions and Problems

In a few problems, you are given more data than you actually need; in a few other problems, you are required to supply data from your general knowledge, outside sources, or informed estimate.

Interpret as significant all digits in numerical values that have trailing zeros and no decimal points.

For all problems, use $g = 9.80 \text{ m/s}^2$ for the free-fall acceleration due to gravity. Neglect friction and air resistance unless instructed to do otherwise.

• Basic, single-concept problem
•• Intermediate-level problem, may require synthesis of concepts and multiple steps
••• Challenging problem
SSM *Solution is in Student Solutions Manual*

Conceptual Questions

1. •Aluminum is more dense than plastic. You are given two identical, closed, and opaque boxes. One contains a piece of aluminum and the other contains a piece of plastic. Without opening the boxes, is it possible to tell which box contains the plastic and which box contains the aluminum? Explain your answer.

2. •Two identically shaped containers in the shape of a truncated cone are placed on a table, but one is inverted such that the small end is resting on the table. The containers are filled with the same height of water. The pressure at the bottom of each container is the same. However, the weight of the water in each container is different. Explain why this statement is correct.

3. •A dam will be built across a river to create a reservoir. Does the pressure in the reservoir at the base of the dam depend on the shape of the dam, given that the depth of the reservoir will be the same regardless of the choice of dam shape? Explain your answer. SSM

4. •**Medical** After sitting for many hours during a trans-Pacific flight, a passenger jumps up quickly as soon as the "fasten seat belt" light is turned off, and immediately falls to the floor, unconscious! Within seconds of being in the horizontal position, however, consciousness is restored. What happened?

5. •**Medical** Usually blood pressure is measured on the arm at the same level as the heart. How would the results differ if the measurement were made on the leg instead?

6. •**Medical** When you cut your finger badly, why might it be wise to hold it high above your head?

7. •**Medical** When you donate blood, is the collection bag held below or above your body? Why?

8. •An ice cube floats in a glass of water so that the water level is exactly at the rim. After the ice cube melts, will all the water still be in the glass? Explain your answer.

9. •The salinity of the Great Salt Lake varies from place to place and from about two to as much as eight times the salinity of ocean water. Is it easier or harder for a person to float in the Great Salt Lake compared to floating in ocean water? Why? SSM

10. •A wooden boat floats in a small pond, and the level of the water at the edge of the pond is marked. Will the level of the water rise, fall, or stay the same when the boat is removed from the pond?

11. •You are given two objects of identical size, one made of aluminum and the other of lead. You hang each object separately from a spring balance. Because lead is denser than aluminum, the lead object weighs more. Now you weigh each object while it is submerged in water. Will the difference between the weight of the aluminum object and weight of the lead object be greater than, less than, or the same as it was when the objects were weighed in air? Explain your answer.

12. •A river runs through a wide valley and then through a narrow channel. How do the velocities of the flows of water compare between the wide valley and the narrow channel?

13. •A dam holds back a very long, deep lake. If the lake were twice as long, but still just as deep, how much thicker would the dam need to be? Why?

14. •The wind is blowing from west to east. Should landing airplanes approach the runway from the west or the east? Explain your answer.

15. •Use Bernoulli's equation to explain why a house roof is easily blown off during a tornado or hurricane. SSM

16. •Why does the stream of water from a faucet become narrower as it falls?

17. •A cylindrical container is filled with water. If a hole is cut on the side of the container so that the water shoots out, what is the direction of the water flow the instant it leaves the container?

Multiple-Choice Questions

18. •Object A has density ρ_1. Object B has the same shape and dimensions as object A, but it is three times as massive. Object B has density ρ_2 such that

   A. $\rho_2 = 3\rho_1$.
   B. $\rho_2 = \dfrac{\rho_1}{3}$.
   C. $\rho_2 = \rho_1$.
   D. $\rho_2 = 2\rho_1$.
   E. $\rho_2 = \dfrac{\rho_1}{2}$.

19. •If the gauge pressure is doubled, the absolute pressure will
   A. be halved.
   B. be doubled.
   C. be unchanged.
   D. be increased, but not necessarily doubled.
   E. be decreased, but not necessarily halved. SSM

20. •A toy floats in a swimming pool. The buoyant force exerted on the toy depends on the volume of
   A. water in the pool.
   B. the pool.
   C. the toy under water.
   D. the toy above water.
   E. none of the above choices.

21. •An object floats in water with 5/8 of its volume submerged. The ratio of the density of the object to that of water is
    A. 8/5.
    B. 5/8.
    C. 1/2.
    D. 2/1.
    E. 3/8.

22. •An ice cube floats in a glass of water. As the ice melts, what happens to the water level?
    A. It rises.
    B. It remains the same.
    C. It falls by an amount that cannot be determined from the information given.
    D. It falls by an amount proportional to the volume of the ice cube.
    E. It falls by an amount proportional to the volume of the ice cube that was initially above the water line.

23. •Water flows through a 0.5-cm-diameter pipe connected to a 1-cm-diameter pipe. Compared to the speed of the water in the 0.5-cm pipe, the speed in the 1-cm pipe is
    A. one-quarter the speed in the 0.5-cm pipe.
    B. one-half the speed in the 0.5-cm pipe.
    C. the same as the speed in the 0.5-cm pipe.
    D. double the speed in the 0.5-cm pipe.
    E. quadruple the speed in the 0.5-cm pipe. SSM

24. •**Medical** Blood flows through an artery that is partially blocked. As the blood moves from the wider region into the narrow region, the blood speed
    A. increases.
    B. decreases.
    C. stays the same.
    D. drops to zero.
    E. alternately increases and then decreases.

25. •Bernoulli's equation, $p + \frac{1}{2}\rho v^2 + \rho g y = $ constant, is a statement of
    A. the conservation of energy for a moving fluid.
    B. the conservation of linear momentum for a moving fluid.
    C. Newton's third law for a moving fluid.
    D. the equation of continuity for a moving fluid.
    E. the conservation of mass for a moving fluid.

26. •An ideal fluid flows through a pipe of variable cross section without any friction. The fluid completely fills the pipe. As the fluid traverses the pipe, it has a constant
    A. kinetic energy.
    B. potential energy.
    C. total energy.
    D. velocity.
    E. pressure.

27. •Two wooden boxes of equal mass but different density are held beneath the surface of a large container of water. Box A has smaller average density than box B. When the boxes are released, they accelerate upward to the surface. Which box has the greater acceleration?
    A. Box A
    B. Box B
    C. They are the same.

    D. We need to know the actual densities of the boxes in order to answer the question.
    E. It depends on the contents of the boxes. SSM

Estimation/Numerical Analysis

28. •Estimate the volume of water consumed in a major Canadian city each day.

29. •Estimate the lift that a human body might experience in hurricane-force winds. SSM

30. •Estimate the mass of Earth if all the water in the oceans were replaced with mercury.

31. •Estimate the depth in fresh water that increases the absolute pressure by 1 atm. How does the depth change for seawater? What about for a pool of mercury? SSM

32. •Estimate the difference in buoyancy for a boat in fresh water versus the same boat in seawater.

33. •Estimate the maximum load that you might be able to lift with a simple hydraulic jack.

34. •**Medical** Estimate the pressure (in pascals) generated by the left ventricle of a human heart during contraction.

Problems

11-1 Liquids and gases are both examples of fluids

11-2 Density measures the amount of mass per unit volume

35. •Determine the mass of a cube of iron that is 2 cm × 2 cm × 2 cm in size.

36. •What is the radius of a sphere made of aluminum, if its mass is 24 kg?

37. •(a) Determine the average density of a cylinder that is 20 cm long, 1 cm in radius, and has a mass of 37 g. (b) Referring to Table 11-1, of what material might the cylinder be made? (c) What is the specific gravity of the material? SSM

38. •How long are the sides of an ice cube if its mass is 0.35 kg?

39. •**Biology** Approximately 65% of a person's body weight is water. What is the volume of water in a 65-kg man?

40. ••A set of density rods is designed to illustrate the concept of density. The idea is to create cylinders of equal diameters and masses, but varying lengths, to show which have the largest and smallest densities. (a) Derive a formula that will predict the ratio of the length of one rod to the length of another rod, as a function of the densities of the two rods. Assume the radius and mass of each cylinder are the same and express your answer in terms of the specific gravity of each rod. (b) If you want to design a set of five density rods (made of aluminum, iron, copper, brass, and lead), determine the ratios of the lengths of each rod to the length of the lead rod, the densest material in the group. The specific gravities of the elements are approximately $SG_{alum} = 2.7$, $SG_{iron} = 7.8$, $SG_{copper} = 8.9$, $SG_{brass} = 8.5$, $SG_{lead} = 11.3$.

41. •**Astronomy** When a star reaches the end of its life, it is possible for a supernova to occur. This may result in the formation of a very small, but very dense, neutron star. The density of such a stellar remnant is about the same as a neutron. Determine the radius of a neutron star that has the mass of our Sun and the same density as a neutron. A neutron has a mass of 1.7×10^{-27} kg and an approximate radius of 1.2×10^{-15} m. Assume that both the neutron star and the neutron itself are spherical in shape. SSM

42. •Assuming that Earth is a perfect sphere of radius 6380 km and mass 5.98×10^{24} kg, determine the average density of our planet.

11-3 Pressure in a fluid is caused by the impact of molecules

43. •(a) An object of mass m_1 is supported by a square surface area of side s_1. Find the equation for the mass m_2 of a second object that will produce the same pressure when supported by a square surface area of side s_2. (b) What is the ratio of m_2 to m_1 if $s_2 = 5s_1$?

44. •An elephant that has a mass of 6000 kg evenly distributes her weight on all four feet. (a) If her feet are approximately circular and each has a diameter of 50 cm, estimate the pressure on each foot. (b) Compare the answer in part (a) with the pressure on each of your feet when you are standing up. Make some rough but reasonable assumptions about the area of your feet.

45. •The head of a nail is 0.32 cm in diameter. You hit it with a hammer with a force of 25 N. (a) What is the pressure on the head of the nail? (b) If the pointed end of the nail, opposite to the head, is 0.032 cm in diameter, what is the pressure on that end? SSM

11-4 In a fluid at rest, pressure increases with increasing depth

46. •Calculate the pressure at the bottom of a graduated cylinder that is half full of mercury and half full of water. Assume the height of the cylinder is 0.25 m and don't forget about atmospheric pressure.

47. •A swimming pool 5.0 m wide by 10 m long is filled to a depth of 10 m. What is the pressure on the bottom of the pool?

48. •A diver is 10.0 m below the surface of the ocean. The surface pressure is 1 atm. What is the absolute pressure and gauge pressure he experiences?

49. •What is the difference in blood pressure (mmHg) between the top of the head and bottom of the feet of a 1.75-m-tall person standing vertically? The density of blood is 1.06×10^3 kg/m^3. SSM

50. •At 25°C the density of ether is 72.7 kg/m^3 and the density of iodine is 4930 kg/m^3. A cylinder is filled with iodine to a depth of 1.5 m. How tall would a cylinder filled with ether need to be so that the pressure at the bottom is the same as the pressure at the bottom of the cylinder filled with iodine?

11-5 Scientists and medical professionals use various units for measuring fluid pressure

51. •**Medical** Suppose that your pressure gauge for determining the blood pressure of a patient measured absolute pressure instead of gauge pressure. How would you write the normal value of systolic blood pressure, 120 mmHg, in such a case? SSM

52. •Convert the following units of pressure to the SI unit of pascals (Pa), where 1 Pa $= 1$ N/m^2.

    A. 1500 kPa = _____ Pa
    B. 35 psi   = _____ Pa
    C. 2.85 atm = _____ Pa
    D. 883 torr = _____ Pa

53. •Assuming the atmospheric pressure is 1 atm at sea level, determine the atmospheric pressure at Badwater (in Death Valley, California) where the elevation is 85 m below sea level.

54. •Elaine wears her wide-brimmed hat at the beach. If the atmospheric pressure at the beach is exactly 1 atm, determine the weight of the imaginary column of air that "rests" on her hat if its diameter is 45 cm.

55. •What is the *absolute* pressure of the air inside a bicycle tire that is inflated with a hand pump to 65 psi? Give your answer in pascals (Pa).

11-6 A difference in pressure on opposite sides of an object produces a net force on the object

56. •A rectangular swimming pool is 8.0 m $\times 35$ m in area. The depth varies uniformly from 1.0 m in the shallow end to 2.0 m in the deep end. (a) Determine the pressure at the bottom of the deep end of the pool and at the shallow end. (b) What is the net force on the bottom of the pool due to the water in the pool? (Ignore the effects of the air above the pool for this part.)

57. •What is the net force on an airplane window of area 1000 cm^2 if the pressure inside the cabin is 0.95 atm and the pressure outside is 0.85 atm? SSM

58. •What force must the surface of a basketball withstand if it is inflated to a pressure of 8.5 psi? Assume the ball has a diameter of 23 cm.

59. •Suppose that the hatch on the side of a Mars lander is built and tested on Earth so that the internal pressure just balances the external pressure. The hatch is a disk 50.0 cm in diameter. When the lander goes to Mars, where the external pressure is 650 N/m^2, what will be the net force (in newtons and pounds) on the hatch, assuming that the internal pressure is the same in both cases? Will it be an inward or an outward force? SSM

60. •What is the net force on the walls of a 55-gal drum that is on the bottom of the ocean (the specific gravity of the ocean is 1.025) at a depth of 250 m? Assume the drum is a cylinder that has a height of $34\frac{1}{2}$ in and a diameter of 21-5/8 in. (Remember to convert inches to meters!) Consider the interior pressure of the drum to be 1 atm.

11-7 A pressure increase at one point in a fluid causes a pressure increase throughout the fluid

61. •What is the maximum weight that can be raised by the hydraulic lift shown in Figure 11-42?

Figure 11-42 Problem 61

62. •A hydraulic lift is designed to raise a 900-kg car. If the "large" piston has a radius of 35.0 cm and the "small" piston has a radius of 2.00 cm, determine the minimum force exerted on the small piston to accomplish the task.

63. •(a) What force will the large piston provide if the small piston in a hydraulic lift is moved down as shown in Figure 11-43? (b) If the small piston is depressed a distance of Δy_1, by how much will the large piston rise? (c) How much work is done in slowly pushing down the small piston compared to the work done in raising the large piston if $\Delta y_1 = 0.20$ m? SSM

Figure 11-43 Problem 63

64. •A hydraulic lift has a leak so that it is only 75% efficient in raising its load. If the large piston exerts a force of 150 N when the small piston is depressed with a force of 15.0 N and the radius of the small piston is 5.00×10^{-2} m, what is the radius of the large piston?

11-8 Archimedes' principle helps us understand buoyancy

65. •A rectangular block of wood, 10 cm × 15 cm × 40 cm, has a specific gravity of 0.6. (a) Determine the buoyant force that acts on the block when it is placed in a pool of fresh water. *Hint:* Draw a free-body diagram labeling all of the forces on the block. (b) What fraction of the block is submerged? (c) Determine the weight of the water that is displaced by the block.

66. •A block of wood will sink 10 cm in fresh water. How far will it sink in seawater? (The specific gravity of seawater is 1.025.)

67. ••A cube of side s is completely submerged in a pool of fresh water. (a) Derive an expression for the pressure difference between the bottom and top of the cube. (b) After drawing a free-body diagram, derive an algebraic expression for the net force on the cube. (c) What is the weight of the displaced water when the cube is submerged? Your expressions may include some or all of the following quantities: atmospheric pressure, the density of fresh water, the length of the side of the cube, the mass of the cube, and the acceleration due to gravity.

68. •Tom and Huck fashion a river raft out of logs. The raft is 3.00 m × 4.00 m × 0.150 m and is made from trees that have an average density of 700 kg/m³. How many people can stand on the raft and keep their feet dry, assuming an average person has a mass of 70 kg?

69. •A crown that is supposed to be made of solid gold is under suspicion. When the crown is weighed in air, it has a weight of 5.15 N. When it is suspended from a digital balance and lowered into water, its apparent weight is measured to be 4.88 N. Given that the specific gravity of gold is 19.3, comment on the authenticity of the crown. SSM

70. •A woman floats in a region of the Great Salt Lake where the water is about four times saltier than the ocean and has a density of about 1130 kg/m³. The woman has a mass of 55 kg, and her density is 985 kg/m³ after exhaling as much air as possible from her lungs. Determine the percentage of her volume that will be above the waterline of the Great Salt Lake.

11-9 Fluids in motion behave differently depending on the flow speed and the fluid viscosity

71. •(a) A hose is connected to a faucet and used to fill a 5.0-L container in a time of 45 s. Determine the volume flow rate in m³/s. (b) Determine the velocity of the water in the hose in part (a) if it has a radius of 1 cm. SSM

72. •How fast is the water leaving the nozzle of a hose with a volume flow rate of 0.45 m³/s? Assume there are no leaks and the nozzle has a circular opening with diameter of 7.5 mm.

73. •Determine the time required for a 50-L container to be filled with water when the speed of the incoming water is 25 cm/s and the cross-sectional area of the hose carrying the water is 3.0 cm².

74. •Medical A cylindrical blood vessel is partially blocked by the buildup of plaque. At one point, the plaque decreases the diameter of the vessel by 60.0%. The blood approaching the blocked portion has speed v_0. Just as the blood enters the blocked portion of the vessel, what will be its speed in terms of v_0?

75. •Medical You inject your patient with 2.5-mL of medicine. If the inside diameter of the 31-gauge needle is 0.114 mm and the injection lasts 0.65 s, determine the speed of the fluid as it leaves the needle. SSM

76. •In July of 1995, a spillway gate broke at the Folsom Dam in California. During the uncontrolled release, the flow rate through the gate peaked at 40,000 ft³/s and about 1.35 billion gallons of water were lost (nearly 40% of the reservoir). Estimate the time that the gate was open.

77. •The return-air ventilation duct in a home has a cross-sectional area of 900 cm². The air in a room that has dimensions 7.0 m × 10.0 m × 2.4 m is to be completely circulated in a 30-min cycle. What is the speed of the air in the duct?

11-10 Bernoulli's equation helps us relate pressure and speed in fluid motion

78. ••Water flows from a fire truck through a hose that is 11.7 cm in diameter and has a nozzle that is 2 cm in diameter. The firemen stand on a hill 5 m above the level of the truck. When the water leaves the nozzle, it has a speed of 20 m/s. Determine the minimum gauge pressure in the truck's water tank.

79. •At one point, Hurricane Katrina had maximum sustained winds of 175 mi/h (240 km/h) and a low pressure in the eye of 666.52 mmHg (0.877 atm). Using the given air speed, compare the atmospheric pressure that would be predicted by Bernoulli's equation to the measured value. Comment on any discrepancies. Assume the pressure of the air is normally 1 atm. SSM

80. •When the atmospheric pressure is 1.00 atm, a water fountain ejects a stream of water that rises to a height of 5.00 m. There is a 1.00-cm-radius pipe that leads from a pressurized tank to the opening that ejects the water. What would happen if the fountain were operating when the eye of a hurricane passes through? Assume that the atmospheric pressure in the eye is 0.877 atm and the tank's pressure remains the same.

81. ••A cylinder that is 20 cm tall is filled with water (Figure 11-44). If a hole is made in the side of the cylinder, 5 cm below the top level, how far from the base of the cylinder will the stream land? Assume that the cylinder is large enough so that the level of the water in the cylinder does not drop significantly.

Figure 11-44 Problem 81

11-11 Viscosity is important in many types of fluid flow

82. •Water flows through a horizontal tube that is 30.0 cm long and has an inside diameter of 1.50 mm at 0.500 mL/s. Determine the pressure difference required to drive this flow if the viscosity of water is 1.00 mPa · s. Assume laminar flow.

83. •Biology Blood takes about 1.50 s to pass through a 2.00-mm-long capillary. If the diameter of the capillary is 5.00 μm and the pressure drop is 2.60 kPa, calculate the viscosity of blood. Assume laminar flow. SSM

84. ••A very large tank is filled to a depth of 250 cm with oil that has a density of 860 kg/m³ and a viscosity of 180 mPa · s. If the container walls are 5.00 cm thick, and a cylindrical hole of radius 0.750 cm has been bored through the base of the container, what is the initial volume flow rate (in L/s) of the oil through the hole?

85. •Water is supplied to an outlet from a pumping station 5.00 km away. From the pumping station to the outlet there is a net vertical rise of 19 m. Take the coefficient of viscosity of water to be 0.0100 poise. The pipe leading from the pumping station to the outlet is 1.00 cm in diameter, and the gauge pressure in the pipe at the point where it exits the pumping station is 520 kPa. At what volume flow rate does water flow from the outlet?

General Problems

86. •Medical The human body contains about 5.0 L of blood that has a density of 1060 kg/m³. Approximately 45% (by mass) of the blood is cells and the rest is plasma.

The density of blood cells is approximately 1125 kg/m³, and about 1% of the cells are white blood cells, the rest being red blood cells. The red blood cells are about 7.5 μm across (modeled as spheres). (a) What is the mass of the blood in a typical human? (b) Approximately how many blood cells (of both types) are in the blood?

87. •In August 2009 a person in Bagnone, Italy, won the largest lottery prize in European history, 146.9 million euros, which at the time was worth 211.8 million U.S. dollars. Gold at the time was worth $953 per troy ounce, and silver was worth $14.16 per troy ounce. A troy ounce is 31.1035 g, the density of gold is 19.3 g/cm³, and the density of silver is 10.5 g/cm³. (a) If the lucky lottery winner opted to be paid in a single cube of pure gold, how high would the cube be? Could he carry it home? (b) What would be the height of a silver cube of the same value? Try to solve this part by using proportional reasoning with the results of part (a) instead of just repeating the same procedure you used in (a).

88. •A hybrid car travels about 50 mi/gal of gasoline. The density of gasoline is 737 kg/m³ and 1 gal equals 3.788 L. Express the car's mileage in miles per kilogram (mi/kg) of gas.

89. •Medical Blood pressure is normally expressed as the ratio of the *systolic* pressure (when the heart just ejects blood) to the *diastolic* pressure (when the heart is relaxed). The measurement is made at the level of the heart (usually at the middle of the

upper arm), and the pressures are given in millimeters of mercury, although the units are not usually written. Normal blood pressure is typically 120/80. How would you write normal blood pressure if the units of pressure used were (a) pascals, (b) atmospheres, or (c) pounds per square inch (lb/in², psi)? (d) Is the blood pressure, as typically stated, the absolute pressure or the gauge pressure? Explain your answer. SSM

90. •Astronomy Evidence from the Mars rover *Discovery* suggests that oceans as deep as 0.50 km once may have existed on Mars. The acceleration due to gravity on Mars is 0.379*g*. (a) If there were any organisms in the Martian ocean in the distant past, what pressure (absolute and gauge) would they have experienced at the bottom, assuming the surface pressure was the same as it is on present-day Earth? Assume that the salinity of Martian oceans was the same as oceans on Earth. (b) If the bottom-dwelling organisms in part (a) were brought from Mars to Earth, how deep could they go in our ocean without exceeding the maximum pressure they experienced on Mars?

91. ••A diver is located 60 m below the surface of the ocean (the specific gravity of seawater is 1.025). To raise a treasure chest that she discovered, the diver inflates a plastic, spherical buoy with her compressed air tanks. The radius of the buoy is inflated to 40 cm. (a) If the treasure chest has a mass of 200 kg, what is the acceleration of the buoy and treasure chest when they are tethered together and released? Assume the chest is 20 cm × 40 cm × 10 cm in size, and neglect the tether's mass and volume. (b) What happens to the radius of the buoy as it ascends in the water? If there are any changes, determine them numerically. How does this change your answer in part (a)?

92. •Medical Blood pressure is normally taken on the upper arm at the level of the heart. Suppose, however, that a patient has both arms in casts so that you cannot take his blood pressure in the usual way. If you have him stand up and take the blood pressure at his calf, which is 95.0 cm below his heart, what would normal blood pressure be? The density of blood is 1060 kg/m³.

93. •Medical A syringe which has an inner diameter of 0.6 mm is attached to a needle with an inner diameter of 0.25 mm. A nurse uses the syringe to inject fluid into a patient's artery where blood pressure is 140/100. Assume the liquid is an ideal fluid. What is the minimum force the nurse needs to apply to the syringe? SSM

94. •A spherical water tank is being filled by a 1-cm-diameter hose. The water in the hose has a uniform speed of 15 cm/s. Meanwhile, the tank springs a leak at the bottom of the sphere. The hole has a diameter of 0.5 cm. Determine the equilibrium level of the water in the tank if water continues flowing through the hose and into the tank at the same rate.

95. •A large water tank is 18 m above the ground (Figure 11-45). Suppose a pipe with a diameter of 8 cm is connected to the tank and leads down to the ground. How fast does the water rush out of the pipe at ground level? Assume that the tank is open to the atmosphere.

Figure 11-45 Problem 95

96. •**Medical** The aorta is approximately 25 mm in diameter. The mean pressure there is about 100 mmHg, and the blood flows through the aorta at approximately 60 cm/s. Suppose that at a certain point a portion of the aorta is blocked so that the cross-sectional area is reduced to 3/4 of its original area. The density of blood is 1060 kg/m^3. (a) How fast is the blood moving just as it enters the blocked portion of the aorta? (b) What is the gauge pressure (in mmHg) of the blood just as it has entered the blocked portion of the aorta?

97. •••An equilateral prism of wood (the specific gravity is 0.6) is placed into a freshwater pool (Figure 11-46). Determine the ratio y_d/y_u of the depth of submersion when the prism is pointed down to the depth of submersion when the prism is pointed up. Assume the prism has a side of s.

Figure 11-46 Problem 97

98. ••**Sports** The air around the spinning baseball in Figure 11-47 (top view) experiences a faster speed on the left than the right side and hence a smaller pressure on the left than the right. Suppose the ball is traveling forward in the x direction at 38.0 m/s and it breaks 15.0 cm to the left in the $-y$ direction (neglect the pull of gravity in the z direction). Determine the pressure difference between the right and left sides of the ball. Assume the ball has a mass of 142 g and a radius of 3.55 cm. In addition, assume it travels at a constant speed of 38 m/s in the x direction from the pitcher's mound to home plate (60.5 ft = 18.44 m). *Hint:* The pressure difference equals the leftward force multiplied by the cross-sectional area of the ball, πr^2.

Figure 11-47 Problem 98

12

Oscillations

In this chapter, your goals are to:

- (12-1) Define oscillation.
- (12-2) Describe the key properties of oscillations, including what makes oscillation happen.
- (12-3) Explain the connection between Hooke's law and the special kind of oscillation called simple harmonic motion.
- (12-4) Discuss how kinetic energy and potential energy vary during an oscillation.
- (12-5) Explain what determines the period, frequency, and angular frequency of a simple pendulum.
- (12-6) Explain what determines the period, frequency, and angular frequency of a physical pendulum.
- (12-7) Describe what happens in underdamped, critically damped, and overdamped oscillations.
- (12-8) Identify the circumstances under which resonance occurs in a forced oscillation.

To master this chapter, you should review:

- (2-4) How to interpret x–t, v_x–t, and a_x–t graphs.
- (6-5, 6-6) The force exerted by an ideal spring that obeys Hooke's law and the potential energy stored in such a spring.
- (3-8, 8-2) The relationships among speed, angular speed, and centripetal acceleration in circular motion.
- (8-6) Newton's second law for rotational motion and how to calculate the torque exerted by a force.

What do you think?

The destructive force of an earthquake results from the side-to-side and up-and-down oscillation of the ground. Consider an earthquake that moves the ground 2.0 mm up and 2.0 mm down, making one up-and-down cycle every 0.80 s. Compared to the maximum acceleration of the ground in this earthquake, what is the maximum acceleration of the ground in a second earthquake that makes the ground move up and down the same distance but takes only 0.40 s per cycle? (a) $\frac{1}{4}$ as great; (b) $\frac{1}{2}$ as great; (c) the same; (d) twice as great; (e) four times as great.

12-1 We live in a world of oscillations

Try sitting by yourself in your room and keeping absolutely still. If no one else is in the room, it may seem as though there is no motion anywhere around you. Not so! Your heart is in continuous motion, pulsing at a rate of about one cycle per second. Your eardrums are also vibrating softly in response to the sound of your breathing. And in the electrical wires within the walls of your room, electrons move back and forth about 60 times per second as part of the processes that supply energy to the room lights, your computer, and other appliances. These are just three examples of a kind of motion called **oscillation,** in which an object moves back and forth around a position of *equilibrium*—that is, a point at which it experiences zero net force. (We introduced the idea of equilibrium in Section 4-3.) As an example, your eardrum is in equilibrium when it is relaxed and displaced neither inward nor outward. Figure 12-1 shows three examples of oscillations in nature and technology.

Figure 12-1 **Oscillations** The kind of motion that we call oscillation is commonplace (a) in nature, (b) in technology, and (c) in medicine.

The wings of common hummingbirds oscillate up and down about 50 times per second.

(a)

The timekeeper at the heart of most wristwatches is a tiny piece of quartz that oscillates 32,768 times per second.

(b)

This MRI image is made by mapping how protons oscillate within molecules in the brain in response to radio waves.

(c)

We'll begin this chapter by studying the causes of oscillation. We'll find that oscillation is possible only when an object experiences a *restoring force*—one that always pushes or pulls the object toward the equilibrium position. We'll find that the oscillations are of a particularly simple nature if the restoring force is directly proportional to how far the object is displaced from equilibrium. This proves to be an important special case that's a very good approximation to many kinds of oscillation.

Just as for other kinds of motion, we'll find that it's useful to describe oscillations in terms of kinetic and potential energy. We'll see that this approach gives us important insights into what happens during oscillations. The energy approach will also help us to understand the role of *damping* in oscillations—for example, what happens to make the oscillations of a swinging pendulum die out, so that the pendulum eventually ends up at rest. Finally, we'll examine *forced* oscillations, in which a rhythmic force is applied to an object to sustain its oscillations even when damping is present. The ideas of forced oscillation will help us understand how the right kind of sound can break a wine glass, how some insects fly, and why architects must design buildings to avoid catastrophic vibrations.

Take-Home Message for Section 12-1

✔ Oscillation is a kind of motion in which an object moves back and forth around an equilibrium position.

12-2 Oscillations are caused by the interplay between a restoring force and inertia

Figure 12-2 shows one of the simplest ways to make an object oscillate. A block is attached to a horizontal spring and is free to slide back and forth. (For simplicity, we'll assume that there's no friction between the block and the surface over which it slides.) We'll call the horizontal direction along which the block can move the x axis, and let $x = 0$ be the point at which the spring is relaxed (Figure 12-2a). Then the quantity x represents the *position* of the block as well as the *displacement* of the block from equilibrium.

When the spring is stretched, corresponding to $x > 0$, it exerts a force on the block that points in the negative x direction so $F_x < 0$ (Figure 12-2b). If instead the spring is compressed, corresponding to $x < 0$, it exerts a force on the block that points in the positive x direction so $F_x > 0$ (Figure 12-2c). In other words, no matter which way the block is displaced from equilibrium, the spring exerts a force that tends to pull or push the block back toward the equilibrium position. A force of this kind is called a **restoring force**.

To start the block in Figure 12-2 oscillating, move the block so as to stretch the spring by a distance A, then release it (Figure 12-3a). The restoring force of the spring pulls the block back toward the equilibrium position at $x = 0$, so the block accelerates and continues to gain speed as it moves back toward equilibrium (Figure 12-3b). The block reaches its maximum speed as it passes through equilibrium (Figure 12-3c). Even though there is zero net force on the block at the equilibrium position, the block's inertia causes it to overshoot this point. As a result, the block compresses the spring, so the

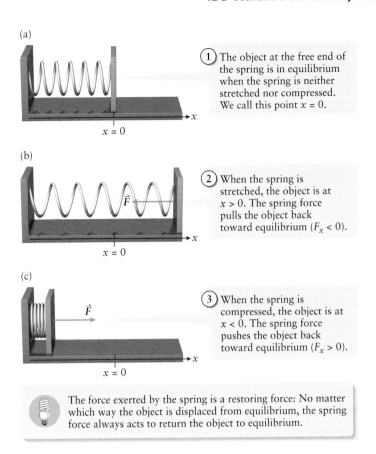

(a)

① The object at the free end of the spring is in equilibrium when the spring is neither stretched nor compressed. We call this point $x = 0$.

$x = 0$

(b)

② When the spring is stretched, the object is at $x > 0$. The spring force pulls the object back toward equilibrium ($F_x < 0$).

$x = 0$

(c)

③ When the spring is compressed, the object is at $x < 0$. The spring force pushes the object back toward equilibrium ($F_x > 0$).

$x = 0$

The force exerted by the spring is a restoring force: No matter which way the object is displaced from equilibrium, the spring force always acts to return the object to equilibrium.

Figure 12-2 **A restoring force** In order for oscillations to take place, there must be a force that always acts to return the oscillating object to equilibrium.

restoring force is now directed opposite to the block's motion as it slows down (Figure 12-3d). Thus, the block eventually comes momentarily to rest with the spring compressed (Figure 12-3e). The restoring force of the spring still acts, so the block again starts moving and gains speed as it heads back toward the equilibrium position (Figure 12-3f). The object reaches equilibrium a second time and again overshoots the equilibrium position (Figure 12-3g). The block stretches the spring as it overshoots, and the restoring force causes the block to slow down (Figure 12-3h). The block ends up once again at its initial position with zero speed (Figure 12-3i). The cycle then repeats. If there is no friction, the oscillation will go on forever!

Not every oscillation involves a spring, but *every* oscillation follows the same general sequence of steps as in Figure 12-3. This figure shows that the two key ingredients for oscillation are a restoring force that always draws the oscillating object back toward the equilibrium position, and inertia that causes the object to overshoot equilibrium.

Oscillation Period and Frequency

The time for one complete cycle of an oscillation is called the **period** of the oscillation. We'll use the symbol T for period. Intuition should tell you that a stiffer spring (which will exert a stronger restoring force) will push and pull the block more rapidly through the steps shown in Figure 12-3 and so will cause the period to be shorter. That same intuition will tell you that a more massive block, which has more inertia, will go through the steps more slowly and hence have a longer period. We'll verify that these ideas are correct later in this section.

A quantity related to the oscillation period is the **frequency** f of the oscillation. The frequency is equal to the number of cycles per unit time. The unit of frequency is the **hertz** (abbreviated Hz): 1 Hz = 1 cycle per second. A pendulum that oscillates once per second has a frequency $f = 1$ Hz. If you play the A4 key on a piano (A above middle C, also called "concert A"), the piano string vibrates 440 times per second, so the frequency is $f = 440$ Hz. The vibrating string compresses the air at this same frequency, which is the frequency of sound that you hear.

Figure 12-3 A cycle of oscillation
Nine stages in the oscillation of a block attached to a spring.

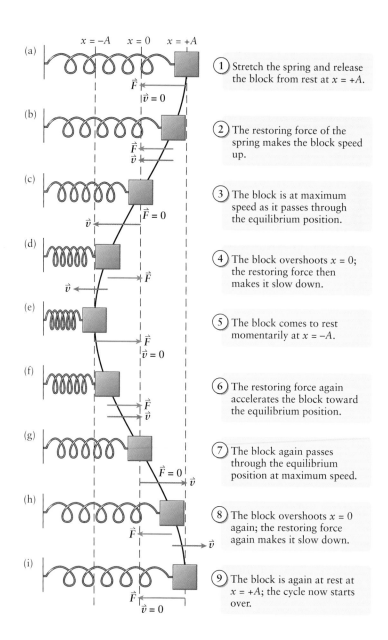

$x = -A$ $x = 0$ $x = +A$

(a)

$\vec{F}$
$|\vec{v} = 0$

① Stretch the spring and release the block from rest at $x = +A$.

(b)

$\vec{F}$
$\vec{v}$

② The restoring force of the spring makes the block speed up.

(c)

$\vec{v}$
$|\vec{F} = 0$

③ The block is at maximum speed as it passes through the equilibrium position.

(d)

$\vec{v}$
$\vec{F}$

④ The block overshoots $x = 0$; the restoring force then makes it slow down.

(e)

$\vec{F}$
$|\vec{v} = 0$

⑤ The block comes to rest momentarily at $x = -A$.

(f)

$\vec{F}$
$\vec{v}$

⑥ The restoring force again accelerates the block toward the equilibrium position.

(g)

$\vec{F} = 0$ $\vec{v}$

⑦ The block again passes through the equilibrium position at maximum speed.

(h)

$\vec{F}$
$\vec{v}$

⑧ The block overshoots $x = 0$ again; the restoring force again makes it slow down.

(i)

$\vec{F}$
$\vec{v} = 0$

⑨ The block is again at rest at $x = +A$; the cycle now starts over.

Since period T is the number of seconds that elapse per cycle and frequency f is the number of cycles that happen per second, it follows that these quantities are the reciprocals of each other:

Frequency and period
(12-1)

Period T of an oscillation

$$f = \frac{1}{T} \quad \text{and} \quad T = \frac{1}{f}$$

Frequency f of the oscillation

Example 12-1 Frequency and Period

(a) What is the oscillation period of your eardrum when you are listening to the A4 note on a piano (frequency 440 Hz)? (b) A bottle floating in the ocean bobs up and down once every 2.00 min. What is the frequency of this oscillation?

Set Up

We'll use Equation 12-1 to find the period T from the frequency f and vice versa.

Frequency and period:

$$f = \frac{1}{T} \quad \text{and} \quad T = \frac{1}{f} \qquad (12\text{-}1)$$

Solve

(a) The period of this oscillation is the reciprocal of the frequency. Note that a cycle is not a true unit but simply a way of counting, so we can remove it from the final answer as needed.

$$T = \frac{1}{f} = \frac{1}{440\ \text{Hz}} = \frac{1}{440\ \text{cycles/s}} = \frac{1}{440}\frac{\text{s}}{\text{cycle}}$$
$$= 2.27 \times 10^{-3}\ \text{s}$$

(b) The frequency of this oscillation is the reciprocal of the period. To get a result in Hz, we must first convert the period to seconds. Note that the period is the number of seconds per cycle, so we can add "cycle" to the calculation as needed.

$$T = 2.00\ \text{min} \times \frac{60\ \text{s}}{1\ \text{min}} = 120\ \text{s}$$
$$f = \frac{1}{T} = \frac{1}{120\ \text{s}} = \frac{1}{120\ \text{s/cycle}} = \frac{1}{120}\frac{\text{cycle}}{\text{s}}$$
$$= 8.33 \times 10^{-3}\ \text{Hz}$$

Reflect

Since frequency and period are the reciprocals of each other, a large value of f (high frequency) corresponds to a small value of T (short period) as in (a) and a small value of f (low frequency) corresponds to a large value of T (long period) as in (b).

Oscillation Amplitude

If the spring in Figures 12-2 and 12-3 exerts the same magnitude of force when it is stretched a certain distance as when it is compressed the same distance, the block in Figure 12-3 will move as far to the left of equilibrium ($x < 0$) as it does to the right of equilibrium ($x > 0$). In this chapter we'll consider only restoring forces that have this symmetric property. In this case the block will oscillate between $x = +A$ and $x = -A$, as shown in Figure 12-3. The distance A is called the **amplitude** of the oscillation. It's equal to the maximum displacement of the object from equilibrium. The amplitude is *always* a positive number, never a negative one.

> **! Watch Out! The amplitude of oscillation is the maximum displacement from equilibrium.**
>
> It's tempting to think of amplitude as the distance from where the spring is stretched the most (Figure 12-3a) to where the spring is compressed the most (Figure 12-3e). That's not correct: The amplitude A equals the distance from the *equilibrium* position to the point of maximum stretch, and it also equals the distance from the equilibrium position to the point of maximum compression. Keep this principle in mind to avoid giving answers that are wrong by a factor of 2.

Period, frequency, and amplitude are just part of a complete description of an oscillation. In the following section we'll see how to get such a complete description for an important special kind of oscillation.

> **? Got the Concept? 12-1** **Heartbeats**
>
> Jess has a resting pulse of 50 heartbeats per minute. When Jess sprints down the track, her pulse increases to 150 beats per minute. Compared to when she is at rest, the oscillation period of her heart when she is sprinting is (a) 9 times as great; (b) 3 times as great; (c) the same; (d) 1/3 as great; (e) 1/9 as great.

Take-Home Message for Section 12-2

✔ Oscillation is caused by a restoring force that returns an object to its equilibrium position (where it experiences zero net force) and by inertia that makes the object overshoot equilibrium.

✔ The period of an oscillation is the time for one complete cycle. The frequency, which is the reciprocal of the period, is the number of cycles per second.

✔ The amplitude of an oscillation equals the maximum displacement from equilibrium.

12-3 The simplest form of oscillation occurs when the restoring force obeys Hooke's law

To have a complete description of what happens during an oscillation, we need to know the position, velocity, and acceleration of the oscillating object at all times during its motion. We can actually find these for the case in which the restoring force is *directly proportional* to the distance that the object is displaced from equilibrium. This relationship is called **Hooke's law** for the force exerted by an ideal spring (Section 6-5). Hooke's law is important because experiment shows that if you stretch a spring by a relatively small amount, the force that the spring exerts on you is directly proportional to the amount of stretch:

Force exerted by an ideal spring   Spring constant of the spring (a measure of its stiffness)

Hooke's law
(6-11)

$$F_x = -kx$$

Extension of the spring ($x > 0$ if spring is stretched, $x < 0$ if spring is compressed)

The minus sign in Equation 6-11 tells us that if the spring is stretched, $x > 0$, it exerts a force in the negative x direction so $F_x < 0$. It also tells us that if the spring is compressed, $x < 0$, it exerts a force in the positive x direction so $F_x > 0$. That's exactly the relationship between displacement x and spring force F_x shown in Figure 6-17.

As we did in Section 6-5, we'll call a spring that obeys Equation 6-11 an *ideal* spring. Real springs deviate from Hooke's law a little. But experiment shows that if the value of x is kept small enough, so that the oscillations have small amplitude, almost every spring obeys Hooke's law quite faithfully.

If the spring in Figures 12-2 and 12-3 is an ideal one, then the net force on the block in Figures 12-2 and 12-3 is equal to the spring force given by Equation 6-11. (There's also a downward gravitational force on the block plus an upward normal force exerted by the surface over which it slides. But these forces cancel each other so that the net force on the block has zero vertical component.) Newton's second law for the x motion of the block tells us that this net force is equal to the mass m of the block multiplied by the block's acceleration a_x:

$$-kx = ma_x$$

If we divide both sides of this equation by the mass m of the block, we get

(12-2)
$$a_x = -\left(\frac{k}{m}\right)x$$

Equation 12-2 tells us that *if a block oscillates because it is attached to an ideal spring that obeys Hooke's law, the acceleration of the block is proportional to the negative of the displacement*. The acceleration is negative when the displacement x is positive, positive when the displacement is negative, and zero when the displacement is zero (that is, when the block is at equilibrium).

Because the acceleration of the block is not constant, we *cannot* describe the motion of the block in Figure 12-3 using the equations from Chapter 2 for straight-line motion with constant acceleration. (Those are nice, simple equations, but they simply don't apply here.) Instead we'll have to solve Equation 12-2 to find x, v_x, and a_x as functions of time t. This sounds like a complicated mathematical problem, but it turns out that we can solve it by using what we know about another, seemingly unrelated kind of motion: an object moving around a circle at constant speed.

Uniform Circular Motion and Hooke's Law

Figure 12-4a shows an object of mass m moving at constant speed v around a circular path of radius A. (We'll see shortly why we choose this symbol for radius.) The object travels once around the circle, an angle of 2π radians, in a time T, so the object's constant *angular* speed is $\omega = 2\pi/T$.

How does this uniform circular motion relate to oscillation? Imagine that you view the circular path edge-on, so that all you can see is the x component of the object's

(a)

① An object of mass m moves at a constant speed around a circle of radius A. It completes one trip around the circle in time T.

② The angular speed of the object is $\omega = 2\pi/T$. The angle θ increases at a rate ω: $\theta = \omega t + \phi$ (ϕ is the value of θ at $t = 0$).

③ If you view the object's motion edge-on...

④ ...you'll see the object oscillating back and forth between $x = +A$ and $x = -A$.

(b)

The x component of uniform circular motion looks like straight-line oscillation around an equilibrium position at $x = 0$.

Figure 12-4 **Oscillation and uniform circular motion** If you look at one component of uniform circular motion, what you see is an oscillation.

motion (Figure 12-4b). From this vantage point you'll see the object oscillating back and forth along a straight-line path, moving a distance A to the left of center and the same distance A to the right of center (Figure 12-4b). The object will take a time T for one back-and-forth cycle. So what you'll see is the object moving in the same way as the block on a spring in Figure 12-3, with period T and amplitude A.

Let's show that the x component of the uniform circular motion obeys Equation 12-2, so that the x component of the object's acceleration is proportional to the object's x coordinate. To do this, we'll use three important facts about uniform circular motion. From Section 8-2 the *linear* speed v of an object in uniform circular motion is equal to the *angular* speed ω multiplied by the radius of the circle. The radius of the circle in Figure 12-4a is A, so the speed of the object's circular motion is

$$v = \omega A \tag{12-3}$$

We also know from Section 3-8 that an object in uniform circular motion has a centripetal acceleration (that is, an acceleration directed toward the center of the circle). This acceleration has a constant magnitude a_{cent} equal to the square of the speed v divided by the radius of the circle, which in this case is equal to A. Using Equation 12-3, we can write the magnitude of the centripetal acceleration as

$$a_{\text{cent}} = \frac{v^2}{A} = \frac{(\omega A)^2}{A} = \frac{\omega^2 A^2}{A} = \omega^2 A \tag{12-4}$$

Finally, from Equation 8-18 we have the following equation for the angle θ from the positive x axis for the angular position of an object at time t, assuming that the object has constant angular acceleration:

$$\theta = \theta_0 + \omega_{0z}t + \frac{1}{2}\alpha_z t^2 \tag{8-18}$$

In Equation 8-18 α_z is the angular acceleration of the object, which is indeed constant in this case: The constant is zero because the motion is uniform and the angular velocity is constant. The quantity ω_{0z} is the initial angular velocity of the object, which is equal to the object's constant angular speed ω. (Figure 12-4a shows that the object moves around the circle in the positive, counterclockwise direction, so the angular velocity is positive and equal to the angular speed.) The angle θ_0 is the value of θ at time $t = 0$; we'll use the symbol ϕ (the Greek letter "phi") for this quantity. Then we can write Equation 8-18 as $\theta - \phi = \omega t$, or

$$\theta = \omega t + \phi \tag{12-5}$$

Now let's put all of these pieces together. Figure 12-5a shows that the x coordinate of the object as it moves around the circle is $x = A \cos \theta$. From Equation 12-5, we can

(a)
① The vector from the center of the circle to the object has length A and is at an angle θ from the $+x$ axis.

② The x coordinate of the object is $x = A \cos \theta = A \cos (\omega t + \phi)$.

(b)
③ The object's velocity vector has magnitude $v = \omega A$ and is at an angle $90° + \theta$ from the $+x$ axis.

④ The x component of the object's velocity is
$v_x = v \cos (90° + \theta) = -v \sin \theta$
or $v_x = -\omega A \sin (\omega t + \phi)$.

(c)
⑤ The object's acceleration vector has magnitude $a_{cent} = \omega^2 A$ and is at an angle $180° + \theta$ from the $+x$ axis.

⑥ The x component of the object's acceleration is
$a_x = a_{cent} \cos (180° + \theta) = -a_{cent} \cos \theta$
or $a_x = -\omega^2 A \cos (\omega t + \phi)$.

 Compare the equations for x and a_x: You'll see that $a_x = -\omega^2 x$. That's the same relationship as for Hooke's law, $a_x = -(k/m)x$, with $\omega^2 = k/m$. So the x component of uniform circular motion is the same as the simple harmonic motion of an object oscillating on the end of an ideal, Hooke's law spring.

Figure 12-5 Oscillation, uniform circular motion, and Hooke's law Finding the x components of the position, velocity, and acceleration in uniform circular motion reveals an important connection to simple harmonic motion.

write this as

$$(12\text{-}6) \qquad x = A \cos (\omega t + \phi)$$

Figure 12-5b shows that the x velocity of the object is $v_x = -v \sin \theta$. From Equation 12-3 and Equation 12-5, we can write this as

$$(12\text{-}7) \qquad v_x = -\omega A \sin (\omega t + \phi)$$

From Figure 12-5c, the x acceleration of the object is $a_x = -a_{cent} \cos \theta$. Equation 12-4 and Equation 12-5 together tell us that we can write the x acceleration as

$$(12\text{-}8) \qquad a_x = -\omega^2 A \cos (\omega t + \phi)$$

√x̄ *See the Math Tutorial for more information on trigonometry*

Here's the payoff for all of this mathematics: If we compare Equation 12-6 and Equation 12-8, we see that the x acceleration of an object in uniform circular motion is directly proportional to the object's x coordinate:

$$(12\text{-}9) \qquad a_x = -\omega^2 x$$

That's *precisely* the relationship between acceleration a_x and displacement x that we found for an object of mass m attached to a spring with spring constant k that obeys Hooke's law: $a_x = -(k/m)x$ (Equation 12-2). The two equations are identical if we set the square of the angular speed ω in Figure 12-4 and Figure 12-5 equal to the ratio of the quantities k/m:

$$(12\text{-}10) \qquad \omega^2 = \frac{k}{m} \quad \text{or} \quad \omega = \sqrt{\frac{k}{m}}$$

In other words, Equation 12-9 and Equation 12-10 tell us something quite profound and unexpected: *A block of mass m attached to an ideal, Hooke's law spring of spring constant k, oscillates in precisely the same way as the x coordinate of an object in uniform circular motion with angular speed ω, provided that $\omega = \sqrt{k/m}$.* We made the detour into analyzing uniform circular motion so that we could arrive at this insight.

With this observation in mind, we can now go back and write a complete description of how an object oscillates when acted on by a restoring force that obeys Hooke's law.

Simple Harmonic Motion: Angular Frequency, Period, and Frequency

We've seen that the period T of the oscillation in Figure 12-4b is the same as the time T that it takes the object in uniform circular motion in Figure 12-4a to travel once around the circle. The angular speed ω equals $2\pi/T$, so T equals $2\pi/\omega$. Using Equation 12-10 for the value of ω along with Equation 12-1 for the relationship between period T and frequency f, we get the following results for the oscillations of a block of mass m attached to an ideal, Hooke's law spring of spring constant k:

Angular frequency
$$\omega = \sqrt{\frac{k}{m}}$$

k = Spring constant of the spring

m = Mass of the object connected to the spring

Period
$$T = \frac{2\pi}{\omega} = 2\pi\sqrt{\frac{m}{k}}$$

Frequency
$$f = \frac{1}{T} = \frac{1}{2\pi}\sqrt{\frac{k}{m}} = \frac{\omega}{2\pi}$$

Angular frequency, period, and frequency for a block attached to an ideal spring
(12-11)

In the first of Equations 12-11 we've introduced a new quantity called the **angular frequency**. We give this the same symbol as the angular *speed* of the circular motion in Figure 12-4, and indeed it has the same value as the angular speed. That's because our analysis of Figure 12-4 showed that the back-and-forth motion of a block attached to an ideal spring is equivalent to the x component of uniform circular motion. If you find this confusing to remember, just keep in mind that the ordinary frequency f equals $\omega/2\pi$, or equivalently $\omega = 2\pi f$ (see the third of Equations 12-11). As we'll see, the quantity ω appears naturally in the equations for oscillation, which is why we use it.

The second of Equations 12-11 tells us that the period of oscillation T is proportional to the square root of the mass m and inversely proportional to the square root of the spring constant k. This means that increasing the mass m makes the period longer, while increasing the spring constant k makes the period shorter. That's exactly what we predicted in Section 12-2 for the oscillations of a block attached to a spring. The last of Equations 12-11 is just the statement that the frequency f is the reciprocal of the period T. This equation says that increasing the mass causes the frequency to decrease, while increasing the spring constant makes the frequency increase.

Just as important as what ω, T, and f depend on is what they do *not* depend on. Note that the amplitude A does not appear in Equations 12-11, which means that the angular frequency, period, and frequency of an oscillation are *independent* of the amplitude if the restoring force obeys Hooke's law. This property is called the **harmonic property**. This may come as a surprise, since doubling the amplitude means the oscillating object has to cover twice as much distance during an oscillation and so should take a longer time to complete an oscillation. But doubling the amplitude also means that the object reaches larger displacements x and so experiences a stronger Hooke's law restoring force $F_x = -kx$. This effect makes the object move faster during the oscillation. The net result is that the period T, the time for one oscillation, is unaffected by changing the amplitude. That means the frequency $f = 1/T$ and the angular frequency $\omega = 2\pi f = 2\pi/T$ are unaffected as well. This is *only* the case if the restoring force obeys Hooke's law. If the restoring force depends on displacement in a different way, the oscillations do not have the harmonic property.

The word "harmonic" sounds like a musical term, and indeed the harmonic property is important in musical instruments. We'll learn in Chapter 13 that the pitch of a musical sound is determined primarily by the frequency of oscillation of the musical instrument that makes the sound, while the loudness of the sound is determined primarily by the amplitude. If changing the amplitude caused a change in frequency, playing the same key on a piano would make a different pitch if you pressed the key softly or pushed hard on the key. That would render a piano almost completely useless. But because the strings of a piano have the harmonic property, they vibrate and have the same frequency, producing sounds of the same pitch whether they are played soft or loud.

As we've described, the harmonic property is a direct result of the restoring force being directly proportional to the displacement from equilibrium (Hooke's law, Equation 6-11). For this reason the kind of oscillation that results from a Hooke's law restoring force is called **simple harmonic motion (SHM)**. Later in this chapter we'll encounter kinds of oscillations that are not simple harmonic motion; the oscillations of a pendulum are one example. We'll see that in many such cases, however, these kinds of oscillations are *approximately* SHM if the amplitude of oscillation is sufficiently small.

> **Watch Out!** **Simple harmonic motion is not the same as circular motion.**
>
> Even though we describe simple harmonic motion in terms of an *angular* frequency, the oscillating object is *not* actually moving in a circle! As we've seen, we can *visualize* simple harmonic motion as one component of the motion of an object moving in a circle with an angular speed ω, but there doesn't need to be an object that's actually moving in a circle.

Example 12-2 SHM I: Angular Frequency, Period, and Frequency

An object of mass 0.80 kg is attached to an ideal horizontal spring of spring constant 1.8×10^2 N/m and set into oscillation as in Figure 12-3. (a) Calculate the angular frequency, period, and frequency of the object. (b) Calculate the angular frequency, period, and frequency if the mass of the object is quadrupled to 4×0.80 kg = 3.2 kg.

Set Up

The spring is ideal and therefore obeys Hooke's law, so the oscillations are simple harmonic motion. This means that in part (a) we can use Equations 12-11 to calculate the angular frequency ω, period T, and frequency f from the spring constant $k = 1.8 \times 10^2$ N/m and the mass $m = 0.80$ kg. Note that ω and f are both inversely proportional to the square root of m, while T is directly proportional to the square root of m. In part (b) we'll use these relationships to determine how the values of ω, T, and f change when we change the value of the mass m.

Angular frequency, period, and frequency:

$$\omega = \sqrt{\frac{k}{m}}$$

$$T = \frac{2\pi}{\omega} = 2\pi\sqrt{\frac{m}{k}}$$

$$f = \frac{1}{T} = \frac{1}{2\pi}\sqrt{\frac{k}{m}} = \frac{\omega}{2\pi} \qquad (12\text{-}11)$$

Solve

(a) Substitute the given values for the mass m and spring constant k into the first of Equations 12-11 to calculate the angular frequency.

$$\omega = \sqrt{\frac{k}{m}} = \sqrt{\frac{1.8 \times 10^2 \text{ N/m}}{0.80 \text{ kg}}}$$

Recall that $1 \text{ N} = 1 \text{ kg} \cdot \text{m/s}^2$, so

$$\frac{1 \text{ N/m}}{\text{kg}} = \frac{1 \text{ kg/s}^2}{\text{kg}} = \frac{1}{\text{s}^2} = \frac{1 \text{ rad}^2}{\text{s}^2}$$

(A radian is a way of counting, not a true unit, so we can insert it or remove it as needed.) Then

$$\omega = \sqrt{\frac{k}{m}} = \sqrt{\frac{1.8 \times 10^2}{0.80} \frac{\text{rad}^2}{\text{s}^2}} = 15 \text{ rad/s}$$

Then use the second and third of Equations 12-11 to find the period and frequency.

If the angular frequency ω is in rad/s, the period T will be in s:

$$T = \frac{2\pi}{\omega} = \frac{2\pi}{15 \text{ rad/s}} = 0.42 \text{ s}$$

The reciprocal of the period in s is the frequency in Hz:

$$f = \frac{1}{T} = \frac{1}{0.42 \text{ s}} = 2.4 \text{ Hz}$$

(b) We could substitute the new value of the mass m into Equations 12-11 to find the new values of ω, T, and f. Instead, we use proportional reasoning to find the new values from the old ones.

The relationships $\omega = \sqrt{\dfrac{k}{m}}$ and $f = \dfrac{1}{2\pi}\sqrt{\dfrac{k}{m}}$ tell us that the angular frequency and the frequency are inversely proportional to the square root of the mass. The new mass is 4 times greater than the old mass, so the new values of ω and f are $1/\sqrt{4} = 1/2$ the old values:

$$\omega_{\text{new}} = \frac{\omega_{\text{old}}}{\sqrt{4}} = \frac{\omega_{\text{old}}}{2} = \frac{15 \text{ rad/s}}{2} = 7.5 \text{ rad/s}$$

$$f_{new} = \frac{f_{old}}{2} = \frac{2.4 \text{ Hz}}{2} = 1.2 \text{ Hz}$$

In the same way, the relationship $T = 2\pi\sqrt{\dfrac{m}{k}}$ tells us that the period T is directly proportional to the square root of the mass. Again the mass has increased by a factor of 4, so the new period is

$$T_{new} = \sqrt{4}\, T_{old} = 2T_{old} = 2(0.42 \text{ s}) = 0.84 \text{ s}$$

Reflect

Our results show that when the mass of the oscillating object increases, the frequency decreases and the period increases. You can check our results by confirming that f_{new} is equal to $\omega_{new}/2\pi$ and that T_{new} is equal to $1/f_{new}$. Are both of these statements true?

Simple Harmonic Motion: Position, Velocity, and Acceleration

Let's now look in more detail at the position x, velocity v_x, and acceleration a_x of an object moving in simple harmonic motion. From Equation 12-6, the position is given by

Position of an object in SHM at time t

Amplitude of the oscillation = maximum displacement from the equilibrium position

$$x = A\cos(\omega t + \phi)$$

Angular frequency of the oscillation $(\omega = 2\pi f = 2\pi/T)$

Phase angle

Position as a function of time for simple harmonic motion

(12-12)

Let's see what Equation 12-12 tells us. The cosine function has values from $+1$ to -1. So Equation 12-12 says that the value of x varies from $x = A$ (when the oscillating object is at its most positive displacement from equilibrium) through $x = 0$ (the equilibrium position) to $x = -A$ (when the object is at its most negative displacement from equilibrium). The cosine is one of the simplest of all oscillating functions, which helps justify the name *simple* harmonic motion. The cosine and sine functions are called **sinusoidal functions** (from the Latin word *sinus*, meaning "bent" or "curved") because of their shape.

The angular frequency ω is measured in rad/s and time t is measured in s, so the product ωt in Equation 12-12 is in radians—just as the argument of the cosine function should be. One cycle of oscillation lasts a time T, over which time the product ωt varies from 0 at $t = 0$ to ωT at $t = T$. But since $T = 2\pi/\omega$ from the second of Equations 12-11, it follows that $\omega T = \omega(2\pi/\omega) = 2\pi$. So over the course of one cycle the value of ωt varies from 0 to $\omega T = 2\pi$. The cosine function goes through one complete cycle when its value increases by 2π, so this tells us that the position x goes through one complete cycle when the time increases by T. That's just what we mean by saying that T is the period of the oscillation.

The one quantity in Equation 12-12 that seems a bit mysterious is the **phase angle** ϕ, which is measured in radians. To explain its significance, recall from our comparison between uniform circular motion and oscillation that ϕ represents the angular position at $t = 0$ of an object in uniform circular motion. For oscillation, the value of ϕ tells us where in the oscillation cycle the object is at $t = 0$. As an example, if $\phi = 0$ Equation 12-12 becomes

$$x = A\cos\omega t \text{ (simple harmonic motion, phase angle } \phi = 0) \qquad (12\text{-}13)$$

Figure 12-6a is the x–t graph that corresponds to Equation 12-13. This graph of x versus t is an ordinary cosine function, which has its most positive value ($x = +A$) when the argument of the function is zero (at $t = 0$) and its most negative value ($x = -A$) one-half cycle later (at $t = T/2$). You can see that the slope of this x–t graph is zero at

(a)

(1) The blue curve graphs the first full cycle of the function $x = A \cos \omega t$, from $t = 0$ to $t = T$. This corresponds to values of ωt from $\omega t = 0$ to $\omega t = \omega T = (2\pi/T)T = 2\pi$.

$t = T/2$
$\omega t = \pi$

$t = T$
$\omega t = 2\pi$

(2) With $x = A \cos \omega t$, the value of x at $t = 0$ is A.

(3) To graph the function $x = A \cos (\omega t + \phi)$, just shift the axes to the right by a distance that corresponds to $\omega t = \phi$.

(b)

$t = T/2$
$\omega t = \pi$

$\omega t = \phi$

$t = T$
$\omega t = 2\pi$

(4) With $x = A \cos (\omega t + \phi)$, the value of x at $t = 0$ is $A \cos \phi$.

Figure 12-6 **Phase angle** The two cycles shown in blue differ by a phase angle ϕ.

$t = 0$, which means that the object has zero velocity at $t = 0$. In other words, the value $\phi = 0$ corresponds to starting the object at rest at $t = 0$ at the position $x = A$. That's just the motion that we depicted in Figure 12-3.

By comparison, Figure 12-6b is the graph that corresponds to Equation 12-12, $x = A \cos (\omega t + \phi)$, for a case in which ϕ is *not* zero but has a positive value. As the figure shows, you can think of the phase angle as shifting the axes to the right if ϕ is positive, as in Figure 12-6b, or to the left when ϕ is negative. Note that in this x–t graph the value of x at $t = 0$ is *not* $+A$; rather, from Equation 12-12 it is equal to

$$x(0) = A \cos (0 + \phi) = A \cos \phi$$

So for an object in simple harmonic motion the value of the phase angle ϕ tells you the point in the oscillation cycle that corresponds to $t = 0$. Note that Figures 12-6a and 12-6b really depict the *same* oscillation, with the same amplitude A and period T; the only difference is the point in the cycle that we call $t = 0$.

The phase angle also appears in the expressions for velocity and acceleration in simple harmonic motion (Equations 12-7 and 12-8), which we found by analogy with uniform circular motion:

Velocity as a function of time for simple harmonic motion (12-14)

Velocity of an object in SHM at time t

Amplitude of the oscillation = maximum displacement from the equilibrium position

$$v_x = -\omega A \sin (\omega t + \phi)$$

Angular frequency of the oscillation ($\omega = 2\pi f = 2\pi/T$)   **Phase angle**

Acceleration as a function of time for simple harmonic motion (12-15)

Acceleration of an object in SHM at time t

Amplitude of the oscillation = maximum displacement from the equilibrium position

$$a_x = -\omega^2 A \cos (\omega t + \phi)$$

Angular frequency of the oscillation ($\omega = 2\pi f = 2\pi/T$)   **Phase angle**

In the case $\phi = 0$, Equations 12-14 and 12-15 become

(12-16)

$$v_x = -\omega A \sin \omega t$$
$$a_x = -\omega^2 A \cos \omega t$$

(simple harmonic motion, phase angle $\phi = 0$)

Figure 12-7 graphs x versus t from Equation 12-13 as well as v_x versus t and a_x versus t from Equations 12-16. In this case the x–t graph is a cosine function, the v_x–t graph is a negative sine function and the a_x–t graph is a negative cosine function. You can confirm that these graphs are consistent with each other by recalling from Section 2-4 that the slope of the x–t graph equals the velocity v_x and the slope of the v_x–t graph equals the acceleration a_x. Note also that the a_x–t graph looks like the negative of the x–t graph. That's what we expect from Hooke's law, $a_x = -(k/m)x$ (Equation 12-2), which tells us that the acceleration in simple harmonic motion is proportional to the negative of the displacement x.

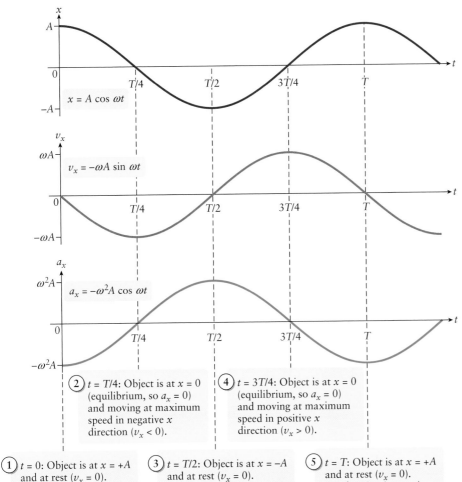

1) $t = 0$: Object is at $x = +A$ and at rest ($v_x = 0$). Acceleration is negative (toward $x = 0$).

2) $t = T/4$: Object is at $x = 0$ (equilibrium, so $a_x = 0$) and moving at maximum speed in negative x direction ($v_x < 0$).

3) $t = T/2$: Object is at $x = -A$ and at rest ($v_x = 0$). Acceleration is positive (toward $x = 0$).

4) $t = 3T/4$: Object is at $x = 0$ (equilibrium, so $a_x = 0$) and moving at maximum speed in positive x direction ($v_x > 0$).

5) $t = T$: Object is at $x = +A$ and at rest ($v_x = 0$). Acceleration is negative (toward $x = 0$).

Figure 12-7 Displacement, velocity, and acceleration in SHM These graphs show displacement x (Equation 12-13) as well as velocity v_x and acceleration a_x (Equations 12-16) for simple harmonic motion for the case $\phi = 0$. Compare to Figure 12-3, which shows the same motion.

If the phase angle ϕ is not equal to zero, the vertical axes of all of the graphs in Figure 12-7 are shifted to the left or right as in Figure 12-6. In this case the velocity at $t = 0$ is equal to

$$v_x(0) = -\omega A \sin(0 + \phi) = -\omega A \sin \phi$$

If $\phi = 0$, the velocity at $t = 0$ is zero and the oscillating object is at rest at that instant (see Figure 12-7). If ϕ is not zero, at $t = 0$ the velocity may not be zero. Figure 12-6b illustrates this: In this case the x–t graph has a negative slope at $t = 0$, which shows that the velocity at that instant is not zero.

Go to Interactive Exercise 12-1 for more practice dealing with simple harmonic motion

---

Example 12-3 SHM II: Position, Velocity, and Acceleration

As in Example 12-2, an object of mass 0.80 kg is attached to an ideal horizontal spring of spring constant 1.8×10^2 N/m and set into oscillation (see Figure 12-3). The amplitude of the motion is 2.0×10^{-2} m, and the phase angle is $\phi = \pi/2$. (a) Find the maximum speed of the object and the maximum magnitude of its acceleration during the oscillation. (b) Find the position, velocity, and acceleration of the object at $t = 0$. (c) Sketch graphs of the position, velocity, and acceleration of the object as functions of time.

Set Up

We can use the simple harmonic motion equations because the spring is ideal (it obeys Hooke's law). From Example 12-2 we know that the angular frequency is $\omega = \sqrt{k/m} = 15$ rad/s, and we are given

Position as a function of time in SHM:

$$x = A \cos(\omega t + \phi) \qquad (12\text{-}12)$$

Velocity as a function of time in SHM:

$$v_x = -\omega A \sin(\omega t + \phi) \qquad (12\text{-}14)$$

the values of the amplitude $A = 2.0 \times 10^{-2}$ m and the phase angle $\phi = \pi/2$. Notice that a_x from Equation 12-15 is equal to $-\omega^2$ times x from Equation 12-12.

Acceleration as a function of time in SHM:

$$a_x = -\omega^2 A \cos(\omega t + \phi) \qquad (12\text{-}15)$$

Solve

(a) Equation 12-14 tells us the velocity v_x as a function of time. The sine function has values from $+1$ to -1, so v_x has values from $+\omega A$ to $-\omega A$. The maximum speed is therefore ωA.

Since $v_x = -\omega A \sin(\omega t + \phi)$, the maximum value of the speed is

$$v_{max} = \omega A = (15 \text{ rad/s})(2.0 \times 10^{-2} \text{ m}) = 0.30 \text{ m/s}$$

(A radian is not a true unit, so we can insert it or remove it as needed.)

In the same way, Equation 12-15 tells us the acceleration a_x as a function of time. The cosine varies from $+1$ to -1, so a_x has values from $+\omega^2 A$ to $-\omega^2 A$ and the maximum magnitude of a_x is $\omega^2 A$.

Since $a_x = -\omega^2 A \cos(\omega t + \phi)$, the maximum value of the acceleration is

$$a_{max} = \omega^2 A = (15 \text{ rad/s})^2 (2.0 \times 10^{-2} \text{ m}) = 4.5 \text{ m/s}^2$$

(b) To find the values of x, v_x, and a_x at $t = 0$, substitute the values of A, ω, and ϕ as well as $t = 0$ into Equations 12-12, 12-14, and 12-15. Note that $\cos(\pi/2) = 0$ and $\sin(\pi/2) = 1$.

Position at $t = 0$:

$$x(0) = A \cos(0 + \phi) = (2.0 \times 10^{-2} \text{ m}) \cos(\pi/2)$$
$$= (2.0 \times 10^{-2} \text{ m})(0) = 0$$

Velocity at $t = 0$:

$$v_x(0) = -\omega A \sin(0 + \phi) = -(15 \text{ rad/s})(2.0 \times 10^{-2} \text{ m}) \sin(\pi/2)$$
$$= -(15 \text{ rad/s})(2.0 \times 10^{-2} \text{ m})(1) = -0.30 \text{ m/s}$$

Acceleration at $t = 0$:

$$a_x(0) = -\omega^2 A \cos(0 + \phi) = -(15 \text{ rad/s})^2 (2.0 \times 10^{-2} \text{ m}) \cos(\pi/2)$$
$$= -(15 \text{ rad/s})^2 (2.0 \times 10^{-2} \text{ m})(0) = 0$$

(c) To draw the x–t graph, recognize that this graph must be sinusoidal and that the slope of the x–t graph is the velocity v_x. The values of x and v_x at $t = 0$ that we found in part (b) tell us that at $t = 0$ the x–t graph has value 0 and a negative slope. The value of x oscillates between $+A = +2.0 \times 10^{-2}$ m and $-A = -2.0 \times 10^{-2}$ m. The graph repeats itself after a time t equal to the period $T = 0.42$ s.

The v_x–t graph is also sinusoidal, and its slope is the acceleration a_x. The values of v_x and a_x at $t = 0$ tell us that at $t = 0$ the v_x–t graph has a negative value and zero slope. From part (a), the value of v_x oscillates between $+v_{max} = +0.30$ m/s and $-v_{max} = -0.30$ m/s. The graph repeats itself after a time t equal to the period $T = 0.42$ s.

Finally, comparing Equations 12-12 and 12-15 shows that $a_x = -\omega^2 x$, so the a_x–t graph looks like the negative of the x–t graph (compare Figure 12-7). From part (a), the value of a_x oscillates between $+a_{max} = +4.5$ m/s^2 and $-a_{max} = -4.5$ m/s^2. The graph repeats itself after a time t equal to the period $T = 0.42$ s.

Reflect

To start an oscillation going so that the graphs look like what we have drawn, begin with the block at rest at equilibrium ($x = 0$) and give it a sharp hit with your hand in the negative x direction so that it starts with a negative x velocity v_x. Note that the x–t, v_x–t, and a_x–t graphs look like those in Figure 12-7 but with the vertical axis shifted to the right by a quarter-cycle. That's what we would expect: Figure 12-6 shows that the effect of a phase angle ϕ is to shift the vertical axis horizontally by ϕ, and $\pi/2$ is one-quarter of 2π (the number of radians in a complete cycle).

(a)

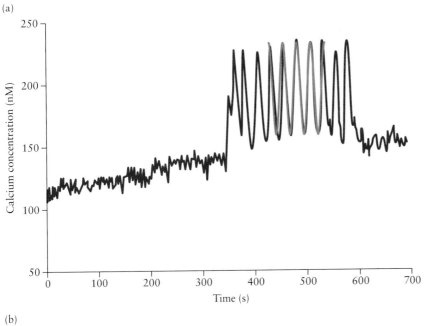

Figure 12-8 **Simple harmonic motion in physiology** (a) The concentration of calcium ions (Ca^{2+}) within a cell can oscillate under certain conditions. A sinusoidal curve (red) is a good match to these oscillations. (b) This graph shows the volume of air in a person's lungs as a function of time. The oscillations in lung volume are also well matched to a sinusoidal curve (red).

(b)

Our discussion of simple harmonic motion has concentrated on blocks attached to springs. But the same basic equations, and the sinusoidal graph of the oscillation as a function of time, apply to many different oscillating systems. **Figure 12-8a** shows an example of an oscillation in cell biology. In some cells the intracellular concentration of calcium ions (Ca^{2+}) oscillates sinusoidally. (These oscillations can regulate enzyme activity, mitochondrial metabolism, or gene expression.) The red sinusoidal curve drawn on top of the data matches these oscillations well. **Figure 12-8b** shows another biological example, the volume of air in a person's lungs as a function of time. Again we've drawn a red sinusoidal curve on top of the data; the close match between the curves shows that the oscillations are essentially simple harmonic motion.

> **Got the Concept? 12-2** Changing the Amplitude
>
> Suppose you were to increase the amplitude of the oscillation in Example 12-3 by a factor of 4, from 2.0×10^{-2} m to 8.0×10^{-2} m. The spring constant and mass remain the same as in Example 12-3. This would cause the frequency of the oscillation to (a) increase by a factor of 4; (b) increase by a factor of 2; (c) decrease by a factor of 1/4; (d) decrease by a factor of 1/2; (e) remain unchanged.

> **Got the Concept? 12-3** Changing the Spring Constant
>
> Suppose you were to increase the spring constant of the spring in Example 12-3 by a factor of 4, from 1.8×10^2 N/m to 7.2×10^2 N/m. The mass and amplitude remain the same as in Example 12-3. This would cause the maximum speed of the block during the oscillation to (a) increase by a factor of 4; (b) increase by a factor of 2; (c) decrease by a factor of 1/4; (d) decrease by a factor of 1/2; (e) remain unchanged.

Got the Concept? 12-4 Changing the Phase Angle

Suppose you were to change the phase angle in Example 12-3 to $\phi = \pi$. The spring constant, mass, and amplitude remain the same as in Example 12-3. This would cause the displacement x of the block at $t = 0$ to be (a) $A = 2.0 \times 10^{-2}$ m; (b) positive, but less than A; (c) zero; (d) $-A = -2.0 \times 10^{-2}$ m; (e) negative, but between zero and $-A$.

Take-Home Message for Section 12-3

✔ The amplitude of an oscillation is the maximum positive displacement from equilibrium.

✔ An object oscillating under the influence of a Hooke's law restoring force is called simple harmonic motion (SHM). The angular frequency, period, and frequency in SHM are unaffected by changes in the oscillation amplitude.

✔ SHM is identical to the projection onto the x axis of the motion of an object in uniform circular motion.

✔ Graphs of the position, velocity, and acceleration in SHM are sinusoidal curves. In each of these graphs, the phase angle shifts the location of the vertical axis (where time equals zero) to the right or left.

12-4 Mechanical energy is conserved in simple harmonic motion

We've been discussing how a spring can provide the restoring force necessary for oscillation to take place. But as we learned in Section 6-6, a spring can also be used to store *potential energy*. One creature that applies this principle to oscillation is the kangaroo (Figure 12-9). A kangaroo's tendons act like springs to store spring potential energy, which is transformed into kinetic energy as the animal hops; this increases the efficiency of movement. Dolphins use a similar mechanism in swimming. Even when a dolphin increases its speed by beating its tail faster, there is hardly any change in the rate at which it consumes oxygen (an indication of the dolphin's power output). The explanation is that the tissue in a dolphin's tail acts much like a spring, storing potential energy as the tail flips either up or down and then transforming the potential energy into kinetic energy. As a result, the dolphin can swim efficiently at high speeds.

These observations suggest that it's worthwhile to look at oscillations again from an energy perspective. To do this, we'll study the interplay between kinetic energy and potential energy for a block connected to the free end of an ideal, Hooke's law spring, oriented horizontally as in Figures 12-2 and 12-3.

Our starting point is the expression from Section 6-6 for the potential energy stored in an ideal spring:

Spring potential energy
(6-19)

| **Spring potential energy** of a stretched or compressed spring | **Spring constant** of the spring |

$$U_{spring} = \frac{1}{2} k x^2$$

Extension of the spring ($x > 0$ if spring is stretched, $x < 0$ if spring is compressed)

Figure 12-9
Spring potential energy When stretched, tendons in a kangaroo's legs store potential energy in much the same way as a spring.

The tendons on the backs of this kangaroo's legs are fully stretched. As such they store spring potential energy...

...which is released during a hop, as the kangaroo straightens its legs and lets its tendons relax...

...and the released spring potential energy is converted into kinetic energy of the kangaroo.

This equation tells us that the potential energy stored in a spring varies during a cycle of oscillation. When the object is at equilibrium ($x = 0$), the spring is neither stretched nor compressed and the spring potential energy is zero: $U_{spring} = 0$. Whenever the spring is stretched ($x > 0$) or compressed ($x < 0$), the spring potential energy is greater than zero. The potential energy is greatest when the spring is either at its maximum extension (when $x = A$) or maximum compression ($x = -A$). At either of those points $U_{spring} = \frac{1}{2}kA^2$.

The *kinetic* energy of the oscillating block, $K = \frac{1}{2}mv^2$, also varies during an oscillation cycle. The block has its maximum speed v_{max} when passing through the equilibrium position, so the kinetic energy has its maximum value $K = \frac{1}{2}mv_{max}^2$ there as well. At any other point in the oscillation the block is moving more slowly than when it passes through equilibrium, so the kinetic energy is less than its maximum value. The kinetic energy has its minimum value $K = 0$ when the oscillating block is momentarily at rest; this happens when the spring is at maximum extension ($x = A$) or maximum compression ($x = -A$).

This analysis shows that for a block oscillating on an ideal spring, the kinetic energy is maximum where the spring potential energy is minimum (at $x = 0$), and the kinetic energy is minimum where the spring potential energy is maximum (at $x = A$ and $x = -A$). This is just what we would expect! If there are no nonconservative forces such as friction acting, the total mechanical energy E (the sum of the kinetic energy of the block and the potential energy of the spring) should remain constant and energy will be transformed back and forth between its kinetic and potential forms as the block oscillates.

To analyze this in more detail, let's look at the expression for the total mechanical energy E of the system of block and spring:

$$E = K + U_{spring} = \frac{1}{2}mv^2 + \frac{1}{2}kx^2 \tag{12-17}$$

Let's use our results from Section 12-3 to see how E, K, and U_{spring} change during the course of an oscillation.

From Equation 12-12, the position as a function of time is $x = A \cos(\omega t + \phi)$, so the spring potential energy as a function of time is

$$U_{spring} = \frac{1}{2}kx^2 = \frac{1}{2}kA^2 \cos^2(\omega t + \phi) \tag{12-18}$$

Since the value of $\cos(\omega t + \phi)$ ranges from $+1$ through zero to -1, you can see that the value of $\cos^2(\omega t + \phi)$ ranges from 0 to 1. Hence the value of U_{spring} ranges from 0 to a maximum value $\frac{1}{2}kA^2$, just as we mentioned above.

Equation 12-14 tells us that the velocity as a function of time is $v_x = -\omega A \sin(\omega t + \phi)$. The velocity can be negative, but the square of the velocity is positive and equal to the square of the speed. Hence the kinetic energy as a function of time is

$$K = \frac{1}{2}mv^2 = \frac{1}{2}m\omega^2 A^2 \sin^2(\omega t + \phi)$$

From the first of Equations 12-11, we know that the angular frequency for a block oscillating on the end of an ideal spring is $\omega = \sqrt{k/m}$. So $m\omega^2 = m(k/m) = k$, and we can rewrite our expression for the kinetic energy as a function of time as

$$K = \frac{1}{2}mv^2 = \frac{1}{2}kA^2 \sin^2(\omega t + \phi) \tag{12-19}$$

Like the cosine function, the value of $\sin(\omega t + \phi)$ ranges from $+1$ through zero to -1 and the value of $\sin^2(\omega t + \phi)$ ranges from 0 to 1. So just like the spring potential energy, the kinetic energy of the block ranges in value from 0 to a maximum value $\frac{1}{2}kA^2$.

$\sqrt{x}$ *See the Math Tutorial for more information on trigonometry*

We can now insert our expressions for K from Equation 12-19 and U_{spring} from Equation 12-18 into Equation 12-17 for the total mechanical energy E. We get

$$E = K + U_{spring} = \frac{1}{2}kA^2 \sin^2(\omega t + \phi) + \frac{1}{2}kA^2 \cos^2(\omega t + \phi)$$

$$= \frac{1}{2}kA^2\left[\sin^2(\omega t + \phi) + \cos^2(\omega t + \phi)\right] \tag{12-20}$$

Equation 12-20 looks like a complicated function of time. But we can simplify it thanks to an important result from trigonometry:

$$\sin^2\theta + \cos^2\theta = 1 \quad \text{for any value of } \theta$$

Then Equation 12-20 becomes

Total mechanical energy of a mass oscillating on an ideal spring
(12-21)

Total mechanical energy of the oscillating mass–spring system

Spring constant

$$E = K + U_{spring} = \frac{1}{2}kA^2$$

Amplitude of the oscillation

During the oscillation, the kinetic energy K and spring potential energy U_{spring} both change...

...but their sum, the total mechanical energy E, always has the same value.

Because both k and A are constant for a specific motion of a given oscillator, the total energy of the oscillating system is constant. This is a statement of the conservation of energy: The energy of the system transforms between the kinetic and potential forms, but the total mechanical energy remains constant (Figure 12-10).

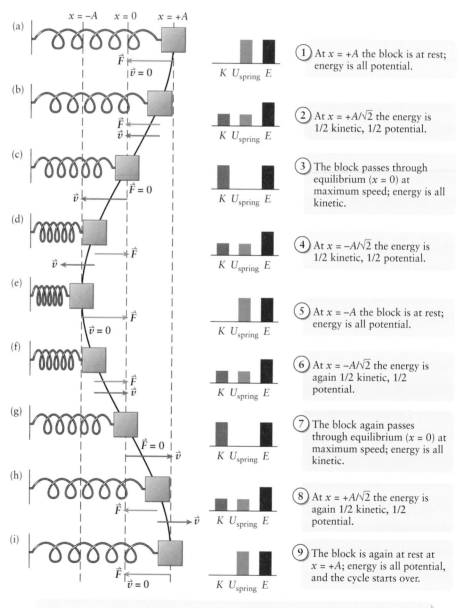

(a)

① At $x = +A$ the block is at rest; energy is all potential.

(b)

② At $x = +A/\sqrt{2}$ the energy is 1/2 kinetic, 1/2 potential.

(c)

③ The block passes through equilibrium ($x = 0$) at maximum speed; energy is all kinetic.

(d)

④ At $x = -A/\sqrt{2}$ the energy is 1/2 kinetic, 1/2 potential.

(e)

⑤ At $x = -A$ the block is at rest; energy is all potential.

(f)

⑥ At $x = -A/\sqrt{2}$ the energy is again 1/2 kinetic, 1/2 potential.

(g)

⑦ The block again passes through equilibrium ($x = 0$) at maximum speed; energy is all kinetic.

(h)

⑧ At $x = +A/\sqrt{2}$ the energy is again 1/2 kinetic, 1/2 potential.

(i)

⑨ The block is again at rest at $x = +A$; energy is all potential, and the cycle starts over.

Figure 12-10 Energy during a cycle of oscillation The bar graphs show the kinetic energy K, spring potential energy U_{spring}, and total mechanical energy $E = K + U_{spring}$ at nine stages in the oscillation of a block attached to a spring (compare Figure 12-3).

The kinetic energy K and potential energy U_{spring} change during a cycle of oscillation, but the total mechanical energy $E = K + U_{spring}$ remains constant.

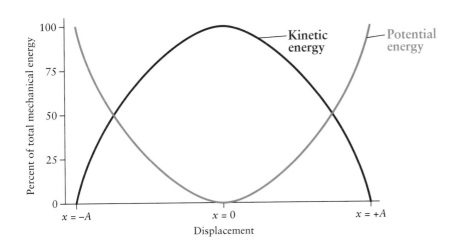

Equations 12-18 and 12-19 give the spring potential energy and kinetic energy as functions of time. It's also helpful to write these relationships as functions of the displacement x. We know from Equation 6-19 that the spring potential energy is $U_{spring} = (1/2)kx^2$; the graph of this as a function of x is a parabola with its minimum value at $x = 0$ (Figure 12-11). From Equation 12-21, the kinetic energy K is equal to the total mechanical energy $E = (1/2)kA^2$ (a constant) minus the potential energy U_{spring}:

$$K = E - U_{spring} = \frac{1}{2}kA^2 - \frac{1}{2}kx^2 \qquad (12\text{-}22)$$

This is an "upside-down" parabola that has its *maximum* value at $x = 0$, as Figure 12-11 shows.

Note that U_{spring} is greatest at the two extremes of displacement ($x = +A$ and $x = -A$) and zero at equilibrium ($x = 0$). The kinetic energy K is zero at the two extremes, where the block momentarily comes to a stop to reverse direction, and greatest as the object passes through $x = 0$. So at $x = 0$ the energy is 100% kinetic and 0% potential, while at $x = +A$ and $x = -A$ the energy is 0% kinetic and 100% potential.

Example 12-4 SHM III: Kinetic and Potential Energy

As in Example 12-3, an object of mass 0.80 kg is attached to an ideal horizontal spring of spring constant 1.8×10^2 N/m. The object is initially at rest at equilibrium. You then start the object oscillating with amplitude 2.0×10^{-2} m. (a) How much work do you have to do on the object to set it into oscillation? (b) What is the speed of the object when the spring is compressed by 1.0×10^{-2} m? (c) How far is the object from equilibrium when the kinetic energy of the object equals the potential energy in the spring?

Set Up

We'll use energy ideas to answer these questions. Equation 12-21 will let us find the (constant) total mechanical energy E of the system from the given spring constant and amplitude. Equation 6-19 will let us find the spring potential energy for any displacement x; we can then find the kinetic energy K using Equation 12-21, and from that find the speed for that value of x.

Total mechanical energy of a mass oscillating on an ideal spring:

$$E = K + U_{spring} = \frac{1}{2}kA^2 \qquad (12\text{-}21)$$

Spring potential energy:

$$U_{spring} = \frac{1}{2}kx^2 \qquad (6\text{-}19)$$

Solve

(a) Initially the system has zero kinetic energy and zero potential energy. You can start the oscillation by pulling the object so that you stretch the spring by a distance $A = 2.0 \times 10^2$ m from equilibrium. The work you do goes into the potential energy of the spring.

(Work you do) = (Change of potential energy of the spring as you stretch it from $x = 0$ to $x = A$)

Initial potential energy

$$= \frac{1}{2}k(0)^2 = 0$$

Final potential energy $= \frac{1}{2}kA^2$

So the work you do is

$$W = \frac{1}{2}kA^2 - 0$$
$$= \frac{1}{2}(1.8 \times 10^2 \text{ N/m})(2.0 \times 10^{-2} \text{ m})^2$$
$$= 3.6 \times 10^{-2} \text{ N} \cdot \text{m} = 3.6 \times 10^{-2} \text{ J}$$

(b) When the spring is compressed by 1.0×10^{-2} m, the displacement is $x = -1.0 \times 10^{-2}$ m. The first step in determining the block's speed at this value of x is to determine its kinetic energy.

From (a), the total mechanical energy is

$$E = \frac{1}{2}kA^2 = 3.6 \times 10^{-2} \text{ J}$$

From Equation 6-19, the spring potential energy for $x = -1.0 \times 10^{-2}$ m is

$$U_{\text{spring}} = \frac{1}{2}kx^2$$
$$= \frac{1}{2}(1.8 \times 10^2 \text{ N/m})(-1.0 \times 10^{-2} \text{ m})^2$$
$$= 9.0 \times 10^{-3} \text{ J}$$

So from Equation 12-21, the kinetic energy at this value of x is

$$K = E - U_{\text{spring}} = 3.6 \times 10^{-2} \text{ J} - 9.0 \times 10^{-3} \text{ J}$$
$$= 2.7 \times 10^{-2} \text{ J}$$

Given the kinetic energy K of the block and its mass $m = 0.80$ kg, calculate the speed of the block.

Solve for the speed v:

Kinetic energy is $K = \frac{1}{2}mv^2$, so

$$v^2 = \frac{2K}{m}$$

$$v = \sqrt{\frac{2K}{m}} = \sqrt{\frac{2(2.7 \times 10^{-2} \text{ J})}{0.80 \text{ kg}}} = 0.26 \text{ m/s}$$

(Recall from Chapter 6 that if the kinetic energy is in joules and the mass is in kilograms, the speed is in meters per second.)
The *velocity* of the block could be $+0.26$ m/s or -0.26 m/s, depending on what direction it is moving as it passes through this point.

(c) Use the same ideas as in part (b) to solve for the value of x at which the kinetic energy K equals the spring potential energy U_{spring}.

From above, the total mechanical energy is

$$E = \frac{1}{2}kA^2 = 3.6 \times 10^{-2} \text{ J}$$

The spring potential energy is

$$U_{\text{spring}} = \frac{1}{2}kx^2$$

and the kinetic energy is

$$K = E - U_{spring}$$

At the value of x for which $K = U_{spring}$,

$$\frac{1}{2}kA^2 - \frac{1}{2}kx^2 = \frac{1}{2}kx^2$$

Multiply both sides by $2/k$ and solve for x:

$$A^2 - x^2 = x^2 \quad \text{so} \quad 2x^2 = A^2 \quad \text{and} \quad x^2 = \frac{A^2}{2}$$

$$x = \pm \sqrt{\frac{A^2}{2}} = \pm \frac{A}{\sqrt{2}}$$

$$= \pm \frac{2.0 \times 10^{-2}\,\text{m}}{\sqrt{2}} = \pm 1.4 \times 10^{-2}\,\text{m}$$

Note that x can be either positive (the spring is stretched by 1.4×10^{-2} m) or negative (the spring is compressed by 1.4×10^{-2} m).

Reflect

The result for part (b) would have been very difficult to find without using the energy approach. You would have needed to use the equations from Section 12-3 to solve for the time t at which the block passes through $x = -1.0 \times 10^{-2}$ m, then use this value of t to find the velocity of the block at that time. The energy approach makes this much easier.

Note that the points $x = \pm A/\sqrt{2} = \pm 0.71A$ where the kinetic and potential energies are equal are shown in Figure 12-10 (see parts (b), (d), (f), and (h) of that figure). These points are *not* halfway between the equilibrium position ($x = 0$) and the extremes of the motion ($x = \pm A$); they are actually closer to the extremes. Can you show that at $x = \pm A/2$, the energy is 75% kinetic and 25% potential? (*Hint:* See the solution to part (b).)

? Got the Concept? 12-5   Rank the Energies

Consider four different systems, each made of a block attached to an ideal horizontal spring. Rank them in order of their total mechanical energy, from largest to smallest value. (a) Block mass 0.50 kg and spring constant 5.0×10^2 N/m, with amplitude 0.020 m; (b) block mass 0.60 kg and spring constant 3.0×10^2 N/m, with speed 1.0 m/s when passing through equilibrium; (c) block mass 1.2 kg and spring constant 4.0×10^2 N/m, with speed 0.50 m/s when passing through $x = -0.010$ m; (d) block mass 2.0 kg and spring constant 2.0×10^2 N/m, with speed 0.20 m/s when passing through $x = 0.050$ m.

Take-Home Message for Section 12-4

✔ Energy is transformed back and forth from kinetic energy to potential energy in systems which contain mechanical or biological springs.

✔ When an object attached to a spring is at its maximum displacement, the energy of the system of spring and object is entirely potential energy.

✔ When the object passes through equilibrium, the energy of the system of spring and object is entirely kinetic energy.

✔ The total energy of the system, the maximum potential energy, and the maximum kinetic energy are all equal to $(1/2)kA^2$.

12-5 The motion of a pendulum is approximately simple harmonic

You've probably had a physician strike the patellar tendon just below your kneecap with a hammer, then watched your lower leg swing upward and back (Figure 12-12a). For a physician this is a test of your patellar reflex: Hitting that tendon sends a signal directly to your spinal cord, which in turn sends a signal to the quadriceps muscle

(a)

(b)

Figure 12-12 **Swinging leg, swinging pendulum** The motions of both (a) your lower leg in a physician's office and (b) a mass hanging from a string have the ingredients for oscillation: a restoring force (gravity) that tends to pull the object toward equilibrium (hanging straight down), and inertia that causes the object to overshoot equilibrium.

on your upper thigh. This makes that muscle flex and makes the lower leg move. But to a physicist this is an example of the same kind of motion as a mass swinging at the end of a string (Figure 12-12b). When allowed to move freely, both your leg and the mass would hang straight down in their equilibrium positions thanks to the influence of gravity. When either your leg or the mass is displaced from equilibrium, released, and allowed to move freely, the force of gravity pulls it back toward equilibrium—that is, gravity serves as a restoring force. And in either case inertia causes the object (leg or mass) to overshoot the equilibrium position. What results in both cases is an oscillation. Both a swinging leg and a mass on the end of a string are examples of **pendulums**—systems that oscillate back and forth due to the restoring force of gravity.

Since pendulums actually *rotate* around a point, we'll describe them using the language of rotational motion that we developed in Chapter 8. So instead of relating a restoring force to the acceleration that it produces, as we did in Section 12-3 for the simple harmonic motion of a block attached to an ideal spring, we'll describe pendulum motion in terms of a restoring *torque* that produces an *angular* acceleration.

In this section we'll explore oscillations of a **simple pendulum**. This is one in which all of the mass is concentrated at a single point. It's an idealized version of the mass-and-string arrangement shown in Figure 12-12b in which the string of length L has zero mass and all of the mass m is compressed to a point. (In Section 12-6 we'll look at other, less idealized pendulums.)

Figure 12-13a shows a simple pendulum. In equilibrium the string hangs straight down; the figure shows the pendulum displaced by an angle θ from the vertical. The blue dashed curve shows the path that the object of mass m at the end of the pendulum will take to return to equilibrium. Figure 12-13b shows the free-body diagram for this object. The two forces that act on this object are a tension force of magnitude T exerted by the string and a gravitational force of magnitude mg. The tension force points along the radial line from the pivot point to the object, so it exerts no torque around that point: It does nothing to make the pendulum rotate around the pivot. The gravitational force does exert a torque, however. From Section 8-6, its magnitude is the magnitude of the vector $\vec{L}$ from the pivot to where the force is applied (that is, the distance L) multiplied by the magnitude mg of the gravitational force and the sine of

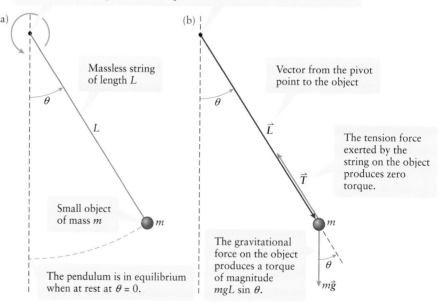

Pivot point: The positive z axis (the rotation axis of the pendulum) points outward from this point. We take positive rotation to be counterclockwise.

(a)

Massless string of length L

θ

L

Small object of mass m

m

The pendulum is in equilibrium when at rest at $\theta = 0$.

(b)

Vector from the pivot point to the object

θ

$\vec{L}$

$\vec{T}$

The tension force exerted by the string on the object produces zero torque.

m

The gravitational force on the object produces a torque of magnitude $mgL \sin \theta$.

θ

$m\vec{g}$

Figure 12-13 **A simple pendulum** (a) Layout of a simple pendulum. (b) The forces on a simple pendulum.

the angle θ (which is the angle between the directions of $\vec{L}$ and $m\vec{g}$). Hence we can write the torque as:

$$\tau_z = -mgL \sin \theta \qquad (12\text{-}23)$$

The subscript z indicates that the pendulum tends to rotate around the z axis shown in Figure 12-13a. The minus sign in Equation 12-23 indicates that this is a *restoring* torque. If the pendulum swings to the right of vertical (counterclockwise) so that θ and $\sin \theta$ are positive, as in Figure 12-13a, the torque will be negative (clockwise): That means it acts to decrease θ and so return the pendulum to the equilibrium position $\theta = 0$. If the pendulum swings instead to the left of vertical (clockwise) so that θ and $\sin \theta$ are negative, the torque will be positive (counterclockwise) and so will again act to restore the pendulum to equilibrium.

The torque in Equation 12-23 is the only torque that acts on the pendulum, so this is also the *net* torque. Newton's second law for rotational motion (Section 8-6) says that the net torque on an object is equal to the moment of inertia multiplied by the angular acceleration. For an object made up of a single point of mass m a distance L from the rotation axis, the moment of inertia is $I = mL^2$. Using the torque from Equation 12-23, we have

$$-mgL \sin \theta = mL^2 \alpha_z$$

If we divide both sides of this equation by mL^2 and rearrange, we get

$$\alpha_z = -\frac{g}{L} \sin \theta \qquad (12\text{-}24)$$

Let's see whether Equation 12-24 is equivalent to Hooke's law. If it is, that means the oscillations of simple pendulums are simple harmonic motion and we can use all of our results from Section 12-3. We saw in Section 12-3 that we can write Hooke's law for straight-line oscillation as

$$a_x = -\omega^2 x$$

That is, the acceleration is directly proportional to the displacement, and the proportionality constant is the negative of the square of the angular frequency ω. From Section 8-5, the quantities x and a_x for straight-line motion correspond to the quantities θ and α_z, respectively, for rotational motion. So the rotational version of Hooke's law is

$$\alpha_z = -\omega^2 \theta \qquad (12\text{-}25)$$

The difference between Equation 12-24 for the pendulum and Equation 12-25, the rotational version of Hooke's law, is that Equation 12-24 involves $\sin \theta$ rather than θ. So in general the oscillations of a simple pendulum do *not* obey Hooke's law, and so the motion of the pendulum is *not* simple harmonic motion.

If, however, the angle θ is relatively small and we measure θ in radians, it turns out that $\sin \theta$ is *approximately* equal to θ (Figure 12-14):

$$\sin \theta \approx \theta \quad \text{when } \theta \text{ is small}$$

(You can confirm this with your calculator. Try calculating $\sin \theta$ for $\theta = 1$ rad, 0.5 rad, 0.2 rad, 0.1 rad, and 0.01 rad. You'll find that as you try smaller values of θ, the value of $\sin \theta$ gets closer and closer to θ.) With this approximation, Equation 12-24 for the simple pendulum becomes

$$\alpha_z \approx -\frac{g}{L} \theta \quad \text{if } \theta \text{ is small} \qquad (12\text{-}26)$$

Compare this to Hooke's law for rotational motion, Equation 12-25, and you'll see that the oscillations of a pendulum *with small amplitude* (so that θ is always small) obey Hooke's law, and that the angular frequency of the simple pendulum's oscillations is given by

$$\omega^2 = \frac{g}{L} \quad \text{or} \quad \omega = \sqrt{\frac{g}{L}}$$

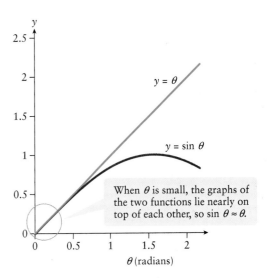

Figure 12-14 **Approximating $\sin \theta$** If the value of θ is small, $\sin \theta$ is approximately equal to θ (measured in radians).

As in Section 12-3, the period T is equal to $2\pi/\omega$ and the frequency f is equal to $1/T$ or $\omega/2\pi$. So we can write the following results for the small-amplitude oscillations of a simple pendulum:

Angular frequency, period, and frequency for a simple pendulum (small amplitude)
(12-27)

Angular frequency $\quad \omega = \sqrt{\dfrac{g}{L}}$

g = Acceleration due to gravity

L = Length of the simple pendulum

Period $\quad T = \dfrac{2\pi}{\omega} = 2\pi\sqrt{\dfrac{L}{g}}$

Frequency $\quad f = \dfrac{1}{T} = \dfrac{1}{2\pi}\sqrt{\dfrac{g}{L}} = \dfrac{\omega}{2\pi}$

 Go to Picture It 12-1 for more practice dealing with simple pendulums

Equations 12-27 show that the angular frequency, period, and frequency for a simple pendulum do *not* depend on the mass of the object at the end of the pendulum. That's because the restoring torque is provided by the gravitational force. Doubling the mass doubles the moment of inertia, which by itself would make the oscillations happen more slowly, but it also doubles the restoring torque, which by itself would make the oscillations happen more rapidly. The two effects cancel each other out so that ω, T, and f are unaffected by changes in the pendulum mass.

Because the small-amplitude oscillations of a simple pendulum obey Hooke's law, it also follows that the angular frequency, period, and frequency do not depend on the *amplitude* of the oscillations. Here the amplitude is the maximum angle from the vertical that the pendulum attains. If you were to pull the simple pendulum in Figure 12-13a to an angle $\theta = 0.1$ rad—about 6°—and let it go, the pendulum would oscillate between $\theta = +0.1$ rad (to the right of vertical) and $\theta = -0.1$ rad (to the left of vertical), and the amplitude of the oscillation would be 0.1 rad.

⚠ Watch Out! **Large-amplitude oscillations of a simple pendulum are *not* simple harmonic motion.**

The results in Equations 12-27 only apply if the angle θ reached by the pendulum is always small enough that $\sin\theta$ is approximately equal to θ. Figure 12-14 shows that this is not a good approximation if θ is greater than about 0.5 rad (about 30°). If the amplitude is larger than this, the motion is *not* simple harmonic and the values of ω, T, and f *do* depend on the amplitude. As an example, if the amplitude is $\pi/2$ (90°), the period of oscillation is about 18% greater than the value given by the second of Equations 12-27. Another difference is that for small-amplitude oscillations, θ is a sinusoidal function of time, just like the oscillations of a block on an ideal spring (Section 12-3). If the amplitude is large, however, the function is a more complicated one.

Example 12-5 Changing a Pendulum

You make a simple pendulum by hanging a small 60-g marble from an elastic thread of negligible mass. With the marble attached, the thread is 40 cm long. (a) Find the period when the marble is pulled a small angle to one side and released. (b) You replace the marble by another small one of mass 260 g. When you do this, the thread stretches an additional 10 cm. Find the new period.

Set Up
We'll use the second of Equations 12-27 to find the period of this simple pendulum.

Period of a simple pendulum:

$$T = 2\pi\sqrt{\dfrac{L}{g}} \qquad (12\text{-}27)$$

Solve

(a) Find the period of the pendulum with the initial length $L = 40$ cm. Be sure to first convert L to meters.

Length of pendulum $L = 40$ cm $\times \left(\dfrac{1 \text{ m}}{100 \text{ cm}}\right) = 0.40$ m

Then the period is

$$T = 2\pi\sqrt{\frac{L}{g}} = 2\pi\sqrt{\frac{0.40 \text{ m}}{9.80 \text{ m/s}^2}} = 2\pi\sqrt{\frac{0.40 \text{ s}^2}{9.80}} = 1.3 \text{ s}$$

(b) Repeat the calculation with the new value of the length.

The new length of the pendulum is

$L_{new} = 40$ cm $+ 10$ cm $= 50$ cm $= 0.50$ m

So the new period is

$$T_{new} = 2\pi\sqrt{\frac{L_{new}}{g}} = 2\pi\sqrt{\frac{0.50 \text{ m}}{9.80 \text{ m/s}^2}} = 1.4 \text{ s}$$

Reflect

Although the mass of the marble changed, we did *not* have to use its mass in the calculation. As we've seen, the period of a simple pendulum depends only on its length, not on its mass.

Note that we know the value of g to three significant figures, but our answers for the period are given to only two significant figures. Can you see why? (*Hint:* Review Section 1-4 if you're not sure.)

? Got the Concept? 12-6 Simple Pendulum I

A small marble is attached to a thread that has a negligible mass and is hung from a support. When the marble is pulled back a small distance and released, it swings in simple harmonic motion with a frequency of 0.60 Hz. What is the frequency of the pendulum after the length of the thread is increased by a factor of 4 but the marble is released in the same way? (a) 2.4 Hz; (b) 1.2 Hz; (c) 0.60 Hz; (d) 0.30 Hz; (e) 0.15 Hz.

? Got the Concept? 12-7 Simple Pendulum II

A small marble is attached to a thread that has a negligible mass and is hung from a support. When the marble is pulled back a small distance and released, it swings in simple harmonic motion with a frequency of 0.60 Hz. If the marble is replaced by one that has four times the mass of the original one, and the new marble is pulled back by half the distance of the original marble before being released, what is the new frequency? Assume that the length of the thread remains the same. (a) 2.4 Hz; (b) 1.2 Hz; (c) 0.60 Hz; (d) 0.30 Hz; (e) 0.15 Hz.

? Got the Concept? 12-8 Pendulum on an Asteroid

A small marble is attached to a thread that has a negligible mass and is hung from a support. When the marble is pulled back a small distance and released, it swings in simple harmonic motion with a frequency of 0.60 Hz. What is the frequency of the pendulum if it is transported to the surface of a small asteroid, where the acceleration due to gravity is only 1/100 that on Earth's surface? (a) 60 Hz; (b) 6.0 Hz; (c) 0.60 Hz; (d) 0.060 Hz; (e) 0.0060 Hz.

Take-Home Message for Section 12-5

✔ In a simple pendulum, all of the mass of the pendulum is concentrated a fixed distance from a rotation point.

✔ The angular frequency ω, the period T, and the frequency f of a simple pendulum depend on the length of the pendulum and the acceleration due to gravity. They do not depend on the pendulum mass.

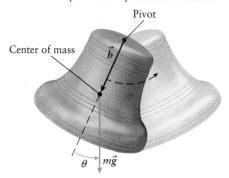

The z axis points perpendicular to the plane of the pendulum's rotation.

Pivot

Center of mass

$\vec{h}$

l

θ $m\vec{g}$

Figure 12-15 **A physical pendulum** The forces on a physical pendulum (one whose mass is not all concentrated in a single small blob, unlike the simple pendulum shown in Figure 12-13).

12-6 A physical pendulum has its mass distributed over its volume

We began the previous section by comparing two examples of pendulum motion: the swing of your lower leg when a physician tests your patellar reflex (Figure 12-12a), and the motion of a mass on the end of a string (Figure 12-12b). The mass on a string is nearly an ideal simple pendulum, since all of the mass is concentrated into a very small volume. But your lower leg is *not* a simple pendulum, because its mass is distributed along the entire distance from the knee to the foot. A pendulum like your lower leg whose mass is distributed throughout its volume is called a **physical pendulum.** Other examples of physical pendulums include a swinging church bell, a chandelier swaying back and forth after an earth tremor, and the pendulum of an old-fashioned grandfather clock. Let's see how to find the angular frequency, period, and frequency for the oscillations of a physical pendulum.

Figure 12-15 shows an example of a physical pendulum of mass m. Two forces act on the pendulum, a gravitational force of magnitude mg that acts at the center of mass of the pendulum, a distance h from the pivot point, and a support force that acts at the pivot. We haven't drawn the support force because it acts at the pivot point and so exerts no torque around that point. The torque exerted by the gravitational force is equal to h (the magnitude of the vector $\vec{h}$ from the pivot to the center of mass) multiplied by the magnitude mg of the gravitational force and the sine of the angle θ between the directions of $\vec{h}$ and $m\vec{g}$:

$$\tau_z = -mgh \sin \theta \tag{12-28}$$

Just as for the torque on a simple pendulum, the minus sign in Equation 12-28 means that this is a restoring torque that always acts to pull the pendulum back toward its equilibrium position $\theta = 0$, with the center of mass directly below the pivot.

The torque in Equation 12-28 is the only torque on the pendulum and so is equal to the net torque $\Sigma\tau_z$. From Newton's second law for rotation (Section 8-6), $\Sigma\tau_z = I\alpha_z$, we have

$$-mgh \sin \theta = I\alpha_z \tag{12-29}$$

In Equation 12-29 the quantity I is the moment of inertia of the pendulum around the pivot point. Just as for the simple pendulum, if the angle θ is small then $\sin \theta$ is approximately equal to θ (measured in radians). To this approximation we can rewrite Equation 12-29 as

$$\alpha_z \approx -\left(\frac{mgh}{I}\right)\theta \quad \text{if } \theta \text{ is small} \tag{12-30}$$

Compare Equation 12-30 to the corresponding equation for the simple pendulum that we derived in Section 12-5, $\alpha_z \approx -(g/L)\theta$ (Equation 12-26): The equation is identical except that g/L has been replaced by mgh/I. So we conclude that just as for the simple pendulum, the oscillations of a physical pendulum are simple harmonic motion provided that the amplitude is relatively small. To find the angular frequency, period, and frequency of a physical pendulum, we simply take Equations 12-27 for a simple pendulum and replace g/L with mgh/I:

Angular frequency, period, and frequency for a physical pendulum (small amplitude) (12-31)

Angular frequency $\omega = \sqrt{\dfrac{mgh}{I}}$

Period $T = \dfrac{2\pi}{\omega} = 2\pi \sqrt{\dfrac{I}{mgh}}$

Frequency $f = \dfrac{1}{T} = \dfrac{1}{2\pi}\sqrt{\dfrac{mgh}{I}} = \dfrac{\omega}{2\pi}$

m = Mass of physical pendulum

g = Acceleration due to gravity

h = Distance from pivot point to center of mass of physical pendulum

I = Moment of inertia of physical pendulum about pivot

Here's a check on our results for a physical pendulum. If all of the mass of the physical pendulum is concentrated at the center of mass, then the moment of inertia of the physical pendulum around the pivot is $I = mh^2$. Then the quantity mgh/I in Equations 12-31 becomes

$$\frac{mgh}{I} = \frac{mgh}{mh^2} = \frac{g}{h}$$

(12-32)

If we change the symbol for the distance from the pivot to the center of mass from h to L, the quantity in Equation 12-32 becomes g/L. Then, from the first of Equations 12-31, the angular frequency for a physical pendulum with all of its mass concentrated at the center of mass becomes $\omega = \sqrt{g/L}$. That's exactly the result we found in Section 12-5 for a simple pendulum, which is just a physical pendulum with all of its mass concentrated a distance L from the pivot (see Figure 12-13 and the first of Equations 12-27). So our results for a *physical* pendulum give us the correct answers for the special case of a *simple* pendulum, just as they should.

 Go to Interactive Exercise 12-2 for more practice dealing with physical pendulums

Example 12-6 An Oscillating Rod

A uniform rod has a length L and a mass m, and is supported so that it can swing freely from one end. Derive an expression for the period of oscillation when the rod is pulled slightly from the vertical and released.

Set Up
Equations 12-31 tell us the period of a physical pendulum. The center of mass of a uniform rod is at its center, and its moment of inertia around one end is given in Table 8-1 (Section 8-3).

Period of a physical pendulum:

$$T = 2\pi \sqrt{\frac{I}{mgh}} \quad \text{(Second of Equations 12-31)}$$

Moment of inertia for a uniform rod of mass m and length L rotating about one end:

$$I = \frac{1}{3}mL^2$$

center of mass

m, L

Solve
Given the moment of inertia I and the distance h, solve for the period.

The center of mass is a distance $L/2$ from the pivot, so

$$h = \frac{L}{2}$$

Substitute I and h into the expression for the period T from Equations 12-31:

$$T = 2\pi \sqrt{\frac{(1/3)mL^2}{mg(L/2)}} = 2\pi \sqrt{\frac{2mL^2}{3mgL}}$$

$$= 2\pi \sqrt{\frac{2L}{3g}}$$

Reflect
Compared to the period of a simple pendulum of length L, $T_{\text{simple pendulum}} = 2\pi \sqrt{L/g}$, the period of a uniform rod free to rotate about its end is smaller by a factor of $\sqrt{2/3} = 0.816$. In other words, the physical pendulum oscillates more quickly. That may seem surprising if you just compare the torques on the two objects. The center of mass of the rod is a distance $h = L/2$ from the pivot, so from Equation 12-28 the torque on the rod is $\tau_z = -mgh \sin \theta = -(mgL/2) \sin \theta$. By contrast, for a simple pendulum all of the mass m is a distance L from the pivot, so $h = L$ and the torque on the pendulum is $\tau_z = -mgh \sin \theta = -mgL \sin \theta$. So the rod experiences half as much torque pulling it back toward equilibrium as does the simple pendulum. Why, then, does the rod oscillate more rapidly?

To see the explanation, we also need to compare the moment of inertia of the rod ($I = mL^2/3$) to the moment of inertia of the simple pendulum ($I = mL^2$). So while the rod experiences half as much torque as the simple pendulum, the rod has only one-third as much inertia as does the simple pendulum. Because its moment of inertia is so small, the rod ends up oscillating faster.

Example 12-7 Moment of Inertia of a Human Leg

How you walk is affected in part by how your legs swing around the rotation axis created by your hip joints. Because your leg has a complex shape and contains a combination of bone, muscle, skin, and other materials, it would be very difficult to calculate the moment of inertia I of a leg around the hip using the definition of the moment of inertia. Instead, I can be found experimentally by measuring the period of the leg when allowed to swing freely. In a clinical study, a person's leg of length 0.88 m is estimated to have a mass of 6.5 kg and a center of mass 0.37 m from the rotation axis through the hip. When allowed to swing freely, it oscillates with a period of 1.2 s. Determine the moment of inertia of the leg in rotation around the axis through the hip. Compare your answer to a uniform rod that has the same mass and length (see Example 12-6).

Set Up

The expression for the period T of a physical pendulum depends on the moment of inertia I for rotation around the pivot, the mass m, and the distance h from pivot to center of mass. We're given the values of $T = 1.2$ s, $m = 6.5$ kg, and $h = 0.37$ m, so we can solve for I. We'll then compare our result to a uniform rod with the same mass ($m = 6.5$ kg) and length ($L = 0.88$ m) as a leg.

Period of a physical pendulum:

$$T = 2\pi\sqrt{\frac{I}{mgh}} \text{ (Second of Equations 12-31)}$$

Moment of inertia for a uniform rod of mass m and length L rotating about one end:

$$I = \frac{1}{3}mL^2$$

Solve

Rearrange the expression for period T to find a formula for the moment of inertia I, then substitute the known values.

Begin with the expression

$$T = 2\pi\sqrt{\frac{I}{mgh}}$$

Square both sides to get rid of the square root, then solve for I:

$$T^2 = \frac{4\pi^2 I}{mgh} \text{ so } I = \frac{mghT^2}{4\pi^2}$$

Substitute numerical values:

$$I = \frac{(6.5 \text{ kg})(9.80 \text{ m/s}^2)(0.37 \text{ m})(1.2 \text{ s})^2}{4\pi^2} = 0.86 \text{ kg} \cdot \text{m}^2$$

As a comparison, find the moment of inertia of a uniform rod with the same mass and length of the leg rotating about one end:

For a rod rotating around one end,

$$I = \frac{1}{3}mL^2 = \frac{1}{3}(6.5 \text{ kg})(0.88 \text{ m})^2 = 1.7 \text{ kg} \cdot \text{m}^2$$

Reflect

The moment of inertia of the uniform rod is *twice* as large as the moment of inertia of that leg. Is that reasonable? Consider that your upper leg (above the knee) is more massive than your lower leg, as suggested by the sketch above, so more of the leg's mass is above the knee than below the knee. By contrast, the mass of a uniform rod is distributed uniformly along its length. We learned in Section 8-3 that the farther an object's mass lies from the rotation axis, the greater the moment of inertia for that axis. So it's not surprising that the uniform rod, which has more of its mass farther from the rotation axis, has a greater moment of inertia than the leg.

? Got the Concept? 12-9 Period of a Rod

A uniform rod has the same length and mass as the leg in the previous example. When supported at one end and allowed to rotate, would the period of this rod be (a) greater than the period of the leg; (b) the same as the period of the leg; (c) less than the period of the leg; or (d) not enough information given to decide?

? Got the Concept? 12-10 Frequency of a Physical Pendulum

You measure the oscillation frequency of a physical pendulum when it is pivoted at one end. You then rearrange the experiment so that the physical pendulum is pivoted around its center of mass. Compared to the frequency when it is pivoted at one end, the frequency when it is pivoted at the center of mass is (a) greater; (b) the same; (c) less, but not zero; (d) zero; (e) not enough information given to decide. (*Hint:* Think about how the pendulum will move when supported at its center of mass.)

Take-Home Message for Section 12-6

✔ A physical pendulum has its mass distributed throughout its volume. Unlike a simple pendulum, it cannot be treated as a point object suspended at the end of a string of negligible mass.

✔ The gravitational torque that arises when the pendulum is displaced from equilibrium acts as a restoring torque that causes the pendulum to return to its equilibrium position.

✔ The angular frequency, period, and frequency of a physical pendulum depend on its mass, the distance from the pivot point to the pendulum's center of mass, and the pendulum's moment of inertia around that point.

12-7 When damping is present, the amplitude of an oscillating system decreases over time

Stand up and let one arm hang limp by your side. With the other hand, pull the limp arm forward, then let it go. The limp arm will swing back and forth like a pendulum, but within a few swings the oscillations die out and your arm is once again hanging by your side. In the same way the vibrations of your eardrum, in response to a source of sound, quickly die away when the source is cut off, as do the vibrations of a cymbal after it has been struck with a drumstick. In all of these cases, the oscillations are diminished or *damped* by some kind of friction force. Let's examine the properties of these **damped oscillations**.

In Section 5-3 we learned about the kinetic friction force that arises when one object slides over another. In that section we assumed that the friction force did not depend on the speed of the sliding. For many oscillating systems, however, it turns out to be a better description to say that the force that causes damping *does* depend on speed. The simplest such damping force is one that is proportional to the speed of the oscillating object:

$$\vec{F}_{\text{damping}} = -b\vec{v} \tag{12-33}$$

The minus sign says that the damping force always opposes the motion of the object: If the object moves to the left, the damping force is to the right, and so on. The quantity b is called the **damping coefficient**. Its value depends on various physical characteristics of a particular system. For example, think of a mass–spring combination that's immersed in a fluid such as air, water, or oil. The value of b in this case depends on the viscosity of the fluid as well as on the size of the oscillating object. The units of force are newtons, where $1\,\text{N} = 1\,\text{kg} \cdot \text{m/s}^2$, and the units of velocity are m/s, so it follows that the units of the damping coefficient b are $\text{N}/(\text{m/s}) = (\text{kg} \cdot \text{m/s}^2)(\text{s/m}) = \text{kg/s}$.

Let's consider an object of mass m attached to an ideal, Hooke's law spring of spring constant k that oscillates along the x axis as in Figure 12-2. The force exerted by the spring has only an x component, equal to $-kx$. If the object is also subject to a damping force given by Equation 12-33, that force also has only an x component (because the velocity has only an x component): $F_{\text{damping}, x} = -bv_x$. The net force on the object is the sum of the spring and damping forces, so Newton's second law for the object is

$$ma_x = -kx - bv_x \tag{12-34}$$

Equation 12-34 is a difficult equation to solve, so we'll just present the solution for x as a function of time. It turns out that the character of the solution depends on the size of the damping coefficient b, and that there are three distinct solutions that depend on whether the damping coefficient is relatively small, equal to a certain critical value, or greater than that critical value.

Underdamped Oscillations

If b is relatively small (less than $2\sqrt{km}$), the system still oscillates but with ever-decreasing amplitude. (This is what you observed in the experiment we described at the beginning of this section about letting your arm swing.) This is called **underdamped oscillation**. If the amplitude when the oscillation begins at $t = 0$ is A, the amplitude at a later time t is

Amplitude of an underdamped oscillation (12-35)

The amplitude of an underdamped oscillator at time t after it is set in motion...

...equals the initial amplitude A at $t = 0$...

$$A(t) = Ae^{-(b/2m)t}$$

...multiplied by an exponential function that decreases with time.

Damping coefficient   Mass of the oscillating object

Figure 12-16 is a graph of this function. The decreasing amplitude means that the oscillating object makes smaller and smaller excursions around the equilibrium position as time goes by.

The presence of the damping force also changes the oscillation angular frequency from the value $\omega = \sqrt{k/m}$ without damping. With damping present, the angular frequency is

Angular frequency of an underdamped oscillation (12-36)

Angular frequency of an underdamped mass-spring combination

Spring constant of the spring

$$\omega_{damped} = \sqrt{\frac{k}{m} - \left(\frac{b}{2m}\right)^2}$$

Damping coefficient

Mass of the oscillating object

The presence of the term $(b/2m)^2$ inside the square root in Equation 12-36 means that the angular frequency is less with damping present than if there is no damping. The presence of the damping force acts to slow down the motion, so it makes sense that damping should decrease the angular frequency and so increase the oscillation period.

If we combine the information in Equations 12-35 and 12-36, we get the following expression for the displacement x as a function of time for a mass–spring combination that is underdamped, that is, that has a relatively small damping force:

(12-37)

$$x = Ae^{-(b/2m)t} \cos\left(\omega_{damped}t + \phi\right)$$

Figure 12-16 **Amplitude of an underdamped oscillation** If an oscillating system has relatively little damping, its oscillations are like simple harmonic motion but with an amplitude $A(t)$ that decreases with time.

The cosine function in Equation 12-37 tells us that an underdamped mass-spring combination oscillates with angular frequency ω_{damped}; the exponential function tells us that the amplitude of those oscillations decreases with time. Equation 12-35 tells us that the greater the value of the damping coefficient b, the more rapidly the amplitude decreases; Equation 12-36 tells us that a greater value of b makes the value of the angular frequency ω_{damped} smaller and so makes the oscillations happen more slowly (smaller frequency and greater period).

Figure 12-17 shows a real-life underdamped oscillation. The blue curve shows measurements of the displacement of a frog's eardrum after it is set into oscillation by a burst of sound. The red curve is an exponential function like that in Equations 12-35 and 12-37. There is a close match between the theoretical red curve and the peaks of the experimental blue curve, which shows that the amplitude decays just as we would expect in an underdamped oscillation. Indeed, Equation 12-37 turns out to be an accurate description of the shape of the blue curve.

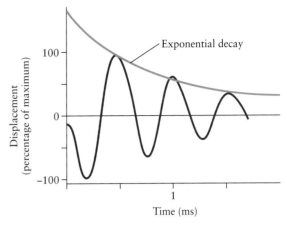

Figure 12-17 Damped oscillations of a frog's eardrum When stimulated by a burst of sound, the eardrum of a frog oscillates with decreasing amplitude (blue curve). The red curve is a decreasing exponential function like that shown in Figure 12-16.

Example 12-8 Oscillations in the Inner Ear

As we discussed in Section 3-10, special sensory cells in the human inner ear play a role in detecting acceleration and in enabling you to balance. In response to a prolonged stimulus, these cells send out an oscillating signal that can resemble the blue curve in Figure 12-18. The red dashed line follows Equation 12-35; for the data shown, $b/2m = 42$ s^{-1} and the period of the oscillations is about 3.2×10^{-3} s. Calculate the time it takes for the amplitude of the oscillations to fall to 20% of the initial amplitude. Express the answer in seconds and as a multiple of the oscillation period.

Figure 12-18 Damped oscillations in the inner ear The blue curve shows a signal sent out by sensory cells in the human inner ear. The red dashed line shows the decay in the amplitude of these signals.

Set Up

The signal oscillates with a decaying amplitude, so this is an underdamped oscillation. Our goal is to find the time t when $A(t)$ equals 0.20 times the initial amplitude A. We'll use Equation 12-35 for amplitude as a function of time.

Amplitude of an underdamped oscillation:

$$A(t) = Ae^{-(b/2m)t} \qquad (12\text{-}35)$$

Solve

Set the time-dependent amplitude equal to 0.20 of the original amplitude and solve for t. To eliminate the exponential, use the properties of the natural logarithm function.

We want the value of t that satisfies the equation

$$A(t) = 0.20A = Ae^{-(b/2m)t}$$

Divide through by the initial amplitude A:

$$0.20 = e^{-(b/2m)t}$$

To get an expression for the time t, we need to "undo" the exponential function. We can do this using the natural logarithm function (ln), which has the property that

$$\ln e^x = x \text{ for any } x$$

With this in mind, take the natural logarithm of both sides of the above equation:

$\ln 0.20 = \ln e^{-(b/2m)t}$, so
$\ln 0.20 = -(b/2m)t$

Then solve for t:

$$t = -\frac{\ln 0.20}{(b/2m)} = -\frac{(-1.6)}{(42\ \text{s}^{-1})} = \frac{1.6}{42}\ \text{s} = 0.038\ \text{s}$$

Express the answer in terms of the period of the oscillation.

The period of the oscillation is 3.2×10^{-3} s, so we can write the time t as

$$t = (0.038\ \text{s}) \times \left(\frac{1\ \text{period}}{3.2 \times 10^{-3}\ \text{s}}\right) = 12\ \text{periods}$$

Reflect

Our results show that the time for the signal amplitude to decay to 0.20 of its initial value corresponds to about 12 complete oscillations. You can use a ruler to make measurements on Figure 12-18 to verify the height of the peak (that is, the amplitude) of the twelfth cycle in the data is close to 20% of the height of the first peak.

Note that the signal shown in Figure 12-18 is an *electrical* signal, not a mechanical one, yet it obeys the same rules as mechanical oscillations. This suggests that the key physics behind oscillation also applies to nonmechanical oscillations. In later chapters we will discover the tremendous importance of electrical oscillations for understanding how power is transmitted over wires and how radio communication works.

Critically Damped and Overdamped Oscillations

Equation 12-36 shows that the angular frequency of oscillation gets smaller and smaller as the damping coefficient b is increased. You can see that the angular frequency becomes *zero* if the quantity under the square root in Equation 12-36 becomes zero. Zero angular frequency means that there are *no* cycles of oscillation per second, which means that the system does not oscillate at all! In this situation we say that the oscillations are **critically damped**: When displaced from equilibrium, the system returns smoothly to equilibrium with *no* overshoot, so there is no oscillation. The suspension of an automobile is designed to give nearly critical damping. (The damping is provided by the shock absorbers.) If the suspension were underdamped, as can happen if the shock absorbers are worn out, an automobile that drove over a bump would oscillate up and down on its suspension several times before settling down, which would make for a very uncomfortable ride.

The value of b that corresponds to critical damping is the value that makes $\omega_{\text{damping}} = 0$ in Equation 12-36. This will happen if

$$\frac{k}{m} - \left(\frac{b}{2m}\right)^2 = 0 \quad \text{or} \quad \left(\frac{b}{2m}\right)^2 = \frac{k}{m}$$

To solve this equation for the value of b for which $\omega_{\text{damped}} = 0$, take the square root of both sides and multiply both sides by $2m$:

$$\frac{b}{2m} = \sqrt{\frac{k}{m}} \quad \text{and so} \quad b = 2m\sqrt{\frac{k}{m}}$$

Simplifying, we get

(12-38) $b = 2\sqrt{km}$ (condition for critical damping)

As an example, in Examples 12-2, 12-3, and 12-4 (Section 12-3) we considered an object of mass 0.80 kg oscillating on a spring of spring constant 1.8×10^2 N/m. From Equation 12-38, this system will be critically damped if we add a damping force for which the damping coefficient b is

$$b = 2\sqrt{km} = 2\sqrt{(1.8 \times 10^2\ \text{N/m})(0.80\ \text{kg})}$$
$$= 2\sqrt{(1.8 \times 10^2\ \text{kg/s}^2)(0.80\ \text{kg})}$$
$$= 24\ \text{kg/s}$$

(We used the definition of the newton: $1\ \text{N} = 1\ \text{kg} \cdot \text{m/s}^2$, so $1\ \text{N/m} = 1\ \text{kg/s}^2$.)

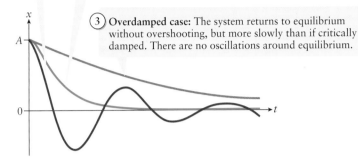

(1) **Underdamped case:** The system oscillates around the equilibrium position, and the amplitude continually decreases.

(2) **Critically damped case:** The system returns to equilibrium without overshooting. There are no oscillations around equilibrium.

(3) **Overdamped case:** The system returns to equilibrium without overshooting, but more slowly than if critically damped. There are no oscillations around equilibrium.

Figure 12-19 **Underdamped, critically damped, and overdamped oscillations** The motion of a damped oscillating system depends on whether it is underdamped ($b < 2\sqrt{km}$), critically damped ($b = 2\sqrt{km}$), or overdamped ($b > 2\sqrt{km}$). In each case the system is displaced from equilibrium by a distance A and then released.

If b has a value greater than $2\sqrt{km}$, the oscillations are **overdamped**. If an overdamped system is displaced from equilibrium, it again returns to equilibrium without overshooting, so again there are no oscillations. But now the damping is so great that the system takes even longer to return to equilibrium than in the critically damped case. If a system is critically damped, it returns to equilibrium in the shortest possible time. Figure 12-19 illustrates underdamped, critically damped, and overdamped oscillations.

Go to Picture It 12-2 for more practice dealing with damped oscillations

---

? Got the Concept? 12-11 Underdamped, Critically Damped, or Overdamped?

A block is attached to an ideal spring. The system of block and spring is critically damped: When the block is displaced from equilibrium and released, the block returns smoothly to equilibrium in the minimum time possible and does not overshoot equilibrium. If you replace the block with a new one of twice the mass, but the damping coefficient and spring constant remain the same, what kind of oscillations will result? (a) Underdamped; (b) critically damped; (c) overdamped; (d) not enough information given to decide.

Take-Home Message for Section 12-7

✔ A damping force is proportional to the velocity of an oscillating object and opposes its motion.

✔ If the damping is light so that the system is underdamped, the object oscillates in periodic motion with an amplitude that decreases with time. The frequency is less than if damping were absent.

✔ Heavier damping can cause critical damping or overdamping, in which case the system returns to equilibrium without overshooting.

12-8 Forcing a system to oscillate at the right frequency can cause resonance

As you did at the beginning of Section 12-7, stand up and let one arm hang limply by your side. With the other hand, again pull the limp arm forward and let it go, and note the frequency at which the arm tends to oscillate on its own. Now put the other hand in your pocket and swing the limp arm back and forth as you might do while walking. Try making it swing at a low frequency, a moderate frequency, and a high frequency. You'll find that it's easiest to make the arm swing at a frequency close to that at which it oscillates on its own, and that it's harder to make it swing at a slower frequency or higher frequency.

What you've just demonstrated are some of the properties of **forced oscillations**. In a forced oscillation, a periodic driving force causes a system to oscillate at the frequency of that driving force. The experiment with your arm shows that it's easiest to force the system to oscillate if the *driving* frequency is near the system's *natural* frequency, which is the frequency at which it would oscillate on its own.

A periodic driving force can take many forms. In some cases it's a single push per cycle, such as what happens when a parent pushes a child on a swing. It turns out that the simplest case to analyze is a *sinusoidal* driving force. Let's see what happens when such a driving force acts on a damped mass–spring combination.

We saw in Section 12-7 that if an underdamped mass–spring combination is displaced from equilibrium, it oscillates with an ever-decreasing amplitude and an angular frequency

(12-39)
$$\omega_{\text{damped}} = \sqrt{\frac{k}{m} - \left(\frac{b}{2m}\right)^2} = \sqrt{\omega_0^2 - \left(\frac{b}{2m}\right)^2}$$

In Equation 12-39 we use the symbol ω_0 for the quantity $\sqrt{k/m}$. We recognize this from Section 12-3 as the angular frequency that the mass–spring combination would have if there were *no* damping (see the first of Equations 12-11). We'll call ω_0 the **natural angular frequency** for the combination of mass and spring. (The natural *frequency* measured in Hz is ω_0 divided by 2π.) Now let's apply a sinusoidal driving force to the mass:

(12-40)
$$F(t) = F_0 \cos \omega t$$

The angular frequency ω of the driving force, called the **driving angular frequency,** can have any value. As an example, consider the human eardrum, which behaves like a damped mass–spring system. Sound entering the ear acts as a driving force that makes the eardrum oscillate; the sound can have any of a wide range of frequencies.

With the driving force $F(t)$ from Equation 12-40 acting along with the force of the spring and the damping force, Newton's second law for the object of mass m attached to the spring is

(12-41)
$$ma_x = -kx - bv_x + F_0 \cos \omega t$$

As was the case for Equation 12-34, the equation for damped oscillations without a driving force that we presented in Section 12-7, solving Equation 12-41 is beyond our scope. But here's what the solutions are like: When the driving force is first applied, the motion is a complicated combination of an oscillation at the angular frequency ω_{damped} given by Equation 12-39 and an oscillation at the driving angular frequency ω. The oscillation at ω_{damped} quickly dies away (it's a damped oscillation), and the system is left oscillating at the driving angular frequency ω. The amplitude of these oscillations is

Amplitude of a damped, driven oscillation
(12-42)

Although we've discussed the case of an underdamped system only, Equation 12-42 turns out to be valid no matter how large the value of b.

Equation 12-42 shows that for a given driving force magnitude F_0, the oscillation amplitude A depends on the driving angular frequency ω. The amplitude is largest when the denominator in Equation 12-42 is smallest. That happens when b is small (so there is very little damping) and when ω is close to the natural angular frequency ω_0 so $\omega_0^2 - \omega^2$ is close to zero. In other words, a system oscillates with large amplitude if you drive at close to its natural angular frequency, and the amplitude is particularly large if the system is only lightly damped. This phenomenon is called **resonance.** Figure 12-20 shows resonance in the eardrum of a frog.

Why does resonance happen? It turns out that if the driving angular frequency ω is equal to the natural angular frequency ω_0, the velocity v_x of the oscillating object is *in phase* with the driving force given by Equation 12-40. That is, the object is passing through equilibrium and has its maximum positive velocity v_x at the time when the force $F(t) = F_0 \cos \omega t$ has its maximum positive value; the object is at its maximum displacement and momentarily at rest ($v_x = 0$) when $F(t)$ equals zero; and so on. The net result is that when ω and ω_0 are equal, the driving force $F_0 \cos \omega t$ (which is in the same direction of the velocity) is the *negative* of the damping force $-bv_x$ (which is always opposite to the velocity). So at this driving angular

Figure 12-20 Resonance This graph shows a quantity related to the oscillation amplitude of a frog's eardrum (on the vertical axis) as a function of the frequency of sound waves causing the oscillation. The peak around 1800 Hz corresponds to the eardrum being forced at the eardrum's natural frequency of 1800 Hz.

frequency the driving force *cancels* the damping force! In this case Equation 12-41 becomes

$$ma_x = -kx$$

That's the same equation obeyed by a mass attached to an ideal spring with *no* damping and *no* driving force. Such a system oscillates freely at angular frequency $\omega_0 = \sqrt{k/m}$.

Figure 12-21 shows a dramatic example of resonance. A crystal wine glass is placed directly in front of a loudspeaker, and the tone emitted by the speaker is tuned— that is, its angular frequency ω is adjusted—to match the natural angular frequency ω_0 of the glass. The oscillations of the glass have little damping, as you can verify by holding such a glass by the stem and tapping the glass with a fingernail: The glass rings for quite a long time, showing that the oscillations are only lightly damped by the internal friction of the glass, and so the damping coefficient b is small. As a result, the amplitude of the oscillations when driven at the natural angular frequency is very large—so large that the glass literally tears itself apart. (This doesn't work if you use an ordinary drinking glass. Even if the loudspeaker is tuned to the natural angular frequency of the glass, the larger internal friction makes b greater than for a crystal wine glass, and the amplitude of oscillation of the driven drinking glass isn't large enough to break the glass.)

One example of resonance in nature is the flight of flies, wasps, and bees. These insects use resonance to help them beat their wings. Their bodies are equipped with special flight muscle cells that can apply cyclic forces at frequencies as high as 1000 Hz or more. These high frequencies correspond to the natural frequencies of the system of an insect's thorax and wings. The special flight muscle cells force the wings of the insect to oscillate at these natural frequencies. The result is that the wings oscillate with large amplitude A even though the force exerted by the flight muscle cells has a small magnitude F_0 (see Equation 12-42).

Figure 12-21 Destructive resonance When forced to oscillate at its natural angular frequency, a crystal wine glass can vibrate with such a large amplitude that it shatters.

 Got the Concept? 12-12   Mosquitoes Listening for Each Other

The sounds made by male mosquitoes in flight are close to 650 Hz, while those made by females are close to 400 Hz. The antennae of mosquitoes differ from male to female (Figure 12-22): The natural frequency of a male's antennae is about 400 Hz, while that of the female's is about 200 Hz. Biologists suspect that some mosquitoes can detect the presence of others based on nerve signals generated when their antennae vibrate. Would you expect that (a) male mosquitoes can detect other males, (b) females can detect other females, (c) males can detect females, (d) females can detect males; (e) more than one of these, or (f) none of these?

Male mosquito   Female mosquito

Figure 12-22 **Mosquito antennae** Mosquitoes may be able to use their antennae to detect oscillations produced by other mosquitoes. What does the physics of resonance tell us about this?

Take-Home Message for Section 12-8

✔ An oscillating system can be forced to oscillate at any frequency.

✔ When the driving angular frequency is the same as the natural angular frequency of the system, the amplitude of oscillations becomes large, and especially large if the damping force is small. This is called resonance.

Key Terms

amplitude
angular frequency
critically damped oscillations
damped oscillations
damping coefficient
driving angular frequency
forced oscillations
frequency

harmonic property
hertz
Hooke's law
natural angular frequency
oscillation
overdamped oscillations
pendulum
period

phase angle
physical pendulum
resonance
restoring force
simple harmonic motion (SHM)
simple pendulum
sinusoidal function
underdamped oscillation

Chapter Summary

Topic	Equation or Figure

Oscillations: A system will oscillate if there is (a) a restoring force that always pulls the system back toward equilibrium and (b) inertia that causes the system to overshoot equilibrium. The period T is the time for one oscillation cycle; the frequency $f = 1/T$ is the number of cycles per second (measured in Hz); the angular frequency ω equals $2\pi f$; and the amplitude A is the maximum displacement from equilibrium.

(Figure 12-12b)

Simple harmonic motion: Oscillations are particularly simple if the restoring force obeys Hooke's law, $F_x = -kx$. In this case, called simple harmonic motion, the angular frequency, period, and frequency are independent of the oscillation amplitude.

Angular frequency
$$\omega = \sqrt{\frac{k}{m}}$$

k = Spring constant of the spring

m = Mass of the object connected to the spring

Period
$$T = \frac{2\pi}{\omega} = 2\pi\sqrt{\frac{m}{k}}$$

Frequency
$$f = \frac{1}{T} = \frac{1}{2\pi}\sqrt{\frac{k}{m}} = \frac{\omega}{2\pi}$$

(12-11)

Equations of simple harmonic motion: In simple harmonic motion the position, velocity, and acceleration are all sinusoidal functions of time. The phase angle ϕ describes where in the oscillation cycle the system is at $t = 0$. We can understand this by comparing uniform circular motion to the motion of a block attached to an ideal spring.

Position of an object in SHM at time t

Amplitude of the oscillation = maximum displacement from the equilibrium position

$$x = A\cos(\omega t + \phi)$$

(12-12)

Angular frequency of the oscillation ($\omega = 2\pi f = 2\pi/T$)

Phase angle

Velocity of an object in SHM at time t

Amplitude of the oscillation = maximum displacement from the equilibrium position

$$v_x = -\omega A\sin(\omega t + \phi)$$

(12-14)

Angular frequency of the oscillation ($\omega = 2\pi f = 2\pi/T$)

Phase angle

Acceleration of an object in SHM at time t

Amplitude of the oscillation = maximum displacement from the equilibrium position

$$a_x = -\omega^2 A\cos(\omega t + \phi)$$

(12-15)

Angular frequency of the oscillation ($\omega = 2\pi f = 2\pi/T$)

Phase angle

Energy in simple harmonic motion: If there is no friction, the total mechanical energy of a system in simple harmonic motion is conserved. At equilibrium, the kinetic energy is maximum and the spring potential energy is zero; at the extremes of the motion, the kinetic energy is zero and the spring potential energy is maximum.

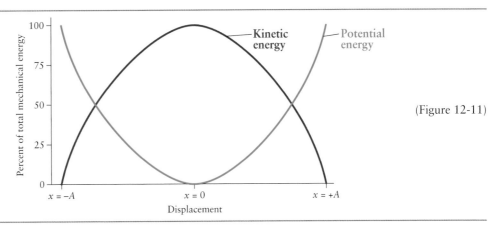

(Figure 12-11)

The simple pendulum: The oscillations of a simple pendulum are simple harmonic motion if the amplitude of oscillation is small. In this case the angular frequency of oscillation of a simple pendulum of length L is $\omega = \sqrt{g/L}$; this does not depend on the mass m.

Pivot point: The positive z axis (the rotation axis of the pendulum) points outward from this point. We take positive rotation to be counterclockwise.

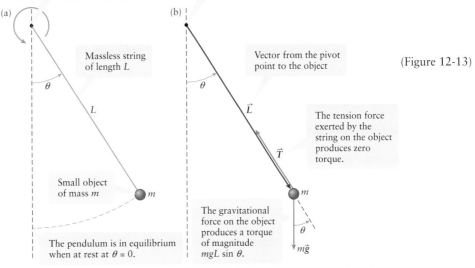

(Figure 12-13)

(a)

Massless string of length L

L

θ

Small object of mass m

m

The pendulum is in equilibrium when at rest at $\theta = 0$.

(b)

Vector from the pivot point to the object

$\vec{L}$

$\vec{T}$

The tension force exerted by the string on the object produces zero torque.

m

The gravitational force on the object produces a torque of magnitude $mgL \sin \theta$.

θ

$m\vec{g}$

The physical pendulum: A pendulum of arbitrary shape also oscillates in simple harmonic motion if the amplitude is small. The angular frequency of oscillation in this case is $\omega = \sqrt{mgh/I}$ for a physical pendulum with mass m whose center of mass is a distance h from the pivot. The pendulum's moment of inertia around the pivot is I.

The z axis points perpendicular to the plane of the pendulum's rotation.

Pivot

Center of mass

$\vec{h}$

θ

$m\vec{g}$

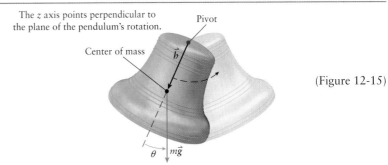

(Figure 12-15)

Damped oscillations: In most cases a damping force acts on an oscillating system. This force can be approximated as being proportional to the oscillating object's speed. The character of the motion depends on the magnitude of the damping coefficient b.

① **Underdamped case:** The system oscillates around the equilibrium position, and the amplitude continually decreases.

② **Critically damped case:** The system returns to equilibrium without overshooting. There are no oscillations around equilibrium.

③ **Overdamped case:** The system returns to equilibrium without overshooting, but more slowly than if critically damped. There are no oscillations around equilibrium.

(Figure 12-19)

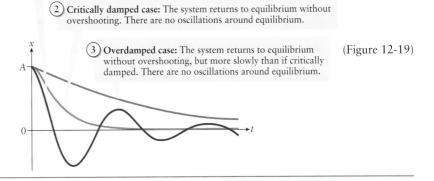

Driven oscillations: Even if damping is present, a system can be driven to oscillate at any angular frequency ω. The amplitude of the resulting oscillation is largest if b is small and the driving angular frequency is close to ω_0, the angular frequency the system would have if there were no damping. This is called resonance.

Amplitude of a mass-spring system driven by a force $F(t) = F_0 \cos \omega t$

Maximum magnitude of the driving force

Damping coefficient

Mass of the oscillating object

Natural angular frequency

Driving angular frequency

$$A = \frac{F_0}{\sqrt{m^2(\omega_0^2 - \omega^2)^2 + b^2\omega^2}} \tag{12-42}$$

Answer to What do you think? Question

(e) The maximum acceleration of an object oscillating in simple harmonic motion is $a_{max} = \omega^2 A$, where A is the amplitude of the oscillation and ω is the angular frequency (see Example 12-3 in Section 12-3). The angular frequency is in turn inversely proportional to the period T: $\omega = 2\pi/T$ (see Equations 12-11). The two oscillations in the problem have the same amplitude $A = 2.0$ mm, but the second one has one-half the period ($T = 0.40$ s versus $T = 0.80$ s). Because ω is inversely proportional to T, the second oscillation has double the angular frequency of the first one. Since a_{max} is proportional to the square of ω, it follows that the second oscillation has $2^2 = 4$ times the maximum acceleration of the first one.

Answers to Got the Concept? Questions

12-1 (d) The number of beats per unit time is just the oscillation frequency of the heart. The oscillation period is the reciprocal of the frequency, so when the frequency increases by a factor of 3 (from 50 beats/min to 150 beats/min) the period decreases to $1/3$ of its original value.

12-2 (e) This oscillation is an example of simple harmonic motion, which means that the frequency is unaffected by changes in the amplitude (the harmonic property).

12-3 (b) From Example 12-3, the maximum speed of the block is $v_{max} = \omega A$. The angular frequency is $\omega = \sqrt{k/m}$ (see the first of Equations 12-11). So increasing the spring constant k by a factor of 4 increases ω and $v_{max} = \omega A$ by a factor of $\sqrt{4} = 2$.

12-4 (d) From Equation 12-12, the displacement at $t = 0$ is $x(0) = A \cos(0 + \phi) = A \cos \pi$. Since $\cos \pi = -1$, it follows that $x(0) = -A$.

12-5 (b), (d), (c), (a) The total mechanical energy of a block oscillating on an ideal spring is $E = K + U_{spring} = \frac{1}{2}mv^2 + \frac{1}{2}kx^2 = \frac{1}{2}kA^2$. In case (a) the spring constant is $k = 5.0 \times 10^2$ N/m and the amplitude is $A = 0.020$ m, so $E = \frac{1}{2}kA^2 = \frac{1}{2}(5.0 \times 10^2 \text{ N/m})$ $(0.020 \text{ m})^2 = 0.10$ J. In case (b) the mass is $m = 0.60$ kg, $k = 3.0 \times 10^2$ N/m, and $v = 1.0$ m/s at $x = 0$. At $x = 0$ the spring potential energy is zero, so the energy is purely kinetic: $E = K = \frac{1}{2}mv^2 = \frac{1}{2}(0.60 \text{ kg})(1.0 \text{ m/s})^2 = 0.30$ J. In case (c) there is both kinetic energy ($m = 1.2$ kg and $v = 0.50$ m/s) and spring potential energy ($k = 4.0 \times 10^2$ N/m and $x = -0.010$ m). So $E = K + U_{spring} = \frac{1}{2}mv^2 + \frac{1}{2}kx^2 = \frac{1}{2}(1.2 \text{ kg})(0.50 \text{ m/s})^2 + \frac{1}{2}(4.0 \times 10^2 \text{ N/m})(-0.010 \text{ m})^2 = 0.17$ J. Similarly, in case (d) there is both kinetic energy ($m = 2.0$ kg and $v = 0.20$ m/s) and potential energy ($k = 2.0 \times 10^2$ N/m and $x = 0.050$ m), so $E = K + U_{spring} = \frac{1}{2}mv^2 + \frac{1}{2}kx^2 = \frac{1}{2}(2.0 \text{ kg})(0.20 \text{ m/s})^2 + \frac{1}{2}(2.0 \times 10^2 \text{ N/m})(0.050 \text{ m})^2 = 0.29$ J.

12-6 (d) The last of Equations 12-27 tells us that $f = (1/2\pi)\sqrt{g/L}$, so the frequency is inversely proportional to the square root of the length L of the pendulum. If L is increased by a factor of 4, the frequency changes by a factor of $1/\sqrt{4} = 1/2$. So the frequency is halved from 0.60 Hz to 0.30 Hz when the length of the pendulum increases by a factor of 4.

12-7 (c) The frequency $f = (1/2\pi)\sqrt{g/L}$ is independent of the mass of the pendulum and independent of the amplitude. So the frequency of the new pendulum is the same as before: $f = 0.60$ Hz.

12-8 (d) The frequency $f = (1/2\pi)\sqrt{g/L}$ is proportional to the square root of g, the acceleration due to gravity. The value of g on the asteroid is $1/100$ as great as on Earth, so the frequency of oscillation there is different by a factor of $\sqrt{1/100} = 1/10$. So the new frequency on the surface of the asteroid is $(1/10)(0.60 \text{ Hz}) = 0.060$ Hz.

12-9 (a) We know from Equations 12-31 that the period of a physical pendulum is $T = 2\pi\sqrt{I/mgh}$, so it is proportional to the square root of the ratio I/h. For a uniform rod of length 0.88 m (the same as the length of the leg), the center of mass is at the center of the rod. So the distance from the pivot point at one end of the rod to the center of mass is one-half of 0.88 m, or 0.44 m. For the leg the corresponding distance is 0.37 m, so h is greater for the rod by a factor of $(0.44 \text{ m})/(0.37 \text{ m}) = 1.2$. In Example 12-7 we found that the moment of inertia I of the rod is twice as large as that for the leg when both rotate around one end. So the period of the rod is greater than that of the leg by a factor of $\sqrt{(2/1.2)} = 1.3$. The effect of the greater moment of inertia overwhelms the effect of the greater distance h, so the rod has a greater period of oscillation and takes longer to complete one back-and-forth swing.

12-10 (d) A physical pendulum supported at its center of mass is in equilibrium no matter what its orientation. That's because the gravitational force acts at the support point, so there is no net torque around that point. (In terms of Equations 12-31, that means $h = 0$: There is zero distance from the pivot point to the center of mass.) Hence the pendulum does not oscillate at all. It goes through *zero* cycles per second, and the frequency is zero.

12-11 (a) From Equation 12-38, the condition for critical damping is $b = 2\sqrt{km}$. This condition was satisfied for the original block. With the new block the mass m is twice as great, so the quantity $2\sqrt{km}$ has increased by a factor of $\sqrt{2}$. How-

ever, the damping coefficient still has the same value, so now b is less than $2\sqrt{km}$ and the damping is less than the critical value. So the oscillations are now underdamped.

12-12 (c) The frequency of sound made by the female in flight is well tuned to the natural frequency of a male's antennae, so his antennae will exhibit large-amplitude vibrations (resonance) in the presence of a female mosquito. This matching of natural frequency of antennae and frequency of flight sounds does not occur between pairs of male or pairs of female mosquitoes.

Questions and Problems

In a few problems, you are given more data than you actually need; in a few other problems, you are required to supply data from your general knowledge, outside sources, or informed estimate. Interpret as significant all digits in numerical values that have trailing zeros and no decimal points.
For all problems, use $g = 9.80 \text{ m/s}^2$ for the free-fall acceleration due to gravity. Neglect friction and air resistance unless instructed to do otherwise.
• Basic, single-concept problem
•• Intermediate-level problem, may require synthesis of concepts and multiple steps
••• Challenging problem
SSM *Solution is in Student Solutions Manual*

Conceptual Questions

1. •Not all oscillatory motion is simple harmonic, but simple harmonic motion is always oscillatory. Explain this statement and give an example to support your explanation. SSM

2. •The fundamental premise of simple harmonic motion is that a force must be proportional to an object's displacement. Is anything else required?

3. •List several examples of simple harmonic motion that you have observed in everyday life.

4. •Explain the difference between a simple pendulum and a physical pendulum.

5. •If the rise and fall of your lungs is considered to be simple harmonic motion, how would you relate the period of the motion to your breathing rate (breaths per minute)? SSM

6. •Explain how *either* a cosine or a sine function can describe simple harmonic motion.

7. •(a) What are the units of ω? (b) What are the units of ωt?

8. •Galileo was one of the first scientists to observe that the period of a simple harmonic oscillator is independent of its amplitude. Explain what it means that the period is independent of the amplitude. Be sure to mention how the requirement that simple harmonic motion undergo small oscillations is affected by this supposition.

9. •Compare $x(t) = A \cos(\omega t)$ to $x(t) = A \cos(\omega t + \phi)$. What is the phase angle ϕ, and how does it change the simple harmonic motion?

10. •What are three factors that can help you distinguish between a simple pendulum and a physical pendulum?

11. •Explain how you could do an experiment to measure the elevation of your location through the use of a simple pendulum. SSM

12. •In the case of the damped harmonic oscillator, what are the units of the damping constant, b?

13. •Explain the difference between the frequency of the driving force and the natural frequency of an oscillator. SSM

14. •The application of an external force other than gravity on a simple pendulum can create many different outcomes, depending on how frequently the force is applied. Explain what will happen to the amplitude of the motion if an external force is applied to a simple pendulum at the same frequency as the natural frequency of the pendulum.

Multiple-Choice Questions

15. •A block is attached to a horizontal spring, the spring stretched so the block is located at $x = A$, and released. At what point in the resulting simple harmonic motion is the speed of the block at its maximum?
    A. $x = A$ and $x = -A$
    B. $x = 0$
    C. $x = 0$ and $x = A$
    D. $x = 0$ and $x = -A$
    E. $x = 0$, $x = -A$, and $x = A$ SSM

16. •A block is attached to a horizontal spring, the spring stretched so the block is located at $x = A$, and released. At what point in the resulting simple harmonic motion is the magnitude of the acceleration of the block at its maximum?
    A. $x = A$ and $x = -A$
    B. $x = 0$
    C. $x = 0$ and $x = A$
    D. $x = 0$ and $x = -A$
    E. $x = 0$, $x = -A$, and $x = A$

17. •A small object is attached to a horizontal spring, pushed to position $x = -A$, and released. In one full cycle of its motion, the total distance traveled by the object is
    A. $A/2$.
    B. $A/4$.
    C. A.
    D. $2A$.
    E. $4A$.

18. •A small object is attached to a horizontal spring and set in simple harmonic motion with amplitude A and period T. How long does it take for the object to travel a total distance of $6A$?
    A. $T/2$.
    B. $3T/4$.
    C. T.
    D. $3T/2$.
    E. $2T$.

19. •An object–spring system undergoes simple harmonic motion. If the mass of the object is doubled, what will happen to the period of the motion?
   A. The period will increase.
   B. The period will decrease by an unknown amount.
   C. The period will not change.
   D. The period will decrease by a factor of 2.
   E. The period will decrease by a factor of 4. SSM

20. •An object–spring system undergoes simple harmonic motion. If the amplitude increases but the mass of the object is not changed, the total energy of the system
   A. increases.
   B. decreases.
   C. doesn't change.
   D. undergoes a sinusoidal change.
   E. decreases exponentially.

21. •You can double the maximum speed of a simple harmonic oscillator by
   A. doubling the amplitude.
   B. reducing the mass to one-fourth its original value.
   C. increasing the spring constant to four times its original value.
   D. all of the above.
   E. none of the above.

22. •Replacing an object on a spring with an object having one-quarter the original mass will have the result of changing the frequency of the vibrating spring by a factor of
   A. $\frac{1}{4}$.
   B. $\frac{1}{2}$.
   C. 1 (no change).
   D. 2.
   E. 4.

23. •A uniform rod of length L hangs from one end and oscillates with a small amplitude. The moment of inertia for a rod rotating about one end is $I = \frac{1}{3}ML^2$. What is the period of the rod's oscillation?
   A. $2\pi\sqrt{\dfrac{L}{g}}$
   B. $2\pi\sqrt{\dfrac{2L}{3g}}$
   C. $2\pi\sqrt{\dfrac{L}{2g}}$
   D. $2\pi\sqrt{\dfrac{L}{3g}}$
   E. $2\pi\sqrt{\dfrac{L}{6g}}$

24. •If the period of a simple pendulum is T and we increase its length so that it's four times longer, what will the new period be?
   A. $T/2$
   B. T
   C. $2T$
   D. $4T$
   E. It is unchanged.

Estimation/Numerical Analysis

25. •(a) Plot a graph of the cosine function, cos (x), using a graphing calculator or software program. (b) How does the plot change when a phase angle of 30° is introduced, that is, cos $(x + 30°)$?

26. •Estimate the period of motion for your car's windshield wipers on (a) the low setting and (b) the high setting.

27. •Estimate the period of motion for a child swinging on a playground swing. SSM

28. •Estimate the period for normal, human eye blinking.

29. •Estimate the frequency of a hummingbird's wings.

30. •Estimate the frequency of a dog's panting on a hot summer day.

31. •Estimate the period of motion for a small coin tied to the end of a shoelace when it swings in simple harmonic motion.

32. •Estimate the frequency of a copy machine making (a) one-sided copies and (b) two-sided copies.

33. •Estimate the effect on the frequency of a grandfather clock pendulum if a 0.01-g fly lands on the very end of the pendulum's bob. SSM

34. •Estimate the energy (both potential and kinetic) associated with the pendulum of a ticking grandfather clock.

35. ••Estimate the period of a kitchen broom allowed to swing in small oscillations while suspended from the end of the handle.

36. ••A force is measured with a force sensor at the times listed in the accompanying table. (a) Make a plot of force versus time and determine if the force obeys simple harmonic motion. (b) If it is simple harmonic motion, determine the period of the motion.

t (s)	F (N)	t (s)	F (N)
0	−20	1.3	+10
0.1	−10	1.4	0
0.2	0	1.5	−10
0.3	+10	1.6	−20
0.4	+20	1.7	−10
0.5	+10	1.8	0
0.6	0	1.9	+10
0.7	−10	2.0	+20
0.8	−20	2.1	+10
0.9	−10	2.2	0
1.0	0	2.3	−10
1.1	+10	2.4	−20
1.2	+20	2.5	−10

37. ••The "ENSO" cycle (El Niño/Southern Oscillation) describes how the subsurface temperature of the Pacific Ocean changes. Figure 12-23 indicates cold episodes with blue shading and warm episodes with red shading for one region of the Pacific. Estimate the periodic pattern for the effect. SSM

Figure 12-23 Problem 37

38. •A simple pendulum that has a length of 1.25 m and a bob with a mass of 4 kg is pulled an angle θ from its natural equilibrium position (hanging straight down). Use a spreadsheet or programmable calculator to calculate the maximum potential energy of the Earth–pendulum system and complete the table.

Using the small-angle approximation, determine the largest angle that applies. *Note:* This formula only works for angles in radians!

Maximum angle from vertical	Maximum potential energy of bob (J)	Maximum speed of bob (m/s)
5°		
10°		
15°		
20°		
25°		
Largest "valid" angle		

Problems

12-2 Oscillations are caused by the interplay between a restoring force and inertia

39. •The period of a simple harmonic oscillator is 0.0125 s. What is its frequency?

40. •A simple harmonic oscillator completes 1250 cycles in 20 min. Calculate (a) the period and (b) the frequency of the motion.

41. •An object on the end of a spring oscillates with a frequency of 15 Hz. Calculate (a) the period of the motion and (b) the number of oscillations that the object undergoes in 2 min. SSM

12-3 The simplest form of oscillation occurs when the restoring force obeys Hooke's law

42. ••High tide occurs at 8:00 A.M. and is 1 m above sea level. Six hours later, low tide is 1 m below sea level. After another 6 h, high tide occurs (again 1 m above sea level), then finally one last low tide (6 h later, 1 m below sea level). (a) Write a mathematical expression that would predict the level of the ocean at this beach at any time of day. (b) Find the times in the day when the ocean level is exactly at sea level.

43. •Plot the following functions for two periods: (a) $x(t) = A \cos (2\pi t)$, (b) $x(t) = A \cos (2\pi t + \pi/2)$, and (c) $x(t) = A \cos (\pi t + \pi/4)$.

44. •What is the mass of an object that is attached to a spring with a force constant of 200 N/m if 14 oscillations occur each 16 s?

45. •A 200-g object is attached to the end of a 55 N/m spring. It is displaced 10 cm to the right of equilibrium and released on a horizontal, frictionless surface. Calculate the period of the motion.

12-4 Mechanical energy is conserved in simple harmonic motion

46. •An object on a spring slides on a horizontal frictionless surface with simple harmonic motion. Determine where the object's kinetic energy and potential energy are the same. Assume the maximum displacement of the object is A so that it oscillates between $+A$ and $-A$.

47. ••A 250-g object attached to a spring oscillates on a frictionless horizontal table with a frequency of 4.00 Hz and an amplitude of 20.0 cm. Calculate (a) the maximum potential energy of the system, (b) the displacement of the object when the potential energy is one-half of the maximum, and (c) the potential energy when the displacement is 10.0 cm. SSM

48. ••The potential energy of an object on a spring is 2.4 J at a location where the kinetic energy is 1.6 J. If the amplitude of the simple harmonic motion is 20 cm, (a) calculate the spring constant and (b) find the largest force that the object experiences.

49. ••The potential energy of a simple harmonic oscillator is given by $U = \frac{1}{2}kx^2$. (a) If $x(t) = A \cos (\omega t)$, plot the potential energy versus time for three full periods of motion. (b) Write the expression for the velocity, $v(t)$, and (c) add the plot of the kinetic energy, $K = \frac{1}{2}mv^2$, to your graph. SSM

12-5 The motion of a pendulum is approximately simple harmonic

50. •A simple pendulum is 1.24 m long. What is the period of its oscillation?

51. •The period of a simple pendulum is 2.25 s. Determine its length.

52. •In 1851, Jean Bernard Léon Foucault suspended a pendulum (later named the Foucault pendulum) from the dome of the Panthéon in Paris. The mass of the pendulum was 28.00 kg and the length of the rope was 67.00 m. The acceleration due to gravity in Paris is 9.809 m/s². Calculate the period of the pendulum.

53. •Geoff counts the number of oscillations of a simple pendulum at a location where the acceleration due to gravity is 9.80 m/s², and finds that it takes 25.0 s for 14 complete cycles. Calculate the length of the pendulum. SSM

54. •**Astronomy** What is the period of a 1-m-long simple pendulum on each of the planets in our solar system? You will need to look up the acceleration due to gravity on each planet.

55. •(a) What is the period of a simple pendulum of length 1.000 m at the top of Mount Everest, 8848 m above sea level? (b) Express your answer as a number times T_0, the period at sea level where h equals 0. The acceleration due to gravity in terms of elevation is $g = g_0 \left(\dfrac{R_E}{R_E + h} \right)^2$ where g_0 is the average acceleration due to gravity at sea level, R_E is Earth's radius, and h is the elevation above sea level. Take g_0 to be 9.800 m/s² and Earth's radius R_E to be 6.380×10^6 m.

56. ••A simple pendulum of length 0.350 m starts from rest at a maximum displacement of 10° from the equilibrium position. (a) At what time will the pendulum be located at an angle of displacement of 8°? (b) What about 5°? (c) When will the pendulum return to its starting position?

57. ••A simple pendulum oscillates between ±8° (as measured from the vertical). The length of the pendulum is 0.50 m. Compare the time intervals between ±8° and ±4°. SSM

12-6 A physical pendulum has its mass distributed over its volume

58. •A pendulum made of a uniform rod with a length of 30 cm is set into harmonic motion about one end. Calculate the period of its motion.

59. •A physical pendulum consists of a uniform spherical bob that has a mass M of 1.0 kg and a radius R of 0.50 m suspended from a massless string that has a length L of 1.0 m. What is the period T of small oscillations of the pendulum?

60. ••A thin, round disk made of acrylic plastic with a density of 1.1 g/cm³ is 20 cm in diameter and 1.0 cm thick (Figure 12-24). A very small hole is drilled through the disk at a point $d = 8.0$ cm from the center. The disk is hung from the hole on a nail and set into simple harmonic motion with a maximum angular displacement (measured from vertical) of $\theta = 7.0°$. Calculate the period of the motion.

Figure 12-24   Problem 60

61. •A solid sphere, made of acrylic plastic with a density of 1.1 g/cm³, has a radius of 5.0 cm (Figure 12-25). A very small "eyelet" is screwed into the surface of the sphere and a horizontal support rod is passed through the eyelet, allowing the sphere to pivot around this fixed axis. If the sphere is displaced slightly from equilibrium, find the period of its harmonic motion when it is released. SSM

Figure 12-25   Problem 61

12-7 When damping is present, the amplitude of an oscillating system decreases over time

62. •An oscillator that has a mass of 100 g experiences damped harmonic oscillation. The amplitude decreases to 36.8% of its initial value in 10.0 s. What is the value of the damping coefficient b?

63. •A 500-g object is attached to a spring with a force constant of 2.5 N/m. The object rests on a horizontal surface that has a viscous, oily substance spread evenly on it. The object is pulled 15 cm to the right of the equilibrium position and set into harmonic motion. After 3 s, the amplitude has fallen to 7 cm due to frictional losses in the oil. (a) Calculate the natural frequency of the system, (b) the damping constant for the oil, and (c) the frequency of oscillation that will be observed for the motion. (d) How much time will it take before the oscillations have died down to one-tenth of the original amplitude (1.5 cm)?

12-8 Forcing a system to oscillate at the right frequency can cause resonance

64. •A forced oscillator is driven at a frequency of 30.0 Hz with a peak force of 16.5 N. The natural frequency of the physical system is 28.0 Hz. If the damping constant is 1.25 kg/s and the mass of the oscillating object is 0.750 kg, calculate the amplitude of the motion.

65. ••An oscillating system has a natural frequency of 50 rad/s. The damping coefficient is 2.0 kg/s. The system is driven by a force $F(t) = (100\,\text{N})\cos((50\,\text{rad/s})t)$. What is the amplitude of the oscillations? SSM

66. •A 5.0-kg object oscillates on a spring with a force constant of 180 N/m. The damping coefficient is 0.20 kg/s. The system is driven by a sinusoidal force of maximum value 50 N, and an angular frequency of 20 rad/s. (a) What is the amplitude of the oscillations? (b) If the driving frequency is varied, at what frequency will resonance occur?

General Problems

67. •The acceleration of an object that has a mass of 0.025 kg and exhibits simple harmonic motion is given by $a(t) = (10\,\text{m/s}^2)\cos(\pi t + \pi/2)$. Calculate its velocity at $t = 2$ s, assuming the velocity of the object is $v = 3.18$ m/s at $t = 0$. SSM

68. •Show that the formulas for the period of an object on a spring $(T = 2\pi\sqrt{m/k})$ and a simple pendulum $(T = 2\pi\sqrt{L/g})$ are dimensionally correct.

69. •The position for a particular simple harmonic oscillator is given by $x(t) = (0.15\,\text{m})\cos(\pi t + \pi/3)$. What are (a) the velocity of the oscillator at $t = 1$ s and (b) its acceleration at $t = 2$ s? SSM

70. •A simple harmonic oscillator is observed to start its oscillations at the maximum amplitude when $t = 0$. Devise a function for the position that is consistent with this initial condition. Repeat when the oscillations start at the equilibrium position when $t = 0$.

71. ••A 200-g object is attached to a spring that has a force constant of 75.0 N/m. The object is pulled 8.00 cm to the right of equilibrium and released from rest to slide on a horizontal, frictionless table. (a) Calculate the maximum speed of the object. (b) Find the location of the object when its velocity is one-third of the maximum speed heading toward the right.

72. ••A 100-g object is fixed to the end of a spring that has a spring constant of 15.0 N/m. The object is displaced 15.0 cm to the right and released from rest at $t = 0$ to slide on a horizontal, frictionless table. (a) Calculate the first three times when the object is at the equilibrium position. (b) What are the first three times when the object is 10.0 cm to the left of equilibrium? (c) What is the first time that the object is 5.00 cm to the right of equilibrium, moving toward the left?

73. ••A damped oscillator with a period of 30 s shows a reduction of 30% in amplitude after 1.0 min. Calculate the percent loss in mechanical energy per cycle. SSM

74. •A system consisting of a small 1.20-kg object attached to a light spring oscillates on a smooth, horizontal surface. A graph of the position x of the object as a function of time is shown in Figure 12-26. Use the graph to answer the following questions. (a) What are the angular velocity ω_0 and the frequency of the motion? (b) What is the spring constant of the spring? (c) What is the maximum speed of the object? (d) What is the maximum acceleration of the object?

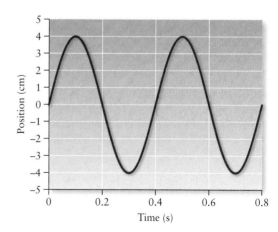

Figure 12-26   Problem 74

75. ••A pendulum made of a uniform rod with a length L_0 of 85 cm hangs from one end and is allowed to oscillate (Figure 12-27). (a) What length of a simple pendulum L_1 will have the same period of simple harmonic motion? (b) A second pendulum made of a uniform rod hangs from a point that is 5.0 cm from its end. What total length L_2 should it have to give it the same period as the first pendulum?

Figure 12-27
Problem 75

76. •(a) Using conservation of energy, derive a formula for the speed of an object that has a mass M, is on a spring that has a force constant k, and is oscillating with an amplitude of A, as a function of position $v(x)$. (b) If M has a value of 250 g, the spring constant is 85 N/m, and the amplitude is 10 cm, use the formula to calculate the speed of the object at $x = 0$ cm, 2.0 cm, 5.0 cm, 8.0 cm, and 10 cm.

77. ••When a small ball swings at the end of a very light, uniform bar, the period of the pendulum is 2.00 s. What will be the period of the pendulum if (a) the bar has the same mass as the ball and (b) the ball is removed and only the bar swings?

78. ••Devise a "correction" to the formula for the period of a pendulum due to a change in altitude (and the corresponding change in the gravitational field). Your answer should provide the percent change in the period for each 1000-m increase (or decrease) in elevation.

79. •••Two identical objects are released from rest at the same height on either side of a symmetric, frictionless ramp. They collide elastically as shown in Figure 12-28. (a) Find the period of the cyclic process in terms of g, the angle θ, the distance x_0, and the starting height y_0. (b) Calculate the numerical value for the period if $y_0 = 2.00$ m, $\theta = 30.0°$, and $x_0 = 5$ m.

Figure 12-28 Problem 79

80. ••**Astronomy** Your spaceship lands on a satellite of a planet around a distant star. As you initially circled the satellite, you measured its diameter to be 5480 km. After landing, you observe that a simple pendulum that had a frequency of 3.50 Hz on Earth now has a frequency of 1.82 Hz. (a) What is the mass of the satellite? Express your answer in kilograms and as a multiple of our Moon's mass. (b) Could you have used the vibrations of a spring–object system to determine the satellite's mass? Explain your reasoning.

81. •A bungee jumper who has a mass of 80 kg leaps off a very high platform. A crowd excitedly watches as the jumper free-falls, reaches the end of the bungee cord, then gets "yanked" up by the elastic cord, again and again. One observer measures the time between the low points for the jumper to be 9.5 s. Another observer realizes that simple harmonic motion can be used to describe the process because several of the subsequent bounces for the jumper require 9.5 s also. Finally, the jumper comes to rest a distance of 40 m below the jump point. Calculate (a) the effective spring constant for the elastic bungee cord and (b) its unstretched length.

82. •**Biology** Spiderwebs are quite elastic, so when an insect gets caught in the web, its struggles cause the web to vibrate. This alerts the spider to a potential meal. The frequency of vibration of the web gives the spider an indication of the mass of the insect. (a) Would a rapidly vibrating web indicate a large (massive) or a small insect? Explain your reasoning. (b) Suppose that a 15-mg insect lands on a horizontal web and depresses it 4.5 mm. If we model the web as a spring, what would be its effective spring constant? (c) At what rate would the web in part (b) vibrate, assuming that its mass is negligible compared to that of the insect? (d) Would the vibration rate differ if the web were not horizontal?

83. ••Two springs are attached end to end to a box of mass M as shown in Figure 12-29. Determine an expression that describes the period of motion for the box attached to this combination of springs. The two individual springs have spring constants of k_1 and k_2, respectively. SSM

Figure 12-29 Problem 83

84. ••Two springs are attached side by side to a box of mass M as shown in Figure 12-30. Determine an expression that describes the period of the motion of the box attached to this combination of springs. The two individual springs have spring constants of k_1 and k_2, respectively.

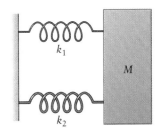

Figure 12-30 Problem 84

85. ••A 2.0-kg object is attached to a spring and undergoes simple harmonic motion. At $t = 0$, the object starts from rest, 10 cm from the equilibrium position. If the force constant of the spring k is equal to 75 N/m, calculate (a) the maximum speed and (b) the maximum acceleration of the object. (c) What is the velocity of the object at $t = 5$ s?

86. •••A 475-kg piece of delicate electronic equipment is to be hung by a 2.80-m-long steel cable. If the equipment is disturbed (such as by being bumped), the vertical vibrational frequency must not exceed 25.0 Hz. (a) What is the maximum diameter the cable can have? (b) Would the piece of equipment cause the cable to stretch appreciably?

13

Waves

In this chapter, your goals are to:

- (13-1) Describe what a mechanical wave is.
- (13-2) Explain the key properties of transverse, longitudinal, and surface waves.
- (13-3) Define the relationship between simple harmonic motion and what happens in a sinusoidal wave.
- (13-4) Explain what determines the propagation speed of a mechanical wave.
- (13-5) Describe what happens when two sinusoidal waves from different sources interfere with each other.
- (13-6) Define the properties of standing waves on a string that is fixed at both ends.
- (13-7) Explain the nature of standing sound waves in open and closed pipes.
- (13-8) Describe how beats arise from combining two sound waves of slightly different frequencies.
- (13-9) Explain what is meant by the intensity and sound intensity level of a sound wave.
- (13-10) Recognize why the frequency of a sound changes if the source and listener are moving relative to each other.

To master this chapter, you should review:

- (6-2)   The relationship between work, force, and displacement.
- (9-2, 9-4)   The nature of the Young's modulus and bulk modulus of a substance.
- (11-2)   The definition of density.
- (12-2, 12-3,   The properties of simple harmonic motion and forced oscillations.
  12-4, 12-8)

13-1 Waves are disturbances that travel from place to place

If you point your index finger downward and flex your wrist repeatedly, your finger oscillates up and down. That's the kind of motion we discussed in Chapter 12: Your finger has an equilibrium position, and it oscillates on either side of that position. But if you dip your finger in a pool of water and repeat this motion, something new happens: A series of ripples spreads away from your finger. The disturbance that you create in this way is called a **wave**. It's actually made up of countless miniature oscillations, since each part of the water's surface oscillates as the wave passes by (Figure 13-1a).

What's remarkable about waves is that the *disturbance* travels a substantial distance across the water's surface, but the individual water molecules stay in pretty much the same place. The same thing is true for *sound* waves. When you sit in an hour-long lecture, sound waves flow continuously from the lecturer to the back of the lecture hall, but there's no overall flow of air from the front to the back of the hall (Figure 13-1b). If there were, by the end of the hour the air would be denser at the back of the lecture hall than at the front!

In this chapter our subject is disturbances of this kind, called **mechanical waves**. In a mechanical wave a disturbance propagates through a material substance that we call the **medium** for the wave. The medium could be a liquid like water (Figure 13-1a), a gas like air (Figure 13-1b), or a solid. (If you live in a residence hall or an apartment, you certainly know that sound waves can travel through solid walls.) Not all waves are mechanical: As we'll learn in Chapter 22, *electromagnetic* waves such as radio signals, light rays, and X-ray beams don't require a medium to propagate and actually propagate fastest in a vacuum.

We'll begin this chapter by looking at the basic properties of mechanical waves. We'll see how to describe waves using mathematics, and we'll discover what determines the speed at which mechanical waves propagate. We'll go on to investigate what happens when two waves overlap and interfere with each other. In some cases the result is a *standing* wave in which the disturbance no longer propagates; in other cases we get a wave that propagates but whose frequency varies with time in a curious way. We'll study the manner in which we perceive sound waves, and we'll see how the properties of sound change when the source, the listener, or both are in motion.

(a) A disturbance at one place in the water, such as a falling drop...

...causes a wave to spread outward over the water's surface.

(b) Sound waves from the lecturer travel through the classroom, but the air doesn't move along with them.

Figure 13-1 Mechanical waves Two examples of mechanical waves: (a) one in a liquid and (b) one in a gas. Mechanical waves can also travel through solids.

Take-Home Message for Section 13-1

✔ In a mechanical wave, a disturbance travels through and displaces a material medium (gas, liquid, or solid). There is no net flow of matter with the disturbance.

13-2 Mechanical waves can be transverse, longitudinal, or a combination of these

Most mechanical waves are of one of the two types shown in Figure 13-2. The wave shown in Figure 13-2a is called a **transverse wave** because the individual parts of the wave medium (the rope) move in a direction *perpendicular* to the direction in which the

(a) ① If the hand holding the rope moves up and down, a **transverse wave** travels along the rope.

② The wave disturbance propagates (moves along the rope) horizontally...

③ ...but individual parts of the rope (the wave medium) move up and down, perpendicular (transverse) to the propagation direction.

(b) ① If the hand holding the spring moves back and forth, a **longitudinal wave** travels along the spring.

② The wave disturbance propagates (moves along the spring) horizontally...

③ ...but individual parts of the spring (the wave medium) move back and forth, parallel (longitudinal) to the propagation direction.

Figure 13-2 Transverse and longitudinal waves These two types of waves differ in how the parts of the wave medium (the material carrying the wave) move relative to the direction that the wave propagates.

The "wave" propagates horizontally through the stadium...

...but individual members of the crowd (the wave medium) move up and down, transverse to the propagation direction.

Figure 13-3 A transverse "wave" Sports fans call this "doing the wave," but a more descriptive name would be "doing the transverse wave."

① Clapping your hands rhythmically at the opening of a tube filled with air...

② ...makes a sound wave propagate down the tube in the form of a series of pressure pulses.

③ The air within the tube is pushed into the higher-pressure regions, so the disturbance of the air is longitudinal (along the same direction as the wave propagation).

Figure 13-4 A longitudinal wave A sound wave is a longitudinal wave.

wave propagates. By contrast, in the **longitudinal wave** shown in Figure 13-2b the individual parts of the wave medium (the spring) move in the direction *parallel* to the direction of wave propagation.

You've participated in a kind of transverse wave if you've been to a crowded sports stadium and "done the wave," in which fans jump up section by section and then sit back down (Figure 13-3). The disturbance moves horizontally through the crowd, but individual parts of the wave medium—that is, the individual fans in the crowd—move up and down, perpendicular to the direction that the "wave" propagates. (Note that this "wave" has the key property of waves that we described in Section 13-1: The disturbance moves through the crowd, but the members of the crowd don't move along with it.)

You can easily make a longitudinal wave just by clapping your hands (Figure 13-4). If you clap your hands together sharply at the opening of a tube, your hands squeeze on the air between them. As a result, the air pressure between your hands increases to a higher level than the pressure of the air that surrounds your hands. When you release your hands, this higher-pressure air pushes on the air around it, causing the surrounding air to compress and undergo a pressure increase. The air behind the newly compressed air then relaxes back to its normal pressure. The result is that a pulse of increased pressure travels down the tube. (There's no net flow of air down the tube, just a disturbance in pressure.) If you clap your hands rhythmically, a series of pressure pulses propagates down the tube. We call this propagating disturbance a **sound wave**.

Here's how you can see that a sound wave is a longitudinal wave. Within each pressure pulse of the sound wave, air molecules are squeezed together; as a pulse passes, the molecules move apart again. The net result is that within the tube, air molecules slosh back and forth parallel to the axis of the tube and so parallel to the direction of wave propagation. That's just our definition of a longitudinal wave (see Figure 13-2b). Because sound waves in a tube consist of regions of higher and lower pressure, physicists sometimes refer to sound and other longitudinal waves as **pressure waves**. (You probably have noticed that your ears, which you use to detect sound waves, are sensitive to changes in air pressure.)

When an earthquake occurs, it produces *both* transverse *and* longitudinal waves that propagate through the body of Earth. The longitudinal waves travel at about twice the speed of the transverse waves, so a seismic monitoring station some distance away from the earthquake site (the *epicenter*) will receive the longitudinal waves before the transverse waves. The more distant the location from the epicenter, the greater the time delay, so by measuring the time delay at a given location scientists can determine how far from that location the earthquake took place. By correlating such measurements made at three or more locations, they can triangulate the position of the epicenter.

A third variety of wave is a **surface wave**, which as the name suggests is a wave that propagates on the surface of a medium. Two common examples are waves on the surface of the ocean and the waves that spread away from a disturbance in a pond (Figure 13-1a). A surface wave is actually a *combination* of a transverse wave and a longitudinal wave. As a surface wave propagates parallel to the (horizontal) surface of the water, particles near the surface move both vertically and horizontally—that is, both transverse and longitudinal to the direction of wave propagation. You can see this behavior by watching a buoy floating in a harbor: As waves pass by the buoy, the buoy bobs up and down (transverse motion) and moves back and forth (longitudinal motion). Surface waves can occur on the surface of solids as well as liquids. As an example, earthquakes produce not only transverse and longitudinal waves that travel through the body of Earth but also waves that travel along Earth's surface. The surface waves are often the most destructive (see the photo that opens Chapter 12, which shows an example of the devastation caused by the surface waves of a powerful earthquake.)

While there are essential differences among transverse, longitudinal, and surface waves, they all have this characteristic in common: The wave propagates through its medium thanks to *restoring forces* that tend to return the medium to its undisturbed state. As an example, for the transverse wave on a rope shown in Figure 13-2a, the restoring force is due to the tension in the rope. To see the importance of tension, imagine detaching the rope from the post on the right-hand side of Figure 13-2a and placing the rope on top of a table. Since the rope is now slack, there is zero tension. If you now wiggle one end of the rope, that end will move in response but *no* wave will travel along the length of the rope. With no restoring force due to tension, the medium (the rope) doesn't resist being disturbed and there is no wave propagation.

The restoring force is different for different types of waves. For the longitudinal waves on a spring shown in Figure 13-2b, it's the Hooke's law force that opposes the spring being either stretched or compressed. In the case of sound waves in air (Figure 13-4), the pressure of the air itself provides the restoring force. A region of higher pressure pushes against the neighboring regions, thus expanding and lowering its pressure back to the equilibrium value; a region of lower pressure contracts due to pressure from its neighbors, thus raising its pressure toward equilibrium. And for surface waves in water the restoring force is the gravitational force, which tends to make the water surface smooth and level and so opposes the kind of disturbance shown in Figure 13-1a.

We saw in Section 12-2 that the presence of a restoring force was also an essential ingredient for *oscillation*. This suggests that there are deep connections between the physics of oscillation that we studied in Chapter 12 and the physics of waves. We'll explore these connections in the next several sections.

? Got the Concept? 13-1 **Restoring Forces in Waves**

Choose the selection that correctly fills in the blanks in the following sentence: In the wave shown in Figure 13-2a the restoring force on a piece of the rope acts in the _____ direction, and in the wave shown in Figure 13-2b the restoring force on a piece of the spring acts in the _____ direction. (a) vertical, vertical; (b) horizontal, vertical; (c) vertical, horizontal; (d) horizontal, horizontal; (e) any of these, depending on circumstances.

Take-Home Message for Section 13-2

✔ In a transverse wave, the elements of the medium are disturbed in the direction perpendicular to the direction in which the wave propagates.

✔ In a longitudinal wave, the elements of the medium are disturbed along the direction in which the wave propagates.

✔ Surface waves propagate on the surface of a medium and are a combination of a transverse and longitudinal wave.

✔ In mechanical waves of all types, a restoring force must be present to make the wave propagate.

13-3 Sinusoidal waves are related to simple harmonic motion

Just as we found it useful to have a mathematical description of what happens in an oscillation as a function of time, it helps to use mathematics to describe what happens in a wave. In general, waves can be very complicated. For example, when you're having a conversation with a friend, the sound waves coming from your mouth spread out in all directions, and the character of the wave changes from one moment to another as you vary the pitch and volume of your voice and pronounce different vowels and consonants. Instead of beginning with complicated cases such as these, we'll start by considering a simple but important kind of wave.

Our first simplification is to restrict ourselves for now to **sinusoidal waves,** in which the wave pattern at any instant is a sinusoidal function (a sine or cosine). This restriction may seem very limiting, but in fact it isn't: It turns out that *any* wave pattern can be formed by combining sinusoidal waves. That's the principle behind some types of musical *synthesizer*. By making combinations of sinusoidal sound waves with different characteristics, a synthesizer can simulate the sound of other musical instruments or create wholly new sounds.

We'll also restrict ourselves to waves that travel along a straight line, like the transverse and longitudinal waves shown in Figure 13-2 and the sound wave in a tube in Figure 13-4. We call these **one-dimensional waves** since they propagate along a single dimension of space.

**Figure 13-5 A wave "snapshot":
Wavelength** The wavelength of a
wave is the distance over which the
wave repeats itself.

① The "snapshot" of the wave at a given instant is a graph at time t of the displacement y of the medium versus the coordinate x along the length of the medium.

② This is a sinusoidal wave: The graph of displacement y versus coordinate x is a sinusoidal function (sine or cosine).

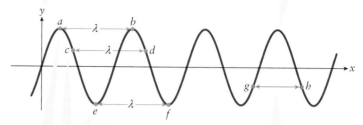

③ Points a and b are one wavelength λ apart: The distance between them corresponds to one complete cycle of the wave. The same is true for points c and d and for points e and f.

④ The displacement is the same at points g and h, but these points are not one wavelength apart: The distance between them does not correspond to a complete cycle.

To be specific, let's consider a sinusoidal, one-dimensional wave on a rope. This is actually what's drawn in Figure 13-2a. If the hand holding the left-hand end of the rope in Figure 13-2a moves up and down in simple harmonic motion with frequency f and period T, the position of the hand as a function of time is a sinusoidal function (see Section 12-3). The wave that propagates down the rope will then also be a sinusoidal function. Let's look at the properties of such a sinusoidal, one-dimensional wave.

Sinusoidal Waves: Wavelength, Amplitude, Period, Frequency, and Propagation Speed

There are two ways to visualize a wave. One is to imagine taking a "snapshot" or "freeze-frame" of the wave to see what the wave as a whole looks like at a given time. The other is to concentrate on a given piece of the medium and see how that piece moves as a function of time. (For the wave on a rope shown in Figure 13-2a, that would mean focusing on a single small piece of the rope and watching its motion.)

In **Figure 13-5** we show a "snapshot" of a sinusoidal wave on a rope at a given instant of time. This "snapshot" is a graph of the displacement y of the medium (the rope) from equilibrium versus position x along the length of the medium. For a transverse wave on the rope, the displacement y is indeed perpendicular to x as shown in Figure 13-5. We can also use Figure 13-5 to depict a "snapshot" of a longitudinal wave like that in Figure 13-2b; in that case y represents the displacement *in the x direction* of pieces of the medium from their undisturbed, equilibrium positions.

Figure 13-5 shows that the **wavelength** λ (the Greek letter "lambda") is the distance the disturbance travels over one full cycle of the wave. You can measure λ from one *crest* (high point) of the wave to the next crest, one *trough* (low point) to the next trough, or any specific point in the cycle to the analogous point in the next cycle. A wavelength is a distance, so its units in the SI system are meters.

Figure 13-6, another "snapshot" of a sinusoidal wave, shows the **amplitude** A of the wave. Just like the amplitude of an oscillation, A is the maximum displacement from equilibrium that occurs as the wave moves through its medium. It is *not* the difference between the maximum positive and maximum negative displacement.

To help us understand how a wave propagates over time, imagine a series of "snapshots" of a sinusoidal wave equally spaced in time like the frames of a movie. **Figure 13-7** shows such a series. As the wave moves through the medium, an individual piece of the

① The "snapshot" of the wave at a given instant is a graph at time t of the displacement y of the medium versus the coordinate x along the length of the medium.

② The amplitude A of the wave is the maximum magnitude of the wave disturbance.

③ The length of the red arrow (from crest to trough) is not equal to the amplitude: This length is equal to $2A$.

Figure 13-6 A wave "snapshot": Amplitude The amplitude of a wave is the maximum displacement from equilibrium.

The red arrow tracks the position of one of the wave crests.
The blue dot shows one individual piece of rope.

(1) A "snapshot" of a sinusoidal wave at a given instant

The wave propagates in the +x direction.

(2) The piece of the rope marked by the blue dot has moved downward toward its equilibrium position ($y = 0$). The crest has moved to the right.

(3) The piece of the rope marked by the blue dot has overshot equilibrium and is still moving downward. The crest continues moving to the right.

(4) The piece of the rope marked by the blue dot has reached its low point and is now moving upward. The crest continues moving to the right.

(5) The piece of the rope marked by the blue dot has again overshot equilibrium and continues upward. The crest continues moving to the right.

(6) The piece of the rope marked by the blue dot has gone through a complete cycle of oscillation and returned to its initial position. The crest has moved one full wavelength and continues moving to the right.

Figure 13-7 Scenes from a wave "movie" These successive "snapshots" of a wave in motion reveal the connection between the period of a wave and the wavelength. The elapsed time from (a) to (f) is one period T.

 During one period of oscillation T of the wave medium, the wave travels a distance of one wavelength λ.

medium (like the blue dot in Figure 13-7) oscillates up and down. Just as in Section 12-2, we use the term **period** and the symbol T for the time required for each piece of the medium to go through a complete oscillation cycle. Furthermore, just as in Sections 12-2 and 12-3 the **frequency** f (in hertz, or Hz) is the number of cycles that a piece of the medium goes through per second, and the **angular frequency** ω (in rads/s) equals the frequency multiplied by 2π:

Period of an oscillation

$$f = \frac{1}{T} \quad \text{and} \quad T = \frac{1}{f}$$

Frequency of the oscillation

Frequency and period of a wave
(12-1)

Angular frequency of a wave

$$\omega = 2\pi f = \frac{2\pi}{T}$$

Angular frequency of a wave
(13-1)

The values of T, f, and ω are the same *everywhere* in the medium where the wave is present, so these quantities are properties of the wave as a whole. The frequency of a sound wave helps determine its pitch: The higher the frequency, the higher the pitch.

Figure 13-7 also shows something remarkable about waves: *During the time that it takes an individual piece of the medium to complete one cycle of oscillation, the wave travels a distance of one wavelength through the medium.* We can use this observation to relate the wavelength and frequency to the *speed* of the wave. Since the wave travels a distance λ in a time T, the **propagation speed** v_{p} of the wave is

$$v_{\mathrm{p}} = \frac{\lambda}{T}$$

From Equations 12-1, the reciprocal $1/T$ of the period is just the frequency f. So we can rewrite the propagation speed as

Propagation speed, frequency, and wavelength of a wave (13-2)

Propagation speed of a wave

$$v_{\mathrm{p}} = f\lambda$$

Frequency   Wavelength

⚠ Watch Out! Be careful relating propagation speed, frequency, and wavelength.

Equation 13-2 may give you the impression that by changing the frequency or wavelength of a wave, you can change the propagation speed. In general this is *not* true! For many common types of waves, including sound waves in air and waves on a rope, the propagation speed is the *same* no matter what the frequency. If sound waves of different frequencies traveled at different speeds, a concertgoer sitting in the back row of a theater would hear a time delay between notes of low frequency (like those from a tuba) and notes of high frequency (like those from a flute); experience tells us that this isn't the case. For waves that propagate at a given speed v_{p}, increasing the frequency f decreases the wavelength λ and vice versa so that the product $f\lambda$ keeps the same value.

⚠ Watch Out! Propagation speed is not the same as the speed of pieces of the medium.

Be careful not to confuse v_{p}, the speed of the *wave*, with the speed of individual pieces of the medium. As Figure 13-7 shows, such pieces oscillate up and down in a transverse wave (or back and forth in a longitudinal wave), and so their speed is continuously changing in magnitude. By contrast, the speed of a wave through a uniform medium (one that has the same properties throughout) stays the same at all times. The magnitude of the propagation speed can also be very different from the speed of pieces of the wave medium. As an example, sound travels through dry air at a temperature of 20°C at $v_{\mathrm{p}} = 343$ m/s (about 1230 km/h, or 767 mi/h). But for a typical sound wave produced by a person speaking, the maximum speed of the air as the wave passes through is less than 10^{-4} m/s, or one-tenth of a millimeter per second.

Example 13-1 Wave Speed on a Sperm's Flagellum

The photograph that opens this chapter shows a sea urchin spermatozoon (sperm cell) in motion. These cells move by beating a long, tail-like flagellum against the surrounding fluid. Although some aspects of the motor that drives the flagellum are distributed along the length of the flagellum, we can approximate the flagellum as behaving like a uniform rope with a transverse wave moving along it. The flagellum is 40 μm long, the period of oscillation of the flagellum is 0.030 s, and there are approximately two complete cycles of the wave in the length of the flagellum. Estimate the speed of the transverse wave as it propagates along the flagellum.

Set Up

We are given the oscillation period T and information about the wavelength λ. We use Equation 12-1 to determine the frequency of oscillation of the flagellum. Given this, we use Equation 13-2 to find the wave speed.

Period and frequency:

$$f = \frac{1}{T} \qquad (12\text{-}1)$$

Propagation speed, frequency, and wavelength of a wave:

$$v_{\mathrm{p}} = f\lambda \qquad (13\text{-}2)$$

Solve

Find the frequency from the period.

From $T = 0.030$ s, the frequency is

$$f = \frac{1}{T} = \frac{1}{0.030 \text{ s}} = 33 \text{ Hz}$$

Two wavelengths fit into the length of the flagellum, so the wavelength is one-half of the 40-μm length. Use this to determine v_p.

Wavelength of the wave:

$$\lambda = \frac{1}{2} \times 40\ \mu\text{m} \times \frac{10^{-6} \text{ m}}{1\ \mu\text{m}} = 2.0 \times 10^{-5} \text{ m}$$

Then the wave speed is

$$v_\text{p} = f\lambda = (33 \text{ Hz})(2.0 \times 10^{-5} \text{ m}) = 7 \times 10^{-4} \text{ m/s}$$

to one significant figure.

Reflect

A wave moving at this propagation speed would travel about 2 m per hour. To put this in perspective, the world record holder in the World Snail Racing Championships (held annually in Congham, England) covered the 13-in. course in 2 min, which is just under 10 m/h. The propagation speed on the flagellum is only a factor of 5 slower—not bad for something 1000 times smaller than a snail.

Convert v_p to meters per hour:

$$v_\text{p} = 7 \times 10^{-4} \text{ m/s} \times \frac{3600 \text{ s}}{1 \text{ h}} = 2 \text{ m/h}$$

Sinusoidal Waves: Displacement as a Function of Position and Time

For a complete description of a wave, we need to know the displacement y of the medium at every position x and every time t. A function that provides this description is called the **wave function** $y(x,t)$. As its symbol suggests, y is a function of *both* x and t.

To obtain this function for a sinusoidal wave, let's start with a "snapshot" of such a wave with amplitude A and wavelength λ. Figure 13-8a shows such a "snapshot" at a given instant of time, which we'll call $t = 0$. Since the wave is sinusoidal and repeats itself over the distance from $x = 0$ to $x = \lambda$, we can write the wave function at $t = 0$ as

$$y(x,0) = A \cos\left(\frac{2\pi x}{\lambda} + \phi\right) \tag{13-3}$$

The factor $2\pi x/\lambda$ varies from 0 at $x = 0$ to 2π at $x = \lambda$, so the cosine function goes through a complete cycle over a distance of one wavelength. The **phase angle** ϕ tells us what point in the cycle corresponds to $x = 0$. (We used a phase angle ϕ in a similar way in our description of simple harmonic motion in Section 12-3.) In Figure 13-8a $\phi = 0$, so the function is a cosine that has its maximum value at $x = 0$. In Figure 13-7a, which shows a different sinusoidal wave at $t = 0$, $\phi = -\pi/2$ (the function is shifted by $\pi/2$ radians, or one-quarter cycle, compared to the wave function in Figure 13-8a).

How can we get the wave function for *any* time t from Equation 13-3? Let's suppose that the wave is propagating in the positive x direction at speed v_p. As Figure 13-8b shows, we can get the wave function at time t by replacing x in the wave function at $t = 0$ with $x - v_\text{p}t$:

$$y(x,t) = A \cos\left[\frac{2\pi}{\lambda}(x - v_\text{p}t) + \phi\right]$$

$$= A \cos\left(\frac{2\pi x}{\lambda} - \frac{2\pi v_\text{p}t}{\lambda} + \phi\right)$$

We can simplify this expression by using Equation 13-2 for the propagation speed, $v_\text{p} = f\lambda$. Dividing both sides of Equation 13-2 by λ tells us that $v_\text{p}/\lambda = f$. Then the wave function becomes

$$y(x,t) = A \cos\left(\frac{2\pi x}{\lambda} - 2\pi ft + \phi\right) \tag{13-4}$$

 See the Math Tutorial for more information on trigonometry

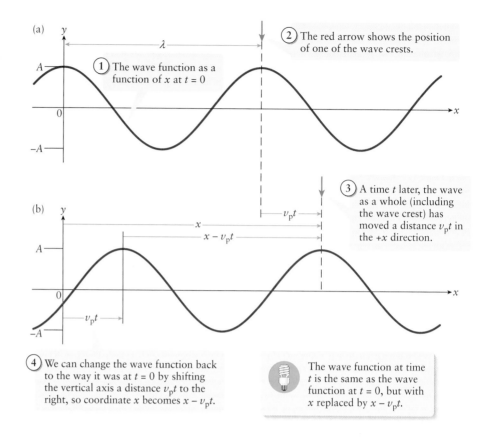

The quantity $2\pi f$ is the angular frequency ω of the wave (see Equations 13-1), and the combination $2\pi/\lambda$ in Equation 13-4 is called the **angular wave number**. We use the symbol k for this quantity:

Angular wave number
(13-5)

Angular wave number

$$k = \frac{2\pi}{\lambda} \quad \text{Wavelength}$$

Since 2π represents the number of radians in one cycle and wavelength λ is in meters, the angular wave number k is measured in radians per meter (rad/m). We use the adjective *angular* since the term "wave number" is typically used for $1/\lambda$, the reciprocal of the wavelength. This quantity multiplied by 2π is the angular wave number $k = 2\pi/\lambda$, in the same fashion that frequency f multiplied by 2π is the angular frequency $\omega = 2\pi f$.

In terms of angular wave number, we can rewrite Equation 13-4 as

Wave function for a sinusoidal wave propagating in the +x direction
(13-6)

Wave function for a sinusoidal wave propagating in the +x direction   Angular wave number of the wave = $2\pi/\lambda$

$$y(x,t) = A \cos{(kx - \omega t + \phi)} \quad \text{Phase angle}$$

Amplitude of the wave   Angular frequency of the wave = $2\pi f$

As an aid to using Equation 13-6, note that the angular frequency $\omega = 2\pi f$ and the angular wave number $k = 2\pi/\lambda$ are related by the propagation speed. To see this relationship, note that $f = \omega/2\pi$ and $\lambda = 2\pi/k$. Then, from Equation 13-2,

$$v_p = f\lambda = \left(\frac{\omega}{2\pi}\right)\left(\frac{2\pi}{k}\right)$$

or

| Propagation speed of a wave | Angular frequency of the wave |

$$v_p = \frac{\omega}{k}$$ Angular wave number of the wave

Propagation speed, angular frequency, and angular wave number
(13-7)

For the waves we are considering, the propagation speed v_p is the same no matter what the angular frequency: Increasing ω causes the angular wave number k to increase (that is, causes the wavelength $\lambda = 2\pi/k$ to decrease) so that the ratio $v_p = \omega/k$ stays the same.

We can use Equation 13-6 to verify a statement that we made earlier: If the wave is sinusoidal, each party of the medium oscillates in simple harmonic motion. To see that this is true, think of x as a constant (so that we are considering a single piece of the wave medium). Then Equation 13-6 becomes

$$y(x,t) = A \cos(kx - \omega t + \phi) = A \cos[-\omega t - (-kx - \phi)]$$
$$= A \cos[\omega t + (-kx - \phi)] \qquad (13\text{-}8)$$

In the last step we used the trigonometric identity $\cos(-\theta) = \cos\theta$. Equation 13-8 looks *exactly* like Equation 12-12 for simple harmonic motion, $x = A \cos(\omega t + \phi)$, if we interpret the quantity $-kx - \phi$ as the phase angle of the simple harmonic oscillation of the wave medium at position x. Equation 13-8 shows that all parts of the medium oscillate with the same amplitude A and the same angular frequency ω, but with a phase angle that depends on the position x within the medium. Two pieces of the medium oscillate together—that is, they are *in phase*—if they are a whole number $(1, 2, 3, \ldots)$ of wavelengths apart, and oscillate opposite to each other—that is, they are *out of phase*—if they are $\frac{1}{2}, 1\frac{1}{2}, 2\frac{1}{2}, \ldots$ wavelengths apart.

We developed Equation 13-6 for a wave propagating in the positive x direction. If the wave propagates instead in the *negative* x direction, in time t it moves a distance $v_p t$ to the *left* in Figure 13-8, and the wave function at time t is the same as the wave function at time $t = 0$, with x replaced by $x + v_p t$. The result is that the wave function for a sinusoidal wave propagating in the negative x direction is the same as Equation 13-6, but with $kx - \omega t$ replaced by $kx + \omega t$.

Example 13-2 A Wave on a Rope

A wave travels down a stretched rope. The wave has amplitude 2.00 cm and wavelength 15.0 cm, and each part of the rope goes through a complete cycle once every 0.400 s. (a) Find the frequency, angular frequency, angular wave number, and propagation speed for this wave. (b) If the wave has phase angle $\phi = 0$, find the displacement of the rope at $x = 1.80$ m (a point 1.80 m from the end of the rope) at time $t = 3.40$ s.

Set Up

We are given the amplitude $A = 2.00$ cm, the oscillation period $T = 0.400$ s, and the wavelength $\lambda = 15.0$ cm. We use Equations 12-1 and 13-1 to determine the frequency and angular frequency, Equation 13-5 to find the angular wave number, and either Equation 13-2 or Equation 13-7 to find the propagation speed. We can find the displacement at any position x and any time t using Equation 13-6.

Period, frequency, and angular frequency:

$$f = \frac{1}{T} \text{ and } \omega = 2\pi f \quad (12\text{-}1 \text{ and } 13\text{-}1)$$

Angular wave number:

$$k = \frac{2\pi}{\lambda} \qquad (13\text{-}5)$$

Propagation speed of a wave:

$$v_p = f\lambda \qquad (13\text{-}2)$$

$$v_p = \frac{\omega}{k} \qquad (13\text{-}7)$$

Wave function of a sinusoidal wave:

$$y(x,t) = A \cos(kx - \omega t + \phi) \qquad (13\text{-}6)$$

$y(x,0) = A \cos kx$

Solve

(a) Calculate the frequency f, angular frequency ω, angular wave number k, and propagation speed v_p.

We know $T = 0.400$ s, so the frequency and angular frequency are

$$f = \frac{1}{T} = \frac{1}{0.400 \text{ s}} = 2.50 \text{ Hz}$$

$$\omega = 2\pi f = (2\pi)(2.50 \text{ Hz}) = 15.7 \text{ rad/s}$$

The angular wave number is

$$k = \frac{2\pi}{\lambda} = \frac{2\pi}{15.0 \text{ cm}}\left(\frac{100 \text{ cm}}{1 \text{ m}}\right) = 41.9 \text{ rad/m}$$

From Equation 13-2, the propagation speed is

$$v_p = f\lambda = (2.50 \text{ Hz})(15.0 \text{ cm})\left(\frac{1 \text{ m}}{100 \text{ cm}}\right) = 0.375 \text{ m/s}$$

Alternatively, from Equation 13-7

$$v_p = \frac{\omega}{k} = \frac{15.7 \text{ rad/s}}{41.9 \text{ rad/m}} = 0.375 \text{ m/s}$$

(b) Find the displacement y at $x = 1.80$ m at time $t = 3.40$ s.

We take the direction of wave propagation to be the $+x$ direction. Then, since $\phi = 0$,

$$y(x,t) = A \cos(kx - \omega t)$$
$$= (2.00 \text{ cm}) \cos\left[(41.9 \text{ rad/m})(1.80 \text{ m}) - (15.7 \text{ rad/s})(3.40 \text{ s})\right]$$
$$= (2.00 \text{ cm}) \cos(75.4 \text{ rad} - 53.4 \text{ rad})$$
$$= (2.00 \text{ cm}) \cos(22.0 \text{ rad}) = (2.00 \text{ cm})(-1.00)$$
$$= -2.00 \text{ cm} = -0.0200 \text{ m}$$

Reflect

The displacement at $x = 1.80$ m and $t = 3.40$ s is equal to the negative of the amplitude A, which means that at this point and this time the rope is at its maximum negative displacement. Here's why this makes sense: $x = 1.80$ m is 12 wavelengths away from $x = 0$, so there are 12 complete wave cycles between this point and the end of the rope. So at any time the displacement at $x = 1.80$ m is the same as at $x = 0$ (these points oscillate in phase). Furthermore, the time $t = 3.40$ s is equal to eight and a half periods of oscillation. At $x = 0$ the wave function is most positive ($y = A = +2.00$ cm) at $t = 0$, and most negative ($y = -A = -2.00$ cm) at times equal to a half period, one and half periods, and so on. So at $t = 3.40$ s, the wave function is at its most negative at $x = 0$ and at $x = 1.80$ m, which is just what we found.

Compared to the wavelength $\lambda = 15.0$ cm $= 0.150$ m, the distance from the end of the rope ($x = 0$) to the point $x = 1.80$ m is

$$\frac{x}{\lambda} = \frac{1.80 \text{ m}}{0.150 \text{ m/cycle}} = 12.0 \text{ cycles}$$

So there are a whole number of wavelengths (12) between $x = 0$ and $x = 1.80$ m, and these two points oscillate in phase.

Compared to the period $T = 0.400$ s, the time $t = 3.40$ s is

$$\frac{t}{T} = \frac{3.40 \text{ s}}{0.400 \text{ s/cycle}} = 8.50 \text{ cycles}$$

So the wave has gone through $8\frac{1}{2}$ cycles of oscillation since $t = 0$, and points that were at their most positive displacement at $t = 0$ are at their most negative displacement at $t = 3.40$ s.

Sinusoidal Sound Waves

We've described sinusoidal waves in terms of their displacement y as a function of position x and time t. For sound waves in air it's usually more convenient to describe them in terms of *pressure variations* as a function of x and t. Humans hear by detecting very small variations of pressure on the eardrum. The ear can detect pressure changes as small as 2×10^{-5} Pa, equivalent to a change in atmospheric pressure of 1 part in 5 *billion* (5×10^9). If you've ever had difficulty getting your ears to "pop" when driving from the mountains down to sea level or on an airliner descending to land, you know how sensitive to pressure differences your ears can be.

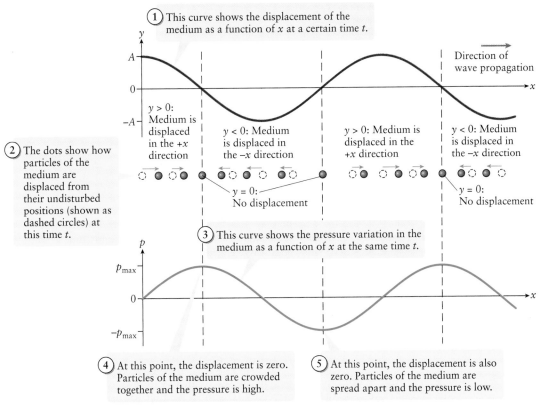

Figure 13-9 Pressure and displacement in a sinusoidal sound wave The pressure variation from normal in a sound wave is greatest where the displacement is zero, and is zero where the displacement is greatest.

Since a sound wave is a longitudinal wave, a positive value of $y(x,t)$ means that the medium is displaced in the positive x direction, while a negative value of $y(x,t)$ means that the medium is displaced in the negative x direction (Figure 13-9). As a result, as a sound wave propagates it squeezes together air molecules at some places along the wave, resulting in regions of air that have higher density and higher pressure. Adjacent regions of air are slightly depleted of air molecules and therefore have lower density and lower pressure. As Figure 13-9 shows, the pressure is greatest or least at points where the displacement is *zero*. So while the pressure is also described by a sinusoidal function, it is shifted by one quarter-cycle from the wave function for displacement $y(x,t)$. That's why we've drawn the displacement graph in Figure 13-9 as a *cosine* curve but the pressure variation graph as a *sine* curve. In particular, if the displacement is described by Equation 13-6,

$$y(x,t) = A \cos (kx - \omega t + \phi)$$

the pressure variation is given by

Pressure variation for a sinusoidal sound wave propagating in the +x direction | Angular wave number of the wave = $2\pi/\lambda$

$$p(x,t) = p_{max} \sin (kx - \omega t + \phi)$$ — Phase angle

Pressure amplitude of the wave | Angular frequency of the wave = $2\pi f$

Pressure variation for a sinusoidal sound wave propagating in the +x direction (13-9)

The quantity p_{max} is the **pressure amplitude**. It represents the maximum pressure variation above or below the pressure of the undisturbed air. A positive value of $p(x,t)$ corresponds to regions of compression (higher density and pressure), while negative values indicate regions of expansion (lower density and pressure).

Watch Out! Pressure variation is not the same as pressure.

Note that $p(x, t)$ in Equation 13-9 is not the total air pressure, but rather represents the pressure *variation* in the sound wave relative to the pressure of the undisturbed air. At any point in the air, the pressure is equal to the pressure of the undisturbed air (normally around 10^5 Pa) plus $p(x,t)$.

Got the Concept? 13-2   Human Hearing

A person with normal hearing can hear sound waves that range in frequency from approximately 20 Hz to 20 kHz (1 kHz = 1 kilohertz = 10^3 Hz). Compared to a 20-Hz sound wave, a 20-kHz sound wave has (a) a shorter wavelength and a faster propagation speed; (b) a longer wavelength and a faster propagation speed; (c) a shorter wavelength and a slower propagation speed; (d) a longer wavelength and a faster propagation speed; (e) none of these.

Take-Home Message for Section 13-3

✔   In a sinusoidal wave, each part of the wave medium goes through simple harmonic motion.

✔   The wavelength λ is the distance the disturbance travels over one full cycle of the wave. In one period T, the wave travels (propagates) a distance of one wavelength.

✔   For many common types of wave, the propagation speed is the same no matter what the frequency. Increasing the wave frequency decreases the wavelength and vice versa.

✔   The wave function $y(x,t)$ describes the displacement of the wave medium at any position x and at any time t. For a sinusoidal wave, $y(x,t)$ is a sinusoidal function.

13-4 The propagation speed of a wave depends on the properties of the wave medium

As we discussed in the previous section, for many common kinds of mechanical waves the propagation speed does not depend on the frequency or wavelength. So what *does* it depend on? We can see the answer by remembering that for a mechanical wave to propagate through a medium, there must be a *restoring force* that tends to return the medium to equilibrium when it's disturbed. The greater the magnitude of this restoring force, the more rapidly the medium goes back to equilibrium and the faster the wave will propagate. At the same time, the *inertia* of the medium acts to slow down the wave propagation. If the same restoring force is applied to a more sluggish medium with more inertia (think of water compared to maple syrup), the medium will return to equilibrium more slowly and the wave will propagate at a lower speed.

Let's look at how the competition between restoring force and inertia determines the propagation speed of transverse waves on a rope and of longitudinal waves in a fluid or solid.

Speed of a Transverse Wave on a String

For a transverse wave on a rope, the restoring force is provided by the *tension* in the rope. We'll denote this by the symbol F. (We used T as the symbol for tension in earlier chapters, but in this chapter we're using T to denote the period of a wave.) If you pluck a rope, the wave that you create will move more rapidly if you pull on the end of the rope to increase the tension.

The inertia of the rope depends on its *mass per unit length* or **linear mass density** (SI units kg/m), which we denote by the Greek letter μ ("mu"). If the rope is uniform, μ is just equal to the mass of the rope divided by its length. A thick rope has more mass per unit length than does a piece of ordinary string and so has more inertia. As the mass per unit length of a rope increases, the wave propagation speed decreases.

If we take both restoring force and inertia into account, we find that the propagation speed v_p of a transverse wave on a rope is

Go to Interactive Exercise 13-1 for more practice dealing with tension

Speed of a transverse wave on a rope (13-10)

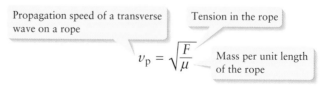

Propagation speed of a transverse wave on a rope

Tension in the rope

$$v_p = \sqrt{\frac{F}{\mu}}$$

Mass per unit length of the rope

Equation 13-10 can be derived by applying Newton's second law to a segment of a rope; however, the derivation is beyond our scope.

Example 13-3 Tension in a Sperm's Flagellum

We found in Example 13-1 (Section 13-3) that transverse waves propagate along the flagellum of a spermatozoon at a speed of about 7×10^{-4} m/s. A flagellum is about 40 μm in length and 0.25 μm in radius, and the material of which the flagellum is made has a density of 1100 kg/m^3 (slightly greater than the density of water). Estimate the tension in the flagellum.

Set Up

We can determine the tension F in the flagellum from the propagation speed v_p and the linear mass density μ. To determine μ (in kg/m), we'll use the definition of *ordinary* density ρ (mass per unit volume introduced in Section 11-2) to find the total mass of the flagellum, then divide it by the flagellum length $L = 40$ μm.

Speed of a transverse wave on a rope (or flagellum):

$$v_\mathrm{p} = \sqrt{\frac{F}{\mu}} \qquad (13\text{-}10)$$

Definition of density:

$$\rho = \frac{m}{V} \qquad (11\text{-}1)$$

40 μm

radius = 0.25 μm

Solve

The flagellum is like a circular cylinder of radius $r = 0.25$ μm and length $L = 40$ μm. Its volume is the cross-sectional area *multiplied by* the length. From the definition of density, the mass of the flagellum is its density multiplied by its volume. The linear mass density equals the mass *divided* by the flagellum's length. So the length drops out of the calculation.

Cross-sectional area of a cylinder of radius $r = 0.25$ μm:

$$A = \pi r^2 = \pi \left[0.25 \ \mu\mathrm{m} \times \left(\frac{10^{-6}\ \mathrm{m}}{1 \ \mu\mathrm{m}} \right) \right]^2 = 2.0 \times 10^{-13}\ \mathrm{m}^2$$

The volume of the flagellum (a cylinder with this cross-sectional area and length $L = 40$ μm) is $V = AL$.

Mass of the flagellum:

$$m = \rho V = \rho A L$$

The linear mass density of the flagellum is its mass divided by its length L:

$$\begin{aligned} \mu &= \frac{m}{L} = \frac{\rho A L}{L} = \rho A \\ &= (1.1 \times 10^3\ \mathrm{kg/m}^3)(2.0 \times 10^{-13}\ \mathrm{m}^2) \\ &= 2.2 \times 10^{-10}\ \mathrm{kg/m} \end{aligned}$$

Given the propagation speed v_p and the linear mass density μ, we can calculate the tension F.

The speed of transverse waves on the flagellum is

$$v_\mathrm{p} = \sqrt{\frac{F}{\mu}}$$

To solve for F, square both sides:

$$v_\mathrm{p}^2 = \frac{F}{\mu}$$

$$\begin{aligned} F = \mu v_\mathrm{p}^2 &= (2.2 \times 10^{-10}\ \mathrm{kg/m})(7 \times 10^{-4}\ \mathrm{m/s})^2 \\ &= 1 \times 10^{-16}\ \mathrm{kg \cdot m/s}^2 = 1 \times 10^{-16}\ \mathrm{N} \end{aligned}$$

to one significant figure.

Reflect

The tension in the flagellum is truly miniscule, about 1/10 of a millionth of a billionth of a newton. Trying to measure such an infinitesimal force directly is almost impossible. But as this example shows, we can determine such forces indirectly by using the properties of waves.

The Speed of Longitudinal Waves

Just as for a transverse wave on a rope, the speed of a *longitudinal* wave in a medium depends on the restoring force and the inertia of the medium. For a longitudinal wave in a fluid (a gas or a liquid), we call a longitudinal wave a *sound* wave. The disturbance associated with the wave corresponds to changes in the pressure of the fluid. We saw in Section 9-4 that the *bulk modulus B* of a material is a measure of how it responds to pressure changes. A larger bulk modulus means the material is more difficult to compress, which means that it has a greater tendency to return to its original volume when the pressure is released. In other words, the value of B tells us about the restoring force that acts within a fluid when disturbed by the pressure changes associated with a longitudinal wave. A measure of the inertia of the material is its density ρ, equal to its mass per volume (see Example 13-3 above). A detailed analysis using Newton's laws shows that the speed of sound waves in a fluid is

Speed of a longitudinal wave in a fluid (13-11)

The greater the bulk modulus B, the faster the propagation speed; the greater the density ρ, the slower the propagation speed.

The speed of longitudinal waves in a *solid* is given by a different expression than Equation 13-11. If we just consider one-dimensional waves such as those that might travel the length of a solid rod, what matters is not the *bulk* modulus B but rather *Young's modulus Y*. We learned in Section 9-2 that Young's modulus tells us how difficult it is to stretch or compress a piece of material along its length; those are just the kind of stresses experienced in a rod with a longitudinal wave propagating down its long axis. So Y tells us about the restoring force in this case, and the propagation speed is

Speed of a longitudinal wave in a solid rod (13-12)

One particularly important case of a longitudinal wave is a sound wave in air. The bulk modulus B and density ρ of air both depend on temperature and humidity, so Equation 13-11 tells us that the speed of sound in air depends on both of these quantities. For most calculations we will use the speed of sound in dry air at 20°C:

(13-13)
$$v_{\text{sound}} = 343 \text{ m/s}$$

The speed of sound is slower in colder air. For example, at the altitude where most jetliners fly (about 11,000 m, or 36,000 ft, above sea level), the average temperature is about −55°C and the speed of sound is only about 295 m/s.

We've stated that the propagation speed of waves is independent of frequency or wavelength in many important cases. One notable exception to this general rule is the speed of *surface* waves in water: For such waves the propagation speed turns out to be greater for waves with longer wavelength λ. As an example, waves with $\lambda = 1.0$ m travel at about 1.2 m/s, while longer-wavelength waves with $\lambda = 10$ m move at about 3.9 m/s.

Example 13-4 Propagation Speeds

Calculate the speed of propagation of two longitudinal waves: (a) A sound wave in room-temperature water, which has bulk modulus 2.2×10^9 N/m² and density 1.0×10^3 kg/m³; (b) a wave traveling along a steel rail of a railroad track, with Young's modulus 2.1×10^{11} N/m² and density 8.0×10^3 kg/m³.

Set Up

We use Equation 13-11 to calculate the wave speed in water (a fluid) and Equation 13-12 for the wave speed along the steel rod (an example of a solid rod).

Speed of a longitudinal wave in water (a fluid):

$$v_p = \sqrt{\frac{B_{water}}{\rho_{water}}} \tag{13-11}$$

Speed of a longitudinal wave along a solid steel rod:

$$v_p = \sqrt{\frac{Y_{steel}}{\rho_{steel}}} \tag{13-12}$$

Solve

(a) For water, use $B_{water} = 2.2 \times 10^9 \text{ N/m}^2$ and $\rho_{water} = 1.0 \times 10^3 \text{ kg/m}^3$.

Speed of sound in water:

$$v_p = \sqrt{\frac{B_{water}}{\rho_{water}}} = \sqrt{\frac{2.2 \times 10^9 \text{ N/m}^2}{1.0 \times 10^3 \text{ kg/m}^3}}$$

$$= \sqrt{2.2 \times 10^6 \frac{\text{N} \cdot \text{m}^3}{\text{kg} \cdot \text{m}^2}} = 1.5 \times 10^3 \sqrt{\frac{\text{N} \cdot \text{m}}{\text{kg}}}$$

Since $1 \text{ N} = 1 \text{ kg} \cdot \text{m/s}^2$,

$$v_p = 1.5 \times 10^3 \sqrt{\frac{\text{kg} \cdot \text{m}}{\text{s}^2} \frac{\text{m}}{\text{kg}}} = 1.5 \times 10^3 \sqrt{\frac{\text{m}^2}{\text{s}^2}}$$

$$= 1.5 \times 10^3 \text{ m/s}$$

For the steel rod, use $Y_{steel} = 2.1 \times 10^{11} \text{ N/m}^2$ and $\rho_{steel} = 8.0 \times 10^3 \text{ kg/m}^3$.

Speed of longitudinal waves on the rail:

$$v_p = \sqrt{\frac{Y_{steel}}{\rho_{steel}}} = \sqrt{\frac{2.1 \times 10^{11} \text{ N/m}^2}{8.0 \times 10^3 \text{ kg/m}^3}}$$

$$= \sqrt{2.6 \times 10^7 \frac{\text{m}^2}{\text{s}^2}} = 5.1 \times 10^3 \text{ m/s}$$

Reflect

Even though water is almost a thousand times denser than air ($\rho_{water} = 1.0 \times 10^3 \text{ kg/m}^3$ versus $\rho_{air} = 1.2 \text{ kg/m}^3$), sound travels over four times faster in water (1.5×10^3 m/s versus 343 m/s in air). The explanation is that the bulk modulus B of water is over *ten thousand* times greater than that for air, $2.2 \times 10^9 \text{ N/m}^2$ versus $1.4 \times 10^5 \text{ N/m}^2$ (which says that water is much more difficult to compress than air). The bulk modulus factor thus overwhelms the density factor so that the wave speed $v_p = \sqrt{B/\rho}$ is greater in water than in air.

In the same way, Young's modulus for steel ($2.1 \times 10^{11} \text{ N/m}^2$) is about 100 times greater than the bulk modulus for water ($2.2 \times 10^9 \text{ N/m}^2$), which says that steel is *very* difficult to compress and there is a tremendous restoring force when it is disturbed by a wave. This more than makes up for steel being eight times denser (and so having eight times more inertia) than water. So longitudinal waves travel even faster along a steel rail than they do in water.

❓ Got the Concept? 13-3   Crack of a Bat

The speed of sound in air is about 343 m/s, while the speed of *light* in air is 3.0×10^8 m/s. While sitting in the stands at a baseball game, you hear the crack of the bat hitting the ball 0.20 s after you see the batter swing. About how far is your seat from the batter? (a) about 70 m; (b) about 140 m; (c) about 340 m; (d) about 680 m; (e) about 1700 m.

Take-Home Message for Section 13-4

✔   The propagation speed of a mechanical wave depends on the strength of the restoring force in the medium (which makes the wave propagate faster) and on the inertia of the medium (which makes the wave propagate more slowly).

✔   For transverse waves on a rope, the propagation speed depends on the ratio of the tension in the rope to its linear mass density (mass per unit length).

✔   The propagation speed of longitudinal waves (sound waves) in a fluid depends on the ratio of the bulk modulus of the fluid to the density of the fluid. For waves traveling along a solid rod, the speed is determined by the ratio of Young's modulus to the density.

13-5 When two waves are present simultaneously, the total disturbance is the sum of the individual waves

So far in our study of waves we've considered only single waves in isolation. But in the real world we are bombarded by multiple waves simultaneously. If you are reading this book outside, you may hear sound waves from the conversations of others, from the wind blowing through the leaves, and from vehicles such as buses or airplanes. How can we describe what happens when more than one wave is present in a given medium?

In most cases, what happens when more than one wave is present in a medium is this: Nothing unusual happens! If you hear the sound of a singer's voice at the same time as the sound of a piano, each sound wave is unaffected by the other. What you hear is simply the *sum* of the two sound waves. That observation is at the heart of an important physical principle called the *principle of superposition:*

> *When two waves are present simultaneously, the total wave is the sum of the two individual waves.*

Where the principle of superposition can lead to surprising results is if the two waves have the *same frequency.* As we discussed in Section 13-3, we can write the wave function of a one-dimensional sinusoidal wave as $y(x,t) = A \cos (kx - \omega t + \phi)$, where A is the amplitude, $k = 2\pi/\lambda$ is the angular wave number, $\omega = 2\pi f$ is the angular frequency, and ϕ is the phase angle (Equation 13-6). Since the propagation speed is $v_p = \omega/k$ (Equation 13-7), two waves with the same frequency f and hence the same angular frequency ω will have the same angular wave number k and wavelength λ. Suppose we add two waves of the same amplitude and angular frequency but different phase angles. If wave 1 has phase angle zero and wave 2 has phase angle ϕ, we can think of ϕ as the **phase difference** for the two waves (that is, the difference between their phase angles). The wave function of the total wave is

 See the Math Tutorial for more information on trigonometry

$$
\begin{aligned}
y_{\text{total}}(x,t) &= y_1(x,t) + y_2(x,t) \\
&= A \cos (kx - \omega t) + A \cos (kx - \omega t + \phi) \\
&= A[\cos (kx - \omega t) + \cos (kx - \omega t + \phi)]
\end{aligned}
$$

To add the two cosine functions in this equation, we use the trigonometric identity for the sum of two cosines found in the Math Tutorial in the back of the book. After a little simplification, we find

(13-14)
$$
y_{\text{total}}(x,t) = 2A \cos \left(\frac{\phi}{2}\right) \cos \left(kx - \omega t + \frac{\phi}{2}\right)
$$

In other words, the total wave has the *same* angular frequency ω and angular wave number k as each individual wave, but has amplitude $2A \cos (\phi/2)$. Let's look at three examples.

(1) *Two waves in phase ($\phi = 0$).* If the phase difference is zero, then the two waves are in phase with each other: Their crests, or high points, occur at the same time t as do their troughs, or low points (Figure 13-10a). Since $\cos 0 = 1$, Equation 13-14 tells us that the total wave has amplitude $2A \cos 0 = 2A$. In other words, the waves reinforce each other so that the amplitude of the total wave is twice that of either individual wave. We call this **constructive interference.** Since each wave repeats itself once per cycle, constructive interference also happens if the phase difference corresponds to a whole number of cycles: $\phi = 2\pi, 4\pi, 6\pi, \ldots$

(2) *Two waves π out of phase ($\phi = \pi$).* Since 2π radians corresponds to one complete cycle, a phase difference of π radians means that the two individual waves are one-half cycle out of step with each other (Figure 13-10b). The waves are *out of phase:* a crest of the first wave occurs at the same time as a trough of the second wave, and vice versa. In this case the two waves cancel each other, so from Equation 13-14 the amplitude of the total wave is $2A \cos \pi/2 = 0$ (recall that $\cos \pi/2 = 0$). This situation is called **destructive interference.** Destructive interference also occurs if the phase difference corresponds to a half cycle plus any whole number of cycles, or π plus an integer multiple of 2π: $\phi = 3\pi, 5\pi, 7\pi, \ldots$

(3) *Two waves with an intermediate phase difference.* If the two waves are neither in phase nor out of phase (Figure 13-10c), we simply say that there is **interference** between the two waves: It is neither completely constructive nor completely destructive.

Figure 13-10 Superposition: combining two waves with the same frequency When two waves arrive at the same location, the total wave is the sum of the two individual waves. The properties of the total wave depend on whether the individual waves are (a) in phase, (b) out of phase, or (c) something in between.

Figure 13-11 shows a real-life example of such interference. Two oscillating fingers dip in unison into a tank of water, producing two sets of surface waves like those in Figure 13-1a with the same amplitude, same frequency, and same wavelength. In certain locations, some of which are shown by the yellow dots in Figure 13-11, the two waves arrive in phase: A crest of the first wave arrives at the same time as a crest of the second wave. There is constructive interference at these locations, and the total wave has a large amplitude. At other locations, some of which are shown by the red dots, a crest of one wave arrives at the same time as a trough of the other wave. The two waves are out of phase, and there is destructive interference. At these locations the two waves essentially cancel each other, so that the total wave is nearly zero.

The interference effect shown in Figure 13-11 may seem surprising, since the two wave *sources* are oscillating in phase. It turns out that in this case what matters are the *distances* from each source to the point where the waves meet and interfere. The same principle applies to waves of all kinds, so in **Figure 13-12** we've drawn two loudspeakers that emit sinusoidal sound waves of the same amplitude A, the same wavelength λ, and the same frequency f. We've drawn the sound waves as sinusoidal functions that indicate the displacement of air along the direction of propagation. The two loudspeakers oscillate *in phase*, so they both emit the exact same waves at any time t. A listener is at point P, a distance D_1 from speaker 1 and a distance D_2 from speaker 2. We call these distances the *path lengths* from either speaker to point P. The **path length difference**

① This photograph shows a tank of water viewed from above.

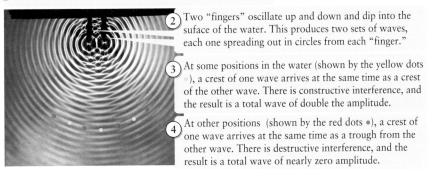

② Two "fingers" oscillate up and down and dip into the suface of the water. This produces two sets of waves, each one spreading out in circles from each "finger."

③ At some positions in the water (shown by the yellow dots ●), a crest of one wave arrives at the same time as a crest of the other wave. There is constructive interference, and the result is a total wave of double the amplitude.

④ At other positions (shown by the red dots ●), a crest of one wave arrives at the same time as a trough from the other wave. There is destructive interference, and the result is a total wave of nearly zero amplitude.

Figure 13-11 Combining water waves Circular surface waves in water spread outward from two sources that oscillate in unison.

Figure 13-12 Combining sound waves Two sinusoidal sound waves of the same amplitude and wavelength travel different distances D_1 and D_2 to point P. How they interfere at P depends on how many wavelengths fit into the path length difference Δ_{pl}.

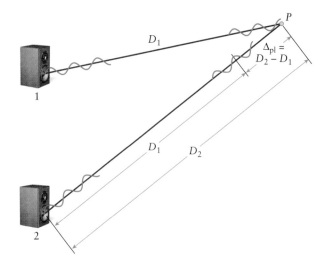

Δ_{pl} ("delta-sub-p-l") for the two waves is the difference between these two distances: $\Delta_{pl} = D_2 - D_1$, so $D_2 = D_1 + \Delta_{pl}$.

At the instant shown in Figure 13-12, wave 1 happens to reach a peak of a cycle at point P. Notice that wave 2 travels farther to reach P. The additional distance is the path length difference Δ_{pl}. Because the two waves are emitted in phase, each wave hits a peak a distance D_1 from its source. So, to determine what happens when the two waves overlap at P, we only need to ask how many cycles of wave 2 fit into the extra distance Δ_{pl}.

If exactly one wavelength λ fits into Δ_{pl} then wave 2 will be at a peak at point P, just as if it were at distance D_1 from the source. The same is true if 2λ, 3λ, 4λ, or *any* integer number of full wavelengths fit into Δ_{pl}. (It's also true if $\Delta_{pl} = 0$, which is the case if point P is equal distances from the two speakers.) And because we've already established that wave 1 is at the same point in its cycle at point P as wave 2 is at D_1 from source 2, we can make this comparison regardless of where in the cycles the waves are at P. If an integer number of wavelengths fit into Δ_{pl}, the two waves will rise and fall together as they arrive at point P. The two waves are therefore *in phase* at point P, and constructive interference takes place there (see Figure 13-10a).

Suppose instead that exactly one-half of a wavelength, or an odd number of half wavelengths ($\lambda/2$, $3\lambda/2$, $5\lambda/2$, . . .) fits into the path length difference Δ_{pl} shown in Figure 13-12. In this case, when wave 2 is at a peak at distance D_1 from the source it will be at a trough in its cycle at point P. So waves 1 and 2 will be *out of phase* at point P, resulting in destructive interference. If the amplitudes of the two waves at P are equal, the total wave will be zero as in Figure 13-10b. (The cancellation isn't complete for the situation shown in Figure 13-11. That's because the amplitude of each surface wave decreases with distance from the source. So at points where D_1 and D_2 are different, the two waves have slightly different amplitudes.)

If the path length difference Δ_{pl} is neither a whole number of wavelengths nor an odd number of half-wavelengths, the interference is neither completely constructive nor completely destructive (Figure 13-10c). Because interference of the surface waves occurs at all points in Figure 13-11, we call the overall pattern in that figure an **interference pattern**.

Here's a summary of the conditions that must be met for constructive and destructive interference:

Path length difference from the two wave sources to the point where interference occurs   Wavelength

Conditions for constructive and destructive interference of waves from two sources (13-15)

Constructive interference: $\Delta_{pl} = n\lambda$ where $n = 0, 1, 2, 3,...$

Destructive interference: $\Delta_{pl} = \left[n + \dfrac{1}{2}\right]\lambda$ where $n = 0, 1, 2, 3,...$

Note that for constructive interference, $n = 0$ refers to the case where there is *zero* path length difference, so the two waves naturally arrive in phase. This is the situation for the center yellow dot in Figure 13-11.

> ## ! Watch Out! Interference effects require special conditions.
>
> A sound system with two speakers resembles the setup in Figure 13-12. Based on our discussion of interference, you might expect that such a system would have "dead spots" where there is destructive interference between the sound waves coming from the two speakers (like the red dots in Figure 13-11) and "loud spots" where there is constructive interference (like the yellow dots in Figure 13-11). But even if you have such a system, you've probably never noticed any such "dead spots" or "loud spots." One reason is that the positions where destructive interference occurs change if the wavelength changes (see Equations 13-15). Music contains sounds
>
> of many different frequencies and hence many different wavelengths, and places that are "dead" or "loud" spots for one of the wavelengths will not be "dead" or "loud" for other wavelengths. Another reason is that in a stereo system, the signals coming from the left-hand speaker are not identical to those from the right-hand speaker. A final reason is that you also receive sound waves that come from the speakers and bounce off the walls or ceiling before reaching you. These have different path lengths than the waves that reach you directly from the speakers, and so they can "smooth out" any interference between the waves that reach you directly.

Example 13-5 Stereo Problems

Your sound system consists of two speakers 2.50 m apart. You sit 2.50 m from one of the speakers so that the two speakers are at the corners of a right triangle. As a test, you have both speakers emit the same *pure tone* (that is, a sinusoidal sine wave). The speakers emit in phase. At your location, what is the lowest frequency for which you will get (a) *destructive* interference? (b) *constructive* interference?

Set Up

There is a path length difference for the two waves that reach your ear: One travels a distance $D_1 = 2.50$ m; the other travels a longer distance D_2 equal to the hypotenuse of the right triangle. Since the product of frequency and wavelength equals the constant speed of sound, the *lowest* frequency for each kind of interference corresponds to the *longest* wavelength.

Constructive interference:
$$\Delta_{pl} = n\lambda \text{ where } n = 0, 1, 2, 3,...$$

Destructive interference:
$$\Delta_{pl} = \left(n + \frac{1}{2}\right)\lambda$$
where $n = 0, 1, 2, 3,...$ (13-15)

Propagation speed of a sound wave:
$$v_{sound} = f\lambda \quad (13\text{-}2)$$

Speed of sound in dry air at 20°C:
$$v_{sound} = 343 \text{ m/s} \quad (13\text{-}13)$$

Solve

(a) The path length difference Δ_{pl} is equal to the difference between the two path lengths D_2 and D_1.

Path length from speaker 2 to the listener:
$$D_2 = \sqrt{D_1^2 + L^2} = \sqrt{(2.50 \text{ m})^2 + (2.50 \text{ m})^2}$$
$$= 3.54 \text{ m}$$

Path length difference:
$$\Delta_{pl} = 3.54 \text{ m} - 2.50 \text{ m} = 1.04 \text{ m}$$

The longest wavelength for which there is destructive interference is the one for which one half-wavelength fits into the distance Δ_{pl}. This corresponds to $n = 0$ in the destructive-interference relation in Equations 13-15.

If one half-wavelength fits into the distance Δ_{pl},
$$\Delta_{pl} = \frac{1}{2}\lambda$$
$$\lambda = 2\Delta_{pl} = 2(1.04 \text{ m}) = 2.08 \text{ m}$$

The frequency of a sound wave with this wavelength is
$$f = \frac{v_{sound}}{\lambda} = \frac{343 \text{ m/s}}{2.08 \text{ m}}$$
$$= 165 \text{ s}^{-1} = 165 \text{ Hz}$$

If the sound has this frequency, there will be destructive interference at the listener's position and the sound level will be diminished.

(b) The longest wavelength for which there is constructive interference is the one for which one full wavelength fits into the distance Δ_{pl}. This corresponds to $n = 1$ in the constructive-interference relation from Equations 13-15. Note that $n = 0$ is possible only if the path length difference is zero, which in this case it is not.

If one wavelength fits into the distance Δ_{pl},

$$\Delta_{pl} = \lambda = 1.04 \text{ m}$$

The frequency of a sound wave with this wavelength is

$$f = \frac{v_{sound}}{\lambda} = \frac{343 \text{ m/s}}{1.04 \text{ m}}$$
$$= 330 \text{ s}^{-1} = 330 \text{ Hz}$$

If the sound has this frequency, there will be constructive interference at the listener's position and the sound level will be elevated.

Reflect

The frequencies that we found are of musical importance: 165 Hz is E below middle C (E3 in musical nomenclature) and 330 Hz is E above middle C (or E4). Note that the higher frequency is exactly double that of the lower frequency. In music, two such tones are said to be an *octave* apart.

Notice that we didn't consider the number of wavelengths that fit into the distance between you and either speaker. All that matters is the *difference* between the two paths. Can you show that in the destructive case the listener is 1.20 wavelengths away from speaker 1 and 1.70 wavelengths away from speaker 2? Can you also show that in the constructive case the numbers are 2.40 wavelengths and 3.40 wavelengths?

? Got the Concept? 13-4 Interference Pattern

If you increase the frequency at which the fingers in Figure 13-11 dip into the water, would the interference pattern (a) move outward away from the fingers, (b) move inward toward the fingers, (c) remain unchanged, or (d) any of these, depending on the value of the frequency?

Take-Home Message for Section 13-5

✔ When two waves from different sources interfere with each other, they obey the principle of superposition. At every point where more than one wave passes simultaneously, the net disturbance of the medium equals the sum of the displacements that each wave would have caused individually.

✔ If two waves are in phase at some location, the two waves reinforce each other and there is constructive interference. If the two waves are out of phase at some location, they cancel each other and there is destructive interference.

13-6 A standing wave is caused by interference between waves traveling in opposite directions

Each of the six strings of a guitar is the same length, and yet each string produces a sound of different pitch when plucked. Why is this? When you turn one of the tuning keys to tighten a string, its pitch goes up. Why? And when one of the strings is pinched against the fingerboard, the pitch also goes up. Again, why?

The answers to these questions will help explain the operation of stringed musical instruments of all kinds, including guitars, violins, harps, and pianos. The basic physics is interference, which we introduced in the last section. But instead of looking at interference between waves coming from two different sources, we'll consider the interference between waves traveling in *opposite directions* along a stretched string.

Standing Waves on a String: Modes

To see how such a situation could arise, consider what happens when you use your hand to send a single pulse down a string tied to a pole (Figure 13-13a). When the pulse reaches the fixed end, the string exerts an upward force on the pole. The pole must then exert a downward force on the string as required by Newton's third law. This action reflects an inverted pulse back along the string (Figure 13-13b).

If you were to wiggle the end of the string up and down periodically, instead of a pulse you would create a sinusoidal wave on the string. The reflection would be an inverted sinusoidal wave traveling back toward you with the same amplitude, wavelength, and frequency as the incoming wave.

Let's see what happens when we add together two sinusoidal waves traveling in opposite directions. From Equation 13-6, the wave function for such a wave traveling in the positive x direction is $y(x,t) = A \cos(kx - \omega t + \phi)$. For simplicity, we'll choose the phase angle ϕ to be zero. As we discussed in Section 13-3, a wave traveling in the *negative* x direction has the same wave function but with $kx - \omega t$ replaced by $kx + \omega t$. We'll also use $\phi = 0$ for this wave, but add a minus sign in front of the amplitude to indicate that the wave is inverted. From the principle of superposition, the total wave is the sum of these two sinusoidal waves with the same amplitude A, angular wave number $k = 2\pi/\lambda$, and angular frequency $\omega = 2\pi f$:

$$y_{\text{total}}(x,t) = A \cos(kx - \omega t) + [-A \cos(kx + \omega t)]$$
$$= A[\cos(kx - \omega t) - \cos(kx + \omega t)]$$

We can again use a trigonometric identity to simplify the difference of the two cosine functions (see the Math Tutorial), arriving at

$$y_{\text{total}}(x,t) = 2A(\sin kx)(\sin \omega t) \tag{13-16}$$

The wave function in Equation 13-16 describes a wave pattern unlike any we've seen yet. Note that the x and t terms do not appear in the same sinusoidal function. As a result, the crests of the wave do *not* move from place to place: The wave is maximum at points where $\sin kx$ equals either $+1$ or -1, and at those points the value of y_{total} oscillates between $+2A$ and $-2A$ as the function $\sin \omega t$ varies between $+1$ and -1. At the points where $\sin kx = 0$, the wave is *always* zero! Because the wave does not move but simply stays in the same place, we call it a **standing wave**. By contrast, a wave of the form $y(x,t) = A \cos(kx - \omega t)$ is referred to as a **traveling wave**. Note that we formed the standing wave by combining two traveling waves that propagate in opposite directions. The two traveling waves each carry a disturbance; when we add them together, the result is that the disturbance stays in the same place. Note that pieces of the string still move, but the *pattern* created by the interference between two traveling sinusoidal waves—the standing wave—remains stationary.

Now think again about the string in Figure 13-13. Let L be the length of the string, take $x = 0$ to be at the end of the string you hold in your hand, and let $x = L$ be at the end of the string attached to the pole. Note from Equation 13-16 that at $x = 0$, $y_{\text{total}} = 0$ (because $\sin k(0) = \sin 0 = 0$). The end that you hold in your hand moves very little compared to the amplitude of the wave on the string, so it's quite accurate to say that the amplitude of the wave at your hand is zero. So waves will reflect from *both* ends of the string, and a steady standing wave can be set up. At the other end of the string at $x = L$, the transverse displacement y must also be zero at all times because that end is rigidly attached to the pole. So $y_{\text{total}}(L,t) = 0$ for all values of t. Equation 13-16 tells us that this will be true only if $\sin kL = 0$. Now, $\sin \theta$ is equal to zero if $\theta = 0, \pi, 2\pi, 3\pi, \ldots$ So it must be true that

$$kL = n\pi \text{ where } n = 1, 2, 3, \ldots \tag{13-17}$$

(We can't have $kL = 0$, since that would mean either that the string has zero length or the angular wave number $k = 2\pi/L$ is zero, corresponding to the wave having an infinite wavelength.) Equation 13-17 is the condition that the displacement of the string is zero at both ends. Since $k = 2\pi/\lambda$, we can rewrite Equation 13-17 as

$$\frac{2\pi L}{\lambda} = n\pi$$

or, simplifying,

Length of a string held at both ends   Wavelength of a standing wave on the string

$$L = \frac{n\lambda}{2} \quad \text{where } n = 1, 2, 3, \ldots$$

Wavelengths for a standing wave on a string
(13-18)

Here λ represents the wavelength of both the standing wave and also the original wave we created on the string. So according to Equation 13-18, a whole number n of half-wavelengths must fit onto the string to generate the standing wave pattern described by Equation 13-16. **Figure 13-14** shows the patterns for $n = 1$ (for which half of a wavelength fits), $n = 2$ (for which two half-wavelengths, or one full wavelength, fits), and $n = 3$ (for which three half-wavelengths, or one and a half full wavelengths, fits). Each of these patterns is called a **standing wave mode**.

(a) As the pulse arrives at the pole, the string exerts an upward force on the pole...

(b) ...so the pole exerts a downward force on the string. This causes the pulse to become inverted as it is reflected.

Figure 13-13 Reflecting a wave
(a) A single pulse moves down a stretched string tied to a pole. (b) The pulse reflects back from the pole.

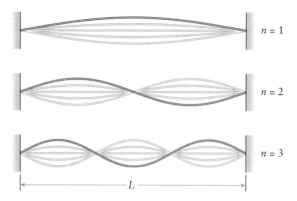

Figure 13-14 **Standing waves on a string I** These illustrations show the first three standing wave modes of a string connected to two supports. The mode number n counts the number of half-wavelengths that fit into the length of the string.

Figure 13-15 **Standing waves on a string II** These photographs show the first three standing wave modes on a string.

Figure 13-15 shows photographs of the $n = 1, 2$, and 3 standing wave modes on a real string. In these photographs the movement of the end of the string that creates the standing waves is extremely slight. This justifies treating the end of this string as fixed, as we described above.

Figure 13-14 and Figure 13-15 show that for all modes except $n = 1$, there are other positions besides the ends at which the displacement of the string is zero for all times. These are the points where $\sin kx = 0$ in Equation 13-16, so the wave function $y_{\text{total}}(x,t)$ equals zero. Any point where the displacement is always zero is called a **node** of the standing wave. For the $n = 1$ standing wave mode there are nodes at each end of the string; for the $n = 2$ mode there is an additional node at the center of the string, $x = L/2$; and for the $n = 3$ mode there are two nodes at $x = L/3$ and $x = 2L/3$.

Positions along the standing wave at which the oscillation of the string is maximal are called **antinodes**. These lie halfway between adjacent nodes. For the $n = 1$ mode in Figure 13-14 and Figure 13-15 there is one antinode at the center of the string ($x = L/2$); for the $n = 2$ mode there are two antinodes, at $x = L/4$ and $x = 3L/4$; and for the $n = 3$ mode there are three antinodes, at $x = L/6$, $x = L/2$, and $x = 5L/6$.

Standing Waves on a String: Frequencies and Musical Sound

We learned in Section 13-4 that the propagation speed of a *traveling* wave on a string under tension F and with linear mass density μ is $v_{\text{p}} = \sqrt{F/\mu}$ (Equation 13-10). Furthermore, the frequency f and wavelength λ of a traveling wave are related by $v_{\text{p}} = f\lambda$ (Equation 13-2). Because a standing wave on a string is a superposition of two traveling waves, we can use these two relationships to find the *frequencies* associated with each of the standing wave modes on a string fixed at both ends.

By combining Equations 13-2 and 13-10, we get the following relationship between the frequency f and wavelength λ of a wave on a string:

$$f\lambda = \sqrt{\frac{F}{\mu}} \quad \text{or} \quad f = \frac{1}{\lambda}\sqrt{\frac{F}{\mu}}$$

To make this specific to *standing* waves on a string, we use the relation $L = n\lambda/2$ from Equation 13-18, which we can rewrite as $(1/\lambda) = n/(2L)$. Substituting this into the above equation, we get

Frequencies for a standing
wave on a string
(13-19)

nth possible frequency of a standing wave on a string held at both ends

Tension in the string

$$f_n = \frac{n}{2L}\sqrt{\frac{F}{\mu}} \quad \text{where } n = 1, 2, 3, \ldots$$

Length of the string

Linear mass density of the string

The subscript n on the symbol f_n in Equation 13-19 denotes the frequency of the nth standing wave mode (see Figure 13-14 or Figure 13-15). Each of these frequencies represents a *natural* frequency of the string, at which it will oscillate if displaced from equilibrium and released. To make the string oscillate at the $n = 1$ frequency, displace it into the $n = 1$ shape shown in Figure 13-14 and let it go; to make it oscillate at the $n = 2$ frequency, displace it into the $n = 2$ shape; and so on. They are also the *resonant* frequencies of the string. If one end of the string is set into oscillation at one of the frequencies given by Equation 13-19, the string will oscillate with large amplitude (see Figure 13-15). If the end of the string is forced to oscillate at a frequency other than those given by Equation 13-19, the result will be a jumble of small-amplitude wiggles rather than a well-behaved standing wave.

The frequency f_1, which is the lowest natural frequency of the string, is called the **fundamental frequency**. The corresponding ($n = 1$) standing wave mode is called the **fundamental mode**. Equation 13-19 shows that the fundamental frequency is equal to

$$f_1 = \frac{1}{2L}\sqrt{\frac{F}{\mu}}$$

(13-20)

Go to Picture It 13-1 for more practice dealing with overtones

The fundamental frequency is proportional to the square root of the string tension F, inversely proportional to the string's linear mass density μ, and inversely proportional to the length L of the string.

Equation 13-20 answers the questions we posed at the beginning of this section about the strings of a guitar. For stringed instruments like a guitar, plucking a string normally causes it to vibrate primarily at its fundamental frequency. If it's an acoustic guitar, the oscillation of the string acts as a driving force that causes the body of the guitar to oscillate at the same frequency (see Section 12-8). The oscillations of the body in turn produce a sound wave of the same frequency in the surrounding air, which is what reaches the listener's ear. (If it's an electric guitar, the pickups on the guitar detect the oscillation of the string and generate an electrical signal of the same frequency. This is then amplified in a loudspeaker to produce sound.) So Equation 13-20 is really an equation for the sound frequencies produced by a stringed musical instrument. It shows that for strings of a given length L, the frequency and hence the pitch of the sound is greater for strings with less mass per unit length μ. That's why the first string on a guitar, which has a fundamental frequency of 329.6 Hz, is much thinner than the sixth string, which has a fundamental frequency of 82.4 Hz. It also shows that if you increase the tension F on a string, the frequency and pitch increase. And it explains what happens when you pinch one of the strings against the fingerboard: This shortens the length of string that's free to vibrate, thereby causing the frequency and pitch to go up.

Equation 13-19 shows that all of the other natural frequencies of a string held at both ends are integer multiples of f_1:

$$f_n = \frac{n}{2L}\sqrt{\frac{F}{\mu}} = n\left(\frac{1}{2L}\sqrt{\frac{F}{\mu}}\right) = nf_1$$

The $n = 2$ frequency f_2, called the *second harmonic* (or *first overtone*), is equal to $2f_1$; the $n = 3$ frequency f_3, called the *third harmonic* (or *second overtone*) is equal to $3f_1$; and so on.

The word *harmonic* should make you think of music, and indeed stringed musical instruments are an important application of the standing wave modes of a string. When you pluck a guitar string, the string actually vibrates in a *superposition* of standing waves with $n = 1$, $n = 2$, $n = 3$, and so on. (Just as two sinusoidal traveling waves can be present simultaneously on a string and combine to make a sinusoidal standing wave, more than one standing wave can be present on a string at the same time.) If it's an acoustic guitar, the guitar body is forced to oscillate simultaneously at the frequencies $f_1, f_2, f_3, \ldots$ and so produces a sound wave that is a superposition of sinusoidal waves at these frequencies. You might think that this would produce a hopeless jumble of sound. In fact, the result is a *nonsinusoidal* sound wave with the same frequency f_1

Figure 13-16 Adding harmonics
(a) A sound wave is produced by a string oscillating simultaneously at its fundamental frequency f_1, its second harmonic f_2, and its third harmonic f_3.
(b) The total sound wave has frequency f_1 but is not a sinusoidal wave.

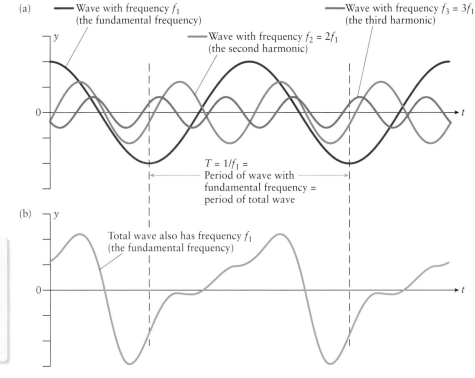

(a) — Wave with frequency f_1 (the fundamental frequency)

— Wave with frequency $f_2 = 2f_1$ (the second harmonic)

— Wave with frequency $f_3 = 3f_1$ (the third harmonic)

$T = 1/f_1 =$
Period of wave with fundamental frequency = period of total wave

(b) Total wave also has frequency f_1 (the fundamental frequency)

• Adding waves of frequencies $f_1, f_2, f_3,...$ (the harmonics of f_1) produces a wave of frequency f_1 with a non-sinusoidal wave function.
• The shape of the sound wave produced by a musical instrument determines the tone quality of the sound.

as the fundamental frequency of the string (Figure 13-16). The shape of the wave function of this nonsinusoidal wave—which depends on the relative amplitudes and phases of the sinusoidal waves at frequencies $f_1, f_2, f_3, \ldots$—determines the *tone quality* or *timbre* of the sound. Different musical instruments playing the same note all generate sound waves of the same frequency, but with different amounts of the various harmonics. As a result, different instruments produce sound waves with differently shaped wave functions and hence different tone qualities, which is why they sound different.

Example 13-6 G-String Physics

The third string on an electric guitar is 0.640 m long and has a linear mass density of 1.14×10^{-3} kg/m. This string is to play a note of frequency 196 Hz (to a musician, this note is G3 or G below middle C). (a) What must be the tension in the string? (b) What is the wavelength of the fundamental standing wave on the string? (c) What is the speed of transverse waves on this string? (d) What is the wavelength of the sound wave produced by the wave?

Set Up

We are given the string length $L = 0.640$ m and the mass per length of the string $\mu = 1.14 \times 10^{-3}$ kg/m. We'll use Equation 13-19 to find the tension F that gives a fundamental frequency $f_1 = 196$ Hz. We'll use Equation 13-18 to find the wavelength λ of the standing wave, and use this along with Equation 13-2 to find the speed of waves on the string. The sound wave produced by the guitar has the same *frequency* as the standing wave on the string. We'll find the *wavelength* of the sound wave using Equations 13-2 and 13-13.

Frequencies for a standing wave on a string:

$$f_n = \frac{n}{2L}\sqrt{\frac{F}{\mu}} \text{ where } n = 1, 2, 3, \ldots$$
(13-19)

Wavelengths for a standing wave on a string:

$$L = \frac{n\lambda}{2} \text{ where } n = 1, 2, 3, \ldots$$
(13-18)

Propagation speed, frequency, and wavelength of a wave:

$$v_p = f\lambda$$
(13-2)

Speed of sound in dry air at 20°C:

$$v_{sound} = 343 \text{ m/s}$$
(13-13)

Solve

(a) The fundamental frequency is given by Equation 13-19 with $n = 1$. Solve this equation for the string tension F.

The fundamental frequency ($n = 1$) is

$$f_1 = \frac{1}{2L}\sqrt{\frac{F}{\mu}}$$

To solve for the string tension F, first square both sides to get rid of the square root:

$$f_1^2 = \frac{1}{4L^2}\frac{F}{\mu}$$

Multiply both sides by $4L^2\mu$:

$$
\begin{aligned}
F &= 4L^2\mu f_1^2\\
&= 4(0.640\ \text{m})^2(1.14 \times 10^{-3}\ \text{kg/m})(196\ \text{Hz})^2\\
&= 71.8\ \text{kg}\cdot\text{m}\cdot\text{Hz}^2 = 71.8\ \text{kg}\cdot\text{m/s}^2\\
&= 71.8\ \text{N}
\end{aligned}
$$

(Recall that $1\ \text{Hz} = 1\ \text{s}^{-1}$.)

(b) For the fundamental mode (the $n = 1$ standing wave) of a string held at both ends, the length of the string equals one half-wavelength.

From Equation 13-18,

$$L = \frac{\lambda}{2}\ \text{for } n = 1$$

$$\lambda = 2L = 2(0.640\ \text{m}) = 1.28\ \text{m}$$
(wavelength of the standing wave on the string)

(c) Find the wave speed on the string using Equation 13-2.

Speed of transverse waves on this string:

$$
\begin{aligned}
v_p &= f\lambda\\
&= (196\ \text{Hz})(1.28\ \text{m})\\
&= 251\ \text{m/s}
\end{aligned}
$$

(d) Use Equations 13-2 and 13-13 to find the wavelength of the sound wave produced by the guitar.

For the sound wave,

$$v_{\text{sound}} = f\lambda$$

The frequency of the sound wave is the same as the frequency of the standing wave on the spring, but the wavelength is different because the wave speed is different:

$$\lambda = \frac{v_{\text{sound}}}{f} = \frac{343\ \text{m/s}}{196\ \text{Hz}} = \frac{343\ \text{m/s}}{196\ \text{s}^{-1}}$$

$$= 1.75\ \text{m}$$

Reflect

There are six strings on the guitar, each of which is under about the same tension. So the total force that acts on the guitar at the points where the strings are attached is about $6 \times 71.8\ \text{N} = 431\ \text{N}$ (about 97 lb). The guitar must be of sturdy construction to withstand these forces.

You can check our result for the speed of transverse waves on the string by using Equation 13-10, $v_p = \sqrt{F/\mu}$, and the value of F that we found in part (a). Do you get the same answer this way?

Note that our answer for part (d) is reasonable. The wavelength λ of the sound wave is greater than the wavelength of the standing wave on the string because, although the frequency f is the same for both waves, the propagation speed v_p is greater for the sound wave and $v_p = f\lambda$.

Got the Concept? 13-5   Changing the String Tension I

If the tension in a guitar string is increased by a factor of 2, the wavelength of the $n = 1$ (fundamental) standing wave mode will (a) increase to twice its previous value; (b) increase, but by a factor different than 2; (c) decrease to 1/2 of its previous value; (d) decrease but by a factor different than 1/2; (e) none of these.

? Got the Concept? 13-6 Changing the String Tension II

If the tension in a guitar string is increased by a factor of 2, the frequency of the $n = 1$ (fundamental) standing wave mode will (a) increase to twice its previous value; (b) increase, but by a factor different than 2; (c) decrease to $1/2$ of its previous value; (d) decrease, but by a factor different than $1/2$; (e) none of these.

Take-Home Message for Section 13-6

✔ Two identical waves traveling in opposite directions can interfere and form a standing wave. In a standing wave, the points where there is zero displacement (the nodes) always remain at the same places in the medium.

✔ For a stretched string held down at both ends, the only allowed standing waves are those that have an integer number of half-wavelengths in the length of the string.

✔ The length, linear mass density, and tension of a string determine the standing wave frequencies for that string.

13-7 Wind instruments, the human voice, and the human ear use standing sound waves

You've probably noticed that your singing voice sounds much better in the shower than in the open. You may have also noticed that a flute (a musical instrument based on a long tube) produces lower notes than a piccolo (which uses a shorter tube). And you know that the sound of fingernails on a chalkboard is a particularly unpleasant one—so much so that just thinking about that sound may make you cringe.

We can help to explain all of these effects by again invoking the idea of *standing waves*, which we introduced in the last section. The standing waves we need to consider are not waves on a string, but rather standing *sound* waves that result from traveling sound waves that reflect from the ends of an enclosure or tube.

Figure 13-17 shows an example of such a standing sound wave. Sound waves travel horizontally through the transparent tube and are reflected when they strike the ends, just as transverse waves on a string are reflected at the fixed ends of the string. Sound is a longitudinal wave, so the motion of the air caused by the wave moving horizontally through the tube is also in the horizontal direction. The solid ends of the tube prevent this motion from taking place there, so there is zero displacement at the ends. This is just like the situation for a string with both ends fixed (see Figure 13-14). So just as for a standing wave on a string, a standing *sound* wave will be set up if a whole number of half-wavelengths of the wave fit into the length of the tube (Equation 13-18). In

Figure 13-17 **Visualizing a standing sound wave** The small white spheres inside this apparatus (known as *Kundt's tube* after the German physicist who devised it in the nineteenth century) help to identify the locations of the antinodes of a standing sound wave in air, which would otherwise be invisible.

1 A loudspeaker (shown in gray) produces a sinusoidal sound wave. This flows into the transparent tube (a soft drink bottle) through an L-shaped pipe.

2 The sound wave bounces back and forth between the left- and right-hand ends of the tube. If the wave frequency is just right, a standing sound wave is set up.

Node — Antinode — Node — Antinode — Node

3 The longitudinal motion of air molecules (shown by the yellow arrows) is greatest at the antinodes of the standing wave. This causes the small white spheres to gather in the region of the antinodes and tends to lift them up.

Figure 13-17 the frequency of sound waves provided by the loudspeaker has been adjusted so that two half-wavelengths (one full wavelength) fit into the tube's length, corresponding to $n = 2$ in Figure 13-14 and Equation 13-18.

Note that we can use Figure 13-14 for the displacement in a standing wave on a string to depict the displacement in a standing *sound* wave in a tube like the one shown in Figure 13-17. The difference is that because sound is a longitudinal wave, the displacement is now measured *along* the direction of wave propagation (see Figure 13-9).

Note also that the *pressure variation* in a traveling sound wave is a quarter-cycle out of phase with the displacement. Figure 13-9 shows this for a traveling sound wave, but the same is true for a standing sound wave. So where there is zero displacement in a standing sound wave (a displacement node) is where the pressure variation is maximum (a pressure antinode); where the displacement oscillates with maximum amplitude (a displacement antinode) is where the pressure variation is zero, so the pressure is always equal to the undisturbed air pressure (a pressure node).

Each standing wave sound frequency corresponds to a natural frequency of the tube. That means that if you produce a sound in the tube at one of those natural frequencies, *resonance* will take place and a strong standing wave will be set up at that frequency. The net result will be that the sound wave you produce will be enhanced, just like the oscillation of a mass–spring combination is enhanced if you force it to oscillate at its natural frequency (see Section 12-8). That explains what happens when you sing in the shower. In the $n = 1$ standing wave mode, half a wavelength will fit between the walls of a shower stall. A typical shower stall is about 1 m wide, so the wavelength of the $n = 1$ mode is about 2 m. The frequency f_1 of this mode is related to the wavelength λ and the propagation speed v_{sound} for sound waves by $v_{sound} = f_1\lambda$ (Equation 13-2), so

$$f_1 = \frac{v_{sound}}{\lambda} = \frac{343 \text{ m/s}}{2 \text{ m}} \approx 170 \text{ Hz}$$

So if you sing at a frequency near 170 Hz (E or F below middle C), the shower stall will resonate and your voice will sound much fuller than it would outside the shower. The same will happen at frequencies that are multiples of 170 Hz (340 Hz, 510 Hz, 680 Hz, etc.).

Standing Waves and Wind Instruments: Closed Pipes

Just as a guitar or other stringed instrument produces tones by using standing waves on a string, a *wind* instrument makes use of standing waves in an air-filled tube. These instruments are played by setting the air within the tube into oscillation. In a brass instrument like a trumpet or trombone, the musician does this by making a buzzing sound with her lips; in a woodwind like a clarinet or saxophone, the musician blows into a reed that vibrates the air in the instrument. In order for the sound to get out of the instrument, it has to be *open* at one or both ends. (When a sound wave traveling down the tube reaches the open end, part of it is reflected back. So the ingredients for making a standing wave are still present.) This means that a wind instrument has a different set of standing wave modes than those shown in Figure 13-14.

Most wind instruments behave like a **closed pipe**, in which one end is closed and the other is open to the air. The end that the musician blows into behaves like a closed end: The displacement is essentially zero, and the pressure variation has its maximum amplitude. (This is analogous to what happens at the left-hand end of the string in Figure 13-15. It's at that end that a force is applied to make the string oscillate, but the displacement there is very small. In the same way, there is very little displacement of the air at the musician's end of a brass instrument or woodwind, but there is a large pressure variation due to the musician either buzzing her lips or making a reed vibrate.) The other end of the tube is open to the air. As a result, the pressure there is essentially equal to the pressure of the surrounding air, so the pressure variation is close to zero and the displacement amplitude is large. In other words, a closed tube has a displacement node at the closed end but a displacement antinode at the open end.

Figure 13-18 shows the first three standing wave modes in a closed pipe. We represent the magnitude of the displacement of the air from

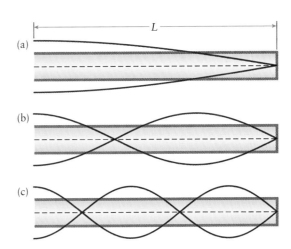

Figure 13-18 Standing sound waves in a closed pipe I (a), (b), and (c) show the displacement patterns for the first three standing sound wave modes of a pipe closed at its right-hand end and open at its left-hand end. There is a displacement node at the closed end and a displacement antinode at the open end.

equilibrium by the separation of the blue curves from the dashed centerline. Figure 13-18a shows that in the fundamental mode of this closed pipe, only *one-quarter* of a wavelength fits in the length of the pipe. You can see this more clearly in Figure 13-19a, in which we've extended the sinusoidal representation of the fundamental mode out beyond the open end to show one full wavelength. For a closed pipe, then, the relationship between the length of the tube L and the wavelength λ of the sound wave that sets up the fundamental mode of the standing wave interference is

$$L = \frac{1}{4}\lambda$$

! Watch Out! **The standing sound wave in a closed pipe does not extend far beyond the pipe.**

This extension of the wave pattern that we've drawn in Figure 13-19a does *not* represent the standing wave; the standing wave exists inside the pipe only. We've drawn this only to allow you to compare the wavelength of the sound with the length of the pipe.

Figures 13-18b and 13-18c show the next two standing wave modes of a closed pipe, and Figure 13-19 shows the displacement patterns extended outside the pipe. You can see that three quarters (3/4) and five quarters (5/4) of a wavelength, respectively, fit into the pipe for these modes. You can also see that the general relationship between L and λ for a closed pipe is

Wavelengths for a standing sound wave in a closed pipe
(13-21)

Length of a closed pipe (open at one end, closed at the other)   Wavelength of a standing wave in the pipe

$$L = \frac{n\lambda}{4} \quad \text{where } n = 1, 3, 5, \ldots$$

Notice that only the *odd* harmonics ($n = 1, 3, 5, \ldots$) can exist in a pipe closed at one end. From $v_{\text{sound}} = f\lambda$ (Equation 13-2 for sound) the corresponding natural frequencies for a closed pipe are

(13-22)

$$f_n = \frac{v_{\text{sound}}}{\lambda} = \frac{v_{\text{sound}}}{(4L/n)} = n\left(\frac{v_{\text{sound}}}{4L}\right) \text{where } n = 1, 3, 5, \ldots$$

You can see from Equation 13-22 that the fundamental frequency of a closed pipe of length L is $f_1 = v_{\text{sound}}/4L$. The next harmonic is the *third* harmonic, $f_3 = 3(v_{\text{sound}}/4L) = 3f_1$; the next harmonic after that is the *fifth* harmonic, $f_5 = 5f_1$; and so on. For a closed pipe, the even harmonics are absent.

Just like what happens when you pluck a guitar string, blowing into a closed-pipe wind instrument produces standing sound waves at more than one of the natural frequencies given by Equation 13-22. As a result, the sound that emanates from the

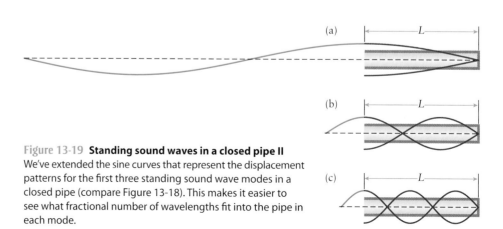

Figure 13-19 Standing sound waves in a closed pipe II
We've extended the sine curves that represent the displacement patterns for the first three standing sound wave modes in a closed pipe (compare Figure 13-18). This makes it easier to see what fractional number of wavelengths fit into the pipe in each mode.

instrument will be a combination of sinusoidal sound waves at frequencies $f_1, f_3, f_5, \ldots$, and the net result will be a nonsinusoidal wave with frequency f_1 (see Figure 13-16). The particular combination of harmonics is different for different wind instruments playing the same note, which gives each instrument its own distinctive tone quality. Equation 13-22 tells us that to change the fundamental frequency of a closed pipe, you must change the pipe length L. For a brass instrument this is done either with a slide (as in a trombone) or with valves that open and close air passages (as in a trumpet or tuba). For a woodwind like a clarinet or oboe, this is done by opening holes in the pipe that effectively shorten the length of the vibrating air column.

You actually have closed pipes on either side of your head. These are the *auditory canals* of your left and right ears, which extend a distance of about 2.5 cm = 0.025 m from the outer ear (an open end) to the eardrum (a closed end). From Equation 13-22, the fundamental frequency ($n = 1$) of this short closed pipe is

$$f_1 = \frac{v_{\text{sound}}}{4L} = \frac{343 \text{ m/s}}{4(0.025 \text{ m})} = 3430 \text{ Hz}$$

This suggests that if a sound wave with a frequency of about 3430 Hz enters your ear, it will cause resonance to take place and the sound wave will be enhanced. In fact, a person with normal hearing is most sensitive to sounds around this frequency. And an important reason why the sound of fingernails scraping across a chalkboard is so unpleasant is that this is a sound in the range from 2000 to 4000 Hz—precisely where your hearing is the most sensitive.

Your vocal tract, which extends from the vocal folds in your throat to your lips, is also a closed pipe (closed at the vocal folds, which behave rather like the reed in a clarinet or oboe, and open at the lips). Unlike other musical instruments, you can reshape your vocal tract by the way that you hold your tongue and your lips. This changes the natural frequencies of the vocal tract (so that they no longer obey Equation 13-22) and makes each spoken sound distinct. To demonstrate this, try saying "a, e, i, o, u" and notice how your tongue and lips change position. Then use your fingers to hold your lips together and repeat the experiment; without the ability to reshape your vocal tract, all five vowels will now sound almost the same.

Example 13-7 An Amorous Frog

The male tree-hole frog of Borneo (*Metaphrynella sundana*) attracts females by croaking out a simple call dominated by a tone of a single frequency. To amplify his call and enhance his attractiveness to potential mates, he finds a tree with a cavity in its trunk, sits inside the cavity, and adjusts the frequency of his call to match the fundamental frequency of the cavity. If the cavity is cylindrical and 11 cm deep, at what frequency should the frog make his mating call?

Set Up

The cavity in the tree trunk acts like a closed pipe (open on the outside of the tree, closed on the inside). Equation 13-22 gives the frequency of the fundamental ($n = 1$) mode of this cavity.

Frequencies for a standing sound wave in a closed pipe:

$$f_n = n\left(\frac{v_{\text{sound}}}{4L}\right) \text{ where } n = 1, 3, 5, \ldots$$

$$(13\text{-}22)$$

11 cm

Solve

Calculate the fundamental frequency using $n = 1$ and $v_{\text{sound}} = 343$ m/s.

The fundamental frequency ($n = 1$) is

$$f_1 = \frac{v_{\text{sound}}}{4L} = \frac{343 \text{ m/s}}{4(11 \text{ cm})}\left(\frac{100 \text{ cm}}{1 \text{ m}}\right)$$

$$= 780 \text{ s}^{-1} = 780 \text{ Hz}$$

Reflect

Our calculated result is close to the measured value of the frequency of a male tree-hole frog's mating call in a cavity 11 cm deep. These frogs have been observed to match the natural frequency of tree cavities from 10 to 15 cm in depth.

Standing Waves and Wind Instruments: Open Pipes

Unlike most other wind instruments, a *flute* is a tube that is open at *both* ends. This is called an **open pipe**. A flautist plays this instrument by blowing across the top of a hole in the pipe; this causes a pressure variation that causes the air inside the pipe to oscillate.

Because this pipe is open at each end, there is a displacement antinode (pressure node) at each end. Figure 13-20 shows the displacement patterns for the first three standing wave modes of such a pipe. (Just as at the open end of a closed pipe, a sound wave traveling through an open pipe is partially reflected at each open end. The traveling waves moving in opposite directions through the pipe give rise to a standing wave.) You can see that in Figure 13-20a one half-wavelength fits in the length L of the pipe. This represents the fundamental mode of the pipe, so the wavelength λ of the fundamental mode is given by

$$L = \frac{1}{2}\lambda$$

Similarly, the standing wave modes in Figures 13-20b and 13-20c have two half-wavelengths (one full wavelength) and three half-wavelengths, respectively, in the length of the pipe. In general, the relationship between L and λ for an open pipe is

Wavelengths for a standing sound wave in an open pipe (13-23)

Length of an open pipe (open at both ends)   Wavelength of a standing wave in the pipe

$$L = \frac{n\lambda}{2} \quad \text{where } n = 1, 2, 3, \ldots$$

This is the same relationship as for standing waves on a string held at both ends (Equation 13-18) or for a pipe *closed* at both ends (see Figure 13-17). Although the wavelengths are the same as in those two cases, an open pipe has antinodes, not nodes, at its two ends.

The corresponding natural frequencies are

(13-24)

$$f_n = \frac{v_{\text{sound}}}{\lambda} = \frac{v_{\text{sound}}}{(2L/n)} = n\left(\frac{v_{\text{sound}}}{2L}\right) \text{where } n = 1, 2, 3, \ldots$$

Unlike a closed pipe (Equation 13-22), an open pipe has *all* harmonics of its fundamental ($n = 1$) frequency. Note that for a given length L, the fundamental frequency of a closed pipe (from Equation 13-22, $f_1 = v_{\text{sound}}/4L$) is one-half of the fundamental frequency of an open pipe (from Equation 13-24, $f_1 = v_{\text{sound}}/2L$). If you cover one end of an open pipe while blowing into it, you change it into a closed pipe and the sound it produces will be lower in frequency and pitch.

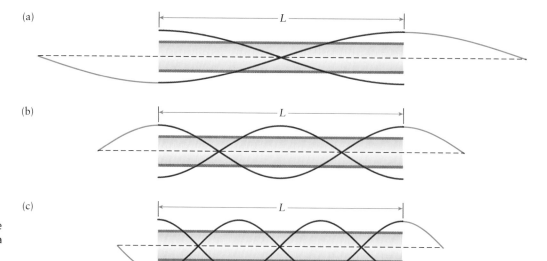

(a)

(b)

(c)

Figure 13-20 Standing sound waves in an open pipe (a), (b), and (c) show the displacement patterns for the first three standing sound wave modes of a pipe open at both ends. There is a displacement antinode at each open end.

? Got the Concept? 13-7 Filling a Water Bottle

Imagine that you gently tap the side of a water bottle as you fill it. As the water level rises, the pitch of the sound made by the bottle as you tap it (a) increases; (b) decreases; (c) first increases, then decreases; (d) first decreases, then increases; (e) stays the same.

Take-Home Message for Section 13-7

✔ Traveling sound waves in a pipe can interfere to form a standing sound wave.

✔ A displacement node always appears at a closed end of the pipe, and a displacement antinode always appears at an open end.

✔ For a closed pipe (open at one end, closed at the other), the standing wave frequencies are odd multiples of the fundamental frequency. For an open pipe (open at both ends), the standing wave frequencies include both even and odd multiples of the fundamental frequency.

13-8 Two sound waves of slightly different frequencies produce beats

You might hear a sound something like "wah wah wah" when a guitar player tunes her instrument by plucking two strings at the same time. As she adjusts the tension on one string, the time between the "wahs" gets so long that they can no longer be heard. This phenomenon, known as **beats**, arises from the interference between sound waves. Beats are most pronounced when two waves of nearly identical frequencies interfere.

To see how beats arise, let's see what happens when we combine two sinusoidal waves with the same amplitude A but with slightly different frequencies f_1 and f_2. Figure 13-21 shows the result: The total wave is also a sinusoidal wave whose frequency f is the average of f_1 and f_2, but with an amplitude that varies between 0 and $2A$. We use the term beats for this up-and-down variation in amplitude. The frequency of the beats, also called the **beat frequency**, is equal to the *absolute value* of the difference between the two frequencies:

Beat frequency heard when sound waves of two similar frequencies interfere

Frequencies of the individual sound waves

$$f_{\text{beats}} = |f_2 - f_1|$$

Beat frequency
(13-25)

(The absolute value ensures that we get a positive value for f_{beats}. We do this because a negative frequency has no meaning.) For example, if the two individual sound waves have frequencies $f_1 = 200$ Hz and $f_2 = 202$ Hz, what you will hear is a tone at a frequency of 201 Hz (the average of 200 Hz and 202 Hz) with an amplitude that rises and falls at frequency $f_{\text{beats}} = |f_2 - f_1| = |202 \text{ Hz} - 200 \text{ Hz}| = 2$ Hz. That is, the amplitude will rise and fall twice per second, or once every 1/2 s.

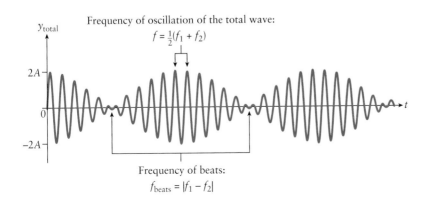

Frequency of oscillation of the total wave:
$f = \frac{1}{2}(f_1 + f_2)$

Frequency of beats:
$f_{\text{beats}} = |f_1 - f_2|$

Figure 13-21 **Beats** When two sinusoidal waves of nearly the same frequency are added together, the total wave has a rising and falling amplitude, or beats.

The greater the difference between the frequencies f_1 and f_2, the greater the beat frequency and the more rapid the beats. If the frequency difference is large enough, the beats are no longer perceptible and you will hear two distinct frequencies.

Example 13-8 Guitar Tuning

You have just replaced the first string on your guitar and wish to tune it to the correct frequency of 329.6 Hz (the note E4). To do this, you pluck both this string and the sixth (E2) string, which you know is properly tuned to 82.4 Hz. You hear one beat every 2.50 s. How far out of tune (in Hz) is the first string?

Set Up

The frequencies 82.4 Hz and 329.6 Hz are far apart, so it may seem surprising that you would get beats when both are sounded. But remember that a plucked string oscillates not only at its fundamental frequency but also at the higher *harmonics* of the string. So what you hear is beats between the sound made by the first string and one of the harmonics of the sixth string.

Beat frequency:

$$f_{beats} = |f_2 - f_1| \qquad (13\text{-}25)$$

Frequencies for a standing wave on a string:

$$f_n = \frac{n}{2L}\sqrt{\frac{F}{\mu}} \text{ where } n = 1, 2, 3, \dots$$
$$(13\text{-}19)$$

6th string
1st string

Solve

The harmonics of the sixth string are at integer multiples of its fundamental frequency.

For the sixth string, $f_1 = 82.4$ Hz

The harmonics are

$f_2 = 2f_1 = 164.8$ Hz
$f_3 = 3f_1 = 247.2$ Hz
$f_4 = 4f_1 = 329.6$ Hz

So if the guitar is properly tuned, the fundamental frequency of the first string is the same as the fourth harmonic frequency of the sixth string. If the first string is mistuned, the frequencies will be different and you will hear beats.

Find the beat frequency and how far out of tune the first string is.

There is one beat per 2.50 s, so the beat frequency (the number of beats per second) is

$$f_{beats} = \frac{1}{2.50 \text{ s}} = 0.400 \text{ s}^{-1} = 0.400 \text{ Hz}$$

This is equal to the difference between the fundamental frequency of the first string and the fourth harmonic frequency of the sixth string:

$$f_{beats} = 0.400 \text{ Hz} = |f_{1 \text{ for first string}} - f_{4 \text{ for sixth string}}|$$
$$= |f_{1 \text{ for first string}} - 329.6 \text{ Hz}|$$

So the first string is out of tune by 0.400 Hz.

Reflect

With just the information given, we don't know whether the first string is tuned 0.400 Hz too high (in which case its frequency is 330.0 Hz) or too low (in which case its frequency is 329.2 Hz). To find out, try increasing the tension on the first string to raise its fundamental frequency. If the beats slow down, the beat frequency is getting closer to zero as you bring the first string into tune, so the first string must have been tuned too low. Keep increasing the tension until the beats stop altogether, at which point the first string is properly tuned. If instead the beats become more rapid, the beat frequency is increasing and so the tuning of the first string is getting worse. This means the first string was tuned too high, so you should decrease the tension on the first string to lower its fundamental frequency and bring it into tune.

? Got the Concept? 13-8 Tuning Forks

When you strike two tuning forks simultaneously, you hear 3 beats per second. The frequency of the first tuning fork is 440 Hz. What is the frequency of the second tuning fork? (a) 446 Hz; (b) 443 Hz; (c) 437 Hz; (d) 434 Hz; (e) not enough information is given to decide.

Take-Home Message for Section 13-8

✔ When two waves of nearly identical frequencies and wavelengths interfere, the result is a total wave whose amplitude rises and falls periodically. This phenomenon is called beats.

✔ The frequency of the beats equals the absolute value of the difference in frequency between the two waves.

13-9 The intensity of a wave equals the power that it delivers per square meter

Humans hear sounds over a wide range of volumes, from very faint sounds (such as leaves rustling in a gentle breeze) to sounds so loud that they can cause pain (such as the sound of the siren on an emergency vehicle driving nearby). Let's analyze the physical differences between loud sounds and faint sounds.

Wave Energy, Power, and Intensity

An important factor in determining the loudness of a sound is the energy carried by the sound wave. To see why this is so, note that in order for the ear to detect a sound, the sound wave must exert a force on the eardrum that makes the eardrum move (be displaced). This means that the sound wave must do *work* on the eardrum (recall from Section 6-2 that work is done when a force acts over a distance). Doing work involves the transfer of energy, and in this case the energy comes from the wave itself. So we can think of the ear as a device for detecting the energy in a sound wave.

The ear is particularly sensitive to the *rate* at which sound wave energy is delivered to it. As an analogy, imagine having someone pour a pitcher of water over your outstretched hand. You'll feel very little effect if the water falls on you very slowly, a drop at a time. But if the pitcher is turned over so that all of the water hits your hand in a short time, your hand will feel pushed down. In the same way, your ear has a greater response if sound wave energy is delivered to your ear at a rapid rate.

The rate at which energy is transferred is called **power**. The unit of power is the joule per second, or **watt** (abbreviated W): 1 W = 1 J/s. As an example, a 50-W light bulb is designed so that when it is in operation, 50 J of energy is delivered to it every second by the electric circuit to which the bulb is connected. If you are using a stationary exercise bicycle at the gym, a reading of 200 W on the bike's display means that you are doing 200 joules of work on the pedals every second. Other common units of power are the *kilowatt* (1 kW = 1000 W) and the *horsepower* (1 hp = 746 W is the rate at which a typical horse can do work by pulling a plow). We'll usually denote power by the symbol P.

Let's apply these ideas about energy and power to a sinusoidal sound wave. We've seen that in a sinusoidal wave, pieces of the wave medium undergo simple harmonic motion. In Section 12-4 we learned that if an object of mass m is attached to an ideal spring of spring constant k and oscillates in simple harmonic motion with amplitude A, the total mechanical energy of the mass–spring system is

$$E = \frac{1}{2}kA^2 \qquad (12\text{-}21)$$

We also learned in Section 12-3 that the angular frequency for an object oscillating on an ideal spring is $\omega = \sqrt{k/m}$, so $\omega^2 = k/m$ and $k = m\omega^2$. If we insert this into Equation 12-21, we get

$$E = \frac{1}{2}m\omega^2 A^2 \qquad (13\text{-}26)$$

Let's see what this says about a sinusoidal sound wave in air with angular frequency ω and displacement amplitude A. (Remember that for a sound wave A represents the maximum longitudinal displacement of the air as the wave passes through it.) According to Equation 13-26, if this wave is present in a chunk of air of mass m, the *wave energy* present in that chunk is $E = (1/2)m\omega^2 A^2$. The wave carries that energy along with it as it propagates. To get a measure of the *power* associated with the wave, let's imagine a cubical volume in the air with sides of length L (Figure 13-22). If

This volume of air has mass $m = \rho L^3$. A sound wave of angular frequency ω and amplitude A is present throughout the volume.

(a)

(b)

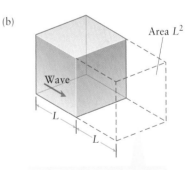

Area L^2

The volume L^3 of wave energy travels a distance L in time $t = L/v_{\text{sound}}$. The power equals the wave energy E in the volume divided by t. The intensity is the power divided by L^2.

Figure 13-22 **Power and intensity in a sound wave** (a) This cubical volume encloses a quantity of air with a sound wave propagating through it. (b) If we imagine the volume moving along with the wave, we can find the power and intensity associated with the wave.

the air has density (mass per volume) ρ, the mass of air in this volume equals the density ρ multiplied by the volume L^3 of the cube: $m = \rho L^3$. From Equation 13-26, the wave energy contained in this volume is

(13-27)
$$E = \frac{1}{2}\rho L^3 \omega^2 A^2$$

The energy in this volume moves along with the wave at propagation speed v_{sound}, so the time required for this volume of energy to move through its own length L is $t = L/v_{sound}$. So the rate at which this energy crosses through an imaginary square of side L (Figure 13-22)—that is, the *power P* delivered across this surface—equals the energy E given by Equation 13-27 divided by the time $t = L/v_{sound}$:

(13-28)
$$P = \frac{E}{t} = \frac{(1/2)\rho L^3 \omega^2 A^2}{L/v_{sound}} = \frac{1}{2}\rho L^2 v_{sound}\omega^2 A^2$$

> **Watch Out!   In a wave there is a flow of energy, not of material.**
>
> Note that in Figure 13-22 what moves a distance L in time t is the *wave energy* contained within the cubical volume of side L. The wave and its associated energy move together, but the wave *medium* doesn't go anywhere: Each piece of the medium just oscillates around its equilibrium position.

Equation 13-28 says that the power associated with the wave is proportional to the square of the wave amplitude A. This turns out to be a general attribute of waves of all kinds, not just sound waves. Note also that the power is proportional to L^2, which is the cross-sectional area through which the wave energy passes. The power *divided* by the cross-sectional area L^2 is called the **intensity** I of the wave, measured in watts per square meter (W/m^2). From Equation 13-28, this is

Sound wave intensity in terms of displacement amplitude A
(13-29)

Intensity of a sound wave   Density of the wave medium (usually air)

$$I = \frac{1}{2}\rho v_{sound}\,\omega^2\,A^2$$

Displacement amplitude of the wave

Speed of sound waves in the medium   Angular frequency of the wave

If you increase the displacement amplitude A of a sound wave of a given frequency, the intensity of the sound will increase. For an ear or other sound detector of a given size, the amount of sound wave power that is received equals the intensity I multiplied by the area of the detector. So increasing the intensity means more sound power enters your ear, and you will perceive the sound to be louder.

Note that the total power (intensity times area) reaching your eardrum would increase if it had a larger cross-sectional area. That's why many nocturnal animals such as bats and coyotes have large external ears: This maximizes the cross-sectional area over which they can collect low-amplitude sound waves coming from potential prey or predators. The larger collected power is then directed to their eardrums, improving their sensitivity. Intensity is a useful measure of the strength of a sound wave because the area factor has been divided out: A coyote may have more sensitive ears than yours (because of the increased collection area of its outer ears), but if you both are exposed to the same sound wave your external ears both experience the same intensity.

Equation 13-29 is expressed in terms of the displacement amplitude A. However, our ears are more directly sensitive to the *pressure* variations in a sound wave. The displacement amplitude A in a sound wave is related to the pressure amplitude p_{max}, or maximum pressure variation, by

(13-30)
$$A = \frac{p_{max}}{\rho v_{sound}\omega}$$

If we substitute Equation 13-30 for A into Equation 13-29, we get an alternative expression for the intensity of a sound wave:

$$I = \frac{1}{2}\rho v_{\text{sound}}\omega^2 \left(\frac{p_{\text{max}}}{\rho v_{\text{sound}}\omega}\right)^2 = \frac{p_{\text{max}}^2}{2}\frac{\rho v_{\text{sound}}\omega^2}{\rho^2 v_{\text{sound}}^2 \omega^2}$$

or, simplifying,

Intensity of a sound wave   Pressure amplitude of the wave

$$I = \frac{p^2{}_{\text{max}}}{2\rho v_{\text{sound}}}$$

Density of the wave medium (usually air)   Speed of sound waves in the medium

Sound wave intensity in terms of pressure amplitude p_{max} (13-31)

Equation 13-31 says that for sound waves in a medium with density ρ for which the speed of sound is v_{sound}, the intensity is proportional to the square of the pressure amplitude.

Our ears can detect sounds with frequencies from 20 Hz to 20,000 Hz. If they were equally sensitive to all frequencies in this range, greater intensity would imply greater loudness. However, our ears are *not* equally sensitive across the audible range: As we learned in Section 13-7, a person with normal hearing is most sensitive to frequencies around 3400 Hz, and less sensitive at higher and lower frequencies. At 1000 Hz, the lowest intensity that a person with normal hearing can sense (the *threshold of hearing*) is about 10^{-12} W/m². The threshold of hearing is substantially higher at frequencies to which the ear is less sensitive, about 10^{-11} W/m² at 10,000 Hz and about 10^{-8} W/m² at 100 Hz. At most frequencies the greatest intensity that a person can tolerate without pain (the *threshold of pain*) is about 1 W/m².

Example 13-9 Loud and Soft

The amplitude of the motion of your eardrum in response to a sound wave more or less matches the amplitude of the motion of nearby air molecules. (a) What is the oscillation amplitude of your eardrum when you hear a tone that has a frequency of 1000 Hz and an intensity of 1.00 W/m², near the threshold of pain? What is the pressure amplitude of this sound? (b) What about a 1000-Hz tone with an intensity of only 1.00×10^{-12} W/m², at the threshold of hearing? Use $\rho = 1.20$ kg/m³ for the density of air and $v_{\text{sound}} = 343$ m/s for the speed of sound in air.

Set Up

We'll use Equations 13-29 and 13-31 to relate the intensity of a sound wave to its displacement amplitude A and pressure amplitude p_{max}. The problem statement tells us that the displacement amplitude of the eardrum is about the same as that of the air.

Sound wave intensity in terms of displacement amplitude A:

$$I = \frac{1}{2}\rho v_{\text{sound}}\omega^2 A^2 \tag{13-29}$$

Sound wave intensity in terms of pressure amplitude p_{max}:

$$I = \frac{p_{\text{max}}^2}{2\rho v_{\text{sound}}} \tag{13-31}$$

Solve

(a) Rearrange Equation 13-29 to find an expression for the displacement amplitude.

From Equation 13-29,

$$A^2 = \frac{2I}{\rho v_{\text{sound}}\omega^2}$$

We are given $f = 1000$ Hz, so substitute $\omega = 2\pi f$:

$$A^2 = \frac{2I}{\rho v_{\text{sound}}(2\pi f)^2} = \frac{2I}{4\pi^2 \rho v_{\text{sound}} f^2} = \frac{I}{2\pi^2 \rho v_{\text{sound}} f^2}$$

Take the square root of both sides and substitute $I = 1.00$ W/m^2, $\rho = 1.20$ kg/m^3, $v_{sound} = 343$ m/s, and $f = 1000$ Hz:

$$A = \sqrt{\frac{I}{2\pi^2 \rho v_{sound} f^2}} = \sqrt{\frac{1.00 \text{ W/m}^2}{2\pi^2 (1.20 \text{ kg/m}^3)(343 \text{ m/s})(1000 \text{ Hz})^2}}$$

$$= 1.11 \times 10^{-5} \sqrt{\frac{\text{W} \cdot \text{s}}{\text{kg} \cdot \text{Hz}^2}}$$

Note that 1 W = 1 J/s and 1 J = 1 N·m = 1 kg·m^2/s^2, and 1 Hz = 1/s = 1 s^{-1}. So

$$1 \sqrt{\frac{\text{W} \cdot \text{s}}{\text{kg} \cdot \text{Hz}^2}} = 1 \sqrt{\frac{\text{J} \cdot \text{s}^2}{\text{kg}}} = 1 \sqrt{\frac{\text{kg} \cdot \text{m}^2}{\text{kg}}} = 1 \text{ m}$$

The units of the displacement amplitude A are therefore meters, as they should be:

$$A = 1.11 \times 10^{-5} \text{ m}$$

Use the same approach with Equation 13-31 to find the pressure amplitude p_{max}.

From Equation 13-31,

$$I = \frac{p_{max}^2}{2\rho v_{sound}}$$

Solve for p_{max}:

$$p_{max}^2 = 2\rho v_{sound} I$$

$$p_{max} = \sqrt{2\rho v_{sound} I} = \sqrt{2(1.20 \text{ kg/m}^3)(343 \text{ m/s})(1.00 \text{ W/m}^2)}$$

$$= 28.7 \sqrt{\frac{\text{kg} \cdot \text{W}}{\text{m}^4 \cdot \text{s}}}$$

Again note that 1 W = 1 J/s, 1 J = 1 N·m, and 1 N = 1 kg·m/s^2. So 1 W = 1 N·m/s and 1 kg = 1 N·s^2/m, and the units of our answer are

$$1 \sqrt{\frac{\text{kg} \cdot \text{W}}{\text{m}^4 \cdot \text{s}}} = 1 \sqrt{\frac{1}{\text{m}^4 \cdot \text{s}} \frac{\text{N} \cdot \text{s}^2}{\text{m}} \frac{\text{N} \cdot \text{m}}{\text{s}}} = 1 \sqrt{\frac{\text{N}^2}{\text{m}^4}} = 1 \text{ N/m}^2$$

The units of p_{max} are newtons per square meter or pascals (1 N/m^2 = 1 Pa), which is correct for pressure:

$$p_{max} = 28.7 \text{ N/m}^2 = 28.7 \text{ Pa}$$

(b) To find the displacement amplitude A and pressure amplitude p_{max} for the new intensity, we don't have to redo the above calculations. Instead, we notice from our calculations that A and p_{max} are both proportional to the square root of the intensity I.

The new intensity is 1.00×10^{-12} W/m^2, which is 10^{-12} times the previous intensity. Since A and p_{max} are both proportional to $\sqrt{I}$, the new amplitudes are equal to the previous values multiplied by $\sqrt{10^{-12}} = 10^{-6}$:

$$A = (1.11 \times 10^{-5} \text{ m}) \times 10^{-6} = 1.11 \times 10^{-11} \text{ m}$$

$$p_{max} = (28.7 \text{ N/m}^2) \times 10^{-6} = 2.87 \times 10^{-5} \text{ N/m}^2 = 2.87 \times 10^{-5} \text{ Pa}$$

Reflect

For the painfully loud sound at 1000-Hz, the eardrum oscillates with an amplitude slightly larger than 10 μm, or about 50% larger than the diameter of a human red blood cell. At the threshold of hearing the oscillation amplitude of the eardrum to a 1000 Hz tone is about 10^{-11} m, about one-tenth the diameter of a hydrogen atom. The pressure amplitudes are also very small: 28.9 Pa is about the difference in atmospheric pressure between the floor and ceiling of your room, and 2.89×10^{-5} Pa is about the same pressure that would be exerted on your eardrum by the weight of a single wing of a fly. These remarkable numbers illustrate the exquisite sensitivity of human hearing.

Sound and the Inverse-Square Law

If you've ever convinced a teacher to hold class outside on a warm spring day, you may have noticed that the teacher's voice is much more difficult to hear outdoors than indoors. That's because when a source of sound (like the teacher's voice) radiates sound waves in all directions without anything getting in the way of the waves, the *intensity* of the waves decreases with increasing distance. In contrast, inside the lecture hall, sound bounces off the walls, back toward the audience, so the intensity does not decrease as quickly with increasing distance from the source.

Figure 13-23 shows how this comes about. Since waves carry energy, a source of sound waves is a source of energy. The rate at which the source emits energy in the form of waves is the *power* of the source. None of the power is lost as the waves spread away from the source, but at greater distances the power is distributed over a greater area. Hence the wave intensity (power divided by area) and the perceived loudness of the sound both decrease with increasing distance. If the source has power P_0 and emits equally in all directions as shown in Figure 13-23, at a distance r from the source the power is spread uniformly over a spherical surface of radius r. The area of such a surface is $4\pi r^2$, so the intensity equals

Figure 13-23 **The inverse-square law for sound waves** A source of sound waves has power P_0. At greater distances from the source this power is spread over a greater area, so the intensity is less.

At a distance r_1, the power is spread over area $4\pi r_1^2$.

Wave source, power P_0 r_2 r_1

At a greater distance r_2, the power is spread over a greater area $4\pi r_2^2$.

Intensity of a sound wave at a distance r from a source that emits in all directions

Power output of the sound source

$$I = \frac{P_0}{4\pi r^2}$$

Distance from the source to the point where the intensity is measured

Inverse-square law for sound waves
(13-32)

Equation 13-32 says that the intensity is inversely proportional to the square of the distance from the source, so this is called the **inverse-square law** for waves.

The inverse-square law explains what happens when class is held outdoors: Compared to the intensity of the teacher's voice at a distance of 1 m, the intensity at 2 m is $(1/2)^2 = 1/4$ as great and the intensity at 3 m is $(1/3)^2 = 1/9$ as great. So with increasing distance, the teacher becomes increasingly difficult to hear. The inverse-square law doesn't apply indoors because sound reflects off the walls and ceiling, so sound energy that would be lost outdoors is reflected back toward you and the other members of the audience.

Example 13-10 Delivering Energy to an Eardrum

You are at an outdoor concert, standing 20 m from a speaker tower that generates 2500 W of sound power. How much sound energy from the speaker tower strikes one of your eardrums per second? A typical human eardrum has a surface area of 55 mm². Assume that the speaker tower emits sound uniformly in all directions.

Set Up
The inverse-square law for sound waves tells us the intensity of the sound that reaches you. To find the power (energy per time) delivered to your eardrum, we use the idea that intensity equals power per area, so power equals intensity times area.

Inverse-square law for sound waves:

$$I = \frac{P_0}{4\pi r^2} \quad (13\text{-}32)$$

2500 W   20 m   area = 55 mm²

sound power into ear
= (intensity of sound) × (area of eardrum)

Solve
Use Equation 13-32 to find the sound intensity at your position.

At a distance $r = 20$ m from a source with power $P_0 = 2500$ W,

$$I = \frac{P_0}{4\pi r^2} = \frac{2500 \text{ W}}{4\pi(20 \text{ m})^2} = 0.50 \text{ W/m}^2$$

The sound power that strikes one of your eardrums equals the sound intensity multiplied by the area of the eardrum.

Power (energy per time) on your eardrum:

$$P = I \times (\text{area of eardrum})$$

$$= (0.50 \text{ W/m}^2)(55 \text{ mm}^2)\left(\frac{1 \text{ m}}{10^3 \text{ mm}}\right)^2$$

$$= 2.7 \times 10^{-5} \text{ W} = 2.7 \times 10^{-5} \text{ J/s}$$

Reflect

The intensity of the sound is close to the threshold of pain, so you would be advised to stand farther away from the sound tower. But notice that even at this very high volume, the power that reaches the ear is very small (about one *millionth* the amount of power needed to light a 25-watt light bulb). This is another testament to the sensitivity of the human ear.

Sound Intensity Level

The range of sound intensities that we can hear spans the range from about 10^{-12} W/m^2 to about 1 W/m^2. It's convenient to compress this broad range of numbers by using *logarithms*. This leads to an alternative way to describe the intensity of a sound wave in terms of *sound intensity level*.

The idea behind logarithms is that any positive number x can be written as $x = b^y$, where b is called the *base*. In this language, we say that y is "the logarithm of x to the base b." As an example, 3 is the logarithm of 8 to the base 2: $8 = 2^3$. We write this relationship as follows:

$$\text{If } x = b^y, \text{ then } y = \log_b x$$

So if x equals b raised to the power y, then y is the logarithm to the base b of x.

A common choice for the base b is 10. With this choice, the above relationship becomes

$$\text{If } x = 10^y, \text{ then } y = \log_{10} x$$

For example, the logarithm to the base 10 of $1000 = 10^3$ is $\log_{10} 10^3 = 3$ and the logarithm to the base 10 of $0.01 = 10^{-2}$ is $\log_{10} 10^{-2} = -2$. (Any number raised to power 0 equals 1, so the logarithm of 1 is 0 in *any* base.) On your calculator the base-10 logarithm is probably denoted by a function key named "log."

Note that the logarithm isn't just for numbers that are multiples of 10. As an example, a number between 1 and 10 has a base-10 logarithm that is between 0 (the logarithm of 1) and 1 (the logarithm of $10 = 10^1$). So $\log_{10} 2 = 0.30$, $\log_{10} 3 = 0.48$, and so on.

Let's now see how the logarithm is used for describing the intensity of a sound. The argument of the logarithm must be a pure number without dimensions or units. We satisfy this requirement by taking the ratio of the intensity I of a sound to 10^{-12} W/m^2, the intensity of a 1000-Hz tone at the threshold of hearing. The **sound intensity level** of a sound with intensity I equals the base-10 logarithm of this ratio multiplied by 10:

Sound intensity level
(13-33)

Sound intensity level of a sound wave   Intensity of the sound

$$\beta = (10 \text{ dB}) \log_{10}\left[\frac{I}{10^{-12} \text{ W/m}^2}\right]$$

Reference intensity

The factor of 10 that multiplies the logarithm in Equation 13-33 is there for convenience. The units of sound intensity level are the **decibel** (dB), named after the

Scottish-born scientist and inventor Alexander Graham Bell. The sound intensity level for a 1000-Hz tone at the threshold of hearing is then

$$\beta = (10 \text{ dB}) \log_{10}\left(\frac{10^{-12} \text{ W/m}^2}{10^{-12} \text{ W/m}^2}\right) = (10 \text{ dB}) \log_{10}(1) = 0 \text{ dB}$$

The sound intensity level for a tone at the threshold of pain is

$$\beta = (10 \text{ dB}) \log_{10}\left(\frac{1 \text{ W/m}^2}{10^{-12} \text{ W/m}^2}\right) = (10 \text{ dB}) \log_{10}(10^{12}) = 120 \text{ dB}$$

So by using sound intensity level we express the intensities of sound in human hearing by the range from 0 dB to 120 dB rather than from 10^{-12} W/m^2 to 1 W/m^2. Table 13-1 lists the sound intensity level of a range of sounds.

Table 13-1
Sound Intensity Levels

Sound	Sound level (dB)
jet engine at 25 m	150
live amplified music	120
car horn at 1 m	110
jackhammer	100
city street	90
vacuum cleaner	70
quiet conversation	50
rustling leaves	20
breathing	10

! Watch Out! A sound intensity level of 0 dB is not the absence of sound.

We are used to thinking of a quantity with a value of zero as being nothing at all. But a sound with sound intensity level 0 dB, while faint, is still a sound. The zero value just means that this is the faintest sound that someone with normal hearing can hear at a frequency of 1000 Hz.

Example 13-11 Double the Intensity

When the intensity of a sound doubles, how does the sound intensity level change?

Set Up
Equation 13-33 relates the sound intensity I to the sound intensity level β. We'll use this to compare two sounds, one of intensity I_1 and the other of intensity $I_2 = 2I_1$.

Sound intensity level:

$$\beta = (10 \text{ dB}) \log_{10}\left(\frac{I}{10^{-12} \text{ W/m}^2}\right) \qquad (13\text{-}33)$$

Solve
Write expressions for the two sound intensity levels.

For sound 1,

$$\beta_1 = (10 \text{ dB}) \log_{10}\left(\frac{I_1}{10^{-12} \text{ W/m}^2}\right)$$

For sound 2,

$$\beta_2 = (10 \text{ dB}) \log_{10}\left(\frac{I_2}{10^{-12} \text{ W/m}^2}\right) = (10 \text{ dB}) \log_{10}\left(\frac{2I_1}{10^{-12} \text{ W/m}^2}\right)$$

Use an important property of logarithms to compare β_1 and β_2.

The logarithm of the *product* of two numbers A and B is equal to the *sum* of their logarithms:

$$\log_{10}(AB) = \log_{10} A + \log_{10} B$$

Using this property, we can express β_2 as

$$\beta_2 = (10 \text{ dB}) \log_{10}\left(\frac{2I_1}{10^{-12} \text{ W/m}^2}\right) = (10 \text{ dB}) \log_{10}\left[2\left(\frac{I_1}{10^{-12} \text{ W/m}^2}\right)\right]$$

$$= (10 \text{ dB})\left[\log_{10} 2 + \log_{10}\left(\frac{I_1}{10^{-12} \text{ W/m}^2}\right)\right]$$

$$= (10\text{ dB}) \log_{10} 2 + (10\text{ dB}) \log_{10}\left(\frac{I_1}{10^{-12}\text{ W/m}^2}\right)$$

$$= (10\text{ dB}) \log_{10} 2 + \beta_1$$

So *multiplying* the intensity by 2 is the same as *adding* $(10\text{ dB}) \log_{10} 2$ to the sound intensity level.

Find the *difference* of the two sound intensity levels.

The difference of the two values of β is

$$\beta_2 - \beta_1 = (10\text{ dB})\log_{10} 2 = (10\text{ dB})(0.30)$$
$$= 3.0\text{ dB}$$

Reflect

A factor of 2 increase in intensity corresponds to adding 3.0 dB to the sound intensity level. Increasing the intensity by a factor of $4 = 2 \times 2$ means adding $3.0\text{ dB} + 3.0\text{ dB} = 6.0\text{ dB}$ to the sound intensity level; increasing intensity by $8 = 2 \times 2 \times 2$ means adding $3.0\text{ dB} + 3.0\text{ dB} + 3.0\text{ dB} = 9.0\text{ dB}$ to the sound intensity level; and so on.

? Got the Concept? 13-9   From One Fan to Two

You measure the sound intensity level of an electric fan to be 60 dB. What is the sound intensity level when a second identical fan is turned on, at the same distance from you as the first one? (a) 120 dB; (b) 90 dB; (c) 66 dB; (d) 63 dB; (e) 62 dB.

Take-Home Message for Section 13-9

✔ The intensity of a sound wave is the power (energy per time) that the wave delivers per unit area. The intensity does not depend on the ear or device used to detect the sound.

✔ The power delivered by a sound wave is equal to the intensity of the wave multiplied by the collecting area.

✔ In the absence of obstructions or reflections, the intensity of sound from a source decreases in inverse proportion to the distance from the source.

✔ The sound intensity level involves the logarithm of a sound wave's intensity divided by a reference value of intensity.

13-10 The frequency of a sound depends on the motion of the source and the listener

Until now, we have only considered waves generated by stationary emitters and observed by stationary listeners. Everyday experience, however, suggests that something curious happens when a moving object creates a sound. As a police car with sirens blaring zooms by you, for example, the frequency of the sound is higher as the car approaches and lower after it passes. Even without a siren, a fast-moving car generates a characteristic high-to-low frequency sound (something like "neee-urrrr") as it approaches and passes you. And although we don't often get the chance to experience this phenomenon in reverse, if you were to move at high speed toward a stationary police car with its sirens blaring, the sound of the siren would follow a similar high-to-low frequency shift as you approached and then passed it. This effect is known as the **Doppler effect**, named for the Austrian physicist Christian Doppler who first proposed this phenomenon associated with waves in 1842.

The Doppler Effect and Frequency Shift

In Figure 13-24a, a police siren emits a periodic sound wave that has a fixed frequency and a fixed wavelength. Because the car is stationary, each wave crest—that is, each region of highest pressure along the wave, shown as arcs of circles—is centered on the siren. On the left side of Figure 13-24b the car moves from left to right. The wave crest

(a)

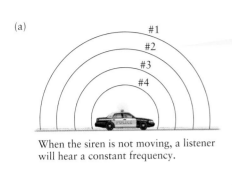

When the siren is not moving, a listener
will hear a constant frequency.

Wave crests spread outward from
the siren. The numbers on the crests
show the sequence in which they
were emitted: First #1, then #2, then
#3, then #4, so the most recently
emitted crest is closest to the siren.

Listener

**Figure 13-24 The Doppler effect:
A moving source** A police car siren
emits a periodic sound wave that
has a fixed frequency and a fixed
wavelength. (a) The police car is
stationary, so each region of highest
pressure along the wave, shown as
arcs of circles, is centered on the siren.
(b) The car moves from left to right.
Because the source of the sound
waves moves as the waves propagate,
the wave crests are closer together as
the car approaches a listener's ear and
farther apart as the car recedes from
the listener.

(b)

As the siren approaches the listener,
the sound frequency is higher.

Listener

The frequency is lower as the siren
moves away from the listener.

associated with the largest circle originated first, when the car was somewhere to the
left, and the circle of the smallest radius represents the most recently generated wave
crest. Because the car moves to the right as the sound wave propagates, the siren emits
each new wave crest closer to the previous one than if the car were stationary. Because
the distance between wave crests determines the wavelength heard by a stationary listener, someone standing in front of the car detects a shorter wavelength than the siren
generates. The opposite is true on the right side of Figure 13-24b, in which the car
moves away from the listener.

The relationship $f = v_{sound}/\lambda$ (Equation 13-2 for sound) tells us that a shorter
wavelength results in a higher frequency. So the listener in Figure 13-24b hears a higher
frequency than the siren generates as the car approaches. Analogously, because
the wave crests are spread further apart behind the car, the observed wavelength lengthens, resulting in the listener hearing a lower frequency.

In **Figure 13-25** we expand the view of the moving police car to
show the car at two instants in time separated by the period T of
the tone created by the siren. A crest of the sound wave was created when the car was at the location marked by the red
dashed line; in the time T the wave crest has propagated as
indicated by the red semicircle. That distance is given by the
product of the speed of sound v_{sound} and T, as shown. The
distance the car moves in that time is $v_{car}T$, where v_{car} is the
speed of the car. This new location is where the car will
emit the next wave crest. So a stationary listener in front of
the car detects $\lambda_{listener}$ (the distance between two successive
wave crests) as the wavelength of the siren's tone. As seen
in the figure these three distances—the distance the sound
moves, the distance the car moves, and the distance between
two successive wave crests at the place where the listener
sits—are related by

$$v_{car}T + \lambda_{listener} = v_{sound}T$$

or

$$\lambda_{listener} = v_{sound}T - v_{car}T \qquad (13\text{-}34)$$

Although this equation mathematically describes the
Doppler effect, by convention we write the relationship as

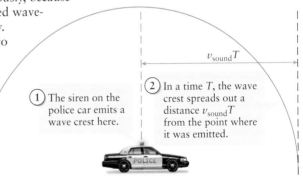

① The siren on the
police car emits a
wave crest here.

② In a time T, the wave
crest spreads out a
distance $v_{sound}T$
from the point where
it was emitted.

$v_{sound}T$

③ In the same time T, the police
car travels a distance $v_{car}T$.

$v_{car}T$ $\lambda_{listener}$

**Figure 13-25 The Doppler
effect: A moving source II**
The wavelength of the sound
heard by a stationary listener
as a source of sound approaches
depends on the distance
the wave travels in a
certain time and the
distance the source
travels in that same time.

Because of the car's motion, a
listener in front of the police car
hears a shortened wavelength.

one between the actual and the observed frequency relative to the speed of the emitter rather than the speed of sound v. To write the expression, we use $T = 1/f$ and Equation 13-2 for sound waves:

$$\lambda_{\text{listener}} = \frac{v_{\text{sound}}}{f_{\text{listener}}}$$

Combining these equations with Equation 13-34 gives

$$\frac{v_{\text{sound}}}{f_{\text{listener}}} = \frac{v_{\text{sound}}}{f} - \frac{v_{\text{car}}}{f}$$

or, rearranging,

$$f_{\text{listener}} = \left(\frac{v_{\text{sound}}}{v_{\text{sound}} - v_{\text{car}}}\right)f$$

Because v_{car} is a positive number, the fraction in parentheses must be greater than 1. So when the car is moving toward a stationary listener, $f_{\text{listener}} > f$ (the listener hears a higher frequency).

We can apply a similar approach to determine the observed frequency as the source moves away from a stationary listener, as well as for the cases in which the listener moves relative to a stationary source. Using "source" instead of "car" as a more general way to indicate the source of the sound, here's a single equation for the frequency heard by the listener no matter how the source and listener are moving:

The Doppler effect
(13-35)

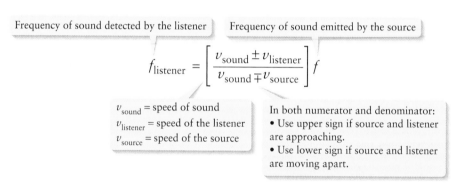

Frequency of sound detected by the listener   Frequency of sound emitted by the source

$$f_{\text{listener}} = \left[\frac{v_{\text{sound}} \pm v_{\text{listener}}}{v_{\text{sound}} \mp v_{\text{source}}}\right] f$$

v_{sound} = speed of sound
v_{listener} = speed of the listener
v_{source} = speed of the source

In both numerator and denominator:
• Use upper sign if source and listener are approaching.
• Use lower sign if source and listener are moving apart.

Notice that the plus sign is above the minus sign in the numerator but below it in the denominator. In Equation 13-35, we use the upper sign when the source or listener approaches the other and the lower sign when it retreats from the other. Equation 13-35 can be used for more than one case simultaneously; for example, if the source and listener are both approaching each other, the observed frequency is

$$f_{\text{listener}} = \left(\frac{v_{\text{sound}} + v_{\text{listener}}}{v_{\text{sound}} - v_{\text{source}}}\right)f$$

In this case, the numerator is larger than the speed of sound v_{sound} and the denominator is smaller than v_{sound}; both factors result in the listener hearing a higher frequency than the one emitted by the source.

The speed of a moving object can be determined by measuring the shift in frequency associated with the Doppler effect. A common way to do this is to create a wave of known frequency and then bounce it off the moving object to be studied. A *radar speed gun* uses this principle: It sends out a *radio* wave of a known frequency and compares it to the frequency of the wave after it is reflected by a moving car. (Because this device uses radio waves rather than sound waves, v_{sound} in Equation 13-35 is replaced by the speed of light c.) Bats and dolphins use the same technique with sound waves to track the motion of prey.

Measuring velocity using a Doppler shift has become important in medical applications, too—for example, to measure blood flow and to record real-time images of a moving fetus. Because the frequencies of sound used for this kind of imaging, between 2 and 10 MHz, are well above the range of human hearing, this technique is called *ultrasonic imaging*.

Consider the process by which ultrasound is used to determine the speed of blood flow through a heart valve. (An obstructed valve is often characterized by an increase in the speed of the blood flow.) A probe that emits a low-intensity sound wave of (high) frequency f_{emitted} is placed over the chest and focused on a region localized around one heart valve. Because the blood is moving, it experiences a wave of frequency f' that has been shifted according to the Doppler effect for a moving listener. Using Equation 13-35, we write

$$f' = \left(\frac{v_{\text{sound}} \pm v}{v_{\text{sound}}} \right) f_{\text{emitted}}$$

In this expression v is the speed of the blood, and the upper sign applies to motion toward the probe and the lower sign to motion away from the probe. The speed of sound in human tissue is about $v_{\text{sound}} = 1540$ m/s.

The sound wave reflects off the blood and returns to the probe. This reflected wave leaves the blood with frequency f', so it's equivalent to the blood emitting sound at frequency f'. So we again apply Equation 13-35, treating the blood as a moving source. The frequency f'' of the reflected ultrasound detected by the probe is then

$$f'' = \left(\frac{v_{\text{sound}}}{v_{\text{sound}} \mp v} \right) f'$$

$$= \left(\frac{v_{\text{sound}}}{v_{\text{sound}} \mp v} \right)\left(\frac{v_{\text{sound}} \pm v}{v_{\text{sound}}} \right) f_{\text{emitted}} \qquad (13\text{-}36)$$

$$= \left(\frac{v_{\text{sound}} \pm v}{v_{\text{sound}} \mp v} \right) f_{\text{emitted}}$$

Equation 13-36 says that when a wave of frequency f_{emitted} from a probe hits blood or another object moving with speed v, the wave that is reflected back to the probe is received with frequency f''. As for Equation 13-35, the upper signs apply to motion toward the probe and the lower signs to motion away from the probe.

Example 13-12 Diagnostic Ultrasound

A certain ultrasound device can measure a fetal heart rate as low as 50 beats per minute. This corresponds to the surface of the heart moving at about 4.0×10^{-4} m/s. If the probe generates ultrasound that has a frequency of 2.0 MHz (1 MHz = 1 megahertz = 10^6 Hz), what frequency shift must the machine be able to detect? Use $v_{\text{sound}} = 1540$ m/s for the speed of sound in human tissue.

Set Up

We are given the frequency $f_{\text{emitted}} = 2.0$ MHz of the sound waves that the probe emits. The frequency *shift* is the difference between f_{emitted} and the frequency f'' of the waves that the probe receives after they reflect from the heart.

Frequency received after reflecting from a moving object:

$$f'' = \left(\frac{v_{\text{sound}} \pm v}{v_{\text{sound}} \mp v} \right) f_{\text{emitted}} \quad (13\text{-}36)$$

heart

ultrasound probe

Solve

Let's begin by considering a region of the heart that is moving toward the probe. Then we use the upper sign in the numerator and denominator of Equation 13-36.

If the heart wall is approaching the probe,

$$f'' = \left(\frac{v_{\text{sound}} + v}{v_{\text{sound}} - v} \right) f_{\text{emitted}}$$

The numerator $v_{\text{sound}} + v$ is greater than the denominator $v_{\text{sound}} - v$, so the quantity in parentheses is greater than 1 and f'' will be greater than f_{emitted}.

Write an expression for the difference between f'' and f_{emitted}.

The frequency shift is

$$f'' - f_{\text{emitted}} = \left(\frac{v_{\text{sound}} + v}{v_{\text{sound}} - v}\right)f_{\text{emitted}} - f_{\text{emitted}}$$

$$= \left(\frac{v_{\text{sound}} + v}{v_{\text{sound}} - v} - 1\right)f_{\text{emitted}}$$

Substitute $v = 4.0 \times 10^{-4}\,\text{m/s}$, $v_{\text{sound}} = 1540\,\text{m/s}$, and $f_{\text{emitted}} = 2.0 \times 10^{6}\,\text{Hz}$:

$$f'' - f_{\text{emitted}} = \left(\frac{1540\,\text{m/s} + 4.0 \times 10^{-4}\,\text{m/s}}{1540\,\text{m/s} - 4.0 \times 10^{-4}\,\text{m/s}} - 1\right)(2.0 \times 10^{6}\,\text{Hz})$$

$$= 1.0\,\text{s}^{-1} = 1.0\,\text{Hz}$$

The wave received by the probe is 1.0 Hz higher in frequency than the wave emitted by the probe.

Reflect

You should repeat the above calculation for a region of the heart that is moving *away* from the probe. Then you'll use the *lower* sign in the numerator and denominator of Equation 13-36. You should find that the frequency shift in this case is $f'' - f_{\text{emitted}} = -1.0$ Hz (that is, the wave received by the probe is 1.0 Hz *lower* in frequency than the wave emitted by the probe). So an ultrasound device must be able to measure a frequency shift that is rather small compared to the emitted frequency $f_{\text{emitted}} = 2.0 \times 10^{6}$ Hz.

Our calculation shows that the frequency shift is proportional to the frequency emitted by the probe. Larger frequency shifts make it easier to detect smaller velocities, so an ultrasound device that operates at a higher frequency has a greater sensitivity. One constraint on this is that absorption of ultrasound waves by human tissue increases with frequency, so higher frequencies cannot penetrate as deeply into the body.

Sound from a Supersonic Source

Something curious occurs when a source of sound moves faster than the speed of sound (that is, the source is *supersonic*). In Figure 13-26a a jet airplane sits on the ground before taking off; the concentric circles centered on the airplane represent the spherical wave crests of the sound it generates. The three drawings in parts (b), (c), and (d) of Figure 13-26 show the airplane flying at increasingly faster speeds. As the airplane increases its speed, it catches up to the sound it generated earlier in the motion, squeezing the wave crests closer together ahead of the airplane. But notice that if the airplane moves at the same speed as the sound, as in Figure 13-26c, the airplane and the sound it generates travel the same distance in any time interval. In this case, the crests of all of the sound waves bunch together. If the airplane is supersonic, so that its speed exceeds the speed of sound as in Figure 13-26d, the airplane moves farther in any time interval than the sound that it emits.

Figure 13-27a shows an expanded view of what happens when the airplane is supersonic. Each circle represents the spherical wave crest of a sound generated when the airplane was at the center of the circle. Notice that all of the sound wave crests generated over the time Δt that the airplane has moved from its initial position (the lighter-colored image to the left) to its final position (the image on the right) interfere constructively. This constructive interference takes place on the surface of a cone, known as the **Mach cone** after the Austrian physicist Ernst Mach who first explained this phenomenon in 1877. In Figure 13-27a (which is only two-dimensional), we represent the cone by the two black lines. Note that there is *no* sound to the right of the Mach cone in Figure 13-27a. An observer to the right of the cone will be able to see the airplane but will not be able to hear it: No sound from the airplane will have reached him yet.

Because all of the wave crests pile up at the Mach cone, this is a region of substantially higher pressure than the surrounding air. If you are standing on the ground when a supersonic airplane flies over, you experience this as a **shock wave** (so called because there is no advance warning that it is coming) or as a **sonic boom**. The pressure increase in a shock wave from an airplane is in the range of 5 to 50 Pa. The shock wave is relatively

Crests of sound waves are expanding spheres, drawn as circles.

(a)

The airplane is stationary on the ground.

(b)   (c)   (d)

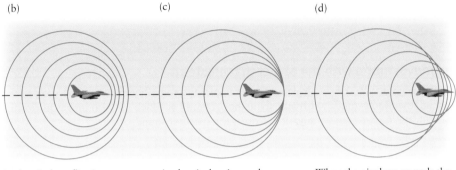

As the airplane flies it catches up to the sound crests it created earlier.

As the airplane's speed increases it catches up with more sound crests.

When the airplane exceeds the speed of sound, it overtakes previously created sound crests.

Figure 13-26 To the speed of sound—and beyond (a) Concentric circles centered on a stationary jet plane represent the spherical wave fronts of the sound it generates. As the speed of the plane increases after takeoff, the plane catches up to the sound wave fronts. (b) The plane is not moving as fast as the sound waves propagate. (c) When the plane moves at the speed of the sound waves, it just exactly catches up to the wave fronts. (d) When the speed of the plane exceeds the speed of sound, the plane moves farther in any time interval than the corresponding sound wave front.

(a)

Mach cone

(b)

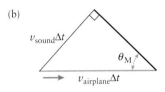

$v_{sound}\Delta t$

θ_M

$v_{airplane}\Delta t$

Figure 13-27 Faster than sound (a) In an expanded view of a plane flying faster than the speed of sound, each circle represents the spherical wave crest of a sound generated when the plane was at the center of the circle. The crests of all of the sound waves generated during the time that the plane has moved from its initial position to its final position interfere constructively on the surface of the Mach cone. (b) Relating the Mach angle to the speed of sound and the speed of the airplane.

narrow in extent, as you can see in **Figure 13-28**. This is a photograph of an X-15 air-craft in a wind tunnel with air moving at more than twice the speed of sound. In the figure, a number of separate shock waves, each originating from various discontinuities on the airplane's surface, are made evident by a photographic technique that reveals regions of differing air density. Notice that each of these regions is only a fraction of the length of the airplane. For this reason, you would hear a sharp, explosive sound from each shock wave as this aircraft passed overhead.

Note that the sonic boom is *not* the amplified sound of the aircraft engine. As Figure 13-28 shows, shock waves spread out from several parts of the airplane and are not associated with the engine at all. If an airplane is still flying supersonically after it runs out of fuel, it still produces a sonic boom.

The angle of the Mach cone depends on the airplane's speed, which we call $v_{airplane}$. To see how to calculate this angle, inspect parts (a) and (b) of Figure 13-27. In a time Δt the airplane travels a distance $v_{airplane}\Delta t$; this is shown by a blue line in Figure 13-27a and **Figure 13-27b**. The distance $v_{airplane}\Delta t$ forms the hypotenuse of a right triangle, one leg of which is the distance $v_{sound}\Delta t$ that the sound travels in time Δt. The sine of the angle θ_M in Figure 13-27b, known as the **Mach angle**, equals the side opposite this angle ($v_{sound}\Delta t$) divided by the hypotenuse ($v_{airplane}\Delta t$). The factors of Δt cancel, leaving

Angle of the Mach cone made by a supersonic airplane

Speed of sound

$$\sin \theta_M = \frac{v_{sound}}{v_{airplane}}$$

Speed of the airplane

Mach angle
(13-37)

Figure 13-28 **Shock waves** This photograph shows air moving over an X-15 aircraft at more than twice the speed of sound in a supersonic wind tunnel. Shock waves originate from various discontinuities on its surface.

If an airplane is flying at the speed of sound, the ratio $v_{\text{sound}}/v_{\text{airplane}}$ equals 1. Since $\sin 90° = 1$, the Mach angle at this speed is $\theta_M = 90°$. As an object's speed increases above v_{sound}, θ_M decreases and the Mach cone lies more tightly around the path of the airplane.

For the case shown in Figure 13-27b, the Mach angle is 45°; in this case, Equation 13-37 tells us that $v_{\text{sound}}/v_{\text{airplane}} = \sin 45° = 0.71$, so $v_{\text{airplane}} = v_{\text{sound}}/0.71 = 1.4 v_{\text{sound}}$ (the airplane is flying at 1.4 times the speed of sound). The ratio of an airplane's speed to the speed of sound is called the **Mach number**: $M = v_{\text{airplane}}/v_{\text{sound}}$. So you can see that $M = 1.4$ for the airplane shown in Figure 13-27b (it is said to be flying "at Mach 1.4"). In terms of the Mach number, we can rewrite Equation 13-37 as $\sin \theta_M = 1/M$.

! **Watch Out!** The Mach cone moves along with the object that creates it.

Although the individual sound waves that go into making a sonic boom travel at the speed of sound, the Mach cone on which the crests pile up moves along with the supersonic airplane. For example, the sonic boom associated with a jet airplane flying horizontally at Mach 1.4 also moves horizontally at 1.4 times the speed of sound.

Example 13-13 Sonic Boom

You are at an air show when a supersonic airplane flies directly over you at an altitude of 1.20 km and a Mach number of 1.10. How long after the airplane was directly overhead do you hear the sonic boom? Use 343 m/s for the speed of sound in air.

Set Up

Mach 1.10 means that the speed of the airplane is 1.10 times the speed of sound. You hear the sonic boom when the Mach cone passes over you, a time Δt after the airplane is overhead. As the sketch shows, when this happens the airplane flying at altitude $H = 1.20$ km has flown past you a distance $v_{\text{airplane}}\Delta t$, where $v_{\text{airplane}} = 1.10 v_{\text{sound}}$. We'll use Equation 13-37 and trigonometry to solve this problem.

Mach angle:

$$\sin \theta_M = \frac{v_{\text{sound}}}{v_{\text{airplane}}} \qquad (13\text{-}37)$$

Solve

Since we know the speed of the airplane, we can use Equation 13-37 to find the Mach angle θ_M.

The speed of the airplane is $v_{\text{airplane}} = 1.10 v_{\text{sound}}$, so Equation 13-37 becomes

$$\sin \theta_M = \frac{v_{\text{sound}}}{v_{\text{airplane}}} = \frac{v_{\text{sound}}}{1.10 v_{\text{sound}}} = \frac{1}{1.10}$$

So θ_M is the angle whose sine is equal to $1/1.10$:

$$\theta_M = \sin^{-1}\left(\frac{1}{1.10}\right) = \sin^{-1} 0.909 = 65.4°$$

The figure above shows that the distances H and $v_{\text{airplane}}\Delta t$ are two sides of a right triangle. Since H is opposite to the angle θ_M and $v_{\text{airplane}}\Delta t$ is adjacent to θ_M, their ratio is the tangent of θ_M.

From the figure,

$$\tan\theta_M = \frac{H}{v_{\text{airplane}}\Delta t}$$

We know the values of $\theta_M = 65.4°$, $H = 1.20$ km, $v_{\text{airplane}} = 1.10v_{\text{sound}}$, and $v_{\text{sound}} = 343$ m/s, so we can solve for Δt:

$$\Delta t = \frac{H}{v_{\text{airplane}}\tan\theta_M} = \frac{H}{1.10v_{\text{sound}}\tan\theta_M}$$

$$= \frac{1.20\text{ km}}{1.10\,(343\text{ m/s})\tan 65.4°}\left(\frac{10^3\text{ m}}{1\text{ km}}\right)$$

$$= 1.46\text{ s}$$

The sonic boom reaches you 1.46 s after the airplane flies overhead.

Reflect

Note that if the airplane emits a sound wave when it is directly above you at altitude $H = 1.20$ km $= 1200$ m, that sound would need a time $H/v_{\text{sound}} = (1200\text{ m})/(343\text{ m/s}) = 3.49$ s to reach you. The sonic boom reaches you *before* that, just 1.46 s after the airplane is directly above you. That's because the shock wave is made up of wave crests that were emitted by the airplane *before* the airplane was directly above you (see Figure 13-27a) and so the wave crests have had more time to reach you.

? Got the Concept? 13-11 Sound from a Supersonic Airplane

When an airplane is traveling at Mach 2.0 (twice the speed of sound), at what speed do sound waves spread away from the point where the airplane emits them? (a) 2.0 times the speed of sound; (b) faster than the speed of sound, but slower than 2.0 times the speed of sound; (c) the speed of sound; (d) slower than the speed of sound.

Take-Home Message for Section 13-10

✔ The frequency of a sound wave heard by a listener is higher if the listener and source are moving toward each other and is lower if they are moving apart. This is called the Doppler effect.

✔ If a source of sound waves moves through the air faster than the speed of sound, a shock wave (sonic boom) is produced.

Key Terms

amplitude	inverse-square law	pressure wave
angular frequency	linear mass density	(longitudinal wave)
angular wave number	longitudinal wave (pressure wave)	propagation speed
antinode	Mach angle	shock wave
beat frequency	Mach cone	sinusoidal wave
beats	Mach number	sonic boom
closed pipe	mechanical wave	sound intensity level
constructive interference	medium	sound wave
decibel	node	standing wave
destructive interference	one-dimensional wave	standing wave mode
Doppler effect	open pipe	surface wave
frequency	path length difference	transverse wave
fundamental frequency	period	traveling wave
fundamental mode	phase angle	watt
intensity	phase difference	wave
interference	power	wave function
interference pattern	pressure amplitude	wavelength

Chapter Summary

Topic	Equation or Figure

Mechanical waves: A mechanical wave is a disturbance that propagates through a material medium. There is no net flow of material through the medium. Mechanical waves can be transverse, longitudinal, or a combination of the two.

(a)

① If the hand holding the rope moves up and down, a **transverse wave** travels along the rope.

② The wave disturbance propagates (moves along the rope) horizontally...

③ ...but individual parts of the rope (the wave medium) move up and down, perpendicular (transverse) to the propagation direction.

(Figure 13-2)

(b)

① If the hand holding the spring moves back and forth, a **longitudinal wave** travels along the spring.

② The wave disturbance propagates (moves along the spring) horizontally...

③ ...but individual parts of the spring (the wave medium) move back and forth, parallel (longitudinal) to the propagation direction.

Sinusoidal waves: In a sinusoidal wave, each piece of the medium undergoes simple harmonic motion with the same amplitude and frequency. At any instant the wave pattern repeats itself over a distance λ known as the wavelength. The product of the frequency and wavelength equals the propagation speed of the wave.

Propagation speed of a wave

$$v_{\text{p}} = f\lambda \qquad (13\text{-}2)$$

Frequency　　Wavelength

Wave function for a sinusoidal wave propagating in the $+x$ direction

Angular wave number of the wave $= 2\pi/\lambda$

$$y(x,t) = A\cos(kx - \omega t + \phi) \qquad (13\text{-}6)$$

Phase angle

Amplitude of the wave　　Angular frequency of the wave $= 2\pi f$

Propagation speed of a wave: The speed at which a wave travels through a medium depends on the type of wave and the properties of the medium.

Propagation speed of a transverse wave on a rope

Tension in the rope

$$v_{\text{p}} = \sqrt{\frac{F}{\mu}} \qquad (13\text{-}10)$$

Mass per unit length of the rope

Propagation speed of a longitudinal wave in a fluid

Bulk modulus of the fluid

$$v_{\text{p}} = \sqrt{\frac{B}{\rho}} \qquad (13\text{-}11)$$

Density of the fluid

Propagation speed of a longitudinal wave along a solid rod

Young's modulus of the solid

$$v_{\text{p}} = \sqrt{\frac{Y}{\rho}} \qquad (13\text{-}12)$$

Density of the solid

Superposition and interference: When two waves are present simultaneously in a medium, the total wave is the sum of the two individual waves. If the two waves have the same frequency but emanate from different places, there will be positions where constructive and destructive interference occur.

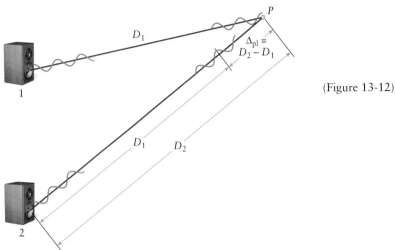

(Figure 13-12)

Standing waves on a string: When sinusoidal waves reflect back and forth from the ends of a string, the result can be a standing wave. Standing waves are possible only if a whole number of half-wavelengths fit into the length of the string. Each standing wave mode has its own natural frequency.

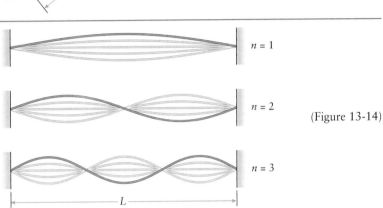

(Figure 13-14)

nth possible frequency of a standing wave on a string held at both ends

Tension in the string

$$f_n = \frac{n}{2L}\sqrt{\frac{F}{\mu}} \quad \text{where } n = 1, 2, 3,\ldots \qquad (13\text{-}19)$$

Length of the string

Linear mass density of the string

Standing sound waves in a pipe: Standing waves can also occur when sinusoidal sound waves reflect back and forth from the ends of a pipe. The allowed wavelengths and frequencies depend on whether the pipe is closed

Closed pipe:

(Figure 13-18a)

(closed at one end and open at the other) or open (open at both ends).

Open pipe:

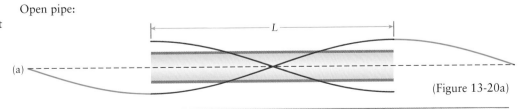

(Figure 13-20a)

Beats: When two sound waves of similar frequencies f_1 and f_2 interfere, the result is a total wave with a frequency $(f_1 + f_2)/2$ and an amplitude that rises and falls at the beat frequency.

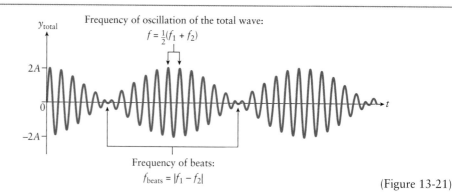

Frequency of oscillation of the total wave:
$$f = \tfrac{1}{2}(f_1 + f_2)$$

Frequency of beats:
$$f_{beats} = |f_1 - f_2|$$

(Figure 13-21)

Beat frequency heard when sound waves of two similar frequencies interfere

Frequencies of the individual sound waves

$$f_{beats} = |f_2 - f_1|$$

(13-25)

Wave intensity: The intensity of a sound wave is the amount of power (energy per unit time) that the wave delivers per unit area. It can be expressed in terms of the displacement amplitude or pressure amplitude of the wave. If the wave source emits equally in all directions, the intensity decreases with distance according to an inverse-square law. Sound intensity level is an alternative way to express intensity using a logarithmic scale.

Intensity of a sound wave

Pressure amplitude of the wave

$$I = \frac{p^2_{max}}{2\rho v_{sound}}$$

(13-31)

Density of the wave medium (usually air)

Speed of sound waves in the medium

Intensity of a sound wave at a distance r from a source that emits in all directions

Power output of the sound source

$$I = \frac{P_0}{4\pi r^2}$$

Distance from the source to the point where the intensity is measured

(13-32)

The Doppler effect: If a source of sound emits waves with frequency f, a listener will hear a different frequency if the source and listener are moving relative to each other.

Frequency of sound detected by the listener

Frequency of sound emitted by the source

$$f_{listener} = \left[\frac{v_{sound} \pm v_{listener}}{v_{sound} \mp v_{source}} \right] f$$

(13-35)

v_{sound} = speed of sound
$v_{listener}$ = speed of the listener
v_{source} = speed of the source

In both numerator and denominator:
• Use upper sign if source and listener are approaching.
• Use lower sign if source and listener are moving apart.

Sonic booms: If an object moves through the air faster than the speed of sound, the sound waves from the object combine to form a conical shock wave. The angle of this cone depends on the speed of the object.

(a)

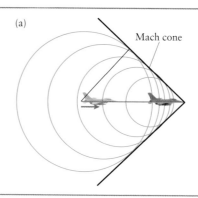

Mach cone

(Figure 13-27a)

Answer to What do you think? Question

(b) We learn in Section 13-3 that the speed of waves on a string (or a flagellum) does not depend on the frequency of the wave.

If the frequency increases, the speed remains the same but the wavelength (the distance from one crest to the next) decreases.

Answers to Got the Concept? Questions

13-1 (c) In the transverse wave shown in Figure 13-2a the individual pieces of rope (the wave medium) move vertically. So the restoring force that influences their motion must also act vertically. In the same way, since the pieces of the spring in Figure 13-2b move horizontally, the restoring force that acts on them must be in the horizontal direction.

13-2 (e) The propagation speed v_p of sound waves does not depend on the frequency f. The frequency and the wavelength λ are related by Equation 13-2, $v_p = f\lambda$, so increasing the frequency makes the wavelength shorter but has *no* effect on the propagation speed.

13-3 (a) The speed of light is so great that you *see* the batter swing a tiny fraction of a second after the swing took place. The speed of sound is relatively slow by comparison. From the relationship $d = v_{sound}t$ with distance d, propagation speed v_{sound}, and time t, the distance that sound travels in $t = 0.20$ s is $d = (343 \text{ m/s})(0.20 \text{ s}) = 69$ m. Note that the time for light to travel this same distance is $t_{light} = d/v_{light} = (69 \text{ m})/(3.0 \times 10^8 \text{ m/s}) = 2.3 \times 10^{-7}$ s, or about $1/4$ of a microsecond (1 microsecond = 1 μs = 10^{-6} s).

13-4 (b) Increasing the frequency decreases the wavelength. The wavelength sets the scale for the entire interference pattern (the positions of destructive and constructive interference depend on the wavelength), so decreasing the wavelength will make all of the distances smaller and the interference pattern will shrink inward toward the two fingers.

13-5 (e) From Equation 13-18 the wavelength of the $n = 1$ standing wave mode on a string of length L is given by $L = \lambda/2$, so $\lambda = 2L$. This does not depend on the tension in the string, so the wavelength remains the same.

13-6 (b) From Equation 13-19 the frequency of each standing wave mode on the string is proportional to the square root of the tension F. So doubling the tension will cause the frequency to increase not by a factor of 2, but by a factor of $\sqrt{2} = 1.41$.

13-7 (a) The bottle is like an air-filled pipe that is open at the top and closed on the bottom (at the surface of the water). The fundamental frequency of this pipe is inversely proportional to the length of the pipe (see Equation 13-22). As you fill the bottle, the length of the air-filled pipe decreases so that the fundamental frequency goes up. The pitch of the sound from the bottle depends on the fundamental frequency, so the pitch goes up as well.

13-8 (e) The beat frequency equals the difference between the frequencies of the two waves that interfere. The beat frequency here is 3 Hz, so the second tuning fork has a frequency of either 440 Hz + 3 Hz = 443 Hz or 440 Hz − 3 Hz = 437 Hz. Without more information we can't tell which of these two is correct.

13-9 (d) The sound waves from each fan carry the same power, so at any distance from the fans the intensity from each fan is the same. Thus the total intensity doubles when both fans are running. We saw in Example 13-11 that doubling the intensity corresponds to adding 3.0 dB to the sound intensity level. So the sound intensity level due to both fans is 60 dB + 3.0 dB = 63 dB.

13-10 (a) The frequency you hear is higher while you're running compared to when you're standing still. Because you are moving toward the source of the sound, you will intercept more wave crests in a given amount of time than you would were you standing still. The qualitative approach we took using Figure 13-24 for a moving source of sound and a stationary listener applies equally well for a stationary source and a moving listener.

13-11 (c) No matter how a source of sound waves is moving, the waves spread outward at the speed of sound from the point where they were emitted. We used this idea in drawing Figure 13-26.

Questions and Problems

In a few problems, you are given more data than you actually need; in a few other problems, you are required to supply data from your general knowledge, outside sources, or informed estimate. Interpret as significant all digits in numerical values that have trailing zeros and no decimal points.

For all problems, use $g = 9.80$ m/s^2 for the free-fall acceleration due to gravity. Neglect friction and air resistance unless instructed to do otherwise.

* Basic, single-concept problem
** Intermediate-level problem, may require synthesis of concepts and multiple steps
*** Challenging problem

SSM *Solution is in Student Solutions Manual*

Conceptual Questions

1. •Explain the difference between longitudinal waves and transverse waves and give two examples of each.

2. •Discuss several ways that the human body creates or responds to waves.

3. •When you talk to your friend, are the air molecules that reach his ear the same ones that were in your lungs? Explain your answer. SSM

4. •Draw a sketch of a transverse wave and label the amplitude, wavelength, a crest, and a trough.

5. •If a tree falls in the forest and no humans are there to hear it, was any sound produced?

6. •Are water waves longitudinal or transverse? Explain your answer.

7. •A sound wave passes from air into water. Give a qualitative explanation of how these properties change: (a) wave speed, (b) frequency, and (c) wavelength of the wave. SSM

8. •Two solid rods have the same Young's modulus, but one has larger density than the other. In which rod will the speed

of longitudinal waves be greater? Explain your answer, making reference to the variables that affect the wave speed.

9. •Earthquakes produce several types of wave. The most significant are the primary wave (or P wave) and the secondary wave (or S wave). The primary wave is a longitudinal wave that can travel through liquids and solids. The secondary wave is a transverse wave that can only travel through solids. The speed of a P wave usually falls between 1000 m/s and 8000 m/s; the speed of an S wave is around 60–70% of the P wave speeds. For any given seismic event, discuss the damage that might be due to P waves and how that would differ when compared to the damage due to S waves.

10. •(a) What is a transverse standing wave? (b) For a string stretched between two fixed points, describe how a disturbance on the string might lead to a standing wave.

11. •Explain the differences and similarities between the concepts of frequency f and angular frequency ω. SSM

12. •Search the Internet for the words *rarefaction*, *phonon*, and *compression* in the context of longitudinal waves. Describe how a longitudinal wave is made up of phonons and explain the connection between rarefaction and compression in such a wave.

13. •If you stand beside a railroad track as a train sounding its whistle moves past, you will experience the Doppler effect. Describe any changes in the perceived sound that a person riding on the train will hear.

14. •(a) Describe in words the nature of a sonic boom. (b) Now, referring to the formula for the Doppler shift, explain the phenomenon.

15. •Explain the concept of phase difference, ϕ, and predict the outcome of two identical waves interfering when $\phi = 0°$, $\phi = 90°$, $\phi = 180°$, $\phi = 270°$, and $\phi = 300°$.

16. •Two pianists sit down to play two identical pianos. However, a string is out of tune on Elizabeth's piano. The $G_3^{\#}$ key (208 Hz) appears to be the problem. When Greg plays the note on his piano and Elizabeth plays hers, a beat frequency of 6 Hz is heard. Luckily, a piano tuner is present, and she is ready to correct the problem. However, in all the confusion, she inadvertently increases the tension in Greg's $G_3^{\#}$ string by a factor of 1.058. Now, both pianos are out of tune! Yet oddly, when Elizabeth plays her $G_3^{\#}$ note and Greg plays his $G_3^{\#}$, there is no beat frequency. Explain what happened.

17. •How does the length of an organ pipe determine the fundamental frequency?

18. •Why do the sounds emitted by organ pipes that are closed on one end and open on the other *not* have even harmonics? Include in your explanation a sketch of the resonant waves that are formed in the pipe.

19. •(a) Explain the differences and similarities among the concepts of intensity, sound level, and power. (b) What happens to intensity as the source of sound moves closer to the observer? (c) What happens to sound level? (d) What happens to power? SSM

20. •A car radio is tuned to receive a signal from a particular radio station. While the car slows to a stop at a traffic signal, the reception of the radio seems to fade in and out. Use the concept of interference to explain the phenomenon. *Hint:* In broadcast technology, the phenomenon is known as multipathing.

Multiple-Choice Questions

21. •A visible disturbance propagates around a crowded soccer stadium when fans, section by section, jump up and then sit back down. What type of wave is this?
   A. longitudinal wave
   B. transverse wave
   C. polarized wave
   D. spherical wave
   E. polarized spherical wave

22. •Two point sources produce waves of the same wavelength that are in phase. At a point midway between the sources, you would expect to observe
   A. constructive interference.
   B. destructive interference.
   C. alternating constructive and destructive interference.
   D. constructive or destructive interference depending on the wavelength.
   E. no interference.

23. •Standing waves are set up on a string that is fixed at both ends so that the ends are nodes. How many nodes are there in the fourth mode?
   A. 2
   B. 3
   C. 4
   D. 5
   E. 6 SSM

24. •Which of the following frequencies are higher harmonics of a string with fundamental frequency of 80 Hz?
   A. 80 Hz
   B. 120 Hz
   C. 160 Hz
   D. 200 Hz
   E. 220 Hz

25. •A trombone has a variable length. When a musician blows air into the mouthpiece and causes air in the tube of the horn to vibrate, the waves set up by the vibrations reflect back and forth in the horn to create standing waves. As the length of the horn is made shorter, what happens to the frequency?
   A. The frequency remains the same.
   B. The frequency will increase.
   C. The frequency will decrease.
   D. The frequency will increase or decrease depending on how hard the horn player blows.
   E. The frequency will increase or decrease depending on the diameter of the horn.

26. •Two tuning forks of frequency 480 Hz and 484 Hz are struck simultaneously. What is the beat frequency resulting from the two sound waves?
   A. 964 Hz
   B. 482 Hz
   C. 4 Hz
   D. 2 Hz
   E. 0 Hz

27. •If a source radiates sound uniformly in all directions, and you triple your distance from the sound source, what happens to the sound intensity at your new position?
   A. The sound intensity increases to three times its original value.

B. The sound intensity does not change.

C. The sound intensity drops to 1/3 its original value.

D. The sound intensity drops to 1/9 its original value.

E. The sound intensity drops to 1/27 its original value. SSM

28. •If the amplitude of a sound wave is tripled, the intensity will

A. decrease by a factor of 3.

B. increase by a factor of 3.

C. remain the same.

D. decrease by a factor of 9.

E. increase by a factor of 9.

29. •A certain sound level is increased by an additional 20 dB. By how much does the intensity increase?

A. The intensity increases by a factor of 2.

B. The intensity increases by a factor of 20.

C. The intensity increases by a factor of 100.

D. The intensity increases by a factor of 200.

E. The intensity does not increase.

30. •A person sitting in a parked car hears an approaching ambulance siren at a frequency f_1, and as it passes him and moves away he hears a frequency f_2. The actual frequency f of the source is

A. $f > f_1$

B. $f < f_2$

C. $f_2 < f < f_1$

D. $f = f_2 + f_1$

E. $f = f_2 - f_1$

Estimation/Numerical Analysis

31. •Estimate the size of the human voice box using the fact that the human ear is most sensitive to sounds of about 3000 Hz. SSM

32. •(a) Estimate the distance that sound waves travel in 10 s. (b) Explain why you might get ±5% of the calculated distance on any given day that you perform an experiment to measure the speed of sound.

33. •Estimate the number of beats per second of a hummingbird's wings.

34. •(a) Estimate the speed of a human wave like those seen at a large sports venue. (b) How would you define the corresponding concepts of wavelength, frequency, and amplitude for the human wave?

35. •Describe how you might estimate the speed of the transverse waves on a violin string. SSM

36. •**Biology** Peristalsis is the rhythmic, wavelike contraction of smooth muscles to propel material through the digestive tract. A typical peristaltic wave will only last for a few seconds in the small intestine, traveling at only a few centimeters per second. Estimate the wavelength of the digestive wave.

37. •Estimate the difference in time required for the sound of the "crack" of the bat to reach the left field bleacher seats on a calm day compared to a blustery day with a stiff breeze blowing out to left field.

38. •(a) Estimate the amplitude, frequency, and wavelength of a typical ocean wave, far at sea, away from coastlines. (b) What is the typical speed of ocean waves?

39. •(a) Using a graphing calculator, spreadsheet, or graphing program, graph the wave function, $y(x)$, that describes the traveling wave described by the data shown. Assume the data were taken at time $t = 0$ s. (b) Write a mathematical function that describes the traveling wave if the period of the motion is 2 s.

x (m)	y (m)	x (m)	y (m)
0	0	7	−4.5
1	4.5	8	−7.8
2	7.8	9	−9
3	9	10	−7.8
4	7.8	11	−4.5
5	4.5	12	0
6	0		

Problems

13-1 Waves are disturbances that travel from place to place

13-2 Mechanical waves can be transverse, longitudinal, or a combination of these

13-3 Sinusoidal waves are related to simple harmonic motion

40. •The period of a sound wave is 0.01 s. Calculate the frequency f and the angular frequency ω.

41. •A wave on a string propagates at 22 m/s. If the frequency is 24 Hz, calculate the wavelength and angular wave number. SSM

42. ••A transverse wave on a string has an amplitude of 20 cm, a wavelength of 35 cm, and a frequency of 2.0 Hz. Write the mathematical description of the displacement from equilibrium for the wave if (a) at $t = 0$, $x = 0$ and $y = 0$; (b) at $t = 0$, $x = 0$ and $y = +20$ cm; (c) at $t = 0$, $x = 0$ and $y = -20$ cm; and (d) at $t = 0$, $x = 0$ and $y = 12$ cm.

43. •Show that the dimensions of speed (distance/time) are consistent with both versions of the expression for the propagation speed of a wave: $v_p = \dfrac{\omega}{k}$ and $v_p = \lambda f$.

44. ••Write the wave equation for a periodic transverse wave traveling in the positive x direction at a speed of 20 m/s if it has a frequency of 10 Hz and an amplitude in the y direction of 0.10 m.

45. •A wave on a string is described by the equation $y(x,t) = (0.5 \text{ m}) \cos [(1.0 \text{ rad/m})x - (10 \text{ rad/s})t]$. What are (a) the frequency, (b) wavelength, and (c) speed of the wave? SSM

46. ••The pressure wave that travels along the inside of an organ pipe is given in terms of distance and time by the following function $p(x,t) = (1.0 \text{ atm}) \sin [(6.0 \text{ rad/m})x - (4.0 \text{ rad/s})t]$. (a) What is the pressure amplitude of the wave? (b) What is the wave number of the wave? (c) What is the frequency of the wave? (d) What is the speed of the wave? (e) What is the corresponding spatial displacement, $s(x,t)$, from equilibrium for the pressure wave, assuming the maximum displacement is 2.0 cm?

47. ••The equation for a particular wave is $y(x,t) = (0.1 \text{ m})\cos (kx - \omega t)$. If the frequency of the wave is 2.0 Hz, what is the value of y at $x = 0$ when $t = 4.0$ s?

48. •Using the graph in Figure 13-29, write the mathematical description of the wave if the period of the motion is 4 s and the wave moves to the right (toward the positive x direction).

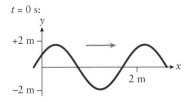

Figure 13-29 Problem 48

49. •Write a mathematical description of the wave using the graphs in Figure 13-30. SSM

Figure 13-30 Problem 49

13-4 The propagation speed of a wave depends on the properties of the wave medium

50. •If the Young's modulus for liquid A is twice that of liquid B, and the density of liquid A is one-half of the density of liquid B, what does the ratio of the speeds of sound in the two liquids (v_A/v_B) equal?

51. •A string that has a mass of 5.0 g and a length of 2.2 m is pulled taut with a tension of 78 N. Calculate the speed of transverse waves on the string. SSM

52. •A long rope is shaken up and down by a rodeo contestant. The transverse waves travel 12.8 m in a time of 2.1 s. If the tension in the rope is 80 N, calculate the mass per unit length for the rope.

53. ••The violin is a four-stringed instrument tuned so that the ratio of the frequencies of adjacent strings is 3 to 2. (This is the ratio when taken as high frequency to lower frequency.) If the diameter of the E string (the highest frequency) on a violin is 0.25 mm, find the diameters of the remaining strings (A, D, and G), assuming they are tuned as indicated (what musicians call intervals of a perfect fifth), they are made of the same material, and they all have the same tension.

54. •At room temperature the bulk modulus of glycerine is about $4.35 \times 10^9 \, \text{N/m}^2$ and the density of glycerine is about $1260 \, \text{kg/m}^3$. Calculate the speed of sound in glycerin.

55. •The Young's modulus of water is $2.2 \times 10^9 \, \text{N/m}^2$. The density of water is $1000 \, \text{kg/m}^3$. Calculate the speed of sound in water. SSM

56. •When sound travels through the ocean, where the Young's modulus is $2.34 \times 10^9 \, \text{N/m}^2$, the wavelength associated with 1000 Hz waves is 1.51 m. Calculate the density of seawater.

57. •What is the speed of sound in gasoline? The Young's modulus for gasoline is $1.3 \times 10^9 \, \text{N/m}^2$. The density of gasoline is 0.74 kg/L.

13-5 When two waves are present simultaneously, the total disturbance is the sum of the individual waves

58. •Two waves interfere at the point x in Figure 13-31. The resultant wave is shown. Draw the three possible shapes for the two waves that interfere to produce this outcome. In each case one wave should head toward the right and one wave should head toward the left.

Figure 13-31 Problem 58

59. •In Figure 13-32, rectangular waveforms are approaching each other. For each case, use the ideas of interference to predict the superposed wave that results when the two waves are coincident. Describe the superposed wave graphically and with text. SSM

Figure 13-32 Problem 59

60. •Construct the resultant wave that is formed when the two waves shown in each case occupy the same space and interfere (Figure 13-33).

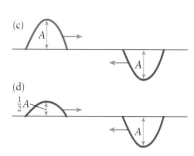

Figure 13-33 Problem 60

61. ••Two identical speakers (1 and 2) are playing a tone with a frequency of 171.5 Hz, in phase (Figure 13-34). The speakers are located 6 m apart. Determine what points (A, B, C, D, or E, all separated by 1 m) will experience constructive interference along the line that is 6 m in front of the speakers. Point A is directly in front of speaker 1. The speed of sound is 343 m/s. SSM

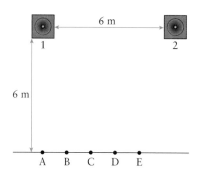

Figure 13-34 Problem 61

13-6 A standing wave is caused by interference between waves traveling in opposite directions

62. •A string is tied at both ends, and a standing wave is established. The length of the string is 2 m, and it vibrates in the

fundamental mode ($n = 1$). If the speed of waves on the string is 60 m/s, calculate the frequency and wavelength of the waves.

63. •A string is fixed on both ends with a standing wave vibrating in the fourth harmonic. Draw the shape of the wave and label the location of antinodes (A) and nodes (N).

64. •A 2.35-m-long string is tied at both ends and it vibrates with a fundamental frequency of 24 Hz. Find the frequencies and make a sketch of the next four harmonics. What is the speed of waves on the string?

65. •A string that is 1.25 m long has a mass of 0.0548 kg and a tension of 200 N. The string is tied at both ends and vibrated at various frequencies. (a) What frequencies would you need to apply to excite the first four harmonics? (b) Make a sketch of the first four harmonics for these standing waves. SSM

66. ••A string of length L is tied at both ends, and a harmonic mode is created with a frequency of 40 Hz. If the next successive harmonic is at 48 Hz and the speed of transverse waves on the string is 56 m/s, find the length of the string. Note that the fundamental frequency is not necessarily 40 Hz.

67. ••An object of mass M is used to provide tension in a 4.5-m-long string that has a mass of 0.252 kg, as shown in Figure 13-35. A standing wave that has a wavelength equal to 1.5 m is produced by a source that vibrates at 30 Hz. Calculate the value of M.

Figure 13-35 Problem 67

68. ••A guitar string has a mass per unit length of 2.35 g/m. If the string is vibrating between points that are 60 cm apart, find the tension when the string is designed to play a note of 440 Hz (A4).

69. ••An E string on a violin has a diameter of 0.25 mm and is made from steel (density of 7800 kg/m³). The string is designed to sound a fundamental note of 660 Hz, and its unstretched length is 32.5 cm. Calculate the tension in the string. SSM

13-7 Wind instruments, the human voice, and the human ear use standing sound waves

70. •An organ pipe of length L sounds its fundamental tone at 40 Hz. The pipe is open on both ends, and the speed of sound in air is 343 m/s. Calculate (a) the length of the pipe and (b) the frequency of the first four harmonics.

71. •An organ pipe sounds two successive tones at 228.6 Hz and 274.3 Hz. Determine whether the pipe is open at both ends or open at one end and closed at the other. SSM

72. •A narrow glass tube is 0.40 m long and sealed on the bottom end. It is held under a loudspeaker that sounds a tone at 220 Hz, causing the tube to radically resonate in its first harmonic. Find the speed of sound in the room.

73. •The third harmonic of an organ pipe that is open at both ends and is 2.25 m long excites the fourth harmonic in another organ pipe. Determine the length of the other pipe and whether it is open at both ends or open at one end and closed at the other. Assume the speed of sound is 343 m/s in air.

74. •**Biology** If the human ear canal with a typical length of about 2.8 cm is regarded as a tube open at one end and closed at

the eardrum, what is the fundamental frequency that we should hear best? Assume that the speed of sound is 343 m/s in air.

75. •**Biology** A male alligator emits a subsonic mating call that has a frequency of 18 Hz by taking a large breath into his chest cavity and then releasing it. If the hollow chest cavity of an alligator behaves approximately as a pipe open at only one end, estimate its length. Is your answer consistent with the typical size of an alligator?

76. •**Biology** The trunk of a very large elephant may extend up to 3 m! It acts much like an organ pipe only open at one end when the elephant blows air through it. (a) Calculate the fundamental frequency of the sound the elephant can create with its trunk. (b) If the elephant blows even harder, the next harmonic may be sounded. What is the frequency of the first overtone?

77. •The longest pipe in the Mormon Tabernacle Organ in Salt Lake City has a "speaking length" of 9.75 m; the smallest pipe is 1.91 cm long. Assuming that the speed of sound is 343 m/s, determine the range of frequencies that the organ can produce if both open and closed pipes are used with these lengths. SSM

13-8 Two sound waves of slightly different frequencies produce beats

78. •The sound from a tuning fork of 440 Hz produces beats against the unknown emissions from a vibrating string. If beats are heard at a frequency of 4 Hz, what is the vibrational frequency of the string?

79. •A guitar string is "in tune" at 440 Hz. When a standardized tuning fork rated at 440 Hz is simultaneously sounded with the guitar string, a beat frequency of 5 Hz is heard. (a) How far out of tune is the string? (b) What should you do to correct this?

80. •Two tuning forks are both rated at 256 Hz, but when they are struck at the same time, a beat frequency of 4 Hz is created. If you know that one of the tuning forks is in tune (but you are not sure which one), what are the possible values of the "out-of-tune" fork?

81. •A guitar string has a tension of 100 N and is supposed to have a frequency of 110 Hz. When a standard tone of that value is sounded while the string is plucked, a beat frequency of 2 Hz is heard. The peg holding the string is loosened (decreasing the tension), and the beat frequency increases. What should the tension in the string be in order to achieve perfect pitch? SSM

82. ••Two identical guitar strings under 200 N of tension produce sound with frequencies of 290 Hz. If the tension in one string drops to 196 N, what will be the frequency of beats when the two strings are plucked at the same time?

13-9 The intensity of a wave equals the power that it delivers per square meter

83. •By what factor should you move away from a point source of sound waves in order to lower the intensity by (a) a factor of 10? (b) A factor of 3? (c) A factor of 2? (d) Discuss how this problem would change if it were a point source that was radiating into a hemisphere instead of a sphere.

84. •Calculate the ratio of the acoustic power generated by a blue whale (190 dB) compared to the sound energy generated by a jackhammer (105 dB). Assume that the receiver of the sound is the same distance from the two sources of sound.

85. ••The steady drone of rush hour traffic persists on a stretch of freeway for 4 h each day. A nearby resident undertakes a plan to harness the wasted sound energy and use it for her home. She mounts a 1-m^2 "microphone" that absorbs 30% of the sound that hits it. If the ambient sound level is 100 dB at the microphone, calculate the amount of sound energy that is collected. Do you think her plan is "sound"? How could you improve it? SSM

86. •A longitudinal wave has a measured sound level of 85 dB at a distance of 3 m from the speaker that created it. (a) Calculate the intensity of the sound at that point. (b) If the speaker were a point source of sound energy, find its power output.

87. •Biology A single goose sounds a loud warning when an intruder enters the farmyard. Some distance from the goose, you measure the sound level of the warning to be 88 dB. If a gaggle of 30 identical geese is present, and they are all approximately the same distance from you, what will the collective sound level be if they all sound off simultaneously? Neglect any interference effects.

88. •Two sound levels, β_1 and β_2, can be compared relative to each other (rather than to some standardized intensity threshold). Find a formula for this by calculating $\Delta \beta = \beta_2 - \beta_1$. You will need to employ your knowledge of basic logarithm operations to derive the formula.

89. •By what factor must you increase the intensity of a sound in order to hear (a) a 1-dB rise in the sound level? (b) What about a 20-dB rise? SSM

90. •Biology The intensity of a certain sound at your eardrum is 0.003 W/m^2. (a) Calculate the rate at which sound energy hits your eardrum. Assume that the area of your eardrum is about 55 mm^2. (b) What power output is required from a point source that is 2 m away in order to create that intensity?

91. •Biology The area of a typical eardrum is 5.0×10^{-5} m^2. Find the sound power incident on an eardrum at the threshold of pain.

13-10 The frequency of a sound depends on the motion of the source and the listener

92. •A fire engine's siren is 1600 Hz when at rest. What frequency do you detect if you move with a speed of 28 m/s (a) toward the fire engine, and (b) away from it? Assume that the speed of sound is 343 m/s in air.

93. •Medical An ultrasound machine can measure blood flow speeds. Assume the machine emits acoustic energy at a frequency of 2.0 MHz, and the speed of the wave in human tissue is taken to be 1500 m/s. What is the beat frequency between the transmitted and reflected waves if blood is flowing in large arteries at 0.020 m/s directly away from the sound source?

94. ••A car sounding its horn (rated by the manufacturer at 600 Hz) is moving at 20 m/s toward the east. A stationary observer is standing due east of the oncoming car. (a) What frequency will he hear assuming that the speed of sound is 343 m/s? (b) What if the observer is standing due west of the car as it drives away?

95. ••A bicyclist is moving toward a sheer wall while holding a tuning fork rated at 484 Hz. If the bicyclist detects a beat frequency of 6 Hz (between the waves coming directly from the tuning fork and the echo waves coming from the sheer wall), calculate the speed of the bicycle. Assume the speed of sound is 343 m/s. SSM

96. ••Medical An ultrasonic scan uses the echo waves coming from something moving (such as the beating heart of a fetus) inside the body and the waves that are directly received from the transmitter to form a measurable beat frequency. This allows the speed of the internal structure to be isolated and analyzed. What is the beat frequency detected when waves with a frequency of 5 MHz are used to scan a fetal heartbeat (moving at a speed of $\pm$ 10 cm/s)? The speed of the ultrasound waves in tissue is about 1540 m/s.

97. ••Biology A bat emits a high-pitched squeal at 50,000 Hz as it approaches an insect at 10 m/s. The insect flies away from the bat, and the reflected wave that echoes off the insect returns to the bat at a frequency of 50,050 Hz. Calculate the speed of the insect as it tries to avoid being the bat's next meal. (A bat can eat over 3000 mosquitoes in one night!) SSM

General Problems

98. ••A large volcanic eruption triggers a tsunami. At a seismic station 250 km away, the instruments record that the time *difference* between the arrival of the tidal wave and the arrival of the sound of the explosion is 9.25 min. Tsunamis typically travel at approximately 800 km/h. (a) Which sound arrives first, the sound in the air or in the water? Prove your answer numerically. (b) How long after the explosion does it take for the first sound wave to reach the seismic station? (c) How long after the explosion does it take for the tsunami to reach the seismic station?

99. ••A transverse wave is propagating according to the following wave function:
$y(x,t) = (1.25 \text{ m}) \cos \left[(5.00 \text{ rad/m})x - (4.00 \text{ rad/s})t \right]$ (a) Plot a graph of y versus x when $t = 0$ s. (b) Repeat when $t = 1$ s.

100. •Medical A diagnostic *sonogram* produces a picture of internal organs by passing ultrasound through the tissue. In one application, it is used to find the size, location, and shape of the prostate in preparation for surgery or other treatment. The speed of sound in the prostate is 1540 m/s, and a diagnostic sonogram uses ultrasound of frequency 2.00. MHz. The density of the prostate is 1060 kg/m^3. (a) What is the wavelength of the sonogram ultrasound? (b) What is Young's modulus for the prostate gland?

101. ••You may have seen a demonstration in which a person inhales some helium and suddenly speaks in a high-pitched voice. Let's investigate the reason for the change in pitch. At 0°C, the density of air is 1.40 kg/m^3, the density of helium is 0.1786 kg/m^3, the speed of sound in helium is 972 m/s, and the speed of sound in air is 331 m/s. (a) What is the bulk modulus of helium at 0°C? (b) If a person produces a sound of frequency 0.500 kHz while speaking with his lungs full of air, what frequency sound will that person produce if his respiratory tract is filled with helium instead of air? (c) Use your result to explain why the person sounds strange when he breathes in helium. SSM

102. •Biology When an insect ventures onto a spiderweb, a slight vibration is set up alerting the spider. The density of spider silk is approximately 1.3 g/cm^3, and its diameter varies considerably depending on the type of spider, but 3.0 mm is typical. If the web is under a tension of 0.50 N when a small beetle crawls onto it 25 cm from the spider, how long will it take for the spider to receive the first waves from the beetle?

103. ••If two musical notes are an *octave* apart, the frequency of the higher note is twice that of the lower note. The note concert A usually has a frequency of 440 Hz (although there is some variation). (a) What is the frequency of a note that is two octaves above (higher than) concert A in pitch? (b) If a certain string on a viola is tuned to middle C by adjusting its tension to T, what should be the tension (in terms of T) of the string so that it plays a note one octave below middle C? SSM

104. •••In Western music, the octave is divided into 12 notes as follows: C, $C^#/D^b$, D, $D^#/E^b$, E, F, $F^#/G^b$, G, $G^#/A^b$, A, $A^#/B^b$, C′. Note that some of the notes are the same, such as $C^#$ and D^b. Each of the 12 notes is called a *semitone*. In the ideal *tempered* scale, the ratio of the frequency of any semitone to the frequency of the note below it is the same for all pairs of adjacent notes. So, for example, $f_D/f_{C#}$ is the same as $f_{A#}/f_A$. (a) Show that the ratio of the frequency of any semitone to the frequency of the note just below it is $2^{1/12}$. (b) If A is 440 Hz, what is the frequency of $F^#$ in the tempered scale? (c) If you want to tune a string from B^b to B by changing only its tension, by what ratio should you change the tension? Should you increase or decrease the tension?

105. •Find the temperature in an organ loft in Vancouver, British Columbia, if the 5th *overtone* associated with the pipe that is resonating corresponds to 1500 Hz. The pipe is 0.7 m long, and its type (open–open or open–closed) is not specified. The speed of sound in air depends on the centigrade temperature (T) according to the following:

$$v(T) = \sqrt{109{,}700 + 402T}.$$

106. •**Biology** An adult female ring-necked duck is typically 16 in long, and the length of her bill plus neck is about 5.0 cm long. (a) Calculate the expected fundamental frequency of the quack of the duck. For a rough but reasonable approximation, assume that the sound is only produced in the neck and bill. (b) An adult male ring-necked duck is typically 18 in long. If its other linear dimensions are scaled up in the same ratio from those of the female, what would be the fundamental frequency of its quack? (c) Which would produce a higher-pitch quack, the male or female?

107. •When a worker puts on earplugs, the sound level of a jackhammer decreases from 105 dB to 75 dB. Then the worker moves twice as far from the sound. Determine the sound level at the new location with the earplugs.

108. ••**Medical** High-intensity focused ultrasound (HIFU) is one treatment for certain types of cancer. During the procedure, a narrow beam of high-intensity ultrasound is focused on the tumor, raising its temperature to nearly 90°C and killing it. A range of frequencies and intensities can be used, but in one treatment a beam of frequency 4.0 MHz produced an intensity of 1500 W/cm². The energy was delivered in short pulses for a total time of 2.5 s over an area measuring 1.4 mm by 5.6 mm. The speed of sound in the soft tissue was 1540 m/s, and the density of that tissue was 1058 kg/m³. (a) What was the wavelength of the ultrasound beam? (b) How much energy was delivered to the tissue during the 2.5-s treatment? (c) What was the maximum displacement of the molecules in the tissue as the beam passed through?

109. •Many natural phenomena produce very high-energy, but inaudible, sound waves at frequencies below 20 Hz

(*infrasound*). During the 2003 eruption of the Fuego volcano in Guatemala, sound waves of frequency 10 Hz (and even less) with a sound level of 120 dB were recorded. (a) What was the maximum displacement of the air molecules produced by the waves? (b) How much energy would such a wave deliver to a 2.0 m by 3.0 m wall in 1.0 min? Assume the density of air is 1.2 kg/m³. SSM

110. ••Two identical 375-g speakers are mounted on parallel springs, each having a spring constant of 50.0 N/cm. Both speakers face in the same direction and produce a steady tone of 1.00 kHz. Both sounds have an amplitude of 35.0 cm, but they oscillate 180° out of phase with each other. What is the highest frequency of the beat that a person will hear if she stands in front of the speakers?

111. •A jogger hears a car alarm and decides to investigate. While running toward the car, she hears an alarm frequency of 869.5 Hz. After passing the car, she hears the alarm at a frequency of 854.5 Hz. If the speed of sound is 343 m/s, calculate the speed of the jogger.

112. •••A rescuer in an all-terrain vehicle (ATV) is tracking two injured hikers in the desert, each of whom has an emergency locator transmitter (ELT) stored in his backpack (**Figure 13-36**). The beacons give off radio signals at 121.5 MHz, in phase, and there is a receiver in the ATV that is tuned to that frequency. The speed of the radio waves is 300,000,000 m/s. The ATV is traveling due east, 200 m north of the hikers, and the hikers are 100 m apart. If the ATV moves at a constant speed of 15 m/s, how many times per second will the driver detect constructive interference between the two signals?

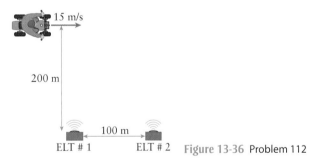

Figure 13-36 Problem 112

113. •••Speaker A is sounding a single tone in phase with speaker B (**Figure 13-37**). The two speakers are separated by 8 m. What intensity level will you hear if you are located 6 m in front of speaker A and the frequency of the tone is 857.5 Hz? Assume that the 40-W speakers can be approximated as point sources and the speed of sound is 343 m/s. SSM

Figure 13-37 Problem 113

14

Thermodynamics I

What do you think?

Fire beetles (*Melanophila acuminata*) converge on burning forests from distances of up to 10 km to lay their eggs in trees weakened by fires. These insects can detect a fire from so far away because they are equipped with special chambers that serve as sensitive thermometers. When heated even by a small amount, the fluid inside the chambers expands and causes the pressure within to increase; sensory neurons respond to the pressure change. As the fluid expands in response to the temperature increase, do you think the chamber walls (a) expand by a greater amount; (b) expand by the same amount; (c) expand by a smaller but nonzero amount; (d) maintain the same size; or (e) contract?

In this chapter, your goals are to:

- (14-1) Define what thermodynamics is.
- (14-2) Explain the meaning of temperature and thermal equilibrium.
- (14-3) Describe the origin of pressure in an ideal gas, and explain the relationship between molecular kinetic energy and gas temperature.
- (14-4) Explain how objects change in size when their temperature changes.
- (14-5) Examine the relationship between the quantity of heat that flows into or out of an object and the temperature change of that object.
- (14-6) Explain how heat must flow in order to cause a substance to change between the solid, liquid, and gas phases.
- (14-7) Describe the key properties of heat transfer by radiation, convection, and conduction.

To master this chapter, you should review:

- (7-3) The relationship between force, collision time, and momentum change in a collision.
- (9-2) The meaning of tensile and compressive stress.
- (11-8) Archimedes' principle for buoyancy.

14-1 A knowledge of thermodynamics is essential for understanding almost everything around you—including your own body

Thermodynamics, broadly defined, is the branch of physics that deals with relationships among properties of substances such as temperature, pressure, and volume, as well as the energy and flow of energy associated with these properties. If that sounds pretty abstract, that's because thermodynamics is such a general subject that it applies to almost *everything* in your surroundings. Thermodynamics explains how the temperature of the light bulb in your reading lamp is related to the amount of light that it emits. Thermodynamics explains how the ice cubes slowly melting in your beverage keep the beverage cold. And thermodynamics even explains how the clothing you wear keeps you warm. Your body is an example of a complex thermodynamic system: Some of the energy released by digesting food goes into maintaining the temperature of your body at a healthy value, and some of the energy is transferred to your surroundings and warms the air around you. Indeed, to understand any aspect of nature or technology that involves the idea of *temperature,* we have to invoke thermodynamic concepts.

A liquid-in-glass thermometer works on the principle that substances like the liquid expand as the temperature increases.

(a)

This ice cube melts because heat flows into it, but its temperature remains at a constant 0°C until it has completely melted.

(b)

These cold-blooded iguanas lose heat by convection but take heat in by radiation from the Sun and by conduction from the hot rock beneath them.

(c)

Figure 14-1 **Thermodynamics** The subject matter of thermodynamics includes (a) the meaning of temperature and how it is measured, (b) what heat is and what happens when heat flows into or out of an object, and (c) the ways in which heat is transferred from one object to another.

Thermodynamics is such a broad subject that it will take us this chapter and the next to introduce and apply its key concepts. We'll begin this chapter by defining what we mean by the temperature of an object, and we'll see that the temperature of a gas has a particularly simple interpretation. We'll go on to examine how objects change their dimensions when the temperature changes (Figure 14-1a). We'll define *heat* as energy that flows from one place to another due to a temperature difference, and we'll see how to analyze the energy flow that takes place when a substance changes phase such as from solid to liquid (Figure 14-1b). We'll conclude this chapter by looking at the ways in which heat can flow from one object to another (Figure 14-1c).

14-2 Temperature is a measure of the energy within a substance

One of the most fundamental quantities in thermodynamics is the *temperature* of an object. We are used to the idea that we can raise the temperature of an object like a piece of chicken or a slice of eggplant by heating it, say in a frying pan. We also know that we can lower the temperature of an object by cooling it, as in a refrigerator or freezer. But these everyday experiences fail to answer an important question: What *is* temperature?

One way to define what we mean by the temperature of a substance is in terms of what happens on the *microscopic* level—that is, how the individual molecules that make up the substance behave. (In *monatomic* substances, such as helium, the molecules are actually individual atoms. In *polyatomic* substances the molecules are made up of combinations of atoms: For example, in water each molecule is made up of two hydrogen atoms and an oxygen atom. We'll use the term *molecule* to refer to the constituents of both monatomic and polyatomic substances.)

Molecules in any substance are always in motion. In a gas or liquid, molecules move in every direction with a range of speeds. A molecule in a solid has an equilibrium position, but it constantly wiggles back and forth around that equilibrium position. We can define **temperature** as a measure of the kinetic energy associated with molecular motion. As the temperature of a given substance increases, so does the average kinetic energy of a molecule in that substance.

This microscopic definition of temperature isn't very helpful, however. For one thing, it isn't very precise: The relationship between the average kinetic energy of a molecule and the temperature is different for gases, liquids, and solids, and often depends on what type of molecule makes up the substance. What's more, this definition doesn't tell us how to *measure* temperature, since it's not very practical to analyze individual molecules in a substance to determine the temperature of that substance.

A practical approach to measuring temperature is to say that *temperature is the property that you measure with a* **thermometer**. There are many kinds of thermometers that work in different ways, but they're all based on the principle that certain substances change their properties when the temperature changes. For example, nearly all liquids increase in volume as temperature increases. A liquid thermometer uses a column of alcohol or mercury inside a glass tube, and the height of that column goes up as the temperature increases and the liquid expands (see Figure 14-1a).

Thermometer, temperature T_1

Object, temperature T_2

Thermometer and object are both at the same intermediate temperature T_{final}; they are in thermal equilibrium.

Figure 14-2 Using a thermometer
When a thermometer is placed in contact with an object and allowed to come to thermal equilibrium, the thermometer and the object end up at the same temperature.

Strictly speaking, a thermometer measures its *own* temperature. The reason you can use a thermometer to measure the temperature of an object (for instance, the temperature of a turkey in the oven or the temperature of the air inside your house) is the phenomenon of *thermal equilibrium*. Experiment shows that when two objects that have different temperatures are in **thermal contact**, so that energy can flow from one to the other, energy flows until both objects reach the same temperature. This final temperature lies between the two original temperatures of the objects. This kind of energy flow that happens due to a temperature difference is what we call *heat transfer*. (We'll present a careful definition of what we mean by *heat* in Section 14-5.) For example, when you take a scoop of ice cream from the freezer and put it in a room-temperature dish, energy flows from the dish into the ice cream. As a result, the temperature of the dish decreases and the temperature of the ice cream rises. (Note that two objects can be in *thermal* contact without being in *physical* contact. An example is a roast placed in an electric oven: Energy flows from the hot, glowing coils of the oven to the roast, even though the roast does not touch the coils. We'll explore this kind of heat transfer in Section 14-7.) The energy flow stops when the two objects are at the *same* temperature. At this point we say the two objects are in **thermal equilibrium**, and we say that *two objects in thermal equilibrium are at the same temperature*. If one of those objects is a thermometer, the reading on the thermometer indicates the temperature of both the thermometer *and* the object with which it is in contact (Figure 14-2).

A good measurement of any property is one that doesn't change the property being measured. (If you want to know what your pet cat does when you're not around, you won't find out by following it around the house.) Unfortunately, any thermometer causes a change in the temperature of the object being measured. That's because some heat transfer has to take place between the object and the thermometer, and this will cause the object's temperature to either increase or decrease. A good thermometer is one that minimizes the amount of heat transfer, so that the temperature of the object hardly changes before the thermometer and object are in thermal equilibrium. Then the thermometer reading is very close to the temperature that the object had before you made it interact with the thermometer.

Now imagine we put a thermometer C in thermal contact with object A (Figure 14-3a). Heat flows until they reach thermal equilibrium and the reading on the thermometer tells us the temperature of object A. We now also put the thermometer C in thermal contact with object B, allowing heat transfer between the thermometer and object B until they come to thermal equilibrium (Figure 14-3b). The reading on the thermometer then tells us the temperature of *both* A and B, so at this point the two objects have the same temperature. Finally, we put A and B into thermal contact with each other (Figure 14-3c). When we do this last step, we find that nothing changes: There is no heat flow between A and B, which means that these two objects at the same temperature must have been in thermal equilibrium *before* we put them in direct contact with each other. In other words, *two objects at the same temperature must be in thermal equilibrium, even if they do not interact*. If we combine this observation with our previous observations about thermal equilibrium, we end up with a single statement called the **zeroth law of thermodynamics**:

> *If two objects are each in thermal equilibrium with a third object, they are also in thermal equilibrium with each other.*

From the zeroth law of thermodynamics we can draw the important conclusion that *temperature is a property of objects in general*, not just of special devices called ther-

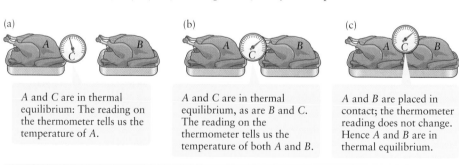

(a) A and C are in thermal equilibrium: The reading on the thermometer tells us the temperature of A.

(b) A and C are in thermal equilibrium, as are B and C. The reading on the thermometer tells us the temperature of both A and B.

(c) A and B are placed in contact; the thermometer reading does not change. Hence A and B are in thermal equilibrium.

Figure 14-3 The zeroth law of thermodynamics If objects A and B are both at the same temperature, they are in thermal equilibrium.

 The **zeroth law of thermodynamics:** If two objects A and B are in thermal equilibrium with a third object C, then A and B are also in thermal equilibrium with each other.

If a gas did not liquefy at low temperature, its pressure would become zero at –273.15°C (absolute zero).

Gas liquefies.

Pressure

Gas 3

Gas 2

Gas 1

Temperature (°C)

Temperature (K)

Figure 14-4 **Ideal gases and absolute zero** The rate at which pressure in a sealed volume of gas decreases as temperature decreases depends on the amount of gas present. However, extrapolating the graphs shows that pressure would become zero for *all* gases at the same temperature. That temperature, −273.15°C, is termed absolute zero.

mometers. (There are also a *first* and a *second* law of thermodynamics; we'll study these in Chapter 15.) To measure temperature, the tube of a liquid thermometer has numbers marked on it to help measure the volume of the liquid. The values associated with the markings are arbitrary, and throughout history a variety of schemes have been used to determine what the numbers on a thermometer should be.

The most common temperature scale in everyday life is the **Celsius scale**, based on the work of the eighteenth-century Swedish astronomer Anders Celsius. In this scale the freezing point of water is approximately 0°C and the boiling point is approximately 100°C (both values are at a standard pressure of 1 atm). By contrast, the official temperature scale used in the United States, the Cayman Islands, and Belize is the **Fahrenheit scale**, originated by the German scientist Daniel Fahrenheit (who also invented the alcohol thermometer and mercury thermometer). On this scale water freezes at 32°F and boils at 212°F at a pressure of 1 atm. These curious values arise in part because one of the points that Fahrenheit used to fix his scale was determined by the reading of a thermometer when placed in a person's mouth.

The range of Fahrenheit temperatures between freezing and boiling (212°F − 32°F = 180°F) corresponds almost exactly to a difference of 100°C on the Celsius scale. So a change of 1°C is nearly equivalent to $(100/180)$°F, or $(5/9)$°F. If we combine this with the observation that 0°C corresponds to 32°F, we get an approximate conversion between Fahrenheit and Celsius scales:

$$T_C = \frac{5}{9}(T_F - 32) \quad \text{and} \quad T_F = \frac{9}{5}T_C + 32 \tag{14-1}$$

You should use Equations 14-1 to verify that 0°C corresponds to 32°F and 100°C corresponds to 212°F.

The Celsius and Fahrenheit scales were based on the properties of a particular substance (water) under particular circumstances (normal atmospheric pressure on Earth). A scale that has its basis in much more fundamental physics is the **Kelvin scale**, first proposed by the nineteenth-century Scottish physicist William Thomson (1st Baron Kelvin). The Kelvin scale is based on the relationship between pressure and temperature of low-density gases. (In Section 14-3 we'll see why it's important that the density be low.) Experiment shows that the pressure in a sealed volume of gas decreases as temperature decreases, and that a graph of pressure versus temperature is a straight line (Figure 14-4). For a given volume, both the slope of this line and the pressure at a given temperature depend on the quantity of gas in the volume. But no matter what kind of gas or what quantity of gas is used, if we extrapolate the lines in Figure 14-4 to low temperatures and pressures, we find that the pressure goes to zero at the *same* temperature. (We have to *extrapolate* each line because at sufficiently low temperatures, any gas becomes a liquid.) This temperature is called **absolute zero** because a lower temperature is not physically possible. Zero temperature in the Kelvin scale is absolute zero, so temperatures in the Kelvin scale are never negative.

The unit of temperature used in the Kelvin scale is the **kelvin**, abbreviated K. The value of the kelvin is based on an easily reproduced temperature that can be precisely measured, which is the temperature of the **triple point** of water. The triple point of a substance is the pressure and temperature of that substance at which the solid, liquid, and vapor phases of the substance all coexist. (We'll learn more about the phases of matter in Section 14-6.) For water the triple point pressure is 0.00603 atm, and the triple point temperature of water is defined to be 273.15 K. With this choice of the value of the kelvin, a change of 1 degree Celsius is *exactly* equal to a change of 1 kelvin. The triple point of water turns out to be at 0.01°C, so 0°C corresponds to 273.15 K and 0 K (absolute zero) corresponds to −273.15°C. To convert from a temperature in kelvins to degrees Celsius, you simply *subtract* 273.15, and to convert a Celsius temperature to a Kelvin temperature you *add* 273.15:

$$(14\text{-}2) \qquad T_C = T_K - 273.15 \text{ and } T_K = T_C + 273.15$$

Water freezes at approximately 0°C = 273.15 K and boils at approximately 100°C = 373.15 K. (The precise values of these temperatures depend on the atmospheric pressure.)

! Watch Out! Temperature is in kelvins, not "degrees Kelvin."

It's correct to say that an object has a temperature of a certain number of degrees Celsius or of degrees Fahrenheit, as in "20 degrees Celsius." But in the Kelvin scale we say an object has a temperature of a certain number of kelvins, as in "293 kelvins." We do *not* say, "293 degrees kelvin." Note also that the name of the scale (Kelvin) is capitalized but the unit (kelvin) is not.

 Go to Picture It 14-1 for more practice dealing with temperature scales

As we will see in the following section, the Kelvin scale is a natural one to use for many purposes in physics. Here's an example of how to convert among temperature values in Fahrenheit, Celsius, and Kelvin.

Example 14-1 Cold, Hot, and In Between

On the Fahrenheit scale, a cold day might be 5°F. A comfortable temperature is 68°F, which is widely accepted as "room temperature," and a hot day might be 95°F. Express all three temperatures in degrees Celsius and kelvins.

Set Up

We can use the first of Equations 14-1 to convert from degrees Fahrenheit to degrees Celsius and the second of Equations 14-2 to convert from degrees Celsius to temperatures on the Kelvin scale.

Conversion between Celsius and Fahrenheit:

$$T_C = \frac{5}{9}(T_F - 32) \text{ and } T_F = \frac{9}{5}T_C + 32 \qquad (14\text{-}1)$$

Conversion between Celsius and Kelvin:

$$T_C = T_K - 273.15 \text{ and } T_K = T_C + 273.15 \qquad (14\text{-}2)$$

Solve

Convert the cold temperature of 5°F to degrees Celsius and to kelvins.

$$T_{C,\text{cold}} = \frac{5}{9}(T_{F,\text{cold}} - 32) = \frac{5}{9}(5 - 32)$$
$$= -15°C$$
$$T_{K,\text{cold}} = -15 + 273.15$$
$$= 258 \text{ K}$$

Do the conversions for the comfortable room temperature of 68°F.

$$T_{C,\text{room}} = \frac{5}{9}(T_{F,\text{room}} - 32) = \frac{5}{9}(68 - 32)$$
$$= 20°C$$
$$T_{K,\text{room}} = 20 + 273.15$$
$$= 293 \text{ K}$$

Finally, convert the hot temperature of 95°F to the Celsius and Kelvin scales.

$$T_{C,\text{hot}} = \frac{5}{9}(T_{F,\text{hot}} - 32) = \frac{5}{9}(95 - 32)$$
$$= 35°C$$
$$T_{K,\text{hot}} = 35 + 273.15$$
$$= 308 \text{ K}$$

Reflect

Our calculations show that typical temperatures on Earth's surface are close to 300 K. That's a good reference number to keep in mind. Another more precise equivalence to remember is that a typical room temperature is 68°F = 20°C = 293 K.

Got the Concept? 14-1 Ranking Temperatures

Rank these temperatures from coldest to warmest: (a) 280 K, (b) −13°C, (c) −13°F.

Take-Home Message for Section 14-2

✔ The temperature of an object is a measure of the kinetic energy of the molecules of which that object is made.

✔ If two objects with different temperatures are in thermal contact so that energy can flow from one to the other, energy will flow until the two objects are at the same temperature. This final state is called thermal equilibrium.

✔ Two objects are in thermal equilibrium if, and only if, they are at the same temperature.

14-3 In a gas, the relationship between temperature and molecular kinetic energy is a simple one

We said in Section 14-2 that the temperature of an object is related to the kinetic energy of its individual molecules. Let's take a look at this relationship in more detail for the case of *gases*, which are in many ways the simplest form of matter. In a liquid or solid, adjacent molecules nearly touch each other, so the forces between molecules are strong. But in a low-density gas the average distance between molecules is large compared to the size of a molecule (see Example 11-3 in Section 11-2). Because gas molecules are very far apart on average, the forces they exert on each other are so weak that we can ignore them. As we'll see, that leads to tremendous simplifications in the relationship between the temperature of a gas and the kinetic energy of its molecules. The insights we'll gain from studying gases will help us better understand the meaning of temperature for liquids and solids as well.

The Ideal Gas Law

Figure 14-4 shows that for a low-density gas at a constant volume, the graph of pressure versus temperature is a straight line and the pressure p is zero when the Kelvin temperature T is zero. This means that the pressure is directly proportional to the Kelvin temperature. We can write this in equation form as

$$p = (\text{constant}) \times T$$

(14-3)

(low–density gas at constant volume)

The pressure of a given quantity of gas also depends on the volume V that the gas occupies. For example, think of a quantity of gas in a flexible container whose volume we can change. Experiment shows that if the temperature of the gas is held constant and the volume is decreased, the pressure increases. In fact, the pressure turns out to be *inversely* proportional to the volume, or in equation form

$$p = \frac{(\text{constant})}{V}$$

(14-4)

(low–density gas at constant temperature)

 See the Math Tutorial for more information on direct and inverse proportions

We also find that for a given kind of gas, if the volume and temperature are held fixed but the *mass* of gas in a container is increased, the pressure increases in direct proportion to the mass. Increasing the mass means increasing the number N of molecules present in the gas, so we can write this relationship as

$$p = (\text{constant}) \times N$$

(14-5)

(low–density gas at constant volume and temperature)

We can combine all three equations, 14-3, 14-4, and 14-5, together into a single relationship:

$$p = (\text{constant}) \times \frac{NT}{V}$$

This relationship is most commonly written in the form

Ideal gas law in terms of number of molecules (14-6)

| Volume occupied by the gas | Number of molecules present in the gas |

| Pressure of an ideal gas | $pV = NkT$ | Temperature of the gas on the Kelvin scale |

Boltzmann constant

The constant k in Equation 14-6, called the **Boltzmann constant**, turns out to have the same value for *all* gases. To four significant figures,

$$k = 1.381 \times 10^{-23}\,\text{J/K}$$

Equation 14-6 is called the **ideal gas law**, and a gas that would obey this equation exactly is called an **ideal gas**. Real gases are *not* ideal: They do not obey this equation exactly, especially at high pressures or at temperatures close to the point at which the gases become liquids. At relatively low gas densities, however, the ideal gas law does a good job of representing the relationship between pressure, volume, and temperature for real gases. That's why an ideal gas is a useful idealization.

Given the very large number of molecules in most samples of gas, it's often more convenient to write Equation 14-6 in terms of the number of *moles* of a gas. One **mole** of a substance contains as many molecules as there are atoms in exactly 12 grams of carbon-12, the variety of carbon that has six protons and six neutrons in its nucleus. To four significant figures the mole, abbreviated mol, contains 6.022×10^{23} molecules. This value is called Avogadro's number N_A:

$$N_A = 6.022 \times 10^{23}\ \text{molecules/mol}$$

The number N of molecules in a substance is therefore equal to the number of moles n multiplied by Avogadro's number: $N = nN_A$. Then Equation 14-6 becomes

$$pV = nN_A kT$$

The product $N_A k$ has a special name: We call it the **ideal gas constant** and give it the symbol R. To four significant figures,

$$R = N_A k = 8.314\ \text{J/(mol} \cdot \text{K)}$$

With this definition, the ideal gas law (Equation 14-6) becomes

Ideal gas law in terms of number of moles (14-7)

| Volume occupied by the gas | Number of moles present in the gas |

| Pressure of an ideal gas | $pV = nRT$ | Temperature of the gas on the Kelvin scale |

Ideal gas constant

The quantities pressure p, volume V, and temperature T characterize the physical state of a system. A relationship among these quantities, like Equation 14-6 or Equation 14-7 for an ideal gas, is called an **equation of state**. The equation of state for a real gas, a liquid, or a solid is substantially more complicated than that for an ideal gas.

Example 14-2 An Ideal Gas at Room Temperature

At ordinary room temperature (20°C) and a pressure of 1 atm (1.013×10^5 Pa $= 1.013 \times 10^5$ N/m^2), how many molecules are there in 1.00 m^3 of an ideal gas? How many moles are there?

Set Up

We can use the two forms of the ideal gas law to determine the number of molecules N and number of moles n. Note that the temperature in the ideal gas law is the *Kelvin* temperature, but we're given the value of the *Celsius* temperature. We'll have to convert the temperature using the second of Equations 14-2.

Ideal gas law in terms of number of molecules:

$$pV = NkT \qquad (14\text{-}6)$$

Ideal gas law in terms of number of moles:

$$pV = nRT \qquad (14\text{-}7)$$

Conversion between Celsius and Kelvin:

$$T_C = T_K - 273.15 \text{ and}$$

$$T_K = T_C + 273.15 \qquad (14\text{-}2)$$

$p = 1$ atm
$V = 1.00$ m^3
$T = 20°C$
$N = ?$

Solve

First convert the temperature to the Kelvin scale.

From the second of Equations 14-2, a temperature of 20°C corresponds to a Kelvin temperature of

$$T = 20 + 273.15 = 293 \text{ K}$$

Solve Equation 14-6 for the number of molecules N and substitute numerical values.

From Equation 14-6,

$pV = NkT$ so

$$N = \frac{pV}{kT} = \frac{(1.013 \times 10^5 \text{ N/m}^2)(1.00 \text{ m}^3)}{(1.381 \times 10^{-23} \text{ J/K})(293 \text{ K})}$$

$$= 2.50 \times 10^{25} \frac{\text{N} \cdot \text{m}}{\text{J}}$$

Since $1 \text{ N} \cdot \text{m} = 1 \text{ J}$, N has *no* units: It is a pure number (in this case, the number of molecules in 1.00 m^3). So

$$N = 2.50 \times 10^{25} \text{ molecules}$$

In a similar way, find the number of moles using Equation 14-7.

From Equation 14-7,

$pV = nRT$ so

$$n = \frac{pV}{RT} = \frac{(1.013 \times 10^5 \text{ N/m}^2)(1.00 \text{ m}^3)}{(8.314 \text{ J/(mol·K)})(293 \text{ K})}$$

$$= 41.6 \frac{\text{N} \cdot \text{m} \cdot \text{mol}}{\text{J}} = 41.6 \text{ mol}$$

Reflect

We can check our results by confirming that the number of molecules equals the number of moles multiplied by Avogadro's number (the number of molecules per mole). To put our result into perspective, the number of *stars* in the observable universe is estimated to be between 3×10^{22} and 10^{24}. The number of molecules in a cubic meter of gas is truly astronomical!

We can also calculate N from the number of moles n and Avogadro's number N_A:

$$N = nN_A = (41.6 \text{ mol})(6.022 \times 10^{23} \text{ molecules/mol})$$

$$= 2.50 \times 10^{25} \text{ molecules}$$

Temperature and Translational Kinetic Energy

With the ideal gas law in hand, let's now see the relationship between pressure, volume, and the *average translational kinetic energy* of molecules in a gas in a container. We'll see that the pressure arises from the forces that individual molecules exert when they collide with the walls of the container.

Figure 14-5 shows a cubical box that has sides of length L and contains N molecules of an ideal gas. Each molecule has mass m. When the gas is in equilibrium, the gas as a whole exhibits no net motion. Although every molecule is moving and has momentum, the *total* momentum of all molecules in the gas averages to zero. In Figure 14-5, one representative molecule has just collided with and bounced off the left wall. We'll follow this molecule for the time Δt that it takes for the single molecule to return to this same position after colliding with the wall on the right side of the container. We'll assume that the molecule doesn't collide with any other molecules during this round trip. (Later in this section we'll see why this is a reasonable assumption to make.) For simplicity, we'll initially consider the molecule to be moving in the x direction only. We'll also make the simplifying assumptions that the walls of the container are rigid and the gas molecules behave like hard spheres, so that the collisions are *elastic* and no energy is lost when a molecule collides with a wall.

When the molecule in Figure 14-5 hits the right-hand wall of the box, it reverses direction but loses no kinetic energy, so its velocity changes from $+v_x$ (to the right) to $-v_x$ (to the left) and its momentum changes from $+mv_x$ to $-mv_x$. So the *change* in the molecule's momentum is $(-mv_x) - (+mv_x) = -2mv_x$. This momentum change occurs

The gas molecule shown has just collided with and been reflected from the wall on the left.

The molecule, moving in the positive x direction, travels a distance L, collides with the right wall, and travels a distance L again before returning to this same position. This round trip takes a time Δt.

Figure 14-5 The origin of gas pressure A cubical container contains a gas. This figure shows one representative gas molecule that has just bounced off the left-hand wall. The combined effect of all molecules bouncing off the walls gives rise to the pressure of the gas.

thanks to the force that the wall exerts on the molecule during the hit. The hit lasts just a short time, and there is one such hit by the right-hand wall on the molecule per time Δt (the time needed for the molecule to make a round trip and return to the right-hand wall). If we call $F_{\text{wall on molecule},x}$ the *average* force that the right-hand wall exerts on the molecule over the time Δt, Equation 7-24 (Section 7-6) says that this force multiplied by Δt equals the change in momentum that the molecule undergoes due to its interaction with the right-hand wall:

$$F_{\text{wall on molecule},x}\Delta t = -2mv_x \quad \text{so} \quad F_{\text{wall on molecule},x} = -\frac{2mv_x}{\Delta t}$$

This is negative because the right-hand wall pushes the molecule to the left, in the negative x direction. By Newton's third law, the average force that the *molecule* exerts on the *wall* is the opposite of this and is *positive* (the molecule exerts a force on the wall in the positive x direction):

$$F_{\text{molecule on wall},x} = -F_{\text{wall on molecule},x} = \frac{2mv_x}{\Delta t}$$

We emphasize that this is the *average* force that this molecule exerts on the wall: During an actual hit the force is large, and the rest of the time (when the molecule is not in contact with the wall) the force is zero. Now, Δt is the time it takes the molecule moving at speed v_x to move a distance $2L$ (back and forth across the length L of the box). Since time equals distance divided by speed, it follows that $\Delta t = 2L/v_x$. Substituting this into our expression for $F_{\text{molecule on wall},x}$ we get

(14-8)
$$F_{\text{molecule on wall},x} = \frac{2mv_x}{(2L/v_x)} = \frac{mv_x^2}{L}$$

Equation 14-8 tells us the average force on the right-hand wall from *one* molecule. However, there are N molecules of mass m in the box shown in Figure 14-5, and each of them collides periodically with the right-hand wall. If every molecule had the same value of v_x, the total force from all gas molecules combined would just be N times the force in Equation 14-8. This is extremely unlikely to be the case, however. So we get the total force that the gas as a whole exerts on the wall by replacing v_x^2 in Equation 14-8 with the *average value* of v_x^2 (that is, averaged over its value for each individual molecule) and then multiplying by N:

(14-9)
$$F_{\text{gas on wall},x} = \frac{Nm(v_x^2)_{\text{average}}}{L}$$

⚠ Watch Out! The average of the square is not the square of the average.

The quantity $(v_x^2)_{\text{average}}$ in Equation 14-9 is the *average value* of the *square* of the quantity v_x. Since the square of a quantity is always positive, it follows that $(v_x^2)_{\text{average}}$ has a positive value. Suppose instead that you calculated the *square* of the *average value* of v_x. You might think this would give you the same answer, but it doesn't: On average there are as

many molecules moving to the left in Figure 14-5 as there are moving to the right, so there are as many with a positive value of v_x as with a negative value. So the average value of v_x is zero, and the square of that is also zero. When we say to take the average value of the square, we mean square first, *then* average!

What we actually measure is the *pressure* that the gas exerts on the walls of the box. The right-hand wall is a square of side L and area L^2, so the pressure (force divided by area) on the right-hand wall is

(14-10)
$$p = \frac{F_{\text{gas on wall},x}}{L^2} = \frac{Nm(v_x^2)_{\text{average}}}{L^3} = \frac{Nm(v_x^2)_{\text{average}}}{V}$$

In Equation 14-10 we've used the symbol V for the volume L^3 of the cubical container of side L.

In general, the gas molecules are moving in the y and z directions as well as the x direction. Since there's no preferred direction inside the box, we expect that the average values of v_y^2 and v_z^2 are the same as the average value of v_x^2: $(v_x^2)_{\text{average}} = (v_y^2)_{\text{average}} = (v_z^2)_{\text{average}}$. Furthermore, the square of the *speed* v of a given molecule is the sum of the squares of its velocity components: $v^2 = v_x^2 + v_y^2 + v_z^2$. If we put these observations together, we can write an expression for the average value of the square of the speed of gas molecules:

$$(v^2)_{\text{average}} = (v_x^2)_{\text{average}} + (v_y^2)_{\text{average}} + (v_z^2)_{\text{average}} = 3(v_x^2)_{\text{average}} \qquad (14\text{-}11)$$

Equation 14-11 tells us that the quantity $(v_x^2)_{\text{average}}$ in Equation 14-10 is equal to one-third of the average value of the square of the speed: $(v_x^2)_{\text{average}} = (v^2)_{\text{average}}/3$. Then we can rewrite Equation 14-10 for the gas pressure as

$$p = \frac{Nm(v^2)_{\text{average}}}{3V} \qquad (14\text{-}12)$$

Now, $K_{\text{translational}} = (1/2)mv^2$ is the translational kinetic energy of a single molecule. (We emphasize *translational* since the molecule could also be rotating around its axis and have rotational kinetic energy. Its constituent atoms could also be vibrating within the molecule, so there could be vibrational kinetic energy as well.) So $K_{\text{translational, average}} = (1/2)m(v^2)_{\text{average}}$ is the *average* translational kinetic energy of a single molecule in the gas. In terms of this we can rewrite Equation 14-12 as

$$p = \frac{Nm(v^2)_{\text{average}}}{3V} = \frac{2N}{3V}\left[\frac{1}{2}m(v^2)_{\text{average}}\right] = \frac{2N}{3V}K_{\text{translational, average}} \qquad (14\text{-}12)$$

Equation 14-12 tells us something important: *The pressure of a given quantity of ideal gas is directly proportional to the average translational kinetic energy of a molecule of the gas.* The more kinetic energy that the molecules have on average, the greater the pressure.

We can learn something no less important by comparing Equation 14-12 with the ideal gas law in terms of number of molecules, Equation 14-6: $pV = NkT$, or $p = (N/V)kT$. In order for both Equations 14-6 and 14-12 to be correct, it must be true that $(2/3)K_{\text{translational, average}} = kT$, or

| Average translational kinetic energy of a molecule in an ideal gas | Average value of the square of a gas molecule's speed | Temperature of the gas on the Kelvin scale |

$$K_{\text{translational, average}} = \frac{1}{2}m(v^2)_{\text{average}} = \frac{3}{2}kT$$

| Mass of a single gas molecule | Boltzmann constant |

Temperature and average translational kinetic energy of an ideal gas molecule (14-13)

In words, Equation 14-13 says that *the average translational kinetic energy of a molecule in an ideal gas is directly proportional to the Kelvin temperature of the gas.* This justifies the statement we made in Section 14-2 about the physical meaning of temperature. Equation 14-13 also relates a *microscopic* property of an ideal gas (the average kinetic energy of an individual gas molecule) to a *macroscopic* property (the temperature of the gas, something you might measure with an ordinary thermometer).

Equation 14-13 also gives us a microscopic interpretation of absolute zero. If the temperature is 0 K, then the average translational kinetic energy of a single gas molecule must also be zero. This is possible only if the speed of the molecule is zero. So absolute zero is the temperature at which all molecular motion would cease.

Note from Equation 14-13 that the average translational kinetic energy of a gas molecule does *not* depend on the *mass* of the molecule, just on the temperature. For example, the air around you is composed almost entirely of molecules of nitrogen (N_2) and oxygen (O_2). A mole of N_2 molecules has a mass of 28.0 g and a mole of O_2 molecules has a mass of 32.0 g, so the mass m of an individual N_2 molecule is $(28.0/32.0) = 0.875$, the mass of an individual O_2 molecule. Nonetheless, on average each kind of molecule in the air has the *same* translational kinetic energy: An average nitrogen molecule must therefore be moving faster than an average oxygen molecule.

A measure of how fast gas molecules move on average is the **root-mean-square speed** or **rms speed**. To see how this is defined, first imagine finding the average value of v^2, the square of the speed v, for all the molecules in a gas that have a given mass m. This is the quantity that we've called $(v^2)_{\text{average}}$. Another word for average is *mean*, which is why $(v^2)_{\text{average}}$ is called the *mean-square* of the speed. The *root*-mean-square speed is the square root of the mean-square:

$$v_{\text{rms}} = \sqrt{(v^2)_{\text{average}}} \qquad (14\text{-}14)$$

 Go to Interactive Exercise 14-1 for more practice dealing with rms speed

Note that v_{rms} has units of m/s. From Equation 14-13, $(1/2)m(v^2)_{average} = (3/2)kT$, so $(v^2)_{average} = 3kT/m$. If we substitute this into Equation 14-14, we get

Root-mean-square speed of
molecules in an ideal gas
(14-15)

Root-mean-square speed of
a molecule in an ideal gas

Boltzmann constant

$$v_{rms} = \sqrt{\frac{3kT}{m}}$$

Temperature of the gas
on the Kelvin scale

Mass of a single gas molecule

Watch Out! The root-mean-square value is not the same as the average value.

We use the root-mean-square speed v_{rms} as a measure of the typical molecular speed in a gas because it follows naturally from Equation 14-13, which relates temperature to translational kinetic energy. It is *not*, however, the same as the *average* molecular speed. To see the difference, consider a gas with just five molecules that have speeds 1.00 m/s, 2.00 m/s, 3.00 m/s, 4.00 m/s, and 5.00 m/s. The average of these speeds is

$$v_{average} = \frac{\left[\begin{array}{c} 1.00 \text{ m/s} + 2.00 \text{ m/s} + 3.00 \text{ m/s} \\ + 4.00 \text{ m/s} + 5.00 \text{ m/s} \end{array} \right]}{5}$$

$$= 3.00 \text{ m/s}$$

but the rms speed is

$$v_{rms} = \sqrt{(v^2)_{average}}$$

$$= \sqrt{\frac{\left[\begin{array}{c} (1.00 \text{ m/s})^2 + (2.00 \text{ m/s})^2 + (3.00 \text{ m/s})^2 \\ + (4.00 \text{ m/s})^2 + (5.00 \text{ m/s})^2 \end{array} \right]}{5}}$$

$$= 3.32 \text{ m/s}$$

It turns out that the average value of any collection of numbers is *always* less than the rms value. For the special case of an ideal gas, a detailed analysis shows that the average speed is $\sqrt{8/(3\pi)} = 0.921$ of the rms speed.

Example 14-3 Oxygen at Room Temperature

Calculate (a) the average translational kinetic energy and (b) the root-mean-square speed of an oxygen molecule in air at room temperature (20°C). One mole of oxygen molecules has a mass of 32.0 g $= 32.0 \times 10^{-3}$ kg.

Set Up

Equation 14-13 tells us the average translational kinetic energy, and Equation 14-15 tells us the rms speed of molecules. Note that we're given the mass per mole of O_2, but we'll need to convert this to m, the mass per molecule. We'll also need to convert the temperature from Celsius to Kelvin.

Temperature and average translational kinetic energy of an ideal gas molecule:

$$K_{translational,average} = \frac{1}{2}m(v^2)_{average} = \frac{3}{2}kT \quad (14\text{-}13)$$

Root-mean-square speed of molecules in an ideal gas:

$$v_{rms} = \sqrt{\frac{3kT}{m}} \quad (14\text{-}15)$$

Conversion between Celsius and Kelvin:

$$T_C = T_K - 273.15 \text{ and } T_K = T_C + 273.15 \quad (14\text{-}2)$$

oxygen molecules

Solve

(a) First find the mass per molecule m and the Kelvin temperature T.

The number of molecules per mole is Avogadro's number, $N_A = 6.022 \times 10^{23}$ molecules/mol. So the mass per O_2 molecule is

$$m = \frac{(32.0 \times 10^{-3} \text{ kg/mol})}{(6.022 \times 10^{23} \text{ molecules/mol})}$$

$$= 5.31 \times 10^{-26} \text{ kg/molecule}$$

From the second of Equations 14-2, the Kelvin temperature that corresponds to 20°C is

$$T = 20 + 273.15 = 293 \text{ K}$$

Use Equation 14-13 to find the average kinetic energy per molecule.

From Equation 14-13,

$$K_{\text{translational,average}} = \frac{3}{2}kT = \frac{3}{2}(1.381 \times 10^{-23}\,\text{J/K})(293\,\text{K})$$
$$= 6.07 \times 10^{-21}\,\text{J}$$

(b) Use Equation 14-15 to find the rms speed of an O_2 molecule.

From Equation 14-15,

$$v_{\text{rms}} = \sqrt{\frac{3kT}{m}} = \sqrt{\frac{3(1.381 \times 10^{-23}\,\text{J/K})(293\,\text{K})}{5.31 \times 10^{-26}\,\text{kg}}}$$
$$= 478\,\text{m/s}$$

Reflect

The rms speed of O_2 molecules is tremendous, 478 m/s = 1720 km/h = 1070 mi/h. Note that very few O_2 molecules in the air travel at precisely that speed: Their speeds range from nearly zero to many times faster than 478 m/s.

Note that the nitrogen (N_2) molecules in air at 20°C have the *same* translational kinetic energy (which does not depend on the mass m of the molecules) but a *different* rms speed (which is proportional to the reciprocal of $\sqrt{m}$). As we discussed above, an N_2 molecule has 0.875 the mass of an O_2 molecule, so the rms speed for N_2 is $1/\sqrt{0.875} = 1.07$ times faster than the rms speed for O_2.

Degrees of Freedom

The factor of three in Equation 14-13 for the average translational kinetic energy of a molecule, $K_{\text{translational,average}} = (1/2)m(v^2)_{\text{average}} = (3/2)kT$, is actually rather significant. It arises because $(v^2)_{\text{average}}$ is the sum of three terms, one for each component of molecular motion (Equation 14-11): $(v^2)_{\text{average}} = (v_x^2)_{\text{average}} + (v_y^2)_{\text{average}} + (v_z^2)_{\text{average}}$. As we discussed above, each of these terms has the same value. That means we can write the average kinetic energy of a molecule as the sum of three equal terms:

$$\frac{1}{2}m(v^2)_{\text{average}} = \frac{1}{2}m(v_x^2)_{\text{average}} + \frac{1}{2}m(v_y^2)_{\text{average}} + \frac{1}{2}m(v_z^2)_{\text{average}} = \frac{3}{2}kT$$

In other words, on average the translational kinetic energy is shared equally between energies associated with the motions in each of the three possible directions. Each direction of motion available to the molecule contributes an average translational kinetic energy of one-third of $(3/2)kT$, or $(1/2)kT$. We refer to each of these possible directions of motion as a **degree of freedom** of the system. (An object that could move only along a straight line would have one degree of freedom, and one that could move only in a plane would have two degrees of freedom. An object that can move in all three dimensions of space has three degrees of freedom.)

The number of degrees of freedom of a gas can be more than simply the number of directions in which gas molecules can translate. If the molecules contain more than one atom, the molecule can have energy of motion even if its translational velocity is zero. As an example, **Figure 14-6** shows possible motions of the ammonia molecule (NH_3). The entire ammonia molecule can rotate, and it can vibrate in two ways: The bonds between the nitrogen (N) and hydrogen (H) atoms can be stretched along the length of the bond and then oscillate, and the hydrogen atoms can be disturbed so that the angle of the bonds oscillates. Each of these also represents a possible degree of freedom of the

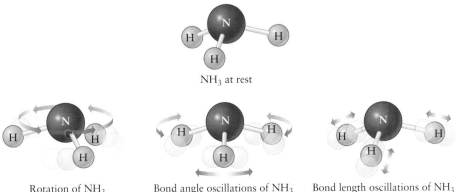

NH_3 at rest

Rotation of NH_3 Bond angle oscillations of NH_3 Bond length oscillations of NH_3

Figure 14-6 **Motions of an ammonia molecule** If a gas is made of molecules with two or more atoms, a molecule can have energy of motion even if the translational velocity of the molecule is zero. For an ammonia (NH_3) molecule, the molecule can rotate, and both the bond angle and the bond length can oscillate. This means that NH_3 has more degrees of freedom than just the three translational degrees of freedom.

gas molecule, and each can contribute an additional $(1/2)kT$ to the average energy per molecule. Thus, the average energy per molecule is likely to be more than $(3/2)kT$ for a gas that is composed of polyatomic molecules. For example, for O_2 and N_2 at room temperature the total energy per molecule is actually close to $(5/2)kT$ because the molecules can both translate (for which there are three degrees of freedom) and rotate (for which there are two degrees of freedom: If the long axis of the O_2 molecule is the z axis, one degree of freedom corresponds to rotation around the x axis and the other to rotation around the y axis). The fact that the energy of a molecule is shared equally among each degree of freedom is called the **equipartition theorem**.

Mean Free Path

Figure 14-7 Stomata on the epidermis of a leaf This photomicrograph shows fine details on the leaf of an elder tree (*Sambucus nigra*). The size of the stomata, through which the leaf exchanges gases with the atmosphere, is related to the mean free path of gas molecules.

In our analysis of what happens in an ideal gas at the microscopic level, we considered what happens when a gas molecule hits one of the container walls but we ignored the effects of collisions between gas molecules. How frequently do such collisions between molecules occur? One way to answer this question is in terms of the **mean free path** of a gas molecule. This is the average distance that a molecule travels from the time at which it collides with one molecule to when it collides with another molecule. If this distance is large compared to the size of the container that holds the gas, we can conclude that a molecule is unlikely to have any collisions with other molecules as it bounces back and forth between the container walls. But if the mean free path is short, a molecule may undergo many collisions with other molecules during a single trip across the container.

The mean free path depends on how densely packed the gas molecules are. If there are very few gas molecules in the volume of the container, collisions between molecules are unlikely and the mean free path is long. If, however, there are many molecules in the container, the likelihood of a collision is greater and the mean free path is short. The mean free path also depends on the *size* of the molecules: The larger the gas molecules are, the bigger "targets" the molecules are for other molecules, the more likely they are to undergo collisions, and the shorter the mean free path.

If we model the molecules as spheres of radius r, the mean free path (to which we give the symbol λ, Greek letter lambda) turns out to be

(14-16)
$$\lambda = \frac{1}{4\sqrt{2}\pi r^2 (N/V)}$$

In Equation 14-16 the volume that the gas occupies is V and the number of gas molecules in that volume is N. Note that just as we expected, the mean free path is short if r is large (the molecules are large in size) or if N/V is large (there are many molecules present per volume, so the molecules are close together). Equation 14-6 tells us that $pV = NkT$, which we can rearrange to read $N/V = p/kT$, so Equation 14-16 becomes

(14-17)
$$\lambda = \frac{kT}{4\sqrt{2}\pi r^2 p}$$

We invite you to use Equation 14-17 to calculate the mean free path for oxygen (O_2) molecules, which are about 2.0×10^{-10} m in radius, at ordinary room temperature (20°C or 293 K) and a pressure of 1 atm $= 1.013 \times 10^5$ N/m². You'll find that $\lambda = 5.6 \times 10^{-8}$ m, a distance that is large compared to the size of a molecule but hundreds of millions of times smaller than the size of a typical container for air. An O_2 molecule trying to travel from one side to another of a room 2 m wide would undergo tens of millions of collisions along the way! How, then, can we justify the assumption we made earlier in this section that we can *ignore* collisions between molecules? The explanation is that a given molecule collides with other molecules that are moving in *all* directions. Some collisions make the molecule speed up, and others make it slow down; some deflect it to the left, and others deflect it to the right. The result is that the effects of all these collisions largely cancel out, so on average we can treat molecules as if they were unaffected by collisions. Note that collisions also tend to *randomize* the velocities of the molecules that make up the gas, which justifies our assumption that the average values of v_x^2, v_y^2, and v_z^2 are all the same.

The concept of mean free path plays an important role in botany. The leaves of plants "breathe" through their pores or *stomata*, tiny apertures through which they exchange gas molecules with the surrounding air (Figure 14-7). In photosynthesis carbon dioxide (CO_2) is taken in through the pores and oxygen (O_2) is released, in respiration O_2 is taken in and CO_2 is released, and in transpiration water vapor (H_2O) is released. Each pore is like a narrow tube, and gas molecules passing through the tube experience collisions with the walls of the tube as well as with each other. When the diameter of the tube is large compared to the mean free path of the gas molecules, gas molecules collide mostly with each other and only infrequently with the tube walls. As a result, gas can flow relatively easily through the tube. But if the tube diameter is about the same as the mean free path, collisions with the walls become more frequent and the rate of gas flow slows dramatically. For this reason the pores are able to expand when conditions require increased gas flow (for example, when intense sunlight shines on the leaf and the rate of photosynthesis goes up).

? Got the Concept? 14-2 Comparing

A small fraction of the molecules in air are atoms of helium. A mole of helium has a mass of 4.00 g, and a helium atom has a radius of about 3×10^{-11} m. State whether each of the following quantities will be greater, less, or the same for helium than for oxygen (O_2, with a mass of 32.0 g/mol

and a radius of about 2.0×10^{-10} m) in a given quantity of air: (a) the average translational kinetic energy per molecule; (b) the total energy of all kinds per molecule; (c) the rms speed; (d) the mean free path.

Take-Home Message for Section 14-3

✔ The ideal gas law relates the pressure, volume, temperature, and number of molecules (or number of moles) for a low-density gas.

✔ The pressure that a gas exerts on the walls of its container is due to collisions that the gas molecules make with the walls.

✔ The temperature of a gas is a measure of the average translational kinetic energy per molecule. In a gas at Kelvin

temperature T, this energy is $(3/2)kT$. This does not depend on the mass of the molecule. Molecules with more than one atom can have additional energy associated with rotation or vibration.

✔ The average distance that a molecule travels between collisions with other molecules is called the mean free path. The larger the molecule and the more densely molecules are packed, the shorter the mean free path.

14-4 Most substances expand when the temperature increases

Nearly all objects and substances expand when heated and contract when cooled. For example, the lid on a jar of pickles may be too tight to unscrew when you first take the jar from the refrigerator, but when the jar warms up the lid expands and is easier to remove. This phenomenon is known as **thermal expansion**. Thermal expansion is the basis of many thermometers, including liquid thermometers that use alcohol or mercury (see Section 14-2 and Figure 14-1a).

In a solid, thermal expansion happens because with increasing temperature the molecules that comprise the solid not only oscillate with greater amplitude around their equilibrium positions, but also shift their equilibrium positions so that they are farther away from their neighbors. In a liquid or gas, increasing temperature means that adjacent molecules collide with each other with greater momentum; this pushes adjacent molecules farther apart and increases the volume of the liquid or gas.

Linear Expansion

Experiment shows that if the temperature change ΔT of a solid object is not too great, the change in each dimension of the object is proportional to ΔT. In particular, if a solid object initially has length L_0, the change ΔL in its length when the temperature changes by ΔT is

Change in the length of an object ⌐ Length of the object before the temperature change ⌐

$$\Delta L = \alpha L_0 \Delta T$$

Coefficient of linear expansion of the substance of which the object is made   Temperature change of the object that causes the length change

Change in length due to a temperature change
(14-18)

Table 14-1 Linear Expansion Coefficients

Substance	Linear Expansion Coefficient (α) $K^{-1} \times 10^{-6}$	Substance	Linear Expansion Coefficient (α) $K^{-1} \times 10^{-6}$
aluminum	22.2	iron, cast	10.4
antimony	10.4	iron, forged	11.3
beryllium	11.5	iron, pure	12.0
brass	18.7	lead	28.0
brick	5.5	marble	12
bronze	18.0	plaster	25
carbon—diamond	1.2	platinum	9.0
cement	10.0	porcelain	3.0
concrete	14.5	quartz, fused	0.59
copper	16.5	rubber	77
glass, hard	5.9	silver	19.5
glass, plate	9.0	solder	24.0
glass, pyrex	4.0	steel	13.0
gold	14.2	wood, oak parallel to grain	4.9
graphite	7.9		

The quantity α (Greek letter alpha) in Equation 14-18 is called the **coefficient of linear expansion**. It depends on what the object is made of, but not on the shape or size of the object. Table 14-1 lists the coefficient of linear expansion for a number of substances. Notice in Equation 14-18 that α has dimensions of inverse temperature (often K^{-1}), so that the dimensions of $\alpha L_0 \, \Delta T$ on the right side of the equation match those of ΔL on the left side.

! Watch Out! **The coefficient of linear expansion can have different units.**

The units of α can be $(^\circ C)^{-1}$ as well as K^{-1}. That's because the sizes of $1^\circ C$ and 1 K are defined to be the same, so the temperature *change* ΔT has the same value whether the temperature is measured on the Celsius scale or the Kelvin scale.

Equation 14-18 and Table 14-1 explain why you can loosen a tight-fitting steel lid on a glass jar of pickles by running hot water over the lid. Initially, the steel lid and the glass mouth of the jar have the same diameter L_0. The hot water makes both the steel and the glass undergo the same temperature change ΔT, but the steel lid expands more (ΔL is greater) because the coefficient of thermal expansion is greater for steel ($\alpha = 13.0 \times 10^{-6} \, K^{-1}$) than for glass ($\alpha = 4 \times 10^{-6}$ to $9 \times 10^{-6} \, K^{-1}$). That makes the fit less snug and makes it easier to unscrew the lid.

Equation 14-18 should remind you of Equation 9-3 (Section 9-2), which says that the change ΔL in length of an object due to a tensile or compressive *stress* (force per unit area) is proportional to the initial length L_0 and the stress F/A:

Go to Picture It 14-2 for more practice dealing with linear expansion

$$\frac{F}{A} = Y\frac{\Delta L}{L_0} \quad \text{or} \quad \Delta L = \left(\frac{1}{Y}\right)L_0\frac{F}{A}$$

We saw in Section 9-2 that this direct proportionality between stress and length change is valid if the stress is not too great. In the same fashion, the direct proportionality between ΔL and ΔT given by Equation 14-18 is valid if ΔT is not too great. (If the temperature change is too great, the direct proportionality between ΔL and ΔT breaks down, and we have to treat α as a function of temperature. The character of this function is different for different substances.)

Example 14-4 An Expanding Bridge

Bridges are constructed with expansion joints (Figure 14-8) to allow the bridge to expand on hot days without buckling. Suppose the bridge is made in two halves, each of which is made of steel and is 10.0 m long when the temperature is 18.0°C. The left-hand end of the left half is held in place and cannot move, as is the right-hand end of the right half. How large a gap should there be between the two halves at 18.0°C so that the structure does not buckle on an exceptionally hot day when the temperature is 45.0°C?

Figure 14-8 **A thermal expansion joint** Bridges are built with thermal expansion joints such as these to account for expansion and contraction of the bridge in hot and cold conditions.

Set Up

At 18.0°C each half of the bridge has length $L_0 = 10.0$ m. We want to choose the gap d between them so that at 45.0°C the gap just closes. For this to happen, each half must increase in length by a distance $d/2$ as the temperature increases. We use Equation 14-18 for the length increase of each half of the bridge. Table 14-1 gives the coefficient of thermal expansion α for steel.

Change in length due to a temperature change:

$$\Delta L = \alpha L_0 \Delta T \qquad (14\text{-}18)$$

Solve

Write an expression for the length change of each bridge half when the temperature increases from 18.0°C to 45.0°C.

From Table 14-1,

$$\alpha = 13.0 \times 10^{-6} \text{ K}^{-1} \text{ for steel}$$

The temperature change is

$$\Delta T = 45.0°\text{C} - 18.0°\text{C} = 27.0 \text{ K}$$

(Recall that a temperature change of 1°C is the same as a temperature change of 1 K.)

Then from Equation 14-18, the length change of each bridge half is

$$\Delta L = \alpha L_0 \Delta T$$
$$= (13.0 \times 10^{-6} \text{ K}^{-1})(10.0 \text{ m})(27.0 \text{ K})$$
$$= 3.51 \times 10^{-3} \text{ m} = 3.51 \text{ mm}$$

The length change ΔL of each bridge half is equal to $d/2$ (half the gap at 18.0°C), so d is equal to $2\Delta L$.

The necessary gap between the two bridge halves at 18.0°C is

$$d = 2 \Delta L = 2(3.51 \text{ mm})$$
$$= 7.02 \text{ mm} = 0.276 \text{ in.}$$

Reflect

This gap is small enough that it offers no resistance to a car's tire or a pedestrian's foot. Without a sufficiently large expansion joint, the bridge halves in this problem would push against each other on a hot day and eventually warp or buckle as shown.

Watch Out!   Holes in an object expand when heated.

Example 14-4 may lead you to conclude that when the temperature of an object increases, the substance of which it is made expands to fill any holes in the object. Not so! *Every* dimension of the object increases, which means the size of the hole also increases (Figure 14-9). That's what happens when you warm the metal lid on a jar to loosen it: The inner diameter of the lid (the size of the "hole" on the inside of the lid) increases so that it no longer fits so tightly on the mouth of the glass jar.

① This solid object has a circular hole cut in it.

② If the temperature increases, the object expands overall and the size of the hole expands.

Thermal expansion affects all dimensions of an object equally.

Figure 14-9 **Heating a hole** When a block with a hole is heated, the hole and the block both expand.

Volume Expansion

When the temperature of a solid object changes, its length, width, and height change according to the linear thermal expansion relationship of Equation 14-18. As a result, its *volume* expands as well. A fluid (a liquid or gas) has no fixed dimensions, however, so Equation 14-18 doesn't apply, but fluids also change their volume when the temperature changes. An equation that describes the volume change with temperature for solids and fluids alike is

Change in volume due to a temperature change (14-19)

Change in the volume of a quantity of substance

Volume of the substance before the temperature change

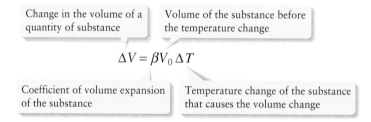

$$\Delta V = \beta V_0 \, \Delta T$$

Coefficient of volume expansion of the substance

Temperature change of the substance that causes the volume change

The **coefficient of volume expansion** β (Greek letter beta) also has units of K^{-1} or $(^\circ C)^{-1}$.

For solids it turns out that the coefficient of volume expansion is just three times the coefficient of linear expansion: $\beta = 3\alpha$. (The factor of three arises because volume expansion involves all three dimensions of space, while linear expansion involves just one dimension.) So you can find the value of β for solids by multiplying the values of α in Table 14-1 by three.

Table 14-2 lists values of β for selected liquids. Note that for ethanol, the liquid used in most alcohol thermometers, $\beta = 750 \times 10^{-6} \, K^{-1}$. Contrast this to the volume expansion coefficient for glass from Table 14-1: α is between $4.0 \times 10^{-6} \, K^{-1}$ and $9.0 \times 10^{-6} \, K^{-1}$ for glass, so $\beta = 3\alpha$ is between $12 \times 10^{-6} \, K^{-1}$ and $27 \times 10^{-6} \, K^{-1}$. That explains how an alcohol thermometer works: When the temperature goes up, the glass tube of the thermometer and the ethanol inside the tube both expand, but the ethanol expands much more (because it has such a large value of β) and so the ethanol rises within the tube. The same is true for a mercury thermometer, since mercury also has a large value of β (see Table 14-2).

We don't list the value of β for gases in Table 14-2. That's because it's most convenient to use Equation 14-7 (the ideal gas law, $pV = nRT$) rather than Equation 14-19 to keep track of the changes in the volume of a gas with temperature.

For nearly all substances β is positive, so the volume increases (the substance expands and $\Delta V > 0$) when the temperature increases ($\Delta T > 0$), and the volume decreases (the substance contracts and $\Delta V < 0$) when the temperature decreases ($\Delta T < 0$). But liquid water is a conspicuous exception to this rule at temperatures below 4°C. Below that temperature, liquid water actually *expands* as the temperature decreases further (Figure 14-10). So water is less dense at 0°C (the freezing point) than at slightly warmer temperatures. As a result, as the water in rivers and lakes gets cold

Table 14-2 Volume Expansion Coefficients for Liquids

Substance	Volume Expansion Coefficient (β) $K^{-1} \times 10^{-6}$
gasoline	905
ethanol	750
water	207
mercury	182

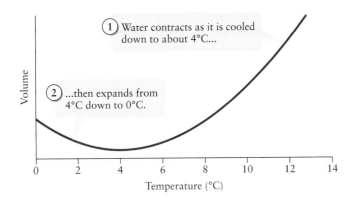

Figure 14-10 **The strange case of cold water**
Although most substances expand when heated and contract when cooled, water is different. As water is cooled below 4°C, it stops contracting and actually expands as the temperature decreases from 4°C to the freezing point.

during the winter, the coldest water (closest to the freezing point) floats to the surface, while denser, warmer water sinks to the bottom. This means that the surface water freezes first and that rivers and lakes freeze from the surface down. Were water like most substances, the coldest water would be denser than warmer water and would sink to the bottom, and bodies of water would freeze from the bottom up. In this case rivers and lakes could freeze throughout their volume during extended periods of cold temperatures, possibly destroying aquatic life. Life on Earth might not have been able to survive if water did not exhibit the unusual property seen in Figure 14-10.

Figure 14-10 shows another aspect of water that affects life on Earth: Above 4°C, an increase in temperature causes liquid water to expand. The average global temperature on Earth has been increasing for decades due to the burning of fossil fuels such as coal and gasoline, which releases carbon dioxide (CO_2) in the atmosphere and causes a temperature increase. (We'll discuss the physics of this process in Section 14-7.) As a result, the water in the oceans is expanding which causes the sea level to rise. At present the rate of rise is about 3 mm/y (millimeters per year), about half of which is due to thermal expansion of seawater; the rest is caused by the melting of land-based ice such as glaciers, causing water to run off into the ocean.

Got the Concept? 14-3   Warming a Cube

A piece of solid aluminum is in the shape of a cube. If the temperature of the cube is increased so that the length of each side increases by 0.0010 (that is, by 0.10%), by how much does the volume of the cube increase? (a) 0.0010; (b) 2 × 0.0010 = 0.0020; (c) 3 × 0.0010 = 0.0030; (d) (0.0010)^2 = 1.0 × 10^{-6}; (e) (0.0010)^3 = 1.0 × 10^{-9}; (f) the mean free path.

Take-Home Message for Section 14-4

✔ Nearly all substances and objects undergo thermal expansion: They expand when their temperature increases, and they contract when their temperature decreases. Liquid water below 4°C is a notable exception.

✔ If the change in temperature is relatively small, the change in the length of an object or the volume of a quantity of substance is proportional to the change in temperature.

14-5 Heat is energy that flows due to a temperature difference

We've seen that the temperature of an object is a measure of the average kinetic energy of its molecules. We've also seen that if two objects at different temperatures are placed in contact, their temperatures eventually come to the same value. So there must be a *flow* of energy between objects at different temperatures. We use the term **heat** and the symbol Q for the energy that flows from one object to another as a result of a temperature difference. Since heat is a form of energy, it has units of joules (J). If heat flows into an object, the value of Q for that object is positive; if heat flows out of an object, the value of Q for that object is negative (Figure 14-11).

Watch Out! Objects do not contain heat.

We emphasize that the term *heat* applies only to energy that is in the process of flowing between objects at different temperatures. We use a different term, **internal energy**, for the energy within an object due to the kinetic *and* potential energies associated with the individual molecules that comprise the object. Note also that *temperature* (a measure of the kinetic energy per molecule) and *heat* (energy flowing due to a temperature difference) are *not* the same quantity. The word "hot" doesn't mean "high heat," but rather "high temperature."

---

(1) If two objects at different temperatures *T* are in contact, energy flows between them due to the temperature difference. This kind of energy flow is called heat (symbol *Q*).

(2) Energy flows into the lower-temperature object, so for this object the heat *Q* is positive.

Object at high *T*

Heat

Object at low *T*

(3) Energy flows out of the higher-temperature object, so for this object the heat *Q* is negative.

Figure 14-11 **Heat flow in thermal contact** Energy in the form of heat (*Q*) flows from the higher-temperature object to the lower-temperature one until the two objects are in thermal equilibrium at the same temperature.

You can understand how heat flows between two objects in contact by considering what happens on the molecular level. Where the two objects touch, molecules on the surfaces of the two objects can interact and bump into each other—that is, they collide. The molecules in the higher-temperature object have more kinetic energy than those in the lower-temperature object. As a result, collisions between surface molecules in the two objects end up transferring kinetic energy from the molecules in the higher-temperature object to those in the lower-temperature object. Collisions between neighboring molecules in each object share these energy transfers among all of the object's molecules. The net result is that energy is transferred from the higher-temperature object to the lower-temperature one.

Experiment shows that in most circumstances the flow of heat into or out of an object changes the object's temperature. (The exception is when the object undergoes a *phase change* such as from solid to liquid, liquid to solid, liquid to gas, or gas to liquid. In the next section we'll discuss what happens in a phase change.) If the quantity of heat *Q* that flows into an object is relatively small, the resulting temperature change ΔT turns out to be *directly* proportional to *Q* and *inversely* proportional to the mass *m* of the object. In other words, the greater the quantity of heat *Q* that flows into an object, the more its temperature changes; the more massive the object and so the more material that makes up the object, the smaller the temperature change for a given quantity of heat *Q*. (The same quantity of heat that will cook a single meatball will cause hardly any temperature change in a pot roast.) We can write this relationship as

$$\Delta T = (\text{constant}) \times \frac{Q}{m}$$

The constant in this equation depends on the substance of which the object is made. It's conventional to express this equation as

Quantity of heat and the resulting temperature change (14-20)

Quantity of heat that flows into (if $Q > 0$) or out of ($Q < 0$) an object

Specific heat of the substance of which the object is made

$$Q = mc\,\Delta T$$

Temperature change of the object that results from the heat flow

Mass of the object

Go to Picture It 14-3 for more practice dealing with specific heat

The quantity *c* is called the **specific heat** of the material that makes up the object. Its units are joules per kilogram per Kelvin (J/(kg·K) or J·kg⁻¹·K⁻¹). For example, the value of *c* for aluminum is 910 J/(kg·K); this means that 910 J of heat must flow into a 1-kg block of aluminum to raise its temperature by 1 K (or, equivalently, 1°C). Table 14-3 lists the values of specific heats for a range of substances. The value of the specific heat for any substance varies somewhat with the temperature; however, over the range of temperatures we typically experience, these variations are small enough that we'll ignore them.

Equation 14-20 says that if heat flows *into* an object, so $Q > 0$, it will cause the temperature to increase so $\Delta T > 0$. That's what happens when you warm a saucepan of water on the stove: Heat flows from the stove's electric heating element or gas flame into the saucepan (so $Q > 0$ for the saucepan), and the saucepan's temperature increases (so $\Delta T > 0$ for the saucepan). If heat flows *out* of an object, so $Q < 0$, it will cause the temperature to decrease, so $\Delta T < 0$. This happens to the saucepan when you take it off the stove and allow it to cool: Heat flows from the saucepan to its surroundings (so $Q < 0$ for the saucepan) and the saucepan's temperature decreases (so $\Delta T < 0$ for the saucepan). Example 14-5 shows how to use Equation 14-20 to find the temperature change of an object due to a certain amount of heat flow.

A slightly more complicated application of Equation 14-20 is to find the final temperature of two objects that begin at different temperatures and are placed in contact (for example, hot coffee poured into a cold container). Example 14-6 shows how to solve this sort of problem. In problems of this kind we'll make the simplifying assumption that the two objects are *thermally isolated*: That is, they can exchange energy with each other but don't exchange energy with anything in their environment. So the amount of energy that flows out of the higher-temperature object is equal to the amount of energy that flows into the lower-temperature object.

Table 14-3 Specific Heats

Substance	Specific Heat ($J \cdot kg^{-1} \cdot K^{-1}$)
air (50°C)	1046
aluminum	910
benzene	1750
copper	387
glass	840
gold	130
ice	(−10°C to 0°C) 2093
iron/steel	452
lead	128
marble	858
mercury	138
methyl alcohol	2549
silver	236
steam (100°C)	2009
water (0°C to 100°C)	4186
wood	1700

Example 14-5 Camping Thermodynamics

A certain camping stove releases 5.00×10^4 J of energy per minute from burning propane. (This requires that it uses up the propane at a rate of about 1 g/min.) If half of the released energy is transferred to 2.00 kg of water in a pot above the flame, how much does the temperature of the water change in 1.00 min? (The other half of the energy released by the stove goes into warming the surrounding air and the material of the pot.)

Set Up
Energy flows from the stove into the water because of the temperature difference between them, so this is the kind of energy that we call heat. In one minute heat Q equal to one-half of 5.00×10^4 J flows into the water. Our goal is to find the resulting temperature change ΔT of the water.

Quantity of heat and the resulting temperature change:

$$Q = mc\,\Delta T \qquad (14\text{-}20)$$

Solve
We are given the values of Q and m, and Table 14-3 lists the value of c for water. Use this and Equation 14-20 to find the temperature change of water in 1.00 min.

Solve Equation 14-20 for the temperature change ΔT:

$$\Delta T = \frac{1}{mc}Q$$

The mass is $m = 2.00$ kg, $c = 4186$ $J \cdot kg^{-1} \cdot K^{-1}$ for water from Table 14-3, and $Q = (1/2) \times (5.00 \times 10^4\,J)$. So

$$\Delta T = \frac{(1/2)(5.00 \times 10^4\,J)}{(2.00\ kg)(4186\ J \cdot kg^{-1} \cdot K^{-1})} = 2.99\ K = 2.99°C$$

If the water starts at a temperature of 20.0°C, after 1.00 min its temperature will be 20.0°C + 2.99°C = 23.0°C. After another 1.00 min, its temperature will be 23.0°C + 2.99°C = 26.0°C, and so on.

Reflect
If you've ever used a camping stove, you know that it takes quite a while to bring water to a boil. Using the numbers in this problem, it would take roughly 27 min to increase the temperature of 2.00 kg of water (corresponding to a volume of 2.00 L) from 20°C to 100°C. That's because water has a very large specific heat, so it takes a lot of heat to raise its temperature by a given amount.

Example 14-6 Cooling Coffee

Your expensive coffee maker produces coffee at a temperature of 95.0°C (203°F), which you find is a bit too warm to drink comfortably. To cool the coffee, you pour 0.350 kg of brewed coffee (mostly water) at 95.0°C into a 0.250-kg aluminum cup that is initially at room temperature (20.0°C). What is the final temperature of the coffee and cup? Assume that the coffee and cup are thermally isolated.

Set Up

There are three unknown quantities in this problem: the quantity of heat Q_{cup} that flows into the cup; the quantity of heat Q_{coffee} that flows into the coffee (which will be negative since heat flows *out* of the coffee); and the final temperature T_f of the two objects (which is what we want to find). So we need three equations that relate these quantities.

We can get two equations by writing Equation 14-20 twice, once for the cup and once for the coffee. To get a third equation, we'll use the idea that the two objects are thermally isolated, so the energy that flows *out* of the hot coffee must equal the energy that flows *into* the cool aluminum cup. So Q_{coffee} (for the coffee) and Q_{cup} (for the cup) both involve the same number of joules. However, Q is negative for the coffee (heat flows out of it) and positive for the cup (heat flows into it), so Q_{coffee} is equal to the negative of Q_{cup}.

Quantity of heat and the resulting temperature change:

$$Q = mc\,\Delta T \qquad (14\text{-}20)$$

Energy is conserved:

$$Q_{coffee} = -Q_{cup}$$

coffee
95.0°C
0.350 kg

cup
20.0°C
0.250 kg

coffee in cup;
temperature
$T_f = ?$

Solve

We are given the masses and initial temperatures of both the cup and the coffee, and we can get the specific heats from Table 14-3. Write equations for the three unknowns Q_{cup}, Q_{coffee}, and T_f. Note that for each object, ΔT is the difference between the final and initial temperatures for that object.

The cup has mass $m_{cup} = 0.250$ kg and initial temperature $T_{cup,i} = 20.0°C$, is made of aluminum with $c_{Al} = 910$ J·kg^{-1}·K^{-1}, and ends up at temperature T_f. Equation 14-20 for the cup says

$$Q_{cup} = m_{cup}c_{Al}\,\Delta T_{cup} = m_{cup}c_{Al}(T_f - T_{cup,i})$$

Note that the final temperature T_f will be greater than $T_{cup,i}$ (the cup gets warmer), so $T_f - T_{cup,i} > 0$ and Q_{cup} will be positive.

The coffee has mass $m_{coffee} = 0.350$ kg and initial temperature $T_{coffee,i} = 95.0°C$, is made almost completely of water with $c_{water} = 4186$ J·kg^{-1}·K^{-1}, and ends up at the same final temperature T_f as the cup. Equation 14-20 for the coffee says

$$Q_{coffee} = m_{coffee}c_{water}\,\Delta T_{coffee} = m_{coffee}c_{water}(T_f - T_{coffee,i})$$

The final temperature T_{final} will be less than $T_{coffee,i}$ (the coffee gets cooler), so $T_f - T_{coffee,i} < 0$ and Q_{coffee} will be negative.

The equation of energy conservation is

$$Q_{coffee} = -Q_{cup}$$

Combine these three equations to get a single equation for T_f, the quantity we are trying to find.

Substitute Q_{cup} and Q_{coffee} from the first two equations into the third equation for energy conservation:

$$Q_{coffee} = -Q_{cup}$$

$$m_{coffee}c_{water}(T_f - T_{coffee,i}) = -m_{cup}c_{Al}(T_f - T_{cup,i})$$

The only unknown quantity in this equation is the final temperature T_f.

Solve for the final temperature T_f.

Multiply out both sides of the equation:

$$m_{coffee}c_{water}T_f - m_{coffee}c_{water}T_{coffee,i} = -m_{cup}c_{Al}T_f + m_{cup}c_{Al}T_{cup,i}$$

Rearrange so that all the terms with T_f are on the same side of the equation:

$$m_{coffee}c_{water}T_f + m_{cup}c_{Al}T_f = m_{coffee}c_{water}T_{coffee,i} + m_{cup}c_{Al}T_{cup,i}$$

or

$$(m_{coffee}c_{water} + m_{cup}c_{Al})\,T_f = m_{coffee}c_{water}T_{coffee,i} + m_{cup}c_{Al}T_{cup,i}$$

Solve for T_f:

$$T_f = \frac{m_{coffee}c_{water}T_{coffee,i} + m_{cup}c_{Al}T_{cup,i}}{m_{coffee}c_{water} + m_{cup}c_{Al}}$$

$$= \frac{\left[\begin{array}{l}(0.350\ kg)(4186\ J\cdot kg^{-1}\cdot K^{-1})(95.0°C) \\ \qquad + (0.250\ kg)(910\ J\ kg^{-1}\ K^{-1})(20.0°C)\end{array}\right]}{(0.350\ kg)(4186\ J\cdot kg^{-1}\cdot K^{-1}) + (0.250\ kg)(910\ J\cdot kg^{-1}\cdot K^{-1})}$$

$$= 84.9°C$$

(Recall that a temperature change of 1°C is equivalent to a temperature change of 1 K. This explains why we can exchange kelvins and degrees Celsius in the above equation.)

The coffee cools from 95.0°C to 84.9°C (close to the ideal drinking temperature preferred by coffee aficionados) and the aluminum cup warms from 20.0°C to 84.9°C.

Reflect

The temperature of the coffee decreases and the temperature of the cup increases, just as we expected. We can check our results by calculating Q_{cup} and Q_{coffee}. This calculation shows that $Q_{coffee} = -Q_{cup}$, which must be true for energy to be conserved.

Note that the final temperature of 84.9°C is closer to the initial temperature of the coffee (95.0°C) than to the initial temperature of the cup (20.0°C). That's because the mass and the specific heat are both greater for the coffee than for the cup, so a given quantity of heat produces a smaller temperature change in the coffee than in the cup.

The temperature change for the cup is

$$\Delta T_{cup} = T_f - T_{cup,i} = 84.9°C - 20.0°C = +64.9°C = +64.9\ K$$

(Recall that 1°C and 1 K represent the same temperature change.) The heat that flows into the cup is

$$Q_{cup} = m_{cup}c_{Al}(T_f - T_{cup,i})$$
$$= (0.250\ kg)(910\ J\cdot kg^{-1}\cdot K^{-1})(+64.9\ K)$$
$$= 1.48 \times 10^4\ J$$

The temperature change for the coffee is

$$\Delta T_{coffee} = T_f - T_{coffee,i} = 84.9°C - 95.0°C = -10.1°C = -10.1\ K$$

The heat that flows into the coffee is

$$Q_{coffee} = m_{coffee}c_{water}\Delta T_{coffee}$$
$$= (0.350\ kg)(4186\ J\ kg^{-1}\cdot K^{-1})(-10.1\ K)$$
$$= -1.48 \times 10^4\ J$$

This is negative because heat flows *out* of the coffee.

In Examples 14-5 and 14-6 we used the SI unit of heat, the joule. However, other units are also commonly used. The **calorie** (cal), equal to 4.186 J, is defined as the quantity of heat required to increase the temperature of one gram (1 g) of pure water from 14.5°C to 15.5°C. So in terms of calories, the specific heat of water at 14.5°C is $c = 1\ cal\cdot g^{-1}\cdot K^{-1}$. The energy content of foods are given in *food* calories, often denoted by a capital C, equal to 1000 calories or 1 kilocalorie: 1 C = 1 kcal = 4186 J = 4.186 kJ. In countries other than the United States, the energy content on food labels is given in units of kilojoules (Figure 14-12).

The unit of heat in the English system is the **British thermal unit** (BTU), defined as the quantity of heat required to increase the temperature of 1 lb of pure water from 63°F to 64°F. The energy flow of air conditioners and heaters is often given in BTUs. One BTU is equal to 1055 J, 252 cal, or 0.252 kcal.

Vaniljasokeri

Aitoa vaniljaa sisältävä vaniljasokeri. Aitouden erotat pienistä mustista pilkuista ja oikeasta vaniljanväristä. Sopii käytettäväksi mausteen tavoin jälkiruokakastikkeisiin, kermavaahtoon, leivonnaisiin ja jälkiruokiin.
Ainekset: Tomusokeri, vanilja-aromi, perunatärkkelys, vanilja.

Ravintosisältö/100 g:

Energiaa	1700 kJ/400 kcal
Proteiinia	0 g
Hiilihydraattia	99 g
Rasvaa	0 g

Nettopaino: 170 g
Säilytys: Kuivassa.
Parasta ennen: Pakkauksen takasivu.

Suomen Sokeri Oy, FI-02460 Kantvik
Kuluttajapalvelu/Konsumentservice:
Puh/Tel. 0800-0-4400, klo/kl 12–15
kuluttajapalvelu@dansukker.fi
www.dansukker.fi

Figure 14-12 **Counting calories and kilojoules** The label on a package of flavored sugar from Finland lists the energy content in both kilojoules (kJ) and food calories (1 food calorie = 1 kilocalorie = 1 kcal).

14-6 Energy must enter or leave an object in order for it to change phase

If you add energy to an object, will its temperature increase? The best answer is "Maybe." If you warm (add heat to) an ice cube to its melting point of 0°C, then continue to warm it, the temperature of the ice cube will *remain* at 0°C until the ice has all melted (Figure 14-1b). The solid, liquid, and gaseous states of water are called its **phases**, and what happens when you boil water is that the water undergoes a **phase change**. Energy must either be absorbed or released in order for a substance to change from one phase to another, but the temperature of the substance stays the same during a phase change. For example, in boiling water at 100°C the energy that the water absorbs goes entirely into rearranging the organization of the water molecules to effect the phase change, with none left over to raise the temperature. You can verify this by putting a thermometer in a pot of water and heating the pot on a stove. The water temperature increases until it reaches 100°C and the water begins to boil. As the water boils away, the temperature will remain at 100°C; at this temperature, all of the heat flowing into the water goes into changing the phase of the water.

You're familiar with several kinds of phase change. When a liquid becomes a solid, the process is called freezing; when a solid becomes a liquid, the process is called melting or **fusion**. Other common phase changes include from liquid to gas, or **vaporization**, and from gas to liquid, or **condensation**. Some substances can change from solid to gas without an intermediate liquid phase. A common example is carbon dioxide (CO_2); at room temperature atmospheric pressure CO_2 goes from a solid form, commonly known as *dry ice*, directly to CO_2 gas. A phase change from solid directly to gas is called **sublimation**; the reverse process, from gas directly to solid, is called **deposition**. Phase changes can also occur between different arrangements of molecules in the crystalline structures of certain solids. For example, if the crystalline form of carbon, called graphite (like that found in pencil lead), is placed under very high pressure, the crystalline structure of the carbon atoms rearranges to form a more valuable kind of crystal known as diamond.

For a given substance at a given pressure, there is a specific temperature at which a phase change occurs. For example, at 1 atmosphere of pressure water can change between its solid and liquid forms at 0°C. This is the temperature at which these two phases can *coexist.* If you allow heat to flow into ice at 0°C, it will begin to melt and the just-melted water will be at the same temperature of 0°C. As heat continues to flow, the temperature of the ice-water mixture will remain at 0°C until all of the ice has melted. Only then will an additional heat flow cause a temperature increase in the liquid water that remains. If you reverse the process and allow heat to flow out of water at 0°C, it will begin to freeze and you'll have a mixture of liquid water and solid ice at 0°C. If heat continues to flow out of the system, the mixture stays at 0°C until the water is converted completely to ice, after which point the temperature can drop below 0°C.

Latent Heat

Suppose a quantity of substance is at the temperature at which a phase change can occur; for example, think of a quantity of liquid water at 100°C (at which temperature it can become a gas) or at 0°C (at which temperature it can become a solid). The amount of heat per unit mass that must flow into or out of the substance to cause the phase change is called the **latent heat**. For liquid water at 100°C, the latent heat is the amount of heat per kilogram that must flow into the water to vaporize it; for liquid water at 0°C, the latent heat is the amount of heat per kilogram that must flow *out* of the water to freeze it. The units of latent heat are joules per kilogram (J/kg).

The value of the latent heat depends on the substance as well as on the kind of phase change. For example, 2.47×10^5 J of heat must flow into a 1-kg block of iron to melt it at its melting temperature of 1811 K, but even more heat (3.34×10^5 J) must flow into a 1-kg block of ice to melt it at its melting temperature of 273 K. We say that the **latent heat of fusion** (that is, melting) is $L_F = 2.47 \times 10^5$ J/kg for iron and $L_F = 3.34 \times 10^5$ J/kg for water. The **latent heat of vaporization** for water is $L_V = 2.26 \times 10^6$ J/kg; this means that 2.26×10^6 J of heat must flow into 1 kg of liquid water at its vaporization temperature of 100°C in order to vaporize it. The values of L_F and L_V for water show that it takes about seven times more energy to vaporize a kilogram of water at 100°C than it does to melt a kilogram of ice at 0°C.

Note that the latent heat of fusion is also the energy *released* per unit mass when a substance changes from a liquid to a solid, and the latent heat of vaporization is the energy *released* per unit mass when a substance changes from gas to liquid. Table 14-4 lists the latent heat of fusion and the latent heat of vaporization for various substances.

Table 14-4 Melting and Boiling Temperatures (T_F and T_V) and Latent Heats of Fusion and Vaporization (L_F and L_V) for Various Substances at 1 atm of Pressure

Substance	T_F (K)	T_V (K)	L_F (J/kg) $\times 10^3$	L_V (J/kg) $\times 10^3$
alcohol (ethyl)	159	351	104	830
aluminum	933	2792	397	10,900
copper	1357	2835	209	4730
gold	1337	3129	63.7	1645
hydrogen (H_2)	14	20	59.5	445
iron	1811	3134	247	6090
lead	600	2022	24.5	866
nitrogen (N_2)	63	77	25.3	199
oxygen (O_2)	54	90	13.7	213
water	273	373	334	2260

The amount of energy needed to cause a phase change to occur is proportional to the mass m of substance. The more massive a block of ice or iron, for example, the more energy is required to melt it. We can summarize these relationships in a single equation:

Quantity of heat that flows into or out of a quantity of substance to cause a phase change

Use + sign if heat flows into the substance; use − sign if heat flows out of the substance.

Heat required for a phase change (14-21)

$$Q = \pm mL$$

Latent heat for the phase change

Mass of the substance

Equation 14-21 applies to all phase changes. For example, if the phase change is fusion (a solid becomes a liquid), then L is the latent heat of fusion L_F and we use the plus sign so Q is positive (heat is added to the substance to make it melt). If the phase change is condensation (a gas becomes a liquid), L is the latent heat of vaporization L_V and we use the minus sign so Q is negative (heat is released by the substance as it condenses).

> **Watch Out!** Equation 14-21 describes what happens in the phase change, not what it takes to get there.
>
> Remember that a phase change can only happen if the substance is at the appropriate temperature (for example, it must be at the vaporization temperature for vaporization or condensation to take place). Equation 14-21 does *not* include the heat that must flow into or out of a substance to get the substance to that temperature. To calculate that, you must use Equation 14-20, $Q = mc\,\Delta T$. So if you want to know how much heat would be needed to vaporize a quantity of liquid water initially at 20°C, you would first use Equation 14-20 to find the amount of heat needed to raise the water temperature from 20°C to 100°C, then use Equation 14-21 to find the amount of heat needed to vaporize that water at 100°C.

Equation 14-21 says that energy in the form of heat must flow into a substance to cause a phase change from solid to liquid or from liquid to gas. Often the source of that energy is a second object in thermal contact with the first. For example, as the sweat on our skin evaporates on a hot day, energy flows from our bodies to the beads of perspiration. This process results in the temperatures of our bodies decreasing just a bit. Although other effects can come into play, energy must be conserved, so whatever energy leaves our bodies appears as energy added to the sweat. There is heat flow *into* the sweat, so $Q_{sweat} > 0$, and heat flow *out of* the body, so $Q_{body} < 0$. Energy conservation says that the number of joules of heat that flows out of the body equals the number of joules that flows into the sweat, so $Q_{body} = -Q_{sweat}$. The energy lost from the body to the sweat causes a decrease in the temperature of the body (which, unlike the sweat, does not undergo a phase change). In other words, perspiration helps us to cool off. A typical person perspires about 0.60 kg of sweat per day, and sweat has a latent heat of vaporization of about 2.43×10^6 J/kg. From Equation 14-21, the heat that flows into one day's worth of sweat to make it evaporate is

$$Q_{sweat} = mL_V = (0.60\ \text{kg})(2.43 \times 10^6\ \text{J/kg}) = 1.5 \times 10^6\ \text{J}$$

The heat flow into the body is $Q_{body} = -Q_{sweat} = -1.5 \times 10^6$ J to two significant figures, so the body *loses* 1.5×10^6 J of energy by sweating. Recall from Section 14-5 that one food calorie (1 kcal) equals 4186 J, so the amount of energy that the body loses by sweating is $(1.5 \times 10^6\ \text{J})(1\ \text{kcal}/4186\ \text{J}) = 350$ kcal. So you must consume at least 350 kcal daily to compensate for the energy lost by sweating. (You also need to drink at least 0.60 kg of water, with a volume of 0.60 L, to compensate for the water lost.)

Go to Interactive Exercise 14-2 for more practice dealing with phase changes

We can apply the same approach to what happens when an ice cube is dropped into a glass of water. Heat is transferred from the water (so $Q_{water} < 0$) into the ice (so $Q_{ice} > 0$) in order for the ice to melt: The number of joules of energy that leaves the water equals the number of joules that enters the ice, so $Q_{water} = -Q_{ice}$. The temperature of the water decreases, and if the water loses enough energy, some or all of it could even freeze.

The following examples illustrate how to solve some typical problems that involve phase changes.

Example 14-7 Melting Ice I

A 1.00-kg block of ice initially at a temperature of 0°C is placed inside an experimental apparatus that allows 250 kJ of heat to flow into the ice. What fraction of the ice melts as a result? What is the final temperature of the melted ice?

Set Up

In this problem the ice starts at the melting temperature, so no heat has to be added to the ice to get it to that temperature. Heat must be added to melt the ice, so $Q_{ice} > 0$. From Table 14-4, the latent heat of fusion for water is $L_F = 334\ \text{kJ/kg} = 334 \times 10^3$ J/kg, so it would take 334 kJ of heat to completely melt 1.00 kg of ice. The heat supplied is less than that, so only part of the ice will melt. We'll use Equation 14-21 to determine the fraction that melts.

Heat required to melt a mass m of ice:

$$Q_{ice} = +mL_F \qquad (14\text{-}21)$$

Solve

Find the mass that melts as a number of kilograms and as a fraction of the total amount of ice.

From Equation 14-21, the mass that melts is

$$m = \frac{Q_{ice}}{L_F} = \frac{250\ kJ}{334\ kJ/kg} = 0.749\ kg$$

Express this as a fraction of the total amount of ice, $m_{total} = 1.00\ kg$:

$$Fraction\ of\ ice\ that\ melts = \frac{m}{m_{total}} = \frac{0.749\ kg}{1.00\ kg} = 0.749$$

Almost three-quarters of the ice melts. Because all of the heat goes into melting the ice, we end up with solid ice and liquid water that are both at the initial temperature of 0°C.

Reflect

If 334 kJ of heat were transferred to the block of ice, it would completely melt. Any more heat added would go into raising the temperature of the resulting liquid water to a value greater than 0°C.

Example 14-8 Melting Ice II

A chunk of ice at −10.0°C is placed in an insulated container that holds 1.00 kg of water at 20.0°C. When the system comes to thermal equilibrium, all of the ice has melted and the entire system is at a temperature of 0.0°C. What was the initial mass of the ice?

Set Up

Three processes occur as the system reaches thermal equilibrium: (a) The temperature of the water decreases from 20.0°C to 0.0°C, so heat flows out of the water; (b) the temperature of the ice increases from −10.0°C to 0.0°C, so heat flows into the ice; and (c) the ice melts at 0°C, so additional heat flows into the ice. Equation 14-20 describes the heat flows associated with the temperature changes, and Equation 14-21 describes the heat flow associated with melting the ice. Energy conservation says that the heat that flows into the ice equals the heat that flows out of the water. Our goal is to the find the initial mass of ice, m_{ice}.

Quantity of heat and the resulting temperature change:

$$Q = mc\ \Delta T \qquad (14\text{-}20)$$

Heat required to melt a mass m of ice:

$$Q_{ice} = +mL_F \qquad (14\text{-}21)$$

Energy is conserved:

$$Q_{ice} = -Q_{water}$$

Solve

Write Equation 14-20 for the water and for the ice, and write Equation 14-21 for the ice. The specific heats for water and ice are given in Table 14-3, and the latent heat of fusion is given in Table 14-4.

Q_{water} is negative: Heat flows *out* of the water to make its temperature decrease.

Q_{ice} positive (both processes require that heat flows into the ice). Note that the term that involves melting the ice is about 16 times larger than the term that involves raising the temperature of the ice from −10.0°C to 0.0°C.

The heat flow into the water that is required to lower its temperature from 20.0°C to 0.0°C:

$$\begin{aligned}
Q_{water} &= m_{water}c_{water}\ \Delta T_{water} \\
&= (1.00\ kg)(4186\ J \cdot kg^{-1} \cdot K^{-1})(0.0°C - 20.0°C) \\
&= (1.00\ kg)(4186\ J \cdot kg^{-1} \cdot K^{-1})(-20.0\ K) \\
&= -8.37 \times 10^4\ J
\end{aligned}$$

(Recall that temperature changes in degrees Celsius are equivalent to temperature changes in kelvins.)

The heat flow into the ice is the sum of the heat required to raise its temperature by −10.0°C to 0.0°C and the heat required to melt it at 0.0°C:

$$\begin{aligned}
Q_{ice} &= m_{ice}c_{ice}\ \Delta T_{ice} + m_{ice}L_F = m_{ice}(c_{ice}\ \Delta T_{ice} + L_F) \\
&= m_{ice}\big[\,(2093\ J \cdot kg^{-1} \cdot K^{-1})\big[0.0°C - (-10.0°C)\big] \\
&\quad + 3.34 \times 10^5\ J/kg\big]
\end{aligned}$$

$$= m_{ice}(2.093 \times 10^4 \, J/kg + 3.34 \times 10^5 \, J/kg)$$
$$= m_{ice}(3.55 \times 10^5 \, J/kg)$$

Use energy conservation to relate Q_{water} and Q_{ice}, then solve for m_{ice}.

The energy flow into the ice equals the negative of the (negative) energy flow into the water:

$$Q_{ice} = -Q_{water}$$
$$m_{ice}(3.55 \times 10^5 \, J/kg) = -(-8.37 \times 10^4 \, J)$$

Solve for m_{ice}:

$$m_{ice} = \frac{8.37 \times 10^4 \, J}{3.55 \times 10^5 \, J/kg} = 0.236 \, kg$$

Reflect

The amount of ice required has a mass of 0.236 kg. In more familiar terms, 1 kg is the mass of 1 L of water, and an ice cube from a typical ice cube tray has a mass of about 0.04 kg (40 g). So it would take about six ice cubes to reproduce the process described in this problem, which doesn't seem unreasonable.

Note that if the container that holds the ice and water were *not* insulated, we would also have to worry about heat flow between the water and the container and between the ice and the container. Using an insulated container allows us to avoid this complication.

Example 14-9 All Ice, All Water, or a Mixture?

A 0.150-kg chunk of ice at $-10.0°C$ is placed in an insulated container that holds 1.00 kg of water at 20.0°C. When the system comes to thermal equilibrium, what is its temperature? How much ice and how much water are present?

Set Up

There are three possible outcomes of this experiment: We could end up with all ice at 0°C or colder, a mixture of ice and liquid water at 0°C, or all liquid water at 0°C or warmer. We'll consider all three possibilities. As in Example 14-8, we'll use Equation 14-20 to describe what happens in any temperature changes and Equation 14-21 to describe what happens in any phase changes. Since the system is isolated, the only heat flow is from the water into the ice. Energy conservation then says that Q_{ice} (which is positive) equals the negative of Q_{water} (which is negative).

Quantity of heat and the resulting temperature change:

$$Q = mc \, \Delta T \qquad (14\text{-}20)$$

Heat required to melt a mass m of ice:

$$Q_{ice} = +mL_F \qquad (14\text{-}21)$$

Energy is conserved:

$$Q_{ice} = -Q_{water}$$

ice
−10.0°C
0.150 kg

water
20.0°C
1.00 kg

final state
= ?

Solve

The energy conservation equation says that the sum of the (positive) heat flow into the ice and the (negative) heat flow into the water must be zero. The simplest way to proceed is to first see how much heat would have to flow out of the water to lower its temperature to 0°C and how much heat would have to flow into the ice to raise its temperature to 0°C. The discrepancy between these tells us what must actually happen.

Energy conservation says that

$$Q_{ice} = -Q_{water}$$

or

$$Q_{ice} + Q_{water} = 0$$

To warm the ice to 0°C requires

$$Q_{ice} = m_{ice}c_{ice} \, \Delta T_{ice}$$
$$= (0.150 \, kg)(2093 \, J \cdot kg^{-1} \cdot K^{-1})[0.0°C - (-10.0°C)]$$
$$= +3.14 \times 10^3 \, J$$

(That is, the ice must absorb 3.14×10^3 J of energy.)

(Recall that temperature changes in degrees Celsius are equivalent to temperature changes in kelvins.)

To cool the water to 0°C requires

$$Q_{water} = m_{water}c_{water}\Delta T_{water}$$
$$= (1.00 \text{ kg})(4186 \text{ J} \cdot \text{kg}^{-1} \cdot \text{K}^{-1})(0.0°C - 20.0°C)$$
$$= -8.37 \times 10^4 \text{ J}$$

(That is, the water must release 8.34×10^4 J of energy.)

The sum of these is $+3.14 \times 10^3$ J $+ (-8.37 \times 10^4$ J$) = -8.06 \times 10^4$ J, which is *not* zero. To satisfy $Q_{ice} + Q_{water} = 0$, we need an extra positive quantity of heat equal to $+8.06 \times 10^4$ J. So the final state is *not* simply 0.150 kg of ice at 0.0°C and 1.00 kg of water at 0.0°C.

Consider the possibility that the final state is at a temperature of 0°C or lower and that some or all of the liquid water has frozen. We can use what we've learned so far to rule this out.

If a mass m of the water were to freeze at 0.0°C, there would be an additional heat flow into the water of

$$-mL_F = -m(3.34 \times 10^5 \text{ J/kg})$$

This is negative because heat must flow *out* of the water to freeze it. But to satisfy the energy conservation equation $Q_{ice} + Q_{water} = 0$ we need an extra *positive* quantity of heat equal to $+8.06 \times 10^4$ J, so this is impossible. We conclude that *none* of the liquid water freezes.

A second possibility is that the final temperature is 0°C, but a portion of the 0.150 kg of ice melts. We can rule this out by seeing how much ice would melt.

The extra $+8.06 \times 10^4$ J of heat could go into melting some or all of the 0.150 kg of ice. The mass m of ice that this could melt is given by

$$Q = 8.06 \times 10^4 \text{ J} = mL_F = m(3.34 \times 10^5 \text{ J/kg}) \text{ so}$$

$$m = \frac{8.06 \times 10^4 \text{ J}}{3.34 \times 10^5 \text{ J/kg}} = 0.241 \text{ kg}$$

But there is only 0.150 kg of ice to melt. So we conclude that *all* of the ice melts, and there is only liquid water in the final state. There is then heat "left over" to raise the temperature of the water above 0°C.

The only possibility that remains is that all of the ice melts, and the final temperature is greater than 0°C.

The extra $+8.06 \times 10^4$ J of heat goes into melting all of the 0.150 kg of ice, then raising the temperature of the remaining water (1.00 kg that was originally water plus 0.150 kg of melted ice) from 0°C to a final temperature T_{final}:

$$8.06 \times 10^4 \text{ J} = m_{ice}L_F + m_{total}c_{water}(T_{final} - 0.0°C) \text{ so}$$

$$8.06 \times 10^4 \text{ J} = (0.150 \text{ kg})(3.34 \times 10^5 \text{ J/kg})$$
$$+ (1.15 \text{ kg})(4186 \text{ J kg}^{-1} \text{ K}^{-1})(T_{final} - 0.0°C)$$
$$= 5.01 \times 10^4 \text{ J} + (4.81 \times 10^3 \text{ J/K})(T_{final} - 0.0°C)$$

Solve for T_{final}:

$$T_{final} - 0.0°C = \frac{8.06 \times 10^4 \text{ J} - 5.01 \times 10^4 \text{ J}}{4.81 \times 10^3 \text{ J/K}} = 6.34 \text{ K}$$

Since a temperature difference of 1 kelvin is the same as a temperature difference of 1 Celsius degree,

$$T_{final} = 6.34°C$$

In the final state, all of the ice has melted and we have liquid water at 6.34°C.

Reflect

We found our answer by assuming that the 1.00 kg cooled from 20.0°C to 0°C, then warmed again to 6.34°C. That's not what the water actually does, but the net effect on the water is the same. We can check our result by calculating the net heat flow into the ice (to warm it from −10.0°C to 0°C, melt it completely, and warm the melted ice to 6.34°C) and the net heat flow into the water (to cool it from 20.0°C to 6.34°C).

Heat flow into 0.150 kg of ice to warm it from −10.0°C to 0°C, melt it, and warm the melted water to 6.34°C:

$$Q_{ice} = m_{ice}c_{ice}[0.0°C - (-10.0°C)] + m_{ice}L_F$$
$$+ m_{ice}c_{water}(6.34°C - 0.0°C)$$
$$= (0.150\ kg)(2093\ J\cdot kg^{-1}\cdot K^{-1})[0.0°C - (-10.0°C)]$$
$$+ (0.150\ kg)(3.34 \times 10^5\ J/kg)$$
$$+ (0.150\ kg)(4186\ J\cdot kg^{-1}\cdot K^{-1})(6.34°C - 0.0°C)$$
$$= 3.14 \times 10^3\ J + 5.01 \times 10^4\ J + 3.98 \times 10^3\ J$$
$$= 5.72 \times 10^4\ J$$

Each of these steps requires heat flow *into* the ice, so the total value of Q_{ice} is positive.

Heat flow into 1.00 kg of water to cool it from 20.0°C to 6.34°C:

$$Q_{water} = m_{water}c_{water}(6.34°C - 20.0°C)$$
$$= (1.00\ kg)(4186\ J\ kg^{-1}\ K^{-1})(6.34°C - 20.0°C)$$
$$= -5.72 \times 10^4\ J$$

This is negative because heat flows *out of* the water as it cools.

Note that $Q_{ice} = -Q_{water}$ and so $Q_{ice} + Q_{water} = 0$, as required for energy to be conserved.

Another check on our result is to make a comparison with Example 14-8. In that example we also started with 1.00 kg of water at 20.0°C but with a larger mass of ice (0.236 kg) at −10.0°C. In that case we also ended up with all liquid water, but at a final temperature of 0.0°C. So our result above is reasonable: If we start with a smaller mass of ice, 0.150 kg, the ice will all melt *and* the system will end up at a temperature above 0.0°C.

We invite you to try this calculation yourself for a somewhat different situation: Again start with 1.00 kg of water at 20.0°C, but add to it 150 kg of ice at −10.0°C (so now there is much more ice than liquid water). Can you show that in this case all of the water freezes and the final temperature of the system is −8.73°C?

Phase Diagrams

A useful tool for visualizing the possible phase changes for a particular substance is a **phase diagram**. This is a graph of pressure versus temperature for the substance. For example, Figure 14-13 is the phase diagram for water. The three red curves in the figure show the boundaries in terms of pressure and temperature between phases. Each point on one of the red curves represents a combination of pressure and temperature at which two phases can coexist and a phase change can take place. For example, at a pressure of 1 atm solid ice and liquid water can coexist at 0°C; this is the melting temperature of ice at that pressure. Similarly, at 1 atm pressure liquid water and water vapor can coexist at 100°C, the temperature at which water boils and vaporizes. The phase diagram shows that at different pressures the phase changes occur at different temperatures. For example, if the pressure is less than 1 atm, the boundary between liquid water and water vapor is at a temperature less than 100°C. That's why water boils at only 95°C at the elevation of Denver or Albuquerque (1610 m or 5280 ft), where air pressure is only about 0.82 atm. Due to the reduced boiling temperature, chefs at such elevations know that foods prepared in boiling water have to be cooked longer than they would be at sea level.

In Section 14-2 we introduced the idea of the *triple point* of the substance, which is the particular combination of pressure and temperature at which the solid, liquid, and gas phases can all coexist. In Figure 14-13 the triple point is where the three red curves meet. If the pressure is greater than the triple-point pressure, the substance can exist in either the solid, liquid, or gas (vapor) phase depending on the temperature. That's the case for water at sea level on Earth: The triple point of water is 0.00603 atm and 0.01°C, so at normal atmospheric pressure (1 atm) water can exist in any of the three phases. Atmospheric pressure decreases with increasing altitude, so very high

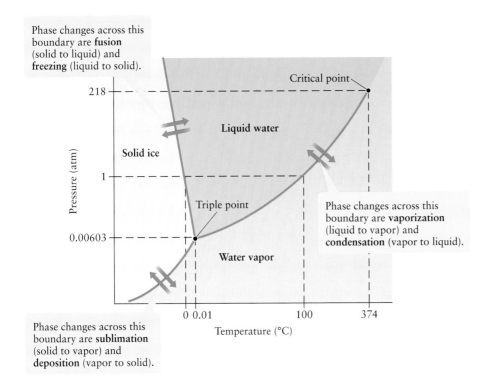

Phase changes across this boundary are **fusion** (solid to liquid) and **freezing** (liquid to solid).

Phase changes across this boundary are **vaporization** (liquid to vapor) and **condensation** (vapor to liquid).

Phase changes across this boundary are **sublimation** (solid to vapor) and **deposition** (vapor to solid).

Figure 14-13 The phase diagram for water A phase diagram shows the relationship between pressure, temperature, and the phase of the substance. Each of the three red curves in the figure marks a boundary between two phases and shows the temperature at which a phase change is possible as a function of pressure.

in the atmosphere the pressure is near or below the triple-point pressure. That's why stratus and cumulus clouds, which are made of droplets of liquid water, are found mostly at low altitudes where the pressure of the air is well above the triple-point pressure. By contrast, the most common clouds in the upper atmosphere are cirrus clouds made of ice crystals; the low pressures at such altitudes make it more difficult for water to be in the liquid phase.

Figure 14-13 shows that the red curve that forms the boundary between the liquid and gas (vapor) phases comes to an end at a certain point, which for water occurs at 218 atm and 374°C. This special combination of pressure and temperature is called the **critical point**. If the pressure is greater than the critical-point pressure, the temperature is greater than the critical-point temperature, or both, there is no sharp dividing line between gas and liquid: The substance exists in a single phase called a *supercritical fluid*. Above the critical temperature, unlike below it, no increase in pressure will cause a gas to condense into liquid form.

? Got the Concept? 14-6   Ranking Energies for Water

Use the information in Tables 14-3 and 14-4 to rank the following from largest to smallest: (a) the energy needed to raise the temperature of 1 kg of ice from −5°C to −4°C; (b) the energy needed to melt 1 kg of ice at 0°C; (c) the energy needed to raise the temperature of 1 kg of liquid water from 20°C to 21°C; (d) the energy needed to boil 1 kg of water at 100°C; and (e) the energy needed to raise the temperature of 1 kg of steam from 110°C to 111°C.

Take-Home Message for Section 14-6

✔ Energy in the form of heat must either be absorbed or released in order for a substance to change from one phase to another.

✔ The latent heat of fusion is the amount of heat per unit mass required to cause a substance to undergo a phase change between the solid and liquid phases. Similarly, the latent heat of vaporization is the amount of heat per unit mass required to cause a substance to undergo a phase change between the liquid and gaseous phases.

✔ The triple point is the particular combination of pressure and temperature at which the solid, liquid, and gas phases of a substance can coexist.

14-7 Heat can be transferred by radiation, convection, or conduction

Animals have evolved to live in a broad range of climates. The jackrabbit in **Figure 14-14a** has a scrawny body, long skinny legs, enormous ears, and thin fur, all of which promote heat loss and enables the animal to survive in the desert. In contrast, the arctic hare's compact body, stubby legs, relatively small ears, and thick insulating fur help prevent heat loss (**Figure 14-14b**).

The iguanas shown in Figure 14-1c are cold-blooded, so they must use different strategies for controlling their body temperature: After a cold swim in the Pacific Ocean, these reptiles warm themselves by lying in the tropical sun atop rocks that have already been heated by the Sun. In this section, we'll look at how heat is transferred from one place to another, such as from a jackrabbit to its environment or from a hot rock to a cold iguana.

Heat can be transferred from one object to another through three processes: *radiation, convection,* and *conduction.*

Radiation is energy transfer by the emission (or absorption) of electromagnetic waves. Some examples of electromagnetic waves are visible light, infrared radiation, and microwaves. (We'll see in Chapter 23 that all of these are different manifestations of the same physical phenomenon.) You use radiation when you lie out on a sunny day or warm yourself under a heat lamp. The iguanas in Figure 14-1c are using radiation to gather energy directly from the sun.

Convection is energy transfer by the motion of a liquid or gas (such as air). Convection is what happens in a pot of water boiling on the stove: Warm water from the bottom of the pot rises, carrying energy to the cooler water at the top of the pot. Convection carries energy away from the arctic hare in Figure 14-14b, as the air warmed by the hare's body rises away from the animal.

Conduction is energy transfer by the collision of particles in one object with the particles in another. It requires physical contact between the two objects. If you use an electric blanket to keep warm on a cold winter's night, the energy flows from the blanket into your body by conduction. The iguanas in Figure 14-1c also use conduction to take in energy from the hot rock on which they are lying.

Let's look at each of these processes of heat transfer individually.

Radiation

Both convection and conduction rely on molecules bumping against one another, but radiation does not. The energy emitted by the Sun reaches Earth after passing through 150 million kilometers of almost completely empty space.

Experiment shows that *any* object emits energy in the form of radiation. The rate at which radiation is emitted by an object—that is, the radiated *power P* in joules per second or watts—is proportional to the object's surface area A and to the fourth power of the Kelvin temperature T of the object:

(a)

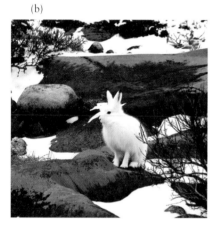

(b)

Figure 14-14 Controlling heat transfer Both (a) jackrabbits and (b) arctic hares belong to the same genus (*Lepus*). However, jackrabbits evolved to radiate heat in the hot desert environment, while arctic hares evolved to conserve heat in the cold conditions of the Arctic.

Rate of energy flow in radiation
(14-22)

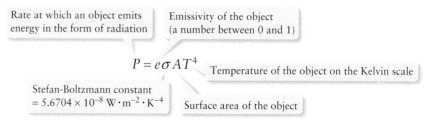

Rate at which an object emits energy in the form of radiation

Emissivity of the object (a number between 0 and 1)

$$P = e\sigma A T^4$$

Temperature of the object on the Kelvin scale

Stefan-Boltzmann constant
$= 5.6704 \times 10^{-8} \text{ W} \cdot \text{m}^{-2} \cdot \text{K}^{-4}$

Surface area of the object

The **Stefan-Boltzmann constant** σ (the Greek letter sigma) has the same value for all objects. The quantity e is the **emissivity** of the surface; its value indicates how well or how poorly a surface radiates. A surface with a value of e close to 1 is a good radiator of thermal energy.

The factor of T^4 in Equation 14-22 means that the radiated power can change substantially with a change in temperature. For example, a kiln for making ceramic pots can easily reach temperatures of 600 K; a pot at this temperature will radiate energy at $2^4 = 16$ times the rate as when the pot is at room temperature of about 300 K. (The red glow from the heating element in an electric toaster is an example of radiation of this

Figure 14-15 **Radiation from a human hand** A special infrared camera was used to record these images of a person's right hand before (left) and after (right) smoking a cigarette. The intensity of the radiation from different parts of the hand, and hence the temperature of those parts, is indicated by colors from red (warmest) through yellow, green, and blue (coldest). The temperature of the fingers drops after smoking because the nicotine in the tobacco causes blood vessels to contract and reduces blood circulation to the extremities.

kind.) The factor A in Equation 14-22 shows that for a given surface temperature T, an object will radiate energy at a greater rate if it has a larger surface area. That's why it's useful for the jackrabbit in Figure 14-14a to have a lanky frame and big ears; this maximizes its surface area and makes it easier for the jackrabbit to get rid of excess energy in the hot desert. The more compact arctic hare in Figure 14-14b has much less surface area for its volume, and so it radiates away less of its internal energy to its frigid surroundings.

Just as for jackrabbits and arctic hares, radiation plays a significant role in heat loss from the human body. Under typical conditions, approximately half of the energy transferred from the body to the environment is in the form of radiation. This radiation is emitted almost entirely in the form of infrared light to which your eye is not sensitive, so you can't see yourself glowing in the dark. But specialized devices can detect this radiation (Figure 14-15). One such device now in common use in medicine is the *temporal artery thermometer*. The nurse runs the thermometer over your head in the region of the temporal artery, and the circuitry in the thermometer detects the power radiated by the blood in the artery. This gives a very accurate measurement of body temperature while being noninvasive.

Radiation and Climate

Radiation is also the mechanism that keeps Earth from freezing. Our planet's interior releases very little heat, so what keeps the surface warm is energy that reaches us from the Sun in the form of electromagnetic radiation. In equilibrium the rate at which Earth *absorbs* solar energy (about 1.21×10^{17} W) must be equal to the rate at which it *emits* energy into space as given by Equation 14-22. Since the emission rate depends on the surface temperature, this is what determines our planet's average surface temperature T. If Earth had no atmosphere, T would be about 254 K ($= -19°C = -2°F$), so cold that oceans and lakes around the world should be frozen over. In fact, Earth's actual average surface temperature is a much more livable 287 K ($= 14°C = 57°F$). The explanation for this discrepancy is called the **greenhouse effect**: Our atmosphere prevents some of the radiation emitted by Earth's surface from escaping into space. Certain gases in our atmosphere called **greenhouse gases**, among them water vapor and carbon dioxide, are transparent to visible light but not to infrared radiation. Consequently, visible sunlight has no trouble entering our atmosphere and warming the surface. But the infrared radiation coming from the heated surface is partially trapped by the atmosphere and cannot escape into space. This lowers Earth's net emissivity e in Equation 14-22. In order to have the power radiated into space equal to the power received from the Sun, the factor of T^4 in Equation 14-22 must be greater to compensate for the reduced value of e. The net effect is that Earth's surface is some 33°C (59°F) warmer than it would be without the greenhouse effect, and water remains unfrozen over most of the planet.

The warming caused by the greenhouse effect gives our planet the moderate temperatures needed for the existence of life. For more than a century, however, our technological civilization has been adding greenhouse gases to the atmosphere at an unprecedented rate. Figure 14-16 shows how the concentration of carbon dioxide (CO_2) has varied in our atmosphere over the past 400,000 years. (Data from past centuries comes from analyzing bubbles of air trapped in ancient ice in the Antarctic.) While there

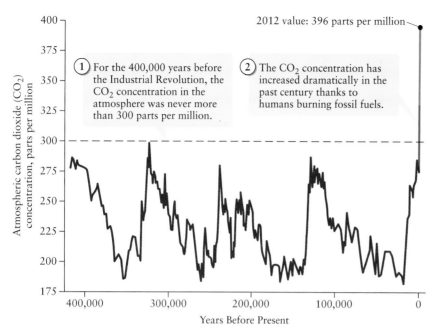

2012 value: 396 parts per million

(1) For the 400,000 years before the Industrial Revolution, the CO_2 concentration in the atmosphere was never more than 300 parts per million.

(2) The CO_2 concentration has increased dramatically in the past century thanks to humans burning fossil fuels.

Figure 14-16 **Carbon dioxide in the atmosphere** Because carbon dioxide (CO_2) absorbs infrared radiation emitted by Earth's surface, its presence in our atmosphere decreases Earth's emissivity and causes the average surface temperature to increase. Thanks to the burning of fossil fuels, the level of CO_2 in our atmosphere is now greater than it has been any time in the past 400,000 years.

is natural variation in the CO_2 concentration, the value has skyrocketed since the beginning of the Industrial Revolution thanks to our burning fossil fuels such as coal and petroleum. The result has been an amplification of the greenhouse effect and an increase in the average surface temperature, an effect known as **global warming** (Figure 14-17). Other explanations for global warming have been proposed, such as changes in the sun's brightness, but these do not stand up to close scrutiny. Only greenhouse gases produced by human activity can explain the steep temperature increase shown in Figure 14-17.

The effects of global warming can be seen around the world. Nine of the 10 warmest years on record have occurred since 2000, and we have seen increasing numbers of droughts, water shortages, and unprecedented heat waves. Glaciers worldwide are receding, the size of the ice cap around the North Pole has decreased by 20% since 1979, and a portion of the Antarctic ice shelf has broken off. Unfortunately, global warming is predicted to intensify in the decades to come. The UN Intergovernmental Panel on Climate Change predicts that if nothing is done to decrease the rate at which we add greenhouse gases to our atmosphere, the average surface temperature will continue to rise by an additional 1.4 to 5.8°C during the twenty-first century. What is worse, temperatures will rise in some regions and decline in others and the patterns of rainfall will be substantially altered. Agriculture depends on rainfall, so these changes in rainfall patterns can cause major disruptions in the world food supply. Studies suggest that the climate changes caused by a 3°C increase in the average surface temperature would cause a worldwide drop in cereal crops of 20 to 400 million tons, putting 400 million more people at risk of hunger.

The solution to global warming will require concerted and thoughtful action. Global warming cannot be stopped completely: Even if we were to immediately halt all production of greenhouse gases, the average surface temperature would increase an additional 2°C by 2100 thanks to the natural inertia of Earth's climate system. Instead, our goal is to minimize the effects of global warming by changing the ways in which we produce energy, making choices about how to decrease our requirements for energy, and searching for ways to remove CO_2 from the atmosphere and trap it in the oceans or beneath our planet's surface. Confronting global warming is perhaps the greatest challenge to face our civilization in the twenty-first century.

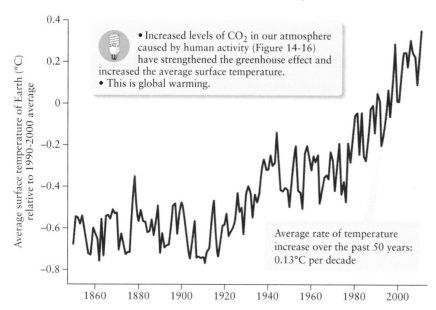

• Increased levels of CO_2 in our atmosphere caused by human activity (Figure 14-16) have strengthened the greenhouse effect and increased the average surface temperature.
• This is global warming.

Average rate of temperature increase over the past 50 years: 0.13°C per decade

Figure 14-17 **Earth's average surface temperature is increasing** The increase in greenhouse gases shown in Figure 14-16 has led to elevated temperatures averaged over our planet's surface. The rate of increase has accelerated over recent decades.

① In convection, a quantity of heated air rises from the radiator...

② ...transfers energy to the surrounding air, cooling off in the process...

28°C   26°C   25°C   23°C

35°C

21°C

19°C

17°C

16°C

③ ...and sinks to the floor, where it returns to the radiator to start the process all over again.

Figure 14-18 **A convection current**
A continuous circulating flow forms when warm air rises, forcing the air above it to move out of the way and then downward somewhere else.

Convection

You probably learned long ago that "hot air rises." It does, and the rising air carries energy with it from one region to another in a process called convection. Figure 14-18 shows a *convection current* in a room: a continuously circulating flow that forms when rising air forces the air above it to move out of the way and then downward somewhere else.

Convection is possible because fluids (gases and liquids) expand when heated. As a region of fluid expands it becomes less dense than its surroundings, and so is buoyed up according to Archimedes' principle (Section 11-8). The hot air "floats" in cooler air, and the cooler air sinks.

Convection plays an important role in driving motions in the atmosphere. People who live near the coasts of large bodies of water often experience a breeze that blows toward the shore in late afternoon and toward the water in early morning (Figure 14-19). Because the specific heat of land is much lower than the specific heat of water, the land heats up and cools down more quickly than the water. Especially when it is hot and the

Late afternoon

Return flow

Warm

Cool

Sea breeze

Early morning

Return flow

Cool

Warm

Land breeze

Figure 14-19 **Seaside convection**
Because the specific heat of land is much lower than the specific heat of water, land heats up and cools down more quickly than the water. This creates onshore sea breezes in late afternoon and offshore land breezes during early morning.

sky is clear, the temperature of the land becomes higher than the temperature of the water as the day progresses; the air above the land gets warmer and less dense. As this warm air rises, it is replaced by cooler air from above the water, resulting in an onshore, or sea breeze. In the early morning, after the land and the air above it have cooled to a temperature below the temperature of the water, air rises above the relatively warmer water, and cooler air from above the land flows to replace it. The result is an offshore, or land breeze.

Conduction

Perhaps you've made the mistake of touching the handle of a metal spoon that has been resting in a pot of soup on the stove. Even though the handle is touching neither the stove nor the soup, it can get hot enough to hurt your fingers if you touch it. A physical connection to the source of the heat exists, of course: The end you hold is connected to the other end of the spoon, which is in the soup, which is touching the pan, which is touching the stove.

The temperature of an object is a measure of the average kinetic energy of its constituent particles. The energetic particles of the hot soup can collide with particles in the end of the spoon in the liquid. As those collisions impart some of the soup's energy to the spoon, that end of the spoon gets hotter. That increased energy gets passed along the spoon, from atom to atom, as collisions between metal atoms occur. Through this process of conduction, the end of the spoon farthest from the soup eventually will also be hot.

Figure 14-20 shows an idealized situation in which conduction takes place. The cylinder of length L and cross-sectional area A is in thermal contact at one end with a hot region at temperature T_H and in thermal contact at the other end with a cold region at temperature T_C. Experiment shows that the rate of heat transfer is proportional to the temperature difference $T_H - T_C$ (the greater the temperature difference, the more rapidly heat flows). The rate of heat transfer is also greater if the cylinder is short (L is small) and wide (A is large). We can put these observations together into a single equation:

(1) The rate H of heat transfer through the cylinder is proportional to the temperature difference $T_H - T_C$.

(2) The rate of heat transfer through the cylinder is greater when its length L is small and its cross-sectional area A is large.

Figure 14-20 **Conduction** The rate of heat exchange by conduction between two objects depends on the temperature difference as well as on the cross-sectional area and length of the contact region between them.

Rate of heat transfer H in conduction = quantity of heat Q that flows divided by the time Δt it takes to flow

Temperature difference of the two places between which heat flows

Rate of energy flow in conduction
(14-23)

$$H = \frac{Q}{\Delta t} = k \frac{A}{L} (T_H - T_C)$$

Thermal conductivity of the material through which the heat flows

Cross-sectional area and length of the material through which the heat flows

The quantity k, called the **thermal conductivity**, is a constant that depends on the material of which the cylinder is made. The units of $H = Q/\Delta t$ are watts (1 W = 1 J/s), so the units of k are watts per meter per kelvin ($W \cdot m^{-1} \cdot K^{-1}$). Table 14-5 lists the thermal conductivity of various substances. A good thermal *conductor* has a high value of k; the thermal conductivity of aluminum, for example, is 235 $W \cdot m^{-1} \cdot K^{-1}$. Materials that are poor thermal conductors—those that make good thermal *insulators*—have k values less than 1 $W \cdot m^{-1} \cdot K^{-1}$. You can actually feel the difference between thermal conductors and thermal insulators. If you pick up a room-temperature aluminum rod ($k = 235$ $W \cdot m^{-1} \cdot K^{-1}$) with one hand and a room-temperature wooden stick ($k = 0.12$ $W \cdot m^{-1} \cdot K^{-1}$) of the same size with the other hand, the aluminum rod will feel colder. Both objects are at the same temperature (which is lower than the temperature of your hand), but the much higher thermal conductivity of the aluminum means that heat can flow into it from your hand at a faster rate.

Table 14-5 shows that the thermal conductivity of air is relatively low. This small value makes air, in particular air trapped between other materials, a good insulator. Most animals rely on air trapped between fur or feathers to slow the rate of heat loss in cold conditions. This phenomenon is even more developed in polar bears. The hair that makes up their fur is hollow; the air trapped within the hair shafts makes it a good thermal insulator. Clothing, particularly that made from cotton, wool, and other woven cloth, keeps us warm primarily because of the air trapped between the fibers. Animal

Go to Picture It 14-4 for more practice dealing with thermal conductivity

Table 14-5 Thermal Conductivities

Material	Thermal Conductivity k ($W \cdot m^{-1} \cdot K^{-1}$)	Material	Thermal Conductivity k ($W \cdot m^{-1} \cdot K^{-1}$)
air	0.024	hydrogen	0.168
aluminum	235	nitrogen	0.024
brick	0.9	plywood	0.13
copper	401	sand (dry)	0.35
cotton	0.03	silver	429
earth (dry)	1.5	steel	46
human fat	0.2	styrofoam	0.033
fiberglass	0.04	water	0.58
glass (window)	0.96	wood (white pine)	0.12
granite	1.7 − 4.0	wool	0.04
gypsum (plaster) board	0.17		

fat is also a good insulator. A typical value of thermal conductivity for human fat is $0.2 \ W \cdot m^{-1} \cdot K^{-1}$, which is about the same as whale blubber and nearly a third smaller than the value of water ($k = 0.58 \ W \cdot m^{-1} \cdot K^{-1}$). That's one reason why blubber is so important to marine mammals in frigid polar waters.

Example 14-10 Heat Loss Through a Window

Windows are a major source of heat loss from a house. That's because of the materials typically used in construction, glass has one of the highest thermal conductivities. Determine the rate of heat loss for a house on an evening when the temperatures of the outer and inner surfaces of the windows are 14.0°C and 15.0°C, respectively. Take the total window area of the house to be 28.0 m² and the thickness of the windows to be 3.80 mm.

Set Up
The rate of heat flow H through all of the windows combined is the same as if there were a single window with area $A = 28.0 \ m^2$ and thickness $L = 3.80 \ mm = 3.80 \times 10^{-3} \ m$. We use Equation 14-23 to calculate the value of H.

Rate of energy flow in conduction:

$$H = k\frac{A}{L}(T_H - T_C) \qquad (14\text{-}23)$$

Solve
Substitute values into Equation 14-23.

From Table 14-5, the thermal conductivity of window glass is $k = 0.96 \ W \cdot m^{-1} \cdot K^{-1}$. The rate of energy flow through the windows is

$$H = k\frac{A}{L}(T_H - T_C)$$

$$= (0.96 \ W \cdot m^{-1} \cdot K^{-1})\left(\frac{28.0 \ m^2}{3.80 \times 10^{-3} \ m}\right)(15.0°C - 14.0°C)$$

$$= 7.1 \times 10^3 \ W = 7.1 \ kW$$

(Recall that a temperature difference of 1.0°C is the same as a temperature difference of 1.0 K.)

Reflect

To maintain the interior of the house at the same temperature, energy has to be provided to the interior by the heating system at a rate of 7.1×10^3 W or 7.1 kW. To put that into perspective, a typical microwave oven or portable hair dryer requires about 1 kW of power to operate. So keeping this house warm with electric heat will require the same amount of electric power as seven microwave ovens or seven hair dryers running continuously.

One way to keep heating costs down is to replace the windows in this house with *dual-pane* or *triple-pane* windows. These windows have two or three sheets of glass separated by a gap of 1 to 2 cm, with gas filling the gap. The greater thickness of glass increases the value of L in Equation 14-23, and the gas between the panes reduces the overall thermal conductivity k.

? Got the Concept? 14-7 Which Plate Is Which?

The photograph in Figure 14-21 was taken 30 s after identical ice cubes were placed on each of two black plates. The plates are the same size and were initially at the same temperature. Which of the following is the most likely composition of the two plates? (a) Left-hand plate is wood, right-hand plate is aluminum; (b) left-hand plate is aluminum, right-hand plate is wood; (c) left-hand plate is brick, right-hand plate is glass; (d) left-hand plate is glass, right-hand plate is brick; (e) not enough information to decide.

Figure 14-21 **Melting ice cubes** An ice cube placed on the left-hand plate melts more rapidly than one placed on the right-hand plate. What does this tell you about the compositions of the two plates?

Take-Home Message for Section 14-7

✔ Heat transfer from one place or object to another can occur through three processes: radiation, convection, and conduction.

✔ In radiation, energy flows from one object to a cooler one in the form of electromagnetic waves. The rate at which an object emits energy in the form of radiation is proportional to its surface area and to the fourth power of its Kelvin temperature.

✔ In convection, energy is carried through a liquid or gas by the motion of that liquid or gas.

✔ In conduction, energy flows within an object through collisions between the particles that make up that object. The rate of heat flow through an object by conduction depends on the dimensions of the object and on the temperature difference between its ends.

Key Terms

absolute zero	fusion	phase diagram
Boltzmann constant	global warming	radiation
British thermal unit	greenhouse effect	root-mean-square speed
calorie	greenhouse gas	(rms speed)
Celsius scale	heat	specific heat
coefficient of linear expansion	ideal gas	Stefan-Boltzmann constant
coefficient of volume expansion	ideal gas constant	sublimation
condensation	ideal gas law	temperature
conduction	internal energy	thermal conductivity
convection	kelvin	thermal contact
critical point	Kelvin scale	thermal equilibrium
degree of freedom	latent heat (of fusion or	thermal expansion
deposition	vaporization)	thermodynamics
emissivity	mean free path	thermometer
equation of state	mole	triple point
equipartition theorem	phase	vaporization
Fahrenheit scale	phase change	zeroth law of thermodynamics

Chapter Summary

Topic	Equation or Figure

Temperature and thermal equilibrium: The temperature of an object is a measure of the kinetic energy of its molecules. Two objects are in thermal equilibrium (so no energy flows from one to the other) if and only if they are at the same temperature. We use both the Celsius and Kelvin temperature scales; on the Kelvin scale, zero temperature is absolute zero.

Thermometer, temperature T_1

Object, temperature T_2

Thermometer and object are both at the same intermediate temperature T_{final}; they are in thermal equilibrium.

(Figure 14-2)

Ideal gases: In an ideal gas, there are no interactions between molecules of the gas. The ideal gas law relates the pressure, volume, and Kelvin temperature of the gas; it can be expressed in terms of either the number of molecules or the number of moles.

Volume occupied by the gas   Number of molecules present in the gas

Pressure of an ideal gas $pV = NkT$ Temperature of the gas on the Kelvin scale   (14-6)

Boltzmann constant

Volume occupied by the gas   Number of moles present in the gas

Pressure of an ideal gas $pV = nRT$ Temperature of the gas on the Kelvin scale   (14-7)

Ideal gas constant

Molecular motion in an ideal gas: The average translational kinetic energy of a molecule of the gas is directly proportional to the Kelvin temperature T. The root-mean-square molecular speed is proportional to the square root of T. If the gas molecules contain more than one atom, there can also be energy in the vibration or rotation of the molecules.

Average translational kinetic energy of a molecule in an ideal gas   Average value of the square of a gas molecule's speed   Temperature of the gas on the Kelvin scale

$$K_{\text{translational, average}} = \frac{1}{2} m(v^2)_{\text{average}} = \frac{3}{2}kT$$ (14-13)

Mass of a single gas molecule   Boltzmann constant

Root-mean-square speed of a molecule in an ideal gas   Boltzmann constant

$$v_{\text{rms}} = \sqrt{\frac{3kT}{m}}$$ Temperature of the gas on the Kelvin scale   (14-15)

Mass of a single gas molecule

Thermal expansion: The length of a solid object changes with temperature, as does the volume of a solid or liquid. In most cases the dimensions increase with increasing temperature; liquid water between 0°C and 4°C is an exception.

Change in the length of an object | Length of the object before the temperature change

$$\Delta L = \alpha L_0 \Delta T \tag{14-18}$$

Coefficient of linear expansion of the substance of which the object is made | Temperature change of the object that causes the length change

Change in the volume of a quantity of substance | Volume of the substance before the temperature change

$$\Delta V = \beta V_0 \Delta T \tag{14-19}$$

Coefficient of volume expansion of the substance | Temperature change of the substance that causes the volume change

Heat and temperature change: Heat is energy that flows from one place to another due to a temperature difference. If there is no change in the phase of an object, heat flow into or out of the object causes a temperature change ΔT.

Quantity of heat that flows into (if $Q > 0$) or out of ($Q < 0$) an object | Specific heat of the substance of which the object is made

$$Q = mc\Delta T \tag{14-20}$$

Temperature change of the object that results from the heat flow

Mass of the object

Heat and phase change: Solid, liquid, and gas are the different possible phases of a substance. At a given pressure, there is a specific temperature at which a substance can change from one phase to another. Each phase change requires heat to flow into or out of the substance. For one particular combination of pressure and temperature, called the triple point, the three phases can coexist.

Quantity of heat that flows into or out of a quantity of substance to cause a phase change | Use + sign if heat flows into the substance; use − sign if heat flows out of the substance.

$$Q = \pm mL \tag{14-21}$$

Latent heat for the phase change

Mass of the substance

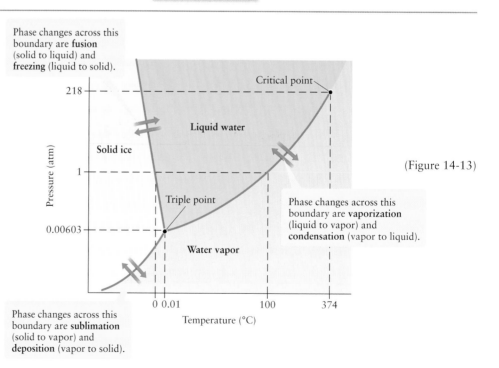

Phase changes across this boundary are **fusion** (solid to liquid) and **freezing** (liquid to solid).

Phase changes across this boundary are **vaporization** (liquid to vapor) and **condensation** (vapor to liquid).

Phase changes across this boundary are **sublimation** (solid to vapor) and **deposition** (vapor to solid).

(Figure 14-13)

Radiation, convection, and conduction: Energy can flow from place to place by radiation (electromagnetic waves), convection (circulation of a liquid or gas), or conduction (direct contact between solid objects). The rate at which an object emits energy by radiation is proportional to the fourth power of the object's Kelvin temperature. The rate at which energy flows through an object by conduction depends on the temperature difference between the ends of the object, the dimensions of the object, and the object's thermal conductivity.

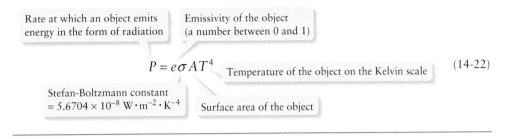

Rate at which an object emits energy in the form of radiation

Emissivity of the object (a number between 0 and 1)

$$P = e\sigma AT^4$$

Temperature of the object on the Kelvin scale

(14-22)

Stefan-Boltzmann constant
$= 5.6704 \times 10^{-8} \ \mathrm{W \cdot m^{-2} \cdot K^{-4}}$

Surface area of the object

① In convection, a quantity of heated air rises from the radiator...

② ...transfers energy to the surrounding air, cooling off in the process...

28°C 26°C 25°C 23°C

35°C

21°C

(Figure 14-18)

19°C

17°C

16°C

③ ...and sinks to the floor, where it returns to the radiator to start the process all over again.

Rate of heat transfer H in conduction = quantity of heat Q that flows divided by the time Δt it takes to flow

Temperature difference of the two places between which heat flows

$$H = \frac{Q}{\Delta t} = k\frac{A}{L}\left(T_\mathrm{H} - T_\mathrm{C}\right)$$

(14-23)

Thermal conductivity of the material through which the heat flows

Cross-sectional area and length of the material through which the heat flows

Answer to What do you think? Question

(c) Almost every substance expands in response to a temperature increase, so we expect that the chamber walls will expand. If they expanded as much or more than the fluid inside the chambers, we would expect that the pressure of the fluid against the chamber walls would stay the same or decrease. Because the pressure increases, it must be that the chamber walls expand by a smaller amount than the fluid. A liquid-in-glass thermometer uses the same basic principle: A temperature increase makes the liquid expand more than the glass tube that contains the liquid, so the liquid level rises in the tube.

Answers to Got the Concept? Questions

14-1 (c), (b), (a) To compare these three temperatures, convert them all to the Kelvin scale. Temperature (b) is -13°C or, with the second of Equations 14-2, $T_\mathrm{K} = T_\mathrm{C} + 273.15 = (-13) + 273.15 = 260$ K. Temperature (c) is -13°F, which from the first of Equations 14-1 is $T_\mathrm{C} = \frac{5}{9}(T_\mathrm{F} - 32) = \frac{5}{9}(-13 - 32) = \frac{5}{9}(-45) = -25$°C and from the second of Equations 14-2 is $T_\mathrm{K} = T_\mathrm{C} + 273.15 = (-25) + 273.15 = 248$ K. So temperature (c) (248 K) is coldest, temperature (b) (260 K) is second coldest, and temperature (a) (280 K) is warmest.

14-2 (a) the same, (b) less, (c) greater, (d) greater. The average translational kinetic energy per molecule $K_\mathrm{translational,\ average} = (3/2)kT$ (Equation 14-13) depends on the temperature but not on the kind of molecule, so this is the same for helium as for oxygen in air at a given temperature. Because oxygen is a diatomic molecule, it can rotate as well as translate, and so the average energy per O_2 molecule is about $(5/2)kT$; helium is monatomic, so it has only translational kinetic energy with an average value of $(3/2)kT$ per molecule. The rms speed

$v_{rms} = \sqrt{3kT/m}$ (Equation 14-15) is greater for helium because helium has a smaller mass per molecule m. Finally, the mean free path λ (Equation 14-16) is inversely proportional to the square of the molecular radius r, so λ is greater for helium than for oxygen.

14-3 (c) The statement of the problem tells us that if the initial length of one side of the cube is L, the change in length due to the temperature increase is $\Delta L = 0.0010L$. From Equation 14-18, $\Delta L = \alpha L \Delta T$; this says that $\alpha L \Delta T = 0.0010L$, and so $\alpha \Delta T = 0.0010$. For solids the coefficient of *volume* expansion β equals 3α, so $\beta \Delta T = 3\alpha \Delta T = 0.0030$. So if the initial volume of the cube is V, the change in its volume due to the temperature increase is given by Equation 14-19: $\Delta V = \beta V \Delta T = (\beta \Delta T)V = 0.0030V$: That is, the volume increases by 0.0030. To check this, note that if the length of each side changes by $\Delta L = 0.0010L$, the new length is $L + \Delta L = L + 0.0010L = 1.0010L$. The volume of the cube then changes from L^3 to $(1.0010L)^3 = (1.0010)^3 L^3$. You can use your calculator to show that $(1.0010)^3 = 1.0030$, so the new volume is $1.0030L^3$—that is, the volume has increased by 0.0030 of its initial volume L^3.

14-4 (a) When two objects are made of the same substance, the final temperature is closer to the initial temperature of the more massive object. Let's check this conclusion using Equation 14-20. For the two objects, this equation says $Q_A = m_A c_A \Delta T_A$ and $Q_B = m_B c_B \Delta T_B$. If the two objects exchange energy with each other only, $Q_A = -Q_B$ (see Example 14-5), so $m_A c_A \Delta T_A = -m_B c_B \Delta T_B$. The two objects are made of the same substance and so have the same specific heat ($c_A = c_B$); thus our equation simplifies to $m_A \Delta T_A = -m_B \Delta T_B$. Since m_A is much greater than m_B, for this equation to be true it must be that ΔT_A is much smaller in absolute value than ΔT_B. In other words, the temperature of A changes much less than does the temperature of B, and the final temperature is closer to the initial temperature of A.

14-5 (a) When two objects have the same mass, the final temperature is closer to the initial temperature of the object with the greater specific heat. Let's check this conclusion using Equation 14-20. For the two objects this equation says $Q_A = m_A c_A \Delta T_A$ and $Q_B = m_B c_B \Delta T_B$. If the two objects exchange energy with each other only, $Q_A = -Q_B$ (see Example 14-5), so $m_A c_A \Delta T_A = -m_B c_B \Delta T_B$. The two objects have the same mass ($m_A = m_B$), so our equation simplifies to $c_A \Delta T_A = -c_B \Delta T_B$. Since c_A is much greater than c_B, for this equation to be true it must be that ΔT_A is much smaller in absolute value than ΔT_B. In other words, the temperature of A changes much less than does the temperature of B, and the final temperature is closer to the initial temperature of A.

14-6 (d), (b), (c), (a), (e) The specific heat of a substance (listed in Table 14-3) is the amount of energy needed to raise the temperature of 1 kg of substance by 1°C (or 1 K). This is 2093 $J \cdot kg^{-1} \cdot K^{-1}$ for ice, 4186 $J \cdot kg^{-1} \cdot K^{-1}$ for water, and 2009 $J \cdot kg^{-1} \cdot K^{-1}$ for steam. The latent heat of fusion and the latent heat of vaporization are, respectively, the amounts of energy needed to melt and vaporize 1 kg of substance at its melting and boiling temperatures. From Table 14-4, the values of these for water are $L_F = 3.34 \times 10^5$ J/kg and $L_V = 2.26 \times 10^6$ J/kg. So the rank of the energies from largest to smallest is (d) energy to boil 1 kg (2.26×10^6 J), (b) energy to melt 1 kg (3.34×10^5 J), (c) energy to raise the temperature of water by 1°C (4186 J), (a) energy to raise the temperature of ice by 1°C (2093 J), and (e) energy to raise the temperature of steam by 1°C (2009 J).

14-7 (b) The ice cube on the left melts much more rapidly because it is placed on a plate with a high thermal conductivity. Table 4-5 shows that the thermal conductivity of aluminum ($k = 235$ $W \cdot m^{-1} \cdot K^{-1}$) is much greater than that of wood ($k = 0.12$ $W \cdot m^{-1} \cdot K^{-1}$), so this is a possibility. By contrast, the thermal conductivities of brick ($k = 0.9$ $W \cdot m^{-1} \cdot K^{-1}$) and glass ($k = 0.96$ $W \cdot m^{-1} \cdot K^{-1}$) are almost identical, so we wouldn't expect much difference between the melting rate of ice cubes placed on a brick plate and a glass plate.

Questions and Problems

In a few problems, you are given more data than you actually need; in a few other problems, you are required to supply data from your general knowledge, outside sources, or informed estimate. Interpret as significant all digits in numerical values that have trailing zeros and no decimal points. For all problems, use $g = 9.80$ m/s^2 for the free-fall acceleration due to gravity. Neglect friction and air resistance unless instructed to do otherwise.

• Basic, single-concept problem
•• Intermediate-level problem, may require synthesis of concepts and multiple steps
••• Challenging problem
SSM *Solution is in Student Solutions Manual*

Conceptual Questions

1. •The phrase "temperature measures kinetic energy" is somewhat difficult to understand and can be seen as contradictory. Give a few reasons why the explanation actually makes sense and a few reasons why it seems contradictory.

2. •If ideal gas A is thermally in contact with ideal gas B for a significant time, what can you say (if anything) about the following variables: P_A versus P_B, V_A versus V_B, and T_A versus T_B? (P, V, and T stand for pressure, volume, and temperature, respectively.)

3. •A skunk is threatened by a great horned owl and emits its foul-smelling fluid in order to get away. Will the odor be more easily detected on a day when it is cooler or when it is warmer? Explain your answer. SSM

4. •A careful physics student is reading about the concept of temperature and has what she thinks is a bright idea. While reading the text, she discovers that the Celsius temperature scale and the Kelvin temperature scale both have the *same* increments for equal temperature differences. However, the Fahrenheit scale was described as having *larger* increments for the same temperature differences. From this information, the student determines that Celsius (or Kelvin) thermometers will always be *shorter* than Fahrenheit thermometers. Explain the parts of her idea that are valid and the parts that are not.

5. •A physics student has decided that reading the textbook is very time-consuming and has decided that she will simply attempt the problems in the book without any prior background reading. During the completion of one problem that

involves a temperature conversion, the student concludes that the answer is $-508°F$. Discuss the validity of the answer.

6. •Search the Internet for *temperature scales*. How many different temperature scales can you find?

7. •The average normal human body temperature falls within the range of $37 \pm 0.5°C$ or $98.6 \pm 0.9°F$. Discuss (a) the difficulties in determining an exact value for normal body temperature and (b) why there is a range of values.

8. •You have probably heard the old saying: "It ain't the heat, it's the humidity that's so unbearable." Discuss what this *really* means and try to include some reference to the definitions of heat and temperature that we have established in this chapter.

9. •(a) Which is hotter: a kilogram of boiling water or a kilogram of steam? (b) Which one can cause a more severe burn? Why? Assume the steam is at the lowest temperature possible for the corresponding pressure. SSM

10. •Describe some possible uses for the following thermometers whose temperature ranges are provided in kelvins.

Thermometer A: 200–270 K
Thermometer B: 230–370 K
Thermometer C: 300–550 K
Thermometer D: 300–315 K

11. •"Temperature is the physical quantity that is measured with a thermometer." Discuss the limitations of this working definition.

12. •A very old mercury thermometer is discovered in a physics lab. All the markings on the glass have worn away. How could you recalibrate the thermometer?

13. •Using the concepts of heat, temperature changes, and heat capacity, give a simplistic explanation of the global demographic factoid that 90% of the world's population lives within 100 km of a coastline.

14. ••In Section 14-3, we show that $K_{translational,average} = (3/2)kT$. The result is valid for a three-dimensional collection of atoms. (a) Discuss any changes in the formula that would correspond to a one-dimensional system. (b) What change would be necessary for a 10-dimensional space?

15. •In warm regions, highway repair work is often completed in the summer months. Describe why this is thermodynamically sound.

16. •Why are some sidewalks often formed in small segments, separated by a small gap between the segments?

17. •Older mechanical thermostats use a bimetallic strip to open and close a mercury switch that turns the heat on or off. A bimetallic strip is made of two different metals fastened together. One side is made of one metal, and the other side is made of a different metal. Describe how a bimetallic strip functions in such a thermostat. SSM

18. •There are several different units besides the joule used to measure thermal energy. (a) List the various units associated with thermal energy and (b) indicate in which area of science or technology they are used.

19. •The ideal gas law can be written as $PV = NkT$ or $PV = nRT$. (a) Explain the different contexts in which you might use one or the other, and (b) define all the variables and constants.

20. •Explain the term *latent* as it applies to phase changes.

21. •Describe the sequence of thermodynamic steps that a very cold block of ice (below 0°C) will undergo as it transforms into steam at a temperature above 100°C.

22. •Write a brief definition of the three different modes of heat transfer: radiation, convection, and conduction.

23. •Describe how convection causes hot air to rise in a room.

24. •Explain how a light material, such as fiberglass insulation, makes an effective barrier to keep a home warm in the winter and cool in the summer.

25. •State the zeroth law of thermodynamics and explain how it is used in physics.

Multiple-Choice Questions

26. •Two objects that have different sizes, masses, and temperatures come into close contact with each other. Thermal energy is transferred
   A. from the larger object to the smaller object.
   B. from the object that has more mass to the one that has less mass.
   C. from the object that has the higher temperature to the object that has the lower temperature.
   D. from the object that has the lower temperature to the object that has the higher temperature.
   E. back and forth between the two objects until they come to equilibrium.

27. •If you halve the value of the root-mean-square velocity or v_{rms} of an ideal gas, the absolute temperature must be
   A. reduced to one-half its original value.
   B. reduced to one-quarter its original value.
   C. unchanged.
   D. increased to twice its original value.
   E. increased to four times its original value. SSM

28. •Two gases each have the same number of molecules, same volume, and same atomic radius, but the atomic mass of gas B is twice that of gas A. Compare the mean free paths.
   A. The mean free path of gas A is four times larger than gas B.
   B. The mean free path of gas A is four times smaller than gas B.
   C. The mean free path of gas A is the same as gas B.
   D. The mean free path of gas A is two times larger than gas B.
   E. The mean free path of gas A is two times smaller than gas B.

29. •If you heat a thin, circular ring so that its temperature is twice what it was originally, the ring's hole
   A. becomes larger.
   B. becomes smaller by an unknown amount.
   C. remains the same size.
   D. becomes four times smaller.
   E. becomes two times smaller.

30. •If you add heat to water at 0°C, the water will decrease in volume until it reaches
   A. 1°C.
   B. 2°C.
   C. 3°C.
   D. 4°C.
   E. 100°C.

31. •Two objects that are not initially in thermal equilibrium are placed in close contact. After a while,
   A. the specific heats of both objects will be equal.
   B. the thermal conductivity of each object will be the same.
   C. the temperature of the cooler object will rise the same amount that the hotter one drops.
   D. the temperature of each object will be the same.
   E. the temperature of the cooler object will rise twice as much as the temperature of the hotter one drops. SSM

32. •When a substance goes directly from a solid state to a gaseous form, the process is known as
   A. vaporization.
   B. fusion.
   C. melting.
   D. condensation.
   E. sublimation.

33. •Which heat transfer process(es) is (are) important in the transfer of energy from the Sun to Earth?
   A. radiation
   B. convection
   C. conduction
   D. conduction and radiation
   E. conduction, radiation, and convection

34. •A clay pot at room temperature is placed in a kiln, and the pot's temperature doubles. How much more heat per second is the pot radiating when hot compared to when cool?
   A. 2 times
   B. 4 times
   C. 8 times
   D. 16 times
   E. 32 times

35. •If the thickness of a uniform wall is doubled, the rate of heat transfer through the wall is
   A. quadrupled.
   B. doubled.
   C. halved.
   D. unchanged.
   E. one-fourth as much. SSM

Estimation/Numerical Analysis

36. •Estimate the hottest and coldest day on Earth for your location and for the planet as a whole.

37. •Estimate the largest temperature drop in a 24-h interval for the last 100 years of weather records in the United States.

38. •Estimate the hottest and coldest ocean temperatures.

39. •Estimate the difference in annual temperature changes in a coastal region (such as the Seattle area) compared to temperature changes in a landlocked state (such as Kansas or Nebraska).

40. •Estimate how much heat is required to melt a typical ice cube taken from your freezer.

41. •Estimate the time you have before you succumb to hypothermia if you fall through the ice into a lake. SSM

42. •Estimate the time required for a kettle of water to boil on a natural gas stove.

43. •Estimate how much more heat a person loses on a cold winter day when she doesn't wear a hat compared to when she does wear one.

44. •If 100 physics students each give off 100 W as they sit in the classroom taking an exam, estimate the temperature increase of the room during the hour-long test. Assume that 1% of the heat goes into raising the air temperature.

45. •In the final stages in the life of a star (such as our Sun), the radiated power decreases by one-half. Estimate the temperature change that would accompany such a shift.

46. ••**Biology** Although many mechanisms help large mammals (such as elephants) keep cool in hot climates, the size of ears is a big factor. The Asian elephant's ears are about 20% smaller than the ears of the African elephant. If the radiant loss of heat through the billions of capillaries in elephant ears is the primary means of staying cool, estimate the relative temperature difference between the territory of Asian elephants versus the territory of African elephants.

47. •Estimate the fraction of heat that is given off by radiation versus conduction when a person lies down in the snow. SSM

48. •A 1.0-g sample of metal is slowly heated. The temperature increase for each increment of heat added is tabulated in the table. Plot a graph for the data and predict the specific heat for this common metal. If the measurements are ±10%, make a guess as to the type of metal it might be.

Heat (J)	Temperature change (°C)
0	0
3.9	10
7.9	20
20	50
40	100

49. •Ordinary ice (frozen H_2O) is cold, dry ice (solid CO_2) is very cold, liquid nitrogen is extremely cold, and liquid helium is almost unimaginably cold! The cost of each is approximately exponentially proportional to the temperature at which they change states. The temperature of dry ice is −78.5°C, and it costs about $1/kg. The temperature of liquid nitrogen is −196°C, and it costs about $2/kg. The temperature of liquid helium is −268°C, and it costs about $100/kg. (a) Predict the cost of 1 kg of ordinary ice. Before you make the estimate, consider the most appropriate temperature scale to use! (b) Check the price of a bag or block of ice at your local grocery or convenience store. How close is your estimate?

50. •(a) Plot water density as a function of temperature for the data listed in the table. (b) Using the graph, discuss how changes in water's density affect the freezing of lakes in the winter.

Density (g/cm³)	Temperature (°C)
0.99990	8.0
0.99996	6.0
1.00000	4.0
0.99996	2.0
0.99988	0.0

Problems

14-1 A knowledge of thermodynamics is essential for understanding almost everything around you—including your own body

14-2 Temperature is a measure of the energy within a substance

51. •Convert the following temperatures:
   A. 28°C = _____ °F
   B. 58°F = _____ °C
   C. 128 K = _____ °F
   D. 78°F = _____ K
   E. 37°C = _____ °F

52. •Convert the following temperatures and comment on any physical significance of each:
   A. 0°C = _____ °F
   B. 212°F = _____ °C

C. 273 K = _____ °F

D. 68°F = _____ K

53. •Explain the physical significance of the value −273.15°C.

54. •Starting from $T_C = 5/9(T_F - 32)$ (the first of Equations 14-1), derive a formula for converting from °C to °F (the second of Equations 14-1).

55. •The highest temperature ever recorded on Earth is 56.7°C, in Death Valley, California, in 1913. The lowest temperature on record is −89.2°C, measured at Vostok Research Station in Antarctica in 1983. Convert these extreme temperatures to °F and kelvin.

56. •In adults the normal range for oral (under the tongue) temperature is approximately 36.7°C to 37.0°C. Calculate the range and differences in °F and in kelvins.

57. •Explain why there must exist a numerical value that is the same on the Celsius scale as on the Fahrenheit scale. Show the calculation that yields this special value. SSM

58. •A thermally isolated system has a temperature of T_A. The temperature of a second isolated system is T_B. When the two systems are placed in thermal contact with each other, they come to an equilibrium temperature of T_C. Describe all the possibilities regarding the relative magnitudes of T_A and T_B when (a) $T_C < T_A$, and (b) $T_C > T_A$.

14-3 In a gas, the relationship between temperature and molecular kinetic energy is a simple one

59. •One mole of an ideal gas is at a pressure of 1.00 atm and occupies a volume of 1.00 L. (a) What is the temperature of the gas? (b) Convert the temperature to °C and °F.

60. •Calculate the energy of a sample of 1.00 mol of ideal oxygen (O_2) gas molecules at a temperature of 300 K. Assume that the molecules are free to rotate, vibrate, and move in three dimensions.

61. •A 55.0-g sample of a certain gas occupies 4.13 L at 20.0°C and 10.0 atm pressure. What is the gas? SSM

62. •The boiling point of water at 1.00 atm is 373 K. What is the volume occupied by water gas due to evaporation of 10.0 g of liquid water at 1.00 atm and 373 K?

63. •An ideal gas is confined to a container at a temperature of 300 K. What is the average kinetic energy of an atom of the gas?

64. •Calculate v_{rms} for a helium atom if 1.00 mol of the gas is confined to a 1.00-L container at a pressure of 10.0 atm.

65. •Two gases present in the atmosphere are water vapor (H_2O) and oxygen (O_2). What is the ratio of their rms speeds? SSM

66. •State-of-the-art vacuum equipment can attain pressures as low as 7.0×10^{-11} Pa. Suppose that a chamber contains helium at that pressure and at room temperature (300 K). Estimate the mean free path for helium in the chamber. Assume the diameter of a helium atom is 1.0×10^{-10} m.

67. •The mean free path for O_2 molecules at a temperature of 300 K and at 1.00 atm pressure is 7.10×10^{-8} m. Use this data to estimate the size of an O_2 molecule. SSM

14-4 Most substances expand when the temperature increases

68. •Calculate the temperature change needed for a cylinder of gold to increase in length by 0.1%.

69. •Calculate the coefficient of linear expansion for a 10.0-m-long metal bar that shortens by 0.500 cm when the temperature drops from 25.0°C to 10.0°C.

70. •By how much would a 1.00-m-long aluminum rod increase in length if its temperature were raised 8.00°C?

71. •A silver pin is exactly 5.00 cm long when its temperature is 180°C. How long is the pin when it cools to 28.0°C? SSM

72. •A sheet of lead has an 8.00-cm-diameter hole drilled through it while at a temperature of 8.00°C. What will be the diameter of the hole if the sheet is heated to 208.00°C?

73. ••A thin sheet of copper 80.00 cm by 100.00 cm at 28.0°C is heated to 228°C. What will be the new area of the sheet?

74. ••A sheet of copper at a temperature of 0°C has dimensions of 20.0 cm by 30.0 cm. (a) Calculate the dimensions of the sheet when the temperature rises to 45.0°C. (b) By what percent does the area of the sheet of copper change?

75. ••A 5.00-m-long cylinder of solid aluminum has a radius of 2.00 cm. (a) If the cylinder is initially at a temperature of 5.00°C, how much will the length change when the temperature rises to 30.0°C? (b) Due to the temperature increase, by how much would the density of the aluminum cylinder change? (c) By what percentage does the volume of the cylinder increase? SSM

76. ••A cube of iron is heated uniformly to 100°C. At that temperature, the volume of the iron is 20.0 cm^3. Find the dimensions of the cube (a) at 100°C and (b) at 20°C.

77. ••A sphere of gold has an initial radius of 1.00 cm when the temperature is 20.0°C. (a) If the temperature is raised to 80.0°C, calculate the new radius of the sphere. (b) What is the percent change in the volume of the sphere?

14-5 Heat is energy that flows due to a temperature difference

78. •What is the specific heat of a 500-g metal sample that rises 4.80°C when 307 J of heat is added to it?

79. •You wish to heat 250 g of water to make a hot cup of coffee. If the water starts at 20.0°C and you want your coffee to be 95.0°C, calculate the minimum amount of heat required. SSM

80. •In a thermodynamically sealed container, 20.0 g of 15.0°C water is mixed with 40.0 g of 60.0°C water. Calculate the final equilibrium temperature of the water.

81. •How much heat is transferred to the environment when the temperature of 2.00 kg of water drops from 88°C to 42°C?

82. •A copper pot has a mass of 1.00 kg and is at 100°C. How much heat must be removed from it to decrease its temperature to precisely 0.00°C?

83. •A lake has a specific heat of 4186 J/(kg·K). If we transferred 1.70×10^{14} J of heat to the lake and warmed the water from 10.0°C to 15.0°C, what is the mass of the water in the lake? Neglect heat released to the surroundings. SSM

84. •Calculate the temperature increase in a 1.00-kg sample of water that results from the conversion of gravitational potential energy directly to heat energy in the world's tallest waterfall, the 807-m-tall *Salto Angel* in Canaima National Park, Venezuela.

85. •A superheated iron bar that has a mass of 5.00 kg absorbs 2.50×10^6 J of heat from a blacksmith's fire. Calculate the temperature increase of the iron.

86. •A 200-g block of ice is at −10.0°C. How much heat must be removed to lower its temperature to −40.0°C?

87. ••A 250-g sample of copper is heated to 100°C and placed into a cup containing 300 g of water initially at 30.0°C. Ignoring the container holding the water, find the final equilibrium temperature of the copper and water, assuming no heat is lost or gained to the environment.

88. ••A 50.0-g calorimeter cup made from aluminum contains 100 g of water. Both the aluminum and the water are at 25.0°C. A 300-g cube of some unknown metal is heated to 150°C and placed into the calorimeter; the final equilibrium temperature for the water, aluminum, and metal sample is 41.0°C. Calculate the specific heat of the unknown metal and make a guess as to its composition.

89. •A hacksaw is used to cut a 20.0-g steel bolt. Each stroke of the saw supplies 30.0 J of energy. How many strokes of the saw will it take to raise the temperature of the bolt from 20.0°C to 80.0°C? Assume none of the energy goes into heating the surroundings. Of course, it will take significantly more than this to also cut the metal! SSM

14-6 Energy must enter or leave an object in order for it to change phase

90. •Calculate the amount of heat required to change 25.0 g of ice at 0°C to 25.0 g of water at 0°C.

91. •How much heat is required to change 25.0 g of ice at −40.0°C to 25.0 g of steam at 140°C?

92. •A sealed container (with negligible heat capacity) holds 30.0 g of 120°C steam. Describe the final state if 100,000 J of heat is removed from the steam.

93. •How much heat is required to melt a 400-g sample of copper that starts at 20.0°C? SSM

94. ••Suppose 20.0 g of ice at −10.0°C is placed into 300 g of water in a 200-g copper calorimeter. If the final temperature of the water and copper calorimeter is 18.0°C, what was the initial common temperature of the water and copper?

95. ••What mass of ice at −20.0°C must be added to 50.0 g of steam at 120°C to end up with water at 40.0°C?

96. •A 60.0-kg ice hockey player is moving at 8.00 m/s when he skids to a stop. If 40% of his kinetic energy goes into melting ice, how much water is created as he comes to a stop? Assume that the surface layer of the ice in the hockey rink has a temperature of 0°C.

97. •You have 50.0 g of iron at 120°C, 60.0 g of copper at 150°C, and 30.0 g of water at 40.0°C. Which of those would melt the most ice, starting at −5.00°C? How much ice does each melt? SSM

14-7 Heat can be transferred by radiation, convection, or conduction

98. •A heated bar of gold radiates at a temperature of 300°C. (a) By what factor does the radiated heat increase if the temperature is increased to 600°C? (b) What if it's increased to 900°C? (c) If the surface area of the gold bar is also doubled, how will the answers be affected?

99. •**Astronomy** An astrophysicist determines the surface temperature of a distant star is 12,000 K. The surface temperature of the Sun is about 5800 K. If the surface temperature of the Sun were to suddenly increase to 12,000 K, by how much would the radiated heat increase?

100. •**Astronomy** A star radiates 3.75 times less heat than our own Sun. What is the ratio of the temperature of the star to the temperature of our Sun?

101. •**Astronomy** A distant star radiates 1000 times more energy than our own Sun, even though the temperature of the star is only 70% of the Sun's. If both stars have an emissivity of 1, estimate the radius of the distant star. Recall, the radius of the Sun is 6.96×10^8 m. SSM

102. ••**Biology** The skin temperature of a nude person is 34.0°C and the surroundings are at 20.0°C. The emissivity of skin is 0.900, and the surface area of the person is 1.50 m². (a) What is the rate at which energy radiates from the person? (b) What is the net energy loss from the body in 1 min by radiation?

103. •Calculate the heat through a glass window that is 30.0 cm × 150 cm in area and 1.20 mm thick. Assume the temperature on the inside of the window is 25.0°C while the outside temperature is 8.00°C. SSM

General Problems

104. •What is the average kinetic energy for an ideal gas made up of diatomic molecules that can move in two dimensions when the temperature is 75.0°F?

105. ••**Astronomy** Is the Sun likely to lose its atomic hydrogen? (a) Calculate the escape velocity for hydrogen atoms from the surface (the *photosphere*) of our Sun. Recall, the radius of the Sun is 6.96×10^8 m. (b) If the root-mean-square speed of the hydrogen atoms were equal to the speed you found in part (a), what would be the temperature of the Sun's photosphere? The mass of a hydrogen atom is 1.68×10^{-27} kg. (c) Given that the actual temperature of the photosphere is 5800 K, is the Sun likely to lose its atomic hydrogen?

106. •**Astronomy** Titan, a satellite of Saturn, has a nitrogen atmosphere with a surface temperature of −179°C and pressure of 1.5 atm. The mass of a nitrogen molecule is 4.7×10^{-26} kg, and we can model it as a sphere of diameter 2.4×10^{-10} m. The average temperature of Earth's atmosphere is about 10°C. (a) What is the density of particles in the atmosphere of Titan? (b) Which has a denser atmosphere, Titan or Earth? Justify your answer by calculating the ratio of the particle density on Titan to the particle density on Earth. (c) What is the average distance that a nitrogen molecule travels between collisions on Titan? How does this result compare with the distance for oxygen calculated in Section 14-3? Is your result reasonable?

107. •A brick wall is composed of 19.0-cm-long bricks ($\alpha = 5.5 \times 10^{-6}$ K^{-1}) and 1.00-cm-long sections of mortar ($\alpha = 8.0 \times 10^{-6}$ K^{-1}) in between the bricks. Describe the expansion effects on a 20.0-m-long section of wall that undergoes a temperature change of 25.0°C. SSM

108. •Derive an approximate formula for the area expansion (ΔA) that a sheet of material undergoes as the temperature changes from T_i to T_f. Assume the linear coefficient of expansion is α for the material.

109. •A 1.00-cm-diameter sphere of copper is placed concentrically over a 0.99-cm-diameter hole in a sheet of aluminum (Figure 14-22). Both the copper and the aluminum start at a temperature of 15.0°C. Describe one set of conditions (if any) in which the copper sphere will pass through the hole in the aluminum.

Figure 14-22   Problem 109

110. •A 20.0-m-long bar of steel expands due to a temperature increase. A 10.0-m-long bar of copper also gets longer due to the same temperature rise. If the two bars were originally separated by a gap of 1.5 cm, calculate the change in temperature and the distances that the steel and copper stretch if the gap is exactly "closed" by the expanding bars. Assume the steel and copper bars are fixed on the ends, as shown in **Figure 14-23**.

Figure 14-23   Problem 110

111. •Suppose a person who lives in a house next to a busy urban freeway attempts to "harness" the sound energy from the nonstop traffic to heat the water in his home. He places a transducer on his roof, "catches" the sound waves, and converts the sound waves into an electrical signal that warms a cistern of water. However, after running the system for 7 days, the 5 kg of water increases in temperature by only 0.01°C! Assuming 100% transfer efficiency, calculate the acoustic power "caught" by the transducer. SSM

112. •**Biology** Susan ordinarily eats 2000 kcal of food per day. If her mass is 60 kg and her height is 1.7 m, her surface area is probably close to 1.7 m². Although the body is only about two-thirds water, we will model it as being all water. (a) Typically, 80% of the calories we consume are converted to heat. If Susan's body has no way of getting rid of the heat produced, by how many degrees Celsius would her body temperature rise in a day? (b) Would this be a noticeable increase? (c) How does her body prevent the increase from happening? (See Table 14.3 as needed.)

113. •Helium condenses at −268.93°C and has a latent heat of vaporization of 21,000 J/kg. If you start with 5.00 g of helium gas at 30.0°C, calculate the amount of heat required to change the sample to liquid helium. The specific heat of helium is 5193 J/(kg·K) at 300 K. SSM

114. ••**Biology** Jane's surface area is approximately 1.5 m². At what rate is heat released from her body when the temperature difference across the skin is 1.00°C? Assume the average thickness of the skin is 1.00 mm.

115. •The Arctic perennial sea ice does not melt during the summer and thus lasts all year. NASA found that the perennial sea ice decreased by 14% between 2004 and 2005. The melted ice covered an area of 720,000 km² (the size of Texas!) and was 3.00 m thick on average. The ice is pure water (not salt water) and is 92% as dense as liquid water. Assume that

the ice was initially at −10.0°C and see Tables 14-3 and 14-4 as needed. (a) How much heat was required to melt the ice? (b) Given that 1.0 gal of gasoline releases 1.3×10^8 J of energy when burned, how many gallons of gasoline contain as much energy as in part (a)? (c) A ton of coal releases around 21.5 GJ = 21.5×10^9 J of energy when burned. How many tons of coal would need to be burned to produce the energy to melt the ice?

116. ••**Sports, Biology** A person can generate about 300 W of power on a treadmill. If the treadmill is inclined at 3.00° and a 70.0-kg man runs at 3.00 m/s for 45.0 min, (a) calculate the percentage of the power output that goes into heating up his body and the percentage that keeps him moving on the treadmill. (b) How much water would that heat evaporate?

117. ••**Biology** A 1.88-m (6 ft 2 in.) man has a mass of 80.0 kg, a body surface area of 2.1 m² and a skin temperature of 30°C. Normally, 80% of the food calories he consumes go to heat, the rest going to mechanical energy. To keep his body's temperature constant, how many food calories should he eat per day if he is in a room at 20°C and he loses heat only through radiation? Does the answer seem reasonable? His emissivity e is 1 because his body radiates almost entirely nonvisible infrared energy, which is not affected by skin pigment. (*Careful*! His body at 30°C radiates into the air at 20°C, but the air also radiates back into his body. The *net* rate of radiation is $P_{net} = P_{body} - P_{air}$.) SSM

118. •**Astronomy** Calculate the total power radiated by our Sun. Assume it is a perfect emitter of radiation ($e = 1$) with a radius of 6.96×10^8 m and a temperature of 5800 K.

119. •••**Biology** You may have noticed that small mammals (such as mice) seem to be constantly eating, whereas some large mammals (such as lions) eat much less frequently. Let us investigate the phenomenon. For simplicity we can model an animal as a sphere. (a) Show that the heat energy stored by an animal is proportional to the cube of its radius, but the rate at which the animal radiates energy away is proportional to the square of its radius. (b) Show that the fraction of the animal's stored energy that it radiates away per second is inversely proportional to the animal's radius. (c) Use the result in part (b) to explain why small animals must eat much more per gram of body weight than very large animals.

120. ••**Astronomy** About 65 million years ago an asteroid struck Earth in the area of the Yucatán Peninsula and wiped out the dinosaurs and many other life forms. Judging from the size of the crater and the effects on Earth, the asteroid was about 10 km in diameter (assumed spherical) and probably had a density of 2.0 g/cm³ (typical of asteroids). Its speed was at least 11 km/s. (a) What is the maximum amount of ocean water (originally at 20°C) that the asteroid could have evaporated if all of its kinetic energy were transferred to the water? Express your answer in kilograms and treat the ocean as though it were freshwater. (b) If the water were formed into a cube, how high would it be? (See Tables 14-3 and 14-4 as needed.)

121. ••A spherical container is constructed from steel and has a radius of 2.00 m at 15.0°C. The container sits in the Sun all day, and its temperature rises to 38.0°C. The container is initially filled completely with water, but it is not sealed. Describe what will happen to the water after the temperature increase.

15

Thermodynamics II

In this chapter, your goals are to:

- (15-1) Explain the general ideas of the laws of thermodynamics.
- (15-2) Define and be able to apply the first law of thermodynamics.
- (15-3) Describe the nature of isobaric, isothermal, adiabatic, and isochoric processes.
- (15-4) Explain why different amounts of heat are required to change the temperature of a gas depending on whether the gas is held at constant temperature or constant pressure.
- (15-5) Define the second law of thermodynamics and its application to heat engines and refrigerators.
- (15-6) Explain the concept of entropy and the circumstances under which entropy changes.

To master this chapter, you should review:

- (6-2) The significance of positive and negative work.
- (14-3) The properties of ideal gases.
- (14-5) The relationship between the quantity of heat added to an object and the resulting temperature change.

15-1 The laws of thermodynamics involve energy and entropy

In Chapter 14 we learned about the zeroth law of thermodynamics, which basically says that the concept of temperature is a useful one. But what are the other laws of thermodynamics, and what do they tell us?

In this chapter we'll begin by learning about the *first law of thermodynamics*, which is a generalized statement about the conservation of energy. This law tells us about the interplay between the internal energy of an object or system, the work that the system does on its surroundings, and the heat that flows into or out of the system (Figure 15-1a). We'll use the first law to analyze a variety of *thermodynamic processes* in which the state of a system—as measured by its pressure, volume, and temperature—changes due to external influences.

According to the first law, some very remarkable things could happen: Room-temperature water could spontaneously lower its temperature and freeze at the same time that the room-temperature glass holding the water spontaneously raises its temperature and melts. The *second law of thermodynamics* describes why such remarkable things are never observed in the real world. It also places a firm limit on the efficiency of *heat engines*, devices that convert heat into work: It tells us that no matter

A cat demonstrates the first law of thermodynamics: The energy it takes in as food is either stored (as fat), converted into work, or released to its surroundings as heat.

An aircraft engine demonstrates the second law of thermodynamics: The burning of fuel releases energy in the form of heat, but it is impossible to convert 100% of this heat into useful work.

(a)

(b)

Figure 15-1 **The laws of thermodynamics** The laws of thermodynamics are universal: They apply to (a) natural systems such as living organisms and (b) manufactured devices such as engines.

how carefully the engine is designed or built, only part of that heat can be converted to work. Most vehicles in our technological society use a heat engine, so this aspect of the second law is of tremendous importance (Figure 15-1b).

We'll finish the chapter with a discussion of *entropy*, a physical quantity that measures the amount of disorder in a system. We'll find that as a result of the second law of thermodynamics, entropy is not conserved: The total amount of entropy in the universe is increasing.

Take-Home Message for Section 15-1

✔ The first law of thermodynamics relates changes in a system's internal energy to the work that the system does and the heat that flows into the system.

✔ The second law of thermodynamics describes what thermodynamic processes are possible. It says that heat cannot of itself flow from one object to a hotter object and that the universe tends toward ever-greater disorder.

15-2 The first law of thermodynamics relates heat flow, work done, and internal energy change

Suppose you take some unpopped kernels of popcorn at room temperature, put them in a pot with cooking oil, and put a lid on the pot. You then put the pot on the stove and warm it. In a few minutes the popcorn has popped and expanded so much that it has lifted the lid off the pot (Figure 15-2). By popping the popcorn, you've changed its volume (each kernel has expanded), its temperature (which has increased), and its **internal energy**, which is the sum of all of the kinetic and potential energies of the molecules that make up a system such as the popcorn (the chemical reaction involved in popping the kernels requires that each kernel absorb energy, so the internal energy has increased). Quantities such as volume, temperature, pressure, and internal energy are called **state**

① Heat flows into the popcorn, so $Q > 0$.

② The internal energy of the popcorn increases (the kernels of corn absorb energy to pop), so $\Delta U > 0$.

③ The popcorn pushes up on the lid and does work on it, so $W > 0$.

Figure 15-2 **A thermodynamic process** In a general thermodynamic process, the internal energy of a system changes, heat enters or leaves the system, and work is done by or on the system.

When we studied mechanical energy, we used the symbol U to represent the *potential energy* associated with a system. It's a little confusing that the same symbol U is used in thermodynamics to represent the *internal energy* of a system, because these two kinds of energy are *not* the same. In thermodynamics the value of U includes the kinetic energy of its molecules and the potential energy of their interactions with each other, but U does *not* include the gravitational potential energy of the system as a whole. For example, if you carry the popcorn in Figure 15-2 to your neighbor's apartment above you, the gravitational potential energy associated with the popcorn increases (the popcorn is at a greater height) but the popcorn's internal energy stays the same. In this chapter and throughout your study of thermodynamics, keep the new definition of the quantity U in mind.

variables because they depend on the state or condition of the popcorn. Any process that changes the state of a system such as the popcorn is called a **thermodynamic process**.

Note that the values of the state variables of a system do *not* depend on the system's history—that is, the details of how the system got to that state. For example, you can pop popcorn on the stove as in Figure 15-2 or in a microwave oven, and in either case the results are the same. The state of a glass of water at room temperature is the same whether the water came out of the tap at room temperature, was heated in a pot and allowed to cool, or was originally a collection of ice cubes that gradually warmed and melted. In other words, the state variables of a system in a given state do not depend on the particular thermodynamic processes that led to that state.

Figure 15-2 shows that in popping the popcorn, heat flows into the popcorn from the stove; the internal energy of the popcorn increases; and the popcorn does work on its surroundings as it lifts the lid of the pot. All three of these processes involve *energy* in one way or another, so let's look at each of them more closely. We'll then see how they're related.

We'll use the same convention as in Chapter 14 that heat Q is positive if it flows *into* a system and negative if heat flows *out of* a system (see Section 14-5). Since heat flows into the popcorn in Figure 15-2 from the stove, $Q > 0$ for the popcorn.

We use the symbol U for the *internal* energy of the popcorn. Since the internal energy of the popcorn increases, its change is positive and $\Delta U > 0$ (the popcorn has more internal energy at the end of the process than at the beginning). Generally speaking, if the temperature of a system increases in a thermodynamic process, the internal energy also increases and so $\Delta U > 0$. If the system temperature decreases, the internal energy generally decreases and so $\Delta U < 0$.

As in earlier chapters, we use W as the symbol for work; in thermodynamics we'll use this symbol to represent the work done *by* a system on its surroundings. For the process shown in Figure 15-2, the popcorn does positive work on the lid: The popcorn exerts an upward force on the lid, and the lid's displacement is also upward. Hence $W > 0$ for the popcorn. In general, $W > 0$ for a system if that system expands and pushes against its surroundings, as in Figure 15-2. If the system is compressed, like air being compressed in a bicycle pump, positive work is done *on* the air (the system in question), so $W < 0$. Remember that if an object does negative work on a second object, it means that the second object does positive work on the first one (see Section 6-2). You do positive work on the air on the bicycle pump to compress it, so the air does negative work on you. (Note that in most discussions of thermodynamics in chemistry textbooks, W is defined to be the work done *on* a system, which is the exact opposite of how it's defined in physics. Keep this in mind if you're taking physics and chemistry at the same time!) Figure 15-3 shows the conventions that we use for the sign of Q and the sign of W.

For the popcorn shown in Figure 15-2, heat flows into the popcorn ($Q > 0$), the internal energy of the popcorn increases ($\Delta U > 0$), and the popcorn does work on its surroundings ($W > 0$). Careful measurement shows that the heat flow into the system is *exactly* equal to the sum of the change in internal energy plus the work done. In other words, the energy that enters the popcorn in the form of heat goes either into changing the popcorn's internal energy or into doing work. None of the energy is lost. We can write this statement as an equation:

(15-1)
$$Q = \Delta U + W$$

It's conventional to rearrange this equation with ΔU on one side and Q and W on the other side:

During a thermodynamic process, the change in the internal energy of a system...

The first law of thermodynamics
(15-2)

$$\Delta U = Q - W$$

...equals the heat that flows into the system during the process...   ...minus the work that the system does during the process.

Equation 15-2 is a mathematical statement of the **first law of thermodynamics**. It's a generalization of the law of conservation of energy. It says that the internal energy of a system can change *only* if the system gains energy from its surroundings (if heat flows in from the surroundings, or its surroundings do positive work on the system) or if the system loses energy to its surroundings (if heat flows out to the surroundings, or the system does positive work on surroundings). No exception to this rule has ever been found.

Figure 15-3 **The signs of work and heat** A quantity of heat Q is considered positive if it enters a system, negative if it leaves. The sign of the work W for a system depends on which object does positive work.

Heat flows into the system: $Q > 0$.

Heat flows out of the system: $Q < 0$.

System does positive work on its surroundings: $W > 0$.

System has positive work done on it by its surroundings: $W < 0$.

For the system shown in Figure 15-2, the quantity of heat that flows into the popcorn is greater than the amount of work that the popcorn does to lift the lid. So while Q and W are both positive, Q is greater than W and $\Delta U = Q - W$ is positive. In other situations the quantities ΔU, Q, and W have different signs. For example, think of your body as a thermodynamic system that you are exercising on a stationary bicycle in the gym. You do work on the pedals of the bicycle ($W > 0$), and heat flows out of your body ($Q < 0$). Since Q is negative and W is positive, $\Delta U = Q - W$ is negative and you lose internal energy. That's the thermodynamic explanation of why exercise helps you lose weight: The internal energy you lose is extracted from energy stored in your body, part of which is in the form of fat (see Example 15-1).

It's important to remember that the internal energy U is a state function that depends only on the current state of the system, not on how it got into that state. To see what this implies, let's consider two *different* thermodynamic processes that take a system from the *same* initial state to the same final state. To be specific, let's consider two ways to change the state of a system made up of a quantity of gas.

In Figure 15-4a a cylinder with a moveable piston encloses a quantity of gas. The gas has an initial pressure, volume, and temperature. We use a candle to let heat flow slowly into the gas (so $Q > 0$) and allow the piston to move, so that the gas expands. In so doing, the gas does positive work on the piston (the gas pushes the piston to the right as the piston moves to the right), so $W > 0$. If we regulate how fast the piston moves, we can arrange it so that the rate at which the gas does work on the piston is exactly the same as the rate at which heat flows into the gas. Then $Q = W$, and from the first law of thermodynamics (Equation 15-2) the internal energy of the gas will remain unchanged: $\Delta U = Q - W = 0$. For an ideal gas the average energy per molecule is proportional to the Kelvin temperature T of the gas (see Section 14-3), so the internal energy U—the average energy per molecule, multiplied by the number of molecules—is also proportional to T. Since U remains constant for the process shown in Figure 15-4a, the temperature of the gas also remains constant.

Now imagine a second thermodynamic process that starts with the gas in the same initial state. In Figure 15-4b we use the same quantity of gas as in Figure 15-4a, and the gas starts at the same pressure, volume, and temperature. The difference is that now the cylinder is equipped with a thin barrier of lightweight material instead of a piston, and there is a vacuum between the barrier and the other end of the cylinder. If we puncture the barrier, the gas expands freely and fills the entire cylinder. Since the gas doesn't push against anything as it expands (it expands into a vacuum), the gas does no work so $W = 0$. Furthermore, if we insulate the walls of the cylinder so that no heat can flow into or out of the gas, $Q = 0$ for this process. So the first law of thermodynamics tells us that in this process as well the internal energy of the gas will not change: $\Delta U = Q - W = 0 - 0 = 0$. And since U is proportional to Kelvin temperature T for an ideal gas, it follows that the temperature of the gas remains constant for this process. In other words, *both* the processes shown in Figure 15-4 take the same quantity of gas from the same initial volume to the same final volume while leaving the temperature unchanged. (The ideal gas law $pV = nRT$, Equation 14-7, tells us that the final pressure p will also be the same. That's because the final volume V, final temperature T, and number of moles n are the same in both processes.)

The two very different processes shown in Figure 15-4 take the system from the same initial state to the same final state, but follow different thermodynamic *paths*. The first path required heat to be added to the system and the system to do positive work on its surroundings. The second path required neither of these things. This is why we cannot say a particular state of a system contains work or heat. Rather, the amount of heat or work required depends on the path the system takes. For any thermodynamic process that takes a system between the same two states, the change in internal energy is the *same*, independent of the path.

(a) When energy is added slowly to gas trapped in a cylinder with a moveable piston...

Gas   Air

...the gas expands, pushing the piston back.

Gas

The gas has done work on the piston.

(b) A thin barrier of lightweight material separates a gas from a vacuum.

Gas   Vacuum

When the barrier ruptures, the gas expands to fill the entire cylinder. No energy was added to the gas in this case, but the final pressure and volume are the same as in part (a).

Gas

Figure 15-4 **Two thermodynamic paths** (a) If heat is added to an expanding gas at just the right rate, the gas temperature remains constant. (b) The gas temperature is also unchanged in a free expansion. So both of these processes have the same initial and final thermodynamic states but follow different paths between these states.

Example 15-1 Cycling It Off

At the end of a 15-minute session on a stationary bicycle at the gym, the bike's display indicates that you have delivered 165 kJ of energy to the bike in the form of work. Your heart rate monitor shows that you have "burned off" 165 food calories of energy. How much energy has your body lost to your surroundings in the form of heat?

Set Up

In this problem your body is the thermodynamic system. You do work on your surroundings (the bicycle), so W is positive and equal to 165 kJ. The 165 food calories (165 kcal) that you have "burned off" represent a decrease in your body's internal energy, so ΔU is negative and equal to -165 kcal. We'll use the first law of thermodynamics to determine the heat Q that flows out of your body.

First law of thermodynamics:

$$\Delta U = Q - W \qquad (15\text{-}2)$$

Your body does work on the bicycle: $W > 0$.

system = your body

Heat flows out of your body: $Q < 0$.

Solve

First convert ΔU from kilocalories to kilojoules.

1 kcal = 4186 J = 4.186 kJ, so

$$\Delta U = -165 \text{ kcal} \left(\frac{4.186 \text{ kJ}}{1 \text{ kcal}} \right) = -691 \text{ kJ}$$

Rearrange Equation 15-2 to solve for the quantity of heat Q that flows *into* your body. A negative value of Q means that heat flows *out of* your body.

From Equation 15-2,

$$Q = \Delta U + W$$
$$= -691 \text{ kJ} + 165 \text{ kJ}$$
$$= -526 \text{ kJ}$$

This is negative, so 526 kJ of energy flows out of your body in the form of heat as you exercise.

Reflect

Let's look at the energy "accounting" for this exercise session. Your body expended 691 kJ of internal energy, of which 165 kJ went into doing work and 526 kJ was lost in the form of heat. One way to look at these numbers is that only $(165 \text{ kJ})/(691 \text{ kJ}) = 0.239$, or 23.9%, of the energy that you expended went into doing work, so your body has an *efficiency* of 23.9% in this situation.

Another instructive number is that 3500 kcal is the energy content of one pound (0.45 kg) of fat. If all of the 165 kcal that you expended came from stored fat, the net result of your exercise is that you will have lost an amount of fat equal to $(165 \text{ kcal})/(3500 \text{ kcal/lb}) = 0.047 \text{ lb} (0.021 \text{ kg, or } 0.75 \text{ ounce})$. Losing weight requires a *lot* of exercise!

❓ Got the Concept? 15-1 An Expanding Ideal Gas

An ideal gas is enclosed in a thermally isolated cylinder, so that no heat can flow into or out of the gas. One end of the cylinder is sealed by a moveable piston like that shown in Figure 15-4a. If you allow the gas to expand slowly by pulling back the piston, what will happen to the temperature of the gas? (a) The temperature increases; (b) the temperature decreases; (c) the temperature stays the same; (d) the temperature increases to begin with, then decreases; (e) the temperature decreases to begin with, then increases.

Take-Home Message for Section 15-2

✔ The internal energy of a system (the sum of the kinetic energy and potential energy of every atom and molecule in the system) describes the state of a system in a way that does not depend on the specific thermodynamic processes that lead to it.

✔ By itself, heat flow into a system increases the internal energy of a system.

✔ Energy leaves a system when that system does positive work.

✔ The first law of thermodynamics relates the change in internal energy of a thermodynamic system to the heat that enters the system and the work done by that system.

15-3 A graph of pressure versus volume helps to describe what happens in a thermodynamic process

A thermodynamic process involves a change in the state of a system. In most cases this involves a change in the pressure of the system, the volume that the system occupies, or both. That's the case for the popping popcorn in Figure 15-2 and the gas that expands against a piston in Figure 15-4a. In this section we'll use the first law of thermodynamics to help us analyze four special but important kinds of thermodynamic processes:

- **Isobaric process:** The pressure of the system remains constant.
- **Isothermal process:** The temperature of the system remains constant.
- **Adiabatic process:** There are no heat transfers into or out of the system.
- **Isochoric process:** The volume of the system remains constant.

Many thermodynamic processes do not fit into any of these simple categories. But by analyzing these four special cases, we'll learn general rules that can be applied to *any* thermodynamic process.

Isobaric Processes

Isobaric processes occur with no change in pressure. An example is when you cook food in a frying pan without a lid: Heat flows into the food and its temperature increases, but the pressure that the atmosphere exerts on the food remains constant.

Let's consider an isobaric process in which work is done. Suppose our system is a quantity of gas inside a cylinder that's sealed with a moveable piston of negligible mass, as in Figure 15-5. At equilibrium the upward force on the piston due to the pressure of the gas equals the downward force due to atmospheric pressure. This condition doesn't change when the gas is heated gradually and expands slowly, so that the piston moves up at constant velocity: The net force on the piston remains zero. Since atmospheric pressure doesn't change, the pressure in the gas must remain constant as well. The process of adding heat to the gas is therefore isobaric. The heat that flows into the gas results in increased volume, but the pressure of the gas remains constant.

To make it easier to visualize and understand what happens in this process, it's useful to make a ***pV* diagram**. This is a graph that plots the pressure of a system on the vertical axis versus the volume of the system on the horizontal axis. On a *pV* diagram, an isobaric process is represented by a horizontal line (Figure 15-6).

In Figure 15-5 the expanding gas does work W on the piston to lift it. To calculate how much work is done, let the constant pressure of the gas be p and the surface area of the piston be A. Figure 15-5 shows that the original length of the cylinder containing the gas is ℓ_i and the final length of the cylinder after the gas has expanded is ℓ_f. Recall that pressure is force per unit area, so force is pressure multiplied by area. This means that the force that the gas exerts on the piston has magnitude $F_{gas} = pA$. This force acts upward, the same direction that the piston moves, and the piston moves a distance $\ell_f - \ell_i$. So the total work done by the gas as it expands is

$$W = F(\ell_f - \ell_i) = pA(\ell_f - \ell_i) = p(A\ell_f - A\ell_i)$$

(15-3)

The volume of a cylinder is equal to the area of its base multiplied by its height. So $A\ell_i$ and $A\ell_f$ are, respectively, the initial volume V_i and final volume V_f occupied by the gas, and we can rewrite Equation 15-3 as

Work that a system does in an isobaric process | Volume of the system at the end of the process

$$W = p(V_f - V_i)$$

Constant pressure of the system | Volume of the system at the beginning of the process

The piston reaches its equilibrium position when the pressure of the gas in the cylinder equals atmospheric pressure.

Heating the gas causes it to expand.

Air $\vec{F}_{air}$ Area A $\vec{F}_{gas}$ Gas ℓ_i

Air $\vec{F}_{air}$ $\vec{F}_{gas}$ ℓ_f Gas

Even after the gas expands, the gas pressure must equal atmospheric pressure. Because neither gas pressure nor atmospheric pressure has changed, the expansion is isobaric.

Figure 15-5 An isobaric expansion The piston exerts a constant pressure on the gas as it is heated, so the pressure of the gas itself remains constant.

Area under the *pV* curve = work W done by the system in an isobaric process

Pressure | p | V_i | V_f | 0 | Volume

Figure 15-6 Work done in an isobaric expansion On a *pV* diagram (a graph of pressure versus volume) for a thermodynamic process, the area under the curve represents the work done by the system.

 Go to Picture It 15-1 for more practice dealing with pV diagrams

Work done in an isobaric (constant-pressure) process (15-4)

The work done by the gas in this isobaric process is the pressure p multiplied by the change in volume $(V_f - V_i)$. Figure 15-6 shows that this is the *area* under the straight line on the pV diagram that represents the process. Note that this area is a rectangle with height p and length $V_f - V_i$, and so its area equals its height multiplied by its length or $p(V_f - V_i)$.

Equation 15-4 is valid for an isobaric process whether the volume increases or decreases. If $V_f > V_i$ so that the system expands like the gas in Figure 15-5, then $V_f - V_i$ is positive and the system does positive work on its surroundings. Such a process is called an *isobaric expansion*. If instead $V_f < V_i$, which would be like the process in Figure 15-5 in reverse, then $V_f - V_i$ is negative and the system does *negative* work on its surroundings—that is, the surroundings (in Figure 15-5, the piston) do positive work on the system. This is called an *isobaric compression*.

We emphasize that Equation 15-4 is valid only for the case of constant pressure. But it turns out to be true in general that in *any* process, the work done is the area under the curve that represents the process on a pV diagram. We'll use this idea later in this section.

Example 15-2 Boiling Water Isobarically

Boiling 1.00 g (1.00 cm³) of water at 1.00 atm results in 1671 cm³ of water vapor. A cylinder like that shown in Figure 15-5 contains 1.00 g of water at 100°C. The pressure on the outside of the piston is 1.00 atm. Determine the change in internal energy of the water when just enough heat is added to the water to boil all of the liquid.

Set Up

In this process heat flows into the water to change its phase from liquid to vapor, and the vapor does work on the piston as it expands. The pressure on the outside of the piston is constant, so the pressure that the piston exerts on the water (liquid plus vapor) is also constant. So this is an isobaric process. We'll apply the first law of thermodynamics to determine the change in internal energy.

First law of thermodynamics:

$$\Delta U = Q - W \qquad (15\text{-}2)$$

Work done in an isobaric (constant-pressure) process:

$$W = p(V_f - V_i) \qquad (15\text{-}4)$$

Heat required for a phase change:

$$Q = \pm mL \qquad (14\text{-}21)$$

The water vapor pushes upward and does work on the piston: $W > 0$.

Heat flows into the water to boil it: $Q > 0$.

system = water

Solve

Use Equation 14-21 to find the heat Q that flows into the water to vaporize it.

Heat flows into the water, so Q in Equation 14-21 is positive. The mass of water is $m = 1.00$ g and the latent heat of vaporization is $L_V = 2260 \times 10^3$ J/kg $= 2.26 \times 10^6$ J/kg (from Table 14-4). So

$$Q = mL_V$$
$$= (1.00\,\text{g})\left(\frac{1\,\text{kg}}{10^3\,\text{g}}\right)(2.26 \times 10^6\,\text{J/kg})$$
$$= 2.26 \times 10^3\,\text{J}$$

Use Equation 15-4 to find the work W that the expanding water vapor does on the piston.

The pressure of the water vapor is $p = 1.00$ atm $= 1.01 \times 10^5$ Pa $= 1.01 \times 10^5$ N/m² and remains constant in this isobaric expansion.
The volume occupied by the water increases from $V_i = 1.00$ cm³ in the liquid state to $V_f = 1671$ cm³ in the vapor state. In calculating the work done by the expanding vapor, we must convert cm³ to m³ using the relationship 1 m $= 10^2$ cm:

$$W = p(V_f - V_i)$$
$$= (1.01 \times 10^5\,\text{N/m}^2)(1671\,\text{cm}^3 - 1.00\,\text{cm}^3)\left(\frac{1\,\text{m}}{10^2\,\text{cm}}\right)^3$$
$$= (1.01 \times 10^5\,\text{N/m}^2)(1670 \times 10^{-6}\,\text{m}^3)$$
$$= 169\,\text{N}\cdot\text{m} = 169\,\text{J}$$

Substitute the values for Q and W into Equation 15-2, the first law of thermodynamics. This tells us the change in internal energy of the water in this process.

$$\Delta U = Q - W$$
$$= 2.26 \times 10^3 \text{ J} - 169 \text{ J}$$
$$= 2.09 \times 10^3 \text{ J}$$

Reflect

We have to add 2.26×10^3 J of energy to boil the water. Of this energy, 2.09×10^3 J goes into increasing the internal energy of the system. The rest of the energy (169 J) leaves the system in the form of work done on the piston.

Isothermal Processes

In an isothermal process, temperature remains constant. Although the process in Example 15-2 is isobaric (constant pressure), it is also isothermal: When a substance freezes or boils, the phase transition occurs with no change in temperature.

Gases can also expand or be compressed in such a way as to maintain a constant temperature, even though no phase transition occurs. As we discussed in Section 15-2, the internal energy U of an ideal gas is directly proportional to the Kelvin temperature of the gas. So if the temperature of an ideal gas remains constant during a thermodynamic process, the internal energy U remains constant as well and there is zero change in the internal energy: $\Delta U = 0$. The first law of thermodynamics, Equation 15-2, tells us that $\Delta U = Q - W$, so for an isothermal process that involves an ideal gas we have

$$0 = Q - W$$

or

$$Q = W \quad \text{(15-5)}$$

(isothermal process for an ideal gas)

So *when an ideal gas undergoes an isothermal process, the quantity of heat Q added to the gas is equal to the work W done by the gas.* Put another way, whatever energy is added to the gas in the form of heat appears as work done by the gas. If heat flows into the gas so that $Q > 0$, it must be that $W > 0$: The gas does positive work on its surroundings, which means it must expand. This is called an *isothermal expansion*. If heat flows out of the gas so that $Q < 0$, then $W < 0$ and the gas does negative work on its surroundings. This means that the surroundings do positive work on the gas, so the volume of the gas decreases. This is called an *isothermal compression*.

How much work is done by a gas that undergoes an isothermal expansion or compression? To get insight into the answer, let's use a pV diagram to depict such a process. The ideal gas law (which we studied in Section 14-3) says that the pressure p, volume V, and temperature T of n moles of an ideal gas are related by

$$pV = nRT \quad \text{(14-7)}$$

In an isothermal process T is constant, so the product pV is likewise constant. If the gas expands and the volume V increases, the pressure p must decrease; if the gas compresses and the volume V decreases, the pressure p must increase. Figure 15-7a shows three **isotherms**, or curves of constant temperature, on a graph of pressure versus volume.

On a pV diagram, the area under the curve represents the work W done by the gas; Figure 15-7b shows this area for an isothermal expansion. Unlike the isobaric case shown in Figure 15-6, the area under the curve is *not* a rectangle, so we cannot find W simply by multiplying the pressure and the change in volume. Using calculus, it can be shown that the work that the gas does as the volume changes is

(a)

(b)

Area under the pV curve = work W done by the gas in an isothermal process

Figure 15-7 Isothermal processes in an ideal gas (a) This pV diagram shows isotherms (curves of constant temperature) for an ideal gas. (b) The work done by an ideal gas in an isothermal expansion.

Number of moles of gas   Ideal gas constant

Work that an ideal gas does in an isothermal process $W = nRT \ln \dfrac{V_f}{V_i}$ Volume of the gas at the end of the process

Kelvin temperature of the gas   Volume of the gas at the beginning of the process

Work done by an ideal gas in an isothermal (constant-temperature) process (15-6)

$\sqrt{x}$ *See the Math Tutorial for more information on logarithms*

Go to Interactive Exercise 15-1 for more practice dealing with internal energy

(15-7)

In Equation 15-6 "ln" is the natural logarithm function. It has the properties that ln x is positive if x is greater than 1 and ln x is negative if x is less than 1; if $x = 1$, then ln $x = $ ln $1 = 0$. So Equation 15-6 says that the gas does positive work ($W > 0$) if the gas expands, so V_f is greater than V_i and V_f/V_i is greater than 1. The gas does negative work (that is, positive work is done on the gas by its surroundings) if the gas is compressed, so V_f is less than V_i and V_f/V_i is less than 1. An alternative version of Equation 15-6 in terms of the number of molecules N present in the gas is

$$W = NkT \ln \frac{V_f}{V_i}$$

Example 15-3 An Isothermal Expansion

A cylinder sealed with a moveable piston as in Figure 15-5 contains 0.100 mol of an ideal gas at a temperature of 295 K. Heat is transferred slowly into the gas, and it is allowed to expand isothermally from an initial volume of 1.00×10^{-3} m^3 to 3.00×10^{-3} m^3 (that is, from 1.00 L to 3.00 L). (a) What are the initial and final pressures of the gas? (b) How much heat is transferred into the gas during this process?

Set Up

Since this is an ideal gas, we can use the ideal gas equation to determine the pressure p from the volume V, number of moles n, and temperature T. The internal energy of an ideal gas does not change if the temperature remains constant, so $\Delta U = 0$ and Q (the quantity of heat that flows into the gas, which is what we're trying to find) equals the work W done by the gas. We'll find W and hence Q with Equation 15-6.

Ideal gas law:

$$pV = nRT \qquad (14\text{-}7)$$

Isothermal process for an ideal gas:

$$Q = W \qquad (15\text{-}5)$$

Work done by an ideal gas in an isothermal (constant-temperature) process:

$$W = nRT \ln \frac{V_f}{V_i} \qquad (15\text{-}6)$$

The gas pushes upward and does work on the piston: $W > 0$.

Heat flows into the gas to make it expand: $Q > 0$.

system = gas

Solve

(a) Use Equation 14-7 to find the initial and final pressures.

The ideal gas law says that $pV = nRT$. Rewrite this to solve for the pressure:

$$p = \frac{nRT}{V}$$

The pressure p_i when the gas occupies the initial volume $V_i = 1.00 \times 10^{-3}$ m^3 is

$$p_i = \frac{nRT}{V_i} = \frac{(0.100 \text{ mol})\left[8.314 \text{ J/(mol·K)}\right](295 \text{ K})}{1.00 \times 10^{-3} \text{ m}^3}$$

$$= 2.45 \times 10^5 \frac{\text{J}}{\text{m}^3}\left(\frac{1 \text{ N·m}}{1 \text{ J}}\right)$$

$$= 2.45 \times 10^5 \text{ N/m}^2 = 2.45 \times 10^5 \text{ Pa}$$

(We used the relationship that 1 joule = 1 newton-meter.) The pressure when the gas occupies the final volume $V_f = 3.00 \times 10^{-3}$ m^3 is

$$p_f = \frac{nRT}{V_f} = \frac{(0.100 \text{ mol})\left[8.314 \text{ J/(mol·K)}\right](295 \text{ K})}{3.00 \times 10^{-3} \text{ m}^3}$$

$$= 8.18 \times 10^4 \text{ Pa}$$

(b) From the first law of thermodynamics, the quantity of heat that enters the gas equals the work done by the gas.

Use Equation 15-6 to calculate the work done by the gas and so the quantity of heat that is added to the gas.

For an isothermal process for an ideal gas, $\Delta U = 0$ and $Q = W$.

The heat that flows into the gas equals the work that the gas does as it expands.

From Equation 15-6, the work done by the gas is

$$W = nRT \ln \frac{V_f}{V_i}$$

$$= (0.100 \text{ mol}) \left[8.314 \text{ J}/(\text{mol} \cdot \text{K}) \right] (295 \text{ K}) \times \ln \left(\frac{3.00 \times 10^{-3} \text{ m}^3}{1.00 \times 10^{-3} \text{ m}^3} \right)$$

$$= (245 \text{ J}) \ln 3.00 = (245 \text{ J})(1.10)$$

$$= 269 \text{ J}$$

Since $Q = W$, the quantity of heat added to the gas is $Q = 269$ J.

Reflect

For an ideal gas that expands isothermally, all of the heat that is transferred into the gas (in this case, 269 J) is converted to work done by the gas on its surroundings.

Note that to keep the temperature constant, the gas pressure must decrease during the expansion. To make this happen, it's not enough to add heat slowly to the gas: The pressure on the other side of the piston must also decrease as the volume increases to match the desired pressure of the gas (so that the piston moves slowly and doesn't accelerate). This tells us that an isothermal expansion or compression of an ideal gas requires rather special circumstances.

Adiabatic Processes

An adiabatic process is one in which there is no heat transfer in or out of a system. An important system that undergoes adiabatic processes is our atmosphere. Air is a very poor conductor of heat (see Section 14-7), so there is little heat flow into or out of a mass of air as its pressure and volume change. This helps explain why many mountain ranges have a relatively wet climate on one side while the other side has a dry climate (Figure 15-8).

When winds carry air up and over mountains, the lower pressure at higher altitudes causes the air mass to expand and do work on the surrounding air ($W > 0$). This expansion occurs nearly adiabatically thanks to the low thermal conductivity of air, so we let Q be zero. From the first law of thermodynamics, Equation 15-2, the change in the internal energy of the air is

$$\Delta U = Q - W = 0 - W \quad \text{or} \quad \Delta U = -W \text{ (adiabatic process)} \qquad (15\text{-}8)$$

Since $W > 0$, it follows that $\Delta U < 0$: The internal energy U of the air decreases as it is pushed up the flanks of the mountains. For an ideal gas U is proportional to the Kelvin temperature of the gas, so the air temperature drops by as much as 10°C for every 1 km of elevation gained. As the temperature decreases, water vapor in the air

Prevailing wind direction

Figure 15-8 **The adiabatic winds of Moloka'i** The prevailing winds push air up and over the mountains that form the backbone of the Hawaiian island of Moloka'i. The temperature of the uplifted air drops and airborne moisture falls as rain, creating the lush rainforest visible as bright green in this satellite photograph. The air that descends on the southwestern side of the mountains is dry, resulting in an arid plain on the southern and western parts of the island.

condenses into clouds and falls as rain, which helps to promote lush vegetation on the windward side of the mountains. By the time the air reaches the other side of the mountains, it has been depleted of moisture and so little rain falls on that side.

The air we have described expands as it is pushed up the slopes of the mountains, so this process is called an *adiabatic expansion*. In an *adiabatic compression* the volume of the gas decreases, so $W < 0$ (the surroundings do work on the gas) and $\Delta U > 0$ (the internal energy of the gas increases, so its temperature increases as well).

!   Watch Out!   Remember that heat and temperature are not the same thing.

Even though no heat flows into or out of air pushed up a range of mountains, the temperature of the air changes. If this statement seems contradictory, it's probably because you're still thinking of *heat* as meaning approximately the same thing as *temperature*. Remember that these two concepts are actually quite different: Heat is energy that flows into or out of an object due to a temperature difference, while temperature is a measure of the kinetic energy of an object's molecules. The temperature can change even if there is *no* heat flow, provided work is done by (or done on) the object.

Isochoric Processes

An isochoric process is one for which the volume remains constant. As an example, consider a quantity of gas sealed inside a rigid container. If heat flows into the gas, the pressure and temperature of the gas will increase but the volume of the gas will remain the same because the container cannot expand.

The pressure of the gas exerts forces on the walls of its container, but since the walls do not move (there is no moveable piston) there is zero displacement. Work is force multiplied by displacement, so the gas does *zero* work in an isochoric process: $W = 0$. From the first law of thermodynamics, Equation 15-2,

(15-9)
$$\Delta U = Q - W = Q - 0 \quad \text{or} \quad \Delta U = Q \,(\text{isochoric process})$$

This says that for an isochoric process, any heat flow into or out of a system goes entirely into changing the internal energy of the system. If Q is positive so that heat flows into the system, the process is called *isochoric heating*; if Q is negative and heat flows out of the system, the process is called *isochoric cooling*.

Example 15-4 Two Thermodynamic Processes: Isochoric and Isobaric

The pV diagram in **Figure 15-9** shows two thermodynamic processes that occur in an ideal diatomic gas, for which the internal energy is $U = (5/2)nRT$. The gas is in a cylinder with a moveable piston (see Figure 15-5) and is initially in the state labeled A on the diagram, at pressure $p_i = 3.03 \times 10^5$ Pa and volume $V_i = 1.20 \times 10^{-3}$ m³. The piston is first locked in place so that the volume of the gas cannot change, and the cylinder is cooled so that the temperature and pressure of the gas both decrease. When the gas is in state B, the pressure of the gas is $p_f = 1.01 \times 10^5$ Pa = 1.00 atm, the same as the air pressure outside the cylinder. The piston is then unlocked so it is free to move, and the cylinder is slowly heated so that the gas expands at constant pressure. The temperature of the gas increases until in the final state (C in Figure 15-9), when the gas is at the same temperature as in the initial state A.
(a) What is the final volume of the gas? (b) Find the values of W, ΔU, and Q for the isochoric process $A \rightarrow B$. (c) Find the values of W, ΔU, and Q for the isobaric process $B \rightarrow C$. (d) Find the values of W, ΔU, and Q for the net process $A \rightarrow B \rightarrow C$.

Process $A \rightarrow B$ isochoric (constant volume)

The light blue curve is an isotherm.

Process $B \rightarrow C$ isobaric (constant pressure)

Figure 15-9 Isochoric cooling and isobaric expansion In this two-step process for an ideal gas, how much work is done, how much heat flows into the gas, and by how much does the internal energy change?

Set Up

We'll use the ideal gas law to determine the final volume of the gas. For the isochoric (constant-volume) process $A \rightarrow B$, the gas does no work, so the quantity of heat Q that enters the gas is equal to the internal energy change ΔU of the gas. (The gas is *cooled* in this process, so $Q < 0$ and $\Delta U < 0$.) We'll determine ΔU from the temperature change. For the isobaric (constant-pressure) process $B \rightarrow C$, the work W that the gas does is given by Equation 15-4; this is positive because the gas expands. The internal energy change ΔU is again given by the temperature change. We'll then determine Q for this process from the first law of thermodynamics.

Ideal diatomic gas:

$$U = \frac{5}{2}nRT$$

Ideal gas law:

$$pV = nRT \qquad (14\text{-}7)$$

First law of thermodynamics:

$$\Delta U = Q - W \qquad (15\text{-}2)$$

Work done in an isobaric (constant-pressure) process:

$$W = p(V_f - V_i) \qquad (15\text{-}4)$$

Isochoric (constant-volume) process:

$$\Delta U = Q \qquad (15\text{-}9)$$

Process $A \rightarrow B$

The volume of the gas is constant: $W = 0$.

system = gas

Heat flows out of the gas: $Q < 0$.

Process $B \rightarrow C$

The gas pushes upward and does work on the piston: $W > 0$.

Heat flows into the gas to make it expand: $Q > 0$.

system = gas

Solve

(a) Use the ideal gas law to find the final volume V_f.

The initial pressure and volume of the gas are

$p_i = 3.03 \times 10^5$ Pa

$V_i = 1.20 \times 10^{-3}$ m^3

From the ideal gas law, Equation 14-7,

$p_i V_i = nRT_i$

where T_i is the initial temperature of the gas in state A.

The final pressure of the gas is

$p_f = 1.01 \times 10^5$ Pa

The ideal gas law tells us that

$p_f V_f = nRT_f$

where T_f is the final temperature of the gas in state C. The initial and final temperatures are the same ($T_i = T_f$) and so

$p_i V_i = p_f V_f$

$$V_f = \frac{p_i V_i}{p_f} = \frac{(3.03 \times 10^5 \text{ Pa})(1.20 \times 10^{-3} \text{ m}^3)}{1.01 \times 10^5 \text{ Pa}} = 3.60 \times 10^{-3} \text{ m}^3$$

The final pressure is one-third of the initial pressure, and the final volume is three times the initial volume.

(b) For the isochoric process $A \rightarrow B$ the work done is $W_{A \rightarrow B} = 0$. Find the change in internal energy ΔU and quantity of heat Q for this process.

The change in internal energy U is the difference between the value of U in state B and the value of U in state A:

$$\Delta U_{A \rightarrow B} = U_B - U_A = \frac{5}{2}nRT_B - \frac{5}{2}nRT_i$$

We don't know the number of moles of gas n, nor do we know the temperatures T_i (in the initial state A, for which the pressure is p_i and the volume is V_i) and T_B (in state B, for which the pressure is p_f and the volume is V_i). But from the ideal gas law $pV = nRT$, so

$p_i V_i = nRT_i$ and $p_f V_i = nRT_B$

So the change in internal energy is

$$\Delta U_{A \rightarrow B} = \frac{5}{2}p_f V_i - \frac{5}{2}p_i V_i = \frac{5}{2}(p_f - p_i)V_i$$

$$= \frac{5}{2}(1.01 \times 10^5 \text{ Pa} - 3.03 \times 10^5 \text{ Pa})(1.20 \times 10^{-3} \text{ m}^3)$$

$$= -606 \text{ J}$$

(Remember that $1 \text{ Pa} = 1 \text{ N/m}^2$ and $1 \text{ N} \cdot \text{m} = 1 \text{ J}$.) From Equation 15-9 for an isochoric process,

$$Q_{A \to B} = \Delta U_{A \to B} = -606 \text{ J}$$

Heat flows out of the gas and the internal energy of the gas decreases.

(c) Find W, ΔU, and Q for the isobaric process $B \to C$.

The work done in an isobaric process is given by Equation 15-4. The constant pressure is $p_f = 1.01 \times 10^5 \text{ Pa}$, and the volume increases from $V_i = 1.20 \times 10^{-3} \text{ m}^3$ to $V_f = 3.60 \times 10^{-3} \text{ m}^3$:

$$
\begin{aligned}
W_{B \to C} &= p_f (V_f - V_i) \\
&= (1.01 \times 10^5 \text{ Pa}) (3.60 \times 10^{-3} \text{ m}^3 - 1.20 \times 10^{-3} \text{ m}^3) \\
&= +242 \text{ J}
\end{aligned}
$$

The gas does positive work as it expands. As in part (b), we calculate the internal energy change with the aid of the ideal gas law:

$$
\begin{aligned}
\Delta U_{B \to C} &= U_C - U_B = \frac{5}{2} nRT_f - \frac{5}{2} nRT_B \\
&= \frac{5}{2} p_f V_f - \frac{5}{2} p_f V_i = \frac{5}{2} p_f (V_f - V_i)
\end{aligned}
$$

This is just $5/2$ times the above expression for $W_{B \to C}$, so

$$\Delta U_{B \to C} = \frac{5}{2} W_{B \to C} = \frac{5}{2}(+242 \text{ J}) = +606 \text{ J}$$

From the first law of thermodynamics, the heat that flows into the gas in this process is

$$
\begin{aligned}
Q_{B \to C} &= \Delta U_{B \to C} + W_{B \to C} = (+606 \text{ J}) + (+242 \text{ J}) \\
&= +848 \text{ J}
\end{aligned}
$$

(d) Find the values of W, ΔU, and Q for the combined process $A \to B \to C$.

The total amount of work done by the gas is

$$W_{A \to B} + W_{B \to C} = 0 + (+242 \text{ J}) = +242 \text{ J}$$

The total change in internal energy of the gas is

$$\Delta U_{A \to B} + \Delta U_{B \to C} = (-606 \text{ J}) + (+606 \text{ J}) = 0$$

The total quantity of heat that flows into the gas is

$$Q_{A \to B} + Q_{B \to C} = -606 \text{ J} + (+848 \text{ J}) = +242 \text{ J}$$

Reflect

For the combined process, there is *zero* net change in the internal energy U of the ideal gas. That's because U depends only on the number of moles of gas and the temperature, which have the same values in the final state C as in the initial state A. In the combined process 242 J of heat flows into the gas, and the gas uses this energy to do 242 J of work.

? Got the Concept? 15-2 Ranking Thermodynamic Processes

The pV diagram in **Figure 15-10** shows four thermodynamic processes for a certain quantity of an ideal gas: (i) $a \to b$, (ii) $a \to c$, (iii) $a \to d$, and (iv) $a \to e$. All four processes start in the same initial state a. The volume is the same for states b, c, and d. Process $a \to c$ lies along an isotherm. (a) Rank these four processes according to the internal energy change ΔU of the gas, from most positive to most negative. If two processes have the same value of ΔU, say so. (b) Rank these four processes according to the work W done by the gas, from most positive to most negative. If two processes have the same value of W, say so.

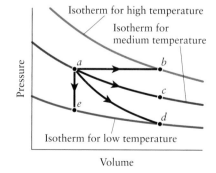

Figure 15-10 Four thermodynamic processes What are the properties of the processes $a \to b$, $a \to c$, $a \to d$, and $a \to e$?

The pV diagram in Figure 15-10 shows four thermo-dynamic processes for a certain quantity of an ideal gas: $a \rightarrow b$, $a \rightarrow c$, $a \rightarrow d$, and $a \rightarrow e$. All four processes start in the same initial state a. The volume is the same for states b, c, and d. Process $a \rightarrow c$ lies along an isotherm. One of these processes could be adiabatic. Which one is it? (a) $a \rightarrow b$; (b) $a \rightarrow c$; (c) $a \rightarrow d$; (d) $a \rightarrow e$; (e) not enough information given to decide.

Take-Home Message for Section 15-3

✔ A pV diagram can be used to describe thermodynamic processes that take a system from one state to another.

✔ Isobaric processes occur with no change in pressure.

✔ Temperature remains constant in isothermal processes.

✔ There is no heat flow into or out of a system during an adiabatic process.

✔ Isochoric processes occur with no change in volume.

15-4 More heat is required to change the temperature of an ideal gas isobarically than isochorically

Our discussion in Section 15-3 of various types of thermodynamic processes was fairly general. Let's now look more closely at some of these processes for the special case in which the thermodynamic system is an ideal gas. This special case has a tremendous number of applications: It will help us understand why a bicycle pump gets warm when you use it to inflate a tire, why the gas emerging from a carbon dioxide (CO_2) fire extinguisher gets extremely cold, and how a diesel engine can make a fuel–air mixture ignite even though there are no spark plugs in such an engine.

Specific Heats of an Ideal Gas

Suppose you have a quantity of ideal gas. How much heat does it take to raise the temperature of the gas to a new, higher temperature? The best answer is "It depends on how you do it." The pV diagram in Figure 15-11 helps us understand why this is so.

This figure shows two possible ways that an ideal gas in a cylinder with a moveable piston can be slowly heated from a lower temperature to a higher one. Process $A \rightarrow B$ is *isochoric*: It takes place at constant volume (the moveable piston is locked in position), so the pressure of the gas increases as you heat the gas. Process $A \rightarrow C$ is *isobaric*: It takes place at constant pressure. The piston is allowed to move so that the gas expands

Process $A{\rightarrow}B$ is isochoric (constant volume) so no work is done.

Isotherm for high temperature

Process $A{\rightarrow}C$ is isobaric (constant pressure). The ideal gas does work.

The temperature change and internal energy change are each the same for the two processes.

Isotherm for low temperature

For a given temperature change, more heat must flow into the ideal gas in process $A{\rightarrow}C$ than in process $A{\rightarrow}B$.

Figure 15-11 Two ways to increase temperature Processes $A \rightarrow B$ and $A \rightarrow C$ for an ideal gas lead to different final states but the same final temperature.

as it is heated, and the pressure inside the cylinder remains equal to the pressure on the other side of the piston. The final temperature is the same for both processes because both state B and state C are on the same isotherm in Figure 15-11.

The internal energy U of an ideal gas depends only on the number of moles and the temperature, so the internal energy change ΔU is the same for both processes. But the amount of work W done by the gas is *different* for the two processes: $W = 0$ for process $A \rightarrow B$ (the gas does no work if the volume it occupies doesn't change), while $W > 0$ for process $A \rightarrow C$ (the expanding gas does work on the piston to make it move). From the first law of thermodynamics, Equation 15-2,

$$\Delta U = Q - W \quad \text{so} \quad Q = \Delta U + W$$

Because ΔU is the same for both processes, *more* heat is required for process $A \rightarrow C$ (in which positive work is done) than for process $A \rightarrow B$ (for which $W = 0$). So the heat required to increase the temperature of an ideal gas is greater if the temperature is increased at constant pressure than if it is increased at constant volume.

Let's be more quantitative about the quantity of heat required to change the temperature of a certain quantity of ideal gas by a given amount. In Section 14-5 we wrote an equation for the heat required to change the temperature of a mass m of substance by an amount ΔT:

(14-20)
$$Q = mc\,\Delta T$$

In Equation 14-20 the quantity c is the *specific heat* of the substance. For an ideal gas we usually write the internal energy U in terms of the number of *moles* of gas present rather than the amount of mass. We follow the same approach for the quantity of heat Q, so we write

Quantity of heat and the resulting temperature change in terms of molar specific heat
(15-10)

Quantity of heat that flows into (if $Q > 0$) or out of (if $Q < 0$) an object   Molar specific heat of the substance of which the object is made

$$Q = nC\Delta T$$

Number of moles present of the substance   Temperature change of the object that results from the heat flow

The quantity C in Equation 15-10 is called the **molar specific heat** of the substance (in the case we're discussing, an ideal gas). It has units of joules per mole per kelvin, or $J/(mol \cdot K)$.

! Watch Out! Don't confuse specific heat and molar specific heat.

It's important to recognize the difference between the specific heat c that appears in Equation 14-20 and the molar specific heat C in Equation 15-10. Specific heat c (lowercase) tells you the number of joules of heat required to raise the temperature of one *kilogram* of a substance by one kelvin.

Molar specific heat C (uppercase) tells you the number of joules of heat required to raise the temperature of one *mole* of the substance by one kelvin. If the substance has a molar mass (mass per mole) of M, the two quantities are related by $C = Mc$.

We've seen that the quantity of heat Q required to make an ideal gas undergo a temperature change ΔT is different if the pressure p is held constant than if the volume V is held constant. To keep track of this difference, we use the symbol C_p for the **molar specific heat at constant pressure** and the symbol C_V for the **molar specific heat at constant volume**. Then we can write Equation 15-10 for these two special cases as

(15-11)
$$Q = nC_p\Delta T \quad \text{(constant pressure)}$$
$$Q = nC_V\Delta T \quad \text{(constant volume)}$$

Our discussion of Figure 15-11 showed that for a given temperature increase ΔT, the value of Q was greater for a constant-pressure process than for a constant-volume process. So we conclude that C_p, the molar specific heat at constant pressure, must be greater than the molar specific heat at constant volume, C_V. Table 15-1, which lists experimental values of C_p and C_V for various gases, shows that this is indeed the case.

Table 15-1 Molar Specific Heats of Gases (in J/(mol·K) for a gas at $T = 300$ K and $p = 1$ atm, except where otherwise indicated)

	Gas	C_p	C_V	$C_p - C_V$	$\gamma = C_p/C_V$
Monatomic	Ar	20.8	12.5	8.28	1.66
	He	20.8	12.5	8.28	1.66
	Ne	20.8	12.7	8.08	1.63
Diatomic	H_2	28.8	20.4	8.37	1.41
	N_2	29.1	20.8	8.33	1.40
	O_2	29.4	21.1	8.33	1.39
	CO	29.3	21.0	8.28	1.39
Triatomic	CO_2	37.0	28.5	8.49	1.30
	SO_2	40.4	31.4	9.00	1.29
	H_2O (373 K)	34.3	25.9	8.37	1.32

Notice the following from Table 15-1:

(a) The *difference* $C_p - C_V$ between the two different molar specific heats has almost the same value for *all* gases.
(b) The value of C_V is nearly the same for all monatomic gases, nearly the same for all diatomic gases, and nearly the same for all triatomic gases. The value increases as the number of atoms increases.

We can understand the first of these observations by using Equation 15-10, the first law of thermodynamics ($\Delta U = Q - W$), and the ideal gas law ($pV = nRT$). For a constant-volume process $W = 0$, so from the second of Equations 15-11 the internal energy change for n moles of an ideal gas that undergoes a given temperature change ΔT is

$$\Delta U = Q - W = nC_V\Delta T - 0 = nC_V\Delta T \tag{15-12}$$
(ideal gas, constant volume)

For a constant-*pressure* process that starts at the same temperature, the gas changes its volume by ΔV and does an amount of work

$$W = p\Delta V = p(V_f - V_i) = pV_f - pV_i$$

where V_f and V_i are the final and initial volumes of the gas. But from the ideal gas law,

$$pV_f = nRT_f \quad \text{and} \quad pV_i = nRT_i$$

where T_f and T_i are the final and initial temperatures of the gas, respectively. The temperature change of the gas is $\Delta T = T_f - T_i$, so we can write the work done by the gas in a constant-pressure process as

$$W = pV_f - pV_i = nRT_f - nRT_i = nR(T_f - T_i) = nR\Delta T \tag{15-13}$$
(ideal gas, constant pressure)

Using Equation 15-13 and the first of Equations 15-11, we can now write the internal energy change for this constant-pressure process as

$$\Delta U = Q - W = nC_p\Delta T - nR\Delta T = n(C_p - R)\Delta T \tag{15-14}$$
(ideal gas, constant volume)

Equation 15-12 for a constant-volume process and Equation 15-14 for a constant-pressure process look rather different from each other. But we know that the internal energy change ΔU for an ideal gas is the *same* in both cases, as long as the number of moles n and the temperature change ΔT are the same for both processes. So ΔU in Equation 15-12 is equal to ΔU in Equation 15-14:

$$nC_V\Delta T = n(C_p - R)\Delta T$$

For this to be true it must be that $C_V = C_p - R$, or

Molar specific heats of
an ideal gas
(15-15)

Molar specific heat of an ideal gas at constant pressure

$$C_p - C_V = R$$ Ideal gas constant

Molar specific heat of an ideal gas at constant volume

Equation 15-15 says that for an ideal gas, C_p is greater than C_V by $R = 8.314 \, \text{J}/(\text{mol} \cdot \text{K})$, the ideal gas constant. The experimentally determined values of $C_p - C_V$ given in Table 15-1 for *real* gases are very close to this theoretical prediction.

How can we understand our second observation from Table 15-1, that the value of C_V is essentially the same for all gases with the same number of atoms? To see the answer, note from Equation 15-12 that for an ideal gas with constant volume $\Delta U = nC_V \Delta T$. In other words, C_V tells us about the change in internal energy of a gas that results from a temperature change. We learned something important about the internal energy of an ideal gas in Section 14-3: On average, each molecule in an ideal gas at temperature T has energy $(1/2)kT$ for each of its *degrees of freedom*. (Recall that k is the Boltzmann constant, equal to the ideal gas constant R divided by Avogadro's number N_A.) A monatomic gas has three degrees of freedom, corresponding to its ability to move in the x, y, and z directions. A diatomic gas at room temperature has two additional degrees of freedom that correspond to its ability to rotate around either of two axes perpendicular to the long axis of the molecule, and a triatomic gas (which at room temperature can both rotate and vibrate) has even more degrees of freedom.

We'll use the symbol D to represent the number of degrees of freedom. Then the average energy per gas molecule is $(D/2)kT$. One mole of the gas contains Avogadro's number of molecules, so the energy per mole is $N_A(D/2)kT = (D/2)(N_Ak)T = (D/2)RT$. (Again, recall that $k = R/N_A$, so $R = N_Ak$.) Then the internal energy of n moles of ideal gas is

$$U = n\left(\frac{D}{2}R\right)T$$

(ideal gas, D degrees of freedom)

If the temperature of the gas changes by ΔT, it follows from Equation 15-16 that the internal energy change is

$$\Delta U = n\left(\frac{D}{2}R\right)\Delta T$$

(ideal gas, D degrees of freedom)

But we saw above that for an ideal gas, $\Delta U = nC_V \Delta T$. Comparing this to Equation 15-17, we see that

Molar specific heat at constant
volume for an ideal gas
(15-18)

Number of degrees of freedom for a molecule of the gas

Molar specific heat of an ideal gas at constant volume $$C_V = \left(\frac{D}{2}\right)R$$ Ideal gas constant

Let's see how well Equation 15-18 works for the real gases listed in Table 15-1. For a monatomic gas there are three degrees of freedom per molecule, so $D = 3$ and Equation 15-18 becomes

$$C_V = \frac{3}{2}R = \frac{3}{2}(8.314 \, \text{J}/(\text{mol} \cdot \text{K})) = 12.47 \, \text{J}/(\text{mol} \cdot \text{K}) \quad \text{(monatomic gas)}$$

Table 15-1 shows that this is a very close fit to the experimental values of C_V for argon, helium, and neon. For a diatomic gas with five degrees of freedom ($D = 5$), we expect

$$C_V = \frac{5}{2}R = \frac{5}{2}(8.314 \, \text{J}/(\text{mol} \cdot \text{K})) = 20.79 \, \text{J}/(\text{mol} \cdot \text{K}) \quad \text{(diatomic gas)}$$

This is also a very close fit to the experimental values for the diatomic atoms listed in Table 15-1. Indeed, this is how we know that such molecules have five degrees of freedom! Experiments show that at temperatures well above room temperature, the value of C_V for diatomic molecule increases and becomes closer to $7R/2 = 29.10\,\text{J}/(\text{mol}\cdot\text{K})$. What's happening is that at higher temperatures it becomes possible for these molecules to vibrate, giving each molecule two additional degrees of freedom (one for the kinetic energy of vibration, the other for the potential energy of vibration).

We encourage you to use Equation 15-18 to determine the number of degrees of freedom for the triatomic gases listed in Table 15-1.

The molar specific heat at constant pressure C_p also depends on D, the number of degrees of freedom. Since $C_p - C_V = R$ (Equation 15-15) and $C_V = (D/2)R$ (Equation 15-18), you can see that

$$C_p = C_V + R = \left(\frac{D}{2}\right)R + R = \left(\frac{D+2}{2}\right)R \tag{15-19}$$

We can get an expression for the number of degrees of freedom D by taking the *ratio* of C_p to C_V. This **ratio of specific heats** is denoted by the Greek letter γ (gamma):

$$\gamma = \frac{C_p}{C_V} \quad \text{(ratio of specific heats)} \tag{15-20}$$

If we substitute Equation 15-18 for C_V and Equation 15-19 for C_p into Equation 15-20, we get

$$\gamma = \frac{C_p}{C_V} = \frac{\left(\dfrac{D+2}{2}\right)R}{\left(\dfrac{D}{2}\right)R} = \frac{D+2}{D} \quad \text{(ideal gas)} \tag{15-21}$$

You can check Equation 15-21 against the experimental values for γ given in Table 15-1. For example, for a monatomic ideal gas with three degrees of freedom ($D = 3$), Equation 15-21 predicts

$$\gamma = \frac{3+2}{3} = 1.67$$

which is a very good match to the experimental values for argon, helium, and neon. Try Equation 15-21 for a diatomic gas with $D = 5$; how well does the predicted value of γ compare to the experimental values in Table 15-1?

Adiabatic Processes for an Ideal Gas

The ratio of specific heats $\gamma = C_p/C_V$ for an ideal gas plays an important role in *adiabatic* processes in which there is zero heat flow into or out of the gas. If we have a quantity of gas in a cylinder with a moveable piston and then allow the piston to move in or out, the gas will compress or expand adiabatically if the cylinder and piston are made of an insulating material that does not allow heat to flow through it. It can be shown that if an ideal gas expands or contracts adiabatically, the pressure p and volume V of the gas are related by

Pressure of an ideal gas   Volume of an ideal gas

$$pV^\gamma = \text{constant}$$

Ratio of specific heats of the gas $= C_p/C_V$

The quantity pV^γ has the same value at all times during an adiabatic process for an ideal gas.

Pressure and volume for ideal gas, adiabatic process
(15-22)

As long as the thermodynamic changes that take place in an ideal gas are adiabatic, the product of pressure and volume to the power γ remains the same. As volume increases in an adiabatic expansion, pressure decreases; as volume decreases in an adiabatic compression, pressure increases.

The ideal gas law $pV = nRT$ also applies to this gas, so $p = nRT/V$. If we substitute this expression for the pressure p into Equation 15-22, we get

$$\frac{nRT}{V}V^\gamma = nRTV^{\gamma-1} = \text{constant}$$

Since the number of moles n does not change (no gas enters or leaves the system) and R is itself a constant, we can rewrite this expression as

Temperature and volume for ideal gas, adiabatic process (15-23)

Kelvin temperature of an ideal gas   Volume of an ideal gas

$$TV^{\gamma-1} = \text{constant}$$

Ratio of specific heats of the gas = C_p/C_V

The quantity $TV^{\gamma-1}$ has the same value at all times during an adiabatic process for an ideal gas.

The value of γ is greater than 1 for all gases (see Table 15-1), so $\gamma - 1$ is greater than zero. So as volume increases in an adiabatic expansion, temperature decreases; as volume decreases in an adiabatic compression, temperature increases.

Equation 15-23 explains what happens when you use a bicycle pump to inflate a tire: The pump rapidly becomes warm to the touch. Although the pump is not made of an insulating material, the air in the pump cylinder is compressed so rapidly that there's no time for heat to flow into or out of the air during the compression. As a result the compression is adiabatic, so the temperature of the gas (and the pump that holds it) increases as the air is compressed.

When you use a fire extinguisher, the compressed gas inside the metal cylinder of the extinguisher expands very rapidly. As for the bicycle pump, a rapid process means that there is no time for heat to flow, so the expansion of the gas is adiabatic. In accordance with Equation 15-23, this means that the temperature of the expelled gas drops. (You can demonstrate this same effect using your own breath. If you open your mouth and breathe on the back of your hand, you can feel that the expelled breath is warm. But the same breath feels cold if you form your lips into a small "O" and then breathe on the back of your hand. In the latter case the air expands rapidly as it exits through the small aperture through your lips, and this expansion is nearly adiabatic.)

Example 15-5 Burning Paper Without Heat

In a classroom physics demonstration, a piece of paper is placed in the bottom of a test tube with a sealed plunger. When the plunger is quickly depressed, compressing the air inside, the paper combusts. How is this possible? Let the initial volume of the gas in the test tube be 10.0 cm³ and the final volume be 1.00 cm³, and let the initial temperature be room temperature (20°C). Calculate the final temperature of the gas in the test tube. Assume that air is an ideal, diatomic gas.

Set Up

Because the compression happens quickly, there is no time for any heat transfer into or out of the air in the tube. So we can consider this to be an adiabatic process. We use Equation 15-23 to relate volume and temperature for this process, and we use Equation 15-21 to find the ratio of specific heats γ for air. For diatomic gases, there are five degrees of freedom.

Ideal gas, adiabatic process:

$$TV^{\gamma-1} = \text{constant} \quad (15\text{-}23)$$

Ratio of specific heats for an ideal gas with D degrees of freedom:

$$\gamma = \frac{C_p}{C_V} = \frac{D+2}{D} \quad (15\text{-}21)$$

V_i = 10.0 cm³
20°C

paper

V_f = 1.00 cm³
temperature = ?

Solve

First find the value of γ for the gas and convert the temperature from Celsius to Kelvin.

From Equation 15-21 with $D = 5$,

$$\gamma = \frac{C_p}{C_V} = \frac{5 + 2}{5} = \frac{7}{5} = 1.40$$

The initial temperature of the air is 20.0°C or

$$T_i = (20 + 273.15) \text{ K} = 293 \text{ K}$$

We know the initial values of the temperature ($T_i = 293$ K) and volume ($V_i = 10.0$ cm^3) and the final value of the volume ($V_f = 1.00$ cm^3). Use these in Equation 15-23 to solve for the final value of temperature.

Equation 15-23 says that the quantity $TV^{\gamma-1}$ has the same value after the compression as before the compression, so

$$T_f V_f^{\gamma-1} = T_i V_i^{\gamma-1}$$

Solve for the final temperature T_f:

$$T_f = \frac{T_i V_i^{\gamma-1}}{V_f^{\gamma-1}} = T_i \left(\frac{V_i}{V_f}\right)^{\gamma-1}$$

$$= (293 \text{ K})\left(\frac{10.0 \text{ cm}^3}{1.00 \text{ cm}^3}\right)^{\left(\frac{7}{5}-1\right)}$$

$$= (293 \text{ K})(10.0)^{\frac{2}{5}}$$

$$= 736 \text{ K or } 463°\text{C}$$

Reflect

The final temperature is above the flash point of paper (the temperature at which paper catches fire—around 450°C), so the paper will burn until the supply of paper or oxygen is used up. This same process is used in diesel engines: A mixture of fuel and air is rapidly compressed in the cylinders of the engine, raising the temperature to such a high value that the mixture spontaneously ignites without a spark plug (as is used in a conventional gasoline engine).

? Got the Concept? 15-4 Heating Helium

A quantity of helium gas at room temperature is placed in a cylinder with a moveable piston. If the cylinder is locked in place so that the volume cannot change and a quantity of heat Q_0 is added to the gas, the temperature of the gas increases by ΔT_0. Now the gas is cooled to its original temperature and the piston is unlocked so that the gas is free to expand. If the pressure exerted on the gas by the piston is held constant and the same quantity of heat Q_0 is added to the gas, what will be the temperature change of the gas? (a) ΔT_0, the same as before; (b) less than ΔT_0; (c) more than ΔT_0.

? Got the Concept? 15-5 Helium versus Nitrogen

Two cylinders, each equipped with a moveable piston, contain equal numbers of moles of a gas. One cylinder contains helium (He), while the other contains nitrogen (N$_2$). If the same quantity of heat Q is added to each gas and each is allowed to expand at constant pressure, what can you say about the temperature change ΔT and amount of work done W for the two gases? (a) ΔT and W are the same for both gases; (b) ΔT and W are both less for He than for N$_2$; (c) ΔT and W are both greater for He than for N$_2$; (d) ΔT is less for He than for N$_2$, but W is greater for He than for N$_2$; (e) ΔT is greater for He than for N$_2$, but W is less for He than for N$_2$; (f) none of these.

Take-Home Message for Section 15-4

✔ More heat must be added to a gas at constant pressure than at constant volume in order to produce the same change in temperature.

✔ Thermodynamic processes that are carried out quickly are often adiabatic because heat transfer is relatively slow.

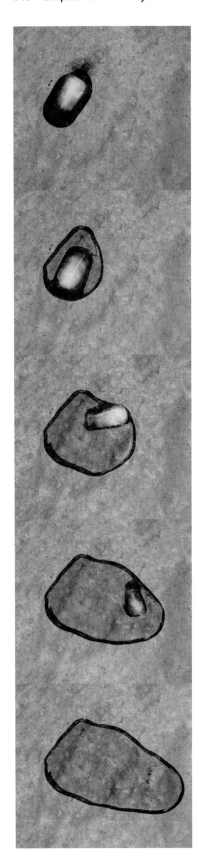

15-5 The second law of thermodynamics describes why some processes are impossible

Figure 15-12 shows two frames from a video in which someone inflates a balloon until it pops. How do you know that the left frame happens before the right one? None of the physical laws that we have studied so far preclude a set of balloon fragments from flying toward each other and reassembling as an intact balloon.

Figure 15-12 **Bursting your balloon** Both images were taken from a video of a person blowing up a balloon until it pops. How do you know that the left frame happens before the right one?

For example, neither conservation of energy nor momentum would be violated were the balloon fragments to reassemble. What about the pictures of an ice cube melting on a piece of granite in Figure 15-13? Each image was taken before the one below it, but would it be possible for this sequence to run in reverse? Here again, the reverse process would be permitted by the fundamental laws we know. The total energy of the system would be conserved if the granite drew enough energy from the water to cause it to freeze: The amount of energy required to melt a chunk of ice is exactly the same as the energy needed to freeze the resulting water. Yet we have declared that heat transfer is always from a hotter to a cooler object. Why?

For both the balloon in Figure 15-12 and the ice cube in Figure 15-13, events happen in a sequence that tends to decrease the level of *organization* or *order*. In Figure 15-12 the air that was confined within the balloon in an orderly way spreads out across the room when the balloon is popped, and the balloon itself breaks into a collection of random fragments. In Figure 15-13 the water molecules begin in an ordered state in which they are locked into the crystalline structure of the ice cube, and they end up free to move in a disordered way within the puddle of melted water. The reverse processes, in which air and balloon fragments spontaneously coalesce into a filled balloon or water spontaneously freezes, never occur in nature. That is, natural events always happen in a direction from ordered to random. We can generalize this observation to the **second law of thermodynamics**, which tells us that randomness in systems tends to increase:

The amount of disorder in an isolated system either always increases or, if the system is in equilibrium, stays the same.

We emphasize that a system described by the second law of thermodynamics must be *isolated*. This is to ensure that nothing outside the system can cause its state to change in an unnatural way. For example, we could manually sort out the fragments of the balloon in Figure 15-12, carefully reassemble them, and then inflate the reassembled balloon. The balloon system would experience increasing order, but only as a result of our external intervention; we could not treat the balloon as isolated. The most general example of an isolated system is the entire universe. Thus the second law of thermodynamics predicts that the amount of randomness in the universe always increases until it reaches equilibrium.

Let's see how to use the second law of thermodynamics to analyze systems that convert heat to work or work to heat. We'll look in particular at mechanical systems such as the internal combustion engine in a car (which takes the heat released by burning fuel and converts it to work) and a kitchen refrigerator (which takes work done by the refrigerator motor and uses it to transfer heat out of the refrigerator's contents). We'll see that the second law imposes strict limits on how efficient an engine can be and on how much performance you can get from a refrigerator. Keep in mind, however, that the second law also applies to living systems such as the human body, in which energy derived from food powers muscle contractions (converting heat to work) and produces sweat, which in turn cools the body down (converting work to heat that flows out of the body through perspiration).

Heat Engines and the Second Law

A system or device that converts heat to work is a **heat engine** or simply an *engine*. Heat engines are cyclic: Some part of the system absorbs energy, work is done, and the system returns to its original state in order for the cycle to begin again. Although the term "engine" might call to mind the complex device that powers an automobile, in thermodynamics a heat engine can be as simple as gas in a piston that expands as heat is added and contracts as the gas cools. There are also tiny molecular engines in living cells. Though much smaller than a piston or the engine in a car, these engines perform the same function, transforming energy into motion. In the mitochondria of all human cells hydrogen ions flow through ATP synthase, a curious enzyme that has a structure not unlike a waterwheel. The hydrogen ions cause the stalk of the ATP synthase to spin, which in turn pushes phosphate ions and adenosine diphosphate molecules together to form adenosine triphosphate (ATP). ATP synthase is in many ways analogous to an engine that converts the kinetic energy of hydrogen ions into a high-energy chemical bond that stores energy in a form that can be used by all cells. Enzymes such as ATP synthase follow a cycle, using energy to do work and then returning to their original state so that the cycle can start again.

We can describe heat engines of all kinds by a simple generic model (Figure 15-14). The engine is thermally connected to a *reservoir* of higher (hotter) temperature (T_H) and to a reservoir of lower (cooler) temperature (T_C). A **reservoir** is a part of a system large enough either to absorb or supply heat without a change in temperature. In an old-time steam engine, for example, the furnace serves as the hot reservoir and the surrounding atmosphere acts as the cold reservoir. Energy Q_H flows from the hot reservoir into the engine; during this process some of the energy goes into work W, and the remainder $|Q_C|$ flows out of the engine and into the cold reservoir in the form of heat.

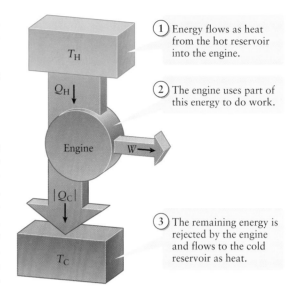

1. Energy flows as heat from the hot reservoir into the engine.

2. The engine uses part of this energy to do work.

3. The remaining energy is rejected by the engine and flows to the cold reservoir as heat.

Figure 15-14 What a heat engine does A generic heat engine, represented by a circle, is thermally connected to a reservoir of higher temperature (T_H) and to a reservoir of lower temperature (T_C). Energy Q_H flows from the hot reservoir into the engine in the form of heat. The engine uses some of the energy to do work W; the remaining energy is rejected as heat to the cold reservoir. (Note that Q_C is negative because it is heat that *leaves* the engine, so the energy that enters the cold reservoir is $|Q_C|$.)

! Watch Out! The quantity Q_C is negative.

Remember our convention that Q is positive if it flows into the object in question and negative if it flows out of the object. So for our engine Q_H is positive (heat flows into the engine from the hot reservoir) and Q_C is negative (heat flows out of the engine into the cold reservoir). However, in analyzing the engine in Figure 15-14 we'll be interested in how much energy flows *into* the *cold reservoir*. So we've labeled Figure 15-14 with $|Q_C|$ (the absolute value of Q_C, which is positive) to indicate the positive quantity of energy that flows into the cold reservoir in the form of heat.

A perfect engine would be one in which *all* of the energy Q_H taken in from the hot reservoir is converted to work, with no heat at all going into the cold reservoir (that is, $Q_C = 0$ in Figure 15-14). This would be a 100% efficient engine: None of the energy from the hot reservoir would be "thrown away" to the cold reservoir. Unfortunately, the second law of thermodynamics says that such a perfect engine is *impossible*. To see why, note that there is an increase in order of the hot reservoir: Because energy flows out of this reservoir, some of the molecules of the reservoir must lose their random motion and so become more orderly. Over one cycle of operation the engine itself returns to its original state, so it has zero net change in order, and there is no change at all in the cold reservoir (because no energy flows into it). So the net result would be that over one cycle the system of engine plus reservoirs undergoes an increase in order. But this violates the second law of thermodynamics, which says that the order of an isolated system can decrease or stay the same, but cannot increase! We conclude that you simply cannot build a perfect engine that's 100% efficient. The *Kelvin-Planck statement* is a rewording of the second law of thermodynamics that describes the inherent inefficiency of heat engines:

> *No process is possible in which heat is absorbed from a reservoir and converted completely into work.*

In order for a heat engine to satisfy the second law of thermodynamics, some heat *must* flow into the cold reservoir in order to make the cold reservoir less ordered. (This happens because the energy added to the cold reservoir increases the random motion of the reservoir's molecules.) The decrease in order of the cold reservoir can then compensate for the increase in order of the hot reservoir. So not all of the energy that flows from the hot reservoir can be converted to work; some of this energy must flow into the cold reservoir and cannot be recovered. That's what happens in a car's gasoline engine: Only about a quarter of the energy released by burning gasoline gets converted into work to propel the car. The remainder goes into heating up the engine and the exhaust gases. Similarly, in the human body only about 27% at best of the energy in food is actually used by your cells to do work. The rest of the energy appears as body heat.

Let's apply the *first* law of thermodynamics, Equation 15-2, to the generic engine shown in Figure 15-14. In one cycle of the engine it takes in an amount of energy Q_H from the hot reservoir in the form of heat and sends an amount of energy $|Q_C|$ to the cold reservoir in the form of heat, so the *net* quantity of heat that goes into the engine is $Q = Q_H - |Q_C|$. In that same cycle the engine does an amount of work W. Because the engine goes through a cycle that returns it to its initial state at the beginning of the cycle, there is zero net change in its internal energy: $\Delta U = 0$. So the first law of thermodynamics, $\Delta U = Q - W$, becomes

$$0 = Q_H - |Q_C| - W$$

or

Work done by a heat engine
(15-24)

Heat that flows from the hot reservoir into the engine in one cycle

Work done by a heat engine in one cycle

$$W = Q_H - |Q_C|$$

Heat that flows from the engine to the cold reservoir in one cycle

The amount of work done equals the difference between the amount of energy taken in from the hot reservoir and the amount of energy discarded into the cold reservoir. The **efficiency** of the engine is defined as the useful work W divided by the amount of energy Q_H taken in to do the work:

(15-25)

$$e = \frac{W}{Q_H}$$

If all the input energy were converted to work, then W would equal Q_H and the efficiency would be 100%, or $e = 1$. But the Kelvin-Planck form of the second law of thermodynamics tells us this is impossible. The best combustion engines, such as the ones found in automobiles, operate at an efficiency of $e \approx 0.30$ (about 30%). Similarly, when human muscles contract, only about 25% of the input energy does work, with the rest lost as heat, so $e \approx 0.25$. Using Equation 15-24, we can express the efficiency of a heat engine (Equation 15-25) in terms of the heat taken in from the hot reservoir and the heat rejected to the cold reservoir:

> Go to Picture It 15-2 for more practice dealing with efficiency

(15-26)

$$e = \frac{W}{Q_H} = \frac{Q_H - |Q_C|}{Q_H} = 1 - \frac{|Q_C|}{Q_H} \quad \text{(efficiency of a heat engine)}$$

Example 15-6 Efficiency of an Engine

The combustion of gasoline in a lawnmower engine releases 44.0 J of energy per cycle. Of that, 31.4 J are lost to warming the body of the engine and the surrounding air. (a) How much work does the lawnmower engine do per cycle? (b) What is the efficiency of the engine?

Set Up

We use Equation 15-24 to determine the work done by the engine and Equation 15-26 to find the efficiency.

Work done by a heat engine:

$$W = Q_H - |Q_C| \qquad (15\text{-}24)$$

Efficiency of a heat engine:

$$e = \frac{W}{Q_H} = \frac{Q_H - |Q_C|}{Q_H} = 1 - \frac{|Q_C|}{Q_H} \qquad (15\text{-}26)$$

$Q_H = 44.0$ J

engine

$W = ?$
$e = ?$

$|Q_C| = 31.4$ J

Solve

(a) The work done by the engine equals the difference between the heat Q_H taken in by burning gasoline and the heat $|Q_C|$ that is lost by the engine.

We are given that in one cycle,

$$Q_H = 44.0 \text{ J}$$
$$|Q_C| = 31.4 \text{ J}$$

From Equation 15-24, the work that the engine does in one cycle is

$$W = Q_H - |Q_C|$$
$$= 44.0 \text{ J} - 31.4 \text{ J} = 12.6 \text{ J}$$

(b) The efficiency of the engine equals the work done divided by the heat taken in. It's also equal to 1 minus the ratio of heat thrown away to heat taken in.

From Equation 15-26, the efficiency is

$$e = \frac{W}{Q_H} = \frac{12.6 \text{ J}}{44.0 \text{ J}} = 0.286$$

Alternatively,

$$e = 1 - \frac{|Q_C|}{Q_H} = 1 - \frac{31.4 \text{ J}}{44.0 \text{ J}}$$
$$= 1 - 0.714 = 0.286$$

Reflect

An efficiency of around 0.25 to 0.30 (25 to 30%) is typical for a gasoline engine.

Figure 15-15 shows the pV diagram for the cyclic process (called the *Otto cycle*) used in a typical automobile engine. (The process is somewhat simplified in this figure. The aircraft engine shown in Figure 15-1b uses this same cycle.) Beginning at the state marked 1, a mixture of fuel and air is rapidly compressed in a cylinder with a moveable piston. Because the compression is rapid, step $1 \rightarrow 2$ is adiabatic and there is no heat flow into the fuel–air mixture. However, work is done *on* the mixture by the piston, so for this step the work done *by* the fuel–air mixture is negative: $W_{1 \rightarrow 2} < 0$. At state 2 a spark ignites the fuel, resulting in heat Q_H flowing into the system. The associated increase in pressure and temperature from state 2 to state 3 occurs so rapidly that the

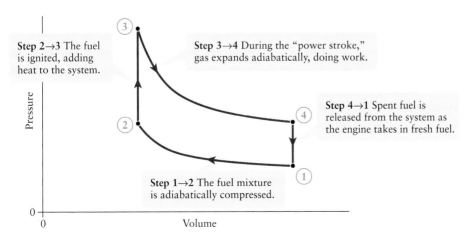

Step 2→3 The fuel is ignited, adding heat to the system.

Step 3→4 During the "power stroke," gas expands adiabatically, doing work.

Step 4→1 Spent fuel is released from the system as the engine takes in fresh fuel.

Step 1→2 The fuel mixture is adiabatically compressed.

Pressure

Volume

Figure 15-15 A simplified otto cycle
This *pV* diagram shows a simplified version of the cycle used in most automobile engines. It is named for the nineteenth-century German engineer Nicolaus Otto, who was the first to build an engine that worked on this cycle.

volume of the gas in the piston remains nearly constant, so no work is done. At state 3, the high pressure causes the gas to expand rapidly and so adiabatically. Because $Q = 0$ in an adiabatic process, the first law of thermodynamics ($\Delta U = Q - W$) tells us that all of the change in internal energy in step $3 \rightarrow 4$ results in positive work done by the gas on the piston: $W_{3 \rightarrow 4} > 0$. As the system returns to its initial state (step $4 \rightarrow 1$, for which the volume again remains constant so no work is done) exhaust is expelled and new fuel is injected into the piston.

The net work output in the cycle is the sum of the positive work in step $3 \rightarrow 4$ (in which the gas pushes against the piston) and the negative work in step $1 \rightarrow 2$ (in which the piston pushes on the gas). Remember that the work done equals the area under the curve in a pV diagram; step $3 \rightarrow 4$ happens at higher pressure than step $1 \rightarrow 2$, so there is more area under the curve for step $3 \rightarrow 4$ than for step $1 \rightarrow 2$ and there is more positive work than negative work. So the net work output of the engine over one cycle is positive. This work is used to turn the driveshaft of the automobile and make the wheels turn.

The Carnot Cycle

The cycle shown in Figure 15-15 is not the only cycle used in heat engines, nor does it have the highest efficiency. It turns out that the most efficient of all possible cyclic processes in a heat engine is the **Carnot cycle** (pronounced "car-noe"), first proposed in the early 1800s by French engineer Sadi Carnot. Carnot based his cycle on a requirement that all of the processes that comprise the cycle be **reversible processes**—that is, the reverse process is physically possible. Let's explore what this means.

Most thermodynamic processes are **irreversible processes**: They can proceed in only one direction. An example is what happens when ice at 0°C is placed in a large metal pot at 20°C. Heat flows from the pot into the ice, so the ice begins to melt and the temperature of the pot begins to drop. When the ice and pot come to equilibrium, the ice has completely melted and the pot and melted water both reach the same final temperature. The reverse of this process—in which liquid water in a pot spontaneously freezes, and the pot warms up—never happens in nature.

An example of a reversible process is ice at 0°C placed in a large metal pot that is also at 0°C. If a small amount of heat is made to flow from the pot into the ice, the ice will partially melt and the pot will contain ice and liquid water at 0°C. Because the amount of heat is so small, the temperature of the pot changes hardly at all and is still 0°C. If the same small amount of heat is now made to flow from the water–ice mixture back into the pot, the water will freeze back to ice and the ice and pot will both be at 0°C. In general, a process that involves heat flow will be reversible *only* if the objects between which heat flows are at the same temperature. If they are at different temperatures, the heat flow will always be from the higher-temperature object to the lower-temperature object and the process will be irreversible.

A process can also be reversible if it involves *no* heat flow ($Q = 0$). An example is a *slow* adiabatic expansion or compression, such as would happen with gas in an insulated cylinder. If the gas is allowed to expand slightly, it does a small amount of positive work on the piston ($W > 0$) and the internal energy of the gas decreases slightly (from the first law of thermodynamics, $\Delta U = Q - W$ is negative because Q is zero and W is positive). In the reverse process, the gas is compressed slightly and does negative work on the piston ($W < 0$, meaning that the piston does work on the gas), and the internal energy of the gas increases. The system then returns to its initial state. By contrast a free expansion of a gas, in which a gas under pressure suddenly expands to a larger volume (as in Figure 15-4b), is *irreversible*. It is not possible to return the system to the initial pressure and volume without adding energy by doing work.

Carnot understood that energy is conserved in both reversible and irreversible processes. But he also understood that in an irreversible process, much of the energy becomes *unavailable*. For example, when energy flows in the form of heat from the 20°C pot into the 0°C ice to melt it, the energy that went into the ice cannot be returned to the pot. In order not to "lose" energy in this way, Carnot realized that the most efficient heat engine cycle possible must therefore involve only reversible processes. As we've seen, this means either slow processes that involve heat flow with zero temperature difference or slow adiabatic processes.

Figure 15-16 shows the pV diagram for the Carnot cycle. The system is an ideal gas in a cylinder with a moveable piston. In state 1 the cylinder is in contact and in equilibrium with the cold reservoir at temperature T_C, so the gas is also at temperature T_C. Here are the four *reversible* steps that make up the cycle:

- **Step 1 → 2: Adiabatic compression.** You take the cylinder filled with gas and wrap it with a perfect insulator so there can be no heat flow into or out of the gas, and you do work on the moveable piston to slowly push it inward (so the gas does negative work). As the gas is compressed, its temperature increases from T_C to T_H.

- **Step 2 → 3: Isothermal expansion.** You remove the insulation and put the cylinder in contact with the hot reservoir at temperature T_H (which is the same as the current temperature of the gas). You now allow the gas to expand so that it does positive work on the piston. The temperature remains equal to T_H because the gas and hot reservoir are in equilibrium.

- **Step 3 → 4: Adiabatic expansion.** You again wrap the cylinder with a perfect insulator and allow the gas to expand. The expanding gas does more positive work on the piston, and the temperature of the gas decreases from T_H back down to T_C.

- **Step 4 → 1: Isothermal compression.** You again remove the insulation, but now you put the cylinder in contact with the cold reservoir at temperature T_C (which is the same as the current temperature of the gas). You do work on the piston to slowly push it inward, so the gas does negative work. The temperature remains equal to T_C because the gas and cold reservoir are in equilibrium. You stop when the gas is once again in state 1, with the same values of pressure, volume, and temperature as initially.

You can see from the description that the Carnot cycle is an idealization (like a massless rope or a frictionless ramp) and is *not* a practical cycle for a real engine. The Carnot cycle is nonetheless tremendously important. Because all four of its processes are reversible, the Carnot cycle is the *most efficient* heat engine cycle possible. It therefore represents the standard against which all other cycles should be compared. Let's see how to determine the efficiency of a Carnot engine.

From Equation 15-26, the efficiency of any heat engine is $e = 1 - |Q_C|/Q_H$. For the Carnot cycle depicted in Figure 15-16, Q_H is the heat that flows into the ideal gas

 The Carnot cycle consists of:
- Two adiabatic processes, for which no heat is transferred in or out of the system.
- Two isothermal processes, one at the temperature of the hot reservoir and one at the temperature of the cold reservoir.

Isotherm for temperature T_H (temperature of the hot reservoir)

Isotherm for temperature T_C (temperature of the cold reservoir)

Step 1→2: Adiabatic compression
Cylinder is insulated so no heat can flow in or out. The gas in the cylinder is compressed adiabatically ($Q = 0$), the temperature of the gas increases from T_C to T_H, and the gas does negative work $W_{1\rightarrow2}$.

Step 2→3: Isothermal expansion at T_H
Cylinder at temperature T_H is in contact with the hot reservoir at temperature T_H. The gas in the cylinder expands isothermally ($\Delta U = 0$), heat Q_H flows into the gas, and the gas does positive work $W_{2\rightarrow3} = Q_H$.

Step 3→4: Adiabatic expansion
Cylinder is insulated so no heat can flow in or out. The gas in the cylinder is allowed to expand adiabatically ($Q = 0$), the temperature of the gas drops from T_H to T_C, and the gas does work $W_{3\rightarrow4}$.

Step 4→1: Isothermal compression at T_C
Cylinder at temperature T_C is in contact with the cold reservoir at temperature T_C. The gas in the cylinder is compressed isothermally ($\Delta U = 0$), heat $|Q_C|$ flows into the gas, and the gas does negative work $W_{4\rightarrow1} = -|Q_C|$.

Figure 15-16 **The Carnot cycle** The most efficient cycle possible for a heat engine is made up of four reversible steps.

during step $2 \to 3$, when the gas cylinder is in contact with the hot reservoir at temperature T_H, and Q_C is the (negative) heat that flows into the gas during step $4 \to 1$, when the gas cylinder is in contact with the cold reservoir at temperature T_C. Both of these processes are isothermal, so $Q = W$ (Equation 15-5): The quantity of heat Q that enters the gas equals the work W done by the gas. Furthermore, we know from Equation 15-6 that the work done by n moles of an ideal gas in an isothermal process at temperature T is $W = nRT \ln (V_f/V_i)$, where V_i and V_f are the volume of the gas at the beginning and end of the process, respectively. So for the two isothermal steps in the Carnot cycle we have

$$Q_H = W_{2 \to 3} = nRT_H \ln \left(\frac{V_3}{V_2} \right)$$

$$Q_C = W_{4 \to 1} = nRT_C \ln \left(\frac{V_1}{V_4} \right)$$

Note that Q_C is negative for step $4 \to 1$. To see this, notice that V_1, the volume in state 1, is less than V_4, the volume in state 4 (see Figure 15-16). So the ratio V_1/V_4 is less than 1, and the natural logarithm of a number less than 1 is negative. Since $\ln (1/x) = -\ln x$, we can write the absolute value of Q_C as

$$|Q_C| = -Q_C = nRT_C \ln \left(\frac{V_4}{V_1} \right)$$

Then we can write the efficiency of the Carnot cycle using Equation 15-26 as

(15-27)
$$e_{\text{Carnot}} = 1 - \frac{|Q_C|}{Q_H} = 1 - \frac{nRT_C \ln \left(\dfrac{V_4}{V_1} \right)}{nRT_H \ln \left(\dfrac{V_3}{V_2} \right)}$$

Equation 15-27 looks rather messy, but we can simplify it by using Equation 15-23, which says that $TV^{\gamma-1} = \text{constant}$ for any adiabatic process. If we apply this to the adiabatic steps $1 \to 2$ and $3 \to 4$, we get

$$\text{Step } 1 \to 2 : T_C V_1^{\gamma-1} = T_H V_2^{\gamma-1} \quad \text{or} \quad \frac{T_C}{T_H} = \frac{V_2^{\gamma-1}}{V_1^{\gamma-1}}$$

$$\text{Step } 3 \to 4 : T_C V_4^{\gamma-1} = T_H V_3^{\gamma-1} \quad \text{or} \quad \frac{T_C}{T_H} = \frac{V_3^{\gamma-1}}{V_4^{\gamma-1}}$$

If we set the two expressions for T_C/T_H equal to each other and rearrange, we get

$$\frac{V_2^{\gamma-1}}{V_1^{\gamma-1}} = \frac{V_3^{\gamma-1}}{V_4^{\gamma-1}} \quad \text{so} \quad \frac{V_2}{V_1} = \frac{V_3}{V_4} \quad \text{and} \quad \frac{V_4}{V_1} = \frac{V_3}{V_2}$$

The last of these tells us that the quantities $\ln (V_4/V_1)$ and $\ln (V_3/V_2)$ in Equation 15-27 are equal and so cancel out, as do the factors of nR. So we're left with a very simple expression for the efficiency of a Carnot engine:

Efficiency of a Carnot engine   Kelvin temperature of the cold reservoir

Efficiency of a Carnot engine
(15-28)
$$e_{\text{Carnot}} = 1 - \frac{T_C}{T_H}$$

Kelvin temperature of the hot reservoir

The efficiency of an ideal Carnot heat engine depends *only* on the hot and cold temperatures between which the engine operates. Equation 15-28 is the maximum theoretical efficiency of *any* heat engine operating between temperatures T_H and T_C. It is impossible for any engine to do better than this.

The efficiency of an ideal Carnot engine can be made closer and closer to $e_{\text{Carnot}} = 1$ (100% efficiency) by decreasing T_C and increasing T_H. In order for the efficiency to be exactly one, T_C must equal 0 K. It is not possible, however, to attain a temperature of absolute zero. This statement is referred to as the **third law of thermodynamics**:

Go to Interactive Exercise 15-2 and 15-3 for more practice dealing with efficiency

> *It is possible for the temperature of a system to be arbitrarily close to absolute zero, but can never reach absolute zero.*

A consequence of the third law of thermodynamics is that it is impossible to make a heat engine that is 100% efficient.

Example 15-7 Carnot Efficiency and Actual Efficiency

An automotive engine is designed to operate between 290 K and 450 K. The engine produces 1.50×10^2 J of mechanical energy for every 6.00×10^2 J of heat absorbed from the combustion of fuel. Calculate (a) the actual efficiency of this engine and (b) the theoretical maximum efficiency of a Carnot engine operating between these temperatures.

Set Up

We'll use Equation 15-26 to determine the actual efficiency and Equation 15-28 to find the efficiency of a Carnot engine operating between 290 K and 450 K.

Efficiency of a heat engine:

$$e = \frac{W}{Q_H} = \frac{Q_H - |Q_C|}{Q_H} = 1 - \frac{|Q_C|}{Q_H}$$

(15-26)

Efficiency of a Carnot engine:

$$e_{Carnot} = 1 - \frac{T_C}{T_H}$$

(15-28)

Solve

(a) We are given $W = 1.50 \times 10^2$ J and $Q_H = 6.00 \times 10^2$ J. Use this and the first expression in Equation 15-26 to find the actual efficiency of the engine.

Actual efficiency:

$$e = \frac{W}{Q_H} = \frac{1.50 \times 10^2 \text{ J}}{6.00 \times 10^2 \text{ J}} = 0.250$$

(b) Compare the answer to (a) to the Carnot efficiency for $T_C = 290$ K and $T_H = 450$ K.

Efficiency for a theoretical Carnot engine operating between these temperatures:

$$e_{Carnot} = 1 - \frac{T_C}{T_H} = 1 - \left(\frac{290 \text{ K}}{450 \text{ K}}\right) = 0.356$$

Reflect

This engine is substantially less efficient than a Carnot engine. Note that even a Carnot engine—the most efficient heat engine that could possibly operate between these temperatures—is not terribly efficient: $e_{Carnot} = 0.356$ means that only 35.6% of the energy released by combustion can be used to do work. The other 64.4% is thrown away in the form of heat. This is one reason why electric cars, which are powered by electric motors that are not subject to the limitations of heat engines, are much more energy-efficient than gasoline-powered cars. The main disadvantage of electric cars is that present-day batteries hold much less energy per kilogram than does gasoline, so the range of a fully charged electric car is substantially less than that of a gasoline-powered car with a full tank of fuel.

Refrigerators

A **refrigerator** is a device that takes in energy and uses it to transfer heat from an object at low temperature to an object at high temperature. An ordinary kitchen refrigerator works this way: Energy is supplied to the refrigerator in the form of electricity, and the refrigerator extracts heat from the contents of the refrigerator (which you want to keep cold) and exhausts heat into the kitchen (normally through the back of the refrigerator, which is why it's warm back there). In many ways, a refrigerator is simply an engine running backward. Like heat engines, refrigerators are cyclic, and like heat engines, refrigerators are constrained by the second law of thermodynamics. The *Clausius form*

Figure 15-17 **What a refrigerator does** A generic refrigerator, represented by a circle, extracts heat Q_C from a cold reservoir at temperature T_C. To do this, work must be done on the refrigerator (so W, the work done *by* the refrigerator is negative and the work done *on* the refrigerator is $|W|$). All of the energy added to the engine as heat and by work is rejected to the hot reservoir at temperature T_H. Here Q_H is negative (it represents heat that *leaves* the refrigerator), so the heat that is rejected *into* the hot reservoir is $|Q_H|$.

③ The energy extracted from the cold reservoir, plus the energy delivered to the refrigerator as work, is rejected to the hot reservoir.

② For this to happen, work must be done on the refrigerator.

① Energy is extracted from the cold reservoir into the refrigerator.

of the second law of thermodynamics, named after the nineteenth-century German physicist Robert Clausius, says that:

No process is possible in which heat is absorbed from a cold reservoir and transferred completely to a hot reservoir.

In other words, it isn't possible to make a perfect refrigerator.

The diagram of a generic refrigerator shown in Figure 15-17 looks similar to the generic heat engine shown in Figure 15-14, but with an important difference: All of the arrows are in the opposite direction. Work is an *input* to this device; as a result, heat Q_C is made to go from the colder region to the hotter one. This transfer is, of course, exactly what you'd want in order to cool down a container in which to store food (a refrigerator) or a building (an air conditioner). A heat pump, a device used to warm up a building, is identical to a refrigerator; the difference is that a heat pump transfers heat from the cold exterior of the building into the warm interior to keep it warm.

Figure 15-18 shows the cycle used in a typical kitchen refrigerator, which uses the inert compound R134a (chemical formula CH_2FCF_3). R134a in the liquid state is forced through a tube (the evaporator coil) that passes through the freezer and refrigerator compartments. The R134a absorbs energy from the air in these compartments to cool them, which raises the temperature of the R134a and turns it into a gas. A compressor pump then pressurizes the R134a gas, which drives the gas around the system again and also increases its temperature even more. As the hot gas passes through the long, narrow condenser coil tube (usually in the back of the refrigerator), heat is transferred from the gaseous R134a to the cooler air in the kitchen. This part of the process cools the gas enough to cause it to liquefy, and the liquid R134a is further cooled by letting it expand rapidly as it passes through a valve from a narrow tube to a much wider one. The cold liquid then makes its way back to the evaporator coil to start the process again. In this way, energy is removed from the interior of the refrigerator and delivered to the surroundings.

A typical kitchen refrigerator uses the inert compound R134a (chemical formula CH_2FCF_3). The R134a is used to remove energy from the interior of the refrigerator and deliver it to the surroundings.

① R134a in the liquid state is forced through a tube (the evaporator coil) that passes through the freezer and refrigerator compartments.

② The R134a is at a lower temperature than the air in the freezer or refrigerator compartments. Hence the R134a absorbs energy from the air in these compartments, cooling them. This raises the temperature of the R134a and turns it into a gas.

③ A compressor pump then pressurizes the R134a gas. This drives the gas around the system, and increases its temperature even more.

④ As the hot gas passes through the long, narrow condenser coil tube (usually in the back of the refrigerator), heat is transferred from the gaseous R134a to the cooler air in the kitchen. This part of the process cools the gas enough to cause it to liquefy.

⑥ The cold liquid then makes its way back to the evaporator coil to start the process again.

⑤ The liquid R134a is further cooled by letting it expand rapidly as it passes through a valve from a narrow tube to a much wider one.

Compressor

Heat in

Evaporator coil

Cool gas

Evaporation

Compression

Cool liquid

Hot gas

Expansion

Condensation

Hot liquid

Expansion valve

Condenser coil

Heat out

Figure 15-18 **Inside a refrigerator** This simplified diagram shows the cyclic process that cools a kitchen refrigerator. This process involves compressing and expanding a refrigerant that transitions between being a liquid and a gas.

The less work required to extract heat Q_C from the cold reservoir, the more efficient the refrigerator. A perfect refrigerator would require no work to be done in order to cause heat to be transferred from the cold to the hot reservoir, but this process isn't possible according to the second law of thermodynamics. The efficiency of a refrigerator is given by the **coefficient of performance**, for which we use symbol CP:

$$CP = \frac{|Q_C|}{|W|} \tag{15-29}$$

As with efficiency, CP is essentially what you get out in terms of what you put in. The smaller the amount of work W for a given quantity of heat Q_C extracted from the cold reservoir, the larger the coefficient of performance CP. A typical value for CP for a kitchen refrigerator or a home air conditioner is 3.

The first law of thermodynamics requires that in one cycle, the total energy that goes into the refrigerator (in the form of work $|W|$ done on it and heat $|Q_C|$ extracted from the cold reservoir) equals the amount of energy that comes out (in the form of heat $|Q_H|$ delivered to the hot reservoir). So

$$|Q_C| + |W| = |Q_H| \quad \text{or} \quad |W| = |Q_H| - |Q_C| \text{ (refrigerator)} \tag{15-30}$$

Equation 15-29 then becomes

$$CP = \frac{|Q_C|}{|W|} = \frac{|Q_C|}{|Q_H| - |Q_C|} \tag{15-31}$$

(coefficient of performance of a refrigerator)

The maximum possible coefficient of performance of a refrigerator is obtained when the system is based on the Carnot cycle run in reverse. In an analogous way to how we found the efficiency of a Carnot engine, it can be shown that the coefficient of performance of a Carnot refrigerator is

$$CP_{Carnot} = \frac{T_C}{T_H - T_C} \tag{15-32}$$

(coefficient of performance of a Carnot refrigerator)

Like the Carnot cycle for engines, a Carnot refrigerator is not a practical device. The significance of Equation 15-32 is that it tells us the theoretical maximum coefficient of performance of a refrigerator operating between cold temperature T_C and hot temperature T_H.

Example 15-8 Kitchen Refrigerator

A kitchen refrigerator has a coefficient of performance of 3.30. When the refrigerator pump is running, it removes energy from the interior of the refrigerator at a rate of 760 J/s. (a) How much work must be done per second to extract this energy? (b) How much energy is rejected into the kitchen per second in this process? (c) If the refrigerator operates between 2°C (the interior of the refrigerator) and 25°C (the kitchen), what is the theoretical maximum coefficient of performance?

Set Up

The energy removed from the cold interior of the refrigerator is represented by $|Q_C|$, and the work done to remove that energy is represented by $|W|$. We can relate these to the coefficient of performance by using Equation 15-31, and to the energy $|Q_H|$ rejected into the warm kitchen by using Equation 15-30. The theoretical maximum value of CP is the Carnot value, given by Equation 15-32.

Coefficient of performance of a refrigerator:

$$CP = \frac{|Q_C|}{|W|} = \frac{|Q_C|}{|Q_H| - |Q_C|} \tag{15-31}$$

Energy relationships for a refrigerator:

$$|Q_C| + |W| = |Q_H| \text{ or}$$

$$|W| = |Q_H| - |Q_C| \tag{15-30}$$

Coefficient of performance of a Carnot refrigerator:

$$CP_{Carnot} = \frac{T_C}{T_H - T_C} \tag{15-32}$$

Solve

(a) Use Equation 15-31 to determine the amount of work that must be done per second.

In 1 s, an amount of energy $|Q_C| = 760$ J is removed from the interior of the refrigerator. The amount of work $|W|$ that must be done to make this happen depends on $|Q_C|$ and the coefficient of performance:

$$CP = \frac{|Q_C|}{|W|}$$

$$|W| = \frac{|Q_C|}{CP} = \frac{760\ \text{J}}{3.30} = 230\ \text{J}$$

So the rate at which work must be done is 230 J/s.

(b) Find the rate at which energy is rejected into the kitchen.

From Equation 15-30, the amount of heat $|Q_H|$ rejected into the kitchen in 1 s is

$$|Q_H| = |Q_C| + |W| = 760\ \text{J} + 230\ \text{J} = 990\ \text{J}$$

So the rate at which the refrigerator rejects heat is 990 J/s.

(c) Calculate the coefficient of performance of a Carnot refrigerator operating between the same hot and cold temperatures.

The temperatures between which the refrigerator operates are

2°C or $T_C = (273.15 + 2)$ K $= 275$ K and

25°C or $T_H = (273.15 + 25)$ K $= 298$ K

The coefficient of performance of a Carnot refrigerator operating between these temperatures is

$$CP_{\text{Carnot}} = \frac{T_C}{T_H - T_C} = \frac{275\ \text{K}}{298\text{K} - 275\ \text{K}} = \frac{275\ \text{K}}{23\ \text{K}}$$
$$= 12$$

Reflect

The coefficient of performance CP is substantially less than what could be achieved by an ideal Carnot refrigerator. Notice that the higher the actual value of CP, the less work must be done to achieve the same amount of cooling inside the refrigerator. Less work means less waste, and as a result, less heating of the kitchen. This actual refrigerator rejects heat into the kitchen at a rate of 990 J/s or 990 W, about the same as the power output of an electric space heater.

 ## Got the Concept? 15-6   A Super Engine

A fellow student announces that he has invented a gasoline engine that is 90% efficient. He claims that he gets such efficiency by running the engine at very high temperatures.

The cylinders of his engine are made of titanium, which has a melting temperature of 1941 K. If he asks you to invest in this engine, should you agree?

Take-Home Message for Section 15-5

✔ One statement of the second law of thermodynamics is that randomness in systems tends to increase over time.

✔ A system or device that converts heat to work is a heat engine. It is not possible to create an engine or process in which heat is absorbed from a reservoir and converted completely into work.

✔ A refrigerator is a heat engine in reverse. It uses work to move heat from a cold reservoir to a hot reservoir.

✔ The third law of thermodynamics states that the temperature of a system can never attain absolute zero.

15-6 The entropy of a system is a measure of its disorder

The second law of thermodynamics uses the concept of the *order* of a system. How can we quantify just how ordered or disordered a system is? Searching for the answer to this question will lead us to introduce a new physical quantity called *entropy* that plays an essential role in thermodynamics.

To get the best understanding of how ordered or disordered a thermodynamic system is, you would have to note the position and behavior of every one of its molecules. That's a challenging task for a system even as small as a single drop of water, which contains about 10^{22} H_2O molecules. (That's roughly 1000 times more molecules than there are grains of sand on all of Earth's beaches.) Instead, let's look at a system with a much smaller number of constituents. Imagine that your sock drawer is an unorganized jumble of an equal number of blue socks and red socks. If you grab four socks without looking at their colors, what distribution of colors within the four-sock "thermodynamic system" are you most likely to have?

There is only one way to end up with four red socks: Each individual selection must be a red sock. There are four ways to have three red socks and one blue one, however. One way is to get a red sock during each of the first three selections and then get one blue one. Another way is for the first sock chosen to be blue and the last three red. We can summarize the possible ways to get three red and one blue sock this way:

$$(\circ \bullet \bullet \bullet), (\bullet \circ \bullet \bullet), (\bullet \bullet \circ \bullet), \text{ and } (\bullet \bullet \bullet \circ)$$

Table 15-2 summarizes all 16 possible four-sock combinations. The most probable grouping is two red socks and two blue socks (6 of the 16 possible combinations). This is also the most randomly distributed, least ordered four-sock state. The most ordered state would be one that was made of either four red socks or four blue socks. Table 15-2 shows that such states are also the least likely ones.

These conclusions about socks taken from a drawer turn out to be true in general: *The most probable final or equilibrium state of a system is the one that is the least ordered.* For example, a hot object and a cold object put into thermal contact come to the same final temperature not because no other possibility is allowed, but because this state is the least ordered and therefore the most probable. Energy would still be conserved if, say, the hot object got hotter while the cold one got colder. But this would be highly improbable because this is a highly ordered state (the energy of the system ends up concentrated in the hot object rather than being spread between the two objects).

Table 15-2 Possible combinations of red and blue socks

Blue	Red	Combinations	Number
0	4	$(\bullet \bullet \bullet \bullet)$	1
1	3	$(\circ \bullet \bullet \bullet), (\bullet \circ \bullet \bullet), (\bullet \bullet \circ \bullet), (\bullet \bullet \bullet \circ)$	4
2	2	$(\circ \circ \bullet \bullet), (\circ \bullet \circ \bullet), (\circ \bullet \bullet \circ), (\bullet \circ \circ \bullet),$ $(\bullet \circ \bullet \circ), (\bullet \bullet \circ \circ)$	6
3	1	$(\bullet \circ \circ \circ), (\circ \bullet \circ \circ), (\circ \circ \bullet \circ), (\circ \circ \circ \bullet)$	4
4	0	$(\circ \circ \circ \circ)$	1

To represent order, we must take the list of variables that describe the state of a system—its temperature T, pressure p, volume V, and internal energy U—and add to it a new variable that we call **entropy**. Entropy, which for historical reasons we give the rather unexpected symbol S, is defined so that the larger its value, the *less order* and the *more disorder* is present in a system. So we can think of entropy S as a measure of *disorder*. The second law of thermodynamics therefore states that *the entropy of an isolated system must either remain constant or increase.* The second law of thermodynamics also predicts that the entropy of the universe—in other words, all things and all processes—must increase until equilibrium is reached.

The second law of thermodynamics suggests that what matters most is not the *amount* of order in a system, but rather how much *change* in order there is in a thermodynamic process. The first law of thermodynamics says the same thing about internal energy. The first law tells us that the change in internal energy, ΔU, must be equal to $Q - W$ (the quantity of heat that enters the system minus the work that the system does). Let's see how to express the entropy change for the special case of a system that undergoes a process that happens at a constant temperature T. To be specific, we'll look at the reversible isothermal expansion of an ideal gas.

Figure 15-19 shows a quantity of ideal gas at temperature T confined within a cylinder with a moveable piston. We put the cylinder in thermal contact with a large reservoir at the same temperature T, then allow the gas to expand. Because the gas is in

Figure 15-19 **Entropy changes in an isothermal expansion** In a reversible isothermal expansion of an ideal gas, the entropy of the gas increases; the entropy of the reservoir with which the gas is in contact decreases by an equal amount.

Gas in a cylinder, temperature T

Reservoir, temperature T

Q

1. If you allow the gas to expand at constant temperature...

2. ...the entropy change of the gas is $\Delta S_{gas} = Q/T$...

3. ...and the entropy change of the reservoir is $\Delta S_{reservoir} = -Q/T$.

In this reversible process, the net entropy change of the system of gas plus reservoir is zero: $\Delta S_{net} = \Delta S_{gas} + \Delta S_{reservoir} = 0$.

thermal contact with the reservoir, its temperature remains constant and so the internal energy of the gas does not change: $\Delta U = 0$. The gas does work on the piston as it expands, so $W > 0$. From the first law of thermodynamics, $\Delta U = Q - W$ and $Q = \Delta U + W$, or in this case (since ΔU is zero) $Q = W$. This says that energy must flow into the gas from the reservoir in the form of heat Q in order that the gas can do work on the piston.

As the gas expands, the volume V that the gas occupies increases, and the molecules of the gas are now more spread out. This makes the gas more disordered, just as taking socks from a drawer and strewing them around the larger volume of your bedroom makes the socks more disordered. The greater the quantity of heat that enters the gas, the more the gas expands, and the greater the increase in disorder. So in this isothermal expansion, the entropy change ΔS of the gas is *proportional* to the quantity of heat Q that flows into the gas.

The entropy change ΔS in an isothermal expansion also depends on the temperature T. For a given quantity of heat Q, the increase in disorder is greater if the system is at a low temperature (so the molecules are moving slowly and are relatively well ordered to start with) than if the system is at a high temperature (so the molecules are moving rapidly in a relatively disordered state). We conclude that the entropy change ΔS in this reversible isothermal process is *inversely proportional* to the Kelvin temperature T.

Putting these ideas together, we *define* the entropy change ΔS in a reversible isothermal process as

Entropy change in a reversible isothermal process
(15-33)

Heat that flows into the system ($Q > 0$ if heat flows in, $Q < 0$ if heat flows out)

Entropy change of a system in a reversible isothermal process

$$\Delta S = \frac{Q}{T}$$

Kelvin temperature of the system

Equation 15-33 shows that the units of entropy are the units of heat (that is, energy) divided by the units of temperature, or joules per kelvin (J/K).

We can also apply Equation 15-33 to the *reservoir* with which the gas cylinder is in contact. If a positive quantity of heat $Q > 0$ flows *into* the gas *from* the reservoir, the heat that flows into the reservoir from the gas is $-Q$. (This says that the quantity of heat that enters the gas equals the quantity of heat that leaves the reservoir.) The gas and reservoir are both at the same temperature T, so the *net* entropy change of the system of gas plus reservoir is

$$\Delta S_{net} = \Delta S_{gas} + \Delta S_{reservoir} = \frac{Q}{T} + \frac{(-Q)}{T} = 0$$

In a reversible isothermal expansion, the entropy of the gas increases (it becomes more disordered), but the entropy of the reservoir decreases (it becomes *less* disordered because it has transferred some of its random thermal energy to the gas). The net change in entropy is zero.

Example 15-9 Calculating Entropy Change

A cylinder containing n moles of an ideal gas at temperature T changes its volume isothermally from an initial volume V_i to a final volume V_f. Find expressions for (a) the entropy change of the gas and (b) the entropy change of the thermal reservoir with which the gas is in contact. (c) Evaluate these for the special case in which 0.050 mol of gas at 20.0°C has an initial volume of 1.00×10^{-3} m³ (equal to 1.00 L) and expands to a final volume of 2.00×10^{-3} m³.

Set Up

Equation 15-33 tells us the entropy change of the gas in terms of its temperature T and the heat Q that flows into the gas during the volume change. From Equation 15-5 the quantity of heat Q equals the work W that the gas does. Equation 15-6 tells us the work done in this process. We'll put all of these pieces together to find the entropy changes of the gas and the thermal reservoir.

Entropy change in a reversible isothermal process:

$$\Delta S = \frac{Q}{T} \qquad (15\text{-}33)$$

Isothermal process for an ideal gas:

$$Q = W \qquad (15\text{-}5)$$

Work done by an ideal gas in an isothermal process:

$$W = nRT \ln \frac{V_f}{V_i} \qquad (15\text{-}6)$$

Solve

(a) Find an expression for the entropy change of the gas.

If we combine Equation 15-5 and Equation 15-6, we find that the quantity of heat that enters the gas equals the work done by the gas:

$$Q_{gas} = W = nRT \ln \frac{V_f}{V_i}$$

From Equation 15-33, the entropy change of the gas in this process is

$$\Delta S_{gas} = \frac{Q_{gas}}{T} = \frac{nRT}{T} \ln \frac{V_f}{V_i} = nR \ln \frac{V_f}{V_i}$$

If the gas expands so that the final volume is greater than the initial volume, the ratio V_f/V_i is greater than 1 and ΔS_{gas} is positive (the entropy of the gas increases). If the gas is compressed so that the final volume is less than the initial volume, the ratio V_f/V_i is less than 1 and ΔS_{gas} is negative (the entropy of the gas decreases).

(b) Find an expression for the entropy change of the reservoir.

The heat that enters the gas comes from the reservoir, so the value of Q for the reservoir equals the negative of the value of Q for the gas:

$$Q_{reservoir} = -Q_{gas} = -nRT \ln \frac{V_f}{V_i}$$

The entropy change of the reservoir is then

$$\Delta S_{reservoir} = \frac{Q_{reservoir}}{T} = -\frac{nRT}{T} \ln \frac{V_f}{V_i} = -nR \ln \frac{V_f}{V_i}$$

If we compare this to the result from part (a), we see that

$$\Delta S_{reservoir} = -\Delta S_{gas}$$

(c) Calculate the numerical values of ΔS_{gas} and $\Delta S_{reservoir}$.

Our expression for ΔS_{gas} doesn't depend on the temperature T, so we don't need to convert 20.0°C into a Kelvin temperature.

With $n = 0.050$ mol, $V_i = 1.00 \times 10^{-3}$ m^3, and $V_f = 2.00 \times 10^{-3}$ m^3, we get

$$\Delta S_{gas} = nR \ln \frac{V_f}{V_i}$$

$$= (0.050 \text{ mol})\left(8.314 \frac{J}{\text{mol·K}}\right) \ln\left(\frac{2.00 \times 10^{-3} \text{ m}^3}{1.00 \times 10^{-3} \text{ m}^3}\right)$$

$$= (0.416 \text{ J/K}) \ln 2.00$$

$$= 0.288 \text{ J/K}$$

$$\Delta S_{reservoir} = -\Delta S_{gas} = -0.288 \text{ J/K}$$

The net entropy change of the system of gas and reservoir is

$$\Delta S_{net} = \Delta S_{gas} + \Delta S_{reservoir}$$

$$= 0.288 \text{ J/K} + (-0.288 \text{ J/K}) = 0$$

Reflect

Note that the expression $\Delta S_{gas} = nR \ln (V_f/V_i)$ just depends on the number of moles n and the ratio of the final and initial volumes occupied by the gas. This is consistent with the idea that a change in entropy corresponds to a change in disorder: The greater the increase in volume, the more disordered the system becomes; the greater the number of moles (and hence the greater the number of molecules) that expand into the new volume, the greater the increase in disorder. To see why the number of moles matter, think of taking socks from your sock drawer and strewing them around your bedroom. If there are only two socks involved, the amount of disorder isn't great; if there are a hundred socks, it's a hugely disordered mess.

In Example 15-9 the gas and reservoir together make up an *isolated* system: The gas and reservoir are in thermal contact with each other, but are not in thermal contact with anything else. In this case, in which the thermodynamic process is *reversible*, the entropy of that isolated system remains constant.

Let's now consider a different isothermal process that's *irreversible*. In Figure 15-20 a metal bar is used to put a hot reservoir at temperature T_H in thermal contact with a cold reservoir at temperature T_C. Heat flows from the hot reservoir to the cold one, but the reservoirs are so large that their temperatures remain essentially unchanged. Just as we did for the reservoir in Example 15-9, we can calculate the entropy change of each

① A quantity of heat $Q = 1.20 \times 10^3$ J flows through the metal rod from the hot reservoir to the cold reservoir.

Hot reservoir
$T_H = 400$ K

Heat

Cold reservoir
$T_C = 300$ K

② Entropy change of the hot reservoir:

$$\Delta S_H = \frac{(-Q)}{T_H} = \frac{(-1.20 \times 10^3 \text{ J})}{400 \text{ K}} = -3.00 \text{ J/K}$$

③ Entropy change of the cold reservoir:

$$\Delta S_C = \frac{(+Q)}{T_C} = \frac{(+1.20 \times 10^3 \text{ J})}{300 \text{ K}} = +4.00 \text{ J/K}$$

Figure 15-20 Entropy changes in irreversible heat flow In irreversible heat flow from a hot object to a cold one, the *net* entropy of the two objects together increases.

The net entropy change in this irreversible process is positive: $\Delta S_{net} = \Delta S_H + \Delta S_C = (-3.00 \text{ J/K}) + (+4.00 \text{ J/K}) = +1.00 \text{ J/K}$. The net entropy always increases in an irreversible process.

reservoir using Equation 15-33, $\Delta S = Q/T$. If a quantity of heat Q is transferred between the reservoirs, then $Q_C = +Q$ (heat flows *into* the cold reservoir from the hot one) and $Q_H = -Q$ (an equal quantity of heat flows *out* of the hot reservoir into the cold one). The entropy of the metal bar doesn't change: As much heat enters one end of the bar as leaves the other. The entropy changes of the two reservoirs are then

$$\text{Cold reservoir: } \Delta S_C = \frac{(+Q)}{T_C} \text{ (positive)}$$

$$\text{Hot reservoir: } \Delta S_H = \frac{(-Q)}{T_H} \text{ (negative)}$$

$$\text{Net entropy change: } \Delta S_{net} = \Delta S_C + \Delta S_H = \frac{(+Q)}{T_C} + \frac{(-Q)}{T_H}$$

As in Example 15-9, the entropy of one object (the cold reservoir) increases while the entropy of the other object (the hot reservoir) decreases. The difference is that the process shown in Figure 15-20 is *irreversible* because the two objects are at *different* temperatures T_C and T_H: By itself heat will flow only from the high-temperature object at T_H to the low-temperature one at T_C, never the other way, so the process cannot run in reverse. And because the two temperatures are different, the entropy changes ΔS_C and ΔS_H in this irreversible process do *not* cancel. To be specific, suppose a quantity of heat $Q = 1.20 \times 10^3$ J flows from a hot reservoir at $T_H = 400$ K to a cold reservoir at $T_C = 300$ K, as shown in Figure 15-20. In this case

$$\text{Cold reservoir: } \Delta S_C = \frac{(+Q)}{T_C} = \frac{1.20 \times 10^3 \text{ J}}{300 \text{ K}} = +4.00 \text{ J/K}$$

$$\text{Hot reservoir: } \Delta S_H = \frac{(-Q)}{T_H} = \frac{-1.20 \times 10^3 \text{ J}}{400 \text{ K}} = -3.00 \text{ J/K}$$

Net entropy change: $\Delta S_{net} = \Delta S_C + \Delta S_H = 4.00 \text{ J/K} + (-3.00 \text{ J/K}) = +1.00 \text{ J/K}$

For this irreversible process the cold reservoir gains more entropy than the hot reservoir loses, so there is a *net increase* in the entropy of the system of two reservoirs. So the system becomes increasingly disordered. While energy is conserved, the energy becomes less available to do useful work (for instance, to run a heat engine between the temperatures of the high and low reservoirs). In general we can say that

In a reversible process there is no net change in entropy. In an irreversible process, the net entropy increases.

This is the *entropy statement* of the second law of thermodynamics.

> **Watch Out!** **The entropy of a system can go down, but only through a process that raises the entropy of another system.**
>
> For both the reversible isothermal expansion of an ideal gas (Figure 15-19) and the irreversible flow of heat from a hot reservoir to a cold one (Figure 15-20), one of the objects undergoes a *decrease* in entropy. This may seem to contradict the statement that entropy stays the same in a reversible process and increases in an irreversible process. In fact there's no contradiction, because this statement is about *net* entropy.
>
> Whenever an object undergoes a decrease in entropy, it's because there's a second object that undergoes an *increase* in entropy (the gas in the example of the reversible isothermal expansion, and the cold reservoir in the example of irreversible heat flow). When all of the interacting objects are taken into account, the *net* entropy never decreases.

The entropy statement of the second law of thermodynamics gives us additional insight into the Carnot cycle, which is the most efficient heat engine theoretically possible. Each step in the Carnot cycle—an isothermal compression, an adiabatic compression, an isothermal expansion, and an adiabatic expansion—is *reversible*. So there is no net entropy change of the system of a Carnot engine, a hot reservoir, and a cold reservoir. (In Example 15-9 we saw that $\Delta S_{net} = 0$ for an isothermal expansion; the same is true for an isothermal compression, in which the gas loses entropy and the reservoir with which it is in contact gains an equal amount of entropy. There is no heat flow at all in a reversible adiabatic compression or expansion, so the entropy does not change in either of these steps.) At the end of each cycle the system is just as ordered as it was at the beginning of the cycle. By contrast, if we use a heat engine that utilized irreversible processes (like the idealized automotive engine cycle shown in Figure 15-15), there is a net increase in entropy—and hence in disorder—per cycle. So the *most efficient* engine is also the one that gives rise to the *least* increase in net entropy.

? Got the Concept? 15-7   Melting versus Vaporization

For water the latent heat of fusion (melting) is $L_F = 3.34 \times 10^5$ J/kg and the latent heat of vaporization is $L_V = 2.26 \times 10^6$ J/kg. Which involves a greater change in entropy? (a) Melting 1.00 kg of ice at 0°C; (b) vaporizing 1.00 kg of liquid water at 100°C; (c) the entropy change is the same for both.

We've considered only situations in which the entropy of objects changes due to the transfer of heat between objects. One situation in which there is *no* heat flow is the free expansion of a gas shown in Figure 15-4b. This process is irreversible: After the barrier has ruptured and the expansion has taken place, it would be impossible for all of the gas molecules to spontaneously reassemble on the left-hand part of the cylinder in Figure 15-4b. So we would expect that the entropy of the gas increases in the irreversible free expansion. However, we can't use Equation 15-33 to calculate the entropy change; there is no heat flow into the gas (the cylinder that encloses the gas is insulated), so the equation $\Delta S = Q/T$ predicts incorrectly that there would be *zero* entropy change. The reason why Equation 15-33 doesn't work is that it assumes that the process occurs slowly enough that the system is never far from equilibrium, which is definitely not the case for the sudden rush of gas in a free expansion. Instead, we find the entropy change by noting that the final state—pressure, volume, and temperature—of the gas after a free expansion is the same as if it had undergone a reversible isothermal expansion to the same final volume (compare parts a and b of Figure 15-4). We saw in Example 15-9 that the entropy of the gas increases in such a process, and we saw how to calculate ΔS_{gas}. Because entropy is a state variable whose value does not depend on the history of the system, the change in entropy ΔS_{gas} must be the same for a free expansion. In a reversible isothermal expansion the gas is in thermal contact with a reservoir at the same temperature, and the entropy of the reservoir decreases by as much as the entropy of the gas increases so that the net entropy change is zero. But for a free expansion the cylinder is isolated, so the only entropy change is the increase in entropy ΔS_{gas} of the gas. So there is indeed a net entropy increase, just as we expect for an irreversible process.

It's instructive to ask what the entropy statement of the second law of thermodynamics says about the existence and evolution of life. Living organisms such as the cat shown in Figure 15-1a undergo a decrease in entropy as they develop. For example, humans start out as a single cell and grow into a highly ordered network of cells by rearranging raw materials (food) from the environment. Complex organisms are more efficient, require less energy, and are thereby better able to survive in an environment of limited resources. The processes, like evolution, by which complex organisms arise from simpler ones necessarily introduce more order and therefore lower entropy. Does this mean that they violate the second law of thermodynamics?

The answer to this question is no: Life most definitely does *not* violate the second law of thermodynamics. While the entropy of a living organism decreases as it develops, the entropy of its surroundings *increases*. That's because when an organism consumes and metabolizes food, it uses some of the energy from the food to do work (for example, to grow), but also wastes some of that energy, too. It is this inefficiency that causes the *net* effect to be an increase in the entropy of the universe. Another way to say this is that the entropy of an organism decreases, but the entropy of its waste products—for example, the carbon dioxide that you exhale, the perspiration that you release from your skin, and the liquid and solid material that you excrete—increases more than the entropy of the organism decreases.

The second law of thermodynamics also tells us about the distant future of our universe. If we consider the universe as a whole as a thermodynamic system, the entropy statement of the second law says that *the entropy S of the universe can never decrease.* Reversible processes in the universe cause no change in *S*, while irreversible processes cause *S* to increase.

Our present-day universe is rather well ordered, with most ordinary matter clumped into *stars* that are at much higher temperatures than their surroundings and that radiate light energy into space. (In our own solar system, more than 99% of the mass is concentrated in our local star, the Sun. The light energy that we receive from the Sun powers all of our weather and is the ultimate source of energy for plant life, which in turn is the source of energy for animal life—including our own.) But over time even the longest-lived stars will eventually cease to shine, the internal energy that they once contained finally spread in a disordered way across the cosmos. In this far-distant, high-entropy future, everything in the universe will approach the same final temperature, which will itself approach absolute zero. This dismal but inescapable state of affairs, which lies perhaps 10^{100} years in our future—many, many times greater than the current age of the universe, which is about 1.37×10^{10} years—is called the *heat death of the universe*.

Take-Home Message for Section 15-6

✔ The entropy of a system is a measure of the disorder of the system. Systems with a low value of entropy are more ordered.

✔ The most probable final state of a system is the one that is the most disordered and has the highest entropy.

✔ In a process in which two objects interact, it's possible for the entropy of one object to decrease. However, the *net* entropy remains constant in a reversible process and increases in an irreversible process.

Key Terms

adiabatic process
Carnot cycle
coefficient of performance
efficiency
entropy
first law of thermodynamics
heat engine
internal energy
irreversible process

isobaric process
isochoric process
isotherm
isothermal process
molar specific heat
molar specific heat at constant
    pressure
molar specific heat at constant
    volume

pV diagram
ratio of specific heats
refrigerator
reservoir
reversible process
second law of thermodynamics
state variable
thermodynamic process
third law of thermodynamics

Chapter Summary

Topic	Equation or Figure

The first law of thermodynamics:
In any thermodynamic process, the change in internal energy of the system is related to the heat Q that enters the system and the work W that the system does during the process. There are simple rules for the signs of Q and W.

During a thermodynamic process, the change in the internal energy of a system...

$$\Delta U = Q - W \qquad (15\text{-}2)$$

...equals the heat that flows into the system during the process...

...minus the work that the system does during the process.

Heat flows into the system: $Q > 0$.

Heat flows out of the system: $Q < 0$.

System does positive work on its surroundings: $W > 0$.

System has positive work done on it by its surroundings: $W < 0$.

(Figure 15-3)

Thermodynamic processes: Four important types of thermodynamic processes are isobaric (constant pressure), isothermal (constant temperature), adiabatic (no heat flow), and isochoric (constant volume). In *any* process, the work done is represented by the area under the curve of the pV diagram for the process. There are simple expressions for the work done in an isobaric process and for the work done by an ideal gas in an isothermal process. In an isochoric process, zero work is done.

Work that a system does in an isobaric process | Volume of the system at the end of the process

$$W = p(V_f - V_i)$$

(15-4)

Constant pressure of the system | Volume of the system at the beginning of the process

Number of moles of gas | Ideal gas constant

Work that an ideal gas does in an isothermal process

$$W = nRT \ln \frac{V_f}{V_i}$$

Volume of the gas at the end of the process

(15-6)

Kelvin temperature of the gas | Volume of the gas at the beginning of the process

Molar specific heats of a gas: The molar specific heat is the energy required to raise the temperature of one mole of substance by one kelvin. For an ideal gas, the molar specific heats at constant pressure (C_p) and constant volume (C_V) differ by a fixed amount; the value of C_V depends on the number of degrees of freedom of a gas molecule.

Quantity of heat that flows into (if $Q > 0$) or out of (if $Q < 0$) an object | Molar specific heat of the substance of which the object is made

$$Q = nC\Delta T$$

(15-10)

Number of moles present of the substance | Temperature change of the object that results from the heat flow

Molar specific heat of an ideal gas at constant pressure

$$C_p - C_V = R$$ Ideal gas constant

(15-15)

Molar specific heat of an ideal gas at constant volume

Number of degrees of freedom for a molecule of the gas

Molar specific heat of an ideal gas at constant volume

$$C_V = \left(\frac{D}{2}\right)R$$ Ideal gas constant

(15-18)

Adiabatic processes for an ideal gas: How pressure, volume, and temperature change in an adiabatic process for an ideal gas depends on the value of the ratio of specific heats for the gas, $\gamma = C_p/C_V$.

Pressure of an ideal gas | Volume of an ideal gas

$$pV^\gamma = \text{constant}$$

(15-22)

Ratio of specific heats of the gas = C_p/C_V

The quantity pV^γ has the same value at all times during an adiabatic process for an ideal gas.

Kelvin temperature of an ideal gas | Volume of an ideal gas

$$TV^{\gamma-1} = \text{constant}$$

(15-23)

Ratio of specific heats of the gas = C_p/C_V

The quantity $TV^{\gamma-1}$ has the same value at all times during an adiabatic process for an ideal gas.

The second law of thermodynamics: The second law says that the amount of order in an isolated system cannot increase. This implies that a heat engine—a device that converts heat into work—cannot be 100% efficient but can convert only part of its heat intake Q_H (from a high-temperature source) into work. The rest is rejected as heat $|Q_C|$ to the engine's low-temperature surroundings. The efficiency is $e = W/Q_H$.

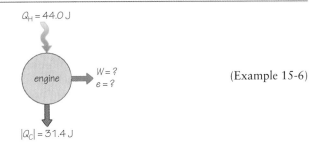

(Example 15-6)

The Carnot cycle: The most efficient heat engine theoretically possible is a Carnot engine. It uses the Carnot cycle, which is based on two reversible adiabatic processes and two reversible isothermal processes. No other engine can have a greater efficiency. A Carnot engine run in reverse is also the best-performing refrigerator theoretically possible.

Efficiency of a Carnot engine   Kelvin temperature of the cold reservoir

$$e_{Carnot} = 1 - \frac{T_C}{T_H}$$

Kelvin temperature of the hot reservoir   (15-28)

Entropy: The entropy of a system is a measure of the amount of disorder present in the system. In a reversible process in which two objects interact with each other, the entropy of one object increases while the entropy of the other object decreases by the same amount. In an irreversible process, the entropy changes do not cancel and there is a net increase in entropy.

Heat that flows into the system ($Q > 0$ if heat flows in, $Q < 0$ if heat flows out)

Entropy change of a system in a reversible isothermal process

$$\Delta S = \frac{Q}{T}$$

Kelvin temperature of the system   (15-33)

Answer to What do you think? Question

(c) The gas escapes very rapidly through the opening in the beetle's abdomen, moving from the high-pressure reaction chamber into the low-pressure air. The gas expands when it encounters lower pressure, but due to its high speed it has no time to exchange heat with the surrounding air. So the expansion of this gas is adiabatic, which means that its temperature drops even though there is no heat flow (see Section 15-4). The droplets of hot liquid do not expand, however, so they maintain their high temperature and deliver a painful (or even fatal) shock to any insect that dares attack the bombardier beetle.

Answers to Got the Concept? Questions

15-1 (b) We can answer this question using the first law of thermodynamics, $\Delta U = Q - W$. In this situation $Q = 0$ because there is no heat flow into or out of the gas. The gas pushes on the moving piston in the same direction that the piston moves, so the gas does positive work on the piston and W is positive. So $\Delta U = Q - W$ is equal to zero minus a positive number, and ΔU is negative—that is, the internal energy U of the gas decreases. For an ideal gas, the internal energy U is directly proportional to the Kelvin temperature T, so a decrease in internal energy means that the gas temperature decreases.

15-2 (a) (i), (ii), (iii) and (iv) (tie) The internal energy U of an ideal gas is directly proportional to its Kelvin temperature. So the internal energy change ΔU is positive if the temperature increases, as is the case for the isobaric process $a \rightarrow b$; ΔU is zero if the temperature stays the same, as for the isothermal process $a \rightarrow c$; and ΔU is negative if the temperature decreases, as for the processes $a \rightarrow d$ and $a \rightarrow e$. The final temperature is the same for processes $a \rightarrow d$ and $a \rightarrow e$ (states d and e are both on the same isotherm), so ΔU has the same negative value for both processes $a \rightarrow d$ and $a \rightarrow e$. (b) (i), (ii), (iii), (iv) The work done in each process is indicated by the area under the curve for that process in the pV diagram. This is greatest for $a \rightarrow b$, smaller for $a \rightarrow c$, and even smaller for $a \rightarrow d$. For all three of these processes the volume increases and $W > 0$. For the isochoric process $a \rightarrow e$ there is no volume change, so the gas does no work at $W = 0$.

15-3 (c) The first law of thermodynamics, Equation 15-2, tells us that $\Delta U = Q - W$ or $Q = \Delta U + W$. For an adiabatic process

$Q = 0$ and so $\Delta U = -W$. For process $a \rightarrow b$ we have $\Delta U > 0$ (the internal energy increases because the temperature increases) and $W > 0$ (the gas expands), so $Q = \Delta U + W$ is positive and the process cannot be adiabatic. For process $a \rightarrow c$ we have $\Delta U = 0$ (the internal energy remains the same because the temperature is constant) and $W > 0$ (the gas expands), so again $Q = \Delta U + W$ is positive and the process cannot be adiabatic. For process $a \rightarrow e$ $\Delta U < 0$ (the internal energy decreases because the temperature decreases) and $W = 0$ (the volume does not change and so the gas does zero work), so $Q = \Delta U + W$ is negative and the process cannot be adiabatic. The only process that could be adiabatic is $a \rightarrow d$, for which $\Delta U < 0$ (the internal energy decreases because the temperature decreases) and $W > 0$ (the gas expands). For the process the quantity $Q = \Delta U + W$ could be adiabatic.

15-4 (b) For the first, constant-volume process the relationship between heat and temperature change is $Q = nC_V\Delta T$, while for the second, constant-pressure process the relationship is $Q = nC_p\Delta T$ (see Equations 15-11). The relationship $C_p - C_V = R$ (Equation 15-15) tells us that C_p is greater than C_V, so for a given quantity of heat Q the temperature change ΔT will be less for a constant-pressure process. You can get the same result from the first law of thermodynamics, $\Delta U = Q - W$ or $Q = \Delta U + W$. For the constant-volume process $W = 0$ and $Q = \Delta U$: All of the heat goes into increasing the internal energy of the gas and so into raising its temperature. But for the constant-pressure process, the expanding gas must do positive work W on the piston. Some of the heat goes into doing this work, so only a fraction of Q is available to increase the internal energy of the gas.

15-5 (c) From Equations 15-11 the relationship between heat and temperature change for these constant-pressure processes is $Q = nC_p\Delta T$. Table 15-1 shows that the molar specific heat at constant pressure C_p has a smaller value for He than for N_2,

so for a given quantity of heat Q the temperature change ΔT is greater for He than for N_2. Equation 15-13 tells us that the work done by an ideal gas in a constant-pressure process is $W = nR\,\Delta T$; the number of moles n is the same for both gases and R is the ideal gas constant, so more work is done by the gas that undergoes the greater temperature change ΔT (in this example, helium).

15-6 No. A gasoline engine uses ambient temperature (about 20°C or 293 K) as the cold temperature. The engine your fellow student has designed uses a hot temperature that must be less than 1941 K, the melting temperature of titanium, or else the cylinders would melt. The efficiency of a Carnot cycle operating between $T_C = 293$ K and $T_H = 1941$ K is $e_{Carnot} = 1 - (T_C/T_H) = 1 - [(293\,\text{K})/(1941\,\text{K})] = 1 - 0.151 = 0.849$, or 84.9%. Your fellow student is claiming an even higher efficiency, which is impossible because no heat engine can have greater efficiency than a Carnot engine. This would be a poor investment!

15-7 (b) Both melting and vaporization take place at a constant temperature, so we can use Equation 15-33, $\Delta S = Q/T$, to calculate the entropy change in each process. For melting at 0°C or $T = 273.15$ K, $Q = mL_F = (1.00\,\text{kg})(3.34 \times 10^5\,\text{J/kg}) = 3.34 \times 10^5$ J and $\Delta S_{melting} = Q/T = (3.34 \times 10^5\,\text{J})/(273.15\,\text{K}) = 1.22 \times 10^3$ J/K. For vaporization at 100°C or $T = (100 + 273.15)$ K $= 373.15$ K, $Q = mL_V = (1.00\,\text{kg})(2.26 \times 10^6\,\text{J/kg}) = 2.26 \times 10^6$ J and $\Delta S_{vaporization} = Q/T = (2.26 \times 10^6\,\text{J})/(373.15\,\text{K}) = 6.06 \times 10^3$ J/K. The entropy change is about five times greater for vaporization than for melting, which agrees with the idea that entropy is a measure of disorder. The molecules of liquid water are able to move while those of ice cannot, so the entropy of liquid water is greater than that of ice. But the molecules of water vapor are free to move over a much greater volume, and so the entropy of water vapor is *very* much greater than that of liquid water.

Questions and Problems

In a few problems, you are given more data than you actually need; in a few other problems, you are required to supply data from your general knowledge, outside sources, or informed estimate. Interpret as significant all digits in numerical values that have trailing zeros and no decimal points. For all problems, use $g = 9.80\,\text{m/s}^2$ for the free-fall acceleration due to gravity. Neglect friction and air resistance unless instructed to do otherwise.

• Basic, single-concept problem

•• Intermediate-level problem, may require synthesis of concepts and multiple steps

•••• Challenging problem

SSM *Solution is in Student Solutions Manual*

Conceptual Questions

1. •Clearly define and give an example of each of the following thermodynamic processes: (a) isothermal, (b) adiabatic, (c) isobaric, and (d) isochoric. SSM

2. •Can a system absorb heat without increasing its internal energy? Explain.

3. •Why does the temperature of a gas increase when it is quickly compressed?

4. •Why is it possible for the temperature of a system to remain constant even though heat is released or absorbed by the system?

5. •When we say "engine," we think of something mechanical with moving parts. In such an engine, friction always reduces the engine's efficiency. Why? SSM

6. •There are people who try to keep cool on a hot summer day by leaving the refrigerator door open, but you can't cool your kitchen this way! Why not?

7. •If the coefficient of performance is greater than 1, do we get more energy out than we put in, violating conservation of energy? Why or why not?

8. •How does the time required to freeze water vary with each of the following parameters: mass of water, power of the refrigerator, and temperature of the outside air?

9. •By how much is the entropy of the universe changed when heat is released from a hotter object to a colder one? In what sense does this correspond to energy becoming unavailable for doing work? SSM

10. •In a slow, steady isothermal expansion of an ideal gas against a piston, the work done is equal to the heat input. Is this consistent with the first law of thermodynamics?

11. •If a gas expands freely into a larger volume in an insulated container so that no heat is added to the gas, its entropy increases. Using the definition of ΔS, explain this statement.

12. •Why do engineers designing a steam-electric generating plant always try to design for as high a feed-steam temperature as possible?

13. •Conduction across a temperature difference is an irreversible process, but the object that lost heat can always be rewarmed, and the one that gained heat can be recooled. An object sliding across a rough table slows down and warms up as mechanical energy dissipates. This process is irreversible, but the object can be cooled and set moving again at its original speed. So in just what sense are these processes "irreversible"? SSM

14. •The frictional drag of the atmosphere causes an orbiting satellite to move closer to Earth and to gain kinetic energy. In what way does energy become unavailable for doing work in this irreversible process?

15. •Is a process necessarily reversible if there is no exchange of heat between the system in which the process takes place and its surroundings?

16. •Is the operation of an automobile engine reversible?

17. •In discussing the Carnot cycle, we say that extracting heat from a reservoir isothermally does not change the entropy of the universe. In a real process, this is a limiting situation that can never quite be reached. Why not? What is the effect on the entropy of the universe? SSM

18. •A pot full of hot water is placed in a cold room, and the pot gradually cools. How does the entropy of the water change?

19. •If you drop a glass cup on the floor, it will shatter into fragments. If you then drop the fragments on the floor, why will they not become a glass cup?

20. •Why is the entropy of 1 kg of liquid iron greater than that of 1 kg of solid iron? Explain your answer.

Multiple-Choice Questions

21. •An ideal gas trapped inside a thermally isolated cylinder expands slowly by pushing back against a piston. The temperature of the gas
   A. increases.
   B. decreases.
   C. remains the same.
   D. increases if the process occurs quickly.
   E. remains the same if the process occurs quickly. SSM

22. •A gas is compressed adiabatically by a force of 800 N acting over a distance of 5.0 cm. The net change in the internal energy of the gas is
   A. +800 J.
   B. +40 J.
   C. −800 J.
   D. −40 J.
   E. 0.

23. •An ideal gas is contained in a cylinder of fixed length and diameter. Eighty joules of heat is added while the piston is held in place. The work done by the gas on the walls of the cylinder is
   A. 80 J.
   B. 0 J.
   C. less than 80 J.
   D. more than 80 J.
   E. not specified by the information given.

24. •In an isothermal process, there is no change in
   A. pressure.
   B. temperature.
   C. volume.
   D. heat.
   E. internal energy *and* pressure.

25. •In an isobaric process, there is no change in
   A. pressure.
   B. temperature.
   C. volume.
   D. internal energy.
   E. internal energy *and* pressure. SSM

26. •In an isochoric process, there is no change in
   A. pressure.
   B. temperature.
   C. volume.
   D. internal energy.
   E. internal energy *and* pressure.

27. •A gas quickly expands in an isolated environment. During the process, the gas exchanges no heat with its surroundings. The process is
   A. isothermal.
   B. isobaric.
   C. isochoric.
   D. adiabatic.
   E. isotonic.

28. •The statement that no process is possible in which heat is absorbed from a cold reservoir and transferred completely to a hot reservoir is
   A. not always true.
   B. only true for isothermal processes.
   C. the first law of thermodynamics.
   D. the second law of thermodynamics.
   E. the zeroth law of thermodynamics.

29. •Carnot's heat engine employs
   A. two adiabatic processes and two isothermal processes.
   B. two adiabatic processes and two isobaric processes.
   C. two adiabatic processes and two isochoric processes.
   D. two isothermal processes and two isochoric processes.
   E. two isothermal processes and two isobaric processes. SSM

30. •Compare two methods to improve the theoretical efficiency of a heat engine: lower T_C by 10 K or raise T_H by 10 K. Which one is better?
   A. Lower T_C by 10 K.
   B. Raise T_H by 10 K.
   C. Both changes would give the same result.
   D. The better method would depend on the difference between T_C and T_H.
   E. There is nothing you can do to improve the theoretical efficiency of a heat engine.

Estimation/Numerical Analysis

31. •(a) Estimate the work (in J) done in raising a book from the floor to the table. (b) Estimate the temperature rise in a glass of water if that amount of energy were added to it.

32. •(a) Estimate the work (in J) done in driving a car across America. (b) If the energy required to do that work were added to an Olympic-sized swimming pool, how much would the temperature of the water rise?

33. •Estimate the internal energy increase in a 1.00-L sample of oxygen that increases in temperature from 20°C to 100°C. Assume that the volume of this ideal gas is constant in the process. SSM

34. •Estimate the pressure acting on a 2-L sample of nitrogen, an ideal gas, when it is held at 300 K.

35. •**Biology** Estimate how far up a granite monolith a 70-kg student can climb if she uses 50% of the energy from a 4000-kcal meal to scale the cliff. (The other 50% supports her resting metabolic rate.) Is your answer reasonable?

36. •Estimate the efficiency of an average internal combustion engine in Canada.

37. •Estimate the distance a car can be driven on a tank of gas. Assume that the gas releases 125,000 BTU of energy per gallon. SSM

38. •Estimate the amount of energy that is wasted each day in Europe due to an additional inefficiency of 5% (on top of the thermodynamic efficiency) from cars that are not lubricated properly. You will have to make some assumptions about how many cars are poorly maintained, how far Europeans drive each day, and so on.

39. •**Biology** Estimate the efficiency of the human body acting as a heat engine.

Problems

15-1 The laws of thermodynamics involve energy and entropy

15-2 The first law of thermodynamics relates heat flow, work done, and internal energy change

40. •If 800 J of heat is added to a system that does no external work, how much does the internal energy of the system increase?

41. •Five hundred joules of heat is absorbed by a system that does 200 J of work on its surroundings. What is the change in the internal energy of the system?

15-3 A graph of pressure versus volume helps to describe what happens in a thermodynamic process

42. •Calculate the amount of work done on a gas that undergoes a change of state described by the pV diagram shown in Figure 15-21.

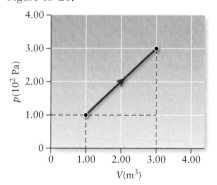

Figure 15-21
Problem 42

43. •Calculate the amount of work done on a gas that undergoes a change of state described by the pV diagram shown in Figure 15-22.

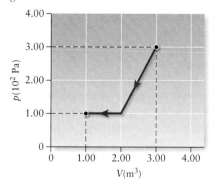

Figure 15-22
Problem 43

44. •A gas is heated and is allowed to expand such that it follows a horizontal line path on a pV diagram from its initial state $(1.0 \times 10^5$ Pa, 1.0 m$^3)$ to its final state $(1.0 \times 10^5$ Pa, 2.0 m$^3)$. Calculate the work done by the gas on its surroundings.

45. •A gas is heated such that it follows a vertical line path on a pV diagram from its initial state $(1.0 \times 10^5$ Pa, 3.0 m$^3)$ to its final state $(2.0 \times 10^5$ Pa, 3.0 m$^3)$. Calculate the work done by the gas on its surroundings. SSM

46. •A sealed cylinder has a piston and contains 8000 cm^3 of an ideal gas at a pressure of 8.0 atm. Heat is slowly introduced, and the gas isothermally expands to 16,000 cm^3. How much work does the gas do on the piston?

47. •An ideal gas expands isothermally, performing 8.80 kJ of work in the process. Calculate the heat absorbed during the expansion. SSM

48. •Heat is added to 8.00 m^3 of helium gas in an expandable chamber that increases its volume by 2.00 m^3. If in the isothermal expansion process 2.00 kJ of work is done by the gas, what was its original pressure?

49. •A cylinder that has a piston contains 2.00 mol of an ideal gas and undergoes a reversible isothermal expansion at 400 K from an initial pressure of 12.0 atm down to 3.00 atm. Determine the amount of work done by the gas.

50. •A gas contained in a cylinder that has a piston is kept at a constant pressure of 2.80×10^5 Pa. The gas expands from 0.500 m^3 to 1.50 m^3 when 300 kJ of heat is added to the cylinder. What is the change in internal energy of the gas?

51. •The pressure in an ideal gas is slowly reduced to 1/4 its initial value, while being kept in a container with rigid walls. In the process, 800 kJ of heat leaves the gas. What is the change in internal energy of the gas during this process? SSM

52. •An ideal gas is compressed adiabatically to half its volume. In doing so, 1888 J of work is done on the gas. What is the change in internal energy of the gas?

53. •Two moles of an ideal monatomic gas expand adiabatically, performing 8.00 kJ of work in the process. What is the change in temperature of the gas during the expansion?

15-4 More heat is required to change the temperature of an ideal gas isobarically than isochorically

54. ••One mole of an ideal monatomic gas ($\gamma = 1.66$), initially at a temperature of 0.00°C, undergoes an adiabatic expansion from a pressure of 10.0 atm to a pressure of 2.00 atm. How much work is done on the gas?

55. •A container holds 32.0 g of oxygen gas at a pressure of 8.00 atm. How much heat is required to increase the temperature by 100°C at constant pressure?

56. •A container holds 32.0 g of oxygen gas at a pressure of 8.00 atm. How much heat is required to increase the temperature by 100°C at constant volume?

57. •The temperature of 4.00 g of helium gas is increased at constant volume by 1.00°C. Using the same amount of heat, the temperature of what mass of oxygen gas will increase at constant volume by 1.00°C? SSM

58. •Heat is added to 1.00 mol of air at constant pressure, resulting in a temperature increase of 100°C. If the same amount of heat is instead added at constant volume, what is the temperature increase? The molar specific heat ratio $\gamma = C_p/C_V$ for the air is 1.4.

59. ••The volume of a gas is halved during an adiabatic compression that increases the pressure by a factor of 2.6. What is the molar specific heat ratio $\gamma = C_p/C_V$?

60. ••The volume of a gas is halved during an adiabatic compression that increases the pressure by a factor of 2.5. By what factor does the temperature increase?

61. ••What ratio of initial volume to final volume, V_i/V_f, will raise the temperature of air from 27.0°C to 857°C in an adiabatic process? The molar specific heat ratio $\gamma = C_p/C_V$ for air is 1.4. SSM

62. ••A monatomic ideal gas at a pressure of 1.00 atm expands adiabatically from an initial volume of 1.50 m³ to a final volume of 3.00 m³. What is the new pressure?

15-5 The second law of thermodynamics describes why some processes are impossible

63. •An engine doing work takes in 10 kJ and exhausts 6 kJ. What is the efficiency of the engine? SSM

64. •What is the theoretical maximum efficiency of a heat engine operating between 100°C and 500°C?

65. •A heat engine operating between 473 K and 373 K runs at about 70% of its theoretical maximum efficiency. What is its efficiency?

66. •An engine operates between 10.0°C and 200°C. At the very best, how much heat should we be prepared to supply in order to output 1000 J of work?

67. •A furnace supplies 28.0 kW of thermal power at 300°C to an engine and exhausts waste energy at 20.0°C. At the very best, how much work could we expect to get out of the system per second? SSM

68. •A kitchen refrigerator extracts 75.0 kJ per second of energy from a cool chamber while exhausting 100 kJ per second to the room. What is its coefficient of performance?

69. •What is the coefficient of performance of a Carnot refrigerator operating between 0.00°C and 80.0°C?

70. •An electric refrigerator removes 13.0 MJ of heat from its interior for each kilowatt-hour of electric energy used. What is its coefficient of performance?

71. •A certain refrigerator requires 35.0 J of work to remove 190 J of heat from its interior. (a) What is its coefficient of performance? (b) How much heat is ejected to the surroundings at 22.0°C? (c) If the refrigerator cycle is reversible, what is the temperature inside the refrigerator? SSM

15-6 The entropy of a system is a measure of its disorder

72. •A reservoir at a temperature of 400 K gains 100 J of heat from another reservoir. What is its entropy change?

73. •What is the minimum change of entropy that occurs in 0.200 kg of ice at 273 K when 6.68×10^4 J of heat is added so that it melts to water? SSM

74. •If, in a reversible process, enough heat is added to change a 500-g block of ice to water at a temperature of 273 K, what is the change in the entropy of the ice/water system?

75. •A room is at a constant 295 K maintained by an air conditioner that pumps heat out. What is the entropy change of the room for each 5.00 kJ of heat removed?

76. •One mole of ideal gas expands isothermally from 1.00 m³ to 2.00 m³. What is the entropy change for the gas?

77. •An 1800-kg car traveling at 80.0 km/h crashes into a concrete wall. If the temperature of the air is 27.0°C, what is the entropy change of the universe as a result of the crash? Assume all of the car's kinetic energy is converted into heat. SSM

78. •A 1000-kg rock at 20.0°C falls 100 m into a large lake, also at 20.0°C. Assuming that all of the rock's kinetic energy on entering the lake converts to thermal energy absorbed by the lake, what is the change in entropy of the lake?

79. •**Astronomy** The surface of the Sun is about 5700 K, and the temperature of Earth's surface is about 293 K. What entropy change occurs when 8000 J of energy is transferred by heat from the Sun to Earth?

80. ••You have a cup containing 220 g of freshly brewed coffee which, at 75.0°C, is too warm to drink. If you cool the coffee a little by pouring 60.0 g of tap water at 26.0°C into the cup, estimate how much the entropy of the universe increases.

81. •In a vacuum bottle, 350 g of water and 150 g of ice are initially in equilibrium at 0.00°C. The bottle is not a perfect insulator. Over time, its contents come to thermal equilibrium with the outside air at 25.0°C. How much does the entropy of universe increase in the process? SSM

General Problems

82. •••A vertical metal cylinder contains an ideal gas. The top of the cylinder is closed off by a piston of mass m that is free to move up and down with no appreciable friction. The piston is a height h above the bottom of the cylinder when the gas alone supports it. Sand is now very slowly poured onto the piston until the weight of the sand is equal to the weight of the piston. Find the new height of the piston (in terms of h) if the ideal gas in the cylinder is (a) oxygen O_2, (b) helium He, or (c) hydrogen H_2.

83. •A Carnot engine on a ship extracts heat from seawater at 18.0°C and exhausts the heat to evaporating dry ice at −78.0°C. If the ship's engines are to run at 8000 horsepower, what is the minimum amount of dry ice the ship must carry for the ship to run for a single day? SSM

84. •A Carnot engine removes 1200 J of heat from a high-temperature source and dumps 600 J to the atmosphere at 20.0°C. (a) What is the efficiency of the engine? (b) What is the temperature of the hot reservoir?

85. ••A certain engine has a second-law efficiency of 85.0%. During each cycle, it absorbs 480 J of heat from a reservoir at 300°C and dumps 300 J of heat to a cold temperature reservoir. (a) What is the temperature of the cold reservoir? (b) How much more work could be done by a Carnot engine working between the same two reservoirs and extracting the same 480 J of heat in each cycle?

86. •A refrigerator is rated at 370 W. Its interior is at 0°C, and its surroundings are at 20°C. If the second law efficiency of its cycle is 66%, how much heat can it remove from its interior in 1 min?

87. ••**Medical** During a high fever, a 60.0-kg-patient's normal metabolism is increased by 10.0%. This results in an increase of 10.0% in the heat given off by the person. When the person slowly walks up five flights of stairs (20.0 m), she normally releases 100 kJ of heat. Compare her efficiency when she has a fever to when her temperature is normal. SSM

88. ••A rigid 5.50-L pressure cooker contains steam initially at 100°C under a pressure of 1.00 atm. Consult Table 15-1 as needed and assume that the values given there remain constant. The mass of a water molecule is 2.99×10^{-26} kg. (a) To what temperature (in °C) would you have to heat the steam so that its pressure was 1.25 atm? (b) How much heat would you need in part (a)? (c) Calculate the specific heat of the steam in part (a) in units of J/(kg·K).

89. ••You have a cup containing 220 g of freshly brewed coffee which, at 75°C, is too warm to drink. If you cool the coffee a little by pouring 60 g of tap water at 26°C into the cup, estimate how much the entropy of the universe increases.

90. ••A certain electric generating plant produces electricity by using steam that enters its turbine at a temperature of 320°C and leaves it at 40°C. Over the course of a year, the plant consumes 4.40×10^{16} J of heat and produces an average electric power output of 600 MW. What is its second-law efficiency?

91. ••As we drill down into the rocks of Earth's crust, the temperature typically increases by 3.0°C for every 100 m of depth. Oil wells are commonly drilled to depths of 1830 m. If water is pumped into the shaft of the well, it will be heated by the hot rock at the bottom and the resulting heated steam can be used as a heat engine. Assume that the surface temperature is 20°C. (a) Using such a 1830-m well as a heat engine, what is the maximum efficiency possible? (b) If a combination of such wells is to produce a 2.5-MW power plant, how much energy will it absorb from the interior of Earth each day? SSM

92. •••The energy efficiency ratio (or rating)—the EER—for air conditioners, refrigerators, and freezers is defined as the ratio of the input rate of heat ($|Q_C|/t$, in BTU/h) to the output rate of work (W/t, in W): $\text{EER} = \dfrac{Q_C/t\,(\text{BTU/hr})}{W/t\,(\text{W})}$. (a) Show that the EER can be expressed as $\dfrac{Q_C\,(\text{BTU})}{W\,(\text{W}\cdot\text{h})}$ and is therefore nothing more than the coefficient of performance CP expressed in mixed units. (b) Show that the EER is related to the coefficient of performance CP by the equation $CP = \text{EER}/3.412$. (c) Typical home freezers have EER ratings of about 5.1 and operate between an interior freezer temperature of 0.00°F and an outside kitchen temperature of about 70.0°F. What is the coefficient of performance for such a freezer, and how does it compare to the coefficient of performance of the best possible freezer operating between those temperatures? (d) What is the EER of the best possible freezer in part (c)?

93. ••Your energy efficient home freezer has an EER of 6.50 (see Problem 15-98). In preparation for a picnic, you put 1.50 L of water at 20.0°C into the freezer to make ice at 0.00°C for your ice chest. (See Tables 11-1, 14-3, and 14-4 as needed.) (a) How much electrical energy (which runs the freezer) is required to make the ice? Express your answer in J and kWh. (b) How much heat is ejected into your kitchen, which is at 22.0°C? (c) How much does making the ice change the entropy of your kitchen?

94. ••Biology The volume of air taken in during a typical breath is 0.5 L. The inhaled air is heated to 37°C (the internal body temperature) as it enters the lungs. Because air is about 80% nitrogen N_2, we can model it as an ideal gas. Suppose that the outside air is at room temperature (20°C) and that you take two breaths every 3.0 s. Assume that the pressure does not change during the process. (a) How many joules of heat does it take to warm the air in a single breath? (b) How many food calories (kcal) are used up per day in heating the air you breathe? Is this a significant amount of typical daily caloric intake?

95. ••A heat engine works in a cycle between reservoirs at 273 K and 490 K. In each cycle, the engine absorbs 1250 cal of heat from the high-temperature reservoir and does 475 J of work. (a) What is its efficiency? (b) By how much is the entropy of the universe changed when the engine goes through one full cycle? (c) How much energy becomes unavailable for doing work when the engine goes through one full cycle? SSM

96. •••You have a cabin on the plains of central Saskatchewan. It is built on a 8.50-m by 12.5-m rectangular foundation with walls 3.00 m tall. The wooden walls and flat roof are made of white pine that is 9.00 cm thick. To conserve heat, the windows are negligibly small. The floor is well insulated so you lose negligible heat through it. The cabin is heated by an electrically powered heat pump operating on the Carnot cycle between the inside and outside air. When the outside temperature is a frigid −10.0°F, how much electrical energy does the heat pump consume per second to keep the interior temperature a steady and toasty 70.0°F? Assume that the surfaces of the walls and roof are at the same temperature as the air with which they are in contact and neglect radiation. (Consult Table 14-5 as needed.)

97. •Sports In an international diving competition, divers fall from a platform 10.0 m above the surface of the water into a very large pool. The diver leaves the platform with negligible initial speed. What is the maximum change in the entropy of the water in the pool at 25.0°C when a 75.0-kg diver executes his dive? Does the pool's entropy increase or decrease?

98. ••A heat engine works in a cycle between reservoirs at 273 K and 490 K. In each cycle the engine absorbs 1250 J of heat from the high-temperature reservoir and does 475 J of work. (a) What is its efficiency? (b) What is the change in entropy of the universe when the engine goes through one complete cycle? (c) How much energy becomes unavailable for doing work when the engine goes through one complete cycle?

99. ••Biology A 68.0-kg person typically eats about 2250 kcal per day, 20.0% of which goes to mechanical energy and the rest to heat. If she spends most of her time in her apartment at 22.0°C, how much does the entropy of her apartment change in one day? Does entropy increase or decrease? SSM

100. •••Consider an engine in which the working substance is 1.23 mol of an ideal gas for which $\gamma = 1.41$. The engine runs reversibly in the cycle shown on the pV diagram (Figure 15-23). The cycle consists of an isobaric (constant-pressure) expansion a at a pressure of 15.0 atm, during which the temperature of the gas increases from 300 K to 600 K, followed by an isothermal expansion b until its pressure becomes 3.00 atm. Next is an isobaric compression c at a pressure of 3.00 atm, during which the temperature decreases from 600 K to 300 K, followed by an isothermal compression d until its pressure returns to 15 atm. Find the work done by the gas, the heat absorbed by the gas, the internal energy change, and the entropy change of the gas, first for each part of the cycle and then for the complete cycle.

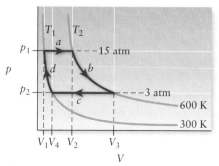

Figure 15-23 Problem 100

16

Electrostatics I: Electric Charge, Forces, and Fields

In this chapter, your goals are to:
- (16-1) Explain why studying electric phenomena is important.
- (16-2) Describe how objects acquire a net electric charge.
- (16-3) Recognize the differences between insulators, conductors, and semiconductors.
- (16-4) Use Coulomb's law to quantitatively describe the force that one charged particle exerts on another.
- (16-5) Explain the relationship between electric force and electric field.
- (16-6) Describe the connection between enclosed charge and electric flux described by Gauss's law.
- (16-7) Apply Gauss's law to symmetric situations and to the distribution of excess charge on conductors.

To master this chapter, you should review:
- (3-2, 3-3, How to add vectors and how to do vector calculations using components. and 3-4)
- (4-2) Newton's second law.

What do you think?

A shark can detect the electric field produced by a small, electrically charged object. If a charged object 2 m from a shark's nose is moved to be only 1 m from the nose, the magnitude of the electric field that the shark detects will (a) decrease; (b) double; (c) increase by a factor of 4; (d) increase by a factor of 8; (e) increase by a factor of 16.

16-1 Electric forces and electric charges are all around you—and within you

You may think of *electricity* as something that gives you a shock on a dry day when you walk across a carpet and then touch a metal doorknob. Or perhaps it's just a commodity that you purchase from the power company. The reality is that electric phenomena are all around you, from the behavior of grains of pollen to the drama of a thunderstorm (Figure 16-1).

Electricity is an essential part of how you learn physics. As you read this sentence, your eye casts an image of the text onto your retina, and this image is transmitted to your brain along the optic nerve as a stream of electrical impulses. Electricity even explains why you don't fall through the floor: The molecules on the surface of the floor exert electric forces that repel the molecules on the underside of your shoes, and these forces are strong enough to balance Earth's downward gravitational force on you.

Electric phenomena are important because *all* ordinary matter is made of electrically charged objects. That's why we'll spend the next several chapters learning about electric charges and their physics. The simplest place to begin our study of electricity is with *electrostatics*, the branch of physics that deals with electric charges at rest and how they interact with each other. In this chapter we'll first learn about the different kinds

Figure 16-1 **Electric charges and forces** Electrostatics—the physics that describes how opposite charges attract and like charges repel—plays an important role in (a) biology and (b) the weather.

(a)

Grains of pollen wafting through the air carry a small amount of electric charge. This attracts them to the oppositely charged stigma of a flower and so aids in pollination.

(b)

The motion of air in a thundercloud causes positive and negative charges to separate and build up within the cloud. The release of these charges causes lightning.

Take-Home Message for Section 16-1

✔ Electric phenomena are important because all ordinary matter is made of electrically charged objects.

✔ Electrostatics is the study of electric charges at rest and the forces that they exert on each other.

of electrical charge in nature, and describe the forces that two electrically charged objects exert on each other. We'll see how these forces manifest themselves in two important classes of materials called conductors and insulators. We'll go on to learn about the concept of an *electric field*, which will give us a powerful way to understand how electric charges can exert forces on each other even over a distance. We'll conclude this chapter with a look at *Gauss's law*, an important tool for understanding electric fields.

16-2 Matter contains positive and negative electric charge

Figure 16-2 shows some simple experiments that demonstrate the nature of electric charge. If you hold two rubber rods next to each other, they neither attract nor repel each other. The same is true for two glass rods held next to each other, or for a rubber rod and a glass rod held next to each other (Figure 16-2a). But if you rub each rubber rod with fur and each glass rod with silk, we find that the rubbed ends of the rubber rods repel each other and the rubbed ends of the glass rods repel each other, but the rubbed ends of the rubber and glass rod attract each other (Figure 16-2b). What's more, the rubbed end of the rubber rod attracts the piece of fur used to rub it, and the rubbed end of the glass rod attracts the piece of silk used to rub it (Figure 16-2c). In each case where there is a repulsion or an attraction, the repulsive or attractive force is stronger the closer the objects are held to each other.

Here's how we explain these experiments and others like them:

(1) *Matter has electric charge.* In addition to having mass, matter also possesses a property called **electric charge**. This charge comes in two forms, positive and negative. An object that has a net electric charge (more positive than negative, or more negative than positive) is **charged**. Most matter, however, contains equal amounts of positive and negative charge and is electrically **neutral**. In Figure 16-2a the rubber and glass rods are electrically neutral, as are the pieces of fur and silk.

(2) *Electric charge is a property of the constituents of atoms.* All ordinary matter is made up of atoms. Atoms are in turn composed of more fundamental particles called electrons, protons, and (except for the most common type of hydrogen atom) neutrons. Electrons carry a negative charge, while protons carry an equally large positive charge; neutrons are neutral. Protons and neutrons have about the same mass as each other and are found in the dense nucleus at the center of an atom. A negatively charged electron has only about 0.05% the mass of a proton,

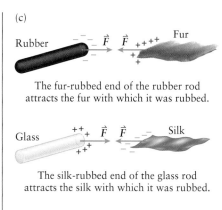

(a)

Rubber   Rubber

Neutral rubber rods:
no attraction or repulsion

Glass   Glass

Neutral glass rods:
no attraction or repulsion

Rubber   Glass

Neutral rubber rod and neutral glass rod:
no attraction or repulsion

(b)   Rub with fur   Rub with silk

Rubber rod   Glass rod

Rubber $\vec{F}$ $\vec{F}$ Rubber

The fur-rubbed ends of
these two rubber rods repel each other.

Glass $\vec{F}$ $\vec{F}$ Glass

The silk-rubbed ends of
these two glass rods repel each other.

Rubber $\vec{F}$ $\vec{F}$ Glass

The fur-rubbed end of
the rubber rod attracts the silk-rubbed
end of the glass rod.

(c)   Fur

Rubber $\vec{F}$ $\vec{F}$

The fur-rubbed end of the rubber rod
attracts the fur with which it was rubbed.

Glass $\vec{F}$ $\vec{F}$ Silk

The silk-rubbed end of the glass rod
attracts the silk with which it was rubbed.

Figure 16-2 Experiments in electrostatics Electric charge can be transferred from one object to another by rubbing. Electrically charged objects exert forces on each other.

so the electrons move around the massive, positively charged nucleus (Figure 16-3). A normal atom contains as many electrons as it does protons and so is electrically neutral.

(3) *Charge can be transferred between objects.* When dissimilar materials are rubbed together, negatively charged electrons can be transferred from one material to the other. As an example, consider the rubber rod and fur shown in Figure 16-2b. Initially, the rod and fur are electrically neutral, so each has equal amounts of positive and negative charge. But when the rubber rod and fur are rubbed together, electrons are transferred from the fur to the rubber. (This is a consequence of the internal structures of the two materials. It turns out that electrons can lower their electric potential energy by moving from the fur to the rubber, so they move in that direction. In the same way, a ball rolls from the top of a hill to the bottom because that's the direction that lowers its gravitational potential energy. We'll discuss electric potential energy in detail in Chapter 17.) This leaves the fur with more positive charge than negative and the rubber with more negative charge than positive. So the fur ends up with a *net* positive charge, and the rubber rod ends up with a *net* negative charge. By contrast, when the glass rod and silk in Figure 16-2b (both of which are initially neutral) are rubbed together, electrons are transferred from the glass to the silk. So the silk ends up with a net negative charge and the glass rod with a net positive charge. In Figure 16-2b we use plus and minus signs to indicate the net charge on each object (+ for positive, − for negative).

(4) *Electrically charged objects exert forces on each other.* Objects with electric charges of the same sign (both positive or both negative) repel each other, while objects with electric charges of opposite sign (one positive and the other negative) attract each other (Figure 16-2c). The force between charges is called the **electric force**. The magnitude of the force depends on the amount of charge on each object and on the distance between the objects. The force increases for a greater amount of charge, and it increases if the charged objects are brought closer to each other.

(5) *Charge is never created or destroyed.* In the experiments shown in Figure 16-2 charge is *transferred* between objects. Although charge moves between the rubber rod and the fur or between the glass rod and the silk, in each case the *total* charge of the two objects remains the same as before they were rubbed together. That is, charge is *conserved;* it is never created or destroyed. No one has ever observed a process in which charge is not conserved, so to the best of our knowledge the conservation of electric charge is an absolute law of nature.

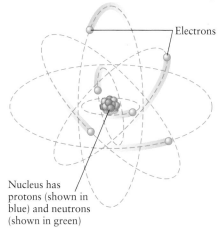

Electrons

Nucleus has
protons (shown in
blue) and neutrons
(shown in green)

Figure 16-3 A simplified model of an atom Negatively charged electrons orbit the atom's nucleus, which contains most of the atom's mass. The nucleus contains two types of particles, positively charged protons and uncharged neutrons.

The character of the electric force explains the remarkable experiment shown in Figure 16-4a. A balloon is first rubbed against the girl's sleeve, causing electrons to transfer from her sleeve onto the rubber surface of the balloon (just like the rubber rod and fur in Figure 16-2b). When the negatively charged balloon is held next to the girl's head, electric forces attract the hair to the balloon—even though the hair is *neutral*. What happens is that the negatively charged electrons on the balloon repel the electrons in the atoms that comprise the hair and attract the positively charged nuclei of these atoms. The electrons and nuclei remain within their atoms but end up slightly displaced from each other (Figure 16-4b). This effect is called **polarization**, and we say that the hair becomes *polarized*. As we described above, the electric force is greater if charged objects are close to each other than if they are far apart. Figure 16-4b shows that the nuclei in the polarized hair are slightly closer to the negatively charged balloon than are the electrons in the hair. So the attractive force between the hair nuclei and the balloon is slightly greater than the repulsive force between the hair electrons and the balloon. The result is that the hair feels a net attractive force toward the balloon.

The unit of electric charge is the **coulomb** (C), named after the eighteenth-century French physicist Charles-Augustin de Coulomb who uncovered the fundamental law that governs the interaction of charges. (We'll discuss this law in Section 16-4.) One coulomb turns out to be quite large compared to the amount of charge on a single electron or proton. As we mentioned above, electrons and protons have the same magnitude of electric charge; we call this magnitude e. Precise measurements show that

$$e = 1.60217657 \times 10^{-19} \text{ C}$$

We use q or Q as the symbol for the charge of an object, so the charge on a proton is (to four significant figures) $q_{\text{proton}} = +e = +1.602 \times 10^{-19}$ C and the charge on an electron is $q_{\text{electron}} = -e = -1.602 \times 10^{-19}$ C. No free particle has ever been detected with a charge smaller in magnitude than e. For that matter, no object has ever been found whose charge was not a multiple of e such as $+2e$, $-3e$, and so on. We summarize this by saying that charge is *quantized*: The charge of an object is always increased or decreased by an amount equal to an integer multiple of the fundamental charge e. It is impossible to add a fraction of a proton or electron to an object. (There is strong evidence that protons and neutrons are composed of more fundamental particles called *quarks* that have charges of $+2e/3$ and $-e/3$. However, no isolated quarks have ever been observed outside of a larger particle such as a proton or neutron. We'll learn more about quarks in Chapter 28.)

Note that while electrons and protons have opposite signs, it's completely arbitrary whether we choose electrons to have negative charge and protons to have positive charge or the other way around. The choice of sign is actually due to the American scientist and statesman Benjamin Franklin, who decided in the mid-eighteenth century

(a)

(b)

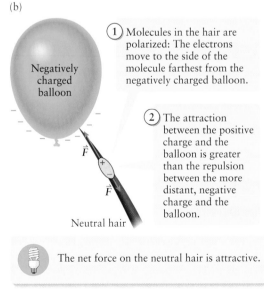

Negatively charged balloon

$\vec{F}$

$\vec{F}$

Neutral hair

① Molecules in the hair are polarized: The electrons move to the side of the molecule farthest from the negatively charged balloon.

② The attraction between the positive charge and the balloon is greater than the repulsion between the more distant, negative charge and the balloon.

The net force on the neutral hair is attractive.

Figure 16-4 A hair-raising experiment (a) Rubbing a balloon on your sleeve gives the balloon an electric charge. A charged balloon can attract your hair and make it stand up, even though your hair has no net charge. (b) The nature of the electric force explains why this attraction happens.

that the sign of charge on a glass rod rubbed with silk (see Figure 16-2b) is positive. The electron and proton were not discovered until much later (1897 and 1919, respectively).

Example 16-1 Electrons in a Raindrop

A water molecule is made up of two hydrogen atoms, each of which has one electron, and an oxygen atom, which has eight electrons. One mole of water has a mass of $18.0 \text{ g} = 18.0 \times 10^{-3}$ kg. How many electrons are there in a single raindrop with a radius of $1.00 \text{ mm} = 1.00 \times 10^{-3}$ m? What is the total charge of all of these electrons? The density of liquid water is $1.00 \times 10^3 \text{ kg/m}^3$.

Set Up

Each water molecule has 10 electrons (two from the hydrogen atoms and eight from the oxygen atom). So we need to determine the number of water molecules in the raindrop and multiply by 10 to find the number of electrons. We'll use the definition of density from Section 11-2 and the number of molecules in a mole (Avogadro's number) from Section 14-3. We'll also need the formula for the volume of a sphere of radius r.

Definition of density:

$$\rho = \frac{m}{V} \qquad (11\text{-}1)$$

Number of molecules in one mole:

$$N_A = 6.022 \times 10^{23} \text{ molecules/mol}$$

Charge of an electron:

$$q_{\text{electron}} = -e = -1.602 \times 10^{-19} \text{ C}$$

Volume of a sphere of radius r:

$$V = \frac{4\pi}{3} r^3$$

Solve

First find the mass of the raindrop, then determine the number of moles of water that corresponds to this mass.

Volume of the raindrop of radius $r = 1.00 \times 10^{-3}$ m:

$$V = \frac{4\pi}{3} r^3 = \frac{4\pi}{3}(1.00 \times 10^{-3}\text{ m})^3 = 4.19 \times 10^{-9}\text{ m}^3$$

From Equation 11-1, the mass of such a raindrop is

$$m = \rho V = (1.00 \times 10^3\text{ kg/m}^3)(4.19 \times 10^{-9}\text{ m}^3) = 4.19 \times 10^{-6}\text{ kg}$$

The number of moles of water in this mass is

$$n = \frac{4.19 \times 10^{-6}\text{ kg}}{18.0 \times 10^{-3}\text{ kg/mol}} = 2.33 \times 10^{-4}\text{ mol}$$

Then determine the number of molecules in the raindrop, and from that determine the number of electrons.

Each mole contains N_A molecules, so the total number of molecules in the raindrop is

$$nN_A = (2.33 \times 10^{-4}\text{ mol})(6.022 \times 10^{23}\text{ molecules/mol})$$
$$= 1.40 \times 10^{20}\text{ molecules}$$

The number of electrons in the raindrop is

$$N = (1.40 \times 10^{20}\text{ molecules})(10\text{ electrons/molecule})$$
$$= 1.40 \times 10^{21}\text{ electrons}$$

To find the charge of this number of electrons, multiply by the charge per electron.

Total charge of this number of electrons:

$$q = Nq_{\text{electron}} = (1.40 \times 10^{21}\text{ electrons})(-1.602 \times 10^{-19}\text{ C/electron})$$
$$= -224\text{ C}$$

Reflect

How large a number is 1.40×10^{21}? The human body contains about 10^{14} cells. Even if you include all of the cells in all of the approximately 9 million (9×10^6) people in New York City, that's only about 9×10^{20} cells—still fewer than the number of electrons in a single raindrop.

The charge of -224 C is quite substantial, but remember that for every electron in a water molecule there is also one proton (one in each hydrogen atom and eight in each oxygen atom). Since a proton carries exactly as much positive charge as an electron carries negative charge, our raindrop has zero *net* charge. In Section 16-4 we'll see how difficult it would be to separate the positive and negative charges of this raindrop.

> **Got the Concept? 16-1   Transferring Charge**
>
> Consider the rubber rod and glass rod in Figure 16-2b. Compared to their masses before they are rubbed with fur and silk, respectively, what are their masses after being rubbed? (a) Both rods have more mass; (b) both rods have less mass; (c) the rubber rod has more mass and the glass rod has less mass; (d) the rubber rod has less mass and the glass rod has more mass; (e) the masses of both rods are unchanged.

Take-Home Message for Section 16-2

✔ Electric charge is quantized. The smallest amount of charge that can be added to or removed from an object is equal to the fundamental charge $e = 1.602 \times 10^{-19}$ C.

✔ All ordinary matter contains positive charge in the form of protons, which have a charge of $+e$, and negative charge in the form of electrons, which have a charge of $-e$. An object is electrically neutral if it contains equal amounts of positive and negative charge. If these amounts are not equal, the object has a net charge.

✔ Charge can neither be created nor destroyed. However, charge can be transferred from one object to another, for example, by moving electrons between objects.

✔ Objects with a net charge exert electric forces on each other. These forces become weaker with increasing distance. If the objects have the same sign of charge (both positive or both negative), the forces are repulsive. If the objects have opposite signs of charge (one positive and one negative), the forces are attractive.

16-3 Charge can flow freely in a conductor but not in an insulator

All substances contain positive and negative charges. But how *mobile* those charges are depends on the specific material. The rubber, glass, silk, and fur shown in Figure 16-2 are all examples of **insulators**, substances in which charges are not able to move freely. All of the electrons in an insulator are bound tightly to the nuclei of atoms, and any excess charge added to an insulator tends to stay wherever it is placed. So when electrons get placed on one end of a rubber rod by rubbing it with fur, the excess electrons stay on that end (Figure 16-5a). The electrons cannot redistribute themselves along the rod, so there is no excess charge on the other, unrubbed end of the rod to attract the positively charged fur. (Due to a polarization effect like that shown in Figure 16-4, there is still a very weak attraction between the positively charged fur and the neutral, unrubbed end of the rubber rod.) Most nonmetals are insulators.

By contrast, a metallic substance such as copper is an example of a **conductor**, a substance in which charges *can* move freely. In copper the outermost, or valence, electron of an atom can easily be dislodged from that atom. (The valence electron is relatively far from the positively charged nucleus, and the many electrons closer to the nucleus tend to shield the valence electron from the charge of the nucleus.) As a result, the valence electrons can move between copper atoms relatively freely. Excess charges

(a)

The fur-rubbed end of the rubber rod attracts the fur with which it was rubbed...

...but the end of the rubber rod that was not rubbed does not feel a strong attraction.

(b)

The nylon-rubbed end of the copper rod attracts the nylon with which it was rubbed...

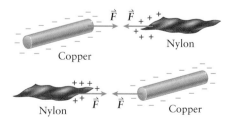

...and the end of the copper rod that was not rubbed also feels a strong attraction.

Figure 16-5 Insulators versus conductors (a) If you place excess charge at one location on an insulator, it remains at that location. (b) If you place excess charge at one location on a conductor, the excess charge can move freely through the conductor.

placed on a conductor can also move freely through the material. This explains what happens when you rub one end of a copper rod with nylon (Figure 16-5b). Electrons are transferred from the nylon to the copper, giving the copper rod a net negative charge and the nylon a net positive charge. But after one end of the copper rod has been rubbed, the nylon attracts *both* ends of the copper rod (rubbed and unrubbed) equally. That's because the excess electrons deposited on one end of the copper rod can easily move within the rod. When the positively charged nylon is brought close to *either* end of the copper rod, the excess electrons on the copper rush to that end. As a result, that end has a net negative charge and is attracted to the nylon.

Conductors and insulators are an essential part of all electric circuits, which are systems in which there is an ongoing current (a flow of charge) around a closed path. Electric circuits are at the heart of any device that uses a battery (such as a mobile phone, a flashlight, or an electric vehicle) or that you plug into a wall socket (such as a desktop computer, a toaster, or an electric fan). An electric circuit uses moving charges (typically electrons) to transfer energy along a conductor from one point in a circuit to another. In a flashlight, for example, electrons flowing through a copper wire carry energy from the battery (which is a repository of *electric potential energy*) to the light bulb, where the energy is converted into visible light. The electrons then return to the battery through a second copper wire to pick up more energy and repeat the process. Insulators play a crucial role in this process: Each conducting wire is clad in a sheath made of an insulator, which helps ensure that the electrons flow only along the length of the wires. (The visible part of an ordinary extension cord or power cord is actually the insulating sheath. The copper wires are contained within the sheath.) We'll explore the idea of electric potential energy in detail in Chapter 17, and we'll devote Chapters 18 and 21 to exploring various important kinds of electric circuits.

Most metals are good electrical conductors *and* also good conductors of heat, with large values of thermal conductivity (see Section 14-7). That's because the flow of electric charge within a material and the flow of heat within that material both require that particles of the material be free to move. In Section 14-3 we learned that the temperature of a material is related to the kinetic energy of that material's particles. For heat to flow from one part of a material to another, the faster-moving particles in the high-temperature part of the material must transfer kinetic energy to the slower-moving particles in the low-temperature part of the object. This can only happen if particles such as electrons are free to move from the high-temperature part of the material to the low-temperature part, where they collide with atoms and transfer their kinetic energy. So the presence of free electrons makes metals good thermal conductors as well as good conductors of electricity. Materials that are electrical insulators, in which the electrons are generally not free to move between atoms, also tend to be thermal insulators with low thermal conductivity.

Not all electric conductors are metals. In biological systems a very important conductor of electricity is water. That's because in nearly all biological systems, electric charges are carried by *ions*—atoms with an excess or deficit of electrons. These ions are suspended in water, that is, in aqueous solution. Water is particularly good at holding ions in solution because the water molecule (H_2O), while electrically neutral, has slightly more negative charge at the oxygen atom of the molecule and slightly more positive charge at the hydrogen atoms. So when an ionic compound such as sodium chloride (NaCl) is dissolved in water, the positive ions (Na^+) are attracted to the negative (oxygen) end of H_2O molecules and the negative ions (Cl^-) are attracted to the positive (hydrogen) end of H_2O molecules. Because the H_2O molecules to which the ions are attached are free to move, the aqueous solutions which make up living things are conductors. It doesn't matter whether charge is carried by an electron or by an ion. As we'll see in Chapter 18, it also doesn't matter whether the moving charges are positive or negative: In either case there is a flow of charge.

? Got the Concept? 16-2 Sodium in Water

A normal atom of sodium (chemical symbol Na) has 11 electrons and is electrically neutral. But in the compound sodium chloride (NaCl) the sodium atom is actually an ion of charge $+e$. How does a sodium atom acquire this charge? (a) by annihilating one of its electrons; (b) by creating a new electron; (c) by transferring an electron to another atom or molecule; (d) by acquiring an electron from another atom or molecule; (e) by acquiring a proton from another atom or molecule.

There's an important third class of substances called **semiconductors**. These substances have electrical properties that are intermediate between those of insulators and conductors. A common example of a semiconductor is silicon. A silicon atom has four outer electrons as compared to just one for copper, which might suggest that it would be a good conductor. However, in pure silicon each of those electrons is part of a chemical bond with a neighboring silicon atom, so the outer electrons have limited mobility. As a result, pure silicon conducts electricity far worse than a conductor such as copper, though still far better than an insulator such as rubber.

Semiconductors turn out to be of tremendous practical use in electric circuits. That's because it's possible to adjust their electrical properties by *doping*—that is, by adding a small amount of a second substance. Here's an example: If we take pieces of silicon that have been doped in different ways and put them in contact, we can arrange it so that charges will flow through the combination in one direction but will *not* flow in the opposite direction! Such a combination, called a *diode*, plays the same role in an electric circuit as the valves in the human heart, which allow blood to flow through the heart in one direction only. In Chapter 21 we'll look at some of the applications of semiconductors to modern technologies such as light-emitting diodes (LEDs), solar cells, and integrated circuits.

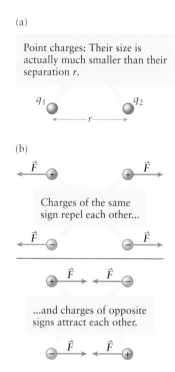

(a)

Point charges: Their size is actually much smaller than their separation *r*.

q_1 q_2

←——— r ———→

(b)

$\vec{F}$ +   + $\vec{F}$

Charges of the same sign repel each other...

$\vec{F}$ −   − $\vec{F}$

+ $\vec{F}$→ ←$\vec{F}$ −

...and charges of opposite signs attract each other.

− $\vec{F}$→ ←$\vec{F}$ +

Figure 16-6 Coulomb's law
(a) Coulomb's law describes the electric force that two point charges (not drawn to scale) exert on each other. (b) The direction of the electric force between point charges depends on the signs (positive or negative) of the charges.

> **Take-Home Message for Section 16-3**
>
> ✔   Charges are free to move within a conductor but can move very little in an insulator.
>
> ✔   In a metal conductor such as copper the moving charges are typically electrons. In biological systems water acts as a conductor, with ions as the moving charges.
>
> ✔   Semiconductors have electrical properties intermediate between those of conductors and insulators.

16-4 Coulomb's law describes the force between charged objects

We learned in Section 16-2 that electrically charged objects, or *charges* for short, exert forces on each other (see Figure 16-2). Careful measurements reveal that the force between two charges is directly proportional to the amount, or magnitude, of each of the interacting charges. The greater the amount of charge on the objects, the larger the force that acts on each charge. The force also depends on the distance between the charged objects; the closer the charges, the larger the force.

Coulomb's law is a summary in mathematical form of the results of these measurements. Specifically, this law tells us about the force between two **point charges**, which are very small charged objects whose size is much smaller than the separation between the charges (Figure 16-6a).

A point charge is an idealization, just like a massless rope or a frictionless incline, but it's a good description in many situations where charged objects interact with each other. Coulomb's law tells us the magnitude of the electric force that two point charges q_1 and q_2 separated by a distance r exert on each other:

Coulomb's law
(16-1)

Any two point charges q_1 and q_2 exert equally strong electric forces on each other.

Coulomb constant

Absolute values of the point charges

$$F_{q_1 \text{ on } q_2} = F_{q_2 \text{ on } q_1} = \frac{k|q_1||q_2|}{r^2}$$

Distance between the point charges

The value of the **Coulomb constant** k in Equation 16-1 is to three significant figures:

$$k = 8.99 \times 10^9 \text{ N} \cdot \text{m}^2/\text{C}^2$$

Note that Equation 16-1 just tells you the *magnitude* of the electric force between two point charges. As Figure 16-6b shows, the *direction* of the electric force is such that charges of the same sign (both positive or both negative) repel each other, while charges of opposite sign (one positive and one negative) attract each other. Figure 16-7 shows an application of this principle.

(a) Normal red blood cells (b) Red blood cells with excess charge removed

10 µm

Figure 16-7 **Coulomb's law and red blood cells** Red blood cells carry oxygen from your lungs to other parts of your body through the circulatory system. (a) Each red blood cell has a slight excess of electrons that gives it a net negative charge. Since all cells are negatively charged, they exert repulsive electric forces on each other that help keep the cells apart. (b) The red blood cells in this photo have been treated with an enzyme that removes the excess electrons. Without electric forces to keep them apart, the red blood cells tend to clump. If red blood cells in your body behaved like this, their flow through your circulatory system would be impeded and your body would be starved for oxygen.

You should notice the similarity between Coulomb's law and Newton's law of universal gravitation:

Gravitational constant (same for any two objects)   Masses of the two objects

Any two objects (1 and 2) exert equally strong gravitational forces on each other.

$$F_{1 \text{ on } 2} = F_{2 \text{ on } 1} = \frac{Gm_1m_2}{r^2}$$

Center-to-center distance between the two objects

The gravitational forces are attractive: $\vec{F}_{1 \text{ on } 2}$ pulls object 2 toward object 1 and $\vec{F}_{2 \text{ on } 1}$ pulls object 1 toward object 2.

Newton's law of universal gravitation
(10-2)

In both Coulomb's law (Equation 16-1) and the law of universal gravitation (Equation 10-2), the force that one object exerts on the other is inversely proportional to the square of the distance between them. In addition, the gravitational force is proportional to the product of the masses of the two particles, while the electric force is proportional to the product of the charges of the two particles. As remarkable as these similarities are, there is one essential difference between the two laws: Newton's law of universal gravitation tells us that two objects with mass always attract each other, but Coulomb's law states that two charged objects can attract or repel each other, depending on the sign of the charges they carry.

The electric force also shares some properties with every other force we've discussed. The electric force is a vector and has a direction. The net electric force on an object is the vector sum of every separate electric force that acts on it. Furthermore, the electric forces that two charged objects exert on each other obey Newton's third law. When point objects with charges q_1 and q_2 interact, the force that object 1 exerts on object 2 is equal in magnitude to the force that object 2 exerts on object 1, but the two forces are in opposite directions (see Figure 16-6b).

Example 16-2 Calculating Electric Force

(a) What is the electric force (magnitude and direction) between two electrons separated by a distance of 10.0 cm = 0.100 m? (b) Suppose you could remove all the electrons from a drop of water 1.00 mm in radius (see Example 16-1 in Section 16-2) and clump them into a ball 1.00 mm in radius. If this ball of electrons is 10.0 cm from the drop of water from which they were removed, what is the magnitude of the electric force between the drop of water and the ball of electrons?

Set Up

The two electrons repel because both have a negative charge $q = -e = -1.602 \times 10^{-19}$ C. From Example 16-1, the combined charge of all of the electrons in a water drop of this size is -224 C; the water drop was initially neutral, so the charge of the water drop after all of the electrons have been removed is $+224$ C. Since the ball of electrons and the water drop (with electrons removed) have opposite signs of charge, they attract each other.

We can use Coulomb's law (Equation 16-1) in both parts of this problem. That's because in both cases the charged objects are much smaller than the distance that separates them, so we can treat them as point charges. (Indeed, electrons are very small even compared to the dimensions of an atom.)

Coulomb's law:

$$F_{q_1 \text{ on } q_2} = F_{q_2 \text{ on } q_1} = \frac{k|q_1||q_2|}{r^2}$$

$$(16\text{-}1)$$

(a)

(b)

Solve

(a) Find the magnitude of the force that each electron exerts on the other.

For the two electrons, the charges are

$$q_1 = q_2 = -e = -1.602 \times 10^{-19} \text{ C}$$

The distance between the electrons is $r = 0.100$ m. From Equation 16-1, the magnitude of the force that each electron exerts on each other is

$$F = \frac{(8.99 \times 10^9 \text{ N} \cdot \text{m}^2/\text{C}^2)|-1.602 \times 10^{-19} \text{ C}||-1.602 \times 10^{-19} \text{ C}|}{(0.100 \text{ m})^2}$$
$$= 2.31 \times 10^{-26} \text{ N}$$

(b) Find the magnitude of the force between the ball of electrons and the water drop from which they were extracted.

For the ball of electrons and the water drop with electrons removed, the charges are

$$q_1 = -224 \text{ C}, q_2 = +224 \text{ C}$$

The distance between the two objects is $r = 0.100$ m. From Equation 16-1, the two objects exert forces on each other of magnitude

$$F = \frac{(8.99 \times 10^9 \text{ N} \cdot \text{m}^2/\text{C}^2)|-224 \text{ C}||+224 \text{ C}|}{(0.100 \text{ m})^2}$$
$$= 4.51 \times 10^{16} \text{ N}$$

Reflect

The repulsive force between the two electrons is tiny because each particle carries only a tiny amount of charge. By contrast, the attractive force between the ball of electrons and the electron-free water drop is immense. To put this force into perspective, a solid cube of lead with a weight of 4.51×10^{16} N would be 7.4 *kilometers* on a side! This is the magnitude of force that you would have to exert to keep the electrons from flying back into the water drop. There is no known way to produce a force of this magnitude, which is why you'll never see an object with all of its electrons removed. It's relatively easy to remove a small fraction of an object's electrons, as for the fur and the glass rod in Figure 16-2b. But removing *all* of the electrons from a piece of fur or a glass rod is not a practical thing to do.

Example 16-3 Three Charges in a Line

A particle with negative charge q is placed halfway between two identical particles, each of which carries the same positive charge: $Q_1 = Q_2 = +Q$. The distance between adjacent charges is d. If each of the three particles experiences a net electric force of zero, what is the magnitude of charge q in terms of Q?

Set Up

We want the net force on each point charge—that is, the *vector* sum of the forces on that charge due to the other two charges—to be equal to zero. We'll use Coulomb's law, Equation 16-1, to solve for the magnitude of the force of one charge on another. We'll also use the idea that charges of the same signs repel while charges of opposite signs attract.

Coulomb's law:

$$F_{q_1 \text{ on } q_2} = F_{q_2 \text{ on } q_1} = \frac{k|q_1||q_2|}{r^2}$$

(16-1)

Solve

Let's start by considering the forces on positive charge Q_2. The other positive charge, Q_1, exerts a repulsive force $\vec{F}_{Q_1 \text{ on } Q_2}$ that pushes Q_2 away from Q_1, that is, to the right. The negative charge q exerts an attractive force $\vec{F}_{q \text{ on } Q_2}$ that pulls Q_2 toward q, that is, to the left. In order for the net force on Q_2 to be zero, these two forces must have the same magnitude.

The net force on charge Q_2 must be zero:

$$\vec{F}_{Q_1 \text{ on } Q_2} + \vec{F}_{q \text{ on } Q_2} = 0$$

For this to be true, $\vec{F}_{Q_1 \text{ on } Q_2}$ and $\vec{F}_{q \text{ on } Q_2}$ must have the same magnitude:

$$F_{Q_1 \text{ on } Q_2} = F_{q \text{ on } Q_2}$$

Use Coulomb's law (Equation 16-1) to find the magnitudes $F_{Q_1 \text{ on } Q_2}$ and $F_{q \text{ on } Q_2}$. Set these equal to each other and solve for the magnitude (absolute value) of q.

The distance between Q_1 and Q_2, each of which has a charge of magnitude Q, is $2d$. From Equation 16-1, the force of Q_1 on Q_2 has magnitude

$$F_{Q_1 \text{ on } Q_2} = \frac{k|Q_1||Q_2|}{(2d)^2} = \frac{kQ^2}{4d^2}$$

d is the distance between Q_1 and q, and also between Q_2 and q. Notice that Q_1 and Q_2 are separated by distance $2d$. Remember that q is negative, so we need to keep its absolute value.

The distance between q and Q_2 is d, so the magnitude of the force of q on Q_2 is

$$F_{q \text{ on } Q_2} = \frac{k|q||Q_2|}{d^2} = \frac{k|q|Q}{d^2}$$

In order for the forces to have the same magnitude,

$$\frac{kQ^2}{4d^2} = \frac{k|q|Q}{d^2}$$

Solve for the absolute value of q:

$$|q| = \frac{Q}{4}$$

Reflect

The value $|q| = Q/4$ satisfies the condition that there is zero net force on Q_2. Because Q_1 is twice as far from Q_2 as q, and because the electric force is inversely proportional to the square of the distance, the charge Q_1 must be $(2)^2 = 4$ times greater than the magnitude of q in order for the forces these charges exert on Q_2 to have the same magnitude.

You can see that since Q_1 and Q_2 have the same charge, the forces on Q_1 are the mirror images of those on Q_2 (a repulsive force to the *left* exerted by Q_2, which is a distance $2d$ from Q_1, and an attractive force to the *right* exerted by q, which is a distance d from Q_1). So the net force on Q_1 will be zero, too.

You can see that the net force on the negative charge q is also guaranteed to be zero. This charge is the same distance d from the two equal positive charges Q_1 and Q_2, so the force from Q_1 that pulls q to the left is just as great as the force from Q_2 that pulls q to the right.

Example 16-4 Three Charges in a Plane

Charges Q_1 and Q_3 are both positive and equal to 1.50×10^{-6} C; charge Q_2 is negative and equal to -1.50×10^{-6} C. Charges Q_1 and Q_2 are placed at a fixed position a distance $D = 6.00$ cm apart, and Q_3 is placed at a fixed position a distance $H = 4.00$ cm above the midpoint of the line that connects Q_1 and Q_2. Calculate the magnitude and direction of the force on Q_3 due to the other two charges.

Set Up

The net force on positive charge Q_3 is the vector sum of $\vec{F}_{1 \text{ on } 3}$, the *repulsive* force that the positive charge Q_1 exerts on Q_3, and $\vec{F}_{2 \text{ on } 3}$, the *attractive* force that the negative charge Q_2 exerts on Q_3. We'll use Coulomb's law to find the magnitude of each of these forces. We'll then add the two force vectors using components.

Coulomb's law:

$$F_{q_1 \text{ on } q_2} = F_{q_2 \text{ on } q_1} = \frac{k|q_1||q_2|}{r^2} \qquad (16\text{-}1)$$

Solve

Use Equation 16-1 to find the magnitudes of the forces $\vec{F}_{1 \text{ on } 3}$ and $\vec{F}_{2 \text{ on } 3}$.

The figure above shows that the distance from Q_1 to Q_3 is the same as the distance from Q_2 to Q_3:

$$r_{13} = r_{23} = \sqrt{\left(\frac{D}{2}\right)^2 + H^2} = \sqrt{\left(\frac{6.00 \text{ cm}}{2}\right)^2 + (4.00 \text{ cm})^2}$$

$$= 5.00 \text{ cm} = 5.00 \times 10^{-2} \text{ m}$$

All three charges have the same magnitude:

$$|Q_1| = |Q_2| = |Q_3| = 1.50 \times 10^{-6} \text{ C}$$

So from Equation 16-1, $\vec{F}_{1 \text{ on } 3}$ and $\vec{F}_{2 \text{ on } 3}$ have the same magnitude:

$$F_{1 \text{ on } 3} = \frac{k|Q_1||Q_3|}{r_{13}^2}$$

$$= \frac{(8.99 \times 10^9 \text{ N} \cdot \text{m}^2/\text{C}^2)(1.50 \times 10^{-6} \text{ C})^2}{(5.00 \times 10^{-2} \text{ m})^2}$$

$$= 8.09 \text{ N}$$

$$F_{2 \text{ on } 3} = \frac{k|Q_2||Q_3|}{r_{23}^2} = F_{1 \text{ on } 3} = 8.09 \text{ N}$$

Choose the positive x direction to be to the right and the positive y direction to be upward. Then find the x and y components of $\vec{F}_{1 \text{ on } 3}$ and $\vec{F}_{2 \text{ on } 3}$, and use these to calculate the components of the net force on Q_3.

The components of $\vec{F}_{1 \text{ on } 3}$ and $\vec{F}_{2 \text{ on } 3}$ are

$$F_{1 \text{ on } 3,x} = F_{1 \text{ on } 3} \cos \theta$$
$$F_{1 \text{ on } 3,y} = F_{1 \text{ on } 3} \sin \theta$$
$$F_{2 \text{ on } 3,x} = F_{2 \text{ on } 3} \cos \theta$$
$$F_{2 \text{ on } 3,y} = -F_{2 \text{ on } 3} \sin \theta$$

Since the magnitudes $F_{1 \text{ on } 3}$ and $F_{2 \text{ on } 3}$ are equal, the components of the net force on Q_3 are

$$F_{\text{net on } 3,x} = F_{1 \text{ on } 3,x} + F_{2 \text{ on } 3,x}$$
$$= F_{1 \text{ on } 3} \cos \theta + F_{2 \text{ on } 3} \cos \theta$$
$$= 2F_{1 \text{ on } 3} \cos \theta$$

$$F_{\text{net on } 3,y} = F_{1 \text{ on } 3} \sin\theta + (-F_{2 \text{ on } 3} \sin\theta)$$
$$= F_{1 \text{ on } 3} \sin\theta - F_{1 \text{ on } 3} \sin\theta = 0$$

From the figure,

$$\cos\theta = \frac{(D/2)}{r_{13}} = \frac{3.00 \text{ cm}}{5.00 \text{ cm}} = 0.600$$

So

$$F_{\text{net on } 3,x} = 2(8.09 \text{ N})(0.600) = 9.71 \text{ N}$$
$$F_{\text{net on } 3,y} = 0$$

So the net force on Q_3 is to the right and has magnitude 9.71 N.

Reflect

The two individual forces on Q_3 add to a net force that is neither directly away from Q_1 nor directly toward Q_2.

Got the Concept? 16-3 Electric Force

In part (b) of Example 16-2 we imagined removing all of the electrons from a drop of water and moving them to a given distance from the water drop. We then calculated the electric force between the drop and the electrons. Suppose instead we removed only one-half of the electrons from the water drop, then moved them to the same distance as in Example 16-2. Compared to the force we calculated in part (b) of Example 16-2, what would be the force between the electrons and the water drop in this case? (a) the same; (b) $1/\sqrt{2}$ as great; (c) 1/2 as great; (d) 1/4 as great; (e) 1/16 as great.

Take-Home Message for Section 16-4

✔ Coulomb's law tells us the magnitude of the electric force that two point charges exert on each other. This magnitude is proportional to the product of the magnitudes of the two charges and inversely proportional to the square of the distance between them.

✔ The electric force between two point charges is repulsive if the two charges have the same sign (both positive or both negative) and attractive if the two charges have opposite signs (one positive and one negative).

16-5 The concept of electric field helps us visualize how charges exert forces at a distance

Most forces in our daily experience arise only when one object is in direct contact with another object. Two examples are the normal force that acts on your body when you sit in a chair or when you push directly on an object. Nevertheless, some forces, such as the gravitational force and the Coulomb force, appear to act even between two objects separated by a distance. The fundamental theory of interactions between particles suggests that objects exert forces on each other by exchanging small units of energy or matter. For our purposes, however, a more useful approach employs the concept of the *field*. In this view, every charged object modifies all of space by producing an electric field, which is strongest closest to the object but extends infinitely far away. A second charged object senses this change in space, interacting with the electric field and experiencing an electric force (Figure 16-8).

If we place a particle carrying charge q in an electric field $\vec{E}$, the force experienced by the particle is

If a particle with charge q is placed at a position where the electric field due to other charges is $\vec{E}$...

$$\vec{F} = q\vec{E}$$

...then the electric force on the particle is $\vec{F} = q\vec{E}$.

Electric field and electric force
(16-2)

Figure 16-8 Electric field and electric force The electric field concept helps us visualize how a charge Q exerts an electric force on a second charge q.

1. To explain how charge Q exerts an electric force on charge q at a point P some distance from charge Q...

2. ...we picture charge Q as producing an electric field at point P. This field is present whether or not there is any charge at point P.

3. If we place a charge q at point P, it senses the electric field due to Q and experiences a force as a result.

4. The force on charge q is in the same direction as the electric field if q is positive...

5. ...and the force on charge q is in the direction opposite to the electric field if q is negative.

An equivalent way to write Equation 16-2 is

$$\vec{E} = \frac{\vec{F}}{q}$$

(16-3)

Equation 16-3 tells us that we can interpret the electric field $\vec{E}$ at a certain point as the *electric force per charge* that acts on a charged object placed at that point. If an object with double the charge is placed at that point, it will experience double the force.

Watch Out! **The direction of *force* versus the direction of *field*.**

Although we can think of the electric field as the electric force per unit charge, you must be careful about the direction of the force. In particular, the direction of the electric force that a charge experiences depends on the *sign* of the charge as well as the *direction* of the electric field. Equation 16-2 tells us that a positive charge ($q > 0$) experiences a force in the same direction as the electric field $\vec{E}$, but a negative charge ($q < 0$) experiences a force in the direction opposite to $\vec{E}$ (Figure 16-8). So the electric field at a certain point is in the direction of the electric force that would be exerted on a *positive* charge placed at that point.

From Equation 16-3 we see that the SI units of electric field are newtons per coulomb, or N/C. If a 1-C charge experiences a 1-N force at a certain point in space, then at that point in space there is an electric field with a magnitude of 1 N/C.

Note that Equations 16-2 and 16-3 are strictly valid *only* if the particle of charge q is a *point* particle (that is, one with a very small size). That's because the value of $\vec{E}$ can be different at different places. If the charge q occupied a large volume (say, spread over a sphere 1 m in diameter), the value of $\vec{E}$ could be different at different points within that volume. In that case it wouldn't be clear which value of $\vec{E}$ to use in Equation 16-2 or 16-3. But if the charge q is within a point particle, it's clear what value of $\vec{E}$ to use: The value at the point where that particle is located.

Although this is the first time we've introduced the idea of a field, we've actually used the concept before. In Chapter 4 we found that we could express the gravitational force $\vec{w}$ on an object of mass m as $\vec{w} = m\vec{g}$, where $\vec{g}$ is the acceleration due to gravity. But we can also think of $\vec{g}$ as the *gravitational field* of Earth. In this picture, Earth sets up a field in the space around it, and $\vec{g}$ represents the value of that field vector (magnitude and direction) at a given point. An object of mass m placed at that point then experiences a gravitational force $\vec{w} = m\vec{g}$ (compare to Equation 16-2). Just as the concept of an electric field gives us a way to visualize how two charges can interact over a distance, the concept of a gravitational field helps us visualize how two objects with mass (Earth and the object of mass m) can interact without touching each other.

 Go to Interactive Exercise 16-1 for more practice dealing with electric fields

Example 16-5 Determining Charge-to-Mass Ratio

When released from rest in a uniform electric field of magnitude 1.00×10^4 N/C, a certain charged particle travels 2.00 cm in 2.88×10^{-7} s in the direction of the field. You can ignore any nonelectric forces acting on the particle. (a) What is the *charge-to-mass ratio* of this particle (that is, the ratio of its charge q to its mass m)? (b) Other experiments show that the mass of this particle is 6.64×10^{-27} kg. What is the charge of this particle?

Set Up

The only force that acts on the particle is the electric force given by Equation 16-2. Since the particle accelerates in the direction of the electric field $\vec{E}$, the force on the particle must also be in the direction of $\vec{E}$. So the charge on the particle must be positive. Since $\vec{E}$ is uniform (it has the same value at all points), the force on the particle will be constant. Its acceleration a_x will be constant as well, so we can use one of the constant-acceleration equations from Chapter 2 to determine a_x. We'll use this with Newton's second law and Equation 16-2 to learn what we can about this particle.

Electric field and electric force:
$$\vec{F} = q\vec{E} \qquad (16\text{-}2)$$

Straight-line motion with constant acceleration:
$$x = x_0 + v_{0x}t + \frac{1}{2}a_x t^2 \qquad (2\text{-}9)$$

Newton's second law:
$$\sum \vec{F}_{\text{ext}} = m\vec{a} \qquad (4\text{-}2)$$

$q > 0$

Solve

(a) We are given that the particle travels 2.00 cm = 2.00×10^{-2} m in 2.88×10^{-7} s. Use this to determine the particle's constant acceleration.

Take the positive x direction to be the direction in which the particle moves. The particle begins at rest, so $v_{0x} = 0$. If we take the initial position of the particle to be $x_0 = 0$, then Equation 2-9 becomes

$$x = \frac{1}{2}a_x t^2$$

Solve for the acceleration:

$$a_x = \frac{2x}{t^2} = \frac{2(2.00 \times 10^{-2}\,\text{m})}{(2.88 \times 10^{-7}\,\text{s})^2} = 4.82 \times 10^{11}\,\text{m/s}^2$$

Relate the acceleration to the net external (electric) force on the particle and solve for the charge-to-mass ratio.

The net force on the particle of charge q is the electric force in the x direction, which from Newton's second law is equal to the mass m of the particle multiplied by the acceleration a_x:

$$qE_x = ma_x$$

This says that the acceleration of a particle in an electric field depends on the particle's charge-to-mass ratio:

$$a_x = \frac{q}{m}E_x$$

In this example we know both a_x and E_x, so the charge-to-mass ratio is

$$\frac{q}{m} = \frac{a_x}{E_x} = \frac{4.82 \times 10^{11}\,\text{m/s}^2}{1.00 \times 10^4\,\text{N/C}}$$

Since 1 N = 1 kg·m/s², this is

$$\frac{q}{m} = 4.82 \times 10^7\,\text{C/kg}$$

(b) Given the charge-to-mass ratio and the mass of the particle, determine the charge q.

The charge of the particle is

$$q = m\left(\frac{q}{m}\right) = (6.64 \times 10^{-27}\,\text{kg})(4.82 \times 10^7\,\text{C/kg})$$
$$= 3.20 \times 10^{-19}\,\text{C}$$

The charge on a proton is $e = 1.60 \times 10^{-19}$ C; the charge on this particle is $2e$.

Reflect

The particle in this example has about four times the mass of a proton but only double the charge of a proton. For historical reasons it's known as an *alpha particle*; in fact, it's the nucleus of a helium atom, which contains two protons (each with charge e) and two neutrons (each with nearly the same mass as a proton but with zero charge).

Figure 16-9 Paper electrophoresis
This analytical technique used by chemists makes use of the electric field concept.

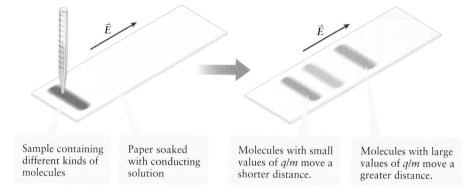

Sample containing different kinds of molecules

Paper soaked with conducting solution

Molecules with small values of q/m move a shorter distance.

Molecules with large values of q/m move a greater distance.

An important application of the force produced by an electric field is *electrophoresis*. Chemists use this technique to separate molecules of different kinds according to their charge and mass. In the simplest kind of electrophoresis, a small amount of a sample containing molecules of different kinds is placed on a strip of filter paper, and the paper is soaked with a solution that conducts electricity (Figure 16-9). An electric field of magnitude E is then applied along the length of the strip. If the molecules could move in the solution without fluid resistance, they would behave like the particle in Example 16-5: Each molecule would accelerate in response to the field, and that acceleration would be proportional to the charge-to-mass ratio q/m of the molecule. As a result, molecules with different values of q/m would move to different locations on the paper. In fact, there *is* fluid resistance on the molecules, but the net result is the same: Molecules with larger values of q/m move farther along the paper than do those with small values of q/m. The many applications of this specific technique, called *paper electrophoresis*, include analyzing currency to determine whether it is counterfeit (a forger's ink may have a different chemical composition than the ink used in legal currency) and looking for the presence of cancer antibodies or human immunodeficiency virus (HIV) in blood.

A different sort of electrophoresis is used for DNA profiling (also called genetic fingerprinting), which is an essential part of modern forensic science. A sample of human DNA is treated with an enzyme that breaks the long DNA strand into shorter segments. The sizes of these segments are characteristic of the person's genetic code, so measuring the segment sizes is a powerful technique for forensic identification. Unfortunately, the ratio of q/m for a segment of DNA is nearly the same for segments of any size, so paper electrophoresis isn't useful. Instead a sample containing the DNA segments is placed in a special gel that is permeated by many microscopic pores. When an electric field is applied, all of the segments move in response, but the smaller segments move through the gel pores more easily than large ones. The result is that the DNA segments are spread out according to their size, allowing a genetic "fingerprint" to be made. Similar techniques are used in medical research for studying both DNA and proteins.

Electric Field of a Point Charge

Equation 16-2 tells us how a charge q responds to a given electric field $\vec{E}$. It also tells us how to determine the value of $\vec{E}$ at any point. As an example, Figure 16-10 shows how we might determine the electric field around a positive point charge Q. To do this,

Figure 16-10 Mapping the electric field We can map out the electric field surrounding a point charge Q—in this case a positive charge—by placing a positive test charge $+q$ at various locations around Q.

• To measure the electric field at a given location due to the charge Q, place a positive test charge q at that location and measure the force $\vec{F}$ on test charge q.

• The electric field at that location is $\vec{E} = \vec{F}/q$.

$q > 0$

Far from positive charge Q, the electric field has a small magnitude.

Close to positive charge Q, the electric field has a large magnitude.

$Q > 0$

$q > 0$

$\vec{E}$

$q > 0$

At all distances from positive charge Q, the electric field points directly away from Q.

(a) Positive point charge: electric field vectors

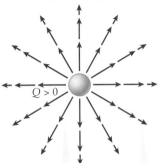

(b) Positive point charge: electric field lines

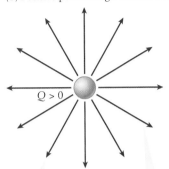

(c) Negative point charge: electric field lines

| Field due to a positive charge points away from the charge. | Field strength decreases with increasing distance from the charge. | Field due to a positive charge points away from the charge. | Farther from the charge, where the field strength is weaker, field lines are farther apart. | Field lines due to a negative charge point toward the charge. | Farther from the charge, where the field strength is weaker, field lines are farther apart. |

Figure 16-11 **Electric field and electric field lines** The electric field around a charged object can be represented by (a) electric field vectors or (b), (c) electric field lines.

we place a small positive charge q (which we call a *test charge*) at various locations around the charge Q and measure the force $\vec{F}$ on that small charge. The electric field at each location is given by Equation 16-3, $\vec{E} = \vec{F}/q$; since q is positive, the electric field is in the same direction as the force on the test charge. The Coulomb force exerted by Q repels a positive test charge q at any location; thus, the direction of force at each location—and so the direction of the electric field at each location, shown by the blue vectors—is radially away from Q. As the lengths of the vectors show, the magnitude of the electric field decreases with increasing distance from Q. That's because the force between Q and q decreases with increasing distance in accordance with Coulomb's law (Section 16-4).

Figure 16-11 shows two ways we can represent the entire electric field around a positive charge Q. In Figure 16-11a we draw vectors to represent the electric field at a large number of points around Q. Figure 16-11b shows a simpler approach that's easier to draw: We connect adjacent vectors to form lines, called **electric field lines.** The direction of the field line passing through any point represents the direction of the field at that point. The magnitude of the electric field is shown by the *density* of the field lines—that is, how close they are to each other. In regions where the field lines are close together, such as close to Q, the field has a large magnitude. Where the field lines are far apart, such as far from Q, the magnitude of the electric field is smaller. If the charge Q is negative, a positive test charge q would experience a force $\vec{F}$ toward Q, and so the electric field $\vec{E} = \vec{F}/q$ due to charge Q is directed *toward* that charge (Figure 16-11c).

! Watch Out! **Electric fields are three-dimensional.**

Figure 16-11 may give you the incorrect impression that the electric field and electric field lines of a point charge Q lie only on the plane of the page. Not so! The electric field completely surrounds the charge; it is three-dimensional. The field lines are arranged around the charge rather like the spines of a sea urchin (Figure 16-12).

Figure 16-12 **An electric field analogy** The electric field lines of a point charge are arranged radially around the charge in three dimensions, much like the spines on a sea urchin.

We can use Coulomb's law, Equation 16-1, to write an expression for the *magnitude* of the electric field due to a point charge Q. If we place a test charge q a distance r from charge Q, Equation 16-1 tells us that the magnitude of the Coulomb force on q is $F = k|q||Q|/r^2$. From Equation 16-2, we can also write this force magnitude as

$F = |q|E$, where E is the magnitude of the electric field due to charge Q at the position of test charge q. Setting these two expressions for F equal to each other, we get

$$|q|E = \frac{k|q||Q|}{r^2}$$

or

Magnitude of the electric field due to a point charge
(16-4)

Magnitude of the electric field due to a point charge Q

Coulomb constant   Absolute value of charge Q

$$E = \frac{k|Q|}{r^2}$$

Distance between point charge Q and the location where the field is measured

The *magnitude* of the electric field due to a point charge Q decreases with increasing distance r from the charge. As Figure 16-11 shows, the *direction* of the electric field depends on the sign of the charge Q. The field points radially outward from a positive point charge and radially inward toward a negative point charge.

Electric Field of an Arrangement of Charges

Go to Picture It 16-1 for more practice dealing with electric fields

The results in Figure 16-11 and Equation 16-4 describe the electric field due to a single point charge (positive or negative). If several point charges $Q_1, Q_2, Q_3, \ldots$ are present, experiment shows that the *net* electric force $\vec{F}$ that these charges exert on a test charge q at any location is just the vector sum of the forces $\vec{F}_1, \vec{F}_2, \vec{F}_3, \ldots$ that these charges *individually* exert on q. If we use the symbol $\vec{E}$ for the net electric field produced at a given location by $Q_1, Q_2, Q_3, \ldots$ together, and the symbols $\vec{E}_1, \vec{E}_2, \vec{E}_3, \ldots$ for the electric fields that these charges produce individually, we can use Equation 16-2 to express this experimental result as

$$\vec{F} = \vec{F}_1 + \vec{F}_2 + \vec{F}_3 + \cdots \quad \text{or} \quad q\vec{E} = q\vec{E}_1 + q\vec{E}_2 + q\vec{E}_3 + \cdots$$

If we divide both sides of the second of these equations by q, we get

(16-5)

$$\vec{E} = \vec{E}_1 + \vec{E}_2 + \vec{E}_3 + \cdots$$

In other words, *when there are two or more point charges present, the electric field at any point in space is the vector sum of the fields due to each charge separately.* The following examples illustrate how to use this principle.

Example 16-6 Where *Is* the Electric Field Zero?

A point charge $Q_1 = +4.00$ nC (1 nC = 1 nanocoulomb = 10^{-9} C) is placed 0.500 m to the left of a point charge $Q_2 = +9.00$ nC. Find the position between the two point charges where the net electric field is zero.

Set Up

At any point between the two charges, the electric field $\vec{E}_1$ due to Q_1 points to the right (away from this positive charge) and the electric field $\vec{E}_2$ due to Q_2 points to the left (away from this positive charge). We want to find the point P where the total field $\vec{E} = \vec{E}_1 + \vec{E}_2$ equals zero. We'll use the symbol D for the 0.500-m distance between the two charges and x for the distance from Q_1 to point P. Then the distance from Q_2 to point P is $D - x$. Our goal is to find the value of x for which $\vec{E} = 0$.

Magnitude of the electric field due to a point charge Q:

$$E = \frac{k|Q|}{r^2} \quad (16\text{-}4)$$

$Q_1 = +4.00$ nC $\vec{E}_2$ P $\vec{E}_1$ $Q_2 = +9.00$ nC

x

$D = 0.500$ m

Total electric field:

$$\vec{E} = \vec{E}_1 + \vec{E}_2 \quad (16\text{-}5)$$

Solve

If the net electric field at P is zero, then $\vec{E}_1$ (to the right) and $\vec{E}_2$ (to the left) must have equal magnitudes so that these two vectors cancel. Use Equation 16-4 to write this statement in equation form.

In order for the net electric field at P to be zero,

$$E_1 = E_2$$

The distance from Q_1 to P is x, and the distance from Q_2 to P is $D - x$, so from Equation 16-4

$$E_1 = \frac{k|Q_1|}{x^2} \quad \text{and} \quad E_2 = \frac{k|Q_2|}{(D - x)^2}$$

Solve this equation for x.

If these are equal to each other,

$$\frac{k|Q_1|}{x^2} = \frac{k|Q_2|}{(D-x)^2}$$

The factors of k cancel in the above equation, so

$$\frac{|Q_1|}{x^2} = \frac{|Q_2|}{(D-x)^2} \quad \text{or}$$

$$|Q_1|(D-x)^2 = |Q_2|x^2$$

Multiply out the quantity $(D-x)^2$ and rearrange:

$$|Q_1|(D^2 - 2Dx + x^2) = |Q_2|x^2$$

$$(|Q_2| - |Q_1|)x^2 + (2D|Q_1|)x + (-D^2|Q_1|) = 0$$

We can simplify this if we divide through by $|Q_1|$:

$$\left(\frac{|Q_2|}{|Q_1|} - 1\right)x^2 + 2Dx + (-D^2) = 0$$

This is a quadratic equation of the form $ax^2 + bx + c = 0$, with
$a = |Q_2|/|Q_1| - 1 = |9.00\text{ nC}|/|4.00\text{ nC}| - 1 = 1.25$,
$b = 2D = 2(0.500\text{ m}) = 1.00\text{ m}$, and $c = -D^2 = -(0.500\text{ m})^2 = -0.250\text{ m}^2$. The solutions are

$$x = \frac{-b \pm \sqrt{b^2 - 4ac}}{2a}$$

$$= \frac{-(1.00\text{ m}) \pm \sqrt{(1.00\text{ m})^2 - 4(1.25)(-0.250\text{ m}^2)}}{2(1.25)}$$

$$= \frac{-(1.00\text{ m}) \pm \sqrt{2.25\text{ m}^2}}{2.50} = \frac{-(1.00\text{ m}) \pm (1.50\text{ m})}{2.50}$$

$$= +0.200\text{ m or } -1.00\text{ m}$$

We want a positive value of x to correspond to a point to the right of Q_1, so the solution we want is $x = +0.200$ m. We conclude that point P is a distance $x = 0.200$ m to the right of charge Q_1 and a distance $D - x = 0.500\text{ m} - 0.200\text{ m} = 0.300$ m to the left of charge Q_2.

Reflect

Because charge Q_1 is smaller than Q_2, the location of the point where the net electric field is zero must be closer to Q_1 than to Q_2. That's just what we found. You can check the result $x = 0.200$ m by substituting this value into the above expressions for E_1 and E_2 and confirming that $E_1 = E_2$ for this value of x.

But what's the significance of the second solution, $x = -1.00$ m? This refers to a point 1.00 m to the *left* of charge Q_1 and 1.00 m + 0.500 m = 1.50 m to the left of charge Q_2. Our calculation shows that this point E_1 is equal to E_2. However, at this point $\vec{E}_1$ and $\vec{E}_2$ *both* point to the *left* (both fields point away from the positive charges that produce them). So at this point the electric fields $\vec{E}_1$ and $\vec{E}_2$ do *not* cancel, and the total field is not zero.

Example 16-7 Field of an Electric Dipole

A combination of two point charges of the same magnitude but opposite signs is called an **electric dipole**. Figure 16-13 shows an electric dipole made up of a point charge $+q$ and a point charge $-q$ separated by a distance $2d$. Derive expressions for the magnitude and direction of the net electric field due to these two charges at a point P a distance y along the midline of the dipole.

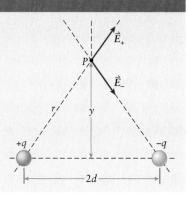

Figure 16-13 **An electric dipole** The field produced by an electric dipole at any point is the vector sum of the fields $\vec{E}_+$ and $\vec{E}_-$ caused by the positive charge $+q$ and the negative charge $-q$, respectively.

Set Up

The net field is the vector sum of the field $\vec{E}_+$ due to the charge $+q$ (which points away from $+q$) and the field $\vec{E}_-$ due to the charge $-q$ (which points toward $-q$). Note that this problem is very similar to Example 16-4 in Section 16-4, in which we used vector addition to find the net electric *force* exerted by two charges (one positive and one negative) on a third charge; here we use vector addition to find the net electric *field* due to the positive and negative charge. As in Example 16-4, we'll choose the positive x direction to be to the right and the positive y axis to be upward and add the two vectors using components.

Magnitude of the electric field due to a point charge Q:

$$E = \frac{k|Q|}{r^2} \qquad (16\text{-}4)$$

Total electric field:

$$\vec{E} = \vec{E}_1 + \vec{E}_2 \qquad (16\text{-}5)$$

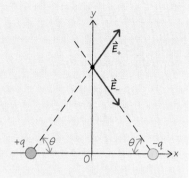

Solve

Use Equation 16-4 to find the magnitudes of the fields $\vec{E}_+$ and $\vec{E}_-$ at P.

The distance from $+q$ to point P is the same as the distance from $-q$ to P. Call this distance r:

$$r = \sqrt{y^2 + d^2}$$

Since $+q$ and $-q$ have the same magnitude (q, which is positive) and are the same distance from P, Equation 16-4 tells us that the fields that the two charges produce at P have the same magnitude:

$$E_+ = E_- = \frac{kq}{r^2} = \frac{kq}{y^2 + d^2}$$

Find the x and y components of $\vec{E}_+$ and $\vec{E}_-$, and use these to calculate the components of the net field at P.

The components of $\vec{E}_+$ and $\vec{E}_-$ are

$$E_{+,x} = E_+ \cos \theta$$
$$E_{+,y} = E_+ \sin \theta$$
$$E_{-,x} = E_- \cos \theta$$
$$E_{-,y} = -E_- \sin \theta$$

Since the magnitudes E_+ and E_- are equal, the components of the net field at P are

$$E_x = E_{+,x} + E_{-,x} = E_+ \cos \theta + E_- \cos \theta$$
$$= \frac{2kq}{y^2 + d^2} \cos \theta$$

$$E_y = E_{+,y} + E_{-,y} = E_+ \sin \theta + (-E_- \sin \theta)$$
$$= \frac{kq}{y^2 + d^2} \sin \theta - \frac{kq}{y^2 + d^2} \sin \theta = 0$$

From the figure,

$$\cos \theta = \frac{d}{r} = \frac{d}{\sqrt{y^2 + d^2}}$$

So the components of the net electric field are

$$E_x = \frac{2kq}{(y^2 + d^2)} \frac{d}{\sqrt{y^2 + d^2}} = \frac{2kqd}{(y^2 + d^2)^{3/2}}$$
$$E_y = 0$$

The net electric field at point P is to the right and has magnitude $E = 2kqd/(y^2 + d^2)^{3/2}$.

Reflect

We can check our result by substituting $y = 0$, so that the point P is directly between the two charges and a distance d from each charge. Then $\vec{E}_+$ and $\vec{E}_-$ both point to the right, and the magnitude of the net electric field should be equal to the sum of the magnitudes of $\vec{E}_+$ and $\vec{E}_-$.

At $y = 0$, the net electric field has magnitude

$$E = \frac{2kqd}{(0 + d^2)^{3/2}} = \frac{2kqd}{d^3} = \frac{2kq}{d^2} = 2\left(\frac{kq}{d^2}\right)$$

This is just twice the magnitude of the field due to each individual charge:

$$E_+ = E_- = \frac{kq}{d^2}$$

Note that at points very far from the dipole, so that y is much greater than d, the magnitude of the field is inversely proportional to the *cube* of y: At double the distance, the field of a dipole is $(1/2)^3 = 1/8$ as great. This is a much more rapid decrease with distance than the field of a single point charge, for which E is inversely proportional to the *square* of the distance: At double the distance, the field of a point charge is $(1/2)^2 = 1/4$ as great. The dipole field decreases much more rapidly because the fields of $+q$ and $-q$ partially cancel each other.

If y is much greater than d, $y^2 + d^2$ is approximately equal to y^2. Then the magnitude of the net electric field due to the dipole is approximately

$$E_{net} = \frac{2kqd}{(y^2)^{3/2}} = \frac{2kqd}{y^3}$$

By using techniques like the ones we employed in Example 16-7, it's possible to calculate and map out the electric field at *all* points around an electric dipole. Figure 16-14 shows the field lines. Note that as you move away from the dipole along its midline, the field lines become farther apart. This is a graphical way of showing that the magnitude of the field decreases with increasing distance, just as we found in Example 16-7.

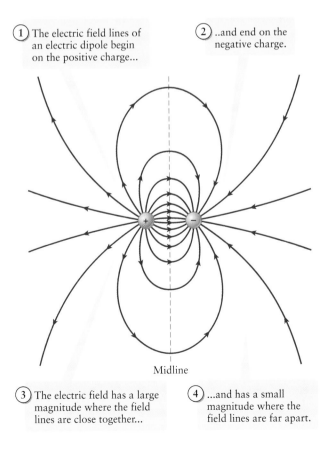

(1) The electric field lines of an electric dipole begin on the positive charge...

(2) ...and end on the negative charge.

Midline

(3) The electric field has a large magnitude where the field lines are close together...

(4) ...and has a small magnitude where the field lines are far apart.

Figure 16-14 Field lines of an electric dipole At any point, the electric field due to an electric dipole is the vector sum of the field due to the positive charge and the field due to the negative charge.

? Got the Concept? 16-4 Electric Field I

The positive charge in the dipole shown in Figure 16-14 is attracted to the negative charge. To find the force of this attraction, the electric field $\vec{E}$ to use in Equation 16-2 is (a) the field due to the positive charge; (b) the field due to the negative charge; (c) the net field due to both charges; (d) none of these.

? Got the Concept? 16-5 Electric Field II

Suppose both of the charges in Figure 16-13 were negative and had the same magnitude. At point P in that figure, the net electric field due to these charges would (a) point to the left; (b) point to the right; (c) point straight up; (d) point straight down; (e) be zero.

Take-Home Message for Section 16-5

✔ Any charged object produces an electric field in the space around it. A second charged object responds to this electric field; this is the origin of the electric force that the first object exerts on the second.

✔ The electric field of a positive point charge points directly away from that charge; the electric field of a negative point charge points directly toward that charge.

✔ The net electric field due to two or more charges is the vector sum of the electric fields due to the individual charges.

Figure 16-15 A protein molecule This illustration shows the structure of a particular protein molecule, a long chain of amino acids that coils on itself in a complex way. The coiling takes place because different parts of the chain carry different amounts of electric charge. The electric forces between the parts pull the chain into the complex shape shown here. Understanding the details of protein folding requires knowing the electric field at any point due to the arrangement of charges along the chain. This very complicated problem can only be solved using a computer.

16-6 Gauss's law gives us more insight into the electric field

Example 16-7 in the previous section shows how we can find the net electric field due to two point charges. In principle, we can extend this approach to calculate the net electric field due to a collection of any number of point charges. If there are many such charges, however, the calculations can become very complex (Figure 16-15).

Happily, there's an alternative and a much easier approach that we can use to find the electric field if the charges are arranged in a very *symmetrical* fashion—for example, uniformly distributed over a spherical volume. This approach uses a principle called *Gauss's law*, which is an alternative way to express Coulomb's law (Equation 16-1). We'll develop Gauss's law in this section and apply it to a variety of physical situations in the following section.

To understand Gauss's law, we first need to define a new quantity called *electric flux*. We'll do this by making an analogy between electric fields and the flow of water.

Water Flux and Electric Flux

Figure 16-16 shows water flowing through a pipe. The vectors labeled $\vec{v}$ in Figure 16-16a represent the velocity of the water at each point. For simplicity we've assumed that the water velocity is the same everywhere. Now imagine that we place a rectangular wire frame of area A in the flow. We define the *flux* of water through this wire frame as the product of (i) the area A of the frame and (ii) the component of flow velocity $\vec{v}$ that's perpendicular to the plane of the frame. If we orient the frame so that it's face-on to the

(a)

Flux = Av

(b)

Flux = 0

(c)

Flux = $Av \cos \theta$

Figure 16-16 Flux of water The flux of water through a rectangular wire frame depends on the velocity $\vec{v}$ of the water, the area A of the wire frame, and the angle between the direction of $\vec{v}$ and the perpendicular to the plane of the frame.

water flow as in Figure 16-16a, then $\vec{v}$ is perpendicular to the plane of the frame and the perpendicular component is just v. The flux is then equal to Av. If instead we orient the frame so that it is edge-on to the flow as in Figure 16-16b, the flow velocity $\vec{v}$ has no component perpendicular to the plane of the frame. In this case the flux is zero. If we orient the frame so that a line perpendicular to the frame is at an angle θ to the direction of $\vec{v}$ as in Figure 16-16c, the perpendicular component of $\vec{v}$ is $v \cos \theta$ and the flux is $A(v \cos \theta) = Av \cos \theta$.

Note that we've actually encountered the concept of flux before. In Section 11-9 we learned that if an incompressible fluid is in steady flow through a pipe of varying cross-sectional area A, the product of the area and the flow speed v has the same value at any two points 1 and 2 along the pipe: $A_1 v_1 = A_2 v_2$ (Equation 11-19). In the language we've just introduced, this says that the *flux* of the fluid through the entire pipe maintains the same value even if the cross-sectional area of the pipe changes.

Figure 16-17 shows how we extend the idea of flux to the electric field. Instead of a pipe carrying a fluid, let's look at a region of space where there is an electric field $\vec{E}$. We saw in Section 16-5 that the value of $\vec{E}$ can vary from point to point, so we consider a small enough region that we can treat $\vec{E}$ as having essentially the same value over that region. We then imagine a small rectangular area A that we can orient however we like. By analogy to the flux of water in Figure 16-16, we define the **electric flux** Φ (the upper-case Greek letter phi) through the area A as follows:

Electric flux $\Phi = AE$

Electric flux $\Phi = 0$

Electric flux through a surface — $\Phi = AE_\perp = AE \cos \theta$

Area of the surface

Magnitude of the electric field

The component of electric field perpendicular to the surface

Angle between the electric field and the perpendicular to the surface

Electric flux (16-6)

In Figure 16-17a we orient the area so that it is face-on to the direction of the electric field $\vec{E}$. Then the electric field is perpendicular to the surface and the angle $\theta = 0$. Therefore $E_\perp$ is equal to the field magnitude E and the electric flux through the surface is $\Phi = AE_\perp = AE$; alternatively, since $\theta = 0$, $\Phi = AE \cos 0 = AE(1) = AE$. In Figure 16-17b the area is edge-on to the electric field, so the electric field has zero component perpendicular to the area A. Then $E_\perp = 0$ and so $\Phi = AE_\perp = 0$. Alternatively, with this orientation $\theta = 90°$ and so $\Phi = AE \cos 90° = AE (0) = 0$. Finally, in Figure 16-17c the area is oriented at an angle θ between 0 and 90°, so the component of the electric field perpendicular to the area is $E_\perp = E \cos \theta$. Then the electric flux $\Phi = AE \cos \theta$ has a value between AE and zero.

Note that unlike the flow of water in Figure 16-16, there's nothing "flowing" through the area A in Figure 16-17. Unlike velocity $\vec{v}$, the electric field $\vec{E}$ does *not* represent motion of any kind. But we can still use the analogy between $\vec{v}$ and $\vec{E}$ as expressed by Figures 16-16 and 16-17 to define electric flux Φ in the manner given by Equation 16-6.

Figure 16-17 **Electric flux** The electric flux through a small rectangular surface depends on the electric field $\vec{E}$, the area A of the surface, and the angle between the direction of $\vec{E}$ and the perpendicular to the plane of the surface. (Compare Figure 16-16.)

Watch Out! In calculating electric flux, the area is "imaginary."

In Figure 16-16 we measured the flux of water through an area outlined by a real, physical wire frame. But we really didn't need the frame: It was simply there to help us visualize the area in question. In defining electric flux as in Figure 16-17, we've done away with the wire frame entirely. If we actually used a frame made of a conducting wire such as copper, the mobile charges in the wire would move in response to the electric field, and the field of these charges themselves could modify the field that we're trying to analyze. You can think of the area A in Figure 16-17 and Equation 16-6 as "imaginary" in the sense that there's no physical object outlining the area.

Electric Flux through a Closed Surface: Gauss's Law

Why is the idea of electric flux through a surface a useful one? To see the answer, let's consider a *closed* surface—that is, one that encloses a volume. For example, in Figure 16-18a we've drawn a spherical surface of radius r that is centered on and encloses a positive point charge q. To find the electric flux through this surface, first note

(a)

(b)

(c)

(d)

Net charge enclosed by
closed surface: $q > 0$

Net charge enclosed by
closed surface: $q < 0$

Net charge enclosed by
closed surface: 0

Net charge enclosed by
closed surface: 0

Electric flux through
closed surface: $\Phi > 0$

Electric flux through
closed surface: $\Phi < 0$

Electric flux through
closed surface: $\Phi = 0$

Electric flux through
closed surface: $\Phi = 0$

Figure 16-18 **Electric flux through a closed surface** The net electric flux through a closed spherical surface is (a) positive if a positive charge is enclosed by the surface, (b) negative if a negative charge is enclosed by the surface, (c) zero if equal amounts of positive and negative charge are enclosed by the surface, and (d) zero if no charge at all is enclosed by the surface.

from Equation 16-4 that the electric field $\vec{E}$ due to the point charge has the same magnitude $E = kq/r^2$ at every point on the surface, because every point is the same distance r from the point charge. However, $\vec{E}$ points in different directions at different points on the spherical surface: straight upward at the top of the surface, to the left at the leftmost point on the surface, and so on. However, if we look at a very small rectangular portion of the surface, then $\vec{E}$ points in essentially the same direction at every point on that rectangle. In fact, $\vec{E}$ is perpendicular to the rectangle of area ΔA, so $\theta = 0$ in Equation 16-6 and the flux through that rectangle is $(\Delta A)E = (\Delta A)(kq/r^2)$. If we now imagine that the entire spherical surface is made up of a very large number of such rectangles of area $\Delta A_1, \Delta A_2, \Delta A_3, \ldots, \Delta A_N$, the *total* electric flux through the spherical surface as a whole is just the sum of the fluxes through the individual rectangles:

$$\Phi = (\Delta A_1)\left(\frac{kq}{r^2}\right) + (\Delta A_2)\left(\frac{kq}{r^2}\right) + (\Delta A_3)\left(\frac{kq}{r^2}\right) + \cdots + (\Delta A_N)\left(\frac{kq}{r^2}\right)$$

(16-7)
$$= (\Delta A_1 + \Delta A_2 + \Delta A_3 + \cdots + \Delta A_N)\left(\frac{kq}{r^2}\right)$$

In Equation 16-7 the quantity $\Delta A_1 + \Delta A_2 + \Delta A_3 + \cdots + \Delta A_N$ is the sum of the areas of all of the individual rectangles that make up the spherical surface, and so is equal to the total area A of the surface. From the Math Tutorial the surface area of a sphere of radius r is $A = 4\pi r^2$, so Equation 16-7 becomes

(16-8)
$$\Phi = (4\pi r^2)\left(\frac{kq}{r^2}\right) = 4\pi kq$$

Notice that the radius of the spherical surface surrounding the point charge q cancels out in this equation. That's because the magnitude of the electric field decreases as the square of the sphere's radius r and the surface area increases at the same rate. So their product—the electric flux Φ—does not depend on the radius and is directly proportional to the charge q enclosed within the spherical surface. This result is a direct consequence of Coulomb's law (Equation 16-1) and the definition of electric field (Equation 16-4), which describe the $1/r^2$ behavior of electric force and electric field for a point charge.

Equation 16-8 also holds true if the charge q is negative (Figure 16-18b). The equation then tells us that the electric flux through the closed surface is *negative* in this case. The interpretation is that the flux is positive if the electric field points out of the closed surface as in Figure 16-18a, but negative if the electric field points into the closed surface as in Figure 16-18b.

What happens if we replace the single charge q with an electric dipole like that shown in Figure 16-14, with both a positive charge and a negative charge of equal

? Got the Concept? 16-6
Electric Flux I

When a certain charged particle is placed at the center of a sphere, the net electric flux through the surface of the sphere is Φ_0. If the radius of the sphere is doubled, what would be the new flux through the sphere? (a) $\Phi_0/4$; (b) $\Phi_0/2$; (c) Φ_0; (d) $2\Phi_0$; (e) $4\Phi_0$.

magnitude? In Figure 16-18c the spherical surface is centered on the dipole and encloses both the positive and negative charges, so the *net* enclosed charge is zero. The figure shows that for each small rectangle on the surface where the electric field $\vec{E}$ points outward, giving a positive contribution to the flux, there is another small rectangle elsewhere on the surface where $\vec{E}$ points inward, giving an equally large negative contribution to the flux. These positive and negative contributions to the flux cancel, so the net electric flux through this surface—which encloses zero net charge—is zero. The same cancellation also happens for the spherical surface in Figure 16-18d, which does not enclose either charge. In this case as well, the net enclosed charge is zero and the net electric flux through the surface is zero.

Here's what we've concluded so far from Figure 16-18:

- Closed surfaces that enclose a point charge q, as in Figure 16-18a and Figure 16-18b, have a nonzero electric flux through them. This flux is proportional to the enclosed charge q, as in Equation 16-8.

- Closed surfaces that enclose zero net charge—in Figure 16-18c because the surface encloses equal amounts of positive and negative charge, in Figure 16-18d because the surface encloses no charge at all—have zero net electric flux through them. This is consistent with Equation 16-8, but with $q = 0$.

We were able to draw these conclusions because the closed surfaces in the figure are spherical in shape and placed symmetrically with respect to the charges inside them. But it can be shown that the same conclusions hold true for a closed surface of *any* shape or placement. We can summarize these conclusions by rewriting Equation 16-8 with q replaced by q_{encl}, which represents the *net* charge enclosed by the closed surface:

Electric flux through a closed surface

Net amount of charge enclosed within the surface

$$\Phi = \frac{q_{encl}}{\varepsilon_0}$$

Permittivity of free space = $1/(4\pi k)$

Gauss's law
(16-9)

This relationship is called **Gauss's law** after the scientist who first deduced it, the nineteenth-century German mathematician and physicist Carl Friedrich Gauss. In honor of Gauss, a closed surface used to enclose charge in order to apply Gauss's law is referred to as a **Gaussian surface**. Equation 16-9 holds true for *any* Gaussian surface (Figure 16-19), no matter what its shape or size and no matter where the charges are located inside the surface. As we mentioned previously, such surfaces are imaginary: The surface does not need to be made of any physical substance.

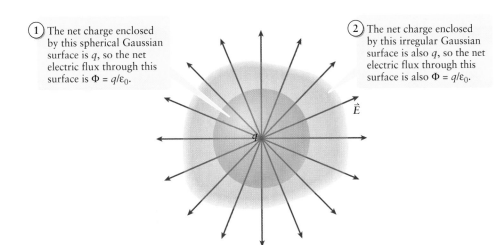

① The net charge enclosed by this spherical Gaussian surface is q, so the net electric flux through this surface is $\Phi = q/\varepsilon_0$.

② The net charge enclosed by this irregular Gaussian surface is also q, so the net electric flux through this surface is also $\Phi = q/\varepsilon_0$.

$\vec{E}$

The net electric flux through a Gaussian surface depends only on the net charge that it encloses, not the shape or size of the surface.

Figure 16-19 **Gauss's law** Two different Gaussian surfaces that enclose the same net charge.

? Got the Concept? 16-7 Electric Flux II

When a certain charged particle is placed at the center of a sphere, the net electric flux through the surface of the sphere is Φ_0. If the sphere were elongated into an oblate spheroid (such as a rugby ball or an American football) but still enclosed the same charge, what would be the new electric flux through the surface? (a) Less than Φ_0; (b) Φ_0; (c) more than Φ_0; (d) not enough information given to decide.

In Equation 16-9 we have replaced the combination $4\pi k$ that appears in Equation 16-8 with $1/\varepsilon_0$. Here ε_0, called the **permittivity of free space** for historic reasons, is equal to $1/(4\pi k) = 8.85 \times 10^{-12}\,\mathrm{C^2/(N \cdot m^2)}$ to three significant figures. So we can state Gauss's law as

The net electric flux through any closed surface equals the net charge enclosed by that surface divided by the permittivity ε_0. Charges outside the surface have no effect on the net electric flux through the surface.

This law holds true because of the $1/r^2$ character of the electric field due to a point charge (see the discussion following Equation 16-8).

We'll see in the following section how we can use Gauss's law to determine the electric field due to certain charge distributions, and what Gauss's law tells us about how charges distribute themselves in a conductor.

? Got the Concept? 16-8 Electric Flux III

When a certain charged particle is placed at the center of a sphere, the net electric flux through the surface of the sphere is Φ_0. If a second, identical charged particle is placed outside the sphere, what would be the new electric flux through the surface? (a) Less than Φ_0; (b) Φ_0; (c) more than Φ_0; (d) not enough information given to decide.

Take-Home Message for Section 16-6

✔ The electric flux through a surface is analogous to the flux of water through a wire frame. Electric flux depends on the magnitude of the electric field, the area of the surface, and the relative orientation of the field and the surface.

✔ For a closed surface (one that encloses a volume), an electric field $\vec{E}$ that points out of the closed surface makes a positive contribution to the electric flux. An electric field that points into the closed surface makes a negative contribution to the electric flux.

✔ Gauss's law states that the net electric flux through a closed surface is proportional to the amount of charge enclosed by the surface. If the net enclosed charge is zero, the net electric flux through the surface is zero.

16-7 In certain situations, Gauss's law helps us to calculate the electric field and to determine how charge is distributed

Gauss's law by itself doesn't tell us the value of the electric field $\vec{E}$ at any one point. Rather, it tells us something about the values of $\vec{E}$ at *every* point on a closed Gaussian surface. For this reason, Gauss's law is useless for finding the value of the electric field at points on the closed surfaces shown in Figures 16-18c and 16-18d: While we know the value of the net electric flux through these surfaces, that isn't enough to tell us the value of $\vec{E}$ at any one point on the surface. Yet we *can* use Gauss's law to determine $\vec{E}$ in cases where the charge that produces the field is distributed in a particularly symmetric way. Let's look at a couple of examples.

Electric Field of a Spherical Charge Distribution

In Figure 16-20 charge Q is distributed uniformly throughout a spherical volume of radius R. (This could be a model of how electric charge is distributed over the volume of an atomic nucleus.) This distribution is *spherically symmetric*: You can rotate the sphere through any angle around its center and it looks exactly the same. Hence the electric field $\vec{E}$ caused by the charge distribution must also be spherically symmetric. This implies that the direction of the electric field must be either radially inward or radially outward, like the sea urchin spines shown in Figure 16-12. (If the field pointed in any other direction, the field lines would look different after rotating the sphere through some angle. The spherical symmetry says that's impossible.) So at any point $\vec{E}$ can have only a radial component E_r, which points either directly away from the center of the sphere ($E_r > 0$) or directly toward the center of the sphere ($E_r < 0$). That's why we've drawn the electric field in Figure 16-20 as pointing in a purely radial direction. This must be true for points inside the sphere as well as outside the sphere.

The spherical symmetry of the charge distribution in Figure 16-20 tells us something more: The value of E_r at a given point can depend only on the radial distance r from the center of the sphere. It can't depend on where around the sphere the point is. (If it did, that would mean that the electric field would look different after rotating the sphere through some angle. Spherical symmetry says that, too, is impossible.)

Given what spherical symmetry tells us about the electric field for the situation in Figure 16-20, what more can we learn by using Gauss's law? In Figure 16-21a we've drawn a spherical Gaussian surface that's centered on the sphere and that encloses the entire sphere. This Gaussian surface has radius $r > R$ and surface area $A = 4\pi r^2$. Just like the spherical surface in Figure 16-18a or Figure 16-18b, the electric field is perpendicular to the surface at every point and has the same magnitude at every point. Using the same reasoning that we used for Equation 16-8, we can say that the net electric flux through this surface is just the area of the surface multiplied by the radial electric field:

$$\Phi = AE_r = 4\pi r^2 E_r \qquad (16\text{-}10)$$

This flux is positive if the electric field points outward (so $E_r > 0$) and negative if the electric field points inward ($E_r < 0$). Since the entire charged sphere is enclosed within the

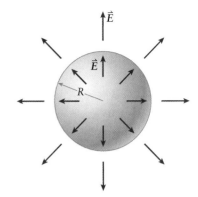

Charge Q is uniformly distributed throughout the volume of this sphere of radius R.

Figure 16-20 A uniformly charged sphere The spherical symmetry of this charge distribution tells us that the electric field $\vec{E}$ that it produces must be radial and that the magnitude of $\vec{E}$ can depend only on the distance from the center of the sphere.

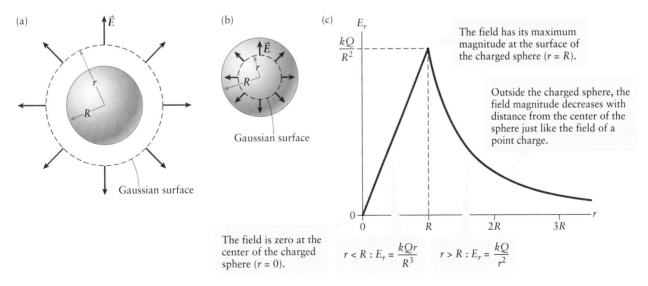

Figure 16-21 Finding the electric field of a uniformly charged sphere To find how $\vec{E}$ depends on distance from the center of the sphere of charge Q, we use (a) one Gaussian surface that encloses the entire sphere and (b) a second Gaussian surface that encloses only part of the sphere. (c) The radial electric field E_r as a function of the distance r from the center, graphed for the case $Q > 0$.

Gaussian surface, the enclosed charge is $q_{encl} = Q$. Gauss's law, Equation 16-9, tell us that the flux is also equal to q_{encl}/ε_0. Equating Equations 16-9 and 16-10 yields

$$(16\text{-}11) \qquad 4\pi r^2 E_r = \frac{Q}{\varepsilon_0} \quad \text{and} \quad E_r = \frac{Q}{4\pi\varepsilon_0 r^2} = \frac{kQ}{r^2} \quad (r > R)$$

Equation 16-11 says that at points outside the sphere, the electric field is *exactly the same* as the field due to a point charge Q (Equation 16-4). The field is purely radial, is inversely proportional to the square of the distance r, and is proportional to the charge Q on the sphere. The field points radially outward ($E_r > 0$) if the charge Q is positive, and points radially inward ($E_r < 0$) if the charge Q is negative. (Compare Figure 16-11.)

We can also use Gauss's law to tell us about the electric field at points *inside* the sphere. In **Figure 16-21b** we've drawn another spherical Gaussian surface of radius r and surface area $A = 4\pi r^2$, but with a radius r that's less than the radius R of the charged sphere. Again the net electric flux through this Gaussian surface is given by Equation 16-10. But now the enclosed charge is less than the total charge Q on the sphere. Since the charge is distributed uniformly, the fraction of charge that's enclosed by the Gaussian surface is just equal to the ratio of the volume within the Gaussian surface (a sphere of radius r, with volume $4\pi r^3/3$) to the total volume occupied by the charge Q (a sphere of radius R, with volume $4\pi R^3/3$). So Gauss's law applied to the Gaussian surface in Figure 16-21b tells us

$$4\pi r^2 E_r = \frac{q_{encl}}{\varepsilon_0} = \frac{1}{\varepsilon_0}\left[Q\left(\frac{4\pi r^3/3}{4\pi R^3/3}\right)\right] = \frac{Qr^3}{\varepsilon_0 R^3}$$

If we divide through by $4\pi r^2$, we get

$$(16\text{-}12) \qquad E_r = \frac{Qr^3}{4\pi\varepsilon_0 r^2 R^3} = \frac{Qr}{4\pi\varepsilon_0 R^3} = \frac{kQr}{R^3} \quad (r < R)$$

Equation 16-12 tells us that inside the charged sphere, the direction of the electric field is the same as outside the sphere: $E_r > 0$ (an outward field) if Q is positive and $E_r < 0$ (an inward field) if Q is negative. It also says that inside the sphere, the magnitude of the field *increases* with increasing distance r from the center of the sphere. At the surface of the charged sphere, $r = R$, both Equation 16-11 and Equation 16-12 give the same result: $E_r = kQ/R^2$. At the very center of the sphere ($r = 0$) the electric field is zero. **Figure 16-21c** shows a graph of E_r as a function of r for the case of a positively charged sphere ($Q > 0$).

These conclusions about the electric field of a charged sphere would have been *very* difficult to obtain without using Gauss's law. (The alternative approach is to divide the charged sphere into a very large number of small segments, treating each segment as an individual point charge, and using vector addition to add the individual electric fields produced by all of the segments. That would take a lot of strenuous mathematics.) The relative ease with which we came to these conclusions shows the power of Gauss's law.

Electric Field of a Large, Flat, Charged Disk

Figure 16-22a shows a charge distribution with a different kind of symmetry: a uniformly charged plate or disk. (We'll see later that charged disks of this kind are found in an important device called a *capacitor*, used in many electric circuits.) This charge distribution has *rotational symmetry*, which means that it looks the same if you rotate it through any angle around an axis that passes vertically through the center of the disk. However, the electric field $\vec{E}$ due to this charge distribution can (and does) vary in a complicated way as you move from the center of the disk toward the edges.

To simplify the problem, let's just consider what the electric field is like at points around the disk near the disk center. We imagine that the edges of the disk are so far away that we can regard them as being infinitely distant. Then our problem is that of finding the electric field due to an *infinite sheet* of charge (**Figure 16-22b**).

We'll use the symbol σ (the lowercase Greek letter sigma) for the amount of charge per unit area on the sheet, also called the **surface charge density**. The sheet is uniformly

Figure 16-22 Finding the electric field of a uniformly charged disk
(a) A uniformly charged disk; (b) to find the electric field of the disk at points close to the center of the disk, we can replace the disk by an infinitely large charged sheet.

charged, so σ has the same value everywhere on the sheet. The units of σ are coulombs per square meter (C/m²).

Our infinite sheet of charge has *translational* symmetry: No matter which way or how far you move parallel to the disk, the charge distribution looks exactly the same. The same must therefore be true of the electric field produced by the charge distribution. So if the disk lies in the xy plane, the electric field $\vec{E}$ at any point cannot depend on the x or y coordinate of that point. The field can depend only on the z coordinate, which is the coordinate measured perpendicular to the plane in Figure 16-22.

Translational symmetry also tells us that $\vec{E}$ must be *perpendicular* to the plane of the sheet. This means that a point charge q placed in that field will feel a force $\vec{F} = q\vec{E}$ either directly toward or directly away from the sheet, depending on the sign of q. (If there were a component of $\vec{E}$ in some direction parallel to the plane of the sheet, a positive point charge would be pushed in that direction. This would only be the case if the point charge were repelled or attracted by one part of the sheet. But since the charge distribution is the same everywhere on the sheet, no part attracts or repels the positive charge more than any other part. So there can't be any component of $\vec{E}$ parallel to the sheet.) Thus $\vec{E}$ can depend only on the z coordinate and can have only a z component.

The infinite sheet also has *reflection* symmetry: It looks the same if we flip the sheet upside down. The same must be true of the electric field. So if the field points upward above the sheet, it must point downward below the sheet, as we've indicated in Figure 16-22b.

To find the electric field at a certain distance h from the plane of the sheet, we'll use a cylindrical Gaussian surface as in Figure 16-22b. The top and bottom faces of the cylinder each have area A, and each is the same distance h from the sheet. The symmetries we have described tell us that the electric field $\vec{E}$ is perpendicular to the top and bottom faces and has the same value everywhere on each of these faces. Because $\vec{E}$ is parallel to the sides of the cylinder, there is *zero* electric flux through the sides: $\Phi_{\text{sides}} = 0$. The flux through the top and bottom faces of the cylinder, however, is not zero. If E_z is the z component of electric field a distance h above the infinite sheet, the flux through the top face of the cylinder is $\Phi_{\text{top}} = AE_z$. Note that this flux is positive if E_z is positive, which means that the electric field above the sheet is upward and points out of the Gaussian surface; this flux is negative if E_z is negative, which means that the electric field above the sheet is downward and points into the Gaussian surface. The reflection symmetry tells us that the flux through the bottom face is the same, so $\Phi_{\text{top}} + \Phi_{\text{bottom}} = 2\Phi_{\text{top}} = 2AE_z$. The net electric flux through the Gaussian surface in Figure 16-22b is therefore

$$\Phi = \Phi_{\text{sides}} + \Phi_{\text{top}} + \Phi_{\text{bottom}} = 0 + 2AE_z = 2AE_z \tag{16-13}$$

The area of the sheet enclosed within the Gaussian surface is A, so the amount of charge enclosed within the surface is the charge per unit area σ multiplied by the area A: $q_{\text{encl}} = \sigma A$. Using this and Equation 16-13 in Gauss's law, Equation 16-9, gives us an expression for the electric field component E_z a distance h above the sheet:

$$2AE_z = \frac{\sigma A}{\varepsilon_0} \quad \text{or} \quad E_z = \frac{\sigma}{2\varepsilon_0} \tag{16-14}$$

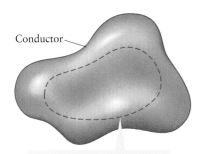

Conductor

There can be no electric field inside the conductor, so the flux through this Gaussian surface must be zero.

Figure 16-23 **A charged conductor** Gauss's law tells us that any excess charge on a conductor must reside on the surface of the conductor.

Equation 16-14 tells us that E_z has the same sign as the surface charge density σ. So the electric field $\vec{E}$ above the sheet points upward (away from the sheet) if the surface charge density is positive ($\sigma > 0$); $\vec{E}$ points downward (toward the sheet) if the surface charge density is negative ($\sigma < 0$). This agrees with the idea that electric fields point away from positive charges and toward negative charges.

Equation 16-14 also tells us that the value of E_z at a point a distance h above the sheet does *not* depend on h. (Note that h doesn't appear anywhere in this equation.) So for an infinite sheet of charge, the electric field is the same at all distances from the sheet.

These results are only approximate, since there's no such thing as a truly infinite sheet of charge. But they are valid for a charged disk at points that are relatively close to the disk, so the height h above the disk is small compared to the radius of the disk. We'll make use of Equation 16-14 in later chapters.

Excess Charge on Conductors

Gauss's law leads to a remarkable conclusion about conducting materials to which excess charge is added so that the conductor has a net charge. Charges are free to move in a conductor, so if we add excess charges they will move in the conductor until they come to rest in equilibrium. In this situation the net force on each added charge is zero. Because the electric force on a charge q is directly proportional to the electric field $\vec{E}$ (Equation 16-2), $\vec{E}$ inside the conductor must be *zero*. If it were not, excess charges inside the conductor would experience a force and be pushed to some new location. Note that this statement only applies *inside* the volume of the conductor. Outside the charged block of conductor the electric field need not be zero.

Let's see what Gauss's law tells us in this situation. Imagine a Gaussian surface that lies completely inside the volume of a conductor that carries excess charge (**Figure 16-23**). Since $\vec{E} = 0$ everywhere inside the conductor, the net electric flux Φ through this surface is zero. From Gauss's law, Equation 16-9, Φ is equal to the net charge q_{encl} enclosed by the surface divided by ε_0. So the net charge inside the Gaussian surface is zero. This holds true for any Gaussian surface, no matter how small, that lies entirely within the conductor. So there can be *no* excess charge within the volume of the conductor. Instead, *all of the excess charge on a conductor in equilibrium must reside on the surface*. That's why we depicted the charged copper rod in Figure 16-5b with its excess charge spread over the surface of the rod, not its interior.

Our conclusion that $\vec{E} = 0$ inside a conductor holds true *only* if all of the charges are at rest. We will see in later chapters that if an electric current is present inside a conductor, there must be a nonzero electric field to sustain the flow of electric charge.

Example 16-8 Gauss's Law and Surface Charge

A conducting sphere of radius R_1 carries excess charge $+7$ C. This sphere is enclosed within a concentric spherical conducting shell of inner radius R_2 and outer radius R_3. The conducting shell carries a net charge $+2$ C. How much charge is on the inner surface of the conducting shell? How much is on the outer surface?

Set Up
In equilibrium the electric field inside the volume of the conducting shell must be zero. So if we imagine a spherical Gaussian surface that lies inside the shell, so that its radius r is intermediate between R_2 and R_3, the net electric flux through that surface will be zero. From Gauss's law, that means that the net charge enclosed by the Gaussian surface must be zero. The $+2$-C charge on the shell will arrange itself on the surfaces of the shell in order to make that happen.

Gauss's law:

$$\Phi = \frac{q_{encl}}{\varepsilon_0} \qquad (16-9)$$

+7 C on solid sphere

R_1
R_2
R_3

+2 C on shell   Gaussian surface

Solve

The charge enclosed within our Gaussian surface includes the charge of the central sphere ($q_{sphere} = +7$ C) and whatever charge q_{inner} is present on the inner surface of the shell. These charges must add to zero.

For the Gaussian surface,

$$q_{encl} = q_{sphere} + q_{inner} = 0$$

So the charge on the inner surface of the shell equals the negative of the charge on the central sphere:

$$q_{inner} = -q_{sphere} = -7 \text{ C}$$

$q_{sphere} = +7$ C
(on outer surface of solid sphere)

$q_{inner} = -7$ C
(on inner surface of shell)

$q_{outer} = +9$ C
(on outer surface of shell)

The total charge on the shell is $q_{shell} = +2$ C. Because all of the excess charge on a conductor resides on its surfaces, q_{shell} is the sum of the charge on the inner and outer surfaces.

$$q_{shell} = q_{inner} + q_{outer}$$

So

$$
\begin{aligned}
q_{outer} &= q_{shell} - q_{inner} \\
&= (+2 \text{ C}) - (-7 \text{ C}) \\
&= +9 \text{ C}
\end{aligned}
$$

Reflect

It may seem odd that while the shell as a whole carries a *positive* excess charge of +2 C, the inner surface of the shell has a *negative* charge. What's happened is that when the positively charged sphere is placed inside the shell, some of the free electrons in the shell are drawn to the shell's inner surface, giving it a negative charge of −7 C. This leaves a deficit of electrons—a positive charge of +7 C—on the outside surface. This in turn adds to the +2 C of excess charge to give the outer surface of the shell a charge of +9 C.

? Got the Concept? 16-9 Size of a Gaussian Surface

In our derivation of Equation 16-13 for the electric field due to an infinite charged sheet, we used a Gaussian surface in the shape of a cylinder whose top and bottom faces had area A. If we used a larger cylinder with top and bottom faces of area $2A$, how would this change our result for the electric field? (a) E_z would be four times larger; (b) E_z would be twice as large; (c) E_z would be the same; (d) E_z would be one-half as great; (e) E_z would be one-fourth as great.

Take-Home Message for Section 16-7

✔ Gauss's law can be used to calculate the electric field in certain cases where the charge distribution has a high degree of symmetry. These include a spherical distribution of charge and a very large, uniformly charged sheet.

✔ Gauss's law tells us that when excess charge added to a conductor is allowed to come to rest in equilibrium, the excess charge resides only on the surfaces of the conductor.

Key Terms

charged
conductors
coulomb
Coulomb's constant
Coulomb's law
electric charge
electric dipole

electric field lines
electric flux
electric force
insulators
Gauss's law
Gaussian surface
neutral

permittivity of free space
point charges
polarization
semiconductors
surface charge density

Chapter Summary

Topic	Equation or Figure

Electric charge: Ordinary matter contains equal amounts of positive and negative charge. Charge can be transferred from one object to another, for example, by rubbing. In this and all other processes, charge is conserved: It can be moved from place to place but can neither be created nor destroyed.

The fur-rubbed ends of these two rubber rods repel each other.

The silk-rubbed ends of these two glass rods repel each other.

The fur-rubbed end of the rubber rod attracts the silk-rubbed end of the glass rod.

(Figure 16-2b)

Conductors, insulators, and semiconductors: In a conductor, charges are free to move with ease; in an insulator, charges can move very little. Semiconductors have properties intermediate between those of conductors and insulators.

The nylon-rubbed end of the copper rod attracts the nylon with which it was rubbed...

...and the end of the copper rod that was not rubbed also feels a strong attraction.

(Figure 16-5b)

Coulomb's law: The electric forces that two point charges exert on each other are proportional to the magnitudes of the charges and inversely proportional to the square of the distance between the charges. These forces are attractive if the two charges have opposite signs, and repulsive if the two charges have the same sign.

Any two point charges q_1 and q_2 exert equally strong electric forces on each other.

Coulomb constant

Absolute values of the point charges

$$F_{q_1 \text{ on } q_2} = F_{q_2 \text{ on } q_1} = \frac{k|q_1||q_2|}{r^2}$$

Distance between the point charges

(16-1)

Electric field: We can regard the interaction between charges as a two-step process: One charge sets up an electric field, and the other charge responds to that field. The electric field points away from

If a particle with charge q is placed at a position where the electric field due to other charges is $\vec{E}$...

$$\vec{F} = q\vec{E}$$

...then the electric force on the particle is $\vec{F} = q\vec{E}$.

(16-2)

a positive charge and toward a negative charge. The electric field of a single point charge is given by a simple equation; the field due to a combination of charges is the vector sum of the fields due to the individual charges.

Magnitude of the electric field due to a point charge Q

Coulomb constant

Absolute value of charge Q

$$E = \frac{k|Q|}{r^2}$$ (16-4)

Distance between point charge Q and the location where the field is measured

Gauss's Law: The electric flux through a surface equals the area of that surface multiplied by the component of electric field perpendicular to the surface. Gauss's law states that the net electric flux through a closed surface (one that encloses a volume) is proportional to the net charge enclosed within that volume. Gauss's law can be used to determine the electric field in situations where the charge distribution is highly symmetric. It also tells us that any excess charge on a conductor resides on the surfaces of the conductor.

Electric flux through a closed surface

Net amount of charge enclosed within the surface

$$\Phi = \frac{q_{encl}}{\varepsilon_0}$$ (16-9)

Permittivity of free space = $1/(4\pi k)$

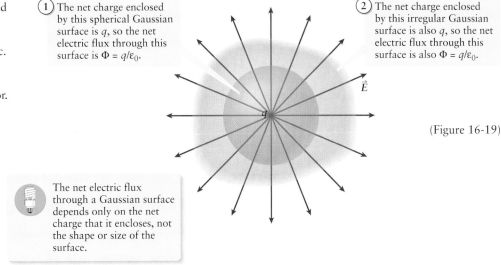

(1) The net charge enclosed by this spherical Gaussian surface is q, so the net electric flux through this surface is $\Phi = q/\varepsilon_0$.

(2) The net charge enclosed by this irregular Gaussian surface is also q, so the net electric flux through this surface is also $\Phi = q/\varepsilon_0$.

$\vec{E}$

(Figure 16-19)

The net electric flux through a Gaussian surface depends only on the net charge that it encloses, not the shape or size of the surface.

Answer to What do you think? Question

(c) The magnitude of the electric field of a charged object measured at a distance r from the object is proportional to $1/r^2$ (see Section 16-5). If r is made one-half as great (decreased from $r = 2$ m to $r = 1$ m), the electric field magnitude changes by a factor of $1/(1/2)^2 = 1/(1/4) = 4$.

Answers to Got the Concept? Questions

16-1 (c) When the rubber rod is rubbed with fur, electrons are transferred to the rod from the fur. The electrons have mass, so the rod gains a little mass and the fur loses an equal amount of mass. By contrast, electrons are transferred from the glass rod to the silk when these two objects are rubbed together. As a result, the glass rod loses a little mass and the silk gains an equal amount of mass. The amount of mass involved is very small but is not zero.

16-2 (c) A sodium atom is neutral because it has 11 protons in its nucleus (each of charge $+e$) and 11 electrons (each of charge $-e$). If a sodium atom loses one of its 11 electrons by transferring it to another atom, it is left with 11 protons with a combined charge of $+11e$ and 10 electrons with a combined charge of $-10e$, and so it has a net positive charge of $+e$. In NaCl, the electron is transferred to the chlorine atom, which then has a net negative charge of $-e$.

16-3   (d) Equation 16-1 tells us that the magnitude of the electric force between two charged objects is directly proportional to the product of the two charges. If we remove only half of the electrons from the neutral water drop, the ball of electrons has half the negative charge as before and the water drop has half the positive charge as before. So the electric force between the water drop and the ball of electrons will be $(\frac{1}{2}) \times (\frac{1}{2}) = \frac{1}{4}$ as great as before.

16-4   (b) Equation 16-2, $\vec{F} = q\vec{E}$, tells us the force $\vec{F}$ that acts on a charge q due to the electric field $\vec{E}$ produced by *other* charges. So to find the force that acts on the positive charge in Figure 16-14 due to the negative charge, in Equation 16-2 we let q be the positive charge (the charge that experiences the force) and let $\vec{E}$ be the electric field produced at the position of the positive charge by the negative charge (the other charge that exerts the force).

16-5   (d) If both charges were negative, the electric field at point P due to each charge would point directly toward that charge. So the electric field due to the right-hand charge would point down and to the right, while the electric field due to the left-hand charge would point down and to the left. Since point P is the same distance from each charge, and each charge has the same magnitude, the electric fields due to the two charges would have the same magnitude. The horizontal components of the two fields cancel (one points left and the other points right), so what remains is a net electric field that points straight down.

16-6   (c) The flux remains the same. According to Gauss's law, the net electric flux due to an enclosed charge does not depend on the size of the surface that encloses the charge.

16-7   (b) The flux remains the same. According to Gauss's law, the net electric flux due to an enclosed charge does not depend on the shape of the surface that encloses the charge.

16-8   (b) The flux remains the same. According to Gauss's law, the electric flux through a closed surface depends only on the charge enclosed *within* the surface. A charge outside the surface will cause positive flux on one part of the surface (where its electric field points out of the surface) and negative flux on another part of the surface (where its electric field points into the surface), but will have no net effect on the flux through the surface as a whole.

16-9   (c) The result does not depend on the size of the cylinder we choose. If we double the area, the flux through the top and bottom faces would double, but the amount of enclosed charge would double as well. In the derivation of Equation 16-14 these factors would cancel, so our result for E_z would be the same.

Questions and Problems

In a few problems, you are given more data than you actually need; in a few other problems, you are required to supply data from your general knowledge, outside sources, or informed estimate.

Interpret as significant all digits in numerical values that have trailing zeros and no decimal points.

For all problems, use $g = 9.80 \text{ m/s}^2$ for the free-fall acceleration due to gravity. Neglect friction and air resistance unless instructed to do otherwise.

• Basic, single-concept problem

•• Intermediate-level problem, may require synthesis of concepts and multiple steps

••• Challenging problem

SSM Solution is in Student Solutions Manual

Conceptual Questions

1. •Discuss the similarities and differences between the gravitational and electric forces.

2. •Why is the gravitational force usually ignored in problems on the scale of particles such as electrons and protons?

3. •How, if at all, would the physical universe be different if the proton were negatively charged and the electron were positively charged?

4. •How, if at all, would the physical universe be different if the proton's charge was very slightly larger in magnitude than the electron's charge?

5. •When an initially electrically neutral object acquires a net positive charge, does its mass increase or decrease? Why? SSM

6. •When you remove socks from a hot dryer, they tend to cling to everything. Two identical socks, however, usually repel. Why?

7. •Describe a set of experiments that might be used to determine if you have discovered a third type of charge other than positive and negative.

8. •How does a person become "charged" as he or she shuffles across a carpet, wearing cloth slippers, on a dry winter day?

9. •After combing your hair with a plastic comb, you find that when you bring the comb near a small bit of paper, the bit of paper moves toward the comb. Then, shortly after the paper touches the comb, it moves away from the comb. Explain these observations. SSM

10. •After combing your hair with a plastic comb, you find that when you bring the comb near an empty aluminum soft-drink can that is lying on its side on a nonconducting table-top, the can rolls toward the comb. After being touched by the comb, the can is still attracted by the comb. Explain these observations.

11. •(a) A positively charged glass rod attracts a lighter object suspended by a thread. Does it follow that the object is negatively charged? (b) If, instead, the rod repels it, does it follow that the suspended object is positively charged?

12. •Some days it can be frustrating to attempt to demonstrate electrostatic phenomena for a physics class. An experiment that works beautifully one day may fail the next day if the weather has changed. Air-conditioning helps a lot while demonstrating the phenomena during the summer. Why?

13. •(a) What are the advantages of thinking of the force on a charge at a point P as being exerted by an electric field at P, rather than by other charges at other locations? (b) Is the convenience of the field as a calculation device worth inventing a new physical quantity? Or is there more to the field concept than that? SSM

14. •Do electric field lines point along the trajectory of positively charged particles? Why or why not?

15. •An electron and a proton are released in a region of space where the electric field is vertically downward. How do the electric forces acting on the electron and proton compare?

16. •Inside a uniform spherical charge distribution, why is it that as one moves out from the center, the electric field increases as r rather than decreases as $1/r^2$?

17. •Is the electric field $\vec{E}$ in Gauss's law only the electric field due to the charge inside the Gaussian surface, or is it the total electric field due to all charges both inside and outside the surface? Explain your answer. SSM

18. •If the net electric flux out of a closed surface is zero, does that mean the charge density must be zero everywhere inside the surface? Explain your answer.

Multiple-Choice Questions

19. •Electric charges of the opposite sign
   A. exert no force on each other.
   B. attract each other.
   C. repel each other.
   D. repel and attract each other.
   E. repel and attract each other depending on the magnitude of the charges.

20. •If two uncharged objects are rubbed together and one of them acquires a negative charge, then the other one
   A. remains uncharged.
   B. also acquires a negative charge.
   C. acquires a positive charge.
   D. acquires a positive charge equal to twice the negative charge.
   E. acquires a positive charge equal to half the negative charge.

21. •Metal sphere A has a charge of $-Q$. An identical metal sphere B has a charge of $+2Q$. The magnitude of the electric force on B due to A is F. The magnitude of the electric force on A due to B is
   A. $F/4$.
   B. $F/2$.
   C. F.
   D. $2F$.
   E. $4F$. SSM

22. •A balloon can be charged by rubbing it with your sleeve while holding it in your hand. You can conclude from this that the balloon is a(n)
   A. conductor.
   B. insulator.
   C. neutral object.
   D. Gaussian surface.
   E. semiconductor.

23. •A positively charged rod is brought near one end of an uncharged metal bar. The end of the metal bar farthest from the charged rod will be charged

   A. positively.
   B. negatively.
   C. neutral.
   D. twice as much as the end nearest the rod.
   E. none of the above ways. SSM

24. •A free positive charge released in an electric field will
   A. remain at rest.
   B. accelerate in the direction opposite to the electric field.
   C. accelerate in the direction perpendicular to the electric field.
   D. accelerate in the same direction as the electric field.
   E. accelerate in a circular path.

25. •Consider a point charge $+Q$ located outside a closed surface such as a sphere bound by the black circle in Figure 16-24. What is the net electric flux through the closed surface?

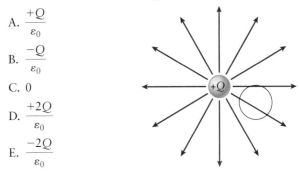

   A. $\dfrac{+Q}{\varepsilon_0}$

   B. $\dfrac{-Q}{\varepsilon_0}$

   C. 0

   D. $\dfrac{+2Q}{\varepsilon_0}$

   E. $\dfrac{-2Q}{\varepsilon_0}$

Figure 16-24 Problem 25

26. •If a charge is located at the center of a spherical volume and the electric flux through the surface of the sphere is Φ, what would be the flux through the surface if the radius of the sphere were tripled?
   A. 3Φ
   B. 9Φ
   C. Φ
   D. $\Phi/3$
   E. $\Phi/9$

27. •A point charge $+Q$ is at the center of a spherical conducting shell of inner radius R_1 and outer radius R_2, as shown in Figure 16-25. The charge on the inner surface of the shell is
   A. $+Q$.
   B. $-Q$.
   C. 0.
   D. $+Q/2$.
   E. $-Q/2$. SSM

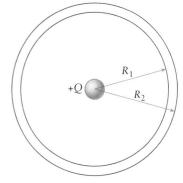

Figure 16-25 Problem 27

Estimation/Numerical Analysis

28. ••(a) Estimate the positive charge in you due to the protons in the molecules present in your body. (b) What is the net charge in your body?

29. • Estimate the amount of charge needed on both a comb and on a bit of tissue paper in order to generate an electric force of sufficient magnitude to support the weight of the paper.

30. •(a) Give a rough value for the force between two charges that possess microcoulombs of charge. (b) What if the charges are in the nanocoulomb range? Assume distances of separation in the centimeter range.

31. •For 10-cm distances of separation, what approximate charges will lead to electrostatic forces of ~10 N? SSM

32. •Estimate the electric field required to levitate a 1-g plastic sphere carrying a net charge of 10 μC near Earth's surface.

33. •Estimate the electric flux passing through the passenger window of your car when you become charged up after sliding into your vehicle.

34. •The magnitude of the repulsive force (F) between two $+2.5$-μC charges as a function of the distance of separation (r) is listed in the following table. Empirically derive a relationship between F and r by doing a curve fit to find the power n of r in the following formula:

$$F = \frac{kq_1q_2}{r^n}$$

Use a graphing calculator or spreadsheet.

r (m)	F (N)	r (m)	F (N)
0.003	5500	0.080	6
0.004	3000	0.100	5
0.005	2000	0.200	1
0.010	600	0.300	0.5
0.020	175	0.400	0.35
0.040	30	0.500	0.25
0.050	10	0.600	0.15

Problems

16-1 Electric forces and electric charges are all around you—and within you

16-2 Matter contains positive and negative electric charge

35. •The nucleus of a copper atom has 29 protons and 35 neutrons. What is the total charge of the nucleus?

36. •Five electrons are added to 1.00 C of positive charge. What is the net charge of the system?

37. ••How many coulombs of negative charge are there in 0.500 kg of water? SSM

38. •An ion has 17 protons, 18 neutrons, and 18 electrons. What is the net charge of the ion?

39. ••The charge per unit length on a glass rod is 0.00500 C/m. If the rod is 1 mm long, how many electrons have been removed from the glass rod?

40. •How many electrons must be transferred from an object to produce a charge of 1.60 C?

16-3 Charge can flow freely in a conductor but not in an insulator

41. •Suppose 2.00 C of positive charge is distributed evenly throughout a sphere of 1.27-cm radius. (a) What is the charge per unit volume for this situation? (b) Is the sphere insulating or conducting? How do you know?

42. •The maximum amount of charge that can be collected on a Van de Graaff generator's conducting sphere (30-cm diameter) is about 30 μC. Calculate the surface charge density, σ, of the sphere in C/m^2.

43. •**Biology** Most workers in nanotechnology are actively monitored for excess static charge buildup. The human body acts like an insulator as one walks across a carpet, collecting -50 nC per step. (a) What charge buildup will a worker in a manufacturing plant accumulate if she walks 25 steps? (b) How many electrons are present in that amount of charge? (c) If a delicate manufacturing process can be damaged by an electrical discharge of greater than 10^{12} electrons, what is the maximum number of steps that any worker should be allowed to take before touching the components? SSM

16-4 Coulomb's law describes the force between charged objects

44. •Two point charges are separated by a distance of 20.0 cm. The numerical value of one charge is twice that of the other. If each charge exerts a force of magnitude 45.0 N on the other, find the magnitude of the charges.

45. •The mass of an electron is 9.11×10^{-31} kg. How far apart would two electrons have to be in order for the electric force exerted by each on the other to be equal to the weight of an electron? SSM

46. •Charge A, $+5.00$ μC, is positioned at the origin of a coordinate system. Charge B, -3.00 μC, is fixed on the x axis at $x = 3.00$ m. (a) Determine the magnitude and direction of the force that charge B exerts on charge A. (b) What is the magnitude and direction of the force that charge A exerts on charge B?

47. ••Point charge A with charge $q_A = +3.00$ μC is located at the origin. Point charge B with charge $q_B = -4.00$ μC is on the x axis at $x = 3.00$ m. Point charge C with charge $q_B = -2.00$ μC is on the x axis at $x = 6.00$ m. And point charge D with charge $q_D = +6.00$ μC is on the x axis at $x = 8.00$ m. What is the net electric force on point charge A due to the other three charges?

48. ••A charge of $+3.00$ μC is located at the origin, and a second charge of -2.00 μC is located on the $x-y$ plane at the point (30.0 cm, 20.0 cm). Determine the electric force exerted by the -2.00 μC charge on the 3.00 μC charge.

49. ••A point charge with charge $q_1 = +5.00$ nC is fixed at the origin. A second point charge with charge $q_2 = -7.00$ nC is located on the x axis at $x = 5.00$ m. Where along the x axis will a third point charge of $q = +2.00$ nC charge need to be for the net electric force on it due to the two fixed charges to be equal to zero? SSM

50. ••Two charges lie on the x axis, a -2.00-μC charge at the origin and a $+3.00$-μC charge at $x = 0.100$ m. At what position along the x axis, if any, should a third $+4.00$-μC charge be placed so that the net force on the third charge is equal to zero?

51. ••Point charge A with a charge of $+3.00$ μC is located at the origin. Point charge B with a charge of $+6.00$ μC is located on the x axis at $x = 7.00$ cm. And point charge C with a charge of $+2.00$ μC is located on the y axis at $y = 6.00$ cm. What is the net force (magnitude and direction) exerted on each charge by the others? SSM

52. •A charge q_1 equal to 0.600 μC is at the origin, and a second charge q_2 equal to 0.800 μC is on the x axis at 5.00 cm. (a) Find the force (magnitude and direction) that each charge exerts on the other. (b) How would your answer change if q_2 were -0.800 μC?

16-5 The concept of electric field helps us visualize how charges exert forces at a distance

53. •At point *P* in Figure 16-26, the electric field is zero. (a) What are the signs of q_1 and q_2? (b) Describe their magnitudes.

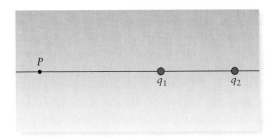

Figure 16-26 Problem 53

54. •Near the surface of Earth, an electric field points radially downward and has a magnitude of approximately 100 N/C. What charge (magnitude and sign) would have to be placed on a penny that has a mass of 3.11 g to cause it to rise into the air with an upward acceleration of 0.190 m/s^2?

55. ••Two charges are placed on the *x* axis, +5.00 μC at the origin and −10.0 μC at *x* = 10.0 cm. (a) Find the electric field on the *x* axis at *x* = 6.00 cm. (b) At what point(s) on the *x* axis is the electric field zero?

56. ••In Figure 16-27, the electric field at the origin is zero. If q_1 is 1.00×10^{-7} C, what is q_2?

Figure 16-27 Problems 56 and 57

57. •In Figure 16-27, if $q_1 = 1.00 \times 10^{-7}$ C and $q_2 = 2.00 \times 10^{-7}$ C, (a) what is the electric field $\vec{E}$ at the point (*x*, *y*) = (0.00 cm, 3.00 cm)? (b) What is the force $\vec{F}$ acting on an electron at that position?

58. •In Figure 16-27, if $q_1 = 1.00 \times 10^{-7}$ C and $q_2 = 2.00 \times 10^{-7}$ C, (a) what is the electric field $\vec{E}$ at the point (*x*, *y*) = (6.00 m, 3.00 m)? (b) What is the force $\vec{F}$ acting on a proton at that position?

59. ••In the Bohr model, the hydrogen atom consists of an electron in a circular orbit of radius $a_0 = 5.29 \times 10^{-11}$ m around the nucleus. Using this model, and ignoring relativistic effects, what is the speed of the electron?

16-6 Gauss's law gives us more insight into the electric field

60. •A rectangular area is rotated in a uniform electric field, from a position where the maximum electric flux goes through it to an orientation where only half the maximum flux goes through it. What is the angle of rotation?

61. •A point charge of 4.00×10^{-12} C is located at the center of a cubical Gaussian surface. What is the electric flux through each face of the cube?

62. •The net electric flux through a cubic box with sides that are 20.0 cm long is 4.80×10^3 N·m^2/C. What charge is enclosed by the box?

63. ••A 10.0-cm-long uniformly charged plastic rod is sealed inside a plastic bag. The net electric flux through the bag is 7.50×10^5 N·m^2/C. What is the linear charge density (charge per unit length) on the rod? SSM

64. ••Figure 16-28 shows a prism-shaped object that is 40.0 cm high, 30.0 cm deep, and 80.0 cm long. The prism is immersed in a uniform electric field of 500 N/C directed parallel to the *x* axis. (a) Calculate the electric flux out of each of its five faces and (b) the net electric flux out of the entire closed surface. (c) If in addition to the given electric field the prism also enclosed a point charge of −2.00 μC, qualitatively how would your answers above change, if at all?

Figure 16-28 Problem 64

16-7 In certain situations, Gauss's law helps us to calculate the electric field and to determine how charge is distributed

65. ••Use Gauss's law to find an expression for the electric field just outside the surface of a sphere carrying a uniform surface charge density σ (charge per unit area). SSM

66. •Determine the charge density for each of the following cases (assume that all densities are uniform): (a) a solid cylinder that has a length *L*, has a radius *R*, and carries a charge *Q* throughout its volume; (b) a flat plate (very thin) that has a width *W*, has a length *L*, and carries a charge *Q* on its surface area; (c) a solid sphere of radius *R* carrying a charge *Q* throughout its volume; and (d) a hollow sphere of radius *R* carrying a charge *Q* over its surface area.

67. ••An electric field of magnitude 400 N/C exists at all points just outside the surface of a 2.00-cm-diameter steel ball bearing. Assuming the ball bearing is in electrostatic equilibrium, (a) what is the total charge on the ball? (b) What is the surface charge density on the ball?

68. ••Consider an infinite plane with a uniform charge distribution σ. (a) Use Gauss's law to find an expression for the electric field due to the plane. (b) What field would be created by two equal but oppositely charged parallel planes? Consider the region between the planes as well as the two regions outside the planes. The simplest way to express your answers is in terms of the surface charge density σ (the charge per unit area) on the plane.

69. ••A −3.20-μC charge sits in static equilibrium in the center of a conducting spherical shell that has an inner radius of

2.50 cm and an outer radius of 3.50 cm. The shell has a net charge of $-5.80\ \mu C$. Determine the charge on each surface of the shell and the electric field just outside the shell.

General Problems

70. ••A spherical party balloon that is 25 cm in diameter contains helium at room temperature (20°C) and at a pressure of 1.3 atm. If one electron could be stripped from every helium atom in the balloon and removed to a satellite orbiting Earth 22,000 mi (32,187 km) above the planet, with what force would the balloon and the satellite attract each other?

71. ••A plutonium-242 atom has a nucleus of 94 protons and 148 neutrons and has 94 electrons. The diameter of its nucleus is approximately 15×10^{-15} m. (a) Make a reasonable physical argument as to why we can treat the nucleus as a point charge for points outside of it. (b) Plutonium decays radioactively by emitting an *alpha particle* from its nucleus. The mass of the alpha particle is 6.6×10^{-27} kg, and the particle has two protons and two neutrons. If the alpha particle comes from the surface of the ^{242}Pu nucleus, what is its greatest acceleration?

72. ••When a test charge of +5.00 nC is placed at a certain point, the force that acts on it has a magnitude of 0.0800 N and is directed northeast. (a) If the test charge were −2.00 nC instead, what force would act on it? (b) What is the electric field at the point in question?

73. ••**Biology** A red blood cell may carry an excess charge of about -2.5×10^{-12} C distributed uniformly over its surface. The cells, modeled as spheres, are approximately 7.5 μm in diameter and have a mass of 9.0×10^{-14} kg. (a) How many excess electrons does a typical red blood cell carry? (b) Does the mass of the extra electrons appreciably affect the mass of the cell? To find out, calculate the ratio of the mass of the extra electrons to the mass of the cell without the excess charge. (c) What is the surface charge density σ on the red blood cell? Express your answer in C/m^2 and in electrons/m^2. SSM

74. ••Three point charges are placed on the $x-y$ plane: a +50.0 nC charge at the origin, a −50.0 nC charge on the x axis at 10.0 cm, and a +150 nC charge at the point (10.0 cm, 8.00 cm). (a) Find the total electric force on the +150 nC charge due to the other two. (b) What is the electric field at the location of the +150 nC charge due to the presence of the other two charges?

75. ••Two small spheres each have a mass m of 0.100 g and are suspended as pendulums by light insulating strings from a common point, as shown in Figure 16-29. The spheres are given the same electric charge, and the two come to equilibrium when each string is at an angle of $\theta = 3.00°$ with the vertical. If each string is 1.00 m long, what is the magnitude of the charge on each sphere?

Figure 16-29 Problem 75

76. ••A small 1.00-g plastic ball that has a charge q of 1.00 C is suspended by a string that has a length L of 1.00 m in a uniform electric field, as shown in Figure 16-30. If the ball is in equilibrium when the string makes a 9.80° angle with the vertical as indicated by θ, what is the electric field strength?

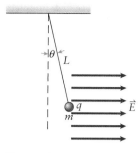

Figure 16-30 Problem 76

77. ••**Biology** The 9-inch-long elephant nose fish in the Congo River generates a weak electric field around its body using an organ in its tail. When small prey (or even potential mates) swim within a few feet of the fish, they perturb the electric field. The change in the field is picked up by electric sensor cells in the skin of the elephant nose. These remarkable fish can detect changes in the electric field as small as $3.0\ \mu N/C$. (a) How much charge (modeled as a point charge) in the fish would be needed to produce such a change in the electric field at a distance of 75 cm? (b) How many electrons would be required to create the charge? SSM

78. •••Three charges (q_A, q_B, and q_C) are placed at the vertices of the equilateral triangle that has sides of length s in Figure 16-31. Derive expressions for the electric field at (a) X (at the center of the triangle), (b) Y (at the midpoint of the side between q_B and q_C), and (c) Z (at the midpoint of the side between q_A and q_C). (d) Now use the following numerical values and calculate the electric field at those same points: $s = 10.0$ cm, $q_A = +20.0$ nC, $q_B = -8.00$ nC, and $q_C = -10.0$ nC.

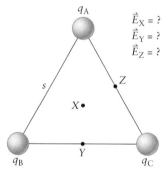

Figure 16-31 Problem 78

79. ••Calculate the electric field at the center of the hexagon shown in Figure 16-32. Assume the sides of the hexagon are all 5.00 cm long. SSM

Figure 16-32 Problem 79

80. ••Electric fields up to 2.00×10^5 N/C have been measured inside of clouds during electrical storms. Neglect the drag force due to the air in the cloud and any collisions with air molecules. (a) What acceleration does the maximum electric field produce

for protons in the cloud? Express your answer in SI units and as a fraction of g. (b) If the electric field remains constant, how far will the proton have to travel to reach 10% of the speed of light $(3.00 \times 10^8 \text{ m/s})$ if it started with negligible speed? (c) Can you neglect the effects of gravity? Explain your answer.

81. ••An electron with an initial speed of $5.00 \times 10^5 \text{ m/s}$ enters a region in which there is an electric field directed along its direction of motion. If the electron travels 5.00 cm in the field before being stopped, what are the magnitude and direction of the electric field?

82. ••An electron, released in a region where the electric field is uniform, is observed to have an acceleration of $3.00 \times 10^{14} \text{ m/s}^2$ in the positive x direction. (a) Determine the electric field producing the acceleration. (b) Assuming the electron is released from rest, determine the time required for it to reach a speed of 11,200 m/s, the escape speed from Earth's surface.

83. ••**Chemistry** The iron atom (Fe) has 26 protons, 30 neutrons, and 26 electrons. The diameter of the atom is approximately 1.0×10^{-10} m, while the diameter of its nucleus is about 9.2×10^{-15} m. (You can reasonably model the nucleus as a uniform sphere of charge.) What are the magnitude and direction of the electric field that the nucleus produces (a) just outside the surface of the nucleus and (b) at the distance of the outermost electron? (c) What would be the magnitude and direction of the acceleration of the outermost electron due only to the nucleus, neglecting any force due to the other electrons? SSM

84. •••An electron with kinetic energy K is traveling along the $+x$ axis, which is along the axis of a cathode-ray tube as shown in Figure 16-33. There is an electric field $E = 12.00 \times 10^4 \text{ N/C}$ pointed in the $+y$ direction between the deflection plates, which are 0.0600 m long and are separated by 0.0200 m. Determine the minimum initial kinetic energy the electron can have and still avoid colliding with one of the plates.

Figure 16-33 Problem 84

85. ••In the famous Millikan oil-drop experiment, tiny spherical droplets of oil are sprayed into a uniform vertical electric field. The drops get a very small charge (just a few electrons) due to friction with the atomizer as they are sprayed. The field is adjusted until the drop (which is viewed through a small telescope) is just balanced against gravity and therefore remains stationary. Using the measured value of the electric field, we can calculate the charge on the drop and from this calculate the charge e of the electron. In one apparatus, the drops are 1.10 μm in diameter and the oil has a density of 0.850 g/cm^3. (a) If the drops are negatively charged, which way should the electric field point to hold them stationary (up or down)? (b) Why? (c) If a certain drop contains four excess electrons, what magnitude electric field is needed to hold it stationary? (d) You measure a balancing field of 5183 N/C for another drop. How many excess electrons are on this drop?

86. •••The electric field is zero everywhere except in the region $0 \le x \le 3.00$ cm, where there is a uniform electric field of 100 N/C in the $+y$ direction. A proton is moving in the $+x$ direction with a speed of $v = 1.00 \times 10^6 \text{ m/s}$. When the proton passes through the region $0 \le x \le 3.00$ cm, the electric field exerts a force on it. (a) When the x coordinate of the proton's position is 3.00 cm, what is its velocity and what is the y coordinate of its position? (b) When the x coordinate of its position equals 10.0 cm, what is its velocity and what is the y coordinate of its position?

87. •••Two hollow, concentric, spherical shells are covered with charge (Figure 16-34). The inner sphere has a radius R_i and a surface charge density of $+\sigma_i$, while the outer sphere has a radius R_o and a surface charge density of $-\sigma_o$. Derive an expression for the electric field in the following three radial regions: (a) $r < R_i$, (b) $R_i < r < R_o$, and (c) $r > R_o$. SSM

Figure 16-34 Problem 87

88. ••A charge $q_1 = +2q$ is at the origin, and a charge $q_2 = -q$ is on the x axis at $x = a$. Find expressions for the total electric field on the x axis in each of the regions (a) $x < 0$; (b) $0 < x < a$; and (c) $a < x$. (d) Determine all points on the x axis where the electric field is zero. (e) Use a graphing calculator or spreadsheet to make a plot of E_x versus x for all points on the x axis, and (f) qualitatively discuss what happens for $-\infty < x < \infty$.

17 Electrostatics II: Electric Potential Energy and Electric Potential

In this chapter, your goals are to:

- (17-1) Explain the significance of energy in electrostatics.
- (17-2) Discuss how the work done on a charged particle by the electric field relates to changes in electric potential energy.
- (17-3) Explain the difference between electric potential and electric potential energy.
- (17-4) Recognize why equipotential surfaces are perpendicular to electric field lines.
- (17-5) Explain what is meant by capacitance, and describe how the capacitance of a parallel-plate capacitor depends on the size of the plates and their separation.
- (17-6) Calculate the electric energy stored in a capacitor.
- (17-7) Explain how to treat capacitors attached in series and in parallel as a single equivalent capacitance.
- (17-8) Describe how the capacitance of a capacitor increases when an insulating material other than a vacuum is placed between the plates of the capacitor.

To master this chapter, you should review:

- (6-2)   The work done by a force on a moving object.
- (6-6)   The relationship between a conservative force and the potential energy associated with that force.
- (10-3)   The generalized expression for gravitational potential energy.
- (16-5, 16-7) The electric field due to a point charge and to a sheet of charge.

What do you think?

A cardiac defibrillator works by delivering an electric shock to a malfunctioning heart to jump-start it back into its normal rhythm. Electric energy is stored for this purpose in the defibrillator by separating positive charge $+q$ from an equal amount of negative charge $-q$. To release this energy to the heart, conducting paddles are placed on the patient's chest, and charge $-q$ in the form of electrons is allowed to flow through the paddles and patient until it reaches the stored charge $+q$ within the defibrillator. If the value q of the charge stored in a defibrillator is doubled, by what factor will the stored energy increase? (a) $\sqrt{2}$; (b) 2; (c) 4; (d) 8; (e) 16.

17-1 Electric energy is important in nature, technology, and biological systems

Everyone is familiar with the idea that *electricity* implies *energy*. The energy to run your computer, lighting, and television is delivered to your home in the form of electricity. A bolt of lightning releases so much energy that it heats air to a temperature of 30,000°C, causing the air to glow with the characteristic light that we call a lightning flash (see Figure 16-1b). A defibrillator saves lives by delivering a sharp punch of electric energy to a malfunctioning heart (see the photo that opens this chapter). When you purchase an ordinary electric battery, you are really paying for the electric energy that the battery can deliver to whatever electric circuit you plug it into (Figure 17-1a). Some specialized species of fish such as electric rays (Figure 17-1b) are equipped with organic batteries; they can deliver an intense burst of electric energy to stun their prey or ward off predators.

In this chapter we'll make clear what is meant by electric potential energy. We'll gain insight into this new kind of energy by considering the similarities to and differ-

(a)

An ordinary battery is a source of electric energy. Devices that use multiple batteries have greater energy requirements.

(b)

An electric ray (order *Torpediniformes*) is equipped with a large number of organic batteries that work together to deliver intense electric shocks.

Figure 17-1 **Electric energy** Sources of electric energy in (a) technology and (b) nature.

ences from gravitational potential energy. Just as there is a change in gravitational potential energy when a massive object moves up or down in the presence of Earth's gravitational field, there is a change in electric potential energy when a charged object moves along with or opposite to an electric field. We'll go on to introduce the useful concepts of electric potential, or electric potential energy per unit charge, and voltage, which is the difference in the value of electric potential at two positions. We'll also learn about equipotential surfaces, which are surfaces on which the electric potential has the same value at every point.

An important device for storing electric energy is a capacitor. In its simplest form a capacitor is just two pieces of metal, called capacitor plates, placed close to each other but not in contact. We'll examine the key properties of capacitors, including how to combine two or more of them for even greater energy storage. We'll conclude the chapter by seeing how capacitors can be made even more effective by inserting an insulating material between the plates. In Chapter 18 we'll learn how batteries like those shown in Figure 17-1a provide electric energy to the components of an electric circuit.

> ## Take-Home Message for Section 17-1
>
> ✔ Electric potential energy associated with a point charge is analogous to the gravitational potential energy associated with a massive object.
>
> ✔ Electric potential is electric potential energy per charge.
>
> ✔ A capacitor is a device for storing electric energy.

17-2 Electric potential energy changes when a charge moves in an electric field

We learned in Section 6-6 that Earth's gravitational force is a *conservative* force: As an object moves from one position to another in the presence of the gravitational force, the work done on the object by the gravitational force depends only on where the object starts and where it ends up, not on how it gets there. This means that we can express the work done by gravity W_{grav} in terms of a change in the gravitational potential energy U_{grav} of the system of Earth and object:

$$W_{grav} = -\Delta U_{grav} \tag{6-16}$$

The minus sign means that if the object moves downward so that gravity does positive work (the gravitational force and the object's displacement are in the same direction), there is a negative change in gravitational potential energy (U_{grav} decreases). If the object moves upward so that gravity does negative work (force and displacement are in opposite directions), there is a positive change in gravitational potential energy (U_{grav} increases). Note that what matters is the *change* in gravitational potential energy as the object moves from one place to another, not the value of U_{grav} at either place. Once you've chosen the value of U_{grav} at a certain position, you can use Equation 6-16 to tell you the value at any other position.

To be specific, suppose an object of mass m moves in a region where the acceleration $\vec{g}$ due to Earth's gravity is the same at all positions, so the gravitational force $\vec{F} = m\vec{g}$ on the object is uniform. The object's displacement is $\vec{d}$, and that displacement is at an angle θ to the direction of the force $\vec{F} = m\vec{g}$ and so at the same angle θ to the direction of $\vec{g}$ (Figure 17-2a). Then the work done by gravity is $W = Fd \cos \theta$ (Equation 6-2), and the change in gravitational potential energy is

$$\Delta U_{grav} = -W_{grav} = -mgd \cos \theta \tag{17-1}$$

 See the Math Tutorial for more information on trigonometry

Figure 17-2 Change in gravitational potential energy When an object of mass m moves in the presence of gravity, the gravitational force can do work on it and there can be a change in gravitational potential energy.

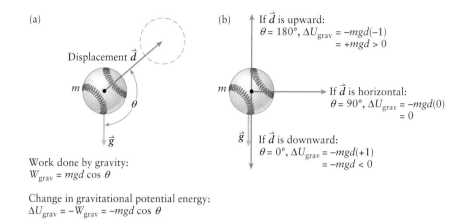

(a)

Displacement $\vec{d}$

m

θ

$\vec{g}$

Work done by gravity:
$W_{\text{grav}} = mgd \cos \theta$

Change in gravitational potential energy:
$\Delta U_{\text{grav}} = -W_{\text{grav}} = -mgd \cos \theta$

(b)

If $\vec{d}$ is upward:
$\theta = 180°$, $\Delta U_{\text{grav}} = -mgd(-1)$
$= +mgd > 0$

m

If $\vec{d}$ is horizontal:
$\theta = 90°$, $\Delta U_{\text{grav}} = -mgd(0)$
$= 0$

$\vec{g}$

If $\vec{d}$ is downward:
$\theta = 0°$, $\Delta U_{\text{grav}} = -mgd(+1)$
$= -mgd < 0$

Equation 17-1 looks a bit different from the way that we wrote the change in gravitational potential energy in Chapter 6, but we can verify that it makes sense (Figure 17-2b). If the object moves a distance d straight upward, opposite to the direction of the gravitational force, $\theta = 180°$ and $\cos \theta = \cos 180° = -1$. In this case gravity does negative work on the object, and the gravitational potential energy increases: $\Delta U_{\text{grav}} = -mgd(-1) = +mgd$. If the object moves a distance d straight downward, in the direction of the gravitational force, $\theta = 0$ and $\cos \theta = \cos 0° = 1$. Then gravity does positive work on the object and the gravitational potential energy decreases: $\Delta U_{\text{grav}} = -mgd(+1) = -mgd$. Gravity does zero work, and there is no change in gravitational potential energy, if the object moves horizontally: Then $\theta = 90°$ and $\Delta U_{\text{grav}} = -mgd \cos 90° = 0$. These results are the same ones that we found in Section 6-6.

We can apply the same concepts to the idea of *electric potential* energy. That's because like gravity, the electric force due to the interaction between charged objects is a conservative force. You can see this easily for the special case in which an object moves in a region of space where there is a *uniform* electric field $\vec{E}$—that is, where the value of $\vec{E}$ is the same at all positions (Figure 17-3). The electric force on an object of charge q moving in this region is constant and equal to $\vec{F} = q\vec{E}$. That's exactly like the situation in Figure 17-2, which shows an object of mass m moving in a region where $\vec{g}$ is the same at all positions, so the gravitational force $\vec{F} = m\vec{g}$ on the object is uniform. We know that this uniform gravitational force is conservative, so the force $\vec{F} = q\vec{E}$ due to a uniform electric field must be conservative as well. Hence we can express the work done by the electric force in terms of a change in *electric* potential energy.

Electric Potential Energy in a Uniform Field

Go to Picture It 17-1 for more practice dealing with electric potential energy

This analogy between gravitational force and electric force tells us how to write the change in electric potential energy for an object of charge q that undergoes a displacement $\vec{d}$ in the presence of a uniform electric field $\vec{E}$ (Figure 17-3a). Following the same steps that we used to find Equation 17-1 above, you can see that if θ is the angle between the directions of $\vec{d}$ and $\vec{E}$, then the work done on the charge by the electric force $\vec{F} = q\vec{E}$ is $W_{\text{electric}} = qEd \cos \theta$. The change in **electric potential energy** equals the negative of the electric work done on the charge:

The change in electric potential energy for an object of charge q that moves in a uniform electric field $\vec{E}$...

...equals the negative of the work done on the object by the electric force.

Electric potential energy for a charge in a uniform electric field
(17-2)

$$\Delta U_{\text{electric}} = -W_{\text{electric}}$$
$$= -qEd \cos \theta$$

Charge of the object

Angle between the displacement and the direction of the electric field

Magnitude of the electric field

Straight-line displacement of the object

(a)

Displacement $\vec{d}$

q +

θ

$\vec{E}$

Work done by electric force:
$W_{electric} = qEd \cos \theta$

Change in electric potential energy:
$\Delta U_{electric} = -W_{electric} = -qEd \cos \theta$

(b)

If $\vec{d}$ is opposite of $\vec{E}$:
$\theta = 180°$, $\Delta U_{electric} = -qEd(-1)$
$= +qEd > 0$

$q > 0$ +

If $\vec{d}$ is perpendicular to $\vec{E}$:
$\theta = 90°$, $\Delta U_{electric} = -qEd(0)$
$= 0$

$\vec{E}$

If $\vec{d}$ is in the same direction as $\vec{E}$:
$\theta = 0°$, $\Delta U_{electric} = -qEd(+1)$
$= -qEd < 0$

(c)

If $\vec{d}$ is opposite of $\vec{E}$:
$\theta = 180°$, $\Delta U_{electric} = -qEd(-1)$
$= +qEd < 0$

$q < 0$ ⊖

If $\vec{d}$ is perpendicular to $\vec{E}$:
$\theta = 90°$, $\Delta U_{electric} = -qEd(0)$
$= 0$

$\vec{E}$

If $\vec{d}$ is in the same direction as $\vec{E}$:
$\theta = 0°$, $\Delta U_{electric} = -qEd(+1)$
$= -qEd > 0$

Figure 17-3 **Change in electric potential energy** When an object of charge q moves in the presence of a uniform electric field $\vec{E}$, the electric force can do work on it and there can be a change in electric potential energy (compare Figure 17-2).

Just as for the gravitational case, Equation 17-2 tells us how much the electric potential energy *changes* when the charge is displaced as shown in Figure 17-3a. The value of the initial electric potential energy $U_{electric}$ can have any value you choose; once you've chosen that value, the value of $U_{electric}$ at the final position equals the initial value plus $(-qEd \cos \theta)$. Note also that the electric potential energy is a shared property of the charge q and the other charges that produce the electric field $\vec{E}$.

Let's examine Equation 17-2 more closely (Figure 17-3b). Suppose q is positive, so that the force $\vec{F} = q\vec{E}$ on the charged object is in the *same* direction as the uniform electric field $\vec{E}$. If this positive charge moves a distance d opposite to $\vec{E}$, then $\theta = 180°$ and $\cos \theta = -1$. In this case the electric force does negative work on the charge, $\Delta U_{electric} = (-qEd)(-1) = +qEd$ (the negative of the work done by the electric force) is positive, and the electric potential energy of the system increases. That's exactly what happens to *gravitational* potential energy when a massive object moves upward from Earth's surface, in the direction opposite to the gravitational force (Figure 17-2b). If the positive charge q instead moves in the same direction as the electric field, and so in the same direction as the electric force, then $\theta = 0$ and $\cos \theta = +1$. Then the electric force does positive work on the object, so $\Delta U_{electric} = (-qEd)(+1) = -qEd$ is negative and the electric potential energy of the system decreases. That's the same thing that happens when a massive object falls toward Earth's surface, in the same direction as the gravitational force on the object: Gravitational potential energy decreases (Figure 17-2b).

Equation 17-2 also applies to the case of an object with *negative* charge ($q < 0$), so that the force $\vec{F} = q\vec{E}$ on this object is in the direction *opposite* to the electric field $\vec{E}$ (Figure 17-3c). If such a negative charge moves a distance d opposite the direction of $\vec{E}$ so that $\theta = 180°$ and $\cos \theta = -1$ in Equation 17-2, the electric force does *positive* work on the charge because the force and displacement are in the same direction. Then, because $q < 0$, $\Delta U_{electric} = +qEd$ is *negative* because q is negative and the electric potential energy of the system decreases. That's exactly the opposite of what happens for a positive charge that moves a distance d in the direction opposite to the uniform electric field. In the same way, if a negative charge moves a distance d in the direction of $\vec{E}$ so that $\theta = 0$ and $\cos \theta = +1$ in Equation 17-2, the electric force does *negative* work on the object (the electric force is opposite to $\vec{E}$ and so opposite the displacement). The electric potential energy change in this case is $\Delta U_{electric} = (-qEd)(+1) = -qEd$, which is positive because q is negative. So the electric potential energy of the system increases. Again, that's exactly opposite to what happens for a positive charge that moves a distance d in the direction of the electric field.

Example 17-1 Electric Potential Energy Difference in a Uniform Field

An electron (charge $q = -e = -1.60 \times 10^{-19}$ C, mass $m = 9.11 \times 10^{-31}$ kg) is released from rest in a uniform electric field. The field points in the positive x direction and has magnitude 2.00×10^2 N/C. Find the speed of the electron after it has moved 0.300 m.

Set Up

Because the electron has a negative charge, the force $\vec{F} = q\vec{E}$ on the electron is directed opposite to the electric field. So the displacement of the electron will be at an angle $\theta = 180°$ to the direction of the electric field.

If the conservative electric force is the only force acting on the electron, then mechanical energy is conserved. We'll find the change in electric potential energy using Equation 17-2, and from this find the change in kinetic energy of the electron. The electron's initial kinetic energy is zero because it starts at rest; once we know the final kinetic energy, we can determine the electron's final speed.

Electric potential energy for a charge in a uniform electric field:

$$\Delta U_{\text{electric}} = -qEd \cos\theta \qquad (17\text{-}2)$$

Conservation of mechanical energy:

$$K_i + U_{\text{electric,i}} = K_f + U_{\text{electric,f}} \qquad (6\text{-}23)$$

Kinetic energy:

$$K = \frac{1}{2}mv^2 \qquad (6\text{-}8)$$

$E = 2.00 \times 10^2$ N/C

$d = 0.300$ m $\longleftarrow$ o $-e$

$\longrightarrow +x$

Solve

Use Equation 17-2 to solve for the change in electric potential energy.

The change in electric potential energy equals the difference between the final and initial electric potential energy:

$$\Delta U_{\text{electric}} = U_{\text{electric,f}} - U_{\text{electric,i}}$$

From Equation 17-2,

$$\begin{aligned}
\Delta U_{\text{electric}} &= U_{\text{electric,f}} - U_{\text{electric,i}} \\
&= -qEd \cos\theta \\
&= -(-1.60 \times 10^{-19}\,\text{C})(2.00 \times 10^2\,\text{N/C})(0.300\,\text{m}) \cos 180° \\
&= -(-9.60 \times 10^{-18}\,\text{N}\cdot\text{m})(-1) \\
&= -9.60 \times 10^{-18}\,\text{N}\cdot\text{m} = -9.60 \times 10^{-18}\,\text{J}
\end{aligned}$$

Find the final kinetic energy and the final speed of the electron.

The initial kinetic energy of the electron is $K_i = 0$. Solve the energy conservation equation for the final kinetic energy of the electron:

$$K_f = K_i + U_{\text{electric,i}} - U_{\text{electric,f}} = 0 - (U_{\text{electric,f}} - U_{\text{electric,i}})$$

$$= 0 - (-9.60 \times 10^{-18}\,\text{J}) = 9.60 \times 10^{-18}\,\text{J}$$

Finally, solve for the final speed of the electron:

$$K_f = \frac{1}{2}mv_f^2 \text{ so}$$

$$v_f = \sqrt{\frac{2K_f}{m}} = \sqrt{\frac{2(9.60 \times 10^{-18}\,\text{J})}{9.11 \times 10^{-31}\,\text{kg}}} = 4.59 \times 10^6\,\text{m/s}$$

Reflect

The electric potential energy decreases when we release the electron in the electric field, in the same way that the gravitational potential energy decreases when you release a ball in the presence of Earth's gravity. In both situations, the kinetic energy increases by the same amount that the potential energy decreases.

You should verify that the force on the electron is very small, only 3.2×10^{-17} N in magnitude. The electron has only a tiny mass, however, and our results show that it acquires a ferocious speed (about 1.5% of the speed of light) after moving just 0.300 m.

Electric Potential Energy of Point Charges

Electric potential energy is particularly important for the case of two point charges interacting with each other. For example, many key quantities in chemistry are impossible to understand without first grasping the concept of electric potential energy. An example is the dissociation energy of an ionic compound such as sodium chloride (NaCl)—that is, the energy that must be given to the molecule to break it into its component atoms. The dissociation energy is determined in large part by the change in electric potential energy required to separate the positive sodium ion (Na^+) and the negative chloride ion (Cl^-), both of which behave much like point charges, as well as by the change in electric potential energy required to move an electron from the Cl^- ion to the Na^+ ion to make the atoms neutral.

Just as for a charge moving in a uniform electric field, we can use our knowledge of gravitation to find an expression for the electric potential energy of two point charges q_1 and q_2 separated by a distance r. In Section 10-2 we saw the following expression for the attractive *gravitational* force between two objects with *masses* m_1 and m_2 separated by a distance r:

Gravitational constant (same for any two objects)   Masses of the two objects

Any two objects (1 and 2) exert equally strong gravitational forces on each other.

$$F_{1\ on\ 2} = F_{2\ on\ 1} = \frac{Gm_1 m_2}{r^2}$$

Center-to-center distance between the two objects

The gravitational forces are attractive: $\vec{F}_{1\ on\ 2}$ pulls object 2 toward object 1 and $\vec{F}_{2\ on\ 1}$ pulls object 1 toward object 2.

Newton's law of universal gravitation (10-2)

The gravitational potential energy of these two objects is given by Equation 10-4 in Section 10-3:

Gravitational constant (same for any two objects)   Masses of the two objects

Gravitational potential energy of a system of two objects (1 and 2)

$$U_{grav} = -\frac{Gm_1 m_2}{r}$$

Center-to-center distance between the two objects

The gravitational potential energy is zero when the two objects are infinitely far apart. If the objects are brought closer together (so r is made smaller), U_{grav} decreases (it becomes more negative).

Gravitational potential energy (10-4)

Figure 17-4a graphs the gravitational potential energy given by Equation 10-4. We choose the point at which potential energy U_{grav} is zero to be where the two objects are infinitely far apart, so $r \to \infty$. The gravitational potential energy is negative for any finite value of r and increases—that is, becomes less negative—as the objects move farther apart. That's because the work done by the gravitational force and the change in gravitational potential energy are negatives of each other: $\Delta U_{grav} = -W_{grav}$ (see Equation 6-16 at the beginning of this chapter section). If we hold object m_1 stationary and move object m_2 farther away, increasing the distance r, the attractive gravitational force does negative work. Then $W_{grav} < 0$, so $\Delta U_{grav} > 0$ and the gravitational potential energy increases, as Figure 17-4a shows.

(a) Gravitational potential energy

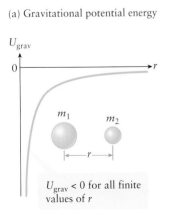

$U_{grav} < 0$ for all finite values of r

(b) Electric potential energy, charges of opposite sign

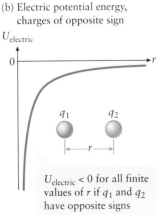

$U_{electric} < 0$ for all finite values of r if q_1 and q_2 have opposite signs

(c) Electric potential energy, charges of the same sign

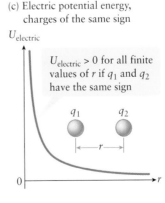

$U_{electric} > 0$ for all finite values of r if q_1 and q_2 have the same sign

Figure 17-4 Potential energy for two masses and for two charges The electric potential energy $U_{electric}$ for two point charges is similar to the gravitational potential energy for two masses. The sign of $U_{electric}$ depends on the signs of the two charges.

Now compare Equation 10-2 to Coulomb's law for the electric force between two point charges, Equation 16-1:

**Coulomb's law
(16-1)**

Any two point charges q_1 and q_2 exert equally strong electric forces on each other.

Coulomb constant

Absolute values of the point charges

$$F_{q_1 \text{ on } q_2} = F_{q_2 \text{ on } q_1} = \frac{k|q_1||q_2|}{r^2}$$

Distance between the point charges

If we replace m and G in Equation 10-2 with q and k, we see that Equation 16-1 is identical to Equation 10-2 for the gravitational force, but with an important difference: The electric force is *attractive* (like the gravitational force) if the two charges q_1 and q_2 have opposite signs (one negative and the other positive), but *repulsive* if q_1 and q_2 have the same sign (either both positive or both negative). Here's an expression for the electric potential energy of two point charges that accounts for both of these possibilities:

**Electric potential energy
of two point charges
(17-3)**

Coulomb constant

Values of the two charges

Electric potential energy of two point charges

$$U_{\text{electric}} = \frac{kq_1q_2}{r}$$

Distance between the point charges

This expression is very similar to Equation 10-4 for gravitational potential energy. Equation 17-3 shows that U_{electric} is inversely proportional to the distance r, so the electric potential energy is zero when the two charges are infinitely far apart ($r \rightarrow \infty$). But unlike gravitational potential energy, U_{electric} can be either negative or positive depending on the signs of the two charges. If q_1 and q_2 have different signs (one positive and one negative) so that the two charges attract each other, then $U_{\text{electric}} < 0$ for any finite distance r between the charges (**Figure 17-4b**). This makes sense: If we hold charge q_1 at rest and move charge q_2 farther away, the attractive electric force on q_2 does negative work (the force on q_2 is opposite to the displacement of q_2). In this case the change in electric potential energy is positive and the electric potential energy increases (becomes less negative) with increasing distance r, just like the gravitational potential energy of two masses. But if q_1 and q_2 have the same sign (both positive or both negative) so that the two charges repel each other, then $U_{\text{electric}} > 0$ for any finite distance r between the charges (**Figure 17-4c**). In this case when q_2 moves away from q_1 the repulsive electric force on q_2 does positive work (the force on q_2 is in the same direction as the displacement of q_2). Then the change in electric potential energy is negative and the electric potential energy *decreases* (becomes less positive) with increasing distance r.

Here's a useful way to interpret U_{electric} as given by Equation 17-3:

The electric potential energy of a pair of point charges equals the amount of work you would have to do to bring the charges to their current positions from infinitely far away.

If the two charges have opposite signs as in Figure 17-4b, you would have to do *negative* work (you would push the charges away from each other as they move toward each other) to oppose the attractive electric force that pulls the two charges together. (If you didn't exert a force to do this work, the electric attraction would make the charges crash into each other instead of stopping a distance r apart.) So in this case the electric potential energy of the two charges is negative, as Figure 17-4b shows. By contrast, if the two charges have the same sign as in Figure 17-4c, you would have to do positive work to push the two charges together (you would push the two charges toward each other as they move toward each other) to overcome the repulsive electric force that pushes the two charges apart. So the electric potential energy of these two charges is positive, as depicted in Figure 17-4c.

The same idea holds for an assemblage of three or more point charges. To put charges q_1, q_2, and q_3 into proximity to each other, you would first have to do work to bring q_1 and q_2 from infinity to a distance r_{12} from each other. If you then brought in the third charge q_3 while keeping the other two charges stationary, you would have to do additional work against the electric force that q_1 exerts on q_3 *and* against the electric force that q_2 exerts on q_3. If q_3 ends up a distance r_{13} from q_1 and a distance r_{23} from q_2, the electric potential energy of the assemblage is the total amount of work that you did:

$$U_{\text{electric}} = \frac{kq_1q_2}{r_{12}} + \frac{kq_1q_3}{r_{13}} + \frac{kq_2q_3}{r_{23}}$$ (17-4)

(electric potential energy of three charges)

The total electric potential energy of a system of three charges is the sum of three terms, one for each pair of charges in the system (q_1 and q_2, q_1 and q_3, and q_2 and q_3). Each such term is the same as Equation 17-3. You can easily extend this idea to an assemblage made up of any number of point charges.

The following examples show how to do calculations using Equations 17-3 and 17-4.

> ▶ *Go to Interactive Exercise 17-1 for more practice dealing with electric potential energy*

Example 17-2 Electric Potential Energy and Nuclear Fission

When a nucleus of uranium-235 (92 protons and 143 neutrons) absorbs an additional neutron, it undergoes a process called *nuclear fission* in which it breaks into two smaller nuclei. One possible fission is for the uranium nucleus to divide into two palladium nuclei, each of which has 46 protons and is 5.9×10^{-15} m in radius. The palladium nuclei then fly apart due to their electric repulsion. If we assume that the two palladium nuclei begin at rest and are just touching each other, what is their combined kinetic energy when they are very far apart?

Set Up

We can treat the two spherical nuclei as though they were point charges of $q = +46e$ located at the centers of the two nuclei. (To motivate this, recall from Section 16-7 that the electric field outside a sphere of charge Q is the same as that of a point charge Q located at the sphere's center.) Equation 17-3 then tells us the electric potential energy of the two palladium nuclei when they begin at rest. We'll then use energy conservation to find the combined kinetic energy when the palladium nuclei are very far apart.

Electric potential energy of two point charges:

$$U_{\text{electric}} = \frac{kq_1q_2}{r}$$ (17-3)

Conservation of mechanical energy:

$$K_i + U_{\text{electric,i}} = K_f + U_{\text{electric,f}}$$ (6-23)

Solve

Use Equation 17-3 to solve for the initial electric potential energy when the two nuclei are just touching.

Each nucleus has charge $+46e$:

$$q_1 = q_2 = +46(1.60 \times 10^{-19}\text{ C}) = +7.36 \times 10^{-18}\text{ C}$$

The separation between the charges is twice the radius of either nucleus:

$$r = 2(5.9 \times 10^{-15}\text{ m})$$

The electric potential energy is

$$U_{\text{electric,i}} = \frac{kq_1q_2}{r} = \frac{(8.99 \times 10^9\text{ N}\cdot\text{m}^2/\text{C}^2)(7.36 \times 10^{-18}\text{ C})^2}{2(5.9 \times 10^{-15}\text{ m})}$$

$$= 4.1 \times 10^{-11}\text{ N}\cdot\text{m} = 4.1 \times 10^{-11}\text{ J}$$

Use energy conservation to find the combined final kinetic energy of the two palladium nuclei.

The palladium nuclei begin at rest, so the initial kinetic energy is zero:

$$K_i = 0$$

The palladium nuclei end up very far apart, so their separation is essentially infinite ($r \to \infty$). The final electric potential energy is therefore zero:

$$U_{\text{electric,f}} = 0$$

From the energy conservation equation, the final kinetic energy is

$$K_f = K_i + U_{electric,i} - U_{electric,f}$$
$$= 0 + 4.1 \times 10^{-11} \text{ J} - 0 = 4.1 \times 10^{-11} \text{ J}$$

Reflect

All of the initial electric potential energy is converted into kinetic energy of the palladium nuclei. The energy released by the fission of a single uranium-235 nucleus, 4.1×10^{-11} J, is very small. But imagine that you could get 1.0 kg of uranium-235, which contains about 2.6×10^{24} uranium atoms, to undergo fission at once. (This is the principle of a *fission bomb*.) The released energy would be $(2.6 \times 10^{24}) \times (4.1 \times 10^{-11} \text{ J}) = 1.1 \times 10^{14}$ J, equivalent to the energy given off by exploding 26,000 tons of TNT. This gives an inkling of the terrifying amount of energy that can be released by a fission weapon.

Example 17-3 Electric Potential Energy of Three Charges

A particle with charge $q_1 = +4.30 \ \mu C$ is located at $x = 0$, $y = 0$. A second particle with charge $q_2 = -9.80 \ \mu C$ is located at $x = 0$, $y = 4.00$ cm, and a third particle with charge $q_3 = +5.00 \ \mu C$ is located at position $x = 3.00$ cm, $y = 0$. (Note that $1 \ \mu C = 1$ microcoulomb $= 10^{-6}$ C.) What is the total electric potential energy of these three charges?

Set Up

We'll use Equation 17-4 to find the value of $U_{electric}$. We're given the values of the three charges; we'll use the positions of the charges to find the distances r_{12}, r_{13}, and r_{23} between them.

Electric potential energy of three charges:

$$U_{electric} = \frac{kq_1q_2}{r_{12}} + \frac{kq_1q_3}{r_{13}} + \frac{kq_2q_3}{r_{23}}$$

(17-4)

Solve

The figure above shows that charges 1 and 2 are $r_{12} = 4.00$ cm apart, and that charges 1 and 3 are $r_{13} = 3.00$ cm apart. The distance between charges 2 and 3 is the hypotenuse of a right triangle of sides r_{12} and r_{13}.

From the figure above,

$$r_{12} = 4.00 \text{ cm} = 4.00 \times 10^{-2} \text{ m}$$
$$r_{13} = 3.00 \text{ cm} = 3.00 \times 10^{-2} \text{ m}$$

From the Pythagorean theorem,

$$r_{23} = \sqrt{r_{12}^2 + r_{13}^2}$$
$$= \sqrt{(4.00 \times 10^{-2} \text{ m})^2 + (3.00 \times 10^{-2} \text{ m})^2}$$
$$= 5.00 \times 10^{-2} \text{ m}$$

Calculate each term in the expression for electric potential energy, Equation 17-4.

We can write Equation 17-4 as

$$U_{electric} = U_{12} + U_{13} + U_{23}$$

Each term on the right-hand side of this equation represents the contribution to the electric potential energy due to a specific pair of point charges. The contribution due to the interaction between charges q_1 and q_2 is

$$U_{12} = \frac{kq_1q_2}{r_{12}}$$

$$= \frac{(8.99 \times 10^9 \, \text{N} \cdot \text{m}^2/\text{C}^2)(+4.30 \times 10^{-6} \, \text{C})(-9.80 \times 10^{-6} \, \text{C})}{4.00 \times 10^{-2} \, \text{m}}$$

$$= -9.47 \, \text{J}$$

The contribution due to the interaction between charges q_1 and q_3 is

$$U_{13} = \frac{kq_1q_3}{r_{13}}$$

$$= \frac{(8.99 \times 10^9 \, \text{N} \cdot \text{m}^2/\text{C}^2)(+4.30 \times 10^{-6} \, \text{C})(+5.00 \times 10^{-6} \, \text{C})}{3.00 \times 10^{-2} \, \text{m}}$$

$$= +6.44 \, \text{J}$$

The contribution due to the interaction between charges q_2 and q_3 is

$$U_{23} = \frac{kq_2q_3}{r_{23}}$$

$$= \frac{(8.99 \times 10^9 \, \text{N} \cdot \text{m}^2/\text{C}^2)(-9.80 \times 10^{-6} \, \text{C})(+5.00 \times 10^{-6} \, \text{C})}{5.00 \times 10^{-2} \, \text{m}}$$

$$= -8.81 \, \text{J}$$

Finally, calculate the total electric potential energy.

The total electric potential energy is the sum of the three terms calculated above:

$$U_{\text{electric}} = U_{12} + U_{13} + U_{23}$$

$$= (-9.47 \, \text{J}) + (+6.44 \, \text{J}) + (-8.81 \, \text{J})$$

$$= -11.82 \, \text{J}$$

Reflect

The contributions U_{12} and U_{23} are negative because these pairs of charges (q_1 and q_2 for U_{12}, q_2 and q_3 for U_{23}) have opposite signs. The members of these pairs attract each other, so you must do negative work against each attractive force to move the charges from infinity to the positions shown in the figure. The contribution U_{13}, however, is positive because charges q_1 and q_3 have the same sign (both positive). These two charges repel, so you must do positive work against the repulsion to move these charges from infinity to their positions. The total potential energy is negative, which shows that the total amount of work you would do to move all three charges from infinity is negative.

? Got the Concept? 17-1   Electric Potential Energy

Suppose you reversed the signs of the three point charges in Example 17-3 so that $q_1 = -4.30 \, \mu\text{C}$, $q_2 = +9.80 \, \mu\text{C}$, and $q_3 = -5.00 \, \mu\text{C}$. If the positions of the charges remain unchanged, what would be the total electric potential energy of this assemblage? (a) More negative than $-11.82 \, \text{J}$; (b) $-11.82 \, \text{J}$; (c) between $-11.82 \, \text{J}$ and $+11.82 \, \text{J}$; (d) $+11.82 \, \text{J}$; (e) more positive than $+11.82 \, \text{J}$.

Take-Home Message for Section 17-2

✔ The electric potential energy associated with a point charge can change if the charge changes position in an electric field.

✔ The electric potential energy of a pair of point charges equals the amount of work you would have to do to move those charges from infinity to their present positions.

✔ The electric potential energy of an assemblage of three or more point charges is the sum of the electric potential energies for each pair of charges in the assemblage.

17-3 Electric potential equals electric potential energy per charge

Our discussion in Section 17-2 shows that if a point charge q changes position, the potential energy change $\Delta U_{\text{electric}}$ depends on both the magnitude and the sign (positive or negative) of q (see Figure 17-3). We can simplify things by considering the potential energy *per charge*—that is, the electric potential energy for a charge at a given position divided by the value of that charge. We call this quantity the **electric potential** and denote it by the symbol V:

Electric potential related to electric potential energy (17-5)

The electric potential at a given position...

...equals the electric potential energy for a charge q_0 at that position...

$$V = \frac{U_{\text{electric}}}{q_0}$$

...divided by the charge q_0.

Electric potential equals electric potential energy per unit charge.

We call the charge q_0 the **test charge**: Its charge has such a small magnitude that it doesn't affect the other charges that create the electric field in which q_0 moves. Because we divide out the value of q_0, the value of the potential V at a given position does *not* depend on the value of the point charge q_0 that we place there. Instead, V is determined by the other charges that produce the electric field at the position where we place the test charge.

Note that electric potential V has the same relationship to electric potential energy U_{electric} as electric field $\vec{E}$ has to electric force $\vec{F}$: V is electric potential energy per charge, just as $\vec{E}$ is electric force per charge. Like electric potential energy, but unlike electric field, potential V is a *scalar* quantity.

For electric potential energy, the value of U_{electric} for a charge at a given position is not as important as the potential energy *difference* $\Delta U_{\text{electric}}$ when the charge moves from a point a to a different point b. The same is true for electric potential. From Equation 17-5, the **electric potential difference** ΔV between two points is

Electric potential difference related to electric potential energy difference (17-6)

The difference in electric potential between two positions...

...equals the change in electric potential energy for a charge q_0 moved between these two positions...

$$\Delta V = \frac{\Delta U_{\text{electric}}}{q_0}$$

...divided by the charge q_0.

Electric potential difference equals electric potential energy difference per unit charge.

The SI unit of electric potential and electric potential difference is the **volt** (V), named after the Italian scientist Alessandro Volta. For example, a common AA or AAA flashlight battery has "1.5 volts" written on its side. This means that the electric potential at the positive terminal of the battery (labeled +) is 1.5 V greater than the electric potential at the negative terminal of the battery (labeled −). In other words, 1.5 V is the electric potential *difference* between the terminals of the battery. In Chapter 18 we'll see how this electric potential difference causes electric charge to flow when a battery is included in an electric circuit. (Note that Volta invented the electric battery in 1800.) Equations 17-5 and 17-6 show that 1 volt is equal to 1 joule per coulomb, and we know that 1 joule is equal to 1 newton multiplied by 1 meter. So

$$1\,\text{V} = 1\,\frac{\text{J}}{\text{C}} = 1\,\frac{\text{N} \cdot \text{m}}{\text{C}}$$

This means that if the electric potential at point b is 1 V higher than at point a, it takes 1 J of work to move a charge of +1 C from a to b. If a charge of +1 C at point b is released from rest and moves to point a, the electric potential that the charge experiences decreases by 1 V, the electric potential energy associated with the charge decreases by 1 J, and the charge acquires 1 J of kinetic energy.

We saw in Chapter 16 that the SI units of electric field are newtons per coulomb, or N/C. Because $1 \text{ V} = 1 \text{ N} \cdot \text{m/C}$, it follows that $1 \text{ V/m} = 1 \text{ N/C}$. So an equally good set of units for electric field is V/m (volts per meter).

We'll often abbreviate the terms *electric potential* and *electric potential difference* as simply *potential* and *potential difference*, respectively. Since the unit of electric potential is the volt, it's also common to refer to electric potential difference as **voltage**.

 Watch Out! **Don't confuse the symbol *V* for electric potential difference and the abbreviation V for volts.**

In this chapter and others you'll see mathematical statements such as "$V = 10$ V." Such statements are perfectly legal because V and V are different symbols. V (italicized) represents the electric potential at a point in space. V (not italicized) is an abbreviation for the unit of electric potential, the volt. In this textbook, you can tell the difference by noticing which font is used and by paying close attention to the context in which V and V are used. But it's pretty hard to handwrite something in italics, so make sure you know the distinction between V and V in your own work on your homework assignments and exams.

Watch Out! **Electric potential and electric potential energy are not the same.**

Remember that electric potential V and electric potential energy U_{electric} are related but different quantities. Electric potential energy U_{electric} refers to the energy associated with a particular amount of charge at a given position. Electric potential V is the energy associated with a *unit* charge at that position. Note that while V and U_{electric} can both be positive or negative, they do not have a direction associated with them. So electric potential and electric potential energy are both *scalar* quantities, not vector quantities.

Electric Potential in a Uniform Electric Field

A simple application of Equation 17-6 is finding the electric potential difference between two points a and b in a uniform electric field (**Figure 17-5**). From Equation 17-2, the change or difference in electric potential energy when a charge q_0 is moved from a to b is $\Delta U_{\text{electric}} = -q_0 E d \cos \theta$. Equation 17-6 tells us that the electric potential difference between a and b is $\Delta U_{\text{electric}}$ divided by q_0, or the electric potential energy change per unit charge:

$$\Delta V = \frac{\Delta U_{\text{electric}}}{q_0} = \frac{-q_0 E d \cos \theta}{q_0}$$
$$= -E d \cos \theta \qquad (17\text{-}7)$$

Equation 17-7 shows that ΔV is positive if $\cos \theta$ is negative, which is the case if the angle θ is greater than 90° as depicted in Figure 17-5. In other words, *if you move in a direction opposite to the electric field, the electric potential increases.* If the angle θ is less than 90°, $\cos \theta$ is positive and ΔV is negative; *if you move in the direction of the electric field, the electric potential decreases.*

We know that the electric force on a positive charge is in the direction of the electric field $\vec{E}$, and the electric force on a negative charge is in the direction opposite to $\vec{E}$. So our observations about how electric potential changes with position tell us that

If an object has positive charge, the electric force on that object pushes it toward a region of lower electric potential. If an object has negative charge, the electric force on that object pushes it toward a region of higher electric potential.

As we'll see below, these observations hold true whether or not the electric field is uniform.

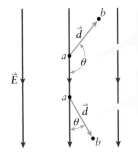

If you move in a direction opposite to the electric field ($\theta > 90°$), the electric potential increases ($\Delta V > 0$).

If you move in the direction of the electric field ($\theta < 90°$), the electric potential decreases ($\Delta V < 0$).

 If you move from point a to point b in a uniform electric field $\vec{E}$, the change in electric potential is $\Delta V = -Ed \cos \theta$.

Figure 17-5 **Change in electric potential** Calculating the difference in electric potential between two points in a uniform electric field $\vec{E}$.

Comparing Equations 17-2 and 17-7 shows that the right-hand side of Equation 17-7 equals the negative of the work done by the electric field ($q_0Ed \cos \theta$) divided by the charge q_0. So another way to think of the potential difference between two points is as the negative of the work done by the electric field per unit charge when a charged object is moved between those points. Alternatively, the potential difference between two points equals the work that *you* must do per unit charge against the electric force to move a charged object between those points. So if you take a charge of $+1$ C that is at rest at point a and move it to point b where it is again at rest, and the potential at b is 1 V higher than the potential at a, the electric field does -1 J of work on the charge and you do $+1$ J of work on that charge.

> Go to Picture It 17-2 for more practice dealing with electric potential

According to Equation 17-7, for a uniform electric field the electric potential difference between two points depends only on the electric field $\vec{E}$ and the displacement $\vec{d}$ between those two points. So knowing how the electric potential varies over a region of space enables us to determine how any charged object will move in that region, regardless of the magnitude of its charge.

Example 17-4 Electric Potential Difference in a Uniform Field I

A uniform electric field points in the positive x direction and has magnitude 2.00×10^2 V/m. Points a and b are both in this field: Point b is a distance 0.300 m from a in the negative x direction. Determine the electric potential difference $V_b - V_a$ between points a and b.

Set Up

We apply Equation 17-7 to the path shown in the figure. Note that the magnitude of the displacement is $d = 0.300$ m, and the angle between the electric field and the displacement is $\theta = 180°$. Note also that the potential difference ΔV equals the potential at the *end* of the displacement $\vec{d}$ (that is, at point b) minus the potential at the *beginning* of the displacement (that is, at point a).

Potential difference between two points in a uniform electric field:

$$\Delta V = V_b - V_a = -Ed \cos \theta \quad (17\text{-}7)$$

Solve

Use Equation 17-7 to solve for the potential difference.

Calculate the potential difference from the electric field magnitude E, the displacement d, and the angle θ:

$$\begin{aligned} \Delta V = V_b - V_a &= -Ed \cos \theta \\ &= -(2.00 \times 10^2 \text{ V/m})(0.300 \text{ m}) \cos 180° \\ &= -(60.0 \text{ V})(-1) \\ &= +60.0 \text{ V} \end{aligned}$$

Reflect

We can check our result by comparing with Example 17-1 in Section 17-2, where we considered the change in electric potential *energy* $\Delta U_{electric}$ for an electron that undergoes the same displacement in this same electric field. Using Equation 17-6, we find the same value of $\Delta U_{electric}$ as in Example 17-1.

The positive value of $\Delta V = V_b - V_a$ means that point b is at a higher potential than point a. This agrees with our observation above that if you travel opposite to the direction of the electric field, the electric potential increases. The value $E = 2.00 \times 10^2$ V/m means that the electric potential increases by 2.00×10^2 V for every meter that you travel opposite to the direction of $\vec{E}$.

If a charge $q_0 = -1.60 \times 10^{-19}$ C travels from a to b, the charge in electric potential energy is given by Equation 17-6:

$$\Delta V = \frac{\Delta U_{electric}}{q_0}$$

so

$$\begin{aligned} \Delta U_{electric} = q_0 \Delta V &= (-1.60 \times 10^{-19} \text{ C})(+60.0 \text{ V}) \\ &= -9.60 \times 10^{-18} \text{ V} \cdot \text{C} = -9.60 \times 10^{-18} \text{ J} \end{aligned}$$

(Recall from above that 1 V = 1 J/C.)

Example 17-5 Electric Potential Difference in a Uniform Field II

Determine the electric potential difference $\Delta V = V_c - V_a$ between points a and c in the uniform electric field of Example 17-4. Point c is a distance 0.500 m from point a, and the straight-line path from a to c makes an angle of 126.9° with respect to the electric field.

Set Up

Again we'll use Equation 17-7 to calculate the potential difference between the two points. Since the displacement from point a to point c points generally opposite to the direction of the electric field, we expect that $\Delta V = V_c - V_a$ will be positive, just like $\Delta V = V_b - V_a$ in Example 17-4.

Potential difference between two points in a uniform electric field:

$$\Delta V = V_c - V_a = -Ed \cos \theta \qquad (17\text{-}7)$$

$E = 2.00 \times 10^2$ V/m

$d = 0.500$ m $\quad \theta = 126.9°$

Solve

Use Equation 17-7 to solve for the potential difference.

Calculate the potential difference from the electric field magnitude E, the displacement d, and the angle θ:

$$\begin{aligned} \Delta V = V_c - V_a &= -Ed \cos \theta \\ &= -(2.00 \times 10^2 \text{ V/m})(0.500 \text{ m}) \cos 126.9° \\ &= -(2.00 \times 10^2 \text{ V/m})(0.500 \text{ m})(-0.600) \\ &= +60.0 \text{ V} \end{aligned}$$

Reflect

The potential difference between points a and c is the *same* as the potential difference between points a and b in Example 17-4. Equation 17-7 tells us why this should be: The potential difference $\Delta V = -Ed \cos \theta$ involves the magnitude E of the electric field multiplied by $d \cos \theta$, which is the component of the displacement $\vec{d}$ in the direction of $\vec{E}$. In both examples the electric field magnitude has the same value (2.00×10^2 V/m), as does the component of displacement in the direction of the electric field (-0.300 m).

Another way to come to this same conclusion is to recognize that the displacement from a to c can be broken down into two parts: a displacement in the negative x direction from a to b, followed by a displacement from b to c in the y direction. The potential difference for the displacement from a to b is $V_b - V_a = +60.0$ V as we calculated in Example 17-4; the potential difference for the displacement from b to c is $V_c - V_b = -Ed \cos 90° = 0$ since that displacement is perpendicular to the electric field. So the net potential difference between a and c is $V_c - V_a = (V_c - V_b) + (V_b - V_a) = +60.0$ V + 0 V = +60.0 V.

Example 17-6 Transmission Electron Microscope

A *transmission electron microscope* forms an image by sending a beam of fast-moving electrons rather than a beam of light through a thin sample. As we will see in Chapter 26, such fast-moving electrons behave very much like a light wave. If the electrons have sufficiently high energy, the image that they form can show much finer detail than even the best optical microscope. The electrons are emitted from a heated metal filament and are then accelerated toward a second piece of metal called the *anode* that is at a potential 2.50 kV (1 kV = 1 kilovolt = 10^3 V) higher than that of the filament. If the electrons leave the filament initially at rest, how fast are the electrons traveling when they pass the anode?

Set Up

As the electrons move through the potential difference between the filament and the anode, the electric potential energy will change in accordance with Equation 17-6. Each electron has a negative charge $q_0 = -e$, so an *increase* in electric potential ($\Delta V > 0$) means a *decrease* in electric potential energy ($\Delta U_{\text{electric}} < 0$). The total mechanical energy (kinetic energy plus potential energy) is conserved as the electron moves because there are no forces acting on it other than the conservative electric force, so the electron kinetic energy will increase as the potential energy decreases.

Electric potential difference related to electric potential energy difference:

$$\Delta V = \frac{\Delta U_{\text{electric}}}{q_0} \qquad (17\text{-}6)$$

Mechanical energy is conserved:

$$E = K + U_{\text{electric}} = \text{constant}$$

filament

electrons

anode

$\Delta V = V_{\text{anode}} - V_{\text{filament}} = 2.50$ kV

Solve

Solve Equation 17-6 for the change in electric potential energy as the electron moves from the filament to the anode, which is at a potential 2.50 kV higher than the filament.

From Equation 17-6,

$$\Delta U_{\text{electric}} = q_0 \Delta V$$

The electron has change $q_0 = -e$, so

$$\Delta U_{\text{electric}} = -e\,\Delta V$$
$$= -(1.60 \times 10^{-19}\ \text{C})(+2.50 \times 10^3\ \text{V})$$
$$= -4.00 \times 10^{-16}\ \text{J}$$

(Recall that 1 V = 1 J/C, so 1 J = 1 C·V.)

The conservation of mechanical energy tells us that the change in the kinetic energy of the electron is equal to the negative of the change in the electric potential energy.

Mechanical energy is conserved:

$$E = K + U_{\text{electric}} = \text{constant}$$

So the *change* in mechanical energy is zero:

$$\Delta E = \Delta K + \Delta U_{\text{electric}} = 0$$

The change in the kinetic energy of the electron is

$$\Delta K = -\Delta U_{\text{electric}} = -(-4.00 \times 10^{-16}\ \text{J})$$
$$= +4.00 \times 10^{16}\ \text{J}$$

Each electron begins with zero kinetic energy, so the change in its kinetic energy is equal to its final kinetic energy as it reaches the anode.

Since the electron begins with zero kinetic energy at the filament, the change in its kinetic energy is

$$\Delta K = +4.00 \times 10^{-16}\ \text{J} = K_{\text{anode}} - K_{\text{filament}} = K_{\text{anode}}$$

Use this to find the speed of the electron at the anode:

$$K_{\text{anode}} = \frac{1}{2} m_{\text{electron}} v_{\text{anode}}^2 \text{ so}$$

$$v_{\text{anode}} = \sqrt{\frac{2K_{\text{anode}}}{m_{\text{electron}}}} = \sqrt{\frac{2(4.00 \times 10^{-16}\ \text{J})}{9.11 \times 10^{-31}\ \text{kg}}}$$

$$= 2.96 \times 10^7\ \text{m/s}$$

Reflect

The electrons are accelerated to nearly one-tenth of the speed of light ($c = 3.00 \times 10^8$ m/s).

Example 17-6 is just one of many situations in which an object with a charge of $-e$ (such as an electron) or $+e$ (such as a proton) moves through a potential difference. A common unit for the potential energy change in such situations is the **electron volt** (eV), which is equal to the magnitude e of the charge on the electron multiplied by 1 volt. Since $e = 1.60 \times 10^{-19}$ C, it follows that

$$1\ \text{eV} = (1.60 \times 10^{-19}\ \text{C})(1\ \text{V}) = 1.60 \times 10^{-19}\ \text{C·V} = 1.60 \times 10^{-19}\ \text{J}$$

In Example 17-6, the electron moves through a potential difference of $+2.50 \times 10^3$ V, so the change in electric potential energy is -2.50×10^3 eV and the kinetic energy that the electron acquires is $+2.50 \times 10^3$ eV. We also use the abbreviations 1 keV = 10^3 eV, 1 MeV = 10^6 eV, and 1 GeV = 10^9 eV. (The largest particle accelerator in the world, the Large Hadron Collider at the European Organization for Nuclear Research CERN near Geneva, Switzerland, accelerates protons to a kinetic energy of 7×10^{12} eV = 7 TeV. This is equivalent to making the protons pass through a potential difference of 7×10^{12}, or 7 trillion, volts.) In later chapters we'll see that the electron volt is a useful unit for expressing energies on the atomic or nuclear scale.

Electric Potential Due to a Point Charge

Note that Equation 17-7 is useful only in the case of a uniform electric field. Another important case is the electric potential due to a point charge Q. We know from Equation

17-3 that if we place a test charge q_0 a distance r from a point charge Q, the electric potential energy of the system of two charges is

$$U_{electric} = \frac{kq_0Q}{r}$$

Equation 17-5 tells us that to find the electric potential due to the point charge Q, we must divide $U_{electric}$ by the value of the test charge q_0:

Electric potential due to a point charge Q Coulomb constant

$$V = \frac{kQ}{r}$$

Value of the point charge

Distance from the point charge Q to the location where the potential is measured

Electric potential due to a point charge
(17-8)

Equation 17-8 says that all points that are the same distance r from a point charge have the same electric potential due to that charge. It also says that if $Q > 0$, the electric potential due to the charge is positive and decreases (becomes less positive) as you move farther away from the charge so that r increases. If $Q < 0$, the electric potential due to the charge is negative and decreases (becomes more negative) as you move closer to the charge. For either sign of Q, the electric potential goes to zero at an infinite distance from the point charge.

These observations about Equation 17-8 are consistent with our previous statements about electric potential and electric force. A positive test charge q_0 placed near a positive charge Q feels an electric force that pushes it farther away from Q, toward regions where the potential V due to Q is lower (less positive). If instead that positive test charge is placed near a negative charge Q, the test charge feels an electric force that pulls it toward Q—again, toward regions where the potential V is lower (in this case, more negative).

> **! Watch Out! Don't confuse the formulas for electric potential and electric field due to a point charge.**
>
> Be sure that you recognize the differences between Equation 17-8, $V = kQ/r$, and Equation 16-4 for the magnitude of the electric field due to a point charge Q, $E = k|Q|/r^2$. Equation 17-8 says that the potential V due to a point charge is inversely proportional to r and can be positive or negative, depending on the sign of Q. By contrast, Equation 16-4 tells us that the magnitude E of the field due to a point charge is inversely proportional to the *square* of r. Furthermore, because E is the magnitude of a vector, it is always positive (it is proportional to the absolute value of Q).

If there is not a single point charge but an assemblage of charges, the total electric potential at a given position due to these charges is the sum of the individual potentials. For example, for the case of three charges Q_1, Q_2, and Q_3, the potential at a point that is a distance r_1 from the first charge, a distance r_2 from the second charge, and a distance r_3 from the third charge is

$$V = \frac{kQ_1}{r_1} + \frac{kQ_2}{r_2} + \frac{kQ_3}{r_3}$$ (17-9)

(electric potential of three charges)

> **? Got the Concept? 17-2 Electric Potential Difference**
>
> Four point charges are each moved from one position to another position where the electric potential has a different value. Rank the four charges in order of the electric potential energy change that takes place, from most positive to most negative. (a) A +0.0010 C charge that moves through a potential increase of 5.0 V. (b) A +0.0020 C charge that moves through a potential decrease of 2.0 V. (c) A −0.0015 C charge that moves through a potential decrease of 4.0 V. (d) A −0.0010 C charge that moves through a potential increase of 2.5 V.

Take-Home Message for Section 17-3

✔ The electric potential at a certain position equals the electric potential energy per unit charge for a test charge at that position. Electric potential is a scalar, not a vector, quantity. Electric potential decreases as you move in the direction of the electric field.

✔ The electric potential due to a point charge is positive if the charge is positive, and negative if the charge is negative.

As you move farther from an isolated point charge, the electric potential becomes closer to zero.

✔ The electric potential due to a collection of charges is the sum of the potentials due to the individual charges.

✔ The electric potential difference between two points equals the difference in electric potential energy per unit charge between those points.

17-4 The electric potential has the same value everywhere on an equipotential surface

In Examples 17-4 and 17-5 in the previous section, we looked at the potential differences between two pairs of points in an electric field, a and b in Example 17-4 and a and c in Example 17-5. Although the electric field is the same in both examples, the distance from a to c in Example 17-5 is clearly longer than the distance from a to b in Example 17-4. So you might have expected that the potential difference $V_c - V_a$ in Example 17-5 would be greater in magnitude than the potential difference $V_b - V_a$ in Example 17-4. In fact we found that the potential differences were equal, which tells us that the potential is the *same* at points b and c. You can see why from Equation 17-7, $\Delta V = -Ed \cos \theta$. A displacement $\vec{d}$ from point b to point c is perpendicular to the electric field $\vec{E}$, so the angle in Equation 17-7 is $\theta = 90°$ and $\cos \theta = \cos 90° = 0$. Thus the potential difference ΔV between points b and c must be zero.

In general, the electric potential will be the same at any two points that lie along a curve perpendicular to electric field lines. Such a curve is called an *equipotential curve* or simply an **equipotential**. You can see that for the case of a uniform electric field, the electric potential will have the same value anywhere on a plane that's perpendicular to the electric field. Such a plane is an example of an **equipotential surface**, one on which the electric potential has the same value at all points (Figure 17-6). No work is required to move a charge from one point to another along any path on an equipotential surface. As we described in Section 17-3, the electric potential decreases as you move in the direction of the electric field $\vec{E}$, so the value of the potential V is lower for equipotential surfaces that are "downstream" in the electric field than on surfaces that are "upstream."

Figure 17-7 shows both electric field lines and equipotentials for the case of a *nonuniform* electric field. Note that the equipotential surfaces are perpendicular at *all* points to the field lines, just as for the case of a uniform field in Figure 17-6. But since

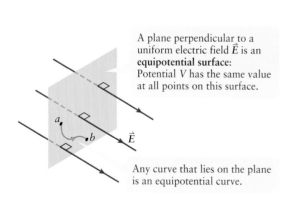

A plane perpendicular to a uniform electric field $\vec{E}$ is an **equipotential surface:** Potential V has the same value at all points on this surface.

Any curve that lies on the plane is an equipotential curve.

Figure 17-6 **Equipotential surfaces I** In a uniform electric field, equipotential surfaces are planes perpendicular to the electric field lines.

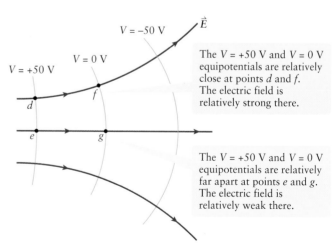

$V = -50$ V

$V = 0$ V

$V = +50$ V

$\vec{E}$

The $V = +50$ V and $V = 0$ V equipotentials are relatively close at points d and f. The electric field is relatively strong there.

The $V = +50$ V and $V = 0$ V equipotentials are relatively far apart at points e and g. The electric field is relatively weak there.

Figure 17-7 **Equipotential surfaces II** In a nonuniform electric field, equipotential surfaces are curved surfaces (seen here from the side) that are everywhere perpendicular to the electric field lines.

the electric field lines are not parallel lines, the equipotential surfaces are not flat planes. In general, *any* surface that is everywhere perpendicular to the electric field is an equipotential surface. Whether the field is uniform or not, the value of the potential V on an equipotential surface is lower the farther "downstream" in the electric field that surface is.

In Figure 17-7 points d and e are both on the equipotential for which $V = +50$ V, and points f and g are both on the equipotential for which $V = 0$ V. So the potential difference between points d and f is the same as the potential difference between points e and g:

$$V_d - V_f = V_e - V_g = (+50 \text{ V}) - (0 \text{ V}) = +50 \text{ V}$$

However, the distance between points d and f is less than that between points e and g. Equation 17-7 tells us that the potential difference between two points is proportional to the distance d between the points and the electric field magnitude E. (This equation is strictly valid only for a uniform field, but is still approximately true for a nonuniform field.) So the electric field must be greater between the points d and f that are closer together, and less between the points e and g that are farther apart. This is an example of a general rule:

Where two adjacent equipotential surfaces are close together, the electric field is relatively strong. Where these surfaces are far apart, the electric field is relatively weak.

Figure 17-8 shows an application of this idea. For a positive point charge (Figure 17-8a) or a negative point charge (Figure 17-8b), the electric field points radially outward or inward. The equipotential surfaces are everywhere perpendicular to the field

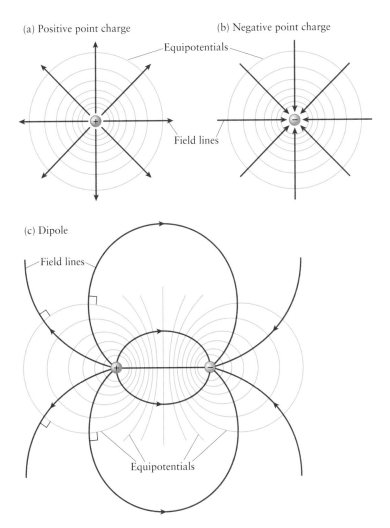

Figure 17-8 Equipotential surfaces
III The equipotential surfaces for a point charge are spheres centered on the point charge.

lines, so they are spheres centered on the point charge. (You could also conclude this from Equation 17-8 for the potential due to a point charge, $V = kQ/r$. This says that V has the same value at all points that are the same distance r from the point charge Q—that is, at all points on a sphere of radius r centered on the point charge.) The radial distance from one spherical equipotential surface to the next is the same no matter where you are around the sphere, so the electric field magnitude is the same at all points a given distance from the point charge. This agrees with Equation 16-4 for the field magnitude E due to a point charge, $E = k|Q|/r^2$; the value of E depends only on the distance from the charge, not on where you are around the charge. For an electric dipole, however, the situation is different (Figure 17-8c). The field lines arc from the positive charge to the negative one, and the equipotential surfaces are neither spherical nor centered on the point charges. (They are, however, everywhere perpendicular to the field lines.) Adjacent equipotential surfaces are close together between the two charges because the electric field is strong there. To the left of the left-hand charge or to the right of the right-hand charge, the electric field is relatively weak and adjacent equipotential surfaces are farther apart.

The equipotential concept is helpful for understanding the electric field around a charged conductor. We learned in Section 16-7 that if we put excess charge on a conductor and allow the individual excess charges to move to their equilibrium positions, all of the excess charge will end up on the conductor's surface and the electric field $\vec{E}$ will be zero everywhere inside the conductor. Since $\vec{E}$ is uniform inside the conductor (it has the same value at all points), we can use Equation 17-7 to calculate the potential difference between two points inside the conductor separated by a distance d: $\Delta V = -Ed \cos \theta = 0$ because $E = 0$. In other words, *the electric potential has the same value everywhere inside a conductor in equilibrium*. We say that a conductor in equilibrium is an **equipotential volume**. That's why we can make statements like "This conductor is at a potential of +20 V"—the value of potential is the same everywhere throughout the volume of the conductor. When we say that each of the batteries in Figure 17-1a has a voltage of 1.5 V, we mean that the potential of the conductor at the positive end of the battery is 1.5 V higher than the potential of the conductor at the negative end. The potential difference is the same between any point on the positive terminal and any point on the negative terminal.

The electric field *outside* a charged conductor is *not* zero. If the excess charge on the conductor is positive, the electric field will point away from the surface of the conductor; if the excess charge is negative, the electric field will point toward the surface. Because the surface of the conductor is part of the equipotential volume, it is itself an equipotential surface. Because field lines and equipotential surfaces are always perpendicular, we conclude that *the electric field just outside a conductor in equilibrium must be perpendicular to the surface of the conductor*. Since the electric field always points toward lower electric potential, we can also conclude that *a positively charged conductor is at a higher electric potential than an adjacent negatively charged conductor*. We'll use these ideas about conductors in the following section to help us understand an important device called a *capacitor*.

? Got the Concept? 17-3 Equipotentials and Electric Field

The orange vertical lines in Figure 17-9 represent equipotential curves in some region of space. Which statement is correct about the electric field $\vec{E}$ at point A compared to the electric field at point B? (a) At A the field $\vec{E}$ points to the right and has a greater magnitude than at B; (b) at A the field $\vec{E}$ points to the right and has a smaller magnitude than at B; (c) at A the field $\vec{E}$ points to the left and has a greater magnitude than at B; (d) at A the field $\vec{E}$ points to the left and has a smaller magnitude than at B; (e) none of these.

Figure 17-9 **What equipotentials tell you about $\vec{E}$** What can you infer from this figure about the electric field at A and B?

17-5 A capacitor stores equal amounts of positive and negative charge

The surface of every cell in your body is a *membrane* composed of a phospholipid bilayer that separates the intracellular fluid (inside the cell) and the extracellular fluid (outside the cell). Negative charge accumulates on the membrane's intracellular (interior) surface, and this attracts positive charge onto the extracellular (exterior) surface. The result is a potential difference between the inner and outer surfaces of the membrane, and an electric field within the membrane that points from the outside in. This field and associated potential help drive essential ions through apertures in the membrane. They are also the source of the electrical signal used by the specialized cells called neurons to code, process, and transmit information.

A system or device that can store positive and negative charge like a cell membrane is called a **capacitor**. In technological applications, a capacitor does not use a membrane per se but instead uses two pieces of metal called **plates**. One plate holds a positive charge q, and the other carries a negative charge $-q$. (Note that the *net* charge on the capacitor is zero.) It takes work to separate the positive and negative charges against the electric forces that attract them to each other, and this work goes into increasing the electric potential energy of the system of charge. So a capacitor is a device for storing electric potential energy. As we'll see in the following section, this stored energy is analogous to the elastic potential energy stored in a stretched or compressed spring. We often need to draw capacitors in diagrams that represent electric circuits. The standard symbol for a capacitor in the diagram of a circuit is

The two closely spaced parallel lines represent the two plates of the capacitor, and the straight horizontal lines represent wires that connect the capacitor to the rest of the circuit.

The simplest geometry for a capacitor is two large parallel plates, one with charge $+q$ and the other with charge $-q$. **Figure 17-10a** shows these two plates separated from each other. We saw in Section 16-7 that close to a large charged plate and far from its edges the electric field due to that plate is uniform, is perpendicular to the plane of the plate, and has magnitude $E = \sigma/(2\varepsilon_0)$ (from Equation 16-14). In this expression σ is the charge per unit area, equal to the charge q divided by the area A of the plate: $\sigma = q/A$. Since each plate has the same magnitude of charge, the field $\vec{E}_+$ due to the charge on the positive plate has the same magnitude as the field $\vec{E}_-$ due to the charge on the negative plate.

For a capacitor the *net* electric field is the vector sum of $\vec{E}_+$ and $\vec{E}_-$: $\vec{E} = \vec{E}_+ + \vec{E}_-$. **Figure 17-10b** shows the two plates moved into position to form a **parallel-plate capacitor**. Because the magnitude of each field does not depend on the distance from the plate that generates the field, $\vec{E}_+$ cancels $\vec{E}_-$ in the region above the upper plate and below the lower plate. Between the plates the fields $\vec{E}_+$ and $\vec{E}_-$ have the same magnitude and point in the same direction, so the net field between the plates has twice the magnitude of the field due to either plate by itself:

$$E = 2\left(\frac{\sigma}{2\varepsilon_0}\right) = \frac{\sigma}{\varepsilon_0} = \frac{q}{\varepsilon_0 A} \qquad (17\text{-}10)$$

(electric field in a parallel-plate capacitor)

(a)

Two large plates (viewed from the side) carry charge +q and −q. Close to the plates the electric fields are nearly constant, so we represent them by straight, parallel field lines.

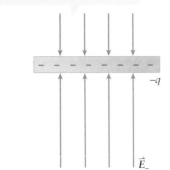

(b)

Because the fields are nearly constant, the magnitude of the field due to each plate is the same at any point near the plates...

(c)

... so when the plates are placed close together, the fields cancel in the region outside the plates. The fields add in between the plates.

Figure 17-10 **Electric field of a parallel-plate capacitor** The field due to two oppositely charged plates is the vector sum of the fields due to each plate.

Note that the electric field points from the positive plate to the negative plate, just as we described in our discussion of conductors in Section 17-4.

(Equation 17-10 and the claim that $\vec{E}_+$ and $\vec{E}_-$ cancel outside the capacitor are strictly true only if the plates are large and close together, and when we consider points in space far from the edges of the capacitor. This idealization is physically reasonable for the kinds of problems we will encounter.)

We can substitute Equation 17-10 into Equation 17-7 to calculate the *potential difference* between the plates of a parallel-plate capacitor. The electric field points from the positive plate to the negative plate. If we let d be the distance between the plates, and we travel from the negative plate to the positive plate, the angle between the electric field and the displacement is $\theta = 180°$. The potential difference is therefore

$$V = V_+ - V_- = -Ed\cos\theta = -Ed(-1)$$

$$= Ed = \left(\frac{q}{\varepsilon_0 A}\right)d$$

(17-11)

$$= \frac{qd}{\varepsilon_0 A}$$

! Watch Out! The symbol *V* sometimes stands for potential, sometimes for potential difference.

Previously in this chapter we've used V to denote the electric potential at a given point and ΔV to denote the difference in electric potential between two points. In Equation 17-11, and throughout our discussion of capacitors, we'll follow common practice and use V as the symbol for the potential difference, or voltage, between the two capacitor plates. Just remember "for capacitors, V means voltage." We'll frequently refer to V as the "voltage *across* the capacitor."

For a given capacitor of fixed plate area A and plate separation d, the potential difference V between the plates is proportional to the magnitude of the charge q on each plate.

We can rewrite Equation 17-11 as an expression for the amount of charge on each plate. To charge an initially uncharged capacitor, we apply a voltage V between its plates as in **Figure 17-11**. Electrons are driven to one of the plates, giving it a charge $-q$; the plate from which the electrons were taken is left with a charge $+q$. (As we mentioned previously, the net charge on the capacitor remains zero.) Equation 17-11 tells us that the magnitude q of the charge that each plate acquires is proportional to the applied voltage V:

$$q = \frac{\varepsilon_0 A}{d} V$$

(17-12)

(charge on a parallel-plate capacitor)

The quantity $\varepsilon_0 A/d$ in Equation 17-12 is called the **capacitance** of the capacitor. We use the symbol C for capacitance:

Capacitance of a parallel-plate capacitor   Permittivity of free space = $1/(4\pi k)$

$$C = \frac{\varepsilon_0 A}{d}$$

Area of each capacitor plate

Distance between the capacitor plates

Capacitance of a parallel-plate capacitor
(17-13)

For a parallel-plate capacitor, C depends only on the area A of the plates, the distance d between them, and the material between them. We've assumed that the plates are separated by vacuum; in Section 17-8 we'll explore what happens if the space between the capacitor plates is filled with a different material. Capacitance is therefore a compact way to summarize the electrical properties of a capacitor. In particular, capacitance tells us the amount of charge that can be stored on a capacitor held at a given voltage. From Equations 17-12 and 17-13,

A capacitor carries a charge $+q$ on its positive plate and a charge $-q$ on its negative plate.   The magnitude of q is directly proportional to V, the voltage (potential difference) between the plates.

$$q = CV$$

The constant of proportionality between charge q and voltage V is the capacitance C of the capacitor.

> Go to Picture It 17-3 for more practice dealing with capacitance

Charge, voltage, and capacitance for a capacitor
(17-14)

This equation says that the magnitude of the charge on the plates of a capacitor is directly proportional to the voltage between the plates. The greater the capacitance, the more charge is present for a given voltage. Note that while Equations 17-12 and 17-13 are valid for a parallel-plate capacitor only, Equation 17-14 is valid for capacitors of *any* geometry. In the problems at the end of this chapter you'll analyze some other simple types of capacitor.

Equation 17-14 shows that the unit of capacitance is the coulomb per volt, also known as the **farad** (symbol F): $1\ \text{F} = 1\ \text{C/V}$. The farad is named for the nineteenth-century English physicist Michael Faraday. The capacitors you'll find in your neighborhood electronics supply store are typically in the range of 10 pF (10×10^{-12} F) to 1000 μF (1000×10^{-6} F); 1 F is an extremely large capacitance. Using $1\ \text{F} = 1\ \text{C/V}$, $1\ \text{V} = 1\ \text{J/C}$, and $1\ \text{J} = 1\ \text{N} \cdot \text{m}$, we see that $1\ \text{F} = (1\ \text{C})/(1\ \text{J/C}) = 1\ \text{C}^2/\text{J} = 1\ \text{C}^2/(\text{N} \cdot \text{m})$. We can express the value of the constant ε_0 (the permittivity of free space) as

$$\varepsilon_0 = 8.85 \times 10^{-12}\ \frac{\text{C}^2}{\text{N} \cdot \text{m}^2} = 8.85 \times 10^{-12}\ \frac{\text{F}}{\text{m}}$$

These units are useful in calculations of capacitance, as we'll see below.

When this battery is connected to the plates of a capacitor, it creates a potential difference V between the plates...

Battery

$+q$ $-q$

...which drives electrons from one plate, through the battery, and onto the other plate. The plate that lost electrons ends up with charge $+q$, and the other plate ends up with charge $-q$.

Figure 17-11 Charging a capacitor The charges that appear on the two capacitor plates have the same magnitude but opposite signs.

Figure 17-12 Capacitive touchscreens Mobile devices such as these use the physics of capacitors to determine where your finger touches the screen.

An everyday application of Equation 17-13 is the touchscreen on a mobile device such as a smartphone or tablet (**Figure 17-12**). Behind the device's glass screen is a layer of a special transparent conductor called indium tin oxide (ITO), which is actually a solid mixture of indium oxide, In_2O_3, and tin oxide, SnO_2. When you touch your finger to the screen, the conducting ITO layer acts as one plate of a capacitor and your finger—which is also a conductor—acts as the other plate. Sensor circuits in the mobile device detect where on the screen a capacitance appears due to this capacitor, which is how the device "knows" where on the screen it has been touched. (To verify that the object touching the screen has to be a conductor, try using the rubber eraser on a pencil to touch the screen of a mobile device. Because rubber is an insulator, not a conductor, the screen won't respond.) The sensor circuits are adjusted so that they will only register if the capacitance C is above a certain minimum value. That explains why you have to physically touch the screen: According to Equation 17-13, C increases as the distance d between the plates decreases, so the capacitance is largest when your finger is touching the screen and so closest to the ITO layer. Your finger still acts as a capacitor plate if you hold it a slight distance away from the screen, but the capacitance is now too low to trigger the sensor circuits.

Example 17-7 A Parallel-Plate Capacitor

Two square, parallel conducting plates each have dimensions 5.00 cm by 5.00 cm and are placed 0.100 mm apart. Determine the capacitance of this configuration.

Set Up

We'll use Equation 17-13 to determine the value of C for this capacitor.

Capacitance of a parallel-plate capacitor:

$$C = \frac{\varepsilon_0 A}{d} \qquad (17\text{-}13)$$

Solve

The area of each plate is the product of the length of the two sides, and the plate separation is given. We need to convert all dimensions into SI units.

Area $A = (5.00 \times 10^{-2} \text{ m})(5.00 \times 10^{-2} \text{ m}) = 2.50 \times 10^{-3} \text{ m}^2$

Plate separation $d = 1.00 \times 10^{-4} \text{ m}$

Using Equation 17-13,

$$C = \frac{(8.85 \times 10^{-12} \text{ F/m})(2.50 \times 10^{-3} \text{ m}^2)}{1.00 \times 10^{-4} \text{ m}} = 2.21 \times 10^{-10} \text{ F}$$
$$= 221 \text{ pF}$$

(Recall that the prefix "p" or pico– represents 10^{-12}.)

Reflect

Capacitors with capacitances of a few hundred picofarads are well within the range available from your local electronics supply store and are likely found in calculators, cell phones, and portable music players.

To make a 1-F capacitor with the same separation $d = 0.100$ mm between plates, we would have to increase the plate area by a factor of $(1 \text{ F})/(2.21 \times 10^{-10} \text{ F}) = 4.52 \times 10^9$. The length of each side would have to be increased by a factor of the square root of 4.52×10^9, or 6.73×10^4. The sides of the plates would be $(6.73 \times 10^4)(5.00 \times 10^{-2} \text{ m}) = 3.36 \times 10^3$ m, or 3.36 *kilometers* (about 2 miles). One farad is a *very* large capacitance.

Example 17-8 Insulin Release

The hormone insulin minimizes variations in blood glucose levels. Pancreatic beta cells ("β-cells") synthesize insulin and store it in *vesicles*, bubble-like organelles approximately 150 nm in radius within the cytoplasm of the cells. To release insulin, vesicles fuse with the membrane of the β-cell. This increases the surface area of the β-cell by the surface area of the fused vesicles (Figure 17-13). The thickness of the cell membrane does not change, so the increase in surface area increases the capacitance of the β-cell membrane. Experiment shows that the membrane capacitance increases at 1.6×10^{-13} F/s during insulin release. If the membrane capacitance is approximately 1 μF per square centimeter of surface area, estimate the number of vesicles that fuse with the cell membrane per second during insulin release.

An insulin-producing beta cell from the pancreas

Red circles outline vesicles containing insulin.

Cell membrane

4. The vesicle has reformed and is ready to be filled with insulin.

3. The vesicle is reforming.

1. One vesicle is fusing with the cell membrane.

2. Now the vesicle has released its insulin to the outside of the cell. The vesicle membrane is part of the cell membrane.

Figure 17-13 **Changing membrane, changing capacitance** To study this important process in a pancreatic β-cell, scientists monitor changes in the capacitance of the cell membrane.

Set Up

Although the cell membrane is not flat like the parallel-plate capacitor shown in Figure 17-10, we can treat it as such because the size of the cell is large compared to the thickness of the cell membrane. (It's like being above Earth's surface at a height that's much smaller than Earth's radius. While Earth is approximately spherical, when seen from such a short distance it appears to be flat.) We'll use Equation 17-13 to calculate the rate at which the area A of the cell membrane must increase to cause the measured rate of capacitance increase. This increase in area comes from fusing vesicles.

Capacitance of a parallel-plate capacitor:

$$C = \frac{\varepsilon_0 A}{d} \qquad (17\text{-}13)$$

Surface area of a sphere of radius r:

$$A_{\text{sphere}} = 4\pi r^2$$

Solve

Find the rate at which the membrane area must increase to cause this rate of capacitance increase.

Rate of change of the capacitance of the membrane:

$$\frac{\Delta C_{\text{m}}}{\Delta t} = 1.6 \times 10^{-13}\ \text{F/s}$$

Equation 17-13 tells us that the capacitance C_{m} is directly proportional to the membrane surface area A_{m}. We are told that the capacitance per unit area is approximately 1 μF/cm^2, so the change in capacitance ΔC_{m} that corresponds to a given change in area ΔA_{m} is

$$\Delta C_{\text{m}} = \left(1\ \frac{\mu\text{F}}{\text{cm}^2}\right)\Delta A_{\text{m}}$$

Since the capacitance increases by 1.6×10^{-13} F in 1 s, the increase in area of the membrane in 1 s must be

$$\begin{aligned}
\Delta A_{\text{m}} &= \frac{\Delta C_{\text{m}}}{1\ \mu\text{F/cm}^2} \\
&= (1.6 \times 10^{-13}\ \text{F})\left(1\ \frac{\text{cm}^2}{\mu\text{F}}\right)\left(\frac{1\ \mu\text{F}}{10^{-6}\ \text{F}}\right)\left(\frac{1\ \text{m}}{100\ \text{cm}}\right)^2 \\
&= 1.6 \times 10^{-11}\ \text{m}^2
\end{aligned}$$

(We used 1 μF = 1 microfarad = 10^{-6} F and 1 m = 100 cm.)

Now we can calculate how many vesicles must fuse with the membrane per second to cause this increase in area.

The surface area of a single vesicle is

$$A_{\text{vesicle}} = 4\pi r_{\text{vesicle}}^2 = 4\pi (150 \text{ nm})^2 = 4\pi (150 \times 10^{-9} \text{ m})^2$$
$$= 2.8 \times 10^{-13} \text{ m}^2$$

The number of vesicles that must add their area to the membrane in 1 s to cause an area increase $\Delta A_m = 1.6 \times 10^{-11} \text{ m}^2$ is

$$\frac{\Delta A_m}{A_{\text{vesicle}}} = \frac{1.6 \times 10^{-11} \text{ m}^2}{2.8 \times 10^{-13} \text{ m}^2/\text{vesicle}} = 57 \text{ vesicles}$$

Our final answer should have just one significant figure, since we were given the capacitance per unit area 1 μF/cm^2 to just one significant figure. So our final answer is that about 60 vesicles fuse with the membrane wall per second.

Reflect

The ability to detect small changes in capacitance makes it possible to study the molecular mechanisms of hormone release from single cells and to verify previous biochemical measurements of insulin release from β-cells. After insulin release, new vesicles form by pinching off from the cell membrane and are refilled with insulin. By recycling the vesicle membrane, β-cells maintain their size over the long term.

? Got the Concept? 17-4 Capacitors

A parallel-plate capacitor has a potential difference V between its plates. If the potential difference is increased to $2V$, what effect does this have on the capacitance C? (a) C increases by a factor of 4; (b) C increases by a factor of 2; (c) C becomes $\frac{1}{2}$ as great; (d) C becomes $\frac{1}{4}$ as great; (e) C is unchanged.

Take-Home Message for Section 17-5

✔ A capacitor has two plates, one with charge $+q$ and the other with charge $-q$.

✔ For a given capacitor the potential difference between the plates is proportional to the magnitude of the charge q on each plate. The proportionality constant, called the capacitance, depends on the geometry of the plates and on the material in the space between the plates.

17-6 A capacitor is a storehouse of electric potential energy

In electric circuits, capacitors are most useful because of their ability to store electric potential energy. An applied voltage V such as that supplied by the battery in Figure 17-11 charges a capacitor by effectively pulling negative charges from one of the plates and depositing them on the other. To move the negative charges away from the positive charges requires work, and it is this work that results in electric potential energy being stored in the capacitor. At a later time, the potential energy can be transferred by charge leaving the capacitor and passed on to other parts of the circuit. (That's what happens in the electronic flash unit in a camera or mobile phone. The device's battery charges a capacitor, and the energy stored in the charged capacitor is used to produce a short, intense burst of light.)

Let's see how to calculate the amount of electric potential energy stored in a capacitor that has charge $+q$ and $-q$ on its positive and negative plates, respectively. This is equal to the amount of electric potential energy that's added to the capacitor if we start with both plates uncharged (which we can regard as a state of zero potential energy) and move charge $+q$ from the first plate to the second one, leaving charge $-q$ on the first plate. If the potential difference between the plates had a constant value ΔV,

Equation 17-6 tells us that the change in electric potential energy $\Delta U_{electric}$ in this process would be

$$\Delta V = \frac{\Delta U_{electric}}{q} \quad \text{so} \quad \Delta U_{electric} = q\,\Delta V$$

However, the potential difference between the plates (that is, the voltage across the capacitor) does *not* stay constant as we transfer charge from one plate to the other! Equation 17-14 tells us that the potential difference between the plates is proportional to the amount of charge on the positive plate. So as we transfer more charge from one plate to the other, the potential difference across which the charge must move increases from zero (its starting value) to a final value V given by Equation 17-14: $q = CV$, so $V = q/C$. To correctly calculate the amount of potential energy stored in the capacitor when it is charged, we have to replace ΔV in Equation 17-6 by the *average* value of the potential difference during the charging process. Because potential difference increases in direct proportion to the charge, this average value is just the average of the starting potential difference and the final potential difference V:

$$\Delta U_{electric} = q\,\Delta V_{average}$$
$$= q\left[\frac{(\text{starting potential difference}) + (\text{final potential difference})}{2}\right]$$
$$= q\left(\frac{0 + V}{2}\right) = \frac{1}{2}qV \tag{17-15}$$

Equation 17-14 tells us that $q = CV$ and $V = q/C$, so we can also write Equation 17-15 as

$$\Delta U_{electric} = \frac{1}{2}(CV)V = \frac{1}{2}CV^2 \quad \text{or} \quad \Delta U_{electric} = \frac{1}{2}q\left(\frac{q}{C}\right) = \frac{q^2}{2C} \tag{17-16}$$

If we say that the electric potential energy of the initial uncharged capacitor was zero, the final potential energy $U_{electric}$ is just equal to the increase in potential energy $\Delta U_{electric}$ given by Equation 17-15 or Equation 17-16. So we can write the potential energy stored in the capacitor in three ways:

The electric potential energy stored in a charged capacitor...

$$U_{electric} = \frac{1}{2}qV = \frac{1}{2}CV^2 = \frac{q^2}{2C}$$

...can be expressed in three ways in terms of the charge q, potential difference V, and capacitance C.

Electric potential energy stored in a capacitor
(17-17)

Equation 17-17 says that the energy stored in a charged capacitor is proportional to the *square* of the charge q or, equivalently, to the square of the potential difference (voltage) V across the capacitor. These results are true for capacitors of all kinds, not just the simple parallel-plate capacitor that we discussed in Section 17-5.

The last of the three expressions for electric potential energy in Equation 17-17, $U_{electric} = q^2/(2C)$, is very similar to the equation for *spring* potential energy that we learned in Section 6-6:

Spring potential energy of a stretched or compressed spring   Spring constant of the spring

$$U_{spring} = \frac{1}{2}kx^2$$

Extension of the spring ($x > 0$ if spring is stretched, $x < 0$ if spring is compressed)

Spring potential energy
(6-19)

The only differences between $U_{electric} = q^2/(2C)$ from Equation 17-17 and the expression in Equation 6-19 is that the spring displacement x is replaced by the charge

q and the spring constant k is replaced by the reciprocal of the capacitance, $1/C$. This similarity isn't surprising. To add potential energy to a spring by stretching it, you have to pull against the force of magnitude $F = kx$ that the spring exerts on you. The greater the distance that the spring is already stretched, the more force it exerts and the harder it is to stretch it further. In exactly the same way, to add potential energy to a capacitor by increasing the magnitude of charge on the two plates, you have to transfer charge against a voltage $V = (1/C)q$. The greater the charge that is already on the plates, the greater the voltage and the harder it is to increase q. In later chapters we'll make more use of this analogy between displacement x and force $F = kx$ for a spring and charge q and voltage $V = (1/C)q$ for a capacitor.

Example 17-9 A Defibrillator Capacitor

A defibrillator, like the one shown in the photograph that opens this chapter, is essentially a capacitor that is charged by a high-voltage source and then delivers the stored energy to a patient's heart. (a) How much charge does the 80.0-μF capacitor in a certain defibrillator store when it is fully charged by applying 2.50 kV? (b) How much energy can this defibrillator deliver?

Set Up

We're given the capacitance $C = 80.0$ μF (recall 1 μF = 1 microfarad = 10^{-6} F) and the potential difference $V = 2.50$ kV (recall 1 kV = 1 kilovolt = 10^3 V) between the capacitor plates. We'll use Equation 17-14 to determine the magnitude q of the charge on each capacitor plate, and Equation 17-17 to find the potential energy $U_{electric}$ stored in the charged capacitor. If we assume that no energy is lost in the process of being transferred to the patient, this is equal to the energy that the defibrillator delivers.

Charge, voltage, and capacitance for a capacitor:

$$q = CV \tag{17-14}$$

Electric potential energy stored in a capacitor:

$$U_{electric} = \frac{1}{2}qV = \frac{1}{2}CV^2 = \frac{q^2}{2C} \tag{17-17}$$

Solve

(a) Substitute the given values of C and V into Equation 17-14 to solve for the charge q.

Charge on the capacitor plates:

$$q = CV = (80.0 \ \mu\text{F})(2.50 \text{ kV})$$
$$= (80.0 \times 10^{-6} \text{ F})(2.50 \times 10^3 \text{ V})$$
$$= 0.200 \text{ F} \cdot \text{V} = 0.200 \text{ C}$$

(Recall that 1 F = 1 C/V, so 1 F$\cdot$V = 1 C.)

(b) Since the values of C and V are given, let's use the second of the three relationships in Equation 17-17 to find the stored electric potential energy.

Energy stored in the capacitor:

$$U_{electric} = \frac{1}{2}CV^2$$
$$= \frac{1}{2}(80.0 \times 10^{-6} \text{ F})(2.50 \times 10^3 \text{ V})^2$$
$$= 2.50 \times 10^2 \text{ F} \cdot \text{V}^2$$
$$= 2.50 \times 10^2 \text{ J}$$

(Recall that 1 V = 1 J/C and 1 F = 1 C/V, so 1 F$\cdot$V^2 = 1 (C/V)V^2 = 1 C$\cdot$V = 1 C$\cdot$(J/C) = 1 J.)

Reflect

The American Heart Association recommends that a defibrillator shock should deliver between 40 and 360 J in order to be effective, so our numerical result is in the recommended range.

We can double-check our answers by using the other two relationships in Equation 17-17. Happily, by using the value of q that we

One alternative way to calculate the energy stored in the capacitor:

$$U_{electric} = \frac{1}{2}qV$$
$$= \frac{1}{2}(0.200 \text{ C})(2.50 \times 10^3 \text{ V})$$
$$= 2.50 \times 10^2 \text{ C} \cdot \text{V}$$
$$= 2.50 \times 10^2 \text{ J}$$

calculated in part (a) we get the same result for $U_{electric}$ in part (b) as we found above.

Remember that in solving any problem, you should *always* take advantage of alternative ways to find the answer in order to check your results.

Another alternative way to calculate the energy stored in the capacitor:

$$U_{electric} = \frac{q^2}{2C}$$

$$= \frac{(0.200\ \text{C})^2}{2(80.0 \times 10^{-6}\ \text{F})}$$

$$= 2.50 \times 10^2 \frac{\text{C}^2}{\text{F}}$$

$$= 2.50 \times 10^2\ \text{J}$$

(Recall that $1\ \text{V} = 1\ \text{J/C}$ and $1\ \text{F} = 1\ \text{C/V}$. You should verify that $1\ \text{C}^2/\text{F} = 1\ \text{J}$.)

? Got the Concept? 17-5 Spreading the Plates of a Capacitor I

Suppose you increase the distance between the plates of a charged parallel-plate capacitor without changing the amount of charge stored on the plates. What will happen to the energy stored in the capacitor? (a) It will decrease; (b) it will remain the same; (c) it will increase; (d) not enough information given to decide.

? Got the Concept? 17-6 Spreading the Plates of a Capacitor II

Suppose you increase the distance between the plates of a parallel-plate capacitor while holding the potential difference between the plates constant. (You could do this by keeping the plates connected to a battery, as in Figure 17-11.) What will happen to the energy stored in the capacitor? (a) It will decrease; (b) it will remain the same; (c) it will increase; (d) not enough information given to decide.

Take-Home Message for Section 17-6

✔ A charged capacitor stores electric potential energy. The amount of energy stored is proportional to the square of the magnitude of the charge on each plate, and also proportional to the square of the potential difference between the plates.

17-7 Capacitors can be combined in series or in parallel

In both biological systems and electric circuits, it is not uncommon for more than one capacitor to be connected together in some way. The net result is that the capacitor combination behaves as though it were a *single* capacitor, with an **equivalent capacitance** that depends on the properties of the individual capacitors actually present. (An analogy is lifting a heavy conference table to move it across the room. Four people of normal strength could do the job, or it could be done by a single weightlifter. We would say that the weightlifter has an "equivalent strength" equal to that of the combination of four normal people.) Our goal in this section is to find the equivalent capacitance in different situations.

Capacitors in Series

Figure 17-14 shows three initially uncharged capacitors with capacitances C_1, C_2, and C_3 that are connected end to end. The capacitors become charged when the combination is connected to a battery of voltage V as shown in the figure. Note that the negative plate of one capacitor is connected to the positive plate of the next capacitor in the combination. Capacitors connected in this way are said to be in **series**.

What is the equivalent capacitance of this series combination? To answer this question, let's first determine the charges q_1, q_2, and q_3 on the individual capacitors and the

Figure 17-14 **Capacitors in series**
What is the equivalent capacitance of
this series combination?

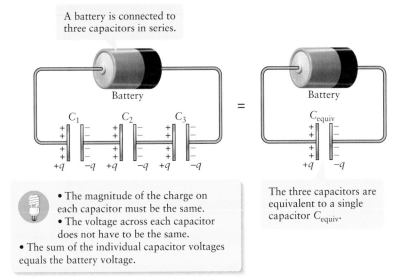

A battery is connected to
three capacitors in series.

• The magnitude of the charge on
each capacitor must be the same.
• The voltage across each capacitor
does not have to be the same.
• The sum of the individual capacitor voltages
equals the battery voltage.

The three capacitors are
equivalent to a single
capacitor C_{equiv}.

voltages V_1, V_2, and V_3 across the individual capacitors. For each capacitor, the magnitudes of the charge on the positive and negative plates must be equal. So as the battery draws negative charge from the left-hand plate of C_1, whatever positive charge $+q$ that plate acquires must be balanced by charge $-q$ on the right plate. The charging of the right plate of C_1 occurs as negative charge is drawn from the left plate of C_2, and because this whole section is initially uncharged, the left plate of C_2 acquires charge $+q$. If we apply the same reasoning to C_3, we see that all three capacitors acquire the *same* charge:

(17-18)
$$q_1 = q_2 = q_3 = q$$
(capacitors in series)

Thus the series combination of three capacitors is equivalent to a single capacitor with charge q. You can think of the charge on the negative plate of C_1 as canceling the charge on the positive plate of C_2, and likewise for the charges on the negative plate of C_2 and the positive plate of C_3. So the three capacitors are equivalent to a single capacitor with charge q.

The charges and voltages for each capacitor are also given by Equation 17-14, $q = CV$. If we substitute this into Equation 17-18, we get

$$q = C_1 V_1 = C_2 V_2 = C_3 V_3$$
(capacitors in series)

which we can rewrite as expressions for the voltages across the individual capacitors:

(17-19)
$$V_1 = \frac{q}{C_1} \quad V_2 = \frac{q}{C_2} \quad V_3 = \frac{q}{C_3}$$
(capacitors in series)

Now, the voltage V of the battery equals the voltage across the combination of three capacitors. This is just the sum of the voltages across the individual capacitors:

(17-20)
$$V = V_1 + V_2 + V_3$$
(capacitors in series)

If we substitute Equations 17-19 into Equation 17-20, we get a relationship between the charge q on each capacitor and the voltage V across the combination—that is, between the charge q on the equivalent capacitor and the voltage V across the equivalent capacitor:

(17-21)
$$V = \frac{q}{C_1} + \frac{q}{C_2} + \frac{q}{C_3} = q\left(\frac{1}{C_1} + \frac{1}{C_2} + \frac{1}{C_3}\right)$$
(capacitors in series)

For the equivalent capacitor alone, of capacitance C_{equiv}, Equation 17-14 says that $q = C_{equiv}V$ or $V = q/C_{equiv}$. If we compare this to Equation 17-21, we see that

 If capacitors are in series, the reciprocal of the equivalent capacitance is the sum of the reciprocals of the individual capacitances.

Equivalent capacitance of capacitors in series (17-22)

$$\frac{1}{C_{equiv}} = \frac{1}{C_1} + \frac{1}{C_2} + \frac{1}{C_3}$$

Equivalent capacitance of capacitors in series

Capacitances of the individual capacitors

If there are more than three capacitors in series, the same rule given in Equation 17-22 applies.

Here's how to follow the prescription of Equation 17-22: (1) Take the reciprocal of each individual capacitance in the series combination, (2) add these reciprocals to find $1/C_{equiv}$, then (3) take the reciprocal of that result to find C_{equiv}. The equivalent capacitance of a series combination is always *less* than the smallest capacitance of any of the individual capacitors.

Capacitors in Parallel

Figure 17-15 shows an alternative way to connect the three initially uncharged capacitors C_1, C_2, and C_3 to a battery with voltage V. Capacitors connected in this way are said to be in **parallel**. Notice the difference in the arrangement of the capacitors in parallel (Figure 17-15) compared to capacitors in series (Figure 17-14). In a series arrangement, the right-hand plate of one capacitor is connected to the left-hand plate of the capacitor to its right. In a parallel arrangement, all of the right-hand plates are connected, and all of the left-hand plates are connected.

To find the equivalent capacitance of capacitors in parallel, first note that all of the right-hand capacitor plates are connected to one terminal of the battery and all of the left-hand plates are connected to the other terminal. So each of the voltages V_1, V_2, and V_3 across the individual capacitors is equal to the voltage V across the battery:

$$V = V_1 = V_2 = V_3$$

(capacitors in parallel)

(17-23)

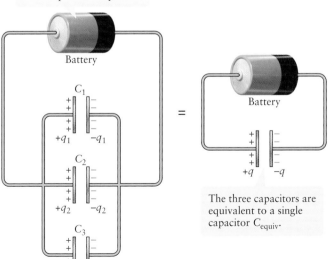

A battery is connected to three capacitors in parallel.

The three capacitors are equivalent to a single capacitor C_{equiv}.

 • The voltage across each capacitor must be the same.
• The charges on each capacitor do not have to be the same.
• The sum of the individual capacitor charges equals the charge q on the equivalent capacitor.

Figure 17-15 Capacitors in parallel
What is the equivalent capacitance of this parallel combination?

Equation 17-23 coupled with Equation 17-14, $q = CV$, then tells us the charges q_1, q_2, and q_3 on the individual capacitors:

(17-24)
$$q_1 = C_1 V \quad q_2 = C_2 V \quad q_3 = C_3 V$$
$$\text{(capacitors in parallel)}$$

The *total* charge acquired by all three capacitors is the sum of the charges q_1, q_2, and q_3. From Equation 17-24,

(17-25)
$$q = q_1 + q_2 + q_3 = C_1 V + C_2 V + C_3 V$$
$$= (C_1 + C_2 + C_3) V$$
$$\text{(capacitors in parallel)}$$

For the equivalent capacitor of capacitance C_{equiv} that corresponds to the three capacitors in parallel, Equation 17-14 says that $q = C_{equiv} V$. Comparing this to Equation 17-25 shows that

Equivalent capacitance of capacitors in parallel
(17-26)

Equivalent capacitance of capacitors in parallel   Capacitances of the individual capacitors

$$C_{equiv} = C_1 + C_2 + C_3$$

If capacitors are in parallel, the equivalent capacitance is the sum of the individual capacitances.

> **! Watch Out!**
>
> **Capacitors in series and parallel have different properties.**
>
> Here's a summary of the differences between series and parallel combinations of capacitors. In a *series* combination, each capacitor has the same charge, but there are different voltages across capacitors with different capacitances. In a *parallel* combination, there is the same voltage across each capacitor, but there are different charges on capacitors with different capacitances.

If there are more than three capacitors in parallel, the same rule given in Equation 17-26 applies. The equivalent capacitance of a parallel combination is always *greater* than the smallest capacitance of any of the individual capacitors.

Example 17-10 shows how to do calculations with capacitors in series and in parallel. (We'll see a biological application of these calculations in the following section.) Many real networks of capacitors are more complex: They have a mixture of series and parallel combinations. To find the equivalent capacitance of such a network, we identify any small grouping of capacitors that are either entirely in series or entirely in parallel, find the equivalent capacitance of each group, and then combine them in larger and larger groupings, using the series and parallel rules, until we have accounted for all of the capacitors in the network. Example 17-11 illustrates how to do this.

Example 17-10 Two Capacitors in Series or in Parallel

(a) If two capacitors are connected in series, find their equivalent capacitance for the case when the capacitors have different capacitances $C_1 = 2.00 \ \mu F$ and $C_2 = 4.00 \ \mu F$ and for the case where both have the same capacitance $C_1 = C_2 = 2.00 \ \mu F$. (b) Repeat part (a) for the two capacitors connected in parallel.

Set Up

We'll use Equations 17-22 and 17-26 to find the equivalent capacitance C_{equiv} in each case. Since there are only two capacitors in each combination, we drop the C_3 term from these equations.

Two capacitors in series:

$$\frac{1}{C_{equiv}} = \frac{1}{C_1} + \frac{1}{C_2} \qquad \text{(17-22)}$$

Two capacitors in parallel:

$$C_{equiv} = C_1 + C_2 \qquad \text{(17-26)}$$

series
C_1 C_2

parallel
C_1
C_2

Solve

(a) We first apply Equation 17-22 to the case where $C_1 = 2.00\ \mu F$ and $C_2 = 4.00\ \mu F$.

With capacitors $C_1 = 2.00\ \mu F$ and $C_2 = 4.00\ \mu F$ in series, Equation 17-22 becomes

$$\frac{1}{C_{equiv}} = \frac{1}{2.00\ \mu F} + \frac{1}{4.00\ \mu F}$$

$$= 0.500\ \mu F^{-1} + 0.250\ \mu F^{-1} = 0.750\ \mu F^{-1}$$

To find C_{equiv}, take the reciprocal of $1/C_{equiv}$:

$$C_{equiv} = \frac{1}{0.750\ \mu F^{-1}} = 1.33\ \mu F$$

Note that C_{equiv} is less than either C_1 or C_2.

Now repeat the calculation for the case where $C_1 = C_2 = 2.00\ \mu F$.

Follow the same steps, but with both capacitances equal to $2.00\ \mu F$:

$$\frac{1}{C_{equiv}} = \frac{1}{2.00\ \mu F} + \frac{1}{2.00\ \mu F}$$

$$= 0.500\ \mu F^{-1} + 0.500\ \mu F^{-1} = 1.00\ \mu F^{-1}$$

$$C_{equiv} = \frac{1}{1.00\ \mu F^{-1}} = 1.00\ \mu F$$

For this case of identical capacitors in series, C_{equiv} is exactly one-half of $C_1 = C_2 = 2.00\ \mu F$.

(b) Apply Equation 17-26 to the case where $C_1 = 2.00\ \mu F$ and $C_2 = 4.00\ \mu F$.

With capacitors $C_1 = 2.00\ \mu F$ and $C_2 = 4.00\ \mu F$ in parallel, Equation 17-26 becomes

$$C_{equiv} = 2.00\ \mu F + 4.00\ \mu F = 6.00\ \mu F$$

Note that C_{equiv} is greater than either C_1 or C_2.

Now repeat the calculation for the case where $C_1 = C_2 = 2.00\ \mu F$.

Follow the same steps, but with both capacitances equal to $2.00\ \mu F$:

$$C_{equiv} = 2.00\ \mu F + 2.00\ \mu F = 4.00\ \mu F$$

For this case of identical capacitors in parallel, C_{equiv} is exactly twice as great as $C_1 = C_2 = 2.00\ \mu F$.

Reflect

Our results illustrate the following general results: Connecting capacitors in series reduces the capacitance, while connecting them in parallel increases the capacitance.

Example 17-11 Multiple Capacitors

Find the equivalent capacitance of the three capacitors shown in Figure 17-16. The individual capacitances are $C_1 = 1.00\ \mu F$, $C_2 = 2.00\ \mu F$, and $C_3 = 6.00\ \mu F$.

Figure 17-16 **A capacitor network** These three capacitors are neither all in series nor all in parallel.

Set Up

Whenever capacitors are combined in ways other than purely in series or purely in parallel, we look for groupings of capacitors that *are* either in parallel or in series, and then we combine the groups one at a time.

Two capacitors in series:

$$\frac{1}{C_{equiv}} = \frac{1}{C_1} + \frac{1}{C_2}$$ (17-22)

Replace the parallel capacitors C_1 and C_2 by their equivalent capacitor C_{12}:

Then find the equivalent capacitance of C_{12} and C_3 in series.

Notice in Figure 17-16 that C_1 and C_2 are in parallel because their two right plates are directly connected, as are their two left plates. We can therefore use Equation 17-26 to find C_{12} (the equivalent capacitance of the combination of C_1 and C_2) by using our relationship for capacitors in parallel.

Capacitor C_3 is in series with C_{12}, so we can find their combined capacitance by using Equation 17-22. This result is C_{123}, the equivalent capacitance of all three capacitors.

Two capacitors in parallel:

$$C_{equiv} = C_1 + C_2 \qquad (17\text{-}26)$$

Solve

First find the equivalent capacitance of the parallel capacitors C_1 and C_2.

For $C_1 = 1.00\ \mu F$ and $C_2 = 2.00\ \mu F$ in parallel, the equivalent capacitance C_{12} is given by Equation 17-26:

$$C_{12} = C_1 + C_2 = 1.00\ \mu F + 2.00\ \mu F = 3.00\ \mu F$$

Then find C_{123}, the equivalent capacitance of the series capacitors C_{12} and C_3. This is the equivalent capacitance of the entire network of C_1, C_2, and C_3.

Since $C_{12} = 3.00\ \mu F$ and $C_3 = 6.00\ \mu F$ are in series, their equivalent capacitance C_{123} is given by Equation 17-22:

$$\frac{1}{C_{123}} = \frac{1}{C_{12}} + \frac{1}{C_3} = \frac{1}{3.00\ \mu F} + \frac{1}{6.00\ \mu F}$$

$$= 0.333\ \mu F^{-1} + 0.167\ \mu F^{-1} = 0.500\ \mu F^{-1}$$

Take the reciprocal of this to find C_{123}:

$$C_{123} = \frac{1}{0.500\ \mu F^{-1}} = 2.00\ \mu F$$

Reflect

As we described previously, when capacitors are connected in parallel, the equivalent capacitance is always greater than the greatest individual capacitor. That's why C_{12} is greater than either C_1 or C_2. When capacitors are connected in series, the equivalent capacitance is always less than the least individual capacitor, which is why C_{123} is less than either C_{12} or C_3.

? Got the Concept? 17-7 Energy in a Capacitor Combination

Capacitor 1 has capacitance $C_1 = 1.0\ \mu F$, and capacitor 2 has capacitance $C_2 = 2.0\ \mu F$. You connect the initially uncharged capacitors to each other, then connect the capacitor combination to a battery. Which capacitor stores the greater amount of electric potential energy if the two capacitors are connected in series? If they are connected in parallel?

(a) Capacitor 1 for both the series and parallel cases; (b) capacitor 2 for both the series and parallel cases; (c) capacitor 1 for the series case, capacitor 2 for the parallel case; (d) capacitor 2 for the series case, capacitor 1 for the parallel case; (e) not enough information given to decide.

Take-Home Message for Section 17-7

✔ Whenever two or more capacitors are connected, the equivalent capacitance is the capacitance of a single capacitor that is the equivalent of the combined capacitors.

✔ Capacitors are connected in series when they are connected one after another. In a series combination, all capacitors have the same charge, and the equivalent capacitance is less than that of any of the individual capacitors.

✔ Capacitors are connected in parallel when all of their right-hand plates are directly connected to each other, and all of their left-hand plates are directly connected to each other. In a parallel combination, the voltage is the same across all capacitors, and the equivalent capacitance is greater than that of any of the individual capacitors.

17-8 Placing a dielectric between the plates of a capacitor increases the capacitance

So far in our discussion of capacitors we've assumed that there is only vacuum between the capacitor plates. In most situations, however, the two plates are separated by a layer of a **dielectric**, a material that is both an insulator and *polarizable*—that is, in which there is a separation of positive and negative charge within the material when it's exposed to an electric field. Dielectrics used in commercial capacitors include glass, ceramics, and plastics such as polystyrene. These dielectrics not only help to keep the positive and negative plates from touching each other, but also increase the capacitance of the capacitor. In this section we'll see how dielectrics make this possible.

Let's consider an isolated parallel-plate capacitor with charges $+q$ and $-q$ on its plates and with vacuum in the space between its plates (Figure 17-17a). The charge creates a uniform electric field $\vec{E}_0$ between the plates. We now insert a dielectric material that fills the space between the plates of this capacitor. What happens then depends on the kind of molecules that make up the dielectric. If the molecules are *polar*—that is, if one end of the molecule has a positive charge and the other end has a negative charge of the same magnitude—the molecules will orient themselves so that their positive ends are pointed toward the negatively charged plate and their negative ends toward the positively charged plate, as in Figure 17-17b. (The most common molecule in your body, the water molecule H_2O, is a polar molecule. Others include ammonia, NH_3, and sucrose, $C_{12}H_{22}O_{11}$.) If the molecules are not polar, so there normally is no separation of charge within the molecule, the electric field between the plates of the capacitor will *induce* a slight separation of the positive and negative charges in each molecule. (We described this process in Section 16-2.) The molecules will then orient

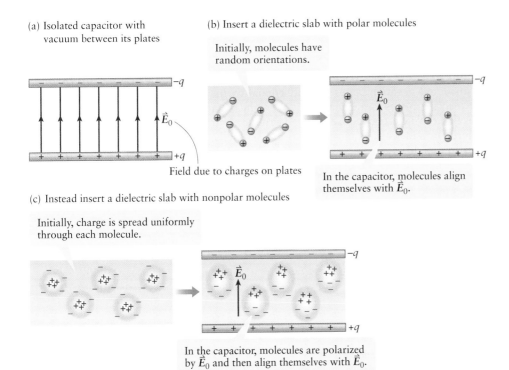

(a) Isolated capacitor with vacuum between its plates

(b) Insert a dielectric slab with polar molecules

Initially, molecules have random orientations.

Field due to charges on plates

In the capacitor, molecules align themselves with $\vec{E}_0$.

(c) Instead insert a dielectric slab with nonpolar molecules

Initially, charge is spread uniformly through each molecule.

In the capacitor, molecules are polarized by $\vec{E}_0$ and then align themselves with $\vec{E}_0$.

(d) With either type of dielectric, the result is layers of positive and negative charge on the dielectric surfaces. These produce a field $\vec{E}_{dielectric}$.

Zero net interior charge

Layer of positive charge

Layer of negative charge

Figure 17-17 A dielectric in a parallel-plate capacitor A dielectric slab inserted between the plates of an isolated capacitor reduces the electric field between the plates.

themselves in the same manner as polar molecules would (Figure 17-17c). In either case we say that the dielectric becomes *polarized* once it has been inserted between the plates of the capacitor.

In the interior of the polarized dielectric in Figure 17-17b or 17-17c, there are as many positive ends of molecules as there are negative ends, so the interior of the dielectric is neutral. But there *is* a net charge at the surfaces of the dielectric: There is a layer of positive charge on the surface next to the negatively charged plate, and a layer of negative charge on the surface next to the positively charged plate. (The dielectric as a whole is neutral, so these two layers have the same magnitude of charge.) These two layers of charge create an electric field $\vec{E}_{\text{dielectric}}$ that points opposite to the electric field $\vec{E}_0$ created by the charges on the plates of the capacitor (Figure 17-17d). Hence $\vec{E}_{\text{dielectric}}$ partially cancels $\vec{E}_0$, and the *net* electric field $\vec{E} = \vec{E}_0 + \vec{E}_{\text{dielectric}}$ between the plates is less than $\vec{E}_0$. So the effect of the dielectric is to *reduce* the electric field between the plates. We can express this as

Electric field in an isolated
parallel-plate capacitor
with a dielectric
(17-27)

Electric field in an isolated parallel-plate capacitor with dielectric between the plates

Electric field in that same capacitor with no dielectric between the plates

$$E = \frac{E_0}{\kappa}$$

Dielectric constant: note that $\kappa \geq 1$

For an isolated charged capacitor, a dielectric reduces the electric field between the plates.

Table 17-1
Dielectric Constants
(at 20°C and 1 atm)

Material	κ
vacuum	1
air	1.00058
lipid	2.2
paraffin	2.2
paper	2.7
ceramic (porcelain)	5.8
water	80

The quantity κ (the Greek letter kappa) is the **dielectric constant** of the material. The greater the value of κ, the more the dielectric is polarized when it is placed between the plates of a charged capacitor, so the greater the magnitude of the field $\vec{E}_{\text{dielectric}}$ due to the dielectric and the smaller the magnitude E of the net field. Table 17-1 lists values of the dielectric constant for a variety of materials.

What does Equation 17-27 tell us about how the dielectric affects the capacitance of the capacitor? We saw in Section 17-5 that the potential difference V between the positive and negative plates is proportional to the magnitude E of the electric field between the plates (see Equation 17-11, which states that $V = Ed$). Equation 17-27 says that the dielectric reduces the value of the electric field by a factor $1/\kappa$, so V is also reduced by a factor $1/\kappa$. Now, Equation 17-14 tells us that the capacitance C is related to potential difference V and the magnitude q of the charges on the plates by $q = CV$, or $C = q/V$. While the dielectric reduces V by a factor $1/\kappa$, it has no effect on the value of q. (Since we specified that the capacitor is isolated, no charge can leave either plate.) Because the capacitance $C = q/V$ is inversely proportional to the potential difference V, which is reduced by a factor $1/\kappa$, it follows that C *increases* by a factor of $1/(1/\kappa) = \kappa$. If C_0 is the capacitance without the dielectric, the capacitance with the dielectric is

Capacitance of a parallel-plate
capacitor with a dielectric
(17-28)

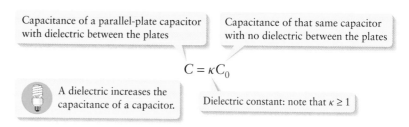

Capacitance of a parallel-plate capacitor with dielectric between the plates

Capacitance of that same capacitor with no dielectric between the plates

$$C = \kappa C_0$$

A dielectric increases the capacitance of a capacitor.

Dielectric constant: note that $\kappa \geq 1$

As an example, Table 17-1 tells us that the dielectric constant of porcelain is $\kappa = 5.8$. From Equation 17-28, the capacitance of a capacitor with porcelain filling the space between its plates is 5.8 times greater than an identical capacitor with vacuum between its plates. That's fundamentally because the electric field in the porcelain-filled capacitor is only $1/5.8 = 0.17$ as great as for an identical vacuum capacitor carrying the same charge (Equation 17-27).

Example 17-12 shows how to apply these ideas to the membrane of a cell, which we can regard as a capacitor with multiple layers of dielectric between its plates.

Example 17-12 Cell Membrane Capacitance

In all cells, it is easier for positive potassium ions (K^+) to flow out of the cell than it is for negative ions. As a result, there is negative charge on the inside of the cell membrane and positive charge on the outside of the membrane, much like a capacitor. Consider a typical cell with a membrane of thickness 7.60 nm = 7.60×10^{-9} m. (a) Find the capacitance of a square patch of membrane 1.00 μm = 1.00×10^{-6} m on a side, assuming that the membrane has dielectric constant $\kappa = 1$. (b) The actual structure of the membrane is a layer of lipid surrounded by layers of a polarized aqueous solution and layers of water (Figure 17-18). Taking account of this structure, find the capacitance of a square patch of membrane 1.00 μm on a side.

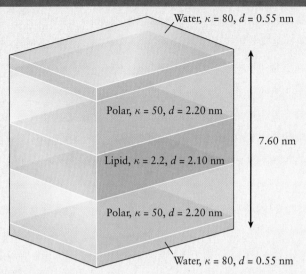

Figure 17-18 **Membrane capacitance** A membrane acts as a capacitor filled with a dielectric. What is the capacitance of a membrane that consists of a layer of lipid surrounded by layers of a polarized aqueous solution and water?

Set Up

A dielectric constant $\kappa = 1$ corresponds to vacuum, so in part (a) we can find the capacitance C_0 of the membrane under the assumption $\kappa = 1$ by using Equation 17-13 from Section 17-5.

In part (b) we must deal with the more complicated situation shown in Figure 17-18. We can't simply use Equation 17-28 to find the capacitance, because there's not a single value of κ for the arrangement of layers that make up the membrane. Instead we'll imagine that there's a very thin conducting sheet separating each layer from the next. If there are charges $+q$ and $-q$ on the outer and inner surfaces of the multilayer membrane, there will also be charges $+q$ and $-q$ on the surfaces of these conducting sheets. This is exactly like the situation with capacitors in series (Section 17-7). So we'll treat each of the five layers in Figure 17-18 as an individual capacitor, then use Equation 17-22 to find the capacitance of the combination.

Parallel-plate capacitor with vacuum between the plates:

$$C_0 = \frac{\varepsilon_0 A}{d} \qquad (17\text{-}13)$$

Parallel-plate capacitor with dielectric:

$$C = \kappa C_0 \qquad (17\text{-}28)$$

Five capacitors in series:

$$\frac{1}{C_{equiv}} = \frac{1}{C_1} + \frac{1}{C_2} + \frac{1}{C_3} + \frac{1}{C_4} + \frac{1}{C_5} \qquad (17\text{-}22)$$

Solve

(a) First use Equation 17-13 to find the capacitance assuming that the membrane has $\kappa = 1$ (equivalent to vacuum).

The area A for the capacitor of interest is a square 1.00 μm on a side:

$$A = (1.00 \ \mu m)^2 = (1.00 \times 10^{-6} \ m)^2$$
$$= 1.00 \times 10^{-12} \ m^2$$

A parallel-plate capacitor with this area and with $d = 7.60 \times 10^{-9}$ m has capacitance

$$C_0 = \frac{\varepsilon_0 A}{d} = \frac{(8.85 \times 10^{-12} \ F/m)(1.00 \times 10^{-12} \ m^2)}{7.60 \times 10^{-9} \ m}$$
$$= 1.16 \times 10^{-15} \ F$$

(b) Calculate the capacitance of each of the five layers separately using Equations 17-13 and 17-28.

The capacitance of the first layer of water is $\kappa_1 = 80$ times the capacitance of a vacuum capacitor of thickness $d_1 = 0.55$ nm:

$$C_1 = \kappa_1 \left(\frac{\varepsilon_0 A}{d_1} \right) = (80) \frac{(8.85 \times 10^{-12} \ F/m)(1.00 \times 10^{-12} \ m^2)}{0.55 \times 10^{-9} \ m}$$
$$= 1.3 \times 10^{-12} \ F$$

Similarly, for the second layer of polarized aqueous solution with $\kappa_2 = 50$ and thickness $d_2 = 2.20$ nm the capacitance is

$$C_2 = \kappa_2 \left(\frac{\varepsilon_0 A}{d_2} \right)$$

$$= (50) \frac{(8.85 \times 10^{-12}\ \text{F/m})(1.00 \times 10^{-12}\ \text{m}^2)}{2.20 \times 10^{-9}\ \text{m}}$$

$$= 2.0 \times 10^{-13}\ \text{F}$$

The capacitance of the third lipid layer with $\kappa_3 = 2.2$ and thickness $d_3 = 2.10$ nm is

$$C_3 = \kappa_3 \left(\frac{\varepsilon_0 A}{d_3} \right)$$

$$= (2.2) \frac{(8.85 \times 10^{-12}\ \text{F/m})(1.00 \times 10^{-12}\ \text{m}^2)}{2.10 \times 10^{-9}\ \text{m}}$$

$$= 9.3 \times 10^{-15}\ \text{F}$$

The fourth layer of polarized aqueous solution is identical to the second layer, and the fifth water layer is identical to the first layer. So

$$C_4 = C_2 = 2.0 \times 10^{-13}\ \text{F}$$
$$C_5 = C_1 = 1.3 \times 10^{-12}\ \text{F}$$

Calculate the net capacitance of the five layers in series using Equation 17-22.

The equivalent capacitance C_{equiv} of the five-layer stack is given by

$$\frac{1}{C_{\text{equiv}}} = \frac{1}{C_1} + \frac{1}{C_2} + \frac{1}{C_3} + \frac{1}{C_4} + \frac{1}{C_5}$$

Since $C_4 = C_2$ and $C_5 = C_1$, this is

$$\frac{1}{C_{\text{equiv}}} = \frac{1}{C_1} + \frac{1}{C_2} + \frac{1}{C_3} + \frac{1}{C_2} + \frac{1}{C_1} = \frac{2}{C_1} + \frac{2}{C_2} + \frac{1}{C_3}$$

$$= \frac{2}{1.3 \times 10^{-12}\ \text{F}} + \frac{2}{2.0 \times 10^{-13}\ \text{F}} + \frac{1}{9.3 \times 10^{-15}\ \text{F}}$$

$$= 1.2 \times 10^{14}\ \text{F}^{-1}$$

The reciprocal of this is C_{equiv}:

$$C_{\text{equiv}} = \frac{1}{1.2 \times 10^{14}\ \text{F}^{-1}} = 8.4 \times 10^{-15}\ \text{F}$$

Reflect

The equivalent capacitance of the stack of five layers is less than that of any individual layer. This is just what we saw in Section 17-7 for capacitors in series.

The capacitance $C_{\text{equiv}} = 8.4 \times 10^{-15}$ F is greater than the capacitance $C_0 = 1.16 \times 10^{-15}$ F calculated assuming $\kappa = 1$ by a factor $C_{\text{equiv}}/C_0 = (8.4 \times 10^{-15}\ \text{F})/(1.16 \times 10^{-15}\ \text{F}) = 7.2$. So the effective dielectric constant of the membrane is 7.2, intermediate between the largest ($\kappa_1 = 80$) and smallest ($\kappa_3 = 2.2$) values of dielectric constant for the individual layers.

? Got the Concept? 17-8 Inserting a Dielectric into a Capacitor

An isolated parallel-plate capacitor (one that is not connected to anything else) has vacuum between its plates and has charges $+q$ and $-q$ on its plates. If you insert a slab of dielectric with dielectric constant κ that fills the space between the plates, the capacitance increases. What happens to the energy stored in the capacitor as you insert the dielectric slab? Will you have to push the slab into the capacitor, or will you feel the capacitor pulling the slab in? (a) Stored energy increases, you will have to push the slab in; (b) stored energy increases, the slab will be pulled in; (c) stored energy decreases, you will have to push the slab in; (d) stored energy decreases, the slab will be pulled in; (e) not enough information given to decide.

Take-Home Message for Section 17-8

✔ When a dielectric material is placed in an electric field $\vec{E}_0$, it becomes polarized. This produces an additional electric field that partially cancels $\vec{E}_0$ and so reduces the net field in the dielectric. The dielectric constant is a measure of how much the field is reduced.

✔ If a dielectric material fills the space between the plates of a capacitor, the capacitance is greater than if there is vacuum between the plates.

Key Terms

capacitance
capacitor
dielectric
dielectric constant
electric potential
electric potential
    difference

electric potential energy
electron volt
equipotential
equipotential surface
equipotential volume
equivalent capacitance
farad

parallel (capacitors)
parallel-plate capacitor
plates
series (capacitors)
test charge
volt
voltage

Chapter Summary

Topic	Equation or Figure

Electric potential energy: Like the gravitational force, the electric force is a conservative force and has an associated potential energy. The change in electric potential energy when a charged object moves from one point to another depends on the sign of the object's charge. The sign of the electric potential energy of two point charges depends on whether the two charges have the same sign or different signs.

The change in electric potential energy for an object of charge q that moves in a uniform electric field $\vec{E}$...

...equals the negative of the work done on the object by the electric force.

$$\Delta U_{\text{electric}} = -W_{\text{electric}}$$
$$= -qEd\cos\theta$$

Charge of the object

Angle between the displacement and the direction of the electric field

Magnitude of the electric field

Straight-line displacement of the object

(17-2)

Coulomb constant   Values of the two charges

Electric potential energy of two point charges

$$U_{\text{electric}} = \frac{kq_1q_2}{r}$$

Distance between the point charges

(17-3)

Electric potential: The electric potential at a given position equals the electric potential energy for a point charge q_0 at that position, divided by the value of q_0. If you move in a direction opposite to the electric field, the electric potential increases; if you move in the direction of the electric field, the electric potential decreases. The electric potential due to a point charge is inversely proportional to the distance from the charge. Voltage is the

If you move in a direction opposite to the electric field ($\theta > 90°$), the electric potential increases ($\Delta V > 0$).

If you move in the direction of the electric field ($\theta < 90°$), the electric potential decreases ($\Delta V < 0$).

(Figure 17-5)

 If you move from point a to point b in a uniform electric field $\vec{E}$, the change in electric potential is $\Delta V = -Ed\cos\theta$.

difference in electric potential between two locations.

Electric potential due to a point charge Q | Coulomb constant

$$V = \frac{kQ}{r}$$ — Value of the point charge

(17-8)

Distance from the point charge Q to the location where the potential is measured

---

Equipotentials: The electric potential has the same value everywhere on an equipotential surface. An equipotential surface is everywhere perpendicular to the electric field. The electric potential has the same value throughout the volume of a conductor in equilibrium.

A plane perpendicular to a uniform electric field $\vec{E}$ is an **equipotential surface:** Potential V has the same value at all points on this surface.

a b $\vec{E}$

Any curve that lies on the plane is an equipotential curve.

(Figure 17-6)

Capacitors: A capacitor has two conducting plates that store charges $+q$ and $-q$, of the same magnitude but opposite sign. The potential difference V between the plates is proportional to the charge q; the proportionality constant, the capacitance C, depends only on the geometry of the capacitor and the substance between the plates.

A capacitor carries a charge $+q$ on its positive plate and a charge $-q$ on its negative plate. | The magnitude of q is directly proportional to V, the voltage (potential difference) between the plates.

$$q = CV$$

(17-14)

The constant of proportionality between charge q and voltage V is the capacitance C of the capacitor.

Energy stored in a capacitor: A charged capacitor stores electric potential energy. The stored energy can be expressed by two of the three quantities: capacitance C, charge q, and potential difference V.

The electric potential energy stored in a charged capacitor...

$$U_{\text{electric}} = \frac{1}{2}qV = \frac{1}{2}CV^2 = \frac{q^2}{2C}$$

(17-17)

...can be expressed in three ways in terms of the charge q, potential difference V, and capacitance C.

Capacitors in series and parallel: A collection of capacitors in a circuit behaves as though it were a single capacitor, with an equivalent capacitance C_{equiv}. The equivalent capacitance is different for capacitors in series (with the positive plate of one capacitor connected to the negative plate of another) than for capacitors in parallel (with positive plates connected to positive plates and negative plates to negative plates).

 If capacitors are in series, the reciprocal of the equivalent capacitance is the sum of the reciprocals of the individual capacitances.

$$\frac{1}{C_{\text{equiv}}} = \frac{1}{C_1} + \frac{1}{C_2} + \frac{1}{C_3}$$

(17-22)

Equivalent capacitance of capacitors in series | Capacitances of the individual capacitors

Equivalent capacitance of capacitors in parallel | Capacitances of the individual capacitors

$$C_{\text{equiv}} = C_1 + C_2 + C_3$$

(17-26)

If capacitors are in parallel, the equivalent capacitance is the sum of the individual capacitances.

Dielectrics: A dielectric is an insulator that becomes polarized when placed in an electric field. When the space between the plates of a capacitor is filled with a dielectric, the electric field between the plates decreases (for a given charge q on the plates) and the capacitance increases.

Capacitance of a parallel-plate capacitor with dielectric between the plates

Capacitance of that same capacitor with no dielectric between the plates

A dielectric increases the capacitance of a capacitor.

$$C = \kappa C_0 \qquad (17\text{-}28)$$

Dielectric constant: note that $\kappa \geq 1$

Answer to What do you think? Question

(c) The energy stored by separating charge $+q$ from charge $-q$ in a capacitor is proportional to q^2 (see Section 17-6, especially Equation 17-17). So doubling the value of q increases the stored energy by a factor of $2^2 = 4$.

Answers to Got the Concept? Questions

17-1 (b) Although q_1, q_2, and q_3 have all reversed sign, the signs of the *products* q_1q_2, q_1q_3, and q_2q_3 in Equation 17-4 remain the same. So if you change all of the positive charges in an assemblage to negative and vice versa, there is no effect on the electric potential energy of the assemblage.

17-2 (c), (a), (d), (b) From Equation 17-6, the potential energy change $\Delta U_{\text{electric}}$ for a point charge q_0 is related to the potential change ΔV by $\Delta V = \Delta U_{\text{electric}}/q_0$, or $\Delta U_{\text{electric}} = q_0\,\Delta V$. For the four cases we have (a) $\Delta U_{\text{electric}} = (+0.0010\ \text{C})(5.0\ \text{V}) = +0.0050\ \text{C}\cdot\text{V} = +0.0050$ J; (b) $\Delta U_{\text{electric}} = (+0.0020\ \text{C})(-2.0\ \text{V}) = -0.0040$ J; (c) $\Delta U_{\text{electric}} = (-0.0015\ \text{C})(-4.0\ \text{V}) = +0.0060$ J; (d) $\Delta U_{\text{electric}} = (-0.0010\ \text{C})(+2.5\ \text{V}) = -0.0025$ J.

17-3 (b) In the vicinity of A, the potential decreases by 1 V (from $V = 0$ V to $V = -1$ V) in the 2-m distance between $x = 0$ and $x = 2$ m. The electric field $\vec{E}$ points in the direction of decreasing potential, which is to the right (the positive x direction) at both points. In the vicinity of B, the equipotentials are much closer together; the potential decreases by 1 V (from $V = -2$ V to $V = -3$ V) in the 0.5-m distance from $x = 3$ m to $x = 3.5$ m. Where equipotentials are farther apart, as at A, the electric field has a smaller magnitude.

17-4 (e) Equation 17-13 shows that the capacitance of a parallel-plate capacitor depends on its geometry only. It does not depend on the amount of charge on the plates or on the potential difference between the plates.

17-5 (c) The stored energy increases. The positive and negative charges on the two plates attract each other, so to pull the plates apart you must do positive work on the system. The work you do increases the electric potential energy stored in the capacitor. To verify this conclusion, note from Equation 17-13 that if you increase the spacing d between the plates, the capacitance $C = \varepsilon_0 A/d$ will decrease. Equation 17-17, $U_{\text{electric}} = q^2/2C$, then tells us that if the charge q remains constant and the capacitance C decreases, the stored energy U_{electric} will increase.

17-6 (a) The stored energy decreases. Equation 17-13 tells us that as you increase the spacing d between the plates, the capacitance $C = \varepsilon_0 A/d$ decreases. Equation 17-17, $U_{\text{electric}} =$ $(1/2)CV^2$, then tells us that if the potential difference V remains constant and C decreases, the stored energy must decrease. Note that in the situation of Got the Concept? 17-5, the stored energy *increases* when the plates are pulled apart. Why is the answer different here? The explanation is that in Got the Concept? 17-5 the charge q remained constant. In the current situation, however, the charge q has to change in accordance with Equation 17-14, $q = CV$: The charge q decreases as the capacitance C decreases. (Electrons flow from the negative plate through the battery and onto the positive plate, so the magnitude of charge on both plates decreases.) Equation 17-17 also tells us that we can express the stored energy as $U_{\text{electric}} = (1/2)qV$, so the stored energy will decrease if q decreases while V remains the same.

17-7 (c) Equation 17-17 gives us two useful expressions for the electric potential energy stored in a capacitor with capacitance C: $U_{\text{electric}} = (1/2)CV^2$ (which says that for a given voltage V, the stored energy is proportional to C) and $U_{\text{electric}} = q^2/2C$ (which says that for a given charge q, the stored energy is inversely proportional to C). In a series combination, both capacitors carry the same charge q, so $U_{\text{electric}} = q^2/2C$ tells us that the capacitor with the smaller capacitance ($C_1 = 1.0\ \mu\text{F}$) stores the greater amount of energy. In a parallel combination, the voltage V is the same for both capacitors, so $U_{\text{electric}} = (1/2)CV^2$ tells us that the capacitor with the greater capacitance ($C_2 = 2.0\ \mu\text{F}$) stores the greater amount of energy. We can draw these conclusions without knowing the specific values of q for the series case or V for the parallel case.

17-8 (d) Because the capacitor is isolated, the charge q does not change when the dielectric slab is inserted. So among the expressions for stored energy given in Equation 17-17, the one to use is $U_{\text{electric}} = q^2/2C$. Since q remains constant but capacitance C increases as you insert the slab, it follows that U_{electric} decreases. Just as a ball is pulled downward by the gravitational force, in the direction that decreases gravitational potential energy, the slab must be pulled into the capacitor by an electric force because motion in that direction decreases electric potential energy U_{electric}.

Questions and Problems

In a few problems, you are given more data than you actually need; in a few other problems, you are required to supply data from your general knowledge, outside sources, or informed estimate.

Interpret as significant all digits in numerical values that have trailing zeros and no decimal points. For all problems, use $g = 9.80 \text{ m/s}^2$ for the free-fall acceleration due to gravity. Neglect friction and air resistance unless instructed to do otherwise.

• Basic, single-concept problem
•• Intermediate-level problem, may require synthesis of concepts and multiple steps
••• Challenging problem
SSM Solution is in Student Solutions Manual

Conceptual Questions

1. •What is the difference between electric potential and electric field?

2. •What is the difference between electric potential and electric potential energy?

3. •Explain why electric potential requires the existence of only one charge, but a finite electric potential energy requires the existence of two charges.

4. •An electron is released from rest in an electric field. Will it accelerate in the direction of increasing or decreasing potential? Why?

5. •Does it make sense to say that the voltage at some point in space is 10.3 V? Explain your answer. SSM

6. ••Explain why an electron will accelerate toward a region of lower electric potential energy but higher electric potential.

7. •Discuss how a topographical map showing various elevations around a mountain is analogous to the equipotential lines surrounding a charged object.

8. •How much work is required to move a charge from one end of an equipotential path to the other? Explain your answer.

9. •(a) If the electric potential throughout some region of space is zero, does it necessarily follow that the electric field is zero? (b) If the electric field throughout a region is zero, does it necessarily follow that the electric potential is zero? SSM

10. •Explain why capacitance depends neither on the stored charge Q nor on the potential difference V between the plates of a capacitor.

11. •Describe three methods by which you might increase the capacitance of a parallel-plate capacitor.

12. •If the voltage across a capacitor is doubled, by how much does the stored energy change?

13. ••The capacitance of several capacitors in series is less than any of the individual capacitances. What, then, is the advantage of having several capacitors in series?

14. •What is the advantage to arranging several capacitors in parallel?

15. ••You charge a capacitor and then remove it from the battery. The capacitor consists of large movable plates with air between them. You pull the plates a bit farther apart. What happens to the stored energy? SSM

16. •Which way of connecting (series or parallel) three identical capacitors to a battery would store more energy?

17. •Qualitatively explain why the equivalent capacitance of a parallel combination of identical capacitors is larger than the individual capacitances.

18. •Does inserting a dielectric into a capacitor increase or decrease the energy stored in the capacitor? Explain your answer.

19. •What are the benefits, if any, of filling a capacitor with a dielectric other than air?

20. ••Capacitors A and B are identical except that the region between the plates of capacitor A is filled with a dielectric. As shown in **Figure 17-19**, the plates of these capacitors are maintained at the same potential difference by a battery. Is the electric field magnitude in the region between the plates of capacitor A smaller, the same, or larger than the field in the region between the plates of capacitor B? Explain your answer.

Figure 17-19 Problem 20

Multiple-Choice Questions

21. ••For a positive charge moving in the direction of the electric field,

    A. its potential energy increases and its electric potential increases.
    B. its potential energy increases and its electric potential decreases.
    C. its potential energy decreases and its electric potential increases.
    D. its potential energy decreases and its electric potential decreases.
    E. its potential energy and its electric potential remain constant. SSM

22. ••If a negative charge is released in a uniform electric field, it will move
    A. in the direction of the electric field.
    B. from high potential to low potential.
    C. from low potential to high potential.
    D. in a direction perpendicular to the electric field.
    E. in circular motion.

23. •An equipotential surface must be
    A. parallel to the electric field at every point.
    B. equal to the electric field at every point.
    C. perpendicular to the electric field at every point.
    D. tangent to the electric field at every point.
    E. equal to the inverse of the electric field at every point.

24. •A positive charge is moved from one point to another point along an equipotential surface. The work required to move the charge
    A. is positive.
    B. is negative.
    C. is zero.
    D. depends on the sign of the potential.
    E. depends on the magnitude of the potential.

25. •The electric potential measured at a point equidistant from two particles that have charges equal in magnitude but of opposite sign is
- A. larger than zero.
- B. smaller than zero.
- C. equal to zero.
- D. equal to the average of the two distances times the charges.
- E. equal to the net electric field.

26. •Four point charges of equal magnitude but differing signs are arranged at the corners of a square (Figure 17-20). The electric field E and the potential V at the center of the square are
- A. $E = 0$; $V \neq 0$.
- B. $E = 0$; $V = 0$.
- C. $E \neq 0$; $V \neq 0$.
- D. $E \neq 0$; $V = 0$.
- E. $E = 2V^{1/2}$.

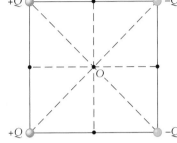

Figure 17-20 Problem 26

27. ••A capacitor consists of a set of two parallel plates of area A separated by a distance d. This capacitor carries a charge Q. If the separation between the plates is doubled, the electrical energy stored in the capacitor will be
- A. halved.
- B. doubled.
- C. unchanged.
- D. quadrupled.
- E. quartered. SSM

28. ••A capacitor consists of a set of two parallel plates of area A separated by a distance d. This capacitor is connected to a battery that maintains a constant potential difference across the plates. If the separation between the plates is doubled, the electrical energy stored in the capacitor will be
- A. halved.
- B. doubled.
- C. unchanged.
- D. quadrupled.
- E. quartered.

29. •When capacitors are connected in series, they have the same
- A. charge.
- B. voltage.
- C. dielectric.
- D. surface area.
- E. separation.

30. •When capacitors are connected in parallel, they have the same
- A. charge.
- B. voltage.
- C. dielectric.
- D. surface area.
- E. separation.

Estimation/Numerical Analysis

31. •If a source charge is in the microcoulomb range, how far from the charge should you be to have an electric potential in the millivolt range as compared to the potential a long way from the charge?

32. •Estimate the number of 100 μF capacitors, connected in parallel, that would provide enough energy to get an electric car moving at 20 m/s (the mass of the car equals 1000 kg, the mass of a 1 μF capacitor equals 0.005 g). Assume the voltage across the capacitors is 12 V.

33. •Estimate the electric potential at the location of an electron bound to the nucleus of an atom. SSM

Problems

17-1 Electric energy is important in nature, technology, and biological systems

17-2 Electric potential energy changes when a charge moves in an electric field

34. ••A point charge q_0 that has a charge of 0.500 μC is at the origin. (a) A second particle q that has a charge of 1.00 μC and a mass of 0.0800 g is placed at $x = 0.800$ m. What is the potential energy of this system of charges? (b) If the particle with charge q is released from rest, what will its speed be when it reaches $x = 2.00$ m?

35. ••A uniform electric field of 2.00 kN/C points in the $+x$ direction. (a) What is the change in potential energy of a $+2.00$ nC test charge, $U_{\text{electric},b} - U_{\text{electric},a}$, as it is moved from point a at $x = -30.0$ cm to point b at $x = +50.0$ cm? (b) The same test charge is released from rest at point a. What is its kinetic energy when it passes through point b? (c) If a negative charge instead of a positive charge were used in this problem, qualitatively how would your answers change? SSM

36. ••**Biology** Two red blood cells each have a mass of 9.0×10^{-14} kg and carry a negative charge spread uniformly over their surfaces. The repulsion arising from the excess charge prevents the cells from clumping together. One cell carries -2.50 pC of charge and the other -3.10 pC, and each cell can be modeled as a sphere 7.5 μm in diameter. (a) What speed would they need when very far away from each other to get close enough to just touch? Assume that there is no viscous drag from any of the surrounding liquid. (b) What is the maximum acceleration of the cells in part (a)?

17-3 Electric potential equals electric potential energy per charge

37. •A uniform electric field of magnitude 28 V/m makes an angle of 30° with a displacement of length 10 m. What is the potential difference of the final position relative to the initial position of this displacement?

38. •At a certain point in space, there is a potential of 800 V relative to zero. What is the potential energy of the system when a $+1.0$ μC charge is placed at that point in space?

39. •How much work is required to move a 2.0-C positive charge from the negative terminal of a 9.0-V battery to the positive terminal? SSM

40. •**Biology** A potential difference exists between the inner and outer surfaces of the membrane of a cell. The inner surface is negative relative to the outer surface. If 1.5×10^{-20} J of work is required to eject a positive sodium ion (Na^+) from the interior of the cell, what is the potential difference between the inner and outer surfaces of the cell?

41. •**Chemistry** What is the electric potential due to the nucleus of hydrogen at a distance of 5.00×10^{-11} m? Assume the potential is equal to zero as $r \to \infty$.

42. •(a) What is the electric potential due to a point charge of $+2.00 \ \mu C$ at a distance of 0.500 cm? (b) How will the answer change if the charge has a value of $-2.00 \ \mu C$? Assume the potential is equal to zero as $r \to \infty$.

43. •The electric potential has a value of -200 V at a distance of 1.25 m from a point charge. What is the value of that charge? Assume the potential is equal to zero as $r \to \infty$.

44. •At point P in Figure 17-21 the electric potential is zero. (As usual, we take the potential to be zero at infinite distance.) (a) What can you say about the two charges? (b) Are there any other points of zero potential on the line connecting P and the two charges?

Figure 17-21 Problem 44

45. •Two point charges are placed on the x axis: $+0.500 \ \mu C$ at $x = 0$ and $-0.200 \ \mu C$ at $x = 10.0$ cm. At what point(s), if any, on the x axis is the electric potential equal to zero? SSM

46. •A charge of $+2.00 \ \mu C$ is at the origin and a charge of $-3.00 \ \mu C$ is on the y axis at $y = 40.0$ cm. (a) What is the potential at point a, which is on the x axis at $x = 40.0$ cm? (b) What is the potential difference $V_b - V_a$ when point b is at (40.0 cm, 30.0 cm)? (c) How much work is required to move an electron at rest from point a to rest at point b?

47. ••Calculate the electric potential at the origin O due to the point charges in Figure 17-22.

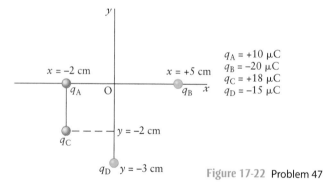

Figure 17-22 Problem 47

17-4 The electric potential has the same value everywhere on an equipotential surface

48. •Electric field lines for a system of two point charges are shown in Figure 17-23. Reproduce the figure and draw on it some equipotential lines for the system.

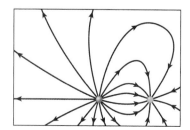

Figure 17-23 Problem 48

49. •In Figure 17-24, equipotential lines are shown at 1-m intervals. What is the electric field at (a) point A and (b) point B?

Figure 17-24 Problem 49

50. •Equipotential lines for some region of space are shown in Figure 17-25. What is the approximate electric field at (a) point A and (b) point B?

Figure 17-25 Problem 50

51. ••Draw the (a) equipotential lines and (b) electric field lines surrounding pairs of charges with the same sign charge (Figure 17-26). SSM

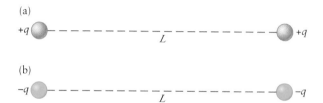

Figure 17-26 Problem 51

52. ••Draw the (a) equipotential lines and (b) electric field lines surrounding a dipole ($+q$ is a distance L from $-q$) (Figure 17-27). All charges are "points" of very small (negligible) dimensions.

Figure 17-27 Problem 52

53. ••Draw the electric field lines and the electric equipotential lines for the following charge distribution (Figure 17-28).

Figure 17-28 Problem 53

17-5 A capacitor stores equal amounts of positive and negative charge

54. •Using a single 10.0-V battery, what capacitance do you need to store 10.0 μC of charge?

55. •A 2.00-μF capacitor is connected to a 12.0-V battery. What is the magnitude of the charge on each plate of the capacitor?

56. •A parallel-plate capacitor has a plate separation of 1.00 mm. If the material between the plates is air, what plate area is required to provide a capacitance of 2.00 pF?

57. •A parallel-plate capacitor has square plates that have edge lengths equal to 1.00×10^2 cm and are separated by 1.00 mm. What is the capacitance of this device?

58. •An air-filled parallel-plate capacitor has plates measuring 10.0 cm × 10.0 cm and a plate separation of 1.00 mm. If you want to construct a parallel-plate capacitor of the same capacitance but with plates measuring 5.00 cm × 5.00 cm, what plate separation do you need?

59. •A parallel-plate capacitor has square plates that have edge length equal to 1.00 m. If the material between the plates is air, what separation distance is required to provide a capacitance of 8850 pF? SSM

17-6 A capacitor is a storehouse of electric potential energy

60. •Using a single 10.0-V battery, what capacitance do you need to store 1.00×10^{-4} J of electric potential energy?

61. •A parallel-plate capacitor has square plates that have edge length equal to 1.00×10^2 cm and are separated by 1.00 mm. It is connected to a battery and is charged to 12.0 V. How much energy is stored in the capacitor?

62. •You charge a 2.00-μF capacitor to 50.0 V. How much additional energy must you add to charge it to 100 V?

63. •A capacitor has a capacitance of 80.0 μF. If you want to store 160 J of electric energy in this capacitor, what potential difference do you need to apply to the plates?

64. ••(a) You want to store 1.00×10^{-5} C of charge on a capacitor, but you only have a 100-V voltage source with which to charge it. What must be the value of the capacitance? (b) You want to store 1.00×10^{-3} J of energy on a capacitor, and you only have a 100-V voltage source with which to charge it. What must be the value of the capacitance?

65. •**Medical** A defibrillator containing a 20.0-μF capacitor is used to shock the heart of a patient by holding it to the patient's chest. Just prior to discharging, the capacitor has a voltage of 10.0 kV across its plates. How much energy is released into the patient, assuming no energy losses? SSM

17-7 Capacitors can be combined in series or in parallel

66. ••How should four 1.0-pF capacitors be connected to have a total capacitance of 0.75 pF?

67. •Three capacitors have capacitances 10.0 μF, 15.0 μF, and 30.0 μF. What is their effective capacitance if the three are connected (a) in parallel and (b) in series?

68. ••A series circuit consists of a 0.50-μF capacitor, a 0.10-μF capacitor, and a 220-V battery. Determine the charge on each of the capacitors.

69. ••Two capacitors provide an equivalent capacitance of 8.00 μF when connected in parallel and 2.00 μF when connected in series. What is the capacitance of each capacitor? SSM

70. ••A 2.00-μF capacitor is first charged by being connected across a 6.00-V battery. It is then disconnected from the battery and connected across an uncharged 4.00-μF capacitor. Calculate the final charge on each of the capacitors.

71. •A 0.0500-μF capacitor and a 0.100-μF capacitor are connected in parallel across a 220-V battery. Determine the charge on each of the capacitors.

72. •What is the equivalent capacitance of the network of three capacitors shown in **Figure 17-29**?

Figure 17-29 Problem 72

73. •Calculate the equivalent capacitance between a and b for the combination of capacitors shown in **Figure 17-30**.

Figure 17-30 Problem 73

74. ••A 10.0-μF capacitor, a 40.0-μF capacitor, and a 100.0-μF capacitor are connected in parallel across a 12.0-V battery. (a) What is the equivalent capacitance of the combination? (b) What is the charge on each capacitor? (c) What is the potential difference across each capacitor?

75. ••A 10.0-μF capacitor, a 40.0-μF capacitor, and a 100.0-μF capacitor are connected in series across a 12.0-V battery. (a) What is the equivalent capacitance of the combination? (b) What is the charge on each capacitor? (c) What is the potential difference across each capacitor? SSM

76. ••For the capacitor network shown in **Figure 17-31**, the potential difference across ab is 75.0 V. How much charge and how much energy are stored in this system?

Figure 17-31 Problem 76

17-8 Placing a dielectric between the plates of a capacitor increases the capacitance

77. •What is the dielectric constant of the material that fills the gap between a parallel-plate capacitor with plate area of 20.0 cm^2 and plate separation of 1.00 cm if the capacitance is measured to be 0.0142 μF?

78. •A parallel-plate capacitor has plates of 1.00 cm by 2.00 cm. The plates are separated by a 1.00-mm-thick piece of paper. What is the capacitance of this capacitor? The dielectric constant for paper is 2.7.

79. ••A 2800-pF air-filled capacitor is connected to a 16-V battery. If you now insert a ceramic dielectric material ($k = 5.8$) that fills the space between the plates, how much charge will flow from the battery? SSM

80. ••A parallel-plate capacitor has square plates that have edge lengths equal to 1.00×10^2 cm and are separated by 1.00 mm. It is connected to a battery and charged to 12.0 V. How much energy would be stored in the capacitor if a ceramic dielectric material (k is 5.8) fills the space between the plates?

81. •••(a) Determine the capacitance of the parallel-plate capacitor shown in Figure 17-32. The dielectric with constant κ_1 fills up one-quarter of the area, but the full separation of the plates. The materials with constants κ_2 and κ_3 fill the other three-quarters of the area, and divide the separation of the plates in half. (b) What happens to the total capacitance if the material with dielectric constant κ_3 is replaced by air?

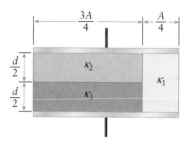

Figure 17-32 Problem 81

82. ••A parallel-plate capacitor that has a plate separation of 0.50 cm is filled halfway with a slab of dielectric material (k is 5.0) (Figure 17-33). If the plates are 1.25 cm by 1.25 cm in area, what is the capacitance of this capacitor?

Figure 17-33 Problem 82

General Problems

83. ••A parallel-plate capacitor has a plate separation of 1.5 mm and is charged to 600 V. If an electron leaves the negative plate, starting from rest, how fast is it going when it hits the positive plate?

84. ••Consider a 1.00-m³ cube that has +2.00-μC charges located at seven of its corners as shown in Figure 17-34. (a) Find the potential at the vacant corner. (b) How much work by an external agent is required to bring an additional +2.00-μC charge from rest at infinity to rest at the vacant corner? (c) How does the problem change, if at all, if a −2.00-μC charge is brought in to fill the empty corner rather than a positive charge?

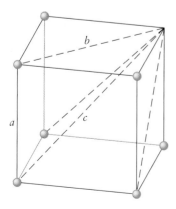

Figure 17-34 Problem 84

85. •••As shown in Figure 17-35, three particles, each with charge q, are at different corners of a rhombus with sides

of length a and with one diagonal of length a and the other of length b. (a) What is the electric potential energy of the charge distribution? (b) How much work by an external agent is required to bring a fourth particle, also of charge q, from rest at infinity to rest at the vacant corner of the rhombus? (c) What is the total electric potential energy of the four charges? SSM

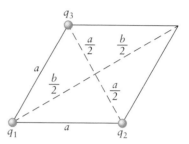

Figure 17-35 Problem 85

86. ••A lightning bolt transfers 20 C of charge to Earth through an average potential difference of 30 MV. (a) How much energy is dissipated in the bolt? (b) How much water (at a temperature of 100°C) can be turned into steam with this energy?

87. ••In 2004, physicists at the Stanford Linear Accelerator Center (SLAC) in California fired electrons toward each other at very high speeds so that they came within 1.0×10^{-15} m of each other (approximately the diameter of a proton). (a) What was the electrical force on each electron at closest approach? (b) Would this force be large enough to move you? (c) How much energy did it take to get the electrons that close together? (d) Ignoring relativistic effects, how fast must the electrons have been traveling initially, when far from each other, to get that close? (e) Do you notice anything suspicious about your answer?

88. ••Biology Under certain circumstances, potassium ions (K⁺) move across the 8.0-nm-thick cell membrane from the inside to the outside. The potential inside the cell is −70.0 mV, and the potential outside is zero. (a) What is the change in the electrical potential energy of the potassium ions as they move across the membrane? Does their potential energy increase or decrease as they move from the inside to the outside?

89. ••Calculate the equivalent capacitance of the combination in Figure 17-36. SSM

Figure 17-36 Problem 89

90. ••Suppose you are supplied with five identical capacitors (each with a capacitance of 10.0 μF). Determine all of the unique combinations that use all five capacitors and the equivalent capacitance of each combination.

91. ••Determine the equivalent capacitance of the combination in Figure 17-37.

Figure 17-37 Problem 91

92. ••The following arrangement of four capacitors has an equivalent capacitance of 8.00 μF (Figure 17-38). Calculate the value of C_x.

Figure 17-38 Problem 92

93. ••Calculate the charge stored on each capacitor in the circuit shown in Figure 17-39.

Figure 17-39 Problem 93

94. ••A parallel-plate capacitor is made by sandwiching 0.100-mm sheets of paper (dielectric constant 2.7) between three sheets of aluminum foil (A, B, and C in Figure 17-40) and rolling the layers into a cylinder. A capacitor that has an area of 10 m^2 is fabricated this way. (To be practical, it would then have to be folded up so as to fit in a small package.) What is the capacitance of this capacitor?

Figure 17-40 Problem 94

95. ••A parallel-plate capacitor with a capacitance of 5.00 μF is charged with a 12.0-V battery. After fully charging the plates, the battery is removed. How much work is required to increase the separation between the plates by a factor of 3?

96. ••An air-filled, parallel-plate capacitor with area A and gap width d is connected to a battery that maintains the plates at potential difference V. (a) The plates are pulled apart, doubling the gap width, while they remain in electrical contact with the battery terminals. By what factor does the potential energy of the capacitor change? (b) If the capacitor is removed from the battery and thus isolated, what happens to the stored potential energy when the gap width is doubled? Explain your answer.

97. ••An air-filled parallel-plate capacitor is attached to a battery with a voltage V. While attached to the battery, the area of the plates is doubled and the separation of the plates is halved. During this process, what happens to (a) the capacitance, (b) the charged stored on the positive plate of the capacitor, (c) the potential across the plates of the capacitor, and (d) the potential energy stored in the capacitor, as compared to the original configuration? (e) How would your answers change if, once the capacitor was charged by the battery, it was disconnected from the battery while the area and separation were changed as above?

98. •••You have a bucketful of capacitors, each with a capacitance of 1.00 μF and a maximum voltage rating of 250 V. You are to come up with a combination that has a capacitance of 0.75 μF and a maximum voltage rating of 1000 V. What is the minimum number of capacitors you need?

99. •••A parallel-plate capacitor has area A and separation d. (a) How is its capacitance affected if a *conducting* slab of thickness $d' < d$ is inserted between, and parallel to, the plates as shown in Figure 17-41? (b) Does your answer depend on where the slab is positioned vertically between the plates? SSM

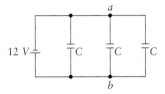

Figure 17-41 Problem 99

100. •••Three 0.18-μF capacitors are connected in parallel across a 12-V battery, as shown in Figure 17-42. The battery is then disconnected. Next, one capacitor is carefully disconnected so that it doesn't lose any charge and is reconnected backward, that is, with its positively charged side and its negatively charged side reversed. (a) What is the potential difference across the capacitors now? (b) By how much has the stored energy of the combination of capacitors changed in the process?

Figure 17-42 Problem 100

101. •(a) Calculate the charge and energy stored on the 25-μF capacitor when the switch S is placed at position A in Figure 17-43. (b) Repeat for both the 25-μF and the 20-μF capacitors after the switch is then placed at position B.

Figure 17-43 Problem 101

102. ••Figure 17-44 shows equipotential curves for 30 V, 10 V, and -10 V. A proton's speed as it passes point A is 80 km/s. It follows the path shown in the figure. What is the proton's speed at point B?

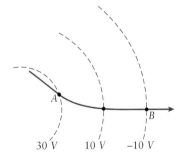

Figure 17-44 Problem 102

103. ••A parallel-plate, air-filled capacitor has a charge of 20.0 μC and a gap width of 0.100 mm. The potential difference between the plates is 200 V. (a) What is the electric field in the region between the plates? (b) What is the surface charge density on the positive plate? (c) If the plates of the capacitor are moved closer together while the charge remains constant, how are the electric field, surface charge density, and potential difference going to change, if at all? Explain your answers.

18

Electric Charges in Motion

In this chapter, your goals are to:

- (18-1) Recognize why moving electric charges are important.
- (18-2) Explain the meaning of current and drift speed, and the difference between direct and alternating current.
- (18-3) Describe the relationships among voltage, current, resistance, and resistivity for charges moving in a wire.
- (18-4) Calculate the resistance of a resistor and the current that a given voltage produces in that resistor.
- (18-5) Discuss Kirchhoff's rules and how to apply them to single-loop and multiloop circuits.
- (18-6) Calculate the power into or out of a circuit element.
- (18-7) Explain what happens when a capacitor in series with a resistor is charged or discharged.

To master this chapter, you should review:

- (5-5) How fluids exert drag forces on objects moving through them.
- (12-3) How to describe the position of an object oscillating with simple harmonic motion.
- (13-9) How power is the rate at which energy is transferred.
- (16-3) How the loosely bound electrons in metals allow them to conduct electricity.
- (16-7) Why the electric field outside a uniformly charged sphere is the same as if all the charge were located at the center of the sphere.
- (17-3) How electric field and potential difference are related, and how potential difference and electric potential energy difference are related.
- (17-5, The relationship among charge, voltage, and capacitance; the energy stored
  17-6, in a capacitor; and the equivalent capacitance of capacitors attached in
  17-7) series and parallel.

18-1 Life on Earth and our technological society are only possible because of charges in motion

In the previous two chapters, we've examined a variety of topics in the general category of electrostatics. For example, we determined the electric field that a point charge or combination of charges generates at various points in space. In doing so, we considered the charges to be fixed in place. But in many important situations in nature and technology electric charges are in *motion*. You are able to read these words thanks to electric charges that travel along the optic nerve from your eye to your brain, transmitting the

(a)
Wires and cables are made of conductors that allow moving charges to flow along their length.

(b)
The current in a mobile device is provided by a battery (a source of emf).

(c)
A camera's electronic flash uses energy stored in a capacitor to produce a burst of light.

Figure 18-1 **Charges in motion** (a) An essential part of any electric circuit. (b) and (c) Two common devices that use currents (moving electric charges).

image of those words in the form of a coded electrical signal. If you are reading these words after sunset, you are either looking at a printed page illuminated by a light bulb that's powered by moving electric charges, or else reading them on a tablet or other electronic device that operates using complex electric circuitry.

In this chapter we'll look at the basic physics of electric charges in motion. We'll introduce the idea of *current*, which measures the rate at which charges move through a conductor (Figure 18-1a). The value of current will prove to be related to the speed at which moving charges drift through the conductor. Ordinary conductors have *resistance* to the flow of charge, so it's necessary to set up a voltage between the ends of a conductor in order to produce a current. This is the role of a *source of emf*, the most common example of which is an ordinary battery (Figure 18-1b). We'll analyze simple circuits that include a source of emf and one or more *resistors* (circuit elements that have resistance), and see how to treat combinations of resistors.

Fundamentally, an electric circuit is used to transfer energy from one place to another (for instance, from a battery to a light bulb, as in the photograph that opens this chapter). We'll see how to describe the *power*, or rate of energy transfer, associated with any circuit element. Finally, we'll study circuits that include a capacitor, which make it possible to deliver energy in a quick burst (Figure 18-1c).

> **Take-Home Message for Section 18-1**
>
> ✔ Technological devices and biological systems depend on electric charges in motion.
>
> ✔ An electric circuit is fundamentally a means of transferring energy.

18-2 Electric current equals the rate at which charge flows

Figure 18-2 shows a common situation in which electric charges are in motion. What sets charges into motion is the **battery**, also known as an *electrochemical cell*. Inside the cell are two different substances that, due to their different chemical properties, undergo a chemical reaction so that each substance ends up with an excess or deficit of electrons. In an ordinary alkaline battery, like an AA or D cell, the two substances are zinc and manganese dioxide. The zinc ends up with an electron excess, while the manganese dioxide ends up with an electron deficit.

The two terminals of the battery are each connected to one of these substances. Electrons can flow between each substance and the metal terminal to which it is attached. As a result, the terminal attached to the substance with an electron excess also has an electron excess and is called the *negative* terminal. The other terminal, attached to the substance with an electron deficit, also has an electron deficit and is called the *positive* terminal. These terminals are marked on the battery by a minus sign and a plus sign, respectively. Because of this charge imbalance, the positive terminal is at a higher electric potential than the negative terminal. The potential difference, or voltage, between the terminals depends on the two substances within the battery. For zinc and manganese dioxide, the voltage is 1.5 V, a number that you will see written on the case of any alkaline battery.

Figure 18-2 Current in a circuit
Charge flows in a wire loop due to the potential difference (voltage) supplied by a battery.

1. A simple electric circuit is made up of a battery connected to a wire and a device (such as a light bulb), forming a closed circuit.

Battery

2. There is a potential difference between the terminals of the battery. This gives rise to an electric field in the wire and device.

3. The electric field causes mobile charges in the wire to flow. The current—the rate at which charge flows past a given point in the wire—is *i*.

4. Charge does not pile up at any point in the circuit. So the current has the same value *i* at all points in the circuit, including inside the battery, in the wire, and inside the device.

Device

We know from Section 17-3 that charges tend to flow between two points when there is a potential difference between those points: The electric force pushes positive charges from high to low potential, and negative charges from low to high potential. If a battery is isolated and not connected to anything, there is no way for charge to travel outside the battery from one terminal to another. So in this case there is no charge flow. But charge *can* flow if a metallic wire is used to connect the two terminals to each other as in Figure 18-2. (As we saw in Section 16-3, metals are especially good electrical conductors because one or more of the electrons associated with a metal atom are only weakly bound to that atom. As a result, these loosely bound electrons can move with relative freedom within the metal.) So the battery and wire form a complete loop or **circuit**, and charge flows continuously through the circuit from one terminal of the battery to the other. Note that the circuit *must* be complete in order for charges to move. If the wire in Figure 18-2 is broken or disconnected from the battery, the flow of charge stops.

Here's another way to see why charges move in the wire. The potential difference between the battery terminals means that there is an electric *field* $\vec{E}$ within the wire. This field points along the length of the wire in the direction from the positive terminal to the negative terminal. A mobile charge with charge q within the wire will feel a force $\vec{F} = q\vec{E}$ from the electric field, and this force is what pushes the charges through the wire. This force is necessary because mobile charges within the wire collide very frequently with the atoms that make up the wire. The net effect of the collisions is to slow or retard the motion of the mobile charges through the wire, rather like how a ball falling through the air or an algal spore moving through water is retarded by fluid resistance (see Section 5-5). The speed at which charge flows is determined by the balance between the retarding force due to collisions and the forward electric force $\vec{F} = q\vec{E}$.

Later in this chapter we'll see how the flow of charge delivers energy to a device (like a light bulb) that's part of the circuit. For now, however, let's concentrate on the properties of the charge flow itself.

Current

See the Math Tutorial for more information on direct and inverse proportions

The **current** in a circuit like that in Figure 18-2 equals the rate at which charge flows past any point in the circuit. In particular, if an amount of charge Δq moves past a certain point in a time Δt, the current *i* is

Current in a circuit

Amount of **charge** that flows past a certain point in the circuit

Definition of current
(18-1)

$$i = \frac{\Delta q}{\Delta t}$$

Time required for that amount of charge to flow past that point

The SI unit of current is the **ampere**, named after the French scientist and mathematician André Ampère. One ampere (abbreviated amp or A) is equivalent to one coulomb of charge passing a given point per second: 1 A = 1 C/s.

In much the same way as we treated fluid flow in Chapter 11, we'll begin by limiting our discussion of currents to a *steady* flow of charge. Then the current i has the same value at all *times*. In addition, the current has the same value at all *points* in a simple circuit like that in Figure 18-2 in which charges move around a single loop. The moving charges cannot "pile up" or accumulate at any point in the circuit (if they did, their mutual electrostatic repulsion would make them spread apart again). There is also no way for more moving charges to join the flow or for charges to leave the flow. So the value of the current is the same everywhere in the circuit.

Note that current is *not* a vector quantity. For example, in Figure 18-2 the current is to the left in the upper part of the circuit, downward in the left-hand part of the circuit, to the right in the lower part of the circuit, and upward in the right-hand part of the circuit. So there is no single vector that describes the direction of current in every part of the circuit. Instead, we simply say that the current in Figure 18-2 is counterclockwise around the circuit. If we reversed the battery so that the positive terminal was on the right rather than on the left, the current would be clockwise.

 Watch Out! **The direction of current is chosen to be the direction in which *positive* charges would flow.**

In ordinary wires and in common electric devices such as light bulbs and toasters, the charges that are free to move are negatively charged electrons. In an electric circuit such as that shown in Figure 18-2, electrons tend to flow through the wire from low potential to high potential, and so from the negative terminal of the battery toward the positive terminal. But in Figure 18-2 we show the current flowing through the wire from the battery's *positive* terminal to its *negative* terminal. That's because the convention is to take current to flow in the direction that positively charged objects would move, regardless of whether the moving objects are positively or negatively

charged. We'll use this convention throughout this book. (This convention is often attributed to the eighteenth-century American scientist and statesman Benjamin Franklin. The discovery that the moving charges in wires are negatively charged came decades after Franklin's death.) Note that in most biological systems such as neurons and muscle cells, the moving charges are in fact positive (they are positive ions, atoms that have lost one or more electrons each). But no matter what the nature of the moving charges, the principles governing current are the same.

Because an electron has a very small charge ($q = -e = -1.60 \times 10^{-19}$ C), typical currents involve the flow of a very large number of electrons. For example, suppose the current i in the circuit shown in Figure 18-2 is 1.00 A or 1.00 C/s. (That's roughly the current in a large flashlight.) Then the rate at which electrons move past any specific point on the wire is

$$1.00 \text{ A} = 1.00 \frac{\text{C}}{\text{s}} = \left(1.00 \frac{\text{C}}{\text{s}}\right)\left(\frac{1 \text{ electron}}{1.60 \times 10^{-19} \text{ C}}\right) = 6.25 \times 10^{18} \frac{\text{electron}}{\text{s}}$$

(Here we're considering the *magnitude* of the current, so we're ignoring the negative sign on the charge of the electron.) This result says that if we were to pass an imaginary plane through the cross section of the wire, we would find about 6×10^{18} electrons crossing that plane per second.

Example 18-1 Charging a Sphere

A large, hollow metal sphere is electrically isolated from its surroundings, except for a wire that can carry a current to charge the sphere. Initially, the sphere is uncharged and is at electrical potential zero. If the sphere has a radius of 0.150 m and the current is a steady 5.00 μA = 5.00×10^{-6} A, how long does it take for the sphere to attain a potential of 4.00×10^5 V?

Set Up

The electric potential at the surface of a charged sphere of radius R depends on the amount of excess charge Q on the sphere. In Section 16-7 we learned that the electric *field* outside a uniformly charged sphere is identical to that of a particle with the same charge, located at the center of the sphere. So the electric *potential* at a point just outside the sphere must be given by Equation 17-8, the equation for the potential of a charged particle with total charge Q located at the center of the sphere. We'll rearrange this equation to solve for the amount of charge required to generate the given electric potential. Then we'll find the time required for this charge to reach the sphere.

Electric potential of a charged sphere:

$$V = \frac{kQ}{R} \qquad (17\text{-}8)$$

Definition of current:

$$i = \frac{\Delta q}{\Delta t} \qquad (18\text{-}1)$$

0.150 m

$i = 5.00\ \mu A$

hollow sphere

Solve

Use Equation 17-8 to solve for the final charge on the sphere.

From Equation 17-8,

$$Q = \frac{VR}{k} = \frac{(4.00 \times 10^5\ \text{V})\,(0.150\ \text{m})}{(8.99 \times 10^9\ \text{N} \cdot \text{m}^2/\text{C}^2)}$$

$$= 6.67 \times 10^{-6} \frac{\text{V} \cdot \text{C}^2}{\text{N} \cdot \text{m}}$$

Since $1\ \text{V} = 1\ \text{J/C} = 1\ \text{N} \cdot \text{m/C}$, this becomes

$$Q = \left(6.67 \times 10^{-6} \frac{\text{V} \cdot \text{C}^2}{\text{N} \cdot \text{m}} \right)\left(\frac{1\ \text{N} \cdot \text{m/C}}{1\ \text{V}} \right)$$

$$= 6.67 \times 10^{-6}\ \text{C} = 6.67\ \mu\text{C}$$

Our result $Q = 6.67\ \mu\text{C}$ is the amount of charge Δq that must flow onto the sphere in a time Δt. Use Equation 18-1 to solve for Δt. Recall that $1\ \text{A} = 1\ \text{C/s}$.

From Equation 18-1,

$$\Delta t = \frac{\Delta q}{i} = \frac{6.67 \times 10^{-6}\ \text{C}}{5.00 \times 10^{-6}\ \text{A}} = \frac{6.67 \times 10^{-6}\ \text{C}}{5.00 \times 10^{-6}\ \text{C/s}}$$

$$= 1.33\ \text{s}$$

Reflect

A charged sphere like this is used in a Van de Graaff generator, which you may have seen demonstrated in your physics class. If you have, you know that when the generator is turned on to charge the sphere, the sphere can begin to throw off sparks within a second or so. So a result for Δt on the order of 1 s is reasonable.

Drift Speed

The value of the current i tells us what quantity of charge flows past a given point in a circuit per second. This is related to the **drift speed** v_{drift}, which is the average speed at which charges move ("drift") through the circuit. Let's see how to relate these two quantities.

Figure 18-3 shows a wire that has a cross-sectional area A and carries a current i. Charges are moving ("drifting") through the green region at an average speed of v_{drift}. At any time, the total moving charge in that region is Δq. This charge can be expressed in terms of n (the number of moving charges per volume), the volume $A\,\Delta x$ of the green region (a cylinder of area A and length Δx), and the amount of charge e on each moving charge:

(18-2)
$$\Delta q = n(\text{Volume})e = n(A\Delta x)e$$

If the moving charges are electrons, each has a charge $-e$ rather than e. But since we take the direction of current to be the direction in which positive charges would flow, we'll use the convenient fiction that the charge is positive. The time required for this volume of charge to drift the distance Δx along the length of the wire is $\Delta t = \Delta x / v_{\text{drift}}$

(1) Current i is present in the wire of cross-sectional area A.

(2) Within the wire there are n mobile charges per unit volume. Each has a charge e.

(3) The mobile charges drift through the wire with speed v_{drift}, and travel a distance Δx in a time $\Delta t = \Delta x/v_{drift}$.

Figure 18-3 Drift speed The current i in a wire is proportional to the speed v_{drift} at which moving charges drift through the wire.

(4) A length Δx of the wire (shown in green) has volume $A\Delta x$. This length contains $n(A\Delta x)$ mobile charges, with total charge $\Delta q = n(A\Delta x)e$.

(5) The current in the wire equals the amount of charge Δq that passes this point divided by the time Δt it takes them to pass this point:

$$i = \frac{\Delta q}{\Delta t} = \frac{n(A\Delta x)e}{\Delta x/v_{drift}} = nAev_{drift}$$

(time equals distance divided by speed). So from Equations 18-1 and 18-2, the current in the wire is

$$i = \frac{\Delta q}{\Delta t} = \frac{n(A\Delta x)e}{\Delta x/v_{drift}}$$

or, simplifying,

Current in a wire   Number of moving charges per unit volume

$$i = nAev_{drift}$$

Speed at which charges drift through the wire

Cross-sectional area of the wire   Magnitude of the charge on each moving charge

Current and drift speed (18-3)

The number of moving charges per volume (n) is different for different materials. Equation 18-3 tells us that for a wire made of a given material and with a given cross-sectional area A, the current i is directly proportional to the drift speed.

! Watch Out!   The drift speed is not the same as the speed at which individual charges move.

Even if there is no current through a wire, the mobile charges within that wire are still in motion. However, their motions are in random directions, so that there is no *net* motion of charge. It's rather like a swarm of bees flying around a hive: Individual bees move in different directions, but the swarm as a whole stays in the same place. If the swarm moves to a different hive, the motions of individual bees will be different but the swarm as a whole will "drift" together to the new hive. In the same way, if a current is present in the wire in Figure 18-3, the individual charges within the green volume can be moving at different speeds and in different directions, but this "swarm" of charge drifts along the wire at speed v_{drift}.

Example 18-2 Electron Drift Speed in a Flashlight

In a large flashlight, the distance from the on-off switch to the light bulb is 10.0 cm. How long does it takes electrons to drift this distance if the flashlight wires are made of copper, are 0.512 mm in radius, and carry a current of 1.00 A? There are 8.49×10^{28} atoms in 1 m^3 of copper, and one electron per copper atom is able to move freely through the metal.

Set Up

We'll use Equation 18-3 to determine the drift speed from the information given about the number of mobile electrons, the radius of the wire, and the current. From this we'll be able to find the drift time by using the familiar relationship between speed, distance, and time.

Current and drift speed:

$$i = nAev_{drift} \qquad (18\text{-}3)$$

Solve

Calculate the drift speed of the electrons in the wire.

Solve Equation 18-3 for the drift speed:

$$v_{drift} = \frac{i}{nAe}$$

There is one mobile electron per atom and 8.49×10^{28} atoms/m^3, so the value of n is 8.49×10^{28} electrons/m^3. The wire has a circular cross section with radius $r = 0.512$ mm $= 0.512 \times 10^{-3}$ m, so its cross-sectional area is

$$A = \pi r^2 = \pi(0.512 \times 10^{-3} \text{ m})^2 = 8.24 \times 10^{-7} \text{ m}^2$$

The magnitude of the charge per electron is $e = 1.60 \times 10^{-19}$ C/electron, and the current is $i = 1.00$ A $= 1.00$ C/s. So the drift speed is

$$v_{drift} = \frac{i}{nAe}$$

$$= \frac{1.00 \text{ C/s}}{(8.49 \times 10^{28} \text{ electrons/m}^3)(8.24 \times 10^{-7} \text{ m}^2)(1.60 \times 10^{-19} \text{ C/electron})}$$

$$= 8.94 \times 10^{-5} \text{ m/s} = 0.0894 \text{ mm/s}$$

Then calculate how long it takes electrons to drift the distance from switch to light bulb.

At this drift speed, the time it takes electrons to travel a distance $d = 10.0$ cm $= 0.100$ m from the flashlight on-off switch to the light bulb is

$$t = \frac{d}{v_{drift}} = \frac{0.100 \text{ m}}{8.94 \times 10^{-5} \text{ m/s}} = 1.12 \times 10^3 \text{ s}$$

$$= (1.12 \times 10^3 \text{ s})\left(\frac{1 \text{ min}}{60 \text{ s}}\right) = 18.6 \text{ min}$$

Reflect

The phrase "a snail's pace" refers to something that moves very slowly. But an ordinary snail moves at about *twice* the drift speed of electrons in this wire. The drift speed is so slow because electrons in the wire are continually colliding with the copper atoms, which slows their progress tremendously. (More sophisticated physics shows that an electron in copper moves in *random* motion at an average speed of about 10^6 m/s, about 10^{10} times faster than the drift speed. In the analogy we made earlier between electrons and a swarm of bees, you should think of the electrons in this wire as *very* fast-moving bees within a swarm that's drifting very, very slowly.)

At their slower-than-a-snail's pace, it takes electrons more than a quarter of an hour to travel from the on-off switch to the light bulb. Why, then, does the flashlight turn on immediately when you move the switch to the "on" position?

The explanation is that the wire is full of mobile electrons, and these electrons drift in response to the electric field in the wire. With the switch in the off position, there is no electric field and so no drift. An electric field is only set up when the switch is put in the on position, making a complete circuit like that shown in Figure 18-2. Changes in the electric field propagate through the wire at close to the speed of light (3×10^8 m/s), so the field is set up throughout the circuit, and the electrons begin to drift, in a tiny fraction of a second. That's why the light comes on nearly instantaneously.

Direct Current and Alternating Current

In the circuit shown in Figure 18-2 the current always flows around the circuit in the same direction, as shown by the arrows labeled i. Current of this kind is called **direct current** or **DC** for short. You'll find direct current in any device that's powered by a battery, such as a flashlight, a television remote control, or a mobile phone. That's because the potential difference between the two terminals of the battery that powers the circuit always has the same sign: The positive terminal is always at a higher potential than the negative terminal.

Something very different happens in a toaster or a table lamp that you plug into a wall socket. The potential difference between the two terminals in a wall socket is not constant, but instead oscillates or *alternates*. At one instant the left-hand terminal is at a higher potential than the right-hand terminal; a short time later the left-hand terminal is the one at the lower potential, and a short time after that the left-hand terminal is again at the higher potential. As a result, the current in a device plugged into a wall socket alternates direction (**Figure 18-4**). This is called **alternating current** or **AC** for short. (The third terminal found in most wall sockets, called the *ground*, remains at a constant potential and is not directly involved in producing the current.)

The potential difference or voltage between the two terminals of a wall socket varies with time in a sinusoidal way, just as does the position of an object in simple harmonic motion (Section 12-3). We can write this voltage as

$$V(t) = V_0 \sin \omega t = V_0 \sin 2\pi f t \qquad (18\text{-}4)$$

This expression says that the potential difference between the left-hand and right-hand terminals in a wall socket varies between $+V_0$ and $-V_0$. In Equation 18-4 f is the frequency at which the voltage oscillates, and $\omega = 2\pi f$ is the corresponding angular frequency. In North America, Central America, and much of South America, the frequency used is $f = 60$ Hz; in most of the rest of the world, $f = 50$ Hz is used. The current in a circuit driven by such a wall socket oscillates with the same frequency. So in an AC circuit, electrons just oscillate back and forth around an equilibrium position. That's very different from a DC circuit, in which electrons plod slowly in the same direction around the circuit.

If $f = 60$ Hz, the *period* of oscillation of the current is $T = 1/f = 1/(60\ \text{Hz}) = 1/60$ s. This means that the current in the circuit shown in Figure 18-4 moves in one direction for $(1/2) \times (1/60)\ \text{s} = 1/120$ s, then moves in the opposite direction for $1/120$ s, and so on. Since the drift speed of electrons in a wire is typically very slow (see Example 18-2), electrons can move only a very short distance (typically around 10^{-6} m or less) in $1/120$ s.

In Chapter 21 we'll study alternating current in detail, learn how an alternating voltage is generated, and see why it's used instead of direct current (DC) for wall sockets. For the remainder of this chapter we'll concentrate exclusively on DC circuits.

The current flows in this direction when the left-hand terminal is at a higher potential than the right-hand terminal...

...and flows in the opposite direction when the left-hand terminal is at a lower potential than the right-hand terminal.

 The alternating voltage of the wall socket produces an **alternating current**.

Figure 18-4 Alternating current The potential difference between the terminals of a wall socket varies sinusoidally. As a result, the current in a circuit that contains this socket alternates direction.

? Got the Concept? 18-1 Current in a Wire

Suppose that part of the wire in Example 18-2 were only half the thickness of the rest of the wire, with a radius of 0.256 mm instead of 0.512 mm. Compared to the rest of the wire, would the current in the thinner part be (a) four times greater, (b) twice as great, (c) the same, (d) one-half as great, or (e) one-fourth as great?

? Got the Concept? 18-2 Drift Speed in a Wire

Suppose that part of the wire in Example 18-2 were only half the thickness of the rest of the wire, with a radius of 0.256 mm instead of 0.512 mm. Compared to the rest of the wire, would the drift speed in the thinner part be (a) four times faster, (b) twice as fast, (c) the same, (d) one-half as fast, or (e) one-fourth as fast?

Take-Home Message for Section 18-2

✔ An electric field applied in a wire results in an electric current (a net flow of charge in the wire).

✔ The SI unit of current is the ampere (A): 1 A = 1 C/s.

✔ Current has a magnitude and a direction, but it is not a vector.

✔ By convention, the direction assigned to a current is the direction in which positive charge carriers would move. In typical metals like those used in wires, it is the negative electrons that actually move and carry current.

✔ Direct current (DC) always travels the same direction around a circuit. Alternating current (AC) continually changes direction.

18-3 The resistance to current through an object depends on the object's resistivity and dimensions

We saw in Section 18-2 that a current can flow in a wire only if there is a potential difference between the ends of the wire. This gives rise to an electric field inside the wire, and this field exerts a force that causes mobile charges to move. However, the motion of these mobile charges is slowed due to collisions between the charges and the atoms of the wire. The net result is that charges drift through the wire at a relatively slow speed. To better understand current, we need to answer three questions:

(1) How is the electric field in a current-carrying wire related to the potential difference between the ends of the wire?
(2) How is the resulting current related to the electric field in the wire?
(3) How large is the current in the wire as a consequence of the potential difference between the ends of the wire?

The first of these questions is easily answered for a straight wire of uniform cross-sectional area A and length L (Figure 18-5). If there is a potential difference V between the ends of the wire, the electric field $\vec{E}$ points along the length of the wire from the high-potential end toward the low-potential end. Since the wire is uniform, we expect that the magnitude E of the field will be uniform as well. From Chapter 17, the potential difference V is just equal to the field magnitude multiplied by the length of the wire:

Figure 18-5 **Inside a current-carrying wire** The electric field in a current-carrying wire points from the higher-potential end toward the lower-potential end. The current is in the same direction.

(18-5)
$$V = EL \quad \text{or} \quad E = \frac{V}{L}$$

This is the same as Equation 17-7, $\Delta V = -Ed \cos \theta$. We've changed the symbol for potential difference from ΔV to V, replaced the distance d by L, and used $\theta = 180°$ for the angle between the direction of $\vec{E}$ and the direction that we imagine traveling along the length of the wire to measure the potential difference. With this choice the potential difference V is positive. Remember that potential always increases as we travel opposite to $\vec{E}$ and decreases as we travel in the direction of $\vec{E}$. Remember also that the direction of current, which we choose to be the direction in which positive charges would move, is in the direction of $\vec{E}$ and so from high potential to low potential. For example, if there is a 1.5-V potential difference ($V = 1.5$ V) between the ends of a wire 10 cm in length ($L = 10$ cm $= 0.10$ m), Equation 18-5 tells us that the electric field inside the wire has magnitude $E = V/L = (1.5 \text{ V})/(0.10 \text{ m}) = 15 \text{ V/m}$.

For the answer to the second question, we must turn to experiments on current-carrying wires. For many materials (including common conductors such as copper), experiments show that the current i that arises in a wire when an electric field is present inside the wire is directly proportional to both the electric field magnitude E and the cross-sectional area A of the wire. We can write this relationship as

(18-6)
$$i = \frac{EA}{\rho}$$

In Equation 18-6 the quantity ρ (the Greek letter rho) is called the **resistivity**. The value of ρ depends on the material of which the wire is made and tells us how well or poorly this material inhibits the flow of electric charge. Equation 18-6 says that for a given cross-sectional area A and a given electric field magnitude E, a *greater* value of the resistivity means a *smaller* amount of current i. (It's unfortunate that the same Greek letter that we use as the symbol for density is also used as the symbol for resistivity. We promise never to use density and resistivity in the same equation!)

The units of resistivity are voltmeters per ampere, or V · m/A. For reasons that we will see below, the unit V/A (volts per ampere) appears very often and is given its own name, the **ohm** (symbol Ω, the uppercase Greek letter omega): $1 \Omega = 1 \text{ V/A}$. In terms of this, the units of resistivity can be written as ohmmeters, or $\Omega \cdot \text{m}$.

For copper, which is a good conductor of electricity, the resistivity is very low: $\rho = 1.725 \times 10^{-8}\ \Omega \cdot$ m at 21°C. For hard rubber, which is a very poor conductor (and a good insulator), $\rho = 10^{13}\ \Omega \cdot$ m at 21°C. The explanation for the huge ratio between these two values of resistivity is that copper has many mobile electrons per cubic meter, while hard rubber has hardly any. The value of resistivity also depends on temperature. In metals, atoms move more rapidly and are likely to be less well organized at higher temperatures compared to lower temperatures. As a result, moving charges suffer more collisions with the atoms in a material when the temperature is higher. Consequently, the resistivity of most metals increases as temperature increases. In other materials, such as ceramics, resistivity *decreases* with increasing temperature. Table 18-1 lists the values of resistivity for a variety of substances at 21°C.

In practice, it's more useful to know the answer to the third question: how the current i in a straight wire is related to the potential difference V between the ends of the wire, rather than the electric field E inside the wire. (That's because electrical meters measure potential difference directly, not electric field.) To obtain such a relationship, substitute the expression $E = V/L$ from Equation 18-5 into Equation 18-6:

$$i = \frac{EA}{\rho} = \left(\frac{V}{L}\right)\left(\frac{A}{\rho}\right) = V\left(\frac{A}{\rho L}\right) \quad \text{or} \quad V = i\left(\frac{\rho L}{A}\right) \qquad (18\text{-}7)$$

We define the **resistance** R of a wire as

Resistance of a wire

Resistivity of the material of which the wire is made

$$R = \frac{\rho L}{A}$$

Length of the wire

Cross-sectional area of the wire

In terms of this new quantity, we can rewrite Equation 18-7 as

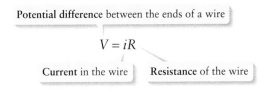

Potential difference between the ends of a wire

$$V = iR$$

Current in the wire   **Resistance** of the wire

Equation 18-9 says the potential difference, or voltage, V required to produce a current i in a wire is proportional to i and to the resistance of the wire. The greater the resistance, the greater the voltage required for a given current. Equation 18-8 further tells us that the resistance of a wire depends on the resistivity of the material of which the wire is made, the length of the wire, and the cross-sectional area of the wire. For a given material, the resistance is greater for a wire that is long (large L) and thin (small A) than for a wire that is short (small L) and thick (large A). You can see an example by looking inside the slots of an ordinary kitchen toaster. The wire that makes up the toaster's heating coils is very thin, and if uncoiled the wire would be very long. This tells us that the coils have a high resistance. The resistance is made even higher by making the wire out of nichrome, which has a resistivity about 10^2 times greater than that of copper (see Table 18-1).

Since resistivity ρ has units of ohmmeters ($\Omega \cdot$ m), length L has units of meters, and area A has units of meters squared, Equation 18-8 says that the units of resistance R are ohms. This agrees with Equation 18-9, since $1\ \Omega = 1$ V/A: To produce a 1-A current in a wire with a resistance of $1\ \Omega = 1$ V/A, a voltage of 1 V is required.

An ohm is a relatively small resistance. The heating coils of a toaster have a resistance R of about 10 to 20 Ω. A typical **resistor**—a circuit component intended to add resistance to the flow of current—such as you will find for sale in an electronics store will likely have a resistance in the range from 1 kΩ (1 kΩ = 1 kilohm = $10^3\ \Omega$) to 10 MΩ

Table 18-1 Resistivity of Some Conductors and Insulators at 21°C

Conductor	$\rho\ (\Omega \cdot m)$
aluminum	2.733×10^{-8}
copper	1.725×10^{-8}
gold	2.271×10^{-8}
iron	9.98×10^{-8}
nichrome	150×10^{-8}
nickel	7.2×10^{-8}
silver	1.629×10^{-8}
titanium	43.1×10^{-8}
tungsten	5.4×10^{-8}

Insulator	$\rho\ (\Omega \cdot m)$
glass	10^{12}
hard rubber	10^{13}
fused quartz	7.5×10^{17}

Definition of resistance
(18-8)

Relationship among potential difference, current, and resistance
(18-9)

$(1\ M\Omega = 1\ \text{megohm} = 10^6\ \Omega)$. The resistance of a human body measured on the skin can be more than $0.5\ M\Omega$. The standard symbol for a resistor is a jagged line:

Equation 18-9 is often referred to as "Ohm's law," after the nineteenth-century Bavarian physicist Georg Ohm whose pioneering experiments increased our understanding of electric current (and for whom the ohm, or volt per ampere, is named). By itself it suggests that voltage and current are directly proportional to each other. This proportionality holds true if the resistance R remains constant as the voltage is changed, and this is in fact the case for many conducting materials over a wide range of voltages. Materials that have this property are referred to as *ohmic*. However, for many materials (including those used in the filament of an incandescent light bulb as well as in a variety of electronic devices), the value of the resistance changes as the potential difference across the material changes. We can still use Equation 18-9 for such *nonohmic* materials, provided we keep in mind that R is not a constant.

Example 18-3 Stretching a Wire

A 10.0-m-long wire has a radius of 2.00 mm and a resistance of 50.0 Ω. If the wire is stretched to 10.0 times its original length, what will be its new resistance?

Set Up

Equation 18-8 tells us that resistance of the wire depends on its resistivity (which is a property of the material of which the wire is made, and doesn't change if the dimensions change). It also depends on the length and cross-sectional area, both of which change when the wire is stretched. To find the new cross-sectional area, we'll use the idea that the volume of the wire (the product of its length and cross-sectional area) does not change as it's stretched.

Definition of resistance:

$$R = \frac{\rho L}{A} \qquad (18\text{-}8)$$

Solve

Find the cross-sectional area of the wire after it has been stretched.

The original cross-sectional area A_1 of the wire of radius $r_1 = 2.00$ mm $= 2.00 \times 10^{-3}$ m is

$$A_1 = \pi r_1^2 = \pi (2.00 \times 10^{-3}\ \text{m})^2 = 1.26 \times 10^{-5}\ \text{m}^2$$

The volume of the wire is $A_1 L_1$, where $L_1 = 10.0$ m is the wire's initial length. If we stretch the wire to a new length $L_2 = 10.0 L_1 = 1.00 \times 10^2$ m, the cross-sectional area will change to a new value A_2, but the volume will be the same:

$$A_2 L_2 = A_1 L_1$$

$$A_2 = \frac{A_1 L_1}{L_2} = \frac{(1.26 \times 10^{-5}\ \text{m}^2)(10.0\ \text{m})}{1.00 \times 10^2\ \text{m}} = 1.26 \times 10^{-6}\ \text{m}^2$$

The new cross-sectional area is $1/10.0$ of the initial cross-sectional area.

Calculate the new resistance of the wire.

The initial resistance of the wire (before being stretched) is

$$R_1 = \frac{\rho L_1}{A_1} = 50.0\ \Omega$$

The resistance of the wire after being stretched is

$$R_2 = \frac{\rho L_2}{A_2}$$

If we take the ratio of the two resistances, the unknown value of resistivity will cancel out:

$$\frac{R_2}{R_1} = \frac{\rho L_2/A_2}{\rho L_1/A_1} = \frac{L_2 A_1}{L_1 A_2}$$

$$= \left(\frac{1.00 \times 10^2 \text{ m}}{10.0 \text{ m}}\right)\left(\frac{1.26 \times 10^{-5} \text{ m}^2}{1.26 \times 10^{-6} \text{ m}^2}\right)$$

$$= (10.0)(10.0) = 1.00 \times 10^2$$

The length has increased by a factor of 10.0 and the cross-sectional area has decreased by a factor of 10.0, so the new value of resistivity is greater than the old value by a factor of $(10.0)^2 = 1.00 \times 10^2$:

$$R_2 = 1.00 \times 10^2 \, R_1 = (1.00 \times 10^2)(50.0 \, \Omega)$$

$$= 5.00 \times 10^3 \, \Omega = 5.00 \text{ k}\Omega$$

Reflect

Stretching the wire makes it longer and thinner. A longer wire has more resistance than a shorter one when both are made from the same material, and a thinner wire has more resistance than a thicker one. So, we should expect the stretched wire in this problem to have a much higher resistance than the wire had initially.

Example 18-4 Calculating Current

If a 12.0-V potential difference is set up between the ends of each wire in Example 18-3, how much current will flow in each wire?

Set Up

We know the resistance of each wire from Example 18-3, and so we can use Equation 18-9 to solve for the current i in each wire.

Relationship between potential difference, current, and resistance:

$$V = iR \qquad (18-9)$$

Solve

Rewrite Equation 18-9 as an expression for the current in terms of the voltage and resistance. Then solve for the current in each case.

From Equation 18-9,

$$i = \frac{V}{R}$$

For the wire before it is stretched, $R = R_1 = 50.0 \, \Omega$. The current that results from a 12.0-V potential difference between the ends of this wire is

$$i_1 = \frac{V}{R_1} = \frac{12.0 \text{ V}}{50.0 \, \Omega} = 0.240 \frac{\text{V}}{\Omega}$$

Recall that $1 \, \Omega = 1 \text{ V/A}$, so $1 \text{ A} = 1 \text{ V/}\Omega$. So the current in the wire before it is stretched is

$$i_1 = 0.240 \text{ A}$$

After the wire is stretched, the resistance is $R = R_2 = 5.00 \times 10^3 \, \Omega$. A 12.0-V potential difference between the ends of this wire produces a current

$$i_2 = \frac{V}{R_2} = \frac{12.0 \text{ V}}{5.00 \times 10^3 \, \Omega} = 2.40 \times 10^{-3} \text{ A} = 2.40 \text{ mA}$$

Reflect

The stretched wire has a greater resistance than the original wire, so the same potential difference produces a smaller current. Note that the milliampere ($1 \text{ mA} = 10^{-3}$ A) is a commonly used unit of current, as are the microampere ($1 \text{ } \mu\text{A} = 10^{-6}$ A), the nanoampere ($1 \text{ nA} = 10^{-9}$ A), and the picoampere ($1 \text{ pA} = 10^{-12}$ A).

❓ Got the Concept? 18-3 Is It Ohmic?

A wire is made of a certain conducting material. You apply different potential differences V across the wire and measure the current i that results. Your results are $V = 2.0$ V, $i = 0.15$ A; $V = 4.0$ V, $i = 0.28$ A; $V = 8.0$ V, $i = 0.50$ A. Is the material of which the wire is made (a) ohmic or (b) nonohmic?

Take-Home Message for Section 18-3

✔ Resistivity ρ is a measure of how well or poorly a particular material inhibits an electric current. The SI units of resistivity are voltmeters per ampere or ohmmeters.

✔ The value of resistivity differs from material to material. The resistivity is low for conductors and high for insulators.

✔ The resistance R of an object is a measure of the current through the object for a given potential difference between its ends. The value of R depends on the object's shape and on the resistivity of the material from which it is made. A long, narrow wire has a much higher resistance than a short, thick one.

The circuit elements with colored bands are resistors. The particular colors on each resistor indicate the value of its resistance.

Figure 18-6 **Resistors in a circuit** A typical electronic circuit is likely to contain many resistors.

18-4 Resistance is important in both technology and physiology

Electrical resistance can be found in every technological device, from the wires in an automobile ignition system to the resistive elements (resistors) in the circuits of a computer or mobile phone. In electronic devices, resistors are often small and cylindrical with colored bands (Figure 18-6). Other resistors look more like tiny, black cubes with the number of ohms etched on one face.

What purpose does a resistor serve? As we have seen, a potential difference V between two points in a conducting material causes a current i. But according to Equation 18-9, $V = iR$, the amount of current that the potential difference produces depends on the resistance of the conducting material. The greater the resistance R, the smaller the current i. Stated another way, the resistance allows us to control the current due to any particular applied voltage.

An important application of this idea takes place in every one of the millions of cells in your body. In order for a cell to live, there must be a higher concentration of positively charged potassium ions (K^+) inside the cell than in the surrounding fluid. This difference in concentration means that K^+ ions tend to leak out of the cell through pathways called *potassium channels* (Figure 18-7). The flow of K^+ ions constitutes a current, and each potassium channel acts like a resistor. For a given potential difference between the interior and exterior of the cell, the amount of current that flows through these channels depends on their resistance. So the flow of potassium through the membranes of your cells is determined by the electrical resistance of the membrane channels.

Why doesn't the flow of K^+ continue until there is equal concentration of these ions inside and outside the cell? Figure 18-7 shows the reason: As positive ions leave the cell, the cell interior is left with a net negative charge and a lower potential than the outside of the cell. This potential difference, called the *membrane potential*, gives rise to an electric field across the membrane that points from the outside to the inside of the cell. This field opposes additional flow of K^+ ions out of the cell. There is still some random flow of K^+ ions in and out of the cell, but the *net* flow stops when the membrane potential reaches an equilibrium value.

As the following example shows, we can use Equation 18-9 to determine the resistance of the membrane to potassium ion flow.

①Potassium ions (shown as green circles) cannot diffuse through a membrane.

②Potassium channels embedded in the membrane allow only potassium ions to diffuse out of the cell.

Cell membrane

Ions

⑤At equilibrium, the membrane potential prevents any additional net movement of positively charged potassium ions out of the cell.

③Positively charged potassium ions leave the cell but negative charges (orange circles) are unable to follow.

④The result is a potential difference (called the membrane potential) across the membrane.

Figure 18-7 **Membrane potential** The concentration of positively changed potassium ions (K⁺) is always higher inside cells than outside, which causes K⁺ ions to leak out. This flow of K⁺ ions is a current; the channels that allow K⁺ ions to leak out of the cell behave like resistors.

Example 18-5 Resistance of a Potassium Channel

Using an instrument called a patch clamp, scientists are able to control the electrical potential difference across a tiny patch of cell membrane and measure the current through individual potassium channels. In one experiment a voltage of 0.120 V was applied across a patch of membrane, and as a result K⁺ ions carried 6.60 pA of current (1 pA = 1 picoampere = 10^{-12} A). What is the resistance of this K⁺ channel?

Set Up
Whether the mobile charges are negative electrons or positive ions, we can use Equation 18-9 to relate potential difference (voltage), current, and resistance.

Relationship among potential difference, current, and resistance:

$$V = iR \qquad (18\text{-}9)$$

Solve
Rewrite Equation 18-9 to solve for the resistance.

From Equation 18-9,

$$R = \frac{V}{i}$$

The current is $i = 6.60$ pA $= 6.60 \times 10^{-12}$ A, so

$$R = \frac{0.120 \text{ V}}{6.60 \times 10^{-12} \text{ A}} = 1.82 \times 10^{10} \ \Omega$$

Reflect

This is an immensely high resistance compared to the values found in circuits like that shown in Figure 18-6. Yet it is very characteristic of the channels in cell membranes, which typically have resistances in the range from 10^9 Ω to 10^{11} Ω. A potassium channel is only about 10^{-9} m wide—so small that K^+ ions must pass through it in single file—so it's not surprising that the resistance is so high.

Although the current through a single potassium channel is very small, the electric field required to produce that current is tremendous. The thickness of the cell membrane is only about 7.5 nm $= 7.5 \times 10^{-9}$ m. Can you use Equation 18-5 to show that a potential difference of 0.120 V across this distance corresponds to an electric field magnitude of 1.6×10^7 V/m? (By comparison, the electric field inside the wires of a flashlight is only about 10 V/m.)

An important application of the membrane potential is in the nervous system. When a nerve signal propagates along an axon—a long, cable-like fiber that extends from a nerve cell—it does so in the form of a *variation* in the membrane potential of the axon. This variation, which travels along the length of the axon, is called an *action potential*. At rest, the baseline membrane potential is lower on the inside compared to the outside surface of a cell. But if the potential on the interior of the membrane becomes just a little less negative, sodium ion (Na^+) channels in the membrane open. Because the concentration of Na^+ is always higher outside of cells compared to inside, Na^+ ions rush into the axon. This flow is so great that the interior surface of the axon membrane ends up with a positive charge and the exterior with a negative charge, just the reverse of what's shown in Figure 18-7. This inversion of charge is the action potential. The Na^+ channels then start closing as potassium (K^+) channels begin to open, allowing K^+ ions to flow out of the axon and restore the resting polarity of the cell membrane. You can think of an action potential as a momentary voltage "flip" that propagates along the length of the axon like a wave pulse along a stretched string.

The speed with which an action potential can propagate along an axon depends in part on the resistance of the axon to current flowing along its length. As Equation 18-8 tells us, this longitudinal resistance depends on both the length and diameter of the axon. The larger the diameter of the axon, for example, the lower the longitudinal resistance and the faster the electrical signal propagates. (In mammals, the signal propagates at about 10 m/s in axons of 3 μm diameter, but at about 50 m/s in axons of 10 μm diameter.) Some axons, such as the giant ones that mediate the escape reflex in squid, have exceptionally large diameters.

Example 18-6 Giant Axons in Squid

Running along each side of the back of a squid is a tube-like structure that can be as large as 1.50 mm in diameter in some species. Originally thought to be blood vessels, these structures are actually giant axons that are part of the squid's nervous system. Although the vast majority of axons in the squid range in diameter from about 10.0 μm to 50.0 μm, as squid develop, axons from about 30,000 neurons fuse together to form these giant axons. Compare the resistance of a giant axon to current along its length to the resistance of an axon with the same length but a more typical diameter of 15.0 μm.

Set Up

Equation 18-8 tells us the resistance of an axon in terms of its resistivity, length, and cross-sectional area. We'll use this to express the ratio of the resistance of a giant axon to that of an ordinary axon of the same composition (and hence same resistivity) and length but of smaller cross-sectional area.

Definition of resistance:

$$R = \frac{\rho L}{A} \qquad (18\text{-}8)$$

brain

giant axon

Solve

Rewrite Equation 18-8 in terms of the diameter of an axon.

An axon has a circular cross section of radius r, so its cross-sectional area is

$$A = \pi r^2$$

The radius is equal to one-half the diameter d, so

$$A = \pi \left(\frac{d}{2}\right)^2 = \frac{\pi d^2}{4}$$

If we substitute this into Equation 18-8, we get an expression for the resistance of an axon of length L and diameter d:

$$R = \frac{\rho L}{(\pi d^2/4)} = \frac{4\rho L}{\pi d^2}$$

Write the ratio of the resistance of a giant axon to that of a typical axon.

Let d_{giant} be the diameter of a giant axon and $d_{typical}$ be the diameter of a typical axon. If the two axons have the same length L and contain the same material of resistivity ρ,

$$R_{giant} = \frac{4\rho L}{\pi d_{giant}^2}$$

$$R_{typical} = \frac{4\rho L}{\pi d_{typical}^2}$$

The ratio of these two resistances is

$$\frac{R_{giant}}{R_{typical}} = R_{giant} \times \frac{1}{R_{typical}} = \frac{4\rho L}{\pi d_{giant}^2} \times \frac{\pi d_{typical}^2}{4\rho L}$$

The factors of 4, ρ, L, and π cancel, so

$$\frac{R_{giant}}{R_{typical}} = \frac{d_{typical}^2}{d_{giant}^2} = \left(\frac{d_{typical}}{d_{giant}}\right)^2$$

Substitute the numerical values of the diameters of the two axons.

We are given $d_{giant} = 1.50$ mm $= 1.50 \times 10^{-3}$ m and $d_{typical} = 15.0\ \mu$m $= 15.0 \times 10^{-6}$ m $= 1.50 \times 10^{-5}$ m. So the ratio of resistances of the two axons is

$$\frac{R_{giant}}{R_{typical}} = \left(\frac{1.50 \times 10^{-5}\ \text{m}}{1.50 \times 10^{-3}\ \text{m}}\right)^2 = (1.00 \times 10^{-2})^2$$

$$= 1.00 \times 10^{-4} = \frac{1}{1.00 \times 10^4}$$

The resistance of the giant axon is one ten-thousandth as great as that of a typical axon.

Reflect

When a squid recognizes danger, it sends electrical signals (action potentials) along the giant axons to trigger muscle contraction. Because the longitudinal resistance along an axon determines the speed at which nerve signals propagate, signals get to the muscle as much as 10,000 times more quickly through the giant axon than they would if the squid's nervous system was comprised entirely of ordinary nerve cells with small-diameter axons.

? Got the Concept? 18-4 Resistance and Diameter

Two copper wires have the same length, but one has four times the diameter of the other. Compared to the wire that has the smaller diameter, the wire that has the larger diameter has a resistance that is (a) 16 times greater; (b) 4 times greater; (c) the same; (d) 1/4 as great; (e) 1/16 as great.

Take-Home Message for Section 18-4

✔ Electrical resistance is important in technology and in the physiology of cells.

✔ For a given applied voltage, the greater the resistance in an electrical system, the smaller the current.

18-5 Kirchhoff's rules help us to analyze simple electric circuits

Many simple electric circuits are made up of a source of electric potential difference and one or more resistors. An example is a light like that shown in the photograph that opens this chapter: The batteries provide the potential difference, and the filament of the light bulb acts as a resistor. We'll refer to batteries and resistors collectively as **circuit elements**. (Later in this chapter we'll consider circuits that also include capacitors as circuit elements.)

In this section we'll see how to analyze circuits made up of a battery and one or more resistors. In particular, we'll see how to determine the voltage across each circuit element as well as the current through each circuit element.

A Single-Loop Circuit and Kirchhoff's Loop Rule

Figure 18-8a shows a battery connected to a single resistor of resistance R. In fact, there are *two* resistors in this circuit; the other one, which we label r, is the **internal resistance** of the battery itself. This reflects the resistance that mobile charges encounter as they pass through the battery. So we can think of the battery as having two components, its **emf** (pronounced "ee-em-eff")—the aspect of the battery that causes charges in the circuit to move—and its internal resistance. Although we draw these as separate entities in Figure 18-8a, they cannot in fact be separated. When we say that a D or AA cell is a "1.5-volt battery" or that the battery in an automobile is "a 12-volt battery," we're actually stating the value of the battery's emf. We use the symbol ε, an uppercase script "e," for emf. So $\varepsilon = 1.5$ V for a D or AA cell and $\varepsilon = 12$ V for a standard automotive battery. (Note that the term "emf" comes from the older term "electromotive force." Although an emf is what pushes mobile charges through the circuit, it has units of volts, not newtons. So it's not accurate to call an emf a "force.") We'll often refer to a battery as a **source of emf**. In later chapters we'll encounter other sources of emf.

The symbol in Figure 18-8a for a source of constant emf is similar to the symbol for a capacitor (see Section 17-5), but with two parallel lines of unequal length:

The longer of the two parallel lines represents the positive terminal of the source. Since we regard current as flowing in the direction that positive charges would move, such a source of emf causes current to flow out of its positive terminal and into its negative terminal (see Figure 18-2).

We call the circuit in Figure 18-8a a **single-loop circuit** because there's only a single path that moving charges can follow around the circuit. Think about what happens to such a charge as it travels through this circuit in the direction of the current i. (We'll continue to use the convenient fiction that these are positive charges.) As the charge passes through the source of emf (the battery) from the negative terminal to the positive terminal, it experiences an *increase* in electric potential (a *voltage rise*) of ε. When it moves through the internal resistance, however, the charge experiences a *decrease* in electric potential (a *voltage drop*) of ir. (Remember that the current moves in the direction of the electric field, and the electric field points in the direction from high potential to low potential. So the potential decreases as you move with the current through a resistor.) The charge experiences an additional decrease in potential (voltage drop) of iR when it moves through the resistor of resistance R.

There's also resistance in the wires that connect the battery and the resistor. However, the resistance of the connecting wires is generally quite small compared to the values of r and R. So we'll ignore the wire resistance and

(a)

A battery has an emf ε...   ...and an internal resistance r.   The battery is connected to a resistor of resistance R.

The connecting wires have negligible resistance.

The sum of the potential changes around the closed loop of this circuit must be zero.

(b)

The potential increases by ε from the negative terminal to the positive terminal of the emf.

The potential drops by ir across the internal resistance and drops by iR across the resistor.

Figure 18-8 Kirchhoff's loop rule (a) A circuit made up of a battery (which has an emf ε and an internal resistance r) and a resistor R. (b) The changes in electric potential around the circuit.

assume that a moving charge experiences no change in potential as it traverses the wires.

The current in Figure 18-8a is steady and does not change with time. So when the charge finishes a complete trip around the circuit and returns to where it started, the value of the potential it experiences at the starting point must have the same value as when the charge left that point. In other words, the *net change* in potential for a round trip around the loop must be *zero* (Figure 18-8b). This idea was first proposed by the Prussian physicist Gustav Kirchhoff in the mid-nineteenth century and is often referred to as **Kirchhoff's loop rule:**

> *The sum of the changes in potential around a closed loop in a circuit must equal zero.*

In equation form, we can write Kirchhoff's loop rule for the circuit in Figure 18-8a as

$$\varepsilon - ir - iR = 0 \qquad\qquad (18\text{-}10)$$

We can rearrange Equation 18-10 to solve for the current in the circuit:

$$\varepsilon = ir + iR = i(r + R)$$
$$i = \frac{\varepsilon}{r + R}$$

To give a specific numerical example, suppose $\varepsilon = 12.0$ V, $r = 1.00\ \Omega$, and $R = 19.0\ \Omega$. Then the current is

$$i = \frac{12.0\ \text{V}}{1.00\ \Omega + 19.0\ \Omega} = \frac{12.0\ \text{V}}{20.0\ \Omega} = 0.600\ \text{A}$$

(Recall that $1\ \text{A} = 1\ \text{V}/\Omega$.) You can see that if the battery had a greater internal resistance r, the current would be smaller. As an example, the internal resistance r of a disposable battery in a flashlight or television remote control increases as the battery is used. Eventually r becomes so great that the current becomes too small to make the device work, which means that it's time to replace the battery. The emf ε of the used battery is almost the same as when it was new; it's the internal resistance that makes the battery no longer useful.

Note that for this numerical example, the voltage drop across the internal resistance is $ir = (0.600\ \text{A})(1.00\ \Omega) = 0.600$ V and the voltage drop across the 19.0-Ω resistor is $iR = (0.600\ \text{A})(19.0\ \Omega) = 11.4$ V. The sum of the potential changes is zero, just as Kirchhoff's loop rule says it must be:

$$\varepsilon - ir - iR = 12.0\ \text{V} - 0.600\ \text{V} - 11.4\ \text{V} = 0$$

For this single-loop circuit, the *current* $i = 0.600$ A is the same through the internal resistance r as through the resistor R. That's because no charges can appear or disappear at any place in the circuit (see Section 18-2). However, the *voltage drops* are different for r and R because the values of resistance are different.

! Watch Out! **The voltage across a battery in a circuit is less than the emf.**

The example we have just given shows that when a battery is in a circuit, the voltage V across the battery (that is, the potential difference between its terminals) is *not* equal to the emf ε. Rather, the voltage across the battery is equal to the emf *minus* the potential drop ir across the internal resistance of the battery. For the battery with emf $\varepsilon = 12.0$ V described above, the voltage is $V = \varepsilon - ir = 12.0\ \text{V} - (0.600\ \text{A})(1.00\ \Omega) =$ 12.0 V $-$ 0.600 V $=$ 11.4 V. The only time when the voltage $V = \varepsilon - ir$ across a battery is equal to the emf is when $i = 0$: that is, when the battery is disconnected from the circuit, so there is no current flowing through the battery. So a 1.5-V battery has a 1.5-V potential difference between its terminals only when the battery isn't connected to anything!

Resistors in Series

An important application of Kirchhoff's loop rule is to resistors in **series**, so that the resistors are connected end to end. (We used the same nomenclature for capacitors in

(a)

The current through each resistor in series is the same.

(b)

• The current i through R_{equiv} is the same as through each of the resistors in series.
• The voltage drop V across R_{equiv} is the same as across the combination of resistors in series.

Figure 18-9 Resistors in series
(a) A circuit contains three resistors connected in series to a source of emf. (b) The three resistors have been replaced by a single, equivalent resistor.

series in Section 17-7.) **Figure 18-9a** shows a circuit that has three resistors R_1, R_2, and R_3 in series connected to a source of emf such as a battery with voltage V. This voltage includes the emf and internal resistance of the battery. Imagine we replace the three separate resistors with an **equivalent resistance**—that is, a single resistor of a resistance R_{equiv} that gives the same current as the series combination, as shown in **Figure 18-9b**. What is the equivalent resistance in terms of R_1, R_2, and R_3?

For R_{equiv} to have the same effect in the circuit as R_1, R_2, and R_3 together, it must give rise to the same current i and the same voltage drop. As we discussed above, the voltage drop across a resistance R that carries current i is iR. The same current is present through each of the three resistors shown in Figure 18-9a, and the total voltage drop across the three resistors in series is the sum of the individual voltage drops: $iR_1 + iR_2 + iR_3$. The voltage drop through the equivalent resistance is iR_{equiv}, so

$$iR_{\text{equiv}} = iR_1 + iR_2 + iR_3 = i(R_1 + R_2 + R_3)$$

So the equivalent resistance of the three resistors in series is

$$R_{\text{equiv}} = R_1 + R_2 + R_3$$

For example, if the three resistors have resistances $R_1 = 25.0\ \Omega$, $R_2 = 12.0\ \Omega$, and $R_3 = 36.0\ \Omega$, they are equivalent to a single resistor with resistance $R_{\text{equiv}} = 25.0\ \Omega + 12.0\ \Omega + 36.0\ \Omega = 73.0\ \Omega$. This means that if we replace the three resistors by a single 73.0-Ω resistor, the current in the circuit will be exactly the same. The net voltage drop is also the same. If the current in our example is $i = 1.00$ A, the voltage drops across the individual resistors are $V_1 = iR_1 = (1.00\ \text{A})(25.0\ \Omega) = 25.0$ V, $V_2 = iR_2 = (1.00\ \text{A})(12.0\ \Omega) = 12.0$ V, and $V_3 = iR_3 = (1.00\ \text{A})(36.0\ \Omega) = 36.0$ V, and the net voltage drop is $25.0\ \text{V} + 12.0\ \text{V} + 36.0\ \text{V} = 73.0$ V. The voltage drop across the equivalent resistance is $iR_{\text{equiv}} = (1.00\ \text{A})(73.0\ \Omega) = 73.0$ V, the same as for the three resistors in series.

In general, if there are N resistors arranged in series, the equivalent resistance is

Equivalent resistance of resistors in series
(18-11)

Equivalent resistance of N resistors in series   Resistances of the individual resistors

$$R_{\text{equiv}} = R_1 + R_2 + R_3 + ... + R_N$$

The equivalent resistance of N resistors in series is the sum of the individual resistances.

① At junction A, current i splits into current i_1 and current i_2.

② At junction B, current i_1 and current i_2 recombine to current i.

Figure 18-10 Kirchhoff's junction rule At the circuit junctions A and B, the net current into the junction must equal the net current out of that junction.

Equation 18-11 tells us that by combining resistors in series, we create a circuit with a higher equivalent resistance than that of any of the individual resistors. A special case is when we put two identical resistors R in series. The equivalent resistance is

$$R_{\text{equiv}} = R + R = 2R$$

The equivalent resistance of two identical resistors in series is twice that of each individual resistor.

Our analysis tells us that for resistors in series, the *current* is the same through each resistor, but the *voltage drop* is different for different resistors. As we will see, this is not the case if the resistors are in an arrangement other than series. To demonstrate this, we'll need to introduce the second of Kirchhoff's laws.

Kirchhoff's Junction Rule and Resistors in Parallel

Figure 18-10 shows a circuit with two resistors R_1 and R_2 connected in **parallel** to a battery. (As in Figure 18-9, the potential V includes both the emf and the internal resistance of the battery.) Unlike the single-loop circuits shown in Figures 18-8 and 18-9, this is a **multiloop circuit**: There is more than one pathway that a moving charge can take from the positive terminal of the battery through the circuit to the negative terminal. In particular, the circuit in Figure 18-10 has two **junctions** at A and B where the current either breaks into two currents (as at A) or comes together (as at B). What is the relationship among the current i that passes through the battery, the current i_1 that passes through resistor R_1, and the current i_2 that passes through resistor R_2?

One condition on i, i_1, and i_2 is that charge can neither be created nor destroyed, nor can it pile up anywhere in the circuit. This means that the rate at which charge *arrives* at a junction must be equal to the rate at which charge *leaves* that junction. This is our second rule of electric circuits. Like the loop rule, this was also proposed by Kirchhoff and is often referred to as **Kirchhoff's junction rule:**

> *The sum of the currents flowing into a junction equals the sum of the currents flowing out of it.*

Let's apply this rule to the junctions shown in Figure 18-10. Current i flows into junction A, and currents i_1 and i_2 flow out of it. So the junction rule tells us that i (the sole current flowing into junction A) must equal $i_1 + i_2$ (the sum of the currents flowing out of A). At junction B, the sum of the currents flowing in is $i_1 + i_2$ and the sole current flowing out is i. So by analyzing either junction we can conclude that

$$i = i_1 + i_2 \qquad (18\text{-}12)$$

This says that the current divides itself into i_1 and i_2 when it reaches junction A, with no extra current being added and no current being lost. These currents rejoin at junction B.

Equation 18-12 tells us that the current splits up when it reaches junction A, but by itself it doesn't tell us how much of current i takes the branch through resistor R_1 (as current i_1) and how much takes the branch through resistor R_2 (as current i_2). To determine this, let's apply the *loop* rule to two different loops through the circuit in Figure 18-10. First consider a loop that starts at the negative terminal of the battery, passes through the battery to the positive terminal (voltage rise V), then follows the path of current i_1 through resistor R_1 (voltage drop i_1R_1), and returns to the negative terminal of the battery. (As before, we'll ignore the resistance of the wires, so there is no voltage drop as a charge traverses the wires.) From the loop rule, the net change in electric potential for this loop is zero:

$$V - i_1R_1 = 0 \qquad (18\text{-}13)$$

The second loop we'll consider also starts at the negative terminal of the battery and passes through the battery to the positive terminal (voltage rise V), but then follows the path of current i_2 through resistor R_2 (voltage drop i_2R_2) before returning to the battery's negative terminal. The loop rule says that the net change in electric potential is also zero for this loop:

$$V - i_2R_2 = 0 \qquad (18\text{-}14)$$

If you compare Equations 18-13 and 18-14, you'll see that these equations can both be true only if

$$i_1R_1 = i_2R_2 \qquad (18\text{-}15)$$

In other words, the voltage drop must be the *same* for each of the resistors in parallel. If the resistances R_1 and R_2 are different, the currents i_1 and i_2 will be different; the current will be greater in the resistor with the smaller resistance and smaller in the resistor with the greater resistance. So for resistors in parallel, the *voltage drop* is the same for both resistors, but the *currents* are different for different resistors. (Compare this to resistors in series, for which the current is the same but the voltage drops are different for different resistors.)

As an illustration, suppose $V = 12.0$ V, $R_1 = 3.00\ \Omega$, and $R_2 = 6.00\ \Omega$. From Equation 18-13, the current i_1 through resistor R_1 is given by

$$V - i_1R_1 = 0 \quad \text{so} \quad i_1R_1 = V \quad \text{and} \quad i_1 = \frac{V}{R_1} = \frac{12.0\text{ V}}{3.00\ \Omega} = 4.00\text{ A}$$

The voltage drop across each resistor in parallel is the same.

• The current i through R_{equiv} is the same as through the combination of resistors in parallel.
• The voltage drop V across R_{equiv} is the same as across each of the resistors in parallel.

Figure 18-11 Resistors in parallel
(a) A circuit contains three resistors connected in parallel to a source of emf. (b) The three resistors have been replaced by a single, equivalent resistor.

Go to Picture It 18-1 for more practice dealing with resistors in combination

We can then find the current i_2 using Equation 18-15:

$$i_1 R_1 = i_2 R_2 \quad \text{and} \quad i_2 = \frac{i_1 R_1}{R_2} = \frac{(4.00\ \text{A})(3.00\ \Omega)}{6.00\ \Omega} = 2.00\ \text{A}$$

Current $i_1 = 4.00$ A is twice as great as current $i_2 = 2.00$ A because resistance $R_1 = 3.00\ \Omega$ is half as great as resistance $R_2 = 6.00\ \Omega$. Note that the total current i that passes through the battery is $i = i_1 + i_2 = 4.00\ \text{A} + 2.00\ \text{A} = 6.00\ \text{A}$.

We now have the tools that we need to find the equivalent resistance of a set of resistors in parallel. Figure 18-11a shows three resistors R_1, R_2, and R_3 connected in parallel to a battery with voltage V (including the emf and internal resistance). The currents through these three resistors are i_1, i_2, and i_3, respectively. Figure 18-11b shows the three resistors replaced by an equivalent resistance R_{equiv}. As we did for the case of three resistors in series, we'll determine R_{equiv} by demanding that the net current i and the voltage drop be the same for the actual set of resistors in Figure 18-11a and the equivalent resistance in Figure 18-11b. From our discussion above, we see that the voltage drop through each of the resistors in Figure 18-11a is equal to V:

$$V = i_1 R_1, \quad V = i_2 R_2, \quad V = i_3 R_3$$

If we divide each of these equations by R_1, R_2, and R_3 respectively, we get expressions for the current through each resistor:

$$(18\text{-}16) \qquad i_1 = \frac{V}{R_1}, \quad i_2 = \frac{V}{R_2}, \quad i_3 = \frac{V}{R_3}$$

The junction rule tells us that the total current that passes through the battery is the sum of the currents through the individual resistors: $i = i_1 + i_2 + i_3$. From Equations 18-16, we can write this as

$$(18\text{-}17) \qquad i = \frac{V}{R_1} + \frac{V}{R_2} + \frac{V}{R_3} = V\left(\frac{1}{R_1} + \frac{1}{R_2} + \frac{1}{R_3}\right)$$

The total current must be the same for the circuit in Figure 18-11b with the equivalent resistance. If we apply the loop theorem to this circuit, we get $V - iR_{equiv} = 0$, so $iR_{equiv} = V$ or

$$(18\text{-}18) \qquad i = \frac{V}{R_{equiv}} = V\left(\frac{1}{R_{equiv}}\right)$$

Since Equations 18-17 and 18-18 are both expressions for the total current i, they can both be valid only if the right-hand sides of these equations are equal to each other. This gives us an equation for the equivalent resistance that corresponds to the three resistors in Figure 18-11a:

$$(18\text{-}19) \qquad \frac{1}{R_{equiv}} = \frac{1}{R_1} + \frac{1}{R_2} + \frac{1}{R_3}$$

As an illustration, suppose the three resistors in Figure 18-11a are $R_1 = 25.0\ \Omega$, $R_2 = 12.0\ \Omega$, and $R_3 = 36.0\ \Omega$. According to Equation 18-19, they are equivalent to a single resistor with resistance R_{equiv} given by

$$\frac{1}{R_{equiv}} = \frac{1}{25.0\ \Omega} + \frac{1}{12.0\ \Omega} + \frac{1}{36.0\ \Omega} = 0.151\ \Omega^{-1}$$

$$R_{equiv} = \frac{1}{0.151\ \Omega^{-1}} = 6.62\ \Omega$$

This is *less* than the resistance of any one of the individual resistors. If the net current through the battery is 1.00 A, the voltage drop across the equivalent resistance is $iR_{equiv} = (1.00\ \text{A})(6.62\ \Omega) = 6.62\ \text{V}$. The voltage drop across each of the individual resistors in parallel must be the same, so $6.62\ \text{V} = i_1 R_1 = i_2 R_2 = i_3 R_3$. You can use these relationships to show that $i_1 = 0.265$ A, $i_2 = 0.551$ A, and $i_3 = 0.184$ A (note that the current is greatest through resistor R_2, which has the smallest of the three resistances). The net current through the battery is $i = i_1 + i_2 + i_3 = 1.00$ A, just as for the battery connected to the equivalent resistance.

We can generalize Equation 18-19 to the case where we have N resistors arranged in parallel:

 The reciprocal of the equivalent resistance of N resistors in parallel is the sum of the reciprocals of the individual resistances.

$$\frac{1}{R_{\text{equiv}}} = \frac{1}{R_1} + \frac{1}{R_2} + \frac{1}{R_3} + ... + \frac{1}{R_N}$$

Equivalent resistance of resistors in parallel (18-20)

Equivalent resistance of N resistors in parallel

Resistances of the individual resistors

Equation 18-20 tells us that by combining resistors in parallel, we create a circuit with a smaller equivalent resistance than any of the individual resistors. For the special case of two identical resistors R in parallel, the equivalent resistance is given by

$$\frac{1}{R_{\text{equiv}}} = \frac{1}{R} + \frac{1}{R} = \frac{2}{R} \quad \text{so} \quad R_{\text{equiv}} = \frac{R}{2}$$

The equivalent resistance of two identical resistors in parallel is one-half that of each individual resistor.

Watch Out! Resistors do not combine in the same way as capacitors.

Be careful to distinguish between the rules for equivalent *resistance* that we've developed in this section and the rules for equivalent *capacitance* that we found in Section 17-7. For resistors in series, we find the equivalent resistance by adding the individual resistances ($R_{\text{equiv}} = R_1 + R_2 + ...$); for resistors in parallel, we find the reciprocal of the equivalent resistance by adding the reciprocals of the individual resistances ($1/R_{\text{equiv}} = 1/R_1 + 1/R_2 + ...$). These rules are reversed for capacitors. For capacitors in series, we find the reciprocal of the equivalent capacitance by adding the reciprocals of the individual capacitances ($1/C_{\text{equiv}} = 1/C_1 + 1/C_2 + ...$); for capacitors in parallel, we find the equivalent capacitance by adding the individual capacitances ($C_{\text{equiv}} = C_1 + C_2 + ...$).

The following examples illustrate some applications of the relationships we've developed in this section. In the second example, we'll see how to analyze resistors arranged in a combination that is neither purely series nor purely parallel.

Example 18-7 Giant Axons in Squid Revisited

As we saw in Example 18-6 (Section 18-4), in a squid axons of approximately 30,000 nerve cells fuse together to form each giant axon. A typical axon has a diameter of 15.0 μm, is 10.0 cm long, and has a resistivity of about 3100 Ω·m. Find the resistance of a giant squid axon by considering it as 30,000 separate axons in parallel.

Set Up
We can find the resistance of a typical axon by using Equation 18-8. Each of these individual axons acts as a separate conducting path that mobile charges can follow between a point of high potential and low potential. That's just like the three resistors in parallel shown in Figure 18-11a, so we can use Equation 18-20 to determine the equivalent resistance of the giant axon as a whole in terms of the resistances of the individual axons.

Definition of resistance:

$$R = \frac{\rho L}{A} \quad (18\text{-}8)$$

Equivalent resistance of resistors in parallel:

$$\frac{1}{R_{\text{equiv}}} = \frac{1}{R_1} + \frac{1}{R_2} + \frac{1}{R_3} + ... + \frac{1}{R_N} \quad (18\text{-}20)$$

same potential difference across all axons

Solve

Calculate the resistance of an individual axon.	Each individual axon has resistivity $\rho = 3100 \ \Omega \cdot m$, length $L = 10.0$ cm $= 0.100$ m, and diameter $15.0 \ \mu m = 15.0 \times 10^{-6}$ m. The radius r is one-half of the diameter:

$$r = \frac{1}{2}(15.0 \times 10^{-6} \, m) = 7.50 \times 10^{-6} \, m$$

If the axon has a circular cross section, its cross-sectional area is $A = \pi r^2$. So from Equation 18-8 the resistance is

$$R = \frac{\rho L}{A} = \frac{\rho L}{\pi r^2} = \frac{(3100 \ \Omega \cdot m)(0.100 \, m)}{\pi (7.50 \times 10^{-6} \, m)^2} = 1.75 \times 10^{12} \ \Omega$$

This resistance is very large because the axon is long and thin and the axon resistivity is much higher than that of metallic conductors (see Table 18-1).

Calculate the resistance of the giant axon, as if it were 30,000 individual axons in parallel.

If N axons are in parallel and each has the same resistance R, there are N identical terms on the right-hand side of Equation 18-20. So

$$\frac{1}{R_{equiv}} = \frac{1}{R_1} + \frac{1}{R_2} + \frac{1}{R_3} + \dots + \frac{1}{R_N} = \frac{N}{R}$$

Take the reciprocal of both sides:

$$R_{equiv} = \frac{R}{N}$$

There are $N = 30{,}000$ individual axons, each of which has resistance $R = 1.75 \times 10^{12} \ \Omega$, so the equivalent resistance of the giant axon is

$$R_{equiv} = \frac{1.75 \times 10^{12} \ \Omega}{30{,}000} = 5.85 \times 10^7 \ \Omega$$

Reflect

In Example 18-6, we found that the resistance of a giant squid axon is about 10,000 times smaller than that of a normal axon. But in this example we've found that the equivalent resistance of a giant axon is 30,000 times smaller than that of an individual axon. Why do our answers differ by a factor of 3?

The explanation is that in this example, we made the implicit assumption that the total cross-sectional area of the giant axon is 30,000 times the cross-sectional area of a small axon. However, in an actual squid the cross-sectional area of the giant axon with a diameter of 1.50 mm is smaller than the total cross-sectional area of 30,000 small axons each of diameter 15.0 μm. Although about 30,000 cells contribute to the formation of the giant axon, the process by which the giant axon forms is *not* an actual fusing together of 30,000 fully formed smaller axons. Nevertheless, it's encouraging that our calculations in Example 18-6 and this problem are pretty close.

Example 18-8   Resistors in Combination

Figure 18-12 shows two different combinations of three identical resistors, each with resistance R. Find the equivalent resistance of the combination in (a) Figure 18-12a and (b) Figure 18-12b.

Figure 18-12 **Two combinations of three identical resistors** What is the equivalent resistance of each combination?

Set Up

Neither combination in Figure 18-12 is a simple series or parallel arrangement of resistors. But in Figure 18-12a resistors 1 and 2 are in parallel with each other, and that combination is in series with resistor 3. Similarly, in Figure 18-12b resistors 4 and 5 are in series with each other, and that combination is in parallel with resistor 6. So we can use Equations 18-11 and 18-20 together to find the equivalent resistance of both arrangements of resistors.

Equivalent resistance of resistors in series:

$$R_{equiv} = R_1 + R_2 + R_3 + \ldots + R_N \quad (18\text{-}11)$$

Equivalent resistance of resistors in parallel:

$$\frac{1}{R_{equiv}} = \frac{1}{R_1} + \frac{1}{R_2} + \frac{1}{R_3} + \ldots + \frac{1}{R_N} \quad (18\text{-}20)$$

resistors in series

resistors in parallel

Solve

(a) For the arrangement in Figure 18-12a, first find the equivalent resistance of resistors 1 and 2.

Resistors 1 and 2 in Figure 18-12a are in parallel, so their equivalent resistance R_{12} is given by Equation 18-20:

$$\frac{1}{R_{12}} = \frac{1}{R} + \frac{1}{R} = \frac{2}{R}$$
$$R_{12} = \frac{R}{2}$$

The combination of resistors 1 and 2 is in series with resistor 3. This tells us the overall equivalent resistance.

Equivalent resistor R_{12} is in series with resistor 3. The equivalent resistance R_{123} of the entire combination is given by Equation 18-11:

$$R_{123} = R_{12} + R = \frac{R}{2} + R = \frac{3R}{2}$$

(b) For the arrangement in Figure 18-12b, first find the equivalent resistance of resistors 4 and 5.

Resistors 4 and 5 in Figure 18-12b are in series, so their equivalent resistance R_{45} is given by Equation 18-11:

$$R_{45} = R + R = 2R$$

The combination of resistors 4 and 5 is in parallel with resistor 6. This tells us the overall equivalent resistance.

Equivalent resistor R_{45} is in parallel with resistor 6. The equivalent resistance R_{456} of the entire combination is given by Equation 18-20:

$$\frac{1}{R_{456}} = \frac{1}{R_{45}} + \frac{1}{R} = \frac{1}{2R} + \frac{1}{R} = \frac{3}{2R}$$
$$R_{456} = \frac{2R}{3}$$

Reflect

If we had more than three resistors, or if the resistors had different values, we could create a large number of combinations and equivalent resistances.

? Got the Concept? 18-5
Combinations of Resistors I

Rank the four circuits shown in Figure 18-13 in order of their equivalent resistance, from highest to lowest.

(a)

(b)

(c)

(d)

Figure 18-13 **Rank the circuits** How do these four circuits compare in their equivalent resistances? In the net current through their sources of emf?

? Got the Concept? 18-6   **Combinations of Resistors II**

Rank the four circuits shown in Figure 18-13 in order of the current through the source of emf V, from highest to lowest.

18-6 The rate at which energy is produced or taken in by a circuit element depends on current and voltage

The aspects of electric circuits that we've concentrated on so far are voltage, current, and resistance. But an electric circuit is fundamentally a way to transfer *energy* from one place to another, such as from a battery to a flashlight bulb (where the energy is converted into visible light) or from a wall socket to a toaster (where the energy is used to heat your morning bread or bagel). In most applications what's of interest is the *rate* at which energy is transferred into or out of a circuit element. For example, in order for a toaster to be useful, it must heat the bread rapidly enough that it becomes toast in a minute or so, not an hour.

As we learned in Section 13-9, **power** is the rate at which energy is transferred into or out of an object. The unit of power is the joule per second, or watt (abbreviated W): $1\ \mathrm{W} = 1\ \mathrm{J/s}$. You can see the importance of power in electric circuits from the numbers that are used to describe various electric devices: An amplifier for a home audio system is rated by its power output (perhaps 75 to 100 W), and any light bulb is stamped with the power that must be supplied to it for normal operation (say, 13 or 60 W).

In this section we'll see how to calculate the power *output* of a source of emf such as a battery, which is fundamentally a source of electric potential energy. We'll also see how to calculate the power *input* of a resistor, which absorbs electric potential energy and converts it into other forms of energy.

Power in a Circuit Element

The key to understanding energy and power in electric circuits is that there is a potential difference across each circuit element, which means that a change takes place in electric potential energy when a moving charge traverses a circuit element. Remember from Section 17-3 the relationship between electric potential difference and electric potential energy difference:

> The difference in electric potential between two positions...

> ...equals the change in electric potential energy for a charge q_0 moved between these two positions...

Electric potential difference related to electric potential energy difference (17-6)

$$\Delta V = \frac{\Delta U_{\text{electric}}}{q_0}$$

> ...divided by the charge q_0.

 Electric potential difference equals electric potential energy difference per unit charge.

Let's rewrite this equation for the case in which a small quantity Δq of moving charge moves from one end of a circuit element to the other. If the potential difference between the ends of the element is ΔV, then Equation 17-6 becomes

(18-21)
$$\Delta V = \frac{\Delta U_{\text{electric}}}{\Delta q} \quad \text{or} \quad \Delta U_{\text{electric}} = (\Delta q)\,\Delta V$$

Charges moving through the emf undergo a potential change of $+\varepsilon$, so electric potential energy increases; energy is extracted from the emf.

Charges undergo a potential change of $-ir$ moving through the internal resistance and $-iR$ moving through the resistor. Electric potential energy decreases; energy goes into the resistances.

Figure 18-14 **Energy and power in a single-loop circuit** Energy flows from the emf into the moving charges; energy flows from the moving charges into the internal resistance and the resistor.

We'll continue to use the idea that current is in the direction in which positive charges would flow, so the moving charge is positive: $\Delta q > 0$. Then Equation 18-21 tells us that there is an *increase* in electric potential energy ($\Delta U_{electric} > 0$) if the charge Δq traverses a circuit element from low potential to high potential, so $\Delta V > 0$. That's the case for a charge that travels through the source of emf in Figure 18-14 from the negative terminal to the positive terminal. Since energy is conserved, it must be that the amount of energy extracted from the source is equal to the increase in electric potential energy.

There is a *decrease* in electric potential energy ($\Delta U_{electric} < 0$) if the charge Δq traverses a circuit element from high potential to low potential, so $\Delta V < 0$. That's what happens when charge Δq travels through the resistor R in Figure 18-14 in the direction of the current. The lost electric potential energy is deposited into the resistor, which causes an increase in the resistor's temperature. If the resistor is the filament of a conventional flashlight bulb, the increased temperature causes the filament to emit radiation, some of which is in the form of visible light (see Section 14-7).

Watch Out! **Potential energy may change as charges move around a circuit, but current does not.**

It's a common misconception that current is "used up" when it passes through a resistor, and that current is "added to" when it passes through a source of emf. In fact, there is *no* change in the current as it passes through either a resistor or a source: Moving charges leave any circuit element at the same rate as they enter the element. All that changes is the electric potential energy associated with the charges.

With a current i through the circuit, the power P for each circuit element is just the rate at which electric potential energy changes in that element. This equals the change in electric potential energy $\Delta U_{electric}$ for a charge Δq that enters the element, as given by Equation 18-21, divided by the time Δt that it takes each new bit of charge Δq to enter the element:

$$P = \frac{\Delta U_{electric}}{\Delta t} = \frac{\Delta q \, \Delta V}{\Delta t} = \left(\frac{\Delta q}{\Delta t}\right)\Delta V = (i)\,\Delta V \qquad (18\text{-}22)$$

In the last part of Equation 18-22 we've used the idea that the ratio $\Delta q/\Delta t$ equals the rate at which charge enters the circuit element—in other words, this ratio equals the current i through the element (see Equation 18-1).

Equation 18-22 states that the power can be positive or negative depending on the sign of the potential difference ΔV between the ends of the circuit element. Instead of worrying about these signs, we'll replace ΔV in Equation 18-22 with the voltage V across the circuit element, which we'll regard as the absolute value of the potential difference between the ends of the element. Then P is always positive, and we can write

Power produced by or transferred into a circuit element

$$P = iV$$

Current through the circuit element

Voltage (absolute value) across the circuit element

Power for a circuit element
(18-23)

 Source of emf: Power flows out of the source and into the moving charges.
Resistor: Power flows out of the charges and into the resistor.

Equation 18-23 applies to *any* circuit element: The amount of power that flows into or out of a circuit element is equal to the product of the current through the element multiplied by the voltage across the element. For a given voltage V, each small amount of charge Δq that traverses the circuit element transfers the same amount of energy into or out of the element; the more charge that traverses the element per unit time and so the greater the current i, the greater the *rate* of energy transfer P.

! Watch Out! The units of power take time into account.

The units of power sometimes cause confusion because it seems that watts require an additional time measurement. For example, to find the power in watts that goes into a flashlight bulb, a student might ask "Find the power for what amount of time?" That's not a sensible question: Time is already included in the units of power, since 1 watt is equal to 1 joule *per second*. When a light bulb is rated at 120 W, that means it requires 120 J of energy every second to operate. Time is already taken into account.

Note that the power company charges its customers based not on how much *power* they use at a given time, but on the total amount of *energy* that they use in one billing period. Since power is energy per time, the units of energy are the units of power multiplied by the units of time. That's why the power company bills on the number of kilowatt-hours (kWh) that a customer uses: 1 kWh = 1000 watt-hours, or the amount of energy it takes to run a device that uses 1000 W of power (typical for a microwave oven) for one hour. Since 1 h = 3600 s, you can see that 1 kWh = (1000 W)(3600 s) = 3.6×10^6 W·s = 3.6×10^6 J.

For the special case where the circuit element is a resistor with resistance R, Equation 18-9 tells us that the voltage V across the resistor is equal to the product of the current and the resistance: $V = iR$, or equivalently $i = V/R$. We can use these two expressions to rewrite Equation 18-23 in two equivalent forms for the special case of a resistor:

$$P = i(iR) \quad \text{or} \quad P = \left(\frac{V}{R}\right)V$$

We can simplify these to

Power for a resistor
(18-24)

Power into a resistor   Current through the resistor

$$P = i^2R = \frac{V^2}{R}$$

Voltage across the resistor

Resistance of the resistor

The expression $P = i^2R$ is useful if we know the current through a resistor of known resistance, while $P = V^2/R$ is useful if we know the voltage across that resistor. The following examples show how to use Equations 18-23 and 18-24.

Example 18-9 Power in a Single-Loop Circuit

A battery with emf 12.0 V and internal resistance 1.00 Ω is connected to a resistor with resistance 19.0 Ω. Find (a) the rate at which energy is supplied by the emf, (b) the rate at which energy flows into the internal resistance, and (c) the rate at which energy flows into the resistor.

Set Up

We can find the current in the circuit using Kirchhoff's loop rule (the sum of the changes in potential around a closed loop in a circuit

Relationship among potential difference, current, and resistance:

$$V = iR \qquad (18-9)$$

$\varepsilon = 12.0\,V \qquad r = 1.00\,\Omega \qquad R = 19.0\,\Omega$

must equal zero). Equation 18-9 then tells us the voltage across either resistance. We'll use Equation 18-23 to determine the power for each element of the circuit, and check our results for the two resistances using Equations 18-24.

Power for a circuit element:

$$P = iV \qquad (18\text{-}23)$$

Power for a resistor:

$$P = i^2R = \frac{V^2}{R} \qquad (18\text{-}24)$$

Solve

(a) First apply Kirchhoff's loop rule to determine the current i. Start at the point a in the circuit and go around in the direction of the current.

There is a voltage rise of $\varepsilon = 12.0$ V going through the emf, a voltage drop of ir going through the internal resistance $r = 1.00\ \Omega$, and a voltage drop of iR going the resistor with resistance $R = 19.0\ \Omega$. The sum of the potential changes around the circuit is zero:

$$+\varepsilon + (-ir) + (-iR) = 0$$

Rearrange this to solve for the current i:

$$\varepsilon - i(r + R) = 0, \text{ so } i(r + R) = \varepsilon \text{ and}$$

$$i = \frac{\varepsilon}{r + R} = \frac{12.0\text{ V}}{1.00\ \Omega + 19.0\ \Omega} = \frac{12.0\text{ V}}{20.0\ \Omega} = 0.600\text{ A}$$

(Recall that $1\text{ A} = 1\text{ V}/\Omega$.)

Use Equation 18-23 to find the power extracted from the emf.

The voltage across the emf itself is $\varepsilon = 12.0$ V. The rate at which energy is extracted from the emf is

$$P_{\text{emf}} = i\varepsilon = (0.600\text{ A})(12.0\text{ V}) = 7.20\text{ A} \cdot \text{V}$$

Since $1\text{ A} = 1\text{ C/s}$, $1\text{ V} = 1\text{ J/C}$, and $1\text{ W} = 1\text{ J/s}$,

$$P_{\text{emf}} = 7.20\frac{\text{C}}{\text{s}} \cdot \frac{\text{J}}{\text{C}} = 7.20\frac{\text{J}}{\text{s}} = 7.20\text{ W}$$

(b) First use Equation 18-9 to find the potential difference across the internal resistance $r = 1.00\ \Omega$. Then find the power in the internal resistance using Equation 18-23.

From Equation 18-9, the voltage across the internal resistance is

$$V_r = ir = (0.600\text{ A})(1.00\ \Omega) = 0.600\text{ V}$$

From Equation 18-23, the rate at which energy flows into the internal resistance is

$$P_r = iV_r = (0.600\text{ A})(0.600\text{ V}) = 0.360\text{ W}$$

This power into the internal resistance goes into heating the battery.

(c) Repeat part (b) for the resistor of resistance $R = 19.0\ \Omega$.

The voltage across the resistor is

$$V_R = iR = (0.600\text{ A})(19.0\ \Omega) = 11.4\text{ V}$$

The rate at which energy flows into the resistor is

$$P_R = iV_R = (0.600\text{ A})(11.4\text{ V}) = 6.84\text{ W}$$

Reflect

Note that the rate at which energy is extracted from the source of emf is equal to the *net* rate at which energy flows into the internal resistance and the resistor. This is equivalent to saying that energy is conserved in the circuit.

The net rate of energy flow into the two resistances is

$$P_r + P_R = 0.360\text{ W} + 6.84\text{ W} = 7.20\text{ W}$$

This is the same as the rate at which energy flows out of the source of emf, $P_{\text{emf}} = 7.20$ W.

We can check our result $P_R = 6.84$ W for the power into the resistor by showing that we get the same results using Equations 18-24. Can you use the same approach to check the result $P_r = 0.360$ W for the internal resistance?

From the first of Equations 18-24, the power into the 19.0-Ω resistor is

$$P_R = i^2R = (0.600 \text{ A})^2(19.0 \text{ }\Omega) = 6.84 \text{ W}$$

(Note that $1 \text{ A}^2 \cdot \Omega = 1 \text{ A} \cdot \text{V} = 1 \text{ W}$.)

To use the second of Equations 18-24, use the voltage $V_R = 11.4$ V across the resistor:

$$P_R = \frac{V_R^2}{R} = \frac{(11.4 \text{ V})^2}{19.0 \text{ }\Omega} = 6.84 \text{ W}$$

(Note that $1 \text{ V}^2/\Omega = 1 \text{ V} \cdot (\text{V}/\Omega) = 1 \text{ V} \cdot \text{A} = 1 \text{ W}$.)

This agrees with the result for P_R found above.

Example 18-10 Power in Series and Parallel Circuits

Two resistors, one with $R_1 = 2.00$ Ω and one with $R_2 = 3.00$ Ω, are both connected to a battery with emf $\varepsilon = 12.0$ V and negligible internal resistance. Find the power delivered by the battery and the power absorbed by each resistor if the resistors are connected to the battery (a) in series and (b) in parallel.

Set Up

We'll use the same tools as in the previous example, plus Equations 18-11 and 18-20 for the equivalent resistance of resistors in series and in parallel. In each case we'll use the equivalent resistance to find the current through the battery, then use Equation 18-23 to determine the power provided by the battery. If the resistors are in series, the current through each is the same as the current through the battery, so we'll use the first of Equations 18-24 ($P = i^2/R$) to determine the power into each resistor. For resistors in parallel the voltage is the same across each resistor, so in that case we'll find the power into each resistor using the second of Equations 18-24 ($P = V^2/R$).

Relationship among potential difference, current, and resistance:

$$V = iR \tag{18-9}$$

Equivalent resistance of two resistors in series:

$$R_{\text{equiv}} = R_1 + R_2 \tag{18-11}$$

Equivalent resistance of two resistors in parallel:

$$\frac{1}{R_{\text{equiv}}} = \frac{1}{R_1} + \frac{1}{R_2} \tag{18-20}$$

Power for a circuit element:

$$P = iV \tag{18-23}$$

Power for a resistor:

$$P = i^2R = \frac{V^2}{R} \tag{18-24}$$

Solve

(a) The two resistors in series are equivalent to a single resistor R_{equiv}. This is connected directly to the terminals of the battery, across which the voltage is ε (we're told to ignore the internal resistance). So the voltage across R_{equiv} is also equal to ε, which tells us the current through the circuit. Equation 18-23 then tells us the power delivered by the battery.

From Equation 18-11, the equivalent resistance of the two resistors in series is

$$R_{\text{equiv}} = R_1 + R_2 = 2.00 \text{ }\Omega + 3.00 \text{ }\Omega = 5.00 \text{ }\Omega$$

The voltage drop across this equivalent resistance is $V = iR_{\text{equiv}}$ from Equation 18-9, which is also equal to the emf $\varepsilon = 12.0$ V of the battery. So the current through the equivalent resistance is given by

$$\varepsilon = iR_{\text{equiv}} \quad \text{or} \quad i = \frac{\varepsilon}{R_{\text{equiv}}} = \frac{12.0 \text{ V}}{5.00 \text{ }\Omega} = 2.40 \text{ A}$$

This is also the current through the battery. Since the voltage across the battery is equal to $\varepsilon = 12.0$ V, the power delivered by the battery is

$$P_{\text{battery}} = i\varepsilon = (2.40 \text{ A})(12.0 \text{ V}) = 28.8 \text{ W}$$

This must be equal to the power that goes into the two resistors.

The current $i = 2.40$ A is the same through both resistors in this series circuit. Use this to calculate the power that goes into each resistor.

Using the first of Equations 18-24, the power into resistor $R_1 = 2.00$ Ω is

$$P_1 = i^2 R_1 = (2.40 \text{ A})^2 (2.00 \text{ }\Omega) = 11.5 \text{ W}$$

The power into resistor $R_2 = 3.00$ Ω is

$$P_2 = i^2 R_2 = (2.40 \text{ A})^2 (3.00 \text{ }\Omega) = 17.3 \text{ W}$$

The net power into the two resistors is equal to the power supplied by the battery, as it should be:

$$P_1 + P_2 = 11.5 \text{ W} + 17.3 \text{ W} = 28.8 \text{ W} = P_{\text{battery}}$$

(b) Follow the same steps as in part (a) to find the equivalent resistance of the two resistors in parallel, the current through the battery connected to that parallel arrangement, and the power delivered by the battery in this situation.

From Equation 18-20, the equivalent resistance of the two resistors in parallel is given by

$$\frac{1}{R_{\text{equiv}}} = \frac{1}{R_1} + \frac{1}{R_2} = \frac{1}{2.00 \text{ }\Omega} + \frac{1}{3.00 \text{ }\Omega} = 0.833 \text{ }\Omega^{-1}$$

$$R_{\text{equiv}} = \frac{1}{0.833 \text{ }\Omega^{-1}} = 1.20 \text{ }\Omega$$

Equation 18-9 tells us that the voltage drop across this equivalent resistance is $V = iR_{\text{equiv}}$; since this equivalent resistance is connected to the terminals of the battery, the voltage drop is also equal to the battery emf $\varepsilon = 12.0$ V. So the current through the equivalent resistance and through the battery is given by

$$\varepsilon = iR_{\text{equiv}} \text{ or } i = \frac{\varepsilon}{R_{\text{equiv}}} = \frac{12.0 \text{ V}}{1.20 \text{ }\Omega} = 10.0 \text{ A}$$

From Equation 18-23, the power delivered by the battery is

$$P_{\text{battery}} = i\varepsilon = (10.0 \text{ A})(12.0 \text{ V}) = 1.20 \times 10^2 \text{ W}$$

Note that this is more than four times as much power as the same battery delivers to the resistors in series.

The voltage is the same across resistors in parallel. Each resistor is effectively connected directly to the terminals of the battery, so the voltage across each resistor is $V = \varepsilon = 12.0$ V. Use this to calculate the power that goes into each resistor.

Using the second of Equations 18-24, we find that the power into resistor $R_1 = 2.00$ Ω is

$$P_1 = \frac{V^2}{R_1} = \frac{\varepsilon^2}{R_1} = \frac{(12.0 \text{ V})^2}{2.00 \text{ }\Omega} = 72.0 \text{ W}$$

The power into resistor $R_2 = 3.00$ Ω is

$$P_2 = \frac{V^2}{R_2} = \frac{\varepsilon^2}{R_2} = \frac{(12.0 \text{ V})^2}{3.00 \text{ }\Omega} = 48.0 \text{ W}$$

As for the series case, the net power into the two resistors is equal to the power supplied by the battery:

$$P_1 + P_2 = 72.0 \text{ W} + 48.0 \text{ W} = 1.20 \times 10^2 \text{ W} = P_{\text{battery}}$$

Reflect

Although the same battery and same resistors are used in both circuits, the power provided by the battery is *much* different in the two circuits. That's because the current through the battery is different for the two circuits: $i = 2.40$ A for the series circuit, $i = 10.0$ A for the parallel circuit.

What's more, the power into each resistor is very different in the two circuits, because the voltage and current for each resistor are greater for the parallel circuit than for the series circuit. If the resistors are light bulbs that take in power and use it to produce light, the lights

Use Equation 18-9 to find the voltage across each resistor in the series circuit:

$$V_1 = iR_1 = (2.40 \text{ A})(2.00 \text{ }\Omega) = 4.80 \text{ V}$$
$$V_2 = iR_2 = (2.40 \text{ A})(3.00 \text{ }\Omega) = 7.20 \text{ V}$$

(compared to $V = \varepsilon = 12.0$ V for each resistor in the parallel circuit) will glow brighter in the parallel circuit than in the series circuit.

Use Equation 18-9 to find the current through each resistor in the parallel circuit:

$$i_1 = \frac{\varepsilon}{R_1} = \frac{12.0 \text{ V}}{2.00 \text{ } \Omega} = 6.00 \text{ A}$$

$$i_1 = \frac{\varepsilon}{R_2} = \frac{12.0 \text{ V}}{3.00 \text{ } \Omega} = 4.00 \text{ A}$$

(compared to $i = 2.40$ A for each resistor in the series circuit)

Note that the current is the same for both resistors in the series circuit, so more power goes into the resistor with the greater resistance ($P_2 = 17.3$ W into $R_2 = 3.00$ Ω versus $P_1 = 11.5$ W into $R_1 = 2.00$ Ω). That follows from the relationship $P = i^2R$ for resistors. By contrast, the voltage is the same for the two resistors in the parallel circuit, so more power goes into the resistor with the smaller resistance ($P_1 = 72.0$ W into $R_1 = 2.00$ Ω versus $P_2 = 48.0$ W into $R_2 = 3.00$ Ω). That agrees with the relationship $P = V^2/R$ for resistors. So if the resistors are light bulbs, the light bulb with $R_2 = 3.00$ Ω is the brighter one in the series circuit, but the bulb with $R_1 = 2.00$ Ω is the brighter one in the parallel circuit! When comparing the power in resistors, choose wisely among the relationships $P = iV$, $P = i^2R$, and $P = V^2/R$.

We've seen how to apply Equation 18-23, $P = iV$, and Equations 18-24, $P = i^2R = V^2/R$, to DC circuits in which there is a steady current that does not vary with time. But these same equations also apply to circuits in which the current is *not* constant and varies. In the following section, we'll use Equations 18-23 and 18-24 to help us understand the time-varying current in a circuit that includes both a resistor and a capacitor.

❓ Got the Concept? 18-7 Batteries in Series

Consider a resistor R connected to a single source of emf ε and negligible internal resistance (Figure 18-15a). If the same resistor is instead connected to two sources of emf ε in series, each with negligible internal resistance (Figure 18-15b), by what factor does the power into the resistor increase? (a) $\sqrt{2}$; (b) 2; (c) 4; (d) 8; (e) 16.

Figure 18-15 **One emf or two** How does adding a second source of emf affect the power delivered to the resistor?

❓ Got the Concept? 18-8 Ranking the Power

Five identical resistors, A, B, C, D, and E, are connected to a source of emf as shown in Figure 18-16. The source has negligible internal resistance. Rank the five resistors in order of the amount of power that goes into each resistor, from greatest to smallest. If the power in two resistors is the same, indicate as such.

Figure 18-16 **Rank the resistors** How do these five identical resistors compare in the power that they absorb?

Take-Home Message for Section 18-6

✔ Power is the rate at which energy is transferred into or out of a system. The unit of power is the watt (1 W = 1 J/s).

✔ The power into or out of any circuit element equals the current through the element multiplied by the voltage across the element.

✔ The power into a resistor is proportional to the square of the current through the resistor or, equivalently, the square of the voltage across the resistor.

18-7 A circuit containing a resistor and capacitor has a current that varies with time

In an ordinary DC circuit, the battery provides a steady current and delivers energy to the other circuit elements at a steady rate. In some circuits, however, what's required is a short burst of energy. That's the case for the electronic flash in a camera or mobile phone (Figure 18-1c): Energy has to be delivered to the flash lamp in a very brief time interval to produce a short-duration, high-intensity flash.

The simplest way to deliver a short burst of electric potential energy to a circuit element is by using a *capacitor* as an energy source. (This would be a good time to review our discussion of capacitors in Sections 17-5 and 17-6.) We'll begin by examining a circuit in which a battery is used to charge a capacitor. Once we've done this, we'll see what happens when the charged capacitor is discharged and its stored energy is delivered to a resistor.

A Series *RC* Circuit: Charging the Capacitor

Figure 18-17a shows a circuit with a resistor of resistance R and a capacitor of capacitance C connected in series to a battery of emf ε. (We will assume that the internal resistance of the battery is so small compared to R that it can be ignored.) Such a circuit that contains both a resistor and capacitor in series is called a **series *RC* circuit**.

Initially, the capacitor in Figure 18-17a is uncharged. If the switch in this circuit is moved to the up position (Figure 18-17b), the circuit is completed and the battery will cause charge to begin to flow. We'll call $t = 0$ the time when the switch is thrown. As time passes, positive charge $+q$ builds up on the upper capacitor plate, and an equal amount of negative charge $-q$ builds up on the lower capacitor plate. (The two charges must be of equal magnitude since the current is the same throughout the circuit. Hence positive charge leaves the initially uncharged lower plate at the same rate that it arrives at the initially uncharged upper plate, leaving as much negative charge on the lower plate as there is positive charge on the upper plate.) So the circuit in Figure 18-17b is a *charging* series *RC* circuit.

Let's apply Kirchhoff's loop rule to the circuit shown in Figure 18-17b. In Section 17-5 we found that the magnitude of the charge q on the capacitor plates is proportional to the voltage V across the capacitor:

A capacitor carries a charge $+q$ on its positive plate and a charge $-q$ on its negative plate.

The magnitude of q is directly proportional to V, the voltage (potential difference) between the plates.

$$q = CV$$

The constant of proportionality between charge q and voltage V is the capacitance C of the capacitor.

Charge, voltage, and capacitance for a capacitor
(17-14)

(a) The position of this switch determines whether or not the source of emf ε is part of the circuit.

(b) With the switch in the up position, the emf causes charge to flow. This current charges the capacitor, so q increases.

Figure 18-17 Charging a series *RC* circuit (a) In this circuit a resistor and an initially uncharged capacitor are connected in series to a source of emf. (b) The switch is moved to the up position at $t = 0$, beginning the charging process.

We can rewrite Equation 17-14 as $V = q/C$. If we start at point p in Figure 18-17b and move in a clockwise round trip through the circuit, we encounter a voltage rise of $+\varepsilon$ as we pass through the source of emf, a voltage drop $-iR$ as we pass through the resistor, and a voltage drop $-q/C$ as we pass through the capacitor from the positive plate (which is at higher potential) to the negative plate (which is at lower potential). Kirchhoff's loop rule tells us that the sum of these voltages must be zero:

$$\varepsilon + (-iR) + \left(-\frac{q}{C}\right) = 0 \tag{18-25}$$

If we solve Equation 18-25 for the current i in the circuit, we get

$$i = \frac{\varepsilon}{R} - \frac{q}{RC} \tag{18-26}$$

Equation 18-26 tells us that the current in the circuit of Figure 18-17b *cannot* be constant. As charge builds up on the capacitor, the value of q increases. As a result, the right-hand side of Equation 18-26 must decrease with time, so the current i must decrease with time as well. Physically what's happening is that the voltage $V = q/C$ across the capacitor increases as the charge increases. This voltage is opposed to that of the source of emf, so the current decreases. Since the current is what's causing the charge to increase, this means that q increases at an ever-slower rate as time goes by.

We'd like to know the capacitor charge q and the current i as functions of time. Solving Equation 18-26 for these functions is a problem in calculus that's beyond our scope. Instead, we'll present the solutions and see that they make sense:

Capacitor charge and current in a charging series *RC* circuit (18-27)

Capacitor charge as a function of time

Capacitance

$$q(t) = C\varepsilon(1 - e^{-t/RC})$$

Source emf

The product RC (resistance multiplied by capacitance) is the **time constant** of the circuit.

$$i(t) = \frac{\varepsilon}{R}e^{-t/RC}$$

Current as a function of time

Resistance

 In these equations, $t = 0$ is when the switch in Figure 18-17b is moved to the up position.

$\sqrt{x}$ *See the Math Tutorial for more information on exponents and logarithms*

Figure 18-18 graphs the charge q and current i as given by Equations 18-27. Both of these equations involve the **exponential function**, the irrational number $e = 2.71828\ldots$ raised to a power. (Note that e is *not* the same as the magnitude of the charge on the electron, for which we unfortunately use the same symbol.) The number e has special properties: If a population has N_0 members and grows at a rate r per year (for example, if the population grows by 2% per year, $r = 0.02$), then after t years the population will be $N(t) = N_0 e^{rt}$. In both of Equations 18-27 the exponential function has a *negative* exponent, which means that this function decreases with time. In particular, $e^{-t/RC}$ decreases by a factor of $1/e = 0.36787\ldots$ every time the quantity t/RC increases by 1—that is, whenever time t increases by RC. At $t = 0$ (when the switch in Figure 18-17

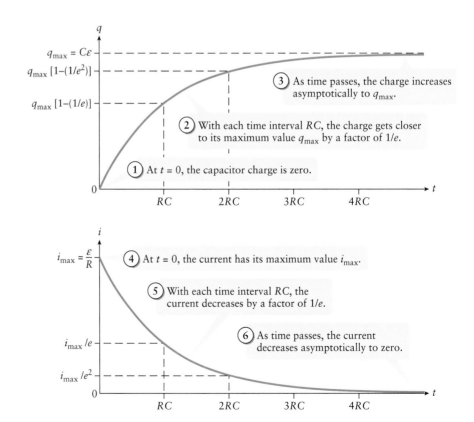

Figure 18-18 Charge and current in a charging series *RC* circuit Capacitor charge q starts at zero and approaches a maximum value; current i starts at a maximum value and approaches zero.

is closed and charge begins to flow), $e^{-t/RC} = e^0 = 1$; at $t = RC$, $e^{-t/RC} = e^{-1} = 1/e = 0.368$ to three significant figures; at $t = 2RC$, $e^{-t/RC} = e^{-2} = 1/e^2 = 0.135$; and so on.

The quantity RC is called the **time constant** of a series RC circuit. (Note that the product RC has units of ohms times farads. Since $1\ \Omega = 1\ V/A$, $1\ F = 1\ C/V$, and $1\ A = 1\ C/s$, it follows that $1\ \Omega \cdot F = 1\ (V/A)(C/V) = 1\ C/A = 1\ s$. So the quantity RC does indeed have units of time.) The smaller the time constant, the more rapidly the charge q approaches its maximum value q_{max} and the more rapidly the current decreases to its final value of zero. This makes sense: A smaller resistance R (and so a smaller value of RC) allows a greater current, which means that the capacitor can accumulate charge at a faster rate. A smaller capacitance C also decreases the time constant because the capacitor can store less charge for a given voltage and so can be charged more rapidly.

No matter what the value of RC, at $t = 0$ the capacitor is uncharged, so there is zero voltage across the capacitor. As a result, at $t = 0$ the voltage iR across the resistor is equal to the voltage ε across the source, so $\varepsilon = iR$ and $i = i_{max} = \varepsilon/R$. After a very long time the current has dropped to zero, so the voltage iR across the resistor is zero. As a result, the voltage q/C across the capacitor is equal to the voltage ε across the source, so $\varepsilon = q/C$ and $q = q_{max} = C\varepsilon$.

A Series RC Circuit: Discharging the Capacitor

Suppose a long time has elapsed since the switch in Figure 18-17b was thrown to the up position, so the capacitor is charged to a charge q_{max}. (This may be less than $C\varepsilon$, depending on how long the source has had to charge the capacitor.) We now throw the switch to the down position as in Figure 18-19 and restart our clock so that $t = 0$ is the time when the switch is moved to the new position. Now the emf is no longer part of the circuit, so the positive charge on the upper plate of the capacitor is free to move counterclockwise around the circuit to cancel the negative charge on the lower plate. So the value of the capacitor charge q decreases, and the electric potential energy stored in the capacitor is transferred into the resistor. We call this a *discharging* series RC circuit.

Kirchhoff's loop rule for the discharging circuit is now the same as Equation 18-25, but with the emf ε removed:

$$\left(-iR \right) + \left(-\frac{q}{C} \right) = 0 \tag{18-28}$$

Solving Equation 18-28 for the current i in the circuit gives

$$i = -\frac{q}{RC} \tag{18-29}$$

The minus sign in Equation 18-29 means that the current flows in the direction opposite to that in the charging RC circuit of Figure 18-17b. (You can see this in Figure 18-19.) Equation 18-29 says that as the capacitor discharges and the charge q decreases, the current i will decrease in magnitude. The charge and current as functions of time are

Capacitor charge as a function of time

$$q(t) = q_{max}\, e^{-t/RC}$$

Capacitor charge at $t = 0$

The product RC (resistance multiplied by capacitance) is the **time constant** of the circuit.

$$i(t) = -\frac{q_{max}}{RC}\, e^{-t/RC}$$

Current as a function of time

With the switch in the down position, the voltage across the capacitor causes a current. This current discharges the capacitor, so q decreases.

Figure 18-19 Discharging a series RC circuit When the switch in the circuit of Figure 18-17 is moved to the down position, the discharging process begins.

Capacitor charge and current in a discharging series RC circuit
(18-30)

 In these equations, $t = 0$ is when the switch in Figure 18-19 is moved to the down position.

Figure 18-20 Charge and current in a discharging series *RC* circuit
Capacitor charge *q* starts at a maximum value and approaches zero; current *i* starts at a maximum (negative) value and approaches zero.

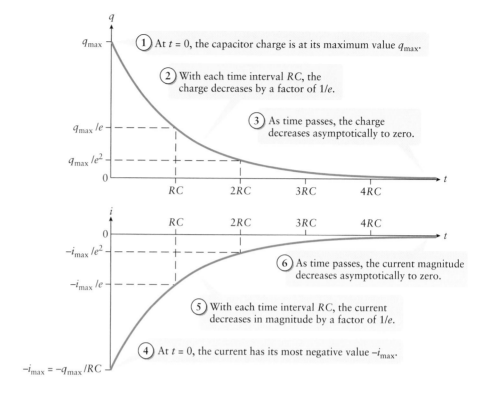

1. At $t = 0$, the capacitor charge is at its maximum value q_{max}.

2. With each time interval RC, the charge decreases by a factor of $1/e$.

3. As time passes, the charge decreases asymptotically to zero.

6. As time passes, the current magnitude decreases asymptotically to zero.

5. With each time interval RC, the current decreases in magnitude by a factor of $1/e$.

4. At $t = 0$, the current has its most negative value $-i_{max}$.

$-i_{max} = -q_{max}/RC$

 Go to Interactive Exercise 18-1 and 18-2 for more practice dealing with RC circuits

 Go to Interactive Exercise 18-3 for more practice dealing with time constants

The graphs in Figure 18-20 show the charge q and current i as given by Equations 18-30. Both functions are proportional to $e^{-t/RC}$, so both decrease by a factor of $1/e$ whenever time t increases by one time constant RC. So the value of RC determines both how rapidly the capacitor charges and how rapidly it discharges.

Example 18-11 A Charging Series *RC* Circuit

A 10.0-MΩ resistor is connected in series with a 5.00-μF capacitor. When a switch is thrown, these circuit elements are connected to a 24.0-V battery of negligible internal resistance. The capacitor is initially uncharged. (a) What is the current in the circuit immediately after the switch is moved so that charging begins? (b) What is the charge on the capacitor once it is fully charged? (c) Find the capacitor charge, current, power provided by the battery, power taken in by the resistor, and power taken in by the capacitor at $t = 50.0$ s. (d) When the capacitor is fully charged, find the total energy that has been delivered by the battery and the total energy that has been delivered to the capacitor.

Set Up

We are given $R = 10.0$ MΩ $= 10.0 \times 10^6$ Ω, $C = 5.00\ \mu$F $= 5.00 \times 10^{-6}$ F, and $\varepsilon = 24.0$ V. Equations 18-27 tell us the capacitor charge and current at any time, including at $t = 0$ (when the switch is first closed) and $t \rightarrow \infty$ (long after the switch is closed, so the capacitor is fully charged). We'll use Equations 18-23 and 18-24 to find the power out of the battery and into the resistor and capacitor. (Equation 17-14 will help us in this.) In order to charge the capacitor to its maximum charge q_{max}, the total charge that must pass through the battery is q_{max}; we'll use this and Equation 17-6 to find the total energy delivered by the battery. Equation 17-17 tells us the total energy that is stored in the charged capacitor.

Capacitor charge and current in a charging series *RC* circuit:

$$q(t) = C\varepsilon(1 - e^{-t/RC})$$
$$i(t) = \frac{\varepsilon}{R}e^{-t/RC} \qquad (18\text{-}27)$$

Power for a circuit element:

$$P = iV \qquad (18\text{-}23)$$

Power for a resistor:

$$P = i^2R = \frac{V^2}{R} \qquad (18\text{-}24)$$

Charge, voltage, and capacitance for a capacitor:

$$q = CV \qquad (17\text{-}14)$$

$\varepsilon = 24.0$ V $R = 10.0$ MΩ
switch closed at $t = 0$
$C = 5.00\ \mu$F

Electric potential difference related to electric potential energy difference:

$$\Delta V = \frac{\Delta U_{\text{electric}}}{q_0} \qquad (17\text{-}6)$$

Electric potential energy stored in a capacitor:

$$U_{\text{electric}} = \frac{1}{2}qV = \frac{1}{2}CV^2 = \frac{q^2}{2C} \qquad (17\text{-}17)$$

Solve

(a) Find the current at $t = 0$.

From the second of Equations 18-27, the current when the switch is first closed at $t = 0$ is

$$i(0) = \frac{\varepsilon}{R}e^{-(0)/RC} = \frac{\varepsilon}{R}e^0$$

Since any number raised to the power 0 equals 1, we have $e^0 = 1$ and

$$i(0) = i_{\text{max}} = \frac{\varepsilon}{R} = \frac{24.0\ \text{V}}{10.0 \times 10^6\ \Omega}$$
$$= 2.40 \times 10^{-6}\ \text{A} = 2.40\ \mu\text{A}$$

(b) Find the capacitor charge long after the switch is closed ($t \to \infty$).

The first of Equations 18-27 tells us the capacitor charge $q(t)$. As $t \to \infty$, the exponent $-t/RC \to -\infty$. Any number raised to the power $-\infty$ is zero, so

$$e^{-t/RC} \to 0$$

$$q(t) = C\varepsilon(1 - e^{-t/RC}) \to q_{\text{max}} = C\varepsilon(1 - 0) = C\varepsilon$$
$$= (5.00 \times 10^{-6}\ \text{F})(24.0\ \text{V})$$
$$= 1.20 \times 10^{-4}\ \text{C} = 0.120\ \text{mC}$$

(c) The time constant for this circuit is $RC = 50.0$ s, so we are actually being asked about the behavior of the circuit one time constant after the switch is closed. Use this to find charge q, current i, and the power out of or into each circuit element.

The time constant for this circuit is

$$RC = (10.0 \times 10^6\ \Omega)(5.00 \times 10^{-6}\ \text{F}) = 50.0\ \text{s}$$

so at $t = 50.0$ s, $t/RC = (50.0\ \text{s})/(50.0\ \text{s}) = 1.00$

From Equations 18-27,

$$q = C\varepsilon(1 - e^{-1.00}) = (5.00 \times 10^{-6}\ \text{F})(24.0\ \text{V})(1 - 0.368)$$
$$= 7.58 \times 10^{-5}\ \text{C} = 0.632 q_{\text{max}}$$

$$i = \frac{\varepsilon}{R}e^{-1.00} = \frac{24.0\ \text{V}}{10.0 \times 10^6\ \Omega}(0.368)$$
$$= 8.83 \times 10^{-7}\ \text{A} = 0.368 i_{\text{max}}$$

The voltage across the battery is $\varepsilon = 24.0$ V, so from Equation 18-23 the power out of the battery is

$$P_{\text{battery}} = i\varepsilon = (8.83 \times 10^{-7}\ \text{A})(24.0\ \text{V})$$
$$= 2.12 \times 10^{-5}\ \text{W} = 21.2\ \mu\text{W}$$

From the first of Equations 18-24, the power into the resistor is

$$P_R = i^2R = (8.83 \times 10^{-7}\ \text{A})^2(10.0 \times 10^6\ \Omega)$$
$$= 7.80 \times 10^{-6}\ \text{W} = 7.80\ \mu\text{W}$$

Equation 17-14, $q = CV$, tells us that the voltage across the capacitor is $V = q/C$. Combining this with Equation 18-23 gives the power into the capacitor:

$$P_C = i\left(\frac{q}{C}\right) = (8.83 \times 10^{-7}\text{A})\left(\frac{7.58 \times 10^{-5}\ \text{C}}{5.00 \times 10^{-6}\ \text{F}}\right)$$
$$= 1.34 \times 10^{-5}\ \text{W} = 13.4\ \mu\text{W}$$

(d) Use the maximum charge stored by the capacitor, which is the total charge moved across the battery, and Equation 7-6 to calculate the change in electric potential energy imparted by the battery. Use Equations 17-7 to calculate the electric potential energy stored in the capacitor.

Note that the net power into the resistor and capacitor combined equals the power out of the battery:

$$P_R + P_C = 7.80 \ \mu W + 13.4 \ \mu W = 21.2 \ \mu W = P_{battery}$$

Long after the switch is closed, the total amount of charge that has passed through the battery and to the positive capacitor plate is $q_{max} = 1.20 \times 10^{-4}$ C. From Equation 17-6, the potential energy change that was imparted by moving this charge across the 24.0-V emf of the battery is

$$\Delta U_{battery} = q_{max} \, \varepsilon = (1.20 \times 10^{-4} \text{ C})(24.0 \text{ V})$$
$$= 2.88 \times 10^{-3} \text{ J} = 2.88 \text{ mJ}$$

The last of Equations 17-17 tells us the amount of energy that went into the capacitor to store charge q_{max} there:

$$U_C = \frac{q_{max}^2}{2C} = \frac{(1.20 \times 10^{-4} \text{ C})^2}{2(5.00 \times 10^{-6} \text{ F})}$$
$$= 1.44 \times 10^{-3} \text{ J} = 1.44 \text{ mJ}$$

So exactly one-half of the energy taken from the battery goes into the capacitor: $U_C = (1/2)\Delta U_{battery}$.

Reflect

Our results for charge q and current i in part (c) agree with Figure 18-18: After one time constant the capacitor charge has reached $[1 - (1/e)] = 0.632 = 63.2\%$ of its fully charged value q_{max}, and the current has decreased to $1/e = 0.368 = 36.8\%$ of its initial value i_{max}. Can you show that after 5 time constants ($t = 5RC = 250$ s) the charge will have reached 99.3% of q_{max} and the current will have decreased to just 0.674% of i_{max}?

The power calculations in part (c) show that all of the power extracted from the battery is accounted for: Part of the energy extracted from the battery goes into the resistor, and the rest goes into adding to the electric potential energy stored in the capacitor. We've shown this for a specific instant, but it's true at *all* times during the charging process.

These results from part (c) also help us understand our calculations in part (d): Only one-half of the energy extracted from the battery goes into the capacitor, so the other half must have gone into the resistor. This is a general result for charging *any* series *RC* circuit.

Axon (stained white) seen end-on.

Myelin (stained-blue) seen end-on.

Figure 18-21 A myelinated axon In vertebrates, special cells wrap themselves around some axons forming a thick insulating layer called myelin. This decreases the effective capacitance of the axon and increases the speed at which nerve signals can propagate along the length of the axon.

The physics of capacitors in circuits helps explain what happens in the propagation of action potentials along axons, which we discussed in Section 18-4. All biological membranes, including the axonal membrane, act like a capacitor. Under resting conditions, the inner surface of the membrane is negatively charged and the outer surface is positively charged (see Figure 18-7). As we described in Section 18-4, as an action potential propagates along an axon the resting charge distribution reverses: At the peak of an action potential, the inner surface of the membrane is positively charged and the outer surface is negatively charged. When the membrane returns to its initial charge state, it's analogous to a capacitor discharging as in the circuit of Figure 18-19. The value of C is the capacitance of a segment of axon membrane, and the value of R is the resistance of that segment to charge flowing through channels in the membrane. (This is different from the resistance we discussed in Section 18-4, especially Example 18-6. There we considered the *longitudinal* resistance for current flowing along the length of the axon; the value of R we're considering here is the *transverse* resistance to charges flowing across the axon membrane, perpendicular to the axon's length.)

The value of the time constant RC determines the rate of discharge: The smaller the value of RC, the faster the capacitance of the membrane discharges and the more rapidly the signal propagates along the axon. We saw in Section 18-4 that some invertebrates such as squid have large-diameter axons to allow action potentials to propagate quickly from the brain to the muscles that mediate escape reflexes. Another way to make signals propagate more rapidly along an axon is to decrease the capacitance C of the membrane, thus reducing the value of RC. In vertebrates, special cells wrap themselves around some axons, forming a thick insulating layer called *myelin* (Figure 18-21). The myelin acts as a capacitor between the surface of the axon and its environment. This additional capacitance is in series with the capacitance of the axon's cell membrane and so decreases the effective capacitance of the axon. (Recall from Section 17-7 that when capacitors are placed in series, the effective capacitance is less than that of any individual capacitor.)

Only certain sections of the axon are coated with myelin. The action potential in the nonmyelinated gaps, or *nodes*, produces a signal that propagates rapidly along the myelinated regions of the axon. The signal weakens in strength in the myelinated region where no action potential is generated, but is reinvigorated when it reaches the next node.

? Got the Concept? 18-9   Discharging an *RC* Circuit

The switch in the circuit of Figure 18-19 is moved to the down position, causing the capacitor to discharge. Suppose that the resistor is a light bulb and that its brightness is proportional to the power into the resistor. Compared to the brightness of the bulb when the switch is moved to the down position at $t = 0$, the brightness of the bulb at $t = RC$ is (a) the same; (b) $1 - (1/e^2) = 0.865$ as great; (c) $1 - 1/e = 0.632$ as great; (d) $1/e = 0.368$ as great; (e) $1/e^2 = 0.135$ as great.

Take-Home Message for Section 18-7

✔ A circuit containing a resistor and a capacitor connected in series is a series *RC* circuit.

✔ Connecting the resistor and an uncharged capacitor to a source of emf causes a current that charges the capacitor. Switching the circuit to remove the source of emf causes the capacitor to discharge through the resistor. In either case, an exponential function describes how the current and the capacitor charge vary with time.

✔ The rate of charge or discharge in a series *RC* circuit depends on the time constant, equal to the product RC. In a time interval RC, the current decreases by a factor of $1/e$.

Key Terms

AC (alternating current)
alternating current (AC)
ampere
battery
circuit
circuit element
current
DC (direct current)
direct current (DC)
drift speed

emf
equivalent resistance
exponential function
internal resistance
junction
Kirchhoff's junction rule
Kirchhoff's loop rule
multiloop circuit
ohm
parallel (resistors)

power
resistance
resistivity
resistor
series (resistors)
series *RC* circuit
single-loop circuit
source of emf
time constant

Chapter Summary

Topic	Equation or Figure
Current: Electric charge flows around a circuit in response to an electric potential difference, such as that provided by a battery (a source of emf). Current is the rate of charge flow, and is related to the speed at which charges drift through the circuit. In ordinary metals the moving charges are negatively charged electrons, but it's conventional to take the direction of the current to be the direction in which positive charges would flow.	Current in a circuit. Amount of **charge** that flows past a certain point in the circuit. $$i = \frac{\Delta q}{\Delta t} \quad (18\text{-}1)$$ Time required for that amount of charge to flow past that point. Current in a wire. Number of moving charges per unit volume. $$i = nAev_{\text{drift}} \quad (18\text{-}3)$$ Speed at which charges drift through the wire. Cross-sectional area of the wire. Magnitude of the charge on each moving charge.

Resistance: Resistivity is a measure of how difficult it is for charges to flow through a material. The resistance of a wire or circuit element depends on the dimensions of the object as well as the resistivity of the material of which the object is made. Resistance and resistivity are not constants, but vary with temperature. A resistor is a circuit element whose most important property is its resistance.

Resistance of a wire   Resistivity of the material of which the wire is made

$$R = \frac{\rho L}{A}$$ Length of the wire

Cross-sectional area of the wire

(18-8)

Voltage, current, and resistance: In order for current to exist in a conductor with resistance, there must be a potential difference (voltage) between the ends of the conductor. For a given resistance, a greater voltage produces a greater current.

Potential difference between the ends of a wire

$$V = iR$$

Current in the wire   Resistance of the wire

(18-9)

Rules for circuits: Kirchhoff's loop rule states that the sum of the changes in electric potential around a closed loop in a circuit must equal zero. Kirchhoff's junction rule states that sum of the currents into a junction equals the sum of the currents out of it. These rules allow us to analyze the currents and voltages in electric circuits.

The potential increases by ε from the negative terminal to the positive terminal of the emf.

The potential drops by ir across the internal resistance and drops by iR across the resistor.

(Figure 18-8b)

Resistors in series and parallel: A collection of resistors in a circuit behaves as though it were a single resistor, with an equivalent resistance R_{equiv}. The equivalent resistance is different for resistors in series (all of which carry the same current) than for

Equivalent resistance of N resistors in series   Resistances of the individual resistors

$$R_{equiv} = R_1 + R_2 + R_3 + \ldots + R_N$$

 The equivalent resistance of N resistors in series is the sum of the individual resistances.

(18-11)

resistors in parallel (all of which have the same voltage).

The reciprocal of the equivalent resistance of N resistors in parallel is the sum of the reciprocals of the individual resistances.

$$\frac{1}{R_{equiv}} = \frac{1}{R_1} + \frac{1}{R_2} + \frac{1}{R_3} + ... + \frac{1}{R_N} \qquad (18\text{-}20)$$

Equivalent resistance of N resistors in parallel

Resistances of the individual resistors

Power in circuits: Power is the rate of energy transfer. In an electric circuit, energy flows from a source of emf into the other circuit elements. The power into a resistor can be expressed in terms of the resistance and either the current through the resistor or the voltage across the resistor.

Power produced by or transferred into a circuit element

$$P = iV \qquad (18\text{-}23)$$

Current through the circuit element

Voltage (absolute value) across the circuit element

Source of emf: Power flows out of the source and into the moving charges.
Resistor: Power flows out of the charges and into the resistor.

Power into a resistor   Current through the resistor

$$P = i^2 R = \frac{V^2}{R} \qquad (18\text{-}24)$$

Voltage across the resistor

Resistance of the resistor

Series RC circuits: If a resistor R and capacitor C are connected in series to a source of emf, the capacitor charge increases toward a maximum value. The current in the circuit (which carries the charge to the capacitor) begins with a large value and gradually decreases to zero. If the source is taken out of the circuit, the capacitor discharges. The current in the circuit now carries the charge away from the capacitor, and again gradually decreases to zero. The rate at which the current decreases depends on the time constant of the circuit, equal to the product RC.

With the switch in the up position, the emf causes charge to flow. This current charges the capacitor, so q increases.

(Figure 18-17b)

With the switch in the down position, the voltage across the capacitor causes a current. This current discharges the capacitor, so q decreases.

(Figure 18-19)

Answer to What do you think? Question

(b) When electrons pass through the battery, they gain electric potential energy. They lose most of this potential energy as they pass through the filament of the light bulb, and this lost energy goes into heating the filament and causing it to glow. The electrons lose the rest of the potential energy as they pass through the wires that connect the battery and light bulb. (This is a relatively small amount of energy because the connecting wires have low resistance.) If electrons lost *kinetic* energy at a certain point in the circuit, they would slow down and create an electron "traffic jam." The electric repulsion between electrons prevents such "jams" from happening, so the electrons must maintain the same average speed and so the same average kinetic energy as they travel around the circuit.

Answers to Got the Concept? Questions

18-1 (c) The current i in a simple circuit (in which the moving charges travel around a single loop) has the same value at all points in the circuit. This is true whether the thickness of the wire varies or is the same at all points.

18-2 (a) As we saw in the answer to the previous Got the Concept? question, the current i has the same value at all points in the circuit. Equation 18-3 shows that for this to be true, the product Av_{drift} (the cross-sectional area of the wire multiplied by the drift speed) must also have the same value at all points. (The quantity n, the number of mobile charges per unit volume, depends only on what the wire is made of, not on its dimensions.) The thinner wire has a radius r that is half as great and a cross-sectional area $A = \pi r^2$ that is one-quarter as great as the rest of the wire. So the drift speed of the electrons must be four times greater in the thinner part of the wire.

18-3 (b) For an ohmic material, the current and voltage are directly proportional, so doubling the voltage should cause a doubling of current. That is *not* the case for this material: Doubling the voltage from 2.0 V to 4.0 V increases the current by a factor of only $(0.28\ A)/(0.15\ A) = 1.9$, and doubling the voltage again from 4.0 V to 8.0 V increases the current by a factor of only $(0.50\ A)/(0.28\ A) = 1.8$. So this material is nonohmic.

18-4 (e) As in Example 18-6, the resistance of wire of resistivity ρ, length L, and diameter d is $R = 4\rho L/\pi d^2$. This says that the resistance is inversely proportional to the square of the diameter. So if the diameter is increased by a factor of 4 while leaving the resistivity and length the same, the resistance will change by a factor of $1/4^2 = 1/16$.

18-5 (c), (a), (b), (d) Combining resistors in series results in a circuit with larger equivalent resistance; combining them in parallel results in a smaller equivalent resistance. Therefore circuits (a) and (c) have higher resistance than circuits (b) and (d). For the same reason, the equivalent resistance of (c) with three resistors in series is higher than that of circuit (a) with two resistors in series, and the equivalent resistance of circuit (b) with two resistors in parallel is higher than that of circuit (d) with three resistors in parallel. So in order of equivalent resistance from highest to lowest, the circuits are (c), (a), (b), and (d). This conclusion doesn't depend on how the value of R_3 compares to the values of R_1 or R_2: Adding any resistance in series to a group of resistors increases the equivalent resistance, and adding any resistance in parallel to a group of resistors decreases the equivalent resistance.

18-6 (d), (b), (a), (c) The larger the equivalent resistance, the smaller the current for a fixed voltage. So a ranking of the circuits in order of decreasing current is just the opposite of a ranking in order of decreasing equivalent resistance. So the ranking in this question is the opposite of the ranking in Got the Concept? 18-5.

18-7 (c) Placing two sources of emf in series is equivalent to increasing the emf from ε to 2ε. This doubles the voltage V across the resistor, which from $V = iR$ (Equation 18-9) means that the current i through the resistor doubles as well. From Equations 18-24, $P = i^2R = V^2/R$, the power into the resistor is proportional to either the square of the current i or the square of the resistor voltage V. So the power into the resistor increases by a factor of $2^2 = 4$. A device such as a flashlight or television remote control that uses two batteries uses four times as much power as one with a single battery; a device with four batteries provides $4^2 = 16$ times as much power.

18-8 $P_A = P_E > P_D > P_B = P_C$ The full current that passes through the source also passes through resistors A and E. This current divides up in order to pass through two branches—one with resistors B and C, one with resistor D—so only a fraction of the full current passes through resistors B, C, and D. Since the power into a resistor is given by $P = i^2R$ (the first of Equations 18-24), it follows that the same power goes into A and E ($P_A = P_E$), and that this is greater than the power into any of the other three resistors. The voltage across the branch with resistors B and C is the same as that across the branch with resistor D (the branches are in parallel). All of this voltage is across resistor D, but only half of this voltage is across resistor B and half across resistor C. From the second of Equations 18-24, $P = V^2/R$, this means that there is more power into D than into B or C, but equal amounts into B and C (so $P_D > P_B = P_C$). So $P_A = P_E > P_D > P_B = P_C$. If the resistors are light bulbs, their ranking by brightness will be the same as this ranking by power.

18-9 (e) The second of Equations 18-30 shows that the current in a discharging series RC circuit is proportional to $e^{-t/RC}$, so at $t = RC$ the current has decreased by a factor of $e^{-1} = 1/e = 0.368$ compared to its value at $t = 0$ (when $e^{-t/RC} = e^0 = 1$). The power into a resistor is $P = i^2R$ (Equations 18-24). Since the power is proportional to the square of i, and i is $1/e$ as great as at $t = 0$, the power is $1/e^2 = (0.368)^2 = 0.135$ as great as at $t = 0$.

Questions and Problems

In a few problems, you are given more data than you actually need; in a few other problems, you are required to supply data from your general knowledge, outside sources, or informed estimate.

Interpret as significant all digits in numerical values that have trailing zeros and no decimal points.

For all problems, use $g = 9.80\ m/s^2$ for the free-fall acceleration due to gravity. Neglect friction and air resistance unless instructed to do otherwise.

• Basic, single-concept problem

•• Intermediate-level problem, may require synthesis of concepts and multiple steps

••• Challenging problem

SSM *Solution is in Student Solutions Manual*

Conceptual Questions

1. •We distinguish the direction of current in a circuit. Why don't we consider it a vector quantity?

2. •Is current dissipated when it passes through a resistor? Explain your answer.

3. •We justified a number of electrostatic phenomena by the argument that there can be no electric field in a conductor. Now we say that the current in a conductor is driven by a potential difference and thus there is an electric field in the conductor. Is this statement a contradiction? SSM

4. •Two wires, A and B, have the same physical dimensions but are made of different materials. If A has twice the resistance of B, how do their resistivities compare?

5. •The average drift velocity of electrons in a wire carrying a steady current is constant even though the electric field within the wire is doing work on the electrons. What happens to this energy?

6. •Under ordinary conditions, the drift speed of electrons in a metal is around 10^{-4} m/s or less. Why doesn't it take a long time for a light bulb to come on when you flip the wall switch that is several meters away?

7. •For a given source of constant voltage, will more heat develop in a large external resistance connected across it or a small one? SSM

8. •An ammeter measures the current through a particular circuit element. (a) How should it be connected with that element, in parallel or in series? (b) Should an ammeter have a very large or a very small resistance? Why?

9. •Biology When a bird lands on a high voltage wire and grabs the wire with its feet, will the bird be electrocuted? Explain your answer.

10. •If the only voltage source you have is 36 V, how could you light some 6-V light bulbs without burning them out?

11. ••Many ordinary strings of Christmas-tree lights contain about 50 bulbs connected in parallel across a 110 V line. Sixty years ago most strings contained 50 bulbs connected in series across the line. What would happen if you could put one of the old-style bulbs into a modern Christmas-tree light set? (The light sockets are made differently to prevent this.) SSM

12. •Biology Explain how an action potential is generated.

13. •Give a simple physical explanation for why the charge on a capacitor in an *RC* circuit can't be changed instantaneously.

14. •(a) Does the time required to fully charge a capacitor through a given resistor with a battery depend on the voltage of the battery? (b) Does it depend on the total amount of charge to be placed on the capacitor? Explain your answers.

Multiple-Choice Questions

15. •If a current-carrying wire has a cross-sectional area that gradually becomes smaller along the length of the wire, the drift velocity
    A. increases along the length of the wire.
    B. decreases along the length of the wire.
    C. remains the same along the length of the wire.
    D. increases along the length of the wire if the resistance increases too.
    E. decreases along the length of the wire if the resistance decreases too. SSM

16. •What causes an electric shock?
    A. current
    B. voltage
    C. both current and voltage

    D. resistance and current
    E. resistance and voltage

17. •Two copper wires have the same length, but one has twice the diameter of the other. Compared to the one that has the smaller diameter, the one that has the larger diameter has a resistance that is
    A. larger by a factor of 2.
    B. larger by a factor of 4.
    C. the same.
    D. smaller by a factor of $1/2$.
    E. smaller by a factor of $1/4$.

18. ••A wire has a length L and a resistance R. It is stretched uniformly to a length of $2L$. The resistance of the wire after it has been stretched is
    A. $(1/4)\, R$.
    B. $(1/2)\, R$.
    C. R.
    D. $2\, R$.
    E. $4\, R$.

19. •When a thin wire is connected across a voltage of 1 V, the current is 1 A. If we connect the same wire across a voltage of 2 V, the current is
    A. $(1/4)$ A.
    B. $(1/2)$ A.
    C. 1 A.
    D. 2 A.
    E. 4 A. SSM

20. •When a wire that has a large diameter and a length L is connected across the terminals of an automobile battery, the current is 40 A. If we cut the wire to half of its original length and connect one piece that has a length $L/2$ across the terminals of the same battery, the current will be
    A. 10 A.
    B. 20 A.
    C. 40 A.
    D. 80 A.
    E. 160 A.

21. •A charge flows from the positive terminal of a 6-V battery, through a light bulb, and through the battery back to the positive terminal. The total voltage drop experienced by the charge is
    A. 1 V.
    B. 6 V.
    C. 0 V.
    D. -1 V.
    E. -6 V.

22. •When a second bulb is added in series to a circuit with a single bulb, the resistance of the circuit
    A. increases.
    B. decreases.
    C. remains the same.
    D. doubles.
    E. triples.

23. •When a bulb is added in parallel to a circuit with a single bulb, the resistance of the circuit
    A. increases.
    B. decreases.
    C. remains the same.
    D. doubles.
    E. triples. SSM

24. •If we use a 2-V battery instead of a 1-V battery to charge the capacitor shown in Figure 18-22, the time constant will
  A. be four times greater.
  B. double.
  C. remain the same.
  D. be half as much.
  E. be four times less.

Figure 18-22 Problem 24

Estimation/Numerical Analysis

25. •Choose three appliances that you use on a daily basis and estimate the amount of electric current that is drawn by each.

26. •Estimate the current in a high voltage transmission line such as you might see in rural areas, sometimes close to remote interstate highways.

27. •Estimate the resistance of the electric coils in your toaster.

28. ••Estimate the electric energy usage of a citizen of a developed country such as Canada or the United States compared to a citizen of a developing nation.

29. •Estimate the current provided by the battery in a cellular phone.

30. •Estimate the electric current of a typical lightning bolt.

31. •Estimate the value of resistors and capacitors that are used in a common flash attachment of a disposable camera. SSM

Problems

18-1 Life on Earth and our technological society are only possible because of charges in motion

18-2 Electric current equals the rate at which charge flows

32. •A steady current of 35 mA exists in a wire. How many electrons pass any given point in the wire per second?

33. •A light bulb requires a current of 0.50 A to emit a normal amount of light. If the light is left on for 1 h, how many electrons pass through the bulb?

34. •During a thunderstorm, a lightning bolt carries current between a cloud and the ground below. If a lightning bolt transports a total charge of 80 C in 0.001 s, what is the magnitude of the average current?

35. •A synchrotron radiation facility consists of a circular ring that has a 40.0-m radius and creates an electron beam with a current of 487 mA when the electrons have a speed approximately equal to the speed of light. How many electrons pass a given point in the accelerator per hour? SSM

36. ••A copper wire that has a diameter of 2.00 mm carries a current of 10.0 A. Assuming that each copper atom contributes one free electron to the metal, find the drift velocity of the electrons in the wire. The molar mass of copper is 63.5 g/mol and the density of copper is 8.95 g/cm^3.

37. •**Biology** 2.00×10^{-3} mol of potassium ions pass through a cell membrane in 4.00×10^{-2} s. (a) Calculate the electric current and (b) describe its direction relative to the motion of the potassium ions.

18-3 The resistance to current through an object depends on the object's resistivity and dimensions

38. •If a copper wire has a resistance of 2.00 Ω and a diameter of 1.00 mm, how long is it?

39. •Calculate the resistance of a piece of copper wire that is 1.00 m long and has a diameter of 1.00 mm.

40. ••The resistance ratio of two conductors that have equal cross-sectional areas and equal lengths is 1:3. What is the ratio of the resistivities of the materials from which they are made?

41. ••An 8.00-m-long length of wire has a resistance of 4.00 Ω. The wire is uniformly stretched to a length of 16.0 m. Find the resistance of the wire after it has been stretched. SSM

42. ••When 120 V is applied to the filament of a 75-W light bulb, the current drawn is 0.63 A. When a potential difference of 3.0 V is applied to the same filament, the current is 0.086 A. Is the filament made of an ohmic material? Explain your answer.

43. •A power transmission line is made of copper that is 1.80 cm in diameter. What is the resistance of 1 mi of the line?

18-4 Resistance is important in both technology and physiology

44. •A common resistor used in a class lab has a color code shown in Figure 18-23. Write the numerical value of the resistor and give its *tolerance* (the uncertainty in the stated value). You may need to look up the resistor code using your favorite online search engine.

Red   Brown

Yellow   Gold   **Figure 18-23** Problem 44

45. ••There is a current of 112 pA when a certain potential is applied across a certain resistor. When that same potential is applied across a resistor made of the identical material but 25 times longer, the current is 0.044 pA. Compare the effective diameters of the two resistors.

46. •What are the first three color codes depicting a resistor with a value of 20 GΩ? You may need to look up the resistor code using your favorite online search engine.

47. ••Electric cables often consist of a large number of strands of conducting wire. Due to variances in manufacturing, cables from a certain company can have between 850 and 950 separate strands, each with a mean diameter of 0.72 ± 0.07 mm. Determine the ratio of the (a) lowest and (b) highest possible resistance of one of these cables to the average resistance of many individual strands of conducting wire. SSM

48. ••A certain flexible conducting wire changes shape as environmental variables, such as temperature, change. If the diameter of the wire increases by 25% while the length decreases by 12%, by what factor does the resistance of the wire change?

49. ••**Biology** Cell membranes contain channels that allow ions to cross the phospholipid bilayer. A particular K$^+$ channel carries a current of 1.9 pA. How many K$^+$ ions pass through it in 1.0 ms?

50. ••**Biology** Cell membranes contain channels that allow K$^+$ ions to leak out. Consider a channel that has a diameter of 1.0 nm and a length of 10 nm. If the channel has a resistance of 18 GΩ, what is the resistivity of the solution in the channel?

18-5 Kirchhoff's rules help us to analyze simple electric circuits

51. •If a light bulb draws a current of 1.0 A when connected to a 12-V circuit, what is the resistance of its filament?

52. •If a flashlight bulb has a resistance of 12.0 Ω, how much current will the bulb draw when it is connected to a 6.0-V circuit?

53. •A light bulb has a resistance of 8.0 Ω and a current of 0.5 A when it is connected to a voltage. At what voltage is it operating?

54. •Calculate the voltage difference $V_A - V_B$ in each of the situations shown in Figure 18-24.

Figure 18-24 Problem 54

55. •An 18.0-Ω resistor and a 6.00-Ω resistor are connected in series. What is the equivalent resistance of the resistors?

56. •An 18.0-Ω resistor and a 6.00-Ω resistor are connected in parallel. What is the equivalent resistance of the resistors?

57. ••A 9.00-Ω resistor and a 3.00-Ω resistor are connected in series across a 9.00-V battery. Find (a) the current through each resistor and (b) the voltage drop across each resistor. SSM

58. ••A 9.00-Ω resistor and a 3.00-Ω resistor are connected in parallel across a 9.00-V battery. Find (a) the current through each resistor and (b) the voltage drop across each resistor.

59. ••A potential difference of 3.6 V is applied between points a and b in Figure 18-25. Find (a) the current in each of the resistors and (b) the total current the three resistors draw from the power source.

Figure 18-25 Problem 59

60. ••The four resistors in Figure 18-26 have an equivalent resistance of 8 Ω. Calculate the value of R_x.

Figure 18-26 Problem 60

61. ••Find the equivalent resistance of the combination of resistors shown in Figure 18-27. SSM

Figure 18-27 Problem 61

62. ••A metal wire of resistance 48-Ω is cut into four equal pieces that are then connected side by side to form a new wire which is one-quarter of the original length. What is the resistance of the new wire?

63. ••Two resistors A and B are connected in series to a 6.0-V battery; the voltage across resistor A is 4.0 V. When A and B are connected in parallel across a 6.0-V battery, the current through B is 2.0 A. What are the resistances of A and B? The batteries have negligible internal resistance.

64. ••A potential difference of 7.50 V is applied between points a and c in Figure 18-28. (a) Find the difference in potential between points b and c. (b) Is the current through the 60-Ω resistor larger or smaller than that through the 35-Ω resistor? Why?

Figure 18-28 Problem 64

18-6 The rate at which energy is produced or taken in by a circuit element depends on current and voltage

65. •A heater is rated at 1500 W. How much current does it draw when it is connected to a 120-V voltage source? SSM

66. •A 4.0-Ω resistor is connected to a 12-V voltage source. What is the power dissipated by the resistor?

67. •A coffeemaker has a resistance of 12 Ω and draws a current of 15 A. How much power does it use?

68. ••When connected in parallel across a 120-V source, two light bulbs consume 60 W and 120 W, respectively. What powers do the light bulbs consume if instead they are connected in series across the same source? Assume the resistance of each light bulb is constant.

69. •A transmission line carries 1200 A and has a resistance of 40 Ω. Calculate the energy lost per second due to *joule heating*, the transformation of electrical energy to thermal energy when current through wires encounters resistance.

70. •A stereo speaker has a resistance of 8 Ω. If the power output is 40 W, calculate the current passing through the speaker wires.

71. •If your local power company charges $0.11 per kW·h, what would it cost to run a 1500-W heater continuously during an 8-h night? SSM

72. ••A house is heated by a 24-kW electric furnace using resistance heating, and the local power company charges $0.10 per kW·h. The heating bill for January is $218. How long must the furnace have been running on an average January day?

18-7 A circuit containing a resistor and capacitor has a current that varies with time

73. •A 4.00-MΩ resistor and a 3.00-μF capacitor are connected in series with a power supply. What is the time constant for the circuit? SSM

74. •A capacitor of 20.0 μF and a resistor of 100 Ω are quickly connected in series to a battery of 6.00 V. What is the charge on the capacitor 0.00100 s after the connection is made?

75. •A 10.0-μF capacitor has an initial charge of 100.0 μC. If a resistance of 20.0 Ω is connected across it, what is the initial current through the resistor?

76. ••A 10.0-μF capacitor carries an initial charge of 80.0 μC. (a) If a resistance of 25.0-Ω is connected across it, what is the

initial current in the resistor? (b) What is the time constant of the circuit?

77. ••A 12.5-μF capacitor is charged to a potential of 50.0 V and then discharged through a 75.0-Ω resistor. (a) How long after discharge begins does it take for the capacitor to lose 90.0% of its initial (i) charge and (ii) energy? (b) What is the current through the resistor at both times in part (a)?

78. ••**Biology** A single ion channel is selectively permeable to K+ and has a resistance of 1.0 GΩ. During an experiment the channel is open for approximately 1.0 ms while the voltage across the channel is maintained at +80 mV with a patch clamp. How many K+ ions travel through the channel?

General Problems

79. ••How much power is dissipated in each resistor shown in Figure 18-29?

Figure 18-29 Problem 79

80. •Determine the current through each resistor in Figure 18-30.

Figure 18-30 Problem 80

81. •••An electric heater consists of a single resistor connected across 110 V. It is used to heat 200.0 g of water in a coffee cup from 20°C to 90°C in 2.70 min. (a) Assuming that 90% of the energy drawn from the power source goes into heating the water, what is the resistance of the heater? (b) Assuming no other heat losses, how much longer will it take to heat your water if you had to power the water heater with your 12.0-V car battery?

82. •••Measurements made during severe electrical storms reveal that lightning bolts can carry as much as 30 C of charge and can travel between a cloud and the ground in time intervals of around 100 μs (and sometimes even shorter). Potential differences have been measured as high as 400 million volts. (a) What is the current in such a lightning strike? How does it compare with typical household currents? (b) What is the resistance of the air during such a strike? (c) How much energy is transferred during a severe strike? (d) What mass of water at 100°C could the lightning bolt in part (c) evaporate?

83. ••In the circuit shown in Figure 18-31, a potential difference of 5.00 V is applied between points *a* and *b*. Determine (a) the equivalent total resistance, (b) the current in each resistor, and (c) the power dissipated in each resistor. (d) How does the amount of power dissipated in the 20-Ω resistor compare to power dissipated in the other two?

Figure 18-31 Problem 83

84. ••**Biology** Giant electric eels can deliver a voltage shock of 500 V and up to 1.0 A of current for a brief time. For a snorkeler swimming in salt water, the resistance of her skin is negligible, so her body resistance is about 600 Ω. A current of about 500 mA can cause heart fibrillation and death if it lasts too long. (a) What is the maximum power a giant electric eel can deliver to its prey? (b) If the snorkeler is unfortunate enough to be struck by the eel, what current will pass through her body? Is this large enough to be dangerous? (c) What power does the snorkeler receive from the eel?

85. ••**Biology** The resistance of the body is made up of two basic parts: the resistance of the skin (see the following problem) and the resistance of the interior of the body. The internal resistance varies somewhat, but about 500 Ω measured between the two hands is typical. We can model this part of the body as a cylinder 1.6 m long and 14 cm in diameter. (a) What is the average internal resistivity of the body? (b) How much power will be delivered to the body of a person who accidentally grabs the ends of wires connected across a 110-V power source?

86. ••**Biology** Most of the resistance of the human body comes from the skin, as the interior of the body contains aqueous solutions that are good electrical conductors. For dry skin, the resistance between a person's hands is measured at typically 500 kΩ. The skin varies in thickness, but on the average it is about 2.0 mm thick. We can model the body between the hands as a cylinder 1.6 m long and 14 cm in diameter with the skin wrapped around it. (a) What is the resistivity of the skin? (b) Compare your answer with that found in part (a) of the previous problem for the internal resistivity of the body. How do you explain the fact that the resistance of the skin is about 1000 times greater than the internal resistance of the body, even though the resistivity of the skin is only about 60 times that of the interior of the body?

87. ••The capacitor in the flash of a disposable camera has a value of 160 μF. What is the resistance of the filament in the bulb if it takes 10 s to charge the capacitor to 80% of its maximum charge?

88. ••A discharging capacitor starts with a maximum charge and exponentially decays to zero. (a) How much time (in terms of the time constant RC) will it take before a discharging capacitor holds only 50% of the maximum charge? (b) What percentage of the original charge will the capacitor hold at a time that is 3 times the time constant?

89. ••A 3.0-μF capacitor is put across a 12-V battery. After a long time ($\sim$20 time constants), the capacitor is disconnected and placed in series through an open switch, with a 200-Ω resistor. (a) Determine the charge on the capacitor before it is discharged. (b) What is the initial current through the resistor

when the switch is closed? (c) At what time will the current reach 37% of its initial value?

90. ••You are working late on a project and find that you need a 75-Ω resistor, but unfortunately you only have a box of 50-Ω resistors on hand. All the electronics shops are closed, so you cannot buy the needed resistor. (a) How can you make a 75-Ω resistor using the resistors you have on hand? (b) How could you use your 50-Ω resistors to make a 60-Ω resistor? (c) Suppose you have only 50-μF capacitors. How could you use them to make a 75-μF capacitor and (d) to make a 60-μF capacitor?

91. ••A circuit probe is any device, such as a meter or an oscilloscope, that gives information about the circuit. Oscilloscopes and voltmeters are designed to measure the voltage across a circuit element, so they are connected across that element. Ideally, the probe should not disturb the circuit in any way by introducing resistance or capacitance, but in reality we cannot avoid some disturbance. A probe should disturb the circuit as little as possible. (a) When it is connected across a circuit element, is the probe in series or in parallel with that element? (b) Should a probe connected in this way have (i) a very large or a very small resistance, (ii) a very large or a very small capacitance? Explain your reasoning and use the properties of series and parallel connections to justify your answer.

92. ••For most purposes, we store electrical energy in batteries. But there are drawbacks to batteries: They release their energy rather slowly and are very damaging environmentally. Capacitors would be much cleaner for the environment and can be quickly recharged. Unfortunately they don't store much energy. (a) A new 1.5-V AAA battery has a "capacity" (*not* capacitance) of 1250 mA · h. What does this "capacity" actually represent? Express it in standard SI units. (b) How many joules of energy can be stored in the AAA battery? (c) At a steady current of 400 mA, how many hours will the AAA battery last? (d) How much energy can be stored in a typical 10-μF capacitor charged to a potential of 1.5 V? How does that compare to the energy stored in the AAA battery?

93. ••An *ultracapacitor* is a very high-capacitance device capable of storing much more energy than an ordinary capacitor. It is designed so that the spacing of the plates is around 1000 times smaller than in ordinary capacitors. Furthermore the plates contain millions of microscopic nanotubes, which increase their effective area 100,000 times. (a) If the plate separation and effective area of a 10-μF capacitor are changed as described above to make an ultracapacitor, what is its new capacitance? (b) How much energy does the ultracapacitor store if charged to 1.5 V? Compare this to the energy stored in an ordinary 10-μF capacitor at that potential. (c) Compare the energy stored in the ultracapacitor to that of the AAA battery in the previous problem. (d) If the ultracapacitor is to take 1.0 min to decrease to $1/e$ of its initial maximum charge, what resistance must it discharge through?

19

Magnetism

What do you think?

The aurora borealis ("northern lights") is caused by fast-moving, electrically charged subatomic particles ejected from the Sun. Earth's magnetic field exerts a magnetic force on these particles that steers them toward our planet's north magnetic pole. When these particles enter Earth's upper atmosphere, they collide with the atoms there and cause the atoms to emit an eerie glow. (A similar effect in the southern hemisphere is called the aurora australis.) In what direction are these subatomic particles moving when the magnetic force on them is strongest? (a) In the same direction as the magnetic field; (b) opposite to the magnetic field; (c) perpendicular to the magnetic field; (d) either (a) or (b); (e) the magnetic force doesn't depend on the direction of motion.

In this chapter, your goals are to:
- (19-1) Recognize that magnetic forces can act over large distances.
- (19-2) Recognize that magnetism is fundamentally an interaction between moving electric charges.
- (19-3) Calculate the magnitude and direction of the magnetic force on a charged particle.
- (19-4) Describe how a mass spectrometer uses magnetic fields to sort atoms according to their mass.
- (19-5) Calculate the magnetic force on a current-carrying wire.
- (19-6) Explain why a current loop in a uniform magnetic field experiences a net torque but zero net force.
- (19-7) Describe the principle of Ampère's law and how to use it.
- (19-8) Calculate the magnetic force that parallel current-carrying wires exert on each other.

To master this chapter, you should review:
- (5-6)   Uniform circular motion.
- (8-6)   The torque generated by a force.
- (16-5) The properties of electric field lines and the nature of electric dipoles.
- (18-2) The relationship between the current in a wire and the drift speed of charges in the wire.
- (18-6) Power into a current-carrying resistor.

19-1 Magnetic forces are interactions between two magnets

If you rub a balloon on your head, then move the balloon a few centimeters away from your head, the hairs on your head will stand up (see Figure 16-4). This phenomenon is a result of *electric* forces. During the rubbing, electrons are transferred between your hair and the balloon, giving one a net negative charge and the other a net positive charge; these attract each other, even over a distance, and this attraction makes your hair stand up. The effect is rather feeble, however, and only the finest hairs on your head will respond noticeably to these electric forces.

Figure 19-1a shows another force that acts at a distance like the electric force, but can be *much* stronger than that between the balloon and your hair. Certain objects called **magnets**, made of one of a handful of special materials such as iron, cobalt, and nickel, can exert strong **magnetic forces** on other magnets. (The name *magnet* comes

(a)

(b)

(c)

Figure 19-1 **Magnetic forces** (a) The force between two bar magnets. (b) A compass needle interacting with Earth's magnet. (c) A large electromagnet.

The north pole of the left-hand bar magnet...

...attracts the south pole of the right-hand bar magnet.

The magnetized compass needle always points toward Earth's magnetic north pole.

The magnetic field required to pick up pieces of iron at a scrap yard comes from an electromagnet—a device that generates a magnetic field when there is current through its wires.

from the region of ancient Greece known as Magnesia, where these objects were discovered more than 2500 years ago.) Just as we use the umbrella term *electricity* to refer to interactions between electrically charged objects, we use the term **magnetism** to describe the interactions between magnets. One application of the magnetic force is the compass (Figure 19-1b). Earth's core acts like a giant magnet. The magnetic compass needle interacts with Earth's magnet in such a way that the compass needle always points toward the north pole. We will see that moving charges such as those in the large electromagnet in Figure 19-1c create magnetic fields.

Our goal in this chapter is to understand magnetism. We begin in the next section by investigating the properties of magnets, and realizing that they are created by moving charges. From there, we develop a full understanding of magnetic forces, which requires us to understand two things: (1) the nature of the magnetic field that moving charges *produce* and (2) how moving charges *respond* to the magnetic fields produced by other moving charges. It turns out to be easiest to look at the second of these first. We'll analyze the magnetic force that acts on a moving charge placed in a magnetic field, as well as the magnetic force on a wire that carries a current (a collection of charges moving in the wire) and is placed in a magnetic field. Later in the chapter we'll see how to calculate the magnetic field produced by a given collection of charges in motion.

> ## Take-Home Message for Section 19-1
>
> ✔ Magnetic forces can act over large distances, much like electric forces.

19-2 Magnetism is an interaction between moving charges

Like the electric force, magnetic forces become stronger as the objects are moved closer together. However, the magnetic force is not simply a form of the electric force, because the attracting magnets in Figure 19-1a are *not* electrically charged: Their atoms are made of positively charged nuclei and negatively charged electrons, but their net charges are zero. Any electric forces between these magnets are very weak and are not responsible for the strong attraction shown in Figure 19-1a.

As we did for the electric force, we can explain how the magnetic force acts at a distance by invoking the idea of a field. Just as an electrically charged object sets up an electric field in the space around it, a magnet sets up a **magnetic field** in the space around it (Figure 19-2). A second magnet placed in this field experiences a magnetic force that depends on the magnitude and direction of the field. We use the symbol $\vec{B}$ for magnetic field. Unlike the electric field $\vec{E}$ of a point charge, which points either directly away from or directly toward the charge, the magnetic field $\vec{B}$ of a magnet points away from one end of a magnet toward the other end. These two ends are called the **magnetic poles** of the magnet, one of which is called the *north pole* and the other the *south pole*. (The meaning of the names is that Earth itself acts like a giant magnet. If allowed to swing freely, a magnet will orient itself so that its north

Bar magnets interact because each magnet produces a magnetic field, to which the other magnet responds.

Iron filings align with the magnetic field, making it visible.

Figure 19-2 The magnetic field of a bar magnet.

(a) These magnets attract.

(b) These magnets repel.

(c) If we cut a magnet in half, each half has a north and south pole.

Figure 19-3 Bar magnets and magnetic poles (a) The opposite poles of these magnets attract. (b) Like poles of these magnets repel. (c) Every magnet has both a north and south pole; they cannot be separated.

pole is toward the north and its south pole is toward the south, as in Figure 19-1b.) By convention we choose the direction of the magnetic field $\vec{B}$ produced by a magnet to be such that $\vec{B}$ points away from the magnet's north pole and toward the magnet's south pole. This should remind you of an electric dipole (see Section 16-5) made up of a positive charge $+q$ and a negative charge $-q$, for which the electric field $\vec{E}$ points away from the positively charged end and toward the negatively charged end. Indeed, a magnet like that shown in Figure 19-2 is often called a **magnetic dipole**.

The magnetic forces between magnets can be either attractive or repulsive. If the north pole of one magnet is close to the south pole of a second magnet, the force attracts the two magnets toward each other (Figure 19-3a); if the north poles are close together or the south poles are close together, the force makes the two magnets repel each other (Figure 19-3b). This is very different from the behavior of electrically charged objects, but analogous to the way in which electric dipoles interact. However, there is an important distinction between electric and magnetic dipoles. You can take an electric dipole apart by separating its component positive and negative charges, but you *cannot* separate the north and south poles of a magnet. If you cut a magnet in half, each half has a north pole and a south pole (Figure 19-3c). The same is true no matter how many small pieces you cut a magnet into; a very small piece produces only a weak magnetic field, but is still a magnetic dipole with both a north pole and a south pole. (Physicists have speculated about the existence of *magnetic monopoles*, particles that have the properties of an isolated north or south magnetic pole. Many experiments have been performed to look for evidence of a magnetic monopole. None has been found.)

What is it about magnets that causes them to produce and respond to magnetic fields? And why is it impossible to separate their north and south poles? The answers to these questions were revealed by a set of crucial experiments in the nineteenth century. Figure 19-4a shows a version of one of these experiments. A coil of copper wire loops through a flat piece of clear plastic, and iron filings are spread over the plastic. Since copper is not magnetic, the filings lie wherever they were placed. But when the coil is connected to a source of emf that establishes a current through the coil, the filings line up just as they do around the magnet in Figure 19-2. This demonstrates that the moving charges that make up the current in the coil *produce* a magnetic field. The field points out of the coil at one end, which is the "north pole" of the coil, and points into the other end, which is the coil's "south pole."

We can verify that the coil produces a magnetic field by carrying out the experiment shown in Figure 19-4b, in which we've replaced one of the two magnets from Figure 19-3a with a coil. When the current in the coil is turned on, the coil and the magnet are attracted to each other. This can only happen if the current-carrying coil is indeed producing a magnetic field, and the magnet is responding to that field. If we flip the coil over as shown in Figure 19-4c, the coil and the magnet now repel each other.

(a) The magnetic field created by current in a coil.

(b) This coil and magnet attract.

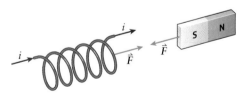

(c) This coil and magnet repel.

(d) These coils attract, just like two magnets.

Figure 19-4 A current-carrying coil acts like a magnet (a) The field of a current-carrying coil is very similar to that of a bar magnet (Figure 19-1a). (b), (c) Such a coil interacts with a bar magnet just as though it were a magnet itself. (d) Two current-carrying coils interact like two bar magnets.

This is just what would happen if the coil were an iron magnet that we flipped over to interchange the north and south poles (see Figures 19-3a and 19-3b).

In order for the coil in Figures 19-4b and 19-4c to be attracted to or repelled from the magnet, it must also be true that the moving charges that make up the current in the coil respond to the magnetic field of the magnet. In other words, a current-carrying coil and a magnet are fundamentally the same, in that both objects *produce* as well as *respond to* magnetic fields. Figure 19-4d shows an experiment that verifies this: Two current-carrying coils with the same orientation attract each other, just as do two magnets with the same orientation.

The series of experiments shown in Figure 19-4 suggests that *magnetism is an interaction between charges in motion.* In order for two objects to exert magnetic forces on each other, there must be moving charges in both objects. We use the umbrella term **electromagnetism** to include both electricity and magnetism, since both involve interactions between charges. The distinction between electricity and magnetism is that two charges exert *electric* forces on each other whether or not the charges are moving, while two charges exert *magnetic* forces on each other only if both charges are in motion. (The objects in the experiments shown in Figure 19-4 are all electrically neutral. So there are no electric forces in those experiments, only magnetic forces.)

You may be wondering how magnetism can involve charges in motion, since the ordinary magnets shown in Figures 19-1, 19-2, and 19-3 are not attached to sources of emf and so do not carry currents. The answer is that there *are* charges in motion inside an ordinary iron magnet: The moving charges are the electrons within the atoms of the magnet, and their motions within the atom are like that of electrons in the circular coils of Figure 19-4. Each individual atom in a magnet produces only a tiny magnetic field. But because a large fraction of the atoms that make up the magnet are oriented so that their electron motions are in the same direction as in the surrounding atoms, their magnetic fields add together to make a substantial total field. This explains why cutting a magnet into pieces doesn't leave you with a separate north pole and south pole: Each piece is simply a smaller version of the original magnet.

? Got the Concept? 19-1 Electric and Magnetic Forces

Two identical objects each have a positive charge Q. One of the objects is held in place, while the other object is in motion a short distance from the first object. What kinds of forces do the two objects exert on each other? (a) Both electric and magnetic forces; (b) electric forces but not magnetic forces; (c) magnetic forces but not electric forces; (d) neither electric forces nor magnetic forces; (e) answer depends on how the second object is moving.

Take-Home Message for Section 19-2

✔ Magnetism is an interaction between moving charged particles. A moving charged particle produces a magnetic field, and a moving charged particle in a magnetic field experiences a force. A stationary charged particle neither produces nor responds to a magnetic field.

✔ In a magnet, charges are in motion at the atomic level to produce a magnetic field.

19-3 A moving point charge can experience a magnetic force

We'll begin our study of magnetic forces by considering the force on a single charged particle moving in a magnetic field $\vec{B}$. For example, this could be an electron moving in a current-carrying wire in the vicinity of a magnet, or a moving proton in Earth's upper atmosphere that is acted on by our planet's magnetic field.

Here's what experiments tell us about the magnetic force on such a moving charged particle:

(1) A charged particle can experience a force when placed in a magnetic field, but *only when it is moving.*

(2) The magnetic force depends on the direction of the charged particle's velocity relative to the direction of the magnetic field. The charged particle does not experience a magnetic force when its velocity is parallel to or opposite to the magnetic field.

(3) The magnitude of the force is proportional to the charge on the particle, to the magnitude of the magnetic field, and to the speed of the particle.

(4) The direction of the force is perpendicular to both the direction of motion of the charged particle and the direction of the magnetic field.

(5) The direction of the force depends on the sign of the charge.

Figure 19-5a shows the magnetic force on a particle with positive charge q moving with velocity $\vec{v}$ in the presence of a magnetic field $\vec{B}$. If θ is the angle between the velocity of the charged particle and the magnetic field, the magnitude of the magnetic force $\vec{F}$ is

Magnitude of magnetic force on a moving charged particle (19-1)

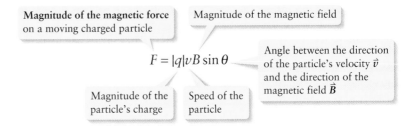

$$F = |q|vB \sin\theta$$

Magnitude of the magnetic force on a moving charged particle

Magnitude of the magnetic field

Angle between the direction of the particle's velocity $\vec{v}$ and the direction of the magnetic field $\vec{B}$

Magnitude of the particle's charge

Speed of the particle

The SI units of magnetic field are **tesla** (T). In Equation 19-1, if charge q is in coulombs (C), speed v is in meters per second (m/s), and magnetic field magnitude B is in tesla (T), the force F is in newtons (N). So 1 T is the same as $1\,\text{N}\cdot\text{s}/(\text{C}\cdot\text{m})$ or $1\,\text{N}/(\text{A}\cdot\text{m})$. (Recall that one ampere equals one coulomb per second: $1\,\text{A} = 1\,\text{C/s}$.) The strongest magnetic field most of us will experience directly is the roughly 2-T field inside a magnetic resonance imaging (MRI) scanner. Other magnetic fields in our environment are much weaker: The strength of Earth's magnetic field is about 5×10^{-5} T, the electrical impulses that drive the contraction and relaxation of your heart produce

(a) Magnetic force on a positive charge

Your right hand helps determine the direction of the magnetic force.

The force $\vec{F}$ is perpendicular to both the velocity $\vec{v}$ and the magnetic field $\vec{B}$.

(b) Magnetic force on a negative charge

If $q < 0$, the magnetic force is opposite to the direction given by your right hand.

Again, the force $\vec{F}$ is perpendicular to both the velocity $\vec{v}$ and the magnetic field $\vec{B}$.

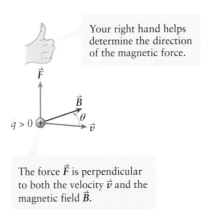

(c) Magnetic force on a positive charge, $\theta = 90°$

For a given speed v, the magnetic force is greatest if the velocity $\vec{v}$ is perpendicular to the magnetic field $\vec{B}$.

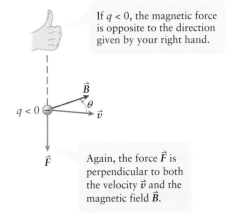

(d) Magnetic force on a positive charge, $\theta = 0$ or $180°$

$\theta = 0$

$\theta = 180°$

In these cases, the magnetic force is zero.

Figure 19-5 Magnetic force on a moving charged particle The direction of the magnetic force on a particle with charge q depends on whether (a) q is positive or (b) q is negative. The magnitude of the force $F = |q|vB \sin\theta$ goes from (c) a maximum value if $\theta = 90°$ to (d) zero if $\theta = 0$ or $\theta = 180°$.

magnetic fields of about 5×10^{-11} T, and the magnetic fields in your brain are on the order of 10^{-13} T. An alternative unit for magnetic field is the *gauss* (G): $1\ G = 10^{-4}$ T.

The direction of the force on the charge is given by a **right-hand rule** (Figure 19-5a). First extend the fingers of your right hand along the direction of the velocity $\vec{v}$, and orient your hand so that the palm is facing the magnetic field vector $\vec{B}$. With your right thumb extended as though you were giving the "thumbs-up" signal, swivel your hand as though you were slapping the magnetic field vector with your open palm. If the particle has a positive charge, so $q > 0$, your thumb points in the direction of the force $\vec{F}$. If the particle has a negative charge, so $q < 0$ (Figure 19-5b), the force $\vec{F}$ points in the direction opposite to that given by the right-hand rule. In either case, the force $\vec{F}$ is perpendicular to the velocity $\vec{v}$ *and* perpendicular to the magnetic field $\vec{B}$. If we draw the vectors $\vec{v}$ and $\vec{B}$ with their tails together, they form a plane; the force $\vec{F}$ is perpendicular to that plane, with a direction given by the right-hand rule. (We will encounter a number of other right-hand rules for magnetism in this chapter.)

Note that Equation 19-1 involves the magnitude or absolute value of the charge, $|q|$, which is always positive. So the magnitude F of the magnetic force does *not* depend on whether the charge is positive or negative.

 Watch Out! The magnetic force on a moving charged particle is never in the same direction as the magnetic field.

From Chapter 16, you're used to the idea that the electric force on a particle with charge q placed in an electric field $\vec{E}$ is $\vec{F}_{\text{electric}} = q\vec{E}$. This force is in the same direction as $\vec{E}$ if q is positive; if q is negative, it is in the direction opposite to $\vec{E}$.

Figures 19-5a and 19-5b show that the magnetic force on a moving charged particle is very different: This force is *perpendicular* to the direction of the magnetic field. Electric and magnetic forces are quite different from each other!

Equation 19-1 tells us that the magnitude of the magnetic force on a moving charged particle depends on the angle θ between the directions of $\vec{v}$ and $\vec{B}$. For a given particle speed v, the magnetic force has its greatest magnitude if the velocity $\vec{v}$ is perpendicular to the magnetic field $\vec{B}$; then $\theta = 90°$, $\sin \theta = 1$, and $F = |q|vB$ (Figure 19-5c). If $\theta = 0$ or $\theta = 180°$, so the particle is moving either in the same direction as $\vec{B}$ or in the direction opposite to $\vec{B}$, $\sin \theta = 0$ and the force on the particle is *zero*. Thus a charged particle moving in the direction of the magnetic field, or in the direction opposite to the magnetic field, experiences no magnetic force (Figure 19-5d).

We've shown the vectors $\vec{v}$, $\vec{B}$, and $\vec{F}$ in perspective in Figure 19-5. Drawing in perspective isn't easy to do, so we'll often use a simple convention for drawing vectors that are pointed either into or out of the pages of this book (Figure 19-6). Think of a vector as an arrow, with a sharp point at its head and feathers at its tail. If a vector is directed perpendicular to the plane of the page and pointed toward you—that is, *out of* the page—we'll depict it with the symbol $\odot$. The dot in the center of this symbol represents the sharp point of the arrowhead. If a vector is directed perpendicular to the plane of the page and pointed away from you—that is, *into* the page—we'll depict it with the symbol $\otimes$. The "X" in the center of this symbol represents the feathers on the tail of the arrow.

 Go to Interactive Exercise 19-1 and 19-2 for more practice dealing with magnetic forces

(a)

If $q > 0$, the force vector in this situation points out of the page (as indicated by the circle with a dot).

(b)

If $q < 0$, the force vector in this situation points into the page (as indicated by the circle with an X).

Figure 19-6 Vectors out of the page and into the page We use the symbols $\odot$ and $\otimes$ to denote vectors that point out of the page and into the page, respectively.

Example 19-1 Magnetic Forces on a Proton and an Electron

At a location near our planet's equator, the direction of Earth's magnetic field is horizontal (that is, parallel to the ground) and due north, and the magnitude of the field is 2.5×10^{-5} T. Find the direction and magnitude of the magnetic force on a particle moving at 1.0×10^4 m/s if the particle is (a) a proton moving horizontally and due east, (b) an electron moving horizontally and due east, and (c) a proton moving horizontally in a direction 25° east of north. Recall that a proton has charge $e = 1.60 \times 10^{-19}$ C and an electron has charge $-e$.

Set Up

In each case we'll use Equation 19-1 to find the magnitude of the force on the moving proton or electron. The right-hand rule (Figure 19-5) will tell us the direction of the magnetic force.

Magnetic force on a moving charged particle:

$$F = |q|vB \sin \theta \qquad (19\text{-}1)$$

Solve

(a) The velocity vector $\vec{v}$ of the proton is perpendicular to the magnetic field vector $\vec{B}$, so in Equation 19-1 the angle $\theta = 90°$ and $\sin \theta = 1$. The vectors $\vec{v}$ and $\vec{B}$ both lie in a horizontal plane; the magnetic force vector $\vec{F}$ must be perpendicular to this plane, so $\vec{F}$ is vertical. The right-hand rule tells us that the force points vertically upward.

Charge on the proton:

$$q = e = 1.60 \times 10^{-19} \text{ C}$$

The proton velocity vector is perpendicular to the magnetic field vector ($\theta = 90°$), so the magnitude of the magnetic force on the proton is

$$\begin{aligned} F &= |q|vB \sin \theta = evB \sin \theta \\ &= (1.60 \times 10^{-19} \text{ C})(1.0 \times 10^4 \text{ m/s})(2.5 \times 10^{-5} \text{ T})\sin 90° \\ &= 4.0 \times 10^{-20} \text{ N} \end{aligned}$$

(b) The electron has the same magnitude of charge as the proton and the same velocity, so it experiences the same magnitude of magnetic force. But its charge is negative, so the direction of the magnetic force $\vec{F}$ on the electron is *opposite* to the direction given by the right-hand rule. Hence the force $\vec{F}$ points vertically downward.

Charge on the electron:

$$q = -e = -1.60 \times 10^{-19} \text{ C}$$

The electron velocity vector is perpendicular to the magnetic field vector ($\theta = 90°$), so the magnitude of the magnetic force on the electron is

$$\begin{aligned} F &= |q|vB \sin \theta = evB \sin \theta \\ &= (1.60 \times 10^{-19} \text{ C})(1.0 \times 10^4 \text{ m/s})(2.5 \times 10^{-5} \text{ T})\sin 90° \\ &= 4.0 \times 10^{-20} \text{ N} \end{aligned}$$

(c) The proton velocity $\vec{v}$ and the magnetic field $\vec{B}$ again both lie in a horizontal plane, but now the angle between these vectors is $\theta = 25°$. So the magnitude of the magnetic force is less than in part (a). The direction of the force is the same as in part (a), however.

The proton velocity vector is at an angle $\theta = 25°$ to the magnetic field vector, so the magnitude of the magnetic force on the proton is

$$\begin{aligned} F &= |q|vB \sin \theta = evB \sin \theta \\ &= (1.60 \times 10^{-19} \text{ C})(1.0 \times 10^4 \text{ m/s}) \\ &\quad \times (2.5 \times 10^{-5} \text{ T}) \sin 25° \\ &= 1.7 \times 10^{-20} \text{ N} \end{aligned}$$

This is smaller than in part (a) because $\sin 25° = 0.42$ compared to $\sin 90° = 1$.

Reflect

This example illustrates how the magnetic force on a moving charged particle depends on the direction in which the particle is moving. Note that the force magnitudes in parts (a), (b), and (c) are very small because a single electron or proton carries very little charge. These particles also have very small mass, however (1.67×10^{-27} kg for the proton and 9.11×10^{-31} kg for the electron), so the resulting *accelerations* are tremendous. Can you use Newton's second law to show that the proton in part (a) and the electron in part (b) have accelerations of 2.4×10^7 m/s^2 and 4.4×10^{10} m/s^2 respectively?

? Got the Concept? 19-2   A Proton in a Magnetic Field

A proton is fired into a region of uniform magnetic field pointing into the page (Figure 19-7). The proton's initial velocity is shown by the blue vector, which lies in the plane of the page. In which direction does the proton's trajectory bend? (a) Toward the top of the figure; (b) toward the bottom of the figure; (c) out of the figure; (d) into the figure; (e) answer depends on the speed of the proton.

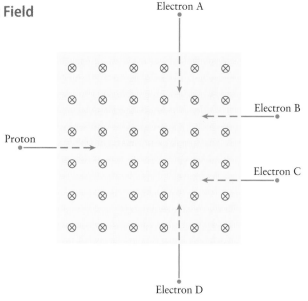

Figure 19-7 **Charged particles in a magnetic field** How will each particle be deflected when it enters this region of uniform magnetic field?

? Got the Concept? 19-3   Electrons in a Magnetic Field

Four electrons, A, B, C, and D, are fired into a region of uniform magnetic field pointing into the page (Figure 19-7). The initial velocities of the electrons are shown by the red vectors, which lie in the plane of the page. Each electron will follow a trajectory that is bent by the magnetic force. For which electron could that trajectory lead to the point on the left-hand side where the proton enters the field region? (There may be more than one correct answer.) (a) Electron A; (b) electron B; (c) electron C; (d) electron D; (e) none of the electrons.

Take-Home Message for Section 19-3

✔ A charged particle moving in a magnetic field can experience a magnetic force. The magnitude of this force depends on the angle θ between the particle's velocity $\vec{v}$ and the direction of the magnetic field $\vec{B}$. The force is maximum if $\theta = 90°$ ($\vec{v}$ and $\vec{B}$ are perpendicular) and zero if $\theta = 0$ or $180°$ ($\vec{v}$ and $\vec{B}$ are either in the same direction or opposite directions).

✔ The magnitude of the magnetic force on a charged particle is proportional to the amount of charge, to the speed of the charged particle, and to the magnitude of the field.

✔ The direction of the magnetic force is perpendicular to both the particle's velocity $\vec{v}$ and the direction of the magnetic field $\vec{B}$, and depends on the sign of the charge. A right-hand rule helps tell us the force direction.

✔ The SI unit of magnetic field is the tesla (T).

19-4 A mass spectrometer uses magnetic forces to differentiate atoms of different masses

An important application of the magnetic force on a moving charged particle is the **mass spectrometer,** a device used by chemists to determine the masses of individual atoms and molecules. Figure 19-8 shows a simplified version of one type of mass spectrometer. A sample to be analyzed is first vaporized and its atoms and molecules are ionized by removing one or more electrons, so all of the ions have a positive charge. A beam of the moving ions then passes through a *velocity selector*, a region where there is *both* an electric field $\vec{E}$ and a magnetic field $\vec{B}$. The fields $\vec{E}$ and $\vec{B}$ are oriented perpendicular to the ion beam as well as perpendicular to each other. You should be able to show in Figure 19-8 that in this region the electric force on a positive ion acts to the left while the magnetic force acts to the right. An ion will pass through this region without deflection only if these two forces cancel so that the *net* force on the ion is zero. For an ion of positive charge q, the electric force has magnitude $F_{electric} = qE$ and the magnetic force has magnitude $F_{magnetic} = qvB \sin 90° = qvB$ (the ion velocity and the magnetic field are perpendicular, so $\theta = 90°$ in Equation 19-1). So the condition for an ion to continue through this region without being deflected is

$$(19\text{-}2) \qquad qE = qvB \quad \text{or} \quad v = \frac{E}{B}$$

(speed of ions emerging from a velocity selector)

③ In this region ions follow a circular path under the influence of a magnetic field. For ions with the same charge, the trajectory depends on the ion mass.

$\odot \vec{B}$

Low-mass ion ⟋   ⟍ High-mass ion

$\vec{v}$

$\vec{E}$ $\vec{E}$

$\vec{v}$

$\vec{B} \odot$ $\odot \vec{B}$

$\vec{v}$

② Only ions with speed $v = E/B$ pass through the aperture: Slow ions are deflected to the left of the aperture, fast ions to the right.

① Positive ions move upward through the velocity selector.

Figure 19-8 **A mass spectrometer** Electric and magnetic forces are used in this device to separate different ions according to their mass.

If an ion has a speed different from $v = E/B$, it will be deflected out of the beam. This is why we call this arrangement of fields a velocity selector: After passing through the $\vec{E}$ and $\vec{B}$ fields, the only ions that remain in the beam are those with a speed given by Equation 19-2.

As Figure 19-8 shows, the ion beam then passes into a second region with a magnetic field as before but no electric field. The beam deflects to the right as a result of the magnetic force and continues to deflect. That's because as the direction of the velocity vector changes, the direction of the magnetic force also changes in order to remain perpendicular to the ion velocity $\vec{v}$. Because $\vec{v}$ and $\vec{B}$ remain perpendicular, the angle θ in Equation 19-1 remains equal to 90° as the ions deflect and the magnitude of the magnetic force remains the same, $F_{magnetic} = qvB \sin 90° = qvB$. You probably recognize that what's going on here is exactly the situation that we described in Section 5-6. Because an ion is acted on by a force of constant magnitude that points perpendicular to the ion's velocity, the ion moves at a constant speed in a circular path—that is, in uniform circular motion. We can use Newton's second law to find the radius r of the circular path followed by an ion of charge q and mass m that moves with speed v. The acceleration in uniform circular motion has magnitude $a = v^2/r$, and the net force on the ion has magnitude qvB, so

$$(19\text{-}3) \qquad qvB = \frac{mv^2}{r} \quad \text{or} \quad r = \frac{mv^2}{qvB} = \frac{mv}{qB}$$

(radius of circular path followed by charged particles in a uniform magnetic field)

Equation 19-3 is the key to understanding how the mass spectrometer works. All of the ions are moving at the same speed v (thanks to the velocity selector), and all are exposed to the same magnitude B of the magnetic field. But ions of different mass m (and the same charge q) will follow paths with different radii and so will land at different locations on the detector in Figure 19-8. By counting how many ions land at each location, we can learn about the composition of the sample being analyzed. Example 19-2 illustrates how this works.

Example 19-2 Measuring Isotopes with a Mass Spectrometer

Most oxygen atoms are the isotope ^{16}O ("oxygen-16"), which contains eight electrons, eight protons, and eight neutrons. The mass of this atom is 16.0 u, where 1 u = 1 atomic mass unit = 1.66×10^{-27} kg. The second most common isotope is ^{18}O ("oxygen-18"), which has two additional neutrons and so is more massive than an atom of ^{16}O: Each atom has a mass of 18.0 u. To determine the relative abundances of ^{16}O and ^{18}O, you send a beam of singly ionized oxygen atoms (^{16}O$^+$ and ^{18}O$^+$, each with a charge $+e = +1.60 \times 10^{-19}$ C) through a mass spectrometer like that shown in Figure 19-8. The magnetic field strength in both parts of the spectrometer is 0.0800 T, and the electric field strength in the velocity selector is 4.00×10^3 V/m. (a) What is the speed of the beam that emerges from the velocity selector? (b) How far apart are the points where the ^{16}O and ^{18}O ions land?

Set Up

We use Equation 19-2 to find the speed v of ions that pass undeflected through the velocity selector, and Equation 19-3 to find the radius of the circular path that each isotope follows. The distance from where each ion enters the region of uniform magnetic field to where it strikes the detector is the diameter (twice the radius) of the circular path.

Speed of ions emerging from a velocity selector:

$$v = \frac{E}{B} \qquad (19\text{-}2)$$

Radius of circular path followed by charged particles in a uniform magnetic field:

$$r = \frac{mv}{qB} \qquad (19\text{-}3)$$

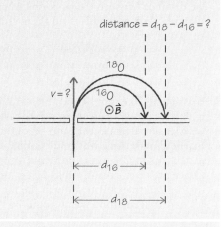

Solve

(a) Calculate the speed of ions that emerge from the velocity selector. Note that this speed does not depend on the charge or mass of the ion, so the $^{16}O^+$ and $^{18}O^+$ ions both emerge with this speed.

From Equation 19-2,

$$v = \frac{E}{B} = \frac{4.00 \times 10^3 \text{ V/m}}{0.0800 \text{ T}} = 5.00 \times 10^4 \frac{\text{V}}{\text{T} \cdot \text{m}}$$

From above, $1 \text{ T} = 1 \text{ N} \cdot \text{s}/(\text{C} \cdot \text{m})$, so $1 \text{ T} \cdot \text{m} = 1 \text{ N} \cdot \text{s}/\text{C}$. We also recall from Chapter 17 that $1 \text{ V} = 1 \text{ J/C} = 1 \text{ N} \cdot \text{m/C}$. So we can write the speed as

$$v = 5.00 \times 10^4 \frac{\text{V}}{\text{T} \cdot \text{m}} = 5.00 \times 10^4 \left(\frac{\text{N} \cdot \text{m}}{\text{C}} \right) \left(\frac{\text{C}}{\text{N} \cdot \text{s}} \right)$$
$$= 5.00 \times 10^4 \text{ m/s}$$

(b) Calculate the radius r and diameter d of the circular path followed by each isotope.

The masses of the two atoms are

For ^{16}O: $m_{16} = (16.0 \text{ u})(1.66 \times 10^{-27} \text{ kg/u}) = 2.66 \times 10^{-26} \text{ kg}$

For ^{18}O: $m_{18} = (18.0 \text{ u})(1.66 \times 10^{-27} \text{ kg/u}) = 2.99 \times 10^{-26} \text{ kg}$

The mass of each positive ion ($^{16}O^+$ and $^{18}O^+$) is slightly less than the mass of the neutral atom; the difference is the mass of one electron, which is $9.11 \times 10^{-31} \text{ kg} = 0.0000911 \times 10^{-26} \text{ kg}$. This difference is so small that we can ignore it.

For ^{16}O,

$$r_{16} = \frac{m_{16}v}{qB} = \frac{(2.66 \times 10^{-26} \text{ kg})(5.00 \times 10^4 \text{ m/s})}{(1.60 \times 10^{-19} \text{ C})(0.0800 \text{ T})}$$
$$= 0.104 \frac{\text{kg} \cdot \text{m}}{\text{T} \cdot \text{C} \cdot \text{s}}$$

Since $1 \text{ T} = 1 \text{ N} \cdot \text{s}/(\text{C} \cdot \text{m})$ and $1 \text{ N} = 1 \text{ kg} \cdot \text{m/s}^2$, it follows that $1 \text{ T} = \text{kg}/(\text{C} \cdot \text{s})$ and $1 \text{ T} \cdot \text{C} \cdot \text{s} = 1 \text{ kg}$. So for ^{16}O we have

$$r_{16} = 0.104 \frac{\text{kg} \cdot \text{m}}{\text{kg}} = 0.104 \text{ m}$$

$$d_{16} = 2r_{16} = 0.208 \text{ m} = 20.8 \text{ cm}$$

For ^{18}O,

$$r_{18} = \frac{m_{18}v}{qB} = \frac{(2.99 \times 10^{-26} \text{ kg})(5.00 \times 10^4 \text{ m/s})}{(1.60 \times 10^{-19} \text{ C})(0.0800 \text{ T})}$$
$$= 0.117 \text{ m}$$

$$d_{18} = 2r_{18} = 0.234 \text{ m} = 23.4 \text{ cm}$$

The distance between the positions where the ^{16}O and ^{18}O ions land is the difference between the two diameters.

The distance between where the ^{16}O and ^{18}O ions land is

$d_{18} - d_{16} = 23.4$ cm $- 20.8$ cm $= 2.6$ cm

This is a substantial distance, so the mass spectrometer does a good job of separating the two isotopes.

Reflect

Experiments like these show that, on average, 99.8% of the oxygen atoms are ^{16}O and 0.2% are ^{18}O. (Making up a small fraction of a percent is a third isotope, ^{17}O.)

Measurements of the ratio of ^{18}O to ^{16}O are important to the science of *paleoclimatology*, the study of Earth's ancient climate. One way to determine the average temperature of the planet in the distant past is to examine ancient ice deposits in Greenland and Antarctica. These deposits endure for hundreds of thousands of years; deposits near the surface are more recent, while deeper deposits are older. The ice comes from ocean water that evaporated closer to the equator and then fell as snow in the far north or far south. Each molecule of water is made up of two hydrogen atoms and one oxygen atom, which could be ^{16}O or ^{18}O. A water molecule can more easily evaporate if it contains lighter ^{16}O than if it contains heavier ^{18}O, so the water that evaporated and fell on Greenland and Antarctica as snow contains an even smaller percentage of ^{18}O than ocean water. This deficiency becomes even more pronounced for colder climates. It has been shown that a decrease of one part per million of ^{18}O in ice indicates a 1.5°C drop in sea-level air temperature at the time it originally evaporated from the oceans.

Using mass spectrometers to analyze ancient ice from Greenland and Antarctica, paleoclimatologists have been able to determine the variation in Earth's average temperature over the past 160,000 years. They have also analyzed the amount of atmospheric carbon dioxide (CO_2) that was trapped in the ice as it froze. An important result of these studies is that higher levels of atmospheric CO_2 have gone hand-in-hand with elevated temperatures for the last 160,000 years, which is just what we would expect from our discussion of global warming in Section 14-7. In the same way, the tremendous increase in CO_2 levels in the past century due to burning fossil fuels has gone hand-in-hand with recent dramatic increases in our planet's average temperature.

? Got the Concept? 19-4 Ions in a Mass Spectrometer

When passed through the mass spectrometer of Example 19-2, which of the following ions would follow nearly the same path as a ^{16}O$^+$ ion? Assume that all ions are moving at the speed given by Equation 19-2. (a) A doubly charged oxygen-16 ion (^{16}O^{2+}); (b) a singly charged sulfur-32 ion (^{32}S$^+$); (c) a doubly charged sulfur-32 ion (^{32}S^{2+}); (d) more than one of these; (e) none of these.

Take-Home Message for Section 19-4

✔ In a mass spectrometer, a magnetic field causes ions of the same speed and charge but different masses to follow different paths.

✔ In a velocity selector, the only charged objects that pass through undeflected are those traveling at the speed for which the electric and magnetic forces have equal magnitudes but opposite directions.

19-5 Magnetic fields exert forces on current-carrying wires

The magnetic force that we've described may seem to apply only in certain very special circumstances. But in fact you use magnetic forces whenever you listen to recorded music through earbuds (**Figure 19-9a**). Within each earbud is a small but powerful magnet adjacent to a flexible plastic cone with a coil of wire attached to it (**Figure 19-9b**). This coil is connected through the earbud wires to your MP3 player, which sends the musical signal to the coil in the form of a varying electric current. Charges within the coil are thus set into motion, and these moving charges experience magnetic forces exerted by the magnet. These forces pull on the coil that contains the charges and on the plastic cone to which the coil is attached. We learned in Section 19-3 that the direction of magnetic force depends on the direction in which charges move. So the force on the charges,

(a)

(b)

Front cover

Transparent plastic cone

Coil (attached to plastic cone)   Magnet (plastic cone is attached to this at its edges)

Figure 19-9 **Earbud physics** (a) Earbuds and other speakers use magnetic forces to produce sound. (b) Internal construction of an earbud.

coil, and plastic cone reverses whenever the current in the coil changes direction. The result is that the plastic cone oscillates back and forth in response to the signal coming from your MP3 player. This oscillation pushes on the surrounding air, producing a sound wave—the sound of music—that travels to your eardrum.

Let's see how to find the magnitude of the magnetic force on a current-carrying wire, such as a segment of the coil in Figure 19-9b. Figure 19-10 shows a straight wire of length ℓ that carries a current i. A magnetic field $\vec{B}$ points at an angle θ to the direction of the current, and has the same value along the entire length of the wire. We learned in Section 18-2 that the current in the wire is related to the speed at which individual charges drift through the wire:

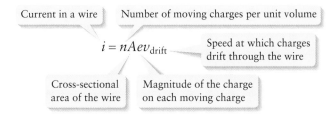

Current in a wire   Number of moving charges per unit volume

$$i = nAev_{\text{drift}}$$

Speed at which charges drift through the wire

Cross-sectional area of the wire   Magnitude of the charge on each moving charge

From Equation 19-1, the magnetic force on an individual charge e moving through the wire at speed v_{drift} has magnitude $ev_{\text{drift}}B \sin \theta$. Each such moving charge feels a force of the same magnitude and in the same direction. The total number of such moving charges in the wire shown in Figure 19-10 is n (the number of moving charges per unit volume) multiplied by the volume V of the wire, where $V = A\ell$ (the cross-sectional area of the wire multiplied by its length). So the magnitude of the *net* magnetic force on all of the moving charges in the wire is

$$F = (nA\ell)(ev_{\text{drift}}B \sin \theta)$$

If we rearrange the terms in this equation, we get

$$F = (nAev_{\text{drift}})\ell B \sin \theta \tag{19-4}$$

The quantity in parentheses in Equation 19-4 is just the current i as given by Equation 18-3. So the magnitude of the magnetic force on a current-carrying wire is

Magnitude of the magnetic force on a current-carrying wire   Magnitude of the magnetic field (assumed uniform over the length of the wire)

$$F = i\ell B \sin \theta$$

Angle between the direction of the current and the direction of the magnetic field $\vec{B}$

Current in the wire   Length of the wire

The force $\vec{F}$ on a current-carrying wire in a magnetic field $\vec{B}$ is perpendicular to both $\vec{B}$ and the length of the wire. The direction is given by a right-hand rule.

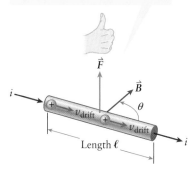

Figure 19-10 **Magnetic force on a current-carrying wire** The force that a magnetic field exerts on this wire is the sum of the forces on all the moving charges within the wire.

Current and drift speed (18-3)

Magnitude of magnetic force on a current-carrying wire (19-5)

Just as for the magnetic force on a moving charged particle, a right-hand rule tells you the direction of the magnetic force on a current-carrying wire. Extend the fingers of your right hand in the direction of the current, and orient your hand so that the palm is facing the magnetic field vector $\vec{B}$. With your right thumb extended, swivel your hand as though you were slapping the magnetic field vector with your open palm. Your outstretched thumb points in the direction of the magnetic field exerted on the wire (Figure 19-10).

Equation 19-5 says that there is *no* magnetic force on the wire if the axis of the wire lies along the direction of the magnetic field $\vec{B}$: that is, if $\vec{B}$ points either in the same direction as the current ($\theta = 0$) or in the direction opposite to the current ($\theta = 180°$). In either case, $\sin \theta = 0$ and $F = 0$. For a given magnetic field of magnitude B, the force is greatest if $\vec{B}$ points perpendicular to the current so $\theta = 90°$ and $\sin \theta = \sin 90° = 1$. This idea is used in the design of the earbuds shown in Figure 19-9. The wires in each earbud are curved into a circular coil, not straight as in Figure 19-10. But we can treat the coil as being made up of many short segments, each of which is effectively a straight piece of wire. As **Figure 19-11a** shows, the magnetic field from the magnet in each earbud is perpendicular to each such segment. The forces on different segments are in different directions, but the vector sum of these forces is toward the magnet. If the current is in the reverse direction as in **Figure 19-11b**, all of the individual forces also reverse direction and the vector sum of the forces is away from the magnet. The current from the MP3 player continually reverses direction, so the coil and attached diaphragm oscillate back and forth, producing a sound wave.

In the following section we'll see how to use Equation 19-5 to help us understand how electric motors work. For now, let's see how to use a magnetic field to levitate a current-carrying wire.

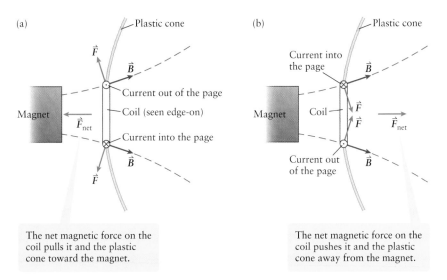

The net magnetic force on the coil pulls it and the plastic cone toward the magnet.

The net magnetic force on the coil pushes it and the plastic cone away from the magnet.

Figure 19-11 Magnetic forces in an earbud (a) The magnetic field produced by an earbud magnet is not uniform, so the field exerts a net force on the coil and the plastic cone to which it is attached. (b) Reversing the direction of the current reverses the direction of the net force.

Example 19-3 Magnetic Levitation

You set up a uniform horizontal magnetic field that points from south to north and has magnitude 2.00×10^{-2} T. (This is about 400 times stronger than Earth's magnetic field, but easily achievable with common magnets.) You want to place a straight copper wire of diameter 0.812 mm in this field, then run enough current through the wire so that the magnetic force will make the wire "float" in midair. This is called *magnetic levitation*. What minimum current is required to make this happen? The density of copper is 8.96×10^{3} kg/m^{3}.

Set Up

In order to make the wire "float," there must be an upward magnetic force on the wire that just balances the downward gravitational force. We know from Equation 19-5 that to maximize the magnetic force, the current direction should be perpendicular to the magnetic field $\vec{B}$. The right-hand rule then shows that the current should flow from west to east so that the magnetic force is directed upward. We're not given the mass of the wire, but we can express the mass (and hence the gravitational force on the wire) in terms of its density. We're also not given the length of the wire; as we'll see, this will cancel out of the calculation.

Magnetic force on a current-carrying wire:

$$F = i\ell B \sin \theta \qquad (19\text{-}5)$$

Definition of density:

$$\rho = \frac{m}{V} \qquad (11\text{-}1)$$

Volume of a cylindrical wire of cross-sectional area A and length ℓ:

$$V = A\ell$$

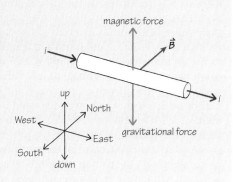

Solve

Write expressions for the two forces (magnetic and gravitational) that act on the wire.

Assume the wire has length ℓ. Since the current flows in a direction perpendicular to the magnetic field, the angle θ in Equation 19-5 is 90°. So the magnitude of the upward magnetic force is

$$F = i\ell B \sin 90° = i\ell B$$

The magnitude of the downward gravitational force on the wire of mass m is

$$w = mg$$

From Equation 11-1, the mass equals the density of copper multiplied by the volume of the wire:

$$m = \rho V = \rho A\ell$$

The cross-sectional area A of the wire is that of a circle of radius r:

$$A = \pi r^2 \quad \text{so} \quad m = \rho A\ell = \rho(\pi r^2)\ell$$

So the magnitude of the gravitational force is

$$w = mg = \rho(\pi r^2)\ell g$$

If the wire is floating in equilibrium, the upward magnetic force must just balance the downward gravitational force. Use this to solve for the required current i.

In equilibrium the net vertical force on the wire is zero:

$$F - w = 0, \text{ so } F = w \text{ and } i\ell B = \rho(\pi r^2)\ell g$$

The length ℓ of the wire cancels out of this equation (both the magnetic force and the gravitational force are proportional to ℓ):

$$iB = \rho(\pi r^2)g$$

Solve for the current i:

$$i = \frac{\rho(\pi r^2)g}{B}$$

$$= \frac{(8.96 \times 10^3 \text{ kg/m}^3)(\pi)(0.406 \times 10^{-3} \text{ m})^2(9.80 \text{ m/s}^2)}{2.00 \times 10^{-2} \text{ T}}$$

$$= 2.27 \frac{\text{kg}}{\text{T} \cdot \text{s}^2} = 2.27 \text{ A}$$

[Check on units: We know from Section 19-3 that $1 \text{ T} = 1 \text{ N}/(\text{A} \cdot \text{m})$, and we also know that $1 \text{ N} = 1 \text{ kg} \cdot \text{m/s}^2$. Therefore $1 \text{ T} = 1 \text{ kg}/(\text{A} \cdot \text{s}^2)$, and so $1 \text{ kg}/(\text{T} \cdot \text{s}^2) = 1 \text{ A}$.]

Reflect

A current of 2.27 A is relatively small, so this experiment in magnetic levitation is not too difficult to perform. Note that the required current i is inversely proportional to the magnitude B of the magnetic field. You can see that if you tried to make a wire "float" using Earth's magnetic field, which is about 1/400 as strong as the field used here, you would need to use an immense current of $400 \times 2.27\ \text{A} = 909\ \text{A}$. That's not practical because a current of that magnitude would cause the wire in this example to melt! (Recall from Equation 18-24 in Section 18-6 that the power into a resistor with resistance R that carries current i is $P = i^2R$. The wire in this example has a small cross-sectional area, so its resistance R will be fairly large. The power delivered to the wire by a 909-A current will quickly increase its temperature to above the melting point of copper, 1085°C.) So you needn't worry about any of your electrical devices floating in midair when you turn on the current.

A practical application of magnetic levitation is train design. By using magnetic forces to make a train float just above the track, the rolling friction between the wheels and the track can be completely eliminated and very high speeds achieved. (Magnetic forces are also used to propel the train forward.) A train of this type in commercial operation in Shanghai, China reaches a top speed of 431 km/h (268 mi/h). Such train lines require special magnets and wires capable of sustaining very high currents.

? Got the Concept? 19-5 Direction of Magnetic Force on a Wire

A long, straight wire carrying a current can be placed in various orientations with respect to a constant magnetic field as shown in Figure 19-12a, b, c, d, e, and f. What is the direction of the force in each case? Give your answers in terms of the positive and negative x, y, and z directions. If the force is zero, say so. (In each case the positive z direction is out of the plane of the figures.)

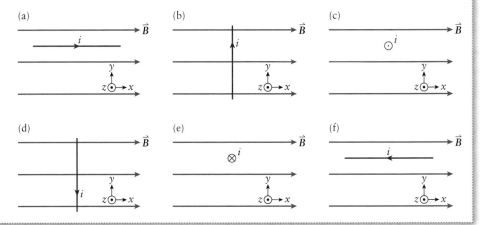

Figure 19-12 **Which way is the force?** What is the direction of the magnetic force on the wire in each case?

Take-Home Message for Section 19-5

✔ The current-carrying wire in a magnetic field experiences a magnetic force that is perpendicular to both the current direction and the magnetic field direction.

✔ The magnitude of this magnetic force is maximum if the current and magnetic field directions are perpendicular, and zero if the wire axis is along the magnetic field.

19-6 A magnetic field can exert a torque on a current loop

A common everyday application of magnetic forces on current-carrying wires is an electric motor. An electric motor is at the heart of a kitchen blender, a vacuum cleaner, the starter for an internal-combustion automobile, and many other devices (Figure 19-13a). Inside any electric motor you'll find a rotating portion (called the *rotor*) that's wrapped with coils of wire (Figure 19-13b), as well as magnets in the stationary part of the motor. When you turn the motor on, causing a current through the coils, the magnets exert forces on the current-carrying wire of the coils. The net effect is that there is a magnetic *torque* that makes the rotor spin. Let's look at a simplified version of this process to see how such a magnetic torque arises.

Figure 19-14a shows a straight wire bent into a single rectangular loop of wire with sides of length L and W. The loop carries a current i provided by a source of emf (not shown), so we call it a **current loop**. This loop is immersed in a uniform magnetic field of magnitude B and is free to rotate around an axis (shown in green). You should apply the right-hand rule for magnetic forces on a current-carrying wire (see Section 19-5) to each side of this loop. You'll see that the left-hand side of the loop experiences a force to the left, the right-hand side feels a force to the right, the top of the loop feels an upward force, and the bottom of the loop feels a downward force, as Figure 19-14a shows. Each segment of the loop carries the same current and is in the same magnetic field. Since the left- and right-hand sides are the same length and at the same angle to the magnetic field, the forces on these two sides have the same magnitude but opposite directions. Thus these forces cancel, and there is zero net force to the left or the right. The forces on the top and bottom segments of the wire also cancel for the same reason. So the net *force* on this rectangular loop is zero. (You can convince yourself that the same would be true if we reversed the direction of the current around the loop or the direction of the magnetic field, or changed the angle between the direction of the field and the plane of the loop.) This result is not just true for rectangular loops like the one shown in Figure 19-14a. It turns out that there is zero net magnetic force on *any* closed current-carrying loop in a uniform magnetic field, no matter what the shape of the loop.

Although the net magnetic force on the current loop in Figure 19-14a is zero, the net magnetic *torque* around the axis is not. Figure 19-14b is a side view of the current

(a)

(b)

Figure 19-13 **Electric motors and magnetic torque** (a) This fan uses an electric motor to rotate the fan blades. (b) The key components of any electric motor are current-carrying coils and a source of magnetic field. The magnetic field exerts forces on the current-carrying wires of the coils, and these produce a torque that makes the rotating part of the motor spin.

> **Watch Out!**
>
> A current-carrying coil can feel a net magnetic force if the $\vec{B}$ field is not uniform.
>
> In Figure 19-14a we assumed that the magnetic field is uniform (its magnitude and direction are the same at all points), and found that the net magnetic force on the current loop is zero. But if the magnetic field magnitude were greater at the left-hand side of the loop than at the right-hand side, then the left-hand side would experience a greater magnetic force. This would result in a net force on the loop to the left. In this chapter we'll restrict our discussion to the simple case in which the field is uniform.

(a) Perspective view

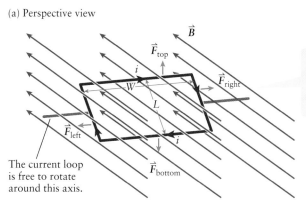

There is zero net magnetic force on a current loop in a uniform magnetic field:

$$\vec{F}_{top} + \vec{F}_{bottom} + \vec{F}_{left} + \vec{F}_{right} = 0$$

The current loop is free to rotate around this axis.

(b) Side view

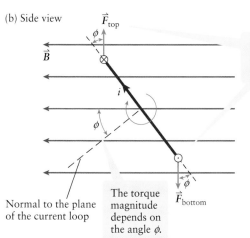

There can be a nonzero net magnetic torque on a current loop in a uniform magnetic field.

Normal to the plane of the current loop

The torque magnitude depends on the angle ϕ.

Figure 19-14 **A current loop in a uniform magnetic field** (a) The magnetic forces on the sides of the current loop. (b) These forces can give rise to a net magnetic torque.

loop; the axis shown in green in Figure 19-14a is perpendicular to the plane of this figure and passes through the center of the loop. The forces on the near and far sides of the loop, which point out of and into the page, respectively, are directed parallel to this axis and so produce no torque. However, the forces that act on the top and bottom sides of the loop both give rise to a torque. For the situation shown in Figure 19-14b, both of these forces tend to make the loop rotate clockwise around the axis, so the net torque is clockwise.

Let's calculate the magnitude of the magnetic torque on the loop in Figure 19-14b. First note that the magnetic field is perpendicular to the current in both the top side of the loop and the bottom side of the loop. So in Equation 19-5 for the magnetic force on a current-carrying wire the angle θ equals $90°$. Both the top and bottom sides of the loop have length W (see Figure 19-14a), so the magnitude of the magnetic force on each of these sides is

$$(19\text{-}6) \qquad\qquad F = iWB \sin 90° = iWB$$

√x̄ *See the Math Tutorial for more information on trigonometry*

To find the torque around the axis that each of these forces produces, we use Equation 8-18:

Magnitude of torque
(8-18)

Magnitude of the **torque** produced by a force acting on an object

Magnitude of the force

$$\tau = rF \sin \phi$$

Distance from the rotation axis of the object to where the force is applied

Angle between the vector $\vec{r}$ (from the rotation axis to where the force is applied) and the force vector $\vec{F}$

In Figure 19-14b the distance r is one-half of the length L of the near or far side of the loop, and ϕ is the angle between the direction of the near or far side of the current loop and the force exerted on either the top or bottom of the loop. This angle phi is also equal to the angle between the direction of the magnetic field and an imaginary line that's perpendicular to the plane of the current loop. We call this imaginary line the **normal** to the plane of the loop. From Equations 8-18 and 19-6, the magnitude of the torque due to the force on either the top or bottom side of the loop is

$$(19\text{-}7) \qquad\qquad \tau_{\text{one side}} = \left(\frac{L}{2}\right)F \sin \phi = \left(\frac{L}{2}\right)(iWB) \sin \phi = \frac{1}{2}i(LW)B \sin \phi$$

The product LW (length times width) in Equation 19-7 is just the area of the current loop: $A = LW$. As we mentioned above, the torque from the top of the loop and the torque from the bottom of the loop both act in the same direction, so the *net* torque on the loop is just double the torque on one side given by Equation 19-7. Using $A = LW$, we have

$$\tau = 2\tau_{\text{one side}} = 2\left(\frac{1}{2}\right)i(LW)B \sin \phi = 2\left(\frac{1}{2}\right)iAB \sin \phi$$

or

Magnitude of magnetic torque
on a current loop
(19-8)

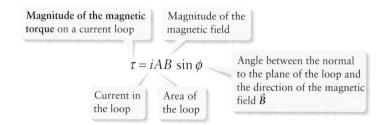

Magnitude of the **magnetic torque** on a current loop

Magnitude of the magnetic field

$$\tau = iAB \sin \phi$$

Angle between the normal to the plane of the loop and the direction of the magnetic field $\vec{B}$

Current in the loop

Area of the loop

Although we've assumed a rectangular loop, Equation 19-8 applies to a current loop of area A of *any* shape.

Typically, the rotating coil in an electric motor is not just a single loop of wire, but has many *turns* (equivalent to many single coils stacked on top of each other). If a coil has N turns, the magnetic torque on it is N times greater than the value given by Equation 19-8.

Example 19-4 Angular Acceleration of a Current Loop

A length of copper wire is formed into a square loop with 50 turns. The loop is free to turn about a frictionless axis that lies in the plane of the loop and passes through its center. Each side of the loop is 2.00 cm long, and the moment of inertia of the loop about the axis of rotation is 4.00×10^{-6} kg·m². The loop lies in a region where there is a uniform magnetic field of magnitude 1.50×10^{-2} T that is perpendicular to the rotation axis of the loop. The current in the loop is 0.500 A. Find the angular acceleration of the loop (magnitude and direction) (a) when the loop is released from rest from the orientation shown in Figure 19-15, (b) after the loop has rotated 90°, and (c) after the loop has rotated 180°.

Figure 19-15 **A square current loop in a magnetic field** When this square current loop is released from rest, how will it begin to rotate?

Set Up

For each orientation we'll use Equation 19-8 to find the magnitude of the magnetic torque on the loop. There is no other torque on the loop (there is no friction, and gravity exerts zero torque since the center of mass of the loop lies on the rotation axis). So the magnetic torque is also the net torque, and we can use Equation 8-20 to find the magnitude of the angular acceleration. We'll find the direction of the angular acceleration by looking at the directions of the magnetic forces on the individual sides of the loop. Figure 19-15 shows that forces on the sides parallel to the rotation axis tend to affect rotation. The forces on the other sides cause no torque (compare Figure 19-14a).

Magnitude of magnetic torque on a current loop:

$$\tau = iAB \sin \phi \qquad (19\text{-}8)$$

Newton's second law for rotational motion:

$$\sum \tau_z = I\alpha_z \qquad (8\text{-}20)$$

Solve

(a) First find the direction of the magnetic torque, and hence the direction of the angular acceleration.

The right-hand rule for the magnetic force on a current-carrying wire shows that the forces on the wire tend to cause a clockwise rotation. So the angular acceleration is clockwise, and when the loop is released it will begin to rotate in the clockwise direction.

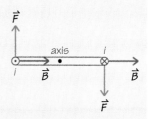

Find the magnitude of the angular acceleration.

The normal to the loop is perpendicular to the magnetic field, so in Equation 19-8 $\sin \phi = \sin 90° = 1$. The loop is square, so the cross-sectional area of the loop is just the square of the length of one side (2.00 cm = 0.0200 m). Since there are 50 turns, the total torque is $N = 50$ times greater than that given by Equation 19-8:

$$\tau = NiAB \sin \phi$$
$$= (50)(0.500 \text{ A})(0.0200 \text{ m})^2 (1.50 \times 10^{-2} \text{ T})(1)$$
$$= 1.50 \times 10^{-4} \text{ T·A·m}^2 = 1.50 \times 10^{-4} \text{ N·m}$$

(Recall that 1 T = 1 N/(A·m), so 1 T·A·m² = 1 N·m.)

This is the net torque on the loop, so from Equation 8-20 the magnitude of the loop's angular acceleration is

$$\alpha = \frac{\tau}{I} = \frac{1.50 \times 10^{-4}\,\text{N} \cdot \text{m}}{4.00 \times 10^{-6}\,\text{kg} \cdot \text{m}^2}$$

$$= 37.5\,\text{rad/s}^2$$

(If the torque is in $\text{N} \cdot \text{m}$ and the moment of inertia is in $\text{kg} \cdot \text{m}^2$, the angular acceleration in Equation 8-20 is in rad/s^2.)

When released, the loop will begin to rotate in the clockwise direction as shown above. Note that as the loop rotates, the angle ϕ and the value of $\sin \phi$ will decrease, so the torque and angular acceleration will decrease: This is *not* a situation with constant angular acceleration.

(b) Find the angular acceleration when the loop has rotated 90° from its initial orientation.

When the loop has rotated 90°, the normal to the loop is in the same direction as the magnetic field so $\phi = 0$ and $\sin \phi = 0$. From Equation 19-8 it follows that there is zero torque on the loop at this point in its rotation. We can also see this using the right-hand rule for the magnetic forces on the wires of the loop: These forces do not exert any torque around the axis. Therefore this orientation represents an equilibrium position for the loop, and the angular acceleration is zero. Note that the loop will be in motion as it passes through this position (there has been an angular acceleration ever since the loop was released). As a result, the loop doesn't stop at this position but keeps on rotating.

(c) Find the angular acceleration when the loop has rotated by 180° from its initial orientation.

At the 180° position, the normal to the loop is again perpendicular to the direction of the magnetic field, just as in part (a). So again the angle $\phi = 90°$, and again the magnitude of the angular acceleration is $\alpha = 37.5\,\text{rad/s}^2$. However, since the loop has been flipped over relative to its original orientation, the directions of the forces are reversed. So the torque and angular acceleration are now *counterclockwise*. In fact, the angular acceleration has been increasingly counterclockwise ever since the loop moved past the position in (b). Since passing that position, the loop has been rotating in a clockwise direction but has been slowing down due to the counterclockwise angular acceleration.

Reflect

The motion of the loop in this example should remind you of the motion of a pendulum (Section 12-5). When displaced from equilibrium and released, the pendulum will swing toward its equilibrium orientation (hanging straight down), but overshoot that equilibrium and swing to the other side of equilibrium. If there is no friction, the pendulum will keep swinging back and forth indefinitely. The same is true for this current loop: If the axis on which it rotates is frictionless, it will oscillate back and forth between the orientation in part (a) and the orientation in part (c).

In an electric motor we want the coil to continue rotating in the same direction, not oscillate back and forth like the coil in Example 19-4. To make this happen, the connection between the coil and the source of emf is arranged so that when the coil is at its equilibrium position (as in part (b) of Example 19-4), the direction of the current *reverses*. As a result, when the coil moves past this equilibrium position, the torque is now in the same direction as the rotation and the rotation continues to speed up. The current reverses again after another half-rotation, so the torque is always in the same direction.

With this arrangement, the coil would continue to gain rotational speed without limit if there were no other torques acting on it. In practice there are other torques that oppose the rotation, and the rotational speed reaches an upper limit. That's the case for the electric fan in Figure 19-13a: Air resistance on the fan blades increases as the fan turns faster, and the fan speed stabilizes when the torque due to air resistance just balances the torque of the electric motor.

? Got the Concept? 19-6 Magnetic Torque

Suppose the number of turns in the current loop of Example 19-4 were increased from 50 to 100. Would this make the maximum angular acceleration of the loop (a) Four times greater, (b) twice as great, (c) 1/2 as great, (d) 1/4 as great, or (e) none of these?

Take-Home Message for Section 19-6

✔ There is zero net force on a current loop in a uniform magnetic field.

✔ A uniform magnetic field can exert a torque on a current loop. The torque is maximum if the normal to the plane of the loop is perpendicular to the magnetic field direction.

19-7 Ampère's law describes the magnetic field created by current-carrying wires

So far in our discussion of magnetism we've looked at the forces and torques that a magnetic field exerts on a current-carrying wire. But current-carrying wires also *produce* magnetic fields (see Figure 19-1c, and Figure 19-4). As we described in Section 19-2, all magnetic fields are produced by electric charges in motion, whether it's a current in the coils of the electromagnet shown in Figure 19-1c, electrons in motion within the atoms of an iron bar magnet, or electric currents in the human brain as shown in Figure 19-16. To complete our understanding of magnetic forces, we need to be able to calculate the magnetic field produced by an arrangement of charges in motion. This is much like Chapter 16, where we needed to learn how to calculate the electric field due to an arrangement of charges in order to complete our understanding of electric forces.

We saw in Section 16-5 that the electric field that is due to a charge distribution is just the vector sum of the electric fields due to all of the charges in the distribution. These calculations can be rather challenging unless the charge distribution is very simple. When we look at the analogous problem of finding the *magnetic* field due to a distribution of moving charges, we find that the problem is even more complicated. That's because the magnetic field due to even a single moving charged particle is itself rather complex: The field does not point directly away from or toward the moving charge, but in a direction determined in part by the velocity (and perpendicular to the velocity vector). Rather than looking at how to do calculations of this kind, we'll just look at the result for one important situation, the magnetic field due to a long, straight, current-carrying wire. We'll then see an alternative approach for calculating a magnetic field using *Ampère's law*. This law is a very powerful one, but like Gauss's law for electric fields (Sections 16-6 and 16-7) it can be used for field calculations only in certain simple situations. We'll conclude the section with a look at the magnetic field produced by a current loop, as well as some of the applications of this field.

Electric currents in the human brain generate weak magnetic fields. The colors in this magnetoencephalogram represent the strength of the magnetic field produced in different regions.

Figure 19-16 **Currents as sources as magnetic field** Electric currents in biological systems produce magnetic fields.

A Long, Straight Wire and Ampère's Law

Consider a very long, straight wire that carries a constant current i. Experiment and calculation both show that the magnetic field due to this current has the properties shown in Figure 19-17. Note that the wire and the magnetic field that it produces have *cylindrical symmetry*: The wire and the field pattern look exactly the same if you rotate the wire around its length. The magnitude of the field is given by

Magnitude of magnetic field due to a long, straight wire (19-9)

> Magnitude of the magnetic field due to a long, straight wire
>
> Permeability of free space
>
> $$B = \frac{\mu_0 i}{2\pi r}$$
>
> Current in the wire
>
> Distance from the wire to the location where the field is measured

Equation 19-9 and the field properties shown in Figure 19-17 are strictly correct only if the wire is infinitely long. But they are very good approximations if the distance r is small compared to the length of the wire.

The constant μ_0 in Equation 19-9, called the **permeability of free space** for historic reasons, plays a role in magnetism that's comparable to the role of the constant ε_0, the *permittivity* of free space, in electricity (see Section 16-6). Its value is *exactly* $\mu_0 = 4\pi \times 10^{-7}\,\text{T}\cdot\text{m/A}$. The value is known exactly because of the way that the tesla is defined: At a distance of 1 m from a long, straight wire carrying a current of 1 A, the magnetic field strength is exactly

$$B = \frac{\mu_0 i}{2\pi r} = \frac{(4\pi \times 10^{-7}\,\text{T}\cdot\text{m/A})(1\,\text{A})}{2\pi(1\,\text{m})} = 2 \times 10^{-7}\,\text{T}$$

① The magnetic field lines due to a long, straight, current-carrying wire are circles that lie in planes perpendicular to the axis of the wire.

② The magnetic field vectors are tangential to the circular magnetic field lines, and perpendicular to the axis of the wire.

③ The magnitude of the field is proportional to the current i and inversely proportional to the distance r from the axis of the wire.

④ Right-hand rule for the field direction: If you point your right thumb in the direction of the current and curl your fingers, the magnetic field curls around the field lines in the direction of the curled fingers of your right hand.

Figure 19-17 Magnetic field of a long, straight, current-carrying wire The magnitude of this field is given by Equation 19-9.

! Watch Out! Remember that vectors are straight, never curved.

When drawing the magnetic field around a long, straight wire, it may be tempting to draw curved arrows to represent how the magnetic field lines curl around the wire. But a vector always denotes a *single* direction and so *cannot* be curved.

At any point along a magnetic field line, the direction of the field is always along the *tangent* to the field line as shown in Figure 19-17.

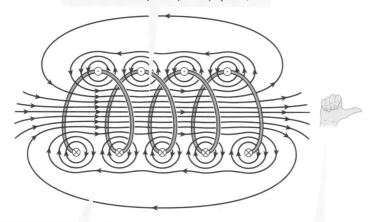

① The magnetic field in the interior of a long, straight solenoid is essentially uniform (the field lines are very nearly evenly spaced).

② The magnetic field outside the solenoid is very weak (the field lines are far apart).

③ Right-hand rule for the field direction: If you curl the fingers of your right hand around the solenoid in the direction of the current, the magnetic field inside the solenoid points in the direction of your right thumb.

Figure 19-18 **Magnetic field of a solenoid** Compare this illustration to the photograph of a solenoid and its field in Figure 19-4a.

The magnetic field around current-carrying wires with other geometries is much more complicated. As an example, Figure 19-18 shows some of the magnetic field lines for a straight helical coil of wire. Such a coil is called a **solenoid**. Close to an individual wire, the field lines resemble those around the long, straight wire shown in Figure 19-17. In the space outside the solenoid the magnetic field is very weak, as you can see from the large spacing between adjacent field lines. (Recall from Section 16-5 that the same is true for electric fields: Where field lines are far apart, the field magnitude is small.) But in the interior of the solenoid the magnetic field lines are close together and nearly evenly spaced, indicating that the magnetic field there is strong and nearly uniform.

This property of solenoids explains why a conventional magnetic resonance imaging (MRI) scanner is in the form of a long tube inside which the patient lies (Figure 19-19). This tube is actually the interior of a solenoid like that shown in Figure 19-18, so the patient is bathed in a strong, uniform magnetic field—which is just what MRI requires. (In Chapter 27 we'll learn more about the physics of MRI.)

Can we use Equation 19-9 to calculate the field inside a solenoid? Not directly, no, because the wires that make up the solenoid are not straight. But we can use Equation 19-9 to illustrate a useful principle about magnetic fields and their sources, and then use that principle to determine the solenoid field. Imagine that we draw a circle of radius r around a long, straight wire as shown in Figure 19-20. Imagine further that we break the circle into a number of segments of length $\Delta \ell$. If $\Delta \ell$ is sufficiently small, we can treat each segment as being straight. Then for each segment, take the component $B_\parallel$ of magnetic field parallel to that segment and multiply it by the segment length $\Delta \ell$. If we add up the values of these products for every segment in the circle, the result is a quantity called the **circulation** of the magnetic field around the circle:

$$\text{Circulation} = \sum B_\parallel \Delta \ell \qquad (19\text{-}10)$$

For the circle shown in Figure 19-20, Equation 19-9 tells us that $B_\parallel$ is equal to $\mu_0 i/(2\pi r)$ at every point around the circle. That's because the magnetic field is everywhere tangent to the circle and so parallel to a short segment of length on the circle. Therefore the circulation of the magnetic field as defined by Equation 19-10 is

$$\text{Circulation} = \sum \left(\frac{\mu_0 i}{2\pi r} \right) \Delta \ell = \frac{\mu_0 i}{2\pi r} \sum \Delta \ell \qquad (19\text{-}11)$$

In Equation 19-11 we've taken the quantity $\mu_0 i/(2\pi r)$ outside the sum because it has the same value everywhere around the circle and so in all terms of the sum.

Figure 19-19 **Magnetic resonance imaging (MRI)** The medical imaging technique known as MRI requires that the patient be immersed in a strong, uniform magnetic field. In this MRI device this is done by having the patient lie inside a solenoid.

Figure 19-20 **Ampère's law and circulation** Ampère's law states that the circulation of magnetic field around a closed path (called an *Amperian loop*) is proportional to the current that passes through that path.

Figure 19-20 **Ampère's law and circulation** Ampère's law states that the circulation of magnetic field around a closed path (called an *Amperian loop*) is proportional to the current that passes through that path.

The quantity $\sum \Delta \ell$ is the sum of the lengths of all of the segments that make up the circle—that is, the circumference of the circle, which is equal to $2\pi r$. So the circulation in Equation 19-11 is equal to

(19-12)
$$\text{Circulation} = \frac{\mu_0 i}{2\pi r}(2\pi r) = \mu_0 i$$

The circulation as given by Equation 19-12 does *not* depend on the radius r of the circle. (If the circle is larger, the magnetic field has a smaller magnitude, but it takes more segments of length $\Delta \ell$ to go all the way around the circle.) Remarkably, the same result holds true even if we draw a noncircular path around the wire: The circulation around *any* path that encloses the wire is equal to $\mu_0 i$. This is an example of **Ampère's law**, which was discovered by the French physicist André-Marie Ampère (pronounced "ahm-pair") in 1826:

Ampère's law
(19-13)

Circulation of magnetic field around an Amperian loop   Permeability of free space

$$\sum B_{||}\Delta \ell = \mu_0 i_{\text{through}}$$

Current through the Amperian loop

An **Amperian loop** is simply a closed path in space; the circle in Figure 19-20 is an example. The subscript "through" reminds us that the right-hand side of Equation 19-13 should only include current that passes through the interior of the Amperian loop.

It can be shown that Ampère's law is true for *any* magnetic field and *any* Amperian loop, no matter what the geometry of the current that produces the magnetic field. (The proof is beyond our scope.) However, it's only in certain very symmetric situations that Ampère's law helps us calculate the value of magnetic field. (This is much like Gauss's law for electric fields. We saw in Sections 16-6 and 16-7 that Gauss's law is always true but is only useful for electric field calculations in certain situations.) Happily, one such situation is the field of a solenoid.

Using Ampère's Law: Magnetic Field of a Solenoid

As Figure 19-18 shows, inside the solenoid the fields from each loop add to create a total field that runs parallel to the central axis; this is especially noticeable close to the axis and far from the ends. Outside the solenoid the fields nearly cancel, especially close to the solenoid and far from the ends. The fields outside the solenoid cancel more completely when the length of the solenoid is large compared to its diameter and when the coils of the solenoid are tightly wound. If there are N turns or *windings* of wire in the solenoid, the *winding density* is $n = N/L$. (The units of n are windings per meter.) Let's see how to use Ampère's law to find the magnetic field of a long, narrow, tightly wound (ideal) solenoid of length L, diameter D, and winding density n carrying a current i. In particular, we'll apply Ampère's law to find the field inside the coil and far from the ends—that is, where we expect the field to be relatively uniform.

To use Ampère's law effectively, we must first select an Amperian loop *through* which current flows and *around* which we can calculate the magnetic field. The point at which we want to determine the field—in this case, a point inside the solenoid—must lie on the Amperian loop. Figure 19-21 shows our choice of Amperian loop on a cutaway view of a section of the solenoid. This view is similar to Figure 19-18, in which the current is shown coming out of the page along the top part of the windings and going into the page along the bottom. We picked a rectangle as the Amperian loop and positioned it so that the bottom of the loop is parallel to one of the field lines of the uniform field inside the solenoid. The left-hand side of Ampère's law, Equation 19-13, can then be written as

$$\sum B_{\parallel} \Delta \ell = B_{\parallel 1} \ell_1 + B_{\parallel 2} \ell_2 + B_{\parallel 3} \ell_3 + B_{\parallel 4} \ell_4 \tag{19-14}$$

Side 4 is in the region of zero magnetic field outside the solenoid, so $B_{\parallel 4} = 0$ and $B_{\parallel 4} \ell_4 = 0$. Side 1 runs partially through this region of zero field, so $B_{\parallel 1} = 0$ there; inside the solenoid the field is nonzero but is perpendicular to side 1, so $B_{\parallel 1} = 0$ there as well. The same is true for side 3, so in Equation 19-14 $B_{\parallel 1} \ell_1 = B_{\parallel 3} \ell_3 = 0$. The only side of the Amperian loop that makes a nonzero contribution to the path integral is side 2. Here the magnetic field of magnitude B is parallel to the side of length ℓ_2, so $B_{\parallel 2} = B$ and Equation 19-14 becomes

$$\sum B_{\parallel} \Delta \ell = B\ell_2 \tag{19-15}$$

On the right-hand side of the Ampère's law equation, we need to evaluate i_{through}, the current that passes through the loop. This quantity is *not* just the current in the solenoid i, because every winding of the coil that passes through the loop brings a contribution i to i_{through}. The length of solenoid enclosed by the loop is ℓ_2 and there are n windings per meter, so there are $n\ell_2$ windings that pass through the

① These are the windings of the solenoid. The current points out of the page along the top and into the page along the bottom.

② We use a rectangular Amperian loop. Sides 1, 3, and 4 make zero contribution to the circulation around this loop (the field is either zero or perpendicular to the loop on these sides).

③ The only contribution to the circulation is from side 2, of length ℓ_2:

$$\sum B_{\parallel} \Delta \ell = B\ell_2$$

Figure 19-21 Ampère's law and the field of a solenoid The Amperian loop shown here helps us to calculate the magnetic field inside a long, straight solenoid.

loop. Each winding carries current i, so the total current through the loop is $n\ell_2$ multiplied by i:

(19-16)
$$i_{\text{through}} = n\ell_2 i$$

We can now substitute Equations 19-15 and 19-16 into the two sides of Equation 19-13 for Ampère's law:

$$B\ell_2 = \mu_0(n\ell_2 i)$$

The length ℓ_2 of the Amperian loop cancels, and we are left with

Magnetic field inside a long,
straight solenoid
(19-17)

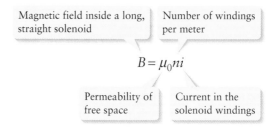

In deriving Equation 19-17, we've assumed that the field inside the solenoid is perfectly uniform and parallel to the solenoid axis and that the field outside the solenoid is exactly zero. These assumptions are strictly valid only for an infinitely long solenoid. But Equation 19-17 is a good approximation at points near the middle of any solenoid, especially one whose length is large compared to its diameter.

Note that Ampère's law also tells us the *direction* of the magnetic field inside the solenoid. Just as for the case of a long, straight wire (Figure 19-17), point your right thumb in the direction of the current through the Amperian loop in Figure 19-21. This current points out of the page, so you should point your thumb in that direction. If you curl the fingers of your right hand, they will curl in a counterclockwise direction: from left to right below the enclosed windings, and from right to left above the enclosed windings. That's consistent with the direction of the magnetic field inside the solenoid, which is from left to right. (The field has zero magnitude above the windings and outside the solenoid, so the direction is meaningless there.)

Equation 19-17 tells us that the magnitude of the uniform field created by a long solenoid is proportional to n, the number of windings per length. The more windings that can be packed into a length of the solenoid, the greater the field magnitude. A typical solenoid used for electronic applications is therefore more likely to look like the one in Figure 19-22, with many layers of tightly packed windings, than the one shown in Figure 19-18.

In the following example, we use Ampère's law to find the magnetic field due to a rather different distribution of current.

Figure 19-22 **A real-life solenoid** When the current to this solenoid is turned on, the iron rod that sticks out from its end experiences a strong magnetic force and is pulled into the solenoid. Such a device can be used to unlock a security door, as well as many other applications.

Example 19-5 Magnetic Field Due to a Coaxial Cable

A coaxial cable consists of a solid conductor of radius R_1 surrounded by insulation, which in turn is surrounded by a thin conducting shell of radius R_2 made of either fine wire mesh or a thin metallic foil (Figure 19-23). The combination is enclosed in an outer layer of insulation. The inner conductor carries current in one direction, and the outer conductor carries it back in the opposite direction. For a coaxial cable that carries a constant current i, find expressions for the magnetic field (a) inside the inner conductor at a distance $r < R_1$ from its central axis, (b) in the space between the two conductors, and (c) outside the coaxial cable. Assume that the moving charge in the inner conductor is distributed uniformly over the volume of the conductor.

Figure 19-23 **A coaxial cable** Equal amounts of current flow in opposite directions in the inner and outer conductors of this cable.

Set Up

Both the inner conductor separately and the coaxial cable as a whole have the same cylindrical symmetry as a long, straight wire (Figure 19-17). So we expect that the field lines are circles concentric with the axis of the cable. Just as for the long, straight wire, this means that it's natural to choose circular paths concentric with the cable axis as the Amperian loops. To find the field in the three regions, we'll choose the radius r of the Amperian loop to be less than R_1 in part (a), between R_1 and R_2 in part (b), and greater than R_2 in part (c).

Ampère's law:

$$\sum B_\parallel \Delta \ell = \mu_0 i_{\text{through}} \quad (19\text{-}13)$$

Dashed circles labeled I, II, and III: Amperian loops for parts (a), (b), and (c) respectively

Solve

(a) Find the field inside the inner conductor by using an Amperian loop of radius $r < R_1$.

Inside the inner conductor, the magnetic field has magnitude B_{inner} and points tangent to the Amperian loop, so $B_\parallel = B_{\text{inner}}$. The left-hand side of the Ampère's law equation is

$$\sum B_\parallel \Delta \ell = B_{\text{inner}} \sum \Delta \ell = B_{\text{inner}} (2\pi r)$$

The Amperian loop encloses area πr^2, which is less than the cross-sectional area πR_1^2 of the inner conductor. The current through the loop is therefore a fraction $(\pi r^2)/(\pi R_1^2)$ of the total current i in the inner conductor:

$$i_{\text{through}} = i\left(\frac{\pi r^2}{\pi R_1^2}\right) = i\frac{r^2}{R_1^2}$$

Insert these into Equation 19-13 and solve for B_{inner}:

$$B_{\text{inner}} (2\pi r) = \mu_0 i \frac{r^2}{R_1^2}$$

$$B_{\text{inner}} = \mu_0 i \frac{r^2}{2\pi r R_1^2} = \frac{\mu_0 i r}{2\pi R_1^2}$$

(b) Find the field between the conductors by using an Amperian loop of radius r, where $R_1 < r < R_2$.

Between the two conductors the magnetic field of magnitude B_{between} also points tangent to the Amperian loop, so as in part (a) the left-hand side of Equation 19-13 is

$$\sum B_\parallel \Delta \ell = B_{\text{between}} (2\pi r)$$

The Amperian loop encloses the entire inner conductor, so $i_{\text{through}} = i$. Insert these into Equation 19-13 and solve for B_{between}:

$$B_{\text{between}} (2\pi r) = \mu_0 i$$

$$B_{\text{between}} = \frac{\mu_0 i}{2\pi r}$$

(c) Find the field outside the cable by using an Amperian loop of radius $r > R_2$.

Just as in parts (a) and (b), outside the outer conductor the magnetic field of magnitude B_{outer} points tangent to the Amperian loop, so

$$\sum B_\parallel \Delta \ell = B_{\text{outer}} (2\pi r)$$

The Amperian loop encloses both conductors, each of which carries current i. Since the currents flow in opposite directions, the *net* current through the loop is $i_{\text{through}} = 0$. So Equation 19-13 tells us

$$B_{\text{outer}} (2\pi r) = \mu_0 (0)$$

$$B_{\text{outer}} = 0$$

Reflect

Our result from (a) says that the magnetic field is zero at the center of the inner conductor ($r = 0$), then increases in direct proportion to r with increasing distance from the center. The field reaches its maximum value at the outer surface of the inner conductor ($r = R_1$). Between the conductors the field is inversely proportional to r, so the magnitude decreases with increasing distance from the center of the cable. Outside the outer conductor there is *zero* magnetic field.

Coaxial cables are often referred to as "shielded" cables. The arrangement of the two conductors eliminates the presence of stray magnetic fields outside the cable. The shielding also serves to isolate the inner conductor from external electromagnetic signals. You'll find a coaxial cable connected to the back of most television sets (it's the "cable" in the term "cable TV"); the signal carried by this cable involves an alternating current and hence a varying magnetic field rather than a steady one, but the shielding principle is the same.

Magnetic Field of a Current Loop

An important special case for which Ampère's law is *not* helpful is the magnetic field produced by a current loop (a current-carrying wire bent into a circle). **Figure 19-24** shows some of the magnetic field lines for such a loop.

Unlike the case for a long, straight wire (Figure 19-17) or for a coaxial cable (Example 19-5), the magnetic field does *not* have the same magnitude at all points on a field line: The magnitude B is greater where the lines are closer together. So choosing an Amperian loop that coincides with a field line will not give us a simple equation for the magnitude B, as was the case in Example 19-5. To calculate the magnetic field at a given point in this situation, it's necessary to find the contribution to the field due to each short segment of the loop, then add those contributions using vector arithmetic.

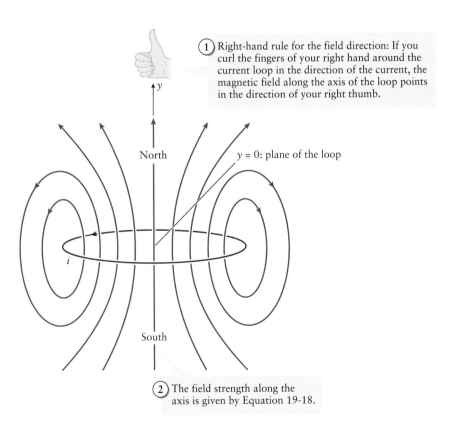

Figure 19-24 Magnetic field due to a current loop This magnetic field pattern is similar to the electric field pattern of an electric dipole (Figure 16-14).

Such a calculation is beyond our scope. Here's the result for the magnitude of the magnetic field along the axis of the current loop, labeled y in Figure 19-24:

$$B = \frac{\mu_0 i}{2} \frac{R^2}{(R^2 + y^2)^{3/2}}$$ (19-18)

In Equation 19-18 i is the current in the loop, R is the radius of the loop, and y is the coordinate along the y axis, where $y = 0$ represents the plane of the loop. If we substitute $y = 0$ into Equation 19-18, we get the field magnitude at the very center of the loop. At points far from the loop, so y is much greater than R, we can replace $R^2 + y^2$ with y^2 to good approximation. Equation 19-18 then becomes

$$B = \frac{\mu_0 i}{2} \frac{R^2}{(y^2)^{3/2}} = \frac{\mu_0 i}{2} \frac{R^2}{|y|^3}$$ (19-19)

(We've added the absolute value signs because y can be positive or negative, but the field magnitude B must be positive.) So at large distances from a current loop, the magnetic field is inversely proportional to the *cube* of the distance from the loop.

This result is reminiscent of the *electric* field of an electric dipole (a combination of a positive charge q and a negative charge $-q$): We found in Example 16-7 (Section 16-5) that at large distances from an electric dipole, the electric field due to that dipole is inversely proportional to the cube of the distance. The overall magnetic field pattern of a current loop also has some similarities to the electric field pattern of an electric dipole. (Compare Figure 19-24 and Figure 16-14; if you rotate Figure 16-14 clockwise 90°, the similarities will be more evident.)

As a result of these similarities, we use the term *magnetic dipole* to refer to a current loop. The two "poles" of a magnetic dipole are the points just above and just below the loop, as Figure 19-24 shows. We call these poles north and south by analogy to the poles of a bar magnet: The magnetic field points away from the current loop at its north pole and points toward the current loop at its south pole, just as for a bar magnet (see Section 19-2).

Note that unlike the two charges that make up an electric dipole, the north and south poles of a current loop can never be separated: The current loop must always have two sides! As we discussed in Section 19-2, a permanent magnet such as a bar magnet acts as a magnetic dipole. That's because a permanent magnet is really just a collection of *atomic* current loops, each the result of electron motions within the atom. Their combined effect is the same as electrons moving around the circular loop of wire in Figure 19-24. The poles of such a magnet can no more be separated than can the two sides of a current loop.

Earth's magnetic field is nearly that of a dipole, with the axis of the field tilted about 11° from Earth's rotation axis. (As a result, the magnetic poles—the place on Earth's surface where the field lines point straight and vertical to the surface—are displaced by several hundreds of kilometers from Earth's geographic poles.) The magnetic field is produced because molten material in the outer regions of Earth's core is in a state of continuous motion, and this motion gives rise to electric currents that generate the field. The photo that opens this chapter illustrates one dynamic consequence of our planet having a magnetic field.

Anyone who uses a compass to navigate makes use of Earth's magnetic field, which points generally from south to north. Other living organisms also take advantage of Earth's field to guide them from location to location. Pigeons, honeybees, and sea turtles among others rely to some extent on an internal magnetic compass to navigate. Sea turtles, for example, have been observed to travel hundreds of kilometers and still find their way back to their nesting sites along relatively direct paths. Yet when the turtles are transported away from their nests after a magnet has been attached to their heads, they take wildly circuitous routes back to the nesting site. The field of the attached magnet clearly disrupts the turtles' ability to determine their position using Earth's magnetic field.

Magnetic Materials

While there are circulating electrons within every kind of atom, not all materials have the same magnetic properties. In some materials there is a net rotation of electron charge within the atom, so each atom behaves like a current loop. In most cases these atomic current loops are randomly oriented, so their effects cancel out. But if the material is placed in a strong magnetic field, the atomic current loops experience a torque and align themselves with the magnetic field (see Figure 19-14b). As a result, the material behaves like a much larger current loop. If the magnetic field is turned off, random thermal motion will cause the atomic current loops to return to their original, nonaligned orientations. Materials that display this behavior are called **paramagnetic**. Everyday paramagnetic materials include aluminum and sodium. The net magnetic effect in a paramagnetic material is generally quite small; while an empty can made of (paramagnetic) aluminum acts like a current loop when brought next to a magnet, the magnetic force on the aluminum can is so small that a magnet can't pick it up.

In a handful of materials, the interactions between adjacent atomic current loops are very strong. As a result, once the material is placed in a magnetic field, the atomic current loops not only align with the field but can *remain* aligned after the field is turned off, leaving the material permanently magnetized. Iron is the most common of these materials, which are called **ferromagnetic** ("ferro" derives from the Latin word for iron). Any permanent magnet, such as one you might use to attach notes to a refrigerator door, is made of a ferromagnetic material. A permanent magnet can pick up objects made of a ferromagnetic material, such as a steel paper clip. The field of the permanent magnet causes the atomic current loops in the paper clip to align, making the paper clip a magnet itself. The magnetized paper clip is then attracted to the permanent magnet.

! Watch Out!   Earth is not a permanent magnet.

Our planet's core is made primarily of iron and nickel, both of which are ferromagnetic materials. It's common to conclude from this that the core is magnetized like a permanent magnet and that this gives rise to our planet's magnetic field. However, this cannot be true. Any ferromagnetic material loses its magnetism if it is heated above a certain temperature specific to that material: This critical temperature is 773°C for iron and 354°C for nickel. The temperature in Earth's core is in excess of 4400°C, so the iron and nickel in the core do *not* act like ferromagnetic materials. Instead, Earth's magnetic field is caused by electric currents in the molten material that makes up the outer regions of the core.

Most materials are neither paramagnetic nor ferromagnetic because their atoms have zero net electron current. When placed in a magnetic field, a small amount of atomic current appears, but the current loops end up aligned in the direction *opposite* to what happens for paramagnetic or ferromagnetic materials. (This is a consequence of *electromagnetic induction*, which we'll discuss in Chapter 20.) As a result, these materials, called **diamagnetic**, are slightly repelled by magnets rather than being attracted. In most cases, however, the repulsion is very weak.

? Got the Concept? 19-7   Ampère's Law

The field lines in Figure 19-24 are closed curves. If the distance around one such curve is L and the current in the loop is i, what is the average value around the closed curve of the component of magnetic field $B_{\parallel}$ parallel to the curve? (a) $\mu_0 i$; (b) $\mu_0 i/L$; (c) $2\mu_0 i$; (d) $2\mu_0 i/L$; (e) not enough information given to decide.

Take-Home Message for Section 19-7

✔ Ampère's law relates the current through a wire to the magnetic field it generates.

✔ Current through a long, straight wire produces a magnetic field with circular field lines centered on the wire.

✔ Current through a solenoid (a straight, helical coil of wire) produces a relatively uniform magnetic field along its axis that is proportional to the winding density as well as the current.

✔ A current loop produces a more complicated magnetic field. A magnetic material can be thought of as a collection of atomic current loops.

19-8 Two current-carrying wires exert magnetic forces on each other

We've seen that a current-carrying wire experiences a force when placed in a magnetic field, and also that a current-carrying wire generates a magnetic field. Let's put these ideas together and look at the magnetic interaction between *two* current-carrying wires. (Note that these two wires do not exert *electric* forces on each other. That's because each wire has as much positive charge as negative charge, and so is electrically neutral.)

André-Marie Ampère was the first to study the magnetic interaction between current-carrying wires theoretically and experimentally. He was also the first to show that two parallel, straight wires carrying current in the same direction attract each other, and that two parallel, straight wires carrying current in opposite directions repel. Let's see why this is the case.

Figure 19-25 shows the situation. Wires 1 and 2 are long, straight, and parallel to each other and separated by a distance d. The current i_1 in wire 1 sets up a magnetic field $\vec{B}_1$ at the position of wire 2, which carries current i_2. The magnitude B_1 of this field is given by Equation 19-20:

$$B_1 = \frac{\mu_0 i_1}{2\pi d} \tag{19-20}$$

The right-hand rule for the field produced by a long, straight wire (Section 19-7) tells us that at the position of wire 2, $\vec{B}_1$ points upward and perpendicular to wire 2. To find the direction of the force $\vec{F}_{1\,on\,2}$ that this field exerts on wire 2, use the right-hand rule for the direction of the magnetic force on a current-carrying wire (Section 19-5): This tells us that $\vec{F}_{1\,on\,2}$ points toward wire 1, so the force attracts wire 2 to wire 1. The magnitude of the force on wire 2, of length ℓ_2, is given by Equation 19-5 with $\theta = 90°$ (since the direction of the current in wire 2 is perpendicular to the direction of $\vec{B}_1$):

$$F_{1\,on\,2} = i_2\ell_2 B_1 \sin 90° = i_2\ell_2 B_1 \tag{19-21}$$

If we substitute B_1 from Equation 19-20 into Equation 19-21, we get

$$F_{1\,on\,2} = i_2\ell_2\left(\frac{\mu_0 i_1}{2\pi d}\right) = \frac{\mu_0 i_1 i_2 \ell_2}{2\pi d} \tag{19-22}$$

The force per unit length on wire 2 is $F_{1\,on\,2}$ (given by Equation 19-22) divided by the length ℓ_2 of wire 2:

Magnetic force per unit length exerted by wire 1 on wire 2 $= F_{1\,on\,2}/\ell_2 = \dfrac{\mu_0 i_1 i_2}{2\pi d}$ (19-23)

We can use the same procedure to find the magnetic force per unit length that wire 2 exerts on wire 1. The field $\vec{B}_2$ that the current i_2 in wire 2 produces at the position of wire 1 has magnitude $B_2 = \mu_0 i_2/(2\pi d)$ and points *downward* in Figure 19-25. From the right-hand rule for the force on a current-carrying wire, the force $\vec{F}_{2\,on\,1}$ on wire 1 points toward wire 2 (the force is attractive); its magnitude is $F_{2\,on\,1} = i_1\ell_1 B_2 = i_1\ell_1[\mu_0 i_2/(2\pi d)] = \mu_0 i_1 i_2 \ell_1/(2\pi d)$, where ℓ_1 is the length of wire 1. The force per unit length on wire 1 is then $F_{1\,on\,2}$ divided by ℓ_1:

Magnetic force per unit length exerted by wire 2 on wire 1 $= F_{2\,on\,1}/\ell_1 = \dfrac{\mu_0 i_1 i_2}{2\pi d}$ (19-24)

The force magnitudes per unit length in Equations 19-23 and 19-24 are equal, and the forces $\vec{F}_{1\,on\,2}$ and $\vec{F}_{2\,on\,1}$ are opposite in direction. That's just what we would expect from Newton's third law.

What changes if we reverse the direction of the current i_1 in wire 1? The force *magnitudes* given by Equations 19-23 and 19-24 won't be affected, but the force *directions* will be. This will reverse the direction of the magnetic field $\vec{B}_1$ that wire 1 produces at the position of wire 2, and so will reverse the direction of the force $\vec{F}_{1\,on\,2}$ on wire 2. So in this case wire 2 will be pushed away from wire 1 (it will be repelled). Reversing the direction

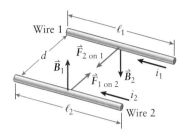

$\vec{B}_1$ = Magnetic field due to wire 1 at the position of wire 2

$\vec{B}_2$ = Magnetic field due to wire 2 at the position of wire 1

Figure 19-25 Magnetic forces between two current-carrying wires These two parallel wires carry current in the same direction and exert attractive magnetic forces on each other. If we reverse the direction of one of the currents, the forces become repulsive.

of i_1 will also reverse the direction of the force $\vec{F}_{2\,\text{on}\,1}$ that wire 2 exerts on wire 1, so this force will push wire 1 away from 2 (again, it will be repelled). So we conclude that

> *Two parallel current-carrying wires attract each other if they carry current in the same direction, and repel each other if they carry current in opposite directions.*

Example 19-6 Wires in a Computer

The two long, straight wires that run along the back of a computer case to power the cooling fan carry 0.110 A in opposite directions. The wires are separated by 5.00 mm. (a) Find the force per unit length (magnitude and direction) that these wires exert on each other. (b) The mass per unit length of the wire is 5.00×10^{-3} kg/m. What acceleration does one of the wires experience due to this force?

Set Up

We'll use Equation 19-23 to find the force per unit length that one wire exerts on the other. (As we saw with Equation 19-24, the force per unit length has the same magnitude for either wire.) If we assume that this force equals the net external force on the wire, we can use Newton's second law to calculate the acceleration of the wire.

Magnetic force per unit length exerted by wire 1 on wire 2:

$$F_{1\,\text{on}\,2}/\ell_2 = \frac{\mu_0 i_1 i_2}{2\pi d} \qquad (19\text{-}23)$$

Newton's second law:

$$\sum \vec{F}_{\text{ext}} = m\vec{a} \qquad (4\text{-}2)$$

Solve

(a) The currents are in opposite directions, so the force is repulsive (it pushes the two wires apart). Use Equation 19-23 to find the magnitude of the force per unit length.

The two wires are separated by $d = 5.00$ mm $= 5.00 \times 10^{-3}$ m and carry currents with the same magnitude: $i_1 = i_2 = 0.110$ A. The force per unit length on either wire is

$$= \frac{(4\pi \times 10^{-7}\,\text{T}\cdot\text{m/A})(0.110\,\text{A})(0.110\,\text{A})}{2\pi(5.00 \times 10^{-3}\,\text{m})}$$
$$= 4.84 \times 10^{-7}\,\text{T}\cdot\text{A} = 4.84 \times 10^{-7}\,\text{N/m}$$

(Recall that $1\,\text{T} = 1\,\text{N}/(\text{A}\cdot\text{m})$.)

(b) Use Newton's second law to find the acceleration of the wire.

Our result for part (a) says that a 1-m length of wire would experience a force of magnitude 4.84×10^{-7} N. Since this wire has mass per unit length 5.00×10^{-3} kg/m, a 1-m length would have mass 5.00×10^{-3} kg. The acceleration is

$$a = |\vec{a}| = \frac{|\sum \vec{F}_{\text{ext}}|}{m} = \frac{4.84 \times 10^{-7}\,\text{N}}{5.00 \times 10^{-3}\,\text{kg}}$$
$$= 9.68 \times 10^{-5}\,\text{m/s}^2$$

Reflect

The force and acceleration are both very gentle, so the effect on these wires will be almost imperceptible. In applications with very large currents, however, the magnetic forces between conductors can be substantial.

? Got the Concept? 19-8 Forces on a Current-carrying Coil

A very flexible helical coil is suspended as shown in Figure 19-26. What will happen when a sizable current i is sent through the coil? (a) The coils will be pulled together; (b) the coils will be pushed apart; (c) some of the coils will be pulled together, while others will be pulled apart; (d) there will be no net effect on the coils.

Figure 19-26 **A hanging coil** What happens to this coil when the current is turned on?

Take-Home Message for Section 19-8

✔ Two wires attract each other when carrying current in the same direction and repel each other when carrying currents in opposite directions.

✔ The forces per unit length on the wires are equal in magnitude and opposite in direction, exactly as required by Newton's third law.

Key Terms

Ampère's law
Amperian loop
circulation
current loop
diamagnetic
electromagnetism
ferromagnetic

magnet
magnetic dipole
magnetic field
magnetic force
magnetic poles
magnetism
mass spectrometer

normal
paramagnetic
permeability of free space
right-hand rule
solenoid
tesla

Chapter Summary

Topic	Equation or Figure

Magnetism and magnetic forces: Magnetic forces are present whenever moving charged objects interact with each other. (By comparison, electric forces are present whenever charged objects interact with each other, whether moving or not.) A magnet is an object that contains charges in continuous motion. A magnet sets up a magnetic field in the space around it; a second magnet responds to that field and can be attracted or repelled, depending on its orientation.

(a) These magnets attract.

(b) These magnets repel.

(Figure 19-3 a/b)

Magnetic force on a moving charged particle: A single charged particle can experience a magnetic force when moving in a magnetic field. The magnitude of the force depends on both the speed of the particle and the direction of the particle relative to the magnetic field. The direction of the force is perpendicular to both the velocity $\vec{v}$ and the magnetic field $\vec{B}$, and is given by a right-hand rule.

Magnitude of the magnetic force on a moving charged particle

Magnitude of the magnetic field

$$F = |q|vB \sin\theta$$

Angle between the direction of the particle's velocity $\vec{v}$ and the direction of the magnetic field $\vec{B}$

(19-1)

Magnitude of the particle's charge

Speed of the particle

(a)

$\vec{F} \odot$ θ $\vec{B}$ $\vec{v}$

(b)

$\vec{F} \otimes$ θ $\vec{B}$ $\vec{v}$

(Figure 19-6)

If $q > 0$, the force vector in this situation points out of the page (as indicated by the circle with a dot).

If $q < 0$, the force vector in this situation points into the page (as indicated by the circle with an X).

Particle trajectories in a magnetic field: A charged particle moving in a magnetic field and subject to no other forces can move in a circular trajectory whose radius depends on its speed, mass, and charge as well as the magnetic field magnitude. This is the principle of the mass spectrometer.

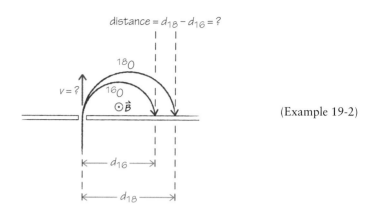

(Example 19-2)

Magnetic forces on current-carrying wires: If a wire carries a current and is placed in a magnetic field, it experiences a magnetic force. This force is the sum of the magnetic forces acting on the individual moving charges within the wire. The force magnitude depends on the amount of current and the orientation of the wire relative to the magnetic field; its direction is given by a right-hand rule.

Magnitude of the magnetic force on a current-carrying wire

Magnitude of the magnetic field (assumed uniform over the length of the wire)

$$F = i\ell B \sin\theta$$

Angle between the direction of the current and the direction of the magnetic field $\vec{B}$

Current in the wire

Length of the wire

(19-5)

The force $\vec{F}$ on a current-carrying wire in a magnetic field $\vec{B}$ is perpendicular to both $\vec{B}$ and the length of the wire. The direction is given by a right-hand rule.

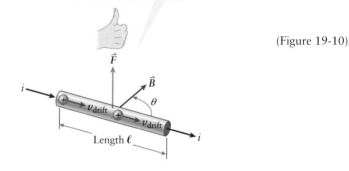

(Figure 19-10)

Magnetic torque on a current loop: A current-carrying loop of wire can experience a torque when placed in a magnetic field. The magnitude and direction of the torque depend on how the current loop is oriented relative to the direction of the magnetic field. Electric motors make use of this principle.

Magnitude of the magnetic torque on a current loop

Magnitude of the magnetic field

$$\tau = iAB \sin\phi$$

Angle between the normal to the plane of the loop and the direction of the magnetic field $\vec{B}$

Current in the loop

Area of the loop

(19-8)

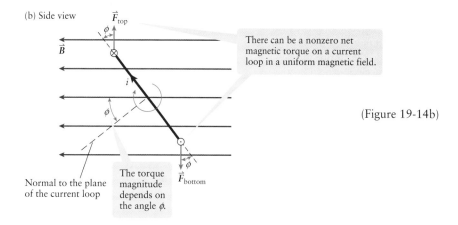

(Figure 19-14b)

(b) Side view

There can be a nonzero net magnetic torque on a current loop in a uniform magnetic field.

The torque magnitude depends on the angle ϕ.

Normal to the plane of the current loop

Ampère's law and the field produced by moving electric currents: A long, straight, current-carrying wire produces a relatively simple magnetic field in the space around it. Ampère's law—which relates the circulation of magnetic field around a closed loop to the amount of current through that loop—can be used to find the magnetic field produced by currents with other simple geometries.

Magnitude of the magnetic field due to a long, straight wire

Permeability of free space

$$B = \frac{\mu_0 i}{2\pi r}$$

Current in the wire

Distance from the wire to the location where the field is measured

(19-9)

Circulation of magnetic field around an Amperian loop

Permeability of free space

$$\sum B_{\parallel} \Delta \ell = \mu_0 i_{\text{through}}$$

Current through the Amperian loop

(19-13)

(1) We draw an Amperian loop that encircles the current-carrying wire. (This particular loop is a circle, and so coincides with a field line.)

Segment of Amperian loop of length $\Delta \ell$

(2) For each segment of the loop, calculate the product of $B_{\parallel}$ (the component of magnetic field parallel to the segment) and the segment length $\Delta \ell$.

Wire

(3) The circulation of magnetic field around the loop is the sum of all these products for the entire loop:

$$\sum B_{\parallel} \Delta \ell$$

(Figure 19-20)

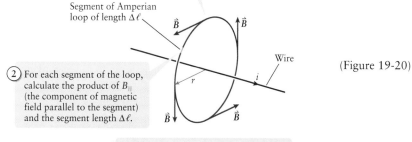

Current loops and magnetic materials: A current loop is called a magnetic dipole because the magnetic field that it produces is similar to the electric field produced by an electric dipole. A permanent magnet is a material in which the atoms behave like individual current loops, many of which are oriented in the same direction so that their individual magnetic fields add to make a strong field.

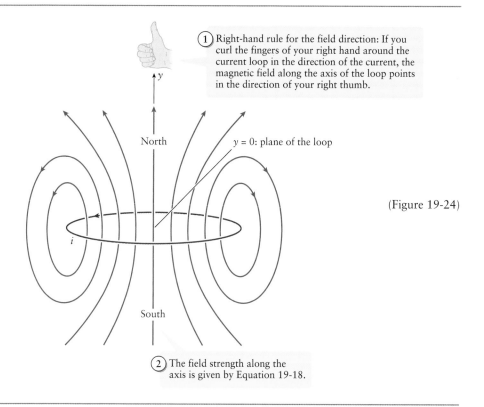

1) Right-hand rule for the field direction: If you curl the fingers of your right hand around the current loop in the direction of the current, the magnetic field along the axis of the loop points in the direction of your right thumb.

$y = 0$: plane of the loop

North

South

(Figure 19-24)

2) The field strength along the axis is given by Equation 19-18.

Force between current-carrying wires: Two parallel current-carrying wires exert magnetic forces on each other: The current in one wire produces a magnetic field, and the current in the other wire responds to that field. The two wires attract if the currents are in the same direction and repel if the currents are in opposite directions.

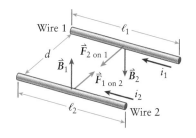

(Figure 19-25)

$\vec{B}_1$ = Magnetic field due to wire 1 at the position of wire 2

$\vec{B}_2$ = Magnetic field due to wire 2 at the position of wire 1

Answer to What do you think? Question

(c) Equation 19-1 (Section 19-3) gives the magnitude of the magnetic force on a charged particle moving in a magnetic field. The magnitude is proportional to sin θ, where θ is the angle between the magnetic field and the velocity of the particle. The sine function is greatest when $\theta = 90°$, in which case the particle is moving perpendicular to the field. This is in stark contrast to the *electric* force on a charged particle, which does not depend on the direction or magnitude of the particle's velocity.

Answers to Got the Concept? Questions

19-1 (b) Two charged objects exert *electric* forces on each other whether or not the objects are moving. But in order for these objects to exert *magnetic* forces on each other, *both* objects must be in motion. (One must be in motion to produce a magnetic field, and the other must be in motion to experience a force due to that field.) Since only one object is in motion, there is no magnetic force between the two objects.

19-2 (a) To apply the right-hand rule to the proton in Figure 19-7, start by pointing the fingers of your right hand in the direction of the proton's initial velocity. Orient your palm so that when you make a "slapping" motion with your hand, your palm points in the direction of the magnetic field (into the page). If you then stick your right thumb out straight, it points toward the top of the page. This is the direction of the force on the proton. This force makes the proton's trajectory bend upward in the figure.

19-3 (a), (c) Electrons have a negative charge, so the direction of the magnetic force each electron experiences is opposite to the direction your thumb points when applying the right-hand rule. For electron A, point the fingers of your right hand in the direction of the electron's initial velocity, then orient your palm so that when you make a "slapping" motion with your hand, your palm points in the direction of the magnetic field (into the page). If you then stick your right thumb out straight, it points to the right, which means the electron feels a force to the left. So electron A feels a force toward the point at which the proton enters the field. For electron B, the right-hand rule has your right thumb pointing toward the bottom of the page, so the force on the electron is toward the top of the page. It does not bend toward the proton's entry point. The right-hand rule predicts the same direction for the magnetic force on electron C, but in this case a force toward the top of the page does bend the electron's trajectory toward the point where the proton enters the field. Finally, when you apply the right-hand rule to electron D, your right thumb sticks out to the left. For the negatively charged electron the magnetic force is therefore to the right, so the trajectory of electron D does not bend toward the proton's entry point into the field.

19-4 (c) Equation 19-3 shows that for a given speed v, the radius of the circular path followed by an ion in a mass spectrometer is $r = mv/(qB)$. This is directly proportional to the ratio of the ion mass m to its charge q. Compared to the value of the ratio m/q for a $^{16}O^+$ ion ($m = 16$ u, $q = e$), the value for a $^{16}O^{2+}$ ion is $1/2$ as great ($m = 16$ u, $q = 2e$), the value for a $^{32}S^+$ ion is twice as great ($m = 32$ u, $q = e$), and the value for a $^{32}S^{2+}$ ion is the same ($m = 32$ u, $q = 2e$).

19-5 (a) Force is zero; (b) $-z$ direction; (c) $+y$ direction; (d) $+z$ direction; (e) $-y$ direction; (f) force is zero. The force on a current-carrying wire is zero if the wire axis lies along the direction of the magnetic field, as in cases (a) and (f). In cases (b), (c), (d), and (e), we use the right-hand rule for the magnetic force on a current-carrying wire to find the direction of the force: Swing the extended fingers of your right hand, palm first, from the direction of the current to the direction of $\vec{B}$. Your extended right thumb then points in the direction of the force on the wire.

19-6 (e) Doubling the number of turns of wire will double the magnetic torque on the current loop. But this also doubles the mass and the moment of inertia of the current loop, so the angular acceleration—equal to the torque divided by the moment of inertia—will be unaffected. For a real electric motor, however, the moment of inertia is due partially to the mass of the coil and partially to the mass of what the motor is turning, such as the fan blades in Figure 19-13a. As a result, doubling the number of turns will increase the maximum torque by a factor of two but increase the moment of inertia by less than a factor of two, and the maximum angular acceleration will in fact increase.

19-7 (b) The net current through the closed curve is i, since the current loop passes once through the plane of the curve. From Ampère's law the circulation of the magnetic field around the closed curve is $\sum B_\parallel \Delta \ell = \mu_0 i_{\mathrm{through}} = \mu_0 i$. The left-hand side of this equation is the average value of $B_\parallel$ multiplied by the total distance around the closed curve, so $(B_\parallel)_{\mathrm{average}} L = \mu_0 i$ and $(B_\parallel)_{\mathrm{average}} = \mu_0 i/L$.

19-8 (a) Each segment of the coil is a piece of wire and is attracted to the piece of wire in the coils directly above and below it (in each of which the current flows in the same direction). Each piece of wire is also repelled by the pieces of wire on the opposite side of the coil above it and the opposite side of the coil below it. But these pieces are at a greater distance d, so these repulsive forces are smaller than the attractive forces (see Equation 19-23). The net result is that the coils attract each other and so pull together.

Questions and Problems

In a few problems, you are given more data than you actually need; in a few other problems, you are required to supply data from your general knowledge, outside sources, or informed estimate.

Interpret as significant all digits in numerical values that have trailing zeros and no decimal points.

For all problems, use $g = 9.80 \text{ m/s}^2$ for the free-fall acceleration due to gravity. Neglect friction and air resistance unless instructed to do otherwise.

• Basic, single-concept problem

•• Intermediate-level problem, may require synthesis of concepts and multiple steps

••• Challenging problem

SSM *Solution is in Student Solutions Manual*

Conceptual Questions

1. • You are given three iron rods. Two of them are magnets but the third one is not. How could you use the two magnets to find that the third rod is not magnetized? SSM

2. • If a magnetic field exerts a force on moving charged particles, is it capable of doing work on the particles? Explain your answer.

3. • A current-carrying wire is in a region where there is a magnetic field, but there is no magnetic force acting on the wire. How can this be?

4. • How is it possible for an object that experiences no net magnetic force to experience a net magnetic torque?

5. •• A velocity selector consists of crossed electric and magnetic fields, with the magnetic field directed toward the top of the page. A beam of positively charged particles passing through the velocity selector from left to right is undeflected by the fields. (a) In what direction is the electric field? (left, right, toward the top of the page, toward the bottom of the page, into the page, out of the page) (b) The direction of the particle beam is reversed so that it travels from right to left. Is it deflected? If so, in what direction? (c) A beam of electrons (negatively charged) moving with the same speed is passed through from left to right. Is it deflected? If so, in what direction? SSM

6. •Physicists refer to crossed electric and magnetic fields as a *velocity selector*. In the same sense, the deflection of charged particles in a strong magnetic field perpendicular to their motion can be thought of as a *momentum selector*. Why?

7. •A long, straight current-carrying wire is placed in a cubic region that has a uniform magnetic field as shown in **Figure 19-27**. Does the force on the wire depend on the width of the magnetic field? Explain your answer.

Figure 19-27 Problem 7 |←——Width——→|

8. •In a lightning strike, there is a negative charge moving rapidly from a cloud to the ground. In what direction is a lightning strike deflected by Earth's magnetic field?

9. •In telephone lines, two wires carrying currents in opposite directions are twisted together. How does this reduce the magnetic fields surrounding the wires? SSM

10. •A power cord for an electronic device consists of two parallel straight wires carrying currents in opposite directions. Is there any force between them? Explain your answer.

11. •Parallel wires exert magnetic forces on each other. What about perpendicular wires? Explain your answer.

Multiple-Choice Questions

12. •The magnetic force on a charged moving particle
   A. depends on the sign of the charge on the particle.
   B. depends on the magnetic field at the particle's instantaneous position.
   C. is in the direction which is mutually perpendicular to the direction of motion of the charge and the direction of the magnetic field.
   D. is proportional both to the charge and to the magnitude of the magnetic field.
   E. is described by all of the above options, A through D.

13. •A proton traveling to the right enters a region of uniform magnetic field that points into the page. When the proton enters this region, it will be
   A. deflected out of the plane of page.
   B. deflected into the plane of page.
   C. deflected toward the top of the page.
   D. deflected toward the bottom of the page.
   E. unaffected in its direction of motion. SSM

14. •An electron is moving northward in a magnetic field. The magnetic force on the electron is toward the northeast. What is the direction of the magnetic field?
   A. up
   B. down
   C. west
   D. south
   E. This situation cannot exist because of the orientation of the velocity and force vectors.

15. •A proton with a velocity along the $+x$ axis enters a region where there is a uniform magnetic field $\vec{B}$ in the $+y$ direction. You want to balance the magnetic force with an electric field so that the proton will continue along a straight line. The electric field should be in the
   A. $+x$ direction.
   B. $-x$ direction.
   C. $+z$ direction.
   D. $-z$ direction.
   E. $-y$ direction.

16. •A circular flat coil that has N turns, encloses an area A, and carries a current i has its central axis parallel to a uniform magnetic field $\vec{B}$ in which it is immersed. The net force on the coil is
   A. zero.
   B. $NiAB$.
   C. NiB.
   D. iBA.
   E. NiA.

17. •A circular flat coil that has N turns, encloses an area A, and carries a current i, has its central axis parallel to a uniform magnetic field $\vec{B}$ in which it is immersed. The net torque on the coil is
   A. zero.
   B. $NiAB$.
   C. NiB.
   D. iBA.
   E. NiA. SSM

18. •A very long, straight wire carries a constant current. The magnetic field a distance d from the wire and far from its ends varies with distance d according to
   A. d^{-3}.
   B. d^{-2}.
   C. d^{-1}.
   D. d.
   E. d^2.

19. •A solenoid carries a current. If the radius of the solenoid were doubled, and all other quantities remained the same, the magnetic field inside the solenoid would
   A. remain the same.
   B. be twice as strong as initially.
   C. be half as strong as initially.
   D. be one-quarter as strong as initially.
   E. be four times as strong as initially.

20. ••Two parallel wires carry currents in opposite directions as shown in **Figure 19-28**. Which of the following statements is correct?

Figure 19-28 Problem 20

   A. The force on the i_2 wire is upward, and the force on the i_1 wire is upward.
   B. The force on the i_2 wire is downward, and the force on the i_1 wire is upward.
   C. The force on the i_2 wire is upward, and the force on the i_1 wire is downward.
   D. The force on the i_2 wire is downward, and the force on the i_1 wire is downward.
   E. Neither wire experiences a net force.

21. ••Two current-carrying wires are perpendicular to each other. One wire lies horizontally with the current directed toward the east. The other wire is vertical with the current directed upward.

What is the direction of the net magnetic force on the horizontal wire due to the vertical wire?

   A. east
   B. west
   C. south
   D. north
   E. zero force SSM

Estimation/Numerical Analysis

22. ••Give an estimate of the force per unit length acting on a pair of high-voltage transmission lines that carry current from a power plant to a distant substation for commercial use (assume that the wires carry current in the same direction).

23. •Estimate the magnetic field at the ground level beneath standard power lines in your neighborhood.

24. •Estimate the magnetic field needed to separate two uranium ions (one has a mass of 235 u, one has a mass of 238 u) into circular paths with radii separated by 1 cm. Assume the two ions enter the magnetic field with the same velocity and the same charge.

25. •Estimate the time required for an electron to complete a circular orbit of 10 cm radius in Earth's magnetic field when it moves at a speed that is of the order of 10^5 m/s. SSM

26. ••Estimate the maximum torque on a coil in a typical electric drill motor.

27. •The magnetic field due to a current-carrying cylinder of radius 1 cm is measured at various points ($r < 1$ cm and $r > 1$ cm). Graph the magnitude of the magnetic field B as a function of r and use this graph to find the functional relationship between the magnetic field and the radial distance. *Hint:* The magnetic field will be described by two different functions—one for inside the cylinder and one for outside the cylinder. After making an initial graph, you may want to graph the data for the inside and outside separately.

r(m)	B(T)	r(m)	B(T)
0.001	0.00050	0.015	0.00353
0.002	0.00100	0.020	0.00250
0.003	0.00152	0.025	0.00200
0.004	0.00200	0.030	0.00180
0.005	0.00252	0.035	0.00143
0.006	0.00300	0.040	0.00125
0.007	0.00350	0.045	0.00110
0.008	0.00401	0.050	0.00103
0.009	0.00453	0.100	0.000502
0.010	0.00500		

Problems

19-1 Magnetic forces are interactions between two magnets

19-2 Magnetism is an interaction between moving charges

19-3 A moving point charge can experience a magnetic force

28. •Convert the units for the following expressions for magnetic fields as directed:

   A. 5.00 T = _____ G
   B. 25,000 G = _____ T
   C. 7.43 mG = _____ μT
   D. 1.88 mT = _____ G

29. •Determine the directions of the magnetic forces that act on positive charges moving in the magnetic fields as shown in **Figure 19-29**. SSM

Figure 19-29
Problem 29

30. •Determine the direction of the missing vector, $\vec{v}$, $\vec{B}$, or $\vec{F}$, in the scenarios shown in **Figure 19-30**. All moving charges are positive.

Figure 19-30
Problem 30

31. •A +1 C charge moving at 1 m/s makes an angle of 45° with a uniform, 1-T magnetic field. What is the magnitude of the magnetic force that the charge experiences?

32. •An electron is moving with a speed of 18 m/s in a direction parallel to a uniform magnetic field of 2.0 T. What are the magnitude and direction of the magnetic force on the electron?

33. •A proton P travels with a speed of 18 m/s toward the top of the page through a uniform magnetic field of 2.0 T directed into the page as shown in Figure 19-31. What are the magnitude and direction of the magnetic force on the proton? SSM

Figure 19-31 Problem 33

34. •A proton is propelled at 2×10^6 m/s perpendicular to a uniform magnetic field. If it experiences a magnetic force of 5.8×10^{-13} N, what is the strength of the magnetic field?

35. •An electron moves with a velocity of 10^7 m/s in the x–y plane at an angle of 45° to both the $+x$ and $+y$ axes. There is a magnetic field of 3.0 T in the $+y$ direction. Calculate the magnetic force (magnitude and direction) on the electron. SSM

36. ••There is a uniform magnetic field of magnitude 2.2 T in the $+z$ direction. Find the force on a particle of charge -1.2 nC if its velocity is (a) 1.0 km/s in the y–z plane in a direction that makes an angle of 40° with the z axis and (b) 1.0 km/s in the x–y plane in a direction that makes an angle of 40° with the x axis.

19-4 A mass spectrometer uses magnetic forces to differentiate atoms of different masses

37. ••A beam of protons is directed in a straight line along the $+z$ direction through a region of space in which there are

crossed electric and magnetic fields. If the electric field is 500 V/m in the $-y$ direction and the protons move at a constant speed of 10^5 m/s, what must be the magnitude and direction of the magnetic field such that the beam of protons continues along its straight-line trajectory?

38. ••A beam of particles (each particle has a charge $q = -2e$ and a kinetic energy of 4.00×10^{-13} J) is deflected by the magnetic field of a bending magnet as shown in Figure 19-32. The radius of curvature of the beam is 20.0 cm, and the strength of the magnetic field is 1.50 T. (a) What is the mass of the particles making up the beam? (b) Sketch the path for the given ions in the given magnetic field as a reference path. Then sketch a path for a more massive doubly ionized negative ion and a less massive doubly ionized positive ion, both with the same speed as the given ions, for comparison.

Figure 19-32 Problem 38

39. •A proton moves in a circle with a speed of 280 m/s through a uniform magnetic field of 2.0 T directed perpendicular to the circular path. What is the orbital radius of the proton?

19-5 Magnetic fields exert forces on current-carrying wires

40. •A 1.5-m length of straight wire experiences a maximum force of 2.0 N when in a uniform magnetic field that is 1.8 T. What current must be passing through it?

41. •A straight segment of wire 35.0 cm long carrying a current of 1.40 A is in a uniform magnetic field. The segment makes an angle of 53° with the direction of the magnetic field. If the force on the segment is 0.200 N, what is the magnitude of the magnetic field? SSM

42. •A straight wire of length 0.50 m is conducting a current of 2.0 A and makes an angle of 30° with a 3.0-T uniform magnetic field. What is the magnitude of the force exerted on the wire?

43. •A wire of length 0.50 m is conducting a current of 8.0 A in the $+x$ direction through a 4.0-T uniform magnetic field directed parallel to the wire. What are the magnitude and direction of the magnetic force on the wire?

44. •A wire of length 0.50 m is conducting a current of 8.0 A toward the top of the page and through a 4.0-T uniform magnetic field directed into the page as shown in Figure 19-33. What are the magnitude and direction of the magnetic force on the wire?

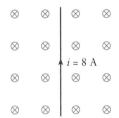

Figure 19-33 Problem 44

45. •A straight wire is positioned in a uniform magnetic field so that the maximum force on it is 4.0 N. If the wire is 80 cm long and carries a current that is 2 A, what is the magnitude of the magnetic field?

19-6 A magnetic field can exert a torque on a current loop

46. ••A square loop 10 cm on a side consists of 100 turns of wire that experiences a minimum torque of zero and a maximum

torque of 0.045 N · m. If the current in the loop is 2.82 A, calculate the magnetic field strength that the loop rests in.

47. ••What is the torque on a round loop of wire that carries a current of 100 A, has a radius of 10 cm, and whose plane makes an angle of 30° with a magnetic field of 0.244 T? Describe how the answer changes if the angle decreases to 10° and increases to 50°. SSM

19-7 Ampère's law describes the magnetic field created by current-carrying wires

48. ••A long, straight wire carries current in the $+z$ direction (out of the page). Determine the direction of the magnetic field due to the current at the points O, P, Q, and R (Figure 19-34).

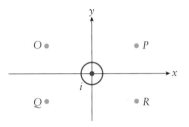

Figure 19-34 Problem 48

49. ••A long, straight wire carries current in the $+x$ direction. Determine the direction of the magnetic field due to the current at the points O, P, Q, and R (Figure 19-35).

Figure 19-35 Problem 49

50. ••Using Figure 19-36, derive an expression for the magnetic field at the point C located at the center of the two circular, current-carrying arcs and the connecting radial lines. Assume the radii of the small and large arcs are r_1 and r_2, respectively.

Figure 19-36 Problem 50

51. ••Derive an expression for the magnetic field at the point C at the center of the circular, current-carrying wire segments shown in Figure 19-37. SSM

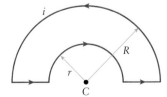

Figure 19-37 Problem 51

52. ••Calculate the magnitude of the magnetic field at a perpendicular distance of 2.2 m from a long, copper pipe that has a diameter of 2 cm and carries a current of 20 A.

53. ••Jerry wants to predict the magnetic field that a high-voltage line creates in his apartment. A current of 100 A passes through a wire that is 5 m from his window. Calculate the magnetic field.

How does the field compare to the magnitude of Earth's magnetic field of about 5×10^{-5} T in New York City? SSM

54. •A solenoid with 25 turns per centimeter carries a current of 25 mA. What is the magnetic field in the interior of the coils?

55. •You want to wind a solenoid that is 3.5 cm in diameter, is 16 cm long, and will have a magnetic field of 0.0250 T when a current of 3.0 A is in it. What total length of wire do you need?

56. •••A coaxial cable consists of a solid inner conductor of radius R_i, surrounded by a concentric outer conducting shell of radius R_o. Insulating material fills the space between the conductors. The inner conductor carries current to the right, and the outer conductor carries the same current to the left down the outer surface of the cable, as shown in Figure 19-38. Using Ampère's law, derive an expression for the magnetic field in three separate regions of space: inside the inner conductor, between the two conductors, and outside of the outer conductor.

Figure 19-38 Problem 56

19-8 Two current-carrying wires exert magnetic forces on each other

57. •If wire 1 carries 2.00 A of current north, wire 2 carries 3.60 A of current south, and the two wires are separated by 1.40 m, calculate the force (magnitude and direction) acting on a 1.00-cm section of wire 1 due to wire 2. SSM

58. •What is the net force on the rectangular loop of wire that is 2.00 cm wide, is 6.00 cm long, and is located 2.00 cm from a long, straight wire that carries $i = 40.0$ A of current as shown in Figure 19-39? Assume a current of 20.0 A is in the loop.

Figure 19-39 Problem 58

59. ••The fasteners on overhead power lines are 50.0 cm long. What force must they be able to withstand if two high-voltage lines are 2.00 m apart, each carrying 2500 A in the same direction?

General Problems

60. ••Horizontal electric power lines supported by vertical poles can carry large currents. Assume that Earth's magnetic field runs parallel to the surface of the ground from south to north with a magnitude of 0.50×10^{-4} T and that the supporting poles are 32 m apart. Find the magnitude and direction of the force that Earth's magnetic field exerts on a 32-m segment of wire carrying 95 A if the current runs (a) from north to south, (b) from east to west, or (c) toward the northwest making an angle of 30° north

of east. (d) Are any of the above forces large enough to have an appreciable effect on the power lines?

61. ••A levitating train is three cars long (180 m) and has a mass of 100 metric tons (1 metric ton = 1000 kg). The current in the superconducting wires is about 500 kA, and even though the traditional design calls for many small coils of wire, assume for this problem that there is a 180-m-long wire carrying the current. Find the size of the magnetic field needed to levitate the train.

62. ••An electron and a proton have the same kinetic energy upon entering a region of constant magnetic field and their velocity vectors are perpendicular to the magnetic field. Suppose the magnetic field is strong enough to allow the particles to circle in the field. What is the ratio of the radii of their circular paths r_p/r_e?

63. •••In Figure 19-40, which shows a mass spectrometer, a particle with charge $-e = -1.60 \times 10^{-19}$ C enters a region of magnetic field that has a strength of 0.00242 T, into the page. The velocity of the particle is confirmed with a velocity selector. The electric field is 90,000 V/m (down) and the magnetic field is 0.0053 T (into page) in the velocity selector. If the radius of curvature of the particle is 4.00 cm, use the information in this problem to calculate the mass of the particle. SSM

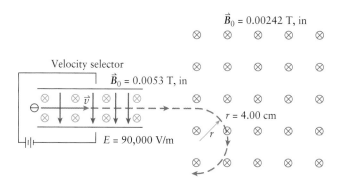

Figure 19-40 Problem 63

64. ••Biology The National High Magnetic Field Laboratory holds the world record for creating the largest magnetic field. Their long-pulse magnet produced a magnetic field of 60 T. To see if such a strong magnetic field could pose health risks for nearby workers, calculate the maximum acceleration the field could produce on Na^+ ions (of mass 3.8×10^{-26} kg) in blood traveling through the aorta. The speed of blood is highly variable, but 50 cm/s is reasonable in the aorta. Does your result indicate that it would be dangerous to expose workers to such a large magnetic field?

65. ••During electrical storms, a bolt of lightning can transfer 10 C of charge in 2.0 μs (the amount and time can vary considerably). We can model such a bolt as a very long current-carrying wire. (a) What is the magnetic field 1.0 m from such a bolt? What is the field 1.0 km away? How do the fields compare with Earth's magnetic field? (b) Compare the fields in part (a) with the magnetic field produced by a typical household current of 10 A in a very long wire at the same distances from the wire as in (a). (c) How close would you have to get to the wire in part (b) for its magnetic field to be the same as the field produced by the lightning bolt at 1.0 km from the bolt?

66. •A straight wire carries a current of 8.00 A toward the top of the page. What are the magnitude and direction of the magnetic field at point *P*, which is 8.00 cm to the right of the wire as shown in **Figure 19-41**?

Figure 19-41 Problem 66

67. ••A long, straight wire carries a current as shown in **Figure 19-42**. A charged particle moving parallel to the wire experiences a force of 0.80 N at point *P*. Assuming the same charge and same velocity, what would be the magnitude of the magnetic force on the charge at point *S*?

Figure 19-42 Problem 67

68. ••Two long, straight wires parallel to the *x* axis are at $y = \pm2.5$ cm (**Figure 19-43**). Each wire carries a current of 16 A in the $+x$ direction. Calculate the magnetic field on the *y* axis at (a) $y = 0$, (b) $y = 1.0$ cm, and (c) $y = 4.0$ cm.

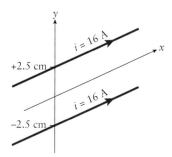

Figure 19-43 Problem 68

69. ••**Medical** Transcranial magnetic stimulation (TMS) is a noninvasive method to stimulate the brain using magnetic fields. It is used in treating strokes, Parkinson's disease, depression, and other physical conditions. In the procedure, a circular coil is placed on the side of the forehead to generate a magnetic field inside the brain. Although values can vary, a typical coil would be about 15 cm in diameter and contain 250 thin circular windings. The magnetic field in the cortex (3.0 cm from the coil measured along a line perpendicular to the coil at its center) is typically 0.50 T. (a) What current in the coil is needed to produce the desired magnetic field inside the brain? (b) What is the magnetic field at the center of the coil at the forehead? (c) If the current needed in part (a) seems too large, how could you easily achieve the same magnetic field with a smaller current?

70. ••A wire of mass 40 g slides without friction on two horizontal conducting rails spaced 0.8 m apart. A steady current of 100 A is in the circuit formed by the wire and the rails. A uniform magnetic field of 1.2 T, directed into the plane of the drawing, acts on it. (a) In which direction in **Figure 19-44** will the wire accelerate? (b) What is the magnetic force on the wire? (c) How long must the rails be if the wire, starting from rest, is to reach a speed of 200 m/s? (d) If the magnetic field were directed out of the page, how would your answers differ?

(e) What if the magnetic field were directed toward the top of the drawing?

Figure 19-44 Problem 70

71. ••A small 20-turn current loop with a 4.00-cm diameter is suspended in a region with a magnetic field of 1000 G, with the plane of the loop parallel with the magnetic field direction. (a) What is the current in the loop if the torque exerted by the magnetic field on the loop is 4.00×10^{-5} N · m? (b) Describe the subsequent motion of the loop if it is allowed to rotate.

72. ••A long, straight wire carries a current of 1.2 A toward the south. A second, parallel wire carries a current of 3.8 A toward the north and is 2.8 cm from the first wire. What is the magnetic force per unit length each wire exerts on the other?

73. •••Two straight conducting rods, which are 1.0 m long, exactly parallel, and separated by 0.85 mm, are connected by an external voltage source and a 17-Ω resistance, as shown in **Figure 19-45**. The 0.5-Ω rod "floats" above the 2.5-Ω rod, in equilibrium. If the mass of each rod is 25 g, what must be the potential of the voltage source? SSM

Figure 19-45 Problem 73

74. ••**Medical** When operated on a household 110-V line, typical hair dryers draw about 1650 W of power. We can model the current as a long, straight wire in the handle. During use, the current is about 3.0 cm from the user's head. (a) What is the current in the dryer? (b) What is the resistance of the dryer? (c) What magnetic field does the dryer produce at the user's head? Compare the field with Earth's magnetic field to decide if we should have health concerns about the magnetic field created when using a hair dryer.

75. ••Three very long, straight wires lie at the corners of a square of side *d*, as shown in **Figure 19-46**. The magnitudes of the currents in the three wires are the same, but the two diagonally opposite currents are directed into the page while the other one is directed outward. Derive an expression for the magnetic field (magnitude and direction) at the fourth corner of the square.

Figure 19-46 Problem 75

76. ••A 2.0-m lamp cord leads from the 110-V outlet to a lamp having a 75-W lightbulb. The cord consists of two insulated parallel wires 4.0 mm apart and held together by the insulation. One wire carries the current into the bulb, and the other carries it out. What is the magnitude of the magnetic field the cord produces (a) midway between the two wires and (b) 2.0 mm from one of the wires in the same plane in which the two wires lie? (c) Compare each of the fields in parts (a) and (b) with Earth's magnetic field (0.5×10^{-4} T). (d) What magnetic force (magnitude and direction) do the two wires exert on one another? Is the force large enough to stress the insulation holding the wires together?

77. ••Some people have raised concerns about the magnetic fields produced by current-carrying high-voltage lines in residential neighborhoods. Currents in such lines can be up to 100 A. Suppose you have such a line near your house. If the wires are supported horizontally 5.0 m above the ground on vertical poles and your living room is 12 m from the base of the poles, what magnetic field strength does the wire produce in your living room if it carries 100 A? Express your answer in teslas and as a multiple of Earth's magnetic field. Does the magnetic field from such wires seem strong enough to cause health concerns? SSM

78. ••**Medical** Magnetoencephalography (MEG) is a technique for measuring changes in the magnetic field of the brain caused by external stimuli such as touching the body or viewing images of food. Such a change in the field occurs due to electrical activity (current) in the brain. During the process, magnetic sensors are placed on the skin to measure the magnetic field at that location. Typical field strengths are a few femtoteslas (1 femtotesla = 1 fT = 10^{-15} T). An adult brain is about 140 mm wide, divided into two sections (called hemispheres although the brain is not truly spherical) each about 70 mm wide. We can model the current in one hemisphere as a circular loop, 65 mm in diameter, just inside the brain. The sensor is placed so that it is along the axis of the loop 2.0 cm from the center. A reasonable magnetic field is 5.0 fT at the sensor. According to this model, (a) what is the current in the brain and (b) what is the magnetic field at the center of the hemisphere of the brain?

79. ••Helmholtz coils are composed of two coils of wire that have their centers on the same axis, separated by a distance that is equal to the radius of the coils (**Figure 19-47**). The coils have N turns of wire that carry a current of i in the same direction. If one coil is centered at the origin, and the other at $x = R$, derive expressions for the net magnetic field due to the coils at the points (a) $x = R/2$ and (b) $x = 2R$.

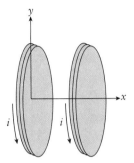

Figure 19-47 Problem 79

80. ••Geophysicists may use the gauss unit for magnetic field (10^4 G = 1 T). Earth's magnetic field at the equator can be taken as 0.7 G directed north. At the center of a flat circular coil that has 10 turns of wire and is 1.4 m in diameter, the coil's magnetic field exactly cancels Earth's field. (a) What must be the current in the coil? (b) How should the coil be oriented?

81. •••**Biology** Migratory birds use Earth's magnetic field to guide them. Some people are concerned that human-caused magnetic fields could interfere with bird navigation. Suppose that a pair of parallel high-voltage lines, each carrying 100 A, are 3.00 m apart and lie in the same horizontal plane. Find the magnitude and direction of the magnetic field the lines produce at a point 15.0 m above them equidistant from both lines in each of the following cases. (a) The lines run in the north–south direction and both currents run from north to south. (b) Both lines run in the north–south direction and the current in the eastern line runs northward while the current in the western line runs southward. (c) The lines run in the east–west direction, and both currents run from west to east. (d) Is it reasonable to think that the fields caused by the wires are likely to interfere with bird migration?

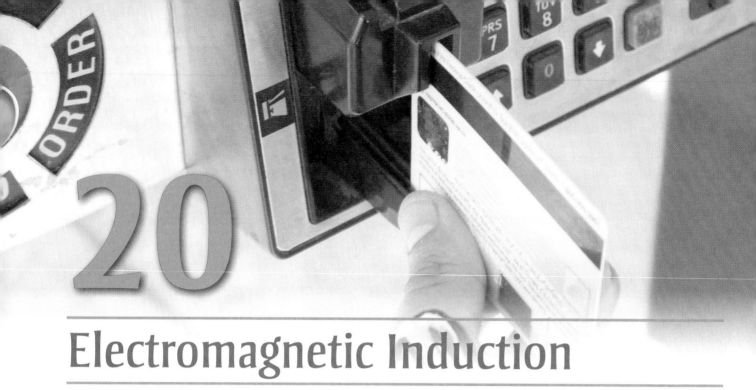

20 Electromagnetic Induction

What do you think?

The stripe on the back of a credit card is magnetized in a pattern that encodes your account information. A credit card reader contains a loop of wire, and when you swipe the card through the reader, the magnetized card's motion generates an electric current in the wire that sends a signal to the credit card company. To make this current flow, what kind of force must act on electrons in the wires of the card reader? (a) A magnetic force; (b) an electric force; (c) a combination of electric and magnetic forces.

In this chapter, your goals are to:
- (20-1) Explain the importance of electromagnetic induction.
- (20-2) Describe what is meant by a motional emf and an induced emf.
- (20-3) Explain what determines the magnitude and direction of an emf in a circuit with a changing magnetic flux.
- (20-4) Define the key properties of an ac generator.

To master this chapter, you should review:
- (6-2) The work done by a constant force.
- (12-3) Simple harmonic motion.
- (16-6) The electric flux through an area.
- (18-6) The electric power for a resistor.
- (19-3, The magnetic force on a moving charged particle and on a
- 19-5) current-carrying wire.
- (19-7) The magnetic field produced by a current-carrying loop.

20-1 The world runs on electromagnetic induction

We've discussed electric circuits in which the current is caused by the emf provided by a battery. But many of the electric circuits around you are *alternating-current* circuits in which the current constantly changes direction. That includes the current in light fixtures, toasters, electric fans, and other devices plugged into wall sockets. (Alternating current also indirectly powers mobile devices like cell phones and laptop computers. These devices have batteries, but the batteries are recharged by plugging them into a wall socket.) What kind of emf produces an alternating current?

The answer to this question comes from a remarkable discovery made by physicists around 1830: *If the magnetic field in a region of space changes, the change gives rise to an electric field.* This electric field, called an *induced* field, is very different in character from the electric field produced by point charges that we described in Chapter 16: An induced electric field does not point away from positive charges and toward negative charges, but instead has field lines that form closed loops like magnetic field lines. That's just what's needed for that induced electric field to push charges around a loop of wire and generate an electric current. As we'll see later in this chapter, it's easy to make this induced electric field flip its direction back and forth, which makes a current that flips back and forth—in other words, an alternating current. The vast amount of electric current used by our technological civilization is produced in this way (Figure 20-1a).

We use the term **electromagnetic induction** for the process whereby a changing magnetic field induces an electric field. (The word *electromagnetic* shows that this

An electric generator produces current by electromagnetic induction: Coils of wire move relative to a magnetic field, which generates an emf in the coils. The motion can be powered by the wind, as in these wind turbines.

A changing magnetic field applied to the brain induces an electric field there, causing electric currents. Areas in red are where the currents are strongest.

Figure 20-1 **Electromagnetic induction** Two examples of the phenomenon of electromagnetic induction, in which electric currents are induced by the presence of a changing magnetic flux.

(a)

(b)

process involves both electric and magnetic fields.) Electromagnetic induction has many applications beyond producing an alternating current to be delivered to wall sockets. It's how a credit card reader decodes the information on the card's magnetized strip (see the photo that opens this chapter). It's also at the heart of a relatively new medical technique called *transcranial magnetic stimulation* (TMS), which allows physicians to stimulate electrical activity in the brain without sticking electrodes to the scalp or inserting them through the skull. In TMS, a time-varying magnetic field is produced inside the brain by current-carrying coils around the head. This causes an induced electric field, which in turn causes currents to flow within the brain (Figure 20-1b). TMS has been used with some success to treat cases of depression that have not responded to more conventional therapy.

In this chapter we'll begin by describing the relationship between a changing magnetic flux and the electric field that it induces. We'll introduce two important laws that describe electromagnetic induction. The first of these, Faraday's law, will tell us how the emf that appears in a closed loop (such as an electric circuit) due to an induced electric field is related to the rate of change of the magnetic flux through the loop. The second, Lenz's law, will tell us the direction of this induced emf. We'll see how induced emf makes possible the important device called a *generator*, which converts mechanical energy into electric energy and creates an alternating emf. (Each of the wind turbines shown in Figure 20-1 uses its spinning blades to run a generator.) In Chapter 21 we'll see how all of these ideas explain the behavior of alternating-current circuits.

> **Take-Home Message for Section 20-1**
>
> ✔ In electromagnetic induction, a time-varying magnetic flux in a certain region gives rise to an electric field in that same region.
>
> ✔ Electromagnetic induction is used to produce an alternating current.

20-2 A changing magnetic flux creates an electric field

Figure 20-2 shows an experiment that we can understand with the physics we already know. A loop of wire with an attached ammeter (a device for measuring the current in the loop) is moved toward the south pole of a stationary magnet. No current flows if the loop is held stationary. That's not surprising, since there's no source of emf connected to the loop. But a current *does* flow in the loop when it is moved toward the magnet's south pole (Figure 20-2a), and flows in the opposite direction when the loop is moved away from the magnet's south pole (Figure 20-2b). What's happening is that the mobile charges within the loop are moving along with the loop through the magnetic field of the bar magnet and so experience a magnetic force that pushes the charges around the loop (Figure 20-2c). Reversing the direction in which the loop and its charges move also reverses the direction of the magnetic force, so the charges are pushed in the opposite direction and the current direction reverses (Figure 20-2d). In either case we say that the magnetic force on the mobile charges is equivalent to an emf that makes the current flow. There is no magnetic force, and hence no emf, if the loop and its charges are at rest. (Recall from Section 19-2 that magnetic forces only act on *moving* charges.) Because the loop must be in motion in order for the emf to appear, we call it a **motional emf**.

Figure 20-2 A loop of wire moving with respect to a magnet If a loop of wire moves toward or away from a magnet, a current flows in the loop. The current is caused by magnetic forces.

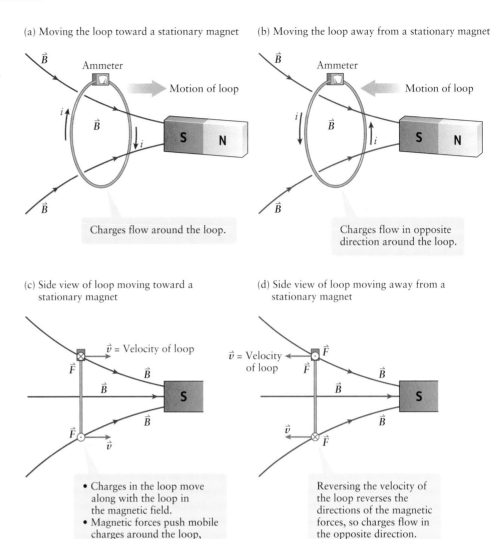

(a) Moving the loop toward a stationary magnet

Charges flow around the loop.

(b) Moving the loop away from a stationary magnet

Charges flow in opposite direction around the loop.

(c) Side view of loop moving toward a stationary magnet

• Charges in the loop move along with the loop in the magnetic field.
• Magnetic forces push mobile charges around the loop, causing a current.

(d) Side view of loop moving away from a stationary magnet

Reversing the velocity of the loop reverses the directions of the magnetic forces, so charges flow in the opposite direction.

Figure 20-3 shows a very similar experiment that involves entirely new and different physics. Now we hold the loop stationary and move the south pole of the magnet either toward the loop (Figure 20-3a) or away from the loop (Figure 20-3b). In this case there can be no magnetic force on the mobile charges within the loop, because those charges are at rest in the stationary loop. Nonetheless, there is an emf in the loop and a current flows around the loop in response, but only when the magnet is moving relative to the loop. Since there is no magnetic force in this situation, it must be that the emf is due to an *electric* force on the mobile charges (Figures 20-3c and 20-3d). What's happening is that when the magnet is moving, the magnetic field strength at the location of the loop is changing: It increases when the magnet's south pole moves toward the loop (Figure 20-3a) and decreases when the magnet's south pole moves away from the loop (Figure 20-3b). So this experiment shows that an electric field is *induced* by the changing magnetic field. For this reason we call the emf in the experiment of Figure 20-3 an **induced emf**. We use the term *electromagnetic induction* for any situation in which a changing magnetic field causes, or induces, an electric field.

Although the experiments in Figures 20-2 and 20-3 are different, they have the *same* result: Whether the loop moves toward the stationary magnet at 1 m/s as in Figure 20-2a or the magnet moves toward the stationary loop at 1 m/s as in Figure 20-3a, the same emf appears in the loop. In fact, the same emf appears if the magnet and loop are both moving, as long as the magnet and loop approach each other at a relative speed of 1 m/s. Since the result is the same in each of these cases, we should be able to describe all of these effects in terms of a single equation. But what equation is that?

(a) Moving the magnet toward a stationary loop

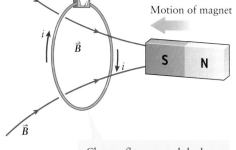

Motion of magnet

Charges flow around the loop.

(b) Moving the magnet away from a stationary loop

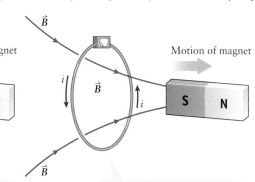

Motion of magnet

Charges flow in the opposite direction around the loop.

Figure 20-3 A magnet moving with respect to a loop of wire If a magnet moves toward or away from a loop of wire, a current flows in the loop. Magnetic forces cannot explain why this happens, so electric forces must be present to produce the current.

(c) Side view of magnet moving toward a stationary loop

$\vec{v}$ = Velocity of magnet

(d) Side view of magnet moving away from a stationary loop

$\vec{v}$ = Velocity of magnet

- Charges in the loop experience electric forces.
- These forces push mobile charges around the loop, causing a current.

Reversing the velocity of the magnet reverses the directions of the electric forces, so charges flow in the opposite direction.

It turns out that a simple way to describe the emf in any of these situations is in terms of the change in *magnetic flux* through the loop in Figures 20-2 and 20-3. We define this in the same way that we defined *electric* flux in Section 16-6: It's the area A of the surface outlined by the loop, multiplied by $B \cos \theta$, the component of the magnetic field that's perpendicular to that surface (see part (a) of **Figure 20-4**). In equation form, the **magnetic flux** Φ_B ("phi-sub-B") through the loop is

Area of the surface

Angle between the magnetic field and the perpendicular to the surface

Magnetic flux through a surface

$$\Phi_B = AB_\perp = AB \cos \theta$$

The component of magnetic field perpendicular to the surface

Magnitude of the magnetic field

Magnetic flux (20-1)

(The subscript B reminds us that this is the flux of the magnetic field $\vec{B}$.) As parts (b) and (c) of Figure 20-4 show, the flux Φ_B can be positive or negative. Note that the choice of positive x direction is arbitrary; in Figure 20-4 we chose the positive x direction to be upward, so Φ_B is positive for the case shown in Figure 20-4b and negative for the case shown in Figure 20-4c. Had we chosen the positive x direction to be downward, we would have had $\Phi_B < 0$ in Figure 20-4b and $\Phi_B > 0$ in Figure 20-4c. It doesn't matter which one we choose, since the physics will turn out to be the same in either case. (It's much as in Chapter 2, where we had to make a choice of positive x direction for analyzing motion in a straight line. The actual motion didn't depend on which direction we chose to be positive and which to be negative.)

$\sqrt{x}$ *See the Math Tutorial for more information on trigonometry*

Figure 20-4 Magnetic flux (a) The magnetic flux through a loop. The flux is (b) most positive when $\vec{B}$ points along the perpendicular to the loop and (c) most negative when $\vec{B}$ points opposite to the perpendicular.

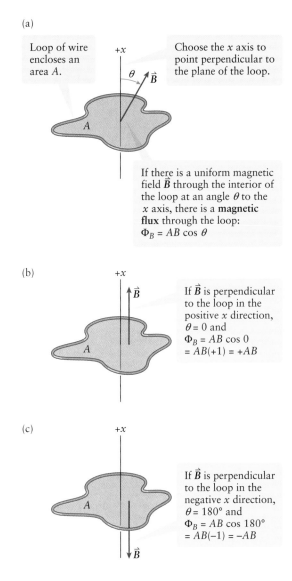

(a)

Loop of wire encloses an area A.

Choose the x axis to point perpendicular to the plane of the loop.

If there is a uniform magnetic field $\vec{B}$ through the interior of the loop at an angle θ to the x axis, there is a **magnetic flux** through the loop:
$\Phi_B = AB \cos \theta$

(b)

If $\vec{B}$ is perpendicular to the loop in the positive x direction, $\theta = 0$ and
$\Phi_B = AB \cos 0$
$= AB(+1) = +AB$

(c)

If $\vec{B}$ is perpendicular to the loop in the negative x direction, $\theta = 180°$ and
$\Phi_B = AB \cos 180°$
$= AB(-1) = -AB$

In Figures 20-2 and 20-3 the magnetic field is not uniform over the area enclosed by the loop, and so the perpendicular component $B_\perp = B \cos \theta$ has different values at different points on this area. In such a case $B_\perp$ in Equation 20-1 is the perpendicular component of the magnetic field *averaged* over the area A enclosed by the loop. Note that if the loop is actually a coil with N turns of wire, the net magnetic flux through the coil is N multiplied by the flux through one turn of the coil.

If the magnet and loop in Figures 20-2 and 20-3 are not moving with respect to each other, the magnetic flux through the loop remains the same. In this case there is no emf and no current in the loop. The flux changes, however, when either the loop moves relative to the magnet (Figure 20-2) or the magnet moves relative to the loop (Figure 20-3). In these cases there *is* an emf in the loop and the current. This suggests that *an emf appears in a loop when the magnetic flux through that loop changes*. This observation is known as **Faraday's law of induction**, named for the nineteenth-century English physicist Michael Faraday:

Magnitude of the induced or motional emf in a loop

Change in the magnetic flux through the surface outlined by the loop

Faraday's law of induction
(20-2)

$$|\varepsilon| = \left| \frac{\Delta \Phi_B}{\Delta t} \right|$$

Time interval over which the change in magnetic flux takes place

This law states that the magnitude of the emf that appears in a loop is equal to the magnitude of the *rate of change* of the magnetic flux through the loop. If a large change in flux $\Delta\Phi_B$ happens in a short time interval Δt, the resulting emf has a large magnitude; if the change in flux is relatively small and happens over a long time interval, the resulting emf has a small magnitude.

Note that Equation 20-2 tells us only the *magnitude* of the emf, not its direction. In the following section we'll see how the direction is determined.

> **Watch Out!** It's not the magnetic flux that causes an emf, but the rate at which the flux changes.
>
> The mere presence of magnetic flux through a loop does not cause an emf to appear in the loop. If a flux is present but does not change, such as what happens when a magnet and loop are held stationary with respect to each other, there is no resulting emf. An emf only appears when the flux *changes*, such as when the magnet and loop in Figures 20-2 and 20-3 move either toward or away from each other.

In the following example we'll check Faraday's law. We'll do this by considering a situation in which we can use our knowledge of magnetic forces to calculate the emf, then compare this to the emf calculated using Equation 20-2.

Go to Interactive Exercise 20-1 for more practice dealing with motional emf

Example 20-1 Changing Magnetic Flux I: A Sliding Bar in a Magnetic Field

A copper bar of length L slides at a constant speed v along stationary, U-shaped copper rails (Figure 20-5). A uniform magnetic field of magnitude B is directed perpendicular to the plane of the bar and rails. The moving bar and stationary rails form a closed circuit, and an emf is produced in this circuit because the wire is moving in a magnetic field. Determine the emf in the circuit (a) by using the expression for the magnetic force on a charge in the moving wire and (b) by using Faraday's law of induction, Equation 20-2.

Copper bar slides on the rails at constant velocity $\vec{v}$.

A uniform magnetic field $\vec{B}$ points perpendicular to the plane of the rails.

Figure 20-5 A sliding copper bar What emf is generated in the bar as it slides in the presence of a magnetic field $\vec{B}$?

Set Up

For a battery, the magnitude of the emf equals the change in electric potential (potential energy per charge) for a charge that traverses the battery. That is, it's equal to the *work per charge* that the battery does on charges that travel from one terminal to the other. We'll use the same idea in part (a) to calculate the emf in terms of the work done by the magnetic force on a charged particle that travels the length of the moving bar. In part (b) we'll find the emf by instead using Equation 20-2. While the magnetic field doesn't change, the area of the loop outlined by the moving bar and the rails *does* change, and so the magnetic flux through this loop changes.

Magnetic force on a moving charged particle:

$$F = |q|vB \sin\theta \qquad (19\text{-}1)$$

Work done by a constant force that points in the same direction as the straight-line displacement:

$$W = Fd \qquad (6\text{-}1)$$

Magnetic flux:

$$\Phi_B = AB_\perp = AB \cos\theta \qquad (20\text{-}1)$$

Faraday's law of induction:

$$|\varepsilon| = \left|\frac{\Delta\Phi_B}{\Delta t}\right| \qquad (20\text{-}2)$$

Solve

(a) Find the magnetic force on a charged particle moving along with the copper bar.

For a positive charge q moving with the bar, the direction of the velocity $\vec{v}$ is perpendicular to the direction of the magnetic field $\vec{B}$. So $\theta = 90°$ in Equation 19-1, and the magnetic force $\vec{F}$ on such a charge has magnitude

$$F = qvB \sin 90° = qvB (1) = qvB$$

The direction of $\vec{F}$ is perpendicular to the directions of both $\vec{v}$ and $\vec{B}$, and so is directed along the length of the moving bar.

Use the magnetic force on a charged particle to find the emf produced in the bar.

The magnetic force $\vec{F}$ on a charge q causes it to move along the length L of the bar. Since $\vec{F}$ is in the same direction as the displacement of the charge, the work done on the charge as it travels this length is

$$W = FL = qvBL$$

The magnitude of the emf in the bar equals the work done per charge:

$$|\varepsilon| = \frac{W}{q} = \frac{qvBL}{q} = vBL$$

(b) Find the emf using Faraday's law of induction.

The magnetic field $\vec{B}$ points perpendicular to the plane of the loop outlined by the moving copper bar and the copper rails. If the area of this loop is A and we take the positive x direction to point out of the plane of the above figure (in the same direction as $\vec{B}$), then $\theta = 0$ in Equation 20-1. The magnetic flux through the loop is then

$$\Phi_B = AB \cos 0 = AB(1) = AB$$

The magnetic field is constant, but the area A changes with time because the bar moves. The speed v of the bar is just the distance Δd that the bar moves divided by the time Δt that it takes to move that distance, so

$$v = \frac{\Delta d}{\Delta t} \quad \text{and} \quad \Delta d = v \Delta t$$

During time Δt the area A of the loop outlined by the moving bar and rails increases by an amount $\Delta A = L \Delta d = Lv \Delta t$. Therefore the change in magnetic flux through the loop during this time is

$$\Delta \Phi_B = (\Delta A)B = (Lv \Delta t)B = vBL \Delta t$$

From Equation 20-2, the magnitude of the emf in the loop is

$$|\varepsilon| = \left| \frac{\Delta \Phi_B}{\Delta t} \right| = \left| \frac{vBL \Delta t}{\Delta t} \right| = vBL$$

Reflect

We find the same expression for the emf in both parts (a) and (b), as we must. We certainly haven't *proved* that Equation 20-2 is correct in all cases where an emf appears due to a wire moving in a magnetic field (a motional emf) or due to a changing magnetic field (an induced emf). But we do have added confidence that Equation 20-2 is valid, and a host of experiments backs up this conclusion.

Example 20-2 Changing Magnetic Flux II: A Varying Magnetic Field

A uniform magnetic field of magnitude $B = 1.50$ T is directed at an angle of 60.0° to the plane of a circular loop of copper wire. The loop is 3.50 cm in diameter. (a) What is the magnetic flux through the loop? What is the induced emf in the loop if the magnetic field decreases to zero (b) in 10.0 s or (c) in 0.100 s?

Set Up

The magnetic flux is given by Equation 20-1. Note that θ in this equation is the angle between the direction of magnetic field $\vec{B}$ and the *perpendicular* to the loop, so $\theta = 90.0° - 60.0° = 30.0°$. The magnetic flux through the loop changes when the field magnitude changes, so an emf will be induced in the loop. We'll use Equation 20-2 to calculate the magnitude of this induced emf.

Magnetic flux:

$$\Phi_B = AB_\perp = AB \cos \theta \qquad (20\text{-}1)$$

Area of a circle of radius r:

$$A = \pi r^2$$

Faraday's law of induction:

$$|\varepsilon| = \left| \frac{\Delta \Phi_B}{\Delta t} \right| \qquad (20\text{-}2)$$

Solve

(a) Find the area of the loop, then use Equation 20-1 to calculate the magnetic flux through the loop.

The radius r of the loop is one-half of the diameter:

$$r = \frac{1}{2}(3.50 \text{ cm}) = 1.75 \text{ cm} = 1.75 \times 10^{-2} \text{ m}$$

The area of the loop is

$$A = \pi r^2 = \pi (1.75 \times 10^{-2} \text{ m})^2 = 9.62 \times 10^{-4} \text{ m}^2$$

From Equation 20-1, the magnetic flux through the loop is

$$\Phi_B = AB \cos \theta = (9.62 \times 10^{-4} \text{ m}^2)(1.50 \text{ T}) \cos 30.0°$$
$$= 1.25 \times 10^{-3} \text{ T} \cdot \text{m}^2$$

(b) The change in magnetic flux is the final value (zero) minus the initial value that we found in (a). Equation 20-2 tells us that to find the magnitude of the induced emf, we divide this change by the time $\Delta t = 10.0$ s over which the flux change takes place.

The change in magnetic flux is

$$\Delta \Phi_B = (\text{final flux}) - (\text{initial flux})$$
$$= 0 - 1.25 \times 10^{-3} \text{ T} \cdot \text{m}^2 = -1.25 \times 10^{-3} \text{ T} \cdot \text{m}^2$$

If the flux decreases to zero in $\Delta t = 10.0$ s, the magnitude of the induced emf is

$$|\varepsilon| = \left| \frac{\Delta \Phi_B}{\Delta t} \right| = \left| \frac{-1.25 \times 10^{-3} \text{ T} \cdot \text{m}^2}{10.0 \text{ s}} \right|$$

$$= 1.25 \times 10^{-4} \text{ T} \cdot \text{m}^2/\text{s} = 1.25 \times 10^{-4} \text{ V}$$

(c) Repeat part (b) with $\Delta t = 0.100$ s.

If the flux decreases to zero in just $\Delta t = 0.100$ s, the magnitude of the induced emf is

$$|\varepsilon| = \left| \frac{\Delta \Phi_B}{\Delta t} \right| = \left| \frac{-1.25 \times 10^{-3} \text{ T} \cdot \text{m}^2}{0.100 \text{ s}} \right|$$

$$= 1.25 \times 10^{-2} \text{ T} \cdot \text{m}^2/\text{s} = 1.25 \times 10^{-2} \text{ V}$$

Reflect

The induced emf is 100 times greater in part (c) than in part (b) because the same flux change takes place in 1/100 as much time. The faster the flux change, the greater the induced emf that results. Note that the emf is induced *only* during the time when the magnetic flux is changing. There is zero emf when the magnetic field is at its original value of 1.50 T, and there is zero emf when the magnetic field has stabilized at its final value of zero.

The emf in both cases is quite small because there is only a single turn of wire in the loop. If we replace the loop by a coil of the same diameter with 500 turns of wire, the induced emf is 500 times greater: $500 \times 1.25 \times 10^{-4}$ V = 0.0625 V in part (b), $500 \times 1.25 \times 10^{-2}$ V = 6.25 V in part (c). The key to generating a large induced emf is to have many turns of wire and a rapid change in magnetic flux.

In this example we chose the positive x direction to be upward, so that the angle θ between the magnetic field and the perpendicular to the loop was 30.0°. Can you show that we would have found the same results for emf had we chosen the positive x direction to be downward, so that $\theta = 150.0°$?

Suppose the loop in Example 20-2 were made out of wood rather than copper wire, but the magnetic field changes in the same manner as in part (b) of Example 20-2. Compared to the emf calculated in part (b) of Example 20-2, the emf induced in the wooden loop would be (a) zero; (b) much smaller, but not zero; (c) slightly less; (d) the same; (e) greater.

Take-Home Message for Section 20-2

✔ A motional emf appears in a conductor that moves in a magnetic field. The force that produces the emf is a magnetic one.

✔ An induced emf appears in any loop subjected to a changing magnetic field. The force that produces the emf is an electric one.

✔ Both motional emfs and induced emfs can be described by Faraday's law of induction: The magnitude of the emf in a loop is equal to the absolute value of the change in magnetic flux through the loop, divided by the time over which the change takes place.

20-3 Lenz's law describes the direction of the induced emf

Equation 20-2 tells us the *magnitude* of the emf that appears in a loop when there is a change in magnetic flux through that loop: $|\varepsilon| = |\Delta\Phi_B/\Delta t|$. It does not, however, tell us the *direction* of that emf—that is, the direction in which the emf tends to make current flow around that loop. As we'll see, there's a simple rule for determining this direction that works for both motional emfs (caused by a conductor moving in a magnetic field) and induced emfs (caused by a conductor being exposed to a changing magnetic field).

To learn about this rule, let's think again about the loop of wire in Figure 20-2. We saw in Section 20-2 that when the loop is moved toward or away from a bar magnet an emf is set up in the loop and a current flows. That's because the mobile charges in the wire experience magnetic forces as they move with the wire in the presence of the magnet's field $\vec{B}_{\text{magnet}}$. That's not the only magnetic field present in this situation, however. As we learned in Section 19-7, a current-carrying loop produces a magnetic field of its own. The direction of the field $\vec{B}_{\text{loop}}$ due to the loop depends on the direction of the current around the loop, and is given by a right-hand rule: Curl the fingers of your right hand around the loop in the direction of the current, and the extended thumb of your right hand will point in the direction of $\vec{B}_{\text{loop}}$ in the interior of the loop (see part (a) of Figure 20-6). So whenever an emf appears in a loop—either a motional emf as in Figure 20-2 or an induced emf as in Figure 20-3—the current produced by that emf generates a magnetic field $\vec{B}_{\text{loop}}$ whose direction depends on the direction of the current and emf. We call $\vec{B}_{\text{loop}}$ an **induced magnetic field**.

The field $\vec{B}_{\text{loop}}$ itself produces a magnetic flux through the loop, and it's the sense of this flux that will tell us the direction of the emf in the loop. Let's choose the positive x direction for the loop in Figure 20-6 to point to the right, perpendicular to the plane of the loop. If the loop is close to the south pole of a bar magnet as in Figure 20-6b, the field of the magnet causes a positive magnetic flux through the loop (the field $\vec{B}_{\text{magnet}}$ points generally to the right, in the positive x direction). If the loop moves toward the magnet as in the left-hand side of Figure 20-6b, the field $\vec{B}_{\text{magnet}}$ inside the loop increases and the positive flux increases. Experiment shows that the current induced in the loop gives rise to an induced magnetic field $\vec{B}_{\text{loop}}$ within the loop which points in the *opposite* direction to $\vec{B}_{\text{magnet}}$. So while the flux due to $\vec{B}_{\text{magnet}}$ becomes more positive, $\vec{B}_{\text{loop}}$ gives rise to a negative flux that opposes the change in the flux of $\vec{B}_{\text{magnet}}$. If instead the loop moves away from the magnet as in the right-hand side of Figure 20-6b, the field $\vec{B}_{\text{magnet}}$ inside the loop decreases and the positive flux decreases. In this case the direction of the induced current in the loop is reversed, as is the direction of the induced magnetic field $\vec{B}_{\text{loop}}$: Now $\vec{B}_{\text{loop}}$ inside the loop points in the *same* direction as $\vec{B}_{\text{magnet}}$. The magnetic flux due to $\vec{B}_{\text{loop}}$ is now positive, which opposes the negative change (decrease) in the flux of $\vec{B}_{\text{magnet}}$.

In both cases shown in Figure 20-6b the induced magnetic field is in a direction opposite to the *change* in flux of the external magnetic field (in this case, the field due to the bar magnet). Many experiments show that this is always the case, no matter whether the induced magnetic field is due to a motional emf, an induced emf, or a combination

(a)

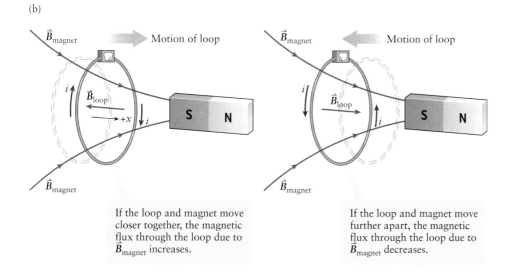

Figure 20-6 **Lenz's law** The current
induced in a loop by a change in flux
always acts to oppose the flux change.

- A current-carrying loop generates a magnetic field $\vec{B}_{\text{loop}}$.
- To find the direction of $\vec{B}_{\text{loop}}$, curl the fingers of your right hand around the loop in the direction of the current i. Your extended right thumb points in the direction of $\vec{B}_{\text{loop}}$ in the interior of the loop.
- $\vec{B}_{\text{loop}}$ itself causes a magnetic flux through the loop.

(b)

If the loop and magnet move closer together, the magnetic flux through the loop due to $\vec{B}_{\text{magnet}}$ increases.

If the loop and magnet move further apart, the magnetic flux through the loop due to $\vec{B}_{\text{magnet}}$ decreases.

of the two. The nineteenth-century Russian physicist Heinrich Lenz summarized these observations in a principle that we now call **Lenz's law**:

The direction of the magnetic field induced within a conducting loop opposes the change in magnetic flux that created it.

It's common to combine Faraday's law and Lenz's law into a single equation:

Induced or motional emf in a loop

Change in the magnetic flux through the surface outlined by the loop

$$\varepsilon = -\frac{\Delta \Phi_B}{\Delta t}$$

Time interval over which the change in magnetic flux takes place

The minus sign indicates that the current caused by the emf induces a magnetic field which opposes the change in flux.

Faraday's law and Lenz's law for induction
(20-3)

We can check Lenz's law by revisiting the sliding copper bar from Example 20-1 (Section 20-2). The upward external magnetic field of magnitude B causes a positive magnetic flux through the loop formed by the sliding bar and the rails on which it slides (Figure 20-7). The area enclosed by this loop increases as the bar slides to the right, so the positive flux increases as well. By Lenz's law an induced current will flow in the loop in order to generate an induced magnetic field that opposes this change in flux. So this induced magnetic field must point downward, and to produce that induced field the current in the loop must be clockwise as seen from above the loop. That's just the direction of current flow that we depicted in the figure that accompanies Example 20-1. So this situation is consistent with Lenz's law.

The sliding copper bar in Figure 20-7 illustrates another aspect of Lenz's law. Once the induced current is flowing in the bar, the external magnetic field exerts a force on that current. Using the right-hand rule for this force (see Section 19-5), we see that this force points opposite to the direction in which the bar is moving. In other words, this force *opposes* the motion that gives rise to the change in flux through the loop made up of the bar and rails. That's always the case when a conductor moves through a magnetic field: A current is induced in the conductor, and the magnetic field exerts a force on the current that opposes the motion of the conductor. We can summarize this in an alternative statement of Lenz's law:

When the magnetic flux through a loop changes, current flows in a direction that opposes that change.

In Example 20-1 we assumed that the bar slides on the rails at a constant speed. Our discussion shows that the bar won't do this on its own: Since a magnetic force opposes the motion of the bar, we need to apply an external force to keep the bar in motion. If we make the bar move faster, the magnetic flux through the loop changes more rapidly, the emf and resulting current in the loop are greater, and the magnetic force opposing the motion of the bar is greater. (The magnetic force on the bar turns out to be proportional to the speed of the bar, just like the drag force on a microscopic object moving through a fluid; see Section 5-5.) So we must apply a greater force to make the bar slide at a faster speed.

1 As the bar slides to the right, the upward magnetic flux through the loop increases.

Figure 20-7 A sliding copper bar revisited Lenz's law helps explain the direction in which current flows in this situation.

2 The induced current i produces an induced magnetic field $\vec{B}_{\text{loop}}$ that opposes the change in flux.

3 The magnetic force on the current in the moving bar opposes the bar's motion.

This same effect explains the phenomenon of *magnetic braking*. If you try to make a magnet move past a conductor or a conductor move past a magnet, currents appear in the conductor. (These are called *eddy currents*, since their pattern resembles that of eddies in a body of water. The conductor does *not* need to be in the form of a loop for these currents to appear.) The magnetic force that the magnet exerts on the eddy currents opposes the motion of the conductor relative to the magnet, and so by Newton's third law there is a force that opposes the motion of the magnet relative to the conductor. One important application of this is to amusement park rides where it's necessary to slow down a fast-moving object such as a roller coaster car. When the car enters the part of the ride where it's supposed to slow down, a copper fin on the car passes through powerful permanent magnets mounted on the track. Eddy currents arise in the fin, and the interaction between the eddy currents and the field of the permanent magnets causes a force that smoothly brings the car to a slow speed. The car is then stopped by conventional mechanical braking.

Eddy currents are also used in an *electromagnetic flowmeter*, a device that can measure the rate of blood flow in an artery. Blood is an electrical conductor; eddy currents are induced in the blood as it flows past magnets in the flowmeter. The device records the small but measurable magnetic fields due to these currents and uses them to determine the rate of flow. The advantage of an electromagnetic flowmeter over other methods for measuring blood flow rate is that it is noninvasive: No component of the device need be surgically introduced into the body.

Another application of eddy currents is magnetic induction tomography, a relatively new experimental technique for medical imaging. In this technique, changing magnetic fields created by coils placed near a part of the body induce eddy currents. Observing the fields produced by these eddy currents is a way to monitor brain swelling. Eddy currents can also be used for the controlled, repeated delivery of medication. A capsule containing the drug is implanted in the body; the capsule is made from a gel that heats up slightly when there are eddy currents, opening pores through which the medication is released. The advantage of this approach is that no implanted electronics are required.

? Got the Concept? 20-2 Induced Current I

In Figure 20-8 a rectangular loop of wire moves to the right into a region of constant, uniform magnetic field. The field points into the plane of the figure, in a direction perpendicular to the plane of the loop. When the loop is entering the field region as in Figure 20-8a, what is the direction of the current around the loop? (a) clockwise; (b) counterclockwise; (c) the current is zero; (d) not enough information given to decide.

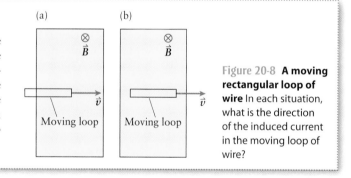

Figure 20-8 **A moving rectangular loop of wire** In each situation, what is the direction of the induced current in the moving loop of wire?

? Got the Concept? 20-3 Induced Current II

In Figure 20-8 a rectangular loop of wire moves to the right into a region of constant, uniform magnetic field. The field points into the plane of the figure, in a direction perpendicular to the plane of the loop. When the loop is moving and completely inside the field region as in Figure 20-8b, what is the direction of the current around the loop? (a) clockwise; (b) counterclockwise; (c) the current is zero; (d) not enough information given to decide.

Take-Home Message for Section 20-3

✔ An emf induced by a changing magnetic flux tends to cause a current to flow. This current generates a magnetic field of its own, called the induced magnetic field.

✔ The induced magnetic field is in a direction that opposes the change in flux that created the emf that gave rise to the induced field.

✔ Eddy currents arise whenever a conducting material, even a nonmagnetic one, moves relative to a magnetic field.

As the coil rotates with angular speed ω, the angle θ between the magnetic field $\vec{B}$ direction and the perpendicular to the coil changes: $\theta = \omega t + \phi$.

Figure 20-9 An ac generator As the coil rotates, an oscillating emf is generated in the turns of wire that make up the coil.

$\sqrt{x}$ *See the Math Tutorial for more information on trigonometry*

20-4 Faraday's law explains how alternating currents are generated

We learned in Section 18-2 about the importance of alternating current in technology. (If you're reading these words in a room lit by electric light, the light bulbs are powered by alternating current. If you're reading on a mobile device such as a tablet, the device's battery was charged by plugging it into a wall socket and using the alternating current delivered by that socket.) We now have the physics we need to understand how alternating current is produced.

Let's look at a coil of wire with N turns, each of which has area A. As Figure 20-9 shows, this coil is free to rotate around an axis. We place the coil in a region of uniform magnetic field $\vec{B}$, then rotate the coil at a constant angular speed ω. What happens? As the coil rotates, the magnetic flux through each turn of the coil changes, and so an emf is generated. The total emf is N times greater than that due to a single turn of wire. As we will see, this is an alternating emf of just the sort required to generate an alternating current. That's why a rotating coil of the sort shown in Figure 20-9 is called an **ac generator**.

We begin by writing an equation for the magnetic flux through the rotating coil. The angle θ between the magnetic field $\vec{B}$ and the perpendicular to the coil changes as the coil rotates:

$$\theta = \omega t + \phi \tag{20-4}$$

In Equation 20-4 ϕ is the value of the angle at $t = 0$. From Equation 20-1, the magnetic flux through the N turns of the coil is

$$\Phi_B = NAB \cos \theta = NAB \cos(\omega t + \phi) \tag{20-5}$$

When $\theta = \omega t + \phi = 0$ so $\cos \theta = 1$, the perpendicular to the coil is in the same direction as $\vec{B}$ and the flux has its most positive value $\Phi_B = NAB$; when $\theta = \omega t + \phi = \pi/2$ so $\cos \theta = 0$, the coil is edge-on to the magnetic field and the flux is zero; when $\theta = \omega t + \phi = \pi$ and $\cos \theta = -1$, the perpendicular to the coil points opposite to $\vec{B}$ and the flux has its most negative value $\Phi_B = -NAB$; and so on. So the magnetic flux varies with time, and it follows that there will be an emf in the coil.

Faraday's law and Lenz's law (Equation 20-3) tell us that the emf is equal to the negative of the rate of change of Φ_B. We actually know how to find the rate of change of a cosine function like that in Equation 20-5. In Section 12-3 we saw that the position of an object undergoing simple harmonic motion with amplitude A is given by

$$x = A \cos(\omega t + \phi) \tag{12-6}$$

The rate of change of position x is just the velocity v_x, which we found was equal to

$$v_x = -\omega A \sin(\omega t + \phi) \tag{12-7}$$

You can see that Equation 20-5 for magnetic flux is identical to Equation 12-6 for position, with amplitude A replaced by NAB (note that A in Equation 20-5 denotes area, not amplitude). Making the same replacement in Equation 12-7 tells us that the rate of change of magnetic flux through the rotating coil is

$$\frac{\Delta \Phi_B}{\Delta t} = -\omega NAB \sin(\omega t + \phi) \tag{20-6}$$

Substituting Equation 20-6 into Equation 20-3 then gives us the emf in the rotating coil:

Emf in an ac generator (20-7)

Angular speed of the rotating coil   Time   Angle of the coil at $t = 0$

Emf produced by an ac generator

$$\varepsilon = \omega NAB \sin(\omega t + \phi)$$

Number of turns in the coil   Area of the coil   Magnitude of the magnetic field to which the coil is exposed

The emf alternates with angular frequency ω, the same as the angular speed of the rotating coil. The maximum value of the emf is $\varepsilon_{max} = \omega NAB$, which shows that we can increase the maximum emf by increasing the angular speed ω, the number of turns N, the coil area A, the magnetic field magnitude B, or a combination of these.

While the emf produced by an ac generator changes from positive to negative, the power delivered by the generator does not. As an example, suppose an ac generator is connected to a circuit device (such as a light bulb or a toaster) that we can represent as a resistor with resistance R. If we ignore the internal resistance of the coil, the emf is equal to the voltage drop across the resistor: $\varepsilon = iR$. The current in the resistor is therefore

$$i = \frac{\varepsilon}{R} = \frac{\omega NAB}{R} \sin(\omega t + \phi) \tag{20-8}$$

The current in the resistor alternates with the same angular frequency ω as the emf. From Section 18-6, the power into such a resistor is

$$P = i^2 R \tag{18-24}$$

If we substitute Equation 20-8 into Equation 18-24, we get

$$P = \left(\frac{\omega NAB}{R} \sin(\omega t + \phi) \right)^2 R = \frac{\omega^2 N^2 A^2 B^2}{R} \sin^2(\omega t + \phi) \tag{20-9}$$

Figure 20-10 shows graphs of the emf ε (Equation 20-7) and resistor power P (Equation 20-9) as functions of time. The power P is *never* negative, which means that energy always flows from the ac generator into the resistor, never the other way. The average value of the function $\sin^2(\omega t + \phi)$ is $\frac{1}{2}$, so the average power into the resistor is

$$P_{\text{average}} = \frac{\omega^2 N^2 A^2 B^2}{2R} \tag{20-10}$$

It may seem like the power given by Equation 20-10 comes "for free": You let the coil rotate, and an emf is generated that makes power flow into the resistor. Alas, this power comes at a price. As we discussed in Section 20-3, whenever a conductor (such as the coil of an ac generator) moves in the presence of a magnetic field, the conductor experiences a magnetic force that opposes its motion. So left to itself, the coil would quickly slow to a halt. To keep the coil in motion, you must apply a torque that just balances the effects of this magnetic force. At an electric generating station, this torque is applied to the blades of a turbine that is connected to the coil. The blades can be turned by the force of the wind (Figure 20-1a), by the force of flowing water at a hydroelectric plant, or by the force of fast-moving steam at a coal-fired or nuclear power plant (where heat from burning fossil fuels or radioactive decay is used to boil water and produce steam). Part of the mechanical power used to make the turbine spin goes

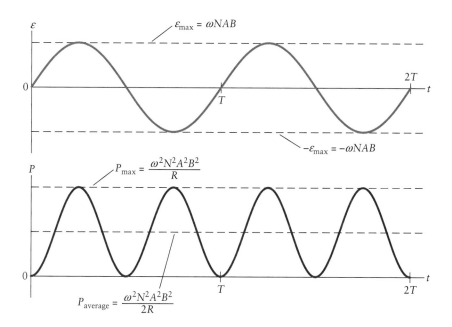

Figure 20-10 **An ac generator: Emf and power** These graphs show the emf ε generated in the coil shown in Figure 20-9, and the power P that this emf delivers to a resistor R connected to the coil. We assume $\phi = 0$ in Equations 20-7 and 20-9. Note that T is the time it takes for the coil to complete one rotation.

Go to Interactive Exercise 20-2 for more practice dealing with coils

into the electric power provided by the generator; the rest is lost due to friction in the turbine and generator.

The ac generator is just part of what's needed for a system of power delivery based on alternating current. In Chapter 21 we'll explore in more detail the physics of alternating current in circuits.

Example 20-3 Lighting the Gym with a Bicycle

You attach the coil of an ac generator to an exercise bicycle, so that as you work the pedals the coil turns and an emf is generated. The generator is geared so that it makes 10 rotations for each rotation of the pedals. The coil has an area of 6.40×10^{-3} m², has 1200 turns of wire, and is in a magnetic field of magnitude 0.100 T. How many times a second must you turn the pedals in order to deliver an average power of 60.0 W to a light bulb with a resistance of 80.0 Ω?

Set Up

The situation is as shown in Figure 20-9. We'll use Equation 20-10 to solve for the angular speed ω of the generator coil. Since the coil makes 10 rotations for every rotation of the pedals, the angular speed of the pedals is equal to ω divided by 10.

Average power delivered by an ac generator to a resistor:

$$P_{\text{average}} = \frac{\omega^2 N^2 A^2 B^2}{2R} \tag{20-10}$$

Solve

Rewrite Equation 20-10 to solve for ω.

Find the angular speed of the generator coil from Equation 20-10:

$$\omega^2 = \frac{2RP_{\text{average}}}{N^2 A^2 B^2}$$

$$\omega = \frac{\sqrt{2RP_{\text{average}}}}{NAB} = \frac{\sqrt{2\,(80.0\ \Omega)\,(60.0\ \text{W})}}{(1200)\,(6.40 \times 10^{-3}\ \text{m}^2)\,(0.100\ \text{T})}$$

$$= 128\ \text{rad/s}$$

Convert this from radians per second to revolutions per second:

$$\omega = \left(128\ \frac{\text{rad}}{\text{s}}\right)\left(\frac{1\ \text{rev}}{2\pi\ \text{rad}}\right) = 20.3\ \text{rev/s}$$

The generator turns 10 times faster than the pedals, so the pedals must turn at a rate of

$$(20.3\ \text{rev/s})/10 = 2.03\ \text{rev/s} = 122\ \text{rev/min}$$

Reflect

A cycling cadence of 122 rev/min isn't difficult for an amateur cyclist, so you can certainly power a light bulb in this way. Exercise bicycles with generators of this kind are commercially available and are used to return power to the electrical grid in the same manner as residential solar panels.

? Got the Concept? 20-4 A Flickering Fluorescent Lamp

Certain types of fluorescent lamps flicker rapidly. That's because these lamps emit a pulse of light every time a burst of electric power is provided to the lamp. If such a lamp is powered by a source of emf that oscillates at 60 Hz, what is the frequency at which the lamp will flicker? (a) 30 Hz; (b) 60 Hz; (c) 120 Hz; (d) 240 Hz; (e) 3600 Hz.

Take-Home Message for Section 20-4

✔ An ac generator consists of a coil that rotates in a magnetic field.

✔ The emf produced by an ac generator oscillates at an angular frequency that equals the angular speed of the rotating coil.

Key Terms

ac generator
electromagnetic induction
Faraday's law of induction

induced emf
induced magnetic field
Lenz's law

magnetic flux
motional emf

Chapter Summary

Topic	Equation or Figure

Motional emf: An emf appears in a loop when that loop moves in the presence of a magnetic field. The emf is a result of magnetic forces on the mobile charges within the loop.

(c) Side view of loop moving toward a stationary magnet

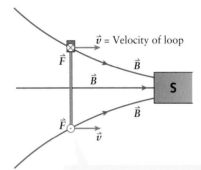

(Figure 20-2c)

- Charges in the loop move along with the loop in the magnetic field.
- Magnetic forces push mobile charges around the loop, causing a current.

Induced emf: An emf also appears in a loop when the magnetic field within the loop changes. Here the forces that create the emf are not magnetic, but electric; an electric field is produced by the changing magnetic field.

(c) Side view of magnet moving toward a stationary loop

(Figure 20-3c)

- Charges in the loop experience electric forces.
- These forces push mobile charges around the loop, causing a current.

Magnitude of the induced or motional emf in a loop

Change in the magnetic flux through the surface outlined by the loop

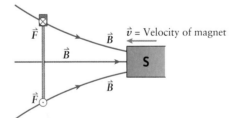

$$|\varepsilon| = \left| \frac{\Delta \Phi_B}{\Delta t} \right|$$

(20-2)

Time interval over which the change in magnetic flux takes place

Lenz's law: The direction of an emf caused by a change in magnetic flux is such as to oppose the flux change. The induced current causes its own flux (which helps compensate for the change), and a conductor and magnet that move relative to each other experience magnetic forces that oppose this relative motion.

Induced or motional emf in a loop

Change in the magnetic flux through the surface outlined by the loop

$$\varepsilon = -\frac{\Delta\Phi_B}{\Delta t}$$ (20-3)

Time interval over which the change in magnetic flux takes place

The minus sign indicates that the current caused by the emf induces a magnetic field which opposes the change in flux.

Alternating current and an ac generator: To produce an alternating emf (the sort needed to cause an alternating current), rotate a coil in the presence of a constant magnetic field. The changing flux causes an emf that oscillates sinusoidally.

Angular speed of the rotating coil   Time   Angle of the coil at $t = 0$

Emf produced by an ac generator

$$\varepsilon = \omega NAB \sin(\omega t + \phi)$$ (20-7)

Number of turns in the coil

Area of the coil

Magnitude of the magnetic field to which the coil is exposed

Answer to What do you think? Question

(b) The electrons in the wire are initially at rest and so do not experience a magnetic force. (Recall that a magnetic field exerts a force only on a charged object that is in motion.) So it must be an *electric* force that sets the electrons into motion. This is a consequence of electromagnetic induction: As you swipe the credit card through the reader, the wire loop is exposed to a varying magnetic field from the stripe on the back of the card. This causes a changing magnetic flux through the loop, which induces an electric field and an emf. Electrons move in the loop in response to this emf.

Answers to Got the Concept? Questions

20-1 (d) The induced emf does *not* depend on what the loop is made of. (Note that Equation 20-2 makes no reference to the properties of the loop material.) So the emf will be exactly the same whether the loop is made of copper, wood, silver, rubber, or even air. The difference is that because copper is a good conductor while wood is a very poor conductor, a current will be generated in the copper loop but not in the wooden loop.

20-2 (b) As the loop in Figure 20-8a moves into the field region, there is an increasing magnetic flux through the loop due to the magnetic field directed into the plane of the figure. According to Lenz's law, current will flow in the loop to induce a magnetic field $\vec{B}_{loop}$ that will oppose this increase, so $\vec{B}_{loop}$ in the interior of the loop must point out of the plane in Figure 20-8a. The right-hand rule depicted in Figure 20-6a tells us that to induce such a field, current must flow counterclockwise around the loop. (You can confirm this by using the right-hand rule for the magnetic force on a moving charge. A positive charge in the right-hand leg of the moving loop feels an upward magnetic force, and this force drives current in a counterclockwise direction around the loop. There are also magnetic forces on charges in the top and bottom legs of the loop, but these forces have zero component along the length of the wire and so do not induce a current.)

20-3 (c) Although the loop in Figure 20-8b is moving, the magnetic flux through the loop remains constant because it is moving through a region of constant, uniform magnetic field. Since there is no flux change, Faraday's law tells us that no emf is induced and so no current will be generated. (You can confirm this by using the right-hand rule for the magnetic force on a moving charge. A positive charge in the right-hand leg of the moving loop feels an upward magnetic force, and this force by itself would drive current in a counterclockwise direction around the loop. But a positive charge in the left-hand leg of the moving loop also feels an upward magnetic force, which by itself would drive current in a clockwise direction around the loop. There are also magnetic forces on charges in the top and bottom legs of the loop, but these forces have zero component along the length of the wire and so do not induce a current. The net effect is that there is *zero* current in the loop.)

20-4 (c) Figure 20-10 shows that the power delivered by an ac generator goes through two up-and-down cycles during the time T required for the emf to go through a single cycle. So if the emf varies at 60 Hz, the power delivered to the fluorescent lamp varies at 2×60 Hz = 120 Hz.

Questions and Problems

In a few problems, you are given more data than you actually need; in a few other problems, you are required to supply data from your general knowledge, outside sources, or informed estimate.

Interpret as significant all digits in numerical values that have trailing zeros and no decimal points.

For all problems, use $g = 9.80 \text{ m/s}^2$ for the free-fall acceleration due to gravity. Neglect friction and air resistance unless instructed to do otherwise.

• Basic, single-concept problem

•• Intermediate-level problem, may require synthesis of concepts and multiple steps

••• Challenging problem

SSM *Solution is in Student Solutions Manual*

Conceptual Questions

1. •A common physics demonstration is to drop a small magnet down a long, vertical aluminum pipe. Describe the motion of the magnet and the physical explanation for the motion. SSM

2. ••Figure 20-11 depicts an electron in between the poles of an electromagnet. Explain how the electron is accelerated if the magnetic field is gradually being increased.

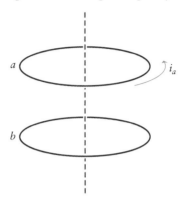

Figure 20-11 Problem 2

3. ••In a popular demonstration of electromagnetic induction, a metal plate is suspended in midair above a large electromagnetic coil, as shown in Figure 20-12. (a) How does this work? (b) If your professor does the demonstration, one thing you'll notice is that the plate gets quite hot. (In fact, you can end the demonstration by frying an egg on the plate!) Why does the plate become hot? (c) Would the trick work if the plate were made of an insulating material?

Metal plate

Figure 20-12
Electromagnetic coil   Problem 3

4. •**Medical** In hospitals with magnetic resonance imaging facilities and at other locations where large magnetic fields are present, there are usually signs warning people with pacemakers and other electronic medical devices not to enter. Why?

5. •Two conducting loops with a common axis are placed near each other, as shown in Figure 20-13. Initially the currents in both loops are zero. If a current is suddenly set up in loop *a* in the direction shown, is there also a current in loop *b*? If so, in which direction? What is the direction of the force, if any, that loop *a* exerts on loop *b*? Explain your answer.

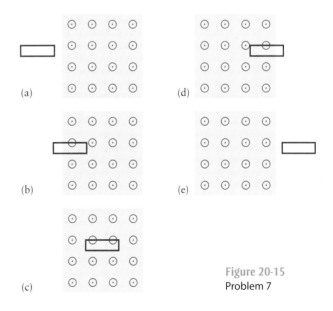

Figure 20-13 Problem 5

6. •A conducting rod slides without friction on conducting rails in a magnetic field as shown in Figure 20-14. The rod is given an initial velocity $\vec{v}$ to the right. Describe its subsequent motion and justify your answer.

Figure 20-14 Problem 6

Multiple-Choice Questions

7. •Figure 20-15 shows a sequence of sketches depicting a rectangular loop passing from left to right through a region of constant magnetic field. The field points out of the page and perpendicular to the plane of the loop. In which one of the sequences is the magnetic flux through the loop decreasing? SSM

    A. from left to right approaching the magnetic field
    B. entering the magnetic field
    C. inside the magnetic field
    D. leaving the magnetic field
    E. from left to right moving away from the magnetic field

Figure 20-15
Problem 7

8. •On which variable does the magnetic flux depend?
   A. the magnetic field
   B. the area of a region through which the magnetic field passes
   C. the orientation of the field with respect to the region through which it passes
   D. all of the above
   E. none of the above

9. •Two metal rings with a common axis are placed near each other, as shown in **Figure 20-16**. If current i_a is suddenly set up and is increasing in ring a as shown, the current in ring b is
   A. zero.
   B. parallel to i_a.
   C. antiparallel to i_a.
   D. alternatively parallel and antiparallel to i_a.
   E. perpendicular to i_a. SSM

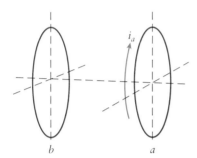

b   a   **Figure 20-16** Problem 9

10. ••**Figure 20-17** shows two coils wound around an iron ring, which directs the magnetic field of each coil around the ring. Current appears in the second coil
    A. the moment the battery is connected by closing the switch.
    B. the entire time the battery is connected with the switch closed.
    C. the moment the battery is disconnected by opening the switch.
    D. the moment the battery is connected by closing the switch and the moment the battery is disconnected by opening the switch.
    E. the entire time the battery is disconnected with the switch open.

Figure 20-17 Problem 10

11. •The copper ring of radius R in **Figure 20-18** lies in a magnetic field pointed into the page. The field is uniformly decreasing in magnitude. The induced current in the ring is
    A. clockwise and constant.
    B. clockwise and changing.
    C. zero.
    D. counterclockwise and constant.
    E. counterclockwise and changing.

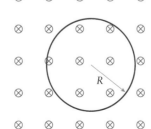

Figure 20-18 Problem 11

12. •A conducting loop moves at a constant speed parallel to a long, straight, current-carrying wire, as shown in **Figure 20-19**.

Figure 20-19 Problem 12

    A. The induced current in the loop will be clockwise.
    B. The induced current in the loop will be only parallel to the current i.
    C. The induced current in the loop will be counterclockwise.
    D. The induced current in the loop will be alternately clockwise and then counterclockwise.
    E. There will be no induced current in the loop.

Estimation/Numerical Analysis

13. •Estimate the electric current in a generator in a large hydroelectric dam (such as Hoover Dam or the Oahe Dam).

14. •Estimate how many turbines (such as the ones at Hoover Dam) would be required to supply enough energy to power the United States.

15. •Give an estimate of the induced voltage created in trans-Atlantic communication cables due to fluctuations in Earth's magnetic field.

16. •Estimate the magnitude of the fluctuations in Earth's geomagnetic field during times of solar flares.

17. ••The induced voltage versus time for a coil that has 100 circular turns of wire with radii 25 cm is given in the table. Plot $V(t)$ and use this graph to predict the graph of the magnetic field as a function of time $B(t)$ that is passing through the loop (assume that the angle between the magnetic field and the area of the loop is 0°).

t(s)	V(V)	t(s)	V(V)
0	0	9	2
1	2	10	4
2	4	11	2
3	2	12	0
4	0	13	−2
5	−2	14	−4
6	−4	15	−2
7	−2	16	0
8	0		

Problems

20-1 The world runs on electromagnetic induction

20-2 A changing magnetic flux creates an electric field

18. •A single-turn circular loop of wire that has a radius of 5.0 cm lies in the plane perpendicular to a spatially uniform magnetic field. During a 0.12-s time interval, the magnitude of the field increases uniformly from 0.2 T to 0.4 T. Determine the magnitude of the emf induced in the loop during the time interval.

19. •A circular coil that has 100 turns and a radius of 10.0 cm lies in a magnetic field that has a magnitude of 0.0650 T directed perpendicular to the coil. (a) What is the magnetic flux through the coil? (b) The magnetic field through the coil is increased steadily to 0.100 T over a time interval of 0.500 s. What is the magnitude of the emf induced in the coil during the time interval?

20. •A 30-turn coil with a diameter of 6.00 cm is placed in a constant, uniform magnetic field of 1.00 T directed perpendicular to the plane of the coil. Beginning at time $t = 0$ s, the field is increased at a uniform rate until it reaches 1.30 T at $t = 10.0$ s. The field remains constant thereafter. What is the magnitude of the induced emf in the coil at (a) $t < 0$ s, (b) $t = 5.00$ s, and (c) $t > 10.0$ s? (d) Plot the magnetic field

and the induced emf as functions of time for the range $-5.00 \text{ s} < t < 15.0 \text{ s}$.

20-3 Lenz's law describes the direction of the induced emf

21. •Determine the direction of the induced current in the loop for each case shown in **Figure 20-20**.

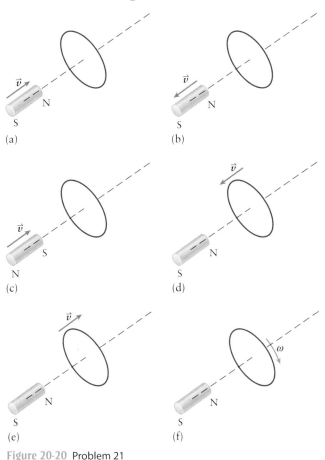

(a)   (b)

(c)   (d)

(e)   (f)

Figure 20-20 Problem 21

22. •A bar magnet is moved steadily through a wire loop as shown in **Figure 20-21**. Make a qualitative sketch of the induced emf in the loop as a function of time (be sure to include the times t_1, t_2, and t_3). Consider the direction of positive emf to be as indicated in the figure.

positive emf direction

Figure 20-21
Problems 22 and 23

23. •A bar magnet is moved steadily through a wire loop as shown in **Figure 20-21**, except that the leading edge of the magnet is the south pole instead of the north pole. Make a qualitative sketch of the induced voltage in the loop as a function of time (be sure to include the times t_1, t_2, and t_3). Consider the direction of positive emf to be as indicated in the figure. SSM

24. ••A square, 30-turn coil 10.0 cm on a side with a resistance of 0.820 Ω is placed between the poles of a large electromagnet. The electromagnet produces a constant, uniform magnetic field of 0.600 T directed into the page. As suggested by **Figure 20-22**,

the field drops sharply to zero at the edges of the magnet. The coil moves to the right at a constant velocity of 2.00 cm/s. What is the current through the wire coil (a) before the coil reaches the edge of the field, (b) while the coil is leaving the field, and (c) after the coil leaves the field? (d) What is the total charge that flows past a given point in the coil as it leaves the field? (e) Plot the induced current in the loop as a function of the horizontal position of the right side of the current loop. Let the right-hand edge of the magnetic field region be $x = 0$. Your plot should be in the range of $-5.00 \text{ cm} < x < 20.0 \text{ cm}$.

$\vec{B}$ into the page   30-turn coil   **Figure 20-22** Problem 24

25. ••(a) Determine the magnitude and direction of the force on each side of the coil in Problem 24 for situations (a) through (c). (b) As the loop enters the field region from the left, what is the direction of the induced current and the resulting force on each segment of the coil?

20-4 Faraday's law explains how alternating currents are generated

26. ••A rectangular coil with sides 0.10 m by 0.25 m has 500 turns of wire. It is rotated about its long axis in a magnetic field of 0.58 T. At what frequency must the coil be rotated for it to generate a maximum potential of 110 V?

27. ••An electromagnetic generator consists of a coil that has 100 turns of wire, has an area of 400 cm², and rotates at 60 rev/s in a magnetic field of 0.25 T. What is the magnitude of the emf induced in the coil? SSM

28. •••A 50-turn square coil with a cross-sectional area of 5.00 cm² has a resistance of 20.0 Ω. The plane of the coil is perpendicular to a uniform magnetic field of 1.00 T. The coil is suddenly rotated about the axis shown in **Figure 20-23** through an angle of 60° over a period of 0.200 s. (a) What charge flows past a point in the coil during that time? (b) If the loop is rotated a full 360° around the axis, what is the net charge that passes the point in the loop? Explain your answer.

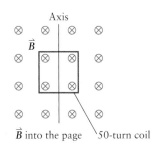

Axis

$\vec{B}$

$\vec{B}$ into the page   50-turn coil

Figure 20-23 Problem 28

29. ••Perhaps it has occurred to you that we could tap Earth's magnetic field to generate energy. One way to do this would be to spin a metal loop about an axis perpendicular to Earth's magnetic field. Suppose that the metal loop is a square that is 45.0 cm on each side and that we want to generate an electric potential in the loop of amplitude 120 V at a place where Earth's magnetic field is 0.50×10^{-4} T. At what angular

speed (in rev/s) would we have to spin the coil? Does this appear to be a feasible method to extract energy from Earth's magnetic field?

General Problems

30. •••A long, rectangular loop of width w, mass m, and resistance R is being pushed into a magnetic field by a constant force $\vec{F}$ (Figure 20-24). Derive an expression for the speed of the loop while it is entering the magnetic field.

Figure 20-24 Problem 30

31. ••A magnetic field of 0.45 G is directed straight down, perpendicular to the plane of a circular coil of wire that is made up of 250 turns and has a radius of 20 cm. (a) If the coil is stretched, in a time of 15 ms, to a radius of 30 cm, calculate the emf induced in the coil during the process. (b) Assuming the resistance of the coil is a constant 25 Ω, what is the induced current in the coil during the process? (c) What is the direction of the induced current in the coil (clockwise or counterclockwise, as viewed from above)? SSM

32. ••**Astronomy** Activity on the Sun, such as solar flares and coronal mass ejections, hurls large numbers of charged particles into space. When the particles reach Earth, they can interfere with communications and the power grid by causing electromagnetic induction. As one example, a current of millions of amps (known as the *auroral electrojet*) that runs about 100 km above Earth's surface can be perturbed. The change in the current causes a change in the magnetic field it produces at Earth's surface, which induces an emf along Earth's surface and in the power grid (which is grounded). Induced electric fields as high as 6.0 V/km have been measured. We can model the circuit at Earth's surface as a rectangular loop made up of the power lines completed by a path through the ground

beneath. We can treat the magnetic field created by the electrojet as being uniform (but not constant). Consider a 1.0-km-long stretch of power line that is 5.0 m above the surface of Earth. If the induced emf in the Earth–power line loop is 6.0 V, at what rate must the magnetic field through the loop be changing?

33. ••**Medical** During transcranial magnetic stimulation (TMS) treatment, a magnetic field typically of magnitude 0.50 T is produced in the brain using external coils. During the treatment, the current in the coils (and hence the magnetic field in the brain) rises from zero to its peak in about 75 μs. Assume that the magnetic field is uniform over a circular area of diameter 2.0 cm inside the brain. What is the magnitude of the average induced emf around this area in the brain during the treatment?

34. •A permanent bar magnet with the north pole pointing downward is dropped into a solenoid. (a) Determine the direction of the induced current that would be measured in the ammeter shown in Figure 20-25. (b) If the magnet is suddenly pulled upward through the solenoid, what is the direction of the induced current that would be measured in the ammeter?

Figure 20-25 Problem 34

35. ••A pair of parallel conducting rails that are 12 cm apart lies at right angles to a uniform magnetic field of 0.8 T directed into the page, as shown in Figure 20-26. A 15-Ω resistor is connected across the rails. A conducting bar is moved to the right at 2 m/s across the rails. (a) What is the current in the resistor? (b) What direction is the current in the bar (up or down)? (c) What is the magnetic force on the bar? SSM

Figure 20-26 Problem 35

21 Alternating-Current Circuits

In this chapter, your goals are to:

- (21-1) Explain the importance of alternating current.
- (21-2) Describe what is meant by the root mean square value.
- (21-3) Calculate the voltage change produced by a transformer.
- (21-4) Describe why an inductor opposes changes in the current passing through it.
- (21-5) Explain the flow of energy in an *LC* circuit.
- (21-6) Describe what happens in a driven series *LRC* circuit when the driving frequency changes.
- (21-7) Discuss why current can flow in only one direction in a *pn* junction diode.

To master this chapter, you should review:

- (12-3, 12-4) Simple harmonic motion and the energy of a mass–spring system.
- (12-8) How a damped oscillator responds to different driving frequencies.
- (17-5, 17-6) The definition of capacitance and the electric energy stored by capacitors.
- (18-3, 18-6) The current through and voltage across a resistor, and the power into a resistor.
- (18-5) Using Kirchhoff's loop rule to analyze circuits.
- (19-7) The magnetic field created by a solenoid.
- (20-2, 20-3) How Faraday's law and Lenz's law describe the induced emf that opposes a change in magnetic flux through a loop.
- (20-4) How ac generators work and the power they generate.

What do you think?

These transformers use Faraday's law to raise and lower the voltage of alternating current. Can they also be used to raise or lower the voltage of *direct* current? (a) Yes; (b) yes, but only to raise the voltage; (c) yes, but only to lower the voltage; (d) no.

21-1 Most circuits use alternating current

In Chapter 20 we learned the principles of electromagnetic induction and how they can be used to *generate* an alternating current. In this chapter we'll learn how to *manipulate* and *use* alternating current. Most of the electrical power on our planet is transmitted and used in the form of an alternating current, so by studying this chapter you'll learn an important aspect of how the world around you works.

We'll see how *mutual inductance*—in which a changing emf in one coil makes it possible to induce an emf in another coil—is key for understanding how electric power can be transmitted efficiently over long distances. This same principle explains how the relatively high voltage of 120 to 240 V available from a wall socket can be used to charge a cell phone that operates at low voltage, typically 5 V or less (Figure 21-1a). We'll also introduce *self-inductance*, an effect in which a changing emf in a coil produces an emf reaction in the coil itself. Self-inductance is at the heart of an important device called an *inductor* that has many applications in circuits.

Figure 21-1 **Alternating current**
When you (a) use the transformer in your mobile phone charger or (b) tune your television to a different channel, you are using the physics of alternating current.

(a)

(b)

This transformer uses mutual inductance—in which a changing emf in one coil induces an emf in a second coil nearby—to reduce the voltage from a wall socket to a lower value suitable for charging a battery.

When you change the channel on a television, you're telling the TV tuning circuit to change its capacitance. This changes the natural frequency of the circuit so that it matches the carrier frequency of the channel you want to watch.

Many circuits that are connected to an ac source (such as the ac voltage provided by a wall socket) can be modeled as a combination of resistors, capacitors, and inductors. We'll see what happens when any one of these circuit elements by itself is connected to an ac source. We'll then go on to examine what happens in an *LRC series circuit* in which all three of these circuit elements are present. We'll find that such circuits hold the key to understanding what happens when you tune a radio or television to receive a particular station (Figure 21-1b). Finally, we'll take a brief look at *semiconductors*, a class of material that plays an important role in many circuits. Semiconductors are essential for the operation of two other important classes of circuit elements, called *diodes* and *transistors*.

Take-Home Message for Section 21-1

✔ The same principles of electromagnetic induction that explain how to produce an alternating current (ac) also tell us how to manipulate and use such currents.

✔ Many circuits that include an ac source can be modeled as a combination of resistors, capacitors, and inductors (a third type of circuit element).

21-2 We need to analyze ac circuits differently than dc circuits

Current arises in a circuit as a result of an applied voltage. The batteries that power your mobile phone or your flashlight are sources of (approximately) constant voltage. A 9-V battery, for example, introduces a roughly constant potential difference of 9 V between the two points at which it connects to a circuit. By convention, we refer to a circuit driven by a fixed voltage source, or one that does not change direction, as **a direct current**, or **dc** circuit. However, when you plug an electrical device into a wall socket, you are accessing an **alternating current**, or **ac** source.

The voltage from an ac source varies with time in a sinusoidal fashion, as we discussed in our description of ac generators in Section 20-4. In that section we wrote the emf delivered by an ac generator as

Emf in an ac generator
(20-7)

Angular speed of the rotating coil   Time   Angle of the coil at $t = 0$

Emf produced by an ac generator

$$\varepsilon = \omega NAB \sin(\omega t + \phi)$$

Number of turns in the coil   Area of the coil   Magnitude of the magnetic field to which the coil is exposed

The value V of this ac voltage oscillates between V_0 (the voltage amplitude) and $-V_0$.

The period T of this ac voltage equals the reciprocal of the frequency f:

$$T = \frac{1}{f} = \frac{2\pi}{\omega}$$

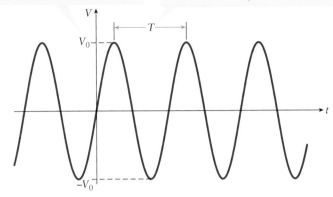

Figure 21-2 **An ac voltage** This figure graphs the ac voltage given by Equation 21-1. Note that at $t = 0$ the voltage is zero and increasing.

Let's choose the time $t = 0$ to be when the angle of the coil is $\phi = 0$, use the symbol V_0 for the combination of factors ωNAB, and use the symbol $V(t)$ for the time-varying emf. (We use V since emf is measured in volts.) If the generator is connected to two terminals, like the two terminals of a wall socket, then $V(t)$ represents the voltage between those terminals. We can then rewrite Equation 20-7 as a general equation that we'll use for ac sources of all kinds:

Time-varying voltage provided by an ac source

Angular frequency of the voltage

$$V(t) = V_0 \sin \omega t$$ Time

Voltage amplitude = maximum positive value of $V(t)$

Voltage of an ac source
(21-1)

Figure 21-2 graphs the voltage $V(t)$ as a function of time. The angular frequency ω of the voltage (in rad/s) is related to the frequency f of the voltage (in Hz) by the same relationship we used in Section 12-3 for simple harmonic motion:

$$\omega = 2\pi f \qquad (21\text{-}2)$$

The period T of the oscillation is equal to $1/f$. For example, in the United States and Canada ac voltage is applied at a frequency $f = 60$ Hz, so the period of oscillation is $T = 1/f = 1/(60\,\text{Hz}) = 0.017\,\text{s}$ and the angular frequency is $\omega = 2\pi f = (2\pi\,\text{rad})(60\,\text{Hz}) = 3.8 \times 10^2\,\text{rad/s}$.

If we attach a source of ac voltage described by Equation 21-1 to a resistor of resistance R, we can still use Equation 18-24 to calculate the power that flows into the resistor:

Power into a resistor

Current through the resistor

$$P = i^2 R = \frac{V^2}{R}$$ Voltage across the resistor

Resistance of the resistor

Power for a resistor
(18-24)

The only difference between a resistor in a dc circuit and one in an ac circuit is that because the voltage varies with time, the power into the resistor also varies with time. The *instantaneous* power into the resistor at time t is

$$(21\text{-}3) \qquad P(t) = \frac{V^2(t)}{R} = \frac{V_0^2 \sin^2(\omega t)}{R}$$

The value of $P(t)$ oscillates between zero (when $\sin \omega t = 0$) and V_0^2/R (when $\sin \omega t = 1$ or -1).

Often it's convenient to talk not about the instantaneous power $P(t)$ but the *average* power P_{average}. For example, if an appliance is designed to be powered by an ac voltage, its power rating in watts (such as a 1000-W microwave oven or a 1500-W hair dryer) is always stated in terms of the average power delivered to that appliance when in operation. The voltage amplitude V_0 and the resistance R are constants, so to find P_{average} we only have to figure out the average value of $\sin^2(\omega t)$. As we discussed in Section 20-4, this average value is $\frac{1}{2}$ (see Figure 20-10). So from Equation 21-3, the average power into the resistor is

$$(21\text{-}4) \qquad P_{\text{average}} = \frac{1}{2}\frac{V_0^2}{R}$$

The average power given by Equation 21-4 is one-half of the maximum value of the instantaneous power given by Equation 21-3.

Equation 21-4 is the basis of an alternative way to describe the voltage provided by an ac source. Comparing this equation to Equation 21-3, we can write

$$\left(\frac{V^2(t)}{R}\right)_{\text{average}} = \frac{1}{2}\frac{V_0^2}{R}$$

If we multiply both sides of this equation by the resistance R, we get

$$(V^2(t))_{\text{average}} = \frac{V_0^2}{2}$$

The left-hand side of this equation is called the *mean square value* of the ac voltage: We take the square of the voltage, then calculate the average (or *mean*) of that quantity. The square root of the mean square is called the **root mean square value**, or **rms value**, of the voltage:

The root mean square (rms) value of $V(t)$...   ... is the square root of the average value of $V^2(t)$.

Root mean square value
(21-5)

$$V_{\text{rms}} = \sqrt{(V^2(t))_{\text{average}}} = \frac{V_0}{\sqrt{2}}$$

If $V(t)$ is a sinusoidal function, its rms value equals the maximum value of $V(t)$ (the amplitude) divided by $\sqrt{2}$.

As an example, in the United States the standard value for the ac voltage supplied by a wall socket is 120 V; this is actually the rms voltage, so $V_{\text{rms}} = 120$ V. The voltage amplitude, or peak voltage, is larger by a factor of $\sqrt{2}$, so $V_0 = V_{\text{rms}}\sqrt{2} = (120\ \text{V})\sqrt{2} = 170$ V.

In terms of the rms voltage, we can write the average power from Equation 21-4 as

$$(21\text{-}6) \qquad P_{\text{average}} = \frac{1}{2}\frac{V_0^2}{R} = \left(\frac{V_0^2}{2}\right)\frac{1}{R} = \left(\frac{V_0}{\sqrt{2}}\right)^2\frac{1}{R} = \frac{V_{\text{rms}}^2}{R}$$

This says that Equation 18-24, $P = V^2/R$, tells us the *average* power if we replace V by the rms value V_{rms} of the voltage.

Watch Out! The average voltage is zero, but the average power is not.

The average voltage of an ac source described by Equation 21-1 is zero. But the average power delivered by that source is *not* zero because power is proportional to the square of the voltage, which is always positive.

Example 21-1 Traveling Abroad with Your Hair Dryer

Seasoned travelers know that an electric device that works in one country may not work in another. A certain hair dryer made in the United States, where the rms wall voltage is 120 V, is rated at 1.5 kW. Find the power output of the hair dryer when connected to a wall outlet in Australia, where the voltage amplitude is 325 V. Treat the resistance of the hair dryer as the same regardless of the wall voltage. (In reality, the resistance depends somewhat on the temperature of the dryer's heating elements, which depends on the operating voltage.)

Set Up

We'll use Equation 21-6 to find the resistance of the hair dryer from the given values of $P_{average}$ and V_{rms} in the United States. We'll then use this same equation to find the average power in Australia. To do this, we'll need to know the rms voltage in Australia; we'll find this from the given value of the voltage amplitude V_0 by using Equation 21-5.

Average power into a resistor:

$$P_{average} = \frac{V_{rms}^2}{R} \tag{21-6}$$

Root mean square (rms) voltage:

$$V_{rms} = \sqrt{(V^2(t))_{average}} = \frac{V_0}{\sqrt{2}} \tag{21-5}$$

Solve

Use Equation 21-6 to determine the resistance of the hair dryer. We assume this has the same value no matter what the operating voltage.

Solve Equation 21-6 for resistance R:

$$R = \frac{V_{rms}^2}{P_{average}}$$

Substitute the values in the United States, $V_{rms} = 120$ V and $P_{average} = 1.5$ kW $= 1.5 \times 10^3$ W:

$$R = \frac{(120\,\text{V})^2}{1.5 \times 10^3\,\text{W}} = 9.6\,\Omega$$

(Recall that $1\,\text{W} = 1\,\text{V}^2/\Omega$.)

Find the value of V_{rms} in Australia; then use this to determine the average power into the hair dryer when used in Australia.

In Australia the voltage amplitude is $V_0 = 325$ V, so the rms voltage is

$$V_{rms} = \frac{V_0}{\sqrt{2}} = \frac{325\,\text{V}}{\sqrt{2}} = 230\,\text{V}$$

With this value of V_{rms}, the average power into the hair dryer is

$$P_{average,Australia} = \frac{V_{rms,Australia}^2}{R} = \frac{(230\,\text{V})^2}{9.6\,\Omega} = 5.5 \times 10^3\,\text{W} = 5.5\,\text{kW}$$

Reflect

Our result of 5.5 kW is *considerably* more power than the hair dryer is designed to take in. You may know how hot the air from a 1500-W hair dryer can be, or perhaps you've felt how hot a 100-W bulb can get after it's been on for a while. So you can probably imagine how hot 5500 W would make the heating element of the hair dryer. To radiate that much power, the required temperature of the heating element might well exceed the melting point of the material! We'll see in the following section how this hair dryer can be used safely even with the higher voltage provided in Australia.

❓ Got the Concept? 21-1 Average and Instantaneous Power

A resistor is connected to a source of ac voltage described by Equation 21-1. At which of the following times is the instantaneous power into the resistor equal to the average power into the resistor? (a) $t = 0$; (b) $t = T/8$; (c) $t = T/4$; (d) more than one of these; (e) none of these.

Take-Home Message for Section 21-2

✔ The arithmetic mean of a sinusoidally varying voltage is zero because it is negative as often as it is positive. The average power is not zero because it is proportional to the square of the voltage, which cannot be negative.

✔ It is common to characterize AC voltage by its root mean square (rms) value. The peak voltage is $\sqrt{2}$ times the rms voltage.

Figure 21-3 Power lines When electric energy is transmitted over long distances in the form of an alternating current, it is most efficient to use very high voltage (typically 110 kV or higher). The power lines shown here are elevated so that people and vehicles cannot touch them, which would present a safety hazard.

21-3 Transformers allow us to change the voltage of an ac power source

All ac circuits are intended to transfer energy from one location to another. For example, if you plug your mobile phone's charger into a wall socket, energy from an ac generator that may be hundreds of kilometers away flows through power lines (Figure 21-3) into your home and into your phone. The *voltage* associated with this energy has different values at different places in the circuit, however; the voltage in the power lines is typically hundreds of kilovolts, the voltage provided by a wall socket in the United States or Canada is 120 V, and the voltage supplied to your phone by the charger is 5 V. In this section we'll see the reason why different voltages are used in this way, and we'll learn about an important device called a *transformer* that makes it possible to raise or lower an alternating-current voltage.

To understand why high voltages are used in power lines, recall this relationship from Section 18-6:

Power for a circuit element
(18-23)

Power produced by or transferred into a circuit element

$$P = iV$$

Current through the circuit element

Voltage (absolute value) across the circuit element

Source of emf: Power flows out of the source and into the moving charges.
Resistor: Power flows out of the charges and into the resistor.

Equation 18-23 tells us that the same amount P of electric power can be delivered at any voltage V, provided that the product of current and voltage remains the same. This is true for ac circuits as well as dc circuits. For a power line, it's best to use high voltage and low current. The reason is that a long power line has a substantial resistance R, and so some of the energy being carried by the current goes into heating the power line rather than being transmitted to the end user. The rate at which energy is dissipated in a resistor with resistance R is given by Equation 18-24 (see Section 21-2), which we can write as $P = i^2R$. To minimize this energy loss, the current i should be as small as possible. It then follows from Equation 18-23 that the voltage V must be as large as possible.

> **! Watch Out!** In power lines, don't confuse the voltage *between* adjacent cables with the voltage *across* the length of a single cable.
>
> You might look at Equation 18-24 and think "It also says that $P = V^2/R$ for a resistor. So why isn't it preferable to have the voltage V be small to minimize energy loss?" The explanation is that in Equation 18-23, $P = iV$, V represents the voltage between the *two* cables that make up a power line. (You can see in Figure 21-3 that the cables come in pairs.) You need both cables to make a complete circuit, just as the power cord for a household appliance has two wires in it (one wire is connected to one prong of the plug at the end of the cord, and the other wire to the other prong). This is the voltage that has to have a large value in order to make the current small. By contrast, in Equation 18-24 the quantity V is the potential difference between two ends of a *single* cable and is related to the current in the cable by the relationship $V = iR$ for resistors (Equation 18-9) that we learned in Section 18-3. This voltage is low if the current is small, so the power $P = i^2R = V^2/R$ that goes into heating the resistor is small.

In the home, however, the voltage must be kept small. That's because there is a risk that a person could be exposed to that voltage (for instance, if a person were to touch an appliance whose internal wiring had failed). If a voltage V is applied between two parts of your body, the resulting current through your body is proportional to V.

② The alternating current in the primary coil creates an alternating magnetic field of the same angular frequency ω. The field lines are "trapped" by the iron core and all pass through the secondary coil.

③ The alternating magnetic flux through the windings of the secondary coil induces an alternating emf, or output voltage, of the same angular frequency ω but of amplitude V_s.

① An input ac voltage with amplitude V_p and angular frequency ω causes an alternating current in the primary coil.

Figure 21-4 **A transformer** This device uses two coils and a piece of magnetic material such as iron to raise or lower the voltage from an ac source.

Primary coil, N_p windings

Secondary coil, N_s windings

Input voltage V_p

Output voltage V_s

Iron core

The amplitude V_s of the output voltage equals (N_s/N_p) times the amplitude V_p of the input voltage.
• If $N_s > N_p$, then $V_s > V_p$. This is a step-up transformer.
• If $N_s < N_p$, then $V_s < V_p$. This is a step-down transformer.

A current of just 0.1 A can cause ventricular fibrillation, and a current of 0.2 A or more can cause severe burns and stop the heart altogether. To reduce the risk of accident, the voltage supplied to the home has to be kept at a much lower value (120 to 240 V) than that used in power lines (more than 110 kV, or about a thousand times higher than what is safe for home use).

A device that can raise or lower an ac voltage to a desired value is called a **transformer**. The transformer shown in Figure 21-4 consists of two coils formed by winding separate wires around a piece of iron. The coil on the left, called the **primary coil**, is connected to the input voltage. The coil on the right, the **secondary coil**, is the source of the output voltage, even though there's no direct electric connection between the two coils. Let's see how this works.

When an ac voltage is applied to the primary coil in the transformer, the current in the windings gives rise to a magnetic field. This field oscillates with the same angular frequency ω as the ac voltage and current, and so creates a time-varying magnetic flux through the windings of the primary coil. Because iron is a magnetic material, the iron core confines the magnetic field lines so that the same flux that passes through each winding of the primary coil also passes through each winding of the secondary coil. As a result, there is a time-varying magnetic flux through the secondary coil. Faraday's law (see Sections 20-2 and 20-3) then tells us that a time-varying emf is induced in the secondary coil, which means this coil acts as a voltage source. The emf in the secondary coil oscillates with the same angular frequency as the current in the primary coil, so the output voltage produced by the secondary coil oscillates at the same rate as the input voltage that feeds into the primary coil. This effect, in which a change in the current in one coil induces an emf and current in a second coil, is called **mutual inductance**.

The *amplitude* of the output voltage in Figure 21-4 will be different from that of the input voltage—that is, the amplitude will be "transformed" by the transformer— if there are different numbers of windings in the primary and secondary coils (N_p and N_s, respectively, in Figure 21-4). To see how this can be, first notice that the time-varying magnetic flux Φ_B in the primary coil induces an emf there. From Equation 20-2, the magnitude of the emf induced in each of the windings of the primary coil is $|\Delta\Phi_B/\Delta t|$, the magnitude of the rate of change of the magnetic flux through that winding. There are N_p windings in the primary coil, so the total emf in that coil has magnitude $N_p|\Delta\Phi_B/\Delta t|$. By Kirchhoff's loop rule (Section 18-5), the sum of the voltage drops around the left-hand circuit that includes the primary coil must be zero, so the emf in the primary coil must have the same magnitude as the input voltage $V_p(t)$. (We're ignoring any voltage drops due to the resistance of the wires in this circuit.) So we can write

$$(21\text{-}7) \qquad |\text{input voltage}| = |V_p(t)| = N_p \left| \frac{\Delta \Phi_B}{\Delta t} \right|$$

Since the iron core ensures that there is the same magnetic flux Φ_B through each winding of the secondary coil as through each winding of the primary coil, the rate of change of the flux is the same and so the emf per winding is the same as well. There are N_s windings in the secondary coil, so the total emf in that coil has magnitude $N_s |\Delta \Phi_B / \Delta t|$. This emf acts as the voltage source for the circuit attached to the secondary coil (the right-hand circuit in Figure 21-4), so the magnitude of the output voltage $V_s(t)$ is

$$(21\text{-}8) \qquad |\text{output voltage}| = |V_s(t)| = N_s \left| \frac{\Delta \Phi_B}{\Delta t} \right|$$

If we divide Equation 21-8 by Equation 21-7, the factors of $|\Delta \Phi_B / \Delta t|$ cancel and we are left with

$$(21\text{-}9) \qquad \frac{|\text{output voltage}|}{|\text{input voltage}|} = \frac{|V_s(t)|}{|V_p(t)|} = \frac{N_s}{N_p}$$

Equation 21-9 is valid for the *instantaneous* values of the input and output voltages, so it must also be true for the *maximum* values. These are the voltage amplitudes, which we call V_p and V_s for the input (primary) voltage and output (secondary) voltage, respectively. Equation 21-9 is also true for the *rms* values of these voltages. So we are left with the result

Input and output voltages for a transformer (21-10)

Amplitudes of the input (p) and output (s) voltages $\Biggl\{ \dfrac{V_s}{V_p} = \dfrac{V_{s,\text{rms}}}{V_{p,\text{rms}}} = \dfrac{N_s}{N_p}$ Number of windings in the primary coil (p) and secondary coil (s)

Rms values of the input (p) and output (s) voltages

In other words, in a transformer the ratio of the number of windings in the secondary coil (N_s) to the number of windings in the primary coil (N_p) determines the output voltage relative to the input voltage. In a **step-up transformer**, N_S is greater than N_P, so the output voltage is greater than the input voltage. In a **step-down transformer**, N_S is less than N_P, which results in an output voltage less than the input voltage. A step-up transformer is used at an electric power generation station to raise the voltage provided by the generator (which is connected to the primary coil) to a much larger value in the transmission lines (which are connected to the secondary coil). Close to where the electric power is to be used in home or industry, step-down transformers are used to reduce the voltage to a safe value. The charger that you use for recharging your mobile phone or other electronic device is also a step-down transformer that lowers the voltage provided by the wall socket to a much lower value suitable for the battery to be recharged.

The *current* in the secondary coil is also different from that in the primary coil. If we neglect any energy losses in the transformer (for instance, due to heating of the iron core by eddy currents), conservation of energy requires that the rate at which energy is delivered to the primary coil by the input voltage must equal the rate at which energy is transferred from the primary to the secondary coil. The rate of energy delivery is power and power equals current times voltage (Equation 18-23), so

input power in primary coil = output power into secondary coil

$$(21\text{-}11) \qquad i_p(t) V_p(t) = i_s(t) V_s(t)$$

In Equation 21-11 $i_p(t)$ and $V_p(t)$ are the current and voltage in the primary coil at time t, and $i_s(t)$ and $V_s(t)$ are the corresponding quantities in the secondary coil. If we rearrange Equation 21-11 and compare to Equation 21-9, we see that

$$\frac{|\text{output current}|}{|\text{input current}|} = \frac{|i_s(t)|}{|i_p(t)|} = \frac{|V_p(t)|}{|V_s(t)|} = \frac{N_p}{N_s} \qquad \textbf{(21-12)}$$

Compare Equation 21-12 with Equation 21-10. For a step-up transformer, for which N_s is greater than N_p, the output voltage is greater than the input voltage but the output current is smaller than the input current. The reverse is true for a step-down transformer.

> *Go to Interactive Exercise 21-1 for more practice dealing with coils and current*

Example 21-2 A High-Voltage Transformer

Each of the 17 generators employed in the hydroelectric power plant at Hoover Dam in Colorado can generate up to 133 MW of average power. This power is delivered at 8.00 kV rms to a transformer that connects to a long-distance transmission line that operates at 5.00×10^2 kV rms. (a) What is the ratio of the number of windings in the secondary coil of the transformer to the number in the primary coil? (b) What is the rms current in the high-voltage transmission line?

Set Up

In part (a) we'll use Equation 21-10 to relate the ratio N_s/N_p (the number of windings in the secondary coil divided by the number in the primary coil) to the input and output rms voltages. In part (b) we'll assume that the transmission line delivers its power to a resistor, so we can relate the current, voltage, and power using Equations 18-9 and 18-23.

Input and output voltages for a transformer:

$$\frac{V_s}{V_p} = \frac{V_{s,\text{rms}}}{V_{p,\text{rms}}} = \frac{N_s}{N_p} \qquad (21\text{-}10)$$

Relationship among potential difference, current, and resistance:

$$V = iR \qquad (18\text{-}9)$$

Power for a circuit element:

$$P = iV \qquad (18\text{-}23)$$

$V_{p,\text{rms}} = 8.00 \text{ kV} \qquad V_{s,\text{rms}} = 5.00 \times 10^2 \text{ kV}$

Solve

(a) We know both the primary and secondary rms voltages, so we can rearrange Equation 21-10 to solve for the ratio of the number of windings.

From Equation 21-10,

$$\frac{N_s}{N_p} = \frac{V_{s,\text{rms}}}{V_{p,\text{rms}}} = \frac{5.00 \times 10^2 \text{ kV}}{8.00 \text{ kV}} = 62.5$$

There are 62.5 times as many windings in the secondary coil as in the primary coil (or, equivalently, 125 windings in the secondary for every two windings of the primary).

(b) Since the resistance R is a constant, the current and voltage both have the same sin ωt time dependence. We use this to relate the average power $P_{\text{average}} = 133$ MW to the rms values of the current and voltage in the transmission line.

If the voltage is $V(t) = V_0 \sin \omega t$, from Equation 18-9 the current is

$$i(t) = \frac{V(t)}{R} = \frac{V_0 \sin \omega t}{R} = \frac{V_0}{R} \sin \omega t = i_0 \sin \omega t$$

In this expression i_0 is the amplitude of the current. From Equation 18-23 the instantaneous power is

$$P(t) = i(t)V(t) = (V_0 \sin \omega t)(i_0 \sin \omega t) = i_0 V_0 \sin^2 \omega t$$

To find the average power P_{average}, replace $\sin^2 \omega t$ by its average value $\tfrac{1}{2}$:

$$P_{\text{average}} = \frac{i_0 V_0}{2} = \left(\frac{i_0}{\sqrt{2}}\right)\left(\frac{V_0}{\sqrt{2}}\right) = i_{\text{rms}} V_{\text{rms}}$$

The average power is the product of the rms current and the rms voltage. Since $i(t)$ has the same time dependence as $V(t)$, the rms value of current is equal to its maximum value divided by $\sqrt{2}$, just as for the voltage. From this expression, the rms current in the transmission line is

$$i_{s,rms} = \frac{P_{average}}{V_{s,rms}} = \frac{133 \text{ MW}}{5.00 \times 10^2 \text{ kV}} = \frac{133 \times 10^6 \text{ W}}{5.00 \times 10^5 \text{ V}} = 266 \text{ A}$$

Reflect

In the process of delivering power to the end user, the voltage must ultimately be stepped down to 120 V. This process is not normally done with a single transformer. One reason is that if only one transformer were used for this stepping-down process, there would need to be more than 4000 windings in the primary coil for every one in the secondary.

Ratio of coil windings to step down 5.00×10^2 kV to 120 V:

$$\frac{N_p}{N_s} = \frac{V_p}{V_s} = \frac{5.00 \times 10^2 \text{ kV}}{120 \text{ V}} = 4170$$

We found a current of 266 A in the transmission line. Although that sounds large, it is only about a factor of 10 more than the current in household wiring. In addition, the power loss in the transmission wire is relatively low at this current. A few hundred kilometers of transmission wire might have a resistance of 25 Ω. The loss in such a line would be about 1.8 MW. Although in absolute terms this is a significant power loss, it represents only 1.4% of the total power transmitted.

The voltage between the two ends of the transmission line is $V_{ends} = iR$, where $R = 25$ Ω is the resistance of the line. Use the formula we derived in part (b) to find the power lost in the transmission line:

$$\begin{aligned} P_{lost,average} &= i_{rms}V_{ends,rms} = i_{rms}(i_{rms}R) \\ &= i_{rms}^2 R = (266 \text{ A})^2 (25 \text{ }\Omega) = 1.8 \times 10^6 \text{ W} = 1.8 \text{ MW} \end{aligned}$$

Express this as a percentage of the power that is transmitted:

$$\begin{aligned} \text{percentage} &= \frac{\text{power lost}}{\text{power transmitted}} \times 100\% \\ &= \frac{1.8 \text{ MW}}{133 \text{ MW}} \times 100\% = 1.4\% \end{aligned}$$

? Got the Concept? 21-2   Transforming a Transformer

A certain step-up transformer has 100 windings in its primary coil and 250 windings in its secondary coil. You reverse the connections to the transformer so that the primary coil becomes the secondary and vice versa. If you now apply an ac input voltage of 120 V rms to the reversed transformer, what will be the rms output voltage? (a) 40 V; (b) 48 V; (c) 100 V; (d) 250 V; (e) 300 V.

Take-Home Message for Section 21-3

✔   A transformer uses mutual inductance to raise or lower an ac voltage.

✔   In a step-up transformer, there are more windings in the secondary coil than in the primary coil. The output voltage is greater than the input voltage, and the output current is less than the input current.

✔   In a step-down transformer, there are fewer windings in the secondary coil than in the primary coil. The output voltage is less than the input voltage, and the output current is greater than the input current.

21-4 An inductor is a circuit element that opposes changes in current

We saw in Section 21-3 that a transformer works by the mutual inductance of two coils: A change in current in one coil causes a change in the magnetic flux through the other coil, which induces an emf. The same physics applies equally well to individual windings within a *single* coil. You can think of each turn of the coil as a separate loop; as a changing current passes through any loop, the changing magnetic field that arises induces an emf in the other loops. This induced emf, according to Lenz's law, opposes the change in flux that created it. So if the current is increasing in the coil, the induced emf will oppose an increase in current. If the current is decreasing, the induced emf will be directed so that the current is augmented. This **self-inductance** has the net effect of opposing a change in current in a coil. Let's see how to determine the emf induced in this way.

Inductance of a Coil

Consider a coil of N windings in which there is a current i. This current causes the coil to produce a magnetic field, and the flux of this field through each winding of the coil is Φ_B. The total flux through all N windings is then $N\Phi_B$. We define the **inductance** of the coil (symbol L) as the total flux divided by the current that produces it:

Definition of inductance
(21-13)

The units of inductance are henrys, abbreviated as H: $1\,\text{H} = 1\,\text{T}\cdot\text{m}^2/\text{A}$.

The magnetic field is directly proportional to the current i that produces it, and the same is true of the flux of that magnetic field. So the numerator in Equation 21-13 is proportional to the current i. Since the denominator in Equation 21-13 is equal to i, the current will cancel out when we calculate the inductance L. The inductance therefore does not depend on i, but only on geometrical factors such as the dimensions of the coil and physical constants. As an example, let's calculate the inductance of a long, straight coil or solenoid. We learned in Section 19-7 that the magnetic field of an ideal solenoid (one whose length is much greater than its diameter) is uniform, and has a magnitude given by Equation 19-17:

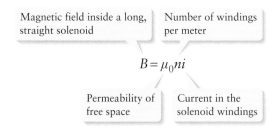

Magnetic field inside a long, straight solenoid
(19-17)

If the solenoid has length ℓ, the quantity n in Equation 19-17 equals the total number of windings N divided by ℓ. We can then write the magnetic flux through the cross-sectional area A of each winding of the solenoid as

$$\Phi_B = BA = (\mu_0 ni)A = \left(\frac{\mu_0 Ni}{\ell}\right)A$$

If we substitute this into Equation 21-13, we get the following expression for the inductance of the solenoid:

$$L = \frac{N\Phi_B}{i} = \frac{N}{i}\left(\frac{\mu_0 Ni}{\ell}\right)A = \frac{\mu_0 N^2 A}{\ell} \qquad (21\text{-}14)$$

(inductance of a solenoid)

For the solenoid, as for any coil, the inductance depends only on its dimensions and a physical constant (μ_0, the permeability of free space); inductance does not depend on current.

The quantity $\mu_0 = 4\pi \times 10^{-7}\,\text{T·m/A}$ appears in all expressions for the inductance of a coil. Since $1\,\text{H} = 1\,\text{T·m}^2/\text{A}$, it follows that $1\,\text{T·m/A} = 1\,\text{H/m}$. So an alternative way to express the permeability of free space is $\mu_0 = 4\pi \times 10^{-7}\,\text{H/m}$. This is useful for problems that involve inductance, like the following example.

Example 21-3 How Large Is One Henry?

You decide to create a solenoid with inductance of 1.00 H by tightly wrapping wire around a plastic pipe. The wire has a diameter of 2.60 mm, and the pipe has an outside radius of 3.00 cm. How long a pipe will you need? Is 1.00 H a large or a small amount of inductance?

Set Up

Winding the wire tightly around the pipe will create a solenoid. The length of the solenoid may likely be large compared to its diameter, so we'll treat it as ideal. Then we can use Equation 21-14 to calculate the inductance of this solenoid. The pipe has a circular cross section, so to find A we'll use the expression for the area of a circle.

Inductance of a solenoid:

$$L = \frac{\mu_0 N^2 A}{\ell} \qquad (21\text{-}14)$$

Area of a circle of radius r:

$$A = \pi r^2$$

Solve

We don't know how many windings the solenoid will have. However, because the solenoid is tightly wrapped we can write the number of windings as the total length of the solenoid divided by the diameter of the wire. We substitute this expression for N into the inductance equation, and then solve for the length of the pipe.

The number of windings that will fit equals the length ℓ of the pipe divided by the diameter D_W of the wire:

$$N = \frac{\ell}{D_W}$$

Substitute this into Equation 21-14 for the inductance of the solenoid:

$$L = \frac{\mu_0 (\ell/D_W)^2 A}{\ell} = \frac{\mu_0 \ell A}{D_W^2}$$

The length of the pipe is therefore

$$\ell = \frac{L D_W^2}{\mu_0 A}$$

The cross-sectional area of the pipe of radius 3.00 cm is

$$A = \pi r^2 = \pi (3.00\,\text{cm})^2 = \pi (3.00 \times 10^{-2}\,\text{m})^2 = 2.83 \times 10^{-3}\,\text{m}^2$$

We are given $L = 1.00\,\text{H}$, $D_W = 2.60 \times 10^{-3}\,\text{m}$, and $\mu_0 = 4\pi \times 10^{-7}\,\text{H/m}$, so

$$\ell = \frac{(1.00\,\text{H})\,(2.60 \times 10^{-3}\,\text{m})^2}{(4\pi \times 10^{-7}\,\text{H/m})\,(2.83 \times 10^{-3}\,\text{m}^2)}$$

$$= 1.90 \times 10^3\,\text{m} = 1.90\,\text{km}$$

Reflect

We would need a pipe nearly 2 km long to construct a 1.00-H inductor! Practical inductors have much smaller values of inductance. (Note that the length we determined is indeed much greater than the radius of the pipe, so we were justified in treating this as an ideal solenoid.)

The emf of an Inductor

An inductor in a circuit produces an emf if the current through the inductor changes. We can find an expression for this emf if we combine the definition of inductance,

Equation 21-13, with Faraday's and Lenz's laws (Section 20-3). From Equation 21-13, the total flux through an inductor is

$$N\Phi_B = Li$$

Faraday's and Lenz's laws tell us that the emf produced by an inductor is equal to the negative of the rate of change of the total flux through the inductor (Equation 20-3). So we can write the induced emf in the inductor as

$$\varepsilon = -\frac{\Delta(N\Phi_B)}{\Delta t} = -\frac{\Delta(Li)}{\Delta t}$$

(21-15)

Let's ignore the resistance of the wire that makes up the inductor, so this is an *ideal* inductor. Then ε in Equation 21-15 is also equal to the voltage V across the inductor (there is no additional voltage drop due to resistance, since there is zero resistance). Since the inductance L does not change with time, we can write Equation 21-15 as

Voltage across an inductor   Inductance of the inductor

$$V = -L\frac{\Delta i}{\Delta t}$$

Rate of change of the current i in the inductor

Voltage across an inductor
(21-16)

The negative sign means that the voltage opposes any change in the current.

Let's examine Equation 21-16 to see what it means. In Figure 21-5a an inductor (symbolized by a coil) carries a constant current i. The rate of change of this constant current is zero, so from Equation 21-16 there is zero voltage across the inductor: $V = 0$. (Remember, we are ignoring the resistance of the wires that make up the inductor.) In Figure 21-5b the current through the inductor increases, so in Equation 21-16 $\Delta i/\Delta t > 0$ and $V < 0$. The negative value of V means that there is a voltage *drop* from where the current enters the inductor to where it leaves the inductor. That's like the voltage drop for current that passes through a resistor, which means that the inductor is now resisting the current—or, more properly, resisting the increase in current. So in this case the voltage opposes the change in current. In Figure 21-5c the current through the inductor decreases, so in Equation 21-16 $\Delta i/\Delta t < 0$ and $V > 0$. The positive value of V means that there is a voltage *gain* from where the current enters the inductor to where it leaves. That's like the voltage gain for current directed through a battery (a source of emf) from the negative terminal to the positive terminal, so in this case the inductor is assisting the current and so is trying to prevent the current from decreasing.

(a) An inductor with constant current

- The symbol for an inductor is a coil.
- An ideal inductor has zero resistance.

$i \longrightarrow$

If the current in the inductor is constant, there is zero voltage across the inductor: $V = 0$. This includes the case where there is no current.

(b) An inductor with increasing current

The voltage *drops* from left to right along the inductor.

i at time $t \longrightarrow$
i at time $t + \Delta t \longrightarrow$

If current in the inductor is increasing so $\Delta i/\Delta t > 0$, there is negative voltage across the inductor: $V < 0$. This voltage opposes the increase in the current.

(c) An inductor with decreasing current

The voltage *rises* from left to right along the inductor.

i at time $t \longrightarrow$
i at time $t + \Delta t \longrightarrow$

If current in the inductor is decreasing so $\Delta i/\Delta t < 0$, there is positive voltage across the inductor: $V > 0$. This voltage opposes the decrease in the current.

Figure 21-5 **Voltage across an inductor** The voltage across an ideal inductor (a coil with no resistance) depends on whether the current through the inductor is (a) constant, (b) increasing, or (c) decreasing.

Again, the voltage opposes the change in current. We can summarize these observations by saying that

The voltage across an inductor opposes any change in the current through the inductor. If the current is not changing, the voltage is zero.

This observation is just what we would expect from Lenz's law, which says that the induced emf in any coil (including an inductor) always acts to oppose any changes. A useful rule is that V in Equation 21-16 represents the voltage *gain* across the inductor when traveling in the direction of the current. If V is negative, there is a voltage drop.

❗ Watch Out! Don't confuse inductors, capacitors, and resistors.

● It's useful to contrast an inductor with two other devices used in circuits, a capacitor (Section 17-5) and a resistor (Section 18-3). The voltage across a capacitor is $V = q/C$, where q is the magnitude of the charge on either plate of the capacitor and C is the capacitance (a quantity that, like the inductance of an inductor, depends on the geometry of the capacitor). The greater the amount of charge on each capacitor plate, the greater the capacitor voltage. The voltage across a resistor that carries current i is $V = iR$, where R is the resistance of the resistor. This voltage is proportional to the rate at which charge moves through the resistor, that is, the current i. The greater the current, the greater the rate at which charge flows through the resistor and the greater the resistor voltage. By contrast, for an inductor Equation 21-16 tells us that the voltage is proportional to the rate of change of current—that is, to the rate of change of the rate at which charge flows through the inductor.

Ferrite inductor

Figure 21-6 Inductor on a cable The ferrite inductor on this monitor cable reduces the interference from external high-frequency electromagnetic signals.

Our observations show that an inductor in a circuit acts to oppose changes in the current within the circuit. The more rapid the change in current—that is, the greater the value of the quantity $\Delta i/\Delta t$ in Equation 21-16—the greater the voltage that will oppose the change. Some computer cables have a built-in inductor (Figure 21-6) that is designed to deal with high-frequency interference from signals radiated from other devices. These high-frequency signals would cause rapidly changing currents in the cables that could compromise the operation of the computer, so it's important to suppress them. If such a signal appears, the inductor will set up a voltage that opposes the signal. The inductor is made of a special material called a *ferrite* that also has a large resistance to high-frequency currents, so the energy in the stray signal is absorbed and dissipated as heat.

As we'll see in the following sections, inductors aren't just for suppressing currents. In the right circumstances, they can be used for *sustaining* an alternating current of just the right frequency. This will help us understand what's involved in tuning a television or radio receiver.

Example 21-4 Inductor Voltage

A 0.500-mH inductor is in a dc circuit that carries a current of 0.500 A. If the current increases to 0.900 A in 0.150 ms due to a fault in the circuit, how large is the voltage that appears across the inductor? From the perspective of a positive charge moving through the inductor, is there a voltage rise or drop across the inductor?

Set Up

We'll use Equation 21-16 to calculate the voltage induced across the inductor. To decide whether there's a voltage rise or drop, we'll use the idea that the voltage across the inductor acts to oppose the change in current.

Voltage across an inductor:

$$V = -L\frac{\Delta i}{\Delta t} \qquad (21\text{-}16)$$

$i = 0.500\ A$
$i\ increasing$

Solve

Find the voltage that appears in the inductor.

The current increases from 0.500 A to 0.900 A in 0.150 ms $= 0.150 \times 10^{-3}$ s, so

$$\frac{\Delta i}{\Delta t} = \frac{0.900\ \text{A} - 0.500\ \text{A}}{0.150 \times 10^{-3}\ \text{s}} = 2.67 \times 10^3\ \text{A/s}$$

From Equation 21-16, the voltage across the inductor is

$$V = -L\frac{\Delta i}{\Delta t} = -(0.500 \times 10^{-3}\,\text{H})(2.67 \times 10^3\,\text{A/s})$$
$$= -1.33\,\text{H}\cdot\text{A/s} = -1.33\,\text{V}$$

The magnitude of the voltage is 1.33 V. The value of V is negative, which means that there is a voltage *drop* of 1.33 V across the inductor. Thus, the voltage opposes the flow of current and so opposes the increase in current (compare Figure 21-5b).

Reflect

The voltage induced in the inductor is comparable to that produced by a household AA or AAA battery. This voltage is only present during the time when the current is *changing*, however; when the current is constant, the inductor voltage is zero.

? Got the Concept? 21-3 Inductors vs. Capacitors vs. Resistors

For which of the following devices does the voltage across that device depend on the current that flows into that device? (a) An inductor; (b) a capacitor; (c) a resistor; (d) more than one of these; (e) none of these.

Take-Home Message for Section 21-4

✔ The inductance of a coil equals the net magnetic flux through the coil due to the current in the coil, divided by the current.

✔ An inductor is a circuit device that opposes any change in the current through that device. The voltage across an inductor is proportional to its inductance and to the rate of change of current through the inductor.

21-5 In a circuit with an inductor and capacitor, charge and current oscillate

Figure 21-7 shows a circuit made up of an inductor of inductance L and a capacitor of capacitance C connected by ideal, zero-resistance wires. This is called an **LC circuit**. With the switch open, positive charge $+Q_0$ is placed on the upper plate of the capacitor and negative charge $-Q_0$ is placed on the lower plate. This can be done by transferring a number of electrons from the upper plate to the lower plate. The switch is then closed, completing the circuit so that charge can flow. What happens? Remarkably, we'll see that the charge in this circuit behaves very much like the block attached to an ideal spring that we studied in Section 12-3: The charge *oscillates* back and forth in simple harmonic motion. Among other applications, this effect is used to generate the oscillating electric field that a microwave oven uses to cook food.

An *LC* Circuit and Simple Harmonic Motion

You might think that the excess electrons would move along the wires from the lower plate to the upper plate until the two plates are electrically neutral, at which point the motion of electrons would stop. Because there's an inductor in the circuit, however, what happens is dramatically different and far more interesting. Figure 21-8 shows four steps in the behavior of the LC circuit. Once the switch is closed (Step 1 in Figure 21-8), a current is established around the circuit in the counterclockwise direction. (Remember that by convention, the direction of current is that in which positive charges would flow.) The current can't suddenly increase, however, because a voltage appears across the inductor to oppose the increase in current. Instead the current increases gradually and

The capacitor is charged before the switch is closed.

Figure 21-7 An *LC* circuit An inductor (inductance L) and a capacitor (capacitance C) are connected as shown. Figure 21-8 shows what happens when we close the switch.

Figure 21-8 Oscillations of an *LC* circuit When the switch in Figure 21-7 is closed, the capacitor charge oscillates back and forth through the circuit. These electrical oscillations are directly analogous to the mechanical oscillations of a block attached to an ideal spring (Section 12-3).

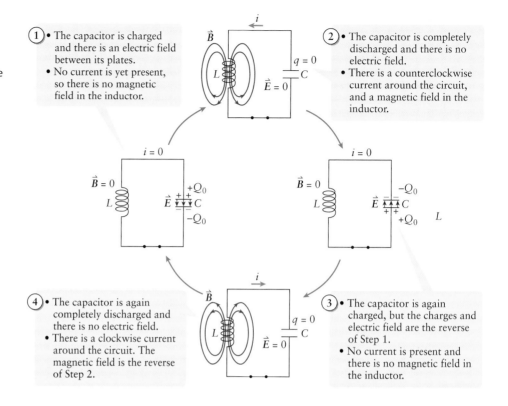

Figure 21-8 Oscillations of an *LC* circuit When the switch in Figure 21-7 is closed, the capacitor charge oscillates back and forth through the circuit. These electrical oscillations are directly analogous to the mechanical oscillations of a block attached to an ideal spring (Section 12-3).

reaches a maximum value when the capacitor is fully discharged (Step 2 in Figure 21-8). The current can't just come to a sudden stop, however; the inductor always opposes any change in the current, so once the current starts to decrease a voltage will appear across the inductor to slow that decrease. As a result the motion of charge continues. When the current finally decreases to zero, the capacitor is again charged but with the opposite polarity to its initial configuration (Step 3 in Figure 21-8). At this point a current is established just as it was between Steps 1 and 2, but in the opposite direction: The current is clockwise, increasing gradually until the current is maximum and the capacitor is again fully discharged (Step 4 in Figure 21-8). Again the inductor keeps the current from coming to a sudden stop, and instead the current decreases gradually until the capacitor is again fully charged and has returned to the configuration in Step 1. The whole process then starts over!

You can see that what's happening here is an *oscillation* of charge and current. Let's show that these oscillations are another example of *simple harmonic motion*, the special kind of oscillatory motion that we studied in Section 12-3. To see this, let's apply Kirchhoff's loop rule to the *LC* circuit in Figure 21-8. This says that if we travel around the circuit and measure the voltage across each element of the circuit, the sum of those voltage changes must be zero.

We'll begin our trip around the circuit at the upper right-hand corner, and move around the circuit clockwise so that we first pass downward through the capacitor. If we let q be the charge on the upper plate of the capacitor at a given instant, the charge on the lower plate at that same instant is $-q$. So if we start at the upper right-hand corner of the circuit and travel downward through the capacitor, we'll encounter a voltage drop

(21-17)
$$V_C = -\frac{q}{C} \quad (LC \text{ circuit})$$

This is negative if q is positive, since then we travel from the positive charge to the negative charge and so will encounter a decrease in electric potential (that is, a voltage drop). If q is negative, so that there's negative charge on the upper plate and positive charge on the lower plate, we'll encounter a voltage rise.

As we continue around the circuit, we'll encounter zero voltage across the wires (which have zero resistance). We next pass upward through the inductor on the left-hand side of the circuit. We'll take the current i to be positive if it also flows upward through the inductor (that is, clockwise around the circuit). If the current is positive, positive charge will flow onto the upper plate of the capacitor. The rate at which the charge q on the upper plate increases, measured in coulombs per second or amperes, is just equal to the current:

$$i = \frac{\Delta q}{\Delta t} \quad (LC \text{ circuit}) \tag{21-18}$$

From Equation 21-16, the voltage across the inductor is

$$V_L = -L\frac{\Delta i}{\Delta t} \quad (LC \text{ circuit}) \tag{21-19}$$

If the current through the inductor is positive (upward, or clockwise around the circuit) and increasing in magnitude (becoming more positive), then $\Delta i/\Delta t$ is positive and V_L is negative: We'll encounter a voltage drop as we move upward through the inductor. The same is true if the current through the inductor is negative (downward, or counterclockwise around the circuit) and decreasing in magnitude (becoming less negative). If instead the current through the inductor is either positive (clockwise) and decreasing or negative (counterclockwise) and becoming more negative, then $\Delta i/\Delta t$ is negative and V_L is positive: We'll encounter a voltage rise as we move upward through the inductor.

Kirchhoff's loop rule says that the sum of the voltages V_C from Equation 21-17 and V_L from Equation 21-19 must be zero:

$$V_C + V_L = -\frac{q}{C} - L\frac{\Delta i}{\Delta t} = 0$$

If we add $L(\Delta i/\Delta t)$ to both sides of this equation, we get

$$L\frac{\Delta i}{\Delta t} = -\frac{q}{C} \quad (LC \text{ circuit}) \tag{21-20}$$

On the face of it Equation 21-20 looks like a very difficult equation to solve. Both the capacitor charge q and the current i depend on time, and Equation 21-18 tells us that the current is equal to the rate of change of the capacitor charge. But in fact this is an equation that we've solved before, although with different symbols. Recall from Section 12-3 that if a block of mass m is attached to an ideal spring of spring constant k and displaced from equilibrium by x, the force that the spring exerts on the block is $F_x = -kx$. (Positive x means that the spring is stretched, and negative x means that the spring is compressed.) If the block is then released, it oscillates. The velocity of the block is the rate of change of the displacement x:

$$v_x = \frac{\Delta x}{\Delta t} \quad (\text{block and ideal spring}) \tag{21-21}$$

Newton's second law says that force $-kx$ on the block is equal to the mass of the block multiplied by its acceleration a_x. Acceleration is the rate of change of velocity, so we can write Newton's second law for the block as

$$m\frac{\Delta v_x}{\Delta t} = -kx \quad (\text{block and ideal spring}) \tag{21-22}$$

You can see that Equations 21-21 and 21-22 for a block and ideal spring are the *same* as Equations 21-18 and 21-20 for an LC circuit, with the names of the variables changed as listed in the first four rows of Table 21-1.

For a block attached to an ideal spring, the spring provides a restoring *force*: Whether the spring is compressed or stretched, this force tries to return the system to equilibrium. The block, however, has *inertia*: Once in motion, it tends to remain in motion, As a result, when the spring reaches the equilibrium position, it does not stop but instead overshoots. As a result, the block oscillates back and forth around its equilibrium position. In a similar way, the capacitor in an LC circuit provides a restoring *voltage* $-q/C$; whether q is positive or negative, this voltage drives charge around the circuit in a direction that tries to neutralize both plates. The inductor opposes changes in current; once a current is in motion, the inductor tends to keep it in motion. As a result, when the capacitor is in equilibrium with both of its plates neutral, the current "overshoots"

Table 21-1 Comparing a block on an ideal spring to an *LC* circuit

Quantity for a block on an ideal spring	Corresponding quantity for an *LC* circuit
spring displacement, x	capacitor charge, q
block velocity, $v_x = \Delta x / \Delta t$	current, $i = \Delta q / \Delta t$
spring constant of the spring, k	reciprocal of the capacitance, $1/C$
mass of the block, m	inductance, L
oscillation amplitude, A	maximum capacitor charge, Q_0
potential energy of the spring, $U_{\text{spring}} = \dfrac{1}{2}kx^2$	electric energy in the capacitor, $U_E = \dfrac{q^2}{2C}$
kinetic energy of the block, $K = \dfrac{1}{2}mv_x^2$	magnetic energy in the inductor, $U_B = \dfrac{1}{2}Li^2$

and the capacitor ends up charged again with reversed polarity. The result is an oscillation that's *exactly* like the simple harmonic motion of a block on an ideal spring. It's like watching the same play but with different actors in the cast: The inductor plays the role of the block, and the capacitor plays the role of the spring.

We can use Table 21-1 to tell us the angular frequency, period, and frequency for the oscillations of an *LC* circuit. From Equation 12-11, these quantities for a block on a spring are

Angular frequency, period, and
frequency for a block attached
to an ideal spring
(12-11)

Angular frequency $\quad \omega = \sqrt{\dfrac{k}{m}}$

k = Spring constant of the spring

m = Mass of the object connected to the spring

Period $\quad T = \dfrac{2\pi}{\omega} = 2\pi\sqrt{\dfrac{m}{k}}$

Frequency $\quad f = \dfrac{1}{T} = \dfrac{1}{2\pi}\sqrt{\dfrac{k}{m}} = \dfrac{\omega}{2\pi}$

Table 21-1 tells us that k corresponds to $1/C$ and m corresponds to L. So the angular frequency, period, and frequency for the oscillations of an *LC* circuit are

Angular frequency, period,
and frequency for an *LC* circuit
(21-23)

Angular frequency $\quad \omega = \sqrt{\dfrac{1}{LC}}$

C = Capacitance

Period $\quad T = \dfrac{2\pi}{\omega} = 2\pi\sqrt{LC}$

L = Inductance

Frequency $\quad f = \dfrac{1}{T} = \dfrac{1}{2\pi}\sqrt{\dfrac{1}{LC}} = \dfrac{\omega}{2\pi}$

The smaller the product LC of inductance and capacitance, the greater the angular frequency and frequency of the oscillations and the shorter the oscillation period.

As an example, imagine an *LC* circuit made with a 2.00-μH inductor and a 10.0-nF capacitor. Then $L = 2.00 \times 10^{-6}$ H and $C = 10.0 \times 10^{-9}$ F, and from the last of Equations 21-23 the oscillation frequency is

$$f = \frac{1}{2\pi}\sqrt{\frac{1}{LC}} = \frac{1}{2\pi}\sqrt{\frac{1}{(2.00 \times 10^{-6}\,\text{H})(10.0 \times 10^{-9}\,\text{F})}}$$

$$= 1.13 \times 10^6\,\text{Hz} = 1.13\,\text{MHz}$$

The charges in this circuit oscillate back and forth 1.13 million times per second and complete one oscillation in a time $T = 1/f = 8.89 \times 10^{-7}\,\text{s} = 0.889\,\mu\text{s}$. Such oscillations are much more rapid than those of a large mechanical oscillator such as a block attached to a spring.

The capacitor charge q is analogous to the displacement x for a block on a spring, so the maximum capacitor charge Q_0 is analogous to the amplitude A (the maximum displacement of the block on a spring). We can use this observation to write expressions for the capacitor charge q and current i as functions of time. In Section 12-3 we found that the displacement x and velocity v_x for a block on a spring are given by

$$x(t) = A \cos(\omega t + \phi) \quad \text{(block and ideal spring)} \tag{12-6}$$

$$v_x(t) = -\omega A \sin(\omega t + \phi) \quad \text{(block and ideal spring)} \tag{12-7}$$

Since A is analogous to Q_0, displacement x is analogous to q, and velocity v_x is analogous to i, we can write the following expressions for an LC circuit:

$$q(t) = Q_0 \cos(\omega t + \phi) \quad \text{(LC circuit)} \tag{21-24}$$

$$i(t) = -\omega Q_0 \sin(\omega t + \phi) \quad \text{(LC circuit)} \tag{21-25}$$

The angular frequency ω is given by the first of Equations 21-23: $\omega = \sqrt{1/LC}$. The cosine is maximum when the sine is zero and vice versa, so the capacitor charge is maximum when the current is zero and the capacitor charge is zero when the current is maximum. That's just what Figure 21-8 shows.

Since $\sin(\omega t + \phi)$ has values between $+1$ and -1, the maximum value of the current in Equation 21-25 is

$$i_{\text{max}} = \omega Q_0 = \frac{Q_0}{\sqrt{LC}} \quad \text{(LC circuit)} \tag{21-26}$$

As an example, consider the LC circuit we described above with $L = 2.00\,\mu\text{H} = 2.00 \times 10^{-6}\,\text{H}$ and $C = 10.0\,\text{nF} = 10.0 \times 10^{-9}\,\text{F}$. If the maximum capacitor charge is $Q_0 = 0.400\,\mu\text{C} = 4.00 \times 10^{-7}\,\text{C}$, the maximum current in the LC circuit is

$$i_{\text{max}} = \frac{Q_0}{\sqrt{LC}} = \frac{4.00 \times 10^{-7}\,\text{C}}{\sqrt{(2.00 \times 10^{-6}\,\text{H})(10.0 \times 10^{-9}\,\text{F})}} = 2.83\,\text{A}$$

Even though only a tiny amount of charge oscillates back and forth between the capacitor plates, the oscillation is so rapid that the maximum current is appreciable.

Energy in an LC Circuit

An electric circuit is first and foremost a means of transferring energy from one part of the circuit to another. The same is true for an LC circuit. To see what kinds of energy are involved, let's first look at the total mechanical energy E in a system made up of a block attached to an ideal spring. From Section 12-4, this is the sum of the kinetic energy K of the moving block and the elastic potential energy U_{spring} in the spring:

$$E = K + U_{\text{spring}} = \frac{1}{2}mv_x^2 + \frac{1}{2}kx^2$$

The kinetic and potential energies change, but the total energy E is constant and equal to $(1/2)kA^2$ (A is the amplitude, or maximum displacement).

Table 21-1 tells us how to find the analogous expression for the total energy of an LC circuit: Just replace m with L, k with $1/C$, x with q, and v_x with i. The result is

Energy in an LC circuit

Magnetic energy U_B in the inductor

Electric energy U_E in the capacitor

$$E = \frac{1}{2}Li^2 + \frac{q^2}{2C}$$

Charge on the capacitor

Inductance of the inductor

Current in the inductor

Capacitance of the capacitor

Magnetic and electric energies in an LC circuit

(21-27)

We recognize the second term on the right-hand side of Equation 21-27, $q^2/2C$, from Section 17-6: It's just the electric potential energy stored in the capacitor. Since a capacitor plays the same role in an LC circuit as the spring does in a block–spring combination, this electric potential energy is analogous to the elastic potential energy of a spring. We use the symbol U_E for this electric energy. The subscript E reminds us that an $\vec{E}$-field is involved; you can think of U_E as the energy required to take an uncharged capacitor and move charges $+q$ and $-q$ to the plates of the capacitor, thereby setting up an electric field $\vec{E}$ between the plates.

The first term on the right-hand side of Equation 21-27, $(1/2)Li^2$, is one that we haven't seen before. The presence of the inductance L in this term tells us that it represents energy stored in the inductor as a result of the presence of current. To see how this energy arises, recall from Section 21-4 that an inductor sets up an emf that opposes any change in the current through the inductor. If we want to make current flow through an inductor where none was flowing before, we have to do work against that emf. The quantity $(1/2)Li^2$ is exactly equal to the amount of work we have to do. By building up the current from zero to i, we also create a magnetic field $\vec{B}$, so we can think of $(1/2)Li^2$ as the energy required to set up a magnetic field in and around the inductor. That's why we call this **magnetic energy** and denote it by the symbol U_B (the subscript B reminds us that a $\vec{B}$-field is involved).

! Watch Out! **Magnetic energy is not the same as kinetic energy.**

Table 21-1 shows that the magnetic energy in an inductor, $U_B = (1/2)Li^2$, is analogous to the kinetic energy $K = (1/2)mv_x^2$ of the block in an oscillating block–spring system. This magnetic energy is only present if charges are in motion in the inductor, so i is nonzero. However, U_B is *not* the kinetic energy of the moving charges. That kinetic energy is very small because the moving electrons have very little mass. Instead, U_B is the energy stored in the magnetic field of the inductor. The inductor current i appears in the expression for U_B because it is this current that gives rise to the magnetic field.

In an LC circuit the energy oscillates between the electric and magnetic forms, just as the energy in a block–spring combination oscillates between the potential and kinetic forms (see Figure 12-10 in Section 12-4). In Figure 21-8 the energy is purely electric in Steps 1 and 3 (where the capacitor charge is maximum and the current is zero) and purely magnetic in Steps 2 and 4 (where the capacitor charge is zero and the current is maximum). If we substitute $q(t)$ from Equation 21-24 and $i(t)$ from Equation 21-25 into Equation 21-27, we get an expression for the energy of the LC circuit at any time:

$$E = U_B + U_E = \frac{1}{2}L[-\omega Q_0 \sin(\omega t + \phi)]^2 + \frac{[Q_0 \cos(\omega t + \phi)]^2}{2C}$$

(21-28)
$$= \frac{1}{2}L\omega^2 Q_0^2 \sin^2(\omega t + \phi) + \frac{Q_0^2}{2C}\cos^2(\omega t + \phi)$$

The first of Equations 21-23 tells us that $\omega = 1/\sqrt{LC}$, so $\omega^2 = 1/LC$ and $L\omega^2 = 1/C$. If we substitute this into the first term on the right-hand side of Equation 21-28 and recall that $\sin^2\theta + \cos^2\theta = 1$, we get

$$E = \frac{Q_0^2}{2C}\sin^2(\omega t + \phi) + \frac{Q_0^2}{2C}\cos^2(\omega t + \phi)$$

$$= \frac{Q_0^2}{2C}(\sin^2(\omega t + \phi) + \cos^2(\omega t + \phi))$$

(21-29)
$$= \frac{Q_0^2}{2C} \quad (LC \text{ circuit})$$

The electric and magnetic energies in an oscillating LC circuit both vary with time, but the total energy $E = Q_0^2/2C$ remains constant.

Example 21-5 Analyzing an *LC* Circuit

An oscillating *LC* circuit is made of a 2.00–μH inductor and a 10.0–nF capacitor. The maximum charge on the capacitor is 0.400 μC. (a) Find the total energy in the circuit. (b) At an instant when one-quarter of the total energy is electric energy in the capacitor, find the absolute values of the capacitor charge and the current in the inductor.

Set Up

Equation 21-29 tells us the total energy of the *LC* circuit. This equals the sum of the magnetic and electric energies, which depend on the current *i* and capacitor charge *q* as Equation 21-27 tells us. We'll use this to find the absolute values of *i* and *q* at the instant in question.

Energy in an *LC* circuit:

$$E = \frac{Q_0^2}{2C} \quad (21\text{-}29)$$

Magnetic and electric energies in an *LC* circuit:

$$E = U_B + U_E = \frac{1}{2}Li^2 + \frac{q^2}{2C} \quad (21\text{-}27)$$

$Q_0 = 0.400\ \mu C$

$L = 2.00\ \mu H$

$C = 10.0\ nF$

Solve

(a) Use Equation 21-29 to find the total energy.

The maximum capacitor charge is $Q_0 = 0.400\ \mu C = 0.400 \times 10^{-6}\ C$, and the capacitance is $C = 10.0\ nF = 10.0 \times 10^{-9}\ F$. The total energy of the oscillating circuit is

$$E = \frac{Q_0^2}{2C} = \frac{(0.400 \times 10^{-6}\ C)^2}{2(10.0 \times 10^{-9}\ F)} = 8.00 \times 10^{-6}\ J = 8.00\ \mu J$$

(b) The total energy remains constant. So if one-quarter of the energy is in the electric form, the other three-quarters must be in the magnetic form. Use this to determine the absolute values of the current and capacitor charge.

The magnetic energy is $\frac{3}{4}$ of the total energy:

$$U_B = \frac{1}{2}Li^2 = \frac{3}{4}E = \frac{3}{4}(8.00 \times 10^{-6}\ J) = 6.00 \times 10^{-6}\ J$$

The inductance is $2.00\ \mu H = 2.00 \times 10^{-6}\ H$. Solve for the absolute value of the current:

$$i^2 = \frac{2U_B}{L} = \frac{2(6.00 \times 10^{-6}\ J)}{2.00 \times 10^{-6}\ H} = 6.00\ A^2$$

$$|i| = \sqrt{i^2} = \sqrt{6.00\ A^2} = 2.45\ A$$

The electric energy is $\frac{1}{4}$ of the total energy:

$$U_E = \frac{q^2}{2C} = \frac{1}{4}E = \frac{1}{4}(8.00 \times 10^{-6}\ J) = 2.00 \times 10^{-6}\ J$$

Solve for the absolute value of the capacitor charge:

$$q^2 = 2CU_E = 2(10.0 \times 10^{-9}\ F)(2.00 \times 10^{-6}\ J)$$
$$= 4.00 \times 10^{-14}\ C^2$$

$$|q| = \sqrt{q^2} = \sqrt{4.00 \times 10^{-14}\ C^2} = 2.00 \times 10^{-7}\ C = 0.200\ \mu C$$

Reflect

We can check our result for $|q|$ by noting that U_E is proportional to q^2. If the electric energy U_E has its maximum value when $q = Q_0 = 0.400\ \mu C$, then U_E will have $\frac{1}{4}$ of this value when $q = Q_0/2 = 0.200\ \mu C$.

Note that all that we can determine in this problem are the absolute values of *i* and *q*. That's because the magnetic and electric energies are proportional to the squares of *i* and *q*, respectively. If the current were negative (counterclockwise in Figure 21-8) so that $i = -2.45\ A$, the magnetic energy would be the same as if $i = +2.45\ A$ (clockwise current in Figure 21-8); if the capacitor charge were negative (so the upper capacitor plate in Figure 21-8 were negatively charged) so $q = -0.400\ \mu C$, the electric energy would be the same as if $q = +0.400\ \mu C$ (the upper capacitor plate were positively charged).

You use the physics of *LC* circuits whenever you use a microwave oven to heat food. At the heart of any microwave oven is a device called a *cavity resonator*, which is basically a hollow metal tube closed at both ends by metal caps. When equal amounts of positive and negative charges are placed on the caps, the charge flows back and forth between the caps along the inner surfaces of the tube. This gives rise to time-varying electric and magnetic fields inside the tube. The electric field is greatest when the magnetic field is zero and vice versa, just as in Figure 21-8. (The geometry of these fields is more complicated than in Figure 21-8, but the basic physics is the same.) The frequency at which the fields oscillate—typically 2.45 GHz, or 2.45×10^9 Hz, in a home microwave oven and 0.915 GHz in a large commercial oven—is determined by the size and shape of the cavity resonator. A small hole in the cavity resonator is connected to one end of a metal pipe, and the other end leads into the interior of the oven. The oscillating fields "flow" along the pipe into the oven, where the energy of the electric field is absorbed by water molecules in the food. This sets the molecules into vibration and raises the temperature of the food, cooking it.

There is resistance in a cavity resonator, just as there is in any real circuit. As a result, the oscillations will die away just as do the oscillations of a block on a spring when friction is present. To sustain the oscillations of a circuit, we need to *drive* the circuit with an alternating voltage, in much the same way you sustain the back-and-forth oscillations of a child on a playground swing by pushing on the child once per cycle. In the following section, we'll analyze what happens in a circuit that contains an inductor, a capacitor, a resistor, and a source of alternating voltage.

> **? Got the Concept? 21-4**
> **Doubling the Charge in an *LC* Circuit**
>
> A certain *LC* circuit oscillates at frequency *f* when the maximum capacitor charge is Q_0. If you double the value of Q_0, the new frequency of oscillation is (a) $2f$; (b) $f\sqrt{2}$; (c) $f/\sqrt{2}$; (d) $f/2$; (e) none of these.

Take-Home Message for Section 21-5

✔ An *LC* circuit, made up of an inductor connected to a capacitor, is the electrical analog of a block attached to a spring. The inductor plays the role of the block, and the capacitor plays the role of the spring.

✔ In an *LC* circuit the capacitor charge and inductor current both oscillate with a frequency determined by the values of the inductance *L* and capacitance *C*.

✔ As the charge and current oscillate, the energy in the circuit oscillates between magnetic energy in the inductor and electric energy in the capacitor. If there is no resistance in the circuit, the energy remains constant.

21-6 When an ac voltage source is attached in series to an inductor, resistor, and capacitor, the circuit can display resonance

When you turn on the radio in a car, you expect to listen to only one station at a time. But the car antenna is being simultaneously bombarded by signals from *all* of the local radio stations. How does the radio "know" which signal to play through the car's speakers and which signals to ignore? The explanation is that the radio circuit is essentially a combination of an inductor, resistor, and capacitor in series, and this circuit is driven by an ac voltage coming from the radio signal. As we'll see, such a **series *LRC* circuit** can be designed to give a large current in response to a voltage at one particular frequency, while responding very little to voltages at other frequencies. When you tune the radio to a station with a particular frequency, you're adjusting the radio circuit so that the frequency at which it has the greatest response matches the frequency of the station you want to hear.

A driven series *LRC* circuit behaves in much the same way as a damped, driven mechanical oscillator like the one we studied in Section 12-8. (This would be a good time to review that section.) In order to understand the properties of a driven series *LRC* circuit, it's useful to first look at three simpler ac circuits: one with just an ac source and a resistor, one with just an ac source and a capacitor, and one with just an ac source and an inductor.

An ac Source and a Resistor

In **Figure 21-9a** an ac source is connected to a resistor of resistance R. The voltage provided by the source is

$$V(t) = V_0 \sin \omega t \qquad (21\text{-}30)$$

What current $i(t)$ is developed in the circuit when we close the switch, and how much power does the source deliver to the resistor? To answer these questions, let's apply Kirchhoff's loop rule, which states that the sum of the voltage drops around the circuit is zero. The voltage across the resistor is $i(t)$ multiplied by R, so the loop rule says that

$$V(t) - i(t)R = 0$$

  See the Math Tutorial for more information on trigonometry

(a) An ac source connected to a resistor

- Current i is in phase with source voltage V.
- Since i and V always have the same sign, the power $P = iV$ delivered by the source is always positive.

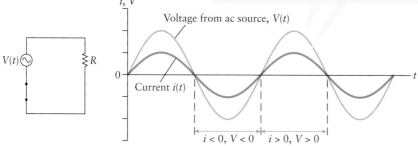

(b) An ac source connected to a capacitor

- Current i leads the source voltage V by 1/4 cycle.
- Half of the time i and V have the same sign, so the power $P = iV$ delivered by the source is positive; the other half of the time i and V have opposite signs and P is negative.

(c) An ac source connected to an inductor

- Current i lags the source voltage V by 1/4 cycle.
- Half of the time i and V have the same sign, so the power $P = iV$ delivered by the source is positive; the other half of the time i and V have opposite signs and P is negative.

Figure 21-9 Three ac circuits The graphs show the source voltage and currents for three circuits: an ac source connected to (a) a resistor, (b) a capacitor, and (c) an inductor.

and so

(21-31)
$$i(t) = \frac{V(t)}{R} = \frac{V_0}{R} \sin \omega t \quad \text{(resistor and ac source)}$$

The graph of $V(t)$ and $i(t)$ versus time in Figure 21-9a shows that the current is in phase with the source voltage. From Equation 18-23, the power that the source delivers to the circuit (in this case, to the resistor) is equal to the product of the current through the source multiplied by the voltage across the source: $P(t) = i(t)V(t)$. The graph in Figure 21-9a shows that $i(t)$ and $V(t)$ always have the same sign (both positive or both negative), so the product $i(t)V(t)$ is always positive. Thus power is always being transferred from the ac source into the resistor.

An ac Source and a Capacitor

The circuit shown in **Figure 21-9b** is the same as in Figure 21-9a, except that we've replaced the resistor by a capacitor. The voltage provided by the source is still given by Equation 21-30, but the voltage across the capacitor is $q(t)/C$, where $q(t)$ is the capacitor charge. The loop rule now says that

$$V(t) - \frac{q(t)}{C} = 0$$

The capacitor charge is therefore

(21-32)
$$q(t) = CV(t) = CV_0 \sin \omega t \quad \text{(capacitor and ac source)}$$

The capacitor charge oscillates between $+CV_0$ and $-CV_0$.

To find the current in the circuit, two trigonometric identities that will be of use are $\sin \theta = \cos(\theta - \pi/2)$ and $\cos \theta = -\sin(\theta - \pi/2)$. Using the first of these, we can rewrite Equation 21-32 as

$$q(t) = CV_0 \cos\left(\omega t - \frac{\pi}{2}\right) \quad \text{(capacitor and ac source)}$$

The current $i(t)$ is the rate of change of the capacitor charge $q(t)$, just as it was for the LC circuit that we discussed in Section 21-5. In that section we saw that if $q(t) = Q_0 \cos(\omega t + \phi)$, then $i(t) = -\omega Q_0 \sin(\omega t + \phi)$ (see Equations 21-24 and 21-25). That's the same situation we have here, with Q_0 replaced by CV_0 and ϕ equal to $-\pi/2$. So the current in the circuit of Figure 21-9b is

$$i(t) = -\omega CV_0 \sin\left(\omega t - \frac{\pi}{2}\right)$$

Using the second trigonometric identity that we stated above, we can write this as

(21-33)
$$i(t) = \omega CV_0 \cos \omega t \quad \text{(capacitor and ac source)}$$

From Equation 21-32, the maximum charge on the capacitor is CV_0 no matter what the frequency. If the frequency is low and the period long, there's plenty of time for the charge to build up from zero to CV_0, so the required current will be low. Equation 21-33 shows the same thing: If the frequency is low, the angular frequency ω is likewise low and the current amplitude ωCV_0 is small. So a capacitor connected to an ac source acts to reduce the current amplitude at low frequency.

The graph in Figure 21-9b shows the source voltage and the current versus time. We say that the current *leads* the voltage by 1/4 cycle: The graph of current has its first peak at $t = 0$, but the graph of voltage reaches its first peak 1/4 cycle later. As a result, for half of the time the current and voltage have the same sign, while for the other half of the time the signs of $i(t)$ and $V(t)$ are opposite. Therefore for half of the time there is positive power $P(t) = i(t)V(t)$ out of the source and into the capacitor, while for the other half of the time the power is negative and energy is flowing out of the capacitor back into the source. What's happening is that the capacitor is alternately charging and discharging; when it's charging the electric energy U_E in the capacitor is increasing, and when it's discharging the electric energy is decreasing. Over one complete cycle, there's *zero* net flow of energy out of the source.

An ac Source and Inductor

Figure 21-9c shows a third circuit, one that includes only an ac source and an inductor. Again the source voltage is given by Equation 21-30. The voltage drop across the inductor is $L(\Delta i / \Delta t)$, so the loop rule says that

$$V(t) - L\frac{\Delta i(t)}{\Delta t} = 0$$

We can solve this for $\Delta i(t)/\Delta t$, which is the rate of change of the current:

$$\frac{\Delta i(t)}{\Delta t} = \frac{V(t)}{L} = \frac{V_0}{L}\sin\omega t \quad \text{(inductor and ac source)} \tag{21-34}$$

Given Equation 21-34 for the rate of change of current, what is the current itself? As we did for the capacitor circuit shown in Figure 21-9b, let's think for a minute about Equation 21-24, $q(t) = Q_0\cos(\omega t + \phi)$, and Equation 21-25, $i(t) = -\omega Q_0\sin(\omega t + \phi)$. In these equations $i(t)$ is the rate of change of $q(t)$. So these equations tell us that if the rate of change of a function is given by a constant multiplied by $\sin(\omega t + \phi)$, the function itself is given by the same constant divided by $-\omega$ and multiplied by $\cos(\omega t + \phi)$. Using this with Equation 21-34, in which the constant is V_0/L and $\phi = 0$, we conclude that the current for the circuit in Figure 21-9c is

$$i(t) = -\frac{V_0}{\omega L}\cos\omega t \quad \text{(inductor and ac source)} \tag{21-35}$$

Equation 21-35 says that the amplitude of the current is $V_0/(\omega L)$. Since ω is in the denominator, the current amplitude is small when the frequency, and hence the angular frequency ω, is high. That agrees with the idea that an inductor opposes changes in current. High frequency corresponds to rapid changes in current, which the inductor suppresses by making the current small. So an inductor connected to an ac source acts to reduce the current amplitude at high frequency. That's in sharp contrast to a capacitor, which acts to reduce the current amplitude at low frequency.

The graph in Figure 21-9c shows $V(t)$ and $i(t)$ versus time for the circuit with an inductor and an ac source. In this circuit the current *lags* behind the voltage by 1/4 cycle; if you look at any peak of the voltage, you'll see that a peak of the current occurs 1/4 cycle later. Just as for the capacitor circuit in Figure 21-9b, for half of the time the current and voltage have the same sign so power flows out of the source and adds energy to the inductor. In this case it's *magnetic* energy that's being added as the current through the inductor increases in magnitude. For the other half of the time, current and voltage have opposite signs, the source power is negative, and energy flows out of the inductor as the current decreases in magnitude. As for the capacitor, over one cycle there is zero net energy delivered to the inductor.

A Driven Series *LRC* Circuit

Let's now combine all of the devices shown in Figure 21-9 into a single circuit (Figure 21-10). Again the voltage of the ac source is given by Equation 21-30, $V(t) = V_0\sin\omega t$. Just as in the three simpler cases depicted in Figure 21-9, we expect that when the switch is closed there will be an oscillating current in the circuit with angular frequency ω. We can also expect that at low frequencies the presence of the capacitor will keep the current amplitude small, while at high frequencies the current amplitude will be small due to the presence of the inductor. At some frequency that's not too low and not too high, the current amplitude will be largest. That's the frequency where the voltage of the ac source produces the greatest response. One of our tasks is to find just what this frequency is.

If we apply Kirchhoff's loop rule to the circuit shown in Figure 21-10, we get the following equation:

$$V(t) - L\frac{\Delta i(t)}{\Delta t} - i(t)R - \frac{q(t)}{C} = 0 \quad \text{(driven series } LRC \text{ circuit)} \tag{21-36}$$

This is a complicated equation, since it involves the capacitor charge $q(t)$; the current $i(t)$, which is the rate of change of the capacitor charge; and the rate of change of the current, $\Delta i(t)/\Delta t$. It is possible to solve Equation 21-36 using some tricks of trigo-

Figure 21-10 A driven series *LRC* circuit When the switch is closed, an oscillating current is set up in this circuit. The amplitude and phase of this current depend on the values of the inductance *L*, resistance *R*, and capacitance *C*, as well as the amplitude V_0 and angular frequency ω of the voltage provided by the ac source.

nometry, but it's a rather strenuous exercise. Instead, let's just present the result for the current $i(t)$ and see what it tells us:

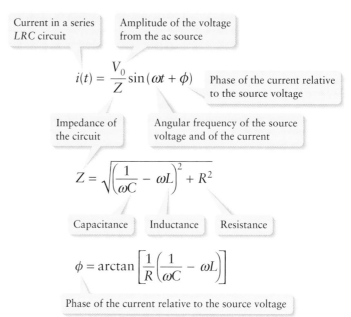

Current in a driven *LRC* circuit
(21-37)

The first of Equations 21-37 shows that the greater the value of the **impedance** Z, the smaller the amplitude V_0/Z of the current. Like resistance, impedance has units of ohms. So you can think of it as similar to an "effective resistance" of the circuit to an ac current. Unlike resistance, however, impedance depends on the angular frequency as given by the second of Equations 21-37. The quantity $[1/(\omega C) - \omega L]^2$ is large at both low and high angular frequencies; that's because the term $1/(\omega C)$ (due to the capacitor) gets very large for low values of ω, while the term ωL (due to the inductor) gets very large for high values of ω. So the impedance Z is large and the current amplitude V_0/Z is small for very low angular frequencies thanks to the capacitor, as well as for very high angular frequencies thanks to the inductor. That's just what we predicted above.

The impedance is smallest, and the current amplitude V_0/Z largest, when the quantity $[1/(\omega C) - \omega L]^2$ equals zero and so

$$\frac{1}{\omega C} - \omega L = 0$$

To solve for the angular frequency at which this happens, multiply this equation by ω/L:

$$\frac{\omega}{L}\left(\frac{1}{\omega C} - \omega L\right) = \frac{1}{LC} - \omega^2 = 0$$

So $\omega^2 = 1/(LC)$, or

(21-38)
$$\omega = \sqrt{\frac{1}{LC}}$$

We saw this same angular frequency in Equation 21-23: It's the angular frequency at which an *LC* circuit oscillates. We'll refer to $\sqrt{1/(LC)}$ as the **natural angular frequency** of the circuit and give it the symbol ω_0. It's the angular frequency at which the current would oscillate if the ac source and resistor weren't in the circuit at all!

In Section 12-8 we saw this same effect, called **resonance**, for an oscillating mechanical system. Equation 21-38 tells us that the current in a driven series *LRC* circuit is greatest, or in resonance, if the *driving* angular frequency ω equals the *natural* angular frequency $\omega_0 = \sqrt{1/(LC)}$. When $\omega = \omega_0 = \sqrt{1/(LC)}$, the impedance in Equation 21-37 is equal to R and the current amplitude is $V_0/Z = V_0/R$.

Why does resonance happen in a series LRC circuit?. The explanation is that at low frequencies the capacitor suppresses the current, and at high frequencies the inductor

(a) Amplitude of the current

(b) Phase of the current

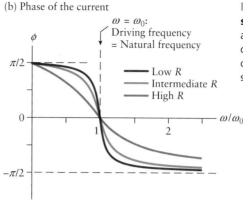

Figure 21-11 **Resonance in a driven series *LRC* circuit** (a) The amplitude and (b) the phase of the current in a driven series *LRC* circuit both depend on the angular frequency ω of the source voltage.

- The current amplitude is maximum at $\omega = \omega_0$ (resonance).
- The smaller the resistance, the greater the current amplitude at resonance.

- At $\omega = \omega_0$ (resonance), $\phi = 0$ and the current is in phase with the source voltage.
- If $\omega < \omega_0$, $\phi > 0$ and the current leads the source voltage. At very low frequencies, ϕ approaches $\pi/2$ (current leads voltage by 1/4 cycle).
- If $\omega > \omega_0$, $\phi < 0$ and the current lags behind the source voltage. At very high frequencies, ϕ approaches $-\pi/2$ (current lags voltage by 1/4 cycle).

suppresses the current. But at one special frequency—the natural frequency of the circuit—the effects of the capacitor and inductor cancel exactly so that the current in the circuit has its maximum amplitude. **Figure 21-11a** shows the current amplitude as a function of the driving frequency ω for three different values of the resistance R. For any value of R the current amplitude is maximum when $\omega/\omega_0 = 1$ and $\omega = \omega_0 = \sqrt{1/(LC)}$. As R decreases, the peak becomes higher (the maximum current amplitude increases).

The third of Equations 21-37 describes the phase ϕ of the current (see **Figure 21-11b**). The value of ϕ tells us how much the current leads the source voltage. At resonance, where $\omega/\omega_0 = 1$ and $\omega = \omega_0 = \sqrt{1/(LC)}$, we have $(1/(\omega C)) - \omega L = 0$ and $\phi = \arctan 0 = 0$. So at resonance the current is in phase with the source voltage, just as happens in a circuit with only an ac source and a resistor (Figure 21-9a).

For very low angular frequencies ω, the quantity $1/(\omega C)$ is large while ωL is small, so $(1/(\omega C)) - \omega L$ is large and positive. In this case ϕ is near $\pi/2$ radians, so at low frequencies the current leads the voltage by about 1/4 of a cycle (recall that there are 2π radians in a cycle). That's just like the behavior of a circuit with only an ac source and a capacitor (Figure 21-9b). By contrast, at very high angular frequencies the quantity $1/(\omega C)$ is small while ωL is large. Then $(1/(\omega C)) - \omega L$ is large and negative, and ϕ is near $-\pi/2$ radians or $-1/4$ cycle. The negative value of ϕ means that at high frequencies the current *lags* the source voltage by about 1/4 cycle. The circuit with just an ac source and an inductor in Figure 21-9c behaves in the same way.

As Figure 21-11b shows, changing the resistance doesn't affect the angular frequency at which $\phi = 0$. This always happens when $\omega = \omega_0 = \sqrt{1/(LC)}$. Changing the value of R does change the shape of the graph of ϕ versus ω, however; the smaller the resistance, the closer the driving angular frequency ω must be to the natural angular frequency ω_0 in order for ϕ to be close to zero.

These ideas show what's involved in tuning a radio. The signal from a broadcast station is at a particular frequency. The radio antenna detects that signal and converts it to an ac voltage with that same frequency. In order for the circuit of the radio receiver to respond to that frequency, the natural frequency of the receiver circuit must match the driving frequency of the signal from the radio station—that is, the radio receiver must be *tuned* to be in resonance with the station to which you want to listen. Other radio signals from other stations will be present in the circuit as well, but their driving frequencies won't match the natural frequency of the circuit. Hence these undesired signals will produce very little response in the radio (see Figure 21-11a), and you'll hear only the sound of the station to which you've tuned the radio. The following example illustrates this idea.

Go to Interactive Exercise 21-2 for more practice dealing with LRC circuits

Example 21-6   Tuning an FM Radio

The tuner knob on an FM radio moves the plates of an adjustable capacitor. This capacitor is in series with a $0.130\text{-}\mu H$ inductor and a net resistance of 755 Ω. The peak current induced in this circuit by a radio wave becomes large when the natural frequency of the circuit matches the carrier frequency of the radio wave. (a) What is the frequency of the FM station that is tuned in when the capacitor in the radio is adjusted to 19.6 pF? (b) If the peak operating voltage in the tuning circuit is 9.00 V, what is the peak current?

Set Up

The tuning circuit resonates when driven by a radio wave with an angular frequency ω that equals the natural angular frequency ω_0 of the circuit. We'll use Equation 21-38 to determine the value of ω_0 for this circuit, and convert it to an ordinary frequency in Hz. We'll find the peak current, or current amplitude, using Equations 21-37.

Natural angular frequency of the tuning circuit:

$$\omega_0 = \sqrt{\frac{1}{LC}} \qquad (21\text{-}38)$$

Relationship between frequency and angular frequency:

$$f = \frac{\omega}{2\pi}$$

Amplitude of the oscillating current:

$$i_{0,max} = \frac{V_0}{Z}$$

$$Z = \sqrt{\left(\frac{1}{\omega C} - \omega L\right)^2 + R^2} \qquad (21\text{-}37)$$

R = 755 Ω

V(t) from radio station: f = ?

C = 19.6 pF

L = 0.130 μH

Solve

(a) Use the given values of capacitance and inductance to determine the natural frequency of the circuit.

We are given $L = 0.130\ \mu H = 0.130 \times 10^{-6}$ H and $C = 19.6$ pF $= 19.6 \times 10^{-12}$ F. From Equation 21-38 the natural angular frequency is $\omega_0 = \sqrt{1/(LC)}$, and the natural frequency is ω_0 divided by 2π :

$$f_0 = \frac{\omega_0}{2\pi} = \frac{1}{2\pi}\sqrt{\frac{1}{LC}} = \frac{1}{2\pi}\sqrt{\frac{1}{(0.130 \times 10^{-6}\,\text{H})(19.6 \times 10^{-12}\,\text{F})}}$$

$$= 99.7 \times 10^6\ \text{Hz} = 99.7\ \text{MHz}$$

(b) Find the amplitude of the oscillating current.

At resonance the term $(1/(\omega C)) - \omega L$ in the expression for impedance is equal to zero. Then Equation 21-37 tells us that $Z = R = 755\ \Omega$. If the voltage amplitude is 9.00 V, the current amplitude is

$$i_{0,max} = \frac{V_0}{Z} = \frac{9.00\ \text{V}}{755\ \Omega} = 0.0119\ \text{A} = 11.9\ \text{mA}$$

Reflect

The carrier frequencies of FM radio stations lie in the megahertz (MHz) range. So the frequency we found, 99.7×10^6 Hz, is 99.7 MHz on your FM radio dial. The peak current, about 10 mA, is typical for a portable FM radio.

Note that you tune a television set in the same way. When you use the remote control to change the channel (Figure 21-1b), you're commanding a circuit in the television to change its capacitance. This adjusts the natural frequency of the circuit to match the carrier frequency of the channel you want to watch.

? Got the Concept? 21-5   Modifying a Series *LRC* Circuit

We've discussed the behavior of a series *LRC* circuit with $R = 1.00\ \Omega$, $C = 5.00\ \mu F$, $L = 20.0\ \mu H$, and $V_0 = 1.00$ V. If we increased the resistance to 2.00 Ω but kept all the other values the same, which of the following would be affected?

(a) The natural angular frequency of the circuit; (b) the current amplitude at resonance; (c) the current amplitude when the driving angular frequency is twice the natural angular frequency; (d) two of (a), (b), and (c); (e) all of (a), (b), and (c).

Take-Home Message for Section 21-6

✔ A driven series LRC circuit is made up of an inductor, capacitor, and resistor connected in series to a source of ac voltage.

✔ The response of a driven series LRC circuit depends on the frequency of the ac source. At low frequencies, the capacitor dominates the circuit and the current is small. The current is also small at high frequencies, where the inductor dominates the circuit. When the frequency of the source equals the natural frequency of the circuit, the current is large and maximum power flows from the source into the resistor. This is resonance.

✔ As the charge and current oscillate, the energy in the circuit oscillates between magnetic energy in the inductor and electric energy in the capacitor. If there is no resistance in the circuit, the energy remains constant.

21-7 Diodes are important parts of many common circuits

We've just about come to the end of our discussion of electric circuits. We've seen two different types of voltage sources (batteries that provide a constant emf and ac sources that provide a time-varying emf) and three kinds of circuit elements (resistors, capacitors, and inductors). Before leaving the subject of circuits, however, let's take a look at another important circuit device called a *diode*. This device is possible because of *semiconductors*, a class of materials whose electrical properties are intermediate between those of conductors and insulators.

A common semiconductor is the element silicon (chemical symbol Si). Each silicon atom has four outer or *valence* electrons. In a conducting material such as copper or silver the valence electrons are free to move throughout the material, so the resistivity of the material is low. In silicon, however, the atoms are formed into a crystal structure in which all four of an atom's valence electrons are involved in chemical bonds with adjacent silicon atoms. As a result, the valence electrons are able to move only with great difficulty. That's why pure silicon has about 10^{10} times the resistivity of copper (though only about 10^{-13} the resistivity of an insulating material like rubber). That can change dramatically by **doping** the silicon—that is, by adding small amounts of a different kind of atom to solid silicon. Two common elements used for this purpose are phosphorous and boron.

Figure 21-12a shows a schematic illustration of a silicon crystal doped with a small amount of phosphorous (chemical symbol P), so that the phosphorous atoms replace a few of the silicon atoms. An atom of phosphorous has five valence electrons, four of which form bonds to the adjacent silicon atoms. The fifth electron can move relatively easily through the material, and so the doped silicon has much lower resistivity than does pure silicon. Adding just one part per million of phosphorous can decrease the resistivity by several powers of ten. Since the mobile charges in phosphorous-doped silicon are negatively charged electrons, we call such a material an **n-type semiconductor** (n for negative).

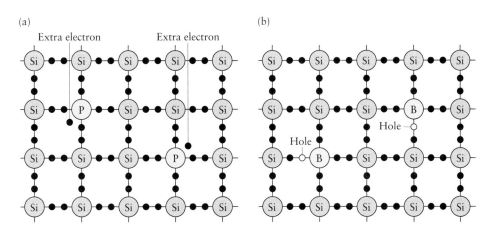

Figure 21-12 Doped semiconductors (a) Silicon (Si) doped with phosphorous (P) is an *n*-type semiconductor. Because phosphorous has five valence electrons, there is an extra, weakly bound electron that can contribute to electrical conduction. (b) Silicon doped with boron (B) is a *p*-type semiconductor. Because boron has only three valence electrons, there is a hole in one of its bonds. The hole can move through the semiconductor as though it were a positive charge, contributing to electrical conduction.

Figure 21-12b shows a different kind of doping in which some of the silicon atoms have been replaced with atoms of boron (chemical symbol B). Boron has only three valence electrons, so for each boron atom there is a "hole" in the electron population. These **holes** are actually free to travel through the boron-doped silicon. (A very rough analogy is to think of these holes as traveling like bubbles of carbon dioxide through a carbonated beverage.) Since a hole represents an absence of negative charge, it's equivalent to a *positive* charge. For this reason boron-doped silicon is called a ***p*-type semiconductor** (*p* for positive). Adding holes by doping the silicon with even a small amount of boron also causes a substantial decrease in resistivity.

We can make a novel kind of device if we take a crystal of silicon and dope one side of the crystal with boron and one side with phosphorous. The side with boron is the *p* side and the side with phosphorous is the *n* side (the two sides are *p*-type and *n*-type semiconductors, respectively). The region where the two sides meet is called a ***pn* junction**. Some of the mobile holes from the *p* side diffuse across the junction to the *n* side, and some of the mobile electrons from the *n* side diffuse to the *p* side. The semiconductor isn't a particularly good conductor, so neither the electrons nor the holes get very far from the junction. The net result is that there's a double layer of charge around the junction, a positive layer of holes on the *n* side of the junction and a negative layer of electrons on the *p* side of the junction (Figure 21-13).

To see what makes a *pn* junction useful, imagine placing it in a dc circuit with a source of emf ε and a resistor. If the polarity of the source is as shown in Figure 21-14a, so that the emf tries to make current flow from the *p* side to the *n* side, we find that a current does indeed flow through the junction and around the circuit. What happens is that the source creates an electric field within the *pn* junction that points from left to right, which helps to drive positively charged holes to the right across the junction and negatively charged electrons to the left across the junction. This enhanced diffusion of electrons and holes gives rise to a net current from left to right in the semiconductor. In this case the *pn* junction is said to be *forward biased*. If we reverse the polarity of the source as shown in Figure 21-14b, however, the source creates an electric field that points from right to left within the *pn* junction. This tends to push the holes leftward (back into the *p* side from which they came) and the electrons rightward (back into the *n* side from which they came). In this case the *pn* junction is said to be *reverse biased*: The emf suppresses the diffusion of electrons and holes, and there is little or no current. Essentially the junction conducts in only one direction! A single-junction semiconductor device like this is called a **diode**.

Diodes have many uses, one of which is converting alternating current into direct current. If we replace the source of emf in Figure 21-14 with an ac source, the diode will conduct electricity when the alternating voltage is positive (forward bias) but not when the alternating voltage is negative (reverse bias). In this case the current through the resistor in Figure 21-14 won't be constant, but it will be in one direction only.

Another use for *pn* junctions is in **photovoltaic solar cells**. Light shining on the *p* side of the junction can excite electrons and produce new holes in the process. If the electrons happen to migrate to the junction, they will be accelerated into the *n* side by the electric field between the double layer of charge at the junction. The result is an excess negative charge on the *n* side and an excess positive charge on the *p* side. This charge imbalance produces a potential difference between the two regions. If one terminal of a resistor is connected to the *p* side and the other terminal to the *n* side, a current will flow through the resistor due to the potential difference and energy will be transferred to the

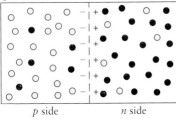

Figure 21-13 A *pn* junction The two sides of this semiconductor are doped with different atoms. Holes diffuse from the *p* side to the *n* side, and electrons diffuse from the *n* side to the *p* side. The result is a double layer of charge at the junction between the two sides.

Figure 21-14 A *pn*-junction diode This device is like a one-way valve for electric current. (a) Current will flow through the *pn* junction if the emf is applied as shown here (forward bias). (b) Little or no current will flow through the *pn* junction if the emf is reversed (reverse bias).

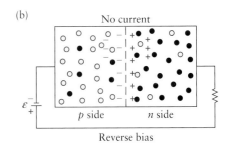

Forward bias

Reverse bias

resistor. The net effect is that the energy of sunlight is converted to electric energy. All solar cells designed for home and industrial use operate on this basic principle.

The basic process used in solar cells can also be run in reverse. In certain kinds of *pn* junctions, a forward bias like that shown in Figure 21-14a produces large concentrations of electrons on the *p* side and holes on the *n* side. When the electrons and holes diffuse across the barrier and recombine, energy is released in the form of light. Such a device is called a **light-emitting diode** or **LED**. LEDs are extremely efficient light sources: They produce much more light for a given power input than do incandescent light bulbs or fluorescent lamps. A television remote control (Figure 21-1b) sends commands to the television in the form of infrared light emitted by an LED.

Many other important semiconductor devices are used in circuits. In a *transistor*, a weak electrical current is used to modulate a stronger current. For example, the alternating current from an MP3 player carries all the musical information about the song you want to hear, but the current is too feeble to drive a speaker or even a pair of earbuds. By using transistors, however, this feeble current can be used to modulate a much stronger current from the MP3 player's battery. This modulated current *is* large enough to drive a speaker or earbuds, and that's what produces the music that you hear.

Take-Home Message for Section 21-7

✔ A semiconductor can be made a better conductor of electricity by doping it with a small amount of a different kind of atom. In an *n*-type semiconductor, there are extra electrons that are able to move through the material and carry a current. In a *p*-type semiconductor, the mobile charges are holes where there is an electron missing. Holes behave like positively charged objects.

✔ In a pn junction one side of the semiconductor is p-type and the other side is n-type. This has the property that it is much easier to establish a current through the junction in one direction compared to the opposite direction.

Key Terms

alternating current (ac)	magnetic energy	root mean square value
diode	mutual inductance	(rms value)
direct current (dc)	*n*-type semiconductor	secondary coil
doping	natural angular frequency	self-inductance
hole	*p*-type semiconductor	series *LRC* circuit
impedance	photovoltaic solar cell	step-down transformer
inductance	*pn* junction	step-up transformer
LC circuit	primary coil	transformer
light-emitting diode (LED)	resonance	

Chapter Summary

Topic	Equation or Figure
Root mean square values for alternating current: To find the root mean square or rms value of a quantity, first find the average (mean) value of the square of that quantity, then take the square root of that average. Alternating voltages are often described in terms of their rms values rather than their amplitudes.	The root mean square (rms) value of $V(t)$... ... is the square root of the average value of $V^2(t)$. $$V_{\text{rms}} = \sqrt{(V^2(t))_{\text{average}}} = \frac{V_0}{\sqrt{2}} \qquad (21\text{-}5)$$ If $V(t)$ is a sinusoidal function, its rms value equals the maximum value of $V(t)$ (the amplitude) divided by $\sqrt{2}$.

Transformers: A transformer uses electromagnetic induction to raise or lower the voltage of an alternating current. The ratio of the output voltage to the input voltage depends on the number of windings in the coils of the transformer. Raising the voltage lowers the current and vice versa. In an ideal transformer, no power is lost in this process.

Amplitudes of the input (p) and output (s) voltages

Rms values of the input (p) and output (s) voltages

Number of windings in the primary coil (p) and secondary coil (s)

$$\frac{V_s}{V_p} = \frac{V_{s,rms}}{V_{p,rms}} = \frac{N_s}{N_p}$$

(21-10)

Inductors: The simplest inductor is a coil of wire. If the current in the coil changes, there will be a change in the magnetic flux through the coil and an emf will be induced to oppose that change. So an inductor in a circuit always acts to oppose any change in the current in that circuit. The inductance of a coil depends on the coil's geometry.

Inductance of a coil   Number of windings in the coil

$$L = \frac{N\Phi_B}{i}$$

Magnetic flux through each winding of the coil due to the field produced by the coil itself

Current in the coil

(21-13)

Voltage across an inductor   Inductance of the inductor

$$V = -L\frac{\Delta i}{\Delta t}$$

Rate of change of the current i in the inductor

The negative sign means that the voltage opposes any change in the current.

(21-16)

LC circuits: A circuit made up of an inductor and capacitor is the electric analog of a block oscillating at the end of an ideal spring. The angular frequency of the oscillation is $\omega = \sqrt{1/(LC)}$. The energy in the LC circuit oscillates between electric energy in the capacitor and magnetic energy in the inductor.

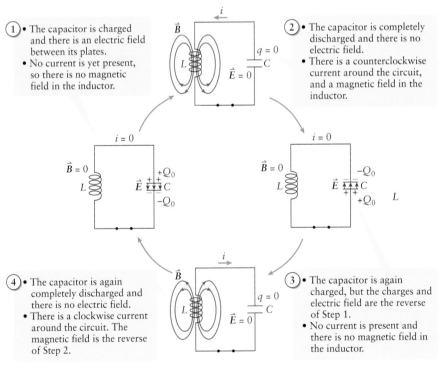

(1) • The capacitor is charged and there is an electric field between its plates.
• No current is yet present, so there is no magnetic field in the inductor.

(2) • The capacitor is completely discharged and there is no electric field.
• There is a counterclockwise current around the circuit, and a magnetic field in the inductor.

(3) • The capacitor is again charged, but the charges and electric field are the reverse of Step 1.
• No current is present and there is no magnetic field in the inductor.

(4) • The capacitor is again completely discharged and there is no electric field.
• There is a clockwise current around the circuit. The magnetic field is the reverse of Step 2.

(Figure 21-8)

Driven series *LRC* circuits: If an ac source is connected in series to an inductor, resistor, and capacitor to make a circuit, the current in the circuit oscillates at the angular frequency of the source. The voltage across the inductor leads the current by 1/4 cycle, the voltage across the resistor is in phase with the current, and the voltage across the capacitor lags the current by 1/4 cycle.

(Figure 21-10)

ic circuit resonance: The current in a driven series *LRC* circuit has its maximum amplitude when the source (driving) angular frequency equals the natural angular frequency $\omega_0 = \sqrt{1/(LC)}$ of the circuit. When this happens, the circuit is in resonance. At resonance the current is in phase with the ac source voltage, and maximum power is delivered to the resistor. In addition, at resonance the voltages across the inductor and capacitor have equal amplitude but are 1/2 cycle out of phase with each other, so their voltages cancel.

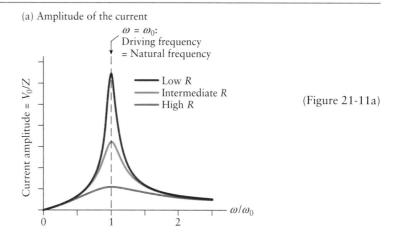

(a) Amplitude of the current

(Figure 21-11a)

Semiconductors and diodes: A semiconductor can be made a better conductor by adding impurities that contribute mobile electrons (an *n*-type semiconductor) or mobile holes (a *p*-type semiconductor). A semiconductor with one side that is *p*-type and one side that is *n*-type can act as a diode that conducts current easily from the *p* side to the *n* side, but conducts poorly in the opposite direction.

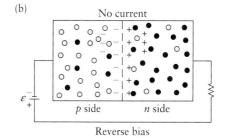

(Figure 21-14)

Answer to What do you think? Question

(d) As we learned in Chapter 20, Faraday's law only comes into play when currents are changing. If the current is constant, as in the case of direct current, Faraday's law has no effect. (See Section 21-3.)

Answers to Got the Concept? Questions

21-1 (b) The voltage provided by the ac source is $V(t) = V_0 \sin \omega t$, where the angular frequency ω is related to the period T by $\omega = 2\pi/T$. The instantaneous power into the resistor is given by Equation 21-3, $P(t) = V^2(t)/R$. At $t = 0$, $V(0) = V_0 \sin 0 = 0$, so $P(0) = 0$. At $t = T/8$, $\omega t = (2\pi/T)(T/8) = \pi/4$ so $V(T/8) = V_0 \sin(\pi/4) = V_0 (1/\sqrt{2})$ and $P(T/8) =$ $(V_0/\sqrt{2}^2)/R = V_0^2/(2R)$. At $t = T/4$, $\omega t = (2\pi/T)(T/4) = \pi/2$ so $V(T/4) = V_0 \sin(\pi/2) = V_0 (1) = V_0$ and $P(T/4) = V_0^2/R$. Equation 21-4 tells us that the average power is $P_{\text{average}} = V_0^2/(2R)$, which is equal to the instantaneous power at $t = T/8$ and not at the other times. Note also that at $t = T/8$, the instantaneous voltage V is equal to the rms value $V_{\text{rms}} = V_0/\sqrt{2}$.

21-2   (b) With the connections reversed, the number of windings in the primary coil is $N_p = 250$ and the number of windings in the secondary coil is $N_s = 100$. With $V_{p,rms} = 120$ V, Equation 21-10 tells us that the output rms voltage is $V_{s,rms} = V_{p,rms}(N_s/N_p) = (120 \text{ V})(100/250) = 48$ V.

21-3   (c) The voltage across an inductor depends on the rate at which the current through the inductor is changing, not on the value of current itself. The voltage across a capacitor depends on the amount of charge on either plate, not on the current. (The current determines how rapidly the capacitor charge is changing and so how rapidly the voltage is changing, but does not affect the present value of the voltage.) The voltage $V = iR$ across a resistor is directly proportional to the current i, so this does depend on the value of current.

21-4   (e) As Equations 21-23 show, the oscillation frequency of an LC circuit depends on the values of inductance and capacitance alone. It does not depend on the amount of charge placed on the capacitor plates. This is the direct analog of the behavior of a block attached to an ideal spring, which we studied in Section 12-3: The oscillation frequency depends on the spring constant and the mass of the block, but does not depend on the amplitude of the oscillation.

21-5   (d) The natural angular frequency $\sqrt{1/(LC)}$ does not depend on the resistance. The other two quantities, however, do. You can see this from Figure 21-11a: Increasing the resistance decreases the current amplitude at *all* angular frequencies, not just at resonance.

Questions and Problems

In a few problems, you are given more data than you actually need; in a few other problems, you are required to supply data from your general knowledge, outside sources, or informed estimate. Interpret as significant all digits in numerical values that have trailing zeros and no decimal points. For all problems, use $g = 9.80 \text{ m/s}^2$ for the free-fall acceleration due to gravity. Neglect friction and air resistance unless instructed to do otherwise.

- Basic, single-concept problem
- •• Intermediate-level problem, may require synthesis of concepts and multiple steps
- ••• Challenging problem
SSM *Solution is in Student Solutions Manual*

Conceptual Questions

1. •What does this statement mean: The voltage drop across an inductor leads the current by 1/4 cycle? SSM

2. •Why does a transformer whose primary coil has 10 times as many turns as its secondary coil normally deliver about 10 times more voltage than it receives?

3. •Does Equation 18-9 apply to alternating currents? If not, is there any manner in which it can be amended so that it will be valid?

4. •Explain why ac voltage is often described using the root mean square value rather than the average voltage.

5. •Search the Internet to determine the root mean square value of voltage in a common wall receptacle for five countries that are not mentioned in this chapter.

6. •Give a simple explanation as to why an electric appliance, which is supposed to be operated with a certain root mean square voltage, operated with a slightly increased root mean square voltage will lead to catastrophic results.

7. •Examine the label on the power converter for a laptop computer, digital camera, or cell phone. If you took the converter to a country where the rms voltage is 240 V, would you need a power transformer? Explain your answer.

8. •(a) What is a transformer? (b) How does it change the voltage input to some different voltage output? (c) Will a transformer work with a dc input?

9. •**Chemistry** Some of the most toxic substances that have been widely used in the United States (and many other countries in the world) are known as polychlorinated biphenyls or PCBs. (PCBs are a class of organic compounds that have two to 10 chlorine atoms attached to biphenyl, a molecule composed of two benzene rings.) Liquid PCBs were often used to fill the interior of transformers. Research PCBs and explain why they were used in transformers.

10. •Why is electric power for domestic use in the United States, Canada, and most of the Western Hemisphere transmitted at very high voltages and stepped down to 120 V by a transformer near the point of consumption?

11. •Discuss the storage of energy in an ideal LC circuit with no losses. SSM

12. •What change must you make in the current in an inductor to double the energy stored in it?

13. •Compare the expressions for the energy stored in an inductor and the energy stored in a capacitor and explain the similarities.

14. •Is the current through a resistor in an ac circuit always in phase with the potential applied to the circuit? Why or why not?

15. •A given length of wire is wound into a solenoid. How will its self-inductance be changed if it is rewound into another coil of (a) twice the length or (b) twice the diameter? SSM

16. •When the switch S is opened in the RL circuit shown in **Figure 21-15**, a spark jumps between the switch contacts. Why?

Figure 21-15 Problem 16

17. •Define the concept of impedance for an LRC circuit. What are the units of impedance?

Multiple-Choice Questions

18. •The most important advantage of ac over dc electrical signals is that
  A. electric power can't be delivered by a dc source.
  B. dc could only be used in the early days of electrical power distribution.
  C. dc results in more power loss in wire than ac.

D. it is relatively straightforward to change the voltage delivered by an ac source.

E. ac is safer.

19. •In a sinusoidal ac circuit with rms voltage V, the peak-to-peak voltage equals
A. $\sqrt{2}V$.
B. $2V$.
C. $V/\sqrt{2}$.
D. $2\sqrt{2}V$.
E. $V/2$. SSM

20. •The common electrical receptacle voltage in North America is often referred to as "120 volts ac." One hundred twenty volts is
A. the arithmetic mean of the voltage as it varies with time.
B. the root mean square (rms) average of the voltage as it varies with time.
C. the peak voltage from an ac wall receptacle.
D. the average voltage over many weeks of time.
E. one-half the peak voltage.

21. •If a power utility were able to replace an existing 500 kV transmission line with one operating at 1 MV, it would change the amount of heat produced in the transmission line to
A. 1/4 of the previous value.
B. 1/2 of the previous value.
C. 2 times the previous value.
D. 4 times the previous value.
E. 0.

22. •Two solenoids have the same cross-sectional area and length, but the first one has twice as many turns per unit length as the second one. The ratio of the inductance of the second to the first is
A. 1:1.
B. $1:\sqrt{2}$.
C. 1:1/2.
D. 1:4.
E. 2:1.

23. •For an LC circuit, when the charge on the capacitor is 1/2 of the maximum charge, the energy stored in the capacitor is
A. the total energy.
B. 1/2 of the total energy.
C. 1/4 of the total energy.
D. 1/8 of the total energy.
E. twice the total energy. SSM

24. •If the current through an inductor were doubled, the energy stored in the inductor would be
A. halved.
B. the same.
C. doubled.
D. quadrupled.
E. 1/4 as much.

25. •The voltage leads the current
A. in circuits with an ac source and a resistor.
B. in circuits with an ac source and a capacitor.
C. in circuits with an ac source and an inductor.
D. in any ac circuit.
E. in circuits with an ac source and both a capacitor and an inductor.

Estimation/Numerical Analysis

26. •Estimate the power lost in a length of wire when the same power is transmitted by dc compared to ac.

27. •Estimate the ac current in an average household appliance. How much current does an average U.S. household draw? SSM

28. •Estimate the number of turns of the secondary compared to the number of turns of the primary for a transformer that is used to power your hair dryer that you purchased in the United States and used in Europe.

29. •The voltage applied to a series LRC circuit is shown in accompanying table. Predict and plot the current as a function of time if $L = 100$ mH, $C = 133$ μC, and $R = 50$ Ω.

t(s)	V(V)	t(s)	V(V)
1	12	14	12
2	12	15	12
3	12	16	−12
4	12	17	−12
5	12	18	−12
6	−12	19	−12
7	−12	20	−12
8	−12	21	12
9	−12	22	12
10	−12	23	12
11	12	24	12
12	12	25	12
13	12		

Proble.ms

21-1 Most circuits use alternating current

21-2 We need to analyze ac circuits differently than dc circuits

30. •A sinusoidally varying voltage is represented by $V(t) = (75.0 \text{ V})\sin(120\pi t)$. What are its frequency and peak voltage?

31. •Write an expression for the instantaneous voltage delivered by an ac generator supplying 120 V (rms) at 60 Hz?

32. •What is the rms current provided to a 60-W light bulb that is plugged into a 120-V rms wall receptacle?

33. •The maximum potential difference across the terminals of a 60.0-Hz sinusoidal ac source is +17.0 V at $t = 1/4$ cycle. If at $t = 0$ the potential difference is zero, calculate the potential difference at $t = 2.00$ ms. SSM

34. •An ac voltage is represented by $V(t) = (200 \text{ V})\sin(120\pi t)$. What is its rms voltage?

35. •The rms current passing through a 50.0-Ω resistor in a sinusoidal ac circuit is 12.0 A. What is the maximum voltage drop across the resistor?

36. •The peak-to-peak current passing through a 150-Ω resistor is 24.0 A. Find the maximum voltage across the resistor and the rms current through the resistor.

37. ••Derive a relationship between the rms current through and the maximum voltage across a resistor R. Apply your result to the following situations: (a) $R = 100$ Ω, $V_{max} = 50.0$ V, $i_{rms} = ?$, (b) $R = 200$ Ω, $i_{rms} = 2.50$ A, $V_{max} = ?$, and (c) $V_{max} = 28.0$ V, $i_{rms} = 127$ mA, $R = ?$

21-3 Transformers allow us to change the voltage of an ac power source

38. •The primary coil of a transformer makes 240 turns around its core, and the secondary coil of that transformer makes

80 turns. If the primary voltage is 120 V (rms), what is the secondary voltage?

39. •The 400-turn primary coil of a step-down transformer is connected to an ac line that is 120 V (rms). The secondary coil voltage is 6.50 V (rms). Calculate the number of turns in the secondary coil. SSM

40. •The primary coil of a transformer makes 240 turns, and the secondary coil of that transformer makes 80 turns. If an alternating current of 3.00 A (rms) passes through the primary coil of the transformer, what current passes through the secondary coil of that transformer? Assume the transformer is ideal.

41. •An ideal transformer produces an output voltage that is 500% larger than the input voltage. If the input current is 10 A (rms), what is the output current?

42. •A neon sign in a shop operates at around 12 kV (rms). A transformer is to step up the 120 V (rms) line voltage to that value. The secondary coil of the transformer has 20,000 turns. How many turns must be placed into the primary coil?

43. ••The 400-turn primary coil of a step-down transformer is connected to an ac line that is 120 V (rms). The secondary coil is to supply 15.0 A at 6.30 V (rms). Assuming no power loss in the transformer, calculate (a) the number of turns in the secondary coil and (b) the current in the primary coil. SSM

44. ••The ratio of the number of turns in the primary to the number of turns in the secondary of a step-down transformer is 25:1. If the input voltage across the primary coil is 750 V (rms) and the current in the output circuit is 25.0 A (rms), how much power is delivered to the secondary? Assume the transformer is 100% efficient.

45. ••**Chemistry** A high-voltage discharge tube is often used to study atomic spectra. The tubes require a large voltage across their terminals to operate. To get the large voltage, a step-up transformer is connected to a line voltage (120 V rms) and is designed to provide 5000 V (rms) to the discharge tube and to dissipate 75.0 W. (a) What is the ratio of the number of turns in the secondary to the number of turns in the primary? (b) What are the rms currents in the primary and secondary coils of the transformer? (c) What is the effective resistance that the 120-V source is subjected to?

21-4 An inductor is a circuit element that opposes changes in current

46. •How much voltage is produced by an inductor of value 25 μH if the time rate of change of the current is 58 mA/s?

47. ••Uncle Leo tunes an old-fashioned radio that has an antenna that is made from a 3.0-cm-long solenoid with a cross-sectional area of 0.50 cm^2, composed of 300 turns of fine copper wire. Calculate the inductance of the coil assuming it is air-filled. SSM

48. •What energy is stored in a 250-mH inductor with a current of 0.055 A?

49. ••A tightly wound solenoid of 1600 turns, cross-sectional area of 6.00 cm^2, and length of 20.0 cm carries a current of 2.80 A. (a) What is its inductance? (b) If the cross-sectional area is doubled, does anything happen to the value of the inductance? Explain your answer.

21-5 In a circuit with an inductor and capacitor, charge and current oscillate

50. •You have a 1.0-mH inductor. What size capacitor should you choose to make an oscillator with a natural frequency of 980 kHz?

51. •An LC circuit is formed with a 15-mH inductor and a 1000-μF capacitor. Calculate the frequency of oscillation f for the circuit.

52. •A 200-pF capacitor is charged to 120 V and then quickly connected to an inductor. Calculate the maximum energy stored in the magnetic field of the inductor as the circuit oscillates.

53. •LC circuits are used for filters in electronics. The selectivity of an LC circuit is defined as the ratio L/C. Calculate the selectivity of the bandwidth for an LC circuit composed of an inductor ($L = 0.250$ H) and a capacitor ($C = 875$ μF).

54. ••If the ratio of the energy stored in a capacitor compared to the total energy stored in an LC circuit is 0.5, calculate the ratio of the charge stored on the capacitor compared to the maximum charge stored on the capacitor in that circuit.

55. ••When the charge on the capacitor in an LC circuit is one-half of the maximum stored charge, calculate the ratio of the energy stored in the capacitor compared to the total energy in both the inductor and the capacitor.

21-6 When an ac voltage source is attached in series to an inductor, resistor, and capacitor, the circuit can display resonance

56. •An LRC circuit contains a 1.00-μF capacitor, a 5.00-mH inductor, and a 100-Ω resistor. What is its resonant frequency?

57. •An LRC circuit contains a 500-Ω resistor, a 5.00-H coil, and an unknown capacitor. The circuit resonates at 1000 Hz. What is the value of the capacitance? SSM

58. •The resonant frequency of an LRC circuit is 250 Hz. If the resistance is 200 Ω and the capacitance is 125 nF, what is the value of the inductance?

59. •A sinusoidal voltage of 120 V (rms) and a frequency of 60 Hz are applied to a 50.0-μF capacitor. Calculate the peak value of the current.

60. •A sinusoidal voltage that is 120 V (rms) and has a frequency of 60 Hz is applied to a 0.20 H inductor. Calculate the peak value of the current.

61. •A sinusoidal voltage of 50.0 V (peak) at a frequency of 400 Hz is applied to a capacitor of unknown capacitance. The current in the circuit is 400 mA (rms). (a) What is the capacitance? (b) If the frequency of the voltage is increased, what, if anything, will happen to the rms value of the current in the circuit? Why?

62. •A 100-Ω resistor is connected across a 120-V rms, 60-Hz ac power line. Calculate (a) i_{rms}, (b) i_{max}, and (c) the average power dissipated in the resistor.

63. ••A sinusoidal voltage of 40.0 V rms and a frequency of 100 Hz is applied to (a) a 100-Ω resistor, (b) a 0.200-H inductor, and (c) a 50.0-μF capacitor. Calculate the peak value of the current and the average power delivered in each case. SSM

64. •A potential of 40.0 V (rms) and a frequency of 100 Hz is applied to (a) a 0.200-H inductor and (b) a 50.0-μF capacitor. In each case, find the peak value of the current.

65. ••In an *LRC* series circuit, the inductance is 250 mH, the resistance is 20 Ω, and the capacitance is 350 μF. If the ac voltage applied across the circuit is given by $V(t) = (10\ V)\sin(12\pi t)$, calculate the voltage across each element at a time of $t = 0.04$ s. SSM

66. ••A 35-mH inductor with 0.20-Ω resistance is connected in series to a 200-μF capacitor and a 60-Hz, ac, 45-V source. Calculate the (a) rms current and (b) phase angle for the circuit.

67. ••Assume that the circuit in Figure 21-16 has L equal to 0.60 H, R equal to 250 Ω, and C equal to 3.5 μF. At a frequency of 60 Hz, what are the impedance and the phase angle between the current and voltage?

68. ••Assume that the circuit in Figure 21-16 has L equal to 0.60 H, R equal to 280 Ω, and C equal to 3.5 μF. The amplitude of the driving voltage is 150 V (rms). At a frequency of 60 Hz, what is the rms current in the circuit?

Figure 21-16
Problems 67 & 68

69. ••In an *LRC* circuit, the voltage amplitude and frequency of the source are 100 V and 500 Hz, respectively. The resistance has a value of 500 Ω, the inductance has a value of 0.20 H, and the capacitance has a value of 2.0 μF. (a) What is the impedance of the circuit? (b) What is the amplitude of the current from the source? (c) If the voltage of the source is given by $V(t) = (100\ V)\sin(1000\pi t)$, how does the current vary with time?

70. ••Compare the rms current that is created in a circuit with only a 75-nF capacitor if the frequency of the 120 V rms source is 60 Hz versus 100 Hz.

71. ••The tuner knob on an FM radio moves the plates of an adjustable capacitor that is in series with a 0.400-μH inductor and a net resistance of 1000 Ω. The peak current induced in the circuit by a radio wave of a specific carrier frequency becomes large when the natural frequency of the circuit matches the carrier frequency. What is the frequency of the FM station that is tuned in when the capacitor in the radio is adjusted to 5.80 pF? If the peak operating voltage in the tuning circuit is 9.00 V, what is the peak current?

72. ••A series *LRC* tuning circuit in a TV receiver resonates at 58 MHz. The circuit uses an 18-pF capacitor. What is the inductance of the circuit?

73. ••An *LRC* series circuit contains a 500-Ω resistor, a 5.00-H inductor, and a capacitor. What value of capacitance will cause the circuit to resonate at 1000 Hz? SSM

General Problems

74. ••A 150-Ω resistor connected across a 60-cycle ac power supply of voltage amplitude 75 V produces heat in the resistor at a certain rate. If you want to replace the ac source with a dc power supply and still produce the same rate of heating, what should be the voltage of the dc source?

75. •• You construct an *LRC* ac circuit using a 125-Ω resistor, a 12.5-mH inductor, and a parallel plate capacitor having a plate separation of 2.10 mm with a plastic material completely filling the region between the plates. The rectangular capacitor plates each measure 4.25 cm by 6.20 cm. (a) If you want the maximum rms current through the circuit at an ac frequency of 55.0 Hz, what should be the dielectric constant of the plastic in the capacitor? (b) Consult Table 17-1 to see if it appears feasible to achieve the desired results for the circuit, and explain why or why not. Would the use of an ultracapacitor (which can have a capacitance of up to several farads) allow you to achieve the desired results?

76. ••In Europe, the standard voltage is 240 V (rms), ac, and 60 cycles/s. Suppose you take your 5.00-W electric razor to Rome and plug it into the receptacle (with an adapter to fit the receptacle but not to change the voltage). (a) What power will it draw in Rome? (b) What rms current will run through the razor in the United States and in Rome? Is the razor in danger of being damaged by using it in Rome without a voltage adapter? (c) If you want to use the razor in Rome without damaging it, what type of transformer would you need? Be as quantitative as you can. (d) What is the resistance of your razor?

77. ••Medical A dc current of 60 mA can cause paralysis of the body's respiratory muscles and hence interfere with breathing, but only 15 mA (rms) of ac current will do the same thing. Suppose a person is working with electrical power lines on a warm humid day and therefore has a low body resistance of 1000 Ω. What dc and what ac (amplitude and rms) potentials would it take to cause respiratory paralysis?

78. ••A power cord has a resistance of 8.00×10^{-2} Ω and is used to deliver 1500 W of power. (a) If the power is delivered at 12.0 V (rms), how much power is dissipated in the power cord (assuming the current and voltage are in phase)? (b) If the power is delivered at 120 V rms, how much power is dissipated in the power cord (again assuming the current and voltage are in phase)? (c) Which voltage would you prefer to use to power your electrical device? Why?

79. •••An ac electrical generator is made by turning a flat coil in a uniform constant magnetic field of 0.225 T. The coil consists of 33 square windings and each winding is 15.0 cm on each side. It rotates at a steady rate of 745 rpm about an axis perpendicular to the magnetic field passing through the middle of the coil and parallel to two of its opposite sides. An 8.50-Ω light bulb is connected across the generator. (a) Find the voltage and current amplitudes for the light bulb. (b) At what average rate is heat generated in the light bulb? (c) How much energy is consumed by the light bulb every hour? SSM

80. ••A small ac heating coil consisting of 750 windings is 8.50 cm long. It has a diameter of 1.25 cm and a resistance of 2.15 Ω. The coil is connected in series with a 2240-μF ultracapacitor, and the combination is plugged into a household outlet (60.0 Hz and 120 V rms). (a) What is the impedance of the circuit? (b) What is the rms current through the resistor? (c) What is the maximum (or peak) current through the resistor?

81. ••Using the series *LRC* circuit in Figure 21-17, determine the maximum voltages V_R, V_C, and V_L across the resistor, capacitor, and inductor, respectively, (a) at a frequency of 100 Hz and (b) at resonance. (c) Explain why the sum of the maximum voltages in each case is larger than the maximum voltage of the applied

potential. (d) Why is the maximum voltage across the inductor equal to the maximum voltage across the capacitor at resonance?

Figure 21-17 Problem 81

82. ••An *LRC* circuit consists of a 15.0-μF capacitor, a resistor, and an inductor connected in series across an ac power source of variable frequency having a voltage amplitude of 25.0 V. You observe that when the power source frequency is adjusted to 44.5 Hz, the rms current through the circuit has its maximum value of 65.0 mA. What will be the rms current if you change the frequency of the power source to 60.0 Hz?

83. ••The circuit in **Figure 21-18** is known as a low-pass filter because it allows low-frequency signals to pass and it attenuates higher frequencies. Suppose its input is an ac signal that is composed of a broad range of frequencies. In this case, the voltage across the capacitor is the output that is detected. Show that the ratio of the output voltage to the input voltage is

$$\frac{V_o}{V_i} = \frac{1}{\sqrt{1 + (\omega RC)^2}}. \text{ SSM}$$

Figure 21-18 Problem 83

84. ••The circuit in **Figure 21-19** is known as a high-pass filter because it allows high-frequency signals to pass and it attenuates lower frequencies. Suppose its input is an ac signal that is composed of a broad range of frequencies. The voltage across the resistor is the output that is detected. Show that the ratio of the output voltage to the input voltage is $\dfrac{V_o}{V_i} = \dfrac{1}{\sqrt{1 + 1/(\omega RC)^2}}$.

Figure 21-19 Problem 84

22 Electromagnetic Waves

In this chapter, your goals are to:

- (22-1) Define an electromagnetic wave.
- (22-2) Discuss how speed, frequency, and wavelength are related for electromagnetic waves, and describe the structure of an electromagnetic plane wave.
- (22-3) Explain what Maxwell's equations are and what they tell us about electromagnetic waves.
- (22-4) Calculate the energy density and intensity of an electromagnetic wave, and the energy of a photon.

To master this chapter, you should review:

- (13-2, 13-3, and 13-4) The properties of mechanical waves
- (16-6) Electric flux and Gauss's law for the electric field
- (17-5, 17-6) Capacitors
- (19-7) Ampère's law
- (20-2, 20-3) Magnetic flux and Faraday's law
- (21-2) Root-mean-square (rms) values
- (21-4, 21-5, and 21-6) Inductors

What do you think?

Our eyes are sensitive to the light from the setting sun, while the radio telescope in this photograph is sensitive to radio waves coming from distant objects in space. Both visible light and radio waves are kinds of electromagnetic waves. Compared to radio waves, visible light has (a) much higher frequency and much faster speed; (b) much lower frequency and much slower speed; (c) about the same frequency and about the same speed; (d) much higher frequency and about the same speed; (e) much lower frequency and about the same speed.

22-1 Light is just one example of an electromagnetic wave

What is light? The answer to this question was not discovered until the nineteenth century, when the Scottish physicist James Clerk Maxwell realized that light is an **electromagnetic wave**—a traveling disturbance that, unlike a sound wave, does not require a physical material through which to propagate. Instead, an electromagnetic wave involves oscillating electric and magnetic fields. These can exist even in the vacuum of space, which is why we can see the light from distant stars (**Figure 22-1a**).

In this chapter we'll study the properties of electromagnetic waves. We'll examine the broad variety of electromagnetic waves, which also includes x rays, microwaves, and radio waves. We'll see how wavelength, frequency, and speed are related for electromagnetic waves that propagate in a vacuum. We'll also look at the inner workings of a particularly simple kind of electromagnetic wave called a *sinusoidal plane wave*. We'll discover how such waves are possible by examining the fundamental equations that govern electric and magnetic fields. We'll then use these equations to help us understand

905

Figure 22-1 Electromagnetic waves Unlike sound waves or water waves, electromagnetic waves do not require the oscillation of any material substance. Instead, what oscillates are electric and magnetic fields. This explains (a) why these waves can propagate in a vacuum and (b) what determines their intensity.

We can see the light from this cluster of stars even though it is separated from us by 100,000 light years (about 10^{18} km) of nearly empty space. This is because electromagnetic waves, including visible light, can propagate in a vacuum.

(a)

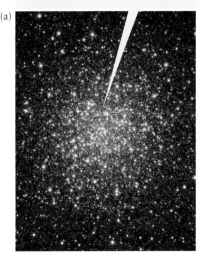

The intensity of an electromagnetic wave—including this laser beam used in ophthalmic surgery—depends on the amplitudes of the electric and magnetic fields that make up the wave.

(b)

Take-Home Message for Section 22-1

✔ Visible light is an example of an electromagnetic wave. The properties of electromagnetic waves are explained by the equations of electricity and magnetism.

the amount of energy carried by an electromagnetic wave and the wave intensity (Figure 22-1b). We'll find that the energy of an electromagnetic wave comes in small packets called *photons*, whose properties help explain why certain kinds of electromagnetic waves can be harmful while others are not.

22-2 In an electromagnetic plane wave, electric and magnetic fields both oscillate

Experiment shows that in a vacuum, all electromagnetic waves—including radio waves, x rays, and others—propagate at the same speed. This is the **speed of light**, to which we give the symbol c:

(22-1)
$$c = 2.99792458 \times 10^8 \text{ m/s} \ (= 3.00 \times 10^8 \text{ m/s to 3 significant figures})$$

Different kinds of electromagnetic waves have different frequencies and wavelengths. In Section 13-3 we learned that for a mechanical wave, the frequency f and wavelength λ are related to the propagation speed of the wave v_p by $v_p = f\lambda$ (Equation 13-2). The same relationship holds for electromagnetic waves in a vacuum with v_p related by c:

Propagation speed, frequency, and wavelength of an electromagnetic wave (22-2)

Speed of light in a vacuum   Frequency of an electromagnetic wave

$$c = f\lambda$$

Wavelength of the wave in vacuum

Equation 22-2 tells us that the product of frequency f and wavelength λ has the same value, c, for *all* electromagnetic waves in a vacuum. The longer the wavelength, the lower the frequency; the shorter the wavelength, the higher the frequency.

Electromagnetic waves of any wavelength are possible. Figure 22-2a shows the names given to different wavelength ranges, which we refer to collectively as the **electromagnetic spectrum**. The human eye is sensitive to only a very narrow range of wavelengths known as **visible light** (Figure 22-2b). Visible light encompasses wavelengths from about $\lambda = 380$ nm to about $\lambda = 750$ nm (1 nm = 1 nanometer = 10^{-9} m). We perceive light of different wavelengths as having different colors; the shortest-wavelength light we

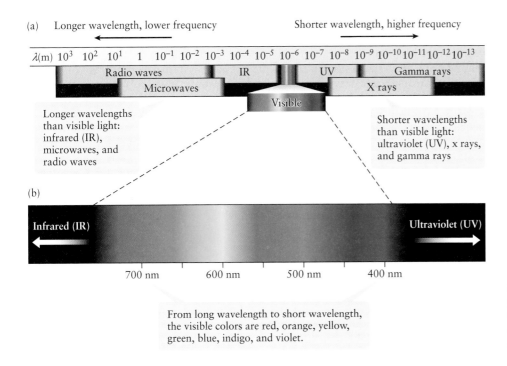

(a) Longer wavelength, lower frequency   Shorter wavelength, higher frequency

λ(m) 10^3 10^2 10^1 1 10^{-1} 10^{-2} 10^{-3} 10^{-4} 10^{-5} 10^{-6} 10^{-7} 10^{-8} 10^{-9} 10^{-10} 10^{-11} 10^{-12} 10^{-13}

Radio waves   IR   UV   Gamma rays

Microwaves   X rays

Visible

Longer wavelengths than visible light: infrared (IR), microwaves, and radio waves

Shorter wavelengths than visible light: ultraviolet (UV), x rays, and gamma rays

(b)

Infrared (IR)   Ultraviolet (UV)

700 nm   600 nm   500 nm   400 nm

From long wavelength to short wavelength, the visible colors are red, orange, yellow, green, blue, indigo, and violet.

Figure 22-2 The electromagnetic spectrum (a) We classify electromagnetic waves according to their wavelength. (b) Visible light makes up a tiny portion of the entire electromagnetic spectrum.

can see is violet, and the longest-wavelength light we can see is red. At wavelengths shorter than visible light are ultraviolet light (UV), x rays, and gamma rays. At wavelengths longer than visible light are infrared light (IR), microwaves, and radio waves.

Other species can detect wavelengths longer or shorter than those visible to humans. Certain snakes (including pythons and rattlesnakes) have special pit organs on their heads that can sense infrared light. This enables these snakes to detect the radiation that both predators and prey emit due to their body temperature (see Section 14-7). Other species, such as damselfish, are able to sense ultraviolet light (Figure 22-3).

Note that in a medium other than a vacuum, electromagnetic waves propagate at speeds slower than c. For example, visible light travels at about 2.2×10^8 m/s $(0.73c)$ in water and at about $0.9998c$ in air. The propagation speed in a medium other than vacuum also depends on the wave frequency: For example, in ordinary glass blue light travels slightly slower than does red light. (We'll see in Chapter 23 that this explains why a prism is able to break white light into colors.) In a vacuum, however, electromagnetic waves of all frequencies propagate at c.

Male Ambon damselfish
(*Pomacentrus amboinensis*)

Seen in ultraviolet light

Male lemon damselfish
(*Pomacentrus moluccensis*)

Seen in ultraviolet light

Figure 22-3 Using ultraviolet light for face recognition The Ambon damselfish (*Pomacentrus amboinensis*, a reef fish native to the western Pacific) has the ability to detect ultraviolet light. Where you see only dark and light bands on a fish's face, an Ambon sees an intricate pattern. This enables the territorial male Ambon damselfish (top) to identify and attack another Ambon in order to defend its territory, but ignore a male lemon damselfish (*Pomacentrus moluccensis*, bottom) with its slightly different facial pattern.

The structure of electromagnetic waves can be quite complex. For example, the waves that make up the beam of laser light shown in Figure 22-1b are strong near the center of the beam, then taper off in strength toward the edge of the beam. An idealized kind of wave that's much simpler to analyze but has all of the key properties of a more general electromagnetic wave is a **sinusoidal plane wave** (Figure 22-4a). As the name suggests, the disturbance in such a wave oscillates in a sinusoidal fashion. There are actually two disturbances in this wave, an electric field $\vec{E}$ with amplitude E_0 and a magnetic field $\vec{B}$ with amplitude B_0. Both of these fields are *transverse*: They are perpendicular to the direction of propagation, just like the disturbance for waves propagating along a stretched rope or string (Sections 13-3 and 13-4). The fields are also perpendicular to each other. In a snapshot of the wave as shown in Figure 22-4a, the $\vec{E}$ and $\vec{B}$ fields repeat over the same distance and so have the same wavelength λ. At a given point in space, as the wave passes by that point the $\vec{E}$ and $\vec{B}$ fields both oscillate with the same frequency f. Equation 22-2 then tells us that both fields propagate at the same speed $c = f\lambda$.

Figure 22-4 A sinusoidal electromagnetic plane wave
(a) The characteristics of a simple electromagnetic wave. This illustration shows two complete wavelengths of the wave. (b) How the electric field $\vec{E}$ and magnetic field $\vec{B}$ extend through space.

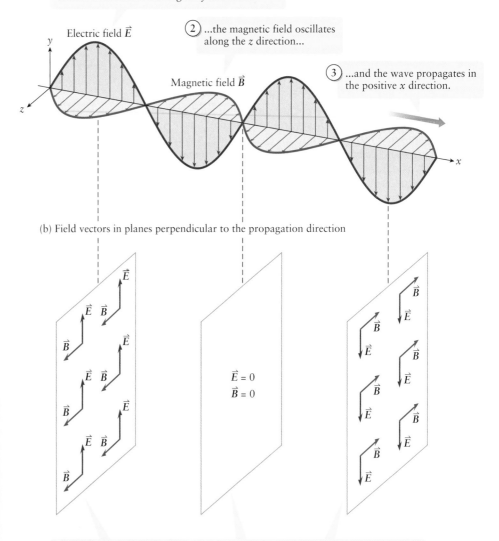

(a) An electromagnetic plane wave propagating in the positive x direction

① In this sinusoidal electromagnetic plane wave, the electric field oscillates along the y direction...

② ...the magnetic field oscillates along the z direction...

③ ...and the wave propagates in the positive x direction.

Electric field $\vec{E}$

Magnetic field $\vec{B}$

(b) Field vectors in planes perpendicular to the propagation direction

$\vec{E} = 0$
$\vec{B} = 0$

• An electromagnetic wave is transverse: The electric and magnetic fields (the wave disturbances) are perpendicular to the propagation direction.
• In this sinusoidal plane wave, the electric and magnetic fields oscillate in phase.
• This is a plane wave because on any plane perpendicular to the direction in which the wave propagates, $\vec{E}$ has the same value at all points and $\vec{B}$ has the same value at all points.

④ At any instant, the electric field vector has the same value at all points on a plane perpendicular to the direction in which the wave propagates (for this wave, any plane perpendicular to the x axis). The same is true for the magnetic field vector.

> ## ⚠ Watch Out! The fields of an electromagnetic plane wave extend beyond the axis of propagation.
>
> Figure 22-4a may give you the misleading impression that the $\vec{E}$ and $\vec{B}$ fields are present only along the x axis (the axis along which the wave propagates). Such a wave would be like an infinitely narrow laser beam. In fact, in a plane wave the fields have the same value at *all* points on a plane perpendicular to the direction of propagation (Figure 22-4b). That's the origin of the term *plane wave*. A true plane wave would extend infinitely far beyond the x axis in Figure 22-4a, so this is an idealization like a frictionless incline or a massless rope. But the fields shown in Figure 22-4 are a good approximation of the actual fields found near the center of the laser beam in Figure 22-1b.

In Section 13-3 we wrote a *wave function* that describes the disturbance associated with a wave on a rope. In the same fashion we can write wave functions for the electric and magnetic fields depicted in Figure 22-4a:

$$E_y(x,t) = E_0\cos(kx - \omega t + \phi)$$
$$B_z(x,t) = B_0\cos(kx - \omega t + \phi)$$

(22-3)

(sinusoidal electromagnetic plane wave)

In Equations 22-3 we use the same symbols that we used for waves on a rope in Section 13-3: $k = 2\pi/\lambda$ is the angular wave number, $\omega = 2\pi f$ is the angular frequency, and ϕ is the phase angle (which tells us what point in the oscillation cycle corresponds to $x = 0$, $t = 0$). Note that $E_y(x, t)$ and $B_z(x, t)$ both depend on position x and time t in the same way, which tells us that the electric and magnetic fields oscillate in phase with the same wavelength and frequency. In addition, the electric field amplitude E_0 and the magnetic field amplitude B_0 in a plane wave are directly proportional to each other:

$$B_0 = \frac{E_0}{c}$$

(22-4)

(sinusoidal electromagnetic plane wave)

Example 22-1 A Radio Wave

A certain FM radio station broadcasts at a frequency of 98.7 MHz (1 MHz $= 10^6$ Hz). In the wave that reaches the radio in your car, the electric field amplitude is 6.00×10^{-2} V/m. Calculate the wavelength of the wave and the amplitude of the magnetic field.

Set Up

We are given the wave frequency f and the electric field amplitude E_0. We use Equation 22-2 to find the wavelength λ and Equation 22-4 to find the magnetic field amplitude B_0.

Propagation speed, frequency, and wavelength of an electromagnetic wave:

$$c = f\lambda$$

(22-2)

Relation between the electric and magnetic field amplitudes in an electromagnetic wave:

$$B_0 = \frac{E_0}{c}$$

(22-4)

electric field, amplitude E_0

magnetic field, amplitude B_0

direction of wave propagation

wavelength λ

Solve

Use Equation 22-2 and the given frequency $f = 98.7$ MHz $= 98.7 \times 10^6$ Hz to solve for the wavelength.

From Equation 22-2,

$$\lambda = \frac{c}{f} = \frac{3.00 \times 10^8 \text{ m/s}}{98.7 \times 10^6 \text{ Hz}} = 3.04 \frac{\text{m}}{\text{s} \cdot \text{Hz}}$$

Recall that 1 Hz $= 1$ s^{-1}, so the units of s and Hz cancel:

$$\lambda = 3.04 \text{ m}$$

Use Equation 22-4 and the value $E_0 = 6.00 \times 10^{-2}$ V/m to solve for the magnetic field amplitude.

From Equation 22-4,

$$B_0 = \frac{E_0}{c} = \frac{6.00 \times 10^{-2}\,\text{V/m}}{3.00 \times 10^8\,\text{m/s}} = 2.00 \times 10^{-10}\left(\frac{\text{V}}{\text{m}}\right)\left(\frac{\text{s}}{\text{m}}\right)$$

We learned in Section 17-3 that 1 V/m = 1 N/C, and in Section 19-3 we learned that $1\,\text{T} = 1\,(\text{N} \cdot \text{s})/(\text{C} \cdot \text{m})$. So

$$B_0 = 2.00 \times 10^{-10}\left(\frac{\text{N}}{\text{C}}\right)\left(\frac{\text{s}}{\text{m}}\right) = 2.00 \times 10^{-10}\,\frac{\text{N} \cdot \text{s}}{\text{C} \cdot \text{m}}$$

$$= 2.00 \times 10^{-10}\,\text{T}$$

Reflect

Because the speed of light c has such a large value in m/s, the magnetic field amplitude B_0 in tesla (T) is much smaller than the electric field amplitude E_0 in volts per meter (V/m). As we'll see later in the chapter, however, the electric and magnetic fields prove to be equally important in an electromagnetic wave in vacuum.

In this example we've seen how to relate the units of magnetic field (T) to those of electric field (V/m): $1\,\text{T} = 1\,(\text{V/m}) \cdot (\text{s/m}) = 1\,\text{V} \cdot \text{s/m}^2$. We'll make use of this result in later examples.

Why must an electromagnetic wave propagating in vacuum be transverse? Would it be possible to have a longitudinal component of the wave, with an oscillating electric or magnetic field along the direction of propagation? For that matter, why is it necessary for an electromagnetic wave to include both electric and magnetic fields? Couldn't there be a wave that included an oscillating electric field but no magnetic field, or an oscillating magnetic field but no electric field? To answer these questions, we need to look at the fundamental equations that govern electric and magnetic fields.

 Got the Concept? 22-1 Electromagnetic Wave Speeds

Four electromagnetic waves in vacuum have different frequencies. Which of these propagates at the fastest speed? (a) $f = 3.95 \times 10^6$ Hz; (b) $f = 2.44 \times 10^7$ Hz; (c) $f = 1.26 \times 10^{11}$ Hz; (d) $f = 2.26 \times 10^8$ Hz; (e) all have the same speed.

Take-Home Message for Section 22-2

✔ Electromagnetic waves in vacuum propagate at the speed of light.

✔ Different kinds of electromagnetic waves have different wavelengths and frequencies. The human eye can detect only a very narrow range of wavelengths.

✔ In a sinusoidal electromagnetic plane wave, the electric and magnetic fields both oscillate in phase with the same wavelength and frequency. The field directions are perpendicular to each other and perpendicular to the direction of propagation.

22-3 Maxwell's equations explain why electromagnetic waves are possible

By the middle of the nineteenth century, scientists understood a great deal about electricity and magnetism. The work of Gauss, Ampère, and Faraday had established fundamental relationships that describe electric and magnetic phenomena; for example, it was understood that electric charges give rise to electric fields and that electric currents give rise to magnetic fields. It was the Scottish physicist James Clerk Maxwell who added to these fundamental relationships and forged our understanding of electricity and magnetism into a unified theory. In this section we'll look at four basic equations, known as **Maxwell's equations**, which describe *all* electromagnetic phenomena. We'll then see how these equations help us understand the nature of electromagnetic waves like the sinusoidal plane wave that we discussed in Section 22-2.

Gauss's Laws for Electricity and Magnetism

The first of Maxwell's equations is **Gauss's law for the electric field**, which we first encountered in Section 16-6. It states that the net electric flux through a closed surface (called a *Gaussian surface*) is proportional to the total amount of electric charge enclosed within that surface:

Electric flux through a closed surface

Net amount of charge enclosed within the surface

$$\Phi_E = \frac{q_{encl}}{\varepsilon_0}$$

Permittivity of free space = $1/(4\pi k)$

Gauss's law for the electric field
(16-9)

In this equation we've added a subscript E to remind us that the quantity on the left-hand side is the flux of the electric field $\vec{E}$.

Figure 22-5a illustrates Gauss's law for the electric field. If a surface encloses a net positive charge, as for Gaussian surface 1 in Figure 22-5a, there is a net outward (positive) electric flux and electric field lines point out of the surface. If instead there is a net negative charge inside the surface, as for Gaussian surface 2 in Figure 22-5a, the

(a) Gauss's law for the electric field: $\Phi_E = q_{encl}/\varepsilon_0$

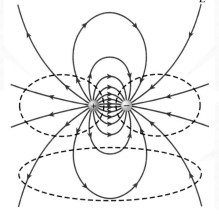

$\vec{E}$

Gaussian surface 1 encloses positive charge. Field lines point out of this surface, and there is a net outward (positive) electric flux.

Gaussian surface 2 encloses negative charge. Field lines point into this surface, and there is a net inward (negative) electric flux.

Gaussian surface 3 encloses zero charge. Each field line that points into this surface at one place points out at another place. There is zero net electric flux.

Figure 22-5 Gauss's laws for the electric and magnetic fields (a) The electric flux through a closed surface depends on the charge enclosed by that surface. (b) The magnetic flux through any closed surface is zero.

(b) Gauss's law for the magnetic field: $\Phi_B = 0$

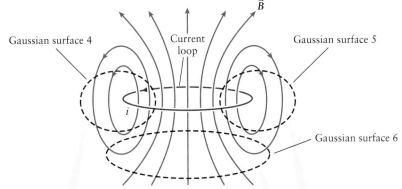

$\vec{B}$

Gaussian surface 4

Current loop

Gaussian surface 5

i

Gaussian surface 6

Gaussian surfaces 4 and 5 enclose part of the current loop. Gaussian surface 6 encloses none of the current loop. For each of these surfaces, each field line that points into the surface at one place points out at another place. There is zero net magnetic flux for each surface.

• In a region of space where there are no electric charges, there is zero net electric flux through any Gaussian surface in that region.
• In any region of space, there is zero net magnetic flux through any Gaussian surface.

net electric flux is inward (negative) and electric field lines point into the surface. If there is no charge at all inside the surface, as for Gaussian surface 3 in Figure 22-5a, there is zero net electric flux: Each field line that enters the surface at one point exits it at another point.

In addition to Gauss's law for the electric field, there is **Gauss's law for the magnetic field**. This states that for *any* closed Gaussian surface, there is *zero* net flux of the magnetic field $\vec{B}$ through that surface:

Gauss's law for the magnetic field
(22-5)

$$\Phi_B = 0$$

As an example, Figure 22-5b shows three Gaussian surfaces in the magnetic field of a current loop. For all three surfaces, each field line that enters the surface at one point exits it at another point. This is true whether there is current enclosed within the Gaussian surface (as for surfaces 4 and 5) or if there is no enclosed current (as for surface 6). Just as for the electric flux for Gaussian surface 3 in Figure 22-5a, this implies that there is zero net flux of magnetic field for all three surfaces. (There *would* be a nonzero net magnetic flux through a Gaussian surface if the surface enclosed an isolated north magnetic pole that had no associated south pole, or an isolated south pole that had no associated north pole. These would be the magnetic analogs of an isolated positive or negative electric charge. Physicists have searched for decades for such isolated poles, called *magnetic monopoles*. No confirmed observations have yet been made.)

What Gauss's Laws Tell Us about Electromagnetic Waves

Equations 16-9 and 22-5 are valid not just for static situations in which the electric and magnetic fields are constant, but also in situations where the $\vec{E}$ and $\vec{B}$ fields are changing. So Gauss's laws for the electric and magnetic fields must also hold true for electromagnetic waves. In Figure 22-6a we've drawn a Gaussian surface that encloses part of the sinusoidal plane wave shown in Figure 22-4. Because the wave is transverse, there is no electric or magnetic flux through the front or back face of the Gaussian surface. Although the fields change, at any instant there is as much outward flux of $\vec{E}$ or $\vec{B}$ on one edge of the Gaussian surface as there is inward flux on the opposite edge. So the net electric flux and the net magnetic flux through this surface is zero, and both of Gauss's laws are obeyed.

Gauss's laws also help us understand why electromagnetic waves in vacuum *must* be transverse. In Figure 22-6b we've sketched part of an electromagnetic wave with an oscillating *longitudinal* electric field (one that points along or opposite to the direction in which the wave propagates). For the Gaussian surface that we've chosen and at the instant of time shown, there is a net nonzero outward flux of electric field. But the wave is in a vacuum, so there can be no charge enclosed by the surface. Equation 16-9 then tells us that there *cannot* be a net electric flux through the surface in Figure 22-6b. We're forced to conclude that the longitudinal wave shown in Figure 22-6b is impossible because it contradicts Gauss's law for the electric field. Likewise, it would be impossible for an electromagnetic wave to have a longitudinal magnetic field, since this would violate Gauss's law for the magnetic field as given by Equation 22-5.

We see that Gauss's laws for the electric and magnetic fields explain why an electromagnetic wave must be transverse. Let's now examine the two remaining members of Maxwell's equations and see what they tell us about the nature of electromagnetic waves.

(a) Gauss's laws say that a transverse electromagnetic wave is permitted.

This edge:
• outward electric flux
• zero magnetic flux

This edge:
• zero electric flux
• inward magnetic flux

Direction of
wave propagation

Front and back faces:
• zero electric flux
• zero magnetic flux

This edge:
• inward electric flux
• zero magnetic flux

This edge:
• zero electric flux
• outward magnetic flux

• The net electric flux through this Gaussian surface is zero: $\Phi_E = 0$.
• The net magnetic flux through this Gaussian surface is zero: $\Phi_B = 0$.
• This agrees with Gauss's laws.

(b) Gauss's laws say that a longitudinal electromagnetic wave is not permitted.

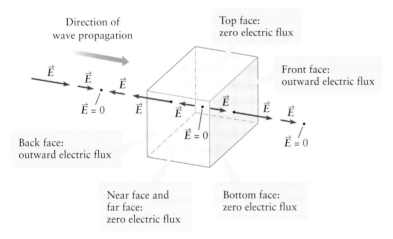

Direction of
wave propagation

Top face:
zero electric flux

Front face:
outward electric flux

$\vec{E} = 0$

$\vec{E} = 0$

Back face:
outward electric flux

Near face and
far face:
zero electric flux

Bottom face:
zero electric flux

• The net electric flux through this Gaussian surface is outward, so $\Phi_E \neq 0$.
• This disagrees with Gauss's law for the electric field.

Figure 22-6 **Gauss's laws applied to a sinusoidal electromagnetic plane wave** (a) A transverse electromagnetic wave in vacuum is compatible with Gauss's laws, but (b) a longitudinal electromagnetic wave in vacuum is not.

Faraday's Law: A Changing Magnetic Field Generates an Electric Field

The third of Maxwell's equations is **Faraday's law,** which we introduced in Sections 20-2 and 20-3. It states that an emf is induced in a loop if the magnetic flux through that loop changes:

Induced or motional
emf in a loop

Change in the magnetic flux through
the surface outlined by the loop

$$\varepsilon = -\frac{\Delta\Phi_B}{\Delta t}$$

Time interval over which the change
in magnetic flux takes place

The negative sign indicates that the current caused by the emf
induces a magnetic field which opposes the change in flux.

Faraday's law and Lenz's law
for induction
(20-3)

Figure 22-7 **A changing $\vec{B}$ produces a circulating $\vec{E}$** (a) Faraday's law says that an emf is induced in the loop when the magnetic field changes. (b) Fundamentally what happens when the magnetic field changes is that a circulating electric field is produced.

(a) A wire loop in a changing magnetic field

(b) A changing magnetic field produces a circulating electric field

Electromagnet

If the upward magnetic field $\vec{B}$ between the poles of the electromagnet increases...

...an emf is induced in the wire loop because the magnetic flux through the loop changes.

If the upward magnetic field $\vec{B}$ between the poles of the electromagnet increases...

...a circulating electric field $\vec{E}$ is produced. If a wire loop is placed here, the electric field gives rise to an emf in the loop.

As an example, Figure 22-7a shows a wire loop placed between the poles of an electromagnet. As the current in the electromagnet increases, the magnetic field increases and the increasing magnetic flux through the wire loop induces an emf in the loop. It's important to note that the emf is present whether the loop is made of a conductor like copper wire, a semiconductor like silicon, or an insulator like wood; the only difference is the amount of current that's established in response to the emf. The emf is even present if there is no material substance there at all!

Fundamentally, what happens is that the changing magnetic field generates a circulating electric field $\vec{E}$, as Figure 22-7b shows. The emf around a loop is just the *circulation* of the electric field around the loop. We define this in exactly the same way that we defined the circulation of magnetic field in Section 19-7. First imagine breaking the loop into a number of small segments of length $\Delta\ell$; then find the component $E_\parallel$ of the electric field that's tangent to each segment; then sum the products $E_\parallel\Delta\ell$:

$$\text{(22-6)} \qquad \text{Circulation of the electric field} = \sum E_\parallel\Delta\ell$$

(A particularly simple case is the circulating electric field shown in Figure 22-7b. Here $\vec{E}$ points tangential to the circular loop of radius r, so the circulation is just the magnitude E multiplied by the total distance around the loop—that is, the circumference $2\pi r$ of the loop.)

We can now rewrite Faraday's law by replacing the induced emf ε in Equation 20-3 with the circulation of the electric field as given by Equation 22-6:

Faraday's law in terms of circulation (22-7)

Circulation of electric field around a loop

Change in the magnetic flux through the surface outlined by the loop

$$\sum E_\parallel\Delta\ell = -\frac{\Delta\Phi_B}{\Delta t}$$

Time interval over which the change in magnetic flux takes place

Equation 22-7 tells us that a changing magnetic flux through a loop causes an electric field that circulates around that loop. This is true even if there is no material substance at the location of the loop. The minus sign in Equation 22-7 tells us the direction of the circulating electric field: If a conducting wire is present around the loop, the electric field will cause charges to flow, and the magnetic field due to those moving charges will oppose the change in magnetic field that caused the change in magnetic flux. (This is Lenz's law, which we introduced in Section 20-3.)

Example 22-2 An Electric Field Due to a Changing Magnetic Field

The uniform magnetic field shown in Figure 22-7b decreases in magnitude from 1.50 T to zero in a time t, inducing an electric field. What is the magnitude of this electric field around a loop 3.50 cm in diameter if (a) $t = 10.0$ s and (b) $t = 0.100$ s?

Set Up

Equation 20-1 tells us the magnetic flux through the loop of diameter 3.50 cm. The magnetic field $\vec{B}$ is perpendicular to the plane of the loop, so θ (the angle between the direction of $\vec{B}$ and the perpendicular to the loop) is $\theta = 0$.

The electric field in this case has the same magnitude E all the way around the circle and is tangent to the circle, so $E_{\parallel}$ in Equation 22-7 is equal to E.

Magnetic flux:

$$\Phi_B = AB_{\perp} = AB \cos\theta \qquad (20\text{-}1)$$

Faraday's law in terms of circulation:

$$\sum E_{\parallel}\Delta\ell = -\frac{\Delta\Phi_B}{\Delta t} \qquad (22\text{-}7)$$

Area of a circle of radius r:

$$A = \pi r^2$$

Circumference of a circle of radius r:

$$C = 2\pi r$$

Solve

(a) First determine the initial and final values of magnetic flux and the change in magnetic flux for a circle of diameter 3.50 cm.

The radius of the loop is half the diameter:

$$r = \frac{1}{2}(3.50 \text{ cm}) = 1.75 \text{ cm} = 1.75 \times 10^{-2} \text{ m}$$

The area of the loop is

$$A = \pi r^2 = \pi (1.75 \times 10^{-2} \text{ m})^2 = 9.62 \times 10^{-4} \text{ m}^2$$

From Equation 20-1, the initial magnetic flux is

$$\Phi_B = AB \cos 0 = (9.62 \times 10^{-4} \text{ m}^2)(1.50 \text{ T})(1)$$
$$= 1.44 \times 10^{-3} \text{ T} \cdot \text{m}^2$$

The final magnetic field is zero, so the final magnetic flux is zero as well. The change in magnetic flux is

$$\Delta\Phi_B = (\text{final flux}) - (\text{initial flux}) = 0 - 1.44 \times 10^{-3} \text{ T} \cdot \text{m}^2$$
$$= -1.44 \times 10^{-3} \text{ T} \cdot \text{m}^2$$

Use Equation 22-7 to calculate the circulation of the electric field in the case where $\Delta t = 10.0$ s. Since the field magnitude E has the same value around the circle and $E_{\parallel} = E$, we can use this to calculate E.

The circulation of the electric field is equal to $-\Delta\Phi_B/\Delta t$:

$$\text{Circulation of the electric field} = \sum E_{\parallel}\Delta\ell = -\frac{\Delta\Phi_B}{\Delta t}$$

$$= -\frac{-1.44 \times 10^{-3} \text{ T} \cdot \text{m}^2}{10.0 \text{ s}} = 1.44 \times 10^{-4} \frac{\text{T} \cdot \text{m}^2}{\text{s}}$$

In Example 22-1 (Section 22-2) we saw that

$$1 \text{ T} = 1 \frac{\text{V} \cdot \text{s}}{\text{m}^2} \text{ so the magnitude of the circulation is}$$

$$1.44 \times 10^{-4} \frac{\text{T} \cdot \text{m}^2}{\text{s}} = 1.44 \times 10^{-4} \left(\frac{\text{V} \cdot \text{s}}{\text{m}^2}\right)\left(\frac{\text{m}^2}{\text{s}}\right) = 1.44 \times 10^{-4} \text{ V}$$

Since $E_{\parallel} = E$ and E has the same value at all points around the circle, we can write the circulation as

$$\sum E_{\parallel}\Delta\ell = \sum E\Delta\ell = E\sum \Delta\ell$$

The sum $\sum \Delta \ell$ is the total distance around the loop, equal to the loop circumference $2\pi r$. So

$$E\,(2\pi r) = 1.44 \times 10^{-4}\ \text{V}$$

$$E = \frac{1.44 \times 10^{-4}\ \text{V}}{2\pi r} = \frac{1.44 \times 10^{-4}\ \text{V}}{2\pi\,(1.75 \times 10^{-2}\ \text{m})} = 1.31 \times 10^{-3}\ \text{V/m}$$

(b) Repeat the calculation for the case where $\Delta t = 0.100$ s

Equation 22-7 tells us that the circulation of the electric field, and hence the electric field itself, is inversely proportional to the time Δt over which the magnetic flux changes. If the magnetic field drops to zero in $\Delta t = 0.100$ s rather than $t = 10.0$ s, the elapsed time is smaller by a factor of

$$\frac{0.100\ \text{s}}{10.0\ \text{s}} = 1.00 \times 10^{-2}$$

and so the induced field is larger by a factor of

$$\frac{1}{1.00 \times 10^{-2}} = 1.00 \times 10^{2}$$

Therefore the electric field in the case where $\Delta t = 0.100$ s is

$$E = (1.00 \times 10^{2})\,(1.31 \times 10^{-3}\ \text{V/m}) = 0.131\ \text{V/m}$$

Reflect

Our results show that the more rapid the change in magnetic field, the greater the magnitude of the electric field that is induced.

If a circular loop of conducting wire were placed along the circular path of diameter 3.50 cm, a current would be generated so as to produce a magnetic field that would oppose the change in magnetic flux. The upward magnetic field in the figure decreases, so the magnetic field produced in this way would have to be upward. The induced current that produces this magnetic field is in the same direction as the circulating electric field. So the electric field and current must both have the direction shown.

If a wire loop were placed here, current would be induced to produce an upward $\vec{B}$.

The Maxwell–Ampère Law: A Changing Electric Field Generates a Magnetic Field

Equation 22-7 tells us that a circulating electric field is produced by a magnetic field that changes over time. In Section 19-7 we learned that a circulating *magnetic* field is produced by electric charges in motion, that is, by a current. The mathematical expression of this statement is *Ampère's law*:

Ampère's law
(19-13)

Circulation of magnetic field around an Amperian loop

Permeability of free space

$$\sum B_{\parallel}\Delta\ell = \mu_0 i_{\text{through}}$$

Current through the Amperian loop

Figure 22-8a shows an application of Ampère's law that we introduced in Section 19-7: the magnetic field due to a long, straight, current-carrying wire. The current through each loop in the figure is equal to the current in the wire, so for each loop $i_{\text{through}} = i$. As a result, there is a magnetic field that circulates around each loop, and the circulation $\sum B_{\parallel}\Delta\ell$ of the magnetic field is equal to $\mu_0 i$.

Now suppose we break the wire in Figure 22-8a and insert two metal disks to form a parallel-plate capacitor (Figure 22-8b). If the same steady current exists as in Figure 22-8a, positive charge will build up on the lower plate and negative charge will build up on the upper plate. As a consequence, the electric field between the two plates will

(a) A current-carrying wire

Wire

$\vec{B}$ $\vec{B}$

$\vec{B}$ $\vec{B}$

i

The current produces a circulating magnetic field $\vec{B}$.

Current i

$\vec{B}$ $\vec{B}$

$\vec{B}$ $\vec{B}$

i

The magnetic field direction is given by a right-hand rule: Point your right thumb in the direction of the current, and the $\vec{B}$ field circulates in the direction of your fingers.

(b) A current-carrying wire with a capacitor

i

Increasing negative charge $-q$

Increasing electric field $\vec{E}$

$\vec{B}$ $\vec{B}$

$\vec{B}$ $\vec{B}$

i

Increasing positive charge $+q$

There is no current between the plates, but the changing electric field $\vec{E}$ produces a circulating magnetic field $\vec{B}$.

Figure 22-8 **A changing $\vec{E}$ produces a circulating $\vec{B}$** (a) Ampère's law says that a magnetic field circulates around a current-carrying wire. (b) A circulating magnetic field can also be produced by a changing electric field.

increase in magnitude. However, there is no current from the lower plate to the upper plate and so $i_{\text{through}} = 0$ for the loop between the plates in Figure 22-8b. So Equation 19-13 predicts that there should be no circulating magnetic field between the plates. Yet experiment shows that there *is* a circulating magnetic field between the plates! How can this be?

James Clerk Maxwell's great insight was to propose that if a changing magnetic field could produce a circulating electric field, then a changing *electric* field could produce a *magnetic* field. That's what's happening between the capacitor plates shown in Figure 22-8b: The electric field is increasing in magnitude as charge builds on the plates, and a circulating magnetic field results. To explain this effect, Maxwell expanded on Ampère's law as given by Equation 19-13 to include an additional term on the right-hand side. The result is called the **Maxwell-Ampère law**:

Circulation of magnetic field around an Amperian loop

Permittivity of free space

Change in the electric flux through the surface outlined by the loop

$$\sum B_{\parallel} \Delta \ell = \mu_0 \left(i_{\text{through}} + \varepsilon_0 \frac{\Delta \Phi_E}{\Delta t} \right)$$

Permeability of free space

Current through the Amperian loop

Time interval over which the change in electric flux takes place

Maxwell-Ampère law
(22-8)

The electric flux Φ_E through a loop, calculated using Equation 16-6, is defined in precisely the same manner as the magnetic flux Φ_B through a loop. The quantity $\varepsilon_0 (\Delta \Phi_E / \Delta t)$ has units of amperes and is called the **displacement current**. Experiment confirms Equation 22-8: A circulating magnetic field can be produced by an electric current, by a changing electric field, or a combination.

We saw in Section 17-5 that we can write the permittivity of free space as $\varepsilon_0 = 8.85 \times 10^{-12}$ F/m. Since 1 F = 1 C/V and 1 A = 1 C/s, we can write this as

$$\varepsilon_0 = 8.85 \times 10^{-12} \frac{\text{F}}{\text{m}} = 8.85 \times 10^{-12} \frac{\text{C}}{\text{V} \cdot \text{m}} = 8.85 \times 10^{-12} \frac{\text{A} \cdot \text{s}}{\text{V} \cdot \text{m}} \qquad (22\text{-}9)$$

We'll make use of this equation in the following example.

Example 22-3 A Magnetic Field Due to a Changing Electric Field

A parallel-plate capacitor like that shown in Figure 22-8b has circular plates 5.00 cm in diameter. The electric field between the plates increases by 8.00×10^5 V/m in 1.00 s, inducing a magnetic field. What is the magnitude of that magnetic field around a loop 3.50 cm in diameter in the space between the capacitor plates?

Set Up

No charge actually moves through the loop in question, so $i_{\text{through}} = 0$ in Equation 22-8. However, the electric flux through the loop changes as the electric field changes, so the term $\Delta\Phi_E/\Delta t$ in Equation 22-8 is not zero and a circulating magnetic field will result. This example is very similar to Example 22-2, except that now we need to calculate the change in *electric* flux to determine the magnitude of the circulating *magnetic* field.

Equation 16-6 tells us the electric flux through the 3.50-cm diameter loop; the electric field $\vec{E}$ is perpendicular to the plane of the loop, so $\theta = 0$. The magnetic field has the same magnitude B all the way around the loop and is tangent to the loop, so $B_{\parallel} = B$ in Equation 22-8.

Electric flux:

$$\Phi_E = AE_{\perp} = AE\cos\theta \quad (16\text{-}6)$$

Maxwell-Ampère law:

$$\sum B_{\parallel}\Delta\ell = \mu_0\left(i_{\text{through}} + \varepsilon_0\frac{\Delta\Phi_E}{\Delta t}\right)$$
$$(22\text{-}8)$$

Permittivity of free space:

$$\varepsilon_0 = 8.85 \times 10^{-12}\frac{\text{A}\cdot\text{s}}{\text{V}\cdot\text{m}} \quad (22\text{-}9)$$

Permeability of free space:

$$\mu_0 = 4\pi \times 10^{-7}\,\text{T}\cdot\text{m/A}$$

Area of a circle of radius r:

$$A = \pi r^2$$

Circumference of a circle of radius r:

$$C = 2\pi r$$

Solve

Find the displacement current $\varepsilon_0(\Delta\Phi_E/\Delta t)$ associated with the change in electric flux through the loop.

The change in electric flux in a time $\Delta t = 1.00$ s is equal to the area of the loop multiplied by the change in electric field in that time (recall that $\theta = 0$). The loop has radius $r = (1/2) \times (3.50\,\text{cm}) = 1.75\,\text{cm} = 1.75 \times 10^{-2}$ m, so

$$\Delta\Phi_E = A(\Delta E)\cos 0 = A(\Delta E)(1)$$
$$= (\pi)(1.75 \times 10^{-2}\,\text{m})^2(8.00 \times 10^5\,\text{V/m})(1)$$
$$= 7.70 \times 10^2\,\text{V}\cdot\text{m}$$

The displacement current through the loop is

$$\varepsilon_0\frac{\Delta\Phi_E}{\Delta t} = \left(8.85 \times 10^{-12}\frac{\text{A}\cdot\text{s}}{\text{V}\cdot\text{m}}\right)\left(\frac{7.70 \times 10^2\,\text{V}\cdot\text{m}}{1.00\,\text{s}}\right)$$
$$= 6.81 \times 10^{-9}\,\text{A}$$

Use Equation 22-8 to determine the magnitude of the circulating magnetic field.

Since $i_{\text{through}} = 0$, the circulation of the magnetic field is equal to μ_0 times the displacement current:

$$\text{Circulation of the magnetic field} = \sum B_{\parallel}\Delta\ell = \mu_0\left(\varepsilon_0\frac{\Delta\Phi_E}{\Delta t}\right)$$

$$= \left(4\pi \times 10^{-7}\frac{\text{T}\cdot\text{m}}{\text{A}}\right)(6.81 \times 10^{-9}\,\text{A}) = 8.56 \times 10^{-15}\,\text{T}\cdot\text{m}$$

Since $B_{\parallel} = B$ and B has the same value at all points around the circle, we can write the circulation as

$$\sum B_{\parallel}\Delta\ell = \sum B\,\Delta\ell = B\sum\Delta\ell$$

The sum $\sum \Delta \ell$ is the total distance around the loop, equal to the loop circumference $2\pi r$. So

$$B(2\pi r) = 8.56 \times 10^{-15}\ \text{T} \cdot \text{m}$$

$$B = \frac{8.56 \times 10^{-15}\ \text{T} \cdot \text{m}}{2\pi(1.75 \times 10^{-2}\ \text{m})} = 7.78 \times 10^{-14}\ \text{T}$$

Reflect

The induced magnetic field is very weak (7.78×10^{-14} T) because the displacement current that produces it is very small (6.81×10^{-9} A). If the electric field between the plates were to change more rapidly, the displacement current would be greater and the induced magnetic field stronger.

The displacement current is in the same direction as the current that brings positive charge to the lower plate of the capacitor. The right-hand rule for using Ampère's law (Section 19-7) tells us that the induced magnetic field is in the direction shown.

The magnetic field due to an increasing $\vec{E}$ circulates in the same direction as the electric field due to a decreasing $\vec{B}$ (see Example 22-2).

In a vacuum, where no electric currents are present, we can write Faraday's law and the Maxwell-Ampère law as

$$\sum E_{\parallel}\Delta \ell = -\frac{\Delta \Phi_B}{\Delta t}$$

$$\sum B_{\parallel}\Delta \ell = +\mu_0 \varepsilon_0 \frac{\Delta \Phi_E}{\Delta t} \qquad (22\text{-}10)$$

Notice that the first of Equations 22-10 (Faraday's law) has a minus sign, while the second of these equations (the Maxwell-Ampère law) does not. This says that the circulating electric field produced by a *decreasing* magnetic flux (so $\Delta \Phi_B / \Delta t < 0$) is in the same direction as the circulating magnetic field produced by an *increasing* electric flux (so $\Delta \Phi_E / \Delta t > 0$). That's why the electric field that we found in Example 22-2 due to a decreasing magnetic field circulates in the same direction as the magnetic field that we found in Example 22-3 due to an increasing electric field.

What Faraday's Law and the Maxwell–Ampère Law Tell Us about Electromagnetic Waves

Faraday's law tells us that a varying magnetic field gives rise to a circulating electric field, and the Maxwell-Ampère law tells us that a varying electric field gives rise to a circulating magnetic field. Taken together, these two laws tell us how electromagnetic waves are possible, and why they involve both electric and magnetic fields.

Imagine that you take an electric charge and oscillate it up and down. This will cause the electric field due to the charge to oscillate as well. By the Maxwell-Ampère law, it follows that a magnetic field will be produced which will circulate in one direction when the electric field is increasing and in the other direction when the electric field is decreasing. In other words, the magnetic field will itself oscillate. Faraday's law then tells us that this magnetic field will itself generate an electric field whose direction changes, circulating in one direction when the magnetic field is increasing and in the other direction when the magnetic field is decreasing. These two laws together tell us that a combination of an oscillating electric field and an oscillating magnetic field can sustain each other, and will continue to sustain each other even after the original source of the oscillating fields—the oscillating charge—has stopped moving.

Let's look at this in a little more detail for the electromagnetic plane wave depicted in Figure 22-4a. **Figure 22-9a** shows five snapshots of the wave as it propagates from left to right in the positive x direction. In each snapshot we're looking at the xy plane, and in each snapshot we've drawn a stationary rectangular loop one-half of a wavelength in

Figure 22-9 Flux and circulation in a sinusoidal electromagnetic plane wave (a) As an electromagnetic plane wave propagates past the dashed rectangular loop, the electric field circulates around the loop when the magnetic flux through the loop changes (Faraday's law). (b) For this loop, the magnetic field circulates around the loop when the electric flux through the loop changes (the Maxwell-Ampère law).

(a) Viewing the plane of the $\vec{E}$ field

(b) Viewing the plane of the $\vec{B}$ field

Magnetic flux through loop is maximum outward; zero circulation of $\vec{E}$.

Electric flux through loop is maximum outward; zero circulation of $\vec{B}$.

Magnetic flux through loop is changing from outward to inward; counterclockwise circulation of $\vec{E}$.

Electric flux through loop is changing from outward to inward; clockwise circulation of $\vec{B}$.

Magnetic flux through loop is maximum inward; zero circulation of $\vec{E}$.

Electric flux through loop is maximum inward; zero circulation of $\vec{B}$.

Magnetic flux through loop is changing from inward to outward; clockwise circulation of $\vec{E}$.

Electric flux through loop is changing from inward to outward; counterclockwise circulation of $\vec{B}$.

Again magnetic flux through loop is maximum outward; zero circulation of $\vec{E}$.

Again electric flux through loop is maximum outward; zero circulation of $\vec{B}$.

width. Because the magnetic field has only a z component, which is perpendicular to the plane of the loop, as the wave propagates there is a varying magnetic flux Φ_B through this loop. When the magnetic flux Φ_B is changing, there is a circulation of electric field around the loop; when the magnetic flux Φ_B has its maximum value either into or out of the xy plane, the flux is instantaneously not changing and there is zero circulation of electric field. That's just what Faraday's law tells us must be true.

Figure 22-9b shows five snapshots of the wave at the same instants as in Figure 22-9a, but in these snapshots we're looking at the xz plane. The rectangular loop in this part of the figure is the same size as those in part (a), but there's a varying *electric* flux Φ_E though this loop because the electric field has only a y component and so is perpendicular to the plane of this loop. When the magnetic flux Φ_E is changing, there is a circulation of magnetic field around the loop; when the magnetic flux Φ_E has its maximum value either into or out of the xz plane, the flux is instantaneously not changing and there is zero circulation of magnetic field. That's in perfect agreement with the Maxwell-Ampère law. Notice also that the circulation of the electric field in Figure 22-9a is counterclockwise when the magnetic flux Φ_B through the loop is changing from outward to inward, while the circulation of the magnetic field in Figure 22-9b is counterclockwise when the electric flux Φ_E is changing from inward to outward. That's a consequence of there being a minus sign in Faraday's law but no minus sign in the Maxwell-Ampère law, as we mentioned above in our discussion of Equations 22-10.

Faraday's law and the Maxwell-Ampère law show why the electric field and magnetic field are both necessary for the propagation of a wave: The varying electric field sustains the magnetic field, and the varying magnetic field sustains the electric field. Once an electromagnetic wave is started, it will continue to propagate through vacuum even across immense distances (Figure 22-1a). These laws also show why the electric and magnetic fields are naturally perpendicular to each other, and why the two fields oscillate together with the same frequency.

Using a more mathematical treatment of Faraday's law and the Maxwell-Ampère law, it's possible to calculate the speed c at which such a wave should propagate through a vacuum. It turns out that the speed is determined by the values of the permittivity of free space ε_0 and the permeability of free space μ_0, both of which appear in Equations 22-10:

$$c = \frac{1}{\sqrt{\mu_0 \varepsilon_0}}$$

If we substitute $\varepsilon_0 = 8.85 \times 10^{-12}\ (\text{A} \cdot \text{s})/(\text{V} \cdot \text{m})$ and $\mu_0 = 4\pi \times 10^{-7}\ \text{T} \cdot \text{m}/\text{A}$, we get

$$c = \frac{1}{\sqrt{\left(4\pi \times 10^{-7}\dfrac{\text{T} \cdot \text{m}}{\text{A}}\right)\left(8.85 \times 10^{-12}\dfrac{\text{A} \cdot \text{s}}{\text{V} \cdot \text{m}}\right)}} = 3.00 \times 10^8 \sqrt{\frac{\text{V}}{\text{T} \cdot \text{s}}}$$

These are very odd units! Note, however, that $1\ \text{V} = 1\ \text{N} \cdot \text{m}/\text{C}$ and $1\ \text{T} = 1\ \text{N} \cdot \text{s}/(\text{C} \cdot \text{m})$, so

$$1\sqrt{\frac{\text{V}}{\text{T} \cdot \text{s}}} = 1\sqrt{\left(\frac{\text{N} \cdot \text{m}}{\text{C}}\right)\left(\frac{\text{C} \cdot \text{m}}{\text{N} \cdot \text{s}}\right)\left(\frac{1}{\text{s}}\right)} = 1\sqrt{\frac{\text{m}^2}{\text{s}^2}} = 1\frac{\text{m}}{\text{s}}$$

The above expression for the speed of an electromagnetic wave then becomes

Speed of light in a vacuum

$$c = \frac{1}{\sqrt{\mu_0 \varepsilon_0}} = 3.00 \times 10^8\ \text{m/s}$$

Permeability of free space   Permittivity of free space

Speed of light in a vacuum
(22-11)

This agrees with Equation 22-1 for the speed of light in a vacuum. The same mathematical analysis that leads to Equation 22-11 also relates the amplitudes E_0 and B_0 of the electric and magnetic fields in the wave: The result is that $B_0 = E_0/c$, the same result that we stated in Section 22-2 (Equation 22-4).

In the following section we'll use our insight into the nature of electromagnetic waves to help us analyze the energy carried by such waves.

> **! Watch Out!** The speed of light in a medium other than a vacuum is less than *c*.
>
> As we noted in Section 22-2, electromagnetic waves propagate at speed *c* only in a vacuum. We determined the value of *c* in Equation 22-11 using ε_0, the permittivity of free space, and μ_0, the permeability of free space; "free space" is equivalent to "in a vacuum." Different materials have different values of permittivity and permeability, which is why the speed of light is different in them.

> **? Got the Concept? 22-2** Maxwell's Equations
>
> According to Maxwell's equations, which of the following situations is *possible*? (a) A closed surface that has a net outward magnetic flux through its surface. (b) A closed surface that has a net outward electric flux through its surface. (c) A loop that has zero electric flux through the interior of the loop and has a magnetic field that circulates around the loop. (d) More than one of (a), (b), and (c). (e) None of (a), (b), or (c).

Take-Home Message for Section 22-3

✔ Maxwell's equations are the four basic equations of electromagnetism.

✔ Gauss's law for the electric field says that the net electric flux through a closed surface is proportional to the charge enclosed by that surface. Gauss's law for the magnetic field says that the net magnetic flux through any closed surface must be zero.

✔ Gauss's laws explain why an electromagnetic wave in a vacuum must be a transverse wave.

✔ Faraday's law says that a circulating electric field is produced around a loop by a time-varying magnetic flux through the loop. The Maxwell-Ampère law states that a circulating magnetic field is produced around a loop by a current through the loop or a time-varying electric flux through the loop.

✔ Faraday's law and the Maxwell-Ampère law explain how an electromagnetic wave sustains itself, and why the electric and magnetic fields are mutually perpendicular.

22-4 Electromagnetic waves carry both electric and magnetic energy, and come in packets called photons

Electromagnetic waves carry energy. You can feel the energy delivered to your skin by sunlight (one kind of electromagnetic wave) on a sunny day. A microwave oven is useful for cooking because the water molecules found in food of all kinds absorb the energy in microwaves, which are at wavelengths between infrared and radio (Figure 22-2). And the energy in a laser beam is so tightly concentrated that it can be used as a surgical tool (Figure 22-1b).

The energy in an electromagnetic wave is actually contained within the electric and magnetic fields themselves. To see what this means, let's return to the physics of capacitors (Sections 17-5 and 17-6) and inductors (Sections 21-4 and 21-5). What we learn from these devices will give us insight into the energy content of electromagnetic waves.

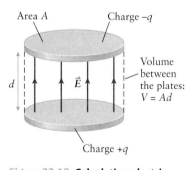

Figure 22-10 Calculating electric energy density The energy stored in this charged capacitor can be thought of as residing in the electric field $\vec{E}$ between the plates.

Energy in Electric and Magnetic Fields

Figure 22-10 shows a parallel-plate capacitor with plates of area *A* separated by a distance *d*. If the two plates are closely spaced, the electric field between the plates is approximately uniform and fills the volume between the plates (that is, there is very little field outside this volume). With a charge $+q$ on one plate and a charge $-q$ on the other plate, the magnitude of this field is

(17-10)

$$E = \frac{q}{\varepsilon_0 A}$$

It takes work to separate the charges $+q$ and $-q$, and the work that went into this goes into the electric potential energy U_E stored in the capacitor. The amount of stored energy is

$$U_E = \frac{q^2}{2C} \tag{17-17}$$

where C, the capacitance of the capacitor, is

$$C = \frac{\varepsilon_0 A}{d} \tag{17-13}$$

We can think of the electric energy in the capacitor as being stored in the electric field itself. To motivate this idea, let's substitute Equation 17-13 into Equation 17-17 and rearrange:

$$U_E = \frac{q^2}{2}\left(\frac{d}{\varepsilon_0 A}\right) = \frac{1}{2}\varepsilon_0\left(\frac{q^2}{\varepsilon_0^2 A^2}\right)Ad = \frac{1}{2}\varepsilon_0\left(\frac{q}{\varepsilon_0 A}\right)^2 Ad \tag{22-12}$$

The quantity $q/(\varepsilon_0 A)$ in parentheses on the far right-hand side of Equation 22-12 is just the electric field magnitude E from Equation 17-10. The quantity Ad is the volume V that the electric field occupies. So we can rewrite Equation 22-12 as

$$U_E = \left(\frac{1}{2}\varepsilon_0 E^2\right)V \tag{22-13}$$

Equation 22-13 tells us that the energy stored in the capacitor is equal to the volume V occupied by the electric field multiplied by a quantity $(1/2)\varepsilon_0 E^2$ that depends on the electric field magnitude E. This quantity has units of energy per volume (J/m^3) and is called the **electric energy density**:

$$u_E = \frac{1}{2}\varepsilon_0 E^2$$

Electric energy density
(22-14)

Equation 22-14 says that wherever there is an electric field, there is energy. This motivates the idea that the energy stored in a capacitor is stored in the field itself. We derived Equation 22-14 for the special case of a parallel-plate capacitor, but it turns out to be valid in any situation where an electric field is present.

We can come to a similar conclusion about the magnetic energy stored in an inductor like the one shown in Figure 22-11. Table 21-1 (Section 21-5) tells us that if an inductor has inductance L and carries a current i, the magnetic energy stored in the inductor is

$$U_B = \frac{1}{2}Li^2 \tag{22-15}$$

For an inductor like that in Figure 22-11, which is a long solenoid with N turns of wire, length ℓ, and cross-sectional area A, the inductance is

$$L = \frac{\mu_0 N^2 A}{\ell} \tag{21-14}$$

Like the electric field inside the parallel-plate capacitor in Figure 22-10, the magnetic field inside the solenoid in Figure 22-11 is nearly uniform and confined to the volume inside the solenoid. From Equation 19-17, the magnitude of this magnetic field is $B = \mu_0 n i$, where n is the number of turns of wire per meter. This is just the total

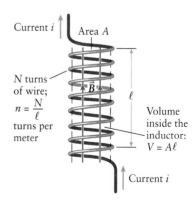

Figure 22-11 Calculating magnetic energy density The energy stored in this current-carrying inductor can be thought of as residing in the magnetic field $\vec{B}$ inside the inductor.

number of turns N divided by the length ℓ of the solenoid: $n = N/\ell$. So we can write the magnitude of the magnetic field inside the solenoid as

$$B = \frac{\mu_0 Ni}{\ell}$$ (22-16)

Let's substitute Equation 21-14 for L into Equation 22-15 for the energy in the solenoid, then rearrange:

$$U_B = \frac{1}{2}\left(\frac{\mu_0 N^2 A}{\ell}\right)i^2 = \frac{1}{2\mu_0}\left(\frac{\mu_0^2 N^2 i^2}{\ell^2}\right)A\ell = \frac{1}{2\mu_0}\left(\frac{\mu_0 Ni}{\ell}\right)^2 A\ell$$ (22-17)

The quantity $\mu_0 Ni/\ell$ in parentheses on the far right of Equation 22-17 is the magnitude B of the magnetic field inside the solenoid. The quantity $A\ell$ is the volume V inside the solenoid, which is also the volume that the magnetic field occupies. So Equation 22-17 becomes

$$U_B = \left(\frac{B^2}{2\mu_0}\right)V$$ (22-18)

Compare this to Equation 22-13 for the electric energy U_E. We see that according to Equation 22-18, the energy stored in the inductor equals the volume V occupied by the magnetic field multiplied by a quantity $B^2/(2\mu_0)$ that depends on the magnetic field magnitude B and has units J/m^3. We call $B^2/(2\mu_0)$ the **magnetic energy density**:

Magnetic energy density   Magnetic field magnitude

Magnetic energy density
(22-19)

$$u_B = \frac{B^2}{2\mu_0}$$

Permeability of free space

Just as Equation 22-14 tells us that there is electric energy wherever there is an electric field, Equation 22-19 tells us that there is magnetic energy wherever there is a magnetic field. This is true for an inductor, so we can think of the energy stored in a current-carrying inductor as being stored in the magnetic field within the inductor. But Equation 22-19 is valid wherever there is a magnetic field.

Energy in an Electromagnetic Plane Wave

Let's apply Equations 22-14 and 22-19 for the electric and magnetic energy densities to the sinusoidal electromagnetic plane wave that we introduced in Section 22-2. From Equation 22-3, in this plane wave the electric field has only a y component and the magnetic field has only a z component:

$$E_y(x,t) = E_0\cos(kx - \omega t + \phi)$$
(22-3)
$$B_z(x,t) = B_0\cos(kx - \omega t + \phi)$$

Substituting these into Equations 22-14 and 22-19, we find that the electric and magnetic energy densities in the plane wave are

$$u_E = \frac{1}{2}\varepsilon_0 E^2 = \frac{1}{2}\varepsilon_0 E_0^2\cos^2(kx - \omega t + \phi)$$

(22-20)
$$u_B = \frac{B^2}{2\mu_0} = \frac{B_0^2}{2\mu_0}\cos^2(kx - \omega t + \phi)$$

Note that u_E and u_B both depend on position x and time t in the same way. It may appear from Equation 22-20 that there are different amounts of energy in the electric and magnetic forms, since the coefficients $(1/2)\varepsilon_0 E_0^2$ and $B_0^2/2\mu_0$ are different. But we know from Equations 22-4 and 22-11 that $B_0 = E_0/c$ and $c = 1/\sqrt{\mu_0\varepsilon_0}$, so

(22-21)
$$\frac{B_0^2}{2\mu_0} = \frac{(E_0/c)^2}{2\mu_0} = \frac{(E_0\sqrt{\mu_0\varepsilon_0})^2}{2\mu_0} = \frac{1}{2}\left(\frac{\mu_0\varepsilon_0}{\mu_0}\right)E_0^2 = \frac{1}{2}\varepsilon_0 E_0^2$$

In other words, the coefficients of u_E and u_B in Equation 22-20 are equal. This means that at any position x and at any time t, an electromagnetic wave in vacuum has equal amounts of electric energy density and magnetic energy density:

$$u_E = u_B = \frac{1}{2}\varepsilon_0 E_0^2 \cos^2(kx - \omega t + \phi) = \frac{B_0^2}{2\mu_0}\cos^2(kx - \omega t + \phi) \qquad (22\text{-}22)$$

The *total* energy density u in the wave is the sum of u_E and u_B. Equation 22-22 tells us that $u_E = u_B$, so u is equal to $2u_E$ or $2u_B$:

$$u = u_E + u_B = \varepsilon_0 E_0^2 \cos^2(kx - \omega t + \phi) = \frac{B_0^2}{\mu_0}\cos^2(kx - \omega t + \phi) \qquad (22\text{-}23)$$

The value of u at any position varies with time, so it's often more useful to state its *average* value. The average value of the cosine function squared is $1/2$, so

Average energy density in an electromagnetic wave · Electric field magnitude · Electric field rms value · Magnetic field magnitude · Magnetic field rms value

$$u_{\text{average}} = \frac{1}{2}\varepsilon_0 E_0^2 = \varepsilon_0 E_{\text{rms}}^2 = \frac{B_0^2}{2\mu_0} = \frac{B_{\text{rms}}^2}{\mu_0}$$

Permittivity of free space · Permeability of free space

Average energy density in an electromagnetic wave
(22-24)

In Equation 22-24 we've used the root-mean-square (rms) values of the oscillating electric and magnetic fields, $E_{\text{rms}} = E_0/\sqrt{2}$ and $B_{\text{rms}} = B_0/\sqrt{2}$ (see Section 21-2).

An even more useful way to express the energy carried by an electromagnetic wave is in terms of the wave **intensity**, or average power per unit area. **Figure 22-12** shows a portion of a wave that has cross-sectional area A and length ℓ. The energy in this portion of the wave is u_{average} from Equation 22-24 multiplied by the volume $A\ell$ of this portion. This entire portion of the wave moves at speed c through the cross-sectional area A in a time t. The power equals the energy in the wave portion divided by the time $t = \ell/c$ that it takes this portion of the wave to travel at speed c through the cross-sectional area A. The intensity, to which we give the symbol S_{average}, equals the power divided by the area A. So

$$S_{\text{average}} = \frac{\text{energy}}{\text{time}} \times \frac{1}{\text{area}} = \frac{(u_{\text{average}}A\ell)}{\ell/c} \times \frac{1}{A} = u_{\text{average}}c$$

The electromagnetic wave energy in this volume moves with the wave at speed c.

Area A

Direction of wave propagation

Figure 22-12 Calculating wave intensity The intensity of an electromagnetic wave equals the amount of wave energy that crosses an area A per unit time, divided by the area A.

Using Equation 22-24, we can rewrite this as

Intensity of an electromagnetic wave · Speed of light · Magnetic field rms value

$$S_{\text{average}} = c\varepsilon_0 E_{\text{rms}}^2 = \frac{cB_{\text{rms}}^2}{\mu_0} = \frac{E_{\text{rms}}B_{\text{rms}}}{\mu_0}$$

Permittivity of free space · Electric field rms value · Permeability of free space

Intensity of an electromagnetic wave
(22-25)

(To write the last expression in Equation 22-25, we used the result that since $B_0 = E_0/c$, it follows that $B_{\text{rms}} = E_{\text{rms}}/c$.)

The units of intensity are watts per square meter, or W/m^2. An everyday example is the intensity of sunlight that reaches Earth, about $1.36 \times 10^3 \text{ W/m}^2$. The following example shows that intensities of other common electromagnetic waves can be much smaller.

Example 22-4 Energy Density and Intensity in a Radio Wave

In Example 22-1 (Section 22-2) we considered an FM radio wave of frequency 98.7 MHz with an electric field amplitude 6.00×10^{-2} V/m. We found that the magnetic field has amplitude 2.00×10^{-10} T. Calculate the rms values of the electric and magnetic field, the average energy density in the wave, and the wave intensity.

Set Up

Each rms value is just equal to the amplitude divided by $\sqrt{2}$. Given the rms values, we'll use Equation 22-24 to calculate the energy density and Equation 22-25 to calculate the intensity.

Root-mean-square values:

$$E_{\text{rms}} = \frac{E_0}{\sqrt{2}}$$

$$B_{\text{rms}} = \frac{B_0}{\sqrt{2}}$$

Average energy density in an electromagnetic wave:

$$u_{\text{average}} = \varepsilon_0 E_{\text{rms}}^2 = \frac{B_{\text{rms}}^2}{\mu_0} \quad (22\text{-}24)$$

Intensity of an electromagnetic wave:

$$S_{\text{average}} = c\varepsilon_0 E_{\text{rms}}^2 = \frac{cB_{\text{rms}}^2}{\mu_0} = \frac{E_{\text{rms}}B_{\text{rms}}}{\mu_0} \quad (22\text{-}25)$$

Permittivity of free space:

$$\varepsilon_0 = 8.85 \times 10^{-12} \frac{\text{C}}{\text{V} \cdot \text{m}} \quad (22\text{-}9)$$

Permeability of free space:

$$\mu_0 = 4\pi \times 10^{-7} \, \text{T} \cdot \text{m/A}$$

electric field, amplitude E_O

magnetic field, amplitude B_O

direction of wave propagation

wavelength λ

Solve

Calculate the rms values of the electric and magnetic fields.

We are given $E_0 = 6.00 \times 10^{-2}$ V/m and $B_0 = 2.00 \times 10^{-10}$ T. The corresponding rms values are

$$E_{\text{rms}} = \frac{E_0}{\sqrt{2}} = \frac{6.00 \times 10^{-2} \, \text{V/m}}{\sqrt{2}} = 4.24 \times 10^{-2} \, \text{V/m}$$

$$B_{\text{rms}} = \frac{B_0}{\sqrt{2}} = \frac{2.00 \times 10^{-10} \, \text{T}}{\sqrt{2}} = 1.41 \times 10^{-10} \, \text{T}$$

Use the value of E_{rms} to calculate the average energy density in the wave.

From Equation 22-24,

$$u_{\text{average}} = \varepsilon_0 E_{\text{rms}}^2 = \left(8.85 \times 10^{-12} \frac{\text{C}}{\text{V} \cdot \text{m}}\right)\left(4.24 \times 10^{-2} \frac{\text{V}}{\text{m}}\right)^2$$

$$= 1.59 \times 10^{-14} \frac{\text{C} \cdot \text{V}}{\text{m}^3}$$

A coulomb times a volt is a joule: 1 C · V = 1 J. So

$$u_{\text{average}} = 1.59 \times 10^{-14} \, \text{J/m}^3$$

Find the intensity of the wave.

Comparing Equations 22-24 and 22-25 shows that the wave intensity is c times the average energy density:

$$S_{\text{average}} = c\varepsilon_0 E_{\text{rms}}^2 = cu_{\text{average}}$$

$$= (3.00 \times 10^8 \, \text{m/s})(1.59 \times 10^{-14} \, \text{J/m}^3)$$

$$= 4.78 \times 10^{-6} \frac{\text{J}}{\text{m}^2 \cdot \text{s}}$$

A joule per second is a watt: 1 J/s = 1 W. So

$$S_{\text{average}} = 4.78 \times 10^{-6} \, \text{W/m}^2$$

Reflect

The energy density and intensity are both very small quantities. It's a testament to the sensitivity of radio receivers that such a wave is quite easy to detect.

We can check our results by using the alternative expressions for $u_{average}$ and $S_{average}$ given in Equations 22-24 and 22-25. As an example, here's a check on the value of $S_{average}$.

From Equation 22-25,

$$S_{average} = \frac{E_{rms}B_{rms}}{\mu_0} = \frac{(4.24 \times 10^{-2}\,\text{V/m})(1.41 \times 10^{-10}\,\text{T})}{4\pi \times 10^{-7}\,\text{T}\cdot\text{m/A}}$$

$$= 4.78 \times 10^{-6}\,\frac{\text{V}\cdot\text{A}}{\text{m}^2}$$

One volt times one ampere is one watt $(1\,\text{V}\cdot\text{A} = 1\,\text{W})$, so

$$S_{average} = 4.78 \times 10^{-6}\,\text{W/m}^2$$

This agrees with our calculation above, as it must.

Photons

Equation 22-25 says that the intensity of an electromagnetic wave depends on the strength of the electric and magnetic fields that make up the wave, but not on the wave frequency. (The frequency f doesn't appear anywhere in this equation.) But everyday experience suggests that wave frequency *does* play a role in the energy carried by an electromagnetic wave. As an example, ultraviolet light can trigger a chemical reaction in the skin that causes a suntan or sunburn, but visible light cannot. (That's why sunscreen contains a substance that allows visible light to pass but blocks ultraviolet light.) X rays, with even higher frequency than ultraviolet light, can pierce soft tissue but not bone; as a result, an x-ray image allows a physician to diagnose a broken bone and a dentist to see cavities in your teeth. Gamma rays, with higher frequency than x rays, can damage DNA, cause cancer, and even kill cells. How can we explain these differences?

The explanation is that the energy of an electromagnetic wave propagates as small, individual packets of energy called **photons**. The energy of an individual photon is proportional to the wave frequency, and the proportionality constant h is called **Planck's constant**:

Energy of a photon　　　　Wave frequency

$$E = hf$$

Planck's constant $= 6.62606957 \times 10^{-34}\,\text{J}\cdot\text{s}$

Energy of a photon
(22-26)

To three significant figures, $h = 6.63 \times 10^{-34}\,\text{J}\cdot\text{s}$.

Equation 22-26 explains why ultraviolet light causes a suntan or sunburn, but light in the visible spectrum does not. In order for tanning or burning to take place in your skin, individual molecules must absorb a certain minimum amount of energy from light to trigger a chemical change. A given molecule must absorb this energy in the form of a single photon, and a visible-light photon lacks sufficient energy to trigger this chemical change. An ultraviolet photon, by contrast, can trigger the change because it has a shorter wavelength, a higher frequency, and more energy per photon. An x-ray photon is more energetic still, which is why it is able to penetrate soft tissue.

Gamma-ray photons, x-ray photons, and short-wavelength, high-frequency ultraviolet photons have enough energy that they can dislodge an electron from an atom. Such **ionizing radiation** breaks apart molecules by pulling electrons from the chemical bonds that hold atoms together. Although ionizing radiation can directly break DNA molecules in living tissue, it's more likely to disrupt some other, more common molecule, such as water, to create highly reactive free radicals that then damage DNA. Depending on the severity of the damage, the cell may be able to recover. However, if the damage cannot be repaired, or if it is repaired incorrectly, the resulting mutations may be lethal. These effects generally go unnoticed until the next time the cell tries to divide. Because cancerous cells divide more frequently than most other cells in the body, they are more susceptible to radiation damage than most healthy cells.

Planck's constant is very small, so a single photon carries only a miniscule amount of energy. As an example, a photon of red light with wavelength $\lambda = 750$ nm $= 7.50 \times 10^{-7}$ m has frequency $f = c/\lambda = (3.00 \times 10^8 \text{ m/s})/(7.50 \times 10^{-7} \text{ m}) = 4.00 \times 10^{14}$ Hz and energy $E = hf = (6.63 \times 10^{-34} \text{ J} \cdot \text{s})(4.00 \times 10^{14} \text{ Hz}) = 2.65 \times 10^{-19}$ J. (Recall that 1 Hz $= 1 \text{ s}^{-1}$.) That's so small that you don't notice individual photons in the light from a lamp, just as you don't notice individual air molecules in a breeze against your face.

It's common to express photon energies in electron volts (eV). We introduced this unit in Section 17-6: 1 eV $= 1.60 \times 10^{-19}$ J. For a red photon of wavelength 750 nm, the energy is $E = (2.65 \times 10^{-19} \text{ J})/(1.60 \times 10^{-19} \text{ J/eV}) = 1.66$ eV. As the following example shows, radio photons have even less energy.

Example 22-5 Photons in a Radio Wave

For the radio wave of Examples 22-1 and 22-4, calculate (a) the energy per photon, (b) the number of photons per cubic meter, and (c) the number of photons per second that strike a receiver antenna of area 10.0 cm².

Set Up

The radio wave has frequency 98.7 MHz $= 98.7 \times 10^6$ Hz. We'll use this and Equation 22-26 to determine the energy of a single radio photon. From Example 22-4 we know that the energy density (energy per unit volume) of the wave is $u_{\text{average}} = 1.59 \times 10^{-14} \text{ J/m}^3$ and the intensity (energy per area per time) is $S_{\text{average}} = 4.78 \times 10^{-6} \text{ W/m}^2$. We'll use these and our calculated value of the photon energy to determine the number of photons per unit volume and the number of photons striking the antenna per time.

Energy of a photon:

$$E = hf \quad\quad\quad (22\text{-}26)$$

antenna, area 10.0 cm²

wave

Solve

(a) Calculate the energy of an individual photon of frequency 98.7 MHz.

From Equation 22-26,

$$E = hf = (6.63 \times 10^{-34} \text{ J} \cdot \text{s})(98.7 \times 10^6 \text{ Hz})$$
$$= 6.54 \times 10^{-26} \text{ J} \cdot \text{s} \cdot \text{Hz}$$

Since 1 Hz $= 1 \text{ s}^{-1}$, 1 J $\cdot$ s $\cdot$ Hz $= 1$ J and so

$$E = 6.54 \times 10^{-26} \text{ J or}$$

$$E = \frac{6.54 \times 10^{-26} \text{ J}}{1.60 \times 10^{-19} \text{ J/eV}} = 4.08 \times 10^{-7} \text{ eV}$$

This is much smaller than the energy of a visible-light photon (2.65×10^{-19} J $= 1.66$ eV for red light) because the frequency of the radio wave is much less than the frequency of visible light (4.00×10^{14} Hz for red light).

(b) Calculate the photon density (number of photons per unit volume).

The energy density in the wave is $u_{\text{average}} = 1.59 \times 10^{-14} \text{ J/m}^3$ and the energy per photon is $E = 6.54 \times 10^{-26}$ J/photon. The number of photons per unit volume is

$$\frac{\text{photons}}{\text{volume}} = \frac{\text{energy}}{\text{volume}} \times \frac{\text{photon}}{\text{energy}} = \frac{\left(\dfrac{\text{energy}}{\text{volume}}\right)}{\left(\dfrac{\text{energy}}{\text{photon}}\right)}$$

$$= \frac{1.59 \times 10^{-14} \text{ J/m}^3}{6.54 \times 10^{-26} \text{ J/photon}} = 2.43 \times 10^{11} \text{ photons/m}^3$$

Each cubic meter of this wave contains 2.43×10^{11} (243 billion) photons.

(c) Calculate the number of photons that strike an area of 10.0 cm² in 1.00 s.

The intensity (energy per area per time) of the wave is $S_{average} = 4.78 \times 10^{-6}$ W/m², so the rate at which energy arrives at the antenna of area $A = 10.0$ cm² is

$$\frac{energy}{area \cdot time} \times area = S_{average}A$$

$$= (4.78 \times 10^{-6}\ \text{W/m}^2)(10.0\ \text{cm}^2)\left(\frac{1\ \text{m}}{100\ \text{cm}}\right)^2$$

$$= 4.78 \times 10^{-9}\ \text{W} = 4.78 \times 10^{-9}\ \text{J/s}$$

The rate at which photons arrive at the antenna is

$$\frac{photons}{time} = \frac{energy}{time} \times \frac{photon}{energy} = \frac{\left(\dfrac{energy}{time}\right)}{\left(\dfrac{energy}{photon}\right)}$$

$$= \frac{4.78 \times 10^{-9}\ \text{J/s}}{6.54 \times 10^{-26}\ \text{J/photon}} = 7.30 \times 10^{16}\ \text{photons/s}$$

In one second, 7.30×10^{16} (73 quadrillion) photons arrive at the antenna.

Reflect

Even this relatively low-intensity wave contains a tremendous number of photons per cubic meter and delivers an astronomical number of photons per second to a receiver.

Our results give us insight into the concerns that some people have expressed about mobile phones causing cancer. The frequencies used by mobile phones are about 7 to 27 times higher (about 700 to 2700 MHz), but even those frequencies correspond to very low photon energies (about 2.9×10^{-6} to 1.1×10^{-5} eV). As we described above, the sort of ionizing radiation that can cause cancer has very high frequency and very high photon energy of several electron volts. The photon energies associated with mobile phones are millions of times smaller, which should be far too low to have any carcinogenic effect.

Watch Out! Photons are both particles and waves.

A common incorrect way to think about photons is to visualize them as small particles like miniature marbles, and to imagine that a large number of photons acting together behave like a wave. The reality is far different! Each individual photon has aspects of *both* wave and particle, and those particles are very different in character from ordinary objects such as marbles. We'll learn more about the curious properties of photons in Chapter 26.

Got the Concept? 22-3 Photons

Three lasers have equal power output. The first emits a pure violet light, the second emits a pure green light, and the third emits a pure red light. Which laser emits the greater number of photons per second? (a) The violet laser; (b) the green laser; (c) the red laser; (d) all emit the same number of photons per second; (e) answer depends on the value of the power output.

Take-Home Message for Section 22-4

✔ Energy is associated with both electric and magnetic fields. An electromagnetic wave in a vacuum has equal amounts of electric energy and magnetic energy per volume.

✔ The intensity of an electromagnetic wave is the average power per unit area. In a vacuum, the intensity equals the average energy per volume in the wave multiplied by the speed of light c.

✔ The energy of an electromagnetic wave comes in packets called photons. The energy of a single photon is proportional to the wave frequency.

Key Terms

displacement current
electric energy density
electromagnetic spectrum
electromagnetic wave
Faraday's law
Gauss's law for the electric field

Gauss's law for the magnetic field
intensity
ionizing radiation
magnetic energy density
Maxwell-Ampère law
Maxwell's equations

photon
Planck's constant
sinusoidal plane wave
speed of light
visible light

Chapter Summary

Topic	Equation or Figure

Speed of electromagnetic waves:
In a vacuum, all electromagnetic
waves propagate at the same speed
$c = 3.00 \times 10^8$ m/s. The shorter
the wavelength, the higher the frequency
of the wave. Our eyes are sensitive to
only a narrow band of wavelengths
known as the visible spectrum.

Speed of light in a vacuum   Frequency of an electromagnetic wave

$$c = f\lambda \qquad (22\text{-}2)$$

Wavelength of the wave in vacuum

Electromagnetic plane waves: The
simplest electromagnetic wave in
vacuum is a sinusoidal plane wave.
The electric and magnetic fields
oscillate in phase, are perpendicular
to each other, and are transverse (both
are perpendicular to the direction of
wave propagation). The amplitude
B_0 of the magnetic field equals the
amplitude E_0 of the electric field
divided by the speed of light c.

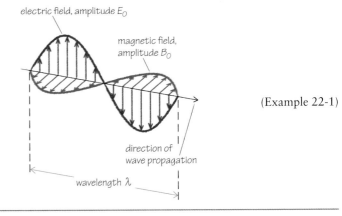

(Example 22-1)

electric field, amplitude E_0

magnetic field, amplitude B_0

direction of wave propagation

wavelength λ

Maxwell's equations: Four equations
govern the behavior of electric and
magnetic fields in all situations.
The two Gauss's laws explain why
electromagnetic waves in vacuum
are transverse. Faraday's law and the
Maxwell-Ampère law explain how
the oscillations of the magnetic field
produce the electric field, and how
the oscillations of the electric field
produce the magnetic field. As a result,
the wave must have both electric and
magnetic aspects, and the electric
and magnetic fields are naturally
perpendicular to each other. Maxwell's
equations also successfully predict the
value of the speed of light in terms of
the permittivity of free space ε_0 and
the permeability of free space μ_0.

Electric flux through a closed surface   Net amount of charge enclosed within the surface

$$\Phi_E = \frac{q_{\text{encl}}}{\varepsilon_0} \qquad (16\text{-}9)$$

Permittivity of free space = $1/(4\pi k)$

Magnetic flux through a closed surface   There is zero magnetic flux through any closed surface, no matter what the size or shape of the surface or what it contains.

$$\Phi_B = 0 \qquad (22\text{-}5)$$

Circulation of electric field around a loop   Change in the magnetic flux through the surface outlined by the loop

$$\sum E_{\parallel}\Delta\ell = -\frac{\Delta\Phi_B}{\Delta t} \qquad (22\text{-}7)$$

Time interval over which the change in magnetic flux takes place

Circulation of magnetic field around an Amperian loop | Permittivity of free space | Change in the electric flux through the surface outlined by the loop

$$\sum B_{\parallel}\Delta\ell = \mu_0\left(i_{\text{through}} + \varepsilon_0\frac{\Delta\Phi_E}{\Delta t}\right) \qquad (22\text{-}8)$$

Permeability of free space | Current through the Amperian loop | Time interval over which the change in electric flux takes place

Electric and magnetic field energy in electromagnetic waves: The energy density (energy per volume) associated with an electric field is $u_E = (1/2)\varepsilon_0 E^2$, and the energy density associated with a magnetic field is $u_B = B^2/2\mu_0$. In an electromagnetic wave in vacuum, there are equal amounts of electric energy and magnetic energy. The average energy density in an electromagnetic wave can be expressed in terms of either the field amplitudes or their rms values. The intensity of the wave is the average power per unit area of the wave.

Average energy density in an electromagnetic wave | Electric field magnitude | Electric field rms value | Magnetic field magnitude | Magnetic field rms value

$$u_{\text{average}} = \frac{1}{2}\varepsilon_0 E_0^2 = \varepsilon_0 E_{\text{rms}}^2 = \frac{B_0^2}{2\mu_0} = \frac{B_{\text{rms}}^2}{\mu_0} \qquad (22\text{-}24)$$

Permittivity of free space | Permeability of free space

Intensity of an electromagnetic wave | Speed of light | Magnetic field rms value

$$S_{\text{average}} = c\varepsilon_0 E_{\text{rms}}^2 = \frac{cB_{\text{rms}}^2}{\mu_0} = \frac{E_{\text{rms}}B_{\text{rms}}}{\mu_0} \qquad (22\text{-}25)$$

Permittivity of free space | Electric field rms value | Permeability of free space

Photons: The energy of an electromagnetic wave comes in packets called photons that have properties of both wave and particle. The higher the wave frequency, the more energy there is per photon.

Energy of a photon | Wave frequency

$$E = hf \qquad (22\text{-}26)$$

Planck's constant = $6.62606957 \times 10^{-34}$ J $\cdot$ s

Answer to What do you think? Question

(d) As we describe in Section 22-2, in a vacuum all varieties of electromagnetic wave propagate at the same speed. Visible light has a much shorter wavelength (λ = about 400 to 700 nm) than radio waves (λ = a few centimeters to several meters) and so has a much higher frequency.

Answers to Got the Concept? Questions

22-1 (e) No matter what the frequency of an electromagnetic wave, its propagation speed in a vacuum is the same: the speed of light $c = 3.00 \times 10^8$ m/s.

22-2 (d) Situation (a) is impossible: Gauss's law for the magnetic field states that the net magnetic flux through any closed surface must be zero. Situation (b) is possible; according to Gauss's law for the electric field, there will be a net outward electric flux through a closed surface that encloses positive charge. Situation (c) is also possible: One example is the loop around the current-carrying wire in Figure 22-8a. There is zero electric field and hence zero electric flux through the interior of the loop, but the current gives rise to a magnetic field that circulates around the loop.

22-3 (c) All three lasers emit the same amount of electromagnetic wave energy per second. However, the energy per photon is different because each laser emits light of a different wavelength and frequency. Figure 22-2 shows that violet has the shortest wavelength, and so the highest frequency and highest photon energy; red has the longest wavelength, and so the lowest frequency and lowest photon energy. To emit the same amount of energy per second, the red laser must emit more of its low-energy photons per second than the other lasers.

Questions and Problems

In a few problems, you are given more data than you actually need; in a few other problems, you are required to supply data from your general knowledge, outside sources, or informed estimate.

Interpret as significant all digits in numerical values that have trailing zeros and no decimal points.

For all problems, use $g = 9.80 \text{ m/s}^2$ for the free-fall acceleration due to gravity. Neglect friction and air resistance unless instructed to do otherwise.

• Basic, single-concept problem

•• Intermediate-level problem, may require synthesis of concepts and multiple steps

••• Challenging problem

SSM *Solution is in Student Solutions Manual*

Conceptual Questions

1. •(a) Rank the following electromagnetic waves from the lowest to the highest wavelength: (a) microwaves, (b) red light, (c) ultraviolet light, (d) infrared light, and (e) gamma rays. (b) Which wavelength has the highest energy per photon? Which has the lowest?

2. •James Clerk Maxwell is credited with compiling the three laws of electricity and magnetism (Gauss's law, Ampère's law, and Faraday's law), adding his own law (also called Gauss's law for magnetism), modifying Ampère's law, and understanding the connections between electricity, magnetism, and optics. Were Maxwell's efforts more important than the individual discoveries of Gauss, Ampère, and Faraday? Explain your answer.

3. •Changing electric fields create changing magnetic fields. These oscillating fields propagate at the speed of light. Describe the orientation (directions) of the fields and the velocity of the electromagnetic wave. SSM

4. •Does a wire connected to a DC source, such as a battery, emit an electromagnetic wave?

5. •Describe how the frequency at which the changing electric and magnetic fields oscillate in electromagnetic waves is related to the speed of light.

6. •Describe how the frequency of an electromagnetic wave is related to the energy of the photons of that wave.

7. •The energy of an ultraviolet light photon is unrelated to the speed of the fundamental electromagnetic waves that make up such radiation. Explain how this is possible. SSM

8. •Match the equations that were conceived of by Carl Friedrich Gauss, André Ampère, Michael Faraday, and James Clerk Maxwell with the corresponding written statements:

i. $\sum B_{\parallel} \Delta \ell = \mu_0 \left(i_{\text{through}} + \varepsilon_0 \dfrac{\Delta \Phi_E}{\Delta t} \right)$

ii. $\sum E_{\parallel} \Delta \ell = -\dfrac{\Delta \Phi_B}{\Delta t}$

iii. $\Phi_B = 0$

iv. $\Phi_E = \dfrac{q_{\text{encl}}}{\varepsilon_0}$

A. The source of an electric field is an electric charge.

B. The source of a magnetic field is an electric current.

C. Changing magnetic fields induce changing electric fields.

D. Changing electric fields induce changing magnetic fields.

9. • Name three types of electromagnetic energy that you used today.

Multiple-Choice Questions

10. •In comparison to x rays, visible light has

A. a speed that is faster.

B. wavelengths that are longer.

C. wavelengths that are equal.

D. wavelengths that are shorter.

E. frequencies that are equal.

11. •X rays and gamma rays

A. have the same frequency.

B. have the same wavelength.

C. have the same speed.

D. have the same "color."

E. None of the above SSM

12. •In comparison to radio waves, visible light has

A. a speed that is faster.

B. wavelengths that are longer.

C. wavelengths that are equal.

D. wavelengths that are shorter.

E. frequencies that are equal.

13. •Which of the following requires a physical medium through which to travel?

A. radio waves

B. light

C. x rays

D. sound

E. gamma rays SSM

14. •In an *RC* circuit, the capacitor begins to discharge. In the region of space between the plates of the capacitor,

A. there is an electric field but no magnetic field.

B. there is a magnetic field but no electric field.

C. there are both electric and magnetic fields.

D. there are no electric and magnetic fields.

E. there is an electric field whose strength is one-half that of the magnetic field.

15. •Maxwell's equations apply

A. to both electric fields and magnetic fields that are constant over time.

B. only to electric fields that are time-dependent.

C. only to magnetic fields that are constant over time.

D. to both electric fields and magnetic fields that are time-dependent.

E. to both time-independent and time-dependent electric and magnetic fields. SSM

16. •The phase difference between the electric and magnetic fields in an electromagnetic wave is

A. 90°.

B. 180°.

C. 0°.

D. alternately 90° and 180°.

E. alternately 0° and 90°.

Estimation/Numerical Analysis

17. •Estimate how long it would take for a bird to circumnavigate Earth traveling at 0.1c. (This would be one fast bird!)

18. •Estimate the average wavelength of radio waves that are received by (a) an AM radio and (b) an FM radio.

19. •Estimate the photon energy associated with the visible light (green) to which the human eye is most sensitive. SSM

20. •Estimate a simple conversion factor between joules and electron volts.

21. •Estimate the wavelength of electromagnetic radiation that would potentially be classified as ionizing radiation.

22. •Estimate the number of photons that are emitted in the 1000-h lifetime of a 100-W light bulb.

23. •An important news announcement is transmitted by radio waves to people who are 300 km away and sitting next to their radios and also by sound waves to people sitting 3 m from the newscaster in a newsroom. Who receives the news first? Explain your answer. SSM

24. •••Use a computer-based, graphical program to plot the graphs of the electric field (E) versus time (t) and the magnetic field (B) versus time (t) on a three-dimensional graph (see the table). Let t be on the x axis, E be on the y axis, and B be on the z axis. Explain the shape of the graph.

E (N/C)	B ($\times 10^{-9}$ T)	t(s)
100	333	0
70.7	236	$\pi/4$
0	0	$\pi/2$
−70.7	−236	$3\pi/4$
−100	−333	π
−70.7	−236	$5\pi/4$
0	0	$3\pi/2$
70.7	236	$7\pi/4$
100	333	2π
70.7	236	$9\pi/4$
0	0	$5\pi/2$
−70.7	−236	$11\pi/4$
−100	−333	3π
−70.7	−236	$13\pi/4$
0	0	$7\pi/2$
70.7	236	$15\pi/4$
100	333	4π
70.7	236	$17\pi/4$
0	0	$9\pi/2$
−70.7	−236	$19\pi/4$
−100	−333	5π
−70.7	−236	$21\pi/4$
0	0 11	$\pi/2$
70.7	236	$23\pi/4$
100	333	6π

Problems

22-1 Light is just one example of an electromagnetic wave

22-2 In an electromagnetic plane wave, electric and magnetic fields both oscillate

25. ••Calculate the wavelengths of the electromagnetic waves with the following frequencies and classify the electromagnetic radiation of each (x ray, radio, etc.).
    A. $f = 4.14 \times 10^{15}$ Hz
    B. $f = 7.00 \times 10^{14}$ Hz
    C. $f = 8.00 \times 10^{16}$ Hz
    D. $f = 3.00 \times 10^{13}$ Hz
    E. $f = 9.00 \times 10^{12}$ Hz
    F. $f = 3.44 \times 10^{17}$ Hz
    G. $f = 8.23 \times 10^{15}$ Hz
    H. $f = 6.00 \times 10^{15}$ Hz

26. •Calculate the wavelengths of the electromagnetic waves with the following frequencies.
    A. $f = 7.50 \times 10^{15}$ Hz
    B. $f = 6.00 \times 10^{14}$ Hz
    C. $f = 5.00 \times 10^{14}$ Hz
    D. $f = 4.29 \times 10^{14}$ Hz
    E. $f = 7.50 \times 10^{16}$ Hz
    F. $f = 2.66 \times 10^{16}$ Hz
    G. $f = 8.23 \times 10^{17}$ Hz
    H. $f = 6.00 \times 10^{18}$ Hz

27. •Calculate the frequencies of the electromagnetic waves that have the following wavelengths:
    A. $\lambda = 700$ nm
    B. $\lambda = 600$ nm
    C. $\lambda = 500$ nm
    D. $\lambda = 400$ nm
    E. $\lambda = 100$ nm
    F. $\lambda = 0.0333$ nm
    G. $\lambda = 500$ μm
    H. $\lambda = 63.3$ pm SSM

28. •Calculate the frequencies of the electromagnetic waves that have the following wavelengths:
    A. $\lambda = 800$ nm
    B. $\lambda = 650$ nm
    C. $\lambda = 550$ nm
    D. $\lambda = 450$ nm
    E. $\lambda = 2.22$ nm
    F. $\lambda = 1.10 \times 10^{-8}$ m
    G. $\lambda = 50.0$ μm
    H. $\lambda = 33.4$ mm

29. •Calculate the range of wavelengths that are received by the typical FM radio in a car.

30. •The antenna for an AM radio station is a 75-m-high tower whose height is equivalent to one-quarter wavelength. At what frequency does the station transmit?

31. •How far does light travel in a vacuum in 10 ns? SSM

32. •How long does it take light to travel 300 km in a vacuum?

33. •How long does it take a radio signal from Earth to reach the Moon, which has an orbital radius of approximately 3.84×10^8 m?

34. •The basic formula relating the frequency and wavelength of an electromagnetic wave to the speed of light is given by

$$c = f\lambda$$

Starting with this expression, derive a similar relationship between the speed of light, the angular frequency ($\omega = 2\pi f$), and the wave number ($k = 2\pi/\lambda$).

35. •• (a) Calculate the wave number of an electromagnetic wave that has an angular frequency of 6.28×10^{15} rad/s. (b) Calculate the angular frequency, the frequency, and the wavelength of a photon that has a wave number of $k = 4\pi \times 10^6$ rad/m. SSM

36. ••The magnetic field of an electromagnetic wave is given by

$$B(x,t) = (0.7\,\mu\text{T})\sin\big[\,(8\pi \times 10^6\,\text{m}^{-1})x$$
$$- (2.40\pi \times 10^{15}\,\text{s}^{-1})t\,\big]$$

Calculate (a) the amplitude of the electric field, (b) the speed, (c) the frequency, (d) the period, and (e) the wavelength.

37. ••Suppose the electric field associated with the radio transmissions of a medical helicopter is given by

$$E(x,t) = (400\,\mu\text{N/C})\cos\big[\,(40\pi\,\text{nm}^{-1})x - (12\pi\,\text{s}^{-1})t\,\big]$$

Determine (a) the wave number, (b) the angular frequency, (c) the wavelength, and (d) the frequency of the electromagnetic wave associated with the electric field.

22-3 Maxwell's equations explain why electromagnetic waves are possible

38. ••The electric field in a region of space increases from 0 to 3000 N/C in 5.00 seconds. What is the magnitude of the induced magnetic field around a circular area with a diameter of 1.00 m oriented perpendicular to the electric field?

39. •••A parallel-plate capacitor has closely spaced plates. Charge is flowing onto the positive plate and off the negative plate at the rate $i = \Delta q/\Delta t = 2.8$ A. What is the displacement current through the capacitor between the plates? SSM

40. ••An 8-cm-diameter parallel-plate capacitor has a 1.0-mm gap. The electric field between the plates is increasing at the rate 1.0×10^6 V/(m·s). What is the magnetic field strength between the plates of the capacitor a distance of 5.0 cm from the axis of the capacitor?

41. ••Charge flows onto the positive plate of a 6.0-cm-diameter parallel-plate capacitor at the rate $i = \Delta q/\Delta t = 1.5$ A. What is the magnetic field between the plates at a distance of 3.0 cm from the axis of the plates?

22-4 Electromagnetic waves carry both electric and magnetic energy, and come in packets called photons

42. ••An electromagnetic plane wave has an intensity $S_{\text{average}} = 200$ W/m². (a) What are the rms values of the electric and magnetic field? (b) What are the amplitudes of the electric and magnetic fields?

43. ••The amplitude of an electromagnetic wave's electric field is 200 V/m. Calculate (a) the amplitude of the wave's magnetic field and (b) the intensity of the wave.

44. ••The rms value of an electromagnetic wave's magnetic field is 400 T. Calculate (a) the amplitude of the wave's electric field and (b) the intensity of the wave.

45. ••Calculate the wavelengths and frequencies of photons that have the following energies.
   - A. $E_{\text{photon}} = 2.33 \times 10^{-19}$ J
   - B. $E_{\text{photon}} = 4.50 \times 10^{-19}$ J
   - C. $E_{\text{photon}} = 3.20 \times 10^{-19}$ J
   - D. $E_{\text{photon}} = 8.55 \times 10^{-19}$ J
   - E. $E_{\text{photon}} = 63.3$ eV
   - F. $E_{\text{photon}} = 8.77$ eV
   - G. $E_{\text{photon}} = 1.98$ eV
   - H. $E_{\text{photon}} = 4.55$ eV

46. ••Calculate the wavelengths and frequencies of the photons that have the following energies.
   - A. $E_{\text{photon}} = 3.45 \times 10^{-19}$ J
   - B. $E_{\text{photon}} = 4.80 \times 10^{-19}$ J
   - C. $E_{\text{photon}} = 1.28 \times 10^{-18}$ J
   - D. $E_{\text{photon}} = 4.33 \times 10^{-20}$ J
   - E. $E_{\text{photon}} = 931$ MeV
   - F. $E_{\text{photon}} = 2.88$ keV
   - G. $E_{\text{photon}} = 7.88$ eV
   - H. $E_{\text{photon}} = 13.6$ eV

General Problems

47. ••**Biology** A recent study found that electrons having energies between 3.0 and 20 eV can cause breaks in a DNA molecule even though they do not ionize the molecule. If the energy were to come from light, (a) what range of wavelengths (in nanometers) could cause DNA breaks, and (b) in what part of the electromagnetic spectrum does the light lie?

48. ••**Medical** A dental x ray typically affects 200 g of tissue and delivers about 4.0 μJ of energy using x rays that have wavelengths of 0.025 nm. What is the energy (in electron volts) of such x ray photons, and how many photons are absorbed during the dental x ray? Assume the body absorbs all of the incident x rays.

49. ••A HeNe laser is made up of a cylindrical beam of light with a diameter of 0.750 cm. The energy is pulsed, lasting for 1.50 ns, and each burst contains an energy of 2.00 J. (a) What is the length of each pulse of laser light? (b) What is the average energy per unit volume for each pulse? SSM

50. •• (a) What is the energy of a photon of green light that has a wavelength of 525 nm? Give your answer in joules and electron volts. (b) What is the wave number of the photon?

23 Wave Properties of Light

In this chapter, your goals are to:

- (23-1) Describe some key properties of light.
- (23-2) Explain Huygens' principle and what it tells us about the laws of reflection and refraction.
- (23-3) Recognize the special circumstances under which total internal reflection can take place.
- (23-4) Explain how a prism is able to break white light into its component colors.
- (23-5) Calculate how the intensity of light is affected by passing through a polarizing filter.
- (23-6) Use the idea of path length difference to calculate what happens in thin-film interference.
- (23-7) Explain why light spreads out when it passes through a narrow opening.
- (23-8) Calculate how the angular resolution of an optical device is limited by diffraction.

To master this chapter, you should review:

- (13-5) Constructive and destructive interference of waves
- (22-2) Plane waves and the electromagnetic nature of light
- (22-4) Photons

What do you think?

Honeybees are able to navigate with respect to the Sun, even though the Sun may not be directly visible to them. Which aspect of the wave nature of light do they exploit to do this? (a) The wavelength of light is shorter in air than in vacuum; (b) light is a transverse wave; (c) light spreads out when it passes through a narrow opening; (d) all of these; (e) none of these.

23-1 The wave nature of light explains much about how light behaves

In Chapter 22 we explored how light is an electromagnetic wave, with electric and magnetic fields that oscillate in phase and that carry equal amounts of energy in vacuum. In this chapter we'll explore several of the consequences of the wave nature of light. For most of this exploration we won't need the details about electric and magnetic fields; what's important is simply that in many cases light can be treated as a wave. As a result, many of the properties of light waves that we'll encounter apply equally well to sound and other types of waves.

We'll begin our discussion by introducing *Huygens' principle*, a simplified model that will help us understand how waves propagate through space. We'll use Huygens' principle to understand the laws of reflection (Figure 23-1a) and of *refraction*—the bending of light when it moves from one transparent material to another. We'll see that in certain circumstances light can be trapped inside a transparent material, just as if that material had mirrored surfaces. This effect, called *total internal reflection*, is essential for the medical technique of endoscopy. We'll see that the speed of light not only

Figure 23-1 **Light waves in nature**
(a) Reflection, (b) dispersion, and
(c) interference are among the many
phenomena that light waves exhibit in
the natural world.

Cats can see even in very low light levels thanks to reflection by a layer called the *tapetum lucidum* at the back of each eye. Incoming light that isn't absorbed by the retina reflects straight back, and some of the reflected light is detected on the second pass.

The colors of the rainbow are caused by dispersion: The speed of light in water depends on the frequency of the light. As a result, each color of sunlight follows a different path as it enters a raindrop and undergoes refraction, reflects off the back of the raindrop, and undergoes refraction again as it exits the raindrop.

The colors of this soap film are caused by interference. Some light reflects from the front surface of the film, and some enters the film and reflects from the back surface. If the wavelength is just right, the two halves interfere constructively and produce a bright band.

(a)   (b)   (c)

Take-Home Message for Section 23-1

✔ Many of the key properties of light can be understood simply by using the idea that light can be treated as a wave.

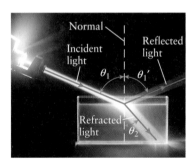

Figure 23-2 **Reflection and refraction** When a beam of incident light strikes the surface of water at an angle θ_1 from the normal, some light is reflected at the same angle ($\theta_1' = \theta_1$) and some light goes into the water at a different angle θ_2.

depends on the material through which the light is traveling, but also on the wavelength of the light. This phenomenon, called *dispersion*, explains the vivid colors of a rainbow (Figure 23-1b).

One aspect of light that depends on its being a transverse wave is its *polarization*, which describes how the electric field vector of the wave is oriented. We'll see how light can become polarized by scattering or reflection, and we'll examine how polarizing filters work and why they're used in sunglasses.

We'll look at the phenomenon of *interference*, in which two light waves can add together constructively or destructively. Interference explains the colors seen in a thin film of soapy water (Figure 23-1c), as well as why cats and other animals have reflective eyes (see Figure 23-1a). We'll finish with a discussion of *diffraction*, an important effect in which light waves spread out when they pass through a small aperture.

23-2 Huygens' principle explains the reflection and refraction of light

We're used to the idea that light travels in straight lines. This is true if the material through which the light travels, called the medium, is uniform in its properties. But the direction in which light propagates changes when the light strikes a *boundary* between two different media, such as that between air and water (Figure 23-2). In general, some of the light reflects off the boundary, while the remainder travels into the second material at a different angle. The **law of reflection** states that the angle of the reflected light is the same as the angle of the incoming, or **incident**, light: $\theta_1' = \theta_1$. We use the term **refraction** to refer to the change in direction of the light that travels into the second medium so that the angle θ_2 for the refracted light is not equal to the angle θ_1 for the incident light.

⚠ Watch Out! **In reflection and refraction, angles are always measured from the normal to the boundary between the one medium and another.**

Note that in Figure 23-2 the angles θ_1, θ_1', and θ_2 are all measured relative to the **normal** to the boundary, which is a line in the direction perpendicular to the boundary. A common mistake is to measure these angles relative to the boundary itself. If you make that mistake, you'll end up getting the wrong answer when you use the formulas that we'll derive in this section!

Why does the law of reflection hold true? And what determines how the direction of the light changes when it travels from one medium into another? We'll answer both of these questions using a model of waves introduced by the seventeenth-century Dutch scientist Christiaan Huygens. (Huygens' model precedes by two centuries Maxwell's complete description of light as an electromagnetic wave, but is consistent with it.) In particular, we'll see that what determines the difference between the incident and refracted angles are the *speeds* at which light travels in the two media. Refraction isn't just for visible light, but occurs for waves of all kinds: Radio waves, sound waves, and water waves may refract when crossing from one medium to another under the right circumstances.

Huygens' Principle and Reflection

Huygens considered waves that travel in two dimensions (like ripples on the surface of a pond) or in three dimensions (like light waves). He suggested that each point on a wave crest, or **front**, at time t can be treated as a source of tiny **wavelets** that themselves move at the speed of the wave (**Figure 23-3**). The wave front at a later time $t + \Delta t$ is then the superposition of all of these wavelets emitted at time t, and is tangent to the leading edges of the wavelets. This idea is called **Huygens' principle**.

As Figure 23-3 shows, Huygens' principle helps explain how circular waves in water retain their shape as they propagate outward from a splash in a pond, and how light waves spread out in spherical wave fronts from a light source. To analyze what's happening to the light beams in Figure 23-2, let's apply Huygens' principle to a *plane* wave like the ones we introduced in Section 22-2. A plane wave propagates in a single direction, and so it is a good description of the light beams shown in Figure 23-2. For each beam in Figure 23-2, the **ray** is an arrow that points in the direction of light propagation. Note that the ray is always perpendicular to the wave front.

Figure 23-4a shows how to apply Huygens' principle to understand the law of reflection. A plane wave with wave front *ABC* is directed at an angle toward the boundary between medium 1 (say, air) and medium 2 (say, water or glass). At time t point A on the wave front has just arrived at the boundary. A time Δt later, the wavelets from points A, B, and C have each spread outward by a distance $v_1 \Delta t$, where v_1 is the speed at which waves propagate in medium 1. The wavelets from points B and C propagate forward through medium 1, while the wavelet from point A is reflected at the boundary and so propagates *backward* from the boundary into medium 1. (We haven't drawn the wavelets that propagate into medium 2. We'll return to those a little later to help us understand refraction. For now, we're concentrating on the light that's reflected back into medium 1.)

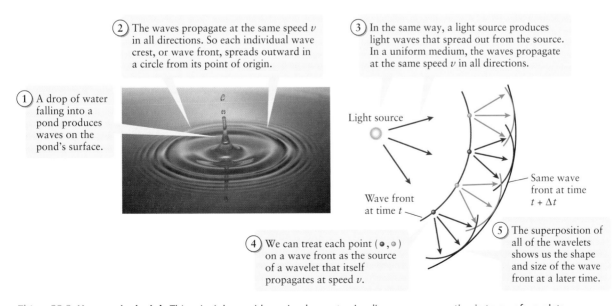

② The waves propagate at the same speed v in all directions. So each individual wave crest, or wave front, spreads outward in a circle from its point of origin.

③ In the same way, a light source produces light waves that spread out from the source. In a uniform medium, the waves propagate at the same speed v in all directions.

① A drop of water falling into a pond produces waves on the pond's surface.

Light source

Wave front at time t

Same wave front at time $t + \Delta t$

④ We can treat each point (●, ○) on a wave front as the source of a wavelet that itself propagates at speed v.

⑤ The superposition of all of the wavelets shows us the shape and size of the wave front at a later time.

Figure 23-3 **Huygens' principle** This principle provides a simple way to visualize wave propagation in terms of wavelets.

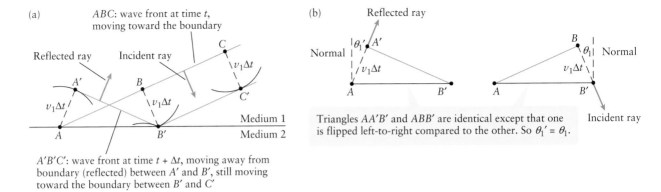

(a)

ABC: wave front at time *t*, moving toward the boundary

Reflected ray   Incident ray

C

$v_1\Delta t$

A'   B   C'

$v_1\Delta t$ $v_1\Delta t$

A   B'   Medium 1   Medium 2

A'B'C': wave front at time *t* + Δt, moving away from boundary (reflected) between A' and B', still moving toward the boundary between B' and C'

(b)   Reflected ray

θ_1' A'

Normal

$v_1\Delta t$

A   B'

B

θ_1 Normal

$v_1\Delta t$

A   B'

Incident ray

Triangles AA'B' and ABB' are identical except that one is flipped left-to-right compared to the other. So $\theta_1' = \theta_1$.

Figure 23-4 **Huygens' principle and reflection** (a) A wave front reflected at a boundary between two media. (b) Finding the law of reflection.

See the Math Tutorial for more information on trigonometry

If we draw a new wave front that's tangent to the leading edges of the wavelets that emanate from points A, B, and C, the result is A'B'C'. The wave front from B' to C' is still propagating toward the boundary; this represents the light still incident on the boundary. But the wave front from A' to B' is propagating away from the boundary and so represents the light reflected from the boundary.

The line BB' in Figure 23-4a is perpendicular to the incident wave front and so points in the direction of the incident ray. Likewise, the line AA' is perpendicular to the reflected wave front and so points in the direction of the reflected ray. We can determine how these directions are related to each other by noticing that the triangles ABB' and AA'B' are both right triangles, both have the same hypotenuse of length AB', and both have one side of length $v_1\Delta t$ (Figure 23-4b). You can see that these two right triangles are identical, except that triangle AA'B' has been flipped left-to-right compared to triangle ABB'. So the angle θ_1' of the line AA' measured from the vertical (that is, from the normal to the boundary) must be the same as the angle θ_1 of the line BB' measured from the vertical. We conclude that

The law of reflection
(23-1)

When light reflects at the boundary between two media, the angle of the reflected ray from the normal...

$$\theta_1' = \theta_1$$

...is equal to the angle of the incident ray from the normal.

This is just the law of reflection that we mentioned above. We'll use Equation 23-1 extensively in Chapter 24 when we study the properties of mirrors.

Huygens' Principle and Refraction

We can also use Huygens' principle to determine the direction of the refracted ray in Figure 23-2. Figure 23-5a is similar to Figure 23-4a, except that for point A we've drawn only the wavelet that emanates from that point and propagates into medium 2. (We've already dealt with the reflected wave, so we don't need to draw that in Figure 23-5a.) We've assumed that the wave speed v_2 in medium 2 is slower than in medium 1, so in a time Δt the wavelet that propagates into medium 2 travels a shorter distance than those propagating in medium 1.

If we again draw a new wave front that's tangent to the leading edges of the wavelets from A, B, and C, the result is A''B'C'. As in Figure 23-4a, the wave front from B' to C' represents incident light in medium 1 that is still propagating toward the boundary at speed v_1. The wave front from A'' to B' represents *refracted* light that is propagating in medium 2 at speed v_2. The angle of the wave front, and hence the angle of the ray that's perpendicular to the wave front, has changed because the wave speed has changed.

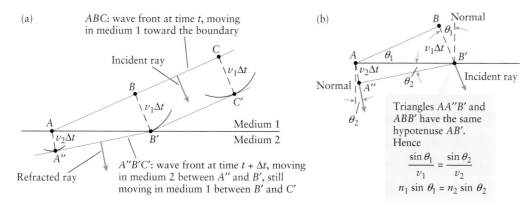

Figure 23-5 **Huygens' principle and refraction** (a) A wave front refracted at a boundary between two media. (b) Finding the law of refraction.

In Figure 23-5b we've redrawn the right triangles ABB' and $AA''B'$ from Figure 23-5a. Both triangles have the same hypotenuse of length AB', but the angles of the two triangles are different. Side BB' of triangle ABB' has length $v_1\Delta t$, points in the direction of the incident ray, and is at an angle θ_1 from the normal to the boundary. Because ABB' is a right triangle, you can see that the angle of side AB from the horizontal is also θ_1, the same as the angle of side BB' from the vertical (the normal to the boundary). If you look now at triangle $AA''B'$, you'll see that side AA'' has length $v_2\Delta t$, points in the direction of the refracted ray, and is at a different angle θ_2 from the normal to the boundary. And because $AA''B'$ is a right triangle, the angle of side $A''B'$ from the horizontal is θ_2, the same as the angle of side AA'' from the normal.

Recall that the sine of an angle in a right triangle equals the length of the side opposite to that angle divided by the length of the hypotenuse. For the angle θ_1 in triangle ABB' this statement about the sine function tells us that

$$\sin\theta_1 = \frac{\text{length of side } BB'}{\text{length of side } AB'} = \frac{v_1\Delta t}{\text{length of side } AB'} \quad \text{so} \quad \frac{\sin\theta_1}{v_1} = \frac{\Delta t}{\text{length of side } AB'} \qquad (23\text{-}2)$$

The same idea applied to the angle θ_2 in triangle $AA''B'$ tells us that

$$\sin\theta_2 = \frac{\text{length of side } AA''}{\text{length of side } AB'} = \frac{v_2\Delta t}{\text{length of side } AB'} \quad \text{so} \quad \frac{\sin\theta_2}{v_2} = \frac{\Delta t}{\text{length of side } AB'} \qquad (23\text{-}3)$$

If you compare Equations 23-2 and 23-3, you can see that

$$\frac{\sin\theta_1}{v_1} = \frac{\sin\theta_2}{v_2} \qquad (23\text{-}4)$$

Equation 23-4 tells us that the relationship between the angles θ_1 and θ_2 is determined by the speeds v_1 and v_2 of the wave in medium 1 and medium 2, respectively.

It's common to express the speed of light in a given medium in terms of a quantity called the **index of refraction**:

Index of refraction of a medium   Speed of light in vacuum

$$n = \frac{c}{v}$$

Index of refraction
(23-5)

Speed of light in the medium

The index of refraction of vacuum is 1, since light travels at the speed of light c so $v = c$ and $n = c/c = 1$. In any material medium, light travels slower than c, so $v < c$ and $n > 1$. The greater the value of the index of refraction n in a given medium, the slower the speed v at which light propagates in that medium. Table 23-1 lists the index of refraction of some common materials. Note that the index of refraction of air is equal to one to three significant digits, so we'll often take $n_{air} = 1$ in calculations.

Equation 23-5 tells us that $1/v = n/c$, so we can rewrite Equation 23-4 as

$$\left(\frac{n_1}{c}\right) \sin \theta_1 = \left(\frac{n_2}{c}\right) \sin \theta_2$$

If we cancel the factors of c on both sides of this equation we get

Snell's law of refraction
(23-6)

Angle of the incident ray from the normal   Angle of the refracted ray from the normal

$$n_1 \sin \theta_1 = n_2 \sin \theta_2$$

Index of refraction for the medium with the incident light   Index of refraction for the medium with the refracted light

Go to Interactive Exercise 23-1 for more practice dealing with refraction

Equation 23-6 is known as **Snell's law of refraction**. (The law is so named because it was deduced by the seventeenth-century Dutch scientist Willebrord Snellius. In fact, Equation 23-6 was first discovered by the Persian scientist Ibn Sahl in 984, more than 600 years before Snellius.)

Snell's law tells us that when a ray of light crosses from one medium to another, the product of the index of refraction and the sine of the angle the ray makes to the normal remains constant. When light passes into a material of higher index of refraction—for example, from air into glass—so that the speed of light is slower in the second medium and $n_2 > n_1$, the sine of the refracted angle and the angle itself both decrease. In this case $\theta_2 < \theta_1$ and the light bends closer to the normal (Figure 23-6a). When light instead passes into a material of lower index of refraction—for example, from glass into air—so that the speed of light is faster in the second medium and $n_2 < n_1$, the sine of the refracted angle and the angle itself both increase. In this situation $\theta_2 > \theta_1$ and the light bends away from the normal (Figure 23-6b).

The fraction of incident light that is reflected and the fraction that is refracted depend in part on the indices of refraction of the two media. (They also depend on the incident angle and on how the electric field vectors in the light wave are oriented relative to the boundary.) The index of refraction of a medium is often a function of the medium's density; one example is blood plasma, the density and index of refraction of which depend on the concentration of dissolved protein. Veterinarians can use this to estimate protein levels in livestock at the clinic or on the farm by measuring how much light refracts as it passes through a sample of an animal's plasma. Winemakers determine the amount of sugar in their grapes by using the same technique.

(a) Refraction from one medium into a slower one

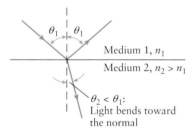

θ_1 θ_1

Medium 1, n_1
Medium 2, $n_2 > n_1$

$\theta_2 < \theta_1$:
Light bends toward the normal

(b) Refraction from one medium into a faster one

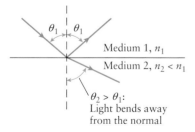

θ_1 θ_1

Medium 1, n_1
Medium 2, $n_2 < n_1$

$\theta_2 > \theta_1$:
Light bends away from the normal

Figure 23-6 **Refraction toward and away from the normal** Which way the refracted ray bends depends on whether the speed of light in the second medium is (a) slower or (b) faster than in the first medium.

Table 23-1 Indices of Refraction	
Material	**Index of Refraction**
vacuum	1.00000
air at 20 °c, 1 atm pressure	1.00029
ice	1.31
water at 20 °c	1.33
acetone	1.36
ethyl alcohol	1.36
eye, cornea	1.38
eye, lens	1.41
sugar water (high concentration)	1.49
Plexiglas	1.49
typical crown glass	1.52
sodium chloride	1.54
sapphire	1.77
diamond	2.42

Example 23-1 Seeing under Water

A surveyor looking at an aqueduct is just able to see the underwater edge where the far wall meets the bottom (Figure 23-7). If the aqueduct is 4.2 m wide and her line of sight to the near, top edge is 25° above the horizontal, find the depth of the aqueduct.

Figure 23-7 **A refracted view** If the surveyor just sees the bottom edge of the far wall of the aqueduct, how deep is the aqueduct?

Set Up

The light beam from the far edge of the bottom of the aqueduct refracts when it reaches the boundary between the water (medium 1) and the air (medium 2). Figure 23-7 shows that the angle of the refracted ray from the *normal* (shown as a vertical dashed line) is $\theta_2 = 90° - 25° = 65°$. We'll first use Snell's law to determine the angle θ_1 of the incident ray, and then use trigonometry and the given width of the aqueduct (4.2 m) to find the depth D.

Snell's law of refraction:

$$n_1 \sin \theta_1 = n_2 \sin \theta_2 \qquad (23\text{-}6)$$

Solve

Find the angle θ_1 of the incident ray using Snell's law.

Solve Equation 23-6 for the sine of the incident angle θ_1:

$$\sin \theta_1 = \frac{n_2}{n_1} \sin \theta_2$$

Figure 23-7 shows that $\theta_2 = 90° - 25° = 65°$, and from Table 23-1 we see that $n_1 = n_{water} = 1.33$ and $n_2 = n_{air} = 1.00$. So

$$\sin \theta_1 = \frac{1.00}{1.33} \sin 65° = 0.68$$

$$\theta_1 = \sin^{-1} 0.68 = 43°$$

Use trigonometry to determine the depth D of the aqueduct.

The incident ray that travels from the far edge of the aqueduct's bottom to the near, top edge is the hypotenuse of a right triangle with vertical dimension D and horizontal dimension 4.2 m. The side of length 4.2 m is the side opposite the angle θ_1, and the side of length D is the side adjacent to this angle. The tangent of θ_1 equals the opposite side divided by the adjacent side:

$$\tan \theta_1 = \frac{4.2 \text{ m}}{D}$$

Solve for the distance D:

$$D = \frac{4.2 \text{ m}}{\tan \theta_1} = \frac{4.2 \text{ m}}{\tan 43°} = 4.5 \text{ m}$$

The aqueduct is 4.5 m deep.

Reflect

The refracted angle $\theta_2 = 65°$ is larger than the incident angle $\theta_1 = 43°$, just as in Figure 23-6b. This makes sense since $n_2 < n_1$ (the index of refraction for air is smaller than the index for water).

Our brains are used to the idea that light travels in straight lines. If we extend the refracted ray backwards, we see that to the surveyor's eye the light from the far edge of the bottom of the aqueduct appears to be coming from a shallower depth than $D = 4.5$ m. You can easily see this effect in a swimming pool.

The red line represents a ray of light that bounces off the bottom of the pond and arrives at your eyes.

Your brain traces the light ray back along the blue dashed line...

...so that the bottom of the pond appears to you to be here.

Figure 23-8 A refracted chopstick
Due to refraction, the submerged part of the chopstick on the right appears displaced from its actual position.

The situation shown in **Figure 23-8** involves the same effect that makes the aqueduct in Example 23-1 appear shallower than it really is. When light from the submerged part of the chopstick passes from water to air at the boundary between the two, the light rays refract. As a result, it appears to our eyes that the submerged part is in a different position than its true location.

Frequency and Wavelength in Refraction

When a wave travels from one medium to another, the frequency of the wave remains the same. (In a given time interval, as many crests arrive at the boundary as leave the boundary. If this were not true, there would be a "traffic jam" of wave crests at the boundary.) However, since the wave speed is different in the two media, the wavelength must change. This follows from the relationship among the propagation speed v of the wave, the frequency f, and the wavelength λ. From Equation 13-2

$$v = f\lambda \quad \text{so} \quad \lambda = \frac{v}{f}$$

In a vacuum light waves travel at speed $v = c$, so the wavelength is

(23-7)
$$\lambda_{\text{vacuum}} = \frac{c}{f}$$

In a medium with index of refraction n, the wave speed from Equation 23-5 is $v = c/n$. Then we can write the wavelength of light in a medium as

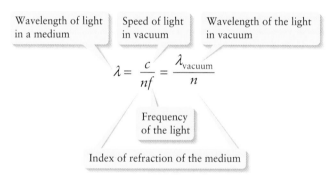

Wavelength of light in a medium
(23-8)

Equation 23-8 says that the wavelength is shorter in a medium with a higher index of refraction, where the propagation speed is slower. For example, red light that has a wavelength $\lambda_{\text{vacuum}} = 750$ nm in vacuum has a wavelength in water ($n = 1.33$) equal to $\lambda = \lambda_{\text{vacuum}}/n = (750 \text{ nm})/(1.33) = 564$ nm. The frequency of this light is the same in both media: $f = c/\lambda_{\text{vacuum}} = (3.00 \times 10^8 \text{ m/s})/(750 \times 10^{-9} \text{ m}) = 4.00 \times 10^{14}$ Hz in vacuum and $f = v/\lambda = c/(n\lambda) = (3.00 \times 10^8 \text{ m/s})/((1.33)(564 \times 10^{-9} \text{ m})) = 4.00 \times 10^{14}$ Hz in water.

We learned in Section 22-4 that the energy of an electromagnetic wave comes in packets called *photons*. The energy of an individual photon is given by Equation 22-26, $E = hf$, where h is a constant called Planck's constant. This equation shows that the energy of a photon does not change when it passes from one medium to another, even though the speed of the photon changes: The frequency f remains constant, so the photon energy $E = hf$ is unchanged. This demonstrates one way that photons are very different from ordinary particles such as marbles, whose kinetic energy changes when their speed changes.

❓ Got the Concept? 23-1 Refraction

A beam of light in air travels into a transparent, flat-walled container made of Plexiglas. The incident angle is 5.00°. The light then travels from the Plexiglas into the water inside the container. In each refraction, does the ray bend closer to the normal or farther away from it? (a) Closer in both refractions; (b) farther away in both refractions; (c) closer going from air to Plexiglas, farther away going from Plexiglas to water; (d) farther away going from air to Plexiglas, closer going from Plexiglas to water; (e) in at least one of the refractions, the light does not bend at all.

Take-Home Message for Section 23-2

✔ Huygens' principle says that each point on a wave front acts as a source of wavelets. The new wave front is the superposition of the individual wavelets.

✔ When waves encounter a boundary between two media in which the wave speed is different, the waves can bounce back into the first medium (reflect) or pass into the second medium at a different angle (refract).

✔ The angle of the reflected ray is the same as the angle of the incident ray (law of reflection).

✔ Snell's law describes the direction of the refracted ray. If the wave speed is lower in the second medium than in the first, the refracted ray bends toward the normal. If the wave speed is faster in the second medium, the refracted ray bends away from the normal.

✔ The index of refraction is a measure of the speed of light in a medium relative to the speed of light in vacuum. The slower light travels in a medium, the larger its index of refraction.

23-3 In some cases light undergoes total internal reflection at the boundary between media

In the photograph shown in Figure 23-2, light in air encounters a boundary with water on the other side. Some of the incident light is reflected at the boundary, and some of it is refracted from the first medium (air) into the second medium (water). There are situations, however, in which *none* of the light is refracted into the second medium. Figure 23-9 shows a light beam in glass that encounters a boundary with air on the other side. As the photograph shows, 100% of the light is reflected back into the glass. This effect is called **total internal reflection**.

Figure 23-10 shows how this effect arises for the case of light in glass that reaches a boundary with air on the other side. Light travels more slowly in glass than air, so the index of refraction of glass is higher than the index of refraction of air. As light crosses the boundary from glass to air, it is bent away from the normal as in Figure 23-10a. As the incident angle of the light increases (Figure 23-10b), the refracted light gets farther from the normal and decreases in intensity. When the incident angle equals the **critical angle** θ_c, the refracted light lies exactly in the plane of the surface (Figure 23-10c). At this angle the intensity of the refracted light is zero. If the incident angle is greater than the critical angle, as in Figure 23-10d, the light is completely reflected back into the glass. This is total internal reflection.

All of the light reflects at the boundary between glass and air; none is refracted into the air. This is total internal reflection.

Figure 23-9 Total internal reflection There is nothing unusual about the place where the light beam strikes the glass, yet none of the light escapes into the air on the other side.

(a) Light refracts as it passes from glass into air. The index of refraction of glass is greater than the index of refraction of air, so $\theta_2 > \theta_1$.

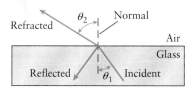

(b) As the angle θ_1 of the incident light increases, so does the angle θ_2 of the refracted light.

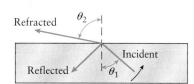

(c) When the angle θ_1 of the incident light equals the critical angle θ_c, the refracted angle is $\theta_2 = 90°$. The intensity of the refracted light becomes zero.

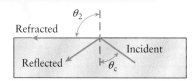

(d) When the angle θ_1 of the incident light is greater than the critical angle θ_c, the light is completely reflected back into the glass. This is total internal reflection.

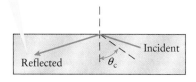

Figure 23-10 Approaching total internal reflection (a) and (b) Light approaches a boundary between glass and air at an incident angle θ_1 less than the critical angle θ_c. (c) When $\theta_1 = \theta_c$, the light ray is refracted along the surface. (d) Total internal reflection occurs for incident angles greater than the critical angle.

Total internal reflection is possible only when the first medium (in Figure 23-10, glass) has a higher index of refraction than the second medium (in Figure 23-10, air), so $n_1 > n_2$. Then the refracted angle θ_2 is greater than the incident angle θ_1, and the refracted angle can reach 90° as in Figure 23-10c. If the first medium has a lower index of refraction than the second medium, so $n_1 < n_2$, the refracted angle θ_2 is less than the incident angle θ_1, and the refracted angle can never reach 90°.

We can calculate the critical angle θ_c using Snell's law of refraction, Equation 23-6. When the incident angle θ_1 equals the critical angle θ_c, the refracted angle θ_2 equals 90°. If we substitute these into Equation 23-6 and recall that sin 90° = 1, we get

$$(23\text{-}9) \qquad n_1 \sin \theta_c = n_2 \sin 90° = n_2 \quad \text{so} \quad \sin \theta_c = \frac{n_2}{n_1}$$

Note that the sine of an angle between 0 and 90° is between 0 and 1. If $n_1 > n_2$, the ratio n_2/n_1 is less than 1, and there will be some angle θ_c for which Equation 23-9 is satisfied. In this case total internal reflection is possible. But if $n_1 < n_2$, the ratio n_2/n_1 is greater than 1 and Equation 23-9 has no solution. This is another way of seeing that total internal reflection is possible only if $n_1 > n_2$.

If we solve Equation 23-9 for the critical angle θ_c, we get

Critical angle for total internal reflection (23-10)

Critical angle for light in medium 1 that encounters a boundary with medium 2 with a lower index of refraction

Index of refraction of medium 2

$$\theta_c = \sin^{-1}\left(\frac{n_2}{n_1}\right)$$

Index of refraction of medium 1

 If the incident angle is greater than the critical angle, there is total internal reflection.

 Go to Picture It 23-1 for more practice dealing with refraction and reflection

Notice that the critical angle depends on the indices of refraction of the media on *both* sides of a boundary.

Example 23-2 Critical Angles

(a) A laser is aimed from under the water toward the surface, as in Figure 23-11. Find the critical angle of the light incident in the water beyond which total internal reflection occurs.
(b) Find the critical angle if the liquid in the tank were replaced by water containing a high concentration of dissolved sugar.

The light undergoes total internal reflection

Air

Water

θ_1

Incident light

Reflected light

Normal

Figure 23-11 Total internal reflection in water Light from a laser aimed from under the water toward the surface is totally internally reflected. What is the minimum incident angle for which total internal reflection will occur?

Set Up

Before hitting the surface (the boundary between water and air), the light is propagating in water, so this is medium 1 with index of refraction n_1. In part (a), medium 1 is ordinary water with $n_1 = 1.33$; in part (b), medium 1 is sugar water with $n_1 = 1.49$. In both parts, medium 2 on the other side of the surface is air with index of refraction $n_2 = 1.00$. We'll use Equation 23-10 to solve for the critical angle in each case.

Critical angle for total internal reflection:

$$\theta_c = \sin^{-1}\left(\frac{n_2}{n_1}\right) \qquad (23\text{-}10)$$

Solve

(a) Find the critical angle if medium 1 is water.

With $n_1 = 1.33$ and $n_2 = 1.00$, the critical angle is

$$\theta_c = \sin^{-1}\left(\frac{1.00}{1.33}\right) = \sin^{-1} 0.752 = 48.8°$$

If the angle of incidence θ_1 is 48.8° or greater, the light will undergo total internal reflection and no light will go into the air. (Note that θ_1 in Figure 23-11 is approximately 60°, which is indeed greater than 48.8°.)

(b) Find the critical angle if medium 2 is sugar water.

With $n_1 = 1.49$ and $n_2 = 1.00$, the critical angle is

$$\theta_c = \sin^{-1}\left(\frac{1.00}{1.49}\right) = \sin^{-1} 0.671 = 42.2°$$

Reflect

Adding sugar to water results in a lower speed of light, which increases the index of refraction. The minimum angle of incidence for which total internal reflection occurs is therefore smaller for sugar water than for pure water. The smaller the critical angle, the larger the range of angles at which light experiences total internal reflection.

Total internal reflection explains what happens when you look down the highway on a hot day and see what appear to be puddles of water on the road. You might even see the reflection of cars and other objects in these "puddles," as in Figure 23-12. The explanation is that air sits in layers above the road, each layer a bit warmer, less dense, and with a lower index of refraction than the one above it. Light from the blue sky that propagates down toward the road is refracted as it encounters the boundary between one layer of air and the next. Because the index of refraction of the layer of air closer to the road is lower, the light is bent farther from the normal. The normal direction in these refractions is vertical, so the light is refracted closer to horizontal, as Figure 23-13 shows. Light that strikes the boundary between layers at a large angle with respect to the normal (a grazing angle as measured from the air layer boundary) can experience total internal reflection and reflect back up into the higher layer. Your eyes trace the light rays back along straight lines, so that the light appears to be coming from a point close to the road. What looks like a puddle is actually a refracted image of the blue sky.

Endoscopy is a medical procedure used to see inside the body. It relies on a light fiber, an optical device used to carry light and sometimes data encoded in pulses of light, from one place to another. A beam of light sent down a light fiber experiences total internal reflection at the surface of the fiber, which results in multiple reflections that keep the beam inside the fiber. The bent bar of Plexiglas in Figure 23-14 carries light in

Figure 23-12 **A mirage** What causes these shimmering patches on the road that look like puddles?

1. Light from a region of sky is refracted as it passes through layers of air above the road.

2. Light travels faster in the layers of warmer air closer to the road, so it is bent closer to horizontal.

3. Total internal reflection occurs for very shallow angles with respect to the air layer boundaries.

4. An image of the region of sky is formed close to the ground that gives the appearance of shimmery, blue puddles on the road.

Figure 23-13 **Explaining a mirage** The "puddles" in Figure 23-12 are an illusion caused by total internal reflection.

Figure 23-14 Light trapped by total internal reflection Light propagates through the interior of a curved bar of Plexiglas by a series of total internal reflections.

a similar way. Because light experiences total internal reflection when it encounters the surface, no light is lost as the beam is reflected back. Notice in Figure 23-14 that no light leaks out of the bar at the points where the beam hits the surface. Most light fiber is made by surrounding a central core with either one or two layers of a "cladding" made from a material of lower index of refraction than the core. The index of refraction of the core and the cladding is chosen to adjust the critical angle at the core-cladding boundary in order to optimize the light-carrying properties of the light fiber. Many endoscopes actually use bundles of several fibers. Light is sent down some fibers to illuminate the subject. Other fibers carry the image back to a camera.

As the following example shows, light fibers can also be used to deliver light energy to the interior of a patient's body in order to relieve the pain of kidney stones.

Example 23-3 Laser Lithotripsy

In a common technique used by urologists to remove kidney stones from the urinary tract, light from a powerful laser is directed down a light fiber inserted into a patient's body through a catheter. The energy of the light is absorbed by the stone, pulverizing it so that the small fragments can safely be passed by the patient. A commonly used light fiber consists of a glass-like core of diameter 2.00 mm and an index of refraction of 1.55. It is surrounded by a cladding of index of refraction 1.46. What is the minimum radius of curvature at which the fiber can be bent before light, initially traveling parallel to the axis of the fiber, will begin to leak out of the fiber (**Figure 23-15**)?

The ray of light colored blue strikes the surface at an angle greater than the critical angle, and experiences total internal reflection.

The ray of light colored green strikes the surface at an angle greater than, but closer to, the critical angle and experiences total internal reflection.

The ray of light colored red strikes the surface at an angle less than the critical angle, so it does not experience total internal reflection and leaves the light fiber.

Figure 23-15 A bent light fiber What is the minimum radius of curvature r of this light fiber to keep light from leaking out?

Set Up

Light leaks out of the fiber when it strikes the surface of the fiber at an angle less than the critical angle. As Figure 23-15 shows, leakage is more likely to happen the deeper into the bend that light strikes the surface of the fiber. So when the fiber is bent to the radius at which light just begins to leak out, the light that strikes the surface farthest into the bend hits at an incident angle just equal to the critical angle. To understand the geometry of this ray, we consider the triangle formed by it and the radius of the bend, as the figure shows. We labeled the radius r_{min} to indicate that light would leak out were the light fiber bent at a smaller radius. We'll use Equation 23-10 to calculate the critical angle.

Critical angle for total internal reflection:

$$\theta_c = \sin^{-1}\left(\frac{n_2}{n_1}\right) \qquad (23\text{-}10)$$

Solve

First use Equation 23-10 to find the critical angle θ_c for light in the core of the fiber reflecting off the boundary with the cladding.

The core in which the light travels has index of refraction $n_1 = 1.55$. The light reflects from the boundary with the cladding, which has index of refraction $n_2 = 1.46$. The critical angle is

$$\theta_c = \sin^{-1}\left(\frac{1.46}{1.55}\right) = \sin^{-1} 0.942 = 70.4°$$

If the incident angle at which light strikes the cladding is more than 70.4°, the light undergoes total internal reflection. If the incident angle is less than 70.4°, light will leak out of the fiber.

Use trigonometry and the calculated value of θ_c to determine the minimum radius of curvature r_{min}.

The figure above shows a right triangle with one side of length r_{min} and a hypotenuse of length $r_{min} + D$. The angle opposite the side of length r_{min} is the critical angle θ_c. The sine of this angle equals the length r_{min} divided by the length of the hypotenuse:

$$\sin \theta_c = \frac{r_{min}}{r_{min} + D}$$

Solve this equation for r_{min}:

$$(r_{min} + D)\sin \theta_c = r_{min}$$
$$r_{min} \sin \theta_c + D \sin \theta_c = r_{min}$$
$$r_{min}(1 - \sin \theta_c) = D \sin \theta_c$$
$$r_{min} = D\left(\frac{\sin \theta_c}{1 - \sin \theta_c}\right)$$

Substitute $D = 2.00$ mm and the calculated value $\theta_c = 70.4°$:

$$r_{min} = (2.00 \text{ mm})\left(\frac{\sin 70.4°}{1 - \sin 70.4°}\right) = (2.00 \text{ mm})\left(\frac{0.942}{1 - 0.942}\right)$$
$$= 32.4 \text{ mm} = 3.24 \text{ cm}$$

Reflect

Our calculation shows that such a light fiber can be bent with a radius of curvature as small as 3.25 cm before light leaks out. This radius is more than adequate to accommodate the twists and turns a fiber would make under normal circumstances in the process of being inserted into a patient.

? Got the Concept? 23-2 Total Internal Reflection

It's possible for a beam of light in Plexiglas to undergo total internal reflection at a boundary if the material on the other side of the boundary is (a) ethyl alcohol; (b) sapphire; (c) diamond; (d) more than one of these; (e) none of these.

Take-Home Message for Section 23-3

✔ When light traveling in a medium with index of refraction n_1 reaches a boundary with a second medium of index of refraction n_2, total internal reflection can happen if $n_1 > n_2$.

✔ Total internal reflection takes place only if the incident angle measured from the normal at the boundary is greater than the critical angle θ_c given by Equation 23-10. In this case, none of the light is refracted into the second medium.

23-4 The dispersion of light explains the colors from a prism or a rainbow

White light is a mixture of all the colors of the visible spectrum. You can see these colors by allowing sunlight to pass through a glass prism, as in Figure 23-16: The different colors emerge in different directions. This happens because the speed of light in a medium other than vacuum, such as the glass in a prism, is different for different frequencies of light. (In vacuum the speed is equal to c for all frequencies.) This is a result of how a light wave interacts with the atoms of a transparent material through which the wave passes. This variation of speed with frequency is called **dispersion**.

Since the speed v of light waves in a medium depends on the frequency, the index of refraction $n = c/v$ (Equation 23-5) depends on frequency as well. In most transparent materials the speed decreases with increasing frequency, from red to yellow to violet (see Figure 22-2): Yellow light travels slightly more slowly than red light, and blue light travels slightly more slowly than yellow light. This means that the index of refraction n increases with increasing frequency. Note that Equation 23-7 tells us that the wavelength in vacuum is inversely proportional to frequency: $\lambda_{vacuum} = c/f$. So we

Figure 23-16 Dispersion Light of different frequencies, and hence different colors, propagates at different speeds through the glass of which this prism is made. As a result, different colors refract along slightly different paths.

Figure 23-17 **Dispersion in different materials** The index of refraction in glass varies with the vacuum wavelength of light and with the type of glass.

can also say that the value of *n* decreases with increasing vacuum wavelength. (We specify *vacuum* wavelength since the wavelength in the medium depends on the value of *n*; see Equation 23-8.) Figure 23-17 shows how the index of refraction varies with vacuum wavelength for four different transparent materials. Note that the indices of refraction given in Table 23-1 are for yellow light, near the middle of the visible spectrum.

Snell's law of refraction, Equation 23-6, tells us that the angle at which light refracts as it crosses the boundary between two transparent media depends on their indices of refraction. So it follows that different colors of light, with different vacuum wavelengths, refract at different angles. Figure 23-18 shows this for light passing from vacuum into glass. The higher the index of refraction of the second medium, the more the refracted light is bent toward the normal. In common glass, the index of refraction is about 1.51 for red light, about 1.52 for yellow light, and about 1.53 for blue light. Because the index of refraction of short-wavelength blue light is higher than for long-wavelength red light, the blue light bends more toward the normal than does the red light. This causes the different colors of light to be spread out or dispersed. (This is the origin of the term *dispersion*.)

The same effect explains the appearance of a rainbow (Figure 23-1b). When raindrops in midair are illuminated by the Sun, sunlight enters each raindrop, is partly reflected off the back of the drop, and then exits out the front of the drop. The index of refraction of water is different for different wavelengths, so each color of light emerges in a slightly different direction to form a rainbow.

The variation of the index of refraction *n* over the visible spectrum characterizes the dispersion of light in that material. In glass, for example, the index of refraction varies by 0.02 from red (*n* = 1.51) to blue (*n* = 1.53), while for diamond the index of refraction varies by 0.04 from red (*n* = 2.41) to blue (*n* = 2.45). As a result, the colors of white light are spread out over a wider angle by a cut diamond than by a piece of glass cut to the same shape. This high value of dispersion contributes to the "sparkly" character of a cut diamond.

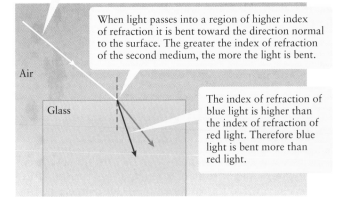

White light is composed of light across all wavelengths (colors) in the visible spectrum. The colors spread apart when light crosses the boundary between two light transmitting media.

When light passes into a region of higher index of refraction it is bent toward the direction normal to the surface. The greater the index of refraction of the second medium, the more the light is bent.

Air

Glass

The index of refraction of blue light is higher than the index of refraction of red light. Therefore blue light is bent more than red light.

Figure 23-18 **Analyzing dispersion** The difference in refracted angle between the red and blue light is greatly exaggerated for clarity.

Example 23-4 Dispersion in Dense Flint Glass

A narrow beam of white light enters a rectangular block of dense flint glass at an angle of 60.0° from the normal. The block is 0.500 m on a side. Calculate how far apart the red and blue parts of the visible spectrum will be when the light leaves the glass. The index of refraction of dense flint glass is 1.75 for red light and 1.79 for blue light.

Set Up

Both colors of light are incident on the block at the same angle: $\theta_1 = 60.0°$. However, the red and blue refract at different angles because the index of refraction is different for the two colors. We'll use Snell's law, Equation 23-6, to calculate the angles θ_{red} and θ_{blue}, then use trigonometry to find the distances d_{red} and d_{blue} shown in the figure. The difference between these distances tells us how far apart the points are where the two colors emerge from the glass.

Snell's law of refraction:

$$n_1 \sin \theta_1 = n_2 \sin \theta_2 \qquad (23-6)$$

Solve

Find the refracted angles θ_{red} and θ_{blue} for the two colors.

For both colors $n_1 = n_{air} = 1.00$ and $\theta_1 = 60.0°$. For red light $n_2 = 1.75$, so Equation 23-6 becomes

$$1.00 \sin 60.0° = 1.75 \sin \theta_{red}$$

$$\sin \theta_{red} = \frac{1.00 \sin 60.0°}{1.75} = 0.4948$$

$$\theta_{red} = \sin^{-1} 0.4948 = 29.66°$$

(We've kept an extra significant digit in our result; we'll round off at the end of the calculation.) Do the same calculation for blue light, for which $n_2 = 1.79$:

$$1.00 \sin 60.0° = 1.79 \sin \theta_{blue}$$

$$\sin \theta_{blue} = \frac{1.00 \sin 60.0°}{1.79} = 0.4838$$

$$\theta_{blue} = \sin^{-1} 0.484 = 28.93°$$

Find the distances d_{red} and d_{blue} for the two colors of light, and from these find the separation between the two colors as they exit the glass.

For each color of light, the ray that extends from where the light enters the block of glass to where it exits the block forms the hypotenuse of a right triangle. The other two sides are the vertical dimension of the block, $w = 0.500$ m, and the distance d_{red} or d_{blue} that the light is displaced horizontally. In each case the side of length w is adjacent to the angle θ_{red} or θ_{blue}, and the side of length d_{red} or d_{blue} is opposite to that angle. In a right triangle, the length of the opposite side divided by the length of the adjacent side equals the tangent of the angle, so

$$\tan \theta_{red} = \frac{d_{red}}{w}$$

$$\tan \theta_{blue} = \frac{d_{blue}}{w}$$

Solve for the distances d_{red} and d_{blue} using the angles that we calculated above:

$$d_{red} = w \tan \theta_{red} = (0.500 \text{ m}) \tan 29.66° = 0.2847 \text{ m}$$
$$d_{blue} = w \tan \theta_{blue} = (0.500 \text{ m}) \tan 28.93° = 0.2764 \text{ m}$$

The distance between where the red light exits the glass and where the blue light exits the glass is

$$d_{red} - d_{blue} = 0.2847 \text{ m} - 0.2764 \text{ m} = 0.0083 \text{ m} = 8.3 \text{ mm}$$

The separation between the two colors is fairly substantial, so this block of glass does a good job of spreading white light into its constituent colors.

In this example we used a block made of flint glass, sometimes called "lead glass" because lead is often added during the glass-making process. We invite you to repeat this calculation for crown glass, the kind of glass commonly used to make windows, for which $n_{red} = 1.51$ and $n_{blue} = 1.53$. Since crown glass has a smaller index of refraction than flint glass, and because the difference between the values of the two indices is smaller for crown glass than for flint glass, you'll find that the distance $d_{red} - d_{blue}$ is smaller for crown glass. Which type of glass would be a better choice for a prism intended to spread apart the different colors of light, as in Figure 23-16?

? Got the Concept? 23-3 Dispersion

A flash of white light (containing all of the colors of the visible spectrum) in air shines straight down on the surface of a pond of water. Which color of light from the flash reaches the bottom of the pond first? (a) The blue light; (b) the yellow light; (c) the red light; (d) all reach the bottom at the same time.

Take-Home Message for Section 23-4

✔   The speed of light in a material medium depends on the frequency of the light. This is called dispersion. In most materials, the index of refraction for visible light increases from the red end of the spectrum (low frequency, long wavelength) to the blue end of the spectrum (high frequency, short wavelength).

✔   When light crosses a boundary into a medium of different index of refraction, different colors refract by different angles. This causes the colors to spread apart by an amount that depends on how strongly the index of refraction varies with wavelength.

23-5 In a polarized light wave, the electric field vector points in a specific direction

When a honeybee finds nectar, it communicates the location to other bees in the hive. In the 1940s Austrian ethologist Karl von Frisch established that if bees can see even a small patch of blue sky, they can use the position of the Sun to describe the path back to the food from the hive. (For his work on animal behavior, von Frisch received the Nobel Prize in Physiology or Medicine in 1973.) How is it that bees can know the position of the Sun even if they can't see it directly?

The explanation is that light is a transverse electromagnetic wave, with an oscillating electric field $\vec{E}$ and magnetic field $\vec{B}$ that are perpendicular to each other and to the direction of wave propagation (see Figure 22-4). The orientation of the $\vec{E}$ field is called the **polarization** of the light wave. (We don't need to separately state the orientation of $\vec{B}$, since we know that it's perpendicular to both the direction of propagation and the orientation of $\vec{E}$.) Natural light such as that emitted by the Sun or an ordinary light bulb is **unpolarized**: The orientation of the electric field changes randomly from one moment to the next. For example, if the wave is propagating in the positive x direction, at one moment $\vec{E}$ may be oriented along the y axis, a short time later it may be oriented along the z axis, a short time after that it may be oriented at 23.7° to the y axis, and so on. The reason for this is that a source of natural light emits light in the form of a stream of photons (see Section 22-4), and the orientation of $\vec{E}$ varies randomly from one photon to another.

When sunlight scatters from molecules or small particles in the atmosphere, however, the scattered light that we see has its $\vec{E}$ field oriented predominantly in one direction (Figure 23-19). (Scattering is stronger for short-wavelength light than for long-wavelength light, which is why the color of the sky is dominated by short-wavelength blue light.) Light in which the orientation of the $\vec{E}$ field changes randomly,

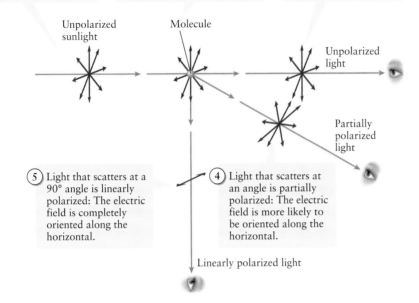

① The blue arrows indicate the orientation of the electric field. In unpolarized light, this orientation changes randomly.

② When light strikes a molecule in the atmosphere, the polarization and direction of propagation can both change.

③ Light that scatters in the forward direction (that is, is not deflected) remains unpolarized.

Figure 23-19 Polarization by scattering The extent to which sunlight is polarized by scattering depends on the scattering angle.

Unpolarized sunlight

Molecule

Unpolarized light

Partially polarized light

⑤ Light that scatters at a 90° angle is linearly polarized: The electric field is completely oriented along the horizontal.

④ Light that scatters at an angle is partially polarized: The electric field is more likely to be oriented along the horizontal.

Linearly polarized light

but is more likely to be in one orientation than in other orientations, is called **partially polarized**. Light for which the $\vec{E}$ field is oriented *completely* along one direction is called **linearly polarized**. For example, the $\vec{E}$ field for the light wave shown in Figure 22-4 has only a y component, so we say this light is linearly polarized along the y axis. Bees have the ability to detect the polarization of light coming from the sky, and by using this they can infer the position of the Sun. (Human eyes, by contrast, are only weakly sensitive to polarization.)

Polarizing Light with a Polarizing Filter

A simple way to make polarized light from unpolarized light is by using a **polarizing filter.** This is a transparent sheet which contains long-chain molecules that are all oriented in the same direction. These molecules absorb light whose polarization direction is along the axis of the molecules, but have no effect on light that is polarized perpendicular to that direction. An equivalent way to think of a polarizing filter is as a series of slits that allow waves to pass that are polarized along the slits, but block waves that are polarized perpendicular to the slits (**Figure 23-20**). If we send unpolarized light into

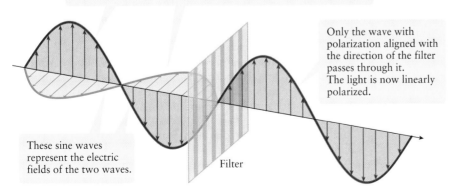

Two waves of different polarizations encounter a polarizing filter.

Only the wave with polarization aligned with the direction of the filter passes through it. The light is now linearly polarized.

These sine waves represent the electric fields of the two waves.

Filter

Figure 23-20 A linear polarizing filter I A filter of this kind allows only light with an electric field component aligned in a certain direction to pass through it.

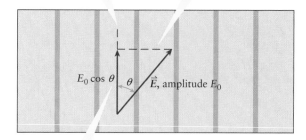

1) The polarizing filter allows light polarized along this direction to pass. It blocks light polarized in the perpendicular direction.

2) As a result, this component of the electric field of a light wave is blocked by the filter...

- The transmitted light is linearly polarized along the polarization direction of the filter.
- The electric field amplitude of the transmitted light equals the incident amplitude E_0 multiplied by $\cos\theta$.
- The intensity of the transmitted light equals the incident intensity I_0 multiplied by $\cos^2\theta$.

$E_0 \cos\theta$ θ $\vec{E}$, amplitude E_0

3) ...and only this component is allowed to pass through the filter.

Figure 23-21 A linear polarizing filter II What happens to light that enters a polarizing filter with its electric field $\vec{E}$ at an angle to the polarization direction?

(a) Photographed without a filter

(b) Photographed with a polarizing filter oriented vertically, to block light with horizontal polarization

Figure 23-22 Reducing reflections with a polarizing filter Reflected light is linearly polarized. The polarizing lenses often used for sunglasses can dramatically reduce glare from reflected light.

the filter, we can think of the electric field $\vec{E}$ at any instant as having a component along the direction of the filter and a component perpendicular to that direction. Only the component of $\vec{E}$ along the direction of the filter will pass through, so the light that emerges from the filter will be linearly polarized.

Since a polarizing filter absorbs some of the light that falls on it, the light exiting the filter is in general less intense than the incident light that falls on it. Suppose the incident light has an oscillating electric field with magnitude E_0 that is oriented at an angle θ to the polarization direction of the filter (Figure 23-21). The component of this field that will be allowed to pass through the filter is the component aligned with the filter direction:

$$(23\text{-}11) \qquad E_{\text{aligned}} = E_0 \cos\theta$$

The intensity of the light is proportional to the square of the electric field amplitude. The amplitude is E_0 for the incident light and (from Equation 23-11) $E_0 \cos\theta$ for the transmitted light, so the intensity I of the transmitted light equals $\cos^2\theta$ times the intensity I_0 of the incident light:

$$(23\text{-}12) \qquad I = E_0^2 \cos^2\theta = I_0 \cos^2\theta$$

If the incident light is unpolarized, the value of the angle θ will vary randomly between 0 and 360°. The average value of $\cos^2\theta$ over this range is $1/2$, so if unpolarized light incident on a polarizing filter has intensity I_0, the intensity of the light that emerges from the filter will be $I = I_0/2$.

Polarizing Light by Reflection

Another way to convert unpolarized light into light that is at least partially polarized is by *reflection*. When light strikes the boundary between two media, a fraction of the light is reflected and the remainder is refracted. The fraction that is reflected depends not only on the incident angle of the light, but also on the orientation of the electric field of the incident light—that is, on the polarization. In general, light polarized parallel to the boundary surface is reflected more strongly than light polarized in the perpendicular direction. If the incident light is unpolarized, that means the reflected light will be at least partially polarized in the orientation parallel to the boundary surface.

As an example, sunlight that reflects from the windshield and the hood of the car in Figure 23-22a is partially polarized parallel to the reflecting surface, so the electric field of the reflected light has a strong horizontal component and a weak vertical component. In Figure 23-22b we've placed a polarizing filter in front of the camera with its polarizing direction in the vertical direction, so light with horizontal polarization is blocked. You can see that the reflected light is greatly suppressed. Polarizing sunglasses use this same principle to minimize reflections from the road or the surface of a lake or ocean: Sunlight reflected from these horizontal surfaces is predominantly polarized in the horizontal direction, so the filters that make up the sunglass lenses are oriented to block light with a horizontal polarization. If you hold a pair of polarizing sunglasses in front of your eyes and slowly rotate them by 90° until the left lens is above the right lens, you'll see that the reflections reappear because the filter direction now aligns with the polarization direction of sunlight reflected from the ground.

For incident unpolarized light at one particular value of the angle of incidence, the reflected light is *completely* polarized in the direction parallel to the boundary between the two media. The angle of incidence θ_1 that results in this special condition is called **Brewster's angle θ_B**. When $\theta_1 = \theta_B$, it turns out that the sum of the incident angle θ_1 and the refracted angle θ_2 equals 90° (**Figure 23-23**):

$$\theta_1 + \theta_2 = 90° \quad \text{when } \theta_1 = \theta_B \tag{23-13}$$

We can use this to solve for the value of Bewster's angle θ_B in terms of the indices of refraction n_1 and n_2 of the two media. Snell's law of refraction, Equation 23-6, gives us this relationship between θ_1 and θ_2:

$$n_1 \sin \theta_1 = n_2 \sin \theta_2 \tag{23-6}$$

If θ_1 equals Brewster's angle θ_B, Equation 23-13 tells us that

$$\theta_2 = 90° - \theta_1 = 90° - \theta_B$$

If we substitute this into Equation 23-6, we get

$$n_1 \sin \theta_B = n_2 \sin (90° - \theta_B)$$

We know from trigonometry that $\sin (90° - \theta_B) = \cos \theta_B$. So

$$n_1 \sin \theta_B = n_2 \cos \theta_B$$

Divide both sides of this equation by n_1, then divide both sides by $\cos \theta_B$. The result is

$$\frac{\sin \theta_B}{\cos \theta_B} = \frac{n_2}{n_1}$$

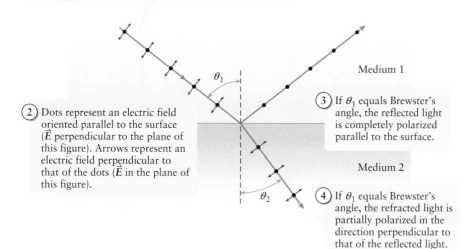

① Unpolarized light propagating in medium 1 strikes the boundary with medium 2 at an incident angle θ_1.

② Dots represent an electric field oriented parallel to the surface ($\vec{E}$ perpendicular to the plane of this figure). Arrows represent an electric field perpendicular to that of the dots ($\vec{E}$ in the plane of this figure).

Medium 1

③ If θ_1 equals Brewster's angle, the reflected light is completely polarized parallel to the surface.

Medium 2

④ If θ_1 equals Brewster's angle, the refracted light is partially polarized in the direction perpendicular to that of the reflected light.

Figure 23-23 **Polarization by reflection** Light reflected from a surface is partially polarized and becomes completely polarized when the incident angle equals Brewster's angle.

The sine of an angle divided by its cosine equals the tangent of the angle. So $\tan \theta_B = n_2/n_1$, or

Brewster's angle for polarization by reflection (23-14)

Brewster's angle for light in medium 1 that encounters a boundary with medium 2

$$\theta_B = \tan^{-1}\left(\frac{n_2}{n_1}\right)$$

Index of refraction of medium 2

Index of refraction of medium 1

If the incident angle equals Brewster's angle, the reflected light is completely polarized in the direction parallel to the surface of the boundary.

Go to Interactive Exercise 23-2 for more practice dealing with polarization

If the angle of incidence for unpolarized light is something other than θ_B, the reflected ray is partly polarized. If unpolarized light strikes the boundary perpendicular to it, so $\theta_1 = 0$, there is no change in polarization of the reflected light.

Example 23-5 Brewster's Angle for Air to Water

At what incident angle must light strike the surface of a pond so that the reflected light is completely polarized?

Set Up
This is the situation shown in Figure 23-23, with air as medium 1 and water as medium 2. The reflected light will be completely polarized if the incident angle θ_1 is equal to Brewster's angle θ_B given by Equation 23-14. Table 23-1 tells us the value of the indices of refraction: $n_1 = n_{air} = 1.00$ and $n_2 = n_{water} = 1.33$.

Brewster's angle for polarization by reflection:

$$\theta_B = \tan^{-1}\left(\frac{n_2}{n_1}\right) \qquad (23\text{-}14)$$

Solve
Use Equation 23-14 to find Brewster's angle for this situation.

With $n_1 = 1.00$ and $n_2 = 1.33$, Brewster's angle is

$$\theta_B = \tan^{-1}\left(\frac{1.33}{1.00}\right) = 53.1°$$

The reflected light will be completely polarized if the incident angle θ_1 is equal to $\theta_B = 53.1°$.

Reflect
The boundary between the two media (air and water) is the horizontal surface of the pond, so the normal to this surface is vertical. Our result tells us that if light from the sky strikes the surface at an angle of 53.1° from the vertical, the reflected light will be completely polarized. Light striking close to this angle will be strongly polarized but not 100% polarized.

You should repeat this calculation for light coming from below the water (say, from a diver's flashlight) and striking the surface of the pond from below. Can you show that in this case, the light that reflects back into the water will be completely polarized if the incident light is at an angle of 36.9° to the vertical?

? Got the Concept? 23-4 Polarizing Filters I

Two polarizing filters, *A* and *B*, are placed one behind the other with their transmission directions perpendicular to each other. A beam of unpolarized light is directed at filter *A*. What fraction of the original light intensity will remain after the light passes through both filters *A* and *B*? (a) 1/2; (b) 1/4; (c) 1/8; (d) zero; (e) none of these.

Two polarizing filters, *A* and *B*, are placed one behind the other with their transmission directions perpendicular to each other. A third polarizing filter, *C*, is placed in between them. The transmission direction of *C* is halfway between those of filters *A* and *B* (that is, at 45° to that of filter *A* and at 45° to that of filter *B*). A beam of unpolarized light is directed at filter *A*. What fraction of the original light intensity will remain after the light passes through filters *A*, *B*, and *C*? (a) 1/2; (b) 1/4; (c) 1/8; (d) zero; (e) none of these.

Take-Home Message for Section 23-5

✔   The orientation of the oscillating electric field in a light wave tells you the polarization of that wave.

✔   In natural light, the direction of the electric field changes randomly and is equally likely to be in any direction perpendicular to the propagation direction of the wave. Such light is called unpolarized.

✔   Light that has its electric field oriented in one specific direction is called linearly polarized. Unpolarized light can be polarized by scattering, by passing it through a polarizing filter, or by reflection.

23-6 Light waves reflected from the layers of a thin film can interfere with each other, producing dazzling effects

The wings of the butterfly *Morpho menelaus* (Figure 23-24) show brilliant, almost glowing colors. Yet the material of which the wings are made is colorless! The explanation for this seeming contradiction is that the colors are produced by the interference of light, a process similar to the interference of sound waves we investigated in Chapter 13.

In Section 13-5 we saw that sound waves interfere constructively or destructively depending on how the peaks and troughs of the two waves align. The same is true for light waves. Let's consider the process that occurs when light of a single wavelength strikes a layer of a transparent material. (Light that has a single definite wavelength is called **monochromatic**.) An example of a transparent layer of this sort is the thin *tapetum lucidum* ("shining carpet") that lines the back of some animals' eyes behind the retina (see Figure 23-1a). The material behind the *tapetum lucidum* is opaque (light cannot pass through it), so we can think of the *tapetum lucidum* as a thin layer against an opaque backing. This thin layer, often called a **thin film**, is of thickness *D*.

As Figure 23-25a shows, some of the light waves that strike the outer surface of the thin film are reflected. The remaining light enters the thin film (Figure 23-25b), then strikes the boundary between the film and the opaque backing, where it is reflected back up. (Some light is also absorbed by the backing.) As Figure 23-25c shows, the light that is reflected from the front of the thin film and the light that is reflected from the opaque backing both end up traveling upward in the same direction.

What was originally a single light wave striking a thin layer of a transparent material has been split into two waves that have traveled different paths. The light that enters the layer and reflects off the inner surface travels farther than the light reflected off the outer surface. For this reason the two light waves, which had to be in phase initially because they were part of the same wave before striking the upper surface, may not be in phase when they recombine. The interference that occurs depends on the number of wave cycles that fit into the extra distance traveled by the light that enters the thin layer. If an integer number of cycles (1, 2, 3, ... cycles) fit into that extra distance, then the two outgoing waves are in phase and constructively interfere. The surface of the film appears bright. If an odd number of half cycles (1/2, 3/2, 5/2, ... cycles) fit into the extra distance, however, the two outgoing waves are 180° out of phase and destructively interfere. (We specify an *odd* number of half cycles because an even number of half cycles is the same as an integer number of full cycles: for example,

Figure 23-24 **Butterfly interference** The iridescent colors on the wings of this *Morpho menelaus* butterfly result from the interference of light waves that reflect from the wing surfaces.

(a)

Some of the light that strikes the surface of a thin transparent layer is reflected.

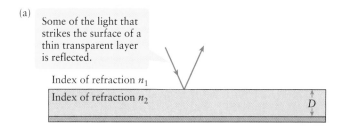

Index of refraction n_1

Index of refraction n_2

D

(b)

Some of the light enters the layer and is refracted...

...then reflected by the bottom surface and finally refracted again as it exits the layer.

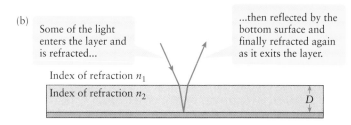

Index of refraction n_1

Index of refraction n_2

D

(c)

Those light waves that were first reflected, and those that entered the thin layer...

...leave in the same direction and interfere with each other.

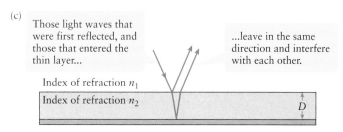

Index of refraction n_1

Index of refraction n_2

D

Figure 23-25 Interference from a thin film For clarity in this figure we've drawn light rays that reach the surface of a thin film at an angle. In our calculations we'll assume that the light hits the surface face-on.

$4/2 = 2$. This case gives constructive, not destructive, interference.) When destructive interference occurs, the two outgoing waves cancel each other out and the surface of the film appears dark.

Let's consider the case in which the incident light is normal to the surface of the thin film (that is, the light strikes the film face-on). Then the path length difference Δ_{pl} for the two waves—one that reflects off the front of the film and the other that reflects off the opaque backing—is twice the thickness of the film:

(23-15) $$\Delta_{\mathrm{pl}} = 2D$$

Constructive interference occurs when an integer number of wavelengths of the light exactly fit into this path length difference of $2D$. Destructive interference occurs when an odd number of half-wavelengths fit into the distance $2D$.

However, the wavelength of light inside the film is not the same as the wavelength outside the film. Recall from Section 23-2 that the wavelength of light in a medium with index of refraction n is

(23-8) $$\lambda = \frac{\lambda_{\mathrm{vacuum}}}{n}$$

As in Figure 23-25, let's say that the material outside the film has index of refraction n_1, and the material of which the film is made has index of refraction n_2. Then Equation 23-8 tells us that the wavelengths in the two materials are

$$\lambda_1 = \frac{\lambda_{\mathrm{vacuum}}}{n_1} \text{ outside the film}$$

$$\lambda_2 = \frac{\lambda_{\mathrm{vacuum}}}{n_2} \text{ inside the film}$$

Comparing these two, we see that

(23-16) $$\lambda_2 = \frac{n_1 \lambda_1}{n_2}$$

We now know everything we need to determine how the light reflected from the outer surface of the thin film interferes with the light that enters the film and is reflected from the inner surface. Constructive interference occurs when the path difference equals an integer number of wavelengths λ_2 (the wavelength of light inside the film):

(23-17) $$2D = m\lambda_2 = m\frac{n_1 \lambda_1}{n_2}, \quad m = 1, 2, 3, \ldots$$

(constructive interference, thin film with an opaque backing)

The case $m = 1$ in Equation 23-17 tells us the minimum thickness of a thin film that results in constructive interference when light of wavelength λ_1 strikes the surface face-on:

(23-18) $$D_{\min} = \frac{n_1 \lambda_1}{2n_2}$$

(minimum thickness for constructive interference, thin film with an opaque backing)

Destructive interference occurs when the path difference equals an odd number of one-half the wavelength λ_2 inside the film:

(23-19) $$2D = (2m - 1)\frac{\lambda_2}{2} = (2m - 1)\frac{n_1 \lambda_1}{2n_2}, \quad m = 1, 2, 3, \ldots$$

(destructive interference, thin film with an opaque backing)

The case $m = 1$ in Equation 23-19 tells us the minimum thickness of a thin film that results in destructive interference when light of wavelength λ_1 strikes the surface face-on:

$$D_{min} = \frac{n_1 \lambda_1}{4n_2} \qquad (23\text{-}20)$$

(minimum thickness for destructive interference,
thin film with an opaque backing)

The *tapetum lucidum* of an animal's eye appears shiny because it preferentially reflects certain wavelengths—to be specific, those that satisfy Equation 23-17, where n_2 is the index of refraction of the material of which the *tapetum lucidum* is made. This gives rise to the phenomenon of *eyeshine* that you can see in Figure 23-1a. The *tapetum lucidum* for the cat in that photo preferentially reflects green light because an integer number of wavelengths of that color fit into the path difference (twice the thickness of the *tapetum lucidum*). Other colors with other wavelengths do not satisfy that relationship perfectly, so they are not reflected as strongly. The eyes of different animals shine with different colors depending on the thickness of the *tapetum lucidum*.

The same effect explains the colors of the *Morpho* butterfly shown in Figure 23-24. The wings of *Morpho* are covered with microscopic scales that act like a thin film. The thickness of these scales is such that there is constructive interference for reflected light at wavelengths in the blue-green part of the spectrum. As a result, *Morpho* appears to glow at those wavelengths.

 Go to Interactive Exercise 23-3 for more practice dealing with films

Example 23-6 A Soapy Film

Monochromatic light that has wavelength 560 nm in air strikes a layer of soapy water, which has an index of refraction of 1.40 and rests on a bathroom tile. (a) If the layer of soapy water is 700 nm thick, does constructive interference, destructive interference, or neither occur when the light strikes the surface close to the normal? (b) What is the minimum thickness of soapy water that would result in no (or minimum) reflection from the surface?

Set Up

The situation is the same as in Figure 23-25. Interference occurs between (i) light that is reflected from the top surface of the soapy layer and (ii) light that enters the soapy layer and is eventually reflected back out. In part (a) we'll compare the given values of wavelength and film thickness to Equations 23-17 and 23-19 to decide whether the interference is constructive, destructive, or something in between. In part (b) we'll use Equation 23-20 to find the minimum thickness for destructive interference. In both parts, Equation 23-16 will help us relate the wavelength of the light in air to its wavelength in the soapy water.

Constructive interference:

$$2D = m\lambda_2 = m\frac{n_1\lambda_1}{n_2}, \quad m = 1, 2, 3, \dots \qquad (23\text{-}17)$$

Destructive interference:

$$2D = (2m - 1)\frac{\lambda_2}{2} = (2m - 1)\frac{n_1\lambda_1}{2n_2}, \quad m = 1, 2, 3, \dots \qquad (23\text{-}19)$$

Minimum thickness for destructive interference:

$$D_{min} = \frac{n_1\lambda_1}{4n_2} \qquad (23\text{-}20)$$

Wavelength in two different media:

$$\lambda_2 = \frac{n_1\lambda_1}{n_2} \qquad (23\text{-}16)$$

Solve

(a) In this situation medium 1 is air ($n_1 = 1.00$) and medium 2, of which the film is made, is soapy water ($n_2 = 1.40$). The wavelength in the soapy water is therefore shorter than in air.

Wavelength in air: $\lambda_1 = 560$ nm

Wavelength in soapy water:

$$\lambda_2 = \frac{n_1\lambda_1}{n_2} = \frac{(1.00)(560 \text{ nm})}{1.40} = 400 \text{ nm}$$

Find how many wavelengths of the wavelength λ_2 in the soapy water fit into the path length difference $\Delta_{pl} = 2D$, where $D = 700$ nm is the film thickness.

The path length difference between the waves that reflect off the top and bottom surfaces of the film is

$$\Delta_{pl} = 2D = 2(700 \text{ nm}) = 1400 \text{ nm}$$

The number of wavelengths that fit into this path length difference equals Δ_{pl} divided by λ_2:

$$\frac{\Delta_{pl}}{\lambda_2} = \frac{1400\text{ nm}}{400\text{ nm}} = 3.5 = \frac{7}{2}$$

The path length difference is an odd number of half wavelengths. We conclude that there is destructive interference between the light that reflects from the top surface of the soapy water and the light that reflects from the bottom surface (where the soapy water touches the tile).

(b) The minimum thickness required for destructive interference is such that the path length difference $2D$ is one half-wavelength, so $2D = \lambda_2/2$ and $D = \lambda_2/4$.

From Equation 23-20, the minimum thickness for destructive interference is

$$D_{min} = \frac{n_1\lambda_1}{4n_2} = \frac{(1.00)(560\text{ nm})}{4(1.40)} = 100\text{ nm}$$

Alternatively, since $\lambda_2 = n_1\lambda_1/n_2$ from Equation 23-16,

$$D_{min} = \frac{\lambda_2}{4} = \frac{400\text{ nm}}{4} = 100\text{ nm}$$

Reflect

When light of wavelength 560 nm in air strikes the soapy layer close to the normal, destructive interference occurs both when the layer is 100 nm thick (so twice the thickness is 200 nm, or 1/2 the wavelength in the soapy water) and when the layer is 700 nm thick (so twice the thickness is 1400 nm, or 7/2 the wavelength in the soapy water). For these thicknesses, reflections from the surface would be minimized, and the surface would look dark.

Destructive interference always occurs when twice the thickness of the layer is an odd multiple of one-half of the wavelength. Can you see that destructive interference would also occur if the film of soapy water were either 300 nm thick or 500 nm thick?

Figure 23-1c shows another example of thin-film interference. This film was made by dipping an open ring into soapy water, then holding the ring vertically. Some of the light that strikes the soap film is reflected from the front surface, while some passes into the film before being reflected at the back surface. When these two light waves recombine, the wavelength of light (the color) that results in constructive interference appears bright. The thickness of the film increases from top to bottom, so the path difference for the two waves is different at different places on the film. That's why the brightest color you see (corresponding to the wavelength for which there is constructive interference) is different at different positions. The thickness of the film is relatively constant *across* the film, however, so the colors appear in bands.

Note that the very top of the soap film in Figure 23-1c appears dark. That may come as a surprise because the top of the film is very thin (far thinner than a wavelength of visible light) so the path difference between light that reflects from the front and back surfaces should be negligible. As a result, there should be constructive interference at the top of the film, and the top should appear bright rather than dark. Why is our prediction incorrect?

To see the explanation, we need to go back to our discussion in Chapter 13 of how waves are reflected from a boundary. In Section 13-6 we saw that a wave pulse on a rope is inverted as it reflects from a fixed boundary. This inversion is equivalent to a phase shift of one-half of a wavelength; the position along the wave that arrived at the boundary as a peak has been reflected as a trough. In general, any wave is inverted when reflected, either partially or completely, from a boundary going from a material of higher wave speed to one of lower wave speed. (For the rope, the wave speed is zero on the other side of the boundary, which is definitely lower than the speed along the rope.) So when light traveling in air is partially reflected from the surface of the soap film, the reflected light wave is inverted. This does not happen, however, to the light that enters the soap film and is reflected from the back surface. At that boundary, light is moving from a medium of lower speed (the soap film) to one of higher speed (air), so no inversion occurs. Thus, even if there were no path length difference between the light wave that reflects from the front surface than the one that reflects from the back surface, these two waves would be 180° out of phase because one is inverted upon reflection but the other is not. This would result in destructive interference. That's just what we see at the top of the soap film in Figure 23-1c, where the film is very thin compared to the wavelength of the light. This explains the dark band across the top of the film.

Thanks to the additional half-wavelength phase shift for a film like that in Figure 23-1c, Equation 23-17 no longer tells us the condition for constructive interference and Equation 23-19 no longer tells us the conditions for destructive interference. Instead, the roles of these equations are reversed: Equation 23-17 is now the condition for *destructive* interference, and Equation 23-19 is now the condition for *constructive* interference.

Example 23-7 Reducing the Reflection

The glass in an LCD display is sometimes given a thin coating to reduce glare. Reflection of light incident on the display, particularly light that strikes close to the normal to the plane of the display, is minimized by means of thin-film interference. Zirconium acrylate, a plastic doped with zirconium that has an index of refraction of 1.54, is often used in antireflective coatings. What is the minimum thickness of zirconium acrylate that will accomplish the desired reduction in reflection for light that has wavelength 560 nm in air? Note that the index of refraction of zirconium acrylate is higher than that of glass.

Set Up

We want the light reflected from the surface of the coating to interfere destructively with the light reflected from the zirconium acrylate-to-glass boundary. This requires that when these two light waves recombine they are shifted by an odd number of half-wavelengths. One half-wavelength shift occurs because the light in air is inverted when it reflects off the surface of the zirconium acrylate, but the light in zirconium acrylate is not inverted when it reflects off the glass. (That's because light travels more slowly in zirconium acrylate than in air, but faster in glass than in zirconium acrylate.) Any additional shift arises from the path difference of $2D$ between the two waves. For the total shift to be equivalent to an odd number of half-wavelengths, the shift due to the path difference must be an *integer* number of wavelengths. The minimum thickness corresponds to $2D$ equal to one wavelength λ_2, where λ_2 is the wavelength in the zirconium acrylate as given by Equation 23-16.

Wavelength in two different media:

$$\lambda_2 = \frac{n_1\lambda_1}{n_2} \qquad (23\text{-}16)$$

Solve

First calculate the wavelength of the light in zirconium acrylate.

We are given the wavelength in air ($n_1 = 1.00$): $\lambda_1 = 560$ nm. The wavelength in zirconium acrylate ($n_2 = 1.54$) is given by Equation 23-16:

$$\lambda_2 = \frac{n_1\lambda_1}{n_2} = \frac{(1.00)(560 \text{ nm})}{1.54} = 364 \text{ nm}$$

The minimum film thickness $D_{\min}$ for destructive interference is such that $2D_{\min}$ equals λ_2. Use this to solve for $D_{\min}$.

The condition for the minimum thickness that leads to destructive interference is

$$2D_{\min} = \lambda_2 = 364 \text{ nm}$$

$$D_{\min} = \frac{364 \text{ nm}}{2} = 182 \text{ nm}$$

Reflect

For most people, light sensitivity peaks in the range of 555 nm to 565 nm, which we perceive as yellow. Antireflective coatings are usually optimized for yellow light (which includes the 560-nm wavelength we've used here) for that reason.

In this section we've emphasized interference due to light reflecting from a *thin* film. Why is it important to specify this? The explanation is that in this section we've assumed that a steady, continuous train of light waves is incident on the film. However, the light from ordinary sources such as light bulbs and the Sun is emitted in a sequence of short bursts, each of which is a segment of wave no more than a few micrometers to about a millimeter in length. This is called the *coherence length* of the light. The phase of the wave changes randomly from one burst to the next. If the thickness of the film is small compared to the coherence length, then the two waves that interfere—the light that reflects from the back of the film and the light that reflects from the front of the film—are part of the same burst, and so the phase relationships we have developed in this section (which assumed a steady train of waves) are valid. But if the thickness of the film is large compared to the coherence length, the two waves are likely to be from different wave bursts and will differ in phase by a random and rapidly changing amount. As a result, the interference between the waves will be neither always constructive nor always destructive, and any interference effects will be wiped out. That's why you won't see interference effects like those we've described in this section from a thick film like an ordinary pane of glass, which is several millimeters deep. (However, you *can* see interference effects for a glass pane if the light source is a laser. A laser produces light in a very different way from an ordinary light bulb, and the coherence length can be several meters.)

? Got the Concept? 23-6 Inversion on Reflection

Figure 23-26 shows light shining on a thin layer of oil that has an index of refraction of 1.4. The oil layer is atop a piece of glass that has an index of refraction of 1.5. On the underside of the glass is air. At which boundary or boundaries does the reflected light undergo an inversion? (a) The air–oil boundary; (b) the oil–glass boundary; (c) the glass–air boundary; (d) more than one of these; (e) none of these.

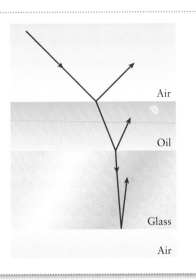

Figure 23-26 **Layers of reflection** At which boundary or boundaries does the reflected light undergo an inversion?

Take-Home Message for Section 23-6

✔ Light waves can interfere constructively or destructively depending on how the peaks and troughs of two waves align when they combine.

✔ When a single beam of light strikes a thin layer of a transparent material, some of the light is immediately reflected while some enters the layer and is reflected off its inner, lower surface. Because these two light rays travel a different distance, they may not be in phase when they recombine, resulting in interference. Whether there is destructive interference, constructive interference, or neither depends on the number of wave cycles that fit into the extra distance traveled by the light that enters the thin layer.

23-7 Diffraction is the spreading of light when it passes through a narrow opening

We saw in Section 23-2 that Huygens' principle—the notion that each point on a wave front itself acts as a source of waves—helped us explain the laws of reflection and refraction. Huygens' principle will also allow us to understand **diffraction**, in which waves tend to spread out when they pass through a narrow opening or near the sharp edge of an object.

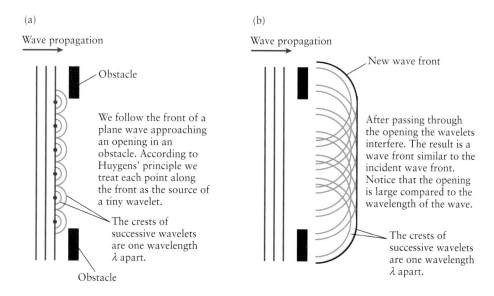

Figure 23-27 **Diffraction I: A wide opening** Huygens' principle predicts that if the width of the opening is large compared to the wavelength, most of the wave continues straight ahead through the opening. A slight amount diffracts to the sides.

(a)

Wave propagation

Obstacle

We follow the front of a plane wave approaching an opening in an obstacle. According to Huygens' principle we treat each point along the front as the source of a tiny wavelet.

The crests of successive wavelets are one wavelength λ apart.

Obstacle

(b)

Wave propagation

New wave front

After passing through the opening the wavelets interfere. The result is a wave front similar to the incident wave front. Notice that the opening is large compared to the wavelength of the wave.

The crests of successive wavelets are one wavelength λ apart.

Consider a wave front of a plane wave that passes through an opening in an obstacle, as in Figure 23-27a. The opening is wide compared to the wavelength of the wave. Many of the wavelets pass through the opening, as in Figure 23-27b. The resulting wave on the other side of the obstacle is mostly a new plane wave, though the ends of the wave front are curved. This means that most of the wave energy continues straight through the opening, with only a small fraction "leaking" to the sides.

Something rather different happens when the opening is comparable in size to or smaller than the wavelength. That's the situation in Figure 23-28a, in which the opening is much narrower than in Figure 23-27a. (It's not necessary for the opening to be exactly the same size as the wavelength, or smaller than the wavelength, or to bear any particular relationship to the wavelength other than the two being *about* the same size.) Because the opening is narrow, only a very few of the wavelets that comprise each wave front pass through it. And because so few wavelets get through, they cannot reproduce the straight wave front that was incident on the opening. After passing through the narrow opening, the wave spreads out; it has undergone diffraction (Figure 23-28b). Diffraction is also present in Figure 23-27b, as shown by the waves that "leak" to the side of the opening, but to a much smaller extent.

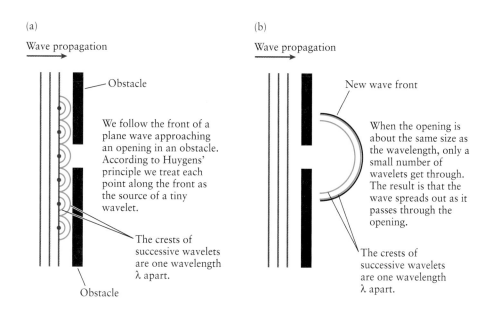

(a)

Wave propagation

Obstacle

We follow the front of a plane wave approaching an opening in an obstacle. According to Huygens' principle we treat each point along the front as the source of a tiny wavelet.

The crests of successive wavelets are one wavelength λ apart.

Obstacle

(b)

Wave propagation

New wave front

When the opening is about the same size as the wavelength, only a small number of wavelets get through. The result is that the wave spreads out as it passes through the opening.

The crests of successive wavelets are one wavelength λ apart.

Figure 23-28 **Diffraction II: A narrow opening** If the width of the opening is comparable to the wavelength, the wave spreads out substantially after exiting the opening. (Compare Figure 23-27.)

Figure 23-29 **Water wave diffraction**
Compare these photographs to
Figures 23-27 and 23-28.

(a) Water waves pass through a wide opening

(b) Water waves pass through a narrow opening

Plane waves enter the opening

Plane waves enter the opening

• The width of the opening is large compared to the wavelength λ.
• Most of the wave energy continues straight ahead, so there is very little diffraction.

• The width of the opening is comparable in size to the wavelength λ.
• The wave spreads out after passing through the opening; diffraction is important.

Figure 23-29 shows these effects for water waves passing through an opening in an obstacle. If the width of the opening is large compared to the wavelength, as in Figure 23-29a, there are almost no effects of diffraction. But if the opening is comparable in size to the wavelength as in Figure 23-29b, the wave spreads out. This explains why you hear someone talking on the other side of an open door, even if you're not directly in front of it. The wavelengths of sound used in human speech are in the range of a few meters, comparable in size to the width of a typical door (about one meter). As a result sound waves emerging from a door spread out like the water waves in Figure 23-29b, making it easy to eavesdrop on conversations. However, you can't *see* through an open door if you stand to one side because the wavelengths of visible light (around 550 nm, or 5.5×10^{-7} m) are very small compared to the width of the door. So light waves passing through the door behave like the water waves in Figure 23-29a.

There's much more to diffraction than how much waves spread out after passing through an opening. To consider diffraction quantitatively, imagine that we send a beam of light of a single wavelength λ through a long, narrow opening or *slit*. The slit has width w. After passing through the slit, the light falls on a screen a distance L away (Figure 23-30). You might expect that the pattern on the screen would be a single blob of light. But as the photo in Figure 23-30 shows, what actually appears is a series of bright and dark patches called **fringes**. This **diffraction pattern** arises because the light that reaches a given spot on the screen is a superposition of

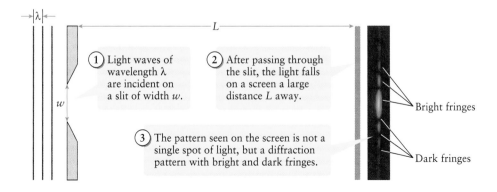

Figure 23-30 **Diffraction through a slit** A diffraction pattern arises when monochromatic light passes through a narrow slit.

① Light waves of wavelength λ are incident on a slit of width w.

② After passing through the slit, the light falls on a screen a large distance L away.

③ The pattern seen on the screen is not a single spot of light, but a diffraction pattern with bright and dark fringes.

Bright fringes

Dark fringes

Huygens wavelets from each part of the slit. At some locations, these wavelets interfere destructively; these are the locations of the dark fringes. At locations between the dark fringes, the wavelets interfere more or less constructively, so at these locations we see bright fringes.

Let's see how to determine the positions of the dark fringes. The first dark fringe is found where light waves from the upper half of the slit, of width $w/2$, and the lower half, also of width $w/2$, interfere destructively. This means that as these waves travel from the slit to the screen, the waves from one half of the slit must travel one half-wavelength farther than the waves from the other half, so the path length difference Δ_{pl} equals $\lambda/2$. We can use this to easily determine the position of the first dark fringe if we assume that the distance L to the screen is much greater than the slit width w. With this assumption, **Figure 23-31** shows that for a given position on the screen, Δ_{pl} is related to the angle θ between the normal to the slit and a line to that position:

$$\Delta_{pl} = \left(\frac{w}{2}\right)\sin\theta$$ (23-21)

> √x̄ *See the Math Tutorial for more information on trigonometry*

To find the angle for the first dark fringe, substitute $\Delta_{pl} = \lambda/2$ (the condition for destructive interference) into Equation 23-21:

$$\frac{\lambda}{2} = \left(\frac{w}{2}\right)\sin\theta$$

so

$$\sin\theta = \frac{\lambda}{w}$$ (23-22)

(first dark fringe)

There are two of these first dark fringes, one on either side of the center of the pattern (see Figure 23-31).

To see how the second dark fringe arises, imagine breaking the slit into quarters, each of width $w/4$. Destructive interference occurs when light from the first quarter arrives at the screen out of phase with light from the second quarter, and light from the third quarter arrives at the screen out of phase with light from the fourth quarter.

1. If the distance L to the screen is much greater than the slit width w, we can treat the screen as being infinitely far away. Then rays from different parts of the slit to a given point on the screen are parallel.

2. As measured from the normal to the slit, all of these rays point at an angle θ.

Δ_{pl} (shown in blue)

1st dark fringes

3. To produce the first dark fringe in the diffraction pattern, the light from the bottom half of the slit must arrive at the screen one half-cycle out of phase with the light from the top half of the slit. So the path length difference Δ_{pl} between the two halves must be equal to 1/2 of a wavelength: $\Delta_{pl} = \lambda/2$.

4. To find the angle θ for the first dark fringe, note that this right triangle has hypotenuse $w/2$ and angle θ opposite the side of length Δ_{pl}. So: $\Delta_{pl} = (w/2)\sin\theta$
$\lambda/2 = (w/2)\sin\theta$
$\sin\theta = \lambda/w$

Figure 23-31 Calculating the single-slit diffraction pattern Dark fringes are found where light from each part of the slit interferes destructively with light from another part.

The path length difference Δ_{pl} between light from adjacent quarters is given by Equation 23-21 with $w/2$ replaced by $w/4$. The condition that $\Delta_{pl} = \lambda/2$ then tells us that

$$\frac{\lambda}{2} = \left(\frac{w}{4}\right) \sin \theta$$

If we solve this for $\sin \theta$, we get

(23-23)
$$\sin \theta = \frac{2\lambda}{w}$$

(second dark fringe)

This gives a larger value for $\sin \theta$, and hence for θ, than for the first dark fringe given by Equation 23-22. For the third dark fringe the factor of 2 in Equation 23-23 is replaced by a 3, for the fourth dark fringe it is replaced by a 4, and so on. In general, the angle of the mth dark fringe is given by

Angle between the normal to the slit and the location of the mth dark fringe

Number of the dark fringe: $m = 1, 2, 3, \ldots$

Dark fringes in diffraction through a slit
(23-24)

$$\sin \theta = \frac{m\lambda}{w}$$

Wavelength of the light

Width of the slit

Equations 23-22 and 23-23 are special cases of Equation 23-24, with $m = 1$ and $m = 2$ respectively.

The middle of the central *bright* fringe (at the center of the diffraction pattern in Figure 23-30 or Figure 23-31) is where all of the waves from the slit arrive in phase, since they all travel essentially the same distance to this point. This point, which corresponds to $\theta = 0$, is where the intensity is maximum. The next bright fringe, located between the first and second dark fringes, is fainter than the central bright fringe. Roughly speaking, at this bright fringe the light from the upper third of the slit interferes destructively with the light from the middle third of the slit, canceling it out. What remains is the light from the lower third of the slit. This wave has one-third the amplitude and hence $(1/3)^2 = 1/9$ the intensity of the wave that reaches the middle of the central bright fringe. (Recall from Section 22-4 that the intensity of an electromagnetic wave is proportional to the square of the amplitude of the electric field.) Successive bright fringes are even fainter. Note that the point of greatest intensity in the central bright fringe is at its center; for the other bright fringes, the point of greatest intensity is close to (but slightly displaced from) a point halfway between the adjacent dark fringes.

Diffraction of light by a slit is compelling evidence that light is a wave. If light were a stream of Newtonian particles, like miniature billiard balls, sending the light through a narrow slit would simply produce a narrower stream. The presence of bright and dark fringes like those shown in Figures 23-30 and 23-31 can only be explained by the wave nature of light.

 Go to Interactive Exercise 23-4 for more practice dealing with diffraction

Example 23-8 Diffraction through a Slit

A green laser pointer emits light at a wavelength of 532 nm. You aim the beam from this laser at a slit 1.50 μm wide. Find the angles of the first, second, and third dark fringes in the diffraction pattern.

Set Up

We are given the wavelength λ and the slit width w, and we want to find the value of the angle θ for the $m = 1, 2,$ and 3 dark fringes. We'll use Equation 23-24 for this purpose.

Dark fringes in diffraction through a slit:

$$\sin \theta = \frac{m\lambda}{w} \quad \text{(23-24)}$$

Solve

Find the angle of the first dark fringe ($m = 1$).

We have $\lambda = 532$ nm $= 5.32 \times 10^{-7}$ m and $w = 1.50$ μm $= 1.50 \times 10^{-6}$ m. From Equation 23-24 with $m = 1$,

$$\sin \theta_1 = \frac{\lambda}{w} = \frac{5.32 \times 10^{-7}\,\text{m}}{1.50 \times 10^{-6}\,\text{m}} = 0.355$$

$$\theta_1 = \sin^{-1} 0.355 = 20.8°$$

Find the angle of the second dark fringe ($m = 2$).

From Equation 23-24 with $m = 2$,

$$\sin \theta_2 = \frac{2\lambda}{w} = \frac{2(5.32 \times 10^{-7}\,\text{m})}{1.50 \times 10^{-6}\,\text{m}} = 0.709$$

$$\theta_2 = \sin^{-1} 0.709 = 45.2°$$

Find the angle of the third dark fringe ($m = 3$).

From Equation 23-24 with $m = 3$,

$$\sin \theta_3 = \frac{3\lambda}{w} = \frac{3(5.32 \times 10^{-7}\,\text{m})}{1.50 \times 10^{-6}\,\text{m}} = 1.06$$

This equation has *no* solution! The sine of an angle cannot be greater than 1, so there is no value of θ_3 that satisfies this equation. We are forced to conclude that the diffraction pattern in this situation has a first dark fringe at $\theta_1 = 20.8°$ and a second dark fringe at $\theta_2 = 45.2°$, but there is no third dark fringe before the end of the pattern at $\theta = 90°$.

Reflect

The number of dark fringes present in the diffraction pattern of a slit depends on the relative sizes of the wavelength λ and the slit width w. We explore this further below.

Figure 23-32 shows the intensity in the diffraction pattern of a slit as a function of the angle θ. As the width of the slit is increased from $w = \lambda$ (Figure 23-32a) to $w = 4\lambda$ (Figure 23-32b) to $w = 8\lambda$ (Figure 23-32c), the pattern becomes narrower. Note that if $w = \lambda$ as in Figure 23-32a, the first dark fringe corresponds to $\sin \theta = \lambda/w = 1$ so $\theta = \sin^{-1} 1 = 90°$; there are no dark fringes at smaller angles. The light intensity is

(a) Slit width w = wavelength λ

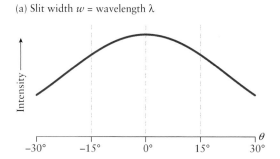

(b) Slit width w = 4 × wavelength λ

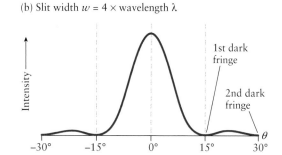

(c) Slit width w = 8 × wavelength λ

Figure 23-32 Intensity in single-slit diffraction The intensity in the diffraction pattern from a narrow slit depends on the relative size of the slit width w and the wavelength λ.

spread out very broadly over all angles, much like what happens to the water waves in Figure 23-29b. If the slit width is large compared to the wavelength, as in Figure 23-32c, most of the intensity goes into the central bright maximum centered at $\theta = 0$. In this case, the vast majority of the light emerging from the slit goes straight ahead or very nearly so. That's just like what happens to the water waves in Figure 23-29a, for which there is very little diffraction.

In this section we've concentrated on the diffraction that takes place when waves, including light waves, pass through a narrow opening. But diffraction can also happen when waves encounter an obstacle. One example is a sound wave coming from one side of your head. As we mentioned above, sound waves used in speech have wavelengths of a meter or more, which is large compared to the diameter of a typical human head. As a result, these sound waves are able to diffract around your head, so you can hear the sound with both ears. Because the sound wave must travel a greater distance to one ear than to the other, there will be a phase difference between the waves that the two ears detect. Your brain detects and processes this information about phase, and uses this to help determine the direction from which the sound is coming.

? Got the Concept? 23-7 Comparing Three Slits

The photographs in Figure 23-33 show the diffraction pattern that is created when red laser light passes through a narrow slit. The wavelength of the light is the same in all three photographs, but the width of the slit is different. Order the photographs from the widest slit to the narrowest one.

(a)   (b)   (c)

Figure 23-33 **Three diffraction patterns** Which pattern was produced by the widest slit? By the narrowest slit?

Take-Home Message for Section 23-7

✔ Waves passing through a narrow opening tend to spread out, or diffract. The diffraction is more important the smaller the size of the opening.

✔ The diffraction pattern caused by waves passing through a narrow slit has bright and dark fringes. The positions of these depend on the relative size of the wavelength and the slit width.

Figure 23-34 **Diffraction by a circular aperture I** Compare the diffraction pattern from a circular aperture with that for a narrow slit (Figure 23-30).

23-8 The diffraction of light through a circular aperture is important in optics

An important real-life application of diffraction is the case of light passing through a *circular* aperture. That's what happens whenever light enters the lens of a microscope, the circular mirror of an astronomical telescope, or the pupil of a human eye. Figure 23-34 shows the diffraction pattern produced by red laser light passing through a circular aperture. Like the diffraction pattern of a slit (Section 23-7), there are bright and dark fringes. But because the aperture is circular, the diffraction pattern has circular symmetry.

Figure 23-35 shows how we define the angle θ of a point in the diffraction pattern of a circular aperture of diameter D through which passes light of wavelength λ. For a narrow slit, we found that the diffraction pattern depends on the relative sizes of the wavelength λ and the slit width w; in the same way, the diffraction pattern of a circular

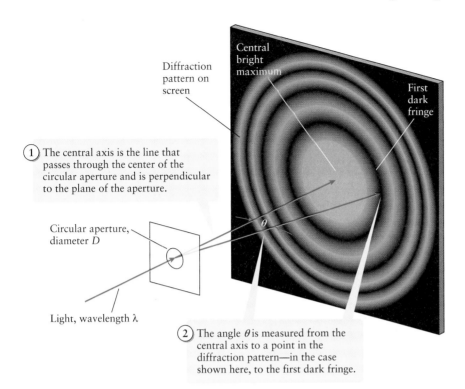

Diffraction pattern on screen

Central bright maximum

First dark fringe

(1) The central axis is the line that passes through the center of the circular aperture and is perpendicular to the plane of the aperture.

Circular aperture, diameter D

θ

Light, wavelength λ

(2) The angle θ is measured from the central axis to a point in the diffraction pattern—in the case shown here, to the first dark fringe.

Figure 23-35 **Diffraction by a circular aperture II** The size of the first dark fringe—and hence the size of the central bright maximum that it surrounds—depends on the ratio of wavelength λ to aperture diameter D.

aperture depends on the relative sizes of λ and D. In particular, the location of the center of the first dark fringe is given by

$$\sin \theta = 1.22 \frac{\lambda}{D} \qquad (23\text{-}25)$$

(circular aperture, first dark fringe)

This is similar to Equation 23-22 for the first dark fringe formed by light passing through a narrow slit of width w, with w replaced by the diameter D. The factor of 1.22 results from the different geometry of a circular opening versus a rectangular one.

Figure 23-36 shows the diffraction pattern made by two pointlike objects as the objects are moved closer and closer together. In Figure 23-36a the two objects are so far apart we see only one object and its associated diffraction pattern in the field of view. In Figure 23-36b a second object has been brought close to the first; the diffraction patterns of the two objects overlap but are still distinct. In Figure 23-36c, however, the two objects are very close together. Their diffraction patterns overlap so much that it is barely possible to tell the two objects apart. We have run into the limit on our ability to **resolve**, or optically distinguish, the two objects.

(a)   (b)   (c)

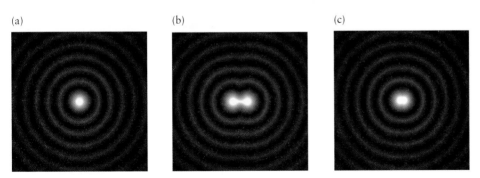

Figure 23-36 **Angular resolution** (a) Light from a single point source gives rise to a diffraction pattern when it passes through a circular aperture. (b) These diffraction patterns from two distant point sources partially overlap but are distinct. (c) At the limit of our ability to resolve two distant point sources, the diffraction patterns formed as their light passes through a circular aperture overlap and are barely distinguishable.

The nineteenth-century English physicist John William Strutt, 3rd Baron Rayleigh, proposed the following criterion for resolvability: Two distant, pointlike objects observed through a circular aperture can be resolved when the central maximum of one coincides with the center of the first dark fringe of the other. The angle θ_R that separates two point objects that are just barely resolved through a circular aperture, known as the **angular resolution** of the aperture, is then just the angle given by Equation 23-25:

Rayleigh's criterion for resolvability
(23-26)

Angle between two pointlike objects that can barely be resolved through an optical device

Wavelength of the light

$$\sin \theta_R = 1.22 \frac{\lambda}{D}$$

Diameter of the circular aperture of the device

 A physician's eye chart is just a device for measuring the value of θ_R for each of your eyes. If you have normal vision, your unaided eye can distinguish objects (such as the lines that make up the letter "E" on an eye chart) that are separated by an angle of as small as $1/60$ of a degree. So $\theta_R = (1/60)°$ for a person with normal vision. The smaller the value of θ_R, the better the resolution and the smaller the details that can be resolved.

Example 23-9 The Hubble Space Telescope

The Hubble Space Telescope (HST) has a circular aperture 2.4 m in diameter. What is the theoretical angular resolution of the HST for light of wavelength 550 nm?

Set Up
Equation 23-26 gives the angular resolution, the smallest angular separation of two objects that can be resolved as a result of diffraction effects.

Rayleigh's criterion for resolvability:

$$\sin \theta_R = 1.22 \frac{\lambda}{D} \qquad (23\text{-}26)$$

Solve
We are given $\lambda = 550$ nm and $D = 2.4$ m. We calculate θ_R from these using Equation 23-26.

From Equation 23-26,

$$\sin \theta_R = 1.22 \frac{(550 \times 10^{-9}\,\text{m})}{(2.4\,\text{m})} = 2.8 \times 10^{-7}$$

$$\theta_R = \sin^{-1}(2.8 \times 10^{-7}) = 1.6 \times 10^{-5} \text{ degree}$$

Reflect
The photograph shown here is a Hubble Space Telescope image of the minor planet Pluto and its largest moon, Charon. Pluto and Charon are separated by about 25×10^{-5} degrees in this image. They are easily resolved by HST, for which $\theta_R = 1.6 \times 10^{-5}$ degrees. By contrast, a telescope of the same diameter on Earth would have a much poorer resolution of about 0.03 degrees due to the blurring effects of the atmosphere. Such a telescope would not be able to resolve Pluto and Charon. This illustrates one important rationale for orbiting telescopes, which operate high above the atmosphere.

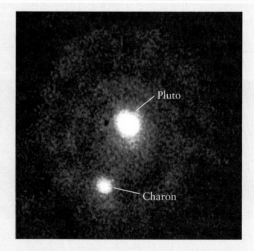

? Got the Concept? 23-8   Angular Resolution

Rank the following telescopes from best to worst angular resolution. Assume that diffraction is the only limiting factor. (a) A radio telescope with an effective diameter of 27 km that observes waves at wavelength 21 cm. (b) A telescope in orbit that has a mirror of 0.85 m diameter and that observes infrared light of wavelength 4.5 μm. (c) An inexpensive telescope for amateur astronomers with a lens of 5.0 cm diameter that observes visible light of wavelength 550 nm.

Take-Home Message for Section 23-8

✔   The angular resolution of an optical device is limited by diffraction, which blurs the images of even pointlike objects.

✔   Rayleigh's criterion states that two pointlike objects can just be resolved if the center of the bright maximum for one object coincides with the first dark fringe for the second object.

Key Terms

angular resolution	incident	ray
Brewster's angle	index of refraction	refraction
critical angle	law of reflection	resolve
diffraction	linearly polarized	Snell's law of refraction
diffraction pattern	monochromatic	thin film
dispersion	normal	total internal reflection
fringe	partially polarized	unpolarized
front	polarization	wavelet
Huygens' principle	polarizing filter	

Chapter Summary

Topic	Equation or Figure	
Speed of light in a medium: In a medium (transparent material) other than vacuum, the speed of light is less than c. This is described in terms of the index of refraction n of the material. The value of n is different for different materials. The wavelength also changes when light enters a medium.	Index of refraction of a medium Speed of light in vacuum $$n = \frac{c}{v}$$ Speed of light in the medium	(23-5)
	Wavelength of light in a medium Speed of light in vacuum Wavelength of the light in vacuum $$\lambda = \frac{c}{nf} = \frac{\lambda_{\text{vacuum}}}{n}$$ Frequency of the light Index of refraction of the medium	(23-8)

Huygens' principle, reflection, and refraction: Each point on a wave front (or wave crest) acts as a source of spherical waves called wavelets. This principle helps us explain the laws of reflection and refraction, which describe what happens when light encounters the boundary between two media. The angle of the reflected light is always equal to the angle θ_1 of the incident light, and the angle θ_2 of the refracted light is given by Snell's law.

(a) Refraction from one medium into a slower one

Medium 1, n_1

Medium 2, $n_2 > n_1$

$\theta_2 < \theta_1$:
Light bends toward the normal

(Figure 23-6a)

Angle of the incident ray from the normal   Angle of the refracted ray from the normal

$$n_1 \sin \theta_1 = n_2 \sin \theta_2 \qquad (23\text{-}6)$$

Index of refraction for the medium with the incident light   Index of refraction for the medium with the refracted light

Total internal refraction: If light in one medium reaches a boundary with a second medium of lower index of refraction ($n_1 > n_2$), total internal reflection is possible. It will only take place if the incident angle is greater than the critical angle for the two media.

Critical angle for light in medium 1 that encounters a boundary with medium 2 with a lower index of refraction

Index of refraction of medium 2

$$\theta_c = \sin^{-1}\left(\frac{n_2}{n_1}\right) \qquad (23\text{-}10)$$

Index of refraction of medium 1

 If the incident angle is greater than the critical angle, there is total internal reflection.

Dispersion: For a given material, the index of refraction depends on the frequency of the light (or, equivalently, the wavelength in vacuum). This is the reason why a prism or water droplets can break white light into its constituent colors.

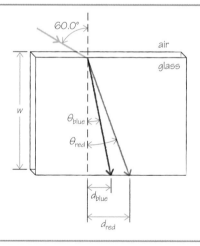

60.0°

air

glass

w

θ_{blue}

θ_{red}

d_{blue}

d_{red}

(Example 23-4)

Polarization: The polarization of a light wave is a description of the orientation of its electric field vector. In unpolarized light, this orientation changes randomly. In linearly polarized light, the orientation is in a fixed direction. Unpolarized light can become polarized by scattering from the atmosphere, by passing through a polarizing filter, or by reflection at Brewster's angle.

Brewster's angle for light in medium 1 that encounters a boundary with medium 2

Index of refraction of medium 2

$$\theta_B = \tan^{-1}\left(\frac{n_2}{n_1}\right) \qquad (23\text{-}14)$$

Index of refraction of medium 1

 If the incident angle equals Brewster's angle, the reflected light is completely polarized in the direction parallel to the surface of the boundary.

Thin-film interference: If a thin, transparent film is illuminated with monochromatic light, the light that reflects from the back surface of the film interferes with light that reflects from the front surface. If the two waves emerge in phase, the interference is constructive; if they are out of phase, it is destructive. The details of the interference depend on whether there is an inversion of the wave on each reflection.

(Example 23-7)

Diffraction: When monochromatic light illuminates a narrow slit, a pattern of bright and dark fringes results. The dark fringes appear where light from any one part of the slit interferes destructively with light from some other part of the slit, so that zero net electromagnetic wave reaches the position of the dark fringe. The narrower the width of the slit, the broader the diffraction pattern.

Angle between the normal to the slit and the location of the mth dark fringe   Number of the dark fringe: $m = 1, 2, 3, ...$

$$\sin\theta = \frac{m\lambda}{w}$$ Wavelength of the light   (23-24)

Width of the slit

Diffraction by a circular aperture: Light also diffracts when it passes through a circular aperture. This sets a fundamental limit on the angular resolution of an optical device: If two objects are closer together than an angle θ_R, it will be impossible to tell with the device whether they are two objects or a single object.

Angle between two pointlike objects that can barely be resolved through an optical device   Wavelength of the light

$$\sin\theta_R = 1.22\,\frac{\lambda}{D}$$ (23-26)

Diameter of the circular aperture of the device

Answer to What do you think? Question

(b) Honeybees use the polarization of sunlight scattered by the atmosphere to determine the position of the Sun in the sky. Light is a transverse wave, with the field vectors perpendicular to the propagation direction; the polarization of the wave tells us the particular orientation of the electric field vector $\vec{E}$ in the wave. If light were a longitudinal wave like sound waves, $\vec{E}$ would always be along the propagation direction and the idea of polarization would not apply. See Section 23-5.

Answers to Got the Concept? Questions

23-1 (c) For the first refraction, medium 1 is air and medium 2 is Plexiglas. Table 23-1 shows that the index of refraction of Plexiglas (1.49) is greater than that of air (1.00), so $n_2 > n_1$. Snell's law of refraction (Equation 23-6) tells us that in this situation $\theta_2 < \theta_1$, so the angle θ_2 that the light makes to the normal in Plexiglas is less than the angle θ_1 the light makes in air. So the light bends toward the normal as it crosses the boundary from air into Plexiglas. For the second refraction, medium 1 is Plexiglas and medium 2 is water. Since water has a lower index of refraction (1.33) than Plexiglas (1.49), in this case $n_2 < n_1$ and Snell's law tells us that in this situation $\theta_2 > \theta_1$. The angle θ_2 that the light makes to the normal in water is greater than the angle θ_1 the light makes in Plexiglas, so the light bends away from the normal as it crosses the boundary from Plexiglas into water. Can you show that the angle is 3.35° in Plexiglas and 3.76° in water?

23-2 (a) Total internal reflection at a boundary between media is possible only if the second medium has a lower index of refraction than the first medium. Here the first medium is Plexiglas, so from Table 23-1 $n_1 = 1.49$. Total internal reflection is possible for ethyl alcohol, for which $n_2 = 1.36$ is less than n_1. It is not possible for sapphire ($n_2 = 1.77$) or diamond ($n_2 = 2.42$), since both of these have an index of refraction greater than $n_1 = 1.49$.

23-3 (c) For water, like most materials, the index of refraction n is greater, and so the wave speed $v = c/n$ is slower for light of greater frequency and shorter wavelength. This means that the blue light is slowest and the red light is fastest, so the red light reaches the bottom of the pond slightly before the other colors.

23-4 (d) Once the light has passed through filter A, it will have one-half the intensity of the incident unpolarized light and will be completely polarized in the transmission direction of that filter. Filter B is set so that its transmission direction is perpendicular to that of filter A. So the angle between the polarization direction of the light that reaches filter B and the transmission direction of filter B is $\theta = 90°$. So from Equation 23-12 the intensity of the light that emerges from filter B will be the intensity of light reaching it from filter A multiplied by $\cos^2 90° = 0$. In other words, *no* light emerges from filter B.

23-5 (c) Once the light has passed through filter A, it will have one-half the intensity of the incident unpolarized light and will be completely polarized in the transmission direction of that filter. The transmission direction of filter C is at 45° to that of filter A, so from Equation 23-12 the light that emerges from filter C is reduced in intensity by an additional factor of $\cos^2 45° = (1/\sqrt{2})^2 = 1/2$. This light is polarized in the transmission direction of filter C. This light now enters filter B, which has a transmission direction at 45° to the direction of filter C. So the light that emerges from filter B is polarized in the transmission direction of filter B and has $\cos^2 45° = (1/\sqrt{2})^2 = 1/2$ the intensity of the light that reached it from filter C. So compared to the unpolarized light that was incident on filter A, the polarized light that emerges from filter B has $(1/2) \times (1/2) \times (1/2) = 1/8$ the intensity.

23-6 (d) When light is reflected from a boundary going from a material of higher wave speed to one of lower wave speed, the wave is inverted. No inversion occurs when light is reflected from a boundary where the transition is from a medium of lower speed to one of higher speed. The higher a material's index of refraction, the lower the speed of light is in that material.

Another way to state the rule is that a light wave is inverted when it is reflected from a boundary going from a material that has a lower index of refraction to one that has a higher index of refraction. So here, the speed of light is highest in air, lower in the oil, and lowest in glass. Light striking the air-to-oil boundary is therefore inverted upon reflection, as is light striking the oil-to-glass boundary. In both cases, the boundary separates a material of higher light speed from one of lower light speed. No inversion occurs at the glass-to-air boundary, however, because the speed of light in glass is lower than the speed in air.

23-7 (b), (c), (a) The narrower the slit, the more the diffracted light is spread out (see Figure 23-32). A good way to compare the three photographs is by looking at the width of the central bright maximum. The central bright maximum is widest in (a), so this is the narrowest slit. Of the other two photos, (c) has the wider central maximum, so the slit width is narrower in photo (c) than in photo (b). Hence the order from the widest to the narrowest slit is (b), (c), (a).

23-8 (b), (a), (c) The smaller the value of θ_R as given by Equation 23-26, the better the diffraction-limited angular resolution. For (a) $\lambda = 21$ cm $= 0.21$ m and $D = 27$ km $= 2.7 \times 10^4$ m, so $\sin \theta_R = 1.22\lambda/D = 9.5 \times 10^{-6}$ and $\theta_R = 5.4 \times 10^{-4}$ degrees. (Note that 27 km is not the diameter of a single telescope. To improve the angular resolution, multiple radio telescopes many kilometers apart are linked together so that they act like a single, gigantic telescope.) For (b) $\lambda = 4.5$ μm $= 4.5 \times 10^{-6}$ m and $D = 0.85$ m, so $\sin \theta_R = 6.5 \times 10^{-6}$ and $\theta_R = 3.7 \times 10^{-4}$ degrees. For (c) $\lambda = 550$ nm $= 550 \times 10^{-9}$ m and $D = 5.0$ cm $= 0.050$ m, so $\sin \theta_R = 1.3 \times 10^{-5}$ and $\theta_R = 7.7 \times 10^{-4}$ degrees. (The actual resolution would be worse due to atmospheric turbulence.) So (b) is the best, (a) is second, and (c) is worst.

Questions and Problems

In a few problems, you are given more data than you actually need; in a few other problems, you are required to supply data from your general knowledge, outside sources, or informed estimate. Interpret as significant all digits in numerical values that have trailing zeros and no decimal points. For all problems, use $g = 9.80$ m/s^2 for the free-fall acceleration due to gravity. Neglect friction and air resistance unless instructed to do otherwise.

• Basic, single-concept problem

•• Intermediate-level problem, may require synthesis of concepts and multiple steps

••• Challenging problem

SSM *Solution is in Student Solutions Manual*

Conceptual Questions

1. •What is Huygens' principle, and why is it necessary to understand Snell's law of refraction?

2. •Why do you expect the last color of the sunset to be on the red end of the visible spectrum?

3. •Explain why the Moon appears to change colors during a total lunar eclipse (when Earth's shadow completely blocks the light coming from the Sun). SSM

4. •Does the depth of a pool determine the critical angle that a light ray will have as it travels from the bottom of the pool and heads toward the air above the water? Explain your answer.

5. •Does the refraction of light make a swimming pool seem deeper or shallower? Explain your answer.

6. •Give two common uses of total internal reflection.

7. •In your own words, explain why the phenomenon of total internal reflection only occurs when light moves from a medium with a larger index of refraction toward a medium with a smaller index of refraction.

8. •Describe the physical interactions that take place when unpolarized light is passed through a polarizing filter. Be sure to describe the electric field of the light before and after the filter as well as the incident and transmitted intensities of the light source.

9. •Recently, researchers have created materials with a negative index of refraction. Explain what happens to the angle of refraction if light enters such a material from air. SSM

10. •Describe how polarized sunglasses work. Why do such sunglasses have *vertically* polarized lenses (as opposed to *horizontally* polarized lenses)?

11. •Give two or three examples of thin-film interference.

12. •A thin layer of gasoline floating on water appears brightly colored in sunlight. From where do the colors come?

13. •Does the phenomenon of diffraction apply to wave sources

other than light? Give an example if it does.

14. •Why was diffraction discovered in the lab after the theory that explains it was developed?

15. •Sunlight striking a diamond throws rainbows of color in every direction. From where do the colors come? SSM

16. •Linearly polarized light is incident at Brewster's angle on the surface of an optical medium. What can be said about the refracted and reflected beams if the incident beam is polarized (a) parallel to the plane of the surface and (b) perpendicular to the plane of the surface?

Multiple-Choice Questions

17. •Which kind of wave can refract when crossing from one medium to another with the wave having a different speed in the two media?
    A. electromagnetic waves
    B. sound waves
    C. water waves
    D. electromagnetic, sound, and water waves
    E. only electromagnetic and sound waves

18. •When light enters a piece of glass from air with an angle of θ with respect to the normal to the boundary surface,
    A. it bends with an angle larger than θ with respect to the normal to the boundary surface.
    B. it bends with an angle smaller than θ with respect to the normal to the boundary surface.
    C. it does not bend.
    D. it bends with an angle equal to two times θ with respect to the normal to the boundary surface.
    E. it bends with an angle equal to one-half θ with respect to the normal to the boundary surface.

19. •Which phenomenon would cause monochromatic light to enter the prism and follow along the path as shown in **Figure 23-37**?

Figure 23-37 Problem 19

    A. reflection
    B. refraction
    C. interference
    D. diffraction
    E. polarization

20. •Which color of light, red or blue, travels faster in crown glass?
    A. red
    B. blue
    C. their speeds are the same
    D. it depends on the material surrounding the glass
    E. blue if the glass is thin

21. •Two linear polarizing filters are placed one behind the other, so that their transmission directions are parallel to one another. A beam of unpolarized light of intensity I_0 is directed at the two filters. What fraction of the light will pass through both filters?
    A. 0
    B. $(1/2)I_0$
    C. I_0
    D. $(1/4)I_0$
    E. $2I_0$ SSM

22. •Two linear polarizing filters are placed one behind the other, so that their transmission directions form an angle of 45°. A beam of unpolarized light of intensity I_0 is directed at the two filters. What fraction of the light will pass through both?
    A. 0
    B. $(1/2)I_0$
    C. I_0
    D. $(1/4)I_0$
    E. $2I_0$

23. •A monochromatic light passes through a narrow slit and forms a diffraction pattern on a screen behind the slit. As the wavelength of the light decreases, the diffraction pattern
    A. shrinks with all the fringes getting narrower.
    B. spreads out with all the fringes getting wider.
    C. remains unchanged.
    D. spreads out with all the fringes getting alternately wider and then narrower.
    E. becomes dimmer.

24. •A monochromatic light passes through a narrow slit and forms a diffraction pattern on a screen behind the slit. As the slit width increases, the diffraction pattern
    A. shrinks with all the fringes getting narrower.
    B. spreads out with all the fringes getting wider.
    C. remains unchanged.
    D. spreads out with all the fringes getting alternately wider and then narrower.
    E. becomes dimmer.

25. •**Figure 23-38** shows two single-slit diffraction patterns. The distance between the slit and the viewing screen is the same in both cases. Which of the following is true about the width of the slits, w_a and w_b?

(a)

(b)

Figure 23-38 Problem 25

    A. $w_a > w_b$
    B. $w_a < w_b$
    C. $w_a = w_b$
    D. $w_a = (1/2)w_b$
    E. $w_a = (1/4)w_b$ SSM

Estimation/Numerical Analysis

26. •Estimate the speed of light in (a) air, (b) water, and (c) glass.

27. •Estimate the range of values for the index of refraction that you will use in this class.

28. •Estimate the time required for light to travel from (a) the Moon to Earth, (b) the Sun to Earth, and (c) Earth to Alpha Centauri (the nearest star to our solar system).

29. •Estimate the distance that light travels in (a) one second, (b) one minute, and (c) one year. SSM

30. •Estimate the range of wavelengths of visible light in water.

31. •A beam of light travels from medium 1 to medium 2 in the x–y plane. Medium 1 is found in quadrants 2 and 3; medium 2 is in quadrants 1 and 4. The beam touches each of the points in the x–y plane given in the table below. Calculate the ratio of the index of refraction of medium 2 to medium 1.

x (cm)	y (cm)	x (cm)	y (cm)
−4	−2.00	+1	+0.296
−3	−1.52	+2	+0.595
−2	−1.02	+3	+0.901
−1	−0.514	+4	+1.20
0	0		

Problems

23-1 The wave nature of light explains much about how light behaves

23-2 Huygens' principle explains the reflection and refraction of light

32. •The speed of light in a newly developed plastic is 1.97×10^8 m/s. Calculate the index of refraction.

33. ••The index of refraction for a vacuum is 1.00000. The index of refraction for air is 1.00029. Determine the ratio of time required for light to travel through 1000 m of air to the time required for light to travel through 1000 m of vacuum.

34. •Calculate the speed of light for each of the following materials:
   A. ice
   B. acetone
   C. Plexiglas
   D. sodium chloride
   E. sapphire
   F. diamond
   G. water
   H. crown glass

35. ••The speed of light in methylene iodide is 1.72×10^8 m/s. The index of refraction of water is 1.33. Through what distance of methylene iodide must light travel such that the time to travel through the methylene iodide is the same as the time required for light to travel through 1000 km of water? SSM

36. ••Light travels from air toward water. If the angle that is formed by the light beam in air with respect to the normal line between the two media is 27°, calculate the angle of refraction of the light in the water.

37. •Determine the unknown angle in each of the situations in Figure 23-39.

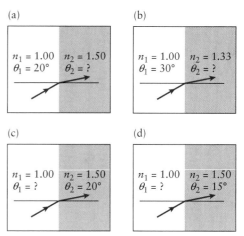

(a) $n_1 = 1.00$ $n_2 = 1.50$ $\theta_1 = 20°$ $\theta_2 = ?$

(b) $n_1 = 1.00$ $n_2 = 1.33$ $\theta_1 = 30°$ $\theta_2 = ?$

(c) $n_1 = 1.00$ $n_2 = 1.50$ $\theta_1 = ?$ $\theta_2 = 20°$

(d) $n_1 = 1.00$ $n_2 = 1.50$ $\theta_1 = ?$ $\theta_2 = 15°$

Figure 23-39 Problem 37

38. •Determine the unknown index of refraction in each of the situations in Figure 23-40.

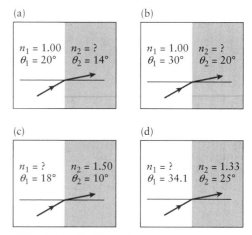

(a) $n_1 = 1.00$ $n_2 = ?$ $\theta_1 = 20°$ $\theta_2 = 14°$

(b) $n_1 = 1.00$ $n_2 = ?$ $\theta_1 = 30°$ $\theta_2 = 20°$

(c) $n_1 = ?$ $n_2 = 1.50$ $\theta_1 = 18°$ $\theta_2 = 10°$

(d) $n_1 = ?$ $n_2 = 1.33$ $\theta_1 = 34.1°$ $\theta_2 = 25°$

Figure 23-40 Problem 38

23-3 In some cases light undergoes total internal reflection at the boundary between media

39. •Calculate the critical angle for the following:
   A. Light travels from plastic ($n = 1.50$) to air ($n = 1.00$).
   B. Light travels from water ($n = 1.33$) to air ($n = 1.00$).
   C. Light travels from glass ($n = 1.56$) to water ($n = 1.33$).
   D. Light travels from air ($n = 1.00$) to glass ($n = 1.55$). SSM

40. •For each of the critical angles given, calculate the index of refraction for the optical materials that light travels out of toward air ($n = 1.00$):
   A. $\theta_c = 48.5°$
   B. $\theta_c = 47.0°$
   C. $\theta_c = 42.6°$
   D. $\theta_c = 35.0°$
   E. $\theta_c = 55.7°$
   F. $\theta_c = 38.5°$
   G. $\theta_c = 22.2°$
   H. $\theta_c = 75.0°$

41. •What is the critical angle for light traveling from sapphire to air?

42. ••What is the largest angle θ_1 that will ensure that light is totally internally reflected in the fiber-optic pipe made of acrylic ($n = 1.50$) shown in Figure 23-41?

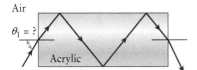

Figure 23-41 Problem 42

43. ••At what angle with respect to the vertical must a scuba diver look in order to see her friend standing on the very distant shore? Take the index of refraction of the water to be $n = 1.33$. SSM

44. ••A point source of light is 2.50 m below the surface of a pool. What is the diameter of the circle of light that a person above the water will see? Assume the water has an index of refraction of $n = 1.33$.

45. ••A block of glass that has an index of refraction of 1.55 is completely immersed in water ($n = 1.33$). What is the critical angle for light traveling from the glass to the water?

23-4 The dispersion of light explains the colors from a prism or a rainbow

46. ••For a certain optical medium, the speed of light varies from a low value of 1.90×10^8 m/s for violet light to a high value of 2.00×10^8 m/s for red light. (a) Calculate the range of the index of refraction of the material for visible light. (b) A white light is incident on the medium from air, making an angle of 30.0° with the normal. Compare the angles of refraction for violet light and red light. (c) Repeat the previous part when the incident angle is 60.0°.

47. •••A beam of light shines on an equilateral glass prism at an angle of 45° to one face (Figure 23-42a). (a) What is the angle at which the light emerges from the opposite face given that $n_{glass} = 1.57$? (b) Now consider what happens when dispersion is involved (Figure 23-42b). Assume the incident ray of light spans the spectrum of visible light between 400 nm and 700 nm (violet to red, respectively). The index of refraction for violet light in the glass prism is 1.572, and it is 1.568 for red light in the glass prism. Find the distance along the right face of the prism between the points where the red light and violet light emerge back into air. Assume the prism is 10.0 cm on a side and the incident ray hits the midpoint of the left face.

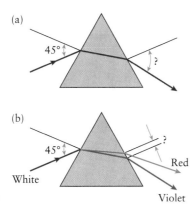

Figure 23-42 Problem 47

48. ••A light beam strikes a piece of glass with an incident angle of 45.0°. The beam contains two colors: 450 nm and an unknown wavelength. The index of refraction for the 450 nm light is 1.482. Determine the index of refraction for the unknown wavelength if the angle between the two refracted rays is 0.275°. Assume the glass is surrounded by air.

49. •••Blue light (500 nm) and yellow light (600 nm) are incident on a 12-cm-thick slab of glass as shown in Figure 23-43. In the glass, the index of refraction for the blue light is 1.545, and for the yellow light it is 1.523. What distance along the glass slab (side AB) separates the points at which the two rays emerge back into air? SSM

Figure 23-43 Problem 49

23-5 In a polarized light wave, the electric field vector points in a specific direction

50. •Unpolarized light is passed through an optical filter that is oriented in the vertical direction. If the incident intensity of the light is 78 W/m², what are the polarization and intensity of the light that emerges from the filter?

51. •What angle(s) does vertically polarized light make relative to a polarizing filter that diminishes the intensity of the light by 25%? SSM

52. ••Light that passes through a series of three polarizing filters emerges from the third filter horizontally polarized with an intensity of 250 W/m². If the polarization angle between the filters increases by 25° from one filter to the next, find the intensity of the incident beam of light, assuming it is initially unpolarized.

53. ••Vertically polarized light that has an intensity of 400 W/m² is incident on two polarizing filters. The first filter is oriented 30.0° from the vertical while the second filter is oriented 75.0° from the vertical. Predict the intensity and polarization of the light that emerges from the second filter.

54. •What is Brewster's angle when light in water is reflected off a glass surface? Assume $n_{water} = 1.33$ and $n_{glass} = 1.55$.

55. •The critical angle between two optical media is 60.0°. What is Brewster's angle at the same interface between the two media?

56. •(a) What would Brewster's angle be for reflections off the surface of water when the light source is beneath the surface? (b) Compare that answer to the angle for total internal reflection when light starts in water and reflects off air.

57. ••At what angle θ above the horizontal is the Sun when a person observing its rays reflected off water finds them linearly polarized along the horizontal (Figure 23-44)? SSM

Figure 23-44 Problem 57

23-6 Light waves reflected from the layers of a thin film can interfere with each other, producing dazzling effects

58. ●●A ray of light is reflected from a thin film back into air. If the film is actually a coating on a slab of glass ($n_{film} < n_{glass}$), describe the phase changes that the reflected ray undergoes (a) as it reflects off the front surface of the film and (b) as it reflects off the back surface of the film (the film–glass interface).

59. ●What is the wavelength of red light (700 nm in air) when it is inside a glass slab with $n = 1.55$?

60. ●●When white light illuminates a thin film with normal incidence, it strongly reflects both indigo light (450 nm in air) and yellow light (600 nm in air) (Figure 23-45). Calculate the minimum thickness of the film if it has an index of refraction of 1.28 and it sits atop a slab of glass that has $n = 1.50$.

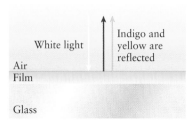

Figure 23-45 Problem 60

61. ●●When white light illuminates a thin film normal to the surface, it strongly reflects both blue light (500 nm in air) and red light (700 nm in air) (Figure 23-46). Calculate the minimum thickness of the film if it has an index of refraction of 1.35 and it "floats" on water with $n = 1.33$. SSM

Figure 23-46 Problem 61

62. ●●A soap bubble is suspended in air. If the thickness of the soap is 625 nm and both blue light (500 nm in air) and red light (700 nm in air) are *not* observed to reflect from the soap film, what is the index of refraction of the thin film?

63. ●●A thin film of cooking oil ($n = 1.38$) is spread on a puddle of water ($n = 1.33$). What are the minimum and the next three thicknesses of the oil that will strongly reflect blue light having a wavelength in air of 518 nm?

64. ●●What is the minimum thickness of a nonreflective coating of magnesium chloride ($n = 1.39$) so that no light centered around 550 nm in air will reflect back off a glass lens ($n = 1.56$)?

65. ●●Water ($n = 1.33$) in a shallow pan is covered with a thin film of oil that is 450 nm thick and has an index of refraction of 1.45. What visible wavelengths will *not* be present in the reflected light when the pan is illuminated with white light and viewed from straight above? SSM

23-7 Diffraction is the spreading of light when it passes through a narrow opening

66. ●Light that has a wavelength of 550 nm is incident on a single slit that is 10.0 μm wide. Determine the angular location of the first three dark fringes that are formed on a screen behind the slit.

67. ●Light that has a wavelength of 475 nm is incident on a single slit that is 800 nm wide. Calculate the angular location of the first three dark fringes that are formed on a screen behind the slit.

68. ●What is the highest order dark fringe that is found in the diffraction pattern for light that has a wavelength of 633 nm and is incident on a single slit that is 1500 nm wide?

69. ●The highest order dark fringe found in a diffraction pattern is 6. Determine the wavelength of light that is used with the single slit that has a width of 3500 nm.

70. ●When blue light ($\lambda = 500$ nm) is incident on a single slit, the central bright spot has a width of 8.75 cm. If the screen is 3.55 m distant from the slit, calculate the slit width.

71. ●●A He–Ne laser illuminates a narrow, single slit that is 1850 nm wide. The first dark fringe is found at an angle of 20.0° from the central peak. Determine the wavelength of the light from the laser. SSM

72. ●●Yellow light that has a wavelength of 625 nm produces a central maximum peak that is 24.0 cm wide on a screen that is 1.58 m from a single slit. Calculate the width of the slit.

23-8 The diffraction of light through a circular aperture is important in optics

73. ●Light from a helium–neon laser with a wavelength of 633 nm passes through a 0.180-mm-diameter hole and forms a diffraction pattern on a screen 2.0 m behind the hole. Calculate the diameter of the central maximum.

74. ●**Biology** The average pupil is 5.0 mm in diameter, and the average normal-sighted human eye is most sensitive at a wavelength of 555 nm. What is the eye's angular resolution in radians?

75. ●**Astronomy** The telescope at Mount Palomar has an objective mirror that has a diameter of 508 cm. What is the angular limit of resolution for 560-nm light in degrees and radians?

76. ●**Astronomy** The Hubble Space Telescope has a diameter of 2.4 m. What is the angular limit of resolution due to diffraction when a wavelength of 540 nm is viewed?

77. ●The distance from the center of a circular diffraction pattern to the first dark ring is 15,000 wavelengths on a screen that is 0.85 m away. What is the size of the aperture? SSM

78. ●●**Biology** Assume your eye has an aperture diameter of 3.00 mm at night when bright headlights are pointed at it. At what distance can you see two headlights separated by 1.50 m as distinct? Assume a wavelength of 550 nm, near the middle of the visible spectrum.

General Problems

79. ●●One way of describing the speed of light in an optical material is to specify the ratio of the time that is required for light to travel through a vacuum to the time required for light to travel through the same length of the optical material. For example, if light travels through a material in 150% of the time for light to travel through a vacuum, the speed of light in the material would be $2/3 = 1/1.5$ that in a vacuum. Complete the table by giving the speed of light and the index of refraction

for each of the following optical materials, listed with the corresponding percentage.

Optical material with percentage of time required for light to pass through compared to an equal length of vacuum	Speed of light	Index of refraction
100%		
125%		
150%		
200%		
500%		
1000%		

80. ••(a) Determine the index of refraction for medium 2 if the distance between points B and C in Figure 23-47 is 0.75 cm. Assume the index of refraction in medium 1 is 1.00. (b) Suppose $n_2 = 1.55$. Calculate the distance between points B and C.

Medium 1
$n_1 = 1.00$

45°

Medium 2 A
$n_2 = ?$

2 cm

B   C

Figure 23-47 Problem 80

81. ••Prove that in the case where there are more than two optically different media sandwiched together, with air on the left and air on the right, the angle at which light returns to air is independent of the indices of refraction of the interior media (Figure 23-48). In other words, the refraction angle, θ_n, is *only* dependent on n_1, θ_1, and n_i (not n_2, n_3, n_4, . . .).

n_1 n_2 n_3 n_4 n_5 $\cdots$ n_i n_1

θ_1

Air   Air

θ_i

Figure 23-48 Problem 81

82. ••One of the world's largest aquaria is the Monterey Bay Aquarium. The viewing wall is made of acrylic and is 0.33 m thick, and the tank holds 1.2 million gallons of water (Figure 23-49). If a ray of light is directed into the plastic from air at an angle of 40°, calculate the angle that the ray will make (a) when it enters the plastic and (b) when it enters the seawater. The indices of refraction for air, acrylic, and seawater are listed on the figure.

Air   Acrylic   Seawater

1.00   1.50   1.37

40°

Figure 23-49 Problem 82

83. ••A flat glass surface ($n = 1.54$) has a layer of water ($n = 1.33$) of uniform thickness directly above the glass. At what minimum angle of incidence must light in the glass strike the glass–water interface for the light to be totally internally reflected at the water–air interface? SSM

84. •••Light rays fall normally on the vertical surface of a glass prism ($n = 1.55$) as shown in Figure 23-50. (a) What is the largest value of θ such that the ray is totally internally reflected at the slanted face? (b) Repeat the calculation if the prism is immersed in water with $n = 1.33$.

θ

Figure 23-50 Problem 84

85. ••The object in Figure 23-51 is a depth $d = 0.85$ m below the surface of clear water. (a) How far from the end of the dock, distance D in the figure, must the object be if it cannot be seen from any point on the end of the dock? The index of refraction of water is 1.33. (b) If you could change the index of refraction of the water, how would you change it so that the object could be seen at any distance from the dock?

Dock

D

$d = 0.85$ m

Water ($n = 1.33$)

Object

Figure 23-51 Problem 85

86. ••The polarizing angle for light that passes from water ($n = 1.33$) into a certain plastic is 61.4°. What is the critical angle for total internal reflection of the light passing from the plastic into air?

87. •••A baseball is hit into a round pool of water that is 4.00 m deep and 17.0 m across (Figure 23-52). It lands right in the center of the pool. A large round raft shaped like a lily pad is floating in the pool, concentrically on top of the location of the ball. What minimum diameter must the raft have in order to completely obscure the ball from sight? Assume that water has an index of refraction of 1.33.

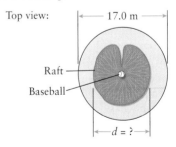

Top view: 17.0 m

Raft

Baseball

$d = ?$

Side view: $d = ?$

4.00 m

17.0 m

Figure 23-52 Problem 87

88. ••A glass lens that has an index of refraction equal to 1.57 is coated with a thin layer of transparent material that has an index of refraction equal to 2.10. If white light strikes the lens at near-normal incidence, light of wavelengths 495 nm in air and 660 nm in air are absent from the reflected light. What is the thinnest possible layer of material for which this can be accomplished?

89. ••Unpolarized light of intensity 100 W/m² is incident on two ideal polarizing sheets that are placed with their transmission axes perpendicular to each other. An additional polarizing sheet is then placed between the two, with its transmission axis oriented at 30° to that of the first. (a) What is the intensity of the light passing through the stack of polarizing sheets? (b) What orientation of the middle sheet enables the three-sheet combination to transmit the greatest amount of light? SSM

90. ••Unpolarized light that has an intensity of 850 W/m² is incident on a series of polarizing filters as shown in Figure 23-53. If the intensity of the light after the final filter is 75 W/m², what is the orientation of the second filter relative to the x axis? *Hint*: $\cos(90 - \theta) = \sin\theta$ and $2\sin\theta\cos\theta = \sin 2\theta$.

Figure 23-53 Problem 90

91. ••A thin film of soap solution ($n = 1.33$) has air on either side and is illuminated normally with white light. Interference minima are visible in the reflected light only at wavelengths of 400, 480, and 600 nm in air. What is the minimum thickness of the film?

92. ••A brass sheet has a thin slit scratched in it. At room temperature (22.0 °C) a laser beam is shined on the slit and you observe that the first dark diffraction spot occurs at ± 25.0° on either side of the central maximum. The brass sheet is then immersed in liquid nitrogen at 77.0 K until it reaches the same temperature as the nitrogen. It is removed and the same laser is shined on the slit. At what angle will the first dark spot now occur? Consult Table 14-1 for the thermal properties of brass.

93. ••A wedge-shaped air film is made by placing a small slip of paper between the edges of two thin plates of glass 12.5 cm long. Light of wavelength 600 nm in air is incident normally on the glass plates. If interference fringes with a spacing of 0.200 mm are observed along the plate, how thick is the paper? This form of interferometry is a very practical way of measuring small thicknesses. SSM

94. ••A thin layer of SiO, having an index of refraction of 1.45, is used as a coating on certain solar cells. The refractive index of the cell itself is 3.5. (a) What is the minimum thickness of the coating needed to cancel visible light of wavelength 400 nm in the light reflected from the top of the coating in air? Are any other visible wavelengths also canceled? (b) Suppose that technological limitations require you to make the coating 3.0 times as thick as in part (a). Which, if any, visible wavelengths in the reflected light will be canceled in air and which, if any, will be reinforced?

95. ••You want to coat a pane of glass that has an index of refraction of 1.54 with a 155-nm-thick layer of material that has an index of refraction greater than that of the glass. The purpose of the coating is to cancel light reflected off the top of the film having a wavelength (in air) of 550 nm. The coating material is very expensive, so you want to use the thinnest possible layer. (a) What should be the index of refraction of the coating? (b) If, due to technological difficulties, you cannot achieve a uniform coating at the desired thickness, what are the next three thicknesses of the coating you could use?

96. ••Two point sources of light each of which has a wavelength of 500 nm are photographed from a distance of 100 m using a camera with a 50.0-mm focal length lens. The camera aperture is 1.05 cm in diameter. What is the minimum separation of the two sources if they are to be resolved in the photograph, assuming the resolution is diffraction limited?

97. ••In 2009, researchers reported on evidence that a giant tsunami had hit the eastern coast of the Mediterranean Sea (present-day Lebanon and Israel) around 1600 BCE, causing huge damage to the civilizations located there. It is believed that the tsunami was caused by the eruption of the Thera volcano near the island of Crete. The waves would have passed through the 100-mile-wide opening between Crete and Rhodes, which would cause them to diffract and spread out. Satellite observations of tsunamis show that the waves measure about 250 mi from a crest to the adjacent trough, and the time between successive crests is typically 60 min. (a) How fast do tsunami waves travel? (b) How long after the eruption of Thera would the tsunami reach the eastern shore of the Mediterranean Sea, 600 mi from Thera? (c) For these waves, could we apply the formula $w \sin\theta = m\lambda$ to find the angles at which the waves cancel after passing through the 100-mile "slit" between Crete and Rhodes? Explain why or why not. SSM

98. ••**Biology** The pupil (the opening through which light enters the lens) of a house cat's eye is round under low light but ciliary muscles narrow it to a thin vertical slit in very bright light. Assume that bright light of wavelength 550 nm in air is entering the eye perpendicular to the lens and that the pupil has narrowed to a slit that is 0.500 mm wide. What are the three smallest angles on either side of the central maximum at which no light will reach the cat's retina (a) if we imagine the eye is filled with air, and (b) if we take into consideration that in reality the eye is filled with a fluid having index of refraction of approximately 1.4? (c) Would the cat be aware of the pattern of alternating dark and light fringes? Why or why not?

99. ••If you peek through a 0.75-mm-diameter hole at an eye chart, you will notice a decrease in visual acuity. Calculate the angular limit of resolution if the wavelength is taken as 575 nm. Compare the result to a 4-mm pupil of the eye that has an angular resolution of 1.75×10^{-4} rad.

100. ••**Biology** The pupil of the eye is the circular opening through which light enters. Its diameter can vary from about 2.0 mm to about 8.0 mm to control the intensity of the light reaching the retina. (a) Calculate the angular resolution, θ_R, of the eye for light that has a wavelength of 550 nm in both bright light and dim light. In which light can you see more sharply, dim or bright? (b) You probably have noticed that when you squint, objects that were a bit blurry suddenly become somewhat clearer. In light of your results in part (a), explain why squinting helps you see an object more clearly.

101. ••**Biology** Under bright light, the pupil of the eye (the circular opening through which light enters) is typically 2.0 mm in diameter. The diameter of the eye is about 25 mm. Suppose you are viewing something with light of wavelength 500 nm. Ignore the effect of the lens and the vitreous humor in the eye. (a) At what angles (in radians and degrees) will the first three diffraction dark rings occur on either side of the central bright spot on the retina at the back of the eye? (b) Approximately how far (in millimeters) from the central bright spot would the dark rings in part (a) occur? (c) Explain why we do not actually observe such diffraction effects in our vision.

102. •••**Astronomy** Sometime around 2022, astronomers at the European Southern Observatory hope to begin using the E-ELT (European Extremely Large Telescope), which is planned to have a primary mirror 42 m in diameter. Let us assume that the light it focuses has a wavelength of 550 nm. (a) What is the most distant Jupiter-sized planet the telescope could resolve, assuming it operates at the diffraction limit? Express your answer in meters and light-years. (b) The nearest known exoplanets (planets beyond the solar system) are around 20 light-years away. What would have to be the minimum diameter of an optical telescope to resolve a Jupiter-sized planet at that distance using light of wavelength 550 nm? (1 light-year = 9.461×10^{15} m)

103. ••**Astronomy** Under the best atmospheric conditions at the premium site for land-based observing (Mauna Kea, Hawaii, elevation ~4.27 km), an optical telescope can resolve celestial objects that are separated by one-fourth of a second of arc (arcsec). The viewing never gets any better than this because of atmospheric turbulence, which makes the images jitter.

(a) What minimum diameter aperture is necessary to provide arcsec resolution due to diffraction? (b) Is there ever any point in building a telescope much bigger than this? Explain your answer. SSM

104. ••**Astronomy** The Herschel infrared telescope, launched in 2009, made observations from 2010 to 2013. Its primary mirror is 3.5 m in diameter, and the telescope focuses infrared light in the range of 55 μm to 672 μm. (a) What wavelength in its observing range will give the maximum angular resolution? What is that maximum resolution (in radians and seconds, $1° = 60'$ and $1' = 60'$)? (b) To achieve the same resolution as in part (a) using visible light of wavelength 550 nm, what should be the mirror diameter of an optical telescope? (c) What is the smallest infrared source that the Herschel infrared telescope can resolve at a distance of 150 light-years? (A light year is the distance that light travels in one year—about 9.461×10^{15} m.)

105. ••**Astronomy** The world's largest refracting telescope is at Yerkes Observatory in Williams Bay, Wisconsin. Its objective is 1.02 m in diameter. Suppose you could mount the telescope on a spy satellite 200 km above the ground. (a) Assuming that the resolution is diffraction limited, what minimum separation of two objects on the ground could it resolve? Take 550 nm as a representative wavelength for visible light. (b) Because of atmospheric turbulence, objects on the surface of Earth can be distinguished only if their angular separation is at least 1.00 arcsec. How far apart would two objects on Earth's surface be if they subtended an angle of 1.00 arcsec as measured from the satellite? Compare this with your answer to part (a).

24

Geometrical Optics

What Do You Think?

Many older adults can see distant objects clearly but must wear corrective eyeglasses to see nearby objects (for example, to read a book). Are the lenses of these eyeglasses (a) thicker at the middle, (b) thicker at the edges, or (c) of uniform thickness?

In this chapter, your goals are to:

- (24-1) Explain the importance of optical devices.
- (24-2) Describe how a plane mirror forms an image.
- (24-3) Use ray diagrams to explain how the image formed by a concave mirror depends on the position of the object.
- (24-4) Calculate the position and height of an image made by a concave mirror.
- (24-5) Explain the differences between the images made by a convex mirror and a concave mirror.
- (24-6) Calculate the position and height of an image made by a concave mirror.
- (24-7) Describe how the curved surfaces of a lens make light rays converge or diverge.
- (24-8) Calculate the focal length of a lens based on its composition and shape.

To master this chapter, you should review:

- (3-8) Calculating the length of a circular arc.
- (23-2) The law of reflection and Snell's law of refraction.

24-1 Mirrors or lenses can be used to form images

You use optical devices every time you see something. The simplest optical device is a piece of reflective material (a *mirror*) or transparent material (a *lens*) shaped so that it changes the direction of light in a regular way. Mirrors and lenses can be used to change the apparent size of objects (**Figure 24-1a**); the lens of your eye is an essential part of vision and needs to be replaced if it becomes clouded with age (**Figure 24-1b**).

To understand the physics of such optical devices, all we need are the laws of reflection and of refraction that we learned in Chapter 23 along with a little bit of geometry. We won't need to refer at all to the wave properties of light. (Indeed, much of the basic physics of mirrors and lenses was deduced before it was understood that light is a wave.) For this reason we use the term **geometrical optics** to refer to the science of mirrors and lenses.

We'll begin by considering a simple plane mirror. We'll see how the law of reflection explains the kind of image that it forms. We'll then use similar ideas to understand

This dentist uses a curved mirror to make a magnified image of a patient's tooth. He can also get a magnified view by using the lenses attached to his eyeglasses.

(a)

The human eye contains a transparent lens that helps focus images onto the retina. Many people develop cataracts as the clear lens gradually becomes cloudy. The treatment is to surgically remove the lens and replace it with an artificial one.

(b)

Figure 24-1 Mirrors and lenses Mirrors and lenses are two different devices used to form images.

the kind of images formed by a mirror with a surface that's curved either inward or outward. In contrast to mirrors, lenses use the refraction of light to form an image: Light rays can change direction when they enter a lens and again when they exit the lens. Happily, we'll find that many of the same ideas that we'll develop by considering curved mirrors apply equally well to lenses.

24-2 A plane mirror produces an image that is reversed back to front

Our visual system can detect only objects that emit or reflect light. (We can't see in the dark!) Although it's easy to find examples of luminous things, such as the Sun, a light bulb, or the screen of a mobile device, most of what we see only reflects light. As we learned in Section 23-2, a ray of light that strikes a surface always reflects in such a way that the angle of incidence equals the angle of reflection. (This is the law of reflection.) However, reflected light is usually **diffuse** because it reflects from an object's surface in many random directions. This is because most surfaces are uneven (**Figure 24-2a**).

If an object has a flat surface, however, light rays that strike that surface are all reflected in the same general direction (**Figure 24-2b**). Such a flat, reflecting surface is called a **plane mirror**, and reflections from such a surface are called specular (from the Latin word for mirror, *speculum*). Your reflection in a bathroom mirror is an example of **specular reflection**. Let's look more closely at how a plane mirror creates an image of an object.

Figure 24-3 shows how your eye and brain interpret light coming from an **object** (a term that refers to anything that acts as a source of light rays for an optical device). Some of the light rays coming from the object go to your eyes. Your brain traces those rays backward to a common origin and interprets that point as the location of the object. **Figure 24-4** shows a similar situation, except that we have added a plane mirror. Some of the light from the object strikes the mirror and is reflected toward your eye. These rays appear to be coming from a point behind the mirror, so your brain interprets the light as coming from that point. We say that the mirror has formed an **image** of the object, and this image lies behind the mirror.

As you can see in Figure 24-4, no light rays actually pass through the location of the image. For this reason, the image formed by a plane mirror is said to be a **virtual image**. We will shortly encounter some optical devices that cause light rays to bend toward each other, so that the image forms where light rays do actually meet. An image formed by light rays coming together is called a **real image**.

(a)

Light that reflects from an object's surface in many random directions is called diffuse. Uneven surfaces produce diffuse light even when the incident rays come from the same direction.

(b)

Light that reflects from a smooth surface is called specular. Light rays coming from the same general direction all reflect in the same general direction.

Figure 24-2 Diffuse and specular reflection Light reflecting from (a) an uneven surface and (b) a smooth surface.

Figure 24-3 Locating an object
When light strikes our eyes, we trace the rays of light back along straight lines to an apparent common source.

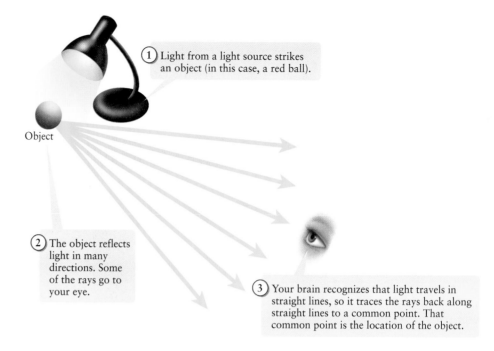

① Light from a light source strikes an object (in this case, a red ball).

Object

② The object reflects light in many directions. Some of the rays go to your eye.

③ Your brain recognizes that light travels in straight lines, so it traces the rays back along straight lines to a common point. That common point is the location of the object.

We can determine the position of the image made by a plane mirror by using a **ray diagram** like that in Figure 24-5. In such a diagram, we draw a few light rays coming from the object and show how they reflect from the mirror. We've drawn the object as a red arrow of height h_O (the **object height**) located a distance d_O (the **object distance**) from the mirror. To determine the position of the image, we must draw at least two rays that emanate from the tip of the object arrow. (We've drawn three in Figure 24-5.) When each ray strikes the mirror, it obeys the law of reflection: The angle of the reflected ray equals the angle of the incident ray. Note that the horizontal ray, which strikes the mirror face-on, is reflected back in a horizontal direction toward the tip of the object arrow.

The reflected rays diverge from each other and never actually meet. But if we trace these rays back to where they would meet, as shown by the dashed lines in Figure 24-5,

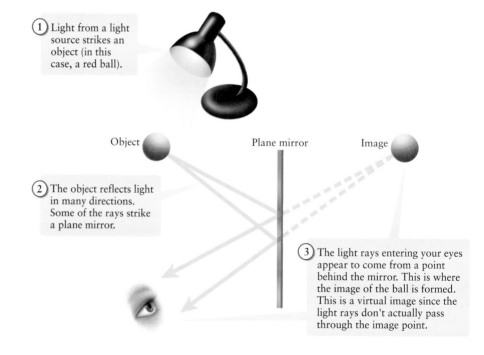

① Light from a light source strikes an object (in this case, a red ball).

Object   Plane mirror   Image

② The object reflects light in many directions. Some of the rays strike a plane mirror.

③ The light rays entering your eyes appear to come from a point behind the mirror. This is where the image of the ball is formed. This is a virtual image since the light rays don't actually pass through the image point.

Figure 24-4 Locating an image
When light from a mirror strikes our eyes, we use the same technique as in Figure 24-3 to determine the position of the image made by the mirror.

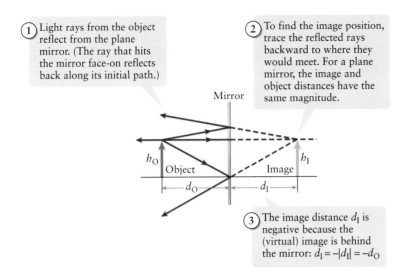

① Light rays from the object reflect from the plane mirror. (The ray that hits the mirror face-on reflects back along its initial path.)

② To find the image position, trace the reflected rays backward to where they would meet. For a plane mirror, the image and object distances have the same magnitude.

③ The image distance d_I is negative because the (virtual) image is behind the mirror: $d_I = -|d_I| = -d_O$

Mirror

h_O Object   Image h_I

d_O d_I

Figure 24-5 **A ray diagram for a plane mirror** This diagram helps us determine the position, orientation, and size of the image.

we find the position of the tip of the image arrow. The geometry of the light rays requires that the image be as far behind the front of the mirror as the object is in front of the mirror. In other words, the **image distance** d_I has the same magnitude as the object distance d_O. We'll use the convention that a point on the reflective side of the mirror (to the left of the mirror in Figure 24-5) is at a positive distance, while a point on the back side of the mirror (to the right of the mirror in Figure 24-5) is at a negative distance. So in Figure 24-5 the object distance d_O is positive but the image distance d_I is negative. We can write the relationship between the image and object distances for a plane mirror as

The image distance is negative.   The object distance is positive.

$$d_I = -|d_I| = -d_O$$

The negative value of d_I indicates that the image is on the opposite side of the mirror from the object.

Image distance for a plane mirror
(24-1)

For example, if you stand a distance $d_O = 1.0$ m in front of a plane mirror, your image is at $d_I = -1.0$ m—that is, 1.0 m behind the mirror.

Figure 24-5 also shows that the **image height** h_I is the same as the object height h_O. We define the **lateral magnification** m as the ratio of the image height to the object height. (We will often refer to m simply as the "magnification.")

Lateral magnification   Image height

$$m = \frac{h_I}{h_O}$$

Object height

Lateral magnification
(24-2)

For a plane mirror, $h_I = h_O$, so the magnification is $m = 1$. For an optical device that results in magnification greater than 1, the image is larger than the object. Such a device is commonly called a *magnifier*; it forms a magnified image of the object. When m is less than one, the image formed by the optical device is smaller than the object. As we'll see in later sections, a curved mirror can form an image that is either larger or smaller than an object placed in front of it.

Go to Picture It 24-1 for more practice dealing with mirrors

> **! Watch Out!** **The image formed by a plane mirror appears *behind* the mirror.**
>
> The image does not form "on" a plane mirror, but rather behind it. This is evident from the ray diagrams in Figure 24-5. But if this diagram doesn't convince you, you can prove it to yourself by taping a bit of paper to a plane mirror, then looking at your reflection in the mirror from about 1 m away.
>
> You'll find it difficult, likely impossible, to focus your eyes on both your image in the mirror and the piece of paper at the same time. That's because your image in the mirror is twice as far from your eyes as the paper on the surface of the mirror. The image is behind the mirror, not on it.

> **! Watch Out!** **The image formed by a plane mirror is reversed back to front, *not* left to right.**
>
> It's a common misconception that your image in a plane mirror is reversed left to right. A better description is that your image is reversed back to front. As an example, in Figure 24-6 a rectangular box *ABCDEFGH* sits in front of a plane mirror, making an image *A'B'C'D'E'F'G'H'*. Note that the face *A'B'C'D'* of the image has the same orientation as the face *ABCD* of the object and is the same distance from the mirror; the same is true of the face *E'F'G'H'* of the image and the corresponding face *EFGH* of the object. You can see that the net result is that the image is identical to the object but flipped from back to front.
>
>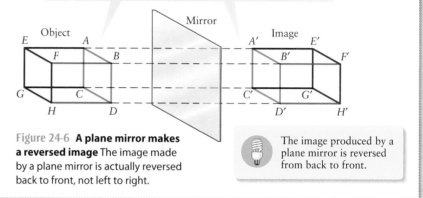
>
> Each point on the image behind the mirror is directly opposite the corresponding point on the object in front of the mirror: *A'* opposite *A*, *B'* opposite *B*, and so on.
>
> **Figure 24-6 A plane mirror makes a reversed image** The image made by a plane mirror is actually reversed back to front, not left to right.
>
> The image produced by a plane mirror is reversed from back to front.

> **? Got the Concept? 24-1** **See You, See Me I**
>
> You look into a mirror hanging near the corner of a hallway and see the eyes of someone standing around the corner.
>
> Is she able to see you? (a) Yes; (b) no; (c) not enough information given to decide.

> **? Got the Concept? 24-2** **See You, See Me II**
>
> You look into a mirror hanging near the corner of a hallway and see the right hand of someone standing around the
>
> corner but not his eyes. Is he able to see you? (a) Yes; (b) no; (c) not enough information given to decide.

Take-Home Message for Section 24-2

✔ When light rays coming from the same general direction hit a plane mirror, they tend to be reflected in the same general direction.

✔ If an object is placed in front of a plane mirror, the image is as far behind the mirror as the object is in front.

The image is the same size as the object, but reversed from back to front.

✔ A plane mirror makes a virtual image; the light rays coming from the image do not actually pass through the image position.

24-3 A concave mirror can produce an image of a different size than the object

Figure 24-7 shows a jalapeño pepper placed in front of two curved mirrors. The mirror in Figure 24-7a is **convex** (its reflective surface is curved outward) and produces an image that is smaller than the object. The mirror in Figure 24-7b is **concave** (its reflective surface

(a) Convex mirror

(b) Concave mirror

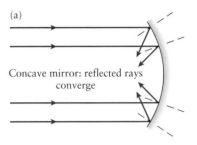

Figure 24-7 **Images from curved mirrors** A curved mirror can produce an image that is a different size than the object.

is curved inward, or "caved in") and produces an image that is larger than the object. This is in contrast to the plane mirror that we studied in Section 24-2, which always produces an image of the same size as the object. What accounts for the difference?

Figure 24-8 shows ray diagrams for parallel light rays striking two *spherical* mirrors—that is, mirrors that are shaped like a section cut from a complete sphere. Figure 24-8a shows that parallel light rays converge after they strike a concave mirror, while Figure 24-8b shows that parallel light rays diverge after they strike a convex mirror. By comparison, parallel light rays that strike a plane mirror remain parallel after striking it (see Figure 24-2b). It's important to consider parallel light rays as we examine various types of mirrors and lenses because light rays that come from distant objects are either parallel or nearly so. The Sun's rays, for example, are essentially parallel when they strike Earth. You can see this from the crisp shadows cast by an object placed in the Sun, such as the hanging frame in Figure 24-9a. In contrast, the shadow cast by a light bulb in Figure 24-9b is fuzzy because the light rays from the light bulb are not parallel.

The concave mirror is of particular interest because it has many practical uses. For example, a bathroom mirror used for applying makeup or for shaving is concave so that it gives an enlarged image of your face. Telescopes used by professional and amateur astronomers have a large concave mirror that brings the light from distant objects to a focus, forming an image. (The dish of the radio telescope in the photograph that opens Chapter 22 is a concave mirror for radio waves. The waves are brought to a focus at a radio receiver, mounted on struts above the telescope dish.) Automobile headlights use the same principle in reverse: A light bulb is placed in front of a concave mirror, and the mirror reflects the light forward to illuminate the road ahead. In this section and the next, we'll look at the concave mirror in detail; we'll return to the convex mirror in Sections 24-5 and 24-6.

(a)

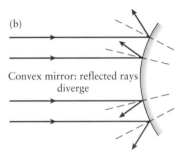

Concave mirror: reflected rays converge

(b)

Convex mirror: reflected rays diverge

Figure 24-8 **Concave and convex mirrors** (a) Parallel light rays converge after reflecting from a concave mirror, but (b) diverge after reflecting from a convex mirror.

(a)

Rays of light from the distant Sun strike the hanging frame. Notice the sharp edges on all of the shadows, including those of the strings holding the frame.

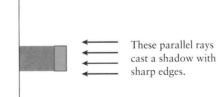

These parallel rays cast a shadow with sharp edges.

(b)

Light from a lamp strikes the frame. Because the light bulb is close to the frame, the central region of the shadow is darker than the outer regions.

These non-parallel rays cast a shadow with fuzzy edges.

Figure 24-9 **Parallel and non-parallel light rays** These photographs show the difference between light rays that are (a) parallel and (b) non-parallel.

• A concave, spherical mirror causes parallel light rays to nearly converge along the principal axis of the mirror.

• If we consider only rays close to the principal axis, or if the mirror is only a small arc of the complete sphere, the light rays all converge to essentially a single point.

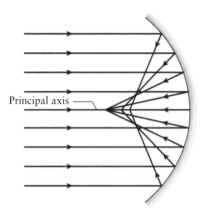

Figure 24-10 Reflection from a spherical mirror How parallel light rays behave when they strike a concave, spherical mirror.

Figure 24-10 shows what happens when a series of parallel light rays strike a concave mirror formed from a fairly large section of a sphere. The incoming rays are parallel to each other and also parallel to the **principal axis** of the mirror, the axis that runs through the center of the sphere and also the center of the mirror. The law of reflection tells us that the angles from the normal to the mirror of the incident and reflected rays are equal at the point where each ray strikes. Notice that while the reflected rays generally converge along the principal axis of the mirror, they do not converge to the exact same point. This characteristic of spherical mirrors is referred to as *spherical aberration*. Only those incoming rays that are relatively close to the axis reflect through a point close enough together for us to say that they are focused on a point. Therefore, we limit the reflective surface of the mirrors we consider to a relatively small section of a sphere. Here "relatively small" means that the size of the reflective surface is small compared to the radius of the sphere. There is no specific cut-off value; rather, the smaller the mirror compared to the radius, the more tightly focused the reflected rays will be. For the rest of this chapter, we will deal with spherical mirrors small enough that we will treat them as if all rays parallel to the principal axis are focused to a single point.

Figure 24-11 defines many of the variables we use to describe the physics of a concave, spherical mirror. The **focal point** of the mirror is the point F along the principal axis at which incident rays parallel to the principal axis converge and come to a common focus when they reflect off the mirror. Although the mirror is only a small section of a full sphere, the point C—the **center of curvature** of the mirror— corresponds to the center of that sphere, and the distance from C to any point on the mirror is r, the radius of the sphere. The distance r is also called the **radius of curvature** of the mirror. The distance from the focal point to the center of the mirror is f, the **focal length**.

A glance at Figure 24-11 suggests that the focal length is about half as great as the radius of curvature. In fact, for a concave mirror small enough that all rays parallel to the principal axis are focused at the focal point, the focal length is *exactly* half of the radius:

Focal length of a spherical mirror

(24-3)

Focal length of a spherical mirror   Radius of curvature of the mirror

$$f = \frac{r}{2}$$

Equation 24-3 says that the tighter the curve of a spherical mirror and hence the smaller the radius of curvature r, the shorter the focal length f. (We'll prove the relationship $f = r/2$ in Section 24-4.)

To see how a concave mirror forms an image, let's put our standard arrow at a point far from the mirror, as in **Figure 24-12a**. "Far" in this case means that the object distance d_O is greater than the radius of the mirror r; in other words, the base of the arrow is farther from the mirror, along the principal axis, than the center of curvature C. Now let's trace two rays of light from the tip of the arrow, as they strike and then are reflected from the mirror. The image of the arrow's tip forms where those two rays intersect. Although any two light rays that originate at the tip of the arrow and that strike the mirror will work, we chose the two used in Figure 24-12 that are particularly convenient. In **Figure 24-12b**, we trace a ray that starts parallel to the principal axis because all light rays parallel to the principal axis are reflected through the focal point. In **Figure 24-12c** we add the trace of a ray that strikes the center of the mirror. Because the normal to the surface at this point lies along the principal axis, it is easy to apply the law of reflection; the incident and reflected rays are symmetric around the axis of the mirror.

Where does the image of the base of the arrow form? The base of the arrow is on the principal axis, which is by definition the normal to the mirror's surface at the center of the mirror. So a light ray coming from the base of the arrow is reflected straight back from the center of the mirror, which means the image of the base of the arrow forms along the principal axis. **Figure 24-12d** shows the final image of the arrow. This is an **inverted image**: It's flipped upside down compared to the object. The image is also smaller than the object. Finally, the image is real; that is, it forms in front of the mirror where light rays reflected from different parts of the mirror's surface meet.

r is the radius of curvature of the full sphere.

f is the focal length.

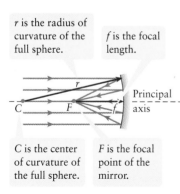

C is the center of curvature of the full sphere.

F is the focal point of the mirror.

Figure 24-11 Mirror nomenclature This drawing defines many of the variables we use to describe a concave, spherical mirror.

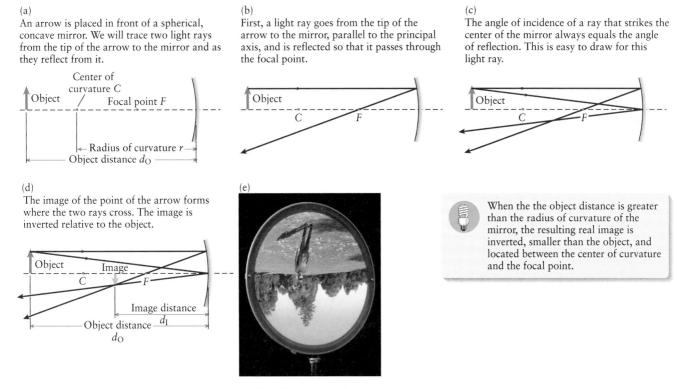

(a)
An arrow is placed in front of a spherical, concave mirror. We will trace two light rays from the tip of the arrow to the mirror and as they reflect from it.

(b)
First, a light ray goes from the tip of the arrow to the mirror, parallel to the principal axis, and is reflected so that it passes through the focal point.

(c)
The angle of incidence of a ray that strikes the center of the mirror always equals the angle of reflection. This is easy to draw for this light ray.

(d)
The image of the point of the arrow forms where the two rays cross. The image is inverted relative to the object.

(e)

When the the object distance is greater than the radius of curvature of the mirror, the resulting real image is inverted, smaller than the object, and located between the center of curvature and the focal point.

Figure 24-12 **Ray diagram for a concave mirror I** (a) A distant object in front of a concave mirror. (b), (c), (d) Locating the image of this object. (e) The image of a person standing far from a concave mirror.

Figure 24-12d shows both the object distance d_O and the image distance d_I; both distances are positive, since the object and image are both on the reflective side of the mirror. It also shows that if d_O is large, the image is closer to the mirror than the object is, so $d_I < d_O$. Note that the image distance is greater than the focal length (the distance from the mirror to the focal point F). This is how a concave mirror is used in a telescope: The object is very far away, while the image is formed very close to the mirror and is much smaller than the object. (For example, the Moon is 3.84×10^5 km distant and 1738 km in radius, but the Moon's image made by an amateur astronomer's telescope is formed only a meter or so from the mirror and is less than a centimeter in radius.) Figure 24-12e shows the inverted image of one of the authors of this book standing far away from a concave mirror.

Let's see what happens if we move the object closer and closer to the mirror. Figure 24-13a shows the arrow object placed at the center of curvature C, so the object distance equals the radius of curvature r. From Equation 24-3 the focal length $f = r/2$, so for the case shown in Figure 24-13 $d_O = r = 2f$. We trace the same two light rays as in Figure 24-12; now where the two rays meet—that is, where the image forms—is farther from the mirror. This image is the same size as the object and, as in the previous case, is both real (the light rays pass through the image) and inverted. Notice that when the object is placed at the center of curvature, the image forms at the center of curvature, so $d_I = d_O$. In Figure 24-13b one of the authors of this book is standing at the center of curvature of a concave mirror; note that his inverted image is larger than that shown in Figure 24-12e.

In Figure 24-14a we've moved the arrow closer still to the mirror, so that it sits between the center of curvature C and the focal point F. In this case the

Figure 24-13 **Ray diagram for a concave mirror II** (a) We move the object from Figure 24-12 to the center of curvature of the concave mirror. (b) The image of a person standing at the center of curvature of a concave mirror.

(a)

(b)

When the object is located at the radius of curvature of the mirror, the resulting real image is inverted, the same size as the object, and located at the radius of curvature.

(a)

Object distance d_O

Object

C   F

Image

Image distance d_I

(b)

When the object is located between the focal length and the radius of curvature of the mirror, the resulting real image is inverted, larger than the object, and located outside the radius of curvature.

Figure 24-14 Ray diagram for a concave mirror III (a) We move the object from Figures 24-12 and 24-13 to a point between the center of curvature and the focal point of the concave mirror. (b) The image of a person standing at such a point.

(a)

Object distance d_O

Object

Image   C   F

(b)

When the object is located at the focal point of the mirror, the reflected rays are parallel. These never meet and so no image is formed.

Figure 24-15 Ray diagram for a concave mirror IV (a) We move the object from Figures 24-12, 24-13, and 24-14 to the focal point of the concave mirror. (b) The image of a person standing near the focal point.

object distance is between $2f$ and f: $2f > d_O > f$. Again we've traced the same two light rays that we considered in the previous two cases. The image is still both real and inverted but has moved farther still from the mirror, with the net result that it is now farther from the mirror than the object (so $d_I > d_O$) and larger than the object. Figure 24-14b shows such an image of one of the authors of this book; compare Figures 24-12e and 24-13b.

Comparing Figures 24-12, 24-13, and 24-14 shows that the image is getting larger and moving farther from the mirror as we move the object closer to the mirror. Figure 24-15a presents the limiting case: We place the object at the focal point so that the object distance equals the focal length, or $d_O = f$. After reflection, light rays that emanate from the tip of the arrow are parallel. (This is how a concave mirror is used in an automobile headlight: The lamp itself is placed close to the focal point of the curved mirror behind it, and the reflected light forms a beam of nearly parallel light rays.) Because the reflected rays are parallel, they never meet; therefore, no image forms when the object is placed at the focal point. When the object is slightly farther from the mirror than the focal point, the image formed by the mirror is extremely large and extremely far from the mirror. The author in Figure 24-15b is standing close to the focal point of the concave mirror; there is no sharp image.

What happens when the object is placed even closer to the mirror, inside the focal point? Then the object distance is less than the focal length ($d_O < f$). As Figure 24-16a shows, in this case the reflected rays never actually meet but rather appear to meet at a point behind the mirror. This means that the image is virtual, like the image formed by the plane mirror of Section 24-2, and the image distance d_I is negative: $d_I = -|d_I| < 0$. The image is larger than the object and is an **upright image** (its orientation is the same as that of the object). That's the kind of enlarged image you see when you look in a curved bathroom mirror for shaving or applying makeup. Figure 24-16b shows

(a)

Object distance d_O

Object

C   F

Image

Image distance $d_I = -|d_O| < 0$

(b)

When the object is closer to the mirror than the focal point, the resulting virtual image is upright, larger than the object, and located behind the mirror.

Figure 24-16 Ray diagram for a concave mirror V (a) We move the object from Figures 24-12, 24-13, 24-14, and 24-15 to a point inside the focal point of the concave mirror. (b) The image of a person standing at such a point.

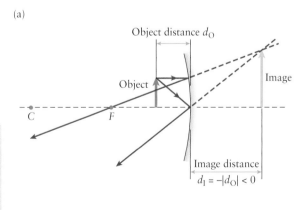

such an enlarged image of one of the authors of this book (compare Figures 24-12e, 24-13b, 24-14b, and 24-15b). The photograph in Figure 24-7b shows another such image.

So far we've investigated the formation of images by concave mirrors entirely by drawing light rays. In the following section we'll take a more quantitative look at how the position of an object placed in front of a concave mirror determines the position and size of the resulting image.

? Got the Concept? 24-3 A Soup Spoon

A shiny spoon is not so different in shape than a spherical mirror: It's concave on one side and convex on the other. Your reflection from the concave side of the spoon, when held at arm's length, is upside down and appears to float in front of the spoon. When you hold the spoon about 6 cm from your eye you see only a blur reflected in the spoon, but when you hold it about 4 cm from your eye your reflection is right side up and appears to be behind the spoon. What is the approximate focal length of the spoon? (a) More than 6 cm; (b) 6 cm; (c) between 4 and 6 cm; (d) 4 cm; (e) less than 4 cm.

? Got the Concept? 24-4 Covering a Concave Mirror

You place a light bulb oriented vertically (with its base on the bottom) just outside the focal point of a concave mirror. The resulting real image of the light bulb falls on a wall far from the mirror. This image is inverted and larger than the light bulb. If you were to paint the bottom half of the mirror black, so that light rays that strike this half of the mirror would not be reflected, the image would show (a) only the top of the light bulb; (b) only the bottom of the light bulb; (c) only the left side of the light bulb; (d) only the right side of the light bulb; (e) the entire light bulb.

Take-Home Message for Section 24-3

✔ A concave spherical mirror is in the shape of the inner surface of a section of a sphere.

✔ When an object is outside the focal point of a concave mirror, the image is outside the focal point, real and inverted.

✔ As the object is moved closer to the focal point, the image becomes larger and forms farther from the mirror.

✔ When the object is at the focal point, the reflected rays are parallel. Effectively, the image is at infinity and infinitely large.

✔ If the object is placed inside the focal point, the image is virtual and upright.

24-4 Simple equations give the position and magnification of the image made by a concave mirror

Let's return to the concave spherical mirror that we considered in the previous section. We'll see that given the radius of the mirror and the object distance, we can determine exactly how far from the mirror the image forms and how much magnification the mirror provides. All we need are a little geometry and the law of reflection.

The Mirror Equation for a Concave Mirror

To find the mathematical relationship among the object distance d_O, image distance d_I, and the radius of curvature r, it's convenient to imagine that the object is a point located on the principal axis of the mirror as in **Figure 24-17**. Then the image will also lie along the principal axis. (The explanation is the same one we used in Section 24-3 to show why the image of the base of the arrow in Figure 24-12 must lie on the principal axis.) Figure 24-17 also shows an arbitrarily chosen ray of light coming from the object and reflecting off the mirror. The image I forms where this reflected ray intercepts the principal axis.

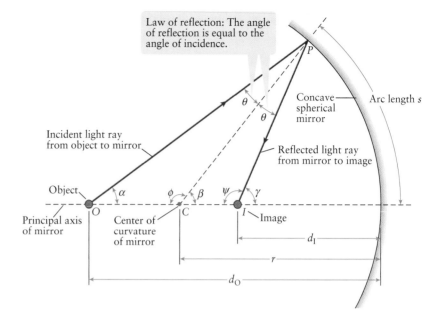

Law of reflection: The angle of reflection is equal to the angle of incidence.

> ! **Watch Out!** The path from object to mirror to image isn't just for one special light ray.
>
> It's tempting to look at Figure 24-17 and think that there's something special about the light ray we've drawn. But *any* ray that emanates from the object point O in Figure 24-17 will reflect off the mirror and pass through the *same* image point I, provided the ray is at a shallow enough angle α to the principal axis of the mirror. So every part of
>
> the mirror contributes to forming the image. (Note that in Figure 24-17 we've drawn the angle α as fairly large. We've done this just to make the figure easier to see. If we drew α as a realistically small angle, the incident and reflected rays would be so close to the principal axis that it would be hard to see the angles in the figure.)

√x̄ *See the Math Tutorial for more information on geometry*

As Figure 24-17 shows, the light ray we've drawn goes from the object point O to a point P on the mirror, then to the image point I. We can find a relationship among d_O, d_I, and r by first finding a relationship among the angles in Figure 24-17 labeled α (the angle between the principal axis and the light ray from O to P), β (the angle between the principal axis and a line from the center of curvature C to P), and γ (the angle between the principal axis and the light ray from P to I). Since we're considering α to be a small angle, then necessarily β and γ are small angles as well. For that reason we can treat each of the three regions formed by one of these angles and the arc length s of the mirror as a sector (a pie-like slice) of a circle. The arc length is common to all three sectors. The length of the arc of a circle of radius r subtended by an angle θ equals $r\theta$ (see Section 3-8), provided the angle θ is in radians. So in Figure 24-17

(24-4)
$$s = d_O\alpha; \quad s = r\beta; \quad s = d_I\gamma$$

Note also that the sum of the angles in any triangle equals 180° or π radians. For the triangle OPC we have

(24-5)
$$\alpha + \theta + \phi = \pi$$

However, the angles ϕ and β in Figure 24-17 must add to 180°, or π radians (together they make up half a circle). So $\phi + \beta = \pi$ and $\phi = \pi - \beta$, and Equation 24-5 becomes

(24-6)
$$\alpha + \theta + \pi - \beta = \pi \quad \text{or} \quad \theta = \beta - \alpha$$

Similarly, for the triangle OPI the sum of the angles is π:

(24-7)
$$\alpha + 2\theta + \psi = \pi$$

Figure 24-17 shows that $\psi + \gamma = \pi$, so $\psi = \pi - \gamma$. Triangle CPI shows that $\beta + \theta + \psi = \pi$. Comparing with Equation 24-7, this means it must be true that $\alpha + 2\theta = \beta + \theta$. Equation 24-7 can then be written as

(24-8)
$$\beta + \theta + \pi - \gamma = \pi \quad \text{or} \quad \theta = \gamma - \beta$$

Equations 24-6 and 24-8 are two different expressions for the angle θ in Figure 24-17. If we set these equal to each other, we get

$$\beta - \alpha = \gamma - \beta \quad \text{or} \quad \alpha + \gamma = 2\beta \tag{24-9}$$

From Equations 24-4, we have $\alpha = s/d_O$, $\beta = s/r$, and $\gamma = s/d_I$. Substituting these into Equation 24-9 gives

$$\frac{s}{d_O} + \frac{s}{d_I} = 2\frac{s}{r}$$

To simplify we divide through by the arc length s, giving us the relationship we've been seeking between the object distance, image distance, and radius of curvature of the mirror:

$$\frac{1}{d_O} + \frac{1}{d_I} = \frac{2}{r} \tag{24-10}$$

To help interpret Equation 24-10, recall from Figure 24-11 that if the incident light rays are parallel, they come to a focus at the focal point a distance f from the mirror. So in this case $d_I = f$. The incident rays will be parallel if the object is infinitely far away, so $d_O \to \infty$ and $1/d_O \to 0$. Then Equation 24-10 becomes

$$0 + \frac{1}{f} = \frac{2}{r} \quad \text{or} \quad f = \frac{r}{2}$$

This justifies Equation 24-3: The focal length of a concave spherical mirror is one-half of the radius of curvature.

If we replace $2/r$ with $1/f$ in Equation 24-10, we get the final form of the **mirror equation**:

$$\frac{1}{d_O} + \frac{1}{d_I} = \frac{1}{f}$$

Object distance — d_O; Image distance — d_I; Focal length — f

Mirror equation and lens equation (24-11)

We also call Equation 24-11 the *lens equation* because, as we shall see in Section 24-8, it's also applicable to the image formed by a lens.

The focal length f of a concave mirror is taken to be positive because the center of curvature C of the mirror is in front of the mirror, that is, on its reflective side (to the left in Figure 24-17). Likewise, since the object point O is in front of the mirror, the object distance d_O is positive. The image distance d_I, however, can be positive if the image is real (in front of the mirror) or negative if the image is virtual (behind the mirror). To see when the image distance is positive and when it is negative, let's rewrite Equation 24-11 to solve for d_I:

$$\frac{1}{d_I} = \frac{1}{f} - \frac{1}{d_O} = \frac{d_O}{d_O f} - \frac{f}{d_O f} = \frac{d_O - f}{d_O f} \quad \text{or} \quad d_I = \frac{d_O f}{d_O - f} \tag{24-12}$$

In Equation 24-12 d_O and f are both positive for a concave mirror, so the numerator $d_O f$ is positive. However, the denominator $d_O - f$ can be positive or negative depending on whether d_O is larger or smaller than f.

If the object is outside the focal point so that $d_O > f$, then the denominator $d_O - f$ in Equation 24-12 is positive and the image distance is positive. Therefore, in this case the image made by the mirror is real. As the object moves closer to the focal point, the difference between d_O and f gets smaller and so d_I given by Equation 24-12 gets larger. Hence the image moves father away from the mirror. If the object is inside the focal point, however, then $d_O < f$ and the denominator $d_O - f$ is negative. Then d_I is negative as well, and the image is virtual. That's exactly the behavior that we deduced in Section 24-3 by analyzing ray diagrams.

As a further check on Equations 24-11 and 24-12, note that if the object is exactly two focal lengths from the mirror so $d_O = 2f$, the image distance is

$$d_I = \frac{d_O f}{d_O - f} = \frac{(2f)f}{2f - f} = \frac{2f^2}{f} = 2f$$

Figure 24-18 **Magnification for a concave spherical mirror** We replace the point object in Figure 24-17 with an object arrow.

- The right triangles $OO'P'$ and $II'P'$ both include the same angle θ.
- So tan $\theta = h_O/d_O = |h_I|/d_I$ and $|h_I|/h_O = d_I/d_O$.
- Since h_I is negative, $h_I = -|h_I|$ and $m = h_I/h_O = -|h_I|/h_O = -d_I/d_O$.

So when the object is a distance $2f$ from the mirror—which, because $r = 2f$, is at the center of curvature—the image is at the same position. That's the same conclusion we came to by using the ray diagram in Figure 24-13.

Magnification for a Concave Mirror

We can also use simple geometry to find an expression for the lateral magnification of the image produced by a concave spherical mirror. In Figure 24-18 we've replaced the point object at O with an upright arrow of height h_O that extends from O (on the principal axis) to O'. Just as in Figure 24-12, we draw two rays coming from the tip of the object arrow at O' to determine the position I' of the tip of the image arrow.

Since the object in Figure 24-18 is outside the focal point F, the image is real and inverted and so the height of the image is negative: $h_I = -|h_I|$. By the law of reflection, the ray from O' to the point P' at the center of the mirror makes the same angle θ with the mirror's principal axis (shown as a dashed line in Figure 24-18) as does the reflected ray from P' to I'. If you look at the right triangle $OO'P'$, you'll see that the tangent of θ (the opposite side divided by the adjacent side) is tan $\theta = h_O/d_O$; if you do the same for the right triangle $II'P'$, you'll see that tan $\theta = |h_I|/d_I$. Setting these two expressions equal to each other, we see that

$$\frac{h_O}{d_O} = \frac{|h_I|}{d_I} \quad \text{or} \quad \frac{|h_I|}{h_O} = \frac{d_I}{d_O}$$

Since $h_I = -|h_I|$, we can rewrite this as

(24-13)

$$-\frac{h_I}{h_O} = \frac{d_I}{d_O} \quad \text{or} \quad \frac{h_I}{h_O} = -\frac{d_I}{d_O}$$

From Equation 24-2, the lateral magnification is $m = h_I/h_O$. So Equation 24-13 tells us that

Lateral magnification
for a mirror or lens
(24-14)

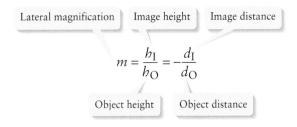

$$m = \frac{h_I}{h_O} = -\frac{d_I}{d_O}$$

Go to Interactive Exercise 24-1 for more practice dealing with concave mirrors

A negative value of the magnification m means that the image is inverted, as in Figure 24-18. If m is positive, the image is upright. (As we'll see in Section 24-8, the same equation also applies to lenses.)

We've derived Equation 24-14 for the case in which the image is in front of the mirror (the same side as the object) and hence real, but it's also true when the image is on the back side of the mirror and hence virtual. When the object is far from the mirror and the image is close to the focal point, d_I is positive and small compared to d_O, so m is small and negative; the mirror produces a reduced, inverted image (see Figure 24-12). As the object distance decreases, the image distance increases and the ratio $m = -d_I/d_O$ increases in absolute value. As we saw above, when $d_O = 2f$ the image distance d_I is also equal to $2f$; then $m = -1$ and the inverted image is as large as the object (see Figure 24-13). If we move the object even closer to the focal point, but still outside it, the image distance is greater than the object distance and the absolute value of the magnification is greater than 1. Hence the inverted image is larger than the object (see Figure 24-14). If we move the object inside the focal point so that $d_O < f$, the image distance is negative (the image is behind the mirror) and the image is virtual. In this case Equation 24-14 tells us that m is positive, so the virtual image is upright (see Figure 24-16). We see that Equation 24-14 gives us the same results as we deduced from the ray diagrams in Section 24-3.

Table 24-1 summarizes when the radius of curvature r, focal length f, image distance d_I, image height h_I, and magnification m are positive and when they are negative.

Table 24-1 Sign Conventions for Mirrors

mirror radius of curvature r	• positive for a concave mirror • negative for a convex mirror
focal length f	• positive for a concave mirror • negative for a convex mirror
image distance d_I	• positive if on the reflective side of the mirror (the same side as the object); the image is then a real image • negative if on the non-reflective side of the mirror (the opposite side from the object); the image is then a virtual image
image height h_I	• positive if the image is upright (the same orientation as the object) • negative if the image is inverted (flipped upside down compared to the object)
lateral magnification m	• positive if the image is upright (the same orientation as the object) • negative if the image is inverted (flipped upside down compared to the object)

Example 24-1 Images Made by a Concave Mirror

An object is 1.50 cm tall and is placed in front of a spherical concave mirror that has a radius of curvature equal to 20.0 cm. Find the image distance and height if the object is (a) 14.0 cm from the mirror; (b) 6.00 cm from the mirror.

Set Up

Our mathematical tools are the expression for the focal length of the mirror, the mirror equation, and the equation for lateral magnification. We're given the radius of curvature $r = 20.0$ cm and the object height $h_O = 1.50$ cm; our goal is to find the values of the image distance d_I and image height h_I for the cases $d_O = 14.0$ cm and $d_O = 6.00$ cm.

Focal length of a spherical mirror:

$$f = \frac{r}{2} \tag{24-3}$$

Mirror equation:

$$\frac{1}{d_O} + \frac{1}{d_I} = \frac{1}{f} \tag{24-11}$$

Lateral magnification of a mirror

$$m = \frac{h_I}{h_O} = -\frac{d_I}{d_O} \tag{24-14}$$

Solve

First calculate the focal length of the mirror.

From Equation 24-3,

$$f = \frac{r}{2} = \frac{20.0 \text{ cm}}{2} = 10.0 \text{ cm}$$

(a) The object distance $d_O = 14.0$ cm is greater than the focal length $f = 10.0$ cm but less than $2f = 20.0$ cm. That is, the object is inside the center of curvature but outside the focal point. We've drawn a ray diagram that's similar to Figure 24-14. This tells us to expect that the image will be real, inverted, farther from the mirror than the object is, and larger than the object.

Calculate the image distance using the mirror equation.

From Equation 24-11,

$$\frac{1}{d_I} = \frac{1}{f} - \frac{1}{d_O} = \frac{1}{10.0 \text{ cm}} - \frac{1}{14.0 \text{ cm}}$$

$$= 0.1000 \text{ cm}^{-1} - 0.0714 \text{ cm}^{-1} = 0.0286 \text{ cm}^{-1} \text{ so}$$

$$d_I = \frac{1}{0.0286 \text{ cm}^{-1}} = 35.0 \text{ cm}$$

The image distance is positive, so the image is 35.0 cm in front of the mirror. An image that forms in front of the mirror is a real image.

Calculate the image height using the magnification equation.

From Equation 24-14,

$$m = \frac{h_I}{h_O} = -\frac{d_I}{d_O} = -\frac{35.0 \text{ cm}}{14.0 \text{ cm}} = -2.50$$

The image is 2.50 times larger than the object and, as the minus sign shows, inverted. Solve for the image height h_I:

$$h_I = mh_O = (-2.50)(1.50 \text{ cm}) = -3.75 \text{ cm}$$

The inverted image is 3.75 cm high.

(b) Now the object distance $d_O = 6.00$ cm is less than the focal length $f = 10.0$ cm, so the object is inside the focal point. We've drawn a ray diagram that's similar to Figure 24-16. This tells us to expect that the image will be virtual, upright, farther from the mirror, and larger than the object.

Calculate the image distance using the mirror equation.

From Equation 24-11,

$$\frac{1}{d_I} = \frac{1}{f} - \frac{1}{d_O} = \frac{1}{10.0 \text{ cm}} - \frac{1}{6.00 \text{ cm}}$$

$$= 0.1000 \text{ cm}^{-1} - 0.1667 \text{ cm}^{-1} = -0.0667 \text{ cm}^{-1} \text{ so}$$

$$d_I = \frac{1}{-0.0667 \text{ cm}^{-1}} = -15.0 \text{ cm}$$

The image distance is negative, so the image is 15.0 cm behind the mirror. An image that forms behind the mirror is a virtual image.

Calculate the image height using the magnification equation.

From Equation 24-14,

$$m = \frac{h_I}{h_O} = -\frac{d_I}{d_O} = -\frac{(-15.0 \text{ cm})}{6.00 \text{ cm}} = +2.50$$

Again the image is 2.50 times larger than the object, but is now upright as shown by the plus sign. Solve for the image height h_I:

$$h_I = mh_O = (+2.50)(1.50 \text{ cm}) = +3.75 \text{ cm}$$

The upright image is 3.75 cm high.

Reflect

In both parts, the position and size of the image are consistent with our ray diagrams. It's always a good idea to draw such diagrams as a check on your calculations using the mirror equation and magnification equation.

Take-Home Message for Section 24-4

✔ The mirror equation relates the focal length of a concave mirror and the positions of the object and image.

✔ A positive value of the image distance d_I indicates that the image is in front of the mirror and is real.

A negative value of d_I indicates that the image is behind the mirror and virtual (the light rays never actually go there).

✔ The magnification of the image is positive if the image is upright and negative if the image is inverted.

24-5 A convex mirror always produces an image that is smaller than the object

Let's now turn our attention to images produced by a convex mirror. As Figure 24-7a shows, if an object is held next to a convex mirror, the resulting image is smaller than the object. The same is true if an object is far away from a convex mirror. Figure 24-19 shows the reflection of a Ferris wheel in the convex surface of a person's eye. Although the Ferris wheel is tens of meters in diameter, its image is only about a centimeter in diameter—smaller than the iris of the eye. In this section we'll use ray diagrams to understand the nature of the images formed by a convex mirror.

Recall from Figure 24-8 the key difference between concave and convex mirrors: Parallel light rays that reflect from a concave mirror converge toward a point in front of the mirror, while parallel light rays that reflect from a convex mirror diverge from a point on the back side of the mirror. (If the mirrors are spherical, the rays don't truly converge on or diverge from a single point. But this is a good description of what happens if the rays are all close to the principal axis of the mirror. We'll make this assumption—the same that we made in Sections 24-3 and 24-4 for concave mirrors—throughout this section.)

Because the focal point of a convex mirror is behind the mirror, we say that the focal length f is negative. For a convex mirror, we call the focal point *virtual* because parallel light rays that reflect from the mirror seem to emanate from that point but don't actually pass through it.

Figure 24-20 shows an object placed a distance d_O in front of a convex mirror. The focal point F lies a distance $|f|$ behind the mirror. (Since the focal length f is negative, the distance is the absolute value of f.) The center of curvature C is also behind the mirror, so the radius of curvature r is also negative. It turns out that the focal length f is equal to one-half of the radius of curvature r, just as for a concave mirror:

$$f = \frac{r}{2}$$

(24-3)

(We'll justify this statement in Section 24-6.) For a concave mirror, f and r are both positive; for a convex mirror, f and r are both negative.

To find the location of the image in Figure 24-20, we draw two rays that emanate from the tip of the object arrow, just as we did for the ray diagrams in Section 24-3 for a concave mirror. The image of the arrow tip forms where the two reflected rays appear to meet. The image of the base of the arrow must lie along the principal axis. (A light ray coming from the base of the arrow and traveling along the principal axis strikes the mirror normal to the surface, and so is reflected straight back. The image of the base of the arrow must therefore form somewhere on the principal axis.) As Figure 24-20 shows, the image is upright. The image is virtual because it forms behind the mirror, just like the image formed by a plane mirror (Section 24-2): The reflected rays don't actually

Figure 24-19 Reflections in a golden eye A Ferris wheel can be seen reflected from the surface of this person's eye. The eye is relatively spherical, so its outer surface acts like a convex mirror.

Figure 24-20 **Ray diagram for a convex mirror** How the image is formed for an object in front of a convex mirror.

• A convex mirror has a negative focal length: $f = -|f|$.
• For any object distance d_O, a convex mirror produces a virtual image behind the mirror.
• The image distance d_I is negative: $d_I = -|d_I|$.
• The virtual image is upright and smaller than the object.

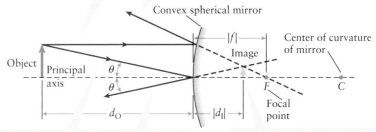

① A light ray that starts off parallel to the principal axis is reflected so that when we trace the ray back behind the mirror, it appears to pass through the virtual focal point F.

Convex spherical mirror

Object

Principal axis

θ
θ

d_O

$|f|$

Center of curvature of mirror

Image

$|d_I|$

Focal point

F

C

② A light ray that strikes the center of the mirror at an angle θ from the principal axis reflects at the same angle.

③ Trace the two reflected rays to where they appear to cross behind the mirror. This is where the virtual image forms.

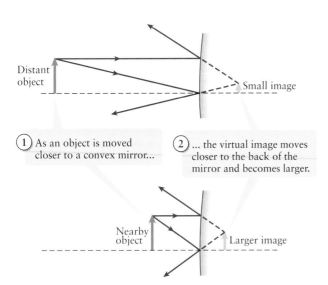

Distant object

Small image

① As an object is moved closer to a convex mirror...

② ... the virtual image moves closer to the back of the mirror and becomes larger.

Nearby object

Larger image

Figure 24-21 **Moving closer to a convex mirror** As the object far from a convex mirror is moved closer to the mirror, the image increases in size.

cross there. Hence the image distance d_I is negative. We saw in Section 24-3 that a concave mirror produces a virtual image only if the object is inside the focal point; a convex mirror produces a virtual image for *any* position of the object.

The image in Figure 24-20 is smaller than the object, no matter what the object distance is. To show this, note that the height of the image arrow is determined in part by the angle of the ray that emerges from the tip of the object arrow moving parallel to the principal axis. The dashed line from where this ray hits the mirror to the focal point F slopes downward toward F, so the image must be smaller than the object. Figure 24-20 also shows that the image formed by the convex mirror will always be upright, always be smaller than the object, and always be closer to the mirror than the virtual focal point.

Figure 24-21 shows how the image size and position change as the object is moved closer to the mirror. As the object distance d_O decreases, the image becomes larger and closer to the mirror, but remains virtual and upright. If the object were moved all the way to the surface of the mirror, the image would be exactly the same size as the object.

Because a convex mirror makes objects appear smaller, they provide a wide-angle view. Rear-view mirrors on automobiles and trucks often include a convex mirror to allow the driver to see as much of the area behind the vehicle as possible. (Any mirror with the label "Objects in mirror are closer than they appear" is a convex mirror.)

In the following section, we'll look at these ideas more quantitatively and see how to calculate the image size and position for a convex mirror.

Got the Concept? 24-6 Solar Cooking

The Sun is so far from Earth that rays of sunlight are effectively parallel. Sunlight reflected from a mirror can be focused onto a pot, raising its temperature enough to pasteurize water in the pot or cook food. What kind of spherical mirror could be used for this purpose? (a) A convex mirror; (b) a concave mirror; (c) either a convex or concave mirror.

Take-Home Message for Section 24-5

✔ Parallel light rays that strike a convex mirror diverge and appear to emanate from a virtual focal point behind the mirror.

✔ If an object is placed anywhere in front of a convex mirror, the resulting image is virtual, upright, closer to the mirror than the object is, and smaller than the object.

24-6 The same equations used for concave mirrors also work for convex mirrors

Just as we did for the concave mirror in Section 24-4, we can use geometry and the law of reflection to find an equation that relates the object and image distances and the radius of curvature for a convex mirror. We'll also find an equation that relates the sizes of the image and object for a convex mirror. Remarkably, we'll see that these equations are exactly the same as those for a concave mirror, provided we're careful with the signs of the radius of curvature, focal length, and image distance for a convex mirror.

The Mirror Equation for a Convex Mirror

In Figure 24-22 we've placed a point object on the principal axis of a convex mirror with the (negative) radius of curvature r. This is analogous to Figure 24-17, in which we placed a point object on the principal axis of a concave mirror. The object is at position O, a distance d_O from the mirror. We've drawn an arbitrarily chosen light ray that travels away from the object at an angle α from the principal axis and reflects off the mirror at P; if we extend the reflected ray backward, the extension (shown as a dashed blue line) crosses the principal axis at I. A second light ray (not shown) that travels away from the object along the principal axis will be reflected straight back along that axis. If we extend this reflected ray backward, it will meet the extension of the first reflected ray at I. Hence I is the position of the image made by the mirror. As we expect, this image is behind the mirror, so the image distance is negative. The center of curvature C of the mirror also lies behind the mirror, so the radius of curvature is also negative. Mathematically, $d_I = -|d_I| < 0$ and $r = -|r| < 0$.

Note that the red dashed line CP in Figure 24-22 is normal to the mirror at P, so by the law of reflection the incident ray and the reflected ray are both at the same angle θ relative to this normal. It follows that θ is also the angle between the line CP and the backward extension PI of the reflected ray.

To relate the object distance d_O, image distance d_I, and radius of curvature r, we'll first find a relationship among α, the angle between the principal axis and the light ray incident on the mirror; β, the angle between the principal axis and the reflected ray; and γ, the angle between the principal axis and the red dashed line CP that defines the normal at the point P where the light ray is reflected. Notice that each of these three angles is part of a right triangle for which one side is the thick black line PQ in Figure 24-22: triangle OPQ for angle α, triangle IPQ for angle β, and triangle CPQ for angle γ. In each case the line PQ, of length h, is the side opposite the angle. Strictly speaking, we're only considering light rays that are very close to the principal axis, or equivalently

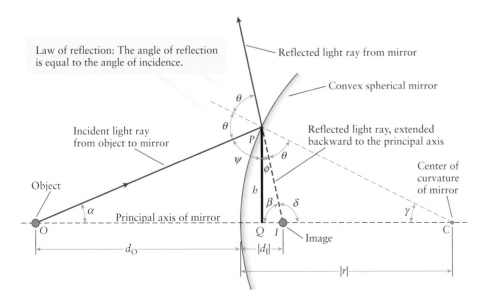

Figure 24-22 **Analyzing a convex spherical mirror** A ray diagram for a point object on the principal axis of a convex spherical mirror.

$\sqrt{x}$ *See the Math Tutorial for more information on trigonometry*

a mirror of very large radius so that we can regard the mirror's curved surface as nearly flat. As a result, we can treat d_O as the base of triangle OPQ, $|d_I|$ as the base of triangle IPQ, and $|r|$ as the base of triangle CPQ. For each triangle the tangent of the angle equals the length h of the side opposite the angle, divided by the length of the triangle's base. So

$$(24\text{-}15) \qquad \tan \alpha = \frac{h}{d_O}, \quad \tan \beta = \frac{h}{|d_I|}, \quad \tan \gamma = \frac{h}{|r|}$$

If the incident ray OP is at a small angle to the principal axis, then α, β, and γ are all small angles. (We've drawn the angle α fairly large in Figure 24-22 to make the geometry easier to visualize. In reality, it must be quite small to conform to the approximation that the rays are nearly parallel to the principal axis.) The tangent of a small angle is approximately equal to the angle in radians, so Equation 24-15 becomes

$$(24\text{-}16) \qquad \alpha = \frac{h}{d_O}, \quad \beta = \frac{h}{|d_I|}, \quad \gamma = \frac{h}{|r|}$$

To relate the angles α, β, and γ, we'll do as in Section 24-4 and use the result that the sum of the angles of any triangle must be 180°, or π radians. For the triangle IPC that connects the image point I, reflection point P, and center of curvature C, the three angles are γ, θ, and δ. So

$$(24\text{-}17) \qquad \gamma + \theta + \delta = \pi$$

Figure 24-22 shows that the angles β and δ must add to π radians (together they make up half a circle around the point I). So $\beta + \delta = \pi$, $\delta = \pi - \beta$, and Equation 24-17 becomes

$$(24\text{-}18) \qquad \gamma + \theta + \pi - \beta = \pi \quad \text{or} \quad \theta = \beta - \gamma$$

For the triangle OPC that connects the object point O, reflection point P, and center of curvature C, the angles are α, $(\psi + \theta)$, and γ, so we have

$$(24\text{-}19) \qquad \alpha + (\psi + \theta + \phi) + \gamma = \pi$$

We can simplify Equation 24-19 by noting from Figure 24-22 that the angles θ, ψ, ϕ and θ form a half-circle around the point P, so their sum is π radians: $\theta + \psi + \phi + \theta = \pi$, or $\psi + \theta + \phi = \pi - \theta$. If we substitute this expression for $(\psi + \theta + \phi)$ into Equation 24-19, we get

$$(24\text{-}20) \qquad \alpha + \pi - \theta + \gamma = \pi \quad \text{or} \quad \theta = \alpha + \gamma$$

Equations 24-18 and 24-20 are both expressions for the angle θ. If we set these equal to each other, we get

$$(24\text{-}21) \qquad \beta - \gamma = \alpha + \gamma \quad \text{or} \quad \alpha - \beta = -2\gamma$$

Equation 24-21 is the relationship among the angles α, β, and γ we've been looking for. We can now get a relationship among the object distance d_O, image distance d_I, and radius of curvature r by substituting the expressions for α, β, and γ from Equation 24-16 into Equation 24-21:

$$\frac{h}{d_O} - \frac{h}{|d_I|} = -\frac{2h}{|r|}$$

If we divide through by the height h of the black line in Figure 24-22 and recall that the image distance and radius of curvature are both negative, so that $d_I = -|d_I|$ and $r = -|r|$, this becomes

$$(24\text{-}22) \qquad \frac{1}{d_O} + \frac{1}{d_I} = \frac{2}{r}$$

Equation 24-22 is *exactly* the same as Equation 24-10, which we derived for a *concave* mirror. It's reassuring that we get the same expression for both kinds of mirrors.

Note that if the object is infinitely far away, so that $d_O \to \infty$ and $1/d_O \to 0$, the rays from the object to the mirror will all be parallel to the axis and the virtual image will be formed at the focal point F, a distance $|f|$ behind the mirror. Then $d_I = -|f| = f$ (recall that the focal length f is negative). For this situation, Equation 24-22 becomes

$$\frac{1}{f} = \frac{2}{r} \quad \text{or} \quad f = \frac{r}{2}$$

This result is exactly the same as that for a concave spherical mirror: The focal length f is equal to one-half of the radius of curvature r (Equation 24-3). The only difference is that for a convex mirror, f and r are both negative.

If we substitute $1/f = 2/r$ into Equation 24-22, we get the mirror equation for a convex mirror:

$$\frac{1}{d_O} + \frac{1}{d_I} = \frac{1}{f} \tag{24-11}$$

This is Equation 24-11, the same mirror equation that we derived for a *concave* mirror in Section 24-4. This equation works equally well whether the focal length is positive (for a concave mirror) or negative (for a convex mirror).

We can use Equation 24-11 to explore the properties of the image made by a convex mirror. We saw in Section 24-4 that this equation can be rewritten as

$$d_I = \frac{d_O f}{d_O - f} \tag{24-12}$$

Using $f = -|f|$ for the negative focal length of a convex mirror, Equation 24-12 becomes

$$d_I = \frac{d_O(-|f|)}{d_O - (-|f|)} = -\left(\frac{d_O}{d_O + |f|}\right)|f| \tag{24-23}$$

The right-hand side of Equation 24-23 is always negative, so the image distance d_I for a convex mirror will always be negative (the image will always be behind the mirror). Note that the fraction in parentheses is always less than or equal to 1, so the image distance is always between 0 and $-f$. That is, the image always forms somewhere between the mirror and the focal point.

Magnification for a Convex Mirror

Figure 24-23 again shows the image made by a convex spherical mirror, but now an upright arrow of height h_O is the object. This arrow is a distance d_O in front of the mirror. Just as for a concave mirror (see Figure 24-18 in Section 24-4), we draw two rays coming from the tip of the object arrow at O'. One ray is parallel to the principal axis of the mirror; after reflection, this travels away from the mirror as though it had been emitted from the focal point F. The other ray bounces off the center of the mirror at P', and the reflected ray makes the same angle θ with the principal axis as the incident ray from O' to P'. If we extend this reflected ray backward, the extension is at the same angle θ to the principal axis. This extension meets the extension of the other reflected ray at I', the position of the tip of the image arrow. The base of the image arrow is at I, directly underneath I' on the principal axis. The image is behind the mirror, so the image distance d_I is negative. This image is also upright, so the image height h_I is positive.

To relate the image and object heights, note that the right triangles $OO'P'$ and $II'P'$ both include the same angle θ. For $OO'P'$ the tangent of θ (the opposite side divided by the adjacent side) equals h_O/d_O; for $II'P'$ the tangent of θ equals $h_I/|d_I|$. These two expressions for $\tan\theta$ must be equal, so

$$\frac{h_O}{d_O} = \frac{h_I}{|d_I|} \quad \text{or} \quad \frac{h_I}{h_O} = \frac{|d_I|}{d_O} = -\frac{d_I}{d_O} \quad (\text{since } d_I = -|d_I|)$$

The lateral magnification m equals h_I/h_O, so it follows that for a convex mirror

$$m = \frac{h_I}{h_O} = -\frac{d_I}{d_O} \tag{24-14}$$

- The right triangles $OO'P'$ and $II'P'$ both include the same angle θ.
- So $\tan\theta = h_O/d_O = h_I/|d_I|$ and $h_I/h_O = |d_I|/d_O$.
- Since d_I is negative, $d_I = -|d_I|$ and $m = h_I/h_O = |d_I|/d_O = -d_I/d_O$.

Go to Interactive Exercise 24-2 for more practice dealing with concave and convex mirrors

This is the same expression for magnification as for a concave mirror. Since the image distance d_I is negative for a convex mirror, Equation 24-14 tells us that the magnification is positive and so the image is upright. In addition, for a convex mirror the image is closer to the mirror than is the object, so $|d_I| < d_O$ and the value of m is less than 1. That is, the image made by a convex mirror is always smaller than the object, just as we saw in Section 24-5.

Watch Out! Positive magnification indicates that an image is upright.

Remember that the sign of the magnification of a mirror doesn't indicate whether the image is larger or smaller than the object, only whether the image is upright or inverted. An upright image, for example, is always associated with a positive magnification, regardless of whether the image is larger than or smaller than the object.

Example 24-2 An Image Made by a Convex Mirror

An object is 1.50 cm high and is placed in front of a spherical convex mirror with a radius of curvature of magnitude 48.0 cm. Find the image distance and height if the object is (a) 68.0 cm from the mirror; (b) 3.00 cm from the mirror.

Set Up

This is similar to Example 24-1 in Section 24-4. The key difference is that the mirror is now convex, so the radius of curvature is negative: $r = -48.0$ cm. We're given the object height $h_O = 1.50$ cm, and want to find the values of the image distance d_I and image height h_I for the cases $d_O = 68.0$ cm and $d_O = 3.00$ cm. Our tools are Equations 24-3, 24-11, and 24-14, which apply to convex mirrors as well as concave ones.

Focal length of a spherical mirror:

$$f = \frac{r}{2} \qquad (24\text{-}3)$$

Mirror equation:

$$\frac{1}{d_O} + \frac{1}{d_I} = \frac{1}{f} \qquad (24\text{-}11)$$

Lateral magnification of a mirror

$$m = \frac{h_I}{h_O} = -\frac{d_I}{d_O} \qquad (24\text{-}14)$$

Solve

Use Equation 24-3 to calculate the focal length of the mirror.

From Equation 24-3,

$$f = \frac{r}{2} = \frac{-48.0 \text{ cm}}{2} = -24.0 \text{ cm}$$

The negative value of focal length means that the focal point is behind the mirror.

In both cases, we expect that the image will be virtual (behind the mirror), smaller than the object, and closer to the mirror than the object is. The specific position and size of the image will be different in the two cases, however.

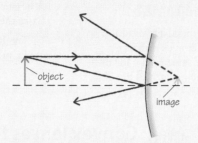

(a) With an object distance $d_O = 68.0$ cm, we use Equation 24-11 to find the image distance and Equation 24-14 to find the image size.

From the mirror equation (Equation 24-11),

$$\frac{1}{d_I} = \frac{1}{f} - \frac{1}{d_O} = \frac{1}{(-24.0 \text{ cm})} - \frac{1}{68.0 \text{ cm}}$$

$$= -0.0417 \text{ cm}^{-1} - 0.0147 \text{ cm}^{-1} = -0.0564 \text{ cm}^{-1} \text{ so}$$

$$d_I = \frac{1}{(-0.0564 \text{ cm}^{-1})} = -17.7 \text{ cm}$$

The image distance is negative, so the image is 17.7 cm behind the mirror. An image that forms behind the mirror is a virtual image. The magnification of the image is, from Equation 24-14,

$$m = \frac{h_I}{h_O} = -\frac{d_I}{d_O} = -\frac{(-17.7 \text{ cm})}{68.0 \text{ cm}} = +0.261$$

Since $m > 0$, the image is upright. The image is 0.261 as tall as the object, so its height is

$$h_I = mh_O = (+0.261)(1.50 \text{ cm}) = 0.391 \text{ cm}$$

(b) Repeat the calculations of part (a) with $d_O = 3.00$ cm.

Calculate the image distance:

$$\frac{1}{d_I} = \frac{1}{f} - \frac{1}{d_O} = \frac{1}{(-24.0 \text{ cm})} - \frac{1}{3.00 \text{ cm}}$$

$$= -0.0417 \text{ cm}^{-1} - 0.333 \text{ cm}^{-1} = -0.375 \text{ cm}^{-1} \text{ so}$$

$$d_I = \frac{1}{(-0.375 \text{ cm}^{-1})} = -2.67 \text{ cm}$$

Again the image distance is negative. Note that with a smaller object distance than in (a), the image distance is also smaller.

The magnification of the image is

$$m = \frac{h_I}{h_O} = -\frac{d_I}{d_O} = -\frac{(-2.67 \text{ cm})}{3.00 \text{ cm}} = +0.889$$

Again $m > 0$ and the image is upright. The image is 0.889 as tall as the object; its height is

$$h_I = mh_O = (+0.889)(1.50 \text{ cm}) = +1.33 \text{ cm}$$

Reflect

As the object is moved closer to the convex mirror, the image moves closer to the mirror and increases in size.

? Got the Concept? 24-7   A Convex Mirror

If the image made by a convex mirror of focal length f is $1/2$ the height of the object, the distance from the object to the mirror must be equal to (a) $4|f|$; (b) $2|f|$; (c) $|f|$; (d) $|f|/2$; (e) $|f|/4$.

Take-Home Message for Section 24-6

✔ The mirror equation that relates the image distance, object distance, and focal length of a convex mirror is the same as for a concave mirror. The same is true for the equation that relates the heights of the image and the object to the image and object distances, and the equation that then relates the focal length and radius of curvature.

✔ The fundamental difference between concave and convex mirrors is that a convex mirror has a negative radius of curvature and so a negative focal length.

24-7 Convex lenses form images like concave mirrors and vice versa

A curved mirror forms images by reflection. A **lens**—a piece of glass or other transparent material with a curved surface on its front side, back side, or both sides—forms images by the *refraction* of light as the light enters and leaves the lens. Just as for a curved mirror, the images made by a lens can be larger or smaller than the object (Figure 24-24). In this section we'll explore how lenses form images.

The key idea that we need to understand lenses is the law of refraction. As we learned in Section 23-2, a light ray changes direction when it moves from one transparent material or medium to a second medium in which light travels at a different speed. The ray bends toward the normal if the speed of light is slower in the second medium (Figure 24-25a); this happens, for example, when light moves from air into glass. The ray bends away from the normal if the speed of light is faster in the second medium, as when light moves from glass into air (Figure 24-25b).

Figure 24-24 Lenses can magnify or shrink Different types of lenses can make (a) large or (b) small images.

This rodent appears larger when viewed through a magnifying glass, a lens that is convex on both sides.

The physicist appears smaller than actual size when viewed through this lens, which is concave on both sides.

(a)   (b)

Figure 24-25 The law of refraction A light ray crossing the boundary between two transparent media can refract either (a) toward or (b) away from the normal, depending on how the speed of light compares in the two media.

(a) Refraction from one medium into a slower one

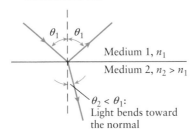

θ_1 θ_1

Medium 1, n_1
Medium 2, $n_2 > n_1$

$\theta_2 < \theta_1$:
Light bends toward the normal

(b) Refraction from one medium into a faster one

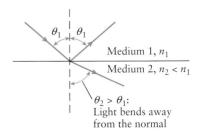

θ_1 θ_1

Medium 1, n_1
Medium 2, $n_2 < n_1$

$\theta_2 > \theta_1$:
Light bends away from the normal

(a) Parallel light rays entering a glass sphere

Each dashed line represents the normal to the surface at the point where a light ray enters the sphere.

The incident angle θ_1 and the refracted angle θ_2 obey the law of refraction.

θ_2 is less than θ_1 for light crossing from air to glass, so the rays are bent toward the principal axis of the sphere. Hence the light rays converge as they enter the sphere.

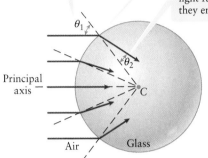

(b) Parallel light rays exiting a glass sphere

θ_2 is greater than θ_1 for light crossing from glass to air, so the rays are bent toward the principal axis of the sphere. Hence the light rays converge as they exit the sphere.

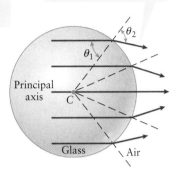

Figure 24-26 Refraction by a glass sphere If a glass sphere is surrounded by air, parallel light rays converge whether they (a) enter the sphere or (b) exit the sphere.

Figure 24-26 shows how parallel light rays refract when they enter or exit a glass sphere (in which the speed of light is relatively slow) surrounded by air (in which the speed of light is almost as fast as in vacuum). We say that both the front and back surfaces of the sphere are convex (they bulge outward). Part (a) of this figure shows that light rays converge when they enter through the convex surface of the sphere; part (b) shows that parallel rays also converge when they exit through the sphere's convex surface. Figure 24-27 shows what happens when parallel light rays enter or exit a piece of glass with a concave surface (one that bulges inward). In part (a) the parallel rays diverge as they cross the concave surface into the glass, and in part (b) the rays diverge as they exit through the concave surface of the glass.

In Figures 24-26 and 24-27 we've considered only what happens when light enters or leaves a glass object with a curved surface. In a lens the light enters from outside, passes through the lens, then exits. So each ray of light refracts *twice* as it travels into and out of the lens. Figure 24-26 shows that the refractions will make the rays converge if each surface is convex, and Figure 24-27 shows that the refractions will make the rays diverge if each surface is concave. So a lens with two convex surfaces—called a *convex lens*—will be a **converging lens** that takes incoming parallel light rays and makes them

(a) Parallel light rays entering a piece of glass with a spherical cutout

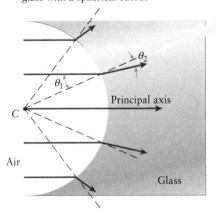

θ_2 is less than θ_1 for light crossing from air to glass, so the rays are bent away from the principal axis of the glass. Hence the light rays diverge as they enter the glass.

(b) Parallel light rays exiting a piece of glass with a spherical cutout

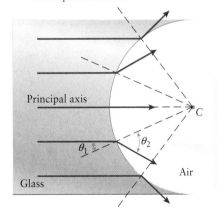

θ_2 is greater than θ_1 for light crossing from glass to air, so the rays are bent away from the principal axis of the glass. Hence the light rays diverge as they exit the glass.

Figure 24-27 Refraction by glass with a spherical cutout If a piece of glass with a spherical cutout is surrounded by air, parallel light rays diverge whether they (a) enter the glass through the cutout or (b) exit the glass through the cutout.

Figure 24-28 **Converging and diverging lenses** Two examples of converging lenses and two examples of diverging lenses.

These are converging lenses: Parallel light rays that enter either of these lenses will exit the lens converging toward each other.

These are diverging lenses: Parallel light rays that enter either of these lenses will exit the lens diverging away from each other.

Convex   Plano-convex   Concave   Plano-concave

converge toward the principal axis. The same is true for a lens with one convex surface and one flat surface, called a *plano-convex* lens. The refraction at the flat surface by itself causes neither convergence nor divergence by itself. Similarly, a lens with two concave surfaces—called a *concave* lens—will be a **diverging lens** that takes incoming parallel light rays and makes them diverge away from the principal axis. A lens with one concave surface and one flat surface, called a *plano-concave* lens, will also be a diverging lens (**Figure 24-28**).

Watch Out! **The curvature of a piece of glass has the opposite effect to the same curvature in a mirror.**

We saw in Section 24-3 that a concave mirror causes light rays to converge on reflection. By contrast, a concave lens causes light rays to diverge as they pass through. Likewise, while we saw in Section 24-5 that a convex mirror causes light rays to diverge on reflection, a convex lens causes light rays to converge as they pass through. Mirrors and lenses are different!

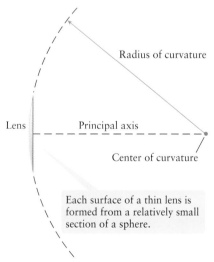

Radius of curvature

Lens

Principal axis

Center of curvature

Each surface of a thin lens is formed from a relatively small section of a sphere.

Figure 24-29 **A thin lens** Analyzing image formation by a lens is much easier if we assume that the lens is thin and has spherical surfaces.

A lens with spherical surfaces suffers from the same spherical aberration that we noted in Section 24-3 for spherical mirrors: Parallel light rays do not all focus to the same point for a converging lens, or appear to originate from a single point for a diverging lens. However, we can neglect this effect if the rays of light are all close to the principal axis. We can assure this by using only a small section of a large spherical surface to form each surface of the lens (**Figure 24-29**). In addition we'll assume that there is very little thickness of material between the front and back surfaces of the lens. The result is called a **thin lens**. We'll consider only thin lenses for the rest of this chapter, so that we can neglect spherical aberration and treat each lens as if parallel rays are focused to a single point. Eyeglasses and contact lenses are everyday examples of thin lenses.

Ray Diagrams for Converging Lenses

We saw earlier that ray diagrams are powerful tools for visualizing how a curved mirror produces an image. Let's see how to draw a ray diagram to help us locate the position of the image made by a converging lens.

Figure 24-30 shows a thin convex lens, created by placing two thin spherical sections such as the one shown in Figure 24-29 back-to-back. Notice that we have marked two points as a focal point *F*. For a thin lens the focal length, the distance from the center of the lens to the focal point, is the same on both sides of the lens, even if the two surfaces have a different radius of curvature. That's why we've drawn

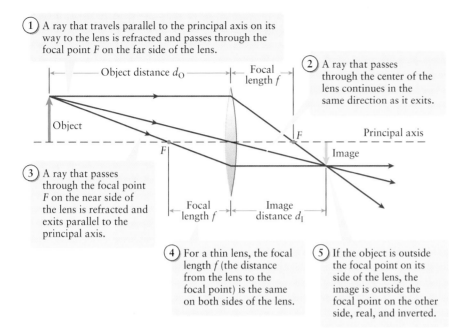

① A ray that travels parallel to the principal axis on its way to the lens is refracted and passes through the focal point *F* on the far side of the lens.

Object distance d_O

Focal length *f*

② A ray that passes through the center of the lens continues in the same direction as it exits.

Object

F

F

Principal axis

Image

③ A ray that passes through the focal point *F* on the near side of the lens is refracted and exits parallel to the principal axis.

Focal length *f*

Image distance d_I

④ For a thin lens, the focal length *f* (the distance from the lens to the focal point) is the same on both sides of the lens.

⑤ If the object is outside the focal point on its side of the lens, the image is outside the focal point on the other side, real, and inverted.

Figure 24-30 **Ray diagram for a converging lens I** How the image is formed for an object placed outside the focal point of a converging lens.

the two focal points *F* in Figure 24-30 the same distance from the geometrical center of the lens.

In Figure 24-30 we've drawn a red arrow as our object on the left-hand side of the lens, and placed this arrow outside the focal point. We've also drawn three representative light rays emanating from the tip of the object arrow. We've drawn the rays as if they refract only once, along the centerline of the lens (the line perpendicular to the principal axis that runs through the center of the lens). Notice how these three rays behave:

Go to Picture It 24-2 for more practice dealing with converging lenses

(1) A ray that arrives at the lens traveling parallel to the principal axis is refracted so that it passes through the focal point *F* on the far (right-hand) side of the lens.

(2) A ray that strikes the lens directly at its center continues in a straight line as it exits. This is only an approximation because it assumes that the ray undergoes no refraction on entering or leaving the lens. But this is a good approximation for a thin lens, which is nearly flat at its very center.

(3) A ray that passes through the near (left-hand) focal point *F* on its way to the lens exits the lens traveling parallel to the principal axis. To see why this is the case, imagine that we could record a video of light traveling along this path, then run the video backward. Then we would see a light ray coming to the far right in Figure 24-30 and traveling parallel to the principal axis. After this ray passes through the lens from right to left, it would naturally pass through the focal point *F* on the left-hand side. If we now run that same video forward, we see light from the object following the path shown in Figure 24-30.

The image of the tip of the arrow in Figure 24-30 forms where the rays coming from the tip cross. The image of the base of the arrow must form along the principal axis, because a ray that comes from the base and travels along the axis strikes the center of the lens and therefore continues in the same direction. You can see that the image of the arrow is real (the light rays actually cross at the image point) and is inverted.

Note that for the case shown in Figure 24-30, the object is relatively far from the lens (the object distance d_O is greater than twice the focal length *f*) and the resulting image is real, inverted, *and* smaller than the object. That's exactly the same result we found for a concave mirror in Section 24-3 (see Figure 24-12). This reinforces the idea that a convex lens behaves similarly to a concave mirror. Figure 24-31 shows an example of a small, inverted image formed when light from a distant object passes through a

Figure 24-31 **A real, inverted image made by a converging lens** The lens in the person's hand makes a real, inverted image of a park bench.

convex lens. You can see the same phenomenon in Figure 11-39 (Section 11-12), in which a sphere of water acts as a convex lens.

> **! Watch Out!** If a lens forms a real image, it must be on the side of the lens opposite to the object.
>
> We've defined a real image as one that forms where reflected or refracted light rays converge. A concave mirror can cause light rays to converge only on the reflective side of the mirror, which is where we would put an object, so this is the only side on which a real image can form. A lens, however, can only cause light rays to converge on the side of the lens *opposite* to the object, as in Figure 24-30. As we'll see below, only a converging lens can produce a real image, and only if the object is outside the focal point as in Figure 24-30.

Recall that for mirrors our convention was that the image distance is positive if the image is real and so is on the same side of the mirror as the object. For a lens we'll also say that the image distance is positive if the image is real. This means that for a lens, a positive image distance d_I implies that the image is on the *opposite* side of the lens from the object. For example, the image distance is positive in Figure 24-30.

In **Figure 24-32** we've moved the standard object to a point between the lens and the focal point, so the object distance is less than the focal length: $d_O < f$. To locate the image, we've drawn just two light rays from the tip of the arrow. One ray moves parallel to the principal axis of the lens and therefore passes through the focal point after being refracted by the lens. The other ray we have drawn strikes the center of the lens and so continues straight. (In Figure 24-30 we drew a third ray through the focal point on the same side of the lens as the object. We don't draw that ray here, since it leads away from the lens rather than toward it.) Notice that these two rays do not meet. But if we extend the rays backward as shown by the dashed lines, they appear to meet on the same side of the lens as the object. Where they meet is the location of the image. The rays do not actually cross there, so this is a *virtual* image. Because the image is on the same side of the lens as the object, the image distance is negative: $d_I < 0$.

As in Figure 24-30, the base of the image arrow must lie on the principal axis of the lens. It follows that the image is upright. Note that the image is also larger than the object. This is the kind of image shown in Figure 24-24a; when we view a rodent by holding a magnifier (a convex lens) close to the rodent (so that the rodent is inside the focal point of the lens), we see an enlarged, upright image of the rodent. This is very similar to the image made by a concave mirror when an object is placed inside the focal point of the mirror (see Figure 24-16).

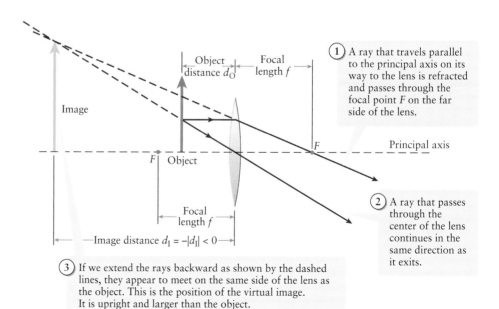

① A ray that travels parallel to the principal axis on its way to the lens is refracted and passes through the focal point F on the far side of the lens.

② A ray that passes through the center of the lens continues in the same direction as it exits.

③ If we extend the rays backward as shown by the dashed lines, they appear to meet on the same side of the lens as the object. This is the position of the virtual image. It is upright and larger than the object.

Object distance d_O | Focal length f

Image

F Object

Focal length f

Image distance $d_I = -|d_I| < 0$

Principal axis

Figure 24-32 Ray diagram for a converging lens II How the image is formed for an object placed inside the focal point of a converging lens.

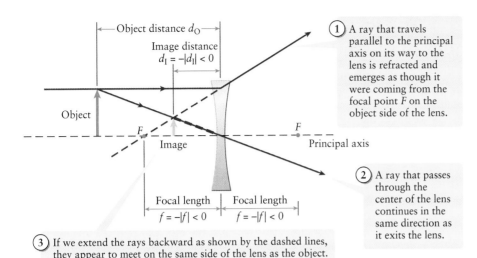

Figure 24-33 **Ray diagram for a diverging lens** How the image is formed for an object placed in front of a diverging lens.

① A ray that travels parallel to the principal axis on its way to the lens is refracted and emerges as though it were coming from the focal point F on the object side of the lens.

② A ray that passes through the center of the lens continues in the same direction as it exits the lens.

③ If we extend the rays backward as shown by the dashed lines, they appear to meet on the same side of the lens as the object. This is the position of the virtual image. It is upright and smaller than the object.

Ray Diagrams for Diverging Lenses

We can also use ray diagrams to learn about the image made by a diverging lens. In Figure 24-33 we've placed an object arrow in front of a thin lens with two concave surfaces. Since this lens causes parallel light rays to diverge, we say that the focal length is negative: $f = -|f| < 0$. (The focal length of a convex mirror, which also causes parallel light rays to diverge, is also negative.)

We've drawn two light rays to determine where the image forms, and as we did for the thin, convex lens, we've drawn the rays as if they refract only once along the center-line of the lens. The refracted rays don't actually meet, but if we extend these rays backward, we find the location where the extensions meet. The image of the tip of the arrow forms at this point; the image is virtual (since the rays don't actually meet there), upright, and smaller than the object. This is the same behavior we saw in Section 24-5 for convex mirrors. As for a convex mirror, the image is virtual, upright, and smaller no matter what the object distance.

Figure 24-24b shows an image made by a concave lens. Just like the image in Figure 24-33, this image is upright and smaller than the object (the physicist standing behind the lens).

Got the Concept? 24-8 A Lens in Sugar Water

You make a lens with two convex surfaces out of ice ($n = 1.31$). You then submerge the lens in a large tank of concentrated sugar water ($n = 1.49$). If you place an object in the tank and in front of the lens, an image is formed at a position inside the tank. What kind of image is this? (a) A real image; (b) a virtual image that is larger than the object; (c) a virtual image that is smaller than the object; (d) either (a) or (b), depending on the distance from the object to the lens; (e) any of (a), (b), or (c), depending on the distance from the object to the lens.

Take-Home Message for Section 24-7

✔ When parallel light rays enter one side of a convex lens, they exit the lens converging toward the focal point on the other side of the lens.

✔ When parallel light rays enter a concave lens, they exit the lens diverging away from the focal point on the same side of the lens that the rays entered.

✔ A convex lens produces a real image if the object is outside the focal point, and produces a virtual image if the object is inside the focal point.

✔ A concave lens produces a virtual image no matter what the position of the object.

24-8 The focal length of a lens is determined by its index of refraction and the curvature of its surfaces

As we did for concave mirrors and convex mirrors, we'd like to find equations for the focal length of a lens; for the relationship among the focal length of a lens, the object distance, and the image distance; and for the magnification of an image produced by a lens. As we'll see, the latter two equations turn out to be identical to those for curved mirrors. The expression for the focal length, however, is a little more complicated and requires a bit of interpretation.

Focal Length of a Thin Lens

The focal length f of a thin lens depends on the index of refraction n of the material of which it is made. The greater the value of n, the more sharply a light ray is bent as it passes either from the surrounding air (for which the index of refraction is essentially 1) into the lens or from the lens into the air. The value of f also depends on how the front and back surfaces of the lens are curved. The mathematical expression of these relationships for a lens in air is called the **lensmaker's equation:**

Lensmaker's equation for the focal length of a thin lens (24-24)

Focal length of a lens surrounded by air

Index of refraction of the lens material

$$\frac{1}{f} = (n - 1)\left(\frac{1}{R_1} - \frac{1}{R_2}\right)$$

Radius of curvature of lens surface 1 (the surface closer to the object)

Radius of curvature of lens surface 2 (the surface farther from the object)

Equation 24-24 can be derived by applying Snell's law of refraction (Equation 23-6) to a ray of light refracted by both surfaces of a lens. The derivation is beyond our scope, however.

The values of the radii of curvature R_1 and R_2 depend on how sharply and in what direction the two surfaces of the lens are curved. As **Figure 24-34** shows, we take a radius to be positive if the center of curvature is on the other side of the lens from the object, but negative if the center of curvature is on the same side as the object. For example, in Figure 24-34 the radius R_1 of surface 1 is positive, but the radius R_2 of surface 2 is negative. The following examples illustrate how to use Equation 24-24.

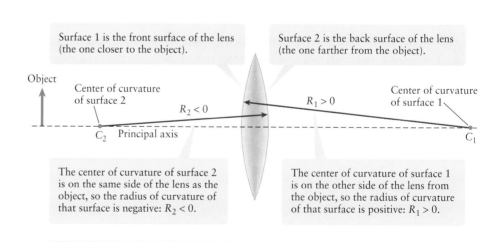

Surface 1 is the front surface of the lens (the one closer to the object).

Surface 2 is the back surface of the lens (the one farther from the object).

Object

Center of curvature of surface 2

$R_2 < 0$

$R_1 > 0$

Center of curvature of surface 1

C_2 Principal axis

C_1

The center of curvature of surface 2 is on the same side of the lens as the object, so the radius of curvature of that surface is negative: $R_2 < 0$.

The center of curvature of surface 1 is on the other side of the lens from the object, so the radius of curvature of that surface is positive: $R_1 > 0$.

Figure 24-34 Interpreting the lensmaker's equation For each surface of a thin lens, the sign of the radius of curvature depends on where the center of curvature is located.

- If the center of curvature of a lens surface is on the other side of the lens from the object, the radius of curvature R of that surface is positive.
- If the center of curvature of a lens surface is on the same side of the lens as the object, the radius of curvature R of that surface is negative.
- A flat surface has an infinite radius of curvature R, so $1/R = 0$ for that surface.

Example 24-3 Calculating Focal Length for a Convex Lens

In Figure 24-34 the front surface (surface 1) of the lens has a radius of curvature of magnitude 15.0 cm, and the back surface (surface 2) has a radius of curvature of magnitude 25.0 cm. The lens is made of crown glass with an index of refraction 1.520. (a) Calculate the focal length of the lens. (b) Next flip the orientation of the lens so that the front surface is now the one with a radius of curvature of magnitude 25.0 cm, and the back surface is now the one with a radius of curvature of magnitude 15.0 cm. Calculate the focal length of the lens in this case.

Set Up

For each situation we'll draw the lens and determine on which side of the lens the centers of curvature lie; that will tell us whether R_1 and R_2 are positive or negative. We'll then use Equation 24-24 to calculate the focal length.

Lensmaker's equation for the focal length of a thin lens:

$$\frac{1}{f} = (n - 1)\left(\frac{1}{R_1} - \frac{1}{R_2}\right) \tag{24-24}$$

Solve

(a) Both surfaces are convex. Hence the center of curvature of each surface is on the other side of the lens from that surface. The center of curvature C_1 of the front surface (on the left in the figure) is on the far side of the lens, so R_1 is positive: $R_1 = +15.0$ cm. The center of curvature C_2 of the back surface (on the right in the figure) is on the near side of the lens, so R_2 is negative: $R_2 = -25.0$ cm.

Calculate the focal length.

From Equation 24-24,

$$\frac{1}{f} = (1.520 - 1)\left(\frac{1}{(+15.0\text{ cm})} - \frac{1}{(-25.0\text{ cm})}\right)$$
$$= 0.520[(0.0667\text{ cm}^{-1}) - (-0.0400\text{ cm}^{-1})]$$
$$= 0.0555\text{ cm}^{-1}$$

$$f = \frac{1}{0.0555\text{ cm}^{-1}} = 18.0\text{ cm}$$

Although R_2 is negative, we subtract rather than add $1/R_2$ in Equation 24-24, so both the $1/R_1$ term and the $1/R_2$ term—that is, both surface 1 and surface 2—contribute to giving $1/f$ a positive value. As a result, the focal length is positive, as we expect for a convex lens.

(b) Because we have flipped the lens around, we have interchanged surfaces 1 and 2. The object is still to the left of the lens, however. As in part (a), R_1 is positive and R_2 is negative, but now $R_1 = +25.0$ cm and $R_2 = -15.0$ cm.

Calculate the focal length.

From Equation 24-24,

$$\frac{1}{f} = (1.520 - 1)\left(\frac{1}{(+25.0\text{ cm})} - \frac{1}{(-15.0\text{ cm})}\right)$$
$$= 0.520[(0.0400\text{ cm}^{-1}) - (-0.0667\text{ cm}^{-1})]$$
$$= 0.0555\text{ cm}^{-1}$$

$$f = \frac{1}{0.0555\text{ cm}^{-1}} = 18.0\text{ cm}$$

Again both the $1/R_1$ term and the $1/R_2$ term contribute to giving $1/f$ a positive value. The focal length has the same positive value as in part (a).

Reflect

The focal length of this thin lens stays the same after we flip it back to front. That's consistent with the statement we made in the previous section that the focal points on either side of the lens are both the same distance (that is, the same focal length) from the lens.

Example 24-4 Calculating Focal Length for a Concave Lens

A certain lens made of crown glass ($n = 1.520$) has concave front and back surfaces. The front surface has a radius of curvature of magnitude 15.0 cm, and the back surface has a radius of curvature of magnitude 25.0 cm. Calculate the focal length of the lens.

Set Up

As in the previous example, we'll first draw the lens and use our drawing to decide whether R_1 and R_2 are positive or negative. Equation 24-24 will then allow us to calculate the focal length.

Lensmaker's equation for the focal length of a thin lens:

$$\frac{1}{f} = (n - 1)\left(\frac{1}{R_1} - \frac{1}{R_2}\right) \tag{24-24}$$

Solve

Both surfaces are concave. Hence the center of curvature of each surface is on the same side of the lens as that surface. The center of curvature C_1 of the front surface (on the left in the figure) is on the near side of the lens, so R_1 is negative: $R_1 = -15.0$ cm. The center of curvature C_2 of the back surface (on the right in the figure) is on the far side of the lens, so R_2 is positive: $R_2 = +25.0$ cm.

Calculate the focal length.

From Equation 24-24,

$$\frac{1}{f} = (1.520 - 1)\left(\frac{1}{(-15.0\,\text{cm})} - \frac{1}{(+25.0\,\text{cm})}\right)$$

$$= 0.520\left[(-0.0667\,\text{cm}^{-1}) - (0.0400\,\text{cm}^{-1})\right]$$

$$= -0.0555\,\text{cm}^{-1}$$

$$f = \frac{1}{(-0.0555\,\text{cm}^{-1})} = -18.0\,\text{cm}$$

The $1/R_1$ term is negative, and we subtract from it the positive $1/R_2$ term. So both terms contribute to giving $1/f$ a negative value so that the focal length is negative.

Reflect

The focal length is negative, which is just what we expect from a concave lens. We encourage you to repeat the calculation with the lens reversed back to front, as in part (b) of Example 24-3; you should get the same result for the focal length. Do you?

Figure 24-35 The human eye Both the cornea and the lens cause light to refract at their curved surfaces. Together, these parts of the eye cause light to be focused on the retina.

Two structures in the human eye focus images on the retina, allowing us to see clearly: the cornea, which makes up the outer surface of the eye, and the lens, which is suspended inside the eye behind the pupil (Figure 24-35). The lens is made of a flexible material. As tiny muscles around the lens contract and relax, the lens becomes more or less round. As the shape of the lens changes, the radius of curvature of its surfaces changes, and this in turn changes the focal length of the lens. This is important because no matter how far away an object is, the image distance is always the same—the distance from the lens to the retina, where images are formed and detected. So the focal length has to change in order to have the image remain on the retina.

By the time we reach middle age, the lenses in our eyes eventually lose some of their elasticity. As a result, the front and back surfaces of the lenses cannot curve as sharply, and light from objects close to the eyes cannot be focused on the retina. This makes it difficult to see objects at close range. This condition, called *presbyopia*, is treated by wearing reading glasses. These glasses are made from convex lenses that help the eye focus the light from a nearby object onto the retina. The lenses of the eyes can also become clouded by cataracts, in which case they are surgically replaced by artificial lenses (see Figure 24-1b).

Image Position and Magnification for a Thin Lens

To see how the image distance is related to the object distance and the focal length for a thin, convex lens, let's look again at a ray diagram like Figure 24-30. We've drawn such a diagram in **Figure 24-36**. Let's see how to use trigonometry to find relationships between the distances of interest.

The shaded regions in Figure 24-36a are similar triangles. That's because the ray from the tip of the object at O' to the tip of the image at I' passes through the center of the lens at C without deflection, so the angle θ is the same in both triangle $O'C'C$ and triangle ICI'. The ratio of the heights of the two triangles is therefore equal to the ratio of their bases; that is

$$\frac{|h_I|}{h_O} = \frac{d_I}{d_O} \tag{24-25}$$

(The height h_I of the image in Figure 24-36a is negative because the image is inverted. That's why we've used $|h_I|$ in Equation 24-25 for the distance from I to I'.) The two shaded regions in Figure 24-36b—the right triangles $FC'C$ and $FI'I$—are also similar triangles. That's because the straight ray from C' to I' passes through the focal point, so the angle ϕ is the same on either side of F. So for these two triangles as well, the ratio of their heights is equal to the ratio of their bases:

$$\frac{|h_I|}{h_O} = \frac{d_I - f}{f} \tag{24-26}$$

If we combine Equation 24-25 and Equation 24-26, we find a relationship between the image distance d_I, the object distance d_O, and the focal length f:

$$\frac{d_I}{d_O} = \frac{d_I - f}{f} \quad \text{or} \quad \frac{d_I}{d_O} = \frac{d_I}{f} - 1 \quad \text{or} \quad \frac{d_I}{d_O} + 1 = \frac{d_I}{f}$$

Divide both sides by d_I:

$$\frac{1}{d_O} + \frac{1}{d_I} = \frac{1}{f} \quad \text{(lens equation)} \tag{24-11}$$

This equation should look familiar; it's the same equation that we deduced for spherical mirrors in Section 24-4. It applies just as well to thin, spherical convex lenses. Now

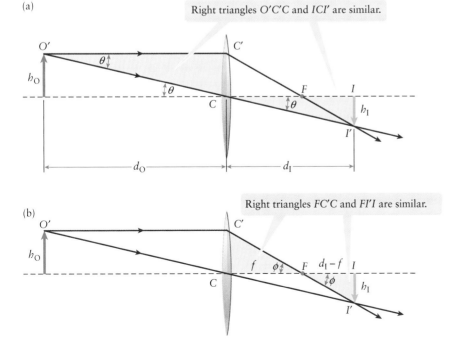

Figure 24-36 Analyzing a converging lens Ray diagrams for an object arrow on the principal axis of a converging lens. The similar triangles in (a) and (b) help us determine the position and magnification of the image.

we see why we were justified in calling Equation 24-11 the mirror and lens equation—it works for both.

The lens equation is expressed in terms of the reciprocals of the object distance d_O, image distance d_I, and focal length f. For that reason it's common, especially among optometrists, to characterize lenses (and also mirrors) in terms of the reciprocal of the focal length:

$$(24\text{-}27) \qquad P = \frac{1}{f}$$

The quantity P is called the **power** of the lens or mirror. The units of P are m^{-1}; $1\ m^{-1}$ is known as 1 **diopter**. The larger the power of a thin, convex lens, the closer to the lens parallel light rays are brought to a focus. A 2-diopter lens brings parallel rays to a focus $1/2$ m (0.5 m) from the lens, while a 5-diopter lens brings parallel rays to a focus $1/5$ m (0.2 m) from the lens.

Equation 24-25 above also tells us the magnification of the image. Since the image height h_I is negative in Figure 24-36a (the image is inverted), h_I is equal to $-|h_I|$ and $|h_I| = -h_I$. If we substitute this into Equation 24-25, we get

$$\frac{(-h_I)}{h_O} = \frac{d_I}{d_O} \quad \text{or} \quad \frac{h_I}{h_O} = -\frac{d_I}{d_O}$$

Lateral magnification is equal to the ratio of image height to object height: $m = h_I/h_O$ (Equation 24-2). So we can write the magnification of the image produced by a thin lens as

$$(24\text{-}14) \qquad m = \frac{h_I}{h_O} = -\frac{d_I}{d_O} \quad \text{(lateral magnification)}$$

That's the same Equation 24-14 that we derived in Section 24-4 for a curved mirror.

We've derived Equations 24-11 and 24-14 for a thin convex lens with a positive focal length, but they turn out to be equally valid for a thin concave lens with a negative focal length. As for mirrors, it's important to keep track of the signs of quantities in these equations. Table 24-2 summarizes when the quantities in the lens-maker's equation (Equation 24-24), the lens equation (Equation 24-11), and the magnification equation (Equation 24-14) are positive and when they are negative.

Because the equations for mirrors and thin lenses are effectively identical, many of the same conclusions that we came to for images made by a curved mirror also apply to images made by a thin lens:

- If the lens has a positive focal length (a converging lens) and an object is placed outside the focal point, the image is real and inverted. Depending on the object distance, the image can be smaller, larger, or the same size as the object.

- If the lens has a positive focal length (a converging lens) and an object is placed inside the focal point of a converging lens, the image is virtual, upright, and larger than the object.

- If the lens has a negative focal length (a diverging lens), the image is virtual, upright, and smaller than the object. This is true for any object distance.

One key difference between mirrors and lenses is in the position of the image. For a mirror a real image is on the same side of the mirror as the object, and a virtual image is on the other side of the mirror. For a lens a real image is on the opposite side of the lens from the object, and a virtual image is on the same side of the lens as the object.

Go to Interactive Exercise 24-3 for more practice dealing with lenses

Table 24-2 Sign Conventions for Lenses

lens surface radius of curvature R_1 or R_2	• positive if the center of curvature is on the side of the lens opposite from the object • negative if the center of curvature is on the same side of the lens as the object
focal length f	• positive for a converging lens • negative for a diverging lens
image distance d_I	• positive if on the side of the lens opposite from the object; the image is then a real image • negative if on the same side of the lens as the object; the image is then a virtual image
image height h_I	• positive if the image is upright (the same orientation as the object) • negative if the image is inverted (flipped upside down compared to the object)
lateral magnification m	• positive if the image is upright (the same orientation as the object) • negative if the image is inverted (flipped upside down compared to the object)

Example 24-5 An Image Made by a Convex Lens

A thin convex lens has a focal length of 15.0 cm. How far from the lens does the image form when an object is placed 9.00 cm from the center of the lens? Is the image virtual or real? Is the image inverted or upright? By what factor is the image magnified relative to the object?

Set Up

We'll begin by drawing a ray diagram to help us visualize the kind of image that will be produced. We'll use Equation 24-11 to calculate the position of this image, and Equation 24-14 to calculate the image height compared to the object height.

Lens equation:

$$\frac{1}{d_O} + \frac{1}{d_I} = \frac{1}{f} \qquad (24\text{-}11)$$

Magnification:

$$m = \frac{h_I}{h_O} = -\frac{d_I}{d_O} \qquad (24\text{-}14)$$

Solve

We begin by drawing a ray diagram. We've drawn one ray from the object that enters the lens parallel to the principal axis, exits the lens, and passes through the focal point F on the other side of the lens. We've also drawn a ray that passes through the center of the lens. The rays never meet on the other side of the lens, but their extensions do meet on the same side of the lens as the object. So the image will be virtual. As the diagram shows, the image is also upright and larger than the object.

Find the image distance using the lens equation.

We are given $d_O = 9.00$ cm and $f = 15.0$ cm. From Equation 24-11,

$$\frac{1}{d_I} = \frac{1}{f} - \frac{1}{d_O} = \frac{1}{15.0 \text{ cm}} - \frac{1}{9.00 \text{ cm}}$$

$$= 0.06667 \text{ cm}^{-1} - 0.111 \text{ cm}^{-1}$$

$$= -0.0444 \text{ cm}^{-1}$$

$$d_I = \frac{1}{(-0.0444 \text{ cm}^{-1})} = -22.5 \text{ cm}$$

The negative value of d_I means that the image is on the same side of the lens of the object, just as the ray diagram shows. It must therefore be a virtual image.

Find the image height using the magnification equation.

From Equation 24-14,

$$m = \frac{h_I}{h_O} = -\frac{d_I}{d_O} = -\frac{(-22.5 \text{ cm})}{9.00 \text{ cm}} = +2.50$$

The plus sign means the image is upright, in agreement with the ray diagram. The image is 2.50 times as large as the object.

Reflect

Although we didn't try to draw the ray diagram to exact scale, by eye the ratio of the focal length to the object distance looks to be about 2 to 1, which is certainly consistent with the actual values $f = 15.0$ cm and $d_O = 9.00$ cm. So we expect that the image distance in the diagram is about one and half times the focal length (22.5 cm compared to 15.0 cm)—and it is. Can you verify that the height of the image in the diagram is about 2.5 times the height of the object?

? Got the Concept? 24-9 Focusing a Camera

Light rays from a distant object are essentially parallel. That's why to focus a digital camera on a distant object, the lens is adjusted so that the distance from the lens to the electronic image sensor (which records the image) is equal to the focal length f. To focus on a nearby object, the lens must be positioned so that the distance from the lens to the image sensor is (a) less than f; (b) more than f; (c) f.

? Got the Concept? 24-10   A Magnifying Glass

By placing an object closer to your eyes, it looks larger and you can see it in more detail. The object has an angular size θ_0 (Figure 24-37a). If you're typical, however, you can focus on an object only if it's about 25 cm or farther from your eyes, which may not allow you to see small details clearly. A magnifying glass, a convex lens with a relatively short focal length, is the solution. When a magnifying glass is placed in between the object and your eye and the object is closer to the lens than the focal point, the image forms with angular size θ_M, which is larger than θ_0. In addition, the image forms farther from your eye than the 25 cm limit so you can focus clearly on it. Draw a ray diagram that shows the principle of a magnifying glass, starting from the sketch in Figure 24-37b.

(a)   When an object is placed close to the eye it spans an angular size θ_0.

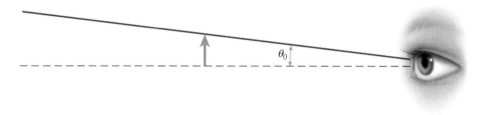

(b)   A magnifying glass is placed between the object and the eye, in order to see more detail without moving the object closer to the eye. Where does the image form?

Figure 24-37 A magnifying glass (a) The angular size of an object. (b) Use this setup to draw a ray diagram that demonstrates the principle of a magnifying glass.

? Got the Concept? 24-11   Microscopes

You've used microscopes many times, but do you know how they work? By applying what you've learned about lenses, you can figure it out for yourself! A simple compound microscope has two lenses, the objective and the eyepiece. An object is placed just beyond the focal point of the objective in order to form a magnified image. Using the sketch in Figure 24-38, determine the location and size of the image by tracing rays from the tip of the arrow to the eye. Is the image real or virtual?

Figure 24-38 A compound microscope Use this setup to draw a ray diagram that demonstrates the principle of a compound microscope.

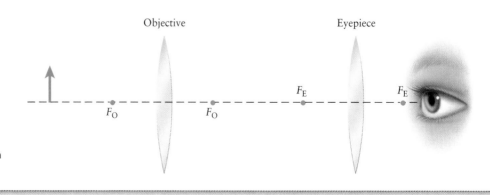

Take-Home Message for Section 24-8

✔ The focal length of a thin lens is determined by the index of refraction of the lens material and the radii of curvature of the front and back surfaces of the lens. These radii can be positive or negative.

✔ The same equation that relates object distance, image distance, and focal length for a spherical mirror also applies

to thin lenses. The magnification equation is also the same for spherical mirrors and thin lenses.

✔ Image distance d_I is positive when the image is real and negative when the image is virtual. The focal length f is positive for a thin, convex lens and negative for a thin, concave lens.

Key Terms

center of curvature
concave
converging lens
convex
diffuse light
diopter
diverging lens
focal length
focal point
geometrical optics
image

image distance
image height
inverted image
lateral magnification
lens equation
lensmaker's equation
mirror equation
object
object distance
object height
plane mirror

power (of a lens or mirror)
principal axis
radius of curvature
ray diagram
real image
specular reflection
thin lens
upright image
virtual image

Chapter Summary

Topic	Equation or Figure

Plane mirrors: A plane mirror makes an upright, virtual image of any object. The image is the same size as the object, so the lateral magnification is $m = 1$. The image is reversed back to front, not side to side.

The image distance is negative.   The object distance is positive.

$$d_I = -|d_I| = -d_O \qquad (24\text{-}1)$$

The negative value of d_I indicates that the image is on the opposite side of the mirror from the object.

Lateral magnification   Image height

$$m = \frac{h_I}{h_O} \qquad (24\text{-}2)$$

Object height

Spherical mirrors: If we consider only parallel light rays that are close to the principal axis of a spherical concave mirror, the reflected rays all converge at the focal point. The distance from the center of the mirror to the focal point is the focal length. If the mirror is convex rather than concave, parallel light rays diverge rather than converge after reflection. The radius of curvature and the focal length are both negative for a convex mirror.

Focal length of a spherical mirror   **Radius of curvature** of the mirror

$$f = \frac{r}{2} \qquad (24\text{-}3)$$

Image formation by a concave mirror:
We can locate the image made by
a concave mirror by drawing a ray
diagram. If the object is outside the focal
point, the image is real and inverted; its
size depends on how far the object is
from the mirror. If the object is inside the
focal point, the image is virtual, upright,
and larger than the object.

(Example 24-1, figure #1)

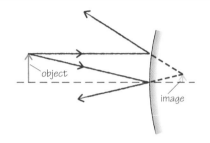

(Example 24-1, figure #2)

Image formation by a convex mirror:
A ray diagram also helps us locate the
image made by a convex mirror. No
matter where the object is placed, the
image is virtual, upright, and smaller
than the object.

(Example 24-2, figure #1)

The mirror equation and lens equation:
The mirror equation and lens equation
relates the object distance, image
distance, and focal length for either
a concave or convex mirror or a
converging or diverging lens. The lateral
magnification depends on the image
and object distances, and can be positive
(if the image is upright) or negative
(if the image is inverted).

$$\frac{1}{d_O} + \frac{1}{d_I} = \frac{1}{f} \quad \text{Focal length}$$

Object distance   Image distance

(24-11)

Lateral magnification   Image height   Image distance

$$m = \frac{h_I}{h_O} = -\frac{d_I}{d_O}$$

Object height   Object distance

(24-14)

Lenses: Due to refraction, light rays
converge as they enter or exit a
converging glass lens and diverge as
they enter or exit a diverging glass lens.
A converging lens behaves similarly to
a concave mirror, and a diverging lens
behaves similarly to a convex mirror.
The focal length of a lens is given by the
lensmaker's equation, which involves the
index of refraction of the lens material
and the radii of curvature of the lens
surfaces. This equation is valid if the lens
is thin.

These are converging lenses:
Parallel light rays that enter either
of these lenses will exit the lens
converging toward each other.

These are diverging lenses:
Parallel light rays that enter either
of these lenses will exit the lens
diverging away from each other.

(Figure 24-28)

Convex   Plano-convex   Concave   Plano-concave

Focal length of a lens
surrounded by air

Index of refraction
of the lens material

$$\frac{1}{f} = (n - 1) \left(\frac{1}{R_1} - \frac{1}{R_2} \right)$$ (24-24)

Radius of curvature of
lens surface 1 (the surface
closer to the object)

Radius of curvature of
lens surface 2 (the surface
farther from the object)

Image formation by lenses: A converging lens produces a real, inverted image if the object is outside the focal point, and a virtual, upright, enlarged image if the object is inside the focal point. A diverging lens always produces a virtual, upright, reduced image. The same equation that relates object distance d_O, image distance d_I, and focal length f for a spherical mirror also applies to thin lenses, as does the equation for lateral magnification.

(Example 24-5)

Answer to What do you think? Question

(a) These eyeglasses are used by people with presbyopia. Their eyes are able to take essentially parallel light rays from distant objects and make them converge onto the retina to form an image, but aren't able to do the same with the diverging light rays coming from a nearby object. The corrective eyeglasses take these diverging light rays and make them nearly parallel, so a converging lens is needed. A converging lens is thicker at the middle than it is at the edges. We discuss the physics of the eye and of lenses in Sections 24-7 and 24-8.

Answers to Got the Concept? Questions

24-1 (a) If you see someone's eyes in a mirror, she can see you as well. This must be true because if light rays can reflect off the mirror from her eyes to yours, then light can follow that path in the opposite direction and reflect from your eyes to hers, too.

24-2 (c) From the information given it's not possible to know whether the person around the corner can see you. We've sketched this situation in Figure 24-39. Light rays that reflect off the mirror from his right hand to your eyes, shown in red, enable you to see his hand. You can't see his eyes because the path that light would need to follow for this to happen, shown by the light blue, dashed line, does not intercept the mirror.

The light ray drawn in red leaves the right hand of the person around the corner, reflects off the mirror, and arrives at your eyes. You can see his right hand.

Mirror

The other person from above

If your right arm is extended, light can follow a path from your hand to the mirror and then to the other person's eyes.

The dashed light blue line indicates the path a light ray would have to travel for you to see his eyes, and for him to see yours. The mirror does not extend far enough for light to reflect in this way.

You from above

Figure 24-39

Whether the other person can see some part of you, however, depends on how far out you are holding your right hand. If it is far enough away from your body, light rays can follow the path drawn in dark blue, from your hand to his eyes.

24-3 (b) When an object is placed farther from a concave mirror than the focal point, the image is real and inverted. Note that a real image forms in front of a mirror; that is, it appears to be in front of the mirror. So when you hold the spoon at arm's length, the object (you!) must therefore be farther from the reflective surface than the focal point. When you hold the spoon 4 cm from your eye, however, you (your eye) must be closer to the spoon than its focal point. An object placed closer to a reflective surface than the focal point forms a virtual, inverted image. Because a virtual image is formed at the point where light rays from any point on an object appear to meet (but don't actually) the image forms behind the mirror and is upright. The focal point of the spoon must be about 6 cm from the spoon. At the focal point no image forms because light rays from any point on your face are reflected parallel to each other.

24-4 (e) A concave mirror makes an image because light rays from a point on the object that strike anywhere on the mirror are all reflected to the same point on the image. If you black out part of the mirror, there are fewer positions on the mirror that contribute to the image, but they still form an image at the same place. This is true for any point on the object, so the image will still show the entire light bulb. The only difference is that the image will be dimmer because only half as much light energy is reflected by the half-painted mirror.

24-5   (b) A real image made by a concave mirror is also an inverted image, so the magnification is $m = -2.00$. Equation 24-14 then tells us the image distance: $m = -d_I/d_O$, so $d_I = -md_O = -(-2.00)(12.0 \text{ cm}) = +24.0 \text{ cm}$. (The positive value of the image distance tells us that the image is in front of the mirror, as must be true for a real image.) The mirror equation, Equation 24-11, then tells us the focal length: $1/f = 1/d_O + 1/d_I = 1/(12.0 \text{ cm}) + 1/(24.0 \text{ cm}) = 0.0833 \text{ cm}^{-1} + 0.0417 \text{ cm}^{-1} = 0.125 \text{ cm}^{-1}$, so $f = 1/(0.125 \text{ cm}^{-1}) = 8.00 \text{ cm}$. Note that the object distance of 12.0 cm is greater than the focal length, as must be the case if the image is to be real.

24-6   (b) A concave mirror can focus parallel light rays; a convex mirror cannot, and so it cannot concentrate solar energy onto a pot for cooking. Another way to see this is to think of the mirror as making an image of the Sun that lies at the position of the pot so as to concentrate the Sun's light there. This is possible with a concave mirror, which makes a real image of a distant object. A convex mirror, by contrast, can only make a virtual image whose rays never actually cross. Hence a convex mirror is no good for concentrating solar energy.

24-7   (c) We can solve this problem using the mirror equation, Equation 24-11, and the expression for magnification, Equation 24-14. The image is one-half the height of the object, so the lateral magnification is $m = h_I/h_O = 1/2$. From Equation 24-14 the magnification m is also equal to $-d_I/d_O$, so $-d_I/d_O = 1/2$ and $d_I = -d_O/2$. That is, the image is half as far from the mirror as the object is and is behind the mirror (because d_I is negative). Substitute $d_I = -d_O/2$ into the mirror equation and solve for d_O:

$$\frac{1}{d_O} + \frac{1}{d_I} = \frac{1}{f} \quad \text{so} \quad \frac{1}{d_O} + \left(-\frac{2}{d_O}\right) = -\frac{1}{d_O} = \frac{1}{f}$$

$$\text{and} \quad d_O = -f = |f|$$

(The focal length of a convex mirror is negative, so $f = -|f|$.) The distance from the object to the mirror equals the distance from the mirror to the focal point.

24-8   (c) The lenses we described in Section 24-7 are made of a material in which light travels more slowly than in the surrounding air—that is, a material with a higher index of refraction than the surroundings. In this situation, however, the lens is made of a material with a *lower* index of refraction

than the surroundings. Hence light rays refract in the opposite sense as they enter and exit the lens, which means that this convex lens is actually a diverging lens. Like the diverging lens in Figure 24-33, the image made by this lens is virtual and smaller than the object.

24-9   (b) As the object approaches the lens, the object distance decreases and so the image distance increases. Hence the sensor must be placed farther from the lens, or equivalently the lens must be farther away from the sensor. On some digital cameras you can actually see the lens move outward from the camera body as the lens focuses on a nearby object.

24-10   Figure 24-40 shows the ray diagram.

The effect of the magnifying glass is to increase the angular size of the image to θ_M.

Figure 24-40

24-11   Figure 24-41 shows the ray diagram.

Notice that the ray that passes through the focal point of the objective exits parallel to the principal axis of the objective, so that this ray enters the eyepiece parallel to the principal axis of the eyepiece. For that reason, this ray passes through the focal point of the eyepiece when it exits.

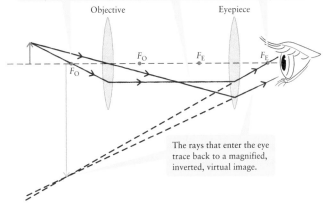

The rays that enter the eye trace back to a magnified, inverted, virtual image.

Figure 24-41

Questions and Problems

In a few problems, you are given more data than you actually need; in a few other problems, you are required to supply data from your general knowledge, outside sources, or informed estimate.

Interpret as significant all digits in numerical values that have trailing zeros and no decimal points.

For all problems, use $g = 9.80 \text{ m/s}^2$ for the free-fall acceleration due to gravity. Neglect friction and air resistance unless instructed to do otherwise.

• Basic, single-concept problem

•• Intermediate-level problem, may require synthesis of concepts and multiple steps

••• Challenging problem

SSM *Solution is in Student Solutions Manual*

Conceptual Questions

1. •A plane mirror seems to invert your image left and right but not up and down. Why is this? SSM

2. •Explain why reflected light is usually diffuse and scattered.

3. •What is the difference between a real image and a virtual image?

4. •When you view a car's side mirror, you see a smaller image than you would if the mirror were flat. Is the mirror concave or convex? Explain your answer.

5. •Explain the meaning, in terms of physics, of the phrase etched on the right side mirror of most cars: "Objects in mirror are closer than they appear."

6. •What is the radius of curvature of a plane mirror? Explain your answer.

7. •For a certain lens in air, both radii of curvature are positive. Is it a converging lens or a diverging lens, or do you need additional information to tell? Explain your answer. SSM

8. •If we move a glass lens from air into water, what will happen to the focal length of the lens? Explain your answer.

9. •A laptop computer is connected to a video projector which projects an image on a screen. If the lens of the projector is half covered, what happens to the image? Explain your answer.

10. •Biology The image focused on your retina is actually inverted (sketch a simple ray trace diagram showing this observation). What does this fact say about our definitions of "right side up" and "upside down"?

11. •Biology Experimental subjects who wear inverting lenses (glasses that invert all images) for several days adapt to their new perception of the world so well that they can even ride a bicycle. Several days after the glasses are removed, their perceptions return to normal. Discuss this phenomenon and comment.

12. •Medical Explain why converging lenses are used to correct farsightedness (hyperopia) while diverging lenses are used for nearsightedness (myopia).

13. •Biology Discuss why nearsightedness is not found in all people, but virtually everyone eventually becomes farsighted as they age.

14. ••Explain why looking through a small opening often provides visual acuity even to an extremely nearsighted person.

Multiple-Choice Questions

15. •Which is true when an object is moved farther from a plane mirror?
  A. The height of the image decreases and the image distance increases.
  B. The height of the image stays the same and the image distance increases.
  C. The height of the image increases and the image distance increases.
  D. The height of the image stays the same and the image distance decreases.
  E. The height of the image decreases and the image distance decreases. SSM

16. •A real image can form in front of
  A. a plane mirror.
  B. a concave mirror.
  C. a convex mirror.
  D. any type of mirror.
  E. no mirrors.

17. •When an object is placed a little farther from a concave mirror than the focal length, the image is
  A. magnified and real.
  B. magnified and virtual.
  C. smaller and real.
  D. smaller and virtual.
  E. smaller and reversed.

18. •If you want to start a fire using sunlight, which kind of mirror would be most efficient?
  A. a plane mirror
  B. a concave mirror

  C. a convex mirror
  D. any type of plane, concave, or convex mirror
  E. It is not possible to start a fire using sunlight and a mirror; you must use a concave lens.

19. •An object is placed at the center of curvature of a concave mirror. Which of the following is true about the image?
  A. real and upright
  B. real and inverted
  C. virtual and upright
  D. virtual and inverted
  E. real, inverted, and reversed SSM

20. •When an object is placed farther from a convex mirror than the focal length, the image is
  A. larger and real.
  B. larger and virtual.
  C. smaller and real.
  D. smaller and virtual.
  E. smaller and reversed.

21. •Medical When a dentist needs a mirror to see an enlarged, upright image of a patient's tooth, what kind of mirror should he use?
  A. a plane mirror
  B. a concave mirror
  C. a convex mirror
  D. either a plane mirror or a concave mirror
  E. either a plane mirror or a convex mirror

22. •A magnifier allows one to look at a very near object by forming an image of it farther away. The object appears larger. To create a magnifier, one would use a
  A. short focal length (< 1 m) converging lens.
  B. short focal length (< 1 m) diverging lens.
  C. long focal length (>1 m) converging lens.
  D. long focal length (>1 m) diverging lens.
  E. either a converging or a diverging lens.

23. •A compound microscope is a two-lens system used to look at very small objects. Which of the following statements is correct?
  A. The objective lens and the eyepiece both have the same focal length, and both serve as simple magnifiers.
  B. The objective lens is a short focal length, converging lens and the eyepiece functions as a simple magnifier.
  C. The objective lens is a long focal length, converging lens and the eyepiece functions as a simple magnifier.
  D. The objective lens is a short focal length, diverging lens and the eyepiece functions as a simple magnifier.
  E. The objective lens is a long focal length, diverging lens and the eyepiece functions as a simple magnifier. SSM

Estimation/Numerical Analysis

24. •Estimate the focal length (in cm) of the corrective lenses in an average pair of glasses.

25. •Estimate the focal length of a convex blind spot mirror that is often added to a vehicle's outside mirror.

26. •Estimate the radius of curvature of a spherical mirror that is typically found in the corridors of busy hospitals, for example, to help prevent collisions when going around a corner.

27. •Give three examples of spherical concave mirrors in your daily life and estimate their approximate focal lengths. SSM

28. •Give three examples of spherical convex mirrors in your daily life and estimate their approximate focal length.

29. •Determine the focal length for an unknown lens with the following object and image distances:

Object Distance (cm)	Image Distance (cm)	Object Distance (cm)	Image Distance (cm)
30	98	60	37
35	67	65	35
40	53	70	34
45	47	75	33
50	42	80	32
55	38		

Problems

24-1 Mirrors or lenses can be used to form images

24-2 A plane mirror produces an image that is reversed back to front

30. •The angle of incidence on a flat mirror is 0°; what is the angle of reflection?

31. •Two flat mirrors are perpendicular to each other. An incoming beam of light makes an angle of $\theta = 30°$ with the first mirror as shown in Figure 24-42. What angle will the outgoing beam make with respect to the normal of the second mirror? SSM

Figure 24-42 Problem 31

32. •A 1.8-m-tall man stands 2.0 m in front of a vertical plane mirror. How tall will the image of the man be?

33. •What must be the minimum height of a plane mirror in order for a 1.80-m-tall person to see a full image of himself?

34. ••A plane mirror is 10 m away from and parallel to a second plane mirror (Figure 24-43). Find the location of the first five images formed by each mirror when an object is positioned exactly in the middle between the two mirrors.

Mirror 1   Mirror 2   Figure 24-43 Problem 34

35. ••A plane mirror is 10 m away from and parallel to a second plane mirror (Figure 24-44). Find the location of the first five images formed by each mirror when an object is positioned 3 m from one of the mirrors. SSM

Mirror 1   Mirror 2   Figure 24-44 Problem 35

36. •At what point(s) A–E will the image of the face be visible in the plane mirror of length L (Figure 24-45)? The distance x

equals $L/2$. The points A–E are collinear and separated by a distance of $3L/4$, and point C lies on a line bisecting the mirror. Assume the face lies directly on point C.

Figure 24-45 Problem 36

37. •Using a ruler, a protractor, and the law of reflection, show the location of the image of your face when you stand a short distance in front of a plane mirror as shown in Figure 24-46.

Figure 24-46 Problem 37

38. ••One person is looking in a plane mirror at the image of a second person (Figure 24-47). Using a ruler, a protractor, and the law of reflection, show the location of the image as seen by the first person.

Figure 24-47 Problem 38

39. ••Suppose an autofocusing camera is positioned 2 m in front of a plane mirror. Describe the self-portrait that is photographed when you snap a picture of yourself. An autofocus camera sends infrared waves from a transmitter and receives the reflected waves that bounce off of the objects in front of the camera to determine the distance at which to focus the lens.

24-3 A concave mirror can produce an image of a different size than the object

40. •Describe the difference between the images seen in a spherical, concave mirror when the object is "up close" (closer to the image than the focal length) compared to "far away" (outside the focal length).

41. •Are there any situations where a real image is formed in a spherical, concave mirror? Describe the location of the object relative to the focal point for such situations. SSM

42. •What is a good way to remember the general shape of a spherical concave mirror?

24-4 Simple equations give the position and magnification of the image made by a concave mirror

43. •An object is placed 8.0 cm in front of a concave mirror that has a 10-cm radius of curvature. Calculate the image distance and the magnification of the image. Determine if the image is real or virtual and whether it is inverted or upright by using (a) a ray trace diagram and (b) the mirror equation. SSM

44. •An object 1.0 cm tall is placed 3.0 cm in front of a spherical concave mirror with a radius of curvature equal to 10.0 cm. Calculate the image distance and height by using (a) a ray trace diagram and (b) the mirror equation.

45. •An object 1.0 cm tall is placed 6 cm in front of a spherical concave mirror with a radius of curvature equal to 10.0 cm. Calculate the image distance and height by using (a) a ray trace diagram and (b) the mirror equation.

46. ••The radius of curvature of a spherical concave mirror is 20 cm. Describe the image formed when a 10-cm-tall object is positioned (a) 5 cm from the mirror, (b) 20 cm from the mirror, (c) 50 cm from the mirror, and (d) 100 cm from the mirror. For each case give the image distance, the image height, the type of image (real or virtual), and the orientation of the image (upright or inverted).

47. ••The radius of curvature of a spherical concave mirror is 15 cm. Describe the image formed when a 20-cm-tall object is positioned (a) 10 cm from the mirror, (b) 20 cm from the mirror, and (c) 100 cm from the mirror. For each case give the image distance, the image height, the type of image (real or virtual), and the orientation of the image (upright or inverted). SSM

48. ••An object is positioned 24 cm from a spherical concave mirror of unknown focal length. The image that is formed is 30 cm from the mirror. (a) Calculate the focal length. (b) Is this answer unique? (c) Is the image real or virtual? (d) If the object is 10 cm tall, determine the height of the image(s).

49. ••Construct the ray trace diagrams to locate the images in the following cases. (a) A 10-cm-tall object is located 5 cm in front of a spherical concave mirror with a radius of curvature of 20 cm. (b) A 10-cm-tall object is located 10 cm in front of a spherical concave mirror with a radius of curvature of 20 cm. (c) A 10-cm-tall object is located 20 cm in front of a spherical concave mirror with a radius of curvature of 20 cm. In each case, start by estimating the height of the image from a sketch.

50. ••Derive a relationship between the radius of curvature of a spherical, concave mirror and the object distance that gives an upright image that is four times as tall as the object.

24-5 A convex mirror always produces an image that is smaller than the object

51. •Describe the difference between the images seen in a spherical, convex mirror when the object is "up close" (a shorter distance from the mirror than the focal distance of the mirror) compared to "far away" (a longer distance from the mirror than the focal distance of the mirror).

52. •Are there any situations where a real image is formed in a spherical, convex mirror? Why or why not?

53. •How can you remember the difference between the shapes of a spherical *concave* mirror and a spherical *convex* mirror?

54. ••Construct ray trace diagrams to locate the images and estimate the image height in each of the following cases. (a) A 10-cm-tall object located 5 cm in front of a spherical convex mirror with a radius of curvature of 20 cm. (b) A 10-cm-tall object located 10 cm in front of a spherical convex mirror with a radius of curvature of 20 cm. (c) A 10-cm-tall object located 20 cm in front of a spherical convex mirror with a radius of curvature of 20 cm.

24-6 The same equations used for concave mirrors also work for convex mirrors

55. ••The radius of curvature of a spherical convex mirror is 20 cm. Describe the image formed when a 10-cm-tall object is positioned (a) 20 cm from the mirror, (b) 50 cm from the mirror, and (c) 100 cm from the mirror. For each case, provide the image distance, the image height, the type of image (real or virtual), and the orientation of the image (upright or inverted). SSM

56. ••The radius of curvature of a spherical convex mirror is 15 cm. Describe the image formed when a 20-cm-tall object is positioned (a) 5 cm from the mirror, (b) 20 cm from the mirror, and (c) 100 cm from the mirror. For each case, provide the image distance, the image height, the type of image (real or virtual), and the orientation of the image (upright or inverted).

57. •A car's convex rearview mirror has a radius of curvature equal to 15 m. What are the magnification, type, and location of the image that is formed by an object that is 10 m from the mirror?

58. •An 18-cm-long pencil is placed beside a convex spherical mirror, and its image is 10.5 cm in length. If the radius of curvature of the mirror is 88.4 cm, find the image distance, the object distance, and the magnification of the pencil.

59. •A 1-cm-long horse fly hovers 1 cm from a shiny sphere with a radius of 25 cm. Describe the location of the image of the fly, its type (real or virtual), and its length.

60. •A spherical convex mirror is placed at the end of a driveway on a corner with a limited view of oncoming traffic. The mirror has a radius of curvature of 1.85 m. Where will the image of a car that is 12.6 m from the mirror appear?

61. ••Using the mirror equation, prove that all images in spherical convex mirrors are virtual. SSM

62. •A girl sees her image in a shiny glass sphere tree ornament that has a diameter of 10 cm. The image is upright and is located 1.5 cm behind the surface of the ornament. How far from the ornament is the child located?

63. •A shiny sphere, 30 cm in diameter, is placed in a garden for aesthetic purposes. Determine the type, location, and height of the image of a 6.00-cm-tall squirrel located 40 cm in front of the sphere.

24-7 Convex lenses form images like concave mirrors and vice versa

64. •Under what circumstances will the images formed by converging or diverging lenses be designated as "real"? Indicate the type or types of lenses and the required position of the object.

65. •A real image that is created due to reflection in a spherical mirror appears in front of the mirrored surface. Is this also the case for a real image that is created due to refraction in a lens? SSM

66. •Where does the bending of light physically take place in a typical biconcave or biconvex lens? Is this how we draw ray trace diagrams? Why or why not?

67. •Which type of lens is used in eyeglasses to correct (a) nearsightedness (myopia)? (b) farsightedness (hyperopia)?

68. •How many rays are required to trace out the image that is formed by a lens in a ray trace diagram?

24-8 The focal length of a lens is determined by its index of refraction and the curvature of its surfaces

69. •A 10-cm-tall object is located in front of a converging lens with a power of 5 diopters. Describe the image created (type, location, height) and draw the ray trace diagrams if the object is located (a) 5 cm from the lens, (b) 10 cm from the lens, (c) 20 cm from the lens, and (d) 50 cm from the lens. SSM

70. ••A 10-cm-tall object is located in front of a diverging lens with a power of −5 diopters. Describe the type, location, and height of the image created, and draw the ray trace diagrams if the object is located (a) 5 cm from the lens, (b) 10 cm from the lens, (c) 20 cm from the lens, and (d) 50 cm from the lens.

71. ••A 2.00-cm-tall object is 18.0 cm in front of a converging lens with a focal length of 30.0 cm. (a) Use the lens equation and (b) a ray trace diagram to describe the type, location, and height of the image that is formed.

72. ••A lens is formed from a plastic material that has an index of refraction of 1.55. If the radius of curvature of one surface is 1.25 m and the radius of curvature of the other surface is 1.75 m, use the lens maker's equation to calculate the focal length and the power of the lens.

73. ••A glass lens ($n = 1.60$) has a focal length of −31.8 cm and a plano-concave shape. (a) Calculate the radius of curvature of the concave surface. (b) If a lens is constructed from the same glass to form a plano-convex shape with the same radius of curvature, what will the focal length be? SSM

74. ••A 2.00-cm-tall object is 30.0 cm in front of a converging lens that has a focal length of 18.0 cm. (a) Use the lens equation and (b) a ray trace diagram to describe the type, location, and height of the image that is formed.

75. •••Biology Calculate the overall magnification of a compound microscope that uses an objective lens with a focal length of 0.50 cm, an eyepiece with a focal length of 2.50 cm, and a distance of 18 cm between the two.

General Problems

Note: In these problems "infinity" means a very large distance compared to the focal length of a lens.

76. ••The opposite walls of a barber shop are covered by plane mirrors, so that multiple images arise from multiple reflections, and you see many reflected images of yourself, receding to infinity. The width of the shop is 6.50 m, and you are standing 2.00 m from the north wall. (a) How far apart are the first two images of you behind the north wall? (b) What is the separation of the first two images of you behind the south wall? Explain your answer.

77. ••An object is 40.0 cm from a concave spherical mirror whose radius of curvature is 32.0 cm. Locate and describe the type and magnification of the image formed by the mirror (a) by calculating the image distance and lateral magnification and (b) by drawing a ray trace diagram. On the ray trace diagram draw an eye in a position from which it can view the image.

78. ••Biology A typical human eye is nearly spherical and usually about 2.5 cm in diameter. Suppose a person first looks at a coin that is 2.3 cm across, located 30.0 cm from her eye, and then looks up at her friend who is 1.8 m tall and 3.25 m away. (a) Find the approximate size of each image (coin and friend) on her retina. (*Hint:* Just look at rays from the top and bottom of the object that pass through the center of the lens.) (b) Are the images in part (a) upright or inverted, and are they real or virtual?

79. ••Biology A typical human lens has an index of refraction of 1.43. The lens has a double convex shape, but its curvature can be varied by the ciliary muscles acting around its rim. At minimum power, the radius of the front of the lens is 10.0 cm,

while that of the back is 6.00 mm. At maximum power the radii are 6.00 mm and 5.50 mm, respectively. (The numbers can vary somewhat.) If the lens were in air, (a) what would be the ranges of its focal length and its power (in diopters)? (b) At maximum power, where would the lens form an image of an object 25 cm in front of the front surface of the lens? (c) Would the image fall on the retina of a human eye? The retina is located approximately 2.5 cm from the lens.

80. ••Biology A typical person's eye is 2.5 cm in diameter and has a near point (the closest an object can be and still be seen in focus) of 25 cm, and a far point (the farthest an object can be and still be in focus) of infinity. (a) What is the range of the effective focal lengths of the focusing mechanism (lens plus cornea) of the typical eye? (b) Is the equivalent focusing mechanism of the eye a diverging or a converging lens? Justify your answer without using any mathematics, and then see if your answer is consistent with your result in part (a).

81. •••A geneticist looks through a microscope to determine the phenotype of a fruit fly. The microscope is set to an overall magnification of 400x with an objective lens that has a focal length of 0.60 cm. The distance between the eyepiece and objective lenses is 16 cm. Find the focal length of the eyepiece lens assuming a near point of 25 cm (the closest an object can be and still be seen in focus). SSM

82. ••A thin lens made of glass that has a refractive index equal to 1.60 has surfaces with radii of curvature that have magnitudes equal to 12.0 and 18.0 mm. What are the possible values for its focal length? Sketch a cross-sectional view of the lens for each possible combination, making sure to label the radii of curvature of each surface of the lens and the associated focal length of the entire lens.

83. ••You are designing lenses that consist of small double convex pieces of plastic having surfaces with radii of curvature of magnitudes 3.50 cm on one side and 4.25 cm on the other side. You want the lenses to have a focal length of 1.65 cm in air. What should be the index of refraction of the plastic to achieve the desired focal length?

84. •••A lens of focal length +15.0 cm is 10.0 cm to the left of a second lens of focal length −15.0 cm. (a) Where is the final image of an object that is 30.0 cm to the left of the positive lens? (b) Is the image real or virtual? (c) How do the image's size and orientation compare to those of the original object? Explain your answer. (d) How must you be oriented to see the image?

85. •••A thin, diverging lens having a focal length of magnitude 45.0 cm has the same principal axis as a concave mirror with a radius of 60.0 cm. The center of the mirror is 20.0 cm from the lens, with the lens in front of the mirror. An object is placed 15.0 cm in front of the lens. (a) Where is the final image due to the lens–mirror combination? (b) Is the final image real or virtual? Upright or inverted? (c) Suppose now that the concave mirror is replaced by a convex mirror of the same radius. Repeat parts (a) and (b) for the new lens–mirror combination. SSM

86. •••When you place a bright light source 36.0 cm to the left of a lens, you obtain an upright image 14.0 cm from the lens and also a faint inverted image 13.8 cm to the left of the lens that is due to reflection from the front surface of the lens. When the lens is turned around, a faint inverted image is 25.7 cm to the left of the lens. What is the index of refraction of the material?

87. •••A thin, converging lens having a focal length of magnitude 25.00 cm is placed 1.000 m from a plane mirror that

is oriented perpendicular to the principal axis of the lens. A flower, 8.400 cm tall, is 1.450 m from the mirror on the principal axis of the lens. (a) Where is the final image of the flower produced by the lens–mirror combination? Is it real or virtual? Upright or inverted? How tall is the image? (b) If the converging lens is replaced by a diverging lens having a focal length of the same magnitude as the original lens, what will be the answers to part (a)?

88. ●●●**Biology** A compound microscope has a tube length of 20.0 cm and an objective lens of focal length 8.0 cm. (a) If it is to have a magnifying power of 200x, what should be the focal length of the eyepiece? (b) If the final image is viewed at infinity, how far from the objective should the object be placed?

89. ●●**Biology** You may have noticed that the eyes of cats appear to glow green in low light. This effect is due to the reflection of light by the *tapetum lucidum*, a highly reflective membrane just behind the retina of the eye. Light that has passed through the retina without hitting photoreceptors is reflected back to the retina, thus enabling the animal to see much better than humans in low light. The eye of a typical cat is about 1.25 cm in diameter. Assume that the light enters the eye traveling parallel to the principal axis of the lens. (a) If some of the light reflected off the *tapetum lucidum* escapes being absorbed by the retina, where will it be focused? (b) The refractive index of the liquid in the eye is about 1.4. How does this affect the location of the image in part (a)? SSM

90. ●●**Medical** A nearsighted eye is corrected by placing a diverging lens in front of the eye. The lens will create a virtual image of a distant object at the far point (the farthest an object can be and still be in focus) of the myopic viewer where it will be clearly seen. In the traditional treatment of myopia, an object at infinity is focused to the far point of the eye. If an individual has a far point of 70 cm, prescribe the correct power of the lens that is needed.

91. ●●**Medical** A farsighted eye is corrected by placing a converging lens in front of the eye. The lens will create a virtual image that is located at the near point (the closest an object can be and still be in focus) of the viewer when the object is held at a comfortable distance (usually taken to be 25 cm). If a person has a near point of 75 cm, what power reading glasses should be prescribed to treat this hyperopia?

92. ●●●**Medical** (a) Prove that when two thin lenses are pressed next to one another, the combined focal length (f combined) of the two lenses, acting together, is given by

$$\frac{1}{f_{combined}} = \frac{1}{f_1} + \frac{1}{f_2}$$

(b) Describe how this relates to a prescription for a contact lens which is placed directly on the eye? (Assume there is no significant separation between the contact lens and the lens of the eye.) (c) Why would an eyeglass prescription that is identical to a contact prescription give a very subtle difference in the image seen?

93. ●●**Medical** An optometrist tests a person and finds that without glasses, he needs to have his eyes 15.0 cm from a book to

read comfortably and can focus clearly only on distant objects up to 2.75 m away, but no farther. A typical normal eye should be able to focus on objects that are between 25.0 cm (the near point) and infinity (the far point) from the eye. (a) What type of correcting lenses does the person need: single focal length or bifocals? Why? (b) What should the optometrist specify as the focal length(s) of the correcting contact lens or lenses? (c) What is the power (in diopters) of the correcting lens or lenses? SSM

94. ●●●**Medical** One of the inevitable consequences of aging is a decrease in the flexibility of the lens. This leads to the farsighted condition called *presbyopia* (elder eye). Almost every aging human will experience it to some extent. However, for the myopic person, at some point, it is possible that far vision will be limited by a subpar far point *and* near vision will be hampered by an expanding near point. One solution is to wear bifocal lenses that are diverging in the upper half to correct the nearsightedness and converging in the lower half to correct the farsightedness.

Suppose one such individual asks for your help. The patient complains that he can't see far enough to safely drive (his far point is 112 cm) and he can't read the font of his smart phone without holding it beyond arm's length (his near point is 83 cm)! Prescribe the bifocals that will correct the visual issues for your patient.

95. ●●A common zoom lens for a digital camera covers a focal length range of 18 mm to 200 mm. For the purposes of this problem, treat the lens as a thin lens. If the lens is zoomed out to 200 mm and is focused on a petroglyph that is 15.0 m away and 38 cm wide, (a) how far is the lens from the photosensor array of the camera and (b) how wide is the image of the petroglyph on the sensors? (c) If the closest that the lens can get to the sensors at its 18 mm focal length is 5.2 cm, what is the closest object it can focus on at that focal length? SSM

96. ●●A macro lens is designed to take very close-range photographs of small objects such as insects and flowers. At its closest focusing distance, a certain macro lens has a focal length of 35.0 mm and forms an image on the photosensors of the camera that is 1.09 times the size of the object. (a) How close must the object be to the lens to achieve this maximum image size? (b) What is the magnification if the object is twice as far from the lens as in part (a)? For this problem, treat the lens as a thin lens.

97. ●**Astronomy** A refracting astronomical telescope, or refractor, consists of an eyepiece lens at one end of a cylindrical tube and an objective lens at the other end. The objective lens gathers light from a distant object (such as a planet) and focuses it at the focal point of the eyepiece lens. The eyepiece basically acts as a simple magnifier to create a virtual image of the objective's image. The overall magnification, M, is found to be $M = -f_o/f_e$, where f_o is the focal length of the objective and f_e is the focal length of the eyepiece. (a) Calculate the magnification of the 36-in refractor at Lick Observatory on Mount Hamilton near San Jose, California. The focal length of the objective lens is 17.37 m, and the focal length of the eyepiece is 22 mm. (b) What is the significance of the negative sign in the magnification equation?

Relativity

25

What Do You Think?

In cancer radiotherapy, a beam of electrons is accelerated to nearly the speed of light. The kinetic energy of the electrons is used to create intense X ray beams that can be accurately targeted on the location of the cancerous tissue. Which requires more energy: (a) accelerating an electron from rest to 90% of the speed of light, or (b) further accelerating that electron from 90 to 99% of the speed of light?

In this chapter, your goals are to:

- (25-1)   Identify some circumstances under which the physics you know breaks down.
- (25-2)   Describe how different observers view the same motion in Newtonian physics.
- (25-3)   Explain how the Michelson-Morley experiment helped rule out the ether model of the propagation of light.
- (25-4)   Describe how the time interval between two events can have different values in different frames of reference.
- (25-5)   Calculate how the dimensions of an object change when it is in motion.
- (25-6)   Explain why the speed of light in a vacuum is an ultimate speed limit.
- (25-7)   Calculate the rest energy of an object with mass.
- (25-8)   Explain what the principle of equivalence tells us about the nature of gravity.

To master this chapter, you should review:

- (2-7)   The motion of objects in free fall.
- (3-6)   Projectile motion.
- (4-2, 4-3) Newton's first and second laws.
- (6-3)   Kinetic energy and the work-energy theorem.
- (7-4)   Elastic collisions.
- (7-6)   The relationship between external forces and momentum change.
- (22-3)   The electromagnetic nature of light.

25-1 The concepts of relativity may seem exotic, but they're part of everyday life

Most of our everyday experiences involve objects that are either not moving with respect to us or are moving at speeds that are slow compared to the speed of light in a vacuum. In the late nineteenth century, scientists began to realize that the laws of physics that we've developed so far in this book don't properly describe light or objects moving at speeds near the speed of light. Albert Einstein first understood the way to extend physics into this regime of extremely high speed.

In this chapter we'll focus on Einstein's *special theory of relativity*. We'll see how discoveries concerning the nature of light helped motivate the central ideas of this theory. We'll also see how a simple postulate—that the speed of light does not depend on the motion of either the emitter or the observer of the light—leads to a radical transformation of our understanding of space and time. We'll discover that the speed of light is an ultimate speed limit, which means that it is impossible to accelerate an object beyond

(a)

In order for a GPS receiver to accurately determine its position, it must use relativity to adjust for time flowing at a different rate aboard a GPS satellite than on Earth.

(b)

Sunlight is a result of reactions deep inside the Sun that convert mass into energy—a process predicted by the special theory of relativity.

Figure 25-1 **Relativity in your world** (a) A GPS-equipped mobile phone and (b) the light from the Sun illustrate applications of the theory of relativity.

that speed. We'll also see that mass is simply another form of energy. We'll conclude with a look at Einstein's *general theory of relativity*, which provides new insights into the nature of gravity.

Although the effects of the special theory of relativity are most pronounced for objects moving at very high speeds, they can be seen in the world around you. Your mobile phone probably has the ability to determine its location using the Global Positioning System, or GPS (Figure 25-1a). A GPS receiver detects signals from a collection of satellites in Earth's orbit and calculates its position by timing those signals. However, the satellites move at about 28,000 km/h (18,000 mi/h) relative to Earth, and special relativity tells us that a moving clock or timekeeper runs at a different rate than a stationary one (see Section 25-4). Your smartphone has to be able to correct for this in order to give you accurate positioning information. Ordinary sunlight is also a consequence of relativity: The Sun shines by converting a fraction of its mass into electromagnetic energy, a direct application of the idea that objects have energy simply as a consequence of having mass (Figure 25-1b).

25-2 Newton's mechanics includes some ideas of relativity

You're on a train in the station, looking out the window at the train right next to yours. One of the trains is moving, but you can't tell which (Figure 25-2). Is your train moving and the other one stationary, or vice versa? Perhaps both are moving. How can you tell?

To address this question, let's return to Newton's first law, which we introduced in Section 4-3:

If the net external force on an object is zero...   ...the object does not accelerate...

$$\text{If } \sum \vec{F}_{ext} = 0 \text{, then } \vec{a} = 0 \text{ and } \vec{v} = \text{constant}$$

...and the velocity of the object remains constant. If the object is at rest, it remains at rest; if it is in motion, it continues in motion in a straight line at a constant speed.

Take-Home Message for Section 25-1

✔ The physics we have learned so far must be modified for objects moving at speeds comparable to the speed of light.

✔ These modifications lead us to new ideas about space, time, and energy.

Figure 25-2 **Relative motion** This is the view of one train as seen from the window of another. Which train is moving?

Newton's first law of motion (4-6)

Figure 25-3 **Two observers** Observers on the platform in a train station use coordinates x, y, and z and measure time t. An observer aboard the train uses coordinates x', y', and z' and measures t'.

An observer aboard the train is in frame of reference S'.

An observer standing on the platform is in frame of reference S.

The train (frame S') moves at constant speed V relative to the platform (frame S) in the positive x direction.

(a)
As measured in S

Net force on the child = 0.
Acceleration of the child = 0.

(b)
As measured in S'

Net force on the child = 0.
Acceleration of the child = 0.

Figure 25-4 **Newton's first law in two frames of reference** The free-body diagram for a child on the train as measured in the two frames of reference shown in Figure 25-3.

The first law states that an object that experiences no net force could *either* be at rest or in motion at a constant velocity. Newton's laws therefore treat both cases identically. So although we might make a distinction between an object at rest and one in (uniform) motion with respect to us, the laws of physics do not. In the case of the two trains, this tells us something profound: If you have no reference to the ground or the tracks on which the trains move, there is *no* way to design an experiment or make a measurement that would tell you whether the other train is moving at a constant velocity with respect to yours or your train is moving a constant velocity with respect to the other one.

A useful way to think about this idea is to introduce the concept of a **frame of reference** (also called a *reference frame* or simply *frame*). This is a coordinate system with respect to which we can make observations or measurements. Figure 25-3 shows two different frames of reference. A person standing on the train platform is in frame S and measures the positions of objects using the coordinates x, y, and z. This person has a watch, and the time of a certain event as measured on this watch is t. A person riding on the train is in frame S' and measures the positions of objects using the coordinates x', y', and z'. The time of an event as measured by this person is t'. If neither frame of reference is accelerating, the message of Newton's first law is that *both* frames are equally good for making measurements.

As an example, let's consider a child sitting in one of the seats on the train (Figure 25-4). The train is on a straight track and is moving relative to the platform at a constant speed V. As measured by a person on the platform (frame of reference S), the child is moving at a constant velocity with zero acceleration, so the net force on the child must be zero: The upward normal force exerted by the seat exactly balances the downward gravitational force that Earth exerts on the child. As measured by another passenger seated on board the train (frame of reference S'), the child is at rest (the child isn't moving relative to that passenger). So as measured in S', the net force on the child must again be zero. The two observers—one in frame of reference S and one in frame of reference S'—disagree about *how* the child moves. But they agree that the child's motion is in accordance with Newton's first law, Equation 4-6.

It's not just Newton's first law that applies in both frames of reference depicted in Figure 25-3. Newton's second law also applies in both frames:

If a **net external force** acts on an object...

...the object accelerates. The acceleration is in the same direction as the net force.

Newton's second law of motion
(4-2)

$$\sum \vec{F}_{\text{ext}} = m\vec{a}$$

The magnitude of acceleration that the net external force causes depends on the mass m of the object (the quantity of material in the object). The greater the mass, the smaller the acceleration.

As an illustration, suppose the child riding on the train is tossing a ball up and down (Figure 25-5). A passenger seated in the train (frame of reference S') sees the motion of the ball as purely vertical (We draw the ball's motion with a slight horizontal displacement to distinguish the up and down motion, but this motion is really only along a vertical line). By contrast, a person on the platform (frame of reference S) sees the ball following a parabolic path: The ball has the same horizontal component of velocity V as the train, and it maintains that horizontal velocity during its flight. As for the child in Figure 25-4, the observers in the two frames of reference disagree about how the ball moves: The motion is along a line as seen in S' but is in a plane as seen in S. Both observers, however, agree that the ball obeys Newton's second law. That's because as observed from both frames of reference, when the ball is in flight only the gravitational force acts on it, and so the acceleration is downward and has magnitude g. In frame S' the straight up-and-down motion is free fall, as we described in Section 2-7; in frame S the ball is in projectile motion, as we described in Section 3-6. Each description is correct for the frame of reference in which the motion is observed.

We refer to a frame of reference attached to an object that does not accelerate as an **inertial frame**. Newton's first law (also called the law of inertia) defines an inertial frame of reference. If, according to an observer, an object at rest tends to remain at rest, and an object in motion maintains the same velocity (speed and direction) unless acted on by a net force, then the object is in an inertial reference frame. If one frame of reference S is inertial, a second frame of reference S' is also inertial if it moves at a constant velocity relative to S. That's the case for the two frames of reference depicted in Figure 25-3.

By contrast, a frame of reference attached to an accelerated object is a **noninertial frame**. To an observer in a noninertial frame, Newton's first law does *not* hold true. An example is a frame of reference attached to a car that is accelerating forward. A ball sitting on the floor of this car has zero net force on it (the upward normal force exerted by the floor balances the downward gravitational force), yet the ball accelerates toward the back of the car. A rotating frame of reference, such as a carnival merry-go-round, is also noninertial because an object that follows a circular path is accelerating. Just like a ball in a car that accelerates forward, a ball placed on the merry-go-round floor has zero net force acting on it, yet this ball will tend to roll to the outside of the merry-go-round. In the frame of reference of a person riding on the merry-go-round, Newton's first law does not hold true.

Strictly speaking, an observer at rest on Earth's surface, such as the person in frame S standing on the platform in Figure 25-3, is in a noninertial frame. That's because Earth rotates on its axis like a merry-go-round and also moves along a roughly circular orbit around the Sun. However, the accelerations involved with those motions are so small (each is a small fraction of g) that for many purposes we can ignore them. As a result, we can safely regard the frame of reference S in Figure 25-3 as an effectively inertial one, and likewise for the frame S' attached to the train.

We've seen that Newton's first and second laws—the fundamental laws of motion—work equally well in both inertial frame S and inertial frame S'. This suggests that the same should be true for *any* inertial frame of reference. This statement is called the **principle of Newtonian relativity**:

The laws of motion are the same in all inertial frames of reference.

The word *relativity* means that measurements made relative to one inertial frame of reference are just as valid as those made relative to another inertial frame. Since the laws of motion don't distinguish between two inertial frames S and S', it's meaningless to ask which frame is "really" moving and which frame is "really" at rest. (You may think that frame S is the one that's really at rest because it's stationary with respect to the platform. But remember that the platform is on Earth and that our entire planet is in motion through the solar system.) So another way to express the principle of Newtonian relativity is:

There is no way to detect absolute motion. Only motion relative to a selected frame of reference can be detected.

Let's apply the principle of Newtonian relativity to the ball shown in Figure 25-5. Suppose you are standing on the platform as the train goes by, so you are in reference frame S. You see the ball following a parabolic path, and you make observations of the x, y, and z coordinates of the ball as functions of time t. The child riding in the train is in reference frame S' and sees the ball moving straight up and down relative to her. As

(a)

As measured in S'

$a_y = -g$

Net force on ball = gravitational force
Ball experiences free fall.

(b)

As measured in S

Net force on ball = gravitational force
Ball experiences projectile motion.

$a_y = -g$

Figure 25-5 A tossed ball in two frames of reference The child on the train from Figure 25-4 tosses a ball straight up and down relative to her.

the ball moves, she measures the x', y', and z' coordinates of the ball as functions of time t'. The two sets of coordinates have the same orientation, as Figure 25-6 shows. To calibrate the two clocks—one in frame S, the other in frame S'—you and the child both set your clocks to read zero at the instant that you pass each other, when the origins of your frames of reference coincide. So at this instant $t = t' = 0$.

Suppose you and the child both measure the same **event**—that is, the ball being at a certain point in its motion, such as being at the high point in its path. In your S frame the coordinates of this event in space and time are x, y, z, and t, and the coordinates of this same event as measured in the S' frame are x', y', z', and t'. (Note that we are thinking of time as a fourth coordinate of an event.) As Figure 25-6 shows, a simple set of equations relates the coordinates of the same event in the two frames:

Galilean coordinate transformation (25-1)

> Inertial frame of reference S' moves at speed V in the positive x direction relative to inertial frame of reference S.

$$x' = x - Vt$$
$$y' = y$$
$$z' = z$$
$$t' = t$$

Coordinates of an event as measured in frame S'

Coordinates of the same event as measured in frame S

This set of equations is known as the **Galilean transformation**. Note that the relative motion of the two frames of reference along the positive x axis does not impact the measured values of the y and z components, which are the same in both reference frames.

We can use the Galilean transformation to compare the velocity of the ball as measured in frame S' to its velocity as measured in frame S. To do this, we'll look at *two* events in the motion of the ball separated by a short time interval from t_1 to t_2 as measured in frame S. During this time interval, the coordinates of the ball as measured in frame S change from x_1, y_1, and z_1 to x_2, y_2, and z_2. The components of the ball's velocity $\vec{v}$ in frame S are

(25-2)

$$v_x = \frac{\Delta x}{\Delta t} = \frac{x_2 - x_1}{t_2 - t_1}$$
$$v_y = \frac{\Delta y}{\Delta t} = \frac{y_2 - y_1}{t_2 - t_1}$$
$$v_z = \frac{\Delta z}{\Delta t} = \frac{z_2 - z_1}{t_2 - t_1}$$

At time t, the coordinate of the ball in S' is $x' = x - Vt$.

At $t = 0$, the origins of frames S and S' coincide.

$t' = 0$

S, S' $y' = y$
$x' = x$
$z' = z$

$t = 0$

S y
x
z

t

S' y'
x'
z'

t'

Figure 25-6 Comparing coordinates in two frames of reference The coordinates of a ball as measured in the two frames of reference shown in Figure 25-3.

For the same two events as measured in frame S' the time interval is from t'_1 to t'_2, and the coordinates change from x'_1, y'_1, and z'_1 to x'_2, y'_2, and z'_2. So in frame S' the components of the object's velocity $\vec{v}'$ are

$$v'_x = \frac{\Delta x'}{\Delta t'} = \frac{x'_2 - x'_1}{t'_2 - t'_1}$$

$$v'_y = \frac{\Delta y'}{\Delta t'} = \frac{y'_2 - y'_1}{t'_2 - t'_1}$$ (25-3)

$$v'_z = \frac{\Delta z'}{\Delta t'} = \frac{z'_2 - z'_1}{t'_2 - t'_1}$$

Now substitute the expressions for x', y', z', and t' from Equations 25-1 into Equations 25-3. We get

$$v'_x = \frac{(x_2 - Vt_2) - (x_1 - Vt_1)}{t_2 - t_1} = \frac{(x_2 - x_1) - V(t_2 - t_1)}{t_2 - t_1} = \frac{(x_2 - x_1)}{t_2 - t_1} - V$$

$$v'_y = \frac{y_2 - y_1}{t_2 - t_1}$$ (25-4)

$$v'_z = \frac{z_2 - z_1}{t_2 - t_1}$$

If we now compare Equations 25-4 for the velocity components in frame S' to Equations 25-2 for the velocity components in frame S, we see that

> Inertial frame of reference S' moves at speed V in the positive x direction relative to inertial frame of reference S.

Velocity components of an object as measured in frame S'

$$v'_x = v_x - V$$
$$v'_y = v_y$$
$$v'_z = v_z$$

Velocity components of the same object as measured in frame S

Galilean velocity transformation
(25-5)

Equations 25-5, which relate the velocity of an object in frame S' to the velocity of the same object in frame S, are called the **Galilean velocity transformation.**

As an example, think again of the ball shown in Figure 25-5. If the ball moves straight up and down as measured in frame S', then in that frame the ball is in free fall with only a y component of velocity. The other two components are zero: $v'_x = v'_z = 0$. As measured in frame S, the velocity of the ball has components

$$v_x = v'_x + V = V$$
$$v_y = v'_y$$
$$v_z = v'_z = 0$$

As measured in frame S, the ball moves up and down along the y direction with the same velocity as measured in frame S': $v_y = v'_y$. At the same time, as measured in frame S the ball maintains a constant velocity V in the x direction. That's just the behavior we expect for a projectile: Its motion is a combination of up-and-down free fall and constant-velocity horizontal motion (see Section 3-6).

❗ Watch Out! There is nothing special about either the S frame or the S' frame.

In Figures 25-5 and 25-6 we've chosen to think of frame S as at rest and frame S' as moving. This selection is purely our choice, because the principle of Newtonian relativity says that *all* inertial frames are equivalent. We could just as well say that frame S' is stationary and frame S is moving with speed V in the negative x direction.

You may wonder why we've spent so much time and effort explaining motion as seen from two different inertial frames of reference. As we'll discover in the next few sections, the reason is that something remarkable happens when the relative speed V

of the two frames is comparable to c, the speed of light in a vacuum. In that case we'll find that the Galilean transformations given by Equations 25-1 and 25-5 do not hold true. For example, as measured in the two different frames, the time interval between events can be different and objects can have different dimensions. These remarkable observations will radically transform our notions of the nature of time and space themselves.

Example 25-1 Two Cars

You observe two race cars approaching you. A red car is in one lane moving at 24 m/s relative to you. In a second lane, a blue car is moving at 36 m/s relative to you. (a) What is the velocity of the red car as measured by the driver of the blue car, relative to her frame of reference? (b) What is the velocity of the blue car as measured by the driver of the red car, relative to his frame of reference?

Set Up

We'll use Equations 25-5 to transform the velocity of a car as measured in one frame of reference to the velocity of the same car as measured in a different frame of reference. Note that these equations assume that frame S' is moving relative to frame S at speed V in the positive x direction. We'll have to keep this in mind when deciding which frame of reference corresponds to S and which to S'.

Galilean velocity transformation:

$$v'_x = v_x - V$$
$$v'_y = v_y$$
$$v'_z = v_z \qquad (25\text{-}5)$$

The given speeds of both cars are measured relative to you, that is, in your frame.

$v_{\text{red},x} = 24$ m/s

$v_{\text{blue},x} = 36$ m/s

We can choose to call your frame the S frame.

Solve

(a) Let's take the positive x direction to be in the direction both cars are moving relative to you. Then we'll take S to be your frame of reference and S' to be the frame of reference of the driver of the blue car. The relative speed of these two frames is $V = 36$ m/s (the speed of the blue car relative to you). All of the motions in this example are along the x axis, so we don't need the y or z members of Equations 25-5.

Use the x equation from Equations 25-5 to relate the velocity of the red car as measured by you ($v_{\text{red},x} = +24$ m/s) to its velocity as measured by the driver of the blue car ($v'_{\text{red},x}$):

$$v'_{\text{red},x} = v_{\text{red},x} - V$$
$$= +24 \text{ m/s} - 36 \text{ m/s}$$
$$= -12 \text{ m/s}$$

$v_{\text{red},x} = 24$ m/s

$v_{\text{blue},x} = 36$ m/s

As measured by the driver of the blue car, the red car is moving in the negative x direction—that is, backwards—at 12 m/s.

(b) Again we take S to be your frame of reference, but now S' is the frame of reference of the driver of the red car. The relative speed of these two frames is $V = 24$ m/s (the speed of the red car relative to you).

Use the x equation from Equations 25-5 to relate the velocity of the blue car as measured by you ($v_{\text{blue},x} = +36$ m/s) to its velocity as measured by the driver of the red car ($v'_{\text{blue},x}$):

$$v'_{\text{blue},x} = v_{\text{blue},x} - V$$
$$= +36 \text{ m/s} - 24 \text{ m/s}$$
$$= +12 \text{ m/s}$$

$v_{\text{red},x} = 24$ m/s

$v_{\text{blue},x} = 36$ m/s

As measured by the driver of the red car, the blue car is moving in the positive x direction—that is, forwards—at 12 m/s.

Reflect

The driver of the blue car sees the red car falling farther and farther behind her at a rate of 12 m/s, while the driver of the red car sees the blue car moving farther and farther in front of him at a rate of 12 m/s. Note that the *magnitude* of the two answers is the same: Both drivers agree that the other driver is moving at a relative speed of 12 m/s.

? Got the Concept? 25-1   Groundspeed versus Airspeed

A typical jet airliner has a cruise airspeed—that is, its speed relative to the air through which it is flying—of 900 km/h. If the wind at the airliner's cruise altitude is blowing at 100 km/h from west to east, what is the speed of the airliner relative to the ground if the airplane is flying from west to east? From east to west? (a) 800 km/h west to east, 1000 km/h east to west; (b) 1000 km/h west to east, 800 km/h east to west; (c) 800 km/h in both directions; (d) 900 km/h in both directions; (e) 1000 km/h in both directions.

Take-Home Message for Section 25-2

✔ Newton's laws of motion treat all nonaccelerating objects identically, whether the objects are in motion or at rest.

✔ The laws of motion are the same in all inertial frames of reference. There is no way to detect absolute motion; only motion relative to a selected frame of reference can be detected.

✔ The Galilean transformations allow you to convert the coordinates and velocity of an object observed in one inertial frame of reference to the coordinates and velocity of the same object observed in a different inertial frame.

25-3 The Michelson-Morley experiment shows that light does not obey Newtonian relativity

We saw in the preceding section that Newton's laws of motion are the same in all inertial frames. Is the same true for the other laws of physics? Physicists asked this very question during the second half of the nineteenth century, specifically about the laws of electromagnetism. As we will see, finding the answer to this question had profound consequences that led to fundamental changes in our understanding of nature.

We learned in Section 22-3 that the laws of electromagnetism explain how electromagnetic waves, including visible light, are possible. These laws also predict that the speed of electromagnetic waves in a vacuum is

Speed of light in a vacuum

$$c = \frac{1}{\sqrt{\mu_0 \varepsilon_0}} = 3.00 \times 10^8 \text{ m/s}$$

Permeability of free space   Permittivity of free space

Speed of light in a vacuum
(22-11)

Our discussion in Section 25-2 tells us that we can measure relative motion but not absolute motion. So when we say that the speed of electromagnetic waves in a vacuum is c, we are forced to ask this question: Relative to what inertial frame of reference is the speed of light equal to c?

In the nineteenth century, the most common answer to this question was to imagine a substance that fills all space. This substance, which was called the *luminiferous ether*, was thought to be the medium for electromagnetic waves, just as air is the medium for sound waves in our atmosphere. This substance must be of extraordinarily low density, so that its presence is almost undetectable. (The word *luminiferous* comes from the Latin for "light-bearing." *Ether* in this phrase has nothing to do with the organic compounds of the same name.) In this model, c is the speed of electromagnetic waves relative to the frame in which the luminiferous ether is at rest.

How can we test whether this model is correct? To see the answer, note that the speed of sound waves in dry air is 343 m/s, but you will measure a different speed if a wind is blowing (that is, the air is moving relative to you). If a sound wave is traveling from west to east and a wind is blowing past you at 10 m/s from west to east, the sound will move relative to you at 343 m/s + 10 m/s = 353 m/s. If the sound wave is traveling from west to east and a 10-m/s wind is blowing from east to west, the speed of the sound wave relative to you will be 343 m/s − 10 m/s = 333 m/s. The same should be true for light waves if the luminiferous ether is moving past you, so that there is an "ether wind." If a light wave is traveling from west to east and the ether is moving from west to east relative to you at 10 m/s, you would measure the speed of the wave to be $c + 10$ m/s; if the ether is instead moving from east to west relative to you at 10 m/s, you would measure the speed of the wave to be $c - 10$ m/s. If we can detect these small changes in the speed of light, that would be evidence that the luminiferous ether really exists.

Nineteenth-century scientists looked to Earth's motion around the Sun as a source of "ether wind." Our planet moves around its orbit at an average speed of 29.8 km/s $= 2.98 \times 10^4$ m/s, or about $10^{-4} c$. If the luminiferous ether is at rest relative to the solar system as a whole, we should experience an "ether wind" that blows past our moving planet at $10^{-4} c$. Depending on the direction of that "ether wind" relative to the direction of light propagation, we would expect the speed of light to vary between $(1 + 10^{-4})c$ and $(1 - 10^{-4})c$. The challenge is to design an experiment that can detect such small changes in the speed of light.

In 1887 the American scientists Albert Michelson and Edward Morley carried out the first definitive experiment of this kind. This seminal experiment is known as the **Michelson-Morley experiment**. Their apparatus, called an *interferometer*, split a beam of light into two, sent the two beams along perpendicular paths, and then allowed them to recombine at a viewing screen (Figure 25-7). What is seen on the viewing screen is an interference pattern between the waves in the two beams. The nature of this pattern depends on the difference in length between the two paths and also on whether the speeds at which light travels along each path are the same or different. If there is an "ether wind" that is more nearly aligned with one leg of the interferometer than the other, the speed of light should indeed be different along the two legs. Their apparatus was sensitive enough that Michelson and Morley should have been able to measure the effects of an "ether wind" due to Earth's motion around the Sun.

Michelson and Morley's results were striking: They found *no* effect due to an "ether wind." They and other scientists refined and repeated the experiment many times, but the results were always the same: There is no evidence for the existence of the luminiferous ether. The conclusion from this and other experiments is that electromagnetic waves do not require the presence of a material medium, but can propagate in a complete vacuum.

Under Newtonian relativity, to explain a constant value of the speed of light in a vacuum required that the equations of electromagnetism hold true only in a specific reference frame, one that is at rest relative to the medium for electromagnetic waves. But if there is no luminiferous ether, there is no such medium and hence no such special frame of reference. So physicists had no choice but to conclude that Newtonian relativity does *not* apply to electromagnetic waves. It was left to Albert Einstein to modify the ideas of Newtonian relativity and find a new way to look at the relationships between measurements made in different inertial frames of reference. We'll explore Einstein's simple yet radical ideas in the following section.

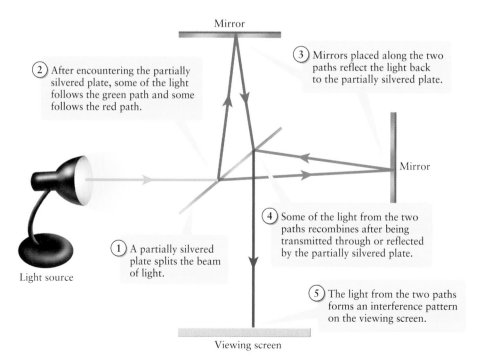

(2) After encountering the partially silvered plate, some of the light follows the green path and some follows the red path.

(3) Mirrors placed along the two paths reflect the light back to the partially silvered plate.

(1) A partially silvered plate splits the beam of light.

(4) Some of the light from the two paths recombines after being transmitted through or reflected by the partially silvered plate.

(5) The light from the two paths forms an interference pattern on the viewing screen.

Light source

Mirror

Mirror

Viewing screen

Figure 25-7 The Michelson-Morley experiment simplified If the luminiferous ether exists and is moving relative to this apparatus, its presence will be apparent in the interference pattern on the viewing screen.

Take-Home Message for Section 25-3

✔ Experiment shows that electromagnetic waves do not require a material medium; they can easily propagate in a perfect vacuum.

✔ As a result, we conclude that electromagnetic waves do not obey Newtonian relativity.

25-4 Einstein's relativity predicts that the time between events depends on the observer

German-born theoretical physicist Albert Einstein published his **special theory of relativity**, or *special relativity* for short, in 1905. Einstein based his theory on two postulates:

- *First postulate:* All laws of physics are the same in all inertial frames.
- *Second postulate:* The speed of light in a vacuum is the same in all inertial frames, independent of both the speed of the source of the light and the speed of the observer.

The adjective "special" means that the theory applies to the special case of inertial frames and constant-velocity motion. Einstein's *general* theory of relativity, which we'll discuss in Section 25-8, extends these ideas to accelerating, noninertial frames.) The first postulate extends the principle of relativity beyond Newton's laws of motion to include thermodynamics and electricity and magnetism, including electromagnetic waves. Einstein's second postulate derives from our conclusion in Section 25-3 that there is no special frame of reference in which the speed of light in a vacuum is equal to $c = 3.00 \times 10^8$ m/s. The implications of this second postulate totally transformed early twentieth-century scientists' understanding of the natural world.

Perhaps the most astounding consequence of the second postulate of special relativity is that the time interval between two events is *not* an absolute. Rather, this time interval depends on the motion of the frame of reference from which time is measured. To see how this comes about, we'll do a thought experiment. Einstein was well known for his ability to solve problems by carrying out these *gedanken*, or thought experiments, some of which were technologically impossible to do as real physical experiments.

Imagine a *light clock*, a special clock that uses light to measure intervals of time (**Figure 25-8**). A laser fires an extremely brief burst, or pulse, of light straight downward. This is reflected by a mirror and arrives at a light-sensitive detector next to the laser. For simplicity, we can treat the laser and detector as being at the same position. One tick of the clock is the time interval between the pulse leaving the laser (event 1) and the pulse arriving at the detector (event 2). In the frame of reference of the clock, these two events occur at the same point in space. We use the term **proper time** for the time interval between two events that occur at the same place, and we denote it by the symbol Δt_{proper}. Another way to think of proper time is that it is the time interval as measured in a frame of reference in which the clock is at rest. You can think of the rest frame of the clock as being "attached" to it.

Figure 25-8 **A light clock** The duration of each "tick" of this clock is the time between the start of the pulse and the time when the reflected light arrives at the detector.

During one tick of this light clock,

Laser   Detector

① A brief light pulse is emitted by the laser...

③ ...and arrives at the light sensitive detector.

Light pulse

D

② ...reflected from the mirror...

Mirror

> **Watch Out!** Every object—including a moving object—has a rest frame.
>
> An object is always at rest with respect to itself, which means that an object is not moving in a reference frame that is attached to it. Notice, however, that the statement is a relative one—the object is not moving *relative* to its own rest frame.
>
> We can still define any number of other frames with respect to which the object *is* in motion. A person standing on the sidewalk is at rest in her own rest frame, but is moving as measured from the frame of reference of a car driving past.

During one tick of our light clock, a light pulse travels the distance D to the mirror and then the same distance back to the detector, for a total distance of $2D$. We imagine that the clock is placed in a vacuum, so that the speed of the light pulse is c. The time interval for the tick is then

$$(25\text{-}6) \qquad \Delta t_{\text{proper}} = \frac{2D}{c}$$

We now let the light clock move at speed V relative to us. In keeping with the way we name frames in discussing Newtonian relativity, we attach a frame S' to the clock and consider ourselves in the S frame. The S' frame therefore moves at speed V relative to the S frame. Figure 25-9 shows the process of a single tick of the clock as observed from our S frame. During the time that it takes for the light pulse to get from the laser to the mirror, the entire clock has moved. And during the time between the reflection from the mirror and the arrival of the light pulse at the detector, the clock has moved again. The total distance L that the clock has moved during this time equals the product of the speed V and the time interval of one clock tick. Be careful, however: We *cannot* assume that the time interval for one tick as measured in S is Δt_{proper} because Δt_{proper} is measured in frame S' at rest with respect to the clock. Instead, we use the symbol Δt for the time interval of one tick as observed from the S frame. So

$$(25\text{-}7) \qquad L = V\Delta t$$

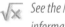 *See the Math Tutorial for more information on trigonometry*

From our vantage point in the S frame, the path followed by the light pulse during time Δt traces out two sides of a triangle (Figure 25-9).

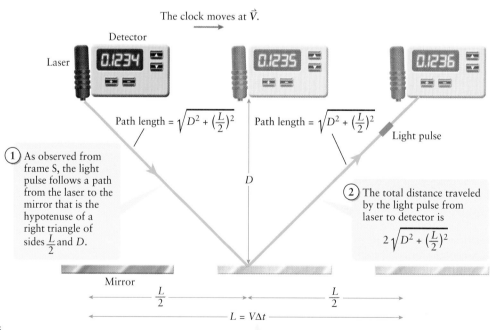

The clock moves at $\vec{V}$.

Detector

Laser

Path length = $\sqrt{D^2 + \left(\frac{L}{2}\right)^2}$ Path length = $\sqrt{D^2 + \left(\frac{L}{2}\right)^2}$

Light pulse

① As observed from frame S, the light pulse follows a path from the laser to the mirror that is the hypotenuse of a right triangle of sides $\frac{L}{2}$ and D.

D

② The total distance traveled by the light pulse from laser to detector is

$$2\sqrt{D^2 + \left(\frac{L}{2}\right)^2}$$

Mirror

$\frac{L}{2}$ $\frac{L}{2}$

$L = V\Delta t$

Figure 25-9 A moving light clock and time dilation When the light clock depicted in Figure 25-8 moves, the distance the light pulse travels is longer than twice the distance from the laser to the mirror.

③ As observed in frame S, $L = V\Delta t$ is the total distance that the clock travels during the travel time Δt of the light pulse.

In our rest frame S the time interval is therefore equal to the sum of the lengths of these two sides—the distance the light pulse travels—divided by the speed at which the light pulse travels in frame S. The second postulate of special relativity assures us that the speed of the light pulse is c in *all* inertial frames, and so is the same in frame S as in frame S'. Thus

$$\Delta t = \frac{2\sqrt{D^2 + \left(\frac{L}{2}\right)^2}}{c} \tag{25-8}$$

We now have two expressions for the time interval between the light pulse leaving the laser and the same pulse arriving at the detector. As measured in the clock rest frame S', this time interval is the proper time $\Delta t_{\mathrm{proper}}$ as given by Equation 25-6; as measured in our rest frame S, the time interval is Δt as given by Equation 25-8. To compare these two time intervals, first note that the distance L does not appear in the expression for $\Delta t_{\mathrm{proper}}$. To eliminate L from the expression for Δt, substitute Equation 25-7 into Equation 25-8:

$$\Delta t = \frac{2\sqrt{D^2 + \left(\frac{V\Delta t}{2}\right)^2}}{c}$$

Square both sides of this equation and rearrange to bring the two Δt terms together:

$$c^2\Delta t^2 = 4\left(D^2 + \left(\frac{V\Delta t}{2}\right)^2\right) = 4D^2 + V^2\Delta t^2$$

$$c^2\Delta t^2 - V^2\Delta t^2 = 4D^2 \quad \text{or} \quad (c^2 - V^2)\Delta t^2 = 4D^2$$

Solve for Δt:

$$\Delta t^2 = \frac{4D^2}{c^2 - V^2} = \frac{4D^2}{c^2\left(1 - \frac{V^2}{c^2}\right)} \quad \text{or} \quad \Delta t = \frac{2D}{c\sqrt{1 - \frac{V^2}{c^2}}} \tag{25-9}$$

If we compare Δt as given by Equation 25-9 to $\Delta t_{\mathrm{proper}}$ as given by Equation 25-6, we get

Time interval between two events as measured in frame S', in which those events occur at the same place.

Time interval between the same two events as measured in frame S

$$\Delta t = \frac{\Delta t_{\mathrm{proper}}}{\sqrt{1 - \frac{V^2}{c^2}}} \tag{25-10}$$

Speed of S' relative to S

Speed of light in a vacuum

Time dilation (25-10)

An observer in S moving relative to the clock measures a time interval Δt for one tick of the light clock. An observer in S' who is at rest with respect to the clock measures the time interval for one tick to be $\Delta t_{\mathrm{proper}}$, regardless of whether the observer and clock are moving with respect to some *other* observer. Equation 25-10 shows that Δt and $\Delta t_{\mathrm{proper}}$ are *not* equal: An observer in the S frame sees time running at a different rate than an observer in the S' frame. This is astounding!

For any nonzero value of V, the speed of one inertial frame relative to another, the denominator in Equation 25-10 is less than 1. It follows that Δt is greater than $\Delta t_{\mathrm{proper}}$. That is, the time interval as measured in S is longer than as measured in S'. We say that the time interval as measured in S has been expanded or *dilated* (the same term used to refer to an increase in size of the pupil of the eye). That's why this effect of special relativity is known as **time dilation**. If $\Delta t_{\mathrm{proper}} = 1$ s, the time interval Δt for one tick as measured in S will be greater than 1 s. Equivalently, if Δt as measured in S equals 1 s, $\Delta t_{\mathrm{proper}}$ as measured in S' will be less than 1 s. So an observer in S says that the light clock, which is moving past her at speed V, is ticking off time slowly: After 1 s has elapsed according to the observer in S, the moving clock has ticked off less than 1 s. So a shorthand way to express Equation 25-10 is that *a moving clock runs slowly*.

Our derivation of Equation 25-10 used the second postulate of relativity, the idea that the speed of light in a vacuum is the same in frame S as in frame S'. The difference between Δt and Δt_{proper} was then a result of the light pulse having to travel different distances in the two frames. As a result, it may seem that Equation 25-10 is valid only for time intervals measured using a light clock. But the first postulate of relativity says that *all* laws of physics are the same in every inertial frame of reference. This implies that time dilation is also valid for time intervals measured using a mechanical clock, such as a grandfather clock that keeps time with an oscillating pendulum or a wristwatch that uses an oscillating piece of quartz (Figure 12-1b). Imagine a pendulum clock, ticking once every time the pendulum makes one full oscillation. If the clock is on your desk, you see it swinging back and forth once every second. If the clock is moving, then the swing of the pendulum is slower, so the clock ticks more slowly. As we will see, however, the effect is very small unless V is very large.

! Watch Out! Time dilation occurs whether or not a clock is present.

You don't need to have a clock per se for the effects of time dilation to occur. Time runs slowly in one frame moving with respect to another frame, even if there is no clock in the moving frame and even if there is no observer in the other frame. Imagine, say, that you can place a *Caenorhabditis elegans* worm (Figure 25-10) on a spacecraft that will fly past Earth at high speed. *C. elegans* is an organism popular among geneticists because it grows to adulthood in a series of easily identifiable developmental stages that all together take less than three days. Each stage lasts eight to twelve hours. Were you to observe a *C. elegans* worm as it moved past you at high speed, each of those stages might take days or even years, measured on a clock at rest with respect to you.

Figure 25-10 **A worm "clock"** The worm *Caenorhabditis elegans* is an organism popular among geneticists because it grows to adulthood in a series of easily identifiable developmental stages each of which lasts a well-defined period of time.

! Watch Out! The effect of time dilation only arises when events in one frame are viewed from a second frame in motion relative to the first.

We imagined, above, a pendulum clock that ticks once every time the pendulum makes one full oscillation. If the clock sits on your desk, you see it swinging back and forth once every second. If you're sitting at your desk and you see the clock move across your desk, you see the pendulum swing more slowly. But if you and your clock are moving together relative to some other specific object or frame, you will see no time dilation effect on your own clock, regardless of how fast you and the clock are moving relative to that other object or frame. You will still see the pendulum swinging back and forth once every second. Although you and the clock are moving relative to the other object or frame, you and the clock are not moving relative to each other.

We do not observe time dilation in everyday life because most objects travel very slowly compared to the speed of light. As an example, in 2006 the *New Horizons* spacecraft was launched toward Pluto at 16,260 m/s = 58,536 km/h = 36,373 mi/h relative to Earth. (This is the greatest launch speed ever given to a spacecraft.) Even this tremendous speed is only 5.42×10^{-5} of the speed of light c, and the factor $1/\sqrt{1 - V^2/c^2}$ in Equation 25-10 is larger than 1 by only 1.47×10^{-9}. Due to time dilation, a clock on board *New Horizons* does indeed run slowly as measured from Earth, but by only one second every 21.5 years! As the following two examples show, however, time dilation can be substantial if the speeds involved are **relativistic speeds**— that is, an appreciable fraction of the speed of light, so that the consequences of Einstein's special theory of relativity are apparent.

Example 25-2 A Moving Clock

A clock moves past you. What must be the speed of the clock relative to you so that you see it as running at one-half (0.500) the rate of the clock on your cell phone in your hand?

Set Up

For a moving clock to be observed as running at 0.500 the rate of a clock at rest with respect to you means making Δt (the time interval measured by you) equal to twice Δt_{proper} (the time interval measured in the rest frame of the moving clock). That implies the factor $1/\sqrt{1 - V^2/c^2}$ in Equation 25-10 must be equal to $1/0.500 = 2.00$. We'll use this to solve for the speed V of the moving clock relative to you.

Time dilation:

$$\Delta t = \frac{\Delta t_{proper}}{\sqrt{1 - \dfrac{V^2}{c^2}}} \qquad (25\text{-}10)$$

clock

cell phone

Solve

Determine the value of V that makes $\Delta t = 2.00 \Delta t_{proper}$.

From Equation 25-10, we want

$$\Delta t = \frac{\Delta t_{proper}}{\sqrt{1 - \dfrac{V^2}{c^2}}} = 2.00 \Delta t_{proper} \quad \text{so} \quad \frac{1}{\sqrt{1 - \dfrac{V^2}{c^2}}} = 2.00$$

Solve for the value of the speed V:

$$\sqrt{1 - \frac{V^2}{c^2}} = \frac{1}{2.00} = 0.500$$

$$1 - \frac{V^2}{c^2} = (0.500)^2 = 0.250$$

$$\frac{V^2}{c^2} = 1 - 0.250 = 0.750$$

$$\frac{V}{c} = \sqrt{0.750} = 0.866$$

$$V = 0.866c$$

$$= 0.866(3.00 \times 10^8 \text{ m/s}) = 2.60 \times 10^8 \text{ m/s}$$

Reflect

For you to observe the moving clock running a factor of 2.00 slower than the clock at rest with respect to you, the relative speed between you and the clock would need to be 86.6% of the speed of light in a vacuum. This is more than 10^4 times faster than the top speed of any craft built by humans.

Example 25-3 Muon Decay

Our planet is continually bombarded by fast-moving subatomic particles from space (mostly protons). When these particles collide with the atoms and molecules that make up Earth's upper atmosphere, they can produce a new sub-atomic particle called the *muon*. These muons travel at high speed, around 0.994c. Muons naturally decay, however; if you create a number of muons in the lab, on average half of them will decay after 1.56 μs (1 μs = 10^{-6} s). This time is known as the *half-life* of the muon. Of the remaining muons, another half will decay after another 1.56 μs, and so on. If 1.00×10^6 muons are created at an altitude of 15.0 km, (a) how many would you expect to strike Earth if time-dilation effects were ignored? (b) How many would you expect to strike Earth when time dilation is taken into account?

Set Up

The production and decay of the muon occur at the same place in the rest frame of the muon, so the half-life of 1.56 μs is a proper time interval in the muon frame. We'll call this frame S'. This frame moves at speed $V = 0.994c$ relative to our frame on Earth, and so we measure a different half-life Δt as given by Equation 25-10. We'll use the idea that the muon population decreases by 1/2 in each half-life to determine how many reach our planet's surface.

Time dilation:

$$\Delta t = \frac{\Delta t_{\text{proper}}}{\sqrt{1 - \dfrac{V^2}{c^2}}} \qquad (25\text{-}10)$$

muon produced

15.0 km

$V = 0.994c$

ground

Solve

(a) If there were no time dilation, the half-life of the muon in the Earth frame S would be $\Delta t = \Delta t_{\text{proper}} = 1.56$ μs, the same as in the muon frame S'. Use this to calculate the number of muons that successfully reach Earth's surface.

Time for a muon to travel a distance $d = 15.0$ km at $V = 0.994$ c:

$$T = \frac{d}{V} = \frac{15.0 \text{ km}}{0.994(3.00 \times 10^8 \text{ m/s})}\left(\frac{10^3 \text{ m}}{1 \text{ km}}\right)$$

$$= 5.03 \times 10^{-5} \text{ s}\left(\frac{1 \text{ }\mu\text{s}}{10^{-6} \text{ s}}\right) = 50.3 \text{ }\mu\text{s}$$

Express this as a multiple of the half-life:

$$\frac{T}{\Delta t_{\text{proper}}} = \frac{50.3 \text{ }\mu\text{s}}{1.56 \text{ }\mu\text{s}} = 32.2 \text{ half-lives}$$

After one half-life, the number of muons has decreased to 1/2 of its initial value; after two-half-lives, to $(1/2) \times (1/2) = 1/2^2$ of its initial value; after three half-lives, to $(1/2) \times (1/2) \times (1/2) = 1/2^3$ of its initial value; and so on. So after 32.2 half-lives, the number of muons remaining would be the original number of 1.00×10^6 multiplied by $1/2^{32.2}$:

$$\text{Muons remaining} = (1.00 \times 10^6)\left(\frac{1}{2^{32.2}}\right)$$

$$= (1.00 \times 10^6)(1.97 \times 10^{-10})$$

$$= 1.97 \times 10^{-4}$$

Much less than 1 muon, on average, survives the trip to Earth's surface.

(b) With time dilation, we first calculate the half-life in the Earth frame using Equation 25-10. We then use the same method as in part (a) to calculate the number of muons that reach Earth's surface.

Accounting for time dilation, the half-life as measured in the Earth frame S is the half-life measured in the muon frame S' divided by $\sqrt{1 - V^2/c^2}$:

$$\Delta t = \frac{\Delta t_{\text{proper}}}{\sqrt{1 - \dfrac{V^2}{c^2}}} = \frac{1.56 \text{ }\mu\text{s}}{\sqrt{1 - \dfrac{(0.994c)^2}{c^2}}} = \frac{1.56 \text{ }\mu\text{s}}{\sqrt{1 - (0.994)^2}}$$

$$= \frac{1.56 \text{ }\mu\text{s}}{\sqrt{0.0120}} = \frac{1.56 \text{ }\mu\text{s}}{0.109}$$

$$= 14.3 \text{ }\mu\text{s}$$

Due to time dilation, the half-life as measured in the Earth frame is about 9 times longer than the half-life as measured in the muon frame.

From part (a), the time for a muon to travel to the surface is 50.3 μs. Expressed as a multiple of the time-dilated half-life, this is

$$\frac{T}{\Delta t} = \frac{50.3\ \mu s}{14.3\ \mu s} = 3.53 \text{ half-lives}$$

The number of muons remaining at the surface is the original number of 1.00×10^6 multiplied by $1/2^{3.53}$:

$$\text{Muons remaining} = (1.00 \times 10^6)\left(\frac{1}{2^{3.53}}\right)$$
$$= (1.00 \times 10^6)(0.0868)$$
$$= 8.68 \times 10^4$$

About one in eleven of the muons produced in the upper atmosphere reaches Earth's surface, far more than would be the case were there no time dilation.

Reflect

One of the earliest confirmations of Einstein's special theory of relativity was a 1941 experiment that compared the number of muons observed in an hour at the top of Mount Washington in New Hampshire (about 2000 m above sea level) to the number observed at the base of the mountain (about 1100 m above sea level). Were there no time dilation, the number of muons observed at the base of the mountain would have been about 10% of the number at the top. The measured rate at the base was over 80%, precisely in accordance with Einstein's prediction. This experiment provided dramatic evidence that the bizarre phenomenon of time dilation is very real.

As we found in this example, the effect of time dilation causes time to run more slowly for the muon than we measure in our own frame, so fewer half-lives elapse for a given distance traveled. Because fewer half-lives have elapsed, fewer muons have decayed.

? Got the Concept? 25-3   Proper Time

A clock is placed aboard Starship *Alpha*, which Albert flies past Earth at half the speed of light relative to Earth. Barbara flies Starship *Beta* alongside *Alpha* at the same velocity. George pilots Starship *Gamma* past Earth at half the speed of light relative to Earth, but in the opposite direction. Elena observes from Earth. For which of these observers is the time interval between ticks of the clock equal to the proper time? (a) Albert; (b) Barbara; (c) George; (d) Elena; (e) more than one of these.

? Got the Concept? 25-4   Comparing Clocks

A clock is placed aboard Starship *Alpha*, which Albert flies past Earth at half the speed of light relative to Earth. Elena observes from Earth, where she has an identical clock. Which pair of words correctly fills in the blanks in this statement: "Elena measures Albert's clock as running _____, and Albert measures Elena's clock as running _____." (a) slow, fast; (b) slow, slow; (c) fast, fast; (d) fast, slow.

Take-Home Message for Section 25-4

✔ Einstein based his special theory of relativity on two postulates: first, that all laws of physics are the same in all inertial frames, and second, that the speed of light in a vacuum is the same in all frames and independent of both the speed of the source of the light and the speed of the observer.

✔ If two events happen at the same place in one frame, the time interval between these events as measured in that frame is called the proper time. As measured from a second frame moving relative to the first one, the time interval between those two events is longer than the proper time. This is called time dilation.

25-5 Einstein's relativity also predicts that the length of an object depends on the observer

We learned in the preceding section that the time interval between two events is not an absolute, but depends on the motion of the observer. As we will see in this section, the *length* of an object is also not an absolute: Different observers will measure the same object as having different dimensions. So the postulates of special relativity tell us that the nature of space and time is very different from what had been thought previous to the work of Einstein.

We'll conclude this section by looking at the *Lorentz transformation*, a set of equations that allows us to convert the space and time coordinates of an event in one inertial frame of reference to the coordinates in a second inertial frame. This transformation is an extension of the Galilean transformation that we explored in Section 25-2. We'll see that the Galilean transformation is actually just a special case of the Lorentz transformation valid for two frames that are moving with respect to each other at a speed far less than *c*.

Length Contraction

Figure 25-11 shows a thought experiment in which we look at the same motion in two different frames of reference, much as we did in Figures 25-8 and 25-9. In Figure 25-11a a rod is moving to the right at speed *V* relative to frame *S*, which you can think of as our frame of reference. To determine the length of the rod, we use our clock to measure the time interval Δt_S required for the rod to travel its own length. The right-hand end of the rod is at $x = 0$ at time $t = 0$, and the left-hand end of the rod is at $x = 0$ at a later time $t = \Delta t_S$. The length *L* of the rod in our frame is therefore the speed *V* of the rod multiplied by the time Δt_S needed to travel its own length:

(25-11)
$$L = V\Delta t_S$$
(length of the rod in frame *S*)

Figure 25-11b shows the same process as observed in the frame of reference *S'* in which the rod is at rest. In this frame the rod has length L_{rest}, and the frame *S* moves to the left at speed *V*. The point $x = 0$ on frame *S* travels from one end of the rod to the other in a time $\Delta t_{S'}$. The length of the rod equals the speed *V* of frame *S* multiplied by the time $\Delta t_{S'}$ that frame *S* needs to travel this length:

(25-12)
$$L_{\text{rest}} = V\Delta t_{S'}$$
(length of the rod in its own rest frame *S'*)

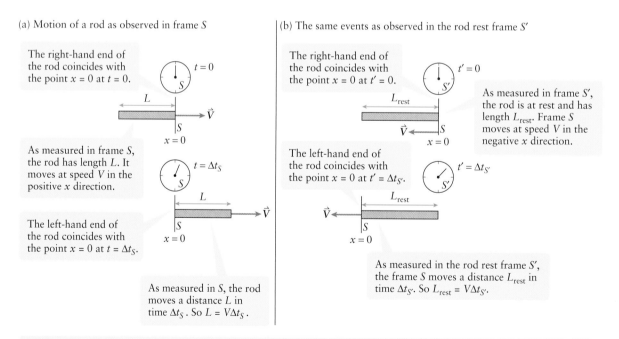

(a) Motion of a rod as observed in frame *S*

The right-hand end of the rod coincides with the point $x = 0$ at $t = 0$.

$t = 0$

As measured in frame *S*, the rod has length *L*. It moves at speed *V* in the positive *x* direction.

The left-hand end of the rod coincides with the point $x = 0$ at $t = \Delta t_S$.

$t = \Delta t_S$

As measured in *S*, the rod moves a distance *L* in time Δt_S. So $L = V\Delta t_S$.

(b) The same events as observed in the rod rest frame *S'*

The right-hand end of the rod coincides with the point $x = 0$ at $t' = 0$.

$t' = 0$

As measured in frame *S'*, the rod is at rest and has length L_{rest}. Frame *S* moves at speed *V* in the negative *x* direction.

The left-hand end of the rod coincides with the point $x = 0$ at $t' = \Delta t_{S'}$.

$t' = \Delta t_{S'}$

As measured in the rod rest frame *S'*, the frame *S* moves a distance L_{rest} in time $\Delta t_{S'}$. So $L_{\text{rest}} = V\Delta t_{S'}$.

- The two events are (1) the right-hand end of the rod coinciding with $x = 0$ and (2) the left-hand end of the rod coinciding with $x = 0$.
- These two events happen at the same place in frame *S*, so Δt_S is the proper time interval between these events. The time interval $\Delta t_{S'}$ must therefore be greater than Δt_S (time dilation).
- The distance L_{rest} must therefore be greater than the distance *L*. So the length *L* of the moving rod is less than the length L_{rest} of the rod in a frame where it is at rest. This is length contraction.

Figure 25-11 **A moving rod and length contraction** A rod as observed in (a) a frame in which the rod is moving along its length and (b) a frame in which the rod is at rest.

To see how the lengths as measured in the two frames compare, note that the length measurements in S and S′ both involve the same pair of events: the right-hand end of the rod coinciding with the point $x = 0$ in frame S, and the left-hand end of the rod coinciding with that same point. These two events happen at the same location in frame S, but at different locations in frame S′. So Δt_S is the proper time interval between these events. The time interval $\Delta t_{S'}$ measured in frame S′ is therefore longer ("dilated") compared to the time interval Δt_S measured in frame S, and the two time intervals are related by Equation 25-10:

$$\Delta t_{S'} = \frac{\Delta t_S}{\sqrt{1 - \dfrac{V^2}{c^2}}} \tag{25-13}$$

Multiply both sides of Equation 25-13 by V, then replace $V\Delta t_S$ by L in accordance with Equation 25-11 and replace $V\Delta t_{S'}$ by L_{rest} according to Equation 25-12:

$$V\Delta t_{S'} = \frac{V\Delta t_S}{\sqrt{1 - \dfrac{V^2}{c^2}}} \quad \text{or} \quad L_{\text{rest}} = \frac{L}{\sqrt{1 - \dfrac{V^2}{c^2}}}$$

We can rewrite this as

Length of an object in a frame of reference S′ in which it is at rest.

$$L = L_{\text{rest}} \sqrt{1 - \frac{V^2}{c^2}}$$

Speed of S′ relative to S

Speed of light in a vacuum

Length of the same object in a frame of reference S in which the object is moving along its length.

Length contraction
(25-14)

If the rod is moving, V is greater than zero and the factor $\sqrt{1 - V^2/c^2}$ is less than 1. So the length L of the moving rod is less than the length L_{rest} of the rod at rest. In other words, *a moving object is shortened along the direction in which it is moving.* This is called **length contraction.**

❗ Watch Out! Length contraction occurs only along the direction of motion.

There is *no* change in length of a moving object in any direction other than the direction of motion. For example, if the rod in Figure 25-11 is moving in the x direction relative to frame S, an observer in S will measure the rod as having a shorter length in the x direction than will an observer in S′ at rest with respect to the rod. But both observers will agree about the height and width of the rod (its dimensions in the y and z directions).

Length contraction gives us an alternative way to understand the results of Example 25-3 in the preceding section, in which we used time dilation to explain how short-lived muons produced at an altitude of 15.0 km are able to survive their trip to Earth's surface. Imagine a vertical rod that extends 15.0 km upward from the ground to where the muons are produced. This rod is stationary relative to Earth, so its length as measured by you on the ground is its rest length: $L_{\text{rest}} = 15.0$ km $= 1.50 \times 10^4$ m. But as seen from the frame of a descending muon, this rod is moving upward along its length at $V = 0.994c$. As measured by a muon, the length of this rod is contracted in accordance with Equation 25-14:

$$L = L_{\text{rest}}\sqrt{1 - \frac{V^2}{c^2}} = (15.0 \text{ km})\sqrt{1 - \frac{(0.994c)^2}{c^2}}$$

$$= (15.0 \text{ km})\sqrt{1 - (0.994)^2}$$

$$= (15.0 \text{ km})\sqrt{0.0120} = (15.0 \text{ km})(0.109)$$

$$= 1.64 \text{ km} = 1.64 \times 10^3 \text{ m}$$

Moving at $V = 0.994c$, this contracted rod travels past the muon in a time

$$\frac{1.64 \times 10^3 \text{ m}}{0.994c} = \frac{1.64 \times 10^3 \text{ m}}{(0.994)(3.00 \times 10^8 \text{ m/s})} = 5.50 \times 10^{-6} \text{ s} = 5.50 \text{ } \mu\text{s}$$

The half-life of the muon in its own rest frame is $1.56 \text{ } \mu\text{s}$, so from the muon's perspective it takes just $(5.50 \text{ } \mu\text{s})/(1.56 \text{ } \mu\text{s}) = 3.53$ half-lives for the contracted rod to move past it—that is, for the muon to move from where it is produced to Earth's surface. That's exactly the result that we found in Example 25-3 using the ideas of time dilation. The ideas of length contraction and time dilation are mutually consistent!

Example 25-4 A Flying Meter Stick I

A meter stick (length 1.00 m) hurtles through space at a speed of $0.800c$ relative to you, with its length aligned with the direction of motion. What do you measure as the length of the meter stick?

Set Up

The meter stick's length along its direction of motion is 1.00 m as measured in its own rest frame S', so $L_{rest} = 1.00$ m. Your frame is frame S, and the two frames are moving relative to each other at $V = 0.800c$. We'll use Equation 25-14 to find the length L as measured in your frame.

Length contraction:

$$L = L_{rest}\sqrt{1 - \frac{V^2}{c^2}} \quad (25\text{-}14)$$

$L_{rest} = 1.00$ m

$V = 0.800c$
= velocity of the meter stick relative to frame S

Solve

Substitute $L_{rest} = 1.00$ m and $V = 0.800c$ into Equation 25-14 and calculate L.

From Equation 25-14,

$$L = L_{rest}\sqrt{1 - \frac{V^2}{c^2}} = (1.00 \text{ m})\sqrt{1 - \frac{(0.800c)^2}{c^2}}$$

$$= (1.00 \text{ m})\sqrt{1 - (0.800)^2} = (1.00 \text{ m})\sqrt{1 - 0.640}$$

$$= (1.00 \text{ m})\sqrt{0.360} = (1.00 \text{ m})(0.600)$$

$$= 0.600 \text{ m} = 60.0 \text{ cm}$$

Reflect

As measured in your frame of reference, the meter stick is only 60.0 cm in length. This is not an optical illusion; the meter stick really is only 60.0% as long in your frame of reference as in the rest frame of the meter stick.

Example 25-5 A Flying Meter Stick II

The meter stick from the preceding example again hurtles through space at a speed of $0.800c$ relative to you, but now it is tilted at an angle of $30.0°$ as measured in its rest frame with respect to the direction of motion. Now what do you measure as the length of the meter stick?

Set Up

As measured in the meter stick's rest frame S', the meter stick is inclined at an angle $\theta' = 30.0°$ to its direction of motion relative to frame S. The x dimension of the stick undergoes length contraction given by Equation 25-14, but the y dimension does not. We'll calculate the x and y dimensions of the stick in your frame S, then use the Pythagorean theorem to find the length of the stick in frame S.

Length contraction:

$$L = L_{rest}\sqrt{1 - \frac{V^2}{c^2}} \quad (25\text{-}14)$$

The meter stick as observed in its rest frame S'

$L_{rest, x}$

$V = 0.800c$
= velocity of the meter stick relative to frame S

$L_{rest} = 1.00$ m

$L_{rest, y}$

$\theta' = 30.0°$

Solve

First calculate the x and y dimensions of the meter stick in its rest frame.

In the rest frame S' of the stick, its dimensions are

$$L_{rest,x} = L_{rest}\cos\theta' = (1.00 \text{ m})\cos 30.0° = 0.866 \text{ m}$$

$$L_{rest,y} = L_{rest}\sin\theta' = (1.00 \text{ m})\sin 30.0° = 0.500 \text{ m}$$

Calculate the x and y dimensions of the meter stick in your frame, in which the stick is moving at $V = 0.800c$ along the x direction.

In your frame S, the x dimension of the stick is contracted:

$$L_x = L_{\text{rest},x}\sqrt{1 - \frac{V^2}{c^2}} = (0.866 \text{ m})\sqrt{1 - \frac{(0.800c)^2}{c^2}}$$

$$= (0.866 \text{ m})\sqrt{1 - 0.640} = (0.866 \text{ m})\sqrt{0.360}$$

$$= 0.520 \text{ m}$$

Length contraction occurs only along the direction of motion, so the y dimension of the stick is *not* contracted:

$$L_y = L_{\text{rest},y} = 0.500 \text{ m}$$

Use the Pythagorean theorem to calculate the length of the meter stick in your frame.

From the Pythagorean theorem, the length of the meter stick in your frame S is

$$L = \sqrt{L_x^2 + L_y^2}$$

$$= \sqrt{(0.520 \text{ m})^2 + (0.500 \text{ m})^2}$$

$$= \sqrt{(0.520 \text{ m})^2 + (0.500 \text{ m})^2}$$

$$= \sqrt{0.520 \text{ m}^2} = 0.721 \text{ m}$$

The meter stick as observed in your frame S

$V = 0.800c$ = velocity of the meter stick relative to frame S

Reflect

Because the meter stick is not aligned with the direction of motion, the amount of contraction is not as great as in Example 25-4, in which the meter stick was completely aligned with the direction of motion. Notice also that the angle θ of the meter stick in your frame is different from the angle $\theta' = 30.0°$ in the stick's rest frame. Can you show that $\theta = 43.9°$?

The Lorentz Transformation

The Galilean transformation that we presented in Section 25-2 is not consistent with the postulates of special relativity. A set of transformation equations that *is* consistent with relativity is the **Lorentz transformation**. As in Figure 25-3, we take frame S' to be moving at speed V in the positive x direction relative to frame S. The origins of the two frames coincide at $t = 0$ in frame S and $t' = 0$ in frame S'. If an event takes place at coordinates x, y, z, t in frame S, the coordinates of that same event in frame S' are

Inertial frame of reference S' moves at speed V in the positive x direction relative to inertial frame of reference S.

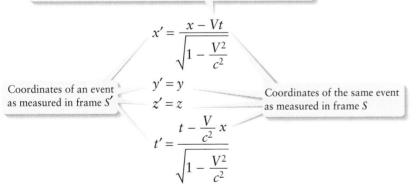

$$x' = \frac{x - Vt}{\sqrt{1 - \frac{V^2}{c^2}}}$$

$$y' = y$$
$$z' = z$$

$$t' = \frac{t - \frac{V}{c^2}x}{\sqrt{1 - \frac{V^2}{c^2}}}$$

Coordinates of an event as measured in frame S'

Coordinates of the same event as measured in frame S

Lorentz transformation
(25-15)

Note that at speeds that are far less than the speed of light, the ratio V/c is very small and can be treated as essentially zero. Then $\sqrt{1 - V^2/c^2}$ is essentially equal to 1, and Equations 25-15 become

$$x' = x - Vt, \quad y' = y, \quad z' = z, \quad t' = t$$

These are just the Galilean transformation equations that we presented in Section 25-2. So at speeds far slower than the speed of light, the equations of Einstein's special theory of relativity reduce to the equations of Newtonian relativity.

Equations 25-15 are useful for finding the coordinates of an event in frame S' if we know the event's coordinates in frame S. If we instead want to determine the coordinates of an event in frame S from the coordinates in frame S', it's most convenient to use the *inverse* Lorentz transformation:

Inverse Lorentz transformation (25-16)

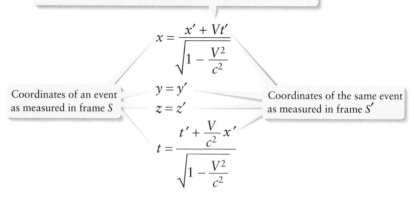

Inertial frame of reference S' moves at speed V in the positive x direction relative to inertial frame of reference S.

$$x = \frac{x' + Vt'}{\sqrt{1 - \dfrac{V^2}{c^2}}}$$

$$y = y'$$
$$z = z'$$

$$t = \frac{t' + \dfrac{V}{c^2}x'}{\sqrt{1 - \dfrac{V^2}{c^2}}}$$

Coordinates of an event as measured in frame S

Coordinates of the same event as measured in frame S'

It's possible to derive the equations for time dilation (Equation 25-10) and length contraction (Equation 25-14) from the Lorentz transformation equations. Instead, let's look at another remarkable result of the special theory of relativity that we can deduce from the Lorentz transformation equations.

Example 25-6 Simultaneity Is Relative

In your reference frame you have a meter stick that is oriented along the x axis, with one end at $x = 0$ and the other end at $x = 1.00$ m. There is a light bulb at each end of the stick, and you make the two bulbs flash simultaneously (as measured by you) at $t = 0$. A spacecraft flies past you at $V = 0.800c$ in the positive x direction. (a) According to an observer in the spacecraft, are the two light flashes simultaneous? If not, which flash happens first as measured by her? (b) On board the spacecraft is an identical meter stick with a light bulb at each end. The observer on board the spacecraft places the two ends of the stick at $x' = 0$ and $x' = 1.00$ m, and she makes the two bulbs flash simultaneously (as measured by her) at $t' = 0$. According to you, are the two light flashes simultaneous? If not, which flash happens first as measured by you?

Set Up

In part (a) we're given the coordinates in frame S of two events, the flash of the left-hand bulb at $x = 0$ and $t = 0$ and the flash of the right-hand bulb at $x = 1.00$ m and $t = 0$. We'll use the t' equation from the Lorentz transformation, Equations 25-15, to determine the times of these two events as measured in the spaceship frame S'. Similarly, in part (b) we're given the coordinates in frame S' of two other events, the flash of the left-hand bulb at $x' = 0$ and $t' = 0$ and the flash of the right-hand bulb at $x' = 1.00$ m and $t' = 0$. We'll find the times of these events as measured in your S frame using the t equation from the inverse Lorentz tranformation, Equations 25-16.

Time equation from the Lorentz transformation:

$$t' = \frac{t - \dfrac{V}{c^2}x}{\sqrt{1 - \dfrac{V^2}{c^2}}} \qquad (25\text{-}15)$$

Time equation from the inverse Lorentz transformation:

$$t = \frac{t' + \dfrac{V}{c^2}x'}{\sqrt{1 - \dfrac{V^2}{c^2}}} \qquad (25\text{-}16)$$

(a) Meter stick at rest in frame S: What does an observer in frame S' measure?

(b) Meter stick at rest in frame S': What does an observer in frame S measure?

Solve

(a) Use the Lorentz transformation to calculate the times of the simultaneous flashes in S as measured in S'.

The left-hand bulb on the meter stick at rest in frame S flashes at $x = 0, t = 0$. In frame S' this bulb flashes at

$$t'_{\text{left}} = \frac{(0) - \dfrac{V}{c^2}(0)}{\sqrt{1 - \dfrac{V^2}{c^2}}} = 0$$

The right-hand bulb on the meter stick at rest in frame S flashes at $x = 1.00$ m, $t = 0$. In frame S' this bulb flashes at

$$t'_{\text{right}} = \frac{(0) - \dfrac{V}{c^2}(1.00 \text{ m})}{\sqrt{1 - \dfrac{V^2}{c^2}}} = \frac{-\dfrac{(0.800c)}{c^2}(1.00 \text{ m})}{\sqrt{1 - \dfrac{(0.800c)^2}{c^2}}}$$

$$= \frac{-0.800 \text{ m}}{c\sqrt{1 - (0.800)^2}} = \frac{-0.800 \text{ m}}{(3.00 \times 10^8 \text{ m/s})(0.600)}$$

$$= -4.44 \times 10^{-9} \text{ s}$$

As observed from the spaceship frame S', the two events are *not* simultaneous: The right-hand bulb flashes 4.44×10^{-9} s before the left-hand bulb.

(b) Use the inverse Lorentz transformation to calculate the times of the simultaneous flashes in S' as measured in S.

The left-hand bulb on the meter stick at rest in frame S' flashes at $x' = 0, t' = 0$. In frame S this bulb flashes at

$$t_{\text{left}} = \frac{(0) + \dfrac{V}{c^2}(0)}{\sqrt{1 - \dfrac{V^2}{c^2}}} = 0$$

The right-hand bulb on the meter stick at rest in frame S' flashes at $x' = 1.00$ m, $t' = 0$. In frame S this bulb flashes at

$$t_{\text{right}} = \frac{(0) + \dfrac{V}{c^2}(1.00 \text{ m})}{\sqrt{1 - \dfrac{V^2}{c^2}}} = \frac{+\dfrac{(0.800c)}{c^2}(1.00 \text{ m})}{\sqrt{1 - \dfrac{(0.800c)^2}{c^2}}}$$

$$= \frac{+0.800 \text{ m}}{c\sqrt{1 - (0.800)^2}} = \frac{+0.800 \text{ m}}{(3.00 \times 10^8 \text{ m/s})(0.600)}$$

$$= +4.44 \times 10^{-9} \text{ s}$$

As observed from your frame S, the two events are *not* simultaneous: The right-hand bulb flashes 4.44×10^{-9} s after the left-hand bulb.

Reflect

This example illustrates yet another counterintuitive consequence of Einstein's special theory of relativity: Two events that are simultaneous to one observer need not be simultaneous to another observer. So even the simple statement "Two things happen at the same time" has to be qualified by stating in which frame of reference it holds true. Time in relativity is not an absolute!

> **? Got the Concept? 25-5 No Contraction?**
>
> A rod with a rest length of 1.00 m whizzes past you at $0.995c$. Is it possible that you could measure its length to be equal to its rest length? (a) Yes; (b) no.

Take-Home Message for Section 25-5

✔ When an object moves relative to an observer, its length in the direction of motion is contracted compared to the length measured in the object's rest frame. This is called length contraction.

✔ The Lorentz transformation allows you to calculate the coordinates of an event measured in one inertial frame based on the coordinates of that event measured in another inertial frame. Unlike the Galilean transformation, the Lorentz transformation is consistent with the postulates of relativity.

25-6 The relative velocity of two objects is constrained by the speed of light, the ultimate speed limit

Suppose you are an outfielder running to catch a batted baseball (Figure 25-12a). The baseball is traveling at 30.0 m/s relative to the ground, and you are running toward the ball at 10.0 m/s relative to the ground. The Galilean velocity transformation that we learned in Section 25-2 says that, relative to you, the baseball travels at 30.0 m/s plus 10.0 m/s, or 40.0 m/s; the velocities simply add. But suppose that instead of being an outfielder running at 10.0 m/s, you are an astronaut flying in your spaceship at 1.00×10^8 m/s as in Figure 25-12b. Instead of moving toward a baseball, you are moving toward a light beam aimed at you by a stationary astronaut. The same idea that we applied to the baseball predicts that relative to you, the light beam travels at $c = 3.00 \times 10^8$ m/s (the speed of the light beam relative to the other astronaut) plus

(a)

As seen by the outfielder, the ball is approaching her at (30.0 m/s) + (10.0 m/s) = 40.0 m/s.

10.0 m/s

Ball

30.0 m/s

(b)

Incorrect Newtonian description:
As seen by the astronaut in the spaceship, the light is approaching her at $(3.00 \times 10^8$ m/s$) + (1.00 \times 10^8$ m/s$) = 4.00 \times 10^8$ m/s.

Light

Frame S

x Frame S' 1.00×10^8 m/s 3.00×10^8 m/s

Figure 25-12 Velocity addition— Newtonian and Einsteinian
(a) An outfielder running toward a batted baseball. (b) An astronaut in her spaceship flying toward a light beam.

Correct Einsteinian description:
As seen by the astronaut in the spaceship, the light is approaching her at 3.00×10^8 m/s.

1.00×10^8 m/s (the speed of your spaceship relative to the other astronaut), or 4.00×10^8 m/s. But that *cannot* be correct: The second postulate of the special theory of relativity says that the speed of light in vacuum is the same to all inertial observers. So the light beam must also travel at speed $c = 3.00 \times 10^8$ m/s relative to you. Clearly, the Galilean transformation for velocities is inadequate. In this section we'll explore the *Lorentz velocity transformation*, which allows us to combine velocities in a way that is consistent with Einsteinian relativity.

It's possible to derive the transformation of velocities from the Lorentz transformation of coordinates that we introduced in Section 25-5 (see Equations 25-15 and 25-16). We'll skip over the derivation and just present the result for the special case in which all motions are along the same line, as in Figure 25-12. Suppose there are two inertial frames of reference, S and S', such that frame S' is moving at speed V in the positive x direction relative to frame S. An object is moving relative to frame S along the x direction, with an x component of velocity v_x. In frame S' the same object has an x component of velocity given by

Inertial frame of reference S' moves at speed V in the positive x direction relative to inertial frame of reference S.

x component of velocity of an object moving along the x axis as measured in frame S'

$$v'_x = \frac{v_x - V}{1 - \dfrac{V}{c^2} v_x}$$

x component of velocity of the same object as measured in frame S

Lorentz velocity transformation
(25-17)

This is called the **Lorentz velocity transformation**. Notice that if the speed V of one frame relative to the other is small compared to c, the ratio V/c is much less than 1 and the denominator is essentially equal to 1. Then Equation 25-17 becomes $v'_x = v_x - V$, which is just the Galilean velocity transformation (the first of Equations 25-5). The same thing happens if the velocity v_x of the object relative to frame S is small compared to c. So if either of the speeds involved is a small fraction of the speed of light, the Lorentz velocity transformation reduces to the Galilean velocity transformation. This justifies our use of the Galilean velocity transformation for slow-moving objects.

Equation 25-17 allows us to find the object's velocity relative to frame S' if we know its velocity relative to frame S. If instead we know the object's velocity relative to frame S' and want to calculate its velocity relative to frame S, we use the **inverse Lorentz velocity transformation**:

Inertial frame of reference S' moves at speed V in the positive x direction relative to inertial frame of reference S.

x component of velocity of an object moving along the x axis as measured in frame S

$$v_x = \frac{v'_x + V}{1 + \dfrac{V}{c^2} v'_x}$$

x component of velocity of the same object as measured in frame S'

Inverse Lorentz velocity transformation
(25-18)

Let's see what the Lorentz velocity transformation tells us about the situation shown in Figure 25-12b. The astronaut with the flashlight is in frame of reference S, and you and your spaceship are in frame of reference S'. You are moving to the right (in the positive x direction), which is just how frame S' must move relative to frame S in order to use Equation 25-17 or 25-18. The relative speed of the two frames is V. We know that the light travels relative to the astronaut with the flashlight at the speed of light in the negative x direction, so its velocity relative to S is $v_x = -c$. We can then use Equation 25-17 to calculate the velocity v'_x of the light relative to you in frame S':

$$v'_x = \frac{v_x - V}{1 - \dfrac{V}{c^2} v_x} = \frac{-c - V}{1 - \dfrac{V}{c^2}(-c)} = \frac{-(c + V)}{1 + \dfrac{V}{c}}$$

We can simplify this by factoring c out of the numerator:

$$v'_x = \frac{-c\left(1 + \dfrac{V}{c}\right)}{1 + \dfrac{V}{c}} = -c$$

This says that as measured by you in frame S', the light travels at the speed of light c in the negative x direction just as in frame S. Note that while $V = 1.00 \times 10^8$ m/s in Figure 25-12b, we didn't have to plug in a numerical value for V to get this result: No matter what the relative speed of the two frames, each observer will see light propagating in a vacuum at the same speed c.

A direct consequence of this calculation with the Lorentz velocity transformation is that *no object can move faster than c, the speed of light in a vacuum, in any inertial frame of reference*. If an object (light) is traveling at speed c in one inertial frame, it is traveling at c in all inertial frames; if an object is traveling slower than c in one inertial frame, it is traveling slower than c in all inertial frames. Thus the speed of light in a vacuum represents an ultimate speed limit.

Example 25-7 Baseball for Superheroes

Suppose the baseball game in Figure 25-12 is being played by superheroes. The outfielder has the power of super speed, and can run at $0.300c$ relative to the ground. The batter has the power of super strength, and can bat the ball with such force that the ball ends up traveling horizontally at $0.900c$ relative to the ground. (The bat and ball are made of super materials that can withstand the tremendous forces required.) How fast is the ball moving relative to the outfielder?

Set Up

This is nearly the same situation that we discussed above with the two astronauts and the beam of light, except that the astronauts have been replaced by (super) baseball players and the beam of light has become a baseball. We use Equation 25-17 to calculate the velocity of the ball relative to the outfielder in frame S'.

Lorentz velocity transformation:

$$v'_x = \frac{v_x - V}{1 - \dfrac{V}{c^2}v_x} \qquad (25\text{-}17)$$

outfielder: frame S' batter: frame S

Solve

Use the velocity of the ball relative to the batter (v_x) and the velocity of the outfielder relative to the batter (V) to find the velocity of the ball relative to the outfielder (v'_x).

The outfielder (frame S') is moving in the positive x direction relative to the batter (frame S) at $V = 0.300c$. The velocity of the ball relative to the batter (frame S) is $v_x = -0.900c$ (negative because the ball is moving in the negative x direction). From Equation 25-17, the velocity of the ball relative to the outfielder is

$$v'_x = \frac{v_x - V}{1 - \dfrac{V}{c^2}v_x} = \frac{-0.900c - 0.300c}{1 - \dfrac{0.300c}{c^2}(-0.900c)}$$

$$= \frac{-1.200c}{1 + (0.300)(0.900)} = \frac{-1.200c}{1.27}$$

$$= -0.945c$$

Relative to the outfielder, the ball is moving at $0.945c$ in the negative x direction (to the left).

Reflect

In the Galilean velocity transformation, the velocity of the ball relative to the outfielder would have been $v'_x = v_x - V = -0.900c - 0.300c = -1.200c$, which is faster than the speed of light in a vacuum. Thanks to the $1 - (V/c^2)v_x$ term in the denominator of Equation 25-17, the actual speed of the ball relative to the outfielder is faster than $0.900c$ but still slower than c. The batter may be super-powered, but the ball cannot exceed the speed of light as measured by any observer.

Suppose the super outfielder in Example 25-7 catches the ball and throws it back toward the super batter, who is still standing at home plate. If the outfielder is still running at 0.300c and she throws the ball at 0.700c relative to her, what is the speed of the ball relative to the batter? (a) 0.331c; (b) 0.506c; (c) 0.826c; (d) 1.00c; (e) 1.26c.

Take-Home Message for Section 25-6

✔ At speeds that are an appreciable fraction of the speed of light, we must use the Lorentz velocity transformation to calculate relative velocities. This transformation respects the rule that the speed of light in a vacuum is the same in all inertial frames of reference.

✔ No object can move faster than c, the speed of light in a vacuum, in any inertial frame of reference.

25-7 The equations for kinetic energy and momentum must be modified at very high speeds

We have seen that the speed of light in a vacuum c is an ultimate speed limit: No object can travel faster than c in any inertial frame of reference. As we'll see in this section, this tells us that the expressions we learned earlier in this book for kinetic energy K (Chapter 6) and momentum $\vec{p}$ (Chapter 7) *cannot* be entirely correct, but fail at speeds that are a reasonable fraction of c. We'll see the reasons why this must be so, and encounter a new kind of energy called *rest energy* that is intrinsic to any object with mass.

In Section 6-3 we introduced kinetic energy through the work-energy theorem:

Work done on an object by the net force on that object

$$W_{net} = K_f - K_i$$

Kinetic energy of the object after the work is done on it

Kinetic energy of the object before the work is done on it

The work-energy theorem
(6-9)

This says that if an object starts at rest so that its initial kinetic energy K_i is zero, the more work the net force on an object does, the greater the final kinetic energy K_f of the object. In principle, there is no limit to how much kinetic energy an object can acquire. There is a problem, however: Using Newtonian physics, we found that the expression for the kinetic energy K of an object of mass m moving at speed v is

$$K = \frac{1}{2}mv^2$$

Since the speed of light in a vacuum c is the maximum speed an object can acquire, this expression says that the maximum kinetic energy that an object can acquire is $(1/2)mc^2$. This contradicts the idea that there should be no limit on an object's kinetic energy. Clearly, we need an improved equation for kinetic energy.

There is a similar problem with the Newtonian expression for momentum. We saw in Section 7-6 that the change in momentum of an object is determined by the external forces on the object and the duration of the time interval over which the forces act:

The sum of all external forces acting on an object

Duration of a time interval over which the external forces act

$$\left(\sum \vec{F}_{external\ on\ object} \right) \Delta t = \vec{p}_f - \vec{p}_i = \Delta\vec{p}$$

External force and momentum change for an object
(7-23)

Change in the momentum $\vec{p}$ of the object during that time interval

Suppose an object starts at rest so that its initial momentum $\vec{p}_i$ is zero and a constant net force acts on it. Then Equation 7-23 says that the longer the time interval Δt that the force acts, the greater the final momentum $\vec{p}_f$ of the object. In principle there is no limit on how long the force can act, so there should be no upper limit on an object's momentum. However, this can't be reconciled with the Newtonian expression for the momentum of an object of mass m with velocity $\vec{v}$:

$$\vec{p} = m\vec{v}$$

According to this expression, the maximum magnitude of momentum that an object of mass m can have is $p = mc$, which would be attained only when an object is moving at the speed of light. This directly contradicts the notion that there should be no upper limit on momentum. Just as for kinetic energy, we need a new expression for momentum that's consistent with the special theory of relativity.

It's possible to derive the correct expressions for K and $\vec{p}$ by looking closely at what happens in an elastic collision, in which both mechanical energy and momentum are conserved (see Section 7-5). The derivation is beyond our scope, so we'll just look at the results. For a particle moving with velocity $\vec{v}$, both the expression for the kinetic energy and the expression for the momentum involve a quantity called **relativistic gamma**:

**Relativistic gamma
(25-19)**

Relativistic gamma for a particle moving at speed v

$$\gamma = \frac{1}{\sqrt{1 - \dfrac{v^2}{c^2}}}$$

Speed of the particle

Speed of light in a vacuum

This dimensionless quantity is equal to 1 when $v = 0$ and becomes infinitely large as v approaches c (Figure 25-13). In terms of relativistic gamma, we can write the correct expressions for kinetic energy and momentum as

**Einsteinian expressions for
kinetic energy and momentum
(25-20)**

Kinetic energy of a particle of mass m and velocity $\vec{v}$

$$K = (\gamma - 1)mc^2$$

$$\vec{p} = \gamma m\vec{v}$$

Relativistic gamma
for speed v

Momentum of a particle of mass m and velocity $\vec{v}$

At speeds that are a small fraction of the speed of light c, these are approximately equal to the Newtonian expressions

$$K = \frac{1}{2}mv^2 \text{ and } \vec{p} = m\vec{v}$$

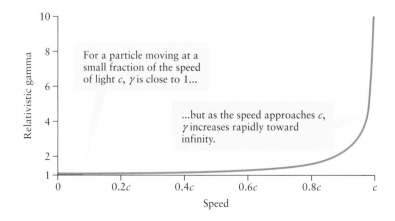

Figure 25-13 Relativistic gamma
The quantity $\gamma = 1/\sqrt{1 - (v^2/c^2)}$ increases dramatically as speed v approaches the speed of light.

For a particle moving at a small fraction of the speed of light c, γ is close to 1...

...but as the speed approaches c, γ increases rapidly toward infinity.

(a) Comparing Newtonian and Einsteinian formulas for kinetic energy   (b) Comparing Newtonian and Einsteinian formulas for momentum

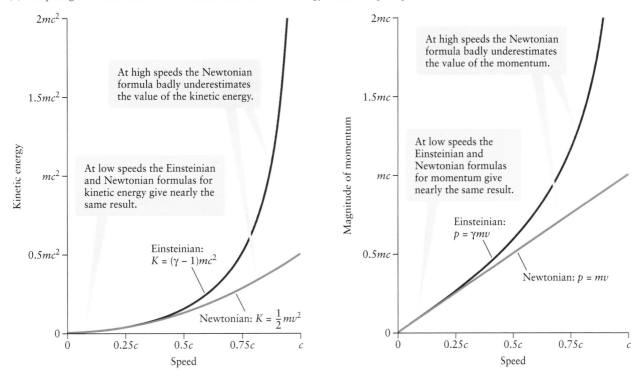

Figure 25-14 Kinetic energy and momentum in relativity These graphs show how the Newtonian and Einsteinian expressions for (a) the kinetic energy of a particle and (b) the momentum of a particle depend on the speed of the particle.

Figure 25-14 compares the kinetic energy K and the magnitude of momentum p from Equations 25-20 to the Newtonian expressions for these quantities. The graphs show that if v is a small fraction of the speed of light, the Einsteinian and Newtonian expressions give essentially identical results. This justifies our use of these expressions in earlier chapters, in which we considered only relatively slow-moving objects. But as the speed v approaches c, the Einsteinian expressions from Equations 25-20 approach infinity. So even though the speed of light is an upper limit to the speed of an object, there is no upper limit on the kinetic energy or momentum of an object.

Example 25-8 The Energy and Momentum Costs of High Speed

Electrons can be accelerated to speeds very close to the speed of light. The mass of an electron is 9.11×10^{-31} kg.
(a) How much kinetic energy must be given to an electron to accelerate it from rest to $0.900c$? How much momentum?
(b) How much additional kinetic energy must be given to the electron to accelerate it from $0.900c$ to $0.990c$? How much additional momentum?

Set Up
We use Equations 25-20 to find the kinetic energy K and magnitude of momentum p for each speed. Equation 25-19 tells us the value of relativistic gamma for each speed.

Relativistic gamma:

$$\gamma = \frac{1}{\sqrt{1 - \dfrac{v^2}{c^2}}} \qquad (25\text{-}19)$$

Einsteinian kinetic energy and momentum:

$$K = (\gamma - 1)\, mc^2$$
$$\vec{p} = \gamma m \vec{v} \qquad (25\text{-}20)$$

Solve

(a) The kinetic energy that must be given to the electron is the difference between its kinetic energy at $v = 0.900c$ and its kinetic energy at $v = 0$, and similarly for the momentum.

At $v = 0$,

$$\gamma = \frac{1}{\sqrt{1 - \dfrac{v^2}{c^2}}} = \frac{1}{\sqrt{1 - 0}} = \frac{1}{1} = 1$$

$$K = (\gamma - 1)\,mc^2 = (1 - 1)\,mc^2 = 0$$
$$p = \gamma mv = (1)\,m\,(0) = 0$$

Just as in Newtonian physics, a particle at rest has zero kinetic energy and zero momentum.

To calculate K and p at nonzero speeds, it's useful to first find the values of mc and mc^2 for an electron:

$$\begin{aligned} mc &= (9.11 \times 10^{-31}\,\text{kg})(3.00 \times 10^8\,\text{m/s}) \\ &= 2.73 \times 10^{-22}\,\text{kg} \cdot \text{m/s} \end{aligned}$$

$$\begin{aligned} mc^2 &= (9.11 \times 10^{-31}\,\text{kg})(3.00 \times 10^8\,\text{m/s})^2 \\ &= 8.20 \times 10^{-14}\,\text{kg} \cdot \text{m}^2/\text{s}^2 \\ &= 8.20 \times 10^{-14}\,\text{J} \end{aligned}$$

At $v = 0.900c$,

$$\gamma = \frac{1}{\sqrt{1 - \dfrac{v^2}{c^2}}} = \frac{1}{\sqrt{1 - \dfrac{(0.900c)^2}{c^2}}} = \frac{1}{\sqrt{1 - (0.900)^2}}$$

$$= \frac{1}{\sqrt{0.190}} = 2.29$$

$$\begin{aligned} K &= (\gamma - 1)mc^2 = (2.29 - 1)(8.20 \times 10^{-14}\,\text{J}) \\ &= 1.06 \times 10^{-13}\,\text{J} \end{aligned}$$

$$\begin{aligned} p &= \gamma mv = (2.29)m(0.900c) = (2.29)(0.900)mc \\ &= (2.29)(0.900)(2.73 \times 10^{-22}\,\text{kg} \cdot \text{m/s}) \\ &= 5.64 \times 10^{-22}\,\text{kg} \cdot \text{m/s} \end{aligned}$$

The electron begins with $K = 0$ and $p = 0$, so it must be given 1.06×10^{-13} J of kinetic energy and 5.64×10^{-22} kg·m/s of momentum to accelerate it from rest to $0.900c$.

(b) Repeat the calculation in part (b) for the additional kinetic energy and momentum that must be given to the electron to accelerate it from $0.900c$ to $0.990c$.

At $v = 0.990c$,

$$\gamma = \frac{1}{\sqrt{1 - \dfrac{v^2}{c^2}}} = \frac{1}{\sqrt{1 - \dfrac{(0.990c)^2}{c^2}}} = \frac{1}{\sqrt{1 - (0.990)^2}}$$

$$= \frac{1}{\sqrt{0.0199}} = 7.09$$

$$\begin{aligned} K &= (\gamma - 1)\,mc^2 = (7.09 - 1)(8.20 \times 10^{-14}\,\text{J}) \\ &= 4.99 \times 10^{-13}\,\text{J} \end{aligned}$$

$$\begin{aligned} p &= \gamma mv = (7.09)\,m\,(0.990c) = (7.09)(0.990)mc \\ &= (7.09)(0.990)(2.73 \times 10^{-22}\,\text{kg} \cdot \text{m/s}) \\ &= 1.92 \times 10^{-21}\,\text{kg} \cdot \text{m/s} \end{aligned}$$

The difference between these values and the values of K and p at $v = 0.900c$ from part (a) tells us the additional kinetic energy and momentum that must be given to the electron:

$$\begin{aligned} \Delta K &= 4.99 \times 10^{-13}\,\text{J} - 1.06 \times 10^{-13}\,\text{J} \\ &= 3.93 \times 10^{-13}\,\text{J} \end{aligned}$$

$$\begin{aligned} \Delta p &= 1.92 \times 10^{-21}\,\text{kg} \cdot \text{m/s} - 5.64 \times 10^{-22}\,\text{kg} \cdot \text{m/s} \\ &= 1.35 \times 10^{-21}\,\text{kg} \cdot \text{m/s} \end{aligned}$$

Reflect
Compared to accelerating an electron from rest to $0.900c$, accelerating that same electron from $0.900c$ to $0.990c$ requires 3.70 times as much additional kinetic energy and 2.40 times as much additional momentum. As the speed gets closer and closer to c, it requires ever-greater amounts of kinetic energy and momentum to cause an ever-smaller speed increase. You can see that an object can never be accelerated from rest to the speed of light. This would require adding *infinite* amounts of kinetic energy and momentum to the object.

We mentioned above that the Einsteinian expressions for kinetic energy and momentum, Equations 25-20, come from an analysis of elastic collisions. In particular, we must demand that if energy and momentum are conserved in one inertial frame of reference, they must be conserved in *all* inertial frames. That's required if energy and momentum are to be consistent with the first of the postulates of special relativity. It turns out that in order for this to be the case, we must also include a term mc^2 in the total energy of a particle of mass m. This quantity is called the **rest energy** of a particle, since it is present even when the particle is not in motion.

Rest energy of a particle   Mass of the particle

$$E_0 = mc^2$$

Speed of light in a vacuum

Rest energy
(25-21)

Equation 25-21 is one of the most famous in science, and one of the most misunderstood. Rest energy is not potential energy; potential energy is associated with a force an object experiences. (For example, gravitational potential energy is associated with the gravitational force.) It is not kinetic energy; kinetic energy is associated with motion. Rest energy is energy that is intrinsic to an object because of its mass.

The physical interpretation of Equation 25-21 is that *mass and energy are equivalent*, or that this mass is simply one possible manifestation of energy. Stated another way, the mass of an object is a measure of its rest energy content. Figure 25-15 is visual evidence of the equivalence of mass and energy. This image shows the result of a head-on collision between two protons, each of which was moving at just under the speed of light. Dozens of new particles appear after the collision. These are not fragments of the colliding protons, but rather new particles that were created in the collision. This is possible because some of the kinetic energy of the colliding protons was converted into the rest energy of these new particles; another portion of this kinetic energy went into the kinetic energies of the new particles, which fly away from the collision site at high speeds.

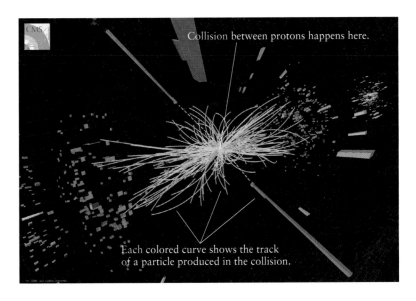

Figure 25-15 **Converting kinetic energy to new particles** This image from the Large Hadron Collider at CERN in Geneva, Switzerland shows dozens of new particles produced by a collision between energetic protons.

You can observe the equivalence of mass and energy in action whenever you go outside on a sunny day or look up at the stars on a clear night. The Sun and stars shine thanks to a process occurring in their interiors in which hydrogen nuclei are fused together to form nuclei of helium. The mass of the products of such a reaction is slightly less than the mass of the hydrogen nuclei present before the reaction. The "lost" mass is converted to energy in the form of electromagnetic radiation, and it is that radiation that we see in the form of sunlight and starlight.

Example 25-9 Converting Mass to Energy in the Sun

The Sun emits 3.84×10^{26} J of energy every second. (a) At what rate (in kg/s) is the Sun's mass decreasing? (b) How much mass has the Sun lost since it was formed 4.56×10^9 years ago? Assume that it has emitted energy at the same rate over its entire history. Compare to the present-day mass of the Sun, 1.99×10^{30} kg.

Set Up

The emitted energy comes from the rest energy of mass that is "lost" in nuclear reactions in the Sun's interior. We use Equation 25-21 to find the amount of mass equivalent to the energy emitted in one second. The total mass lost over the Sun's lifetime equals this amount of mass multiplied by the number of seconds that have elapsed since the Sun formed.

Rest energy:

$$E_0 = mc^2 \qquad\qquad (25\text{-}21)$$

Solve

(a) Calculate the amount of mass lost by the Sun per second.

Mass equivalent of 3.84×10^{26} J:

$$m = \frac{E_0}{c^2} = \frac{3.84 \times 10^{26}\ \text{J}}{(3.00 \times 10^8\ \text{m/s})^2} = 4.27 \times 10^9\ \text{J} \cdot \text{s}^2/\text{m}^2$$

Since $1\ \text{J} = 1\ \text{kg} \cdot \text{m}^2/\text{s}^2$, we can write this as

$$m = 4.27 \times 10^9\ \text{kg}$$

The mass of the Sun decreases at a rate of 4.27×10^9 kg/s.

(b) Calculate the total amount of mass lost by the Sun in its history.

The age of the Sun in seconds is

$$(4.56 \times 10^9\ \text{y})\left(\frac{365.25\ \text{d}}{1\ \text{y}}\right)\left(\frac{24\ \text{h}}{1\ \text{d}}\right)\left(\frac{60\ \text{min}}{1\ \text{h}}\right)\left(\frac{60\ \text{s}}{1\ \text{min}}\right) = 1.44 \times 10^{17}\ \text{s}$$

In this number of seconds, the total mass lost by the Sun is

$$\left(4.27 \times 10^9\ \frac{\text{kg}}{\text{s}}\right)(1.44 \times 10^{17}\ \text{s}) = 6.14 \times 10^{26}\ \text{kg}$$

As a fraction of the Sun's present-day mass, the amount of mass lost is $(6.14 \times 10^{26}\ \text{kg})/(1.99 \times 10^{30}\ \text{kg}) = 3.09 \times 10^{-4} = 0.0309$ percent of the total mass.

Reflect

In more than 4 billion years of producing energy at a prodigious rate, the Sun has lost only a tiny fraction of its total mass. This is a testament to how much energy can be released by converting even a small amount of mass.

? Got the Concept? 25-7 Can We Build a Starship?

The total amount of electric energy produced per year in the United States from all sources is about 1.5×10^{19} J. You propose to use all of this energy to accelerate a spacecraft to $0.990c$ in order to travel to other stars. About how massive could your proposed starship be? (a) About 3×10^6 kg (the mass of an ocean liner); (b) about 3×10^5 kg (the mass of a large airliner); (c) about 3×10^3 kg (the mass of a sport utility vehicle); (d) about 30 kg (the mass of a kayak or canoe); (e) about 3 kg (the mass of a skateboard).

25-8 Einstein's general theory of relativity describes the fundamental nature of gravity

Sitting in a chair in the patent office in Bern, Switzerland, in 1907, a young Albert Einstein had what he would call "the happiest thought of my life." He imagined a man falling freely from the roof of a house and realized that "at least in his immediate surroundings—there exists no gravitational field." If the man released an object, for example, it would accelerate at the same rate as the man accelerated, and because the man would "not feel his own weight," it would appear to him that neither he nor the object was experiencing a gravitational force.

Einstein's thought experiment led him to postulate a new principle called the **principle of equivalence**. This principle states that

A gravitational field is equivalent to an accelerated frame of reference in the absence of gravity.

The principle of equivalence dictates that it is not possible to distinguish experimentally between a system in an accelerating frame and a system under the influence of gravity. In other words, if you were to drop a ball in a windowless elevator car that makes no noise and doesn't shake, you could not tell from the motion of the ball whether the elevator car were sitting stationary on the surface of a planet and experiencing its gravity or accelerating in empty space, far from sources of gravity. For example, if you were standing in this elevator car and experienced an acceleration of 9.80 m/s^2, you wouldn't be able to tell whether the car was stationary on Earth or accelerating at 9.80 m/s^2 in the absence of Earth's gravity.

Let's explore physics in this imaginary elevator car further. In Figure 25-16a a ball is thrown horizontally while the elevator car is stationary near Earth's surface. Due to the force of gravity, the ball accelerates downward, following a familiar parabolic arc.

(a) This elevator car is stationary near the surface of Earth. A ball thrown horizontally follows a parabolic path as it falls.

(b) This elevator car is stationary, far from Earth or any other massive object. A ball thrown horizontally travels in a straight line.

Figure 25-16 Elevator cars on Earth and in space A ball is thrown horizontally in (a) an elevator car on Earth's surface and (b) in an elevator car far from any massive object.

The figure shows the positions of the ball at five instants, spanning four equal time intervals. What if the elevator car were far from Earth and from any other massive object that could exert a noticeable gravitational force on the ball? In that case the ball would travel along a straight line, as shown in Figure 25-16b. No gravity means no acceleration . . . or does it? Consider the situation shown in Figure 25-17. The elevator car is again far from any object that could exert a noticeable gravitational force on the ball, but now the car is accelerating. The direction of the acceleration is "up" (toward the top of the page). Because there is no discernible gravitational force, the ball travels in a straight line as in Figure 25-16b. However, because the elevator car is accelerating, an observer in the car sees the ball trace out a parabolic arc with respect to the walls and floor of the car. Remember that there are no windows in the elevator car, and it makes no noise and does not vibrate as it moves. An observer in the car cannot, therefore, detect its motion. The observer feels the effect of the principle of equivalence: It appears that the ball is falling under the influence of gravity.

Einstein's theory of gravitation is therefore a theory of accelerating frames of reference. Because this is more general than the case of inertial frames, the type that was at the heart of the special theory of relativity, this expanded theory is called the **general theory of relativity**.

To see the real power of Einstein's postulate about the equivalence of acceleration and gravity, substitute a beam of light for the ball in our elevator car thought experiment. We expect that a beam of light travels in a straight line, so in analogy to throwing the ball, shining the light horizontally should result in a horizontal beam of light. Certainly that is the case when the elevator is stationary and far from any massive objects. If the elevator were accelerating, however, as in the case of the ball depicted in Figure 25-17, an observer in the elevator car would *not* see the light move straight toward the far wall. You might need a precise measuring device to detect it, but the light would hit the opposing wall below the height at which it started. Did the light bend, or is it that the elevator car has moved during the time that the light travels from one side of the car to the other? The principle of equivalence tells us that the observer has no way of knowing whether the car is accelerating or whether it is at rest near an object that exerts a gravitational force on it. We are therefore justified in declaring that the car is stationary and that the light is deflected! In addition, we must conclude that the beam's parabolic path results from the influence of a gravitational force. Both the beam of light and the ball accelerate due to a gravitational field.

The deflection of light in the presence of massive objects is small, an effect you might imagine would have been impossible to measure in Einstein's time. Einstein realized, however, that because the Sun's mass is large, if the light from a distant star were to pass close to the Sun, the change in its direction would be measurable. Light passing close to the Sun would only be visible during a total eclipse, so in order to test Einstein's theory the English astronomer Sir Arthur Eddington led an expedition to an island off the west coast of Africa in 1919 to photograph a total eclipse of the Sun. Eddington compared the position relative to other stars of a star cluster that was optically close to the Sun during the eclipse to its position at other times. His measurements confirmed Einstein's theory that massive objects deflect light.

Figure 25-17 An accelerating elevator car in space When a ball is thrown horizontally in an elevator car, which is both far from any massive object and also accelerating, it follows a straight path. An observer in the elevator, however, would see the ball follow a parabolic path with respect to the floor and walls of the elevator car.

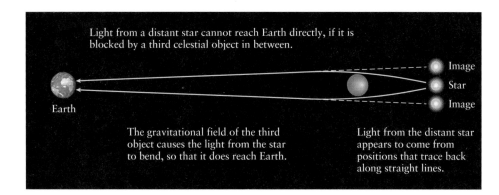

Light from a distant star cannot reach Earth directly, if it is blocked by a third celestial object in between.

Earth

Image

Star

Image

The gravitational field of the third object causes the light from the star to bend, so that it does reach Earth.

Light from the distant star appears to come from positions that trace back along straight lines.

Figure 25-18 **Gravity deflects light**
A massive object positioned between Earth and a distant star bends light from the star so that it can be seen on Earth. This is called gravitational lensing.

A more stunning phenomenon associated with gravitational bending of light occurs when multiple images of a distant star form as light is bent by a closer, massive celestial object, such as the black hole at the center of a galaxy. **Figure 25-18** depicts such *gravitational lensing*, in which a massive object is positioned directly between Earth and a distant star. Light from the star cannot reach Earth directly, but the lensing effect results in light initially not propagating toward Earth to be bent back toward us. In this way light from the star can approach Earth from many directions—for example, the two directions shown in the figure. **Figure 25-19a** presents an example of gravitational lensing showing four distinct images. When light is bent around the intervening object and reaches Earth from a full circle around it, the star's light is spread out into a ring around the lensing object, as in **Figure 25-19b**.

Earlier in this chapter we saw that Einstein's special theory of relativity addresses time dilation; a clock moving at constant speed relative to an observer is seen to be running slowly. Imagine a scenario in which *two* observers moving at constant speed relative to each other can each see a clock carried by the other. Each observes a moving clock, so each measures the other's clock to be running slowly *compared to* his own clock. Is this possible? If the two observers stopped their relative motion and brought the clocks together, certainly both clocks could not be slow relative to the other!

Einstein's general theory of relativity is required to resolve this puzzle. When the two observers are in relative motion at constant speed, their frames are symmetric; that is, either observer can consider the other to be in motion. To bring the two clocks together to compare their times, however, one of the observers must decelerate. The two frames are therefore no longer symmetric. One is inertial and the other, the frame that decelerates, is not. In addition, general relativity must be applied to understand the measurement of time from one frame to the other. Time runs more slowly in the frame that experiences the change in speed.

This issue of acceleration and deceleration is central to the so-called twins paradox, one of the most well-known puzzles in relativity. We'll state it this way: Bertha takes a

(a)   (b)

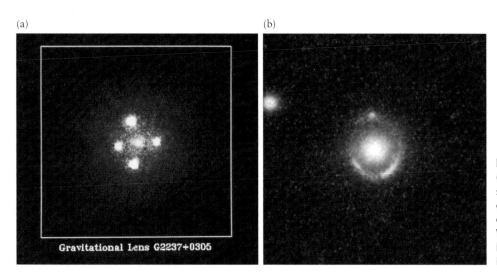

Gravitational Lens G2237+0305

Figure 25-19 **Gravitational lenses**
(a) These four separate images of a single star are formed by a massive gravitational lens. (b) Light leaving a distant star travels in every direction. When that light is bent toward Earth by a massive gravitational lens, the image formed can be a circular ring.

trip to the star Proxima Centauri on a fast spaceship, while her twin Eartha stays at home. Eartha's clock ticks off ten years in the time Bertha is gone. Special relativity suggests that were Eartha to observe Bertha's clock, she would see it running slowly compared to her own. After ten hours have elapsed on Eartha's clock, for example, she observes that only eight hours have elapsed on Bertha's. Eartha expects that when Bertha returns, she will have aged eight years, not ten—Bertha will be younger than Eartha at the end of the trip. But according to the puzzle, Bertha considers herself at rest and sees Eartha moving away and then returning. In the telling of the paradox, the claim is made that the two views are equally valid, so Bertha sees Eartha's clock running slowly and expects that Eartha will be younger than she is at the end of the trip. But the two views are not symmetric! Bertha must accelerate to leave Earth, decelerate when she reaches Proxima Centauri, and then accelerate and decelerate again in order to return home. For this reason her frame can be distinguished from Eartha's. It is simply not correct to declare that each twin can consider the other to be moving in an inertial frame; special relativity does not apply. Although the mathematical details are beyond the scope of this book, general relativity predicts that the clock that accelerates and decelerates (Bertha's clock) will run slowly, so Bertha will be younger than Eartha upon her return.

Take-Home Message for Section 25-8

✔ The principle of equivalence, a central postulate of Einstein's general theory of relativity, declares that a gravitational field is equivalent to an accelerated frame of reference in the absence of gravity.

✔ It is not possible to distinguish between a system in an accelerating frame and a system under the influence of gravity.

✔ One important prediction of general relativity is that light bends as it passes through a gravitational field.

Key Terms

event
frame of reference (reference frame)
Galilean transformation
Galilean velocity transformation
general theory of relativity
inertial frame
inverse Lorentz velocity transformation

length contraction
Lorentz transformation
Lorentz velocity transformation
Michelson-Morley experiment
noninertial frame
principle of equivalence
principle of Newtonian relativity

proper time
reference frame (frame of reference)
relativistic gamma
relativistic speed
rest energy
special theory of relativity
time dilation

Chapter Summary

Topic	Equation or Figure
Newtonian relativity: The principle of Newtonian relativity states that the laws of motion are the same in all inertial frames of reference. The Galilean transformation relates the coordinates of an event in one frame to the coordinates of the same event in another frame, and the Galilean velocity transformation relates the velocity of an object relative to one frame to its velocity relative to another frame. These transformations are valid only for speeds that are small compared to the speed of light c.	Inertial frame of reference S' moves at speed V in the positive x direction relative to inertial frame of reference S. $$\begin{aligned} x' &= x - Vt \\ y' &= y \\ z' &= z \\ t' &= t \end{aligned}$$ Coordinates of an event as measured in frame S' Coordinates of the same event as measured in frame S (25-1)
	Inertial frame of reference S' moves at speed V in the positive x direction relative to inertial frame of reference S. $$\begin{aligned} v_x' &= v_x - V \\ v_y' &= v_y \\ v_z' &= v_z \end{aligned}$$ Velocity components of an object as measured in frame S' Velocity components of the same object as measured in frame S (25-5)

The Michelson-Morley experiment:
In the nineteenth century it was hypothesized that space was filled with a material medium, called the luminiferous ether, that was required in order for light to propagate through space. The Michelson-Morley experiment provided evidence that the ether does not exist, and motivated Einstein's special theory of relativity.

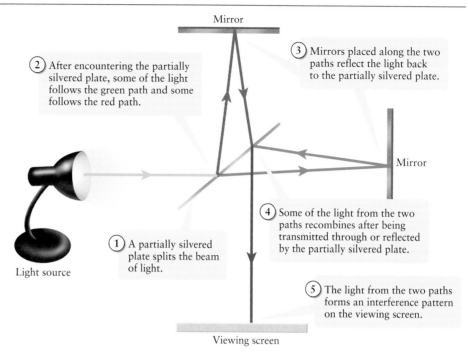

Mirror

(2) After encountering the partially silvered plate, some of the light follows the green path and some follows the red path.

(3) Mirrors placed along the two paths reflect the light back to the partially silvered plate.

Mirror

(4) Some of the light from the two paths recombines after being transmitted through or reflected by the partially silvered plate.

(1) A partially silvered plate splits the beam of light.

Light source

(5) The light from the two paths forms an interference pattern on the viewing screen.

Viewing screen

(Figure 25-7)

The special theory of relativity:
Einstein's special theory of relativity is based on the postulates that all laws of physics are the same in all inertial frames, and the speed of light in a vacuum is the same in all inertial frames. Two consequences are that moving clocks run slow and moving objects are shortened along their direction of motion.

Time interval between two events as measured in frame S', in which those events occur at the same place.

$$\Delta t = \frac{\Delta t_{\text{proper}}}{\sqrt{1 - \dfrac{V^2}{c^2}}}$$

Time interval between the same two events as measured in frame S

Speed of S' relative to S

Speed of light in a vacuum

(25-10)

Length of an object in a frame of reference S' in which it is at rest.

$$L = L_{\text{rest}} \sqrt{1 - \frac{V^2}{c^2}}$$

Length of the same object in a frame of reference S in which the object is moving along its length.

Speed of S' relative to S

Speed of light in a vacuum

(25-14)

The Lorentz transformation:
The Lorentz transformation is a generalization of the Galilean transformation that is valid for all speeds. The Lorentz velocity transformation is a generalization of the Galilean velocity transformation: It shows that the speed of light c is an ultimate speed limit and that an object at rest can never be accelerated to c.

Inertial frame of reference S' moves at speed V in the positive x direction relative to inertial frame of reference S.

$$x' = \frac{x - Vt}{\sqrt{1 - \dfrac{V^2}{c^2}}}$$

$$y' = y$$
$$z' = z$$

$$t' = \frac{t - \dfrac{V}{c^2}x}{\sqrt{1 - \dfrac{V^2}{c^2}}}$$

Coordinates of an event as measured in frame S'

Coordinates of the same event as measured in frame S

(25-15)

Inertial frame of reference S' moves at speed V in the positive x direction relative to inertial frame of reference S.

x component of velocity of an object moving along the x axis as measured in frame S'

$$v_x' = \frac{v_x - V}{1 - \dfrac{V}{c^2} v_x}$$

x component of velocity of the same object as measured in frame S

(25-17)

Kinetic energy, momentum, and rest energy: The formulas for kinetic energy and momentum must be modified to account for c being the ultimate speed limit. The relativity postulates also show that an object with mass m has a rest energy $E_0 = mc^2$ even when it is not in motion.

Kinetic energy of a particle of mass m and velocity $\vec{v}$

$$K = (\gamma - 1)mc^2$$

Relativistic gamma for speed v

$$\vec{p} = \gamma m \vec{v}$$

(25-20)

Momentum of a particle of mass m and velocity $\vec{v}$

At speeds that are a small fraction of the speed of light c, these are approximately equal to the Newtonian expressions

$$K = \frac{1}{2}mv^2 \text{ and } \vec{p} = m\vec{v}$$

The general theory of relativity: The principle of equivalence states that a gravitational field is equivalent to an accelerated frame of reference in the absence of gravity. This principle shows that light is affected by gravity just as objects with mass are.

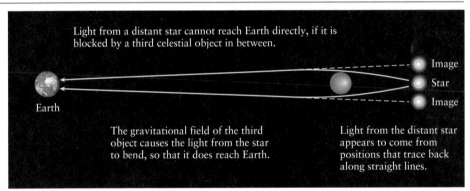

Light from a distant star cannot reach Earth directly, if it is blocked by a third celestial object in between.

Earth

Image
Star
Image

The gravitational field of the third object causes the light from the star to bend, so that it does reach Earth.

Light from the distant star appears to come from positions that trace back along straight lines.

(Figure 25-18)

Answer to What do you think? Question

(b)   As an object approaches the speed of light, it becomes increasingly difficult to further increase its speed. See Example 25-8 in Section 25-7.

Answers to Got the Concept? Questions

25-1   (b) Let S be the frame of reference of an observer on the ground, and let S' be the frame of reference of an observer moving with the air (for example, an observer floating in a balloon). Then S' is moving due east at $V = 100$ km/h, so we take the positive x direction to be to the east. First suppose the airliner is flying west to east, so its velocity relative to the air is $v_x' = +900$ km/h. From the first of Equations 25-5, the velocity of the airplane relative to the ground in this situation is $v_x = v_x' + V = +900$ km/h $+ 100$ km/h $= +1000$ km/h; relative to the ground, the airliner is moving east at 1000 km/h. If instead the airliner is flying east to west, its velocity relative to the air is $v_x' = -900$ km/h and its velocity relative to the ground is $v_x = v_x' + V = -900$ km/h $+ 100$ km/h $= -800$ km/h; the airliner is moving west at 800 km/h relative

to the ground. In North America high-altitude winds typically blow from west to east as in this example, so a west-to-east airliner trip is typically faster than an east-to-west trip between the same two airports.

25-2   (b) This is similar to Got the Concept? Question 25-1. Let S be the frame of reference of the water, and let S' be the frame of reference of the dolphin. The dolphin swims in the positive x direction at speed $V = 10$ m/s. As measured in frame S, the sound wave moves in the positive x direction at velocity $v_x = 1500$ m/s. From the first of Equations 25-5, the velocity of the sound wave relative to S', the frame of reference of the dolphin, is $v_x' = v_x - V = 1500$ m/s $- 10$ m/s $= 1490$ m/s. Because the dolphin is "chasing" the sound wave, the speed of the wave relative to the dolphin is less than its speed relative to the water. As we will see in Section 25-6, light waves do not behave like this: If you shoot a laser beam forward from a fast-moving vehicle, the speed of the light wave relative to the vehicle is $c = 3.00 \times 10^8$ m/s no matter how fast it is moving.

25-3 (e) The proper time is measured in any frame that is at rest with respect to the clock. Albert aboard Starship *Alpha* is at rest with respect to the clock, so he measures the clock's proper time. Although Barbara is not on the same craft as the clock, she is also not moving relative to it, so she also measures the clock's proper time. George's speed is the same as the clock's, but not in the same direction. So George is moving with respect to the clock and therefore does not observe proper time intervals. The same is true for Elena on Earth, who is moving relative to the clock. We conclude that the time interval between clock ticks is the proper time for both Albert and Barbara, but it is not the proper time for either George or Elena.

25-4 (b) The statement of time dilation is that moving clocks run slow. Albert's clock is moving relative to Elena, and Elena's clock is moving at the same speed relative to Albert. So *both* observers will see the other person's clock running slow. There is no contradiction, since the two observers are looking at different pairs of events: Elena is looking at the time interval between two clicks of Albert's clock, while Albert is looking at the time interval between two clicks of Elena's clock.

25-5 (a) The length you measure will be the same as the rest length if the rod is oriented so that its length is perpendicular to the direction of motion. There is no length contraction along

a perpendicular direction. (The *width* of the rod will be contracted along the direction of motion, but that's not what the question is about.)

25-6 (c) The outfielder's frame is S', so the velocity of the ball relative to her is $v'_x = +0.700c$ (positive since the ball is now moving in the positive x direction). She is still moving at $V = 0.300c$ relative to the batter. The velocity of the ball relative to the batter is v_x, given by the inverse Lorentz velocity transformation (Equation 25-18):

$$v_x = \frac{v'_x + V}{1 + \frac{V}{c^2}v'_x} = \frac{0.700c + 0.300c}{1 + \frac{(0.300c)}{c^2}(0.700c)}$$

$$= \frac{1.00c}{1 + 0.210} = 0.826c$$

25-7 (d) The kinetic energy of the spacecraft will be $K = (\gamma - 1)mc^2$. From Example 25-8, $\gamma = 7.09$ if $v = 0.990c$, so $K = (7.09 - 1)mc^2 = 6.09mc^2$. If all of the 1.5×10^{19} J goes into the kinetic energy K of the starship, the mass that can be accelerated to $0.990c$ will be

$$m = \frac{K}{6.09c^2} = \frac{1.5 \times 10^{19}\,\text{J}}{(6.09)(3.00 \times 10^8\,\text{m/s})^2}$$

$$= 27\,\text{J} \cdot \text{s}^2/\text{m}^2 = 27\,\text{kg}$$

That's about the mass of a kayak or canoe, not including any occupants. This calculation shows that it's simply not feasible with current technology to build a spacecraft that can carry humans and travel at speeds approaching the speed of light.

Questions and Problems

In a few problems, you are given more data than you actually need; in a few other problems, you are required to supply data from your general knowledge, outside sources, or informed estimate.
Interpret as significant all digits in numerical values that have trailing zeros and no decimal points.
For all problems, use $g = 9.80$ m/s² for the free-fall acceleration due to gravity. Neglect friction and air resistance unless instructed to do otherwise.
• Basic, single-concept problem
•• Intermediate-level problem, may require synthesis of concepts and multiple steps
••• Challenging problem
SSM *Solution is in Student Solutions Manual*

Conceptual Questions

1. •Why do you think there was so much resistance from the established physics community when Einstein proposed his new theory of relativistic motion in 1905?

2. •How would you change the following Galilean transformation equations in the case where a frame was moving both in the x and the y direction?

$$x' = x - Vt$$
$$y' = y$$
$$z' = z$$
$$t' = t$$

3. •What is a frame of reference? What is an inertial frame of reference? SSM

4. •What kind of reference frame is Earth's surface? Explain your answer.

5. •What does the phrase "all motion is relative, there is no absolute motion" mean?

6. •Describe the Michelson and Morley experiment. Why do you think it was repeated so many times? (It may be the most often performed experiment in the history of physics.)

7. •Explain how the measurement of time enters into the determination of the length of an object. SSM

8. •What are the two postulates of the special theory of relativity?

9. •Is it possible for one observer to find that event A happens after event B and another observer to find that event A happens before event B? Explain your answer.

10. •Is it possible to accelerate an object to the speed of light in a real situation? Explain your answer.

11. •Gene Roddenberry created the popular TV and film series *Star Trek*. Once at a public lecture he was asked if he thought we would ever be able to travel faster than light. He responded, "No, and that's a good thing because it means that we can always do it in science fiction." How have science fiction writers gotten around the cosmic speed limit?

12. •What is the fundamental postulate of the general theory of relativity?

13. •Describe one of the predictions of general relativity.

Multiple-Choice Questions

14. •Which of the following statements are true?

A. The laws of motion are the same in all inertial frames of reference.

B. The laws of motion are the same in all reference frames.

C. There is no way to detect absolute motion.

D. All of the above statements are true.

E. Only two of the above statements are true.

15. •If we used radio waves to communicate with an alien spaceship approaching Earth at 10% of the speed of light, we would receive their signals at a speed of

A. 0.10c.

B. 0.90c.

C. 0.99c.

D. 1.00c.

E. 1.10c. SSM

16. •Time dilation means that

A. the slowing of time in a moving frame of reference is only an illusion resulting from motion.

B. time really does pass more slowly in a frame of reference moving relative to a frame of reference at relative rest.

C. time really does pass more slowly in a frame of reference at rest relative to a frame of reference that is moving.

D. time is unchanging regardless of the frame of reference.

E. no two clocks at rest can ever read the same time.

17. •A meter stick hurtles through space at a speed of 0.95c with its length perpendicular to the direction of motion. You measure its length to be equal to

A. 0 m.

B. 0.05 m.

C. 0.95 m.

D. 1.00 m.

E. 1.05 m.

18. •A particle has an Einsteinian momentum of p. If its speed doubles, the Einsteinian momentum will be

A. greater than $2p$.

B. equal to $2p$.

C. less than $2p$

D. equal to $2p/c$.

E. equal to p.

19. •Consider two atomic clocks, one at the GPS ground control station near Colorado Springs (elevation 1830 m) and the other one in orbit in a GPS satellite (altitude 20,200 km). According to the general theory of relativity, which atomic clock runs slow?

A. The clock in Colorado runs slow.

B. The clock in orbit runs slow.

C. The clocks keep identical time.

D. The orbiting clock is 95% slower than the clock in Colorado.

E. The orbiting clock alternately runs slow and then fast depending on where the Sun is. SSM

Estimation/Numerical Analysis

20. •Estimate the difference in a 10,000-s time interval as measured by a proper observer and a relative observer traveling on a commercial jetliner.

21. •Estimate the minimum speed required to observe a 10% change between the proper time and the relative time.

22. •Estimate the percent error between the Newtonian momentum and the Einsteinian momentum at (a) typical macroscopic speeds and (b) speeds that are a substantial fraction of c.

23. •Are there any numerical values of v/c that lend themselves to relatively simple calculations of γ (without the use of a calculator)?

24. •If all effects due to general relativity are neglected, and the effects of time dilation are cumulative, how many trips into outer space would an astronaut have to make to experience a 10% change in the length of his life (as measured by an observer at rest on Earth)? Is the time longer or shorter by 10% according to the observer on Earth?

25. •Estimate the percentage of the world's population that has a basic understanding of Einstein's special theory of relativity (assume your understanding of the concepts in this chapter constitutes a basic understanding). SSM

26. ••Estimate the increase in rest energy of a copper sample [100 kg, $c = 387 \, \text{J}/(\text{kg} \cdot °\text{C})$] if its temperature is increased 100°C.

27. •This problem is intended to help you to understand the behavior of relativistic variables such as time, length, and momentum. To begin, construct a table (like the one shown below) of the following values for γ versus v/c, in which

$$\gamma = \frac{1}{\sqrt{1 - \left(\dfrac{v}{c}\right)^2}} \qquad c = 3.00 \times 10^8 \, \text{m/s}$$

v/c	γ	v/c	γ
0	0.7	0.4	0.999
0.1	0.8	0.5	0.9999
0.2	0.9	0.6	
0.3	0.99		

Now, plot a graph of the variable γ versus v/c. As long as γ is close to unity, the effects of Einstein's special theory of relativity go unnoticed. (a) From your graph (or your chart) determine the maximum value of v/c for which γ is less than 1% larger than unity (1.0). (b) What numerical value does the slope take at $v/c = 0.1$, $v/c = 0.5$, $v/c = 0.9$, and $v/c = 0.999$?

Problems

25-1 The concepts of relativity may seem exotic, but they're part of everyday life

25-2 Newton's mechanics includes some ideas of relativity

28. ••A bicyclist rides at 8.00 m/s toward the north. A car is moving at 25.0 m/s, also toward the north, and is initially behind the rider. A truck is moving at 15.0 m/s toward the south, approaching the bicycle and the car. (a) Make a sketch of the three vehicles and label their respective velocity vectors, relative to the ground. (b) Calculate the relative velocities of each vehicle compared to the other two. Solve the problem both with vector diagrams and with equations.

29. ••A frame of reference, S, is fixed on the surface of Earth with the x axis pointing toward the east, the y axis pointing toward the north, and the z axis pointing up. A second frame of reference, S', is moving at a constant 4.00 m/s toward the east. (a) Describe mathematically the relationships between x' and x,

y' and y, and z' and z. (b) A picture is taken in the S frame of reference at $t = 4.00$ s at the point (2 m, 1 m, 0 m). Calculate the corresponding values of x', y', and z' for the same event in the S' frame. SSM

30. •A boat sails from the pier at Fisherman's Wharf in San Francisco at 4.00 m/s, directly toward Alcatraz. A kite rider heads directly away from Alcatraz toward the boat at a relative speed of 6.00 m/s, according to the skipper of the sailboat. Calculate the velocity of the kite rider relative to the pier.

31. ••A radio-controlled model car travels at 15.0 m/s, to the right, relative to the parking lot that it is driving on. A girl on her scooter chases after the model car at 4.00 m/s. The parking lot represents reference frame S, the model car is in frame S', and the girl is described by frame S''. Assume that the car and the girl are both at the origin of the parking lot at $t = 0$ s. Write down the Galilean transformation between (a) S and S', (b) S and S'', and (c) S' and S''.

32. ••Assume that the origins of S and S' coincide at $t = t' = 0$ s. An observer in inertial frame S measures the space and time coordinates of an event to be $x = 750$ m, $y = 250$ m, $z = 250$ m, and $t = 2.0$ μs. What are the space coordinates of the event in inertial frame S' which is moving in the $+x$ direction at a speed of $0.01c$ relative to S?

33. ••At time $t' = 4.00 \times 10^{-3}$ s, as measured in S', a particle is at the point $x' = 10$ m, $y' = 4$ m, and $z' = 6$ m. Compute the corresponding values of x, y, and z, as measured in S, for (a) a relative velocity between S' and S of $+500$ m/s and (b) a relative velocity between S' and S of -500 m/s. Assume that the origins of S and S' are coincident at $t = 0$ and that the motion lies along the x and x' axes.

34. ••Suppose that at $t = 6.00 \times 10^{-4}$ s, the space coordinates of a particle are $x = 100$ m, $y = 10$ m, and $z = 30$ m according to coordinate system S. Compute the corresponding values as measured in the frame S' if the relative velocity between S' and S is 150,000 m/s along the x and x' axes. The reference frames start together, with their origins coincident at $t = 0$.

35. •••A float plane lands on a river. Assume the velocity of the airplane relative to the air is 30 m/s, due east; the velocity of the wind is 20 m/s, due north; and the current in the river is 5 m/s, due south. Calculate the velocity of the plane just before it lands relative to the water. SSM

36. •A spaceship moves by Earth at 2.4×10^8 m/s. A satellite moves by Earth in the opposite direction at 1.6×10^8 m/s. Use the Galilean transformation to calculate the speed of the satellite relative to the spaceship and comment on your answer.

25-3 The Michelson-Morley experiment shows that light does not obey Newtonian relativity

37. •The Michelson-Morley experiment was performed hundreds of times in a futile attempt to find the luminiferous ether. Why was the experiment performed on an enormous slab of marble that was floated in a pool of mercury?

38. ••Consider an airplane traveling at 25 m/s airspeed between two points that are 2000 km apart. What is the round-trip time for the plane (a) if there is no wind? (b) if there is a wind blowing at 10 m/s, perpendicular to the line joining the two points? (c) if there is a wind blowing at 10 m/s along the line joining the two points?

39. ••Suppose that the length L in the Michelson-Morley experiment is 20,000 m. What would be the difference in light travel times on the two legs of the Michelson-Morley experiment *if the ether existed* and if Earth moved relative to it at the following speeds: (a) at its orbital speed around the Sun, (b) at $0.01c$, (c) at $0.1c$, (d) at $0.5c$, and (e) at $0.9c$?

25-4 Einstein's relativity predicts that the time between events depends on the observer

40. ••An observer in reference frame S observes that a lightning bolt strikes the origin and 10^{-4} s later a second lightning bolt strikes the same location. What is the time separation between the two lightning bolts determined by a second observer in reference frame S' moving at a speed of $0.8c$ along the collinear x–x' axis?

41. •A radioactive particle travels at $0.80c$ relative to the laboratory observers who are performing research. Calculate the half-life of the particle as measured in the laboratory frame compared to the half-life according to the proper frame of the particle.

42. •Muons at rest in the laboratory have an average lifetime of about 2.2 μs. What is the average lifetime, measured in the laboratory, of muons traveling at $0.99c$ with respect to the laboratory?

43. ••When muons traveled through the laboratory at a speed of $0.98c$, scientists obtained an average lifetime value of 11 μs before a muon decayed. If the muons were at rest in the laboratory, what would be the average lifetime of muons? SSM

44. ••The time dilation effect between two frames of reference is measured in the lab to have a 0.01% difference between the relative time and the proper time $\left[\Delta t = (t - t_{proper})/t_{proper} \times 100\% = 0.01\% \right]$. Calculate the relative speed of the two reference frames.

45. ••**Astronomy** The Andromeda galaxy is a spiral galaxy that is a distance of 2.54 million light-years from Earth. Is there any possible speed that a spaceship can achieve to deliver a human being to this galaxy? Consider the lifetime of a human to be 80 years.

46. ••**Astronomy** The nearest star to our own Sun is Proxima Centauri, 4.24 light-years away. If a spaceship travels at $0.75c$, how much time is required for a one-way trip (a) according to an Earth observer, and (b) according to the captain of the ship?

47. ••A subatomic particle is traveling with a "γ factor," $\gamma = 1/\sqrt{1 - (v/c)^2}$, of 20 as observed by a radiation monitor in a nuclear power plant. The particle is measured to "decay" 30 ns after it is observed by the plant. What is the proper lifetime of such a particle?

48. ••A spaceship travels at $0.95c$ toward Alpha Centauri. According to Earthlings, the distance is 4.37 light-years. (a) From the perspective of the space travelers, how long does it take to reach this star if the ship starts at Earth? (b) How long do Earthlings measure for the trip?

25-5 Einstein's relativity also predicts that the length of an object depends on the observer

49. ••A car travels in the positive x direction in the reference frame S. The reference frame S' moves at a speed of $0.80c$, along the x axis. The proper length of the car is 3.20 m. Calculate the length of the car according to observers in the S' frame. SSM

50. •The length of a spaceship is measured to have a relative length that is two-thirds of its proper length. What is the speed of the spaceship relative to the observer?

51. • A stick moves past an observer at a speed of $0.44c$. According to the observer the stick is oriented parallel to the direction of motion and is 0.88 m long. Determine the proper length of the stick.

52. ••A standard tournament domino is 1.5 in wide and 2.5 in long. Describe how you might orient a domino so that it will measure 1.5 in by 1.5 in as it moves by. What relative speed is required?

53. ••How fast must a pion be moving to travel 100 m (according to the laboratory frame) before it decays? The average lifetime, at rest, of a pion is 2.60×10^{-8} s. Give your answer in units of meters per second (m/s) and as a fraction of the speed of light (in other words, $v = ?$ and $v/c = ?$). SSM

25-6 The relative velocity of two objects is constrained by the speed of light, the ultimate speed limit

54. ••Spaceship A moves at $0.8c$ toward the right, while spaceship B moves in the opposite direction at $0.7c$ (both speeds are measured relative to Earth). (a) Calculate the velocity of Earth relative to spaceship A. (b) Calculate the velocity of Earth relative to spaceship B. (c) Calculate the velocity of spaceship A relative to spaceship B.

55. ••A (very fast) car traveling with a velocity of $+0.35c$ passes an observer sitting on the side of the road. A truck traveling with a velocity of $+0.25c$ passes the same observer. Determine the relative velocity between the car and the truck. Give your answer in terms of "the velocity of the truck relative to the car is . . ." and "the velocity of the car relative to the truck is. . . ."

56. ••A spaceship flies by Earth at $0.92c$. It fires a rocket at $0.75c$ in the forward direction, relative to the spaceship. What is the velocity of the rocket relative to Earth?

57. ••Suppose the spaceship in problem 56 continues to fly by Earth at $0.92c$. This time, however, it fires a rocket at $0.75c$ in the backward direction relative to the spaceship. What is the velocity of the rocket relative to Earth? SSM

58. ••Prove that the relative velocity of a laser fired from a spaceship that is moving at $0.92c$ past Earth will be c from the perspective of Earth.

59. ••A proton travels in the accelerator at Fermilab at 99.999954% of the speed of light. An anti-proton travels in the opposite direction at the same speed. What is the relative velocity of the two particles?

25-7 The equations for kinetic energy and momentum must be modified at very high speeds

60. ••A 2.00-kg object moves at 400,000 m/s. (a) Calculate the Newtonian momentum of the object. (b) Calculate the Einsteinian momentum of the object. (c) Which of the answers is correct? What is the percent difference?

61. ••An electron travels at $0.444c$. Calculate (a) its Einsteinian momentum, (b) its Einsteinian kinetic energy, (c) its rest energy, and (d) the total energy of the electron. SSM

62. •A proton ($m = 1.673 \times 10^{-27}$ kg) is traveling at $0.5c$. Calculate its Einsteinian momentum and its Einsteinian kinetic energy.

63. •A particle is traveling with respect to an observer such that its Einsteinian energy is twice its rest energy. How fast is it moving with respect to the observer?

64. ••A particle has a rest energy of 5.33×10^{-13} J and a total energy of 9.61×10^{-13} J. Calculate the momentum of the particle.

65. ••A proton has a rest energy of 1.50×10^{-10} J and a momentum of 1.07×10^{-19} kg·m/s. Calculate its speed. SSM

25-8 Einstein's general theory of relativity describes the fundamental nature of gravity

66. ••What would an observer measure for the free-fall acceleration in an elevator near the surface of Earth if the elevator accelerates downward at 8 m/s²?

67. ••What would an observer measure for the free-fall acceleration in an elevator near the surface of Earth if the elevator accelerates downward at 18 m/s²? SSM

General Problems

68. ••A super rocket car traverses a straight track 2.40×10^5 m long in 10^{-3} s as measured by an observer next to the track. (a) How much time elapses on a clock in the rocket car during the run? (b) What is the distance traveled in traversing the track as determined by the driver of the rocket car?

69. ••Observers in reference frame S see an explosion located at $x_1 = 580$ m. A second explosion occurs 4.5 μs later at $x_2 = 1500$ m. In reference frame S', which is moving along the $+x$ axis at speed v, the explosions occur at the same point in space. What is the separation in time between the two explosions as measured in S'? SSM

70. ••A spaceship departs from Earth for the star Alpha Centauri, which is 4.37 light-years away. The spaceship travels at $0.77c$. (a) What is the time required to get there as measured by a passenger on the spaceship? (b) How long does it take for the spaceship to arrive at Alpha Centauri as measured on Earth?

71. ••A radioactive nucleus traveling at a speed of $0.8c$ in a laboratory decays and emits an electron in the same direction as the nucleus is moving. The electron travels at a speed of $0.6c$ relative to the nucleus. (a) How fast is the electron moving according to an observer in the laboratory? (b) Rocket A travels away from Earth at $0.6c$, and rocket B travels away from Earth in exactly the opposite direction at $0.8c$. What is the speed of rocket B as measured by the pilot of rocket A? (c) Why did you get the same answer that you did for part (a)?

72. ••A beam of pions has a speed of $0.88c$. Their mean lifetime, as measured in the reference frame of the laboratory, is 2.6×10^{-8} s. What is the distance traveled by the laboratory, as measured by the pion, during its lifetime?

73. •••Muons have a proper lifetime of 2.20×10^{-6} s. Suppose a muon is formed at an altitude of 3000 m and travels at a speed of $0.950c$ straight toward Earth. (a) Does the muon reach Earth's surface before it decays? Complete the problem from both perspectives: the muon's point of view and Earth's reference frame. (b) Calculate the minimum speed of the muon so that it *just barely* reaches Earth's surface as it decays.

74. ••Two students, Nora and Allison, are both the same age when Allison hops aboard a flying saucer and blasts off to achieve a cruising speed of $0.800c$ for 20 years (according

to Allison). Neglecting the acceleration of the ship during blastoff, landing, and turnarounds, find the difference in age between Nora and Allison when they are reunited. Who is younger?

75. ••Suppose a jet plane flies at 300 m/s relative to an observer on the ground. Using only special relativity, determine the distance of the flight, as measured by an observer on the ground, before the clocks aboard the plane are 10 s behind clocks on the ground. Assume the two clocks were originally synchronized to start. SSM

76. ••At the end of the linear accelerator at the Stanford Linear Accelerator Center (SLAC), electrons have a speed of $0.99999999995c$. (a) Calculate the value of γ for an electron at SLAC. (b) What time interval would an observer at rest relative to the accelerator measure for a time interval of 1.66 μs measured from the electron's perspective?

77. ••The proper half-life of a certain subatomic particle is about 1×10^{-8} s. How fast is a beam of these particles moving if one-half of them decay in 6×10^{-8} s as measured in the laboratory?

78. ••Based on experiments in your lab, you know that a certain radioisotope has a half-life of 2.25 μs. As a high-speed spaceship passes your lab, you measure that the same isotope at rest inside the spaceship takes 3.15 s for one-half of it to decay. (a) What is the half-life of the isotope as measured by an astronaut working inside the spaceship? (b) How fast is the spaceship traveling relative to Earth?

79. ••Recent home energy bills indicate that a household used 411 kWh of electrical energy and 201 therms for gas heating and cooking in a period of one month. Given that 1.0 therm is equal to 29.3 kWh, how many milligrams of mass would need to be converted directly to energy each month to meet the energy needs for the home? SSM

80. ••We know 1 kg of trinitrotoluene (TNT) yields an energy of 4.2 MJ. The energy released comes from the chemical bonds in the material. How much mass would be required to create an explosion equivalent to 1.8×10^9 kg TNT? Assume all the energy comes simply from the mass of the material.

81. ••Astronomy High-speed cosmic rays strike atoms in Earth's upper atmosphere and create secondary showers. Suppose a particle in one of the showers is created 25.0 km above the surface traveling downward at 90.0% the speed of light. Consider the following two events: "a particle is created in the upper atmosphere" and "a particle strikes the ground." We can view the events from two reference frames, one fixed on Earth and one traveling with the created particle. (a) In which of the reference frames are the proper time and the rest length between the two events measured? Explain your reasoning. (b) In the particle's reference frame, how long after its creation does it take it to reach the ground? (c) In Earth's reference frame, how long after creation does it take the particle to reach the ground? (d) Show that the times in parts (b) and (c) are consistent with time dilation.

82. •••A rocket 642 m long is traveling parallel to Earth's surface at $0.5c$ from left to right. At time $t = 0$, a light flashes for an instant at the center of the rocket. Detectors at opposite ends of the rocket record the arrival of the light signal. Call event A the light striking the left detector and event B the light striking the right detector. Observers at rest in the rocket and on Earth record the events. (a) What is the speed of the light signal as measured by the observer (i) at rest in the rocket and (ii) at rest on Earth? (b) At what time after the flash do events A and B occur as measured by (i) the observer in the rocket and (ii) the observer at rest on Earth? Which event occurs first in each case? (c) Show that the results in part (b) are consistent with time dilation.

83. ••Biology Twin astronauts, Harry and Larry, have identical pulse rates of 70 beats/min on Earth. Harry remains on Earth, but Larry is assigned to a space voyage during which he travels at $0.75c$ relative to Earth. What will be Larry's pulse rate as measured by (a) Harry on Earth and (b) the doctor in Larry's rocket?

84. ••A rocket is traveling at speed v relative to Earth. Inside a lab in the rocket, two laser beams are turned on, one pointing in the forward direction and the other pointing in the backward direction relative to the rocket's velocity. (a) What is the speed of each laser beam relative to the laboratory in the rocket? (b) Use the Lorentz velocity transformation to find the velocity of each laser beam as measured by an observer at rest on Earth. (c) As observed from Earth, how fast are the two laser beams separating from *each other*?

85. •••A 1000-kg rocket is flying at $0.90c$ relative to your lab. Calculate the kinetic energy of the rocket using the Einsteinian formula and the ordinary Newtonian formula. What is the percent error if we use the Newtonian formula? Does the Newtonian formula overestimate or underestimate the kinetic energy?

86. •••A spaceship is traveling at $0.50c$ relative to Earth. Inside the ship, a cylindrical piston that is 50.0 cm long and 4.50 cm in diameter contains 1.25 mol of ideal gas at 25.0°C under 2.20 atm of pressure. The cylinder is oriented with its axis parallel to the direction in which the spaceship is flying. What is the particle density (in molecules per cubic meter) of the gas in the cylinder as measured by (a) an astronaut in the rocket ship's lab and (b) a scientist in an Earth lab?

87. •••Astronomy In December 2009, the discovery was announced of a planet that may have a large amount of water, and hence would be a good candidate for possible life. The planet, GJ 1214b, orbits a small star that is 42 light-years from Earth. In the future, we might decide to send some astronauts to explore the planet. When they arrive there, we want them to be young enough to perform tests. Suppose that the captain is 25 years old at launch time. (a) What is the minimum speed the spaceship will need for the captain to be no more than 60 years old at arrival? (b) As soon as the spaceship arrives at the planet, the captain has orders to send a radio signal to Earth to notify Mission Control that the trip was successful. How many years after launch from Earth will it be when the signal arrives at Earth? You can ignore acceleration times and any motion of Earth and GJ 1214b. SSM

26

Quantum Physics and Atomic Structure

In this chapter, your goals are to:
- (26-1) Recognize the limitations of classical physics for explaining the properties of light and matter.
- (26-2) Describe how the photoelectric effect and blackbody radiation provide evidence for the photon picture of light.
- (26-3) Explain why the wavelength of a photon increases if it scatters from an electron.
- (26-4) Calculate the wavelength of a particle such as an electron.
- (26-5) Describe why atoms absorb light at only certain wavelengths, and why they emit and abosrb light at the same wavelengths.
- (26-6) Explain how the Bohr model of the atom explains the spectrum of hydrogen.

To master this chapter, you should review:
- (3-8)   Uniform circular motion.
- (4-2)   Newton's second law.
- (8-8)   Angular momentum of a moving particle.
- (14-3)   The energy of molecules in an ideal gas.
- (14-7)   Heat transfer by radiation.
- (17-3)   Electric potential.
- (22-2, 22-3, 22-4)   The electromagnetic nature of light.
- (25-7)   Relativistic kinetic energy and momentum.

26-1 Experiments that probe the nature of light and matter reveal the limits of classical physics

We have uncovered hints that light and other electromagnetic waves have a particle-like nature. Is there strong evidence that light actually comes in the form of photons? Can a photon strike a particle such as an electron and "bounce" or scatter the way a cue ball does when it strikes a billiard ball? If waves have a particle-like nature, do particles ever exhibit properties we associate with waves?

In this chapter we'll see that the answer to each of these questions is "yes." The photoelectric effect (Figure 26-1a), in which light striking a surface causes the surface to eject electrons, can only be understood if light comes in the form of photons. The

Night vision goggles "amplify light" using the photoelectric effect. Even faint light causes a surface to emit electrons, and the current of these electrons can be amplified in a circuit to generate a brighter image that the wearer of the goggles can see.

The characteristic color of neon lights is due to the structure of the neon atom. When excited by an electric current, neon atoms in the light tube jump to a higher energy level. When they return to the starting energy level, they emit photons of a specific frequency, wavelength, and color.

(a)

(b)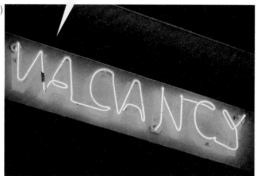

Figure 26-1 **Photons, electrons, and atoms** Two examples of the interaction between light and matter. These can only be understood if we use the ideas that light has particle aspects and matter has wave aspects.

same is true for blackbody radiation, the light emitted by an object as a consequence of its temperature. We'll see direct evidence that photons really do behave like tiny "cue balls" when they scatter from electrons. And we'll learn that particles like electrons also have a wavelike aspect. This wave nature of matter will help us understand the structure of atoms and the manner in which atoms absorb and emit light (Figure 26-1b). We'll find that the energies of atoms are *quantized*—that is, they can have only certain very definite values. The lesson of this chapter is that the microscopic world of atoms and light is very different in character from the macroscopic world of ordinary-sized objects that we see around us.

26-2 The photoelectric effect and blackbody radiation show that light is absorbed and emitted in the form of photons

By the end of the nineteenth century, it was recognized that light was an electromagnetic wave. Maxwell's equations (Section 22-3) describe the properties of these waves in great detail, and so physicists were confident that they had a deep understanding of the nature of light. But experimental studies of two very different phenomena showed that the true nature of light is actually more complex. In one of these phenomena, the *photoelectric effect*, a material absorbs light and the absorbed energy is used to eject electrons; in the other, called *blackbody radiation*, a material emits electromagnetic radiation when it is heated. The discoveries made by studying these two phenomena radically altered how physicists answered the question, "What is light?"

The Photoelectric Effect

When light strikes certain materials, electrons can be ejected from the surface of those materials (Figure 26-2a). This **photoelectric effect**, discovered in 1886, plays an important role in biological research through a technique called *photoemission electron microscopy* or PEEM. In this technique a biological sample is illuminated with ultraviolet light or X rays. Different materials in the surface layer of the sample will emit fewer or greater numbers of electrons in response to this light.

(a)

(b)

Figure 26-2 **The photoelectric effect** (a) In the photoelectric effect, electrons escape from a surface when the surface is illuminated with light. (b) An example of photoemission electron microscopy. Protein interactions with polymers are critical to understanding the compatibility of synthetic materials with blood (such as medical implants). Here the spatial distribution of fibrinogen, a blood protein, is mapped relative to a PS/PMMA polymer substrate, using photoemission electron microscopy (PEEM). Data measured at the Advanced Light Source, Lawrence Berkeley National Laboratory. This image could be made because fibrinogen and the substrate emit different numbers of electrons when illuminated with ultraviolet light.

By recording the differences in the number of emitted electrons, called **photoelectrons**, it's possible to construct an image of the sample surface that shows where the different materials are located. Figure 26-2b shows an example of an image made in this way.

What makes the photoelectric effect so remarkable is that it does not behave in accordance with the idea that light is an electromagnetic wave. It takes energy to liberate an electron from the surface of a material, and in the photoelectric effect this energy is provided by the electric and magnetic energy in the light absorbed by the surface. We learned in Section 22-4 that according to Maxwell's equations, the intensity of such a wave depends on the rms values of the electric and magnetic fields in that wave, but not on the frequency of the wave:

Intensity of an
electromagnetic wave
(22-25)

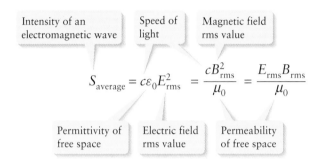

$$S_{\text{average}} = c\varepsilon_0 E_{\text{rms}}^2 = \frac{cB_{\text{rms}}^2}{\mu_0} = \frac{E_{\text{rms}}B_{\text{rms}}}{\mu_0}$$

Equation 22-25 leads us to predict that light of *any* frequency should be able to liberate an electron from the surface of a material, provided the light wave is sufficiently intense. Experiment shows that this is not the case. For example, if the biological sample shown in Figure 26-2 is illuminated with red light, no electrons are ejected no matter how intense the light. But if instead we illuminate the sample with X rays, which have a higher frequency than red light, electrons *are* ejected. (Figure 26-2b was made by using X rays.) This is impossible to understand on the basis of Maxwell's equations.

In 1905, the same year that he published his special theory of relativity, Albert Einstein proposed a simple but radical explanation for the strange behavior of the photoelectric effect. He suggested that light of frequency f comes in small packets, each with an energy E that is directly proportional to the frequency. Today these packets are called **photons**. We first encountered this idea in Section 22-4:

Energy of a photon
(22-26)

$$E = hf$$

We'll see shortly how the value of Planck's constant h is determined from the photoelectric effect.

Let's see how Einstein's idea explains the properties of the photoelectric effect. The minimum amount of energy required to remove a single electron from a material is called the **work function** Φ_0 of the material (Φ is the uppercase Greek letter phi). The value of Φ_0 varies from one material to another; it is small if electrons are easy to remove, and large if electrons are hard to remove. In a given material, some electrons will be more difficult to remove, but Φ_0 represents the energy required to remove the most easily dislodged electron. Einstein proposed that an electron can absorb only a single photon at a time. So for even the most easily dislodged electron to be ejected from the material, it must absorb a photon with an energy equal to or greater than Φ_0. If the energy of the absorbed photon is greater than Φ_0, the energy that remains after the electron is ejected goes into the kinetic energy of the electron as it flies away from the material. Electrons that require more energy to be ejected will emerge from the material with less kinetic energy, but those with *maximum* kinetic energy will be those that were the easiest to dislodge. So in Einstein's picture, the most energetic electrons ejected from the material will emerge with kinetic energy K_{max} given by

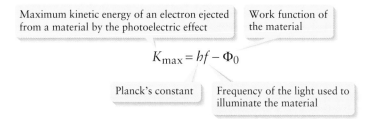

$$K_{max} = hf - \Phi_0$$

Maximum kinetic energy of an electron ejected from a material by the photoelectric effect

Work function of the material

Planck's constant

Frequency of the light used to illuminate the material

Maximum kinetic energy of an electron in the photoelectric effect (26-1)

Equation 26-1 tells us that that a graph of K_{max} as a function of the light frequency f should be a straight line of slope h (see **Figure 26-3**). Since kinetic energy can never be negative, Equation 26-1 also tells us that electrons will be emitted only if $hf - \Phi_0 > 0$, or

$$f > f_0 = \frac{\Phi_0}{h}$$

(26-2)

In words, Equation 26-2 says that electrons will be emitted from the surface only if the light frequency is greater than a threshold frequency f_0 equal to the work function Φ_0 divided by Planck's constant h. This agrees with the observation that no electrons are ejected if a surface is illuminated with light of too low a frequency, no matter how intense the light.

The graph shown in Figure 26-3 turns out to be an excellent match to experimental measurements of the maximum kinetic energy of ejected electrons for different frequencies f. The slope of the graph tells us the value of Planck's constant h. Equation 26-1 also shows that if we extend the graph of K_{max} as a function of f to (unphysical) values of K_{max} less than zero, the graph intercepts the vertical axis at $-\Phi_0$. If we repeat the experimental measurements for a second material with a different work function Φ_0, the straight line intercepts the vertical axis at a different point but has the same slope h as for the first material. This reinforces the idea that Planck's constant is a universal constant associated with the energy of the photons, not the specific properties of the material that absorbs the photons.

The remarkable fit of Einstein's theory to experiment is powerful evidence that light is indeed absorbed in the form of photons with energy $E = hf$ as given by Equation 22-26. In recognition of his achievement, Einstein was awarded the Nobel Prize in Physics in 1921 for his explanation of the photoelectric effect.

Go to Interactive Exercise 26-1 for more practice dealing with the photoelectric effect

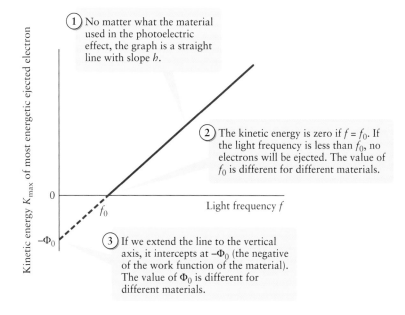

① No matter what the material used in the photoelectric effect, the graph is a straight line with slope h.

② The kinetic energy is zero if $f = f_0$. If the light frequency is less than f_0, no electrons will be ejected. The value of f_0 is different for different materials.

③ If we extend the line to the vertical axis, it intercepts at $-\Phi_0$ (the negative of the work function of the material). The value of Φ_0 is different for different materials.

Figure 26-3 Electron kinetic energy versus frequency in the photoelectric effect The kinetic energy of the most energetic electron ejected in the photoelectric effect depends on the frequency of the light. This cannot be explained using the wave model of light, but can be explained by the photon concept.

> **! Watch Out! Some electrons require more energy than Φ_0 to be ejected.**
>
> The work function Φ_0 is the smallest amount of energy required to eject an electron from a given material under the most favorable conditions. Other electrons in the material require more energy to eject and will emerge from the material with less kinetic energy than the value K_{max} given by Equation 26-1.

Example 26-1 The Photoelectric Effect with Cesium

The work function for a sample of cesium is 3.43×10^{-19} J. (a) What is the minimum frequency of light that will result in electrons being ejected from this sample by the photoelectric effect? (b) What is the maximum wavelength of light that will result in electrons being ejected from this sample by the photoelectric effect?

Set Up

Equation 26-1 tells us that the minimum energy required to eject an electron corresponds to having $K_{max} = 0$, so the electrons just barely make it out of the cesium. We'll use this to find the threshold frequency f_0 that just barely allows an electron to be ejected. We'll find the corresponding wavelength using Equation 22-2.

Maximum kinetic energy of an electron in the photoelectric effect:

$$K_{max} = hf - \Phi_0 \qquad (26\text{-}1)$$

Propagation speed, frequency, and wavelength of an electromagnetic wave:

$$c = f\lambda \qquad (22\text{-}2)$$

light, frequency f and wavelength λ

cesium

Solve

(a) Use Equation 26-1 to calculate the frequency f that corresponds to $K_{max} = 0$.

From Equation 26-1 with $K_{max} = 0$,

$$0 = hf - \Phi_0$$
$$hf = \Phi_0$$

This says that the photon energy hf is just enough to remove the most easily dislodged electron from the material (which requires energy Φ_0), with nothing left over to give the electron any kinetic energy. So $hf = \Phi_0$ is the minimum photon energy that will eject an electron, and the frequency f of this photon is the minimum (threshold) frequency that will do the job:

$$f_0 = f = \frac{\Phi_0}{h}$$
$$= \frac{3.43 \times 10^{-19}\,\text{J}}{6.63 \times 10^{-34}\,\text{J}\cdot\text{s}} = 5.17 \times 10^{14}\,\text{s}^{-1} = 5.17 \times 10^{14}\,\text{Hz}$$

(b) Find the wavelength that corresponds to the frequency that we calculated in part (a).

We can rewrite Equation 22-2 as

$$\lambda = \frac{c}{f}$$

In words, this says that wavelength is inversely proportional to frequency. So the *minimum* frequency of light that will eject an electron corresponds to the *maximum* wavelength that will eject an electron:

$$\lambda_{max} = \frac{c}{f_0} = \frac{3.00 \times 10^8\,\text{m/s}}{5.17 \times 10^{14}\,\text{Hz}}$$
$$= 5.80 \times 10^{-7}\,\text{m} = 580\,\text{nm}$$

(Recall that 1 nm = 10^{-9} m.)

Reflect

Figure 22-2 shows that a wavelength of 580 nm is in the yellow-green part of the visible spectrum. If we illuminate cesium with light of higher frequency and shorter wavelength than this (for example, blue or violet light), the photons will have more energy than the minimum and electrons will be ejected from the cesium. If instead we illuminate cesium with light of lower frequency and longer wavelength (for example, orange or red light), the photons will have less energy than the required minimum and no electrons will be ejected.

Blackbody Radiation

The photoelectric effect shows that light is *absorbed* in the form of photons. If we are to fully believe the photon concept, however, it must also be true that light is *emitted* in the form of photons. We learned in Section 14-7 that ordinary objects emit electromagnetic radiation as a result of their temperature. If we can find evidence that this emission is in the form of photons, we will have further evidence that the photon description of light is the correct one. Let's take a closer look at the detailed properties of radiation of this kind.

Experiment shows that the rate at which an object emits radiation is proportional to its surface area A and to the fourth power of its Kelvin temperature T:

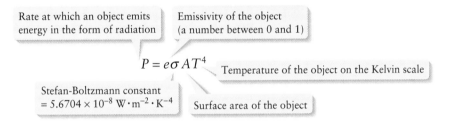

Rate at which an object emits energy in the form of radiation

Emissivity of the object (a number between 0 and 1)

$$P = e\sigma A T^4$$

Temperature of the object on the Kelvin scale

Stefan-Boltzmann constant $= 5.6704 \times 10^{-8}\ \text{W} \cdot \text{m}^{-2} \cdot \text{K}^{-4}$

Surface area of the object

Rate of energy flow in radiation (14-22)

The higher the temperature of an object of a given size, the greater the radiated power P and so the more brightly it glows.

Experiment also shows that the *color* of the radiation emitted by an object depends on its temperature T (Figure 26-4). A heated object emits light at all wavelengths, but emits most strongly at a particular frequency called the *frequency of maximum emission*. As the temperature increases, the frequency of maximum emission increases.

Equation 14-22 shows that the radiated power also depends on a quantity e called the *emissivity*, which depends on the properties of the object's surface. This has its greatest value ($e = 1$) for an idealized type of dense object called a **blackbody**. An ideal blackbody does not reflect any light at all, but absorbs all radiation falling on it. If a blackbody is in thermal equilibrium with its surroundings, it must emit energy at the

① This metal bar heated with a flame emits light at all frequencies, but glows most strongly at red frequencies.

② As the temperature of the bar increases, it glows most strongly at orange frequencies...

③ ...and at even higher temperatures, it glows most strongly at yellow frequencies.

- A hot, dense object emits electromagnetic radiation. The idealized case is called **blackbody radiation**.
- The frequency of maximum emission is directly proportional to the Kelvin temperature T of the object: The higher the temperature T, the greater the frequency of maximum emission.

Figure 26-4 **Radiation from heated objects** The color of the light from a heated object depends on its temperature.

same rate that it absorbs it in order that its temperature T remain constant. So in addition to being a perfect absorber of energy, an ideal blackbody in thermal equilibrium with its surroundings is also a perfect emitter of energy because it emits as much energy as it absorbs.

Ordinary objects, such as tables, textbooks, and people, are not ideal blackbodies; they reflect light, which is why they are visible. (Even a piece of wood darkened with soot or painted a dull black reflects *some* light.) But it is possible to make a nearly ideal blackbody simply by building a box and drilling a small hole in one side (Figure 26-5a). Light that enters the hole will reflect around inside the box, with part of the light energy being absorbed by the walls on each reflection. Eventually all of the light energy will be absorbed, so the interior of the box acts like a perfect absorber and is effectively an ideal blackbody. You can see this effect if you look into another person's eye (Figure 26-5b). The pupil at the center of the iris appears black, even though the tissues that line the interior of the eye are pinkish in color. That's because after multiple reflections, those tissues almost completely absorb light that enters the eye through the pupil.

If the box in Figure 26-5a is in thermal equilibrium at temperature T, the rate at which the walls absorb energy in the form of radiation must be equal to the rate at which the walls emit energy. The cavity in the interior of the box will be filled with this radiation, which will itself be in thermal equilibrium with the walls of the box. Since the walls act as an ideal blackbody, the light that fills the cavity is effectively **blackbody radiation**—the kind of light that would be emitted by a perfect blackbody of emissivity $e = 1$ at temperature T. We can study this light by examining the small fraction of light that emerges from the hole in Figure 26-5a.

Figure 26-6 shows the experimentally observed *spectrum* of blackbody radiation—that is, the relative amount of light energy present at different frequencies—for two different temperatures. Note that the high-temperature curve lies above the low-temperature curve at all frequencies. This tells us that the higher the temperature of a blackbody, the greater the amount of radiation at all frequencies. Note also that as the blackbody temperature increases, the peak of the curve shifts to a higher frequency. This agrees with our observation about how the frequency of maximum emission varies with an object's temperature (Figure 26-4). Figure 26-6 explains why we can't see the radiation from objects at room temperature, about $T = 300$ K. At this relatively low temperature, the frequency of maximum emission is in the infrared, which our eyes cannot see. There is some emission at visible frequencies (in Figure 26-6, to the right of the peak of the curve), but the amount of emission is so low at $T = 300$ K that our eyes can't detect it.

(a)   (b)

• When the box comes to thermal equilibrium at temperature T, it will emit radiation from its inner walls at the same rate that it absorbs radiation.
• This radiation will fill the cavity inside the box.
• Some of the radiation will leak out of the hole. Because the box acts as a perfect blackbody, the radiation that leaks out will be blackbody radiation.

1 Light enters a hole in the box.

2 The light reflects off the inner walls of the box many times. On each reflection, part of the light energy is absorbed by the walls.

3 Eventually all of the light energy is absorbed. Hence the interior of the box (the cavity) acts like a perfect absorber— that is, an ideal blackbody.

View into the interior of the eye

Figure 26-5 **A blackbody cavity** (a) A box with a small hole in one side is a good approximation to an ideal blackbody. (b) The interior of the eye has very similar properties to the box in (a).

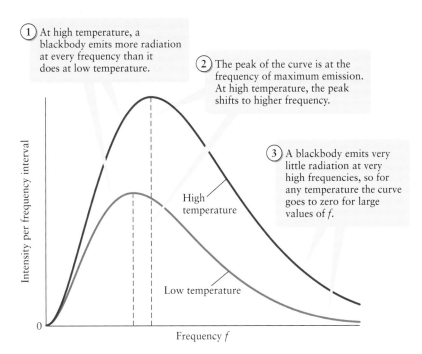

① At high temperature, a blackbody emits more radiation at every frequency than it does at low temperature.

② The peak of the curve is at the frequency of maximum emission. At high temperature, the peak shifts to higher frequency.

③ A blackbody emits very little radiation at very high frequencies, so for any temperature the curve goes to zero for large values of *f*.

High temperature

Low temperature

Intensity per frequency interval

0

Frequency *f*

Figure 26-6 Blackbody spectra The spectrum of light emitted by an ideal blackbody depends on the temperature of the blackbody.

In the late nineteenth century, physicists tried to understand the shape of the blackbody spectrum shown in Figure 26-6 using their knowledge of thermodynamics and electromagnetic waves. Their efforts ended in failure. To understand how they failed, we begin by noting that the electromagnetic waves inside the cavity in Figure 26-5a should be in the form of *standing* waves. That's because the waves will bounce back and forth between the walls of the cavity. We learned in Section 13-6 that when waves bounce back and forth between the ends of a string that's tied down at both ends, steady wave patterns arise for waves of certain wavelengths and frequencies. The same is true for electromagnetic waves in a cavity. A key difference is that while the patterns of nodes and antinodes in standing waves on a string are one-dimensional (along the length of the string), the corresponding patterns for standing waves in a cavity are three-dimensional and so are more complicated. Another difference is that a standing electromagnetic wave involves two varying quantities, the electric field and the magnetic field. For our purposes, however, all we need to know is that these standing waves exist.

The shape of the blackbody spectrum in Figure 26-6 should be indicative of how much energy is present in the standing waves in each frequency range. The general shape of these curves shows that there should be relatively little energy at very low frequencies, more energy at frequencies near the frequency of maximum emission, and again relatively little energy at high frequencies. However, nineteenth-century physics suggested that *every* possible standing wave in the cavity should contain on average the same amount of energy. This conclusion came from the equipartition theorem, which we first encountered in Section 14-3. This theorem states that a molecule in a gas at a Kelvin temperature T has, on average, an amount of energy $(1/2)kT$ for each degree of freedom of the molecule, where $k = 1.381 \times 10^{-23}$ J/K is the Boltzmann constant. Arguments from thermodynamics suggest that for the same reason, a standing wave inside a cavity in thermal equilibrium at temperature T should also possess an average amount of energy equal to $(1/2)kT$ per degree of freedom. There are two degrees of freedom per standing wave, one for the electric field and one for the magnetic field, so the total average energy per standing wave should be kT. It turns out that the number of standing waves in a given frequency interval increases with increasing frequency. So according to nineteenth-century physics, the total energy per frequency interval (equal to the energy kT per standing wave multiplied by the number of standing waves per frequency interval) should increase with increasing frequency and *never* decrease (Figure 26-7). This is in profound disagreement with the experimentally observed shape of the spectrum.

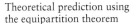

Theoretical prediction using
the equipartition theorem

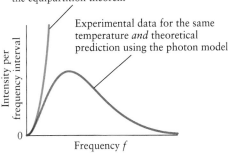

Experimental data for the same
temperature *and* theoretical
prediction using the photon model

Intensity per
frequency interval

0

Frequency *f*

- A photon model accurately describes the spectrum of blackbody radiation.
- The model that does not use the photon concept fails to describe the spectrum.

Figure 26-7 The photon model explains blackbody radiation A model for blackbody radiation that does not use the photon concept predicts (incorrectly) that the intensity should increase without limit as the frequency increases.

If we now introduce the photon concept, however, we *can* match the experimentally observed spectrum. We still use the idea that the average energy available for a standing wave of frequency *f* is *kT*, but now this energy goes into photons of that frequency which each have energy $E = hf$. This energy fundamentally comes from the walls of the box in Figure 26-5a, since these walls are what emit the photons. At low frequencies the photon energy *hf* is small compared to the available energy *kT*, so there will be very many photons present for a low-frequency standing wave. But at high frequencies *hf* is much larger than *kT*, which means that the energy required to produce a photon is larger than the average energy available to produce one. Hence the average number of photons present for that standing wave will be very small. (It need not be zero, since *kT* is only the *average* energy available. From time to time, the available energy will be greater than *kT*, and some photons can be produced.) So even though energy is *available* for a high-frequency standing wave, that energy can't be used to create photons, and so the amount of energy *present* is quite small. That's just the effect we need to make the theoretical curve in Figure 26-7 decline at large frequencies.

Using a somewhat different version of this photon argument, in 1900 the German physicist Max Planck was able to make a theoretical prediction for the blackbody spectrum that was in excellent agreement with the experimental spectrum shown in Figure 26-7. Planck's theoretical formula was the first to involve the new quantity *h* that now bears his name, and the value of *h* given in Equation 22-26 is the one that gives the best match between this formula and the experimental data. Planck was awarded the 1918 Nobel Prize in Physics for his achievement.

The explanation of blackbody spectra in terms of photons is the evidence we were seeking that light is emitted in the form of photons. In the following section we'll see even more compelling evidence for the photon picture of light.

? Got the Concept? 26-1 Blackbody Radiation

Two objects of the same size are both perfect blackbodies. One is at a temperature of 3000 K, so its frequency of maximum emission is in the infrared part of the electromagnetic part of the spectrum; the other is at a temperature of 12,000 K, so its frequency of maximum emission is in the ultraviolet part of the spectrum. Compared to the object at 3000 K, the object at 12,000 K (a) emits more infrared light; (b) emits more visible light; (c) emits more ultraviolet light; (d) two of (a), (b), and (c); (e) all of (a), (b), and (c).

Take-Home Message for Section 26-2

✔ In the photoelectric effect, an electron in a material can absorb light energy that strikes the surface and as a result be ejected from the surface.

✔ For any material, the light must have a certain minimum frequency in order for electrons to be ejected. This is evidence that light comes in the form of photons, with an energy proportional to their frequency.

✔ A perfect blackbody is an ideal absorber of light and also an ideal emitter of light. The spectrum of light emitted by a blackbody depends on its temperature.

✔ The spectrum of light emitted by a blackbody can only be understood if we use the idea that light is emitted in the form of photons.

26-3 As a result of its photon character, light changes wavelength when it is scattered

Blackbody radiation and the photoelectric effect suggest that photons can be treated like tiny bundles. We have therefore made the claim that as quantized units of energy, photons have a particle-like nature. Are there other implications of this claim? For example, an electron absorbs the energy of a photon in the photoelectric effect. But if a photon is like a particle, is it possible that, as in the collisions we studied in Chapter 7, a photon could strike an electron and bounce off? If so, based on our experience with collisions, we ought to expect that linear momentum would be conserved in such an interaction and that the momentum of the photon should change as a result. This effect, called *Compton scattering*, is further evidence that light does indeed come in the form of photons.

Let's first see how to express the momentum of a photon. We saw in Section 25-7 that for a particle of mass m, we can write the kinetic energy and momentum as

Kinetic energy of a particle of mass m and velocity $\vec{v}$

$$K = (\gamma - 1)mc^2$$

Relativistic gamma for speed v

$$\vec{p} = \gamma m \vec{v}$$

Momentum of a particle of mass m and velocity $\vec{v}$

Einsteinian expressions for kinetic energy and momentum
(25-20)

 At speeds that are a small fraction of the speed of light c, these are approximately equal to the Newtonian expressions

$$K = \frac{1}{2}mv^2 \text{ and } \vec{p} = m\vec{v}$$

In these expressions, the quantity γ (relativistic gamma) is

Relativistic gamma for a particle moving at speed v

$$\gamma = \frac{1}{\sqrt{1 - \dfrac{v^2}{c^2}}}$$

Speed of the particle

Speed of light in a vacuum

Relativistic gamma
(25-19)

We also saw that an object of mass m has a rest energy E_0 that is present even when it is not moving:

Rest energy of a particle   Mass of the particle

$$E_0 = mc^2$$

Speed of light in a vacuum

Rest energy
(25-21)

If we combine the first of Equations 25-20 with Equations 25-19 and 25-21, we find that the total energy of a particle (kinetic energy plus rest energy) is

$$E = K + E_0 = (\gamma - 1)mc^2 + mc^2 = \gamma mc^2 = \frac{mc^2}{\sqrt{1 - \dfrac{v^2}{c^2}}} \tag{26-3}$$

From the second of Equations 25-20, the magnitude of the momentum of a particle is

$$p = \gamma mv = \frac{mv}{\sqrt{1 - \dfrac{v^2}{c^2}}} \tag{26-4}$$

Comparing Equations 26-3 and 26-4, we see that

$$(26\text{-}5) \qquad p = \frac{Ev}{c^2} \quad \text{(momentum of a particle of total energy } E\text{)}$$

A photon has zero mass, which is why it can travel at the speed of light. (Any object with nonzero mass would require an infinite amount of kinetic energy to reach $v = c$, as we described in Section 25-7.) As such, we can't apply Equation 26-3 or 26-4 directly to photons. But we can use the combination in Equation 26-5, in which mass does not appear explicitly. Setting $v = c$ in Equation 26-5, we get the following relationship for the momentum of a photon:

$$(26\text{-}6) \qquad p = \frac{Ec}{c^2} = \frac{E}{c} \quad \text{(momentum of a photon)}$$

From Equation 22-26 we can write $E = hf$, and we know that for light waves $c = f\lambda$ (Equation 22-2). If we substitute these into Equation 26-6, we get an alternative expression for the momentum of a photon:

$$p = \frac{hf}{f\lambda}$$

or, simplifying,

Momentum and energy of a photon (26-7)

Magnitude of the momentum of a photon   Energy of the photon

$$p = \frac{E}{c} = \frac{h}{\lambda}$$

Planck's constant

Speed of light in a vacuum   Wavelength of the photon

A photon's momentum is directly proportional to the energy that it carries and inversely proportional to its wavelength. Thus a violet photon of wavelength 400 nm has twice the momentum, as well as twice the energy, of an infrared photon of wavelength 800 nm.

In the early 1920s, American physicist Arthur Compton showed conclusively that photons have momentum and that the momentum is inversely proportional to the wavelength as stated in Equation 26-7. In his experiments, an X ray photon collided with an electron in a carbon atom, a process now called **Compton scattering**. Compton detected both the electron, which is knocked out of the atom, and the scattered photon. Compton could only account for the directions and energies of the electron and the scattered photon by associating a momentum vector with the incoming and outgoing photon and then requiring that momentum be conserved. In other words, he showed that the photon description of light applies not just to the absorption and emission of light, but also to what happens to light when it is scattered. For revealing this fundamental aspect of light, Compton was awarded the Nobel Prize in Physics in 1927.

Compton's results are most concisely expressed in terms of the change in wavelength of the photon as a result of the collision with the electron. Figure 26-8 shows the collision of a photon (symbol γ_i) and a stationary electron (symbol e^-). The electron is scattered at angle ϕ relative to the initial direction of the photon, and the photon scatters at angle θ relative to its initial direction. Although we have labeled the photon γ_f after the collision, the scattered photon is the same photon that collided with the electron. The subscripts "i" for "initial" and "f" for "final" instead imply that the energy, wavelength, and other quantities associated with the photon have changed as a result of the collision. For example, because energy is conserved during

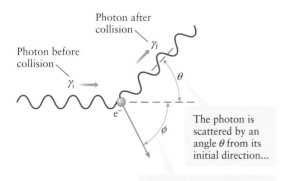

Photon after collision
Photon before collision
γ_i
γ_f
θ
e^-
ϕ

The photon is scattered by an angle θ from its initial direction...

...and the scattered electron moves off at an angle ϕ from the initial direction of the photon.

Figure 26-8 Compton scattering A photon undergoes a wavelength shift when it scatters from an electron that is initially at rest.

the collision and because some of the photon's energy is almost always transferred to the electron, the outgoing photon carries less energy than it had initially. From Equation 26-7, the energy of a photon is

$$E = pc = \frac{hc}{\lambda}$$

Because the photon has less energy after the collision than it had initially, E_f is less than E_i, and the final wavelength λ_f is greater than the initial wavelength λ_i. In other words, as the energy of the photon decreases, its wavelength increases. Compton found that the increase in wavelength $\Delta\lambda$ from λ_i to λ_f is a function of the angle θ at which the photon scatters:

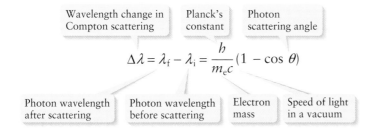

$$\Delta\lambda = \lambda_f - \lambda_i = \frac{h}{m_e c}(1 - \cos\theta)$$

Compton scattering equation
(26-8)

The proportionality constant in Equation 26-8 is known as the Compton wavelength λ_C:

$$\lambda_C = \frac{h}{m_e c}$$

(26-9)

 See the Math Tutorial for more information on trigonometry

 Go to Picture It 26-1 for more practice dealing with Compton scattering

The scattering angle θ of the photon ranges from 0° (straight forward) to 180° (straight back). When the photon continues in the same direction after the collision, so that θ equals 0° and $\cos\theta$ equals 1, $\Delta\lambda$ equals zero. In other words, if $\theta = 0°$ there is no change in the photon's wavelength and no change in the photon's energy.

The maximum change in a photon's wavelength and energy when it undergoes Compton scattering occurs when it scatters straight back, in the direction opposite to the one in which it approached the electron. In this case $\theta = 180°$, so $\cos\theta = -1$ and the term in parentheses in Equation 26-8 equals 2. The maximum possible change in the photon's wavelength is therefore $2\lambda_C$, or twice the Compton wavelength. Using the known values of h, m_e, and c, we find

$$\lambda_C = \frac{h}{m_e c} = \frac{6.63 \times 10^{-34}\,\text{J}\cdot\text{s}}{(9.11 \times 10^{-31}\,\text{kg})(3.00 \times 10^8\,\text{m/s})}$$

$$= 2.43 \times 10^{-12}\,\text{m} = 2.43 \times 10^{-3}\,\text{nm} = 0.00243\,\text{nm}$$

(Recall that 1 nm = 10^{-9} m.) The small value of λ_C means that Compton scattering has a negligible effect on the wavelength of visible-light photons. The wavelength of visible light ranges between about 380 nm and 750 nm; the Compton wavelength is considerably smaller. For example, if a photon of wavelength 400 nm is scattered by an electron, its wavelength changes by a value on the order of 0.00243 nm. Such a tiny change is very difficult to measure, so we can ignore the wavelength change of a visible-light photon due to Compton scattering. But for an X ray photon with a wavelength on the order of 10^{-11} m = 0.01 nm, a wavelength shift of 0.00243 nm corresponds to a large percentage of the initial wavelength. That's why Compton first noticed this effect in the scattering of X rays.

If light did not have a photon aspect, we would expect *no* wavelength change on scattering. A light wave of frequency f and wavelength λ encountering an electron would make the electron oscillate at the same frequency f, and the electron would emit radiation with the same frequency f and hence the same wavelength λ as the initial light wave. The change in wavelength that Compton observed is unambiguous evidence that light does indeed have a particle character.

Example 26-2 Compton Scattering

A photon carries 2.00×10^{-14} J of energy. It undergoes Compton scattering in a block of carbon. What is the largest fractional change in energy the photon can undergo as a result?

Set Up

Given the initial photon energy $E_i = 2.00 \times 10^{-14}$ J, we can calculate its wavelength λ_i using Equation 26-7. We use Equation 26-8 to calculate the change in wavelength due to scattering; this will be maximum if $\theta = 180°$, so $\cos \theta = -1$. Once we know the final wavelength λ_f, we can use Equation 26-7 again to find the final photon energy. Comparing this to the initial photon energy tells us the fractional change in energy.

Momentum and energy of a photon:

$$p = \frac{E}{c} = \frac{h}{\lambda} \qquad (26\text{-}7)$$

Compton scattering equation:

$$\Delta\lambda = \lambda_f - \lambda_i = \frac{h}{m_e c}(1 - \cos \theta) \qquad (26\text{-}8)$$

Before:

photon   electron at rest

After:

scattered photon   recoiling electron

Solve

First calculate the wavelength of the initial photon using Equation 26-7.

From Equation 26-7, the wavelength of the initial photon is

$$\lambda_i = \frac{hc}{E_i} = \frac{(6.63 \times 10^{-34}\,\text{J}\cdot\text{s})(3.00 \times 10^8\,\text{m/s})}{2.00 \times 10^{-14}\,\text{J}}$$

$$= (9.95 \times 10^{-12}\,\text{m})\left(\frac{1\,\text{nm}}{10^{-9}\,\text{m}}\right) = 9.95 \times 10^{-3}\,\text{nm}$$

Calculate the wavelength shift using Equation 26-8.

The maximum wavelength shift is with $\theta = 180°$ and $\cos \theta = -1$:

$$\Delta\lambda_{\text{max}} = \lambda_f - \lambda_i = \frac{h}{m_e c}(1 - \cos 180°)$$

$$= (2.43 \times 10^{-3}\,\text{nm})[1 - (-1)] = 4.86 \times 10^{-3}\,\text{nm}$$

The wavelength of the final photon equals the wavelength of the initial photon plus the shift $\Delta\lambda$. Use this to find the energy of the final photon.

The final wavelength is

$$\lambda_f = \lambda_i + \Delta\lambda = 9.95 \times 10^{-3}\,\text{nm} + 4.86 \times 10^{-3}\,\text{nm}$$

$$= 1.481 \times 10^{-2}\,\text{nm} = 1.481 \times 10^{-11}\,\text{m}$$

The energy of the final photon is

$$E_f = \frac{hc}{\lambda_f} = \frac{(6.63 \times 10^{-34}\,\text{J}\cdot\text{s})(3.00 \times 10^8\,\text{m/s})}{1.481 \times 10^{-11}\,\text{m}}$$

$$= 1.34 \times 10^{-14}\,\text{J}$$

This is less than the energy of the initial photon. The lost energy has gone into the kinetic energy of the scattered electron.

Express the energy change as a fraction of the initial photon energy.

The fractional energy change is the energy change $E_f - E_i$ divided by the initial energy E_i:

$$\text{fractional energy change} = \frac{E_f - E_i}{E_i}$$

$$= \frac{1.34 \times 10^{-14}\,\text{J} - 2.00 \times 10^{-14}\,\text{J}}{2.00 \times 10^{-14}\,\text{J}}$$

$$= -0.328 = -32.8\%$$

Reflect

An initial photon of this high energy and short wavelength can lose as much as 32.8% (nearly one-third) of its initial energy when it undergoes Compton scattering.

Example 26-2 suggests why X rays are useful in cancer radiation therapy. If an X ray photon strikes an electron in a water molecule within a cancerous cell, the photon can scatter and transfer a substantial amount of energy to the electron. This energy is great enough that the electron escapes from the molecule, leaving the water molecule in an ionized state. These ionized water molecules damage the DNA of the cancerous cell and cause cell death.

? Got the Concept? 26-2 Compton Scattering

Suppose a photon has a wavelength equal to the Compton wavelength λ_C. If this photon collides with an electron, and the photon is scattered through an angle of 90°, what will be the wavelength of the photon after the collision? (a) zero; (b) $\lambda_C/2$; (c) λ_C; (d) $2\lambda_C$; (e) $3\lambda_C$.

Take-Home Message for Section 26-3

✔ A photon has zero mass but does have momentum. The magnitude of the momentum is proportional to the photon energy and inversely proportional to the wavelength.

✔ In Compton scattering, a photon scatters from an electron. The photon loses energy and momentum, and these are transferred to the electron. The change in wavelength of the photon depends on the angle through which it is scattered.

26-4 Matter, like light, has aspects of both waves and particles

We have seen that light, previously thought to be a wave, is actually a stream of particles. But these particles (photons) have a wave aspect: Associated with them is a frequency f, which determines the photon energy $E = hf$, and a wavelength λ, which determines the photon momentum $p = h/\lambda$. So light has a dual nature, with attributes of both wave and particle. Is it possible that the same could be true for ordinary matter, which we know is made of particles such as electrons, protons, and neutrons? Could these particles also have a wave aspect?

In 1924, French graduate student Louis de Broglie (pronounced "de broy'") proposed precisely that idea. In particular, he suggested that the relationship $p = h/\lambda$ between momentum p and wavelength λ that applies to photons should also apply to particles such as electrons (Figure 26-9). The wavelength of a particle is called its de Broglie wavelength:

A particle has a de Broglie wavelength...   ...equal to Planck's constant...

$$\lambda = \frac{h}{p}$$

de Broglie wavelength
(26-10)

...divided by the momentum of the particle. The greater the momentum, the shorter the de Broglie wavelength.

How large should we expect the wavelength of an electron to be? Let's examine the case of an electron of charge $q = -e$ that gains its momentum by moving through a potential difference of V, so the electron starts at position a where the potential is zero and moves to a position b where the potential has a positive value V. (You may want to review the discussion of electric potential in Section 17-3.) The electron potential energy then changes from $U_a = qV_a = (-e)(0)$ to $U_b = qV_b = (-e)V = -eV$. The change in electric potential energy is

$$\Delta U = U_b - U_a = (-eV) - 0 = -eV < 0$$

Figure 26-9 **Wave-particle duality** Matter has both particle aspects (speed and momentum) and wave aspects (wavelength).

Particle description	Wave description
Particle, mass m Speed v_1 Momentum $p_1 = mv_1$	Wavelength $\lambda_1 = \dfrac{h}{p_1}$
Particle, mass m Speed $v_2 = 2v_1$ Momentum $p_2 = mv_2 = 2p_1$	Wavelength $\lambda_2 = \dfrac{h}{p_2} = \dfrac{h}{2p_1} = \dfrac{\lambda_1}{2}$

The de Broglie wavelength is inversely proportional to the momentum. If the momentum is doubled, the wavelength decreases by 1/2.

The electric potential energy decreases by an amount eV. Mechanical energy is conserved if the only force acting on the electron is the (conservative) electric force, so the decrease in electric potential energy equals the gain in kinetic energy of the electron:

$$(26\text{-}11) \qquad \Delta K = -\Delta U = -(-eV) = +eV > 0$$

If the electron starts at rest, its initial kinetic energy is zero and its final kinetic energy is $K = (1/2)mv^2$, so $\Delta K = (1/2)mv^2 - 0 = (1/2)mv^2$. (We're assuming that the electron is moving at a speed much slower than the speed of light c, so we don't have to use the Einsteinian expression for kinetic energy.) Then, from Equation 26-11, the final kinetic energy of the electron is

$$K = \frac{1}{2}mv^2 = eV$$

Solve for the final speed of the electron:

$$(26\text{-}12) \qquad v^2 = \frac{2K}{m} = \frac{2eV}{m} \quad \text{so} \quad v = \sqrt{v^2} = \sqrt{\frac{2eV}{m}}$$

The final momentum of the electron is $p = mv$, and its final wavelength is $\lambda = h/p = h/mv$ from Equation 26-10. If we substitute v from Equation 26-12 into the formula for the wavelength of the electron, we get

$$(26\text{-}13) \qquad \lambda = \frac{h}{mv} = \frac{h}{m}\sqrt{\frac{m}{2eV}} = \frac{h}{\sqrt{2meV}}$$

Suppose that the electron is accelerated through a potential difference $V = 50.0$ V. Substituting this into Equation 26-13 along with the values of Planck's constant h, the electron mass m, and the magnitude e of the electron charge, we get

$$\lambda = \frac{6.63 \times 10^{-34}\,\text{J}\cdot\text{s}}{\sqrt{2(9.11 \times 10^{-31}\,\text{kg})(1.60 \times 10^{-19}\,\text{C})(50.0\,\text{V})}}$$

$$= 1.74 \times 10^{-10}\,\text{m} = 0.174\,\text{nm}$$

To see how to measure such a short electron wavelength, note that a photon with this wavelength is in the X ray region of the electromagnetic spectrum (see Figure 22-2). It was known in the 1920s that X rays show interference effects when they reflect from adjacent atoms in a crystal: At certain angles, waves that reflect from one atom will interfere constructively (so the reflected intensity is high) with those that reflect from neighboring atoms, while at other angles they interfere destructively (so the reflected intensity is near zero). This can happen because the spacing between adjacent atoms in a crystal is around 0.1 nm, comparable to the wavelength of the X rays. So if electrons have a wave aspect, we expect that a beam of electrons that have been accelerated from rest through 50.0 V should display the same kind of interference effects as a beam of X rays.

In 1927 the American physicists Clinton Davisson and Lester Germer performed precisely this kind of experiment using a beam of electrons directed at a target of crystalline nickel. They found that the intensity of reflected electrons was greater for certain angles, just as for X rays. What's more, the angles at which this maximum intensity occurred were precisely those expected if the wavelength of electrons was given by the de Broglie relation, Equation 26-10. This groundbreaking result was quickly confirmed in experiments carried out by the British physicist G. P. Thomson. These results resoundingly confirmed de Broglie's remarkable hypothesis and showed that matter does indeed have a wave aspect. (The 1927 Nobel Prize in Physics went to de Broglie; the 1937 prize was shared by Davisson and Thomson.) The dual character of *both* light and matter, which have both wave and particle characteristics, is called **wave-particle duality.**

Wave-particle duality is a surprising and counterintuitive fact about the nature of our universe. It is also of tremendous practical use. One important application that has revolutionized biology is the *electron microscope*. A major limitation of ordinary microscopes is that the smallest detail that can be resolved is about the size of a wavelength of visible light (about 380 to 750 nm). This makes microscopes useless for seeing details of the structure of viruses, for example, which range in size from 5 to 300 nm. But as our above example of the 50.0-V electron shows, the wavelength of electron waves can be a fraction of a nanometer. So images made with an *electron microscope* can reveal details that are forever hidden from an ordinary visible-light microscope. Figure 26-10 is an electron microscope image of an influenza virus, in which details smaller than a nanometer across can be seen.

Because the de Broglie wavelength is inversely proportional to momentum, the wavelength is very small for objects with large momentum. That's why we don't see wave effects for objects in our environment that are large enough to see with the unaided eye: The wavelengths of such objects are infinitesimal. As an example, a dust mote (such as you might see floating in the air when a shaft of sunlight comes in the window) has mass of about 8×10^{-10} kg. If it drifts at a speed of 1 mm/s = 10^{-3} m/s, its momentum is

$$p = mv = (8 \times 10^{-10}\,\text{kg})(10^{-3}\,\text{m/s}) = 8 \times 10^{-13}\,\text{kg}\cdot\text{m/s}$$

and its de Broglie wavelength is

$$\lambda = \frac{h}{p} = \frac{6.63 \times 10^{-34}\,\text{J}\cdot\text{s}}{8 \times 10^{-13}\,\text{kg}\cdot\text{m/s}} = 8 \times 10^{-22}\,\text{m}$$

That's about 10^{-6} of the diameter of a proton! It's impossible to see wave effects from a wave with such a tiny wavelength: To see diffraction of such a wave, we would have to create a slit whose width is much smaller than the width of a single proton. Wave effects are even smaller for larger objects (greater mass m) moving faster (greater speed v). So the wave aspect of matter is generally only noticeable on the atomic or subatomic scale. Particles such as electrons exhibit noticeable wave properties; objects such as dust motes, baseballs, and humans do not.

Figure 26-10 An electron micrograph When a beam of low-energy electrons is shot through a thin slice of a specimen in a transmission electron microscope (TEM), the pattern formed by the diffracted electrons forms an image. A TEM captured this (false-color) image of an influenza virus particle, which is only about 100 nm in diameter. Because the wavelengths of low-energy electrons are so much shorter than those of light, a TEM is capable of significantly better resolution than light microscopes (better than 0.005 nm for a TEM, compared to about 0.2 μm with the most powerful optical microscopes).

Example 26-3 Finding the Wavelength of a Room-Temperature Neutron

A nuclear reactor emits *thermal neutrons*. These are neutrons that behave as though they were particles of an ideal gas at Kelvin temperature T. We learned in Section 14-3 that the average kinetic energy of a particle in an ideal gas at temperature T is $(3/2)kT$, where $k = 1.381 \times 10^{-23}$ J/K is the Boltzmann constant. Calculate the de Broglie wavelength of an average neutron at 293 K (room temperature). The mass of a neutron is 1.67×10^{-27} kg.

Set Up

We'll first calculate the kinetic energy of an average neutron using Equation 14-13, which we learned in Section 14-3. From this we can find the speed and magnitude of momentum of an average neutron. Equation 26-10 will then allow us to calculate the de Broglie wavelength of such a neutron.

de Broglie wavelength:

$$\lambda = \frac{h}{p} \qquad (26\text{-}10)$$

Temperature and average translational kinetic energy of an ideal gas particle:

$$K_{translational,\ average} = \frac{1}{2}m(v^2)_{average} = \frac{3}{2}kT \quad (14\text{-}13)$$

Solve

Calculate the translational kinetic energy, speed, and momentum of an average neutron at $T = 293$ K.

From Equation 14-13,

$$K_{translational,\ average} = \frac{3}{2}kT = \frac{3}{2}(1.381 \times 10^{-23}\ \text{J/K})(293\ \text{K})$$
$$= 6.07 \times 10^{-21}\ \text{J}$$

Calculate the speed of a neutron with this kinetic energy:

$$K_{translational,\ average} = \frac{1}{2}mv^2 \text{ so}$$

$$v = \sqrt{\frac{2K_{translational,\ average}}{m}} = \sqrt{\frac{2(6.07 \times 10^{-21}\ \text{J})}{1.67 \times 10^{-27}\ \text{kg}}}$$
$$= 2.70 \times 10^3\ \text{m/s}$$

The magnitude of momentum of a neutron with this speed is

$$p = mv = (1.67 \times 10^{-27}\ \text{kg})(2.70 \times 10^3\ \text{m/s})$$
$$= 4.50 \times 10^{-24}\ \text{kg} \cdot \text{m/s}$$

Calculate the de Broglie wavelength of such a neutron.

From Equation 26-10,

$$\lambda = \frac{h}{p} = \frac{6.63 \times 10^{-34}\ \text{J} \cdot \text{s}}{4.50 \times 10^{-24}\ \text{kg} \cdot \text{m/s}} = 1.47 \times 10^{-10}\ \text{m} = 0.147\ \text{nm}$$

(Recall that $1\ \text{J} = 1\ \text{kg} \cdot \text{m}^2/\text{s}^2$ and $1\ \text{nm} = 10^{-9}\ \text{m}$.)

Reflect

The de Broglie wavelength of a thermal neutron is about 0.147 nm, a distance that is typical of the size of atoms and of the spacing between atoms within a molecule. For this reason, thermal neutrons are useful for studying the structure of complex molecules such as proteins: When the neutrons scatter from a protein molecule, they diffract and produce a diffraction pattern that is characteristic of the particular arrangement of atoms in the molecule. X rays can have the same wavelength, but they interact with the charges within atoms and so scatter only weakly from the relatively small atoms (with a small amount of internal charge) such as hydrogen, carbon, nitrogen, and oxygen found in proteins. Neutrons, by contrast, are electrically neutral and actually scatter more strongly from smaller atoms than from larger ones. This makes neutrons superior to X rays for studies of protein structure.

Got the Concept? 26-3 Ranking de Broglie Wavelengths

Rank the following objects in order of their de Broglie wavelength, from longest to shortest. (a) A proton moving at 2.00×10^3 m/s; (b) a proton moving at 4.00×10^3 m/s; (c) an electron moving at 2.00×10^3 m/s; (d) an electron moving at 4.00×10^3 m/s.

26-5 The spectra of light emitted and absorbed by atoms show that atomic energies are quantized

We have seen that the late nineteenth and early twentieth centuries were years of tremendous change in physics. Studying the photoelectric effect and blackbody radiation led to the revolutionary concept that light has particle aspects, and de Broglie introduced the no less revolutionary idea that matter has wave aspects. During this same time, a key set of experiments radically transformed our understanding of the nature of atoms.

The Nuclear Atom

The early Greeks introduced the idea of the atom, a unit of matter so small that it could not be subdivided. (The word *atom* is derived from the Greek term for indivisible.) In 1897 the British physicist J. J. Thomson discovered that atoms are not in fact indivisible, but have an internal structure: All atoms contain negatively charged particles (electrons) that can be removed from the atom. It was known that atoms are electrically neutral, so there must also be positively charged material inside an atom. But what form does this positive charge take?

Thomson proposed that most of the mass of the atom is in the form of electrons and that the positively charged material is a low-density sort of jelly in which the electrons are embedded. This model is sometimes called the "plum pudding model," since Thomson envisioned electrons scattered throughout the positive charge much like raisins in the traditional English dessert. (If you're not familiar with plum pudding, think of electrons as pieces of fruit embedded in a gelatin dessert or salad.) A crucial experiment that tested this model was carried out in 1909 at the University of Manchester in England by the New Zealand–born British chemist and physicist Ernest Rutherford with his colleagues Hans Geiger and Ernest Marsden. They fired subatomic particles called *alpha particles* (which were known to be positive helium ions, thousands of times more massive than an electron) at a very thin gold foil. Rutherford expected that if the gold atoms had the structure described in Thomson's model, the alpha particles would be only slightly deflected from their initial direction as a result of passing through the diffuse, positive "pudding" of the atoms. Instead, Rutherford was startled to discover that alpha particles were sometimes scattered at large angles with respect to the initial direction, occasionally leaving the gold foil directly *backward*. (In reflecting on this experiment, Rutherford later said, "It was quite the most incredible event that ever happened to me in my life. It was as incredible as if you fired a 15-in. shell [a large projectile fired from a military weapon] at a piece of tissue paper and it came back and hit you. On consideration, I realized that this scattering backwards must be the result of a single collision, and when I made calculations I saw that it was impossible to get anything of that order of magnitude unless you took a system in which the mass of the atom was concentrated in a minute nucleus."

To account for this, Rutherford proposed a model of the atom in which negatively charged electrons orbit a small, positively charged *nucleus* that contains nearly all of the atom's mass. In Rutherford's model, most of the volume of each atom is empty, so most alpha particles fired at the gold foil would experience only slight deflections as they passed through. But once in a while, about one time out of every 10,000, an alpha particle would approach a gold nucleus almost head on and be scattered at a large angle, sometimes directly backward.

Unlike planets orbiting the Sun, electrons orbiting an atomic nucleus fit into a well-defined organizational structure. We'll explore this structure from three perspectives and in historical order: first, the early clues that hinted at the structure, then the development of mathematical models that describe the structure, and finally (in the following section) the theory that explains it.

The Discovery of Atomic Spectra

In the early part of the nineteenth century, the English scientist William Hyde Wollaston noted the appearance of dark lines in the spectrum of visible light coming from the Sun (Figure 26-11). While conducting experiments on glass-making, a German optician-turned-physicist, Joseph von Fraunhofer, independently discovered these lines. These lines are always in the same locations within the spectrum. Some years later Gustav Kirchhoff, the same physicist we encountered in our study of electric circuits, was able to reproduce these same dark lines in the laboratory. He passed light from a lamp (made to simulate sunlight) through vapors created by heating sodium. The light from the lamp itself had a continuous spectrum like that of a blackbody, but the spectrum of light that had passed through the sodium vapor had two dark lines. Kirchhoff concluded that the dark lines result from certain specific colors of light being absorbed by the sodium vapor. What is more, these lines were at the same position as the closely spaced pair of lines in the yellow-orange region of the Sun's spectrum. (You can easily find these lines in Figure 26-11.) The same mechanism must therefore be happening with sunlight: The light coming from the solar interior has a continuous, blackbody-like spectrum, but certain wavelengths of that light are absorbed by atoms in the Sun's atmosphere. The Sun's atmosphere must contain sodium atoms identical to those in Kirchhoff's laboratory. In light of Kirchhoff's discovery, a spectrum like that shown in Figure 26-11 is called an **absorption spectrum**, and the dark lines are called **absorption lines**.

Scientists soon discovered that each element produces its own characteristic absorption lines when light passes through a vapor containing atoms of that element. Thus an absorption spectrum acts as a "fingerprint" of the chemical composition of the vapor that produced the absorption lines. (This is how we know the chemical composition of the Sun's atmosphere. It's also how we determine the chemical composition of the atmospheres of distant stars like those in the photograph that opens this chapter, and how we know that all stars have basically the same chemical makeup.) What was not understood was *why* atoms should selectively absorb only light of certain wavelengths, and why the absorbed wavelengths should be different for atoms of different elements.

An important clue about the mystery of absorption spectra came from studying the light *emitted* by atoms. Physicists of the nineteenth century discovered that light created by heating a vapor gives rise to an **emission spectrum**, a spectrum that consists only of specific emitted wavelengths. What is more, if the vapor contains atoms of a certain element, the wavelengths in the emission spectrum from those atoms (the **emission lines**) are precisely the same as the wavelengths in the absorption spectrum of that same element (Figure 26-12). To explore this, we'll concentrate on the absorption and

(a) The absorption spectrum produced by passing white light through a gas of hydrogen atoms

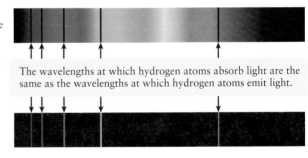

The wavelengths at which hydrogen atoms absorb light are the same as the wavelengths at which hydrogen atoms emit light.

(b) The emission spectrum produced by a heated gas of hydrogen atoms

Figure 26-12 **Absorption and emission spectra of atomic hydrogen** (a) When light passes through a gas, light of specific wavelengths is absorbed, forming dark lines. (b) When a gas is made to glow by passing an electric current through it, it emits only specific wavelengths of light.

• Atoms of each element absorb and emit light at wavelengths that are characteristic of that element.
• The characteristic wavelengths differ from one element to another.
• Hydrogen has the simplest arrangement of characteristic wavelengths of any element.

emission spectra of hydrogen, which has the simplest set of absorption and emission lines of any element. But the underlying physics applies to all elements.

Johann Balmer, a Swiss mathematician, made an analysis of the lines in the absorption and emission spectra of hydrogen. He devised a formula that both reproduced the wavelengths of lines that had been reported and correctly predicted the wavelengths of spectral lines of which Balmer was unaware. This was later extended by the Swedish physicist Johannes Rydberg. The Rydberg formula for the hydrogen spectral lines is

Wavelength of an absorption or emission line in the spectrum of atomic hydrogen

$$\frac{1}{\lambda} = R_{\mathrm{H}}\left(\frac{1}{n^2} - \frac{1}{m^2}\right)$$

Rydberg constant = $1.09737 \times 10^7 \mathrm{\ m^{-1}}$

n and m are integers: n can be 1, 2, 3, 4, ... and m can be any integer greater than n.

Rydberg formula for the spectral lines of hydrogen
(26-14)

The value of the constant R_{H} in Equation 26-14, called the *Rydberg constant*, is chosen to match the experimental data. To four significant figures, $R_{\mathrm{H}} = 1.097 \times 10^7 \mathrm{\ m^{-1}}$. As an example, the hydrogen absorption and emission lines shown in Figure 26-12 all correspond to $n = 2$ in Equation 26-14. The series of wavelengths for which $n = 2$ are called the *Balmer series*. For example, to get the wavelength of the red spectral line in Figure 26-12, set $n = 2$ and $m = 3$ in Equation 26-14:

$$\frac{1}{\lambda} = R_{\mathrm{H}}\left(\frac{1}{2^2} - \frac{1}{3^2}\right) = (1.097 \times 10^7 \mathrm{\ m^{-1}})\left(\frac{1}{4} - \frac{1}{9}\right) = 1.524 \times 10^6 \mathrm{\ m^{-1}}$$

Then take the reciprocal:

$$\lambda = \frac{1}{1.524 \times 10^6 \mathrm{\ m^{-1}}} = 6.563 \times 10^{-7} \mathrm{\ m} = 656.3 \mathrm{\ nm}$$

The spectral line to the left of this one in Figure 26-12 (in the blue-green part of the spectrum) corresponds to $n = 2$ and $m = 4$; you can show that for this spectral line, $\lambda = 486.2$ nm. The wavelengths with $n = 1$ are all in the ultraviolet and are called the *Lyman series*; the wavelengths with $n = 3$ are all in the infrared and are called the *Paschen series*.

What Balmer and Rydberg did not know was *why* the spectral hydrogen lines were given by this relatively simple formula. It was left to the Danish physicist Niels Bohr to provide the explanation.

Energy Quantization

Bohr realized that to fully understand the structure of the hydrogen atom, he had to be able to derive Balmer's formula using the laws of physics. He first made the rather wild assumption that the electron in a hydrogen atom can orbit the nucleus only in certain specific orbits. (This was a significant break with the ideas of Newton, in whose mechanics any orbit should be possible.) Figure 26-13 shows the four smallest of these **Bohr orbits**, labeled by the numbers $n = 1$, $n = 2$, $n = 3$, and so on.

Although confined to one of these allowed orbits while circling the nucleus, an electron can jump from one Bohr orbit to another. For an electron to do this, the hydrogen atom must gain or lose a specific amount of energy. The atom must absorb energy for the electron to go from an inner to an outer orbit; the atom must release energy for the electron to go from an outer to an inner orbit. As an example, Figure 26-14 shows an electron jumping between the $n = 2$ and $n = 3$ orbits of a hydrogen atom as the atom absorbs or emits a photon.

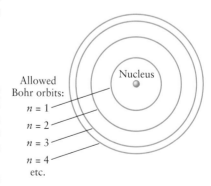

Allowed Bohr orbits:
$n = 1$
$n = 2$
$n = 3$
$n = 4$
etc.

Nucleus

Figure 26-13 **Bohr orbits in the hydrogen atom** In the model devised by Niels Bohr, electrons in the hydrogen atom are allowed to be in certain orbits only. (The radii of the orbits are not shown to scale.)

Figure 26-14 The Bohr model explains absorption and emission spectra When a photon is (a) absorbed or (b) emitted by a hydrogen atom, the electron makes a transition or jump between two allowed orbits. The photon energy equals the difference in energy between the upper and lower electron orbits.

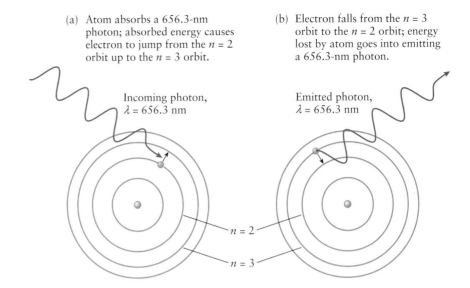

(a) Atom absorbs a 656.3-nm photon; absorbed energy causes electron to jump from the $n = 2$ orbit up to the $n = 3$ orbit.

(b) Electron falls from the $n = 3$ orbit to the $n = 2$ orbit; energy lost by atom goes into emitting a 656.3-nm photon.

Incoming photon, $\lambda = 656.3$ nm

Emitted photon, $\lambda = 656.3$ nm

$n = 2$

$n = 3$

When the electron jumps from one orbit to another, the energy of the photon that is emitted or absorbed equals the difference in energy between these two orbits. This energy difference, and hence the photon energy, is the same whether the jump is from a low orbit to a high orbit (Figure 26-14a) or from the high orbit back to the low one (Figure 26-14b). According to Einstein, if two photons have the same energy E, the relationship $E = hf$ (Equation 22-26) tells us that they must also have the same frequency f and hence the same wavelength $\lambda = c/f$. It follows that if an atom can emit photons of a given energy and wavelength, it can also absorb photons of precisely the same energy and wavelength. Thus, Bohr's picture explains Kirchhoff's observation that atoms emit and absorb the same wavelengths of light.

The Bohr picture also helps us visualize what happens to produce an emission spectrum. When a gas is heated, its atoms move around rapidly and can collide forcefully with each other. These energetic collisions excite the atoms' electrons into high orbits. The electrons then cascade back down to the innermost possible orbit, emitting photons whose energies are equal to the energy differences between different Bohr orbits. In this fashion, a hot gas produces an emission line spectrum with a variety of different wavelengths.

To produce an absorption spectrum, begin with a relatively cool gas, so that the electrons in most of the atoms are in inner, low-energy orbits. If a beam of light with a continuous spectrum is shone through the gas, most wavelengths will pass through undisturbed. Only those photons will be absorbed whose energies are just right to excite an electron to an allowed outer orbit. Hence, only certain wavelengths will be absorbed, and dark lines will appear in the spectrum at those wavelengths.

As in Figure 26-14, the energy of the photon that is absorbed or emitted in a jump between orbits must be equal to the *difference* between the energy of the atom with the electron in the larger-radius, higher-energy orbit and the energy of the atom with the electron in the smaller-radius, lower-energy orbit. Bohr concluded that the numbers n and m in the Rydberg formula correspond to the numbers of the orbits between which an electron jumps as it absorbs or emits a photon. The value of n is the number of the lower orbit, and the value of m is the number of the upper orbit. For example, the jump shown in Figure 26-14 corresponds to $n = 2$ and $m = 3$.

We can better understand Bohr's idea by combining the Rydberg formula, Equation 26-14, with the expressions $E = hf$ and $f = c/\lambda$ for a photon. Together these latter two expressions say that the energy of a photon of wavelength λ is $E = hc/\lambda$. So if we multiply Equation 26-14 by hc, we get an expression for the energy of a photon absorbed or emitted by a hydrogen atom:

$$(26\text{-}15) \qquad E_{\text{photon}} = \frac{hc}{\lambda} = hcR_{\text{H}}\left(\frac{1}{n^2} - \frac{1}{m^2}\right) = \frac{hcR_{\text{H}}}{n^2} - \frac{hcR_{\text{H}}}{m^2} = \left(-\frac{hcR_{\text{H}}}{m^2}\right) - \left(-\frac{hcR_{\text{H}}}{n^2}\right)$$

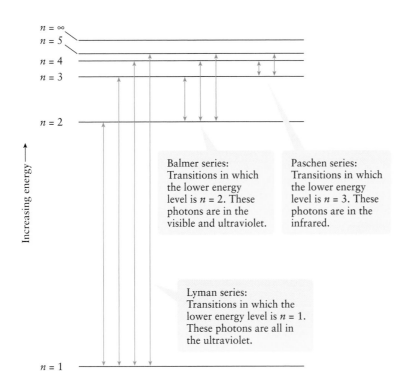

Figure 26-15 **Hydrogen energy levels** This figure shows some of the lower-lying energy levels of the hydrogen atom and possible transitions between those levels. Note that the energy difference is greatest between the $n = 1$ and $n = 2$ levels, less between the $n = 2$ and $n = 3$ levels, and even less between the $n = 3$ and $n = 4$ levels.

If we say that a hydrogen atom has energy $E_{\mathrm{atom},n} = -hcR_{\mathrm{H}}/n^2$ when the electron is in the nth orbit and has energy $E_{\mathrm{atom},m} = -hcR_{\mathrm{H}}/m^2$ when the electron is in the mth orbit, where m is greater than n, then we can rewrite Equation 26-15 as

$$E_{\mathrm{photon}} = E_{\mathrm{atom},m} - E_{\mathrm{atom},n}$$

(26-16)

Equation 26-16 uses the idea that the energy of a hydrogen atom is **quantized**: That is, the energy can only have certain values. These energies are given by

$$E_{\mathrm{atom},n} = -\frac{hcR_{\mathrm{H}}}{n^2} \quad \text{where } n = 1, 2, 3, 4, \ldots$$

(26-17)

Note that the energy of the atom is negative, and greater values of n correspond to energies that are less negative (that is, closer to zero). This agrees with the idea that the larger the orbit and the greater the value of n for that orbit, the higher the energy.

Each quantized value of the energy is called an **energy level**. Figure 26-15 shows several of the energy levels of the hydrogen atom, along with vertical arrows that show the energy of the photon that must be absorbed or emitted in a jump or transition between levels. The transitions that correspond to the Lyman series involve a photon with a very large amount of energy, so these photons have a high frequency and short wavelength: They are all in the ultraviolet part of the spectrum. By contrast, the transitions that correspond to the Paschen series involve a photon with a very small amount of energy, which is why these photons have a low frequency and long wavelength and are in the infrared part of the spectrum. The Balmer series is intermediate between these two; the wavelengths are either in the visible range (380 to 750 nm) or the ultraviolet range.

Elements other than hydrogen also absorb and emit light at specific wavelengths, although those wavelengths do not follow a simple mathematical pattern like the characteristic wavelengths of hydrogen given by Equation 26-14. The conclusion is that there are quantized energy levels for atoms of other elements, but the arrangement of energy levels is more complex than for hydrogen. In the following section we'll see how Niels Bohr justified the quantization of energy for the relatively simple case of the hydrogen atom, and how he was able to reproduce Equation 26-17 for the energy levels. We'll then use these ideas to gain insight into the structure of other atoms.

⚠ Watch Out! Energy quantization is not just an obscure effect in atomic physics.

Discrete energy levels play an important role in modern technology. A *laser* is a device that emits an intense beam of light of a very specific wavelength. This is possible because the laser contains a material with two distinct energy levels. Light of the laser's characteristic wavelength is emitted when transitions take place from the upper level to the lower one. (What makes the laser unique is that these transitions occur coherently rather than at random. Energy is added to the material to pump its molecules into excited states. The excited molecules naturally want to transition to a lower state, but if left on their own, would do so at random times. However, when a photon of energy equal to the difference between two states is sent into the material, it can *stimulate* this transition and cause a second photon of that same energy to be released. This photon can stimulate further emission, and so the number of emitted photons increases. The emitted photons are all in phase and all travel in the same general direction. The net result is an intense beam.) If materials did not have quantized energy levels, the lasers found in Blu-ray and DVD players (which scan the video information encoded on the disc) could not exist. Fluorescent light bulbs also depend on energy quantization. The material inside the bulb emits ultraviolet photons when an electric current passes through it. These photons are absorbed by the white coating on the inner surface of the bulb. Since ultraviolet photons are very energetic, this excites the material of the coating to very high energy levels. The coating then drops down to its initial energy level in a series of small steps. (It's like taking a big leap to the top of a staircase, then coming carefully down the staircase one step at a time.) Each small step between closely spaced energy levels emits a low-energy, visible-light photon. There are so many such energy levels, with a variety of spacing between them, that the net result is that a mixture of almost all visible colors—that is, white light—is emitted from the bulb. These are just two of the many applications of energy quantization.

Example 26-4 Photon Possibilities

A collection of hydrogen atoms is excited to the $n = 3$ energy level. What are the possible wavelengths that these atoms could emit as they return to the lowest-energy ($n = 1$) level?

Set Up

There are two routes that an atom can take from the $n = 3$ level to the $n = 1$ level. One, it could drop down to the $n = 1$ level in a single step by emitting a single photon whose energy is equal to the difference between the energies of the $n = 3$ and $n = 1$ levels. The wavelength of this photon is given by Equation 26-14 with $n = 1$ and $m = 3$. Two, the atom could first drop to the $n = 2$ level by emitting a photon (with a wavelength given by Equation 26-14 with $n = 2$ and $m = 3$), then emit a second photon as it drops from the $n = 2$ level to the $n = 1$ level (with a wavelength given by Equation 26-14 with $n = 1$ and $m = 2$). So three different wavelengths can be emitted by the excited atoms. We'll calculate each of these in turn.

Rydberg formula for the spectral lines of hydrogen:

$$\frac{1}{\lambda} = R_H \left(\frac{1}{n^2} - \frac{1}{m^2} \right) \qquad (26\text{-}14)$$

Solve

Use Equation 26-14 to calculate each of the three possible wavelengths.

For the $n = 3$ to $n = 1$ transition,

$$\frac{1}{\lambda} = R_H \left(\frac{1}{1^2} - \frac{1}{3^2} \right) = (1.097 \times 10^7 \text{ m}^{-1}) \left(1 - \frac{1}{9} \right)$$

$$= 9.751 \times 10^6 \text{ m}^{-1}$$

$$\lambda = \frac{1}{9.751 \times 10^6 \text{ m}^{-1}} = 1.026 \times 10^{-7} \text{ m} = 102.6 \text{ nm}$$

This is an ultraviolet wavelength.

For the $n = 3$ to $n = 2$ transition,

$$\frac{1}{\lambda} = R_\mathrm{H}\left(\frac{1}{2^2} - \frac{1}{3^2}\right) = (1.097 \times 10^7\,\mathrm{m^{-1}})\left(\frac{1}{4} - \frac{1}{9}\right)$$

$$= 1.524 \times 10^6\,\mathrm{m^{-1}}$$

$$\lambda = \frac{1}{1.524 \times 10^6\,\mathrm{m^{-1}}} = 6.563 \times 10^{-7}\,\mathrm{m} = 656.3\,\mathrm{nm}$$

This is a visible wavelength (in the red part of the spectrum).

For the $n = 2$ to $n = 1$ transition,

$$\frac{1}{\lambda} = R_\mathrm{H}\left(\frac{1}{1^2} - \frac{1}{2^2}\right) = (1.097 \times 10^7\,\mathrm{m^{-1}})\left(1 - \frac{1}{4}\right)$$

$$= 8.228 \times 10^6\,\mathrm{m^{-1}}$$

$$\lambda = \frac{1}{8.228 \times 10^6\,\mathrm{m^{-1}}} = 1.215 \times 10^{-7}\,\mathrm{m} = 121.5\,\mathrm{nm}$$

This is another ultraviolet wavelength.

Reflect

Comparing with Figure 26-15 shows that the 656.3-nm wavelength represents an emission line of the Balmer series, while the 102.6-nm and 121.5-nm wavelengths represent emission lines of the Lyman series.

❓ Got the Concept? 26-4 Ranking Hydrogen Transitions

Rank the following transitions between hydrogen energy levels in terms of the energy of the photon involved, from highest to lowest energy. (a) An atom drops from the $n = 4$ level to the $n = 2$ level. (b) An atom rises from the $n = 3$ level to the $n = 5$ level. (c) An atom drops from the $n = 3$ level to the $n = 1$ level. (d) An atom drops from the $n = 4$ to the $n = 3$ level.

Take-Home Message for Section 26-5

✔ Atoms are composed of electrons orbiting a positively charged nucleus that has most of the mass of the atom.

✔ In the Bohr model, an electron's orbits around the nucleus can have only certain well-defined energies. Thus the energy of the atom is quantized and can have only certain values. The atom cannot have energies intermediate between those values.

✔ Electrons that make a transition from one allowed orbit to another either radiate or absorb a photon of a well-defined energy. This gives rise to the lines in emission and absorption spectra.

26-6 Models by Bohr and Schrödinger give insight into the intriguing structure of the atom

The force that pulls the Moon toward Earth is directed toward Earth's center, yet the Moon does not fall into Earth. In the same way, the negatively charged electron in an atom experiences a Coulomb force that points directly toward the positively charged protons at the center of the atom. Why does the electron orbit rather than fall in to the proton? You likely have an intuitive answer that both the Moon and the electron *orbit* rather than fall in. (In a real sense each *is* falling in, but it is always missing the target!) Niels Bohr based his model of the hydrogen atom, for which he received the Nobel Prize in Physics in 1922, on the physics of atomic orbits. The **Bohr model** provides a theoretical foundation for the physics of atomic spectra that we encountered in the previous section.

The Bohr Model

Bohr made two fundamental assumptions in describing the orbit of an electron around a positive atomic nucleus. First, he modeled the orbit as uniform circular motion, that is, as an electron moving at constant speed in a circular path. This is not exactly correct, but more than satisfactory to provide a broad and correct understanding of the atom. Bohr's second assumption was that only specific values are allowed for the angular momentum associated with each orbiting electron. We will return to this second assumption shortly.

Bohr considered a single electron orbiting a nucleus of charge $+Ze$, where Z, the *atomic number of an atom*, is the number of protons in the nucleus. The orbiting electron experiences only one force, the Coulomb attraction between it and the protons in the atomic nucleus. The magnitude of the Coulomb force on an electron orbiting in a circle of radius r is, from Equation 16-1,

$$F = \frac{k(Ze)(e)}{r^2} = \frac{kZe^2}{r^2}$$

Here $k = 8.99 \times 10^9 \, \text{N} \cdot \text{m}^2/\text{C}^2$ is the Coulomb constant. Newton's second law (Equation 4-2) requires that this force equal the mass of the electron m_e multiplied by the acceleration it experiences. For an object in uniform circular motion at speed v, the magnitude of the acceleration is, from Equation 3-17,

$$a = \frac{v^2}{r}$$

Combining the above two equations into Newton's second law gives

$$\frac{kZe^2}{r^2} = \frac{m_e v^2}{r}$$

If we multiply both sides of this equation by r, we get

(26-18)
$$\frac{kZe^2}{r} = m_e v^2$$

Let's set Equation 26-18 aside for a moment and examine Bohr's second assumption—a requirement that only specific values are allowed for the angular momentum associated with the electron. Bohr recognized that the dimensions of Planck's constant h are those of angular momentum, so he constrained the electron's angular momentum to be only multiples of h. Specifically, this requirement is

(26-19)
$$L = n\left(\frac{h}{2\pi}\right) = n\hbar$$

(orbital angular momentum in the Bohr model)

where L is the electron's orbital angular momentum and n is any integer starting from 1. The constant $\hbar$ (pronounced "h bar") is defined to be h divided by 2π.

To relate angular momentum to Equation 26-18, we express L in terms of the mass of the electron m_e, its speed v, and its distance from the center of the atom r using Equation 8-23:

| Magnitude of the angular momentum of a particle | Component of the particle's linear momentum perpendicular to the vector $\vec{r}$ from rotation axis to particle |

Magnitude of the angular momentum of a particle
(8-23)

$$L = rp_\perp = rp \sin \phi$$

Distance from the rotation axis to the particle

Since the electron moves in a circle, the vector from the rotation axis to the particle always has the same radius r and is always perpendicular to the momentum vector. So $\phi = 90°$, $\sin \phi = 1$, and

(26-20)
$$L = rm_e v$$

We can now rewrite Equation 26-18 in terms of the angular momentum L by multiplying the right-hand side by 1 in the form of $(r^2/r^2)(m_e/m_e)$:

$$\frac{kZe^2}{r} = \frac{r^2 m_e^2 v^2}{m_e r^2} = \frac{L^2}{m_e r^2}$$

Bohr's requirement that the electron's angular momentum is an integer multiple of $\hbar$ then gives

$$\frac{kZe^2}{r} = \frac{(n\hbar)^2}{m_e r^2}$$

or

$$r_n = \frac{n^2 \hbar^2}{m_e k Z e^2} \quad \text{where } n = 1, 2, 3, \ldots \tag{26-21}$$

(orbital radii in the Bohr model)

We add the subscript "n" to the variable r to indicate that the radius can take on only specific values and that the allowed values of radius depend on n. Because the values of r_n are proportional to the square of an integer, the orbital radii of electrons in an atom are quantized.

Notice that both n and Z in Equation 26-21 are dimensionless. Because r_n is a distance, all of the other terms on the right-hand side, taken as they appear in the equation, must have dimensions of distance as well. This distance, usually written as a_0 and called the Bohr radius, is

Bohr radius
(26-22)

Using the best measured values for $\hbar$, m_e, k, and e, we find that the value of the Bohr radius a_0 is approximately

$$a_0 = 0.529 \times 10^{-10} \text{ m} = 0.0529 \text{ nm}$$

In terms of a_0, the quantized radii of the electron orbits (Equation 26-21) are

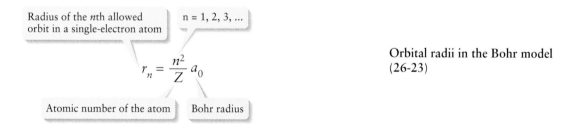

Orbital radii in the Bohr model
(26-23)

The integer n identifies the orbit, where the $n = 1$ orbit is the closest to the nucleus. Because every element is distinguished by the number of protons it carries, the atomic number Z specifies a particular element. So, for example, setting Z equal to 1 gives the radii of the electron orbits in a hydrogen atom, and setting Z equal to 1 and n equal to 1 gives the radius of the first electron orbit in hydrogen. This is the normal state, usually referred to as the ground state, of hydrogen. Moreover, notice that the radius of the ground state orbit of hydrogen is the Bohr radius. In other words, the radius of a typical hydrogen atom is about 0.05 nm. We can also conclude from Equation 26-23 together with the value of the Bohr radius that, in general, atoms are no more than a few nm in radius. The Bohr model sets the scale for atomic sizes.

What is the energy of an electron orbiting an atomic nucleus according to the Bohr model? This is the sum of its kinetic energy and its electric potential energy. For two point charges q_1 and q_2, $U_{electric} = kq_1q_2/r$ (Equation 17-3), so

$$(26\text{-}24) \qquad E = \frac{1}{2}m_ev^2 + \frac{k(-e)(Ze)}{r_n}$$

We can write the kinetic energy term in terms of angular momentum in a way that is similar to our approach in developing the relationship for r_n. Using Equation 26-20 shows that the kinetic energy term becomes

$$\frac{1}{2}m_ev^2 = \frac{1}{2}\frac{L^2}{m_er_n^2} = \frac{n^2\hbar^2}{2m_er_n^2}$$

so the total electron energy from Equation 26-24 is

$$E = \frac{n^2\hbar^2}{2m_er_n^2} - \frac{kZe^2}{r_n}$$

Substituting Equation 26-23 for r_n and Equation 26-22 for a_0 gives the energy in terms of only the physical constants and the counting integer n:

$$E = \frac{n^2\hbar^2}{2m_e}\left(\frac{m_ekZe^2}{n^2\hbar^2}\right)^2 - kZe^2\frac{m_ekZe^2}{n^2\hbar^2}$$

Simplifying this is straightforward when you notice that the numerator of both terms is $m_e(kZe^2)^2$ and that both terms have $n^2\hbar^2$ in the denominator:

$$E = \frac{m_e(kZe^2)^2}{2n^2\hbar^2} - \frac{m_e(kZe^2)^2}{n^2\hbar^2}$$

or

$$(26\text{-}25) \qquad E_n = -\frac{m_e(kZe^2)^2}{2n^2\hbar^2}, \quad n = 1, 2, 3, \ldots$$

(electron energies in the Bohr model)

We add the subscript n to the variable E to indicate that the orbital energy of the electron can take on only specific values, and that the allowed values of energy depend on n. Because the values of E_n are proportional to $1/n^2$, the orbital energy of electrons in an atom is quantized. This is in agreement with our conclusion in the previous section that for atomic spectral lines to occur only at specific, and always the same, wavelengths, electrons must orbit the hydrogen nucleus with specific, well-defined energies. Note also that the energy is equal to a negative constant divided by n^2, exactly in accordance with Equation 26-17. (We'll see below that the numerical value of the constant is the same in Equation 26-25 as in Equation 26-17.)

The value of energy of an electron in orbit around an atomic nucleus is negative, but closer and closer to zero for increasing values of n. In other words, the lowest energy orbit is the one closest to the nucleus, as we would expect. You might imagine that the negative values of energy suggest that the electron is at the bottom of a hole, and its orbital energy is insufficient to allow it to escape. That the electron energy is taken as negative emphasizes that the electron is bound to the nucleus, and that energy must be supplied in order to either move the electron to a higher orbit or to break the electron free from the nucleus altogether.

Because E_n is an energy, and because both n and Z are dimensionless, the combination of other quantities on the right-hand side of Equation 26-25 must have dimensions of energy as well. This energy, usually written as E_0, is called the Rydberg energy:

Rydberg energy
(26-26)

In Equation 26-26 we've given the value of the Rydberg energy in joules and in electron volts (eV). The energy that an electron acquires when it moves through a potential difference of 1 V is 1 eV, or approximately 1.602×10^{-19} J. To give you an idea of the amount of energy 1 eV represents, a photon of visible light carries between about 1.5 and 3 eV.

Using Equation 26-26, we can write Equation 26-25 for the quantized electron orbital energy in terms of the Rydberg energy E_0:

Electron energies in the
Bohr model
(26-27)

Again, the integer n identifies the orbit, and the atomic number Z specifies a particular element. Setting Z equal to 1 and n equal to 1 therefore tells us that the energy of the ground state of hydrogen is -13.6 eV. We can also conclude from Equation 26-27 together with the value of the Rydberg energy that, in general, the energy of electrons in orbit around an atomic nucleus is between about -10 eV and, for the largest elements (for which Z is about 100), -10^5 eV. The Bohr model sets the scale for atomic electron energies.

What does the Bohr model predict for the atomic spectral lines of hydrogen? Every line results from a transition between two electron orbits; that is, the energy of the emitted photon is the energy difference ΔE between two allowed orbits (see Equation 26-16). Since the energy of a photon is hf and its frequency $f = c/\lambda$, the wavelength λ of the photon is then

$$\lambda = \frac{hc}{\Delta E}$$

Recalling that the Rydberg formula is written in terms of the reciprocal of the photon wavelength, we write

$$\frac{1}{\lambda} = \frac{\Delta E}{hc} \qquad (26\text{-}28)$$

Let's consider the transition of an electron from a higher orbit m down to a lower orbit n. We can determine the energy difference between these two orbits by applying Equation 26-27. Atomic number Z equals 1 for hydrogen, so

$$\Delta E = -\frac{1}{m^2}E_0 - \left(-\frac{1}{n^2}\right)E_0$$

or

$$\Delta E = \left(\frac{1}{n^2} - \frac{1}{m^2}\right)E_0$$

Substituting this into Equation 26-28 yields

$$\frac{1}{\lambda} = \frac{E_0}{hc}\left(\frac{1}{n^2} - \frac{1}{m^2}\right)$$

Compare this to the Rydberg formula, Equation 26-14. It has exactly the same form!
How does the value of E_0/hc compare to the value of R_H, which equals approximately $1.10 \times 10^7 \text{ m}^{-1}$? In SI units

$$\frac{E_0}{hc} = \frac{2.18 \times 10^{-18}\,\text{J}}{(6.63 \times 10^{-34}\,\text{J} \cdot \text{s})(3.00 \times 10^8\,\text{m/s})} = 1.10 \times 10^7\,\text{m}^{-1}$$

The ratio E_0/hc equals R_H, so $E_0 = hcR_H$. That's just what we expect if we compare Equation 26-17 (in which we deduced the energies from the Rydberg equation) and Equation 26-27 (in which we derived the energies from the Bohr assumptions). We conclude that the Rydberg formula for the spectral lines of hydrogen is entirely consistent with the Bohr model.

Example 26-5 Lowest Energy Level of a Lithium Ion

Find the (a) radius, (b) energy, and (c) speed of an electron in the lowest energy level of the doubly ionized lithium ion. An atom of lithium $(Z = 3)$ has three electrons, so this ion has just one electron.

Set Up

For this ion, $Z = 3$; for the lowest energy level, $n = 1$. We'll use Equation 26-23 to calculate the radius of this orbit, Equation 26-27 to calculate the energy, and Equation 26-19 for angular momentum to determine the electron speed.

Orbital radii in the Bohr model:

$$r_n = \frac{n^2 a_0}{Z} \quad \text{where } n = 1, 2, 3, \ldots$$
$$(26\text{-}23)$$

Electron energies in the Bohr model:

$$E_n = -\frac{Z^2}{n^2} E_0 \quad \text{where } n = 1, 2, 3, \ldots$$
$$(26\text{-}27)$$

Orbital angular momentum in the Bohr model:

$$L = n\left(\frac{h}{2\pi}\right) = n\hbar \qquad (26\text{-}19)$$

Solve

(a) Calculate the radius of the orbit.

From Equation 26-23 with $Z = 3$ and $n = 1$,

$$r_1 = \frac{1^2 a_0}{3} = \frac{a_0}{3} = \frac{0.0529\,\text{nm}}{3} = 0.0176\,\text{nm}$$

(b) Calculate the energy.

From Equation 26-27 with $Z = 3$ and $n = 1$,

$$E_n = -\frac{3^2}{1^2} E_0 = -9E_0 = -9(13.6\,\text{eV}) = -122\,\text{eV}$$

(c) To find an expression for the electron speed, combine Equation 26-19 with the equation for the angular momentum of a particle moving in a circular orbit.

Equation 26-20 tells us that the angular momentum of an electron of mass m_e moving in an orbit of radius r at speed v is $L = rm_e v$. Set this equal to the expression for L in Equation 26-19:

$$rm_e v = n\hbar \qquad \text{so}$$

$$v = \frac{n\hbar}{rm_e}$$

We are interested in the case of $n = 1$, and calculated r_1 in part (a). Substituting the values for $\hbar = h/(2\pi)$ and the mass of the electron gives:

$$v = \frac{1(6.63 \times 10^{-34} \text{ J·s})}{2\pi (1.76 \times 10^{-11} \text{ m})(9.11 \times 10^{-31} \text{ kg})}$$

$$= 6.58 \times 10^6 \text{ m/s}$$

Reflect

The radius of an electron in the lowest level of the doubly ionized lithium ion ($Z = 3$) is one-third the radius of an electron in the ground state of hydrogen. Because there are three protons in the lithium nucleus, compared to one for hydrogen, the Coulomb force on the electron is greater, so it is reasonable that the orbital radius is smaller. Also, notice that the speed of the electron is about 2% of the speed of light in a vacuum.

Why did we insist that the problem be about a doubly ionized lithium ion, rather than a lithium atom? The difference is that when more than one electron is present, each electron is affected not only by the electric force from the nucleus but also by the electric force from the other electrons. We haven't taken the interaction between electrons into account in any of our calculations: The Bohr model is for *single-electron* atoms and ions only.

Although the Bohr model successfully predicts atomic spectra and other phenomena associated with hydrogen atoms, it nevertheless leaves us with an outstanding question. Why should the electron orbits be quantized in multiples of $\hbar$? For the answer we turn back to Louis de Broglie. Recall that de Broglie postulated that particles, such as electrons, have a wavelike nature. As a result, the electron's wave interferes with itself as the electron makes multiple revolutions around the nucleus. The only allowed orbits are those for which the electron waves constructively interfere and form standing waves.

For a nonrelativistic electron of mass m_e moving at speed v, the momentum has magnitude $p = m_e v$. From the de Broglie relation, Equation 26-10, the wavelength of such an electron is

$$\lambda = \frac{h}{m_e v}$$

For an electron orbiting an atomic nucleus we put this in terms of angular momentum by making use of Equation 26-20:

$$\lambda = \frac{hr}{m_e vr} = \frac{hr}{L}$$

To connect this more directly with the circular path of the orbit, we introduce a factor of 2π:

$$\lambda = \frac{hr}{L} = \frac{2\pi\hbar r}{L}$$

Now let L be an integer multiple of $\hbar$, as Bohr required. Then

$$\lambda = \frac{2\pi\hbar r}{n\hbar}$$

or

$$n\lambda = 2\pi r$$

We recognize $2\pi r$ as the circumference of the orbital path of the electron. An integer number of full electron waves fit into the circumference of the orbit only when Bohr's requirement is met. In a real sense, it is the wavelike nature of particles that results in the quantization of the energy of atomic electrons.

Confirming Energy Quantization

Bohr's model of the atom works relatively well for hydrogen, for a singly ionized helium ion (an atom with Z equal to 2 but only one electron), and for a doubly ionized lithium ion (an atom with Z equal to 3 but only one electron, as in Example 26-5). For atoms with more than one electron, it isn't possible to make calculations of energy levels using Bohr's physics. However, the general picture of the atom it provides, with electrons in quantized energy states, applies to all atoms. This was confirmed experimentally in 1914 by the German physicists James Franck and Gustav Hertz. (Franck and Hertz were awarded the 1925 Nobel Prize in Physics for their work. Gustav Hertz was a nephew of Heinrich Hertz, whom we encountered earlier.)

In what is now known as the *Franck-Hertz experiment*, Franck and Hertz used a device similar to the one shown schematically in Figure 26-16 to measure the effect of bombarding atoms in a gas with electrons. The cathode is heated in order to give off electrons, which are accelerated by a variable voltage toward the mesh grid. Some electrons pass through the grid and arrive at the anode, where the electron current is detected by the ammeter. Notice that a voltage is also applied between the grid and the anode, which acts against the electrons; only electrons that carry sufficient energy as they pass the grid will make it to the anode. These electrical components sit inside a tube filled with low-pressure mercury vapor, so collisions between an electron and a mercury (Hg) atom can occur. Franck and Hertz used mercury vapor because the spectral lines of low-pressure mercury gas were well studied; one prominent ultraviolet spectral line has a wavelength $\lambda = 253.7$ nm. The energy of this photon is

$$E = hf = \frac{hc}{\lambda} = \frac{(6.63 \times 10^{-34}\,\text{J}\cdot\text{s})(3.00 \times 10^{8}\,\text{m/s})}{253.7 \times 10^{-9}\,\text{m}}$$

$$= (7.84 \times 10^{-19}\,\text{J})\left(\frac{1\,\text{eV}}{1.60 \times 10^{-19}\,\text{J}}\right) = 4.90\,\text{eV}$$

This is the energy emitted when an atomic electron falls from an excited energy level state down to a lower energy level. To see the significance of this number, consider what happens in the collision of an electron and a mercury atom in the Franck-Hertz tube. In general, the more kinetic energy an electron carries as it approaches the grid, the more likely it will make it through. So anode current should grow as the voltage between the cathode and the grid is increased. However, if the energy levels of electrons in Hg (and all) atoms are quantized, when the kinetic energy of the incident electron equals the energy difference between two Hg energy levels, the Hg atom can absorb the electron's energy. When this happens it is less likely that the electron will reach the anode, so the anode current should decrease. Figure 26-17 shows a typical curve of current versus voltage from the Franck-Hertz experiment. The general trend, as we would expect, is that the anode current increases as the voltage is increased. But the current drops dramatically at certain values of accelerating voltage, in this case, at 4.9 V, and at 9.8 V and 14.7 V, which are multiples of 4.9 V. This is the very same energy of the mercury spectral line!

When the cathode-grid voltage is set to 4.9 V, the kinetic energy of electrons that leave the cathode reaches 4.9 eV just as they approach the mesh grid. (Recall that the unit of energy eV is the amount of energy gained by an electron when it experiences a potential difference of 1 V.) For this reason, electrons that collide with a mercury atom in close proximity to the grid give up their energy in the process of causing an electron in the atom to jump to a higher energy level. But because the collision occurs close to the grid, there is no opportunity for the electron to undergo another acceleration; in other words, there is no opportunity for the electron to acquire enough energy to reach the anode. For this reason, when the cathode-grid voltage is set to 4.9 V, so that the collisions

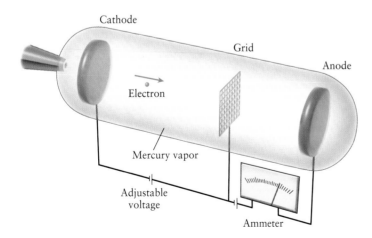

Figure 26-16 The Franck-Hertz experiment In this experiment, electrons are accelerated from a cathode toward a mesh grid in a tube filled with mercury vapor. Some electrons pass through the grid, and the current at the anode is measured by the ammeter.

between electrons and Hg atoms occur near the grid with electron kinetic energy equal to 4.9 eV, the number of electrons reaching the anode decreases. In addition, when the voltage is set to 9.8 V, accelerated electrons that collide with an Hg atom halfway between the cathode and the grid lose their energy, and then accelerate up to a kinetic energy of 4.9 eV again by the time they reach the grid. A collision there once again results in the electron transferring its energy to an Hg atom and being unable to reach the anode. A similar phenomenon occurs when the voltage is set to any integer multiple of 4.9 V. This rise and fall in anode current versus cathode-grid voltage is shown dramatically in Figure 26-17. The underlying explanation of this phenomenon is the quantization of electron energy levels in the atom, as predicted by Bohr.

Beyond the Bohr Model: Quantum Mechanics

As powerful as the Bohr model is at providing an understanding of the atom and atomic spectra, it does not tell the whole story. The Bohr atom treats the electrons that orbit atomic nuclei as particles. Yet as the scientists of the early twentieth century were beginning to learn, electrons exhibit the properties of waves. No theoretical description of the atom can be complete unless it accounts for the wave nature of the electrons. The theoretical underpinning of our understanding of atoms that includes these wave properties is found in an equation developed by Austrian physicist Erwin Schrödinger. The *Schrödinger equation* relies on matter waves to describe the state of a system as a function of time, much like Newton's laws do while treating physical systems as particles. The Schrödinger equation is thus the fundamental equation of **quantum mechanics**, in which matter is treated as intrinsically wavelike in nature. Schrödinger was awarded the 1933 Nobel Prize in Physics for his work. (The Schrödinger equation itself is too mathematically ornate for the purposes of this book.)

Perhaps the most notable difference between Schrödinger's quantum-mechanical description and Newton's classical description of physics is seen in the ability to specify the position and velocity of objects. In Newton's description, at any instant of time we can identify a specific position in space and a specific velocity vector for any particle in a system, for example, an electron orbiting an atomic nucleus. A wave, however, is not localized in space, even after applying advanced mathematical notions that squeeze it into a relatively well-defined region of space. The result is that while Newton's laws predict the position and velocity of an object, the Schrödinger equation predicts the *probability* of finding a certain value of position or velocity. For this reason, electrons in the quantum model of the atom are described not as tiny marbles orbiting the nucleus at fixed radii, but rather as a charge distribution. This distribution, sometimes called a *probability cloud*, gives the probability of finding the electron at any given position; the denser the cloud in some region, the more likely it is that the electron will be found there.

Figure 26-18a shows the probability cloud associated with the ground state of hydrogen. The more dense the color in any region in this figure, the more likely it is that the electron will be found in that region. This probability distribution is spherically symmetric; that is, it only varies as a function of radius from the center of the nucleus. For that reason we can also express the same information in a curve of probability versus radius, as in Figure 26-18b. Notice that the most probable radius of an electron in the ground state of a hydrogen atom is a_0, the Bohr radius.

The Bohr model employs a single integer, or **quantum number**, to describe electron states. For the Bohr atom this integer is n, which determines the energy level of the electron. In the fully quantum-mechanical view of the atom, *four* quantum numbers are required. These are n, the principal quantum number; ℓ, the angular momentum (or orbital) quantum number; m_ℓ, the magnetic quantum number; and m_s, the electron spin quantum number. The specific values of each of these four quantum numbers completely describes the state of an electron in an atom.

The principal quantum number n plays a role in the quantum atom similar to that which n plays in the classical Bohr atom; in particular, it specifies the energy level or electron shell. The lowest energy state, or ground state, corresponds to n equal to 1.

The angular momentum quantum number ℓ is a measure of the angular momentum the electron carries. For any value of n, ℓ varies in integer steps from 0 to $n - 1$; each value of ℓ specifies a subshell, or electron orbital, within the energy level specified by n. The shape of each orbital is different. By convention, we refer to the orbitals with

Figure 26-17 Evidence of energy quantization As the voltage between the cathode and the mesh grid in the Franck-Hertz experiment increases, the anode current increases. When the kinetic energy of the accelerated electrons equals the energy required to excite an electron in a mercury atom to a higher energy level, accelerated electrons lose energy. Not as many electrons reach the anode at the corresponding cathode-grid voltages, so the anode current decreases.

(a)

(b)

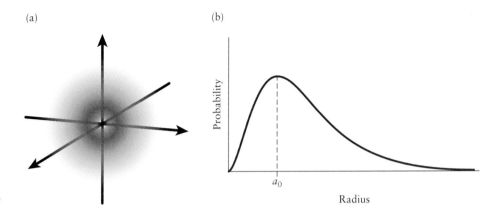

Figure 26-18 The Schrödinger picture of the hydrogen atom (a) In the state of lowest energy, an electron in a hydrogen atom can be found anywhere relative to the nucleus. The darker (denser) the color in a region of the probability cloud, the more likely it is that the electron will be found in that region. (b) The probability cloud in part (a) is spherically symmetric, so we can represent the probability of finding the electron as a function of radius from the center of the nucleus. The probability peaks at a distance from the nucleus equal to a_0, the Bohr radius.

letters rather than integer numbers; the values of ℓ equal to 0, 1, 2, 3, 4, and 5 correspond to the orbitals s, p, d, f, g, and h. It is also standard to refer to an electron subshell by giving both n and this orbital letter code together. For example, an electron in the p subshell of the $n = 2$ energy level is said to be in the $2p$ subshell. The electron's energy is slightly dependent on the value of ℓ, an effect called *fine structure* not found in the Bohr model.

The magnetic quantum number m_ℓ specifies an orientation of an electron's subshell. It is so called because its value determines the (very small) energy associated with the interaction of a moving charge—the electron—with the magnetic field of the nucleus. The larger the value of ℓ, the more orientations are allowed; m_ℓ can take integer values between $-\ell$ and $+\ell$, including 0. Figure 26-19 shows the shapes of a number of electron orbitals.

The fourth quantum number m_s involves a new feature of the electron that was not discovered until the 1920s. Electrons have an intrinsic characteristic called **spin**, which is akin to the angular momentum of a rotating sphere. Even electrons that do not orbit an atomic nucleus possess spin, which can take on one of two values, often called spin "up" and spin "down." To fully describe an atomic electron, then, we must also specify its spin state. This is described by the electron spin quantum number m_s, which for an electron can be equal to either $+1/2$ or $-1/2$.

These quantum numbers play an important role in multi-electron atoms. Each electron in a multi-electron atom has a specific value of n, ℓ, m_ℓ, and m_s. (The details of the

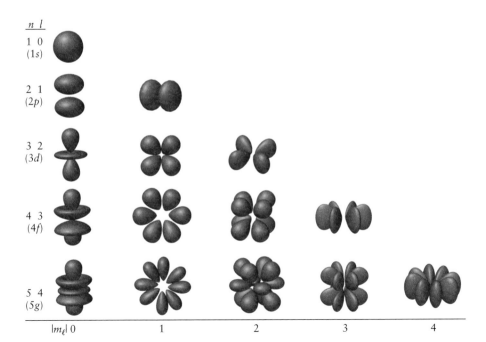

Figure 26-19 Probability clouds for different quantum numbers The probability cloud for each atomic orbital, specified by a specific value of the quantum numbers n, ℓ, and m_ℓ, has a different shape.

orbitals are affected by the presence of other electrons, but the same four quantum numbers still apply.) What is more, it turns out that there can be only *one* electron with a specific combination of these four quantum numbers. This fundamental restriction on electrons is called the **Pauli exclusion principle**, after the Swiss physicist Wolfgang Pauli who deduced this principle in 1925. (Pauli received the 1945 Nobel Prize in Physics for his work.) Let's see what the Pauli exclusion principle tells us about the structure of multi-electron atoms.

For the $n = 1$ shell, only one value of ℓ (equal to 0, which is the s orbital) and therefore only one value of m_ℓ, is allowed. Two values of m_s are always possible, so the maximum number of electrons that can occupy the $n = 1$ shell is $1 \times 2 = 2$, the product of the number of possible m_ℓ values and the number of possible m_s values. That is, two electrons can occupy the 1s orbital. For $n = 2$, ℓ is allowed to be either 0 or 1. When $\ell = 0$, the only possible value of the magnetic quantum number is $m_\ell = 0$. So including the factor of 2 for the electron spin quantum number, one possible value of m_ℓ and two possible values of m_s means two electrons can occupy the 2s orbital. However, when ℓ equals 1 (the p orbital), m_ℓ can be -1, 0, or $+1$. Including the factor of 2 for the electron spin quantum number, that means that the number of electrons that can occupy the 2p orbital is 3×2, or 6. Because two electrons can occupy the 2s orbital and six electrons can occupy the 2p orbital, an atom can have at most eight electrons in the $n = 2$ energy level.

The pattern above repeats for $n = 3$, up through ℓ equals 2, the d orbital. For this orbital, five values $(-2, -1, 0, +1, +2)$ are possible for m_ℓ, so the maximum number of electrons in this orbital is $5 \times 2 = 10$. Thus two electrons can occupy 3s, six can occupy 3p, and ten can occupy 3d. The maximum number of electrons in the $n = 3$ energy shell of an atom is therefore 18.

The arrangement of electrons, according to how many occupy which orbitals, is directly correlated to the chemical properties of the elements. Consider the 18 lightest elements and their electron configurations, listed in Table 26-1. (In the table, the number of electrons that occupy a particular orbital is given as a superscript, for example, $2p^4$ indicates that four electrons occupy the 2p orbital.) In hydrogen, lithium, and sodium (as well as potassium, rubidium, cesium, and francium), the outermost, or valence, electron is a single electron in an s orbital. These *alkali metals* share common chemical properties and occupy a single column in the periodic table.

Three of the *noble gases* are listed in Table 26-1. These are helium, neon, and argon; in each, the outermost subshell is completely full. As a result, all electrons are relatively tightly bound, so these elements do not easily gain, lose, or share electrons. For that reason, the noble gases are relatively inert. Helium, neon, and argon, as well as the other noble gases occupy a single column in the periodic table.

Halogens are elements that are highly reactive; that is, they easily form bonds with certain other elements, especially the alkali metals, to form molecules. Two halogens, fluorine and chlorine, are listed in Table 26-1. The outermost shell in both is one electron short of being full, which means that an atom of one of these elements can readily share an electron with another atom. This is particularly true for an atom of an alkali metal, which has one valence electron that is easily shared. So bring a sodium atom near a chlorine atom, and they will readily bond to form NaCl (table salt).

⚠ Watch Out! **As atomic number increases, electron orbitals do not fill in a continuous fashion.**

● The configuration of the 18 electrons of argon, the heaviest element listed in Table 26-1, is $1s^2 2s^2 2p^6 3s^2 3p^6$. The next heaviest element is potassium, for which the configuration of the 19 electrons is $1s^2 2s^2 2p^6 3s^2 3p^6 4s^1$. Notice that the additional electron does not occupy the 3d orbital, although d follows p in our ordering (s, p, d, f, and so on). Orbitals fill according to the increase in energy required, and for that reason, do not fill according to counting up linearly in ℓ (orbital letters) and m_ℓ. Instead, orbitals fill in this order: 1s, 2s, 2p, 3s, 3p, 4s, 3d, 4p, 5s, 4d, 5p, 6s, 4f, 5d, 6p, 7s, 5f, 6d, 7p. Notice that 4s and not 3d follows the 3p orbital in this sequence, which is why the valence electron in potassium is in a 4s orbital.

The ideas of quantum mechanics find applications on scales even smaller than that of the atom. In the final two chapters of this book we will see how quantum-mechanical ideas help us understand the nature of the atomic nucleus and of the fundamental particles that are the essential building blocks of all ordinary matter.

 Go to Interactive Exercise 26-2 for more practice dealing with atomic energy

Table 26-1 Electron Configurations of Light Elements

Atomic Number	Element	Electron Configuration
1	Hydrogen (H)	$1s^1$
2	Helium (He)	$1s^2$
3	Lithium (Li)	$1s^2 2s^1$
4	Beryllium (Be)	$1s^2 2s^2$
5	Boron (B)	$1s^2 2s^2 2p^1$
6	Carbon (C)	$1s^2 2s^2 2p^2$
7	Nitrogen (N)	$1s^2 2s^2 2p^3$
8	Oxygen (O)	$1s^2 2s^2 2p^4$
9	Fluorine (F)	$1s^2 2s^2 2p^5$
10	Neon (Ne)	$1s^2 2s^2 2p^6$
11	Sodium (Na)	$1s^2 2s^2 2p^6 3s^1$
12	Magnesium (Mg)	$1s^2 2s^2 2p^6 3s^2$
13	Aluminum (Al)	$1s^2 2s^2 2p^6 3s^2 3p^1$
14	Silicon (Si)	$1s^2 2s^2 2p^6 3s^2 3p^2$
15	Phosphorus (P)	$1s^2 2s^2 2p^6 3s^2 3p^3$
16	Sulfur (S)	$1s^2 2s^2 2p^6 3s^2 3p^4$
17	Chlorine (Cl)	$1s^2 2s^2 2p^6 3s^2 3p^5$
18	Argon (Ar)	$1s^2 2s^2 2p^6 3s^2 3p^6$

? Got the Concept? 26-5 Ionization Energy

The *ionization energy* of an atom is the energy required to remove an electron from the atom. In terms of the Bohr model, it is equal to the energy difference between the $n = 1$ energy level (the level of lowest energy, in which the electron is closest to the nucleus) and the $n = \infty$ energy level (which has an infinite radius, so the electron has moved infinitely far away). Compared to the ionization energy of hydrogen, the energy required to remove the last electron from doubly ionized lithium is (a) 3 times greater; (b) 9 times greater; (c) 27 times greater; (d) 81 times greater; (e) 243 times greater.

Take-Home Message for Section 26-6

✔ In the Bohr model of the atom, electrons follow Newtonian orbits around the nucleus but with quantized values of orbital angular momentum. As a result only certain orbital radii and orbital energies are allowed.

✔ The Franck-Hertz experiment confirmed that atomic energies are quantized.

✔ The Schrödinger equation explains the hydrogen atom by describing the electron as a wave. It predicts the probability of finding the electron at a particular location within the atom.

✔ The Pauli exclusion principle allows us to understand the structure of multi-electron atoms.

Key Terms

absorption lines
absorption spectrum
blackbody
blackbody radiation
Bohr model
Bohr orbit
Compton scattering

de Broglie wavelength
emission lines
emission spectrum
energy level
Pauli exclusion principle
photoelectric effect
photoelectrons

photon
quantized
quantum mechanics
quantum number
spin
wave-particle duality
work function

Chapter Summary

Topic	Equation or Figure

The photoelectric effect: When light shines on a surface, the surface can emit electrons. However, no electrons are emitted if the frequency of the light is below a certain critical value. Einstein showed that this could be explained if light is absorbed in the form of photons whose energy is proportional to their frequency: $E = hf$, where h is Planck's constant.

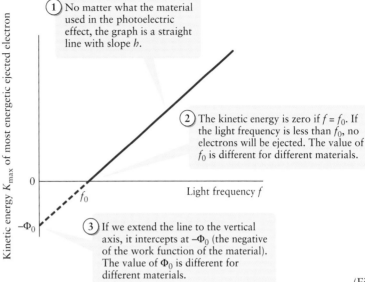

(Figure 26-3)

Blackbody radiation: Objects emit light due to their temperature. An ideal blackbody (one that does a perfect job of absorbing light) is also a perfect emitter of light. The details of the spectrum of a blackbody can be understood only if a blackbody emits light in the form of photons.

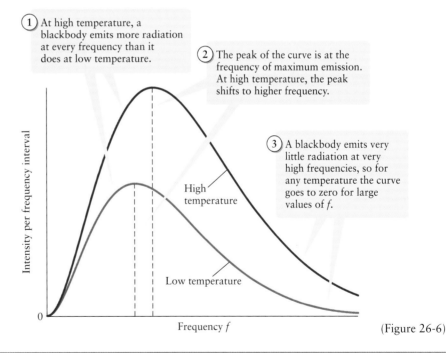

(Figure 26-6)

Compton scattering: Photons have momentum in inverse proportion to their wavelength. This is demonstrated by Compton scattering, in which a photon undergoes an increase in wavelength when it scatters from an electron.

$$p = \frac{E}{c} = \frac{h}{\lambda}$$

Magnitude of the momentum of a photon — Energy of the photon — Planck's constant — Speed of light in a vacuum — Wavelength of the photon

(26-7)

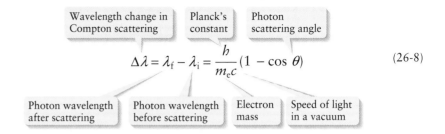

$$\Delta \lambda = \lambda_{\mathrm{f}} - \lambda_{\mathrm{i}} = \frac{h}{m_{\mathrm{e}} c} (1 - \cos \theta) \qquad (26\text{-}8)$$

Wavelength change in Compton scattering | Planck's constant | Photon scattering angle

Photon wavelength after scattering | Photon wavelength before scattering | Electron mass | Speed of light in a vacuum

---

Wave-particle duality: Just as photons have particle aspects, matter has wave aspects. The de Broglie wavelength of a particle is inversely proportional to the momentum (the same relationship between wavelength and momentum as for a photon).

A particle has a de Broglie wavelength... | ...equal to Planck's constant...

$$\lambda = \frac{h}{p} \qquad (26\text{-}10)$$

...divided by the momentum of the particle. The greater the momentum, the shorter the de Broglie wavelength.

Atomic structure and atomic spectra: Alpha particle scattering shows that the atom is made up of a small positive nucleus surrounded by electrons. The energy of an atom is quantized: It can have only certain definite values. The evidence for this comes from the spectra of atoms, which show that atoms absorb only specific wavelengths of light and that they emit the same wavelengths that they absorb.

(a) The absorption spectrum produced by passing white light through a gas of hydrogen atoms

The wavelengths at which hydrogen atoms absorb light are the same as the wavelengths at which hydrogen atoms emit light.

(b) The emission spectrum produced by a heated gas of hydrogen atoms

- Atoms of each element absorb and emit light at wavelengths that are characteristic of that element.
- The characteristic wavelengths differ from one element to another.
- Hydrogen has the simplest arrangement of characteristic wavelengths of any element.

(Figure 26-12)

The Bohr model of the atom: In the Bohr model of hydrogen, a single electron orbits the nucleus much like a satellite orbiting Earth. The difference is that the orbit can have only certain values of angular momentum, radius, and energy. Transitions between the allowed orbits are the cause of absorption and emission spectra.

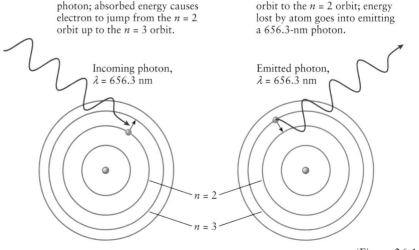

(a) Atom absorbs a 656.3-nm photon; absorbed energy causes electron to jump from the $n = 2$ orbit up to the $n = 3$ orbit.

Incoming photon, $\lambda = 656.3$ nm

(b) Electron falls from the $n = 3$ orbit to the $n = 2$ orbit; energy lost by atom goes into emitting a 656.3-nm photon.

Emitted photon, $\lambda = 656.3$ nm

$n = 2$

$n = 3$

(Figure 26-14)

The Schrödinger equation and the Pauli exclusion principle: In the more complete Schrödinger description of the atom, the electron is described by a wave. Four quantum numbers describe the state of the electron, and a probability cloud describes the probability of finding an electron at different positions within the atom. The Pauli exclusion principle states that there can be only one electron per state; this helps explain the properties of multi-electron atoms.

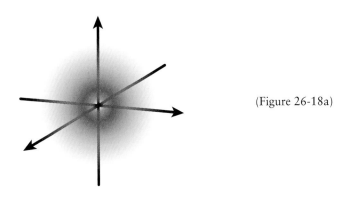

(Figure 26-18a)

Answer to What do you think? Question

(a) The spectrum of light from a star is very similar to the spectrum of an ideal blackbody (Section 26-2). Blue light has a higher frequency than red light, so the blue stars have a frequency of maximum emission (at which they emit most strongly) that is greater than that of the red stars. The frequency of maximum emission of a blackbody increases with increasing temperature, so the blue stars must be hotter than the red stars. To determine the chemical composition of the stars, the color of stars isn't enough information: We need to look at the absorption spectrum of the stars (Section 26-5). This can't be inferred from a photograph like the one that opens this chapter. In fact, it turns out that all of the stars in this image have almost the same chemical composition: predominantly hydrogen and helium, with trace amounts of other elements.

Answers to Got the Concept? Questions

26-1 (e) Figure 26-6 shows that the higher the temperature, the more light a blackbody of a given size emits at *all* frequencies. Note that both the 3000-K blackbody and the 12,000-K blackbody emit light at visible frequencies, not just the invisible frequencies at which they emit most strongly. That's why you can see radiation from these objects. The 3000-K blackbody emits more red light than any other visible color, so it will appear red; the 12,000-K blackbody emits more blue light than any other visible color, so it will appear blue.

26-2 (d) If $\theta = 90°$, then $\cos \theta = \cos 90° = 0$ and the wavelength shift in Compton scattering is $\Delta\lambda = (h/m_e c)(1 - \cos\theta) = (h/m_e c)(1 - 0) = h/m_e c = \lambda_C$. The initial wavelength is λ_C, so the final wavelength is $\lambda_f = \lambda_i + \Delta\lambda = \lambda_C + \lambda_C = 2\lambda_C$. That is, the final photon has twice the wavelength and so half the energy of the initial photon. (The lost energy is transferred to the electron from which the photon scattered.)

26-3 (c), (d), (a), (b) Equation 26-10 tells us that the de Broglie wavelength λ is inversely proportional to the momentum p: $\lambda = h/p$. So a ranking from longest to shortest de Broglie wavelength is the same as a ranking from smallest to largest momentum. A proton has mass 1.67×10^{-27} kg and an electron has mass 9.11×10^{-31} kg, so the momentum in each of the four cases is (a) $(1.67 \times 10^{-27} \text{ kg})(2.00 \times 10^3 \text{ m/s}) = 3.34 \times 10^{-24} \text{ kg} \cdot \text{m/s}$; (b) $(1.67 \times 10^{-27} \text{ kg})(4.00 \times 10^3 \text{ m/s}) = 6.68 \times 10^{-24} \text{ kg} \cdot \text{m/s}$; (c) $(9.11 \times 10^{-31} \text{ kg})(2.00 \times 10^3 \text{ m/s}) = 1.82 \times 10^{-27} \text{ kg} \cdot \text{m/s}$; (d) $(9.11 \times 10^{-31} \text{ kg})(4.00 \times 10^3 \text{ m/s}) =$ 3.64×10^{-27} kg·m/s. So the ranking is (c) slow-moving electron, (d) fast-moving electron, (a) slow-moving proton, (b) fast-moving proton.

26-4 (c), (a), (b), (d) The photon energy is equal to the difference between the energies of the upper energy level of the atom and the lower energy level of the atom. To determine the ranking, just look at Figure 26-15 to see the spacing between the energy levels of the atom. The spacing is (c) greatest between the $n = 3$ and $n = 1$ levels, (a) second greatest between the $n = 4$ and $n = 2$ levels, (b) third greatest between the $n = 5$ and $n = 3$ levels, and (d) least between the $n = 4$ and $n = 3$ levels.

26-5 (b) The ionization energy is equal to $E_{\text{ionization}} = E_\infty - E_1$. From Equation 26-27,

$$E_{\text{ionization}} = E_\infty - E_1 = \left(-\frac{Z^2}{\infty^2}E_0\right) - \left(-\frac{Z^2}{1^2}E_0\right)$$
$$= 0 - (-Z^2 E_0) = Z^2 E_0$$

(The reciprocal of infinity is zero.) A doubly ionized lithium ion is like a hydrogen atom—both have a single electron—but with $Z = 3$ instead of $Z = 1$ for hydrogen. Since the ionization energy is proportional to Z^2, the value for doubly ionized lithium is $3^2 = 9$ times greater than for hydrogen. You can see that for hydrogen $E_{\text{ionization}} = E_0 = 13.6$ eV, while for doubly ionized lithium $E_{\text{ionization}} = 9E_0 = 9(13.6 \text{ eV}) = 122$ eV.

Questions and Problems

In a few problems, you are given more data than you actually need; in a few other problems, you are required to supply data from your general knowledge, outside sources, or informed estimate. Interpret as significant all digits in numerical values that have trailing zeros and no decimal points.

For all problems, use $g = 9.80 \text{ m/s}^2$ for the free-fall acceleration due to gravity. Neglect friction and air resistance unless instructed to do otherwise.

* • Basic, single-concept problem
* •• Intermediate-level problem, may require synthesis of concepts and multiple steps
* ••• Challenging problem

SSM *Solution is in Student Solutions Manual*

Conceptual Questions

1. •Does the de Broglie wavelength of a particle increase or decrease as its kinetic energy increases?

2. •How does the intensity of light from a blackbody change when its temperature is increased? What changes occur in the body's radiation spectrum?

3. •According to classical electromagnetic theory, an accelerated charge emits electromagnetic radiation. What would this mean for the electron in the Bohr atom? What would happen to its orbit?

4. •Are there quantities in classical physics that are quantized?

5. •What is the shortest wavelength of electromagnetic radiation that can be emitted by a hydrogen atom? SSM

6. •Prior to Einstein's description of the photoelectric effect, light was thought to act like a wave. Explain why the existence of a frequency below which photoelectrons are not emitted favors a description of light as a particle instead.

7. •Describe how the number of photoelectrons emitted from a metal plate in the photoelectric effect would change if (a) the intensity of the incident radiation were increased, (b) the wavelength of the incident radiation were increased, and (c) the work function of the metal were increased.

8. •Is it possible to observe photoelectrons emitted from a metal plate with relativistic speeds?

9. •Consider the photoelectric emission of electrons induced by monochromatic incident light. The incoming photons all have the same energy, but the emitted electrons have a range of kinetic energies. Why?

10. •A markedly nonclassical feature of the photoelectric effect is the fact that the energy of the emitted electrons doesn't increase as you increase the intensity of the light striking the metal surface. What change does occur as the intensity is increased?

11. •The Compton effect is practically unobservable for visible light. Why?

12. •Which of the two Compton scattering experiments more clearly demonstrates the particle nature of electromagnetic radiation: a collision of the photon with an electron or a collision with a proton? Explain your answer.

13. •An electron and a proton have the same kinetic energy. Which has the longer wavelength? SSM

14. •Is the wavelength of an electron the same as the wavelength of a photon if both particles have the same total energy?

15. •Why do you think Bohr's model was originally designed for the element hydrogen?

16. •Why do you think that Bohr's model of the hydrogen atom is still taught in undergraduate physics classes?

17. •Why do we never observe the wave nature of particles for everyday objects such as birds or bumblebees, for example? SSM

Multiple-Choice Questions

18. •An element emits a spectrum that
    A. is the same as all other elements.
    B. is evenly spaced.
    C. is unique to that element.
    D. is evenly spaced and unique to that element.
    E. is indistinguishable from most other elements.

19. •An ideal blackbody is an object that
    A. absorbs most of the energy that strikes it and emits a little of the energy it generates.
    B. absorbs a little of the energy that strikes it and emits most of the energy it generates.
    C. absorbs half of the energy that strikes it and emits half of the energy it generates.
    D. absorbs all the energy that strikes it and emits all the energy it generates.
    E. neither absorbs nor emits energy except at ultraviolet ("black light") wavelengths.

20. •The color of light emitted by a hot object depends on
    A. the size of the object.
    B. the shape of the object.
    C. the material from which the object is made.
    D. the temperature of the object.
    E. the color of the object.

21. •Which photon has more energy?
    A. a photon of ultraviolet radiation.
    B. a photon of green light.
    C. a photon of yellow light.
    D. a photon of red light.
    E. a photon of infrared radiation. SSM

22. •Light that has a wavelength of 600 nm strikes a metal surface, and a stream of electrons is ejected from the surface. If light of wavelength 500 nm strikes the surface, the maximum kinetic energy of the electrons emitted from the surface will
    A. be greater.
    B. be smaller.
    C. be the same.
    D. be 5/6 smaller.
    E. be unmeasurable.

23. •In the Compton effect experiment, the change in a photon's wavelength depends on
    A. the scattering angle.
    B. the initial wavelength.
    C. the final wavelength.

D. the density of the scattering material.

E. the atomic number of the scattering material.

24. •The maximum change in a photon's energy when it undergoes Compton scattering occurs when its scatter angle is at

A. 0°.

B. 45°.

C. 90°.

D. 135°.

E. 180°.

25. •As the scattering angle in the Compton effect increases, the energy of the scattered photon

A. increases.

B. stays the same.

C. decreases.

D. decreases by sin θ.

E. increases by sin θ. SSM

26. •The de Broglie wavelength depends only on

A. the particle's mass.

B. the particle's speed.

C. the particle's energy.

D. the particle's momentum.

E. the particle's charge.

Estimation/Numerical Analysis

27. •Estimate the order of magnitude of atomic ionization energies. Compare this with the order of magnitude for the nuclear binding energy, which is in the megaelectron volt (MeV) range.

28. •What is the approximate size of an atom?

29. •Estimate the amount of blackbody energy radiated from your body. SSM

30. •On average, an electron will exist in any given state in the hydrogen atom for about 10^{-8} s before jumping to a lower level. Estimate the number of revolutions about the nucleus that an electron makes in 10^{-8} s.

31. •Estimate the size of the electrostatic forces that hold the atom together compared to the size of the force due to gravity.

32. •Estimate the ratio of the mass of the proton to the mass of the electron.

33. •Estimate the speed of an electron at which the de Broglie wavelength approximates the size of an atom. SSM

34. •In the early twentieth century, Max Planck used an empirical mathematical equation to describe the data that was collected in measuring blackbody radiation. Here's the formula he conceived:

$$\frac{\Delta I}{\Delta \lambda} = \frac{2\pi h c^2}{\lambda^5}\left(\frac{1}{e^{hc/(\lambda k_B T)} - 1}\right)$$

where I is the intensity of light emitted, λ is the wavelength of light emitted, h is Planck's constant (6.63×10^{-34} J · s), c is the speed of light (3.00×10^8 m/s), k is the Boltzmann constant (1.38×10^{-23} J/K), and T is the absolute temperature of the radiating cavity in kelvin. Create a spreadsheet that generates at least 15 values of $\Delta I/\Delta \lambda$ (choose a range of 15+ values of wavelength and calculate the value of the above function for $\Delta I/\Delta \lambda$ for some constant temperature). Once you have the set

of data, plot it in a graph and apply an appropriate curve fit to depict the unique shape of the curve. Now, change the temperature several times to see how the curve changes.

35. •Using Einstein's explanation of the photoelectric effect ($K = hf - \Phi_0$), derive a numerical value for Planck's constant (h) by plotting a graph of the following data.

Wavelength of light (nm)	Stopping potential (V)
400	1.60×10^{-19} J
450	1.06×10^{-19} J
500	6.09×10^{-20} J
550	2.00×10^{-20} J

Problems

26-1 Experiments that probe the nature of light and matter reveal the limits of classical physics

26-2 The photoelectric effect and blackbody radiation show that light is absorbed and emitted in the form of photons

36. ••Suppose a blackbody at 400 K radiates just enough heat in 15 min to boil water for a cup of tea. How long will it take to boil the same water if the temperature of the radiator is 500 K?

37. •Wien's displacement law states that the wavelength at which a blackbody emits the maximum power is given by the following formula:

$$\lambda_{\text{max}} = \frac{0.290 \text{ K} \cdot \text{cm}}{T}$$

At what wavelength (in nanometers) will a blackbody emit its highest value when its temperature is 400°C?

38. ••MIG (metal inert gas) welders can be approximated as blackbodies. At what wavelength will the peak radiation from such a welder be emitted if it operates at a temperature of 4000 K? Compare your answer to the wavelength for peak radiation from a TIG (tungsten inert gas) welder that operates at 6000 K. The peak wavelength is given by Wien's displacement law, shown in problem 37.

39. •An object that approximates a blackbody at a temperature of 300 K radiates heat into its immediate surroundings. Calculate the wavelength at which the maximum intensity per unit wavelength is emitted using Wien's displacement law (see problem 37). SSM

40. •Using Wien's displacement law (see problem 37), calculate the peak wavelength for blackbody radiation from (a) the polar ice cap at −40°C, (b) burning ethyl alcohol at 365 °C, and (c) deep space at 2.7 K.

41. •The Sun emits its maximum power at a wavelength of 475 nm. Using Wien's displacement law (see problem 37), determine the corresponding temperature of the outer layer of the Sun, assuming it is a blackbody.

42. •(a) If the human body acts like a blackbody, use Wien's displacement law (see problem 37) to calculate the wavelength of light for which the maximum amount of radiation is emitted. Assume an average skin temperature of 34°C. (b) In what part of the electromagnetic spectrum is the light?

43. •Calculate the range of photon frequencies and energies in the visible spectrum of light (approximately 380–750 nm). SSM

44. •What is the energy of a low-frequency 2000-Hz photon?

45. •What is the energy of a 0.200-nm photon?

46. •What are the wavelength and frequency of a 3.97×10^{-19}-J photon?

47. ••**Biology** Under most conditions, the human eye will respond to a flash of light if 100 photons hit photoreceptors at the back of the eye. Determine the total energy of such a flash if the wavelength is 550 nm (green light).

48. ••The threshold wavelength for the photoelectric effect for silver is 262 nm. (a) Determine the work function for silver. (b) What is the maximum kinetic energy of an emitted electron if the incident light has a wavelength of 222 nm?

49. ••Light that has a 195-nm wavelength strikes a metal surface, and photoelectrons are produced moving as fast as $0.004c$. (a) What is the work function of the metal? (b) What is the threshold wavelength for the metal above which no photoelectrons will be emitted? SSM

50. •What is the minimum frequency of light required to eject electrons from a metal with a work function of 6.53×10^{-19} J?

51. ••The work functions of aluminum, calcium, potassium, and cesium are 6.54×10^{-19} J, 4.65×10^{-19} J, 3.57×10^{-19} J, and 3.36×10^{-19} J, respectively. For which of the metals will photoelectrons be emitted when irradiated with visible light?

26-3 As a result of its photon character, light changes wavelength when it is scattered

52. ••The quantity $\lambda_C = h/(mc)$ is called the Compton wavelength. Calculate the numerical value of this quantity for (a) an electron, (b) a proton, and (c) a pi meson (which has a mass of 2.50×10^{-28} kg).

53. ••What is the momentum of a photon if the wavelength is (a) 550 nm and (b) 0.0711 nm? SSM

54. ••X rays that have wavelengths of 0.125 nm are scattered off free electrons at an angle of 30.0°. (a) Calculate the wavelength of the scattered electromagnetic radiation. (b) Calculate the *fractional wavelength change* $(\Delta\lambda/\lambda_i = (\lambda_f - \lambda_i)/\lambda_i)$ for the scattered X rays.

55. ••If a photon undergoes Compton scattering and experiences a fractional wavelength change of +7.25%, calculate the angle at which the scattered photons are directed if the original photons have a wavelength of 0.00335 nm.

56. ••Photons that have wavelengths of 0.00225 nm are Compton scattered at 45.0°. What is the energy of the scattered photons?

57. ••X ray photons that have wavelengths of 0.140 nm are scattered off carbon atoms (which possess essentially stationary electrons in their valence shells). What are the wavelengths of the Compton-scattered photons and the kinetic energies of the scattered electrons at angles of (a) 0.00°, (b) 30.0°, (c) 45.0°, (d) 60.0°, (e) 90.0°, and (f) 180°? SSM

58. ••A 0.0750-nm photon Compton scatters off a stationary electron. Determine the maximum speed of the scattered electron.

59. ••A photon Compton scatters off a stationary electron at an angle of 60.0°. The electron moves away with 1.28×10^{-17} J of kinetic energy. Determine the initial wavelength of the photon.

60. ••An X ray source is incident on a collection of stationary electrons. The electrons are scattered with a speed of 4.50×10^5 m/s, and the photon scatters at an angle of 60.0°

from the incident direction of the photons. Determine the wavelength of the X ray source.

61. ••Arthur Holly Compton scattered photons that had wavelengths of 0.0711 nm off a block of carbon during his famous experiment of 1923 at Washington University in St. Louis, Missouri. (a) Calculate the frequency and energy of the photons. (b) What is the wavelength of the photons that are scattered at 90.0°? (c) What is the energy of the photons that are scattered at 90.0°? (d) What is the energy of the electrons that recoil from the Compton scattering with $\theta = 90.0°$?

26-4 Matter, like light, has aspects of both waves and particles

62. •Calculate the de Broglie wavelength of a 0.150-kg ball moving at 40 m/s. Comment on the significance of the result.

63. •Calculate the de Broglie wavelength of an electron that has a speed of $0.00730c$. SSM

64. •What is the de Broglie wavelength of a proton ($m = 1.67 \times 10^{-27}$ kg) moving at 400,000 m/s?

65. ••Restate de Broglie's formula for particle waves in the case that the speeds are relativistic.

66. •A proton ($m = 1.67 \times 10^{-27}$ kg) has a de Broglie wavelength of 1.20×10^{-15} m. Calculate the speed of the proton. Be careful of any relativistic corrections that might apply!

67. ••What is the de Broglie wavelength of an electron that has a kinetic energy of (a) 1.60×10^{-19} J, (b) 1.60×10^{-18} J, (c) 1.60×10^{-17} J, (d) 1.60×10^{-16} J, (e) 1.60×10^{-13} J, and (f) 1.60×10^{-10} J? SSM

68. ••Calculate the de Broglie wavelength of an alpha particle ($m_\alpha = 6.64 \times 10^{-27}$ kg) that has a kinetic energy of (a) 1.60×10^{-13} J, (b) 8.00×10^{-13} J, and (c) 1.60×10^{-12} J.

69. •Calculate the de Broglie wavelength of a thermal neutron that has a kinetic energy of about 6.41×10^{-21} J.

70. •A relativistic electron has a de Broglie wavelength of 346 fm (1 fm = 10^{-15} m). Determine its velocity.

71. ••Write an expression that relates the Newtonian kinetic energy ($K = (1/2)mv^2$) and mass of a nonrelativistic particle to its de Broglie wavelength. (Complete the expression $\lambda(K, m) = ?$)

26-5 The spectra of light emitted and absorbed by atoms show that atomic energies are quantized

72. ••The Balmer formula can be written as follows:

$$\lambda = (364.56 \text{ nm})\left(\frac{m^2}{m^2 - 4}\right)$$

where m is equal to any integer larger than 2. This represents the wavelengths of visible colors that are emitted from the hydrogen atom. Calculate the first four colors (wavelengths) that are observed in the spectrum of hydrogen.

73. ••**Astronomy** The 21-cm line emitted by hydrogen in interstellar gas clouds is the spectral line that is produced when an electron in the ground state of hydrogen switches spin states. Determine the energy difference between the two spin states in this *hyperfine* transition. SSM

74. ••Prove that the Balmer formula is a special case of the Rydberg formula with n set equal to 2.

$$\text{Rydberg formula: } \frac{1}{\lambda} = R_H\left(\frac{1}{n^2} - \frac{1}{m^2}\right)$$

$$R_H = 1.09737 \times 10^7 \, \text{m}^{-1}$$

$$\text{Balmer formula: } \lambda = b\left(\frac{m^2}{m^2 - 4}\right) \quad b = 364.56 \, \text{nm}$$

75. ••A hypothetical atom has four unequally spaced energy levels in which a single electron can be found. Suppose a collection of the atoms is excited to the highest of the four levels. (a) What is the maximum number of unique spectral lines that could be measured as the atoms relax and return to the lowest, ground state? (b) Suppose the previous hypothetical atom has 10 energy levels. Now what is the maximum number of unique spectral lines that could be measured in the emission spectrum of the atom?

76. •The Lyman series results from transitions of the electron in hydrogen in which the electron ends at the $n = 1$ energy level. Using the Rydberg formula for the Lyman series, calculate the wavelengths of the photons emitted in the transitions from the energy states that correspond to n equal to 2 through 6, and indicate the initial and final state of the transition corresponding to each wavelength.

77. •The Balmer series results from transitions of the electron in hydrogen in which the electron ends at the $n = 2$ energy level. Using the Rydberg formula for the Balmer series, calculate the wavelengths of the photons emitted in the transitions from the energy states that correspond to n equal to 3 through 6, and indicate the initial and final state of the transition corresponding to each wavelength. SSM

78. •The Paschen series results from transitions of the electron in hydrogen in which the electron ends at the $n = 3$ energy level. Using the Rydberg formula for the Paschen series, calculate the wavelengths of the photons emitted in the transitions from the energy states that correspond to n equal to 4 through 6, and indicate the initial and final state of the transition corresponding to each wavelength.

79. ••Calculate the shortest wavelength (and the highest energy) associated with emitted photons in the (a) Lyman, (b) Balmer, and (c) Paschen series.

80. ••Express the Balmer formula (See problem 74) in terms of the *frequency* of the photons that are emitted (rather than the wavelength). Extend all numerical values out to five significant figures.

81. ••Express the Rydberg formula in terms of the *frequency* of the photons that are emitted (rather than the wavelength). Extend all numerical values out to five significant figures. SSM

26-6 Models by Bohr and Schrödinger give insight into the intriguing structure of the atom

82. •For an electron in the nth state of the hydrogen atom, write expressions for (a) the angular momentum of the electron, (b) the radius of the electron's orbit, (c) the kinetic energy of the electron, (d) the total energy of the electron, and (e) the speed of the electron.

83. ••Set up a chart for the five quantities listed in problem 82 and calculate the values for $n = 1, 2, 3, 4$, and 5 (4 significant figures, SI units). See the following table.

n	L_n	r_n	K_n	E_n	v_n
1					
2					
3					
4					
5					

84. ••Devise a straightforward method that allows you to calculate (a) the speed and (b) the angular momentum of an electron in the nth Bohr orbit. Your expressions should contain the number of the orbit, n, and constants.

85. ••Using the formula that you devised in problem 84, calculate the speed of an electron and the angular momentum of an electron in the tenth Bohr orbit. SSM

86. ••**Astronomy** Radio astronomers use radio frequency waves to identify the elements in distant stars. One of the standard lines that is often studied is designated the 272α line. This spectral line refers to the transition in hydrogen from $n_i = 273$ to $n_f = 272$. Calculate the wavelength and frequency of the electromagnetic radiation that is emitted for the 272α transition.

87. ••**Astronomy** For carbon ($Z = 6$), the frequencies of spectral lines resulting from a single electron transition are increased over those for hydrogen by the ratio of the Rydberg constants:

$$\frac{R_C}{R_H} = \frac{1 - m_e/m_C}{1 - m_e/m_H}$$

The mass of a hydrogen atom is 1837 times greater than the mass of the electron, and the mass of the carbon atom is 12 times greater than the mass of the hydrogen atom. Find the shift in frequency for the carbon 272α transition compared to the hydrogen 272α transition (see problem 86). Express your answer in megahertz (MHz).

88. ••The Lyman series ($n_f = 1$), the Balmer series ($n_f = 2$), and the Paschen series ($n_f = 3$) are commonly studied in basic chemistry and physics classes. The Brackett series ($n_f = 4$) and the Pfund series ($n_f = 5$) are not so well known. (a) Calculate the shortest and longest wavelengths for the spectral lines that are part of the Brackett series. (b) Calculate the shortest and longest wavelengths for the spectral lines that are part of the Pfund series.

89. •A hydrogen atom that has an electron in the $n = 2$ state absorbs a photon. (a) What wavelength must the photon possess to send the electron to the $n = 4$ state? (b) What possible wavelengths would be detected in the spectral lines that result from the deexcitation of the atom as it returns from $n = 4$ to the ground state? SSM

90. •How much energy is needed to ionize a hydrogen atom that starts in the Bohr orbit represented by $n = 3$? If an atom is ionized, its outer electron is no longer bound to the atom.

91. ••Derive the first 10 energy levels (sketch and label an energy-level diagram) for singly-ionized helium, He$^+$.

General Problems

92. ••**Biology** Vitamin D is produced in the skin when 7-dehydrocholesterol reacts with UVB rays (ultraviolet B) having wavelengths between 270 nm and 300 nm. What is the energy range of the UVB photons?

93. ••A typical HeNe laboratory laser produces light of wavelength 632.8 nm. The laser beam carries a power of 0.50 mW and strikes a target perpendicular to the beam. (a) How many photons per second strike the target? (b) At what rate does the laser beam deliver linear momentum to the target if the photons are all absorbed by the target?

94. ••**Astronomy** In 2009 astronomers detected gamma ray photons having energy ranging from 700 GeV to around 5 TeV coming from supernovae (exploding giant stars) in the galaxy M82. (a) What is the range of wavelengths of the gamma ray photons detected from M82? (b) Calculate the ratio of the energy of the 5 TeV photons to the energy of visible light having a wavelength of 500 nm.

95. •••Derive the Compton scattering formula for the change in wavelength between the scattered photon and the incident photon when they are exposed to a free electron, initially at rest.

96. ••A photon of frequency 4.81×10^{19} Hz scatters off a free stationary electron. Careful measurements reveal that the photon goes off at an angle of 125° with respect to its original direction. (a) How much energy does the electron gain during the collision? (b) What percent of its original energy does the photon lose during the collision?

97. ••**Chemistry** A laboratory oven that contains hydrogen molecules H_2 and oxygen molecules O_2 is maintained at a constant temperature. Each oxygen molecule is 16 times as massive as a hydrogen molecule. Find the ratio of the de Broglie wavelength of the hydrogen molecule to that of the oxygen molecule.

98. ••A hydrogen atom makes a transition from the $n = 5$ state to the ground state and emits a single photon of light in the process. The photon then strikes a piece of silicon, which has a photoelectric work function of 4.8 eV. Is it possible that a photoelectron will be emitted from the silicon? If not, why not? If so, find the maximum possible kinetic energy of the photoelectron.

99. ••Suppose the electron in the hydrogen atom were bound to the proton by gravitational forces (rather than electrostatic forces). Find (a) the radius and (b) the energy of the first orbit.

100. ••**Biology** The *E. coli* bacterium is about 2.0 μm long. Suppose you want to study it using photons of that wavelength or electrons having that de Broglie wavelength. (a) What is the energy of the photon and the energy of the electron? (b) Which one would be better to use, the photon or the electron? Explain why.

101. •••Use the de Broglie wave concept to fit circular standing waves into the orbits of the Bohr model of the hydrogen atom to prove Bohr's hypothesis of the quantization of angular momentum. Assume that in the first Bohr orbit, exactly one de Broglie wavelength matches up with the circumference, in the second orbit, two waves match up, in the third orbit, three waves match up, and so on (Figure 26-20).

$n = 2$ $n = 3$ $n = 4$ $n = 5$

Figure 26-20 Problem 101

27

Nuclear Physics

In this chapter, your goals are to:
- (27-1) Explain why quantum ideas play an important role in nuclear physics.
- (27-2) Describe how we know that the force that holds the nucleus together is both strong and of short range.
- (27-3) Explain how and why the binding energy per nucleon in a nucleus depends on the size of the nucleus.
- (27-4) Calculate the energy released in nuclear fission.
- (27-5) Describe why very high temperatures are needed for nuclear fusion reactions.
- (27-6) Calculate what happens in the decay of a radioactive substance.

To master this chapter, you should review:
- (3-8) Uniform circular motion.
- (11-2) How to calculate the density of an object.
- (22-4) The energy of a photon.
- (25-7) The equivalence of mass and energy.
- (26-5) How an atom in an excited energy level emits a photon when the atom decays to a lower energy level.
- (26-6) The spin of an electron.

What do you think?

This remarkable painting on a wall in the Chauvet-Pont-d'Arc Cave in southern France is known to be 30,000 to 33,000 years old. This age is determined from the radioactive decay of carbon-14 (a type of carbon with 6 protons and 8 neutrons in its nucleus), which has a half-life of 5730 years. Of the carbon-14 that was present when this painting was made, the fraction that remains today is somewhat less than (a) half; (b) 1/4; (c) 1/8; (d) 1/16; (e) 1/32.

27-1 The quantum concepts that help explain atoms are essential for understanding the nucleus

We learned in Chapter 26 that a handful of radical ideas—the notion that energy is quantized, that electromagnetic waves come in packets called photons, and that the laws of quantum mechanics can specify only the probabilities that particles will behave in certain ways—are essential for understanding the nature and behavior of the atom. These same ideas apply on the even smaller scale of the atomic nucleus.

In this chapter we'll learn that unlike the atom, in which negatively charged electrons are bound to the positively charged nucleus by the attractive electric force, nuclei are bound by a *strong nuclear force* that keeps the protons and neutrons bound together. We'll also see that like atoms, nuclei have an intrinsic angular momentum or *spin*; magnetic resonance imaging, or MRI, makes use of how nuclear spins respond to an external magnetic field (**Figure 27-1a**). The interplay between the strong nuclear force and the electric force (which makes all of the protons in a nucleus try to repel each other) means

1109

Figure 27-1 **Applications of nuclear physics** The properties of atomic nuclei explain (a) how magnetic resonance imaging (MRI) works, (b) how the Sun provides energy for life on Earth, and (c) how Earth sustains its internal energy.

When placed in a strong magnetic field, the nuclei of hydrogen atoms will orient their spins with the field. This effect is at the heart of the diagnostic technique called magnetic resonance imaging.

Photosynthesis in plants depends on energy from sunlight. This energy is released by nuclear reactions that take place in the core of the Sun.

More than 50% of the energy that powers our planet's geological activity, including volcanic eruptions, comes from the radioactive decay of unstable nuclei in Earth's interior.

(a)

(b)

(c)

that nuclei of different sizes are more tightly or loosely bound. We'll see that as a result, the largest nuclei are prone to break into smaller fragments through a process called *fission*. We'll also learn that the smallest nuclei can release energy by *fusion*, in which two nuclei join together to form a larger one. Fusion reactions make the Sun shine, and the sunlight that they produce makes life on Earth possible (Figure 27-1b).

Understanding the binding energies of nuclei will also help us understand the three main types of radioactive decay: alpha, beta, and gamma. The energy released by alpha and beta decays in our planet's interior helps power geologic activity such as volcanic eruptions (Figure 27-1c). We'll find that the concept of *half-life* will help us understand the nature of radioactive decays of all kinds.

Take-Home Message for Section 27-1

✔ Many of the same concepts that help us understand atomic physics are also important in nuclear physics.

✔ The balance between the strong nuclear force and the electric force determines the stability of nuclei.

27-2 The strong nuclear force holds nuclei together

As we learned in Chapter 26, an atom has a small, positively charged nucleus at its center. There are two ways you can see that the nucleus must be positively charged. First, because atoms are neutral, positive charge is required to balance the negative charge of the electrons. Second, the Coulomb attraction between the nucleus and the negatively charged electrons provides the force that holds the atom together.

The *repulsive* Coulomb forces between the protons, however, must be large because they are close together inside the nucleus. To see just how large these forces are, note that a typical radius of a nucleus is about 5 fm (1 fm = 1 femtometer = 10^{-15} m). The electric force between two protons (each of charge $+e = 1.60 \times 10^{-19}$ C) separated by a distance $r = 5.00$ fm is

$$F = \frac{k(+e)(+e)}{r^2} = \frac{(8.99 \times 10^9 \text{ N} \cdot \text{m}^2/\text{C}^2)(1.60 \times 10^{-19}\text{C})^2}{(5.00 \times 10^{-15}\text{m})^2}$$
$$= 9.21 \text{N}$$

This may not seem like a lot of force, but remember that this force is applied to a proton, which has a mass of only 1.67×10^{-27} kg. If the electric force were the only force acting on the protons in a nucleus, the nucleus would simply fly apart.

What's more, nuclei also have neutrons, the neutrally charged particle we mentioned briefly in Chapter 16. Neutrons and protons share many similar properties, including similar masses: The masses of the neutron and proton are 1.6749×10^{-27} kg and 1.6726×10^{-27} kg, respectively. Collectively, we refer to protons and neutrons as **nucleons**. Neutrons do not feel the electric force at all, so this force can't be responsible for keeping neutrons within the nucleus.

We conclude that there must be an additional *attractive* force that acts on all nucleons (both protons and neutrons) and that binds them together in the nucleus. This attractive force must be stronger than the repulsive electric force between protons, so we call it the **strong nuclear force**. To explain the properties of the nucleus, it must be that over short distances the strong nuclear force is hundreds of times stronger than the electrostatic force.

If the nuclear force is so strong compared to the electrostatic force, and if protons attract other protons by this force, why are neutrons necessary to help overcome the Coulomb repulsion between protons? The answer lies in the *range* of the strong nuclear force, which is the distance beyond which one nucleon no longer experiences a force due to another. Experiments show that the strong nuclear force diminishes rapidly as the separation between two nucleons increases, and has a range of about 2.0 fm. The radius of a proton or neutron is about 0.85 fm, so two nucleons must almost be touching to experience the strong nuclear force. By contrast, the electrostatic repulsion between protons separated by a distance r is proportional to $1/r^2$, and so is present even if the distance r is very large. We say that the strong nuclear force is a *short-range* force, whereas the electric force is a *long-range* force. As a very rough analogy, you can think of protons and neutrons as tiny spheres coated with very strong Velcro, which makes the nucleons stick together if they are brought close enough to each other.

Because the range of the nuclear force is smaller than the diameter of most nuclei (a few to perhaps 15 fm), each nucleon exerts an attractive nuclear force only on its nearest neighbors. Each proton in a nucleus, however, exerts a repulsive force on *every other* proton. As a result, the nuclear force between neighboring protons cannot overcome the Coulomb repulsion between all of the protons. To prevent a nucleus from spontaneously breaking apart (that is, for it to be *stable*), the nucleus must have about as many neutrons as protons or more (for larger nuclei). An unstable nucleus will eventually undergo a spontaneous transformation, termed a *decay*, in which it either splits apart or gives off energy in some other way. In addition, atoms that have more than about 20 protons require more neutrons than protons to be stable. Figure 27-2 shows the number of neutrons versus the number of protons in known, stable atomic nuclei. Notice that as the number of protons increases, more additional neutrons are required for stability.

Nuclides, Isotopes, and Nuclear Sizes

Atoms of each element have a unique number of protons and the same number of electrons: Hydrogen has one, helium two, lithium three, and so on. Many properties of atoms are related to this number, usually designated as the **atomic number** Z. In a similar way, many properties of nuclei arise from the **neutron number** N, that is, the number of neutrons in the nucleus. Although the value of Z of an elemental species is fixed (changing the number of protons changes the element), the value of N is not fixed for each element. Each combination of N and Z specifies a **nuclide**. For each element, the most common configuration of N and Z corresponds to the most stable nuclide; nuclei of that elemental species with a different number of neutrons are termed **isotopes**. For example, potassium has 19 protons (and 19 electrons). The most stable and most common nuclide of potassium has 20 neutrons, $N = 20$. We denote this nuclide with the symbol ^{39}K. The number of protons ($Z = 19$) is understood from the symbol K for potassium, and the total number of protons and neutrons, termed the **mass number** A, is given in the pre-superscript, 39. This potassium nuclide can also be referred to as potassium-39. Note that the mass number of any nucleus equals the atomic number plus the neutron number: $A = Z + N$.

More than 93% of all potassium atoms have a ^{39}K nucleus. About 7% of potassium atoms have a ^{41}K nucleus, however. These atoms contain 19 electrons orbiting a nucleus with 19 protons and 22 neutrons. We say that ^{39}K and ^{41}K are two isotopes of potassium.

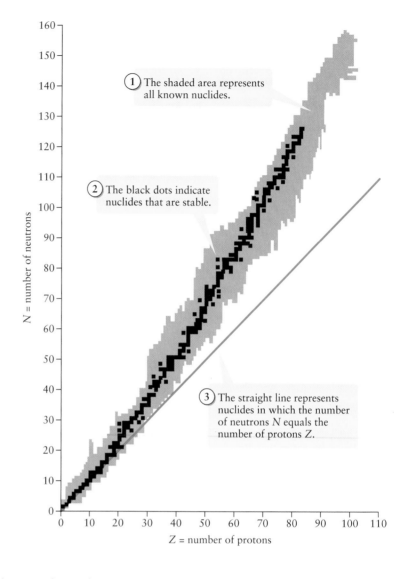

For most nuclides, more neutrons than protons must be present (N must be greater than Z) to prevent the protons from flying apart due to electrostatic repulsion.

The *size* of a nucleus (its radius and volume) is related to the mass number A. Experiments show that all nuclei are approximately spherical and have radii proportional to the cube root of A, or $A^{1/3}$:

Radius of a nucleus (27-1)

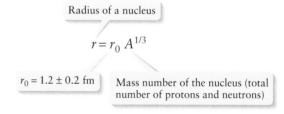

$$r = r_0 A^{1/3}$$

This equation states that if we increase the number of nucleons in a nucleus by a factor of 10, say from $A = 20$ to $A = 200$, the radius of the nucleus will increase by a factor of $10^{1/3} = 2.2$ (Figure 27-3).

The volume of a sphere is proportional to r^3 and therefore proportional to $(A^{1/3})^3$, so the volume of a nucleus is directly proportional to the mass number A. In other words, the volume of a nucleus is proportional to the number of nucleons within that nucleus. This is consistent with our model of nucleons as spheres covered with Velcro. In this model, increasing the number of nucleons by a factor of 10 would result in a ball of nucleons (that is, a nucleus) with 10 times the volume. Because the attractive force is short-range, there is no tendency for the nucleons to be compressed together as the size of the nucleus increases. This is very different from planets, which are held together by the long-range gravitational force of attraction between all of the parts of the planet.

As an example, compare the planets Jupiter and Saturn (which have the same chemical composition): Jupiter has 3.3 times more mass than Saturn, but Jupiter has only 1.7 times greater volume because it is more highly compressed and has a greater density. Nuclei of different sizes do not behave like planets of different sizes: All nuclei have basically the same density (see Example 27-2 below). This is further evidence that the strong nuclear force is short-range rather than long-range.

Can we simply add more protons and more neutrons to make larger and larger nuclei? The answer is "no," and for the same reason that neutrons are required for nuclear stability. We have seen that as we work our way up the periodic table to atoms that have more and more protons, more *additional* neutrons are required for stability. Each additional proton exerts a repulsive force on all the others, but neutrons and protons can only attract their nearest neighbors. Those additional neutrons cause the size of the nucleus to grow, so that eventually, too many neutrons are near the surface of the nucleus and therefore not completely surrounded by neighbors. At that point, the nuclear forces holding the nucleus together are not large enough to overcome the Coulomb repulsion between the protons and the nucleus cannot be stable. The largest stable nuclide is lead-208 (^{208}Pb), which has 82 protons and 126 neutrons.

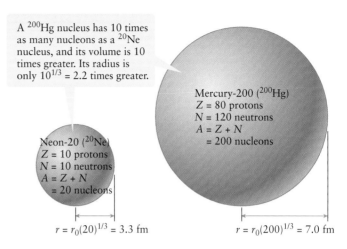

A ^{200}Hg nucleus has 10 times as many nucleons as a ^{20}Ne nucleus, and its volume is 10 times greater. Its radius is only $10^{1/3}$ = 2.2 times greater.

Mercury-200 (^{200}Hg)
Z = 80 protons
N = 120 neutrons
A = Z + N
= 200 nucleons

Neon-20 (^{20}Ne)
Z = 10 protons
N = 10 neutrons
A = Z + N
= 20 nucleons

$r = r_0(20)^{1/3}$ = 3.3 fm $r = r_0(200)^{1/3}$ = 7.0 fm

Figure 27-3 **Nuclear sizes** The volume of an atomic nucleus is proportional to the number of nucleons it contains (the mass number A). The nuclear radius is proportional to the cube root of A.

Example 27-1 Nuclear Radii

Estimate the radius of the nucleus of ^{12}C, a relatively small nucleus; ^{118}Sn, a nucleus of medium size; and ^{236}U, a relatively large nucleus. The nuclides ^{12}C and ^{118}Sn are stable; ^{236}U, like all other isotopes of uranium, is unstable.

Set Up
In each case, we use Equation 27-1 to calculate the radius of the nucleus. The value of A for each nucleus is given by the pre-superscript: A = 12 for the carbon (C) nucleus, A = 118 for the tin (Sn) nucleus, and A = 236 for the uranium (U) nucleus.

Radius of a nucleus:

$$r = r_0 A^{1/3} \qquad (27\text{-}1)$$

Solve
Apply Equation 27-1 to each nuclide.

We'll use $r_0 = 1.2$ fm in our calculations.
For ^{12}C, which has 6 protons and 6 neutrons,

$$r(^{12}\text{C}) = (1.2 \text{ fm})(12)^{1/3} = 2.7 \text{ fm}$$

For ^{118}Sn, which has 50 protons and 68 neutrons,

$$r(^{118}\text{Sn}) = (1.2 \text{ fm})(118)^{1/3} = 5.9 \text{ fm}$$

For ^{236}U, which has 92 protons and 144 neutrons,

$$r(^{236}\text{U}) = (1.2 \text{ fm})(236)^{1/3} = 7.4 \text{ fm}$$

Reflect
This calculation shows that typical nuclei have radii of just a few femtometers. Although ^{236}U has $236/12 = 19.7$ times as many nucleons as ^{12}C, it is only larger in radius by a factor of $(7.4 \text{ fm})/(2.7 \text{ fm}) = 2.7$. That's a consequence of the $A^{1/3}$ factor in Equation 27-1: Note that $(19.7)^{1/3} = 2.7$.

Notice that in carbon, the smallest of the three nuclei, the number of neutrons equals the number of protons. In tin, which has almost 10 times the mass number of carbon, the number of neutrons required for nuclear stability is 36% higher than the number of protons. And even with nearly 60% more neutrons than protons, the relatively large ^{236}U nucleus is not stable. So we see direct evidence that more and more additional neutrons, compared to the number of protons, are required for nuclear stability, and that at some size a nucleus is too large for the strong nuclear force to overcome the Coulomb repulsion between the protons.

Example 27-2 Nuclear Density

Estimate the density (in kg/m^3) of a nucleus that has mass number A.

Set Up

The density of an object is its mass m divided by its volume V. We'll find the volume of a nucleus from Equation 27-1 and the formula for the volume of a sphere. To estimate the mass of a nucleus, we'll multiply the mass number A (the number of nucleons) by the average mass of a nucleon.

Radius of a nucleus:

$$r = r_0 A^{1/3} \qquad (27\text{-}1)$$

Definition of density:

$$\rho = \frac{m}{V} \qquad (11\text{-}1)$$

Volume of a sphere of radius r:

$$V = \frac{4}{3}\pi r^3$$

mass $m = A \times$ (average mass of a nucleon)
radius $r = r_0 A^{1/3}$
volume $V = (4/3)\pi r^3$
density $\rho = m/V$

Solve

Find the volume of a nucleus of mass number A.

Substitute Equation 27-1 into the expression for the volume of a sphere of radius r:

$$V = \frac{4}{3}\pi r^3 = \frac{4}{3}\pi (r_0 A^{1/3})^3 = \frac{4}{3}\pi r_0^3 (A^{1/3})^3$$

$$= \frac{4}{3}\pi r_0^3 A$$

Use $r_0 = 1.2$ fm $= 1.2 \times 10^{-15}$ m as in Example 27-1:

$$V = \frac{4}{3}\pi (1.2 \times 10^{-15}\text{m})^3 A$$

$$= (7.2 \times 10^{-45}\text{m}^3)A$$

Take the average mass of a nucleon to be the average of the proton mass m_p and the neutron mass m_n. Use this to write an expression for the mass of a nucleus of mass number A.

The average mass of a nucleon is

$$m_{avg} = \frac{m_p + m_n}{2} = \frac{(1.6726 \times 10^{-27}\text{ kg}) + (1.6749 \times 10^{-27}\text{ kg})}{2}$$

$$= 1.6738 \times 10^{-27}\text{ kg}$$

A nucleus with A nucleons then has mass

$$m = m_{avg}A = (1.6738 \times 10^{-27}\text{ kg})A$$

Calculate the density of the nucleus.

The density of the nucleus is

$$\rho = \frac{m}{V} = \frac{(1.6738 \times 10^{-27}\text{ kg})A}{(7.2 \times 10^{-45}\text{m}^3)A} = \frac{1.6738 \times 10^{-27}\text{ kg}}{7.2 \times 10^{-45}\text{m}^3}$$

$$= 2.3 \times 10^{17}\text{ kg/m}^3$$

Reflect

Our final expression for the density ρ does not depend on A, the mass number of the nucleus. So the density of atoms of *all* nuclei is about the same. This agrees with our statements about the short-range character of the strong nuclear force. Note also that iridium, the densest of all stable elements, has a density of 22,650 kg/m^3 (22.65 times the density of water). Our calculation shows that nuclei are 10^{13} times denser than iridium. Nuclei are *extremely* dense! This makes sense: Most of the mass of an atom is concentrated in its nucleus, which has a far smaller volume than the atom as a whole. So nuclear density (mass divided by volume) must be far greater than what we think of as the "ordinary" density of matter such as water.

Nuclear Spin and Magnetic Resonance Imaging

We learned in Section 26-6 that electrons have a type of intrinsic angular momentum called *spin*. (This is something of a misnomer because this angular momentum does not correspond directly to a spinning motion of the electrons.) Protons, and neutrons, too, have spin, and like an electron the spin of a proton or neutron can take on one of two values, often referred to as "spin up" and "spin down." In nuclei with an even number of nucleons, typically there are as many "spin up" nucleons as there are "spin down," and most such nuclei have zero net spin. (The orbital angular momentum of nucleons moving inside the nucleus can also contribute to the net spin of the nucleus.) But a nucleus with an odd number of nucleons must have a nonzero net spin. In particular, the nucleus of hydrogen—a single proton—has a net spin.

Measurements that make use of the spin of hydrogen nuclei enable us to localize hydrogen in an object or body, as well as to get information about the material in which those hydrogen atoms are embedded. That's the principle of **magnetic resonance imaging** (MRI). In an MRI scanner, spin information is used to form a three-dimensional map of the density of hydrogen atoms in a body. Because living organisms are composed largely of water—our bodies, for example, are 60 to 70% water—and because each water molecule contains two hydrogen atoms, living organisms are packed full of protons. As such, MRI is an ideal way to probe the internal structures in the body. The MRI scan in Figure 27-4 shows the leg bones rubbing against each other in the knee of a person with osteoarthritis. Figure 27-1a shows an MRI scan of a patient's head.

Protons and neutrons also have associated magnetic fields. This field is related to the spin, so because spin is either up or down, the field is a dipole in nature. Like a bar magnet, this magnetic field has a direction, and that direction is parallel to the direction of the angular momentum vector. As a result, when a nucleus that has an odd number of nucleons A is placed in a uniform external magnetic field, the magnetic force tends to align the spin direction either generally parallel to or antiparallel to the external field. To be precise, the spin direction aligns so that its component along the direction of the external field has a fixed positive or negative value. As such, the spin direction can rotate, or *precess*, around an axis defined by the field direction. Figure 27-5a shows this precession for a nucleus with spin aligned with the external field, and Figure 27-5b shows this precession for a nucleus with spin anti-aligned with (that is, opposed to) the external field.

Consider a large number of hydrogen atoms placed in a uniform magnetic field. About half of the protons will end up with spin aligned with the field and half with spin anti-aligned. Now, the energy of the spin-aligned orientation of a nucleus in an external magnetic field (Figure 27-5a) is higher than the energy of the anti-aligned orientation (Figure 27-5b) by an amount ΔE that depends on the magnetic field

Figure 27-4 **A magnetic resonance image** The red arrows in this MRI image indicate where bones rub together in the knee of a patient suffering from osteoarthritis.

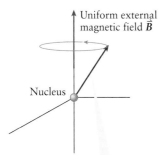

(a) A nucleus with its spin aligned with an external magnetic field

Uniform external magnetic field $\vec{B}$

Nucleus

The spin angular momentum vector of the nucleus traces out a cone, but is generally aligned in the same direction as $\vec{B}$.

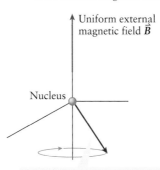

(b) A nucleus with its spin opposed to an external magnetic field

Uniform external magnetic field $\vec{B}$

Nucleus

The spin angular momentum vector of the nucleus traces out a cone, but is generally aligned in the direction opposite to $\vec{B}$.

Figure 27-5 **Nuclear spin** When a nucleus is placed in an external magnetic field, the component of the spin along the direction of the external field is either (a) aligned with the external field or (b) anti-aligned with the external field.

strength. Suppose we now bathe the atoms in an additional alternating magnetic field with frequency f. The alternating field is made up of photons of frequency f and energy hf, where h is Planck's constant (see Section 26-2). If we choose the frequency f so that hf is equal to ΔE, that means the photon energy is just equal to the energy difference between the two spin states. As a result, protons that are initially in the lower energy state, with their spin anti-aligned with the field, can absorb a photon of energy $\Delta E = hf$ and flip their spin to align with the external field. What is more, protons that are initially in the higher energy state, with their spin aligned with the field, can be stimulated by the alternating field to emit a photon of energy $\Delta E = hf$ and so flip their spin to the lower energy, anti-aligned state. (We discussed this process of *stimulated emission* in Section 26-5.)

The difference in energy between the two spin states of a hydrogen atom depends on the strength of the external field. With the high field strength required to be able to clearly observe the spin-flipping phenomenon, typically around 3 T, the energy difference ΔE is about 5×10^{-7} eV. From Equation 22-26, the frequency of a photon of this energy is

$$f = \frac{\Delta E}{h} = \frac{5 \times 10^{-7} \text{ eV}}{4.14 \times 10^{-15} \text{ eV} \cdot \text{s}} = 1.2 \times 10^8 \text{ s}^{-1} = 120 \text{ MHz}$$

(We used the value of h in eV · s.) So the frequency of the oscillating field used to induce the hydrogen atoms to flip their spins in a strong magnetic field is around 100 MHz, which is in the radio-frequency part of the electromagnetic spectrum.

How do we "see" this spin flipping and so form an image of the location of hydrogen? Initially, there will always be more atoms in the lower energy state than the higher energy state (lower energy is more likely for a system than higher energy), so when the hydrogen atoms in an external magnetic field are exposed to radio-frequency waves, there is a net absorption of the electromagnetic energy. When the radio-frequency signal is turned off, the spins begin to return to their initial (equilibrium) state, and in so doing they generate a radio-frequency field. The MRI device detects that radio-frequency field and uses it to form a map of the density of hydrogen atoms in the body.

As we have mentioned, the difference in energy ΔE between the two hydrogen spin states depends on the strength of the external magnetic field. In an MRI device, the magnetic field is made to vary over a body's volume, so that the energy absorbed and then re-emitted in the spin-flip process also varies in different parts of the body. The exact frequencies of the radio energy detected by the MRI device therefore provide the information necessary to create images of high spatial resolution. In addition, the time it takes for the spins of the hydrogen nuclei to return to their equilibrium state depends on the particular molecules in the tissue. So, timing information in an MRI device provides the means to differentiate one type of tissue from another.

? Got the Concept? 27-1 Nuclear Radius and Density

A ^{20}Ne nucleus has 10 protons and 10 neutrons for a total of 20 nucleons, and a ^{160}Dy nucleus has 66 protons and 94 neutrons for a total of 160 nucleons. Compared to a ^{20}Ne nucleus, a ^{160}Dy nucleus has (a) double the radius and a greater density; (b) 8 times the radius and a greater density; (c) double the radius and the same density; (d) 8 times the radius and the same density; (e) double the radius and a lower density.

Take-Home Message for Section 27-2

✔ The strong nuclear force binds nucleons (protons and neutrons) together in the nucleus of an atom.

✔ The volume of a nucleus is proportional to its mass number (the total number of nucleons in the nucleus).

✔ To be stable, a light nucleus must have about as many neutrons as protons. More massive nuclei with more than about 20 protons require more neutrons than protons to be stable. Very large nuclei with mass number greater than 208 are always unstable.

✔ Protons and neutrons have spin. Magnetic resonance imaging uses the difference in energy between a state in which a nuclear spin is aligned with an external magnetic field and the state in which the spin is anti-aligned with the field.

27-3 Some nuclei are more tightly bound and more stable than others

Release a ball at the top of a hill and it rolls down. Pull an object attached to the free end of a spring away from its equilibrium position and it tends to return to that position. In both cases, the systems are finding their way to a more stable configuration. All physical systems do the same; if a more stable configuration exists for a system, it will eventually find itself in that configuration as long as nature provides a mechanism for the transition to take place.

In this context, consider the nucleus of a helium atom, which consists of two protons and two neutrons. The four nucleons remain bound together in a configuration that must be more stable than when they are separate, otherwise the helium nucleus would end up broken apart. This stability results because the attraction of the strong nuclear force between the four nucleons overwhelms the electrostatic repulsive force between the two protons. But let's look at stability from another perspective.

The total mass M_{tot} of the two protons and two neutrons in the nucleus of ^{4}He equals the sum of two proton masses (m_p) and two neutron masses (m_n):

$$M_{tot} = 2m_p + 2m_n$$
$$= 2(1.6726 \times 10^{-27} \text{ kg}) + 2(1.6749 \times 10^{-27} \text{ kg}) = 6.695 \times 10^{-27} \text{ kg}$$

But the actual mass of a helium nucleus is 6.645×10^{-27} kg, which is *less* than the total mass of the two protons and two neutrons. How is this possible? The answer is the key to nuclear stability; the energy equivalent of the difference in mass is tied up in binding the nucleons together. Recall from Section 25-7 that energy and mass are equivalent: An object of mass m has a rest energy $E_0 = mc^2$ (Equation 25-21). Since a ^{4}He nucleus has a smaller mass than its constituent nucleons, it also has a smaller rest energy. The difference between the rest energy of the ^{4}He nucleus and the rest energy of its constituent nucleons is the **binding energy** E_B. You can think of this as the energy that is released when the four nucleons come together to form a ^{4}He nucleus. Alternatively, you can think of the binding energy as the energy that would be required to separate a ^{4}He nucleus into two protons and two neutrons. The greater the binding energy per nucleon in a nucleus, the more tightly the nucleus is bound and therefore the more stable it is.

Figure 27-6 is a graph of the binding energy per nucleon (E_B/A) as a function of mass number. The energy values on the vertical axis are given in MeV, where 1 MeV = 10^6 eV. As we have learned before, one eV, or one electron volt, is the amount of energy acquired by an electron when it experiences a potential difference of one volt: 1 eV = 1.60×10^{-19} J. Figure 27-6 shows that the value of E_B/A for all nuclides is in the range from 1 to 9 MeV, which is why these units are convenient. (By comparison, the binding energy of a hydrogen *atom*—the energy required to separate the single electron in a hydrogen atom from the proton—is 13.6 eV, about 10^{-5} as great as the binding energy of even the most weakly bound nucleus. This indicates how small the forces are on electrons within atoms compared to the forces within the nucleus.)

Figure 27-6 shows that the nuclide with the smallest binding energy per nucleon is ^{2}H, an isotope of hydrogen with one proton and one neutron. (Just 0.0115% of hydrogen atoms are of this isotope.) As A increases, E_B/A increases rapidly because more nucleons are surrounded by other nucleons to which they are attracted and so are more tightly bound. The value of E_B/A peaks at about 8.8 MeV for A in the range of 56 to 62, and then decreases slowly for higher and higher values of A. The decrease happens because the number of protons Z also increases as A increases, and the electric repulsion between protons destabilizes the nucleus. The most stable nuclei are ^{56}Fe and ^{58}Fe (two isotopes of iron) and ^{62}Ni; the binding energy per nucleon of these nuclei places them near the peak of the E_B/A curve in Figure 27-6.

Whenever possible, nuclei will rearrange themselves to maximize their stability and so maximize their binding energy per nucleon. Figure 27-6 shows that nuclei of relatively large values of mass number A can become more stable by decreasing the number of nucleons. One process of this kind is **nuclear fission**, in which nuclei split into smaller pieces. For example, atoms of curium-244 can spontaneously fission into xenon-135 and molybdenum-109. Curium has 96 protons, so ^{244}Cm has 148 neutrons. There are 54 protons in xenon and 42 in molybdenum or 96 total. The total number of

Figure 27-6 **The curve of binding energy** The binding energy per nucleon in a nucleus depends on the mass number *A*.

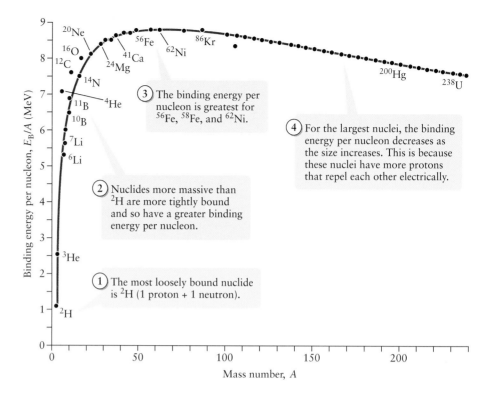

nucleons in ^{135}Xe and ^{109}Mo, 244, equals the number of nucleons in ^{244}Cm. In other words, ^{135}Xe and ^{109}Mo contain the same 96 protons and 148 neutrons as in the original ^{244}Cm; the curium atom has split into two fragments. We'll discuss fission in more detail in Section 27-4.

Figure 27-6 also shows that nuclei with relatively small values of *A* can become more stable by increasing the number of nucleons. One way to do this is by **nuclear fusion**, in which two small nuclei join together to make a larger one. For example, the 12 protons and 12 neutrons in two carbon-12 nuclei can fuse to form a magnesium-24 nucleus. More than one atom can also be formed by fusion processes. For example, when a helium-3 nucleus fuses with a lithium-6 nucleus, the reaction forms two helium-4 nuclei and one hydrogen-1 nucleus. (Count the nucleons: ^{3}He has two protons and one neutron, and ^{6}Li has three protons and three neutrons, for a total of five protons and four neutrons. The two ^{4}He nuclei have two protons and two neutrons each, leaving one more proton to form a ^{1}H atom.) In Section 27-5 we'll discuss nuclear fusion more carefully.

Let's see how to calculate the binding energy per nucleon of a nucleus such as ^{4}He. We can do this by finding the total mass of the protons and neutrons that make up the nucleus, and comparing it to the mass of the actual nucleus. We then convert that difference to the equivalent energy. Instead of measuring mass in kilograms, it's most convenient to use units that take advantage of the equivalence between mass and energy. Since rest energy equals mass multiplied by c^2, we'll measure masses in units of MeV/c^2. Note that $1\ \mathrm{MeV}/c^2 = 1.7827 \times 10^{-30}$ kg.

In these units, the mass of a proton is $938.27\ \mathrm{MeV}/c^2$, the mass of a neutron is $939.57\ \mathrm{MeV}/c^2$, and the mass of a ^{4}He nucleus is $3727.4\ \mathrm{MeV}/c^2$. The difference Δ between (i) the mass of the two protons and two neutrons separately and (ii) the mass of the helium nucleus is

$$\Delta = 2m_\mathrm{p} + 2m_\mathrm{n} - m_\mathrm{He}$$
$$= 2(938.27\ \mathrm{MeV}/c^2) + 2(939.57\ \mathrm{MeV}/c^2) - 3727.4\ \mathrm{MeV}/c^2$$
$$= 28.3\ \mathrm{MeV}/c^2$$

The energy equivalent of any mass is obtained by multiplying it by c^2, so the energy equivalent of this difference is 28.3 MeV. (Notice how straightforward it is to find the energy equivalent of mass when we write mass in units of MeV/c^2.) In other words, the binding energy of ^{4}He is 28.3 MeV. There are four nucleons in the helium nucleus, so E_B/A is about 7.1 MeV. You can verify this result from the curve in Figure 27-6.

The binding energy per nucleon is much higher for ^{4}He than for other light nuclei. (Figure 27-6 shows that E_B/A is about 2.5 MeV for ^{3}He and about 5.3 MeV for ^{6}Li.) Thanks to its relatively high binding energy per nucleon, ^{4}He is far more stable than other light nuclei. For this reason, when large nuclei break apart to transform to a more stable, more energetically favorable state, in many cases, they do so by emitting two protons and two neutrons bound together. In such processes the four bound protons and neutrons are referred to as an *alpha particle* (α particle), and we say that the alpha is emitted as nuclear radiation. Nuclear radiation is the emission by a nucleus of either energy or one of a small number of particles. We'll discuss nuclear radiation in more detail in Section 27-6.

To find the binding energy of ^{4}He, we subtracted the mass of the nucleus from the mass of the two protons and two neutrons separately, and then multiplied by c^2 to find the equivalent energy. In general, for a nucleus consisting of N neutrons and Z protons, E_B is

$$E_B = (Nm_n + Zm_p - m_{nucleus})c^2$$

where m_n is the mass of a neutron, m_p is the mass of a proton, and $m_{nucleus}$ is the mass of the nucleus. In practice, it's easier to measure the masses of neutral *atoms* (including their electrons) than the masses of isolated atomic nuclei. In terms of these masses, we can write the binding energy of a nucleus as

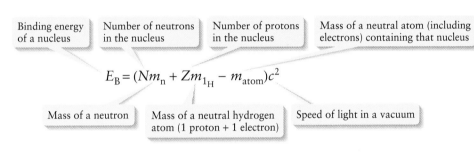

Binding energy of a nucleus
(27-2)

The terms Zm_{1_H} and m_{atom} each include the mass of Z electrons, so the electron masses cancel. The masses of neutral atoms are given in Appendix C. Note that the values in that appendix are given in units of atomic mass units (u or amu), where

$$1\ u = 931.494\ \mathrm{MeV}/c^2$$

? Got the Concept? 27-2
Stability

Rank these nuclides in order from most stable to least stable: (a) ^{11}B, (b) ^{20}Ne, (c) ^{86}Kr, (d) ^{200}Hg.

Example 27-3 The Binding Energy of ^{4}He

Previously, we determined the binding energy per nucleon in the ^{4}He nucleus using the mass of the nucleus. Use the values from Appendix C to determine the binding energy per nucleon (in MeV/c^2) in the ^{4}He nucleus using the atomic mass of ^{4}He.

Set Up

We'll use Equation 27-2 and the values given in Appendix C for the neutron mass, the atomic mass of ^{1}H, and the atomic mass of ^{4}He.

Binding energy of a nucleus:

$$E_B = (Nm_n + Zm_{1_H} - m_{atom})c^2$$

(27-2)

Solve

Calculate the binding energy of the ^{4}He nucleus, which has two neutrons ($N = 2$) and two protons ($Z = 2$).

From Appendix C,

neutron mass = m_n = 1.008665 u

atomic mass of ^{1}H = m_{1_H} = 1.007825 u

atomic mass of ^{4}He = $m_{4_{He}}$ = 4.002602 u

Substitute these into Equation 27-2, with $m_{atom} = m_{4_{He}}$:

$$E_B = (2(1.008665 \text{ u}) + 2(1.007825 \text{ u}) - 4.002602 \text{ u})c^2$$
$$= 0.030378 \text{ u}c^2$$

Since 1 u = 931.494 MeV/c^2,

$$E_B = 0.030378 \text{ u}c^2 \left(\frac{931.494 \text{ MeV}/c^2}{1 \text{ u}} \right)$$

$$= 28.297 \text{ MeV}$$

The binding energy per nucleon equals the binding energy of the nucleus divided by the number of nucleons in the nucleus.

The ^{4}He nucleus has four nucleons (two neutrons and two protons), so the binding energy per nucleon is

$$\frac{E_B}{A} = \frac{28.297 \text{ MeV}}{4} = 7.0742 \text{ MeV}$$

Reflect

Previously, we calculated $E_B/A = 7.1$ MeV to two significant figures using the mass of the ^{4}He nucleus; our new calculation is consistent with this.

Why would we do this kind of calculation using atomic masses rather than nuclear masses? The reason is that in general, the masses of neutral atoms have been well measured, but precise measurements of the masses of atomic nuclei in isolation are difficult to obtain.

Take-Home Message for Section 27-3

✔ The binding energy of a nucleus is the energy that would be required to separate it into its individual nucleons.

✔ The greater the binding energy per nucleon in a nucleus, the more tightly the nucleus is bound and therefore the more stable it is.

✔ The most stable nuclides are ^{56}Fe, ^{58}Fe, and ^{62}Ni. Smaller and larger nuclei have a lower binding energy per nucleon.

27-4 The largest nuclei can release energy by undergoing fission and splitting apart

As we saw in the previous section, nuclei with higher values of binding energy per nucleon (E_B/A) are more stable than those with lower values. Figure 27-6, a plot of the binding energy E_B per nucleon in nuclei versus mass number A, shows that E_B/A decreases as A increases beyond 60 or so. In other words, large nuclei are less stable than smaller ones for A greater than about 60. As a consequence of this instability, these large nuclei can undergo processes that result in the fragmentation or *fission* of the nucleus into smaller nuclei. Fragmentation of a large nucleus can happen spontaneously, or it can be induced by imparting energy to the nucleus through a collision. In either case, the smaller fragments of a large nucleus have a higher value of E_B/A and are therefore more stable.

Let's take a look at one of the most important processes of this kind, called **neutron-induced fission**. As an example, the collision of a neutron with a ^{235}U nucleus will cause it to fission. Figure 27-7 shows one possible result. For a brief time the neutron and ^{235}U nucleus remain stuck together as ^{236}U*. (The asterisk indicates that this is an excited and short-lived state of ^{236}U.) This excited nucleus quickly fissions into fragments. In this particular reaction the fragments are an isotope of tellurium, an isotope of zirconium, and three neutrons. Because these fragments are all more stable than the

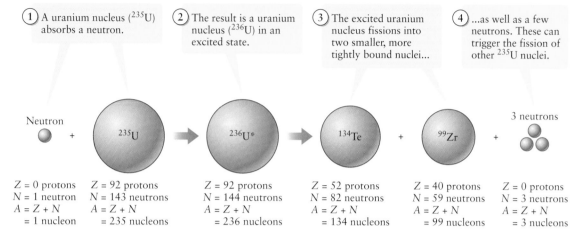

① A uranium nucleus (^{235}U) absorbs a neutron.

② The result is a uranium nucleus (^{236}U) in an excited state.

③ The excited uranium nucleus fissions into two smaller, more tightly bound nuclei...

④ ...as well as a few neutrons. These can trigger the fission of other ^{235}U nuclei.

Neutron

^{235}U

^{236}U*

^{134}Te

^{99}Zr

3 neutrons

Z = 0 protons
N = 1 neutron
A = Z + N
    = 1 nucleon

Z = 92 protons
N = 143 neutrons
A = Z + N
    = 235 nucleons

Z = 92 protons
N = 144 neutrons
A = Z + N
    = 236 nucleons

Z = 52 protons
N = 82 neutrons
A = Z + N
    = 134 nucleons

Z = 40 protons
N = 59 neutrons
A = Z + N
    = 99 nucleons

Z = 0 protons
N = 3 neutrons
A = Z + N
    = 3 nucleons

 Energy is released in this fission reaction: The total kinetic energy of the fission fragments is much greater than the total kinetic energy of the initial neutron and ^{235}U nucleus.

Figure 27-7 Neutron-induced fission
When one of the largest nuclei absorbs a slow-moving neutron, it can fission into smaller, more stable fragments.

original nucleus, energy is released. The process described by Figure 27-7 occurs even when the colliding neutron is moving very slowly and so has essentially zero kinetic energy. So the released energy is almost entirely due to the change in binding energy between the initial ^{235}U nucleus and the fission products.

We can estimate the energy released in the process shown in Figure 27-7 by comparing the binding energy of the ^{235}U nucleus to the binding energies of the ^{134}Te and ^{99}Zr fragments. (There is no binding energy associated with the initial or final neutrons; they are not bound to any other particle.) If you make measurements on the graph in Figure 27-6, you'll see that the binding energy per nucleon E_B/A is about 7.6 MeV for $A = 235$, about 8.4 MeV for $A = 134$, and about 8.7 MeV for $A = 99$. The binding energy of each nucleus (E_B) equals the binding energy per nucleon (E_B/A) multiplied by the number of nucleons (A). The energy released in the fission reaction equals the difference between the total binding energy of the fragments and the binding energy of the initial ^{235}U nucleus:

(energy released)

$= $ (binding energy of ^{134}Te) $+$ (binding energy of ^{99}Zr)

$\quad - $ (binding energy of ^{235}U)

$= (134)(8.4\text{ MeV}) + (99)(8.7\text{ MeV}) - (235)(7.6\text{ MeV})$

$= 200\text{ MeV}$

We've given our result to just one significant figure because the values of E_B/A that we measured from Figure 27-6 are just estimates. The actual amount of energy released during this process is about 185 MeV, which is quite close to our estimate. This illustrates the tremendous amount of energy released in fission. By contrast, combustion (a chemical process that involves the electrons in molecules, not the nuclei of atoms) yields only a few eV for every molecule of fuel consumed. The energy release in fission is greater by a factor of several million!

When a heavy nucleus like ^{235}U undergoes fission, a wide variety of fragments can result. Figure 27-7 shows one possible result. Two others are

$$\text{n} + {}^{235}\text{U} \rightarrow {}^{236}\text{U}^* \rightarrow {}^{143}\text{Ba} + {}^{90}\text{Kr} + 3\text{n}$$

$$\text{n} + {}^{235}\text{U} \rightarrow {}^{236}\text{U}^* \rightarrow {}^{140}\text{Xe} + {}^{92}\text{Sr} + 4\text{n}$$

In each case the total number of protons and the total number of neutrons both remain the same. The ^{235}U nucleus has 92 protons and $235 - 92 = 143$ neutrons. In the first of these two processes, ^{143}Ba has 56 protons and 87 neutrons, and ^{90}Kr has 36 protons and 54 neutrons. The total number of protons after the fission has occurred is then $56 + 36 = 92$. The total number of neutrons before the fission is $143 + 1 = 144$ (including the neutron that starts the process). After the fission, the number of neutrons is $87 + 54 + 3 = 144$ (including the three neutrons released in the process). You can easily verify that the number of protons and the number of neutrons remain the same in the second process above.

Uranium-235 can also undergo *spontaneous* fission, in which the nucleus fragments without undergoing a collision with a neutron. The following example shows how to calculate the energy released in this process.

Example 27-4 Spontaneous Uranium Fission

Determine the energy released when a ^{235}U nucleus spontaneously undergoes fission to ^{140}Xe, ^{92}Sr, and three neutrons. The binding energy per nucleon in the nuclei of ^{235}U, ^{140}Xe, and ^{92}Sr are 7.59 MeV, 8.29 MeV, and 8.65 MeV, respectively.

Set Up

The energy released during the fission process is the difference between the binding energy of ^{140}Xe and ^{92}Sr nuclei and the binding energy of the ^{235}U nucleus. (There is no binding energy associated with the three neutrons.) The binding energy for each nucleus equals the binding energy per nucleon for that nucleus multiplied by the number of nucleons A.

(energy released)

= (total binding energy of fragments)
− (binding energy of original ^{235}U nucleus)

$Z = 92$ protons
$N = 143$ neutrons
$A = Z + N$
= 235 nucleons

$Z = 54$ protons
$N = 86$ neutrons
$A = Z + N$
= 140 nucleons

$Z = 38$ protons
$N = 54$ neutrons
$A = Z + N$
= 92 nucleons

$Z = 0$ protons
$N = 3$ neutrons
$A = Z + N$
= 3 nucleons

Solve

Calculate the energy released.

The binding energies of the individual nuclei are

For ^{235}U: $(235)(7.59 \text{ MeV}) = 1784$ MeV

For ^{140}Xe: $(140)(8.29 \text{ MeV}) = 1161$ MeV

For ^{92}Sr: $(92)(8.65 \text{ MeV}) = 796$ MeV

The energy released in the spontaneous fission is then

(energy released) = (binding energy of ^{140}Xe) + (binding energy of ^{92}Sr)
− (binding energy of ^{235}U)

= 1161 MeV + 796 MeV − 1784 MeV

= 173 MeV

Reflect

This result is consistent with our earlier claim that a typical amount of energy released in the fission of ^{235}U is around 200 MeV.

Spontaneous fission of ^{235}U is a *very* unlikely process: A given ^{235}U nucleus has a 50% chance of decaying in a period of 7.04×10^8 years, and the probability that it will decay by spontaneous fission is only 7.0×10^{-11}. (Here 7.04×10^8 y is the *half-life* for spontaneous fission. We'll discuss this concept more carefully in Section 27-6. In that section we'll see that ^{235}U normally decays by a different process called *alpha emission*.) By contrast, once a ^{235}U nucleus merges with a neutron to form an excited ^{236}U* nucleus as in Figure 27.7, it typically undergoes fission within a fraction of a second.

All of the examples of fission that we've described result in the release of neutrons. Imagine what can happen if a large number of ^{235}U atoms are close to each other. Should one nucleus be struck by a neutron and fission as shown in Figure 27-7, there would then be three neutrons moving through the uranium. Should each of these neutrons strike a ^{235}U nucleus and start a fission process, there would be nine neutrons, so possibly nine more fissions. With a sufficient number of ^{235}U atoms present, this *chain reaction* quickly grows, with an accompanying rapid increase in energy released.

Isotopes that are capable of sustaining a fission chain reaction are used as nuclear fuels. Such isotopes are termed *fissile*; the most common fissile nuclear fuels are ^{233}U, ^{235}U, ^{239}Pu, and ^{241}Pu. The fission reactions they undergo are characterized by the production of, typically, two or three neutrons in addition to larger fragments. In addition, a chain reaction in a fissile material can be induced by a neutron carrying essentially zero kinetic energy. Indeed, in fuels such as ^{235}U, slower, less energetic neutrons are more efficiently absorbed by the fissile nuclei.

The process that produces electricity in most nuclear reactors uses the energy released in a fission chain reaction to heat water and produce steam to drive an electric generator (see Section 20-4). There are several challenges to producing energy in this way. First, a minimum amount, or *critical mass*, of fissile material must be present to sustain a chain reaction. As it happens, only a small percentage, about 0.7%, of the naturally occurring uranium in the world is ^{235}U, and the other three commonly used fissile isotopes do not occur naturally. Most naturally occurring uranium is ^{238}U. To use uranium as a nuclear fuel, then, it is necessary to separate the ^{235}U atoms from the ^{238}U, a costly and difficult process known as *enrichment*. In addition, the ^{238}U atoms that inevitably remain tend to absorb free neutrons and thereby inhibit a chain reaction. Once the critical mass of ^{235}U has been assembled, controlling the chain reaction is another challenge. If too many of the neutrons produced in the fissions result in a second fission, the energy released increases so rapidly that the fuel and whatever vessel is used to contain it can be damaged or even melt. To control a fission chain reaction in a nuclear reactor, control rods made of a substance that is a good absorber of neutrons are inserted between pieces of fuel.

Operating a fission nuclear reactor safely is perhaps the most significant challenge posed by nuclear power generation. First, the fission fragments are radioactive. Many of these fragments, or the fragments produced when they decay, are long-lived and tend to produce dangerous radiation for years, centuries, or even longer. In addition, reactors commonly use water as a *moderator*, a material that tends to slow the free neutrons (in order to make them more easily absorbed by a ^{235}U nucleus). Should the containment vessel rupture, this hot water can be released into the atmosphere in the form of steam carrying radioactive particles. Perhaps the most significant nuclear accident occurred at the Chernobyl nuclear power plant in Ukraine in 1986, in which an uncontrolled chain reaction caused a catastrophic power increase, leading to a series of explosions and the release of large quantities of radioactive steam, fuel, and smoke into the environment.

? Got the Concept? 27-3 Fission

Consider the spontaneous fission process ^{20}Ne $\rightarrow$ ^{10}B + ^{10}B. This process does not occur in nature. Why not? (a) The number of protons does not remain constant; (b) the number of neutrons does not remain constant; (c) both (a) and (b); (d) this process would absorb energy, not release it; (e) this process would neither release not absorb energy.

Take-Home Message for Section 27-4

✔ The binding energy per nucleon of nuclides with more than about 60 neutrons and protons decreases with increasing values of A. For this reason, the fission process, in which a nucleus breaks up into smaller fragments, leads to more stable configurations of the nucleons in bigger nuclei.

✔ Fission can be triggered by allowing a slow-moving neutron to merge with a fissile nucleus.

27-5 The smallest nuclei can release energy if they are forced to fuse together

In the previous section, we explored nuclear fission, processes by which a large nucleus splits into smaller fragments to move to a more stable configuration of the neutrons and protons it contains. Smaller is not always better, however. The larger the binding energy per nucleon (E_B/A) in a nucleus the more stable it is, and on the plot of E_B/A versus mass number (Figure 27-6), the very largest nuclei have lower values of E_B/A than smaller ones when A is greater than about 60. This is not the case, however, for small nuclei. With a few exceptions, as we move up toward a mass number A of around 60, the binding energy per nucleon increases. In other words, for small nuclei, moving to a more stable configuration requires processes that make the nucleus larger. These are *fusion* processes.

Figure 27-8 shows the process by which two ³He nuclei (each with two protons and one neutron) fuse together to form a ⁴He nucleus (with two protons and two neutrons). Two protons are left over, and without more neutrons there is no way for the protons to be bound together in a single nucleus. As a result, these protons fly off separately. Energy is released during this process because the final configuration of the protons and neutrons is more stable than the initial configuration. A photon carries away the energy released.

How much energy is released in the process shown in Figure 27-8? As in fission, the energy released in fusion is the difference between the total binding energy of the final nuclei and the total binding energy of the original nuclei. From Figure 27-6, the binding energy per nucleon for ³He is approximately 2.5 MeV. Each ³He has three nucleons, so the total binding energy of ³He is 3(2.5 MeV) = 7.5 MeV and the two ³He nuclei together have a combined binding energy equal to 7.5 MeV + 7.5 MeV = 15.0 MeV. In Section 27-3 we found that a ⁴He nucleus has a binding energy of 28.3 MeV. The two protons are single particles, so they make no contribution to the binding energy. The energy released in the fusion process is therefore

$$
\begin{aligned}
\text{(energy released)} &= \text{(binding energy of ⁴He nucleus)} \\
&\quad - \text{(binding energy of two ³He nuclei)} \\
&= (28.3\ \text{MeV}) - (15.0\ \text{MeV}) = 13.3\ \text{MeV}
\end{aligned}
$$

The actual value, found using more accurate values of the binding energies, is closer to 12.86 MeV.

The process shown in Figure 27-8 is the final step in the *proton–proton cycle*, the fusion process that is the source of the Sun's energy. The cycle begins with the fusing of two protons (the nuclei of ¹H) to form ²H. This nucleus fuses with another proton, forming ³He, and finally, two ³He nuclei fuse to form ⁴He. We can summarize these three steps as

$$\text{Step 1: } {}^1\text{H} + {}^1\text{H} \rightarrow {}^2\text{H} + e^+ + \nu_e$$

$$\text{Step 2: } {}^2\text{H} + {}^1\text{H} \rightarrow {}^3\text{He} + \gamma$$

$$\text{Step 3: } {}^3\text{He} + {}^3\text{He} \rightarrow {}^4\text{He} + {}^1\text{H} + {}^1\text{H} + \gamma$$

In Step 1, the e^+ particle is a **positron**, a particle with the same mass as an electron but with positive charge $+e$. The particle named ν_e (the Greek letter nu with a subscript e)

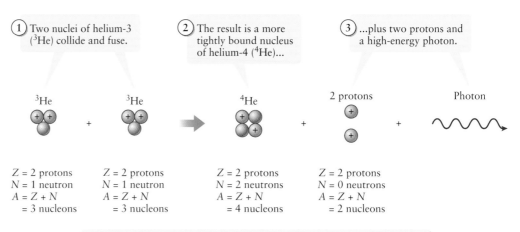

① Two nuclei of helium-3 (³He) collide and fuse.

② The result is a more tightly bound nucleus of helium-4 (⁴He)...

③ ...plus two protons and a high-energy photon.

| ³He | ³He | ⁴He | 2 protons | Photon |

$Z = 2$ protons
$N = 1$ neutron
$A = Z + N$
= 3 nucleons

$Z = 2$ protons
$N = 1$ neutron
$A = Z + N$
= 3 nucleons

$Z = 2$ protons
$N = 2$ neutrons
$A = Z + N$
= 4 nucleons

$Z = 2$ protons
$N = 0$ neutrons
$A = Z + N$
= 2 nucleons

Figure 27-8 Nuclear fusion
The fusion of two ³He nuclei to make a ⁴He nucleus is one of the energy-releasing reactions that takes place in the core of the Sun.

Energy is released in this fusion reaction: The total kinetic energy of the ⁴He nucleus and protons, plus the energy of the photon, is much greater than the total kinetic energy of the initial ³He nuclei.

is a **neutrino**, a nearly massless, neutral particle. Also note that this step involves a proton being converted into a neutron. We'll discuss this conversion, called beta-plus decay, in Section 27-6. Step 1, and the subsequent interaction of the positron with an electron in the Sun (in which the two particles annihilate each other and convert into photons), release 1.44 MeV of energy. The energy released in Step 2 is 5.49 MeV. Both of these steps must occur twice before Step 3 can occur (because Step 3 requires two ^{3}He nuclei). So six protons are used in Steps 1 and 2, and in Step 3 two of those protons are returned along with a ^{4}He nucleus. The net result is therefore that four ^{1}H nuclei disappear and are replaced by one ^{4}He nucleus. The net energy release is 2(1.44 MeV) from the Step 1 happening twice, plus 2(5.49 MeV) from Step 2 happening twice, plus 12.86 MeV from the fusion of two ^{3}He nuclei in Step 3. The sum of these is a net energy release of 26.7 MeV as four ^{1}H nuclei are transformed into a ^{4}He nucleus.

Fission processes release more energy than the proton–proton fusion cycle, around 200 MeV compared to 26.7 MeV. Therefore, it might seem that fission is a more effective way to convert fuel to energy. Consider, however, that while 235 nucleons in ^{235}U are spent in order to release 200 MeV, in the fusion process described above, the 26.7 MeV released come at the expense of only four nucleons. Comparing energy per nucleon (think miles per gallon), fission provides less than 1 MeV per nucleon, while proton–proton fusion gives 26.7 MeV divided by 4, or nearly 7 MeV per nucleon. Fusion processes are more efficient at releasing the energy held in binding nuclei together.

Hydrogen makes up about 75% of the Sun's mass of approximately 2×10^{30} kg. If the proton–proton cycle leads to more stability, why doesn't all of that hydrogen quickly fuse to form ^{4}He, leaving the Sun a gigantic (and cool) ball of helium gas? The answer lies in the same forces at play within nuclei: the Coulomb force that repels protons from each other and the short-ranged strong nuclear force that draws them together. In order for two protons to fuse to form ^{2}H, they must come within a few femtometers of each other, at which point the strong attraction is able to overcome the Coulomb repulsion. This requires the protons to have considerable kinetic energy, which can come from being at high temperature. A temperature of more than 4×10^6 K is required for the proton–proton cycle to start. The temperature at the core of the Sun is around 15×10^6 K, so the proton–proton cycle can and does occur there. Even at that temperature, however, the probability that two nearby protons will fuse is small. This means that only a small fraction—about 4×10^{-19}—of the hydrogen in the Sun is undergoing fusion at any one time. The Sun won't burn out for a long time.

As a star ages, its core temperature increases and additional fusion reactions become possible. For example, three ^{4}He nuclei can fuse to form a ^{12}C nucleus. This requires a temperature of about 10^8 K because the ^{4}He nuclei are more massive than protons and repel each other more strongly due to their greater charge. At even higher temperatures, a ^{4}He nucleus can fuse with a ^{12}C nucleus to form a ^{16}O nucleus, a ^{4}He nucleus can fuse with a ^{16}O nucleus to form a ^{20}Ne nucleus, and so on. So as stars age, they manufacture heavier and heavier chemical elements. In the most massive stars, which have the highest core temperatures, so much kinetic energy is available at the very end of the star's evolution that fusion processes can produce even the heaviest nuclei up to uranium. Making these massive nuclei by fusion absorbs rather than releases energy, which is why it can happen only in very special circumstances.

These fusion reactions in stars make life on Earth possible. Here's why: When the universe first originated some 13.8 billion years ago, almost all ordinary matter was in the form of hydrogen or helium. (We'll discuss the origin of the universe in Chapter 28.) All heavier elements had to be manufactured by fusion within stars. After an aging star produces elements heavier than helium and goes through its final stages of evolution, it disperses much of its material into interstellar space (**Figure 27-9**). This material, which is enriched in heavy elements, can then be incorporated into a later generation of stars. We now understand that our Sun is such a "second-generation" star, with an elevated abundance of elements heavier than helium. As part of the process by which the Sun formed, some of these elements went into forming Earth and the other planets that orbit the Sun. This means that all of the nuclei of carbon in the organic compounds that make up your body, all of the nuclei in the oxygen that you breathe, and all of the nuclei in the silicon in the sand on Earth's beaches were manufactured in stars that died billions of years ago. This is one of the great lessons of nuclear physics: You are made of star-stuff.

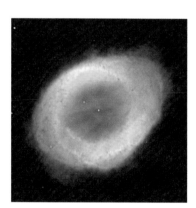

Figure 27-9 **Seeding space with fusion products** The Ring Nebula is a cloud of gas emitted by an aging star. The cloud includes nitrogen (shown in red) and oxygen (shown in green) produced by fusion reactions within the star.

? Got the Concept? 27-4 Fusion

Ordinary hydrogen gas is in the form of diatomic hydrogen (H_2), and more than 99.9% of the atoms in hydrogen gas have a nucleus that is a single proton (^1H). Why don't the two hydrogen nuclei in an H_2 molecule spontaneously undergo fusion as in Step 1 of the proton–proton cycle: $^1H + {}^1H \rightarrow {}^2H + e^+ + \nu_e$? (a) The nuclei are too far apart; (b) the nuclei are moving too slowly relative to each other; (c) the nuclei in an atom are different from those outside an atom; (d) both (a) and (b); (e) all of (a), (b), and (c).

Take-Home Message for Section 27-5

✔ The binding energy per nucleon of nuclides that have fewer than about 60 neutrons and protons is larger for increasing values of mass number A. For this reason, fusion of two small nuclei to form a larger one leads to more stable configuration of the nucleons.

✔ Fusion can only take place if the fusing nuclei come very close to each other. Therefore very high temperatures are required so the nuclei can overcome their mutual electric repulsion.

27-6 Unstable nuclei may emit alpha, beta, or gamma radiation

For many people, phrases such as radioactivity and nuclear radiation have come to be synonymous with danger. Not all nuclear radiation is dangerous, however. In addition, nuclear radiation in our environment is not limited to that released during the explosion of a bomb or an incident at a power plant. In this section we'll explore a number of aspects of nuclear radiation.

All naturally occurring nuclear processes take place because the final state is more stable, more energetically favorable, than the initial state. This is true of fission and fusion processes, and it is true of radiation processes, too. A relatively few nuclides—266 out of over 3000—are stable. All the rest are **radioactive**; that is, they decay into another nuclide by radiating away one or more particles. It's also possible for a nucleus in an excited state to radiate energy in the form of a photon as the nucleus transitions to a less excited state. Depending on the process, this radiation can carry away a small or a large amount of energy.

The three most common modes by which radiation occurs are *alpha*, *beta*, and *gamma* radiation. The terms were coined by Ernest Rutherford, who in his research between 1899 and 1903 classified radiation according to the depth that a radiation particle was able to penetrate other objects. Alpha particles penetrated the least, beta particles more, and gamma particles the most. (Rutherford received the 1908 Nobel Prize in Chemistry for this research, which was the first to show that one element can change into another through radioactive processes.) We now know that alpha particles are the nuclei of ^4He; beta particles are electrons; and gamma particles are photons of very high energy that can be millions of times greater than the energies of visible-light photons.

Before we consider the properties of these specific types of radioactive processes, let's look at a concept that is common to all of them—the idea of *radioactive half-life*.

Radioactive Decay and Half-Life

Nuclear radiation of all kinds—alpha, beta, or gamma—involves physics on the very small scale of the nucleus, and so is governed by quantum mechanics. As we learned in Section 26-6, quantum mechanics cannot tell us the position or velocity of a particular object at any time. It can, however, tell us the *probability* that an object will be at a particular place or have a particular velocity at any given instant. In the same way, quantum mechanics cannot tell us when a given radioactive nucleus will decay, but it can predict the probability that this nucleus will decay within a given time interval. Because all we can state is probabilities, it follows that radioactive decay is a statistical process.

As an example, consider the emission of a beta particle in the decay of ^{137}Cs (cesium), in which a neutron is converted into a proton, which proceeds as

$$^{137}\text{Cs} \rightarrow {}^{137}\text{Ba} + e^- + \bar{\nu}_e$$

The beta particle is the electron (e^-), and $\bar{\nu}_e$ is an **antineutrino**, related to the light, neutral neutrino particle we discussed in the context of fusion in the previous section. Every ^{137}Cs nucleus can, and eventually will, decay radioactively to a barium nucleus (^{137}Ba). In addition, we know that if a sample of ^{137}Cs contains, say, 10,000 atoms, after 30.17 years, only about 5000 will be left. However, if we select any one individual ^{137}Cs atom of those 10,000 atoms, we have no idea when its nucleus will decay. Perhaps it will decay in the next second, or perhaps not for 1000 years or more.

We can't make a definitive claim about when any particular atomic nucleus will decay, but we can quantify the *rate* at which a group of radioactive atoms decays, that is, the number of decays per second. Because radioactive decay is a statistical process, the probability λ that any one nucleus of a given type will decay in the next second is the same for all such nuclei. The quantity λ is called the **decay constant**. It has units of s^{-1}, since it refers to a probability per second. The value of λ is different for different radioactive nuclides: It is greater for nuclides that decay rapidly, and smaller for nuclides that decay slowly.

If we have a sample of N such nuclei, the total number of decays that take place in the next second—that is, the *decay rate*—will be equal to the product of the decay constant λ (the probability that any one nucleus decays in the next second) and N (the number of radioactive nuclei present). So the decay rate of a radioactive sample is greater if the sample is larger (the number of nuclei N in the sample is greater) or the nuclei have a higher decay constant λ. The SI unit of decay rate is the **becquerel** (Bq), after the nineteenth-century French physicist Antoine Henri Becquerel, who along with Marie Skłodowska-Curie and Pierre Curie won the 1903 Nobel Prize in Physics for their discovery of radioactivity. The becquerel is equivalent to one radioactive decay per second. Physicists also commonly use units of curies (Ci) for decay rate; $1 \text{ Ci} = 3.7 \times 10^{10} \text{ Bq} = 3.7 \times 10^{10}$ decays/s.

After an elapsed time of Δt seconds, the total number of decays will be equal to $\lambda N \Delta t$. This means that in a time Δt, the number of radioactive nuclei decreases by $\lambda N \Delta t$. So the *change* in the number of nuclei present is

$$\Delta N = -\lambda N \Delta t \tag{27-3}$$

The minus sign in Equation 27-3 indicates that the number of nuclei decreases as a result of the decays. If we divide both sides of Equation 27-3 by the elapsed time Δt, we get an expression for the rate of change $\Delta N / \Delta t$ of the number of nuclei:

In a sample of radioactive material, the rate of change of the number of radioactive nuclei...

... is negative because the number of nuclei decreases due to decay...

$$\frac{\Delta N}{\Delta t} = -\lambda N$$

Radioactive decay equation
(27-4)

...is proportional to the decay constant (the probability that a given nucleus decays in a one-second interval)...

...and is proportional to the number of radioactive nuclei that remain.

Equation 27-4 tells us that as time goes by, the decay rate will decrease because the number of radioactive nuclei will decrease. Using the tools of calculus, we can solve Equation 27-4 to find the number of nuclei present as a function of time, $N(t)$. The result is

$$N(t) = N_0 e^{-\lambda t} \tag{27-5}$$

In Equation 27-5 N_0 is the number of nuclei present at a specific time that we choose to call $t = 0$. This equation tells us that the number of nuclei present decreases

Figure 27-10 **Nuclear decay and half-life** This exponential curve shows the evolution of a sample that originally contains 10,000 cesium-137 (^{137}Cs) nuclei, which decay to barium-137 (^{137}Ba).

- The half-life of a nuclear decay is the time required for one-half of the nuclei present initially to decay.
- Radioactive decay is a statistical process: It's impossible to predict when any one individual unstable nucleus will decay.

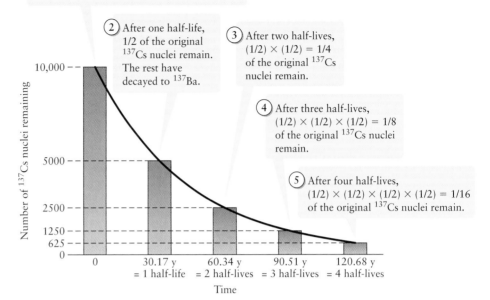

① Initially we have 10,000 ^{137}Cs nuclei. These nuclei are unstable, and decay to ^{137}Ba.

② After one half-life, 1/2 of the original ^{137}Cs nuclei remain. The rest have decayed to ^{137}Ba.

③ After two half-lives, $(1/2) \times (1/2) = 1/4$ of the original ^{137}Cs nuclei remain.

④ After three half-lives, $(1/2) \times (1/2) \times (1/2) = 1/8$ of the original ^{137}Cs nuclei remain.

⑤ After four half-lives, $(1/2) \times (1/2) \times (1/2) \times (1/2) = 1/16$ of the original ^{137}Cs nuclei remain.

exponentially, as Figure 27-10 shows. The number of decays per second at time t is equal to the decay constant λ (the decay probability per second per nucleus), multiplied by $N(t)$, the number of nuclei remaining at time t. We can write this as

$$R(t) = \lambda N(t) = \lambda N_0 e^{-\lambda t}$$

In this equation λN_0 is equal to the decay rate at $t = 0$, which we call R_0. So the decay rate as a function of time is

(27-6)
$$R(t) = R_0 e^{-\lambda t}$$

Equation 27-6 tells us that the decay rate, too, will decrease exponentially as time goes by. With the passage of time, a radioactive sample will undergo fewer and fewer decays.

Figure 27-10 shows that for the beta decay of ^{137}Cs, the number of ^{137}Cs nuclei remaining decreases by one-half every 30.17 years. Because the decay rate is proportional to the number of ^{137}Cs nuclei remaining, the decay rate also decreases by one-half every 30.17 years. This time is called the **half-life** of the radioactive decay, to which we give the symbol $\tau_{1/2}$ (the Greek letter tau). If there are N_0 radioactive nuclei present at $t = 0$, there will be $N_0/2$ present at $t = \tau_{1/2}$. If we substitute this into Equation 27-5, we get

$$\frac{N_0}{2} = N_0 e^{-\lambda \tau_{1/2}}$$

Divide both sides of this equation by N_0, then take the natural logarithm of both sides:

(27-7)
$$\ln\left(\frac{1}{2}\right) = \ln\left(e^{-\lambda \tau_{1/2}}\right)$$

Why do we do this? The reason is that the natural logarithm "undoes" the exponential function: For any x, $\ln(e^x) = x$. Furthermore, the natural logarithm has the property that for any x, $\ln(1/x) = -\ln x$. If we apply these to Equation 27-7, we get

$$-\ln 2 = -\lambda \tau_{1/2}$$

or

$$\tau_{1/2} = \frac{\ln 2}{\lambda} \qquad (27\text{-}8)$$

Equation 27-8 says that the half-life is inversely proportional to the decay constant λ, the probability that a given nucleus of a certain type will decay in a one-second interval. The greater the decay constant, the shorter the half-life and the more rapidly a sample of that nucleus will decay.

The half-life of radioactive sources varies widely, from far less than one second to billions of years or more. Commonly used radioactive sources include ^{32}P, a beta emitter used in DNA research that has a half-life of 14.3 days, ^{241}Am, an alpha emitter often found in household smoke detectors that has a half-life of 432.2 y, and ^{238}U, an alpha emitter with a half-life of 4.47×10^{9} y. Notice that none of these have a half-life on the order of a second or less; radioactive isotopes with half-lives that short aren't terribly useful because they don't stay around long enough.

Example 27-5 Technetium

A form of an isotope of technetium, ^{99m}Tc, undergoes gamma decay with a half-life of 6.01 h. (The "m" stands for "metastable." Technetium-99 is widely used as a radioactive tracer for medical purposes, because its gamma radiation is easily detected and because technetium doesn't stay in the body for long. Hence the total radiation delivered to the patient is low.) (a) What is the decay constant λ, the probability that a nucleus of ^{99m}Tc will decay per second, in this sample? Does λ change as time goes on? (b) What fraction of the initial number of ^{99m}Tc nuclei will be left after 1.00 day? (c) What fraction will be left after 4.00 days have elapsed?

Set Up

We'll use Equation 27-8 to relate the decay constant λ to the half-life. Equation 27-5 will tell us the number of ^{99m}Tc nuclei remaining after a time t in terms of the initial number of nuclei N_0.

Half-life of a radioactive substance:

$$\tau_{1/2} = \frac{\ln 2}{\lambda} \qquad (27\text{-}8)$$

Number of radioactive nuclei present at time t:

$$N(t) = N_0 e^{-\lambda t} \qquad (27\text{-}5)$$

Solve

(a) Determine the decay constant for ^{99m}Tc.

We can rewrite Equation 27-8 as

$$\lambda = \frac{\ln 2}{\tau_{1/2}}$$

Substitute $\tau_{1/2} = 6.01$ h:

$$\lambda = \frac{\ln 2}{(6.01 \text{ h})}\left(\frac{1 \text{ h}}{60 \text{ min}}\right)\left(\frac{1 \text{ min}}{60 \text{ s}}\right) = 3.20 \times 10^{-5} \text{ s}^{-1}$$

The probability that a given ^{99m}Tc nucleus will decay in a one-second interval is 3.20×10^{-5}, corresponding to odds of 1 in $(1/3.20 \times 10^{-5}) = 31{,}200$. This value depends only on the half-life, so it does not vary with time.

(b) To find the fraction of nuclei remaining after $t = 1.00$ d, substitute this value of t into Equation 27-5.

The fraction of ^{99m}Tc nuclei remaining after a time t equals the number remaining $N(t)$ divided by the number N_0 present initially:

$$\frac{N(t)}{N_0} = \frac{N_0 e^{-\lambda t}}{N_0} = e^{-\lambda t}$$

From part (a) we know the value of λ in s^{-1}, so we need to express t in seconds:

$$t = (1.00 \text{ d})\left(\frac{24 \text{ h}}{1 \text{ d}}\right)\left(\frac{60 \text{ min}}{1 \text{ h}}\right)\left(\frac{60 \text{ s}}{1 \text{ min}}\right) = 8.64 \times 10^{4} \text{ s}$$

The fraction of nuclei remaining is then

$$\frac{N(1.00\ \text{d})}{N_0} = e^{-(3.20\times10^{-5}\ \text{s}^{-1})(8.64\times10^{4}\ \text{s})}$$

$$= e^{-2.77} = 0.0628$$

(c) Repeat part (b) with $t = 4.00$ d.

The elapsed time is now

$$t = (4.00\ \text{d})\left(\frac{8.64\times10^{4}\ \text{s}}{1\ \text{d}}\right) = 3.46\times10^{5}\ \text{s}$$

and the fraction of nuclei remaining is

$$\frac{N(4.00\ \text{d})}{N_0} = e^{-(3.20\times10^{-5}\ \text{s}^{-1})(3.46\times10^{5}\ \text{s})}$$

$$= e^{-11.1} = 1.55\times10^{-5}$$

Reflect

We can check our results by noting that $t = 1.00$ d is almost exactly four times the 6.01-h half-life of $^{99\text{m}}$Tc, and $t = 4.00$ d is almost exactly 16 times the half-life. This check agrees with our calculations, as it should.

After each half-life, the number of $^{99\text{m}}$Tc nuclei remaining decreases by one-half. So after four half-lives, the fraction of $^{99\text{m}}$Tc nuclei remaining will be

$$\frac{1}{2} \times \frac{1}{2} \times \frac{1}{2} \times \frac{1}{2} = \frac{1}{2^4} = \frac{1}{16} = 0.0625$$

The fraction actually remaining at $t = 1.00$ d (slightly less than four 6.01-h half-lives) is 0.0628, very close to our estimate.
After 16 half-lives, the fraction of $^{99\text{m}}$Tc remaining will be

$$\frac{1}{2^{16}} = \frac{1}{65,536} = 1.53\times10^{-5}$$

The fraction actually remaining at $t = 4.00$ d (slightly less than 16 times the 6.01-h half-life) is 1.55×10^{-5}, which again is very close to our estimate.

Alpha Radiation

When a large nucleus breaks into smaller fragments during a nuclear fission process, the new configuration of those protons and neutrons is more stable because the total binding energy increases. There are many ways, of course, for a large nucleus to split into smaller pieces, but the more likely decay products would be those that are more stable, that is, those with larger binding energy per nucleon. It is also probable, however, for smaller fragments to be ejected from a large nucleus. The radioactive emission of a ^{4}He nucleus is the most likely decay process for a large nucleus. As Figure 27-6 shows, ^{4}He has a greater binding energy per nucleon than any other nucleus with a small value of A. So the nucleus of the ^{4}He atom is far more stable than other small nuclei and therefore a far more probable decay product of large nuclei. Another name for a ^{4}He nucleus is an **alpha particle** (symbol α), and emission of an alpha particle is called **alpha decay**.

The alpha radiation process reduces the number of protons Z of the initial, or parent, nucleus by two, and reduces the number of neutrons of the parent by two. The result is a daughter nucleus that has an atomic number $Z-2$ and a mass number $A-4$, accompanied by an alpha particle (**Figure 27-11**).

The daughter nucleus and the alpha particle both carry away the energy released in alpha decay. However, the kinetic energy of the alpha particle is far greater than the kinetic energy of the daughter. We can confirm this by looking at the ratio of the kinetic energy K_α of the alpha particle to the kinetic energy K_D of the daughter. The alpha particle has mass m_α and is emitted with speed v_α, and the daughter nucleus has

① This parent nucleus is large and unstable.

② The parent decays into a daughter nucleus with two fewer protons and two fewer neutrons...

③ ...plus an alpha particle (a ^{4}He nucleus).

Alpha (α) particle

Parent nucleus   →   Daughter nucleus   +

Z protons   Z – 2 protons   Z = 2 protons
N neutrons   N – 2 neutrons   N = 2 neutrons
Z + N = A nucleons (Z – 2) + (N – 2)   Z + N = 4 nucleons
                    = A – 4 nucleons

Figure 27-11 **Alpha decay** Large nuclei can increase their stability by emitting an alpha particle and becoming a smaller, more stable daughter nucleus.

Energy is released in this decay: The daughter nucleus is more tightly bound (has a greater binding energy) than the parent.

mass m_D and is emitted with speed v_D. The kinetic energies of the alpha particle and the daughter are then

$$K_\alpha = \frac{1}{2}m_\alpha v_\alpha^2$$

$$K_D = \frac{1}{2}m_D v_D^2$$

The ratio of these kinetic energies is

$$\frac{K_\alpha}{K_D} = \frac{(1/2)m_\alpha v_\alpha^2}{(1/2)m_D v_D^2} = \frac{m_\alpha}{m_D}\left(\frac{v_\alpha}{v_D}\right)^2 \qquad (27\text{-}9)$$

We can relate the speeds v_α and v_D by noting that momentum must be conserved in the alpha decay (because no external forces act on the parent nucleus as it decays). If the parent nucleus is at rest, the total momentum is zero before the decay and so must be zero after the decay. The alpha particle and daughter nucleus must therefore fly off in opposite directions, and each must have the same magnitude of momentum:

$$m_\alpha v_\alpha = m_D v_D \quad \text{so} \quad \frac{v_\alpha}{v_D} = \frac{m_D}{m_\alpha}$$

If we substitute this into Equation 27-9, we find that the ratio of the alpha particle's kinetic energy to that of the daughter nucleus is

$$\frac{K_\alpha}{K_D} = \frac{m_\alpha}{m_D}\left(\frac{v_\alpha}{v_D}\right)^2 = \frac{m_\alpha}{m_D}\left(\frac{m_D}{m_\alpha}\right)^2 = \frac{m_D}{m_\alpha}$$

The mass of the daughter nucleus is much larger than the mass of the alpha particle, so the fraction m_D/m_α is much greater than one and K_α is large compared to K_D.

All nuclei with more than 82 protons are unstable and have some probability of alpha decay. As an example, the element thorium ($Z = 90$ protons) undergoes alpha decay to radium which contains two fewer protons ($Z = 88$). The α decay of ^{228}Th, for example, is

$$^{228}\text{Th} \rightarrow {}^{224}\text{Ra} + \alpha$$

Just as ^{228}Th decays to ^{224}Ra, ^{224}Ra undergoes alpha decay to ^{220}Rn. This process continues until the daughter nucleus has $Z = 82$ or less. In this case the final alpha decay is to lead, with $Z = 82$:

$$^{228}\text{Th} \rightarrow {}^{224}\text{Ra} + \alpha \quad (\tau_{1/2\,\text{Th}} = 1.91\,\text{y})$$
$$\hookrightarrow {}^{220}\text{Rn} + \alpha \quad (\tau_{1/2\,\text{Ra}} = 3.63\,\text{d})$$
$$\hookrightarrow {}^{216}\text{Po} + \alpha \quad (\tau_{1/2\,\text{Rn}} = 55.6\,\text{s})$$
$$\hookrightarrow {}^{212}\text{Pb} + \alpha \quad (\tau_{1/2\,\text{Po}} = 0.145\,\text{s})$$

Note that in each alpha decay the daughter nucleus has two fewer protons and two fewer neutrons than its parent.

Another nucleus that decays by alpha radiation is ^{235}U, which has a half-life $\tau_{1/2} = 7.04 \times 10^8$ y. (In Example 27-4 in Section 27-4 we looked at the spontaneous fission of ^{235}U. This is a very rare decay mode; ^{235}U undergoes alpha decay rather than spontaneous fission almost 100% of the time.) It is now understood that substantial amounts of ^{235}U, ^{238}U ($\tau_{1/2} = 4.47 \times 10^9$ y), and ^{232}Th ($\tau_{1/2} = 1.40 \times 10^{10}$ y) are found in Earth's core, and that the energy released by the alpha decay of these isotopes helps to sustain our planet's high internal temperatures and so keep much of the interior in a fluid state. All of Earth's geologic activity, including earthquakes, volcanic eruptions (Figure 27-1c), and the drifting of continents, is powered by the motions of our planet's fluid interior. So alpha decay plays an important role in Earth's dynamic geology.

Example 27-6 Alpha Decay of ^{238}U

The uranium isotope ^{238}U undergoes alpha decay to ^{234}Th. The binding energy per nucleon is 7.570 MeV in ^{238}U and 7.597 MeV in ^{234}Th. Find the energy released in the process ^{238}U $\rightarrow$ ^{234}Th $+ \alpha$.

Set Up

We'll use the same principle that we used in Example 27-4 (Section 27-4) to find the energy released in fission: The released energy equals the total binding energy of the nuclei present after the decay, minus the binding energy of the original (parent) nucleus. As in that example, we'll find the binding energy for each nucleus by multiplying the binding energy per nucleon times the number of nucleons A.

(energy released)

= (total binding energy of daughter plus alpha particle)
  – (binding energy of original ^{238}U nucleus)

Solve

From Example 27-3 (Section 27-3), the binding energy of a ^{4}He nucleus (an alpha particle) is

$E_B(^4\text{He}) = 28.297$ MeV

The binding energy of a ^{234}Th nucleus ($A = 234$) is

$E_B(^{234}\text{Th}) = (234)(7.597 \text{ MeV}) = 1777.7$ MeV

and the binding energy of a ^{238}U nucleus ($A = 238$) is

$E_B(^{238}\text{U}) = (238)(7.570 \text{ MeV}) = 1801.7$ MeV

The released energy is then

$E_{\text{released}} = E_B(^{234}\text{Th}) + E_B(^4\text{He}) - E_B(^{238}\text{U})$
$= 1777.7 \text{ MeV} + 28.297 \text{ MeV} - 1801.7 \text{ MeV}$
$= 4.3$ MeV

Reflect

The alpha particles emitted by radioactive isotopes with long half-lives, such as ^{238}U, tend to have kinetic energies in the 4 to 5 MeV range.

Beta Radiation

For most possible mass numbers A, there exist a number of nuclides with that same value of A. For example, molybdenum, technetium, ruthenium, and rhodium each have an isotope with 99 nucleons: ^{99}Mo has 42 protons and 57 neutrons, ^{99}Tc has 43 protons and 56 neutrons, ^{99}Ru has 44 protons and 55 neutrons, and ^{99}Rh has 45 protons and 54 neutrons. (It is also possible to create isotopes of other elements with A equal to 99.) The binding energy per nucleon in each is slightly different, however, so that only one is the most stable: For $A = 99$, the most stable isotope is ^{99}Ru. If there were a process whereby ^{99}Tc could convert one of its neutrons into a proton, or ^{99}Rh could convert one of its protons into a neutron, either of these nuclei could transform into the more stable ^{99}Ru.

The process that makes this possible is called **beta decay**. There are actually two varieties of beta decay. In **beta-minus decay** a neutron (charge zero) changes into a proton (charge $+e$). The net charge cannot change, so an electron (charge $-e$), also known as a beta-minus (β^-) particle, is also produced and escapes from the nucleus. To account for other conservation requirements a third particle, the neutral and nearly massless antineutrino ($\bar{\nu}_e$), is also created in this process. The full process, then, is

$$n \rightarrow p + e^- + \bar{\nu}_e \quad (\text{beta-minus decay})$$

In **beta-plus decay** a proton ($+e$) changes into a neutron (charge zero). To conserve charge, a positively charged electron or *positron*, also called a beta-plus (β^+) particle, is also produced and escapes from the nucleus, along with a neutral and nearly massless neutrino (which, for our purposes, is essentially the same particle as an antineutrino). This process is

$$p \rightarrow n + e^+ + \nu_e \quad (\text{beta-plus decay})$$

Figure 27-12a depicts the beta-minus decay of a nucleus with too many neutrons such as ^{99}Tc. We can write this process as

$$^{99}\text{Tc} \rightarrow {}^{99}\text{Ru} + e^- + \bar{\nu}_e$$

The number of nucleons ($A = 99$) is the same before and after the decay, but the number of protons Z has increased by 1 (from 43 to 44) and the number of

(a) Nuclei with too many neutrons can undergo beta-minus (β^-) decay.

(b) Nuclei with too many protons can undergo beta-plus (β^+) decay.

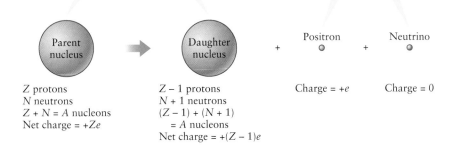

Figure 27-12 **Beta decay** Nuclei can increase their stability by (a) converting one neutron into a proton or (b) converting one proton into a neutron.

neutrons N has decreased by 1 (from 56 to 55). The decay of ^{137}Cs to ^{137}Ba, which we discussed at the beginning of this section, is another example of beta-minus decay. In this case Z increases from 55 to 56 and N decreases from 82 to 81.

One particularly important example of beta-plus decay is the decay of potassium-40 (^{40}K) to argon-40 (^{40}Ar). This process has a very long half-life of 1.25×10^9 y. Since potassium is abundant in Earth's interior, the energy released by this decay makes a substantial contribution to keeping our planet's interior in a fluid state and powering its geologic activity.

Figure 27-12b depicts the beta-plus decay of a nucleus with too many protons such as ^{99}Rh. We can write this process as

$$^{99}\text{Rh} \rightarrow {}^{99}\text{Ru} + e^+ + \nu_e$$

As for beta-minus decay, the number of nucleons remains the same (in this case, $A = 99$). But now the number of protons Z decreases by 1 (from 45 to 44), and the number of neutrons increases by 1 (from 54 to 55).

An important application of beta decay is in carbon-14 dating, a technique used to measure the age of objects that are composed, or partially composed, of organic matter. Almost all carbon atoms in Earth's atmosphere—for example, the carbon in carbon dioxide, CO_2—has a nucleus with a stable isotope of carbon, either ^{12}C (98.9%) or ^{13}C (1.1%). But about 1 in 10^{12} of those carbon atoms has a ^{14}C nucleus. This radioactive isotope of carbon is a β^- emitter with a half-life of 5730 y:

$$^{14}\text{C} \rightarrow {}^{14}\text{N} + e^- + \bar{\nu}_e$$

Carbon-14 is constantly produced in the atmosphere by cosmic rays slamming into ^{14}N nuclei. As a result, even though ^{14}C radioactively decays, the ratio of ^{14}C to ^{12}C in the atmosphere has remained relatively constant for at least tens of thousands of years. The ^{14}C/^{12}C ratio is the same in living organisms, for example, plants that breathe in CO_2, as it is in the atmosphere. However, once an organism dies, it no longer replenishes its supply of carbon, so the ^{14}C/^{12}C ratio decreases as the ^{14}C decays. As an example, a measurement of the ^{14}C/^{12}C ratio in, say, the smoke stains in the Chauvet-Pont-d'Arc Cave in southern France (see the figure that opens this chapter), which contains the earliest known cave paintings, allows a determination of time since the firewood that created the smoke was part of a living tree. Carbon-14 dating tells us that the paintings were made between 30,000 and 33,000 years ago.

Example 27-7 Ötzi the Iceman

In 1991, two German hikers discovered a human corpse in the Ötztal Alps on the border between Austria and Italy. The remains were not those of the victim of a climbing accident, but rather a well-preserved natural mummy of a man who lived during the last Ice Age. The rate of radioactive decay of ^{14}C in the mummy of "Ötzi the Iceman" was measured to be 0.121 Bq per gram. In a living organism, the rate of radioactive decay of ^{14}C is 0.231 Bq per gram. How long ago did Ötzi the Iceman live?

Set Up

Once Ötzi died, his body stopped taking in ^{14}C. After that time the number $N(t)$ of ^{14}C nuclei in his body decreased due to beta-minus decay. The ^{14}C decay rate $R(t)$, which is proportional to $N(t)$, decreased in the same manner. We are given $R(t) = 0.121$ Bq/g for the present-day decay rate, and $R_0 = 0.231$ Bq/g (the decay rate for a living organism and hence the decay rate at time $t = 0$, the last date on which Ötzi was still alive). We'll solve Equation 27-6 for the present time t (the elapsed time since Ötzi died), using Equation 27-8 to find the decay constant λ from the known half-life $\tau_{1/2} = 5730$ y of ^{14}C.

Decay rate as a function of time:

$$R(t) = R_0 e^{-\lambda t} \qquad (27\text{-}6)$$

Half-life of a radioactive substance:

$$\tau_{1/2} = \frac{\ln 2}{\lambda} \qquad (27\text{-}8)$$

Solve

Rearrange Equations 27-6 and 27-8 to find an expression for the time t since Ötzi died.

We know the present-day decay rate $R(t)$ and the initial decay rate in a living organism R_0. We want to find the time t since Ötzi died, so we rearrange Equation 27-6. Divide both sides by R_0:

$$\frac{R(t)}{R_0} = e^{-\lambda t}$$

Take the natural logarithm of both sides and recall that $\ln e^x = x$:

$$\ln\left(\frac{R(t)}{R_0}\right) = \ln e^{-\lambda t} = -\lambda t$$

Divide both sides by $-\lambda$:

$$t = -\frac{1}{\lambda}\ln\left(\frac{R(t)}{R_0}\right)$$

To get an expression for $1/\lambda$, divide both sides of Equation 27-8 by $\ln 2$:

$$\frac{1}{\lambda} = \frac{\tau_{1/2}}{\ln 2}$$

Putting everything together, the time t since Ötzi died is

$$t = -\frac{\tau_{1/2}}{\ln 2}\ln\left(\frac{R(t)}{R_0}\right)$$

Substitute the given values into the expression for t.

We are given $\tau_{1/2} = 5730$ y for ^{14}C, $R(t) = 0.121$ Bq/g, and $R_0 = 0.231$ Bq/g:

$$t = -\frac{(5730\text{ y})}{\ln 2}\ln\left(\frac{0.121\text{ Bq/g}}{0.231\text{ Bq/g}}\right) = -\frac{(5730\text{ y})}{0.693}\ln 0.524$$

$$= -\frac{(5730\text{ y})}{0.693}(-0.647) = 5350\text{ y}$$

Reflect

Our result shows that Ötzi died 5350 y ago. His well-preserved mummy thus gives us a unique look into life in prehistoric Europe.

Carbon-14 dating can only be used on objects less than about 50,000 years old, or about 8 to 10 half-lives of ^{14}C. For older objects the decay rate of ^{14}C has decreased to such a small value that it is difficult to measure accurately, and so any determination of age becomes difficult with this technique. For much older objects such as rocks, a similar approach is used but with isotopes with much longer half-lives. For example, the age of meteorites that fall to Earth is determined by looking at the ratio of uranium to lead (the endpoint of a series of alpha decays that starts with uranium); the oldest of these is more than 4.5×10^9 years old.

Gamma Radiation

A nucleus in an excited state radiates energy in a way analogous to the emission of a photon when an electron in an excited atomic state falls to a state of lower energy (see Section 26-5). Just like atoms, nuclei have excited states of definite energy, and when they transition from an excited state to a less excited one, they will emit a photon of energy equal to the difference in energy between the initial and final states.

The most common way that a nucleus can become excited is following an alpha decay or a beta decay. Although these decay processes result in a more stable

① In gamma (γ) decay, a nucleus in an excited state drops into a less excited state.

② The energy lost by the nucleus goes into a high-energy photon (gamma ray).

Photon

Excited nucleus → Less excited nucleus + ∿∿∿ →

Z protons
N neutrons
Z + N = A nucleons

Z protons
N neutrons
Z + N = A nucleons

In gamma decay, there is no change in the number of protons or the number of neutrons in the nucleus.

Figure 27-13 **Gamma decay** An excited nucleus can lower its energy by emitting a photon.

configuration of the nucleons, the nucleons that remain in the daughter nucleus may not be, initially, in the most stable arrangement for that particular nuclide. This excited daughter nucleus decays to a more stable configuration, giving off energy in the form of a gamma (γ) ray (**Figure 27-13**). This process is called **gamma decay**.

The energy carried away when a nucleus in an excited state decays is on the order of 1 MeV. From Equation 22-26 in Section 22-4, $E = hf$, the frequency and wavelength of a photon of energy $E = 1.00 \text{ MeV} = 1.00 \times 10^6$ eV are

$$f = \frac{E}{h} = \frac{1.00 \times 10^6 \text{ eV}}{4.14 \times 10^{-15} \text{ eV} \cdot \text{s}} = 2.42 \times 10^{20} \text{ Hz}$$

$$\lambda = \frac{c}{f} = \frac{3.00 \times 10^8 \text{ m/s}}{2.42 \times 10^{20} \text{ Hz}}$$

$$= 1.24 \times 10^{-12} \text{ m} = 1.24 \times 10^{-3} \text{ nm}$$

Recall that the wavelength of visible light photons is in the range from 380 to 750 nm; a photon emitted by an excited nucleus is in the gamma radiation range, far from the visible part of the spectrum.

Gamma radiation does not change the atomic number Z or the neutron number N of a nucleus; that is, the number of protons and the number of neutrons remain the same after a γ ray is emitted. As an example, earlier we considered the beta-minus decay of ^{137}Cs to ^{137}Ba. In 95% of those decays, the ^{137}Ba nucleus is formed in an excited state that we denote as ^{137}Ba*:

$$^{137}\text{Cs} \rightarrow {}^{137}\text{Ba*} + \text{e}^- + \bar{\nu}_e$$

The excited barium nucleus then decays to its ground state by emission of a photon of energy 0.662 MeV:

$$^{137}\text{Ba*} \rightarrow {}^{137}\text{Ba} + \gamma$$

The values of $Z = 56$ and $N = 81$ for the barium nucleus do not change in this second step of the radiation process.

❓ Got the Concept? 27-5   Half-Lives

A certain radioactive isotope has a half-life of 5 days. You are given a sample containing a number of nuclei of this isotope. About how long would you have to wait before about 1/1000 of the initial number of nuclei remained? (a) 20 days; (b) 40 days; (c) 50 days; (d) 100 days; (e) 1000 days.

Take-Home Message for Section 27-6

✔ Radioactive decay is a statistical process. The number of nuclei and the decay rate both decrease exponentially with time, and both decrease by one-half in a time equal to one half-life.

✔ The three most common modes by which radiation occurs are alpha, beta, and gamma radiation.

✔ Alpha particles are ^{4}He nuclei and are emitted by large nuclei with $Z > 82$. In alpha emission the proton number and neutron number each decrease by 2.

✔ Beta particles are either negatively-charged electrons or positively-charged positrons. In beta-minus emission a neutron in the nucleus changes into a proton; in beta-plus emission a proton in the nucleus changes into a neutron.

✔ Gamma particles are high-energy photons, typically with energies of about 1 MeV. They are emitted when a nucleus decays from an excited state to a less excited one.

Key Terms

alpha decay
alpha particle
antineutrino
atomic number
becquerel
beta decay
beta-minus decay
beta-plus decay
binding energy

decay constant
gamma decay
half-life
isotope
magnetic resonance imaging
mass number
neutrino
neutron-induced fission
neutron number

nuclear fission
nuclear fusion
nucleon
nuclide
positron
radioactive
strong nuclear force

Chapter Summary

Topic	Equation or Figure

The strong nuclear force and nuclear sizes: The strong nuclear force is a short-range attractive force that acts between nucleons (protons or neutrons). Because the force is short-ranged, the volume of a nucleus is proportional to the mass number (number of nucleons). In larger nuclei, the number of neutrons must exceed the number of protons in order to counterbalance the electric repulsion between protons.

 For most nuclides, more neutrons than protons must be present (N must be greater than Z) to prevent the protons from flying apart due to electrostatic repulsion.

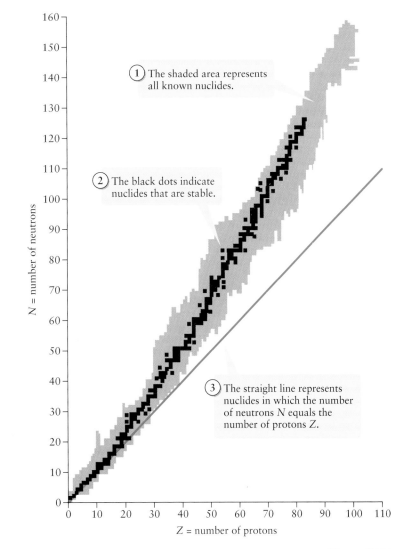

(1) The shaded area represents all known nuclides.

(2) The black dots indicate nuclides that are stable.

(3) The straight line represents nuclides in which the number of neutrons N equals the number of protons Z.

N = number of neutrons

Z = number of protons

(Figure 27-2)

Nuclear binding energy: The binding energy of a nucleus is the energy required to separate it into its constituent nucleons. The binding energy per nucleon is greatest for nuclei with around 60 nucleons; for larger nuclei, the electric repulsion between protons makes nuclei less stable. The binding energy of a particular isotope can be calculated from the mass of a neutral atom containing that isotope.

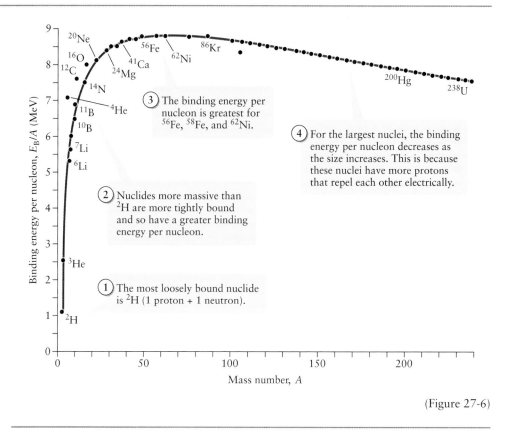

(3) The binding energy per nucleon is greatest for ^{56}Fe, ^{58}Fe, and ^{62}Ni.

(4) For the largest nuclei, the binding energy per nucleon decreases as the size increases. This is because these nuclei have more protons that repel each other electrically.

(2) Nuclides more massive than ^{2}H are more tightly bound and so have a greater binding energy per nucleon.

(1) The most loosely bound nuclide is ^{2}H (1 proton + 1 neutron).

(Figure 27-6)

| Binding energy of a nucleus | Number of neutrons in the nucleus | Number of protons in the nucleus | Mass of a neutral atom (including electrons) containing that nucleus |

$$E_B = (Nm_n + Zm_{1_H} - m_{atom})c^2 \qquad (27\text{-}2)$$

| Mass of a neutron | Mass of a neutral hydrogen atom (1 proton + 1 electron) | Speed of light in a vacuum |

Nuclear fission: When the largest nuclei absorb a neutron, they fragment (fission) into two smaller nuclei plus a few neutrons. The fragments are more tightly bound than the original nucleus, so energy is released in this process. In a sustained fission reaction, the released neutrons trigger other, nearby nuclei to also undergo fission.

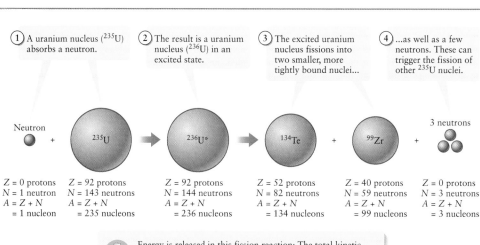

(1) A uranium nucleus (^{235}U) absorbs a neutron.

(2) The result is a uranium nucleus (^{236}U) in an excited state.

(3) The excited uranium nucleus fissions into two smaller, more tightly bound nuclei...

(4) ...as well as a few neutrons. These can trigger the fission of other ^{235}U nuclei.

Neutron + ^{235}U → ^{236}U* → ^{134}Te + ^{99}Zr + 3 neutrons

Neutron	^{235}U	^{236}U*	^{134}Te	^{99}Zr	3 neutrons
$Z = 0$ protons	$Z = 92$ protons	$Z = 92$ protons	$Z = 52$ protons	$Z = 40$ protons	$Z = 0$ protons
$N = 1$ neutron	$N = 143$ neutrons	$N = 144$ neutrons	$N = 82$ neutrons	$N = 59$ neutrons	$N = 3$ neutrons
$A = Z + N$	$A = Z + N$	$A = Z + N$	$A = Z + N$	$A = Z + N$	$A = Z + N$
$= 1$ nucleon	$= 235$ nucleons	$= 236$ nucleons	$= 134$ nucleons	$= 99$ nucleons	$= 3$ nucleons

 Energy is released in this fission reaction: The total kinetic energy of the fission fragments is much greater than the total kinetic energy of the initial neutron and ^{235}U nucleus.

(Figure 27-7)

Nuclear fusion: The smallest nuclei can merge together to form a larger nucleus, releasing energy in the process. These fusion processes require very high temperatures so that the fusing nuclei have enough kinetic energy to overcome their mutual electric repulsion.

① Two nuclei of helium-3 (^{3}He) collide and fuse.

② The result is a more tightly bound nucleus of helium-4 (^{4}He)...

③ ...plus two protons and a high-energy photon.

^{3}He ^{3}He ^{4}He 2 protons Photon

Z = 2 protons
N = 1 neutron
$A = Z + N$
= 3 nucleons

Z = 2 protons
N = 1 neutron
$A = Z + N$
= 3 nucleons

Z = 2 protons
N = 2 neutrons
$A = Z + N$
= 4 nucleons

Z = 2 protons
N = 0 neutrons
$A = Z + N$
= 2 nucleons

 Energy is released in this fusion reaction: The total kinetic energy of the ^{4}He nucleus and protons, plus the energy of the photon, is much greater than the total kinetic energy of the initial ^{3}He nuclei.

(Figure 27-8)

Nuclear decay and half-life: The decay of unstable nuclei is a statistical process. This means that the rate of decay is proportional to the number of unstable nuclei present. As a result, the number of nuclei and the decay rate both decline in an exponential manner. The time for the number of nuclei and the decay rate to decrease by one-half is called the half-life.

• The half-life of a nuclear decay is the time required for one-half of the nuclei present initially to decay.
• Radioactive decay is a statistical process: It's impossible to predict when any one individual unstable nucleus will decay.

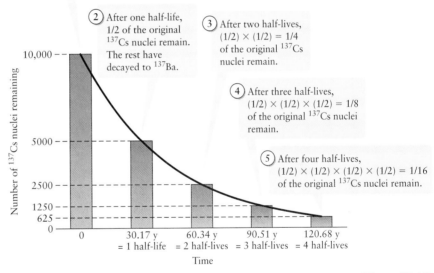

① Initially we have 10,000 ^{137}Cs nuclei. These nuclei are unstable, and decay to ^{137}Ba.

② After one half-life, 1/2 of the original ^{137}Cs nuclei remain. The rest have decayed to ^{137}Ba.

③ After two half-lives, (1/2) × (1/2) = 1/4 of the original ^{137}Cs nuclei remain.

④ After three half-lives, (1/2) × (1/2) × (1/2) = 1/8 of the original ^{137}Cs nuclei remain.

⑤ After four half-lives, (1/2) × (1/2) × (1/2) × (1/2) = 1/16 of the original ^{137}Cs nuclei remain.

Number of ^{137}Cs nuclei remaining

10,000
5000
2500
1250
625
0

0   30.17 y   60.34 y   90.51 y   120.68 y
= 1 half-life = 2 half-lives = 3 half-lives = 4 half-lives

Time

(Figure 27-10)

Alpha, beta, and gamma decays: Large nuclei release energy and become more stable by emitting an alpha particle (a ^{4}He nucleus). Other nuclei with too many neutrons undergo beta-minus decay, in which one neutron changes into a proton; those with too many protons undergo beta-plus decay, in which one proton changes into a neutron. In gamma decay, an excited state of a nucleus (indicated by an asterisk) transitions to a less excited state and emits a gamma-ray photon (γ).

An alpha decay:

$$^{228}\text{Th} \rightarrow {}^{224}\text{Ra} + \alpha$$

A beta-minus decay:

$$^{99}\text{Tc} \rightarrow {}^{99}\text{Ru} + e^- + \bar{\nu}_e$$

A beta-plus decay:

$$^{99}\text{Rh} \rightarrow {}^{99}\text{Ru} + e^+ + \nu_e$$

A gamma decay:

$$^{137}\text{Ba}^* \rightarrow {}^{137}\text{Ba} + \gamma$$

Answer to What do you think? Question

(e) In a radioactive material, the amount that remains decreases by 1/2 after one half-life. After two half-lives, the amount that remains is $(1/2) \times (1/2) = (1/2)^2 = 1/4$; after three half-lives, $(1/2) \times (1/2) \times (1/2) = (1/2)^3 = 1/8$; and so on. The age of the cave painting is between $(30{,}000 \text{ y})/(5730 \text{ y}) = 5.2$ half-lives and $(33{,}000 \text{ y})/(5730 \text{ y}) = 5.8$ half-lives, so more than 5 half-lives have elapsed since the painting was made. Therefore the amount of carbon-14 remaining is less than $(1/2) \times (1/2) \times (1/2) \times (1/2) \times (1/2) = (1/2)^5 = 1/32$ of the original.

Answers to Got the Concept? Questions

27-1 (c) Equation 27-1 tells us that the radius of a nucleus is proportional to $A^{1/3}$, the cube root of the number of nucleons (the mass number). Compared to a ^{20}Ne nucleus, a ^{160}Dy nucleus has $160/20 = 8$ times as many nucleons, so its radius is larger by a factor of $8^{1/3} = 2$. As we discussed in Example 27-2, nuclei with any value of A have the same density.

27-2 (c), (b), (d), (a) A ranking in order of stability is a ranking in order of binding energy per nucleon. Figure 27-6 shows that this is greatest for ^{86}Kr (more than 8.5 MeV), second greatest for ^{20}Ne (slightly more than 8 MeV), third greatest for ^{200}Hg (slightly less than 8 MeV), and least for ^{11}B (about 6.9 MeV).

27-3 (d) The number of protons and the number of neutrons both remain the same: A ^{20}Ne nucleus has 10 protons and 10 neutrons, and each ^{10}B nucleus has 5 protons and 5 neutrons. But the binding energy per nucleon for ^{10}B is *less* than for ^{20}Ne (see Figure 27-6). For fission to occur and energy to be released, the fragments must have a greater binding energy per nucleon than the initial nucleus. The process ^{20}Ne $\rightarrow$ ^{10}B + ^{10}B would require a substantial amount of energy to be spontaneously added to the ^{20}Ne nucleus, and there's no way that can happen.

27-4 (d) In order for two ^{1}H nuclei to fuse, they must come to within a few femtometers (1 fm = 10^{-15} m) of each other. But in a typical molecule, including H$_2$, the separation between nuclei in adjacent atoms is on the order of 10^{-10} m. So the nuclei are normally too far apart to fuse. If they were moving rapidly with respect to each other and so had a large kinetic energy, the nuclei could overcome their mutual Coulomb repulsion and come close enough to fuse. But atomic nuclei move hardly at all within molecules, and so fusion cannot happen this way. Option (c) is incorrect: The properties of a nucleus are affected not at all by the presence or absence of electrons orbiting the nucleus.

27-5 (c) After each 5-day half-life, the number of nuclei decreases by a factor of 1/2. For the number to decrease by a factor of 1/1000 requires about 10 half-lives, since $(1/2)^{10} = 1/2^{10} = 1/1024$.

Questions and Problems

In a few problems, you are given more data than you actually need; in a few other problems, you are required to supply data from your general knowledge, outside sources, or informed estimate. Interpret as significant all digits in numerical values that have trailing zeros and no decimal points.

For all problems, use $g = 9.80$ m/s^2 for the free-fall acceleration due to gravity. Neglect friction and air resistance unless instructed to do otherwise.

- • Basic, single-concept problem
- •• Intermediate-level problem, may require synthesis of concepts and multiple steps
- ••• Challenging problem

SSM *Solution is in Student Solutions Manual*

Conceptual Questions

1. •What is an isotope?

2. •What is the difference between atomic number and mass number?

3. •Describe two characteristics of the binding energy that are comparable to the work function (from the photoelectric effect) and two characteristics that are dissimilar to the concept of the work function.

4. •(a) Describe what is meant by the phrase "larger nuclei are neutron rich." (b) Why do most nuclei contain at least as many neutrons as protons?

5. •A simple idea of nuclear physics can be stated as follows: "The whole nucleus weighs less than the sum of its parts." Explain why.

6. •Describe the basic characteristics of the nuclear force that exists between nucleons. What other competing force is present in the nucleus?

7. •Some historians would claim that without Einstein's special theory of relativity, nuclear physics would never have developed. Explain why. SSM

8. •What is the difference between fission and fusion?

9. •(a) Which elements in the periodic table are more likely to undergo nuclear fission? (b) Which are more likely to undergo nuclear fusion?

10. •**Astronomy** (a) Describe the nuclear reactions that occur in our Sun. (b) Discuss how the equilibrium state of the Sun is not permanent and discuss the eventual future of our solar system.

11. •Explain how conservation of energy and momentum would be violated if a neutrino were not emitted in beta decay. SSM

12. •To date, the decay constant of a radioactive nucleus is just that, *constant*. It does not depend on the size of the nuclear sample or the temperature or any external fields (such as gravity, electricity, or magnetism). Define the decay constant and

comment on how nuclear radioactivity would change if the quantity were dependent on temperature.

13. •At any given instant, a sample of radioactive uranium contains many, many different isotopes of atoms that are *not* uranium. Explain why.

14. •(a) Explain how radioactive ^{14}C is used to determine the age of ancient artifacts. (b) Which types of artifacts can have their age determined in this way and which types cannot?

15. •If atomic masses are used, explain why the mass of a beta particle is *not* accounted for in the basic beta decay

$$n \rightarrow p + e^- + \bar{\nu}_e$$

Assume that the mass of the antineutrino ($\bar{\nu}_e$) is very small and can be neglected. SSM

16. •**Medical** Describe, in broad terms, the health risks associated with the three major forms of radioactivity: alpha, beta, and gamma. Focus on the dangers due to inherent health risks and the ability of each to penetrate shielding material.

Multiple-Choice Questions

17. •In an atomic nucleus, the nuclear force binds _____ together.
   A. electrons
   B. neutrons
   C. protons
   D. neutrons and protons
   E. neutrons, protons, and electrons

18. •The mass of a nucleus is _____ the sum of the masses of its nucleons.
   A. always less than
   B. sometimes less than
   C. always more than
   D. always equal to
   E. sometimes equal to

19. •Which of the following statements is true?
   A. Fusion absorbs energy and fission releases energy.
   B. Fusion releases energy and fission absorbs energy.
   C. Both fusion and fission absorb energy.
   D. Both fusion and fission release energy.
   E. Both fusion and fission can release or absorb energy. SSM

20. •In fission processes, which of the following statements is true?
   A. Only the total number of nuclei remains the same.
   B. Only the total number of protons remains the same.
   C. Only the total number of neutrons remains the same.
   D. The total number of protons and the total number of nuclei both remain the same.
   E. The total number of protons and the total number of neutrons both remain the same.

21. •In a spontaneous fission reaction, the total mass of the products is _____ the mass of the original elements.
   A. greater than
   B. less than
   C. the same as
   D. double
   E. one-half

22. •What is the source of the Sun's energy?
   A. chemical reactions
   B. fission reactions
   C. fusion reactions
   D. gravitational collapse
   E. both fusion reactions and fission reactions

23. •In a spontaneous fusion reaction, the total mass of the products is _____ the mass of the original elements.
   A. greater than
   B. less than
   C. the same as
   D. double
   E. one-half SSM

24. • The decay constant λ depends only on
   A. the number of atoms at the initial time.
   B. the initial decay rate.
   C. the half-life.
   D. the binding energy per nucleon.
   E. whether the decay is alpha, beta, or gamma.

25. • The number of radioactive atoms in a radioactive sample
   A. decreases linearly with time.
   B. increases linearly with time.
   C. decreases exponentially with time.
   D. increases exponentially with time.
   E. remains constant.

26. • The decay rate for any isotope
   A. decreases linearly with time.
   B. increases linearly with time.
   C. decreases exponentially with time.
   D. increases exponentially with time.
   E. remains constant.

Estimation/Numerical Analysis

27. •Estimate the relative size of the nuclear force compared to the electrostatic force between two protons in the nucleus.

28. •Estimate the size of the nucleus compared to the size of the atom.

29. •Estimate the density of an atomic nucleus compared to an atom. SSM

30. •Estimate the energy of a typical nuclear reaction compared to the energy of a typical chemical reaction.

31. •Estimate the ratio of the nuclear force between two nucleons when they are separated by a distance of 0.5 fm compared to a separation distance of 2.0 fm.

32. •Estimate the number of half-lives that must go by before 10% of an isotope remains. What about 1%?

33. •Estimate the mass of a basketball that has the density of nuclear material.

34. •Estimate the number of nuclei that are in a 50-kg human body.

35. •If the half-life of a radioactive isotope is 1 day, (a) estimate how long it takes before the sample is reduced to 62.5% of its original amount and (b) how long before it is reduced to 6.25% of its original amount. SSM

36. •(a) Using a spreadsheet or programmable calculator, calculate the binding energy per nucleon for the following isotopes of the first five elements. Masses given are atomic masses.

hydrogen-1: 1.007825 u	lithium-8: 8.022486 u	boron-8: 8.024605 u
hydrogen-2: 2.014102 u	lithium-9: 9.026789 u	boron-10: 10.012936 u
hydrogen-3: 3.016049 u	lithium-11: 11.043897 u	boron-11: 11.009305 u
helium-3: 3.016029 u	beryllium-7: 7.016928 u	boron-12: 12.014352 u
helium-4: 4.002602 u	beryllium-9: 9.012174 u	boron-13: 13.017780 u
helium-6: 6.018886 u	beryllium-10: 10.013534	boron-14: 14.025404 u
helium-8: 8.033922 u	beryllium-11: 11.021657 u	boron-15: 15.031100 u
lithium-6: 6.015121 u	beryllium-12: 12.026921 u	
lithium-7: 7.016003 u	beryllium-14: 14.024866 u	

(b) Now calculate the binding energy per nucleon for the following isotopes of the last five naturally occurring elements. The masses provided are atomic masses.

radium-221: 221.01391 u	thorium-228: 228.028716 u	uranium-231: 231.036264 u
radium-223: 223.018499 u	thorium-229: 229.031757 u	uranium-232: 232.037131 u
radium-224: 224.020187 u	thorium-230: 230.033127 u	uranium-233: 233.039630 u
radium-226: 226.025402 u	thorium-231: 231.036299 u	uranium-234: 234.040946 u
radium-228: 228.031064 u	thorium-232: 232.038051 u	uranium-235: 235.043924 u
actinium-227: 227.027749 u	thorium-234: 234.043593 u	uranium-236: 236.045562 u
actinium-228: 228.031015 u	protactinium-231: 231.035880 u	uranium-238: 238.050784 u
thorium-227: 227.027701 u	protactinium-234: 234.043300 u	uranium-239: 239.054290 u

(c) Compare your results and comment on any patterns or trends that are obvious.

Problems

Note: In all cases, unless otherwise stated, binding energy, energy released, and the like, are to be expressed in MeV. Also, all atomic masses should be calculated to the nearest 10^{-6}.

27-1 The quantum concepts that help explain atoms are essential for understanding the nucleus

27-2 The strong nuclear force holds nuclei together

37. •Provide the elemental abbreviation, and give the number of protons, the number of neutrons, and the mass number for each of the following isotopes:

    A. hydrogen-3   C. aluminum-26
    B. beryllium-8   D. gold-197

    E. technetium-100   G. osmium-190
    F. tungsten-184   H. plutonium-239

38. ••Calculate the radius of each of the nuclei in problem 37.

39. •Name the element, and give the number of protons, the number of neutrons, and the mass number for each of the following nuclei:

    A. ^{2}H   D. ^{12}C   G. ^{131}I
    B. ^{4}He   E. ^{56}Fe   H. ^{235}U
    C. ^{6}Li   F. ^{90}Sr

40. ••If our Sun (mass = 1.99×10^{30} kg, radius = 6.96×10^{8} m) were to collapse into a neutron star (an object composed of tightly packed neutrons with roughly the same density as neutrons within a nucleus), what would the new radius of our "neutron-sun" be?

41. ••Given that a nucleus is approximately spherical and has a radius $r = r_0 A^{1/3}$ (where r_0 is about 1.2 fm), determine its approximate mass density. Express your answer in SI units and convert to tons per cubic inch, units that might be used in a news report. SSM

27-3 Some nuclei are more tightly bound and more stable than others

42. ••Calculate the atomic mass of each of the isotopes listed below. Give your answer in atomic mass units (u) and in grams (g). The values will include the mass of Z electrons.

    A. ^{1}H   D. ^{12}C   G. ^{131}I
    B. ^{4}He   E. ^{56}Fe   H. ^{238}U
    C. ^{9}Be   F. ^{90}Sr

43. •What is the binding energy of carbon-12? Give your answer in MeV. SSM

44. ••What is the binding energy per nucleon for the following isotopes?

    A. ^{2}H   D. ^{12}C   G. ^{129}I
    B. ^{4}He   E. ^{56}Fe   H. ^{235}U
    C. ^{6}Li   F. ^{90}Sr

45. •What minimum energy is needed to remove a neutron from ^{40}Ca and convert it to ^{39}Ca? The atomic masses of the two isotopes are 39.96259098 u and 38.97071972 u, respectively.

46. •What is the binding energy of the last neutron of carbon-13? The atomic mass of carbon-13 is 13.003355 u.

47. ••**Medical** Iodine-131 is a radioactive isotope that is used in the treatment of cancer of the thyroid. The natural tendency of the thyroid to take up iodine creates a pathway for which radiation (β- and γ) that is emitted from this unstable nucleus can be directed onto the cancerous tumor with very little collateral damage to surrounding healthy tissue. Another advantage of the isotope is its relatively short half-life (8 days). Calculate the binding energy of iodine-131 and the binding energy per nucleon. The mass of iodine-131 is 130.906124 u.

27-4 The largest nuclei can release energy by undergoing fission and splitting apart

48. •Calculate the energy released in the following nuclear fission reaction:

$$^{239}\text{Pu} + \text{n} \rightarrow {}^{98}\text{Tc} + {}^{138}\text{Sb} + 4\text{n}$$

Recall that the atomic masses are ^{239}Pu = 239.052157 u, ^{98}Tc = 97.907215 u, and ^{138}Sb = 137.940793 u.

49. •Complete the following nuclear fission reaction of thorium-232 and calculate the energy released in the reaction: ^{232}Th + n → ^{99}Kr + ^{124}Xe + __? The atomic masses are ^{232}Th = 232.038051 u, ^{99}Kr = 98.957606 u, and ^{124}Xe = 123.905894 u. SSM

50. •Complete the following fission reactions:

A. ^{235}U + n → ^{128}Sb + ^{101}Nb + __?__

B. ^{235}U + n → __?__ + ^{116}Pd + 4n

C. ^{238}U + n → ^{99}Kr + __?__ +11n

D. __?__ + n → ^{101}Rb + ^{130}Cs + 8n

51. •Complete the following fission reactions:

A. ^{242}Am + __?__ → ^{90}Sr + ^{149}La + 4n

B. ^{244}Pa + n → __?__ + ^{131}Sb + 12n

C. __?__ + n → ^{92}Se + ^{153}Sm + 6n

D. ^{262}Fm + n → ^{112}Rh + __?__ + 9n

52. •Calculate the energy (in MeV) released in the following nuclear fission reaction:

$$^{242}\text{Am} + \_\_?\_\_ \rightarrow {}^{90}\text{Sr} + {}^{149}\text{La} + 4\text{n}$$

Start by completing the reaction and use the following nuclear masses: ^{242}Am = 242.059549 u, ^{90}Sr = 89.9077387 u, and ^{149}La = 148.934733 u.

53. ••Assuming that in a fission reactor a neutron loses half its energy in each collision with an atom of the moderator, determine how many collisions are required to slow a 200-MeV neutron to an energy of 0.04 eV.

54. ••Knowing that the binding energy per nucleon for uranium-235 is about 7.6 MeV/nucleon and the binding energy per nucleon for typical fission fragments is about 8.5 MeV/nucleon, find an average energy release per uranium-235 fission reaction in MeV.

55. ••How many kilograms of uranium-235 must completely fission to produce 1000 MW of power continuously for one year? SSM

56. ••Repeat problem 55 in the more realistic case where the fission reactions are about 30% efficient in producing 1000 MW of power over 1 year of continuous operation.

57. ••Calculate the number of fission reactions per second that take place in a 1000-MW reactor. Assume that there are 200 MeV/reaction released.

27-5 The smallest nuclei can release energy if they are forced to fuse together

58. •Complete the following fusion reactions:

A. ^{2}H + ^{3}H → ^{4}He + __?__

B. ^{4}He + ^{4}He → ^{7}Be + __?__

C. ^{2}H + ^{2}H → ^{3}He + __?__

D. ^{2}H + ^{1}H → γ + __?__

E. ^{2}H + ^{2}H → ^{3}H + __?__

59. ••Calculate the energy released in each of the fusion reactions in problem 58. Give your answers in MeV.

60. ••**Astronomy** Consider the proton–proton cycle that occurs in most stars (including our own Sun):

Step 1: ^{1}H + ^{1}H → ^{2}H + e^{+} + ν_e

Step 2: ^{2}H + ^{1}H → ^{3}He + γ

Step 3: ^{3}He + ^{3}He → ^{4}He + 2 ^{1}H + γ

Calculate the net energy released from the three steps. Do *not* ignore the mass of the positron in Step 1. (You may ignore the mass of the neutrino.)

61. ••Each D–T fusion reaction releases about 20 MeV. How much tritium (T or ^{3}H) is needed to create 1014 J of energy, assuming that an endless supply of deuterium (D or ^{2}H) is available? SSM

62. ••How many fusion reactions per second must be sustained to operate a deuterium–tritium fusion power plant that outputs 1000 MW, operating at 33% efficiency?

27-6 Unstable nuclei may emit alpha, beta, or gamma radiation

63. •Complete the following conversions (cpm is counts per minute):

A. 100 μCi = _____ Bq

B. 1500 cpm = _____ Bq

C. 16,500 Bq = _____ Ci

D. 7.55×10^{10} Bq = _____ cpm

64. •The curie unit is defined as 1 Ci = 3.7×10^{10} Bq, which is about the rate at which radiation is emitted by 1.00 g of radium. (a) Calculate the half-life of radium from the definition. (b) What does your calculation tell you about the radiation emission rate of radium?

65. •A certain radioactive isotope has a decay constant of 0.00334 s^{-1}. Find the half-life in seconds and days. SSM

66. ••A radioactive sample is monitored with a radiation detector to produce 5640 counts per minute. Twelve hours later, the detector reads 1410 counts per minute. Calculate the decay constant and the half-life of the sample.

67. •What fraction of a sample of ^{32}P will be left after 4 months? Its half-life is 14.3 days.

68. •What fraction of a radioactive sample will be left after 6 half-lives? What about 7.5 half-lives?

69. ••**Medical** A patient is injected with 7.88 μCi of radioactive iodine-131 that has a half-life of 8.02 days. Assuming that 90% of the iodine ultimately finds its way to the thyroid, what decay rate do you expect to find in the thyroid after 30 days? SSM

70. ••The ratio of carbon-14 to carbon-12 in living wood is 1.3×10^{-12}. How many decays per second are there in 550 g of wood?

71. ••You take a course in archaeology that includes field work. An ancient wooden totem pole is excavated from your archaeological dig. The beta activity is measured at 150 cpm. If the totem pole contains 225 g of carbon and the ratio of carbon-14 to carbon-12 in living trees is 1.3×10^{-12}, what is the age of the pole?

72. ••Twelve centuries after a tree limb is cut, determine the decay rate for 500 g of carbon from the tree.

73. ••How many nuclei of radon-222 are present in a sample with an activity of 485 cpm? SSM

74. ••The ages of rocks that contain fossils can be determined using the isotope ^{87}Rb. This isotope of rubidium undergoes beta decay with a half-life of 4.75×10^{10} y. Ancient samples contain a ratio of ^{87}Sr to ^{87}Rb of 0.0225. Given that ^{87}Sr is a stable product of the beta decay of ^{87}Rb, and there was originally no ^{87}Sr present in the rocks, calculate the age of the rock sample.

Assume that the decay rate is constant over the relatively short lifetime of the rock compared to the half-life of ^{87}Rb.

75. •Complete the following alpha decays:
- A. $^{238}\text{U} \rightarrow \alpha + \underline{\quad?\quad}$
- B. $^{234}\text{Th} \rightarrow \underline{\quad?\quad} + {}^{-?}\text{Ra}$
- C. $\underline{\quad?\quad} \rightarrow \alpha + {}^{236}\text{U}$
- D. $^{214}\text{Bi} \rightarrow \alpha + \underline{\quad?\quad}$

76. •Complete the following beta decays:
- A. $^{14}\text{C} \rightarrow e^- + \bar{\nu}_e + \underline{\quad?\quad}$
- B. $^{239}\text{Np} \rightarrow e^- + \bar{\nu}_e + \underline{\quad?\quad}$
- C. $\underline{\quad?\quad} \rightarrow e^- + \bar{\nu}_e + {}^{60}\text{Ni}$
- D. $^{3}\text{H} \rightarrow e^- + \bar{\nu}_e + \underline{\quad?\quad}$
- E. $^{13}\text{N} \rightarrow e^+ + \underline{\quad?\quad} + \underline{\quad?\quad}$

77. •Complete the following gamma decays:
- A. $^{131}\text{I}^* \rightarrow \gamma + \underline{\quad?\quad}$
- B. $^{145}\text{Pm}^* \rightarrow {}^{145}\text{Pm} + \underline{\quad?\quad}$
- C. $\underline{\quad?\quad} \rightarrow \gamma + {}^{24}\text{Na}$

78. ••Nickel-64 has an excited state 1.34 MeV above the ground state. The atomic mass of the ground state of this isotope of nickel is 63.927967 u. (a) What is the mass of the atom when the nucleus is in this excited state? (b) What is the wavelength of the gamma ray that is emitted when the nucleus decays to the ground state?

General Problems

79. ••(a) What is the approximate radius of the ^{238}U nucleus? (b) What electric force do two protons on opposite ends of the ^{238}U nucleus exert on each other? (c) If the electric force in part (b) were the only force acting on the protons, what would be their acceleration just as they left the nucleus? (d) Why do the protons in part (b) not accelerate apart? SSM

80. ••The semi-empirical binding energy formula is given as follows:

$$E_B = (15.8\,\text{MeV})A - (17.8\,\text{MeV})A^{2/3}$$
$$- (0.71\,\text{MeV})\frac{Z(Z-1)}{A^{1/3}} - (23.7\,\text{MeV})\frac{(N-Z)^2}{A}$$

where A is the mass number, N is the number of neutrons, and Z is the number of protons. Using the formula, calculate the binding energy per nucleon for fermium-252. Compare your answer with the standard common expression for the binding energy: $E_B = (Nm_n + Zm_p - m_{\text{whole}})c^2$.

81. ••The *fissionability parameter* is defined as the atomic number squared divided by the mass number for any given nucleus (Z^2/A). It can be shown that when this parameter is less than 44, a nucleus will be stable against small deformation; essentially, the nucleus will be stable against spontaneous fission. Calculate the value of this parameter for (a) ^{235}U, (b) ^{238}U, (c) ^{239}Pu, (d) ^{240}Pu, (e) ^{246}Cf, and (f) ^{254}Cf.

82. •The stable isotope of sodium is ^{23}Na. What kind of radioactivity would be expected from (a) ^{22}Na and (b) ^{24}Na?

83. ••In 2010, physicists for the first time created the heavy element number 117 by colliding calcium-48 and berkelium-249 at high energy. The result was two isotopes of the new element, one of which had a half-life of 14 ms and contained 176 neutrons. (a) What is the radius of the nucleus of the new element 117? (b) What percent of the newly created isotope was left 1.0 s after its creation? SSM

84. ••Natural uranium is made up of two isotopes: ^{235}U and ^{238}U. The half-life of ^{235}U is 7.04×10^8 y, and the half-life of ^{238}U is 4.47×10^9 y. Assuming that all uranium isotopes were created simultaneously and in equal amounts at the same time that Earth was formed, estimate the age of Earth. The current percent abundance of ^{235}U is 0.72% and for ^{238}U it is 99.28%.

85. ••**Astronomy** The atom technetium (Tc) has no stable isotopes, yet its spectral lines have been detected in red giant stars (stars at the end of their lifetimes). Tc can be produced artificially on Earth. Its longest-lived isotope, ^{98}Tc, has a half-life of 4.2 million years. (a) If any ^{98}Tc was present when Earth formed 4.5×10^9 y ago, what percentage of it is still present? (Careful! You cannot do this calculation with your calculator. You must use logarithms to express the answer in scientific notation.) (b) What percent of the original ^{98}Tc would be present in a red giant that is 10 billion years old? (Careful again! You'll need to use logarithms.) (c) Explain why the detection of technetium in old stars is strong evidence that stars manufacture the atoms in the universe.

86. ••An old wooden bowl unearthed in an archeological dig is found to have one-fourth of the amount of carbon-14 present in a similar sample of fresh wood. Determine the age of the bowl.

87. ••In an attempt to determine the age of the cave paintings in Chauvet-Pont-d'Arc Cave in France, scientists used carbon-14 dating to measure the age of bones of bears found in the cave. The bears are depicted in the paintings, so presumably the bones are approximately the same age as the paintings. The results showed that the level of ^{14}C was reduced to 2.35% of its present-day level. How old were the bones (and presumably the paintings)? SSM

88. ••In one common type of household smoke detector, the radioactive isotope americium-241 decays by alpha emission. The alpha particles produce a small electrical current because they are charged. If smoke enters the detector, it blocks the alpha particles, which reduces the current and causes the alarm to go off. The half-life of ^{241}Am is 433 y, and its atomic weight is 241 g/mol. Typical decay rates in smoke detectors are 690 Bq. (a) Write the decay reaction of ^{241}Am and identify the daughter nucleus. (b) By how much does the alpha particle current decrease in 1.0 y due to the decay of the americium? How much in 50 y? (c) How many grams of ^{241}Am are there in a typical smoke detector?

89. ••In March 2011, a giant tsunami struck the Fukushima nuclear reactor in Japan, resulting in very large radiation leaks, including cesium-137. The isotope has a 30-y half-life and is a beta-minus emitter. (a) What daughter nucleus is left after cesium-137 decays? (b) How long after the release will it take for the decay rate of the cesium-137 to be reduced by 99%?

90. ••Three isotopes of aluminum are given in the following table:

Isotope	Atomic mass (u)	E_B/nucleon	Decay process
^{26}Al	25.986892		
^{27}Al	26.981538		Stable
^{28}Al	27.981910		

Calculate the binding energy per nucleon for each isotope and make a prediction of the decay processes for the unstable isotopes aluminum-26 and aluminum-28.

91. ••**Biology** In February 2010, the discovery of leaks due to aging pipes of the carcinogen tritium (^{3}H) at 27 U.S. nuclear reactors was announced. In one well in Vermont, contaminated water registered 70,500 pCi/L, whereas the federal safety limit was 20,000 pCi/L. Tritium is a β^- emitter with a half-life of 12.3 y. (a) How many protons and neutrons does the tritium nucleus contain? (b) Write out the decay equation for tritium and identify the daughter nucleus. (c) If the leak at the Vermont site is stopped, how long will it take for the water in the contaminated well to reach the federal safety level?

92. ••**Medical** Iodine-125 is used to treat, among other things, brain tumors and prostate cancer. It decays by gamma decay with a half-life of 59.4 days. Patients who fly soon after receiving ^{125}I implants are given medical statements from the hospital verifying such treatment because their radiation could set off radiation detectors at airports. If the initial decay rate was 525 μCi, (a) what will the rate be at the end of the first year, and (b) how many months after the treatment will the decay rate be reduced by 90%?

93. ••**Medical** Ruthenium-106 is used to treat melanoma in the eye. This isotope decays by β^- emission with a half-life of 373.59 days. One source of the isotope is reprocessed nuclear reactor fuel. (a) How many protons and neutrons does the ^{106}Ru nucleus contain? (b) Could we expect to find significant amounts of ^{106}Ru in ore mined from the ground? Why or why not? (c) Write the decay equation for ^{106}Ru and identify the daughter nucleus. (d) How many years after ^{106}Ru is implanted in the eye does it take for its decay rate to be reduced by 75%?

94. ••**Medical** You are asked to prepare a sample of ruthenium-106 for a radiation treatment. Its half-life is 373.59 days, it is a beta emitter, its atomic weight is 106/g/mol, and its density at room temperature is 12.45/g/cm^3. (a) How many grams will you need to prepare a sample having an

activity rate of 125 μCi? (b) If the sample in part (a) is a spherical droplet, what will be its radius?

95. ••Electron capture by a proton is *not* allowed in nature. Explain why. Specifically, describe why the following nuclear reaction does *not* occur (and for good reason!): SSM

$$e^- + p \not\rightarrow n + \nu_e$$

96. ••Taking into account the recoil (kinetic energy) of the daughter nucleus, calculate the energy of the alpha particle in the following decay:

$$^{235}\text{U} \rightarrow \alpha + {}^{231}\text{Th}$$

97. ••Several radioactive decay series are observed in nature. Four of the most well known are as shown here. The neptunium decay series actually is extinct. The first three all end in different, stable isotopes of lead.

    A. Thorium Decay Series: $A = 4n$
        Starting isotope: ^{232}Th Ending isotope: ^{208}Pb
    B. Radium or Uranium Decay Series: $A = 4n + 2$
        Starting isotope: ^{238}U Ending isotope: ^{206}Pb
    C. Actinium Decay Series: $A = 4n + 3$
        Starting isotope: ^{235}U Ending isotope: ^{207}Pb
    D. Neptunium Decay Series: $A = 4n + 1$
        Starting isotope: ^{237}Np Ending isotope: ^{209}Bi

Trace out the pathway (keeping count of the total number of alpha and beta emissions) that terminates with a stable nucleus for each of the radioactive decay series above.

98. ••A friend suggests that the world's energy problems could be solved if only physicists were to pursue the fusion of *heavy* nuclei rather than the fusion of *light* nuclei. To prove his point, he suggests that the following fusion reaction should be considered: ^{157}Nd + ^{80}Ge $\rightarrow$ ^{235}U + 2n.

Using the insights that you have acquired in this chapter, show that his argument is flawed. The atomic mass of neodymium-157 is 156.939032 u, and the mass of germanium-80 is 79.925373 u.

28

Particle Physics and Beyond

In this chapter, your goals are to:

- (28-1) Explain why physicists examine both the smallest and largest objects in the universe.
- (28-2) Describe the difference between hadrons and leptons, and explain what hadrons are made of.
- (28-3) Explain how fundamental particles interact with each other, and the differences among the four fundamental forces.
- (28-4) Calculate the distance to a remote galaxy from its recessional velocity.

To master this chapter, you should review:

- (10-4) How the speed of an object in a gravitational orbit depends on the strength of the gravitational force (distance from the massive central object).
- (13-10) How the Doppler effect describes the shift in frequency of a sound wave coming from a moving object.
- (15-3) How an ideal gas cools when it undergoes an adiabatic expansion.
- (22-4) The energy of a photon.
- (25-7) The equivalence of mass and energy.
- (26-2) How the frequency spectrum of blackbody radiation depends on temperature.
- (26-5) Atomic spectra and Rutherford's discovery of the nucleus.
- (27-6) The process of beta decay.

28-1 Studying the ultimate constituents of matter helps reveal the nature of the universe

"What is the world made of?" "Where did I come from?" You probably asked questions like these when you were a small child. Physicists and astronomers ask these questions throughout their professional lives, in search of ever more sophisticated answers about the nature and origin of the physical universe. In this final chapter we'll take a brief look at our present understanding of **particle physics**, the branch of physics that concerns the fundamental constituents of matter and how they interact. We'll also see evidence that our universe began in a state of tremendously high temperature and immense density some 13.8 billion years ago.

We'll begin by looking at the fundamental particles that make up all of the ordinary matter that you see around you, including the matter that makes up your body.

Oranges are a good source of potassium. A small fraction of the potassium is radioactive ^{40}K, which decays by emitting a positron—a bit of antimatter. This decay also involves a quark, a neutrino, and an exchange particle called a W$^+$.

(a)

When a television is disconnected from the source, about 1% of the "static" on the screen is from cosmic background radiation— the afterglow of the Big Bang at the beginning of time.

(b)

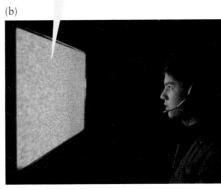

Figure 28-1 **Particle physics and cosmology** Ordinary objects and common technology connect us to (a) particle physics, the study of fundamental particles and their interactions, and (b) cosmology, the study of the nature and evolution of the universe.

These include leptons, of which the electron is the best-known example, and quarks, which have the curious property that their charges are a fraction of the fundamental charge e. We'll see that these fundamental particles interact with each other by exchanging particles back and forth, a process that actually involves violating the law of conservation of energy (but in a way that's nonetheless compatible with the laws of physics). These interactions help explain the strong forces that hold the nucleus together, the electric forces that keep electrons in the atom, and the weak forces that cause radioactive beta decay (Figure 28-1a).

We'll conclude the chapter by redirecting our attention from the smallest particles to some of the largest structures in the universe, the galaxies. We'll learn that our universe is expanding and is filled with electromagnetic radiation that is left over from the first few hundred thousand years of the history of the universe (Figure 28-1b). We'll also find that most of the matter in the universe is in a form whose nature is almost a complete mystery, and that most of the energy in the universe is even more mysterious in its character. There is much we know about the physical universe, but there is a great deal more yet to be learned!

> **Take-Home Message for Section 28-1**
>
> ✔ Ordinary matter such as atoms is composed of a small variety of different fundamental particles.
>
> ✔ Studying distant galaxies tells us about the nature and evolution of our universe.

28-2 Most forms of matter can be explained by just a handful of fundamental particles

By the late nineteenth century, scientists had come to the conclusion that all matter was composed of atoms and that atoms could not be subdivided into more elementary particles. The notion was that a hydrogen atom was fundamentally different from a helium atom, which in turn was fundamentally different from a carbon atom, and so on. As we learned in Section 26-5, this conclusion was incorrect. In 1897 J. J. Thomson discovered the electron, a particle of charge $-e = -1.602 \times 10^{-19}$ C, which turned out to be a constituent of the atoms of every element. In 1909 Ernest Rutherford discovered the atomic nucleus, and in 1917 he found evidence that all nuclei contain a positively charged particle of charge $+e$ that is identical with a hydrogen nucleus—that is, what we now call a proton. In 1932 the English physicist James Chadwick discovered the neutron, which has zero charge. As we learned in Chapter 27, all nuclei are composed of protons and neutrons (referred to collectively as nucleons) and all atoms are made of nuclei plus electrons. So by 1932 it seemed that these three particles—electron, proton, and neutron—were the truly fundamental building blocks of which all matter is made. That conclusion, too, turned out to be wildly incorrect.

Since 1932, literally hundreds of other subatomic particles have been discovered. All of these are unstable and decay to other particles with a radioactive half-life of a

(a)

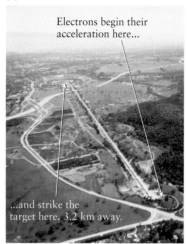

Electrons begin their acceleration here...

...and strike the target here, 3.2 km away.

(b)

When high-energy electrons scatter from protons, a substantial number scatter backwards.

Quarks

Electron

Proton

This is evidence that there are small charged objects (quarks) inside the proton.

Figure 28-2 Discovering quarks
(a) In a seminal experiment at the Stanford Linear Accelerator Center, electrons were accelerated to a kinetic energy of 20 GeV = 2 × 10⁴ MeV and fired into a target containing protons. (b) Measuring how the electrons scattered from the protons provided evidence of the existence of quarks.

fraction of a second. (In this aspect they resemble the neutron: A free neutron that is not incorporated into a nucleus undergoes beta decay with a half-life of about 15 minutes.) But none of these additional particles can be regarded as simple combinations of protons, neutrons, and electrons. They include the neutrino, which has no charge, interacts hardly at all with other particles, and has a mass so close to zero that it has yet to be accurately measured; the muon, which resembles an electron in almost every way except that it is 207 times more massive; the pion, which like the proton and neutron experiences the strong nuclear force but has only about one-seventh the mass of a proton; and the delta, which resembles a proton or neutron but is about 30% more massive and comes in four varieties, with charges $+2e$, $+e$, 0, and $-e$. The discovery of these additional particles forced physicists to once again ask the question: What *are* the fundamental building blocks of matter?

Hadrons and Quarks

To answer this question, it's useful to distinguish between particles that experience the strong nuclear force, including the proton and neutron, and those that do not, such as the electron. Since protons and neutrons are relatively heavy and electrons are relatively light, we use the term **hadrons** (from the Greek word for stout or thick) for particles that experience the strong force and the term **leptons** (from the Greek word for small or delicate) for those that do not. (The photon is considered to be in a special category of its own, to which we will return later.) The vast majority of new particles discovered since 1932 are hadrons, so we'll look at these first.

In 1964 the American physicists Murray Gell-Mann and George Zweig independently proposed that all hadrons are made of more fundamental entities that Gell-Mann whimsically named **quarks**. The first evidence that quarks really exist came from experiments carried out at the Stanford Linear Accelerator Center, or SLAC, in 1967 (**Figure 28-2a**). These experiments were the same in principle as Rutherford's 1909 experiment that led to the discovery of the atomic nucleus. As we saw in Section 26-5, Rutherford aimed a beam of alpha particles at a target of gold. Had the charge inside the atom been distributed more or less uniformly, the alpha particles would have undergone only gentle deflections as they passed through the gold atoms. Instead, Rutherford found that some alpha particles were scattered by very large angles. This was evidence that charge was highly concentrated into a very small object within the atom—namely, the nucleus. The experiment at SLAC used electrons instead of alpha particles and aimed these electrons at a target of protons (the nuclei of hydrogen atoms inside a tank of liquid hydrogen). The 3.2-km-long accelerator gave each electron a tremendous kinetic energy—some 20,000 MeV, compared to the 7 MeV of Rutherford's alpha particles—and a correspondingly large momentum. This was done so that the electron would have a de Broglie wavelength much smaller than the size of the proton and so would be sensitive to fine details of the proton's internal structure as it passed through the proton.

Much as in the Rutherford experiment six decades before, many physicists expected that the electrons would undergo only small-angle deflections because they thought the charge inside the proton was distributed uniformly over its volume. And just as in the Rutherford experiment, what they found was that a substantial number of electrons were scattered by very large angles (**Figure 28-2b**). The conclusion was that the proton's charge is carried by smaller entities inside the proton, which are the quarks.

These experiments and a host of others confirm that Gell-Mann and Zweig were correct and that quarks are the fundamental building blocks of all hadrons. To explain all of the hundreds of hadron varieties currently known, we need six varieties or *flavors* of quarks. These are known as the up (u), down (d), charm (c), strange (s), top (t), and bottom (b) quarks. Table 28-1 lists the six quarks, along with their masses and charges. The quarks are divided into three groups, or *generations*, of two quarks: u and d in the first generation, c and s in the second generation, and t and b in the third generation. As seen in the table, the quarks in each generation are more massive than those in the previous generation. Physicists usually write the quark generations as

$$\begin{pmatrix} u \\ d \end{pmatrix} \begin{pmatrix} c \\ s \end{pmatrix} \begin{pmatrix} t \\ b \end{pmatrix}$$

The quarks along the top row (u, c, and t) all have the same charge, as do the quarks along the bottom row (d, s, and b). However, all six quarks differ not only in mass but also in other subtle properties. (These properties are beyond our scope in this brief introduction.) All attempts to find evidence of a fourth-generation quark have failed; as best we know, there are only three generations of quarks.

Note that each flavor of quark has a charge that is a *fraction* of e, either $+2e/3$ or $-e/3$. The explanation is that the proton, neutron, and other related particles are actually combinations of three quarks. Figure 28-3 shows four examples of such combinations. Any hadron that can be made up of three quarks is called a **baryon**. Baryons always have a net charge that is an integer multiple of e. Two examples are the least massive baryons, the proton (Figure 28-3a) of net charge $+e$ and the neutron (Figure 28-3b) with net charge zero. This picture explains why the neutron, which has zero net charge, nonetheless produces a magnetic field of its own: The u quark and two d quarks within the neutron are each charged, and the motions of these charged particles within the neutron generates a magnetic field.

Note that in Table 28-1 we list only an *approximate* mass for each quark. We know quite precise values of the masses of other particles; for example, the mass of the proton is known to seven significant figures. By contrast, we know only rough values for the masses of the quarks. That's because, unlike protons, neutrons, or electrons, quarks are never found as solitary particles. Instead, they are found only in combinations like those shown in Figure 28-3. This situation is quite unlike that in atoms, in which electrons can be removed by ionization, or in nuclei, in which protons or neutrons can be removed from a nucleus in a sufficiently energetic collision. By contrast, it seems to be impossible to remove an individual quark from a baryon. This is called **quark confinement**: Quarks within baryons are confined there and cannot be removed and isolated.

Note also that the mass of a baryon is generally much greater than the sum of the masses of its constituent quarks. For example, a proton is composed of two u quarks and a d quark, which from Table 28-1 have a combined mass of approximately $2(2\ \text{MeV}/c^2) + 5\ \text{MeV}/c^2 = 9\ \text{MeV}/c^2$. Yet the mass of the proton is $938.1\ \text{MeV}/c^2$. The difference is associated with the forces that bind the quarks together and keep them confined within the proton. We'll explore these forces in the following section.

Other hadrons are made up of a quark and an **antiquark**, the **antimatter** version of a quark. Every matter particle has an antimatter partner that is identical to it in every way except that it is oppositely charged. We've already encountered one example of antimatter, the positron (e^+) produced in β^+ decay (Section 27-5), which has the same mass as the electron. In fact, the positron and electron are identical except for the sign of their charges ($-e$ for the electron, $+e$ for the positron); the electron and the positron are a matter–antimatter pair. Each of the six quarks has an antiquark associated with it. Antiquarks are signified by adding "bar" to the name or placing a bar over the quark's symbol. For example, the antiquark associated with the up quark (u) is the up-bar or $\bar{u}$. The $\bar{u}$ antiquark has charge $-2e/3$, the opposite of the $+2e/3$ charge of the u quark. In the same way, the $\bar{d}$ antiquark carries charge $+e/3$, the opposite of the $-e/3$ charge of the d quark.

Figure 28-4 shows three examples of hadrons made up of a quark and antiquark. Such quark-antiquark combinations are called **mesons**. The charge of a meson is always an integer multiple of e. Pions are the least massive mesons; the π^+ (Figure 28-4a) and the π^- (Figure 28-4b) both have a mass of $139.6\ \text{MeV}/c^2$. There is also a neutral pion (π^0), which is made up of a combination of $u\bar{u}$ and $d\bar{d}$ and has a slightly lower mass of $135.0\ \text{MeV}/c^2$. Pions, like all other mesons, are unstable; they decay with a half-life that is a small fraction of a second.

When a particle and its antimatter partner meet, their total mass can be converted to its equivalent energy. For example, the collision of an electron and a positron results in two or more photons that carry the total energy of the two particles, a process known as *annihilation*. A quark and antiquark can also annihilate each other; we'll see examples of these processes in the next section.

Table 28-1 The Six Quarks

Quark	Symbol	Charge	Approximate Mass
up	u	$+\dfrac{2}{3}e$	$2\ \text{MeV}/c^2$
down	d	$-\dfrac{1}{3}e$	$5\ \text{MeV}/c^2$
charm	c	$+\dfrac{2}{3}e$	$1.3\ \text{GeV}/c^2$
strange	s	$-\dfrac{1}{3}e$	$0.1\ \text{GeV}/c^2$
top	t	$+\dfrac{2}{3}e$	$173\ \text{GeV}/c^2$
bottom	b	$-\dfrac{1}{3}e$	$5\ \text{GeV}/c^2$

Note: $1\ \text{GeV}/c^2 = 10^3\ \text{MeV}/c^2 = 10^9\ \text{eV}/c^2$.

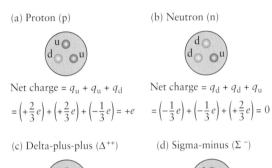

(a) Proton (p)

Net charge $= q_u + q_u + q_d$

$= \left(+\dfrac{2}{3}e\right) + \left(+\dfrac{2}{3}e\right) + \left(-\dfrac{1}{3}e\right) = +e$

(b) Neutron (n)

Net charge $= q_d + q_d + q_u$

$= \left(-\dfrac{1}{3}e\right) + \left(-\dfrac{1}{3}e\right) + \left(+\dfrac{2}{3}e\right) = 0$

(c) Delta-plus-plus (Δ^{++})

Net charge $= q_u + q_u + q_u$

$= \left(+\dfrac{2}{3}e\right) + \left(+\dfrac{2}{3}e\right) + \left(+\dfrac{2}{3}e\right) = +2e$

(d) Sigma-minus (Σ^-)

Net charge $= q_s + q_d + q_d$

$= \left(-\dfrac{1}{3}e\right) + \left(-\dfrac{1}{3}e\right) + \left(-\dfrac{1}{3}e\right) = -e$

Figure 28-3 **Baryons** All baryons, including (a) the proton and (b) the neutron, are made of combinations of three quarks. The proton is the only stable baryon; the neutron and (c), (d), all others decay into simpler particles.

(a) Positive pion (π^+)

Net charge $= q_u + q_{\bar{d}}$

$= \left(+\dfrac{2}{3}e\right) + \left(+\dfrac{1}{3}e\right) = +e$

(b) Negative pion (π^-)

Net charge $= q_d + q_{\bar{u}}$

$= \left(-\dfrac{1}{3}e\right) + \left(-\dfrac{2}{3}e\right) = -e$

(c) Strange D-plus (D_s^+)

Net charge $= q_c + q_{\bar{s}}$

$= \left(+\dfrac{2}{3}e\right) + \left(+\dfrac{1}{3}e\right) = +e$

Figure 28-4 **Mesons** All mesons are made of a quark and an antiquark.

Table 28-2 The Six Leptons

Lepton	Symbol	Charge	Mass
electron	e^-	$-e$	$0.5110 \text{ MeV}/c^2$
electron neutrino	ν_e	0	$<2 \text{ eV}/c^2$
muon	μ^-	$-e$	$105.7 \text{ MeV}/c^2$
muon neutrino	ν_μ	0	$<0.18 \text{ MeV}/c^2$
tau	τ^-	$-e$	$1777 \text{ MeV}/c^2$
tau neutrino	ν_τ	0	$<18.2 \text{ MeV}/c^2$

Just as three quarks make up a baryon, three antiquarks make up an *antibaryon*. For each variety of baryon, there is a corresponding variety of antibaryon. For example, the proton has quark content uud and charge $2e/3 + 2e/3 + (-e/3) = e$; the corresponding antibaryon is the antiproton, which has quark content $\overline{u}\,\overline{u}\,\overline{d}$ and charge $(-2e/3) + (-2e/3) + e/3 = -e$.

Leptons

While all hadrons are composed of quarks or antiquarks, there are other particles that are not composed of quarks at all. The *leptons* are another category of particles that are as fundamental as the quarks; to the best of our knowledge, leptons are not made up of smaller constituents. The electron is a lepton, as is the muon that we encountered in Section 25-4 (see Example 25-3). The electron neutrino that is created in hydrogen fusion (Section 27-5) and in beta decay (Section 27-6) is also a lepton. There are six leptons, listed in Table 28-2, as well as their antimatter partners.

Notice that in Table 28-2 we have listed the leptons in three groups of two. As is the case for the quarks, leptons form three generations, which we usually write as

$$\begin{pmatrix} e^- \\ \nu_e \end{pmatrix} \begin{pmatrix} \mu^- \\ \nu_\mu \end{pmatrix} \begin{pmatrix} \tau^- \\ \nu_\tau \end{pmatrix}$$

As for the quarks listed in Table 28-1, the leptons in each successive generation are more massive than their counterparts in the preceding generation. In many ways, the muon and tau are more massive versions of the electron, so they share many properties and interact with other particles in similar ways. One way in which electrons, muons, and tau particles *are* significantly different (in addition to the differences in mass) is that while the electron is stable and does not decay, the other two are unstable: The muon has a half-life of 1.56 μs (see Example 25-3) and the tau has a half-life of about 2.0×10^{-13} s.

Each lepton also has an antimatter particle associated with it. We have already encountered the electron and positron as a matter–antimatter pair. The antimuon (μ^+) and antitau (τ^+) are identical to the muon and tau in every way except that μ^+ and τ^+ carry positive rather than negative charge.

Unlike quarks, which appear in groups of three to form baryons or in quark-antiquark combinations to form mesons, leptons do not group together to form other particles. In the following section we'll see the reason for this. We'll also discover an essential third class of particles in addition to hadrons and leptons, the *exchange particles*.

Conservation Laws for Hadrons and Leptons

In earlier chapters we encountered a number of important conservation laws, including the conservation of energy and the conservation of momentum. There are several additional conservation laws that govern the behavior of hadrons and leptons.

- *Baryon number is conserved.* Every baryon (composed of three quarks) is assigned *baryon number B* equal to $+1$, and every antibaryon is assigned B equal to -1. Mesons are assigned $B = 0$, as are leptons. Experiments show that in every process that involves baryons, the sum of the values of B for all particles present before the process equals the sum of the values of B for all particles present after the process. Consider, for example, β^- decay of a neutron:

$$n \rightarrow p + e^- + \overline{\nu}_e$$
$$B = 1 \quad 1 \quad 0 \quad 0$$

(28-1)

The neutron and proton are both baryons, so each has $B = +1$. The electron and the antineutrino are leptons, each with $B = 0$. The total baryon number equals 1 before the decay and equals $1 + 0 + 0 = 1$ after the decay, so baryon number is conserved. Quarks have a fractional baryon number: Every quark has $B = +1/3$ and every antiquark has

$B = -1/3$. That's consistent with a baryon with three quarks having $B = 3(+1/3) = +1$ and a meson with a quark and antiquark having $B = (+1/3) + (-1/3) = 0$.

- *Lepton number is conserved.* Every electron (e^-) and electron neutrino (ν_e) is assigned *electron-lepton number* $L_e = +1$, and every positron (e^+) and electron antineutrino ($\bar{\nu}_e$) is assigned L_e equal to -1. Muons, muon neutrinos, tau particles, and tau neutrinos each have a similarly defined *muon-lepton number* L_μ or a *tau-lepton number* L_τ. A particle that is not a lepton is assigned L_e, L_μ, and L_τ equal to zero. Experiment shows that each of these lepton numbers is separately conserved.

As an example, consider the β^- decay of a neutron from Equation 28-1:

$$n \rightarrow p + e^- + \bar{\nu}_e$$
$$L_e = 0 \quad 0 \quad 1 \quad -1 \tag{28-2}$$

Both the neutron and the proton are baryons, so each has $L_e = 0$; the electron has $L_e = +1$ and the electron antineutrino has $L_e = -1$. The total value of L_e before the decay is zero, and afterward it is $0 + 1 + (-1) = 0$. The electron-lepton number is conserved in β^- decay. A second example is the decay of a tau into an electron, an electron antineutrino, and a tau neutrino:

$$\tau^- \rightarrow e^- + \bar{\nu}_e + \nu_\tau$$
$$L_e = 0 \quad 1 \quad -1 \quad 0 \tag{28-3}$$
$$L_\tau = 1 \quad 0 \quad 0 \quad 1$$

The tau (τ^-) and tau neutrino (ν_τ) each have $L_e = 0$ and $L_\tau = 1$, the electron (e^-) has $L_e = 1$ and $L_\tau = 0$, and the electron antineutrino ($\bar{\nu}_e$) has $L_e = -1$ and $L_\tau = 0$. You can see that the total electron-lepton number equals 0 before and after the decay, and the tau-lepton number equals 1 before and after the decay. Both of these lepton numbers are separately conserved in the β^- decay.

Physicists have searched for processes in which either baryon number or one of the lepton numbers is not conserved. No such process has ever been observed. It appears that these four laws—conservation of baryon number, electron-lepton number, muon-lepton number, and tau-lepton number—are as universal and fundamental as the law of conservation of electric charge (which says that the net electric charge has the same value before and after any process).

? Got the Concept? 28-1 Particles That May or May Not Exist

Which of the following particles could possibly exist? (a) A meson with charge $-2e$; (b) a baryon with charge $-2e$; (c) an antibaryon with charge $-2e$; (d) more than one of these; (e) none of these.

? Got the Concept? 28-2 Processes That May or May Not Happen

Electric charge is conserved in each of these processes, but some never occur. Which are possible? (a) $n + p \rightarrow n + p + p + \bar{p}$ ($\bar{p}$ is an antiproton); (b) $n + p \rightarrow n + n + p$; (c) $\pi^- \rightarrow \mu^- + \bar{\nu}_e$; (d) more than one of these; (e) none of these.

Take-Home Message for Section 28-2

✔ Quarks are the constituents of hadrons, the particles that experience the strong nuclear force. There are six varieties of quarks, each of which has a charge that is a fraction of e.

✔ Baryons such as the proton are made up of three quarks. Mesons are made up of a quark and an antiquark.

✔ Leptons, which include electrons and neutrinos, have no constituent particles. They do not experience the strong force.

✔ In the interactions of subatomic particles, baryon number and the three lepton numbers are conserved.

28-3 Four fundamental forces describe all interactions between material objects

Since early in our study of physics we have seen the importance of *forces*, the pushes and pulls that one object exerts on another. We've encountered three fundamental kinds of forces: gravity, the electromagnetic force, and the strong nuclear force. Gravity is an attractive force that draws objects that have mass closer together. The gravitational force attracts you to Earth and keeps Earth in orbit around the Sun. Electric and magnetic forces, two manifestations of the electromagnetic force, cause charged objects to accelerate. As a result, electrons can be bound to atomic nuclei, and atoms can bond together. Any contact force, such as the normal force between two objects that touch or the force of friction are electromagnetic in nature; they arise from the electromagnetic interactions between the atoms of the two surfaces in contact. As we explored in Chapter 27, the strong force binds protons and neutrons together to form atomic nuclei. To this list, we will add a force that we have not yet named but the effects of which we encountered in Section 27-6; this **weak force** is at the heart of the interaction that governs beta decay.

Now that we are exploring the fundamental constituents of matter, we are in a position to ask a central question about force: How do objects exert forces on each other? And what is fundamentally different about the four different kinds of forces: gravitational, electromagnetic, strong, and weak? If we can understand how fundamental entities such as quarks and leptons exert forces of different kinds on each other, we will be closer to answering these questions.

As we will see, the manner in which fundamental particles exert forces on each other—that is, how they *interact*—comes from a remarkable aspect of nature: It is possible to violate the law of conservation of energy, provided we do it for a sufficiently short time.

The Heisenberg Uncertainty Principle

To see how it's possible to violate energy conservation, let's consider the photon. We learned in Section 22-4 that the energy of a photon is proportional to its frequency:

Energy of a photon
(22-26)

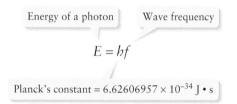

$$E = hf$$

For a photon to have a definite energy, it must therefore have a definite frequency. However, a wave ψ with a definite frequency also has an infinite duration (Figure 28-5a). This means that wave has always been present and will always be present. A more realistic description of a wave is one that has a finite duration: for example, the wave produced when you turn a source of waves (like a laser pointer) on and then off again. Mathematically, a wave of a finite duration Δt can be expressed as a sum of waves of infinite duration like the one shown in Figure 28-5a, but with a range of frequencies of breadth Δf (Figure 28-5b). To make a shorter-duration wave, we have to add together infinite-duration waves from a broader range of frequencies (Figure 28-5c). We can express the relationship between Δt (the duration of a wave) and Δf (the breadth of frequencies that go into that wave) as

(28-4)

$$\Delta f \Delta t \geq \frac{1}{4\pi}$$

Equation 28-4 says that the product of the wave duration Δt and the frequency breadth Δf cannot be less than $1/4\pi$. (This number arises from the specific way in which Δt and Δf are defined mathematically.) It says that to minimize the duration of a wave necessarily means increasing the range of frequencies that make up the wave. So the shorter the duration of a wave, the less precisely we can answer the question "What is the frequency of the wave?" In other words, a wave of finite duration does not have a single definite frequency.

(a)

(b)

(c)

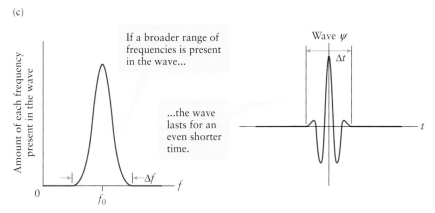

Figure 28-5 **Wave frequency and wave duration** (a) A wave of a single, discrete frequency has an infinite duration. (b), (c) Combining waves over a breadth of frequencies yields a total wave that has a finite duration.

Equation 28-4 is true for waves of all kinds, from ocean waves to sound waves to seismic waves. If we apply it to electromagnetic waves and multiply both sides of the equation by Planck's constant h, we get

$$h\Delta f\Delta t \geq \frac{h}{4\pi} \quad \text{or} \quad \Delta(hf)\Delta t \geq \frac{\hbar}{2}$$ (28-5)

Here $\Delta(hf)$ is the breadth of values of the quantity hf that must be included in the wave, and $\hbar = h/2\pi$. (We introduced $\hbar = h/2\pi$, or "h bar," in Section 26-6.) But Equation 22-26 tells us that $E = hf$ is the energy of a photon associated with the wave. So $\Delta(hf) = \Delta E$, the uncertainty in photon energy, and Equation 28-5 becomes

$$\Delta E\Delta t \geq \frac{\hbar}{2} \text{ for a photon}$$ (28-6)

This means that just as a wave of finite duration does not have a single definite frequency, a photon of finite duration does not have a single definite energy, but includes energy values that extend over a range of breadth ΔE. We can think of ΔE as the *uncertainty* in the energy of the photon. Equation 28-6 says that if a photon has a duration Δt, the product of Δt and uncertainty in energy ΔE of the photon cannot be less than $\hbar/2$, and so ΔE cannot be less than $\hbar/(2\Delta t)$. This energy uncertainty is *not* a result of the limitations of an experimental apparatus that we might use to measure the energy of a photon. Rather, it is intrinsic to photons because of their wave nature.

We have used the equation $E = hf$ to apply to photons only. But this relationship applies to particles of *all* kinds: We can think of anything with an energy E as having an associated frequency f given by $E = hf$. Then Equation 28-6 applies to phenomena in general, not just to photons. This implies that any physical phenomenon that has a finite duration Δt will necessarily have an uncertainty ΔE in energy given by Equation 28-6. The minimum value of this uncertainty is found by replacing the $\geq$ sign (greater than or equal to) in Equation 28-6 with an equals sign. The shorter the duration Δt of the phenomenon, the greater the minimum value of the energy uncertainty ΔE and the more uncertain the energy of the phenomenon. The German physicist Werner Heisenberg first expressed this idea in 1927, which is why it is known as the **Heisenberg uncertainty principle**:

Heisenberg uncertainty principle
(28-7)

The energy of a phenomenon is necessarily uncertain by an amount ΔE.

$$\Delta E \Delta t \geq \frac{\hbar}{2}$$

The shorter the duration Δt of the phenomenon, the greater the energy uncertainty ΔE.

$\hbar = \dfrac{h}{2\pi}$
= Planck's constant divided by 2π

Another way to interpret Equation 28-7 is to say that it places limits on how precisely the law of conservation of energy must be obeyed. Suppose a system undergoes some kind of process that lasts for a time Δt. Equation 28-7 says that the energy of the system is necessarily uncertain during that process, and the minimum energy uncertainty is given by $\Delta E \Delta t = \hbar/2$ or $\Delta E = \hbar/(2\Delta t)$. So it's fundamentally impossible to measure the energy of the system with an uncertainty less than $\hbar/(2\Delta t)$. This means that during the process, the energy of the system could actually vary by as much as $\hbar/(2\Delta t)$, and there would be no way that we could tell that the energy had changed value—that is, that the energy was not conserved. The shorter the duration Δt of the process, the greater the amount $\hbar/(2\Delta t)$ by which energy conservation can be (temporarily) violated during that time Δt. Stated another way, it's acceptable to violate the law of conservation of energy by an amount ΔE, provided the duration of time during which the law is violated is no more than $\Delta t = \hbar/(2\Delta E)$.

Exchange Particles: The Electromagnetic Force

The Heisenberg uncertainty principle helps us understand the following bold statement: *All forces result from the exchange of particles.* To see what we mean by this statement, first consider the electromagnetic force. Up to this point we've used the idea that charged particles exert electromagnetic forces on each other even at a distance, with no physical contact required. But a more sophisticated way to look at this force is to envision that when two charged particles exert an electric or magnetic force on each other, they do so by exchanging a photon: One of the charged particles emits the photon and the other absorbs it. The exchanged photon has energy, and it violates the law of conservation of energy for this photon to spontaneously appear and be emitted by one of the charged particles. But as we have seen, it's perfectly acceptable to violate the law of conservation of energy by an amount ΔE, provided we do so for a time no longer than $\Delta t = \hbar/(2\Delta E)$. So the uncertainty principle proves that what we've described can take place provided the exchanged photon is absorbed by the second particle (and so disappears) within a time $\hbar/(2\Delta E)$ after the photon was emitted by the first particle.

In this picture we say that the electromagnetic force is *mediated* by the exchange of a photon and that the exchanged photon is the *mediator* of the force. The particles that mediate forces are called **exchange particles**. You should try to envision a continuous stream of photons going back and forth between charged particles, so that the two particles continuously exert an electromagnetic force on each other. Any charged particle can and does emit and absorb photons exchanged in this way. These photons are not the same as the photons emitted by a light bulb or a laser, however; they can exist for only a finite time before they must disappear. We call them **virtual particles**.

We can represent the exchange process by a diagram such as the one shown in **Figure 28-6**. In this slightly simplified version of a *Feynman diagram*, invented by American physicist Richard Feynman to visualize and analyze processes that involve fundamental particles, time runs from left to right. The lines associated with each particle do not represent actual paths that the particles take through space, but only indicate which particles interact with which other particles. In Figure 28-6, two electrons exchange a photon, and in so doing each exerts an electromagnetic force on the other. A particle such as an electron is drawn as a solid, straight line in Feynman diagrams. An exchange particle is drawn either as a wavy line (as for the photon) or a spiral line.

This picture helps us understand Coulomb's law, which tells us that the electric force between two charged particles separated by a distance r decreases in proportion to $1/r^2$. In other words, the electric force goes to zero only when the charges are infinitely far apart. This is possible because the photon has zero mass, so its minimum energy $E = hf$ is zero. (If the photon did have a mass m, its minimum energy would be its rest energy mc^2.) If one particle violates conservation of energy by creating and emitting a photon of energy ΔE, the uncertainty principle says that this photon can exist no longer than $\Delta t = \hbar/(2\Delta E)$. Even traveling at the speed of light c, this photon can travel no farther than $c\Delta t = c\hbar/(2\Delta E)$, so that distance is the maximum separation at which two charged particles can interact by exchanging photons of energy ΔE. But because the lower limit on the energy of a photon is zero, the amount ΔE by which the particle violates conservation of energy can be as small as we like. So the distance $c\Delta t = c\hbar/(2\Delta E)$ can be arbitrarily large, and two charged particles can interact via the electromagnetic force at any distance out to infinity. But because only these low-energy photons can be exchanged between charged particles separated by great distances r, the force is quite weak if r is large—just as in Coulomb's law.

Exchange Particles: The Strong Force

We use a similar picture to explain the strong interaction between quarks. The Feynman diagram in **Figure 28-7** shows two quarks that exert forces on each other by exchanging a particle called the **gluon**. This rather whimsical name expresses the idea that the exchange of gluons provides the force that confines, or glues, quarks inside baryons. Gluon exchange is also how the quark and antiquark inside a meson interact with each other and how the antiquarks inside an antibaryon interact.

Like the photon, the gluon has zero mass, so the lower limit on the energy of a gluon is zero. Using the same argument we made above for photons, it follows that quarks or antiquarks separated by any distance, no matter how large, can interact by exchanging gluons. But unlike photons, the kinds of particles that emit and absorb gluons are not simply those with electric charge: They are particles that have a different attribute called *color*. (This is yet another of the light-hearted names associated with quark physics. It has nothing to do with the wavelength of light or the perception of color by the human eye.) Quarks and antiquarks carry color, as do gluons themselves. So unlike photons, gluons can interact with each other by exchanging other gluons. (By contrast, photons have no electric charge and cannot interact directly with other photons.) As a consequence of this

1. One electron (e^-) emits a virtual photon (γ).

2. A second electron (e^-) absorbs the virtual photon.

Charged particles exert electromagnetic forces on each other by exchanging virtual photons.

Figure 28-6 **Photon exchange and the electromagnetic interaction** All electric and magnetic interactions between charged particles involve the exchange of virtual photons.

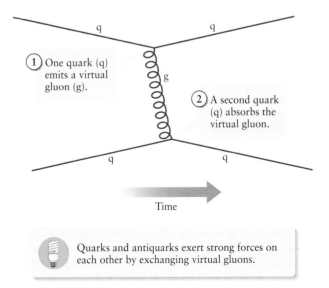

1. One quark (q) emits a virtual gluon (g).

2. A second quark (q) absorbs the virtual gluon.

Quarks and antiquarks exert strong forces on each other by exchanging virtual gluons.

Figure 28-7 **Gluon exchange and the strong interaction between quarks** The forces that bind quarks together inside baryons and mesons are the result of the exchange of virtual gluons.

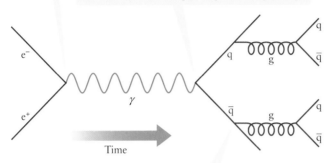

① In electron-positron annihilation, an electron (e⁻) and a positron (e⁺) collide and are transformed into a virtual photon.

② If the e⁻ and e⁺ had sufficient energy, the photon can transform into a quark (q) and antiquark (q̄).

③ The quark and antiquark can emit gluons, which transform into quark-antiquark pairs. The shower of quarks and antiquarks coalesces into hadrons, including baryons (three quarks), antibaryons (three antiquarks), and/or mesons (quark-antiquark pairs).

Figure 28-8 Electron-positron annihilation and hadron production When an electron and positron collide, the result can be a shower of hadrons produced via virtual photons and gluons.

curious aspect of gluons, the force that gluons mediate between quarks gets stronger, not weaker, as the quarks move farther apart. This helps to explain why this force makes it impossible to remove an isolated quark from a hadron.

Since quarks are charged, they also interact electromagnetically by exchanging photons. But these interactions have a relatively small effect compared to the dominant strong interaction mediated by gluons.

As we mentioned in the previous section, when an electron and a positron (matter and antimatter) collide, they annihilate. The Feynman diagram in Figure 28-8 shows one possible outcome of such an annihilation. The electron of charge $-e$ and the positron of charge $+e$ disappear and are replaced by a single photon. This *virtual* photon does not have the proper relationship between energy and momentum that a real photon must have, and so it violates the conservation laws that govern the electron-positron collision. Like an exchange photon, this virtual photon can exist for only a finite time before it must disappear. In some cases the virtual photon will transform back into an electron-positron pair. But as Figure 28-8 shows, it's also possible for the virtual photon to become a quark and an antiquark of the same flavor (for instance, a u quark and a ū antiquark, or an s quark and an s̄ antiquark). The quark and antiquark can themselves emit virtual gluons, which can in turn transform into quark-antiquark pairs. Depending on how much energy is available in the original collision between electron and positron, many such quark-antiquark pairs can be produced. These will sort themselves into combinations of quarks (baryons), combinations of antiquarks (antibaryons), and quark-antiquark pairs (mesons). The result will be a shower of hadrons emanating from the site of the electron-positron collision. The image that opens this chapter shows two "jets" of hadrons emerging from the site of just such a collision. Many varieties of hadrons were first identified in electron-positron collision experiments of this sort.

The notion of gluon exchange also helps us understand the strong force in the context in which we first encountered it in Section 27-2: a force that attracts nucleons (protons or neutrons) to each other. Figure 28-9 shows how this force between nucleons arises. The meson that is produced in this way acts as an exchange particle between the nucleons, and this exchange gives rise to the attractive force between nucleons. The meson exchange particle has a substantial mass $m_{exchange}$, and so the minimum energy that an exchanged meson can have is its rest energy $m_{exchange}c^2$. Producing such a meson means violating the conservation of energy by an amount of at least $\Delta E = m_{exchange}c^2$, which means that the meson can exist for a time no longer than $\Delta t = \hbar/(2\Delta E) = \hbar/2m_{exchange}c^2$. Even moving at the speed of light, the maximum distance that this exchange meson can travel during a time Δt is

(28-8)
$$c\Delta t = \frac{c\hbar}{2m_{exchange}c^2} = \frac{\hbar}{2m_{exchange}c}$$

(range of a force mediated by an exchange particle of mass $m_{exchange}$)

Equation 28-8 tells us the *range* of the force mediated by the exchange meson. There are many types of mesons, but the type whose exchange will have the longest range is the one with the smallest mass. (That's because the range in Equation 28-8 is inversely proportional to the mass of the exchange particle.) The mass of the lightest meson, the neutral pion (π^0), is 135.0 MeV/c^2 = 135.0×10^6 eV/c^2, so the maximum range of the strong force between nucleons should be

$$\frac{\hbar}{2m_{neutral\ pion}c} = \frac{\hbar c}{2m_{neutral\ pion}c^2} = \frac{hc}{4\pi m_{neutral\ pion}c^2}$$

$$= \frac{(4.136 \times 10^{-15}\ eV \cdot s)(3.00 \times 10^8\ m/s)}{4\pi(135.0 \times 10^6\ eV/c^2)c^2}$$

$$= 7.31 \times 10^{-16}\ m = 0.731\ fm$$

①One of the quarks in the proton emits a virtual gluon.

②The virtual gluon transforms into a virtual quark (q) and a virtual antiquark (q̄), which together constitute a virtual meson.

③The virtual quark and antiquark transform back into a virtual gluon, which is absorbed by one of the quarks in the neutron.

Figure 28-9 **The strong force between nucleons** The force that binds protons and neutrons together has its origin in the interaction between quarks and gluons.

• Nucleons (protons and neutrons) exert the strong force on each other by exchanging virtual mesons.
• This exchange is actually due to interactions between quarks and gluons.

Because this range is so small, the strong force between nucleons is a short-range force, just as we discussed in Section 27-2. Indeed, the rough value of 0.731 fm that we calculated here is of the same order of magnitude as the value we gave in Section 27-2 for the range of the strong force between nucleons.

Exchange Particles: The Weak Force and the Gravitational Force

The weak force is mediated by *three* different exchange particles. These are the neutral Z^0 (charge zero) and the positively and negatively charged W particles, W^+ (charge $+e$) and W^- (charge $-e$). (These particles are really three manifestations of the same particle, but have different names for historical reasons.) These particles are not massless: The Z^0 has mass 91.2 GeV/c^2, about 100 times the mass of a proton, and the W^+ and W^- both have mass 80.4 GeV/c^2. The calculation above shows that the range of the force mediated by an exchange particle of mass $m_{exchange}$ is inversely proportional to the mass. So since the Z^0, W^+, and W^- have roughly 600 times the mass of the neutral pion (135.0 MeV/c^2), the range of the weak force is roughly 1/600 that of the strong force between nucleons, or about 10^{-18} m $= 10^{-3}$ fm. The weak force is not only weak, it is of *extremely* short range!

It turns out that any two particles can exert a weak force on each other. For example, Figure 28-10 shows two examples of the weak interaction between a neutrino and an electron. Note that even though the weak interaction does not directly involve electric charge, charge is still conserved. In Figure 28-10a the neutrino remains neutral, and the electron retains its charge of $-e$. In Figure 28-10b the neutrino emits a W^+ of charge $+e$ and becomes an electron of charge $-e$, so charge is conserved. The W^+ combines with an electron of charge $-e$ and becomes a neutrino of charge zero, and again charge is conserved.

Figure 28-11 shows how the weak force gives rise to the β^- decay of a neutron (quark content udd) to a proton (quark content uud):

$$n \rightarrow p + e^- + \bar{\nu}_e$$

Compared to a u quark, a d quark is substantially more massive (see Table 28-1) and so has a substantially greater rest

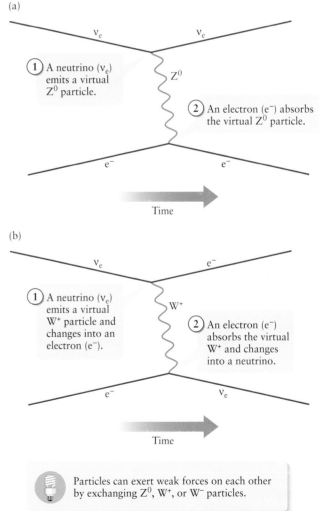

(a)

①A neutrino (ν_e) emits a virtual Z^0 particle.

②An electron (e^-) absorbs the virtual Z^0 particle.

Time

(b)

①A neutrino (ν_e) emits a virtual W^+ particle and changes into an electron (e^-).

②An electron (e^-) absorbs the virtual W^+ and changes into a neutrino.

Time

Particles can exert weak forces on each other by exchanging Z^0, W^+, or W^- particles.

Figure 28-10 **The weak interaction** The weak force between particles involves the exchange of massive virtual particles. These come in both (a) neutral and (b) charged varieties.

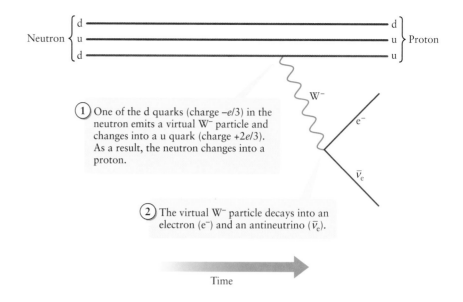

Figure 28-11 Beta decay of a neutron The weak interaction describes how a free neutron decays into a proton, an electron, and an antineutrino.

① One of the d quarks (charge $-e/3$) in the neutron emits a virtual W^- particle and changes into a u quark (charge $+2e/3$). As a result, the neutron changes into a proton.

② The virtual W^- particle decays into an electron (e^-) and an antineutrino ($\bar{\nu}_e$).

Time

energy. It's therefore favorable for the d quark to lower its energy by becoming a u quark. It does this by emitting a W^- particle as shown. This is a very short-lived virtual particle, since the rest energy of the W^- ($80.4\,\text{GeV}/c^2$) is far greater than the rest energy of the original d quark (about $5\,\text{MeV}/c^2 = 5 \times 10^{-3}\,\text{GeV}/c^2$), and so emitting a W^- means that we've violated energy conservation by quite a bit. The W^- of charge $-e$ quickly decays into an electron of charge $-e$ and a neutral antineutrino. (It has to be an *anti*neutrino to conserve electron-lepton number L_e: The W^- is not a lepton and therefore has $L_e = 0$, so the particles into which the W^- decays must also have a net electron-lepton number of zero. The electron, with $L_e = +1$, must therefore be accompanied by a neutral particle with $L_e = -1$, which means an antineutrino rather than a neutrino.)

As we discussed in Section 27-6, in some nuclei it's energetically favorable for β^+ decay to take place, in which a proton changes to a neutron. This is similar to the process shown in Figure 28-11, except that one of the u quarks in a proton changes to a d quark by emitting a W^+ rather than a W^-. The W^+ then decays into a positron (e^+) and a neutrino (ν_e). One nucleus in which this happens is the potassium isotope ^{40}K, which occurs in nature and is found in foods such as oranges (see Figure 28-1a). The bit of antimatter produced in this way—the positron—quickly encounters an atomic electron and annihilates. Happily, this happens very infrequently in your food (and releases very little energy when it does happen). So you need not fear the harmful effects of biting into a bit of antimatter when you eat fruit!

A particle named the *graviton* is thought to mediate the gravitational force. So far, no experimental evidence has confirmed the existence of this particle, although no experimental evidence has excluded it either. Because the gravitational force between two masses separated by a distance r is proportional to $1/r^2$, just like the electric force between two charged particles, the graviton is thought to have the same mass as the photon: zero. The graviton also carries no charge.

Table 28-3 summarizes the four fundamental forces and the exchange particles that mediate these forces. The picture that this table summarizes—in which two classes of fundamental particles, the six quarks and the six leptons, interact by means of six exchange particles, the graviton, the Z^0, the W^+, the W^-, the photon, and the gluon—is called the **Standard Model**. What this very simple table does not reflect is the decades of experimental and theoretical effort (and several Nobel Prizes in Physics) that have gone into constructing this model. A number of questions about the Standard Model remain unanswered and are the subject of active research by physicists around the globe.

Table 28-3 The Forces

Force	Range	Mediator(s)	Strength Relative to the Strong Force
gravity	infinite	graviton	10^{-40}
weak	$\sim 10^{-3}$ fm	Z^0, W^+, W^-	10^{-6}
electromagnetic	infinite	photon (γ)	10^{-2}
strong	~ 1 fm	gluon (g)	1

? Got the Concept? 28-3

A Quark Decay

A c quark can decay into an s quark via the weak force. In this process, what does the c quark emit? (a) A W^+, which decays into a positron and a neutrino; (b) a W^+, which decays into a positron and an antineutrino; (c) a W^-, which decays into an electron and a neutrino; (d) a W^-, which decays into an electron and an antineutrino.

28-4 We live in an expanding universe, and the nature of most of its contents is a mystery

The Standard Model gives us a description of all the normal matter in the world around us. All of the atoms in our bodies and our surroundings are made of leptons and hadrons, the hadrons are all made of quarks, and all of these particles interact by means of exchange particles. Why, you may ask, do we specify that this description applies to "normal" matter only? What other sort of matter could there be, and how much of the contents of the physical universe is so-called normal matter? To answer these questions, we must turn our attention from the smallest fundamental particles to galaxies, some of the largest structures in the universe, and to the nature of the universe itself—the subject of the science called **cosmology**.

The Hubble Law and the Expansion of the Universe

Figure 28-12 is an image made with the Hubble Space Telescope of a small portion of the night sky. At first glance it may appear that the bright dots in this image are individual stars. But closer inspection shows that each is actually a **galaxy**, a collection of a tremendous number of stars (typically 10^{10} to 10^{12}). Our Sun is one of approximately 2×10^{11} stars in the Milky Way, the local galaxy of which we are part.

In the 1920s the American astronomer Edwin Hubble was the first to show that galaxies are very distant. (He did this by identifying within other galaxies certain types of stars that are found in our own galaxy and whose light output is known. These stars appear very dim when seen in other galaxies, so they must be very far away.) In collaboration with the astronomer Milton Humason, he also measured the spectra of many galaxies. These are really the spectra of the combined light from all of the stars that make up each galaxy, and so they have absorption lines (see Section 26-5). Hubble and Humason found that most galaxies show a **redshift** in their spectrum: That is, the absorption lines in the spectra of galaxies are all shifted to longer wavelengths and lower frequencies than in the spectra of nearby stars in our own galaxy. (We use the term *redshift* because in the visible part of the electromagnetic spectrum, red light has the longest wavelength and lowest frequency.) What's more, the greater the distance to a galaxy, the greater the wavelength shift. What did this discovery mean?

To answer this question, recall what we learned in Section 13-10 about the *Doppler effect*: If a source of waves is moving away from us, the wave that we receive from that source is shifted to a lower frequency and a longer wavelength. In Section 13-10 we introduced this idea in the context of sound waves, but the same effect also applies to electromagnetic waves. Hubble and Humason concluded that other galaxies are moving away from us, and so the light that we receive from those galaxies is at a longer wavelength. Their results showed that the speed v at which a distant galaxy is receding from us is directly proportional to the distance d to that galaxy (Figure 28-13):

Figure 28-12 **A universe of galaxies** Each blob of light in this image from the Hubble Space Telescope is a galaxy, a grouping of billions of stars and other matter. The area shown is a very small patch of sky, only about 1/12 the width of the full Moon.

> **Watch Out!**
>
> **A galaxy is not a solar system, nor is it the entire universe.**
>
> In everyday language, many people use the terms *galaxy*, *solar system*, and *universe* interchangeably. In fact, a galaxy is a large collection of stars and other matter, while a solar system is a single star and its retinue of planets. Our galaxy contains some 200 billion stars, many of which have planets, and the observable universe contains literally billions of galaxies.

The speed at which a distant galaxy moves away from us... ...is directly proportional to its distance from us.

$$v = H_0 d$$

Hubble constant = 70 km/s/Mpc = 2.3×10^{-18} s^{-1}

The Hubble law
(28-9)

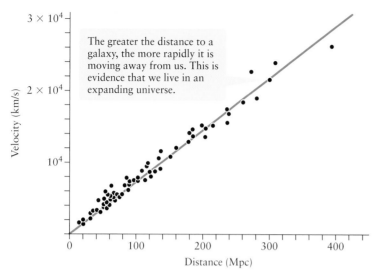

The greater the distance to a galaxy, the more rapidly it is moving away from us. This is evidence that we live in an expanding universe.

Figure 28-13 **The Hubble law** Each black dot in this graph represents the speed at which an individual galaxy is moving away from us, as well as the distance to that galaxy. The straight line is the best fit to that data, corresponding to a value of $H_0 = 70$ km/s/Mpc in Equation 28-9.

This direct proportionality is called the **Hubble law**, and the constant H_0 in Equation 28-9 is called the **Hubble constant**. Astronomers typically measure distances in the cosmos in parsecs (pc), a unit equal to 3.26 light-years. One light-year (ly) is the distance that light travels in one year, equal to 3.09×10^{16} m. The current best value of H_0 is about 70 km/s/Mpc, where 1 Mpc = 1 megaparsec = 10^6 pc = 3.26×10^6 ly.

What can we deduce from the observations that distant galaxies are moving away from us and that the speed at which they move away is proportional to the distance? The interpretation is that because remote galaxies are getting farther and farther apart as time goes on, the universe is expanding. A good analogy is a loaf of raisin bread being baked in an oven. As the loaf expands during baking, the amount of space between the raisins gets larger and larger. In the same way, as the universe expands, the amount of space between widely separated galaxies increases. The expansion of the universe is actually the expansion of space.

! Watch Out! **The universe is expanding, but the galaxies (and you) are not.**

It's important to realize that the expansion of the universe occurs primarily in the vast spaces that separate clusters of galaxies. Just as the raisins in a loaf of raisin bread don't expand as the loaf expands in the oven, galaxies themselves do not expand. Einstein and others have established that an object that is held together by its own gravity, such as a galaxy or a cluster of galaxies, is always contained within a patch of nonexpanding space. A galaxy's gravitational field produces this nonexpanding region. Thus, Earth and your body, for example, are not getting any bigger. Only the distance between widely separated galaxies increases with time.

Although distant galaxies are moving away from us, that does *not* mean that we are at the center of the universe. In an expanding universe, every galaxy moves away from every other galaxy, so an alien astronomer in a distant galaxy would see the same relationship between the speeds and distances of galaxies—that is, the same Hubble law—as does an Earth astronomer. Since every point in the universe appears to be at the center of the expansion, it follows that our universe has no center at all.

! Watch Out! **"If the universe is expanding, what is it expanding into?"**

This commonly asked question arises only if we take too literally our raisin bread analogy, in which the loaf (representing the universe) expands in three-dimensional space into the surrounding air. But the actual universe includes *all* space; there is nothing "beyond" it, because there is no "beyond." Asking "What lies beyond the universe?" is as meaningless as asking "Where on Earth is north of the North Pole?"

The ongoing expansion of space explains why the light from remote galaxies is redshifted. Imagine a photon coming toward us from a distant galaxy. As the photon travels through space, the space is expanding, so the photon's wavelength becomes stretched. When the photon reaches our eyes, we see an increased wavelength: The photon has been redshifted. The greater the distance the photon has had to travel and so the longer the amount of time it has had to travel to reach us, the more its wavelength will have been stretched. Thus, photons from distant galaxies have larger redshifts than those of photons from nearby galaxies, as expressed by the Hubble law.

A redshift caused by the expansion of the universe is properly called a **cosmological redshift**. It is *not* the same as a Doppler shift. Doppler shifts are caused by an object's motion through space, whereas a cosmological redshift is caused by the expansion of space.

Example 28-1   Measuring the Distance to a Galaxy from Its Redshift

Find the distances to the following galaxies: (a) NGC 4889, whose redshifted spectrum shows that it is moving away from us at 6410 km/s (2.14% of the speed of light); (b) 1255-0, which has a larger redshift that shows it to be moving away from us at $0.822c$. Express the distances in megaparsecs and in light-years.

Set Up

For each galaxy we know the speed v at which it is moving away from us due to the expansion of the universe. So we can use the Hubble law to determine the distance d to that galaxy.

The Hubble law:

$$v = H_0 d \qquad (28\text{-}9)$$

Solve

(a) Use Equation 28-9 and the value $H_0 = 70$ km/s/Mpc to calculate the distance to NGC 4889.

Rewrite Equation 28-9 to solve for the distance d:

$$d = \frac{v}{H_0}$$

We are given $v = 6410$ km/s, so

$$d = \frac{6410 \text{ km/s}}{70 \text{ km/s/Mpc}} = 92 \text{ Mpc}$$

$$= (92 \text{ Mpc})\left(\frac{3.26 \times 10^6 \text{ ly}}{1 \text{ Mpc}}\right) = 3.0 \times 10^8 \text{ ly}$$

(b) Repeat the calculations for the galaxy 1255-0, which is moving away at $0.822c$.

For this galaxy,

$$v = 0.822c = 0.822(3.00 \times 10^5 \text{ km/s})$$
$$= 2.47 \times 10^5 \text{ km/s}$$

Use this to calculate the distance to the galaxy as in part (a):

$$d = \frac{2.47 \times 10^5 \text{ km/s}}{70/\text{km/s/Mpc}} = 3.5 \times 10^3 \text{ Mpc}$$

$$= (3.5 \times 10^3 \text{ Mpc})\left(\frac{3.26 \times 10^6 \text{ ly}}{1 \text{ Mpc}}\right) = 1.1 \times 10^{10} \text{ ly}$$

Reflect

NGC 4889 is some 300 million light-years away, so the light we see from NGC 4889 left that galaxy 300 million years ago, before even the first dinosaurs appeared on Earth. Galaxy 1255-0 is far more distant, some 11 *billion* light-years away. When the light we receive from 1255-0 left that galaxy some 11 billion years ago, our Earth—which is a mere 4.56×10^9 years old—had not yet formed. When we use telescopes to look at distant astronomical objects, we are not only looking out into space; we are also looking back in time.

The Big Bang, Cosmic Background Radiation, and the Origin of Matter

If the universe is expanding, it must be that in the past the matter in the universe must have been closer together and therefore denser than it is today. If we look far enough into the very distant past, there must have been a time when the density of matter was almost inconceivably high. This leads us to conclude that some sort of tremendous event caused ultradense matter to begin the expansion that continues to the present day. This event, called the **Big Bang**, marks the beginning of the universe. If we use the observed expansion rate of the universe and work backwards, we find that the age of the universe is approximately 13.8 billion (13.8×10^9) years.

We learned in Section 15-3 that the temperature of an ideal gas decreases when it undergoes an adiabatic expansion (one in which there is no heat transfer to its surroundings). The expansion of the universe is much like an adiabatic expansion, so it follows that the average temperature of the universe has decreased over the past 13.8 billion years. (There are places in the universe that are at very high temperature, such as the interiors of stars. But the average temperature of space is very cold.) If we work backward in time, it follows that the early universe must have been at very high temperatures indeed. The hot early universe must therefore have been filled with many

Watch Out!

It's not correct to think of the Big Bang as an explosion.

When a bomb explodes, pieces of debris fly off into space from a central location. If you could trace all the pieces back to their origin, you could find out exactly where the bomb had been. This process is not possible with the universe, however, because the universe itself always has and always will consist of all space. The present-day universe is infinite, and was infinite when it first originated in the Big Bang.

high-energy photons of high frequency and short wavelength. The properties of this radiation field depended on its temperature, as described by Planck's blackbody law (Section 26-2).

The universe has expanded so much since those ancient times that all those short-wavelength photons have had their wavelengths stretched by a tremendous factor. As a result, they have become low-energy, long-wavelength photons. The temperature of this cosmic radiation field is now only a few degrees above absolute zero, and the black-body spectrum of this radiation has its peak intensity at low frequencies in the micro-wave part of the electromagnetic spectrum (wavelengths of approximately 1 mm). Hence, this radiation field, which fills all of space, is called the **cosmic microwave background** or **cosmic background radiation**. It represents the "afterglow" of the very high-temperature conditions that prevailed when the universe was young.

It's actually possible to detect the cosmic background radiation using an ordinary television (Figure 28-1b). Using much more sensitive detectors, scientists have found that the cosmic background radiation does indeed have a blackbody spectrum with a temperature of 2.725 K, which we can regard as the average temperature of the present-day universe. However, we observe different cosmic background radiation coming from different parts of the sky. Even when the effects of Earth's motion are accounted for, there remain variations in the temperature of the radiation field of about 200 μK (200 microkelvins, or 2×10^{-4} K) above or below the average 2.725 K temperature (Figure 28-14). These tiny temperature variations indicate that matter and radiation were not distributed in a totally uniform way in the early universe. Regions that were slightly denser than average were also slightly cooler than average; less dense regions were slightly warmer. Over time, the denser regions evolved to form the first galaxies, and within them the first stars. By studying these nonuniformities, we are really studying our origins.

The map of the sky shown in Figure 28-14 shows the universe as it was some 380,000 years after the Big Bang, when the universe was less than 0.003% of its present age. Prior to that time, the universe was so dense as to be opaque. (Think of a hot, dense, luminous fog.) Events prior to that date are forever hidden from our direct view. But by using the laws of particle physics that we described in Sections 28-2 and 28-3, we can infer a great deal about what conditions must have been like in the very early universe.

Our best understanding is that the universe began at extremely high temperatures and that the immense energy gave rise to a sea of quarks, antiquarks, leptons, and anti-leptons. As the universe expanded and cooled, by 10^{-6} s after the Big Bang quarks and antiquarks had coalesced into baryons, antibaryons, and mesons. But now we have a dilemma. If there had been perfect symmetry between particles and antiparticles, then for every proton there should have been an antiproton. For every electron, there should likewise have been a positron. By the time the universe was 1 second old, every particle would have been annihilated by an antiparticle, leaving no matter at all in the universe! Obviously, this did not happen.

The resolution to this dilemma is that the laws of physics are very slightly asymmetrical between matter and antimatter: For every 10^9 antimatter particles that were created out of the energy of the Big Bang, 10^9 plus one matter particles were created. When those 10^9 antimatter particles encountered 10^9 matter particles, annihilations resulted in no more particles and lots of energy in the form of photons. (These are the photons that gave rise to the cosmic background radiation that we see today.) That one extra matter particle avoided annihilation. All the normal matter that we see today is a result of the very slight imbalance between matter and antimatter in the early universe. Experiments on particle interactions are consistent with this very slight asymmetry between matter and antimatter.

By 15 minutes after the Big Bang, temperatures had dropped enough that protons and neutrons could coalesce into the first atomic nuclei. Only the four lightest elements (hydrogen, helium, lithium, and beryllium) were present in appreciable numbers. The heavier elements would be formed only much later, once stars had formed and nuclear reactions within those stars could manufacture carbon, nitrogen, oxygen, and all the other elements.

Figure 28-14 Temperature variations in the cosmic microwave background This map shows small variations in the temperature of the cosmic background radiation across the entire sky. Lower-temperature regions (shown in blue) show where the early universe was slightly denser than average.

Keep in mind that only *nuclei* formed in the first 15 minutes of the history of the universe. It would be another 380,000 years before temperatures became low enough for these nuclei to combine with electrons to form atoms. When this happened, the universe became transparent for the first time. The map of the cosmic background radiation in Figure 28-14 shows the universe at that moment in cosmic history.

Dark Matter and Dark Energy

At this point we might feel that we have understood, at least in broad outline, the nature and origin of matter. But have we in fact accounted for all of the matter in the universe? To answer this question we again look at galaxies, in particular *spiral galaxies* like the ones shown in Figure 28-15. These galaxies have a flattened disk shape, and all of the material in the galaxy rotates around the center. Each part of the galaxy is held in its orbit around the center by the gravitational attraction of the other parts of the galaxy; the greater that gravitational attraction on a given part, the faster that part must move to remain in a circular orbit (see Section 10-4). So if we can measure the speed at which parts of the galaxy orbit around the center, we can calculate the total amount of mass in the galaxy. Most of the atoms in the galaxy are in its stars, and we can estimate the combined mass of all the stars from the brightness of the galaxy. If the total amount of mass in the galaxy is a close match to the combined amount of mass in its stars, then we can conclude that ordinary matter accounts for most or all of the mass of the galaxy.

We can measure orbital speeds most directly for spiral galaxies that happen to be oriented edge-on to us, like the one shown in Figure 28-15b. We do this by looking at the spectrum of light from the two sides of the galaxy: The spectral lines will be Doppler shifted toward shorter wavelengths on the side where material is rotating toward us, and toward longer wavelengths on the side where material is rotating away from us. (These shifts are in addition to the cosmological redshift in the galaxy's spectrum as a whole, caused by the expansion of the universe.) The amount of Doppler shift tells us the speeds at which material in various parts of the galaxy are moving around the center.

These measurements have been made for a wide variety of spiral galaxies, and the results are always the same: The total mass of the galaxy deduced from the orbital speeds is about *five times greater* than the combined mass of all of the stars in the galaxy. So ordinary matter, which is concentrated in the galaxy's stars, is only a small fraction of the mass of the galaxy. The remaining mass is in a form that does not emit electromagnetic radiation of any kind, and may not even be composed of the fundamental particles that we described in Sections 28-2 and 28-3. This mysterious matter, which is the dominant form of matter in spiral galaxies and apparently in the universe as a whole, is called **dark matter**. As of this writing, its nature remains a mystery to science.

There is yet another complication to our understanding of the universe. As we look at increasingly distant galaxies, and so look farther back in the history of the universe, we find that as expected these distant galaxies are moving away from us due to the expansion of the universe. But the expansion rate has *not* been constant; observations show that for the past billion years, the expansion of the universe has been *speeding up!* To date, the only viable explanation for this increased speed is that, in addition to ordinary matter and dark matter, the universe is suffused with a curious form of energy that causes an accelerated expansion of the universe. We cannot detect this energy from its gravitational effects (the technique astronomers use to detect dark matter), and it does not emit detectable radiation of any kind. We refer to this curious energy as **dark energy**. The nature of dark energy is even more mysterious than that of dark matter.

Since matter and energy are equivalent through the Einstein relation $E = mc^2$, we can compare the relative importance of ordinary matter, dark matter, and dark energy by asking what fraction of the total energy in the universe each one represents. The graph in Figure 28-16 shows the results: Dark energy represents 68.3% of the total, dark matter another 26.8%, and "ordinary" normal matter just 4.9%. This is a sobering graph, for it tells us that more than 95% of the energy in the universe is in forms that we do not understand! The quest to understand both dark energy and dark matter is one of the most challenging pursuits in contemporary physics.

(a) We see spiral galaxy NGC 3982 face-on.

All of the matter in the galaxy rotates around the center.

(b) We see spiral galaxy NGC 4013 edge-on.

Stars at one edge rotate toward us...

...and stars at the other edge rotate away from us.

Figure 28-15 Measuring the mass of a spiral galaxy (a) The material in a spiral galaxy is held in orbit around the center by the gravitational attraction of all the other material in the galaxy. (b) For a galaxy that is edge-on to us, we can measure the orbital speeds, and hence the mass of the galaxy, using the Doppler effect.

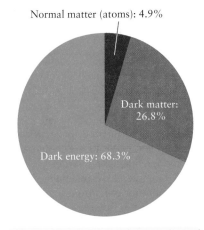

Normal matter (atoms): 4.9%

Dark matter: 26.8%

Dark energy: 68.3%

What we think of as "normal" matter makes up less than 5% of the contents of the universe.

Figure 28-16 Recipe for a universe This pie chart shows the three constituents of the universe as a whole. The numbers show what percentage of the total energy content of the universe each constituent represents.

? Got the Concept? 28-4 Dark Matter

In spiral galaxies like those shown in Figure 28-15, the ratio of dark matter to visible matter is about five to one. The percentage of the light from a spiral galaxy that is emitted by dark matter is closest to (a) 83%; (b) 80%; (c) 20%; (d) 17%; (e) zero.

Take-Home Message for Section 28-4

✔ The redshifts of galaxies reveal that we live in an expanding universe.

✔ The universe began with a Big Bang, with tremendously high temperatures present in the early universe. The cosmic background radiation is the "afterglow" of that early epoch in the history of the universe.

✔ The dominance of matter over antimatter in the universe is the result of a small but important asymmetry in the laws of particle physics.

✔ Most of the matter in the universe is in the form of dark matter, and most of the energy in the universe is in the form of dark energy. The nature of dark matter and the nature of dark energy are unsolved problems in physics.

Key Terms

antimatter
antiquark
baryon
Big Bang
cosmic background radiation
cosmic microwave background
cosmological redshift
cosmology
dark energy

dark matter
exchange particle
galaxy
gluon
hadron
Heisenberg uncertainty principle
Hubble constant
Hubble law
lepton

meson
particle physics
quark
quark confinement
redshift
Standard Model
virtual particle
weak force

Chapter Summary

Topic	Equation or Figure

Hadrons and leptons: Hadrons, including the proton and neutron, are particles that experience the strong force; leptons, including the electron and neutrino, are particles that do not. Hadrons are composed of more fundamental particles called quarks; these are confined to the interior of hadrons and cannot exist in isolation. Hadrons include baryons, which are made of three quarks, and mesons, which are made of a quark and antiquark. Leptons are themselves fundamental particles; they are not made of anything simpler.

Baryons

(a) Proton (p)

Net charge $= q_u + q_u + q_d$

$= \left(+\frac{2}{3}e\right) + \left(+\frac{2}{3}e\right) + \left(-\frac{1}{3}e\right) = +e$

(b) Neutron (n)

Net charge $= q_d + q_d + q_u$

$= \left(-\frac{1}{3}e\right) + \left(-\frac{1}{3}e\right) + \left(+\frac{2}{3}e\right) = 0$

(Figure 28-3)

Mesons

(a) Positive pion (π^+)

Net charge $= q_u + q_{\bar{d}}$

$= \left(+\frac{2}{3}e\right) + \left(+\frac{1}{3}e\right) = +e$

(b) Negative pion (π^-)

Net charge $= q_d + q_{\bar{u}}$

$= \left(-\frac{1}{3}e\right) + \left(-\frac{2}{3}e\right) = -e$

(Figure 28-4)

The four forces and exchange particles: All interactions between particles can be understood in terms of four basic forces. Each of these forces involves the exchange of virtual particles, which is permitted by the Heisenberg uncertainty principle. The strong force between quarks involves the exchange of gluons, and the electromagnetic force involves the exchange of photons; both gluons and photons have zero mass, so these are long-range forces. The weak force responsible for beta decay involves the exchange of massive particles, so this force has a very short range. The gravitational force involves the exchange of gravitons, which have not yet been detected experimentally.

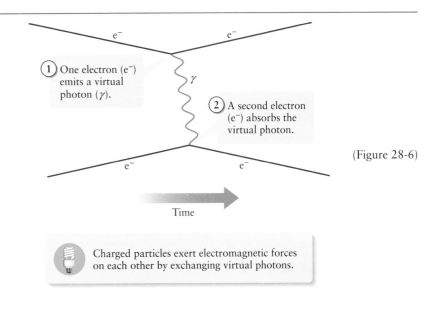

① One electron (e^-) emits a virtual photon (γ).

② A second electron (e^-) absorbs the virtual photon.

Time

(Figure 28-6)

 Charged particles exert electromagnetic forces on each other by exchanging virtual photons.

The energy of a phenomenon is necessarily uncertain by an amount ΔE.

$$\Delta E \Delta t \geq \frac{\hbar}{2}$$

(28-7)

The shorter the duration Δt of the phenomenon, the greater the energy uncertainty ΔE.

$\hbar = \dfrac{h}{2\pi}$

= Planck's constant divided by 2π

Cosmology, dark matter, and dark energy: The Hubble law—the more distant a galaxy is from us, the faster it moves away from us—tells us that the universe is expanding and was once very highly compressed and at very high temperature. The cosmic background radiation is a relic of this ancient epoch. Processes in the early universe had a slight preference for matter over antimatter, which is why the present-day universe contains matter but almost no antimatter. Normal matter is actually just a small component of the universe: Mysterious dark matter is about five times as prevalent. Even more important and even more mysterious is dark energy, which causes the expansion of the universe to speed up.

The speed at which a distant galaxy moves away from us...

...is directly proportional to its distance from us.

$$v = H_0 d$$

(28-9)

Hubble constant = 70 km/s/Mpc = 2.3×10^{-18} s^{-1}

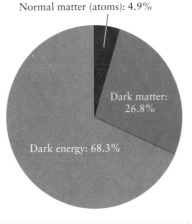

Normal matter (atoms): 4.9%

Dark matter: 26.8%

Dark energy: 68.3%

(Figure 28-16)

 What we think of as "normal" matter makes up less than 5% of the contents of the universe.

Answer to What do you think? Question

(e) A collision such as this can produce other electrons (matter) and positrons (antimatter), but can also produce a shower of quarks and antiquarks. These can group into baryons (particles that are combinations of quarks, which are matter), antibaryons (particles that are combinations of antiquarks, which are antimatter), and mesons (particles that are a combination of a quark and an antiquark, and hence a mixture of matter and antimatter).

Answers to Got the Concept? Questions

28-1 (c) A quark has charge $+2e/3$ or $-e/3$, and an antiquark has charge $-2e/3$ or $+e/3$ (see Table 28-1). Mesons are made up of one quark and one antiquark, and no quark-antiquark combination has a net charge $-2e$. Baryons are made up of three quarks, and no combination of three quarks has a net charge $-2e$. Antibaryons are made up of three antiquarks; if each of the three has charge $-2e/3$, the total charge of the antibaryon will be $(-2e/3) + (-2e/3) + (-2e/3) = -2e$.

28-2 (a) The neutron (n) and proton (p) each have baryon number $B = 1$ and the antiproton ($\bar{p}$) has $B = -1$. Baryon number is conserved in process (a), since total B equals $1 + 1 = 2$ before the process and equals $1 + 1 + 1 + (-1) = 2$ after the process. This process can occur if the initial neutron and proton have sufficient kinetic energy so that, when they collide, this energy can be converted into the rest energy of the additional proton and antiproton. Baryon number is *not* conserved in process (b), since total B equals $1 + 1 = 2$ before the process and $1 + 1 + 1 = 3$ after the process. So (b) cannot occur. In process (c) the π^- is a meson with $L_e = 0$ and $L_\mu = 0$, the muon μ^- has $L_e = 0$ and $L_\mu = 1$, and the electron antineutrino $\bar{\nu}_e$ has $L_e = -1$ and $L_\mu = 0$. The total electron-lepton number is 0 before the process and $0 + -1 = -1$ after the process, and the total muon-lepton number is zero before the process and $1 + 0 = 1$ after the process. So neither electron-lepton number L_e nor muon-lepton number L_μ is conserved in process (c), and process (c) cannot occur.

28-3 (a) Table 28-1 shows that the c quark has charge $+2e/3$ and the s quark has a charge $-e/3$. The quark must therefore emit a W^+ with charge $+e$, so that the total charge of the W^+ and s quark equals the initial charge of the c quark: $(+e) + (-e/3) = +2e/3$. The W^+ must decay into a positron (charge $+e$) to conserve charge. Since the W^+ has electron-lepton number $L_e = 0$ (it's not a lepton) and the positron has $L_e = -1$, the positron must be accompanied by a neutral particle with $L_e = +1$. That must be a neutrino, not an antineutrino (which has $L_e = -1$).

28-4 (e) Dark matter is so called because it emits *no* electromagnetic radiation of any kind.

Questions and Problems

In a few problems, you are given more data than you actually need; in a few other problems, you are required to supply data from your general knowledge, outside sources, or informed estimate.
Interpret as significant all digits in numerical values that have trailing zeros and no decimal points.
For all problems, use $g = 9.80$ m/s² for the free-fall acceleration due to gravity. Neglect friction and air resistance unless instructed to do otherwise.
• Basic, single-concept problem
•• Intermediate-level problem, may require synthesis of concepts and multiple steps
••• Challenging problem
SSM *Solution is in Student Solutions Manual*

Conceptual Questions

1. •Define these terms: (a) baryon, (b) meson, (c) quark, (d) lepton, and (e) antiparticle.

2. •What do exchange particles do?

3. •Discuss the similarities and differences between a photon and a neutrino.

4. •Write the quark content for the antiparticle of each of the following: (a) e, (b) n, (c) p, and (d) π^+.

5. •Considering only the up (u), down (d), and strange (s) quarks, how many unique combinations of quarks resulting in a baryon can be produced (neglect the antimatter baryons) from just these three quarks? SSM

6. •A positron is stable; that is, it does not decay. Why, then, does a positron have only a short existence?

7. •When a positron and an electron annihilate at rest, why must more than one photon be created?

8. •A meson and a baryon come very close to one another. The particles could interact by which of the fundamental forces (gravitational, electromagnetic, weak, or strong)?

9. •Explain the evidence in favor of the existence of dark matter.

10. •Why are scientists convinced that dark energy must exist?

Multiple-Choice Questions

11. •A particle composed of a quark and an antiquark is classified as a
   A. baryon.
   B. meson.
   C. photon.
   D. pion.
   E. particon. SSM

12. •A particle composed of three quarks is classified as a
   A. baryon.
   B. meson.

C. photon.
D. pion.
E. particon.

13. •The quark composition of an antiproton is
A. uud.
B. uud̄.
C. ūūd.
D. ūūd̄.
E. uuu.

14. •The beta decay process is mediated by the
A. gravitational force.
B. electromagnetic force.
C. strong force.
D. weak force.
E. dark force.

15. •Through which force does the electrically neutral pion interact with other particles?
A. strong
B. electromagnetic
C. weak
D. gravitational
E. dark SSM

16. •Through which force does the photon interact with other particles?
A. strong
B. electromagnetic
C. weak
D. gravitational
E. dark

17. •Particles that interact using the strong force are
A. neutrinos.
B. leptons.
C. photons.
D. quarks.
E. gravitons.

18. •Recent observations indicate that the universe is dominated by
A. matter.
B. dark matter.
C. dark energy.
D. photons.
E. none of the above.

19. •A mysterious energy that seems to cause the expansion of the universe to accelerate is
A. gravitational potential energy.
B. electric potential energy.
C. thermal energy.
D. dark energy.
E. kinetic energy.

Estimation/Numerical Analysis

20. •One type of meson that can be exchanged between nucleons is the ρ (rho), with a mass of 775 MeV/c^2. Estimate the range of the interaction due to the exchange of ρ mesons. *Hint:* The range of the meson must be less than $R = c\hbar/(2mc^2)$, and the radius of the nucleus is about 1.5 fm.

21. •Estimate the distance to a galaxy that is moving away from us at one-tenth of the speed of light due to the expansion of the universe.

Problems

28-1 Studying the ultimate constituents of matter helps reveal the nature of the universe

28-2 Most forms of matter can be explained by just a handful of fundamental particles

22. ••Is the reaction $n \rightarrow \pi^+ + \pi^- + \mu^+ + \mu^-$ possible? Explain your answer.

23. ••Is the reaction $p \rightarrow e^+ + \gamma$ possible? Explain your answer. SSM

24. ••Is the reaction $e^- + p \rightarrow n + \bar{\nu}_e$ possible? Explain your answer.

25. ••(a) Describe the particle that is composed of the quark combination uds. (b) How would your answer change if the quark combination were instead uss? Explain your answer.

26. ••What is the quark structure of a π^- meson?

27. ••Two protons collide in a particle accelerator and generate new particles from their kinetic energy. Which of the following reactions is possible? Which is not possible? If a reaction is not possible, state which conservation law(s) is (are) violated.
a. $p + p \rightarrow p + p + p + \bar{p}$
b. $p + p \rightarrow p + p + n + \bar{n}$
c. $p + p \rightarrow p + K^+$

28. ••Which of the following two possibilities for the weak decay of a sigma particle (a baryon) are possible? Why?
a. $\Sigma^- \rightarrow \pi^- + p$
b. $\Sigma^- \rightarrow \pi^- + n$

29. ••Which of the following reactions is possible? If a reaction is not possible, tell which conservation law(s) is (are) violated.
a. $n \rightarrow p + e^- + \bar{\nu}_e$
b. $\mu^- \rightarrow e^- + \bar{\nu}_e + \nu_\mu$
c. $\pi^- \rightarrow \mu^- + \bar{\nu}_\mu$ SSM

30. ••One possible mode of decay of a photon is proton-antiproton pair production:

$$\gamma \rightarrow p + \bar{p}$$

What is the maximum wavelength of such a photon?

31. ••A neutral η (eta) meson at rest decays into two gamma rays according to

$$\eta \rightarrow \gamma + \gamma$$

Calculate the energy, momentum, and wavelength of each of the photons. The mass of the eta particle is 547 MeV/c^2.

32. ••Two protons collide in a particle accelerator, with the same speed, causing the reaction:

$$p + p \rightarrow p + p + \pi^0$$

Calculate the minimum kinetic energy of each of the incident protons.

33. ••A high-energy photon in the vicinity of a nucleus can create an electron-positron pair by pair production:

$$\gamma \rightarrow e^- + e^+$$

(a) What minimum energy photon is required? (b) Why is the nucleus needed? SSM

34. ••How much energy, in the form of gamma rays, would result due to the annihilation of a positron with kinetic energy 34 MeV and an electron with kinetic energy 16 MeV?

35. ••A proton-antiproton annihilation takes place, and the resulting photons have a total energy of 2.5 GeV. Find the kinetic energy of the proton and antiproton if the proton has (a) the same kinetic energy as the antiproton and (b) 1.25 times as much kinetic energy as the antiproton. SSM

36. ••The kinetic energy of a neutral pion (π^0) is 860 MeV. This pion decays to two photons, one of which has energy 640 MeV. Calculate the energy of the other photon.

28-3 Four fundamental forces describe all interactions between material objects

37. ••Draw the Feynman diagram for beta-plus decay wherein a proton changes into a neutron, a positron, and a neutrino.

38. ••Draw the Feynman diagram for the pair production of an electron and a positron from a gamma ray.

39. ••Draw the Feynman diagram for pair annihilation of a proton and an antiproton. SSM

40. ••Draw the Feynman diagram for the beta decay of the antineutron.

41. ••Suppose that a new fundamental force were discovered having a range about equal to the radius of a hydrogen atom. Estimate what you would expect to be the mass (in MeV/c^2) of the mediating particle of the new force. How does the mass compare with the mass of the electron?

28-4 We live in an expanding universe, and the nature of most of its contents is a mystery

42. •A galaxy is observed to recede from Earth with an approximate speed of $0.8c$. (a) Approximately how far from Earth is this galaxy? (b) How long ago was this light emitted by the galaxy?

43. •The galaxy NGC 3982 shown in Figure 28-15a is 6.8×10^7 ly from Earth. Approximately how fast is it receding from Earth?

General Problems

44. ••Suppose that a fifth fundamental force were discovered and that it was mediated by electrons and positrons. Estimate the range of the force.

45. ••(a) What stable nucleus would have a diameter equal to 10 times the approximate range of the strong force? (b) What would be the electric repulsion on a proton at the surface of the nucleus in part (a)? SSM

46. ••According to the U.S. Energy Information Administration, the United States used approximately 4.12×10^{12} kWh of electrical energy during 2010. (a) If we could generate all the energy using a matter–antimatter reactor, how many kilograms of fuel would the reactor need, assuming 100% efficiency in the annihilation? (b) Suppose the fuel consisted of

iron and anti-iron, each of density 7800 kg/m^3. If the iron and anti-iron were each stored as a cubical pile, what would be the dimensions of each cube?

47. •••Suppose that an electron neutrino and an electron anti-neutrino, both of which are just barely moving, encounter each other in space and completely annihilate to form two photons of equal energy. In view of the uncertainty about the mass of the electron neutrino (see Table 28-2), what is the shortest wavelength of light that could be emitted by the annihilation? Would the light be visible to the human eye?

48. ••Baryons are said to be "color neutral." This refers to the fact that each of the three quarks that comprise the baryon has a "color" quantum number (which is either red, green, or blue). (There is no actual color to see with quarks; color is only a quantum characteristic that can be likened to the electric charge of an electron, for example). Just as with visible light, when you mix red with green with blue you get white light, so it is with the color nature of quarks. A proton is not simply made up of uud; rather, it is $u_R u_G d_B$, for example. All the other quantum numbers that you have learned about (charge, baryon number, strangeness, etc.) still apply. The color quantum numbers "add up" to a neutral white (R + G + B = white). Express all the possible color quantum states that might exist for an ordinary proton ($u_R u_G d_B$, $u_B u_R d_G$, etc.).

49. ••Like baryons, mesons are also color neutral. (See problem 48 for a discussion of color neutrality.) However, because mesons are made up of quark-antiquark pairs, it is not the combination of colors that cancels, but rather the subtraction of "anticolor" that creates the color neutrality. For example, a π^+ meson is made up of $u_R \overline{d}_R$. The antidown red quark cancels the up red quark much like the negative charge of an electron is canceled by the positive charge of a positron. Write the various possible color combinations for the three pions (π^+, π^0, π^-).

50. ••**Astronomy** The universe has evolved through several distinct *epochs* over the course of the last 13.8 billion years. The first epoch that occurred after the Big Bang, called the *Planck Epoch*, took place during the first 10^{-43} s after the Big Bang. This time interval is called the *Planck time*, t_P. (To understand what happened during the Planck Epoch, a theory that describes gravity in terms of quantum mechanics is required. No such theory yet exists.) Calculate t_P by first using dimensional analysis and finding the proper combination of the fundamental constants: G, c, and $\hbar$. Then use the current numerical values of each to calculate the precise number for t_P. (Recall that G is Newton's gravitational constant and is equal to 6.6738×10^{-11} N·m^2/kg^2, c is the speed of light and is equal to 2.9979×10^8 m/s, and $\hbar$ is Planck's constant divided by 2π or 1.0546×10^{-34} J·s). Start your calculation by asking what power would each of the three constants need to have in order to yield units of seconds: $[t_P] = [G]^x[c]^y[\hbar]^z$. Solve for x, y, and z to derive the formula for t_P.

51. •••In July 2011, physicists at the Tevatron at Fermilab near Chicago announced the discovery of a long-predicted but short-lived particle, the *xi-sub-b baryon*, Ξ_b. It is made up of a strange quark, an up quark, and a bottom quark, and is so short-lived that it travels less than a millimeter during its lifetime. (a) What is the charge of the Ξ_b baryon? (b) Estimate its lifetime if it travels about 0.5 mm before it decays.

APPENDIX A
SI Units and Conversion Factors

Base Units*

Length	The *meter* (m) is the distance traveled by light in a vacuum in 1/299,792,458 s.
Time	The *second* (s) is the duration of 9,192,631,770 periods of the radiation corresponding to the transition between the two hyperfine levels of the ground state of the ^{133}Cs atom.
Mass	The *kilogram* (kg) is the mass of the international standard body preserved at Sèvres, France.
Mole	The *mole* (mol) is the amount of substance of a system which contains as many elementary entities as there are atoms in 0.012 kg of carbon-12.
Current	The *ampere* (A) is that constant current which, if maintained in two straight parallel conductors of infinite length, of negligible circular cross section, and placed 1 m apart in vacuum, would produce between the conductors a force equal to 2×10^{-7} N/m of length.
Temperature	The *kelvin* (K) is 1/273.16 of the thermodynamic temperature of the triple point of water.
Luminous intensity	The *candela* (cd) is the luminous intensity in a given direction, of a source that emits monochromatic radiation of frequency 540×10^{12} Hz and that has a radiant intensity, in that direction of 1/683 W/steradian.

*These definitions are found on the Internet at http://physics.nist.gov/cuu/Units/current.html.

Derived Units

Force	newton (N)	$1 \text{ N} = 1 \text{ kg} \cdot \text{m/s}^2$
Work, energy	joule (J)	$1 \text{ J} = 1 \text{ N} \cdot \text{m}$
Power	watt (W)	$1 \text{ W} = 1 \text{ J/s}$
Frequency	hertz (Hz)	$1 \text{ Hz} = \text{cy/s}$
Charge	coulomb (C)	$1 \text{ C} = 1 \text{ A} \cdot \text{s}$
Potential	volt (V)	$1 \text{ V} = 1 \text{ J/C}$
Resistance	ohm (Ω)	$1 \text{ }\Omega = 1 \text{ V/A}$
Capacitance	farad (F)	$1 \text{ F} = 1 \text{ C/V}$
Magnetic field	tesla (T)	$1 \text{ T} = 1 \text{ N/(A} \cdot \text{m)}$
Magnetic flux	weber (Wb)	$1 \text{ Wb} = 1 \text{ T} \cdot \text{m}^2$
Inductance	henry (H)	$1 \text{ H} = 1 \text{ J/A}^2$

Conversion Factors

Conversion factors are written as equations for simplicity;
relations marked with an asterisk are exact.

Length

1 km = 0.6214 mi

1 mi = 1.609 km

1 m = 1.0936 yard = 3.281 ft = 39.37 in.

*1 in. = 2.54 cm

*1 ft = 12 in. = 30.48 cm

*1 yard = 3 ft = 91.44 cm

1 light-year = 1 $c \cdot y$ = 9.461 $\times$ 10^{15} m

*1 Å = 0.1 nm

Area

*1 m^2 = 10^4 cm^2

1 km^2 = 0.3861 mi^2 = 247.1 acres

*1 in.^{2} = 6.4516 cm^2

1 ft^2 = 9.29 $\times$ 10^{-2} m^2

1 m^2 = 10.76 ft^2

*1 acre = 43 560 ft^2

1 mi^2 = 640 acres = 2.590 km^2

Volume

*1 m^3 = 10^6 cm^3

*1 L = 1000 cm^3 = 10^{-3} m^3

1 gal = 3.785 L

1 gal = 4 qt = 8 pt = 128 oz = 231 in.^{3}

1 in.^{3} = 16.39 cm^3

1 ft^3 = 1728 in.^{3} = 28.32 L
    = 2.832 $\times$ 10^4 cm^3

Time

*1 h = 60 min = 3.6 ks

*1 d = 24 h = 1440 min = 86.4 ks

1 y = 365.25 day = 3.156 $\times$ 10^7 s

Speed

*1 m/s = 3.6 km/h

1 km/h = 0.2778 m/s = 0.6214 mi/h

1 mi/h = 0.4470 m/s = 1.609 km/h

1 mi/h = 1.467 ft/s

Angle and Angular Speed

*π rad = 180°

1 rad = 57.30°

1° = 1.745 $\times$ 10^{-2} rad

1 rev/min = 0.1047 rad/s

1 rad/s = 9.549 rev/min

Mass

*1 kg = 1000 g

*1 tonne = 1000 kg = 1 Mg

1 u = 1.6605 $\times$ 10^{-27} kg
        931.49 MeV/c^2

1 kg = 6.022 $\times$ 10^{26} u

1 slug = 14.59 kg

1 kg = 6.852 $\times$ 10^{-2} slug

Density

*1 g/cm^3 = 1000 kg/m^3 = 1 kg/L

(1 g/cm^3)g = 62.4 lb/ft^3

Force

1 N = 0.2248 lb = 10^5 dyn

*1 lb = 4.448222 N

(1 kg)g = 2.2046 lb

Pressure

*1 Pa = 1 N/m^2

*1 atm = 101.325 kPa = 1.01325 bar

1 atm = 14.7 lb/in.^{2} = 760 mmHg
        = 29.9 in.Hg = 33.9 ftH$_2$O

1 lb/in.^{2} = 6.895 kPa

1 torr = 1 mmHg = 133.32 Pa

1 bar = 100 kPa

Energy

*1 kW $\cdot$ h = 3.6 MJ

*1 cal = 4.186 J

1 ft $\cdot$ lb = 1.356 J = 1.286 $\times$ 10^{-3} BTU

*1 L $\cdot$ atm = 101.325 J

1 L $\cdot$ atm = 24.217 cal

1 BTU = 778 ft $\cdot$ lb = 252 cal = 1054.35 J

1 eV = 1.602 $\times$ 10^{-19} J

1 u $\cdot$ c^2 = 931.49 MeV

*1 erg = 10^{-7} J

Power

1 horsepower = 550 ft $\cdot$ lb/s = 745.7 W

1 BTU/h = 2.931 $\times$ 10^{-4} kW

1 W = 1.341 $\times$ 10^{-3} horsepower
    = 0.7376 ft $\cdot$ lb/s

Magnetic Field

*1 T = 10^4 G

Thermal Conductivity

1 W/(m $\cdot$ K) = 6.938 BTU $\cdot$ in./(h $\cdot$ ft^2 $\cdot$ °F)

1 BTU $\cdot$ in./(h $\cdot$ ft^2 $\cdot$ °F) = 0.1441 W/(m $\cdot$ K)

APPENDIX B
Numerical Data

Terrestrial Data

Free-fall acceleration g	
Standard value (at sea level at 45° latitude)*	9.806 65 m/s^2; 32.1740 ft/s^2
At equator*	9.7804 m/s^2
At poles*	9.8322 m/s^2
Mass of Earth M_E	5.98×10^{24} kg
Radius of Earth R_E, mean	6.38×10^6 m; 3960 mi
Escape speed	1.12×10^4 m/s; 6.96 mi/s
Solar constant†	1.37 kW/m^2
Standard temperature and pressure (STP):	
Temperature	273.15 K
Pressure	101.3 kPa (1.00 atm)
Molar mass of air	28.97 g/mol
Density of air (273.15 K, 101.3 kPa), ρ_{air}	1.29 kg/m^3
Speed of sound (273.15 K, 101.3 kPa)	331 m/s
Latent heat of fusion of H_2O (0°C, 1 atm)	334 kJ/kg
Latent heat of vaporization of H_2O (100°C, 1 atm)	2.26 MJ/kg

* Measured relative to Earth's surface.

† Average power incident normally on 1 m^2 outside Earth's atmosphere at the mean distance from Earth to the Sun.

Astronomical Data*

Earth	
Distance to the Moon, mean†	3.844×10^8 m; 2.389×10^5 mi
Distance to the Sun, mean†	1.496×10^{11} m; 9.32×10^7 mi; 1.00 AU
Orbital speed, mean	2.98×10^4 m/s
Moon	
Mass	7.35×10^{22} kg
Radius	1.737×10^6 m
Period	27.32 day
Acceleration of gravity at surface	1.62 m/s^2
Sun	
Mass	1.99×10^{30} kg
Radius	6.96×10^8 m

* Additional solar system data are available from NASA at http://nssdc.gsfc.nasa.gov/planetary/planetfact.html.

† Center to center.

Physical Constants*

Universal constant of gravitation	G	$6.673\ 84(80) \times 10^{-11}$ N $\cdot$ m^2/kg^2
Speed of light	c	$2.997\ 924\ 58 \times 10^8$ m/s
Fundamental charge	e	$1.602\ 176\ 565(35) \times 10^{-19}$ C
Avogadro's constant	N_A	$6.022\ 141\ 29(27) \times 10^{23}$ particles/mol
Gas constant	R	$8.314\ 462\ 1(75)$ J/(mol $\cdot$ K)
		$1.987\ 206\ 5(36)$ cal/(mol $\cdot$ K)
		$8.205\ 746(15) \times 10^{-2}$ L $\cdot$ atm/(mol $\cdot$ K)
Boltzmann constant	$k = R/N_A$	$1.380\ 648\ 8(13) \times 10^{-23}$ J/K
		$8.617\ 332\ 4(81) \times 10^{-5}$ eV/K
Stefan-Boltzmann constant	$\sigma = (\pi^2/60)k^4/(\hbar^3 c^2)$	$5.670\ 373(21) \times 10^{-8}$ W/(m^2 $\cdot$ K^4)
Atomic mass constant	$m_u = (1/12)m(^{12}C)$	$1.660\ 538\ 921(73) \times 10^{-27}$ kg = 1 u
Permeability of free space	μ_0	$4\pi \times 10^{-7}$ N/A^2
		$1.256\ 637\ \ldots \times 10^{-6}$ N/A^2
Permittivity of free space	$\epsilon_0 = 1/(\mu_0 c^2)$	$8.854\ 187\ 817\ \ldots \times 10^{-12}$ C^2/(N $\cdot$ m^2)
Coulomb constant	$k = 1/(4\pi\epsilon_0)$	$8.987\ 551\ 787\ \ldots \times 10^9$ N $\cdot$ m^2/C^2
Planck's constant	h	$6.626\ 069\ 57(29) \times 10^{-34}$ J $\cdot$ s
		$4.135\ 667\ 516(91) \times 10^{-15}$ eV $\cdot$ s
	$\hbar = h/(2\pi)$	$1.054\ 571\ 726(47) \times 10^{-34}$ J $\cdot$ s
		$6.582\ 119\ 28(15) \times 10^{-16}$ eV $\cdot$ s
Mass of electron	m_e	$9.109\ 382\ 91(40) \times 10^{-31}$ kg
		$0.510\ 998\ 928(11)$ MeV/c^2
Mass of proton	m_p	$1.672\ 621\ 777(74) \times 10^{-27}$ kg
		$938.272\ 046(21)$ MeV/c^2
Mass of neutron	m_n	$1.674\ 927\ 351(74) \times 10^{-27}$ kg
		$939.565\ 379(21)$ MeV/c^2
Bohr magneton	$m_B = e\hbar/(2m_e)$	$9.274\ 009\ 68(20) \times 10^{-24}$ J/T
		$5.788\ 381\ 806\ 6(38) \times 10^{-5}$ eV/T
Nuclear magneton	$m_n = e\hbar/(2m_p)$	$5.050\ 783\ 53(11) \times 10^{-27}$ J/T
		$3.152\ 451\ 258(99) \times 10^{-8}$ eV/T
Magnetic flux quantum	$\phi_0 = h/(2e)$	$2.067\ 833\ 758(46) \times 10^{-15}$ T $\cdot$ m^2
Quantized Hall resistance	$R_K = h/e^2$	$2.581\ 280\ 744\ 34(84) \times 10^4$ Ω
Rydberg constant	R_H	$1.097\ 373\ 156\ 853\ 9(55) \times 10^7$ m^{-1}
Josephson frequency–voltage quotient	$K_J = 2e/h$	$4.835\ 978\ 70(11) \times 10^{14}$ Hz/V
Compton wavelength	$\lambda_C = h/(m_e c)$	$2.426\ 310\ 238\ 9(16) \times 10^{-12}$ m

* The values for these and other constants may be found on the Internet at http://physics.nist.gov/cuu/Constants/index.html. The numbers in parentheses represent the uncertainties in the last two digits. (For example, 2.044 43(13) stands for 2.044 43 $\pm$ 0.000 13.) Values without uncertainties are exact, including those values with ellipses (such as the value of pi is exactly 3.1415. . .).

APPENDIX C
Periodic Table of Elements[*]

1																	18
1 **H**	2											13	14	15	16	17	2 **He**
3 **Li**	4 **Be**											5 **B**	6 **C**	7 **N**	8 **O**	9 **F**	10 **Ne**
11 **Na**	12 **Mg**	3	4	5	6	7	8	9	10	11	12	13 **Al**	14 **Si**	15 **P**	16 **S**	17 **Cl**	18 **Ar**
19 **K**	20 **Ca**	21 **Sc**	22 **Ti**	23 **V**	24 **Cr**	25 **Mn**	26 **Fe**	27 **Co**	28 **Ni**	29 **Cu**	30 **Zn**	31 **Ga**	32 **Ge**	33 **As**	34 **Se**	35 **Br**	36 **Kr**
37 **Rb**	38 **Sr**	39 **Y**	40 **Zr**	41 **Nb**	42 **Mo**	43 **Tc**	44 **Ru**	45 **Rh**	46 **Pd**	47 **Ag**	48 **Cd**	49 **In**	50 **Sn**	51 **Sb**	52 **Te**	53 **I**	54 **Xe**
55 **Cs**	56 **Ba**	57–71 Lanthanoids	72 **Hf**	73 **Ta**	74 **W**	75 **Re**	76 **Os**	77 **Ir**	78 **Pt**	79 **Au**	80 **Hg**	81 **Tl**	82 **Pb**	83 **Bi**	84 **Po**	85 **At**	86 **Rn**
87 **Fr**	88 **Ra**	89–103 Actinoids	104 **Rf**	105 **Db**	106 **Sg**	107 **Bh**	108 **Hs**	109 **Mt**	110 **Ds**	111 **Rg**	112 **Cn**						

Lanthanoids	57 **La**	58 **Ce**	59 **Pr**	60 **Nd**	61 **Pm**	62 **Sm**	63 **Eu**	64 **Gd**	65 **Tb**	66 **Dy**	67 **Ho**	68 **Er**	69 **Tm**	70 **Yb**	71 **Lu**
Actinoids	89 **Ac**	90 **Th**	91 **Pa**	92 **U**	93 **Np**	94 **Pu**	95 **Am**	96 **Cm**	97 **Bk**	98 **Cf**	99 **Es**	100 **Fm**	101 **Md**	102 **No**	103 **Lr**

[*] From http://old.iupac.org/reports/periodic_table/IUPAC_Periodic_Table-21Jan11.pdf.

Atomic Numbers and Atomic Weights*

Atomic Number	Name	Symbol	Weight	Atomic Number	Name	Symbol	Weight
1	Hydrogen	H	[1.007 84; 1.008 11]	57	Lanthanum	La	138.90547(7)
2	Helium	He	4.002602(2)	58	Cerium	Ce	140.116(1)
3	Lithium	Li	[6.938; 6.997]	59	Praseodymium	Pr	140.90765(2)
4	Beryllium	Be	9.012182(3)	60	Neodymium	Nd	144.242(3)
5	Boron	B	[10.806; 10.821]	61	Promethium	Pm	
6	Carbon	C	[12.009 6; 12.011 6]	62	Samarium	Sm	150.36(2)
7	Nitrogen	N	[14.006 43; 14.007 28]	63	Europium	Eu	151.964(1)
8	Oxygen	O	[15.999 03; 15.999 77]	64	Gadolinium	Gd	157.25(3)
9	Fluorine	F	18.9984032(5)	65	Terbium	Tb	158.92535(2)
10	Neon	Ne	20.1797(6)	66	Dysprosium	Dy	162.500(1)
11	Sodium	Na	22.98976928(2)	67	Holmium	Ho	164.93032(2)
12	Magnesium	Mg	24.3050(6)	68	Erbium	Er	167.259(3)
13	Aluminum	Al	26.9815386(8)	69	Thulium	Tm	168.93421(2)
14	Silicon	Si	[28.084; 28.086]	70	Ytterbium	Yb	173.054(5)
15	Phosphorus	P	30.973762(2)	71	Lutetium	Lu	174.966 8(1)
16	Sulfur	S	[32.059; 32.076]	72	Hafnium	Hf	178.49(2)
17	Chlorine	Cl	[35.446; 35.457]	73	Tantalum	Ta	180.94788(2)
18	Argon	Ar	39.948(1)	74	Tungsten	W	183.84(1)
19	Potassium	K	39.0983(1)	75	Rhenium	Re	186.207(1)
20	Calcium	Ca	40.078(4)	76	Osmium	Os	190.23(3)
21	Scandium	Sc	44.955912(6)	77	Iridium	Ir	192.217(3)
22	Titanium	Ti	47.867(1)	78	Platinum	Pt	195.084(9)
23	Vanadium	V	50.9415(1)	79	Gold	Au	196.966569(4)
24	Chromium	Cr	51.9961(6)	80	Mercury	Hg	200.59(2)
25	Manganese	Mn	54.938045(5)	81	Thallium	Tl	[204.382; 204.385]
26	Iron	Fe	55.845(2)	82	Lead	Pb	207.2(1)
27	Cobalt	Co	58.933195(5)	83	Bismuth	Bi	208.98040(1)
28	Nickel	Ni	58.6934(2)	84	Polonium	Po	
29	Copper	Cu	63.546(3)	85	Astatine	At	
30	Zinc	Zn	65.38 (2)	86	Radon	Rn	
31	Gallium	Ga	69.723(1)	87	Francium	Fr	
32	Germanium	Ge	72.63 (1)	88	Radium	Ra	
33	Arsenic	As	74.92160(2)	89	Actinium	Ac	
34	Selenium	Se	78.96(3)	90	Thorium	Th	232.03806(2)
35	Bromine	Br	79.904(1)	91	Protactinium	Pa	231.03588(2)
36	Krypton	Kr	83.798(2)	92	Uranium	U	238.02891(3)
37	Rubidium	Rb	85.4678(3)	93	Neptunium	Np	
38	Strontium	Sr	87.62(1)	94	Plutonium	Pu	
39	Yttrium	Y	88.90585(2)	95	Americium	Am	
40	Zirconium	Zr	91.224(2)	96	Curium	Cm	
41	Niobium	Nb	92.90638(2)	97	Berkelium	Bk	
42	Molybdenum	Mo	95.96 (2)	98	Californium	Cf	
43	Technetium	Tc		99	Einsteinium	Es	
44	Ruthenium	Ru	101.07(2)	100	Fermiun	Fm	
45	Rhodium	Rh	102.90550(2)	101	Mendelevium	Md	
46	Palladium	Pd	106.42(1)	102	Nobelium	No	
47	Silver	Ag	107.8682(2)	103	Lawrencium	Lr	
48	Cadmium	Cd	112.411(8)	104	Rutherfordium	Rf	
49	Indium	In	114.818(3)	105	Dubnium	Db	
50	Tin	Sn	118.710(7)	106	Seaborgium	Sg	
51	Antimony	Sb	121.760(1)	107	Bohrium	Bh	
52	Tellurium	Te	127.60(3)	108	Hassium	Hs	
53	Iodine	I	126.90447(3)	109	Meitnerium	Mt	
54	Xenon	Xe	131.293(6)	110	Darmstadtium	Ds	
55	Cesium	Cs	132.9054519(2)	111	Roentgenium	Rg	
56	Barium	Ba	137.327(7)	112	Copernicium	Cn	

*Some weights are listed as intervals ([a; b]; a ≤ atomic weight ≤ b) because these weights are not constant but depend on the physical, chemical, and nuclear histories of the samples used. Atomic weights are not listed for some elements because these elements do not have stable isotopes. Exceptions are thorium, protactinium, and uranium. Elements 113 to 118 are not listed in this table although they have been reported (IUPAC has not named them). From *Atomic Weights of the Elements 2009 (IUPAC Technical Report)*, Pure Appl. Chem., Vol. 83(2), pp. 359–396, 2011.

Table of Atomic Masses

Element	Symbol	Mass number (*indicates radioactive)	Atomic mass	Percent abundance	Half-life and decay mode (if unstable)	
(Neutron)	*n*	1*	1.008665		10.4 m	β^-
Hydrogen	H	1	1.007825	99.985		
Deuterium	D	2	2.014102	0.015		
Tritium	T	3*	3.016049		12.33 y	β^-
Helium	He	3	3.016029	0.00014		
		4	4.002602	99.99986		
		6*	6.018886		0.81 s	β^-
		8*	8.033922		0.12 s	β^-
Lithium	Li	6	6.015121	7.5		
		7	7.016003	92.5		
		8*	8.022486		0.84 s	β^-
		9*	9.026789		0.18 s	β^-
		11*	11.043897		8.7 ms	β^-
Beryllium	Be	7*	7.016928		53.3 d	ec
		9	9.012174	100		
		10*	10.013534		1.5×10^6 y	β^-
		11*	11.021657		13.8 s	β^-
		12*	12.026921		23.6 ms	β^-
		14*	14.042866		4.3 ms	β^-
Boron	B	8*	8.024605		0.77 s	β^+
		10	10.012936	19.9		
		11	11.009305	80.1		
		12*	12.014352		0.0202 s	β^-
		13*	13.017780		17.4 ms	β^-
		14*	14.025404		13.8 ms	β^-
		15*	15.031100		10.3 ms	β^-
Carbon	C	9*	9.031030		0.13 s	β^+
		10*	10.016854		19.3 s	β^+
		11*	11.011433		20.4 m	β^+
		12	12.000000	98.90		
		13	13.003355	1.10		
		14*	14.003242		5730 y	β^-
		15*	15.010599		2.45 s	β^-
		16*	16.014701		0.75 s	β^-
		17*	17.022582		0.20 s	β^-

(Continued)

Element	Symbol	Mass number (*indicates radioactive)	Atomic mass	Percent abundance	Half-life and decay mode (if unstable)	
Nitrogen	N	12*	12.018613		0.0110 s	β^+
		13*	13.005738		9.96 m	β^+
		14	14.003074	99.63		
		15	15.000108	0.37		
		16*	16.006100		7.13 s	β^-
		17*	17.008450		4.17 s	β^-
		18*	18.014082		0.62 s	β^-
		19*	19.017038		0.24 s	β^-
Oxygen	O	13*	13.024813		8.6 ms	β^+
		14*	14.008595		70.6 s	β^+
		15*	15.003065		122 s	β^+
		16	15.994915	99.71		
		17	16.999132	0.039		
		18	17.999160	0.20		
		19*	19.003577		26.9 s	β^-
		20*	20.004076		13.6 s	β^-
		21*	21.008595		3.4 s	β^-
Fluorine	F	17*	17.002094		64.5 s	β^+
		18*	18.000937		109.8 m	β^+
		19	18.998404	100		
		20*	19.999982		11.0 s	β^-
		21*	20.999950		4.2 s	β^-
		22*	22.003036		4.2 s	β^-
		23*	23.003564		2.2 s	β^-
Neon	Ne	18*	18.005710		1.67 s	β^+
		19*	19.001880		17.2 s	β^+
		20	19.992435	90.48		
		21	20.993841	0.27		
		22	21.991383	9.25		
		23*	22.994465		37.2 s	β^-
		24*	23.993999		3.38 m	β^-
		25*	24.997789		0.60 s	β^-
Sodium	Na	21*	20.997650		22.5 s	β^+
		22*	21.994434		2.61 y	β^+
		23	22.989767	100		
		24*	23.990961		14.96 h	β^-
		25*	24.989951		59.1 s	β^-
		26*	25.992588		1.07 s	β^-
Magnesium	Mg	23*	22.994124		11.3 s	β^+
		24	23.985042	78.99		
		25	24.985838	10.00		
		26	25.982594	11.01		
		27*	26.984341		9.46 m	β^-
		28*	27.983876		20.9 h	β^-
		29*	28.375346		1.30 s	β^-

Element	Symbol	Mass number (*indicates radioactive)	Atomic mass	Percent abundance	Half-life and decay mode (if unstable)	
Aluminum	Al	25*	24.990429		7.18 s	β^+
		26*	25.986892		7.4×10^5 y	β^+
		27	26.981538	100		
		28*	27.981910		2.24 m	β^-
		29*	28.980445		6.56 m	β^-
		30*	29.982965		3.60 s	β^-
Silicon	Si	27*	26.986704		4.16 s	β^+
		28	27.976927	92.23		
		29	28.976495	4.67		
		30	28.973770	3.10		
		31*	30.975362		2.62 h	β^-
		32*	31.974148		172 y	β^-
		33*	32.977928		6.13 s	β^-
Phosphorus	P	30*	29.978307		2.50 m	β^+
		31	30.973762	100		
		32*	31.973762		14.26 d	β^-
		33*	32.971725		25.3 d	β^-
		34*	33.973636		12.43 s	β^-
Sulfur	S	31*	30.979554		2.57 s	β^+
		32	31.972071	95.02		
		33	32.971459	0.75		
		34	33.967867	4.21		
		35*	34.969033		87.5 d	β^-
		36	35.967081	0.02		
Chlorine	Cl	34*	33.973763		32.2 m	β^+
		35	34.968853	75.77		
		36*	35.968307		3.0×10^5 y	β^-
		37	36.965903	24.23		
		38*	37.968010		37.3 m	β^-
Argon	Ar	36	35.967547	0.337		
		37*	36.966776		35.04 d	ec
		38	37.962732	0.063		
		39*	38.964314		269 y	β^-
		40	39.962384	99.600		
		42*	41.963049		33 y	β^-
Potassium	K	39	38.963708	93.2581		
		40*	39.964000	0.0117	1.28×10^9 y	β^+, ec, β^-
		41	40.961827	6.7302		
		42*	41.962404		12.4 h	β^-
		43*	42.960716		22.3 h	β^-

(Continued)

Element	Symbol	Mass number (*indicates radioactive)	Atomic mass	Percent abundance	Half-life and decay mode (if unstable)	
Calcium	Ca	40	39.962591	96.941		
		41*	40.962279		1.0×10^5 y	ec
		42	41.958618	0.647		
		43	42.958767	0.135		
		44	43.955481	2.086		
		46	45.953687	0.004		
		48	47.952534	0.187		
Scandium	Sc	41*	40.969250		0.596 s	β^+
		43*	42.961151		3.89 h	β^+
		45	44.955911	100		
		46*	45.955170		83.8 d	β^-
Titanium	Ti	44*	43.959691		49 y	ec
		46	45.952630	8.0		
		47	46.951765	7.3		
		48	47.947947	73.8		
		49	48.947871	5.5		
		50	49.944792	5.4		
Vanadium	V	48*	47.952255			
		50*	49.947161	0.25	15.97 d	β^+
		51	50.943962	99.75	1.5×10^{17} y	β^+
Chromium	Cr	48*	47.954033		21.6 h	ec
		50	49.946047	4.345		
		52	51.940511	83.79		
		53	52.940652	9.50		
		54	53.938883	2.365		
Manganese	Mn	53*	52.941292		3.74×10^6 y	ec
		54*	53.940361		312.1 d	ec
		55	54.938048	100		
		56*	55.938908		2.58 h	β^-
Iron	Fe	54	53.939613	5.9		
		55*	54.938297		2.7 y	ec
		56	55.934940	91.72		
		57	56.935396	2.1		
		58	57.933278	0.28		
		60*	59.934078		1.5×10^6 y	β^-
Cobalt	Co	57*	56.936294		271.8 d	ec
		58*	57.935755		70.9 h	ec, β^+
		59	58.933198	100		
		60*	59.933820		5.27 y	β^-
		61*	60.932478		1.65 h	β^-
Nickel	Ni	58	57.935346	68.077		
		59*	58.934350		7.5×10^4 y	ec, β^+
		60	59.930789	26.223		
		61	60.931058	1.140		
		62	61.928346	3.634		
		63*	62.929670		100 y	β^-
		64	63.927967	0.926		

Element	Symbol	Mass number (*indicates radioactive)	Atomic mass	Percent abundance	Half-life and decay mode (if unstable)
Copper	Cu	63	62.929599	69.17	
		64*	63.929765		12.7 h ec
		65	64.927791	30.83	
		66*	65.928871		5.1 m β^-
Zinc	Zn	64	63.929144	48.6	
		66	65.926035	27.9	
		67	66.927129	4.1	
		68	67.924845	18.8	
		70	69.925323	0.6	
Gallium	Ga	69	68.925580	60.108	
		70*	69.926027		21.1 m β^-
		71	70.924703	39.892	
		72*	71.926367		14.1 h β^-
Germanium	Ge	69*	68.927969		39.1 h ec, β^+
		70	69.924250	21.23	
		72	71.922079	27.66	
		73	72.923462	7.73	
		74	73.921177	35.94	
		76	75.921402	7.44	
		77*	76.923547		11.3 h β^-
Arsenic	As	73*	72.923827		80.3 d ec
		74*	73.923928		17.8 d ec, β^+
		75	74.921594	100	
		76*	75.922393		1.1 d β^-
		77*	76.920645		38.8 h β^-
Selenium	Se	74	73.922474	0.89	
		76	75.919212	9.36	
		77	76.919913	7.63	
		78	77.917307	23.78	
		79*	78.918497		$\leq 6.5 \times 10^4$ y β^-
		80	79.916519	49.61	
		82*	81.916697	8.73	1.4×10^{20} y $2\beta^-$
Bromine	Br	79	78.918336	50.69	
		80*	79.918528		17.7 m β^+
		81	80.916287	49.31	
		82*	81.916802		35.3 h β^-
Krypton	Kr	78	77.920400	0.35	
		80	79.916377	2.25	
		81*	80.916589		2.11×10^5 y ec
		82	81.913481	11.6	
		83	82.914136	11.5	
		84	83.911508	57.0	
		85*	84.912531		10.76 y β^-
		86	85.910615	17.3	

(Continued)

Element	Symbol	Mass number (*indicates radioactive)	Atomic mass	Percent abundance	Half-life and decay mode (if unstable)
Rubidium	Rb	85	84.911793	72.17	
		86*	85.911171		18.6 d β^-
		87*	86.909186	27.83	4.75×10^{10} y β^-
		88*	87.911325		17.8 m β^-
Strontium	Sr	84	83.913428	0.56	
		86	85.909266	9.86	
		87	86.908883	7.00	
		88	87.905618	82.58	
		90*	89.907737		29.1 y β^-
Yttrium	Y	88*	87.909507		106.6 d ec, β^+
		89	88.905847	100	
		90*	89.914811		2.67 d β^-
Zirconium	Zr	90	89.904702	51.45	
		91	90.905643	11.22	
		92	91.905038	17.15	
		93*	92.906473		1.5×10^6 y β^-
		94	93.906314	17.38	
		96	95.908274	2.80	
Niobium	Nb	91*	90.906988		6.8×10^2 y ec
		92*	91.907191		3.5×10^7 y ec
		93	92.906376	100	
		94*	93.907280		2×10^4 y β^-
Molybdenum	Mo	92	91.906807	14.84	
		93*	92.906811		3.5×10^3 y ec
		94	93.905085	9.25	
		95	94.905841	15.92	
		96	95.904678	16.68	
		97	96.906020	9.55	
		98	97.905407	24.13	
		100	99.907476	9.63	
Technetium	Tc	97*	96.906363		2.6×10^6 y ec
		98*	97.907215		4.2×10^6 y β^-
		99*	98.906254		2.1×10^5 y β^-
Ruthenium	Ru	96	95.907597	5.54	
		98	97.905287	1.86	
		99	98.905939	12.7	
		100	99.904219	12.6	
		101	100.905558	17.1	
		102	101.904348	31.6	
		104	103.905428	18.6	
Rhodium	Rh	102*	101.906794		207 d ec
		103	102.905502	100	
		104*	103.906654		42 s β^-

Element	Symbol	Mass number (*indicates radioactive)	Atomic mass	Percent abundance	Half-life and decay mode (if unstable)
Palladium	Pd	102	101.905616	1.02	
		104	103.904033	11.14	
		105	104.905082	22.33	
		106	105.903481	27.33	
		107*	106.905126		6.5×10^6 y β^-
		108	107.903893	26.46	
		110	109.905158	11.72	
Silver	Ag	107	106.905091	51.84	
		108*	107.905953		2.39 m ec, β^+, β^-
		109	108.904754	48.16	
		110*	109.906110		24.6 s β^-
Cadmium	Cd	106	105.906457	1.25	
		108	107.904183	0.89	
		109*	108.904984		462 d ec
		110	109.903004	12.49	
		111	110.904182	12.80	
		112	111.902760	24.13	
		113*	112.904401	12.22	9.3×10^{15} y β^-
		114	113.903359	28.73	
		116	115.904755	7.49	
Indium	In	113	112.904060	4.3	
		114*	113.904916		1.2 m β^-
		115*	114.903876	95.7	4.4×10^{14} y β^-
		116*	115.905258		54.4 m β^-
Tin	Sn	112	111.904822	0.97	
		114	113.902780	0.65	
		115	114.903345	0.36	
		116	115.901743	14.53	
		117	116.902953	7.68	
		118	117.901605	24.22	
		119	118.903308	8.58	
		120	119.902197	32.59	
		121*	120.904237		55 y β^-
		122	121.903439	4.63	
		124	123.905274	5.79	
Antimony	Sb	121	120.903820	57.36	
		123	122.904215	42.64	
		125*	124.905251		2.7 y β^-
Tellurium	Te	120	119.904040	0.095	
		122	121.903052	2.59	
		123*	122.904271	0.905	1.3×10^{13} y ec
		124	123.902817	4.79	
		125	124.904429	7.12	
		126	125.903309	18.93	
		128*	127.904463	31.70	$> 8 \times 10^{24}$ y $2\beta^-$
		130*	129.906228	33.87	1.2×10^{21} y $2\beta^-$

(Continued)

Element	Symbol	Mass number (*indicates radioactive)	Atomic mass	Percent abundance	Half-life and decay mode (if unstable)
Iodine	I	126*	125.905619		13 d ec, β^+, β^-
		127	126.904474	100	
		128*	127.905812		25 m β^-, ec, β^+ β^-
		129*	128.904984		1.6×10^7 y
Xenon	Xe	124	123.905894	0.10	
		126	125.904268	0.09	
		128	127.903531	1.91	
		129	128.904779	26.4	
		130	129.903509	4.1	
		131	130.905069	21.2	
		132	131.904141	26.9	
		134	133.905394	10.4	
		136	135.907215	8.9	
Cesium	Cs	133	132.905436	100	
		134*	133.906703		2.1 y β^-
		135*	134.905891		2×10^6 y β^-
		137*	136.907078		30 y β^-
Barium	Ba	130	129.906289	0.106	
		132	131.905048	0.101	
		133*	132.905990		10.5 y ec
		134	133.904492	2.42	
		135	134.905671	6.593	
		136	135.904559	7.85	
		137	136.905816	11.23	
		138	137.905236	71.70	
Lanthanum	La	137*	136.906462		6×10^4 y ec
		138*	137.907105	0.0902	1.05×10^{11} y ec, β^+
		139	138.906346	99.9098	
Cerium	Ce	136	135.907139	0.19	
		138	137.905986	0.25	
		140	139.905434	88.43	
		142	141.909241	11.13	
Praseodymium	Pr	140*	139.909071		3.39 m ec, β^+
		141	140.907647	100	
		142*	141.910040		25.0 m β^-
Neodymium	Nd	142	141.907718	27.13	
		143	142.909809	12.18	
		144*	143.910082	23.80	2.3×10^{15} y α
		145	144.912568	8.30	
		146	145.913113	17.19	
		148	147.916888	5.76	
		150	149.920887	5.64	
Promethium	Pm	143*	142.910928		265 d ec
		145*	144.912745		17.7 y ec
		146*	145.914698		5.5 y ec
		147*	146.915134		2.623 y β^-

Element	Symbol	Mass number (*indicates radioactive)	Atomic mass	Percent abundance	Half-life and decay mode (if unstable)
Samarium	Sm	144	143.911996	3.1	
		146*	145.913043		1.0×10^8 y α
		147*	146.914894	15.0	1.06×10^{11} y α
		148*	147.914819	11.3	7×10^{15} y α
		149	148.917180	13.8	
		150	149.917273	7.4	
		151*	150.919928		90 y β^-
		152	151.919728	26.7	
		154	153.922206	22.7	
Europium	Eu	151	150.919846	47.8	
		152*	151.921740		13.5 y ec, β^+
		153	152.921226	52.2	
		154*	153.922975		8.59 y β^-
		155*	154.922888		4.7 y β^-
Gadolinium	Gd	148*	147.918112		75 y α
		150*	149.918657		1.8×10^6 y α
		152*	151.919787	0.20	1.1×10^{14} y α
		154	153.920862	2.18	
		155	154.922618	14.80	
		156	155.922119	20.47	
		157	156.923957	15.65	
		158	157.924099	24.84	
		160	159.927050	21.86	
Terbium	Tb	158*	157.925411		180 y ec, β^+, β^-
		159	158.925345	100	
		160*	159.927551		72.3 d β^-
Dysprosium	Dy	156	155.924277	0.06	
		158	157.924403	0.10	
		160	159.925193	2.34	
		161	160.926930	18.9	
		162	161.926796	25.5	
		163	162.928729	24.9	
		164	163.929172	28.2	
Holmium	Ho	165	164.930316	100	
		166*	165.932282		1.2×10^3 y β^-
Erbium	Er	162	161.928775	0.14	
		164	163.929198	1.61	
		166	165.930292	33.6	
		167	166.932047	22.95	
		168	167.932369	27.8	
		170	169.935462	14.9	
Thulium	Tm	169	168.934213	100	
		171*	170.936428		1.92 y β^-

(Continued)

Element	Symbol	Mass number (*indicates radioactive)	Atomic mass	Percent abundance	Half-life and decay mode (if unstable)
Ytterbium	Yb	168	167.933897	0.13	
		170	169.934761	3.05	
		171	170.936324	14.3	
		172	171.936380	21.9	
		173	172.938209	16.12	
		174	173.938861	31.8	
		176	175.942564	12.7	
Lutetium	Lu	173*	172.938930		1.37 y ec
		175	174.940772	97.41	
		176*	175.942679	2.59	3.8×10^{10} y β^-
Hafnium	Hf	174*	173.940042	0.162	2.0×10^{15} y α
		176	175.941404	5.206	
		177	176.943218	18.606	
		178	177.943697	27.297	
		179	178.945813	13.629	
		180	179.946547	35.100	
Tantalum	Ta	180	179.947542	0.012	
		181	180.947993	99.988	
Tungsten (Wolfram)	W	180	179.946702	0.12	
		182	181.948202	26.3	
		183	182.950221	14.28	
		184	183.950929	30.7	
		186	185.954358	28.6	
Rhenium	Re	185	184.952951	37.40	
		187*	186.955746	62.60	4.4×10^{10} y β^-
Osmium	Os	184	183.952486	0.02	
		186*	185.953834	1.58	2.0×10^{15} y α
		187	186.955744	1.6	
		188	187.955744	13.3	
		189	188.958139	16.1	
		190	189.958439	26.4	
		192	191.961468	41.0	
		194*	193.965172		6.0 y β^-
Iridium	Ir	191	190.960585	37.3	
		193	192.962916	62.7	
Platinum	Pt	190*	189.959926	0.01	6.5×10^{11} y α
		192	191.961027	0.79	
		194	193.962655	32.9	
		195	194.964765	33.8	
		196	195.964926	25.3	
		198	197.967867	7.2	
Gold	Au	197	196.966543	100	
		198*	197.968217		2.70 d β^-
		199*	198.968740		3.14 d β^-

Element	Symbol	Mass number (*indicates radioactive)	Atomic mass	Percent abundance	Half-life and decay mode (if unstable)
Mercury	Hg	196	195.965806	0.15	
		198	197.966743	9.97	
		199	198.968253	16.87	
		200	199.968299	23.10	
		201	200.970276	13.10	
		202	201.970617	29.86	
		204	203.973466	6.87	
Thallium	Tl	203	202.972320	29.524	
		204*	203.973839		3.78 y β^-
		205	204.974400	70.476	
	(Ra E″)	206*	205.976084		4.2 m β^-
	(Ac C″)	207*	206.977403		4.77 m β^-
	(Th C″)	208*	207.981992		3.053 m β^-
	(Ra C″)	210*	209.990057		1.30 m β^-
Lead	Pb	202*	201.972134		5×10^4 y ec
		204	203.973020	1.4	
		205*	204.974457		1.5×10^7 y ec
		206	205.974440	24.1	
		207	206.975871	22.1	
		208	207.976627	52.4	
	(Ra D)	210*	209.984163		22.3 y β^-
	(Ac B)	211*	210.988734		36.1 m β^-
	(Th B)	212*	211.991872		10.64 h β^-
	(Ra B)	214*	213.999798		26.8 m β^-
Bismuth	Bi	207*	206.978444		32.2 y ec, β^+
		208*	207.979717		3.7×10^5 y ec
		209	208.980374	100	
	(Ra E)	210*	209.984096		5.01 d α, β^-
	(Th C)	211*	210.987254		2.14 m α
	(Ra C)	212*	211.991259		60.6 m α, β^-
		214*	213.998692		19.9 m β^-
		215*	215.001836		7.4 m β^-
Polonium	Po	209*	208.982405		102 y α
	(Ra F)	210*	209.982848		138.38 d α
	(Ac C′)	211*	210.986627		0.52 s α
	(Th C′)	212*	211.988842		0.30 μs α
	(Ra C′)	214*	213.995177		164 μs α
	(Ac A)	215*	214.999418		0.0018 s α
	(Th A)	216*	216.001889		0.145 s α
	(Ra A)	218*	218.008965		3.10 m α
Astatine	At	215*	214.998638		$\approx$100 μs α
		218*	218.008685		1.6 s α
		219*	219.011297		0.9 m α
Radon	Rn				
	(An)	219*	219.009477		3.96 s α
	(Tn)	220*	220.011369		55.6 s α
	(Rn)	222*	222.017571		3.823 d α

(Continued)

Element	Symbol	Mass number (*indicates radioactive)	Atomic mass	Percent abundance	Half-life and decay mode (if unstable)
Francium		221*	221.01425		4.18 m α
	Fr	222*	222.017585		14.2 m β⁻
	(Ac K)	223*	223.019733		22 m β⁻
Radium	Ra	221*	221.01391		29 s α
	(Ac X)	223*	223.018499		11.43 d α
	(Th X)	224*	224.020187		3.66 d α
		225*			14.9 d β⁻
	(Ra)	226*	226.025402		1600 y α
	(MsTh₁)	228*	228.031064		5.75 y β⁻
Actinium	Ac	225*			10 d α
	(Ms Th₂)	227*	227.027749		21.77 y β⁻
		228*	228.031015		6.15 h β⁻
		229*			1.04 h β⁻
Thorium	Th				
	(Rd Ac)	227*	227.027701		18.72 d α
	(Rd Th)	228*	228.028716		1.913 y α
		229*	229.031757		7300 y α
	(Io)	230*	230.033127		75,000 y α, sf
	(UY)	231*	231.036299	100	25.52 h β⁻
	(Th)	232*	232.038051		1.40×10^{10} y α
	(UX₁)	234*	234.043593		24.1 d β⁻
Protactinium	Pa	231*	231.035880		32,760 y α
	(UZ)	234*	234.043300		6.7 h β⁻
Uranium	U	231*	231.036264		4.2 d β⁺
		232*	232.037131		69 y α
		233*	233.039630		1.59×10^5 y α
	(UII)	234*	234.040946	0.0055	2.45×10^5 y α
	(Ac U)	235*	235.043924	0.720	7.04×10^8 y α
	(UI)	236*	236.045562		2.34×10^7 y α
		238*	238.050784	99.2745	4.47×10^9 y α
		239*	239.054290		23.5 m β⁻
Neptunium	Np	235*	235.044057		396 d α
		236*	236.046559		1.54×10^5 y ec
		237*	237.048168		2.14×10^6 y α
Plutonium	Pu	236*	236.046033		2.87 y α, sf
		238*	238.049555		87.7 y α, sf
		239*	239.052157		24,120 y α, sf
		240*	240.053808		6560 y α, sf
		241*	241.056846		14.4 y β⁻
		242*	242.058737		3.7×10^5 y α, sf
		244*	244.064200		8.1×10^7 y α, sf
Americium	Am	240*	240.055285		2.12 d ec
		241*	241.056824		432 y α, sf
Curium	Cm	247*	247.070347		1.56×10^7 y α
		248*	248.072344		3.4×10^5 y α, sf

Element	Symbol	Mass number (*indicates radioactive)	Atomic mass	Percent abundance	Half-life and decay mode (if unstable)
Berkelium	Bk	247*	247.070300		1380 y α
		249*	249.074979		327 d β⁻
Californium	Cm	250*	250.076400		13.1 y α, sf
		251*	251.079580		898 y α
Einsteinium	Es	252*	252.082974		1.29 y α
		253*	253.084817		2.02 d α, sf
Fermium	Fm	253*	253.085173		3.00 d ec
		254*	254.086849		3.24 h α, sf
Mendelevium	Md	256*	256.093988		75.6 m ec, β⁺
		258*	258.098594		55 d α
Nobelium	No	257*	257.096855		25 s α
		259*	259.100932		58 m α, sf
Lawrencium	Lr	259*	259.102888		6.14 s α, sf
		260*	260.105346		3.0 m α, sf
Rutherfordium	Rf	260*	260.160302		24 ms sf
		261*	261.108588		65 s α, sf
Dubnium	Db	261*	261.111830		1.8 s α
		262*	262.113763		35 s α
Seaborgium	Sg	263*	263.118310		0.78 s α, sf
Bohrium	Bh	262*	262.123081		0.10 s α, sf
Hassium	Hs	265*	265.129984		1.8 ms α
		267*	267.131770		60 ms α
Meitnerium	Mt	266*	266.137789		3.4 ms α, sf
		268*	268.138820		70 ms α
Darmstadtium	Ds	269*	269.145140		0.17 ms α
		271*	271.146080		1.1 ms α
		273*	272.153480		8.6 ms α
Roentgenium	Rg	272*	272.153480		1.5 ms α
Copernicium	Cn	277*	?		0.2 ms α
Ununtrium	Unt	284*	?		? α
Ununquadium	Unq	289*	?		? α
Ununpentium	Unp	288*	?		? α
Ununhexium	Unh	292*	?		? α
Ununseptium	Uus				
Ununoctium	Uno	294*	?		? α

Math Tutorial

In this tutorial, we review some of the basic results of algebra, geometry, trigonometry, and calculus. In many cases, we merely state results without proof. Table M-1 lists some mathematical symbols.

M-1 Significant figures

Many numbers we work with in science are the result of measurement and are therefore known only within a degree of uncertainty. This uncertainty should be reflected in the number of digits used. For example, if you have a 1-meter-long rule with scale spacing of 1 cm, you know that you can measure the height of a box to within a fifth of a centimeter or so. Using this rule, you might find that the box height is 27.0 cm. If there is a scale with a spacing of 1 mm on your rule, you might perhaps measure the box height to be 27.03 cm. However, if there is a scale with a spacing of 1 mm on your rule, you might not be able to measure the height more accurately than 27.03 cm because the height might vary by 0.01 cm or so, depending on where you measure the height of the box. When you write down that the height of the box is 27.03 cm, you are stating that your best estimate of the height is 27.03 cm, but you are not claiming that it is exactly 27.030000 . . . cm high. The four digits in 27.03 cm are called **significant figures**. Your measured length, 27.03 cm, has four significant digits. Significant figures are also called significant digits.

The number of significant digits in an answer to a calculation will depend on the number of significant digits in the given data. When you work with numbers that have uncertainties, you should be careful not to include more digits than the certainty of measurement warrants. *Approximate* calculations (order-of-magnitude estimates) always result in answers that have only one significant digit or none. When you multiply, divide, add, or subtract numbers, you must consider the accuracy of the results. Listed below are some rules that will help you determine the number of significant digits of your results.

(1) When multiplying or dividing quantities, the number of significant digits in the final answer is no greater than that in the quantity with the fewest significant digits.

(2) When adding or subtracting quantities, the number of decimal places in the answer should match that of the term with the smallest number of decimal places.

(3) Exact values have an unlimited number of significant digits. For example, a value determined by counting, such as 2 tables, has no uncertainty and is an exact value. In addition, the conversion factor 0.0254000 . . . m/in. is an exact value because 1.000 . . . inches is exactly equal to 0.0254000 . . . meters. (The yard is, by definition, equal to exactly 0.9144 m, and 0.9144 divided by 36 is exactly equal to 0.0254.)

(4) Sometimes zeros are significant and sometimes they are not. If a zero is before a leading nonzero digit, then the zero is not significant. For example, the number 0.00890 has three significant digits. The first three zeroes are not significant digits but are merely markers to locate the decimal point. Note that the zero after the nine is significant.

Table M-1 Mathematical Symbols	
$=$	is equal to
$\neq$	is not equal to
$\approx$	is approximately equal to
$\sim$	is of the order of
$\propto$	is proportional to
$>$	is greater than
$\geq$	is greater than or equal to
$\gg$	is much greater than
$<$	is less than
$\leq$	is less than or equal to
$\ll$	is much less than
Δx	change in x
$|x|$	absolute value of x
$n!$	$n(n-1)(n-2)\ldots1$
Σ	sum

(5) Zeros that are between nonzero digits are significant. For example, 5603 has four significant digits.

(6) The number of significant digits in numbers with trailing zeros and no decimal point is ambiguous. For example, 31,000 could have as many as five significant digits or as few as two significant digits. To prevent ambiguity, you should report numbers by using scientific notation or by using a decimal point.

Example M-1   Finding the Average of Three Numbers

Find the average of 19.90, −7.524, and −11.8179.

Set Up
You will be adding 3 numbers and then dividing the result by 3. The first number has four significant digits, the second number has four, and the third number has six.

Solve
Sum the three numbers.

$$19.90 + (−7.524) + (−11.8179) = 0.55\textit{81}$$

If the problem only asked for the sum of the three numbers, we would round the answer to the least number of decimal places among all the numbers being added—the answer would be 0.56 (0.5581 rounds up to 0.56 to two significant digits). However, we must divide this intermediate result by 3, so we use the intermediate answer with the two extra digits (italicized and red).

$$\frac{0.5581}{3} = 0.18\textit{60333}\ldots$$

Only two of the digits in the intermediate answer, 0.55*81* ..., are significant digits, so we must round the final number to get our final answer. The number 3 in the denominator is a whole number and has an unlimited number of significant digits. Thus, the final answer has the same number of significant digits as the numerator, which is 2.

The final answer is 0.19.

Reflect
The sum in step 1 has two significant digits following the decimal point, the same as the number being summed with the least number of significant digits after the decimal point.

M-2 Equations

An **equation** is a statement written using numbers and symbols to indicate that two quantities, written on either side of an equal sign (=), are equal. The quantity on either side of the equal sign may consist of a single term, or of a sum or difference of two or more **terms**. For example, the equation $x = 1 − (ay + b)/(cx − d)$ contains three terms, x, 1, and $(ay + b)/(cx − d)$.

You can perform the following operations on equations:

(1) The same quantity can be added to or subtracted from each side of an equation.
(2) Each side of an equation can be multiplied or divided by the same quantity.
(3) Each side of an equation can be raised to the same power.

These operations are meant to be applied to each *side* of the equation rather than each term in the equation. (Because multiplication is distributive over addition, operation 2—and only operation 2—of the preceding operations also applies term by term.)

Caution: Division by zero is forbidden at any *stage in solving an equation; results (if any) would be invalid.*

Adding or Subtracting Equal Amounts
To find x when $x − 3 = 7$, add 3 to both sides of the equation: $(x − 3) + 3 = 7 + 3$; thus, $x = 10$.

Multiplying or Dividing by Equal Amounts

If $3x = 17$, solve for x by dividing both sides of the equation by 3; thus, $x = \frac{17}{3}$, or 5.7.

Example M-2 Simplifying Reciprocals in an Equation

Solve the following equation for x:

$$\frac{1}{x} + \frac{1}{4} = \frac{1}{3}$$

Equations containing reciprocals of unknowns occur in many circumstances in physics. Two instances of this are geometric optics and electric circuit analysis.

Set Up

In this equation, the term containing x is on the same side of the equation as a term not containing x. Furthermore, x is found in the denominator of a fraction. We'll start by isolating the $1/x$ term, find common denominators, and then multiply both sides of the equation by appropriate quantities.

Solve

Subtract $\dfrac{1}{4}$ from each side.

$$\frac{1}{x} = \frac{1}{3} - \frac{1}{4}$$

Simplify the right side of the equation by using the lowest common denominator.

Begin by multiplying both terms on the right-hand side by appropriate forms of 1.

$$\frac{1}{x} = \frac{1}{3}\frac{4}{4} - \frac{1}{4}\frac{3}{3} = \frac{4}{12} - \frac{3}{12}$$

$$= \frac{4 - 3}{12} = \frac{1}{12} \quad \text{so} \quad \frac{1}{x} = \frac{1}{12}$$

Multiply both sides of the equation by $12x$ to determine the value of x.

$$12x\frac{1}{x} = 12x\frac{1}{12}$$

$$12 = x$$

Reflect

To check our answer, substitute 12 for x in the left side of original equation.

$$\frac{1}{x} + \frac{1}{4} = \frac{1}{12} + \frac{3}{12} = \frac{4}{12} = \frac{1}{3}$$

M-3 Direct and inverse proportions

When we say variable quantities x and y are **directly proportional**, we mean that as x and y change, the ratio x/y is constant. To say that two quantities are proportional is to say that they are directly proportional. When we say variable quantities x and y are **inversely proportional**, we mean that as x and y change, the ratio xy is constant.

Relationships of direct and inverse proportion are common in physics. Objects moving at the same velocity have momenta directly proportional to their masses. The ideal gas law ($PV = nRT$) states that pressure P is directly proportional to (absolute) temperature T, when volume V remains constant, and is inversely proportional to volume, when temperature remains constant. Ohm's law ($V = IR$) states that the voltage V across a resistor is directly proportional to the electric current in the resistor when the resistance remains constant.

Constant of Proportionality

When two quantities are directly proportional, the two quantities are related by a *constant of proportionality*. If you are paid for working at a regular rate R in dollars per day, for example, the money m you earn is directly proportional to the time t you work;

the rate R is the constant of proportionality that relates the money earned in dollars to the time worked t in days:

$$\frac{m}{t} = R \quad \text{or} \quad m = Rt$$

If you earn \$400 in 5 days, the value of R is \$400/(5 days) = \$80/day. To find the amount you earn in 8 days, you could perform the calculation

$$m = (\$80/\text{day})(8 \text{ days}) = \$640$$

Sometimes the constant of proportionality can be ignored in proportion problems. Because the amount you earn in 8 days is $\frac{8}{5}$ times what you earn in 5 days, this amount is

$$m_{8 \text{ days}} = 8_{\text{days}} \frac{\$400}{5_{\text{days}}} = \$640$$

Example M-3 Painting Cubes

You need 15.4 mL of paint to cover one side of a cube. The area of one side of the cube is 426 cm². What is the relation between the volume of paint needed and the area to be covered? How much paint do you need to paint one side of a cube on which the one side has an area of 503 cm²?

Set Up
To determine the amount of paint for the side whose area is 503 cm² we will set up a proportion.

Solve
The volume V of paint needed increases in proportion to the area A to be covered.

V and A are directly proportional.

That is, $\dfrac{V}{A} = k$ or $V = kA$

where k is the proportionality constant

Determine the value of the proportionality constant using the given values $V_1 = 15.4$ mL and $A_1 = 426$ cm².

$$k = \frac{V_1}{A_1} = \frac{15.4 \text{ mL}}{426 \text{ cm}^2} = 0.0362 \text{ mL/cm}^2$$

Determine the volume of paint needed to paint a side of a cube whose area is 503 cm² using the proportionality constant in step 1.

$$V_2 = kA_2 = (0.0362 \text{ mL/cm}^2)(503 \text{ cm}^2)$$
$$= 18.2 \text{ mL}$$

Reflect
Our value for V_2 is greater than the value for V_1, as expected. The amount of paint needed to cover an area equal to 503 cm² should be greater than the amount of paint needed to cover an area of 426 cm² because 503 cm² is larger than 426 cm².

M-4 Linear equations

A **linear equation** is an equation of the form $x + 2y - 4z = 3$. That is, an equation is linear if each term either is constant or is the product of a constant and a variable raised to the first power. Such equations are said to be linear because the plots of these equations form straight lines or planes. The equations of direct proportion between two variables are linear equations.

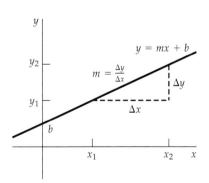

Figure M-1 Graph of the linear equation $y = mx + b$, where b is the y intercept and $m = \Delta y / \Delta x$ is the slope.

Graph of a Straight Line

A linear equation relating y and x can always be put into the standard form

(M-1) $y = mx + b$

where m and b are constants that may be either positive or negative. Figure M-1 shows a graph of the values of x and y that satisfy Equation M-1. The constant b, called the **y intercept**, is the value of y at $x = 0$. The constant m is the **slope** of the line, which equals the ratio of the change in y to the corresponding change in x. In the figure, we have indicated two points on the line, (x_1, y_1) and (x_2, y_2), and the changes $\Delta x = x_2 - x_1$ and $\Delta y = y_2 - y_1$. The slope m is then

$$m = \frac{y_2 - y_1}{x_2 - x_1} = \frac{\Delta y}{\Delta x}$$

If x and y are both unknown in the equation $y = mx + b$, there are no unique values of x and y that are solutions to the equation. Any pair of values (x_1, y_1) on the line in Figure M-1 will satisfy the equation. If we have two equations, each with the same two unknowns x and y, the equations can be solved simultaneously for the unknowns. Example M-4 shows two methods for simultaneously solving two linear equations.

Example M-4 Using Two Equations to Solve for Two Unknowns

Find any and all values of x and y that simultaneously satisfy

$$3x - 2y = 8 \qquad \text{(M-2)}$$
$$\text{and}$$
$$y - x = 2 \qquad \text{(M-3)}$$

Set Up
Graph the two equations. At the point where the lines intersect, the values of x and y satisfy both equations.
  We can solve two simultaneous equations by first solving either equation for one variable in terms of the other variable and then substituting the result into the second equation.

Figure M-2 Graph of Equations M-2 and M-3. At the point where the lines intersect, the values of x and y satisfy both equations.

Solve

Solve Equation M-3 for y.

$$y = x + 2$$

Substitute this value for y into Equation M-2.

$$3x - 2(x + 2) = 8$$

Simplify the equation and solve for x.

$$3x - 2x - 4 = 8$$
$$x - 4 = 8$$
$$x = 12$$

Use your solution for x and one of the given equations to find the value of y.

Return to Equation M-3 and substitute $x = 12$.
$$y - x = 2, \text{ where } x = 12$$
$$y - 12 = 2$$
$$y = 2 + 12 = 14$$

Reflect
An alternative method is to multiply one equation by a constant such that one of the unknown terms is eliminated when the equations are added or subtracted.

We can multiply through Equation M-3 by 2
$$2(y - x) = 2(2)$$
$$2y - 2x = 4$$

Add the result to Equation M-2 and solve for x:

$$2y - 2x = 4$$
$$3x - 2y = 8$$
$$\overline{}$$
$$3x - 2x = 12 \Rightarrow x = 12$$

Substitute into Equation M-3 and solve for y:

$$y - 12 = 2 \Rightarrow y = 14$$

M-5 Quadratic equations and factoring

A **quadratic equation** is an equation of the form $ax^2 + bxy + cy^2 + ex + fy + g = 0$, where x and y are variables and and a, b, c, e, f, and g are constants. In each term of the equation the powers of the variables are integers that sum to 2, 1, or 0. The designation *quadratic equation* usually applies to a much simpler equation of one variable that can be written in the standard form

(M-4)
$$ax^2 + bx + c = 0$$

where a, b, and c are constants. The quadratic equation has two solutions or **roots**— values of x for which the equation is true.

Factoring

We can solve some quadratic equations by **factoring**. Very often terms of an equation can be grouped or organized into other terms. When we factor terms, we look for multipliers and multiplicands—which we now call **factors**—that will yield two or more new terms as a product. For example, we can find the roots of the quadratic equation $x^2 - 3x + 2 = 0$ by factoring the left side to get $(x - 2)(x - 1) = 0$. The roots are $x = 2$ and $x = 1$.

Factoring is useful for simplifying equations and for understanding the relationships between quantities. You should be familiar with the multiplication of the factors $(ax + by)(cx + dy) = acx^2 + (ad + bc)xy + bdy^2$.

You should readily recognize some typical factorable combinations:

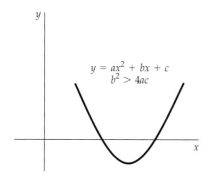

$y = ax^2 + bx + c$
$b^2 > 4ac$

1. Common factor: $2ax + 3ay = a(2x + 3y)$
2. Perfect square: $x^2 - 2xy + y^2 = (x-y)^2$ (If the expression on the left side of a quadratic equation in standard form is a perfect square, the two roots will be equal.)
3. Difference of squares: $x^2 - y^2 = (x + y)(x - y)$

Also, look for factors that are prime numbers (2, 5, 7, etc.) because these factors can help you simplify terms quickly. For example, the equation $98x^2 - 140 = 0$ can be simplified because 98 and 140 share the common factor 2. That is, $98x^2 - 140 = 0$ becomes $2(49x^2 - 70) = 0$, so we have $49x^2 - 70 = 0$.

This result can be further simplified because 49 and 70 share the common factor 7. Thus, $49x^2 - 70 = 0$ becomes $7(7x^2 - 10) = 0$, so we have $7x^2 - 10 = 0$.

Figure M-3 Graph of y versus x when $y = ax^2 + bx + c$ for the case $b^2 > 4ac$. The two values of x for which $y = 0$ satisfy the quadratic equation (Equation M-4).

The Quadratic Formula

Not all quadratic equations can be solved by factoring. However, *any* quadratic equation in the standard form $ax^2 + bx + c = 0$ can be solved by the **quadratic formula**,

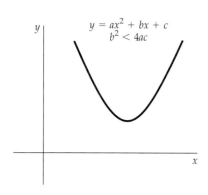

$y = ax^2 + bx + c$
$b^2 < 4ac$

(M-5)
$$x = \frac{-b \pm \sqrt{b^2 - 4ac}}{2a} = -\frac{b}{2a} \pm \frac{1}{2a}\sqrt{b^2 - 4ac}$$

When b^2 is greater than $4ac$, there are two solutions corresponding to the + and − signs, respectively. **Figure M-3** shows a graph of y versus x where $y = ax^2 + bx + c$. The curve, a **parabola**, crosses the x axis twice. (The simplest representation of a parabola in (x, y) coordinates is an equation of the form $y = ax^2 + bx + c$.) The two roots of this equation are the values for which $y = 0$; that is, they are the x intercepts.

When b^2 is less than $4ac$, the graph of y versus x does not intersect the x axis, as is shown in **Figure M-4**; there are still two roots, but they are not real numbers. When $b^2 = 4ac$, the graph of y versus x is tangent to the x axis at the point $x = -b/2a$; the two roots are each equal to $-b/2a$.

Figure M-4 Graph of y versus x when $y = ax^2 + bx + c$ for the case $b^2 < 4ac$. In this case, there are no real values of x for which $y = 0$.

Example M-5 Factoring a Second-Degree Polynomial

Factor the expression $6x^2 + 19xy + 10y^2$.

Set Up

We examine the coefficients of the terms to see whether the expression can be factored without resorting to more advanced methods. Remember that the multiplication $(ax + by)(cx + dy) = acx^2 + (ad + bc)xy + bdy^2$.

Solve

The coefficient of x^2 is 6, which can be factored two ways.

$$ac = 6$$
$$3 \cdot 2 = 6 \quad \text{or} \quad 6 \cdot 1 = 6$$

The coefficient of y^2 is 10, which can also be factored two ways.

$$bd = 10$$
$$5 \cdot 2 = 10 \quad \text{or} \quad 10 \cdot 1 = 10$$

List the possibilities for a, b, c, and d in a table. Include a column for $ad + bc$.

If $a = 3$, then $c = 2$, and vice versa. In addition, if $a = 6$, then $c = 1$, and vice versa. For each value of a there are four values for b.

a	b	c	d	$ad + bc$
3	5	2	2	16
3	2	2	5	19
3	10	2	1	23
3	1	2	10	32
2	5	3	2	19
2	2	3	5	16
2	10	3	1	32
2	1	3	10	23
6	5	1	2	17
6	2	1	5	32
6	10	1	1	16
6	1	1	10	61
1	5	6	2	32
1	2	6	5	17
1	10	6	1	61
1	1	6	10	16

Find a combination such that $ad + bc = 19$. As you can see from the table there are two such combinations.

$$ad + bc = 19$$
$$3 \cdot 5 + 2 \cdot 2 = 19 \text{ and}$$
$$2 \cdot 2 + 5 \cdot 3 = 19$$

It doesn't matter which combination we choose. To finish this problem we will use the combination in the second row of the table to factor the expression in question:

$$6x^2 + 19xy + 10y^2 = (3x + 2y)(2x + 5y)$$

Reflect

As a check, expand $(3x + 2y)(2x + 5y)$ to see if we return to the original equation.

$$(3x + 2y)(2x + 5y) = 6x^2 + 15xy + 4xy + 10y^2$$
$$= 6x^2 + 19xy + 10y^2$$

You should be able to show that the combination in the fifth row is also an acceptable factoring.

M-6 Exponents and logarithms

Exponents

The notation x^n stands for the quantity obtained by multiplying x by itself n times. For example, $x^2 = x \cdot x$ and $x^3 = x \cdot x \cdot x$. The quantity n is called the **power,** or the **exponent,** of x (the **base**). Listed below are some rules that will help you simplify terms that have exponents.

(1) When two powers of x are multiplied, the exponents are added:

$$(x^m)(x^n) = x^{m+n} \tag{M-6}$$

Example: $x^2 x^3 = x^{2+3} = (x \cdot x)(x \cdot x \cdot x) = x^5$.

(2) Any number (except 0) raised to the 0 power is defined to be 1:

(M-7)
$$x^0 = 1$$

(3) Based on rule 2,
$$x^n x^{-n} = x^0 = 1$$

(M-8)
$$x^{-n} = \frac{1}{x^n}$$

(4) When two powers are divided, the exponents are subtracted:

(M-9)
$$\frac{x^n}{x^m} = x^n x^{-m} = x^{n-m}$$

(5) When a power is raised to another power, the exponents are multiplied:

(M-10)
$$(x^n)^m = x^{nm}$$

(6) When exponents are written as fractions, they represent the roots of the base. For example,
$$x^{1/2} \cdot x^{1/2} = x$$

so
$$x^{1/2} = \sqrt{x} \quad (x > 0)$$

Example M-6 Simplifying a Quantity That Has Exponents

Simplify $\dfrac{x^4 x^7}{x^8}$.

Set Up

According to rule 1, when two powers of x are multiplied, the exponents are added.

$(x^m)(x^n) = x^{m+n}$ (M-6)

Rule 4 states that when two powers are divided, the exponents are subtracted.

$\dfrac{x^n}{x^m} = x^n x^{-m} = x^{n-m}$ (M-9)

Solve

Simplify the numerator $x^4 x^7$ using rule 1.

$x^4 x^7 = x^{4+7} = x^{11}$

Simplify $\dfrac{x^{11}}{x^8}$ using rule 4.

$\dfrac{x^{11}}{x^8} = x^{11} x^{-8} = x^{11-8} = x^3$

Reflect

Use the value $x = 2$ to test our answer.

$\dfrac{2^4 2^7}{2^8} = 2^3 = 8$

$\dfrac{2^4 2^7}{2^8} = \dfrac{(16)(128)}{256} = \dfrac{2048}{256} = 8$

Logarithms

Any positive number can be expressed as some power of any other positive number except one. If y is related to x by $y = a^x$, then the number x is said to be the **logarithm** of y to the **base** a, and the relation is written

$$x = \log_a y$$

Thus, logarithms are *exponents*, and the rules for working with logarithms correspond to similar laws for exponents. Listed below are some rules that will help you simplify terms that have logarithms.

(1) If $y_1 = a^n$ and $y_2 = a^m$, then

$$y_1 y_2 = a^n a^m = a^{n+m}$$

Correspondingly,

(M-11)
$$\log_a y_1 y_2 = \log_a a^{n+m} = n + m = \log_a a^n + \log_a a^m = \log_a y_1 + \log_a y_2$$

It then follows that

$$\log_a y^n = n \log_a y \qquad \text{(M-12)}$$

(2) Because $a^1 = a$ and $a^0 = 1$,

$$\log_a a = 1 \qquad \text{(M-13)}$$

and

$$\log_a 1 = 0 \qquad \text{(M-14)}$$

There are two bases in common use: logarithms to base 10 are called **common logarithms,** and logarithms to base e (where $e = 2.718\ldots$) are called **natural logarithms.**

In this text, the symbol ln is used for natural logarithms and the symbol log, without a subscript, is used for common logarithms. Thus,

$$\log_e x = \ln x \quad \text{and} \quad \log_{10} x = \log x \qquad \text{(M-15)}$$

and $y = \ln x$ implies

$$x = e^y \qquad \text{(M-16)}$$

Logarithms can be changed from one base to another. Suppose that

$$z = \log x \qquad \text{(M-17)}$$

Then

$$10^z = 10^{\log x} = x \qquad \text{(M-18)}$$

Taking the natural logarithm of both sides of Equation M-18, we obtain

$$z \ln 10 = \ln x$$

Substituting log x for z (see Equation M-17) gives

$$\ln x = (\ln 10)\log x \qquad \text{(M-19)}$$

Example M-7 Converting between Common Logarithms and Natural Logarithms

The steps leading to Equation M-19 show that, in general, $\log_b x = (\log_b a)\log_a x$, and thus that conversion of logarithms from one base to another requires only multiplication by a constant. Describe the mathematical relation between the constant for converting common logarithms to natural logarithms and the constant for converting natural logarithms to common logarithms.

Set Up
We have a general mathematical formula for converting logarithms from one base to another. We look for the mathematical relation by exchanging a for b and vice versa in the formula.

Solve
We have a formula for converting logarithms from base a to base b.

$$\log_b x = (\log_b a)\log_a x$$

To convert from base b to base a, exchange all a for b and vice versa.

$$\log_a x = (\log_a b)\log_b x$$

Divide both sides of the equation in step 1 by $\log_a x$.

$$\frac{\log_b x}{\log_a x} = \log_b a$$

Divide both sides of the equation in step 2 by $(\log_a b)\log_a x$.

$$\frac{1}{\log_a b} = \frac{\log_b x}{\log_a x}$$

The results show that the conversion factors $\log_b a$ and $\log_a b$ are reciprocals of one another.

$$\frac{1}{\log_a b} = \log_b a$$

Reflect
For the value of $\log_{10} e$, your calculator will give 0.43429. For ln 10, your calculator will give 2.3026. Multiply 0.43429 by 2.3026; you will get 1.0000.

M-7 Geometry

The properties of the most common **geometric figures**—bounded shapes in two or three dimensions whose lengths, areas, or volumes are governed by specific ratios—are a basic analytical tool in physics. For example, the characteristic ratios within triangles give us the laws of *trigonometry* (see Section M-8), which in turn give us the theory of vectors, essential in analyzing motion in two or more dimensions. Circles and spheres are essential for understanding, among other concepts, angular momentum and the probability densities of quantum mechanics.

Basic Formulas in Geometry

Circle The ratio of the circumference of a circle to its diameter is a number π, which has the approximate value

$$\pi = 3.141\ 592$$

The circumference C of a circle is thus related to its diameter d and its radius r by

(M-20) $$C = \pi d = 2\pi r \quad \text{circumference of circle}$$

The area of a circle is (Figure M-5)

(M-21) $$A = \pi r^2 \quad \text{area of circle}$$

Parallelogram The area of a parallelogram is the base b multiplied by the height h (Figure M-6):

$$A = bh$$

Triangle The area of a triangle is one-half the base multiplied by the height (Figure M-7):

$$A = \frac{1}{2}bh$$

Sphere A sphere of radius r (Figure M-8) has a surface area given by

(M-22) $$A = 4\pi r^2 \quad \text{surface area of sphere}$$

and a volume given by

(M-23) $$V = \frac{4}{3}\pi r^3 \quad \text{volume of sphere}$$

Cylinder A cylinder of radius r and length L (Figure M-9) has a surface area (not including the end faces) of

(M-24) $$A = 2\pi r L \quad \text{surface of cylinder}$$

and volume of

(M-24) $$V = \pi r^2 L \quad \text{volume of cylinder}$$

Area of a circle $A = \pi r^2$

Figure M-5 Area of a circle.

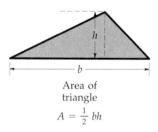

Area of parallelogram
$A = bh$

Figure M-6 Area of a parallelogram.

Area of
triangle
$A = \frac{1}{2} bh$

Figure M-7 Area of a triangle.

Spherical surface area
$A = 4\pi r^2$
Spherical volume
$V = \frac{4}{3}\pi r^3$

Figure M-8 Surface area and volume of a sphere.

Cylindrical surface area
$A = 2\pi r L$
Cylindrical volume
$V = \pi r^2 L$

Figure M-9 Surface area (not including the end faces) and the volume of a cylinder.

Example M-8 Calculating the Volume of a Spherical Shell

An aluminum spherical shell has an outer diameter of 40.0 cm and an inner diameter of 38.0 cm. What is the volume of the aluminum in this shell?

Set Up

The volume of the aluminum in the spherical shell is the volume that remains when we subtract the volume of the inner sphere having $d_i = 2r_i = 38.0$ cm from the volume of the outer sphere having $d_o = 2r_o = 40.0$ cm.

Spherical Volume:

$$V = \frac{4}{3}\pi r^3 \qquad \text{(M-23)}$$

Solve

Subtract the volume of the sphere of radius r_i from the volume of the sphere of radius r_o.

$$V = V_o - V_i = \frac{4}{3}\pi r_o^3 - \frac{4}{3}\pi r_i^3 = \frac{4}{3}\pi (r_o^3 - r_i^3)$$

Substitute 20.0 cm for r_o and 19.0 cm for r_i.

$$V = \frac{4}{3}\pi \left[(20.0 \text{ cm})^3 - (19.0 \text{ cm})^3 \right]$$

$$= 4.78 \times 10^3 \text{ cm}^3$$

Reflect

The volume calculated is less than the volume of the outer sphere.

$$V_o = \frac{4}{3}\pi r_o^3 = \frac{4}{3}\pi (20.0 \text{ cm})^3$$

$$= 3.35 \times 10^4 \text{ cm}^3$$

M-8 Trigonometry

Trigonometry, which gets its name from Greek roots meaning "triangle" and "measure," is the study of some important mathematical functions, called **trigonometric functions**. These functions are most simply defined as ratios of the sides of right triangles. However, these right-triangle definitions are of limited use because they are valid only for angles between zero and 90°. However, the validity of the right-triangle definitions can be extended by defining the trigonometric functions in terms of the ratio of the coordinates of points on a circle of unit radius drawn centered at the origin of the xy plane.

In physics, we first encounter trigonometric functions when we use vectors to analyze motion in two dimensions. Trigonometric functions are also essential in the analysis of any kind of periodic behavior, such as circular motion, oscillatory motion, and wave mechanics.

Angles and Their Measure: Degrees and Radians

The size of an angle formed by two intersecting straight lines is known as its **measure**. The standard way of finding the measure of an angle is to place the angle so that its **vertex**, or point of intersection of the two lines that form the angle, is at the center of a circle located at the origin of a graph that has Cartesian coordinates and one of the lines extends rightward on the positive x axis. The distance traveled *counterclockwise* on the circumference from the positive x axis to reach the intersection of the circumference with the other line defines the measure of the angle. (Traveling clockwise to the second line would simply give us a negative measure; to illustrate basic concepts, we position the angle so that the smaller rotation will be in the counterclockwise direction.)

One of the most familiar units for expressing the measure of an angle is the **degree,** which equals $1/360$ of the full distance around the circumference of the circle. For greater precision, or for smaller angles, we either show degrees plus minutes (') and seconds ("), with $1' = 1°/60$ and $1" = 1'/60 = 1°/3600$; or show degrees as an ordinary decimal number.

For scientific work, a more useful measure of an angle is the **radian** (rad). Again, place the angle with its vertex at the center of a circle and measure counterclockwise rotation around the circumference. The measure of the angle in radians is then defined as the length of the circular arc from one line to the other divided by the radius of the

Figure M-10 The angle θ in radians is defined to be the ratio s/r, where s is the arc length intercepted on a circle of radius r.

circle (Figure M-10). If s is the arc length and r is the radius of the circle, the angle θ measured in radians is

(M-26)
$$\theta = \frac{s}{r}$$

Because the angle measured in radians is the ratio of two lengths, it is dimensionless. The relation between radians and degrees is

$$360° = 2\pi \text{ rad}$$

or

$$1 \text{ rad} = \frac{360°}{2\pi} = 57.3°$$

Figure M-11 shows some useful relations for angles.

The Trigonometric Functions

Figure M-12 shows a right triangle formed by drawing the line segment BC perpendicular to AC. The lengths of the sides are labeled a, b, and c. The right-triangle definitions of the trigonometric functions $\sin \theta$ (the **sine**), $\cos \theta$ (the **cosine**), and $\tan \theta$ (the **tangent**) for an acute angle θ are

(M-27)
$$\sin \theta = \frac{a}{c} = \frac{\text{opposite side}}{\text{hypotenuse}}$$

(M-28)
$$\cos \theta = \frac{b}{c} = \frac{\text{adjacent side}}{\text{hypotenuse}}$$

(M-29)
$$\tan \theta = \frac{a}{b} = \frac{\text{opposite side}}{\text{adjacent side}} = \frac{\sin \theta}{\cos \theta}$$

(**Acute angles** are angles whose positive rotation around the circumference of a circle measures less than 90° or $\pi/2$.) Three other trigonometric functions—the **secant** (sec), the **cosecant** (csc), and the **cotangent** (cot), defined as the reciprocals of these functions—are

(M-30)
$$\csc \theta = \frac{c}{a} = \frac{1}{\sin \theta}$$

(M-31)
$$\sec \theta = \frac{c}{b} = \frac{1}{\cos \theta}$$

(M-32)
$$\cot \theta = \frac{b}{a} = \frac{1}{\tan \theta} = \frac{\cos \theta}{\sin \theta}$$

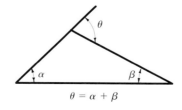

Figure M-11 Some useful relations for angles.

The angle θ, whose sine is x, is called the arcsine of x, and is written $\sin^{-1} x$. That is, if

$$\sin \theta = x$$

then

$$\theta = \arcsin x = \sin^{-1} x \qquad \text{(M-33)}$$

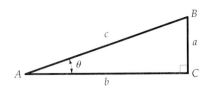

Figure M-12 A right triangle with sides of length a and b and a hypotenuse of length c.

The arcsine is the inverse of the sine. The inverse of the cosine and tangent are defined similarly. The angle whose cosine is y is the arccosine of y. That is, if

$$\cos \theta = y$$

then

$$\theta = \arccos y = \cos^{-1} y \qquad \text{(M-34)}$$

The angle whose tangent is z is the arctangent of z. That is, if

$$\tan \theta = z$$

then

$$\theta = \arctan z = \tan^{-1} z \qquad \text{(M-35)}$$

Trigonometric Identities

We can derive several useful formulas, called **trigonometric identities,** by examining relationships between the trigonometric functions. Equations M-30 through M-32 list three of the most obvious identities, formulas expressing some trigonometric functions as reciprocals of others. Almost as easy to discern are identities derived from the **Pythagorean theorem,**

$$a^2 + b^2 = c^2 \qquad \text{(M-36)}$$

Simple algebraic manipulation of Equation M-36 gives us three more identities. First, if we divide each term in Equation M-36 by c^2, we obtain

$$\frac{a^2}{c^2} + \frac{b^2}{c^2} = 1$$

or, from the definitions of $\sin \theta$ (which is a/c) and $\cos \theta$ (which is b/c),

$$\sin^2 \theta + \cos^2 \theta = 1 \qquad \text{(M-37)}$$

Similarly, we can divide each term in Equation M-36 by a^2 or b^2 and obtain

$$1 + \cot^2 \theta = \csc^2 \theta \qquad \text{(M-38)}$$

and

$$1 + \tan^2 \theta = \sec^2 \theta \qquad \text{(M-39)}$$

Table M-2 lists these last three and many more trigonometric identities. Notice that they fall into four categories: functions of sums or differences of angles, sums or differences of squared functions, functions of double angles (2θ), and functions of half angles ($\frac{1}{2}\theta$). Notice that some of the formulas contain paired alternatives, expressed with the signs $\pm$ and $\mp$; in such formulas, remember to always apply the formula with either all the upper or all the lower alternatives.

Table M-2   Trigonometric Identities

$$\sin(A \pm B) = \sin A \cos B \pm \cos A \sin B$$

$$\cos(A \pm B) = \cos A \cos B \mp \sin A \sin B$$

$$\tan(A \pm B) = \frac{\tan A \pm \tan B}{1 \mp \tan A \tan B}$$

$$\sin A \pm \sin B = 2 \sin\left[\frac{1}{2}(A \pm B)\right]\cos\left[\frac{1}{2}(A \mp B)\right]$$

$$\cos A + \cos B = 2 \cos\left[\frac{1}{2}(A + B)\right]\cos\left[\frac{1}{2}(A - B)\right]$$

$$\cos A - \cos B = 2 \sin\left[\frac{1}{2}(A + B)\right]\sin\left[\frac{1}{2}(B - A)\right]$$

$$\tan A \pm \tan B = \frac{\sin(A \pm B)}{\cos A \cos B}$$

$$\sin^2 \theta + \cos^2 \theta = 1; \ \sec^2 \theta - \tan^2 \theta = 1; \ \csc^2 \theta - \cot^2 \theta = 1$$

$$\sin 2\theta = 2 \sin \theta \cos \theta$$

$$\cos 2\theta = \cos^2 \theta - \sin^2 \theta = 2 \cos^2 \theta - 1 = 1 - 2 \sin^2 \theta$$

$$\tan 2\theta = \frac{2 \tan \theta}{1 - \tan^2 \theta}$$

$$\sin \frac{1}{2}\theta = \pm\sqrt{\frac{1 - \cos \theta}{2}}; \ \cos \frac{1}{2}\theta = \pm\sqrt{\frac{1 + \cos \theta}{2}};$$

$$\tan \frac{1}{2}\theta = \pm\sqrt{\frac{1 - \cos \theta}{1 + \cos \theta}}$$

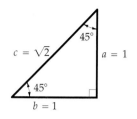

Figure M-13 An isosceles right triangle.

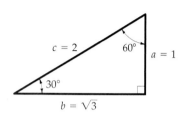

Figure M-14 A 30°–60°–90° right triangle.

Some Important Values of the Functions

Figure M-13 is a diagram of an *isosceles* right triangle (an isosceles triangle is a triangle with two equal sides), from which we can find the sine, cosine, and tangent of 45°. The two acute angles of this triangle are equal. Because the sum of the three angles in a triangle must equal 180° and the right angle is 90°, each acute angle must be 45°. For convenience, let us assume that the equal sides each have a length of 1 unit. The Pythagorean theorem gives us a value for the hypotenuse of

$$c = \sqrt{a^2 + b^2} = \sqrt{1^2 + 1^2} = \sqrt{2} \text{ units}$$

We calculate the values of the functions as follows:

$$\sin 45° = \frac{a}{c} = \frac{1}{\sqrt{2}} = 0.707 \quad \cos 45° = \frac{b}{c} = \frac{1}{\sqrt{2}} = 0.707 \quad \tan 45° = \frac{a}{b} = \frac{1}{1} = 1$$

Another common triangle, a 30°–60°–90° right triangle, is shown in Figure M-14. Because this particular right triangle is in effect half of an *equilateral triangle* (a 60°–60°–60° triangle or a triangle having three equal sides and three equal angles), we can see that the sine of 30° must be exactly 0.5 (Figure M-15). The equilateral triangle must have all sides equal to c, the hypotenuse of the 30°–60°–90° right triangle. Thus, side a is one-half the length of the hypotenuse, and so

$$\sin 30° = \frac{1}{2}$$

To find the other ratios within the 30°–60°–90° right triangle, let us assign a value of 1 to the side opposite the 30° angle. Then

$$c = \frac{1}{0.5} = 2 \qquad\qquad b = \sqrt{c^2 - a^2} = \sqrt{2^2 - 1^2} = \sqrt{3}$$

$$\cos 30° = \frac{b}{c} = \frac{\sqrt{3}}{2} = 0.866 \qquad \tan 30° = \frac{a}{b} = \frac{1}{\sqrt{3}} = 0.577$$

$$\sin 60° = \frac{b}{c} = \cos 30° = 0.866 \qquad \cos 60° = \frac{a}{c} = \sin 30° = \frac{1}{2}$$

$$\tan 60° = \frac{b}{a} = \frac{\sqrt{3}}{1} = 1.732$$

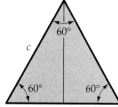

Figure M-15 (a) An equilateral triangle. (b) An equilateral triangle that has been bisected to form two 30°–60°–90° right triangles.

Small-Angle Approximation

For small angles, the length a is nearly equal to the arc length s, as can be seen in Figure M-16. The angle $\theta = s/c$ is therefore nearly equal to $\sin \theta = a/c$:

(M-40) $\qquad\qquad \sin \theta \approx \theta \quad$ for small values of θ

Similarly, the lengths c and b are nearly equal, so $\tan \theta = a/b$ is nearly equal to both θ and $\sin \theta$ for small values of θ:

(M-41) $\qquad\qquad \tan \theta \approx \sin \theta \approx \theta \quad$ for small values of θ

Equations M-40 and M-41 hold only if θ is measured in radians. Because $\cos \theta = b/c$, and because these lengths are nearly equal for small values of θ, we have

(M-42) $\qquad\qquad \cos \theta \approx 1 \quad$ for small values of θ

Figure M-17 shows graphs of θ, $\sin \theta$, and $\tan \theta$ versus θ for small values of θ. If accuracy of a few percent is needed, small-angle approximations can be used only for angles of about a quarter of a radian (or about 15°) or less. Below this value, as the angle becomes smaller, the approximation $\theta \approx \sin \theta \approx \tan \theta$ is even more accurate.

Figure M-16 For small angles, $\sin \theta = a/c$, $\tan \theta = a/b$, and the angle $\theta = s/c$ are all approximately equal.

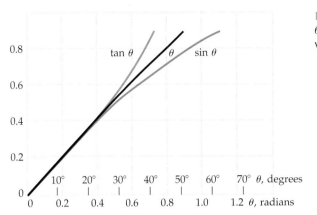

Figure M-17 Graphs of tan θ, θ, and sin θ versus θ for small values of θ.

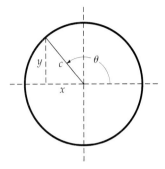

Trigonometric Functions as Functions of Real Numbers

So far we have illustrated the trigonometric functions as properties of angles. Figure M-18 shows an *obtuse* angle with its vertex at the origin and one side along the x axis. The trigonometric functions for a "general" angle such as this are defined by

$$\sin \theta = \frac{y}{c} \tag{M-43}$$

$$\cos \theta = \frac{x}{c} \tag{M-44}$$

$$\tan \theta = \frac{y}{x} \tag{M-45}$$

It is important to remember that values of x to the left of the vertical axis and values of y below the horizontal axis are negative; c in the figure is always regarded as positive. Figure M-19 shows plots of the general sine, cosine, and tangent functions versus θ. The sine and cosine functions have a period of 2π rad. Thus, for any value of θ, $\sin(\theta + 2\pi) = \sin \theta$, and so forth. That is, when an angle changes by 2π rad, the function returns to its original value. The tangent function has a period of π rad. Thus, $\tan(\theta + \pi) = \tan \theta$, and so forth. Some other useful relations are

$$\sin(\pi - \theta) = \sin \theta \tag{M-46}$$

$$\cos(\pi - \theta) = -\cos \theta \tag{M-47}$$

$$\sin\left(\frac{1}{2}\pi - \theta\right) = \cos \theta \tag{M-48}$$

$$\cos\left(\frac{1}{2}\pi - \theta\right) = \sin \theta \tag{M-49}$$

Because the radian is dimensionless, it is not hard to see from the plots in Figure M-21 that the trigonometric functions are functions of all real numbers.

Figure M-18 Diagram for defining the trigonometric functions for an obtuse angle.

(a)

(b)

(c)

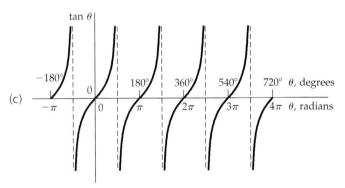

Figure M-19 The trigonometric functions sin θ, cos θ, and tan θ versus θ.

Example M-9 Cosine of a Sum

Using the suitable trigonometric identity from Table M-2, find $\cos(135° + 22°)$. Give your answer with four significant figures.

Set Up
As long as all angles are given in degrees, there is no need to convert to radians, because all operations are numerical values of the functions. Be sure, however, that your calculator is in degree mode. The suitable identity is $\cos(A \pm B) = \cos A \cos B \mp \sin A \sin B$, where the upper signs are appropriate.

Solve

Write the trigonometric identity for the cosine of a sum, with $A = 135°$ and $B = 22°$:

$$\cos(135° + 22°) = (\cos 135°)(\cos 22°) - (\sin 135°)(\sin 22°)$$

Using a calculator, find $\cos 135°$, $\sin 135°$, $\cos 22°$, and $\sin 22°$:

$$\cos 135° = -0.7071$$
$$\cos 22° = 0.9272$$
$$\sin 135° = 0.7071$$
$$\sin 22° = 0.3746$$

Enter the values in the formula and calculate the answer:

$$\cos(135° + 22°) = (-0.7071)(0.9272) - (0.7071)(0.3746)$$
$$= -0.9205$$

Reflect

The calculator shows that $\cos(135° + 22°) = \cos(157°) = -0.9205$.

Figure M-20 Two vectors separated by an angle θ.

(a)

(b)

Figure M-21 The dot product is a measure of how parallel two vectors are. (a) $B \cos \theta$ is the component of $\vec{B}$ that is parallel to $\vec{A}$. (b) $A \cos \theta$ is the component of $\vec{A}$ that is parallel to $\vec{B}$.

M-9 The Dot Product

For two vectors $\vec{A}$ and $\vec{B}$ separated by angle θ, as shown in **Figure M-20**, their dot product C is defined as

(M-50)
$$C = \vec{A} \cdot \vec{B} = AB \cos \theta$$

which you can read as, "C equals A dot B." In Equation M-50, A and B are the magnitudes of vectors $\vec{A}$ and $\vec{B}$ respectively. As a result, the dot product of two vectors is a scalar quantity. This is why $\vec{A} \cdot \vec{B}$ is also called the **scalar product** of $\vec{A}$ and $\vec{B}$.

Physically, the dot product $\vec{A} \cdot \vec{B}$ is a measure of how parallel the two vectors are. We can think of it as the magnitude of vector $\vec{A}$ multiplied by the component of vector $\vec{B}$ that is parallel to $\vec{A}$. Referring to **Figure M-21a**, we see that $B \cos \theta$ is the component of $\vec{B}$ that is parallel to $\vec{A}$. That is, $B \cos \theta$ tells us how much of $\vec{B}$ points in the direction of $\vec{A}$. Alternatively, the dot product $\vec{A} \cdot \vec{B}$ can be thought of as the magnitude of vector $\vec{B}$ multiplied by the component of vector $\vec{A}$ parallel to $\vec{B}$ (**Figure M-21b**).

The dot product is commutative; the order of the vectors in a dot product does not affect the result:

$$\vec{A} \cdot \vec{B} = \vec{B} \cdot \vec{A}$$

The dot product is also distributive, which means

$$\vec{A} \cdot (\vec{B} + \vec{C}) = \vec{A} \cdot \vec{B} + \vec{A} \cdot \vec{C}$$

Three special cases of the dot product are particularly important in physics. First, the dot product of two vectors $\vec{A}$ and $\vec{B}$ that point in the same direction (so $\theta = 0$ and $\cos \theta = \cos 0 = 1$) equals the product of their magnitudes:

(M-51)
$$\vec{A} \cdot \vec{B} = AB \cos 0 = AB$$
(if $\vec{A}$ and $\vec{B}$ point in the same direction)

(As an example, the dot product of a vector $\vec{A}$ with itself is equal to the square of its magnitude: $\vec{A} \cdot \vec{A} = AA \cos 0 = A^2$.)

Second, the dot product of two perpendicular vectors $\vec{A}$ and $\vec{B}$ (so $\theta = 90°$ and $\cos \theta = \cos 90° = 0$) is zero:

(M-52)
$$\vec{A} \cdot \vec{B} = AB \cos 90° = 0$$
(if $\vec{A}$ and $\vec{B}$ are perpendicular)

Third, if two vectors $\vec{A}$ and $\vec{B}$ point in opposite directions (so $\theta = 180°$ and $\cos \theta = \cos 180° = -1$), their dot product equals the *negative* of the product of their magnitudes:

(M-53)
$$\vec{A} \cdot \vec{B} \cos 180° = -AB$$
(if $\vec{A}$ and $\vec{B}$ point in opposite directions)

Finally, it's useful to know how to calculate the dot product of two vectors $\vec{A}$ and $\vec{B}$ that are expressed in terms of their components A_x, A_y, A_z, and B_x, B_y, and B_z:

(M-54)
$$\vec{A} \cdot \vec{B} = A_x B_x + A_y B_y + A_z B_z$$

You can verify that Equation M-54 is correct by thinking of $\vec{A}$ as the sum of three vectors: $\vec{A}_1$, which has only an x-component A_x; $\vec{A}_2$, which has only a y-component A_y; and $\vec{A}_3$, which has only a z-component A_z. From the definition of the dot product, $\vec{A}_1 \cdot \vec{B}$ is equal to A_x multiplied by the component of $\vec{B}$ in the direction of $\vec{A}_1$, or $\vec{A}_1 \cdot \vec{B} = A_x B_x$. Similarly, $\vec{A}_2 \cdot \vec{B} = A_y B_y$ and $\vec{A}_3 \cdot \vec{B} = A_z B_z$. Since $\vec{A} = \vec{A}_1 + \vec{A}_2 + \vec{A}_3$ and the dot product is distributive, it follows that

$$\vec{A} \cdot \vec{B} = (\vec{A}_1 + \vec{A}_2 + \vec{A}_3) \cdot \vec{B} = \vec{A}_1 \cdot \vec{B} + \vec{A}_2 \cdot \vec{B} + \vec{A}_3 \cdot \vec{B} = A_x B_x + A_y B_y + A_z B_z$$

That's the same as Equation M-54. If the vectors have only x- and y-components, Equation M-54 simplifies to $\vec{A} \cdot \vec{B} = A_x B_x + A_y B_y$.

Example M-10   The Dot Product

(a) Calculate the dot product of vector $\vec{A}$ with magnitude 5.00 pointed in a horizontal direction 36.9° north of east and vector $\vec{B}$ of magnitude 1.50 pointed in a horizontal direction 53.1° south of west. (b) What is the dot product of vector $\vec{C}$ with components $C_x = 4.00$, $C_y = 3.00$ and vector $\vec{D}$ with components $D_x = -0.900$, $D_y = -1.20$?

Set Up

In part (a) we know the magnitude and direction of the vectors, so we'll use Equation M-50. In part (b) the vectors are given in terms of components, so we'll evaluate the dot product using Equation M-54.

$$\vec{A} \cdot \vec{B} = AB \cos \theta \qquad \text{(M-50)}$$

Dot product of two vectors in terms of components:

$$\vec{A} \cdot \vec{B} = A_x B_x + A_y B_y + A_z B_z \qquad \text{(M-54)}$$

Solve

(a) The drawing shows that the angle between $\vec{A}$ and $\vec{B}$ is $\theta = 163.8°$. We use this in Equation M-50 to evaluate the dot product.

$$\begin{aligned}
\vec{A} \cdot \vec{B} &= AB \cos \theta \\
&= (5.00)(1.50) \cos 163.8° \\
&= (5.00)(1.50)(-0.960) \\
&= -7.20
\end{aligned}$$

(b) Both $\vec{C}$ and $\vec{D}$ are in the x-y plane and have no z components, so we just need the first two terms in Equation M-54 to calculate their dot product.

$$\begin{aligned}
\vec{C} \cdot \vec{D} &= C_x D_x + C_y D_y \\
&= (4.00)(-0.900) + (3.00)(-1.20) \\
&= -7.20
\end{aligned}$$

Reflect

It's not a coincidence that we got the same result in part (b) as in part (a): Vectors $\vec{A}$ and $\vec{C}$ are the same, as are vectors $\vec{B}$ and $\vec{D}$. (You can verify this by using the techniques from Chapter 3 to calculate the components of the vectors $\vec{A}$ and $\vec{B}$ in part (a). You'll find that the components are the same as those of $\vec{C}$ and $\vec{D}$ in part (b).) This should give you confidence that the method of calculating the dot product using components gives you the same result as the method that involves the magnitudes and directions of the vectors.

Notice that the angle between vectors $\vec{A}$ and $\vec{B}$ is between 90° and 180°, and the dot product is negative.

M-10 The Cross Product

The dot product, described in section M-9, is only one way to multiply two vectors. We can also multiply two vectors $\vec{A}$ and $\vec{B}$ using the **cross product**

(M-55)
$$\vec{C} = \vec{A} \times \vec{B}$$

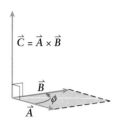

$$\vec{C} = \vec{A} \times \vec{B}$$

$\vec{B}$

ϕ

$\vec{A}$

Figure M-22 The cross product is a vector $\vec{C}$ that is perpendicular to both $\vec{A}$ and $\vec{B}$, and has a magnitude $AB \sin \phi$, which equals the area of the parallelogram shown.

The symbol "×" represents the mathematical operation known as the cross product. As you can see from Equation M-55, the result of taking the cross product of two vectors is also a vector. The magnitude of the resulting vector is the product of the magnitudes of the two vectors and the sine of the angle between them. That is, the magnitude of the cross product of $\vec{A}$ and $\vec{B}$ is

(M-56)
$$C = |\vec{A} \times \vec{B}| = AB \sin \phi$$

where according to convention ϕ is defined as the angle that goes from $\vec{A}$ to $\vec{B}$. $\vec{C}$ points in the direction perpendicular to both $\vec{A}$ and $\vec{B}$ as shown in **Figure M-22**.

The magnitude of the cross product $\vec{A} \times \vec{B}$ can be interpreted as the magnitude of vector $\vec{A}$ multiplied by the component of vector $\vec{B}$ perpendicular to $\vec{A}$, or the magnitude of vector $\vec{B}$ multiplied by the component of vector $\vec{A}$ perpendicular to $\vec{B}$.

Note that the order of the two vectors in a cross product makes a difference. The cross product of $\vec{B}$ and $\vec{A}$ is the negative of the cross product of $\vec{A}$ and $\vec{B}$ or

(M-57)
$$\vec{A} \times \vec{B} = -\vec{B} \times \vec{A}$$

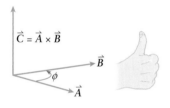

$$\vec{C} = \vec{A} \times \vec{B}$$

$\vec{B}$

ϕ

$\vec{A}$

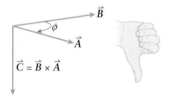

$\vec{B}$

ϕ

$\vec{A}$

$$\vec{C} = \vec{B} \times \vec{A}$$

Figure M-23 (a) To find the direction of , point the fingers of your right hand in the direction of vector $\vec{A}$, then curl them toward vector $\vec{B}$. Your thumb points in the direction of the cross product. (b) The direction of $\vec{B} \times \vec{A}$ points in the opposite direction of.

This results from the definition of the angle ϕ in Equation M-56. Since ϕ is directed from the first vector to the second vector, if you travel the angle from the second vector to the first—in reverse direction-ϕ becomes negative. And the sine of a negative angle is also negative.

In addition, the cross product obeys the distributive law under addition:

(M-58)
$$\vec{A} \times (\vec{B} + \vec{C}) = \vec{A} \times \vec{B} + \vec{A} \times \vec{C}$$

To determine the direction of the cross product $\vec{C} = \vec{A} \times \vec{B}$, you can use the right-hand rule. To apply this rule, point the fingers of your right hand in the direction of the first vector of the cross product (in this case $\vec{A}$). Then curl your fingers toward the second vector, $\vec{B}$. If you stick your thumb straight out, it points in the direction of the cross product, vector $\vec{C}$ (**Figure M-23a**). If you instead want to find the direction of the cross product $\vec{B} \times \vec{A}$, begin by pointing the fingers of your right hand in the direction of vector $\vec{B}$. Then curl them toward vector $\vec{A}$. Your thumb again points in the direction of the cross product (**Figure M-23b**). Note that because you must curl your fingers in the opposite direction as for $\vec{C} = \vec{A} \times \vec{B}$, the cross product of $\vec{B} \times \vec{A}$ points in the opposite direction of $\vec{A} \times \vec{B}$, which is just what we stated in Equation M-58.

There are two special cases of the cross product that are worth pointing out. The first is the cross product for two perpendicular vectors, for which $\phi = 90°$, so $\sin \phi = 1$.

$$|\vec{A} \times \vec{B}| = AB \sin 90° = AB(1) = AB$$

(magnitude of the cross product of two perpendicular vectors)

The second special case is the cross product of two parallel vectors, for which $\phi = 0$, so $\sin \phi = 0$.

$$|\vec{A} \times \vec{B}| = AB \sin 0 = AB(0) = 0$$

(magnitude of the cross product for two parallel vectors)

One example of a cross product of two parallel vectors is the cross product of a vector with itself: $\vec{A} \times \vec{A} = 0$.

Example M-11 The Cross Product

Evaluate $\vec{A} \times \vec{B}$, in which the components of vector $\vec{A}$ are $A_x = 5$, $A_y = 0$, and the components of vector $\vec{B}$ are $B_x = 9$, $B_y = 7$.

Set Up

We will use the definition of the magnitude of the cross product, Equation M-56, to find the magnitude of the cross product, and the right-hand rule to determine the direction of the cross product.

We will have to use the components of vector $\vec{B}$ to determine its magnitude and the angle it makes with the x axis and vector $\vec{A}$.

$$C = |\vec{A} \times \vec{B}| = AB \sin \phi$$

$$(\text{M-56})$$

Finding vector magnitude and direction from vector components:

$$A = \sqrt{A_x^2 + A_y^2}$$

$$\tan \theta = \frac{A_y}{A_x} \qquad (3\text{-}2)$$

Solve

Begin by determining the magnitude and direction of vector $\vec{B}$ using its components and Equations 3-2.

Determine the magnitude of vector $\vec{B}$ from its components:

$$B = \sqrt{B_x^2 + B_y^2} = \sqrt{9^2 + 7^2} = 11.4$$

Determine the angle $\vec{B}$ makes with the x axis (and vector $\vec{A}$) from its components:

$$\tan \phi = \frac{B_y}{B_x} = \frac{7}{9} = 0.778, \text{ so}$$

$$\phi = \arctan 0.778 = 37.9°$$

Because vector $\vec{A}$ has only an x component, its magnitude is equal to its x component, and the angle it makes with the x axis is 0.

Determine the magnitude of vector $\vec{A}$ from its components:

$$A = \sqrt{A_x^2 + A_y^2} = \sqrt{5^2 + 0^2} = 5$$

Because $\vec{A}$ has only an x component, it makes an angle of zero degrees with the x axis.

Now that we know both the magnitude and direction of the vectors, we can use Equation M-56 to determine the magnitude of the cross product.

Apply Equation M-56 to the two vectors:

$$|\vec{A} \times \vec{B}| = AB \sin \phi$$
$$= (5.00)(11.4)\sin 37.9°$$
$$= (5.00)(11.4)(0.614)$$
$$= 35.0$$

Use the right-hand rule to determine the direction of the cross product.

From the figure, if we first point the fingers of our right hand in the direction of $\vec{A}$ (along the x axis), and then curl them toward $\vec{B}$, we see that the thumb points in the positive z direction. So the cross product $\vec{A} \times \vec{B}$ has a magnitude of 35 in the $+z$ direction.

Reflect

The vectors $\vec{A}$ and $\vec{B}$ lie in the xy plane, so the cross product, which must be perpendicular to both vectors, should point along the z axis, which is just what we found.

MCAT® Appendix

The section that follows includes material from previously administered MCAT® items and is reprinted with permission of the Association of American Medical Colleges (AAMC).

Passage 13 (81–85)

Tennis balls must pass a rebound test before they can be certified for tournament play. To qualify, balls dropped from a given height must rebound within a specified range of heights. Measuring rebound height can be difficult because the ball is at its maximum height for only a brief time. It is possible to perform a simpler indirect measurement to calculate the height of rebound by measuring how long it takes the ball to rebound and hit the floor again. The diagram below illustrates the experimental setup used to make the measurement.

The ball is dropped from a height of 2.0 m, and it hits the floor and then rebounds to a height h. A microphone detects the sound of the ball each time it hits the floor, and a timer connected to the microphone measures the time (t) between the two impacts. The height of the rebound is $h = gt^2/8$ where $g = 9.8 \text{ m/s}^2$ is the acceleration due to gravity. Care must be taken so that the measured times do not contain systematic error. Both the speed of sound and the time of impact of the ball with the floor must be considered. Four balls were tested using the method. The results are listed in the table below.

Ball	Time (s)
A	1.01
B	1.05
C	0.97
D	1.09

81. If NO air resistance is present, which of the following quantities remains constant while the ball is in the air between the first and second impacts?
- A. Kinetic energy of the ball
- B. Potential energy of the ball
- C. Momentum of the ball
- D. Horizontal speed of the ball

82. What measurement is made by the timer?
- A. Duration of the impacts
- B. Time that the ball is at maximum height
- C. Time between the first and second bounces
- D. Decrease in time of successive bounces

83. Balls C and D failed the test, while balls A and B passed. A ball that had which of the following measured times would definitely pass the test?
- A. 0.95 s
- B. 0.99 s
- C. 1.03 s
- D. 1.07 s

84. What percentage of its original potential energy did ball C lose between the start of the experiment and its rebound to maximum height?
- A. 24%
- B. 42%
- C. 51%
- D. 58%

85. With what approximate vertical speed does a ball in the experiment strike the floor?
- A. 4 m/s
- B. 6 m/s
- C. 10 m/s
- D. 20 m/s

Passage X (Questions 134–138)

The study of the flight of projectiles has many practical applications. The main forces acting on a projectile are air resistance and gravity. The path of a projectile is often approximated by ignoring the effects of air resistance. Gravity is then the only force acting on the projectile. When air resistance is included in the analysis, another force F_R is introduced. F_R is proportional to the square of the velocity, v. The direction of the air resistance is exactly opposite the direction of motion. The equation for air resistance is $F_R = pv^2$, where p is a proportionality constant that depends on such factors as the density of the air and the shape of the projectile.

Air resistance was studied by launching a 0.5-kg projectile from a level surface. The projectile was launched with a speed of 30 m/s at a 40° angle to the surface. (Note: Assume air resistance is present unless otherwise specified. Acceleration due to gravity is $g = 9.8 \text{ m/s}^2$; $\sin 40° = 0.64$; $\cos 40° = 0.77$.)

134. If a 0.5-kg projectile is launched straight up and is given an initial kinetic energy of 259 J, to what maximum height will it rise? (Note: Assume that the effects of air resistance are negligible.)
- A. 26 m
- B. 51 m
- C. 102 m
- D. 204 m

135. Which of the following statements is (are) true about the kinetic energy of the projectile when it returns to the elevation from which it was launched?
- I. It is the same as when it was launched.
- II. It is dependent on the initial velocity.
- III. It is dependent on the value of p.
- A. II only
- B. I and II only
- C. I and III only
- D. II and III only

136. What is the approximate total kinetic energy of the projectile at the highest point in its path? (Note: Assume that the effects of air resistance are negligible.)

 A. 92 J
 B. 133 J
 C. 184 J
 D. 225 J

137. Which of the following graphs best illustrates the relationship between the total speed of the projectile (v) and its horizontal distance from the launch point (x)? (Note: Assume that the effects of air resistance are negligible and that the left axis represents the location of the launch point.)

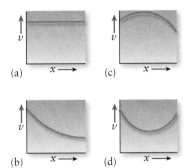

138. What is the magnitude of the horizontal component of air resistance on the projectile at any point during the flight? (Note: v_x = horizontal speed.)

 A. $(pv^2) \cos 40°$
 B. $pv^2/2$
 C. $(pv_x^2) \sin 40°$
 D. pv_x^2

Passage 12 (Questions 73–80)

A pressure difference between the ends of a horizontal, uniform pipe is required to maintain the steady flow of a viscous fluid through the pipe. The fluid pressure at the downstream end of the pipe (P_2) depends on the tube length (L), inside radius of the pipe (r), viscosity (η), volume flow rate (f), and the pressure at the beginning of the pipe (P_1). These quantities are related by Poiseuille's equation $\Delta P = P_2 - P_1 = \dfrac{(8\eta L f)}{\pi r^4}$, where ΔP is the pressure differential.

Two experiments were conducted to investigate the flow of distilled water and glycerin through various pipes.

Experiment 1

Distilled water flowed through pipes that were 5.0 m long and had different radii. The pressure differential between the beginning and end of the pipes was measured while the flow rate was held constant. The results are listed in Table 2. (Note: At 20°C, distilled water has a viscosity of 1×10^{-3} kg/m·s and a density of 1×10^3 kg/m³.)

Trial	L(m)	r(m)	f (m³/s)	ΔP (N/m²)
1	5.0	0.05	0.003	6.0
2	5.0	0.04	0.003	15.0
3	5.0	0.03	0.003	47.0
4	5.0	0.02	0.003	240
5	5.0	0.01	0.003	3820

Experiment 2

Glycerin flowed through pipes that had different lengths but the same radius. The flow rates were measured while the pressure differential between the beginning and end of the pipes was held constant. The results are listed in Table 3. (Note: At 20°C, glycerin has a viscosity of 1.5×10^{-3} kg/m·s and a density of 1.3×10^3 kg/m³.)

Trial	L(m)	r(m)	ΔP (N/m²)	f (m³/s)
1	1.0	0.01	100	2.6×10^{-7}
2	1.5	0.01	100	1.7×10^{-7}
3	2.0	0.01	100	1.3×10^{-7}
4	2.5	0.01	100	1.0×10^{-7}
5	3.0	0.01	100	8.7×10^{-8}

73. When viscosity increases, an increase in pressure differential is required to maintain the same volume flow rate. This is because an increase in viscosity is related to an increase in which of the following factors?

 A. Pipe radius
 B. Friction
 C. Fluid density
 D. Turbulence

74. When fluid flow is compared to electricity, which of the following fluid characteristics is analogous to electrical current?

 A. Pressure differential
 B. Volume flow rate
 C. Viscosity
 D. Flow speed

75. In which trial of Experiment 2 did a unit length of glycerin have the greatest kinetic energy?

 A. Trial 1
 B. Trial 2
 C. Trial 4
 D. Trial 5

76. If an additional trial of Experiment 1 were conducted using a pipe with a radius of 0.06 m, what would be the expected pressure differential?

 A. 0.4 N/m²
 B. 1.0 N/m²
 C. 1.5 N/m²
 D. 2.9 N/m²

77. If water and glycerin flowed through identical pipes and had the same pressure differential, which fluid would have the greater flow rate?

 A. Water, because it has a lower viscosity
 B. Water, because it has a lower density
 C. Glycerin, because it has a higher viscosity
 D. Glycerin, because it has a higher density

78. If ΔP is held constant and r is reduced by 33%, by what percentage does f decrease?

 A. 33%
 B. 56%
 C. 80%
 D. 98%

79. If an additional trial of Experiment 2 were conducted using a pipe that was 4.0 m long, what would be the expected flow rate?

A. 2.6×10^{-8} m³/s
B. 4.3×10^{-8} m³/s
C. 6.5×10^{-8} m³/s
D. 7.8×10^{-8} m³/s

80. Which of the following graphs best shows how the volume flow rate of a fluid flowing out of a uniform pipe varies as the pressure differential between the beginning and end of the pipe is changed?

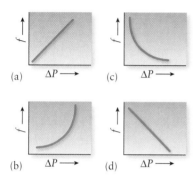

Passage 7 (Questions 41–48)

Three experiments were conducted to examine collisions between masses suspended at the ends of simple pendula. Each pendulum consisted of a mass, or bob, attached to the bottom of a rod of negligible mass. The top of the rod was anchored to a solid surface from which it could swing free of friction. For sufficiently small amplitudes, each pendulum executed simple harmonic motion with a period $T = 2\sqrt{\dfrac{l}{g}}$, where l is the length of the pendulum, and g is the acceleration due to gravity. (Note: Assume air resistance is negligible in the experiments.)

Experiment 1

Two identical pendula with steel balls for bobs were hung next to each other so that their bobs barely touched when they hung vertically. The left pendulum bob was moved to the side and then released. The bobs collided, and immediately after the collision, the left bob was at rest while the right bob moved with the same speed that the left bob had before the collision.

Experiment 2

The steel bobs were replaced with nonidentical balls made of an unknown substance. The left pendulum bob was moved to the same position as in Experiment 1 and then released. After the collision, the right bob moved to the right while the left bob rebounded to the left.

Experiment 3

The bobs were replaced with identical balls made of a deformable, sticky material. The left pendulum bob was moved to the same position as in Experiment 1 and then released. After the collision, the bobs stuck together, and the final speed of the combined bobs was less than the speed of the left bob before the collision.

41. Which of the following diagrams best describes the subsequent motion of a bob that detaches from a simple pendulum? When the bob moves through the lowest point of its arc?

42. Which of the following quantities is NOT conserved in the collision in Experiment 3?

A. Linear momentum
B. Angular momentum
C. Potential energy
D. Kinetic energy

43. Which of the following would occur if the collision in Experiment 1 was perfectly elastic?

A. The right bob would rise to the same height that the left bob started from.
B. The support rod would stretch enough that the right bob would move in a straight line.
C. Both bobs would move away from the impact with equal and opposite velocities.
D. Both bobs would move to the right after the collision.

44. Which of the following accurately describes the difference between the pendulum bobs used in Experiment 2?

A. The left bob was more elastic than the right bob.
B. The left bob was less elastic than the right bob.
C. The left bob weighed less than the right bob.
D. The left hob weighed more than the right bob.

45. If the speed of the left bob in Experiment 3 was v immediately before the collision, what was its speed immediately after the collision?

A. $v/4$
B. $v/2$
C. $v/\sqrt{2}$
D. Approximately equal to but slightly less than v.

46. If the maximum height of the left bob in Experiment 1 was increased by a factor of 2, by what factor would the maximum height of the right bob increase?

A. $\sqrt{2}$
B. $\frac{3}{2}$
C. 2
D. 4

47. The speed with which the left bob rebounds in Experiment 2 is

A. less than its speed before the collision.
B. equal to its speed before the collision.
C. greater than its speed before the collision.
D. equal to the speed of the right bob before the collision.

48. A pendulum bob is replaced with one that weighs 2 times as much. How does the time it takes for the new bob to move from a small angle of displacement to the lowest point of its arc compare to the time it took the old bob?

A. It takes $\frac{1}{2}$ as long.
B. It takes the same amount of time.
C. It takes $\sqrt{2}$ times as long.
D. It takes 2 times as long.

Passage 1 (Questions 1–6)

Ultrasonic waves are used in many applications by analyzing their reflections and refractions from interfaces between different media. Different intensities of reflections of a scanned object can provide a picture or pattern that can be electronically constructed and displayed on a monitor. The ultrasonic wavelength used for investigation should be equal to or smaller than the size of the object being scanned.

Ultrasonic waves are used for diagnostic purposes in medicine. Waves are directed into a body, and reflections occur at interfaces between different tissues or fluids. A practical depth of penetration of this technique for diagnostic scans is about 200 times the wavelength of the incident ultrasonic waves.

Another use of ultrasonic waves is an application of the Doppler effect. Doctors can detect and monitor blood flow speed as blood moves directly toward the incident ultrasonic waves. Calculations of flow toward the incident waves are made by using the relationship $\dfrac{f_o}{f_s} = \dfrac{v}{v - 2v_s}$, where f_o is the observed frequency, f_s is the incident frequency, v is the speed of ultrasonic waves in the medium, and v_s is the speed of the moving blood.

Ultrasonic waves that are reflected from a moving object are shifted in frequency. If the incident and reflected waves are mixed, this change in frequency causes beats to occur at a frequency that is equal to the absolute value of the difference between the incident and the reflected frequency. This phenomenon can also occur when waves that have 2 separate frequencies and that have been emitted from 2 stationary sources are mixed.

1. The speed of sound in tissue for an ultrasonic scan is 1,500 m/s. From the information given in the passage, what maximum frequency could be used for a scan when a depth of investigation of 0.20 m is required?
  A. 1.2×10^3 Hz
  B. 6.0×10^3 Hz
  C. 1.2×10^6 Hz
  D. 1.5×10^6 Hz

2. When ultrasonic waves are detected by a transducer that feeds a signal into a display monitor, which of the following is the best description of the energy transformation that occurs at the transducer?
  A. mechanical to electrical
  B. kinetic to mechanical
  C. potential to kinetic
  D. potential to electrical

3. When a trumpet is tuned by comparison with a 512-Hz note from a piano, a beat frequency of 4 Hz is produced. The trumpet could have produced which of the following pairs of frequencies?
  A. 504 Hz and 508 Hz
  B. 508 Hz and 512 Hz
  C. 508 Hz and 516 Hz
  D. 512 Hz and 516 Hz

4. An ultrasonic wave enters a body with a speed of 1,500 m/s, and a reflection is noted at the same position on the surface 4.0×10^{-5} s later. What is the distance between the surface and the reflecting interface?
  A. 1.3×10^{-8} m
  B. 2.7×10^{-8} m
  C. 3.0×10^{-2} m
  D. 6.0×10^{-2} m

5. According to the passage, what is the lowest wave frequency that should be used to provide an image of an object that is 10^{-3} m on each side? (Note: Assume that the wave travels at 1,500 m/s.)
  A. 1.5 Hz
  B. 1.5×10^6 Hz
  C. 6.7×10^6 Hz
  D. 6.7×10^7 Hz

6. Which of the following best explains why ultrasonic waves are reflected at boundaries within a human body?
  A. Reflections occur at the boundary between objects with different shapes.
  B. Reflections occur at the boundary between objects with different densities.
  C. Reflections occur when the frequency of the ultrasonic wave decreases.
  D. Reflections occur when the frequency of the ultrasonic wave increases.

Passage 2 (Questions 7-13)

A student performed 2 experiments to investigate the behavior of springs.

Experiment 1

The student investigated the stretching of a horizontal spring on a smooth table. One end of the spring was fastened to a vertical wall, and the spring was stretched by a string attached over a pulley to a hanging mass (M) as shown in Figure 1. The experimental results showing how the total spring length (L) changed with variations to M are given in Table 4.

Trial	M (kg)	L (m)
1	0	0.400
2	0.1	0.405
3	0.4	0.420
4	2.0	0.500

Experiment 2

The student slid a mass (m) with speed (v) along a horizontal tabletop with which it had negligible friction. The mass collided with a magnetic bumper plate that was attached to a horizontal spring fastened to a wall, as shown in Figure 2. When the spring was compressed a distance (x), the spring had a potential energy of $1/2kx^2$, where k is the spring constant. Maximum potential energy occurred at maximum recoil distance, x_{max}. Values of mass and speed used in Experiment 2 are given in Table 5.

Trial	m (kg)	v (m/s)
1	1	5
2	2	4
3	3	3
4	4	2
5	5	1

7. What is the value of k for the spring used in Experiment 1?
   A. 4 N/m
   B. 25 N/m
   C. 100 N/m
   D. 200 N/m

8. For which of the following trials of Experiment 2 is the recoil distance the greatest?
   A. Trial 1
   B. Trial 2
   C. Trial 3
   D. Trial 4

9. In Experiment 2, the mass clings to the magnetic bumper plate and vibrates back and forth. Which of the following best compares f_1, the vibration frequency of Trial 1 to f_4, the vibration frequency of Trial 4?(Note: The period of vibration of this system is $T = 2\pi\sqrt{\dfrac{m}{k}}$.)

   A. $f_1 = \dfrac{f_4}{4}$

   B. $f_1 = \dfrac{f_4}{2}$

   C. $f_1 = f_4$

   D. $f_1 = 2f_4$

10. In Experiment 2, what minimum force must exist between the mass and the bumper plate so that the mass can vibrate back and forth?

   A. $\dfrac{k(x_{max})^2}{4}$

   B. $\dfrac{k(x_{max})^2}{2}$

   C. kx_{max}

   D. $k(x_{max})^2$

11. Which of the following graphs best describes the potential energy (PE) of the spring as it is compressed to x_{max} in Experiment 2?

(a)

(b)

(c)

(d)

12. Two identical springs are hung side by side and are attached to the same mass. If each spring has a spring constant of 12 N/m, what is the spring constant of the 2-spring system?
   A. 6 N/m
   B. 12 N/m
   C. 18 N/m
   D. 24 N/m

13. After Trial 3 of Experiment 1, an additional mass of 3.0 kg was added to the 0.4-kg mass that was already attached to the system. How much farther did the mass descend when the 3.0-kg mass was added?
   A. 0.15 m
   B. 0.17 m
   C. 0.55 m
   D. 0.57 m

Passage II (Questions 74–80)

An electromagnetic railgun is a device that can fire projectiles by using electromagnetic energy instead of chemical energy. A schematic of a typical railgun is shown below.

The operation of the railgun is simple. Current flows from the current source into the top rail, through the movable conducting armature into the bottom rail, then back to the current source. The current in the two rails produces a magnetic field directly proportional to the amount of current. This field produces a force on the charges moving through the movable armature. The force pushes the armature and the projectile along the rails.

The force is proportional to the square of the current running through the railgun. For a given current, the force and the magnetic field will be constant along the entire length of the railgun. The detectors placed outside the railgun give off signal when the projectile passes them. This information can be used to determine the exit speed and kinetic energy of the projectile. Projectile mass, rail current, and exit speed are listed in the table below.

Projectile mass (kg)	Rail current (A)	Exit speed (km/s)
0.01	10.0	2.0
0.01	15.0	3.0
0.02	10.0	1.4
0.04	10.0	1.0

74. Which of the following graphs best represents the dependence of exit speed on projectile mass?

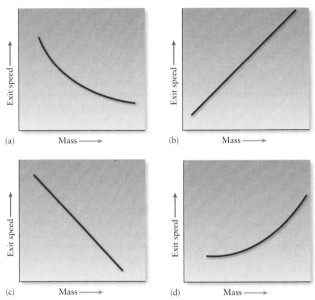

(a)   Mass ⟶

(b)   Mass ⟶

(c)   Mass ⟶

(d)   Mass ⟶

75. What change made to the railgun would reduce power consumption without lowering the exit speeds?
   A. lowering the rail current
   B. lowering the rail resistivity
   C. lowering the rail cross-sectional area
   D. reducing the magnetic field strength

76. Starting from a resting position at the right end of the railgun, the armature applies a constant force of 3.0 N to a projectile with mass of 0.06 kg. How long will it take for the projectile to move 1.0 m?
   A. 0.02 s
   B. 0.04 s
   C. 0.20 s
   D. 0.40 s

77. Lengthening the rails would increase the exit speed because of
   A. an increased rail resistance.
   B. a stronger magnetic field between the rails.
   C. a larger force on the armature.
   D. a longer distance over which the force is present.

78. For a given mass, if the current were decreased by a factor of 2, the exit speed would
   A. increase by a factor of 2.
   B. increase by a factor of $\sqrt{2}$.
   C. decrease by a factor of $\sqrt{2}$.
   D. decrease by a factor of 2.

79. If a projectile leaves a railgun near the surface of Earth with a speed of 2.0 km/s horizontally, how far will it fall in 0.01 s?
   A. 4.9×10^{-4} m
   B. 4.9×10^{-2} m
   C. 9.8×10^{-2} m
   D. 2.0×10^{1} m

80. If a projectile with a mass of 0.1 kg accelerates from a resting position to a speed of 10 m/s in 2 s, what is the average power supplied by the railgun to the projectile?
   A. 0.5 W
   B. 2.5 W
   C. 5.0 W
   D. 10.0 W

Passage 4 (Questions 19-26)

The Hubble telescope was carried into Earth's orbit and released by the space shuttle *Discovery* while orbiting at 7.81×10^{3} m/s. Before releasing the telescope, it was necessary for *Discovery* to achieve an orbit higher than any shuttle had reached in the past. This was because high levels of solar activity had heated Earth's upper atmosphere, causing it to expand outward. In order to avoid atmospheric drag which could cause the telescope to fall back to Earth, the telescope had to be placed as high as possible above the outer fringes of the atmosphere. The Hubble telescope was placed in orbit at an altitude of 6.11×10 m, a distance equivalent to approximately 4.8% of Earth's diameter. This altitude was as high as *Discovery*'s chemically powered engines could lift the 1.1×10^{4}-kg telescope.

The Hubble telescope is the largest telescope ever placed into orbit. Its primary concave mirror has a diameter of 2.4 m and a focal length of approximately 13 m. In addition to having optical detectors, the telescope is equipped to detect ultraviolet light, which does not easily penetrate Earth's atmosphere. (Note: Use $g = 9.8$ m/s^2.)

19. When the Hubble telescope is focused on a very distant object, the image from its primary mirror is
   A. real and erect.
   B. real and inverted.
   C. virtual and erect.
   D. virtual and inverted.

20. Assuming that the Hubble telescope is traveling in a circular orbit, which of the following expressions is equal to its orbital speed? (Note: G is the gravitational constant, M_e is the mass of Earth, M_t is the mass of the telescope, and r is the distance of the telescope from the center of Earth.)
   A. $\dfrac{GM_E}{r}$
   B. $\sqrt{\dfrac{GM_E}{r}}$
   C. $\dfrac{GM_t}{r}$
   D. $\dfrac{GM_t}{r^2}$

21. If the acceleration due to gravity were nearly constant from Earth's surface to the altitude of the Hubble telescope, what would the telescope's approximate potential energy be relative to Earth's surface?
   A. 3.3×10^{9} J
   B. 6.6×10^{9} J
   C. 3.3×10^{10} J
   D. 6.6×10^{10} J

22. The magnification of a telescope is determined by dividing the focal length of the primary mirror by the focal length of the eyepiece. If an eyepiece with a focal length of 2.5×10^{-2} m could be used with the primary mirror of the Hubble telescope, it would produce an image magnified approximately how many times?
   A. 10
   B. 96
   C. 520
   D. 960

23. Which of the following is the best explanation of why ultraviolet light does not penetrate Earth's atmosphere as easily as visible light does?

A. Ultraviolet light has a shorter wavelength and is more readily absorbed by the atmosphere.

B. Ultraviolet light has a lower frequency and is more readily absorbed by the atmosphere.

C. Ultraviolet light contains less energy and cannot travel as far through the atmosphere.

D. Ultraviolet light is reflected away from Earth by the upper atmosphere.

24. As the Hubble telescope was transported into orbit aboard *Discovery*, which of the following best describes the main energy conversion(s) taking place?

A. kinetic to gravitational potential

B. gravitational potential to kinetic

C. gravitational potential to kinetic to chemical

D. chemical to kinetic to gravitational potential

25. What is the approximate kinetic energy of the Hubble telescope while in orbit?

A. 4.3×10^7 J

B. 3.3×10^{11} J

C. 6.6×10^{11} J

D. 4.3×10^{12} J

26. The image of a very distant object that is produced by a mirror such as that used in the Hubble telescope will be at what location in relationship to the mirror and focal point?

A. behind the mirror

B. between the mirror and the focal point

C. at the focal point

D. outside the focal point

Passage IV (Questions 94–99)

Retroreflecting arrays consist of spherical beads. Light is refracted as it enters a bead, then reflected off the back of the bead. Arrays of retroreflectors are attached to flexible sheets used as safety reflectors on clothing and bicycles. Ideal retroreflectors return a beam to its source regardless of the angle of incidence of the beam to it. Each light ray is returned on a path no farther than the diameter of a bead from the source ray. Thus, if a distortion that changes the path of light is placed in front of the retroreflecting array, the incident and reflected rays will pass through the same distortion. When this occurs, the ray perfectly retraces itself, thereby canceling the distortion.

An experiment is conducted with the setup illustrated in Figure 3. A light source covered by a screen with a pinhole in it provides a point source of light. A glass pane acts as a beam splitter. Some of the source light is reflected out of the experiment; the remainder of the light is incident upon the array. Some of the light returning from the array is reflected at a right angle to a viewing screen by the beam splitter. The wave front reflected from a retroreflecting array will be irregular. However, a pinhole image will still appear on the screen because the human eye cannot perceive the separation of the wave fronts.

94. The beam splitter in Figure 3 is set at what angle to the incident beam?

A. 15°

B. 30°

C. 45°

D. 60°

95. Which of the following figures shows a possible path for a ray of light passing through a retroreflecting bead? (Note: Assume that the index of refraction of the bead is greater than that of air.)

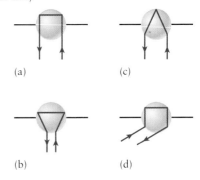

96. The glass that is used as a beam splitter is replaced with glass that is identical except that it has a 10% higher index of refraction. Which of the following changes will occur to the pinhole?

A. It will move.

B. It will become larger.

C. It will become smaller.

D. It will become clearer.

97. What is the approximate number of wavelengths of light that can travel in one direction within a retroreflecting bead that has a diameter of 5×10^{-5} m? (Note: The speed of light = 3×10^8 m/s and its frequency is approximately 10^{15} Hz.)

A. 0.6

B. 1.7×10^2

C. 1.5×10^4

D. 3.3×10^6

98. If a single-wavelength laser is used in place of the light source and pinhole, how will the image on the viewing screen change?

A. It will be larger.

B. It will be less bright.

C. It will be shifted.

D. It will show stronger patterns of interference.

99. With the screen removed, an observer at Point A sees a virtual image of the pinhole. Which of the following indicates that the observer is viewing a virtual image?

A. It moves as the observer changes the angle of view.

B. It is larger than the real image.

C. It is dimmer than the real image.

D. It is fuzzier than the real image.

Answers to Odd Problems

Chapter 1

1. The SI unit for distance is meters. It is defined as the distance traveled by light in a vacuum in 1/299,792,458 of a second. The SI unit for mass is the kilogram. It is defined as the mass of a carefully protected prototype block of platinum and iridium that is stored in France. The SI unit of time is the second. It is defined as the time required for a cesium atom to emit 9,192,631,770 complete cycles of radio waves due to transitions between two particular energy levels of the cesium atom.

3. Scientists prefer using metric prefixes and units because it allows them to apply a simple set of conversions between units based on powers of 10 rather than having to remember many different conversions specific to each case. For example, converting millimeters to kilometers requires you to divide by 10^6, as does milligrams to kilograms. However, converting ounces to pounds requires that you divide by 16, whereas converting inches to feet requires division by 12 in American Standard Units.

5. No. 3 m = 70 m has consistent units (meters) but is clearly false. This is also the case for 1 = 2 (which is unitless).

7. m/s^2

9. B

11. C

13. C

15. D

17. C

19. The centerfield fence in Major League Baseball is about 400 ft or 120 m from home plate. A baseball will travel about 100 mph or 45 m/s as it leaves the pitcher's hand, which is about the speed it leaves the batter's bat. This means the ball takes about 3 s to reach the fence for a line drive.

21. An average person uses about 100 L of water for showering. A total of 10 L of water is used for cooking, drinking, and washing hands; 24 L of water is used in the toilet; and 20 L is used for a load of laundry in a top-loading washer. So, a reasonable estimate of daily water use is about 150 L.

23. The tallest building may be about 10 stories on a campus (as long your campus is not in a large city). A typical floor of a building is 3.5 m high. So, the highest building is probably about 35 m tall.

25. A typical human male has a mass of 80 kg. A person is mainly water, and water has a density of $1000 \ kg/m^3$, so the volume of a human is about $0.08 \ m^3$. We are told that a cell is approximated by a sphere of radius 10^{-5} m, or approximately $4 \times 10^{-15} \ m^3$ in volume. The number of cells in the body is then 2×10^{13} cells.

27. A. 2.37×10^2
    B. 2.23×10^{-3}
    C. 4.51×10^1
    D. 1.115×10^3
    E. 1.487×10^4
    F. 2.1478×10^2
    G. 4.42×10^{-6}
    H. 1.2345678×10^7

29. A. kilo (k)
    B. giga (G)
    C. mega (M)
    D. tera (T)
    E. milli (m)
    F. pico (p)
    G. micro (μ)
    H. nano (n)

31. A. 1.25
    B. 0.233
    C. 0.786
    D. 4.54×10^6
    E. 0.0208
    F. 4.44×10^6
    G. 1.25×10^{-5}
    H. 1.44×10^8

33. A. 49.2
    B. 592
    C. 1.54×10^{-4}
    D. 11.5
    E. 2290
    F. 3580
    G. 6950
    H. 1.05×10^7

35. A. 0.328
    B. 0.112
    C. 2.20×10^6
    D. 4.4300
    E. 0.225
    F. 1.72×10^8
    G. 0.0225300
    H. 2.000×10^9

37. (a) 3×10^5 m; (b) 3.37×10^{-5} m; (c) 7.75×10^{10} W

39. 13 mpg

41. A. 4
    B. 1
    C. 6
    D. 1
    E. 5
    F. 2
    G. 3
    H. 4

43. A. 26.2
    B. -32.3
    C. 74.8
    D. 233

45. The first term in the equation has dimensions of length; the second term has dimensions of length divided and multiplied by time, which is length; the third is again length. Therefore, the equation is consistent.

47. The unit of mass is kg. The unit of speed is m/s, which is squared to give m^2/s^2. The fraction $\frac{1}{2}$ is unitless.

So the units of the right-hand side are then $kg \cdot m^2/s^2$. This must be equal to the units of the joule on the left-hand side.

49. A and E

51. (a) 0.0025 kg; (b) 0.15 mg/mL or .15 kg/m^3; (c) 5.2×10^{-16} m; (d) 0.0081 kg; (e) 2.0×10^{-5} m^3/s; (f) 1400 kg/m^3

53. 4.4 m

55. (a) 5.3 L or 0.0053 m^3; (b) 0.074 kg or 74 g

57. (a) BMI = m/h^2; (b) On Earth there are 2.2046 pounds in a kilogram. There are 39.4 inches per meter. So BMI = $(39.3702 \text{ in}/m)^2/(2.2046 \text{ lb}/kg) \ W/h^2 = 703 \ W/h^2$; (c) 81.3 kg to 97.6 kg

Chapter 2

1. The object's velocity gets closer to zero. The object slows down.

3. The average speed of an object is the total distance traveled by the object divided by the total time. The average velocity of an object is defined as the ratio of displacement, Δx, to the time interval, Δt. Average velocity is a vector (it contains both a magnitude and a direction), while average speed is not.

5. Speed and velocity have the same units. You can interchange them freely if the direction of the velocity is completely clear and constrained to be strictly positive. If the velocity is not fixed in one direction, the two terms must be distinguished.

7. One advantage is that people in countries other than the United States will be more likely to easily understand the distance component of the unit. The disadvantages are that no country lists its speed limits in m/s, so it's hard to figure out how long it takes to get to highway speed. Further, the raw numbers will be smaller than in the case of using another unit system, so careless readers may get the impression that the car has very slow acceleration. It would be better to use km/h/s, as speed limits around the world are generally expressed in km/h.

9. If the object has constant velocity (acceleration is 0), then the average velocity and instantaneous velocity will be the same. The average velocity and instantaneous velocity may otherwise agree for a moment during the interval over which the average is taken. For instance, if an object undergoes constant acceleration, then the average and instantaneous velocity will agree at the midpoint of the time interval over which the average is calculated.

11. The acceleration is constant. The acceleration is determined by the acceleration of gravity (which is approximately constant over the range of heights to which a ball can be thrown). Additional forces of air resistance may also cause acceleration, but these forces are small for the ball.

13. The velocity will be the same. The upward trajectory involves the ball going up and reversing itself, then duplicating the trajectory of the ball launched straight down. This means that the ball launched straight up will be traveling the same speed as the ball shot straight down when the falling ball passes the cannon on the way down to the bottom of the cliff.

15. The choice of "up" and "right" as positive directions is arbitrary. However, this convention is common in mathematics textbooks and allows us to apply common formulas easily. Having any standard coordinate system makes understanding the answers easier.

17. D

19. B

21. C

23. It may take 15 s to accelerate if limited by engine power. Only 6 s may be needed to decelerate by braking strongly (this is also the acceleration time of a fairly fast car).

25. (a) Stopping from 10 m/s in 2 s on a muddy field will have an acceleration of only 5 m/s^2. Stopping from 10 m/s in 0.5 s on a high-traction surface will require an acceleration of about 20 m/s^2; (b) For the male athlete, the accelerations will be approximately the same.

27. A 5-kg cat would need to reach a velocity of roughly 4.4 m/s to jump up to the counter (about 1 m high). If the cat's legs extend about 10 cm while jumping, this would require an acceleration of 98 m/s^2.

29. Cruise ships accelerate very slowly, reaching a cruising speed of 10 m/s over half an hour. This gives an acceleration of about 0.006 m/s^2.

31. (a) The ball goes from 0 m/s to about 45 m/s over the course of about 0.5 s as the pitcher winds up and throws the ball. This would equate to about 90 m/s^2; (b) The soccer ball accelerates from 0 m/s to about 30 m/s over the course of about 0.1 s as the player's foot makes contact with the ball. This means the acceleration is about 300 m/s^2.

33. $x(m) = 6t - 12, 0 \leq t(s) \leq 4.5$
$x(m) = 15, 4.5 \leq t(s) \leq 8$
$x(m) = 1.5t^2 - 22.5t + 99, 8 \leq t(s) \leq 13$
$x(m) = 5(t - 13) + 60, 13 \leq t(s) \leq 21$
$x(m) = 10(21 - t) + 100, 21 \leq t(s) \leq 24$
$x(m) = 70, 24 \leq t(s) \leq 25$

35. A. 108
B. 22.5
C. 201,000
D. 60
E. 44.7

37. 4 km/h

39. (a) Zero average velocity because he ends where he starts; (b) 4 km/h; (c) 2.70 m/s

41. 39.2 km

43. 17 m

45. 0.5 m/s

47. 0.918 s

49. 2.83 m/s^2

51. 28 m for the Bugatti; 33 m for the Saleen S7

53. 20.3 m

55. $x = x_0 + \dfrac{v^2 - v_0^2}{2a}$

57. 22.0 m/s

59. 5.99 m/s

61. (a) 8.2 m/s; (b) +1.6 m/s; (c) 0 m/s. It has already hit the ground; (d) after 1.84 s
63. (a) 58.24 s; (b) 3.53 m; (c) 13°
65. The trains will stop with 62 m between them.
67. (a) 2.9; (b) 0.41 m forward
69. Geoff wins
71. 2.83 m
73. 130 m
75. The payload reaches 3.90 km and takes 64.6 s from launch to landing.
77. (a) 0.500 s; (b) 2.20 m; (c) 0.736 s
79. 0.00230 m/s²
81. (a) 1020 m; (b) (i) 42.4 m/s; (ii) 0 m/s

Chapter 3

1. (a) As long as the magnitudes are unequal, there is no orientation of two vectors that will result in their adding to zero. The only time two vectors can sum to zero magnitude is when they point in opposite directions and have the same magnitude. (b) Three vectors with different magnitudes can sum to zero in any case where two of the vectors sum to be equal in magnitude and opposite in direction to the third.
3. If an object is moving at constant velocity (for example, the magnitude and direction of the velocity vector are the same at all times), the average and instantaneous velocities are identical. If an object's velocity is changing, these two velocity vectors are different.
5. Air resistance can be modeled as a force that depends on the velocity. Increased velocity causes a corresponding increase in drag force. Also, this force opposes motion, so it will point in the direction opposite of velocity. Therefore, the acceleration in the horizontal direction will oppose the direction the projectile is fired, and the projectile will slow down in the horizontal direction as it travels through the air. This is different from the case with no air resistance, where there is no acceleration in the horizontal direction and the projectile travels at a constant horizontal speed. This will result in the object traveling a shorter distance when air resistance is considered. In the vertical direction, if air resistance is considered, the projectile will experience larger downward acceleration as it rises and smaller (but still net downward) acceleration as it falls. As a consequence, the maximum speed in the vertical direction will be smaller, as will the maximum height.
7. A vector is a mathematical construct that incorporates both the magnitude and direction of a quantity. The magnitude is the size or quantity of the vector (its length). The magnitude contains no directional information.
9. (a) The maximum range is achieved by launching at an angle of 45 degrees; (b,c) From Equations 3-12 and 3-13, both the maximum height and longest time of flight are achieved by launching the projectile vertically.
11. Yes, at the highest point in the soccer ball's trajectory, the acceleration vector points downward. At this

point, the soccer ball's vertical component of velocity is changing from upward to downward (and is therefore 0). This means the soccer ball has velocity purely in the horizontal direction, meaning the velocity and acceleration vectors are perpendicular.
13. Yes. The force from the vine is accelerating the ape upward; at the bottom of the swing is when the vertical component of the velocity changes from downward to upward, which requires an acceleration in the upward direction.
15. Yes. You are accelerating because the direction of the velocity vector is changing. The acceleration vector points east.
17. B
19. D
21. D
23. D
25. B
27.

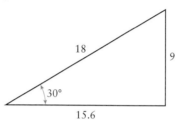

29. The ball peaked at about 110 ft in the vertical direction and about 300 ft in the horizontal direction. The launch angle is approximately 30 degrees. Using an acceleration of 32 ft/s², that corresponds to an initial speed of about 53 m/s. Without air resistance, because the ball reached maximum height at 300 ft, we might expect the ball to travel 600 ft. According to the graph, we expect the ball might travel 540 ft, suggesting that the second half of the ball's flight showed a 20% decrease in flight distance. Accounting for this loss due to drag, we might estimate an initial speed of up to 65 m/s for the baseball.
31. (a) (13,6); (b) (6,21); (c) (13,12); (d) (9.5,25.5)
33. (a) $A_x = 4.3$, $A_y = 2.5$; (b) $A_x = -2.5$, $A_y = 4.3$; (c) $A_x = -4.3$, $A_y = -2.5$
35. 73.5 m long with angle 61 degrees above the $+x$ axis
37. 8.00 m, 90 degrees from $+x$ axis
39. 50 m/s, 53 degrees west of north
41. 8.9 m/s², 40 degrees above the $+x$ axis; no
43. $v_x = 16.7$ m/s, $v_y = 11.3$ m/s
45.

(a)

(b)

(c)

47. (a) 2 travels farthest followed by 1, 3, 4, and 5;
    (b) 1 takes the longest followed by 2, 3, 4, and 5;
    (c) all have equal speed at impact
49. 5.53 m/s
51. 22.5 degrees elevation
53. 13.0 m/s² toward the center of the circle
55. 491 m/s² toward the center of the bit
57. 0.00104 m/s²
59. $\dfrac{a_{\text{Mary}}}{a_{\text{Kelly}}} = \dfrac{r_{\text{Mary}}}{r_{\text{Kelly}}}$ where r is the radius of the respective lane.
61. 8.94 m/s² toward the center of Earth
63. 1.7 km
65. (a) 4.0 s; (b) 140 m; (c) 0.92 s
67. (a) 0.705 s; (b) 1.11 s
69. 0.255 s
71. 6.71 km east and 13.4 km south
73. The balloon thrown down hits 0.186 s before the balloon thrown horizontally. They are both moving at the same speed at impact.
75. 35.3 m/s
77. 5.91 m/s
79. 27.4 m/s
81. (a) 82.2 ft/s; (b) 3.00 s
83. 2.83 times faster
85. Yes, the acceleration is only 5.80g

Chapter 4

1. Yes, the net force vector will determine the direction of the acceleration vector for the mass in question.
3. $[F] = \text{N} = \text{kg} \cdot \text{m/s}^2$
5. This definition agrees with the one given in the book. Each equal quantity of matter (by the measure of mass) resists acceleration to the same degree, so it has the same inertia.
7. Double the rope up. Each of the two strands of rope will then only have to support 425 N of force.
9. Yes, Earth also pulls on the Sun with a force equal in magnitude and opposite in direction to the force of the Sun on Earth. This is in agreement with Newton's third law.
11. Electrical wires hung on utility poles have a tension on them. Keys on a long cord will produce tension in the cord (especially when "swung"). When you walk a dog on a leash, there is a tension present in the leash. There is a tension in the straps of a backpack that is hanging off your shoulders. There is a tension in your shoelaces when you tie them.
13. As the elevator accelerates up, the scale reading increases to $mg + ma$. While ascending at constant speed, the scale again reads mg. As the elevator slows to

a stop, the scale reads $mg - ma$. As the elevator accelerates down, the scale again reads $mg - ma$. For the constant speed portion of the trip, the scale reading is mg. As the elevator slows down to stop, the scale reads $mg + ma$. Once the elevator is at rest, the scale again reads mg.
15. Zero, because the scale remains at rest.
17. 40 N; 100 N
19. Weight is due to gravity. The Moon has less gravity than Earth.
21. During a collision, the car slows down extremely fast while the people inside it continue moving forward due to their inertia. Seat restraints minimize the damage by slowing the people as soon as possible, preventing a buildup in the difference between the speed of the car and its occupants. Conventional restraints can still crush or cause whiplash, especially to children. A rear-facing restraint is tightly attached to the car's frame and will start slowing the infant immediately. The force will be distributed evenly over the baby's whole body, minimizing all of those risks.
23. A bird begins flying by pushing backward against the air with its wings. The air then exerts an equal and opposite force forward on the bird. This forward force propels it forward.
25. B
27. B
29. D
31. D
33. C
35. Apple ≈ 1 N; penny ≈ 0.03 N; textbook ≈ 25 N; calculator ≈ 5 N; 1 L of water ≈ 10 N
37. A baseball throw can be in the range of 40 m/s. A baseball has a mass of around 0.15 kg. The powerful part of the throw lasts about 0.05 s. This gives
$$F = m\frac{\Delta v}{\Delta t} \approx 120\,\text{N}.$$
39. Tennis balls weigh around 57 g. A typical ball launcher sends the ball at 12 m/s. This process takes around 0.1 s. The force is about 7 N.
41. 2,000 to 50,000 N
43. 1 to 5 N
45. The apparent weight of the rider as measured by a spring scale will reach its maximum value during the ascent from the ground floor to the fourth floor. This is because the weight of the rider will be added to the force required to accelerate from 0 m/s to 10 m/s.

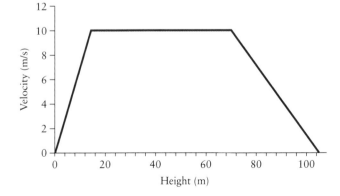

47. 4000 N
49. 12.00 m/s^2
51. (a) 120 kg; (b) 194 N
53. 2450 N
55. 0 N
57.

59.

$F_{\text{winch}} = 4500$ N

$F_{\text{drag}} = 2000$ N $F_{\text{gravity}} = 1960$ N

61. (a) The component of F$_3$ parallel to the +x axis is −210 N. The component of F$_3$ perpendicular to the +x axis is −33.8 N.
(b)

(c) When Player 3's rope brakes, the net force parallel to the +x axis is 170 N. The net force parallel to the +y axis is −3.67 N. The direction of the net force is 1.24 degrees below the +x axis.
(d) The net force is 170 N to three significant figures. This means the mass of the box is 17.0 kg.
63. (a) 45 N in the vertical, upward direction; (b) 10 N in the vertical, upward direction; (c) 0 N
65. 760 N
67. 410 N
69. 10,000 N
71. 481 N
73. 4.20 s
75. 1.50 m/s^2 to the west
77. 3.31 kg
79. 1.70 × 10^4 N
81. (a) 189 N; (b) 294 N; (c) 414 N
83. The scale will initially read 700 N while the elevator is at rest. Then it will read 914 N as the elevator accelerates upward. The scale will again read 700 N as the elevator travels at constant speed. The scale will read 557 N as the elevator slows to a stop. It will then read 0 N as the elevator free-falls to the bottom.

85. (a) $a = 2.10 \times 10^3$ m/s^2, the time is $t = 1.38$ ms
(b) $F_n = 25.9$ mN ↑

$F_g = 0.12$ mN ↓ ●

(c) $F_{\text{ground}} = 25.9$ mN, which is 215 times the weight of the froghopper.
87. (a) 644 N; (b) 92.9 kg
89. (a) 466 N; (b) 537 N
91. $T_1 = 2.49$ N and $T_2 = 7.46$ N
93. $a = 3.36$ m/s^2, $T = 19.3$ N
95. $a = 3.50$ m/s^2, $T_2 = 25.2$ N, $T_1 = 8.40$ N
97. 2910 N or 3.96 times the astronaut's weight on Earth
99. (a) The largest pull force before a string breaks is 73.2 N; (b) $T_A = 26.2$ N; $T_B = 45.0$ N

Chapter 5

1. Sometimes. If the coefficient of static friction is less than 1, the normal force will be larger than the static friction force. If the coefficient of static friction is more than 1, the static friction force can exceed the normal force or not, depending on how much friction is required to prevent slipping.
3. When a pickup truck accelerates forward, the contents will also accelerate forward due to the force of static friction between the box and the truck's bed.
5. (a) Weight stays the same; (b) normal force decreases; (c) frictional force is the same; (d) maximum static frictional force decreases
7. If the water stays in the bucket, it is because the whirling is so fast that at the top of the circle, the bucket is accelerating downward faster than the acceleration of gravity. The bottom of the bucket is needed to pull the water down! The sides of the bucket prevent the water from sloshing ahead or behind with the rest of the water that is going in the same circle. The weight is always pointing straight down (whether at the top or at the bottom), but the normal force N from the bottom of the bucket changes direction, pointing down at the top of the swing and up at the lowest point. Thus, $\sum F_{\text{top}} = mg + N$, while $\sum F_{\text{bottom}} = mg - N$.
9. Examples include an object on a slope; an object in a stack of objects (the lower objects' normal forces are greater than their own weight); an object pressed to a wall; and an object sitting in an elevator as the elevator accelerates.
11. His acceleration decreases because the net force on him decreases. Net force is equal to his weight minus his drag force. The faster an object is moving, the larger the drag force it experiences as a function of its speed. Because drag force increases with increasing speed, net force and acceleration decrease. As the drag force approaches his weight, the acceleration approaches zero.
13. The frictional force between tires and road provides the centripetal force that keeps the car moving in a circle. If the frictional force is not strong enough to keep the car in a circle, the car continues in a straight line and starts to skid.

15. If you know the car's instantaneous speed and the radius of curvature, you can use the formula $a_{cent} = v^2/r$. Another method would be to hang a small object from a light string and measure the angle θ of the string with respect to the vertical. The magnitude of the car's acceleration is the acceleration due to gravity multiplied by the tangent of the angle: $a_{cent} = g \tan \theta$.

17. Banking the curve allows the normal force to help push the car into the turn. The additional normal force also increases the maximum frictional force.

19. Yes. If he lies flat in relation to the wind and she does not, she will have a smaller profile in relation to the wind. Thus, she will experience less drag and be able to catch up.

21. A

23. A

25. A and D are both correct

27. B

29. 0.7 for standard tires, but as high as 0.9 for racing tires

31. Assume the initial speed of the runner is 7 m/s and the slide covers 3 m. The acceleration would be approximately -8 m/s^2. Then $\mu_k = a/g \approx 0.8$.

33. A hockey puck may leave the stick of a player with a speed of 8.0 m/s and slide about 30 m before coming to a stop. Then $\mu_k \approx 0.1$.

35. It takes about 2 s to fall 2 m at a 30 degree angle from the vertical (the length of the slide); with this data, the coefficient of kinetic friction is 0.34.

37. We can plot the force versus time.

Force vs. Time

Then we see that the crate is likely stationary up until $t = 0.3$ s. So we use the average of points at $t = 0.1$ s through $t = 0.25$ s to find the coefficient of static friction. We then use the points at $t = 0.35$ s through $t = 0.5$ s for the coefficient of kinetic friction. So $\mu_s = 0.837$ and $\mu_k = 0.535$.

39. 41.0 N

41. 0.5

43. (a) 245 N; (b) 25.0 N; (c) 0.102

45. 0.565 m/s^2

47. 80.2 N

49. 2.20 kg

51. $a = 2.21 \text{ m/s}^2$; $T = 36.1$ N

53. No motion occurs ($a = 0 \text{ m/s}^2$)

55. $40.0 \text{ } \mu\text{m/s}$

57. 151 N

59. 75.0 m

61. 1.58 N

63. 1.18×10^4 N

65. 8.97 N

67. (a) 0.0337 m/s^2; (b) 0.0217 m/s^2

69. 353 N

71. (a) 6.84 s; (b) The bottom of the tire tends to slip backward relative to the pavement, so the frictional force opposes the backward motion and hence is forward.

73. 3.77 m/s^2, up the slope

75. 0.382

77. (a) 3.63×10^{-5} kg/m; (b) 24.0 m/s

79. 0.409

81. $\theta = \cos\left(\dfrac{g}{L(2\pi N)^2}\right)$

83. 2.10 km

Chapter 6

1. If the magnitude of the force or the magnitude of the displacement is zero, then the work done can be zero. In addition, if the force and displacement are nonzero but perpendicular, then the work done will also be zero.

3. Stepping on the log rather than over it requires additional work to lift the body against gravity. Most of this additional work is not conserved, meaning it is more tiring to step on the log.

5. (a) Yes, she is expending energy; (b) No, she does no work on the boulder. The energy she is expending is being dissipated inside herself.

7. Yes. For example, if you push two boxes along the floor, the lead box is pushed by the normal force of the trailing box on the lead box. Since the contact surface between the two boxes moves, this normal force of the trailing box on the lead box does positive work on the lead box.

9. Yes, every time the kinetic energy decreases from a positive value to a smaller positive value, the change in kinetic energy is negative.

11. The snowboarder walks to the top of the mountain, which requires converting stored chemical energy into heat and kinetic energy, which in turn is converted into gravitational potential energy and more heat (if the snowboarder rides a lift, the source will also include wherever the lift gets its energy). Then, riding down, the gravitational potential energy and some chemical energy will be converted into kinetic energy, which is in turn dissipated into heat.

13. The orbital path of the satellite is around a circle. Its instantaneous displacement vector is tangent to the circle. The gravitational force points toward the center of the circle along the radius. The radius is perpendicular to the tangent of a circle, meaning that the displacement vector is perpendicular to the force. Therefore, no work can be done.

15. (a) When it reaches the bottom; (b) When it reaches terminal velocity. This will occur when the force of air resistance is equal and opposite to the force of gravity. This may or may not be before the rock reaches the bottom.

17. The system of you and Earth has more gravitational potential energy when you are at the top of the hill. It is harder to pedal up the hill because you are converting chemical energy in your body to mechanical energy, which is stored as potential energy as you climb the hill.

19. C
21. C
23. E
25. C
27. An 8-kg suitcase being lifted into a trunk that has an elevation of 0.75 m will gain 60 J of potential energy, but that energy is not the minimum required to get the suitcase in. The lip of the trunk is about 1.1 m above the ground, so the suitcase will at one point have an increase of 90 J in potential energy.
29. A standard estimate of the energy used during a hard jog is 7–8 kcal/kg/hr. For a runner who has a mass of 80 kg and runs 5 km in 25 min, the energy is roughly 1 MJ.
31. The cue ball has a mass of roughly 0.17 kg and travels at a speed of about 1.5 m/s, which yields 0.5 J for the kinetic energy.
33. Pumas have been seen to execute a 5.4-m vertical leap. Supposing that pumas are of average weight (62 kg), the maximum kinetic energy required is about 3300 J.
35. (a) 0.812 J; (b) 2.069 J; (c) 1.257 J; (d) 2.444 J
37. 8700 J
39. Moe does 6000 J of work, Larry does −3600 J of work, and Curly does 0 J of work.
41. (a) 2800 J; (b) −1000 J; (c) −1800 J; (d) 0 J
43. 0.013 J
45. 28.8 m/s
47. 13.3 m/s
49. 0.251
51. 1120 N; The force on the hand will be slightly less, as the glove will compress somewhat, absorbing energy.
53. 4.1 J
55. 2.5 J
57. −1.71 kJ
59. (a) 9.80 cm; (b) 0.960 J
61. 207 J
63. 426 N/m
65. 15.6 m/s
67. 9.66 m
69. 1.81 m/s; the mass impacts the speed only if the mass is too small. If the mass is too small, the mass of the string and the effects of air resistance will become significant.
71. 28.8 m/s
73. 43.8 m/s
75. +3.06 kJ for the rider, −3.06 kJ for the force of gravity
77. (a) $\sqrt{\dfrac{h}{H}}$; (b) 0.866
79. 0.370 m
81. 7.0 m/s
83. (a) 19.9 m; (b) 9.90 m/s
85. No, there was no friction.
87. 0.882
89. (a) 24 m/s; (b) 710 J/kg is lost to nonconservative forces
91. $v = \sqrt{3gR}$

Chapter 7

1. An impulse, commonly speaking, is a brief push; or, psychologically, a spur-of-the moment desire. This fits a common use for the physicist's notion of impulse, which is a collision. The forces in collisions will tend to be brief. Changes in momentum, of course, occur in other situations, and the term makes less sense there.
3. Yes, if the tennis ball moves 18 times faster.
5. The force of the impact is less on carpet, which can be seen by considering the momentum (the impulse is spread over more time) or by considering energy (the work is done over more distance).
7. Pushing off the boat to step onto the pier will push the boat away. You will make less progress than if you are on solid ground and can easily fall in the gap.
9. The momentum of Mars is around 1.5×10^{28} kg·m/s; the momentum of the asteroid is around 7×10^{12} kg·m/s. This is more than 15 orders of magnitude smaller, so no noticeable change to Mars' trajectory could result from the impact.
11. Deploying air bags around the phone allows the air bags to lower the force of the collision by increasing the length of time over which the collision occurs. The lower force is less likely to damage the phone.
13. When two balls are raised and released on a Newton's cradle, the balls collide with the balls at rest on the cradle and transfer their energy and momentum to the two balls on the other side of the collision. The fact that two balls are always moving is required by the combination of conservation of momentum and conservation of energy. If you only applied conservation of momentum, it would be possible for the three stationary balls to move off with a lower speed than the two incoming balls. This does not happen.
15. Part of the force opposing the arrow's advance is friction from the sides, which will depend linearly on how far the arrow has penetrated the target. This force is equivalent to a spring that resists compression but won't rebound. Doubling the speed will quadruple the kinetic energy. The kinetic energy is dissipated when the "spring" has absorbed all of the energy, which occurs at twice the depth. The arrow penetrates twice as far. We could alternately assume that the force is mainly at the front of the arrow and is constant. In this case, the penetration must quadruple for Fd to match the quadrupled kinetic energy. Other assumptions are possible, but they are more difficult to work with.
17. D
19. A
21. B
23. D
25. B
27. A baseball has a mass of about 145 g. A typical fastball is about 90–100 mph or 40–45 m/s. So, the momentum is about 6 kg·m/s.
29. Roughly speaking, it is around your navel. The ratio of the center of mass to height in humans is about 0.55.
31. $p = mv = (6 \times 10^{24}\,\text{kg})(30,000\,\text{m/s}) = 1.8 \times 10^{29}$ kg·m/s.
33. A tennis ball has a mass of 0.057 kg. Supposing an incoming volley is about 40 m/s, we get an impulse of around 5 kg·m/s.

35. (a)

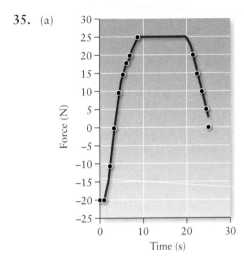

(b) The area under the force versus time curve gives the impulse; this area is approximately equal to the sum of each force value multiplied by the time interval of 1 second. This leads to an impulse of 388 kg·m/s. Because the mass of the object is 2 kg, the velocity will be 199 m/s.

37. 46 m/s

39. 946 kg·m/s

41. (a) 330 kg·m/s; (b) 5 kg

43. 0.8 m/s to the right

45. $v_1 = (1.1v_0, -1.1v_0)$, $v_2 = (0.95v_0, 0.55v_0)$

47. The lighter sheep wins.

49. 6.67 m/s due east

51. 9.81 m/s

53. 5.99 m/s, 45.2° deflected toward the sidelines from the running back's original path.

55. The lighter block goes 9.00 m/s and the heavier block goes 5.00 m/s, both east.

57. $v_{neutron} = 6.67 \times 10^4$ m/s in the reverse direction and $v_{deuteron} = 1.33 \times 10^5$ m/s in the forward direction

59. 160 N

61. 46.2 m/s

63. (a) 10.7 N·s toward the pitcher; (b) 10.7 N·s toward the catcher; (c) 8920 N; (d) The bat is able to dissipate this force by deforming during the collision.

65. The center of mass for the three-body system is at (30.8 cm, 10.8 cm).

67. 4.97 kg·m/s

69. (a) 8.63×10^{10} kg·m/s was temporarily "borrowed" from Earth while the people were falling, but there is no change from before the fall to after the fall; (b) While the people were falling, Earth temporarily moved toward them at a velocity of 1.45×10^{-14} m/s

71. 69.4 mph

73. 421 kg

75. The snowboarder is moving at 2.83 m/s, and the skier is moving at 14.1 m/s.

77. 76.5 km/h at 80.8° North of East.

79. 488 g

81. $v_0 = 5$ m/s, $\theta_1 = 45.5°$, $\theta_2 = 52.4°$

83. (a) $64/289 \approx 0.221$; (b) The oxygen nucleus rebounds in the original direction that the proton was traveling, the proton travels opposite its initial direction.

Chapter 8

1. N·m is the same unit as energy because 1 Joule = $1 \text{ kg} \cdot \text{m}^2 \cdot \text{s}^{-2} = \text{N} \cdot \text{m}$. However, even though the units are the same, we cannot equate torque and energy.

3. Different axes will have different moments. Imagine holding a long stick (4 m × 1 cm × 1 cm). It's easy to spin it around its center around an axis that runs along its length (low moment of inertia), but it is harder to spin it around an axis through its center and perpendicular to the length (high moment of inertia). Swinging it like a pendulum will be even harder.

5. (a) J; (b) kg·m²; (c) kg·m²/s

7. (a) They are leaning to change the torque that the force of gravity acting on them applies to the seesaw. Leaning backward increases the lever arm, and hence the torque exerted by gravity due to the person at the top. Simultaneously, leaning forward decreases the lever arm, and hence the torque exerted by gravity due to the person at the bottom. These two effects combine to provide a net torque that causes the seesaw to rotate so the person at the top descends, and the person at the bottom rises. (b) If the riders are going up and down by this method and are situated equally far from the center, their masses must be quite similar.

9. A tailless cat will have a much harder time. The initial step involves flinging the tail and legs out to the side. This increases its moment of inertia along an axis that the rest of the body lies along. The legs and tail are then spun around that axis. Conservation of angular momentum compels the rest of the body to spin the other way. Once the body is in place, the legs are retracted (lowering their moment of inertia) and oriented properly, then re-extended. Taking the tail away makes the process less effective. The tail (being long) has a large moment of inertia and, just as importantly, is able to counterbalance the legs so that the axis of the turn is placed along the axis of the body.

11. Assuming it's not simply an issue of her being too weak, she is pushing against the door too close to the hinges. This small lever arm does not let the force she applied produce enough torque.

13. The moment of inertia of the turntable–cookie dough system is greater than the turntable alone, yet the angular momentum is the same. Therefore, there is a brief pair of equal and opposite torques to accelerate the cookie dough and decelerate the turntable. The rotational kinetic energy decreases as the collision is inelastic.

15.

Translational motion	Rotational motion
$x = x_0 + v_0t + at^2/2$	$\theta = \theta_0 + \omega_0t + \alpha t^2/2$
$v = v_0 + at$	$\omega = \omega_0 + \alpha t$
$p = mv$	$L = m\omega r$
$\Sigma F = ma = dp/dt$	$\Sigma \tau = I\alpha = dL/dt$
$K = mv^2/2 = p^2/(2m)$	$K_{rot} = I\omega^2/2 = L^2/(2I)$

17. The rotational kinetic energy is proportional to the moment of inertia of the object that rolls without slipping down the inclined plane. The moment of inertia for each of the geometric shapes is $I_{sphere} = (2/5)\, mR^2$; $I_{cylinder} = (1/2)mR^2$; and $I_{ring} = mR^2$. The larger the moment of inertia, the greater the fraction of the initial potential energy that will transform into rotational kinetic energy, and the smaller the fraction that will transform into translational kinetic energy. The winning object will have the maximum translational kinetic energy and the minimum rotational kinetic energy. Because $0.4 < 0.5 < 1.0$, the sphere beats the cylinder beats the ring.

19. One radian is the angle produced by going one radius of length around the edge of a circle. Radians should be included if the resulting quantity is intrinsically angular in nature (e.g., one can include it in angular momentum) but not otherwise. For example, rotational kinetic energy is just energy, so the units are joules, not joules multiplied by radians squared.

21. (a) c; (b) i; (c) a; (d) ii; (e) d; (f) iv;
    (g)

23. B
25. E
27. C
29. B
31. B
33. The radius is around 25 m and the speed is around 15 m/s, so the angular speed is about 0.6 rad/s.
35. A typical door is about 1 m wide. A relatively small force, say 10 N, will open a door with well-maintained hinges if the force is applied perpendicular to the face of the door along the edge far from the hinges. The torque in this case is 10 N·m.
37. Female figure skaters are often around 50 kg. Model her body as a cylinder of mass M_{body} equal to 40 kg and radius R equal to 0.15 m; model her arms as rods each of mass M_{arm} equal to 5 kg and length L equal to 0.50 m. When her arms are extended, the moment of inertia of her body around her central axis is $I = (1/2)M_{body}R^2 = 0.45$ kg·m². Her arms each contribute $I = (1/12)M_{arm}L^2 + M_{arm}h^2$, where h is the distance from her central axis to the center of mass of her arms, approximately halfway from shoulder to hand. Here h equals 0.15 m + (1/2)0.50 m or 0.40 m. Each arm therefore contributes $I = 0.90$ kg·m²; her moment of inertia around her central axis is therefore 0.45 kg·m² + 2(0.90 kg·m²) = 2.3 kg·m². With arms drawn in tightly, let M_{body} equal 50 kg and neglect her arms; $I = 0.56$ kg·m².

39. One rotation per day yields $\omega = 0.000073$ rad/s.
41. If the ball's mass is 0.25 kg, its diameter is negligibly small and the radius of its motion is 1 m, its moment of inertia is 0.25 kg·m². If it completes one revolution per second, the angular moment is 7.2 kg·m²/s.
43. $\omega_{0-10} = 0.350$ rad/s, $\alpha_{15-25} = 0.480$ rad/s², $\tau_{0-10} = 0.000275$ N·m, $\tau_{10-15} = -0.018$ N·m, $\tau_{15-25} = 0.12$ N·m.
45. 1.71 rad/s
47. 2.65×10^{-6} rad/s
49. 2.24 J
51. 4.08 rad/s or 39.0 rpm
53. 86.5 kg·m²
55. $(11/6)\, MR^2$
57. $(3/2)\, MR^2$
59. 858 g·cm²
61. $21.25\, MR^2$
63. 3.32 m/s
65. 14 cm above the top of the loop
67. The translational kinetic energy is $5/2$ of the rotational energy.
69. 2.67×10^{33} J, the ratio is roughly 1.04×10^4
71. 1.05 J
73. 7.5 min
75. 0.335 rad/s², 0.553 m/s
77. 21 rad/s²
79. 74 N·m
81. 9.90 N·m
83. (a) 63.8 N·m; (b) 57.8 N·m; (c) 21.8 N·m; (d) 0 N·m
85. 102 kg
87. (a) 21.5 kg·m²; (b) 5.63 N·m
89. T = 1.63 N
    $\alpha_{pulley} = 13.1$ rad/s²
91. (a) T = 0.248 N
    $\alpha = 2.60 \times 10^2$ rad/s²
    (b) I = 2.38×10^2 rad/s²
93. 2.95 kg·m²/s
95. 7.08×10^{33} kg·m²/s
97. 5390 kg·m²/s
99. $0.63\, ML^2$
101. (a) 147,000 rad/s²; (b) 0.292 rotations
103. 190 rpm
105. (a) 24 spokes; (b) 1.24 kg
107. 2.15 m
109. 0.00114 N·m
111. $F = (196\ \text{N/kg})(1\ \text{kg} + M)$
113. (a) 1.16×10^{-9} rad/d/yr (b) Accumulated debris would take 2270 yr under present conditions.
115. (a) 71% of its current angular momentum, 4200 times as fast; (b) The kinetic energy increases by a factor of 7400.
117. Have the kids all move to the outer edge of the merry-go-round.

119. (a) $t = \dfrac{D}{x_c}\left(\dfrac{7M}{5k}\right)^{\frac{1}{2}}$

    (b) $[t] = \dfrac{[D]}{[x_c]}\left(\dfrac{[M]}{[k]}\right)^{\frac{1}{2}} = \dfrac{m}{m}\left(\dfrac{kg}{\frac{N}{m}}\right)^{\frac{1}{2}} = s$

Chapter 9

1. (a) Young's modulus accounts for the stretching or compressing of an object in one dimension. The bulk modulus describes the expansion or compression of an entire volume; (b) Both of the variables have the same units (Pa, MPa, GPa, etc.).

3. Yes. Real cables have weight, and that weight can be sufficient to break the cable.

5. Young's modulus describes the material's response to linear strain (like pulling on the ends of a wire); the bulk modulus describes the material's response to uniform pressure (acting over the entire volume); and the shear modulus describes the material's response to shearing strains. Determining the type of stress or strain involved (linear strain, uniform pressure, or shearing strain) implies which modulus (Young's, bulk, or shear) applies.

7. Due to the different shape of men's and women's lower bodies (in particular the width of their pelvis), there is different stress on the ACL. Additionally, increased flexibility in women can transfer additional stress to the ACL that may be carried by other muscles and tendons in men.

9. (a) The bottom of the plank is under compression; (b) The top of the plank is under tension; (c) The exact center is neither stretched nor compressed.

11. The brass wire stretches by $\dfrac{4\,mgL}{\pi D^2 Y_{\text{Brass}}}$ and the steel wire stretches $\dfrac{4\,mgL}{\pi D^2 Y_{\text{Steel}}}$

13. The shear modulus is a measure of how much an object will deform under a given stress. The larger the shear modulus, the less it will deform; it is more rigid. So, the term *rigidity* applies because a material will deform less if it has a larger shear modulus.

15. If the strings are hit by the ball, they stretch; if they are hit hard enough, the tensile stress exceeds the ultimate strength, and the strings break.

17. Leg bones need to hold form in order to fulfill their role in holding the body together; they are cushioned by hooves and cartilage. The small strain of the leg bone means that the bones do not change length by a large amount as weight is first placed on a leg and then taken off the leg. Antlers, on the other hand, need to be able to bend a great deal in order to survive the strong impacts to which they are subjected.

19. B
21. C
23. A
25. A
27. A
29. 10 GPa (approximately the same as for oak wood)
31. Assuming the breaking strength is about 10 MPa and the diameter of your bone is about 1 cm, this leads to about 800 N; a value of 1000 N or more is probably accurate.

33. 17,000 N
35.

(a) Yield strength = 250 GPa; (b) ultimate strength = 400 GPa; (c) Young's modulus = 1250 GPa

37. 3400 N
39. F = 950 kN, strain = 0.14
41. brass
43. (a) The strain on the aluminum bar is 2.86 times the strain on the steel bar; (b) The strain is independent of the relative lengths of the bars
45. 1.6 kN
47. 0.27 MPa
49. (a) 64.2 mm; (b) 6.42 mm
51. 2.0×10^8 Pa
53. 4.64 cm
55. $(x/h) = 0.00125$, $\phi = 0.0716°$
57. 1.16×10^{-3} m^3
59. 240 kPa
61. (a) 5; (b) No, they cannot use this rope.
63. 1270 N, 286 lbs
65. (a) 1.2×10^8 strands; (b) 2.2 cm; yes this seems reasonable.
67. (a) $\Delta V = .046$ cm^3 (the diamond increases from 0.11 cm^3 to 0.16 cm^3); (b) $\Delta r = 0.04$ cm (r increases from 0.30 cm to 0.34 cm)
69. (a) 0.035 mm; (b) no; (c) It depends on whether the given length of the bone is for when he is standing or lying down. Include the weight in cases in which the given length is for lying down.
71. (a) 1.12 cm; (b) 2 cm
73. 2.6 mm
75. 51,000 N
77. (a) 9800 N; (b) 0.34 cm^2

Chapter 10

1. Newton reasoned that the Moon, as it orbits, falls back toward the center of Earth due to the pull of gravity. Incrementally, it will move tangent to the orbital path; then it will fall back to Earth. The combined motion leads to the familiar circular path. An apple falls straight toward Earth without the tangential motion. The vertical motion is the same for both the apple and the Moon.

3. (a) When the mass of one object is doubled, the force between two objects doubles; (b) If both masses are halved, the force between two objects is one-fourth the original value.

5. The mass cancels when applying $F = ma$ to get the acceleration.

7. Orbiting the Sun is an incomplete description of the Moon's motion, but the Moon is definitely orbiting the Sun as a part of the Earth–lunar system.

9. The most noticeable effects would be the comparison between the dynamics at relatively small distances (such as the Earth–Moon system) with the dynamics at extremely large distances (such as galaxies and galaxy clusters). The deviation in the inverse square law would result in a different value for G or M. Also, noncircular orbits would not be elliptical, although if the power is close enough to 2, the difference in orbit could be too small to notice without watching for a very long time.

11. The gravitational potential energy is negative because we choose to place the zero point of potential energy at $r = \infty$. With that choice, the gravitational potential energy is negative because the gravitational force is attractive. The two objects will gain kinetic energy as they approach one another.

13. By Kepler's law, the faster an object is moving as it orbits the Sun, the closer it is to the Sun. Thus, Earth is closer to the Sun when the Northern Hemisphere is in winter.

15. Humans had to evolve to support their body against the force of gravity (human legs had to evolve to support the weight of a human). The cardiovascular system had to evolve to be able to move blood back from the legs to the heart against the force of gravity. The way humans run is also evolved to the particular gravity of Earth. There are many other examples.

17. B

19. E

21. A

23. B

25. A

27. Assuming it is possible to measure a force of about 10^{-7} N, about 1 cm center-to-center separation.

29. The potential energy difference between the top of Mount Everest and sea level is only 0.14% when using a constant g model as opposed to using the full law of gravitation.

31. The force between Earth and Jupiter is 1/18,000 of the force between Earth and the Sun. The impact would be small.

33. 4×10^{-10} N, toward the stump

35. 9.4×10^{-16} N

37. The force of attraction to Earth is 9.80 N. The force of attraction to the Moon is 3.44×10^{-5} N.

39. 2.37×10^{20} N toward the Sun

41. 346,000 km from the Earth or 38,400 km from the Moon

43. 49.0 N for the object on Earth's surface versus 49.1 N for the second object. These values are essentially the equal. The small difference arises from the fact that $\dfrac{GM_{\text{Earth}}}{R_{\text{Earth}}^2}$ does not exactly equal 9.80 m/s^2.

45. $+490$ kJ

47. (a) 1450 m/s; (b) 1.05×10^8 J

49. 1.88 Earth years

51. 7730 m/s

53. 4.07×10^7 m

55. 3.59×10^7 m above Earth's surface

57. 3.751×10^8 m

59. (a) The potential energies are -9.37×10^{10} J and -1.42×10^{10} J for nearest and farthest point in the orbit; b) 8.95×10^{10} J are required

61. (a) 7.44 km/s; (b) 8.37 km/s

63. (a) 2.54 s; (b) 9.44 m/s toward the surface of Mars

65. (a) 1.52 hr; (b) 88.3 N, which is 90.1% of the force on the surface of Earth; c) The rest of the space station is falling with the object. Since both the object and the station are in free-fall together, there is no weight relative to the station (if we ignore tidal effects).

67. 5.48×10^{-12} N toward the center ball

69. 25.8 cm from the larger (10 kg) object

Chapter 11

1. No. The pieces could be different sizes.

3. No. The pressure of the water is determined by its depth, gravity, and the pressure pushing down on the surface (air pressure). The ability of the dam to withstand the pressure does of course depend on its shape.

5. The pressure would be higher because of the additional pressure from fluid depth.

7. The collection bag should be held below the body so that the blood can flow down into it.

9. It is easier because the addition of salt to water makes it denser which increases the upward buoyant force of the water on you.

11. The same. Density is intrinsic to a material, weight only depends on mass and gravity, and both blocks will experience the same upward buoyant force from the water because they are submerged.

13. The dam could be the same thickness.

15. The airflow over the roof is very fast, while the airflow inside the house is not. This lowers the exterior pressure. If the roof is not made to hold down against a large part of an atmosphere of pressure pushing it up, it flies off.

17. Horizontal

19. D

21. B

23. A

25. A

27. A

29. A wind that is 33 m/s (barely hurricane level) passing over the top of a 1 m^2 prone body that is on top of still air results in a lift of approximately 700 N.

31. Mercury is 760 mm; water is 13.6 times greater or 10.4 m; and seawater is 10.1 m.

33. Using a 6:1 hydraulic jack operated by hand, a 300-kg object could easily be lifted.

35. 62 g

37. (a) 589 kg/m^3; (b) Perhaps fresh wood; (c) 0.589

39. 42 L

41. 13 km

43. (a) $m_2 = \dfrac{m_1 s_2^2}{s_1^2}$; (b) $m_2 = 25\, m_1$

45. (a) 3.11 MPa; (b) 311 MPa
47. 98 kPa
49. 136 mmHg
51. 880 mmHg
53. 1.01 atm
55. 550 kPa
57. 1.0 kN
59. 19.8 kN; 4440 lb. It will be an outward force.
61. 14,000 N
63. (a) 1940 N; (b) The large piston rises by 0.00825 Δy_1; (c) 3.2 J of work is done either way.
65. (a) 35 N; (b) 60% of the total block volume is submerged; (c) 35 N
67. (a) $\Delta P = 1000sg$; (b) $F_{net} = (1000s^3 - m)g$; (c) weight = $1000s^3g$
69. Based on the measurements, the specific gravity of the crown is 19.1, which may be low enough to induce suspicion. However, the crown could still be a fake with the correct specific gravity if the mixture of metals used has an average specific gravity equal to gold.
71. (a) 1.11×10^{-4} m^3/s; (b) 0.354 m/s
73. 670 s
75. 380 m/s, way too fast
77. 1.04 m/s
79. 0.973 atm. The wind is made to go in a circle by the low pressure in the still center, so most of the pressure drop has to be from a lowered baseline pressure, not the Bernoulli effect.
81. 0.173 m
83. 0.003 Pa·s
85. 2.55×10^{-6} m^3
87. (a) 71 cm, no; (b) 3.54 m
89. (a) $1.59 \times 10^4/1.06 \times 10^4$; (b) 0.158/0.105; (c) 2.32/1.55; (d) Gauge pressure; these pressures are much less than atmospheric pressure. When you are cut, blood comes out rather than air rushing into your body.
91. (a) 4.1 m/s^2; (b) The reduced pressure lets the air in the buoy spread out more. The buoy will displace more water, causing further acceleration during the ascent. The radius at the surface is 0.70 m.
93. 0.0038 N
95. 18.8 m/s
97. 2.11

Chapter 12

1. Oscillatory motion includes simple harmonic motion, but it also includes circular motion, decaying oscillations, and oscillations that have shapes other than pure sine waves.
3. A child on a swing or any resonant musical instrument.
5. Breaths per minute is a frequency. The period is its reciprocal.
7. (a) radians/second; (b) radians
9. It is an offset of where in the oscillation cycle we choose to set the zero time. If, for example, the phase angle is π rather than zero, the solution

starts at $-A$ instead of $+A$. In either case, however, the initial velocity is zero, and the motion is the same.
11. The force of gravity depends on elevation and determines the period of the pendulum. Measuring the period and length of the pendulum will yield enough information to estimate the strength of the gravitational force; doing so very precisely would enable useful comparison to established values.
13. The frequency of the driving force is just how often the applied force repeats. That depends on things outside the oscillator. The natural frequency of the oscillator is the frequency it oscillates at most readily or the frequency it will oscillate at if displaced from equilibrium and released.
15. B
17. E
19. A
21. D
23. B
25. (a)

b) The graph is shifted 30° ($\pi/6$) to the left.
27. Swings are typically around 2 m in length, so we get a period of around 3 s.
29. 50 Hz
31. A shoelace is about 1 m long when removed from a shoe, so the period would be about 2.0 s if we ignore the mass of the shoelace.
33. A 0.01-g fly clinging to the bottom of a pendulum that has a disk bob which is 1 kg, has a radius of 10 cm, and is centered at 1 m from the axis would produce a frequency reduction of around 1 part in 4×10^7.
35. A broom that has a 1.5-m-long, 0.5-kg handle with moment of inertia $1/3\ (mL^2)$ about the end of the broom handle as well as a 0.5-kg broom head with moment of inertia mL^2 will have a period of about 2.3 s.
37. About 3 years
39. 80 Hz
41. (a) 0.067 s; (b) 1800
43.

(a) is the green line, (b) is the blue line, (c) is the red line
45. 0.38 s
47. (a) 3.2 J; (b) 14 cm; (c) 0.79 J

49. (a, c)

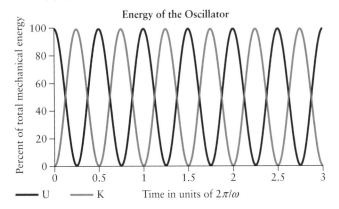

Energy of the Oscillator

— U   — K   Time in units of $2\pi/\omega$

(b) $v(t) = -\omega A \sin(\omega t)$

51. 1.26 m

53. 0.792 m

55. (a) 2.010 s; (b) 1.001 T_0

57. The time between $\pm 8°$ is 0.71 s. The time between $\pm 4°$ is 0.24 s.

59. 2.5 s

61. 0.53 s

63. (a) 0.36 Hz; (b) 0.25; (c) 0.35 Hz; (d) 9.1 s

65. 1.0 m

67. 3.2 m/s

69. (a) 0.41 m/s; (b) -0.74 m/s^2

71. (a) 1.55 m/s; (b) 7.5 cm or -7.5 cm from equilibrium

73. 16% loss per cycle

75. (a) 57 cm; (b) 0.90 m

77. (a) 1.89 s; (b) 1.63 s

79. (a) $T = 2\left(\sqrt{\dfrac{2y_0}{g\sin^2\theta}} + \dfrac{x_0}{2\sqrt{2gy_0}}\right)$; (b) 3.35 s

81. (a) 35 N/m; (b) 17.6 m

83. $T = 2\pi\sqrt{m\left(\dfrac{1}{k_1} + \dfrac{1}{k_2}\right)}$

85. (a) 0.61 m/s; (b) 3.75 m/s^2; (c) 0.44 m/s

Chapter 13

1. Longitudinal waves are those motions where the displacements are along the axis of wave propagation; transverse waves are those where the displacements are perpendicular to that axis. Longitudinal waves include sound and waves along a spring produced by extending and contracting it. Transverse waves include the vibrations of string instruments and "the wave" in a stadium.

3. A very few of them, maybe, especially if he is close by. The air molecules collide many times as they propagate the wave from place to place. The collisions transmit the wave motion without requiring the individual molecules to go the full distance.

5. Yes

7. (a) The wave speed depends entirely on the medium, so wave speed increases as the wave passes from air into water; (b) The frequency is determined by the actual vibrations of the source, so the frequency does not change; (c) The wavelength depends on changes in the wave speed, so the wavelength increases, too.

9. A P wave moves the rock through which it moves along the direction of propagation much like a sound wave through air. This push and pull can cause tall buildings to sway and perhaps topple. S waves cause up–down displacements, which could cause objects to fall off shelves. In earthquakes, the most damage results from waves that propagate along the surface, in a way similar to waves on the surface of the ocean. Surface waves can be transverse undulations or, like ocean waves crashing near the shore, rolling waves that have both a transverse and a longitudinal component.

11. The frequency counts the number of oscillations per time. The angular frequency counts the oscillations per time in units of 2π; one complete oscillation is equivalent to 2π rad. The angular frequency is more natural from a mathematical point of view.

13. A rider on the train, moving at the same speed as the horn was when it emitted the sound, will not experience a Doppler effect on the whistle because of that shared velocity. There can be slight differences in the two velocities, though, from building up speed, braking, or going around a curve. In such cases, there will be a very slight Doppler effect.

15. The phase difference is how two waves line up. If it's 0, then they line up perfectly and add to each other directly, resulting in a wave with double the amplitude of either individual wave. If it's 180°, the two waves cancel perfectly, resulting in no wave. If it's 90° or 270°, then they add to each other, resulting in a wave with $\sqrt{2}$ times the amplitude of a single wave and phase directly in between that of the original two waves. If it's 300°, then again they add differently, but the result is a wave with $\sqrt{3}$ times the original amplitude of either individual wave, and a phase again directly between the two original waves.

17. The time it takes for the wave to make it from one end to the other and back determines the phase difference between one pass and the next. The lowest frequency that produces zero phase difference, and thus total reinforcement, is the fundamental frequency.

19. (a) Intensity is the power per unit area that is emitted by a source of sound. It has nothing to do with the reception of the sound through the process of "hearing." The units are W/m^2. Sound level is a mathematical relationship that puts the intensity onto a logarithmic scale. The units are decibels (dB). Loudness is the physiological response to sound waves. Different frequencies with the same intensity will be more sensitively heard by humans. Power is the energy per unit time emitted by the source. (b) Intensity depends on the inverse of the distance squared, so intensity increases as the source of sound moves closer. (c) Sound level depends on the log of intensity, so sound level increases as the source of sound moves closer. (d) The total power emitted by the source does not change as it moves closer to the observer.

21. B

23. D

25. B

27. D

29. C

31. 2.8 cm (if the voice box is considered to be an open–closed organ pipe).

33. 50 beats/s

35. Measure the pitch of the fundamental frequency (compare to a known standard like A 440 Hz), and measure the length of the string. The speed is twice the length divided by the frequency.

37. No wind: $t = (150\,\mathrm{m})/(343\,\mathrm{m/s}) = 0.44$ s; with wind of 10 m/s: $t = (150\,\mathrm{m})/(353\,\mathrm{m/s}) = 0.43$ s.

39. (a)

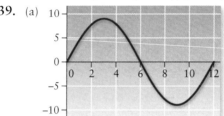

(b) $y = 9 \sin\left(\dfrac{\pi x}{6} + \pi t\right)$

41. $\lambda = 92$ cm, k = 6.85

43. (dimensions of ω)/(dimensions of k) = (inverse time)/(inverse distance) = distance $\times$ (inverse time); (dimensions of λ)(dimensions of f) = (distance)(inverse time) = (distance per time)

45. (a) 1.6 Hz; (b) 6.3 m; (c) 10 m/s

47. 0.1 m

49. $y = \sin(10\pi x - \pi t)$

51. 185 m/s

53. $D_A = 0.38$ mm, $D_D = 0.56$ mm, $D_G = 0.84$ mm

55. 1500 m/s

57. 1300 m/s

59. (a)   (c)

(b)   (d)

(a) A square wave packet with amplitude $2A_1$
(b) Zero
(c) A square wave packet with amplitude $2.5A_1$
(d) A square wave packet with amplitude $0.5A_2$

61. A: partially constructive; B: partially destructive; C: partially constructive; D: perfectly constructive; E: partially destructive

63.

65. (a) $f_1 = 27.0$ Hz; $f_2 = 54.0$ Hz; $f_3 = 81.0$ Hz; $f_4 = 108$ Hz

(b)

67. 12.6 kg

69. 70.5 N

71. Open at both ends

73. The length is 3.38 m, and the pipe is open at both ends.

75. 4.8 m. That's definitely on the large size, but not outrageous.

77. 8.79 Hz to 44.49 kHz

79. (a) 5 Hz; (b) Try tightening the string just a little tiny bit. If that makes the beats faster, loosen it a bit.

81. 104 N

83. (a) 3.16; (b) 1.73; (c) 1.41; (d) No difference, except that you may be able to get a larger factor decrease by moving to the side rather than directly away from the source.

85. 43 J per day. She'd do better by completely replacing the plan with something else. Barring that, she could move the collector closer to the highway (above the sound blocking barrier would be best), or make it much larger (much of the cost would be the electronics rather than the collector). Focusing wouldn't do much in the horizontal direction as the source is diffuse, but vertical focusing reflectors could help.

87. 102.8 dB

89. (a) 1.26; (b) 100

91. 50 μW

93. 53 Hz

95. 2.11 m/s

97. 0.33 m/s

99. (a)

(b)

101. (a) 1.69×10^5 N/m^2; (b) 1.47 kHz; (c) The parts of the resonator that are in the air all have a frequency increase from the substitution of some helium into the air; the parts of the resonator that are in the body do not. This produces a different mix of frequencies and a different general sound.

103. (a) 1760 Hz; (b) T/4

105. 31.8°C

107. 69.0 dB

109. (a) 1.1 mm; (b) 360 J

111. 2.98 m/s

113. 111 dB

Chapter 14

1. It makes sense because the average kinetic energy in each degree of freedom (position, rotation, deformation) is proportional to the temperature. It is a bit contradictory because the individual components can have more or less kinetic energy than average.

3. The warmer the day, the faster the molecules will move, so the sooner the smell will spread.

5. If the temperature is a temperature difference, then it could make sense. Otherwise, a temperature of $-508°F$ is less than absolute zero. The student's only other chance to be correct is if the question is counterfactual.

7. (a) The temperature is different in the various accessible places on the body, and most peripheral temperatures are noticeably cooler than core temperature. If armpit temperature gets as high as 37°C, that's a fever. (b) In addition to the normal measurement variations, the body's temperature is homeostatically regulated only to a range, and the set point of that regulation can shift (it tends to rise in the evening).

9. (a) They are the same temperature. (b) The steam because of its latent heat of vaporization.

11. Supposing that one understands what "thermometer" means and how to use one, the definition is not too bad. One limitation is that temperatures are achievable that cannot be measured with thermometers. Another limitation of the definition is that it doesn't incorporate anything about the underlying phenomenon, though defining temperature in a way that does is difficult.

13. The reason that so many people live near coastal regions (versus in landlocked locales) is related to this thermodynamic argument. The temperature range in landlocked regions is much larger because the specific heat of dirt is so much lower than that of water. The average temperature of Kansas City is about 12°C, and the average in San Francisco is 13°C. However, maximum and minimum temperatures range from below $-18°C$ to above 38°C in the Midwest, while in the San Francisco area, the range is from $-1°C$ to less than 38°C. The water that surrounds coastal cities tends to balance the temperature changes due to the large value for water's specific heat. The average temperature of a coastal city is basically the average temperature of the ocean right off the coast.

15. It makes sense to make highway repairs in the summertime because the material (concrete, asphalt, etc.) will expand to its maximum level when it is first put in place. If you repair a pothole, for example, in the winter months, the asphalt will expand beyond the hole's capacity when the warmer summertime comes around. This causes buckling and bumpy conditions.

17. The two metals must be chosen to have different thermal expansion coefficients. Because the metals are attached directly, thermal expansion will bend the bimetallic strip, which in turn pushes or pulls on the switch.

19. (a) $PV = NkT$ is most appropriate if one is counting molecules (deriving a quantity). $PV = nRT$ is most appropriate if one is counting moles (analyzing lab results). (b) P equals the pressure of the gas, V is the volume the gas occupies, N equals the number of molecules, n is the number of moles of molecules, k is the Boltzmann constant, R is the universal gas constant,

and T is the temperature of the gas.

21. First, the temperature of the ice rises to 0°C [the specific heat of ice is 2090 J/(kg·°C)]. Second, all the ice melts (the heat of fusion is 333,000 J/kg). Third, the water warms up to 100°C [the specific heat of water is 4186 J/(kg·°C)]. Fourth, all the water boils (the heat of vaporization is 2,260,000 J/kg). Finally, the temperature of the steam rises [the specific heat of steam is 2010 J/(kg·°C)].

23. Heated air expands and becomes more buoyant. Cooler, denser air near the ceiling descends. Thus, the warm fluid rises and the cooler fluid falls. The same effect will be found in a pot of heated water as well.

25. If A is in thermal equilibrium with B, and B is in thermal equilibrium with C, then A is in thermal equilibrium with C. This is used to establish that temperature is actually a property of objects.

27. B

29. A

31. D

33. A

35. C

37. A change of 103°F, going from $-54°F$ to 49°F (Loma, MT, in 1972)

39. 40°F on the coast, 80°F in a landlocked area

41. 2 or 3 minutes

43. 30 kJ

45. The final temperature is 84% of the initial temperature.

47. Conduction carries away about 200 times more heat.

49. (a) $0.10 per kg; (b) $0.75 per kg

51. (a) 82°F; (b) 14°C; (c) $-229°F$; (d) 290 K; (e) 99°F

53. The temperature at which the pressure of all gases should become zero is -273.15 K. This value, the same for all gases, sets the zero point of the Kelvin temperature scale.

55. 134°F and $-129°F$; 329.9 K and 184.0 K

57. The degree units on the Celsius and Fahrenheit scales are not the same. So while average kinetic energy per molecule in a gas versus temperature is a straight line using either scale, the lines have a different slope when plotted against Fahrenheit temperatures versus Celsius temperatures. These lines must however cross. $T_{cross} = -40°C$.

59. (a) 12.2 K; (b) $-260.8°C$, $-437.5°F$

61. Oxygen

63. 6.21×10^{-21} J

65. 4:3 (H_2O:O_2)

67. 1.80×10^{-10} m

69. $33.3 \times 10^{-6}/°C$

71. 4.985 cm

73. 8053 cm^2

75. (a) 0.0278 m; (b) final density = $(1 - 6.16 \times 10^{-7})$ (initial density); (c) 0.0000616%

77. (a) 1.0009×10^{-2} m; (b) 0.256%

79. 78.5 kJ

81. 3.85×10^5 J

83. 8.12×10^9 kg

85. 1110°C

87. 35.0°C

89. 19 strokes

91. 79.4 kJ

93. 248 kJ
95. 235 g
97. The iron melts 7.86 g of ice, the copper melts 10.1 g of ice, and the water melts 14.6 g of ice. Water melts the most ice.
99. A factor of 18.32 times
101. 65 solar radii or 4.5×10^{10} m
103. 6.12 kW
105. (a) 618 km/s; (b) 1.55×10^{7} K; (c) Not rapidly, anyway. The solar wind is not driven by thermal escape from the photosphere.
107. The wall lengthens by 0.281 cm
109. Heat up just the aluminum to 470°C, while leaving the copper at room temperature.
111. 346 μW
113. 7870 J must be removed
115. (a) 7.1×10^{20} J; (b) 5.4×10^{12} gal; (c) 3.3×10^{8} tons
117. 3250 kcal, not unreasonable for a man of this size.
119. (a) The stored energy is proportional to the animal's mass, which is proportional to its volume, which is proportional to the cube of its radius $\left(V = \frac{4}{3}\pi R^3 \right)$. The rate at which the animal radiates energy is proportional to its surface area, which is proportional to the square of its radius ($A = 4\pi R^2$). (b) The fraction of its stored energy that it radiates away per second is $(\Delta E / \Delta t)/E$. The numerator is proportional to R^2, and the denominator is proportional to R^3, so the radiated ratio is $\left((\Delta E / \Delta t)/E \propto \left(\dfrac{R^2}{R^3} \right) \propto (1/R) \right)$. (c) For a small animal (small R), the fraction of its energy radiated per second is larger than it is for a large animal. To replace this energy in order to maintain a constant body temperature, the small animal must eat more frequently than the large animal.
121. 0.129 m^3 of water leaks out of the sphere.

Chapter 15

1. (a) Isothermal processes are those in which the temperature remains constant throughout. An example of an isothermal process is when an acid is slowly poured into a base and allowed to equilibrate with a water bath. The work done by isothermal processes (for an ideal gas) is given by $nRT \ln (V_f / V_i)$. (b) Adiabatic processes are those in which there is no heat lost or gained. An example of an adiabatic process is a bicycle pump that is used to increase the pressure and temperature of the air that is inside as it goes into the tire. The work done by an adiabatic process is simply the change in internal energy (because $Q = 0$). (c) Isobaric processes are those in which the pressure remains constant. An example of an isobaric process is a gas in a cylinder that is sealed with a moveable piston. As the gas is heated, the volume will expand to balance out the increase in temperature but the pressure remains constant. (d) Isochoric processes are those in which the volume does not change. An example of an isochoric process is a gas inside a cylinder that cannot expand or contract. If you change the temperature of the gas, it will respond by changing the pressure. No work is done by isochoric processes.

3. The compressing force causes the walls of the container to hit the gas molecules with more force than if the walls were stationary. This causes more acceleration of the molecules, resulting in higher temperature.

5. Kinetic friction saps kinetic energy and converts it into heat. Unless the engine was attempting to generate heat, the heat from friction is energy that won't be going to whatever it was the engine was supposed to accomplish.

7. A coefficient of performance only gauges how efficiently existing energy is shifted from one place to another; it does not indicate violation of conservation of energy.

9. It increases by the amount of the heat divided by the temperature for the cool object (Q/T_c), minus the amount of heat divided by the temperature for the hot object (Q/T_h). When there was a temperature difference, that difference could be harnessed to do work. Once the two objects have equilibrated, that way of extracting work is no longer possible because the difference no longer exists.

11. Before the gas was released, one knew that the gas was entirely in the smaller volume. This is a state of relative order. After the release, the gas can be anywhere in the larger volume, which is a more disordered state than before the expansion. This corresponds to an increase in entropy.

13. The irreversible processes are a bit like one-way streets—you can go around the block, but you cannot take a U-turn. More concretely, general heat loss is undone not by letting the heat back into the hot object, but by finding something even hotter or by doing work on the object to heat it; the halting of a ball that rolled to a stop is not undone by letting the grass kick it back into motion, but by going and fetching the ball. Note that the reversible adiabatic cooling does not let heat escape to the environment, but rather stores the thermal energy as mechanical energy in another part of the system.

15. No. The term *surroundings* is a boundary we draw at our convenience. If we chose the system as Earth and imagined enclosing it in a perfectly reflecting balloon to prevent heat exchanges with its surroundings, would we suddenly be unable to break teacups?

17. As the piston recedes, it will sap energy from the gas molecules striking it. This lowers the gas temperature, requiring it to be reheated by the hot reservoir—but that is then not isothermal. The slower the piston recedes, the less energy it saps, but if the engine is to actually run at all, it does have to move. By not acting isothermally, there is heat, so Q/T will be nonzero, and thus there is an entropy increase.

19. There are relatively few configurations of the cup's components that are a cup, compared to the number of configurations that are not. This ratio is so large that it is difficult to express even with scientific notation. Even if the dropping-on-floor process is changing the state of the glass in random ways instead of preferentially destructive ones, the random drawing will be from the full set of states and cup states are a vanishingly small portion of the set.

21. B

23. B

25. A

27. D

29. A

31. (a) Raising a 1-kg book 1 m would take about 10 J. (b) This would raise the temperature of a glass of water by 0.02°C.

33. Treat the gas as ideal, so $U = 3/2 \, nRT$. One liter of oxygen is about 0.05 mol. Convert the temperatures from °C to K; the change in internal energy is about 40 J.

35. At a typical metabolic 20% efficiency, about 2 km up. The efficiency of the climbing itself is likely to lower this further, so probably less than 1.5 km.

37. 500 km

39. $e = (T_{body} - T_{environment})/T_{body}$; using $T_{body} = 310$ K and $T_{environment} = 293$ K, e is about 5.5%. $[310 - 293]/310 = 5.5\%$. This is far lower than real human body efficiency; the body is not well modeled as a heat engine.

41. 300 J

43. 300 J

45. 0 J

47. 8.8 kJ

49. 9.22 kJ

51. -800 kJ

53. -321 K

55. 2.91 kJ

57. 19.2 g

59. 1.4

61. 27.5

63. 40%

65. 14.8%

67. 13.7 kJ

69. 3.41

71. (a) 5.43; (b) 225 J; (c) -24°C

73. 245 J/K

75. -16.9 J/K

77. 1.48 kJ/K

79. 25.9 J/K

81. 23.1 J/K

83. 1.83×10^6 kg

85. (a) 47.2°C; (b) 32 J

87. The efficiency drops from 10.5% to 9.66%.

89. The room's entropy increases by 25.5 kJ/K.

91. (a) 15.8%; (b) 1.37 TJ

93. (a) 329 kJ = 0.0914 kWh; (b) 956 kJ; (c) 3.24 kJ/K

95. (a) 38%; (b) 0.288 J/K; (c) 78.6 J

97. The water's entropy increases by 24.7 J/K

Chapter 16

1. Similarities: The force varies as $1/r^2$; the force is directly proportional to the product of the masses or charges; the force is directed along the line that connects the two particles.
   Differences: Newton's law includes a minus sign, whereas Coulomb's law does not. Like charges repel; like masses always attract. The gravitational constant G is many orders of magnitude smaller than the Coulomb constant k, the gravitational force is many orders of magnitude weaker than the Coulomb force.

3. There would be no difference. The charges were originally arbitrarily defined as positive and negative.

5. The mass decreases because electrons are removed from the object to make it positively charged.

7. Our current understanding is that like charges repel and opposite charges attract. If a charged insulating object either repels or attracts both charged glass (positive) and charged rubber (negative), then you may have discovered a new kind of charge. However, you may also just be observing polarization (to be discussed in later chapters).

9. When the comb is run through your hair, electrons are transferred to the comb. The paper is polarized by the charged comb. The paper is then attracted to the comb. When they touch, a small amount of charge is transferred to the paper so now the paper and comb are similarly charged and repel each other.

11. (a) No, the object could be attracted after being polarized. (b) Yes, to be repelled, the suspended object should be charged positively.

13. (a) If the charges creating the field move, the fact that the field propagates at the speed of light also allows us to understand the changes in the field, and hence force on the other charged objects. With the electric field, we see that charged particles take some time to experience the effects of other charges moving near them. (b) In electrostatics the field is just a computational device, and using it is merely a matter of convenience. However, in electrodynamics the field is necessary for energy and momentum to be conserved, so it is more than just convenience that leads us to the electric field.

15. The electric forces are equal in magnitude but opposite in direction, and the force on the proton is downward while the force on the electron is upward.

17. The electric field is the total electric field due to all charges both inside and outside the Gaussian surface. However, the charges outside the surface create a net zero electric flux through the surface.

19. B

21. C

23. A

25. C

27. B

29. Around 10^{-11} or 10^{-12} C

31. Around 1–10 μC.

33. About 0.05 N·m^2/C.

35. 4.6×10^{-18} C

37. 2.7×10^7 C

39. 2.7×10^{13} electrons

41. (a) 2.33×10^5 C/m^3; (b) Insulating. If it were conducting, none of the charge would be in the volume of the sphere. Charge would only be on the surface.

43. (a) $-1.25 \, \mu$C; (b) 7.8×10^{12} e$^-$; (c) No more than three steps

45. 5.08 m

47. 0.0110 N to the right

49. -27.3 m

51. $F_A = 36.3$ N at angle $\theta = 24.4°$ below the negative x axis
    $F_B = 43.5$ N at angle $\theta = 10.9°$ below the positive x axis
    $F_C = 25.2$ N at angle $\theta = 67.4°$ above the negative x axis

53. (a) q_1 and q_2 have opposite charges (one is positive and the other is negative). (b) The charge of q_2 is larger in magnitude to counter the effect of being a larger distance away.

55. (a) 6.88×10^7 N/C in the $+x$ direction; (b) -24.1 cm

57. (a) 5.09×10^5 N/C pointing $25.9°$ above the negative x axis; (b) 8.15×10^{-14} N pointing $25.9°$ below the positive x axis

59. 2.18×10^6 m/s

61. 0.075 N·m^2/C

63. 6.64×10^{-5} C/m

65. $E = \sigma/\varepsilon_0$ pointing radially outward.

67. (a) We're not told the direction of the electric field, so the charge could be positive or negative. We'll assume positive. $Q = 1.78 \times 10^{-11}$ C; (b) 3.54×10^{-9} C/m^2

69. $+3.20$ μC on the inner shell, -9.00 μC on the outer shell. The field points radially inward with magnitude 6.61×10^7 N/C

71. (a) With 94 protons confined to a small space, they are likely to be concentrated into an approximately uniform sphere of charge, which is equivalent to a point charge for points outside it. (b) 1.1×10^{29} m/s^2

73. (a) 1.6×10^7 electrons; (b) $m_{el}/m_{cell} = 1.6 \times 10^{-10}$. So the extra mass is not significant. (c) $\sigma = -0.014$ C/m$^2 = 9.0 \times 10^{16}$ electrons/m^2

75. 7.9×10^{-9} C

77. (a) 1.9×10^{-16} C; (b) 1200 electrons

79. 2.16×10^{10} N/C at an angle of $60°$ with respect to the $+x$ axis

81. 14.2 N/C in the direction of travel of the electron

83. (a) 1.8×10^{21} N/C, outward from the center of the nucleus. (b) 1.5×10^{13} N/C, outward from the center of the nucleus. (c) 2.6×10^{24} m/s^2, outward from the center of the nucleus.

85. (a) The electric field is pointing downward. (b) Gravity pulls downward on the drop, so the electric force on it must be upward. Since the drop is negative, the electric field must point downward for the force to point upward. (c) 9070 N/C; (d) 7

87. (a) 0; (b) $\dfrac{\sigma_i R_i^2}{\epsilon_0 r^2}$ pointing radially outward;

(c) $\dfrac{\sigma_i R_i^2 - \sigma_o R_o^2}{\epsilon_0 r^2}$ pointing radially outward

Chapter 17

1. The electric potential is the electric potential energy per unit charge and is a scalar. The electric field is the electric force per unit charge and is a vector. The electric potential depends on both the electric field and the region over which the field extends.

3. Both electric field and potential result from the existence of a charge. If a charge exists, it will create both of these physical quantities. In order to have a nonzero potential energy, a force must be able to do work on an object as it is moved. If only one charge exists, then there is no electric force acting on the charge. If there is no force, then that force can do no work, so there is no potential energy.

5. This statement makes sense only if the zero point of the electric potential has been previously defined.

7. A topographical map details the lines surrounding a mountain (for example) where the elevation is the same. These plots let a hiker know how the terrain changes in elevation as one moves from point A to point B. If the lines of elevation are very close together, that will indicate that the mountain is very steep. Walking along these lines of constant elevation is much easier (no change in gravitational potential energy). With an equipotential line, the quantity that stays the same is the voltage. With no change in voltage, there is no change in electric potential energy (hence, no work is done when an electric charge moves along an equipotential line). These lines will never cross (they would be multivalued and that is not possible), and the closer together they are, the greater the electric field is in that region.

9. (a) Yes, a region of constant potential must have zero electric field. (b) No, if the electric field is zero, the potential need only be constant.

11. Increase plate area, decrease separation, and increase the dielectric constant.

13. Connecting capacitors in series allows the total potential difference to be split among the individual capacitors. Every capacitor has a maximum allowable voltage that cannot be exceeded. If the maximum voltage across a capacitor is exceeded, the resulting electric field will cause dielectric breakdown, destroying the capacitor. By connecting the capacitors in series, each capacitor is kept below its maximum voltage.

15. The energy stored in the capacitor increases.

17. For a given potential across them, the capacitors in parallel have a greater total area and so can store a greater amount of charge, thus having a larger capacitance.

19. The larger dielectric strength increases the maximum voltage that can be applied across the electrodes. The larger dielectric constant decreases the voltage required to store a given amount of charge, thus increasing the capacitance. The dielectric material can also be used to maintain the separation of the electrodes.

21. D

23. C

25. C

27. B

29. A

31. 10^6 m

33. 25 V

35. (a) -3.20×10^{-6} J; (b) 3.20×10^{-6} J; (c) The potential difference between the two points would remain the same. However, if a negative charge were placed at rest at point a, then it would never reach point b unless an external force acted upon it. The charge would accelerate in the $-x$ direction, away from point b.

37. 242 V

39. 18 J

41. 28.8 V

43. -2.78×10^{-8} C

45. 7.14 cm and 16.7 cm

47. 2.13×10^{6} V

49. (a) 1 V/m to the left; (b) 1 V/m to the left

51.

(a)

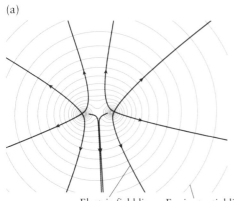

Electric field line   Equipotential line

(b)

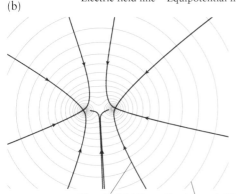

Electric field line   Equipotential line

53.

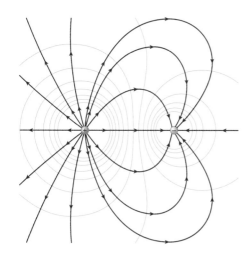

55. 24 μC

57. 8.85×10^{-9} F

59. 1.00 mm

61. 6.37×10^{-7} J

63. 2000 V

65. 1000 J

67. (a) 55.0 μF; (b) 5.00 μF

69. 4.00 μF and 4.00 μF

71. 11.0 μC on the 0.0500 μF capacitor and 22.0 μF on the 0.100 μF capacitor

73. 4.0 μF

75. (a) 7.41 μF; (b) 88.9 μC on each capacitor; (c) $V_{10} = 8.89$ V, $V_{40} = 2.22$, $V_{100} = 0.889$ V

77. 8020

79. 2.15×10^{-7} C

81. (a) $C_{eq} = \dfrac{\epsilon_0 A}{2d}\left(\dfrac{3\kappa_2\kappa_3}{\kappa_2 + \kappa_3} + \dfrac{\kappa_1}{2}\right)$

(b) $\kappa_3 = 1$ so $C_{eq} = \dfrac{\epsilon_0 A}{2d}\left(\dfrac{3\kappa_2}{\kappa_2 + 1} + \dfrac{\kappa_1}{2}\right)$

83. 1.45×10^{7} m/s

85. (a) $U = \dfrac{3kq^2}{a}$

(b) $U = \dfrac{2kq^2}{a} + \dfrac{kq^2}{b}$

(c) $U = \dfrac{5kq^2}{a} + \dfrac{kq^2}{b}$

87. (a) 231 N; (b) Not large enough to move you, but large enough to feel. (c) 2.31×10^{-13} J; (d) 5.04×10^{8} m/s; (e) It is faster than the speed of light!

89. 4.4 pF

91. 1.15 pF

93. 7.2 μC

95. 720 μJ

97. (a) C increases by a factor of 4; (b) Q increases by a factor of 4; (c) V remains constant; (d) The stored potential energy increases by a factor of 4; (e) The capacitance will still increase by a factor of 4, the charge will remain constant, V is reduced by a factor of 4, and the energy is reduced by a factor of 4.

99. (a) $C_{before} = \dfrac{\epsilon_0 A}{d}$, $C_{after} = \dfrac{\epsilon_0 A}{d - d'}$

(b) The effect is independent of the location of the slab.

101. (a) $Q = 75$ μC, $U = 1.1 \times 10^{-4}$ J

(b) $Q_{20} = 33.3$ μC, $Q_{25} = 41.7$ μC, $U_{20} = 27.8$ μJ, $U_{25} = 34.7$ μJ

103. (a) 2.00×10^{6} V/m; (b) $\sigma = 1.77 \times 10^{-5}$ C/m^2; (c) Since the charge remains constant, the surface charge density also remains constant. This means that the electric field also remains constant. The voltage between the plates, however, is reduced because the quantity d is reduced.

Chapter 18

1. Current is the amount of charge passing a point in the circuit per second. In this sense, it is more like a flux than a vector. It has a direction and magnitude, but is not really a vector.

3. There is no contradiction. If a conductor is in electrostatic equilibrium, the electric field within it must be zero. However, any conductor that is carrying a current is definitely not in electrostatic equilibrium.

5. This energy is dissipated as heat in the wire. The amount of energy dissipated is related to the amount of current running through the wire and the resistance of the wire.

7. A small resistance will dissipate more power and generate more heat.

9. The bird will not be electrocuted because there is no potential difference between the bird's feet. The bird grabs only one high-voltage wire, and it is not completing a circuit.

11. The voltage drop across each bulb in the old series string was about 1/50 of 110 V, or 2.2 V. The modern parallel connection puts the full 110 V across each bulb. Placing 110 V across one of the old bulbs, designed to operate at 2.2 V, would result in excessive current in the filament, which would burn out the bulb immediately, perhaps in a spectacular manner.

13. It cannot be changed instantaneously because the resistor in the circuit limits the current (the rate of flow of charge). Because the current is finite, it requires time for the charge to flow on and off of the capacitor plates.

15. A

17. E

19. D

21. C

23. B

25. A laptop computer draws about 2 A of current. A hair dryer draws about 10 A of current. A compact fluorescent light bulb draws about 0.2 A of current.

27. About 10 Ω

29. About 100 mA

31. 1 kΩ, 100 μF

33. 1.12×10^{22} electrons

35. 1.09×10^{22} electrons

37. (a) 4.82×10^3 A; (b) Potassium ions are positive, so the current is in the same direction that the ions flow.

39. 0.0220 Ω

41. 16.0 Ω

43. 0.109 Ω

45. The resistor that carries 112 pA is 10 times larger in diameter than the other.

47. (a) 0.77; (b) 1.3

49. 12,000 K$^+$ ions

51. 12 Ω

53. 4.0 V

55. 24.0 Ω

57. (a) 0.750 A in each resistor; (b) $V_9 = 6.75$ V, $V_3 = 2.25$ V

59. (a) 0.60 A in each of the 6-Ω resistors and 0.30 A in the 12-Ω resistor. (b) 1.5 A

61. 29 Ω

63. $R_A = 6.0\ \Omega$, $R_B = 3.0\ \Omega$

65. 12.5 A

67. 2.7 kW

69. 58 MW

71. $1.32

73. 12.0 s

75. 0.500 A

77. (a) (i) 0.00216 s, (ii) 0.00108 s; (b) (i) 0.0667 A, (ii) 0.211 A

79. 5 Ω: 45 W; 8 Ω: 28 W; 10 Ω: 90 W; 16 Ω: 56 W

81. (a) 30 Ω; (b) 3 hours and 45 minutes longer

83. (a) 16 Ω; (b) 20 Ω: 0.12 A, 12 Ω: 0.20 A, 8 Ω: 0.32 A; (c) 20 Ω: 0.29 W, 12 Ω: 0.49 W, 8 Ω: 0.84 W; (d) It is 18% of the total power dissipation.

85. (a) 4.8 $\Omega \cdot$m; (b) 24 W

87. 39 kΩ

89. (a) 36 μC; (b) 0.060 A; (c) 6.0×10^{-4} s after closing the switch

91. (a) Parallel because both branches (the circuit element and the probe) span the same potential difference; (b) (i) Very large resistance because this will cause the total resistance of the two components in parallel to have approximately the same resistance as the original element, (ii) Very small capacitance so that the time constant is small. The measurements will quickly reach a steady state because many time constants elapse over a short time.

93. (a) 1000 F; (b) 1100 J, or 10^6 times more energy; (c) 17% of the energy of a AAA battery; (d) 0.060 Ω

Chapter 19

1. Use both ends of one iron rod to approach the other iron rods. If both ends of the rod you are holding attract both ends of the other two rods, then the one you are holding is not magnetized iron.

3. The wire is aligned with the magnetic field.

5. (a) The electric field points into the page. (b) The beam is deflected into the page. (c) The electron beam is not deflected.

7. Yes, because the width of the field determines the length of the wire in the magnetic field. The larger the length of wire in the magnetic field, the larger the force exerted on the wire will be.

9. Since the directions of the two currents are opposite, the magnetic field from one wire is opposite to the other. This means the magnetic fields will cancel each other to some extent.

11. There will be no net force on the wires, but there will be a torque. When two wires are perpendicular, each wire will experience a force on one end and another force, equal in magnitude but opposite in direction, on the other end. This results in zero net force. However, the forces will produce a nonzero torque that will make the wires want to align with each other such that the current in each wire is traveling in the same direction as the current in the neighboring wire.

13. C

15. D

17. A

19. A

21. E

23. about 4×10^{-6} T

25. 6 μs

27.

For $r < 0.01$ m: $B(r) = (0.501 \text{ T/m})r$
For $r > 0.01$ m: $B(r) = (0.000050 \text{ T} \cdot \text{m})/r$

29. (a) out of the page; (b) down; (c) down; (d) to the left; (e) out of the page; (f) right

31. 0.7 N

33. 5.8×10^{-18} N to the left

35. 3.4×10^{-12} N in the $-z$ direction

37. 5×10^{-3} T in the $+x$ direction

39. 1.5 μm

41. 0.511 T

43. 0 N

45. 2.5 T

47. 0.664 N·m at 30°
0.755 N·m at 10°
0.493 N·m at 50°

49. B_O and B_P point in the $+z$ direction (out of the page). B_Q and B_R point in the $-z$ direction (into the page).

51. $B = \dfrac{\mu_0 I}{4}\left(\dfrac{R - r}{rR}\right)$ into the page

53. $B = 4 \times 10^{-6}$ T $= 0.08\, B_{\text{Earth}}$

55. 120 m

57. 1.03×10^{-8} N away from wire 2

59. 0.313 N

61. 0.0109 T

63. 9.12×10^{-31} kg

65. (a) $B = 1.0$ T at $r = 1.0$ m, $B = 0.001$ T at $r = 1.0$ km. Compared to Earth's magnetic field, the lightning bolt has a magnetic field 20,000 times as large at 1.0 m and 20 times as large at 1.0 km. (b) $B = 2.0 \times 10^{-6}$ T at $r = 1.0$ m, $B = 2.0 \times 10^{-9}$ T at $r = 1.0$ km. In each case, the field due to the lightning is 500,000 times greater than the household current. (c) $r = 2.0$ mm

67. 0.40 N

69. (a) 298 A; (b) 0.62 T; (c) The easiest way to achieve the same field with less current is to increase the number of windings, N.

71. (a) 15.9 mA; (b) The loop will initially rotate to point its dipole moment in the direction of the magnetic field. At this instant, there is no net torque on the loop, but because of its rotational momentum it will continue to rotate past this point, slowing down. After it momentarily comes to rest, it will rotate back toward its initial position. If the system is frictionless, this harmonic oscillation will continue indefinitely.

73. 650 V

75. $B = \dfrac{\mu_0 i}{2\sqrt{2}\pi d}$ pointing down and to the right so that the vector is 45° below a horizontal line pointing to the right.

77. $B = 1.5 \times 10^{-6}$ T $= 0.031\, B_{\text{Earth}}$. Since the field is so much smaller than the Earth's magnetic field, there should be little or no cause for concern.

79. (a) $B = 0.7155 \dfrac{\mu_0 Ni}{R}$ in the $+x$ direction.

(b) $B = 0.221 \dfrac{\mu_0 Ni}{R}$ in the $+x$ direction.

81. (a) 2.64×10^{-6} T pointing westward; (b) 2.64×10^{-7} T pointing vertically upward; (c) 2.64×10^{-6} T pointing southward; (d) In (a) and (c), B is about 5% of B_{Earth}. This is fairly small, but it could possibly be enough to interfere with navigation. In part (b), B is about 0.5% of B_{Earth}, which seems too small to cause much of a problem.

Chapter 20

1. The falling bar magnet induces a current in the wall of the pipe. In accordance with Lenz's law, the direction of this induced current is such that it produces a magnetic field that exerts a force on the magnet opposing its motion. The speed of the magnet therefore increases more slowly than in free-fall until it reaches a terminal speed at which the magnetic and gravitational forces are equal and opposite. After this point, the magnet continues to fall, but at a constant speed.

3. (a) The magnetic coil produces a rapidly varying magnetic field that flows through the plate. From Lenz's law, this induces a current in the plate such that the magnetic field of the plate opposes the field of the magnetic coil, repelling the plate and causing it to levitate. (b) The large induced current in the plate dissipates a large amount of power in the plate, heating it up. (c) If the plate were an insulating material, this trick would not work because a current could not be induced.

5. A current is induced in loop b while the current in loop a is changing. If the current is in the direction shown and is increasing, the flux of its magnetic field through loop b is upward and increasing. In accordance with Lenz's law, the direction of the induced current in loop b is such that the flux of its magnetic field through loop b is downward, opposing the change in flux that produced it. This means that the current in loop b is in the opposite direction as the current in loop a, and the two loops repel. After the current in loop a stops changing, then the current in loop b becomes 0 and there is no force between the loops.

7. D

9. C

11. A

13. About 16,500 A

15. About 5 V/km or 15,000 V total. This is such a large variation that it would cause the cable to exceed the maximum current allowed and cease to function.

17.

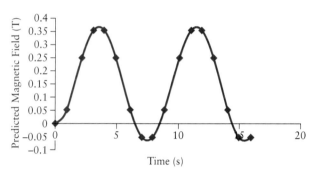

19. (a) 0.204 Wb; (b) 0.220 V
21. (a) counterclockwise; (b) clockwise; (c) clockwise; (d) counterclockwise; (e) clockwise; (f) no induced current
23. V

25. (a) For part a and part c, $F = 0$ on all segments. For part b, using x to represent the length of the given segment still in the magnetic field, $F = 0$ on the right-hand segment, $F = (0.0790$ N/m$)x$ in the upward direction for the top segment, $F = (0.0790$ N/m$)x$ in the downward direction for the bottom segment, and $F = 0.0790$ N to the left for the left-hand segment. (b) The current will be counterclockwise as viewed. The force on the left-hand segment will be zero. The force on the top and bottom segments will be $F = (0.0790$ N/m$)x$ downward and upward, respectively. The force on the right-hand segment will be $F = 0.0790$ N to the left.
27. 380 V
29. 1.9×10^6 rev/s. This is nearly 2 million rev/s, which does not seem feasible.
31. (a) 0.12 V; b) 0.0047 A; (c) counterclockwise
33. 2.1 V
35. (a) 0.01 A; (b) up; (c) 0.001 N

Chapter 21

1. It means that the current peaks one-fourth of a period after the voltage drop peaks. One-fourth of a period corresponds to a phase difference of 90°.
3. Ohm's law ($V = iR$) is not precisely valid for AC circuits. But if you use the rms voltage and the rms current, it can still be used to describe a resistor in a circuit.
5. For example:

Country	V_{rms}	Frequency (Hz)
Angola	220	50
Botswana	231	50
Ecuador	120–127	60
Mexico	127	60
Slovenia	220	50

7. No. These devices usually work over a range of voltages and will not function properly if a transformer is used. They contain "smart" circuitry that senses if the voltage is 120 V or 240 V. (Many people needlessly buy transformers for their laptops. What may be needed, depending on destination, is an adapter plug.)
9. PCBs were widely used for many applications, especially as dielectric fluids in transformers, capacitors, and coolants. PCBs have low water solubility ($0.0027 - 0.42$ ng/L for Aroclors) and low vapor pressures at room temperature, but they have high solubility in most organic solvents, oils, and fats. They have high dielectric constants, very high thermal conductivity, and high flash points (from 170 to 380°C) and are chemically fairly inert, being extremely resistant to oxidation, reduction, addition, elimination, and electrophilic substitution.
11. The electrical energy stored in the capacitor is $U_E = \dfrac{q^2}{2C}$, which varies as $\cos^2 \omega t$, and the magnetic energy stored in the inductor is $U_B = \dfrac{Li^2}{2}$, which varies as $\sin^2 \omega t$. Therefore, when a maximum amount of energy is stored in the capacitor, no energy is stored in the inductor, and vice versa.
13. The capacitor has energy $U_E = \dfrac{q^2}{2C}$ and the inductor has energy $U_B = \dfrac{Li^2}{2}$. We see that both energies are proportional to the square of a quantity related to charge (either i or q). However, the magnetic energy stored is proportional to the inductance, but the electric energy stored is inversely proportional to the capacitance.
15. (a) Self-inductance drops by a factor of 2; (b) self-inductance increases by a factor of 2
17. Impedance describes the overall opposition to the flow of charge in a circuit driven by a time-varying voltage. The SI units of impedance are ohms (Ω).
19. D
21. A
23. C
25. C
27. Most household appliances draw between 1 and 20 amps. Most households have a main circuit breaker that "trips" at 150 A or so.

29. The voltage is graphed in red, oscillating between +12 V and −12 V. The current is shown in black, and oscillates between +0.001 A and −0.001 A.

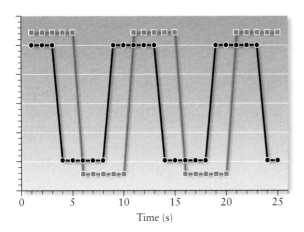

31. $V(t) = 120\sqrt{2}V \sin(120\pi t)$
33. 11.6 V
35. 849 V
37. $V_{max} = \sqrt{2}i_{rms}R$
(a) 0.354 A; (b) 707 V; (c) 156 Ω
39. 22 turns
41. 2 A rms
43. (a) 21 turns; (b) 0.788 A
45. (a) 42; (b) $i_s = 0.0150\ A$, $i_p = 0.625\ A$; (c) 192 Ω
47. 0.19 mH
49. (a) 9.65 mH; (b) The inductance doubles, assuming the number of turns and the length are held constant because the inductance is proportional

to A: $\left(L = \dfrac{\mu N^2 A}{\ell} \right)$.

51. 41 Hz
53. 286 H/F
55. 1/4
57. 5.07 nF
59. 3.2 A
61. (a) 4.50 μF; (b) The rms current will increase. As ω is increased, X_c is reduced, so i_{rms} will increase.
63. (a) $i = 0.566\ A$, $P = 16.0\ W$; (b) $i = 1.45\ A$, $P = 0\ W$; (c) $i = 1.78\ A$, $P = 0\ W$
65. $V_R = 1.00\ V$, $V_C = 10.3\ V$, $V_L = -1.25\ V$
67. 590 Ω, 65°
69. (a) 690 Ω; (b) 0.15 A; (c) $I(t) = (0.15\ A) \sin(1000\ \pi t + 1.56)$
71. 104.5 MHz, $i = 0.009$ A
73. 5.07 nF
75. (a) $\kappa = 6.03 \times 10^7$; (b) Table 17-1 tells us that this is not a feasible dielectric constant since it is much greater than that of ordinary materials. However, the required capacitance ($C = 670\ \mu F$) is easily within the range of ultracapacitors.
77. For DC, $V = 60$ V. For AC, $V_{rms} = 15$ V and $V_0 = 21$ V.
79. (a) $i_0 = 1.53\ A$, $V_0 = 13.0\ V$; (b) 10.0 W; (c) 3.60×10^4 J
81. (a) $V_R = 14.9\ V$, $V_C = 53.9\ V$, $V_L = 23.4\ V$; (b) $V_R = 33.9\ V$, $V_C = 80.9\ V$, $V_L = 80.9\ V$; (c) The sum of the voltages is larger than the applied voltage because the maximum voltages in each circuit element are not reached simultaneously. Since each element

reaches its maximum voltage at a different time, the sum of the maximum voltages is not required to equal the maximum applied potential. (d) At resonance, the impedance of the capacitor is equal to the impedance of the inductor. Both circuit elements have impedance of $\sqrt{L/C}$. Therefore, the maximum voltage of each circuit element will be the same.

Chapter 22

1. (a) e, c, b, d, a; (b) Gamma rays have the highest energy per photon. Microwaves have the lowest energy per photon.
3. The electric field is perpendicular to the magnetic field and the velocity of the wave. That means, for example, that the electric fields will vibrate along the x axis, the magnetic field along the y axis, and the EM radiation will move along the z axis. These three vectors are mutually perpendicular to each other.
5. The speed of light is proportional to the frequency $(c = \lambda f)$.
7. All EM waves move at the same speed ($c = 3.00 \times 10^8$ m/s). However, the wavelength times the frequency equals this constant ($c = \lambda f$). Therefore, the wavelength can vary (smaller/larger) in proportion to the frequency (larger/smaller).
9. For example, using visible light to see in your house, using wireless Internet transmitted as radio waves, and using microwaves to heat food in a microwave
11. C
13. D
15. E
17. 1.3 s
19. 2.25 eV
21. About 10 nm
23. People 300 km away receive the news first. $t_{radio} = 0.001$ s and $t_{sound} = 0.0088$ s.
25. (a) 7.25×10^{-8} m, UV; (b) 4.29×10^{-7} m, Purple Visible; (c) 3.75×10^{-9} m, X ray; (d) 1.00×10^{-5} m, IR; (e) 3.33×10^{-5} m, IR; (f) 8.72×10^{-10} m, X ray; (g) 3.65×10^{-8} m, UV; (h) 5.00×10^{-8} m, UV
27. (a) 4.29×10^{14} Hz; (b) 5.00×10^{14} Hz; (c) 6.00×10^{14} Hz; (d) 7.50×10^{14} Hz; (e) 3.00×10^{15} Hz; (f) 9.01×10^{18} Hz; (g) 6.00×10^{11} Hz; (h) 4.47×10^{18} Hz
29. 2.78 m to 3.41 m
31. 3 m
33. 1.28 s
35. (a) 2.09×10^7 m; (b) $\omega = 3.77 \times 10^{15}$ rad/s, $f = 6.00 \times 10^{14}$ Hz, $\lambda = 5.00 \times 10^{-7}$ m
37. (a) 1.26×10^{11} m^{-1}; (b) $12\pi \times 10^{18}$ rad/s; (c) 4.99×10^{-11} m; (d) 6.02×10^{18} Hz
39. 2.8 A
41. 1.0×10^{-5} T
43. (a) 6.67×10^{-7} T; (b) 53.1 W/m^2
45. (a) $\lambda = 853$ nm, $f = 3.52 \times 10^{14}$ Hz; (b) $\lambda = 442$ nm, $f = 6.79 \times 10^{14}$ Hz; (c) $\lambda = 621$ nm, $f = 4.83 \times 10^{14}$ Hz; (d) $\lambda = 232$ nm, $f = 1.29 \times 10^{15}$ Hz; (e) $\lambda = 19.6$ nm, $f = 1.53 \times 10^{16}$ Hz; (f) $\lambda = 142$ nm, $f = 2.11 \times 10^{15}$ Hz; (g) $\lambda = 627$ nm, $f = 4.78 \times 10^{14}$ Hz; (h) $\lambda = 273$ nm, $f = 1.10 \times 10^{15}$ Hz

47. (a) 62.1 nm to 414 nm; (b) It extends from violet visible light into the UV.

49. (a) 0.45 m; (b) 101,000 J/m^3

Chapter 23

1. Christiaan Huygens suggested that every point along the front of a wave be treated as many separate sources of tiny "wavelets" that themselves move at the speed of the wave. This is important to see how light moves from one medium to another, different, medium and allows you to predict the bending that occurs in Snell's law.

3. The light coming from the Sun is refracted as it passes through Earth's atmosphere. Because of the wavelength dependence of the index of refraction, red light bends less than orange than yellow than green than blue than violet. In addition, bluer light is scattered more than red light as it passes through the atmosphere. Because of these effects, more red/orange colored light can pass into the shadow of the Earth, making the Moon appear red.

5. The swimming pool seems shallower. If you follow a light ray that bounces off the bottom of the swimming pool and ends up entering your eyes, the light exits the water at an angle from the normal larger than the angle at which it arrived at the water–air boundary. This is because the index of refraction of water is greater than that of air. Your brain assumes that light travels in a straight line, so you interpret the origin of the ray on the floor of the swimming pool to be along the line of the light ray as it enters your eyes. The distance you measure to the origin of the light ray is fixed by your stereo vision, so the swimming pool appears to be shallower than it really is.

7. When light moves from a medium of larger index of refraction toward a medium with a smaller index of refraction, the angle of refraction will *increase*.
If you make the incident angle larger and larger, the refracted angle will ultimately approach 90°. After the light moves past this critical value, it is reflected rather than refracted. In mathematical terms, sin θ cannot be larger than 1. When Snell's law would require the sine of the angle of refraction to be greater than one, total internal reflection will occur.

9. When light enters a material with a negative index of refraction, the light refracts "back" away from the normal to the surface as seen in the picture below:

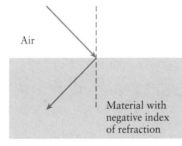

Air

Material with negative index of refraction

11. 1. Soap bubbles reflect different colors. 2. Thin film coatings on photographic lenses ("nonreflective coatings"). 3. Oil floating in a puddle of water will show different colors

13. Yes, diffraction occurs for all wavelike phenomena. Sound waves are diffracted through an open window, and water waves are diffracted around an obstacle in the water, for example.

15. Sunlight includes all of the colors of the rainbow, and one of the delightful aspects of a diamond is its strong dispersion. The diamond bends violet light much more than red light so that sunlight is separated into its different colors as it passes through the diamond surface.

17. D

19. B

21. B

23. A

25. A

27. air–diamond: $\sim (1.0–2.4)$

29. (a) 300,000,000 m; (b) 2×10^{10} m; (c) 9.5×10^{15} m

31. $n_2/n_1 = 1.56$

33. 1.00029

35. 763 km

37. (a) 13.2°; (b) 22.1°; (c) 30.9°; (d) 20.1°

39. (a) 41.8°; (b) 48.8°; (c) 58.5°; (d) no critical angle

41. 41.8°

43. 48.8°

45. 59.1°

47. (a) 59.1°; (b) 0.00793 cm

49. 0.0534 cm

51. 60° and 120°

53. 150 W/m^2; the light is polarized 75° from the vertical

55. 40.9°

57. 36.9°

59. 452 nm

61. 648 nm

63. $t = 93.8$ nm; $t = 282$ nm; $t = 469$ nm; $t = 657$ nm

65. $\lambda = 631$ nm and $\lambda = 473$ nm are not seen in the film.

67. $\theta_1 = 36.4°$, additional fringes are not visible.

69. 583 nm

71. 633 nm

73. 17 mm

75. 7.71×10^{-6} degrees $= 1.34 \times 10^{-7}$ radians

77. 3.46×10^{-5} m

79.

Optical material with percentage of time required for light to pass through compared to an equal length of vacuum	Speed of light	Index of refraction
100%	3.00×10^8 m/s	1.00
125%	2.40×10^8 m/s	1.25
150%	2.00×10^8 m/s	1.50
200%	1.50×10^8 m/s	2.00
500%	6.00×10^7 m/s	5.00
1000%	3.00×10^7 m/s	10.00

81. $n_1 \sin(\theta_1) = n_n \sin(\theta_n)$ is true

83. 40.5°

85. (a) 0.969 m; (b) You would have to change the index of refraction of water to be smaller than the index of refraction of air. Under this condition, total internal reflection cannot occur.

87. 9.14 m

89. (a) 9.38 W/m^2; (b) 45°

91. 902 nm

93. 188 μm

95. (a) 1.77; (b) 310 nm, 465 nm, and 620 nm

97. (a) 500 mi/hr; (b) 1.2 hr; (c) The formula $w\sin\theta = m\lambda$ applies only if the wavelength is smaller than the slit width. In this case, $w = 100$ mi and $\lambda = 500$ mi, so the formula would not apply.

99. 9.35×10^{-4} rad. This is larger than the pupil, which makes sense because the pupil is larger in diameter than the hole.

101. (a) Ring 1 occurs at 3.05×10^{-4} rad $= 1.75 \times 10^{-2}$ degrees, ring 2 occurs at 5.58×10^{-4} rad $= 3.19 \times 10^{-2}$ degrees, ring 3 occurs at 8.10×10^{-4} rad $= 4.64 \times 10^{-2}$ degrees. (b) $x_1 = 7.6 \times 10^{-3}$ mm, $x_2 = 1.4 \times 10^{-2}$ mm, $x_3 = 2.0 \times 10^{-2}$ mm. (c) The dark rings, and hence the bright rings, are so close together that the bright rings are essentially right next to each other and mask the dark rings, thus eliminating the diffraction effect and giving us only bright light.

103. (a) about 55–60 cm; (b) Telescopes are built larger than the diffraction-limited diameter for greater light-collecting power (it allows you to see dimmer objects).

105. (a) 13.1 cm; (b) 96.9 cm. Since the resolution with atmospheric turbulence is less than the diffraction limited resolution, the atmospheric resolution is the limiting factor, so the telescope can resolve only objects separated by about 1 m.

Chapter 24

1. Actually, a plane mirror does neither, but instead inverts objects back to front. If the mirror inverted right and left, then the object's right hand that points east would appear on the image as a right hand pointing toward the west. Because the image is inverted back to front, the object facing north is transformed into an image that faces south. Also, the object's right hand is transformed into a left hand in the image.

3. A real image forms where light rays come together but no light rays actually meet where a virtual image forms.

5. This phrase refers to the fact that the curved mirrors produce images that are not located at the same point as an image in a plane mirror. In fact, the mirrors are designed so that if you see a vehicle in the rearview mirror, you should not change lanes because they are too close.

7. Additional information is needed. In accordance with the lensmaker's equation, if the radius of curvature of the front surface is the larger, it is a diverging lens; if the radius of curvature of the front surface is the smaller, it is a converging lens.

9. The full image formed, but it is dimmer than before because it is formed with half as much light.

11. Since the brain can be "trained" to interpret all the nerve inputs that it receives, it is feasible that upright and inverted could be "redefined." It must be very disconcerting, however, for those several days when "up is down and down is up!"

13. The condition known as presbyopia (farsightedness) is associated with a weakening of the muscles around the eye and inflexibility in the crystalline lens system as a person ages. This loss in adaptive amplitude leads to the inability to focus on objects that are close up. Myopia, on the other hand, is a disorder that affects as many as 50% of the world's population, but it is not brought on by the aging process.

15. B

17. A

19. B

21. B

23. B

25. 3 m

27. For example, a shiny spoon (f about 5 cm), a shiny salad bowl (f about 15 cm), and a reflector in a flashlight (f about 2 cm).

29. About 22.86 cm

31. 60°

33. 0.900 m

35. The first five images to the left are 3 m, 17 m, 23 m, 37 m, and 43 m to the left of the left mirror. The first five images to the right are 7 m, 13 m, 27 m, 33 m, and 47 m to the right of the right mirror.

37.

39. The camera will focus the lens on the surface of the mirror (2 m away from the virtual image). It will be out of focus a little bit.

41. As long as $d_O > f$, the image will be real in a concave, spherical mirror. In this case, the focal point is located between the mirror and the object.

43. (a)

(b) $d_I = 13$ cm, $m = -1.7$. The image is real and inverted.

45. (a)

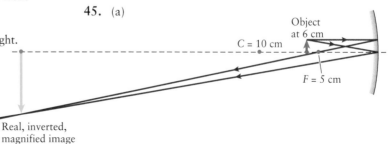

(b) $d_I = 30$ cm, $h = -5.0$ cm

47. (a) $d_I = 30$ cm, $h = 60$ cm, the image is real and inverted; (b) $d_I = 12$ cm, $h = 12$ cm, the image is real and inverted; (c) $d_I = 8.11$ cm, $h = 1.62$ cm, the image is real and inverted

49.

(a)

Virtual, upright, enlarged image

(b)

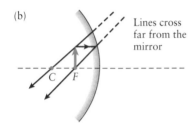

Lines cross far from the mirror

(c)

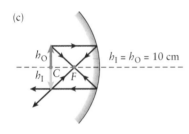

$h_I = h_O = 10$ cm

51. In both cases, the images are virtual. The image of an "up close" object is larger than the image of the same object "far away." In both cases the image is smaller than the object.

53. A convex mirror is the opposite of a concave mirror. Use a phrase such as "The cave goes in" to remember the shape of a concave mirror.

55. (a) $d_I = -6.67$ cm, $h = 3.33$ cm. The image is virtual and upright.
(b) $d_I = -8.33$ cm, $h = 1.67$ cm. The image is virtual and upright.
(c) $d_I = -9.09$ cm, $h = 0.909$ cm. The image is virtual and upright.

57. $d_I = -4.29$ m, $m = 0.429$. The image is virtual and upright.

59. $d_I = -0.962$ cm, length = 0.926 cm. The image is virtual and upright.

63. $d_I = -6.32$ cm, $h = 0.947$. The image is virtual and upright.

65. No, a real image in a converging lens occurs on the opposite side of the lens from the object.

67. (a) Nearsightedness is corrected by a diverging lens.
(b) Farsightedness is corrected by a converging lens.

69. (a) $d_I = -6.7$ cm, $h_I = 13$ cm. The image is virtual and upright.

Upright, virtual, enlarged image

(b) $d_I = -20$ cm, $h_I = 20$ cm. The image is virtual and upright.

Upright, virtual, enlarged image

(c) No image is formed.

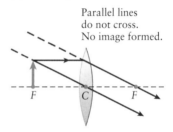

Parallel lines do not cross. No image formed.

(d) $d_I = 33$ cm, $h_I = 6.7$ cm. The image is real and inverted.

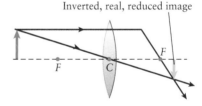

Inverted, real, reduced image

71. (a) $d_I = -45$ cm, $h_I = 5.0$ cm. The image is virtual and upright.

(b)

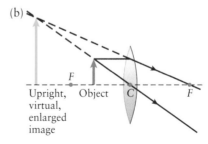

Upright, virtual, enlarged image

73. (a) $R = 0.191$ m; (b) $f = 31.8$ cm
75. 360
77. (a) $d_I = 26.7$ cm, $m = -0.668$

(b)

Object at 40 cm

$F = 16$ cm

$R = 32$ cm

Real, inverted, reduced image at 26.7 cm

79. (a) at minimum power: $f_{min} = 8.72$ mm, $P_{min} = 115$ D; at maximum power: $f_{max} = 6.73$ mm, $P_{max} = 150$ D; (b) 6.92 mm; (c) This image would not fall on the retina of the human eye.
81. 1.67 cm
83. 2.16
85. (a) The image is 750 cm from the mirror on the same side as the object. (b) The image is real and inverted. (c) The image is now 15.3 cm past the mirror on the opposite side from the lens. The image is real and upright.
87. (a) The final image is 43.75 cm behind the mirror. The image is virtual and inverted. $h = 10.5$ cm. (b) The final image is 116.1 cm behind the mirror. The image is virtual and erect. $h = 3.00$ cm.
89. (a) 3.1 mm in front of the retina. (b) Reflection is not affected by the index of refraction, so the answer would be the same as in part (a).
91. 2.67 D
93. (a) Both the near point and far point are too close, so the patient needs bifocals to correct both problems. (b) $f_{near} = 37.5$ cm, $f_{distant} = 275$ cm; (c) $P_{near} = -2.67$ D, $P_{distant} = -0.364$ D
95. (a) 203 mm; (b) 0.51 cm; (c) 27.5 mm
97. (a) -790; (b) The negative sign tells us that the image is inverted when viewed in the eyepiece.

Chapter 25

1. There is always a great deal of resistance to change, in any context, but especially in academia. Physics in this era (c. 1900) was predicated on Newtonian theories regarding motion, gravity, and cosmology. In addition, Maxwell's theory of electromagnetism was firmly in place. These two scientists were held in the highest esteem and were "above reproach." It was heretical for anyone, much less a young, upstart physicist who was not even part of a university, to challenge these time-tested, universally accepted underpinnings of physics. On a much more pragmatic level, it is always a "tough sell" when the new theory is complicated and not intuitive.
3. A frame of reference or reference frame is a coordinate system with respect to which we will make observations or measurements. An inertial frame is one that moves at constant speed relative to another; that is, we refer to a frame of reference attached to a nonaccelerating object as an inertial frame.
5. It means that there is no preferential frame of reference that is "fixed in place." Even the velocity of a car relative to the Earth can be rephrased as the velocity of the Earth relative to the car!

7. If the object is moving relative to you, you measure its length by finding the difference between the coordinates of its endpoints at the same time.
9. Yes, it is possible. See Equation 25-15. If two light bulbs at opposite ends of a meter stick flash simultaneously as measured in a frame at rest relative to the meter stick (one bulb at $x = 0$ and the other at $x = 1$ m), then the order of events can change depending on the circumstances of the observer. An observer moving in the $-x$ direction would measure the bulb at 1 m flashing after the bulb at 0 m, while an observer moving in the $+x$ direction would measure the bulb at 0 m flashing after the bulb at 1 m.
11. Writers like to use travel through higher dimensions, which could presumably shorten the distance traveled, making it appear that the traveler has moved faster than the speed of light. They also often employ wormholes, or connections between two points in space–time, created when the space–time "surfaces" become deformed enough to "touch" each other and become physically connected. These sorts of deformations are possible (at least in theory) where high-mass objects like black holes exist.
13. One important prediction of general relativity is that light bends as it passes through a gravitational field.
15. D
17. D
19. A
21. $0.417c$
23. Yes. If $v/c = 0.6$, then $\gamma = 1.25$. If $v/c = 0.8$, then $\gamma = 1.67$.
25. About 5% of the world population
27.

v/c	γ	v/c	γ
0	1.0000	0.7	1.4003
0.1	1.0050	0.8	1.6667
0.2	1.0206	0.9	2.2942
0.3	1.0483	0.99	7.0888
0.4	1.0911	0.999	22.3663
0.5	1.1547	0.9999	70.7124
0.6	1.2500		

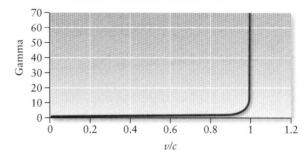

(a) 0.1; (b) $v/c = 0.1$, slope $= 0.102$; $v/c = 0.5$, slope $= 0.770$; $v/c = 0.9$, slope $= 10.9$; $v/c = 0.999$, slope $= 11,200$
29. (a) $x' = x - 4t$, $y' = y$, $z' = z$; (b) $x' = -14$ m, $y' = 1$ m, $z' = 0$ m
31. (a) $x' = x - 15t$, $y' = y$, $z' = z$; (b) $x'' = x - 4t$, $y'' = y$, $z'' = z$; (c) $x' = x'' - 11t$, $y' = y''$, $z' = z''$
33. (a) $x = 12$ m, $y = 4$ m, $z = 6$ m, $t = 4 \times 10^{-3}$ s; (b) $x = 8$ m, $y = 4$ m, $z = 6$ m, $t = 4 \times 10^{-3}$ s

35. 39.1 m/s in the direction of 39.8° north of the east direction
37. The massive slab of marble was used to keep any vibrations from disrupting the light as it moved through the interferometer. The slab needed to be rotated at different points in the experiment, so the mercury made it easier to move.
39. (a) 6.61×10^{-7} μs; (b) 0.00667 μs; (c) 0.675 μs; (d) 23.8 μs; (e) 396 μs
41. 1.67
43. 2.19 μs
45. 0.9999999995c
47. 1.5 ns
49. 1.92 m
51. 0.980 m
53. $v = 2.99 \times 10^8$ m/s, $v/c = 0.997$
55. The velocity of the truck relative to the car is $-0.110c$. The velocity of the car relative to the truck is $0.110c$.
57. 0.548c
59. 0.99999999999989c
61. (a) 1.35×10^{-22} kg·m/s; (b) 9.51×10^{-15} J; (c) 8.20×10^{-14} J; (d) 9.15×10^{-14} J
63. 0.866c
65. 0.209c
67. 8.2 m/s² in the upward direction
69. 3.29 μs
71. (a) 0.946c; (b) 0.946c; (c) Consider part a. If the nucleus is "Earth," then the laboratory goes by at a speed of 0.8c, which corresponds to rocket B in part b. The nucleus emits an electron in the forward direction, at a speed of 0.6c, and this electron corresponds to rocket A in part b. In part a, we determined the speed of the electron relative to the lab frame, which is then equivalent to the speed of rocket A relative to rocket B in this problem. Since two objects must always have the same speed relative to each other, our calculation of the speed of rocket B relative to rocket A better give the same answer.
73. (a) The muon does not make it to Earth's surface. (b) 0.977c
75. 6×10^{15} m
77. 0.986c
79. 0.252 mg
81. (a) The proper time is the time measured by the particle because the two events occur at the same location in that reference frame. The proper length is in the Earth reference frame because the atmosphere and Earth are at rest in that frame. (b) 40.4 μs. (c) 92.6 μs
83. (a) 46.3 beats/min; (b) 70 beats/min
85. $K_{Newton} = 3.645 \times 10^{19}$ J, $K_{Einstein} = 1.647 \times 10^{20}$ J, % error = 69%. The Newtonian expression underestimates the kinetic energy.
87. (a) 0.77c; (b) 96.7 years

Chapter 26

1. The de Broglie wavelength decreases as the kinetic energy increases.
3. The electron in the Bohr atom would be constantly accelerating, and so it would be constantly radiating. As the electron radiates, it would lose energy and slowly spiral into the nucleus.

5. The shortest wavelength is the wavelength that is emitted when a free electron is captured into the lowest energy state. This wavelength is 91.2 nm.
7. (a) As long as the radiation has a frequency above the cutoff value, the greater the intensity the larger the flux of photoelectrons that flow off of the metal plate. If the frequency of the light is below the cutoff, it does not matter how much the intensity is increased. No photoelectrons will be emitted. (b) If the wavelength is increased, the energy of the radiation will decrease. If it slips below the work function of the metal plate, the photoelectric effect will cease. (c) If the work function of the metal is increased, it will eventually grow past the energy of the incident photons and the effect will cease.
9. The exact amount of energy required to free an electron from a surface depends on a variety of factors, for example, the energy level of tht electron and the electron's motion at the moment it is struck by a photon. The kinetic energy of any electron is the difference between the energy of a photon and this varying energy required to liberate the electron.
11. Visible light can Compton scatter. However, because the Compton wavelength is so small compared to the wavelength of visible light (0.0024 nm compared to 400 to 750 nm), the change in the wavelength of a visible photon would be negligibly small.
13. The electron has the longer wavelength.
15. Hydrogen is the first, most elemental, simplest element in the periodic table. Any cogent theory of atoms must describe hydrogen first and then work its way up to the larger, more complicated elements. In addition, because hydrogen only has one electron, it presents no complications to the orbit of an electron due to the interaction of other electrons.
17. Because the rest mass of a macroscopic object is so large, the de Broglie wavelength is too small to observe. The wavelength of everyday objects is many orders of magnitude less than the radius of an atom. This is far too small for us to observe.
19. D
21. A
23. A
25. C
27. 5–25 eV; this is 10^5 times smaller than the nuclear binding energy.
29. Between 500 and 1000 W
31. The electrostatic force is 10^{39} times greater than the gravitational force.
33. 7.3×10^6 m/s
35.

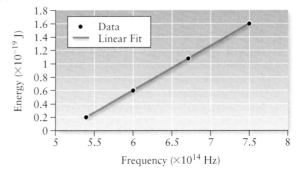

Using this data, we calculate $h = 6.8 \times 10^{-34}$ J·s $= 4.12 \times 10^{-15}$ eV·s

37. 4310 nm

39. 9670 nm

41. 6110 K

43. $f_{violet} = 7.85 \times 10^{14}$ Hz, $f_{red} = 3.85 \times 10^{14}$ Hz; $E_{violet} = 3.27$ eV, $E_{red} = 1.59$ eV

45. $E = 6200$ eV $= 9.94 \times 10^{-16}$ J

47. $E = 225$ eV $= 3.61 \times 10^{-17}$ J

49. (a) $\phi = 2.27$ eV; (b) 546 nm

51. Ca, K, and Cs

53. (a) 1.21×10^{-27} kg·m/s $= 2.25$ eV/c;
    (b) 9.32×10^{-24} kg·m/s $= 17400$ eV/c

55. 25.8°

57. (a) $\lambda = 0.140$ nm, $K = 0$ eV
    (b) $\lambda = 0.14033$ nm, $K = 20.8$ eV
    (c) $\lambda = 0.14071$ nm, $K = 44.7$ eV
    (d) $\lambda = 0.1412$ nm, $K = 75.3$ eV
    (e) $\lambda = 0.14243$ nm, $K = 151$ eV
    (f) $\lambda = 0.14486$ nm, $K = 297$ eV

59. 0.137 nm

61. (a) $f = 4.22 \times 10^{18}$ Hz, $E = 17440$ eV;
    (b) 0.0735 nm; (c) 16,860 eV; (d) 576 eV

63. 3.32×10^{-10} m

65. $\lambda = \dfrac{h}{\gamma m v}$

67. (a) 1.23×10^{-9} m
    (b) 3.88×10^{-10} m
    (c) 1.23×10^{-10} m
    (d) 3.88×10^{-11} m
    (e) 8.80×10^{-13} m
    (f) 1.24×10^{-15} m

69. 1.43×10^{-10} m

71. $\lambda = \dfrac{h}{\sqrt{2Km}}$

73. 5.91×10^{-6} eV

75. (a) 6 lines; (b) 45 lines

77. $n_i = 6 \rightarrow n_f = 2$, $\lambda = 411$ nm
    $n_i = 5 \rightarrow n_f = 2$, $\lambda = 434$ nm
    $n_i = 4 \rightarrow n_f = 2$, $\lambda = 486$ nm
    $n_i = 3 \rightarrow n_f = 2$, $\lambda = 656$ nm

79. $\lambda_{Lyman} = 91.1$ nm
    $\lambda_{Balmer} = 365$ nm
    $\lambda_{Paschen} = 820$ nm

81. $f = (3.2898 \times 10^{15}$ Hz$)\left(\dfrac{1}{n^2} - \dfrac{1}{m^2}\right)$

83.

n	L_n (J·s)	r_n (m)	K_n (J)
1	1.06×10^{-34}	5.29×10^{-11}	2.18×10^{-18}
2	2.11×10^{-34}	2.11×10^{-10}	5.44×10^{-19}
3	3.16×10^{-34}	4.76×10^{-10}	2.42×10^{-19}
4	4.22×10^{-34}	8.46×10^{-10}	1.36×10^{-19}
5	5.27×10^{-34}	1.32×10^{-9}	8.70×10^{-20}

n	E_n (J)	v_n (m/s)
1	-2.18×10^{-18}	2.19×10^{6}
2	-5.44×10^{-19}	1.09×10^{6}
3	-2.42×10^{-19}	7.29×10^{5}
4	-1.36×10^{-19}	5.47×10^{5}
5	-8.70×10^{-20}	4.38×10^{5}

85. $v = 2.19 \times 10^{5}$ m/s, $L = 1.055 \times 10^{-33}$ J·s

87. $\Delta f = 0.2$ MHz

89. (a) 486 nm; (b) 1879 nm, 656 nm, 486 nm, 122 nm, 103 nm, and 97.3 nm

91. $E_{10} = -0.0340$ eV
    $E_9 = -0.0420$ eV
    $E_8 = -0.0531$ eV
    $E_7 = -0.0694$ eV
    $E_6 = -0.0944$ eV
    $E_5 = -0.136$ eV
    $E_4 = -0.213$ eV
    $E_3 = -0.378$ eV
    $E_2 = -0.85$ eV
    $E_1 = -3.40$ eV

93. (a) 1.59×10^{15} photons/s; (b) 1.67×10^{-12} kg·m/s

95. $\lambda_f - \lambda_i = \dfrac{h}{m_e c}(1 - \cos\theta)$

97. $\dfrac{\lambda_H}{\lambda_O} = 4$

99. (a) 1.20×10^{29} m; (b) $E = -4.21 \times 10^{-97}$ J

Chapter 27

1. Isotopes are nuclides with the same atomic number, Z, but a different number of neutrons, N. So, they have different mass numbers, $A = Z + N$.

3. Binding energy is a measure of how difficult it is to break the nucleus into its constituent "pieces," similar to the way that the work function measures the difficulty in removing an electron from the surface of a conductor. Also, the binding energy is different for different isotopes, similar to the way that the work function is tabulated for different conductors studied in the photoelectric effect.
   The work function is usually a few eV (maybe ~ 10 eV at the maximum), while the binding energy in the nucleus is on the order of MeV. There is really no definitive means of predicting the work function. It is measured empirically, whereas for the binding energy we can use Einstein's equation to calculate the expected values ($E = \Delta mc^2$).

5. The whole nucleus weighs less than the sum of its parts because some of that mass is converted to energy when the parts are fused. In order to break apart the nucleus, you must add energy equivalent to the binding energy, which becomes mass after fission.

7. Certainly, the central ideas of binding energy and "Q values" of nuclear reactions would not have been possible to develop without the $E = mc^2$ concept. The Manhattan project in World War II, where nuclear weapons were designed and successfully tested, would not have been possible had it not been for Einstein's theory of the equivalence of mass and energy (as well as his letter to President Roosevelt endorsing this project in the early 1940s).

9. (a) Elements with higher atomic number than iron are more likely to fission. (b) Elements with lower atomic number than iron are more likely to undergo fusion.

11. Consider the typical beta decay, such as the decay of a neutron: n $\rightarrow$ p $+ \beta^- + \nu_e$. If the electron (β^-) were the only decay product, application of conservation of

energy and momentum to the two-body decay would require that the β particle be ejected with a single unique energy. Instead, we observe experimentally that β particles are produced with energies that range from zero to a maximum value. Further, because the original neutron had spin 1/2, conservation of angular momentum would be violated if the final decay products consisted of only the two particles p and β, each with spin 1/2.

13. As uranium begins to decay, the daughter nuclei are themselves often radioactive, decaying by various paths (which all lead down to a stable isotope in the periodic table). So, at any instant there are isotopes from all the many possible decay modes of all the radioactive progeny of the parent nuclei.

15. Because the atomic masses include Z electron masses in their values, it is already taken into account. There is 1 electron mass included in the atomic mass of the proton. There is no need to add in another one to account for the beta particle.

17. D

19. E

21. B

23. B

25. C

27. The nuclear force is about 100 times larger than the electrostatic force.

29. 5×10^{17}

31. About 40 times greater. In some models, the force is actually repulsive for small separation distances (< 0.7 fm) and attractive for larger separation distances.

33. 2×10^{16} kg

35. (a) 0.678 days or 16.3 hours; (b) 4 days

37. (a) H, 1 proton and 2 neutrons, mass number 3
(b) Be, 4 protons and 4 neutrons, mass number 8
(c) Al, 13 protons and 13 neutrons, mass number 26
(d) Au, 79 protons and 118 neutrons, mass number 197
(e) Tc, 43 protons and 57 neutrons, mass number 100
(f) W, 74 protons and 110 neutrons, mass number 184
(g) Os, 76 protons and 114 neutrons, mass number 190
(h) Pu, 94 protons and 145 neutrons, mass number 239

39. (a) Hydrogen, 1 proton and 1 neutron, mass number 2
(b) Helium, 2 protons and 2 neutrons, mass number 4
(c) Lithium, 3 protons and 3 neutrons, mass number 6
(d) Carbon, 6 protons and 6 neutrons, mass number 12
(e) Iron, 26 protons and 30 neutrons, mass number 56
(f) Strontium, 38 protons and 52 neutrons, mass number 90
(g) Iodine, 53 protons and 78 neutrons, mass number 131
(h) Uranium, 92 protons and 143 neutrons, mass number 235

41. 12.7 km

43. 92.2 MeV

45. 15.643 MeV

47. 1100 MeV binding energy, 8.42 MeV/nucleon

49. 10n, 89.95 MeV is released

51. (a) n; (b) ^{102}Zr; (c) ^{250}Cm; (d) ^{142}Cs

53. About 33 collisions

55. 366 kg

57. 3.1×10^{19} reactions/second

59. (a) 17.6 MeV; (b) 19.0 MeV; (c) 3.27 MeV; (d) 5.49 MeV; (e) 4.03 MeV

61. 1.56×10^{-9} g

63. (a) 3.70×10^6 Bq; (b) 25 Bq; (c) 4.46×10^{-7} Ci; (c) 4.53×10^{12} cpm

65. 208 s = 0.00240 days

67. 0.298% of the original sample

69. 0.530 μCi

71. 25,740 years

73. 3.85×10^6 nuclei

75. (a) $^{238}\text{U} \rightarrow {}^{234}\text{Th} + \alpha$
(b) $^{234}\text{Th} \rightarrow {}^{230}\text{Ra} + \alpha$
(c) $^{240}\text{Pu} \rightarrow {}^{236}\text{U} + \alpha$
(d) $^{214}\text{Bi} \rightarrow {}^{210}\text{Tl} + \alpha$

77. (a) $^{131}\text{I}^* \rightarrow {}^{131}\text{I} + \gamma$
(b) $^{145}\text{Pm}^* \rightarrow {}^{145}\text{Pm} + \gamma$
(c) $^{24}\text{Na}^* \rightarrow {}^{24}\text{Na} + \gamma$

79. (a) 7.4 fm; (b) 1.0 N; (c) 6.2×10^{26} m/s^2; (d) The strong nuclear force holds them together.

81. (a) 36; (b) 36; (c) 37; (d) 37; (e) 39; (f) 38

83. (a) 8.0 fm; (b) 3.1×10^{-20}%

85. (a) 10^{-320}%; (b) $10^{-714.7}$%; (c) Since essentially none of the original Tc would be left at the end of the star's lifetime, it must be produced recently in the star. This means that the star is manufacturing the atom.

87. 31,000 years

89. (a) barium-137; (b) 200 years

91. (a) 1 proton and 2 neutrons; (b) $^3\text{H} \rightarrow {}^3\text{He} + e^-$. The daughter is helium-3. (c) 22.4 years

93. (a) 44 protons and 62 neutrons; (b) We would not find any in mined ores. Such ores are many millions of years old (at the least), so if any ruthenium-106 were present initially, it would have decayed to essentially zero. (c) $^{106}\text{Ru} \rightarrow {}^{106}\text{Rh} + e^-$. The daughter is rhodium-106. (d) 2.05 years

95. The Q value for this forbidden reaction is -0.274 MeV. Since $Q < 0$, this reaction cannot occur. If it did, all low-energy electrons could react with protons and turn into neutrons. This would disrupt all chemical reactions, making life impossible.

97. (a) 6 α and 4 e^- particles are emitted; (b) 18 α and 6 e^- particles are emitted; (c) 9 α and 4 e^- particles are emitted; (d) 8 α and 4 e^- particles are emitted

Chapter 28

1. (a) Baryons are hadrons made up of three quarks. (b) Mesons are hadrons made up of quark–antiquark pairs. (c) Quarks are fractionally charged particles that make up hadronic material (baryons and/or mesons). (d) Leptons are particles that are driven by the electroweak force and mediated with photons and W/Z bosons. e) Antiparticles are the negative-energy counterpart to every particle. All particles possess antiparticles that are equal in mass but opposite in charge.

3. The photon and the neutrino are both neutral in charge and possess no baryon quantum number. There are some early models in which the electron neutrino is massless;

in that case, it would travel at the speed of light. These two particles are driven by the electroweak force.

5. uud, udd, ddd, uuu, uus, dds, uds, uss, dss, and sss.

7. If only one photon were created, linear momentum could not be conserved because a zero momentum photon is not possible.

9. Measurements of the orbital speed of spiral galaxies show that the galaxies rotate faster than should be allowed given the amount of visible matter in the galaxy. The mass needed to hold the rotating galaxy together is about six times the total mass of the visible matter in the galaxy. This additional necessary matter is dark matter.

11. B

13. D

15. A

17. D

19. D

21. 430 Mpc

23. No. It is impossible because neither baryon number nor lepton number is conserved.

25. (a) Λ or Σ^0 because these particles have the correct charge and quark configuration.
(b) Ξ_0 because this particle has the correct charge and quark configuration.

27. (a) and (b) are possible, (c) is not possible because baryon number is not conserved.

29. All are allowed.

31. $E_\gamma = 273.5$ MeV, $\lambda = 4.53 \times 10^{-6}$ nm, and $p = 1.46 \times 10^{-19}$ kg·m/s for each photon.

33. (a) 1.02 MeV; (b) The nucleus is required to absorb the momentum so that conservation of momentum is not violated.

35. (a) $K_p = 0.312$ GeV $= K_{p^-}$; (b) $K_p = 0.347$ GeV and $K_{p^-} = 0.277$ GeV

37.

39.

41. $m = 1.87 \times 10^{-3}$ MeV/c^2, so $m_e/m = 270$

43. 1500 km/s

45. (a) Ge; (b) 290 N

47. 620 nm. These photons will appear reddish-orange in color to the human eye.

49. $\pi^+ = (u_R\overline{d_R}, u_B\overline{d_B}, u_G\overline{d_G})$
$\pi^0 = (u_R\overline{u_R}, u_B\overline{u_B}, u_G\overline{u_G})$
$\pi^- = (d_R\overline{u_R}, d_B\overline{u_B}, d_G\overline{u_G})$

51. (a) It is neutral ($Q = 0$). (b) About 2 ps

MCAT® Question Answers

The section that follows includes material from previously administered MCAT® items and is reprinted with permission of the Association of American Medical Colleges (AAMC).

Passage 13 (B)

81. D
82. C
83. C
84. B
85. B

Passage X (G)

134. B
135. D
136. B
137. D
138. D

Passage 12 (A)

73. B
74. B
75. A
76. D
77. A
78. C
79. C
80. A

Passage 7

41. C
42. D
43. A
44. C
45. B
46. C
47. A
48. B

Passage 1

1. D
2. A
3. C
4. C
5. B
6. B

Passage 2

7. D
8. B
9. D
10. C
11. A
12. D
13. A

Passage II (E)

74. A
75. B
76. C
77. D
78. D
79. A
80. B

Passage 4 (C)

19. B
20. B
21. D
22. C
23. A
24. D
25. B
26. C

Passage IV (F)

94. C
95. C
96. A
97. B
98. D
99. A

Credits

Photo Credits

Cover: Kim Taylor/Hotspot Media   p. 1: Masterfile   p. 2: iStockphoto/Thinkstock   p. 4: © BIPM. Reproduced with permission of Bureau international des poids et mesures.   p. 5: NASA   p. 8: David Tauck   p. 20: Martin Sundberg/UpperCut Images/Alamy   p. 21: Fuse/Getty Images   p. 39: Mike Greenslade/Alamy   p. 50: Goodshoot/Thinkstock   p. 51: Richard Megna/Fundamental Photographs   p. 67: Martin Rietze/Westend61 GmbH/Alamy   p. 68 (left): Wojciechbeczynski/Dreamstime.com   p. 68 (center): iStockphoto/Thinkstock   p. 68 (right): iStockphoto/Thinkstock   p. 73: Rob Flynn/USDA ARS   p. 81: iStockphoto/Thinkstock   p. 84: iStockphoto/Thinkstock   p. 87 (top): Toño Labra/AgeFotostock   p. 87 (bottom): NVC ARTS, a Warner Music Group company   p. 91: Richard Megna/Fundamental Photographs   p. 117: Thinkstock   p. 118: Jamie Roach/Shutterstock.com   p. 120: Ryan McVay/Thinkstock   p. 122: Dr. James Grainger   p. 141: Thomas Krämer/age fotostock   p. 157: Doug James/Shutterstock.com   p. 158 (top): iStockphoto/Thinkstock   p. 158 (bottom): Katrina Brown/Dreamstime.com   p. 159: Hemera/Thinkstock   p. 160: iStockphoto/Thinkstock   p. 161 (top): David Tauck   p. 161 (bottom): itsmejust/Shutterstock   p. 174 (left): Nadezhda V. Kulagina/Shutterstock.com   p. 174 (right): Masterfile   p. 177 (left): Filmfoto/Dreamstime.com   p. 177 (right): Daveh900/Dreamstime.com   p. 195: Jean-Paul Ferrero/Auscape/The Image Works   p. 196 (top left): AP Photo/Kevin Wolf   p. 196 (top center): iStockphoto/Thinkstock   p. 196 (top right): Rubberball/Corbis   p. 196 (bottom): Ocean/Corbis   p. 198 (right): J. Hindman/Shutterstock   p. 209: Sampics/Corbis   p. 210: Ken Fisher/Getty Images   p. 213: Emil von Maltitz/Getty Images   p. 219: Lee Jae-Won/Reuters/Corbis   p. 244: Jim Zipp/Science Source   p. 245 (top left): Stephen Mcsweeny/Shutterstock   p. 245 (top right): David Fleetham/Alamy   p. 245 (bottom): prudkov/Shutterstock   p. 252: AP Photo/Dale Davis   p. 261: Raycat/iStockphoto   p. 265: Hemera/Thinkstock   p. 271: Art Directors & TRIP/Alamy   p. 272: AP Photo/Kathy Willens   p. 279: NVC ARTS, a Warner Music Group company   p. 290 (left): AP Photo/Amy Sancetta   p. 290 (right): AP Photo/Amy Sancetta   p. 291 (top left): iStockphoto/Thinkstock   p. 291 (top center): Dr. John Brackenbury/Science Source   p. 291 (top right): NASA/Goddard Space Flight Center   p. 291 (bottom): Imagestate   p. 297: David Tauck   p. 298: Ocean/Corbis   p. 302: Mike Powell/Getty Images   p. 308 (left): George Tiedemann/NewSport/Corbis   p. 308 (bottom): Berenice Abbott/Science Source   p. 321: Joe Belanger/Shutterstock.com   p. 335: AP Photo/Phil O'Brien   p. 339: Agence Nature/Natural History Picture Archive/Photoshot   p. 353 (top): Tim Stelzer/Flickr/Getty Images   p. 353 (bottom): Rachel Torres/Alamy   p. 354 (top right): Nobilior/Fotolia   p. 354 (top center): Lasse Kristensen/Dreamstime   p. 354 (top left): Blend Images/Alamy   p. 354 (bottom left): Muriel de Seze/Getty Images   p. 354 (bottom right): Christoph Wilhelm/Getty Images

p. 357: Lucie Lang/Shutterstock   p. 359: MedicalRF/Science Source   p. 361 (top): Michael Blann/Getty Images   p. 361 (bottom): Exactostock/SuperStock   p. 367: Noria, S., Xu, et al., Assembly and Reorientation of Stress Fibers Drivers Morphological Changes to Endothelial Cells Exposed to Shear Stress American Journal of Pathology (2004) 164: 1211–1223. ©2004 Elsevier.   p. 369: Tom Pantages   p. 373 (bottom): Rachel Torres/Alamy   p. 381: NASA   p. 382 (top left): NASA/NOAA   p. 382 (top center): NASA/JPL/USGS   p. 382 (top right): ESO   p. 382 (bottom): T.A.Rector, I.P.Dell'Antonio/NOAO/AURA/NSF   p. 395: Pat Corkery, United Launch Alliance   p. 399: NASA/University of Arizona/HiRise-LPL   p. 401: Photo by Christina Micek   p. 403: NASA   p. 411: NASA   p. 420: Corbis   p. 421 (left): Stockbyte/Thinkstock   p. 421 (center): SOHO consortium. SOHO is a project of international cooperation between ESA and NASA   p. 421 (right): iStockphoto/Thinkstock   p. 428: Indranil Mukherjee/AFP/Getty Images   p. 429 (top): Roger A. Freedman   p. 429 (bottom): Roger A. Freedman   p. 435: Jupiterimages/Thinkstock   p. 448 (left): Andy Sacks/Getty Images   p. 448 (center): iStockphoto/Thinkstock   p. 448 (right): Images produced by Hal Pierce, Laboratory for Atmospheres, NASA Goddard Space Flight Center.   p. 466: iStockphoto/Thinkstock   p. 469: NASA   p. 481: Fatih Polat/Dreamstime.com   p. 482 (left): iStockphoto/Thinkstock   p. 482 (center): Photodisc/Thinkstock   p. 482 (right): Zephyr/Science Source   p. 496: David Tauck   p. 502 (top): BSIP SA/Alamy   p. 502 (bottom): GIPhotoStock/Science Source   p. 515 (top): George Resch/Fundamental Photographs   p. 515 (bottom left): Eric V. Grave/Science Source   p. 515 (bottom right): Eric V. Grave/Science Source   p. 516 (bottom): GIPhotoStock/Science Source   p. 524: Cosson, J., A Moving Image of Flagella: News and Views on the Mechanisms Involved in Axonemal Beating, Cell Biology International (1996) 20: 2, 83–94.   p. 525 (left): Don Farrall/Getty Images   p. 525 (right): moodboard/Fotolia.com   p. 526: Elijah Light   p. 541: Berenice Abbott/Science Photo Library/Science Source   p. 546: David Tauck   p. 550: Tatsuya Kitamura   p. 570: NASA/Science Photo Library   p. 582: Helmut Schmitz, University of Bonn   p. 583 (left): iStockphoto/Thinkstock   p. 583 (center): iStockphoto/Thinkstock   p. 583 (right): BlueGreen Pictures/SuperStock   p. 594: Andrew Syred/Science Source   p. 597: peacepics/Fotolia.com   p. 604: David Tauck   p. 612 (left): Scott Rheam/U.S. Fish and Wildlife Service   p. 612 (right): Bonnie Fink/Dreamstime.com   p. 613: Robert Markus/Science Photo Library   p. 618: University of Illinois at Urbana-Champaign Physics Department   p. 628: James P. Blair/National Geographic/Getty Images   p. 629 (left): Trevor Hirst/iStockphoto   p. 629 (right): Roger A. Freedman   p. 629 (bottom): iStockphoto/Thinkstock   p. 637: NASA   p. 648 (left): David Tauck   p. 648 (center): Ted Kinsman/Science Source   p. 648 (right): Ted Kinsman/Science Source   p. 673: Exactostock/SuperStock   p. 674 (left): Biophoto Associates/Science Source   p. 674 (right): KingWu/iStockphoto   p. 676: Image Source/Getty Images   p. 681: Kung-Ming Jan and Shu Chien, 1973 Rockefeller University

Press. Originally published in The Journal of General Physiology. 61:638–654. **p. 689:** NOAA **p. 694:** Reprinted by permission from Macmillan Publishers Ltd., Shinoda, T., Ogawa, H., Cornelius, F., Toyoshima, C., Research Collaboratory for Structural Bioinformatics, Crystal structure of the sodium-potassium pump at 2.4 A resolution. Nature (2009) 459: 446-50, copyright 2009. **p. 712:** muratseyit/ iStockphoto **p. 713 (left):** iStockphoto/Thinkstock **p. 713 (right):** NHPA/SuperStock **p. 734:** iStockphoto/Thinkstock **p. 735:** NASA **p. 758:** Charles D. Winters/Science Source **p. 759 (left):** iStockphoto/Thinkstock **p. 759 (center):** Stockbyte/Thinkstock **p. 759 (right):** Asia Images Group Pte Ltd/Alamy **p. 770:** David Tauck **p. 794:** Biophoto Associates/Science Source **p. 804:** iStockphoto/Thinkstock **p. 805 (left):** GIPHOTOSTOCK/Science Photo Library **p. 805 (center):** Todd Ruskell **p. 805 (right):** Cordelia Molloy/Science Photo Library **p. 805 (bottom):** Alchemy/ Alamy **p. 806:** Eli Sidman, Technical Services Group, MIT. **p. 815 (left):** Jupiterimages/Thinkstock **p. 815 (right):** Christina Micek **p. 819 (left):** iStockphoto/Thinkstock **p. 819 (right):** iStockphoto/Thinkstock **p. 823:** Elekta **p. 825:** Arno Massee/Science Photo Library **p. 828 (top):** Paul Silverman/Fundamental Photographs **p. 828 (bottom):** David Tauck **p. 846:** iStockphoto/Thinkstock **p. 847 (left):** Digital Vision/Thinkstock **p. 847 (right):** "Keck, et. al. ""Transcranial magnetic stimulation as a therapeutic tool in psychiatry: what do we know about the neurobiological mechanisms?" Journal of Psychiatric Research 35 (2001) 193–215 **p. 867:** iStockphoto/Thinkstock **p. 868 (left):** iStockphoto/Thinkstock **p. 868 (right):** iStockphoto/ Thinkstock **p. 872:** Peter & Georgina Bowater/Aurora Photos **p. 880:** Todd Ruskell **p. 905:** iStockphoto/ Thinkstock **p. 906 (left):** S.Kafka and K.Honeycutt, Indiana University/WIYN/NOAO/NSF **p. 906 (right):** Will & Deni McIntyre/Science Photo Library/Science Source **p. 907:** Siebeck, et. al. "A Species of Reef Fish that Uses Ultraviolet Patterns for Covert Face Recognition" Current Biology 20 (March 9, 2010) 407–410. **p. 935:** Medioimages/Photodisc/ Thinkstock **p. 936 (left):** David Tauck **p. 936 (center):** iStockphoto/Thinkstock **p. 936 (right):** Carol and Mike Werner/Phototake, Inc. **p. 936 (bottom):** George Resch/ Fundamental Photographs **p. 937:** iStockphoto/Thinkstock **p. 942:** David Tauck **p. 943:** GIPhotoStock/Science Source **p. 944:** GIPhotoStock/Photo Researchers/Getty Images **p. 945:** Kent Wood/Science Source **p. 946:** David Tauck **p. 947:** GIPhotoStock/Science Source **p. 952:** David Tauck **p. 955:** Michael Gray/Dreamstime.com **p. 962 (left):** George Resch/Fundamental Photographs **p. 962 (right):** George Resch/Fundamental Photographs **p. 962 (bottom):** Edward Kinsman/Science Photo Library/Science Source **p. 963:** Edward Kinsman/Science Photo Library/Science Source **p. 966 (left):** Richard Megna/Fundamental Photographs **p. 966 (center):** Richard Megna/Fundamental Photographs **p. 966 (right):** Richard Megna/Fundamental Photographs **p. 966 (bottom):** sciencephotos/Alamy **p. 969:** NASA, ESA, and STScI **p. 980:** Stockbyte/Thinkstock **p. 981 (right):** Syracuse Newspapers/Blume/The Image Works **p. 981 (left):** BananaStock/Thinkstock **p. 985:** David Tauck **p. 985 (top):** David Tauck **p. 985 (bottom):** David Tauck **p. 987 (top):** David Tauck **p. 987 (bottom):** David Tauck **p. 988 (top):** David Tauck **p. 988 (middle):** David Tauck **p. 988 (bottom):** David Tauck **p. 995:** Melissa Gaskell/Alamy **p. 1002 (left):** Monika Graff/The Image Works **p. 1002 (right):** Rachael Lynn Beaton/University of Virginia **p. 1005:** Derrick Alderman/Alamy **p. 1024:** Pixtal/SuperStock **p. 1025 (left):** iStockphoto/Thinkstock **p. 1025 (right):** Comstock/Thinkstock **p. 1025 (bottom):** © Eitan Simanor/ Alamy **p. 1026:** OJO Images/SuperStock **p. 1036:** Sir John Sulston **p. 1053:** © 2011 CERN, for the benefit of the CMS Collaboration **p. 1057 (left):** NASA **p. 1057 (right):** NASA, ESA, A. Bolton (Harvard-Smithsonian CfA) and the SLACS Team **p. 1066:** T.A. Rector (University of Alaska Anchorage), Richard Cool (University of Arizona) and WIYN/NOAO **p. 1067 (left):** U.S. Air Force /Staff Sgt. Jacob Bragg/Alamy **p. 1067 (right):** iStockphoto/Thinkstock **p. 1067 (bottom):** Dr. Adam P. Hitchcock, McMaster University **p. 1071 (left):** Richard Megna/Fundamental Photographs **p. 1071 (center):** Richard Megna/Fundamental Photographs **p. 1071 (right):** Richard Megna/Fundamental Photographs **p. 1072:** iStockphoto/Thinkstock **p. 1081:** Frederick Murphy/CDC **p. 1109:** Stephane Marc/Maxppp/Zuma Press/Newscom **p. 1110 (left):** Dr. Leon Kaufman. University Of California, San Francisco **p. 1110 (center):** Brand X Pictures/Thinkstock **p. 1110 (right):** iStockphoto/Thinkstock **p. 1115:** Science Source **p. 1125:** C. F. Claver/WIYN/NOAO/NSF **p. 1146:** CERN **p. 1147 (left):** iStockphoto/Thinkstock **p. 1147 (right):** Hemera/Thinkstock **p. 1148:** Stanford Linear Accelerator Center/Science Source **p. 1159:** NASA, ESA, R. Ellis (Caltech), and the UDF 2012 Team **p. 1162:** ESA and the Planck Collaboration **p. 1163 (top):** NASA, ESA, and the Hubble Heritage Team (STScI/AURA) **p. 1163 (bottom):** C. Howk (JHU), B. Savage (U. Wisconsin), N.A.Sharp (NOAO)/ WIYN/NOAO/NSF

Illustration and Table Credits

Figure 6-20: Reeves N.D., Narici M.V. and Maganaris C.N., Strength training alters the viscoelastic properties of tendons in elderly humans. Muscle and Nerve (2003) 28: 74–81. Reproduced with permission of John Wiley & Sons, Inc.
Table 11-1: Data for biological materials from Vogel, S., Comparative Biomechanics, Princeton (2003) and Alexander, R.M, Exploring Biomechanics, Scientific American (1992).
Figure 12-8: (a) Young, S.H. and Rozengurt, E., Amino acids and Ca2$^+$ stimulate different patterns of Ca2$^+$ oscillations through the Ca2$^+$-sensing receptor, Am J Physiol Cell Physiol (2002) 282:1414-1422. ©The American Physiological Society (APS). All rights reserved. (b) Coyle, M.A, et al, Evaluation of an ambulatory system for the quantification of cough frequency in patients with chronic obstructive pulmonary disease, Cough (2005) 1:3.
Figure 12-17: Anson, C. P. Hearing in the Frog: Dynamics of the Middle Ear, Proceedings of the Royal Society of London. Series B, Biological Sciences (1981) 212:1189, pp. 459–485. Copyright © 1981, The Royal Society.

Figure 12-18: Armstrong, C. E. and Roberts, W. M., Electrical Properties of Frog Saccular Hair Cells: Distortion by Enzymatic Dissociation, The Journal of Neuroscience (1998) 18(8):2962–2973. ©Society of Neuroscience.

Figure 12-20: From Anson, M., Pinder, A. C., Keating, M. J, and Chung, S. H., 916 Acoustic vibration of the amphibian eardrum studied by white noise analysis and holographic interferometry, Acoust. Soc. Am (1985) 78:3. Reprinted with permission, ©1985 Acoustical Society of America.

Figure 14-16: Graph (Atmospheric Carbon Dioxide) from Skeptical Science Graphics by Skeptical Science.

Figure 14-17: Graph (Various Temperature Measurements) from Skeptical Science Graphics by Skeptical Science.

Figure 23-19: Adapted from OpenStax College, Polarization, Connexions, May 25, 2012, Fig. 11, http://cnx.org/content/m42522/1.2/.

INDEX